The CASSELL
THESAURUS

The CASSELL
THESAURUS

Cassell
Wellington House
125 Strand
London
WC2R 0BB

First published 1998

British Library Cataloguing in Publication Data
A catalogue entry for this book is available from the British Library

ISBN 0–304–34928–3

Printed and bound in Great Britain by Mackays of Chatham PLC, Kent

Contents

Acknowledgements

Compilers	Betty Kirkpatrick David Pickering
Editor	Martin Manser
Proof-reader	Alice Grandison
Database editor	Alex Williams
Database technology	Gentian I.T. Consultants
Typographic consultants	Newton Engert Partnership
Typesetting	Gem Graphics

How to use *The Cassell Thesaurus*

The entry

Each entry in *The Cassell Thesaurus* begins with the headword in bold type followed by the part of speech in italics. A definition is then given in italics within parentheses. This definition is followed by its own list of synonyms or similar expressions, and then by any antonyms or opposite expressions. These lists appear in normal roman type.

Where the headword has more than one meaning, senses are numbered **1**, **2** etc. and each sense number in bold is followed by its definition. A list of synonyms and antonyms applicable to each specific shade of meaning is given after each definition. Senses are ordered on a basis of current frequency. Closely related uses may share a number, subdivided as **a**, **b** etc. Sense numbering starts afresh for a second or subsequent parts of speech.

Organization of entries

Some headwords have more than one part of speech, new parts of speech being marked off on a separate line. Some may also have related expressions or idioms (which continue on the same line at the end of the article). These idioms are phrases that include the headword, and are therefore grouped under it. Idioms are placed immediately after the last sense of the last part of speech of the headword, and are in strict alphabetical order.

A number of headwords only have thesaurus entries relating to an idiom or idioms nested under them. In these cases, the headword is followed by its part of speech as used in the idiom, then the idiom and the list of synonyms and antonyms relating to the idiom itself.

Spellings

Recommended modern British spellings are used. Compounds given in only one form, (solid, e.g. eyesight, hyphenated, e.g. basket-maker, as two words, e.g. hot air) may often quite correctly be spelt in one of the other styles.

Labels

Descriptive labels in brackets have been added where appropriate. They fall into three main categories – stylistic labels, e.g. (*coll.*), (*poet.*), (*offensive*), geographical labels, e.g. (*N Am.*), (*New Zeal.*), and grammatical usage labels, e.g. (*usu. pl.*). A list of abbreviations used appears on p.xiii. In addition, obsolete and archaic words, phrases and meanings are preceded by a dagger sign †.

Proprietary Terms

This book includes some words which are or are asserted to be proprietary names. The presence or absence of such assertions should not be regarded as affecting the legal status of any proprietary name or trade mark.

Chief Abbreviations

All are given here in roman, though some of them may also appear in *italics* as labels.

a.	adjective
adv.	adverb
alln.	allusion
appar.	apparently
attrib.	attributive
augm.	augmentative
Austral.	Australia, Australian
aux.	auxiliary
Biol.	Biology
Bot.	Botany
c.	circa, about
Can.	Canada, Canadian
cent.	century
cents.	centuries
Chem.	Chemistry
coll.	colloquial
collect.	collective
comb.	combination
comp.	comparative
conj.	conjunction
conn.	connected
constr.	construction, constructed
cp.	compare
derog.	derogatory
dial.	dialect, dialectal
emphat.	emphatic, emphatically
esp.	especially
euphem.	euphemistic, euphemistically
exc.	except
facet.	facetious, facetiously
fig.	figuratively

ger.	gerund, gerundive
Gram.	Grammar
Hist.	History
ident.	identical, identified
imper.	imperative
impers.	impersonal
ind.	indicative
inf.	infinitive
int.	interjection
interrog.	interrogative, interrogatively
intr.	intransitive
iron.	ironical, ironically
lit.	literal, literally
Math.	Mathematics
Med.	Medicine
Mil.	Military
Mus.	Music
n.	noun
N Am.	North America, North American
Naut.	Nautical
neg.	negative, negatively
New Zeal.	New Zealand
North.	Northern
obj.	objective
opp.	opposed, opposition
orig.	originally, origin
part.	participle, participial
pass.	passive
perh.	perhaps
pers.	person, personal
pl.	plural
poet.	poetical, poetry
pop.	popular, popularly
poss.	possessive, possibly
p.p.	past participle

pred.	predicative
prep.	preposition
pron.	pronoun, pronounced
ref.	reference, referring
reflex.	reflexive
rel.	related
S Afr.	South Africa, South African
Sc.	Scottish
sing.	singular
sl.	slang
subj.	subjunctive
superl.	superlative
tr.	transitive
usu.	usually
v.	verb
verb.a.	verbal adjective
verb.n.	verbal noun
v.i.	verb intransitive
v.refl.	verb reflexive
v.tr.	verb transitive

THE THESAURUS

abandon v.t. **1** (*to give up completely*) dispense with, give up, relinquish, renounce. ANTONYMS: keep, retain. **2** (*to desert or forsake (a person)*) cast aside, desert, discard, forsake, jilt, leave, leave behind, rejected, (*coll.*) run out on, walk out on. ANTONYMS: maintain, remain with, support. **3** (*to leave or leave behind (a ship)*) evacuate, leave, quit, vacate, withdraw from. ANTONYMS: occupy. **4** (*to surrender (oneself) unreservedly*) give oneself up to, give rein to, give way to, indulge in, lose oneself in, yield to. **5** (*to yield to the control of another person*) abdicate, cede, deliver up, give up, relinquish, renounce, surrender, yield. ANTONYMS: claim, take. **6** (*to give up (something) before it is completed or ended*) cease, desist from, discontinue, drop, forgo, forswear, give up, (*sl.*) jack in, kick, (*coll.*) pack in, stop. ANTONYMS: begin, take up.

~n. (*freedom from conventional restraint, careless freedom of manner*) immoderation, impetuosity, lack of restraint, recklessness, wantonness, wildness. ANTONYMS: inhibition, restraint.

abandoned a. **1** ((*of a person*) *deserted or forsaken*) cast aside, discarded, forlorn, forsaken, jilted, rejected. ANTONYMS: cherished, maintained, supported. **2** ((*of a place etc.*) *left empty, left unused*) deserted, empty, evacuated, unused, vacated. ANTONYMS: occupied, used. **3** (*uninhibited, unrestrained*) immoderate, impetuous, reckless, uninhibited, unrestrained, wanton, wild. ANTONYMS: inhibited, restrained. **4** (*wholly given up to wickedness, profligate*) corrupt, debauched, dissipated, dissolute, immoral, profligate, reprobate, wanton, wicked. ANTONYMS: moral, righteous, virtuous.

abase v.t. (*to humble or degrade*) belittle, bring low, debase, degrade, demean, demote, discredit, disgrace, dishonour, disparage, downgrade, humble, humiliate, lower, mortify, reduce. ANTONYMS: elevate, honour, promote, upgrade.

abashed a. (*embarrassed or ashamed*) ashamed, discomfited, embarrassed, humiliated, mortified, shamefaced, taken aback. ANTONYMS: bold, confident, unashamed.

abate v.t. (*to lessen, esp. to make less violent or intense*) alleviate, appease, assuage, blunt, decrease, diminish, dull, ease, lessen, reduce, soothe. ANTONYMS: increase, intensify.

~v.i. (*to lessen or diminish, esp. to become less violent or intense*) decrease, die down, diminish, ease, ebb, lessen, let up, subside, taper off. ANTONYMS: increase, intensify.

abbey n. (*a building either now or formerly inhabited by a body of monks or nuns*) convent, friary, monastery, priory, religious house.

abbreviate v.t. (*to shorten (esp. a word or phrase) by omitting certain parts of it*) abridge, clip, compress, condense, contract, curtail, cut, cut down, cut short, précis, reduce, shorten, summarize, truncate. ANTONYMS: expand, extend, lengthen.

abbreviation n. **1** (*the act of abridging or contracting*) abridgement, clipping, compressing, condensing, contracting, curtailing, cutting, reduction, shortening, summarizing, truncating. ANTONYMS: expanding, extending, lengthening. **2** (*an abridged or shortened form, esp. of a word*) abridgement, contracted form, contraction, shortened form. **3** (*an abridgement*) abstract, digest, précis, résumé, summary, synopsis. ANTONYMS: expansion, extension.

abdicate v.t. **1** (*to resign, to renounce formally*) abjure, cede, give up, relinquish, renounce, resign from, waive, yield. ANTONYMS: take up. **2** (*to refuse to accept (responsibility)*) abandon, cast aside, give up, neglect, reject, relinquish, renounce, repudiate, turn one's back on, wash one's hands of. ANTONYMS: accept.

~v.i. (*to abandon or relinquish a throne, or other dignity or privilege*) quit, resign, retire, stand down.

abdication n. **1** (*the act of relinquishing a throne or other privilege*) quitting, resignation, retiral, retirement, standing down. **2** (*the act of renouncing something formally*) abjuration, ceding, giving up, relinquishing, relinquishment, renunciation, waiving, yielding. **3** (*the refusal to accept responsibility*) abandonment, giving up, neglect, neglecting, rejection, relinquishing, relinquishment, renunciation.

abdomen n. (*the belly*) belly, (*pl.*) gut, (*pl., coll.*) inside, intestines, paunch, stomach, (*coll.*) tum, (*coll.*) tummy.

abdominal *a.* (*belonging to the abdomen*) gastric, intestinal, stomach, stomachic, visceral.

abduct *v.t.* (*to kidnap; to take away illegally* (*esp. a woman or child*)) carry off, hold hostage, hold to ransom, kidnap, make off with, run off with, seize, snatch.

aberrant *a.* **1** (*deviating from the normal type*) abnormal, anomalous, atypical, deviant, divergent, irregular. ANTONYMS: normal, regular, typical. **2** (*inconsistent with the usual or accepted standard*) abnormal, anomalous, atypical, eccentric, extraordinary, irregular, odd, peculiar, queer, unusual. ANTONYMS: normal, ordinary, regular, typical. **3** (*wandering from the right course or way*) deviant, erring, perverted, wrong. ANTONYMS: righteous.

aberration *n.* **1** (*deviation from, or inconsistency with, the norm*) abnormality, anomaly, deviation, divergence, irregularity, variation. **2** (*a departure from a person's normal behaviour*) abnormality, eccentricity, irregularity, oddness, peculiarity, unusualness. ANTONYMS: normality, regularity. **3** (*deviation from the normal type*) derangement, disorder, vagary.

abet *v.t.* (*to encourage or aid* (*a person*) *in crime or wrongdoing by word or deed*) aid, assist, back, encourage, help, support. ANTONYMS: discourage, hinder, obstruct.

abetter *n.* (*an accessory to a crime*) accessory, accomplice, assistant, associate, backer, confederate, henchman/ henchwoman, second, supporter.

abeyance *n.* **in abeyance** (*suspended, temporarily out of use*) hanging fire, inoperative, on ice, on the back burner, out of use, shelved, suspended. ANTONYMS: in use, operative.

abhor *v.t.* (*to hate extremely, loathe*) abominate, be disgusted by, be revolted by, detest, execrate, hate, loathe, recoil from, shudder at. ANTONYMS: adore, enjoy, like, love.

abhorrence *n.* (*extreme hatred, loathing*) abomination, aversion, detestation, disgust, execration, hate, hatred, horror, loathing, repugnance, revulsion. ANTONYMS: adoration, enjoyment, liking, love.

abhorrent *a.* (*exciting loathing or hatred*) abominable, detestable, disgusting, distasteful, execrable, hated, hateful, heinous, horrible, horrid, loathsome, odious, repellent, repugnant, repulsive, revolting. ANTONYMS: admirable, attractive, likeable.

abide *v.t.* (*to endure, tolerate*) bear, brook, endure, put up with, stand, stomach, suffer, tolerate. **to abide by** (*to comply with, act upon* (*terms, a decision*)) accept, adhere to, comply with, conform to, follow, keep to, obey, observe. ANTONYMS: disobey, ignore, reject.

abiding *a.* (*continuing, permanent*) constant, continuing, durable, enduring, eternal, everlasting, immutable, lasting, permanent, persistent, persisting, stable, steadfast, unchanging, unending. ANTONYMS: ephemeral, fleeting, short-lived, temporary.

ability *n.* **1** (*the capacity or power* (*to do something*)) capability, capacity, competence, facility, faculty, potential, power. ANTONYMS: inability, incapacity. **2** (*physical or mental capacity or talent*) adeptness, adroitness, aptitude, cleverness, competence, competency, dexterity, endowment, expertise, expertness, flair, gift, knack, (*coll.*) know-how, proficiency, qualification, savoir faire, skill, talent. ANTONYMS: incompetence.

abject *a.* **1** (*miserable and wretched*) deplorable, miserable, pitiable, wretched. **2** (*very humble and submissive*) grovelling, humble, obsequious, servile, submissive, sycophantic, toadying. ANTONYMS: arrogant, proud. **3** (*contemptible, low*) base, contemptible, despicable, ignoble, ignominious, low, mean, vile, worthless. ANTONYMS: great, noble, worthy.

abjure *v.t.* **1** (*to renounce or retract upon oath*) abandon, abdicate, deny, disavow, disclaim, forswear, give up, recant, relinquish, renege on, renounce, retract. ANTONYMS: keep to, maintain. **2** (*to vow to avoid or refrain from*) abandon, abnegate, abstain from, eschew, forgo, forsake, give up, (*sl.*) jack in, kick, (*coll.*) pack in, refrain from, renounce. ANTONYMS: take up.

ablaze *adv., pred.a.* **1** (*on fire, in a blaze*) alight, blazing, burning, flaming, on fire. ANTONYMS: extinguished. **2** (*brilliant*) aglow, bright, brilliant, flashing, gleaming, illuminated, lit up. ANTONYMS: dark, dull. **3** (*excited*) animated, aroused, excited, impassioned, passionate. ANTONYMS: apathetic.

able *a.* **1** (*having sufficient power or acquired skill to do something indicated*) capable, competent. ANTONYMS: incapable. **2** (*gifted, active*) accomplished, adept, adroit, apt, capable, clever, competent, dexterous, effective, expert, fit, gifted, proficient, qualified, skilful, skilled, talented. ANTONYMS: incompetent, inept, mediocre, talentless.

able-bodied *a.* (*having a sound, strong body*) fit, healthy, robust, strong, sturdy, vigorous. ANTONYMS: debilitated, frail, ill, weak.

abnegate *v.t.* (*to deny oneself, to renounce*)

abandon, abjure, abstain from, deny oneself, eschew, forgo, forsake, give up, (*sl.*) jack in, kick, (*coll.*) pack in, refrain from, refuse, reject, relinquish, renounce, sacrifice.

abnegation *n.* **1** (*denial, renunciation*) abandonment, abjuration, abstention, eschewal, eschewing, giving up, refusal, rejection, relinquishment, renunciation, sacrifice. **2** (*self-sacrifice*) abstinence, self-denial, self-sacrifice, temperance. ANTONYMS: indulgence, intemperance.

abnormal *a.* (*not normal or typical*) aberrant, anomalous, atypical, curious, deviant, divergent, eccentric, exceptional, extraordinary, irregular, odd, oddball, off the wall, outré, peculiar, queer, singular, strange, uncommon, unnatural, untypical, unusual, weird. ANTONYMS: common, regular, typical, usual.

abnormality *n.* **1** (*departure from the normal or typical*) anomaly, deviation, divergence, eccentricity, irregularity, oddness, peculiarity, queerness, singularity, strangeness, uncommonness, unnaturalness, weirdness. ANTONYMS: commonness, normality, ordinariness, regularity. **2** (*irregularity, deformity*) aberration, anomaly, deformity, deviation, irregularity, malformation.

abode *n.* (*place of residence; a habitation*) accommodation, domicile, dwelling, dwelling-place, habitat, habitation, home, house, lodging, quarters, residence.

abolish *v.t.* **1** (*to do away with, put an end to*) annihilate, axe, destroy, do away with, eliminate, end, eradicate, expunge, exterminate, extirpate, obliterate, overthrow, put an end to, quash, stamp out, terminate, wipe out. **2** (*to cancel or revoke* (*used of laws or offices*)) annul, axe, cancel, invalidate, nullify, repeal, rescind, revoke, void. ANTONYMS: pass, validate.

abolition *n.* **1** (*the act of abolishing or doing away with*) annihilation, axing, destruction, elimination, ending, eradication, expunging, extermination, extirpation, obliteration, overthrow, quashing, termination, wiping out. **2** (*the state of being abolished*) annulment, axing, cancellation, invalidation, nullification, repeal, rescinding, revocation, voiding. ANTONYMS: validation.

abominable *a.* **1** (*very loathsome, hateful*) abhorrent, contemptible, despicable, detestable, disgusting, execrable, hateful, heinous, horrible, loathsome, nasty, nauseous, obnoxious, odious, offensive, repellent, repugnant, repulsive, revolting, unpleasant, vile. ANTONYMS: attractive, delightful, likeable, lovely, pleasant. **2** (*very bad, awful*) awful, bad, (*coll.*)

god-awful, (*coll.*) rotten, (*coll.*) terrible, unfortunate. ANTONYMS: fortunate, good.

abominate *v.t.* (*to loathe, to hate exceedingly*) abhor, detest, execrate, feel disgust for, feel revulsion for, hate, have an aversion to, loathe, recoil from, shudder at. ANTONYMS: admire, adore, like, love.

abomination *n.* **1** (*extreme hatred or loathing*) abhorrence, aversion, detestation, disgust, distaste, execration, hate, hatred, horror, loathing, odium, repugnance, revulsion. ANTONYMS: admiration, liking, love. **2** (*something that is vile or hateful*) anathema, bête noire, bugbear, curse, horror, plague, torment.

aboriginal *a.* (*original, inhabiting a place from the earliest times*) ancient, autochthonous, earliest, first, indigenous, native, original. ANTONYMS: immigrant.

abort *v.t.* **1** (*to cause* (*a foetus*) *to be expelled from the womb before it is able to survive independently*) terminate. **2** (*to terminate prematurely or in the early stages*) axe, call a halt to, call off, end, halt, put a stop to, stop, terminate. ANTONYMS: begin, set up.
~*v.i.* **1** ((*of a foetus*) *to be expelled from the womb prematurely;* (*of a mother*) *to miscarry*) have a miscarriage, have an abortion, miscarry, undergo a termination. **2** (*to end prematurely or unsuccessfully*) come to a halt, end, fail, stop, terminate.

abortion *n.* **1** (*a procedure to induce the premature expulsion of a foetus*) termination. **2** (*the act of miscarrying*) miscarriage. **3** (*anything that fails or is terminated prematurely*) defeat, disappointment, failure, fiasco. ANTONYMS: success, triumph.

abortive *a.* (*fruitless, failing in its effect*) failed, fruitless, futile, ineffective, ineffectual, unavailing, unproductive, unsuccessful, useless, vain, worthless. ANTONYMS: effective, effectual, productive, successful.

abound *v.i.* **1** (*to be present in great quantities*) be plentiful, flourish, proliferate, superabound, thrive. ANTONYMS: be scarce. **2** (*to be rich* (*in*), *to be copiously supplied* (*with*)) be alive (with), be crawling (with), be crowded (with), be full (of), be jammed (with), be packed (with), be rich (in), be thronged (with), overflow (with), swarm (with), teem (with).

abounding *a.* (*plentiful, copious*) abundant, copious, flourishing, luxuriant, plenteous, plentiful, profuse, prolific, rich, superabundant, teeming. ANTONYMS: scarce, sparse.

about *prep.* **1** (*concerning, in connection with*) concerning, connected with, re, referring to, regarding, relating to, respecting, touching on, with reference to, with regard to, with respect to. **2** (*near in time*) almost, approaching, approximately, circa, nearly, roughly. **3** (*near in space*) adjacent to, beside, close by, near, nearby. **4** (*surrounding, around the outside of*) around, encircling, round, surrounding. **5** (*here and there within*) around, over, through, throughout. **6** (*engaged in*) busy with, engaged in, occupied with.

~*adv.* **1** (*approximately; nearly*) almost, approximately, close to, nearly. **2** (*here and there; in different places and, usu., having various experiences*) around, from place to place, here and there, hither and thither, to and fro. **3** (*nearby or present in a particular locality*) about the place, around, hereabouts, in the vicinity, near, nearby. **4** (*in existence, current*) around, current, going around, happening, in circulation, in existence, present, prevalent. **to be about to** (*to be on the point of* (*doing something*)) be intending to, be on the brink of, be on the point of, be on the verge of, be preparing to, be ready to, be soon to.

above *prep.* **1** (*over, at or to a higher point than*) higher than, on top of, over. ANTONYMS: below. **2** (*in excess of, more than*) exceeding, greater than, higher than, in excess of, more than, over, surpassing. ANTONYMS: below, less than, lower than. **3** (*superior to, more important than*) higher than, over, superior to. ANTONYMS: below, lower than, subordinate to. **4** (*too noble for; untouched by because of* (*one's*) *reputation, honesty etc.*) beyond, not liable to, not open to, not subject to. **5** (*beyond the understanding of*) beyond, beyond the understanding of, too difficult for. **6** (*more than and in preference to*) before, in preference to, more than, rather than.

~*adv.* **1** (*in a higher place or position; upstairs, on a higher floor*) aloft, high up, on high, overhead. ANTONYMS: below, low down. **2** (*at a previous point*) before, earlier, previously, prior to this. ANTONYMS: later.

~*a.* (*above-mentioned, given at a previous point in something written*) aforementioned, aforesaid, earlier, foregoing, preceding, previous, prior. ANTONYMS: below, later. **above all** (*principally, before everything else*) before all else, first and foremost, first of all, mainly, most importantly, principally. **above oneself** (*arrogant; conceited*) arrogant, (*coll.*) big-headed, conceited, proud, self-important, stuck-up, supercilious, superior. ANTONYMS: modest, self-effacing.

above board *adv., a.* (*(done) openly; without dishonesty or trickery*) candid, fair, forthright, frank, honest, honourable, open, straight. ANTONYMS: devious, dishonest, furtive, secret.

abrade *v.t.* (*to rub or wear away by friction*) erode, grind, rub away, scour, scrape, wear away, wear down.

abrasion *n.* **1** (*the act of rubbing away or wearing down*) erosion, grinding, rubbing away, scouring, scraping, wearing away, wearing down. **2** (*a superficial lesion of the skin*) graze, scrape, scratch, sore.

abrasive *a.* **1** (*tending to rub; able to polish by abrading*) coarse, erosive, frictional, harsh, rough, scraping, scratching. ANTONYMS: smooth. **2** ((*of a person's manner*) *causing friction or irritation*) aggressive, biting, caustic, cutting, harsh, irritating, rough, sharp, vitriolic. ANTONYMS: smooth, soothing.

abreast *adv.* **1** (*side by side with the fronts in line*) alongside, beside each other, level, shoulder to shoulder, side by side. **2** (*up to date, aware* (*of*)) acquainted (with), au fait (with), aware (of), conversant (with), familiar (with), informed (about), in touch (with), knowledgeable (about), up to date (with). ANTONYMS: ignorant (of), unaware (of), uninformed (about).

abridge *v.t.* (*to reduce the length of* (*a book etc.*)) abbreviate, compress, concentrate, condense, contract, curtail, cut, cut down, decrease, précis, reduce, shorten, summarize, trim, truncate. ANTONYMS: expand, extend, lengthen.

abridgement *n.* **1** (*a condensed version*) abstract, contraction, digest, outline, précis, résumé, summary, synopsis. **2** (*the act of abridging*) abbreviating, abridging, condensation, contraction, curtailment, cutting, reduction, shortening, summarizing, truncation. ANTONYMS: expansion, extension, lengthening.

abroad *adv.* **1** (*in or to a foreign country*) in/ to a foreign country, in/ to foreign parts, out of the country, overseas. ANTONYMS: at/ to home, home, in/ to one's native land. **2** ((*of news, rumour*) *circulating*) circulating, in circulation, publicly.

abrogate *v.t.* (*to annul by an authoritative act; to repeal*) abolish, annul, cancel, countermand, invalidate, nullify, repeal, repudiate, rescind, retract, reverse, revoke, void, withdraw. ANTONYMS: confirm, validate.

abrogation *n.* (*the act of abrogating; repeal*) abolition, annulment, cancellation, countermanding, invalidation, nullification, repeal, repudiation, rescinding, rescission, retraction, reversal, revocation, voiding, withdrawal. ANTONYMS: confirmation, validation.

abrupt *a.* **1** (*sudden, unexpected*) hasty, headlong, hurried, precipitate, quick, rapid, sudden, surprising, swift, unexpected, unforeseen. ANTONYMS: anticipated, expected, gradual, slow. **2** (*brusque, curt*) blunt, brisk, brusque, crisp, curt, gruff, impolite, offhand, rude, short, snappy, terse, unceremonious. ANTONYMS: civil, long-winded, polite. **3** (*very steep, precipitous*) precipitous, sharp, steep, sudden. ANTONYMS: gradual. **4** ((*of writing etc.*) *marked by sudden changes in subject*) disconnected, discontinuous, disjointed, irregular, jerky, rough, uneven. ANTONYMS: elegant, flowing, regular.

abscond *v.i.* (*to go away secretly or in a hurry*) bolt, clear out, decamp, disappear, (*sl.*) do a bunk, (*sl.*) do a runner, escape, flee, fly, make off, run away, (*coll.*) skedaddle, slip away, sneak away, steal off.

absence *n.* **1** (*the state of being absent from a place, event etc.*) absenteeism, nonappearance, non-attendance, truancy. ANTONYMS: appearance, attendance, presence. **2** (*a lack (of); the non-existence (of)*) lack, need, non-existence, omission, unavailability, want. ANTONYMS: existence, presence.

absent *a.* **1** (*away from or not present in a place*) away, elsewhere, gone, missing, not present, off, out, truant. ANTONYMS: present. **2** (*lacking, missing*) lacking, missing, non-existent, unavailable, wanting. ANTONYMS: available, existent, present.

absent-minded *a.* (*inattentive, abstracted in mind from immediate objects or business*) absorbed, abstracted, day-dreaming, distracted, distrait(e), dreaming, dreamy, engrossed, faraway, forgetful, in a brown study, inattentive, preoccupied, unheeding, unthinking. ANTONYMS: alert, attentive, vigilant.

absolute *a.* **1** (*complete, utter*) arrant, complete, consummate, downright, entire, out and out, outright, perfect, pure, sheer, thorough, total, unadulterated, unmitigated, unqualified, utter. ANTONYMS: partial, slight. **2** (*independent, under no restraint*) boundless, full, infinite, supreme, total, ultimate, unbounded, unconditional, unlimited, unrestrained, unrestricted, utter. ANTONYMS: conditional, limited, restricted. **3** (*arbitrary, despotic*) arbitrary, authoritarian, autocratic, autonomous, despotic, dictatorial, tyrannical. ANTONYMS: democratic. **4** (*universally valid, not conditional*) established, fixed, independent, rigid, set. **5** (*not subject to doubt or uncertainty*) actual, categorical, certain, conclusive, decided, decisive, definite, genuine, positive, sure, undoubted, unquestionable. ANTONYMS: doubtful, indefinite, questionable.

absolutely *adv.* **1** (*totally, unconditionally*) completely, entirely, perfectly, purely, thoroughly, totally, utterly, wholly. ANTONYMS: partly, slightly. **2** (*certainly, definitely*) actually, categorically, certainly, conclusively, decidedly, definitely, genuinely, positively, surely, unquestionably, without a doubt. ANTONYMS: doubtfully, questionably. **3** (*in an arbitrary or despotic manner*) arbitrarily, autocratically, autonomously, despotically, dictatorially, tyrannically.

absolution *n.* (*acquittal, forgiveness*) acquittal, deliverance, discharge, exoneration, forgiveness, freeing, liberation, pardoning, remission, reprieve, vindication. ANTONYMS: conviction, guilt, punishment.

absolve *v.t.* (*to pardon; acquit*) acquit, discharge, exonerate, forgive, free, liberate, pardon, reprieve, vindicate. ANTONYMS: convict, find guilty, punish.

absorb *v.t.* **1** (*to suck or soak up*) blot up, drink up, mop up, soak up, suck up. **2** (*to incorporate*) appropriate, assimilate, incorporate, swallow up, take in. **3** (*to fully occupy the attention of, to engross*) captivate, engage, engross, fascinate, grip, hold, immerse, interest, involve, occupy, preoccupy, rivet. ANTONYMS: bore, weary.

absorbed *a.* (*fully engrossed*) captivated, engaged, engrossed, fascinated, gripped, immersed, interested, involved, occupied, preoccupied, rapt, riveted, spellbound, wrapped up. ANTONYMS: bored, uninterested, wearied.

absorbent *a.* (*absorbing, tending to absorb*) absorbing, absorptive, penetrable, permeable, porous, spongelike, spongy. ANTONYMS: impenetrable, impermeable.

absorbing *a.* (*occupying one's complete attention*) captivating, engrossing, fascinating, gripping, interesting, preoccupying, riveting, spellbinding. ANTONYMS: boring, dull, tedious, wearisome.

absorption *n.* **1** (*the act of absorbing*) blotting up, mopping up, soaking up, sucking up. **2** (*the process of being absorbed*) appropriation, assimilation, incorporation, swallowing up, taking in. **3** (*the engrossing of someone's attention*) captivation, concentration, engagement, engrossment, fascination, immersion, intentness, interest, involvement, occupation, preoccupation, raptness. ANTONYMS: boredom, lack of concentration, lack of interest.

abstain *v.i.* **1** (*to keep oneself away, refrain (from)*) avoid, decline (to), desist (from), eschew, forbear (to), forgo, give up, hold back (from), keep (from), refrain (from), refuse.

ANTONYMS: indulge (in). **2** (*to refrain voluntarily from intoxicating liquors*) (*coll.*) be on the wagon, be teetotal, have taken the pledge. ANTONYMS: be an alcoholic, drink, overimbibe.

abstemious *a.* (*sparing, not self-indulgent, esp. in the use of food and strong liquors*) abstinent, ascetic, frugal, moderate, puritanical, self-denying, self-restrained, sober, sparing, temperate. ANTONYMS: immoderate, intemperate, self-indulgent.

abstention *n.* (*the act of abstaining or refraining, esp. from exercising one's right to vote*) abstaining, avoidance, desistance, forbearing, refraining, refusal.

abstinence *n.* (*the act or practice of refraining from some indulgence*) abstemiousness, asceticism, moderation, self-denial, self-restraint, soberness, sobriety, teetotalism, temperance. ANTONYMS: excess, immoderation, indulgence, self-indulgence.

abstract[1] *v.t.* **1** (*to take away, remove*) detach, dissociate, draw away, extract, isolate, remove, separate, take away, take out. ANTONYMS: attach, combine. **2** (*to epitomize, summarize*) abbreviate, abridge, compress, condense, contract, cut down, epitomize, outline, précis, shorten, summarize. ANTONYMS: expand, extend, lengthen.

abstract[2] *a.* **1** (*not related to concrete or particular instances*) conceptual, hypothetical, ideal, intellectual, notional, philosophical, theoretic, theoretical. ANTONYMS: concrete, tangible. **2** (*abstruse*) abstruse, arcane, complex, deep, obscure, profound, recondite, subtle. ANTONYMS: clear, perceptible, plain, self-evident. **3** ((*of art*) *non-representational*) non-realistic, non-representational, unrealistic. ANTONYMS: realistic, true-to-life.

abstracted *a.* (*absent-minded, withdrawn in thought*) absent-minded, absorbed in thought, daydreaming, distracted, distrait(e), dreaming, dreamy, faraway, in a brown study, inattentive, lost in thought, pensive, preoccupied, thoughtful, withdrawn, wool-gathering. ANTONYMS: attentive, concentrating, intent.

abstraction *n.* **1** (*the act of abstracting or separating*) detachment, dissociation, extraction, isolation, removal, separation. ANTONYMS: attachment, combination. **2** (*the state of being engrossed in thought; absent-mindedness*) absent-mindedness, absorption, daydreaming, distraction, dreaming, inattention, inattentiveness, pensiveness, preoccupation, thoughtfulness. ANTONYMS: attentiveness, concentration. **3** (*an abstract idea*) concept, generality, hypothesis, idea, notion, philosophy, theory.

abstruse *a.* (*difficult to understand*) abstract, arcane, complex, deep, difficult, enigmatic, esoteric, hidden, incomprehensible, mysterious, obscure, perplexing, profound, puzzling, recondite, subtle, unfathomable. ANTONYMS: clear, manifest, plain, transparent.

absurd *a.* **1** (*ridiculous, ludicrous*) comical, daft, farcical, funny, idiotic, laughable, ludicrous, ridiculous, silly. ANTONYMS: serious. **2** (*inconsistent with reason; nonsensical*) crazy, foolish, idiotic, illogical, inane, irrational, nonsensical, ridiculous, senseless, silly, stupid, unreasonable. ANTONYMS: logical, rational, sensible, wise.

absurdity *n.* **1** (*the quality or state of being absurd*) craziness, daftness, farce, farcicalness, folly, foolishness, funniness, idiocy, illogicality, inanity, irrationality, ludicrousness, preposterous, ridiculousness, senselessness, silliness, stupidity, unreasonableness. ANTONYMS: cleverness, logic, logicality, sense, seriousness, wisdom. **2** (*an absurd notion or statement*) foolishness, gibberish, nonsense, rubbish, twaddle. ANTONYMS: sense.

abundance *n.* (*a more than sufficient quantity or number* (*of*)) ampleness, amplitude, (*coll.*) bags, copiousness, (*coll.*) heaps, lavishness, (*coll.*) loads, (*coll.*) oodles, plenteousness, plenty, profusion, (*coll.*) stacks, (*coll.*) tons. ANTONYMS: inadequacy, insufficiency, scantness, sparseness.

abundant *a.* (*more than sufficient, ample*) ample, bountiful, copious, generous, great, huge, large, lavish, plentiful, profuse. ANTONYMS: inadequate, insufficient, scanty, sparse.

abuse[1] *v.t.* **1** (*to put to an improper use, misuse*) exploit, misapply, misemploy, misuse, take advantage of. **2** (*to insult, to use coarse language to*) curse, insult, inveigh against, swear at, vilify. ANTONYMS: compliment, disparage, praise. **3** (*to maltreat, act cruelly to*) damage, harm, hurt, ill-treat, ill-use, injure, maltreat, mistreat. ANTONYMS: care for, cherish, protect.

abuse[2] *n.* **1** (*improper treatment, misuse*) exploitation, misapplication, misemployment, misuse. **2** (*a corrupt practice or custom*) corruption, crime, fault, misconduct, misdeed, offence, wrong, wrongdoing. **3** (*insulting or scurrilous language*) curses, cursing, disparagement, insults, invective, revilement, vilification. ANTONYMS: compliments, praise. **4** (*physical maltreatment; sexual mistreatment*) brutality, cruelty, damage, harm, hurt, ill-treatment, ill-use, injury, maltreatment, mistreatment. ANTONYMS: care, protection.

abusive *a.* **1** ((*of language*) *scurrilous or*

insulting) disparaging, insulting, offensive, rude, scathing, scurrilous, vilifying, vituperative. ANTONYMS: complimentary, flattering. **2** (*subjecting others to physical or sexual abuse*) brutal, cruel, damaging, harmful, hurtful, injurious.

abut *v.i.* (*to border* (*on or upon*)) adjoin, be contiguous, be next to, border on, join, meet, touch.

abutting *a.* (*adjacent*) adjacent, adjoining, bordering, contiguous, joining, neighbouring, next.

abysmal *a.* **1** (*extremely bad*) inadequate, pathetic, poor, (*coll.*) terrible, woeful. ANTONYMS: first-class, (*coll.*) marvellous. **2** (*profound, immeasurable*) boundless, complete, deep, extreme, immeasurable, infinite, profound, utter.

abyss *n.* **1** (*a vast physical chasm or cavity*) chasm, gorge, gulf, pit, ravine, void. **2** (*anything conceived of as immensely deep and unfathomable*) chasm, depths, hell, hell-hole.

academic *a.* **1** (*of or relating to a college or university*) educational, pedagogical, scholastic. **2** (*scholarly*) bookish, brainy, erudite, highbrow, intellectual, learned, literary, scholarly, studious, well-read. ANTONYMS: ignorant, lowbrow. **3** (*impractical, unrelated to practical concerns*) abstract, conjectural, hypothetical, impractical, notional, speculative, theoretical. ANTONYMS: concrete, practical. ~*n.* (*a member of the staff of a college or university etc.*) don, (*coll.*) egghead, lecturer, pedagogue, professor, teacher.

accede *v.i.* **1** (*to agree* (*to*), *assent* (*to*)) accept, acquiesce (in), agree (to), assent (to), comply (with), concur (in), consent (to), endorse, go along (with), yield (to). ANTONYMS: disagree (with), refuse, turn one's back (on). **2** (*to come to or attain* (*an office or dignity*)) assume, attain, come to, enter upon, inherit, succeed to. ANTONYMS: abdicate from, give up, resign from.

accelerate *v.t.* (*to increase the speed or rate of progress*) advance, expedite, facilitate, hasten, hurry up, precipitate, quicken, speed up, spur on, (*coll.*) step up, stimulate. ANTONYMS: delay, hinder, impede, slow down. ~*v.i.* (*to increase in velocity or rate of progress*) go faster, hasten, hurry, pick up speed, quicken, speed up. ANTONYMS: brake, slow, slow down.

acceleration *n.* (*the act of accelerating*) advancing, expedition, facilitation, hastening, hurrying up, precipitation, quickening, speeding up, spurring. ANTONYMS: deceleration, slowing down.

accent[1] *n.* **1** (*a manner of speaking or pronunciation peculiar to an individual, a locality or a nation*) enunciation, inflection, intonation, modulation, pronunciation. **2** (*a particular prominence given to a syllable by means of stress or higher musical pitch*) accentuation, emphasis, force, stress. **3** (*a mark used in writing or printing certain languages, usu. placed over particular letters*) diacritic, diacritical mark, mark, sign. **4** (*emphasis or attention given to something*) accentuation, emphasis, highlighting, importance, priority, prominence, stress, underlining.

accent[2] *v.t.* **1** (*to lay stress upon* (*a syllable or word, or a note or passage of music*)) accentuate, emphasize, lay stress on, maximize, place emphasis on, place stress on, put emphasis on, put stress on, stress. **2** (*to mark with emphasis, make conspicuous*) accentuate, draw attention to, emphasize, give prominence to, heighten, highlight, maximize, place emphasis on, point up, put stress on, underline. ANTONYMS: play down, underplay, understate.

accentuate *v.t.* (*to lay stress on, to emphasize*) accent, draw attention to, emphasize, give prominence to, heighten, highlight, lay emphasis on, lay stress on, maximize, place emphasis on, put stress on, underline. ANTONYMS: gloss over, make light of, minimize, underplay, understate.

accept *v.t.* **1** (*to consent to take* (*something offered*)) receive, take, take receipt of. ANTONYMS: decline, refuse, reject. **2** (*to give a positive response to* (*an invitation, recommendation*)) reply in the positive to, say yes to. ANTONYMS: decline, reject, say no to. **3** (*to behave in a friendly or approving way towards*) embrace, receive, welcome. ANTONYMS: reject, repudiate. **4** (*to admit the truth of, to receive as valid*) believe, credit, have faith in, trust. ANTONYMS: disbelieve. **5** (*to admit, to be willing to acknowledge*) acknowledge, admit, recognize. ANTONYMS: reject. **6** (*to be willing to submit to* (*a referee's decision*)) acquiesce in, agree to, bow to, comply with, concur with, consent to, defer to, go along with, submit to, yield to. ANTONYMS: challenge, disagree with, dispute, reject. **7** (*to undertake the responsibilities or duties of*) assume, be responsible for, tackle, take upon oneself.

acceptable *a.* **1** (*adequate, satisfactory*) adequate, all right, fair, good enough, passable, satisfactory, tolerable. ANTONYMS: intolerable, unacceptable, unsatisfactory. **2** (*welcome, pleasing*) agreeable, delightful, gratifying, nice, pleasant, pleasing, welcome. ANTONYMS: disagreeable, nasty, unpleasant, unwelcome.

3 ((*of behaviour*) *approved of and considered normal*) admissible, allowable, tolerable. ANTONYMS: inadmissible, intolerable, unacceptable.

acceptance *n.* **1** (*the act of receiving a thing offered or due*) receipt, receiving, taking. ANTONYMS: refusal, rejection. **2** (*agreement to terms; an act of accepting an invitation etc.*) acquiescence, agreement, compliance, concurrence, consent, deference, submitting, yielding. ANTONYMS: refusal, rejection. **3** (*an act of accepting an invitation etc.*) accepting, reply in the affirmative, saying yes to. ANTONYMS: refusal, rejection. **4** (*friendly or approving behaviour towards*) embrace, reception, warm reception, welcome. ANTONYMS: rejection, repudiation. **5** (*general approval or belief*) approval, belief, credence, currency, trust. ANTONYMS: disbelief. **6** (*admission, acknowledgement*) acknowledgement, admission, recognition. ANTONYMS: rejection. **7** (*the undertaking of responsibilities or duties*) assumption, tackling, undertaking.

accepted *a.* **1** (*generally approved*) acknowledged, admitted, agreed, allowed, approved, disputed, sanctioned. **2** (*generally recognized*) acknowledged, common, conventional, customary, established, expected, normal, recognized, standard, traditional, usual. ANTONYMS: abnormal, uncommon, unconventional, unusual.

access *n.* **1** (*admission to a place or person*) admission, admittance, entrée. **2** (*a means of approach or entry*) approach, channel, entrance, entry, passage, road, way in. **3** (*a sudden, usu. violent, attack of a disease or emotion*) fit, onset, outburst, paroxysm.
~*v.t.* (*to gain access to, esp. to retrieve* (*data*) *from computer storage*) gain, gain access to, get hold of, retrieve.

accessibility *n.* **1** (*the fact that a place can be easily approached*) approachability. ANTONYMS: inaccessibility. **2** (*the fact that something can be easily obtained*) achievability, availability, handiness, nearness, obtainability. ANTONYMS: inaccessibility. **3** (*the fact that someone is approachable*) affability, affableness, approachability, availability, cordiality, friendliness, pleasantness. ANTONYMS: inaccessibility. **4** (*the fact that something is not difficult to understand*) comprehensibility, intelligibility, penetrability. ANTONYMS: impenetrability, incomprehensibility.

accessible *a.* **1** (*capable of being reached; easy to approach*) approachable, reachable. ANTONYMS: far-off, inaccessible. **2** (*easy to reach or obtain*) achievable, at hand, attainable, available, (*coll.*) get-at-able, handy, near,

nearby, obtainable, on hand, reachable, ready, to hand. ANTONYMS: inaccessible, unavailable, unobtainable. **3** ((*of a person*) *readily available* (*esp. to subordinates*); *approachable*) affable, approachable, available, cordial, friendly, pleasant. ANTONYMS: inaccessible, unapproachable. **4** (*not difficult to understand*) comprehensible, fathomable, intelligible, penetrable, understandable. ANTONYMS: impenetrable, incomprehensible.

accession *n.* **1** (*coming to the throne; becoming the holder of an office, rank or dignity*) assumption, attaining, attainment, entering, inheritance, succession. ANTONYMS: abdication, resignation. **2** (*the act of acceding to a treaty, agreement etc.*) acceptance, acquiescence, agreement, assent, compliance, concurrence, consent, endorsement. ANTONYMS: disagreement, refusal. **3** (*an increase, addition, esp. a book added to the stock of a library*) addition, augmentation, enlargement, expansion, extension, increase, increment. ANTONYMS: decrease, diminution.

accessory *n.* **1** (*a supplementary thing*) addition, add-on, adjunct, adornment, appendage, attachment, decoration, extra, fitment, frill, supplement, trim, trimming. **2** (*a person who is involved in a crime without actually being present when it is committed*) abettor, accomplice, assistant, associate, confederate, helper, partner.
~*a.* (*additional; accompanying*) additional, ancillary, auxiliary, contributory, extra, secondary, subordinate, supplemental, supplementary. ANTONYMS: main, principal.

accident *n.* **1** (*a mishap, esp. one that results in danger or injury*) calamity, disaster, misadventure, misfortune, mishap. **2** (*chance*) chance, fate, fortuity, fortune, luck, twist of fate. **3** (*a crash involving vehicles and people*) car accident, car crash, collision, crash, (*coll.*) pile-up, traffic accident. **by accident 1** (*unintentionally*) accidentally, by mistake, inadvertently, unintentionally, unwittingly, without premeditation. ANTONYMS: by design, deliberately, intentionally, on purpose. **2** (*by chance, fortuitously*) accidentally, by chance, fortuitously, unexpectedly, without arrangement, without planning. ANTONYMS: as planned, by arrangement.

accidental *a.* **1** (*occurring by chance or unexpectedly*) adventitious, casual, chance, fortuitous, inadvertent, unexpected, unforeseen, unintended, unintentional, unplanned, unpremeditated, unwitting. ANTONYMS: deliberate, intended, intentional, planned. **2** (*adventitious, non-essential*) incidental, inessential,

non-essential, subsidiary, supplemental. ANTO-
NYMS: essential.

accidentally *adv.* **1** (*unintentionally*) by
accident, by mistake, inadvertently, unintentionally, unwittingly, without premeditation.
ANTONYMS: by design, deliberately, intentionally, on purpose. **2** (*by chance, fortuitously*)
by accident, by chance, fortuitously, unexpectedly, without arrangement, without planning. ANTONYMS: as planned, by arrangement.

acclaim *v.t.* **1** (*to greet or receive with great enthusiasm*) applaud, cheer, commend, eulogize
over, extol, hail, laud, offer congratulations to,
pay homage to, pay tribute to, praise, salute.
ANTONYMS: censure, criticize, disparage, give
flak to. **2** (*to announce publicly and with great
enthusiasm*) announce, declare, hail, proclaim.
~*n.* (*enthusiastic praise or approval*) acclamation, applause, approbation, approval,
bouquets, cheering, cheers, commendation,
congratulations, eulogy, exaltation, homage,
laudation, ovation, plaudits, praise, tribute.
ANTONYMS: criticism, disparagement, flak.

acclamation *n.* **1** (*the act of acclaiming;
enthusiastic approval*) applause, approbation,
approval, cheering, commendation, congratulations, eulogy, exaltation, homage,
laudation, ovation, plaudits, praise, salutation, tribute. **2** (*the act of announcing something publicly and with great enthusiasm*)
announcement, declaration, hailing, proclamation.

acclimatization *n.* (*the act or process of
acclimatizing*) accommodation, adaptation,
adjustment, familiarization, habituation,
inurement, naturalization.

acclimatize *v.t.* (*to habituate to a new climate
or environment*) accustom, adapt, adjust,
familiarize, habituate, inure.
~*v.i.* (*to become used to a new climate or
environment*) accommodate, adapt, adjust,
become accustomed, become familiar, become
inured, become naturalized, become seasoned,
become used, get used, grow used.

acclivity *n.* (*an upward slope, as distinct from
declivity*) ascent, hill, rise, rising ground,
slope. ANTONYMS: declivity, depression.

accommodate *v.t.* **1** (*to provide lodging for*)
board, house, lodge, provide housing for, put a
roof over someone's head, put up, shelter. **2** (*to
have or provide space for*) have room for, have
space for, house, take. **3** (*to fit, adapt or adjust*)
acclimatize, accustom, adapt, adjust, conform,
familiarize, fit, harmonize, modify. **4** (*to do a
favour for, oblige*) aid, assist, do (someone) a
favour, help, oblige. **5** (*to supply or furnish*

(*with*)) afford, furnish, give, grant, provide,
serve, supply. ANTONYMS: deprive.

accommodating *a.* (*obliging, yielding to
others' desires*) complaisant, compliant, cooperative, friendly, helpful, kind, obliging,
pliable, unselfish. ANTONYMS: disobliging, obstructive, uncooperative, unhelpful.

accommodation *n.* **1** (*a place to live or stay,
lodgings*) home, house, housing, lodging,
quarters, residence, shelter. **2** (*space, or a
place, to keep or store something*) capacity,
room, space. **3** (*adjustment; the state of being
fitted or adapted*) acclimatization, adaptation,
adjustment, conformity, familiarization, fitting, harmonization, modification. **4** (*the act of
doing someone a favour*) aid, assistance,
favour, help, obliging. **5** (*the act of supplying or
furnishing something*) affording, furnishing,
giving, granting, provision, serving, supply.

accompaniment *n.* **1** (*something which gives
greater completeness to*) addition, complement, supplement. **2** (*the escorting of someone, attending as a companion*) attendance,
chaperonage, chaperoning, conducting, escorting, squiring, ushering. **3** (*existence alongside
something*) coexistence, coincidence, concurrence.

accompany *v.t.* **1** (*to go with, attend as a companion*) attend, chaperone, conduct, escort, go
along with, go with, keep (someone) company,
squire, usher. **2** (*to exist along with; to be a
characteristic of*) be associated with, be
connected with, be related to, coexist with,
coincide with, go together with, go with, occur
with. **3** (*to supplement*) complement, go with,
supplement. **4** (*to play the instrumental accompaniment for*) play for, play with.

accompanying *a.* (*going with or existing along
with someone or something*) added, additional,
associated, attendant, complementary, concomitant, connected, related, supplementary.

accomplice *n.* (*a partner, esp. in crime*)
abettor, accessory, ally, assistant, associate,
collaborator, colleague, confederate, fellow-
conspirator, helper, henchman/ henchwoman,
partner.

accomplish *v.t.* **1** (*to complete, to finish*) complete, conclude, consummate, effect, finish,
fulfil. ANTONYMS: begin, give up, start. **2** (*to
carry out, achieve*) achieve, bring about, bring
off, carry out, do, effect, effectuate, execute,
fulfil, perform, realize. ANTONYMS: fail.

accomplished *a.* **1** (*complete, finished*)
complete, completed, concluded, effected,
finished, fulfilled. ANTONYMS: incomplete,
unfinished. **2** (*highly skilled, consummate*)

able, adept, consummate, deft, expert, gifted, masterly, polished, practised, proficient, skilful, skilled, talented. ANTONYMS: amateurish, inexpert, poor, talentless.

accomplishment *n.* **1** (*the act of accomplishing or fulfilling*) achievement, effecting, effectuating, execution, fulfilment, performance, realization. ANTONYMS: failure. **2** (*the act of completing or finishing something*) completion, conclusion, consummation, effecting, finishing, fulfilment. **3** (*something achieved*) achievement, attainment, deed, feat, triumph. **4** (*an attainment, esp. a social skill*) ability, art, attainment, gift, proficiency, skill, social skill, talent.

accord *v.t.* (*to grant, to bestow*) allow, bestow, confer, endow, give, grant, offer, present, tender. ANTONYMS: refuse, withhold.
~*v.i.* (*to agree or be in harmony* (*with*)) agree (with), assent (to), be in agreement (with), be in harmony (with), coincide (with), concur (with), conform (to), correspond (with), fit (in with), give one's assent (to), match, tally (with). ANTONYMS: conflict (with), differ (from), disagree (with).
~*n.* (*agreement, assent*) agreement, assent, concord, concurrence, harmony, unison. ANTONYMS: conflict, disagreement, discord, dispute. **according to 1** (*in proportion or relation to*) commensurate with, in proportion to, in relation to. **2** (*as stated or reported by*) as reported by, as stated by, on the authority of, to quote. **3** (*in conformity with*) complying with, in accordance with, in accord with, in conformity with, in keeping with, in line with. **of one's own accord** (*voluntarily*) freely, of one's own free will, voluntarily, willingly. **with one accord** (*with the assent of all*) as one, concertedly, in complete agreement, unanimously, with one voice.

accordance *n.* **in accordance with** (*in conformity with, in such a way as to correspond to*) according to, complying with, in accord with, in conformity with, in keeping with, in line with.

accordingly *adv.* **1** (*suitably, in accordance*) appropriately, correspondingly, fitly, properly, suitably. **2** (*therefore, consequently*) as a consequence, as a result, consequently, hence, in consequence, so, therefore, thus.

accost *v.t.* **1** (*to approach, to speak to*) address, approach, buttonhole, confront, greet, hail, speak to, stop. **2** ((*of a prostitute*) *to solicit*) importune, make overtures to, solicit.

account *v.t.* (*to regard as, to consider*) believe, consider, deem, hold, judge, rate, reckon, regard, think, view.

~*n.* **1** (*a description or narrative*) chronicle, description, explanation, history, narration, narrative, record, report, statement, story, tale, version. **2** (*a facility at a bank etc. that enables a customer to deposit and withdraw money; the amount of money in an account*) bank account, current account, deposit account, savings, savings account. **3** (*a business arrangement whereby a shop etc. allows a customer to buy goods on credit*) credit account, credit arrangement. **4** (*a statement of goods or services supplied with a calculation of money due*) bill, charges, debts, invoice, tally. **5** (*profit, advantage*) advantage, avail, benefit, gain, profit. **6** (*importance, consequence*) consequence, distinction, import, importance, merit, note, significance. ANTONYMS: insignificance, unimportance. **of no account** (*valueless, negligible*) insignificant, minor, negligible, petty, unimportant, valueless, worthless. ANTONYMS: important, significant. **on account of** (*for the sake of, because of*) because of, for the sake of. **on no account** (*by no means*) absolutely not, certainly not, under no circumstances. **to account for 1** (*to give, or to serve as, an explanation of*) elucidate, explain, explain away, give an explanation of/ for, give grounds for, give reasons for, justify, show grounds for. **2** (*to kill or defeat* (*an enemy, opponent*)) destroy, kill, put out of action, put to death. **3** (*to give a satisfactory record of*) be responsible for, be the reason for. **4** (*to constitute, make up*) compose, constitute, make up, represent.

accountable *a.* (*responsible*) answerable, responsible.

accoutrement *n.* (*dress, equipment*) apparatus, appointments, appurtenances, array, (*coll.*) bits and pieces, clothes, clothing, dress, equipment, fittings, furnishings, garb, gear, kit, outfit, paraphernalia, tackle, things, trappings.

accredit *v.t.* **1** (*to attribute* (*a saying, discovery etc.*) (*to a person*)) ascribe, assign, attribute. **2** (*to give official recognition to, sanction*) accept, appoint, authorize, certify, depute, empower, license, sanction, warrant.

accredited *a.* **1** (*recognized officially, generally accepted*) accepted, appointed, approved, authorized, certified, licensed, official, sanctioned, warranted. ANTONYMS: unauthorized, unofficial. **2** (*conforming to an official standard of quality*) attested, certified. ANTONYMS: uncertified.

accretion *n.* **1** (*increase in growth by external additions*) accumulation, enlargement, growth, increase. ANTONYMS: decrease, diminution. **2** (*a part added by one of these processes*) addition, add-on, growth, supplement.

accrue *v.i.* (*to grow, to increase*) accumulate, amass, build up, collect, gather, grow, increase, stockpile.
~*v.t.* (*to amass*) accumulate, amass, build up, collect, gather, hoard, stockpile.

accumulate *v.t.* (*to bring together by degrees, to amass*) accrue, amass, build up, collect, cumulate, gather, heap up, hoard, pile up, stockpile, store. ANTONYMS: disperse, distribute.
~*v.i.* (*to grow in size, number or quantity, by repeated additions*) accrue, build up, collect, gather, grow, heap up, increase, pile up, stockpile. ANTONYMS: decrease, scatter.

accumulation *n.* **1** (*the act of accumulating or amassing*) accrual, accruing, aggregation, build-up, collection, cumulation, gathering, increase, stockpiling. ANTONYMS: decrease, scattering. **2** (*something that has been accumulated*) aggregation, build-up, collection, conglomeration, cumulation, gathering, heap, hoard, mass, pile, stack, stock, stockpile, store.

accuracy *n.* **1** (*the state of being without error or defect*) correctness, exactness, faultlessness, precision, rightness. ANTONYMS: inaccuracy, wrongness. **2** (*exactness; correctness resulting from care*) carefulness, closeness, exactness, faithfulness, meticulousness, precision. ANTONYMS: carelessness, imprecision, inaccuracy, inexactness, looseness.

accurate *a.* **1** (*without error or defect*) (*coll.*) bang on, correct, error-free, exact, fault-free, faultless, precise, right, (*coll.*) spot on. ANTONYMS: inaccurate, wrong. **2** (*careful, precise, exact*) careful, close, exact, faithful, meticulous, painstaking, precise, true, unerring. ANTONYMS: careless, imprecise, inaccurate, inexact, loose.

accursed *a.* **1** (*lying under a curse*) bedevilled, cursed, curse-laden, damned, ill-fated, under a curse. ANTONYMS: blessed. **2** (*execrable, detestable*) abominable, despicable, detestable, execrable, foul, hateful, hellish, horrible, loathsome, nasty, obnoxious, odious, vile. ANTONYMS: lovely, nice, pleasant.

accusation *n.* **1** (*the act of accusing or charging someone with a crime*) accusing, arraigning, arraignment, blaming, charging, citation, citing, impeaching, impeachment, imputation, incriminating, incrimination, indicting, indictment. ANTONYMS: defence. **2** (*the act of accusing or laying the blame formally on someone*) accusing, blaming, censuring, incriminating. ANTONYMS: absolution, absolving, exoneration, vindication. **3** (*a charge brought against someone*) arraignment, blame, charge, citation, impeachment, imputation, incrimination, indictment.

accuse *v.t.* **1** (*to charge with a crime or fault*) arraign, charge, cite, impeach, indict. ANTONYMS: defend. **2** (*to lay the blame formally on (a person or thing)*) attribute blame to, blame, censure, declare guilty, hold responsible, impute blame to, incriminate, lay (something) at the door of, lay the blame on, (*sl.*) stick (something) on. ANTONYMS: absolve, exonerate, vindicate.

accustom *v.t.* (*to habituate (oneself, someone) (to), to make familiar by use*) acclimatize (to), accommodate (to), adapt (to), adjust (to), familiarize (with), get used (to), habituate (to), inure (to), make familiar (with).

accustomed *a.* (*often practised, usual*) common, conventional, customary, established, everyday, fixed, habitual, normal, ordinary, regular, routine, set, traditional, typical, usual, wonted. ANTONYMS: atypical, rare, uncommon, unusual.

ace *n.* (*a person who is particularly skilful or successful in any activity, esp. sport*) adept, champion, expert, genius, (*esp. N Am., coll.*) hotshot, master, star, virtuoso, wizard. ANTONYMS: dud, failure.
~*a.* (*excellent, brilliant*) (*coll.*) A1, adept, brilliant, champion, crack, excellent, fine, first-rate, great, (*esp. N Am., coll.*) hotshot, master, masterly, outstanding, skilful, skilled, superb. ANTONYMS: hopeless, poor, useless.

acerbic *a.* **1** (*sour, astringent*) acetic, acid, acidic, acidulous, acrid, astringent, bitter, pungent, sharp, sour, tart, vinegary. ANTONYMS: sweet. **2** (*bitter or harsh in speech or manner*) acid, acrimonious, biting, bitter, brusque, caustic, harsh, mordant, nasty, rancorous, rude, sarcastic, sharp, stinging, trenchant, unkind, virulent, vitriolic. ANTONYMS: kind, soft, sweet.

ache *v.i.* **1** (*to suffer continuous dull pain; to be the source of an ache*) be painful, be sore, hurt, pound, throb. **2** (*to suffer mental or emotional distress*) be distressed, be miserable, be sad, be sorrowful, be unhappy, grieve, mourn, sorrow, suffer. ANTONYMS: be joyful, rejoice. **3** (*to long (for or to do)*) covet, crave (for), desire, hanker (after), hunger (for), long (for), pine (for), thirst (for), want, wish (for), yearn (for).
~*n.* **1** (*continuous dull pain (in contrast to a twinge)*) dull pain, hurt, pain, pounding, soreness, throbbing. **2** (*mental or emotional distress*) anguish, distress, grief, misery, sadness, sorrow, suffering, unhappiness. ANTONYMS: happiness, joy, rejoicing. **3** (*longing*)

craving, desire, hankering, hunger, longing, thirst, want, wish, yearning.

achievable *a.* (*that can be achieved*) accessible, attainable, feasible, obtainable, possible, practicable, realizable, within one's reach. ANTONYMS: impossible, impracticable, unachievable, unattainable.

achieve *v.t.* **1** (*to accomplish, finish*) accomplish, bring about, bring off, carry out, complete, conclude, consummate, effect, effectuate, execute, finish, fulfil, perform. ANTONYMS: fail in, give up. **2** (*to attain or bring about by an effort*) acquire, arrive at, attain, earn, gain, get, obtain, procure, reach, win.

achievement *n.* **1** (*the act of accomplishing*) acquisition, attainment, earning, gaining, getting, obtaining, procural, procurement, reaching, winning. **2** (*the act of completing or finishing something*) accomplishing, accomplishment, completion, concluding, conclusion, consummation, effecting, effectuating, execution, finishing, fulfilling, fulfilment, performance, performing. ANTONYMS: failing in, giving up. **3** (*the thing achieved*) accomplishment, act, deed, effort, exploit, feat, performance.

acid *a.* **1** (*sour, sharp to the taste*) acetic, acidulous, acrid, pungent, sharp, sour, tart, vinegary. ANTONYMS: sweet. **2** (*sharp or sour in manner or speech*) acerbic, astringent, biting, bitter, caustic, cutting, harsh, mordant, sarcastic, stinging, trenchant, virulent, vitriolic. ANTONYMS: kind, soft, sweet.

acknowledge *v.t.* **1** (*to admit the truth of, accept*) accept, admit, allow, concede, confess, grant, own, recognize. ANTONYMS: deny, disclaim, reject. **2** (*to show awareness or recognition of, e.g. by a gesture*) address, greet, hail, recognize, salute. ANTONYMS: ignore, snub, spurn. **3** (*to confirm receipt of (a letter etc.)*) answer, reply to, respond to. ANTONYMS: disregard, ignore. **4** (*to express appreciation or gratitude for*) express gratitude for, give thanks for, show appreciation for, thank.

acknowledged *a.* (*generally accepted or recognized*) accepted, accredited, admitted, avowed, declared, recognized.

acknowledgement *n.* **1** (*the act of recognizing or accepting something*) acceptance, admission, admitting, allowing, conceding, concession, confessing, granting, owning, recognition. ANTONYMS: denial, disclaiming, rejection. **2** (*the act of showing awareness or recognition of someone, e.g. by a gesture*) addressing, greeting, hailing, recognition, salutation, saluting. ANTONYMS: ignoring, snubbing, spurning. **3** (*the act of confirming receipt*

of a letter etc.) answering of, replying to, responding to. ANTONYMS: disregarding, ignoring. **4** (*confirmation of receipt of a letter etc.*) answer, reply, response. **5** (*the act of expressing gratitude*) giving thanks, showing appreciation, thanking. **6** (*an expression of gratitude, esp.* (*usu. in pl.*)) appreciation, gratitude, thanks.

acme *n.* (*the highest point, perfection* (*of achievement, excellence etc.*)) apex, climax, crest, crown, culmination, height, high point, peak, pinnacle, summit, top, vertex, zenith. ANTONYMS: base, bottom, low point, nadir.

acolyte *n.* (*a faithful follower*) adherent, admirer, assistant, attendant, follower, helper, henchman/ henchwoman.

acquaint *v.t.* (*to make (someone, oneself) aware of or familiar with* (*usu. followed by with*)) advise of, apprise of, enlighten, familiarize with, inform of, let (someone) know, make (someone) aware of, make (someone) conversant with, make (someone) familiar with, tell. ANTONYMS: leave (someone) in ignorance.

acquaintance *n.* **1** (*knowledge of any person or thing*) awareness, familiarity, knowledge, understanding. ANTONYMS: ignorance. **2** (*the state of knowing, or becoming known to, a person*) association, familiarity, intimacy, relationship, social contact. **3** (*a person, or the persons collectively, whom one knows, but with whom one is not intimate*) associate, colleague, contact.

acquainted *a.* **1** (*known to another or each other*) friendly with, known to, on friendly terms with. ANTONYMS: unacquainted with. **2** (*familiar* (*with*)) apprised (of), au fait (with), aware (of), cognizant (of), conscious (of), conversant (with), experienced (in), familiar (with), informed (of), knowledgeable (about), privy (to), versed (in), well-versed (in). ANTONYMS: ignorant (of), unaware (of), unconscious (of), unfamiliar (with).

acquiesce *v.i.* (*to assent, to concur* (*in*)) accede (to), accept, agree (with), assent (to), bow (to), comply (with), concur (with), conform (to), consent (to), go along (with), obey, submit (to), yield (to). ANTONYMS: demur (at), disagree (with), dissent (with), protest (about).

acquiescence *n.* (*tacit acceptance*) acceptance, accession, agreement, assent, compliance, concurrence, conforming, consent, giving in, obedience, submission, submitting, yielding. ANTONYMS: demurral, disagreement, dissent, protest.

acquiescent *a.* **1** (*submissive*) ingratiating,

obsequious, passive, servile, submissive, subordinate, toadying. ANTONYMS: assertive, domineering, imperious, masterful. **2** (*accepting, assenting*) acceding, accepting, agreeable, assenting, compliant, concurrent, conforming, consenting, obedient, submissive, yielding. ANTONYMS: demurring, dissenting, protesting.

acquire *v.t.* (*to gain, or obtain possession of, by one's own exertions or abilities*) achieve, amass, appropriate, attain, buy, collect, come by, earn, gain, gather, get, get possession of, obtain, pick up, procure, purchase, receive, secure, win. ANTONYMS: forfeit, give up, lose, relinquish.

acquirement *n.* **1** (*the act of acquiring*) achievement, achieving, acquisition, amassing, appropriation, attainment, buying, collecting, collection, earning, gaining, gathering, getting, obtaining, procurement, purchase, receiving, securing, winning. ANTONYMS: forfeiture, losing, loss, relinquishment. **2** (*a personal attainment, esp. a mental one*) accomplishment, achievement, attainment, knowledge, qualification, skill.

acquisition *n.* **1** (*the act of acquiring*) achievement, achieving, acquirement, acquiring, amassing, appropriation, attaining, attainment, buying, collection, earning, gaining, gathering, getting, obtaining, procurement, purchase, purchasing, receiving, securing, winning. **2** (*the object acquired*) buy, gain, possession, prize, purchase.

acquisitive *a.* (*eager to acquire possessions; materialistic*) avaricious, covetous, grasping, greedy, materialistic, mercenary, predatory, rapacious. ANTONYMS: bountiful, generous, munificent.

acquisitiveness *n.* (*eagerness to acquire possessions*) avarice, covetousness, graspingness, greed, materialism, predatoriness, rapaciousness, rapacity. ANTONYMS: generosity, munificence.

acquit *v.t.* (*to release from an obligation, suspicion or charge*) absolve, clear, deliver, discharge, exculpate, find innocent, free, liberate, release, relieve, vindicate. ANTONYMS: blame, charge, condemn, convict, find guilty. ~*v.refl.* **1** (*to conduct* (*oneself*) *in a particular way*) act, behave, comport oneself, conduct oneself, perform. **2** (*to discharge* (*oneself*) *of* (*the duties of one's position*)) accomplish, carry out, discharge, effect, execute, perform.

acquittal *n.* **1** (*a deliverance from a charge by legal process; being declared not guilty*) absolution, clearance, clearing, deliverance, delivering, discharge, exculpation, exoneration, freeing, liberation, release, vindication.

ANTONYMS: charging, condemnation, conviction. **2** (*performance*) action, behaviour, comportment, conduct, performance. **3** (*discharge of duty*) accomplishment, conduct, discharge, performance.

acrid *a.* **1** (*pungent, biting to the taste*) acerbic, acetic, acid, astringent, biting, bitter, burning, harsh, irritating, pungent, sharp, sour, stinging, tart, vinegary. **2** (*of irritating temper and manners*) acerbic, acrimonious, bitter, caustic, sarcastic, sharp. ANTONYMS: amiable, friendly. **3** (*extremely critical*) acerbic, acid, acrimonious, astringent, biting, bitter, caustic, critical, cruel, cutting, harsh, mordant, sarcastic, sharp, stinging, trenchant, vitriolic, vituperative. ANTONYMS: friendly, kindly.

acrimonious *a.* (*bad-tempered and recriminating*) acerbic, acid, biting, bitter, caustic, crabbed, cross, cutting, harsh, irascible, mordant, nasty, rancorous, sharp, spiteful, splenetic, tart, testy, trenchant, venomous, virulent, vitriolic. ANTONYMS: affable, friendly, kindly.

acrimony *n.* (*bitterness of feeling, manner or speech*) acerbity, asperity, astringency, bitterness, crabbedness, crossness, harshness, irascibility, mordancy, nastiness, rancour, sharpness, spite, spitefulness, tartness, testiness, trenchancy, venom, virulence, vitriol. ANTONYMS: affability, friendliness, kindliness.

act *n.* **1** (*something that is done or being done, a deed*) accomplishment, achievement, action, deed, exploit, feat, move, operation, performance, undertaking. **2** (*a law or edict of a legislative or judicial body*) bill, decree, dictum, edict, enactment, law, ordinance, ruling, statute. **3** (*any one of the principal divisions of a play*) division, part, section. **4** (*insincere pretending behaviour*) affectation, counterfeit, dissimulation, fake, feigning, pose, posture, pretence, sham. ~*v.t.* **1** (*to perform* (*a play*)) do, enact, perform, present, stage. **2** (*to play the part of*) play, play the part of, portray. **3** (*to impersonate or pretend*) impersonate, mimic. ~*v.i.* **1** (*to take action, to do something*) be active, do, function, move, operate, perform, react, take action. ANTONYMS: be idle, be inactive, do nothing. **2** (*to produce an effect*) be effective, be efficacious, take effect, work. ANTONYMS: be ineffective. **3** (*to behave, to conduct oneself*) acquit oneself, behave, comport oneself, conduct oneself. **4** (*to perform as an actor*) be an actor/ actress, perform, play, tread the boards. **5** (*to pretend to be*) counterfeit, dissimulate, fake, feign, put it on, put on an act, sham. **to act for** (*to be the* (*esp. legal*) *representative of*) be the representative of, deputize for, fill in for, represent, stand in for, substitute for, take the place of. **to act on/ upon 1** (*to follow, to carry out* (*advice, recommendation*)) act in accordance with, carry out, follow, obey, take. ANTONYMS: ignore. **2** (*to have an effect on, to influence*) affect, have an effect, have an impact on, influence, work on. **to act out** (*to represent* (*a scene, one's desires*) *in physical action or by performance*) characterize, enact, mime, portray, represent. **to act up 1** (*to behave badly*) behave badly, be naughty, misbehave, play up. ANTONYMS: be good. **2** (*to function badly, to give trouble*) cause problems, cause trouble, give trouble, malfunction, play up. ANTONYMS: run smoothly.

acting *a.* (*doing temporary duty*) deputy, fill-in, interim, pro tem, provisional, substitute, surrogate, temporary. ANTONYMS: full-time, permanent.

~*n.* **1** (*performance, action*) action, execution, functioning, moving, operation, performance, reaction, taking action. ANTONYMS: inaction. **2** (*dramatic performance*) drama, dramatics, performing, stagecraft, theatricals, the performing arts, the stage, the theatre. **3** (*insincere pretending behaviour*) counterfeiting, dissimulation, faking, feigning, imposture, playacting, posing, posturing, pretence, pretending, putting it on, putting on an act, sham, shamming.

action *n.* **1** (*the condition or fact of acting or doing*) acting, activity, doing, execution, functioning, movement, moving, operation, performance, work, working. ANTONYMS: inaction, inactivity. **2** (*anything done or performed*) act, deed, endeavour, exploit, feat, manoeuvre, move, operation, performance, undertaking. **3** (*energetic activity or forcefulness, esp. as a characteristic of a person*) assertiveness, energy, force, forcefulness, get-up-and-go, liveliness, vigour, (*coll.*) vim, vitality. ANTONYMS: inaction, lethargy, sluggishness. **4** (*an effect or influence*) consequences, effect, influence, result. **5** (*exciting activity*) activity, excitement. **6 a** (*combat, fighting*) battle, combat, conflict, fighting, warfare. ANTONYMS: peace. **b** (*a small-scale military engagement*) affray, battle, clash, conflict, encounter, engagement, fight, skirmish. **7** (*the events constituting the main storyline in a play, novel etc.*) activity, events, incidents. **8** (*a legal process, a lawsuit*) case, lawsuit, legal case, legal proceedings, litigation, prosecution, suit. **out of action** (*not working, unable to operate*) inoperative, (*coll.*) kaput, not working, out of commission, out of order. ANTONYMS: in action, operative, working. **to take action** (*to do something, esp. something decisive or something intended as a*

protest) act, do something, make a move, take steps. ANTONYMS: do nothing.

activate *v.t.* **1** (*to make active, to set going*) actuate, energize, get going, initiate, kick-start, set going, set in motion, start off, switch on, trigger off, turn on. ANTONYMS: deactivate, switch off, terminate, turn off. **2** (*to induce activity in* (*someone*)) actuate, animate, arouse, energize, excite, galvanize, get (someone) going, get (someone) moving, impel, incite, induce, influence, inspire, mobilize, motivate, move, prod, prompt, rouse, spur, stimulate, stir, urge. ANTONYMS: discourage, impede, obstruct.

active *a.* **1** (*busy*) bustling, busy, engaged, occupied, on the go, on the move. ANTONYMS: idle, inactive. **2** (*that involves the performance of actual work; involved in something in this way*) functioning, in action, involved, operative, working. ANTONYMS: inactive. **3** (*able to move about and perform tasks*) energetic, mobile, nimble, sprightly, spry. ANTONYMS: immobile, incapacitated, stiff. **4** (*communicating action, initiating or furthering a process*) effective, effectual, potent. ANTONYMS: inactive, inert. **5** (*in actual operation or capable of actual operation*) functioning, in action, in force, in operation, operational, operative, working. ANTONYMS: inactive, inoperative.

activity *n.* **1** (*the quality or state of being active*) activeness, functioning, involvement. ANTONYMS: inactivity. **2** (*a situation in which many things are happening and people are busy*) animation, bustle, flurry, hurly-burly, hustle, hustle and bustle, liveliness, movement, stir. **3** (*liveliness, vigorous action*) energy, mobility, nimbleness, sprightliness, spryness. ANTONYMS: inactivity, incapacity, stiffness. **4** (*a pursuit, recreation*) endeavour, enterprise, hobby, interest, occupation, pastime, project, pursuit, scheme, undertaking, venture.

actor *n.* **1** (*a performer*) performer, play-actor, player, thespian. **2** (*a doer*) agent, doer, executor, operator, performer, practitioner.

actress *n.* (*a female actor*) perfomer, play-actor, player, thespian.

actual *a.* (*existing in act or reality, real*) authentic, factual, genuine, real, true, veritable. ANTONYMS: hypothetical, theoretical, unreal, untrue.

actually *adv.* **1** (*in fact, in reality*) in fact, literally, really. **2** (*as a matter of fact*) as a matter of fact, indeed, in fact, in point of fact, in reality, in truth, really.

actuate *v.t.* **1** (*to put in action, to cause to operate*) activate, energize, get going, initiate, kick-start, set going, set in motion, set off, start going, switch on, trigger, turn on. ANTONYMS: deactivate, switch off, terminate, turn off. **2** (*to motivate, to induce*) arouse, drive, energize, excite, galvanize, goad, impel, induce, influence, inspire, motivate, move, prod, prompt, rouse, spur, stimulate, stir, urge. ANTONYMS: discourage, impede, obstruct.

acumen *n.* (*acuteness of mind, shrewdness*) acuteness, astuteness, cleverness, discernment, ingenuity, judgement, (*coll.*) nous, penetration, perception, perspicacity, perspicuity, sagacity, sharpness, shrewdness, smartness, wisdom.

acute *a.* **1** (*sharp, penetrating*) discerning, incisive, keen, penetrating, sensitive, sharp. ANTONYMS: dull. **2** (*quick to perceive minute distinctions, sensitive to detail*) astute, clever, discerning, discriminating, judicious, penetrating, perceptive, perspicacious, sagacious, sharp, shrewd, smart. ANTONYMS: dull, obtuse, stupid. **3** ((*of pain*) *sharp, piercing*) excruciating, fierce, intense, keen, penetrating, piercing, severe, sharp, shooting, stabbing. ANTONYMS: dull. **4** ((*of an illness*) *attended with violent symptoms, and coming speedily to a crisis*) intense, severe, short, short and sharp, sudden. ANTONYMS: chronic, long-lasting. **5** ((*of a problem, shortage*) *very serious, requiring urgent attention*) at a crisis, critical, crucial, dangerous, decisive, essential, grave, important, pressing, serious, severe, urgent, vital. ANTONYMS: inconsequential, unimportant.

acutely *adv.* (*very strongly, intensely*) deeply, extremely, intensely, keenly, markedly, painfully, profoundly, very, very much. ANTONYMS: slightly.

acuteness *n.* **1** (*sharpness in one's mind*) discernment, incisiveness, keenness, penetration, sensitivity, sharpness. ANTONYMS: dullness. **2** (*quickness in perceiving minute distinctions, sensitivity to detail*) astuteness, cleverness, discernment, discrimination, judiciousness, penetration, perception, perceptiveness, perspicacity, sagacity, sharpness, shrewdness, smartness. ANTONYMS: dullness, obtuseness, stupidity. **3** (*a sharp intensity of pain*) fierceness, intensity, keenness, severity, sharpness. ANTONYMS: dullness. **4** (*the state of illness being critical*) intensity, severity, shortness, suddenness. ANTONYMS: chronicity. **5** (*the state of a problem being critical*) criticalness, cruciality, crucialness, danger, decisiveness, gravity, importance, seriousness, severity, urgency. ANTONYMS: unimportance.

adage *n.* (*a proverb; a pithy maxim handed down from old time*) aphorism, axiom, dictum, maxim, proverb, saw, saying.

adamant *a.* (*stubbornly determined*) determined, firm, immovable, inexorable, inflexible, insistent, intransigent, obdurate, resolute, resolved, rigid, set, stubborn, unbending, uncompromising, unrelenting, unyielding. ANTONYMS: compliant, flexible, pliable, pliant, tractable.

adapt *v.t.* (*to adjust, to make suitable for a new purpose or conditions*) acclimatize, accommodate, accustom, adjust, alter, change, convert, familiarize, fit, habituate, modify, remodel, shape, suit, tailor, transform. ~*v.i.* (*to change so as to become fit or suitable for new conditions*) acclimatize, accommodate, alter, become accustomed, become habituated, become used, change, comply, conform, familiarize oneself.

adaptable *a.* **1** (*capable of being adapted*) adjustable, convertible, modifiable, variable, versatile. **2** (*able to adapt easily*) compliant, easygoing, flexible, malleable, pliant, resilient, versatile. ANTONYMS: inflexible, set in one's ways.

adaptation *n.* **1** (*the act of adapting or the state of being adapted to new conditions*) acclimatization, accommodation, adjustment, alteration, compliance, conforming, familiarization, habituation. **2** (*a change that is necessary to suit a new purpose*) adjustment, alteration, change, conversion, fitting, tailoring, transformation.

add *v.t.* **1** (*to put together with or join with*) affix, append, attach, include, put in, put on. ANTONYMS: remove, take away. **2** (*to combine* (*numbers*) *in order to make a total*) add up, compute, count up, reckon, total, tot up. ANTONYMS: deduct, subtract. **3** (*to say or write in addition*) go on to say, state further. **to add on** (*to attach as a supplement or extension*) affix, append, attach, put in, put on. ANTONYMS: take away, take off. **to add to** (*to increase*) amplify, augment, exacerbate, increase, intensify, magnify. ANTONYMS: detract from, diminish, reduce. **to add up 1** (*to perform the operation of addition*) add, compute, count, count up, reckon, total, tot up. ANTONYMS: subtract. **2** (*to make sense*) make sense, ring true, seem plausible, stand to reason. **to add up to 1** (*to amount to*) amount to, come to. **2** (*to mean, to have as an effect*) amount to, constitute, imply, indicate, mean, signify.

addendum *n.* (*a thing to be added, an addition*) addition, adjunct, affix, appendix, codicil, postscript, supplement.

addict *n.* **1** (*a person who has become addicted to some habit, esp. the taking of drugs*) drug abuser, (*coll.*) freak, (*esp. in comb., coll.*) head, (*sl.*) junkie, user. **2** (*a person who is extremely devoted to something, esp. a pastime or sport*) adherent, (*coll.*) buff, devotee, enthusiast, fan, follower, (*coll.*) freak, (*sl.*) nut.

addicted *a.* **1** (*dependent, esp. on a narcotic drug*) dependent (on), habituated (to), (*coll.*) hooked (on). **2** (*enthusiastically devoted to something*) dedicated (to), devoted (to), enthusiastic (for), fond (of), (*coll.*) hooked (on), obsessed (with).

addiction *n.* **1** (*a condition of physical dependence on something, esp. a narcotic drug*) craving (for), dependence (on), habit. **2** (*an extreme devotion to something*) dedication (to), devotion (to), enthusiasm (for), fondness (for), obsession (with).

addition *n.* **1** (*the process of combining two or more numbers or quantities into one sum*) adding up, computation, counting up, reckoning, summation, totalling, totting up. ANTONYMS: subtraction. **2** (*a thing that is added*) addendum, additive, add-on, appendage, appendix, extension, extra, gain, increase, increment, supplement. **3** (*the act of adding one thing to another*) adding, affixing, appending, attachment, besides, inclusion. ANTONYMS: removal. **in addition** (*as well, also*) additionally, also, as well, beside, besides, into the bargain, over and above, to boot, too. ANTONYMS: instead.

additional *a.* (*added; supplementary*) added, additional, add-on, appended, extra, further, more, supplemental, supplementary. ANTONYMS: less.

additionally *adv.* (*as well, also, in addition*) also, as well, besides, in addition, into the bargain, over and above, to boot, too. ANTONYMS: instead.

additive *n.* (*something added, esp. a substance added to food to preserve or enhance it*) addition, supplement.

addled *a.* (*mentally confused or deranged*) befuddled, confused, deranged, mixed-up, muddled.

address *n.* **1** (*the place where a person lives or an organization has its premises*) abode, domicile, dwelling, home, house, location, lodging, quarters, residence. **2** (*the written form of this used on letters etc.*) inscription, label, postal directions. **3** (*a speech or discourse delivered to an audience*) diatribe, discourse, disquisition, dissertation, harangue, lecture, oration, philippic, sermon, speech, talk. **4** (*tact, adroitness*) adroitness, deftness, dexterity, diplomacy, discretion, expertise, skilfulness, skill, tact. ANTONYMS: awkwardness, clumsiness, tactlessness.

~*v.t.* **1** (*to write the address on (a letter, envelope)*) direct, inscribe, label. **2** (*to speak to*) approach, greet, hail, salute, speak to, talk to. ANTONYMS: ignore. **3** (*to deliver a speech or discourse to*) deliver an oration to, deliver a sermon to, give a speech to, give a talk to, harangue, lecture, make a speech to, preach to, speak to, talk to. **4** (*to direct (a message, protest etc.) to*) aim, communicate, convey, direct, send. **5** (*to direct one's attention to; to deal with*) apply oneself, attend to, cope with, deal with, focus on, get down to, get to grips with, tackle, undertake. ANTONYMS: neglect. **6** (*to speak to (someone), using a particular title or name*) call, designate, name. **to address oneself to 1** (*to speak to*) speak to, talk to. **2** (*to apply oneself to; to deal with*) apply oneself to, attend to, cope with, deal with, direct one's attention to, focus on, get down to, get to grips with, tackle, undertake. ANTONYMS: neglect.

adduce *v.t.* (*to bring forward as a proof or illustration, to cite*) advance, cite, forward, instance, mention, name, offer, point out, present, proffer, put forward, quote.

adept[1] *a.* (*thoroughly versed, highly skilled*) able, accomplished, adroit, deft, dexterous, expert, masterly, proficient, skilful, skilled, versed, well-versed, wizard. ANTONYMS: amateurish, awkward, clumsy, inept.

adept[2] *n.* (*a person who is completely versed in any science or art*) ace, (*coll.*) dab hand, expert, genius, (*esp. N Am., coll.*) hotshot, master, past master, wizard. ANTONYMS: (*sl.*) duffer.

adequacy *n.* **1** (*sufficiency*) ampleness, enough, sufficiency. ANTONYMS: deficiency, inadequacy. **2** (*the state of being just good enough for something*) acceptability, passableness, satisfactoriness, tolerability, tolerableness. **3** (*competence*) ability, capability, competence, fitness, qualifications, suitability.

adequate *a.* **1** (*equal to a requirement, sufficient*) ample, enough, requisite, sufficient. ANTONYMS: deficient, inadequate, insufficient, not enough, too little. **2** (*competent*) able, capable, competent, fit, qualified, suitable, suited. ANTONYMS: incapable, incompetent, unsuitable. **3** (*barely sufficient, just good enough*) acceptable, fair, passable, satisfactory, tolerable. ANTONYMS: unacceptable, unsatisfactory.

adhere *v.i.* **1** (*to stick (to)*) be attached (to), be fastened (to), be fixed (to), be glued (to), cling (to), stick (to). **2** (*to continue to give support to*) be constant to, be devoted to, be faithful to, be loyal to, be true to, stand by, support. ANTONYMS: abandon, forsake, give up on. **3** (*not to deviate (followed by to)*) abide (by), comply (with), follow, hold (to), keep (to), obey, observe, stand (by), stick (to). ANTONYMS: break (with), deviate (from), disobey, ignore.

adherent *a.* (*sticking*) adhering, adhesive, clinging, gluey, glutinous, gummy, mucilaginous, sticking, tacky, viscous.
~*n.* **1** (*a supporter, a follower*) admirer, advocate, disciple, follower, partisan, protagonist, supporter, upholder, votary. **2** (*a devotee*) addict, admirer, aficionado, (*coll.*) buff, devotee, enthusiast, fan.

adhesive *a.* (*having the power of adhering*) adherent, adhering, clinging, gluey, glutinous, gummy, mucilaginous, sticking, sticky, tacky, viscous.
~*n.* (*a substance used for sticking things together*) cement, fixative, glue, gum, paste.

adieu *int.* (*goodbye, farewell*) farewell, goodbye.
~*n.* (*a farewell*) farewell, goodbye, leave-taking, parting.

adjacent *a.* (*lying next* (*to*); *bordering*) abutting (on), adjoining, attached (to), bordering (on), close (to), contiguous (to), nearby, near (to), neighbouring, next door (to), proximate (to), touching. ANTONYMS: distant (from), far away (from), remote (from).

adjoin *v.t.* (*to be next to and contiguous with*) abut on, be adjacent to, be contiguous to, be next door to, be next to, border on, connect, join, link, neighbour, touch.

adjoining *a.* (*adjacent, neighbouring*) abutting, adjacent, bordering, connected, connecting, contiguous, interconnecting, joined, joining, linking, near, neighbouring, next door, touching. ANTONYMS: distant, separate.

adjourn *v.t.* **1** (*to put off or defer till a later period*) defer, delay, postpone, put off, put on the back burner, shelve. ANTONYMS: bring forward. **2** (*to suspend* (*a meeting*) *in order to meet at a later period or elsewhere*) break off, discontinue, interrupt, suspend. ANTONYMS: continue.
~*v.i.* (*to move elsewhere*) move, retire, withdraw. ANTONYMS: remain, stay.

adjournment *n.* **1** (*the act of adjourning*) adjourning, deferral, delay, postponement, shelving. **2** (*the act of suspending a meeting to a later time or elsewhere*) adjourning, breaking off, discontinuation, interruption, suspension. **3** (*the time during which or to which business or a meeting is postponed*) break, breather, interval, pause, rest, stop.

adjudge *v.t.* (*to pronounce officially or formally*) declare, decree, deem, judge, pronounce.

adjudicate *v.t.* (*to give a decision regarding, to judge*) decide, determine, give a ruling on, settling.
~*v.i.* (*to act as a judge in a competition*) arbitrate, be adjudicator, judge, referee, umpire.

adjudicator *n.* (*a person who adjudicates*) arbitrator, judge, referee, umpire.

adjunct *n.* (*any thing joined to another without being an essential part of it*) accessory, addendum, addition, add-on, appendage, appurtenance, attachment, extension, extra, supplement.

adjust *v.t.* **1** (*to regulate; to make slight alteration to, esp. to achieve greater accuracy*) alter, fix, modify, regulate, tune. **2** (*to arrange; to put in the correct order or position*) arrange, compose, fix, neaten, put in order, rearrange. **3** (*to make suitable or correspondent* (*to*)) accommodate, adapt, alter, fit, modify, shape, suit.
~*v.i.* (*to adapt or conform* (*to a new situation, environment etc.*)) acclimatize, accommodate, accustom oneself, adapt, become accustomed, conform, get used to, orientate, settle in.

adjustable *a.* (*that is capable of being adjusted*) adaptable, alterable, movable.

adjustment *n.* **1** (*the act of adjusting*) alteration, fixing, modification, regulation, tuning. **2** (*the act of arranging or putting in the correct order or position*) arrangement, arranging, fixing, neatening, putting in order, rearrange. **3** (*the act of adapting or conforming to a new situation, environment etc.*) acclimatization, accommodation, accustoming, adjusting, conforming, orientation, settling. **4** (*the state of being adjusted*) adaptation, alteration, modification, rearrangement.

ad-lib *v.i.* (*to extemporize*) extemporize, improvise, speak extemporaneously, speak impromptu, speak off the cuff, (*coll.*) wing it.
~*a.* (*improvised, extempore*) extemporaneous, extempore, improvised, off the cuff, spontaneous, unprepared, unrehearsed. ANTONYMS: prepared, rehearsed.
~*adv.* (*in an improvised manner*) extemporaneously, extempore, impromptu, off the cuff, off the top of one's head, spontaneously, without preparation, without rehearsal.

administer *v.t.* **1** (*to manage or conduct as chief agent*) conduct, control, direct, govern, handle, manage, preside over, run, supervise. **2** (*to superintend the execution of* (*e.g. laws*)) apply, dispense, execute, put into operation. **3** (*to give* (*medicine, remedy*)) dispense, dose, give. **4** (*to provide, give or distribute*) deliver, dispense, distribute, give, hand out, mete out, provide, supply.

administration *n.* 1 (*the act of administering, control*) administering, conducting, control, controlling, direction, government, handling, management, running, supervision. 2 (*the act of administering or distributing something*) delivery, dispensation, distribution, giving, handing out, provision, supplying. 3 (*the act of administering medicine*) dispensation, dosing, giving. 4 (*the act of administering laws etc.*) application, dispensation, execution. 5 (*the management of the affairs of a business, organization etc.*) executive, governing body, management, supervision. 6 (*a government*) government, ministry, regime.

administrative *a.* (*of or relating to administration*) controlling, directorial, executive, governing, governmental, management, managerial, supervisory.

administrator *n.* (*a person who administers or manages*) controller, director, executive, manager, superintendent.

admirable *a.* 1 (*worthy of admiration*) commendable, laudable, praiseworthy, worthy. ANTONYMS: deplorable, despicable. 2 (*excellent, highly satisfactory*) excellent, fine, first-class, first-rate, great, marvellous, masterly, superb. ANTONYMS: mediocre, poor.

admiration *n.* 1 (*pleasure or respect excited by anything pleasing or excellent*) appreciation, approbation, approval, esteem, regard, respect, veneration. ANTONYMS: contempt, scorn. 2 (*pleased contemplation*) appreciation, delight, enjoyment, pleasure. ANTONYMS: displeasure.

admire *v.t.* 1 (*to have a high opinion of, to respect*) appreciate, approve of, esteem, have a high opinion of, hold in esteem, hold in high regard, hold in regard, idolize, look up to, respect, think highly of, value, venerate. ANTONYMS: despise, hold in contempt, scorn. 2 (*to regard with pleasure and approval*) delight in, enjoy, take pleasure in. 3 (*to express admiration of*) commend, compliment, express admiration for, express appreciation of, praise, sing the praises of. ANTONYMS: criticize, denigrate, scorn. 4 (*to be attracted to*) be attracted to, feel affection for, feel love for, love. ANTONYMS: hate.

admirer *n.* 1 (*a person who feels admiration*) aficionado, (*coll.*) buff, devotee, enthusiast, fan, lover, supporter. 2 (*a suitor, lover*) beau, lover, suitor.

admissible *a.* (*capable of being admitted*) acceptable, allowable, permissible, permitted, tolerable, tolerated. ANTONYMS: inadmissible, unacceptable.

admission *n.* 1 (*permission or the right to enter*) access, admittance, entrance, entrée, entry, right of entry. ANTONYMS: exclusion. 2 (*a charge made or paid for entry*) entrance fee, entry charge. 3 (*an acknowledgement, a confession*) acknowledgement, confession, disclosure, divulgence, revelation. ANTONYMS: denial. 4 (*a concession made in an argument*) acknowledgement, concession.

admit *v.t.* 1 (*to concede, to acknowledge*) acknowledge, concede, grant. ANTONYMS: deny, reject. 2 (*to accept as valid or true*) acknowledge, confess, disclose, divulge, own, reveal. ANTONYMS: deny. 3 (*to allow to enter*) allow access to, let in, permit entry to, receive, take in. ANTONYMS: exclude, keep out, refuse entrance to. 4 ((*of a space*) *to have room for, to accommodate*) accommodate, have room for, have space for, hold.

admittance *n.* (*entrance given or permitted*) access, admission, entrance, entry, reception. ANTONYMS: exclusion.

admix *v.t.* 1 (*to mix, to mingle*) blend, combine, merge, mingle, mix. ANTONYMS: separate. 2 (*to add as a further ingredient*) add, include, put in.

admonish *v.t.* 1 (*to reprove gently*) berate, censure, chide, rebuke, reprimand, reprove, scold, (*coll.*) tell (someone) off, upbraid. 2 (*to urge, exhort*) advise, counsel, enjoin, exhort, urge. ANTONYMS: discourage. 3 (*to warn, caution*) caution, warn. ANTONYMS: applaud, commend, congratulate, praise.

admonition *n.* 1 ((*a*) *gentle reproof*) chiding, rebuke, reprimand, reproof, scolding, (*coll.*) telling-off, upbraiding. ANTONYMS: applause, commendation, congratulations, praise. 2 (*a friendly caution or warning*) caution, warning.

admonitory *a.* 1 (*gently reproving*) admonishing, censorious, chiding, rebuking, reprimanding, reproving, scolding, upbraiding. ANTONYMS: commendatory, congratulatory, praising. 2 (*cautionary*) cautionary, warning.

ado *n.* 1 (*activity*) activity, bustle, commotion, excitement, flurry, hurly-burly. 2 (*trouble, difficulty, fuss*) agitation, bother, commotion, difficulty, disturbance, fuss, problems, (*coll.*) to-do, trouble.

adolescence *n.* (*the period between childhood and adulthood*) pubescence, teenage years, teens, youth.

adolescent *a.* 1 (*growing up; between puberty and maturity*) teenage, young. 2 (*immature; silly*) immature, juvenile, puerile, silly. ANTONYMS: mature.

adopt *v.t.* **1** (*to take* (*a child*) *as one's own*) foster, take in. ANTONYMS: abandon, cast aside, disown. **2** (*to embrace, to espouse* (*a principle, cause etc.*)) accept, assume, embrace, espouse, take up. ANTONYMS: abandon, give up, reject. **3** (*to accept* (*a report, accounts*) *officially*) accept, approve, endorse, ratify. ANTONYMS: challenge, dispute, reject. **4** (*to choose as a candidate in an election*) choose, select, vote for. ANTONYMS: deselect, reject.

adoption *n.* **1** (*the act of adopting a child*) fosterage, fostering, taking in. ANTONYMS: abandonment, disowning. **2** (*the act of adopting a candidate in an election*) choice, choosing, selecting, selection, voting for. ANTONYMS: deselection, rejection. **3** (*the act of adopting a principle, cause etc.*) acceptance, assumption, embracing, espousal, taking up. **4** (*the act of accepting reports, accounts officially*) acceptance, approval, endorsement, ratification. ANTONYMS: challenging, disputing, rejection.

adorable *a.* (*charming, delightful*) appealing, attractive, captivating, charming, cute, darling, dear, delightful, enchanting, fetching, lovable, sweet, winning, winsome. ANTONYMS: hateful, horrible, nasty.

adoration *n.* **1** (*ardent love or esteem*) admiration, affection, cherishing, devotion, doting, esteem, idolization, love, reverence, revering, worship. ANTONYMS: contempt, dislike, hate, loathing. **2** (*worship, veneration*) exaltation, glorification, laudation, magnification, praise, praising, reverence, revering, veneration, worship.

adore *v.t.* **1** (*to regard with the utmost respect and affection*) admire, be devoted to, cherish, dote on, esteem, hold dear, idolize, love, revere, worship. ANTONYMS: despise, detest, hate, loathe. **2** (*to worship as a god*) exalt, glorify, laud, magnify, praise, revere, venerate, worship. **3** (*to like very much*) be fond of, delight in, like, love, relish, take pleasure in. ANTONYMS: dislike, have an aversion to.

adorn *v.t.* **1** (*to decorate, ornament*) decorate, embellish, garnish, ornament, trim. **2** (*to add attractiveness to*) beautify, enhance, prettify.

adornment *n.* **1** (*a decoration or ornament*) decoration, embellishment, frills, garnishing, ornament, ornamentation, trimming. **2** (*the act of adorning or decorating*) decorating, decoration, embellishing, garnishing, ornamentation, trimming. **3** (*the act of adorning or making more attractive*) beautification, beautifying, enhancement, prettifying.

adrift *a., adv.* **1** (*detached from its moorings; unfastened*) afloat, drifting, unanchored, unfastened, unmoored, untied. ANTONYMS: anchored, moored. **2** (*wandering, at a loss, at the mercy of circumstances*) aimless, directionless, goalless, purposeless, rootless, rudderless, unsettled, without purpose. ANTONYMS: purposeful, settled. **3** (*inaccurate; not keeping to a course, guideline, schedule etc.*) amiss, awry, off course, wrong. ANTONYMS: on course, right.

adroit *a.* (*dexterous, mentally or physically resourceful*) able, adept, clever, competent, deft, dexterous, expert, ingenious, masterly, nimble, proficient, skilful, skilled, smart. ANTONYMS: clumsy, inept, maladroit, unskilled.

adroitness *n.* (*dexterity, mental or physical resourcefulness*) ability, adeptness, cleverness, competence, dexterity, expertness, ingeniousness, mastery, nimbleness, proficiency, skilfulness, skill, smartness. ANTONYMS: clumsiness, ineptness, maladroitness.

adulation *n.* (*uncritical praise and admiration*) admiration, adoration, fawning, flattery, hero-worship, idolization, praise, worship. ANTONYMS: contempt, revilement, vilification.

adulatory *a.* (*uncritically praising and admiring*) admiring, adoring, fawning, flattering, hero-worshipping, idolizing, praising, worshipping. ANTONYMS: contemptuous, vilifying.

adulterate *v.t.* (*to corrupt or debase* (*something*) *by mixing it with an inferior substance*) bastardize, contaminate, corrupt, debase, doctor, make impure, spoil, taint, vitiate. ANTONYMS: purify.

advance *v.t.* **1** (*to bring or move forward or upwards*) bring forward, move forward, send forward. ANTONYMS: move back, put back. **2** (*to promote, to further*) accelerate, assist, boost, expedite, facilitate, forward, further, give a helping hand to, hasten, help, improve, move on, progress, promote. ANTONYMS: impede, obstruct, retard, set back. **3** (*to put forward for attention*) adduce, introduce, offer, present, proffer, propose, put forward, submit, suggest. ANTONYMS: suppress, withdraw, withhold. **4** (*to set to an earlier time; to bring forward to an earlier date or time*) bring forward, put forward. ANTONYMS: delay, postpone, put back, put off.
~*v.i.* **1** (*to move forward*) go forward, move forward, proceed, step forward. ANTONYMS: go back, move back. **2** (*to progress*) develop, flourish, forge ahead, gain ground, go ahead, go forward, press on, proceed, progress, push forward, thrive. ANTONYMS: go back, lose ground, retreat.
~*n.* **1** (*the act or process of moving forward*) going forward, moving forward, proceeding.

ANTONYMS: going back. **2** (*progress*) advancement, development, furtherance, growth, headway, improvement, progress. ANTONYMS: decline, regression. **3** (*an example of progress or increased sophistication*) advancement, breakthrough, development, discovery, finding. ANTONYMS: setback. **4** (*a payment made beforehand; a loan*) deposit, down payment, loan, prepayment, retainer. **5** (*a rise* (*in price*)) increase, rise. ANTONYMS: reduction. **6** (*pl.*) (*amorous overtures*) approaches, moves, overtures, propositioning. **7** (*promotion*) advancement, betterment, promotion, step up, upgrading. ANTONYMS: demotion, downgrading.
~*a.* **1** (*done, supplied etc. beforehand*) beforehand, earlier, early, previous, prior. ANTONYMS: late, later. **2** ((*of position*) *forward*) foremost, forward, in front, leading. ANTONYMS: back, rear. **in advance** (*beforehand*) ahead of time, beforehand, earlier, previously. ANTONYMS: in arrears, later.

advanced *a.* **1** (*more highly developed, sophisticated etc. than the norm*) ahead of the times, avant-garde, highly developed, modern, progressive, ultra-modern. ANTONYMS: backward, underdeveloped, undeveloped. **2** ((*of a person's age*) *far on*) elderly, old. **3** ((*of a child*) *precocious*) bright, developed, forward, gifted, mature, precocious, talented, well-developed. ANTONYMS: backward, slow. **4** (*dealing with a subject at a difficult, not basic, level*) high-level, senior. ANTONYMS: basic, elementary, low-level.

advancement *n.* **1** (*preferment*) betterment, improvement, preferment, promotion, upgrading. ANTONYMS: demotion, downgrading. **2** (*furtherance, improvement*) advance, development, furtherance, growth, headway, improvement, progress. ANTONYMS: decline, regression.

advantage *n.* **1** (*a favourable condition or circumstance*) asset, benefit, blessing, boon, good point. ANTONYMS: disadvantage, drawback, handicap, hindrance, snag. **2** (*superiority of any kind; a superior or better position*) ascendancy, dominance, precedence, superiority, supremacy, the edge, the trump card, the upper hand. ANTONYMS: inferiority. **3** (*profit, benefit*) avail, benefit, gain, good, profit. ANTONYMS: disadvantage.
~*v.t.* (*to benefit*) aid, assist, benefit, be of use to, do good to, help. ANTONYMS: hinder, impede, obstruct.

advantageous *a.* **1** (*conferring advantage*) dominant, favourable, superior. ANTONYMS: disadvantageous. **2** (*profitable, beneficial*) beneficial, favourable, helpful, of assistance, of benefit, of service, of use, of value, profitable, useful, valuable. ANTONYMS: detrimental, disadvantageous, unfavourable.

advent *n.* (*any arrival, a coming*) appearance, approach, arrival, coming, entrance, occurrence, onset. ANTONYMS: departure, going.

adventitious *a.* **1** (*accidental, casual*) accidental, casual, chance, fortuitous, incidental, unexpected, unintentional, unplanned. ANTONYMS: deliberate, planned. **2** (*extraneous, foreign*) alien, external, extraneous, foreign, outside. ANTONYMS: internal.

adventure *n.* **1** (*an enterprise in which hazard or risk is incurred*) escapade, experience, exploit, feat, venture. **2** (*enterprise and daring*) danger, daring, enterprise, hazard, peril, precariousness, risk. ANTONYMS: caution, safety, security.

adventurer *n.* **1** (*a person who seeks adventures*) daredevil, speculator, venturer. **2** (*a person who seeks to gain social position by false pretences*) charlatan, fortune-hunter, (*sl.*) gold-digger, opportunist, rogue.

adventurous *a.* **1** (*fond of adventure*) audacious, bold, daredevil, daring, intrepid, venturesome. ANTONYMS: cautious, timid, timorous, unadventurous. **2** (*involving risk; hazardous*) dangerous, daring, hazardous, perilous, precariousness, risky. ANTONYMS: safe, secure, unadventurous.

adversary *n.* **1** (*an opponent*) antagonist, fellow-competitor, fellow-contestant, opponent, opposer, opposition, rival. ANTONYMS: team-mate. **2** (*an enemy, a foe*) enemy, foe, rival. ANTONYMS: ally, confederate, friend.

adverse *a.* **1** (*unpropitious, unfavourable*) disadvantageous, inauspicious, unfavourable, unfortunate, unlucky, unpropitious. ANTONYMS: auspicious, favourable, propitious. **2** (*hostile, inimical*) antipathetic, hostile, inimical, negative, unfavourable, unfriendly. ANTONYMS: favourable, friendly, positive. **3** (*harmful, disadvantageous*) dangerous, detrimental, disadvantageous, harmful, hurtful, injurious. ANTONYMS: advantageous, beneficial.

adversity *n.* **1** (*adverse circumstances, misfortune*) affliction, bad luck, calamity, catastrophe, disaster, distress, hardship, hard times, ill luck, misery, mishap, sadness, sorrow, suffering, tribulation, trouble, woe, wretchedness. ANTONYMS: comfort, good fortune, good luck, joy, prosperity. **2** (*an instance of this*) accident, affliction, calamity, catastrophe, disaster, misfortune, mishap, reverse, setback, tragedy, trial. ANTONYMS: blessing, godsend, stroke of luck, windfall.

advertise *v.t.* **1** (*to publicly describe* (*a product, service, vacancy etc.*) *in order to promote awareness, increase sales, invite applications etc.*) crack up, display, (*coll.*) give a plug to, give a puff to, give a push to, give publicity to, (*coll.*) plug, promote, publicize, puff, push, tout. **2** (*to give public notice of; to make publicly known*) announce, make known, make public, publicize. ANTONYMS: hush up, smother, suppress.

advertisement *n.* **1** (*a paid announcement in a newspaper or on radio, television etc.*) (*coll.*) ad, (*coll.*) advert, bill, blurb, commercial, display, placard, (*coll.*) plug, poster, promotion, puff, push, (*usu. in pl.*) small ad. **2** (*the act of advertising*) advertising, cracking up, displaying, (*coll.*) plugging, promotion, publicizing, pushing, touting. **3** (*the act of making something public*) announcement, intimation, notification. **4** (*a public notice*) announcement, notice.

advice *n.* **1** (*counsel, opinion as to a course of action*) counsel, counselling, guidance, help, hints, recommendations, tips. **2** (*a formal or official notice*) communication, data, notice, notification.

advisability *n.* (*the state of being advisable*) appropriateness, aptness, desirability, fitness, judiciousness, propriety, prudence, soundness, suitability, wisdom. ANTONYMS: folly, stupidity.

advisable *a.* (*proper, to be recommended*) appropriate, apt, best, desirable, fit, fitting, judicious, politic, proper, prudent, recommended, seemly, sensible, sound, suitable, wise, wisest. ANTONYMS: foolish, ill-advised, imprudent, inappropriate, unwise.

advise *v.t.* **1** (*to counsel* (*a person*)) commend, counsel, give advice to, give guidance to, give hints to, give tips to, offer suggestions to, recommend, urge. **2** (*to recommend* (*a course of action*)) advocate, commend, recommend, suggest, urge. ANTONYMS: advise against, discourage. **3** (*to inform, to notify*) acquaint, apprise, inform, notify, tell, warn.

adviser *n.* (*a person who advises, esp. in a professional capacity*) aide, confidant, confidante, consultant, counsellor, guide, mentor.

advisory *a.* (*having the function or power to advise*) advising, consultative, counselling.

advocacy *n.* (*verbal support or argument in favour* (*of*)) backing, championing, defence, encouragement, promotion, recommendation, support, upholding. ANTONYMS: discouragement, opposition.

advocate[1] *n.* (*a person who defends or promotes a cause*) backer, champion, defender, promoter, proponent, supporter, upholder. ANTONYMS: opponent.

advocate[2] *v.t.* (*to plead in favour of, recommend*) advise, argue for, back, champion, commend, defend, encourage, favour, prescribe, press for, promote, recommend, subscribe, suggest, uphold, urge. ANTONYMS: advise against, discourage, oppose, take a stand against.

aegis *n.* (*protection, a protective influence*) auspices, backing, patronage, protection, sponsorship, support. **under the aegis of** (*under the auspices of*) sponsored by, under the auspices of, under the patronage of, under the protection of, with the backing of, with the help of, with the protection of, with the support of.

aeon *n.* (*a period of immense duration*) age, ages, eternity, long time.

affability *n.* (*the state of being affable*) agreeableness, amiability, amicability, approachability, civility, congeniality, cordiality, courteousness, friendliness, geniality, good humour, good nature, good temper, kindliness, niceness, pleasantness, sociability, warmth. ANTONYMS: nastiness, rudeness, surliness, unfriendliness.

affable *a.* (*friendly, approachable*) agreeable, amiable, amicable, approachable, civil, congenial, cordial, courteous, friendly, genial, good-humoured, good-natured, good-tempered, kindly, nice, pleasant, sociable, warm. ANTONYMS: nasty, rude, unapproachable, unfriendly, unsociable.

affair *n.* **1** (*a matter, something that is to be done*) business, concern, interest, matter, project, responsibility, undertaking. **2** (*a sexual or romantic relationship, esp. an extramarital one*) adulterous relationship, extramarital relationship, liaison, love affair, relationship, romance. **3** (*an event or sequence of events, esp. one that attains public fame or notoriety*) case, circumstance, episode, event, happening, incident, occurrence. **4** (*a thing*) article, object, something, thing. **5** (*public or private business*) business, business affairs, concerns, finances, personal affairs, transactions. **6** (*a social gathering, party*) (*coll.*) do, function, party, social event, social gathering.

affect[1] *v.t.* **1** (*to have an effect upon, exert an influence upon*) act on/ upon, alter, change, concern, have a bearing on, have an effect on, have an impact on, have an influence on, impinge on, influence, modify, sway, transform, work on. **2** ((*of a disease*) *to attack*) attack, infect, strike at. **3** (*to touch or stir* *emotionally*) disturb, impress, move, overcome, perturb, stir, touch, upset.

affect² *v.t.* **1** (*to make a pretence of, to feign*) counterfeit, fake, feign, pretend, put on, sham, simulate. **2** (*to imitate or assume*) adopt, assume, espouse.

affectation *n.* **1** (*pretentiousness*) affectedness, artificiality, insincerity, posturing, pretentiousness. ANTONYMS: genuineness, sincerity. **2** (*a mannerism, form of behaviour etc. adopted or contrived in order to impress*) air, (*pl.*) airs and graces, pretension. **3** (*assumption, adoption*) adoption, assumption, espousal. **4** (*pretence*) act, facade, fakery, false display, feigning, front, pose, pretence, sham, show, simulation.

affected *a.* **1** (*pretentious, given to affectation*) attitudinizing, camp, insincere, (*coll.*) la-di-da, posing, posturing, pretentious, unnatural. ANTONYMS: down-to-earth, sincere, unaffected. **2** (*artificially adopted, contrived*) counterfeit, fake, feigned, (*coll.*) phoney, put-on, sham, simulated, spurious. ANTONYMS: genuine, sincere. **3** (*mannered, unnatural*) artificial, contrived, mannered, pompous, pretentious, studied, unnatural. ANTONYMS: natural.

affecting *a.* (*touching, moving*) heart-rending, moving, pathetic, poignant, touching, upsetting.

affection *n.* (*fondness, love*) attachment, desire, devotion, fondness, friendliness, liking, love, passion. ANTONYMS: dislike, hatred, loathing.

affectionate *a.* (*of a loving disposition*) caring, devoted, doting, fond, friendly, kind, loving, tender, warm. ANTONYMS: cold, unfeeling.

affiliate *v.i.* (*to become connected or associated, combine (with)*) ally, amalgamate, associate, become associated, become connected, combine, join, merge, unite. ANTONYMS: break away (from), separate (from).

affiliation *n.* **1** (*the act of affiliating; the process of being affiliated*) allying, amalgamating, amalgamation, association, combination, joining, merging, union, uniting. ANTONYMS: breaking up, separation. **2** (*association, link*) association, bond, connection, link, relationship, tie.

affinity *n.* **1** (*a natural attraction to or liking for something*) attraction, empathy, fondness, liking, rapport, sympathy. ANTONYMS: antipathy, aversion, dislike. **2** (*a close connection or structural resemblance*) analogy, likeness, resemblance, similarity, similitude. ANTONYMS: difference, disparity, dissimilarity.

affirm *v.t.* **1** (*to assert positively or solemnly*) assert, attest, aver, avow, declare, proclaim, pronounce, state, swear. **2** (*to confirm, to ratify*) certify, confirm, ratify, testify. ANTONYMS: deny, rebut, refute.

affirmation *n.* **1** (*the act of affirming anything; something which is affirmed*) assertion, attestation, averment, avowal, proclamation, pronouncement, statement, swearing. **2** (*a statement or declaration of the existence, truth, worth etc. of something*) certification, confirmation, ratification, testifying, testimony. ANTONYMS: denial, rebuttal, refutation.

affirmative *a.* (*expressing agreement or consent*) agreeing, assenting, concurring, confirming, consenting, corroborative, positive.

affix *v.t.* **1** (*to fasten, attach*) attach, fasten, fix, glue, paste, put on, stick, tack. ANTONYMS: detach, remove, take off. **2** (*to annex, to subjoin*) add, add on, append, attach, subjoin. ANTONYMS: remove.

afflict *v.t.* (*to inflict bodily or mental pain on; to trouble*) beset, burden, distress, harass, hurt, oppress, plague, rack, torment, trouble, vex, worry, wound.

affliction *n.* **1** (*trouble, misery*) adversity, calamity, distress, harassment, hardship, hurt, misery, misfortune, oppression, pain, suffering, torment, tribulation, trouble, vexation, woe, worry, wretchedness. **2** (*a mental or bodily ailment*) ailment, disease, disorder, illness. **3** (*an unpleasant experience that causes great distress*) burden, ordeal, scourge, torment, trial, trouble.

affluence *n.* (*wealth, prosperity*) opulence, prosperity, riches, wealth. ANTONYMS: poverty.

affluent *a.* (*wealthy, prosperous*) comfortably off, in the money, (*coll.*) loaded, moneyed, opulent, prosperous, rich, wealthy, (*coll.*) well-heeled, well off, well-to-do. ANTONYMS: hard up, impoverished, penniless, poor.

afford *v.t.* **1** (*to have the money, the means etc. to*) have the money for, meet the expense of, pay for. **2** (*to have the time to*) have enough, spare. **3** (*to be able to ignore the disadvantages of*) bear, stand, sustain. **4** (*to provide, supply*) bestow, furnish, give, impart, offer, produce, provide, supply, yield.

affray *n.* (*a fight or disturbance involving two or more persons in a public place*) altercation, brawl, disturbance, fight, fracas, free-for-all, mêlée, quarrel, row, scrap, scuffle, skirmish, tussle.

affront *v.t.* (*to insult openly*) insult, offend, outrage, slight.

~n. (*an open insult*) insult, slap in the face, slight, slur, snub. ANTONYMS: compliment.

aficionado n. (*a keen follower or fan*) adherent, admirer, (*coll.*) buff, devotee, enthusiast, fan, follower, (*coll.*) freak, lover, supporter.

afoot adv. (*in progress, in action*) about, around, circulating, going on, in progress, stirring.

aforesaid a. (*said or mentioned before*) above, aforementioned, earlier, foregoing, preceding, previous.

afraid a. **1** (*filled with fear, terrified*) alarmed, apprehensive, fearful, frightened, intimidated, nervous, scared, terrified. ANTONYMS: fearless, unafraid. **2** (*regretfully admitting or of the opinion*) apologetic, regretful, sorry. ANTONYMS: happy, pleased.

afresh adv. (*again*) again, anew, freshly, once again, once more, over again.

after prep. **1** (*at a later time than*) following, later than, subsequent to. ANTONYMS: before. **2** (*behind*) at the back of, behind. ANTONYMS: in front of. **3** (*in pursuit or search of*) following, in pursuit of, in quest of, in search of. **4** (*in view of, considering*) considering, in the light of, in view of, taking into consideration. **5** (*in spite of*) despite, in spite of, notwithstanding, regardless of. **6** (*concerning*) about, concerning, regarding. **7** (*in imitation of; from an original by*) in imitation of, in the manner of, in the style of, on the model of. **8** ((*in a list*) *following*) at a later point than, below, following. ANTONYMS: before. **9** (*using the name of*) for, in honour of, with the name of.
~adv. **1** (*later, subsequently*) afterwards, following, later, subsequently, thereafter. ANTONYMS: before, beforehand. **2** (*behind*) at the back, behind, in the rear.

afterlife n. (*life after death*) afterworld, hereafter, life after death.

aftermath n. (*consequences or after-effects*) after-effects, consequences, result, upshot.

afterward adv. (*subsequently*) after, later, next, subsequently, then. ANTONYMS: before, beforehand.

again adv. **1** (*a second time, once more*) afresh, anew, another time, a second time, once more. **2** (*in addition*) also, in addition, over and above. **3** (*moreover, besides*) also, besides, further, furthermore, in addition, moreover. **4** (*on the other hand*) conversely, on the contrary, on the other hand. **again and again** (*with frequent repetition, repeatedly*) continually, frequently, often, over and over, persistently, repeatedly, time and again, time and time again.

ANTONYMS: infrequently, occasionally, rarely, seldom.

against prep. **1** (*in opposition to*) averse to, contra, hostile to, in disagreement with, in opposition to, opposed to, versus. ANTONYMS: for, in favour of, pro. **2** (*fighting or competing with*) counter to, in opposition to, resisting. ANTONYMS: with. **3** (*in contrast to*) as a foil to, in contrast to. **4** (*in contact with*) in contact with, touching, up against. **5** (*in preparation or provision for*) as provision for, in anticipation of, in expectation of, in preparation for. **6** (*unfavourable to*) damaging to, detrimental to, disadvantageous to, prejudicial to, unfavourable to. ANTONYMS: in one's favour.

agape a., adv. (*in an attitude or condition of wondering expectation*) agog, amazed, astonished, astounded, dumbfounded, expectant, flabbergasted, (*sl.*) gobsmacked, spellbound, thunderstruck.

age n. **1** (*the length of time that a person or thing has existed*) duration, period, span. **2** (*a period or stage of life*) period, point, stage, time. **3** (*a distinct period of the past; a period of geological time*) epoch, era, generation, period, time. **4** (*usu. pl.*) (*a long time*) (*coll.*) aeons, a long time, (*coll.*) an eternity. **5** (*the latter portion of life*) advancing years, elderliness, old age, seniority. ANTONYMS: youth, youthfulness. **6** ((*legal*) *maturity, majority*) majority, maturity.
~v.i. **1** (*to show the signs of becoming older*) decline, deteriorate. **2** (*to grow old*) become old, become older, get old, get older, grow old, grow older. **3** (*to mature*) mature, mellow, ripen.
~v.t. (*to cause to grow old or to show signs of age*) make old, make older.

aged a. (*old*) ancient, elderly, old. ANTONYMS: young, youthful.

agency n. **1** (*a commercial organization offering a specific service*) business, company, concern, firm, organization. **2** (*a place where an agent conducts business*) bureau, office. **3** (*causative action, instrumentality*) action, activity, effect, force, influence, instrumentality, mechanism, medium, power, vehicle, work. **4** (*immediate or intervening action*) good offices, intercession, intervention, mediation.

agenda n. (*a list of the business to be transacted*) calendar, programme, schedule, timetable.

agent n. **1** (*a person who acts or transacts business on behalf of another*) deputy, emissary, envoy, go-between, negotiator, representative, substitute. **2** (*a person or company that offers a specific service or acts as a broker*) broker, factor, negotiator. **3** (*a person who exerts power*) author, doer, executor, performer, perpetrator. **4** (*something that produces an effect; the material cause or instrument*) agency, cause, force, instrument, means, medium, power, vehicle.

agglomerate *v.i.* (*to gather in a mass*) accumulate, amass, cluster, collect, gather, pile up.

agglomeration *n.* (*a mass, a heap*) accumulation, clump, cluster, collection, heap, jumble, lump, mass, miscellany, pile, stack.

aggrandizement *n.* (*the act of aggrandizing; the state of being aggrandized*) advancement, elevation, ennobling, exaltation, magnification, promotion.

aggravate *v.t.* **1** (*to make worse or more severe*) exacerbate, exaggerate, heighten, increase, inflame, intensify, magnify, make worse, worsen. ANTONYMS: alleviate, decrease, diminish, ease, lessen, reduce. **2** (*to exasperate, to irritate*) anger, annoy, exasperate, (*coll.*) get on one's nerves, infuriate, irk, irritate, provoke, vex. ANTONYMS: pacify, please.

aggravation *n.* **1** (*the intensification of a situation or condition for the worse*) exacerbation, exaggeration, heightening, increase, inflammation, intensification, magnification, worsening. ANTONYMS: alleviation, decrease, diminution, easing, lessening, reduction. **2** (*the act of aggravating or exasperating*) angering, annoyance, exasperating, exasperation, infuriating, irking, irritating, irritation, provoking, vexing. ANTONYMS: pacification, pleasing. **3** (*the state of being aggravated or annoyed*) anger, annoyance, fury, irritation, provocation, vexation. **4** (*something which aggravates or annoys*) irritant, nuisance, pest, thorn in the flesh.

aggregate *n.* **1** (*the total, the whole*) entirety, sum, total, totality, whole. **2** (*a mass formed by the union of individual units or particles*) accumulation, agglomeration, assemblage, clump, cluster, collection, concentration, heap, lass, lump, miscellany, mixture, pile, stack.

aggression *n.* **1** (*forcefulness or self-assertiveness*) aggressiveness, assertiveness, forcefulness, (*coll.*) pushiness, self-assertiveness, vigour. ANTONYMS: diffidence, hesitancy, self-effacement. **2** (*a hostile attitude or outlook*) aggressiveness, antagonism, belligerence, hostility, militance, pugnacity. ANTONYMS: friendliness, pacifism, peacefulness.

aggressive *a.* **1** (*involving an act of aggression*) belligerent, hostile, warring. **2** (*offensive, pugnacious*) argumentative, bellicose, belligerent,

combative, hostile, militant, pugnacious, quarrelsome, warring. ANTONYMS: friendly, peaceful, placatory. **3** (*forceful or self-assertive*) assertive, dynamic, energetic, enterprising, forceful, (*coll.*) pushy, self-assertive, vigorous. ANTONYMS: diffident, self-effacing.

aggressor *n.* (*the person, country etc. that begins hostilities, a quarrel etc.*) assailant, attacker, instigator, invader, provoker.

aggrieved *a.* (*having a grievance*) abused, afflicted, harmed, hurt, ill-used, injured, mistreated, wronged.

aghast *a.* (*appalled, horrified*) amazed, appalled, horrified, horror-struck, shocked, stunned, thunderstruck.

agile *a.* **1** (*having the ability to move quickly and gracefully*) active, limber, lithe, nimble, sprightly, spry, supple. ANTONYMS: awkward, clumsy, lumbering, stiff, ungainly. **2** (*mentally quick, nimble*) active, alert, clever, nimble, quick-witted, sharp. ANTONYMS: dull, slow, slow-witted.

agitate *v.t.* **1** (*to shake or move briskly*) beat, churn, shake, stir, toss, whisk. **2** (*to excite, to disturb*) alarm, arouse, confuse, disconcert, disquiet, disturb, excite, fluster, perturb, ruffle, trouble, upset, work up. ANTONYMS: calm, calm down, pacify, soothe.
~*v.i.* (*to arouse public feeling or opinion for or against something*) argue, campaign, protest.

agitation *n.* **1** (*commotion, perturbation*) alarm, clamour, commotion, confusion, disconcertment, disquiet, disturbance, excitement, ferment, fluster, perturbation, trouble, tumult, turmoil, upheaval, upset. **2** (*attempts to stir up public excitement or to initiate action*) argument, campaigning, debate, protest.

agitator *n.* (*a person who or something which agitates*) agent provocateur, demagogue, firebrand, inciter, rabble-rouser, troublemaker.

agnostic *n.* (*a person who believes that knowledge of the existence of God is impossible*) disbeliever, doubter, doubting Thomas, sceptic. ANTONYMS: believer.

ago *adv.* (*before this time*) before now, before this time, formerly, in the past, in time gone by, since.

agonizing *a.* (*causing agony*) excruciating, harrowing, painful, sore.

agony *n.* **1** (*anguish of mind*) affliction, anguish, distress, misery, pain, suffering, torment, torture, woe, wretchedness. **2** (*extreme physical pain*) affliction, pain, pangs, suffering, torment, torture.

agree *v.i.* **1** (*to be of one mind, to hold the same opinion*) be of the same mind, be of the same opinion, be on the same wavelength, concur. ANTONYMS: disagree. **2** (*to consent, to accede (to)*) accede (to), accept, acquiesce (in), assent (to), consent (to). ANTONYMS: disagree (with). **3** (*to harmonize, to coincide (with)*) accord (with), conform (to), correspond (with), fit, harmonize (with), match, square (with), tally (with). ANTONYMS: be at variance (with), contradict, differ (from), disagree (with). **4** (*to suit; be good for*) be beneficial to, be good for, suit. ANTONYMS: disagree with.
~*v.t.* (*to reach agreement about*) arrange, decide on, settle on.

agreeable *a.* **1** (*pleasing, pleasant*) congenial, delightful, enjoyable, gratifying, nice, pleasant, pleasing, pleasurable, satisfying, to one's liking. ANTONYMS: disagreeable, unpleasant. **2** (*favourable, disposed to*) acquiescent, amenable, assenting, compliant, consenting, in accord, well-disposed, willing. ANTONYMS: in disagreement. **3** (*friendly, pleasant*) amiable, congenial, friendly, genial, good-natured, likeable, nice, pleasant. ANTONYMS: disagreeable, nasty, unfriendly, unpleasant.

agreement *n.* **1** (*the fact of being of one mind; concurrence in the same opinion*) accord, assent, concurrence, harmony, unity. ANTONYMS: disagreement, dispute. **2** (*an arrangement mutually acceptable; a contract duly executed and legally binding*) arrangement, bargain, compact, contract, covenant, deal, pact, settlement, treaty. **3** (*conformity, correspondence*) accordance, coincidence, conformity, congruity, correspondence, harmony, matching, similarity, tallying. ANTONYMS: conflict, disagreement, disparity, dissimilarity, incongruity.

agriculture *n.* (*the science and practice of cultivating the soil, growing crops and rearing livestock*) farming, husbandry.

aground *a., adv.* (*on the shallow bottom of any water*) beached, foundered, grounded, high and dry, stranded, stuck.

ahead *adv.* **1** (*in front, further on*) further on, in front, in the lead, in the vanguard. ANTONYMS: behind, in the rear. **2** (*forward, esp. in a straight line*) forwards, on, onwards. **to be ahead** (*to be in the lead, to be winning*) be in front, be in the lead, be leading, be winning. ANTONYMS: be in the rear, be losing.

aid *v.t.* **1** (*to assist, to help*) abet, assist, give a helping hand to, give assistance to, give help to, help, lend a hand to, succour, support. ANTONYMS: hinder, impede, obstruct. **2** (*to make (a process) easier or quicker*) accelerate, contribute to, encourage, expedite, facilitate, hasten, help, speed up. ANTONYMS: hinder, impede, obstruct.
~*n.* **1** (*help, assistance*) assistance, help, helping hand, support. **2** (*financial or material assistance given by one country to another*) assistance, contribution, help, subsidy. **3** (*a helper or supporter*) aide, assistant, helper, supporter.

ailing *a.* (*affected with illness, sick*) debilitated, ill, incapacitated, indisposed, infirm, invalid, not well, off colour, poorly, sick, sickly, under the weather, unwell. ANTONYMS: well.

ailment *n.* (*a (slight) disorder or illness*) affliction, complaint, disease, disorder, illness, indisposition, infirmity, malady, sickness.

aim *v.t.* **1** (*to point at a target with (a missile or weapon), to level (a gun) at a target*) direct, level, point, train. **2** (*to direct (a blow, remark, criticism) at*) direct, focus, level, point.
~*v.i.* (*to intend, to endeavour (to do)*) aspire (to), attempt (to), endeavour (to), intend (to), mean (to), plan (to), strive (to), try (to).
~*n.* (*an intention, a purpose*) ambition, aspiration, design, end, goal, intention, object, objective, plan, purpose, target, wish.

aimless *a.* (*purposeless, objectless*) directionless, goalless, pointless, purposeless, undirected. ANTONYMS: purposeful, settled.

air *n.* **1** (*the mixture of gases which envelops the earth*) atmosphere. **2** (*a distinctive quality, an aura*) ambience, atmosphere, aura, effect, feeling, flavour, impression, mood, quality, tone. **3** (*manner, appearance*) appearance, bearing, demeanour, gesture, look, manner, mien, style. **4** (*usu. pl.*) (*affectation, haughtiness*) affectations, affectedness, airs and graces, posing, posturing. **5** (*a light wind, a breeze*) breath of air, breeze, draught, wind, (*poet.*) zephyr. **6** (*a tune, melody*) melody, song, tune.
~*v.t.* **1** (*to expose to open or fresh air, to ventilate*) aerate, freshen, ventilate. **2** (*to express publicly (a grievance, an opinion)*) broadcast, circulate, communicate, declare, disclose, divulge, exhibit, express, give expression to, give vent to, make known, make public, proclaim, publicize, publish, reveal, tell, utter, vent, voice. ANTONYMS: conceal, hide, keep secret.

airily *adv.* (*in a nonchalant or offhand way*) blithely, breezily, casually, cheerfully, flippantly, gaily, jauntily, light-heartedly, lightly, nonchalantly.

airiness *n.* **1** (*the state of being well-ventilated*) freshness. **2** (*the state of being spacious*) lightness, openness, spaciousness. ANTONYMS: pokiness. **3** (*the state of being breezy*) breeziness, draughtiness, windiness. ANTONYMS:

calmness. **4** (*flippancy, nonchalance*) blitheness, breeziness, cheerfulness, flippancy,
gaiety, jauntiness, light-heartedness, nonchalance. ANTONYMS: gloom, moroseness, seriousness.

airing n. **1** (*exposure to the free action of the
air or to heat*) aeration, drying, freshening,
ventilating, ventilation. **2** (*a walk or ride
in the open air*) excursion, jaunt, outing,
stroll, walk. **3** (*the public expression of something*) broadcasting, circulation, communication, declaration, disclosure, divulgence,
exposure, expression, proclamation, publicizing, publishing, revelation, telling, utterance,
uttering, venting, voicing. ANTONYMS: concealment.

airless a. (*close, musty*) close, muggy, musty,
oppressive, stale, stifling, stuffy, suffocating,
unventilated. ANTONYMS: airy, fresh, well-
ventilated.

airs and graces n.pl. (*would-be elegant or
genteel mannerisms intended to impress*)
affectation, affectedness, posing, posturing,
pretensions, (*sl.*) swank.

airtight a. (*not allowing air to pass in or out*)
closed, sealed, shut tight.

airy a. **1** (*well-ventilated*) fresh, well-
ventilated. ANTONYMS: musty, stale, stuffy, unventilated. **2** (*spacious; uncluttered*) light,
open, spacious, uncluttered. ANTONYMS:
cluttered, pokey. **3** (*flippant; offhand*) blithe,
breezy, casual, cheerful, flippant, gay, jaunty,
light-hearted, nonchalant. ANTONYMS: gloomy,
morose, serious. **4** (*breezy*) blowy, breezy,
gusty, windy. ANTONYMS: calm.

aisle n. (*a passage between the seats in a
church, theatre, cinema etc.*) corridor, passage,
passageway.

ajar a., adv. ((*of a door*) *partly open*) half-open,
partly open.

akin a. **1** (*allied by blood relationship*) connected, kin, related. **2** (*allied* (*to*) *in properties
or character*) alike, analogous (to), corresponding (to), similar (to).

alacrity n. (*briskness, eagerness*) briskness,
eagerness, enthusiasm, haste, promptness,
readiness, swiftness, willingness. ANTONYMS:
apathy, reluctance, slowness, unwillingness.

alarm n. **1** (*warning of approaching danger*)
alarm bell, alarm signal, distress signal, siren,
tocsin. **2** (*terror mingled with surprise*) agitation, apprehension, consternation, dismay,
disquiet, fear, fright, nervousness, panic,
perturbation, terror, trepidation. ANTONYMS:

calmness, composure, nonchalance, sang-
froid.
~v.t. **1** (*to frighten; to startle*) agitate, dismay,
disquiet, disturb, frighten, panic, perturb,
(*coll.*) put the wind up, scare, startle, terrify,
unnerve. ANTONYMS: calm down, comfort,
reassure. **2** (*to rouse to a sense of danger*) alert,
arouse, warn.

alarmed a. (*frightened, startled*) afraid,
agitated, dismayed, disturbed, frightened, in a
panic, perturbed, scared, startled, terrified,
unnerved. ANTONYMS: calm, composed, cool.

alarming a. (*frightening, disturbing*) disturbing, frightening, perturbing, shocking,
startling, terrifying, unnerving.

alarmist n. (*a person who needlessly spreads
alarm, a scaremonger*) (*coll.*) doom and gloom
merchant, (*coll.*) doom merchant, doomster,
scaremonger, voice of doom.

alcohol n. (*any intoxicating drink containing
alcohol*) alcoholic drink, (*coll.*) booze, liquor,
strong drink.

alcoholic n. (*a person who is addicted to
alcohol*) alcohol addict, (*sl.*) alky, (*coll.*)
boozer, (*coll.*) dipso, dipsomaniac, drunk,
drunkard, hard drinker, heavy drinker, (*sl.*)
lush, sot, tippler, toper, (*sl.*) wino.
~a. **1** (*relating to or containing alcohol*) hard,
inebriating, intoxicating, spirituous, strong.
ANTONYMS: non-alcoholic, soft. **2** (*addicted
to alcohol*) alcohol-addicted, alcohol-depend-
ent, dipsomaniac, drunken. ANTONYMS: teetotal.

alcoholism n. (*addiction to or excessive use
of alcohol*) alcohol abuse, alcohol addiction,
drunkenness, heavy drinking. ANTONYMS:
teetotalism.

alcove n. (*a recess in a wall*) bay, niche, nook,
opening, recess.

alert a. **1** (*watchful, vigilant*) attentive, aware,
circumspect, heedful, observant, on one's
guard, on the lookout, on the qui vive, vigilant, wary, watchful, wide awake. ANTONYMS:
heedless, inattentive, unwary. **2** (*able to think
quickly and clearly*) bright, on one's toes, on
the ball, perceptive, quick, quick off the mark,
quick-thinking, sharp, wide awake. ANTONYMS:
dull, slow.
~n. (*warning of danger*) alarm, alarm signal,
siren, warning.

alertness n. **1** (*watchfulness, vigilance*) attention, attentiveness, awareness, circumspection, heedfulness, vigilance, wariness,
watchfulness. ANTONYMS: inattention, inattentiveness, unwariness. **2** (*the ability to think
quickly and clearly*) brightness, perception,

perceptiveness, quickness, sharpness. ANTO-
NYMS: dullness, slowness.

alias *adv.* (*otherwise* (*named or called*)) also
called, also known as, otherwise, otherwise
known as.
~*n.* (*an assumed name*) assumed name, nom de
plume, pen-name, pseudonym, stage name.

alibi *n.* (*an excuse* (*for failing to do something*))
excuse, explanation, justification, pretext,
reason.

alien *a.* **1** (*unfamiliar; strange*) exotic, incongruous, outlandish, strange, unfamiliar, unknown. ANTONYMS: familiar, known. **2** (*foreign;
belonging to a foreign country*) exotic, foreign,
not native. ANTONYMS: native. **3** (*unacceptable,
repugnant to*) contrary to, hostile to, incompatible with, opposed to, out of keeping with,
repugnant to, unacceptable to. ANTONYMS:
compatible with, in keeping with.
~*n.* **1** (*a foreigner; a foreign-born non-naturalized
resident*) foreigner, outsider, stranger. **2** (*a
being from another world*) extraterrestrial,
(*coll.*) little green man.

alienate *v.t.* **1** (*to cause to become unfriendly
or hostile*) estrange, make hostile, make unfriendly, set against, turn away. ANTONYMS:
endear, make friendly. **2** (*to cause to feel
isolated or estranged*) cut off, divide, divorce,
estrange, isolate, separate, sever. ANTONYMS:
integrate, join, make part of. **3** (*to transfer to
the ownership of another*) convey, transfer.

alienation *n.* **1** (*the act of alienating or turning away*) alienating, estrangement, setting
against, turning away. **2** (*the act of alienating or
isolating*) cutting off, divorce, estrangement,
isolation, separation, severance. ANTONYMS:
integration. **3** (*the feeling of being estranged
from one's social environment*) divorce,
estrangement, isolation, separation, severance.
ANTONYMS: integration, involvement. **4** (*the
transference of ownership to another*) conveyance, transfer, transference, transferring.

alight[1] *v.i.* **1** (*to get down, descend*) descend,
dismount, get down, get off. ANTONYMS: get on,
get up, mount. **2** (*to reach the ground, to settle*)
come to rest, land, settle, touch down.
ANTONYMS: take off. **3** (*to come by chance, to
happen* (*on*)) chance upon, come on by
chance, come upon, discover, encounter,
happen upon, stumble on.

alight[2] *adv., pred.a.* **1** (*on fire*) ablaze, aflame,
burning, ignited, on fire. ANTONYMS: ex-
tinguished. **2** (*illuminated*) illuminated, lit, lit
up. ANTONYMS: dark. **3** ((*of a person's eyes*)
excited and happy) bright, illuminated, lit up,
shining.

align *v.t.* **1** (*to range or place in a line*) arrange,
even up, line up, order, put in order, range,
straighten. **2** (*to place in a position of agreement with others*) affiliate, agree, ally,
associate, cooperate, join, side, sympathize.
ANTONYMS: disagree (with), dissociate (from).

alignment *n.* **1** (*the act of ranging in line or
being ranged*) arrangement, arranging, evening
up, lining up, ordering, ranging, straightening.
2 (*the act of taking a side or associating with
a party, cause, etc.*) affiliation, agreement,
alliance, allying, association, cooperation,
joining, siding, sympathy. ANTONYMS: disagreement, disassociation.

alike *a.* (*similar*) akin, analogous, corresponding, equal, identical, like, parallel,
resembling, similar, the same. ANTONYMS:
different, dissimilar, diverse, unlike.
~*adv.* (*in the same manner, similarly*) equally,
identically, in the same manner, in the same
way, just the same, similarly. ANTONYMS:
differently, dissimilarly.

alimony *n.* (*payment of means of support, esp.
after legal separation or divorce*) keep, maintenance, support.

alive *pred.a.* **1** (*living, existent*) (*coll.*) alive and
kicking, animate, existent, in the land of the
living, live, living. ANTONYMS: dead, deceased,
extinct. **2** (*in force or operation*) active, existent, existing, extant, functioning, going on, in
existence, in force, in operation, operational,
operative, prevalent. ANTONYMS: dead, dead as
a dodo, extinct, inactive. **3** (*lively, active*)
active, alert, animated, energetic, full of life,
full of zest, lively, spirited, sprightly, vigorous,
vital, vivacious. ANTONYMS: apathetic, dull,
lifeless. **4** (*sensitive, responsive* (*to*)) alert (to),
awake (to), aware (of), cognizant (of), conscious (of), sensible (of). ANTONYMS: unaware
(of), unconscious (of). **5** (*swarming* (*with*); *full
of*) abounding (in), bristling (with), bustling
(with), crawling (with), crowded (with), full
(of), jumping (with), overrun (by), packed
(with), swarming (with), teeming (with),
thronged (with). ANTONYMS: empty (of), free
(of).

all *a.* **1** (*the whole* (*quantity, amount or degree*)
of) the complete, the entire, the totality of,
the whole (of). ANTONYMS: a portion of, part.
2 (*every one of*) each, each and every, every,
every one of, every single. **3** (*the greatest possible*) complete, entire, full, greatest, maximum,
total, utter. ANTONYMS: least, little, minimal,
minimum.
~*pron.* **1** (*all the persons concerned; everyone*)
each one, each person, everybody, everyone,
every person, the whole lot. ANTONYMS: some.
2 (*all the things concerned; everything*) each

thing, every thing, lock, stock and barrel, the whole lot. ANTONYMS: some.

~*n.* (*the whole, the totality*) aggregate, entirety, everything, the total amount, the whole amount, totality, whole.

~*adv.* (*entirely, completely*) altogether, completely, entirely, fully, totally, utterly, wholly. ANTONYMS: partially, partly.

allay *v.t.* **1** (*to calm* (*fear*); *to diminish* (*suspicion*)) calm, diminish, lessen, moderate, pacify, quell, quiet, reduce, soothe. ANTONYMS: arouse, increase, intensify. **2** (*to alleviate, to relieve* (*pain*)) abate, alleviate, assuage, blunt, ease, mitigate, reduce, relieve, soothe. ANTONYMS: aggravate, exacerbate.

allegation *n.* (*an assertion without proof, a statement of what one undertakes to prove*) accusation, affirmation, assertion, averment, avowal, charge, claim, declaration, deposition, statement.

allege *v.t.* (*to affirm positively but without or before proof*) affirm, assert, aver, avow, claim, declare, maintain, make an allegation, profess, put forward, state.

alleged *a.* (*supposed*) claimed, declared, ostensible, professed, so-called, stated, supposed. ANTONYMS: genuine, proven.

allegiance *n.* (*loyalty, devotion*) adherence, devotion, faithfulness, fidelity, loyalty. ANTONYMS: disloyalty, infidelity, perfidy.

allegoric *a.* (*relating to or consisting of allegory*) emblematic, figurative, metaphorical, symbolic.

allegory *n.* **1** (*a story, play etc. using symbolic representation*) apologue, fable, parable. **2** (*the technique of symbolic representation*) analogy, metaphor, symbolism.

allergic *a.* **1** (*having an allergic response* (*to*)) affected (by), hypersensitive (to), sensitive (to), susceptible (to). **2** (*averse* (*to*)) antipathetic (to), averse (to), disinclined (to), hostile (to), loath (to), opposed (to).

allergy *n.* **1** (*hypersensitiveness to certain substances inhaled or touched*) hypersensitivity, sensitivity, susceptibility. **2** (*an aversion, antipathy*) antipathy, aversion, disinclination, dislike, hostility, opposition.

alleviate *v.t.* (*to lighten, lessen*) abate, allay, assuage, calm, diminish, ease, lessen, mitigate, moderate, palliate, quell, quiet, reduce, soothe. ANTONYMS: aggravate, exacerbate.

alley *n.* (*a passage, esp. between or behind buildings*) alleyway, backstreet, lane, passage, passageway.

alliance *n.* **1** (*agreement committing two or more states, individuals etc. to act together*) agreement, compact, concordat, pact, treaty. **2** (*union or connection of interests*) affiliation, association, coalition, confederation, federation, league, marriage, partnership, union.

allied *a.* **1** (*united, associated*) affiliated, amalgamated, confederate, joint, united. **2** (*of the same type, related*) associated, connected, kindred, linked, related, similar. ANTONYMS: dissimilar, unconnected, unrelated.

allocate *v.t.* (*to assign, allot*) allot, apportion, assign, bestow, dispense, distribute, dole out, give out, grant, mete out, set aside, share out.

allocation *n.* **1** (*the act of allocating*) allotment, allotting, apportioning, assigning, bestowal, dispensation, distribution, doling out, giving out, granting, meting out, sharing out. **2** (*an amount or thing allocated*) allowance, grant, lot, measure, portion, quota, ration, share.

allot *v.t.* (*to distribute, to assign as one's share*) allocate, apportion, assign, bestow, dispense, distribute, dole out, give out, grant, mete out, share out.

allotment *n.* **1** (*the act of allotting*) allocating, apportioning, assigning, bestowing, dispensation, distribution, doling out, giving out, meting out, sharing out. **2** (*the share assigned*) allowance, grant, lot, measure, portion, quota, ration, share.

allow *v.t.* **1** (*to permit*) authorize, give permission to, give the go-ahead to, (*coll.*) give the green light to, let, permit, sanction. ANTONYMS: disallow, forbid, refuse permission, withhold permission. **2** (*to assign, set aside for a purpose*) allocate, allot, apportion, assign, set aside. **3** (*to give or provide* (*a limited quantity or sum*)) bestow, furnish, give, grant, provide. **4** (*to acknowledge, concede*) acknowledge, concede, confess, give, grant, own. ANTONYMS: deny, refute. **to allow for** (*to make allowance or deduction for*) bear in mind, make allowance for, take into account, take into consideration. ANTONYMS: forget about, ignore.

allowable *a.* (*that can be allowed*) acceptable, admissible, authorized, permissible, sanctioned, tolerable. ANTONYMS: forbidden, inadmissible, unacceptable.

allowance *n.* **1** (*a fixed quantity or sum allowed to a particular person or for a specific purpose*) allocation, apportionment, grant, lot, portion, quota, ration, subsidy. **2** (*a deduction or discount, made in consideration of something*) concession, deduction, discount, rebate, reduction. ANTONYMS: addition, extra. **to make**

allowance/ allowances for 1 (*to take* (*mitigating circumstances*) *into account*) allow for, bear in mind, take into account, take into consideration. ANTONYMS: forget about, ignore. **2** (*to consider, when making a decision*) make adjustments, make concessions, make excuses, take (something) into account, take (something) into consideration.

all right *a., adv.* **1** (*satisfactory, in good condition etc.*) acceptable, adequate, average, fair, fine, good enough, (*coll.*) OK, (*coll.*) okay, passable, satisfactory. ANTONYMS: inadequate, not good enough, unacceptable, unsatisfactory. **2** (*safe and well*) fine, (*coll.*) OK, (*coll.*) okay, safe, safe and sound, sound, unharmed, uninjured, well. ANTONYMS: ill, in danger, injured, unwell.

allude *v.i.* **1** (*to make indirect reference* (*to*), *to hint at*) hint, imply, insinuate, suggest. **2** (*to mention, to refer* (*to*)) make mention of, mention, mention en passant, mention in passing, refer to, speak of, touch upon. ANTONYMS: ignore, pass over.

allure *v.t.* (*to attract or tempt by the offer of some real or apparent good*) attract, beguile, bewitch, captivate, charm, entice, entrance, fascinate, lure, seduce, tempt. ANTONYMS: put off, repel, (*coll.*) turn off.

alluring *a.* (*enticing, attractive*) attractive, beguiling, bewitching, captivating, enchanting, enticing, fascinating, seductive, tempting. ANTONYMS: repellent, repugnant, repulsive, unattractive.

allusion *n.* **1** (*a reference to anything not directly mentioned*) mention, reference. **2** (*a hint*) hint, implication, innuendo, insinuation, suggestion.

ally[1] *v.t.* (*to unite by treaty, confederation, marriage or friendship*) affiliate, associate, band together, collaborate, combine, form an alliance, go into partnership, join forces, join together, marry, unite. ANTONYMS: break up, divorce, separate, split up.

ally[2] *n.* (*a person or group etc. that helps or supports another*) accomplice, associate, collaborator, colleague, confederate, friend, partner. ANTONYMS: adversary, enemy, opponent, rival.

almighty *a.* **1** (*omnipotent*) absolute, all-powerful, omnipotent, supreme. **2** (*very great, very loud*) awful, dreadful, excessive, great, terrible.

almost *adv.* (*nearly, very nearly*) all but, approaching, approximately, as good as, bordering on, close to, just about, nearly, not far from, not quite, on the brink of, on the verge of, practically, verging on, virtually, well-nigh. ANTONYMS: completely, entirely, fully, wholly.

aloft *adv.* (*high up, on high*) high up, in the air, on high, overhead, up, up above. ANTONYMS: down low.

alone *a., adv.* **1** (*with no other present*) by itself, by oneself, solitary, unaccompanied, unattended, unescorted. ANTONYMS: accompanied, escorted, with others. **2** (*without help from others*) by oneself, by one's own efforts, single-handed, unaided, unassisted. ANTONYMS: aided, assisted, with help. **3** (*lonely*) abandoned, deserted, desolate, forlorn, forsaken, isolated, lonely, lonesome, solitary. **4** (*only, solely*) exclusively, only, solely. **5** (*without equal, unique*) incomparable, matchless, peerless, singular, unequalled, unique, unparalleled, unsurpassed. **6** (*not near others*) apart, by itself, detached, separate. ANTONYMS: among others.

along *prep.* **1** (*from one end to the other of*) from one end to the other of, through, throughout the length of. **2** (*beside and extending over the length of*) alongside, beside, by the side of, close to, on the edge of.
~*adv.* **1** (*forward, onward*) ahead, forward, forwards, on, onward, onwards. **2** (*in company with someone or oneself*) as an escort, as a partner, as company. **along with** (*in company or together with*) accompanied by, coupled with, in addition to, in company with, plus, together with, with. ANTONYMS: without.

aloof *adv.* (*away, at a distance, apart*) apart, at a distance, at arm's length, away. ANTONYMS: close, near.
~*a.* (*distant or unsympathetic in manner*) chilly, cold, cool, detached, distant, forbidding, formal, haughty, indifferent, remote, reserved, stand-offish, unapproachable, unfriendly, unresponsive, unsociable, unsympathetic. ANTONYMS: friendly, sociable, warm.

aloud *adv.* (*audibly*) audibly, clearly, distinctly. ANTONYMS: under one's breath.

also *adv., conj.* **1** (*in addition, as well*) as well, besides, in addition, into the bargain, to boot, too. ANTONYMS: instead. **2** (*likewise, besides*) besides, further, furthermore, in addition, moreover.

alter *v.t.* (*to cause to vary or change in some degree*) adapt, adjust, change, convert, metamorphose, modify, remodel, reshape, revise, transform, vary.
~*v.i.* (*to undergo some change*) adapt, adjust, amend, change, metamorphose, suffer a sea change.

alteration *n.* **1** (*the act of altering*) adaptation, adjustment, amendment, changing, conversion, metamorphosis, modification, remodelling, reshaping, revision, transformation, varying. **2** (*the change made*) adaptation, adjustment, amendment, change, conversion, metamorphosis, modification, revision, transformation, variation.

altercation *n.* (*a vehement dispute*) argument, fight, fracas, quarrel, row, (*coll.*) set-to, squabble, wrangle.

alternate[1] *v.i.* (*to happen or succeed one another by turns*) interchange, rotate, take it in turns, take turns.

alternate[2] *a.* **1** (*done or happening by turns, first one and then the other*) by turns, in rotation, interchanging. **2** (*every other, every second*) every other, every second.

alternative *a.* **1** (*being the other of two things open to choice*) another, different, other, second, substitute. **2** (*denoting to a lifestyle, art form etc. which constitutes an alternative to conventional methods or systems*) nonstandard, unconventional, unorthodox. ANTONYMS: conventional, standard, traditional.
~*n.* (*either of two courses which may be chosen*) choice, option, preference, selection.

alternatively *adv.* (*as an alternative, otherwise*) as an alternative, if not, instead, on the other hand, or, otherwise.

although *conj.* (*though, notwithstanding*) despite the fact that, even although, even if, even supposing, even though, notwithstanding the fact that, though, while, whilst.

altitude *n.* (*vertical height*) elevation, height, tallness.

altogether *adv.* **1** (*completely, entirely*) absolutely, completely, entirely, fully, perfectly, quite, totally, utterly, wholly. ANTONYMS: partially, partly, relatively, slightly. **2** (*inclusive of everything*) all told, in all, in toto, taken together. ANTONYMS: separately. **3** (*on the whole, in view of all things*) all in all, all things considered, by and large, in general, in the main, on the whole, taking everything into consideration.

altruism *n.* (*devotion to the good of others* (*as opposed to egoism*)) benevolence, charity, generosity, open-handedness, philanthropy, public-spiritedness, self-sacrifice, unselfishness. ANTONYMS: egoism, meanness, selfishness, self-seeking.

altruistic *a.* (*showing devotion to the good of others*) benevolent, charitable, generous, open-handed, philanthropic, public-spirited, self-sacrificing, unselfish. ANTONYMS: egoistic, mean, selfish, self-seeking.

always *adv.* **1** (*on all occasions, in all cases*) consistently, every time, invariably, regularly, unfailingly, without exception, without fail. ANTONYMS: hardly ever, never, rarely, scarcely ever, seldom. **2** (*repeatedly, regularly*) constantly, continually, forever, incessantly, perpetually, regularly, repeatedly. ANTONYMS: never, rarely, seldom. **3** (*in any event, whatever the circumstances*) come what may, in any case, in any event, no matter what, whatever happens. **4** (*forever; till the end of one's life*) endlessly, eternally, ever, everlastingly, evermore, forever. ANTONYMS: fleetingly, for a time, temporarily.

amalgamate *v.i.* (*to combine, to merge into one*) blend, combine, fuse, integrate, merge, mingle, unite. ANTONYMS: break up, part, separate, split up.

amass *v.t.* (*to collect together, to accumulate*) accumulate, assemble, collect, gather, heap up, hoard, pile up, (*coll.*) stash away, store up.

amateur *n.* (*a person who practises anything as a pastime, as distinguished from one who does so professionally*) dabbler, dilettante, layman/ laywoman/ lay person, non-professional. ANTONYMS: professional.

amateurish *a.* (*not up to the professional standard*) bungling, clumsy, crude, incompetent, inexpert, unprofessional, unskilful, unskilled. ANTONYMS: expert, professional, skilful, skilled.

amaze *v.t.* (*to astound, to overwhelm with wonder*) astonish, astound, bewilder, (*coll.*) bowl over, confound, dumbfound, flabbergast, shock, stagger, startle, stun, stupefy, surprise.

amazement *n.* (*overwhelming surprise*) astonishment, bewilderment, shock, stupefaction, surprise, wonder.

ambassador *n.* **1** (*a high-ranking diplomat*) attaché, consul, diplomat, plenipotentiary. **2** (*a representative; a promoter* (*e.g. of peace*)) agent, deputy, emissary, envoy, legate.

ambience *n.* (*a surrounding atmosphere or influence*) air, atmosphere, aura, character, environment, feel, flavour, impression, milieu, mood, quality, setting, spirit, surroundings, temper, tenor, tone, (*coll.*) vibes, vibrations.

ambiguity *n.* **1** (*the state of being ambiguous*) ambivalence, equivocalness. ANTONYMS: clarity. **2** (*a doubtful or obscure meaning*) abstruseness, doubtfulness, dubiety, dubiousness, indefiniteness, indeterminateness, obscurity, uncertainty, unclearness, vagueness.

ANTONYMS: clarity, explicitness, obviousness, plainness. **3** (*an instance of being ambiguous*) enigma, paradox, puzzle.

ambiguous *a.* **1** (*susceptible to two or more meanings*) ambivalent, equivocal. ANTONYMS: clear, unmistakable. **2** (*of doubtful meaning, equivocal*) abstruse, cryptic, doubtful, dubious, enigmatic, indefinite, indeterminate, obscure, paradoxical, puzzling, uncertain, unclear, vague. ANTONYMS: clear, explicit, obvious, plain.

ambition *n.* **1** (*a desire for power, success etc.*) aspiration, drive, enterprise, force, forcefulness, get-up-and-go, high hopes, striving. **2** (*a strong desire to achieve anything, usu. something advantageous or creditable*) desire, eagerness, hankering, longing, yearning, zeal. ANTONYMS: apathy, disinclination. **3** (*the object of such desire*) aim, aspiration, design, dream, end, goal, hope, object, objective, purpose, wish.

ambitious *a.* **1** (*actuated by ambition*) aspiring, assertive, enterprising, forceful, go-ahead, (*coll.*) on the make, (*coll.*) pushy. ANTONYMS: unambitious. **2** (*highly desirous (of); eager and determined (to do)*) avid (for), covetous (of), desirous (of), determined (to), eager (to), enthusiastic (about), intent (on). ANTONYMS: apathetic (about), unambitious (for), unenthusiastic (about). **3** (*necessitating great effort, resources, skill etc.*) arduous, bold, challenging, demanding, difficult, elaborate, exacting, formidable, grandiose, hard, impressive, pretentious, severe, strenuous. ANTONYMS: easy, simple.

ambivalence *n.* (*the simultaneous existence in the mind of two incompatible feelings or wishes*) clash, conflict, contradiction, doubt, equivocation, fluctuation, hesitancy, indecision, irresolution, uncertainty, vacillation, wavering. ANTONYMS: certainty, decisiveness, resolution, sureness.

ambivalent *a.* (*having or showing ambivalence*) clashing, conflicting, contradictory, debatable, doubtful, equivocal, fluctuating, hesitant, inconclusive, in conflict, in two minds, irresolute, mixed, uncertain, unresolved, unsure, vacillating, warring, wavering. ANTONYMS: certain, decided, resolute, sure.

amble *v.i.* (*to walk at a leisurely relaxed pace*) dawdle, (*esp. N Am., coll.*) mosey, saunter, stroll, wander. ANTONYMS: dash, hasten, rush.

ambush *v.t.* (*to lie in wait for*) ambuscade, lay a trap for, lie in wait for, set a trap for, waylay.

ameliorate *v.t.* (*to make better, to improve*) alleviate, amend, benefit, better, ease, improve, make better, mend, mitigate, relieve. ANTONYMS: aggravate, exacerbate, make worse, worsen.

amenable *a.* (*willing to cooperate, readily persuaded*) acquiescent, adaptable, agreeable, flexible, pliant, responsive, tractable. ANTONYMS: inflexible, obstinate, recalcitrant.

amend *v.t.* **1** (*to alter (a person or thing) for the better, to improve*) ameliorate, better, enhance, fix, improve, make better, reform, remedy, repair. **2** (*to remove errors from, to correct*) alter, correct, rectify, revise.

amendment *n.* **1** (*an alteration*) alteration, correction, revision. **2** (*a change for the better*) amelioration, betterment, enhancement, improvement, reform, remedy, repair. **3** (*something added to a bill or motion; esp. an addition to the US constitution*) addendum, addition, adjunct, alteration, appendage, attachment.

amends *n.* (*reparation, compensation*) atonement, compensation, recompense, redress, reparation, restitution.

amenity *n.* (*a feature or facility conducive to the usefulness or attractiveness of something*) comfort, convenience, facility, resource, service.

amiable *a.* (*friendly, likeable*) affable, agreeable, charming, congenial, delightful, engaging, friendly, genial, good-humoured, good-natured, kindly, likeable, lovable, pleasant, sociable. ANTONYMS: disagreeable, ill-natured, unfriendly, unpleasant.

amicable *a.* (*resulting from friendliness*) civil, cordial, friendly, harmonious, peaceful. ANTONYMS: antagonistic, hostile, unfriendly.

amid *prep.* (*in the midst of, among*) amidst, among, amongst, in the middle of, in the midst of, in the thick of.

amiss *a.* (*faulty, wrong*) awry, faulty, unsatisfactory, unsuitable, wrong. ANTONYMS: all right, right, satisfactory. **to take amiss** (*to be offended by*) be affronted by, be insulted by, (*coll.*) be miffed at, be offended by, be upset by, take umbrage at.

amity *n.* (*friendship, mutual good feeling*) accord, amiability, comradeship, concord, cordiality, fellowship, friendliness, friendship, good will, harmony, kindliness, peacefulness. ANTONYMS: enmity, hostility.

ammunition *n.* (*any projectiles, e.g. bullets, shells, that can be discharged from a weapon*) bullets, cartridges, powder, shells, shot.

amnesty n. (a general pardon) absolution, general pardon, pardon, reprieve.

amok adv. (in a frenzy, esp. as below) berserk, frenziedly, in a frenzy, maniacally, uncontrollably, violently, wildly.

among prep. **1** (in the midst of; surrounded by) amid, amidst, in the middle of, in the midst of, in the thick of, surrounded by. **2** (in the number of) included in, in the company of, in the group of, in the number of, out of. **3** (by sharing or dividing between a group of) between, to each of. **4** (involving a group of) by all of, by the joint action of, by the whole of, jointly, mutually, together, with one another.

amorous a. **1** (naturally inclined to love) affectionate, ardent, loving, passionate. ANTONYMS: cold, frigid, passionless. **2** (lecherous) amatory, erotic, lecherous, lustful, sexual.

amorphous a. **1** (shapeless) formless, inchoate, indefinite, indeterminate, nebulous, shapeless, unformed, vague. ANTONYMS: formed, shaped. **2** (unorganized) disorganized, structureless, unorganized, unstructured, unsystematic. ANTONYMS: organized, structured.

amount v.i. **1** (to mount up (to), to add up (to)) add up to, come to, mount up to, run to, total. **2** (to be equivalent (to)) add up to, approximate to, be equal to, be equivalent to, correspond to. **3** (to grow into) become, come to be, develop into, grow into.
~n. **1** (a (numerical) quantity) expanse, extent, mass, measure, number, quantity, volume. **2** (the sum total) grand total, sum total, total.

ample a. **1** (of large dimensions) big, broad, capacious, commodious, great, large, roomy, spacious, substantial, voluminous, wide. ANTONYMS: narrow, restricted, small. **2** (more than enough) abundant, copious, enough and to spare, generous, lavish, liberal, plentiful, profuse. ANTONYMS: meagre, scant, sparse. **3** (sufficient) adequate, enough, plenty, sufficient. ANTONYMS: inadequate, insufficient.

amplification n. **1** (enlargement or extension) development, dilation, elaboration, expansion, expatiation, extension, lengthening, supplementing. ANTONYMS: abbreviation, abridgement, condensation, reduction. **2** (increase in strength of a signal or sound) augmentation, boost, increase, intensification, magnification. ANTONYMS: decrease, lowering, reduction.

amplify v.t. **1** (to increase, esp. the strength of (a signal) or the loudness of (sound)) augment, boost, increase, intensify, magnify. ANTONYMS: decrease, lower, reduce. **2** (to enlarge or dilate upon) add to, develop, dilate on, elaborate

on, enlarge on, expand, expatiate on, expound on, extend, flesh out, go into detail about, lengthen, supplement. ANTONYMS: abridge, condense, cut, reduce.

amputate v.t. (to cut off (a limb or part of a limb) by surgical operation) cut off, dismember, excise, lop, remove, sever.

amulet n. (anything worn about the person as an imagined preservative against sickness, witchcraft etc.) charm, lucky charm, talisman.

amuse v.t. **1** (to cause to laugh or smile) cheer up, (coll.) crease, excite laughter in, have rolling in the aisles, (coll.) make (someone) fall about, make (someone) laugh, make (someone) smile, make (someone) split their sides. ANTONYMS: depress. **2** (to keep pleasantly occupied, to entertain) divert, entertain, interest, occupy. ANTONYMS: bore, weary.

amusement n. **1** (anything which amuses; diversion) distraction, diversion, entertainment, game, hobby, pastime, recreation. ANTONYMS: employment, job, work. **2** (the act of amusing, the excitement of laughter) diverting, entertaining, entertainment, interesting, occupying. ANTONYMS: boring, wearying. **3** (the state of being amused) fun, hilarity, laughter, merriment, mirth. ANTONYMS: depression, sadness.

amusing a. **1** (entertaining, diverting) diverting, enjoyable, entertaining, interesting. ANTONYMS: boring, tedious, wearisome. **2** (causing laughter or smiles) droll, facetious, farcical, funny, hilarious, humorous, jocular, laughable, ridiculous. ANTONYMS: depressing, sad.

anaemic a. **1** (lacking vitality) colourless, dull, enervated, feeble, impotent, ineffectual, weak. ANTONYMS: vigorous, vital. **2** (pale) ashen, bloodless, colourless, pale, pallid, wan. ANTONYMS: florid, rosy-cheeked, ruddy.

anaesthetic a. (producing anaesthesia) deadening, dulling, narcotic, numbing, opiate.
~n. (a substance which produces anaesthesia (during surgical operations)) narcotic, opiate.

analogous a. (presenting some analogy or resemblance) akin, alike, comparable, corresponding, equivalent, kindred, like, parallel, related, resembling, similar. ANTONYMS: contrasting, different, dissimilar, unlike.

analogy n. (similarity; a comparison used to demonstrate this) correlation, correspondence, equivalence, likeness, parallel, relation, resemblance, similarity, similitude. ANTONYMS: contrast, difference, dissimilarity.

analyse v.t. **1** (to take to pieces, resolve into its constituent elements) break down, decompose, dissect, fractionate, separate. **2** (*to examine closely*) examine, inquire into, investigate, research, scrutinize, study. **3** (*to examine critically*) criticize, evaluate, judge, review, study.

analysis *n.* **1** (*a close examination*) examination, inquiry, investigation, research, scrutiny, study. **2** (*a critical examination*) assessment, criticism, evaluation, judgement, review, study. **3** (*separation into constituent elements*) breakdown, decomposition, dissection, fractionation, separation.

analytic *a.* (*given to or skilled in analysing*) critical, inquiring, inquisitive, investigative, problem-solving, searching.

anarchic *a.* (*opposing all forms of government; lawless*) lawless, revolutionary, ungoverned, without government.

anarchist *n.* (*a person opposed to all forms of government*) nihilist, revolutionary.

anarchy *n.* **1** (*disorder, lawlessness*) chaos, disorder, disorganization, insurrection, lawlessness, rebellion, revolution, riot. ANTONYMS: government, law and order, order. **2** (*absence of government; lack of settled government*) lawlessness, revolution.

anathema *n.* (*an object of loathing*) abomination, aversion, bane, bête noire, bugbear, hate, pet hate.

anatomy *n.* **1** (*the physical structure of an animal or plant or of one of its parts*) composition, make-up, structure. **2** (*the act of dissecting*) cutting up, dismemberment, dissection, vivisection, zootomy. **3** (*a minute examination, analysis*) analysis, examination, inquiry, investigation, research, scrutiny, study.

ancestor *n.* **1** (*any person from whom another person is descended; a progenitor*) forebear, forefather, progenitor. ANTONYMS: descendant. **2** (*any thing or person regarded as the forerunner of a later thing or person*) forerunner, precursor, predecessor.

ancestral *a.* (*derived from or possessed by ancestors*) hereditary, inherited.

ancestry *n.* (*a line of ancestors*) descent, extraction, genealogy, lineage.

anchor *v.t.* (*to fix firmly*) attach, fasten, fix, secure, tie.

ancient *a.* **1** (*of or belonging to time long past*) age-old, bygone, olden, time-worn. ANTONYMS: recent. **2** (*past, former*) earliest, prehistoric, primeval. **3** (*antiquated*) antiquated, archaic, obsolete, old, old-fashioned, outmoded, out-of-date, passé, very old. ANTONYMS: modish, new, novel, state-of-the-art, up to date.

ancillary *a.* (*auxiliary, esp. providing support to a central service or industry*) accessory, additional, attendant, auxiliary, contributory, extra, secondary, subordinate, subsidiary. ANTONYMS: chief, main, primary, principal.

anecdote *n.* (*a brief account of an interesting or amusing fact or incident*) narrative, story, tale, yarn.

angelic *a.* **1** (*resembling or of the nature of an angel*) celestial, cherubic, heavenly, seraphic. **2** (*supremely good, innocent etc.*) good, innocent, pure, saintly, virtuous. ANTONYMS: devilish, evil, wicked.

anger *n.* (*rage, fierce displeasure*) annoyance, displeasure, exasperation, fury, ill humour, ill temper, indignation, ire, irritability, irritation, outrage, pique, rage, resentment, vexation, wrath.

angle[1] *n.* (*a point of view from which something is considered, an approach*) approach, perspective, point of view, position, slant, standpoint, viewpoint.

angle[2] *v.i.* (*to try to elicit, as a compliment*) aim (for), be after, cast about (for), fish (for), invite, look for, seek, solicit.

angry *a.* (*wrathful, expressing anger*) annoyed, cross, enraged, exasperated, furious, hot under the collar, ill-tempered, incensed, indignant, infuriated, irascible, irate, irritated, (*coll.*) mad, (*sl.*) pissed off, raging, resentful, riled, wrathful. ANTONYMS: calm, (*coll.*) laid back.

angst *n.* (*a nonspecific feeling of anxiety and guilt*) anxiety, apprehension, disquiet.

anguish *n.* (*excessive pain or distress of body or mind*) agony, distress, heartache, pain, sorrow, suffering, torment, torture, woe.

angular *a.* (*bony, lacking in plumpness*) bony, gaunt, rangy, raw-boned, scrawny, skinny, spare. ANTONYMS: buxom, plump.

animal *n.* **1** (*any one of the lower animals as distinct from humans*) beast, brute, creature. **2** (*a human being whose animal nature is abnormally strong, a brute*) barbarian, beast, brute, fiend, monster, savage, swine.

animated *a.* (*full of life; lively*) active, buoyant, dynamic, ebullient, energetic, enthusiastic, excited, exhilarated, lively, spirited, vibrant, vigorous, vital, vivacious. ANTONYMS: apathetic, lethargic, lifeless, listless.

animation *n.* (*liveliness, vitality*) action, activity, buoyancy, dynamism, ebullience, energy, enthusiasm, excitement, life, liveliness, sparkle, spirit, verve, vibrancy, vigour, vitality, vivacity, zing. ANTONYMS: apathy, lethargy, lifelessness, listlessness.

animosity n. (*hostility, extreme dislike*) acrimony, animus, antagonism, antipathy, bitterness, dislike, enmity, hate, hatred, hostility, ill will, loathing, malevolence, malice, rancour, resentment, spite. ANTONYMS: friendliness, good will, rapport.

annals n.pl. (*historical records*) archives, chronicles, history, records.

annex v.t. 1 (*to add on to, esp. to something larger*) add, affix, append, attach, connect, join, unite. 2 (*to take possession of* (*territory*)) appropriate, arrogate, capture, occupy, seize, take over.

annexe n. 1 (*an appendix*) addendum, adjunct, appendix, supplement. 2 (*an extension to a main building*) extension, wing.

annihilate v.t. (*to destroy completely*) abolish, decimate, destroy, eradicate, erase, exterminate, extinguish, extirpate, liquidate, obliterate, root out, wipe out.

annihilation n. (*complete destruction*) abolition, decimation, destruction, eradication, erasure, extermination, extinction, extinguishing, extirpation, liquidation, obliteration, rooting out, wiping out.

annotate v.t. (*to make notes or comments upon*) add footnotes to, commentate on, comment on, elucidate, explain, gloss, make observations on.

annotation n. (*an explanatory note*) comment, commentary, elucidation, explanation, footnote, gloss, note, observation.

announce v.t. 1 (*to make known, to proclaim*) advertise, broadcast, declare, disclose, divulge, give out, intimate, make known, proclaim, promulgate, propound, publicize, publish, report, reveal, tell. ANTONYMS: conceal, cover up, keep secret, suppress. 2 (*to make known the approach or arrival of*) give notice of, harbinger, herald, indicate, signal, warn.

announcement n. 1 (*an official statement*) advertisement, broadcast, bulletin, communiqué, declaration, intimation, proclamation, report, revelation, statement. 2 (*the act of making known or proclaiming something*) advertising, broadcasting, declaration, divulgence, intimation, proclamation, promulgation, propounding, publicizing, publishing, reporting, revelation, telling. ANTONYMS: concealment, cover-up, suppression, withholding.

announcer n. (*a person who announces the items of a broadcasting programme, reads news*

summaries etc.*) broadcaster, commentator, newscaster, newsreader, presenter, reporter.

annoy v.t. 1 (*to cause to feel irritated or angry*) (*coll.*) aggravate, anger, exasperate, (*coll.*) get on someone's nerves, (*coll.*) get to, incense, infuriate, madden, provoke, rub (someone) up the wrong way, ruffle, vex. ANTONYMS: appease, calm down, pacify, soothe. 2 (*to tease, to put to inconvenience by repeated or continued acts*) bother, disturb, harass, (*coll.*) hassle, pester, plague, torment, trouble, worry.

annoyance n. 1 (*the state of being annoyed*) (*coll.*) aggravation, anger, exasperation, fury, irritation, provocation, vexation. 2 (*something which annoys*) bother, irritant, nuisance, (*coll.*) pain, (*coll.*) pain in the neck, thorn in the flesh, trial, trouble, worry.

annoying a. 1 (*of a person*) *causing annoyance*) (*coll.*) aggravating, exasperating, infuriating, maddening, vexing. 2 (*of a thing*) *causing anxiety*) bothersome, disturbing, troublesome, worrying.

annual a. (*returning or happening every year*) once a year, yearly.

annually adv. (*yearly*) each year, every year, once a year, per annum, per year, year after year, yearly.

annul v.t. 1 (*to render void, cancel*) abolish, abrogate, cancel, countermand, declare null and void, invalidate, negate, nullify, quash, repeal, rescind, retract, reverse, revoke, void. 2 (*to declare the invalidity of* (*a marriage*)) declare null and void, nullify, void.

anomalous a. (*irregular, abnormal*) aberrant, abnormal, atypical, deviant, eccentric, exceptional, incongruous, inconsistent, irregular, odd, peculiar, rare, strange, unusual. ANTONYMS: normal, regular, typical, usual.

anomaly n. ((*a*) *deviation from the common or established order, abnormality*) aberration, abnormality, departure, deviation, eccentricity, exception, incongruity, inconsistency, irregularity, oddity, peculiarity, rarity.

anonymous a. (*of unknown or unavowed authorship or origin*) incognito, nameless, unacknowledged, undesignated, unidentified, unknown, unnamed, unspecified. ANTONYMS: designated, identified, named, specified.

another a. 1 (*an additional, one more*) additional, further, second. 2 (*a different*) different, some other.

answer n. 1 (*a reply to a question*) reply, response. ANTONYMS: query, question. 2 (*a reply to a charge*) defence, explanation, plea, rebuttal. 3 (*a reply to a letter*) acknowledgement, reply, response. **4** (*a reply to a statement*) comeback, rejoinder, reply, response, riposte. **5** (*the solution to a problem*) explanation, resolution, solution. **6** (*a reaction*) reaction, response.

~*v.t.* **1** (*to reply or respond to* (*a question*)) give an answer to, give a reply to, make response to, reply to, respond to. ANTONYMS: query, question. **2** (*to reply to* (*a letter*)) acknowledge, reply to, respond to, send an acknowledgement to, send a reply to, send a response to. **3** (*to reply to* (*a statement*)) rejoin, reply, respond, retort. **4** (*to act on a signal or summons from*) react to, respond to. **5** (*to solve*) explain, give the solution to, resolve, solve. **6** (*to be sufficient for or suitable to*) fulfil, measure up to, meet, satisfy, suit. **7** (*to fit* (*a particular description*)) agree with, conform to, correspond to, fit, match. **to answer back** (*to reply rudely or cheekily*) argue, be cheeky, be impertinent, be rude, cheek, talk back. **to answer for 1** (*to be responsible or answerable for*) be accountable for, be liable for, be responsible for, be to blame for, take responsibility for, (*coll.*) take the rap for. **2** (*to speak as a representative of*) speak for, speak on behalf of. **3** (*to express one's confidence in; vouch for*) attest to, bear witness to, guarantee, testify to, vouch for. **to answer to 1** (*to correspond, to suit*) agree with, answer, conform to, correspond to, fit, match. **2** (*to be responsible or answerable to*) be accountable to, be answerable to, be responsible to, obey, report to.

answerable *a.* **1** (*responsible to*) accountable to, responsible to. **2** (*liable to be called to account for*) accountable for, liable for, responsible for, to blame for.

antagonism *n.* **1** (*opposition*) animosity, antipathy, dislike, enmity, hostility, opposition. **2** (*conflict, active disagreement*) conflict, friction, ill feeling, rivalry. ANTONYMS: accord, amity, friendship, harmony, peace.

antagonist *n.* (*an opponent; a person who contends or strives with another*) adversary, enemy, foe, opponent, rival.

antagonistic *a.* **1** (*wanting to disagree; unfriendly*) aggressive, antipathetic, belligerent, contentious, hostile, inimical, unfriendly. ANTONYMS: friendly, harmonious, peaceful. **2** (*opposed to*) averse to, hostile to, in conflict with, opposed to. ANTONYMS: in favour of.

antagonize *v.t.* (*to arouse hostility or opposition in*) (*coll.*) aggravate, alienate, annoy, estrange, make hostile, offend, rub (someone) up the wrong way. ANTONYMS: pacify, placate.

antecedent *n.* **1** (*an ancestor*) ancestor,

forebear, forefather, progenitor. **2** (*pl.*) (*past circumstances, background*) background, history, past.

antediluvian *a.* (*old-fashioned, antiquated*) ancient, antiquated, archaic, obsolete, old-fashioned, outmoded, out of date, (*coll.*) out of the ark, passé. ANTONYMS: fashionable, modern, modish.

anteroom *n.* (*a room leading into or forming an entrance to another*) lobby, outer room, reception area, vestibule, waiting room.

anthology *n.* (*any collection of selected poems or other literary pieces*) collection, compendium, compilation, miscellany, selection, treasury.

antic *n.* (*pl.*) (*ridiculous or troublesome behaviour*) buffoonery, capers, clowning, frolics, horseplay, larks, monkey tricks, pranks, (*coll.*) skylarking, tomfoolery, tricks.

anticipate *v.t.* **1** (*to foresee*) await, count on, expect, forecast, foresee, look for, predict, prepare for. **2** (*to forestall, to thwart by acting first*) beat (someone) to it, (*coll.*) beat (someone) to the draw, forestall, intercept, nullify, prevent. **3** (*to cause to happen earlier, to hasten*) antedate, be earlier than, come/ go before. ANTONYMS: come/ go after. **4** (*to look forward to*) await with pleasure, look forward to. ANTONYMS: dread.

anticipation *n.* **1** (*the act of anticipating or foreseeing*) anticipating, awaiting, expectation, forecasting, foreseeing, foresight, prediction, preparation. **2** (*the act of anticipating or forestalling*) anticipating, forestalling, interception, nullification, preventing. **3** (*the act of causing to happen earlier*) antedating, anticipating. **4** (*expectation, foresight*) expectation, foresight, forethought, presentiment.

anticlimax *n.* (*the opposite of climax*) bathos, comedown, disappointment, let-down. ANTONYMS: climax, culmination, height, peak, zenith.

antidote *n.* **1** (*a medicine designed to counteract poison or disease*) antitoxin, antivenin, neutralizer. ANTONYMS: poison, toxin, venom. **2** (*anything intended to counteract something harmful or unpleasant*) corrective, countermeasure, cure, remedy.

antipathetic *a.* (*having an antipathy or contrariety to*) antagonistic to, averse to, hostile to, opposed to. ANTONYMS: fond of.

antipathy *n.* (*hostile feeling towards; aversion*) abhorrence, animosity, animus, antagonism, aversion, dislike, distaste, enmity, hate, hatred, hostility, ill feeling, loathing, odium, opposition, repugnance. ANTONYMS: affection, affinity, friendship, liking.

antiquated *a.* (*old-fashioned, out of date*) ancient, antediluvian, antique, archaic, dated, decrepit, hoary, obsolete, old-fashioned, (*coll.*) old hat, outmoded, out of date, outworn, passé, superannuated. ANTONYMS: fashionable, modern, modish, up to date.

antique *a.* **1** (*ancient, that has been in existence for a long time*) age-old, ancient, elderly, old, time-worn, very old. ANTONYMS: new, recent. **2** (*old-fashioned, antiquated*) ancient, antediluvian, antiquated, archaic, dated, decrepit, hoary, obsolete, old-fashioned, (*coll.*) old hat, outmoded, out of date, outworn, passé. ANTONYMS: current, fashionable, modern, modish, up to date. **3** (*old and valuable*) antiquarian, old, vintage. ANTONYMS: modern, new.
~*n.* (*a piece of furniture, ornament etc., made in an earlier period and valued by collectors*) heirloom, object of virtu, objet de vertu, relic.

antiquity *n.* **1** (*the state of being ancient, great age*) age, ancientness, old age, oldness. ANTONYMS: newness. **2** (*ancient times, esp. the period of European history before the Middle Ages*) ancient times, olden days, time immemorial.

antiseptic *a.* **1** (*counteracting putrefaction, by inhibiting the growth of micro-organisms*) bactericidal, disinfectant, germicidal. **2** (*free from contamination*) aseptic, clean, germ-free, sanitary, sterile, uncontaminated, unpolluted. ANTONYMS: contaminated, dirty, germ-laden, infected, septic. **3** (*lacking interest, warmth or excitement, sterile*) characterless, clinical, cold, colourless, stark, sterile, unexciting. ANTONYMS: characterful, colourful, warm.

antisocial *a.* **1** (*opposed to the interest of society, or to the principles on which society is constituted*) anarchistic, asocial, disorderly, disruptive, lawless, rebellious. ANTONYMS: law-abiding, orderly. **2** (*unsociable*) distant, misanthropic, reserved, retiring, uncommunicative, unfriendly, unsociable, withdrawn. ANTONYMS: companionable, friendly, gregarious, sociable.

antithesis *n.* **1** (*the direct opposite*) contrary, converse, inverse, opposite, reverse, the other extreme. **2** (*opposition, contrast*) contradiction, contrariety, contrast, opposition, reversal, reverse. ANTONYMS: accord, agreement, conformity.

anxiety *n.* **1** (*the state of being anxious*) agitation, angst, apprehension, care, concern,

disquiet, disquietude, edginess, foreboding, misgiving, nervousness, tenseness, trepidation, unease, uneasiness, worry. ANTONYMS: assurance, calmness, nonchalance. **2** (*eager desire*) desire, eagerness, longing, need, wish, yearning.

anxious *a.* **1** (*troubled or fearful about some uncertain or future event*) agitated, apprehensive, concerned, disturbed, fearful, nervous, on edge, tense, troubled, twitchy, uneasy, (*sl.*) wired, worried. ANTONYMS: assured, calm, carefree, nonchalant. **2** (*distressing, worrying*) disturbing, tense, troublesome, uneasy, unsettling, upsetting, worrying. **3** (*eagerly desirous* (*to do something*)) desirous (of), eager (to), impatient (to), keen (to), longing (to), yearning (to). ANTONYMS: disinclined (to), loath (to), reluctant (to).

anyhow *adv.* **1** (*anyway*) anyway, at all events, in any manner, in any way. **2** (*in a disorderly fashion, imperfectly*) carelessly, casually, haphazardly, unmethodically, unsystematically. ANTONYMS: methodically, neatly, systematically. **3** (*anyway, used to express a contrast*) anyway, in any case, in any event.

apace *adv.* (*at a quick pace, fast*) at full speed, fast, post-haste, quickly, rapidly, speedily, swiftly. ANTONYMS: slowly.

apart *adv.* **1** (*parted, at a distance from one another*) at a distance, separate, separated. ANTONYMS: together. **2** (*into two or more pieces or parts*) asunder, in pieces, to bits, to pieces. **3** (*to or on one side*) aside, to one side, to the side. **4** (*not being taken into account*) aside. **5** (*independently*) alone, by itself/ oneself, independently. **apart from** (*with the exception of, leaving out*) aside from, besides, but, except, except for, excluding, leaving aside, not counting, omitting, other than, save. ANTONYMS: counting, including.

apartment *n.* **1** (*a suite of rooms, lodgings*) accommodation, living quarters, lodgings, quarters, rooms, suite. **2** (*a flat*) flat.

apathetic *a.* (*characterized by apathy; indifferent*) cool, dispassionate, emotionless, impassive, indifferent, languid, listless, passive, phlegmatic, torpid, unconcerned, unenthusiastic, uninterested, unmoved, unresponsive. ANTONYMS: enthusiastic, excited, interested, passionate.

apathy *n.* (*absence of feeling or passion*) coolness, impassivity, indifference, inertia, lack of emotion, lack of enthusiasm, lack of interest, languor, listlessness, passiveness, passivity, torpor, unresponsiveness. ANTONYMS: enthusiasm, feeling, interest, passion.

ape v.t. (to imitate or mimic) copy, echo, imitate, mimic, mock, parody, parrot.

aperture n. (an opening, a hole) breach, chink, cleft, crack, fissure, gap, hole, interstice, opening, orifice, passage, perforation, rent, rift, slit, slot, space, tear, vent, window.

apex n. **1** (the top or summit of anything) crest, crown, peak, pinnacle, point, summit, tip, top, vertex. ANTONYMS: base, bottom. **2** (the culmination, climax) acme, apogee, climax, culmination, height, high point, peak, pinnacle, top, zenith. ANTONYMS: bottom, low point, nadir.

aphorism n. (a pithy sentence, containing a maxim or wise precept) adage, axiom, epigram, gnome, maxim, proverb, saw, saying.

aplomb n. (self-possession, coolness) assurance, calmness, composure, confidence, coolness, equanimity, level-headedness, poise, sang-froid, self-assurance, self-confidence, self-possession. ANTONYMS: awkwardness, discomposure, nervousness.

apocalyptic a. (prophesying disaster or doom) ominous, oracular, portentous, prophetic, revelational.

apocryphal a. (probably not true; spurious) fictitious, legendary, mythical, spurious, unauthenticated, unsubstantiated. ANTONYMS: authentic, real, true, verified.

apogee n. (the highest point, the culmination) acme, apex, climax, culmination, height, high point, peak, pinnacle, top, zenith. ANTONYMS: bottom, low point, nadir.

apologetic a. (regretfully acknowledging or excusing an offence) contrite, penitent, regretful, remorseful, repentant, rueful, sorry. ANTONYMS: defiant, unrepentant.

apologist n. (a person who defends or vindicates by reasoned argument) advocate, champion, defender, spokesman/ spokeswoman, spokesperson, supporter, vindicator. ANTONYMS: attacker, detractor, opponent.

apologize v.i. (to make an apology or excuses) ask forgiveness, beg pardon, express regret, make an apology, offer one's apologies, say one is sorry. ANTONYMS: be unrepentant.

apology n. **1** (a regretful acknowledgement of offence) regrets. **2** (an excuse) excuse, excuses, explanation. **3** (a defence, vindication) apologia, argument, defence, excuse, explanation, justification, plea, vindication. **4** (a poor substitute for the real thing) caricature, excuse, imitation, mockery, poor excuse, stopgap, substitute, travesty.

apostasy n. ((a) renunciation of religious faith or political principles) backsliding, defection, desertion, disloyalty, faithlessness, falseness, heresy, inconstancy, infidelity, perfidy, treachery, unfaithfulness. ANTONYMS: constancy, faithfulness, loyalty.

apostate a. (unfaithful to creed or principles) backsliding, disloyal, faithless, false, heretical, inconstant, perfidious, treacherous, unfaithful. ANTONYMS: devoted, faithful, loyal.

apostle n. (the leader of, or an outstanding figure in, a movement, esp. of reform) advocate, champion, crusader, pioneer, proponent, supporter.

appal v.t. (to horrify, to shock) disgust, dismay, horrify, outrage, shock.

appalling a. **1** (horrifying, shocking) awful, disgusting, dreadful, ghastly, grim, horrifying, outrageous, shocking, terrible. **2** (unsatisfactory) inadequate, poor, substandard, unsatisfactory, very bad. ANTONYMS: excellent, very good.

apparatus n. **1** (equipment generally) appliances, equipment, gear, implements, instruments, paraphernalia, tackle, tools. **2** (the administrative workings of a (political) system or organization) organization, set-up, structure, system, workings.

apparel n. (clothes) attire, clothes, clothing, costume, dress, garb, habit, outfit.

apparent a. **1** (plain, obvious) clear, discernible, evident, indubitable, manifest, marked, obvious, overt, patent, plain, unmistakable, visible. ANTONYMS: doubtful, dubious, unclear. **2** (appearing (in a certain way), seeming) ostensible, outward, quasi, seeming, specious, superficial. ANTONYMS: actual, genuine, real.

apparently adv. (to external appearances) it appears that, it seems that, on the face of it, ostensibly, seemingly.

apparition n. (a spectre, ghost) ghost, phantom, revenant, spectre, spirit, (coll.) spook, wraith.

appeal v.i. **1** (to make an earnest request (for)) ask (for), beg (for), petition (for), plead (for), put in a plea (for), request, solicit. **2** (to make an earnest request (to)) beg, beseech, entreat, implore, petition, solicit, sue, supplicate. **3** (to attract or be of interest (to)) attract, be of interest to, charm, fascinate, interest, intrigue. ANTONYMS: bore, repel, revolt. **4** (to refer to some person or thing for corroboration or support) lodge an appeal with.
~n. **1** (reference or recourse to another person or authority, esp. a higher court) challenge,

questioning, referral. **2** (*power of attracting or interesting*) allure, attraction, attractiveness, charm, fascination, interest. ANTONYMS: repulsiveness. **3** (*entreaty*) entreaty, invocation, petition, plea, prayer, request, solicitation, suit, supplication.

appear *v.i.* **1** (*to become or be visible*) arrive, become visible, come into sight, come into view, crop up, emerge, materialize, occur, surface. ANTONYMS: disappear, vanish. **2** (*to be manifest*) be apparent, be clear, be discernible, be evident, be manifest, be obvious, be patent, be plain. ANTONYMS: be doubtful, be unclear. **3** (*to seem*) give the impression of being, look, look alike, look as if, seem, strike one as. **4** (*to present oneself*) attend, be in attendance, be present, present oneself, put in an appearance, show, show up, turn up. ANTONYMS: be absent. **5** (*to be published; to come before the public*) become available, be published, come on the market, come out. **6** (*to take part in a play, film etc.*) act, be on stage, perform, play.

appearance *n.* **1** (*the act of appearing*) advent, arrival, coming, debut, emergence, introduction, materialization, occurrence, surfacing. ANTONYMS: disappearance, vanishing. **2** (*the act of appearing formally or publicly*) attendance, presence, showing, showing up, turning up. ANTONYMS: absence, non-attendance. **3** (*the outward or visible form of a person or thing*) air, aspect, bearing, demeanour, expression, form, impression, look, looks, manner, mien. **4** (*external show, pretence*) front, guise, impression, outward show, pretence, semblance, show.

appease *v.t.* **1** (*to pacify, to calm*) allay, alleviate, assuage, calm, calm down, pacify, quieten, soothe, tranquillize. ANTONYMS: exacerbate, inflame, provoke. **2** (*to conciliate by acceding to demands*) accommodate, conciliate, mollify, pacify, placate, propitiate, reconcile. ANTONYMS: annoy, antagonize, incense, infuriate. **3** (*to satisfy (an appetite, thirst etc.)*) assuage, quench, relieve, satisfy, take the edge off.

appeasement *n.* **1** (*the act of appeasing; the state of being appeased*) allaying, alleviation, assuagement, pacification, quietening, soothing, tranquillization. **2** (*the act of satisfying an appetite, thirst etc.*) assuagement, assuaging, quenching, relief, satisfying. **3** (*the endeavour to preserve peace by giving way to the demands of an aggressor power*) accommodation, concession, conciliation, mollification, pacification, placation, propitiation. ANTONYMS: aggression, belligerence.

appellation *n.* (*a name, designation*) description, designation, epithet, name, sobriquet, style, term, title.

append *v.t.* (*to add or subjoin*) add, adjoin, affix, annex, attach, tack on. ANTONYMS: detach, remove.

appendage *n.* **1** (*something added or appended*) addendum, addition, adjunct, affix, annexe, appendix, appurtenance, attachment, supplement. **2** (*a subordinate or subsidiary organ or process, such as a limb or branch*) extremity, limb, member, projection, protuberance.

appendix *n.* **1** (*a supplement to a book or document containing useful material*) addendum, end matter, postscript, supplement. **2** (*something appended; an adjunct*) addendum, addition, add-on, adjunct, affix, annexe, appendage, appurtenance, attachment, codicil.

appertain *v.i.* **1** (*to relate (to)*) be connected (with), be pertinent (to), be relevant (to), have a bearing (on), have reference (to), have relevance (to), have to do (with), pertain (to), relate (to). ANTONYMS: be irrelevant (to), be unconnected (with), have nothing to do (with). **2** (*to belong to (as a part to a whole or as a privilege)*) belong to, be part of. **3** (*to be suitable or appropriate (to)*) apply (to), be appropriate (for), be proper (for), be suitable (for). ANTONYMS: be inappropriate (for), be unsuitable (for).

appetite *n.* **1** (*desire for food*) hunger. **2** (*inclination or desire for something*) craving, demand, desire, hankering, hunger, inclination, liking, longing, love, need, passion, proclivity, propensity, relish, yearning, zest. ANTONYMS: aversion, disgust, dislike, revulsion.

appetizer *n.* (*a stimulant to appetite, esp. food (or drink) served before or at the beginning of a meal*) antipasto, canapé, hors d'oeuvre, starter.

appetizing *a.* (*stimulating appetite or hunger; delicious*) delicious, inviting, mouth-watering, palatable, (*coll.*) scrumptious, tasty, tempting. ANTONYMS: disgusting, revolting, unappetizing.

applaud *v.i.* (*to express approbation, esp. by clapping the hands*) cheer, clap, give a (big) hand to, give a standing ovation to, (*coll.*) put one's hands together for. ANTONYMS: boo, hiss. ~*v.t.* (*to commend or praise in an audible and significant manner*) acclaim, admire, approve, commend, compliment, eulogize, express admiration for, express approval of, extol, laud, praise. ANTONYMS: censure, condemn, criticize.

applause *n.* **1** (*the act of applauding*) cheering, cheers, clapping, hand, handclapping, standing ovation. ANTONYMS: booing, hissing. **2** (*praise or approval emphatically expressed*) acclaim, acclamation, accolades, admiration, approbation, approval, bouquets, commendation, compliments, eulogy, extolment, laudation, plaudits, praise. ANTONYMS: censure, condemnation, criticism.

appliance n. **1** (*an apparatus or device*) apparatus, device, gadget, implement, instrument, machine, mechanism, tool. **2** (*the act of applying*) administering, application, applying, employment, exercise, use, using, utilization.

applicable a. (*appropriate; relevant*) apposite, appropriate, apt, fit, fitting, germane, pertinent, relevant, suitable, suited, to the point, to the purpose. ANTONYMS: inapplicable, inapposite, inappropriate, irrelevant.

applicant n. (*a person who applies, esp. for a job*) aspirant, candidate, interviewee, suitor.

application n. **1** (*the act of applying, esp. an ointment*) covering, painting, putting on, rubbing on, smearing, spreading. **2** (*an ointment that is applied to the skin*) balm, cream, emollient, lotion, ointment, rub, salve, unguent. **3** ((*a) petition, request*) appeal, claim, demand, inquiry, petition, plea, request, requisition, suit. **4** (*the use to which something is put*) employment, exercise, function, practice, purpose, use. **5** (*relevance*) applicability, appositeness, appropriateness, pertinence, reference, relevance. ANTONYMS: inappropriateness, irrelevance. **6** (*disciplined and sustained work or study*) assiduity, commitment, dedication, diligence, effort, hard work, industry, perseverance, persistence, work.

apply v.t. **1** (*to put to (practical) use, to employ*) administer, bring into effect, bring into play, bring to bear, exercise, put into practice, put to use, use, utilize. **2** (*to bring into operation (a rule, law*)) bring into effect, bring into operation, bring into play, bring to bear, put into practice. **3** (*to put or rub on*) cover with, paint, put on, rub on, smear, spread. ~v.i. **1** (*to offer oneself for a job, position etc.*) make an application for, put in an application for, put in for, try for. ANTONYMS: withdraw from. **2** (*to make a formal request (for*)) appeal, claim, petition, request, solicit, sue, supplicate. **3** (*to be relevant (to*)) appertain (to), be applicable (to), be apposite (to), be germane (to), be pertinent (to), be relevant (to), have a bearing (on), have relevance (to), pertain (to), refer (to), relate (to). ANTONYMS: be inapplicable (to), be irrelevant (to), have nothing to do (with). **to apply oneself** (*to work, study etc. in a concentrated and diligent fashion*) be assiduous, be diligent, be industrious, buckle to, commit oneself, make an effort, persevere, persist, put one's shoulder to the wheel, work hard. ANTONYMS: be idle, slacken off.

appoint v.t. **1** (*to nominate, designate (to a position, office*)) choose, designate, elect, install, name, nominate, select. ANTONYMS: deselect, dismiss, (*coll.*) sack. **2** (*to decide on, to fix (a time, place*)) allot, arrange, choose, designate, determine, establish, fix, set, settle.

appointment n. **1** (*an arrangement to meet at a specific time*) arrangement, assignation, (*coll.*) date, engagement, meeting, rendezvous, tryst. **2** (*the act of appointing, esp. to a position or office*) choosing, designation, election, installation, naming, nominating, selection. ANTONYMS: deselection, dismissal, (*coll.*) sacking. **3** (*the job or position to which someone is appointed*) job, office, place, position, post, situation. **4** (*a person who is appointed to something*) appointee, office-holder. **5** (*equipment, fixtures and fittings*) accoutrements, appurtenances, equipage, equipment, fixtures, furnishings, paraphernalia, trappings.

apportion v.t. (*to share out in just or suitable proportions*) allocate, allot, assign, deal, dispense, distribute, dole out, hand out, measure out, mete out, parcel out, ration out, share out.

apposite a. (*appropriate*) applicable, appropriate, apropos, apt, fitting, germane, pertinent, proper, relevant, suitable, suited, to the point. ANTONYMS: inapposite, inappropriate, unsuitable.

appraisal n. **1** (*an authoritative valuation*) pricing, survey, valuation. **2** (*an estimate of worth*) assessment, estimate, estimation, evaluation, judgement, sizing-up, summing-up.

appraise v.t. **1** (*to estimate the worth, value or quality of*) assay, assess, estimate, evaluate, gauge, give a judgement on, give an assessment of, give an estimate of, give an estimation of, give an evaluation of, judge, size up, sum up. **2** (*to set a price on, to value*) price, survey, value.

appreciable a. (*capable of being appreciated; significant*) clear-cut, considerable, definite, detectable, discernible, distinguishable, evident, goodly, marked, material, noticeable, obvious, perceptible, pronounced, recognizable, significant, substantial, visible. ANTONYMS: imperceptible, insignificant, insubstantial.

appreciate v.t. **1** (*to esteem highly*) admire, cherish, esteem, hold in esteem, hold in high regard, prize, rate highly, respect, think highly of, think much of, treasure, value. ANTONYMS: denigrate, disparage, scorn. **2** (*to feel gratitude for*) be appreciative of, be grateful for, be thankful for, give thanks for. **3** (*to understand*) acknowledge, be aware of, be cognizant of, be conscious of, discern, know, perceive, realize, recognize, understand. ANTONYMS: be unaware of, be unconscious of. **4** (*to raise in value*) inflate, raise in value.

~*v.i.* **1** (*to rise in value*) accumulate, increase in price, rise in value. ANTONYMS: decline in value. **2** ((*of prices*) *to rise*) grow, increase, inflate, rise. ANTONYMS: decrease, fall.

appreciation *n.* **1** (*gratitude or grateful recognition*) acknowledgement, gratefulness, gratitude, indebtedness, thankfulness, thanks. ANTONYMS: ingratitude, ungratefulness. **2** (*admiration, respect*) admiration, enjoyment, esteem, high regard, regard, relish, respect. ANTONYMS: contempt, scorn. **3** (*an estimate or assessment of the worth or value of something*) appraisal, assessment, estimation, evaluation, valuation. **4** (*understanding of or sensitivity to something*) awareness, cognizance, comprehension, discernment, knowledge, perception, realization, recognition, understanding. ANTONYMS: ignorance, incomprehension. **5** (*a rise in value*) escalation, gain, growth, increase, inflation, rise. ANTONYMS: decrease, reduction. **6** (*a critical study or review, esp. a favourable one*) appraisal, assessment, commentary, critical analysis, criticism, critique, review, study.

appreciative *a.* **1** (*feeling or expressing appreciation*) grateful, indebted, thankful. ANTONYMS: ungrateful. **2** (*esteeming favourably*) admiring, approving, enthusiastic, favourable. ANTONYMS: disapproving, unfavourable. **3** (*sensitive* (*to*), *understanding*) aware (of), cognizant (of), conscious (of), mindful (of), responsive (to), sensitive (to). ANTONYMS: insensitive (to), unaware (of), unmindful (of).

apprehend *v.t.* **1** (*to grasp or lay hold of mentally*) appreciate, comprehend, conceive, grasp, realize, recognize, think, understand. ANTONYMS: misapprehend, misconceive, misunderstand. **2** (*to seize, to arrest*) arrest, capture, catch, (*coll.*) collar, detain, (*sl.*) nick, (*coll.*) run in, seize, take. ANTONYMS: free, liberate, release.

apprehension *n.* **1** (*fear, dread of what may happen*) alarm, anxiety, apprehensiveness, (*coll.*) butterflies in the stomach, concern, disquiet, dread, fear, fearfulness, foreboding, misgiving, mistrust, nervousness, suspicion, trepidation, unease, uneasiness, worry. ANTONYMS: boldness, nonchalance, unconcern. **2** (*ability to perceive or grasp mentally*) awareness, grasp, knowledge, perception, understanding. ANTONYMS: misunderstanding, unawareness. **3** (*the act of seizing or arresting*) arrest, capture, catching, (*coll.*) collaring, detention, (*sl.*) nicking, seizure, taking. ANTONYMS: freeing, liberation, release. **4** (*conception, idea*) belief, concept, conception,

idea, notion, opinion, sentiment, thought, view.

apprehensive *a.* (*anticipative of something unpleasant or harmful, fearful*) afraid, alarmed, anxious, concerned, fearful, frightened, mistrustful, nervous, on edge, scared, suspicious, twitchy, uneasy, worried. ANTONYMS: bold, nonchalant, unafraid.

apprentice *n.* (*a learner, a novice*) beginner, learner, neophyte, novice, probationer, pupil, student, trainee, tyro. ANTONYMS: expert, master.

apprise *v.t.* (*to inform, to bring to the notice of*) acquaint, advise, enlighten, inform, let (someone) know, make (someone) aware, notify, tell, warn.

approach *v.i.* (*to come or go near or nearer*) advance, come close, come near, come nearer, draw close, draw near, draw nearer, edge near, edge nearer, go close, go near, go nearer, near. ~*v.t.* **1** (*to come near to*) advance on, catch up, come close, come near, come nearer to, draw near, draw nearer to, edge near, edge nearer to, gain on, go close, go near, go nearer to, move towards, near. ANTONYMS: move away from. **2** (*to communicate with* (*a person*) *with a view to making a proposal*) accost, address, appeal to, greet, hail, make advances to, make overtures to, solicit. **3** (*to begin to deal with* (*a task, problem*)) begin, commence, embark on, enter upon, make a start on, set to, start, tackle. ANTONYMS: complete, finish. **4** (*to resemble; to be equal to*) be like, be similar to, compare with, resemble. ANTONYMS: be dissimilar, be unlike. **5** (*to approximate to, to be close to*) be close to, come close to, come near to. ~*n.* **1** (*the act of drawing near*) advance, advent, coming, drawing near, nearing. ANTONYMS: departure, going. **2** (*avenue, entrance*) access, avenue, passageway, road, street, way. **3** (*a way of dealing with a person or thing*) method, mode, modus operandi, procedure, style, technique, way. **4** (*communication with a person for a particular purpose; sexual advances*) advances, appeal, application, overtures, proposal, proposition.

approachable *a.* **1** (*capable of being approached*) accessible, attainable, passable, reachable. ANTONYMS: inaccessible. **2** (*friendly*) affable, congenial, cordial, friendly, genial, open, sociable. ANTONYMS: aloof, stand-offish, unapproachable.

approaching *a.* (*coming near in time*) advancing, coming, forthcoming, imminent, impending.

approbation *n.* (*approval, commendation*) acceptance, acclaim, admiration, approval, assent, commendation, endorsement, favour, praise, ratification, sanction. ANTONYMS: disapprobation, disapproval, disfavour.

appropriate[1] *v.t.* **1** (*to take e.g. land as one's own, esp. unlawfully or without permission*) annex, arrogate, commandeer, confiscate, expropriate, grab, impound, seize, take over, take possession of. **2** (*to steal*) embezzle, filch, misappropriate, (*sl.*) nick, pilfer, (*coll.*) pinch, purloin, steal. **3** (*to devote to or set apart for a special purpose or use*) allocate, allot, apportion, assign, devote, earmark, set apart.

appropriate[2] *a.* (*suitable, fit*) applicable, apposite, apropos, apt, becoming, correct, fit, fitting, germane, pertinent, proper, relevant, right, seemly, suitable, to the point, to the purpose. ANTONYMS: inappropriate, irrelevant, unsuitable.

approval *n.* **1** (*favourable opinion*) acceptance, acclaim, admiration, appreciation, approbation, assent, commendation, consent, endorsement, esteem, favour, praise, regard, respect. ANTONYMS: disapprobation, disapproval, dislike. **2** (*an act or the act of sanctioning*) agreement, authorization, endorsement, (*coll.*) go-ahead, (*coll.*) green light, imprimatur, (*coll.*) OK, (*coll.*) okay, ratification, sanctioning, validation. ANTONYMS: disapproval, prohibition.

approve *v.t.* (*to sanction, confirm*) accede to, accept, agree to, assent to, authorize, bless, confirm, consent to, endorse, give assent to, give consent to, (*coll.*) give the go-ahead to, (*coll.*) give the green light to, (*coll.*) OK, (*coll.*) okay, ratify, sanction, validate. ANTONYMS: (*coll.*) give the red light to, reject, turn down. ~*v.i.* (*to express a favourable opinion (of)*) acclaim, admire, applaud, appreciate, be pleased (with), commend, esteem, favour, have a good opinion (of), have a high opinion (of), hold in high regard, laud, like, praise, respect, think highly (of). ANTONYMS: censure, condemn, disapprove.

approximate[1] *v.i.* (*to be more or less identical or equal (to)*) approach, be similar (to), border (on), come close (to), come near (to), resemble, verge on.

approximate[2] *a.* **1** (*nearly approaching accuracy*) almost exact, close, near. ANTONYMS: accurate, exact, precise. **2** (*rough, inexact*) estimated, inexact, loose, rough. ANTONYMS: accurate, exact, precise.

approximately *adv.* (*roughly*) about, almost, around, circa, close to, in the neighbourhood of, in the region of, just about, more or less, nearly, not far off, roughly. ANTONYMS: exactly, precisely, (*coll.*) spot-on.

approximation *n.* **1** (*something approximate, esp. a mathematical value that is sufficiently accurate for a purpose though not exact*) conjecture, estimate, (*coll.*) guesstimate, guesswork. **2** (*a likeness, semblance*) correspondence, likeness, semblance, similarity.

appurtenance *n.* **1** (*an accessory, an appendage*) accessory, accompaniment, adjunct, appendage, attachment, supplement. **2** (*pl.*) (*things which belong to something else*) accessories, accoutrements, belongings, equipment, impedimenta, paraphernalia, trappings.

apron *n.* (*a garment worn in front of the body to protect the clothes*) pinafore, (*coll.*) pinny.

apropos *a.* (*appropriate*) applicable, apposite, appropriate, apt, germane, pertinent, relevant, to the point. ANTONYMS: inappropriate, inapt, irrelevant. **apropos of** (*with regard to, concerning*) concerning, in respect of, on the subject of, re, regarding, respecting, with reference to, with regard to, with respect to.

apt *a.* **1** (*suitable, relevant*) applicable, apposite, appropriate, apropos, correct, fit, fitting, germane, pertinent, proper, relevant, seemly, suitable, timely, to the point, to the purpose. ANTONYMS: inappropriate, inapt, unsuitable. **2** (*having a tendency (to), likely*) disposed (to), given (to), inclined (to), liable (to), likely (to), of a mind (to), prone (to), ready (to). ANTONYMS: disinclined (to), unlikely (to). **3** (*quick, ready*) able, bright, clever, gifted, intelligent, quick, quick to learn, sharp, smart, talented. ANTONYMS: inept, slow, stupid.

aptitude *n.* **1** (*a natural talent or ability*) ability, bent, capacity, faculty, flair, gift, knack, proficiency, skill, talent. **2** (*fitness, suitability*) applicability, appositeness, appropriateness, correctness, fitness, pertinence, relevance, seemliness, suitability. ANTONYMS: inappropriateness, irrelevance.

aptness *n.* **1** (*suitability*) applicability, appositeness, appropriateness, correctness, fitness, germaneness, pertinence, relevance, seemliness, suitability, timelessness. ANTONYMS: inappropriateness, inaptness, unsuitability. **2** (*quickness, readiness*) ability, brightness, cleverness, intelligence, quickness, sharpness, smartness, talent. ANTONYMS: dullness, slowness. **3** (*an inclination, tendency*) disposition, inclination, likelihood, likeliness, predilection, proneness, propensity, readiness, tendency. ANTONYMS: disinclination.

aquiline *a.* ((*esp. of noses*) *hooked, curved, like an eagle's bill*) curved, eagle-like, hooked.

arable *a.* ((*of land*) *ploughed or capable of being ploughed*) cultivable, fertile, ploughable, ploughed, productive, tillable, tilled. ANTO-NYMS: infertile, unproductive.

arbiter *n.* **1** (*a judge*) adjudicator, arbitrator, judge, referee, umpire. **2** (*a person who has power to decide according to their absolute pleasure*) authority, controller, determiner, expert, lord, master, ruler.

arbitrary *a.* **1** ((*apparently*) *random, irrational*) capricious, chance, discretionary, erratic, inconsistent, personal, random, subjective, unreasoned, whimsical. ANTONYMS: consistent, objective, reasoned. **2** (*subject to the will or control of no other, despotic*) absolute, autocratic, despotic, dictatorial, dogmatic, domineering, high-handed, imperious, overbearing, peremptory, tyrannical, uncontrolled. ANTONYMS: democratic, limited.

arbitrate *v.t.* (*to decide, to settle*) decide, determine, settle.
~*v.i.* (*to act as arbitrator or umpire*) act as judge, adjudicate, judge, mediate, referee, sit in judgement, umpire.

arbitration *n.* (*the hearing or determining of a dispute by means of an arbitrator*) adjudicating, judgement, mediation, settlement.

arbitrator *n.* (*an umpire, an arbiter*) adjudicator, arbiter, judge, referee, umpire.

arc *n.* (*something curved in shape*) arch, bend, bow, crescent, curve.

arcane *a.* (*secret, esoteric*) abstruse, concealed, covert, cryptic, enigmatic, esoteric, hidden, mysterious, recondite, secret.

arch[1] *n.* **1** (*a curved structure, used as an opening or a support, e.g. for a bridge*) archway, span, vault. **2** (*anything resembling this, a curve*) arc, bend, bow, curvature, curve, dome.
~*v.i.* (*to assume an arched form*) bend, bow, curve.

arch[2] *a.* (*self-consciously teasing or mischievous*) artful, knowing, mischievous, pert, playful, roguish, saucy, sly.

arch- *pref.* (*leading, pre-eminent, esp. in a bad sense, as in arch-enemy; arch-hypocrite*) chief, foremost, greatest, leading, main, pre-eminent, principal.

archaic *a.* **1** (*old-fashioned, antiquated*) ancient, antediluvian, antiquated, antique, obsolete, old-fashioned, (*coll.*) old hat, outmoded, out of date, passé, superannuated. ANTONYMS: fashionable, modern, up to date. **2** (*of or belonging to a much earlier period, ancient*) ancient, bygone, olden.

arched *a.* (*having the form of an arch*) bowed, curved, domed, vaulted.

archetype *n.* **1** (*the primitive or original type or pattern*) original, prototype. **2** (*a typical or perfect example of something*) classic example, exemplar, ideal, model, paradigm, pattern, prime example, standard.

architect *n.* **1** (*a person who plans and draws the designs of buildings, and superintends their erection*) designer, planner. **2** (*a contriver or a designer of something*) author, contriver, creator, deviser, engineer, founder, instigator, inventor, maker, originator, planner, prime mover, shaper.

architecture *n.* **1** (*the art or profession of designing buildings*) building design, construction design, planning. **2** (*the structure or design of anything*) design, framework, makeup, structure, style.

archive *n.* **1** (*a place in which* (*historical*) *records are kept*) museum, record office, registry. **2** ((*historical*) *records officially preserved*) annals, chronicles, records, registers, rolls.

arctic *a.* (*extremely cold*) chilly, cold, freezing, frigid, frosty, frozen, glacial, icy. ANTONYMS: hot, sweltering.

ardent *a.* (*intense, zealous*) avid, eager, earnest, emotional, enthusiastic, fervent, fervid, fierce, hot-blooded, impassioned, intense, keen, passionate, profound, spirited, vehement, warm, zealous. ANTONYMS: apathetic, cold, lukewarm.

ardour *n.* **1** (*intensity of emotion, fervour*) earnestness, fervour, fierceness, fire, hot-bloodedness, impassionedness, intensity, passion, profoundness, spirit, vehemence, warmth. ANTONYMS: coldness. **2** (*zeal, enthusiasm*) avidity, eagerness, enthusiasm, keenness, zeal. ANTONYMS: apathy, indifference, lack of enthusiasm.

arduous *a.* (*laborious, involving a lot of effort*) burdensome, difficult, exhausting, fatiguing, formidable, gruelling, hard, harsh, heavy, Herculean, laborious, punishing, rigorous, severe, strenuous, taxing, tiring, tough. ANTONYMS: easy, painless, undemanding.

area *n.* **1** (*a particular extent of surface, a region*) district, domain, locality, neighbourhood, quarter, region, sector, stretch, territory, tract, zone. **2** (*a section of a larger space or surface or of a building etc., esp. one designated for a particular purpose*) part, portion, section, sector, space. **3** (*the measurable extent of a surface*) compass, expanse, extent, scope, size. **4** (*a sphere of interest or study*) arena, department, discipline, domain, field, province, realm, scene, sphere, territory.

arena n. **1** (*an area enclosed by seating in which sports events or entertainments take place*) amphitheatre, (*esp. N Am.*) bowl, coliseum/ colosseum, field, ground, park, ring, stadium, stage. **2** (*a field of conflict*) battlefield, battleground, field of conflict, theatre of war. **3** (*a sphere of action*) area, department, discipline, domain, field, province, realm, scene, sphere, territory.

argue v.t. **1** (*to (try to) exhibit or prove by reasoning*) assert, claim, contend, expostulate, hold, insist, maintain. ANTONYMS: deny, rebut, refute. **2** (*to discuss, debate*) debate, discourse, discuss. **3** (*to convince by logical methods*) convince, persuade, prevail upon, talk into, talk round. ANTONYMS: dissuade, talk out of.
~v.i. (*to quarrel, to exchange views heatedly*) (*coll.*) argy-bargy, bicker, disagree, dispute, fall out, fight, have an argument, quarrel, squabble, wrangle. ANTONYMS: be reconciled, make up.

argument n. **1** (*an exchange of views, esp. an angry or passionate one*) altercation, bickering, clash, controversy, difference of opinion, disagreement, dispute, falling-out, feud, fight, quarrel, row, squabble, wrangle. **2** ((*a*) *debate, discussion*) debate, discussion, forum. **3** (*a series of reasons or demonstration put forward*) case, defence, line of reasoning, logic, reason, reasoning. **4** (*an abstract or summary of a book*) abstract, outline, précis, summary, synopsis. **5** (*the subject of a discourse*) assertion, claim, contention, declaration. ANTONYMS: rebuttal, refutation. **6** (*the main theme or plot of a story etc.*) gist, plot, story, storyline, subject, subject matter, theme, topic.

argumentative a. **1** (*having a natural tendency to argue*) belligerent, combative, contentious, disputatious. ANTONYMS: accommodating, conciliatory, easygoing. **2** (*controversial*) contentious, controversial, disputed, open to dispute.

arid a. **1** (*dry, without moisture*) desert, dried up, dry, parched, waterless. ANTONYMS: watery, wet. **2** (*barren, bare*) bare, barren, infertile, sterile, unproductive. ANTONYMS: fertile, fruitful, lush. **3** (*dry, uninteresting*) boring, colourless, drab, dreary, dry, dull, flat, jejune, lifeless, monotonous, tedious, uninspired, uninteresting, vapid. ANTONYMS: exciting, interesting, lively.

aridity n. **1** (*dryness, drought*) drought, dryness, parchedness, waterlessness. ANTONYMS: wetness. **2** (*barrenness*) barrenness, infertility, sterility. ANTONYMS: fertility, fruitfulness, lushness. **3** (*absence of interest or appeal*) boredom, colourlessness, drabness, dreariness, dryness, dullness, flatness, jejuneness, lack of interest,

lifelessness, monotony, tedium, vapidness. ANTONYMS: excitement, interest, liveliness.

aright adv. (*correctly, without failure or mistake*) accurately, correctly.

arise v.i. **1** (*to appear, to come into being*) appear, begin, come into being, come into existence, come to light, commence, crop up, emerge, happen, make an appearance, occur, spring up, start, turn up. ANTONYMS: die, disappear. **2** (*to originate (from), to occur as a result*) be caused (by), emanate (from), ensue, follow, originate (from), proceed (from), result (from), stem (from). **3** (*to assume an upright position after lying or sitting, to get up*) get to one's feet, get up, rise, stand up. ANTONYMS: sit down. **4** (*to rise up, to ascend*) ascend, climb, go up, mount, rise up, soar. ANTONYMS: descend.

aristocracy n. (*the nobility*) nobility, patricians, peerage, ruling class, upper class, (*coll.*) upper crust. ANTONYMS: hoi polloi, masses, rabble.

aristocrat n. (*a noble*) grandee, lord/ lady, noble, nobleman/ noblewoman, patrician, peer/ peeress.

aristocratic a. **1** (*of or relating to an aristocracy or to aristocrats*) blue-blooded, high-born, noble, patrician, titled, upper-class, (*coll.*) upper-crust, well-born. ANTONYMS: common, low-born, plebeian. **2** (*grand, stylish*) courtly, dignified, elegant, fine, grand, polished, stylish, well-bred. ANTONYMS: common, unrefined, vulgar.

arm[1] n. **1** (*a division of a service or organization*) branch, department, detachment, division, offshoot, section, sector. **2** (*power, authority*) authority, force, might, power, strength, sway. ANTONYMS: powerlessness.

arm[2] n. **1** (*a weapon*) armament, firearm, gun, ordnance, weapon, weaponry. **2** (*heraldic bearings*) blazonry, coat of arms, crest, device, emblem, escutcheon, heraldic device, insignia.
~v.t. (*to equip with tools or other appliances*) equip, furnish, issue with, provide, supply.
~v.i. (*to prepare for war*) arm oneself, mobilize, prepare for war, take up arms.

armistice n. (*a cessation of fighting for a stipulated time during war*) ceasefire, peace, suspension of hostilities, truce.

armoury n. (*a place for keeping arms, an arsenal*) arms depot, arsenal, magazine, ordnance depot.

army n. **1** (*a body of people organized for land warfare*) armed force, land forces, (*collect.*) military, military force, soldiers, soldiery, troops. **2** (*a multitude, a very large number*) crowd, horde, host, mob, multitude, pack, swarm, throng.

aroma *n.* (*an agreeable odour or smell*) bouquet, fragrance, perfume, redolence, scent, smell. ANTONYMS: (*coll.*) pong, stink.

aromatic *a.* **1** (*fragrant*) fragrant, perfumed, scented, sweet-scented, sweet-smelling. ANTONYMS: (*coll.*) ponging, stinking. **2** (*spicy*) pungent, spicy, tangy. ANTONYMS: bland, mild.

around *prep.* **1** (*on all sides of; enveloping*) about, encircling, enclosing, encompassing, on all sides of, on every side of, surrounding. **2** (*from place to place in*) about, here and there. ~*adv.* **1** (*here and there, at various points; at random*) at random, here and there. **2** (*in existence*) existent, in existence. **3** (*in the vicinity, at hand*) at hand, available, in the vicinity, to hand. ANTONYMS: unavailable. **4** (*approximately*) about, approximately, circa, close to, nearly, near to, roughly. ANTONYMS: exactly, precisely.

arouse *v.t.* **1** (*to stir up, awaken*) awaken, call forth, cause, excite, foment, foster, incite, induce, inspire, instigate, kindle, provoke, spark off, stimulate, stir up, summon up. ANTONYMS: dampen, quell, still. **2** (*to excite, stimulate*) egg on, encourage, excite, goad, incite, inflame, prompt, provoke, rouse, spur on, stimulate, urge. ANTONYMS: discourage, dissuade.

arrange *v.t.* **1** (*to adjust, to put in proper order*) align, array, categorize, classify, dispose, group, line up, marshal, order, organize, position, put in order, range, rank, set out, sort, sort out, systematize, tidy. ANTONYMS: disturb, mess up. **2** (*to work out or agree the order or circumstances of*) agree on, decide on, devise, fix, organize, plan, schedule, set, settle on. ANTONYMS: cancel, postpone. **3** (*to adapt (a musical composition) for other voices or instruments*) adapt, harmonize, instrument, orchestrate, score, set. ~*v.i.* **1** (*to make plans or preparations (for, to)*) make preparations, plan, prepare. **2** (*to come to an agreement (with)*) agree, decide, (*coll.*) fix up, plan.

arrangement *n.* **1** (*the act of arranging, the state of being arranged*) aligning, categorization, classification, disposition, grouping, marshalling, ordering, organization, positioning, ranging, ranking, sorting, systematization, tidying. ANTONYMS: disorganization, disturbance, messing up. **2** (*the manner in which things are arranged*) categorization, classification, disposition, line-up, order, set-up, structure, system. **3** (*an agreement, settlement*) agreement, compact, contract, deal, settlement. **4** (*pl.*) (*dispositions in advance, preparations*) plans, preparations, provisions. **5** (*Mus.*) (*the adaptation of a musical composition for instruments or voices for which it was not written; a piece of music so adapted*) adaptation, harmonization, instrumentation, orchestration, score, setting.

arrant *a.* (*complete, thorough*) absolute, complete, downright, out and out, outright, rank, thorough, thoroughgoing, through and through, total, unmitigated, utter.

array *n.* **1** (*an impressive display or collection*) arrangement, assemblage, collection, display, disposition, exhibition, parade, show. **2** (*dress, attire*) apparel, attire, clothes, clothing, dress, garb. ~*v.t.* **1** (*to adorn, to dress up*) adorn, apparel, attire, clothe, deck, dress, garb, robe. **2** (*to set in order; to marshal (troops) for battle*) arrange, assemble, dispose, group, line up, marshal, muster, order, organize, range.

arrears *n.pl.* (*that which remains unpaid or undone*) balance, debt, deficit, outstanding payment. **in arrear/ arrears** (*behindhand, esp. in payment*) behind, behindhand, in debt, late, overdue.

arrest *v.t.* **1** (*to apprehend and take into legal custody*) apprehend, (*sl.*) bust, capture, catch, (*coll.*) collar, detain, (*sl.*) nab, (*sl.*) nick, (*coll.*) pinch, (*coll.*) run in, seize, take, take into custody, take prisoner. ANTONYMS: let go, release. **2** (*to stop, check*) block, bring to a halt, bring to a standstill, check, end, halt, inhibit, nip (something) in the bud, obstruct, prevent, stop. ANTONYMS: initiate, instigate, precipitate. **3** (*to seize and fix (the sight, mind etc.)*) attract, capture, catch, catch hold of, engage, engross, grip, rivet, seize, take hold of. ~*n.* **1** (*seizure, detention, esp. by legal authority*) apprehension, (*sl.*) bust, (*sl.*) busting, capture, (*coll.*) collaring, detention, (*coll.*) nabbing, (*sl.*) nicking, (*coll.*) pinching, seizure, taking into custody. ANTONYMS: freeing, release. **2** (*a stoppage*) check, end, halt, inhibition, obstruction, preventing, stay, stoppage.

arresting *a.* (*striking, catching the attention*) conspicuous, extraordinary, impressive, outstanding, remarkable, striking. ANTONYMS: ordinary, unimpressive, unremarkable.

arrival *n.* **1** (*the act of coming to a journey's end or destination*) advent, approach, arriving, coming, entrance, entry. ANTONYMS: departure, going. **2** (*the coming to a position, state of mind etc.*) advent, arriving, occurrence, occurring.

arrive *v.i.* **1** (*to reach a destination*) appear, come on the scene, enter, get here/ there, put in an appearance, reach one's destination, show, show up, turn up. ANTONYMS: depart, leave. **2** ((*of an event, time*) *to occur*) crop up, happen, occur, present itself, take place, turn up. **3** (*to attain fame, success or recognition*) achieve success, be successful, gain recognition, make good, (*coll.*) make it, make the grade, reach the top, succeed. ANTONYMS: be unsuccessful, fail.

arrogance *n.* **1** (*the act or quality of being arrogant*) conceit, condescension, disdain, egotism, haughtiness, hauteur, high-handedness, imperiousness, loftiness, lordliness, pride, self-importance, superciliousness, swagger. ANTONYMS: diffidence, humility, modesty. **2** (*undue assumption*) impertinence, insolence, presumption.

arrogant *a.* **1** (*overbearing, haughty*) conceited, condescending, disdainful, egotistic, haughty, high-handed, imperious, lofty, lordly, overbearing, overweening, proud, self-important, stuck-up, supercilious, swaggering, (*coll.*) uppity. ANTONYMS: diffident, humble, modest. **2** (*claiming or assuming too much*) impertinent, insolent, presumptuous.

arrogate *v.t.* (*to make unduly exalted claims to* (*a thing*)) appropriate, commandeer, expropriate, seize, usurp.

arrow *n.* **1** (*a slender, straight, sharp-pointed missile shot from a bow*) bolt, dart, flight, shaft. **2** (*anything resembling an arrow, esp. a sign indicating direction*) indicator, pointer.

arsenal *n.* **1** (*a place for the manufacture and storage of naval and military ammunition*) armoury, arms depot, magazine, ordnance depot. **2** (*a stock or supply of things, e.g. arguments*) stock, stockpile, store, storehouse, supply.

art *n.* **1** (*creative activity concerned with the production of aesthetic objects*) creativity. **2** (*creative activity of a visual kind; visual works of art*) drawing, painting, visual art. **3** (*human skill or workmanship as opposed to nature*) artifice, artistry, craft, skill. **4** (*a method, technique*) method, practice, procedure, process, system, technique, way. **5** (*a facility, knack*) aptitude, facility, flair, gift, knack, talent. **6** (*craft, cunning*) artfulness, artifice, craft, cunning, deceit, duplicity, foxiness, guile, slyness, smartness, trickery, wiles, wiliness. ANTONYMS: ingenuousness, openness, straightforwardness.

artful *a.* (*crafty, cunning*) crafty, cunning, deceitful, designing, duplicitous, foxy, ingenious, intriguing, politic, scheming, sly, smart, tricky, wily. ANTONYMS: artless, ingenuous.

article *n.* **1** (*a thing, an object*) commodity, item, object, thing. **2** (*a prose composition in a newspaper, magazine etc.*) account, feature, item, piece, report, story, write-up. **3** (*a prose composition, complete in itself*) composition, discourse, essay, item, treatise. **4** (*a distinct statement, clause or provision in an agreement, statute or other document*) clause, paragraph, passage, point, portion, section, subsection.

articulate[1] *v.t.* **1** (*to utter* (*words*) *distinctly*) enunciate, pronounce, say, speak, utter. **2** (*to express* (*an idea, thought*) *clearly and coherently*) express, give voice to, pronounce, state, utter, verbalize, voice. ANTONYMS: conceal, suppress.

articulate[2] *a.* **1** (*able to express oneself clearly and coherently*) clear, coherent, communicative, distinct, eloquent, expressive, fluent, lucid, silver-tongued, vocal, well-spoken. ANTONYMS: inarticulate, incoherent, tongue-tied. **2** (*clearly and coherently expressed*) clear, coherent, comprehensible, fluent, intelligible, lucid, understandable. ANTONYMS: incoherent, unclear, unintelligible.

articulation *n.* (*the act or process of speaking*) delivery, diction, enunciation, pronunciation, speaking, speech, talking, verbalization, vocalization.

artifice *n.* **1** (*a clever expedient, a contrivance*) contrivance, device, dodge, expedient, manoeuvre, stratagem, tactic, trick. **2** (*cunning, trickery*) artfulness, chicanery, craft, cunning, deceit, deception, duplicity, foxiness, guile, scheming, slyness, strategy, trickery, wiliness. **3** (*a cunning trick*) dodge, machination, ruse, subterfuge, trick, wile.

artificial *a.* **1** (*made or produced by human agency, not natural*) ersatz, imitation, man-made, manufactured, mock, plastic, simulated, synthetic. ANTONYMS: natural, real. **2** (*not real, fake*) bogus, counterfeit, ersatz, fake, (*coll.*) phoney, sham, specious, spurious. ANTONYMS: authentic, genuine, real. **3** (*affected in manner, insincere*) affected, assumed, contrived, factitious, false, feigned, forced, hollow, insincere, laboured, meretricious, (*coll.*) phoney, pretended, pretentious, strained, unnatural. ANTONYMS: natural, sincere, unaffected.

artisan *n.* (*a skilled manual worker*) artificer, craftsman/ craftswoman, journeyman, skilled worker.

artistic *a.* **1** (*made or done with particular skill or taste; aesthetically pleasing*) aesthetic, attractive, beautiful, creative, decorative, elegant, exquisite, graceful, imaginative, lovely, ornamental, stylish, tasteful. ANTONYMS:

inartistic, tasteless. **2** (*having a natural talent for one or other of the arts, esp. painting*) creative, gifted, imaginative, talented.

artistry *n.* (*skill*) craftsmanship, creativity, flair, skill, talent, workmanship.

artless *a.* (*guileless, simple*) childlike, guileless, ingenuous, innocent, naive, natural, simple, sincere, trusting, unpretentious, unsophisticated. ANTONYMS: contrived, insincere, unnatural.

ascend *v.i.* (*to go or come from a lower to a higher place or degree*) climb, go up, mount, move up, rise, soar, take off, tower. ANTONYMS: descend, drop, go down.

ascendancy *n.* (*controlling influence*) authority, command, control, dominance, domination, dominion, influence, mastery, power, predominance, prevalence, rule, sovereignty, superiority, supremacy, sway.

ascendant *a.* **1** (*moving upwards, rising*) ascending, climbing, mounting, rising. ANTONYMS: descendant, falling. **2** (*predominating, ruling*) authoritative, commanding, controlling, dominant, influential, powerful, predominant, prevailing, ruling, superior, supreme, uppermost. ANTONYMS: subordinate, subservient.

ascent *n.* **1** (*the act or process of ascending, upward motion*) ascending, ascension, climbing, mounting, rising, soaring, taking off. ANTONYMS: descent. **2** (*a slope*) acclivity, gradient, incline, rise, slope, upward slope.

ascertain *v.t.* (*to discover or verify by investigation or experiment*) confirm, determine, discover, establish, ferret out, find out, identify, learn, make certain, settle, verify.

ascetic *a.* (*practising rigorous self-discipline, esp. for spiritual or religious ends*) abstemious, abstinent, austere, celibate, frugal, puritanical, rigorous, self-denying, self-disciplined, Spartan, strict. ANTONYMS: hedonistic, self-indulgent, sensuous.
~*n.* (*any person given to rigorous self-denial and mortification*) anchorite, hermit, recluse, self-denier, solitary.

ascribe *v.t.* (*to attribute, to assign (to)*) accredit, assign, attribute, blame, charge, credit, impute, lay (something) on, put (something) down, set (something) down.

ashamed *a.* **1** (*feeling shame, either abashed by consciousness of one's own error or guilt or on account of some other person or thing*) conscience-stricken, crestfallen, discomfited, embarrassed, guilty, humiliated, mortified, red-faced, remorseful, shamefaced, sheepish,

sorry, with one's tail between one's legs. ANTONYMS: proud, unashamed, unrepentant. **2** (*unwilling or hesitant*) hesitant, loath, unrestrained, unwilling. ANTONYMS: willing.

ashen *a.* (*pale*) anaemic, colourless, grey-faced, pale, pallid, wan, white. ANTONYMS: florid, flushed, ruddy.

asinine *a.* (*stupid, ridiculous*) brainless, daft, (*coll.*) dumb, fatuous, foolish, half-witted, idiotic, inane, moronic, senseless, silly, stupid. ANTONYMS: clever, sensible, wise.

ask *v.t.* **1** (*to inquire of; to put (a question) to*) (*coll.*) grill, inquire of, interrogate, pump, put a question to, query, question, quiz. ANTONYMS: answer, reply to. **2** (*to seek to obtain by words, to request*) appeal for, ask for, beg, beseech, claim, crave, demand, implore, request, seek, solicit. **3** (*to invite*) bid, invite, summon.

askew *adv.* (*out of true, awry*) awry, crooked, out of line, out of true, to one side. ANTONYMS: in line, level, straight.

asleep *adv., pred.a.* (*in or into a state of sleep*) (*coll.*) dead to the world, dormant, fast asleep, sleeping, slumbering, sound asleep. ANTONYMS: awake, wide awake.

aspect *n.* **1** (*a particular element or feature of something*) angle, facet, feature, side. **2** (*a way of regarding or viewing something*) angle, outlook, point of view, slant, standpoint, viewpoint. **3** ((*of a building*) *a position facing in a particular direction*) location, outlook, position, prospect, scene, situation, view. **4** (*a facial expression*) air, appearance, countenance, demeanour, expression, look, mien.

asperity *n.* (*harshness of manner*) acerbity, acrimony, bitterness, harshness, roughness, severity, sharpness, sourness.

aspersion *n.* **to cast aspersions on** (*to make disparaging or slanderous remarks about*) (*coll.*) bad-mouth, decry, defame, denigrate, deprecate, disparage, slander, vilify. ANTONYMS: commend, praise.

asphyxiate *v.t.* (*to suffocate*) choke, smother, stifle, strangle, suffocate, throttle.

aspiration *n.* (*steadfast desire or ambition*) aim, ambition, carving, desire, dream, goal, hankering, longing, objective, wish, yearning.

aspire *v.i.* (*to seek to attain (to)*) aim (to), be ambitious (for), crave (for), desire, dream (of), hanker (after), long (for), wish (for), yearn (for).

aspiring *a.* (*eagerly desirous of some high object, ambitious*) ambitious, aspirant, expectant, hopeful, would-be.

assail *v.t.* **1** (*to attack violently by physical means*) assault, attack, lay into, mug, set about, set upon. **2** (*to attack with abuse, censure etc.*) attack, belabour, bombard, harangue, lambast, tear into.

assailant *n.* (*a person who attacks another physically*) aggressor, assailer, assaulter, attacker, mugger.

assassin *n.* (*a person who kills someone, esp. for money or for fanatical, political etc. motives*) (*sl.*) contract killer, executioner, (*sl.*) hitman, killer, liquidator, murderer, professional killer, slayer, sniper, terrorist.

assassinate *v.t.* (*to kill, esp. for money or for fanatical, political etc. motives*) eliminate, execute, kill, liquidate, murder, slay, (*sl.*) take out.

assault *n.* **1** (*a violent physical or verbal attack*) attack, mugging, onslaught. **2** (*an act of or attempt at rape*) attempted rape, indecent assault, molestation, rape, sexual assault, sexual interference. **3** (*the charge of an attacking body on a fortified place*) act of aggression, attack, charge, offensive, onslaught, storming, strike. ANTONYMS: defence.
~*v.t.* **1** (*to make a violent physical or verbal attack on*) assail, m0attack, hit, mug, set about, set upon, strike. **2** (*to attack (a fortified place) by sudden rush*) attack, charge, launch an offensive on, storm, strike at. ANTONYMS: defend.

assemble *v.t.* **1** (*to call together*) call, collect, convoke, gather, muster, rally, round up, summon. ANTONYMS: disband, dismiss, disperse. **2** (*to bring together*) accumulate, amass, collect, gather, get together, heap up, hoard, marshal, pile up, put together, stockpile, store up. ANTONYMS: disperse. **3** (*to fit together the component parts of*) erect, fit, fit together, piece together, put together, set up. ANTONYMS: disassemble, dismantle, take apart.
~*v.i.* (*to meet or come together*) collect, come together, congregate, convene, flock together, foregather, gather, meet. ANTONYMS: disperse, scatter.

assembly *n.* **1** (*the act of assembling*) erection, piecing together, putting together, setting up. **2** (*a body of people met together for some common purpose*) congregation, congress, convention, crowd, gathering, meeting, multitude, rally. **3** (*a deliberative, legislative or religious body*) congress, council, diet, house, parliament, synod.

assent *v.i.* (*to agree to or sanction something proposed*) accede to, accept, acquiesce in, agree to, allow, approve of, comply with, concur with, consent to, permit, sanction. ANTONYMS: disapprove of, dissent from, reject.

~*n.* (*the act of admitting, agreement*) acceptance, accord, acquiescence, agreement, approval, compliance, concurrence, consent, permission, sanction. ANTONYMS: disagreement, disapproval.

assert *v.t.* **1** (*to affirm, to declare positively*) affirm, allege, announce, aver, avow, contend, declare, maintain, postulate, proclaim, pronounce, state, swear. ANTONYMS: deny, refute, retract. **2** (*to insist on (a claim etc.)*) defend, insist on, press for, push for, stand up for, uphold, vindicate. ANTONYMS: give up. **3** (*to put (oneself) forward, insist on one's rights etc.*) behave aggressively, behave confidently, exert one's influence, make one's presence felt, put (oneself) forward.

assertion *n.* **1** (*the act of asserting*) asserting, defence, insistence, upholding, vindication. **2** (*a positive statement, an affirmation*) allegation, announcement, avowal, contention, declaration, postulation, proclamation, pronouncement, statement.

assertive *a.* (*putting oneself forward, forthright*) aggressive, confident, decisive, determined, dogmatic, emphatic, firm, forceful, positive, (*coll.*) pushy, self-assured, self-confident, strong-willed. ANTONYMS: diffident, meek, self-effacing, shy.

assess *v.t.* **1** (*to judge the quality or worth of; to value*) appraise, estimate, evaluate, gauge, judge, rate, size up, value, weigh up. **2** (*to fix by authority the amount of (a tax, fine etc. for a person or community)*) fix, impose, levy, set.

assessment *n.* **1** ((*an*) *estimation, appraisal*) appraisal, estimation, evaluation, gauging, rating, valuation, weighing up. **2** (*an official valuation for taxation purposes*) charge, evaluation, levy, tariff, tax, toll.

asset *n.* (*a useful or valuable resource*) advantage, aid, benefit, blessing, boon, help, resource, strength, strong point. ANTONYMS: disadvantage, handicap, hindrance, impediment, liability.

assets *n.pl.* (*all the property of a person or company which may be liable for outstanding debts*) belongings, capital, effects, estate, funds, goods, holdings, money, possessions, property, reserves, resources, securities, valuables, wealth.

assiduous *a.* (*hard-working, conscientious*) attentive, conscientious, constant, diligent, hard-working, indefatigable, industrious, laborious, persevering, sedulous, steady, studious, unflagging, untiring, zealous. ANTONYMS: idle, inattentive, indolent, lazy.

assign *v.t.* **1** (*to allot, to apportion*) allocate, allot, apportion, dispense, give, grant. **2** (*to designate for a specific purpose*) appoint, choose, designate, name, nominate, select. **3** (*to name, to fix*) appoint, fix, name, select, set. **4** (*to ascribe, to attribute*) accredit, ascribe, attribute, put down. **5** (*to transfer, to surrender*) convey, make over, transfer.

assignation *n.* (*a meeting, esp. an illicit one between lovers*) clandestine meeting, (*coll.*) date, illicit meeting, meeting, rendezvous, tryst.

assignment *n.* **1** (*the act of assigning; allocation*) allocation, allotment, apportioning, dispensation, giving, granting. **2** (*a specific task or mission*) charge, commission, duty, job, mission, obligation, responsibility, task. **3** (*the act of designating for a specific purpose*) appointment, choice, choosing, designation, naming, nomination, selection. **4** (*a legal transference of right or property*) conveyance, transfer, transference.

assimilate *v.t.* **1** (*to take as nutriment and convert into living tissue*) absorb, digest, ingest. ANTONYMS: reject. **2** (*to take in (information) and comprehend*) absorb, comprehend, grasp, take in, understand. **3** (*to incorporate*) absorb, embrace, include, incorporate, subsume, take in. **4** (*to make similar or alike*) adapt, adjust, homogenize, make like, make similar. ~*v.i.* **1** (*to become absorbed or incorporated*) blend, fit in, fuse, merge, mingle, mix. **2** (*to become similar*) adapt, adjust, become like, become similar, conform.

assist *v.t.* **1** (*to help, to give support to*) abet, aid, back, be of assistance to, collaborate with, give succour to, give support to, help, lend (someone) a hand, lend (someone) a helping hand. ANTONYMS: hamper, hinder, impede, thwart. **2** (*to act as a subordinate to*) be an assistant to, be (someone's) girl Friday, be (someone's) Man Friday, be (someone's) right-hand man, be (someone's) right-hand woman, be subordinate to, relieve, second, support. **3** (*to make (a task) easier or quicker*) aid, benefit, expedite, facilitate, further, promote. ANTONYMS: hamper, hinder, hold up, retard.

assistance *n.* (*help, support*) a hand, a helping hand, aid, backing, collaboration, furtherance, reinforcement, relief, succour, support. ANTONYMS: hindrance, obstruction.

assistant *n.* **1** (*a person who assists another*) abettor, accessory, accomplice, associate, backer, collaborator, confederate, helper, helpmate, partner, supporter. **2** (*an auxiliary*) aide, deputy, girl Friday, henchman, henchwoman, Man Friday, right-hand man, right-hand

woman, second-in-command, subordinate. ANTONYMS: boss, chief.

associate[1] *v.t.* **1** (*to connect in the mind or imagination*) connect, link, relate, think of together. ANTONYMS: dissociate. **2** (*to unite, to combine*) affiliate, ally, combine, join, link, unite. ANTONYMS: dissociate, segregate, separate. ~*v.i.* (*to keep company or mix (with)*) be friends, consort, fraternize, hang around, hobnob, keep company, (*coll.*) run around, socialize. ANTONYMS: avoid, be estranged from, fall out with.

associate[2] *n.* (*a partner, colleague, esp. in business*) collaborator, colleague, confederate, co-owner, friend, mate.

association *n.* **1** (*the act of combining for a common purpose*) affiliation, alliance, combination, combining, joining, linking, uniting. ANTONYMS: dissociation, segregation, separation. **2** (*a society formed for the promotion of some common object*) club, confederation, federation, league, order, organization, society, syndicate, union. **3** (*cooperation, intimacy*) affinity, connection, cooperation, fellowship, friendship, intimacy, liaison, relationship. ANTONYMS: animosity, enmity, hostility. **4** (*mental connection of ideas, memories, etc.*) connection, correlation, link.

assorted *a.* (*of various sorts, miscellaneous*) different, diverse, diversified, heterogeneous, miscellaneous, mixed, motley, sundry, varied, variegated. ANTONYMS: like, same, similar.

assortment *n.* (*a collection of things of various kinds*) hotchpotch, jumble, medley, mélange, miscellany, mishmash, mixed bag, mixture, pot-pourri, variety.

assuage *v.t.* **1** (*to soothe, to lessen the violence or pain of*) allay, alleviate, calm, ease, lessen, mitigate, moderate, mollify, palliate, relieve, soothe, temper. ANTONYMS: aggravate, exacerbate, intensify. **2** (*to appease, satisfy*) appease, blunt, quench, satisfy, slake, take the edge off.

assume *v.t.* **1** (*to take for granted, to accept without proof or as a hypothesis*) believe, expect, fancy, imagine, presume, presuppose, suppose, surmise, take as read, take for granted, think, understand. ANTONYMS: know, know for sure. **2** (*to pretend, feign*) fake, feign, pretend, put on, sham, simulate. **3** (*to take upon oneself, to undertake (a task, office*)) begin, embark upon, enter upon, set about, take on, take responsibility for, take up, take upon oneself, undertake. ANTONYMS: give up, relinquish. **4** (*to take on, adopt (a quality, characteristic*)) adopt, come to have, put on, take on. **5** (*to arrogate, to claim*) appropriate, arrogate, commandeer, expropriate, pre-empt, seize, take, take over, usurp. ANTONYMS: give up, relinquish, yield.

assumed a. (*feigned, false*) affected, bogus, counterfeit, fake, false, feigned, fictitious, imitation, made-up, make-believe, (*coll.*) phoney, pretended, pseudo, sham, simulated, spurious. ANTONYMS: authentic, real, true.

assumption n. 1 (*the act of assuming or undertaking a task etc.*) assuming, beginning, embarking on, entering upon, setting about, taking on, taking up, undertaking. ANTONYMS: giving up, relinquishing. 2 (*the act of assuming or taking on a quality etc.*) adopting, adoption, putting on, taking on. 3 (*the act of assuming, appropriation*) acquisition, appropriation, arrogation, assuming, commandeering, expropriation, pre-empting, seizure, takeover, taking, usurpation. ANTONYMS: giving up, relinquishing, yielding. 4 (*the thing assumed; a supposition*) belief, expectation, guess, hypothesis, inference, postulate, premise, presumption, presupposition, supposition, surmise, thinking, understanding. 5 (*arrogance*) arrogance, conceit, impertinence, impudence, presumption. ANTONYMS: diffidence, modesty.

assurance n. 1 (*a positive declaration*) affirmation, guarantee, oath, pledge, promise, vow, word, word of honour. ANTONYMS: denial. 2 (*certainty, security*) certainty, guarantee, sureness, surety. 3 (*self-confidence, self-reliance*) confidence, self-assurance, self-confidence, self-possession, self-reliance. ANTONYMS: diffidence, self-doubt, self-effacement.

assured a. 1 (*certain, guaranteed*) certain, dependable, guaranteed, reliable, secure, sure. ANTONYMS: insecure, uncertain, unreliable. 2 (*self-confident, full of assurance*) assertive, confident, poised, positive, self-assertive, self-assured, self-confident, self-reliant. ANTONYMS: diffident, self-effacing, self-possessed.

astonish v.t. (*to strike with sudden surprise or wonder, to amaze*) amaze, astound, bewilder, confound, daze, dumbfound, flabbergast, stagger, stun, stupefy, surprise, take one's breath away, take (someone) aback.

astonishing a. (*very surprising*) amazing, astounding, bewildering, breathtaking, impressive, sensational, staggering, stunning, stupefying, surprising, wondrous.

astonishment n. (*the state of being astonished; amazement*) amazement, bewilderment, consternation, stupefaction, surprise, wonder, wonderment.

astound v.t. (*to strike with amazement, to shock with surprise*) amaze, astonish, bewilder, dumbfound, flabbergast, stagger, stun, stupefy, surprise, take one's breath away.

astounding a. (*very surprising*) amazing, astonishing, bewildering, breathtaking, impressive, sensational, staggering, stunning, stupefying, surprising.

astray a., adv. 1 (*in or into sin, crime or error*) into sin, into wrongdoing, to the bad. 2 (*out of or away from the right way*) adrift, off course, off the right track.

astringent a. 1 (*causing contraction of body tissues*) constrictive, contractile, contracting, styptic. 2 (*severe, harsh*) acerbic, caustic, hard, harsh, mordant, rigorous, rough, severe, stern, strict, stringent, trenchant. ANTONYMS: kindly, lenient, mild.

astronaut n. (*a person who is trained to travel into space in a spacecraft*) cosmonaut, spaceman, space traveller, spacewoman.

astute a. 1 (*acute, discerning*) acute, bright, clever, discerning, perceptive, politic, quick, quick-witted, sharp. 2 (*wily, cunning*) artful, clever, crafty, cunning, perception, sharp, shrewd, wily. ANTONYMS: igenuous, naive.

asunder adv. (*apart, in different pieces or places*) apart, into pieces, to bits, to pieces, to shreds. ANTONYMS: together.

asylum n. 1 (*protection from extradition given by one country to a person, esp. a political refugee, from another*) protection, refuge, safekeeping, safety, sanctuary, shelter. 2 (*a shelter, a refuge*) harbour, haven, refuge, retreat, sanctuary, shelter.

asymmetric a. (*not symmetrical; out of proportion*) disproportionate, irregular, misproportioned, uneven. ANTONYMS: even, proportionate, regular, symmetrical.

atheism n. (*disbelief in the existence of a God or gods*) disbelief, heathenism, heresy, nonbelief, scepticism, unbelief. ANTONYMS: belief, faith, religion.

atheist n. (*a person who disbelieves, or denies the existence of a God*) disbeliever, heathen, heretic, infidel, non-believer, sceptic, unbeliever. ANTONYMS: believer.

athletic a. 1 (*of or for athletes or athletics*) sporting, sports. 2 (*physically strong and fit*) active, energetic, fit, muscular, powerful, robust, strapping, strong, sturdy, vigorous. ANTONYMS: frail, inactive, unfit, weak.

atmosphere n. 1 (*the air in any given place*) air. 2 (*mental or moral environment*) background, environment, milieu, surroundings.

3 (*a prevailing mood or tone felt to be present in a place, work of art etc.*) air, ambience, aura, character, feel, feeling, flavour, mood, quality, spirit, tone, (*coll.*) vibes.

atom *n.* (*the smallest particle of matter possessing the properties of an element*) bit, crumb, dot, fragment, grain, iota, jot, mite, molecule, particle, scrap, shred, spot, trace, whit.

atone *v.i.* (*to make expiation or satisfaction for some crime or fault*) compensate, do penance, expiate, make amends, make recompense, make redress, make reparation, pay.

atonement *n.* (*reparation, amends*) amends, compensation, expiation, payment, penance, propitiation, recompense, redress, reparation, restitution, satisfaction.

atrocious *a.* **1** (*very bad, execrable*) appalling, dreadful, horrible, monstrous, outrageous, shocking, terrible, unpleasant. ANTONYMS: admirable, pleasant. **2** (*savagely cruel, wicked*) barbaric, barbarous, brutal, cruel, fierce, inhuman, merciless, ruthless, savage, vicious, villainous, violent, wicked. ANTONYMS: civilized, kindly, merciful.

atrocity *n.* **1** (*an act of extreme cruelty or ruthlessness, esp. against defenceless victims*) act of barbarity, act of brutality, act of cruelty, barbarity, enormity, evil, horror, outrage. **2** (*excessive cruelty or other flagrant wickedness*) barbarity, brutality, cruelty, fierceness, horror, inhumanity, mercilessness, ruthlessness, savagery, viciousness, violence, wickedness.

atrophy *v.i.* (*to waste away*) decay, degenerate, shrink, shrivel, waste, waste away, wilt, wither.

attach *v.t.* **1** (*to connect, affix*) adhere, affix, append, bind, connect, couple, fasten, fix, join, link, secure, stick, tie, unite. ANTONYMS: loosen, separate, uncouple, untie. **2** (*to attribute (importance, significance etc.*)) ascribe, assign, associate, attribute, impute, invest, lay, place, put. ANTONYMS: dissociate. **3** (*to join, to become a member of*) ally oneself with, become affiliated to, become associated with, enlist in, join, join forces with, sign on with, unite with. ANTONYMS: distance oneself from, withdraw from. **4** (*to appoint to an organization, military etc. unit, temporarily*) appoint, assign, detail, second.

attached *a.* **1** (*fond of; liking*) devoted to, fond of. **2** (*married, engaged or in a long-term relationship*) engaged, going steady, in a relationship, married, spoken for. ANTONYMS: free, unattached, unmarried.

attachment *n.* **1** (*the act of attaching*)

adhering, affixing, appendage, binding, connecting, connection, coupling, fastening, fixing, joining, linking, securing, sticking, tie, uniting. ANTONYMS: loosening, separation, uncoupling, untying. **2** (*the means by which something is attached*) clamp, connecter, coupling, junction, link. **3** (*a thing that can be attached, esp. a device that can be fitted to a machine*) accessory, accoutrement, add-on, appendage, appurtenance, extension, extra, fitting, supplement. **4** (*affection, devotion*) affection, affinity, bond, devotion, fidelity, fondness, friendship, liking, love, loyalty, tenderness. ANTONYMS: antipathy, aversion, dislike, hostility. **5** (*a temporary posting or secondment*) appointment, assignment, detailing, secondment.

attack *v.t.* **1** (*to launch a physical or armed assault on*) assail, assault, beset, charge, lay into, mug, pounce upon, rush, set upon, strike. ANTONYMS: defend, guard, protect. **2** (*to criticize or abuse strongly*) abuse, berate, (*coll.*) blast, censure, criticize, denigrate, fulminate against, harangue, (*coll.*) have a go at, impugn, (*coll.*) knock, lambast, revile, (*coll.*) slam, slate, tear into, vilify. ANTONYMS: admire, praise, support. **3** (*to begin (a piece of work) with determination*) embark on, get started on, get to work on, set about, undertake. **4** ((*of a physical agent, disease etc.*) *to exert a destructive or harmful influence on*) affect, have an effect on, infect.
~*n.* **1** (*the act of attacking; an assault*) assault, charge, foray, incursion, mugging, offensive, onset, onslaught, rush, storming, strike. ANTONYMS: defence, protection. **2** (*violent criticism or abuse*) abuse, censure, criticism, denigration, fulmination, harangue, (*coll.*) knocking, lambasting, revilement, (*coll.*) slamming, slating, vilification. ANTONYMS: admiration, laudation, praise. **3** (*a sudden fit of illness, panic etc.*) bout, convulsion, fit, paroxysm, seizure, spasm. **4** (*the beginning of active work on something*) beginning, commencement, onslaught, start, undertaking. **5** (*vigour and decisiveness in undertaking something*) aggression, decisiveness, determination, positiveness, strength, vigour. ANTONYMS: hesitation, weakness.

attacker *n.* **1** (*a person who attacks someone physically*) aggressor, assailant, assaulter, mugger. **2** (*a person who criticizes someone strongly*) abuser, censor, critic, denigrator, haranguer, (*coll.*) knocker, vilifier. ANTONYMS: admirer, supporter.

attain *v.t.* **1** (*to reach, to arrive at*) arrive at, gain, get to, reach. **2** (*to accomplish*) accomplish, achieve, complete, finish, fulfil, realize. **3** (*to obtain*) acquire, gain, get, obtain, procure, realize, secure, win. ANTONYMS: fail to get, lose, miss.

attainable a. **1** ((of a place) that can be reached) accessible, reachable, within reach. ANTONYMS: inaccessible, out of reach. **2** (that can be accomplished) achievable, feasible, likely, obtainable, possible, practicable, probable, procurable, realizable. ANTONYMS: impossible, impracticable, improbable, unattainable.

attainment n. **1** (the act of attaining or reaching something) attaining, reaching. **2** (the act of attaining or accomplishing something) accomplishment, achievement, attaining, completion, finishing, fulfilment, realization. **3** (the act of accomplishing or obtaining something) acquiral, attaining, gaining, getting, obtaining, procuration, procuring, realization, securing, winning. **4** (something which is attained) accomplishment, achievement, acquisition, feat. **5** (a personal achievement or accomplishment) ability, accomplishment, achievement, art, gift, proficiency, skill, talent.

attempt v.t. **1** (to try, endeavour (to do, achieve etc.)) aim, do one's best, endeavour, essay, seek, strive, try, venture. **2** (to make an effort to achieve) (coll.) have a crack at, (coll.) have a go at, (coll.) have a shot at, (coll.) have a stab at, try, try one's hand at, venture to.

~n. (an endeavour, effort) bid, (coll.) crack, effort, endeavour, essay, go, (coll.) shot, (coll.) stab, try, venture.

attend v.t. **1** (to be present at) appear at, be at, be present at, go to, put in an appearance at, show up at, turn up at. ANTONYMS: be absent from, miss. **2** (to go regularly to (church, a school etc.)) be a member of, frequent, go to. **3** (to accompany, escort) accompany, chaperone, escort, squire, usher. **4** (to look after, wait upon) care for, look after, mind, minister to, nurse, take care of, tend. ANTONYMS: neglect. **5** (to result from) arise from, be accompanied by, be associated with, be consequent upon, connected with, follow from, issue from, occur with, result from.

~v.i. **1** (to pay attention, apply the mind (to)) concentrate (on), follow, heed, listen (to), mark, mind, note, notice, observe, pay attention (to), pay heed (to), take note (of), take notice (of), watch. ANTONYMS: disregard, ignore, neglect. **2** (to apply one's efforts or energies (to)) apply oneself (to), cope (with), deal (with), devote oneself (to), give one's attention (to), handle, see (to), take care (of). **3** (to be present) be present, be there, put in an appearance, show, turn up. ANTONYMS: be absent, play truant.

attendance n. **1** (presence) appearance, presence, showing up. ANTONYMS: absence. **2** (the (number of) persons attending) audience, crowd, gate, house, turnout. **in attendance** (waiting, attendant (on)) present, standing by, there.

attendant a. (following as a consequence; accompanying) accompanying, associated, concomitant, consequent, related, resultant. ~n. **1** (a person who attends or accompanies another; a servant) aide, chaperon, chaperone, companion, equerry, escort, flunkey, lackey, squire. **2** (a person employed to assist, guide etc. the general public) assistant, custodian, guard, guide, helper, steward.

attention n. **1** (the act or state of concentrating the mind on some object) attentiveness, concentration, heed, intentness, scrutiny, studying, thinking, thought. ANTONYMS: daydreaming, distraction, inattention. **2** (notice, interest) awareness, consciousness, heed, notice. ANTONYMS: ignorance, unawareness. **3** (consideration, action) action, consideration, investigation. **4** (watchful care) care, ministrations, treatment. **5** (usu. pl.) (an act of courtesy or kindness) civility, courtesy, gallantry, politeness. **6** (usu. pl.) (an act indicating love or the desire to woo) advances, approach, overtures.

attentive a. **1** (paying attention; listening carefully) alert, awake, careful, concentrating, heedful, intent, listening, mindful, observant, vigilant. ANTONYMS: abstracted, careless, heedless, inattentive. **2** (polite, courteous) chivalrous, civil, considerate, courteous, gallant, gracious, kind, polite, thoughtful. ANTONYMS: impolite, rude, thoughtless.

attenuated a. **1** (thin, slender) drawn out, elongated, slender, thin, thinned out, threadlike. **2** (weakened) diminished, enervated, lessened, reduced, weakened. ANTONYMS: increased, strengthened.

attest v.t. **1** (to vouch for, to certify) affirm, bear out, confirm, corroborate, endorse, verify, vouch for. ANTONYMS: contradict, deny, refute. **2** (to give evidence or proof of) demonstrate, evidence, prove, show, substantiate, verify. ANTONYMS: disprove. **3** (to testify, bear witness that) bear witness, give evidence, testify.

attire v.t. (to dress, esp. in fine or formal clothing) apparel, array, clothe, dress, fit out, garb, rig out, robe. ~n. (dress, clothes) apparel, array, clothes, clothing, costume, dress, garb, garments, (coll.) gear, habit, outfit, (coll.) rig-out, robes, (coll.) togs.

attitude n. **1** (a mental position or way of thinking with respect to someone or something) frame of mind, opinion, outlook, perspective, point of view, position, stance, thoughts, viewpoint. **2** (*bearing or gesture, expressing action or emotion*) air, bearing, demeanour, manner. **3** (*a posture or position taken by a person, animal or object*) pose, position, posture, stance.

attract *v.t.* **1** (*to draw to oneself or itself or cause to approach*) draw, magnetize, pull towards. ANTONYMS: repel. **2** (*to arouse interest or fascination in*) allure, appeal to, bewitch, captivate, charm, draw, enchant, entice, fascinate, induce, interest, inveigle, invite, lure, (*sl.*) pull, tempt. ANTONYMS: disgust, put (someone) off, repel, revolt.

attraction *n.* **1** (*the action or power of attracting*) allure, appeal, attractiveness, captivation, charm, enchantment, enticement, fascination, inducement, interest, invitation, lure, (*coll.*) pull, temptation. ANTONYMS: disgust, repulsion, revulsion. **2** (*a person, thing or characteristic that attracts*) draw, feature, inducement, interest, lure. **3** (*a force causing two objects, molecules etc. to be drawn together*) draw, magnetism, pull. ANTONYMS: repulsion.

attractive *a.* (*pleasing to the senses, appealing*) agreeable, alluring, appealing, charming, enticing, fascinating, inviting, pleasant, pleasing, tempting. ANTONYMS: repulsive, revolting, unpleasant.

attribute¹ *n.* (*a quality ascribed or imputed to any person or thing*) aspect, character, characteristic, facet, feature, idiosyncrasy, mark, peculiarity, property, quality, quirk, trait.

attribute² *v.t.* (*to regard as caused by*) ascribe, assign, chalk up to, credit, lay (something) at the door of, put (something) down to, set down to, trace to.

audacious *a.* **1** (*bold, daring*) adventurous, bold, brave, courageous, daredevil, daring, enterprising, fearless, gallant, intrepid, plucky, valiant, venturesome. ANTONYMS: cautious, cowardly, timid, unadventurous. **2** (*impudent, shameless*) brazen, cheeky, defiant, forward, impertinent, impudent, insolent, pert, presumptuous, rude, shameless. ANTONYMS: modest, respectful, timid.

audacity *n.* **1** (*courage, daring*) adventurousness, audaciousness, boldness, bravery, courage, courageousness, daring, enterprise, fearlessness, gallantry, (*coll.*) guts, intrepidity, pluck, valour. ANTONYMS: caution, cowardice, timidity. **2** (*effrontery*) brazenness, cheek, defiance, effrontery, forwardness, front, impertinence, impudence, insolence, pertness,

presumption, rudeness, shamelessness. ANTONYMS: modesty, respectfulness, timidity.

audible *a.* (*clear or loud enough to be heard*) clear, discernible, distinct, hearable, perceptible. ANTONYMS: imperceptible, inaudible, indistinct, unclear.

audience *n.* **1** (*an assembly of hearers or spectators at a play, concert etc.*) house, listeners, spectators, viewers. **2** (*a formal interview granted by a superior to an inferior*) consultation, hearing, interview, meeting, reception.

augment *v.t.* (*to increase*) add to, amplify, boost, build up, enlarge, escalate, expand, extend, heighten, increase, inflate, intensify, magnify, multiply, raise, reinforce, strengthen, swell. ANTONYMS: contract, curtail, decrease, lessen, lower, reduce.

august *a.* (*inspiring reverence and admiration*) dignified, distinguished, exalted, grand, illustrious, imposing, impressive, lofty, majestic, noble, regal, stately. ANTONYMS: base, ignoble, lowly, mean.

aura *n.* (*a distinctive atmosphere or quality*) air, ambience, atmosphere, feel, feeling, mood, quality, spirit, suggestion, tone, (*coll.*) vibes.

auspicious *a.* (*favourable*) bright, encouraging, favourable, felicitous, fortunate, hopeful, lucky, opportune, optimistic, promising, propitious, providential, rosy, timely. ANTONYMS: bleak, hopeless, pessimistic, unfavourable.

austere *a.* **1** (*severely simple, unadorned*) plain, severe, simple, Spartan, stark, unadorned, undecorated, unembellished. ANTONYMS: elaborate, fancy, ostentatious. **2** (*ascetic, abstemious*) abstemious, abstinent, ascetic, chaste, puritanical, self-denying, self-disciplined, sober, Spartan. ANTONYMS: debauched, dissipated, self-indulgent. **3** (*severe, stern*) cold, distant, exacting, forbidding, formal, grim, hard, harsh, inflexible, rigid, serious, severe, solemn, stern, stiff, strict, unrelenting, unyielding. ANTONYMS: affable, friendly, jovial, warm.

authentic *a.* **1** (*of undisputed origin, genuine*) bona fide, genuine, (*coll.*) kosher, legitimate, real, rightful, true, valid. ANTONYMS: counterfeit, false, spurious. **2** (*entitled to acceptance or belief, trustworthy*) credible, dependable, honest, reliable, true, trustworthy, truthful. ANTONYMS: undependable, unreliable, untrustworthy.

authenticate *v.t.* **1** (*to establish the genuineness or credibility of*) certify, confirm, endorse, ratify, validate, warrant. **2** (*to verify the authorship of*) prove, substantiate, verify.

authenticity *n.* **1** (*the fact of being genuine*) genuineness, legitimacy, rightfulness, validity. ANTONYMS: falseness, spuriousness. **2** (*the fact of being trustworthy*) credibility, dependability, honesty, reliability, trustworthiness, truthfulness. ANTONYMS: unreliability, untrustworthiness.

author *n.* **1** (*the composer of a literary work*) poet, writer. **2** (*a person whose profession is writing, esp. books*) novelist, writer. **3** (*the originator or producer of anything*) architect, cause, creator, designer, father, founder, initiator, mother, originator, planner, prime mover.

authoritarian *a.* (*favouring or enforcing strict obedience to authority*) disciplinarian, dogmatic, Draconian, harsh, rigid, severe, stern. ANTONYMS: flexible, lenient, liberal.

authoritative *a.* (*accepted as possessing authority, as being true etc.*) authentic, definitive, dependable, reliable, sound, trustworthy, valid. ANTONYMS: questionable, unreliable.

authority *n.* **1** (*legitimate power to command or act*) jurisdiction, power, prerogative, right. **2** (*delegated power or right to act*) authorization, licence, permission, sanction, say-so, warrant. **3** (*power or influence, derived from character, mental superiority etc.*) ascendancy, command, control, dominance, dominion, force, might, power, supremacy, sway, weight. **4** (*weight of testimony, credibility*) attestation, declaration, deposition, evidence, say-so, testimony, word. **5** (*the standard book or work of reference on any subject*) reference, source. **6** (*an expert, one entitled to speak with authority on any subject*) arbiter, connoisseur, expert, master, pundit, specialist.

authorize *v.t.* **1** (*to give authority to, to empower*) accredit, commission, empower, enable, entitle, give authority to, license. ANTONYMS: debar, forbid, prohibit. **2** (*to sanction*) agree to, allow, approve, give leave to, (*coll.*) give the go-ahead to, (*coll.*) give the green light to, license, permit, ratify, sanction, warrant. ANTONYMS: forbid, prohibit, veto.

autocratic *a.* (*absolute, despotic*) absolute, all-powerful, bossy, despotic, dictatorial, domineering, high-handed, imperious, oppressive, tyrannical. ANTONYMS: lenient.

automatic *a.* **1** (*operating without direct or continuous human intervention*) automated, mechanical, mechanized, push-button, self-acting, self-activating, self-regulating. ANTONYMS: hand-operated, manual. **2** ((*of actions,

behaviour) *spontaneous, reflex*) instinctive, involuntary, mechanical, reflex, spontaneous, unconscious. ANTONYMS: deliberate, intentional, voluntary. **3** (*certain, unavoidable*) certain, ineluctable, inescapable, inevitable, routine, unavoidable. ANTONYMS: avoidable.

autonomous *a.* (*self-governing or partially self-governing*) independent, self-governing, self-ruling. ANTONYMS: dependent, subsidiary.

autonomy *n.* (*the right of self-government*) home rule, independence, self-government, self-rule. ANTONYMS: dependency.

autopsy *n.* (*a post-mortem examination*) post-mortem, post-mortem examination. ANTONYMS: biopsy.

auxiliary *a.* **1** (*helping, aiding*) aiding, assisting, back-up, helping, supporting. **2** (*subsidiary (to)*) additional, ancillary, reserve, secondary, subsidiary, substitute, supplementary. ANTONYMS: main, principal.

available *a.* **1** (*capable of being employed; at one's disposal*) at one's disposal, convenient, handy, near, nearby, on tap, ready, ready for use, to hand. ANTONYMS: unavailable, unobtainable. **2** (*at hand, accessible*) accessible, at hand, attainable, (*coll.*) get-at-able, reachable, within reach. ANTONYMS: inaccessible, unattainable.

avarice *n.* (*excessive desire for wealth; greed*) acquisitiveness, covetousness, greed, greediness, miserliness, rapacity. ANTONYMS: generosity, philanthropy.

avenge *v.t.* (*to take vengeance for*) repay, requite, revenge, take vengeance for.

average *a.* (*medium, ordinary*) commonplace, everyday, fair, middle-of-the-road, middling, normal, ordinary, passable, regular, run-of-the-mill, standard, typical, unexceptional, unremarkable, usual. ANTONYMS: exceptional, remarkable, unusual.

averse *a.* (*unwilling, reluctant (to)*) disinclined, loath, opposed, reluctant, unwilling. ANTONYMS: eager, inclined, willing.

aversion *n.* (*disinclination, dislike*) abhorrence, disgust, disinclination, dislike, hatred, loathing, repugnance, revulsion. ANTONYMS: liking, love.

avid *a.* (*very keen, enthusiastic*) ardent, devoted, eager, enthusiastic, fervent, keen, passionate, zealous. ANTONYMS: apathetic, indifferent, unenthusiastic.

avoid *v.t.* (*to keep at a distance from, to shun*) circumvent, dodge, give a wide berth to, keep away from, keep (someone) at arm's length, shun, steer clear of. ANTONYMS: approach, confront, seek out.

awake v.i. (*to wake from sleep, cease sleeping*) wake, wake up. ANTONYMS: go to sleep.

~v.t. **1** (*to arouse from sleep, or from inaction*) awaken, rouse, wake. **2** (*to excite to action or new life*) animate, enliven, stimulate, vitalize. ANTONYMS: bore, weary. **3** (*to stir up, revive*) activate, arouse, awaken, call forth, excite, fan, kindle, provoke, revive, rouse, wake. ANTONYMS: quench.

~a. **1** (*not asleep; roused from sleep*) wakeful, wide awake. ANTONYMS: asleep, sleeping. **2** (*aware, alive (to)*) alert (to), attentive (to), aware (of), heedful (of), on one's guard (against), vigilant (for), watchful (for). ANTONYMS: heedless (of), inattentive (to).

award v.t. (*to grant or confer, esp. as a prize for merit or as something needed*) bestow, confer, endow, grant, present.

~n. **1** (*a prize that is awarded*) decoration, prize, trophy. **2** (*a sum of money that is awarded*) endowment, grant, handout, presentation.

aware a. (*conscious, cognizant*) acquainted, apprised, cognizant, conscious, informed, in the know. ANTONYMS: unaware, unconscious.

awe n. (*solemn, reverential wonder*) amazement, astonishment, fear, respect, reverence, veneration, wonder.

awful a. **1** (*extremely disagreeable; very bad of its kind*) appalling, deplorable, disagreeable,

dreadful, frightful, ghastly, horrendous, horrible, nasty, shocking, terrible, unpleasant. ANTONYMS: excellent, magnificent, wonderful. **2** (*very great, excessive*) enormous, huge, immense, incredible, vast. ANTONYMS: small, tiny. **3** (*inspiring awe; worthy of profound reverence*) amazing, awe-inspiring, awesome.

awkward a. **1** (*lacking dexterity, clumsy*) bungling, clumsy, (*coll.*) ham-fisted, inept, maladroit. ANTONYMS: dexterous. **2** (*ungraceful, ungainly*) blundering, gauche, inelegant, uncoordinated, ungainly, ungraceful. ANTONYMS: elegant, graceful. **3** (*unhandy, ill-adapted for use*) cumbersome, unhandy, unmanageable, unwieldy. ANTONYMS: handy. **4** (*embarrassed, ill at ease*) embarrassed, ill at ease, uncomfortable. **5** (*embarrassing; not easy to manage or deal with*) delicate, embarrassing, inconvenient, inopportune, sensitive, untimely. **6** (*deliberately uncooperative or unhelpful*) bloody-minded, difficult, disobliging, perverse, troublesome, trying, uncooperative. ANTONYMS: cooperative, obliging.

awry adv. **1** (*obliquely, crookedly*) askew, crookedly, lopsidedly, out of line, out of true, unevenly. ANTONYMS: straight. **2** (*erroneously, amiss*) amiss, wrong. ANTONYMS: right.

axiom n. (*a self-evident or generally accepted truth*) adage, aphorism, dictum, gnome, maxim, truism.

B

babble *v.i.* **1** (*to talk incoherently*) gabble, gibber, jabber, mumble, mutter. **2** (*to talk childishly or inopportunely*) burble, chatter, drivel, prattle, (*coll.*) rabbit on, waffle.

babel *n.* (*noisy confusion*) bedlam, clamour, commotion, confusion, din, disorder, hubbub, hullabaloo, pandemonium, tumult, uproar.

baby *n.* **1** (*an infant; a child in arms*) babe, (*Sc. or North.*) bairn, child, infant, neonate, new-born child, (*coll.*) sprog, tiny tot, tot. **2** (*the youngest person in a family, group etc.*) most junior, youngest.
~*a.* (*small or smaller than usual*) diminutive, dwarf, little, midget, mini, miniature, minute, small, (*coll.*) teeny-weeny, tiny, wee.
~*v.t.* (*to treat like a baby*) coddle, cosset, featherbed, humour, indulge, mollycoddle, over-indulge, pamper, pet, spoil, spoon-feed.

babyish *a.* (*like a baby*) childish, immature, infantile, jejune, juvenile, puerile, spoiled. ANTONYMS: mature.

back *n.* **1** (*the hinder part of the human body*) dorsum, spine. **2** (*the surface of any object opposite to the face or front*) hinder part, hind part, rear, rear end, stern. ANTONYMS: fore, front, head.
~*a.* **1** (*situated behind or in the rear*) hind, hinder, hindmost, rear. ANTONYMS: fore, front. **2** (*behind in time*) bygone, earlier, former, previously.
~*adv.* **1** (*in a direction to the rear*) backwards, behind, rearwards, to the rear. ANTONYMS: frontwards, to the front. **2** (*in return, in retaliation*) in retaliation, in return, in revenge. **3** (*in time past*) ago, before, earlier, previously, since.
~*v.t.* **1** (*to support morally, to uphold*) abet, advocate, aid, assist, champion, encourage, endorse, promote, second, side with, support, uphold. ANTONYMS: discourage, hinder, oppose, thwart. **2** (*to support financially*) finance, give backing to, sponsor, subscribe to, subsidize, underwrite. **3** (*to confirm*) attest to, back up, confirm, corroborate, reinforce, substantiate, support, vouch for. ANTONYMS: contradict, deny, dispute.
~*v.i.* (*to move in a reverse direction*) go backwards, move backwards, reverse. **behind someone's back** (*secretly, surreptitiously*) covertly, deceitfully, secretly, slyly, sneakily, surreptitiously. ANTONYMS: openly. **to back away** (*to withdraw*)

fall back, move back, recede, retire, retreat, withdraw. ANTONYMS: advance, move forward, progress. **to back down/ out** (*to retreat from a difficult situation*) accede, admit defeat, back-pedal, backtrack, climb down, concede, concede defeat, give in, submit, surrender, withdraw, yield. ANTONYMS: persist, stick to one's guns. **to back out of** (*to decide not to do something that one had promised to do*) abandon, (*coll.*) chicken out of, (*coll.*) get cold feet, go back on, pull out of, renege on, retreat from, withdraw from. ANTONYMS: keep, persist with, stay with. **to back up 1** (*to support*) be on the side of, second, side with, stand by, support. ANTONYMS: be against, oppose, thwart. **2** (*to confirm*) attest to, back, confirm, corroborate, reinforce, substantiate, support, vouch for. ANTONYMS: contradict, deny, dispute.

backbiting *n.* (*malicious comments*) abuse, aspersions, (*coll.*) bad-mouthing, calumny, defamation, denigration, detraction, disparagement, gossip, libel, malice, maligning, mudslinging, scandalmongering, slander, slurs, spite, spitefulness, vilification, vituperation. ANTONYMS: praise, praising.

backbone *n.* **1** (*the bony framework of the back*) spinal column, spine, vertebrae, vertebral column. **2** (*a main support or axis*) basis, foundation, framework, mainstay, structure, support. **3** (*strength of character*) (*sl.*) bottle, character, courage, determination, firmness, fortitude, grit, gumption, mettle, nerve, pluck, resolution, resolve, stamina, steadfastness, strength, strength of character, tenacity, toughness, will-power. ANTONYMS: cowardice, indecision, weakness.

backer *n.* **1** (*a person who supports a suggestion, plan etc.*) advocate, champion, promoter, seconder, supporter, upholder. ANTONYMS: critic, detractor. **2** (*a person who supports a project etc. financially*) (*coll.*) angel, benefactor, financer, promoter, sponsor, subsidizer, underwriter.

background *n.* **1** (*that part of a picture or stage-scene which serves as the setting for the chief objects of contemplation*) backcloth, backdrop, scene, setting. **2** (*the setting; relevant information about preceding events etc.*) circumstances, conditions, environment, factors, framework, history. **3** (*a person's upbringing,* *education and history*) breeding, education, family circumstances, history, upbringing.

backhanded *a.* (*indirect*) ambiguous, double-edged, equivocal, indirect, ironic, oblique, two-edged. ANTONYMS: direct, straightforward.

backing *n.* **1** (*supporting, seconding*) aid, approval, assistance, championship, commendation, encouragement, endorsement, espousal, help, promotion, support. ANTONYMS: criticism, detraction, obstruction. **2** (*financial support*) patronage, sponsorship, support, underwriting. **3** (*money supplied for a project by an investor*) finance, funds, subsidy. **4** (*musical accompaniment, esp. for a popular song*) accompaniment, harmony, support.

backlash *n.* (*a strong adverse reaction*) counteraction, counterblast, kickback, reaction, recoil, repercussion, retaliation.

backlog *n.* (*arrears of unfulfilled orders, unfinished work etc.*) accumulation, arrears, build-up, heap, stockpile.

back-pedal *v.i.* (*to reverse a course of action*) back down, backtrack, change one's mind, do an about-face, do a U-turn, shift ground.

backward *a.* **1** (*directed to the back or rear*) rearward. ANTONYMS: forward. **2** (*reluctant, unwilling*) bashful, diffident, hesitant, reluctant, retiring, shrinking, shy, timid, unwilling. ANTONYMS: bold, enthusiastic, forward, willing. **3** (*behind in progress; mentally handicapped*) (*Hist.*) ESN, retarded, slow, with learning difficulties. ANTONYMS: gifted, precocious.

backwards *adv.* **1** (*with the back foremost*) back first, in reverse. ANTONYMS: forwards. **2** (*towards the back or rear*) behind, rearwards, to the back. ANTONYMS: forwards, to the front. **3** (*towards a worse state*) in reverse, into deterioration, retrogressively, worse. ANTONYMS: better, forwards.

backwoods *n.pl.* (*a remote, uncultured area*) the back of beyond, (*coll.*) the middle of nowhere, (*coll.*) the sticks, the wilds.

bad *a.* **1** (*not good, unpleasant*) disagreeable, distressing, dreadful, grim, nasty, terrible, uncomfortable, unfortunate, unlucky, unpleasant, unsatisfactory. ANTONYMS: agreeable, fortunate, lucky, satisfactory. **2** (*defective, faulty*) defective, deficient, erroneous, faulty, imperfect, inadequate, ineffectual, inept, inferior, poor, substandard, unsatisfactory, useless, worthless, wrong. ANTONYMS: adequate, perfect, right, satisfactory. **3** (*evil, morally depraved*) base, corrupt, (*coll.*) crooked, depraved, dishonest, dishonourable, evil, immoral, reprobate, rotten, sinful, villainous, wicked, wrong. ANTONYMS: good, honest, moral, virtuous. **4** (*harmful,*

damaging) damaging, dangerous, deleterious, destructive, detrimental, harmful, hurtful, injurious, unhealthy, unwholesome. ANTONYMS: advantageous, beneficial, healthy, wholesome. **5** (*painful, dangerous*) below par, critical, disastrous, distressing, grave, painful, pernicious, serious, severe, terrible. ANTONYMS: minor. **6** (*disobedient*) disobedient, mischievous, naughty, refractory, unruly, wayward. ANTONYMS: biddable, good, obedient. **7** ((*of food*) *decayed*) decayed, mouldy, off, putrid, rancid, rotten, sour, spoiled. ANTONYMS: fresh. **8** (*in ill health, sick*) ailing, ill, indisposed, not well, sick, under the weather, unhealthy, unwell. ANTONYMS: healthy, well. **9** (*injured, diseased*) damaged, diseased, injured. ANTONYMS: healthy, uninjured, whole. **10** (*sorry for what one has done*) apologetic, conscience-stricken, contrite, guilty, penitent, regretful, remorseful, sad, sorry. ANTONYMS: impenitent, unrepentant.

badge *n.* **1** (*a distinctive mark or token*) emblem, indication, indicator, mark, sign, signal, symbol, token. **2** (*an emblem sewn on clothing*) crest, device, emblem, escutcheon, insignia, shield.

badger *v.t.* (*to worry, to tease*) annoy, bother, (*sl.*) bug, bully, chivvy, goad, harass, harry, (*coll.*) hassle, hound, importune, irritate, nag, pester, plague, torment.

badly *adv.* **1** (*improperly, wickedly*) criminally, evilly, immorally, improperly, naughtily, unethically, wickedly, wrongly. ANTONYMS: ethically, morally, properly, virtuously. **2** (*unskilfully, imperfectly*) carelessly, defectively, faultily, imperfectly, inadequately, incompetently, incorrectly, inefficiently, ineptly, poorly, shoddily, unskilfully, wrongly. ANTONYMS: adequately, competently, efficiently, well. **3** (*unfortunately, disastrously*) disastrously, unfavourably, unfortunately, unhappily, unluckily, unsuccessfully. ANTONYMS: favourably, luckily, well. **4** (*very much, by much*) acutely, deeply, desperately, exceedingly, gravely, greatly, intensely, seriously, severely, very much. ANTONYMS: hardly at all, minimally, very little.

baffle *v.t.* **1** (*to perplex, confound*) astonish, astound, bamboozle, bewilder, confound, confuse, daze, disconcert, dumbfound, flummox, mystify, nonplus, perplex, puzzle, stagger, stump, stun. ANTONYMS: make clear to, make plain to. **2** (*to thwart, defeat*) baulk, block, check, deflect, foil, frustrate, hinder, obstruct, prevent, thwart, upset. ANTONYMS: advance, assist, help, promote.

baggage *n.* (*luggage; belongings packed for travelling*) accoutrements, bags, belongings, effects, gear, luggage, paraphernalia, things, trappings.

baggy *a.* (*loose*) loose, oversize, roomy, sagging, shapeless, slack. ANTONYMS: close-fitting, tight.

bail *n.* (*security, guarantee*) bond, guarantee, pledge, security, surety, warranty. **to bail out** (*to rescue from difficulty*) aid, assist, give a helping hand to, help, relieve, rescue.

bait *v.t.* (*to harass, torment*) (*coll.*) aggravate, annoy, badger, bother, harass, harry, hound, irritate, needle, persecute, pester, plague, provoke, tease, torment, (*coll.*) wind up, worry. ~*n.* (*a temptation, allurement*) allurement, attraction, incentive, inducement, lure, snare, temptation. ANTONYMS: disincentive.

balance *n.* **1** (*a pair of scales*) scales, weighing machine. **2** (*an equality of weight or power*) equilibrium, equipoise, equity, evenness, parity, symmetry. ANTONYMS: disparity, imbalance, unevenness. **3** (*stability*) stability, steadiness. ANTONYMS: instability, unsteadiness. **4** (*harmony of design*) harmony, proportion, symmetry. **5** (*the remainder, the residue*) difference, remainder, residue, rest. **6** (*calmness*) aplomb, calm, calmness, composure, (*coll.*) cool, equanimity, level-headedness, poise, sang-froid. ANTONYMS: agitation, panic.
~*v.t.* **1** (*to compare*) appraise, assess, compare, consider, evaluate, review, weigh up. **2** (*to bring to an equipoise, to steady*) secure, stabilize, support. **3** (*to make* (*two amounts*) *equal*) equalize, even, even up.
~*v.i.* **1** (*to have equal weight or force*) be equal, be even, be level, correspond, match. **2** (*to have the debtor and creditor side equal*) add up, reckon, tally. **in the balance** (*in an uncertain state*) at a critical stage, critical, uncertain, undecided, unsure. **on balance** (*taking all factors into consideration*) all in all, all things considered, considering everything, taking everything into consideration.

balcony *n.* **1** (*a gallery or platform projecting from a house or other building*) terrace, veranda. **2** (*in theatres, a tier of seats between the dress circle and the gallery*) gallery, (*coll.*) the gods, upper circle.

bald *a.* **1** (*without hair upon the crown of the head*) bald-headed, bald-pated, hairless, without hair. ANTONYMS: hairy, hirsute. **2** (*bare, treeless*) bare, barren, bleak, exposed, stark, treeless. ANTONYMS: fertile, tree-covered. **3** (*undisguised, shameless*) blunt, direct, forthright, plain, simple, stark, straightforward, undisguised, unembellished, unvarnished. ANTONYMS: embellished, euphemistic.

baleful *a.* **1** (*full of evil*) evil, malevolent, wicked. ANTONYMS: good, virtuous. **2** (*harmful, deadly*) dangerous, deadly, harmful, injurious, malignant, menacing, noxious, pernicious,

threatening, venomous. ANTONYMS: friendly, helpful.

ball[1] *n.* (*a spherical body of any dimensions*) globe, globule, orb, sphere, spheroid.

ball[2] *n.* (*a social assembly for dancing*) dance, formal dance, masked ball, party.

ballot *n.* (*the method or system of secret voting*) election, poll, polling, vote, voting.

balm *n.* **1** (*fragrant ointment or oil*) cream, emollient, lotion, ointment, salve, unguent. **2** (*anything which soothes pain or distress*) anodyne, comfort, consolation, curative, cure, palliative, remedy, restorative, solace. ANTONYMS: irritant.

balmy *a.* **1** (*fragrant, mild*) clement, fragrant, gentle, mild, soft, temperate. ANTONYMS: harsh, inclement, rough, stormy. **2** (*daft, silly*) (*sl.*) barmy, (*coll.*) batty, crazy, daft, eccentric, foolish, idiotic, insane, (*coll.*) loopy, mad, (*sl.*) nutty, odd, peculiar, silly, stupid, weird. ANTONYMS: normal, sane.

bamboozle *v.t.* **1** (*to mystify for purposes of fraud; to cheat*) cheat, (*sl.*) con, deceive, defraud, delude, dupe, fool, hoax, hoodwink, mislead, swindle, trick. **2** (*to bewilder, confuse*) baffle, bewilder, confound, confuse, mystify, perplex, puzzle, stump.

ban *v.t.* (*to forbid, to proscribe*) bar, black, blackball, block, boycott, debar, disallow, embargo, exclude, forbid, interdict, prohibit, proscribe, suppress, veto. ANTONYMS: allow, authorize, permit, sanction.
~*n.* (*a formal prohibition*) bar, block, boycott, embargo, interdict, prohibition, proscription, suppression, veto. ANTONYMS: approval, authorization, permission, permit, sanction.

banal *a.* (*commonplace, trite*) clichéd, commonplace, hackneyed, humdrum, mundane, (*coll.*) old hat, pedestrian, platitudinous, prosaic, run-of-the-mill, stale, stereotyped, stock, tired, trite, unimaginative, uninspired, unoriginal, vapid. ANTONYMS: fresh, imaginative, novel, original.

band[1] *n.* **1** (*a flat slip of cloth, used to bind together or as part of a garment*) belt, binding, bond, chain, cord, fetter, shackle, strap, tie. **2** (*a transverse stripe*) bar, line, streak, strip, stripe.

band[2] *n.* **1** (*a company of musicians playing together*) (*coll.*) combo, ensemble, group, orchestra. **2** (*an organized group*) association, camp, club, confederate, gang, set, society. **3** (*an assemblage of people*) assemblage, assembly, bevy, body, company, crew, gang, group, horde, mob, pack, party, throng, troop.

band[3] *v.i.* (*to unite, to assemble*) affiliate, ally, combine, confederate, group (together), join (together), merge, team up, unite. ANTONYMS: disband, separate, split up.

bandage *n.* (*a strip of flexible material used to bind up wounds, fractures etc.*) Band-Aid®, dressing, Elastoplast®, gauze, plaster.
~*v.t.* (*to bind up with a bandage*) bind, bind up, cover, dress.

bandit *n.* (*a brigand*) brigand, crook, desperado, gangster, gunfighter, gunman, marauder, outlaw, plunderer, robber, thief.

bandy[1] *v.t.* (*to exchange* (*esp. blows, arguments etc.*)) exchange, interchange, reciprocate, swap, trade.

bandy[2] *a.* (*crooked, bent outwards*) bent, bowed, crooked, curved. ANTONYMS: straight.

bane *n.* (*a cause of ruin or mischief*) affliction, bête noire, blight, burden, calamity, curse, misery, nuisance, pest, plague, scourge, torment, trial, trouble. ANTONYMS: blessing, boon, joy, pleasure.

bang *v.t.* **1** (*to close* (*a door*) *with a loud noise*) clatter, crack, crash, slam. **2** (*to beat with loud blows*) beat, drum, hammer, hit, knock, pound, rap, slap, strike, thump. **3** (*to thump; to handle roughly*) bash, batter, belt, box, drub, hit, punch, slap, smack, strike, thrash, thump, (*coll.*) wallop, whack.
~*v.i.* (*to resound with a loud noise*) boom, burst, clatter, crack, crash, detonate, explode, resound.
~*n.* **1** (*a sudden explosive noise*) boom, burst, clap, detonation, pop, report. **2** (*a resounding blow, a thump*) bash, belt, blow, box, bump, knock, punch, rap, slap, smack, thump, (*coll.*) wallop, whack.
~*adv.* **1** (*with a violent blow or noise*) noisily, violently. **2** (*suddenly, abruptly*) abruptly, all at once, slap, smack, suddenly. **3** (*exactly*) absolutely, completely, dead, right, totally.

bangle *n.* (*a ring-bracelet or anklet*) anklet, bracelet.

banish *v.t.* **1** (*to condemn to exile*) deport, exile, expatriate, expel, outlaw, send into exile. **2** (*to drive out or away*) bar, cast out, dislodge, dismiss, drive away, drive out, eject, evict, exclude, expel, get rid of, oust, remove, send away. ANTONYMS: admit, embrace, receive, welcome.

banishment *n.* **1** (*the act of banishing*) barring, dislodgement, dismissal, ejection, eviction, exclusion, ousting, removal. ANTONYMS: admittance, embracing, receiving, welcoming. **2** (*exile, expatriation*) deportation, exile, expatriation, expulsion.

banister *n.* (*the whole railing protecting the outer side of a staircase*) handrail, railing, rails.

bank[1] *n.* **1** (*a raised area of ground*) mound, ridge, shelf. **2** (*a mound with steeply sloping sides*) embankment, gradient, hillock, incline, knoll, margin, rise, slope. **3** (*the shore of a river*) brink, edge, embankment, margin, shore, side.
~*v.t.* (*to form into a bank*) accumulate, bank up, heap up, pile up, stack up.
~*v.i.* ((*of an aircraft etc.*) *to incline inwards at a high angle in turning*) incline, pitch, slant, slope, tilt.

bank[2] *n.* **1** (*an establishment which deals in money*) commercial bank, financial institution, high-street bank, savings bank. **2** (*in gaming, the money which the proprietor of the table has before them*) kitty, pool, pot. **3** (*any store or reserve of material or information*) accumulation, fund, hoard, repository, reserve, reservoir, stock, stockpile, store, supply.
~*v.i.* (*to count or depend* (*on*)) count (on), depend (on), have confidence (in), pin one's hopes (on), rely (on), trust (in).
~*v.t.* (*to deposit in a bank*) deposit, save.

bankrupt *a.* **1** (*insolvent*) (*coll.*) broke, (*coll.*) bust, failed, impoverished, insolvent, penniless, ruined. ANTONYMS: prosperous, solvent, wealthy. **2** (*lacking some necessary or desirable quality*) bereft of, deficient in, in need of, lacking, wanting, without. ANTONYMS: full of, rich in.
~*v.t.* (*to render insolvent*) beggar, (*coll.*) bust, impoverish, ruin.

bankruptcy *n.* (*the state of being bankrupt*) failure, impoverishment, insolvency, liquidation, pennilessness, penury, ruin, ruination. ANTONYMS: prosperity, solvency, wealth.

banner *n.* (*an ensign or flag painted with some device or emblem*) ensign, flag, pennant, placard, sign, standard, streamer.

banter *n.* (*good-natured raillery*) badinage, chaff, jesting, joking, (*coll.*) kidding, raillery, repartee, teasing.

baptism *n.* **1** (*the act of baptizing*) baptizing, christening, naming. **2** (*an initiation* (*ceremony*)) debut, inauguration, initiation, introduction, launch, rite of passage.

baptize *v.t.* **1** (*to christen, to give a name or nickname to*) christen, name, nickname. **2** (*to initiate into or to introduce to for the first time*) inaugurate, initiate, introduce, launch.

bar[1] *n.* **1** (*a piece of iron or other solid material, long in proportion to breadth; a pole*) batten, pole, rod, spar, stick. **2** (*a straight stripe*) band, belt, line, streak, strip, stripe. **3** (*a small roughly rectangular block of chocolate, soap etc.*) block, cake, lump. **4** (*any thing that constitutes a hindrance or obstruction*) barrier, block, check, deterrent, drawback, hindrance, impediment, obstruction, stop, stumbling-block. ANTONYMS: aid, benefit, help. **5** (*the counter in a public house, hotel or other place of refreshment, across which liquors etc. are sold*) (*coll.*) boozer, pub, public house, (*sl.*) watering hole. **6** (*a rail or barrier*) barrier, rail, railing.

~*v.t.* **1** (*to fasten with a bar or bars*) bolt, fasten, lock, padlock, secure. ANTONYMS: unlock. **2** (*to exclude*) ban, debar, exclude, forbid, keep out, preclude, prohibit. ANTONYMS: let in. **3** (*to hinder, to prevent*) block, check, hinder, impede, obstruct, prevent, restrain, stop. ANTONYMS: aid, assist, facilitate, help.

bar² *prep.* (*except, apart from*) apart from, barring, except, except for, excepting, excluding, leaving out, omitting, other than, with the exception of. ANTONYMS: including.

barb *n.* **1** (*a point, a sting*) needle, point, prickle, prong, spike, sting, thorn. **2** (*a biting or pointed remark or comment*) dig, gibe, insult, sneer.

barbarian *n.* **1** (*a savage*) savage, wild man, wild woman. **2** (*a person destitute of pity or humanity*) brute, monster, savage.

barbaric *a.* **1** (*of or relating to barbarians*) primitive, rude, savage, uncivilized, unsophisticated, wild. ANTONYMS: civilized, sophisticated, wild. **2** (*cruel, inhuman*) barbarous, brutal, cruel, inhuman, inhumane, savage, vicious. ANTONYMS: gentle, humane.

barbarity *n.* **1** (*brutality, cruelty*) brutality, cruelty, inhumaneness, inhumanity, savagery, viciousness. ANTONYMS: gentleness, humaneness, humanity. **2** (*an act of brutality or cruelty*) atrocity, outrage.

barbarous *a.* **1** (*uncivilized*) primitive, savage, uncivilized, unsophisticated, wild. ANTONYMS: civilized, sophisticated. **2** (*uncultured; uncouth*) boorish, coarse, ignorant, uncouth, uncultivated, uncultured, unpolished, unrefined, unsophisticated, vulgar. ANTONYMS: cultivated, cultured, polished, refined. **3** (*cruel*) barbaric, brutal, cruel, inhuman, inhumane, savage, vicious. ANTONYMS: gentle, humane.

barbed *a.* (*hurtful, biting*) cruel, cutting, hurtful, nasty, pointed, scathing, sneering, unkind.

bare *a.* **1** (*unclothed, naked*) (*coll.*) buck naked, in the raw, naked, nude, stark naked, stripped, unclad, unclothed, undressed, without a stitch. ANTONYMS: attired, clad, clothed. **2** (*destitute of natural covering, such as hair, leaves etc.*) barren, bleak, desolate, infertile, treeless. ANTONYMS: fertile, lush. **3** (*simple, undisguised*) bald, basic, mere, plain, simple, stark, undisguised, unembellished, unvarnished. ANTONYMS: embellished. **4** (*meagre*) basic, inadequate, meagre,

mere, scanty. **5** (*unadorned*) austere, basic, plain, spartan, stark, unadorned, unembellished. ANTONYMS: elaborate, fancy, ornamented.

barefaced *a.* (*impudent, shameless*) audacious, blatant, bold, brash, brazen, flagrant, glaring, impudent, insolent, open, shameless, unconcealed, undisguised. ANTONYMS: concealed, hidden, secret, subtle.

barely *adv.* (*hardly, scarcely*) by the skin of one's teeth, hardly, just, only just, scarcely. ANTONYMS: completely, fully.

bargain *n.* **1** (*an agreement between parties, generally concerning a sale*) agreement, arrangement, compact, contract, covenant, deal, pact, pledge, transaction, treaty, understanding. **2** (*an advantageous purchase*) discount, give-away, good buy, good value, reduction, (*coll.*) snip, (*coll.*) steal.

~*v.i.* **1** (*to haggle over terms*) argue terms, discuss terms, haggle, negotiate. **2** (*to make a contract or agreement for purchase or sale*) agree, come to an agreement, come to an understanding, contract, covenant. **into/ in the bargain** (*over and above what is stipulated*) additionally, also, as well, besides, moreover, over and above. **to bargain on/ for** (*to count on, to expect*) allow for, anticipate, be expecting, be prepared for, contemplate, count on, expect, foresee, have in mind, imagine, look for, make allowances for.

barge *n.* (*a flat-bottomed freight-boat used principally on canals*) canal boat, flat boat, houseboat, narrow boat.

~*v.i.* (*to lurch (into), rush (against)*) bump (into), cannon (into), collide (with), crash (into), lurch (against).

bark¹ *v.i.* **1** (*to utter a sharp, explosive cry, like that of a dog*) bay, howl, woof, yap, yelp. **2** (*to speak in an angry, explosive manner*) bawl, shout, shriek, snap, thunder, yell.

~*n.* **1** (*a sharp, explosive cry, orig. of dogs*) howl, woof, yap, yelp. **2** (*talk expressed in an angry, explosive manner*) bawling, shout, shriek, snapping, thundering, yapping, yell.

bark² *n.* (*an outer covering*) casing, coating, cortex, covering, crust, husk, rind, skin.

~*v.t.* (*to graze, to abrade (the shins, elbows etc.)*) abrade, excoriate, graze, rub, scrape, skin.

barmy *a.* (*crazy, silly*) (*sl.*) barking, (*coll.*) barking mad, (*coll.*) batty, (*sl.*) bonkers, (*coll.*) cracked, (*coll.*) crackpot, crazy, daft, (*sl.*) doolally, foolish, idiotic, insane, (*coll.*) loopy, mad, (*coll.*) not all there, (*sl.*) nuts, (*sl.*) nutty, off one's head, (*sl.*) off one's trolley, (*coll.*) out to lunch, (*coll.*) round the bend, (*coll.*) round the twist, silly, stupid, weird. ANTONYMS: (*coll.*) all there, sane, sensible.

barn *n.* (*a covered building for the storage of grain and other agricultural produce*) outbuilding, outhouse, shed.

baron *n.* **1** (*a noble, a peer*) aristocrat, lord, noble, nobleman, peer. **2** (*a powerful head of a business organization*) captain of industry, financier, industrialist, magnate, mogul, tycoon.

baroque *a.* (*flamboyant*) decorated, elaborate, embellished, extravagant, flamboyant, florid, fussy, ornate, ostentatious, overdecorated, rococo, showy. ANTONYMS: plain, simple.

barrack *n.pl.* (*buildings used to house troops*) billet, camp, encampment, garrison, quarters.

barrage *n.* **1** (*a screen of artillery fire to cover an advance, or hinder the enemy*) battery, bombardment, broadside, burst, cannonade, fusillade, gunfire, salvo, shelling, volley. **2** (*heavy or continuous questioning or criticism*) avalanche, burst, deluge, flood, hail, onslaught, plethora, profusion, storm, stream, torrent.

barrel *n.* (*a cylindrical wooden vessel formed of staves held together by hoops*) butt, cask, firkin, hogshead, keg, tun, vat.

barren *a.* **1** (*incapable of producing offspring*) childless, infertile, sterile. ANTONYMS: fecund, fertile. **2** (*bearing no fruit or vegetation*) arid, desert, desolate, infertile, unfruitful, unproductive, waste. ANTONYMS: fertile, fruitful, lush, productive, rich. **3** (*not productive intellectually*) boring, dull, flat, lacklustre, prosaic, stale, uninspiring, uninteresting, uninventive, vapid. ANTONYMS: exciting, interesting, inventive.

barricade *n.* (*a hastily formed rampart erected across a street or passage*) bar, barrier, blockade, bulwark, fence, obstacle, palisade, rampart, roadblock, stockade.
~*v.t.* (*to block or defend with a barricade*) bar, block, blockade, close off, defend, fence in, fortify, obstruct, protect, shut in, shut off.

barrier *n.* **1** (*an obstacle which hinders approach or attack*) bar, barricade, blockade, fence, fortification, railing, rampart, wall. **2** (*a difficulty, an obstruction*) check, difficulty, drawback, handicap, hindrance, hurdle, impediment, obstacle, restraint, restriction, snag, stumbling-block.

barter *v.t.* (*to give* (*anything except money*) *in exchange for some other commodity*) exchange, swap, trade.
~*v.i.* (*to traffic by exchanging one thing for another*) bargain, haggle, swap.
~*n.* (*traffic by exchanging one commodity for another*) bargaining, exchange, haggling, swapping, trade-off, trading.

base[1] *n.* **1** (*the lowest part on which anything rests*) foundation, pedestal, plinth, prop, rest, stand, support. **2** (*the bottom of anything*) bottom, foot. ANTONYMS: apex, top. **3** (*a starting point of an expedition etc.*) camp, centre, headquarters, post, settlement, starting-point, station. **4** (*that on which something essentially depends, a basis*) basis, core, essence, essentials, fundamentals, heart, key, origin, root, source.

base[2] *a.* **1** (*low in the moral scale; despicable*) bad, contemptible, corrupt, despicable, dishonourable, disreputable, disrespectable, evil, foul, ignoble, immoral, infamous, low, mean, nasty, unprincipled, vile, villainous, wicked, wrong. ANTONYMS: good, honourable, moral, noble, virtuous. **2** (*menial, inferior*) inferior, low, lowly, mean, menial, miserable, servile, slavish, subservient, sycophantic, wretched. ANTONYMS: lofty, noble, superior. **3** (*alloyed, debased*) adulterated, alloyed, counterfeit, debased, fake, forged, impure, spurious. ANTONYMS: genuine, pure.

baseless *a.* (*groundless*) foundationless, groundless, unconfirmed, uncorroborated, unfounded, ungrounded, unjustifiable, unjustified, unproven, unsubstantiated, unsupported. ANTONYMS: authenticated, confirmed, substantiated, well-founded.

bashful *a.* (*shy, easily embarrassed*) abashed, blushing, coy, diffident, embarrassed, hesitant, modest, over-modest, reserved, reticent, self-conscious, self-effacing, shamefaced, sheepish, shrinking, shy, timid, timorous. ANTONYMS: bold, brash, confident, immodest.

basic *a.* **1** (*of, relating to or constituting a base, fundamental*) elementary, essential, fundamental, key, primary, rudimentary. ANTONYMS: peripheral, secondary, supplementary. **2** (*without luxury, extras etc.*) (*sl.*) bog standard, no-frills, plain, simple, spartan, standard, stark, unadorned, (*coll.*) without bells and whistles, without frills. ANTONYMS: elaborate, fancy.

basically *adv.* (*fundamentally*) at bottom, at heart, essentially, fundamentally, in essence, intrinsically.

basics *n.pl.* (*fundamental principles*) brass tacks, core, essentials, facts, fundamentals, hard facts, nitty-gritty, nuts and bolts, practicalities, principles, rudiments, the ABC.

basin *n.* **1** (*a hollow* (*usu. circular*) *vessel for holding food being prepared or water, esp. for washing*) bowl, container, receptacle, vessel. **2** (*the tract of country drained by a river and its tributaries*) bed, channel.

basis *n.* **1** (*the base or foundation*) backup, base, footing, foundation, grounds, reason. **2** (*the* fundamental principle or support) chief ingredient, core, essence, fundamental principle, groundwork, main constituent, premise, starting point. **3** (an arrangement, a situation) arrangement, condition, footing, method, position, principle, procedure, situation, system.

bask v.i. **1** (to expose oneself to the influence of warmth) laze, lie, loll, lounge, relax, sunbathe, sun oneself, warm oneself. **2** (to luxuriate (in love, good fortune etc.)) delight (in), enjoy, indulge oneself (in), luxuriate (in), rejoice (in), revel (in), savour, take pleasure (in), wallow (in).

basket n. (a wickerwork vessel of plaited twigs or similar material) container, creel, hamper, pannier, punnet, receptacle.

bass a. (of or relating to the lowest part in harmonized musical composition) deep, deep-pitched, deep-toned, low, low-pitched, low-toned, resonant, sonorous. ANTONYMS: high, high-pitched, squeaky.

bastard n. **1** (an illegitimate child or person) illegitimate child, love child, natural child. **2** (an obnoxious or disagreeable person) (taboo sl.) cunt, (sl.) git, rascal, scoundrel, (taboo sl.) sod, villain.
~a. **1** (born out of wedlock, illegitimate) †base, illegitimate, natural, (coll.) on the wrong side of the blanket. **2** (spurious, not genuine) adulterated, counterfeit, fake, false, hybrid, imperfect, impure, sham, spurious. ANTONYMS: authentic, genuine, pure.

bastardize v.t. (to debase) adulterate, contaminate, debase, defile, degrade, demean, depreciate, devalue.

bastion n. (a defence) bulwark, citadel, defence, fortress, mainstay, prop, protection, stronghold, support.

batch n. **1** (any quantity produced at one operation or treated together) lot, pack, quantity, set. **2** (a group, set) assemblage, bunch, collection, crew, group, pack, set.

bath n. **1** (the act of washing or immersing the body in water) dip, long hot soak, soak, wallow. **2** (a usu. large) container for water for immersing the body for washing) bathtub, hip bath, Jacuzzi®, sitz-bath, tub, whirlpool bath.
~v.t. (to wash or put (usu. a child) in a bath) immerse, wash.

bathe v.i. **1** (to swim in a body of water for pleasure) swim, take a dip. **2** (to take a bath) have a bath, have a long hot soak, soak, take a bath.
~v.t. (to cleanse or soothe (a wound etc.) by applying liquid) clean, cleanse, rinse, wash.

~n. (the act of immersing the body to take a swim (esp. in the sea, a river etc.) or a bath) bathing, dip, plunge, swim.

bathing costume n. (a garment for swimming or sunbathing in) (Austral.) bathers, bathing suit, bikini, (esp. Austral., coll.) cossie, one-piece, one-piece swimsuit, swimming costume, swimming trunks, swimsuit, trunks.

baton n. **1** (a truncheon used as a weapon) stick, truncheon. **2** (a staff or club) club, rod, staff, stick.

battalion n. (a large group of people acting together) crowd, horde, host, mob, multitude, throng.

batter v.t. (to strike with successive blows so as to shake or demolish) abuse, assault, bash, beat, hit, pound, pummel, strike, thrash, thump, (coll.) wallop, whack.
~v.i. (to hammer (at) a door) beat against, buffet, dash against, strike against.

battery n. **1** (a number of pieces of artillery for combined action) artillery, cannonry, cannons, guns. **2** (an assailing by blows) assault, attack, beating, domestic violence, GBH, grievous bodily harm, (coll.) mugging, physical violence, striking, thrashing, thumping. **3** (a connected series of tests) chain, cycle, sequence, series, set, string, succession.

battle n. **1** (a fight or hostile engagement between opposing armies etc.) affray, clash, conflict, encounter, engagement, fray, skirmish, struggle, tussle. **2** (fighting, war) armed conflict, combat, fighting, hostilities, military action, war, warfare. ANTONYMS: accord, armistice, peace, truce. **3** (a persistent struggle) fight, struggle, trial. **4** (an argument) altercation, argument, clash, conflict, disagreement, dispute, feud, fight, strife.
~v.i. **1** (to fight, to contend (with or against)) argue, disagree, feud, fight, quarrel, war, wrangle. **2** (to struggle persistently) contend, fight, labour, strive, struggle.

battleaxe n. (a formidable woman) dragon, fury, harridan, shrew, Tartar, termagant, virago, vixen.

battle-cry n. (a war cry, a slogan) catchphrase, catchword, motto, shibboleth, slogan, war cry, watchword.

battlefield n. (the scene of a battle) battle front, battleground, battle lines, combat zone, field of battle, front, killing field, war zone.

battlement n. (a parapet with openings on the top of a building, orig. for defensive purposes) barbican, bartizan, bulwark, fortification, parapet, rampart.

battleship n. (*a warship*) battlecruiser, capital ship, gunboat, man-of-war, ship of the line, warship.

batty a. (*mentally unstable; crazy*) (*sl.*) barking, (*coll.*) barking mad, (*sl.*) barmy, (*coll.*) bats, (*sl.*) bonkers, (*coll.*) cracked, (*coll.*) crackers, crazy, daft, (*sl.*) doolally, eccentric, foolish, (*coll.*) loopy, mad, (*sl.*) nuts, (*sl.*) nutty, (*sl.*) off one's trolley, (*coll.*) out to lunch, potty, (*coll.*) touched. ANTONYMS: (*coll.*) all there, lucid, rational, sane.

bauble n. (*a gewgaw, a showy trinket*) bagatelle, gewgaw, knick-knack, trifle, trinket.

baulk v.i. (*to refuse to proceed; to hesitate* (*at*)) demur (at), dodge, draw back (from), eschew, flinch (from), hesitate (to/from), jib (at), recoil (from), refuse, resist, shrink (from). ANTONYMS: accept, embrace, welcome.
~v.t. (*to hinder; to disappoint*) baffle, bar, block, check, foil, frustrate, halt, hinder, impede, obstruct, prevent, stop, thwart. ANTONYMS: advance, assist, further, promote.

bawdy a. (*obscene, lewd*) (*sl.*) blue, coarse, crude, dirty, erotic, filthy, impure, indecent, indelicate, lascivious, lewd, libidinous, licentious, near the bone, near the knuckle, obscene, pornographic, prurient, racy, (*coll.*) raunchy, ribald, risqué, rude, smutty, suggestive, titillating, vulgar. ANTONYMS: chaste, clean, pure.

bawl v.i. **1** (*to cry loudly, howl*) blubber, cry, howl, sob, squall, wail, weep. **2** (*to shout at the top of one's voice*) bellow, clamour, howl, roar, shout, yell. ANTONYMS: murmur, whisper.

bay[1] n. (*an inlet of the sea extending into the land, with a wide mouth*) arm of the sea, bight, cove, gulf, inlet, sound.

bay[2] n. (*an opening or recess in a wall*) alcove, niche, nook, opening, recess.

bay[3] v.i. (*to bark hoarsely, as a hound at its prey*) bark, howl, yelp.

bazaar n. **1** (*an Eastern market place*) market, market place, mart, souk. **2** (*a sale of useful or ornamental articles in aid of charity*) bring-and-buy (sale), fair, fête, jumble sale, sale of work.

be v., often aux. **1** (*to exist, to live*) be alive, exist, have being, have life, live. ANTONYMS: be dead, be extinct. **2** (*to become, remain*) continue, endure, last, persist, prevail, remain, stay, survive. **3** (*to happen, occur*) arise, come about, come to pass, crop up, happen, occur, take place, transpire. **4** (*to have come or gone to a certain place*) attend, be present at, go to. ANTONYMS: be absent, stay away from. **5** (*to be situated*) be located, be sited, be situated, dwell, reside.

beach n. (*a sandy or pebbly seashore*) coast, sands, seashore, seaside, shingle, shore, strand.

beached a. (*run aground on a beach*) aground, high and dry, marooned, run aground, stranded.

beacon n. (*a light or a fire, e.g. on a tower, that functions as a signal or warning*) beam, bonfire, flare, lighthouse, rocket, signal fire, smoke signal, warning light.

bead n. **1** (*a small globular perforated body of glass or other material*) ball, pellet. **2** (*a beadlike drop*) blob, bubble, drop, droplet, globule. **3** (*pl.*) (*a necklace*) necklace, necklet, string of beads.

beak n. **1** (*the pointed bill of a bird*) bill, mandible, nib. **2** (*the prow of an ancient war galley, used as a ram*) bow, prow, ram, rostrum.

beam n. **1** (*a large, long piece of timber squared on its sides, esp. one supporting rafters in a building*) board, girder, joist, lath, plank, rafter, spar, support, timber. **2** (*a ray of light or radiation*) bar, flare, flash, gleam, glimmer, glint, glow, ray, shaft, streak, stream. **3** (*a broad smile*) grin, grin from ear to ear, smile.

bear v.t. **1** (*to carry, to show*) carry, display, exhibit, have, show. **2** (*to bring*) bring, carry, convey, move, take, tote, transmit, transport. **3** (*to support the weight of*) bear the weight of, carry, hold, shoulder, sustain. **4** (*to endure, to tolerate*) abide, brook, endure, experience, go through, put up with, stand, stomach, suffer, tolerate, undergo. **5** (*to give birth to*) bring forth, give birth to, produce. **6** (*to produce, to yield*) give, produce, yield. **7** (*to feel an emotion, e.g. hatred, for an extended period*) entertain, harbour, have, hold, possess.
~v.i. (*to take a certain direction* (*as to the point of the compass*)) bend, curve, diverge, fork, go, incline, move, tack, turn, veer. **to bear down on 1** (*to approach purposefully*) advance on, close in on, converge on. **2** (*to make* (*someone*) *worried or depressed*) burden, encumber, oppress, weigh down on. **to bear on** (*to be relevant to*) appertain to, concern, have a bearing on, pertain to, relate to. **to bear out** (*to confirm, to justify*) confirm, corroborate, endorse, give credence to, justify, prove, ratify, substantiate, support, uphold, verify, vindicate. ANTONYMS: contradict, deny, disprove, give the lie to. **to bear up** (*to endure cheerfully*) carry on, cope, endure, grin and bear it, persevere. ANTONYMS: collapse, crack up. **to bear with** (*to put up with, to endure*) be patient with, endure, put up with, show forbearance towards, suffer, tolerate. ANTONYMS: get annoyed at, get impatient with, get irritated at.

bearable a. (*capable of being endured*) endurable, supportable, sustainable, tolerable. ANTONYMS: insufferable, insupportable, unbearable.

beard *n.* (*the hair on the lower part of a man's face, esp. on the chin*) designer stubble, facial hair, five o'clock shadow, growth, stubble, whiskers.

~*v.t.* (*to oppose with resolute effrontery*) brave, challenge, confront, defy, face, stand up to, tackle.

bearded *a.* (*furnished with a beard*) bewhiskered, bristly, hairy, hirsute, stubbly, unshaven, whiskered. ANTONYMS: beardless, cleanshaven, smooth-faced.

bearer *n.* **1** (*a porter*) (*N Am.*) bellboy, (*N Am.*) bellhop, porter. **2** (*a person who holds or presents a cheque*) beneficiary, consignee, payee. **3** (*a bringer of anything*) carrier, conveyor, courier, messenger, runner.

bearing *n.* **1** (*deportment, manner*) air, attitude, behaviour, carriage, demeanour, deportment, gait, manner, mien, posture. **2** (*relation, connection*) connection, pertinence, relation, relevance. **3** (*relative position*) course, location, orientation, position, situation, way, whereabouts.

beast *n.* **1** (*any of the animals other than human beings*) animal, creature, fauna. **2** (*a brutal person*) barbarian, brute, fiend, monster, pig, savage, swine.

beastly *a.* **1** (*like a beast in form or nature*) animal, animal-like, beastlike, theroid. **2** (*disagreeable*) awful, disagreeable, dreadful, foul, horrible, nasty, terrible, unpleasant.

beat *v.t.* **1** (*to strike with repeated blows*) bang, bash, batter, belt, birch, cane, (*sl.*) clobber, clout, flog, give a hiding to, hammer, hit, lash, leather, pound, slap, smack, strike, thrash, thump, (*coll.*) wallop, whack, whip. **2** (*to work* (*metal etc.*) *by striking*) forge, form, hammer, shape, work. **3** (*to mix or agitate by beating*) blend, mix, whip, whisk. **4** ((*of water, wind etc.*) *to dash against*) break against, dash against, strike. **5** (*to conquer, overcome*) best, (*sl.*) clobber, conquer, defeat, (*coll.*) give a pasting to, (*coll.*) lick, outstrip, overcome, rout, (*coll.*) run rings round, triumph over, trounce, vanquish, (*coll.*) wipe the floor with. ANTONYMS: be defeated by, lose to. **6** (*to break or do better than* (*a record*)) break, exceed, outdo, surpass, top, transcend. **7** (*to perplex*) baffle, mystify, nonplus, perplex, puzzle. **8** (*to tread, as a path*) make, tramp, trample, tread, wear.

~*v.i.* **1** (*to pulsate, throb*) palpitate, pulsate, pulse, throb, thud, thump, vibrate. **2** (*to move rhythmically*) flap, flutter.

~*n.* **1** (*a strong musical rhythm*) accent, cadence, measure, rhythm, stress, time. **2** (*a stroke or blow*) bang, belt, blow, clout, hit, slap, smack, stroke, thump. **3** (*a pulsation, a throb*) pounding, pulsation, pulse, throb, throbbing, vibration. **4** (*a certain assigned space regularly traversed at intervals by patrols, police etc.*) circuit, course, round, route, way. **to beat up** (*to injure seriously by beating*) assault, attack, batter, (*sl.*) duff up, knock about, (*coll.*) mug, (*sl.*) rough up, thrash.

beaten *a.* **1** (*defeated*) conquered, defeated, routed, trounced, vanquished. ANTONYMS: triumphant, victorious, winning. **2** (*trodden smooth*) much-trodden, smooth, trampled, trodden, well-trodden, well-used, well-worn, worn. **3** (*mixed for beating, blended*) blended, foamy, frothy, mixed, whipped, whisked.

beating *n.* **1** (*a punishment or chastisement by blows*) belting, birching, caning, chastisement, corporal punishment, flogging, hammering, hiding, lashing, leathering, (*coll.*) pasting, slapping, smacking, thrashing, thumping, (*coll.*) walloping, whacking, whipping. **2** (*pulsation, throbbing*) pounding, pulsation, pulsing, throb, throbbing, vibration. **3** (*an overthrow, defeat*) conquest, defeat, overthrow, rout, routing, trouncing, vanquishing.

beau *n.* **1** (*a woman's lover*) admirer, boyfriend, escort, follower, lover, suitor, swain, sweetheart. **2** (*a man unduly attentive to dress and social fashions*) coxcomb, dandy, fop, popinjay, (*dated coll.*) swell, (*sl.*) toff.

beautiful *a.* (*full of beauty; pleasing to look at*) alluring, appealing, attractive, comely, exquisite, fair, glamorous, good-looking, gorgeous, handsome, lovely, pretty, ravishing, (*sl.*) stunning. ANTONYMS: hideous, repulsive, ugly.

beautify *v.t.* (*to make beautiful*) adorn, decorate, embellish, enhance, garnish, gild, glamorize, ornament, prettify.

beauty *n.* **1** (*that quality which gives the eye or the other senses intense pleasure*) allure, appeal, attractiveness, comeliness, exquisiteness, fairness, glamour, handsomeness, loveliness, prettiness, pulchritude. ANTONYMS: hideousness, ugliness, unsightliness. **2** (*a beautiful person, esp. a woman*) (*sl.*) babe, belle, (*sl.*) cracker, good-looker, (*sl.*) knockout, (*coll.*) lovely, (*sl.*) stunner, Venus. **3** (*a particular aspect that gives satisfaction*) advantage, asset, attraction, benefit, blessing, boon, good thing. ANTONYMS: detraction, disadvantage.

beaver *v.i.* **to beaver away at** (*to work hard at*) concentrate on, hammer away at, keep one's nose to the grindstone, persevere at, plug away at, slog away at.

because *conj.* **1** (*by reason of, on account of*) as a consequence of, as a result of, by reason of, on account of, owing to, thanks to. **2** (*for this reason*) as, inasmuch as, in view of the fact that, owing to the fact that, since.

beckon *v.i.* (*to make a signal by a gesture of the hand or a finger or by a nod*) gesticulate, gesture, make a gesture, make a sign, motion, nod, sign, signal, wave.
~*v.t.* **1** (*to summon or signal to by a motion of the hand, a nod etc.*) call, gesture, motion, signal, summon. **2** (*to attract, to entice*) allure, attract, call, draw, entice, lure, pull, tempt. ANTONYMS: repel.

become *v.i.* (*to pass from one state or condition into another*) come to be, develop into, evolve into, grow into, mature into, metamorphose into, turn out to be.
~*v.t.* **1** (*to be proper* (*to or for*)) befit, be fitting (for), behove, be proper (to/for), be seemly (for), be suitable (for), suit. ANTONYMS: be improper (for), be unseemly (for), be unsuitable (for). **2** (*to look well upon*) enhance, flatter, look good on, look well on, suit. ANTONYMS: detract from, do nothing for. **to become of** (*to happen to*) befall, be the fate of, be the lot of, happen to.

becoming *a.* **1** (*suitable, proper*) appropriate, apt, comme il faut, fitting, proper, seemly, suitable. ANTONYMS: inappropriate, unseemly, unsuitable. **2** (*in harmony or keeping* (*with*)) appropriate (to), befitting, compatible (with), congruous (with), in keeping (with), suitable (for). ANTONYMS: inappropriate (to), incompatible (with), incongruous (for), unsuitable (for). **3** ((*of clothes*) *making one look attractive*) attractive, chic, elegant, enhancing, flattering, lovely, pretty, stylish. ANTONYMS: ugly, unattractive.

bed *n.* **1** (*an article of domestic furniture to sleep on*) bedstead, berth, bunk, cot, couch, divan, hammock, pallet. **2** (*the use of a bed in marriage, conjugal rights*) intimacy, lovemaking, sex, sexual intercourse, sexual relationship. **3** (*a plot of ground in a garden*) border, lot, patch, plot. **4** (*the flat surface on which anything rests*) base, bottom, foundation, substratum, substructure, support.
~*v.t.* **1** (*to plant in a bed or beds*) plant, plant out. **2** (*to have sexual intercourse with*) (*sl.*) bonk, (*taboo sl.*) fuck, go to bed with, have sex with, (*taboo sl.*) lay, make love to, sleep with. **3** (*to embed*) base, bury, embed, establish, fix, found, insert, set.

bedaub *v.t.* (*to daub over, to besmear*) besmear, smear, spatter, splash.

bedclothes *n.pl.* (*sheets, blankets and coverlets for a bed*) bedcovers, bedding, bedlinen, blankets, covers, duvet, sheets.

bedeck *v.t.* (*to deck out, to adorn*) adorn, array, deck out, decorate, embellish, festoon, garnish, ornament, trim.

bedevil *v.t.* (*to torment*) afflict, beset, distress, harass, irritate, pester, plague, torment, trouble, vex, worry.

bedlam *n.* (*a scene of wild uproar*) chaos, clamour, commotion, confusion, furore, hubbub, hullabaloo, pandemonium, tumult, turmoil, uproar.

bedraggled *a.* (*looking untidy and wet or dirty*) dirty, drenched, dripping wet, messy, muddied, muddy, soaked, soaking wet, sodden, soiled, sopping, stained, untidy, wet.

bedridden *a.* (*confined to bed through age or sickness*) confined to bed, flat on one's back, housebound, laid up.

bedrock *n.* **1** (*the rock underlying superficial formations*) rock bed, solid foundation, substratum. **2** (*the fundamental principles*) basic principles, basics, core, elementary principles, fundamentals. **3** (*the lowest possible state*) depths, lowest point, nadir, rock bottom. ANTONYMS: heights, peak, zenith.

beef *v.i.* (*to grumble, to grouse*) complain, gripe, grouse, grumble, moan, mutter, protest.

beefy *a.* **1** (*stolid*) chubby, corpulent, fat, heavy, overweight, plump, podgy, rotund, stolid. ANTONYMS: skinny, slim, thin. **2** (*muscular*) brawny, burly, muscular, powerful, powerfully-built, stalwart, strapping, strongly-built, sturdy. ANTONYMS: frail, puny, weak.

beetling *a.* (*overhanging, prominent*) jutting, overhanging, projecting, protruding, sticking out.

befall *v.i.* (*to happen*) arise, come about, come to pass, happen, materialize, occur, supervene, take place, transpire.

befitting *a.* (*suitable or proper*) appropriate, apt, becoming, fitting, proper, right, seemly, suitable. ANTONYMS: improper, inappropriate, unseemly.

before *prep.* **1** (*in front of, in time*) earlier than, previous to, prior to. ANTONYMS: after, following. **2** (*in front of, in space*) ahead of, in advance of, in front of. ANTONYMS: at the back of, behind. **3** (*in the presence or sight of*) before the very eyes of, in front of, in the presence of, under the nose of. **4** (*in preference to*) in preference to, rather than, sooner than.
~*adv.* **1** (*ahead, in front*) ahead, in advance, in front, in the vanguard. ANTONYMS: behind, in the rear. **2** (*beforehand, in the past*) beforehand, earlier, formerly, hitherto, in advance, in the past, previously. ANTONYMS: after, afterwards, later.

beforehand *adv.* (*in advance, before the time*) ahead of time, before, before the appointed time,

earlier, in advance, previously, sooner. ANTO-
NYMS: afterwards, later.

befriend *v.t.* (*to become a friend of, to help*)
assist, back, give a helping hand to, give support
to, help, look after, make friends with, support.

befuddle *v.t.* **1** (*to confuse, baffle*) bewilder, confuse, disorient, mix up, muddle. **2** (*to stupefy
with drink*) inebriate, intoxicate, make drunk,
stupefy.

beg *v.i.* **1** (*to ask for alms*) ask for alms, ask for
money, (*esp. N Am., coll.*) bum, cadge, (*coll.*)
mooch, (*coll.*) scrounge, seek charity, sponge.
2 (*to make an earnest request*) beseech, entreat,
plead, request.
~*v.t.* **1** (*to ask earnestly, to entreat*) ask, beseech,
entreat, implore, importune, plead with,
request. **2** (*to ask politely or formally for*) crave,
request, seek.

beget *v.t.* **1** (*to generate, to procreate*) father, procreate, sire. **2** (*to cause to come into existence*)
bring about, bring forth, cause, create, effect,
give rise to, occasion, produce, result in.

beggar *n.* **1** (*a person who lives by asking alms*)
(*esp. N Am., coll.*) bum, cadger, mendicant,
(*coll.*) moocher, (*coll.*) scrounger, sponger. **2** (*a
person in indigent circumstances*) (*coll.*) bag
lady, (*coll.*) bagman, derelict, down-and-out,
(*esp. N Am.*) hobo, homeless person, pauper,
tramp, vagrant. **3** (*a fellow*) individual, person,
thing.
~*v.t.* (*to impoverish*) bankrupt, impoverish, make
poor, pauperize, reduce to poverty, ruin.
ANTONYMS: make prosperous, make rich.

beggary *n.* **1** (*the state or condition of a habitual
beggar*) mendicancy, vagrancy. **2** (*extreme
indigence*) bankruptcy, destitution, impecun-
iousness, impoverishment, indigence, need,
neediness, pauperdom, pauperism, pennilessness, penury, vagrancy.

begin *v.i.* **1** (*to come into existence, to start*)
appear, arise, come into being, come into
existence, commence, crop up, dawn, emerge,
happen, occur, originate, spring up, start. ANTO-
NYMS: come to an end, end, finish. **2** (*to start
doing something*) commence, get going, get off
the ground, start, start the ball rolling, start up.
ANTONYMS: cease, finish, stop.
~*v.t.* (*to be the first to do, to commence*) commence,
embark upon, enter upon, inaugurate, initiate,
instigate, institute, (*coll.*) kick-start, set about,
set in motion, start. ANTONYMS: bring to a close,
cease, finish, stop.

beginner *n.* (*a young learner or practitioner*)
apprentice, fledgling, greenhorn, initiate, learner, neophyte, novice, raw recruit, (*sl.*) rookie,
trainee, tyro. ANTONYMS: authority, expert, old
hand, veteran.

beginning *n.* **1** (*the first cause, the origin*) fount,
fountainhead, origin, roots, seeds, source,
starting point. ANTONYMS: end, termination.
2 (*the first state or commencement*) birth,
commencement, dawn, inauguration, inception,
initiation, instigation, (*coll.*) kick-off, onset,
opening, start, starting point. ANTONYMS: close,
death, end, termination. **3** (*the first part of something*) commencement, first part, opening, start.
ANTONYMS: close, conclusion, end, last part.

begrudge *v.t.* **1** (*to grudge*) feel bitter about, give
reluctantly, give unwillingly, resent. ANTONYMS:
give generously, give willingly. **2** (*to envy* (*a person*) *the possession of*) be envious of, be jealous
of, envy, grudge.

beguile *v.t.* **1** (*to deceive, to lead into by fraud*)
cheat, deceive, lead astray, mislead. **2** (*to charm
away the tedium of*) pass, while away. **3** (*to
entertain*) amuse, divert, entertain. ANTONYMS:
bore. **4** (*to bewitch*) allure, bewitch, captivate,
charm, delight, enchant, enthral, seduce. ANTO-
NYMS: put off, repel, revolt.

beguiling *a.* (*deceiving, charming*) alluring, bewitching, captivating, charming, delightful,
enchanting, enthralling, seductive. ANTONYMS:
repulsive, revolting.

behalf *n.* **on behalf of 1** (*on account of, for the
sake of*) for the benefit of, for the good of, in
support of, in the interests of. **2** (*representing*) as
a representative of, for, in place of, in the name
of, representing.

behave *v.i.* **1** (*to conduct oneself*) acquit oneself,
act, comport oneself, conduct oneself, perform.
2 (*to conduct oneself well, to display good manners*) act properly, conduct oneself well, mind
one's manners, mind one's Ps & Qs. ANTONYMS:
be unruly, get up to mischief, misbehave. **3** (*to
function properly*) act, function, operate,
perform, work. ANTONYMS: malfunction.

behaviour *n.* **1** (*manners, conduct*) actions, conduct, manners, response, way of acting, ways.
2 (*the manner in which a thing acts*) action, functioning, operation, performance, working.

behead *v.t.* (*to cut the head off*) decapitate, execute, guillotine.

behest *n.* (*a command, an injunction*) bidding,
command, decree, dictate, direction, injunction,
instruction, mandate, order, request, wish.

behind *prep.* **1** (*at the back of*) at the back of, at
the rear of, on the further side of, on the other
side of. ANTONYMS: in front of. **2** (*inferior to*)
inferior to, less advanced than, slower than,
weaker than. ANTONYMS: in front of, more
advanced than, superior to. **3** (*after, later than*)
after, later than. ANTONYMS: before, earlier than.

4 (*in support of*) backing, for, in agreement with, in support of, on the side of, supporting. ANTONYMS: against, on the other side, working against. **5** (*responsible for the existence or doing of*) at the back of, at the bottom of, responsible for, the cause of, the instigator of, the source of, to blame for. **6** (*in the rear of*) after, at the back of, following, in the wake of, on the heels of, to the rear of. ANTONYMS: before, in front of, preceding. ~*adv.* **1** (*at the back, in the rear*) at the back, at the rear, following, in the rear. ANTONYMS: ahead, in front. **2** (*backwards, on the further side*) backwards, over one's shoulder, to the rear, towards the back, towards the rear. ANTONYMS: frontwards, to the front. **3** (*in arrears*) behindhand, in arrears, in debt, late, overdue. ANTONYMS: in advance, up to date. **4** (*behind schedule*) behindhand, behind schedule, late, slow, tardy. ANTONYMS: ahead of schedule, early, on time.

behindhand *a., adv.* **1** (*dilatory, tardy*) behind, behind schedule, late, slow, tardy. ANTONYMS: ahead of schedule, early, on time. **2** (*backward, old-fashioned*) backward, behind the times, old-fashioned, out of date. ANTONYMS: complete, modern, up to date. **3** (*in arrears*) behind, in arrears, in debt, late, overdue.

behold *v.t.* **1** (*to see*) catch sight of, discern, espy, observe, perceive, see, spot. **2** (*to look attentively at*) consider, contemplate, inspect, look at, observe, regard, scan, study, survey, (*coll.*) take a dekko at, view, watch. ANTONYMS: ignore.

beholden *a.* (*obliged, indebted* (*with to*)) grateful, indebted, obligated, obliged, owing (someone), under an obligation.

behove *v.t.* **1** (*to befit, to suit*) be appropriate, be apt, befit, be fitting, be proper, be seemly, be suitable. ANTONYMS: be inappropriate, be unseemly. **2** (*to be incumbent on*) be advisable for, be essential for, be expected of, be incumbent on, be necessary for, be obligatory for, be the duty of.

beige *a.* (*of a light brownish yellow*) biscuit, biscuit-coloured, buff, ecru, fawn, mushroom, neutral, oatmeal, sandy.

being *n.* **1** (*existence*) existence, existing, life, living. ANTONYMS: death, extinction, non-existence. **2** (*nature, essence*) essence, nature, soul, spirit. **3** (*an animal or person that exists*) animal, creature, human, human being, individual, living thing, mortal, person.

belabour *v.t.* **1** (*to beat, to thrash*) batter, beat, belt, hit, strike, thrash, whip. **2** (*to assault verbally*) attack, berate, blast, censure, criticize, (*coll.*) knock, lambast, lay into, slate, tear into. **3** (*to dwell unduly on*) dwell on, flog to death, over-elaborate on.

belated *a.* (*very late; behind time*) behind schedule, delayed, late, overdue, tardy. ANTONYMS: early, prompt.

belch *v.i.* **1** (*to eject wind noisily by the mouth from the stomach*) break wind, burp, eructate. **2** (*to issue out, as by eructation*) issue, pour, spew. ~*v.t.* (*to eject* (*smoke etc.*)*, to throw out*) discharge, disgorge, eject, emit, expel, give off, issue, pour forth, spew, vent.

beleaguer *v.t.* **1** (*to besiege*) assail, attack, besiege, blockade, lay siege to, surround. **2** (*to harass*) badger, beset, bother, harass, (*coll.*) hassle, nag, pester, plague, set upon, torment.

belie *v.t.* **1** (*to misrepresent*) conceal, disguise, distort, falsify, gloss over, misrepresent. **2** (*to fail to perform or justify*) fail to justify, fail to live up to, fall short of. ANTONYMS: justify, live up to. **3** (*to contradict*) contradict, deny, disprove, give the lie to, refute. ANTONYMS: confirm, corroborate, prove.

belief *n.* **1** (*religion, religious faith*) credo, creed, doctrine, faith, ideology, religion. ANTONYMS: agnosticism, atheism, scepticism. **2** (*reliance, confidence*) confidence, credence, faith, reliance, trust. ANTONYMS: doubt, mistrust, scepticism. **3** (*an opinion firmly held*) conviction, feeling, impression, notion, opinion, theory, view, viewpoint, way of thinking. ANTONYMS: disbelief.

believable *a.* (*capable of being believed*) acceptable, conceivable, creditable, imaginable, likely, plausible, possible, probable, within the bounds of possibility. ANTONYMS: improbable, incredible, unbelievable, unlikely.

believe *v.t.* (*to accept as true*) accept, be convinced by, (*sl.*) buy, credit, regard as true, swallow, trust. ANTONYMS: disbelieve, distrust, doubt. **to believe in** (*to trust in, to rely on*) have confidence in, have faith in, place reliance on, rely on, swear by, trust in. ANTONYMS: distrust, have no faith in.

believer *n.* (*a person who believes*) adherent, convert, devotee, disciple, follower, proselyte, protagonist. ANTONYMS: agnostic, atheist, doubting Thomas, sceptic, unbeliever.

belittle *v.t.* (*to depreciate or undermine verbally*) decry, deprecate, depreciate, deride, derogate, detract from, disparage, downplay, make light of, minimize, play down, scoff at, sneer at, underestimate, underrate, undervalue. ANTONYMS: exaggerate, exalt, praise.

bellicose *a.* (*inclined to war or fighting*) aggressive, belligerent, combative, hawkish, militaristic, pugnacious, quarrelsome, warlike, warmongering. ANTONYMS: pacifist, peaceable, peace-loving.

belligerent *a.* **1** (*carrying on war*) at war, battling, combative, warring. ANTONYMS: at peace. **2** (*aggressive*) aggressive, antagonistic, argumentative, captious, combative, contentious, disputatious, hostile, irascible, militant, pugnacious, quarrelsome, unfriendly, warmongering. ANTONYMS: conciliatory, friendly, peaceable.

bellow *v.i.* (*to emit a loud hollow sound*) bawl, howl, roar, shout, yell. ANTONYMS: murmur, whisper.

belly *n.* (*that part of the human body in front which extends from the breast to the insertion of the lower limbs*) abdomen, (*sl.*) breadbasket, gut, (*coll.*) insides, stomach, (*coll.*) tum, (*coll.*) tummy.

belong *v.i.* **1** (*to be the property* (*of*)) be held (by), be in the ownership (of), be in the possession (of), be owned (by), be the property (of). **2** (*to be a member* (*of*)) be affiliated (to), be allied (to), be a member (of), be associated (with). **3** (*to be part* (*of*), *to be connected* (*with*)) be an adjunct (of), be an appendage (of), be attached (to), be connected (with), be part (of), relate (to). **4** (*to be rightly placed* (*in*)) be at home (in), be part (of), be suited (to), feel at home (in), fit (in). ANTONYMS: be out of place (in).

belongings *n.pl.* (*one's possessions*) accoutrements, appurtenances, (*sl.*) clobber, effects, gear, goods and chattels, paraphernalia, personal effects, personal property, property, stuff, things.

beloved *a.* (*loved greatly*) adored, cherished, darling, dear, dearest, favoured, precious, prized, treasured. ANTONYMS: hated, loathed.

~*n.* (*a person who is greatly loved*) betrothed, boyfriend, darling, dear one, fiancé, fiancée, girlfriend, love, lover, sweetheart.

below *prep.* **1** (*under in place*) further down than, lower than, under, underneath. ANTONYMS: above. **2** (*lower on a scale than*) less than, lower than. ANTONYMS: above, higher than. **3** (*inferior to in rank or excellence*) inferior to, lower than, subordinate to. ANTONYMS: above, further up than, superior to. **4** (*unworthy of, unsuitable to*) beneath, degrading to, inappropriate to, not befitting, unworthy of. ANTONYMS: appropriate to, in keeping with, worthy of.

~*adv.* **1** (*in or to a lower place or rank*) beneath, down below, downstairs, further down, lower down, underneath. ANTONYMS: above, up above. **2** (*lower on the same page, or on a following page*) at a later place, at a later point, further down, further on, later on. ANTONYMS: above, earlier, previously.

belt *n.* **1** (*a broad, flat strip of leather or other material worn around the waist*) band, cummerbund, girdle, sash, waistband. **2** (*a broad strip or stripe*) band, bar, line, stria, strip, stripe. **3** (*a zone or region*) area, district, extent, region, stretch, tract, zone. **4** (*a blow*) bang, blow, clout, punch, smack, thump, (*coll.*) wallop.

~*v.t.* **1** (*to encircle with or as with a belt*) encircle, encompass, gird. **2** (*to thrash with a belt*) flog, lash, (*sl.*) paste, strap, whip. **3** (*to hit very hard*) bash, batter, beat, hit, smack, strike, thrash, thump, (*coll.*) wallop.

bemoan *v.t.* (*to moan over, to deplore*) bewail, complain about, deplore, grieve over, lament, regret, weep over. ANTONYMS: rejoice in.

bemused *a.* (*confused*) bewildered, confused, dazed, disconcerted, muddled, perplexed, puzzled, stunned.

bench *n.* **1** (*a long seat*) form, long seat, pew, settle, stall. **2** (*a carpenter's or other mechanic's work table*) workbench, work table. **3** (*judges or magistrates collectively*) court, judges, judiciary, magistrates.

bend *v.t.* **1** (*to render curved or angular*) arc, arch, bow, contort, crook, curve, flex, twist, warp. ANTONYMS: straighten. **2** (*to direct to a certain point*) aim, direct, point, steer, train, turn. **3** (*to subdue*) compel, direct, force, influence, sway.

~*v.i.* **1** (*to assume the form of a curve or angle*) curve, diverge, incline, loop, swerve, turn, twist, veer. **2** (*to incline from an erect position*) bow, crouch, hunch, lean down, stoop. ANTONYMS: stand up straight, straighten up.

~*n.* **1** (*a bending curve or flexure*) angle, arc, arch, bow, crook, curve, hook, loop, twist. **2** (*a sudden turn in a road or river*) corner, curve, hairpin, meander, twist, zigzag.

beneath *prep.* **1** (*below, under in place or position*) below, lower than, under, underneath. ANTONYMS: above, over. **2** (*unworthy of*) below, unbefitting, unworthy of. **3** (*inferior to in quality*) inferior to, lower than, subordinate to, worse than. ANTONYMS: above, superior to.

~*adv.* (*in a lower place, below*) below, down below, in a lower place, to a lower place, to a lower point, underneath. ANTONYMS: above, up above.

benefactor *n.* **1** (*a person who gives another help or friendly service*) (*coll.*) angel, backer, friend, helper, patron, promoter, sponsor, subsidizer, supporter, sympathizer, well-wisher. **2** (*a person who gives to a religious or charitable institution*) contributor, donor, patron, philanthropist, subscriber.

beneficial *a.* (*advantageous, helpful*) advantageous, expedient, favourable, gainful, profitable, propitious, rewarding, salubrious, useful, valuable. ANTONYMS: detrimental, disadvantageous, harmful.

beneficiary *n.* (*a person who receives a favour*) gainer, heir, inheritor, legatee, lucky one, receiver, recipient, winner.

benefit *n.* **1** (*advantage, gain*) advantage, disadvantage, gain, good, interest, profit, well-being. ANTONYMS: detriment, disadvantage, harm. **2** (*an advantage, something favourable*) advantage, blessing, boon, (*coll.*) perk. **3** (*money or services provided under government social security or private pension schemes etc.*) (*coll.*) dole, income support, jobseeker's allowance, social security, unemployment benefit, welfare.
~*v.t.* (*to do good to*) be advantageous to, be of advantage to, be of service to, better, do good to, help, improve, profit. ANTONYMS: be disadvantageous to, harm.
~*v.i.* (*to derive advantage* (*from*)) gain, make money, profit, reap benefits. ANTONYMS: suffer loss.

benevolence *n.* (*charitable feeling, goodwill*) altruism, charity, compassion, friendliness, generosity, goodness, goodwill, kind-heartedness, kindness, sympathy. ANTONYMS: hostility, ill will, malevolence, unkindness.

benevolent *a.* **1** (*disposed to do good, generous*) altruistic, bountiful, caring, charitable, compassionate, friendly, generous, good, kind, kindhearted, kindly, liberal, philanthropic, sympathetic, warm-hearted. ANTONYMS: hostile, mean, unkind. **2** (*charitable*) alms-giving, charitable, non-profit-making.

benign *a.* **1** (*kind-hearted, gracious*) affable, amiable, friendly, genial, gracious, kind, kindhearted, kindly, sympathetic. ANTONYMS: harsh, unkind. **2** (*mild*) balmy, gentle, healthy, mild, pleasant, salubrious, temperate. ANTONYMS: harsh, severe, unpleasant. **3** (*favourable, propitious*) advantageous, auspicious, beneficial, encouraging, favourable, good, helpful, lucky, opportune, propitious. ANTONYMS: inauspicious, inopportune, unfavourable. **4** ((*of a tumour etc.*) *not malignant*) curable, non-cancerous, nonmalignant. ANTONYMS: cancerous, malignant.

bent *n.* **1** (*an inclination, a bias*) bias, inclination, leaning, partiality, predisposition. **2** (*a disposition, a propensity*) disposition, penchant, proclivity, propensity, tendency, wont. **3** (*an ability, a skill*) ability, aptitude, capability, capacity, facility, flair, forte, genius, gift, knack, skill, talent.
~*a.* **1** (*curved*) angled, arched, contorted, crooked, curved, twisted, warped. ANTONYMS: plumb, straight. **2** (*intent* (*on*), *resolved* (*to*)) determined (to), disposed (to), fixed (on), inclined (to), insistent (on), intent (on), resolved (to), set (on).

ANTONYMS: disinclined (to), loath (to), reluctant (to). **3** (*dishonest*) corrupt, (*coll.*) crooked, dishonest, (*coll.*) dodgy, fraudulent. ANTONYMS: honest, law-abiding, upright. **4** ((*of the body*) *stooped*) bowed, crouching, hunched, stooped. ANTONYMS: straight up, upright.

bequeath *v.t.* **1** (*to leave by will or testament*) bestow, leave, make over, transfer, will. ANTONYMS: inherit. **2** (*to transmit to future generations*) hand down, impart, leave, pass on, transmit. ANTONYMS: inherit.

bequest *n.* **1** (*the act of bequeathing*) bequeathing, bestowal, leaving, willing. **2** (*that which is bequeathed*) endowment, gift, inheritance, legacy, settlement.

berate *v.t.* (*to rebuke or scold vehemently*) blast, castigate, censure, chide, criticize, fulminate against, (*coll.*) give a dressing down to, (*coll.*) give a rocket to, (*coll.*) give a telling-off to, harangue, lambast, rail at, read the riot act to, rebuke, reprimand, reprove, scold, (*coll.*) tear a strip off, upbraid.

bereave *v.t.* (*to deprive or rob of anything*) deprive, dispossess, divest, rob, strip.

bereavement *n.* **1** (*the state of being bereaved*) deprivation, dispossession, loss. **2** (*the loss of a near relative or friend by death*) death, loss.

bereft *a.* (*deprived* (*esp. of something abstract, as hope*)) deprived (of), destitute (of), devoid (of), lacking, robbed (of), wanting, without.

berserk *a., adv.* (*filled with furious rage*) amok, (*N Am.*) ape, beside oneself, crazed, crazy, enraged, frenzied, hysterical, insane, mad, maniacal, manic, out of one's mind, uncontrollable, unrestrainable, violent, wild. ANTONYMS: calm, controlled, restrained, sane.

berth *n.* **1** (*a sleeping place on board ship or in a railway carriage*) bunk, cabin, compartment, couchette. **2** (*a place for a ship at a wharf*) anchorage, dock, mooring.
~*v.t.* (*to moor in a berth*) anchor, dock, land, moor, tie up.
~*v.i.* (*to moor in a berth*) dock, drop anchor, land, moor.

beseech *v.t.* **1** (*to ask earnestly, implore*) appeal to, ask earnestly, beg, entreat, implore, importune, petition, plead with, solicit. **2** (*to ask earnestly for*) appeal for, beg, crave, plead for, pray for, solicit.

beset *v.t.* **1** (*to set upon, to assail*) assail, attack, badger, bedevil, bother, harass, hound, pester, plague, torment, trouble, worry. **2** (*to set or surround* (*with*)) encircle (with), enclose (in), fence (in), hem (in), ring (round), surround (with).

besetting *a.* (*particularly or constantly tempting*) habitual, inveterate, persistent.

beside *prep.* 1 (*by the side of, side by side with*) abreast of, alongside, at the side, by the side of, cheek by jowl with, next to, with. 2 (*in comparison with*) against, compared with, in comparison with, next to. 3 (*near, close to*) adjacent to, by, close to, hard by, near, next to. **beside oneself** (*out of one's wits, with worry etc.*) amok, (*N Am.*) ape, apoplectic, berserk, crazy, demented, distraught, frantic, frenzied, hysterical, in a frenzy, insane, mad, manic, out of one's mind, unbalanced, uncontrollable, unhinged, unrestrained, violent, wild. **beside the point/ question** (*irrelevant*) immaterial, inapplicable, inapposite, inappropriate, irrelevant, neither here nor there, unconnected.

besides *prep.* 1 (*in addition to, over and above*) as well as, in addition to, over and above. 2 (*other than, except*) apart from, except, excluding, not counting, not including, other than, without.
~*adv.* (*moreover, in addition*) additionally, also, as well, further, furthermore, in addition, moreover, too, what is more.

besiege *v.t.* 1 (*to surround (a place) with intent to capture it by military force*) beleaguer, blockade, encircle, lay siege to, surround. 2 (*to crowd round*) crowd, mob, throng. 3 (*to assail importunately*) badger, beset, bother, harass, (*coll.*) hassle, hound, importune, nag, pester, plague, torment, trouble, worry.

besmirch *v.t.* (*to sully the reputation of, to dishonour*) dishonour, slander, smear, sully, tarnish.

besotted *a.* (*infatuated (with)*) bewitched (by), doting (on), infatuated (with), smitten (with), spellbound (by).

bespatter *v.t.* (*to spatter over or about*) bedaub, befoul, begrime, besprinkle, dirty, muddy, spatter, splash, splatter.

bespeak *v.t.* (*to give evidence of*) bear witness to, betoken, demonstrate, denote, display, evidence, evince, exhibit, give evidence of, indicate, manifest, reveal, show, signify, suggest, testify to.

best *a.* 1 (*of the highest quality*) excellent, finest, first-class, first-rate, sublime, superlative, supreme. ANTONYMS: second-class, substandard, third-rate. 2 (*surpassing all others*) chief, finest, foremost, highest, leading, outstanding, principal, top, unexcelled, unsurpassed. ANTONYMS: inferior, lowest, worst. 3 (*most desirable*) correct, most apt, most desirable, most fitting, most suitable, right, wisest. ANTONYMS: least desirable, worst, wrong.

~*adv.* 1 (*in the highest degree*) extremely, greatly, most, most highly, to the greatest extent, to the highest degree. ANTONYMS: worst. 2 (*in a manner that is better than any other*) excellently, in the best way, superlatively, unsurpassedly. ANTONYMS: in the worst way.
~*n.* 1 (*the best thing*) cream, crème de la crème, elite, finest, flower, pick. ANTONYMS: dregs, worst. 2 (*the utmost*) (*coll.*) damnedest, hardest, utmost.
~*v.t.* (*to get the better of*) beat, conquer, defeat, get the better of, (*coll.*) lick, outclass, (*coll.*) outsmart, prevail over, (*coll.*) run rings round, thrash, triumph over, trounce, vanquish, (*coll.*) wipe the floor with, worst. ANTONYMS: be beaten by, suffer defeat at the hands of. **at one's best** (*in prime condition, in one's prime*) in best condition, in peak form, in prime condition, in top form. ANTONYMS: at one's worst.

bestial *a.* 1 (*brutish, inhuman*) barbaric, barbarous, beastly, brutal, brutish, cruel, feral, inhuman, inhumane, savage, violent. ANTONYMS: gentle, mild. 2 (*sexually depraved*) carnal, depraved, lascivious, lecherous, lewd, lustful, sensual, sordid.

bestow *v.t.* (*to give as a present*) accord, allot, assign, bequeath, commit, confer on, donate, endow with, give, grant, hand out, hand over, impart, present.

bestride *v.t.* 1 (*to sit upon with the legs astride*) bestraddle, stand astride, straddle. 2 (*to span, overarch*) cross, extend over, pass over, span, straddle.

bet *n.* 1 (*an act of betting, a wager*) gamble, (*coll.*) punt, venture, wager. 2 (*a sum staked on a contingent event*) ante, pledge, stake, wager. 3 (*an opinion*) belief, expectation, feeling, forecast, guess, opinion, prediction, theory, view. 4 (*a course of action*) alternative, course of action, option, possibility.
~*v.t.* 1 (*to lay a wager (for or against)*) lay a wager, lay odds, put money on, wager. 2 (*to stake on a contingency*) chance, gamble, hazard, pledge, risk, stake, venture, wager. 3 (*to be sure*) aver, be certain, be confident, be sure, say confidently.
~*v.i.* (*to lay a wager*) gamble, lay a wager, (*coll.*) punt, speculate, wager.

bête noire *n.* (*a pet aversion*) abomination, anathema, aversion, bugbear, pet hate.

betoken *v.t.* 1 (*to foreshow, to be an omen of*) augur, bode, forebode, foreshadow, foreshow, portend, presage. 2 (*to indicate*) be as sign of, bespeak, denote, indicate, mean, show, signify, suggest.

betray *v.t.* 1 (*to deliver up a person or thing treacherously*) (*coll.*) blow the whistle on, (*sl.*)

grass on, inform on, (*coll.*) sell (someone) down the river, (*sl.*) shop, (*sl.*) squeal on. ANTONYMS: protect, shield. **2** (*to be false to*) be disloyal to, break faith with, double-cross, (*coll.*) sell (someone) down the river, (*fig.*) stab (someone) in the back, treat (someone) treacherously. ANTONYMS: be faithful to, be loyal to. **3** (*to disclose against one's will; to reveal incidentally*) blab, blurt out, disclose, divulge, give away, let slip, reveal. ANTONYMS: keep secret, keep to one's self. **4** (*to lead astray*) deceive, delude, dupe, hoodwink, lead astray, mislead.

betrayal *n.* **1** (*a treacherous violation of a trust*) act of betrayal, act of disloyalty, breach of faith, breach of trust, double-crossing, treacherous act. **2** (*a revelation or divulging*) disclosure, divulgence, revelation.

betrothal *n.* (*the state of being betrothed*) betrothement, engagement, marriage contract.

betrothed *a.* (*engaged to be married*) affianced, engaged, engaged to be married, promised in marriage.
~*n.* (*a person engaged to be married*) fiancé, fiancée, husband-to-be, (*dated or facet.*) intended, wife-to-be.

better *a.* **1** (*superior, more excellent*) greater, of better quality, of higher quality, superior, worthier. ANTONYMS: inferior, worse. **2** (*more desirable*) more appropriate, more fitting, more suitable, preferable. ANTONYMS: less desirable, worse. **3** (*improved in health*) cured, fitter, healthier, much-improved, on the mend, recovered, stronger. ANTONYMS: unhealthier, weaker, worse.
~*adv.* **1** (*in a superior or more excellent manner*) in a superior way, to a higher standard, to the good. ANTONYMS: to a lower standard, worse. **2** (*in a greater or higher degree*) to a greater degree, to a greater extent. ANTONYMS: the less, worse.
~*v.t.* **1** (*to make better*) advance, ameliorate, amend, correct, enhance, forward, further, improve, make better, promote, rectify, reform, relieve. ANTONYMS: make worse, worsen. **2** (*to surpass, to improve on*) beat, cap, excel, go one better than, improve on, outdo, surpass, top.
~*v.i.* (*to become better, to improve*) ameliorate, become better, grow better, improve, (*coll.*) pick up. ANTONYMS: deteriorate, go downhill, worsen.

betterment *n.* (*improvement*) advance, amelioration, enhancement, furtherance, improvement, rectification, reform, relief.

between *prep.* **1** (*intermediate in relation to*) amidst, in the middle of, (*poet.*) mid. **2** (*related so as to separate*) differentiating, discriminating, distinguishing, separating. **3** (*related so as to*

connect) connecting, joining, linking, uniting. **4** (*among*) among, to each of.

beverage *n.* (*any drink other than water*) aperitif, drink, drop, libation, (*coll.*) poison, refreshment.

bevy *n.* **1** (*a flock of larks or quails*) flight, flock. **2** (*a group of people, esp. women*) assembly, band, bunch, company, crowd, gaggle, gathering, group, troupe.

bewail *v.t.* (*to wail over, to lament for*) bemoan, cry over, deplore, grieve for, lament, mourn, regret, rue, wail over, weep for.

beware *v.i.* (*to be wary, to be on one's guard*) be careful, be cautious, be chary, be on one's guard, be on the alert, be on the lookout, be wary, look out, mind out, take care, watch out. ANTONYMS: be careless, be inattentive, be off one's guard.
~*v.t.* (*to be wary (of), on guard (against)*) be on one's guard (against), be on the alert (for), be on the lookout (for), be wary (of), look out (for), mind out (for), steer clear (of), watch out (for).

bewilder *v.t.* (*to perplex, confuse*) baffle, bamboozle, befuddle, bemuse, confound, confuse, daze, disconcert, flummox, mix up, muddle, mystify, nonplus, perplex, puzzle, stump.

bewildered *a.* (*perplexed, confused*) all at sea, baffled, bemused, confused, disconcerted, muddled, mystified, nonplussed, perplexed, puzzled, taken aback, thrown off balance.

bewildering *a.* (*confusing, puzzling*) baffling, confusing, disconcerting, muddling, perplexing, puzzling. ANTONYMS: clear, crystal clear.

bewitch *v.t.* **1** (*to charm, to fascinate*) beguile, captivate, charm, enchant, entrance, fascinate, hypnotize, mesmerize, spellbind, transfix. ANTONYMS: disgust, repel, revolt. **2** (*to practise witchcraft against*) cast a spell over, enchant, place under a spell, put a spell on.

bewitching *a.* (*alluring, charming*) alluring, beguiling, captivating, charming, enchanting, entrancing, fascinating, spellbinding.

beyond *prep.* **1** (*on or towards the farther side of*) further on than, on the far side of, on the farther side of, on the other side of, over, past. **2** (*past, later than*) after, later than, on the other side of, past. **3** (*exceeding in quantity or amount, more than*) above, exceeding, greater than, in excess of, more than. ANTONYMS: below, less than. **4** (*outside the limit of*) above, beyond the capacity of, beyond the limit of, out of reach of, out of the range of. ANTONYMS: within the range of. **5** (*in addition to, over and above*) apart from, except, in addition to, other than, over and above.

~*adv.* (*farther away, at a greater distance*) at a greater distance, farther away, further on, yonder.

bias *n.* **1** (*a leaning of the mind, inclination*) bent, leaning, partiality, penchant, predilection, predisposition, proclivity, proneness, propensity, tendency. ANTONYMS: aversion, disinclination. **2** (*prejudice, prepossession*) bigotry, discrimination, intolerance, narrow-mindedness, one-sidedness, partiality, prejudice, unfairness. ANTONYMS: fairness, impartiality, objectivity. **3** (*an edge cut slantwise across a strip of material*) angle, cross, diagonal, oblique, slant, slope.
~*v.t.* (*to prejudice, to prepossess*) influence, prejudice, sway, weight.

biased *a.* (*not impartial, prejudiced*) discriminatory, one-sided, partial, prejudiced, unfair. ANTONYMS: fair, impartial, unbiased.

Bible *n.* **1** (*the sacred writings of the Christian religion, comprising the Old and New Testaments*) Holy Writ, the Good Book, the Holy Bible, the Scriptures, the Word, the Word of God. **2** (*a textbook, an authority*) authority, guide, handbook, manual, textbook, vademecum.

bicker *v.i.* (*to quarrel or squabble over petty issues*) argue, dispute, fight, have a disagreement, have a fight, have an argument, have a row, quarrel, row, (*coll.*) scrap, spar, squabble, wrangle.

bicycle *n.* (*a two-wheeled pedal-driven vehicle*) bike, cycle, push-bike.

bid *v.t.* **1** (*to offer, to make a tender of* (*a price*), *esp. at an auction or for work to be undertaken*) make a bid of, make an offer of, offer, proffer, submit, tender. **2** (*to command*) charge, command, direct, enjoin, instruct, order, tell. **3** (*to say*) call, greet, say, tell, wish.
~*n.* (*an offer of a price, e.g. at an auction*) ante, offer, price, submission, tender.

biddable *a.* (*obedient, willing*) amenable, complaisant, cooperative, docile, meek, obedient, tractable. ANTONYMS: disobedient, intractable, refractory.

bidding *n.* **1** (*a bid at an auction*) bid, offer, tender. **2** (*an auction*) auction, sale. **3** (*invitation, command*) behest, command, demand, direction, injunction, instruction, invitation, mandate, order, request, summons.

big *a.* **1** (*large or great in size or intensity*) colossal, enormous, extensive, gigantic, great, huge, hulking, immense, large, mammoth, massive, prodigious, sizeable, spacious, substantial, vast, voluminous. ANTONYMS: diminutive, little, small, tiny. **2** ((*of a person*) *great in size, weight or height*) beefy, brawny, bulky, burly, fat, heavy, huge, hulking, large, muscular, solid, stout, strapping, tall, thickset. ANTONYMS: puny, small, thin, tiny. **3** (*grown up*) adult, full-grown, grown, grown-up, mature. ANTONYMS: juvenile, young. **4** (*important*) critical, crucial, decisive, important, key, major, momentous, of moment, serious, significant, weighty. ANTONYMS: insignificant, minor, unimportant. **5** (*magnanimous*) benevolent, generous, kind, kind-hearted, liberal, magnanimous, unselfish, warm-hearted. ANTONYMS: mean, stingy, unkind. **6** (*boastful, pretentious*) arrogant, boastful, bragging, conceited, haughty, pompous, pretentious, proud. ANTONYMS: humble, modest, self-effacing, unassuming. **7** (*most important, dominant*) distinguished, eminent, foremost, important, leading, main, major, notable, noteworthy, outstanding, powerful, pre-eminent, principal, well-known. ANTONYMS: humble, minor, unimportant, unknown.

bigot *n.* (*a person intolerantly devoted to a particular creed or party*) dogmatist, extremist, fanatic, zealot.

bigoted *a.* (*affected with bigotry*) biased, discriminatory, dogmatic, fanatical, illiberal, intolerant, narrow-minded, partial, partisan, prejudiced, unfair, warped. ANTONYMS: broad-minded, impartial, tolerant.

bigotry *n.* (*the conduct or mental condition of a bigot*) bias, discrimination, dogmatism, fanaticism, intolerance, narrow-mindedness, partiality, prejudice, unfairness. ANTONYMS: broad-mindedness, impartiality, tolerance.

bigwig *n.* (*a person of importance*) (*sl.*) big cheese, (*sl.*) big gun, (*coll.*) big noise, (*coll.*) big shot, celebrity, dignitary, (*sl.*) nob, notable, panjandrum, somebody, VIP. ANTONYMS: cipher, nobody, nonentity.

bilge *n.* (*worthless nonsense*) balderdash, bunkum, claptrap, drivel, gibberish, hogwash, nonsense, (*coll.*) piffle, (*sl.*) poppycock, (*coll.*) rot, rubbish, (*coll.*) tommyrot, (*sl.*) tosh, twaddle.

bilious *a.* **1** (*produced or affected by bile*) ill, liverish, nauseated, out of sorts, queasy, sick. **2** (*peevish, ill-tempered*) bad-tempered, cantankerous, cross, crotchety, grouchy, grumpy, ill-humoured, ill-tempered, irritable, peevish, (*sl.*) ratty, testy, tetchy, touchy. ANTONYMS: even-tempered, good-humoured, well-tempered. **3** ((*of a colour*) *disgusting*) garish, nauseating, violent, vivid.

bilk *v.t.* (*to cheat, to defraud*) cheat, (*sl.*) con, cozen, defraud, diddle, (*coll.*) do, fleece, gull, (*sl.*) rook, swindle.

bill[1] *n.* **1** (*a statement of particulars of goods delivered or services rendered*) account, invoice, reckoning, statement, (*N Am., coll.*) tab, tally. **2** (*a draft of a proposed law*) draft legislation, proposed law, white paper. **3** (*an advertisement or public announcement printed and distributed or posted up*) advertisement, circular, flyer, handbill, handout, leaflet, notice, placard, poster. **4** (*a theatre programme*) list, listing, playbill, programme.
~*v.t.* **1** (*to announce by bills or placards*) advertise, announce, give notice of. **2** (*to put into a programme*) list, schedule, timetable. **3** (*to present an account for payment to*) charge, debit, invoice, present an account to, send (someone) an account, send (someone) an invoice.

bill[2] *n.* (*the horny beak of birds*) beak, mandible.

billow *n.* **1** (*a great swelling wave of the sea*) breaker, roller, wave. **2** (*anything sweeping onwards like a mighty wave*) deluge, flood, outpouring, rush, surge, swell, tide. **3** (*anything curved or swelling like a wave*) cloud, mass.
~*v.i.* **1** (*to surge*) flow, roll, surge, swell. **2** (*to rise in billows*) balloon, belly, puff up, rise up, swell up.

bin *n.* **1** (*a receptacle for storing things*) box, container, receptacle. **2** (*a container for rubbish*) litter bin, (*coll.*) rubbish, rubbish bin, (*N Am.*) trash can, waste bin, waste-paper basket.

bind *v.t.* **1** (*to tie together, to or on something*) attach, fasten, lash, rope, secure, stick, strap, tie, tie up, truss. ANTONYMS: loosen, unfasten, untie. **2** (*to put in bonds, confine*) confine, hamper, hinder, restrain, restrict, shackle. ANTONYMS: free, release. **3** (*to wrap with a cover or bandage*) bandage, cover, dress, wrap. **4** (*to form a border to*) border, edge, finish, hem, trim. **5** (*to oblige, to compel*) compel, constrain, force, necessitate, obligate, oblige, require. ANTONYMS: free, release from.

binding *a.* (*obligatory*) compulsory, irrevocable, mandatory, obligatory, unalterable. ANTONYMS: discretionary, optional, voluntary.

binge *n.* **1** (*a drinking spree*) (*sl.*) bender, (*coll.*) blinder, drinking bout, (*sl.*) jag, (*coll.*) session. **2** (*over-indulgence in anything*) orgy, overload, spree.

biography *n.* (*the history of the life of a person*) (*coll.*) bio, life, life history, life story, profile.

birth *n.* **1** (*the bearing of offspring*) childbirth, confinement, parturition. **2** (*parentage, lineage, esp. high*) ancestry, blood, descent, extraction, genealogy, heritage, line, lineage, origin, parentage, pedigree, race, stock, strain. **3** (*origin, beginning*) beginning, commencement, fountainhead, genesis, source, start. ANTONYMS: conclusion, death, end.

birthmark *n.* (*a mark formed on the body of a child at birth*) blemish, discoloration, naevus.

birthright *n.* (*a basic right. e.g. as a member of a family*) due, heritage, inheritance, patrimony, right.

bisect *v.t.* (*to divide into two (equal) parts*) cut in half, cut in two, divide in two, halve, separate into two parts, split down the middle, split in two.

bisexual *a.* **1** (*having both sexes combined in one individual*) androgynous, hermaphrodite. **2** (*attracted sexually to both sexes*) (*sl.*) AC/DC, (*sl.*) ambidextrous, (*sl.*) bi, (*sl.*) swinging both ways. ANTONYMS: heterosexual, homosexual.

bit[1] *n.* **1** (*a small portion*) (*coll.*) smidgen, soupçon, taste. **2** (*a morsel, a fragment*) chunk, fragment, lump, morsel, mouthful, piece, portion, section, segment, slice, small piece. **3** (*the smallest quantity, a jot*) atom, crumb, grain, hint, iota, jot, mite, particle, scrap, shred, speck, suggestion, tinge, trace, whit. **4** (*a brief period of time*) flash, instant, (*coll.*) jiffy, little, little while, minute, moment, second, (*coll.*) tick, two shakes of a lamb's tail.

bit[2] *n.* (*the iron part of the bridle inserted in the mouth of a horse*) curb, restraint, snaffle. **to take the bit between one's teeth** (*to act decisively*) get down to it, get serious, get stuck in, put one's shoulder to the wheel, set to.

bitch *n.* (*a malicious or spiteful woman*) harpy, hell-cat, she-devil, shrew, termagant, virago, vixen.
~*v.i.* **1** (*to moan, complain*) (*sl.*) beef, (*coll.*) bellyache, carp, cavil, complain, gripe, grouse, grumble, moan, whine. **2** (*to make unpleasant remarks*) be malicious, be spiteful, speak maliciously, speak slanderously.
~*v.t.* (*to mess up, botch*) botch, bungle, mess up, ruin, (*sl.*) screw up, spoil, wreck.

bitchy *a.* (*spiteful*) catty, malicious, mean, nasty, shrewish, snide, spiteful, venomous, vindictive. ANTONYMS: kindly, nice, pleasant.

bite *v.t.* **1** (*to cut or crush with the teeth*) chew, gnaw at, munch, nibble. **2** (*to tear at with the teeth*) nip, sink one's teeth into, tear at. **3** (*to pierce (as) with the teeth, to sting*) pierce, prick, puncture, sting. **4** (*to hold fast, as an anchor or screw*) clamp, grip, take hold. **5** (*to corrode*) burn, corrode, eat away at, eat into, erode, wear away.
~*v.i.* **1** (*to take a bait*) be enticed, be lured, be tempted, rise to the bait, take the bait. **2** (*to have an effect*) have results, take effect, work.
~*n.* **1** (*a wound made by the teeth*) lesion, nip, puncture, wound. **2** (*a mouthful, a small quantity*) bit, morsel, mouthful, piece, taste.

3 (*pungency*) edge, kick, piquancy, punch, pungency, sharpness, spice, spiciness. **4** (*a small meal, a snack*) a bite to eat, a little something, meal, refreshment, snack.

biting *a.* **1** (*sharp, keen*) bitterly cold, cutting, keen, penetrating, piercing, sharp, stinging. **2** (*stinging, sarcastic*) acid, caustic, cutting, incisive, mordant, sarcastic, sharp, stinging, trenchant, vitriolic, withering.

bitter *a.* **1** (*sharp or biting to the taste*) acid, acrid, astringent, harsh, sharp, sour, tart, unsweetened, vinegary. ANTONYMS: sugary, sweet. **2** (*angry and resentful*) acrimonious, begrudging, embittered, grudging, rancorous, resentful, sour. ANTONYMS: forgiving, gracious. **3** (*painful, distressing*) distressing, harrowing, painful, poignant, unhappy. ANTONYMS: happy, pleasant. **4** (*piercingly cold*) biting, cutting, harsh, intensely cold, keen, penetrating, piercing, sharp, stinging. **5** (*harsh, virulent*) acrimonious, hostile, malevolent, rancorous, vicious, virulent. ANTONYMS: amicable, friendly.

bitterness *n.* **1** (*sharpness of taste*) acidity, acridity, acridness, astringency, harshness, sharpness, sourness, tartness, vinegariness. ANTONYMS: sugariness, sweetness. **2** (*anger, resentment*) acrimony, embitteredness, grudge, grudgingness, rancour, resentment, sourness. ANTONYMS: grace, happiness. **3** (*great distress*) agony, distress, pain, painfulness, poignancy, unhappiness. **4** (*intense cold*) bite, harshness, keenness, sharpness, sting. **5** (*malevolence*) acrimony, hostility, malevolence, rancour, viciousness, virulence. ANTONYMS: amicability.

bizarre *a.* (*odd, strange*) abnormal, comical, curious, deviant, eccentric, extraordinary, freakish, grotesque, irregular, ludicrous, odd, oddball, (*coll.*) offbeat, off the wall, outlandish, outré, peculiar, queer, ridiculous, (*sl.*) rum, strange, unconventional, unusual, (*sl.*) wacky, weird, zany. ANTONYMS: normal, run-of-the-mill, usual.

blab *v.t.* (*to reveal indiscreetly*) blurt out, disclose, divulge, let slip, reveal, tell.
~*v.i.* (*to talk indiscreetly, to tell secrets*) let the cat out of the bag, (*sl.*) sing, squeal, tell, tell tales. ANTONYMS: keep a secret, keep one's mouth shut, keep (something) under wraps.

black *a.* **1** (*intensely dark in colour*) coal-black, dark, dusky, ebony, inky, jet-black, pitch-black, raven, sable. ANTONYMS: light, milk-white, white. **2** (*dark-skinned, esp. of African descent*) coloured, dark-skinned, Negro, Negroid. ANTONYMS: Caucasian, white. **3** ((*of the sky*) *heavily overcast*) cloudy, dark, gloomy, murky, overcast. ANTONYMS: bright, clear. **4** (*having no light*) moonless, pitch-dark, starless, unlit. **5** (*angry*) aggressive, angry, belligerent, enraged, furious,

hostile, menacing, sullen, threatening. ANTONYMS: calm, friendly, peaceful. **6** (*atrociously wicked*) bad, corrupt, criminal, depraved, evil, immoral, iniquitous, nefarious, sinful, vile, villainous, wicked. ANTONYMS: good, moral, pure, virtuous. **7** (*dismal, mournful*) depressing, disastrous, dismal, distressing, doleful, gloomy, melancholy, mournful, negative, ominous, sad, sombre, unfortunate, unhappy. ANTONYMS: bright, cheerful, happy, positive. **8** (*dirty*) dingy, dirty, filthy, grimy, grubby, muddy, soiled, sooty, stained, unclean. ANTONYMS: clean, spotless. **9** ((*of humour*) *macabre*) cynical, dark, macabre, sick.
~*v.t.* **1** (*to soil*) besmirch, dirty, muddy, stain, sully. **2** (*to place under a trade union ban*) ban, bar, blacklist, boycott, embargo. **in the black** (*having money*) in credit, in funds, solvent, without debt. ANTONYMS: in debt, in the red.

black and white *a.* **1** (*recorded in writing or print*) clearly defined, in print, in writing, written down. ANTONYMS: spoken, vague. **2** (*divided into two extremes, not admitting of compromise*) absolute, categorical, uncompromising, unequivocal. ANTONYMS: grey.

blackball *v.t.* (*to exclude*) ban, bar, blacklist, debar, exclude, ostracize, reject, repudiate, shut out, vote against. ANTONYMS: vote for, welcome.

blacken *v.t.* **1** (*to make black, to darken*) begrime, darken, make black, make dirty, make sooty, soil, stain. **2** (*to sully, to defame*) (*coll.*) bad-mouth, besmirch, calumniate, decry, defame, denigrate, drag through the mud, rubbish, (*sl.*) slag off, slander, smear, speak ill of, stain, sully, taint, tarnish, vilify.

blackguard *n.* (*a scoundrel*) (*dated*) cad, rascal, (*coll.*) rat, rogue, (*coll.*) rotter, scoundrel, swine, villain.

blacklist *v.t.* (*to ban or prohibit* (*books etc.*)) ban, bar, blackball, boycott, debar, exclude, preclude, prohibit, reject, repudiate.

black magic *n.* (*magic, necromancy*) black art, magic, necromancy, occultism, sorcery, the occult, voodoo, witchcraft, wizardry.

blackmail *n.* **1** (*any payment extorted by intimidation*) (*sl.*) hush money, protection money, ransom. **2** (*the use of threats or pressure to influence someone's actions*) extortion, intimidation.
~*v.t.* **1** (*to levy blackmail on*) extort money from, hold to ransom, milk money from. **2** (*to threaten*) coerce, compel, force, threaten.

blackout *n.* **1** (*a temporary loss of consciousness*) coma, faint, (*coll.*) flaking-out, loss of consciousness, passing-out, swoon, unconsciousness. **2** (*an electrical power failure*)

electricity failure, power cut, power failure. **3** (*a suppression of communications*) censorship, non-communication, suppression of information, withholding of information.
~*v.t.* **1** (*to censor or suppress* (*a broadcast etc.*)) censor, suppress, withhold. **2** (*to obscure* (*windows*), *extinguish* (*lights etc.*)) cloak, conceal, cover, shade.
~*v.i.* (*to suffer a temporary loss of consciousness*) collapse, faint, (*coll.*) flake out, lose consciousness, pass out, swoon.

black sheep *n.* (*a bad member of a group or family*) disgrace, ne'er-do-well, prodigal, reprobate, wastrel.

blame *v.t.* **1** (*to censure, to find fault with*) accuse, admonish, censure, chide, condemn, criticize, find fault with, reproach, reprove, scold, upbraid. ANTONYMS: acclaim, commend, praise. **2** (*to hold responsible*) ascribe, attribute, hold accountable, hold liable, hold responsible, impute, lay (something) at the door of, pin (something) on, (*sl.*) stick (something) on. ANTONYMS: absolve, acquit, exonerate, vindicate.
~*n.* **1** (*the expression of censure*) accusation, censure, condemnation, criticism, fault-finding, recrimination, reproach. ANTONYMS: acclaim, commendation, credit, praise. **2** (*responsibility, accountability*) accountability, culpability, fault, guilt, liability, (*coll.*) rap, responsibility. ANTONYMS: absolution, acquittal, exoneration, vindication. **to be to blame** (*to be culpable*) be at fault, be blameworthy, be culpable, be guilty. ANTONYMS: be blameless, be innocent.

blameless *a.* (*free from blame*) above reproach, above suspicion, guiltless, innocent, in the clear, irreproachable, not guilty, not responsible, not to blame, (*coll.*) squeaky-clean. ANTONYMS: at fault, culpable, guilty, responsible.

blameworthy *a.* (*deserving blame*) at fault, culpable, guilty, to blame. ANTONYMS: blameless, innocent.

blanch *v.t.* (*to bleach, to make pale*) bleach, fade, make pale, make pallid, whiten.
~*v.i.* (*to become white*) become white, go pale, grow pale, lose colour. ANTONYMS: blush, go red.

bland *a.* **1** (*having very little taste*) flavourless, insipid, tasteless. ANTONYMS: flavoursome, sapid, tasty. **2** (*dull, insipid*) boring, dull, flat, humdrum, insipid, monotonous, nondescript, tedious, unexciting, uninspiring, uninteresting, vapid. ANTONYMS: exciting, inspiring, interesting, stimulating. **3** (*mild, gentle*) balmy, gentle, mild, soft, soothing. ANTONYMS: harsh, rough, severe. **4** (*genial, affable*) affable, amiable, courteous, genial, placid, smooth, suave, undemonstrative, urbane. ANTONYMS: rough, volatile.

blandishment *n.* (*cajolery, charm*) blarney, cajolery, compliment, flattery, ingratiation, (*coll.*) soft soap, (*coll.*) sweet talk. ANTONYMS: insult.

blank *a.* **1** (*empty, vacant*) bare, clear, empty, unfilled, vacant, void. **2** (*without expression*) deadpan, empty, expressionless, impassive, poker-faced, vacant, vacuous. ANTONYMS: expressive. **3** (*not written or printed on*) bare, clean, empty, uncompleted, unmarked, white. ANTONYMS: filled-in, marked, written-on. **4** (*confused, dispirited*) bewildered, confused, nonplussed, perplexed, puzzled, uncomprehending. ANTONYMS: comprehending, understanding. **5** (*pure, downright*) absolute, categorical, downright, outright, unqualified, utter. ANTONYMS: qualified.
~*n.* **1** (*a blank space in a written or printed document*) box, space. **2** (*a vacant space, a void*) emptiness, empty space, space, vacuum, void.

blanket *n.* **1** (*a piece of woollen or other warm material, used as bed-covering*) bedcover, bedspread, cover, covering, coverlet, rug, spread. **2** (*a thick covering of, e.g. snow*) carpet, cloak, coat, coating.
~*a.* (*covering all conditions or cases*) across-the-board, comprehensive, general, inclusive, overall, sweeping, universal, wide-ranging. ANTONYMS: limited, restricted.
~*v.t.* **1** (*to cover with or as with a blanket*) carpet, coat, cover, overlay. **2** (*to stifle*) eclipse, extinguish, obscure, stifle, suppress.

blare *v.i.* **1** (*to roar, bellow*) bellow, blast, boom, resound, roar, scream. ANTONYMS: murmur, whisper. **2** (*to sound as a trumpet*) honk, toot, trumpet.

blarney *n.* (*smooth, flattering speech*) blandishment, flattery, honeyed words, smooth talk, (*coll.*) soft soap, (*coll.*) sweet talk.

blasé *a.* (*dulled in sense or emotion*) apathetic, bored, indifferent, jaded, uncaring, unexcited, uninterested, unmoved, world-weary. ANTONYMS: eager, enthusiastic, excited, interested.

blaspheme *v.t.* (*to utter profane language against* (*God or anything sacred*)) desecrate, profane. ANTONYMS: respect, revere.
~*v.i.* (*to utter blasphemy, to rail*) curse, (*coll.*) cuss, swear, utter oaths, utter profanities.

blasphemous *a.* (*grossly irreverent or impious*) godless, impious, irreligious, irreverent, profane, sacrilegious, ungodly, unholy. ANTONYMS: godly, holy, pious, reverent.

blasphemy *n.* **1** (*profane language towards God or about sacred things*) curses, oaths, profanities, swearing. **2** (*impious irreverence*) desecration, godlessness, impiety, irreverence, profaneness, profanity, sacrilege, ungodliness. ANTONYMS: godliness, holiness, piety.

blast *n.* **1** (*a violent gust of wind*) draught, gale, gust, rush, squall, storm, tempest. **2** (*the sound of a trumpet or the like*) bellow, blare, blaring, boom, roar. **3** (*a blowing by explosive*) blowing-up, detonation, explosion. **4** (*a severe reprimand*) (*sl.*) bollocking, castigation, chiding, rebuke, reprimand, reproof, scolding. ANTONYMS: commendation, praise.

~*v.t.* **1** (*to blow or breathe on so as to wither*) blight, destroy, kill, ruin, shrivel, spoil, wither, wreck. ANTONYMS: foster, help. **2** (*to blow up with explosive*) blow up, demolish, explode, raze to the ground. **3** (*to reprimand*) (*sl.*) bollock, castigate, chide, criticize, lambast, rebuke, reprimand, reprove, scold, (*coll.*) tear off a strip. ANTONYMS: commend, praise.

~*v.i.* (*to emit a blast*) bellow, blare, boom, roar.

blasted *a.* (*blighted*) benighted, blighted, destroyed, devastated, ruined, shrivelled, spoiled, wasted, withered, wrecked. ANTONYMS: flourishing, thriving.

blast-off *n.* (*the launch of a rocket-propelled missile or space vehicle*) launch, lift-off, take-off.

blatant *a.* (*very obvious, palpable*) barefaced, brazen, conspicuous, flagrant, glaring, manifest, noticeable, obtrusive, obvious, overt, pronounced, shameless. ANTONYMS: discreet, subtle, unobtrusive.

blaze *n.* **1** (*a bright glowing flame*) flame, flames. **2** (*a large dangerous fire*) conflagration, fire, flames, inferno. **3** (*a glow of bright light or colour*) beam, flare, flash, glare, glitter, glow. **4** (*an outburst of display, splendour*) display, outburst. **5** (*an outburst of passion*) burst, eruption, explosion, flare-up, outbreak, outburst, rush, storm, torrent.

~*v.i.* **1** (*to burn with a bright flame*) be ablaze, burn, flame, flare up. **2** (*to shine, to glitter*) beam, flash, gleam, glitter, glow, shine. **3** (*to be bright with colour*) be brightly coloured, be brilliant, be colourful, be resplendent, be vibrant, glow.

blazing *a.* **1** (*emitting flame or light*) ablaze, alight, burning, flaming, on fire. **2** (*radiant, lustrous*) ablaze, aglow, alight, illuminated, lit up, lustrous, radiant, shining. **3** (*very angry*) enraged, fuming, furious, hot under the collar, in a temper, in a towering rage, incensed, infuriated, livid, raging, wrathful.

blazon *v.t.* (*to proclaim, to trumpet*) advertise, broadcast, proclaim, publicize, trumpet. ANTONYMS: conceal, keep secret, suppress.

bleach *v.t.* (*to make white by exposure to the sun or by chemical agents*) blanch, decolorize, fade, lighten, make pale, make paler, make white, make whiter, pale, wash out, whiten.

~*v.i.* (*to grow white*) blanch, fade, grow pale, grow paler, grow white, grow whiter, lighten.

bleak *a.* **1** (*bare of vegetation*) arid, bare, barren, desolate, exposed, unproductive, unsheltered, waste. ANTONYMS: fertile, productive, sheltered. **2** (*desolate, cheerless*) cheerless, comfortless, dark, depressing, desolate, disheartening, dismal, drab, dreary, gloomy, hopeless, joyless, miserable, sombre, wretched. ANTONYMS: bright, cheerful, cosy.

bleary *a.* **1** ((*of eyes*) *looking tired or as if one has been crying*) rheumy, sleep-filled, sleepy, tired, watery. **2** (*unclear, blurred*) blurred, blurry, cloudy, dim, foggy, fuzzy, hazy, indistinct, misty, murky, unclear. ANTONYMS: clear, distinct.

bleed *v.i.* **1** (*to emit or discharge blood*) lose blood, run with blood, shed blood. **2** (*to feel acute mental pain*) ache, agonize, be distressed, grieve, hurt, mourn, sorrow, suffer.

~*v.t.* (*to extort money from*) extort, extract, fleece, milk, squeeze.

blemish *v.t.* **1** (*to spoil the appearance of*) damage, deface, discolour, disfigure, impair, mar, mark, scar, spoil. **2** (*to tarnish, to sully*) blot, damage, flaw, stain, sully, taint, tarnish.

~*n.* **1** (*a physical stain, an imperfection*) birthmark, blotch, discoloration, disfigurement, mark, naevus, scar, spot. **2** (*a moral defect, a flaw*) blot, defect, fault, flaw, stain, taint.

blench *v.i.* (*to shrink back, to draw back*) flinch, recoil, shy, start, wince.

blend *v.t.* (*to mix, to mingle* (*e.g. teas or other food*)) amalgamate, combine, fuse, intermix, merge, mingle, mix, mix together, synthesize, unite. ANTONYMS: separate.

~*v.i.* (*to form a harmonious union or compound*) complement each other, fit together, go well, harmonize. ANTONYMS: clash.

~*n.* (*a mixture of various qualities* (*of teas, wines etc.*)) admixture, alloy, amalgam, amalgamation, combination, composite, compound, fusion, mix, mixture, synthesis, union.

bless *v.t.* **1** (*to consecrate, to hallow*) consecrate, hallow, sanctify. ANTONYMS: curse. **2** (*to extol, worship*) exalt, extol, glorify, magnify, praise. **3** (*to thank*) be grateful to, give thanks to. ANTONYMS: curse. **4** (*to give a special quality to*) bestow, endow, favour, furnish, give, grant, provide.

blessed *a.* **1** (*consecrated by religious rites*) consecrated, divine, hallowed, holy, sacred, sanctified. ANTONYMS: cursed. **2** (*worthy of veneration*) extolled, revered, venerated. **3** (*joyful, blissful*) blissful, glad, happy, joyful. ANTONYMS: miserable, unhappy.

blessing *n.* **1** (*consecration*) consecration, hallowing, sanctification, sanctifying. ANTONYMS: cursing. **2** (*a cause of happiness*) advantage, benefit, boon, bounty, favour, gift, godsend, good fortune. ANTONYMS: curse, disadvantage. **3** (*grace before or after meat*) benediction, grace. **4** (*approval, support*) approbation, approval, backing, consent, endorsement, favour, permission, sanction, support, (*coll.*) the green light, thumbs up. ANTONYMS: disapproval, rejection, (*coll.*) the red light, thumbs down.

blight *n.* **1** (*a disease affecting the growth of plants*) canker, disease, infestation, plague. **2** (*any spoiling or malignant influence*) affliction, bane, calamity, curse, evil, ill luck, misfortune, pestilence, plague, scourge, tribulation, trouble. ANTONYMS: blessing, good fortune.
~*v.t.* **1** (*to affect with blight*) blast, destroy, kill, shrivel, wither. **2** (*to mar, frustrate*) crush, dash, destroy, frustrate, mar, ruin, spoil, undo, wreck.

blind *a.* **1** (*destitute of sight*) sightless, (*dated*) stone-blind, unseeing, unsighted, visually challenged. ANTONYMS: seeing, sighted. **2** (*unseen, dark*) concealed, hidden, obscured, unseen. **3** (*having no outlet*) blocked off, closed off, deadend, exitless. **4** (*destitute of understanding or foresight*) dense, dim, imperceptive, insensitive, obtuse, slow, undiscerning. ANTONYMS: discerning, perceptive. **5** (*reckless, heedless*) careless, frantic, heedless, impetuous, mindless, rash, reckless, thoughtless, uncontrolled, unrestrained, unthinking, wild. ANTONYMS: careful, cautious. **6** (*without thinking, undiscerning*) indiscriminate, instinctive, intuitive, uncritical, undiscerning, unreasoned, unthinking. ANTONYMS: reasoned.
~*n.* **1** (*a pretence, a pretext*) camouflage, cloak, cover, disguise, facade, front, mask, screen, smokescreen. **2** (*a window-screen or shade, esp. one on rollers for coiling up*) roller blind, screen, shade, shutter, venetian blind.
~*v.t.* **1** (*to make blind (permanently or temporarily)*) dazzle, deprive of sight, get in (someone's) line of sight, make blind, obscure (someone's) vision. **2** (*to deceive*) deceive, delude, hoodwink. **3** (*to darken the understanding of*) bamboozle, bewilder, confound, confuse, muddle. **blind to** (*incapable of appreciating*) heedless of, ignorant of, inattentive to, oblivious to, unaware of, unconscious of, unmindful of. ANTONYMS: aware of, conscious of.

blindly *adv.* **1** (*without sight*) sightlessly, unseeing, without sight. **2** (*recklessly, heedlessly*) carelessly, frantically, heedlessly, impetuously, mindlessly, rashly, recklessly, thoughtlessly, uncontrolledly, unrestrainedly, wildly. ANTONYMS: carefully, cautiously. **3** (*without thinking, undiscerningly*) indiscriminately, instinctively, intuitively, uncritically, undiscerningly, without thinking. ANTONYMS: rationally.

blink *v.i.* **1** (*to open and shut the eyes*) nictitate, wink. **2** (*to look with winking eyelids, to look unsteadily*) peer, squint, wink. **3** (*to shine fitfully*) flash, flicker, glimmer, glitter, sparkle, twinkle, waver, wink.
~*v.t.* (*to shut the eyes to*) condone, connive at, disregard, ignore, overlook, shut one's eyes to, take no notice of, turn a blind eye to.

bliss *n.* (*happiness of the highest kind*) (*coll.*) cloud nine, delight, ecstasy, elation, euphoria, happiness, joy, rapture, seventh heaven. ANTONYMS: despondency, gloom, misery.

blissful *a.* **1** (*full of bliss*) cock-a-hoop, delighted, ecstatic, elated, enraptured, euphoric, in ecstasies, in raptures, in seventh heaven, joyful, joyous, (*coll.*) on cloud nine, over the moon. ANTONYMS: despondent, gloomy, miserable, wretched. **2** (*causing bliss*) glorious, great, marvellous, terrific, wonderful.

blister *n.* **1** (*a swelling raised on the skin caused by some injury, burn etc. and containing a watery fluid*) abscess, bleb, boil, carbuncle, cyst, pustule, swelling, vesicle, wen. **2** (*any similar swelling on metal, a painted surface etc.*) bubble, bulge, protuberance, swelling.

blithe *a.* **1** (*cheerful, joyous*) carefree, cheerful, (*coll.*) chirpy, frisky, gay, happy, jolly, joyful. ANTONYMS: depressed, despondent. **2** (*merry, sprightly*) jolly, light-hearted, merry, sprightly. **3** (*casual, indifferent*) blasé, careless, casual, indifferent, nonchalant, uncaring, unconcerned, untroubled, unworried. ANTONYMS: careful, concerned.

blitz *n.* **1** (*intense enemy onslaught, esp. an air raid*) air raid, assault, attack, bombardment, offensive, onslaught, raid, strike. **2** (*intensive activity*) all-out effort, assault, attack, onslaught.

blizzard *n.* (*a furious storm of snow and wind*) snow squall, snowstorm.

bloat *v.t.* (*to cause to swell*) balloon, blow up, dilate, distend, enlarge, extend, inflate, puff, swell.

blob *n.* **1** (*a globular drop of liquid*) bead, bubble, drop, droplet, globule. **2** (*any vague, soft form*) lump, mass.

bloc *n.* (*a combination of parties, or of nations*) alliance, cabal, clique, coalition, combination, combine, coterie, faction, federation, group, league, party, ring, schism, syndicate, union, wing.

block *n.* **1** (*a solid unshaped mass of any material*) bar, brick, cake, chunk, cube, hunk, lump, mass, piece, square, wedge. **2** (*a large building, esp. one that is divided*) building, complex, department. **3** (*a hindrance, an impediment*) bar,

barrier, check, hindrance, hurdle, impediment, obstacle, stumbling-block. **4** (*an obstruction, a blockage*) blockage, obstruction, occlusion, stoppage. **5** (*a quantity of things treated as a unit*) band, batch, cluster, group, quantity, set.
~*v.t.* **1** (*to stop up, to obstruct*) bung up, choke, clog, obstruct, plug, stop up. ANTONYMS: clear, unblock. **2** (*to impede (progress or advance)*) arrest, check, deter, frustrate, halt, hinder, impede, obstruct, stand in the way, stop, thwart. ANTONYMS: expedite, facilitate, promote. **3** (*to shape (a hat) on the block*) fashion, form, mould, shape.

blockade *n.* **1** (*the besieging of a place, so as to compel surrender by starvation*) beleaguerment, investment, siege. **2** (*anything that prevents access or progress*) barricade, barrier, obstacle, obstruction.

blockage *n.* (*an obstruction*) block, obstruction, occlusion, stoppage.

bloke *n.* (*a man, a fellow*) (*coll.*) bod, (*coll.*) chap, (*coll.*) customer, fellow, (*coll.*) geezer, (*coll.*) guy, man, (*coll.*) punter.

blond, blonde *a.* **1** (*fair or light in colour*) fair, flaxen, golden, light. ANTONYMS: dark. **2** (*having light hair and a fair complexion*) fair, fair-haired, golden-haired, light-haired. ANTONYMS: brunette.

blood *n.* **1** (*lineage, descent*) ancestry, birth, descent, extraction, family, genealogy, heritage, line, lineage, origin, pedigree, race, stock, strain. **2** (*temperament, passion*) disposition, humour, kidney, nature, passion, spirit, temper, temperament.

blood-curdling *a.* (*horrifying*) chilling, dreadful, hair-raising, horrendous, spine-chilling, terrifying.

bloodless *a.* **1** (*without effusion of blood*) nonviolent, peaceful. **2** (*very pale*) anaemic, colourless, pale, pallid, wan. **3** (*spiritless*) apathetic, emotionless, languid, listless, passionless, phlegmatic, sluggish, torpid, unemotional, unfeeling. ANTONYMS: emotionless, passionate.

bloodshed *n.* (*the act of shedding blood*) carnage, killing, massacre, murder, slaughter, slaying.

bloodthirsty *a.* (*eager to shed blood*) homicidal, murderous, savage, warlike.

bloody *a.* **1** (*stained or running with blood*) bleeding, blood-soaked, blood-spattered, bloodstained, unstaunched. **2** (*cruel, murderous*) bloodthirsty, cruel, homicidal, murderous, savage, vicious.

bloom *n.* **1** (*a flower*) blossom, efflorescence,

flower. **2** (*flush, glow*) flush, freshness, glow, lustre, radiance. **3** (*prime, perfection*) heyday, peak, perfection, prime, strength, vigour.
~*v.i.* **1** (*to blossom, to come into flower*) be flowering, be in bloom, be in flower, blossom, come into flower, come out, flower, open out. ANTONYMS: fade, wilt, wither. **2** (*to develop to the highest point of perfection or beauty*) blossom, do well, flourish, get on well, prosper, succeed, thrive. ANTONYMS: decline, do badly, fade.

blossom *n.* (*a flower*) bloom, efflorescence, flower.
~*v.i.* **1** (*to bloom*) be in bloom, be in flower, bloom, flower. **2** (*to flourish*) bloom, burgeon, do well, flourish, get on well, prosper, succeed, thrive. ANTONYMS: decline, do badly, fade.

blot *n.* **1** (*a stain of ink or other discolouring matter*) blotch, mark, patch, smear, smudge, splodge, spot, stain. **2** (*a disgrace, defect*) blemish, defect, disgrace, fault, flaw, imperfection, scar, stain, taint, tarnishing.
~*v.t.* **1** (*to stain with ink or other discolouring matter*) blotch, mark, smear, smudge, spot, stain. **2** (*to dry or remove with a soft paper or cloth*) absorb, dry up, soak up, take up. **3** (*to disfigure, to sully*) besmirch, blacken, damage, disgrace, sully, taint, tarnish. **to blot out** (*to obliterate, to efface*) efface, erase, expunge, obliterate, wipe out.

blotch *n.* **1** (*a mark on the skin*) birthmark, blemish, eruption, mark, naevus, patch, pimple, pustule, spot. **2** (*a blot*) blot, mark, patch, smear, smudge, splodge, spot, stain.

blotchy *a.* (*full of blotches*) blemished, patchy, reddened, spotty.

blow[1] *v.i.* **1** (*to move as a current of air*) flow, waft. **2** (*to send a current of air from the mouth*) breathe, gasp, pant, puff. **3** (*to boast*) boast, brag, crow, talk big.
~*v.t.* **1** (*to drive a current of air upon*) drive, sweep, toss, waft, whirl. **2** (*to sound (a wind instrument or a note on it)*) blare, blast, play, sound, toot, trumpet. **3** (*to spoil (an opportunity)*) botch, bungle, (*coll.*) make a hash of, make a mess of, mar, muff, ruin, (*sl.*) screw up, spoil, wreck. **4** (*to squander*) (*coll.*) binge, dissipate, fritter away, lavish, squander.
~*n.* **1** (*a blast of air*) blare, blast, blowing, sounding, toot. **2** (*a breath of fresh air*) blast of air, breath of fresh air, breeze, draught, gust, puff of wind, wind. **3** (*a boast*) boast, bragging, crowing. **to blow out 1** (*to extinguish by blowing*) douse, extinguish, put out, snuff out. **2** ((*of a tyre*) *to burst*) break open, burst, erupt, explode, puncture, rupture. **to blow over** (*to pass away, to subside*) be forgotten, cease, die down, disappear, end, finish, pass, pass away, sink into

oblivion, subside, vanish. **to blow up 1** (*to inflate*) balloon, distend, enlarge, expand, inflate, puff up, pump up, swell up. ANTONYMS: contract, deflate, let down. **2** (*to explode*) detonate, explode, fragment, go off. **3** (*to destroy by explosion*) blast, bomb, detonate, explode. **4** (*to exaggerate*) colour, embroider, exaggerate, heighten, magnify, overstate. ANTONYMS: minimize, understate. **5** (*to lose one's temper*) become angry, become enraged, blow a fuse, erupt, (*coll.*) fly off the handle, go off the deep end, (*coll.*) hit the roof, (*coll.*) lose one's cool, lose one's temper, see red. ANTONYMS: keep calm, (*coll.*) keep one's cool.

blow² *n.* **1** (*a stroke with the fist or any weapon*) bang, bash, belt, buffet, clout, hit, knock, punch, rap, smack, (*sl.*) sock, thump, thwack, (*coll.*) wallop, whack. **2** (*a severe shock*) bolt from the blue, bombshell, calamity, catastrophe, disaster, jolt, reverse, setback, shock, upset.

blow-out *n.* **1** (*a hearty meal*) banquet, (*sl.*) bash, (*coll.*) beanfeast, (*coll.*) binge, celebration, feast, spree. **2** (*the puncturing of a tyre*) burst tyre, flat, flat tyre, puncture.

blowy *a.* (*windy*) blustery, breezy, draughty, stormy, windy. ANTONYMS: calm, still.

blowzy *a.* **1** (*having a red, bloated face*) florid, red-faced, ruddy, weathered. **2** (*untidy, sluttish*) dishevelled, slatternly, slipshod, slovenly, sluttish, tousled, unkempt, untidy. ANTONYMS: neat, neat and tidy, tidy.

bludgeon *n.* (*a short, thick stick*) blackjack, club, cosh, cudgel, (*Ir.*) shillelagh, truncheon.
~*v.t.* **1** (*to strike with a bludgeon or similar instrument*) beat, club, cosh, cudgel, hit, strike. **2** (*to coerce verbally, or by physical force*) browbeat, (*coll.*) bulldoze, coerce, compel, dragoon, force, pressurize, railroad, steamroller, strong-arm.

blue *a.* **1** (*of the colour of the cloudless sky*) azure, cerulean, cobalt, cyan, indigo, navy, navy-blue, powder-blue, royal blue, sapphire, ultramarine. **2** (*miserable, low-spirited*) dejected, depressed, despondent, downcast, downhearted, down in the dumps, (*coll.*) fed up, gloomy, glum, low, low in spirits, melancholic, miserable, morose, sad, unhappy, wretched. ANTONYMS: cheerful, happy. **3** (*obscene, smutty*) bawdy, coarse, dirty, indecent, lewd, naughty, near the bone, near the knuckle, obscene, risqué, smutty, vulgar. ANTONYMS: clean, decent, respectable. **out of the blue** (*unexpectedly*) all of a sudden, suddenly, unexpectedly, without warning.

blueprint *n.* (*any original plan for future work*) design, draft, guideline, layout, pattern, pilot scheme, plan, prototype, representation, scheme, sketch.

blues *n.pl.* (*low spirits, depression*) dejection, depression, despondency, downheartedness, gloom, glumness, low spirits, melancholy, misery, moroseness, sadness, unhappiness.

bluff¹ *a.* **1** ((*of a cliff, or a ship's bows*) *having a broad, flattened front*) blunt, flat, sheer. **2** (*blunt, outspoken*) abrupt, blunt, brusque, candid, curt, direct, frank, open, outspoken, plain-spoken, short, straightforward. ANTONYMS: diplomatic, subtle, tactful.
~*n.* (*a cliff with a broad, precipitous front*) bank, cape, cliff, headland, promontory, slope.

bluff² *n.* (*an act of bluffing*) cheat, (*sl.*) con, deceit, deception, fake, fraud, pretence, sham, trick.
~*v.t.* (*to hoodwink*) cheat, (*sl.*) con, deceive, delude, hoodwink, mislead, (*coll.*) put one over on, trick.
~*v.i.* (*to make one's adversary believe that one is strong*) fake it, feign, pretend, put it on, sham.

blunder *v.i.* **1** (*to err grossly*) be guilty of an oversight, (*coll.*) blow it, (*coll.*) boob, (*sl.*) drop a clanger, err, make a mistake, (*sl.*) screw up, slip up. **2** (*to flounder, to stumble*) flounder, lurch, stagger, stumble.
~*n.* (*a stupid error*) (*sl.*) bloomer, (*coll.*) boob, (*sl.*) booboo, (*sl.*) clanger, error, faux pas, gaffe, inaccuracy, mistake, oversight, slip, slip-up.

blunt *a.* **1** (*without edge or point*) dull, not sharp, unsharpened. ANTONYMS: sharp. **2** (*abrupt, unceremonious*) abrupt, bluff, brusque, candid, curt, direct, frank, open, outspoken, plain-spoken, short, straightforward. ANTONYMS: diplomatic, indirect, subtle, tactful.
~*v.t.* (*to make less sharp or keen*) dampen, dull, make blunt, take the edge off, weaken. ANTONYMS: sharpen.

blur *n.* (*a smear, a stain*) blot, blotch, smear, smudge, spot.
~*v.t.* **1** (*to smear, to blot*) besmear, blot, blotch, smear, smudge, spot. **2** (*to render misty and indistinct*) bedim, make hazy, make indistinct, make vague. ANTONYMS: make clear, make distinct.

blurred *a.* (*unclear*) blurry, faint, fuzzy, hazy, indistinct, misty, unclear, vague. ANTONYMS: clear, distinct.

blurt *v.t.* (*to utter abruptly* (*usu. with out*)) blab, call out, cry out, disclose, divulge, exclaim, let slip, reveal, tell. ANTONYMS: keep secret, suppress.

blush *v.i.* (*to become red in the face from shame or other emotion*) (*coll.*) burn up, colour, crimson, flush, go crimson, go red, go scarlet, redden, turn crimson, turn red. ANTONYMS: blanch, go pale, pale.

~n. (*the reddening of the face produced by shame, modesty etc.*) colour, flush, glow, reddening, redness, rosiness, ruddiness. ANTONYMS: paleness, pallor, whiteness.

bluster *v.i.* **1** (*to blow boisterously*) blast, gust, roar. **2** (*to swagger, to boast*) act the bully, boast, brag, issue threats, play the bully, rant, swagger, throw one's weight around.
~n. (*empty vaunts and threats*) boasting, bragging, bullying, swaggering, threatening.

blustery *a.* (*blowing boisterously*) blowy, boisterous, gusting, gusty, squally, stormy, tempestuous, wild. ANTONYMS: calm, still.

board *n.* **1** (*a piece of timber of considerable length*) length of wood, panel, piece of timber, piece of wood, plank, slat. **2** (*meals provided in a hotel etc.*) food, keep, meals. **3** (*the people who have the management of some public trust or business concern*) board of directors, committee, directorate, directors, governors, management, panel of trustees, trustees.
~v.t. **1** (*to furnish or cover with boards*) close up, cover up, seal, shut up. **2** (*to provide with daily meals and usu. lodging*) put up, take in. **3** (*to go on (a ship)*) embark, enter, get on, go aboard, go on board, step aboard. ANTONYMS: disembark, get off.
~v.i. (*to have one's meals and usu. lodging at another person's house*) have lodgings, have rooms, live, lodge, room.

boast *n.* **1** (*excessively proud assertion*) bluster, brag, crowing, vaunt. **2** (*an occasion of pride*) jewel, pride, pride and joy, source of joy, source of pride, treasure.
~v.i. (*to praise oneself, to speak ostentatiously*) be boastful, blow one's own trumpet, brag, crow, sing one's own praises, swagger, swank, (*coll.*) talk big, vaunt. ANTONYMS: be humble, be modest.
~v.t. (*to have as worthy of pride*) enjoy, have, own, possess, pride oneself on.

boastful *a.* (*full of boasting*) arrogant, bragging, cocky, conceited, crowing, egotistical, overbearing, swaggering, (*coll.*) swanking, (*coll.*) swollen-headed, vainglorious, vaunting. ANTONYMS: humble, modest, self-effacing, unassuming.

boat *n.* (*a small vessel, propelled by oars or sails*) craft, dinghy, vessel, yacht.

bob *v.t.* (*to move with a short jerking motion*) jerk, nod.
~v.i. (*to have a short jerking motion*) bounce, float, jerk, wobble. **to bob up** (*to emerge suddenly*) appear, arise, emerge, materialize, pop up, spring up, surface, turn up.

bode *v.i.* (*to portend (well or ill)*) augur, forebode, portend, presage.

bodily *adv.* (*wholly, completely*) completely, entirely, totally, wholly.

body *n.* **1** (*the material frame of a person or animal*) build, figure, form, frame, physique, shape. **2** (*the main trunk, excluding the head and limbs*) torso, trunk. **3** (*a corpse, a dead body*) cadaver, carcass, corpse, dead body, remains, skeleton, (*sl.*) stiff. **4** (*a collective mass of something such as water*) expanse, extent, mass, quantity. **5** (*a collective mass of something such as information*) collection, corpus, mass, stock, supply. **6** (*a person*) anybody, human being, individual, man, person, someone, woman. **7** (*a society, a corporation*) association, band, bloc, company, confederation, corporation, group, party, society. **8** (*strength, substantial quality*) density, firmness, shape, solidity, strength, substance. **9** (*the main part*) bulk, majority, mass, preponderance.

bog *n.* (*a marsh, a morass*) fen, marsh, marshland, quagmire, slough, swamp. **to bog down** (*to overwhelm, as with work*) allow no progress, bring to a standstill, make stuck, overwhelm.

bogey *n.* **1** (*a spectre*) apparition, bogeyman, evil spirit, ghost, hobgoblin, phantom, sandman, spectre, spirit, (*coll.*) spook. **2** (*a bugbear*) anathema, bane, bête noire, bugbear, pet hate.

boggle *v.i.* **1** (*to shrink back from*) be reluctant to, demur at, flinch from, hang back from, hesitate to, jib at, shrink back from. **2** (*to be astounded*) be amazed, be astonished, be astounded, (*coll.*) be bowled over, (*coll.*) be fazed, be flabbergasted, (*coll.*) be staggered, be startled.
~v.t. (*to overwhelm (mentally)*) amaze, astonish, astound, flabbergast, overwhelm, shock, startle.

bogus *a.* (*sham, counterfeit*) counterfeit, fake, false, forged, fraudulent, mock, (*coll.*) phoney, (*coll.*) pseudo, sham, spurious. ANTONYMS: authentic, genuine, real, true.

bohemian *n.* (*a person who leads a free, irregular life, despising social conventionalities*) beatnik, hippy, New Age traveller, nonconformist.
~a. (*of or characteristic of social bohemians*) alternative, nonconformist, (*coll.*) offbeat, unconventional, unorthodox. ANTONYMS: conservative, conventional, orthodox.

boil *v.i.* **1** (*to be agitated by the action of heat, as water*) bubble, cook, heat. **2** (*to bubble or seethe like boiling water*) bubble, churn, effervesce, foam, froth, seethe. **3** (*to be agitated with passion*) be enraged, be furious, blow a fuse, (*coll.*) blow one's top, (*coll.*) fly off the handle, foam at the mouth, fulminate, (*coll.*) hit the roof, rage, rave, see red, seethe, storm.
~v.t. (*to cook by heat in boiling water*) bring to the boil, cook, heat, simmer.

boisterous *a.* **1** (*wild, unruly*) active, bouncy, disorderly, energetic, exuberant, frisky, impetuous, lively, loud, noisy, obstreperous, romping, rowdy, rumbustious, uncontrolled, unrestrained, unruly, wild. ANTONYMS: controlled, inactive, restrained, subdued. **2** (*stormy, roaring*) blustery, gusting, gusty, raging, rough, squally, stormy, tempestuous, turbulent, wild, windy. ANTONYMS: calm, still.

bold *a.* **1** (*courageous, daring*) adventurous, brave, courageous, daring, fearless, gallant, heroic, intrepid, lion-hearted, undaunted, valiant, valorous. ANTONYMS: cowardly, fearful, timid, timorous. **2** (*vigorous, striking*) bright, colourful, conspicuous, distinct, eye-catching, flashy, forceful, loud, pronounced, showy, striking, vibrant, vivid. ANTONYMS: pale, subdued, subtle. **3** (*forward, presumptuous*) audacious, barefaced, bold as brass, brash, brazen, cheeky, forward, immodest, impertinent, impudent, pert, (*coll.*) pushy, saucy, unabashed. ANTONYMS: meek, retiring, shy.

bolshie *a.* (*stubborn and argumentative*) awkward, bloody-minded, difficult, obdurate, perverse, stubborn, uncooperative. ANTONYMS: accommodating, cooperative, obliging.

bolster *v.t.* (*to support with or as with a bolster*) aid, assist, boost, brace, buoy up, buttress, help, hold up, prop, reinforce, shore, strengthen, support.

bolt *n.* **1** (*a short thick arrow with a blunt head*) arrow, dart, missile, projectile, shaft. **2** (*a discharge of lightning*) burst, discharge, flash, fork, shaft, sheet, streak, thunderbolt. **3** (*a sliding piece of iron for fastening a door, window etc.*) bar, catch, fastener, hasp, latch, lock. **4** (*a metal pin for holding objects together, frequently screwheaded*) dowel, peg, pin, rivet, rod. **5** (*a sudden start or flight*) dart, dash, escape, flight, run, rush, sprint.
~*v.t.* **1** (*to shut or fasten by means of a bolt*) bar, fasten, latch, lock, secure, shut. ANTONYMS: open, unlock. **2** (*to swallow hastily and without chewing*) devour, gobble, gulp, guzzle, wolf.
~*v.i.* (*to run away* (*as a horse*)) abscond, decamp, escape, flee, hurry, make a break for it, make a dash for it, make a run for it, run away, run off, rush off.

bolt upright *a., adv.* (*straight upright*) erect, ramrod straight, rigid, stiff, straight up, upright.

bomb *n.* (*an explosive device triggered by impact or a timer*) charge, explosive, grenade, incendiary, incendiary device, mine, shell, torpedo.
~*v.t.* (*to attack or destroy with bombs*) blitz, blow up, bombard, shell, strafe, torpedo.

bombard *v.t.* **1** (*to attack with shot and shell*) blitz, blow up, bomb, open fire on, shell, strafe. **2** (*to assail with arguments*) assail, attack, barrage, batter, belabour, beset, besiege, harass, pester, plague.

bombastic *a.* (*using high-sounding words*) blustering, fustian, grandiloquent, grandiose, high-flown, inflated, long-winded, magniloquent, ostentatious, pompous, ranting, turgid, verbose, wordy. ANTONYMS: concise, terse.

bona fide *a.* (*genuine*) authentic, genuine, honest, (*coll.*) kosher, legal, legitimate, real, sound, true. ANTONYMS: bogus, false, (*coll.*) phoney, sham.

bond *n.* **1** (*pl.*) (*chains, imprisonment, captivity*) captivity, chains, fetters, imprisonment, manacles, shackles. ANTONYMS: freedom. **2** (*that which restrains or connects*) attachment, binding, connection, link, tie, union. **3** (*a binding agreement*) agreement, pact, pledge, promise, transaction, treaty.
~*v.t.* (*to bind or connect* (*as bricks or stones*) *firmly together*) bind, cement, connect, fasten, fuse, glue, gum, join, paste.

bondage *n.* (*slavery, captivity*) captivity, enslavement, imprisonment, oppression, servitude, slavery, subjection, subjugation, thraldom, yoke.

bonnet *n.* (*a hat tied beneath the chin*) cap, hat.

bonny *a.* (*beautiful, pretty*) attractive, beautiful, handsome, lovely, pretty. ANTONYMS: ugly, unattractive.

bonus *n.* **1** (*something over and above what is due*) boon, extra, icing on the cake, plus. **2** (*a gratuity over and above a fixed salary*) bounty, commission, gratuity, (*coll.*) perk, perquisite, reward, tip.

bon vivant *n.* (*a person fond of good living*) epicure, (*coll.*) foodie, gastronome, (*dated*) gourmand, gourmet. ANTONYMS: ascetic.

bony *a.* (*very thin, with bones scarcely covered with flesh*) angular, emaciated, gaunt, lean, rawboned, scraggy, scrawny, skeletal, skinny, thin. ANTONYMS: fat, fleshy, plump.

book *n.* **1** (*a collection of sheets printed, written on or blank, bound in a volume*) booklet, exercise book, jotter, notebook, pad. **2** (*a literary composition of considerable extent*) hardback, novel, opus, paperback, publication, textbook, title, tome, volume, work. **3** (*pl.*) (*a set of accounts*) accounts, ledgers, records.
~*v.t.* (*to reserve by payment in advance*) charter, engage, make a booking for, make a reservation for, pre-hire, pre-order, reserve.
~*v.i.* (*to make a reservation*) book, make a booking, make a reservation. **to be in someone's good books** (*to be regarded with favour by someone*) be

favourite, be flavour of the month, be in favour, be someone's blue-eyed boy/ girl, be someone's favourite, have the approval of. ANTONYMS: be in someone's bad books, be in someone's black books.

bookish a. (*learned, studious*) academic, blue-stocking, donnish, (*coll.*) egghead, erudite, high-brow, intellectual, learned, literary, scholarly, studious, well-read. ANTONYMS: illiterate.

boom n. **1** (*a loud, deep sound*) bang, bellow, blare, blast, burst, explosion, reverberation, roar, rumble, thundering. **2** (*a burst of commercial activity and prosperity*) advance, boost, development, expansion, growth, improvement, increase, upsurge, upswing, upturn. ANTONYMS: decline, decrease, slump.

~v.i. **1** (*to make a loud, deep sound*) bang, bellow, blare, blast, explode, resound, reverberate, roar, rumble, thunder. **2** (*to become very prosperous or active*) burgeon, develop, do well, expand, flourish, grow, improve, increase, intensify, mushroom, prosper, succeed, thrive. ANTONYMS: decrease, deteriorate, fail, slump.

boon n. (*a benefit, a blessing*) advantage, blessing, bonus, gain, godsend, good thing, plus. ANTONYMS: bad thing, disadvantage, drawback.

boor n. (*a rude or insensitive person*) bumpkin, churl, (*coll.*) clodhopper, lout, oaf, (*coll.*) peasant, philistine, (*N Am.*) redneck, vulgarian, yob.

boorish a. (*rude, unmannerly*) (*coll.*) clodhopping, coarse, gross, ill-mannered, insensitive, loutish, oafish, rough, rude, uncivilized, un-couth, unrefined, unsophisticated, vulgar, yobbish. ANTONYMS: genteel, refined, sensitive.

boost v.t. **1** (*to push upwards*) elevate, heave up, help up, (*coll.*) hoick, hoist, push up, raise, shove up, thrust up. **2** (*to advertise on a big scale*) advertise, give a puff to, (*coll.*) hype up, (*coll.*) plug, promote, publicize, puff up, write up. **3** (*to promote or encourage*) advance, assist, bolster, develop, encourage, facilitate, foster, further, help, promote. ANTONYMS: impede, obstruct. **4** (*to enlarge or increase*) amplify, enlarge, expand, (*coll.*) hike up, increase, (*coll.*) jack up, magnify, raise. ANTONYMS: decrease, reduce.

~n. **1** (*an upward push*) heave, help, (*coll.*) hoick, hoist, lift, push, shove, thrust. **2** (*encouragement, support*) assistance, encouragement, help, shot in the arm, stimulus, support. ANTONYMS: discouragement, hindrance, impediment. **3** (*an increase*) amplification, enlargement, expansion, (*coll.*) hike, increase, (*coll.*) jacking up, magnification, rise. ANTONYMS: decrease, reduction. **4** (*an advertisement, advertising*) advertisement, (*coll.*) hype, (*coll.*) plug, promotion, publicity, publicizing, puff, write-up.

boot n. (*a kind of shoe that covers the whole foot and the lower part of the leg*) (*sl.*) bovver boot, DM®, Doc Marten®, highleg, wellington.

~v.t. **1** (*to kick*) give a kick to, kick, punt. **2** (*to start a computer program*) running) load, start. **to boot out** (*to dismiss, sack*) dismiss, eject, evict, expel, (*sl.*) give (someone) the push, (*N Am., sl.*) give the bum's rush to, (*coll.*) give the (old) heave-ho to, kick out, oust, put out, (*coll.*) sack, show (someone) the door, throw out, throw (someone) out on their ear.

booth n. **1** (*a stall or tent at a fair, polling station etc.*) counter, stall, stand. **2** (*a compartment or structure containing a telephone, a table in a restaurant etc.*) compartment, cubicle.

bootless a. (*profitless, unavailing*) abortive, fruitless, futile, ineffective, ineffectual, profit-less, unavailing, unproductive, unsuccessful, useless, vain. ANTONYMS: effective, productive, successful.

booty n. **1** (*spoil taken in war*) pillage, plunder, spoil, spoils. **2** (*property carried off by thieves*) (*sl.*) boodle, haul, loot, spoil, spoils, (*sl.*) swag. **3** (*a gain, a prize*) gain, prize, profit, takings, winnings.

bordello n. (*a brothel*) bawdy house, brothel, (*N Am., sl.*) cat-house, house of ill fame, house of ill repute, whorehouse.

border n. **1** (*an edge, margin*) bound, boundary, brim, confines, edge, flange, hem, limit, lip, perimeter, rim, skirt, verge. **2** (*a frontier or frontier region*) boundary, frontier, march.

~v.t. **1** (*to put a border or edging to*) bind, edge, fringe, hem, trim. **2** (*to form a boundary to*) bound, edge, skirt.

~v.i. **1** (*to be contiguous*) abut, adjoin, be adjacent to, be next to, join, neighbour, touch. **2** (*to approximate, resemble*) approach, approximate to, be like, be similar to, come close to, resemble, verge on. ANTONYMS: be dissimilar to, be unlike.

bore[1] v.t. **1** (*to make a hole through*) drill, penetrate, perforate, pierce, puncture, tap. **2** (*to hollow out*) gouge out, hollow out, tunnel.

~n. **1** (*a hole made by boring*) bore hole, hole, shaft, tunnel. **2** (*the diameter of a tube*) calibre, diameter.

bore[2] n. **1** (*a tiresome person*) (*coll.*) anorak, (*coll.*) drag, dull person, tiresome person, (*coll.*) train-spotter, (*coll.*) yawn. **2** (*something that one finds annoying or a nuisance*) bother, (*coll.*) drag, nuisance, (*coll.*) pain in the neck, (*coll.*) yawn.

~v.t. (*to weary with dullness*) be tedious to, bore (someone) to death, bore (someone) to tears, fatigue, jade, make bored, pall on, tire, weary. ANTONYMS: divert, interest, stimulate.

bored a. (*tired and uninterested*) bored stiff, bored to death, bored to tears, ennuyé(e), tired, uninterested, wearied. ANTONYMS: excited, interested.

boredom *n.* **1** (*the condition of being boring*) dullness, flatness, lack of interest, monotony, sameness, tediousness, tedium. **2** (*the condition of being bored*) apathy, ennui, languor, malaise, weariness, world-weariness. ANTONYMS: excitement, interest, stimulation.

boring *a.* (*dull, uninteresting*) dry as dust, dull, flat, humdrum, monotonous, repetitious, routine, (*coll.*) samey, tedious, tiresome, unexciting, uninteresting, wearisome. ANTONYMS: exciting, interesting, stimulating.

borrow *v.t.* **1** (*to obtain under a promise to return*) ask the loan of, (*esp. N Am., sl.*) bum, cadge, have the temporary use of, (*coll.*) mooch, (*coll.*) scrounge, take on loan, (*sl.*) touch (someone) for. ANTONYMS: lend, loan. **2** (*to adopt, to assume from other people*) acquire, adopt, appropriate, obtain, take over. **3** (*to copy, imitate*) appropriate, copy, lift, pirate, plagiarize, steal, take, usurp.

bosom *n.* **1** (*the breast of a human being, esp. of a woman*) (*sl.*) boobs, breast, chest, (*taboo sl.*) knockers, (*taboo sl.*) tits. **2** (*the breast as the seat of emotions*) affections, emotions, feelings, heart, soul. **3** (*the interior of anything*) centre, core, heart, midst, protection.

bosom friend *n.* (*a dearest and most intimate friend*) (*coll.*) best buddy, best friend, (*coll.*) best mate, boon companion, close friend, confidant(e), constant companion, dear friend, intimate.

bosomy *a.* ((*of a woman*) *having large breasts*) busty, chesty, (*sl.*) stacked, (*facet.*) well-upholstered.

boss *n.* **1** (*a supervisor, foreman*) foreman, forewoman, (*coll.*) gaffer, manager, overseer, owner, superintendent, supervisor. ANTONYMS: employee, underling, worker. **2** (*a chief or leader*) (*sl.*) big cheese, chief, director, employer, executive, head, (*N Am., sl.*) honcho, (*coll.*) kingpin, leader, master.
~*v.t.* (*to direct, to control*) be in charge of, control, direct, manage, oversee, run, superintend, supervise.

bossy *a.* (*domineering*) authoritarian, autocratic, bullying, despotic, dictatorial, dominating, domineering, imperious, overbearing, tyrannical. ANTONYMS: meek, timid.

botch *v.t.* (*to do badly or clumsily*) bungle, do (something) badly, make a botch of, (*coll.*) make a hash of, make a mess of. ANTONYMS: do (something) well, make a good job of.

bother *v.t.* **1** (*to annoy, to pester*) disturb, harass, (*coll.*) hassle, molest, nag, pester, plague,

torment, worry. **2** (*to worry*) be of concern to, concern, disturb, perturb, upset, worry. ANTONYMS: be of no concern to, not matter to.
~*v.i.* **1** (*to worry oneself*) be anxious, be concerned, be perturbed, be upset, be worried. ANTONYMS: be unconcerned, not care. **2** (*to take trouble*) go to the trouble (of), inconvenience oneself, make the effort, put oneself out, take pains, trouble.
~*n.* **1** (*trouble, fuss*) effort, exertion, fuss, (*coll.*) hassle, inconvenience, trouble. **2** (*disturbance*) commotion, disturbance, fighting, row, trouble, uproar.

bothersome *a.* (*troublesome, annoying*) annoying, exasperating, infuriating, irritating, nuisance, tiresome, troublesome, vexing.

bottle *n.* **1** (*a vessel with a narrow neck for holding liquids*) balthazar, carafe, decanter, flask, jeroboam, magnum, methuselah, nebuchadnezzar. **2** (*courage, strength of will*) boldness, bravery, courage, daring, (*coll.*) guts, nerve, pluck, spunk, valour. ANTONYMS: cowardice, fear, timidity. **the bottle** (*drinking*) alcohol, alcoholic drink, (*sl.*) booze, hard drink, liquor. **to bottle up** (*to restrain, repress* (*one's emotions*)) conceal, control, curb, keep back, keep in check, restrain. ANTONYMS: give rein to, let go.

bottleneck *n.* (*a constricted outlet*) block, blockage, congestion, constriction, jam, narrowing, obstruction.

bottom *n.* **1** (*the lowest part of anything, the part on which anything rests*) base, basis, floor, foot, foundation, substructure, support, underneath, underside. ANTONYMS: crown, peak, summit, top. **2** (*the buttocks, the posterior*) (*taboo sl.*) arse, (*esp. N Am., taboo sl.*) ass, (*coll.*) backside, behind, (*sl.*) bum, (*N Am., sl.*) buns, (*N Am., sl.*) butt, buttocks, (*coll.*) derrière, (*N Am., sl.*) fanny, hindquarters, (*sl.*) jacksy, posterior, rear, rear end, seat, tail. **3** (*the bed or channel of any body of water*) bed, depths, floor. **4** (*the inmost part, the furthest point of something*) far end, furthest point. ANTONYMS: top end. **5** (*the lowest rank*) lowest level, lowest position, lowest rank. ANTONYMS: top. **6** (*foundation, base*) base, core, essence, foundation, heart, meat, nitty-gritty, substance. **7** (*source, basis*) basis, cause, origin, root, source.
~*a.* (*of or relating to the bottom*) last, lowest.

bottomless *a.* (*fathomless, unfathomable*) boundless, deep, fathomless, immeasurable, infinite, unfathomable, unlimited.

bough *n.* (*a large branch of a tree*) arm, branch, limb.

boulder *n.* (*a water-worn, rounded stone*) (*Geol.*) erratic, rock, (*Geol.*) sarsen, stone.

bounce *v.i.* **1** (*to rebound*) rebound, recoil, ricochet, spring back. **2** (*to bound like a ball*)

bound, caper, hop, jump, leap, prance, romp, skip, spring.
~*v.t.* (*to throw or turn out*) (*sl.*) boot out, (*coll.*) chuck out, eject, evict, expel, kick out, oust, put out, remove, throw out.

bouncing *a.* (*stout, strong*) healthy, robust, strong, thriving, vigorous. ANTONYMS: frail, ill, weak.

bound¹ *n.* (*a leap, a spring*) bounce, hop, jump, leap, skip, spring, vault.
~*v.i.* (*to leap, to spring*) bounce, hop, jump, leap, spring, vault.

bound² *n.* **1** (*a limit, a boundary*) border, boundary, confines, limit, march, perimeter. **2** (*limitation, restriction*) boundary, demarcation, limit, limitation, restriction.
~*v.t.* **1** (*to set bounds to, to confine*) confine, cramp, delimit, limit, place a limit on, restrain, restrict. **2** (*to form the boundary of*) confine, encircle, enclose, fence in, surround, wall in. **out of bounds** ((*of an area etc.*) *forbidden, prohibited*) banned, barred, forbidden, (*coll.*) off-limits, prohibited.

bound³ *a.* **1** (*under obligation, obliged*) committed, compelled, constrained, duty-bound, forced, obligated, obliged, pledged. **2** (*certain* (*to*)) certain, destined, sure, very likely. ANTONYMS: unlikely. **bound up in** (*busy or occupied with*) busy with, concerned with, engrossed in, obsessed with, occupied with, preoccupied with. **bound up with** (*intimately associated with*) allied to, associated with, connected with, tied up with. ANTONYMS: separate from, unconnected with.

boundary *n.* (*a mark indicating a limit*) border, bounds, confines, edge, limit, march, margin, perimeter, periphery, verge.

boundless *a.* (*limitless*) bottomless, endless, immeasurable, immense, incalculable, inexhaustible, infinite, limitless, unending, untold, vast, without limit. ANTONYMS: limited, little, restricted, small.

bountiful *a.* **1** (*liberal, munificent*) benevolent, generous, giving, liberal, magnanimous, munificent, open-handed, philanthropic, unsparing, unstinting. ANTONYMS: mean, niggardly, stingy. **2** (*plenteous, abundant*) abundant, ample, bounteous, bumper, copious, generous, lavish, liberal, plenteous, plentiful, princely, profuse, prolific, superabundant. ANTONYMS: meagre, paltry, scant, sparse.

bounty *n.* **1** (*gracious liberality*) benevolence, generosity, largesse, liberality, magnanimity, munificence, open-handedness, philanthropy. ANTONYMS: meanness, niggardliness, stinginess. **2** (*a gift*) bonus, donation, gift, gratuity, present, reward, tip.

bouquet *n.* **1** (*a bunch of flowers*) bunch of flowers, flower arrangement, nosegay, posy, spray. **2** (*the perfume exhaled by wine*) aroma, fragrance, perfume, redolence, scent, smell. **3** (*a compliment*) commendation, compliment, eulogy, praise, tribute. ANTONYMS: brickbat, censure, criticism.

bourgeois *a.* **1** (*of or relating to the middle class or capitalist classes*) middle-class. ANTONYMS: aristocratic, plebeian, working-class. **2** (*commonplace, unintellectual*) conventional, humdrum, ordinary, philistine, uncreative, uncultured, unimaginative. ANTONYMS: creative, imaginative, unconventional. **3** (*middle-class in outlook*) capitalist, materialistic, money-oriented.

bout *n.* **1** (*a turn, a round*) competition, contest, encounter, match, round. **2** (*a spell of work*) period, run, shift, spell, stint, stretch, time, turn. **3** (*a fit of drunkenness or of illness*) attack, fit, spell.

bovine *a.* **1** (*sluggish*) inactive, lethargic, phlegmatic, slow-moving, sluggish, stolid, torpid. ANTONYMS: active, fleet, lively. **2** (*dull, stupid*) dense, dimwitted, doltish, dull-witted, slow-witted, stupid, thick. ANTONYMS: bright, clever, quick-thinking.

bow¹ *v.i.* **1** (*to bend forward as a sign of submission or salutation*) bend forward, bob, curtsy, make obeisance, salaam. **2** (*to incline the head*) incline the head, nod. **3** (*to submit, to yield*) accept, capitulate, comply, give in, submit, surrender, yield. ANTONYMS: offer resistance, resist, withstand.
~*v.t.* (*to cause to bend*) arch, bend, crook, curve, stoop. ANTONYMS: straighten.
~*n.* (*an inclination of the body or head, as a salute or token of respect*) bob, curtsy, nod, obeisance, salaam. **to bow out** (*to retire, to retreat*) get out, leave, pull out, quit, resign, retire, retreat, stand down, step down, withdraw.

bow² *n.* (*the rounded fore-end of a ship or boat*) fore, front, head, prow, stem. ANTONYMS: stern.

bowdlerize *v.t.* (*to expurgate* (*a book*)) blue-pencil, censor, cut, expurgate.

bowl¹ *n.* **1** (*a hollow* (*usu. hemispherical*) *vessel for holding liquids*) basin, container, dish, receptacle, vessel. **2** (*in geography, a natural basin*) crater, depression, dip, hole, hollow, valley. **3** (*a stadium*) arena, park, stadium.

bowl² *v.i.* (*to move rapidly and smoothly* (*usu. with along*)) drive, go, move, travel, trundle.
~*v.t.* **1** (*to cause to roll along the ground*) pitch, roll, send. **2** (*to deliver* (*as a ball at cricket*)) deliver, fling, hurl, pitch, send, spin, throw. **3** (*to strike the wicket and put* (*a player*) *out*) hit,

box 84 **branch**

(*coll.*) knock over, skittle. **to bowl over 1** (*to knock over*) bring down, fell, floor, knock down, knock over. **2** (*to impress*) amaze, astonish, astound, dumbfound, flabbergast, overwhelm, stagger, startle, stun, surprise.

box[1] *n.* **1** (*a case or receptacle usu. with a lid and rectangular, for holding solids*) bin, carton, case, casket, chest, coffer, container, crate, pack, package, trunk. **2** (*a compartment partitioned off in a theatre, court etc.*) cabin, compartment, cubicle, enclosure, hut, kiosk.
~*v.t.* (*to enclose in a box*) pack, package. **to box in** (*to surround, to enclose*) confine, enclose, fence in, hem in, shut in, surround.

box[2] *v.t.* (*to strike (on the ear etc.) with the open hand*) belt, buffet, clout, hit, punch, slap, smack, (*sl.*) sock, strike, thump, (*coll.*) wallop, whack.
~*v.i.* (*to fight or spar with fists or with gloves*) exchange blows, fight, spar.

boxer *n.* (*a person who boxes*) fighter, prize-fighter, pugilist, sparring partner.

boxing *n.* (*the sport of fist fighting with gloves*) prizefighting, pugilism, the noble art, the ring.

boy *n.* (*a male child*) child, lad, schoolboy, stripling, young man, youngster, youth.

boycott *v.t.* **1** (*to combine to ostracize (a person) on account of their political opinions*) avoid, blackball, blacklist, eschew, give (someone) the cold shoulder, ostracize, send (someone) to Coventry, shun, spurn, stay away from, steer clear of. ANTONYMS: make friends with, welcome. **2** (*to refuse to have dealings with*) ban, bar, debar, embargo, outlaw, place an embargo on, prohibit, proscribe, put an embargo on. ANTONYMS: deal with, trade with.

boyfriend *n.* (*a male friend, esp. a regular partner or lover*) admirer, (*coll.*) date, lover, (*dial., coll.*) man, man friend, partner, (*coll.*) steady, suitor, sweetheart, (*coll.*) toyboy, young man. ANTONYMS: girlfriend, (*coll.*) woman, young woman.

boyish *a.* (*characteristic of or suitable to a boy*) childish, immature, young, youthful. ANTONYMS: adult, grown-up.

brace *n.* **1** (*that which tightens or supports*) clamp, coupling, support, vice. **2** (*a timber to strengthen the framework of a building*) buttress, prop, reinforcement, stanchion, strut, support, truss. **3** (*a couple, a pair*) couple, duo, pair, two.
~*v.t.* (*to strengthen, to fill with firmness*) fortify, get ready, prepare, steady, steel, strengthen, tense.

bracelet *n.* (*an ornamental band for the wrist*) armlet, bangle, torc, wristlet.

bracing *a.* (*imparting tone or strength*) brisk, chilly, cool, crisp, energizing, exhilarating, forti-

fying, fresh, health-giving, healthy, invigorating, refreshing, restorative, reviving, stimulating, strengthening, tonic, vitalizing. ANTONYMS: draining, enervating, exhausting, tiring.

brackish *a.* (*of a saline taste*) bitter, briny, saline, salty. ANTONYMS: fresh.

brag *v.i.* (*to boast*) blow one's own trumpet, boast, crow, show off, sing one's own praises, swagger, (*coll.*) talk big, vaunt.

braggart *n.* (*a boastful person*) (*sl.*) bigmouth, blowhard, boaster, brag, braggadocio, show-off, swaggerer, windbag.

braid *n.* **1** (*plaited hair*) pigtail, plait. **2** (*a woven fabric for trimming*) cord, tape, thread, twine, yarn.
~*v.t.* **1** (*to intertwine, to plait*) interlace, intertwine, interweave, plait, twine, weave. **2** (*to trim or bind with braid*) bind, decorate, edge, fringe, trim.

brain *n.* **1** (*intellectual power*) (*coll.*) grey matter, head, intellect, intellectual powers, intelligence, mental capacity, mental powers, mind. **2** (*an intelligent person*) (*coll.*) brainbox, (*coll.*) egghead, (*coll.*) Einstein, genius, highbrow, intellect, mastermind, mind, polymath, sage, scholar, thinker. ANTONYMS: dunce. **3** (*pl.*) (*intelligence*) acumen, brightness, cleverness, intellect, intelligence, (*coll.*) nous, (*sl.*) savvy, sense, shrewdness, wit.

brainless *a.* (*silly, witless*) dense, (*coll.*) dim, foolish, idiotic, inane, mindless, senseless, stupid, thick, unintelligent, witless. ANTONYMS: bright, clever, sensible.

brainwashing *n.* (*the subjection of a victim to sustained mental pressure in order to induce them to change their views*) conditioning, inculcation, indoctrination.

brainy *a.* (*acute, clever*) bright, brilliant, clever, intelligent, smart. ANTONYMS: dense, stupid.

brake *n.* (*anything that stops or hinders something*) check, constraint, control, curb, rein, restraint.
~*v.i.* (*to apply a brake*) decelerate, hit the brake, put on the brakes, reduce speed, slow, slow down. ANTONYMS: accelerate, speed up.

branch *n.* **1** (*a limb of a tree*) arm, bough, limb, shoot, twig. **2** (*anything considered as an extension of a main trunk, as of a river, road, etc.*) feeder, subdivision, subsidiary, tributary. **3** (*a subdivision*) part, side, subdivision. **4** (*a local office of an organization*) chapter, department, division, local office, section, subdivision, subsection, wing. ANTONYMS: head office, parent firm.
~*v.i.* (*to diverge from a main direction*) depart from, deviate from, diverge from, shoot off from,

turn aside from. **to branch out** (*to broaden one's activities*) add to one's interests, diversify, expand one's range of activities, extend one's field of interests.

brand *n.* **1** (*a particular kind of manufactured article*) kind, line, make, sort, type, variety. **2** (*a trade mark*) brand name, label, registered trade mark, trade mark, trade name. **3** (*class, quality*) cast, class, kind, sort, species, stamp, style, type, variety. **4** (*a mark of identification*) ear-mark, identification, mark, marker, stamp. **5** (*a stigma*) blot, mark, slur, smirch, stain, stigma, taint.
~*v.t.* **1** (*to mark with a brand*) mark, stamp. **2** (*to imprint on the memory*) engrave, fix, impress, imprint, print, stamp. **3** (*to stigmatize*) denounce, label, mark, stigmatize.

brandish *v.t.* (*to wave or flourish about* (*a weapon etc.*)) display, flourish, raise, shake, swing, wag, wave, wield.

brash *a.* **1** (*vulgarly assertive or pushy*) audacious, bold, brazen, cheeky, cocky, forward, impertinent, impudent, insolent, (*coll.*) pushy, self-assertive. ANTONYMS: reserved, self-effacing, timid. **2** (*rash*) careless, foolhardy, hasty, heedless, impetuous, impulsive, incautious, precipitate, reckless. ANTONYMS: careful, cautious, prudent.

brat *n.* (*a child, an infant, usu. one who is badly behaved*) imp, (*dated or facet.*) rapscallion, rascal, scamp, urchin, whippersnapper.

bravado *n.* (*swaggering behaviour*) bluster, blustering, boastfulness, bragging, swaggering, swashbuckling, vaunting.

brave *a.* **1** (*daring, courageous*) bold, courageous, daring, dauntless, doughty, fearless, gallant, game, (*coll.*) gutsy, heroic, intrepid, lion-hearted, mettlesome, plucky, spunky, undaunted, valiant, valorous. ANTONYMS: cowardly, craven, fearful, (*coll.*) yellow. **2** (*excellent, fine*) excellent, fine, showy, spectacular, splendid.
~*v.t.* (*to defy, to challenge*) challenge, confront, dare, defy, endure, face, stand up to. ANTONYMS: give in to, surrender to.

bravery *n.* (*courage*) boldness, courage, daring, doughtiness, fearlessness, gallantry, gameness, (*coll.*) guts, heroism, intrepidity, mettle, pluck, spirit, spunk, valour. ANTONYMS: cowardice, fearfulness, timidity.

brawl *v.i.* (*to quarrel noisily*) argue, battle, clash, exchange blows, fight, have a disagreement, have a dispute, quarrel, (*coll.*) row, (*coll.*) scrap, scuffle, squabble, tussle, wrangle, wrestle.
~*n.* (*a noisy quarrel, disturbance*) affray, altercation, argument, brouhaha, clash, disagreement, dispute, exchange of blows, fight, fisticuffs,

fracas, fray, free-for-all, mêlée, (*coll.*) punch-up, quarrel, row, (*esp. N Am.*) ruckus, (*coll.*) scrap, scrimmage, scuffle, skirmish.

brawn *n.* **1** (*muscle, flesh*) beef, beefiness, brawniness, burliness, sturdiness. **2** (*strength, muscularity*) might, muscle, muscularity, robustness, strength.

brawny *a.* (*muscular, strong*) beefy, burly, mighty, muscular, powerful, powerfully-built, stalwart, strapping, strong, sturdy, thickset, well-built. ANTONYMS: puny, scrawny, weak, (*coll.*) weedy.

brazen *a.* (*shameless, impudent*) audacious, barefaced, bold, brash, brassy, defiant, forward, immodest, impudent, insolent, pert, presumptuous, (*coll.*) pushy, shameless, unabashed, unashamed. ANTONYMS: modest, reserved, retiring, shy.
~*v.t.* (*to face impudently* (*often with out*)) be defiant, be impenitent, be unabashed, be unashamed, be unrepentant, confront, defy, face, put a brave face on it, show a bold front, stand one's ground. ANTONYMS: back down, be ashamed, be repentant.

breach *n.* **1** (*a break, a gap*) aperture, break, chasm, cleft, crack, fissure, fracture, gap, hole, opening, rift, split. **2** (*violation of a law, duty etc.*) contravention, disobedience, infraction, infringement, neglect, transgression, violation. ANTONYMS: adherence, compliance, observance. **3** (*a rupture of friendship or alliance*) disagreement, division, estrangement, (*coll.*) falling-out, parting of the ways, schism, separation. ANTONYMS: reunion, union. **4** (*alienation, a quarrel*) alienation, disaffection, discord, dissension, quarrel.
~*v.t.* **1** (*to make a breach or gap in*) break through, burst through, make a gap in, open up, rupture, split. **2** (*to break* (*a law, contract etc.*)) abrogate, contravene, disobey, infringe, neglect, transgress, violate. ANTONYMS: adhere to, comply with, observe.

bread *n.* (*food*) daily bread, food, provisions, subsistence, sustenance.

breadth *n.* **1** (*measure from side to side*) broadness, span, spread, wideness, width. ANTONYMS: length. **2** (*extent, largeness*) compass, comprehensiveness, degree, expanse, extensiveness, extent, immensity, range, reach, scale, scope, size, sweep, vastness. **3** (*liberality, tolerance*) broad-mindedness, latitude, liberality, magnanimity, open-mindedness, tolerance. ANTONYMS: intolerance, narrow-mindedness, narrowness.

break *v.t.* **1** (*to rend apart, to shatter*) crack, fracture, rend, sever, shatter, smash, snap, splinter, split. ANTONYMS: mend, repair. **2** (*to* perforate or pierce (*skin or other surface*)) penetrate, perforate, pierce, puncture, split. **3** (*to subdue, to tame*) cow, crush, overcome, overpower, subdue, tame. **4** (*to ruin financially*) bankrupt, impoverish, make a pauper of, make bankrupt, make (someone) penniless, ruin. **5** (*to damage, to cause* (*a machine*) *to stop working*) disable, impair, render inoperable. ANTONYMS: mend, repair. **6** (*to destroy* (*someone's spirit*)) bring (someone) to their knees, crush, destroy. **7** (*to disconnect, to interrupt*) discontinue, disturb, interfere with, interrupt, suspend. **8** (*to intercept, to lessen the force of*) cushion, diminish, lessen, soften. **9** (*to disobey, to infringe*) abrogate, breach, burst, contravene, disobey, disregard, infringe, transgress, violate. ANTONYMS: comply with, keep, obey, observe. **10** (*to do better than* (*a record*)) beat, cap, exceed, outdo, outstrip, surpass, top. **11** (*to decipher* (*a code*)) crack, decipher, decode, figure out, solve, unravel. **12** (*to announce* (*news, information etc.*)) announce, disclose, divulge, impart, reveal, tell. ANTONYMS: keep secret, suppress.

~*v.i.* **1** (*to separate into two or more portions*) crack, fracture, fragment, shatter, smash, snap, splinter, split. **2** ((*of a machine*) *to stop working*) become inoperative, be unusable, break down, cease to work, (*coll.*) go kaput, malfunction. **3** (*to stop or pause in an activity*) discontinue, halt, knock off, pause, rest, stop, take a break, take a rest, (*coll.*) take five. **4** (*to show signs of strong emotion, e.g. tears, suddenly*) be overcome, cave in, collapse, (*coll.*) crack, (*coll.*) crack up, crumple, go to pieces. **5** (*to appear with suddenness*) appear, begin, burst out, come into being, erupt, occur. ANTONYMS: die down, disappear, fade.

~*n.* **1** (*an opening, gap*) breach, chink, cleft, crack, fissure, fracture, gap, gash, hole, opening, rent, rift, rupture, split, tear. **2** (*interruption of continuity in time or space*) discontinuation, gap, halt, hiatus, interval, (*coll.*) let-up, lull, pause, stop, suspension. **3** (*a breach in a relationship*) alienation, breach, disaffection, disagreement, dispute, estrangement, rift, rupture, schism, split. **4** (*a pause or interval*) (*coll.*) breather, breathing-space, coffee break, interlude, intermission, playtime, recess, rest, supper break, tea break, time off. **5** (*a rest, holiday*) holiday, rest, time off, vacation. **6** (*irregularity*) alteration, change, variation. **7** (*a lucky opportunity*) advantage, chance, golden opportunity, good luck, opening, opportunity, stroke of luck. ANTONYMS: bad luck, stroke of ill luck. **to break away 1** (*to start away*) decamp, escape, flee, fly, (*coll.*) leg it, make a break for it, make off, run away, run for it, take to one's heels. **2** (*to revolt, to rebel from*) break with, detach oneself from, disassociate oneself from, form a splinter group, leave, part company with, secede from, separate from. ANTONYMS: associate from, join. **to break**

down 1 (*to destroy, to overcome*) crush, defeat, destroy, overcome, overpower, overwhelm, subdue. **2** ((*of a machine*) *to stop working*) break, cease to function, (*coll.*) conk out, fail, (*coll.*) go kaput, seize up, stop, stop going, stop working. ANTONYMS: function, go, operate. **3** (*to collapse, to fail*) collapse, come to nothing, disintegrate, fail, fall through, founder. **4** (*to lose control of oneself*) be overcome, be overcome with emotion, cry, go to pieces, lose control, (*coll.*) lose one's cool, weep. **5** (*to analyse* (*costs etc.*) *into component parts*) analyse, classify, divide up, segregate, separate out. **to break in 1** (*to tame*) tame, train. **2** (*to wear in* (*e.g. shoes*)) baptize, (*coll.*) christen, get used to, wear in. **3** (*to enter a building by using force*) break and enter, burgle, commit burglary, make a forced entry. **to break into 1** (*to enter by force*) break and enter, burgle, enter by force, make a forced entry, rob. **2** (*to interrupt*) butt into, (*sl.*) horn in, interrupt, intervene in. **3** (*to suddenly burst out with*) begin, burst into, commence, give way to, launch into, start. **to break off 1** (*to detach from*) detach, divide, pull off, separate, sever, snap off. ANTONYMS: join, unite. **2** (*to cease, to desist*) bring to an end, call a halt to, cease, desist from, discontinue, end, finish, halt, interrupt, pause, stop, suspend, terminate. ANTONYMS: begin, commence, start. **to break out 1** (*to burst loose, to escape*) abscond, bolt, break loose, burst out, (*sl.*) do a runner, escape, flee, fly, get free. **2** (*to burst forth* (*as a war*)) appear, arise, begin, burst forth, commence, emerge, happen, occur, spring up, start. ANTONYMS: end, terminate. **3** (*to appear* (*as an eruption on the skin*)) appear, burst forth, erupt. ANTONYMS: disappear, fade. **4** (*to exclaim*) call out, cry out, exclaim, utter. **to break through 1** (*to force a way through*) get past, pass through, penetrate, pierce, puncture. **2** (*to achieve success*) be successful, (*coll.*) crack it, make headway, progress, succeed. ANTONYMS: be unsuccessful, fail. **to break up 1** (*to disintegrate*) break in pieces, crumble, decompose, disintegrate, dismantle, dissolve, fall to pieces. **2** (*to dissolve into laughter*) be doubled up with laughter, be in stitches, burst out laughing, (*coll.*) crack up, dissolve into laughter, (*coll.*) fall about, split one's sides. ANTONYMS: break down, burst into tears. **3** (*to separate*) disband, disperse, divorce, go their separate ways, part, scatter, separate, split up. ANTONYMS: come together, convene, get together. **4** (*to cause to separate*) disband, disperse, put to rout, scatter, send off, separate. ANTONYMS: assemble, bring together. **5** (*to come to an end*) adjourn, come to an end, end, finish, stop, terminate. ANTONYMS: convene, open, start off. **6** (*to bring to an end, to destroy*) bring to an end, destroy, end, kill, terminate. ANTONYMS: bring into being, start off.

breakable *a.* (*capable of being broken*) brittle, delicate, flimsy, fragile, frangible, gimcrack, insubstantial, jerry-built. ANTONYMS: durable, solid, tough.

breakaway *a.* (*that is or involves a group that breaks away from a main body*) dissenting, rebel, schismatic, seceding, secessionist.

breakdown *n.* **1** (*downfall, collapse*) collapse, crack-up, disintegration, mental breakdown, mental collapse, mental disintegration, nervous breakdown. **2** (*total failure resulting in stoppage*) collapse, (*coll.*) conking out, failure, (*coll.*) fizzling out, malfunction, non-operation, seizing up, stoppage. **3** (*an analysis*) analysis, categorization, classification, dissection, itemization, separation.

breaker *n.* (*a heavy wave breaking against the rocks or shore*) billow, comber, roller, wave.

break-in *n.* (*an illegal forced entry into premises, esp. for criminal purposes*) breaking and entering, burglary, forced entry, housebreaking, robbery, unlawful entry.

breakneck *a.* ((*of speed*) *very fast*) dangerous, fast, rapid, reckless, speedy, swift. ANTONYMS: cautious, slow.

break of day *n.* (*dawn*) cockcrow, crack of dawn, dawn, daybreak, early morning, first light, sunrise. ANTONYMS: close of day, nightfall, sunset.

breakthrough *n.* (*an advance, a discovery*) advance, development, discovery, find, finding, invention, step forward.

break-up *n.* **1** (*disintegration, dissolution*) breakdown, collapse, disintegration, dissolution, divorce, failure, parting, rift, separation, split, splitting-up. **2** (*dispersal*) disbandment, dispersal, scattering.

breakwater *n.* (*a pier or anything similar, to break the force of the waves*) groyne, jetty, mole, pier, sea wall.

breast *n.* **1** (*either of the organs for the secretion of milk in women*) (*sl.*) boob, bosom, bust, chest, (*taboo sl.*) knocker, (*taboo sl.*) tit. **2** (*the seat of the affections*) being, core, heart, seat of the affections, soul. **3** (*the affections*) affections, emotions, feelings.

breath *n.* **1** (*a single respiration*) exhalation, gasp, gulp of air, inhalation, pant, respiration, wheeze. **2** (*a very slight breeze*) breath of air, breeze, gust, puff of wind, zephyr. ANTONYMS: gale, hurricane. **3** (*respite*) break, (*coll.*) breather, breathing-space, interval, pause, respite, rest. **4** (*an instant*) instant, minute, moment, second. **5** (*a whiff, a trace*) hint, suggestion, suspicion, touch, trace, undertone, whiff. **6** (*a rumour, a whisper*) murmur, rumour, suggestion, whisper. **7** (*breath of air necessary for life*) breath of life, existence, life, puff. **out of breath** (*gasping for air after exercise*) blowing, breathless, gasping, panting, puffing, puffing and blowing, puffing and panting, wheezing, winded.

breathe *v.i.* **1** (*to inhale or exhale air*) inhale and exhale, inspire and expire, respire, take breath. **2** (*to live*) be alive, exist, have life, live. ANTONYMS: be dead. **3** (*to move or sound like breath*) murmur, sigh, whisper.
~*v.t.* **1** (*to utter*) articulate, express, mention, say, speak, tell, utter, voice. **2** (*to utter softly*) murmur, say in an undertone, sigh, whisper. **3** (*to add* (*life, confidence etc.*)) impart, infuse, inject, instil. **4** (*to express, to manifest*) betoken, display, exhibit, express, indicate, intimate, manifest, show, suggest. **to breathe in** (*to inhale*) inhale, inspire. **to breathe out** (*to exhale*) exhale, expire.

breather *n.* (*a rest in order to gain breath*) break, breathing-space, halt, interval, lull, pause, respite, rest, stop.

breathless *a.* **1** (*out of breath*) blowing, gasping, panting, puffing, puffing and blowing, puffing and panting, wheezing, winded. **2** (*excited, eager*) agog, all agog, avid, eager, excited, on edge, on tenterhooks, on the edge of one's seat, with bated breath.

breathtaking *a.* (*astonishing, marvellous*) amazing, astonishing, astounding, awe-inspiring, awesome, impressive, magnificent, moving, overwhelming, spectacular, striking, stunning, thrilling. ANTONYMS: boring, mundane.

breed *v.t.* **1** (*to raise* (*cattle etc.*), *to rear*) farm, raise, rear. **2** (*to give rise to, to produce*) arouse, bring about, cause, create, engender, generate, give rise to, make, originate, produce, stir up. **3** (*to educate, to bring up*) bring up, educate, nurture, raise, rear, train.
~*v.i.* (*to produce offspring*) bring forth young, give birth, multiply, procreate, produce offspring, reproduce.
~*n.* **1** (*family, offspring*) family, line, lineage, pedigree, race, reproduction, stock. **2** (*a sort, kind*) class, kind, sort, strain, variety.

breeding *n.* **1** (*the act of giving birth to young*) procreation, reproduction. **2** (*the raising of a breed*) raising, rearing. **3** (*bringing up, rearing*) bringing up, education, nurturing, raising, rearing, training, upbringing. **4** (*education, good manners*) civility, courtesy, cultivation, culture, gentility, good manners, polish, refinement. ANTONYMS: coarseness, roughness.

breeze *n.* (*a light wind*) breath of wind, current

of air, draught, gentle wind, gust, light wind, puff of wind, zephyr.

~*v.i.* (*to move in a lively way*) glide, sail, sally, stroll, sweep.

breezy *a.* **1** (*windy*) airy, blowy, blustery, fresh, gusty, squally, windy. ANTONYMS: calm, still, windless. **2** (*lively, brisk*) airy, animated, blithe, buoyant, carefree, casual, cheerful, (*coll.*) chirpy, free-and-easy, frisky, genial, informal, jaunty, jovial, light-hearted, lively, sparkling, spirited, sprightly, (*coll.*) upbeat, vivacious. ANTONYMS: dull, lifeless, serious.

brevity *n.* **1** (*briefness, shortness*) briefness, ephemerality, impermanence, shortness, transience, transitoriness. ANTONYMS: length, lengthiness, permanence. **2** (*conciseness*) briefness, compactness, conciseness, crispness, curtness, pithiness, pointedness, shortness, succinctness, terseness. ANTONYMS: discursiveness, wordiness.

brew *v.t.* **1** (*to make* (*beer, ale etc.*) *by steeping and fermenting*) ferment, make, manufacture. **2** (*to prepare* (*other beverages*) *by infusion*) infuse, make, prepare. **3** (*to contrive, to plot*) concoct, contrive, (*coll.*) cook up, devise, foment, hatch, plan, plot, stir up.

~*v.i.* (*to be in preparation*) be imminent, be impending, be in the offing, be threatening, form, gather force, impend, loom, threaten.

~*n.* (*the product of brewing*) ale, beer, beverage, concoction, drink, infusion, tea.

bribe *n.* (*a gift of money etc. offered to anyone to influence their conduct*) (*coll.*) backhander, carrot, enticement, graft, hush money, inducement, kickback, lure, (*coll.*) pay-off, (*esp. N Am.*) payola, sop, sweetener.

~*v.t.* (*to influence in action by means of a gift or other inducement*) buy off, corrupt, (*coll.*) give a backhander to, give an inducement to, give a sop to, (*coll.*) grease the palm of, (*coll.*) oil the palm of, (*coll.*) square, suborn.

bribery *n.* (*the act of giving or receiving bribes*) buying off, corruption, graft, inducement, (*coll.*) palm-greasing, (*coll.*) palm-oiling, (*esp. N Am.*) payola, protection, subornation.

bric-a-brac *n.* (*fancy ware, curiosities*) baubles, bibelots, curios, gewgaws, knick-knacks, objets d'art, ornaments, trinkets.

bridge *n.* (*a structure over a river, road etc. to carry a road or path across*) arch, flyover, overpass, viaduct.

~*v.t.* (*to span or cross with or as with a bridge*) cross, extend across, go over, span, traverse.

brief *a.* **1** (*short in duration*) ephemeral, evanescent, fleeting, impermanent, momentary, pass-

ing, short, short-lived, temporary, transient, transitory. ANTONYMS: enduring, lengthy, long-lasting, permanent, protracted. **2** (*short, concise*) compact, concise, crisp, economic, pithy, short, succinct, terse, to the point. ANTONYMS: lengthy, long-winded, verbose, wordy. **3** (*curt*) abrupt, blunt, brusque, curt, sharp, short.

~*v.t.* (*to give detailed instructions to*) advise, (*sl.*) clue (someone) up, (*coll.*) fill (someone) in, give (someone) instructions, (*coll.*) give (someone) the gen, (*coll.*) give (someone) the low-down, inform, instruct, prime, put (someone) in the picture.

briefly *adv.* **1** (*for a short time*) ephemerally, fleetingly, for a short time, momentarily, temporarily, transiently, transitorily. ANTONYMS: at length, for a long time, permanently. **2** (*concisely*) concisely, crisply, economically, in a few words, in a nutshell, in brief, pithily, succinctly, tersely, to the point. ANTONYMS: at length, verbosely, wordily.

brigade *n.* (*an organized group of soldiers or workers*) band, body, company, contingent, corps, crew, force, group, outfit, squad, team, troop, unit.

brigand *n.* (*a robber, a bandit*) bandit, outlaw, pirate, plunderer, robber.

bright *a.* **1** (*shining*) beaming, brilliant, dazzling, effulgent, flashing, gleaming, glittering, glowing, illuminated, luminous, lustrous, radiant, scintillating, shimmering, shining, sparkling, twinkling. ANTONYMS: dark, dim, dull, gloomy. **2** (*unclouded*) clear, cloudless, fair, fine, sunny, unclouded. ANTONYMS: cloudy, dull, shadowy. **3** (*cheerful, happy*) cheerful, cheery, (*coll.*) chirpy, glad, happy, jolly, joyful, light-hearted, merry, vivacious. ANTONYMS: miserable, sad, unhappy. **4** (*witty, clever*) accomplished, astute, brainy, brilliant, clever, ingenious, intelligent, quick-witted, sharp, smart, witty. ANTONYMS: dense, dull, stupid. **5** ((*of a colour*) *strong and easily seen*) bold, brilliant, glowing, intense, rich, strong, vivid. ANTONYMS: dull, pale, subtle. **6** ((*e.g. of a career or the future*) *likely to be successful, promising*) auspicious, cheerful, favourable, golden, hopeful, optimistic, promising, propitious, rosy. ANTONYMS: dark, gloomy, hopeless, unfavourable.

brighten *v.t.* **1** (*to make bright*) brighten up, lighten up, make bright, make brighter. ANTONYMS: darken, make dull. **2** (*to make happy, hopeful etc.*) (*coll.*) buck up, buoy up, cheer up, gladden, liven up, (*coll.*) perk up. ANTONYMS: cast down, depress, make dejected.

~*v.i.* **1** (*to become bright*) brighten up, illuminate, lighten, light up, make bright, make brighter. ANTONYMS: darken, dull. **2** ((*of the weather*) to *clear up*) become fine, become sunny, clear up, improve. ANTONYMS: cloud over, dull down. **3** (*to become happy, hopeful etc.*) (*coll.*) buck up, cheer up, liven up, (*coll.*) perk up. ANTONYMS: become gloomy, get depressed.

brilliance *n.* **1** (*brightness, sparkle*) beam, blaze, brightness, dazzle, gleam, glitter, luminousness, lustre, radiance, sheen, sparkle. ANTONYMS: darkness, dimness, dullness. **2** (*cleverness, great intelligence*) aptitude, astuteness, braininess, brightness, cleverness, intellect, intelligence, smartness, talent. ANTONYMS: denseness, stupidity. **3** (*splendour, magnificence*) glory, grandeur, impressiveness, intensity, magnificence, (*sl.*) pizazz, splendour, vividness. ANTONYMS: dullness, ordinariness.

brilliant *a.* **1** (*shining, sparkling*) bright, dazzling, gleaming, glittering, luminous, lustrous, radiant, shining, sparkling. ANTONYMS: dark, dim, dull. **2** (*illustrious, distinguished*) celebrated, distinguished, eminent, famous, illustrious, notable, noteworthy, outstanding. ANTONYMS: obscure, undistinguished, unknown. **3** (*extremely clever and successful*) astute, brainy, bright, clever, gifted, intellectual, intelligent, smart, talented. ANTONYMS: dense, slow-witted, stupid, unintelligent. **4** (*splendid, impressive*) glorious, grand, impressive, intense, magnificent, remarkable, splendid, superb, vivid. ANTONYMS: dull, ordinary, unimpressive, unremarkable. **5** (*excellent*) (*coll.*) brill, enjoyable, excellent, fine, marvellous, splendid, superb, wonderful. ANTONYMS: boring, miserable, tedious.

brim *n.* **1** (*the upper edge of a vessel*) edge, lip, rim. **2** (*the brink of a hollow or body of water*) border, brink, edge, margin, skirt, verge. **3** (*the rim of a hat*) edge, rim. ~*v.i.* (*to be full to the brim*) be filled to the top, be full, be full to the brim, overflow, run over.

brim-full *a.* (*full to the brim*) brimming, crammed, filled, full, overflowing. ANTONYMS: empty, vacant.

bring *v.t.* **1** (*to cause to come along with oneself*) conduct, escort, guide, lead, usher. ANTONYMS: lead away, take away. **2** (*to carry, to lead*) bear, carry, deliver, fetch, take, transport. ANTONYMS: collect, take away. **3** (*to influence, to persuade*) compel, force, induce, influence, make, persuade, prevail upon, prompt, sway. **4** (*to produce, result in*) earn, fetch, gross, make, net, produce, yield. **5** (*to cause, to create*) bring about, cause, create, effect, engender, give rise to, occasion, produce, wreak. **to bring about** (*to cause, to bring to pass*) accomplish, achieve, bring, cause, create, effect, engender, give rise to, occasion, produce, wreak. **to bring down 1** (*to lower* (*a price*)) cut, decrease, lower, reduce.

ANTONYMS: increase, put up, raise. **2** (*to depose, to overthrow*) depose, overthrow, put down. **3** (*to make unhappy*) cast down, depress, dispirit, sadden. **to bring in 1** (*to produce, to yield*) bring, earn, fetch, gross, make, net, produce, yield. **2** (*to introduce* (*as an action or bill*)) inaugurate, initiate, introduce, launch. **to bring off** (*to accomplish*) accomplish, achieve, be successful in, bring about, carry off, discharge, execute, perform, pull off. ANTONYMS: fail in. **to bring up 1** (*to educate, to rear*) care for, educate, nurture, raise, rear, train. **2** (*to lay before a meeting*) advance, broach, introduce, move, propose, put forward, submit, suggest, table.

brink *n.* (*the edge or border of a precipice, pit etc.*) border, brim, edge, limit, margin, rim, verge. **on the brink of** (*on the point of*) in danger of, on the edge of, on the point of, on the threshold of, on the verge of.

brisk *a.* **1** (*lively, active*) active, energetic, fast, quick, rapid, sprightly, swift, vigorous. ANTONYMS: slow, sluggish. **2** (*busy*) active, bustling, busy, hectic. **3** (*stimulating, bracing*) bracing, crisp, fresh, invigorating, keen, refreshing. ANTONYMS: enervating, tiring. **4** (*brusque, curt*) abrupt, brusque, curt, sharp, snappy.

brittle *a.* (*liable to break or be broken*) breakable, crisp, fragile, frangible, hard. ANTONYMS: non-breakable, soft.

broach *v.t.* **1** (*to mention, to make public*) bring up, introduce, mention, moot, propose, put forward, raise, raise the subject of, speak of, talk of, touch on. ANTONYMS: withdraw. **2** (*to pierce* (*as a cask*), *so as to allow liquor to flow*) crack, crack open, open, uncork.

broad *a.* **1** (*wide, extended across*) large, wide. ANTONYMS: narrow. **2** (*extensive, expansive*) expansive, extensive, large, spacious, sweeping, vast. ANTONYMS: limited, narrow, small. **3** (*of wide range, general*) broad-ranging, catholic, comprehensive, far-reaching, general, universal, unlimited, wide, wide-ranging. ANTONYMS: limited, narrow. **4** (*concerning the main ideas of something, not detailed*) general, loose, non-specific, undetailed, unspecific, vague. ANTONYMS: detailed, specific. **5** (*tolerant, liberal*) broad-minded, liberal, permissive, progressive, tolerant, unbiased, unprejudiced. ANTONYMS: biased, bigoted, intolerant, narrow-minded. **6** (*coarse, obscene*) (*sl.*) blue, coarse, gross, improper, indecent, indelicate, near the bone, near the knuckle, obscene, vulgar. ANTONYMS: decent, proper, refined.

broadcast *n.* (*anything transmitted to the public by radio or television*) programme, radio show, show, telecast, television show, transmission. ~*v.t.* **1** (*to transmit by radio or television*) air, beam, cable, put on the air, radio, relay, send out, televise, transmit. **2** (*to disseminate widely*) advertise, announce, circulate, communicate, disseminate, make public, proclaim, promulgate, publicize, publish, report, spread. ANTONYMS: conceal, keep secret, suppress.

broaden *v.t.* **1** (*to make broader*) make broader, make wider, widen. ANTONYMS: make narrower, narrow. **2** (*to increase*) amplify, augment, develop, enlarge, expand, extend, increase, supplement, widen. ANTONYMS: narrow, restrict.

broad-minded *a.* (*tolerant, having an open mind*) flexible, forbearing, liberal, open-minded, permissive, progressive, tolerant, unbiased, unprejudiced. ANTONYMS: bigoted, dogmatic, intolerant, narrow-minded.

brochure *n.* (*a small pamphlet*) booklet, circular, handout, leaflet, pamphlet.

broke *a.* (*ruined, penniless*) bankrupt, (*coll.*) bust, (*sl.*) cleaned out, (*coll.*) flat broke, impecunious, impoverished, indigent, insolvent, (*coll.*) on one's beam-ends, (*coll.*) on one's uppers, penniless, penurious, poverty-stricken, ruined, (*sl.*) skint, (*sl.*) stony-broke, (*coll.*) strapped for cash, (*coll.*) without two pennies to rub together. ANTONYMS: flush, rich, solvent, wealthy.

broken *a.* **1** (*in pieces*) burst, cracked, demolished, destroyed, disintegrated, fractured, fragmented, in pieces, in smithereens, rent, ruptured, shattered, smashed, splintered, split. **2** (*not working, not functioning properly*) (*coll.*) bust, damaged, defective, faulty, inoperative, (*coll.*) kaput, non-functioning, not working, (*coll.*) on the blink, out of commission, out of order. ANTONYMS: functioning, in working order, operative, working. **3** (*not whole or continuous*) disconnected, discontinuous, disturbed, fragmentary, incomplete, intermittent, interrupted, spasmodic. ANTONYMS: continuous, uninterrupted. **4** (*crushed, humbled*) beaten, conquered, crushed, defeated, demoralized, discouraged, dispirited, humbled, overpowered, overwhelmed, subdued, vanquished. ANTONYMS: unbeaten, undefeated, victorious. **5** (*transgressed, violated*) contravened, disobeyed, disregarded, flouted, ignored, infringed, transgressed, violated. ANTONYMS: obeyed, observed. **6** (*interrupted, incoherent*) disjointed, faltering, halting, hesitant, incoherent, stammering, stumbling. ANTONYMS: coherent, fluent.

broken-hearted *a.* (*crushed in spirit by grief or anxiety*) bowed down, desolate, devastated, forlorn, grief-stricken, heartbroken, inconsolable, miserable, prostrated, sad, sorrowing, unhappy, wretched. ANTONYMS: ecstatic, euphoric, joyful.

broker *n.* (*an agent, a factor*) agent, dealer,

factor, go-between, intermediary, middleman, negotiator, representative, third party.

brooch *n.* (*an ornamental clasp with a pin, worn on clothing*) clip, pin.

brood *v.i.* (*to meditate moodily*) agonize, fret, meditate, mope, muse, ponder, ruminate, think, worry.

brook[1] *n.* (*a small stream*) beck, burn, rivulet, stream, streamlet.

brook[2] *v.t.* (*to endure, to put up with*) accept, allow, countenance, endure, put up with, stand, stomach, support, tolerate.

brothel *n.* (*premises where prostitutes sell their services*) bawdy house, bordello, (*NAm., sl.*) cathouse, house of ill repute, (*sl.*) knocking shop, whorehouse.

brother *n.* (*a person closely connected with another*) associate, (*coll.*) chum, colleague, companion, comrade, fellow, mate, (*coll.*) pal, partner.

brotherhood *n.* (*a fraternity, an association for mutual service*) alliance, association, clique, coterie, fraternity, guild, league, lodge, order, society, union.

brotherly *a.* (*fraternal*) brotherlike, fraternal.

brow *n.* **1** (*the forehead*) forehead, temple. **2** (*the top of a hill*) crown, peak, summit, top. ANTONYMS: base, bottom.

browbeat *v.t.* (*to intimidate arrogantly*) (*coll.*) bulldoze, bully, coerce, compel, dragoon, force, intimidate, strong-arm, threaten, tyrannize.

browned off *a.* **1** (*disappointed*) (*coll.*) cheesed off, disappointed, discouraged, disgruntled, (*taboo sl.*) pissed off, (*coll.*) sick as a parrot. **2** (*bored, fed up*) bored, (*coll.*) cheesed off, discontented, (*coll.*) fed up, sick and tired.

browse *v.t.* **1** (*to nibble and eat off* (*twigs, young shoots etc.*)) graze, nibble. **2** (*to read in a desultory way*) dip into, flip through, glance through, leaf through, scan, skim.

bruise *v.t.* **1** (*to injure without breaking skin, usu. with discoloration*) blacken, contuse, discolour, make black and blue, mark. **2** (*to batter, grind up*) batter, crush, pound, pulverize. **3** (*to hurt, disable*) distress, hurt, offend, upset, wound. ~*n.* **1** (*a discoloured area of the skin caused by rupture of underlying blood vessels*) black and blue mark, contusion, discoloration. **2** (*a damaged area on a fruit*) blemish, mark.

brunt *n.* (*the shock or force of an attack*) force, full force, impact, main force, pressure, shock, stress, thrust, violence.

brush *n.* **1** (*an instrument for cleaning, generally made of bristles or feathers*) besom, broom, sweeping brush, yard-brush. **2** (*an instrument* *consisting of hairs or bristles attached to a handle, for painting etc.*) paintbrush. **3** (*a brushing*) hit, stroke, touch. **4** (*an attack, a skirmish*) clash, conflict, confrontation, encounter, engagement, fight, fracas, (*coll.*) set-to, skirmish, tussle. **5** (*a thicket of small trees*) brushwood, thicket, undergrowth.

~*v.t.* **1** (*to sweep or scrub with a brush*) scrub, sweep. **2** (*to touch lightly, as in passing*) caress, flick, glance, graze, kiss, scrape, stroke, touch. **to brush aside** (*to dismiss curtly*) dismiss, disregard, shrug off, sweep aside. **to brush up on** (*to refresh one's memory of*) (*sl.*) bone up on, go over, polish up, read up, refresh one's memory of, revise.

brush-off *n.* (*a brusque rebuff*) cold shoulder, (*coll.*) knock-back, rebuff, rejection, repudiation, repulse, slight, snub.

brusque *a.* (*rough or blunt in manner*) abrupt, blunt, curt, discourteous, gruff, offhand, sharp, short, terse, uncivil. ANTONYMS: civil, courteous, effusive, expansive, gracious.

brutal *a.* **1** (*savage, cruel*) barbarous, callous, cruel, murderous, savage, vicious. ANTONYMS: gentle. **2** (*coarse, unrefined*) animal, brutish, carnal, coarse, crude. ANTONYMS: refined.

brute *n.* **1** (*an animal*) animal, beast, wild animal, wild beast. **2** (*a violent or rough person*) beast, devil, fiend, monster, ogre, savage, swine.

bubbly *a.* **1** (*full of bubbles*) carbonated, effervescent, fizzy, sparkling. **2** (*excited, vivacious*) animated, bouncy, buoyant, ebullient, elated, lively, merry, sparkling. ANTONYMS: depressed, downcast.

bucket *n.* (*a vessel with a handle, for carrying water*) pail, pitcher, scuttle.

buckle *n.* **1** (*a link of metal etc., for fastening straps etc.*) catch, clasp, fastener. **2** (*a curl, a twist*) bend, contortion, kink, twist, warp.

~*v.t.* **1** (*to fasten with or as with a buckle*) fasten, secure. **2** (*to bend, to twist*) bend, contort, kink, twist, warp.

bucolic *a.* (*pastoral, rustic*) agricultural, country, (*coll.*) hick, pastoral, rural, rustic.

budding *a.* (*aspiring*) aspiring, developing, embryonic, incipient, potential, (*sl.*) wannabe.

budge *v.i.* **1** (*to move from one's place*) go, move, shift, stir. **2** (*to change one's opinion*) change one's mind, give in, give way, have a change of heart.

~*v.t.* **1** (*to cause to move*) dislodge, move, shift. **2** (*to cause one's opinion to change*) change (someone's) mind, persuade, sway, win over.

budget *n.* (*the amount of money allowed (for a specific item etc.)*) allocation, allowance, quota, ration.

buff *n.* (*an expert on or devotee of a subject*) addict, admirer, aficionado, connoisseur, devotee, enthusiast, expert, fan, (*coll.*) freak.

~*a.* (*light yellow*) beige, sand-coloured, straw-coloured, yellowish, yellowish-brown.

~*v.t.* (*to polish with a piece of leather*) burnish, polish, rub, shine, smooth.

buffet[1] *n.* (*a blow with the hand or fist, a cuff*) bang, blow, box, clout, cuff, slap, smack, thump, (*coll.*) wallop.

~*v.t.* (*to thump, to cuff*) batter, beat against, push against, strike against.

buffet[2] *n.* **1** (*a refreshment bar*) café, cafeteria, refreshment stall, snack bar. **2** (*dishes of food set out on a table from which diners help themselves*) cold meal, cold table, self-service meal, stand-up meal.

buffoon *n.* **1** (*a person who indulges in jests*) clown, comedian, comic, jester, joker, wag. **2** (*a vulgar, clowning fool*) clown, dolt, fool, idiot, nincompoop, (*coll.*) nitwit.

bug *n.* **1** (*any small insect*) (*coll.*) creepy-crawly, insect. **2** (*a viral infection*) disease, germ, illness, infection, virus. **3** (*a secreted radio receiver*) listening device, phone-tap, tap, wire-tap. **4** (*a flaw, esp. in a computer program*) defect, error, failing, fault, flaw, (*coll.*) glitch, (*coll.*) gremlin. **5** (*a temporary craze or fashion*) craze, fad, fashion, fixation, mania, obsession, passion.

bugbear *n.* (*a nuisance*) abomination, anathema, bane, bête noire, bogey, dread, hate, nightmare, pet hate.

build *v.t.* **1** (*to make by putting together parts and materials*) assemble, construct, erect, put up, raise. ANTONYMS: demolish, raze to the ground, tear down. **2** (*to establish, to develop*) develop, establish, found, inaugurate, institute, originate, set up, start up. ANTONYMS: destroy, end.

~*n.* (*shape, figure*) body, figure, form, frame, physique, proportions, shape, structure. **to build up 1** (*to establish or strengthen by degrees*) establish, found, inaugurate, institute, originate, set up, start up. ANTONYMS: destroy, end. **2** (*to increase*) add to, boost, develop, expand, extend, increase, strengthen. ANTONYMS: contract, reduce, weaken. **3** (*to praise*) advertise, (*coll.*) hype up, (*coll.*) plug, praise, promote, publicize, puff. ANTONYMS: criticize, deprecate.

building *n.* **1** (*the act of constructing or erecting*) assembly, construction, erection, putting up, raising. ANTONYMS: demolition, tearing down. **2** (*a structure erected*) edifice, erection, structure.

build-up *n.* **1** (*a creation of favourable publicity*) advertising, advertising campaign, ballyhoo, (*coll.*) hype, (*coll.*) plug, (*coll.*) plugging, promotion, publicity, puff. **2** (*an increase*) escalation, expansion, extension, growth, increase.

ANTONYMS: contraction, decrease, reduction. **3** (*an accumulation*) accretion, accumulation, backlog, heap, pile, stockpile.

built-in *a.* **1** (*part of the main structure*) incorporated, integral, integrated. ANTONYMS: separate, stand-alone. **2** (*fixed, included*) inbuilt, included, incorporated, inherent, integral, intrinsic.

bulge *n.* **1** (*a swelling on a surface*) bump, lump, protrusion, protuberance, swelling. ANTONYMS: cavity, dent, hollow. **2** (*a temporary increase in volume or numbers*) augmentation, boost, increase, rise, surge, swell. ANTONYMS: decrease, lessening, lowering, reduction.
~*v.i.* (*to be protuberant*) bag, balloon, belly, distend, protrude, stick out, swell, swell out.

bulk *n.* **1** (*size, mass*) bigness, bulkiness, dimensions, extent, hugeness, immensity, largeness, magnitude, mass, massiveness, size, volume, weight. **2** (*the greater portion, the main mass*) better part, body, greater part, lion's share, majority, major part, mass, most, preponderance. ANTONYMS: minority.

bulky *a.* **1** (*of great bulk or dimensions*) awkward, cumbersome, heavy, hulking, stout, substantial, unwieldy, weighty. **2** (*large*) big, colossal, enormous, huge, immense, large, massive, vast, very large. ANTONYMS: small, tiny.

bulldoze *v.t.* **1** (*to level or clear* (*ground*) *using a bulldozer*) demolish, flatten, level, raze. **2** (*to force or bully*) bludgeon, browbeat, bully, coerce, dragoon, force, intimidate, railroad, steamroller, strong-arm.

bullet *n.* (*a metal ball or cone used in firearms of small calibre*) ball, pellet, projectile, shot, slug.

bulletin *n.* **1** (*a brief news item on radio or television, a news bulletin*) announcement, communiqué, dispatch, newsflash, news item, news report, report, statement. **2** (*a periodical publication of an organization, society etc.*) journal, leaflet, newsletter, newspaper.

bully *n.* (*a person who intimidates or hurts those who do not stand up for themselves*) aggressor, browbeater, bully boy, intimidator, menace, oppressor, persecutor, thug, tormentor, tyrant.
~*v.t.* (*to oppress, terrorize*) browbeat, cow, intimidate, oppress, persecute, push around, terrorize, torment, tyrannize.

bulwark *n.* **1** (*a rampart or fortification*) bastion, buttress, fortification, outwork, rampart. **2** (*any shelter, protection*) buffer, defence, guard, protection, safeguard, security.

bumbling *a.* (*behaving in a disorganized way, making many mistakes*) blundering, bungling, clumsy, foolish, incompetent, inefficient, inept. ANTONYMS: able, competent, efficient.

bump *n.* **1** (*a thump, a dull, heavy blow*) bang, crash, thud, thump. **2** (*a collision, a crash*) collision, crash, impact, knock, smash. **3** (*a swelling*) lump, protuberance, swelling. **4** (*a short, sudden movement*) bounce, jerk, jolt, shake.
~*v.t.* **1** (*to hurt by striking against something*) bang, hit, hurt, injure, knock, strike. **2** (*to hit* (*against*)) bang, collide with, crash into, hit, knock into, run into, smash into, strike.
~*v.i.* **1** (*to collide*) bang (into), collide (with), crash (into), knock (into), run (into). **2** (*to move along with a bump or succession of bumps*) bounce, jerk, jolt, shake. **to bump into 1** (*to collide with, to hit*) collide with, crash into, hit, knock into, run into, smash into. **2** (*to meet unexpectedly*) chance upon, come across, encounter, happen upon, light upon, meet, meet by chance, run across, run into. **to bump off** (*to murder*) assassinate, (*coll.*) do away with, (*sl.*) do in, kill, murder. **to bump up** (*to increase* (*prices*)) boost, escalate, (*coll.*) hike up, increase, (*coll.*) jack up, raise, step up. ANTONYMS: decrease, lower, reduce.

bumpkin *n.* (*a country lout*) (*coll.*) clodhopper, country bumpkin, (*coll.*) hick, peasant, rustic, yokel.

bumptious *a.* (*disagreeably self-opinionated*) arrogant, cocky, conceited, full of oneself, overbearing, overconfident, presumptuous, self-important, self-opinionated. ANTONYMS: modest, retiring, unassuming.

bumpy *a.* **1** ((*of a journey*) *uncomfortable, because travelling on a rough surface*) bouncy, choppy, jarring, jerky, jolting, jolty, rough. ANTONYMS: smooth. **2** (*full of bumps, uneven*) lumpy, pitted, potholed, rough, rutted, uneven. ANTONYMS: even, smooth.

bunch *n.* **1** (*a cluster of several things of the same kind tied together*) bouquet, posy, sheaf, spray. **2** (*a cluster of things growing together*) clump, cluster, knot, tuft. **3** (*a number of things fastened together*) cluster, collection, set. **4** (*a lot, a collection*) assortment, batch, bundle, collection, heap, lot, mass, pile, stack. **5** (*a group, a herd*) band, cluster, collection, crowd, gang, gathering, group, herd, knot, party.
~*v.i.* **1** (*to come or grow into a cluster or bunch*) bundle, cluster, collect, cram together, gather, group, herd, huddle, pack. **2** (*to gather into folds*) fold, gather, pleat.

bungle *v.t.* (*to botch*) botch, (*sl.*) cock up, (*coll.*) foul up, louse up, make a mess of, mismanage, muff, (*sl.*) screw up.

bungling *a.* (*clumsy, unskilful*) awkward, blundering, (*sl.*) cack-handed, clumsy, (*coll.*) ham-fisted, incompetent, inept, maladroit, unskilful. ANTONYMS: competent, expert, skilful.

buoy n. 1 (*an anchored float indicating a fairway, reef etc.*) float, marker, navigation guide. 2 (*a lifebuoy*) lifebelt, lifebuoy, life jacket. **to buoy up** (*to make cheerful*) boost, cheer up, lift, raise.

buoyant a. 1 (*tending to float*) floatable, floating, light. 2 (*light-hearted*) blithe, bouncy, breezy, bright, carefree, cheerful, (*coll.*) chirpy, happy, jaunty, joyful, light-hearted, lively, merry, sparkling, sprightly, (*coll.*) upbeat, vivacious. ANTONYMS: depressed, downcast, miserable, sad, unhappy.

burden n. 1 (*a load*) cargo, freight, load. 2 (*a load of care, obligation etc.*) anxiety, care, charge, duty, load, obligation, onus, responsibility, strain, stress, trouble, worry. 3 (*the principal theme of a composition*) argument, gist, keynote, substance, text, theme.
~v.t. 1 (*to load*) load, weigh down. 2 (*to oppress, to encumber*) afflict, bother, encumber, oppress, overwhelm, plague, tax, torment, trouble, weigh down, worry.

bureau n. 1 (*a writing table with drawers for papers*) desk, writing desk, writing table. 2 (*an office*) agency, office. 3 (*a government department*) branch, department, division.

bureaucracy n. (*rigid adherence to procedure, inflexible government*) officialdom, red tape.

bureaucrat n. (*a government official*) administrator, civil servant, functionary, jack-in-office, mandarin, official, public servant.

bureaucratic a. (*tending towards bureaucracy*) going by the book, official, red-tape, rigid.

burgeon v.i. (*to begin to grow or develop*) develop, flourish, grow, multiply, mushroom. ANTONYMS: fail, wither.

burglar n. (*a person who breaks into premises with intent to commit a theft*) cat burglar, housebreaker, robber, thief.

burglary n. (*the act of breaking into premises with intent to commit a theft*) breaking and entering, breaking in, forced entry, housebreaking, larceny, robbery, theft.

burial n. 1 (*the act of burying a dead body in the earth*) burying, entombment, interment. 2 (*a funeral with burying of the body*) burial service, exequies, funeral, funeral service, obsequies.

burlesque n. (*mockery, grotesque imitation*) caricature, lampooning, mockery, parody, satire, (*coll.*) send-up, travesty.

burly a. (*stout, corpulent*) beefy, big, brawny, bulky, corpulent, hefty, hulking, large, muscular, powerful, stout, strapping, thickset, well-built. ANTONYMS: slender, small, thin, (*coll.*) weedy.

burn v.t. 1 (*to destroy or scorch by fire*) burn down, char, incinerate, scorch, singe. 2 (*to subject to the action of fire*) ignite, put a match to, set alight, set on fire. 3 (*to corrode, eat into*) bite into, corrode, eat into, wear away.
~v.i. 1 (*to be on fire*) be ablaze, be in flames, be on fire, blaze, flame. 2 (*to be or become intensely hot*) be fevered, be feverish, be hot, feel hot. 3 (*to emit light, to shine*) blaze, gleam, glow, shine. 4 (*to rage, to be inflamed*) be aroused, be excited, be passionate, seethe, smoulder.

burning a. 1 (*in a state of heat*) blazing. 2 (*intensely hot*) boiling, fevered, feverish, hot, roasting, scorching. ANTONYMS: cold, freezing. 3 (*ardent, glowing*) all-consuming, ardent, consuming, eager, fervent, fervid, impassioned, intense, passionate, vehement. 4 (*having a painful stinging sensation*) biting, irritating, prickling, smarting, stinging, tingling. 5 (*urgent, very important*) critical, crucial, key, pressing, urgent, vital.

burrow n. (*a hole in the ground made by rabbits, foxes etc., for a dwelling-place*) den, hole, lair, tunnel.
~v.i. 1 (*to hide oneself*) conceal oneself, go under, hide, nestle, shelter. 2 (*to investigate (into)*) delve (into), dig (for), look (for), search (for).
~v.t. (*to make by means of excavation*) dig, excavate, tunnel.

burst v.t. (*to break with suddenness and violence*) break open, crack, fracture, rend asunder, rupture, shatter, split. ANTONYMS: mend, repair.
~v.i. 1 (*to be broken suddenly from within*) break open, crack, fracture, fragment, rupture, shatter, split open. 2 (*to rush forth with suddenness and force*) gush, pour forth, rush, spout, surge. **to burst in 1** (*to enter suddenly*) barge in, make a sudden entrance. 2 (*to interrupt*) break in, butt in, chime in, cut in, interrupt. **to burst out 1** (*to break out*) break loose, break out, escape. 2 (*to begin suddenly to laugh, cry etc.*) begin, break out, commence, start. 3 (*to exclaim*) call out, cry, exclaim, shout, yell.

bury v.t. 1 (*to place (a corpse) under ground*) consign to the grave, entomb, inter, lay to rest. ANTONYMS: dig up, disinter, exhume. 2 (*to put under ground*) hide under ground, place under ground, put under ground. 3 (*to hide, to cover up*) conceal, cover up, hide, sink, submerge. 4 (*to embed*) drive in, embed, implant, sink.

bush n. 1 (*a thick shrub*) shrub, tree. 2 (*a clump of shrubs*) shrubbery, thicket, undergrowth. 3 (*uncleared land, more or less covered with wood, esp. in Australasia*) backwoods, brush, scrubland, the wild.

bushy a. (*growing like a bush*) fuzzy, shaggy, thick, unruly. ANTONYMS: sparse, thin.

business n. 1 (*employment, profession*) calling,

career, employment, job, line, line of work, métier, occupation, profession, trade, work. **2** (*duty, concern*) affair, concern, duty, function, responsibility, task. **3** (*a particular matter demanding attention*) issue, matter, point, problem, question, subject, theme, topic. **4** (*an affair, a matter*) affair, case, matter, set of circumstances, situation, thing. **5** (*commercial activity*) buying and selling, commerce, commercial activity, dealings, trade, trading, trafficking, transactions. **6** (*a commercial establishment*) commercial concern, commercial enterprise, company, corporation, enterprise, firm, organization, venture.

businesslike *a.* (*methodical, efficient*) efficient, methodical, orderly, organized, professional, systematic. ANTONYMS: disorganized, inefficient, sloppy, unprofessional.

bust *n.* **1** (*a sculptured representation of the head, shoulders and breast of a person*) cameo, head and shoulders, sculpture. **2** (*the upper front part of the body, the bosom, esp. of a woman*) (*sl.*) boobs, bosom, breasts, chest, (*taboo sl.*) knockers, (*taboo sl.*) tits.

bustle *n.* (*agitation, fuss*) activity, agitation, commotion, flurry, fuss, stir, (*coll.*) to-do, tumult.
~*v.i.* (*to be active, esp. with excessive fuss and noise*) busy oneself, dash, fuss, hurry, rush, scurry, scuttle.

busy *a.* **1** (*fully occupied*) engaged, occupied, otherwise engaged, working. ANTONYMS: free, unoccupied. **2** (*actively employed* (*in*)) employed (in), engaged (in), involved (in), occupied (with), preoccupied (with), working (at). **3** (*characterized by great activity*) action-packed, active, exacting, full, hectic, strenuous, taxing, tiring. ANTONYMS: inactive, leisurely, relaxed. **4** (*hard-working*) active, diligent, energetic, hard-working, industrious, (*coll.*) on the go, restless. ANTONYMS: idle, inactive, indolent, lazy. **5** (*meddlesome*) inquisitive, interfering, meddlesome, meddling, (*coll.*) nosy, officious, prying, snooping. **6** (*fussy*) cluttered, fussy, ornate, over-elaborate. ANTONYMS: plain, simple, stark.
~*v.i.* (*to occupy oneself* (*about, in etc.*)) employ, engross, imnvolve, occupy.

busybody *n.* (*a meddler*) gossip, interferer, meddler, (*coll.*) Nosy Parker, pry, pryer, scandalmonger, snoop, snoopy.

butt[1] *n.* **1** (*the thick end of anything, esp. of a tool or weapon*) handle, heft, hilt, shaft, stock. **2** (*the end of a cigarette after most of it has been smoked*) end, (*coll.*) fag end, remnant, stub.

butt[2] *n.* (*a large cask*) barrel, cask, pipe.

butt[3] *n.* (*a target for ridicule or abuse*) Aunt Sally, (*coll.*) mark, (*N Am., sl.*) patsy, scapegoat, target, victim.

butt[4] *v.t.* (*to strike with or as with the head*) buffet, bump, knock, push, ram, shove. **to butt in** (*to interfere, interrupt*) chime in, cut in, interfere in, interrupt, intrude, meddle, (*coll.*) put one's oar in, (*coll.*) stick one's nose in.

buttonhole *v.t.* (*to detain in conversation*) accost, detain, detain in conversation, take aside, waylay.

buttress *n.* **1** (*a structure built against a wall to strengthen it*) abutment, brace, prop, reinforcement, strut, support. **2** (*a prop, support*) cornerstone, mainstay, pillar, prop, support, sustainer.

buxom *a.* ((*of women*) *plump and comely*) bosomy, cuddly, curvaceous, plump, voluptuous, well-rounded.

buy *v.t.* **1** (*to obtain by means of money*) invest in, pay for, purchase, shop for. **2** (*to gain by bribery*) bribe, (*sl.*) fix, (*coll.*) grease the palm of, (*coll.*) square, suborn.
~*n.* (*a purchase*) bargain, deal, purchase.

buzz *n.* **1** (*a sibilant hum, like that of a bee*) buzzing, drone, hum, humming, whir. **2** (*a confused, mingled noise*) hubbub, hum, murmur. **3** (*report, rumour*) chit-chat, gossip, hearsay, news, report, rumour, (*coll.*) the grapevine.

bygone *a.* (*past*) departed, former, gone by, of old, past, previous. ANTONYMS: future, to be, to come.

by-law *n.* (*a private statute made by the members of a local authority*) local regulation, regulation, rule, statute.

bypass *n.* (*a road for the purpose of diverting traffic from crowded areas*) orbital, orbital road, ring road, ring route.
~*v.t.* **1** (*to avoid, evade*) avoid, circumvent, evade, find a way round, get round, pass over. **2** (*to go round*) go round, make a detour round, pass round.

bystander *n.* (*an onlooker, an eyewitness*) eyewitness, looker-on, observer, onlooker, spectator, witness.

byword *n.* **1** (*a person or thing noted for a particular characteristic*) embodiment, example, personification, type. **2** (*a common saying*) catchword, motto, slogan, tag.

C

cabin *n.* **1** (*a small hut*) chalet, cottage, house, hovel, hut, lodge, shack, shanty, shed. **2** (*a room or compartment in a ship or aircraft*) apartment, berth, compartment, quarters, room.

cabinet *n.* **1** (*a piece of furniture with drawers, shelves etc., in which to keep articles*) bureau, chest, closet, commode, cupboard, desk, dresser, escritoire, locker, tallboy. **2** (*a deliberative committee of the principal members of government*) administration, assembly, committee, council, counsellors, ministry, senate.

cache *n.* **1** (*a place in which provisions, arms etc. are hidden*) hiding place, repository, reserve, store, storehouse, treasure-house, treasury, vault. **2** (*the hidden provisions, arms etc.*) accumulation, fund, hoard, nest egg, (*coll.*) stash, stockpile, supply, treasure.
~v.t. (*to hide or conceal in a cache*) bury, conceal, hide, put away, secrete, (*coll.*) stash, store.

cackle *n.* **1** (*the cackling of a hen*) cackling, clucking, squawking. **2** (*silly chatter*) babble, chatter, gabble.
~v.i. **1** (*of a hen) to make a squawking or clucking noise*) cluck, crow, squawk. **2** (*to chatter in a silly manner*) babble, blather, chatter, gabble, gibber, jabber, prate, prattle. **3** (*to giggle*) chuckle, giggle, laugh, snicker, snigger, titter.

cacophonous *a.* (*harsh-sounding, discordant*) deafening, discordant, dissonant, grating, harsh, inharmonious, jarring, raucous, strident. ANTONYMS: harmonious.

cadaverous *a.* **1** (*corpselike*) corpselike, deathly. **2** (*deathly pale*) ashen, blanched, bloodless, gaunt, ghastly, haggard, pale, pallid, wan, white. ANTONYMS: rosy, ruddy.

cage *n.* **1** (*an enclosure of wire or iron bars, in which animals are kept*) box, corral, crate, enclosure, hutch, pen, pound. **2** (*a prison cell*) brig, cell, (*sl.*) clink, prison.
~v.t. **1** (*to confine in or as if in a cage*) confine, coop up, enclose, fence in, hem in, pound, restrain, restrict, shut up. ANTONYMS: free. **2** (*to confine in a prison*) impound, imprison, incarcerate, lock up, shut up.

cajole *v.t.* **1** (*to persuade by flattery*) (*coll.*) butter up, flatter, inveigle, persuade, (*coll.*) soft-soap, (*coll.*) sweet-talk. **2** (*to wheedle, to coax*) coax, entice, entrap, (*coll.*) jolly along, lure, manoeuvre, tempt, wheedle. **3** (*to beguile or deceive*) beguile, deceive, decoy, dupe, mislead, seduce.

calamity *n.* **1** (*extreme misfortune or adversity*) adversity, affliction, cataclysm, catastrophe, devastation, disaster, downfall, misadventure, mischance, misfortune, mishap, reverse, ruin, tragedy, trial, tribulation, trouble. ANTONYMS: blessing. **2** (*great distress or misery*) anguish, distress, hardship, misery, woe, wretchedness.

calculate *v.t.* **1** (*to determine by mathematical process*) add up, assess, compute, count, determine, enumerate, estimate, figure, reckon. **2** (*to ascertain beforehand*) ascertain, evaluate, gauge, judge, measure, rate, value, weigh, work out. **3** (*to plan beforehand*) aim, design, intend, plan. **4** (*to adjust, to arrange*) adjust, arrange.

calculated *a.* **1** (*prearranged, intended*) considered, deliberate, intended, intentional, planned, prearranged, purposeful. ANTONYMS: hasty, impulsive. **2** (*premeditated, cold-blooded*) callous, cold-blooded, deliberate, predetermined, premeditated, wilful. **3** (*suitable, designed (to)*) adapted (for), aimed (at), designed (to), suitable (for).

calculating *a.* **1** (*shrewd, acting with forethought*) acute, canny, cautious, circumspect, far-sighted, penetrating, perspicuous, sharp, shrewd, wary. **2** (*scheming*) conniving, crafty, cunning, designing, devious, manipulative, politic, scheming, sly. ANTONYMS: guileless.

calculation *n.* **1** (*the act of computing or calculating*) assessment, computation, estimation, figuring, valuation, working out. **2** (*the result of this*) amount, answer, computation, estimate, product, result. **3** (*a forecast or projection*) estimation, forecast, projection, reckoning. **4** (*careful planning*) caution, circumspection, deliberation, discretion, foresight, forethought, planning, precaution, prudence. ANTONYMS: rashness.

call *v.t.* **1** (*to name, to designate*) denominate, denote, designate, dub, identify, label, name, style, tag, term. **2** (*to regard or consider as*) consider, estimate, judge, regard, think. **3** (*to summon, to gather*) assemble, bid, collect,

convene, convoke, gather, muster, rally, summon. **4** (*to communicate with or summon by telephone or radio*) buzz, contact, dial, phone, radio, ring up, telephone. **5** (*to command*) bid, command, direct, order, urge. **6** (*to announce or cause to happen*) announce, appoint, declare, decree, elect, ordain, proclaim. **7** (*to rouse from sleep*) arouse, awaken, knock up, rouse, waken, wake up. **8** (*to nominate or summon* (*to a profession etc.*)) invite, nominate, summon. **9** (*to lure* (*birds etc.*) *by imitating their cry*) decoy, lure.
~*v.i.* (*to speak in a loud voice; to shout*) bellow, cry, exclaim, hail, roar, shout, whoop, yell. ANTONYMS: murmur, whisper.
~*n.* **1** (*a loud cry*) bellow, cry, exclamation, hail, roar, scream, shout, whoop, yell. **2** (*a vocal address or supplication*) address, announcement, appeal, command, demand, plea, request, supplication. **3** (*a communication by telephone or radio*) bell, (*sl.*) buzz, (*coll.*) ring, telephone call, (*coll.*) tinkle. **4** (*a summons, an invitation*) bidding, invitation, summons. **5** (*a requirement or demand*) demand, notice, order, requirement. **6** (*necessity, justification*) cause, claim, duty, excuse, grounds, justification, necessity, need, occasion, reason, right, urge. **to call for 1** (*to desire the attendance of*) invite, require, summon. **2** (*to appeal for, to demand*) appeal for, ask for, demand. **3** (*to require, necessitate*) entail, involve, necessitate, need, occasion, order, require, suggest. **4** (*to visit a place to bring* (*a person or thing*) *away*) collect, come for, fetch, get, pick up. **to call off** (*to cancel*) abandon, abolish, break off, cancel, discontinue. **to call on 1** (*to invoke, to appeal to*) appeal to, ask, bid, call upon, entreat, invoke, request, summon, supplicate. **2** (*to pay a short visit to*) drop in on, look in on, look up, see, visit.

calling *n.* **1** (*an occupation or profession*) area, business, career, craft, employment, job, line, métier, occupation, profession, province, pursuit, speciality, trade, walk of life. **2** (*a vocation*) mission, vocation.

callous *a.* (*unfeeling, insensitive*) apathetic, cold, cold-hearted, hardbitten, hardened, hard-hearted, harsh, heartless, indifferent, insensitive, thick-skinned, uncaring, unfeeling, unsympathetic. ANTONYMS: caring, sensitive, sympathetic.

calm *a.* **1** (*still, quiet*) balmy, even, halcyon, mild, pacific, peaceful, placid, quiet, restful, serene, smooth, still, tranquil. ANTONYMS: stormy, turbulent. **2** (*composed, undisturbed*) collected, composed, cool, dispassionate, equable, impassive, imperturbable, relaxed, self-possessed, stoical, undisturbed, unemotional, unexcitable, unexcited, (*coll.*) unfazed,

(*coll.*) unflappable, unmoved, unruffled. ANTONYMS: agitated, disturbed.
~*n.* (*the state of being calm*) calmness, hush, peace, peacefulness, placidity, quiet, repose, serenity, stillness, tranquillity.
~*v.t.* (*to make calm*) allay, alleviate, appease, assuage, hush, lull, pacify, placate, quieten, relax, soothe, still.

camouflage *n.* (*disguise, esp. the concealment of guns, vehicles etc., from the enemy by means of deceptive painting and covering*) blind, cloak, concealment, cover, deception, disguise, front, guise, mask, masking, screen.
~*v.t.* (*to disguise*) cloak, conceal, cover, disguise, hide, mask, obfuscate, obscure, screen, veil. ANTONYMS: expose, unmask.

camp[1] *n.* **1** (*the place where an army is lodged in tents or other temporary structures*) bivouac, cantonment, encampment. **2** (*the temporary quarters of holidaymakers, Scouts or Guides etc., usu. in tents or caravans*) campsite, tents. **3** (*a body of adherents*) adherents, body, clique, coterie, faction, group, party, set, side.

camp[2] *a.* **1** (*affectedly homosexual*) gay, homosexual. **2** (*effeminate*) effeminate, limp-wristed. **3** (*exaggerated, artificial*) affected, artificial, exaggerated, flamboyant, mannered, ostentatious, outrageous, (*sl.*) poncy, posturing, showy, studied, theatrical.

cancel *v.t.* **1** (*to annul, revoke*) abolish, abort, abrogate, annul, break off, call off, countermand, deny, do away with, expunge, invalidate, nullify, obviate, quash, repeal, repudiate, rescind, revoke, void. ANTONYMS: confirm. **2** (*to withdraw or discontinue*) discontinue, refrain from, withdraw. **3** (*to obliterate by drawing lines across*) blot out, cross out, delete, efface, obliterate, scratch out, scribble over, strike out.

cancellation *n.* (*the act of cancelling*) abandonment, abolition, abrogation, annulment, breaking off, calling off, cessation, deletion, elimination, nullification, obliteration, quashing, repeal, rescission, revocation, stoppage, termination, withdrawal. ANTONYMS: confirmation.

candid *a.* **1** (*frank, sincere*) frank, free, guileless, honest, ingenuous, open, sincere, truthful, uncalculating. **2** (*outspoken, freely critical*) blunt, critical, forthright, outspoken, plain, straightforward, unequivocal, (*coll.*) upfront. **3** (*unbiased*) equitable, fair, impartial, just, objective, unbiased, unbigoted, unprejudiced. ANTONYMS: biased, prejudiced.

candidate *n.* **1** (*a person who seeks or is proposed for some office or appointment*) applicant, aspirant, claimant, competitor, contender, contestant, entrant, nominee, runner, solicitant, suitor. **2** (*a person or thing considered likely for a particular end*) possibility, prospect.

candour *n.* **1** (*frankness, sincerity*) artlessness, bluntness, directness, fairness, forthrightness, frankness, guilelessness, honesty, naivety, openness, simplicity, sincerity, straightforwardness, truthfulness. **2** (*freedom from bias*) fairness, impartiality, justice, objectivity, unbias. ANTONYMS: bias, prejudice.

cantankerous *a.* (*bad-tempered; quarrelsome*) argumentative, bad-tempered, contrary, crabby, cross, crotchety, crusty, difficult, grouchy, grumpy, ill-humoured, irascible, irritable, peevish, quarrelsome, (*sl.*) ratty, snappish, surly, testy, tetchy. ANTONYMS: amiable, genial.

capability *n.* (*the quality of being capable*) ability, aptitude, competence, facility, faculty, means, potential, power, proficiency, qualification, skill, talent, wherewithal. ANTONYMS: incompetence, ineptitude.

capable *a.* (*competent, able*) able, accomplished, adept, adequate, apt, clever, competent, effectual, efficient, experienced, expert, fitted, gifted, intelligent, masterly, proficient, qualified, skilful, suited, talented. ANTONYMS: incapable, unskilled.

capacity *n.* **1** (*room, volume*) amplitude, compass, dimensions, extent, magnitude, range, room, size, space, volume. **2** (*capability, ability*) ability, acumen, aptitude, aptness, capability, cleverness, content, efficiency, facility, faculty, gift, intelligence, judgement, perspicacity, power, readiness, sense, strength, talent, understanding. ANTONYMS: inability, ineptitude. **3** (*opportunity, scope*) opportunity, room, scope. **4** (*relative position or office*) appointment, character, duty, function, job, office, place, position, post, province, responsibility, role, service, sphere. **5** (*legal qualification*) competence, qualification.

caper *n.* **1** (*a frolicsome leap*) gambol, hop, jump, leap, skip. **2** (*a high-spirited escapade*) antic, escapade, jape, jest, lark, practical joke, prank, revel, stunt. **3** (*any activity, esp. of questionable legality*) crime, mischief.
~*v.i.* **1** (*to leap*) bound, hop, jump, leap, prance, spring. **2** (*to skip about, to frolic*) bounce, cavort, curvet, dance, frisk, frolic, gambol, romp, skip, trip.

capital *a.* **1** (*chief, most important*) cardinal, central, chief, controlling, essential, foremost, important, key, leading, main, major,

overruling, paramount, pre-eminent, primary, prime, principal, prominent, vital. **2** (*excellent, first-rate*) choice, excellent, extraordinary, fine, first-rate, (*coll.*) great, matchless, outstanding, prime, select, splendid, sterling, superb, superior, world-class. ANTONYMS: poor. **3** (*punishable by death*) fatal, serious.
~*n.* **1** (*money used to start a business or industry*) cash, finance, funds, investment, means, money, principal, savings, wealth, wherewithal. **2** (*the main fund or stock of a corporation or business firm*) assets, property, resources, stock.

capitulate *v.i.* (*to surrender, esp. on stipulated terms*) concede, give in, give up, relent, submit, succumb, surrender, (*coll.*) throw in the towel, yield. ANTONYMS: conquer, resist.

capricious *a.* (*given to unexpected and unpredictable changes*) changeable, erratic, fanciful, fickle, fitful, flighty, impulsive, inconstant, irresolute, mercurial, queer, quirky, uncertain, unpredictable, unreliable, unsteady, variable, wanton, wayward, whimsical. ANTONYMS: predictable, reliable.

captivate *v.t.* (*to fascinate, to charm*) absorb, allure, attract, beguile, bewitch, charm, dazzle, delight, enchant, enrapture, ensnare, enthral, entrance, fascinate, hypnotize, infatuate, lure, mesmerize, ravish, seduce. ANTONYMS: disgust, repel.

captive *n.* (*a person or animal taken prisoner or held in confinement*) convict, detainee, hostage, internee, prisoner, slave.
~*a.* **1** (*taken prisoner*) arrested, caught, ensnared. **2** (*held in confinement or control*) caged, confined, enslaved, imprisoned, incarcerated, locked up, penned, restrained, restricted, subjugated. ANTONYMS: free.

captivity *n.* (*the state of being captive*) bondage, confinement, custody, detention, duress, enslavement, enthralment, imprisonment, incarceration, internment, restraint, servitude, slavery, thraldom. ANTONYMS: freedom.

capture *v.t.* **1** (*to take as a captive*) apprehend, arrest, catch, (*coll.*) collar, detain, take captive, take prisoner. **2** (*to take control of; to seize as a prize*) bag, grab, (*sl.*) nab, secure, seize, take. ANTONYMS: release.
~*n.* (*the act of capturing*) apprehension, arrest, catch, imprisonment, seizure, taking.

cardinal *a.* (*fundamental, chief*) capital, central, chief, essential, first, foremost, fundamental, greatest, highest, important, key, leading, main, necessary, paramount, primary, prime, principal, vital. ANTONYMS: inessential, secondary.

care n. **1** (*anxiety, concern*) anxiety, concern, disquiet, distress, perplexity, sorrow, strain, vexation, woe, worry. ANTONYMS: indifference, pleasure. **2** (*a cause of anxiety*) affliction, burden, hardship, pressure, responsibility, stress, tribulation. **3** (*serious attention, heed*) attention, carefulness, caution, circumspection, consideration, forethought, heed, prudence, punctiliousness, regard, solicitude, vigilance, watch, watchfulness. ANTONYMS: inattention, neglect. **4** (*supervision, protection*) charge, control, custody, direction, guardianship, keeping, management, protection, supervision. **5** (*sorrow*) grief, sorrow, trouble.
~v.i. **1** (*to be concerned*) be bothered, be interested, feel for, mind. **2** (*to be anxious or troubled*) bother, fret, mind, trouble, worry. **3** (*to have respect or liking (for)*) like, love, respect. **4** (*to be desirous, willing or inclined (to)*) desire, wish. **to care for 1** (*to provide for; to look after*) attend, foster, look after, mind, minister to, nurse, protect, provide for, take care of, tend, watch over. ANTONYMS: neglect. **2** (*to like, to be fond of*) be fond of, desire, enjoy, fancy, like, love, prize, take to, want.

career n. **1** (*a course or progress through life, esp. a person's working life*) course, passage, path, procedure, progress, race, walk. **2** (*a person's chosen profession or occupation*) business, calling, craft, employment, job, livelihood, métier, occupation, profession, pursuit, trade, vocation. **3** (*a swift course*) course, running.
~v.i. (*to move in a swift, headlong course*) (*coll.*) barrel along, bolt, dash, fly, hurtle, race, rush, shoot, speed, tear, zoom.

carefree a. (*free from responsibility*) airy, blithe, breezy, buoyant, careless, cheerful, (*coll.*) chirpy, content, easygoing, happy-go-lucky, indifferent, insouciant, jaunty, light-hearted, nonchalant, sunny, trouble-free, unconcerned, untroubled. ANTONYMS: careworn, responsible.

careful a. **1** (*cautious, watchful*) alert, cautious, chary, circumspect, discreet, heedful, judicious, mindful, prudent, thrifty, vigilant, wary, watchful. ANTONYMS: incautious, reckless. **2** (*painstaking, attentive*) accurate, attentive, conscientious, exact, fastidious, fussy, methodical, painstaking, particular, precise, punctilious, scrupulous, systematic, thorough, thoughtful. ANTONYMS: careless, negligent. **3** (*solicitous, concerned*) concerned, protective, solicitous.

careless a. **1** (*heedless, thoughtless*) devil-may-care, hasty, heedless, imprudent, incautious, inconsiderate, indiscreet, irresponsible, lackadaisical, rash, reckless, regardless, thoughtless, uncaring, unconcerned, unguarded, unobservant. ANTONYMS: careful, responsible. **2** (*inattentive, negligent (of)*) absent-minded, inattentive, negligent, remiss, unmindful. **3** (*done without care; inaccurate*) cursory, disorderly, imprecise, inaccurate, incorrect, inexact, neglectful, offhand, perfunctory, slapdash, slipshod, sloppy, untidy. **4** (*casual*) artless, casual, ingenuous, nonchalant, unstudied.

caress n. (*a gentle touch*) cuddle, embrace, fondling, hug, kiss, pat, touch.
~v.t. **1** (*to stroke affectionately*) cuddle, embrace, fondle, hug, kiss, nuzzle, pet, stroke. **2** (*to touch gently*) pat, touch.

cargo n. (*freight carried by ship or aircraft*) baggage, burden, consignment, contents, freight, goods, lading, load, merchandise, shipment, tonnage, truckload, ware.

caricature n. **1** (*a representation of a person exaggerating characteristic traits in a ludicrous way*) distortion, exaggeration, misrepresentation. **2** (*a burlesque, a parody*) burlesque, lampoon, mimicry, parody, satire, (*coll.*) send-up, skit, take-off, travesty.
~v.t. **1** (*to represent in a caricature*) distort, misrepresent. **2** (*to burlesque, to parody*) burlesque, lampoon, mimic, mock, parody, ridicule, satirize, send up, (*coll.*) take off.

carnage n. (*slaughter of a large number human beings*) bloodbath, bloodshed, butchery, holocaust, killing, massacre, mass murder, murder, slaughter.

carnal a. **1** (*bodily, sexual*) animal, bodily, concupiscent, corporeal, erotic, fleshly, lascivious, lecherous, lewd, libidinous, licentious, lustful, prurient, randy, (*coll.*) raunchy, salacious, sensual, sexual, voluptuous. **2** (*temporal, secular*) mundane, secular, temporal. **3** (*worldly, unspiritual*) earthly, physical, unspiritual, worldly. ANTONYMS: spiritual.

carry v.t. **1** (*to transport or convey from one place to another by supporting and moving with the thing conveyed*) bear, convey, drag, fetch, haul, (*coll.*) hump, lift, lug, move, relay, take, transport. **2** (*to conduct or transmit*) announce, broadcast, communicate, conduct, convey, display, disseminate, give, lead, offer, pass on, publish, relay, release, report, stock, transmit. **3** (*to bear or support*) bear, bear up, bolster, hold up, maintain, shoulder, stand, suffer, support, sustain, underpin, uphold. **4** (*to have in or on*) have in, stock, take. **5** (*to imply or

involve) entail, imply, involve. **6** (*to hold*
(*oneself*) *in a particular way*) bear oneself, hold
oneself. **7** (*to extend or cause to move in any
direction in time or space*) drive, impel,
influence, motivate, propel, spur, urge. ANTO-
NYMS: deter. **8** (*to accomplish*) accomplish,
effect. **9** (*to win, to capture*) capture, gain,
secure, take, win. ANTONYMS: lose. **to carry on
1** (*to conduct or engage in* (*a business, a
conversation etc.*)) administer, conduct, engage
in, operate, run. **2** (*to continue*) continue,
endure, go on, keep going, keep on, last,
maintain, perpetuate, persevere, persist,
proceed. ANTONYMS: give up, stop. **3** (*to behave
in a particular way, esp. to flirt outrageously*)
flirt, fool around. **4** (*to make a fuss*) act up,
create, make a fuss, misbehave, play up. **to
carry out 1** (*to perform*) do, perform, undertake. **2** (*to accomplish*) accomplish, achieve,
carry through, complete, conclude, consummate, discharge, effect, execute, fulfil, implement, realize.

carve *v.t.* **1** (*to cut* (*solid material*) *into the shape
of a person, thing etc.*) cut, fashion, form,
model, sculpt, shape. **2** (*to decorate or inscribe
by cutting*) chisel, decorate, engrave, etch,
incise, inscribe. **3** (*to cut* (*letters, patterns etc.*)
into the surface of hard material) chip, cut,
hack, hew, slash, whittle.

case¹ *n.* **1** (*an instance, an occurrence*) example,
instance, occurrence. **2** (*a state of affairs,
situation*) circumstances, condition, context,
contingency, event, plight, position, predicament, situation, state. **3** (*a set of arguments for
or against a particular action or cause*)
argument, line. **4** (*a question at issue*) issue,
point, question. **5** (*the patient suffering from
the disease etc.*) client, invalid, sufferer,
victim. **6 a** (*a cause or suit in a court of law*)
action, cause, dispute, lawsuit, proceedings,
process, suit, trial. **b** (*facts or evidence for
submission to a court*) evidence, plea,
submission, testimony. **c** (*a cause that has been
decided and may be quoted as a precedent*)
example, illustration, instance, occasion,
occurrence, precedent, specimen.

case² *n.* **1** (*a box or other container*) box,
cabinet, canister, capsule, carton, casket,
chest, container, crate, package. **2** (*a covering
or sheath*) capsule, covering, holder, sheath.
3 (*a protective outer shell or cover*) casing,
cover, covering, folder, jacket, pod, protection,
shell, wrapper. **4** (*a suitcase*) bag, suitcase,
trunk.

cash *n.* **1** (*coins and bank notes*) bank notes,
bills, bullion, change, coins, currency, hard
cash, notes, (*coll.*) readies, silver. **2** (*money,
wealth*) (*sl.*) brass, (*sl.*) bread, (*sl.*) dosh, (*sl.*)

dough, funds, (*sl.*) lolly, (*coll.*) loot, money,
(*coll.*) necessary, resources, wealth, wherewithal.

cast *v.t.* **1** (*to throw, to hurl*) chuck, dash, drive,
drop, fling, hurl, impel, launch, lob, pitch,
project, send, shed, shy, sling, throw, thrust,
toss. **2** (*to emit or throw by reflection*) diffuse,
distribute, emit, give, radiate, reflect, scatter,
spread, throw. **3** (*to throw off, to shed*) discard,
shed, throw off. **4** (*to dismiss, to reject*)
dismiss, reject, throw out. **5** (*to assign the parts
in* (*a play, film etc.*)) allot, appoint, assign,
choose, designate, name, pick, select. **6** (*to
found, to mould*) form, found, model, mould,
set, shape. **7** (*to add up, to calculate*) add up,
calculate, compute, figure, forecast, reckon,
total. **8** (*to register* (*a vote etc.*)) record, register.
~*n.* **1** (*a throw*) chuck, fling, lob, pitch, shy,
throw, thrust, toss. **2** (*the set of actors allocated
roles in a play, film etc.*) actors, characters,
company, dramatis personae, players, troupe.
3 (*a mould*) form, model, mould, shape.
4 (*chance, fortune*) chance, fate, fortune. **5** (*a
twist*) irregularity, turn, twist, warp. **6** (*a tinge,
a characteristic quality*) air, appearance, bent,
colouring, complexion, demeanour, inclination, look, manner, mien, semblance, shade,
stamp, style, suggestion, tinge, tone, turn.
7 (*an adding up, a calculation*) calculation,
computation.

castigate *v.t.* **1** (*to chastise, to punish*) beat,
cane, chastise, correct, discipline, flail, flay,
flog, lash, penalize, punish, scourge, thrash,
whip. **2** (*to rebuke or criticize severely*) (*coll.*)
bawl out, berate, (*coll.*) carpet, censure,
chasten, criticize, (*coll.*) dress down, haul over
the coals, lambast, put down, rebuke, reprimand, scold, (*coll.*) tear a strip off, tear into,
(*coll.*) tell off, (*coll.*) tick off, upbraid.

casual *a.* **1** (*happening by chance; accidental*)
accidental, chance, fortuitous, incidental,
serendipitous, unexpected, unforeseen, unintentional, unpremeditated. ANTONYMS: deliberate, intentional. **2** (*occasional, temporary*)
irregular, occasional, part-time, temporary.
3 (*careless, unmethodical*) careless, irregular, random, unmethodical. **4** (*unconcerned,
apathetic*) apathetic, blasé, cool, easygoing,
indifferent, lackadaisical, natural, nonchalant,
perfunctory, relaxed, unconcerned. ANTONYMS:
enthusiastic, passionate. **5** (*informal*) informal, lounge, relaxed, sporty. ANTONYMS:
formal, smart.

casualty *n.* **1** (*a person who is killed or injured
in a war or in an accident*) dead, fatality, loss,
sufferer, victim. ANTONYMS: survivor. **2** (*an
accident, esp. one involving personal injury or*

loss of life) accident, blow, calamity, catastrophe, chance, contingency, disaster, misadventure, mischance, misfortune, mishap.

catastrophe n. **1** (a great misfortune or disaster) adversity, affliction, blow, calamity, cataclysm, devastation, disaster, failure, fiasco, meltdown, mischance, misfortune, mishap, reverse, tragedy, trial, trouble. ANTONYMS: triumph. **2** (a final event, esp. one that brings disaster or ruin) climax, conclusion, culmination, curtains, denouement, end, finale, termination, upshot.

catch v.t. **1** (to grasp, to take hold of) clutch, grab, grasp, grip, snatch, take hold of. ANTONYMS: drop. **2** (to seize, esp. in pursuit) apprehend, arrest, bag, capture, (sl.) nab, seize. **3** (to take in a snare) ensnare, entrap, trap. **4** (to come upon suddenly, to surprise) detect, discover, expose, find out, surprise, take unawares, unmask. **5** (to receive by infection or contagion) come down with, contract, develop, get, go down with, succumb to. **6** (to be in time for) board, get, take. **7** (to check, to interrupt) check, curb, interrupt, restrain, stop. **8** (to cause to become fastened or entangled) entangle, fasten, snag. **9** (to grasp, to apprehend) apprehend, comprehend, discern, fathom, feel, figure out, follow, gather, get, grasp, hear, perceive, recognize, see, sense, take in, (coll.) twig, understand. **10** (to attract, to gain) allure, attract, bewitch, captivate, charm, delight, draw, enchant, enrapture, entice, fascinate, gain, win. ANTONYMS: bore, repel.
~n. **1** (a fastening device) bolt, clasp, clip, fastener, hook, hook and eye, latch, pin, (dial.) sneck. **2** (an acquisition) acquisition, bag, conquest, prize, take, trophy. **3** (a trap, a snare) snag, snare, trap. **4** (a concealed difficulty) difficulty, disadvantage, drawback, hitch, problem, snag, trick. ANTONYMS: benefit.

catching a. **1** (infectious) communicable, contagious, infectious, transferable, transmissible, transmittable. ANTONYMS: non-contagious. **2** (attractive) alluring, attractive, bewitching, captivating, charming, enchanting, enticing, entrancing, fascinating, fetching, taking, winning. ANTONYMS: repulsive.

categorical a. **1** (absolute, unconditional) absolute, downright, emphatic, firm, outright, positive, unconditional, unequivocal, unqualified, unreserved, unrestricted. ANTONYMS: conditional, qualified. **2** (explicit, direct) direct, explicit, express, unambiguous. ANTONYMS: vague.

category n. (an order, a class) area, class, classification, department, division, grade, grouping, head, heading, kind, list, order, rank, section, sort, sphere, type, variety.

cater v.i. **1** (to supply food, entertainment etc. (for)) provision, victual. **2** (to provide what is needed (for)) furnish, outfit, provide, purvey, supply. **3** (to pander (to)) baby, coddle, cosset, gratify, humour, indulge, minister to, mollycoddle, oblige, pamper, pander, satisfy, spoil.

catholic a. **1** (general, comprehensive) all-embracing, all-inclusive, broad, comprehensive, eclectic, general, global, inclusive, universal, wide, worldwide. **2** (liberal, tolerant) broad-minded, charitable, large-hearted, liberal, tolerant, unbiased, unbigoted, unprejudiced. ANTONYMS: intolerant, narrow-minded.

cause n. **1** (that which produces or contributes to an effect) beginning, genesis, origin, root, source, spring. ANTONYMS: effect, outcome. **2** (the agent bringing about something) agent, creator, mainspring, maker, originator, producer. **3** (the reason that justifies some act) basis, ground, incentive, inducement, justification, motivation, motive, object, purpose, reason. **4** (a side or party) faction, movement, party, side. **5** (a set of principles or ideals etc.) belief, conviction, enterprise, ideal, movement, principles, purpose, undertaking. **6** (a matter in dispute) case, concern, issue, matter, question, subject, topic.
~v.t. **1** (to produce; to be the cause of) bring about, create, engender, generate, give rise to, lead to, produce. **2** (to effect) effect, effectuate, result in. **3** (to make or induce to) compel, incite, induce, lead to, make, motivate, occasion, precipitate, provoke. ANTONYMS: deter, prevent.

caustic a. **1** (burning, corrosive) astringent, burning, corrosive, destructive. **2** (bitter, sarcastic) acid, acrimonious, biting, bitter, critical, cutting, harsh, keen, mordacious, mordant, pungent, sarcastic, sardonic, scathing, severe, sharp, stinging, trenchant, virulent, vitriolic. ANTONYMS: bland, temperate.

caution n. **1** (care to avoid injury or misfortune) alertness, care, circumspection, deliberation, discretion, forethought, heed, prudence, vigilance, wariness, watchfulness. ANTONYMS: imprudence, recklessness. **2** (a warning) advice, counsel, warning. **3** (a reprimand and injunction) admonishment, admonition, injunction, reprimand. **4** (something extraordinary, a strange or amusing person) (sl.) card, (coll.) hoot, (coll.) laugh, (coll.) scream.
~v.t. (to warn) admonish, advise, counsel, enjoin, forewarn, tip off, urge, warn.

cautious a. (careful, wary) alert, (coll.) cagey,

careful, chary, circumspect, discreet, guarded, heedful, judicious, prudent, tentative, vigilant, wary, watchful. ANTONYMS: incautious, reckless.

cease v.i. 1 (to come to an end, to stop) break off, bring to an end, conclude, culminate, die away, discontinue, end, fail, finish, halt, stay, stop, terminate. ANTONYMS: begin, start. 2 (to desist (from)) desist, leave off, refrain.

cede v.t. 1 (to give up, to surrender) abandon, abdicate, concede, deliver up, give up, hand over, relinquish, renounce, resign, step down, surrender, turn over. 2 (to yield, to grant) allow, convey, give, grant, transfer, yield.

celebrate v.t. 1 (to observe (a special occasion etc.) with festivities) honour, keep, mark, observe. 2 (to perform (a religious service or ceremony)) administer, consecrate, hallow, sanctify, say, sing. 3 (to praise, to extol) applaud, commend, drink to, eulogize, exalt, extol, glorify, honour, laud, lionize, praise, proclaim, reverence, toast. ANTONYMS: criticize, ignore. 4 (to commemorate) commemorate, honour, remember, ritualize, solemnize.
~v.i. (to mark an occasion with festivities) make merry, party, rejoice, revel.

celebrated a. (famous, renowned) acclaimed, distinguished, eminent, famed, famous, glorious, illustrious, lionized, notable, noted, noteworthy, outstanding, popular, pre-eminent, prominent, renowned, revered, well-known. ANTONYMS: obscure, unpopular.

celebration n. 1 (a special event when something is celebrated) carousal, festival, festivity, frolic, gala, jubilee, merrymaking, party, (coll.) rave, (coll.) rave-up, revelry. 2 (the act of celebrating something, esp. in a religious ceremony) ceremony, commemoration, extolling, hallowing, honouring, observance, observation, performance, remembrance, rite, sanctification, solemnization.

celebrity n. 1 (a famous person) big name, (coll.) celeb, dignitary, hero, heroine, luminary, megastar, name, personage, personality, somebody, star, superstar, VIP. ANTONYMS: nonentity, unknown. 2 (fame, renown) distinction, eminence, fame, glory, honour, notability, note, popularity, pre-eminence, prestige, prominence, renown, reputation, repute, stardom. ANTONYMS: ignominy, obscurity.

celibacy n. 1 (the unmarried state) bachelorhood, singleness, spinsterhood. 2 (abstention from sexual activity) abstinence, chastity, continence, purity, self-denial, virginity.

cement n. 1 (a powdery substance, esp. used to make concrete and hardening like stone) mortar, plaster. 2 (any analogous material, paste etc. for sticking things together) adhesive, glue, gum, paste.
~v.t. (to unite with or as with cement) attach, bind, bond, glue, gum, stick together, unite, weld.

central a. 1 (proceeding from or situated in the centre) inner, middle. 2 (principal, of chief importance) cardinal, chief, dominant, essential, focal, fundamental, important, key, main, primary, prime, principal, significant. ANTONYMS: inessential, subsidiary.

centre n. 1 (the middle point or part) core, heart, kernel, middle, midpoint, midst. ANTONYMS: border, edge. 2 (the point round which something revolves) axis, hub, pivot. 3 (the most important point) crux, focus. 4 (the source from which anything emanates) nucleus, source.
~v.t. 1 (to place in the centre) centralize, middle. 2 (to collect to a point) cluster, concentrate, converge, focus, meet. ANTONYMS: diffuse, spread.

ceremonial a. (of or performed with ceremonies) celebratory, ceremonious, communicative, dignified, formal, liturgical, official, ritual, ritualistic, solemn, stately. ANTONYMS: casual, informal.
~n. 1 (the prescribed order for a ceremony or function) ceremony, observance, rite, ritual. 2 (a polite usage or formality) formality, solemnity. 3 (the rules for ceremonies) etiquette, manners.

ceremony n. 1 (a prescribed rite, esp. in accordance with religion or tradition) ceremonial, commemoration, formality, observance, parade, rite, sacrament. 2 (an occasion when such rites or formalities are performed) function, ritual, service. 3 (a usage of politeness) courtesy, decorum, etiquette, form, lip service, niceties, pomp, propriety, protocol.

certain a. 1 (sure, confident) assured, confident, convinced, positive, satisfied, sure. 2 (undoubtedly true) ascertained, conclusive, established, incontrovertible, indubitable, irrefutable, known, plain, true, undeniable, undoubted, unequivocal, unmistakable, valid. ANTONYMS: dubious. 3 (absolutely determined or fixed) decided, definite, determined, fixed, set, settled. 4 (bound, destined) bound, definite, destined, fated, ineluctable, inescapable, inevitable, inexorable, sure. 5 (unfailing, reliable) assured, constant, dependable, guaranteed, invariable, reliable, stable, staunch, steady, trustworthy, unerring, unfailing,

unquestionable. ANTONYMS: unreliable.
6 (*some*) particular, precise, some, special, specific.

certainty *n.* **1** (*that which is certain*) actuality, fact, reality, (*N Am., coll.*) sure thing, truth. **2** (*absolute assurance*) assurance, authoritativeness, certitude, confidence, conviction, faith, inevitability, positiveness, self-assurance, sureness, trust, validity. ANTONYMS: doubt, uncertainty.

certify *v.t.* (*to attest to, esp. in writing*) affirm, ascertain, assure, attest, authenticate, aver, avow, classify, confirm, corroborate, declare, endorse, establish, guarantee, prove, substantiate, testify, validate, verify, vouch for. ANTONYMS: deny.

chain *n.* **1** (*bond, fetter*) bond, check, coupling, fetter, link, manacle, shackle, union. **2** (*bondage, restraint*) bondage, captivity, enslavement, restraint. **3** (*a connected series*) course, progression, range, sequence, series, set, string, succession, train.
~*v.t.* (*to fasten or bind with a chain or chains*) bind, confine, enslave, fasten, fetter, handcuff, limit, manacle, restrain, secure, shackle, tether, tie. ANTONYMS: release.

challenge *n.* **1** (*an invitation to take part in a contest of any kind*) dare, invitation. **2** (*a difficult task which stretches one's abilities*) demand, problem, task, test, trial. **3** (*a demand for proof or justification*) confrontation, defiance, interrogation, provocation, question, ultimatum.
~*v.t.* **1** (*to invite to take part in a contest of any kind*) accost, confront, dare, defy, throw down the gauntlet. **2** (*to call into question*) demand, doubt, impugn, investigate, question. **3** (*to object to, to contest*) contest, dispute, object to, oppose, take exception to. **4** (*to stimulate, to stretch*) arouse, provoke, stimulate, stretch, tax, test, try.

chamber *n.* **1** (*a legislative assembly*) assembly, congress, council, diet, judicature, legislature, moot, senate. **2** (*a room, esp. a bedroom*) apartment, bedroom, cell, compartment, cubicle, hall, room. **3** (*a cave or underground cavity*) cave, cavern, cavity, hollow, niche, nook, recess.

champion *n.* **1** (*a person who defeats all competitors*) challenger, combatant, conqueror, fighter, hero, victor, winner. **2** (*a person who supports a person or a cause*) backer, defender, guardian, patron, protagonist, protector, upholder.
~*v.t.* **1** (*to defend as a champion*) defend, fight for. **2** (*to support* (*a cause*)) advocate, back, encourage, endorse, espouse, forward, maintain,

promote, stand up for, stick up for, support, sustain, uphold.

chance *n.* **1** (*a risk, a possibility*) gamble, hazard, jeopardy, opening, opportunity, possibility, prospect, risk, scope, window. ANTONYMS: certainty, impossibility. **2** (*likelihood, probability*) liability, likelihood, odds, probability. ANTONYMS: improbability, unlikelihood. **3** (*an unplanned result or occurrence*) accident, coincidence, contingency. **4** (*fortune, luck*) fortune, luck, misfortune. **5** (*fate, the indeterminable course of events*) destiny, fate, fortuity, providence.
~*v.t.* (*to risk*) bet, endanger, gamble, hazard, imperil, jeopardize, risk, speculate, stake, try, venture, wager.
~*v.i.* (*to happen, to come to pass*) befall, betide, come about, come to pass, fall out, happen, occur, take place.
~*a.* (*accidental, unforeseen*) accidental, casual, contingent, fortuitous, inadvertent, incidental, random, serendipitous, unexpected, unforeseeable, unforeseen, unintentional, unlooked-for, unplanned, unpremeditated. ANTONYMS: deliberate, intentional.

change *v.t.* **1** (*to make different, to alter*) alter, convert, diversify, fluctuate, make different, moderate, modify, reform, remodel, reorganize, restyle, shift, vary. **2** (*to exchange*) alternate, barter, displace, exchange, interchange, replace, substitute, swap, switch, trade.
~*v.i.* **1** (*to become different*) alter, develop, vary. **2** (*to pass from one state or phase to another*) metamorphose, mutate, shift, transform, transmute.
~*n.* **1** (*alteration, variation*) alteration, difference, innovation, modification, permutation, variation. ANTONYMS: invariability, stability. **2** (*shifting, transition*) conversion, metamorphosis, mutation, shift, transformation, transition, transmutation. ANTONYMS: immutability. **3** (*an exchange; something substituted for another*) exchange, interchange, replacement, substitute, switch, trade. **4** (*small coins given in return for other money*) cash, coins, coppers, currency, silver. **5** (*novelty, variety*) break, departure, diversion, novelty, variation, variety.

changeable *a.* **1** (*liable to change, variable*) fluid, irregular, mobile, mutable, shifting, uncertain, uneven, unpredictable, unreliable, unsettled, unstable, unsteady, variable. ANTONYMS: stable, unchanging. **2** (*inconstant, fickle*) capricious, erratic, fickle, fitful, inconstant, mercurial, temperamental, undependable, vacillating, versatile, volatile, wavering. ANTONYMS: steadfast.

changeless *a.* (*unchanging*) abiding, consistent, constant, eternal, everlasting, fixed, immutable, inevitable, permanent, perpetual, reliable, settled, stable, steadfast, steady, unalterable, unchanging, uniform, unvarying. ANTONYMS: changeable.

channel *n.* 1 (*the bed of a stream or an artificial watercourse*) aqueduct, bed, canal, ditch, moat, sluice, watercourse, waterway. 2 (*the deep or navigable part of an estuary, river etc.*) fairway, passage, route. 3 (*a narrow piece of water joining two seas*) narrows, neck, strait. 4 (*a tube or duct for the passage of liquids or gases*) conduit, duct, main, tube. 5 (*a course or line*) course, direction, line, way. 6 (*a band of frequencies on which radio and television signals can be transmitted*) band, frequency, programme. 7 (*a furrow*) fluting, furrow, groove.
~*v.t.* (*to guide or direct*) conduct, convey, direct, guide, lead, transmit.

chaos *n.* (*confusion, disorder*) anarchy, bedlam, confusion, disorder, disorganization, havoc, lawlessness, pandemonium, tumult, turmoil. ANTONYMS: order.

chaotic *a.* (*confused, disordered*) anarchic, confused, deranged, disordered, disorganized, frenzied, haphazard, hectic, incoherent, jumbled, lawless, riotous, topsy-turvy, tumultuous, uncontrolled, unruly, wild. ANTONYMS: ordered, organized.

chap *n.* (*a man, a fellow*) (*coll.*) bloke, character, fellow, (*coll.*) geezer, (*coll.*) guy, individual, lad, man, person, (*coll.*) type.

character *n.* 1 (*the distinctive qualities peculiar to a person or thing*) attribute, characteristic, distinction, feature, idiosyncrasy, mark, peculiarity, quality, trait. 2 (*the sum of a person's mental and moral qualities*) attributes, bent, calibre, cast, complexion, constitution, disposition, individuality, kidney, kind, make-up, nature, personality, quality, temper, type. 3 (*moral excellence*) courage, goodness, honesty, honour, integrity, morality, rectitude, strength, uprightness. ANTONYMS: disrepute. 4 (*reputation or standing, esp. good reputation*) reputation, respectability, standing, status. 5 (*position, capacity*) capacity, position, rank, role. 6 (*a person*) fellow, (*coll.*) guy, individual, person, personage, (*coll.*) sort, (*coll.*) type. 7 (*an eccentric person*) eccentric, (*sl.*) loony, (*sl.*) nut, oddball, oddity, (*coll.*) weirdo. 8 (*a personality created by a novelist, poet etc.*) creation, personality. 9 (*an actor's role*) part, persona, role. 10 (*a letter or other mark made by writing, printing etc.*) cipher, device, emblem, figure,

hieroglyph, letter, logo, mark, monogram, number, rune, seal, sign, stamp, symbol, type.

characteristic *n.* (*a typical or distinctive quality or feature*) attribute, character, earmark, faculty, feature, idiosyncrasy, mark, peculiarity, property, quality, quirk, trait.
~*a.* (*constituting or exhibiting a characteristic*) distinctive, distinguishing, emblematic, idiosyncratic, individual, peculiar, representative, singular, special, specific, symbolic, symptomatic, typical. ANTONYMS: uncharacteristic, unrepresentative.

charge *v.t.* 1 (*to ask as a price*) ask, claim, demand, expect, require. 2 (*to debit (to)*) bill, debit, invoice. 3 (*to accuse*) accuse, allege, arraign, assert, blame, censure, impeach, incriminate, indict, involve. ANTONYMS: clear, pardon. 4 (*to enjoin, to command*) bid, command, demand, enjoin, exhort, instruct, order. 5 (*to entrust*) commit, entrust. 6 (*to rush on and attack*) assail, assault, attack, rush, storm. ANTONYMS: retreat. 7 (*to load, to fill*) burden, fill, lade, load, tax. 8 (*to saturate, to pervade*) imbue, permeate, pervade, saturate.
~*n.* 1 (*a price demanded, a cost*) amount, cost, (*sl.*) damage, expenditure, expense, fee, outlay, payment, price, rate. 2 (*a financial liability, a tax*) demand, liability, tax. 3 (*a formal accusation of crime*) accusation, allegation, imputation, indictment. ANTONYMS: acquittal, reprieve. 4 (*a duty or obligation*) duty, obligation, office, responsibility. 5 (*a command, a commission*) command, commission, mission. 6 (*care, custody*) care, concern, control, custody, guardianship, jurisdiction, protection, safe keeping, supervision, ward. 7 (*attack, onrush*) assault, attack, onrush, onset, onslaught, raid, rush, sally, sortie. ANTONYMS: retreat. 8 (*instructions, directions*) command, direction, exhortation, injunction, instruction, mandate, order, precept. 9 (*a load, a burden*) burden, cargo, load, onus, weight. 10 (*a thrill*) (*sl.*) rush, thrill.

charitable *a.* 1 (*relating to or supported by charity*) humanitarian, philanthropic. 2 (*generous to those in need*) bountiful, generous, lavish, liberal, munificent. ANTONYMS: mean, tight-fisted. 3 (*benevolent, kindly*) beneficent, benevolent, broad-minded, compassionate, considerate, favourable, forgiving, gracious, humane, indulgent, kindly, large-hearted, lenient, magnanimous, sympathetic, tolerant, understanding. ANTONYMS: intolerant, unkind.

charity *n.* 1 (*generosity to those in need, alms-giving*) alms-giving, assistance, generosity, largesse, munificence, philanthropy. 2 (*the money etc. so given*) alms, benefaction, contribution, donation, endowment, fund, gift, handout, relief. **3** (*kindness, goodwill*) benevolence, bounty, compassion, generosity, goodness, goodwill, humanity, kindness, pity. ANTONYMS: meanness, selfishness. **4** (*tolerance of faults and offences*) indulgence, leniency, liberality, tolerance. ANTONYMS: intolerance. **5** (*love of one's fellow human beings*) affection, fellow feeling, love, tenderness. ANTONYMS: malice.

charm *n.* **1** (*a power of alluring, fascinating etc.*) allure, appeal, draw, pull. **2** (*a pleasing or attractive feature*) attraction, desirability, fascination, magnetism. **3** (*a spell, an enchantment*) enchantment, magic, sorcery, spell. **4** (*an article worn to avert evil or ensure good luck*) amulet, fetish, talisman.
~*v.t.* **1** (*to attract, to delight*) allure, attract, delight, enamour, enrapture, enthral, please, ravish, transport, win over. ANTONYMS: alienate, repel. **2** (*to enchant, to fascinate*) absorb, beguile, bewitch, cajole, captivate, enchant, entrance, fascinate, hypnotize, mesmerize.

charming *a.* (*highly pleasing; delightful*) alluring, appealing, attractive, bewitching, captivating, delightful, engaging, eye-catching, fascinating, fetching, irresistible, likeable, lovely, pleasant, pleasing, seductive, winning. ANTONYMS: repulsive, unappealing.

chase *v.t.* **1** (*to pursue, esp. at speed*) follow, pursue, run after, tail, trail. **2** (*to hunt*) hound, hunt, track. **3** (*to drive away*) drive away, expel. **4** (*to put to flight*) put to flight, rout, wing. **5** (*to try to achieve or obtain*) aim for, strive after.
~*n.* **1** (*the act of chasing*) pursuit, race, trail. **2** (*the hunting of wild animals*) hunt, hunting.

chasm *n.* **1** (*a deep cleft in the ground*) abyss, cleft, crater, crevasse, fissure, gorge, gulf, hollow, opening, ravine, rent, rift, split. **2** (*a breach or division between persons or parties*) alienation, breach, division. **3** (*a gap or void*) cavity, gap, void.

chaste *a.* **1** (*abstaining from all sexual intercourse, or from sex outside marriage*) abstinent, celibate. **2** (*innocent, virginal*) immaculate, incorrupt, innocent, modest, moral, pure, stainless, uncontaminated, undefiled, unsullied, vestal, virginal, virtuous, wholesome. ANTONYMS: corrupt, immoral. **3** (*free from obscenity*) clean, decent, decorous, elegant, refined. ANTONYMS: obscene. **4** (*simple, unadorned*) austere, quiet, restrained, severe, simple, unadorned, unaffected, undecorated, unembellished.

chastity *n.* **1** (*virginity*) innocence, maidenhead, maidenhood, virginity, virtue. **2** (*celibacy*) abstemiousness, abstinence, celibacy,

continence, forbearance, restraint. ANTONYMS: debauchery, promiscuity. **3** (*purity of taste and style*) modesty, purity, simplicity.

chat *v.i.* (*to talk easily and familiarly*) chatter, confabulate, converse, gossip, have a heart-to-heart, (*coll.*) jaw, natter, prattle, (*coll.*) rabbit, talk.
~*n.* (*easy, familiar talk*) chatter, (*coll.*) chinwag, chit-chat, colloquy, (*coll.*) confab, conversation, gossip, heart-to-heart, natter, small talk, talk.

cheap *a.* **1** (*low in price*) bargain, budget-priced, cut-price, economical, economy, inexpensive, low-cost, low-priced, reasonable, reduced, sale. ANTONYMS: dear, expensive. **2** (*worth more than its price or cost*) under-priced, undervalued. **3** (*of poor quality*) common, inferior, low-quality, paltry, poor, second-rate, (*coll.*) tacky, trashy, worthless. **4** (*despicable*) base, contemptible, despicable, low, mean, seedy, shabby, sleazy, sordid, tatty, tawdry, vulgar.

cheat *v.t.* **1** (*to defraud, to deprive*) defraud, deprive, diddle, (*coll.*) do, (*coll.*) fiddle, fleece, foil, frustrate, (*coll.*) rip off, (*sl.*) stiff, swindle, thwart. **2** (*to deceive, to trick*) bamboozle, beguile, (*sl.*) con, deceive, delude, (*coll.*) double-cross, dupe, fool, hoax, hoodwink, (*coll.*) kid, mislead, take in, trick. **3** (*to escape, esp. by luck or skill*) avoid, escape.
~*n.* **1** (*a person who cheats*) charlatan, cheater, con artist, (*sl.*) conman, deceiver, fraud, fraudster, impostor, rogue, swindler, trickster. **2** (*a trick or deception*) artifice, deceit, deception, imposture, (*N Am., sl.*) scam, trick. **3** (*a fraud, a swindle*) fraud, (*coll.*) rip-off, (*N Am., sl.*) scam, swindle.

check *n.* **1** (*a test for accuracy, quality etc.*) examination, inspection, investigation, research, scrutiny, test. **2** (*a sudden stoppage or restraint*) constraint, control, curb, damper, hold-up, inhibition, limitation, stoppage. **3** (*a person or thing that stops or restrains motion*) bar, barrier, hindrance, impediment, obstacle, obstruction. **4** (*a reverse, a rebuff*) blow, disappointment, frustration, rebuff, rejection, repulse, reverse, setback. **5** (*a pause*) break, halt, pause, stoppage. **6** (*restraint*) repression, restraint, suppression. **7** (*a mark put against items in a list*) line, mark, stroke, tick. **8** (*a token by which the correctness or authenticity of a document etc. may be ascertained*) criterion, model, norm, standard, yardstick.
~*v.t.* **1** (*to test the accuracy, quality etc. of*) check out, examine, inspect, investigate, look at, look over, monitor, probe, research, scrutinize, study, test, vet. ANTONYMS: ignore, overlook. **2** (*to confirm*) confirm, corroborate, prove,

verify. **3** (*to cause to stop or slow down*) arrest, delay, halt, retard, slow down, stop. ANTO-NYMS: accelerate, speed up. **4** (*to restrain, to curb*) bridle, control, curb, hinder, impede, inhibit, limit, obstruct, rein, repress, restrain, thwart. **5** (*to rebuke*) admonish, blame, (*coll.*) carpet, chide, rebuff, rebuke, reprimand, reprove, scold, (*coll.*) tell off. **6** (*to mark with a tick etc.*) mark, tick, tick off.

cheek *n.* (*impudence, sauciness*) assurance, audacity, brass, brazenness, effrontery, front, gall, impertinence, impudence, insolence, (*sl.*) lip, (*coll.*) neck, nerve, sauciness, temerity.

cheerful *a.* **1** (*contented*) blithe, bright, buoyant, (*coll.*) chirpy, contented, gay, glad, happy, jaunty, jolly, joyous, light-hearted, merry, sunny. ANTONYMS: cheerless, dismal. **2** (*full of good spirits*) enthusiastic, hearty, spirited. **3** (*lively, animated*) animated, invigorated, lively, sparkling, sprightly. ANTONYMS: dull, lifeless.

cherish *v.t.* **1** (*to treat with affection, to protect lovingly*) care for, comfort, cosset, cultivate, foster, harbour, hold dear, love, nourish, nurse, nurture, preserve, prize, protect, shelter, support, sustain, tend, treasure. ANTONYMS: despise, dislike. **2** (*to hold closely to, to cling to*) cleave to, cling to, hold onto. ANTONYMS: abandon, desert.

chest *n.* **1** (*a large strong box*) box, casket, coffer, strongbox, trunk. **2** (*a case for holding particular commodities*) case, crate. **3** (*the fore part of the human body from the neck to the waist*) bosom, breast.

chew *v.t.* **1** (*to grind with the teeth*) bite, champ, crunch, gnaw, grind, masticate, munch, nibble. **2** (*to ruminate on, to digest mentally*) consider, deliberate, digest, meditate, mull, muse, ponder, reflect, review, ruminate, think, weigh.

chic *n.* **1** (*smartness, style*) elegance, smartness, style. **2** (*the best fashion or taste*) fashion, taste, tastefulness.
~*a.* (*stylish, elegant*) elegant, fashionable, modish, (*coll.*) sexy, smart, sophisticated, tasteful, (*coll.*) trendy, up-to-date. ANTONYMS: inelegant, unfashionable.

chief *a.* **1** (*principal, first*) capital, cardinal, central, essential, first, foremost, premier, primary, prime, principal. ANTONYMS: least. **2** (*most important, main*) key, leading, main, outstanding, paramount, predominant, prevailing, ranking, superior, supreme, uppermost.
~*n.* **1** (*a leader, esp. of a clan*) captain, chieftain, commander, leader, lord, master, ringleader,

ruler. ANTONYMS: follower, subject. **2** (*the head of a department*) boss, director, governor, head, manager, overseer, principal, superintendent.

chiefly *adv.* **1** (*principally, especially*) above all, especially, essentially, predominantly, primarily, principally. **2** (*for the most part*) as a rule, by and large, for the most part, in general, in the main, largely, mainly, mostly, on the whole, usually.

child *n.* **1** (*a young person*) adolescent, (*Austral., N Am., sl.*) ankle-biter, (*Sc. or North.*) bairn, boy, brat, girl, juvenile, (*coll.*) kid, little one, minor, (*sl.*) nipper, stripling, teenager, toddler, tot, young person, youngster, youth. ANTONYMS: adult. **2** (*a son or daughter*) daughter, issue, offspring, progeny, son. **3** (*an infant, a baby*) babe, baby, infant, suckling. **4** (*an unborn baby*) embryo, foetus. **5** (*an inexperienced or childish person*) dolt, greenhorn.

childish *a.* **1** (*of or befitting a child*) babyish, boyish, girlish, young. ANTONYMS: adult, grown-up. **2** (*silly, puerile*) foolish, frivolous, immature, infantile, juvenile, puerile, silly, simple, trifling, weak. ANTONYMS: sensible.

chill *n.* **1** (*coldness*) cold, coldness. **2** (*a cold*) cold, flu, influenza, sniffles. **3** (*coldness of the air etc.*) bite, bleakness, cold, coldness, coolness, crispness, iciness, nip, rawness, sharpness. ANTONYMS: warmth. **4** (*coldness of manner etc.*) aloofness, frigidity, hostility, remoteness, unfriendliness.
~*v.t.* **1** (*to make cold*) cool, cool down. **2** (*to preserve (meat etc.) by cold*) freeze, ice, preserve, refrigerate. ANTONYMS: defrost, warm up. **3** (*to depress, to discourage*) dampen, deject, depress, discourage, dishearten, dispirit, distress. ANTONYMS: encourage. **4** (*to frighten*) alarm, frighten, scare.
~*v.i.* (*to hang around*) hang around, loiter, relax.
to chill out (*to relax*) calm down, relax, take it/ things easy.

chilly *a.* **1** (*rather cold*) bleak, cold, cool, crisp, draughty, fresh, frosty, icy, (*coll.*) nippy, (*coll.*) parky, penetrating, raw, sharp, wintry. ANTONYMS: balmy, warm. **2** (*cold in manner; unfriendly*) aloof, cold, distant, frigid, frosty, hostile, remote, unemotional, unenthusiastic, unfriendly, unresponsive, unsympathetic, unwelcoming. ANTONYMS: friendly, welcoming.

chip *n.* **1** (*a small piece of wood, stone etc. detached*) bit, flake, fragment, morsel, paring, piece, scrap, shard, shaving, sliver, splinter, wafer. **2** (*the place from which such a piece has been removed*) damage, defect, dent, flaw, nick, notch, scrape, scratch. **3** (*a very small piece of silicon, with an integrated circuit printed on it*) microchip, silicon chip.

~*v.t.* (*to cut or break a chip or chips off*) chisel, cut, damage, dent, gash, hew, nick, whittle.

chivalrous *a.* **1** (*gallant, noble*) bold, brave, courageous, gallant, heroic, high-minded, intrepid, knightly, noble, valiant. ANTONYMS: cowardly, ungallant. **2** (*courteous*) courteous, courtly, gracious, polite, well-mannered.

choice *n.* **1** (*the power or act of choosing*) adoption, choosing, election, selection. **2** (*the range to choose from*) selection, variety. **3** (*selection, preference*) discrimination, preference, selection. **4** (*an alternative*) alternative, option. **5** (*the best part*) best part, cream, elite, flower, pick, select.
~*a.* **1** (*selected, chosen with care*) chosen, hand-picked, picked, preferred, selected. ANTONYMS: rejected. **2** (*of great value or superior quality*) best, desirable, excellent, exquisite, first-rate, precious, prime, prize, rare, select, special, superior. ANTONYMS: inferior.

choke *v.t.* **1** (*to block the windpipe* (*of*), *so as to prevent breathing*) asphyxiate, garrotte, strangle, throttle. **2** (*to smother, to stifle*) restrain, smother, stifle. **3** (*to repress, to silence*) gag, prohibit, repress, silence. **4** (*to stop up, to block*) block, bung, clog, congest, constrict, dam, obstruct, stop up.
~*v.i.* **1** (*to be partially suffocated; to be unable to breathe*) cough, fight for breath, gag, gasp, retch. **2** (*to die*) die, (*sl.*) snuff it.

choose *v.t.* **1** (*to select from a number*) adopt, cull, designate, elect, go for, opt for, pick, prefer, select, settle on, single out. ANTONYMS: reject. **2** (*to prefer* (*to do something rather than something else*)) feel inclined, prefer, wish. **3** (*to decide willingly* (*to do*)) decide, determine, make up one's mind.

choosy *a.* (*hard to please, particular*) demanding, difficult, discerning, discriminating, exacting, finicky, fussy, hard to please, particular, (*coll.*) picky, selective. ANTONYMS: undiscriminating.

chop *v.t.* **1** (*to cut with a sharp blow*) cleave, cut, hack, hew, slash. **2** (*to cut or strike off*) crop, cut off, lop, sever, shear, strike off, truncate. **3** (*to cut* (*meat, vegetables etc.*) *into parts or small pieces*) cube, cut up, dice, hash, mince, slice. **4** (*to reduce or abolish*) abolish, axe, reduce.
~*n.* **1** (*a cutting stroke or blow*) blow, cut, stroke. **2** (*dismissal from a job*) (*sl.*) axe, (*sl.*) boot, dismissal, (*coll.*) heave-ho, (*coll.*) sack.

chronic *a.* **1** ((*of a disease, social problem etc.*) *of long duration, or apt to recur*) incurable, lasting, lingering, long-lasting, persistent, recurring. ANTONYMS: curable, temporary. **2**

(*habitual*) confirmed, deep-rooted, deep-seated, habitual, hardened, ingrained, inveterate, persistent. **3** (*very bad, severe*) abysmal, appalling, atrocious, awful, dreadful, extreme, severe, very bad.

chubby *a.* (*plump, rounded*) ample, buxom, chunky, dumpy, fat, flabby, fleshy, overweight, plump, podgy, portly, rounded, stocky, stout, stubby, stumpy, thickset, tubby. ANTONYMS: lean, thin.

chuckle *v.i.* (*to laugh quietly to oneself*) cackle, chortle, giggle, laugh, snigger, titter.
~*n.* (*a quiet laugh*) cackle, chortle, giggle, laugh, snigger, titter.

churn *v.t.* (*to agitate with violence or continued motion* (*often with up*)) agitate, beat, disturb, stir up, whip.
~*v.i.* ((*of waves etc.*) *to swirl about*) boil, convulse, foam, froth, seethe, swirl about, toss.

circle *n.* **1** (*a ring, a round figure or object*) band, circumference, coil, cordon, disc, hoop, loop, perimeter, periphery, revolution, ring, round, wheel. **2** (*a class, a set*) assembly, class, clique, club, company, coterie, crowd, fellowship, fraternity, group, order, school, set, society. **3** (*a sphere of action or influence*) area, compass, domain, field, orbit, province, realm, region, scene, sphere. **4** (*a circular route*) circuit, lap, orbit. **5** (*a cycle*) cycle, period, series. **6** (*a round body, a sphere*) ball, globe, orb, sphere.
~*v.t.* **1** (*to move round*) circumnavigate, travel round, wheel round. **2** (*to surround*) belt, circumscribe, compass, encircle, encompass, gird, surround.
~*v.i.* (*to move in a circle*) coil, pivot, revolve, ring, rotate, whirl.

circuit *n.* **1** (*the line enclosing a space, the distance round about*) boundary, bounds, circumference, edge, limit, margin, perimeter, periphery. **2** (*the space enclosed within certain limits*) ambit, area, compass, district, range, region. **3** (*the act of revolving or moving round*) lap, orbit, perambulation, revolution, rotation, round. **4** (*a circular route or itinerary followed by a salesperson, politician etc.*) beat, course, itinerary, journey, milk round, route, tour.

circuitous *a.* (*indirect, roundabout*) direct, indirect, labyrinthine, meandering, oblique, rambling, roundabout, serpentine, tortuous, winding. ANTONYMS: direct, unswerving.

circulate *v.i.* **1** (*to pass from place to place or person to person*) go about, move about, travel. **2** ((*of blood in the body etc.*) *to pass through certain channels and return to the starting point*) course, flow, pump, run. **3** (*to move*

round) move round, orbit, revolve, rotate. **4** (*to move from person to person at a social gathering*) mingle, mix, socialize.
~*v.t.* (*to spread, to diffuse*) air, announce, broadcast, diffuse, disseminate, distribute, divulge, issue, make known, proclaim, promulgate, propagate, publicize, publish, put about, report, spread.

circumstance *n.* **1** (*an incident, an occurrence*) accident, affair, contingency, episode, event, happening, incident, occasion, occurrence, particular. **2** (*pl.*) (*the facts and other conditions that affect an act or an event*) details, elements, factors, facts, particulars, points. **3** (*ceremony, fuss*) ceremony, fuss, pomp.

citizen *n.* **1** (*a member of a state having political rights*) denizen, householder, inhabitant, national, native, resident, subject, taxpayer, voter. **2** (*a dweller in a town or city*) burgess, burgher, city-dweller, suburbanite, town-dweller, townsman, townswoman, villager.

city *n.* (*a large and important town*) borough, burgh, conurbation, metropolis, municipality, town.
~*a.* (*of or relating to a city*) civic, metropolitan, municipal, urban.

civil *a.* **1** (*domestic, not foreign*) domestic, home, internal. ANTONYMS: foreign. **2** (*commercial, legislative*) civic, commercial, legislative, municipal, political. **3** (*of or relating to social, commercial and administrative affairs*) administrative, civilian, commercial, lay, secular, social. **4** (*polite, courteous*) accommodating, affable, civilized, complaisant, courteous, courtly, formal, obliging, polished, polite, proper, refined, respectful, suave, urbane, well-bred, well-mannered. ANTONYMS: ill-mannered, impolite.

civilization *n.* **1** (*a civilized society or people of the past*) culture, nation, people, society. **2** (*the act or process of civilizing*) cultivation, development, edification, education, enlightenment, polish, progress, refinement, sophistication. ANTONYMS: barbarism.

civilize *v.t.* **1** (*to bring out of barbarism*) domesticate, elevate, humanize, tame. **2** (*to instruct in the refinements of civilized society*) edify, educate, enlighten, polish, refine, school, teach.

claim *v.t.* **1** (*to demand as a right*) appropriate, ask, call for, challenge, collect, commandeer, demand, exact, require, requisition. **2** (*to assert that one has or has done* (*something*)) allege, assert, declare, profess, state. **3** (*to affirm, to maintain*) affirm, contend, hold, insist,

maintain, uphold. **4** (*to take or have as a consequence*) account for, cost, take.
~*n.* **1** (*a demand for something due*) call, demand, request, requirement. **2** (*an assertion*) affirmation, allegation, application, assertion, declaration, petition, profession, protestation. **3** (*a real or supposed right*) privilege, right.

clan *n.* **1** (*a tribe or number of families bearing the same name, descended from a common ancestor*) race, tribe. **2** (*a large extended family*) dynasty, family, house, line. **3** (*a clique, a set*) band, brotherhood, circle, clique, coterie, crowd, faction, fellowship, fraternity, gang, group, order, party, ring, sect, set, sisterhood, society, sorority.

clandestine *a.* (*secret, underhand*) cloak-and-dagger, closet, concealed, covert, fraudulent, furtive, illegal, private, secret, sly, stealthy, surreptitious, underground, underhand. ANTONYMS: open.

clap *v.t.* **1** (*to strike together noisily*) clash, strike together. **2** (*to applaud, by striking the hands together*) acclaim, applaud, cheer. ANTONYMS: boo, jeer. **3** (*to strike quickly or slap with something flat*) bang, pat, punch, slap, strike, (*coll.*) wallop, whack. **4** (*to put or place suddenly*) place, put, slap.

clarify *v.t.* **1** (*to make easier to understand*) clear up, elaborate, elucidate, enlighten, explain, explicate, illuminate, interpret, make plain, resolve, shed light on, simplify. ANTONYMS: confuse, obscure. **2** (*to clear from visible impurities*) cleanse, filter, purify, refine, strain. ANTONYMS: pollute.

clarity *n.* (*clearness*) clearness, comprehensibility, definition, distinctness, explicitness, intelligibility, lucidity, pellucidity, precision, purity, simplicity, transparency, unambiguousness, understandability. ANTONYMS: murkiness, obscurity.

clash *v.i.* **1** (*to make a loud noise by striking together*) bang, clang, clank, clatter, crash, jangle, jar, rattle. **2** (*to come into collision*) collide, crash. **3** (*to disagree; to conflict*) argue, battle, conflict, differ, disagree, dispute, feud, fight, grapple, quarrel, squabble, war, wrangle. ANTONYMS: agree. **4** ((*of colours*) *to be in disharmony*) conflict, jar. ANTONYMS: go together, match.
~*n.* **1** (*the noise produced by the violent collision of two bodies*) bang, clang, clatter, crash, rattle. **2** (*opposition, conflict*) altercation, argument, battle, brush, conflict, confrontation, difference, disagreement, discord, dispute, fight, opposition, quarrel, showdown, squabble, struggle. **3** (*a collision*) collision, crash, (*coll.*) pile-up, smash. **4** (*disharmony of colours*) conflict, disharmony, jarring.

class n. **1** (a number of persons or things ranked together) group, kind, rank, set. **2** (a social rank) echelon, level, order, rank, stratum. **3** (the system of social ranking) caste, social order, social ranking, social standing, standing. **4** (a number of pupils or students taught together) form, grade, group, set, year. **5** (an occasion when they are taught) lesson, seminar, session. **6** (a division according to quality) category, classification, denomination, division, group, league. **7** (high quality or merit) bearing, breeding, distinction, excellence, importance, merit, pedigree, prestige, quality, refinement, taste.
~v.t. (to assign to a class or classes) arrange, assort, brand, categorize, classify, codify, designate, dispose, grade, group, label, order, rank, rate, type.

classic n. (any recognized masterpiece) exemplar, masterpiece, model, paradigm, paragon, prototype.
~a. **1** (of the first rank, esp. in literature or art) best, consummate, deathless, enduring, finest, first-class, immortal, legendary, masterly, notable, outstanding, superior, time-honoured, world-class. ANTONYMS: inferior, second-rate. **2** (outstandingly typical) characteristic, regular, representative, standard, typical, usual. **3** (harmonious, well-proportioned) balanced, harmonious, well-balanced, well-proportioned. **4** (pure, restrained) pure, refined, restrained. **5** (of standard authority) archetypal, definitive, exemplary, model, quintessential, standard.

classify v.t. **1** (to distribute into classes or divisions) arrange, assort, catalogue, categorize, class, codify, dispose, distribute, file, grade, group, pigeon-hole, rank, rate, sort, systematize, tabulate. **2** (to restrict the availability of (information), esp. for security reasons) restrict, withhold.

clean a. **1** (free from dirt, contamination etc.) fresh, hygienic, purified, sanitary, spotless, stainless, sterile, unblemished, uncontaminated, undefiled, unpolluted, unsoiled, unspotted, unstained, unsullied, washed. ANTONYMS: dirty, filthy. **2** (clear, unused) blank, clear, unmarked, unobstructed, unused. **3** (free from errors, defects etc.) faultless, flawless, immaculate, impeccable, perfect. ANTONYMS: used. **4** (free from ceremonial defilement) cleansed, holy, pure. **5** (free from evidence of criminal activity) above board, even-handed, fair, legal, proper. **6** (not carrying a gun) unarmed, weaponless. **7** (free from sexual references, innuendo etc.) blameless, chaste, decent, innocent, moral, pure, respectable, undefiled, virtuous. **8** (smooth, streamlined) shapely, smooth, streamlined. **9** (adroit, dexterous) adroit, dexterous, unerring. **10** (complete) complete, conclusive, decisive, entire, final, perfect, thorough, total, whole.
~v.t. **1** (to make clean) bath, cleanse, dust, launder, mop, polish, rinse, scour, sponge, sweep, wash, wipe. ANTONYMS: dirty, soil. **2** (to cleanse, to purify) cleanse, decontaminate, disinfect, purge, purify, sanitize. ANTONYMS: adulterate.

clear a. **1** (free from darkness or dullness) light, undimmed. ANTONYMS: dark, dull. **2** (luminous, bright) bright, luminous, lustrous, shiny, sparkling. **3** (transparent, translucent) crystalline, glassy, limpid, pellucid, see-through, translucent, transparent. ANTONYMS: opaque. **4** ((of the sky etc.) free from clouds or mist) cloudless, fair, fine, halcyon, sunny, unclouded. ANTONYMS: cloudy, murky. **5** (distinctly audible) audible, distinct, sharp, well-defined. ANTONYMS: inaudible, indistinct. **6** (evident, easy to see) apparent, blatant, conspicuous, evident, explicit, express, manifest, noticeable, obvious, palpable, patent, perceptible, plain, pronounced, recognizable, visible. ANTONYMS: hidden, obscure. **7** (lucid, easy to understand) coherent, comprehensible, logical, lucid, understandable. **8** (indisputable, unambiguous) incontrovertible, indisputable, unambiguous, unequivocal, unquestionable. ANTONYMS: ambiguous, confused. **9** (certain, unmistaken) certain, convinced, decided, definite, positive, resolved, sure, unmistaken. **10** (irreproachable, guiltless) blameless, clean, guileless, guiltless, innocent, irreproachable, pure, sinless, stainless, unblemished, undefiled, untarnished. **11** (unobstructed) empty, open, smooth, unhampered, unhindered, unimpeded, unobstructed. ANTONYMS: blocked, obstructed. **12** (free, unentangled) free, unentangled, unshackled. **13** (complete) absolute, complete, entire, whole.
~v.t. **1** (to make clear) unblock, unclog. **2** (to liberate, to disengage) disengage, disentangle, extricate, free, liberate, loosen, unload. **3** (to acquit, to exonerate) absolve, acquit, excuse, exonerate, justify, vindicate. **4** (to pass or leap over without touching) jump, leap, pass over, vault. **5** (to gain, to realize as profit) acquire, earn, gain, make, realize, reap, secure.
~v.i. **1** (to become clear or unclouded) brighten, improve, lighten. **2** (to dissipate, disappear etc.) disappear, dissipate, fade, thin. **to clear out 1** (to empty) empty, sort, tidy up. **2** (to depart) clear off, decamp, depart, get out, leave, retire, run off, slope off, withdraw. **to clear up 1** (to elucidate) answer, clarify, eliminate, elucidate, explain, remove, resolve,

settle, solve, straighten out, unravel. **2** (*to tidy up*) order, rearrange, tidy up.

clearly *adv.* **1** (*in a clear, lucid manner*) coherently, comprehensibly, logically, lucidly, understandably. **2** (*distinctly, audibly*) audibly, distinctly. **3** (*plainly, evidently*) evidently, manifestly, markedly, obviously, openly, overtly, plainly, starkly. **4** (*certainly, undoubtedly*) beyond doubt, certainly, definitely, incontestably, incontrovertibly, indubitably, undeniably, undoubtedly, unequivocally, unquestionably.

clemency *n.* (*mercy*) compassion, forbearance, forgiveness, gentleness, humanity, indulgence, kindness, leniency, mercy, mildness, moderation, pity, quarter, tenderness, tolerance. ANTONYMS: cruelty, harshness.

clergyman *n.* (*a person who is ordained for the Christian Church, a member of the clergy*) chaplain, churchman, cleric, curate, dean, ecclesiastic, evangelist, man of God, man of the cloth, minister, padre, parson, pastor, preacher, priest, rector, reverend, vicar. ANTONYMS: layman.

clergywoman *n.* (*a female member of the clergy*) chaplain, churchwoman, cleric, curate, dean, ecclesiastic, evangelist, minister, mother, padre, parson, pastor, preacher, priest, rector, reverend, vicar, woman of God, woman of the cloth. ANTONYMS: laywoman.

clerical *a.* **1** (*of or relating to the clergy*) churchly, ecclesiastical, ministerial, pastoral, priestly, sacerdotal. **2** (*of or relating to a clerk or office worker*) bookkeeping, office, secretarial.

clever *a.* **1** (*intelligent*) astute, brainy, bright, canny, deep, discerning, intelligent, keen, knowledgeable, perceptive, quick, quick-witted, rational, sagacious, sensible, shrewd, smart. ANTONYMS: dense, stupid. **2** (*dexterous, skilful*) able, adroit, capable, dexterous, expert, skilful. ANTONYMS: awkward, inept, inexpert. **3** (*talented*) endowed, gifted, talented. **4** (*ingenious*) creative, ingenious, inventive, resourceful. **5** (*cunning*) artful, crafty, cunning, foxy, guileful, sly, wily.

cliché *n.* (*a hackneyed phrase*) banality, bromide, (*coll.*) chestnut, old saw, platitude, stereotype, truism.

client *n.* (*a customer*) buyer, consumer, customer, habitué, patron, regular, shopper, user.

cliff *n.* **1** (*a high, steep rock face, esp. on the coast*) bluff, crag, escarpment, face, headland, overhang, rock face, scar. **2** (*a precipice*) drop, precipice.

climax *n.* (*the highest point, culmination*) acme, apex, apogee, crest, crisis, culmination, head, height, highlight, high point, maximum, peak, summit, top, turning point, zenith.

climb *v.t.* (*to ascend, esp. by means of the hands and feet*) ascend, clamber, mount, scale, scramble up, shin up, top. ANTONYMS: descend. ~*v.i.* (*to rise*) go up, rise, soar.

cling *v.i.* (*to adhere closely, esp. by grasping or embracing*) adhere, attach, clasp, cleave, clutch, embrace, fasten, fix, grasp, grip, hold fast, hug, stick, twine round. ANTONYMS: separate.

clip *v.t.* **1** (*to cut with shears or scissors*) cut, dock, lop, shear. **2** (*to trim*) crop, pare, prune, shorten, trim. **3** (*to cut out*) cut away, cut out. **4** (*to cut* (*a word*) *short by omitting letters, syllables etc.*) curtail, cut short. **5** (*to hit sharply*) clout, cuff, punch, slap, smack, strike, thump, (*coll.*) wallop, whack.

cloak *n.* **1** (*a loose, wide, outer garment, usu. sleeveless*) cape, coat, mantle, overcoat, poncho, robe, shawl, wrap. **2** (*a covering*) cover, mask, shield, shroud, veil. **3** (*a disguise, a pretext*) blind, disguise, excuse, front, pretext. ~*v.t.* **1** (*to cover with or as with a cloak*) cover, mantle, veil. **2** (*to disguise*) camouflage, disguise. **3** (*to hide*) conceal, cover up, hide, mask, obscure, screen. ANTONYMS: expose, reveal.

clog *v.t.* **1** (*to obstruct*) block, bung, obstruct, stop up. **2** (*to choke up*) choke up, congest, dam up, jam. **3** (*to hinder*) hinder, impede. **4** (*to encumber or hamper with a weight*) burden, encumber, fetter, hamper, weigh down.

close¹ *a.* **1** (*near in time or space*) adjacent, adjoining, alongside, approaching, at hand, hard by, imminent, impending, near, nearby, neighbouring, †nigh, pending, upcoming. ANTONYMS: distant, remote. **2** (*intimate, familiar*) confidential, dear, devoted, familiar, inseparable, intimate, loving. ANTONYMS: aloof, indifferent. **3** (*nearly alike*) akin, alike, similar. **4** (*solid, dense*) congested, cramped, crowded, dense, impenetrable, jam-packed, packed, solid, thick, tight. ANTONYMS: empty, uncrowded. **5** (*concise, compressed*) compact, compressed, concise. **6** (*attentive, concentrated*) alert, assiduous, attentive, careful, concentrated, detailed, dogged, earnest, fixed, intense, intent, keen, minute, painstaking, rigorous, searching, thorough. **7** (*following the original closely*) conscientious, exact, faithful, literal, strict. **8** (*accurate, precise*) accurate, exact, minute, precise. **9** (*without ventilation, stifling*) airless, confined, fuggy, heavy, humid, muggy, musty, oppressive, stagnant, stale, stifling, stuffy, suffocating, sweltering, thick, unventilated. ANTONYMS: airy, fresh. **10** (*of the weather*) *warm and damp*) humid, muggy, oppressive, sweltering. **11** (*closed, shut fast*) closed, fast, secure, shut fast. **12** (*confined, shut in*) confined, enclosed, shut in. **13** (*restricted, limited*) limited, reserved, restricted. **14** (*retired, secret*) guarded, hidden, private, reticent, retired, secluded, secret, secretive, silent, taciturn, tight-lipped, uncommunicative, unforthcoming. **15** (*parsimonious, miserly*) mean, miserly, near, niggardly, parsimonious, penny-pinching, penurious, stingy, tight-fisted, ungenerous. ANTONYMS: extravagant, magnanimous.

close² *v.t.* **1** (*to shut*) fasten, secure, shut. **2** (*to fill (up) an opening*) bar, block, bung, choke, clog, cork, fill, obstruct, plug, seal, stop up. ANTONYMS: clear, unblock. **3** (*to enclose, to shut in*) confine, enclose, shut in. **4** (*to bring or unite together*) bring together, come together, connect, couple, fuse, join, unite. ANTONYMS: disconnect, separate. **5** (*to be the end of, to conclude*) conclude, culminate, discontinue, end, finish, shut down, terminate, wind up. ANTONYMS: begin, start. **6** (*to complete*) complete, finish, settle.
~*v.i.* **1** (*to come to an end, to cease*) cease, come to an end. **2** (*to stop doing business, esp. at the end of the working day*) put up the shutters, shut up shop. **3** (*to agree, to come to terms*) agree, come to terms, negotiate. **4** (*to come to hand-to-hand fighting*) contend with, fight, grapple.
~*n.* (*an end, a conclusion*) cessation, completion, conclusion, culmination, denouement, end, ending, finale, finish, termination.

clothes *n.pl.* (*garments, dress*) apparel, attire, (*sl.*) clobber, clothing, costume, dress, (*sl.*) duds, ensemble, garb, garments, (*coll.*) gear, get-up, (*coll.*) glad rags, outfit, (*coll.*) togs, vestments, wardrobe, wear.

cloudy *a.* **1** (*consisting of or covered with clouds*) clouded, overcast. ANTONYMS: clear. **2** (*not transparent*) blurred, dim, hazy, misty, muddy, murky, nebulous, opaque. ANTONYMS: transparent. **3** (*obscure, confused*) confused, indefinite, indistinct, obscure, vague. **4** (*dull, gloomy*) dismal, dull, dusky, gloomy, grey, leaden, louring, lustreless, sombre, sullen, sunless.

clown *n.* **1** (*a comic entertainer in a circus or pantomime*) comedian, comic, fool, harlequin, jester, pierrot. **2** (*a buffoon*) buffoon, joker, prankster. **3** (*a clumsy or foolish person*) dolt, fool, idiot, (*sl.*) jerk. **4** (*a rough, ill-bred person*) boor, lout, oaf, peasant.

~*v.i.* (*to play silly jokes*) act the fool, caper, fool around, horse around, mess about, (*taboo, sl.*) piss around, play the fool.

club¹ *n.* (*a piece of wood with one end thicker and heavier than the other, used as a weapon*) baton, cosh, cudgel, staff, truncheon.
~*v.t.* (*to beat with a club*) bash, batter, beat, bludgeon, (*sl.*) clobber, clout, cosh, cudgel, hammer, lambast, pommel, pummel, strike, thrash.

club² *n.* **1** (*an association of persons combined for some common object, such as politics, sport etc.*) alliance, association, circle, clique, company, consortium, federation, fellowship, fraternity, group, guild, league, lodge, order, organization, set, society, sorority, union. **2** (*a nightclub*) cabaret, disco, nightclub.

clue *n.* (*anything that serves as a guide or hint for the solution of a problem or crime*) evidence, guide, hint, indication, information, inkling, intimation, key, lead, pointer, sign, suggestion, suspicion, tip, tip-off, trace.

clump *n.* **1** (*a thick cluster of shrubs or flowers*) cluster, copse, group, spinney, thicket, wood. **2** (*a thick mass of small objects*) assemblage, bunch, bundle, chunk, clod, gathering, hunk, lump, mass, wad.
~*v.i.* **1** (*to walk or tread in a heavy and clumsy fashion*) clomp, lumber, plod, stamp, stomp, stump, thud, thump, tramp, trudge. **2** (*to form or gather into a clump or clumps*) agglutinate, assemble, bunch, cluster, gather. ANTONYMS: disperse.

clumsy *a.* **1** (*awkward, ungainly*) awkward, blundering, bovine, bumbling, bungling, (*coll.*) butter-fingered, gauche, gawky, (*coll.*) ham-fisted, inept, inexpert, lumbering, oafish, ponderous, uncoordinated, uncouth, ungainly, ungraceful, unskilful. ANTONYMS: adept, deft. **2** (*ill-constructed, difficult to use*) awkward, ill-constructed, inconvenient, unwieldy. **3** (*rude, tactless*) rough, rude, tactless, undiplomatic.

cluster *n.* **1** (*a number of things of the same kind growing or joined together*) clump, tuft. **2** (*a bunch*) accumulation, agglomeration, batch, bunch, bundle, collection. **3** (*a group, a crowd*) aggregation, assembly, band, body, company, crowd, gathering, group, knot, swarm.
~*v.i.* (*to come or to grow into a cluster or clusters*) accumulate, aggregate, assemble, band, bunch, collect, congregate, crowd, flock, gather, group, mass, throng. ANTONYMS: disperse.

clutch *n.* **1** (*a grip, a grasp*) clasp, embrace, grasp, grip, hold, snatch. **2** (*the paw or talon of* a *rapacious animal*) hands, paws, talons. **3** (*pl.*) (*grasping hands, tyrannical power*) claws, control, domination, influence, possession, power.

~*v.t.* **1** (*to seize or grip with the hand*) catch, clasp, cling to, embrace, fasten, grapple, grasp, grip, seize, take. **2** (*to snatch*) grab, snatch.

clutter *v.t.* (*to fill or strew with clutter*) disarrange, litter, mess up, scatter, strew, untidy.

~*n.* **1** (*a mess, a disorderly collection of things*) disarray, disorder, jumble, litter, lumber, mess, muddle, rubbish, untidiness. **2** (*a confused noise*) clamour, din, hubbub, noise. **3** (*bustle, confusion*) bustle, chaos, confusion.

coach *n.* **1** (*a long-distance bus*) bus, charabanc, omnibus, vehicle. **2** (*a railway carriage*) car, carriage. **3** (*a four-wheeled, horse-drawn vehicle*) carriage, hackney, hansom, phaeton, trap, wagon. **4** (*a person who trains sports players*) manager, trainer. **5** (*a tutor who prepares students for examinations*) teacher, tutor. **6** (*any specialized instructor*) handler, instructor, mentor, teacher, trainer.

~*v.t.* **1** (*to train*) drill, train. **2** (*to prepare for an examination*) cram, prepare. **3** (*to instruct or advise in preparation for any event*) advise, direct, guide, instruct, school, tutor.

coarse *a.* **1** (*large in size or rough in texture*) bristly, large, prickly, rough, scaly, scratchy, uneven. ANTONYMS: fine, smooth. **2** (*rude, rough*) brutish, gruff, loutish, rough, rude, uncivil, vulgar. **3** (*unpolished, unrefined*) crude, impure, rough-hewn, unfinished, unpolished, unpurified. ANTONYMS: polished, refined. **4** (*indecent, obscene*) bawdy, earthy, foul-mouthed, gross, immodest, improper, indecent, indelicate, lascivious, obscure, offensive, ribald, rude, smutty, vulgar. ANTONYMS: decent, proper. **5** (*common, of inferior quality*) average, common, inferior, low-quality, second-rate, shoddy, tawdry, trashy.

coast *n.* **1** (*that part of the border of a country where the land meets the sea*) beach, coastline, seaboard. **2** (*the seashore*) seashore, shore, strand.

~*v.i.* (*to proceed without any positive effort*) cruise, drift, freewheel, glide, sail.

coat *n.* **1** (*an outer garment with sleeves*) blazer, cape, great coat, jacket, overcoat. **2** (*the fur or natural external covering of an animal*) fleece, fur, hair, hide, pelt, skin, wool. **3** (*any covering*) covering, husk, integument, rind, shell, skin, tunic. **4** (*a layer of any substance covering another*) blanket, coating, dusting, film, glaze, lamination, layer, membrane, overlay, patina, sheet, skin, varnish, veneer.

~*v.t.* **1** (*to cover*) blanket, cover, envelop,

laminate, mantle, overlay. **2** (*to spread with a layer of anything*) apply, paint, plaster, smear, spread.

coax *v.t.* **1** (*to persuade by flattery*) allure, beguile, cajole, charm, decoy, entice, flatter, implore, induce, inveigle, (*coll.*) jolly along, lure, persuade, prevail upon, (*coll.*) soft-soap, soothe, (*coll.*) sweet-talk, talk into, urge, wheedle. ANTONYMS: coerce, force. **2** (*to handle with care and patience*) handle, manipulate.

cocky *a.* (*self-important, conceited*) arrogant, brash, cheeky, cocksure, conceited, egotistical, haughty, lordly, overconfident, proud, saucy, self-important, swaggering, vain. ANTONYMS: modest, self-effacing.

code *n.* **1** (*a series of symbols, letters etc. used for the sake of secrecy*) cipher, encoding. **2** (*a collection of laws systematically arranged*) canon, laws, regulations, rules, system. **3** (*the principles accepted in any sphere of art, conduct etc.*) convention, criteria, custom, ethics, etiquette, manners, maxim, practice, principles.

coerce *v.t.* **1** (*to restrain by force*) constrain, hold back, restrain. **2** (*to enforce by compulsion*) browbeat, (*coll.*) bulldoze, bully, compel, constrain, dragoon, drive, enforce, force, impel, intimidate, oblige, press, pressurize, (*esp. N Am.*) railroad.

coherent *a.* **1** (*articulate, intelligible*) articulate, clear, comprehensible, intelligible, lucid, understandable. ANTONYMS: incoherent, unintelligible. **2** (*logically connected, consistent*) congruous, connected, consistent, logical, orderly, organized, rational, reasoned, systematic. ANTONYMS: inconsistent, irrational.

coil *v.t.* **1** (*to wind (a rope etc.) into rings*) curl, loop, twine, wind. **2** (*to twist into a spiral shape*) convolute, entwine, snake, spiral, twist, wrap, wreathe, writhe.

coincide *v.i.* **1** (*to correspond in time, place etc.*) accord, come together, correspond, harmonize, match, square, tally. ANTONYMS: clash. **2** (*to happen at the same time*) coexist, happen together, synchronize. **3** (*to agree, to concur*) acquiesce, agree, concur. ANTONYMS: conflict, disagree.

coincidence *n.* **1** (*the act or condition of coinciding*) concomitance, concurrence, conjunction, contemporaneity, correlation, correspondence, simultaneity, synchronism. **2** (*an instance of this*) accident, chance, eventuality, fluke, fortuity, happenstance, luck, stroke of luck. ANTONYMS: design.

coincidental *a.* **1** (*that coincides*) coincident,

concomitant, concurrent, simultaneous, synchronous. **2** (*of the nature of or resulting from coincidence*) accidental, casual, chance, fluky, fortuitous, lucky, unforeseen, unintentional, unplanned, unpredictable. ANTONYMS: calculated, deliberate.

cold *a.* **1** (*low in temperature, esp. in relation to normal temperature*) arctic, biting, bitter, bleak, chill, chilly, cool, freezing, frigid, frosty, frozen, harsh, icy, inclement, keen, (*coll.*) nippy, (*coll.*) parky, polar, raw, wintry. ANTONYMS: hot, warm. **2** (*suffering from a sensation of lack of heat*) benumbed, chilled, chilly, freezing, frozen, numbed, shivery. **3** (*without ardour, indifferent*) apathetic, indifferent, lacklustre, lukewarm, passionless, phlegmatic, unconcerned. ANTONYMS: enthusiastic. **4** (*lacking friendliness, unwelcoming*) aloof, distant, frigid, glacial, inhospitable, remote, reserved, stand-offish, stony, unfeeling, unfriendly, unmoved, unresponsive, unsympathetic, unwelcoming. ANTONYMS: friendly, sympathetic. **5** (*sad, depressing*) bleak, cheerless, depressing, discouraging, disheartening, dismal, dispiriting, gloomy, sad. **6** (*dead*) dead, stiff. **7** (*unconscious*) comatose, unconscious. **8** (*unrehearsed*) unprepared, unrehearsed.
~*n.* **1** (*absence of warmth*) chill, frigidity, frostiness, iciness. ANTONYMS: warmth. **2** (*a viral infection of the mucous membranes of the respiratory tract*) flu, influenza, sniffles.

cold-blooded *a.* (*unfeeling, callous*) barbarous, brutal, callous, cruel, dispassionate, hardened, heartless, indifferent, inhuman, insensitive, merciless, pitiless, ruthless, stonyhearted, thick-skinned, unemotional, unfeeling, unmoved, unresponsive, vicious. ANTONYMS: kind, sensitive.

collaborate *v.i.* **1** (*to work jointly with another*) cooperate, join forces, participate, partner, team up, work together. ANTONYMS: compete. **2** (*to cooperate with an enemy in occupation of one's own country*) collude, conspire, cooperate, fraternize.

collapse *v.i.* **1** (*to fall in, to give way*) cave in, crack up, crumple, deflate, disintegrate, dissolve, fall down, fall in, give way, subside, tumble down. **2** (*to break down, to suffer from physical or nervous illness*) break down, crack up, drop, faint, go to pieces, (*coll.*) keel over, pass out, (*poet.*) swoon. ANTONYMS: recover. **3** (*to come to nothing*) come to nothing, evaporate, fail, fall flat, fall through, fizzle out, founder, go under.
~*n.* **1** (*the act or an instance of collapsing*) cave-in, disintegration, downfall, ruin, subsidence. **2** (*complete failure*) failure, flop. **3** (*a sudden physical or nervous illness*) breakdown, (*coll.*) crack-up, exhaustion, faint, prostration.

colleague *n.* (*a fellow worker*) ally, assistant, associate, collaborator, companion, comrade, confederate, fellow, mate, partner, workmate. ANTONYMS: opponent, rival.

collect *v.t.* **1** (*to gather together into one mass or place*) accumulate, aggregate, amass, assemble, compile, flock together, gather together, heap, hoard, save, stockpile. **2** (*to gather from a number of sources*) gather, raise, secure, solicit. **3** (*to call for, to fetch*) call for, fetch, pick up. **4** (*to concentrate, to bring under control*) assemble, concentrate, control, convene, draw, muster, rally, summon.

collection *n.* **1** (*the act of collecting*) gathering, putting aside, stockpiling, storing. **2** (*that which is collected*) accumulation, anthology, assemblage, assortment, cluster, compilation, gathering, group, heap, hoard, mass, pile, set, stockpile, store. **3** (*money contributed for religious, charitable or other purposes*) alms, contribution, donation, offering, offertory, (*coll.*) whip-round.

collide *v.i.* (*to come into collision or conflict*) clash, conflict, crash, hit, (*sl.*) prang, smash.

collision *n.* **1** (*the act of striking violently together*) accident, bump, crash, encounter, impact, (*coll.*) pile-up, (*sl.*) prang, smash, wreck. **2** (*opposition*) antagonism, conflict, opposition. ANTONYMS: accord. **3** (*the clashing of interests*) battle, clash, conflict, confrontation, skirmish.

colossal *a.* **1** (*huge*) big, elephantine, enormous, gargantuan, giant, gigantic, (*coll.*) ginormous, Herculean, huge, immense, mammoth, massive, monstrous, monumental, mountainous, prodigious, titanic, vast. ANTONYMS: minuscule, tiny. **2** (*remarkable*) extraordinary, great, incredible, overwhelming, prodigious, remarkable, spectacular, staggering, stupendous, tremendous, wonderful.

colour *n.* **1** (*any one of the hues into which light can be resolved, or a mixture of these*) hue, shade, tincture, tint. **2** (*that which is used for colouring, a paint*) coloration, dye, paint, pigment, tincture. **3** (*the use or effect of colour in drawings, photography etc.*) coloration, colouring. **4** (*the complexion of the face, esp. a healthy hue*) bloom, blush, complexion, flush, glow, hue, rosiness, ruddiness. **5** (*pigmentation of the skin, esp. dark pigmentation*) pigment, pigmentation. **6** (*often pl.*) (*appearance, esp. false appearance*) appearance, disguise, facade, guise, semblance. **7** (*pl.*) (*a flag*) banner, ensign, flag, pennant, standard.

8 (*excuse*) excuse, pretence, pretext. 9 (*quality of tone*) timbre, tone. 10 (*general character, quality*) character, disposition, make-up, quality. 11 (*mood*) disposition, mood, temper, temperament. 12 (*vividness, animation*) animation, brilliance, richness, vividness.

~*v.t.* 1 (*to give or apply colour to*) stain, tinge, tint, wash. 2 (*to paint, to dye*) crayon, dye, paint. 3 (*to misrepresent*) bias, disguise, distort, falsify, garble, gloss over, misrepresent, pervert, prejudice, (*N Am.*) put a spin on, slant, taint, twist, warp. 4 (*to exaggerate*) embroider, exaggerate, varnish. 5 (*to influence*) affect, influence.

~*v.i.* (*to turn red, to blush*) blush, burn, crimson, flush, go red, redden. ANTONYMS: pale, whiten.

colourless *a.* 1 (*without colour*) neutral, uncoloured. ANTONYMS: colourful. 2 (*pale, subdued in tone*) anaemic, ashen, blanched, bleached, faded, neutral, pale, pallid, pasty, sallow, sickly, wan, washed out, waxen. ANTONYMS: radiant, ruddy. 3 (*lacking in life and vigour*) bland, boring, characterless, drab, dreary, dull, insipid, lacklustre, lifeless, monotonous, tame, tedious, unenthusiastic, unmemorable, vapid. ANTONYMS: animated, interesting. 4 (*neutral, impartial*) impartial, neutral, unbiased.

column *n.* 1 (*a pillar or solid body of wood or stone, of considerably greater length than thickness*) monolith, monument, obelisk, pilaster, pillar, post, shaft, upright. 2 (*a perpendicular line of figures*) file, line, list, procession, row. 3 (*a regular article in a newspaper or magazine*) article, editorial, feature, piece, review. 4 (*a body of troops in deep files*) file, line, queue, rank, train.

combat *v.i.* (*to fight, to struggle*) battle, clash, contend, contest, defy, duel, engage, fight, oppose, resist, strive, struggle, war, withstand, wrestle. ANTONYMS: acquiesce, surrender.

~*n.* (*a fight, a battle*) action, altercation, battle, conflict, confrontation, contest, controversy, disagreement, dispute, duel, encounter, engagement, feud, fight, quarrel, skirmish, struggle, vendetta, war, warfare. ANTONYMS: peace, truce.

combination *n.* 1 (*the act or process of combining*) amalgamation, blending, coalescence, connection, fusion, mingling. ANTONYMS: separation. 2 (*a combined body or mass*) alloy, amalgam, amalgamation, blend, composite, compound, conglomerate, conjunction, meld, mix, mixture, synthesis. 3 (*a union, an association*) alliance, association, bloc, cabal, cartel, coalition, confederacy, confederation, consortium, conspiracy, federation, league, merger, organization, party, society, syndicate, trust, union.

combine *v.t.* 1 (*to cause to unite or coalesce*) amalgamate, associate, fuse, incorporate, integrate, meld, mix, synthesize, unify, unite. ANTONYMS: dissociate. 2 (*to bring together*) bind, blend, bond, bring together, connect, join, link, marry, merge, put together. ANTONYMS: separate, sever.

come *v.i.* 1 (*to move from a distance to a place nearer to the speaker or hearer*) advance, move. 2 (*to approach*) approach, draw near, move towards. ANTONYMS: depart. 3 (*to reach, to extend*) extend, reach, stretch. 4 (*to arrive*) appear, arrive, enter. 5 (*to arrive at some state or condition*) arrive at, end up. 6 (*to appear*) appear, materialize, show, show up, turn up. 7 (*to happen, to befall*) befall, happen, occur, take place, transpire, turn out. 8 (*to result, to originate (from)*) arise, emanate, emerge, ensue, flow, issue, originate, result. **to come about** (*to result, to come to pass*) arise, come to pass, happen, occur, result. **to come across** (*to meet with accidentally*) bump into, chance upon, discover, encounter, find, happen upon, hit upon, light upon, meet, notice, run across, stumble upon, unearth. **to come at** 1 (*to reach, to gain access to*) attain, discover, find, gain access to, grasp, reach. 2 (*to attack*) assail, assault, attack, charge, descend on, fall upon, fly at, go for, light into, rush, rush at. **to come by** 1 (*to call, to visit*) call, look up, visit. 2 (*to obtain, to gain*) acquire, gain, get, lay hold of, obtain, procure, secure, win. **to come off** 1 (*to take place*) happen, occur, take place. 2 (*to be accomplished*) be effective, be successful, go well, succeed. ANTONYMS: fail. **to come out** 1 (*to be published*) appear, be produced, be published. 2 (*to turn out*) conclude, end up, finish, result, turn out. 3 (*to declare something openly, esp. one's homosexuality*) come out of the closet, declare openly, openly admit.

comedian *n.* 1 (*an entertainer who tells jokes, humorous anecdotes etc.*) clown, comic, entertainer, funny man, humorist, jester, joker, stand-up, wit. 2 (*an actor or writer of comedy*) comic, wit.

comedy *n.* 1 (*a dramatic composition of an entertaining character depicting and often satirizing the incidents of ordinary life*) burlesque, farce, pantomime, revue, satire, (*coll.*) sitcom. ANTONYMS: melodrama, tragedy. 2 (*humour*) badinage, buffoonery, drollery, facetiousness, fun, hilarity, humour, jesting, joking, slapstick, wisecracking. ANTONYMS: seriousness.

comely *a.* 1 (*pleasing in appearance or behaviour*) appealing, attractive, beautiful, blooming, bonny, buxom, elegant, fair, good-looking, graceful, handsome, lovely, pleasing, pretty, wholesome, winsome. ANTONYMS: repulsive, ugly. **2** (*becoming, decent*) becoming, decent, decorous, fit, fitting, proper, seemly, suitable. ANTONYMS: indecorous, unbecoming.

comfort *v.t.* **1** (*to console*) alleviate, assuage, calm, commiserate with, console, ease, reassure, relieve, solace, soothe. ANTONYMS: aggravate, trouble. **2** (*to cheer, to encourage*) cheer, encourage, enliven, gladden, hearten, inspire, invigorate, refresh, strengthen. ANTONYMS: depress.
~*n.* **1** (*consolation*) alleviation, compensation, consolation, relief, solace. ANTONYMS: aggravation, irritation. **2** (*support in time of weakness*) aid, assistance, help, succour, support. **3** (*encouragement*) cheer, encouragement, hopefulness. **4** (*general well-being, absence of trouble*) ease, well-being. ANTONYMS: anxiety, trouble. **5** (*pl.*) (*the material things that contribute to this*) cosiness, creature comforts, luxury, plenty, security, snugness.

comfortable *a.* **1** (*providing comfort or security*) agreeable, ample, (*coll.*) comfy, commodious, convenient, cosy, delightful, easy, enjoyable, homely, luxurious, pleasant, relaxing, restful, roomy, snug. ANTONYMS: uncomfortable. **2** (*at ease, free from trouble or pain*) at ease, carefree, relaxed, serene, tranquil, untroubled. ANTONYMS: disturbed, troubled. **3** (*happy, contented*) complacent, contented, gratified, happy.

comic *a.* **1** (*of or relating to comedy*) absurd, amusing, comical, droll, funny, humorous, jocular, joking, laughable, witty. ANTONYMS: melancholy, serious. **2** (*facetious, intended to provoke laughter*) burlesque, facetious, farcical.
~*n.* **1** (*a comedian*) comedian, funny man, humorist, wag, wit. **2** (*a droll or amusing person*) buffoon, clown.

command *v.t.* **1** (*to order, to call for*) call for, compel, demand, direct, enforce, enjoin, instruct, order, require, tell. ANTONYMS: obey. **2** (*to govern, to exercise authority over*) administer, govern, lead, rule. **3** (*to control, to have at one's disposal*) control, handle, manage, supervise. **4** (*to master, to subjugate*) control, master, subjugate. **5** (*to dominate, to overlook*) dominate, look down on, overlook.
~*n.* **1** (*an order, a mandate*) behest, bidding, canon, commandment, decree, demand, direction, directive, edict, injunction, instruction, mandate, order, precept, requirement, ultimatum. **2** (*power, authority*) authority, charge, direction, dominion, government, influence, leadership, power, rule, sovereignty, stewardship. ANTONYMS: subordination. **3** (*control, mastery*) control, domination, mastery,

supervision. **4** (*a working knowledge* (*of*)) grasp, knowledge.

commander *n.* **1** (*a person who commands or is in authority*) boss, captain, chief, director, head, leader, ruler, top man, top woman. **2** (*a general or leader of a body of troops etc.*) commander-in-chief, commanding officer, general, leader, officer.

commemorate *v.t.* **1** (*to keep in remembrance by some solemn act*) pay tribute to, remember. ANTONYMS: forget, ignore. **2** (*to celebrate the memory of*) celebrate, consecrate, hallow, honour, keep, mark, observe, revere, salute, solemnize, venerate. **3** (*to be a memorial of*) immortalize, memorialize.

commence *v.i.* (*to start, to begin*) begin, embark, enter upon, establish, inaugurate, initiate, instigate, open, start. ANTONYMS: end, stop.

commerce *n.* **1** (*trade, financial transactions*) business, dealing, exchange, merchandising, trade, traffic, trafficking. **2** (*social intercourse*) communication, conversation, dealings, intercourse, relations, socializing.

commercial *a.* **1** (*of or relating to commerce*) business, mercantile, profit-making, trade, trading. ANTONYMS: non-profit-making. **2** (*done for profit*) marketable, mercenary, monetary, pecuniary, profitable, saleable.

commit *v.t.* **1** (*to entrust, to deposit*) commend, confide, consign, delegate, deliver, deposit, entrust, give, hand over, transfer. **2** (*to perpetrate*) carry out, do, enact, execute, perform, perpetrate. **3** (*to send for trial or to prison*) confine, imprison, incarcerate, intern, put away, sentence. ANTONYMS: release. **4** (*to assign, to pledge*) assign, bind, compromise, obligate, pledge, promise, swear, undertake, vouchsafe, vow.

common *a.* **1** (*belonging equally to more than one*) joint, mutual, shared. **2** (*open or free to all*) collective, communal, community, public, universal. ANTONYMS: private. **3** (*ordinary, usual*) accepted, average, commonplace, conventional, everyday, familiar, general, habitual, ordinary, plain, prevailing, prevalent, prosaic, routine, run-of-the-mill, standard, stock, usual. ANTONYMS: outstanding, unusual. **4 a** (*of low rank, position or birth*) inferior, lower-class, plebeian. ANTONYMS: superior, upper-class. **b** (*vulgar*) banal, coarse, hackneyed, stale, trite, vulgar. **c** (*inferior, mean*) base, cheap, inferior, low-grade, mean.

commotion *n.* **1** (*agitation, excitement*) ado, agitation, brouhaha, bustle, disorder, disturbance, excitement, ferment, furore, fuss, hubbub, hullabaloo, racket, rumpus, to-do, tumult, upheaval, uproar. ANTONYMS: calm, peace. **2** (*a popular insurrection*) insurrection, revolution, riot.

communal *a.* **1** (*for common use or benefit*) collective, general, joint, mutual, public, shared. ANTONYMS: individual, private. **2** (*of or relating to the community*) community, local, neighbourhood.

communicate *v.t.* **1** (*to pass on, to transmit*) pass on, send on, share, spread, transmit. **2** (*to impart, to reveal*) acquaint, announce, convey, declare, disclose, disseminate, divulge, impart, inform, make known, proclaim, publish, report, reveal, tell, unfold. ANTONYMS: conceal, suppress.
~*v.i.* **1** (*to convey information, esp. by speech or writing*) call, commune, converse, correspond, talk. **2** (*to establish mutual understanding* (*with someone*)) be on the same wavelength (as), connect (with), get through (to), hit it off (with), relate (to), speak the same language (as).

communication *n.* **1** (*the act of communicating*) dissemination, spreading, transmission. **2** (*that which is communicated*) announcement, bulletin, communiqué, disclosure, dispatch, message, report, statement, word. **3** (*news, information*) information, intelligence, news. **4** (*conversation or correspondence*) conversation, correspondence, discourse, social intercourse. **5** (*a means of passing from one place to another*) conveyance, transport. **6** (*a connecting link*) connection, contact, link, touch.

communicative *a.* **1** (*inclined or ready to communicate*) candid, expansive, forthcoming, frank, informative, open, unreserved. ANTONYMS: uncommunicative. **2** (*talkative, not reserved*) chatty, loquacious, talkative, voluble. ANTONYMS: quiet, taciturn.

community *n.* **1** (*a body of people living in a particular place*) neighbourhood, people, populace, population. **2** (*a body of individuals having common nationality etc.*) commonwealth, nation, state. **3** (*society at large, the public*) public, society. **4** (*an organized body, social or political*) association, body, brotherhood, company, organization, sisterhood. **5** (*fellowship*) fellowship, interdependence. **6** (*similarity of nature or character*) affinity, agreement, identity, similarity.

compact *a.* **1** (*closely packed or fitted together*) close, compressed, dense, packed. ANTONYMS: dispersed, loose. **2** (*small and practical*) neat, portable, small, snug. **3** (*solid*) compacted, concentrated, condensed, firm, impenetrable,

impermeable, solid, thick. **4** (*succinct*) brief, concise, condensed, epigrammatic, laconic, pithy, succinct, terse. ANTONYMS: long-winded, verbose.
~*v.t.* **1** (*to consolidate*) concentrate, consolidate. **2** (*to join or pack closely and firmly together*) compress, cram, pack, stuff.

companion *n.* **1** (*a person who associates with or accompanies another*) assistant, attendant, chaperon, chaperone, escort. **2** (*a comrade*) acquaintance, (*coll.*) buddy, comrade, crony, friend, mate, partner. **3** (*a partner*) accomplice, ally, associate, colleague, confederate, counterpart, fellow, match, mate, twin.

companionship *n.* (*fellowship, company*) association, brotherhood, camaraderie, company, comradeship, conviviality, fellow feeling, fellowship, fraternity, friendship, rapport, sisterhood, society, togetherness.

company *n.* **1** (*society, companionship*) companionship, fellowship, society. **2** (*a number of people associated together for carrying on a business*) association, business, concern, corporation, establishment, firm, house, institution, partnership, syndicate. **3** (*a number of people assembled*) assemblage, assembly, audience, band, body, camp, circle, convention, crowd, ensemble, gathering, group, league, meeting, party, set, throng. **4** (*guests, visitors*) callers, guests, visitors. **5** (*a body of actors etc.*) band, cast, outfit, troupe.

compare *v.t.* **1** (*to liken* (*one thing to another*)) correlate, equate, liken, parallel, resemble. **2** (*to see how* (*one thing*) *agrees with or resembles another*) balance, contrast, juxtapose, set against, weigh.
~*v.i.* (*to bear comparison* (*with*)) approach, approximate (to), bear comparison (with), come up (to), compete (with), equal, match, rival, vie (with).

comparison *n.* **1** (*the act of comparing*) collation, juxtaposition. **2** (*a simile or illustration*) analogy, illustration, simile. **3** (*similarity*) analogy, comparability, correlation, correspondence, kinship, likeness, match, relation, resemblance, similarity. ANTONYMS: contrast.

compassion *n.* (*sympathy for the sufferings and sorrows of others*) charity, clemency, commiseration, compunction, condolence, fellow feeling, heart, humanity, kindliness, mercy, pity, quarter, soft-heartedness, sorrow, sympathy, tenderness. ANTONYMS: indifference, ruthlessness.

compatible *a.* **1** (*well-matched or well-suited*) co-existing, congenial, like-minded, well-matched, well-suited. ANTONYMS: incompatible, unsuited. **2** (*consistent, harmonious*) accordant, agreeable, congruous, consistent, consonant, harmonious, reconcilable.

compelling a. 1 (convincing) cogent, conclusive, convincing, forceful, irrefutable, persuasive, powerful, strong, telling, weighty. ANTONYMS: unconvincing, unpersuasive. 2 (arousing strong interest or admiration) alluring, enchanting, enthralling, gripping, hypnotic, irresistible, mesmeric, riveting, spellbinding. ANTONYMS: boring, uninteresting. 3 (urgent) binding, compulsive, imperative, overpowering, overriding, pressing, urgent.

compensate v.t. 1 (to recompense) indemnify, pay back, recompense, refund, remunerate, repay. 2 (to make amends for) atone, expiate, make amends, make good, make reparation, requite, reward, satisfy. 3 (to counterbalance) balance, cancel out, counteract, counterbalance, equalize, even up, neutralize, nullify, offset, redress, square.

compete v.i. 1 (to contend as a rival (with)) challenge, contend, contest, fight, oppose, rival, vie. 2 (to strive in emulation) emulate, strive, struggle. 3 (to take part (in a race, contest etc.)) go in (for), join in, participate, take part.

competent a. 1 (qualified, capable) able, adept, appropriate, capable, clever, fit, knowledgeable, prepared, proficient, qualified, skilled, suitable. ANTONYMS: incompetent, unsuitable. 2 (sufficient, adequate) acceptable, adequate, equal, satisfactory, sufficient. ANTONYMS: inadequate, insufficient.

competition n. 1 (the act of competing) contention, rivalry. 2 (a competitive game, contest etc.) championship, contest, event, game, head-to-head, match, meet, puzzle, quiz, race, tournament. 3 (rivalry) rivalry, strife, struggle. 4 (the people or organizations competing against one) adversaries, challengers, field, opponents, opposition, rivals.

complacent a. 1 (smug, self-satisfied) self-righteous, self-satisfied, smug, unconcerned. 2 (satisfied, gratified) contented, gratified, pleased, satisfied, serene. ANTONYMS: discontent, unsatisfied.

complain v.i. 1 (to express dissatisfaction or objection) (sl.) beef, (coll.) bellyache, bemoan, bewail, (sl.) bitch, bleat, carp, cry, find fault, fuss, gripe, groan, grouch, grouse, growl, grumble, kick up a fuss, murmur, whine, whinge. 2 (to make a charge) accuse, allege, charge. 3 (to express grief) grieve, lament, moan, wail.

complaint n. 1 (an expression of grievance or dissatisfaction) annoyance, (sl.) beef, (sl.)

bitch, dissatisfaction, grievance, gripe, grouch, grouse, grumble, lament, †plaint, protest, quibble, remonstrance, trouble, wail. 2 (an ailment) affliction, ailment, disease, disorder, illness, indisposition, malady, sickness, upset. ANTONYMS: health. 3 (an accusation) accusation, allegation, charge, criticism.

complete a. 1 (finished) concluded, ended, finished, over, settled, terminated. ANTONYMS: incomplete, unfinished. 2 (entire, free from deficiency) entire, faultless, flawless, full, intact, integral, perfect, unabridged, unbroken, undiminished, undivided, unimpaired, whole. ANTONYMS: deficient, imperfect. 3 (absolute) absolute, consummate, downright, dyed-in-the-wool, out-and-out, outright, perfect, pure, thorough, total, unmitigated, utter. ANTONYMS: partial. 4 (skilled, highly accomplished) accomplished, expert, skilled.
~v.t. 1 (to finish) accomplish, achieve, bring to an end, cap, close, conclude, discharge, do, end, finalize, finish, fulfil, perform, realize, settle, terminate, wrap up. ANTONYMS: begin, start. 2 (to bring to a state of perfection) perfect, polish, round off. 3 (to fill in the required information on (a questionnaire, a form etc.)) answer, fill in, fill out.

completion n. (the act of finishing) accomplishment, achievement, attainment, close, conclusion, consummation, culmination, end, execution, expiration, finalization, finish, fruition, fulfilment, performance, realization. ANTONYMS: beginning.

complex a. 1 (composed of several parts, composite) composite, compound, heterogeneous, manifold, multifarious, multiple. 2 (complicated) circuitous, complicated, convoluted, elaborate, intricate, involved, knotty, labyrinthine, mingled, mixed, tangled, tortuous.

complicate v.t. (to make complex or intricate) confound, confuse, entangle, interweave, involve, make intricate, mess up, mix up, muddle, ravel, (sl.) screw up, snarl up, tangle. ANTONYMS: clear up, simplify.

complicated a. (having many different parts and therefore difficult to understand) Byzantine, complex, compound, confused, convoluted, elaborate, intricate, involved, knotty, labyrinthine, perplexing, problematic, puzzling, tangled. ANTONYMS: simple, straightforward, uncomplicated.

complication n. 1 (the state of being complicated) complexity, confusion, convolution, entanglement, intricacy, involvement. ANTONYMS: simplicity. 2 (a complicated or complicating circumstance) difficulty, drawback, embarrassment, hitch, obstacle, obstruction, predicament, problem, snag. **3** (*a disease or condition arising in the course of another*) condition, disease, side effect.

compliment[1] *n.* **1** (*pl.*) (*ceremonious greetings, respects*) courtesy, felicitation, greeting, regard, respect, salutation. **2** (*pl.*) (*praise*) bouquet, eulogy, favour, flattery, homage, honour, praise, tribute. ANTONYMS: insult.

compliment[2] *v.t.* (*to congratulate, to praise*) commend, congratulate, extol, flatter, laud, pay tribute to, praise, salute, sing the praises of, speak highly of. ANTONYMS: abuse, insult.

complimentary *a.* **1** (*expressing praise*) adulatory, appreciative, approving, commendatory, congratulatory, eulogistic, flattering, laudatory. ANTONYMS: insulting, rude, uncomplimentary. **2** (*given free of charge*) courtesy, free of charge, gratis, gratuitous, on the house.

comply *v.i.* **1** (*to act or be in accordance (with rules, wishes etc.)*) abide (by), accord (with), adhere (to), conform (to), defer (to), follow, meet, obey, observe, respect, satisfy. ANTONYMS: defy, violate. **2** (*to assent, to agree*) accede, acquiesce, agree, assent, concur, consent, submit, yield.

component *a.* (*serving to make up a compound or a larger whole*) constituent, integral, intrinsic.
~*n.* (*a constituent part*) bit, constituent, element, ingredient, item, part, piece, unit. ANTONYMS: whole.

compose *v.t.* **1** (*to make, esp. by putting together several parts to form one whole*) arrange, build, compile, construct, fashion, form, make, put together. ANTONYMS: demolish, destroy. **2** (*to make up by combination*) compound, comprise, constitute, make up. **3** (*to write or produce (a literary or musical work etc.)*) author, construct, contrive, create, devise, formulate, frame, imagine, invent, originate, produce, think up, write. **4** (*to arrange artistically*) arrange, design. **5** (*to calm, to soothe*) appease, assuage, calm, collect, control, pacify, placate, quell, quiet, reconcile, regulate, resolve, settle. ANTONYMS: disorganize.

composition *n.* **1** (*the act of composing or putting together to form a whole*) compilation, creation, fabrication, fashioning, formation, formulation, invention, making, manufacture, mixture, origination, production. **2** (*the thing composed, esp. a literary or musical work*) creation, opus, piece, study, work. **3** (*an essay*) article, essay, exercise, story, treatise. **4** (*structural arrangement, style*) arrangement, balance, concord, configuration, consonance,

constitution, design, disposition, form, formation, harmony, layout, organization, proportion, structure, style, symmetry. **5** (*the arrangement of different figures in a picture*) arrangement, group, grouping. **6** (*a combination of several parts or ingredients*) aggregate, alloy, amalgam, combination, composite, compound, mix, mixture. **7** (*constitution*) constitution, disposition, make-up. **8** (*character, nature*) character, nature, temperament.

composure *n.* (*tranquillity, esp. of the mind*) aplomb, calm, calmness, (*coll.*) cool, dignity, ease, equanimity, imperturbability, placidity, poise, self-assurance, self-possession, serenity, tranquillity. ANTONYMS: discomposure, perturbation.

compound[1] *a.* (*collective, combined*) collective, combined, complex, composite, conglomerate. ANTONYMS: simple, unmixed.
~*n.* **1** (*a combination, a mixture*) amalgam, blend, combination, composite, composition, conglomerate, consolidation, fusion, medley, meld, merger, mix, mixture, synthesis. **2** (*a combination of two or more elements by chemical action*) alloy, amalgam.

compound[2] *v.t.* **1** (*to make into a whole by the combination of several constituent parts*) amalgamate, blend, coalesce, combine, concoct, fuse, intermingle, mass, meld, mingle, mix, synthesize, unite. ANTONYMS: separate. **2** (*to make up or form (a composite)*) concoct, form, formulate, make up, put together. **3** (*to intensify or complicate*) add to, aggravate, augment, complicate, enhance, exacerbate, heighten, intensify, magnify, multiply, worsen. ANTONYMS: decrease, moderate. **4** (*to adjust by agreement*) adjust, arrange, compose, negotiate, settle.

comprehend *v.t.* **1** (*to grasp mentally, to understand*) appreciate, apprehend, assimilate, conceive, discern, fathom, get, grasp, know, make out, perceive, realize, see, take in, understand. ANTONYMS: misapprehend, misconstrue. **2** (*to comprise, to include*) comprise, contain, embody, embrace, enclose, encompass, include, involve, take in. ANTONYMS: exclude.

comprehensive *a.* **1** (*including all or most things; thorough*) all-embracing, all-encompassing, all-inclusive, blanket, complete, encyclopedic, exhaustive, full, inclusive, thorough, universal. ANTONYMS: incomplete, restricted. **2** (*extending widely*) broad, extensive, sweeping, wide.

compress *v.t.* **1** (*to squeeze or press together*) cram, crowd, crush, knit, pack, press together, squash, squeeze together. **2** (*to bring into narrower *limits*) constrict, contract, narrow, wedge. **3** (*to condense*) abbreviate, abridge, compact, concentrate, condense, shorten, summarize. ANTONYMS: expand.

compromise *n.* **1** (*a settlement by mutual concession*) concession, settlement. **2** (*adjustment of opposing opinions or purposes by a partial surrender*) accommodation, accord, adjustment, agreement, concession, give and take, negotiation, trade-off. ANTONYMS: controversy, dispute. **3** (*a medium between conflicting courses of action*) balance, half measure, medium, middle ground.
~*v.t.* **1** (*to place in a position of difficulty or danger*) endanger, expose, hazard, imperil, implicate, jeopardize. ANTONYMS: protect. **2** (*to expose to risk of disgrace*) discredit, disgrace, dishonour, embarrass, prejudice.
~*v.i.* (*to make a compromise*) accommodate, adjust, agree, arbitrate, concede, give and take, meet halfway, negotiate, relent, settle. ANTONYMS: argue, disagree.

compulsory *a.* **1** (*required by law, regulations etc.*) binding, forced, imperative, mandatory, obligatory, required, requisite. ANTONYMS: discretionary, voluntary. **2** (*necessary, essential*) essential, necessary, unavoidable.

comrade *n.* **1** (*a friend, a companion*) (*coll.*) buddy, (*coll.*) chum, companion, crony, friend, mate, (*coll.*) pal. **2** (*an intimate associate*) ally, associate, colleague, confederate, fellow, partner.

conceal *v.t.* **1** (*to hide or cover from sight or observation*) camouflage, cover, disguise, hide, mask, obscure, screen. ANTONYMS: expose, lay bare. **2** (*to keep secret*) bury, dissemble, keep secret, secrete. **3** (*to keep back from publicity or utterance*) keep dark, keep quiet, suppress. ANTONYMS: disclose, reveal.

concede *v.t.* **1** (*to give up, to surrender*) abandon, cede, deliver, give up, hand over, relinquish, resign, surrender, waive, yield. ANTONYMS: fight, resist. **2** (*to admit, to grant*) accept, acknowledge, admit, allow, confess, grant, own, recognize. ANTONYMS: deny, dispute.

conceit *n.* **1** (*a vain opinion of oneself*) arrogance, boastfulness, egotism, narcissism, pride, self-esteem, self-importance, self-love, swagger, vainglory, vanity. ANTONYMS: modesty. **2** (*a whim, a fanciful idea*) belief, caprice, concept, fancy, fantasy, idea, imagination, notion, quip, thought, vagary, whim, whimsy.

conceited *a.* (*full of conceit, vain*) arrogant, (*coll.*) big-headed, boastful, cocky, complacent, egocentric, egotistical, immodest,

narcissistic, proud, puffed up, self-centred, self-important, smug, snobbish, stuck-up, swaggering, vain. ANTONYMS: modest, unassuming.

conceivable *a.* (*capable of being conceived in the mind, imaginable*) believable, credible, imaginable, possible, thinkable. ANTONYMS: incredible, unbelievable.

conceive *v.t.* **1** (*to form, as an idea or concept, in the mind*) appreciate, apprehend, comprehend, conceptualize, conjure up, dream up, envisage, fancy, grasp, perceive, picture, realize, see, understand. **2** (*to think*) imagine, speculate, suppose, think. **3** (*to formulate*) contrive, create, design, develop, devise, form, formulate, frame, hatch, plan, plot, produce, project, purpose, think up.

concentrate *v.i.* **1** (*to come to a common focus or centre*) accumulate, assemble, centre, cluster, collect, congregate, converge, crowd, focus, gather, group, muster. ANTONYMS: disperse. **2** (*to direct all one's thoughts or efforts to one end*) apply oneself, attend, consider, focus on, meditate, pay attention, ponder, think. ANTONYMS: drift, wander.

conception *n.* **1** (*the impregnation of the ovum followed by implantation in the womb*) fertilization, germination, impregnation, insemination. **2** (*origin, beginning*) beginning, birth, commencement, genesis, inauguration, inception, initiation, introduction, launch, origin, outset, start. **3** (*a concept*) comprehension, concept, design, idea, image, impression, inkling, notion, perception, picture, plan, thought, understanding.

concern *v.t.* **1** (*to relate or belong to*) appertain to, apply to, bear on, belong to, pertain to, refer to, regard, relate to. **2** (*to affect*) affect, impact, influence. **3** (*to disturb, to worry*) bother, disquiet, distress, perturb, trouble, unsettle, upset, worry. **4** (*to involve* (*oneself*)) affect, involve, touch.
~*n.* **1** (*interest, regard*) bearing, importance, interest, regard, relation, relevance. **2** (*anxiety, solicitude*) anxiety, apprehension, attention, burden, care, consideration, disquiet, disquietude, distress, heed, regard, responsibility, solicitude, sympathy, worry. ANTONYMS: indifference. **3** (*a business, a firm*) business, company, corporation, enterprise, establishment, firm, house, organization. **4** (*an affair, a thing*) affair, business, charge, duty, job, matter, problem, responsibility, task, thing.

concerning *prep.* (*with respect to*) about, apropos, as regards, as to, re, regarding, relating to, respecting, touching, with respect to.

conciliatory a. (*showing that one is willing to reconcile conflicting parties, views etc.*) appeasing, disarming, friendly, mollifying, pacific, peaceable, placatory, propitiative, reconciliatory, soothing, winning.

concise a. (*condensed, brief*) abbreviated, abridged, brief, compact, compressed, condensed, curtailed, epigrammatic, laconic, pithy, short, succinct, summary, terse, trenchant. ANTONYMS: long-winded, rambling.

conclude v.t. 1 (*to bring to an end, to finish*) cease, close, complete, end, finish, round off, terminate, wind up, wrap up. ANTONYMS: begin, start. 2 (*to determine, to settle*) accomplish, bring about, carry out, clinch, decide, determine, effect, establish, fix, resolve, settle, work out. 3 (*to gather as a consequence from reasoning, to infer*) assume, construe, deduce, gather, guess, infer, judge, presume, reckon, suppose, surmise.

conclusion n. 1 (*an end, a finish*) close, completion, end, ending, finale, finish, termination. ANTONYMS: beginning. 2 (*a result*) consequence, culmination, effect, issue, outcome, result, sequel, upshot. 3 (*an inference*) assumption, deduction, guess, inference, opinion, supposition, surmise. 4 (*a final decision or judgement*) decision, judgement, resolution, verdict. 5 (*settlement (of terms etc.*)) agreement, settlement.

concrete a. 1 (*existing, real*) actual, existing, factual, literal, material, physical, real, solid, substantial, tangible. ANTONYMS: abstract, insubstantial. 2 (*specific, definite*) clearcut, definite, explicit, particular, precise, specific. ANTONYMS: vague. 3 (*formed by the union of many particles in one mass*) conglomerated, consolidated.
~n. (*coarse gravel and sand mixed with water*) cement, mortar.

concur v.i. 1 (*to coincide*) coincide, combine. 2 (*to agree*) accede, acquiesce, approve, assent, consent. 3 (*to act in conjunction (with*)) act in conjunction, collaborate, cooperate, harmonize, join, join forces.

condemn v.t. 1 (*to censure, to blame*) blame, censure, criticize, damn. 2 (*to pronounce guilty, to give judgement against*) denounce, disparage, pronounce guilty, rebuke, reprehend, reprimand, reprove, scold, upbraid. ANTONYMS: acclaim, applaud. 3 (*to doom (to), to force into a particular state*) doom, force.

condemnation n. 1 (*the act of condemning*) blame, censure, denunciation, disapprobation, disapproval, reproach, reprobation, reproof, stricture. 2 (*the state of being condemned*) banning, conviction, damnation, doom, judgement, prohibition, proscription, sentence. ANTONYMS: acquittal.

condescending a. (*patronizing*) arrogant, contemptuous, disdainful, haughty, highhanded, imperious, lofty, lordly, overbearing, patronizing, pompous, snobbish, (*coll.*) snooty, (*sl.*) snotty, supercilious, superior, (*sl.*) toffee-nosed. ANTONYMS: humble, respectful.

condition n. 1 (*a stipulation, a requirement*) contingency, demand, limitation, modification, necessity, prerequisite, provision, proviso, qualification, requirement, requisite, restriction, rider, rule, stipulation. 2 (*a term of a contract*) article, clause, term. 3 (*circumstances or external characteristics*) case, circumstances, plight, position, predicament, shape, situation, state of affairs. 4 (*a (good) state of health or fitness*) fettle, fitness, form, health, order, shape, trim. 5 (*a long-standing ailment*) ailment, complaint, illness, infirmity, malady, problem, weakness. 6 (*rank or position in life*) caste, class, estate, grade, order, position, rank, standing, station, status.
~v.t. 1 (*to make fit*) adapt, educate, equip, make fit, make ready, outfit, prepare, ready, teach, train. 2 (*to accustom*) acclimatize, accustom, habituate. 3 (*to test, to examine*) examine, inspect, test. 4 (*to stipulate*) agree on, stipulate.

condolence n. (*an expression of sympathy*) comfort, commiseration, compassion, consolation, fellow feeling, pity, solace, sympathy.

condone v.t. (*to forgive or overlook (an offence etc.*)) disregard, excuse, forgive, let pass, overlook, pardon, turn a blind eye to, wink at. ANTONYMS: condemn, denounce.

conduct[1] n. 1 (*the way in which anyone acts or lives*) attitude, bearing, behaviour, carriage, comportment, demeanour, deportment, habits, manners, ways. 2 (*management, direction*) administration, command, control, direction, government, handling, management, operation, organization, regulation, running, supervision. 3 (*the act of leading or guiding*) guidance, leadership.

conduct[2] v.t. 1 (*to lead, to guide*) accompany, attend, escort, guide, lead, pilot, steer, usher. 2 (*to manage, to direct*) administer, carry on, control, direct, govern, handle, manage, operate, organize, preside over, regulate, run, supervise. 3 (*to transmit (heat, electricity etc.*)) bear, carry, channel, convey, transmit. 4 (*to behave*) acquit, act, behave, comport.

confer v.t. (*to bestow, to grant*) accord, award, bestow, give, grant, hand out, present, vouchsafe. ANTONYMS: withdraw.

~v.i. (*to consult together*) consult, converse, deliberate, discourse, discuss, parley, talk.

conference n. 1 (*the act of conferring; consultation*) consultation, debate, discussion, talk. 2 (*a meeting for consultation or discussion*) congress, convention, convocation, council, forum, meeting, seminar, symposium. 3 (*a league or association in sport, commerce etc.*) association, league.

confess v.t. 1 (*to acknowledge, to admit*) acknowledge, admit, own, own up. 2 (*to admit reluctantly, to concede*) admit, allow, blurt out, (*coll.*) come clean, concede, confide, disclose, divulge, grant. ANTONYMS: conceal, hush up. 3 (*to reveal, to make manifest*) affirm, assert, attest, aver, avow, confirm, declare, manifest, profess, prove, reveal, testify. ANTONYMS: deny, repudiate.

confidence n. 1 (*trust, faith*) belief, credence, dependence, faith, reliance, trust. ANTONYMS: doubt, mistrust. 2 (*self-reliance, assurance*) aplomb, assurance, audacity, boldness, courage, firmness, nerve, poise, self-assurance, self-possession, self-reliance. ANTONYMS: apprehension, nervousness. 3 (*assuredness, certainty*) assuredness, certainty, certitude, conviction.

confident a. 1 (*full of confidence*) assured, secure, self-assured, self-possessed, self-reliant, unabashed. ANTONYMS: unsure. 2 (*assured, certain*) assured, certain, convinced, positive, satisfied, secure, sure. ANTONYMS: doubtful, uncertain. 3 (*self-reliant, bold*) bold, cocksure, courageous, dauntless, fearless, reliant, self-reliant. ANTONYMS: nervous, timid.

confidential a. 1 (*told or given in confidence*) classified, (*coll.*) hush-hush, off the record, restricted, secret. ANTONYMS: public. 2 (*entrusted with the private concerns of another*) dependable, entrusted, faithful, reliable, trusted, trustworthy. ANTONYMS: unreliable. 3 (*private, intimate*) innermost, intimate, personal, private.

confine v.t. 1 (*to shut up, to imprison*) cage, impound, imprison, incarcerate, intern, pen, shut up. ANTONYMS: release. 2 (*to keep within bounds*) bind, bound, circumscribe, enclose, hem in. 3 (*to limit in application*) hold back, limit, repress, restrict.

confirm v.t. 1 (*to establish the truth or correctness of*) affirm, assure, clinch, establish, fix, settle, support. 2 (*to ratify, to make valid*) accredit, approve, authenticate, authorize, back up, bear out, corroborate, endorse, ratify, recognize, sanction, substantiate, sustain, uphold, validate, verify. ANTONYMS: refute.

3 (*to strengthen*) brace, buttress, fortify, reinforce, strengthen, support.

confirmation n. 1 (*the act of confirming*) acceptance, affirmation, agreement, approval, assent, authentication, corroboration, endorsement, ratification, sanction, substantiation, validation, verification. ANTONYMS: contradiction, refutation. 2 (*corroborative testimony*) authentication, corroboration, evidence, proof, substantiation, testimony, validation, verification.

confiscate v.t. (*to take or seize, esp. as a penalty*) appropriate, commandeer, dispossess, expropriate, forfeit, impound, seize, sequester, sequestrate, take. ANTONYMS: give back, restore.

conflict[1] n. 1 (*a fight, a struggle*) affray, battle, brawl, clash, collision, combat, contention, contest, encounter, engagement, fight, fracas, head-to-head, (*coll.*) set-to, strife, struggle, war, warfare. 2 (*a clash or the opposition of opinions or purposes*) altercation, antagonism, argument, controversy, difference, disagreement, discord, dispute, dissension, friction, interference, opposition, strife, variance. ANTONYMS: accord, agreement.

conflict[2] v.i. 1 (*to come into collision, to clash*) clash, collide. 2 (*to strive or struggle*) combat, contend, contest, fight, strive, struggle. 3 (*to differ, to disagree*) differ, disagree, quarrel. ANTONYMS: agree.

conform v.t. 1 (*to make like in form, to make similar (to)*) assimilate, make similar. 2 (*to accommodate, to adapt*) accommodate, adapt, adjust.
~v.i. 1 (*to comply, to assent*) abide (by), assent, comply, fall in (with), follow, obey, observe, respect, yield. 2 (*to be in harmony or agreement (with)*) accord (with), agree (with), concur (with), correspond (to), harmonize (with), match, square (with), suit, tally (with). ANTONYMS: disagree (with).

confound v.t. 1 (*to throw into confusion*) confuse, upset. 2 (*to perplex, to bewilder*) amaze, astonish, astound, baffle, bewilder, disconcert, dumbfound, flabbergast, flummox, mystify, nonplus, perplex, startle, stun, surprise. 3 (*to mix up, to confuse*) confuse, jumble, mix up. 4 (*to put to shame*) embarrass, shame. 5 (*to defeat, to overthrow*) annihilate, contradict, defeat, demolish, destroy, explode, overthrow, overwhelm, refute, ruin.

confront v.t. 1 (*to face*) encounter, face, face up to. 2 (*to face defiantly*) accost, brave, challenge, defy, oppose, resist, stand up to. ANTONYMS: avoid, evade.

confrontation *n.* (*a dispute*) battle, challenge, conflict, contest, crisis, defiance, encounter, face-off, head-to-head, opposition, resistance, (*coll.*) set-to, showdown.

confuse *v.t.* **1** (*to confound, to perplex*) baffle, bemuse, bewilder, confound, faze, flummox, mystify, nonplus, obscure, perplex, puzzle. **2** (*to jumble up*) botch, derange, disarrange, disorder, entangle, garble, jumble up, mess up, mix up, muddle, ravel, snarl up, tangle. **3** (*to mix or mingle so as to render indistinguishable*) blend, intermingle, mingle, mix. **4** (*to disconcert*) abash, addle, ashame, demoralize, discomfit, discompose, disconcert, discountenance, dismay, disorient, embarrass, fluster, mortify, nonplus, rattle, shame, (*coll.*) throw, unbalance, unnerve, upset.

confusion *n.* **1** (*disorder*) disarrangement, disarray, disorder, disorganization, jumble, mess, mix-up, muddle, shambles, state, tangle, untidiness. ANTONYMS: neatness, order. **2** (*perplexity*) bemusement, bewilderment, disorientation, mystification, perplexity, puzzlement. ANTONYMS: clarification, enlightenment. **3** (*embarrassment*) abashment, chagrin, demoralization, discomfiture, discomposure, embarrassment, mortification, shame. **4** (*disturbance of consciousness*) chaos, disorder, disturbance, turmoil, upheaval. **5** (*commotion*) anarchy, bustle, chaos, clutter, commotion, turmoil.

congenial *a.* **1** (*pleasant, agreeable*) affable, agreeable, companionable, friendly, genial, kindly, pleasant, pleasing. ANTONYMS: disagreeable, unfriendly. **2** (*having similar tastes, character etc.*) compatible, like-minded, sympathetic. **3** (*suitable*) adapted, congruous, consonant, favourable, fit, suitable, well-matched, well-suited.

congested *a.* **1** (*closely crowded, blocked*) blocked, choked, clogged, crammed, crowded, jammed, obstructed, overcrowded, overfilled, overflowing, packed, plugged, stopped, stuffed, teeming. ANTONYMS: clear, unobstructed. **2** (*affected with congestion*) blocked-up, stuffed-up.

congratulate *v.t.* **1** (*to express pleasure or praise to*) acclaim, commend, praise. **2** (*to compliment*) compliment, felicitate.

congratulations *n.pl.* (*an expression of pleasure or praise*) best wishes, bravo, compliments, felicitations, good wishes, greetings.

congregation *n.* **1** (*a body of people gathered together*) assembly, body, crowd, gathering, host, meeting, multitude, muster, throng. **2** (*an assembly of persons for religious worship*) assembly, brethren, church, fellowship, flock, laity, parish, parishioners.

conjecture *n.* (*guess, surmise*) assumption, belief, conclusion, fancy, guess, hypothesis, inference, notion, presumption, speculation, supposition, surmise, suspicion, theory. ~*v.t., v.i.* (*to guess, to surmise*) assume, conclude, deduce, fancy, guess, hypothesize, imagine, infer, suppose, surmise, theorize. ANTONYMS: prove.

conjure *v.t.* **1** (*to effect by or as if by magical influence*) bewitch, charm, enchant, fascinate. **2** (*to effect by jugglery or sleight of hand*) juggle, play tricks, prestidigitate.

connect *v.t.* **1** (*to join or fasten together*) affix, bind, cohere, couple, fasten together, glue, join, link, rivet, secure, stick, tack, tie. ANTONYMS: detach, sever. **2** (*to unite, to correlate*) combine, conjoin, correlate, unite. **3** (*to associate in one's mind*) ally, associate, relate.

connected *a.* **1** (*united, esp. by marriage*) united. **2** (*closely related*) affiliated, akin, allied, associated, related. **3** (*coherent*) coherent, comprehensible, fluent, intelligible. **4** (*joined or linked together*) combined, coupled, joined, linked. ANTONYMS: disconnected.

connection *n.* **1** (*the act of connecting*) bonding, coupling, joining, linking, uniting. **2** (*the place where two parts or things are connected*) coupling, fastening, link. **3** (*a person or thing that connects, a link*) alliance, association, attachment, junction, link, tie, union. **4** (*relationship (esp. by marriage)*) affiliation, affinity, association, interrelation, liaison, link, marriage, relationship. **5** (*a person so connected*) kin, kith, relation, relative. **6** (*a business associate or contact, esp. one with influence*) acquaintance, ally, associate, contact, friend, sponsor.

conquer *v.t.* **1** (*to win or gain, esp. by military force*) acquire, annex, gain, obtain, seize, take possession of, win. ANTONYMS: lose. **2** (*to vanquish, to overcome*) beat, (*sl.*) clobber, crush, defeat, humble, (*coll.*) lick, master, overcome, overpower, overthrow, quell, rout, subjugate, vanquish. ANTONYMS: give in, submit. **3** (*to subdue, to surmount*) master, overcome, subdue, surmount.

conquest *n.* **1** (*the act of conquering*) acquisition, annexation, appropriation, enticement, invasion, occupation, seduction, subjection, subjugation. **2** (*a thing that is conquered*) booty, catch, plunder, prize, spoils, trophy. **3** (*a person whose affection or compliance has been gained*) adherent, admirer, fan, follower, supporter, worshipper. **4** (*the acquisition of sovereignty by force of arms*) coup, overthrow. **5** (*victory, subjugation*) mastery, rout, subjugation, success, triumph, victory.

conscience n. (*moral sense*) ethics, inner voice, integrity, morality, morals, principles, scruples, standards.

conscientious a. **1** (*scrupulous, diligent*) assiduous, careful, cautious, diligent, exacting, faithful, meticulous, painstaking, particular, punctilious, rigorous, scrupulous, thorough. ANTONYMS: careless, slack. **2** (*actuated by strict regard to the dictates of conscience*) fair, good, high-minded, honourable, incorruptible, just, moral, principled, responsible, scrupulous, upright, upstanding. ANTONYMS: unprincipled, unscrupulous.

conscious a. **1** (*fully aware of one's surroundings etc.*) alert, alive to, awake, mindful, responsive, sensible. ANTONYMS: insensible, oblivious. **2** (*having knowledge, aware*) aware, cognizant, knowing, percipient. ANTONYMS: ignorant. **3** (*intentional*) calculated, deliberate, intentional, premeditated, purposeful, rational, reasoning, wilful. ANTONYMS: accidental, unintentional. **4** (*self-conscious*) self-conscious, studied.

consent v.i. (*to agree, to give permission*) accede, acquiesce, agree, allow, approve, assent, cede, comply, concede, concur, conform, give in, permit, submit, yield. ANTONYMS: decline, resist.
~n. **1** (*agreement*) acquiescence, agreement, concurrence. **2** (*permission*) approval, assent, authorization, concession, go-ahead, (*coll.*) green light, (*coll.*) OK, (*coll.*) okay, permission, sanction. **3** (*compliance*) compliance, obedience.

consequence n. **1** (*a result or effect*) aftermath, effect, end, issue, outcome, repercussion, result, upshot. ANTONYMS: cause. **2** (*importance*) account, concern, importance, interest, moment, portent, significance, weight. **3** (*social importance, distinction*) distinction, eminence, importance, influence, note, rank, repute, standing, status. **4** (*a conclusion*) conclusion, deduction, inference.

conservation n. **1** (*the act of conserving*) keeping, saving. **2** (*preservation from waste or decay*) husbandry, maintenance, management, perpetuation, preservation, upkeep. ANTONYMS: decay, waste. **3** (*protection of natural resources and the environment*) custody, guardianship, protection, safeguarding.

conservative a. **1** (*of or relating to the political party that supports private ownership and free enterprise*) right-wing, (*coll.*) Tory. **2** (*moderate, not extreme*) cautious, guarded, hidebound, middle-of-the-road, moderate, reactionary, sober. ANTONYMS: extreme. **3** (*conventional*) conventional, traditional.
~n. **1** (*a person inclined to preserve established things*) moderate, reactionary, traditionalist. ANTONYMS: radical. **2** (*a member or supporter of the Conservative Party*) right-winger, (*coll.*) Tory.

conserve v.t. (*to preserve from decay or loss*) go easy on, hoard, hold on to, husband, keep, nurse, preserve, protect, reserve, save, spare, store up. ANTONYMS: squander, waste.

consider v.t. **1** (*to think about, to contemplate*) chew over, cogitate, contemplate, deliberate, meditate, mull over, muse, ponder, reflect, ruminate, study, think about, weigh. **2** (*to observe and examine*) examine, eye up, note, observe. **3** (*to bear in mind, be mindful of*) bear in mind, keep in mind, turn over in one's mind. **4** (*to estimate, to regard*) believe, deem, estimate, gauge, judge, rate, regard, think. **5** (*to have or show regard for*) care for, esteem, regard, respect. **6** (*to discuss*) consult, discuss.

considerable a. **1** (*large or great*) abundant, ample, appreciable, big, comfortable, decent, fair, goodly, great, large, marked, noticeable, plentiful, reasonable, sizeable, substantial, (*coll.*) tidy, tolerable. ANTONYMS: inconsiderable, insubstantial. **2** (*important, worth consideration*) distinguished, estimable, illustrious, important, influential, notable, noteworthy, remarkable, renowned, respectable, significant, venerable, worthy. ANTONYMS: insignificant, undistinguished.

considerate a. (*characterized by regard for others*) accommodating, attentive, caring, charitable, compassionate, concerned, helpful, kind, kind-hearted, kindly, mindful, obliging, solicitous, sympathetic, tactful, thoughtful, unselfish. ANTONYMS: inconsiderate, thoughtless.

consideration n. **1** (*the act of considering*) analysis, attention, cogitation, contemplation, deliberation, discussion, examination, perusal, reflection, regard, review, scrutiny, study, thought. **2** (*reflection, thought*) contemplation, deliberation, meditation, reflection, rumination, thought. **3** (*regard for others, thoughtfulness*) attentiveness, benevolence, care, compassion, concern, kindliness, kindness, respect, solicitude, tact, thoughtfulness. ANTONYMS: thoughtlessness. **4** (*a motive for action*) ground, motive, reason. **5** (*a recompense, a reward*) compensation, emolument, fee, gratuity, payment, recompense, remuneration, reward, tip.

consist v.i. 1 (*to be composed (of)*) amount (to), be composed (of), be made up (of), comprise, contain, embody, include, incorporate, involve. 2 (*to be compatible or consistent (with)*) accord (with), be consistent (with), conform (to), harmonize (with). ANTONYMS: clash (with).

consistent a. 1 (*congruous, harmonious*) accordant, agreeing, coherent, compatible, congruous, consonant, harmonious, logical. 2 (*uniform in opinion or conduct*) constant, dependable, faithful, loyal, persistent, regular, steadfast, steady, unchanging, undeviating, uniform, unswerving. ANTONYMS: contradictory, inconsistent.

console v.t. (*to comfort or cheer in trouble*) assuage, calm, cheer, comfort, encourage, relieve, solace, soothe, support. ANTONYMS: distress, upset.

consolidate v.t. 1 (*to form into a solid and compact mass*) amalgamate, cement, compact, compress, condense, congeal, fuse, harden, solidify, thicken. 2 (*to strengthen, to reinforce*) fortify, reinforce, secure, stabilize, strengthen. ANTONYMS: undermine, weaken. 3 (*to unite in one whole*) combine, federate, join, unite.

conspicuous a. 1 (*obvious, clearly visible*) apparent, blatant, clear, discernible, evident, manifest, noticeable, obvious, palpable, patent, perceptible, plain, visible. ANTONYMS: indiscernible, unnoticeable. 2 (*attracting or striking the eye*) eye-catching, loud, ostentatious, showy. 3 (*remarkable, extraordinary*) celebrated, distinguished, exceptional, extraordinary, famous, glorious, notable, outstanding, prominent, remarkable, striking. ANTONYMS: humble, obscure.

conspiracy n. 1 (*the act of conspiring*) collaboration, collusion, connivance, treachery. 2 (*a plot*) confederacy, intrigue, machination, plot, scheme, stratagem.

constant a. 1 (*continuous, unceasing*) ceaseless, continuous, endless, eternal, everlasting, incessant, interminable, never-ending, nonstop, perennial, perpetual, persevering, persistent, relentless, sustained, unceasing, uninterrupted, unremitting, untiring. 2 (*continual, occurring frequently*) continual, recurrent, regular. 3 (*unchanging, steadfast*) fixed, habitual, immovable, immutable, invariable, permanent, stable, steadfast, steady, unalterable, unbroken, unchanging, uniform, unvarying. ANTONYMS: changeable, erratic. 4 (*firm, unshaken*) determined, dogged, firm, persevering, resolute, unflagging, unshaken, unwavering. 5 (*faithful in love or friendship*) attached, dependable, devoted, faithful, loyal, stalwart, staunch, true, trustworthy, trusty, unfailing. ANTONYMS: disloyal, fickle.

consternation n. (*anxiety, dismay*) alarm, amazement, anxiety, astonishment, bewilderment, confusion, dismay, distress, dread, fear, horror, panic, shock, terror, trepidation, worry. ANTONYMS: relief.

constitute v.t. 1 (*to make up or compose*) compose, comprise, create, make up. 2 (*to form, to be*) amount to, be, be equivalent to, form, represent. 3 (*to establish*) create, establish, found, set up. ANTONYMS: abolish. 4 (*to elect or appoint to an office*) appoint, authorize, commission, delegate, depute, elect, empower, name, nominate, ordain.

construct v.t. 1 (*to make by putting parts together*) build, compose, create, design, elevate, erect, establish, fabricate, forge, form, formulate, frame, invent, make, manufacture, put up, raise, set up, shape. ANTONYMS: demolish, dismantle. 2 (*to put together, to assemble*) assemble, create, put together.

construction n. 1 (*the act or process of constructing*) assembly, building, composition, creation, fabrication, formation. 2 (*the thing constructed*) building, edifice, erection, fabric, structure. 3 (*a style of structure*) form, mode, style. 4 (*interpretation (of words, conduct etc.)*) analysis, explanation, inference, interpretation, reading, rendering.

constructive a. 1 (*tending to improve or be helpful*) beneficial, helpful, improving, positive, practical, productive, useful, valuable. ANTONYMS: destructive, negative. 2 (*implied by interpretation*) deduced, derived, implicit, implied, inferential, inferred, virtual.

consult v.i. (*to take counsel together, to confer (with)*) commune, confer, debate, deliberate, discuss, take counsel, talk over.
~v.t. 1 (*to ask for advice, an opinion etc.*) ask, canvass, inquire of, interrogate, question. 2 (*to refer to for information*) look up, refer to, turn to. 3 (*to take into account*) regard, respect, take into account, take into consideration.

consume v.t. 1 (*to eat or drink*) bolt, devour, digest, drink, eat, gobble, gulp, guzzle, (*coll.*) polish off, (*coll.*) put away, swallow. 2 (*to use up*) absorb, deplete, drain, eat up, employ, exhaust, expend, finish up, lavish, lessen, reduce, spend, use up, utilize, vanish, wear out. 3 (*to destroy by fire, decomposition etc.*) annihilate, decay, demolish, destroy, devastate, gut, lay waste, ravage, raze, ruin, wreck. 4 (*to waste, to squander*) (*sl.*) blow, dissipate, fritter away, squander, throw away, waste. 5 (*to engross, to obsess*) absorb, devour, dominate, eat up, engross, enthral, fascinate, monopolize, obsess, preoccupy, rivet.

consummation n. **1** (*the completion of something already begun*) accomplishment, achievement, attainment, completion, culmination, end, finale, finish, fulfilment, realization. **2** (*perfect development*) acme, climax, culmination, finish, peak, perfection.

contact n. **1** (*touch, the state of touching*) approximation, contiguity, junction, juxtaposition, touch, union. **2** (*the act or state of meeting or communicating*) association, communication, connection, meeting. **3** (*a business or other acquaintance who can provide one with introductions etc.*) acquaintance, colleague, connection, friend, sponsor. **4** (*a person who has been exposed to an illness and is likely to carry contagion*) carrier, vector.
~v.t. (*to establish contact or communication with*) approach, call, communicate, correspond with, e-mail, fax, get hold of, get in touch with, get onto, get through to, phone, reach, ring, speak to, telephone, write to.

contagious a. **1** (*communicable by contact, communicating disease by contact*) catching, communicable, spreadable, transferable, transmissible. **2** (*infectious*) infectious, pestiferous, pestilential.

contain v.t. **1** (*to hold within fixed limits*) confine, hold, limit. **2** (*to be capable of holding*) accommodate, carry, enclose, hold, seat. **3** (*to comprise, to include*) comprise, embody, embrace, include, involve. **4** (*to restrain*) bridle, check, control, curb, hold back, put down, repress, restrain, stifle, suppress.

contaminate v.t. **1** (*to pollute*) infect, pollute. ANTONYMS: purify. **2** (*to corrupt, to infect*) adulterate, corrupt, decay, infect, poison, rot. **3** (*to defile, to sully*) befoul, besmirch, debase, defile, soil, stain, sully, taint, tarnish.

contemplate v.t. **1** (*to look at, to study*) behold, check out, examine, eye, gaze at, inspect, look at, observe, regard, scan, scrutinize, stare at, study, survey, view, watch. **2** (*to meditate and reflect on*) brood over, chew over, cogitate, consider, deliberate, meditate, mull over, muse over, ponder, reflect on, ruminate. **3** (*to purpose, to intend*) intend, mean, plan, propose, purpose. **4** (*to regard as possible or likely*) envisage, expect, foresee, visualize.

contemplative a. (*thoughtful, studious*) intent, introspective, lost in thought, meditative, musing, pensive, rapt, reflective, ruminative, studious, thoughtful.

contemporary a. **1** (*living at the same time*) coexistent, coincidental, concomitant, concurrent, contemporaneous, synchronous. **2** (*up-to-date, modern*) current, fashionable, modern, modish, new, newfangled, present, recent, stylish, (*coll., sometimes derog.*) trendy, up-to-date, (*coll.*) with it. ANTONYMS: old-fashioned, out-of-date.

contempt n. **1** (*scorn, disdain*) abhorrence, condescension, derision, disdain, disgust, disrespect, hatred, loathing, mockery, neglect, scorn, slight. ANTONYMS: admiration, respect. **2** (*shame, disgrace*) disgrace, dishonour, humiliation, shame. **3** (*disobedience to the rules of a court, legislative body etc.*) disobedience, disregard.

contemptible a. (*worthy of contempt, despicable*) abject, base, degenerate, derisory, despicable, detestable, ignominious, inferior, loathsome, low, mean, miserable, paltry, pitiful, shabby, shameful, vile, worthless, wretched. ANTONYMS: admirable, praiseworthy.

contemptuous a. (*disdainful, scornful*) arrogant, condescending, cynical, derisive, disdainful, disrespectful, haughty, insolent, insulting, scornful, sneering, supercilious, withering. ANTONYMS: civil, respectful.

content[1] a. **1** (*satisfied, pleased*) cheerful, comfortable, contented, fulfilled, glad, happy, pleased, satisfied. ANTONYMS: dissatisfied. **2** (*willing*) agreeable, amenable, willing.
~v.t. (*to satisfy, to make content*) appease, cheer, delight, gladden, gratify, humour, indulge, mollify, placate, please, reconcile, satisfy, soothe, suffice.
~n. (*satisfaction, ease of mind*) comfort, contentment, delight, ease of mind, felicity, gratification, happiness, peace, pleasure, satisfaction, serenity, tranquillity. ANTONYMS: discontent.

content[2] n. **1** (*capacity or power of containing; volume*) capacity, dimensions, load, magnitude, measure, scope, size, volume. **2** (*the meaning (of an utterance etc.*)) burden, essence, gist, ideas, import, matter, meaning, pith, purport, significance, subject, substance, text, theme, thesis, thoughts, topic. ANTONYMS: form.

contentious a. **1** (*quarrelsome, argumentative*) argumentative, bickering, captious, combative, disputatious, factious, peevish, perverse, petulant, pugnacious, quarrelsome, querulous, wrangling. **2** (*controversial, disputed*) controversial, debatable, disputed, litigious.

contest[1] v.t. **1** (*to contend, to strive earnestly for*) compete, contend, fight over, strive for, vie. **2** (*to dispute, to call in question*) argue, call in question, challenge, confute, debate, dispute, doubt, litigate, object to, oppose, question, refute.

contest² *n*. **1** (*a struggle for victory or superiority*) affray, battle, combat, competition, conflict, contention, encounter, fight, shock, strife, struggle, war. **2** (*a dispute, a controversy*) altercation, argument, controversy, debate, disagreement, discord, dispute, quarrel. **3** (*competition, rivalry*) competition, game, match, meeting, race, rivalry, tournament, trial.

contestant *n*. (*a person who contests, a competitor*) adversary, aspirant, candidate, competitor, contender, entrant, opponent, participant, player, rival.

context *n*. **1** (*setting, surroundings*) background, connection, framework, relation, setting, surroundings. **2** (*the relevant circumstances*) circumstances, conditions, environment, situation.

continual *a*. **1** (*frequently recurring*) frequent, recurrent, regular, repeated, repetitive. ANTONYMS: infrequent. **2** (*unbroken, incessant*) constant, continuous, endless, eternal, everlasting, incessant, interminable, non-stop, perpetual, persistent, steady, sustained, unbroken, unceasing, uninterrupted, unremitting. ANTONYMS: erratic, spasmodic.

continue *v.t.* **1** (*to carry on without interruption*) carry on, go on, keep on. ANTONYMS: cease, stop. **2** (*to keep up*) keep up, maintain, prolong, sustain. **3** (*to take up again, to resume*) carry on, proceed, recommence, resume, take up again. **4** (*to extend, to complete*) complete, draw out, ...tend, lengthen, perpetuate, prolong, protract.
~*v.i.* **1** (*to remain, to stay*) remain, rest, stay. **2** (*to last, to remain in existence*) abide, endure, last, persist, survive. **3** (*to persevere*) persevere, persist in, pursue, soldier on, stick at. ANTONYMS: give up.

continuous *a*. **1** (*connected without a break in space or time*) connected, constant, continued, prolonged, unbroken. ANTONYMS: broken, disconnected. **2** (*uninterrupted, unceasing*) ceaseless, endless, everlasting, incessant, interminable, non-stop, perpetual, persistent, sustained, undivided, uninterrupted. ANTONYMS: interrupted, spasmodic.

contract¹ *v.t.* **1** (*to draw together*) draw together, knit. **2** (*to make smaller*) compress, condense, confine, constrict, make smaller, squeeze. **3** (*to abbreviate, to shorten*) abbreviate, abridge, curtail, lessen, shorten. **4** (*to incur, to become liable for*) become liable for, incur, run up. **5** (*to catch (a disease)*) catch, develop, get, go down with, succumb to. **6** (*to agree to by covenant*) agree, covenant, settle. ANTONYMS: disagree. **7** (*to arrange or enter into*

(*a marriage*)) arrange, bargain, come to terms, engage, enter into, negotiate, pledge, promise.
~*v.i.* (*to become smaller or narrower*) diminish, dwindle, narrow, reduce, shrink, shrivel, tighten. ANTONYMS: broaden, expand.

contract² *n*. **1** (*a formal agreement*) agreement, arrangement, bargain, bond, commission, commitment, compact, concordat, convention, covenant, engagement, obligation, pact, settlement, stipulation, treaty, understanding. **2** (*an undertaking to do certain work etc. for a specified sum*) agreement, deal, undertaking.

contradict *v.t.* (*to deny the truth of (a statement etc.*)) belie, challenge, contravene, controvert, counter, deny, dispute, gainsay, impugn, negate, oppose, rebut, refute, reverse. ANTONYMS: agree (with), confirm.

contradictory *a*. **1** (*affirming the contrary*) antithetical, contrary, opposite. **2** (*inconsistent*) conflicting, incongruous, inconsistent. **3** (*logically incompatible*) incompatible, irreconcilable, opposed, paradoxical. **4** (*disputatious*) antagonistic, argumentative, disputatious.

contraption *n*. (*a strange or improvised device*) apparatus, appliance, contrivance, device, gadget, gear, instrument, mechanism, rig, (*coll.*) thingamajig, widget.

contrary¹ *a*. **1** (*opposite*) opposed, opposite. **2** (*opposed, diametrically different*) counter, different, discordant, inconsistent, inimical, opposed, paradoxical. ANTONYMS: consistent, harmonious. **3** (*contradictory*) antagonistic, clashing, contradictory, hostile. **4** ((*of wind etc.*) *unfavourable*) adverse, bad, foul, inauspicious, unfavourable, unlucky, unpropitious.
~*n*. (*the opposite*) antithesis, converse, opposite, reverse.

contrary² *a*. (*wayward, perverse*) argumentative, awkward, cantankerous, difficult, disobliging, headstrong, intractable, obstinate, perverse, refractory, self-willed, (*coll.*) stroppy, stubborn, unaccommodating, unfriendly, wayward, wilful. ANTONYMS: obliging, willing.

contrast¹ *v.t.* (*to set in opposition, so as to show the difference between*) compare, differentiate, discriminate, distinguish, juxtapose, set off. ANTONYMS: liken.
~*v.i.* (*to stand in contrast or opposition*) deviate, differ, diverge, oppose.

contrast² *n*. **1** (*unlikeness of things or qualities*) contrariety, difference, disparity, dissimilarity, distinction, divergence, opposition, polarity. ANTONYMS: similarity. **2** (*the presentation of unlike things with a view to comparison*) comparison, differentiation.

contribute *v.t.* (*to give for a common purpose*) bestow, (*coll.*) chip in, donate, give, grant, provide, subscribe, supply. ANTONYMS: refuse, withhold.

~*v.i.* (*to have a share in any act or effect*) advance, aid, conduce, help, influence, lead, promote, support, tend.

contrite *a.* **1** (*deeply sorry for wrongdoing, full of remorse*) chastened, conscience-stricken, regretful, remorseful, sorrowful, sorry. **2** (*thoroughly penitent*) humble, penitent, remorseful, repentant.

contrived *a.* (*forced, artificial*) artificial, elaborate, forced, laboured, overdone, strained, unnatural. ANTONYMS: natural, spontaneous.

control *n.* **1** (*check, restraint*) brake, check, curb, limitation, regulation, restraint. **2** (*directing and regulating power*) direction, guidance, management, regulation. **3** (*authority, command*) authority, charge, command, government, influence, jurisdiction, leadership, power, rule, superintendence, supervision, supremacy, sway.

~*v.t.* **1** (*to exercise power over, to command*) administer, boss, command, conduct, direct, dominate, govern, hold sway over, lead, oversee, pilot, reign over, rule, steer, superintend, supervise. **2** (*to restrain, to hold in check*) bridle, check, constrain, contain, curb, hold in check, limit, master, put down, regulate, rein in, repress, restrain, subdue, suppress. **3** (*to verify or check*) check, determine, verify. **4** (*to operate or direct* (*a vehicle, machine etc.*)) direct, handle, manage, manipulate, operate, wield.

controversial *a.* **1** (*relating to or arousing controversy*) contentious, debatable, disputable, doubtful, moot, questionable. ANTONYMS: indisputable. **2** (*inclined to argue or dispute*) argumentative, disputatious, factious, litigious, provocative.

controversy *n.* (*a dispute or debate, esp. one carried on in public over a long period of time*) altercation, argument, debate, disagreement, dispute, quarrel, row, (*esp. N Am., coll.*) spat, squabble, tiff. ANTONYMS: agreement.

convalescence *n.* (*recovery of health after illness, surgery etc.*) cure, improvement, recovery, recuperation, rehabilitation, restoration.

convenient *a.* **1** (*suitable, opportune*) appropriate, expedient, fit, opportune, seasonable, suitable, suited, timely, well-timed. ANTONYMS: awkward, inconvenient. **2** (*useful, handy*) beneficial, handy, serviceable, useful. **3** (*at hand, close by*) accessible, at hand, available, close by, nearby, ready. ANTONYMS: inaccessible.

convention *n.* **1** (*an agreement, a treaty*) agreement, bargain, compact, concordat, contract, entente, pact, protocol, stipulation, treaty. **2** (*an accepted usage, code of conduct etc.*) code, custom, etiquette, formality, practice, propriety, protocol, routine, rule, tradition, usage. **3** (*a meeting, a conference*) assembly, conference, congregation, gathering, meeting, seminar, symposium. **4** (*the persons assembled at such a meeting*) assembly, conference, congress, convocation, council, delegates, representatives.

conventional *a.* (*relating to or in accordance with convention*) accepted, agreed, commonplace, correct, customary, established, everyday, expected, habitual, normal, ordinary, orthodox, prevailing, proper, regular, ritual, standard, traditional, usual, wonted. ANTONYMS: unconventional, unorthodox.

converge *v.i.* **1** (*to tend towards one point*) approach, lean towards, tend towards. ANTONYMS: diverge. **2** (*to meet at one point*) blend, combine, come together, concentrate, focus, gather, join, meet, merge, mingle, unite. **3** ((*of opinions, ideas etc.*) *to tend towards the same conclusion*) agree, coincide, concur, correspond.

conversation *n.* **1** (*the act of conversing*) communication, converse, discussion, gossip, talk. **2** (*an instance of this*) chat, (*coll.*) chinwag, colloquy, (*coll.*) confab, confabulation, dialogue, discourse, discussion, exchange, gossip, parley, powwow, talk, tête-à-tête.

converse *v.i.* (*to talk easily and informally* (*with*) *etc.*) chat, chatter, commune, confabulate, confer, discourse, gossip, speak, talk.

conversion *n.* **1** (*change from one state to another*) change, metamorphosis, transfiguration, transmutation. **2** (*change to a new mode of life, religion etc.*) change of heart, persuasion, proselytization, rebirth, regeneration. **3** (*the changing of one kind of unit, security etc. into another kind*) adaptation, alteration, modification, reconstruction, remodelling, reorganization.

convert *v.t.* **1** (*to change from one physical state to another*) alter, change, metamorphose, mutate, transfigure, transform, transmute, transpose, turn. **2** (*to cause to turn from one religion or party to another*) baptize, convince, persuade, proselytize, save, win over. **3** (*to change* (*one kind of securities*) *into another kind*) cash, change. **4** (*to change the structure or use of* (*a building or part of a building*)) adapt, alter, modify, remodel.

convey *v.t.* **1** (*to carry, to transport*) bear, bring, carry, conduct, fetch, forward, move, send, transmit, transport. **2** (*to impart, to communicate*) communicate, disclose, impart, make known, reveal, tell, transmit. **3** (*to transfer (property)*) bequeath, cede, deliver, devolve, grant, lease, transfer, will.

convict[1] *v.t.* **1** (*to prove guilty*) condemn, prove guilty. **2** (*to return a verdict of guilty against*) condemn, find guilty, imprison, pronounce guilty, sentence. ANTONYMS: acquit.

convict[2] *n.* (*a criminal sentenced to a term in prison*) captive, (*sl.*) con, criminal, (*coll.*) crook, culprit, felon, jailbird, lag, malefactor, prisoner, villain.

conviction *n.* **1** (*the act of convicting*) condemnation, judgement, punishment, sentence. **2** (*the state of being convinced*) assurance, certainty, certitude, confidence, earnestness, fervour, firmness, reliance, sureness. ANTONYMS: faith. **3** (*strong belief*) belief, creed, faith, opinion, persuasion, position, principle, tenet, trust, view.

convince *v.t.* **1** (*to satisfy the mind of*) assure, satisfy. **2** (*to persuade, to cause to believe*) bring round, persuade, prevail upon, sway, talk into, win over.

cool *a.* **1** (*slightly or moderately cold*) breezy, chilled, chilling, chilly, cold, fresh, (*coll.*) nippy, refreshing. ANTONYMS: warm. **2** ((*of colours*) *creating a feeling of coolness*) bluish, greenish. **3** (*aloof, unfriendly*) aloof, detached, distant, frigid, offhand, remote, reserved, stand-offish, uncommunicative, unfriendly, unsympathetic, unwelcoming. ANTONYMS: cordial, friendly. **4** (*apathetic, unenthusiastic*) apathetic, incurious, indifferent, lukewarm, unenthusiastic, uninterested, unresponsive. ANTONYMS: enthusiastic. **5** (*dispassionate, not showing emotion*) calm, collected, composed, deliberate, dispassionate, imperturbable, (*coll.*) laid-back, level-headed, phlegmatic, placid, quiet, self-controlled, self-possessed, serene, (*coll.*) together, unemotional, unexcited, (*coll.*) unfazed, (*coll.*) unflappable, unruffled. ANTONYMS: agitated, perturbed. **6** (*calmly impudent or audacious*) audacious, bold, brazen, cheeky, impertinent, impudent, insolent, presumptuous, shameless, unabashed. **7** (*very good, excellent*) excellent, (*coll.*) fantastic, good, marvellous, wonderful. **8** (*fashionable, smart*) cosmopolitan, elegant, fashionable, smart, sophisticated, (*coll., sometimes derog.*) trendy, urbane. **9** (*relaxed*) at ease, relaxed, restful, sedate. **10** ((*of jazz*) *controlled and restrained*) controlled, restrained, understated.
~*n.* **1** (*coolness, moderate temperature*) chill, coolness. **2** (*calmness of emotion*) aplomb,

calmness, composure, control, poise, self-control, self-discipline, self-possession, temper.
~*v.t.* (*to quiet, to calm*) allay, assuage, calm, quiet.
~*v.i.* **1** (*to become cool or cooler*) chill, cool off, freeze, ice, refrigerate. **2** ((*of excitement, enthusiasm etc.*) *to become less*) abate, dampen, diminish, lessen, moderate, quench, reduce, temper.

cooperate *v.i.* **1** (*to work or act with another or others for a common end*) act in concert, collaborate, combine, concur, conspire, interact, join forces, pull together, team up, unite, work together. **2** (*to be helpful or obliging*) abet, accommodate, aid, assist, contribute, help, oblige, participate, pitch in. ANTONYMS: impede, resist.

cooperation *n.* **1** (*the act of cooperating*) collaboration, concert, concurrence, cooperating, interaction, participation, teamwork, unity. ANTONYMS: dissension. **2** (*helpfulness, willingness to oblige another*) assistance, backing, helpfulness, patronage, sponsorship, support. ANTONYMS: hindrance, opposition. **3** (*a form of partnership or association for the production or distribution of goods*) association, cooperative, partnership.

coordinate[1] *a.* (*of the same order, importance etc.*) complementary, correlative, correspondent, equal, equivalent, parallel, synonymous, tantamount.

coordinate[2] *v.t.* (*to correlate, to bring into orderly relation of parts and whole*) arrange, categorize, classify, codify, correlate, dispose, grade, group, match, order, organize, rank, rate, systematize, unify.
~*v.i.* (*to work well together, to produce a good effect*) harmonize, integrate, mesh, pull together, synchronize.

cope *v.i.* **1** (*to encounter, to contend successfully (with)*) contend, deal, encounter, grapple, handle, struggle, tangle, tussle, wrestle. **2** (*to deal (with), manage successfully*) come through, deal, (*coll.*) get by, (*coll.*) make out, make the grade, manage, survive.

copious *a.* **1** (*plentiful, abundant*) abundant, ample, extensive, full, generous, lavish, liberal, plentiful, unstinted. **2** (*producing a plentiful supply*) bounteous, bountiful, exuberant, luxuriant, overflowing, profuse, prolific, rich.

copy *n.* **1** (*a transcript or imitation of an original*) counterfeit, double, duplicate, facsimile, fake, forgery, image, imitation, likeness, photocopy, print, replica, representation,

reproduction, transcript, twin. ANTONYMS: original. **2** (*an example of a particular work or book*) example, issue, sample, specimen. **3** (*in journalism, material for reporting*) material, text, writing. **4** (*a model, a pattern*) model, original, pattern.
~*v.t.* **1** (*to make a copy of*) counterfeit, duplicate, photocopy, plagiarize, replicate, reproduce. **2** (*to follow as pattern or model*) ape, echo, emulate, follow, imitate, impersonate, mimic, mirror, parrot, simulate.

cordial *a.* (*hearty, warm-hearted*) affable, affectionate, amiable, congenial, courteous, earnest, friendly, genial, good-natured, gracious, heartfelt, hearty, pleasant, polite, sincere, sociable, warm-hearted, welcoming. ANTO-NYMS: cold, unfriendly.

core *n.* **1** (*the heart or inner part of anything*) centre, heart, innards, inside, nucleus. **2** (*the hard middle of a fruit, containing the seeds*) kernel, middle. **3** (*the gist, the essence*) crux, essence, gist, marrow, nub, pith, quintessence, substance, sum.

corporeal *a.* **1** (*of or relating to the body*) bodily, fleshly, human. **2** (*material, physical*) material, physical, substantial, tangible. ANTONYMS: mental, spiritual.

corpse *n.* (*a dead body, esp. of a human being*) body, cadaver, carcass, remains, (*sl.*) stiff.

corpulent *a.* (*excessively fat or fleshy*) beefy, big, bulky, burly, fat, fleshy, large, obese, overweight, plump, portly, rotund, stout, tubby, well-padded. ANTONYMS: slim, thin.

correct *v.t.* **1** (*to set right*) put right, rectify, right, set right. **2** (*to remove faults or errors from*) amend, cure, emend, fix, improve, rectify, redress, reform, remedy, repair, right. ANTONYMS: impair, spoil. **3** (*to mark errors in for rectification*) assess, evaluate, grade, mark. **4** (*to punish, to chastise*) admonish, berate, castigate, chasten, chastise, chide, discipline, punish, rebuke, reprimand, reprove, scold. ANTONYMS: compliment, praise. **5** (*to obviate, to counteract*) annul, cancel, counteract, counterbalance, make up for, neutralize, nullify, obviate, offset, reverse. **6** (*to adjust* (*a measuring instrument etc.*) *to register accurately*) adjust, change, modify.
~*a.* **1** (*true, accurate*) accurate, exact, precise, right, strict, true. ANTONYMS: inaccurate, wrong. **2** (*right, proper*) acceptable, appropriate, decent, decorous, diplomatic, fitting, (*coll.*) OK, (*coll.*) okay, proper, right, seemly, suitable. ANTONYMS: improper, inappropriate. **3** (*conforming to a fixed standard*) approved, conventional, customary, established, normal, orthodox, set, standard, traditional, usual.

4 (*free from fault or imperfection*) faultless, flawless, perfect, unerring, unimpeachable. ANTONYMS: faulty, flawed.

correction *n.* **1** (*the act of correcting*) amendment, emendation, modification, rectification, redress, remedy, reparation, righting. **2** (*amendment, improvement*) alteration, amendment, emendation, improvement. **3** (*punishment, chastisement*) admonition, castigation, chastisement, discipline, punishment, reprimand, reproof.

correspond *v.i.* **1** (*to be comparable or equivalent* (*to*)) be equivalent (to), be similar, correlate. **2** (*to fit* (*with*), *to suit*) accord (with), agree (with), be consistent (with), coincide (with), complement, concord, conform (to), fit (with), harmonize (with), match, square (with), suit, tally (with). ANTONYMS: differ (from), disagree (with). **3** (*to communicate by letters sent and received*) communicate, exchange letters, write.

correspondent *a.* (*agreeing or congruous* (*with*)) accordant (with), agreeing (with), analogous (to), comparable (with), congruous (with), corresponding (to), equivalent (to), like, matching, parallel (to), reciprocal, similar (to). ANTONYMS: different (from).
~*n.* **1** (*a person with whom communication is kept up by letters*) letter-writer, penfriend, (*coll.*) pen pal, writer. **2** (*a person who sends news from a particular place or on a particular subject, to a newspaper, radio or TV station etc.*) contributor, journalist, newspaperman, newspaperwoman, reporter, (*coll.*) stringer.

corroborate *v.t.* (*to confirm, to establish*) authenticate, back up, bear out, confirm, document, endorse, establish, ratify, strengthen, substantiate, support, sustain, validate, verify. ANTONYMS: contradict, refute.

corrupt *a.* **1** (*perverted by bribery or willing to be*) (*sl.*) bent, (*coll.*) crooked, dishonest, dishonourable, fraudulent, perverted, unprincipled, unscrupulous, untrustworthy. ANTONYMS: honest, honourable. **2** (*involving bribery or unethical practices*) shady, sharp, underhand, unethical. **3** (*depraved*) abandoned, debased, defiled, degenerate, demoralized, depraved, dissolute, evil, immoral, profligate, wicked. ANTONYMS: virtuous. **4** ((*of a text etc.*) *vitiated by additions or alterations*) adulterated, altered, contaminated, defiled, distorted. **5** (*not genuine*) doctored, fake, falsified. ANTONYMS: genuine, real. **6** (*spoiled, tainted*) contaminated, infected, spoiled, tainted. **7** (*putrid, decomposed*) decayed, decomposed, putrescent, putrid, rotten.
~*v.t.* **1** (*to change from a sound to an unsound*

state) adulterate, debase, warp. **2** (*to make impure or unwholesome*) contaminate, infect. **3** (*to bribe*) bribe, buy off, (*sl.*) fix, suborn. **4** (*to falsify*) doctor, falsify, tamper with. **5** (*to defile*) defile, vitiate. **6** (*to debauch, to seduce*) debauch, deprave, pervert, seduce.

corruption *n.* **1** (*the state of being corrupt*) (*coll.*) crookedness, dishonesty, unscrupulousness. **2** (*bribery or fraud*) bribery, extortion, (*coll.*) fiddling, fraud. **3** (*moral deterioration*) baseness, decadence, degeneration, degradation, depravity, evil, immorality, impurity, iniquity, perversion, profligacy, sinfulness, vice, wickedness. **4** (*a corrupt reading or version*) adulteration, debasement, distortion. **5** (*decomposition, putrefaction*) decay, decomposition, foulness, infection, pollution, putrefaction, putrescence, rot. **6** (*misrepresentation*) distortion, falsification, misrepresentation.

cosmopolitan *a.* **1** (*at home in any part of the world*) well-travelled, worldly, worldly-wise. ANTONYMS: parochial, provincial. **2** (*free from national prejudices and limitations*) broad-minded, catholic, open-minded. ANTONYMS: narrow-minded. **3** (*sophisticated*) sophisticated, suave, urbane.

cost *v.t.* **1** (*to require as the price of possession or enjoyment*) necessitate, require. **2** (*to cause the expenditure of*) be priced at, be valued at, be worth, come to, fetch, get, go for, retail at, sell at, set back. **3** (*to result in the loss of or the infliction of*) deprive, harm, hurt, injure, lose. **4** (*to calculate or set the price of* (*a job etc.*)) estimate, price, quote, value, work out.
~*n.* **1** (*the price charged or paid for a thing*) amount, figure, price, tariff. **2** (*expense, charge*) charge, (*coll.*) damage, expense. **3** (*expenditure of any kind*) expenditure, outlay, payment. **4** (*penalty, loss*) damage, deprivation, detriment, harm, hurt, injury, loss, penalty, sacrifice. **5** (*pain, trouble*) pain, suffering, trouble.

costly *a.* **1** (*of high price*) dear, excessive, exorbitant, extortionate, pricey, (*coll.*) steep, stiff. ANTONYMS: cheap, reasonable. **2** (*valuable*) lavish, luxurious, opulent, precious, priceless, rich, splendid, sumptuous, valuable. **3** (*involving great loss or sacrifice*) catastrophic, damaging, deleterious, disastrous, harmful, ruinous.

costume *n.* (*dress*) apparel, attire, (*coll.*) clobber, dress, ensemble, garb, garments, (*coll.*) gear, get-up, habit, kit, outfit, rags, raiment, (*coll.*) togs, uniform.

cosy *a.* **1** (*comfortable, snug*) comfortable, (*coll.*) comfy, relaxed, secure, sheltered, snug, tucked up, warm. ANTONYMS: exposed,

uncomfortable. **2** (*complacent*) complacent, pleased with oneself, self-satisfied, smug. **3** (*warm and friendly*) close, friendly, intimate, warm. **4** (*showing or resulting from friendship, usu. to the detriment of others*) hand in glove, (*sl.*) in cahoots, in league.

council *n.* **1** (*a number of people met together for deliberation or some administrative purpose*) assembly, board, chamber, committee, conclave, conference, congregation, convention, convocation, counsel, gathering, meeting, panel. **2** (*a higher branch of the legislature*) cabinet, congress, diet, government, house, ministry, parliament.

counsel *n.* **1** (*advice*) admonition, advice, caution, direction, guidance, information, recommendation, suggestion, warning. **2** (*opinion given after deliberation*) consideration, deliberation, opinion. **3** (*a consultation*) consultation, discussion. **4** (*a barrister*) advocate, attorney, barrister, (*coll.*) brief, lawyer, legal adviser, solicitor.
~*v.t.* **1** (*to give advice or counsel to*) be supportive of, encourage, give advice to, help, support. **2** (*to advise*) admonish, advise, advocate, caution, exhort, guide, instruct, prescribe, recommend, urge, warn.

count *v.t.* **1** (*to reckon up in numbers, to total*) add, calculate, check, compute, enumerate, estimate, figure, number, quantify, reckon, score, tally, total, tot up. **2** (*to include*) include, number among, take into account. **3** (*to consider*) consider, deem, impute, judge, rate, think. **4** (*to esteem*) consider, esteem, regard.
~*v.i.* (*to possess a certain value*) carry weight, matter, rate, signify, tell, weigh.
~*n.* **1** (*a reckoning or numbering*) calculation, computation, enumeration, numbering, poll, reckoning. **2** (*the sum* (*of*)) sum, tally. **to count on/ upon** (*to rely on*) bank on, believe in, depend on, figure on, lean on, reckon on, rely on, take for granted, trust.

countenance *n.* **1** (*the face*) face, (*sl.*) mug, visage. **2** (*the features*) features, physiognomy. **3** (*look or expression*) air, appearance, aspect, expression, look, mien. **4** (*favour, support*) aid, approval, assistance, backing, corroboration, endorsement, favour, sanction, support. ANTONYMS: disapproval.
~*v.t.* **1** (*to approve, to permit*) allow, approve, brook, condone, endure, permit, put up with, sanction, stand for, tolerate. ANTONYMS: oppose. **2** (*to abet, to encourage*) abet, aid, back, champion, encourage, endorse, help, support.

counteract *v.t.* **1** (*to act in opposition to*) check, contravene, correct, counterbalance, countervail, cross, defeat, foil, frustrate, hinder, invalidate, negate, obviate, offset, oppose, resist, thwart. **2** (*to neutralize*) annul, cancel, compensate for, counterbalance, make up for, neutralize, nullify.

counterfeit *a.* **1** (*made in imitation with intent to be passed off as genuine*) artificial, bogus, ersatz, fake, fraudulent, imitation, (*coll.*) phoney, (*coll.*) pseudo, spurious. ANTONYMS: authentic, genuine. **2** (*forged*) copied, faked, forged. **3** (*pretend; false*) false, feigned, make-believe, mock, pretend, sham, simulated.
~*n.* **1** (*a counterfeit thing*) copy, fake, forgery, fraud, imitation, (*coll.*) phoney, reproduction, sham. **2** (*a person who pretends to be what they are not, an impostor*) charlatan, con artist, impostor.
~*v.t.* **1** (*to make a counterfeit copy of, to forge*) copy, fabricate, forge. **2** (*to imitate or copy without right and pass off as genuine*) fake, falsify. **3** (*to imitate, to mimic*) imitate, impersonate, mimic. **4** (*to pretend, to simulate*) feign, pretend, put on, sham, simulate.

countless *a.* (*innumerable*) endless, immeasurable, incalculable, infinite, innumerable, legion, limitless, measureless, multitudinous, myriad, numberless, uncounted, untold. ANTONYMS: few, limited.

country *n.* **1** (*a territory or state*) commonwealth, kingdom, nation, realm, state, territory. **2** (*the inhabitants of any territory or state*) citizenry, citizens, community, inhabitants, nation, people, populace, public, society. **3** (*one's native land*) fatherland, homeland, motherland, nationality. **4** (*the rural part as distinct from cities and towns*) countryside, farmland, green belt. ANTONYMS: city, town. **5** (*the rest of a land as distinguished from the capital*) backwoods, provinces, (*coll.*) sticks, wilds. **6** (*a region or area*) area, district, land, part, region, terrain, territory.

couple *n.* **1** (*two*) brace, pair, two. **2** (*a few*) a few, several. **3** (*two people who are engaged, married or in a steady relationship*) (*coll.*) item, twosome. **4** (*two of anything of the same kind considered together*) duo, pair, twins. **5** (*a pair or brace of animals*) brace, pair, team. **6** (*that which joins two things together*) coupling, link.
~*v.t.* **1** (*to connect or fasten together*) bracket, buckle, clasp, combine, connect, fasten together, join, link. ANTONYMS: separate. **2** (*to unite persons together, esp. in marriage*) (*sl.*) hitch, marry, pair, unite, wed, yoke.
~*v.i.* (*to copulate*) breed, copulate, mate.

courage *n.* (*bravery, boldness*) audacity, (*sl.*) balls, boldness, (*sl.*) bottle, bravery, daring, dauntlessness, fearlessness, firmness, fortitude, gallantry, grit, (*coll.*) guts, heroism,

intrepidity, mettle, nerve, pluck, resolution, valour. ANTONYMS: cowardice, timidity.

courageous *a.* (*brave, bold*) audacious, bold, brave, daring, dauntless, fearless, gallant, gritty, hardy, heroic, indomitable, intrepid, plucky, resolute, stalwart, stout-hearted, unafraid, valiant, valorous. ANTONYMS: cowardly, timid.

course *n.* **1** (*continued movement along a path*) advance, continuity, flow, furtherance, headway, march, movement, progress, progression. **2** (*the act of passing from one place to another*) movement, moving, passage, passing. **3** (*the direction in which something moves*) bearing, direction, tack, way. **4** (*the path passed along*) channel, line, orbit, passage, path, road, route, run, track, trail, trajectory, way. **5** (*a period of time passed*) duration, lapse, passage, period, season, spell, sweep, term, time. **6** (*the ground on which a race is run or on which a game (such as golf) is played*) circuit, field, ground, lap, racecourse, round, track. **7** (*the act of running, a race*) race, running. **8** (*a series (of lessons, medical treatments etc.)*) sequence, series, succession. **9** (*a planned programme of study*) classes, lectures, programme, regimen, schedule, studies. **10** (*mode of procedure*) method, mode, plan, policy, practice, procedure, process, routine. **11** (*method of life or conduct*) behaviour, conduct, deportment, manner.
~*v.t.* **1** (*to run after, to pursue*) chase, follow, hunt, pursue, run after. **2** (*to traverse*) cross, pass over, traverse.
~*v.i.* **1** (*to run or move quickly*) bolt, charge, dash, hasten, move apace, race, run, rush, scud, scurry, speed. **2** ((*of blood etc.*) *to flow or circulate*) circulate, flow, gush, pulse, stream, surge.

courteous *a.* (*polite, considerate*) affable, attentive, ceremonious, civil, considerate, courtly, decorous, gallant, gracious, obliging, polished, polite, proper, refined, respectful, urbane, well-behaved, well-bred, well-mannered. ANTONYMS: discourteous, impolite.

courtesy *n.* **1** (*politeness, graciousness*) affability, ceremony, civility, cordiality, courtliness, elegance, formality, gallantry, good breeding, good manners, graciousness, polish, politeness, urbanity. **2** (*favour*) benevolence, consent, consideration, favour, generosity, indulgence, kindness.

cover *v.t.* **1** (*to overlay*) layer, mantle, overlay. **2** (*to overspread with something*) canopy, coat, daub, envelop, overspread. **3** (*to overspread with something so as to protect or conceal*) encase, house, sheathe. **4** (*to clothe*) clothe, dress, put on, swaddle, wrap. **5** (*to hide or screen*) camouflage, cloak, conceal, cover up, disguise, eclipse, enshroud, hide, hood, mantle, mask, obscure, screen, shroud, veil. ANTONYMS: reveal, unmask. **6** (*to lie over so as to shelter or conceal*) defend, guard, protect, reinforce, shelter, shield, watch over. **7** (*to include or deal with*) comprise, contain, deal with, embody, embrace, encompass, include, incorporate, involve. **8** (*to be enough to defray*) compensate for, counter, counterbalance, defray, make up for, offset, pay for. **9** (*to travel across*) cross, range, travel across, traverse. **10** (*to protect by insurance*) insure, protect, provide for. **11** (*to report on for a newspaper, broadcasting station etc.*) describe, detail, investigate, narrate, recount, relate, report, write up. **12** (*to extend over*) engulf, extend over, flood, inundate, submerge. **13** (*to have range or command over*) command, range over. ~*n.* **1** (*anything which covers or hides*) canopy, case, clothing, coating, covering, housing, sheath. **2** (*a lid*) cap, lid, top. ANTONYMS: base, bottom. **3** (*the outside covering of a book*) binding, case, dust jacket, jacket, wrapper. **4** (*anything which serves to conceal or disguise*) camouflage, cloak, concealment, cover-up, disguise, facade, front, mask, screen, veil. **5** (*pretence, pretext*) excuse, guise, pretence, pretext. **6** (*shelter, protection*) defence, guard, hiding place, protection, refuge, retreat, sanctuary, shelter, shield. **7** (*a thicket, woods which conceal game*) thicket, undergrowth, woods. **8** (*the coverage of an insurance policy*) indemnity, insurance, protection. **9** (*a bed covering, blanket*) bed covering, blanket, counterpane, duvet, eiderdown, quilt. **10** (*an envelope or other wrapping for a packet in the post*) envelope, wrapper, wrapping.

covetous *a.* **1** (*eagerly desirous (of)*) craving, desirous, yearning. **2** (*eager to obtain and possess*) avid, eager. **3** (*avaricious*) acquisitive, avaricious, envious, grasping, greedy, jealous, mercenary, rapacious.

cowardly *a.* (*faint-hearted, spiritless*) abject, afraid, (*coll.*) chicken, craven, faint-hearted, fearful, frightened, (*coll.*) gutless, lily-livered, pusillanimous, scared, shrinking, spineless, spiritless, timid, timorous, (*coll.*) yellow. ANTONYMS: brave, courageous.

cower *v.i.* **1** (*to stoop, to crouch*) bend, crouch, stoop. **2** (*to shrink or quail through fear*) cringe, draw back, flinch, grovel, quail, recoil, shrink, skulk, tremble.

coy *a.* **1** (*coquettish*) arch, coquettish, flirtatious, kittenish. **2** (*modest, shrinking from familiarity*) backward, bashful, demure, diffident, modest, prudish, reserved, retiring,

self-conscious, self-effacing, shrinking, shy, timid, unassuming. ANTONYMS: confident, forward. **3** (*annoyingly unforthcoming*) evasive, unforthcoming.

crack *v.t.* **1** (*to break without entire separation of the parts*) break, burst, chip, chop, cleave, craze, fracture, shatter, snap, splinter, split. ANTONYMS: mend. **2** (*to cause to give a sharp, sudden noise*) burst, crash, detonate, explode, pop, ring, snap. **3** (*to cause to break down by stress, torture etc.*) break down, wear down. **4** (*to solve (a problem, code etc.)*) decipher, decode, fathom, solve, unravel, work out. **5** (*to hit sharply and with force*) (*coll.*) clip, clout, cuff, hit, rap, slap, thump, (*coll.*) wallop, whack. **6** (*to open and drink (e.g. a bottle of wine)*) crack open, open, uncork. ~*v.i.* (*to break down under pressure, e.g. of stress*) break down, collapse, fail, give way, go to pieces, lose control, snap, succumb, yield. ~*n.* **1** (*a partial separation of parts*) breach, break, fracture. **2** (*the opening so made*) chink, chip, cleft, cranny, crevice, fissure, gap, hole, opening, rift, slit. **3** (*a sharp sudden sound or report*) bang, burst, clap, crash, explosion, pop, report, shot, snap. **4** (*a defect or flaw, e.g. in personality*) chink, defect, flaw. **5** (*a sarcastic joke*) dig, gag, insult, jibe, joke, quip, wisecrack, witticism. ~*a.* (*excellent, brilliant*) ace, brilliant, choice, elite, excellent, first-class, first-rate, great, superior, top.

craft *n.* **1** (*dexterity, skill*) ability, aptitude, art, artistry, cleverness, dexterity, expertise, flair, genius, ingenuity, knack, (*coll.*) know-how, mastery, skill, talent, technique, workmanship. ANTONYMS: incompetence. **2** (*cunning, deceit*) artfulness, artifice, contrivance, cunning, deceit, deviousness, duplicity, guile, ruse, scheme, shrewdness, stratagem, subterfuge, subtlety, trickery, wiliness. **3** (*a handicraft or trade*) business, calling, employment, handicraft, handiwork, line, occupation, profession, pursuit, trade, vocation, work. **4** (*a boat*) boat, hovercraft, ship, vessel. **5** (*an aircraft or space vehicle*) aeroplane, aircraft, (*N Am.*) airplane, plane, rocket, spacecraft, spaceship.

crafty *a.* (*sly, cunning*) artful, astute, calculating, canny, clever, cunning, designing, devious, foxy, guileful, insidious, knowing, scheming, sharp, shrewd, sly, sneaky, subtle, tricky, wily. ANTONYMS: artless, naive.

cram *v.t.* **1** (*to push or press in so as to fill to overflowing*) compact, compress, crowd, crush, force, jam, overcrowd, overfill, overstuff, pack, pack in, press, push, ram, shove, squeeze, stuff. **2** (*to eat greedily*) glut, gorge, guzzle, (*esp. N Am., sl.*) pig out, put away, stuff.

~*v.i.* (*to learn a subject hastily and superficially, esp. for an examination*) (*coll.*) mug up, revise, study, (*coll.*) swot up.

crank *n.* (*an eccentric*) (*sl.*) case, (*coll.*) character, eccentric, (*coll.*) freak, (*sl.*) nut, (*sl.*) nutcase, (*sl.*) nutter, oddball, (*coll.*) weirdo.

crash *v.t.* **1** (*to cause* (*a vehicle etc.*) *to hit something with great force*) bang, clang, clash, clatter, roar, thunder. **2** (*to hit, drop etc.* (*something*) *so that it makes a loud smashing noise*) drop, hit, smash, throw.

~*v.i.* **1** ((*of a vehicle etc.*) *to hit something with great force*) bang, bump, collide, hit, plough into, smash. **2** ((*of an aircraft*) *to fall with great force to the ground or into the sea*) crash-land, fall, give way, hurtle, lurch, overbalance, pitch, plummet, plunge, sprawl, topple, tumble. **3** (*to move* (*through etc.*) *with great force and violence*) dash, hurtle, precipitate, rush. **4** (*to move, come together etc. with a loud noise, and often also breaking*) break, crumble, dash, fracture, shatter, shiver, smash, splinter. **5** (*to fail, be ruined financially*) collapse, fail, fold, (*coll.*) go bust, go under.

~*n.* **1** (*a loud sudden noise, as of many things broken at once*) bang, blast, boom, clang, clash, clatter, din, explosion, racket, smash, thunder. **2** (*a violent smash*) accident, bump, collision, jar, jolt, (*coll.*) pile-up, (*sl.*) prang, smash, wreck. **3** (*a sudden failure, bankruptcy*) bankruptcy, collapse, debacle, depression, downfall, failure, ruin, smash.

~*a.* (*done rapidly, with urgency*) emergency, immediate, intensive, rapid, urgent.

crass *a.* **1** (*loutish, boorish*) blundering, boorish, coarse, gross, loutish, lumpish, oafish, unrefined, vulgar. **2** (*extremely stupid, obtuse*) asinine, bovine, dense, doltish, obtuse, stupid, thick, witless. ANTONYMS: clever, intelligent. **3** (*extremely tactless or insensitive*) indelicate, insensitive, tactless.

crave *v.t.* **1** (*to long for*) covet, desire, (*coll.*) fancy, hanker after, hunger for, long for, lust after, pine for, sigh for, thirst for, want, yearn for. **2** (*to ask for earnestly and submissively*) ask for, beg, beseech, entreat, implore, petition, plead for, pray for, seek, solicit, supplicate.

crawl *v.i.* **1** (*to move slowly on one's hands and knees*) creep, go on hands and knees. ANTONYMS: walk. **2** ((*of an insect, snake etc.*) *to move slowly with the body on or close to the ground*) slink, slither, squirm, worm, wriggle, writhe. **3** (*to move slowly*) creep, drag, inch, steal. ANTONYMS: run, sprint. **4** (*to assume an abject posture or manner*) cower, cringe, fawn, grovel.

5 (*to get on, e.g. in a career, by obsequious servility*) (*N Am., sl.*) brown-nose, creep, (*N Am., sl.*) kiss ass, pander to, toady to. **6** (*to be covered with crawling things*) abound, swarm, teem.

craze *v.t.* (*to make insane*) bewilder, confuse, dement, derange, distemper, drive mad, enrage, inflame, madden, unbalance, unhinge. ANTONYMS: calm, soothe.

~*n.* **1** (*an extravagant idea or enthusiasm*) enthusiasm, fad, fashion, infatuation, mania, novelty, obsession, passion, rage, trend, vogue. **2** (*madness*) derangement, insanity, madness.

crazy *a.* **1** (*mad, deranged*) (*sl.*) barking, (*sl.*) barmy, (*coll.*) batty, berserk, (*sl.*) bonkers, (*sl.*) crackers, crazed, demented, deranged, insane, (*coll.*) loopy, lunatic, mad, (*coll.*) mental, (*sl.*) nuts, (*coll.*) out to lunch, potty, touched, unbalanced, unhinged. ANTONYMS: rational, sane. **2** (*ridiculous*) absurd, bizarre, eccentric, fantastic, foolhardy, foolish, (*sl.*) half-baked, idiotic, inane, irresponsible, ludicrous, nonsensical, odd, outrageous, peculiar, potty, preposterous, ridiculous, silly, weird. ANTONYMS: prudent, sensible. **3** (*very enthusiastic* (*about*)) ardent, avid, devoted, eager, enamoured, enthusiastic, fanatical, infatuated, (*coll.*) into, keen, mad, passionate, smitten, wild, zealous. ANTONYMS: indifferent, unenthusiastic. **4** (*wild, exciting*) exciting, irrational, outrageous, preposterous, wild.

create *v.t.* **1** (*to produce, to bring into existence*) beget, bring about, coin, contrive, design, develop, devise, (*coll.*) dream up, engender, fabricate, forge, generate, hatch, initiate, invent, make, manufacture, originate, produce, think up. **2** (*to be the occasion of*) cause, lead to, occasion, provoke, start. **3** (*to invest with a new character or office*) appoint, constitute, establish, found, install, invest, make, set up.

creation *n.* **1** (*the act of creating*) birth, conception, formation, generation, genesis, inception, invention, making, origin, procreation, production. ANTONYMS: destruction. **2** (*that which is created or produced*) concoction, handiwork, invention, product, production. **3** (*the world, all created things*) cosmos, life, living world, nature, universe, world. **4** (*the act of investing with a new character or position*) appointment, constitution, foundation, inception, investiture. **5** (*a production of art or intellect*) achievement, brainchild, magnum opus, work.

creative *a.* **1** (*having the ability to create*) fertile, productive. **2** (*imaginative*) artistic, clever, gifted, imaginative, ingenious, inspired, inventive, resourceful, skilled, talented. **3** (*original*) original, stimulating, visionary.

creature *n.* **1** (*a living being*) being, organism. **2** (*an animal*) animal, beast, brute. ANTONYMS: human being. **3** (*a person* (*as an epithet of pity or endearment*)) character, fellow, individual, man, mortal, person, soul, woman. **4** (*a person who owes their rise or fortune to another*) cur, dependant, hanger-on, hireling, lackey, minion, puppet, retainer, thing.

credible *a.* **1** (*deserving of or entitled to belief*) believable, conceivable, imaginable, likely, plausible, possible, probable, reasonable, supposable, tenable, thinkable. ANTONYMS: implausible, incredible. **2** (*convincing; seemingly effective*) convincing, effective, persuasive.

credit *n.* **1** (*belief, trust*) belief, confidence, credence, faith, reliance, trust. ANTONYMS: disbelief. **2** (*credibility, trustworthiness*) credibility, honesty, integrity, probity, trustworthiness. **3** (*a reputation inspiring confidence*) esteem, fame, glory, good name, honour, kudos, prestige, regard, reputation, repute, standing, status. **4** (*an acknowledgement of value*) acclaim, acknowledgement, approval, commendation, merit, praise, recognition, tribute. ANTONYMS: blame. **5** (*anything due to any person*) acknowledgement, ascription, attribution, creditation.
~*v.t.* **1** (*to believe*) accept, bank on, believe, (*sl.*) buy, fall for, rely on, swallow, trust. **2** (*to set to the credit of* (*a person*)) accredit, ascribe to, assign to, attribute to, (*coll.*) chalk up to, impute to, refer to.

creep *v.i.* **1** (*to crawl along the ground*) crawl, slither, squirm, worm, wriggle, writhe. **2** (*to move slowly and imperceptibly*) crawl, dawdle, drag, edge, inch, skulk, slink, sneak, steal, tiptoe. **3** (*to behave with servility; to fawn*) (*coll.*) bootlick, (*N Am., sl.*) brown-nose, fawn, grovel, pander to, (*coll.*) suck up to, toady to. **4** (*to have a sensation of shivering or shrinking, e.g. from fear*) cower, cringe, shiver, shrink.
~*n.* (*an unpleasant or servile person*) (*taboo sl.*) arselicker, (*coll.*) bootlicker, sycophant, toady.

creepy *a.* (*causing the sensation of creeping of the flesh*) disturbing, eerie, forbidding, frightening, ghostly, hair-raising, macabre, menacing, nightmarish, ominous, scary, sinister, terrifying, threatening, weird.

crest *n.* **1** (*a plume on the head of a bird*) comb, plume. **2** (*any tuft on the head of an animal*) topknot, tuft. **3** (*a plume of feathers, esp. affixed to the top of a helmet*) plume, tassel. **4** (*the apex of a helmet*) apex, crest. **5** (*a heraldic figure printed on paper or painted on a building etc.*) badge, bearings, charge, coat of

arms, device, emblem, insignia, seal, shield, symbol. **6** (*the summit of a mountain or hill*) height, peak, pinnacle, ridge, summit, top.

crime *n.* **1** (*an act contrary to human or divine law*) fault, felony, misdeed, misdemeanour, offence, transgression, trespass, violation, wrong. **2** (*wrongdoing, sin*) corruption, delinquency, illegality, iniquity, malefaction, misconduct, sin, sinfulness, unrighteousness, vice, villainy, wickedness, wrongdoing. **3** (*something to be regretted or to be ashamed of*) atrocity, disgrace, outrage.

criminal *a.* **1** (*contrary to law or right*) felonious, illegal, illicit, iniquitous, lawless, nefarious, unlawful, unrighteous, wrong. ANTONYMS: lawful, legal. **2** (*guilty of a crime*) amoral, (*sl.*) bent, corrupt, (*coll.*) crooked, culpable, depraved, disgraceful, dishonest, guilty, immoral, sinful, villainous, wicked. ANTONYMS: scandalous, senseless, shameful.
~*n.* **1** (*a person guilty of a crime*) culprit, delinquent, evildoer, malefactor, miscreant, offender, sinner, transgressor, villain, wrongdoer. **2** (*a convict*) (*sl.*) con, convict, (*coll.*) crook, felon, inmate, jailbird, lag, lawbreaker, outlaw.

cringe *v.i.* **1** (*to shrink back in fear*) blench, cower, draw back, flinch, quail, recoil, shrink back. **2** (*to crouch, to bend humbly*) bend, bow, crouch, duck, stoop. **3** (*to fawn, behave obsequiously to*) crawl, creep, fawn, grovel, pander to, sneak, toady. **4** (*to wince in embarrassment*) quiver, shy, start, tremble, wince.

cripple *v.t.* **1** (*to make lame*) hamstring, lame, maim. **2** (*to deprive of the use of the limbs*) debilitate, disable, enervate, enfeeble, handicap, incapacitate, paralyse, weaken. **3** (*to deprive of or lessen the power of action*) cramp, damage, impair, sabotage, undermine. ANTONYMS: expedite, further.

crisis *n.* **1** (*a momentous point in politics, domestic affairs etc.*) climax, confrontation, critical point, (*coll.*) crunch, crux, culmination, height, moment of truth. **2** (*a time of great danger or difficulty*) calamity, catastrophe, danger, dilemma, disaster, emergency, exigency, extremity, meltdown, mess, plight, predicament, quandary, trouble. **3** (*a turning point, esp. that of a disease indicating recovery or death*) turning point, watershed.

crisp *a.* **1** (*hard, dry and brittle*) brittle, crumbly, dry, friable, hard. ANTONYMS: drooping, soft. **2** ((*of vegetables etc.*) *firm, crunchy*) crispy, crunchy, firm, fresh. ANTONYMS: wilted. **3** ((*of weather etc.*) *cold and invigorating*) bracing, brisk, cold, fresh, invigorating, refreshing, stimulating. **4** ((*of a person's manner*) *brisk*) brisk, businesslike, decisive, no-nonsense. **5** ((*of wording*) *concise*) abrupt, brief, brusque, concise, incisive, pithy, short, succinct, tart, terse, to the point. ANTONYMS: long-winded. **6** ((*of a person's features*) *neat, clean-cut*) clean-cut, neat, orderly, smart, snappy, spruce, tidy, well-groomed. **7** ((*of hair*) *closely curled*) crimped, curly, frizzy. **8** ((*of paper*) *stiff*) crackly, stiff.

critical *a.* **1** (*of or relating to criticism*) analytical, diagnostic, discerning, discriminating, penetrating. **2** (*fastidious, exacting*) captious, carping, censorious, derogatory, disapproving, disparaging, exacting, fastidious, fault-finding, niggling, (*coll.*) nit-picking, scathing. ANTONYMS: easygoing, permissive. **3** (*decisive, vital*) crucial, decisive, essential, important, key, momentous, pivotal, pressing, serious, severe, urgent, vital. ANTONYMS: unimportant. **4** (*attended with danger or risk*) dangerous, grave, (*coll.*) hairy, perilous, precarious, risky, touch-and-go. ANTONYMS: safe.

criticism *n.* **1** (*the act of judging, esp. literary or artistic works*) analysis, appraisal, appreciation, assessment, comment, estimation, examination, judgement, valuation. **2** (*a critical essay or opinion*) commentary, critique, essay, notice, opinion, review. **3** (*an unfavourable judgement*) censure, condemnation, disapproval, disparagement, fault-finding, (*coll.*) flak, objection, (*coll.*) panning, (*coll.*) slam, slating, stricture. ANTONYMS: praise.

criticize *v.t.* **1** (*to examine critically and deliver an opinion on*) analyse, appraise, comment on, discuss, estimate, evaluate, examine, judge, opine, pass judgement on, review, value. **2** (*to censure*) attack, blast, carp, censure, damn, denounce, disapprove of, disparage, excoriate, find fault with, impugn, (*coll.*) knock, lambast, (*coll.*) pan, put down, (*coll.*) slam, slate. ANTONYMS: commend, praise.

croak *v.i.* **1** ((*of e.g. a frog or a raven*) *to make a hoarse low sound in the throat*) caw, gasp, grunt, squawk, wheeze. **2** (*to die*) (*sl.*) buy it, die, expire, (*sl.*) kick the bucket, pass away, (*sl.*) peg out, perish. **3** (*to grumble*) complain, groan, grouse, grumble, moan, murmur, mutter.

crook *n.* **1** (*a shepherd's or bishop's hooked staff*) crosier, staff, stave. **2** (*a curve, a bend*) angle, bend, bow, curve, hook, meander, turn. **3** (*a thief, a swindler*) cheat, criminal, lag, robber, swindler, thief, villain.

crooked *a.* **1** (*bent, curved*) angled, askew, awry, bent, bowed, curved, hooked, slanted, tilted, uneven, unsymmetrical. ANTONYMS: straight. **2** (*twisting, winding*) deviating, meandering, tortuous, turning, twisting, warped, winding, zigzag. **3** (*deformed*) crippled,

deformed, disfigured, distorted, misshapen. **4** (*perverse*) (*sl.*) bent, corrupt, crafty, criminal, deceitful, dishonest, dishonourable, dubious, fraudulent, illegal, illicit, nefarious, perverse, questionable, shady, shifty, treacherous, underhand, unlawful, wrong. ANTONYMS: ethical, honest.

crop *n.* **1** (*the amount cut or gathered from plants*) fruits, gathering, harvest. **2** (*an amount produced*) output, produce, product, yield. **3** (*a group of anything produced, appearing etc. at one time*) batch, group, lot. **4** (*the craw of a fowl, constituting a kind of first stomach*) craw, stomach. **5** (*a short whipstock with a loop instead of a lash*) riding crop, whip. **6** (*a seam of rock*) outcrop, seam, stratum.
~*v.t.* **1** (*to cut off the ends of*) chop, dock, lop, top-and-tail. **2** (*to reap, to gather*) bring in, collect, garner, gather, mow, pick, pluck, reap. **3** ((*of an animal*) *to bite off and eat*) bite off, browse, graze, nibble. **4** (*to cut off, to cut short*) clip, curtail, cut short, pare, prune, reduce, shear, shorten, snip, top, trim. **5** (*to sow*) plant, seed, sow.
~*v.i.* (*to yield a harvest, to bear fruit*) bear fruit, produce, yield.

cross *n.* **1** (*an ancient instrument of execution made of two pieces of timber set transversely*) crucifix, rood. **2** (*the animal or plant resulting from a mixture of two distinct stocks*) crossbreed, cur, hybrid, mongrel. **3** (*a mixture*) amalgam, blend, combination, mixture. **4** (*anything that thwarts or obstructs*) hindrance, impediment, obstruction, stumbling-block. **5** (*trouble, affliction*) affliction, burden, grief, load, misery, misfortune, trial, tribulation, trouble, vexation, woe, worry.
~*a.* **1** (*peevish, angry*) angry, annoyed, bad-tempered, cantankerous, crotchety, crusty, fractious, furious, grouchy, grumpy, ill-tempered, irascible, irate, irritable, (*sl.*) peeved, (*taboo sl.*) pissed off, (*sl.*) ratty, splenetic, testy, tetchy, vexed. ANTONYMS: cheerful, placid. **2** (*transverse, lateral*) crosswise, lateral, oblique, transverse. **3** (*contrary, perverse*) adverse, contrary, opposed, opposing, perverse, unfavourable.
~*v.t.* **1** (*to erase by cross lines, to cancel*) cancel, delete, erase, rub out, strike out, wipe out. **2** (*to pass across, to traverse*) bridge, cross over, ford, pass over, ply, span, traverse. **3** (*to cause to intersect*) criss-cross, entwine, intersect, intertwine, join, lace, meet. **4** (*to cause to interbreed*) cross-breed, hybridize, interbreed, mix. **5** (*to cross-fertilize*) cross-fertilize, cross-pollinate. **6** (*to thwart, to counteract*) block, counteract, deny, foil, frustrate, hinder, impede, interfere, obstruct, oppose, resist, thwart.

crotchety *a.* (*irritable*) angry, awkward, bad-tempered, cantankerous, contrary, crabby, cross, crusty, difficult, disagreeable, fractious, grouchy, grumpy, irascible, irritable, obstreperous, (*sl.*) ratty, surly, testy, touchy. ANTONYMS: affable, good-tempered.

crouch *v.i.* **1** (*to stoop, to bend low*) bend low, bow, duck, hunch, kneel, squat, stoop. **2** (*to cringe, to fawn*) cower, cringe, fawn, grovel, pander.

crowd *n.* **1** (*a number of persons or things collected closely together*) army, assembly, bevy, company, concourse, flock, flood, herd, horde, host, mass, mob, multitude, pack, press, rabble, swarm, throng, troupe. **2** (*the mass, the populace*) (*coll.*) great unwashed, hoi polloi, mass, masses, mob, people, populace, proletariat, public, rabble, rank and file, riff-raff. **3** (*a set, a lot*) (*coll.*) bunch, circle, clique, faction, group, lot, party, set. **4** (*an audience*) attendance, audience, congregation, gate, house, spectators.
~*v.t.* **1** (*to press or squeeze closely together*) compress, cram, jam, pack, press together, squeeze together, stuff. **2** (*to throng or press upon*) congest, cram, pack, press upon, throng. **3** (*to come close to in an aggressive or threatening way*) butt, elbow, jostle, shove.
~*v.i.* **1** (*to press, to throng*) cluster, congregate, flock, huddle, mass, muster, press, push, stream, surge, swarm, throng. ANTONYMS: disperse. **2** (*to collect in crowds*) assemble, collect, gather.

crown *n.* **1** (*the ornamental headdress worn on the head by monarchs as a badge of sovereignty*) chaplet, circlet, coronet, diadem, tiara. **2** (**Crown**) (*the power of the sovereign*) authority, dominion, jurisdiction, power, sovereignty. **3** (*the sovereign*) emperor, empress, government, king, monarch, monarchy, potentate, queen, realm, royalty, ruler, sovereign. **4** (*a garland of honour worn on the head*) bays, garland, laurels, laurel wreath. **5** (*the culmination, glory*) culmination, glory, perfection, ultimate, zenith. **6** (*a reward, distinction*) distinction, honour, prize, reward, trophy. **7** (*the top of anything*) acme, apex, crest, pinnacle, summit, tip, top.
~*v.t.* **1** (*to invest with a crown or regal dignity*) enthrone, invest. **2** (*to surround, or top, as if with a crown*) cap, surmount, surround, top. **3** (*to dignify, to adorn*) adorn, decorate, dignify, festoon, honour. **4** (*to consummate*) complete, consummate, culminate, finish, fulfil, perfect, round off, terminate. **5** (*to hit on the head*) belt, cosh, cuff, punch.

crucial *a.* **1** (*decisive*) conclusive, critical, decisive. **2** (*searching*) searching, testing, trying. **3** (*very important*) central, essential, imperative, important, momentous, pivotal, pressing, significant, urgent, vital. **4** (*excellent*) (*sl.*) ace, (*coll.*) brill, (*coll.*) cool, excellent, great, (*sl.*) wicked.

crude *a.* **1** (*raw, in a natural state*) natural, original, raw, uncooked, unpolished, unprocessed, unrefined. ANTONYMS: refined. **2** (*rude, vulgar*) boorish, coarse, crass, dirty, gross, indecent, lewd, obscene, ribald, rude, smutty, uncouth, vulgar. **3** (*offensively blunt*) blunt, brusque, inconsiderate, indelicate, offensive, tactless. **4** (*rough, unfinished*) approximate, clumsy, coarse, hasty, makeshift, primitive, rough, rudimentary, sketchy, undeveloped, unfinished. **5** (*imperfectly developed*) immature, inexperienced, undeveloped.

cruel *a.* **1** (*disposed to give pain to others*) bloodthirsty, brutal, ferocious, hard, harsh, inexorable, malevolent, merciless, pitiless, relentless, remorseless, ruthless, sadistic, savage, severe, unrelenting, vicious. ANTONYMS: compassionate, merciful. **2** (*unfeeling, hard-hearted*) callous, cold-blooded, flinty, hard-hearted, heartless, inhuman, stony-hearted, unfeeling. **3** (*causing pain, painful*) agonizing, excruciating, fierce, intense, painful.

crumb *n.* **1** (*a small piece, esp. of bread*) bit, bite, fragment, grain, mite, morsel, scrap, shred, sliver, snippet. **2** (*a tiny portion, a particle*) atom, mote, particle, portion, speck.

crumble *v.t.* (*to break into small particles*) break up, bruise, crush, fragment, granulate, grind, pound, powder, pulverize, triturate.
~*v.i.* **1** (*to fall into small pieces*) break up, collapse, disintegrate, fall apart, go to pieces, tumble down. **2** (*to fall into ruin*) decay, decompose, degenerate, deteriorate, moulder, perish.

crusade *n.* **1** (*any of several expeditions undertaken by Christians in the Middle Ages to recover possession of the Holy Land*) holy war, jihad. **2** (*any campaign conducted in a fanatical spirit*) campaign, cause, drive, expedition, movement, push, struggle, war.

crush *v.t.* **1** (*to press or squeeze together between two harder bodies*) press together, squeeze together. **2** (*to crumple*) break, compress, crease, crumple, crunch, flatten, pound, pulverize, smash. **3** (*to overwhelm by superior power*) beat, conquer, defeat, extinguish, overcome, overpower, overwhelm, put down, quell, subdue, vanquish. **4** (*to oppress, to ruin*) oppress, repress, ruin, suppress. **5** (*to dismay or subdue*) abash, browbeat, devastate, disgrace, dismay, embarrass, humiliate, mortify, put down, quash, shame.

~n. 1 (*the act of crushing*) crunch, squash, squeeze. 2 (*a crowd*) crowd, huddle, press, throng. 3 (*a crowded social gathering*) gathering, meeting, party. 4 (*an infatuation or the object of this*) infatuation, obsession, (*sl.*) pash, passion. 5 (*a drink made by or as if by crushing fruit*) cordial, squash.

cry *v.i.* 1 (*to weep*) bawl, blubber, howl, mewl, snivel, wail, weep, yowl. ANTONYMS: laugh, snigger. 2 (*to lament loudly*) bewail, keen, lament. 3 (*to utter inarticulate sounds when weeping*) sob, whimper, whine. 4 (*to make a loud exclamation, esp. because of grief*) ejaculate, exclaim, vociferate. 5 (*to call loudly*) bellow, hail, (*esp. N Am., coll. or dial.*) holler, howl, roar, scream, screech, shout, shriek, whoop, yell. ANTONYMS: mutter, whisper. 6 ((*of animals and birds*) *to make their natural sound*) call, trill. 7 (*to make a proclamation*) advertise, announce, blazon, broadcast, hawk, noise, proclaim, promulgate, publish, trumpet.
~n. 1 (*a loud utterance, usu. inarticulate*) bawl, bellow, call, ejaculation, exclamation, (*esp. N Am., coll. or dial.*) holler, hoot, howl, outcry, roar, scream, screech, shriek, squawk, whoop, yell, yelp. ANTONYMS: laugh. 2 (*an importunate call or prayer*) appeal, call, entreaty, petition, plea, prayer, request, supplication. 3 (*proclamation, public notification*) announcement, notice, proclamation, publication, slogan. 4 (*a catchword*) catchword, phrase, slogan. 5 (*weeping*) bawling, blubbering, crying, snivelling, sobbing, wailing, weeping. 6 (*lamentation*) keening, lament, lamentation, sorrowing.

cryptic *a.* 1 (*hidden, secret*) cabalistic, esoteric, hidden, mystical, occult, secret. 2 (*hard to understand*) abstruse, ambiguous, apocryphal, arcane, coded, dark, enigmatic, inscrutable, mysterious, nebulous, obscure, perplexing, puzzling, recondite, unclear, unintelligible, vague, veiled.

cuddle *v.t.* (*to embrace, to hug*) (*coll.*) canoodle, caress, clasp, embrace, fondle, huddle, hug, (*coll.*) neck, nestle, pet, (*coll.*) smooch, snuggle.
~n. (*a hug, an embrace*) embrace, fondle, hug, pet, snuggle.

cue *n.* 1 (*a signal to an actor*) prompt. 2 (*a signal, e.g. in a piece of music*) indication, nod, sign, signal, wink. 3 (*a hint, reminder*) hint, intimation, reminder, suggestion.
~v.t. (*to give a cue to*) indicate, prompt, remind, signal, wink.

culprit *n.* 1 (*a person who is at fault*) criminal, delinquent, evildoer, malefactor, miscreant, offender, rascal, sinner, transgressor, villain,

wrongdoer. 2 (*a person who is arraigned before a judge on a charge*) accused, felon, prisoner.

cultivate *v.t.* 1 (*to till, to prepare for crops*) farm, plant, plough, prepare, till, work. 2 (*to raise or develop by tilling*) develop, harvest, raise, tend. 3 (*to seek the friendship of*) cherish, court, foster, further, help, nurture, promote, pursue, run after, seek after, woo. 4 (*to improve by labour or study*) ameliorate, better, civilize, discipline, educate, elevate, enrich, improve, polish, promote, refine, train. ANTONYMS: neglect.

culture *n.* 1 (*a state of intellectual and artistic development*) accomplishment, breeding, cultivation, discernment, discrimination, edification, education, elegance, elevation, enlightenment, erudition, gentility, good taste, improvement, polish, politeness, refinement, sophistication, suavity, urbanity. ANTONYMS: barbarism. 2 (*an ethos reflecting this*) civilization, customs, lifestyle, mores, society, way of life. 3 (*intellectual or moral training*) discipline, training. 4 (*the act of tilling*) ploughing, tilling. 5 (*husbandry, farming*) agriculture, agronomy, cultivation, farming, husbandry. 6 (*breeding*) breeding, raising, rearing.

cumbersome *a.* 1 (*unwieldy, unmanageable*) awkward, bulky, clumsy, heavy, hefty, incommodious, unmanageable, unwieldy, weighty. ANTONYMS: compact, handy. 2 (*burdensome, troublesome*) burdensome, inconvenient, oppressive, troublesome. ANTONYMS: convenient.

cunning *a.* (*artful, crafty*) artful, astute, calculating, canny, crafty, deceitful, designing, devious, foxy, guileful, ingenious, knowing, sharp, shifty, shrewd, skilful, sly, tricky, wily. ANTONYMS: guileless, stupid.
~n. 1 (*skill, knowledge acquired by experience*) ability, adroitness, art, artifice, cleverness, craft, deftness, dexterity, finesse, ingenuity, knowledge, skill, subtlety. 2 (*artfulness, subtlety*) artfulness, astuteness, craftiness, deceitfulness, deception, deviousness, foxiness, guile, shrewdness, slyness, subtlety, trickery, wiliness.

curb *n.* (*a check, a restraint*) brake, bridle, check, control, deterrent, limitation, rein, restraint, restriction.
~v.t. (*to restrain, to keep in check*) bridle, check, constrain, control, hinder, impede, inhibit, keep in check, moderate, muzzle, repress, restrain, restrict, retard, subdue, suppress. ANTONYMS: encourage, promote.

cure *n.* 1 (*the act of healing or curing disease*) alleviation, healing, recovery. 2 (*a remedy, a restorative*) antidote, corrective, drug, medication, medicine, nostrum, panacea, prescription, remedy, restorative, specific. **3** (*a course of remedial treatment*) therapy, treatment.

~*v.t.* **1** (*to heal, to make sound or whole*) alleviate, ease, heal, mend, relieve, remedy, restore, treat. ANTONYMS: aggravate. **2** (*to preserve or pickle*) dry, marinate, pickle, preserve, salt, smoke. **3** (*to eliminate or correct* (*a habit or practice*)) corrupt, eliminate, fix, rectify, repair. **4** (*to harden* (*plastic etc.*)) harden, vulcanize.

curious *a.* **1** (*inquisitive, desirous to know*) inquiring, inquisitive, interested, meddlesome, nosy, prying, questioning, searching, snooping. ANTONYMS: indifferent, uninterested. **2** (*extraordinary, odd*) abnormal, bizarre, extraordinary, freakish, intriguing, mysterious, odd, peculiar, puzzling, quaint, queer, remarkable, singular, strange, surprising, unexpected, unorthodox, unusual, weird, wonderful. ANTONYMS: commonplace, ordinary.

current *a.* **1** (*belonging to the present week, month, year*) existing, present. **2** (*passing at the present time*) contemporaneous, contemporary, fashionable, in, latest, (*coll.*) now, stylish, (*coll., sometimes derog.*) trendy, up-to-date, up-to-the-minute. **3** (*in general circulation among the public*) accepted, circulating, common, customary, general, in circulation, known, ongoing, popular, present, prevailing, prevalent, rife, topical, widespread.

~*n.* **1** (*a flowing stream, a body of water, air etc., moving in a certain direction*) course, draught, flow, jet, river, stream, tide, undertow. **2** (*a general drift or tendency*) atmosphere, drift, feeling, inclination, mainstream, mood, tendency, tenor, trend, undercurrent, (*coll.*) vibes.

curse *v.t.* **1** (*to invoke harm or evil upon*) accurse, blast. **2** (*to vex or torment* (*with*)) afflict, blight, burden, injure, plague, saddle, scourge, torment, trouble, vex, weigh down. **3** (*to excommunicate*) damn, denounce, excommunicate.

~*v.i.* (*to swear, to utter imprecations*) blaspheme, swear.

~*n.* **1** (*a solemn invocation of divine vengeance* (*upon*)) imprecation, invocation, malediction. **2** (*a profane oath*) blasphemy, expletive, oath, obscenity, profanity, swear word. **3** (*the evil imprecated*) affliction, bane, burden, calamity, disaster, evil, hardship, misfortune, ordeal, plague, scourge, torment, tribulation, trouble, vexation. **4** (*anything which causes evil or trouble*) jinx, spell. **5** (*a sentence of excommunication*) ban, denunciation, excommunication.

cursory *a.* (*hasty, careless*) brief, careless, casual, desultory, fleeting, hasty, hurried, offhand, passing, perfunctory, quick, rapid, slapdash, slight, summary, superficial. ANTONYMS: thorough.

curt *a.* (*abrupt, esp. rudely terse*) abrupt, blunt, brief, brusque, concise, gruff, laconic, offhand, rude, sharp, short, snappish, succinct, summary, tart, terse, unceremonious, uncivil.

curve *n.* (*a line of which no three consecutive points are in a straight line*) arc, arch, bend, camber, crescent, curvature, loop, turn.

~*v.t.* (*to cause to bend without angles*) arc, arch, bend, bow, coil, curl, hook, inflect, spiral, swerve, turn, twist, wind. ANTONYMS: straighten.

custody *n.* **1** (*guardianship, security*) care, charge, custodianship, guardianship, keeping, protection, safe keeping, security, supervision, trusteeship, ward, watch. **2** (*imprisonment, confinement*) confinement, detention, imprisonment, incarceration.

custom *n.* **1** (*a habitual use or practice*) convention, etiquette, fashion, form, habit, manner, mode, observance, policy, practice, procedure, ritual, routine, rule, style, tradition, usage, use, way, wont. **2** (*frequenting a shop to purchase*) business, clients, customers, patronage, support, trade.

customary *a.* (*habitual, usual*) accepted, accustomed, acknowledged, common, confirmed, conventional, established, everyday, familiar, fashionable, general, habitual, normal, ordinary, popular, regular, routine, traditional, usual, wonted. ANTONYMS: exceptional, unusual.

customer *n.* **1** (*a purchaser*) buyer, client, consumer, purchaser, shopper. **2** (*a person who purchases regularly from a particular shop or business*) patron, regular. **3** (*a person, a fellow*) (*coll.*) bloke, (*coll.*) chap, character, fellow, (*coll.*) guy, person.

cut[1] *v.t.* **1** (*to penetrate or wound with a sharp instrument*) gash, incise, lacerate, nick, notch, open, penetrate, pierce, score, slash, slice, slit, stab, stick, wound. **2** (*to divide with a sharp-edged instrument*) divide, separate. ANTONYMS: join. **3** (*to sever, to hew*) chop, cleave, clip, detach, dock, fell, hack, hew, lop, mow, reap, sever. **4** (*to trim or clip*) carve, clip, slice, trim. **5** (*to form by cutting*) chip, chisel, chop, engrave, fashion, form, inscribe, saw, sculpt, shape, whittle. **6** (*to reduce by cutting*) contract, pare, prune, rationalize, reduce, slash, slim down. ANTONYMS: augment, expand. **7** (*to shorten* (*a play or book*)) abbreviate, abridge, condense, crop, curtail, excise, mutilate, shorten. **8** (*to intersect, to cross*) cross, intersect, meet. **9** (*to divide into two* (*as a pack of cards*)) dissect, divide, part, segment, split. **10** (*to wound deeply*) affront, aggrieve, distress, grieve, hurt, offend, pain, upset, wound. **11** (*to leave, to give up*) abstain from, cut out, give up, leave. **12** (*to ignore deliberately a person that one might be expected to greet*) avoid, cold-shoulder, (*coll.*) freeze out, ignore, rebuff, renounce, send to Coventry, slight, snub, spurn. ANTONYMS: acknowledge, greet. **13** (*to record a song etc. on* (*a master tape, disc etc.*)) (*coll.*) lay down, record.

cut² n. **1** (*an opening or wound made by cutting*) gash, graze, incision, laceration, nick, opening, slash, slit, wound. **2** (*anything done or said that hurts the feelings*) affront, dig, hurt, insult, jibe, offence, slight, snub. **3** (*the omission of a part of a play*) deletion, excision, omission. **4** (*a channel, a groove*) channel, groove, slit, trench. **5** (*a part cut off*) chop, cutback, cutting, reduction. **6** (*the shape in which a thing is cut, style*) configuration, fashion, form, look, mode, shape, style. **7** (*a share, esp. of money*) percentage, piece, portion, (*coll.*) rake-off, share, slice.

cute a. **1** (*attractive, pretty*) adorable, amusing, appealing, attractive, charming, dainty, delightful, engaging, lovable, lovely, pretty, sweet, winning, winsome. ANTONYMS: repulsive. **2** (*cunning, clever*) adroit, astute, canny, clever, crafty, cunning, sharp, shrewd.

cutting a. **1** (*sharp-edged*) keen, penetrating, piercing, sharp. **2** (*wounding the feelings deeply*) distressing, hurtful, offensive, upsetting, wounding. **3** (*sarcastic, biting*) acid, acrimonious, barbed, bitter, caustic, malicious, pointed, sarcastic, sardonic, scathing, sneering, stinging, trenchant, vicious, vitriolic.

cycle n. **1** (*a series of events or phenomena recurring in the same order*) circle, course, sequence, series, succession. **2** (*the period in which a series of events is completed*) phase, revolution, rotation, round. **3** (*a long period, an age*) aeon, age, epoch, era, period.

cynical a. (*bitter, sarcastic*) bitter, contemptuous, derisive, distrustful, ironic, misanthropic, mocking, pessimistic, sarcastic, sardonic, sceptical, scoffing, scornful, sneering, suspicious, unbelieving.

D

dab *v.t.* (*to press with a soft substance*) blot, daub, pat, press, smudge, stipple, tap, touch, wipe.

~*n.* **1** (*a light stroke or wipe with a soft substance*) pat, press, stroke, tap, touch. **2** (*a small amount of a soft substance dabbed*) bit, (*coll.*) dollop, drop, (*coll.*) smidgen, speck, spot, touch, trace.

dabble *v.t.* (*to wet by little dips*) dip, moisten, paddle, spatter, splash, spray, sprinkle, wet.

~*v.i.* (*to do or practise anything in a superficial manner*) dally, dip into, flirt with, play at, scratch the surface of, tinker with, toy with, trifle with.

dabbler *n.* (*a person who dabbles with or in any subject*) amateur, dallier, dilettante, layman, laywoman, potterer, tinkerer, trifler. ANTONYMS: professional.

daft *a.* **1** (*weak-minded, imbecile*) dimwitted, dull-witted, feeble-minded, (*coll.*) not all there, (*coll.*) not the full shilling, simple, simple-minded, slow, slow-witted, (*coll.*) touched. ANTONYMS: bright, clever, intelligent. **2** (*foolish, silly*) absurd, asinine, (*coll.*) cracked, crazy, fatuous, foolish, idiotic, inane, insane, ludicrous, lunatic, mad, nonsensical, ridiculous, senseless, silly, stupid, thoughtless. ANTONYMS: clever, sensible, serious, solemn. **daft about** (*very fond of*) besotted by, (*coll.*) crazy about, doting on, (*coll.*) dotty about, enamoured of, (*sl.*) gone on, infatuated by, (*coll.*) mad about, (*coll.*) nuts about, (*sl.*) nutty about, obsessed by, (*coll.*) potty about, sweet on.

dagger *n.* (*a short two-edged weapon adapted for stabbing*) bayonet, blade, dirk, knife, poniard, stiletto. **at daggers drawn** (*on hostile terms*) at loggerheads, at odds, at war, fighting, hostile, on bad terms, quarrelling, rowing. ANTONYMS: friendly, in harmony, on good terms. **to look daggers** (*to look with fierceness*) frown, glare, glower, look black, lower, scowl. ANTONYMS: grin, smile.

daily *a.* **1** (*happening or recurring every day*) (*formal*) circadian, diurnal, everyday, (*formal*) quotidian. ANTONYMS: weekly, yearly. **2** (*ordinary, usual*) common, commonplace, day-to-day, everyday, habitual, ordinary, regular, routine, usual. ANTONYMS: extraordinary, irregular, uncommon, unusual.

~*adv.* **1** (*day by day*) day after day, day by day, every day, once a day, (*formal*) per diem. **2** (*often*) frequently, often, regularly. ANTONYMS: rarely, seldom.

dainty *a.* **1** (*pretty, delicate*) delicate, elegant, exquisite, fine, graceful, neat, petite, pretty, tasteful. ANTONYMS: awkward, clumsy, inelegant, maladroit, ugly. **2** (*pleasing to the taste, choice*) appetizing, choice, delectable, delicious, flavoursome, luscious, palatable, savoury, tasty, toothsome. ANTONYMS: disgusting, flavourless, unappetizing. **3** (*fastidious, delicate*) (*coll.*) choosy, delicate, discriminating, fastidious, finicky, fussy, meticulous, nice, particular, (*coll.*) picky, refined, scrupulous. ANTONYMS: coarse, uncouth, undiscriminating.

~*n.* (*a delicacy; a choice morsel*) confection, delicacy, fancy, sweetmeat, titbit.

dais *n.* (*a platform*) platform, podium, stage, stand.

dale *n.* (*a valley, esp. in the English Midlands*) glen, vale, valley.

dally *v.i.* **1** (*to trifle (with), to treat frivolously*) flirt (with), (*coll.*) fool around (with), play (with), toy (with), treat frivolously, trifle (with). **2** (*to delay, to waste time*) (*coll.*) cool one's heels, dawdle, delay, (*coll.*) dilly-dally, drag one's feet, hang about, (*coll.*) kick one's heels, kill time, linger, loiter, take one's time, tarry. ANTONYMS: hasten, hurry, make haste.

dam *n.* (*a barrier*) bank, barrage, barricade, barrier, embankment, hindrance, obstruction, wall.

damage *n.* **1** (*injury or detriment to any person or thing*) defacement, detriment, devastation, harm, havoc, hurt, impairment, injury, loss, mischief, mutilation, suffering, vandalism. ANTONYMS: improvement, reparation. **2** (*pl.*) (*reparation in money for injury sustained*) compensation, indemnity, reimbursement, reparation, restitution, satisfaction.

~*v.t.* (*to cause damage to*) be detrimental to, deface, devastate, do damage to, do mischief to, harm, hurt, impair, inflict loss on, injure, mar, mutilate, ruin, spoil, vandalize, wreak havoc on, wreck. ANTONYMS: fix, improve, mend, repair.

damaging *a.* (*harmful*) deleterious, detrimental, disadvantageous, harmful, injurious, prejudicial, ruinous, unfavourable. ANTONYMS: advantageous, favourable, improving.

damn *v.t.* **1** (*to condemn, to criticize harshly*) attack, berate, blast, castigate, censure, condemn, criticize, denounce, inveigh against, lambast, reprimand, reprove, scold, (*sl.*) slam, (*coll.*) slate. ANTONYMS: admire, commend, congratulate, praise. **2** (*to condemn to eternal punishment*) (*formal*) anathematize, curse, doom, excommunicate, execrate, proscribe. ANTONYMS: bless, exalt.
~*v.i.* (*to swear profanely*) blaspheme, curse, swear.
~*n.* (*a negligible amount*) (*sl.*) brass farthing, (*coll.*) hoot, iota, jot, (*coll.*) tinker's curse, (*coll.*) two hoots, whit.

damnable *a.* (*atrocious, despicable*) abominable, atrocious, base, despicable, detestable, disagreeable, execrable, foul, hateful, heinous, hideous, horrendous, horrible, infernal, nasty, objectionable, obnoxious, repugnant, repulsive, revolting, unpleasant. ANTONYMS: admirable, fine, pleasant, praiseworthy, worthy.

damnation *n.* **1** (*condemnation to eternal punishment*) anathema, (*formal*) anathematization, ban, curse, excommunication, execration, proscription. **2** (*eternal punishment*) doom, eternal punishment, hell, perdition. ANTONYMS: eternal life, heaven, salvation. **3** (*condemnation*) berating, castigation, censure, condemnation, criticism, denunciation, lambasting, reprimand, reproof, scolding, (*sl.*) slamming, (*coll.*) slating. ANTONYMS: admiration, commendation, congratulation, praise.

damned *a.* **1** (*condemned to everlasting punishment*) accursed, condemned, cursed, doomed, excommunicated, lost. ANTONYMS: blessed. **2** (*hateful, execrable*) accursed, annoying, confounded, infernal, nasty, uncooperative, wretched.

damning *a.* (*suggesting guilt*) accusatorial, condemnatory, implicating, implicatory, incriminating.

damp *a.* (*slightly wet; clammy*) clammy, dank, dripping, drizzly, humid, moist, rainy, sodden, soggy, wet, wettish. ANTONYMS: bone dry, dry.
~*n.* **1** (*humidity, moisture*) clamminess, dampness, dankness, drizzle, humidity, moistness, sogginess, wet, wetness. ANTONYMS: aridity, dry, dryness. **2** (*discouragement*) check, cloud, (*coll.*) cold water, curb, damper, depression, deterrent, discouragement, gloom, hindrance, impediment, obstacle, pall, restraint. ANTONYMS: encouragement, incentive, inspiration.
~*v.t.* **1** (*to moisten*) dampen, humidify, moisten,

wet. ANTONYMS: dry. **2** (*to check, to depress*) check, chill, cool, curb, dampen, dash, deaden, decrease, depress, diminish, discourage, dispirit, dull, inhibit, lessen, limit, moderate, put a damper on, smother, stifle, throw cold water on. ANTONYMS: encourage, increase, inspire.

damper *n.* **to put a damper on** (*to discourage, to stifle*) check, curb, damp, dampen, dash, depress, discourage, dispirit, limit, smother, stifle, throw cold water on. ANTONYMS: encourage, increase, inspire.

dampness *n.* (*moistness*) clamminess, dankness, drizzle, humidity, moistness, sogginess, wet, wetness. ANTONYMS: aridity, dry, dryness.

dance *v.i.* **1** (*to move, usu. to music, with rhythmical steps*) (*N Am. sl.*) cut a rug, (*sl.*) hoof it, (*coll.*) shake a leg, (*facet.*) trip the light fantastic. **2** (*to frolic, to move in a lively way*) bounce, caper, frolic, gambol, hop, jig, jump, pirouette, prance, romp, skip.
~*n.* (*a dancing party, a ball*) ball, dancing party, disco, (*sl.*) hop, (*sl.*) rave.

dandle *v.t.* (*to bounce* (*a child*) *up and down on one's knees*) bounce, jiggle, ride.

dandy *n.* (*a man extravagantly concerned with his appearance*) beau, coxcomb, (*N Am. sl.*) dude, fop, man about town, popinjay, (*coll.*) sharp dresser, (*sl.*) swell.

danger *n.* **1** (*risk, hazard; exposure to injury or loss*) endangerment, hazard, insecurity, jeopardy, peril, precariousness, risk, vulnerability. **2** (*anything that causes peril*) hazard, menace, peril, pitfall, threat.

dangerous *a.* **1** ((*of a person*) *likely to cause harm*) desperate, harmful, high-risk, reckless, unsafe. ANTONYMS: harmless, innocuous. **2** (*not protected*) chancy, exposed, hazardous, insecure, perilous, precarious, risky, unsafe, vulnerable. ANTONYMS: invulnerable, safe, secure. **3** ((*of a situation*) *in which there is a risk of harm*) menacing, nasty, ominous, threatening, treacherous, ugly. ANTONYMS: harmless, nice.

dangle *v.i.* **1** (*to hang loosely*) hang, hang down, sway, swing, trail. **2** (*to hang about, esp. to obtain some favour*) hang about, hang around, hover.
~*v.t.* **1** (*to cause to dangle*) brandish, flourish, sway, swing, wave. **2** (*to hold out* (*a temptation, bait etc.*)) entice (someone) with, hold out, lure (someone) with, tempt (someone) with.

dangling *a.* (*that dangles*) drooping, hanging, loose, swaying, swinging, trailing.

dank *a.* (*damp, moist*) chilly, clammy, damp, dripping, drizzly, humid, moist, wet. ANTO-NYMS: dry.

dapper *a.* **1** (*spruce, smart*) chic, (*coll.*) natty, out of a bandbox, smart, smartly-dressed, soigné(e), spruce, stylish, tidy, trim, well-groomed, well-turned-out. ANTONYMS: dishevelled, ill-groomed, messy, (*coll.*) sloppy, slovenly, unkempt, untidy. **2** (*brisk, active*) active, agile, brisk, lively, nimble, sprightly, spry. ANTONYMS: clumsy, inactive, stiff.

dapple *v.t.* (*to streak, to variegate*) bedaub, bespeckle, dot, fleck, mottle, speckle, spot, stipple, streak, variegate.

dappled *a.* (*streaked, variegated*) brindled, dotted, flecked, marked, mottled, particoloured, piebald, pied, pinto, speckled, spotted, stippled, streaked, variegated.

dare *v.i.* (*to have the courage or impudence* (*to*)) be brave enough (to), be so bold as (to), have the courage (to), have the impudence (to), have the nerve (to), hazard, make so bold as (to), pluck up courage (to), presume, risk, venture.
~*v.t.* **1** (*to attempt, to venture on*) attempt, brave, confront, face. **2** (*to challenge, to defy*) challenge, defy, goad, taunt, throw down the gauntlet to.
~*n.* (*a challenge to do something dangerous*) challenge, provocation, taunt, ultimatum.

daredevil *n.* (*a fearless, reckless person*) adventurer, desperado, madcap, stuntman, stunt-woman.
~*a.* (*fearless, reckless*) adventurous, audacious, bold, brave, daring, death-defying, fearless, madcap, reckless. ANTONYMS: cautious, (*coll.*) chicken, cowardly, timid.

daring *a.* (*bold; reckless*) adventurous, audacious, bold, brave, daredevil, fearless, intrepid, reckless, undaunted, valiant. ANTO-NYMS: cautious, (*coll.*) chicken, cowardly, timid.

dark *a.* **1** (*without light*) black, dim, gloomy, ill-lit, murky, pitch, pitch-black, pitch-dark, poorly lit, unlighted, unlit. ANTONYMS: bright, brightly lit, lit. **2** (*shaded*) cloudy, dim, shaded, shadowy, shady, sunless. ANTONYMS: bright, sunny. **3** (*dark-haired or dark-skinned*) black, brunette, dark-haired, dark-skinned, dusky, olive-skinned, sallow, swarthy. ANTO-NYMS: blond(e), fair, fair-haired, fair-skinned, light-skinned. **4** (*gloomy, sombre*) dejected, depressed, dismal, doleful, gloomy, grave, grim, joyless, melancholy, miserable, morbid, morose, mournful, pessimistic, sad, sombre. ANTONYMS: cheerful, glad, happy, optimistic. **5** (*obscure, ambiguous*) abstruse, ambiguous,

arcane, baffling, complex, complicated, cryptic, deep, enigmatic, incomprehensible, mysterious, obscure, puzzling, recondite, unfathomable. ANTONYMS: clear, comprehensible, explicit, obvious, plain. **6** (*hidden, concealed*) concealed, hidden, secret, (*coll.*) under wraps, unrevealed. ANTONYMS: exposed, known, open, public, revealed. **7** (*without spiritual or intellectual enlightenment*) benighted, ignorant, uncultivated, uneducated, unenlightened, unlettered, unschooled. **8** (*wicked, evil*) bad, base, criminal, evil, foul, infamous, iniquitous, nefarious, sinful, vile, villainous, wicked. ANTONYMS: good, law-abiding, pure, virtuous. **9** (*cheerless*) bleak, cheerless, dim, dingy, drab, gloomy. ANTONYMS: bright, cheerful. **10** (*sad, sullen*) angry, brooding, dour, forbidding, frowning, glowering, menacing, moody, sulky, sullen, threatening. ANTONYMS: cheerful, friendly, pleasant.
~*n.* **1** (*absence of light*) blackness, darkness, dimness, gloom, murk. ANTONYMS: light. **2** (*night, nightfall*) dead of night, dusk, evening, night, nightfall, night-time, twilight. ANTONYMS: day, daylight, daytime, light. **in the dark** (*in ignorance* (*about*)) ignorant (of), unaware (of), unconscious (of), unenlightened, uninformed. **to keep something dark** (*to keep silent about something*) conceal, cover up, hide, hush up, keep secret. ANTONYMS: disclose, divulge, publicize, reveal.

darken *v.i.* **1** (*to become dark or darker*) blacken, cloud over, dim, grow dark, grow darker, grow dim. ANTONYMS: bright, brighten, grow light, lighten. **2** (*to become gloomy or troubled*) become menacing, become moody, become threatening, grow angry, grow sullen, grow troubled. ANTONYMS: become cheerful, brighten, lighten.
~*v.t.* **1** (*to make dark or darker*) black, blacken, dim, make dark, make darker, tan. ANTONYMS: lighten, light up. **2** (*to render gloomy*) cast a pall over, damp, dampen, deject, depress, dispirit, put a damper on. ANTONYMS: cheer up, enliven, gladden.

darkness *n.* **1** (*the state or quality of being dark*) blackness, dark, dimness, gloom, murk, murkiness, night, nightfall, shade, shadows. ANTONYMS: brightness, daylight, light. **2** (*obscurity*) abstruseness, ambiguity, arcaneness, complexity, complication, incomprehensibility, obscurity. ANTONYMS: clarity, comprehensibility, explicitness, plainness. **3** (*ignorance*) ignorance, lack of education, lack of knowledge. **4** (*wickedness*) badness, baseness, evil, foulness, infamy, iniquity, nefariousness, sin, sinfulness, vileness, villainy, wickedness. ANTONYMS: goodness, virtue.

darling n. **1** (*a person who is dearly loved*) beloved, love, loved one. **2** (*a favourite*) apple of one's eye, blue-eyed boy/ girl, (*N Am.*) fair-haired boy/ girl, favourite, pet. ANTONYMS: bête noire, bugbear, thorn in the flesh. **3** (*a lovable or charming person or thing*) charmer, pet, poppet, sweetheart, (*coll.*) sweetie. ANTONYMS: horror. **4** (*used as a term of endearment*) dear, dearest, (*esp. N Am.*) honey, love, (*coll.*) pet, sweetheart.
~a. **1** (*dearly loved*) adored, beloved, cherished, dear, dearest, loved, much loved, precious. ANTONYMS: hated, loathed. **2** (*charming, de-lightful*) adorable, attractive, captivating, charming, (*coll.*) cute, delightful, enchanting, engaging, lovely, sweet, winsome. ANTONYMS: frightful, horrible, nasty.

darn v.t. (*to mend with stitches that cross or interweave*) mend, patch, repair, sew, stitch.
~n. (*a place mended by darning*) mend, patch, repair.

dart n. **1** (*a short-pointed missile weapon thrown by the hand*) arrow, barb. **2** (*a sudden leap or rapid movement*) bolt, bound, dash, leap, run, (*coll.*) scoot, speed, sprint. ANTO-NYMS: amble, stroll.
~v.t. (*to shoot or send forth suddenly*) cast, fling, send, shoot, throw.
~v.i. (*to run or move swiftly*) bolt, bound, dash, fly, hurry, race, run, rush, (*coll.*) scoot, shoot, speed, sprint, (*coll.*) tear. ANTONYMS: amble, stroll.

dash v.i. **1** (*to strike against something and break*) batter, beat, break, crash, smash, strike. **2** ((*usu. with off or away*) *to run or drive quickly*) bolt, bound, dart, fly, hurry, race, run, rush, (*coll.*) scoot, shoot, speed, sprint, (*coll.*) tear. ANTONYMS: amble, stroll.
~v.t. **1** (*to throw violently or suddenly*) cast, fling, hurl, pitch, slam, sling, smash, throw. **2** (*to frustrate; to confound*) abash, baulk, blight, cast down, confound, daunt, depress, destroy, discourage, dishearten, dispirit, foil, frustrate, put a damper on, ruin, sadden, shatter, spoil, thwart. ANTONYMS: cheer up, encourage, in-spire.
~n. **1** (*a rapid movement*) bolt, bound, dart, race, run, rush, sprint, spurt. **2** (*a small amount*) bit, drop, grain, hint, little, pinch, smack, soup-çon, sprinkling, suggestion, suspicion, tinge, touch, trace. ANTONYMS: lot, (*coll.*) masses, (*coll.*) ton. **3** (*daring; display*) brio, élan, flair, flourish, liveliness, ostentation, panache, (*coll.*) pizazz, spirit, style, verve, vigour, vivacity. ANTONYMS: dullness, tedium.

dashing a. **1** (*daring, spirited*) animated, bold, daring, dazzling, debonair, dynamic, lively, spirited, stylish, swashbuckling. ANTONYMS:

lacklustre, lifeless, stolid, timid. **2** (*showy, smart*) dapper, elegant, flamboyant, jaunty, (*coll.*) natty, showy, smart, (*coll.*) sporty, (*coll.*) swish. ANTONYMS: frumpish, inelegant.

dastardly a. (*cowardly and nasty*) base, con-temptible, cowardly, craven, despicable, low, mean, nasty, (*coll.*) rotten, vile. ANTONYMS: brave, gallant, noble.

data n.pl. (*facts or information from which other things may be deduced*) details, facts, facts and figures, information, material, stat-istics.

date n. **1** (*a fixed point of time*) age, epoch, era, period, stage, time. **2** (*the time at which any-thing happened or is appointed to take place*) day, scheduled time, set time, time. **3** (*a social or other engagement (usu. with a romantic partner)*) appointment, assignation, engage-ment, meeting, rendezvous, tryst. **4** (*a person with whom one has a date*) beau, boyfriend, escort, friend, girlfriend, partner, regular part-ner, steady.
~v.t. **1** (*to note or fix the date of*) assign a date to, determine the date of, put a date to. **2** (*to have a romantic relationship with*) court, go around with, go out with, (*coll.*) go steady with, have a relationship with, see, take out.
~v.i. **1** (*to begin (from)*) begin (from), belong (to), come (from), exist (from), originate (in). **2** (*to become dated*) become dated, become obsol-ete, become old-fashioned, become outmoded, get out of date, show one's age.

dated a. (*old-fashioned*) antiquated, démodé, obsolete, old-fashioned, (*coll.*) old hat, out-dated, out of date, passé, unfashionable. ANTO-NYMS: fashionable, modern, (*coll. sometimes derog.*) trendy, up-to-date.

daub v.t. **1** (*to smear or coat with a soft adhesive substance*) bedaub, besmear, coat, cover, plas-ter, smear, spatter, splatter. **2** (*to apply (colour) in a crude or inartistic style*) plaster, slap on, spatter, splatter.
~n. (*a smear*) blotch, patch, smear, smudge, splodge.

daunt v.t. (*to intimidate, to dishearten*) alarm, deter, dishearten, dispirit, frighten, intimidate, put off, scare, strike fear into, subdue, terrify, unnerve. ANTONYMS: encourage, give heart to, hearten, inspire.

dawdle v.i. (*to be slow, to linger*) be slow, dally, delay, (*coll.*) dilly-dally, go slowly, (*coll.*) hang about, kill time, loiter, move at a snail's pace, take one's time, trail along, walk slowly. ANTO-NYMS: hasten, hurry, rush.

dawn n. **1** (*the break of day*) break of day, cock-crow, crack of dawn, daybreak, daylight, early morning, first light, morning, sunrise, (*N Am.*) sunup. ANTONYMS: (*poet.*) gloaming, nightfall, sunset. **2** (*the first rise or appearance*) advent, appearance, arrival, beginning, birth, commencement, dawning, development, emergence, genesis, inception, onset, origin, outset, rise, start. ANTONYMS: close, death, end. **to dawn upon** (*to be realized gradually by*) be realized, come into one's head, come into one's mind, cross one's mind, enter one's mind, flash across one's mind, occur to one, pass through one's mind, register, strike.

day *n.* **1** (*the time the sun is above the horizon*) broad daylight, daylight, daylight hours, daytime. ANTONYMS: night, night-time. **2** (*a space of twenty-four hours, esp. that commencing at midnight*) calendar day, twenty-four-hour period. **3** (*any specified point or date*) date, scheduled time, set time, time. **4** (*an age*) age, epoch, era, period, time. **5** (*period of vigour or prosperity*) height, heyday, peak, prime, zenith. **day after day** (*with monotonous regularity, every day continuously*) ceaselessly, continually, continuously, persistently, regularly, relentlessly, without respite. **day and night** (*always*) all the time, always, constantly, continually, continuously, incessantly, perpetually. ANTONYMS: now and again, occasionally, periodically. **day by day** (*gradually, every day*) evenly, every day, gradually, progressively, steadily. ANTONYMS: abruptly, all at once, all of a sudden, suddenly.

daybreak *n.* (*the first appearance of daylight*) break of day, cockcrow, crack of dawn, daylight, early morning, first light, morning, sunrise, (*N Am.*) sunup. ANTONYMS: late at night, nightfall, sunset.

daydream *n.* **1** (*a romantic scheme voluntarily indulged in*) castle in Spain, castle in the air, dream, fond hopes, pipe dream, wishful thinking. **2** (*reverie*) musing, reverie, woolgathering.
~*v.i.* **1** (*to have daydreams*) build castles in Spain, build castles in the air, dream, fantasize, have pipe dreams. **2** (*to be in a reverie*) be in a brown study, be lost in thought, dream, indulge in wool-gathering, muse, stare into space.

daydreamer *n.* (*a person who indulges in daydreams*) dreamer, fantasist, pipe dreamer, visionary, Walter Mitty.

daylight *n.* **1** (*the light of day, as opposed to that of the moon or artificial light*) broad daylight, light of day, natural light, sunlight. ANTONYMS: artificial light, darkness. **2** (*dawn*) break of day, cockcrow, crack of dawn, dawn, daybreak, early morning, first light, morning,

sunrise, (*N Am.*) sunup. ANTONYMS: (*poet.*) gloaming, nightfall, sunset. **to see daylight 1** (*to begin to understand*) become aware, (*coll.*) catch on, comprehend, discern, fathom, (*coll.*) get the idea, (*sl.*) get the picture, realize, see the light, (*sl.*) twig, understand. ANTONYMS: be ignorant, be in the dark, be unaware. **2** (*to draw near to the end of a task*) approach the end, be nearly finished, have the end in sight.

daze *v.t.* (*to stupefy, to confuse*) befuddle, bewilder, confuse, muddle, shock, stun, stupefy.
~*n.* (*the state of being dazed*) bewilderment, confusion, shock, state of shock, stupor, trance.

dazzle *v.t.* **1** (*to overpower with a glare of light*) bedazzle, blind. **2** (*to bewilder with rapidity of motion, stupendous number etc.*) amaze, astonish, astound, (*coll.*) bowl over, fascinate, hypnotize, impress, overawe, overpower, overwhelm, stagger, strike dumb, take one's breath away.

dazzling *a.* (*brilliant, very impressive*) brilliant, glittering, glorious, sensational, sparkling, splendid, stunning, superb. ANTONYMS: dull, ordinary, unexceptional.

dead *a.* **1** (*having ceased to live*) deceased, defunct, departed, extinct, gone, late. ANTONYMS: alive, living. **2** (*having no life, lifeless*) inanimate, lifeless. **3** (*benumbed, temporarily deprived of the power of action*) benumbed, insensible, numb, numbed, paralysed. **4** (*unconscious or unappreciative*) apathetic, cold, dispassionate, frigid, indifferent, insensitive, lukewarm, unappreciative, unresponsive, unsympathetic. ANTONYMS: appreciative, passionate, sensitive. **5** (*obsolete, useless*) barren, discontinued, inactive, ineffective, inoperative, invalid, lapsed, obsolete, outdated, outmoded, stagnant, sterile, unprofitable, useless. ANTONYMS: active, effective, fertile, live, operative, profitable. **6** (*extinct*) at an end, ended, extinguished, finished, passed, quelled, quenched, terminated. ANTONYMS: active, alive, living. **7** (*dull, flat*) boring, dull, flat, humdrum, insipid, stale, tedious, uninteresting, vapid. ANTONYMS: fascinating, interesting, sparkling, vivacious. **8** (*certain, unerring*) accurate, exact, on the mark, precise, sure, true, unerring, unfailing. ANTONYMS: imprecise, inaccurate, inexact, uncertain, unsure. **9** (*complete*) absolute, downright, entire, out-and-out, thorough, total, unqualified, utter. **10** (*sudden*) abrupt, hurried, quick, rapid, sudden, swift. ANTONYMS: gradual, slow. **11** (*exhausted*) dead beat, exhausted, fatigued, played out, (*esp. N Am., coll.*) pooped, spent, tired, tired out, worn out. ANTONYMS: energetic, fresh, full of energy, refreshed.

~*adv.* (*absolutely, completely*) absolutely, categorically, completely, entirely, quite, thoroughly, totally, utterly. ANTONYMS: partially, partly.

deaden *v.t.* 1 (*to diminish the vitality or force of*) abate, blunt, check, damp, dampen, diminish, dull, impair, lessen, reduce, smother, stifle, suppress, weaken. ANTONYMS: activate, increase, strengthen. 2 (*to make insensible, to dull*) benumb, desensitize, numb, paralyse.

deadlock *n.* (*a position in which no progress can be made*) cessation, full stop, halt, impasse, stalemate, stand-off, standstill, stop.

deadly *a.* 1 (*causing death; fatal*) dangerous, death-dealing, destructive, fatal, lethal, malignant, mortal, poisonous, toxic, venomous, virulent. ANTONYMS: benign, harmless, safe. 2 (*like death*) ashen, deathlike, deathly, ghastly, ghostly, pale, pallid, wan. ANTONYMS: healthy, red-cheeked, ruddy. 3 (*very boring*) boring, dull, humdrum, lacklustre, monotonous, tedious, uninteresting, wearisome. ANTONYMS: electrifying, fascinating, interesting, riveting. 4 (*implacable, irreconcilable*) (*coll.*) at each other's throats, fierce, grim, hostile, implacable, irreconcilable, mortal, savage, unrelenting. 5 (*intense*) extreme, great, inordinate, intense, marked, strong. ANTONYMS: low-key, mild, weak. 6 (*accurate, unerring*) accurate, on target, on the mark, precise, sure, true, unerring, unfailing. ANTONYMS: imprecise, inaccurate, off the mark.
~*adv.* (*extremely, intensively*) absolutely, categorically, completely, entirely, excessively, extremely, intensively, thoroughly, totally, utterly.

deadpan *a.* (*with an expressionless face or manner*) blank, empty, expressionless, impassive, inexpressive, inscrutable, poker-faced, straight-faced. ANTONYMS: eloquent, expressive.

deaf *a.* 1 (*incapable or dull of hearing*) dull of hearing, hard of hearing, having hearing difficulties, hearing-impaired, stone-deaf, with impaired hearing. ANTONYMS: sharp-eared. 2 (*unwilling to hear, refusing to listen*) heedless, indifferent, oblivious, uncaring, unconcerned, unhearing, unmindful, unmoved. ANTONYMS: concerned, heedful, mindful.

deafen *v.t.* (*to make wholly or partially deaf*) deprive of hearing, impair one's hearing, make deaf.

deafening *a.* (*extremely loud*) booming, ear-splitting, over-loud, overpowering, resounding, reverberating.

deal *n.* 1 (*a bargain, a business transaction*) agreement, arrangement, bargain, business transaction, contract, negotiation, pact, transaction, understanding. 2 (*an indefinite quantity*) amount, degree, extent, quantity. 3 (*a particular form of treatment at a person's hands*) handling, terms, treatment, usage.
~*v.t.* 1 (*to distribute or give in succession (as cards)*) allocate, apportion, assign, dispense, distribute, divide out, dole out, give out, hand out, mete out, share out. 2 (*to administer*) administer, deliver, give. **to deal in** (*to be engaged in; to trade in*) be engaged in, buy and sell, do business in, engage in, trade in, traffic in. **to deal with** 1 (*to take action in respect of, to handle*) attend to, be responsible for, cope with, handle, manage, see to, sort out, tackle, take care of. 2 (*to have to do with*) be about, concern, consider, discuss, have to do with, treat of. 3 (*to behave towards*) act, behave, conduct oneself.

dealer *n.* 1 (*a trader, a merchant*) chandler, merchant, retailer, salesman, salesperson, saleswoman, trader, trafficker, vendor, wholesaler. 2 (*a jobber on the Stock Exchange*) broker, jobber.

dealing *n.* (*behaviour, treatment*) actions, behaviour, business practices, conduct, treatment.

dealings *n.pl.* (*trade*) business, commerce, negotiations, relations, trade, trafficking, transaction, truck. **to have dealings with** (*to deal or associate with*) associate with, deal with, have relations with, have truck with.

dear *a.* 1 (*beloved, cherished*) adored, beloved, cherished, darling, dearest, favourite, precious, prized, treasured, valuable, valued. ANTONYMS: despised, hated, worthless. 2 (*precious, valuable*) cherished, favourite, precious, prized, treasured, valuable, valued. ANTONYMS: despised, hated, worthless. 3 (*costly, of a high price*) at a premium, costly, exorbitant, expensive, high-priced, overpriced, (*coll.*) pricey, (*coll.*) steep, (*coll.*) up-market. ANTONYMS: cheap, inexpensive, low-cost. 4 (*attractive, delightful*) adorable, attractive, captivating, charming, (*coll.*) cute, darling, delightful, enchanting, engaging, lovable, lovely, sweet, winning, winsome. ANTONYMS: frightful, horrible, nasty.
~*n.* 1 (*a term of endearment*) darling, dearest, (*esp. N Am.*) honey, love, (*coll.*) pet, precious, sweet, sweetheart. 2 (*a nice person*) angel, darling, pet, sweetheart. ANTONYMS: monster, (*coll.*) pig, (*coll.*) swine.
~*adv.* (*dearly, at a high price*) at a great cost, at a heavy cost, at a high price, dearly.

dearly *adv.* 1 (*very much*) greatly, profoundly,

very much. **2** (*with affection, sincerely*) affectionately, devotedly, fondly, lovingly, with affection.

dearth *n.* (*a scarcity; lack*) deficiency, inadequacy, insufficiency, lack, meagreness, paucity, scantiness, scarceness, scarcity, shortage, shortness, sparseness, want. ANTONYMS: excess, over-abundance, surfeit, surplus.

death *n.* **1** (*extinction of life; the act of dying*) decease, dying, end, loss of life, passing. ANTONYMS: birth. **2** (*decay, destruction*) annihilation, destruction, end, eradication, extinction, finish, obliteration, ruin, ruination, termination, undoing. ANTONYMS: beginning, emergence, rise. **3** (**Death**) (*the personification of death*) the angel of death, the grim reaper. **4** (*slaughter*) bloodshed, killing, massacre, murder, slaying.

deathless *a.* (*immortal, imperishable*) eternal, everlasting, immortal, imperishable, memorable, perpetual, timeless, undying, unfading. ANTONYMS: ephemeral, fleeting, mortal, transitory.

debacle *n.* (*a complete failure*) catastrophe, collapse, disaster, downfall, failure, fiasco, havoc, ruination.

debar *v.i.* **1** (*to exclude from approach or action*) bar, blackball, deny, exclude, keep out, preclude, refuse admission to, shut out. ANTONYMS: admit, let in. **2** (*to prohibit, to forbid*) bar, disallow, exclude, forbid, prevent, prohibit, proscribe, stop, veto. ANTONYMS: allow, permit.

debase *v.t.* **1** (*to lower in quality or value*) abase, cheapen, degrade, demean, demote, depress, devalue, diminish, disgrace, dishonour, downgrade, drag down, humble, humiliate, lower, reduce, shame. ANTONYMS: enhance, improve. **2** (*to adulterate*) adulterate, bastardize, contaminate, corrupt, defile, depreciate, impair, mar, pervert, poison, pollute, spoil, sully, taint, vitiate. ANTONYMS: purify.

debatable *a.* **1** (*open to discussion or argument*) arguable, borderline, contestable, disputable, doubtful, dubious, (*coll.*) iffy, moot, open, questionable, uncertain, undecided, unsettled, unsure. ANTONYMS: certain, settled. **2** (*contentious*) contentious, controversial, problematic.

debate *v.t.* **1** (*to contend about by words or arguments, esp. publicly*) argue, contend, contest, discuss, question, wrangle. ANTONYMS: agree. **2** (*to consider*) cogitate, consider, deliberate, meditate upon, mull over, ponder, reflect, ruminate, think, weigh.
~*n.* (*a formal or public*) *discussion of a question*) altercation, argument, cogitation, consideration, contention, contest, controversy,

deliberation, discussion, disputation, dispute, meditation, polemic, reflection, row, wrangle. ANTONYMS: agreement.

debauched *a.* (*having loose morals*) abandoned, corrupt, debased, degenerate, depraved, dissipated, dissolute, immoral, licentious, loose, perverted, profligate, sleazy, unprincipled, wanton.

debonair *a.* **1** (*having self-assurance, carefree*) breezy, buoyant, carefree, charming, cheerful, dashing, gay, insouciant, jaunty, light-hearted, nonchalant, self-assured, sprightly, sunny. **2** (*pleasing in manner and bearing*) affable, civil, courteous, dapper, elegant, genial, genteel, gracious, obliging, polite, refined, smooth, suave, urbane, well-bred.

debt *n.* **1** (*something which is owing from one person to another, esp. a sum of money*) arrears, bill, debit, deficit. ANTONYMS: asset. **2** (*obligation, liability*) claim, commitment, due, duty, indebtedness, liability, obligation, responsibility.

debut *n.* (*a first appearance before the public, esp. of a performer*) beginning, bow, coming out, entrance, first appearance, inauguration, initiation, introduction, launch, launching, premiere, presentation.

decadent *a.* **1** (*having low moral or cultural standards*) corrupt, debauched, degenerate, depraved, dissipated, dissolute, immoral. **2** (*self-indulgent, affected*) affected, debased, degenerative, degraded, self-indulgent, waning.

decay *v.i.* **1** (*to rot*) atrophy, corrode, decompose, go off, mortify, moulder, perish, putrefy, rot, spoil, turn. **2** (*to decline in excellence*) decline, degenerate, fall off. **3** (*to fall away, to deteriorate*) crumble, decrease, deteriorate, diminish, disintegrate, dissolve, dwindle, ebb, fall away, shrivel, wane, waste away, wear away, wither.
~*n.* **1** (*gradual failure or decline*) collapse, decline, deterioration, fading, failure. **2** (*wasting away, gradual dissolution*) consumption, decadence, degeneracy, degeneration, dissolution, wasting away. **3** (*decomposition of dead tissue*) atrophy, decomposition, gangrene, mortification, mould, putrefaction, putrescence, rot.

deceit *n.* **1** (*the act of deceiving*) deceiving, deception, dissimulation. **2** (*a tendency to deceive*) craftiness, cunning, deceitfulness, deceptiveness, dishonesty, hypocrisy, slyness, treachery. **3** (*trickery, deception*) cheating, chicanery, deception, dissimulation, double-dealing, duplicity, fraudulence, guile, pretence, trickery. **4** (*a stratagem, a dishonest act*) artifice, blind, cheat, (*sl.*) con, deception, double-cross, fraud, hoax, imposture, lie, manoeuvre, ploy, ruse, (*N Am., sl.*) scam, (*coll.*) sting, stratagem, subterfuge, swindle, trick, wile.

deceitful *a.* **1** (*given to deceit*) artful, crafty, (*coll.*) crooked, cunning, deceptive, designing, dishonest, double-dealing, duplicitous, guileful, hypocritical, insincere, scheming, sly, sneaky, treacherous, tricky, underhand, untrustworthy, wily. ANTONYMS: honest. **2** (*intended to deceive*) counterfeit, false, fraudulent, illusory, (*coll.*) phoney.

deceive *v.t.* (*to mislead deliberately or knowingly*) bamboozle, beguile, cheat, (*sl.*) con, delude, (*coll.*) double-cross, dupe, fool, hoax, hoodwink, lead on, mislead, outwit, (*coll.*) pull a fast one on, (*sl.*) stiff, (*coll.*) sting, swindle, (*coll.*) take for a ride, (*coll.*) take in, trick.

decent *a.* **1** (*becoming, seemly*) appropriate, becoming, befitting, comely, fit, fitting, proper, seemly, suitable. ANTONYMS: inappropriate, unseemly. **2** (*modest; decorous*) chaste, decorous, pure, virtuous. **3** (*respectable*) dignified, nice, polite, presentable, respectable, tasteful. **4** (*passable, tolerable*) acceptable, adequate, all right, ample, average, competent, fair, middling, moderate, passable, reasonable, satisfactory, sufficient, tolerable. ANTONYMS: unacceptable, unsatisfactory. **5** (*kind and honest*) accommodating, considerate, courteous, friendly, generous, gracious, helpful, honest, honourable, kind, nice, obliging, thoughtful.

deception *n.* **1** (*the act of deceiving*) craftiness, cunning, deceit, deceitfulness, deceptiveness, dissimulation, double-dealing, duplicity, fraudulence, guile, hypocrisy, insincerity, sophistry, treachery, trickery. ANTONYMS: candour, honesty. **2** (*something which deceives*) artifice, bluff, cheat, deceit, decoy, fraud, hoax, illusion, imposture, intrigue, lie, manoeuvre, pretence, ruse, sham, stratagem, subterfuge, swindle, trick, wile.

deceptive *a.* (*tending or apt to deceive*) ambiguous, bogus, counterfeit, deceitful, delusive, dishonest, fake, fallacious, false, fraudulent, illusory, misleading, mock, shifty, specious, spurious, unreliable, untruthful.

decide *v.t.* **1** (*to come to a decision about, to determine*) adjudge, adjudicate, choose, decree, determine, elect, judge, make up one's mind, purpose, rule. **2** (*to settle by adjudging* (*victory or superiority*)) conclude, end, resolve, settle, terminate. ANTONYMS: dither, procrastinate.

decided *a.* **1** (*clear, unmistakable*) absolute, categorical, certain, clear, definite, distinct, evident, incontestable, indisputable, irrefutable, marked, obvious, positive, pronounced, settled, sure, unambiguous, unequivocal, unmistakable, unquestionable. ANTONYMS: doubtful. **2** (*determined, firm*) adamant, assertive, decisive, deliberate, determined, emphatic, firm, fixed, resolute, strong-willed, unfaltering, unhesitating, unswerving, unwavering. ANTONYMS: irresolute, undecided.

decision *n.* **1** (*the act or result of deciding*) conclusion, determination, outcome, resolution, result. **2** (*the determination of a trial or contest*) arbitration, decree, finding, judgement, ruling, sentence, settlement, verdict. **3** (*resolution, firmness of character*) character, decisiveness, determination, firmness, purpose, resoluteness, resolution, resolve, steadfastness. ANTONYMS: indecision, irresolution.

decisive *a.* **1** (*determining the outcome of something*) absolute, categorical, conclusive, critical, crucial, deciding, definitive, fateful, final, significant. ANTONYMS: inconclusive. **2** (*able to make decisions quickly*) decided, determined, emphatic, firm, forceful, incisive, resolute, strong-minded, trenchant, unwavering, vacillating. ANTONYMS: indecisive, weakminded.

declaration *n.* **1** (*the act of declaring or proclaiming*) acknowledgement, affirmation, assertion, attestation, averment, avowal, deposition, disclosure, proclamation, profession, promulgation, pronouncement, protestation, publication, revelation. **2** (*something which is declared or proclaimed*) announcement, notification, proclamation, pronouncement. **3** (*an official announcement, esp. of constitutional laws*) announcement, edict, manifesto. **4** (*an affirmation in lieu of oath*) affirmation, statement.

declare *v.t.* **1** (*to assert or affirm positively*) affirm, announce, assert, asseverate, attest, aver, avow, certify, claim, confirm, maintain, ratify, say, state, submit, swear, testify, utter, validate. ANTONYMS: deny. **2** (*to announce publicly*) announce, broadcast, confess, convey, decree, disclose, herald, make known, manifest, proclaim, profess, promulgate, pronounce, publish, reveal, show, trumpet.

decline *v.i.* **1** (*to deteriorate, to decay*) decay, decrease, degenerate, deteriorate, diminish, drop, dwindle, ebb, fade, fail, fall off, flag, lessen, peter out, shrink, sink, subside, taper off, wane, weaken. ANTONYMS: increase. **2** (*to refuse something politely*) abstain, avoid, deny, forgo, refuse, reject, turn down. ANTONYMS:

accept. **3** (*to slope downwards*) descend, dip, incline, sink, slant, slope. ANTONYMS: ascend, rise. **4** (*to droop*) droop, sag, stoop.
~*n.* **1** (*a falling-off*) abatement, downturn, dwindling, ebb, falling-off, lessening, reduction, slump. **2** (*deterioration, decay*) decay, deterioration, diminution, drop. ANTONYMS: improvement. **3** (*gradual approach to extinction or death*) decay, decrepitude, degeneration, deterioration, enfeeblement, failing, senility, weakening, worsening.

decompose *v.t.* **1** (*to resolve into constituent elements*) break up, crumble, disintegrate, dissolve, make fall apart, separate. **2** (*to separate the elementary parts of*) analyse, atomize, break down, dissect.
~*v.i.* (*to become decomposed; to putrefy*) decay, fester, go off, moulder, putrefy, rot, spoil, turn.

decorate *v.t.* **1** (*to make more attractive by ornamentation*) adorn, beautify, bedeck, deck, garnish, grace, ornament. **2** (*to be an embellishment to*) dress up, elaborate, embellish, embroider, festoon, (*sl.*) tart up, trim. **3** (*to confer a medal or other badge of honour on*) cite, honour. **4** (*to paint, paper etc. (a room or house)*) colour, do up, fix up, furbish, paint, paper, renovate, restore, wallpaper.

decoration *n.* **1** (*the act of decorating*) adornment, beautification, elaboration, embellishment, enrichment, garnishing, ornamentation. **2** (*ornamentation, ornament*) bauble, flounce, flourish, frill, ornament, trimming. **3** (*a medal or other badge of honour*) award, badge, citation, colours, laurel, medal, order, ribbon.

decorous *a.* **1** (*behaving in a polite and decent manner*) appropriate, becoming, befitting, comely, correct, decent, dignified, fit, fitting, genteel, polite, proper, respectable, seemly, suitable, well-behaved. ANTONYMS: unfit, unseemly. **2** (*in good taste*) elegant, refined, tasteful.

decoy *n.* (*a bait, an attraction*) attraction, bait, enticement, inducement, lure, trap.
~*v.t.* **1** (*to lure into a trap or snare*) ensnare, entrap. **2** (*to allure, to entice*) allure, attract, bait, entice, inveigle, lure, seduce, tempt, trick.

decrease[1] *v.i.* (*to become less*) abate, contract, decline, diminish, drop, dwindle, ease, fail, fall off, lessen, let up, lower, peter out, reduce, shrink, slacken, subside, wane. ANTONYMS: increase.
~*v.t.* (*to make less, to reduce in size gradually*) curtail, cut, reduce.

decrease[2] *n.* (*lessening, a diminution*) abatement, contraction, curtailment, cut, cutback,

decline, diminution, downturn, dwindling, ebb, falling-off, lessening, loss, lowering, recession, reduction, shrinkage, slackening, subsidence, wane. ANTONYMS: increase.

decree *n.* (*a law or ordinance made by superior authority*) canon, command, decision, demand, dictate, dictum, directive, edict, enactment, injunction, judgement, law, mandate, order, ordinance, precept, proclamation, regulation, ruling, statute.
~*v.t.* **1** (*to command by a decree*) charge, command, demand, dictate, direct, enjoin, lay down, mandate, order, prescribe, proclaim, pronounce, proscribe, rule. **2** (*to ordain or determine*) adjudge, decide, determine, ordain.

decrepit *a.* **1** (*weak from age and infirmities*) aged, ancient, crippled, debilitated, disabled, doddering, elderly, enfeebled, feeble, frail, incapacitated, infirm, old, senile, tottering, unfit, wasted, weak, worn out. ANTONYMS: youthful. **2** (*dilapidated, decayed*) antiquated, battered, broken-down, crumbling, decayed, derelict, deteriorated, dilapidated, ramshackle, rickety, run-down, superannuated, tumbledown, weather-beaten, worn out.

dedicate *v.t.* **1** (*to apply wholly to some purpose, person or thing*) apply, commit, devote, give over to, pledge, surrender, yield. **2** (*to inscribe or address (a work of art) to a friend or patron*) address, assign, inscribe. **3** (*to consecrate solemnly to God or to some sacred purpose*) bless, consecrate, hallow, sanctify, set apart.

dedication *n.* **1** (*devotion to a pursuit or cause*) adherence, allegiance, commitment, devotion, faithfulness, fidelity, loyalty, singlemindedness, wholeheartedness. ANTONYMS: apathy, indifference. **2** (*a dedicatory inscription*) address, inscription, message.

deduce *v.t.* (*to draw as a conclusion by reasoning, to infer*) assume, conclude, derive, divine, draw, gather, glean, infer, presume, reason, suppose, surmise, (*sl.*) suss out, understand, work out.

deduct *v.t.* (*to take away, to subtract*) dock, knock off, reduce by, remove, subtract, take away, take from, take off, take out, withdraw. ANTONYMS: add.

deduction *n.* **1** (*the act of deducting*) abstraction, decrease, diminution, reduction, removal, subtraction, withdrawal. ANTONYMS: addition. **2** (*the act of deducing*) inferring, reasoning, working-out. **3** (*an inference, a consequence*) assumption, conclusion, consequence, finding, inference, result.

deed n. **1** (a thing done with intention) act, action. **2** (an illustrious exploit, an achievement) accomplishment, achievement, exploit, feat. **3** (fact, reality) fact, reality, truth. **4** (a document containing the terms of a contract) agreement, contract, document, instrument, title.

deep a. **1** (extending far down) bottomless, immeasurable, profound, unfathomable, yawning. **2** (having a thickness or measurement back or down) broad, thick. **3** (dark-coloured) dark, intense, rich, strong, vivid. ANTONYMS: light, pale. **4** (profound, penetrating) abstruse, arcane, difficult, discerning, esoteric, impenetrable, incomprehensible, inscrutable, mysterious, obscure, profound, recondite. ANTONYMS: shallow, superficial. **5** (heartfelt, earnest) ardent, earnest, genuine, grave, heartfelt, profound, serious, sincere. **6** (intense, extreme) extreme, great, heinous, intense, profound, serious, severe. **7** (low in pitch, full in tone) bass, booming, full, low, resonant, reverberative, sonorous. **8** (well-versed, sagacious) acute, learned, penetrating, perspicacious, sagacious, well-versed, wise. **9** (artful, secretive) artful, astute, crafty, cunning, devious, insidious, knowing, scheming, secretive, shrewd.
~adv. **1** (deeply, far down) deeply, far down. **2** (profoundly, intensely) heavily, intensely, profoundly.
~n. **1** (anything deep) depth, vastness. **2** (the sea) (coll.) briny, high seas, main, ocean, sea. **3** (a deep place, an abyss) abyss, cavity, gulf. **in deep water** (in trouble) having problems, (coll.) in a jam, in a mess, in a tight corner, in difficulty, in dire straits, in distress, in trouble.

deepen v.t. (to make deeper) burrow, dig out, dredge, excavate, hollow, mine, scrape out, sink.
~v.i. (to become deeper) amplify, augment, concentrate, enhance, expand, grow, increase, intensify, magnify, reinforce, strengthen.

deface v.t. **1** (to spoil the appearance or beauty of) blemish, damage, deform, disfigure, flaw, harm, impair, injure, mar, mutilate, ruin, spoil, sully, tarnish, vandalize. **2** (to erase, to obliterate) destroy, eradicate, erase, obliterate.

defamatory a. (speaking maliciously about a person) abusive, calumnious, denigrating, derogatory, disparaging, injurious, insulting, libellous, maledictory, slanderous, vilifying, vituperative. ANTONYMS: complimentary.

default n. **1** (failure to do something, esp. to meet financial liabilities) dereliction, failure, lapse. **2** (lack, absence) absence, deficit, lack, neglect, omission, oversight, want. **3** (a fault, a defect) defect, deficiency, fault.
~v.i. (to fail to do something, esp. to meet financial liabilities) dishonour, dodge, evade, fail, fall short, neglect, (coll.) rat, swindle, (coll.) welsh.

defeat v.t. **1** (to overthrow, to conquer) beat, conquer, crush, destroy, discomfit, (coll.) lick, master, overpower, overthrow, overwhelm, quell, repulse, rout, subdue, subjugate, thrash, vanquish, whip, worst. ANTONYMS: succumb, yield. **2** (to resist successfully, to frustrate) check, foil, frustrate, thwart. **3** (to baffle) baffle, confound, disappoint.
~n. (overthrow, esp. of an army) conquest, discomfiture, overthrow, (sl.) pasting, repulse, rout, thrashing, trouncing. ANTONYMS: success, victory.

defect[1] n. **1** (absence of something essential to perfection or completeness) absence, lack, shortcoming, shortfall, want. **2** (moral imperfection, failing) failing, foible, frailty, inadequacy, weakness. **3** (blemish) blemish, blotch, error, fault, flaw, imperfection, mark, mistake, spot, taint.

defect[2] v.i. (to desert one's country or cause for the other side) abandon, change sides, desert, forsake, go over, mutiny, rebel, revolt.

defective a. **1** (imperfect, faulty) broken, deficient, faulty, flawed, impaired, imperfect, inadequate, incomplete, insufficient, lacking, (coll.) on the blink, out of order, short, wanting. ANTONYMS: perfect, working. **2** (mentally or physically lacking) abnormal, backward, feeble-minded, retarded, simple, subnormal.

defence n. **1** (the state or act of defending) cover, deterrence, guard, immunity, protection, resistance, safeguard, security, shelter. ANTONYMS: attack. **2** (something which defends) armament, barricade, screen, shield. **3** (pl.) (fortifications, fortified posts) bastion, bulwark, buttress, fortification, rampart. **4** (justification, vindication) argument, exoneration, explanation, extenuation, justification, plea, reason, vindication. ANTONYMS: accusation. **5** (excuse) apology, excuse, explanation, extenuation, justification, plea. **6** (the defendant's reply to the plaintiff's declaration or charges) declaration, denial, plea, pleading, testimony.

defend v.t. **1** (to shield from harm) arm, cover, fend off, fight for, fortify, guard, parry, preserve, protect, safeguard, screen, secure, shelter, shield, ward off, watch over. ANTONYMS: attack. **2** (to maintain by argument) argue for, assert, back, champion, endorse, espouse, justify, maintain, plead, represent, speak up for, stand by, stand up for, stick up for, support, sustain, uphold, vindicate. ANTONYMS: accuse.

defensive *a.* **1** (*serving to defend*) defending, protective, safeguarding. **2** (*over-anxious to defend oneself against* (*expected*) *criticism*) over-anxious, (*coll.*) uptight. **3** (*protective, not aggressive*) on guard, protective, vigilant, watchful. ANTONYMS: aggressive.

defer[1] *v.t.* (*to put off; to postpone*) lay aside, postpone, put off, put on ice, (*coll.*) put on the back burner, set aside, suspend.
~*v.i.* (*to delay; to procrastinate*) adjourn, delay, procrastinate, temporize. ANTONYMS: hasten.

defer[2] *v.i.* (*to yield to the opinion of another*) accede (to), agree (to), bow (to), capitulate (to), cede (to), comply (with), give ground, give in (to), give way (to), respect, submit (to), yield (to). ANTONYMS: oppose, resist.

deference *n.* **1** (*submission to the views or opinions of another*) acquiescence, capitulation, complaisance, compliance, non-resistance, obedience, obeisance, submission, surrender, yielding. ANTONYMS: disobedience, non-compliance. **2** (*respect, regard*) attention, civility, consideration, courtesy, esteem, homage, honour, obeisance, politeness, regard, respect, reverence, thoughtfulness, veneration. ANTONYMS: disrespect, impertinence.

defiant *a.* **1** (*openly disobedient*) disobedient, disrespectful, insolent, insubordinate, mutinous, rebellious, unruly. ANTONYMS: obedient, respectful. **2** (*challenging; hostile in attitude*) aggressive, antagonistic, belligerent, bold, brazen, challenging, hostile, obstinate, opposed, provocative, pugnacious, recalcitrant, self-willed, stubborn, truculent.

deficient *a.* **1** (*defective; falling short*) defective, faulty, flawed, impaired, imperfect, incomplete, weak. ANTONYMS: perfect. **2** (*not fully supplied*) inadequate, insufficient, lacking, meagre, scant, scarce, sketchy, skimpy, wanting. ANTONYMS: abundant.

deficit *n.* (*a falling short of revenue as compared with expenditure*) arrears, default, deficiency, loss, shortage, shortfall. ANTONYMS: surplus.

define *v.t.* **1** (*to state the meaning of* (*a word etc.*)) characterize, clarify, describe, designate, detail, determine, explain, expound, identify, interpret, name, specify, spell out, state. **2** (*to fix with precision* (*as duties etc.*)) delineate, establish, fix, lay down, mark out, outline. **3** (*to determine the limits of*) bound, circumscribe, demarcate, limit.

definite *a.* **1** (*limited, fixed precisely*) determinate, determined, fixed, limited, marked. ANTONYMS: confused, loose. **2** (*exact, clear*) clear, distinct, exact, explicit, obvious,

particular, plain, precise, specific, unambiguous, unequivocal, well-defined. ANTONYMS: inexact, unclear. **3** (*positive, sure*) assured, certain, confirmed, decided, guaranteed, positive, settled, sure.

definitely *adv.* **1** (*in a definite manner*) absolutely, categorically, clearly, decidedly, easily, finally, obviously, patently, plainly, positively, unequivocally, unmistakably, unquestionably. **2** (*certainly*) certainly, indubitably, surely, undoubtedly, without doubt.

definition *n.* **1** (*the act of defining*) delimitation, delineation, demarcation, fixing, outlining, settling, specification. **2** (*a statement of the meaning of a word etc.*) clarification, description, elucidation, explanation, explication, exposition, interpretation, meaning. **3** (*clearness of form, esp. of an image*) clarity, clearness, contrast, distinctness, focus, precision, resolution, sharpness.

definitive *a.* **1** (*decisive; conclusive*) absolute, accurate, categorical, complete, conclusive, decisive, final, positive, ultimate. **2** (*being the best or most authoritative of its kind*) authoritative, best, consummate, exhaustive, perfect, thorough.

deflate *v.t.* **1** (*to let down* (*a pneumatic tyre, balloon etc.*) *by allowing the gas to escape*) collapse, empty, flatten, let down, puncture. ANTONYMS: blow up, inflate. **2** (*to reduce the inflation of* (*currency*)) depreciate, depress, devalue. **3** (*to humiliate*) chasten, disconcert, discourage, dispirit, humble, humiliate, mortify, squash. **4** (*to reduce the importance of*) diminish, reduce.

deflect *v.i.* **1** (*to turn or move to one side*) divert, move aside, turn aside. **2** (*to deviate*) bend, deviate, diverge, glance off, ricochet, shy, slew, swerve, veer.
~*v.t.* **1** (*to cause to turn or deviate*) bounce off, divert, move aside, turn aside. **2** (*to ward off, to avoid* (*criticism etc.*)) avert, avoid, ward off.

deformed *a.* **1** (*misshapen*) bent, blemished, crooked, distorted, malformed, mangled, marred, misbegotten, misshapen, twisted, warped. **2** (*disfigured, ugly*) crippled, disfigured, gross, grotesque, ugly.

defunct *a.* **1** (*dead, deceased*) dead, deceased, departed, extinct, gone. **2** (*no longer in operation or use*) bygone, expired, inoperative, invalid, non-existent, obsolete, outmoded, out of commission, redundant, unusable.

defy *v.t.* **1** (*to disregard openly*) despise, disobey, disregard, flout, scorn, slight, spurn. **2** (*to baffle*) baffle, defeat, elude, foil, frustrate, repel, repulse, resist, thwart, withstand. **3** (*to* *challenge to do or substantiate*) brave, challenge, confront, dare, face, provoke.

degenerate[1] *a.* **1** (*having fallen from a better to worse state*) degraded, deteriorated, fallen, inferior, lapsed. **2** (*having low moral standards*) base, corrupt, debased, debauched, decadent, depraved, dissolute, ignoble, immoral, low, mean, perverted, reprobate, vile.
~*n.* (*a degenerate person or animal*) debauchee, pervert, profligate, rake, reprobate, roué.

degenerate[2] *v.i.* **1** (*to fall off in quality from a better to a worse state*) decay, decline, decrease, deteriorate, fall off, lapse, rot, sink, slip, weaken, worsen. ANTONYMS: improve. **2** (*to revert to a lower type*) backslide, regress, retrogress, revert.

degrade *v.t.* **1** (*to reduce in rank or dignity*) demote, downgrade. ANTONYMS: elevate, promote, raise. **2** (*to remove from office*) break, cashier, depose, unseat. **3** (*to debase, to lower*) abase, cheapen, corrupt, debase, demean, injure, lower, pervert, reduce. ANTONYMS: raise. **4** (*to bring into contempt*) discredit, disgrace, dishonour, disparage, humble, humiliate, mortify, shame. ANTONYMS: exalt. **5** (*to wear away*) disintegrate, wear away, wear down.
~*v.i.* (*to degenerate*) degenerate, depreciate, deteriorate.

degrading *a.* (*humiliating, debasing*) cheapening, contemptible, debasing, demeaning, discreditable, disgraceful, dishonourable, humiliating, shameful, undignified, unworthy.

degree *n.* **1** (*a step in progression or rank*) division, extent, gradation, grade, interval, limit, mark, measure, notch, point, rung, scale, stage, step, unit. **2** (*relative position or rank*) caste, class, estate, grade, level, order, position, rank, situation, standing, station, status. **3** (*relative condition or quality*) ambit, calibre, condition, extent, intensity, level, magnitude, measure, proportion, quality, quantity, range, ratio, scale, scope, severity, standard.

deity *n.* **1** (*divine nature*) divinity. **2** (*a god or goddess*) creator, god, goddess, godhead, idol, immortal, Prime Mover, supreme being. ANTONYMS: mortal.

dejected *a.* (*depressed in spirit*) (*coll.*) blue, crestfallen, depressed, despondent, disconsolate, disheartened, dispirited, doleful, downcast, downhearted, forlorn, gloomy, glum, heartbroken, low-spirited, melancholy, miserable, morose, sad, unhappy. ANTONYMS: cheerful, happy.

delay *v.t.* **1** (*to postpone, to put off*) defer, hold over, postpone, procrastinate, protract, put off, put on hold, put on ice, shelve, stall, suspend,

temporize. **2** (*to hinder, to make* (*someone*) *late*) arrest, bog down, check, detain, halt, hinder, hold back, hold up, impede, obstruct, retard, set back, slow up, stop. ANTONYMS: accelerate, speed up.
~*v.i.* **1** (*to put off action*) hesitate, temporize, vacillate. **2** (*to linger*) dally, dawdle, drag, hang back, lag, linger, loiter, mark time, shilly-shally, tarry.
~*n.* **1** (*postponement, retardation*) deferment, deferral, postponement, procrastination, retardation, stay, suspension. **2** (*time lost before action; hindrance*) break, breather, check, detention, gap, hiatus, hindrance, hold-up, impediment, interlude, interruption, interval, lull, obstruction, setback, stoppage, suspension, wait.

delectable *a.* **1** (*delightful, highly pleasing*) adorable, agreeable, charming, choice, dainty, delightful, enjoyable, enticing, gratifying, inviting, lush, pleasant, pleasing, pleasurable, satisfying. ANTONYMS: disagreeable, unpleasant. **2** (*delicious to the taste*) appetizing, delicious, luscious, (*coll.*) scrumptious, tasty, toothsome, (*coll.*) yummy. ANTONYMS: unappetizing.

delegate[1] *n.* **1** (*a person authorized to transact business*) agent, representative. **2** (*a deputy*) agent, deputy. **3** (*a member of a deputation or committee*) ambassador, commissioner, emissary, envoy, legate, nuncio, plenipotentiary.

delegate[2] *v.t.* **1** (*to depute as an agent or representative, with authority to transact business*) accredit, appoint, authorize, commission, depute, designate, empower, mandate, name, nominate. **2** (*to entrust the performance of or responsibility for* (*a task etc.*) *to another*) assign, charge, commit, consign, devolve, entrust, give, hand down, hand over, pass on, transfer.

delete *v.t.* (*to erase*) blot out, cancel, cross out, cut out, edit, efface, eliminate, erase, excise, expunge, obliterate, remove, rub out, score out, strike out, wipe out.

deliberate[1] *a.* **1** (*done or carried out intentionally*) calculated, conscious, considered, designed, intended, intentional, planned, prearranged, preconceived, premeditated, purposeful, studied, thoughtful, wilful. ANTONYMS: accidental, inadvertent. **2** (*circumspect, cautious*) calm, careful, cautious, circumspect, collected, composed, cool, discreet, fastidious, heedful, methodical, painstaking, prudent, punctilious, systematic, thoughtful, wary. **3** (*leisurely*) even, leisurely, measured, paced, ponderous, regular, slow, steady, sure, unhurried. ANTONYMS: hasty, hurried.

deliberate[2] *v.i.* **1** (*to weigh matters in the mind, to ponder*) cogitate, evaluate, meditate, mull over, ponder, reflect, think, weigh. **2** (*to consider, to discuss*) consider, consult, debate, discuss, take counsel.

deliberately *adv.* (*intentionally*) calculatingly, cold-bloodedly, consciously, determinedly, emphatically, intentionally, knowingly, on purpose, pointedly, purposely, resolutely, studiously, wilfully, wittingly. ANTONYMS: accidentally, unwittingly.

delicacy *n.* **1** (*the quality of being delicate*) elegance, exquisiteness, fineness, grace, gracefulness. **2** (*anything that is subtly pleasing to the senses*) beauty, subtlety. **3** (*a luxury, a choice morsel*) dainty, luxury, morsel, savoury, titbit, treat. **4** (*fineness of texture, design or workmanship*) daintiness, fineness, lightness. ANTONYMS: coarseness. **5** (*fragility, susceptibility to injury*) flimsiness, fragility, frailty, infirmity, susceptibility, weakness. ANTONYMS: robustness. **6** (*accuracy of perception*) discrimination, fastidiousness, scrupulousness. **7** (*fineness, sensitiveness*) sensibility, sensitivity. **8** (*gentleness, consideration for others*) consideration, gentleness, perceptiveness, sensitivity, tact, taste.

delicate *a.* **1** (*exquisite in form or texture*) elegant, exquisite, fine, graceful. **2** (*fine, smooth*) fine, smooth. ANTONYMS: coarse, rough. **3** (*subtle in colour or style*) faint, muted, pastel, soft, subdued, subtle. ANTONYMS: garish, strong. **4** (*easily injured, fragile*) ailing, breakable, debilitated, feeble, flimsy, fragile, frail, perishable, sickly, tender, weak. **5** (*requiring careful treatment; critical*) critical, difficult, (*coll.*) hairy, precarious, sensitive, (*coll.*) sticky, (*coll.*) ticklish, touchy, tricky. **6** (*sensitive, subtly perceptive*) appreciative, perceptive, sensitive. **7** (*fastidious, tender*) dainty, demure, effeminate, fastidious, finicky, nice, prudish, scrupulous, soft, squeamish, tender. **8** (*refined, pure*) chaste, pure, refined. **9** (*gentle, considerate*) considerate, diplomatic, discreet, gentle, sensitive, tactful. **10** (*skilful, dexterous*) accurate, deft, dexterous, ingenious, skilful. **11** (*dainty, palatable*) choice, dainty, delicious, palatable.

delicious *a.* (*giving great pleasure to the sense of taste*) agreeable, amusing, appetizing, charming, choice, delectable, delightful, enjoyable, entertaining, exquisite, luscious, nice, palatable, pleasant, pleasing, (*coll.*) scrumptious, succulent, tasty, toothsome. ANTONYMS: distasteful, unpleasant.

delight *v.t.* (*to please greatly, to charm*) amuse, captivate, charm, divert, enchant, enrapture,

entertain, entrance, excite, fascinate, gladden, gratify, please, ravish, rejoice, satisfy, thrill, tickle. ANTONYMS: disgust, displease.

~*v.i.* (*to be highly pleased; to take great pleasure* (*in*)) adore, appreciate, enjoy, feast (on), glory (in), indulge (in), like, love, luxuriate (in), relish, revel (in), savour.

~*n.* (*a state of great pleasure and satisfaction*) bliss, delectation, ecstasy, elation, felicity, gladness, gratification, happiness, joy, pleasure, rapture, satisfaction, transport. ANTONYMS: displeasure.

delighted *a.* (*extremely pleased and satisfied*) captivated, charmed, ecstatic, elated, enchanted, enraptured, happy, joyous, jubilant, overjoyed, over the moon, pleased, rapt, thrilled. ANTONYMS: dismayed.

delightful *a.* (*very pleasing and satisfying*) agreeable, amusing, captivating, charming, congenial, delectable, diverting, enchanting, engaging, entertaining, exciting, fascinating, gratifying, lovely, pleasant, pleasurable, rapturous, ravishing, thrilling. ANTONYMS: disagreeable, unpleasant.

delinquent *n.* (*an offender, a culprit*) criminal, culprit, defaulter, hooligan, lawbreaker, malefactor, miscreant, offender, villain, wrongdoer.

delirious *a.* **1** (*suffering from wandering in the mind, as a result of fever etc.*) feverish, rambling, wandering. ANTONYMS: clear-headed, lucid. **2** (*raving, madly excited*) crazy, demented, deranged, distracted, disturbed, hysterical, incoherent, insane, irrational, lunatic, mad, maddened, ranting, raving, unhinged, wild. ANTONYMS: sane, sensible. **3** (*frantic with delight or other excitement*) carried away, ecstatic, excited, frantic, frenzied, thrilled.

deliver *v.t.* **1** (*to distribute, to present*) bear, bring, carry, cart, convey, distribute, present, transport. **2** (*to give over, to hand on*) commit, consign, entrust, give over, grant, hand on, hand over, make over, transfer, turn over. **3** (*to free from danger or restraint*) emancipate, free, liberate, loose, redeem, release, rescue, save. **4** (*to assist at the birth of* (*a child*); *to give birth to*) bear, bring forth, give birth to. **5** (*to discharge, to send out*) acquit, discharge, dispense, feed, give forth, produce, provide, purvey, release, send forth, supply. **6** (*to pronounce formally or officially*) announce, broadcast, communicate, declare, enunciate, express, give forth, make known, present, proclaim, promulgate, pronounce, publish, utter. **7** (*to surrender, to give up*) cede, give up, relinquish, surrender, yield. **8** (*to aim successfully* (*a blow to an opponent, a ball to a teammate etc.*)) administer, aim, deal, direct, give, inflict, launch, send, strike, throw.

~*v.i.* (*to fulfil a promise, to live up to expectations*) (*coll.*) do the business, fulfil, perform.

delivery *n.* **1** (*the act of delivering*) consignment, conveyance, dispatch, distribution, shipment, transmission, transportation. **2** (*setting free, rescue*) deliverance, emancipation, escape, liberation, release, rescue. **3** (*transfer*) surrender, transfer. **4** (*a batch of letters etc. delivered*) batch, consignment, shipment. **5** (*the utterance of a speech*) articulation, elocution, enunciation, intonation, speech, utterance. **6** (*childbirth*) childbirth, confinement, labour, parturition.

delusion *n.* **1** (*the act of deluding*) deception, self-deception. **2** (*an error, a fallacy*) error, fallacy, misapprehension, misconception, mistake. **3** (*an erroneous idea in which the subject's belief is unshaken by facts*) fancy, hallucination, obsession, psychosis.

demand *n.* **1** (*an authoritative claim or request*) behest, bidding, claim, command, direction, order, request, requisition. **2** (*the thing demanded, esp. price*) charge, price, requirement. **3** (*a peremptory question*) inquiry, interrogation, question. ANTONYMS: answer. **4** (*desire to purchase or possess*) call, desire, market.
~*v.t.* **1** (*to ask for or claim with authority or as a right*) ask for, call for, claim, request, solicit. **2** (*to ask for in a peremptory manner*) challenge, exact, insist on, order. **3** (*to seek to ascertain by questioning*) interrogate, query, question. ANTONYMS: reply. **4** (*to need, to require*) call for, entail, involve, necessitate, need, require, take, want.

demanding *a.* (*requiring a lot of attention or energy*) challenging, difficult, exacting, exhausting, exigent, hard, laborious, taxing, tough, trying, wearing. ANTONYMS: easy.

democratic *a.* (*governed by the principles of democracy; favouring equality*) autonomous, egalitarian, popular, populist, representative, republican, self-governing. ANTONYMS: autocratic.

demolish *v.t.* **1** (*to pull down; to raze*) bulldoze, dismantle, flatten, knock down, level, pull down, raze, reduce, tear down. ANTONYMS: build, construct. **2** (*to ruin, to destroy*) annihilate, crush, defeat, destroy, devastate, (*coll.*) lick, obliterate, overturn, pulverize, ruin, terminate, (*esp. N Am., coll.*) trash, wreck. **3** (*to refute*) disprove, rebut, refute. **4** (*to eat up*) consume, devour, eat, gobble up, put away.

demon *n.* **1** (*an evil spirit supposed to have the power of taking possession of human beings*) evil spirit, fiend, ghoul. **2** (*a malignant supernatural being*) devil, fallen angel, imp, incubus, succubus. ANTONYMS: angel. **3** (*a very cruel or evil person*) monster, ogre, rogue, scoundrel, villain. **4** (*an extremely clever or skilful person*) ace, addict, fanatic, (*coll.*) freak, genius, master, wizard.

demonstrate *v.t.* **1** (*to show by logical reasoning or beyond the possibility of doubt*) establish, prove, show, testify. **2** (*to describe and prove by means of specimens and experiments*) describe, establish, exhibit, prove. **3** (*to display, to indicate*) display, expose, illustrate, indicate, make clear, manifest.
~*v.i.* (*to organize or take part in a public or military demonstration*) march, parade, picket, protest, rally.

demonstration *n.* **1** (*the act of demonstrating*) exhibition, illustration, indication. **2** (*clear, indubitable proof*) affirmation, confirmation, evidence, proof, substantiation, testimony, validation, verification. **3** (*an outward manifestation of feeling etc.*) expression, manifestation. **4** (*a public exhibition or declaration of principles, feelings etc. by any party*) (*coll.*) demo, lobby, march, parade, picket, protest, rally, sit-in. **5** (*an exhibition and description of objects for the purpose of teaching or showing how something works*) description, exhibition, explanation, exposition, presentation, test, trial.

demonstrative *a.* **1** (*manifesting one's feelings openly*) affectionate, communicative, effusive, emotional, expansive, expressive, gushing, loving, open, unconstrained, unreserved, unrestrained, warm. ANTONYMS: reserved, undemonstrative. **2** (*having the power of exhibiting and proving*) evidential, explanatory, expository, illustrative, indicative, representative, symptomatic. **3** (*conclusive*) absolute, certain, conclusive, convincing, definitive, indisputable, sure.

demoralize *v.t.* (*to lower the morale of, to discourage*) bewilder, crush, daunt, deject, depress, devitalize, disconcert, discourage, dishearten, dispirit, enfeeble, fluster, perturb, rattle, shake, subdue, undermine, unnerve, upset, weaken. ANTONYMS: encourage, hearten.

demure *a.* **1** (*reserved and modest*) decorous, diffident, discreet, grave, modest, reserved, reticent, retiring, sedate, shy, sober, staid, unassuming. ANTONYMS: brash, immodest. **2** (*affectedly modest*) affected, bashful, coy, priggish, prim, prissy, prudish, strait-laced. ANTONYMS: wanton.

denial *n.* **1** (*the act of denying*) contradiction, refusal. **2** (*a negative reply*) rebuff, refusal.

3 (*abjuration, disavowal*) abjuration, disavowal, disclaimer, dismissal, dissent, negation, prohibition, rejection, renunciation, repudiation, repulse, retraction, veto, withdrawal. ANTONYMS: confirmation.

denigrate *v.t.* **1** (*to defame*) asperse, (*coll.*) bad-mouth, belittle, decry, defame, disparage, impugn, (*coll.*) knock, malign, rubbish, run down, (*sl.*) slag off, slander, vilify. ANTONYMS: compliment, praise. **2** (*to blacken*) besmirch, blacken, defile, sully.

denomination *n.* **1** (*a religious group or sect*) belief, body, church, creed, cult, faith, group, order, persuasion, school, sect. **2** (*a kind, esp. of particular units (such as coins)*) body, category, class, classification, genus, group, kind, nature, variety. **3** (*a designation or title*) appellation, designation, identification, label, name, style, tag, term, title.

denounce *v.t.* **1** (*to accuse or condemn publicly*) accuse, arraign, attack, blame, brand, castigate, censure, charge, condemn, decry, denunciate, impugn, pillory, proscribe, rebuke, revile, ridicule, shame, stigmatize, vilify. **2** (*to inform against*) implicate, incriminate, inform against.

dense *a.* **1** (*compact; having its particles closely united*) close, close-knit, compact, compressed, condensed, impenetrable, solid, substantial, thick. **2** (*crowded close together*) crowded, jammed, packed, tight. **3** (*stupid, obtuse*) crass, dim, dull, (*coll.*) dumb, obtuse, slow, stolid, stupid, (*coll.*) thick. ANTONYMS: clever, quick.

dent *n.* **1** (*a depression such as is caused by a blow with a blunt instrument*) cavity, chip, concavity, crater, depression, dimple, dip, hole, hollow, impression, indentation, notch, pit. **2** (*a lessening*) diminution, lessening.
~*v.t.* **1** (*to make a dent in*) depress, dint, gouge, groove, hollow, imprint, indent, notch, press in, push in. **2** (*to have a diminishing effect on*) damage, diminish, reduce.

deny *v.t.* **1** (*to assert to be untrue or non-existent*) contradict, disagree, disprove, dispute, gainsay, oppose, rebuff, refute. ANTONYMS: agree, confirm. **2** (*to disown, to reject*) abjure, disavow, discard, disclaim, disown, forswear, recant, reject, renounce, repudiate, retract, revoke. ANTONYMS: accept, avow. **3** (*to refuse to grant*) begrudge, decline, disallow, forbid, negative, refuse, reject, turn down, veto, withhold. **4** (*to refuse admittance to*) bar, exclude, refuse admittance to. ANTONYMS: admit.

depart *v.i.* **1** (*to go away, to leave*) abscond, absent, check out, decamp, disappear, escape, exit, fly, go, go away, leave, quit, remove, retire, retreat, run off, set out, slope off, start out, vanish, withdraw. ANTONYMS: arrive, turn up. **2** (*to diverge, to deviate (from)*) abandon, break away, deviate, differ, digress, stray, swerve, turn aside, vary, veer. **3** (*to pass away, to die*) die, expire, pass away.

department *n.* **1** (*a separate part or branch of business or administration*) branch, bureau, division, office, part, section, sector, station, subdivision, unit. **2** (*an area of knowledge*) area, bailiwick, concern, domain, function, line, province, realm, responsibility, speciality, sphere, territory. **3** (*any one of the administrative divisions of a country, such as France*) district, division, province, region.

departure *n.* **1** (*the act of departing; leaving*) departing, disappearance, exit, exodus, going, leave-taking, leaving, removal, retirement, withdrawal. ANTONYMS: arrival. **2** (*the starting of a journey*) beginning, launch, start. **3** (*divergence, deviation*) abandonment, branching off, deviation, difference, digression, divergence, variation, veering.

depend *v.i.* **1** (*to be contingent, as to the result, on something else*) be contingent on, hang on, hinge on, pivot on, rest on, revolve around, turn on. **2** (*to rely for support or maintenance*) bank on, count on, lean on, rely on, trust in, turn to. **3** (*to trust, to reckon (on)*) confide (in), reckon (on), rely (on), trust (in).

dependable *a.* (*able to be depended upon*) faithful, loyal, reliable, reputable, responsible, staunch, steady, sure, true, trustworthy, trusty, unfailing. ANTONYMS: undependable, unreliable.

depict *v.t.* **1** (*to paint, to portray*) delineate, draw, illustrate, outline, paint, picture, portray, render, represent, reproduce, sculpt, sketch. **2** (*to describe or represent in words*) characterize, describe, detail, narrate, outline, sketch.

deplete *v.t.* **1** (*to reduce*) decrease, impoverish, lessen, reduce. ANTONYMS: increase. **2** (*to empty, to exhaust*) bankrupt, consume, drain, empty, evacuate, exhaust, expend, use up. ANTONYMS: augment, replenish.

deplorable *a.* **1** (*lamentable*) awful, calamitous, dire, disastrous, distressing, disturbing, grave, grievous, heartbreaking, lamentable, melancholy, miserable, pathetic, pitiable, regrettable, sad, troubling, unfortunate, upsetting, wretched. ANTONYMS: creditable, laudable. **2** (*unacceptably bad*) bad, blameworthy, despicable, discreditable, disgraceful, dishonourable, disreputable, execrable, opprobrious, reprehensible, scandalous, shameful. ANTONYMS: excellent, marvellous.

deport *v.t.* **1** (*to expel from one country to another*) banish, exile, expatriate, expel, extradite, oust, remove, transport. **2** (*to conduct or to behave* (*oneself etc.*)) acquit, act, bear, behave, carry, comport, conduct, hold.

depose *v.t.* **1** (*to remove from a throne or other high office*) demote, dethrone, dismiss, displace, oust, remove, unseat. ANTONYMS: enthrone. **2** (*to bear witness* (*that*), *to testify on oath to*) asseverate, avouch, bear witness, declare, testify.

deposit *v.t.* **1** (*to lay down, to place*) drop, lay down, locate, place, put, set, settle, sit. **2** (*to lodge for safety or as a pledge*) consign, lodge, set aside, store. **3** (*to lodge in a bank account*) bank, hoard, lodge, put away, save, (*coll.*) stash away.
~*n.* **1** (*a pledge, a first instalment*) advance payment, down payment, instalment, part payment, pledge, retainer, security, trust, warranty. **2** (*a sum of money lodged in a bank*) stake, sum. **3** (*matter accumulated or precipitated and left behind*) accumulation, alluvium, deposition, dregs, lees, precipitate, sediment, silt.

depraved *a.* (*corrupt*) abandoned, corrupt, debased, debauched, degenerate, dissolute, evil, immoral, lascivious, lewd, licentious, perverted, profligate, shameless, sinful, vicious, vile, wanton, warped, wicked. ANTONYMS: chaste, virtuous.

depreciate *v.t.* **1** (*to lower the value of*) decrease, deflate, depress, devaluate, diminish, lessen, lower, reduce. ANTONYMS: increase, raise. **2** (*to disparage, to undervalue*) belittle, decry, denigrate, deprecate, deride, detract, discredit, disparage, look down on, malign, play down, ridicule, run down, scorn, slight, sneer at, traduce, underestimate, underrate, undervalue. ANTONYMS: appreciate, praise. **3** (*to reduce the price of*) cheapen, mark down, reduce.

depredation *n.* (*plundering, spoliation*) desolation, despoiling, destruction, devastation, harrying, laying waste, looting, marauding, pillage, plundering, ransacking, rapine, robbery, sacking, spoliation, theft.

depress *v.t.* **1** (*to press down*) flatten, level, lower, press down, push down. **2** (*to lower*) cheapen, depreciate, devaluate, devalue, diminish, downgrade, impair, lessen, lower, reduce. ANTONYMS: raise. **3** (*to dispirit, to make dejected*) burden, cast down, chill, damp,

daunt, deject, desolate, discourage, dishearten, dispirit, oppress, sadden, weigh down. ANTONYMS: cheer, encourage. **4** (*to reduce or keep down the energy or activity of*) debilitate, devitalize, drain, dull, enervate, enfeeble, exhaust, lower, restrain, sap, slow down, weaken. ANTONYMS: enliven, strengthen. **5** (*to humble, to abase*) abase, bring down, humble.

depressed *a.* (*suffering from depression, low in spirits*) (*coll.*) blue, crestfallen, dejected, despondent, discouraged, dispirited, down, downcast, downhearted, fed up, gloomy, glum, low, melancholy, miserable, moody, morose, pessimistic, sad, unhappy. ANTONYMS: cheerful, optimistic.

depressing *a.* (*making one feel sad or dejected*) bleak, daunting, disappointing, discouraging, disheartening, dismal, dispiriting, distressing, dreary, funereal, gloomy, grey, hopeless, melancholy, pessimistic, saddening, sombre. ANTONYMS: cheering, uplifting.

depression *n.* **1** (*lowering of the spirits, dejection*) blues, dejection, despair, despondency, discouragement, dolefulness, downheartedness, dumps, gloom, hopelessness, low spirits, melancholy, sadness, unhappiness. **2** (*slackness of business; a long economic crisis*) decline, downturn, hard times, inactivity, recession, slackness, slowdown, slump, stagnation. ANTONYMS: boom. **3** (*a hollow place on a surface*) cavity, dent, dimple, dip, groove, hollow, impression, indentation, pit, recess, valley.

deprive *v.t.* (*to take from, to dispossess* (*of*)) dispossess, divest, expropriate, rob, strip, take (from), wrest.

deprived *a.* (*lacking adequate social, educational and medical facilities*) badly off, bereft, destitute, forlorn, impoverished, in need, lacking, necessitous, needy, poor, poverty-stricken, under-privileged. ANTONYMS: prosperous, well off.

depth *n.* **1** (*deepness*) deepness, drop, extent, measure. **2** (*a deep place, an abyss*) abyss, chasm, profundity. ANTONYMS: apex, summit. **3** (*the middle or height of a season*) height, middle, midst. **4** (*pl.*) (*the sea*) ocean, sea. **5** (*mental penetration*) acumen, astuteness, discernment, insight, intuition, penetration, perception, perspicacity, profundity, sagacity, shrewdness, understanding, wisdom. **6** (*intensity of colour*) brilliance, intensity, richness, strength, vividness. **7** (*profundity of thought or feeling*) abstruseness, complexity, intricacy, obscurity, profundity, reconditeness. ANTONYMS: superficiality, triviality.

deputy *n.* **1** (*a person who is appointed or sent to act for another or others*) agent, lieutenant, proxy, representative, stand-in, substitute, surrogate. **2** (*a delegate, a member of a deputation*) ambassador, commissioner, delegate, emissary, envoy, legate, nuncio.

deranged *a.* **1** (*insane*) (*coll.*) batty, berserk, (*sl.*) bonkers, (*coll.*) cracked, crazy, delirious, demented, insane, irrational, lunatic, mad, (*coll.*) mental, (*sl.*) nutty, (*coll.*) touched, unbalanced, unhinged. ANTONYMS: lucid, sane. **2** (*mentally disturbed*) distracted, disturbed.

derelict *a.* **1** (*forsaken, abandoned*) abandoned, deserted, discarded, forsaken, left. **2** (*dilapidated, showing neglect*) dilapidated, neglected, ruined, run-down, tumbledown. ~*n.* **1** (*a down-and-out*) (*coll.*) bag lady, (*coll.*) bagman, (*esp. N Am., coll.*) bum, down-and-out, outcast, tramp, vagabond, vagrant. **2** (*anything abandoned* (*esp. a ship at sea*)) ruin, wreck.

deride *v.t.* (*to laugh at, to mock*) abuse, belittle, diminish, disdain, disparage, insult, jeer, (*coll.*) knock, laugh at, mock, poke fun at, ridicule, scoff, scorn, sneer, taunt, tease. ANTONYMS: respect.

derision *n.* (*ridicule, mockery*) abuse, contempt, disdain, disparagement, disrespect, insult, laughter, mockery, ridicule, sarcasm, satire, scoffing, scorn, sneering, taunting.

derisive *a.* **1** (*scoffing, ridiculing*) abusive, insulting, mocking, sarcastic, sneering. **2** (*ridiculous*) contemptible, insulting, laughable, ludicrous, outrageous, preposterous, ridiculous.

derivation *n.* **1** (*the act of deriving*) acquiring, deriving, extraction, getting, obtaining. **2** (*origin, extraction*) ancestry, basis, beginning, cause, descent, extraction, foundation, genealogy, origin, rise, root, source, spring. **3** (*the etymology of a word, the process of tracing a word to its root*) etymology, root, word history, word origin.

derivative *a.* **1** (*derived*) acquired, borrowed, derived, inferred, obtained, procured, transmitted. **2** (*copied from something else*) copied, imitative, plagiaristic, uninventive, unoriginal. ANTONYMS: genuine, original. **3** (*secondary, not original*) rehashed, secondary, second-hand. ~*n.* (*anything derived from a source*) by-product, derivation, descendant, development, offshoot, outgrowth, spin-off.

derive *v.t.* **1** (*to obtain, to get*) acquire, gain, get, obtain, procure, receive, secure. **2** (*to deduce*) deduce, elicit, infer. **3** (*to draw, as from a source or principle*) draw, extract. **4** (*to trace the origin of*) trace, track. **5** (*to deduce or determine from data*) deduce, determine, gather, glean, infer. ~*v.i.* **1** (*to come, to proceed*) come, flow, issue, proceed. **2** (*to originate*) arise, descend, develop (from), emanate, emerge (from), originate, spring (from), stem (from).

derogatory *a.* (*tending to detract from honour or character; disparaging*) belittling, damaging, debasing, defamatory, demeaning, denigrating, depreciatory, detracting, discreditable, dishonourable, disparaging, injurious, insulting, offensive, opprobrious, slighting, unfavourable. ANTONYMS: complimentary, flattering.

descend *v.i.* **1** (*to come or go down*) alight, climb down, come down, dismount, go down. ANTONYMS: ascend, climb. **2** (*to sink, to fall*) drop, fall, plummet, sink, subside, tumble. **3** (*to slope downwards*) dip, gravitate, incline, slant, slope. **4** (*to make an attack*) assail, assault, attack, fall upon, invade, pounce, raid, swoop. **5** (*to originate; to be derived*) derive, issue, originate, proceed, spring. **6** (*to be transmitted from one generation to the next*) hand down, pass down. **7** (*to lower or abase*) abase, condescend, degenerate, deteriorate, lower, stoop.

descendant *n.* (*a person who descends from an ancestor; offspring*) child, issue, offspring, posterity, progeny, successor. ANTONYMS: ancestor.

descent *n.* **1** (*the act of descending*) coming down, descending. **2** (*a slope downwards*) declivity, dip, drop, slant, slope. ANTONYMS: ascent. **3** (*decline in rank or prosperity*) debasement, decadence, decline, degeneration, degradation, deterioration. **4** (*a sudden attack*) assault, attack, foray, incursion, invasion, onslaught, pounce, raid, swoop. **5** (*a fall*) drop, fall, plunge. **6** (*lineage, origin*) ancestry, derivation, extraction, family tree, genealogy, heredity, lineage, origin, parentage, pedigree, stock. **7** (*issue of one generation*) issue, offspring, young.

describe *v.t.* **1** (*to set forth the qualities or properties of in words*) characterize, chronicle, define, depict, detail, explain, express, identify, illustrate, label, narrate, portray, recount, relate, report, represent, set forth, specify, style, tell. **2** (*to draw, to trace out*) delineate, draw, mark out, outline, trace.

description *n.* **1** (*the act of describing*) characterization, delineation, depiction, explanation. **2** (*an account of anything in words*) account, chronicle, history, narrative, portrait, portrayal, report, representation, sketch, story.

3 (*a kind, a sort*) brand, breed, category, character, class, feather, genre, genus, (*coll.*) ilk, kidney, kind, nature, order, sort, species, (*N Am.*) stripe, type, variety.

desert[1] *n.* (*a waste, uninhabited, uncultivated place*) dust bowl, solitude, waste, wilderness, wilds.
~*a.* **1** (*uninhabited, waste*) arid, bare, desolate, empty, lonely, parched, solitary, uninhabited, vacant, waste, wild. **2** (*untilled, barren*) barren, infertile, uncultivated, unproductive, untilled. ANTONYMS: fertile.

desert[2] *v.t.* **1** (*to forsake, to abandon*) abandon, betray, decamp, forsake, jilt, maroon, (*coll.*) run out on, strand, vacate, (*coll.*) walk out on. **2** (*to quit, to leave*) leave, quit, relinquish, renounce, resign.
~*v.i.* (*to abandon the service without permission*) abscond, defect, go absent without leave.

deserted *a.* (*uninhabited, neglected*) abandoned, bereft, cast off, derelict, desolate, empty, forlorn, forsaken, friendless, Godforsaken, isolated, lonely, neglected, solitary, stranded, uninhabited, unoccupied, vacant. ANTONYMS: occupied.

deserve *v.t.* (*to be worthy of, to merit by conduct or qualities*) be worthy of, earn, justify, merit, warrant, win.

deserving *a.* (*merited, worthy*) commendable, creditable, estimable, good, laudable, meritorious, praiseworthy, righteous, worthy. ANTONYMS: undeserving.

design *v.t.* **1** (*to formulate, to project*) conceive, contemplate, contrive, create, devise, fabricate, fashion, forge, formulate, frame, invent, mould, originate, project, think up. **2** (*to draw, to plan*) delineate, describe, draft, draw, lay out, outline, pattern, plan, sketch out, trace. **3** (*to purpose, to intend*) aim, intend, mean, plan, purpose, scheme. **4** (*to devote or apply to a particular purpose*) apply, appropriate, devote.
~*n.* **1** (*a plan, a scheme*) conception, enterprise, plan, project, scheme, undertaking. **2** (*a purpose, an intention*) aim, end, goal, intent, intention, meaning, object, objective, point, purpose, target. **3** (*an arrangement of forms and colours forming a pattern*) arrangement, configuration, figure, form, motif, organization, pattern, shape, style. **4** (*a preliminary sketch, a study*) blueprint, diagram, draft, drawing, outline, sketch, study. **5** (*plot, general idea*) construction, idea, plot.

designate *v.t.* **1** (*to indicate, to mark*) characterize, define, denote, describe, earmark, indicate, mark, particularize, pinpoint, point

out, set forth, show, specify, stipulate. **2** (*to describe (as)*) call, christen, describe, dub, entitle, identify, label, name, nickname, nominate, style, term. **3** (*to select, to appoint*) allot, appoint, assign, choose, delegate, depute, elect, nominate, pick, select.

designer *n.* **1** (*a person who designs*) architect, author, creator, deviser, inventor, originator. **2** (*a person who makes designs for clothing, stage or film sets etc.*) couturier, decorator, stylist.

designing *a.* (*crafty, scheming*) artful, calculating, conniving, conspiring, crafty, (*coll.*) crooked, cunning, deceitful, devious, foxy, intriguing, plotting, scheming, sharp, shrewd, sly, treacherous, tricky, unscrupulous, wily.

desirable *a.* **1** (*worthy of being desired*) coveted, desired, enviable, looked-for, popular, sought-after. **2** (*attractive*) adorable, alluring, attractive, captivating, fascinating, fetching, glamorous, seductive, sexy, winsome. ANTONYMS: repulsive, ugly. **3** (*agreeable*) advantageous, agreeable, beneficial, choice, estimable, excellent, fine, good, pleasing, profitable, superior, worthwhile. ANTONYMS: disagreeable.

desire *v.t.* **1** (*to wish (to do)*) want, wish. **2** (*to wish for the attainment or possession of*) aspire to, covet, crave, die for, fancy, hanker after, hope for, long for, pine for, sigh for, thirst for, wish for, yearn for. **3** (*to express a wish to have, to request*) ask, beseech, command, demand, entreat, importune, order, petition, request, require, solicit, summon.
~*n.* **1** (*an eagerness of the mind to obtain or enjoy some object*) aspiration, craving, eagerness, hankering, hope, inclination, longing, need, thirst, urge, want, wish, yearning, (*coll.*) yen. ANTONYMS: aversion. **2** (*a request, an entreaty*) appeal, entreaty, importunity, order, petition, request, solicitation, supplication. **3** (*sensual appetite, lust*) appetite, concupiscence, lasciviousness, lechery, libido, lust, lustfulness, passion, salaciousness.

desolate *a.* **1** (*forsaken, lonely*) dreary, forsaken, God-forsaken, lonely, remote, solitary, unfrequented. **2** (*deserted, barren*) bare, barren, bleak, deserted, neglected, ruined, uninhabited, waste. **3** (*comfortless; upset*) bereft, dejected, depressed, despondent, disconsolate, dismal, downcast, forlorn, friendless, gloomy, hopeless, inconsolable, lonely, melancholy, miserable, mournful, sad, upset, wretched. ANTONYMS: cheerful, optimistic.

desolation *n.* **1** (*the state of being desolated*) barrenness, bleakness, isolation, loneliness, remoteness, solitude, wildness. **2** (*neglect,* ruin) despoliation, destruction, devastation, havoc, neglect, ruin, waste. **3** (*bitter grief, affliction*) affliction, anguish, bitterness, dejection, despair, despondency, distress, dreariness, gloom, grief, loneliness, melancholy, misery, sadness, sorrow, unhappiness, woe, wretchedness.

despair *v.i.* **1** (*to be without hope*) give up, quit, surrender. **2** (*to give up all hope*) despond, lose heart, lose hope.

~*n.* **1** (*hopelessness*) anguish, dejection, depression, desperation, despondency, discouragement, gloom, hopelessness, melancholy, misery, pessimism, resignation, wretchedness. ANTONYMS: hope. **2** (*a person who or something which causes hopelessness*) burden, cross, hardship, ordeal, pain, trial, tribulation, trouble.

desperate *a.* **1** (*reckless, regardless of danger*) audacious, daring, devil-may-care, fearless, hasty, headstrong, hopeless, impetuous, lawless, rash, reckless. ANTONYMS: cautious. **2** (*affording little hope of success or escape*) despairing, foolhardy, forlorn, hopeless, madcap, wild. **3** (*extremely dangerous*) critical, dangerous, dire, grave, hazardous, perilous, precarious, risky. **4** (*very bad, awful*) awful, bad, wretched. **5** (*wanting very badly to do or have to do something*) aching, covetous, craving, desirous, hungry, longing, pining, thirsty, yearning.

desperation *n.* **1** (*recklessness*) defiance, foolhardiness, frenzy, fury, heedlessness, impetuosity, imprudence, madness, rage, rashness, recklessness. **2** (*hopelessness, despondency*) agony, anguish, anxiety, dejection, depression, despair, despondency, distress, gloom, heartache, hopelessness, melancholy, misery, pain, pessimism, sorrow, torture, trouble, unhappiness, worry. ANTONYMS: hope.

despicable *a.* (*meriting contempt; vile*) abject, base, cheap, contemptible, degrading, detestable, disgraceful, disreputable, hateful, ignoble, ignominious, low, mean, nasty, reprehensible, shabby, shameful, sordid, vile, wretched. ANTONYMS: admirable, noble.

despise *v.t.* (*to regard with contempt*) abhor, deride, detest, disdain, disregard, hate, loathe, look down on, revile, scorn, slight, sneer at, spurn. ANTONYMS: admire, cherish.

despite *prep.* (*in spite of*) against, even with, ignoring, in contempt of, in defiance of, in spite of, notwithstanding, regardless of, undeterred by.

despondent *a.* (*very unhappy, disheartened*) dejected, depressed, despairing, disconsolate, discouraged, disheartened, dispirited, doleful, downcast, downhearted, gloomy, glum, hopeless, low-spirited, melancholy, miserable, morose, sorrowful, unhappy, wretched. ANTONYMS: happy, joyful.

despotic *a.* (*tyrannical, cruel*) absolute, arbitrary, authoritarian, autocratic, cruel, dictatorial, domineering, imperious, oppressive, totalitarian, tyrannical, tyrannous, unconstitutional, unfair. ANTONYMS: democratic.

destination *n.* **1** (*the place to which a person is going or to which a thing is sent*) harbour, haven, journey's end, landing place, stop, stopping place, terminus. ANTONYMS: start. **2** (*the purpose for which a thing is appointed or intended*) aim, ambition, design, end, goal, intention, object, objective, purpose, target.

destined *a.* (*foreordained*) bound, certain, designed, doomed, fated, foreordained, ineluctable, inescapable, inevitable, intended, meant, ordained, predestined, predetermined, sure, unavoidable, written.

destiny *n.* **1** (*the purpose or end to which any person or thing is appointed*) end, purpose. **2** (*fate, fortune*) doom, fate, fortune, karma, lot, portion.

destitute *a.* **1** (*deprived of money and the necessities of life*) badly off, bankrupt, (*coll.*) broke, deprived, (*coll.*) dirt-poor, distressed, down and out, (*coll.*) flat broke, hard up, impecunious, impoverished, indigent, insolvent, in want, necessitous, needy, penniless, penurious, poor, poverty-stricken. ANTONYMS: rich, solvent. **2** (*lacking, bereft (of)*) bereft, depleted, deprived (of), devoid (of), drained, empty (of), lacking, short, wanting, without.

destroy *v.t.* **1** (*to demolish; to pull to pieces*) demolish, dismantle, pull down, raze, tear down. **2** (*to undo, to nullify*) annul, cancel, counteract, disprove, eradicate, neutralize, nullify, overturn, refute, reverse, undermine, undo. **3** (*to annihilate; to lay waste*) annihilate, crush, devastate, lay waste, (*esp. N Am., coll.*) trash, waste, wipe out, wreck. **4** (*to ruin the life or situation of*) ravage, ruin, shatter, smash. **5** (*to kill (a sick animal) humanely*) kill, put down, put to sleep.

destruction *n.* **1** (*the act of destroying*) annihilation, crushing, destroying, devastation, eradication, extermination, extinction, liquidation, overwhelming, razing, ruination, shattering, undoing, wrecking. ANTONYMS: construction, creation. **2** (*the state of being destroyed*) havoc, mayhem, ruin, wreckage. **3** (*demolition, ruin*) collapse, demolition, downfall, ruin. **4** (*death, slaughter*) death, massacre, murder, slaughter.

destructive a. 1 (causing destruction; ruinous) baleful, calamitous, cataclysmic, catastrophic, damaging, deadly, deleterious, detrimental, devastating, fatal, harmful, injurious, lethal, malignant, mischievous, noxious, pernicious, poisonous, toxic, virulent. 2 (serving to confute (arguments); negative) adverse, antagonistic, conflicting, contradictory, contrary, critical, derogatory, disapproving, discouraging, discrediting, disparaging, hostile, invalidating, negative, opposed, subversive, undermining, vicious. ANTONYMS: constructive.

desultory a. 1 (passing quickly from one subject to another) brief, cursory, fitful, haphazard. 2 (loose, disjointed) aimless, chaotic, disconnected, discursive, disjointed, disorderly, erratic, inconsistent, inexact, irregular, loose, rambling, random, roving, spasmodic, unmethodical, unsystematic.

detach v.t. (to disconnect, to separate) cut off, disconnect, disengage, disentangle, disjoin, disunite, free, isolate, loosen, part, remove, segregate, separate, sever, tear off, uncouple, undo, unfasten, unhitch. ANTONYMS: attach, fasten.

detached a. 1 (not personally involved, impartial) aloof, disinterested, dispassionate, impartial, impersonal, neutral, objective, reserved, separate, unbiased, uncommitted, unemotional, uninvolved, unprejudiced. ANTONYMS: involved. 2 ((of a house) not joined to the house next door) divided, free-standing, separate, unconnected. ANTONYMS: semidetached, terraced.

detail n. 1 (an item) aspect, circumstance, component, count, element, fact, factor, feature, item, particular, point, respect, specific, technicality. 2 (pl.) (minute parts of a picture, statue etc., as distinct from the work as a whole) fine points, minutiae, niceties, particulars, specifics. 3 (a minor matter) nicety, trifle, triviality. 4 (a body of soldiers etc. selected for a special duty) body, cadre, detachment, duty, fatigue, force, group, party, squad, team, unit. ~v.t. 1 (to list the particular items of) catalogue, enumerate, itemize, list, particularize, tabulate, tally. 2 (to relate minutely) delineate, depict, describe, narrate, portray, recite, recount, rehearse, relate. 3 (to appoint for a particular service) allocate, appoint, assign, charge, commission, delegate, detach, send.

detailed a. (related in detail, meticulous) complete, comprehensive, exact, exhaustive, full, inclusive, meticulous, minute, particular, precise, thorough. ANTONYMS: cursory, summary.

detain v.t. 1 (to restrain; to keep in custody) arrest, confine, hold, intern, restrain. ANTONYMS: free, release. 2 (to delay, to hinder) check, delay, hinder, hold up, impede, keep, retard, slow up, stay, stop. 3 (to withhold) hold back, keep back, retain, withhold.

detect v.t. 1 (to discover or find out) catch, disclose, discover, expose, find out, reveal, trace, track down, uncover, unearth, unmask. 2 (to observe (radiation or a signal) with a detector) ascertain, catch, descry, discern, distinguish, identify, make out, note, notice, observe, perceive, read, recognize, scent, sense, spot.

detention n. 1 (the act of detaining) hindrance, holding back. 2 (arrest; confinement) arrest, confinement, custody, duress, incarceration, internment, (sl.) porridge, quarantine, restraint, (sl.) time. ANTONYMS: liberty, release.

deter v.t. 1 (to discourage or frighten (from)) caution, damp, daunt, discourage, dissuade, frighten, intimidate, put off, scare off, talk out of, warn. ANTONYMS: encourage. 2 (to hinder or prevent) check, hinder, inhibit, obstruct, prevent, prohibit, restrain, stop, thwart.

deteriorate v.t. (to make inferior) corrupt, debase, impair, injure, lower, spoil.
~v.i. 1 (to become worse) decline, degrade, depreciate, get worse, slump, worsen. ANTONYMS: improve. 2 (to degenerate) crumble, decay, decline, decompose, degenerate, disintegrate, ebb, erode, fade, fall apart, lapse, retrogress, weaken.

determination n. 1 (resolution, strength of mind) backbone, constancy, conviction, dedication, doggedness, drive, firmness, fortitude, (coll.) guts, indomitability, intention, perseverance, persistence, resolution, resolve, single-mindedness, steadfastness, strength of mind, tenacity, will-power. ANTONYMS: indecision, irresolution. 2 (settlement by a judicial decision, conclusion) conclusion, decision, judgement, outcome, pronouncement, purpose, resolution, result, settlement, solution, verdict.

determine v.t. 1 (to ascertain exactly) ascertain, certify, check, detect, discover, find out, infer, learn, verify, work out. 2 (to settle finally, to decide) arbitrate, clinch, decide, fix, judge, resolve, settle. 3 (to direct, to shape) affect, condition, control, decide, dictate, direct, govern, impel, impose, incline, induce, influence, lead, modify, regulate, rule, shape. 4 (to conclude) conclude, end, finish, terminate.
~v.i. (to decide, to resolve) choose, decide, elect, establish, fix, purpose, resolve.

determined a. 1 (resolute) adamant, bent on,

decided, dogged, firm, fixed, immovable, obstinate, persistent, purposeful, resolute, set on, single-minded, stalwart, steadfast, strong-willed, stubborn, tenacious, unfaltering, unwavering. ANTONYMS: irresolute, wavering. **2** (*having a fixed purpose*) fixed, predetermined, settled.

deterrent *n.* (*something which deters*) check, curb, discouragement, disincentive, hindrance, hitch, impediment, obstacle, obstruction, restraint. ANTONYMS: incentive, spur.

detest *v.t.* (*to hate exceedingly, to abhor*) abhor, abominate, despise, dislike, execrate, hate, loathe, recoil from. ANTONYMS: love, relish.

detestable *a.* (*very bad, despicable*) abhorrent, abominable, despicable, disgusting, execrable, hateful, horrible, horrid, loathsome, nasty, obnoxious, obscene, odious, offensive, repugnant, repulsive, revolting, shocking, unpleasant, vile. ANTONYMS: adorable, lovely.

detract *v.i.* **1** (*to diminish, to reduce*) devalue, diminish, lessen, lower, reduce, subtract, take away. ANTONYMS: augment, complement. **2** (*to speak disparagingly*) (*coll.*) bad-mouth, cast aspersions, disparage, slander.

detrimental *a.* (*causing harm or damage*) adverse, baleful, damaging, deleterious, destructive, disadvantageous, harmful, hurtful, inimical, injurious, mischievous, pernicious, unfavourable. ANTONYMS: beneficial, helpful.

devastate *v.t.* **1** (*to lay waste, to ravage*) demolish, desolate, despoil, destroy, flatten, lay waste, level, pillage, plunder, ravage, raze, ruin, sack, spoil, (*esp. N Am., coll.*) trash, waste, wreck. **2** (*to overwhelm, to upset greatly*) confound, crush, discompose, disconcert, (*coll.*) floor, mortify, overpower, overwhelm, shatter, take aback, upset.

devastating *a.* (*overwhelming, very upsetting*) caustic, cutting, deadly, destructive, effective, incisive, keen, mordant, overpowering, overwhelming, penetrating, ravishing, savage, spectacular, stunning, telling, trenchant, upsetting, vitriolic.

develop *v.t.* **1** (*to unfold, to bring to light gradually*) advance, bring forth, disclose, unfold. **2** (*to evolve*) evolve, grow, unfold, work out. **3** (*to bring to completion or maturity by natural growth*) age, complete, cultivate, foster, grow, mature, nurture. **4** (*to begin to have*) acquire, begin, breed, commence, contract, create, generate, originate, pick up, start. ~*v.i.* **1** (*to expand*) amplify, augment, broaden, enlarge, expand. **2** (*to progress*) advance, bloom, blossom, flourish, flower, grow, mature, progress, promote, ripen. **3** (*to come

to light gradually*) appear, come into view, emerge.

development *n.* **1** (*gradual growth and advancement*) advance, advancement, expansion, formation, growth, improvement, increase, progress, progression, spread, unfolding. **2** (*an event which is likely to affect a situation*) change, circumstance, condition, event, happening, incident, issue, occurrence, result, situation, upshot. **3** (*evolution*) evolution, growth. **4** (*completion*) completion, culmination, fruition, maturity, perfection.

deviant *a.* (*deviating from what is socially acceptable*) aberrant, abnormal, (*sl.*) bent, different, divergent, (*coll.*) freaky, heretical, idiosyncratic, (*coll.*) kinky, odd, offbeat, peculiar, perverse, perverted, quirky, sick, strange, twisted, unusual, warped. ANTONYMS: normal, orthodox.

deviate *v.i.* **1** (*to turn aside*) avert, bend, deflect, depart, diverge, divert, turn, turn aside, vary, veer. **2** (*to stray or swerve from the path of duty*) digress, drift, meander, stray, swerve, wander.

device *n.* **1** (*a contrivance, an invention*) apparatus, appliance, contraption, contrivance, gadget, (*coll.*) gizmo, implement, instrument, invention, machine, mechanism, tool, utensil. **2** (*an explosive, a bomb*) bomb, explosive, incendiary. **3** (*a scheme; a stratagem*) artifice, design, dodge, expedient, gambit, improvisation, manoeuvre, plan, ploy, project, purpose, ruse, scheme, shift, stratagem, strategy, stunt, trick, wile. **4** (*a design, a pattern*) design, figure, motif, pattern. **5** (*an emblem or fanciful design*) badge, coat of arms, crest, design, emblem, logo, monogram, motto, seal, slogan, symbol.

devil *n.* **1** (**Devil**) (*Satan, the chief spirit of evil*) Beelzebub, Evil One, Lucifer, (*coll.*) Old Nick, Prince of Darkness, Satan. **2** (*any evil spirit*) demon, evil spirit, fiend, imp, incubus, succubus. ANTONYMS: angel. **3** (*a wicked, malignant or cruel person*) beast, brute, fiend, ghoul, monster, ogre, rogue, savage, terror, villain. **4** (*a person*) beggar, (*coll.*) bloke, (*coll.*) chap, (*coll.*) fellow, (*coll.*) guy, person. **5** (*something troublesome*) nuisance, (*coll.*) pain, trouble. **6** (*a person of extraordinary energy, devoted to mischievous ends*) imp, (*coll.*) monkey, (*coll.*) pickle, rapscallion, rascal, rogue, scamp, scoundrel. **7** (*an unfortunate person, a wretch*) beggar, creature, (*coll.*) thing, unfortunate, wretch. **8** (*energy, unconquerable spirit*) dash, energy, liveliness, vigour.

devious *a.* **1** (*insincere and deceitful*) calculating, crafty, (*coll.*) crooked, deceitful, deceptive, designing, dishonest, double-dealing, furtive, insidious, insincere, misleading, scheming, shifty, sly, surreptitious, treacherous, tricky, underhand, wily. ANTO-NYMS: forthright, honest. **2** (*circuitous, rambling*) circuitous, confusing, crooked, deviating, erratic, excursive, indirect, misleading, rambling, roundabout, serpentine, sinuous, tortuous, wandering, zigzag. ANTO-NYMS: direct, undeviating.

devise *v.t.* **1** (*to invent, to form in the mind*) conceive, concoct, construct, contrive, (*coll.*) cook up, design, draft, dream up, formulate, frame, imagine, invent, originate, plan, plot, prepare, project, scheme, think up, work out. **2** (*to give or assign* (*property*) *by will*) assign, bequeath, bestow, convey, dispose of, give, hand down, transfer, will.

devoid *a.* (*empty* (*of*), *lacking*) barren, bereft, deficient, denuded, destitute, empty, free (from), lacking, vacant, void, wanting, without. ANTONYMS: full.

devote *v.t.* (*to dedicate; to give wholly up* (*to*)) allot, apply, appropriate, assign, commit, concern oneself, consecrate, dedicate, enshrine, give, occupy oneself, pledge, put away, reserve, set apart.

devoted *a.* **1** (*dedicated, ardently attached*) ardent, attached, caring, committed, concerned, constant, dedicated, devout, doting, earnest, enthusiastic, faithful, fond, loving, loyal, staunch, steadfast, true, zealous. ANTONYMS: indifferent, unenthusiastic. **2** (*dedicated, consecrated* (*to*)) committed, consecrated, dedicated.

devotion *n.* **1** (*deep, self-sacrificing loyalty*) adherence, affection, allegiance, attachment, commitment, constancy, faithfulness, fidelity, fondness, love, loyalty. ANTONYMS: apathy, disloyalty. **2** (*pl.*) (*prayers, religious worship*) observance, prayer, ritual, worship. **3** (*religious zeal*) devoutness, godliness, holiness, piety, reverence, sanctity. ANTONYMS: impiety. **4** (*the act of devoting*) commitment, consecration, dedication. **5** (*the state of being devoted*) ardour, earnestness, intensity, passion, zeal.

devour *v.t.* **1** (*to eat up quickly and greedily*) bolt, consume, cram, eat, gobble, gorge, gulp, guzzle, (*esp. N Am., sl.*) pig out on, (*coll.*) polish off, stuff, swallow, wolf. **2** ((*of fire*) *to destroy wantonly, to engulf*) annihilate, consume, demolish, destroy, devastate, engulf, obliterate, ravage, spend, swallow up, waste, wipe out. **3** (*to read eagerly*) drink in, enjoy, feast on, relish, revel in, take in. **4** (*to absorb, to overwhelm*) absorb, engross, overwhelm, preoccupy.

devout *a.* **1** (*deeply religious*) committed, devoted, faithful, godly, orthodox, pious, religious, reverent, saintly. **2** (*pious, filled with devotion*) devotional, faithful, holy, pious, spiritual. ANTONYMS: impious, sacrilegious. **3** (*sincere, genuine*) ardent, deep, devoted, earnest, fervent, genuine, heartfelt, hearty, intense, passionate, profound, serious, sincere, zealous.

dexterity *n.* **1** (*manual skill*) adroitness, agility, aptitude, aptness, competence, craft, deftness, handiness, knack, nimbleness, proficiency, skill, sleight of hand, touch. ANTONYMS: clumsiness, incompetence. **2** (*mental skill, cleverness*) artistry, astuteness, cleverness, cunning, expertise, facility, guile, ingenuity, intelligence, keenness, mastery, sharpness, shrewdness, tact.

diabolical *a.* **1** (*of the devil*) demonic, devilish, diabolic, fiendish, hellish, infernal, satanic. **2** (*very bad, unpleasant*) abominable, appalling, atrocious, bad, cruel, difficult, disastrous, dreadful, evil, excruciating, hideous, horrible, monstrous, nasty, outrageous, shocking, tricky, unpleasant, vile, wicked.

diagnose *v.t.* (*to distinguish, to determine*) analyse, determine, distinguish, identify, interpret, investigate, name, pinpoint, pronounce, recognize.

diagram *n.* **1** (*a drawing made to demonstrate or illustrate some statement or definition*) drawing, illustration. **2** (*an illustrative figure drawn roughly or in outline*) figure, outline, plan, representation, schema, sketch. **3** (*a series of marks or lines representing graphically the results of statistical or other observations*) chart, graph, layout.

dialect *n.* (*a form of language peculiar to a particular district or people*) accent, argot, cant, idiom, jargon, language, (*coll.*) lingo, patois, pronunciation, speech, tongue, vernacular.

dialogue *n.* (*a conversation or discourse*) chat, colloquy, communication, confabulation, conference, conversation, converse, discourse, discussion, duologue, interlocution, (*sl.*) rap, talk.

dictate *v.t.* **1** (*to read or recite to another* (*words to be written*)) read out, recite, say, speak, transmit, utter. **2** (*to prescribe, to lay down with authority*) bid, command, decree, demand, direct, enjoin, establish, impose, lay down, ordain, order, prescribe, pronounce.

dictatorial *a.* **1** (*of or relating to a dictator*) absolute, arbitrary, autocratic, despotic, omnipotent, totalitarian, tyrannical, tyrannous.

ANTONYMS: democratic, egalitarian. **2** (*imperious, overbearing*) authoritarian, bossy, dogmatical, domineering, imperious, magisterial, oppressive, overbearing. ANTONYMS: meek, suppliant.

diction *n.* **1** (*the use of words*) articulation, delivery, elocution, eloquence, enunciation, fluency, inflection, intonation, oratory, presentation, pronunciation, speech. **2** (*manner of expression; style*) expression, language, phraseology, phrasing, rhetoric, style, terminology, usage, vocabulary, wording.

die *v.i.* **1** (*to lose life, to depart this life*) (*sl.*) bite the dust, breathe one's last, decease, depart, expire, (*sl.*) go west, (*sl.*) kick the bucket, lose one's life, pass away, pass on, (*sl.*) peg out, perish, (*sl.*) snuff it. ANTONYMS: live, survive. **2** (*to come to an end; to cease to exist*) cease, come to an end, end, subside. **3** (*to wither, to lose vitality*) break down, decay, decline, disappear, dwindle, fade, lapse, pass, sink, vanish, wane, wilt, wither. **4** (*to fail, to cease to function*) fail, fizzle out, halt, peter out, run down, stop. **5** (*to cease or pass away gradually*) cease, fade, pass away. **6** (*to faint, to languish with affection*) ache, crave, desire, faint, hunger, languish, long, pine for, (*poet.*) swoon, want, yearn.

diet *n.* **1** (*a prescribed course of food followed for health reasons, or to reduce weight*) regime, regimen. **2** (*the food and drink a person usually takes*) aliment, comestibles, edibles, fare, food, intake, nourishment, nutriment, provisions, rations, subsistence, sustenance, viands, victuals.
~*v.i.* (*to take food, esp. according to a prescribed regimen or to reduce weight*) abstain, fast, lose weight, reduce, slim. ANTONYMS: indulge.

differ *v.i.* **1** (*to be dissimilar*) contrast, depart, deviate, diverge, stand apart, vary. **2** (*to disagree in opinion; to quarrel*) argue, conflict, contend, contradict, disagree, dispute, dissent, oppose, quarrel, take issue. ANTONYMS: agree, concur.

difference *n.* **1** (*the state of being unlike or distinct*) contrast, deviation, differentiation, discrepancy, disparity, dissimilarity, divergence, diversity, unlikeness, variation. ANTONYMS: likeness, similarity. **2** (*the quality by which one thing differs from another*) distinction, exception, idiosyncrasy, incongruity, particularity, peculiarity, singularity. **3** (*disproportion between two things*) disproportion, imbalance. **4** (*the remainder of a quantity after another quantity has been subtracted from it*) balance, remainder, residue, rest. **5** (*a disagreement in opinion, a quarrel*) altercation, argument, clash, conflict, contention, contretemps, controversy, debate, disagreement, discordance, dispute, dissension, quarrel, row, (*coll.*) set-to, strife, tiff, wrangle.

different *a.* **1** (*unlike, dissimilar*) at odds, clashing, conflicting, contrary, contrasting, discrepant, disparate, dissimilar, divergent, diverse, inconsistent, opposed, unalike, unlike. **2** (*distinct, not the same*) discrete, distinct, individual, other, separate. **3** (*unusual*) atypical, bizarre, distinctive, exceptional, new, novel, out of the ordinary, peculiar, rare, singular, special, strange, uncommon, unconventional, unique, unusual. ANTONYMS: common, ordinary.

differentiate *v.t.* **1** (*to make different*) adapt, adjust, alter, change, convert, make different, modify, specialize, transform. **2** (*to constitute a difference between, of or in*) contrast, discern, discriminate, distinguish, mark off, oppose, separate, set off, tell apart.

difficult *a.* **1** (*hard to do or carry out*) arduous, burdensome, challenging, demanding, formidable, grim, hard, laborious, onerous, painful, strenuous, toilsome, tough, wearisome. ANTONYMS: easy. **2** (*troublesome*) thorny, ticklish, tiresome, troublesome, trying. **3** (*hard to please*) awkward, contrary, demanding, finicky, fussy, hard to please, intractable, obstreperous, perverse, recalcitrant, refractory, stubborn, unaccommodating. ANTONYMS: accommodating, tractable. **4** (*not easily managed*) awkward, unamenable, unmanageable. **5** (*hard to understand*) abstract, abstruse, baffling, complex, complicated, enigmatical, incomprehensible, intricate, involved, knotty, obscure, perplexing, puzzling, recondite. ANTONYMS: simple, uncomplicated. **6** (*bad-tempered*) bad-tempered, cross, crotchety, fractious, short-tempered. **7** (*full of difficulties or problems*) fraught, involved, problematic.

difficulty *n.* **1** (*the quality of being difficult*) arduousness, awkwardness, hardship, laboriousness, labour, pain, strain, strenuousness. ANTONYMS: ease. **2** (*anything difficult*) trial, tribulation, trouble. **3** (*an obstacle; objection*) complication, hindrance, hurdle, impediment, objection, obstacle, pitfall, problem, protest, snag, stumbling-block. **4** (*scruple*) qualm, reluctance, scruple.

diffident *a.* **1** (*lacking confidence in oneself or one's powers*) hesitant, insecure, nervous, self-conscious. ANTONYMS: confident, self-assured. **2** (*bashful, shy*) backward, bashful, doubtful, humble, meek, modest, reluctant, reserved, self-effacing, sheepish, shrinking, shy, timid, unassertive, unassuming, unobtrusive, withdrawn. ANTONYMS: assertive.

diffuse[1] *v.t.* **1** (*to pour forth*) dispense, pour forth. **2** (*to spread abroad by pouring out*) disperse, distribute, scatter, spread abroad. **3** (*to circulate*) circulate, disseminate, propagate. **4** (*to dissipate*) dispel, dissipate.

diffuse[2] *a.* **1** (*scattered, spread out*) diffused, scattered, spread out, widespread. ANTONYMS: concentrated. **2** (*copious, verbose*) circuitous, circumlocutory, copious, diffusive, digressive, discursive, long-winded, loquacious, meandering, rambling, verbose, wordy. ANTONYMS: concise.

dig *v.t.* **1** (*to excavate or turn up with a spade or similar instrument, or with hands, claws etc.*) break up, excavate, till, turn up, work. **2** (*to thrust or push into something*) drive, force, plunge, punch, push, stab, thrust. **3** (*to obtain by digging*) burrow, disinter, dredge up, exhume, grub, mine, quarry, scoop, unearth. **4** (*to poke*) jab, nudge, poke, prod. **5** (*to approve of or like*) approve of, enjoy, like, understand.
~*v.i.* (*to search*) delve, explore, investigate, probe, research, search.
~*n.* **1** (*a thrust, a poke*) jab, nudge, poke, prod, punch, stab, thrust. **2** (*a cutting remark*) barb, (*coll.*) crack, cutting remark, gibe, insinuation, insult, jeer, quip, slur, sneer, taunt, (*coll.*) wisecrack.

digest[1] *v.t.* **1** (*to break (food) down in the stomach into forms which can be easily assimilated by the body*) break down, dissolve, incorporate, macerate. **2** (*to assimilate, to understand*) absorb, assimilate, grasp, master, take in, understand. **3** (*to arrange under proper heads or titles*) arrange, classify, codify, dispose, methodize, order, organize, systematize, tabulate. **4** (*to think over*) consider, contemplate, meditate, ponder, study, think over, weigh.

digest[2] *n.* (*a compendium or summary*) abbreviation, abridgement, compendium, condensation, epitome, précis, résumé, summary, synopsis.

dignified *a.* (*stately; gravely courteous*) august, courteous, elegant, formal, grand, honourable, imposing, lofty, lordly, majestic, noble, regal, reserved, serious, sober, staid, stately, upright. ANTONYMS: undignified, vulgar.

dignify *v.t.* **1** (*to invest with dignity*) adorn, advance, aggrandize, better, distinguish, elevate, ennoble, exalt, glorify, grace, honour, promote, raise, upgrade, uplift. **2** (*to give the appearance of dignity to*) dress up, (*sl.*) tart up.

dignitary *n.* (*a person who holds a position of dignity*) (*coll.*) big shot, (*coll.*) bigwig, celebrity, (*coll.*) high-up, luminary, notable,

personage, public figure, somebody, VIP, worthy.

dignity *n.* **1** (*a serious and respectable manner*) calm, courtliness, decorum, distinction, formality, grandeur, gravity, hauteur, loftiness, pride, respectability, self-esteem, seriousness, solemnity, stateliness. **2** (*worth, nobility*) majesty, nobility, worth. **3** (*estimation, rank*) estimation, level, position, rank. **4** (*the importance due to rank or position*) greatness, honour, importance, prestige, respect, standing, station, status.

digression *n.* (*a deviation from the main topic*) aside, departure, detour, deviation, divergence, diversion, footnote, irrelevance, obiter dictum, parenthesis, ramble, wandering.

dilapidated *a.* (*ruined; shabby*) battered, broken-down, crumbling, decayed, decaying, decrepit, fallen in, neglected, ramshackle, rickety, ruined, ruinous, run-down, shabby, shaky, tumbledown, worn out, wrecked. ANTONYMS: well-maintained.

dilate *v.t.* (*to expand, to widen*) broaden, distend, enlarge, expand, extend, puff out, stretch, widen. ANTONYMS: compress, deflate.
~*v.i.* **1** (*to expand, to swell*) enlarge, expand, extend, swell. ANTONYMS: compress, deflate. **2** (*to speak at length on a subject*) amplify, develop, dwell on, enlarge, expand, expound.

dilatory *a.* **1** (*causing or tending to cause delay*) delaying, stalling. **2** (*addicted to or marked by procrastination*) procrastinating, putting off. **3** (*slow, tardy*) backward, behindhand, dawdling, laggardly, slack, slow, sluggish, tardy. ANTONYMS: expeditious, prompt.

dilemma *n.* **1** (*a position in which a person is forced to choose between equally unfavourable alternatives*) deadlock, impasse, quandary, stalemate. **2** (*a difficult situation*) bind, difficulty, embarrassment, fix, jam, mess, perplexity, (*coll.*) pickle, plight, predicament, problem, puzzle, spot, tight corner.

diligent *a.* **1** (*assiduous in any business or task*) assiduous, attentive, careful, conscientious, meticulous, punctilious, scrupulous, thorough. ANTONYMS: careless. **2** (*persevering, industrious*) hard-working, indefatigable, industrious, laborious, painstaking, persevering, persistent, sedulous, studious, tireless. ANTONYMS: lazy.

dilute *v.t.* **1** (*to make (a liquid) thin by adding water*) thin, water, weaken. **2** (*to reduce the strength or power of*) adulterate, diffuse, mitigate, reduce, water down.
~*a.* **1** (*diluted, weakened*) adulterated, cut, diluted, thinned, watered down, weakened.

2 (*faded, colourless*) colourless, faded, washed out, watery.

dim *a.* **1** (*lacking in light or brightness*) dark, dusky. ANTONYMS: bright, light. **2** (*obscure; not clear*) bleary, blurred, fuzzy, ill-defined, indistinct, muzzy, obscure, unclear. ANTONYMS: clear. **3** (*indistinct, misty*) cloudy, dusky, faint, foggy, gloomy, indistinct, misty, murky, nebulous, shadowy, tenebrous. **4** (*without lustre, dull*) dingy, dull, lustreless, opaque, sullied, tarnished. ANTONYMS: shiny. **5** (*not clearly understanding or understood*) confused, muddled, obscure, vague. **6** (*stupid, unintelligent*) dense, (*coll.*) dumb, obtuse, slow, stupid, (*coll.*) thick, unintelligent. ANTONYMS: brilliant, smart.
~*v.t.* (*to make dim*) blur, cloud, darken, dull, fade, lower, obscure, tarnish. ANTONYMS: brighten.

diminish *v.t.* **1** (*to make smaller or less*) compress, curtail, cut, lessen, reduce, shorten. ANTONYMS: amplify, enlarge. **2** (*to reduce in power, rank etc.*) demote, downgrade, weaken. **3** (*to taper*) abate, decline, die out, dwindle, ebb, fade, peter out, recede, shrivel, slacken, subside, taper, wane. **4** (*to disparage, to degrade*) belittle, cheapen, degrade, demean, deprecate, depreciate, devalue, discredit, disparage, humiliate, put down. **5** (*to subtract from*) subtract from, take away.
~*v.i.* (*to become less, to decrease*) contract, decrease, shrink.

diminutive *a.* (*small, tiny*) bantam, compact, infinitesimal, little, midget, mini, miniature, minuscule, minute, petite, (*coll.*) pint-sized, pocket, puny, pygmy, small, tiny, (*coll.*) titchy, undersized, (*esp. Sc.*) wee. ANTONYMS: enormous, large.

din *n.* (*a loud and continued noise*) bedlam, bellow, blare, clamour, clangour, clash, clatter, commotion, crash, hubbub, hullabaloo, noise, outcry, pandemonium, racket, roar, row, rumpus, tumult, uproar. ANTONYMS: quiet, tranquillity.

dine *v.i.* (*to take dinner*) banquet, eat, feast, lunch, snack, sup.

dingy *a.* **1** (*soiled, grimy*) dirty, grimy, seedy, shabby, soiled. **2** (*of a dusky or dun colour*) colourless, dark, dim, discoloured, dismal, drab, dreary, dull, dun, dusky, faded, sombre.

dip *v.t.* **1** (*to plunge into a liquid for a short time*) bathe, douse, duck, dunk, immerse, plunge, rinse, souse, submerge. **2** (*to dye by plunging into a liquid*) coat, dye, wash. **3** (*to put (the hand or a ladle) into liquid and scoop out*) ladle, scoop, spoon.

~*v.i.* **1** (*to sink, e.g. below the horizon*) descend, disappear, drop, fade, go down, set, sink, subside. ANTONYMS: rise. **2** (*to bend downwards*) bend, bow, droop, sag, slump. **3** (*to slope or extend downwards*) incline, slope, tilt.
~*n.* **1** (*the act of dipping in a liquid*) ducking, immersion, plunge, soaking. **2** (*a short swim*) bathe, dive, plunge, swim. **3** (*the quantity taken up at one dip or scoop*) scoopful, spoonful. **4** (*sauce, gravy etc. into which something is to be dipped*) gravy, relish, sauce. **5** (*depth or degree of submergence*) basin, cavity, declivity, depression, hole, hollow, incline, slope. **6** (*the angle at which strata slope downwards into the earth*) decline, drop, fall, slip.

diplomacy *n.* **1** (*the art of conducting negotiations between nations*) negotiation, politics, statecraft, statesmanship. **2** (*adroitness, tact*) adroitness, artfulness, delicacy, discretion, savoir faire, skill, subtlety, tact. ANTONYMS: tactlessness, thoughtlessness.

diplomatic *a.* **1** (*of or relating to diplomacy or ambassadors*) ambassadorial, political. **2** (*adroit, tactful*) adept, adroit, courteous, discerning, discreet, judicious, polite, politic, prudent, sensitive, subtle, tactful. ANTONYMS: clumsy, tactless.

dire *a.* **1** (*dreadful, fearful*) dreadful, fearful, frightful, ominous, portentous. **2** (*lamentable, sad*) dismal, gloomy, grim, lamentable, sad. **3** (*of poor quality; terrible*) appalling, awful, low-quality, poor, terrible. **4** (*extreme*) critical, crucial, crying, desperate, drastic, extreme, imperative, pressing, serious, urgent.

direct *a.* **1** (*straight*) straight, unswerving. **2** (*in a straight line from one body or place to another*) non-stop, straight, through, unbroken, uninterrupted. ANTONYMS: circuitous, crooked, curved, roundabout. **3** (*shortest*) nearest, shortest. **4** (*diametrical*) diametrical, exact. **5** (*immediate; not by proxy*) face-to-face, first-hand, head-on, immediate, personal. **6** (*honest, to the point*) candid, downright, frank, honest, open, to the point. ANTONYMS: devious, sly. **7** (*plain, straightforward*) blunt, categorical, explicit, express, plain, point-blank, straightforward, to the point, unambiguous, unequivocal.
~*v.t.* **1** (*to point or turn in a direct line towards any place or object*) aim, point, turn. **2** (*to show the correct road to*) guide, indicate, show. **3** (*to inscribe with an address or direction*) address, label, mail, post, send. **4** (*to speak or write to*) address, speak to, write to. **5** (*to aim, to point*) aim, fix, focus, point, train. **6** (*to guide, to prescribe a course to*) advise, conduct, counsel, escort, guide, pilot, prescribe, steer, usher.

7 (*to order, to command*) bid, charge, command, demand, dictate, enjoin, instruct, order. **8** (*to manage, to act as leader of* (*a group of musicians, film etc.*)) administer, control, govern, handle, head, head up, lead, manage, mastermind, operate, oversee, preside over, regulate, rule, run, superintend, supervise.

direction *n.* **1** (*the act of directing*) administration, charge, conduct, control, directorship, government, guidance, handling, instruction, leadership, management, manipulation, operation, oversight, regulation, rule, running, superintendence, supervision. **2** (*the end or object aimed at*) aim, end, object. **3** (*the course taken*) avenue, bearing, course, line, path, road, route, track, way. **4** (*often pl.*) (*the name or address on a letter or parcel*) address, label. **5** (*an order or instruction*) command, directive, guideline, indication, injunction, instruction, order.

directly *adv.* **1** (*exactly*) exactly, precisely, straight, unswervingly. **2** (*at once*) at once, dead, due, forthwith, immediately, instantaneously, instantly, post-haste, presently, promptly, quickly, right away, soon, speedily, straight away. ANTONYMS: later. **3** (*in a direct manner*) candidly, frankly, honestly, openly, overtly, personally, plainly, point-blank, straightforwardly, truthfully, unequivocally.

director *n.* **1** (*a person who directs or manages*) administrator, boss, captain, chairman, chief, controller, executive, governor, head, leader, manager, organizer, overseer, principal, supervisor. **2** (*an instructor, a counsellor*) adviser, counsellor, instructor. **3** (*anything which controls or regulates*) control, regulator. **4** (*a spiritual adviser, a confessor*) confessor, guru.

dirt *n.* **1** (*foul or unclean matter, matter that soils*) filth, soil. **2** (*mud, dust*) dust, grime, mire, muck, ooze, slime, sludge. **3** (*faeces*) (*taboo sl.*) crap, dung, excrement, faeces, filth, manure, ordure, (*taboo sl.*) shit. **4** (*a worthless thing, refuse*) dross, garbage, junk, leavings, refuse, trash. **5** (*dirtiness*) dirtiness, filthiness. **6** (*earth, soil*) clay, earth, ground, loam, mud, soil. **7** (*obscene or malicious talk*) gossip, indecency, (*coll.*) low-down, obscenity, rumour, scandal, slander, sleaze, smut, talk.

dirty *a.* **1** (*full of or soiled with dirt*) begrimed, filthy, foul, grimy, (*coll.*) grotty, grubby, (*orig. N Am., sl.*) grungy, messy, mucky, muddy, slovenly, soiled, spotted, stained, sullied. **2** (*foul, unclean*) foul, nasty, unclean. **3** (*offensive, obscene*) (*sl.*) blue, coarse, indecent, lascivious, lewd, obscene, off-colour, offensive, pornographic, prurient, ribald, risqué, salacious, sleazy, smutty, sordid, vulgar.

ANTONYMS: respectable, upright. **4** (*mean; contemptible*) base, contemptible, corrupt, cowardly, (*coll.*) crooked, deceitful, despicable, dishonest, fraudulent, ignominious, illegal, low, mean, shabby, treacherous, unfair, unscrupulous, unsporting. ANTONYMS: fair. **5** ((*of weather*) *wet and gusty*) bad, foul, gusty, rainy, rough, squally, stormy, wet, windy. ANTONYMS: fine. **6** ((*of a colour*) *dull*) clouded, dull, unclear. ANTONYMS: bright, clear.

~*v.t.* (*to make dirty, to soil*) befoul, begrime, blacken, defile, foul, mess up, muddy, pollute, smear, smirch, smudge, soil, spoil, stain, sully, tarnish. ANTONYMS: clean.

disability *n.* (*weakness, handicap*) affliction, ailment, complaint, defect, disablement, disorder, disqualification, handicap, helplessness, impairment, impotency, inability, incapacity, incompetence, infirmity, malady, powerlessness, weakness.

disabled *a.* (*handicapped, incapacitated*) bedridden, crippled, damaged, enfeebled, handicapped, impaired, incapacitated, infirm, lame, maimed, mangled, mutilated, paralysed, weak, weakened, wrecked. ANTONYMS: able-bodied, sound.

disadvantage *n.* **1** (*an unfavourable position or condition*) defect, drawback, fault, flaw, handicap, hindrance, impediment, inconvenience, liability, nuisance, setback, shortcoming, snag, trouble, weakness. ANTONYMS: advantage. **2** (*detriment, hurt*) damage, detriment, harm, hurt, injury, loss, prejudice. ANTONYMS: benefit.

disagreeable *a.* **1** (*offensive, unpleasant*) abominable, disgusting, displeasing, distasteful, horrid, nasty, noxious, objectionable, obnoxious, odious, offensive, repellent, repugnant, repulsive, revolting, uninviting, unpalatable, unpleasant, unsavoury, (*coll.*) yucky. ANTONYMS: pleasant. **2** (*ill-tempered*) abrupt, bad-tempered, brusque, churlish, contrary, cross, difficult, disobliging, grouchy, ill-natured, ill-tempered, irritable, nasty, objectionable, peevish, (*sl.*) ratty, rude, surly, tetchy, unlikeable. ANTONYMS: agreeable, good-natured.

disagreement *n.* **1** (*difference of opinion*) difference, discrepancy, disparity, dissimilarity, dissimilitude, divergence, diversity, incongruity, variance. ANTONYMS: similarity. **2** (*a quarrel, a falling out*) altercation, argument, clash, conflict, contention, controversy, debate, difference, discord, dispute, dissension, division, falling out, misunderstanding, quarrel, row, squabble, strife, tiff, wrangle. ANTONYMS: agreement, harmony.

disappear v.i. 1 (*to go out of sight; to become invisible*) depart, ebb, evanesce, fade, recede, vanish, wane, withdraw. ANTONYMS: appear. 2 (*to cease to exist*) cease, die out, dissolve, end, evaporate, expire, melt away, perish. ANTONYMS: materialize.

disappoint v.t. 1 (*to defeat the expectations or desires of*) chagrin, dash, delude, disenchant, dishearten, disillusion, dismay, fail, let down, mortify, sadden. 2 (*to frustrate, hinder (a plan)*) baffle, confound, defeat, foil, frustrate, hamper, hinder, thwart, undo.

disappointment n. 1 (*the failure of one's hopes*) chagrin, discontent, discouragement, disenchantment, disillusionment, dissatisfaction, failure, frustration, mortification, regret. 2 (*something which or a person who disappoints*) blow, calamity, disaster, failure, fiasco, let-down, misfortune, reverse, setback, (*coll.*) wash-out.

disapprove v.t. (*to condemn, as not approved of*) blame, censure, condemn, criticize, decry, denounce, deplore, deprecate, discountenance, dislike, frown on, object to, put down, reject, spurn, take exception to, veto.

disarray n. (*disorder, confusion*) chaos, clutter, confusion, disorder, jumble, mess, muddle, shambles, state, tangle, unruliness, upset. ANTONYMS: harmony, order.

disaster n. 1 (*a sudden misfortune*) accident, affliction, blow, calamity, cataclysm, catastrophe, misadventure, mischance, misfortune, mishap, reverse, tragedy, trouble. 2 (*misfortune, ill luck*) adversity, ill luck, misfortune. 3 (*fiasco*) fiasco, flop, (*coll.*) wash-out.

disastrous a. 1 (*causing or threatening disaster*) cataclysmic, catastrophic, destructive, devastating, dire, harmful, ruinous. 2 (*very unsuccessful*) adverse, awful, calamitous, catastrophic, dire, dreadful, horrendous, ill-fated, terrible, tragic, unfortunate, unlucky, unpropitious, unsuccessful. ANTONYMS: fortunate, successful.

disband v.i. (*to separate, to disperse*) break up, dismiss, disperse, dissolve, part company, scatter, separate. ANTONYMS: assemble, gather.

discard v.t. (*to get rid of, to reject*) abandon, cast aside, (*coll.*) chuck, dismiss, dispense with, drop, dump, get rid of, jettison, junk, reject, relinquish, repudiate, scrap, shed, throw aside, throw out, (*esp. N Am.*) trash. ANTONYMS: keep, save.

discern v.t. (*to perceive distinctly with the senses, to make out*) detect, distinguish, identify, make out, notice, observe, perceive, recognize.

discernible a. (*that can be perceived, apparent*) apparent, appreciable, conspicuous, detectable, distinct, distinguishable, identifiable, noticeable, observable, obvious, palpable, perceivable, perceptible, plain, recognizable, visible. ANTONYMS: invisible.

discharge[1] v.t. 1 (*to unload from a ship, vehicle etc.*) unburden, unload. 2 (*to emit, to let fly*) emit, exude, give off, gush, let fly, let off, ooze, release. 3 (*to dismiss*) cashier, discard, dismiss, eject, expel, (*coll.*) fire, oust, remove, (*coll.*) sack. 4 (*to release from confinement*) free, liberate, release, set free. 5 (*to relieve of a load*) disburden, lighten, relieve. 6 (*to fire (a gun)*) detonate, explode, fire, set off, shoot. 7 (*to empty, to pour out*) dispense, empty, pour out, void. 8 (*to pay off; to settle*) clear, honour, liquidate, meet, pay off, satisfy, settle, square up. 9 (*to perform (a duty)*) accomplish, carry out, do, execute, fulfil, perform. 10 (*to cancel, to annul*) absolve, acquit, annul, cancel, clear, exonerate, pardon.

discharge[2] n. 1 (*unloading*) unburdening, unloading. 2 (*firing (of a gun)*) blast, burst, detonation, explosion, firing, fusillade, report, salvo, shot, volley. 3 (*payment*) payment, satisfaction, settlement. 4 (*dismissal*) dismissal, expulsion, notice, (*coll.*) sack. 5 (*release, liberation*) acquittal, clearance, exoneration, liberation, pardon, release, remittance. 6 (*(of a duty) performance*) accomplishment, achievement, execution, fulfilment, observance, performance. 7 (*a fluid discharged*) emission, excretion, flow, ooze, secretion, seepage.

disciple n. 1 (*a pupil of a leader etc.*) adherent, apprentice, pupil, scholar, student. ANTONYMS: master, teacher. 2 (*a follower of a particular cult, area of interest etc.*) aficionado, apostle, believer, convert, devotee, fan, follower, partisan, votary.

discipline n. 1 (*training of the mental, moral and physical powers to promote order and obedience*) check, control, curb, direction, drill, exercise, government, indoctrination, instruction, regulation, restraint, restriction, schooling, self-control, subjection, training. 2 (*punishment, chastisement*) castigation, chastisement, correction, penalty, punishment. 3 (*order, systematic obedience*) conduct, method, order, regimen, routine. 4 (*a branch of instruction*) area, branch, course, curriculum, field, speciality, subject.
~v.t. 1 (*to train, esp. in obedience and methodical action*) break in, check, coach, condition, control, drill, educate, enlighten, exercise, govern,

inculcate, indoctrinate, inform, instruct, prepare, regulate, restrain, school, teach, train. **2** (*to punish*) castigate, chasten, chastise, correct, criticize, penalize, punish, rebuke, reprimand, reprove.

disclose *v.t.* **1** (*to make known, to reveal*) blurt out, broadcast, communicate, confess, divulge, impart, inform, leak, let slip, make known, make public, publish, relate, report, reveal, tell, utter. ANTONYMS: suppress. **2** (*to uncover; to lay bare*) bare, bring to light, discover, expose, lay bare, reveal, show, uncover, unveil. ANTONYMS: hide, obscure.

discomfort *n.* **1** (*lack of ease or comfort*) ache, affliction, hurt, irritation, pain, soreness, twinge. **2** (*uneasiness, distress*) annoyance, bother, care, difficulty, disquiet, distress, hardship, inconvenience, malaise, nuisance, trouble, uneasiness, unpleasantness, vexation, worry. ANTONYMS: ease.
~*v.t.* (*to cause pain or uneasiness to*) discompose, disquiet, distress, disturb, embarrass, hurt, pain. ANTONYMS: ease, reassure.

discompose *v.t.* **1** (*to disturb, to agitate*) agitate, bewilder, confuse, disconcert, disquiet, disturb, embarrass, faze, fluster, (*coll.*) hassle, perplex, perturb, provoke, rattle, ruffle, unnerve, unsettle, upset, vex, worry. **2** (*to disarrange*) confuse, disarrange, disorder, untidy.

disconcerting *a.* (*making one feel confused or uneasy*) alarming, awkward, baffling, bewildering, bothersome, confusing, dismaying, distracting, disturbing, embarrassing, off-putting, perplexing, puzzling, unnerving, unsettling, upsetting. ANTONYMS: reassuring.

disconnected *a.* **1** (*incoherent, ill-connected*) confused, disjointed, garbled, ill-connected, illogical, incoherent, irrational, jumbled, mixed-up, rambling, random, uncoordinated, unintelligible, wandering. ANTONYMS: coherent. **2** (*separated*) broken off, cut off, interrupted, separated, severed, split, suspended, unattached, unconnected.

disconsolate *a.* (*unable to be consoled or comforted*) crushed, dejected, desolate, despairing, dismal, down, forlorn, gloomy, grief-stricken, heartbroken, hopeless, inconsolable, melancholy, miserable, pessimistic, sad, unhappy, woeful, wretched. ANTONYMS: cheerful, optimistic.

discontented *a.* (*dissatisfied, uneasy*) annoyed, (*sl.*) brassed off, (*sl.*) browned off, (*coll.*) cheesed off, disgruntled, displeased, disquieted, dissatisfied, exasperated, (*coll.*) fed up, fretful, irritated, miserable, petulant, (*taboo sl.*) pissed off, testy, unhappy, vexed. ANTONYMS: content.

discontinue *v.t.* **1** (*to stop producing*) end, finish, halt, stop, terminate. ANTONYMS: continue. **2** (*to break off, to interrupt*) break off, interrupt, pause, suspend. **3** (*to leave off, to cease to use*) cease, leave off, quit. **4** (*to give up*) abandon, drop, give up, kick, refrain from.

discord *n.* **1** (*lack of agreement; contention*) clash, conflict, contention, disagreement, discordance, dispute, dissension, disunity, friction, incompatibility, opposition, row, rupture, strife, variance, wrangling. ANTONYMS: agreement, concord. **2** (*a lack of harmony in a combination of notes sounded together*) cacophony, din, disharmony, dissonance, harshness, jangle, jarring, racket, tumult. ANTONYMS: harmony.

discordant *a.* **1** (*unpleasing, esp. to the ear*) cacophonous, dissonant, grating, harsh, jangling, jarring, shrill, strident, unmelodious, unmusical, unpleasing. ANTONYMS: harmonious, tuneful. **2** (*opposite, contradictory*) adverse, clashing, conflicting, contradictory, contrary, different, disagreeing, dissimilar, divergent, incompatible, incongruous, opposite.

discount[1] *n.* (*a deduction from the amount of a price*) allowance, cut, deduction, markdown, rebate, reduction.

discount[2] *v.t.* **1** (*to deduct a certain sum from (a price)*) deduct, knock off, lower, mark down, rebate, reduce, take off. **2** (*to lend or advance (an amount), deducting interest at a certain rate per cent from the principle*) advance, lend, loan. **3** (*to make allowance for, to disregard*) allow for, dismiss, disregard, gloss over, ignore, leave out, omit, overlook, pass over.

discourage *v.t.* **1** (*to deprive of courage; to dishearten*) abash, cast down, cow, dampen, dash, daunt, deject, demoralize, depress, dishearten, dismay, frighten, intimidate, overawe, unnerve. ANTONYMS: encourage, inspire. **2** (*to dissuade; to deter*) check, curb, deprecate, deter, discountenance, dissuade, divert from, hinder, inhibit, oppose, prevent, put off, restrain, slow, stop, suppress, talk out of.

discourteous *a.* (*impolite, rude*) abrupt, bad-mannered, brusque, curt, disrespectful, ill-bred, ill-mannered, impertinent, impolite, insolent, offhand, rude, uncivil, uncourteous, ungentlemanly, ungracious, unladylike, unmannerly. ANTONYMS: polite, well-mannered.

discover *v.t.* **1** (*to gain the first sight of*) behold, bring to light, see, spot. **2** (*to find out by exploration*) conceive, devise, invent, originate, pioneer. **3** (*to ascertain, to realize suddenly*) ascertain, determine, find out, identify, learn, notice, perceive, realize, recognize, track down. **4** (*to detect*) come across, come upon, detect, dig up, discern, ferret out, find, light upon, locate, turn up, uncover, unearth. **5** (*to disclose, to reveal*) betray, disclose, make known, reveal.

discovery *n.* **1** (*the act of discovering*) ascertainment, detection, exploration, finding, location, origination. **2** (*something which is made known for the first time*) breakthrough, coup, innovation, invention. **3** (*disclosure*) disclosure, manifestation, revelation.

discredit *n.* **1** (*lack or loss of credit*) blame, disgrace, dishonour, disrepute, humiliation. ANTONYMS: credit. **2** (*disrepute, disgrace*) aspersion, censure, disgrace, dishonour, disrepute, ignominy, ill repute, imputation, obloquy, odium, opprobrium, reproach, scandal, shame, slur, smear, stigma. ANTONYMS: approval, credit. **3** (*disbelief; lack of credibility*) disbelief, distrust, doubt, mistrust, question, scepticism, suspicion.
~*v.t.* **1** (*to disbelieve*) challenge, deny, disbelieve, discount, distrust, doubt, mistrust, question. **2** (*to bring into disrepute*) belittle, blacken, blame, bring into disrepute, censure, defame, degrade, deprecate, detract from, disgrace, dishonour, disparage, libel, malign, reproach, slander, slur, smear, sully, vilify. ANTONYMS: commend, praise.

discreditable *a.* (*disreputable, disgraceful*) blameworthy, degrading, disgraceful, dishonourable, disreputable, humiliating, ignoble, ignominious, improper, infamous, reprehensible, scandalous, shameful, unprincipled, unworthy.

discreet *a.* **1** (*prudent, wary*) careful, cautious, chary, circumspect, considerate, diplomatic, discerning, guarded, judicious, politic, prudent, reserved, sagacious, sensible, tactful, wary. ANTONYMS: tactless, undiplomatic. **2** (*subtle*) subdued, subtle, unobtrusive.

discrepancy *n.* (*a difference; an inconsistency*) conflict, deviation, difference, disagreement, discordance, disparity, dissimilarity, dissonance, divergence, gap, incompatibility, incongruity, inconsistency, variance, variation. ANTONYMS: correspondence.

discretion *n.* **1** (*the power or faculty of distinguishing things that differ*) choice, discrimination, inclination, option, predilection, preference, wish. **2** (*discernment, judgement*) care, caution, circumspection, common sense, consideration, diplomacy, discernment, good sense, judgement, judiciousness, prudence, sagacity, tact, wariness. **3** (*freedom of judgement and action*) freedom, independence, leeway, liberty.

discretionary *a.* (*not compulsory, not controlled strictly*) arbitrary, elective, non-mandatory, open, optional, unrestricted, voluntary. ANTONYMS: mandatory.

discriminate *v.i.* **1** (*to make a distinction or difference*) assess, differentiate, discern, distinguish, isolate, judge, segregate, separate, sift, sort. **2** (*to treat (unfairly) a group of people either worse or better than other groups*) disfavour, favour, pick out, single out, victimize.

discursive *a.* (*passing from one subject to another; rambling*) circuitous, circumlocutory, desultory, diffuse, digressive, erratic, long-winded, loose, meandering, rambling, roundabout, verbose, wordy.

discuss *v.t.* **1** (*to debate*) argue, confer, converse, debate, talk about, thrash out. **2** (*to consider or examine by argument*) assess, consider, deliberate, examine, go into, review, sift.

discussion *n.* (*consideration or investigation by argument for and against*) analysis, argument, chat, colloquy, confabulation, conference, consideration, consultation, conversation, debate, deliberation, dialogue, discourse, examination, exchange, investigation, review, scrutiny, talk.

disdainful *a.* (*showing contempt and haughtiness*) aloof, arrogant, contemptuous, derisive, haughty, (*coll.*) high and mighty, hoity-toity, insolent, insulting, mocking, pompous, proud, scornful, sneering, snobbish, stuck-up, supercilious, superior.

disease *n.* **1** (*an illness*) affliction, ailment, (*sl.*) bug, complaint, condition, disorder, illness, indisposition, infection, infirmity, malady, sickness, upset. **2** (*any disorder or morbid condition*) blight, cancer, contagion, contamination, disorder, malady, plague, virus.

disentangle *v.t.* (*to free from entanglement*) detach, disconnect, disengage, extricate, free, loose, separate, sever, undo, unfold, unravel, unsnarl, untangle, untie, untwist.

disfigure *v.t.* (*to spoil the beauty or appearance of*) blemish, damage, deface, deform, distort, impair, injure, maim, mar, mutilate, ruin, scar, spoil.

disgrace *n.* **1** (*the state of being out of favour*) degradation, discredit, dishonour, disrepute, embarrassment, humiliation, ignominy, infamy, obloquy, odium, opprobrium, shame. ANTONYMS: credit, repute. **2** (*the cause of shame*) aspersion, blemish, blot, scandal, slur, smear, smirch, stain, stigma, taint.
~*v.t.* **1** (*to dishonour; to bring disgrace on*) abase, defame, discredit, dishonour, disparage,

humiliate, mortify, reproach, shame, slur, stain, stigmatize, sully, taint, tarnish. **2** (*to dismiss from favour*) debase, degrade.

disgraceful *a.* (*shameful, dishonourable*) blameworthy, contemptible, degrading, despicable, detestable, discreditable, dishonourable, disreputable, embarrassing, humiliating, ignominious, improper, infamous, mean, outrageous, scandalous, shameful, shocking, unseemly, unworthy.

disgruntled *a.* (*annoyed, disappointed*) annoyed, (*esp. N Am.*) cranky, cross, disappointed, discontented, displeased, dissatisfied, exasperated, (*coll.*) fed up, grouchy, grumpy, huffy, peeved, petulant, (*taboo sl.*) pissed off, put out, sulky, sullen, unhappy, vexed.

disguise *v.t.* **1** (*to conceal or alter the appearance of, with unusual dress*) alter, camouflage, cloak, conceal, cover, hide, mask, muffle, screen, secrete, shroud, veil. ANTONYMS: reveal. **2** (*to hide by a counterfeit appearance*) alter, counterfeit, deceive, dissemble, dissimulate, fake, falsify, fudge, gloss over, misrepresent.
~*n.* **1** (*a dress or manner put on to disguise*) camouflage, cloak, concealment, costume, cover, dress, get-up, guise, identify, mask, screen, veil. **2** (*a pretence or show*) appearance, blind, deception, dissimulation, facade, front, pretence, semblance, show, trickery, veneer.

disgust *v.t.* **1** (*to cause loathing or aversion in*) displease, horrify, nauseate, put off, repulse, revolt, sicken. ANTONYMS: delight, please. **2** (*to offend the taste of*) appal, offend, outrage.
~*n.* **1** (*loathing, repulsion*) abhorrence, abomination, animosity, antipathy, aversion, contempt, detestation, dislike, hatefulness, hatred, loathing, repugnance, repulsion, revulsion. ANTONYMS: liking, love. **2** (*a strong feeling of nausea*) distaste, nausea.

dishearten *v.t.* (*to discourage, to disappoint*) cast down, crush, dampen, dash, daunt, deject, depress, deter, disappoint, disconcert, discourage, dismay, dispirit, sadden. ANTONYMS: cheer up, hearten.

dishevelled *a.* **1** ((*of hair*) *hanging loosely and negligently*) disarranged, disordered, loose, ruffled, tousled, uncombed. **2** ((*of a person*) *untidy, unkempt*) bedraggled, blowzy, disarrayed, ill-kempt, messy, rumpled, unkempt, untidy. ANTONYMS: spruce, tidy.

dishonest *a.* (*fraudulent, deceitful*) (*sl.*) bent, cheating, corrupt, (*coll.*) crooked, deceitful, disreputable, fraudulent, guileful, hypocritical, insincere, lying, mendacious, perfidious, shady, underhand, unfair, unprincipled,

unscrupulous, untrustworthy, untruthful. ANTONYMS: honest, straight.

dishonour *n.* **1** (*disgrace, discredit*) abasement, degradation, discredit, disfavour, disgrace, disrepute, ignominy, infamy, obloquy, odium, opprobrium, scandal, shame. **2** (*reproach, disparagement*) abuse, affront, aspersion, defamation, disparagement, insult, libel, outrage, reproach, slander.
~*v.t.* **1** (*to bring disgrace or shame on*) abase, blacken, corrupt, debase, debauch, defame, degrade, discredit, disgrace, humble, humiliate, mortify, shame, sully. **2** (*to refuse to accept or pay* (*a cheque or bill*)) decline, refuse, reject. **3** (*to violate the chastity of*) debauch, defile, deflower, molest, pollute, rape, ravish, seduce, violate.

dishonourable *a.* **1** (*causing dishonour; disgraceful*) contemptible, degrading, despicable, discreditable, disgraceful, ignoble, ignominious, infamous, scandalous, shameful. **2** (*unprincipled; without honour*) base, corrupt, dishonest, disreputable, duplicitous, faithless, hypocritical, mean, perfidious, treacherous, unfaithful, unprincipled, unscrupulous, untrustworthy.

disingenuous *a.* (*lacking in frankness or candour*) artful, calculating, crafty, cunning, deceitful, designing, devious, dishonest, duplicitous, guileful, hypocritical, insidious, insincere, lying, scheming, slick, tricky, underhand, unfair, wily. ANTONYMS: candid, frank.

disintegrate *v.t.* (*to reduce to fragments or powder*) break apart, break up, fragment, powder, pulverize, separate, shatter, splinter.
~*v.i.* (*to fall to pieces, to crumble*) break up, crumble, decay, decompose, fall apart, rot.

disinterested *a.* (*without personal interest or prejudice; unbiased*) detached, dispassionate, equitable, even-handed, fair, impartial, neutral, objective, unbiased, unprejudiced, unselfish. ANTONYMS: biased, prejudiced.

disjointed *a.* (*broken up, incoherent*) aimless, broken up, confused, desultory, disconnected, dislocated, dismembered, disordered, displaced, divided, fitful, incoherent, jumbled, muddled, rambling, separated, spasmodic, split, unconnected.

dislike *v.t.* (*to regard with repugnance or aversion*) abhor, abominate, despise, detest, disapprove of, disfavour, execrate, hate, loathe, object to, scorn, shun. ANTONYMS: like.
~*n.* (*a feeling of repugnance; aversion*) abhorrence, animosity, antagonism, antipathy, aversion, contempt, detestation, disapprobation,

disapproval, disgust, disinclination, displeasure, distaste, enmity, execration, hatred, hostility, loathing, odium, repugnance. ANTONYMS: liking.

disloyal a. (not true to allegiance) disaffected, faithless, false, perfidious, rebellious, seditious, subversive, traitorous, treacherous, treasonable, two-faced, unfaithful, untrue, untrustworthy. ANTONYMS: faithful, loyal.

dismal a. 1 (dark, depressing) bleak, cheerless, dark, depressing, discouraging, doleful, drab, dreary, dull, forlorn, funereal, gloomy, grim, lugubrious, melancholy, miserable, morose, sad, sombre, woeful. ANTONYMS: cheerful, sunny. 2 (depressingly poor) disappointing, poor.

dismay v.t. 1 (to deprive of courage; to dispirit) daunt, depress, disappoint, discourage, dishearten, disillusion, dispirit, put off. 2 (to terrify, to daunt) affright, alarm, disconcert, frighten, horrify, intimidate, paralyse, petrify, scare, terrify, unnerve.
~n. 1 (utter loss of courage or resolution) chagrin, disappointment, discouragement, disillusionment, upset. 2 (a state of terror or fear) alarm, anxiety, apprehension, awe, consternation, dread, fear, fright, horror, panic, shock, terror, trepidation.

dismiss v.t. 1 (to send away; to disband) demobilize, disband, disperse, dissolve, free, let go, release, send away. 2 (to discharge from office or employment) cashier, discharge, (coll.) fire, give notice to, lay off, (coll.) sack. 3 (to reject) put aside, reject, shelve. 4 (to discard) banish, cast off, discard, dispel, disregard, drop, repudiate, spurn.

dismissal n. (discharge from employment) (sl.) boot, discharge, expulsion, (N Am., sl.) kiss-off, (sl.) push, removal, (coll.) sack.

disobedient a. (refusing or neglecting to obey) contrary, defiant, delinquent, headstrong, insubordinate, intractable, mischievous, mutinous, naughty, obstinate, obstreperous, rebellious, recalcitrant, refractory, stubborn, undisciplined, ungovernable, unruly, wayward, wilful. ANTONYMS: obedient, submissive.

disobey v.t. 1 (to neglect or refuse to obey) defy, disregard, ignore, mutiny, oppose, rebel, resist. ANTONYMS: obey, toe the line. 2 (to violate, to transgress) break, contravene, flout, infringe, transgress, violate.

disorder n. 1 (lack of order; confusion) chaos, clutter, confusion, derangement, disarray, disorganization, irregularity, jumble, mess, muddle, shambles, state, tangle, untidiness. 2 (tumult, commotion) bedlam, clamour,

commotion, disturbance, fight, fuss, hubbub, hullabaloo, quarrel, riot, rumpus, scuffle, (coll.) shindig, tumult, turbulence, turmoil, unrest, unruliness, upheaval, uproar. 3 (disease, illness) affliction, ailment, complaint, disease, illness, indisposition, malady, sickness. 4 (neglect of laws or discipline) anarchy, indiscipline, lawlessness. ANTONYMS: order.
~v.t. (to throw into confusion) clutter, confound, confuse, derange, disarrange, discompose, disorganize, disturb, jumble, mess up, mix up, muddle, scatter, scramble, shake up, snarl, tangle, unsettle, untidy, upset.

disorderly a. 1 (confused, disarranged) chaotic, cluttered, confused, disarranged, disordered, disorganized, disturbed, haphazard, jumbled, messy, muddled, scrambled, topsy-turvy, untidy. ANTONYMS: neat, tidy. 2 (causing disturbance, unruly) boisterous, disruptive, lawless, mutinous, noisy, obstreperous, rebellious, refractory, riotous, rowdy, stormy, tumultuous, turbulent, undisciplined, ungovernable, unmanageable, unruly, violent, wild. ANTONYMS: orderly.

disorganize v.t. (to destroy the arrangement of) break up, confuse, derange, destroy, disarrange, discompose, disorder, disrupt, disturb, jumble, mix up, muddle, unsettle, upset. ANTONYMS: organize.

disparage v.t. 1 (to treat or speak of slightingly) (coll.) bad-mouth, belittle, blast, criticize, defame, denigrate, deprecate, depreciate, deride, (coll.) knock, malign, put down, ridicule, rubbish, run down, scorn, (sl.) slag off, slander, slight, vilify. 2 (to discredit, to disgrace) detract from, discredit, disgrace. 3 (to think lightly of, to undervalue) underestimate, underrate, undervalue.

dispassionate a. (calm, impartial) calm, cool, detached, disinterested, impartial, impassive, imperturbable, level-headed, moderate, neutral, objective, self-possessed, serene, temperate, unbiased, unemotional, unexcitable, unmoved, unprejudiced, unruffled. ANTONYMS: emotional, prejudiced.

dispatch v.t. 1 (to send off to some destination, esp. with haste) consign, dismiss, express, forward, hasten, hurry, mail, post, quicken, remit, send, send off, speed, transmit. 2 (to settle, to finish) conclude, discharge, dispose of, expedite, finish, settle. 3 (to put to death) assassinate, butcher, execute, kill, liquidate, murder, put to death, slaughter, slay. 4 (to eat quickly) bolt, cram, eat.
~n. 1 (quickness, speed) alacrity, celerity, expedition, haste, hurry, promptitude, promptness, quickness, rapidity, speed, swiftness.

2 (*a message, esp. an official communication*) account, bulletin, communication, communiqué, document, instruction, item, letter, message, missive, piece, report, story. **3** (*the act or an instance of killing someone*) assassination, execution, killing, slaughter.

dispense *v.t.* **1** (*to deal out, to distribute*) allocate, allot, apportion, assign, deal out, disburse, (*sl.*) dish out, distribute, dole out, give out, hand out, mete out, pass out, share. ANTONYMS: withhold. **2** (*to administer*) administer, apply, carry out, conduct, direct, discharge, enforce, execute, implement, operate, supervise, undertake. **3** (*to prepare and give out* (*medicine*)) administer, measure, mix, prepare, supply. **4** (*to grant a dispensation to*) except, excuse, exempt, exonerate, let off, release, relieve, reprieve. **to dispense with 1** (*to do without*) abstain from, do without, eschew, forgo, forswear, give up, omit, reject, relinquish, renounce, waive. **2** (*to grant exemption from*) except, excuse, exempt, exonerate, let off, release, relieve, reprieve.

disperse *v.t.* **1** (*to drive or throw in different directions*) scatter, send, spread, strew. ANTONYMS: gather. **2** (*to dissipate, to cause to vanish*) diffuse, dispel, dissipate, dissolve. **3** (*to disseminate*) broadcast, circulate, disseminate, spread about.
~*v.i.* **1** (*to be scattered in different directions*) go one's separate ways, part, scatter. **2** (*to break up, to vanish*) break up, disappear, dissolve, vanish.

dispirited *a.* (*discouraged, disheartened*) crestfallen, dejected, depressed, despondent, discouraged, disheartened, down, downcast, gloomy, glum, low, morose, pessimistic, sad. ANTONYMS: cheerful, optimistic.

displace *v.t.* **1** (*to remove from the usual or proper place*) derange, disarrange, dislodge, disturb, misplace, move, relocate, remove, shift, transpose. **2** (*to remove from a position; to dismiss*) depose, discharge, dismiss, (*coll.*) fire, remove, (*coll.*) sack, unseat. **3** (*to put something in the place of, to supersede*) oust, replace, succeed, supersede, supplant, take the place of. **4** (*to banish*) banish, dispossess, eject, evict, exile.

display *v.t.* **1** (*to exhibit, to show*) demonstrate, exhibit, expose, present, show. **2** (*to exhibit ostentatiously*) boast, flaunt, flourish, parade, show off, vaunt. **3** (*to make known, to reveal*) disclose, make known, publicize, reveal, unfold, unveil. ANTONYMS: conceal, veil.
~*n.* **1** (*displaying*) displaying, exposure. **2** (*show, exhibition*) array, demonstration, exhibition, exposition, pageant, parade, presentation,

show. **3** (*a computer screen*) monitor, screen, VDU, visual display unit. **4** (*ostentatious behaviour*) flourish, ostentation, pomp, spectacle.

displeasure *n.* (*a feeling of annoyance or anger*) anger, annoyance, chagrin, disapproval, discontentment, disfavour, disgust, dislike, dissatisfaction, distaste, exasperation, indignation, irritation, offence, pique, resentment, vexation, wrath. ANTONYMS: approval, pleasure.

dispose *v.t.* **1** (*to arrange, to set in order*) arrange, array, group, marshal, order, organize, place, put, range, rank, regulate, set in order, stand. **2** (*to settle*) conclude, deal with, decide, determine, finish, fix, settle. **3** (*to adjust, to incline*) adjust, bias, condition, direct, incline, influence, lead, move, predispose. **4** (*to hand over, to bestow*) allot, apportion, bestow, deal out, dispense, distribute, give out, hand over, parcel out, part with, transfer. **to dispose of 1** (*to put into the hands of someone else*) bestow, give, hand over, make over, transfer. **2** (*to get rid of*) (*coll.*) chuck, destroy, discard, dump, get rid of, jettison, junk, reject, scrap, throw out, unload. **3** (*to sell*) part with, sell. **4** (*to finish, to settle*) conclude, deal with, determine, end, finish, settle. **5** (*to kill*) destroy, do away with, finish off, kill, (*sl.*) knock off, (*coll.*) polish off. **6** (*to use up*) consume, exhaust, spend, use up.

disposed *a.* (*inclined*) apt, given, inclined, leaning (towards), liable, likely, minded, predisposed, prone, ready, subject, tending (towards), willing.

disposition *n.* **1** (*the act of arranging or bestowing*) adjustment, arrangement, bestowing, disposing, distribution, transfer. **2** (*arrangement in general*) arrangement, classification, grouping, ordering, organization. **3** (*inclination, natural tendency*) aptitude, attitude, bent, bias, character, constitution, habit, inclination, leaning, make-up, nature, personality, predisposition, proclivity, propensity, temper, temperament, tendency. **4** (*a caprice, fancy*) caprice, fancy, humour, whim.

disprove *v.t.* (*to prove to be erroneous or unfounded*) confute, contradict, controvert, demolish, discredit, expose, invalidate, negate, overturn, rebut, refute. ANTONYMS: confirm, prove.

dispute *v.i.* **1** (*to quarrel in opposition to another*) altercate, argue, bicker, brawl, clash, contend, quarrel, row, spar, squabble, wrangle. ANTONYMS: agree. **2** (*to debate, to discuss*) argue, confer, converse, debate, discuss, talk.
~*v.t.* **1** (*to oppose, to deny the truth of*) argue,

challenge, contend, contradict, deny, doubt, impugn, oppose, question, rebut. **2** (*to reason upon, to discuss*) argue, discuss, reason, talk about. **3** (*to contend or strive for*) contend, contest, strive for. **4** (*to strive against, to resist*) resist, strive against, withstand.
~*n.* **1** (*contention or strife in argument*) altercation, argument, brawl, contention, controversy, debate, discussion, strife. **2** (*a difference of opinion; a quarrel*) difference, disagreement, discord, disputation, falling out, feud, quarrel, wrangle. **3** (*strife, struggle*) conflict, contest, strife, struggle.

disqualify *v.t.* **1** (*to render unfit, to debar*) debar, disable, incapacitate, invalidate, render unfit. **2** (*to disbar from a competition on account of an irregularity*) ban, debar, eliminate, exclude, preclude, rule out.

disregard *v.t.* **1** (*to take no notice of; to neglect*) brush aside, discount, gloss over, ignore, neglect, overlook, pass over, take no notice of, turn a blind eye to, turn a deaf ear to, wink at. **2** (*to ignore as unworthy of regard*) brush off, cold-shoulder, cut, despise, disdain, dismiss, disparage, ignore, scorn, slight, snub.
~*n.* (*lack of attention or regard*) (*coll.*) brush-off, contempt, disdain, disrespect, heedlessness, inattention, indifference, neglect, negligence, oversight, slight.

disrepair *n.* (*a state of being out of repair*) collapse, decay, decrepitude, deterioration, dilapidation, ruin, ruination.

disreputable *a.* **1** (*of bad repute, not respectable*) abject, base, contemptible, derogatory, discreditable, disgraceful, dishonourable, disorderly, dubious, ignominious, low, mean, notorious, opprobrious, reprehensible, scandalous, shady, shameful, shocking, unprincipled. ANTONYMS: reputable, respectable. **2** (*dirty or shabby in appearance*) bedraggled, dilapidated, dingy, dirty, dishevelled, disordered, down at heel, messy, scruffy, seedy, shabby, sloppy, slovenly, tattered, threadbare, unkempt, worn. ANTONYMS: smart.

disrespectful *a.* (*lacking in respect; rude*) bad-mannered, cheeky, contemptuous, discourteous, forward, (*coll.*) fresh, ill-bred, impertinent, impolite, impudent, indecorous, insolent, insulting, irreverent, misbehaved, pert, rude, saucy, uncivil. ANTONYMS: polite, respectful.

disrupt *v.t.* **1** (*to interrupt, to prevent from continuing*) break in, interfere, interrupt, intrude. **2** (*to tear apart, to break in pieces*) break in pieces, tear apart. **3** (*to upset, to confuse*) agitate, confuse, disconcert, disorder, disorganize, disturb, shake up, spoil, upset.

dissatisfaction *n.* (*a state of discontent, displeasure*) annoyance, chagrin, disappointment, disapproval, discomfort, discontent, dislike, dismay, displeasure, disquiet, distress, exasperation, frustration, irritation, regret, resentment, uneasiness, unhappiness. ANTONYMS: satisfaction.

disseminate *v.t.* **1** (*to spread (information) about*) broadcast, circulate, diffuse, disperse, dissipate, distribute, proclaim, promulgate, publicize, publish, spread about. **2** (*to scatter (seed) about with a view to growth*) propagate, scatter, strew.

dissension *n.* (*disagreement of opinion; strife*) conflict, contention, difference, disagreement, discord, dispute, dissent, friction, quarrel, row, strife. ANTONYMS: agreement.

dissent *v.i.* **1** (*to differ or disagree in opinion*) differ, disagree, dispute, object, oppose, protest. ANTONYMS: agree. **2** (*to withhold assent or approval*) decline, refuse, withhold assent. ANTONYMS: assent.
~*n.* (*difference or disagreement of opinion*) difference, disagreement, discord, dissension, dissidence, objection, opposition, refusal, resistance. ANTONYMS: agreement.

dissident *a.* (*not in agreement; disagreeing*) conflicting, contentious, differing, disagreeing, discordant, dissenting, nonconformist, schismatic.
~*n.* **1** (*a person who dissents from or votes against any motion*) dissenter, nay, protester. **2** (*a person who disagrees with the government; a dissenter*) agitator, dissenter, heretic, rebel, revolutionary, subversive.

dissimilar *a.* (*unlike in nature or appearances*) contrasting, different, discordant, disparate, distinct, divergent, diverse, heterogeneous, manifold, mismatched, unlike, unrelated, various. ANTONYMS: alike, similar.

dissipate *v.t.* **1** (*to scatter; to drive in different directions*) diffuse, drive away, scatter, strew. **2** (*to disperse, to dispel*) diffuse, dispel, disperse, dissolve. **3** (*to squander, to waste*) burn up, consume, deplete, drain, exhaust, expend, fritter away, misspend, run through, spend, squander, throw away, use up, waste.
~*v.i.* **1** (*to be dispersed, to vanish*) disappear, evaporate, vanish, vaporize. **2** (*to indulge in dissolute enjoyment*) carouse, debauch, indulge, lavish, make merry, party, revel, roister.

dissipation *n.* **1** (*the act of dissipating or scattering*) dispersal, dissemination, scattering. **2** (*excessive indulgence in frivolity or vice*) abandon, debauchery, depravity, dissoluteness, drunkenness, indulgence, lavishness, licentiousness, prodigality, profligacy, self-indulgence. **3** (*wasteful expenditure, extravagance*) excess, extravagance, intemperance, squandering, wantonness, waste, wastefulness. ANTONYMS: frugality. **4** (*dispersion, diffusion*) diffusion, disappearance, disintegration, dispersion, dissolution, vanishing.

dissolute *a*. (*loose in morals; debauched*) abandoned, corrupt, debauched, degenerate, depraved, dissipated, hedonistic, immoral, intemperate, lewd, libertine, libidinous, licentious, loose, profligate, wanton, wild. ANTONYMS: chaste, moral.

dissolution *n*. **1** (*the act or process of dissolving, separating etc.*) breakdown, break-up, collapse, decay, decomposition, disintegration, dispersal, dissolving, division, liquefaction, melting, separation. ANTONYMS: amalgamation, consolidation. **2** (*death, the separation of soul and body*) annihilation, death, demise, extinction. **3** (*the official ending of a marriage or other relationship*) break-up, conclusion, disbandment, discontinuation, divorce, end, finish, parting, separation, suspension, termination. **4** (*dissoluteness, corruption*) corruption, debauchery, depravity, dissipation, dissoluteness, intemperance, wantonness.

dissolve *v.t.* **1** (*to diffuse the particles of* (*a substance*) *in a liquid*) diffuse, mix. **2** (*to convert from a solid to a liquid state by heat or moisture*) liquefy, melt. **3** (*to separate; to break up*) break up, destroy, disperse, disunite, divorce, separate, sever. **4** (*to put an end to* (*as a meeting etc.*)) dismiss, disperse, wind up.
~*v.i.* **1** (*to become liquefied*) liquefy, melt, soften, thaw. ANTONYMS: solidify. **2** (*to decompose, to disintegrate*) crumble, decompose, disintegrate. **3** (*to separate*) break up, disintegrate, separate. **4** (*to fade away, to melt away*) dissipate, dwindle, evanesce, evaporate, fade away, fizzle out, melt away, waste away. **5** (*to vanish*) disappear, vanish. **6** (*to be emotionally overcome*) break down, collapse, melt into. **7** (*in films and TV, to fade out one scene and merge in the next*) fade out, merge.

distance *n*. **1** (*extent of separation*) extent, gap, interval, lapse, length, range, reach, separation, space, span, stretch, width. **2** (*the quality of being distant, remoteness*) farness, remoteness, remove. **3** (*reserve, unfriendliness*) aloofness, coldness, constraint, coolness, detachment, frigidity, haughtiness, reserve, restraint, stiffness, unfriendliness. ANTONYMS: friendliness, warmth.

distant *a*. **1** (*separated by intervening space*) apart, dispersed, distinct, scattered, separate,

spaced out. **2** (*remote in space or time*) afar, far, faraway, far-flung, far-off, outlying, out-of-the-way, remote, removed. ANTONYMS: close, nearby. **3** (*not obvious; slight*) faint, indirect, indistinct, obscure, slight, uncertain. ANTONYMS: obvious, plain. **4** (*reserved, cool*) aloof, cold, cool, detached, formal, frigid, haughty, reserved, restrained, reticent, stand-offish, stiff, unapproachable, unfriendly, withdrawn. ANTONYMS: friendly, warm. **5** (*distracted, absent*) absent, distracted.

distaste *n*. (*dislike, disinclination*) abhorrence, antipathy, aversion, detestation, disfavour, disgust, disinclination, dislike, displeasure, horror, loathing, repugnance, revulsion.

distasteful *a*. **1** (*offensive, displeasing*) abhorrent, disagreeable, disgusting, displeasing, foul, hateful, loathsome, nauseating, objectionable, obnoxious, obscene, offensive, repugnant, repulsive, revolting, undesirable, uninviting, unpleasant. ANTONYMS: agreeable. **2** (*unpleasant to the taste*) unpalatable, unsavoury. ANTONYMS: tasty.

distinct *a*. **1** (*clearly distinguished or distinguishable*) contrasting, detached, different, discrete, dissimilar, distinguishable, individual, separate, singular, unconnected, unique, unusual. ANTONYMS: identical, similar. **2** (*unmistakable, clear*) apparent, blatant, clear, decided, definite, evident, explicit, lucid, manifest, marked, obvious, patent, plain, precise, sharp, transparent, unambiguous, unequivocal, unmistakable, well-defined. ANTONYMS: unclear, vague.

distinction *n*. **1** (*a mark or note of difference*) contrast, difference, differential, dissimilarity, division, separation. **2** (*a distinguishing quality*) characteristic, distinctiveness, feature, individuality, mark, particularity, peculiarity, quality, trait. **3** (*the act of distinguishing*) differentiation, discernment, discrimination, distinguishing, penetration, perception, separation. **4** (*honour, rank*) honour, rank, title. **5** (*eminence, superiority*) account, celebrity, consequence, credit, eminence, excellence, fame, glory, greatness, honour, importance, merit, prestige, prominence, quality, renown, repute, significance, superiority, worth. ANTONYMS: insignificance.

distinctive *a*. **1** (*serving to mark distinction or difference*) characteristic, different, distinguishing, extraordinary, idiosyncratic, individual, original, remarkable, singular, special, uncommon, unique. ANTONYMS: commonplace, ordinary. **2** (*distinct*) distinct, separate.

distinguish *v.t.* **1** (*to discriminate, to differentiate*) ascertain, decide, determine, differentiate, discriminate, judge, set apart. **2** (*to indicate the difference of from others by some external mark*) denote, indicate, individualize, mark. **3** (*to classify*) categorize, characterize, classify. **4** (*to discriminate between*) discriminate between, tell apart. **5** (*to perceive the existence of by means of the senses*) detect, discern, identify, know, make out, perceive, pick out, recognize, see, sense, single out, tell. **6** (*to make prominent, or well known*) celebrate, dignify, ennoble, honour, immortalize, make famous, signalize.

distinguished *a.* **1** (*having an air of nobility or dignity*) aristocratic, august, dignified, grand, lordly, majestic, noble, regal, stately. ANTONYMS: common. **2** (*eminent, celebrated*) acclaimed, celebrated, conspicuous, eminent, famed, famous, honoured, illustrious, notable, noted, noteworthy, pre-eminent, prominent, remarkable, renowned, respected, well-known. ANTONYMS: unknown.

distort *v.t.* **1** (*to alter the natural shape of*) alter, bend, buckle, contort, deform, disfigure, misshape, turn, twist, warp, wrench, wrest. **2** (*to pervert from the true meaning*) bias, colour, corrupt, falsify, garble, misrepresent, pervert, slant, (*N Am.*) spin, tamper with, twist, varnish.

distract *v.t.* **1** (*to draw or turn aside*) deflect, divert, draw away, sidetrack, turn aside. **2** (*to confuse, to perplex*) agitate, befuddle, bewilder, confound, confuse, discompose, disconcert, disturb, fluster, mystify, perplex, puzzle, rattle. **3** (*to drive mad, to trouble*) craze, derange, madden, torment, trouble. **4** (*to amuse*) absorb, amuse, beguile, delight, divert, engross, entertain, interest, occupy.

distraught *a.* (*bewildered, agitated*) agitated, anxious, beside oneself, bewildered, crazed, delirious, desperate, distracted, distressed, frantic, hysterical, mad, overwrought, perturbed, raving, stricken, troubled, upset, wild, worked up. ANTONYMS: calm, composed.

distress *n.* **1** (*extreme anguish or pain of mind or body*) ache, affliction, agony, anxiety, depression, desolation, discomfort, grief, heartache, misery, pain, sadness, sorrow, suffering, torment, torture, unhappiness, woe, worry. ANTONYMS: joy. **2** (*misery, poverty*) destitution, hardship, indigence, misery, need, poverty, privation, straits. **3** (*fatigue*) exhaustion, fatigue, tiredness. **4** (*calamity, misfortune*) adversity, calamity, catastrophe, difficulty, disaster, misfortune, tragedy, trial, trouble. **5** (*a state of danger*) danger, jeopardy, peril.
~*v.t.* **1** (*to afflict with anxiety or unhappiness*) afflict, bother, disturb, grieve, harass, harrow,

oppress, pain, perplex, plague, sadden, torment, trouble, upset, vex, worry, wound. **2** (*to tire out*) exhaust, fatigue, tire out.

distribute *v.t.* **1** (*to divide or deal out amongst a number*) administer, allocate, allot, apportion, assign, deal out, (*sl.*) dish out, dispense, dispose, divide, dole out, give, give out, hand out, measure out, mete, parcel out, partition, pass out, share. ANTONYMS: withhold. **2** (*to spread about, to disperse*) diffuse, disperse, disseminate, scatter, spread about, strew. **3** (*to arrange, to classify*) allocate, arrange, assort, categorize, class, classify, file, group, order.

district *n.* **1** (*a portion of territory specially defined for administrative etc. purposes*) area, region, territory. **2** (*a division having its own representative in a legislature, its own district council etc.*) borough, community, constituency, department, neighbourhood, parish, precinct, quarter, sector, ward. **3** (*a region, tract of country*) locale, locality, part, region, tract, vicinity, zone.

distrust *v.t.* (*to doubt, to suspect*) disbelieve, discredit, doubt, misbelieve, mistrust, question, suspect. ANTONYMS: believe, depend.
~*n.* (*suspicion, discredit*) caution, disbelief, discredit, doubt, incredulity, misgiving, mistrust, qualm, question, scepticism, suspicion, uncertainty, wariness. ANTONYMS: confidence, trust.

disturb *v.t.* **1** (*to agitate, to disquiet*) agitate, alarm, confound, discompose, disquiet, distract, distress, excite, fluster, harass, (*coll.*) hassle, perturb, provoke, ruffle, shake, trouble, unsettle, upset, vex, worry. ANTONYMS: calm, soothe. **2** (*to change the position of*) confuse, derange, disarrange, disorder, disorganize, move, muddle, reposition, shift. **3** (*to interrupt, to inconvenience*) bother, disrupt, hinder, inconvenience, interfere with, interrupt, intrude on, pester, put out, rouse, startle.

disturbance *n.* **1** (*interruption of a settled state of things*) agitation, annoyance, bother, confusion, derangement, disarray, disorder, disorganization, distraction, hindrance, inconvenience, interference, interruption, intrusion, molestation, perturbation, upheaval, upset. ANTONYMS: calm. **2** (*public agitation or excitement*) agitation, bother, brawl, commotion, disorder, excitement, fracas, hubbub, hurly-burly, outbreak, outburst, riot, (*esp. N Am.*) ruckus, rumpus, tumult, turbulence, turmoil, uproar, violence.

disturbed *a.* (*emotionally or mentally unstable*) agitated, (*sl.*) bonkers, crazy, depressed, disordered, emotional, insane, mad, maladjusted, nervous, neurotic, (*sl.*) nuts, psychotic,

troubled, unbalanced, unstable, upset. ANTO-
NYMS: balanced, untroubled.

dive v.i. **1** (*to plunge, esp. head first, under
water*) plunge, submerge. **2** (*to descend
quickly*) descend, dip, drop, duck, fall, jump,
leap, nosedive, pitch, plummet, sink, sound,
swoop. **3** (*to enter deeply* (*into any question or
pursuit*)) go into, penetrate, probe.
~n. **1** (*a sudden plunge head first into water*)
plunge. **2** (*a sudden plunge or dart*) dart, dash,
descent, dip, duck, fall, jump, leap, lunge,
nosedive, pitch, plunge, spring, swoop. **3** (*a
disreputable bar or pub*) bar, club, (*sl.*) joint,
nightclub.

diverge v.i. **1** (*to go in different directions from
a common point*) bifurcate, branch off, divide,
fork, part, radiate, separate, split, spread. **2** (*to
vary from a normal form*) depart, digress, drift,
meander, stray, vary, veer, wander. **3** (*to deviate, to differ*) conflict, deviate, differ, disagree,
dissent. ANTONYMS: agree.

diverse a. **1** (*different, unlike*) assorted, different, distinct, diversified, manifold, miscellaneous, mixed, multiform, several, sundry,
unlike, varied, various. **2** (*made up of a variety
of things*) different, differing, discrete, disparate, dissimilar, distinct, divergent, separate, unlike, varying. ANTONYMS: similar.

diversion n. **1** (*the act of diverting or turning
aside*) change, deflection, deviation, digression, diverting, turning aside, variation. **2** (*a
relaxation, amusement*) amusement, delight,
distraction, divertissement, enjoyment, entertainment, fun, game, gratification, hobby, pastime, play, pleasure, recreation, relaxation,
sport. ANTONYMS: business, work. **3** (*a redirection of traffic owing to the temporary closing of
a road*) bypass, detour, deviation, redirection.
4 (*the act of diverting the attention of the enemy
from any design by demonstration or feigned
attack*) decoy, feint, mock attack.

diversity n. **1** (*difference, variance*) difference,
dissimilarity, distinctiveness, unlikeness,
variance. ANTONYMS: similarity. **2** (*variety,
distinctness*) assortment, extent, miscellany,
multiplicity, range, variety.

divert v.t. **1** (*to turn from any course or
direction*) avert, deflect, redirect, switch, turn
aside. **2** (*to draw off, to distract*) detract, distract, draw off, lead astray, sidetrack. **3** (*to
entertain, to amuse*) absorb, amuse, beguile,
delight, engage, entertain, gratify, interest,
occupy, recreate. ANTONYMS: bore.

divide v.t. **1** (*to cut or part in two*) bisect,
branch, cleave, cut, detach, disconnect, disjoin, disunite, fork, part, partition, segregate,

separate, sever, shear, split, subdivide, sunder.
ANTONYMS: join, splice. **2** (*to distribute, to deal
out*) allocate, allot, apportion, deal out, dispense, distribute, dole out, measure out,
parcel out, portion, share. **3** (*to distinguish the
different kinds of, to classify*) arrange, assort,
categorize, classify, dispose, distinguish,
grade, group, order, organize, rank, separate,
sort. **4** (*to destroy unity amongst*) alienate,
break up, come between, disaffect, disunite,
estrange, split.

divine[1] a. **1** (*of or relating to God or gods*) godly.
2 (*appropriate to the service of the Deity,
religious*) consecrated, holy, mystical, religious, sacred, sanctified, spiritual. ANTONYMS:
profane. **3** (*superhuman, godlike*) angelic,
celestial, godlike, heavenly, saintly, superhuman, supernatural. **4** (*wonderful*) awesome,
beautiful, delightful, excellent, glorious, great,
marvellous, splendid, superb, wonderful.

divine[2] v.t. **1** (*to find out by inspiration or
intuition*) infer, intuit. **2** (*to foresee, to presage*)
foresee, foretell, predict, presage, prognosticate, prophesy. **3** (*to conjecture, to guess*)
conjecture, deduce, guess, imagine, suppose,
surmise, suspect.

division n. **1** (*the act of dividing*) cutting up,
detaching, dividing. **2** (*the state of being
divided; separation*) segmentation, separation,
splitting up. **3** (*distribution*) apportionment,
distribution, sharing. **4** (*something which
divides or separates*) divide, divider, dividing
line. **5** (*a boundary, a partition*) border, boundary, demarcation, frontier, partition. **6** (*a separate or distinct part*) allotment, portion,
segment, share. **7** (*a district, an administrative
unit*) department, district, sector, unit. **8** (*a
separate group of people*) community, group.
9 (*a distinct sect or body*) body, branch, sect.
10 (*disagreement, variance*) breach, conflict,
difference, disagreement, discord, disunion,
estrangement, feud, rupture, split, strife,
upset, variance. ANTONYMS: agreement, unity.
11 (*each of the groups of teams of a similar
standard which make up a sports league*) flight,
league. **12** (*a separate kind or variety*) category,
class, distinction, kind, species, variety.
13 (*the part of a county or borough returning a
Member of Parliament*) borough, constituency,
ward.

divorce n. **1** (*the dissolution of a marriage*)
annulment, break-up, decree absolute, decree
nisi, dissolution. ANTONYMS: marriage. **2** (*a separation of things closely connected*) breach,
break, disconnection, disunion, rupture, separation, severance, split-up.
~v.t. **1** (*to dissolve by legal process the bonds
of marriage between*) annul, dissolve. **2** (*to

remove, to separate) detach, disconnect, dissociate, disunite, divide, part, remove, separate, sever, split up, sunder.

divulge v.t. (to make known; to reveal) betray, broadcast, communicate, confess, declare, disclose, expose, impart, leak, let slip, make known, proclaim, promulgate, publish, reveal, (sl.) spill, tell, uncover. ANTONYMS: conceal.

dizzy a. 1 (giddy, dazed) befuddled, dazed, faint, giddy, light-headed, reeling, shaky, staggering, swimming, tipsy, tottering, unsteady, vertiginous, wobbly, (coll.) woozy. ANTONYMS: steady. 2 (causing dizziness, confusing) bewildering, confusing, dizzying. 3 (reeling) reeling, whirling. 4 (foolish, scatterbrained) capricious, empty-headed, feather-brained, fickle, flighty, foolish, frivolous, giddy, scatterbrained, silly. ANTONYMS: sensible, serious.

do v.t. 1 (to perform or carry out (a work, service etc.)) carry out, execute, perform, transact. 2 (to produce, to make) create, make, produce. 3 (to bring to an end, to complete) accomplish, complete, discharge, end, finish, resolve. 4 (to cause, to render) bring about, cause, create, effect, produce, render. 5 (to translate) adapt, render, translate, transpose. 6 (to prepare, to cook) arrange, cook, fix, get ready, make, organize, prepare, see to. 7 (to play the part of) perform, play. 8 (to put on (a play)) act, give, perform, present, produce, put on, stage. 9 (to rob) burgle, rob. 10 (to cheat, to swindle) cheat, (sl.) con, deceive, defraud, diddle, dupe, fleece, hoax, humbug, (sl.) stiff, swindle, trick. 11 (to injure, to kill) hurt, injure, kill, murder. 12 (to tire out) exhaust, fatigue, tire out. 13 (to visit and see the sights of) cover, explore, look at, tour, visit. 14 (to have sexual intercourse with) (sl.) have, (sl.) make, seduce. 15 (to take (a drug)) (sl.) shoot up, take.
~v.i. 1 (to act, to behave) act, bear oneself, carry oneself, conduct oneself. 2 (to perform deeds) achieve, perform. 3 (to finish, to make an end) cease, end, finish. 4 (to fare, to get on (in an undertaking or in health etc.)) fare, get along, get on, make out, manage, proceed. 5 (to be enough, to answer the purpose) answer, pass muster, satisfy, serve, suffice, suit.
~n. (a party, a celebration) affair, celebration, event, function, gathering, occasion, party. **to do away with** (to remove, to abolish) abolish, discard, dispose of, eliminate, remove. **to do up 1** (to renovate, to decorate) decorate, modernize, redecorate, renovate, repair, restore. **2** (to fasten) button, fasten, lace, tie, zip. **to do without** (to dispense with) dispense with, forgo, give up, go without, manage without, relinquish, renounce.

docile a. (tractable; easily managed) amenable, biddable, compliant, ductile, manageable, meek, obedient, passive, pliant, submissive, tractable, yielding. ANTONYMS: intractable, obstinate.

dock n. 1 (an artificial basin for the reception of ships to load and unload) anchorage, basin, dockyard, harbour. 2 (a wharf) jetty, pier, quay, wharf.
~v.t. 1 (to bring into dock) anchor, berth, land, moor, put in, tie up. 2 (to join (a spacecraft) with another) couple, hook up, interlock, join, link up, rendezvous, unite.

doctor n. (a qualified practitioner of medicine or surgery) (coll.) bones, consultant, (coll.) doc, general practitioner, GP, locum, (coll.) medic, medical practitioner, physician, specialist, surgeon.
~v.t. 1 (to treat medically) attend, care for, cure, heal, treat. 2 (to patch up, to mend) botch, cobble, fix, mend, patch up, repair. 3 (to adulterate) adulterate, dilute, mix with, poison, spike, water down. 4 (to falsify) alter, change, disguise, distort, falsify, fudge, misrepresent, modify, pervert, tamper with. 5 (to castrate (a dog or cat)) castrate, neuter, spay, sterilize.

doctrine n. 1 (what is taught) instruction, teaching. 2 (the principles of any church, scientific school etc.) article, belief, canon, concept, conviction, credo, creed, dogma, idea, opinion, precept, principle, tenet, thesis, view.

document[1] n. (a written or printed paper containing information for the establishment of facts) certificate, charter, deed, form, instrument, paper, record, report.

document[2] v.t. 1 (to furnish with the documents necessary to establish any fact) establish, furnish, supply. 2 (to prove by means of documents) authenticate, back up, certify, cite, corroborate, detail, instance, prove, substantiate, support, validate, verify. 3 (to record in a document) chronicle, record.

doddery a. (feeble and worn-out through old age) aged, decrepit, doddering, faltering, feeble, floundering, frail, infirm, old, senile, shaky, shambling, superannuated, tottery, trembly, unsteady, weak.

dodge v.i. 1 (to move aside suddenly) move aside, shift, sidestep, swerve, turn aside, veer. 2 (to move rapidly from place to place so as to elude pursuit etc.) bob, dart, duck, weave.
~v.t. 1 (to escape from by quickly moving aside) avoid, evade, sidestep. 2 (to evade by cunning or deceit) avoid, deceive, elude, escape, evade, fend off, get out of, hedge, parry, shirk, shuffle, trick.

~n. **1** (*a sudden movement to one side*) dart, sidestep, swerve. **2** (*a trick, an artifice*) artifice, deception, feint, machination, plot, ploy, ruse, scheme, stratagem, subterfuge, trick, wile. **3** (*an evasion*) avoidance, evasion. **4** (*a skilful contrivance or expedient*) contrivance, device, expedient.

dodgy a. **1** (*crafty, tricky*) artful, crafty, tricky, untrustworthy. **2** (*uncertain, risky*) chancy, dangerous, delicate, (*coll.*) dicey, difficult, (*coll.*) hairy, (*coll.*) iffy, perilous, problematic, risky, (*coll.*) ticklish, uncertain, unreliable. ANTONYMS: safe.

dogged a. (*stubborn, persistent*) determined, firm, immovable, indefatigable, intent, obstinate, persevering, persistent, pertinacious, resolute, set, single-minded, staunch, steadfast, steady, stubborn, tenacious, unflagging, unshakeable, unwavering. ANTONYMS: irresolute, unsteady.

dogmatic a. **1** (*asserted with authority, positive*) assertive, authoritative, categorical, downright, emphatic, obdurate, positive, stubborn. **2** (*arrogant, dictatorial*) arrogant, dictatorial, domineering, imperious, intolerant, magisterial, overbearing, peremptory, (*coll.*) pushy.

dole n. **1** (*unemployment benefit*) benefit, jobseeker's allowance. **2** (*money or food distributed in charity*) alms, charity, donation, gift, grant, gratuity, handout, largesse.
~v.t. (*to distribute*) administer, allocate, allot, apportion, assign, deal, (*coll.*) dish out, dispense, distribute, divide, give, hand out, mete, share. ANTONYMS: withhold.

doleful a. (*sorrowful, sad*) cheerless, dejected, depressing, disconsolate, dismal, down, forlorn, funereal, gloomy, lugubrious, melancholy, miserable, mournful, pitiful, rueful, sad, sombre, sorrowful, woebegone, wretched.

domain n. **1** (*territory over which authority or control is exercised*) demesne, dominion, empire, kingdom, land(s), province, realm, region, territory. **2** (*one's landed property, estate*) estate, land(s), property. **3** (*sphere of influence or action*) area, bailiwick, concern, department, field, orbit, province, realm, sphere.

domestic a. **1** (*employed or kept at home*) family, home, household, private. **2** (*fond of home*) domesticated, home-loving, homely. **3** (*relating to the internal affairs of a nation; not foreign*) civil, home, internal, native. ANTONYMS: foreign, international. **4** (*of or relating to the home*) home, household.
~n. (*a household servant*) char, charwoman, cleaner, daily, help, housekeeper, maid, menial, servant.

dominant a. **1** (*ruling, governing*) ascendant, assertive, authoritative, commanding, controlling, governing, leading, predominant, presiding, reigning, ruling, superior, supreme. ANTONYMS: subservient. **2** (*overshadowing, prominent*) chief, influential, main, outstanding, overshadowing, paramount, predominant, pre-eminent, prevailing, principal, prominent.

dominate v.t. **1** (*to predominate over*) eclipse, outshine, override, overrule, overshadow, predominate over, prevail over. **2** (*to overlook (as a hill)*) bestride, look down on, loom over, overlook, stand over, tower above. **3** (*to influence controllingly*) command, control, crush, direct, domineer, govern, influence, lead, master, monopolize, overbear, reign over, rule, subdue, subjugate, suppress, tyrannize.

domination n. **1** (*the exercise of authority*) authority, power. **2** (*rule, control*) ascendancy, command, control, despotism, dictatorship, dominion, hegemony, influence, mastery, oppression, repression, rule, subjection, subordination, superiority, suppression, supremacy, sway, tyranny.

domineering a. (*exercising authority arrogantly and tyrannically*) arrogant, authoritarian, autocratic, bossy, despotic, dictatorial, harsh, haughty, high-handed, imperious, lordly, magisterial, masterful, officious, oppressive, overbearing, peremptory, (*coll.*) pushy, strict, tyrannical. ANTONYMS: meek, submissive.

dominion n. **1** (*sovereign authority; control*) ascendancy, authority, command, control, dominance, domination, government, grasp, grip, hegemony, jurisdiction, lordship, mastery, power, pre-eminence, primacy, rule, sovereignty, supremacy, sway. **2** (*uncontrolled right of possession*) possession, prerogative, privilege, right. **3** (*a district or country under one government*) area, country, district, domain, empire, kingdom, province, realm, region, territory.

donate v.t. (*to bestow as a gift*) award, bequeath, bestow, (*coll.*) chip in, confer, contribute, (*sl.*) cough up, give, grant, hand out, pledge, present, provide, subscribe, supply, vouchsafe, will. ANTONYMS: receive.

donation n. **1** (*the act of giving*) bestowal, contribution, giving. **2** (*a gift, a contribution*) alms, award, benefaction, bequest, contribution, gift, grant, gratuity, handout, largesse, offering, present, presentation, stipend, subscription.

donor n. (*a giver*) almsgiver, backer, benefactor, contributor, giver, philanthropist, provider, supplier, supporter. ANTONYMS: recipient.

doom n. **1** (fate (usu. in an evil sense)) destiny, fate, fortune, lot, portion. **2** (ruin, destruction) annihilation, catastrophe, death, destruction, downfall, extinction, perdition, ruin. **3** (judicial decision or sentence) decision, decree, judgement, sentence, verdict. **4** (condemnation, penalty) condemnation, fate, penalty.
~v.t. **1** (to condemn (to do something)) condemn, damn. **2** (to predestine) decree, destine, foreordain, predestine, preordain.

door n. **1** (a frame of wood or metal, usually on hinges, closing the entrance to a building, room etc.) gate, hatch. **2** (means of approach) access, doorway, egress, entrance, entry, exit, ingress, opening, portal. **3** (the means of access (to)) access, beginning, entrance.

dope n. **1** (a stupefying drug) amphetamine, barbiturate, (coll.) downer, drug, hallucinogen, narcotic, opiate, stimulant, (coll.) upper. **2** (a stupid person) (taboo sl.) dickhead, (coll.) dimwit, (sl.) dipstick, dolt, dunce, fool, idiot, (sl.) jerk, (sl.) nerd, (coll.) nitwit, numskull, (sl.) pillock, (sl.) plonker, (sl.) prat, (taboo sl.) prick, simpleton, (coll.) twit, (sl.) wally. **3** (inside information, particulars) data, details, facts, (coll.) gen, (coll.) info, information, (coll.) low-down, particulars.
~v.t. (to drug, to stupefy with drugs) anaesthetize, doctor, drug, inject, knock out, sedate, stupefy.

dormant a. **1** (in a state resembling sleep, inactive) asleep, comatose, dull, hibernating, immobile, inactive, lethargic, resting, sleeping, sluggish, somnolent, still, torpid. ANTONYMS: active, awake. **2** (undeveloped, inoperative) inert, inoperative, undeveloped. **3** (in abeyance) in abeyance, latent, potential, quiescent, suspended.

dose n. **1** (the amount of any medicine which is taken or prescribed to be taken at one time) dosage, draught, prescription. **2** (a quantity or amount of anything offered or given) amount, measure, portion, quantity.

dot n. **1** (a little mark made with a pointed instrument) mark, speck, spot. **2** (a full point) full stop, period, stop. **3** (a tiny thing) atom, bit, dab, fleck, iota, jot, mite, morsel, mote, point, scrap, speck, spot.
~v.t. (to mark with a dot or dots) bespeckle, dab, dabble, fleck, pepper, speckle, spot, sprinkle, stipple, stud.

dote v.i. **to dote on** (to be foolishly fond of) admire, adore, be fond of, cherish, hold dear, idolize, love, prize, treasure. ANTONYMS: detest, hate.

double¹ a. **1** (forming a pair, twofold) coupled, doubled, dual, duplicate, paired, twice, twin,

twofold. **2** (folded) bent back, folded, overlapped. **3** (of two kinds, ambiguous) ambiguous, double-barrelled, dual.

double² n. **1** (a bend or twist (in a road or river)) bend, curve, twist. **2** (a person who almost exactly resembles someone else) clone, copy, counterpart, (coll.) dead ringer, doppelgänger, duplicate, fellow, lookalike, mate, replica, ringer, (coll.) spitting image, twin.
~v.t. **1** (to increase by an equal quantity, to multiply by two) copy, duplicate, enlarge, grow, increase, magnify, multiply, repeat, replicate, twin. ANTONYMS: halve. **2** (to fold down or over) bend, fold down, fold over.

double-cross v.t. (to betray, to cheat) betray, cheat, deceive, defraud, hoodwink, mislead, swindle, trick, (coll.) two-time.

doubt v.t. **1** (to hold or think questionable) query, question. ANTONYMS: accept. **2** (to hesitate to assent to) demur, fluctuate, hesitate, scruple, vacillate, waver. **3** (to suspect or fear) disbelieve, distrust, fear, mistrust, suspect.
~n. **1** (indecision, suspense) hesitancy, hesitation, indecision, irresolution, suspense, uncertainty, vacillation. **2** (distrust, inclination to disbelieve) apprehension, disbelief, disquiet, distrust, fear, incredulity, misgiving, qualm, scepticism, suspicion. ANTONYMS: confidence. **3** (a question, a problem) ambiguity, confusion, difficulty, dilemma, perplexity, problem, quandary, question.

doubtful a. **1** (uncertain, admitting of doubt) improbable, inconclusive, indefinite, indeterminate, uncertain, unconfirmed, unlikely, unsettled. **2** (ambiguous, not clear in meaning) ambiguous, debatable, equivocal, obscure, problematic, unclear, vague. **3** (uncertain, hesitating) distrustful, hesitating, irresolute, perplexed, sceptical, uncertain, unconvinced, undecided, unresolved, unsettled, unsure, vacillating, wavering. ANTONYMS: decided, positive. **4** (suspicious) disreputable, (coll.) dodgy, dubious, hazardous, (coll.) iffy, questionable, shady, suspect, suspicious.

doubtlessly adv. (certainly) absolutely, assuredly, certainly, clearly, doubtless, indisputably, indubitably, naturally, positively, precisely, surely, truly, undoubtedly, unquestionably, without doubt.

dour a. (sullen; stern) adamant, austere, bold, cold, hard, harsh, inflexible, obdurate, obstinate, rigid, rigorous, severe, sour, stern, stubborn, sullen, tough, uncompromising, unfriendly, unyielding. ANTONYMS: genial, jovial.

down a. **1** (moving or directed towards a lower position) downward, slanting, sloping.

2 (*depressed, downcast*) (*coll.*) blue, dejected, depressed, disheartened, dismal, downcast, low, miserable, sad, unhappy.
~*v.t.* **1** (*to strike down, to overcome*) bring down, fell, floor, knock down, overcome, overthrow, prostrate, put down, strike down, subdue, throw down. **2** (*to eat or drink*) consume, drain, drink, eat, gulp, put away, swallow.
~*v.i.* (*to descend*) decline, descend, drop, go down.

down and out *a.* (*utterly destitute and without resources*) (*coll.*) broke, derelict, destitute, (*coll.*) dirt-poor, (*coll.*) flat broke, impoverished, indigent, penniless, poor, poverty-stricken, ruined, short, (*sl.*) skint, without resources. ANTONYMS: rich, wealthy.

downfall *n.* **1** (*a sudden loss of prosperity, rank etc.*) breakdown, collapse, comedown, defeat, descent, disgrace, fall, overthrow, ruin, undoing. ANTONYMS: rise. **2** (*a fall of rain, snow etc.*) cloudburst, deluge, downpour, rainstorm, snowstorm.

downhearted *a.* (*dispirited, dejected*) (*coll.*) blue, chap-fallen, crestfallen, dejected, depressed, despondent, disappointed, discouraged, disheartened, dismayed, dispirited, downcast, low, low-spirited, miserable, pessimistic, sad, sorrowful, unhappy. ANTONYMS: cheerful, jolly.

downright *a.* **1** (*directly to the point; plain*) bluff, blunt, brash, candid, categorical, clear, direct, explicit, flat, forthright, frank, honest, open, outright, outspoken, plain, straightforward, to the point, unequivocal, (*coll.*) upfront. **2** (*complete, utter*) absolute, complete, positive, thoroughgoing, total, utter.
~*adv.* (*thoroughly, absolutely*) absolutely, assuredly, certainly, completely, definitely, entirely, indubitably, profoundly, surely, thoroughly, totally, uncompromisingly, unconditionally, unquestionably, utterly.

doze *v.i.* (*to sleep lightly*) catnap, (*coll.*) drop off, drowse, (*sl.*) kip, nap, (*coll.*) nod off, sleep, slumber, snooze.
~*n.* (*a light sleep; a nap*) catnap, (*coll.*) forty winks, (*sl.*) kip, nap, siesta, snooze.

drab *a.* **1** (*of a dull brown or dun colour*) brown, dun. **2** (*dull, commonplace*) cheerless, colourless, commonplace, dingy, dismal, dreary, dull, flat, gloomy, grey, lacklustre, monotonous, shabby, sombre, uninspired, vapid. ANTONYMS: bright, cheerful.

draft *n.* **1** (*the first outline of any document*) abstract, blueprint, delineation, outline, plan. **2** (*a rough sketch of work to be executed*) rough, sketch. **3** (*a written order for the payment of money*) money order, postal order. **4** (*a cheque or bill drawn, esp. by a department or a branch of a bank upon another*) bill, cheque. **5** (*a number of people selected for some special purpose*) contingent, detachment.
~*v.t.* (*to compose the first form of*) compose, delineate, design, draw, formulate, frame, outline, plan, prepare, put together, rough out, sketch.

drag *v.t.* **1** (*to pull along the ground by main force*) draw, haul, lug, pull, tow, tug, yank. ANTONYMS: push. **2** (*to search (a river etc.) with a grapnel*) search, trawl. **3** (*to perform too slowly*) dawdle, (*coll.*) dilly-dally, lag behind, linger, loiter, straggle, trail behind.
~*v.i.* **1** ((*of a dress etc.) to trail along the ground*) dangle, trail. **2** (*to move slowly or heavily*) crawl, creep, inch, limp along, plod, shamble, shuffle, slog, trudge. ANTONYMS: hasten, hurry. **3** (*to draw on a cigarette*) draw on, inhale, pull. **4** (*to go on at great length*) draw out, extend, go on, keep going, prolong, protract, spin out, stretch out.
~*n.* **1** (*a draw on a cigarette*) draw, inhalation, puff, pull. **2** (*something or someone boring or irritating*) annoyance, bore, bother, (*coll.*) headache, irritation, (*coll.*) pain, pest. **3** (*an impediment*) hindrance, impediment, obstacle.

drain *v.t.* **1** (*to draw off gradually*) bleed, draw off. **2** (*to cause to run off by tapping etc.*) milk, tap. **3** (*to empty by drawing away moisture from*) dry, empty, evacuate, extract, pump off, remove, withdraw. **4** (*to drink up*) consume, drink up, finish, gulp down, quaff, swallow. **5** (*to exhaust or to deprive (of vitality, resources etc.*)) debilitate, deplete, deprive, dissipate, exhaust, sap, tax, use up, weaken, weary.
~*v.i.* (*to flow off gradually*) discharge, drip, ebb, effuse, exude, flow out, leak, ooze, outflow, seep, trickle, well out.
~*n.* **1** (*a strain, heavy demand*) demand, depletion, drag, exhaustion, reduction, sap, strain. **2** (*a channel for conveying water, sewage etc.*) channel, conduit, culvert, ditch, gutter, outlet, pipe, sewer, trench, watercourse.

drama *n.* **1** (*a play, usually intended for performance by living actors on the stage*) dramatization, piece, play, production, scenario, show, work. **2** (*an exciting or distressing event*) crisis, excitement, scene, spectacle, theatrics, turmoil. **3** (*dramatic art*) acting, dramaturgy, histrionics, stagecraft, theatre, the stage.

dramatic *a.* **1** (*of or relating to the stage, theatrical*) theatrical, thespian. **2** (*striking, impressive*) breathtaking, catastrophic, climactic, electrifying, exciting, extraordinary, impressive, powerful, radical, sensational, shocking, startling, striking, sudden, suspenseful, tense, thrilling, vivid. **3** (*over-emotional, meant for effect*) exaggerated, flamboyant, histrionic, melodramatic, overdone, over-emotional, showy.

drastic *a.* (*acting vigorously; effective*) desperate, dire, extreme, fierce, forceful, harsh, intensive, potent, powerful, radical, rigorous, severe, strong, vigorous, violent. ANTONYMS: moderate, reasonable.

draught *n.* **1** (*a current of air*) breath, breeze, current, flow, influx, movement, puff, wind. **2** (*the act of pulling*) dragging, haulage, pulling, traction. **3** (*the quantity of liquor drunk at once*) cup, dram, drink, gulp, nip, quantity, sip, swallow, (*coll.*) swig, tipple, tot. **4** (*a dose of medicine*) dose, measure, portion. **5** (*a preliminary drawing or plan for a work*) design, draft, drawing, plan.

draw *v.t.* **1** (*to draft, to picture*) delineate, depict, design, draft, map out, mark out, outline, paint, picture, portray, sketch, trace. **2** (*to drag or pull*) drag, haul, pull, tow, tug. **3** (*to pull after one*) haul, lug, pull, trail. **4** (*to remove by pulling*) extract, pull out, take out. **5** (*to cause to flow or come forth*) bring forth, flow. **6** (*to elicit*) bring forth, call forth, elicit, entice, induce. **7** (*to receive, to derive*) acquire, derive, get, obtain, procure, receive, secure, take. **8** (*to infer, to deduce*) conclude, deduce, get, glean, infer. **9** (*to take in, to inhale*) breathe in, inhale, inspire, pull, suck, take in. **10** (*to lengthen, to stretch*) elongate, extend, lengthen, protract, pull out, stretch. **11** (*to unsheathe* (*a sword*)) pull out, unholster, unsheathe. **12** (*to attract, to cause to follow one*) allure, attract, entice, invite, lure, (*coll.*) pull, tempt. **13** (*to compose* (*a document*)) compose, draft, formulate, frame, prepare, write. **14** (*to pull* (*curtains*) *open or shut*) close, pull, pull across.
~*v.i.* **1** (*to move, to approach*) advance, approach, come, go, move, proceed. **2** (*to finish a game with equal scores*) be all square, be equal, be even, tie.
~*n.* **1** (*the act or power of drawing*) drawing. **2** (*a pull, a strain*) pull, strain. **3** (*an attraction, a lure*) attraction, charisma, drawing power, enticement, lure, magnetism, (*coll.*) pull. **4** (*the act of drawing lots*) lottery, raffle, sweepstake. **5** (*a drawn game or contest*) dead heat, deadlock, impasse, stalemate, tie. **6** (*a puff on a cigarette*) inhalation, puff, pull.

drawback *n.* (*a disadvantage; an obstacle*) catch, defect, difficulty, disadvantage, downside, fault, shortcoming, snag, stumbling-block, trouble. ANTONYMS: advantage, benefit.

dread *v.t.* **1** (*to fear greatly*) be afraid of, be frightened of, be terrified by, fear. **2** (*to be apprehensive or anxious about*) cringe at, quail at, shrink from, tremble.
~*n.* **1** (*great fear or terror*) alarm, dismay, fear, fright, horror, panic, terror, trepidation. **2** (*apprehension of evil*) anticipation, anxiety, apprehension, apprehensiveness, concern, misgiving, nervousness, perturbation, uneasiness, worry. **3** (*awe, reverence*) awe, fear, holy terror, reverence. **4** (*the person or thing dreaded*) menace, terror.
~*a.* **1** (*exciting great fear or terror*) alarming, dire, dreaded, feared, frightful, horrible, terrifying. **2** (*awe-inspiring*) awe-inspiring, awful, revered.

dreadful *a.* **1** (*inspiring dread; terrible*) alarming, appalling, awful, dire, distressing, fearful, formidable, frightening, frightful, hideous, horrendous, horrible, malevolent, monstrous, scary, shocking, terrible, tragic. **2** (*annoying, disagreeable*) annoying, disagreeable, frightful, horrid, troublesome. **3** (*bad, extreme*) bad, extreme, intense, severe.

dream *n.* **1** (*a vision*) daydream, mirage, vision. **2** (*thoughts and images that pass through the mind of a sleeping person*) delusion, fancy, fantasy, hallucination, illusion, imagination, mirage, reverie, speculation, vagary. **3** (*the state of mind in which these occur*) reverie, trance. **4** (*a visionary idea*) ambition, aspiration, design, desire, goal, hope, notion, target, thirst, vision, wish. **5** (*someone or something beautiful or enticing*) beautiful, delight, gem, joy, marvel, pleasure, treasure.
~*v.i.* **1** (*to have visions*) envisage, (*coll.*) see things. **2** (*to think, to imagine as in a dream*) conceive, conjure up, fancy, fantasize, hallucinate, imagine, think, visualize. **3** (*to waste time in idle thoughts*) daydream, idle.

dreamy *a.* **1** (*habitually daydreaming*) absent, abstracted, daydreaming, faraway, musing, pensive, preoccupied, thoughtful. **2** (*visionary*) dreamlike, faint, fanciful, imaginary, indefinite, intangible, misty, shadowy, speculative, surreal, vague, visionary. **3** (*soft and gentle*) calming, dreamlike, drowsy, gentle, lazy, lulling, peaceful, quiet, relaxing, romantic, soft, soothing, tranquil. **4** (*extremely attractive*) attractive, beautiful, gorgeous, handsome, sublime.

dreary *a.* (*dismal, cheerless*) bleak, cheerless, colourless, depressing, dismal, doleful, downcast, drab, dull, forlorn, funereal, gloomy, glum, humdrum, joyless, melancholy, monotonous, sombre, tedious, tiresome. ANTONYMS: cheerful, interesting.

dress *v.t.* **1** (*to clothe, to attire*) attire, change, clothe, don, garb, put on, robe, slip on. ANTONYMS: disrobe, undress. **2** (*to adorn, to decorate*) adorn, array, bedeck, deck, decorate, drape, embellish, festoon, furbish, ornament, trim. **3** (*to trim, brush etc.*) brush, cleanse, comb, groom, trim. **4** (*to cleanse and treat (a wound)*) attend to, bandage, bind up, cleanse, plaster, strap up, treat. **5** (*to prepare for use, to cook*) cook, get ready, prepare. **6** (*to make straight*) align, straighten. **7** (*to arrange*) arrange, array, order. **8** (*to cut*) cut, prune. **9** (*to square and give a smooth surface to (stone etc.)*) smooth, square. **10** (*to arrange goods attractively in (a shop window)*) arrange, display.
~*n.* **1** (*that which is worn as clothes, esp. outer garments*) costume, ensemble, get-up, outfit, suit. **2** (*garments, apparel*) apparel, attire, clothes, clothing, costume, garb, garments, (*coll.*) togs. **3** (*a lady's gown, a frock*) frock, gown, robe.

drift *n.* **1** (*a driving or compelling force*) current, flow, impulse, rush, sweep. **2** (*the course of movement*) bias, course, direction, flow, movement, tendency, trend. **3** (*meaning, aim*) aim, design, essence, gist, import, intention, meaning, purport, significance, tendency, tenor, thrust. **4** (*a mass (of snow, leaves etc.) driven together*) accumulation, bank, heap, mass, mound, pile. **5** (*deviation of a ship or aircraft from a direct course caused by a current*) deviation, veer.
~*v.i.* **1** (*to be driven into heaps*) accumulate, amass, bank up, pile up. **2** (*to be carried along by or as if by a current*) coast, float, meander, ramble, roam, rove, stray, waft, wander.
~*v.t.* (*to drive along or into heaps*) drive, gather, heap up, pile up.

drill *n.* **1** (*a metal tool for boring holes in hard material*) bit, borer, gimlet. **2** (*constant exercise in any art*) exercise, practice, repetition. **3** (*rigorous training or discipline*) coaching, discipline, instruction, training.
~*v.t.* **1** (*to bore with a pointed tool*) bore, penetrate, perforate, pierce, puncture. **2** (*to train by repeated exercise*) coach, discipline, indoctrinate, instruct, practise, rehearse, school, teach, train, tutor.

drink *v.t.* **1** (*to swallow (a liquid)*) gulp, guzzle, (*coll.*) knock back, quaff, sip, suck, sup, swallow, (*coll.*) swig, swill, take in, toss off, wash down. **2** (*to absorb, suck in*) absorb, imbibe, suck in, take in. **3** (*to empty*) drain, empty, swallow up. **4** (*to take in by the senses*) assimilate, digest, take in. **5** (*to pledge, to toast*) pledge, salute, toast.
~*v.i.* (*to drink alcohol habitually, esp. to excess*) (*coll.*) booze, carouse, (*sl.*) hit the bottle, indulge, tipple, tope.

~*n.* **1** (*something to be drunk*) beverage, cup, dram, draught, glass, gulp, nip, potion, sip, (*coll.*) slug, swallow, (*coll.*) swig, taste, tot. **2** (*intoxicating liquor*) alcohol, (*coll.*) booze, (*coll.*) hard stuff, (*N Am., coll.*) liquor, spirits. **3** (*excessive indulgence in intoxicating liquors*) drunkenness, intemperance.

drip *v.i.* (*to fall in drops*) dribble, drizzle, drop, ooze, seep, splash, sprinkle, trickle.
~*n.* **1** (*the act of dripping, a falling in drops*) dribble, dripping, drop, falling, leak, sprinkle, trickle. **2** (*a stupid or insipid person*) fool, milksop, mummy's boy, (*coll.*) ninny, softie, weakling, (*coll.*) weed, (*coll.*) wet, (*coll.*) wet lettuce, (*coll.*) wimp.

drive *v.t.* **1** (*to push or urge by force*) herd, hurl, impel, press, propel, push, send, urge. **2** (*to guide or direct (a vehicle or horse)*) direct, guide, handle, manage, steer. **3** (*to convey in a vehicle*) convey, motor, run, take, transport. **4** (*to constrain, to compel*) actuate, coerce, compel, constrain, force, motivate, oblige, press, prod, prompt, spur. **5** (*to frighten (game) into an enclosure or towards guns*) chase, hunt. **6** (*to throw*) impel, propel, throw. **7** (*to force (a nail etc.) with blows*) dash, dig, hammer, plunge, ram, sink, stab, strike, thrust. **8** (*to bore (a tunnel etc.)*) bore, cut, dig out, drill.
~*v.i.* **1** (*to dash, to rush violently*) dash, hasten, rush. **2** (*to drift, to be carried*) carry, drift. **3** (*to travel in a vehicle, esp. under one's own direction or control*) motor, ride, travel. **4** (*to control or direct a vehicle, engine etc.*) control, direct, pilot, steer. **5** (*to aim, to intend*) aim, intend, mean, tend.
~*n.* **1** (*a ride in a vehicle*) excursion, jaunt, journey, outing, ride, run, (*coll.*) spin, trip, turn, (*coll.*) whirl. **2** (*a road for driving on, esp. a private carriageway to a house*) byway, carriageway, driveway, lane, road, route, street. **3** (*a concerted effort made for charity etc.*) appeal, campaign, crusade, effort, (*coll.*) push, surge. **4** (*push, energy*) effort, energy, impetus, push, vigour, vim. **5** (*energy, motivation*) ambition, energy, enterprise, enthusiasm, (*coll.*) get-up-and-go, initiative, motivation, (*coll.*) pep, (*coll.*) zip.

drivel *n.* **1** (*slaver; spittle flowing from the mouth*) dribble, saliva, slaver, spit, spittle. **2** (*silly, nonsensical talk*) balderdash, (*sl.*) balls, (*taboo sl.*) bullshit, bunkum, (*sl.*) cobblers, (*sl.*) codswallop, (*taboo sl.*) crap, garbage, gibberish, (*sl.*) hogwash, nonsense, (*coll.*) piffle, (*sl.*) poppycock, rot, rubbish, (*taboo sl.*) shit, (*coll.*) tripe, twaddle, (*coll.*) waffle.
~*v.i.* **1** (*to allow spittle to flow from the mouth*) dribble, drool, slaver, slobber. **2** (*to talk nonsense*) babble, blether, burble, chatter, gab,

gibber, prate, prattle, ramble, talk nonsense, (*coll.*) waffle.

droll *a*. (*ludicrous, laughable*) amusing, clownish, comic, comical, diverting, eccentric, entertaining, facetious, funny, humorous, jocular, laughable, ludicrous, odd, quaint, ridiculous, whimsical. ANTONYMS: serious.

droop *v.i.* **1** (*to lean or bend down*) bend, bow, dangle, drop, hang, lean, sag. **2** ((*of the sun*) *to sink*) fall, go down, set, sink. **3** (*to fail, to lose heart*) decline, diminish, fade, fail, faint, falter, flag, languish, lose heart, slump, weaken, wilt, wither.

drop *n*. **1** (*a globule or small portion of liquid in a spherical form*) bead, bubble, drip, droplet, globule, pearl, tear. **2** (*a very small quantity of a fluid*) dab, dash, dram, mouthful, nip, pinch, shot, sip, spot, taste, tot, trace, trickle. **3** (*the act of dropping*) collapse, descent, fall. **4** (*a reduction, a lowering*) cut, decline, decrease, deterioration, downturn, fall-off, lowering, reduction, slump. ANTONYMS: rise. **5** (*an abrupt fall in a surface*) abyss, chasm, declivity, descent, fall, plunge, precipice, slope.
~*v.t.* **1** (*to allow or cause to fall in drops, as a liquid*) dribble, drip, trickle. **2** (*to take off* (*one's trousers or underpants*)) cast off, doff, take off. **3** (*to lower*) let down, lower. **4** (*to give up*) abandon, dismiss, forsake, give up, kick, quit, relinquish. **5** (*to set down* (*a passenger*) *from a vehicle*) deposit, set down. **6** (*to mention casually*) let fall, mention. **7** (*to bear* (*a foal, calf etc.*)) bear, give birth to. **8** (*to omit*) exclude, leave out, omit. **9** (*to stop* (*doing something*)) break off, cease, discontinue, stop. ANTONYMS: continue. **10** (*to let go*) dismiss, (*coll.*) fire, let go, (*coll.*) sack. **11** (*to sprinkle with drops*) besprinkle, scatter, sprinkle. **12** (*to stop seeing or associating with* (*someone*)) (*coll.*) chuck, cold-shoulder, desert, disown, (*coll.*) ditch, (*coll.*) dump, forsake, ignore, jilt, leave, reject, renounce, repudiate, throw over, (*coll.*) walk out on.
~*v.i.* **1** (*to fall in drops; to drip*) dribble, drip, trickle. **2** (*to fall*) descend, dive, fall, plummet, plunge, sink, tumble. **3** (*to collapse suddenly*) collapse, droop, faint, sink. **4** (*to die*) breathe one's last, die, expire. **5** (*to come to an end*) cease, end, lapse. **6** (*to fall*) decline, decrease, diminish, fall, lessen, slacken, subside, taper. ANTONYMS: rise.

drought *n*. **1** (*dryness*) aridity, dehydration, dryness. **2** (*a protracted lack of something*) dearth, deficiency, insufficiency, lack, scarcity, shortage, want. ANTONYMS: abundance, glut. **3** (*thirst*) need, thirst.

drown *v.t.* **1** (*to submerge, to overwhelm with*

water) deluge, drench, engulf, flood, immerse, inundate, overflow, sink, submerge, swamp. **2** (*to overwhelm, to put an end to*) deaden, muffle, obliterate, overcome, overwhelm, quench, stifle, suppress.

drowsy *a*. **1** (*inclined to sleep, sleepy*) comatose, dozy, half asleep, lethargic, nodding, sleepy, somnolent, tired. ANTONYMS: awake, perky. **2** (*disposing to sleep*) dreamy, hypnotic, restful, soothing, soporific. **3** (*sluggish, stupid*) dazed, (*coll.*) dopey, drugged, groggy, heavy, sluggish, stupid.

drudgery *n*. (*menial or tedious work*) chore, (*coll.*) fag, grind, hard work, labour, slavery, slog, (*coll.*) sweat, toil, travail, work.

drug *n*. **1** (*any substance used as an ingredient in medical preparations*) medicament, medication, medicine, physic, simple. **2** (*a narcotic causing addiction*) amphetamine, analgesic, barbiturate, (*sl.*) dope, hallucinogen, narcotic, opiate, painkiller, sedative, stimulant, tranquillizer.
~*v.t.* **1** (*to administer drugs, esp. narcotics, to*) (*sl.*) dope, dose, medicate, treat. **2** (*to render insensible with drugs*) anaesthetize, (*coll.*) knock out, sedate. **3** (*to deaden*) deaden, dull, numb, stupefy.

drunk *a*. **1** (*intoxicated, overcome with alcoholic liquors*) (*sl.*) blotto, (*sl.*) canned, drunken, inebriated, intoxicated, (*coll.*) legless, (*sl.*) loaded, (*sl.*) paralytic, (*taboo sl.*) pissed, (*sl.*) plastered, (*coll.*) sloshed, (*sl.*) smashed, (*coll.*) soaked, (*coll.*) squiffy, (*sl.*) stoned, (*coll.*) tiddly, (*sl.*) tight, tipsy. ANTONYMS: sober. **2** (*inebriated, highly excited* (*with joy etc.*)) delirious, ecstatic, excited, exhilarated, exuberant, inflamed, invigorated, overjoyed.
~*n*. (*a habitually drunken person*) alcoholic, dipsomaniac, drinker, drunkard, inebriate, (*sl.*) soak, tippler, (*sl.*) wino.

drunkenness *n*. (*the state of being drunk; intemperance*) alcoholism, bibulousness, dipsomania, inebriety, insobriety, intemperance, intoxication. ANTONYMS: sobriety, temperance.

dry *a*. **1** (*devoid of moisture*) moistureless, waterless. **2** (*arid*) arid, barren, desiccated, waterless. ANTONYMS: damp, wet. **3** (*thirsty*) parched, thirsty. **4** (*dried up*) dehydrated, drained, dried up, evaporated. **5** (*lacking interest, dull*) bland, boring, dreary, dull, insipid, lifeless, monotonous, prosaic, tedious, tiresome, uninteresting, wearisome. ANTONYMS: interesting, lively. **6** (*meagre*) bare, meagre, plain. **7** (*sarcastic, ironical*) biting, cutting, cynical, deadpan, droll, ironical, keen, sarcastic, sharp, sly, witty, wry. **8** (*without* sympathy or cordiality) cold, discouraging, harsh, unsympathetic.

~v.t. 1 (to free from or deprive of water or moisture) dehumidify, dehydrate, desiccate, sear. 2 (to drain, to wipe) blot, drain, mop, sponge, towel, wipe.

~v.i. (to lose or be deprived of moisture) dehydrate, harden, mummify, parch, shrink, shrivel up, wilt, wither.

dubious a. 1 (doubtful; wavering in mind) doubtful, hesitant, (coll.) iffy, uncertain, unconvinced, undecided, undetermined, unsure, vacillating, wavering. 2 (of uncertain result or issue) ambiguous, debatable, doubtful, equivocal, indefinite, problematic, uncertain, unsettled. ANTONYMS: certain. 3 (open to suspicion) (coll.) dodgy, (coll.) fishy, (coll.) iffy, questionable, shady, suspect, suspicious, unreliable, untrustworthy. ANTONYMS: trustworthy.

duck v.i. 1 (to plunge under water) dip, dive, plunge, submerge. 2 (to bow) bend, bow, crouch, dodge, stoop.

~v.t. 1 (to dip under water and suddenly withdraw) dip, douse, dunk, immerse, plunge, souse, submerge, wet. 2 (to avoid (a responsibility etc.)) avoid, dodge, elude, evade, shirk, shun, shy away from, sidestep.

due a. 1 (owed, that ought to be paid) in arrears, outstanding, owed, payable, unpaid. 2 (proper, appropriate) apposite, appropriate, apt, becoming, claimable, deserved, fit, fitting, just, meet, obligatory, proper, requisite, right, suitable. 3 (expected, appointed to arrive) anticipated, expected, scheduled. 4 (that may be attributed (to)) ascribable, attributable. 5 (arranged) arranged, planned.

~adv. (exactly, directly) dead, directly, exactly, precisely, straight, undeviatingly.

~n. (a debt, an obligation) debt, obligation, toll, tribute.

dull a. 1 (slow of understanding; not quick in perception) dense, dim, (coll.) dopey, (coll.) dumb, obtuse, slow, stolid, stupid, (coll.) thick, unintelligent. ANTONYMS: clever, perceptive. 2 (without sensibility) apathetic, blank, callous, dead, heavy, indifferent, insensible, insensitive, lifeless, listless, numb, passionless, unresponsive, unsympathetic. 3 (not sharp or acute) blunt, dulled, edgeless, unsharpened. ANTONYMS: sharp. 4 (sluggish, slow of movement) inactive, inert, slack, slow, sluggish, torpid, uneventful. 5 (dim, tarnished) dim, drab, faded, lacklustre, murky, muted, sombre, subdued, tarnished. ANTONYMS: bright. 6 (cloudy, overcast) cloudy, depressing, dim, dismal, gloomy, grey, leaden, opaque, overcast. 7 (uninteresting, tedious) banal, boring,

commonplace, dreary, flat, humdrum, monotonous, plain, prosaic, tedious, tiresome, unimaginative, uninteresting, vapid, wearisome. 8 (hard of hearing) deaf, hard of hearing. 9 (not loud or clear) indistinct, muffled, quiet, subdued, unclear. ANTONYMS: loud.

~v.t. 1 (to make dull or stupid) stupefy. 2 (to render less acute or effective) allay, alleviate, assuage, ease, lessen, mitigate, moderate, palliate, paralyse, reduce, relieve, soften. ANTONYMS: aggravate. 3 (to make blunt) blunt. 4 (to make heavy, to deaden) dampen, deaden, deject, depress, discourage, dishearten, dispirit, sadden. ANTONYMS: cheer. 5 (to tarnish, to dim) blur, cloud, darken, dim, fade, obscure, stain, sully, tarnish.

duly adv. 1 (in a suitable manner; properly) appropriately, becomingly, befittingly, correctly, decorously, deservedly, fittingly, properly, regularly, rightfully, suitably. 2 (punctually) on time, punctually.

dumb a. 1 (unable to utter articulate sounds) inarticulate. ANTONYMS: articulate. 2 (unable to speak, through some physical cause) mute, voiceless, wordless. 3 (silent, (temporarily) speechless) silent, speechless, tongue-tied. 4 (refraining from speaking) reticent, taciturn, unspeaking. 5 (soundless) quiet, silent, soundless, voiceless. 6 (stupid, unintelligent) asinine, dense, dim, (coll.) dopey, dull, foolish, obtuse, stupid, (coll.) thick, unintelligent. ANTONYMS: bright, intelligent.

dumbfound v.t. (to confuse, to astound) amaze, astonish, astound, bewilder, (coll.) bowl over, confound, confuse, flabbergast, floor, flummox, nonplus, overwhelm, perplex, shock, stagger, startle, strike dumb, stun, take aback.

dump n. 1 (a place for depositing rubbish) junkyard, refuse heap, rubbish heap, rubbish tip, scrapyard, tip. 2 (an unpleasant place, esp. a house) (coll.) hole, hovel, (sl.) joint, mess, pigsty, shack, shanty, slum.

~v.t. 1 (to put down carelessly) deposit, let fall, put down. 2 (to unload) offload, tip, unload. 3 (to dispose of) (coll.) chuck away, discard, discharge, dispose of, (coll.) ditch, empty out, get rid of, jettison, junk, reject, scrap, throw away. 4 (to end a relationship with) (coll.) chuck, disown, (coll.) ditch, drop, jilt, leave, reject, renounce, repudiate, throw over, (coll.) walk out on.

duplicate[1] a. 1 (existing in two parts exactly corresponding) double, twin, twofold. 2 (corresponding exactly with another) corresponding, equivalent, identical, matching.

~n. 1 (one of two things exactly similar in

material and form) carbon copy, clone, double, lookalike, match, mate, ringer, twin. **2** (*a reproduction*) copy, facsimile, reproduction. ANTONYMS: original.

duplicate[2] *v.t.* **1** (*to make or be a reproduction of*) clone, copy, imitate, match, replicate, reproduce. **2** (*to double*) double, echo.

durable *a.* (*lasting, firm*) abiding, constant, dependable, enduring, firm, fixed, hard-wearing, indestructible, lasting, long-lasting, permanent, reliable, resistant, sound, stable, stout, strong, sturdy, substantial, tough. ANTONYMS: fragile, perishable.

dutiful *a.* (*careful in performing the duties required by justice or propriety*) attentive, careful, compliant, conscientious, deferential, devoted, diligent, docile, faithful, filial, obedient, obliging, punctilious, reliable, respectful, responsible, reverential, submissive, willing. ANTONYMS: disrespectful.

duty *n.* **1** (*something which is bound or ought to be paid or done*) assignment, bit, calling, charge, chore, engagement, job, mission, onus, part, responsibility, role, task, trust. **2** (*moral or legal obligation*) burden, obligation, onus. **3** (*obedience due to parents or superiors*) allegiance, deference, fidelity, loyalty, obedience, respect, reverence. **4** (*any service or office*) business, office, service. **5** (*a tax charged by a government*) customs, due, excise, impost, levy, tariff, tax, toll. **6** (*office, function*) function, occupation, office, work.

dwarf *n.* **1** (*a human being, animal or plant much below the natural or ordinary size*) bantam, homunculus, manikin, midget, pygmy, runt. ANTONYMS: giant. **2** (*a supernatural being of small stature*) gnome, goblin.

~*a.* **1** (*below the ordinary or natural size*) petite, undersized. **2** (*stunted, tiny*) baby, diminutive, miniature, pocket, puny, small, stunted, tiny.

~*v.t.* **1** (*to stunt the growth of*) check, retard, stunt. **2** (*to cause to look small by comparison*) bestride, dim, diminish, dominate, minimize, overshadow, tower over.

dwelling *n.* (*a residence*) abode, domicile, establishment, habitation, home, homestead, house, lodging, (*coll.*) pad, quarters, residence.

dwindle *v.i.* **1** (*to become smaller*) abate, contract, decrease, die away, diminish, ebb, fade, lessen, peter out, pine, shrink, shrivel, sink, subside, taper off, wane, waste away, weaken. ANTONYMS: increase, magnify. **2** (*to degenerate*) decay, decline, degenerate, fall, wither.

dyed in the wool *a.* (*fixed in one's opinions*) confirmed, diehard, fixed, inflexible, inveterate, set, settled, unchangeable, uncompromising, unshakeable.

dynamic *a.* (*active, energetic*) active, driving, eager, electric, energetic, forceful, go-ahead, lively, magnetic, motive, potent, powerful, spirited, vigorous, vital. ANTONYMS: inactive, listless.

E

each *a., pron.* (*every one* (*of a limited number*) *considered separately*) each and every one, every, every single.

eager *a.* **1** (*excited by an ardent desire to attain or succeed*) agog, anxious, avid, desirous of, hopeful of, hungry, impatient, intent on, interested in, itching, keen, longing, raring, ready, thirsty, wishing, wishing with all one's heart, with one's heart set on, yearning. ANTONYMS: apathetic, reluctant, uninterested in. **2** (*keen, enthusiastic*) ardent, avid, (*coll.*) bright-eyed and bushy-tailed, earnest, enthusiastic, interested, keen, keen as mustard. ANTONYMS: apathetic, half-hearted, indifferent. **3** ((*of a desire or wish*) *strong or impatient*) fervent, impatient, passionate, strong, vehement, wholehearted, zealous.

early *adv.* **1** (*in good time*) in advance, in good time, in plenty of time, promptly, punctually, with time to spare. ANTONYMS: late. **2** (*soon after the beginning of a period*) at the beginning, at the start, early on, initially, near the beginning, near the start, towards the beginning. ANTONYMS: late on, towards the end.
~*a.* **1** (*before the expected or usual time*) advanced, forward, precocious, premature, undeveloped, untimely. ANTONYMS: late, overdue. **2** (*happening or situated near the beginning of a period of development, existence etc.*) first, initial, opening, primeval, primitive, primordial, young. ANTONYMS: end, final, late.

earmark *v.t.* (*to set aside* (*funds etc.*) *for a particular purpose*) allocate, designate, keep back, lay aside, put aside, put away, reserve, set aside.

earn *v.t.* **1** (*to gain* (*money etc.*) *as the reward of labour*) bring in, clear, collect, draw, gain, get, gross, make, net, pocket, procure, pull in, realize, receive, take home. ANTONYMS: inherit, win. **2** (*to merit or become entitled to as the result of any course of conduct*) achieve, attain, be deserving of, be entitled to, be worthy of, deserve, gain, get, merit, obtain, rate, receive, secure, warrant, win. ANTONYMS: be unworthy of.

earnest *a.* **1** (*serious, not joking*) grave, important, serious, solemn. **2** (*eager or zealous in the performance of any act*) ardent, determined, eager, enthusiastic, fervent, intense, keen, passionate, purposeful, vehement, wholehearted, zealous. ANTONYMS: apathetic, different. **3** (*heartfelt, sincere*) deep, fervent, heartfelt, impassioned, intense, passionate, profound, sincere, strong, warm, wholehearted. ANTONYMS: apathetic, dispassionate, half-hearted. **4** (*very serious, esp in one's beliefs*) intense, overserious, pensive, serious, sincere, solemn, staid, steady, studious, thoughtful. ANTONYMS: flippant, frivolous, light-hearted. **in earnest 1** (*seriously, not jokingly*) not joking, serious, sincere. **2** (*with determination*) determinedly, fervently, for real, passionately, wholeheartedly, with commitment, with dedication, with determination, with no holds barred, with zeal, zealously.

earth *n.* **1** (*the globe, the planet on which we live*) globe, planet, sphere, world. **2** (*dry land, as opposed to the sea*) dry land, ground, land, solid ground, terra firma. ANTONYMS: sea, sky. **3** (*soil; the soft material in which plants grow, composed of clay, mould etc.*) clay, dirt, loam, mould, soil, topsoil, turf.

earthenware *n.* (*coarse pottery made of baked clay*) ceramics, crockery, pottery, stoneware, terracotta.

earthly *a.* **1** (*relating to this world, terrestrial*) mundane, tellurian, telluric, terrestrial. ANTONYMS: extraterrestrial, heavenly. **2** (*mortal, human*) anthropoid, human, mortal, natural. ANTONYMS: immortal, supernatural. **3** (*carnal or materialistic, as opposed to spiritual*) carnal, corporeal, fleshly, human, material, materialistic, mortal, non-spiritual, physical, profane, secular, sensual, temporal, worldly. ANTONYMS: immaterial, spiritual, unworldly. **4** (*possible, conceivable*) conceivable, feasible, imaginable, likely, possible, probable.

earthy *a.* **1** (*consisting of, composed of or resembling earth or soil*) claylike, dirtlike, earthlike, soil-like. **2** (*talking about sex in a direct and rude way*) bawdy, (*sl.*) blue, coarse, crude, gross, indecent, obscene, (*coll.*) raunchy, ribald, smutty. ANTONYMS: decent, delicate, refined.

ease *n.* **1** (*a state of freedom from trouble or pain*) affluence, comfort, content, contentment, enjoyment, happiness, leisure,

luxury, opulence, peace, peacefulness, prosperity, quiet, relaxation, repose, rest, restfulness, security, serenity, tranquillity, wealth. ANTONYMS: discomfort, hardship, labour, misery. **2** (*freedom from constraint or formality*) aplomb, casualness, flexibility, freedom, informality, insouciance, naturalness, nonchalance, poise, suaveness, unaffectedness, unceremoniousness, unreservedness, urbanity. ANTONYMS: awkwardness, constraint, formality, reserve. **3** (*absence of effort*) adroitness, dexterity, easiness, effortlessness, facility, proficiency, readiness, simplicity. ANTONYMS: difficulty, effort, exertion.
~*v.t.* **1** (*to free from pain or trouble*) bring comfort to, calm, comfort, console, pacify, quiet, quieten, solace, soothe, tranquillize. ANTONYMS: agitate, upset, worry. **2** (*to make easier or lighter*) abate, allay, alleviate, appease, assuage, calm, diminish, lessen, mitigate, moderate, mollify, palliate, quiet, quieten, reduce, relieve, soothe, still, tranquillize. ANTONYMS: aggravate, agitate, worsen. **3** (*to render less difficult*) accelerate, advance, aid, assist, boost, expedite, facilitate, forward, further, give a boost to, give a helping hand to, help, make easier, oil the wheels of, promote, simplify, smooth, smooth the way of, speed up. ANTONYMS: hinder, obstruct, retard, slow down. **4** (*to make looser, to relax*) loosen, relax, slacken. ANTONYMS: tighten. **5** (*to move slowly and carefully*) edge, guide, inch, manoeuvre, move gently, slide, slip, steer. ANTONYMS: force, manhandle.

easy *a.* **1** (*not difficult, not requiring great exertion or effort*) a piece of cake, (*coll.*) a pushover, child's play, easy as falling off a log, (*coll.*) easy-peasy, effortless, foolproof, idiot-proof, no problem, (*sl.*) no sweat, no trouble, painless, simple, straightforward, trouble-free, uncomplicated, undemanding. ANTONYMS: complex, complicated, difficult, exacting. **2** (*free from pain or discomfort*) anxiety-free, at ease, at peace, calm, carefree, comfortable, content, contented, easeful, leisurely, pain-free, peaceful, relaxed, secure, serene, tranquil, trouble-free, undisturbed, untroubled, unworried. ANTONYMS: anxious, painful, tense, uncomfortable, worried. **3** (*in comfortable circumstances, well-to-do*) affluent, comfortable, (*coll.*) cushy, in clover, moneyed, of means, (*coll.*) on Easy Street, prosperous, rich, wealthy, well-heeled, well-to-do. ANTONYMS: impoverished, penniless, poor. **4** (*free from embarrassment or affectation*) affable, casual, easygoing, free, free and easy, informal, insouciant, (*coll.*) laid-back, natural, nonchalant, relaxed, suave, unaffected, unceremonious, unforced, unreserved, urbane. ANTONYMS:

affected, formal, unnatural, (*coll.*) uptight. **5** (*written, spoken etc. in a natural, unforced way*) even, flowing, fluent, regular, smooth, steady, unforced, unhurried. ANTONYMS: erratic, irregular, uneven, unsteady. **6** (*easily persuaded, compliant*) accommodating, acquiescent, amenable, biddable, compliant, docile, exploitable, gullible, like putty in someone's hands, manageable, obliging, pliant, soft, submissive, suggestible, tractable, trusting, yielding. ANTONYMS: intractable, obdurate, tough, unmanageable. **7** (*indulgent, not exacting*) amenable, easygoing, flexible, forbearing, free and easy, indulgent, (*coll.*) laid-back, lenient, liberal, mild, permissive, tolerant, undemanding, unexacting. ANTONYMS: demanding, exacting, inflexible. **8** (*fitting loosely*) baggy, floppy, loose, loose-fitting, sagging, slack. ANTONYMS: close, tight, tight-fitting.

easygoing *a.* (*taking things in an easy manner*) amenable, amiable, carefree, casual, easy, even-tempered, flexible, happy-go-lucky, indulgent, insouciant, (*coll.*) laid-back, liberal, nonchalant, permissive, placid, relaxed, serene, tolerant, undemanding, unexacting. ANTONYMS: formal, intolerant, tense, (*coll.*) uptight.

eat *v.t.* **1** (*to chew and swallow as food*) bolt, chew, consume, devour, gobble, gulp down, ingest, munch, (*coll.*) scoff, swallow, (*coll.*) tuck into, wolf, wolf down. ANTONYMS: abstain from, drink. **2** (*to wear away, to waste*) corrode, decay, destroy, dissolve, eat away, eat into, erode, gnaw away, rot, rust, waste away, wear away.
~*v.i.* (*to take food*) break one's fast, feed, (*coll.*) graze, have a meal, partake of food, snack, take food. ANTONYMS: diet, fast, starve. **to eat away** (*to destroy, to rust*) corrode, decay, destroy, dissolve, eat, erode, gnaw away, reduce, rot, rust, waste away, wear away. **to eat into 1** (*to corrode*) corrode, dissolve, eat, erode, gnaw away, waste away, wear away. **2** (*to use time or resources, so reducing the amount available*) consume, deplete, expend, get through, make inroads into, use up.

eatable *a.* (*fit to be eaten*) digestible, edible, fit to eat, good to eat, palatable. ANTONYMS: inedible.

eavesdrop *v.i.* (*to listen secretly so as to overhear confidences*) bug, listen in, monitor, overhear, spy, tap.

ebb *n.* **1** (*the flowing back or going out of the tide*) abatement, flowing back, flowing out, going out, receding, recession, reflux, retreat, retrocession, subsiding, withdrawal. ANTONYMS: advance, flowing. **2** (*decline, decay*) decay, decline, decrease, degeneration,

deterioration, diminishing, diminution, dropping away, dwindling, dying away, dying out,
fading, failure, falling away, flagging, lessening, petering out, sinking, wane, weakening.
ANTONYMS: advance, improvement, strengthening, success.
~*v.i.* **1** (*to flow back*) abate, come out, flow back,
flow out, go out, recede, retreat, retrocede,
subside, withdraw. ANTONYMS: advance, flow
in. **2** (*to decline, to decay*) be on one's last legs,
be on the way out, decay, decline, decrease,
degenerate, deteriorate, die away, die out,
diminish, drop away, dwindle, fade away, fail,
flag, grow feeble, lessen, peter out, sink, wane,
weaken. ANTONYMS: advance, be successful,
improve, succeed.

ebullient *a.* (*overflowing with high spirits,
exuberant*) animated, (*coll.*) bubbly, buoyant,
chirpy, effervescent, elated, enthusiastic, euphoric, excited, exuberant, high-spirited, in
high spirits, irrepressible, lively, (*sl.*) on a
high, sparkling, vivacious.

eccentric *a.* **1** (*peculiar or odd in manner or
character*) abnormal, bizarre, (*coll.*) dotty,
freakish, idiosyncratic, non-conformist, (*sl.*)
nutty, odd, (*coll.*) off-beat, off-the-wall, outlandish, outré, peculiar, queer, quirky, (*sl.*)
rum, (*coll.*) screwy, singular, strange, unconventional, unusual, (*esp. N Am., sl.*) wacko,
(*sl.*) wacky, (*coll.*) way-out, weird. ANTONYMS:
conventional, normal, ordinary. **2** (*departing
from the usual practice or established forms or
laws*) aberrant, abnormal, anomalous, atypical,
deviant, exceptional, irregular, odd, peculiar,
rare, unusual. ANTONYMS: normal, regular,
standard, typical.
~*n.* (*a person of odd or peculiar habits*) (*sl.*) card,
(*coll.*) character, crank, freak, (*sl.*) geek, (*esp. N
Am., coll.*) kook, non-conformist, (*sl.*) nut, (*sl.*)
nutter, oddball, oddity, (*coll.*) queer fish, (*esp.
N Am., coll.*) screwball, (*coll.*) weirdo.
ANTONYMS: conformist.

eccentricity *n.* (*odd or whimsical conduct or
character*) aberration, abnormality, bizarre-
ness, (*coll.*) dottiness, foible, freakishness,
idiosyncrasy, non-conformity, (*sl.*) nuttiness,
oddness, (*coll.*) off-beatness, outlandishness,
peculiarity, peculiarness, queerness, quirk,
quirkiness, (*sl.*) rumness, singularity, strangeness, unconventionality, (*esp. N Am., sl.*)
wackiness, weirdness. ANTONYMS: conformity,
conventionality, normality.

ecclesiastic *n.* (*a person in holy orders, a
member of the clergy*) chaplain, churchman,
churchwoman, clergyman, clergywoman,
cleric, deacon, deaconess, divine, holy man,
holy woman, man of the cloth, minister,
parson, pastor, preacher, prelate, priest,

vicar, woman of the cloth. ANTONYMS: lay
person.

ecclesiastical *a.* (*of or relating to the Church
or the clergy*) church, churchly, churchy,
clerical, divine, holy, non-secular, pastoral,
priestly, religious, spiritual. ANTONYMS: lay.

echelon *n.* ((*a group of persons in*) *a level or
grade of an organization etc.*) degree, grade,
level, place, position, rank, stage, tier.

echo *n.* **1** (*the repetition of a sound caused by its
being reflected from some obstacle*) repeat-
ing, repetition, resounding, reverberation. **2** (*a
close imitation; a hearty response*) clone, copy,
duplicate, image, imitation, mirror image,
parallel, parody, reflection, repeat, repetition.
3 (*a reminder of something else*) allusion,
evocation, hint, memory, overtones, remembrance, reminder, suggestion, trace.
~*v.i.* (*to give an echo; to resound*) repeat,
resound, reverberate, ring.
~*v.t.* **1** (*to repeat with approval*) parrot, reiterate,
restate, say again, state again. **2** (*to imitate
closely*) ape, copy, imitate, mimic, mirror,
parody, parrot, recall, reproduce, resemble.

éclat *n.* **1** (*brilliant success*) brilliance, distinction, fame, glory, honour, renown, success.
2 (*acclamation, applause*) acclaim, acclamation, admiration, applause, approbation,
approval, bouquets, commendation, ovation,
plaudits, praise. **3** (*splendour, striking effect*)
display, lustre, magnificence, ostentation, (*sl.*)
pizazz, pomp, show, splendour, theatricality.

eclectic *a.* **1** (*broad, not exclusive*) all-
embracing, broad, broad-based, catholic,
comprehensive, diverse, general, liberal,
multi-faceted, multifarious, varied, wide-ranging. ANTONYMS: exclusive, narrow, restricted.
2 (*selecting from the* (*best of*) *doctrines,
teachings etc. of others*) discriminating,
discriminatory, picking and choosing, selective. ANTONYMS: indiscriminate.

eclipse *n.* **1** (*the obscuration of the light from a
heavenly body by the passage of another body
between it and the eye*) blotting out, conceal-
ing, darkening, dimming, extinction, obscuration, shadowing, veiling. **2** (*a loss of glory or
reputation*) decline, degeneration, deterioration, diminishing, diminution, ebb, failure,
fall, loss, wane, waning, weakening. ANTO-
NYMS: improvement, increase, rise, success.
3 (*the act of being better than another person
or thing*) excelling, outshining, outstripping,
overshadowing, surpassing, transcending.
~*v.t.* **1** (*to intercept the light of, to obscure*) block
out, blot out, cast a shadow over, conceal,
cover, darken, dim, extinguish, obscure,
overshadow, shade, shroud, veil. **2** (*to surpass,*

excel) dwarf, exceed, excel, leave standing, outdo, outrival, outstrip, overshadow, put in the shade, surpass, transcend.

economic *a.* **1** (*relating to the science of economics*) budgetary, financial, fiscal, monetary. **2** (*relating to industrial concerns or commerce*) business, commercial, industrial, mercantile, trade. **3** (*capable of yielding a profit, financially viable*) cost-effective, gainful, money-making, money-spinning, productive, profitable, profit-making, remunerative, viable. ANTONYMS: loss-making, unprofitable. **4** (*thrifty, economical*) budget, cheap, dirt-cheap, inexpensive, low-budget, low-cost, low-price, modest, reasonable, rock-bottom. ANTONYMS: costly, dear, exorbitant, expensive.

economical *a.* **1** (*characterized by economic management; thrifty*) careful, economizing, frugal, penny-pinching, prudent, scrimping, sparing, thrifty. ANTONYMS: extravagant, spendthrift, wasteful. **2** (*cheap*) budget, cheap, dirt-cheap, inexpensive, low-budget, low-cost, low-price, modest, reasonable, rock-bottom. ANTONYMS: costly, dear, exorbitant, expensive.

economize *v.i.* (*to manage domestic or financial affairs with economy*) be economical, be frugal, be thrifty, budget, cut back, cut corners, cut one's coat according to one's cloth, draw in one's horns, pull in one's horns, retrench, save, scrimp, scrimp and save, tighten one's belt. ANTONYMS: be extravagant, (*coll.*) push the boat out.

economy *n.* **1** (*a formalized system for the production and consumption of wealth*) business resources, financial state, financial system. **2** (*a judicious use of money or resources; frugality*) budgeting, carefulness, conservation, frugality, husbandry, parsimony, penny-pinching, prudence, restraint, retrenchment, saving, scrimping, scrimping and saving, thrift, thriftiness. ANTONYMS: extravagance, profligacy.

ecstasy *n.* (*a state of mental exaltation*) bliss, (*coll.*) cloud nine, delight, elation, euphoria, exaltation, exultation, fervour, frenzy, high spirits, joy, jubilation, rapture, rhapsody, seventh heaven, transports. ANTONYMS: depression, misery.

ecstatic *a.* (*excited and extremely happy*) blissful, delighted, delirious, elated, enraptured, euphoric, exalted, exultant, fervent, frenzied, (*coll.*) high, in a frenzy, in seventh heaven, joyful, joyous, jubilant, (*coll.*) on cloud nine, overjoyed, over the moon, rapturous, rhapsodic, transported. ANTONYMS: depressed, desolate, miserable.

eddy *n.* (*a small whirlpool*) maelstrom, vortex, whirlpool.
~*v.i., v.t.* (*to whirl in an eddy*) swirl, whirl.

edge *n.* **1 a** (*the sharp or cutting part of an instrument, such as a sword*) blade, cutting edge. **b** (*the sharpness of this*) keenness, sharpness. ANTONYMS: bluntness. **2** (*the margin or extremity of anything*) border, boundary, brim, brink, contour, flange, fringe, limit, lip, margin, outer limit, outline, perimeter, periphery, rim, side, threshold, verge. ANTONYMS: centre, middle. **3** (*penetrating power; keenness*) acuteness, cleverness, incisiveness, keenness, perceptiveness, perspicacity, quickness, sharpness, smartness. ANTONYMS: apathy, dullness, stupidity. **4** (*acrimony, bitterness*) acerbity, acrimony, bite, bitterness, causticity, force, mordancy, pointedness, pungency, sharpness, sting, trenchancy, virulence. ANTONYMS: blandness, mildness, sweetness.
~*v.t.* **1** (*to sharpen, to put an edge on*) file, hone, put an edge on, sharpen, strop, whet. ANTONYMS: blunt. **2** (*to make an edge or border to*) bind, fringe, hem, rim, trim. **3** (*to be a border to*) border, bound, rim, skirt. **4** (*to move or put forward little by little*) ease, guide, inch, manoeuvre, slide, slip, steer. ANTONYMS: manhandle, thrust.
~*v.i.* (*to move forward or away little by little*) creep, ease oneself, inch, sidle, steal, worm one's way. ANTONYMS: barge, push one's way, thrust. **on edge** (*irritable*) anxious, edgy, ill-at-ease, irascible, like a cat on hot bricks, nervous, nervy, on tenterhooks, restive, tetchy, touchy, twitchy, uneasy, (*coll.*) uptight, (*sl.*) wired. ANTONYMS: calm, cool, calm and collected, (*coll.*) laid-back, nonchalant. **to have the edge on/ over** (*to have an advantage over*) be dominant over, be in the lead over, be superior to, have ascendancy over, have the advantage over, have the upper hand over, have the whip hand over.

edging *n.* (*that which forms the border or edge of anything, such as lace, trimming etc. on a dress*) binding, border, edge, fringe, trim, trimming.

edgy *a.* (*irritable, nervy*) anxious, ill-at-ease, irascible, irritable, like a cat on hot bricks, nervous, nervy, on edge, on tenterhooks, tense, tetchy, touchy, twitchy, uneasy, (*coll.*) uptight, (*sl.*) wired. ANTONYMS: at ease, (*coll.*) laid-back, relaxed.

edible *a.* (*fit for food, eatable*) digestible, eatable, fit to eat. ANTONYMS: inedible, uneatable.

edict *n.* (*a proclamation or decree issued by authority*) act, bill, canon, command, decree, dictate, dictum, enactment, injunction, law, order, proclamation, pronouncement, regulation, rule, ruling, status.

edification n. (*instruction; improving*) coaching, education, enlightenment, guidance, improvement, indoctrination, information, instruction, schooling, teaching, tuition, tutoring, uplifting.

edifice n. (*a building, esp. one of some size and pretension*) building, construction, erection, pile, structure.

edify v.t. (*to instruct; to improve*) build up, coach, educate, enlighten, guide, improve, indoctrinate, inform, instruct, school, teach, tutor, uplift.

edit v.t. **1** (*to prepare for publication or processing by compiling, selecting, etc.*) adapt, check, compile, copy-edit, correct, emend, modify, polish, rephrase, revise, rewrite. **2** (*to censor; to correct*) blue-pencil, bowdlerize, censor, clean up, cut, delete, erase, expurgate. **3** (*to manage (a periodical etc.) by selecting and revising the literary matter*) be in charge of, be responsible for, be the editor of, direct, head, head up.

edition n. **1** (*the form in which a literary work is published*) copy, volume. **2** (*the whole number of copies published at one time*) issue, number, printing, print run.

educate v.t. (*to train and develop the intellectual and moral powers of*) coach, develop, discipline, drill, edify, enlighten, improve, inculcate, indoctrinate, inform, instruct, prepare, prime, school, teach, train, tutor.

educated a. (*having been educated to a high standard*) bluestocking, cultivated, cultured, enlightened, erudite, (*coll., often derog.*) highbrow, informed, knowledgeable, learned, lettered, literate, of letters, polished, refined, schooled. ANTONYMS: ignorant, illiterate, lowbrow, uneducated.

education n. **1** (*the systematic training and development of the intellectual and moral faculties*) coaching, development, drilling, edification, edifying, enlightenment, erudition, inculcation, indoctrination, informing, instruction, preparation, priming, schooling, teaching, training, tuition, tutelage, tutoring. **2** (*the result of a systematic course of training and instruction*) cultivation, culture, enlightenment, erudition, knowledge, letters, literacy, polish, refinement, scholarship, schooling. ANTONYMS: ignorance, illiteracy.

educational a. **1** (*of or relating to education*) academic, didactic, edifying, educative, instructional, learning, pedagogic, pedagogical, scholastic, teaching. **2** (*giving information or knowledge*) edifying, educative, enlightening, heuristic, improving, informative, instructional, instructive. ANTONYMS: uninformative.

educationalist n. (*a person who is versed in educational methods*) academic, coach, educationist, educator, instructor, lecturer, pedagogue, schoolteacher, teacher, trainer, tutor.

eerie a. (*strange and frightening*) chilling, creepy, eldritch, frightening, ghostly, mysterious, scaring, scary, spectral, (*coll.*) spooky, strange, uncanny, unearthly, unnatural, weird.

efface v.t. (*to destroy or remove (something), so that it cannot be seen*) blank out, blot out, delete, eliminate, eradicate, erase, expunge, obliterate, rub out, wipe out.

effect n. **1** (*the result or product of a cause or operation*) aftermath, conclusion, consequence, event, issue, net result, outcome, result, upshot. ANTONYMS: cause. **2** (*efficacy, power of producing a required result*) accomplishment, effectiveness, effectuality, efficacy, efficiency, fulfilment, potency, power, productiveness, success. ANTONYMS: failure, ineffectiveness. **3** (*aim, purpose*) import, meaning, sense, significance, tenor. **4** (*the impression created by a work of art etc.*) impact, impression. **5** (*goods, personal estate*) accoutrements, baggage, belongings, (*coll.*) bits and pieces, equipment, gear, goods, goods and chattels, luggage, possessions, property, tackle, things, trappings. **6** (*the act of putting into operation*) action, enforcement, execution, force, implementation, operation. ANTONYMS: abeyance, suspension.

~v.t. (*to cause to happen*) accomplish, achieve, actuate, bring about, carry out, cause, complete, effectuate, execute, fulfil, give rise to, implement, initiate, make, perform. **in effect** (*in reality, substantially*) actually, effectively, essentially, for all practical purposes, in actual fact, in actual purposes, in reality, in truth, practically, really, substantially. **to take effect** **1** (*to operate*) become functional, become operative, become valid, begin, come into being, come into force, come into operation, function. **2** (*to produce its effect*) become effective, have its effect, have the desired effect, produce results, work.

effective a. **1** (*producing its proper effect*) adequate, capable, competent, effectual, efficacious, efficient, productive, successful. ANTONYMS: ineffective, inefficient, unsuccessful. **2** (*producing a striking impression*) compelling, forceful, impressive, moving, outstanding, persuasive, potent, powerful, remarkable, striking, telling. ANTONYMS: unimpressive, weak. **3** (*real, actual*) actual, genuine, in essence, real, true. ANTONYMS: apparent, ostensible, seeming, supposed. **4** (*starting officially*) active, in force, in operation, in use, operative, valid, with effect. ANTONYMS: inactive, inoperative, invalid.

effectiveness *n.* **1** (*the production of a proper effect*) adequacy, capability, competence, effectuality, effectualness, efficaciousness, efficacy, efficiency, productiveness, productivity, success. **2** (*the production of a striking impression*) force, forcefulness, impressiveness, potency, power. ANTONYMS: ineffectiveness, inefficiency, weakness.

effectual *a.* (*productive of an intended effect*) adequate, capable, competent, effective, efficacious, efficient, productive, successful. ANTONYMS: ineffective, ineffectual, unsuccessful.

effectuate *v.t.* (*to cause to happen*) accomplish, achieve, actuate, bring about, carry out, cause, complete, effect, execute, fulfil, give rise to, implement, initiate, make, perform, produce.

effeminate *a.* ((*of a man*) *womanish; unmanly*) camp, effete, feeble, sissy, unmanly, weak, (*coll.*) wimpish, womanish. ANTONYMS: macho, manly.

effervesce *v.i.* **1** (*to bubble up, from the escape of gas, as fermenting liquors*) bubble, fizz, foam, froth, sparkle. **2** (*to boil over with excitement*) be animated, be buoyant, be exhilarated, be exuberant, be irrepressible, be jubilant, be lively, bubble, bubble over, sparkle.

effervescence *n.* **1** (*bubbling up, from the escape of gas, as fermenting liquors*) bubbliness, carbonation, fizz, fizziness, foam, foaminess, froth, frothiness, sparkle. **2** (*great excitement*) animation, bubbliness, buoyancy, ebullience, enthusiasm, excitement, exhilaration, exuberance, high spirits, irrepressibility, jubilation, liveliness, sparkle, vivacity. ANTONYMS: depression, despondency, low spirits.

effervescent *a.* **1** (*bubbling up, from the escape of gas, as fermenting liquors*) bubbling, bubbly, carbonated, fizzing, fizzy, foamy, frothy, sparkling. ANTONYMS: flat, still. **2** (*very excited*) animated, bubbly, buoyant, ebullient, enthusiastic, excited, exhilarated, exuberant, high-spirited, in high spirits, irrepressible, jubilant, lively, sparkling, vivacious. ANTONYMS: depressed, despondent, in low spirits, lifeless.

effete *a.* **1** (*having lost all vigour and efficiency*) burnt out, decadent, drained, enervated, enfeebled, exhausted, feeble, finished, played out, powerless, spent, weak, weakened, worn out. **2** ((*of a man*) *womanish; unmanly*)

effeminate, feeble, sissy, (*coll.*) wimpish, womanish.

efficacious *a.* (*producing or having power to produce the effect intended*) adequate, capable, competent, effective, effectual, efficient, potent, powerful, productive, successful.

efficiency *n.* (*power to produce a desired result*) ability, adeptness, adequacy, capability, competence, deftness, effectiveness, effectualness, efficacy, expertise, mastery, productiveness, productivity, proficiency, skilfulness, skill. ANTONYMS: clumsiness, inability, incompetence, inefficiency, ineptness.

efficient *a.* (*causing or producing effects or results*) able, adept, adequate, businesslike, capable, competent, deft, effective, effectual, efficacious, organized, productive, proficient, skilful, well-organized, workmanlike. ANTONYMS: clumsy, incompetent, inefficient, inept.

effigy *n.* (*a representation or likeness of a person, as on coins, medals etc.*) bust, dummy, guy, icon, idol, image, likeness, model, representation, statue.

effluent *n.* (*the liquid that is discharged from a sewage tank*) effluvium, pollutant, sewage, waste.

effort *n.* **1** (*an exertion of physical or mental power, an endeavour*) application, elbow grease, endeavour, energy, exertion, force, labour, muscle, power, strain, stress, striving, struggle, work. ANTONYMS: idleness, inertia. **2** (*the result of an effort, something achieved*) accomplishment, achievement, act, attainment, creation, deed, feat, opus, product, production, result.

effortless *a.* (*achieved easily and skilfully*) easy, easy as falling off a log, (*coll.*) easy-peasy, facile, painless, simple, trouble-free, uncomplicated, undemanding, unexacting. ANTONYMS: demanding, difficult, exacting, hard.

effrontery *n.* (*bold, shameless behaviour*) arrogance, audacity, boldness, (*coll.*) brass neck, brazenness, (*coll.*) cheek, (*sl.*) chutzpah, disrespect, (*coll.*) face, gall, impertinence, impudence, incivility, insolence, (*coll.*) neck, nerve, presumption, shamelessness, temerity. ANTONYMS: bashfulness, reserve, shyness.

effulgent *a.* (*shining brightly*) beaming, blazing, bright, brilliant, dazzling, flaming, fluorescent, glowing, incandescent, luminous, lustrous, shining, splendid, vivid. ANTONYMS: dull, lacklustre.

effusion *n.* (*that which is poured out*) discharge, emission, gush, issue, outpouring, shedding, stream.

effusive *a.* (*showing strong feelings in an enthusiastic way*) demonstrative, ebullient, enthusiastic, expansive, extravagant, exuberant, fulsome, gushing, lavish, lyrical, (*coll.*) OTT, over-the-top, profuse, rhapsodic, smarmy, unreserved, unrestrained, verbose, wordy. ANTONYMS: reserved, restrained, understated.

egg *v.t.* (*to incite, to urge* (*on*)) drive, encourage, exhort, goad, incite, prod, prompt, push, spur, urge. ANTONYMS: discourage.

egghead *n.* (*an intellectual*) academic, bluestocking, bookworm, (*coll.*) brain, genius, highbrow, intellectual, know-it-all, pedagogue, pedant, scholar. ANTONYMS: dolt, dunce.

egocentric *a.* (*self-centred*) egoistic, egoistical, egotistic, egotistical, self-centred, selfish.

egoism *n.* (*pure self-interest, systematic selfishness*) egocentricity, egomania, egotism, narcissism, self-absorption, self-centredness, self-importance, self-interest, selfishness, self-love, self-regard, self seeking. ANTONYMS: altruism.

egoist *n.* (*a person who acts from self-interest and selfishness*) egomaniac, egotist, narcissist, self-seeker.

egoistic *a.* (*acting from self-interest and self-ishness*) egocentric, egomaniacal, egotistic, egotistical, full of oneself, narcissistic, self-absorbed, self-centred, self-important, self-seeking. ANTONYMS: altruistic.

egotism *n.* (*an extreme sense of self-importance and obsession with oneself*) arrogance, conceit, egocentricity, egoism, egomania, narcissism, pride, self-admiration, self-conceit, self-esteem, self-glorification, self-importance, self-love, self-praise, superiority, vanity. ANTONYMS: humility, modesty, self-hatred.

egotist *n.* (*a person who is self-important and obsessed with themselves*) (*coll.*) bighead, blowhard, braggart, egocentrist, egoist, egomaniac.

egotistic *a.* (*acting in a way that is self-important and obsessed with oneself*) conceited, egocentric, egoistic, egoistical, egomaniacal, full of oneself, narcissistic, self-admiring, self-conceited, self-important, superior, vain. ANTONYMS: modest.

egregious *a.* (*conspicuously bad, flagrant*) appalling, arrant, blatant, flagrant, glaring, grievous, gross, heinous, infamous, insufferable, intolerable, monstrous, notorious, outrageous, rank, scandalous, shocking. ANTONYMS: slight.

ejaculate *v.t.* **1** (*to utter suddenly and briefly; to exclaim*) blurt out, call out, cry, shout, utter,

vocalize, voice. **2** (*to eject*) discharge, eject, emit, expel, release, spurt.
~*v.i.* **1** (*to utter ejaculations*) burst out, call out, cry, exclaim, shout, yell. **2** (*to emit semen*) climax, (*sl.*) come, have an orgasm, orgasm.

ejaculation *n.* **1** (*an abrupt exclamation*) call, cry, exclamation, shout, utterance. **2** (*the emission of seminal fluid*) climax, (*sl.*) coming, orgasm.

eject *v.t.* **1** (*to cause to come out of e.g. a machine*) discharge, disgorge, emit, excrete, expel, exude, release, spew, vomit. **2** (*to force to leave*) banish, (*sl.*) boot out, cast out, (*coll.*) chuck out, deport, dismiss, dispossess, drive away, evacuate, exile, expel, (*N Am., sl.*) give (someone) the bum's rush, (*coll.*) give (someone) the heave-ho, kick out, put out, remove, throw out, (*coll.*) turf out, turn out. **3** (*to push out or remove forcefully*) propel, throw out, thrust out.

eke *v.t.* **1** (*to produce or maintain with difficulty*) scrape, scratch, scrimp. **2** (*to make up for or supply deficiencies in* (*with out*)) add to, augment, enlarge, increase, stretch out, supplement.

elaborate[1] *a.* **1** (*carefully or highly wrought*) baroque, decorative, extravagant, fancy, flash, flashy, fussy, intricate, ornamented, ornate, ostentatious, rococo, showy. ANTONYMS: minimal, plain, simple, unadorned. **2** (*highly finished*) careful, complete, complex, complicated, detailed, intricate, involved, painstaking, perfected, thorough. ANTONYMS: careless, rough, sketchy, unfinished.

elaborate[2] *v.t.* (*to develop in detail*) develop, improve, perfect, polish, refine, work out.
~*v.i.* (*to go into more detail* (*on*)) add detail to, add flesh to, amplify, enlarge on, expand on, expatiate on, flesh out. ANTONYMS: condense, summarize.

élan *n.* (*energy and confidence*) dash, flair, flourish, (*sl.*) oomph, panache, (*sl.*) pizazz, spirit, style, verve, zest.

elapse *v.i.* ((*esp. of time*) *to glide or pass away*) glide by, go by, go on, pass, pass by, roll by, roll on, slip away, slip by, steal by.

elastic *a.* **1** (*having the quality of returning to that form from which it has been compressed or distorted*) flexible, pliable, pliant, resilient, springy, stretchy, tensile, yielding. **2** ((*e.g. of plans or ideas*) *that can be changed easily*) accommodating, adaptable, adjustable, flexible, fluid, variable. ANTONYMS: fixed, rigid, set.

elasticity *n.* **1** (*the quality of returning to that form from which it has been compressed or* *distorted*) flexibility, give, pliancy, resilience, rubberiness, springiness, stretch, stretchiness. **2** ((*e.g. of plans or ideas) the quality of being able to be changed easily*) adaptability, adjustability, fluidness, variability.

elated *a.* (*extremely happy and excited*) cock-a-hoop, delighted, ebullient, ecstatic, euphoric, excited, exhilarated, exultant, gleeful, in high spirits, in seventh heaven, in transports, joyful, joyous, jubilant, jumping for joy, (*coll.*) on cloud nine, overjoyed, over the moon, rapt, rhapsodic, transported. ANTONYMS: depressed, despondent, in low spirits, miserable.

elation *n.* (*a state of extreme happiness and excitement*) bliss, delight, ebullience, ecstasy, euphoria, excitement, exhilaration, glee, high spirits, joy, joyfulness, jubilation, rapture, rhapsody, transports.

elbow *n.* (*an elbow-shaped* (*usu. obtuse*) *angle or corner*) angle, bend, corner, crook, joint, turning.
~*v.t.* (*to push with the elbows, to jostle*) bump, jostle, knock, nudge, push, shoulder, shove, thrust.

elbow room *n.* (*ample room for action*) breathing space, freedom to act, latitude, leeway, room, room to manoeuvre, scope, space.

elder *a.* (*older*) older, senior. ANTONYMS: junior, younger.

elderly *a.* (*old*) advanced in years, ageing, long in the tooth, old, oldish, senescent. ANTONYMS: young, youngish. **the elderly** (*people who are old*) elderly people, OAPs, old-age pensioners, old people, pensioners, senior citizens. ANTONYMS: the young.

elect *v.t.* **1** (*to choose for any office or employment*) choose, decide on, designate, determine on, opt for, pick, plump for, prefer, select, settle on, vote for. **2** (*to determine on any particular course of action*) choose to, decide on, determine to, opt to.

election *n.* **1** (*the act of choosing from a number of people or things, esp. by vote*) appointing, appointment, choice, choosing, deciding on, designation, opting for, picking, preference, selection, vote, voting. **2** (*the ceremony or process of electing*) ballot, hustings, poll, vote.

elector *n.* (*a person who has the right, power or privilege of electing*) constituent, selector, voter.

electric *a.* (*very exciting*) charged, dramatic, exciting, jolting, magnetic, rousing, startling, stimulating, stirring, tense, thrilling. ANTONYMS: low-key.

electrify *v.t.* (*to thrill with joy or other exciting*

emotion) animate, charge, excite, fire, galvanize, jolt, move, rouse, shock, startle, stimulate, take one's breath away, thrill.

elegance *n.* (*the quality of being pleasing to good taste*) chic, exquisiteness, fashionableness, finesse, grace, gracefulness, modishness, style, stylishness, tastefulness. ANTONYMS: gaucheness, inelegance, tastelessness.

elegant *a.* (*pleasing to good taste*) aesthetic, artistic, chic, debonair, exquisite, fashionable, fine, graceful, modish, stylish, tasteful, well-turned-out. ANTONYMS: gauche, inelegant, tasteless.

elegiac *a.* (*relating to or of the nature of elegies*) dirgelike, doleful, funereal, lamenting, melancholic, mournful, plaintive, sad. ANTONYMS: cheerful, happy.

elegy *n.* (*a lyrical poem or a song of lamentation*) dirge, lament, plaint, requiem, threnody.

element *n.* **1** (*any one of the fundamental parts of which anything is composed*) basis, component, constituent, factor, feature, ingredient, integrand, member, module, part, piece, section, segment, subdivision, trace, unit. **2** (*the proper or natural sphere of any person or thing*) domain, environment, field, habitat, medium, milieu, realm, sphere, world. **3** (*pl.*) (*the rudiments of any science or art*) basics, essentials, foundations, fundamentals, principles, rudiments.

elemental *a.* **1** (*of or like the primitive forces of nature*) atmospheric, environmental, natural. **2** (*of or arising from first principles*) basic, elementary, embryonic, essential, fundamental, primary, primitive, radical, rudimentary. ANTONYMS: advanced.

elementary *a.* **1** (*rudimentary, relating to first principles*) basic, (*sl.*) bog standard, elemental, fundamental, introductory, preparatory, primary, rudimentary. ANTONYMS: advanced, sophisticated. **2** (*easy, simple*) easy, (*coll.*) easy as falling off a log, (*coll.*) easy as pie, facile, rudimentary, simple, straightforward, uncomplicated. ANTONYMS: complicated, difficult.

elevate *v.t.* **1** (*to lift up; to raise higher*) hoist, lift up, raise. ANTONYMS: lower. **2** (*to raise in position or dignity*) advance, aggrandize, give advancement to, give promotion to, promote, upgrade. ANTONYMS: demote, downgrade. **3** (*to make happier*) animate, brighten, buoy up, cheer, elate, exhilarate, give (someone) a boost, gladden, raise (someone's) spirits, uplift. ANTONYMS: depress.

elevation *n.* **1** (*the act of elevating*) hoisting, lifting up, raising. ANTONYMS: lowering. **2** (*the state of being elevated*) advancement, aggrandizement, promotion, upgrading. ANTO-NYMS: demotion. **3** (*an elevated position or ground*) eminence, height, hill, hillock, mound, mountain, rise. **4** (*height above sea level, or any other given level*) altitude, height.

elf *n.* (*a tiny supernatural being*) fairy, imp, pixie, sprite.

elfin *a.* (*very small and delicate*) dainty, diminutive, elfish, elflike, little, small, tiny. ANTONYMS: elephantine, huge, large.

elicit *v.t.* (*to obtain* (*information or a response*), *esp. when this is difficult*) bring forth, bring out, call forth, educe, evoke, exact, extort, extract, obtain, wrest.

eligible *a.* (*fit or deserving to be chosen*) acceptable, appropriate, desirable, fit, qualified, suitable, suited, worthy. ANTONYMS: ineligible, unqualified, unsuitable.

eliminate *v.t.* (*to remove, get rid of*) dispose of, do away with, eradicate, get rid of, remove, stamp out.

elite *n.* (*the best part, the most powerful*) the aristocracy, the cream, the crème de la crème, the elect, the flower, the jewel in the crown, the nobility, the pick. ANTONYMS: the dregs, the riff-raff.

elixir *n.* **1** (*a cordial, a sovereign remedy*) cure-all, nostrum, panacea, sovereign remedy. **2** (*the essential principle or quintessence*) essence, pith, principle, quintessence. **3** (*a distillation or concentrated tincture*) concentrate, essence, extract, potion, solution, syrup, tincture.

elocution *n.* (*the art or manner of speaking or reading*) articulation, delivery, diction, enunciation, oratory, phrasing, pronunciation, rhetoric, speaking, speech, speech-making, utterance, voice production.

elongate *v.t.* (*to make longer*) draw out, extend, lengthen, make longer, prolong, protract, stretch, stretch out. ANTONYMS: make shorter, reduce, shorten.

elope *v.i.* **1** (*to run away with a lover, with a view to a secret marriage*) run away together, run off together. **2** (*to run away in a secret manner, to abscond*) abscond, bolt, decamp, flee, slip away, sneak off, steal away.

eloquence *n.* **1** (*fluent appropriate verbal expression, esp. of emotional ideas*) articulacy, articulateness, command of language, expression, expressiveness, fluency, forcefulness, oratory, persuasiveness, power of speech, rhetoric, (*coll.*) the gift of the gab, way with words. ANTONYMS: hesitancy, inarticulacy. **2** (*a way of expressing something clearly*) emotion,

expressiveness, intensity, significance. ANTONYMS: blankness.

eloquent *a.* **1** (*having the power of expression in fluent and appropriate language*) articulate, expressive, fluent, forceful, glib, persuasive, pithy, silver-tongued, smooth-tongued, well-spoken. ANTONYMS: hesitant, inarticulate, speechless, stumbling. **2** (*full of feeling or interest*) expressive, meaningful, pregnant, revealing, significant, telling, vivid. ANTONYMS: blank, deadpan, inexpressive.

elsewhere *adv.* (*in or to some other place*) away, not here, somewhere else. ANTONYMS: here.

elucidate *v.t.* (*to make clear and easy to understand*) annotate, clarify, explain, explicate, expound, gloss, illuminate, interpret, make clear, make plain, shed light on, throw light on. ANTONYMS: complicate, obscure.

elude *v.t.* **1** (*to escape from by artifice or dexterity*) avoid, bilk, circumvent, dodge, (*coll.*) duck, evade, flee from, get away from, give (someone or something) the slip, lose, shake off, throw off the scent. **2** (*to remain undiscovered or unexplained by*) baffle, be forgotten by, confound, escape, stump. ANTONYMS: come to mind.

elusive *a.* **1** (*difficult to catch or locate*) difficult to make contact with, evasive, slippery. **2** (*difficult to remember*) fleeting, fugitive, indefinable, subtle, transitory. **3** (*difficult to understand or describe*) baffling, deceptive, equivocal, evasive, misleading, puzzling. ANTONYMS: straightforward.

emaciated *a.* (*abnormally and unhealthily thin*) anorexic, atrophied, cadaverous, gaunt, haggard, scrawny, shrivelled, shrunken, skeletal, thin as a rake, undernourished, wasted. ANTONYMS: obese, overweight.

emanate *v.i.* (*to issue or flow as from a source, to originate*) arise, derive, emerge, flow from, issue, originate, proceed, stem.
~*v.t.* (*to emit, to send out*) discharge, emit, exhale, give off, give out, radiate, send forth, send out.

emanation *n.* **1** (*the act of emanating from something, as from a source*) derivation, emergence, origination, proceeding. **2** (*that which emanates, an efflux, an effluence*) discharge, effluence, effluent, efflux, emission, exhalation, radiation.

emancipate *v.t.* (*to release from slavery or oppression*) deliver, discharge, enfranchise, free, let loose, liberate, release, set free, unchain, unfetter, unshackle, unyoke. ANTONYMS: enslave, fetter, shackle.

emancipation n. 1 (the releasing from slavery or oppression) deliverance, discharge, enfranchisement, freeing, liberating, liberation, manumission, release, unchaining, unfettering, unshackling, unyoking. ANTONYMS: enslaving, fettering, shackling. 2 (the state of being freed from any bond or restraint) deliverance, freedom, liberation. ANTONYMS: bondage, servitude, slavery.

emasculate v.t. 1 (to castrate) castrate, desex, neuter. 2 (to deprive of masculine strength or vigour) cripple, debilitate, enervate, enfeeble, make feeble, make weak, weaken. ANTONYMS: make strong, strengthen.

embalm v.t. 1 (to preserve (e.g. a body) from putrefaction by means of spices and aromatic drugs) anoint, mummify, preserve. 2 (to imbue with sweet scents) aromatize, make fragrant, perfume, scent. 3 (to preserve from oblivion) cherish, conserve, enshrine, immortalize, keep in mind, preserve, store, treasure.

embargo n. (a hindrance, impediment) ban, bar, barrier, blockage, check, hindrance, impediment, interdict, obstruction, prohibition, proscription, (coll.) red light, restraint, restriction, stoppage. ANTONYMS: authorization, encouragement, (coll.) green light, permission.
~v.t. (to prohibit, to forbid) ban, bar, block, boycott, check, forbid, impede, interdict, place an embargo on, prohibit, proscribe, restrain, restrict, stop. ANTONYMS: authorize, encourage, (coll.) give (something) the green light, permit.

embark v.i. 1 (to engage or enter (upon any undertaking)) begin, commence, engage upon, enter upon, get going, initiate, institute, launch, set up, start, take up, turn one's hand to, undertake, venture into. ANTONYMS: bring to a close, close, wind up. 2 (to go on board a ship, an aircraft etc.) board, board the aircraft, go on board. ANTONYMS: alight, disembark, land.

embarrass v.t. (to make (someone) feel ashamed or uncomfortable) abash, agitate, confuse, discomfit, discompose, disconcert, distress, fluster, humiliate, make self-conscious, make to feel awkward, make uncomfortable, mortify, perturb, upset.

embarrassed a. (feeling ashamed or uncomfortable) abashed, awkward, bashful, confused, discomfited, disconcerted, distressed, flustered, humiliated, mortified, nonplussed, perturbed, self-conscious, shy, uncomfortable, upset. ANTONYMS: composed, nonchalant.

embarrassing a. (causing embarrassment) awkward, compromising, confusing, (coll.) cringe-making, discomfiting, disconcerting, distressing, humiliating, mortifying, tricky, uncomfortable, upsetting.

embarrassment n. 1 (feeling of shame or uncomfortableness) awkwardness, bashfulness, confusion, discomfiture, discomposure, distress, humiliation, mortification, self-consciousness, uncomfortableness. 2 (financial difficulties) dire straits, financial difficulties, fix, mess, plight, predicament, tight corner.

embed v.t. (to set firmly in surrounding matter) drive in, fix firmly in, hammer in, implant, insert, plant, ram in, set firmly in, sink in.

embellish v.t. 1 (to decorate in order to make more attractive) adorn, beautify, bedeck, bespangle, deck, decorate, dress, dress up, emblazon, enhance, festoon, garnish, gild, ornament, (sl.) tart up, trim. 2 (to add incidents or imaginary accompaniments so as to heighten (a narrative)) add colour to, dress up, elaborate on, embroider, enhance, enlarge on, exaggerate, garnish, gild, overstate, varnish. ANTONYMS: play down, understate.

ember n. (smouldering remnants of a fire or of passion etc.) ashes, cinders, remnant, residue.

embezzle v.t. (to take and use fraudulently (what is committed to one's care)) appropriate, filch, (sl.) have one's hand in the till, make off with, misappropriate, (sl.) nick, pilfer, purloin, (coll.) rip off, rob, steal, thieve.

embezzlement n. (fraudulent taking and using of what is committed to one's care) appropriation, (Law) defalcation, filching, fraud, larceny, misappropriation, (sl.) nicking, peculation, pilfering, purloining, robbery, theft.

embitter v.t. (to make bitter, or more bitter) anger, disaffect, make bitter, make resentful, poison, sour.

emblazon v.t. (to decorate; to make brilliant) adorn, colour, decorate, embellish, illuminate, ornament, paint.

emblem n. (a symbolic figure; a representation of an object symbolizing some other thing or quality) badge, crest, device, figure, image, insignia, mark, representation, sign, symbol, token, type.

emblematic a. (representing something symbolically) figurative, representative, symbolic.

embodiment n. 1 (an expression in concrete form) epitome, example, exemplar, exemplification, expression, incarnation, incorporation, manifestation, personification, realization, reification, representation, symbol, symbolization, type. 2 (incorporation or inclusion) assimilation, collection, combination, concentration, consolidation, encompassing, inclusion, incorporation, integration, organization.

embody *v.t.* **1** (*to express in a concrete form*) body forth, exemplify, express, incarnate, incorporate, manifest, personify, realize, represent, stand for, symbolize, typify. **2** (*to incorporate, to include*) assimilate, bring together, collect, combine, comprise, consolidate, constitute, contain, embrace, encompass, include, incorporate, integrate, organize, take in.

embolden *v.t.* (*to give boldness to*) fire, give courage to, hearten, inflame, invigorate, make bold, make bolder, make brave, make braver, rouse, stir.

embrace *v.t.* **1** (*to enfold in the arms*) clasp, clasp in one's arms, clasp to one's bosom, clutch, cuddle, encircle in one's arms, enfold, give (someone) a bear hug, hold, hold in one's arms, hug, squeeze, take in one's arms. **2** (*to include, comprise*) comprehend, comprise, contain, cover, deal with, embody, encompass, include, incorporate, involve, subsume, take in, take into account. **3** (*to receive, accept eagerly*) accept, accept wholeheartedly, accept with enthusiasm, adopt, espouse, take up, welcome.
~*n.* (*a clasping in the arms*) bear hug, clasp, (*coll.*) clinch, clutch, cuddle, hold, hug, squeeze.

embroider *v.t.* (*to embellish with additions, esp. a narrative with exaggerations or fiction*) add colour to, colour, dress up, elaborate on, embellish, enhance, enlarge on, exaggerate, garnish, gild, overstate. ANTONYMS: play down, understate.

embroidery *n.* **1** (*ornamentation stitched with the needle*) needlepoint, needlework, sewing. **2** (*exaggeration or fiction added to a narrative*) addition, colour, elaboration, embellishment, enhancement, exaggeration, fabrication, gilding, overstatement, tall story. ANTONYMS: understatement.

embroil *v.t.* **1** (*to throw into confusion*) complicate, confuse, disarrange, disorder, disturb, jumble, mix up, muddle, snarl up, throw into confusion. **2** (*to involve* (*someone*) *in a quarrel or contention* (*with another*)) concern, entangle, get (someone) mixed up in, implicate, include, involve.

embryonic *a.* (*in an undeveloped or very early stage of development*) beginning, early, elementary, immature, incipient, primary, rudimentary, seminal, undeveloped, unformed. ANTONYMS: developed, mature.

emend *v.t.* (*to correct, to remove faults from*) alter, amend, censor, correct, edit, improve, polish, rectify, revise, rewrite.

emendation *n.* (*correction, removal of faults*) alteration, amendment, correction, editing, improvement, polishing, rectification, rectifying, revision, rewriting.

emerge *v.i.* **1** (*to rise up out of anything in which a thing has been immersed or sunk*) arise, come to the surface, come up, pop up, rise, spring, surface. ANTONYMS: fall, sink, submerge. **2** (*to appear in sight* (*from below the horizon or from a place of concealment*)) appear, arrive, become visible, come into view, come out, emanate, issue, pop up, proceed, spring up, surface. ANTONYMS: depart, disappear from sight, withdraw. **3** (*to appear, to come out* (*such as facts in an inquiry*)) become apparent, become known, become public, become public knowledge, be disclosed, be exposed, be publicized, come out, come to light. ANTONYMS: be suppressed, remain secret. **4** (*to become apparent*) appear, become apparent, become popular, become prominent, come to the fore, crop up, develop, materialize, surface. ANTONYMS: decline, wane.

emergence *n.* **1** (*the appearance in sight from below the horizon or from a place of concealment*) advent, appearance, arrival, emanation, issuing, surfacing. ANTONYMS: departure, disappearance, withdrawal. **2** (*the rising up of something that has been immersed or sunk*) arising, coming to the surface, rising, surfacing. **3** (*the appearance or coming out of something, e.g. facts in an inquiry*) broadcasting, coming to light, disclosure, exposure, publicizing, unfolding. ANTONYMS: suppression. **4** (*the state of something becoming apparent*) appearance, coming to the fore, development, materialization, surfacing. ANTONYMS: decline, waning.

emergency *n.* (*a sudden occurrence or situation demanding immediate action*) accident, crisis, danger, desperate straits, dire straits, disaster, exigency, extreme difficulty, extremity, panic stations, plight, predicament, state of alarm, state of urgency, unforeseen circumstances, urgent situation.

emergent *a.* (*coming into being, evolving*) budding, developing, embryonic, evolving, rising.

emigrate *v.i.* (*to leave one's country in order to settle in another*) migrate, move abroad, relocate, resettle.

emigration *n.* (*the leaving of one's own country in order to settle in another*) exodus, expatriation, migration, relocation.

eminence *n.* **1** (*a part rising above the rest, or projecting above the surface*) elevation, height, high ground, hill, hillock, knoll, raised ground, rise, rising ground. ANTONYMS: hollow. **2** (*the quality of being famous and respected*) celebrity, distinction, esteem, fame, greatness, high standing, illustriousness, importance, notability, note, pre-eminence, prestige, prominence, rank, renown, reputation, repute, standing, stature, superiority. ANTONYMS: anonymity, lowliness, ordinariness.

eminent *a.* (*famous and respected*) celebrated, distinguished, esteemed, famous, great, high-ranking, illustrious, important, major, notable, noted, noteworthy, of distinction, of note, of repute, outstanding, pre-eminent, prestigious, prominent, remarkable, renowned, reputable, revered, superior, well-known. ANTONYMS: anonymous, ordinary, undistinguished, unknown.

eminently *adv.* ((*used as an intensifier*) *extremely*) exceedingly, exceptionally, extremely, greatly, highly, markedly, outstandingly, remarkably, signally, very, well.

emissary *n.* (*a messenger or agent, esp. one sent on a secret or dangerous mission*) agent, attaché, courier, delegate, deputy, embassy, envoy, go-between, herald, legate, messenger, representative, scout.

emission *n.* **1** (*the act or process of emitting*) discharge, effusion, ejaculation, ejection, excretion, exudation, issue, issuing, ooze, oozing, outpouring. ANTONYMS: absorption, assimilation. **2** (*the thing given off or out*) discharge, effusion, excretion, exhalation, exudate.

emit *v.t.* (*to give out, to utter*) discharge, ejaculate, eject, excrete, exhale, exude, give off, give out, issue, leak, let out, ooze, pour out, send forth, send out, voice. ANTONYMS: absorb, assimilate, take in.

emollient *a.* (*making soft or supple*) demulcent, moisturizing, softening, soothing. ~*n.* (*a substance which soothes and diminishes irritation*) balm, lotion, moisturizer, ointment, salve.

emolument *n.* (*the profit arising from any office or employment*) compensation, earnings, fee, financial reward, gain, income, pay, payment, proceeds, profit, recompense, remuneration, return, revenue, reward, salary, stipend, wages.

emotion *n.* (*a state of excited feeling of any kind, whether of pain or pleasure*) agitation, ardour, excitement, feeling, fervour, heat, passion, reaction, sensation, sentiment, vehemence, warmth. ANTONYMS: apathy, coldness, impassivity.

emotional *a.* **1** (*of or relating to emotion*) affecting, ardent, demonstrative, disturbing, emotive, exciting, fervent, heartrending, impassioned, moving, passionate, pathetic, poignant, sentimental, stirring, tear-jerking, tender, touching, upsetting. ANTONYMS: passionless, undemonstrative, unemotional, unexciting. **2** (*easily affected with emotion*) ardent, demonstrative, excitable, feeling, fervent, hot-blooded, loving, melodramatic, passionate, responsive, sensitive, sentimental, susceptible, temperamental, tender, warm. ANTONYMS: apathetic, cold, unemotional.

emotionless *a.* (*not showing any emotion*) cold, cold-blooded, detached, distant, frigid, glacial, icy, impassive, imperturbable, indifferent, phlegmatic, remote, undemonstrative, unemotional, unfeeling. ANTONYMS: emotional, excitable, hot-blooded, passionate.

emotive *a.* (*tending to produce emotion*) contentious, controversial, critical, delicate, high-profile, sensitive, stirring, touchy. ANTONYMS: low-key, run-of-the-mill.

empathize *v.t.* (*to be able to understand the experience of others*) be in sympathy with, be on the same wavelength as, feel rapport with, identify with, speak the same language as, sympathize with.

empathy *n.* (*the capacity for identifying with the experience of others*) affinity, fellow feeling, rapport, sympathy. ANTONYMS: antipathy, indifference.

emphasis *n.* (*force or intensity of expression, feeling etc.*) accent, accentuation, force, importance, insistence, intensity, power, priority, prominence, significance, strength, stress, underlining, urgency, weight. ANTONYMS: weakness.

emphasize *v.t.* **1** (*to give special prominence to, to distinguish*) accentuate, call attention to, give prominence to, give weight to, highlight, insist on, lay stress on, maximize, place the emphasis on, play up, point up, put the accent on, put the spotlight on, spotlight, strengthen, stress, underline. ANTONYMS: gloss over, minimize, play down. **2** (*to pronounce (a word or syllable) with particular stress*) accentuate, put the accent on, put the stress on, stress.

emphatic *a.* **1** (*behaving or speaking in a forceful way*) certain, decided, definite, determined, direct, earnest, energetic, forceful, forcible, positive, unequivocal, vehement, vigorous. ANTONYMS: equivocal, tentative, undecided. **2** (*using forceful language to show strong, certain feelings*) categorical, certain, definite, determined, earnest, forceful, insistent, positive, sure. ANTONYMS: doubtful, hesitant, uncertain, unsure. **3** ((*e.g. of a victory*) *clear and undoubted*) absolute, categorical, certain, clear, definite, distinct, marked, positive, powerful, pronounced, remarkable, resounding, significant, striking. ANTONYMS: uncertain, unimportant, unremarkable.

empirical *a.* (*founded on experience or observation, not theory*) experiential, experimental, first-hand, hands-on, heuristic, practical, pragmatic. ANTONYMS: academic, hypothetical, theoretical.

employ *v.t.* **1** (*to use, to exercise*) apply, bring to bear, exercise, exert, make use of, ply, use, utilize. **2** (*to keep in one's service, esp. for pay*) commission, engage, enlist, enrol, hire, put on the payroll, sign on, take into employment, take on. ANTONYMS: dismiss, (*coll.*) sack. **3** (*to spend or pass* (*time, oneself etc.*) *in any occupation*) fill, make use of, occupy, put to use, spend, take up, use up.
~*n.* (*occupation, business*) business, employment, occupation, profession, service.

employed *a.* **1** (*working in a job*) having a job, having work, in a job, in employment, in work, working. ANTONYMS: jobless, out of work, unemployed. **2** (*busy, using the time doing* (*something*)) busy, engaged in, occupied in, preoccupied with.

employee *n.* (*a person who is employed regularly in some task or occupation for salary or wages*) hired hand, member of staff, member of the workforce, wage-earner, worker, workman, workwoman. ANTONYMS: boss, director, employer.

employer *n.* (*a person who employs people for salary or wages*) boss, director, (*coll.*) gaffer, (*N Am., sl.*) honcho, manager, owner, proprietor.

employment *n.* **1** (*the act of employing*) commissioning, engagement, enlistment, hire, signing on, taking on. **2** (*regular occupation, trade or profession*) occupation, profession, pursuit, service, trade, vocation, work. ANTONYMS: joblessness, unemployment. **3** (*the act of using*) application, exercise, exertion, use, utilization.

empower *v.t.* **1** (*to authorize*) accredit, allow, authorize, certify, commission, entitle, license, permit, qualify, sanction, warrant. **2** (*to enable*) allow, enable, equip, facilitate, fit, give power to, give the means to. ANTONYMS: disempower.

emptiness *n.* **1** (*an empty space*) vacancy, vacuum, void. **2** (*the state of having nothing in an area or space*) bareness, barrenness, desolation, destitution. **3** (*a feeling of meaninglessness*) aimlessness, fruitlessness, hollowness, idleness, ineffectiveness,

ineffectualness, meaninglessness, purposelessness, shadowiness, uselessness, worthlessness. ANTONYMS: effectiveness, meaningfulness, worth. **4** (*a sense of foolishness*) foolishness, frivolity, frivolousness, inanity, senselessness, stupidity. ANTONYMS: intelligence, sense, wisdom. **5** (*hunger*) desire, hunger, ravening.

empty *a.* **1** (*void, containing nothing*) hollow, unfilled, void. ANTONYMS: filled, full. **2** (*devoid* (*of*)) in need of, lacking, short of, wanting, without. ANTONYMS: full of, rich in, with. **3** (*vacant, unoccupied*) free, uninhabited, unoccupied, untenanted, vacant. ANTONYMS: inhabited, occupied. **4** (*destitute, desolate*) bare, barren, deserted, desolate, destitute. ANTONYMS: fertile, inhabited, populated. **5** (*meaningless, having no effect*) aimless, fruitless, futile, hollow, idle, ineffective, ineffectual, insubstantial, meaningless, purposeless, shadowy, unsubstantial, useless, worthless. ANTONYMS: ineffective, meaningful, purposeful. **6** (*senseless, inane*) foolish, frivolous, inane, senseless, stupid, unintelligent, unwise. ANTONYMS: intelligent, sensible, wise. **7** (*hungry, unsatisfied*) famished, hungry, ravenous, (*coll.*) starving, unfed, unfilled. ANTONYMS: full, sated, (*coll.*) stuffed.
~*v.t.* **1** (*to remove the contents from, to make vacant*) clear, drain, evacuate, unload, unpack, vacate, void. ANTONYMS: fill, pack. **2** (*to remove from a receptacle* (*into another*)) decant, deplete, discharge, drain, pour out. ANTONYMS: fill up, replenish.
~*v.i.* **1** (*to become empty*) become empty, become vacant. ANTONYMS: fill up. **2** (*to discharge* (*as a river*)) discharge, drain, flow out, issue, ooze, pour out.

empty-headed *a.* (*silly, witless*) brainless, (*coll.*) dizzy, (*coll.*) dopey, feather-brained, flighty, giddy, (*coll.*) hare-brained, inane, scatterbrained, scatty, silly, stupid, vacuous. ANTONYMS: clever, level-headed, sensible.

emulate *v.t.* (*to try to equal or excel*) challenge, compete with, copy, follow, imitate, mimic, rival, vie with.

enable *v.t.* **1** (*to authorize, to empower* (*to*)) accredit, allow, authorize, certify, commission, entitle, license, permit, qualify, sanction, warrant. **2** (*to supply with means* (*to do any act*)) allow, empower, equip, facilitate, fit, give the means to, give the power to. ANTONYMS: disable, disempower.

enact *v.t.* **1** (*to decree*) authorize, command, decree, legislate, ordain, order, rule, sanction. ANTONYMS: annul, repeal. **2** (*to represent, act*) act, appear as, depict, impersonate, perform, play, play the part of, portray, represent, stage.

enactment *n.* **1** (*the act or fact of enacting*) authorizing, decreeing, legislating, ordaining, ordering, ruling, sanctioning. ANTONYMS: annulment, repeal. **2** (*something enacted, as a law*) act, authorization, bill, command, commandment, decree, dictate, edict, law, legislation, measure, motion, order, ordinance, proclamation, pronouncement, regulation, statute. **3** (*the performance of e.g. a play*) acting, appearance, depiction, impersonation, performance, portrayal, representation, staging.

enamour *v.t.* **to be enamoured 1** (*to be in love*) be bewitched by, be captivated by, (*coll.*) be crazy about, be fond of, be infatuated with, be in love with, be mad about, (*sl.*) be nuts about, be smitten with, be wild about, (*coll.*) fancy, (*coll.*) have a crush on, love. ANTONYMS: detest, hate. **2** (*to be fond* (*of*)) be addicted to, be fond of, be keen on, be partial to, be wild about, have a fondness for, have a liking for, have a taste for, like. ANTONYMS: dislike, have an aversion to.

encampment *n.* (*a camp*) base, camp, campground, campsite.

encapsulate *v.t.* **1** (*to capture the essence of*) capture, contain, embody, embrace, include. **2** (*to put in a shortened form*) abridge, compress, condense, epitomize, précis, shorten, summarize, sum up. ANTONYMS: elaborate on, enlarge, expand.

enchant *v.t.* (*to make* (*someone*) *feel interested and excited*) beguile, bewitch, captivate, cast a spell on, charm, delight, enrapture, enthral, entrance, fascinate, hold spellbound. ANTONYMS: bore.

enchanter *n.* (*a person who practises enchantment; a magician*) conjuror, magician, necromancer, sorcerer, warlock, witch, wizard.

enchanting *a.* (*very attractive and charming*) alluring, appealing, attractive, beguiling, bewitching, captivating, charming, delightful, engaging, enthralling, entrancing, fascinating, irresistible, lovely, pleasing, ravishing, spellbinding, winsome. ANTONYMS: boring, repulsive, ugly, unattractive.

enchantment *n.* **1** (*a strong feeling of attraction and interest*) allure, appeal, attraction, charm, delight, fascination, glamour, rapture. **2** (*a magic spell*) magic, necromancy, sorcery, witchcraft, wizardry.

enchantress *n.* **1** (*a female magician*) hex, sorceress, witch. **2** (*a woman that men find very attractive and interesting*) femme fatale, seductress, siren, temptress, vamp.

enclose *v.t.* **1** (*to surround or hem in on all sides*) circle, circumscribe, close in, confine, encircle, fence in, hedge, hem in, ring, shut in, surround, wall in. **2** (*to put one thing inside another for transmission or carriage*) include, insert, put in, send with.

enclosure *n.* **1** (*the act of enclosing an area of land*) circling, fencing in, hedging, hemming in, ringing, shutting in, walling in. **2** (*a space of ground enclosed or fenced in*) area, arena, compound, courtyard, pound, stockade. **3** (*anything enclosed in an envelope, wrapper etc.*) insertion.

encompass *v.t.* **1** (*to surround or cover completely*) circle, circumscribe, close in, confine, encircle, enclose, fence in, hedge, hem in, ring, shut in, surround, wall in. **2** (*to include, to contain*) comprise, contain, cover, deal with, embody, embrace, include, incorporate, involve, take in. ANTONYMS: exclude.

encounter *v.t.* **1** (*to meet with, come across, esp. unexpectedly*) bump into, chance upon, come upon, happen upon, meet, meet by chance, run across, run into, stumble upon. **2** (*to meet in a hostile manner*) clash with, combat, come into conflict with, confront, do battle with, engage with, fight, grapple with. **3** (*to confront resolutely, to oppose*) be faced with, confront, contend with, meet face to face with. ANTONYMS: dodge, evade.
~*n.* **1** (*a meeting face to face*) confrontation. **2** (*a hostile meeting, a battle*) action, battle, brush, clash, collision, combat, conflict, confrontation, contest, dispute, engagement, face-off, fight, (*coll.*) run-in, scuffle, (*coll.*) set-to, skirmish, struggle, tussle. **3** (*an unplanned or unexpected meeting*) chance meeting, meeting.

encourage *v.t.* **1** (*to give courage or confidence to*) animate, breathe courage into, buoy up, cheer up, embolden, hearten, inspire, motivate, rally, rouse, stimulate, stir. ANTONYMS: daunt, depress, dishearten. **2** (*to urge, to incite* (*to do*)) bring influence to bear, egg on, exhort, goad, incite, influence, persuade, prompt, spur on, sway, urge. ANTONYMS: discourage, dissuade. **3** (*to cause to happen or to increase* (*trade, opinion etc.*)) advance, aid, assist, promote, stimulate, support. ANTONYMS: discourage, hinder, impede.

encouragement *n.* **1** (*the activity of giving courage or confidence to someone*) animating, animation, buoying up, cheering up, emboldening, heartening, inspiration, inspiring, motivating, motivation, rallying, rousing, stimulating, stimulation, stimulus, stirring. ANTONYMS: daunting, depressing, discouragement. **2** (*the act of urging or inciting someone to do something*) egging on, exhortation, goad, goading, incitement, inciting, influencing, persuading, persuasion, prompting, spur, spurring on, swaying, urging. ANTONYMS: discouragement, dissuasion. **3** (*the act of causing something to happen or to increase*) advancement, aid, aiding, assistance, assisting, backing, boosting, forwarding, fostering, furtherance, furthering, help, helping, promoting, promotion, stimulating, support, supporting. ANTONYMS: discouragement, hindering, hindrance, impediment, impeding.

encouraging *a.* (*giving* (*someone*) *hope and confidence*) bright, cheerful, favourable, heartening, hopeful, optimistic, promising, rosy. ANTONYMS: disheartening, gloomy, pessimistic.

encroach *v.i.* (*to intrude* (*upon*) *what belongs to another*) impinge, infringe, intrude, invade, overrun, overstep, trespass.

encroachment *n.* (*the act of encroaching*) impingement, impinging, incursion, infringement, intrusion, invasion, overrunning, overstepping, trespassing.

encumber *v.t.* (*to impede or embarrass by a burden or difficulty*) burden, cramp, hamper, handicap, hinder, hold back, impede, obstruct, oppress, overload, put a strain on, restrain, retard, saddle, slow down, tax, trammel, weigh down.

encumbrance *n.* (*a hindrance to freedom of action or motion*) burden, constraint, drag, handicap, hindrance, impediment, liability, load, millstone, obstacle, obstruction, restraint, trammel, weight. ANTONYMS: advantage, help, support.

encyclopedic *a.* ((*of knowledge*) *comprehensive; wide-ranging*) all-embracing, all-encompassing, all-inclusive, complete, comprehensive, exhaustive, thorough, universal, vast, wide-ranging.

end *n.* **1** (*the extreme point or boundary of a line or of anything that has length*) border, bound, boundary, edge, extremity, limit, margin, point, terminus, tip. **2** (*the termination or last portion*) cessation, close, closure, completion, conclusion, denouement, ending, expiration, expiry, finale, finish, halting, stopping, winding-up. ANTONYMS: beginning, commencement, start. **3** (*a ceasing to exist*) annihilation, death, demise, destruction, dying, extermination, extinction, passing away. ANTONYMS: birth. **4** (*a result, a natural consequence*) consequence, issue, outcome, resolution, result, upshot. ANTONYMS: cause. **5** (*a purpose, an object*) aim, aspiration, design, end in view, goal, intent, intention, object, objective, purpose, target. **6** (*a remnant*) bit, butt, fragment, oddment, remainder, remnant, scrap, stub, tag end, tail end, vestige.

~*v.i.* **1** (*to come to an end, to cease*) close, conclude, discontinue, end, expire, finish, halt, peter out, stop, terminate, wind up. **2** (*to result* (*in*)) culminate in, end in, terminate in.

~*v.t.* **1** (*to bring to an end*) close, conclude, discontinue, dissolve, end, finish, halt, stop, terminate, wind up. **2** (*to put to an end, to destroy*) abolish, annihilate, bring to an end, close, conclude, discontinue, dissolve, end, exterminate, extinguish, finish, halt, stop, terminate, wind up. ANTONYMS: begin, launch, start. **at the end of one's tether** (*at the limit of one's endurance or patience*) at the limit of one's endurance, at the limit of one's patience, at the limit of one's strength, not coping, not knowing how to deal with, not knowing what to do. **in the end** (*finally*) at last, at length, at long last, eventually, finally, in the long run, ultimately. ANTONYMS: at first, initially. **on end** (*upright, erect*) erect, standing up, upright, vertical. ANTONYMS: horizontal. **to come to an end** (*to end, to be finished*) cease, close, conclude, discontinue, end, finish, halt, stop, terminate, wind up. ANTONYMS: begin, commence, start. **to end up 1** (*to arrive at finally*) arrive finally, come to a halt, come to a stop, (*coll.*) fetch up, finish up, wind up. ANTONYMS: begin, start off. **2** (*to become at last*) finish as, finish up as, turn out to be. ANTONYMS: begin as, start off as. **to put an end to** (*to terminate, to stop*) abolish, annihilate, bring to an end, close, conclude, destroy, discontinue, dissolve, end, exterminate, extinguish, finish, halt, stop, terminate, wind up. ANTONYMS: begin, launch, start.

endanger *v.t.* (*to expose to danger*) expose to danger, imperil, jeopardize, put at risk, put in danger, risk, threaten. ANTONYMS: defend, guard, protect, safeguard.

endear *v.t.* (*to make dear* (*to*)) bind, captivate, charm, engage, win. ANTONYMS: repel.

endearment *n.* (*words or a gesture expressing affection*) loving words, soft words, sweet nothings, sweet talk. ANTONYMS: expletive, insult.

endeavour *v.i.* (*to try, to make an effort* (*to*)) aim, attempt, do one's best, (*coll.*) do one's damnedest, (*coll.*) give it one's best shot, (*sl.*) go for it, (*coll.*) have a crack at, (*coll.*) have a go at, have a shot at, (*coll.*) have a stab at, labour, make an all-out effort, make an effort, strive, struggle, take pains to, try, try one's hand, work at. ANTONYMS: give up, lie back, make no effort.

~*n.* (*an effort, an attempt*) attempt, (*coll.*) crack, effort, enterprise, (*coll.*) go, labouring, shot, (*coll.*) stab, striving, struggle, trial, try, venture.

ending n. (*a conclusion, a termination*) cessation, close, closure, completion, conclusion, denouement, end, expiration, expiry, finale, finish, halting, stopping, termination, winding-up. ANTONYMS: beginning, commencement, start.

endless a. (*seeming to continue for ever*) boundless, continual, everlasting, incessant, infinite, limitless, never-ending, perpetual, unbounded, unbroken, unending, uninterrupted, unlimited, without end.

endorse v.t. **1** (*to write (one's name) on the back of (a cheque) to specify oneself as the payee*) countersign, sign, undersign. **2** (*to ratify, approve*) advocate, approve, authorize, back, champion, confirm, favour, (*coll.*) give (something) the green light, (*coll.*) give (something) the OK/okay, (*coll.*) give (something) the thumbs up, (*coll.*) OK, (*coll.*) okay, promote, ratify, recommend, sanction, subscribe to, support, uphold, warrant. ANTONYMS: attack, disapprove, reject.

endorsement n. (*an action or statement showing approval or support*) advocacy, approbation, approval, authorization, backing, championship, confirmation, favour, (*coll.*) green light, (*coll.*) OK, (*coll.*) okay, promotion, ratification, recommendation, sanction, seal of approval, subscription to, support, thumbs up, warrant. ANTONYMS: attack, disapproval, rejection.

endow v.t. **1** (*to bestow a permanent income upon*) donate money to, finance, fund, pay for, will money to. **2** (*to invest with goods, estate, privileges etc.*) bestow, confer, furnish, gift, give, grant, invest, present, provide, supply.

endowment n. **1 a** (*the act of making permanent provision for the support of any person, institution etc.*) bestowal, conferring, financing, furnishing, giving, granting, investing, presentation, presenting, providing, provision, supply. **b** (*the fund or property so appropriated*) bequest, donation, funding, gift, grant, legacy, provision, settlement. **2** (*pl.*) (*natural gifts, qualities or ability*) abilities, aptitudes, attributes, capabilities, capacities, characteristics, faculties, gifts, powers, qualities, strengths, talents. ANTONYMS: weaknesses.

endurance n. **1** (*the capacity of bearing or suffering with patience*) acceptance, forbearance, fortitude, patience, resignation, stamina, sufferance, toleration. **2** (*continuance, duration*) continuance, durability, duration, immutability, lasting, lasting power, longevity, permanence, persistence, staying power, survival, tenacity. ANTONYMS: impermanence, transience, transitoriness.

endure v.t. **1** (*to undergo, to suffer*) experience, go through, suffer, sustain, undergo. **2** (*to bear, to stand (a test or strain)*) bear, brave, brook, cope with, put up with, stand, (*coll.*) stick, suffer, support, tolerate, weather, withstand.

enduring a. (*continuing to exist for a long time*) abiding, continuing, durable, eternal, immortal, immutable, imperishable, lasting, long-lasting, perennial, permanent, persistent, remaining, surviving. ANTONYMS: fleeting, short-lived, temporary, transient.

enemy n. (*someone hostile to another person, or to a cause etc.*) adversary, antagonist, competitor, foe, hostile party, opponent, rival, the opposition. ANTONYMS: ally, confederate, friend.

energetic a. **1** (*active, vigorously operative*) active, animated, (*coll.*) bright-eyed and bushy-tailed, brisk, indefatigable, lively, (*coll.*) peppy, spirited, sprightly, tireless, vibrant, vigorous, vital. ANTONYMS: idle, inactive, indolent, lethargic, sluggish. **2** (*forcible, powerful*) aggressive, determined, effective, effectual, emphatic, forcible, high-powered, potent, powerful, strenuous, strong, vigorous. ANTONYMS: ineffective, low-key, weak.

energize v.t. (*to give energy to*) activate, animate, enliven, invigorate, motivate, pep up, rouse, stimulate, stir, vitalize. ANTONYMS: debilitate, enervate, exhaust.

energy n. (*force, vigour*) activity, cogency, dash, drive, enthusiasm, exertion, force, forcefulness, liveliness, might, potency, power, push, spirit, stamina, vitality, vivacity, zest, zing. ANTONYMS: inactivity, inertia, lethargy, sluggishness.

enervate v.t. (*to deprive of strength; to weaken*) debilitate, drain, enfeeble, exhaust, fatigue, incapacitate, prostrate, sap, tire, tire out, weaken, wear out, weary. ANTONYMS: energize, invigorate, pep up, vitalize.

enfold v.t. **1** (*to wrap or surround*) encircle, enclose, envelop, fold, shroud, swathe, wrap, wrap up. **2** (*to hold close to oneself*) clasp, cuddle, embrace, enclose, hold, hug.

enforce v.t. **1** (*to bring into effect*) administer, apply, carry out, discharge, execute, implement, put in force. **2** (*to press or urge forcibly (an argument etc.)*) compel, exact, force, insist on, necessitate, oblige, require, urge.

enforced a. (*forced, not voluntary*) compulsory, forced, involuntary, necessitated, prescribed, required, unwilling.

engage v.t. **1** (*to hire, order*) bespeak, book, charter, hire, lease, order, rent, reserve, secure. ANTONYMS: cancel. **2** (*to employ, to occupy the attention of*) absorb, engross, fill, grip, hold,

involve, occupy, preoccupy, rivet, take up.
3 (*to arrange to employ*) appoint, commission, employ, enlist, enrol, hire, put on the
payroll, sign on, take on. ANTONYMS: declare
redundant, (*coll.*) sack. **4** (*to attract* (*someone
or someone's attention*)) arrest, attract, capture,
catch, draw, gain, win.
~v.i. 1 (*to enter into, embark* (*on*)) become
involved in, embark on, enter into, set about,
tackle, undertake. ANTONYMS: give up, leave.
2 (*to begin to fight, to enter into conflict* (*with*))
clash, come into conflict, do battle, engage in
a struggle, enter into combat, fight, grapple,
join battle, struggle, take part in an encounter,
wage war. ANTONYMS: make peace. **3** (*to interlock* (*with*)) dovetail, fit together, interact,
interlock, join, mesh.

engaged *a.* **1** (*pledged to marry*) affianced,
betrothed, engaged to be married, spoken for.
2 (*busy, employed*) occupied, tied up, unavailable. ANTONYMS: available, free. **3** (*occupied*) in use, occupied, unavailable.
ANTONYMS: vacant. **4** ((*of a telephone line*)
already being used) busy, in use, unavailable.
ANTONYMS: available, free.

engagement *n.* **1** (*an obligation, a contract*)
agreement, bond, compact, contract, obligation, pact, pledge, promise, vow. **2** (*a mutual
promise of marriage*) betrothal. **3** (*employment
or occupation of time or attention*) absorption,
engrossment, preoccupation. **4** (*an appointment*) appointment, arrangement, commit-
ment, (*coll.*) date, meeting, rendezvous. **5** (*the
state of being hired*) appointment, employment, job, post, situation, work. **6** (*an action or
battle between armies or fleets*) action, battle,
combat, conflict, confrontation, contest, encounter, face-off, fight, struggle.

engaging *a.* (*pleasing, attractive* (*used of manners or address*)) agreeable, appealing,
attractive, captive, charming, delightful, enchanting, likeable, lovable, pleasant, pleasing,
sweet, winning, winsome. ANTONYMS: disagreeable, nasty, unattractive.

engender *v.t.* **1** (*to cause to happen*) arouse,
bring about, cause, create, effect, excite,
generate, give rise to, induce, instigate, lead to,
make, occasion, produce, provoke, rouse, stir
up. **2** (*to beget*) beget, breed, create, give birth
to, procreate.

engine *n.* (*an apparatus consisting of a number
of parts for applying mechanical power*)
internal-combustion engine, machine, mechanism, motor.

engineer *v.t.* (*to contrive, to manage by tact or
ingenuity*) bring about, cause, concoct, contrive, create, devise, direct, effect, manage,

manipulate, manoeuvre, mastermind, orchestrate, originate, plan, plot, scheme, wangle.

engrave *v.t.* **1** (*to cut figures, letters etc.* (*on*),
with a chisel or graver) carve, chase, chisel, cut,
etch, inscribe. **2** (*to impress deeply and
strongly*) embed, fix, impress, imprint, ingrain,
set, stamp.

engraving *n.* **1** (*the act or art of cutting figures,
letters etc. on wood, stone or metal*) carving,
chasing, chiselling, cutting, etching, inscribing, inscription. **2** (*that which is engraved*)
block, carving, cut, etching, plate, woodcut.
3 (*an impression from an engraved plate, a
print*) etching, impression, print.

engrossed *a.* (*absorbed* (*in, as in reading a
book*)) absorbed, captivated, caught up, deep,
enthralled, entranced, fascinated, gripped, immersed, intent, interested, intrigued, lost, occupied, preoccupied, rapt, riveted. ANTONYMS:
bored.

engrossing *a.* (*absorbing, occupying the
attention completely*) absorbing, captivating,
compelling, enthralling, entrancing, fascinating, gripping, interesting, intriguing, riveting.
ANTONYMS: boring, dull, run-of-the-mill.

engulf *v.t.* (*to swallow up, as in a gulf or
whirlpool*) bury, consume, deluge, drown, envelop, flood, immerse, inundate, overrun,
overwhelm, submerge, swallow up, swamp.

enhance *v.t.* **1** (*to raise in importance, degree
etc.*) add force to, add to, amplify, augment,
boost, elevate, embellish, emphasize,
heighten, improve, increase, intensify, magnify, maximize, raise, reinforce, strengthen,
stress. ANTONYMS: decrease, detract from,
diminish, reduce, take away from. **2** (*to raise in
price*) escalate, (*coll.*) hike up, increase, inflate, (*coll.*) jack, raise. ANTONYMS: lower,
reduce.

enigma *n.* (*an inexplicable or mysterious person or thing*) mystery, paradox, puzzle.

enigmatic *a.* (*mysterious and difficult to
understand*) ambiguous, arcane, baffling,
cryptic, incomprehensible, indecipherable, inexplicable, inscrutable, mysterious, mystifying, obscure, oracular, perplexing, puzzling,
recondite, unfathomable, unintelligible. ANTO-
NYMS: comprehensible, intelligible, straightforward, understandable.

enjoin *v.t.* (*to direct or command* (*a person to do
something*)) advise, bid, call upon, charge,
command, counsel, demand, direct, instruct,
order, prescribe, require, urge, warn.

enjoy *v.t.* **1** (*to take pleasure or delight in*)

appreciate, be amused by, be entertained by, be fond of, be pleased by, (*coll.*) be turned on by, delight in, find pleasure in, have a fancy for, have a liking for, like, love, rejoice in, relish, revel in, savour, take pleasure in. ANTONYMS: be bored by, (*coll.*) be turned off by, dislike, loathe. **2** (*to have the use or benefit of*) be blessed with, be favoured with, benefit from, experience, have, have the advantage of, have the use of, own, possess, reap the benefit of, use. **to enjoy oneself** (*to experience pleasure or happiness*) (*coll.*) have a ball, have a good time, have fun, have the time of one's life, party. ANTONYMS: be bored, be miserable.

enjoyable *a.* (*giving pleasure*) agreeable, amusing, delectable, delicious, delightful, diverting, entertaining, fine, (*coll.*) fun, good, gratifying, great, lovely, nice, pleasant, pleasurable, satisfying, to one's liking. ANTONYMS: boring, hateful, miserable, unpleasant.

enjoyment *n.* **1** (*a feeling of pleasure and satisfaction*) amusement, delectation, delight, diversion, entertainment, fun, gaiety, gladness, gratification, gusto, happiness, joy, merriment, pleasure, recreation, relish, satisfaction, zest. ANTONYMS: boredom, misery. **2** (*the fact of having something such as a right or benefit*) advantage, benefit, blessing, exercise, experience, favour, ownership, possession, use.

enlarge *v.t.* (*to make greater; to extend in dimensions, quantity or number*) add to, amplify, augment, blow up, broaden, dilate, distend, elongate, expand, extend, heighten, increase, inflate, lengthen, magnify, make bigger, make greater, make larger, stretch, swell, widen. ANTONYMS: decrease, make smaller, reduce, shorten.
~*v.i.* **1** (*to become bigger*) expand, grow, grow bigger, grow larger, increase, stretch, swell, wax, widen. ANTONYMS: contract, decrease, grow less, smaller. **2** (*to expatiate* (*upon*), *to give more details about*) amplify, develop, elaborate, expand, expatiate, flesh out, give details.

enlighten *v.t.* (*to give* (*someone*) *information* (*on*)) advise, apprise, edify, educate, illuminate, inform, instruct, make aware, teach.

enlightened *a.* (*having understanding and wisdom; free from ignorance*) broad-minded, civilized, cultivated, educated, informed, knowledgeable, liberal, literate, open-minded, reasonable, refined, sophisticated, wise. ANTONYMS: ignorant, prejudiced, uneducated, uninformed.

enlightenment *n.* (*the state of having understanding and wisdom; freedom from ignorance*) awareness, broad-mindedness, civilization,

cultivation, education, information, insight, instruction, knowledge, learning, liberality, literacy, open-mindedness, refinement, sophistication, teaching, understanding, wisdom. ANTONYMS: ignorance, illiteracy, narrow-mindedness, prejudice.

enlist *v.t.* **1** (*to enrol, esp. to engage for military service*) enrol, recruit, register, sign up. **2** (*to gain the assistance or support of*) acquire, gain, gather, get, muster, obtain.

enliven *v.t.* (*to give spirit or animation to*) animate, arouse, awaken, brighten up, buoy up, cheer up, excite, exhilarate, fire, hearten, inspire, invigorate, pep up, (*coll.*) perk up, revitalize, rouse, stir, vitalize, wake up. ANTONYMS: put a damper on, repress, subdue.

en masse *adv.* (*in a group, all together*) all together, as a group, as one, in a body, in a group, in a mass, together. ANTONYMS: individually, separately.

enmity *n.* (*the state or quality of being an enemy*) acrimony, animosity, animus, antagonism, antipathy, aversion, bad blood, bad feeling, bitterness, hate, hatred, hostility, ill feeling, ill will, malevolence, malice, malignity, rancour, spite, spitefulness, venom. ANTONYMS: friendliness, good will, harmony, love.

ennui *n.* (*lack of interest in things, boredom*) apathy, boredom, dissatisfaction, inertia, languor, lassitude, lethargy, listlessness, melancholy, sluggishness, tedium. ANTONYMS: energy, enthusiasm, interest.

enormity *n.* **1** (*a monstrous crime, an atrocity*) atrocity, crime, disgrace, evil, horror, monstrosity, outrage, transgression, villainy. **2** (*the state or quality of being excessively wicked*) atrociousness, atrocity, badness, dreadfulness, evil, heinousness, hideousness, horror, iniquity, monstrousness, nefariousness, outrageousness, viciousness, vileness, wickedness. ANTONYMS: goodness, virtue, worthiness.

enormous *a.* (*exceedingly great in size, number or quantity*) astronomic, Brobdingnagian, colossal, extra-large, gargantuan, gigantic, Herculean, huge, (*sl., facet.*) humungous, immense, jumbo, mammoth, massive, monstrous, mountainous, prodigious, stupendous, titanic, tremendous, vast. ANTONYMS: diminutive, limited, minute, tiny.

enormously *adv.* (*to a very great extent, extremely*) extremely, hugely, markedly, tremendously, very.

enormousness *n.* (*the state of being enormous*) hugeness, immenseness, immensity, magnitude, massiveness, vastness. ANTONYMS: minuteness.

enough *a.* (*sufficient or adequate for need or demand*) adequate, ample, (*coll.*) plenty, sufficient. ANTONYMS: insufficient.

~*pron.* (*a quantity or amount which satisfies a requirement or desire*) ample supply, full measure, plenty, sufficiency. ANTONYMS: insufficiency.

~*adv.* (*sufficiently, passably*) adequately, amply, fairly, passably, reasonably, satisfactorily, sufficiently, tolerably. ANTONYMS: inadequately, insufficiently.

enrage *v.t.* (*to put in a rage*) anger, annoy, exasperate, incense, inflame, infuriate, irritate, madden, make one's blood boil, make (someone) see red, provoke, throw (someone) into a rage.

enraged *a.* (*very angry*) angry, annoyed, cross, exasperated, fuming, furious, (*coll.*) hopping mad, in a fury, in a rage, incensed, livid, (*coll.*) mad, raging. ANTONYMS: calm, composed.

enraptured *a.* (*feeling extremely pleased and happy*) delighted, ecstatic, elated, euphoric, in raptures, in seventh heaven, joyful, (*coll.*) on cloud nine, overjoyed, over the moon, thrilled, (*coll.*) thrilled to bits, (*coll.*) tickled pink, transported with delight. ANTONYMS: depressed, despondent, in the depths, in the doldrums.

enrich *v.t.* **1** (*to make rich or richer*) feather (someone's) nest, make rich, make richer, make wealthier, make wealthy. **2** (*to add to the quality or value of*) add to, ameliorate, boost, develop, enhance, improve, increase, supplement, upgrade. ANTONYMS: detract from, diminish, lower.

enrol *v.t.* (*to include as a member, to record the admission of*) admit, enlist, enter, register, sign on, sign up.

~*v.i.* (*to enrol oneself (as a member, student etc.)*) enlist, join, sign up.

en route *adv.* (*on the way; on the road*) along the route, along the way, in transit, on the road, on the way.

ensconce *v.t.* (*to settle (oneself) comfortably or securely*) establish, install, settle.

ensemble *n.* **1** (*all the parts of anything taken together*) accumulation, aggregate, assemblage, collection, combination, composite, entirety, set, sum, (*coll.*) the whole caboodle, total, totality, whole. **2** (*an outfit consisting of several (matching) garments*) costume, get-up, outfit, (*coll.*) rig-out, suit. **3** (*a combination of two or more performers or players*) band, cast, company, group, troupe.

enshrine *v.t.* (*to enclose and cherish (something) as if it is sacred*) cherish, conserve, hold sacred, immortalize, preserve, treasure.

ensign *n.* (*a national banner, a standard*) banner, colours, flag, pennant, standard, streamer.

ensnare *v.t.* (*to entrap*) capture, catch, enmesh, entangle, entrap, net, snare, trap. ANTONYMS: free, liberate, set free.

ensue *v.i.* (*to follow in course of time, to succeed*) come after, come next, come to pass, follow, happen after, result, succeed. ANTONYMS: come before, precede.

ensure *v.t.* **1** (*to make certain (that)*) certify, guarantee, make certain, make sure. **2** (*to make safe (against or from any risk)*) guard, make safe, make secure, protect, safeguard, secure.

entail *v.t.* (*to involve, to necessitate*) bring about, call for, give rise to, impose, involve, lead to, necessitate, occasion, require, result in.

entangle *v.t.* **1** (*to ensnare, as in a net*) catch, enmesh, ensnare, entrap, snare, trap. ANTONYMS: extricate, free, liberate. **2** (*to involve in difficulties, obstacles etc.*) embroil, implicate, involve. **3** (*to twist together so that unravelling is difficult*) knot, snarl up, tangle, twist. ANTONYMS: unravel, untangle. **4** (*to make complicated or confused*) complicate, confuse, jumble, mix up, muddle. ANTONYMS: clarify, clear up, simplify.

enter *v.t.* **1** (*to go or come into*) come into, flow into, go into, make an entrance into, move into, pass into. ANTONYMS: exit (from), go out of, leave. **2** (*to pierce, to penetrate*) go through, penetrate, pierce, puncture. **3** (*to associate oneself with, become a member of*) become a member of, enlist in, enrol in, go in for, join, participate in, put one's name down for, sign on for, sign up for, take part in, take up. ANTONYMS: drop out of, leave, pull out of, resign from, withdraw from. **4** (*to insert, to set down in a list, a book etc.*) catalogue, document, file, inscribe, list, log, mark, note down, put down, record, register, set down, write down. **5** (*to present or submit (a proposal, a protest etc.)*) offer, present, proffer, put forward, register, submit, tender. ANTONYMS: cancel, take back, withdraw. **6** (*to start doing something or being involved in something*) become involved in, begin, commence, embark on, engage in, involve oneself in, start, undertake, venture on. ANTONYMS: end, give up, leave.

~*v.i.* (*to become a competitor*) go in, participate in, put one's name down, sign up, take part. ANTONYMS: drop out, pull out, withdraw.

enterprise *n.* **1** (*an undertaking, esp. a bold or difficult one*) adventure, campaign, effort, operation, programme, project, scheme, task, undertaking, venture. **2** (*spirit of adventure,* *boldness*) ambition, boldness, daring, dash, drive, energy, enthusiasm, get-up-and-go, initiative, (*sl.*) oomph, (*coll.*) pep, push, resourcefulness, sense of adventure, spirit, vigour, (*coll.*) vim, zest, (*coll.*) zip. ANTONYMS: apathy, inertia, lack of initiative, timidity. **3** (*a business concern*) company, concern, establishment, firm, organization.

enterprising *a.* (*ready to undertake schemes involving difficulty or hazard*) adventurous, ambitious, bold, daring, dashing, energetic, enthusiastic, entrepreneurial, go-ahead, (*coll.*) peppy, (*coll.*) pushy, resourceful, spirited, vigorous. ANTONYMS: apathetic, cautious, timid, unadventurous.

entertain *v.t.* **1** (*to receive and treat as a guest*) have as one's guest, play host/hostess to, show hospitality to, wine and dine. **2** (*to occupy agreeably; to amuse*) amuse, beguile, delight, divert, give pleasure to, occupy. ANTONYMS: bore. **3** (*to hold in mind, cherish*) accept, consider, contemplate, give consideration to, give thought to, pay attention to, take notice of, think about. ANTONYMS: ignore, reject. ~*v.i.* (*to exercise hospitality, to receive company*) have company, have guests, play host/hostess.

entertainer *n.* (*a person who entertains, esp. a person who performs amusingly at an entertainment*) artist, artiste, performer.

entertaining *a.* (*amusing*) amusing, comical, delightful, diverting, funny, humorous, interesting, pleasant, pleasing, witty.

entertainment *n.* **1** (*a public performance intended to amuse*) performance, presentation, show. **2** (*the pleasure afforded to the mind by anything interesting, amusement*) amusement, distraction, diversion, enjoyment, fun, pleasure, recreation. ANTONYMS: boredom, tedium.

enthral *v.t.* (*to captivate*) absorb, beguile, bewitch, captivate, carry away, charm, delight, enchant, engross, enrapture, entrance, fascinate, grip, hold spellbound, put (someone) into transports of delight, rivet. ANTONYMS: bore, bore to tears.

enthralling *a.* (*extremely interesting*) captivating, charming, delightful, enchanting, entrancing, fascinating, gripping, spellbinding. ANTONYMS: boring, tedious.

enthuse *v.i.* (*to manifest enthusiasm*) be enthusiastic, gush, show enthusiasm, wax lyrical. ANTONYMS: be unenthusiastic.

enthusiasm *n.* **1** (*intense and passionate zeal*) ardour, avidity, commitment, eagerness, exuberance, fanaticism, fervour, frenzy, keenness, passion, vehemence, wholeheartedness, zeal, zest. ANTONYMS: apathy, half-heartedness,

indifference. **2** (*an activity or subject that someone is very interested in*) craze, fad, hobby, interest, passion, pastime, recreation.

enthusiast *n.* (*a person whose mind is completely possessed by any subject*) admirer, aficionado, (*coll.*) buff, devotee, fan, fanatic, follower, (*coll.*) freak, lover, supporter, zealot.

enthusiastic *a.* (*very interested and excited*) ardent, avid, eager, exuberant, fanatical, fervent, keen, passionate, vehement, wholehearted, zealous. ANTONYMS: apathetic, half-hearted, indifferent.

entice *v.t.* (*to try to persuade someone to do something by offering them something*) beguile, cajole, decoy, induce, inveigle, lead astray, lead on, lure, persuade, seduce, tempt, wheedle.

enticement *n.* **1** (*something offered in an attempt to persuade someone to do something*) allurement, attraction, bait, cajolery, (*sl.*) come-on, decoy, inducement, lure, temptation. **2** (*the art of trying to persuade someone to do something*) beguiling, cajolery, cajoling, decoying, inducing, inveigling, leading astray, leading on, luring, persuading, persuasion, seducing, seduction, temptation, tempting, wheedling.

enticing *a.* (*alluring, seductive*) alluring, attractive, beguiling, seductive, tempting.

entire *a.* **1** (*whole, complete*) complete, full, total, whole. ANTONYMS: incomplete, partial. **2** (*unbroken, undivided*) complete, intact, perfect, sound, unbroken, undamaged, undivided, unimpaired, whole. ANTONYMS: broken, damaged, divided. **3** (*unqualified, unreserved*) absolute, full, outright, thorough, total, unmitigated, unmodified, unqualified, unreserved, unrestricted. ANTONYMS: partial, qualified.

entirely *adv.* **1** (*in every part; completely*) absolutely, completely, fully, thoroughly, totally, unreservedly, utterly, without qualification, without reservation. ANTONYMS: in part, partially, with reservations. **2** (*exclusively*) exclusively, only, solely.

entirety *n.* **1** (*entireness, completeness*) completeness, entireness, fullness, totality, unity, wholeness. **2** (*the entire amount or extent*) aggregate, sum, total, whole of. ANTONYMS: division, part.

entitle *v.t.* **1** (*to give a right or claim to anything*) accredit, allow, authorize, empower, enable, equip, give the right to, license, make eligible, permit, qualify, sanction, warrant. **2** (*to give a certain name or title to*) call, christen, designate, dub, give the title of, label, name, style, title.

entity n. (anything that has real existence, a being) being, body, individual, object, organism, quantity, substance, thing.

entourage n. (people following or attending on an important person) associates, attendants, companions, company, cortege, escort, following, retinue, staff, train.

entrails n.pl. (the internal parts of animals; the intestines) bowels, gut, innards, (coll.) insides, internal organs, intestines, viscera.

entrance¹ n. 1 (the act of entering, or an instance of entering) arrival, coming in, entry, going in, ingress. ANTONYMS: departure, exit. 2 (the power, right or liberty of entering) access, admission, admittance, entrée, entry, ingress. 3 (the passage or doorway by which a place is entered) access, approach, avenue, door, doorway, entrance hall, entry, foyer, gate, gateway, hall, ingress, lobby, opening, passage, porch, portal, threshold, way in. ANTONYMS: exit, way out.

entrance² v.t. (to carry away, enrapture) beguile, bewitch, captivate, carry away, charm, delight, enchant, fascinate, hold spellbound, send into raptures, send into transports, transport.

entrant n. 1 (a person entering upon or into a new profession, sphere etc.) beginner, initiate, neophyte, newcomer, new member, novice, probationer, (sl.) rookie, trainee, tyro. 2 (a person entering a competition, examination etc.) applicant, candidate, competitor, contestant, participant, player.

entrap v.t. 1 (to catch in or as in a trap) bag, catch, enmesh, ensnare, snare, trap. ANTONYMS: liberate, set free. 2 (to entangle in contradictions, difficulties etc.) decoy, enmesh, ensnare, entice, inveigle, lead on, lure, seduce, trick.

entreat v.t. (to beseech, to ask earnestly) appeal to, ask earnestly, beg, beseech, crave, implore, importune, petition, plead with, pray, request, solicit, supplicate.

entreaty n. (an urgent request) appeal, importuning, petition, plea, pleading, prayer, request, solicitation, suit, supplication.

entrench v.t. (to put (oneself) in a defensible position) embed, ensconce, establish, fix, implant, install, lodge, root, set, settle.

entrenched a. ((of a person's attitude etc.) fixed, difficult to change by argument etc.) deep-rooted, deep-seated, dyed-in-the-wool, firm, fixed, indelible, ingrained, irremovable, rooted, set, unshakable. ANTONYMS: flexible, fluctuating, variable.

entrepreneur n. (a person who undertakes a (financial) enterprise, esp. one with an element of risk) businessman, business person, businesswoman, financier, magnet, tycoon, (coll.) whiz-kid.

entrust v.t. 1 (to commit or confide (something or someone) to a person's care) assign, commit, consign, deliver, give custody of, hand over, make over. 2 (to charge with (a duty, care etc.)) charge, invest.

entry n. 1 (the act of entering) arrival, coming in, entrance, going in. ANTONYMS: departure, exit. 2 (the passage or other way by which anything is entered) access, approach, avenue, door, doorway, entrance, entrance hall, foyer, gate, gateway, hall, lobby, opening, passage, porch, portal, threshold, way in. ANTONYMS: exit, way out. 3 (the act of entering or inscribing in a book etc.) cataloguing, documenting, filing, inscribing, listing, logging, noting, recording, registering, setting down, writing down. 4 (an item so entered) item, listing, memo, minute, note, record, statement. 5 (a person, animal or thing competing in a race or competition) attempt, effort, go, submission, try. 6 (the right of admission) access, admission, admittance, entrée, entry, permission to enter.

entwine v.t. (to twine or twist together) braid, interlace, intertwine, interweave, plait, twine, twist round, wind round. ANTONYMS: disentangle, unravel, untangle.

enumerate v.t. (to specify the items of) cite, detail, itemize, list, mention, name, quote, recite, recount, relate, specify, spell out.

enunciate v.t. 1 (to pronounce distinctly, articulate clearly) articulate, pronounce, say, sound, speak, utter, vocalize, voice. 2 (to state or announce with formal precision) assert, declare, express, give voice to, proclaim, promulgate, pronounce, propound, state, utter.

envelop v.t. (to surround so as to hide, to enshroud) blanket, cloak, conceal, cover, encase, encircle, enclose, enfold, engulf, enshroud, enwrap, hide, obscure, shroud, surround, swaddle, swathe, veil, wrap.

enviable a. (greatly to be desired) desirable, fortunate, lucky, tempting, to be desired. ANTONYMS: undesirable, unenviable, unlucky.

envious a. (feeling envy) begrudging, covetous, desirous, green, green-eyed, green with envy, grudging, jaundiced, jealous, resentful.

environment n. 1 (that which encompasses, surrounding objects, scenery, etc.) ambience, atmosphere, background, circumstances, conditions, domain, element, habitat, medium, milieu, setting, situation, surroundings, territory, world. **2** (*the whole of the natural world, esp. considered as vulnerable to pollution etc.*) earth, natural world, nature.

envisage *v.t.* (*to contemplate, esp. a particular aspect of*) conceive of, contemplate, imagine, picture, think of, visualize.

envoy *n.* (*a person sent as a messenger*) agent, courier, delegate, deputy, emissary, intermediary, legate, representative.

envy *n.* **1** (*ill will at the success or good fortune of others*) covetousness, enviousness, grudge, grudgingness, jealousy, resentfulness, resentment, the green-eyed monster. **2** (*the object of this feeling*) object of envy, source of envy. ~*v.t.* (*to regard with envy*) be covetous of, be envious of, begrudge, be jealous of, covet, grudge, resent.

ephemeral *a.* (*short-lived, transient*) brief, evanescent, fleeting, fugitive, momentary, passing, short, short-lived, temporary, transient, transitory. ANTONYMS: abiding, enduring, long-lasting.

epic *a.* **1** (*narrating some heroic event in a lofty style*) heroic. **2** (*large-scale*) extraordinary, grand, great, huge, large-scale, massive, vast. ANTONYMS: minuscule, tiny.

Epicurean *a.* (*devoted to pleasure, esp. the more refined varieties of sensuous enjoyment*) gourmandizing, hedonistic, pleasure-loving, self-indulgent, sensualist, sybaritic.

epidemic *a.* (*affecting at once a large number in a community*) extensive, general, prevalent, rampant, rife, sweeping, wide-ranging, widespread. ANTONYMS: limited, restricted.

epigram *n.* (*a pithy or witty saying or phrase*) aphorism, bon mot, quip, saying, witticism.

epigrammatic *a.* (*expressed in a brief, witty way*) brief, concise, crisp, neat, pithy, pointed, pungent, sharp, short, succinct, terse, to the point, well-turned, witty. ANTONYMS: prolix, verbose, wordy.

epilogue *n.* (*the concluding part of a book or speech*) afterword, coda, conclusion, postscript, tailpiece. ANTONYMS: preamble, preface, prologue.

episode *n.* **1** (*an incident or series of events in a story*) chapter, instalment, part, scene, section. **2** (*an incident or closely connected series of events in real life*) circumstance, escapade, event, experience, happening, incident, occasion, occurrence.

episodic *a.* (*occurring as separate incidents*) intermittent, irregular, occasional, sporadic. ANTONYMS: even, regular.

epitaph *n.* (*a commemorative inscription in prose or verse, as for a tomb or monument*) commemoration, dedication, elegy, inscription.

epithet *n.* **1** (*an adjective or phrase denoting any quality or attribute*) adjective, appellation, description, designation, label, name, tag, title. **2** (*an abusive expression*) curse, expletive, four-letter word, oath, obscenity, swear word. **3** (*a nickname*) name, nickname, sobriquet.

epitome *n.* **1** (*a brief summary of a book, document etc.*) abbreviation, abridgement, abstract, compendium, condensation, contraction, digest, précis, resume, summary, synopsis. **2** (*a representation in miniature of something else*) archetype, embodiment, exemplification, incarnation, personification, quintessence, representation, type.

epitomize *v.t.* **1** (*to make a summary or abridgement of*) abbreviate, abridge, condense, contract, cut, précis, reduce, shorten, summarize. ANTONYMS: elaborate on, expand, lengthen. **2** (*to represent in miniature*) be representative of, embody, exemplify, incarnate, personify, represent, symbolize, typify.

epoch *n.* (*a period in history or of a person's life characterized by momentous events*) age, era, period, time.

equable *a.* **1** (*characterized by evenness or uniformity*) consistent, constant, even, regular, stable, steady, unchanging, uniform. **2** (*even-tempered*) calm, composed, cool, cool, calm and collected, easygoing, even-tempered, imperturbable, level-headed, placid, serene, tranquil, unexcitable, (*coll.*) unflappable. ANTONYMS: emotional, excitable, temperamental, volatile. **3** ((*of opinions*) *not extreme; generally considered reasonable*) moderate, non-extreme.

equal *a.* **1** (*the same in size, number etc.*) alike, commensurate, identical, like, proportionate, the same. ANTONYMS: different, disproportionate, unequal, unlike. **2** (*even, not variable*) constant, even, invariable, level, regular, stable, unchanging, uniform. ANTONYMS: changeable, inconstant, irregular, uneven, variable. **3** (*evenly balanced*) even, evenly balanced, evenly matched, fifty-fifty, level pegging. ANTONYMS: ill-matched, unequal, uneven. **4** (*fair, just, impartial*) egalitarian, even-handed, fair, impartial, just, non-partisan, unbiased, unprejudiced. ANTONYMS: biased, partisan, prejudiced, unfair. **5** (*having adequate ability or means (to)*) able, adequate, capable, competent, fit, ready, suitable, suited, up to. ANTONYMS: inadequate, incompetent, unfit, unsuitable.

~n. (*a person of the same or similar age, rank, office, talents or the like*) compeer, counterpart, equivalent, peer.

~v.t. **1** (*to be equal to*) be equal to, be equivalent to, be the same as, correspond to. **2** (*to become equal to, to match*) be equal to, be level with, match, measure up to, parallel.

equality n. (*the state of being equal*) balance, evenness, levelness, likeness, parity.

equanimity n. (*evenness or composure of mind*) aplomb, calm, composure, (*coll.*) cool, equilibrium, even-temperedness, imperturbability, level-headedness, phlegm, placidness, presence of mind, sang-froid, self-control, self-possession, serenity, stability, steadiness, tranquillity, unexcitability, (*coll.*) unflappability. ANTONYMS: emotionalism, excitability, volatility.

equate v.t. (*to regard as equal* (*to*)) associate, bracket together, compare, connect, liken, link.

~v.i. (*to be equal*) be equal to, be equivalent to, correspond to, match, parallel.

equilibrium n. **1** (*a state of equal balance, equipoise*) balance, equipoise, evenness, stability, steadiness. **2** (*mental or emotional balance or stability*) aplomb, calm, composure, (*coll.*) cool, equanimity, even-temperedness, imperturbability, level-headedness, phlegm, placidness, presence of mind, sang-froid, self-control, self-possession, sense of balance, serenity, stability, steadiness, tranquillity, unexcitability, (*coll.*) unflappability.

equip v.t. **1** (*to fit out* (*as a ship*), *to prepare for any particular duty*) attire, fit out, furnish, kit out, outfit, prepare, provide, rig out, supply. **2** (*to qualify*) empower, fit, make fit, make ready, prepare, qualify.

equipment n. (*that which is used in equipping or fitting out*) apparatus, appurtenances, (*coll.*) box of tricks, furnishings, gear, outfit, paraphernalia, supplies, tackle, things, tools.

equitable a. (*acting or done with equity; just*) disinterested, even-handed, fair, fair-minded, impartial, just, non-partisan, open-minded, proper, reasonable, right, unbiased, unprejudiced. ANTONYMS: biased, prejudiced, unfair, unjust.

equity n. (*justice, fairness*) disinterest, disinterestedness, equitableness, even-handedness, fair-mindedness, fairness, fair play, impartiality, justice, justness, open-mindedness, properness, rectitude, rightness. ANTONYMS: bias, discrimination, partiality, prejudice.

equivalent a. (*of equal value, force or weight* (*to*)) commensurate (with), comparable (to), corresponding (to), equal (to), identical (with), interchangeable (with), like, similar (to), the same (as).

equivocal a. (*ambiguous, capable of a twofold interpretation*) ambiguous, ambivalent, circuitous, doubtful, indefinite, misleading, oblique, obscure, uncertain, unclear, vague. ANTONYMS: clear, definite, straightforward, unambiguous.

equivocate v.i. (*to prevaricate*) beat about the bush, dodge the issue, fence, (*coll.*) flannel, hedge, hesitate, hum and haw, (*coll.*) pussyfoot around, quibble, shilly-shally, sidestep the issue, sit on the fence, use evasive tactics, vacillate, (*coll.*) waffle. ANTONYMS: be frank, face facts, speak one's mind.

era n. (*a historical period*) aeon, age, epoch, period, stage, time.

eradicate v.t. (*to root up*) abolish, annihilate, destroy, efface, eliminate, erase, excise, expunge, exterminate, extinguish, extirpate, obliterate, remove, root out, stamp out, uproot, weed out, wipe out.

erase v.t. (*to obliterate, to expunge*) blot out, blue-pencil, cancel, delete, efface, excise, expunge, obliterate, remove, rub out, wipe out.

erect a. (*upright, vertical*) perpendicular, standing, standing up, straight, upright, vertical. ANTONYMS: horizontal, lying.

~v.t. **1** (*to set upright; to raise*) put up, set up, set upright. ANTONYMS: take down. **2** (*to construct, to build*) assemble, build, construct, put up. ANTONYMS: lower, take down. **3** (*to set up, to establish*) create, establish, form, found, institute, organize. ANTONYMS: break up, disband, (*coll.*) wind up.

erection n. **1** (*the act of building, constructing etc.*) assembly, building, constructing, construction, creation, establishment, forming, foundation, founding, instituting, organizing, putting up, setting up. **2** (*a building, a structure*) building, construction, edifice, pile, structure. **3** (*the distension of a part consisting of erectile tissue, esp. the penis*) tumescence, tumidity, turgescence.

erode v.t. (*to eat into or away*) abrade, corrode, deteriorate, eat away, gnaw away, grind down, wear, wear away.

erotic a. (*relating to or causing sexual desire; amatory*) (*euphem.*) adult, amatory, aphrodisiac, (*sl.*) blue, pornographic, (*coll.*) raunchy, sensual, sexually stimulating, sexy, (*sl.*) steamy, suggestive, titillating.

err v.i. **1** (*to blunder; to be incorrect*) be

inaccurate, be incorrect, be in error, be mistaken, be wrong, (*coll.*) boob, get the wrong end of the stick, make a blunder, make a mistake, slip up. ANTONYMS: be correct, be right. **2** (*to sin*) do wrong, go astray, go wrong, misbehave, sin.

errand *n.* (*a short journey to carry a message or perform some other commission, esp. on another's behalf*) assignment, charge, commission, mission.

erratic *a.* **1** (*irregular in movement, unpredictable*) directionless, meandering, wandering, wavering. ANTONYMS: controlled, regular, straight. **2** (*irregular in behaviour*) abnormal, capricious, changeable, fitful, inconsistent, irregular, uneven, unpredictable, unreliable, unstable, variable, wayward, whimsical. ANTONYMS: consistent, predictable, regular.

erroneous *a.* (*mistaken, incorrect*) fallacious, faulty, flawed, inaccurate, incorrect, inexact, invalid, mistaken, specious, spurious, unfounded, unsound, untrue, wrong. ANTONYMS: accurate, correct, right, true.

error *n.* **1** (*a mistake in writing, printing etc.*) erratum, literal, misprint, typing error, typo. **2** (*a deviation from truth or accuracy*) (*sl.*) bloomer, blunder, (*coll.*) boob, (*sl.*) boo-boo, fallacy, flaw, (*coll.*) howler, inaccuracy, miscalculation, misinterpretation, mistake, oversight, slip, slip-up, solecism. ANTONYMS: accuracy, truth. **3** (*a transgression, a sin of a venial kind*) evildoing, misdeed, offence, sin, transgression, wrongdoing.

erudite *a.* (*learned, well-read, well-informed*) cultivated, educated, (*coll., often derog.*) highbrow, intellectual, knowledgeable, learned, literate, scholarly, well-informed, well-read. ANTONYMS: illiterate, uneducated.

erudition *n.* (*learning, extensive knowledge gained by study*) education, knowledge, learning, letters, scholarship.

erupt *v.i.* **1** (*to burst out*) blow up, burst forth, burst out, explode, flare up. **2** ((*of a volcano*) *to emit lava, gases etc.*) belch forth, discharge, gush out, pour forth, spew out, vent.

eruption *n.* **1** (*the act of bursting forth*) explosion, flare-up, outburst. **2** (*the breaking out of pimples, rash etc. upon the skin*) flare-up, outbreak, rash.

escalate *v.i.* (*to increase (rapidly) in intensity or magnitude*) accelerate, be stepped up, develop rapidly, expand, grow, heighten, increase, intensify, mushroom. ANTONYMS: decrease, diminish, wane, wind down.
~*v.t.* (*to cause to escalate*) accelerate, amplify, expand, heighten, increase, intensify, magnify, step up. ANTONYMS: decrease, reduce.

escapade *n.* (*an exciting or daring prank or adventure*) adventure, antics, caper, fling, frolic, lark, prank, spree, stunt.

escape *v.t.* **1** (*to evade, to avoid (a thing or act*)) avoid, circumvent, dodge, (*coll.*) duck, evade, give the slip to, keep out of the way of, sidestep, steer clear of. **2** (*to slip away from, elude recollection of*) baffle, be forgotten by, elude, stump. **3** (*to find an issue from*) discharge, emanate, issue, leak, leakage.
~*v.i.* **1** (*to get free*) abscond, bolt, break free, decamp, (*sl.*) do a bunk, (*sl.*) do a runner, flee, get away, make one's escape, (*coll.*) make one's getaway, run away. **2** (*to find an issue, to leak*) discharge, emanate, issue, seep.
~*n.* **1** (*the act or an instance of escaping*) absconding, bolting, breakout, decampment, fleeing, flight, (*coll.*) getaway, running away. **2** (*a way of avoiding an unpleasant situation*) avoidance, circumvention, dodging, (*coll.*) ducking, sidestepping. **3** (*a leakage (from a gas or water pipe etc.*)) discharge, emanation, emission, leak, leakage. **4** (*something that helps one forget about ordinary life*) distraction, diversion, fantasy, relief.

eschew *v.t.* **1** (*to avoid; to shun*) avoid, evade, give a wide berth to, have nothing to do with, shun, steer clear of. **2** (*to abstain from*) abandon, (*formal*) abjure, abstain from, forgo, forswear, give up, (*sl.*) jack in, kick, (*coll.*) pack in, refrain from, renounce, (*coll.*) swear off.

escort[1] *n.* **1** (*an armed guard attending persons, baggage etc.*) bodyguard, convoy, cortege, entourage, guard, retinue, train. **2** (*a person or persons accompanying another for protection or guidance*) attendant, chaperon, companion, partner.

escort[2] *v.t.* **1** (*to act as escort to*) accompany, chaperone, partner. **2** (*to attend upon*) accompany, chaperone, partner.

esoteric *a.* **1** (*of philosophical doctrines etc., meant for or intelligible only to the initiated*) abstruse, arcane, cryptic, hidden, inscrutable, mysterious, obscure, recondite, secret. ANTONYMS: clear, manifest, obvious, open. **2** (*secret, confidential*) abstruse, arcane, cryptic, hidden, inscrutable, mysterious, obscure, private, secret. ANTONYMS: clear, obvious, open.

especially *adv.* ((*used as an intensifier*) *particularly, exceptionally*) eminently, exceptionally, extraordinarily, markedly, outstandingly, particularly, remarkably, signally, strikingly, supremely, uncommonly, unusually.

espionage *n.* (*the act or practice of spying*) intelligence, reconnaissance, spying, surveillance, undercover work.

espouse *v.t.* (*to adopt, to defend* (*a cause etc.*)) adopt, back, defend, embrace, promote, support, take up. ANTONYMS: abandon, give up.

essay *n.* (*a short informal literary composition or disquisition, usu. in prose*) article, composition, discourse, disquisition, dissertation, paper, piece, tract, treatise.

essence *n.* **1** (*the distinctive quality of a thing*) essential nature, quintessence, soul, spirit, substance. **2** (*a solution or extract obtained by distillation*) concentrate, distillate, extract, tincture. **in essence** (*fundamentally*) basically, essentially, fundamentally, in effect, to all intents and purposes. **of the essence** (*of the greatest importance*) crucial, essential, indispensable, of the greatest importance, of the utmost importance, vital. ANTONYMS: of no importance, unimportant.

essential *a.* **1** (*necessary to the existence of a thing, indispensable* (*to*)) crucial (to), indispensable (to), necessary (for), needed (for), prerequisite (for), vital (for). ANTONYMS: dispensable (to), incidental (to), inessential (to). **2** (*of or relating to the essence of a thing*) basic, characteristic, fundamental, inherent, intrinsic. **3** (*containing the essence or principle of a plant etc.*) concentrated, distilled, extracted. **4** (*being a perfect example of a particular kind of person or thing*) absolute, complete, perfect, quintessential.

establish *v.t.* **1** (*to set upon a firm foundation, to found*) create, form, found, inaugurate, institute, organize, set up, start. ANTONYMS: close, destroy, wind up. **2** (*to settle or secure firmly* (*in office, opinion etc.*)) ensconce, entrench, fix, install, plant, root, secure, settle. ANTONYMS: uproot. **3** (*to substantiate, put beyond dispute*) attest to, authenticate, certify, confirm, corroborate, prove, substantiate, validate, verify. ANTONYMS: contradict, discredit, disprove.

establishment *n.* **1** (*the act of establishing*) creation, formation, founding, inauguration, institution, organization. ANTONYMS: closure, destruction, winding up. **2** (*a public institution or business organization*) business, company, concern, firm, shop. **3** (*a private household*) abode, domicile, dwelling, home, house, household, residence. **4** (*the group of people who are in positions of power and influence in society*) bureaucracy, officialdom, the authorities, the powers that be, the system.

estate *n.* **1** (*property, esp. a landed property*) domain, lands, property. **2** (*a person's assets and liabilities taken collectively*) assets, effects, possessions, property, resources. **3** (*circumstances, standing*) circumstance, condition, lot, position, situation, state.

estate agent *n.* (*an agent concerned with the renting or sale of real estate*) property agent, property dealer, real estate agent, (*N Am.*) realtor.

esteem *v.t.* (*to hold in high estimation, to regard with respect*) admire, hold in high regard, look up to, prize, respect, revere, think highly of, value, venerate. ANTONYMS: despise, look down on, scorn.
~*n.* (*opinion or judgement as to merit or demerit, esp. a favourable opinion*) admiration, high opinion, high regard, regard, respect, reverence, veneration. ANTONYMS: contempt, scorn.

estimate[1] *v.t.* (*to compute the value of, to appraise*) appraise, assess, calculate, compute, count, evaluate, gauge, guess, guesstimate, judge, reckon.

estimate[2] *n.* (*an approximate calculation of the value, number, extent etc. of anything*) appraisal, assessment, calculation, computation, guess, guesstimate, reckoning, rough guess.

estimation *n.* **1** (*the act of estimating*) appraisal, assessment, calculation, computation, guessing, guesstimate, reckoning. **2** (*opinion or judgement*) consideration, feeling, judgement, opinion, view, way of thinking. **3** (*approval*) admiration, approval, esteem, favour, good opinion, high regard, regard, respect. ANTONYMS: contempt, disrespect, scorn.

estrange *v.t.* **1** (*to alienate, to make indifferent*) alienate, break up, disaffect, disunite, divide, set apart, set at odds. ANTONYMS: bring together, make close, reunite, unite. **2** (*to cut off from friendship*) destroy the affection of, destroy the friendship of, divorce, drive apart, make hostile, sever, split up. ANTONYMS: attract, bring together, reunite.

estrangement *n.* **1** (*alienation; the state of being indifferent*) alienation, disaffection. ANTONYMS: unity. **2** (*the state of being cut off from friendship*) break-up, divorce, hostility, parting, separation, split-up. ANTONYMS: reconciliation, unity.

eternal *a.* **1** (*everlasting, perpetual*) abiding, ceaseless, constant, endless, everlasting, infinite, lasting, never-ending, permanent, perpetual, timeless, unceasing, undying, unending, without end. ANTONYMS: ephemeral, fleeting, temporary. **2** (*incessant, constant*) constant, continual, continuous, endless, incessant, interminable, never-ending, nonstop, perpetual, persistent, relentless, unremitting, without respite. ANTONYMS: infrequent, occasional.

eternity *n.* **1** (*eternal duration*) for ever, infinity, time without end. ANTONYMS: transience, transitoriness. **2** (*future life after death*) afterlife, heaven, immortality, life after death, paradise, the hereafter, the next world, the world hereafter, world without end. **3** (*a very long time*) ages, ages and ages, a long time, an age, the duration. ANTONYMS: a minute, a moment, a second, a short time.

ethical *a.* (*conforming to a recognized standard*) correct, decent, fair, good, honest, honourable, just, moral, principled, proper, right, righteous, upright, virtuous. ANTONYMS: bad, dishonourable, unethical, unprincipled.

ethics *n.pl.* (*a system of principles and rules of conduct*) moral code, morals, moral standards, moral values, principles.

ethnic *a.* **1** (*relating to or characteristic of a race or culture*) national, racial, tribal. **2** (*of or relating to the culture or traditions of a particular people*) cultural, folk, traditional. **3** (*belonging to a nation by birth or origin rather than by acquired nationality*) aboriginal, autochthonous, indigenous, native.

ethos *n.* (*the characteristic spirit or character of a people, institution etc.*) character, disposition, flavour, spirit, tenor.

etiquette *n.* (*the conventional rules of behaviour in polite society*) accepted behaviour, civility, code of behaviour, convention, courtesy, decorum, formalities, good form, good manners, manners, politeness, propriety, protocol.

eulogy *n.* (*praise, panegyric*) acclaim, acclamation, accolade, applause, approval, bouquets, commendation, compliment, encomium, extolment, laudation, paean, panegyric, plaudit, praise, tribute. ANTONYMS: censure, condemnation, criticism.

euphemistic *a.* (*using a soft or pleasing term or phrase for one that is harsh or offensive*) genteel, indirect, polite, softened, understated. ANTONYMS: blunt, direct, frank, plain.

euphoria *n.* (*a feeling of well-being, supreme content, esp. exaggerated or baseless*) bliss, ecstasy, elation, exaltation, exhilaration, exultation, glee, joy, jubilation, rapture, transports. ANTONYMS: dejection, despair, misery.

euphoric *a.* (*of or relating to a feeling of well-being, supreme content, esp. exaggerated or baseless*) blissful, buoyant, ecstatic, elated, enraptured, exhilarated, exultant, gleeful, in raptures, in seventh heaven, joyful, (*coll.*) on cloud nine, over the moon, rapturous. ANTONYMS: dejected, despondent, in despair.

evacuate *v.t.* **1** (*to remove inhabitants from (a danger zone)*) clear, pull (someone) out,

remove. **2** (*to withdraw from (esp. of troops)*) abandon, depart from, desert, leave, move out of, pull out of, quit, vacate, withdraw from.

evade *v.t.* **1** (*to avoid or elude by artifice or stratagem*) avoid, dodge, elude, escape from, get away from, give the slip to, keep out of the way of, shake off, steer clear of. **2** (*to avoid (doing something), to shirk*) avoid, dodge, (*coll.*) duck, shirk, sidestep, steer clear of. **3** (*to avoid answering (a question)*) avoid, circumvent, fend off, fudge, hedge, parry.

evaluate *v.t.* (*to determine the value of, to appraise*) appraise, assess, calculate, estimate, gauge, judge, put a price on, put a value on, rate, reckon, value, weigh up.

evaluation *n.* (*a determination of the value of something; appraisal*) appraisal, assessment, calculation, estimation, gauge, judgement, reckoning, valuation.

evanescent *a.* (*fading, fleeting*) brief, ephemeral, fleeting, fugitive, impermanent, short-lived, temporary, transient, transitory. ANTONYMS: everlasting, long-lasting, permanent.

evaporate *v.i.* (*to disappear, to vanish*) dematerialize, disappear, disperse, dissipate, dissolve, evanesce, fade, fade away, melt, melt away, vanish.

evasion *n.* **1** (*the act of evading or escaping (as from a question or charge)*) avoidance, dodging, eluding, escape. **2** (*a subterfuge, an equivocation*) artifice, cunning, deception, dodging, (*coll.*) ducking, equivocation, fencing, (*coll.*) flannel, fudging, hedging, parrying, quibbling, subterfuge, trickery, (*coll.*) waffle. ANTONYMS: directness, straightforwardness.

even[1] *a.* **1** (*level, smooth*) flat, flush, level, plane, smooth, uniform. ANTONYMS: bumpy, uneven. **2** (*equal*) commensurate, comparable, equal, evenly matched, identical, level, level pegging, like, neck and neck, on a par, similar, the same. ANTONYMS: different, disparate, unequal. **3** ((*of a competition*) *having competitors that are equally good*) drawn, equal, level, tied. **4** (*uniform or unvarying in quality*) constant, regular, stable, steady, unchanging, uniform, unvarying. ANTONYMS: changing, irregular, variable. **5** (*unvarying, unruffled*) calm, composed, cool, equable, even-tempered, placid, serene, tranquil, unexcitable, (*coll.*) unflappable, unperturbable, unruffled, well-balanced. ANTONYMS: emotional, excitable, irascible, volatile. **to be/ get even with** (*to revenge oneself on*) be revenged on, get one's own back on, pay (someone) back, revenge oneself on, take one's revenge on, take vengeance on.

even² *v.t.* **1** (*to make smooth or level*) flatten, level, plane, smooth. ANTONYMS: roughen. **2** (*to place on a level*) balance up, equalize, make equal, make even, make level, make the same.

evening *n.* (*the close or latter part of the day*) dusk, late afternoon, night, nightfall, sunset. ANTONYMS: morning, sunrise.

event *n.* **1** (*anything that happens, as distinguished from a thing that exists*) episode, experience, happening, incident, occasion, occurrence. **2** (*any item in a programme of games, contests etc., esp. one on which money is wagered*) bout, competition, contest, game, match, race, round.

eventful *a.* **1** (*full of events*) action-packed, active, busy, lively. ANTONYMS: boring, dull, uneventful. **2** (*attended by important changes*) critical, crucial, historic, important, memorable, momentous, notable, noteworthy, of consequence, remarkable, significant. ANTONYMS: inconsequential, run-of-the-mill, unremarkable.

eventual *a.* (*finally resulting, ultimate*) final, last, resultant, subsequent, ultimate.

eventuality *n.* (*a possible event or result*) case, chance, contingency, event, eventuality, likelihood, possibility, probability.

ever *adv.* **1** (*at all times; always*) always, at all times, constantly, continually, eternally, everlastingly, for ever, perpetually, to the end of time, unendingly. **2** (*at any time*) at any time, under any circumstances.

everlasting *a.* **1** (*lasting for ever, eternal*) abiding, endless, enduring, eternal, immortal, infinite, never-ending, timeless, undying, without end. ANTONYMS: ephemeral, fleeting, transitory. **2** (*continual, unintermittent*) constant, continual, continuous, endless, incessant, never-ending, non-stop, uninterrupted, unremitting. ANTONYMS: intermittent, limited, periodic, sporadic. **3** (*interminable, tiresome*) incessant, interminable, never-ending, non-stop, tedious, wearisome.

every *a.* (*each of a group or collection, all separately*) each, every single.

everyone *pron.* (*everybody*) all, all and sundry, each and every one, each one, each person, everybody, every person, one and all. ANTONYMS: nobody, no one.

everything *pron.* (*all things collectively*) all, every single thing, the lot, the total, (*coll.*) the whole caboodle, the whole lot, (*N Am., sl.*) the whole shebang, (*coll.*) the whole shooting match. ANTONYMS: nothing.

everywhere *adv.* **1** (*in every place*) all around, all over, in every place. ANTONYMS: nowhere. **2** (*in many places*) extensively, far and wide, high and low, the world over.

evict *v.t.* (*to eject from lands or property by law*) (*coll.*) chuck out, eject, expel, kick out, oust, put out, remove, show (someone) the door, throw out, (*coll.*) turf out, turn out.

evidence *n.* **1** (*anything that makes clear or obvious; testimony*) demonstration, indication, manifestation, mark, sign, suggestion, testimony, token, tract. **2** (*information by which a fact is proved or sought to be proved*) affirmation, authentication, confirmation, corroboration, proof, substantiation, verification. **3** (*such statements, proofs etc. as are legally admissible as testimony in a court of law*) affidavit, attestation, declaration, sworn statement, testimony.

evident *a.* (*open or plain to the sight; obvious*) apparent, as plain as the nose on your face, blatant, clear, conspicuous, discernible, manifest, noticeable, obvious, patent, perceptible, plain, plain as a pikestaff, plain as the nose on your face, transparent, unmistakable, visible. ANTONYMS: imperceptible, invisible, vague.

evidently *adv.* **1** (*obviously*) clearly, manifestly, obviously, patently, perceptibly, plainly, transparently, unmistakably, visibly. ANTONYMS: imperceptibly, indiscernibly, vaguely. **2** (*apparently*) apparently, as far as one can judge, as far as one can tell, from all appearances, it appears, it seems, it would appear, it would seem, seemingly.

evil *a.* **1** (*morally bad, wicked*) bad, base, corrupt, depraved, immoral, iniquitous, malevolent, sinful, vile, villainous, wicked, wrong. ANTONYMS: good, moral, virtuous. **2** (*unlucky, producing disastrous results*) adverse, calamitous, dire, disastrous, inauspicious, painful, pernicious, ruinous, sad, unfavourable, unfortunate, unhappy, unlucky. ANTONYMS: favourable, fortunate, happy. ~*n.* **1** (*that which injures or displeases, harm*) calamity, catastrophe, destruction, disaster, harm, injury, misery, misfortune, pain, ruin, sorrow, suffering. ANTONYMS: advantage, benefit, good. **2** (*sin, depravity*) badness, baseness, corruption, depravity, immorality, iniquity, malevolence, sin, sinfulness, vileness, villainy, wickedness, wrong. ANTONYMS: goodness, morality, virtue.

evince *v.t.* (*to show clearly, to indicate*) demonstrate, display, evidence, exhibit, manifest, reveal, show, show signs of. ANTONYMS: conceal, hide.

evocative *a.* (*tending to evoke, esp. feelings or memories*) reminiscent, suggestive.

evoke *v.t.* **1** (*to call up, to summon forth* (*a memory etc.*) *esp. from the past*) awaken, bring to mind, call to mind, call up, conjure up, rekindle, stir up, summon. **2** (*to elicit or provoke*) arouse, bring forth, cause, elicit, give rise to, induce, produce, provoke. **3** (*to cause* (*spirits*) *to appear*) conjure up, invoke, raise, summon up.

evolve *v.i.* (*to develop*) develop, grow, progress, unfold, unroll, work out.

exacerbate *v.t.* (*to aggravate, to increase the violence of* (*as a disease*)) add fuel to the fire, add salt to the wound, aggravate, heighten, increase, intensify, make worse, worsen. ANTONYMS: decrease, improve.

exact[1] *a.* **1** (*accurate, strictly correct*) accurate, (*coll.*) bang on, close, correct, error-free, faithful, faultless, identical, on the nail, precise, right, (*coll.*) spot on, to the letter, true, unerring. ANTONYMS: approximate, imprecise, inexact, rough, wrong. **2** (*precise, strict*) careful, conscientious, exacting, methodical, meticulous, orderly, painstaking, particular, precise, punctilious, rigorous, scrupulous, strict. ANTONYMS: careless, negligent, remiss, slapdash.

exact[2] *v.t.* **1** (*to compel* (*money etc.*) *to be paid or surrendered*) (*coll.*) bleed, bully, coerce, demand, extort, extract, force, milk, (*Austral., N Am., sl.*) put the bite on for, (*coll.*) put the screws on for, squeeze, wrest, wring. **2** (*to insist on, to require authoritatively*) call for, command, compel, demand, insist on, require.

exacting *a.* **1** (*severe or excessive in demanding*) demanding, firm, harsh, imperious, rigid, rigorous, stern, strict, unbending, unsparing, unyielding. ANTONYMS: easygoing, nonchalant, undemanding. **2** (*requiring much effort or skill*) arduous, demanding, difficult, hard, laborious, onerous, stringent, taxing, tiring, tough. ANTONYMS: easy, effortless, simple.

exactly *adv.* **1** (*in an exact manner*) accurately, closely, correctly, identically, precisely, to the letter, truly, unerringly, without error. ANTONYMS: imprecisely, inaccurately. **2** (*precisely, just so* (*in answer to a question or affirmation*)) absolutely, certainly, just so, quite, right. ANTONYMS: certainly not, not at all, no way. **3** (*no more, no less or no different from what is stated*) absolutely, in every detail, in every respect, just, precisely.

exactness *n.* **1** (*the quality of being exact*) accuracy, closeness, correctness, faithfulness, identicalness, precision, rightness, truth. ANTONYMS: imprecision, inexactness, roughness, wrongness. **2** (*carefulness and thoroughness*) care, carefulness, conscientiousness,

methodicalness, meticulousness, orderliness, precision, rigorousness, scrupulousness, strictness. ANTONYMS: carelessness, negligence, sloppiness.

exaggerate *v.t.* **1** (*to overstate, to represent as greater than is in fact the case*) add colour to, amplify, colour, embellish, embroider, heighten, magnify, make a mountain out of a molehill, make a production of, overdo, overemphasize, overestimate, overstate, overstress. ANTONYMS: minimize, underemphasize, understate. **2** (*to increase, intensify, aggravate*) accentuate, aggravate, emphasize, give prominence to, heighten, increase, intensify, maximize, overemphasize, overstress, stress. ANTONYMS: decrease, diminish.

exaggerated *a.* **1** (*represented as greater than is in fact the case*) coloured, embellished, embroidered, exalted, excessive, hyperbolic, inflated, magnified, (*coll.*) OTT, overdone, overemphasized, overstated, over the top. ANTONYMS: muted, underplayed, understated. **2** (*unnatural and intended to impress people*) affected, extravagant, mannered, overdone, pretentious, theatrical. ANTONYMS: genuine, low-key, muted.

exaggeration *n.* **1** (*the act of representing something as greater than is in fact the case*) amplification, embellishment, embroidering, embroidery, magnification, overemphasis, overstatement. ANTONYMS: minimizing, understatement. **2** (*a statement that represents something as greater than is in fact the case*) hyperbole, overstatement, purple prose. ANTONYMS: understatement.

exalt *v.t.* **1** (*to raise in power or position*) advance, aggrandize, dignify, ennoble, honour, promote, raise, upgrade. ANTONYMS: demote, downgrade. **2** (*to praise, glorify*) acclaim, exalt, extol, glorify, idolize, laud, magnify, pay homage to, pay tribute to, praise, reverence, set on a pedestal, worship. ANTONYMS: denigrate, deprecate, disparage.

exaltation *n.* **1** (*the act or instance of praising*) acclamation, extolment, glorification, homage, lauding, magnification, plaudits, praise, reverencing, tribute, worship. ANTONYMS: denigration, deprecation, disparagement. **2** (*elevation in power or position*) advancement, aggrandizement, elevation, ennoblement, promotion, rise, upgrading. ANTONYMS: demotion, downgrading. **3** (*great happiness*) bliss, delight, ecstasy, elation, exultation, happiness, joy, joyfulness, jubilation, rapture, rhapsody, transport. ANTONYMS: depression, despondency, misery.

exalted *a.* **1** (*lofty, noble*) august, dignified,

elevated, eminent, high-born, high-ranking, honoured, lofty, noble, prestigious. ANTONYMS: humble, low-born. **2** (*very happy*) delighted, ecstatic, elated, in raptures, in seventh heaven, joyful, (*coll.*) on cloud nine. ANTONYMS: depressed, in low spirits, miserable.

examination *n.* **1** (*the act of examining, or an instance of examining*) assessment, check-up, inspection. **2** (*careful inspection, scrutiny*) analysis, appraisal, consideration, exploration, inspection, investigation, observation, probing, research, scrutiny, study, survey, test. **3** (*the process of testing the capabilities of a candidate for any post, or the knowledge of a student*) assessment, evaluation, test. **4** (*a careful inquiry into facts by taking evidence*) cross-examination, cross-questioning, (*coll.*) grilling, interrogation, questioning, quizzing.

examine *v.t.* **1** (*to inquire into, scrutinize*) analyse, appraise, check out, conduct tests on, consider, explore, go over, inspect, investigate, look at, look into, observe, probe, research, review, scan, scrutinize, sift, study, survey, take stock of, test, vet, weigh. **2** (*to inspect, to explore*) assess, check, check over, conduct an examination of, give (someone) a check-up, inspect. **3** (*to question* (*e.g. the accused or a witness*)) address questions to, cross-examine, cross-question, (*coll.*) grill, inquire of, interrogate, pump, put questions to, question, quiz. **4** (*to test the capabilities, knowledge of etc., by questions and problems*) assess, evaluate, put (someone) through their paces, subject to examination, test.

example *n.* **1** (*a sample, a specimen*) case, case in point, exemplification, illustration, instance, representative case, sample, specimen. **2** (*a model or pattern*) archetype, criterion, exemplar, ideal, model, norm, paradigm, pattern, precedent, standard. **3** (*a punishment, or the person punished serving as a warning*) admonition, caution, lesson, warning.

exasperate *v.t.* **1** (*to irritate to a high degree; to provoke*) anger, annoy, (*sl.*) bug, enrage, gall, (*coll.*) get on the nerves of, (*coll.*) get to, incense, inflame, infuriate, irk, irritate, madden, (*sl.*) needle, pique, provoke, rile, try the patience of, vex. ANTONYMS: calm, pacify, placate. **2** (*to aggravate, to embitter*) add fuel to the fire, aggravate, exacerbate, intensify, make worse, rub salt in the wound, worsen. ANTONYMS: improve, make better.

excavate *v.t.* **1** (*to form by digging or hollowing out*) cut out, dig, dig out, gouge, hollow out, mine, quarry, scoop out. **2** (*to uncover by digging, to dig out, esp. for archaeological research*) dig up, disinter, exhume, reveal, uncover, unearth.

excavation *n.* **1** (*the act of digging or hollowing out*) digging, gouging, hollowing out, mining, quarrying, scooping out. **2** (*a hole or area of ground that has been dug out*) burrow, cavity, cutting, dig, ditch, dugout, hole, hollow, mine, pit, quarry, shaft, trench, trough.

exceed *v.t.* **1** (*to go or pass beyond*) do more than, go beyond, go beyond the bounds of, go beyond the limits of, go over, go over the limit of, overstep. **2** (*to be more or greater than*) be greater than, be more than, pass, surmount, top. ANTONYMS: be less than. **3** (*to be better than*) beat, be better than, be superior to, better, cap, eclipse, excel, outdistance, outdo, outshine, outstrip, overshadow, (*coll.*) run rings round, surpass, top, transcend.

exceedingly *adv.* (*very much*) enormously, especially, exceptionally, extraordinarily, extremely, greatly, highly, hugely, inordinately, superlatively, supremely, to a great extent, to a marked extent, tremendously, unusually, vastly, very.

excel *v.t.* (*to surpass in qualities*) beat, beat hollow, be better than, be superior to, better, cap, eclipse, outclass, outdo, outrival, outshine, overshadow, (*coll.*) run rings round, surpass, top, transcend.

~*v.i.* (*to be superior, distinguished or pre-eminent* (*in or at*)) be a master (of), be outstanding (at), be proficient (in or at), be skilful (at), be skilled (in), be talented (at), have a gift (for), shine (at), show talent (at).

excellence *n.* (*superiority, pre-eminence*) brilliance, distinction, eminence, quality, skill, superiority, supremacy, transcendence, worthiness. ANTONYMS: incompetence, inferiority.

excellent *a.* (*surpassing others in some good quality*) (*coll.*) A1, accomplished, (*sl.*) ace, admirable, (*coll.*) brill, brilliant, (*coll.*) cracking, distinguished, eminent, exceptional, extraordinary, fine, first-rate, notable, noted, outstanding, pre-eminent, prime, quality, skilful, superb, superior, supreme, top, (*coll.*) topnotch, valuable, very good, world-class, worthy. ANTONYMS: hopeless, incompetent, inferior, poor.

except *v.t.* (*to leave out, to omit*) bar, debar, disallow, exclude, leave out, omit, pass over, reject, rule out. ANTONYMS: allow, include.

~*prep.* (*not including, exclusive of*) apart from, bar, barring, besides, but, excepting, excluding, exclusive of, other than, save, with the exception of. ANTONYMS: including, inclusive of.

exception *n.* **1** (*that which is excepted*) debarment, exclusion, non-inclusion, omission, rejection. ANTONYMS: inclusion. **2** (*an instance* *of that which is excluded from a rule or other generalization*) anomaly, departure, deviant, deviation, freak, inconsistency, irregularity, oddity, peculiarity, quirk, special case. **to take exception** (*to object, to find fault*) be offended, cavil, find fault, object, protest, raise an objection, resent, take offence, take umbrage.

exceptionable *a.* (*objectionable*) abhorrent, disagreeable, nasty, objectionable, obnoxious, offensive, repugnant, unacceptable, undesirable, unpleasant. ANTONYMS: agreeable, pleasant, welcome.

exceptional *a.* **1** (*unusual, unprecedented*) aberrant, abnormal, anomalous, atypical, deviant, divergent, extraordinary, freak, irregular, odd, out of the ordinary, peculiar, rare, singular, special, strange, uncommon, unusual. **2** (*extraordinarily good*) excellent, marvellous, outstanding, phenomenal, prodigious, remarkable, superior, (*coll.*) tremendous, very good. ANTONYMS: inferior, poor.

excerpt *n.* (*an extract or selection from a book, film etc.*) citation, clip, (*esp. N Am.*) clipping, cutting, extract, passage, quotation, quote, section, selection.

excess *n.* **1** (*that which exceeds what is usual or necessary*) enough and spare, extra, glut, overabundance, overkill, plethora, superfluity, surfeit, too much. ANTONYMS: deficiency, scarcity. **2** (*extreme behaviour that is considered unacceptable*) debauchery, dissipation, dissoluteness, extravagance, immoderation, intemperance, lack of restraint, over-indulgence, prodigality. ANTONYMS: moderation, restraint, temperance.
~*a.* (*more than is usual or permitted*) additional, extra, redundant, residual, spare, superfluous, surplus.

excessive *a.* (*more than normal or proper*) exorbitant, extravagant, extreme, immoderate, inordinate, intemperate, needless, (*coll.*) OTT, outrageous, over the top, profligate, superfluous, surplus, too much, uncalled-for, undue, unnecessary, unreasonable, unwarranted. ANTONYMS: deficient, insufficient, too little.

excessively *adv.* (*to an extent that is more than normal or proper*) extravagantly, extremely, immoderately, inordinately, needlessly, unduly, unreasonably. ANTONYMS: inadequately, insufficiently.

exchange *v.t.* **1** (*to hand over for an equivalent in kind*) barter, change, convert into, trade. **2** (*to give and receive in turn, to interchange*) bandy, barter, interchange, reciprocate, swap, switch, trade.
~*n.* **1** (*a parting with one article or commodity for*

an equivalent in kind) changing, conversion. **2** (*the act of giving and receiving reciprocally, interchange*) bandying, barter, bartering, dealing, interchange, reciprocation, reciprocity, swapping, switching, trade, trading. **3** (*the place where merchants, brokers etc. meet to transact business*) money market, Stock Exchange, stock market.

excise *n.* (*a tax or duty on certain articles produced and consumed in a country*) customs, duty, levy, tariff, tax, toll.

excitable *a.* (*susceptible to stimulation*) choleric, edgy, emotional, fiery, highly strung, hot-headed, irascible, mercurial, moody, nervous, nervy, passionate, temperamental, tempestuous, (*coll.*) uptight, volatile. ANTONYMS: imperturbable, (*coll.*) laid-back, phlegmatic.

excite *v.t.* **1** (*to stimulate, to bring into activity*) arouse, awaken, bring about, call forth, cause, evoke, foment, incite, instigate, kindle, provoke, rouse, stir up, wake, waken, whet. **2** (*to stir up the feelings or emotions of* (*a person*)) agitate, animate, arouse, discompose, disturb, electrify, fire, galvanize, incite, inflame, inspire, move, provoke, rouse, stimulate, thrill, titillate, (*coll.*) turn on, (*coll.*) wind up. ANTONYMS: depress, dispirit.

excited *a.* (*having one's feelings stirred up*) agitated, animated, discomposed, disturbed, elated, emotional, enthusiastic, exhilarated, feverish, (*coll.*) high, moved, nervous, nervy, overwrought, roused, stimulated, thrilled, (*coll.*) turned on, worked up, (*coll.*) wound up. ANTONYMS: apathetic, calm, (*coll.*) laid-back.

excitement *n.* **1** (*the state of having one's feelings stirred up*) agitation, animation, anticipation, commotion, discomposure, disturbance, elation, emotion, enthusiasm, exhilaration, ferment, feverishness, nervousness, passion, perturbation, stimulation, tumult. ANTONYMS: apathy, calmness. **2** (*something that stirs up the feelings*) adventure, (*sl.*) buzz, kick, stimulation, thrill.

exciting *a.* (*producing excitement or enthusiasm*) electrifying, exhilarating, inspiring, intoxicating, invigorating, moving, provocative, rousing, (*coll.*) sexy, stimulating, stirring, thrilling. ANTONYMS: boring, dull, monotonous, unexciting.

exclaim *v.i.* (*to cry out abruptly or passionately*) call, call out, cry out, ejaculate, proclaim, roar, shout, shriek, utter, yell.

exclamation *n.* (*an expression of surprise, pain etc.*) call, cry, ejaculation, interjection, proclamation, roar, shout, shriek, utterance, yell.

exclude *v.t.* **1** (*to prevent from participating*)

ban, bar, blackball, boycott, debar, disallow, embargo, forbid, interdict, keep out, ostracize, prevent, prohibit, proscribe, refuse, shut out, veto. ANTONYMS: allow, include, let in, welcome. **2** (*to debar; to expel and keep out*) ban, (*sl.*) boot out, (*sl.*) bounce, (*coll.*) chuck out, drive out, eject, evict, expel, force out, get rid of, keep out, kick out, oust, remove, throw out, turn out. ANTONYMS: admit, let in. **3** (*to reject, to leave out*) count out, eliminate, except, ignore, leave out, omit, pass over, preclude, reject, repudiate, rule out, set aside. ANTONYMS: count in, include.

exclusive *a.* **1** (*fastidious in the choice of associates, snobbish*) choice, clannish, (*coll.*) classy, cliquish, closed, discriminatory, elegant, fashionable, high-class, (*coll.*) posh, private, restricted, restrictive, (*coll.*) ritzy, snobbish, (*coll.*) swish, upmarket. ANTONYMS: open, public, unrestricted. **2** (*not inclusive (of)*) except for, excepting, excluding, leaving out, not counting, not including, omitting, setting aside. ANTONYMS: including, inclusive (of). **3** (*excluding all else*) absolute, complete, entire, full, only, sole, total, undivided, whole. ANTONYMS: partial, shared.

excoriate *v.t.* **1** (*to strip the skin from*) flay, peel, skin, strip. **2** (*to tear off* (*the skin*) *by abrasion*) abrade, gall, scrape, scratch, skin. **3** (*to criticize severely*) attack, berate, blast, castigate, censure, chide, condemn, denounce, (*coll.*) give (someone) a rocket, (*coll.*) give (someone) what for, lambaste, let fly at, read the riot act to, rebuke, reprimand, reprove, revile, scold, (*coll.*) tear a strip off, upbraid, vilify. ANTONYMS: applaud, praise.

excrement *n.* (*refuse matter discharged from the body after digestion, faeces*) excrescence, excreta, faeces, (*used by or to children*) number two, ordure, (*taboo sl.*) shit, stools.

excrete *v.t., v.i.* (*to separate and discharge* (*superfluous matter*) *from the organism*) discharge, eject, eliminate, emit, evacuate, expel, exude, pass, void.

excruciating *a.* (*extremely painful*) acute, agonizing, burning, excessive, extreme, harrowing, insufferable, intense, piercing, racking, searing, severe, unbearable, unendurable, very sore.

excursion *n.* **1** (*a short tour, a trip by an individual or a body of persons*) day trip, expedition, jaunt, journey, outing, tour, trip. **2** (*a wandering from the subject, a digression*) detour, deviation, digression, rambling, straying, wandering.

excusable *a.* (*that can be forgiven*) allowable, condonable, defensible, forgivable, justifiable, pardonable, understandable, venial,

warrantable. ANTONYMS: inexcusable, unforgivable, unpardonable.

excuse¹ *v.t.* **1** (*to free from blame, to lessen the blame attaching to*) absolve, acquit, exculpate, exonerate, forgive, pardon. ANTONYMS: blame, punish. **2** (*to serve as a vindication or apology for, to justify*) be an excuse for, condone, defend, explain, justify, make allowances for, mitigate, pardon, vindicate. **3** (*to relieve of or exempt from an obligation or duty*) discharge, exempt, free, let off, liberate, release, relieve, spare.

excuse² *n.* **1** (*a plea offered in extenuation of a fault or for release from an obligation etc.*) apology, defence, explanation, grounds, justification, mitigation, reason, vindication. **2** (*a pretended reason*) cover, cover-up, fabrication, front, pretext, subterfuge.

execrable *a.* (*abominable*) abominable, atrocious, deplorable, despicable, foul, heinous, horrible, loathsome, nasty, obnoxious, odious, repulsive, revolting, terrible, very bad, vile. ANTONYMS: admirable, excellent, marvellous.

execute *v.t.* **1** (*to perform, to accomplish*) accomplish, achieve, bring off, carry out, complete, discharge, do, effect, enact, finish, fulfil, implement, perform, prosecute, put into effect, realize. ANTONYMS: fail in. **2** (*to play or perform* (*a piece of music, a part in a play*)) perform, play, render. **3** (*to carry out a sentence of death on*) behead, electrocute, guillotine, hang, kill, put before a firing squad, put to death, (*coll.*) send to the chair, (*coll.*) string up.

execution *n.* **1** (*performance, accomplishment*) accomplishment, achievement, completion, discharge, effecting, enactment, finishing, fulfilment, implementation, performance, prosecution, realization. ANTONYMS: failure. **2** (*the carrying out of a death sentence*) capital punishment, death sentence, electrocution, guillotine, hanging, judicial killing, killing, putting to death. **3** (*the mode of performing a work of art, skill*) delivery, performance, presentation, rendition, style, technique.

executioner *n.* (*a person who carries out a death sentence*) hangman, public executioner.

executive *a.* (*having the function or power of executing*) administrative, controlling, directing, governing, managerial.
~*n.* **1** (*the person or body of persons carrying laws, sentences etc. into effect*) administration, government, leadership. **2** (*in business, a senior manager or administrator*) administrator, director, manager, official.

exemplar *n.* **1** (*a pattern or model to be copied*)

benchmark, criterion, epitome, example, ideal, model, paradigm, pattern, standard, yardstick. **2** (*a typical example*) example, exemplification, illustration, instance, sample, specimen, type.

exemplary *a.* **1** (*worthy of imitation*) admiral, commendable, estimable, excellent, fine, good, laudable, meritorious, model, praiseworthy, worthy. ANTONYMS: bad, pathetic, poor, worthless. **2** (*typical, serving to exemplify*) characteristic, illustrative, representational, typical. ANTONYMS: atypical, unrepresentative. **3** (*serving as a warning*) admonitory, cautionary, example-setting, monitory, warning.

exemplify *v.t.* **1** (*to illustrate by example*) demonstrate, depict, illustrate, instance. **2** (*to be an example of*) embody, epitomize, illustrate, personify, represent, serve as an example, typify.

exempt *a.* (*not liable or subject to* (*a tax, obligation etc.*)) excused from, free from, immune from, spared. ANTONYMS: liable to, subject to.
~*v.t.* (*to grant immunity* (*from*)) absolve, discharge, exclude, excuse, free, grant immunity, let off, liberate, release, relieve, spare. ANTONYMS: include.

exemption *n.* (*the state or an instance of being exempt*) absolution, discharge, dispensation, exception, exclusion, freedom, immunity, indemnity, liberation, release, relieve, spare. ANTONYMS: inclusion.

exercise *n.* **1** (*systematic exertion of the body for the sake of health*) drill, exercise regime, gymnastics, keeping-fit, physical training, training, working-out, workout. **2** (*mental practice designed to develop a faculty or skill*) lesson, problem, task, work. **3** (*the act of using or exerting* (*a skill, a right etc.*)) application, employment, exertion, implementation, operation, practice, use, utilization.
~*v.t.* **1** (*to exert, to put in practice or operation*) apply, bring into play, bring to bear, employ, exert, make use of, practise, put into practice, use, utilize, wield. **2** (*to train* (*a person*)) drill, train, work. **3** (*to make anxious or solicitous, to perplex*) agitate, burden, distress, make uneasy, occupy, perplex, preoccupy, trouble, vex, worry. ANTONYMS: calm, soothe, tranquillize.
~*v.i.* (*to take* (*regular*) *physical exercise; to do exercises*) do exercises, train, work out.

exert *v.t.* (*to use* (*strength, power etc.*) *with effort, to put in operation*) apply, bring into play, bring to bear, employ, exercise, expend, make use of, practise, put into practice, set in motion, spend, use, utilize, wield. **to exert oneself** (*to strive, to use effort*) apply oneself,

bend over backwards, do one's best, endeavour, (*coll.*) give it one's best shot, labour, make an all-out effort, make an effort, pull out all the stops, put one's back into, put oneself out, spare no effort, strain, strive, struggle, try, try as hard as one can, work. ANTONYMS: idleness, inertia.

exertion *n.* (*physical or mental effort*) effort, endeavour, exercise, labour, pains, strain, stress, striving, struggle, toil, work. ANTONYMS: idleness, inertia.

exhalation *n.* (*that which is exhaled*) discharge, effluvium, emanation, emission, fog, mist, smoke, steam, vapour.

exhale *v.t.* (*to emit, or cause to be emitted, in vapour*) discharge, eject, emit, expel, give off, issue.
~*v.i.* (*to make an expiration, as distinct from inhale*) breathe out, expire.

exhaust *v.t.* **1** (*to use up the whole of, to consume*) (*sl.*) blow, consume, deplete, dissipate, expend, finish, run through, spend, use up. **2** (*to wear out by exertion*) debilitate, drain, enervate, fatigue, (*coll.*) knacker, overtax, prostrate, sap, (*coll.*) take it out of one, tire out, wear out, weary. ANTONYMS: enliven, invigorate, revitalize. **3** (*to empty by drawing out the contents*) drain, empty, void.

exhausted *a.* (*extremely tired*) (*coll.*) all in, burnt out, dead beat, dog-tired, (*coll.*) done in, drained, fatigued, (*coll.*) knackered, (*esp. N Am., coll.*) pooped, prostrate, ready to drop, spent, tired out, weary, worn out, zonked. ANTONYMS: active, (*coll.*) bright-eyed and bushy-tailed, energetic, full of beans, lively.

exhausting *a.* (*tending to exhaust or tire out completely*) debilitating, draining, enervating, fatiguing, gruelling, (*coll.*) knackering, laborious, punishing, strenuous, taxing, tiring, wearing, wearying. ANTONYMS: enlivening, invigorating, revitalizing.

exhaustion *n.* (*a complete loss of strength*) debilitation, enervation, faintness, fatigue, feebleness, lassitude, tiredness, weakness, weariness. ANTONYMS: energy, liveliness, vigour.

exhaustive *a.* (*tending to exhaust* (*esp. a subject*), *comprehensive*) all-embracing, all-inclusive, all-out, complete, comprehensive, detailed, encyclopedic, extensive, far-reaching, full, full-scale, in-depth, intensive, sweeping, thorough, thoroughgoing, total. ANTONYMS: cursory, incomplete, perfunctory, superficial.

exhibit *v.t.* **1** (*to offer to public view*) demonstrate, display, present, put on display, put on show, set out, show, unveil. ANTONYMS: keep secret, keep under wraps. **2** (*to show, to display*) betray, demonstrate, disclose, evince, expose, express, give away, indicate, make clear, manifest, reveal, show. ANTONYMS: conceal, cover up, hide, suppress.

exhibition *n.* **1** (*a public display of works of art, natural products etc.*) demonstration, display, exhibit, exposition, fair, presentation, show, spectacle. **2** (*the act of allowing to be seen, as temper*) betrayal, demonstration, display, exposure, expression, indication, manifestation, revelation, show. ANTONYMS: concealment, suppression.

exhilarate *v.t.* (*to enliven, to animate*) animate, brighten, cheer up, delight, elate, enliven, excite, gladden, invigorate, lift, pep up, (*coll.*) perk up, raise the spirits of, revitalize, stimulate. ANTONYMS: cast down, depress, dispirit.

exhilarating *a.* (*making one feel very happy and excited*) enlivening, exciting, invigorating, stimulating, thrilling. ANTONYMS: boring, dull.

exhilaration *n.* (*a feeling of great excitement and happiness*) animation, delight, elation, excitement, gaiety, gladness, happiness, high spirits, hilarity, joy, jubilation, liveliness, merriment, vivacity. ANTONYMS: dejection, gloom, low spirits, misery.

exhort *v.t.* (*to advise or encourage by argument*) admonish, advise, caution, counsel, encourage, enjoin, entreat, goad, incite, influence, persuade, press, prompt, push, stimulate, sway, urge, warn.

exhortation *n.* (*the act or practice of exhorting*) admonition, advice, caution, counsel, encouragement, entreaty, goading, incitement, lecture, persuasion, prompting, recommendation, sermon, urging, warning.

exhume *v.t.* (*to dig out, esp. a corpse from its grave*) dig up, disinter, unearth. ANTONYMS: bury, inter.

exigence *n.* **1** (*urgent need, necessity*) demand, necessity, need, requirement. **2** (*a state of affairs demanding immediate action, an emergency*) catastrophe, crisis, difficulty, dire straits, disaster, emergency, extremity, fix, jam, (*coll.*) pickle, plight, predicament, trouble.

exile *n.* **1** (*banishment, expatriation*) banishment, deportation, expatriation, expulsion. **2** (*a person who is banished, or has been long absent from their native country*) deportee, émigré, (*coll.*) expat, expatriate, outcast. ~*v.t.* (*to banish from one's native country, town etc.*) banish, cast out, deport, drive out, eject, expatriate, outcast, refugee.

exist *v.i.* **1** (*to be, to have actual being*) be living, have being, have existence, have life, live. **2** (*to continue to be*) abide, be extant, continue, endure, last, live, prevail, remain, survive. ANTONYMS: be extinct, die out. **3** (*to live or have being under specified conditions*) eke out a living, eke out an existence, live, stay alive, subsist, survive.

existence *n.* **1** (*the state of being or existing*) actuality, being, life, subsistence. ANTONYMS: death. **2** (*continuance of being*) continuance, endurance, subsistence, survival. ANTONYMS: death, dying out, end. **3** (*mode of existing*) lifestyle, way of living.

existent *a.* (*having being or existence, actual*) abiding, current, enduring, existing, extant, in existence, living, obtaining, present, prevailing, remaining, surviving. ANTONYMS: dead, died out, gone, past.

exit¹ *n.* **1** (*a passage or door, a way out*) egress, way out. ANTONYMS: entrance, way in. **2** (*a going out*) departure, exodus, farewell, going, leave-taking, leaving, retirement, retreat, withdrawal. ANTONYMS: arrival, coming, entrance. **3** (*departure, esp. from this life; death, decease*) death, decease, demise, passing away.

exit² *v.i.* (*to depart, to leave a place*) depart, go away, go out, leave, retire, retreat, say farewell, say goodbye, take one's leave, withdraw. ANTONYMS: arrive, come in, enter.

exodus *n.* (*a departure, esp. of a large group of people*) departure, escape, evacuation, exit, fleeing, flight, Hegira, leaving, mass exodus, migration, retreat, withdrawal. ANTONYMS: arrival, entrance.

exonerate *v.t.* **1** (*to free from a charge or blame, to exculpate*) absolve, acquit, clear, declare innocent, discharge, dismiss, exculpate, excuse, let off, pardon, vindicate. ANTONYMS: blame, censure, find guilty, punish. **2** (*to relieve from a duty or liability*) discharge, except, excuse, exempt, free, let off, liberate, release, relieve, set free. ANTONYMS: burden, impose.

exorbitant *a.* **1** (*grossly excessive, extravagant*) beyond the pale, excessive, extravagant, extreme, immoderate, inordinate, monstrous, (*coll.*) OTT, outrageous, over the top, preposterous, ridiculous, unacceptable, undue, unreasonable, unwarranted. ANTONYMS: moderate, reasonable. **2** ((*of prices*) unreasonably high) excessive, extortionate, extravagant, immoderate, inflated, outrageous, overdear, overexpensive, sky-high, (*coll.*) through the roof, unreasonable. ANTONYMS: (*coll.*) dirt-cheap, give-away, rock-bottom.

exorcize *v.t.* **1** (*to expel* (*as an evil spirit*) *by prayers and ceremonies*) cast out, drive out. **2** (*to free or purify from unclean spirits*) clear, free, purify, rid.

exotic *a.* **1** (*introduced from a foreign country*) alien, foreign, imported, non-native. ANTONYMS: native. **2** (*unusual and different in an exciting way*) astonishing, bizarre, colourful, curious, different, extraordinary, extravagant, fascinating, glamorous, impressive, mysterious, outlandish, remarkable, sensational, strange, striking, unfamiliar, unusual. ANTONYMS: dull, ordinary, run-of-the-mill.

expand *v.t.* **1** (*to open or spread out*) open out, spread out, unfurl, unroll. **2** (*to distend, to cause to increase in bulk*) augment, broaden, dilate, distend, enlarge, extend, fill out, increase, lengthen, magnify, stretch, swell, thicken, widen. ANTONYMS: contract, decrease, shorten. **3** (*to write out in full* (*what is condensed or abbreviated*)) amplify, develop, elaborate on, expatiate on, expound, flesh out, go into detail, pad out.
~*v.i.* (*to become more relaxed, to talk more openly*) become chatty, become communicative, become friendlier, become more sociable, become talkative, loosen up, lose one's reserve, relax, talk more. ANTONYMS: become taciturn, clam up, grow tense.

expanse *n.* **1** (*a wide, open extent or area*) opening out, spreading out, unfolding, unfurling, unravelling, unrolling. ANTONYMS: folding. **2** (*expansion or extension*) augmentation, broadening, distension, enlargement, extension, increase, lengthening, stretching, swelling, thickening, widening.

expansive *a.* **1** (*able or tending to expand*) distending, expandable, expanding, extendible, extending, stretching, stretchy. **2** (*extending widely, comprehensive*) all-embracing, broad, comprehensive, encyclopedic, extensive, far-reaching, global, thorough, universal, wide, wide-ranging, widespread. ANTONYMS: limited, narrow, restricted. **3** (*frank, effusive*) communicative, effusive, extrovert, frank, garrulous, loquacious, open, talkative, uninhibited, unreserved. ANTONYMS: reserved, taciturn.

expatiate *v.i.* (*to speak or write copiously* (*on a subject*)) amplify, develop, discourse on, dwell on, elaborate on, embellish, enlarge on, expand on, expound, go into details about.

expatriate *n.* (*a person living away from their own country*) deportee, emigrant, émigré, exile, (*coll.*) expat, refugee.
~*a.* (*living abroad*) banished, deported, emigrant, exiled, (*coll.*) expat, refugee.

expect *v.t.* **1** (*to regard as certain or likely to happen, to anticipate*) anticipate, assume, await, bank on, forecast, foresee, have in prospect, hope for, look for, look forward, predict, presume. **2** (*to require as due*) call for, demand, insist on, look for, require, seek. **3** (*to think, to suppose* (*that*)) assume, believe, calculate, conjecture, guess, imagine, presume, reckon, suppose, surmise, think.

expectancy *n.* **1** (*the act or state of expecting, expectation*) assumption, belief, calculation, conjecture, feeling, forecast, guess, prediction, presumption, reckoning, supposition, surmise, thoughts. **2** (*prospect of possessing, enjoying etc.*) likelihood, outlook, probability, promise, prospect. **3** (*a feeling that something good or exciting is going to happen*) anticipation, anxiety, curiosity, eagerness, expectation, hope, suspense, waiting.

expectant *a.* **1** (*expecting, waiting in expectation of something*) anticipating, anticipatory, anxious, eager, expecting, hopeful, in suspense, on tenterhooks, waiting, watchful. **2** (*pregnant*) enceinte, (*coll.*) expecting, (*sl.*) having a bun in the oven, (*sl.*) in the club, in the family way, pregnant.

expectation *n.* **1** (*the act or state of expecting, anticipation*) assumption, belief, calculation, conjecture, feeling, forecast, guess, prediction, presumption, reckoning, supposition, surmise, thought. **2** (*confident awaiting*) anticipation, expectancy, hope, looking forward, promise. **3** (*the probability of a future event*) chance, likelihood, outlook, possibility, probability, prospect. **4** (*something expected*) hope, prospect, speculation.

expecting *a.* (*pregnant*) enceinte, expectant, (*sl.*) having a bun in the oven, (*sl.*) in the club, in the family way, pregnant.

expedient *a.* (*advantageous, convenient*) advantageous, advisable, beneficial, convenient, desirable, effective, fit, gainful, helpful, judicious, opportune, politic, practical, pragmatic, profitable, suitable, useful. ANTONYMS: deleterious, detrimental, disadvantageous.
~*n.* (*an advantageous way or means*) agency, artifice, contrivance, device, machination, manoeuvre, means, measure, method, plan, plot, resort, resource, scheme, stratagem, trick, way.

expedite *v.t.* (*to facilitate, to assist the progress of*) accelerate, advance, aid, assist, ease, facilitate, further, hasten, help, hurry, precipitate, promote, quicken, rush, speed up, step up, urge on. ANTONYMS: decelerate, hold up, slow down.

expedition *n.* **1** (*any journey or voyage by an*

organized body for some definite object) excursion, exploration, jaunt, journey, mission, odyssey, outing, quest, safari, tour, travels, trek, trip, undertaking, voyage. **2** (the persons with their equipment engaged in this) band, company, crew, explorers, party, team, travellers, troop, voyagers. **3** (speed, promptness) alacrity, celerity, expeditiousness, fastness, haste, hurry, promptness, punctuality, quickness, rapidity, readiness, speed, swiftness, velocity. ANTONYMS: leisureliness, slowness, tardiness.

expeditious a. (speedy, active) brisk, fast, hasty, hurried, immediate, in a hurry, instant, prompt, punctual, quick, rapid, ready, speedy, summary, swift, swift-moving. ANTONYMS: delayed, slow, tardy.

expel v.t. **1** (to drive or force out) belch, discharge, drive out, eject, emit, excrete, force out, spew out. **2** (to eject, to banish) banish, cast out, deport, drive out, evict, exile, expatriate, kick out, oust, outlaw, proscribe, (coll.) send packing, show (someone) the door, (coll.) turf out. ANTONYMS: allow in, let in, welcome. **3** (to turn out formally (as from a school or society)) ban, bar, blackball, debar, dismiss, drum out, evict, exclude, (coll.) give the bum's rush, reject, throw out, (coll.) throw out on one's ear, (coll.) turf out. ANTONYMS: admit, let in, welcome.

expend v.t. **1** (to spend, to lay out) discourse, (coll.) dish out, (coll.) fork out, lavish, lay out, pay out, (coll.) shell out, spend. ANTONYMS: reserve, save. **2** (to consume, to use up) consume, deplete, drain, empty, exhaust, finish off, go through, sap, use, use up. ANTONYMS: conserve, store.

expendable a. (likely to be or intended to be wasted) dispensable, inessential, replaceable, unimportant, unnecessary, unneeded. ANTONYMS: crucial, essential, irreplaceable, vital.

expenditure n. **1** (the act of expending) disbursement, (coll.) dishing out, (coll.) forking out, outlay, paying out, (coll.) shelling out, spending. ANTONYMS: saving. **2** (the amount expended) charge, cost, expense, outgoings, outlay, payment. ANTONYMS: income, saving. **3** (the act of using energy, money etc.) consumption, depletion, draining, exhaustion, finishing off, using, using up. ANTONYMS: conservation.

expense n. **1** (a laying out or expending) disbursement, (coll.) dishing out, expending, (coll.) forking out, laying out, outlay, paying out, (coll.) shelling out, spending. **2** (cost, price paid) charge, cost, expenditure, outgoings, outlay, payment, price. **3** (outlay in

performance of a duty or commission) costs, expenditure, outgoings, outlay. **at the expense of 1** (at the cost of) at the cost of, with the loss of, with the sacrifice of. **2** (to the discredit or detriment of) to the detriment of, to the discomfort of, to the discredit of, to the embarrassment of, to the humiliation of.

expensive a. **1** (costly, requiring a large expenditure) costly, dear, exorbitant, extortionate, high-priced, overpriced, (coll.) steep. ANTONYMS: cheap, (coll.) dirt-cheap. **2** (extravagant, lavish) costly, extravagant, lavish, profligate, spendthrift.

experience n. **1** (practical acquaintance with any matter) acquaintance with, contact with, exposure to, familiarity with, involvement in, participation in. **2** (knowledge gained by observation or trial) expertise, hands-on training, (coll.) know-how, learning, practical knowledge, practice, savoir faire, training, wisdom. **3** (something undergone of an affecting or impressive nature) adventure, affair, case, circumstance, encounter, episode, event, happening, incident, occurrence, ordeal, trial. ~v.t. (to undergo, to feel) be familiar with, be involved in, encounter, endure, face, feel, go through, have experience of, have personal experience of, know, live through, meet, participate in, suffer, sustain, undergo.

experienced a. (practised, skilled) accomplished, adept, capable, competent, expert, knowledgeable, master, mature, practised, professional, proficient, qualified, seasoned, skilful, skilled, trained, veteran, well-versed. ANTONYMS: apprentice, inexperienced, unqualified, untrained.

experiment n. (an act or process designed to discover some unknown truth, or to test a fact) assay, carry out an experimentation, exploration, inquiry, investigation, pilot study, research, test, trial, trial and error, trial run, try-out. ~v.i. (to make an experiment or trial (on or with)) assay, carry out an investigation, carry out tests, conduct an experiment, conduct an inquiry, conduct research, explore, have a trial run, investigate, launch a pilot study, put to the test, test, (coll.) test-drive, trial.

experimental a. (derived from or founded upon experiment) empirical, exploratory, investigative, pilot, preliminary, research, speculative, test, trial, trial-and-error. ANTONYMS: final, finalized.

expert a. (experienced, dexterous from use and experience) able, accomplished, ace, adept, adroit, apt, capable, clever, competent, crack, deft, dexterous, excellent, experienced, knowledgeable, master, masterly, practised, professional, proficient, qualified, skilful, skilled, specialist, trained, well-versed. ANTONYMS: amateur, incapable, inexpert.

~n. (*a person who has special skill or knowledge*) ace, adept, authority, (*coll.*) buff, connoisseur, (*coll.*) dab hand, maestro, master, past master, (*coll.*) pro, pundit, specialist, virtuoso. ANTONYMS: amateur, dabbler.

expertise n. (*expert skill or knowledge*) ability, accomplishment, capability, cleverness, competence, dexterity, excellence, experience, (*coll.*) know-how, knowledge, mastery, professionalism, proficiency, qualification, skilfulness, skill, specialization. ANTONYMS: amateurism, clumsiness, inability, inexperience.

expiate v.t. (*to make reparation or amends for*) atone for, do penance for, make amends for, make redress for, make reparation for, make up for, pay for, redress.

expiration n. (*cessation, termination*) cessation, closure, conclusion, discontinuation.

expire v.i. **1** (*to come to an end*) be invalid, be void, cease, close, come to an end, conclude, discontinue, end, finish, lapse, run out, stop, terminate. ANTONYMS: begin, start. **2** (*to emit the last breath; to die*) breathe one's last, (*sl.*) croak, decease, die, (*sl.*) kick the bucket, pass away, pass on, (*sl.*) peg out, perish, (*sl.*) pop one's clogs. ANTONYMS: be born. **3** (*to breathe out*) breathe out, exhale.

explain v.t. **1** (*to make clear or intelligible*) clarify, decipher, define, demonstrate, describe, elaborate on, elucidate, expound, illuminate, illustrate, interpret, make clear, make plain, shed light on, spell out, throw light on. ANTONYMS: confuse, muddle, obscure. **2** (*to account for*) account for, excuse, give a justification for, give an apologia for, give an explanation for, give a reason for, justify, vindicate.

explanation n. **1** (*the sense or definition given by an interpreter or expounder*) clarification, deciphering, definition, description, elaboration, elucidation, explication, expounding, illumination, illustration, interpretation. ANTONYMS: confusion, muddle. **2** (*that which accounts for anything*) apologia, cause, excuse, justification, reason, vindication.

explanatory a. (*serving to explain*) defining, demonstrative, descriptive, elucidatory, explicative, illuminative, illustratory, interpretative. ANTONYMS: confusing, muddling.

expletive n. (*an interjection or word added for emphasis, esp. a swear word*) curse, ejaculation, exclamation, interjection, oath, obscenity, swear word.

explicable a. (*capable of being explained*) accountable, definable, explainable, intelligible, interpretable, justifiable, understandable. ANTONYMS: inexplicable.

explicate v.t. **1** (*to unfold the meaning of*) analyse, develop, evolve, explain, formulate, work out. **2** (*to make clear, explain the difficulties of* (*a text etc.*)) clarify, decipher, define, describe, elaborate on, elucidate, explain, illustrate, interpret, make clear, make plain, shed light on, spell out, throw light on. ANTONYMS: confuse, muddle, obscure.

explicit a. **1** (*plainly expressed, distinctly stated, as distinct from implicit*) categorical, certain, clear, crystal clear, definite, straightforward. ANTONYMS: implicit, indistinct, unambiguous, unclear, unequivocal. **2** ((*of a person*) *unreserved, outspoken*) candid, direct, forthright, frank, open, outspoken, plain-spoken, uninhibited, unreserved, unrestrained. ANTONYMS: indirect, restrained, vague.

explode v.t. (*to cause to burst with a loud noise*) burst, detonate, shatter.

~v.i. **1** (*to burst with a loud noise*) blow up, burst, detonate, erupt, go bang, go off, shatter. **2** (*to give vent suddenly to strong feelings, esp. anger*) (*coll.*) blow one's cool, (*coll.*) blow one's top, blow up, bluster, (*coll.*) flip one's lid, (*coll.*) fly off the handle, (*coll.*) hit the roof, rage, rant and rave. **3** (*to come to an end as if by bursting, to collapse*) belie, blow sky-high, blow up, debunk, discredit, disprove, give the lie to, invalidate, refute, repudiate. ANTONYMS: confirm, prove.

exploit[1] n. (*a feat, a great achievement*) accomplishment, achievement, adventure, attainment, deed, escapade, feat, stunt.

exploit[2] v.t. **1** (*to make use of, derive benefit from*) capitalize on, (*coll.*) cash in on, gain from, make capital out of, make use of, profit from, put to good use, put to use, take advantage, turn to account, use, use to advantage, utilize. **2** (*to utilize, esp. to make use of or take advantage of for one's own profit*) abuse, impose upon, make use of, take advantage of, take for a ride.

exploration n. **1** (*an inquiry into a subject*) analysis, consideration, examination, inquiry, inspection, investigation, probe, research, review, search, study, survey. **2** (*a journey through a place to find out what it is like*) discovery, investigation, journey of discovery, prospecting, survey, travelling, travels, voyage of discovery.

exploratory *a.* (*undertaken in order to find out more about something*) analytic, analytical, experimental, fact-finding, investigative, preliminary, probing, testing, trial.

explore *v.t.* **1** (*to search or inquire into*) analyse, consider, examine, inquire into, inspect, investigate, look into, probe, research into, review, scrutinize, search into, study, survey, take stock of. **2** (*to travel over* (*a country etc.*) *in order to examine or discover*) go on a journey of discovery, investigate, prospect, range over, recce, reconnoitre, survey, take a look at, tour, travel in, travel round, traverse.

explorer *n.* (*a traveller into unknown or little-known parts*) discoverer, prospector, scout, traveller.

explosion *n.* **1** (*a bursting or exploding with a loud noise*) bang, blast, boom, crack, crash, detonation, eruption, report, rumble. **2** (*a sudden and violent outbreak, as of physical forces, anger etc.*) eruption, fit, flare-up, outbreak, outburst, paroxysm. **3** (*a sudden and very rapid increase or expansion*) acceleration, burgeoning, dramatic rise, escalation, leap, mushrooming, rapid increase, rocketing, speeding-up. ANTONYMS: drop, plummeting, tumbling.

explosive *a.* **1** (*liable to explode or cause explosion*) eruptive, flammable, unstable, volatile. ANTONYMS: non-flammable, stable. **2** ((*of a situation*) *tense, potentially violent*) charged, critical, dangerous, delicate, hazardous, inflammable, perilous, sensitive, tense, ugly, unstable, volatile, volcanic.

exponent *n.* **1** (*a person who sets forth or explains*) demonstrator, elucidator, expounder, illustrator, interpreter. **2** (*a person who promotes a party, principle or cause*) advocate, backer, champion, defender, promoter, proponent, spokesman, spokesperson, spokeswoman, supporter, upholder. ANTONYMS: adversary, opponent. **3** (*a type, a representative*) example, exemplar, illustration, instance, model, pattern, representative, sample, specimen, standard, type. **4** (*a person who performs or interprets a play, dance etc.*) executant, interpreter, performer, player, practitioner, presenter.

export *v.t.* (*to carry or send* (*goods*) *to foreign countries*) dispatch abroad, market abroad, sell abroad, sell on the export market, send overseas.

expose *v.t.* **1** (*to lay bare or open*) display, exhibit, lay bare, make obvious, manifest, present, put on show, unveil. ANTONYMS: cover, hide. **2** (*to leave unprotected or vulnerable*) endanger, imperil, lay bare, leave unprotected,

make vulnerable, put at risk, put in jeopardy. ANTONYMS: protect. **3** (*to subject* (*to any influence or action*)) acquaint with, bring into contact with, familiarize with, introduce, lay open, make acquainted with, make conversant with, make familiar with, subject. ANTONYMS: keep away from. **4** (*to disclose, reveal*) bring to light, disclose, divulge, lay bare, let out, make known, reveal, uncover, unearth. ANTONYMS: conceal, hide, keep quiet, keep secret. **5** (*to unmask, reveal the identity of*) blow the gaff on, (*coll.*) blow the whistle on, denounce, smoke out, unmask, unveil. ANTONYMS: keep quiet about, protect, screen, shield.

exposé *n.* (*a disclosure, an exposure* (*of damning or sensational information*)) disclosure, divulgence, exposure, revelation, uncovering.

exposed *a.* **1** (*laid bare or open*) bare, displayed, exhibited, laid bare, on show, uncovered. ANTONYMS: covered, hidden. **2** (*left unprotected or vulnerable*) open, open to the elements, unprotected, unsheltered, unshielded. ANTONYMS: protected, sheltered. **3** (*vulnerable to* (*attack etc.*)) at risk of, in danger of, in jeopardy, in peril of, left open to, liable to, open to, subject to, vulnerable to. ANTONYMS: protected from, safe from.

exposition *n.* **1** (*an explanation or interpretation of the meaning of an author or a work, a commentary*) commentary, critique, discourse, dissertation, elucidation, exegesis, explanation, explication, interpretation, treatise. **2** (*a public exhibition*) demonstration, display, exhibition, fair, presentation, show.

expostulate *v.i.* (*to reason earnestly* (*with a person*), *to remonstrate*) argue (with), make a protest (to), raise an objection (with), reason (with), remonstrate (with). ANTONYMS: agree (with), placate.

exposure *n.* **1** (*the act of exposing*) endangering, laying bare, putting at risk, putting in jeopardy. **2** (*the state of being unsheltered from cold, heat, sun etc.*) extreme cold, extreme heat, hypothermia, lack of protection, lack of shelter. ANTONYMS: protection, shelter. **3** (*a display, esp. of goods for sale*) demonstration, display, exhibition, exposition, manifestation, presentation, publicity, show, uncovering. ANTONYMS: concealment. **4** (*a disclosure, revelation*) airing, betrayal, disclosure, divulgence, exposé, revelation, uncovering, unmasking. ANTONYMS: concealment, suppression. **5** (*the direction in which a building etc. faces*) aspect, location, outlook, position, setting, view.

expound *v.t.* (*to set out the meaning of in detail*) describe, elucidate, explain, explicate, illustrate, interpret, set forth, spell out, unfold.

express[1] *a.* **1** (*set forth or expressed distinctly*) categorical, certain, clear, clear-cut, definite, direct, distinct, exact, explicit, frank, outright, plain, pointed, precise, specific, unambiguous, unequivocal, unmistakable, well-defined. ANTONYMS: indefinite, indistinct, obscure, uncertain, unclear. **2** (*done, made for a special purpose*) especial, particular, sole, special, specific. ANTONYMS: general, universal. **3** (*travelling quickly*) expeditious, fast, high-speed, prompt, quick, (*coll.*) quickie, rapid, speedy, swift. ANTONYMS: leisurely, slow.

express[2] *v.t.* **1** (*to put into words or symbolize by gestures etc.*) articulate, assert, communicate, couch, declare, enunciate, give vent to, give voice to, phrase, point out, pronounce, put, put into words, say, speak, state, tell, utter, verbalize, voice, word. ANTONYMS: keep quiet, keep secret, suppress. **2** (*to cause to be clearly seen*) communicate, convey, demonstrate, denote, depict, evince, exhibit, illustrate, indicate, intimate, manifest, reveal, show. ANTONYMS: conceal, hide. **3** (*to squeeze or press out; to exude*) extract, force out, press out, squeeze.

expression *n.* **1** (*the act, or an instance, of expressing*) communication, conveyance, demonstration, depicting, evincing, exhibition, illustration, indication, intimation, manifestation, revelation, showing. ANTONYMS: suppression. **2** (*that which is expressed, an utterance*) announcement, articulation, assertion, declaration, enunciation, proclamation, pronouncement, saying, statement, utterance, verbalization, voicing. **3** (*a word, a phrase*) choice of words, idiom, language, phrase, phraseology, phrasing, remark, term, turn of phrase, word. **4** (*the aspect of the face as showing feeling, purpose etc.*) air, appearance, aspect, countenance, face, look, mien. **5** (*intonation of voice*) cadence, inflection, intonation, pitch, timbre, tone. **6** (*the mode of execution that expresses the spirit and feeling of a passage*) ardour, artistry, depth, emotion, feeling, force, intensity, passion, power, spirit, vividness. ANTONYMS: apathy, dispassion.

expressionless *a.* **1** (*not showing one's feelings or thoughts*) blank, deadpan, emotionless, inscrutable, poker-faced, vacuous. ANTONYMS: expressive, mobile. **2** (*without (strong) feeling*) apathetic, boring, dispassionate, dry, dull, emotionless, passionless, spiritless, unimpassioned, wooden. ANTONYMS: expressive, spirited.

expressive *a.* **1** (*serving to express*) demonstrative, indicative of, revealing, showing feeling, suggestive of. **2** (*significant*) meaningful, pointed, pregnant, significant, telling. ANTONYMS: meaningless. **3** (*vividly indicating any expression or emotion*) eloquent, emotional, evocative, graphic, intense, lively, moving, passionate, spirited, striking, sympathetic, vivid. ANTONYMS: apathetic, dull, wooden. **4** ((*of a face or expression*) *showing one's feelings*) animated, mobile. ANTONYMS: deadpan, emotionless.

expressly *adv.* **1** (*very clearly*) absolutely, categorically, clearly, decidedly, definitely, directly, distinctly, explicitly, plainly, positively, precisely, unambiguously, unequivocally. ANTONYMS: indirectly, indistinctly. **2** (*particularly; deliberately*) especially, particularly, purposely, solely, specially, specifically. ANTONYMS: generally.

expropriate *v.t.* ((*of the state*) *to take from an owner, esp. for public use*) appropriate, arrogate, commandeer, confiscate, grab, impound, requisition, seize, take, take away, take over, take possession of, usurp.

expulsion *n.* **1** (*the act, or an instance, of expelling*) banishment, debarment, discharge, dismissal, drumming out, ejection, eviction, exclusion, removal, (*coll.*) sacking. **2** (*ejection*) discharge, ejection, elimination, evacuation, excretion, voiding.

expunge *v.t.* (*to efface, to erase*) blot out, blue-pencil, cancel, cross out, delete, do away with, efface, eliminate, eradicate, erase, excise, get rid of, (*coll.*) get shot of, obliterate, remove, rub out, scratch out, strike out, wipe out. ANTONYMS: leave, stet.

expurgate *v.t.* (*to free from anything offensive or obscene* (*used esp. of books*)) blue-pencil, bowdlerize, censor, clean up, sanitize.

exquisite *a.* **1** (*fine, delicate*) choice, consummate, dainty, delicate, ethereal, fine, flawless, fragile, perfect, subtle. ANTONYMS: clumsy, coarse, flawed, imperfect. **2** (*delicately beautiful*) attractive, choice, dainty, delicate, delightful, elegant, fine, graceful, incomparable, lovely, pretty. ANTONYMS: ugly. **3** (*delicate or refined in perception, fastidious*) cultivated, discerning, discriminating, fastidious, knowing, refined, selective, sensitive. ANTONYMS: coarse, undiscerning, unrefined. **4** ((*of pain or pleasure*) *very strong*) acute, excruciating, intense, keen, piercing, poignant, sharp. ANTONYMS: blunted, deadened, dull.

extant *a.* ((*of a species, document etc.*) *still existing*) alive, (*coll.*) alive and kicking, existent, existing, in existence, living, remaining, subsisting, surviving. ANTONYMS: dead, extinct, gone.

extemporaneous *a.* (*made or done without*

preparation) ad-lib, extempore, impromptu, improvised, makeshift, off the cuff, on-the-spot, spontaneous, unplanned, unpremeditated, without preparation. ANTONYMS: prepared, rehearsed.

extempore *adv.* (*without premeditation or preparation*) extemporaneously, off the cuff, (*coll.*) off the top of one's head, spontaneously, without preparation.
~*a.* (*unstudied, delivered without preparation*) ad-lib, extemporaneous, extempory, impromptu, improvised, off the cuff, on-the-spot, spontaneous, unplanned, unprepared, unrehearsed, unstudied, without preparation. ANTONYMS: prepared, rehearsed.

extemporize *v.t.* (*to compose or produce without preparation*) ad-lib, improvise, make up.
~*v.i.* (*to speak without notes or previous study*) ad-lib, improvise, make it up as one goes along, play it by ear, think on one's feet, (*coll.*) wing it.

extend *v.t.* **1** (*to stretch out; to make larger in space, time or scope*) reach out, spread out, straighten out, stretch out, unfold, unfurl, unroll. ANTONYMS: fold, retract, roll up, withdraw. **2** (*to prolong (as a line, a period etc.*)) drag out, draw out, elongate, increase, lengthen, make longer, prolong, protract, spin out, stretch, stretch out. ANTONYMS: curtail, cut short, decrease, shorten. **3** (*to enlarge*) add to, amplify, augment, broaden, develop, elongate, enlarge, expand, increase, lengthen, stretch, stretch out, supplement, widen. ANTONYMS: decrease, lessen, shorten. **4** (*to hold out, offer*) advance, bestow, confer, give, give out, grant, hold out, impart, present, proffer, put forth, yield. ANTONYMS: withdraw.
~*v.i.* (*to stretch, to reach (in space, time or scope*)) carry on, go on, last, reach, run on, stretch.

extended *a.* **1** (*spread out*) spread out, straightened out, stretched out, unfolded, unfurled, unrolled. ANTONYMS: folded, retracted, rolled up. **2** (*made longer*) drawn-out, elongated, increased, lengthened, long, longer, prolonged, protracted, stretched. **3** (*enlarged*) broad, broadened, enlarged, expanded, extensive, far-reaching, increased, large-scale, wide, widened.

extension *n.* **1** (*the state of being extended; prolongation*) amplification, augmentation, broadening, development, elongation, enlargement, expansion, increase, lengthening, prolongation, protraction, stretching, supplementing, widening. **2** (*an increase of dimension, an addition*) addendum, addition, add-on, adjunct, annexe, appendage,

supplement. **3** (*an extra period of time allowed to complete some activity*) additional time, extra time, increased time, more time.

extensive *a.* **1** (*widely spread or extended, large*) capacious, generous, immense, large, large-scale, sizeable, spacious, spread-out, substantial, vast, wide. **2** (*comprehensive*) broad, catholic, comprehensive, far-reaching, great, large, substantial, thorough, universal, vast, wide, wide-ranging. ANTONYMS: limited, narrow, small.

extent *n.* **1** (*the space or degree to which anything is extended*) area, bounds, compass, expanse, length, range, reach, scope, space, stretch. **2** (*scope, degree*) amount, breadth, comprehensiveness, coverage, degree, distribution, duration, length, magnitude, measure, quantity, range, scope, size, volume, width.

extenuate *v.t.* (*to diminish the seriousness of, by showing mitigating circumstances*) decrease, diminish, justify, lessen, minimize, mitigate, moderate, palliate, play down, qualify, reduce, soften, temper, weaken. ANTONYMS: aggravate, increase, intensify.

extenuating *a.* (*reducing the seriousness of something*) justifying, mitigating, moderating, palliative, serving as an excuse.

exterior *a.* **1** (*external, outer*) external, outer, outermost, outside, outward, superficial, surface. ANTONYMS: inner, innermost, inside, internal. **2** (*coming from without, extrinsic*) alien, external, extraneous, extrinsic, foreign, outside. ANTONYMS: inside, interior.
~*n.* (*the outer surface*) coating, covering, facade, face, outer surface, outside, outward appearance, shell, surface. ANTONYMS: inside, interior.

exterminate *v.t.* (*to eradicate, to destroy utterly, esp. living creatures*) abolish, annihilate, (*coll.*) bump off, destroy, eliminate, eradicate, extirpate, get rid of, (*coll.*) get shot of, kill.

external *a.* **1** (*of or relating to the outside, superficial*) exterior, outer, outermost, outside, outward, superficial, surface, visible. ANTONYMS: inner, innermost, inside, internal. **2** (*extraneous, extrinsic*) alien, exterior, extraneous, extrinsic, foreign, outside. ANTONYMS: inherent, inside, internal, intrinsic.

extinct *a.* **1** ((*of a volcano) that has permanently ceased eruption*) extinguished, inactive. ANTONYMS: active. **2** (*worn out, ended*) antiquated, dead, defunct, ended, finished, gone, obsolete, outworn, terminated. ANTONYMS: alive, current, living. **3** (*come to an end, that has died out (as a family, species etc.*)) defunct, died out, gone, vanished, wiped out. ANTONYMS: existent, extant, living.

extinction *n.* (*extermination, annihilation*) annihilation, death, destruction, dying out, ending, extermination, extinguishing, finishing, obliteration, termination.

extinguish *v.t.* **1** (*to put out, to quench* (*as a light, hope etc.*)) douse, put out, quench, smother, snuff out, stifle. ANTONYMS: kindle, set alight. **2** (*to destroy, to annihilate*) annihilate, (*coll.*) bump off, destroy, eliminate, end, eradicate, erase, expunge, extirpate, get rid of, (*coll.*) get shot of, kill, remove, wipe out.

extirpate *v.t.* (*to root out, to destroy utterly*) annihilate, (*coll.*) bump off, destroy, eliminate, eradicate, erase, excise, expunge, get rid of, (*coll.*) get shot of, remove, uproot, wipe out.

extol *v.t.* (*to praise in the highest terms, to glorify*) acclaim, applaud, commend, compliment, congratulate, cry up, eulogize, exalt, glorify, laud, panegyrize, pay tribute to, praise, praise to the skies, sing the praises of, throw bouquets at. ANTONYMS: denigrate, disparage, vilify.

extort *v.t.* (*to wrest or wring* (*from*) *by force, threats etc.*) (*coll.*) bleed, bully, coerce, exact, extract, milk, obtain by blackmail, (*Austral., N Am., sl.*) put the bite on for, (*coll.*) put the screws on for, squeeze, wrest, wring.

extortion *n.* **1** (*oppressive or illegal exaction*) blackmail, (*coll.*) bleeding, coercion, exaction, force, milking, oppression, squeezing, wresting, wringing. **2** (*a gross overcharge*) daylight robbery, dearness, exorbitance, expensiveness, overcharging, overpricing. ANTONYMS: cheapness, undercharging.

extortionate *a.* **1** ((*of prices*) *exorbitant*) excessive, exorbitant, extravagant, immoderate, inflated, inordinate, outrageous, overdear, overexpensive, overpriced, preposterous, skyhigh, unreasonable. ANTONYMS: dirt-cheap, give-away, rock-bottom. **2** (*characterized by extortion; oppressive*) bloodsucking, exacting, grasping, rapacious, usurious.

extra *a.* **1** (*beyond what is absolutely necessary*) additional, excess, inessential, left over, redundant, reserve, spare, superfluous, supernumerary, supplementary, surplus, to spare, unnecessary, unused. ANTONYMS: just enough, needed, required, with nothing to spare. **2** (*supplementary, additional*) accessory, added, additional, ancillary, auxiliary, fresh, further, more, new, other, subsidiary, supplemental, supplementary. ANTONYMS: basic.

~*adv.* **1** (*over and above what is usual*) especially, extraordinarily, extremely, particularly, remarkably, uncommonly, unusually. **2** (*additionally*) additionally, as well, besides, into the bargain, on top, over and above, to boot.

~*n.* **1** (*something beyond what is absolutely necessary or usual*) add-on, supplement. ANTONYMS: basic price. **2** (*an addition*) accessory, addendum, addition, add-on, adjunct, appendage, appurtenance, attachment, supplement. ANTONYMS: essential.

extract[1] *v.t.* **1 a** (*to draw or pull out*) draw out, extirpate, pluck out, prize out, pull out, remove, root out, take out, tear out, uproot, withdraw, wrest out. ANTONYMS: insert, put in. **b** (*to draw out by mechanical or chemical means*) distil, draw out, express, press, separate, squeeze. **2** (*to select a part from, to quote* (*as a passage from a book etc.*)) abstract, choose, cite, copy, cut out, quote, reproduce, select. **3** (*to extort*) (*coll.*) bleed, bully, coerce, exact, extort, force, milk, obtain by blackmail, (*Austral., N Am., sl.*) put the bite on for, (*coll.*) put the screws on for, squeeze, wrest, wring. **4** (*to deduce* (*from*)) deduce, derive, develop, educe, elicit, evolve.

extract[2] *n.* **1** (*that which is extracted by distillation, solution etc.*) concentrate, decoction, distillate, essence, juice, solution. **2** (*a passage quoted from a book or writing*) abstract, citation, (*esp. N Am.*) clipping, cutting, excerpt, fragment, passage, quotation, quote, selection.

extraction *n.* **1** (*the act, or an instance, of extracting*) drawing out, extirpation, plucking out, prizing out, pulling out, removal, rooting out, taking out, tearing out, uprooting, withdrawal, wresting out. ANTONYMS: insertion. **2** (*descent, derivation*) ancestry, birth, blood, bloodline, derivation, descent, family, lineage, origin, parentage, pedigree, race, stock. **3** (*the act of drawing anything from a substance by chemical or mechanical process*) distillation, expressing, pressing, separation, squeezing.

extradite *v.t.* (*to secure the extradition of*) banish, deport, expel, outlaw.

extradition *n.* (*the surrender of fugitives from justice to the country where the crime was committed*) banishment, deportation, expulsion, outlawing.

extraneous *a.* **1** (*foreign, not belonging to a class, subject etc.*) beside the point, immaterial, inapposite, inappropriate, inapt, irrelevant, not germane, peripheral, unconnected, unrelated. ANTONYMS: germane, material, relevant. **2** (*not intrinsic, external*) alien, exterior, external, extrinsic, foreign, outside. ANTONYMS: inherent, internal, intrinsic. **3** (*not essential*) additional, extra, incidental, inessential, peripheral, redundant, superfluous, supplementary, unnecessary, unneeded. ANTONYMS: essential, necessary, needed.

extraordinary *a.* **1** (*beyond or out of the ordinary course, unusual*) amazing, astounding, bizarre, curious, fantastic, odd, orthodox, peculiar, remarkable, strange, surprising, unconventional, unusual, weird. ANTONYMS: common, ordinary, orthodox, usual. **2** (*of an uncommon degree or kind, remarkable*) exceptional, marvellous, outstanding, peculiar, phenomenal, rare, remarkable, signal, singular, special, striking, surprising, uncommon, unusual, wonderful. ANTONYMS: ordinary, run-of-the-mill, usual. **3** (*additional, extra*) additional, auxiliary, extra, other, subsidiary, supplementary.

extrapolate *v.t.* (*to infer, conjecture from what is known*) deduce, estimate, infer, reason, work out.

extravagance *n.* **1** (*the state or quality of being extravagant*) exaggeration, excess, excessiveness, immoderateness, immoderation, outrageousness, overkill, preposterousness, recklessness, wildness. ANTONYMS: carefulness, moderation, restraint. **2** (*excessive expenditure, prodigality*) excess, improvidence, imprudence, lavishness, overspending, prodigality, profligacy, recklessness, spending money like water, squandering, waste, wastefulness. ANTONYMS: carefulness, frugality, prudence, thrift.

extravagant *a.* **1** (*unrestrained by reason, immoderate*) exaggerated, excessive, immoderate, inordinate, irrational, (*coll.*) OTT, outrageous, over the top, preposterous, reckless, unrestrained, wild. ANTONYMS: moderate, restrained. **2** (*spending money unrestrainedly, wasteful*) improvident, imprudent, lavish, prodigal, profligate, prudent, reckless, spendthrift, thrifty. **3** ((*of prices etc.*) *exorbitant*) costly, dear, excessive, exorbitant, expensive, extortionate, high, overpriced, sky-high, steep, unreasonable. ANTONYMS: cheap, dirt-cheap, low, rock-bottom.

extravaganza *n.* (*a fantastic composition in drama, fiction or other literary form*) display, pageant, show, spectacle, spectacular.

extreme *a.* **1** (*of the highest degree, most intense*) acute, exceptional, extraordinary, great, greatest, high, highest, intense, maximum, severe, supreme, ultimate, utmost, uttermost. ANTONYMS: lowest, minimum. **2** (*beyond what is reasonable, immoderate*) exaggerated, excessive, extraordinary, fanatical, immoderate, inordinate, intemperate, (*coll.*) OTT, outrageous, over the top, unreasonable. ANTONYMS: low-key, moderate, reasonable, usual. **3** (*outermost, farthest*) endmost, farthest, most distant, outermost, remotest. ANTONYMS: innermost, nearest. **4** (*last, final*) final, last,

terminal, ultimate. **5** (*very strict or rigorous*) draconian, drastic, hard, hard as nails, harsh, immoderate, overzealous, radical, relentless, rigid, severe, stern, strict, stringent, unbending, uncompromising, unyielding. ANTONYMS: mild, moderate, soft.
~*n.* **1** (*the utmost or farthest point or limit*) border, boundary, edge, end, extremity, frontier, limit, margin, periphery, pole, verge. **2** (*the utmost or highest degree*) acme, apex, apogee, climax, culmination, height, limit, maximum, ne plus ultra, peak, pinnacle, summit, top, ultimate, zenith. ANTONYMS: bottom, depths, minimum, nadir. **in the extreme** (*in the highest degree*) exceedingly, exceptionally, excessively, extremely, greatly, inordinately, intensely, severely, supremely.

extremely *adv.* (*very, to a great degree*) acutely, (*coll.*) awfully, exceedingly, exceptionally, excessively, extraordinarily, greatly, highly, inordinately, intensely, in the extreme, markedly, severely, (*coll.*) terribly, ultra, uncommonly, unusually, utterly, very. ANTONYMS: moderately, ordinarily, slightly.

extremist *n.* (*a person holding extreme opinions and ready to undertake extreme actions*) diehard, fanatic, radical, zealot. ANTONYMS: moderate.

extremity *n.* **1** (*the utmost point or limit*) border, boundary, bounds, brink, edge, end, frontier, limit, margin, outer limit, periphery, verge. ANTONYMS: centre, middle. **2** (*the greatest degree*) acme, apex, apogee, climax, culmination, extreme, height, maximum, ne plus ultra, peak, pinnacle, summit, top, ultimate, zenith. ANTONYMS: bottom, depths, minimum, nadir. **3** (*a condition of the greatest difficulty or distress*) adversity, bad luck, crisis, danger, dire straits, disaster, distress, emergency, exigency, hardship, hard times, indigence, misfortune, trouble, worry. ANTONYMS: good fortune, happiness, prosperity. **4** (*pl.*) (*the hands and feet*) appendages, feet, fingers, hands, limbs, toes.

extricate *v.t.* (*to disentangle, to set free from any perplexity, difficulty or embarrassment*) deliver, detach, disengage, disentangle, extract, free, get out, liberate, release, remove, rescue, save, set free. ANTONYMS: engage, involve.

extrinsic *a.* **1** (*being outside or external*) exterior, external, outside, outward. **2** (*proceeding or operating from outside*) alien, exterior, external, foreign, outside. ANTONYMS: inherent, inner, internal. **3** (*not essential*) additional, extra, extraneous, incidental, needless, peripheral, redundant, superfluous, supplementary, unnecessary. ANTONYMS: essential, necessary, needed.

extrovert n. (*a lively, sociable person*) gregarious person, outgoing personality, social person. ANTONYMS: introvert.

extrude v.t. (*to thrust or push out or away*) eject, expel, force out, press out, push out, squeeze out, thrust out.
~v.i. (*to become pushed out*) extend, jut out, poke out, project, protrude, stick out.

exuberant a. 1 (*overflowing with vitality, spirits or imagination*) animated, bouncy, bubbly, buoyant, cheerful, ebullient, effervescent, elated, energetic, enthusiastic, excited, exhilarated, full of life, high-spirited, in high spirits, irrepressible, lively, (*sl.*) on a high, spirited, sprightly, vigorous, vivacious. ANTONYMS: apathetic, in low spirits, lifeless. 2 (*effusive*) ebullient, flamboyant, fulsome, lavish, (*coll.*) OTT, over the top, unreserved, unrestrained. ANTONYMS: reserved, restrained. 3 (*overflowing, copious*) abundant, copious, lavish, lush, luxuriant, profuse, rank, rich, superabundant, teeming, thriving. ANTONYMS: scanty, sparse.

exude v.t. 1 (*to emit or discharge through pores, as sweat or other liquid matter*) discharge, drip, emit, excrete, issue, leak, ooze, secrete, sweat. 2 (*to show freely (a feeling, mood etc.)*) display, exhibit, give out, issue, manifest, ooze, radiate, send out, show.
~v.i. (*to ooze or flow out slowly through pores etc.*) discharge, drip, emanate, filter, flow out, issue, leak, ooze, seep, well out. ANTONYMS: gush, pour.

exult v.i. 1 (*to rejoice greatly*) be beside oneself with joy, be delighted, be ecstatic, be elated, be in seventh heaven, be joyful, be jubilant, (*coll.*) be on cloud nine, be overjoyed, be over the moon, celebrate, jump for joy, rejoice. ANTONYMS: be despondent, be in the depths. 2 (*to triumph (over)*) crow (over), gloat (over), triumph (over).

exultant a. (*feeling or displaying exultation*) cock-a-hoop, delighted, ecstatic, elated, enraptured, gleeful, in seventh heaven, joyful, jubilant, (*coll.*) on cloud nine, overjoyed, over the moon, rejoicing, transported, triumphant. ANTONYMS: dejected, depressed, despondent.

eye[1] n. 1 (*sight, ocular perception*) eyesight, observation, sight, vision. 2 (*careful observation, attention*) attention, lookout, notice, observation, surveillance, view, vigilance, watch. ANTONYMS: inattention. 3 (*a mental perception, way of regarding*) appreciation, awareness, discernment, discrimination, judgement, perception, recognition, sensitivity, taste. ANTONYMS: insensitivity, lack of discrimination. 4 (*estimation, judgement (of conduct etc.)*) belief, judgement, mind, opinion, point of view, view, viewpoint. 5 (*a small opening or perforation*) aperture, eyelet, hole, opening. **an eye for an eye** (*strict retaliation*) reprisal, requital, retaliation, retribution, revenge, vengeance. ANTONYMS: forgiveness. **to have an eye for** (*to appreciate*) appreciate, hold in regard, prize, recognize, think highly of, treasure. **to keep an eye on** (*to watch carefully or narrowly*) keep tabs on, keep under surveillance, look after, monitor, observe, scrutinize, supervise, survey, watch, watch over. ANTONYMS: ignore, neglect. **to see eye to eye** (*to be in complete agreement (with)*) agree (with), be in accord (with), be in agreement (with), be in harmony (with), be in sympathy (with), be on the same wavelength (as), concur (with), harmonize (with). ANTONYMS: be at odds (with), disagree (with). **up to the eyes** (*deeply (engaged, in debt etc.)*) engrossed, fully occupied, inundated, overwhelmed, (*coll.*) up to here, (*coll.*) up to the ears, up to the elbows, wrapped up.

eye[2] v.t. (*to watch, to observe (suspiciously, jealously etc.)*) contemplate, gaze at, inspect, look at, observe, ogle, regard, scan, scrutinize, stare at, study, survey, (*coll.*) take a dekko at, take a look at, view, watch.

eye-catching a. (*striking*) arresting, attention-grabbing, attractive, captivating, showy, spectacular.

eyesight n. (*vision, the ability to see*) eye, range of vision, sight, vision.

eyesore n. (*anything offensive to the sight*) blemish, blot on the landscape, disfigurement, excrescence, horror, monstrosity, scar.

eyewitness n. (*a person who sees an event with their own eyes and is able to give evidence*) bystander, observer, onlooker, passer-by, spectator, watcher, witness.

F

fable *n.* **1** (*a story, esp. one in which animals are represented as endowed with speech in order to convey a moral lesson*) allegory, moral, parable, story, tale. **2** (*a legend, a myth*) fairy tale, legend, myth. ANTONYMS: history. **3** (*a fabrication, a falsehood*) fabrication, falsehood, fantasy, fib, fiction, figment, invention, lie, (*rhyming sl.*) porky, romance, story, tall story, untruth, (*sl.*) whopper, (*coll.*) yarn.

fabric *n.* **1** (*felted or knitted material*) cloth, material, stuff, textile, weave. **2** (*the basic structure of a building*) foundations, framework, structure. **3** (*the basic structure, a system of correlated parts*) configuration, constitution, construction, infrastructure, make-up, organization, structure, system, web.

fabricate *v.t.* **1** (*to build, to construct*) assemble, build, construct, erect, put up, raise, set up. ANTONYMS: dismantle. **2** (*to form by art or manufacture*) fashion, form, frame, make, manufacture, produce, shape. **3** (*to invent, to trump up*) coin, concoct, (*coll.*) cook up, counterfeit, create, design, devise, fake, falsify, feign, forge, formulate, hatch, imagine, invent, make up, manufacture, originate, think up, trump up.

fabrication *n.* **1** (*forgery, a falsehood*) concoction, fable, fairy tale, fake, falsehood, fib, fiction, figment, forgery, invention, lie, (*rhyming sl.*) porky, prevarication, tale, untruth, yarn. ANTONYMS: truth. **2** (*manufacture, construction*) assemblage, assembly, building, construction, contrivance, erection, fashioning, formation, formulation, framing, making, manufacture, origination, production.

fabulous *a.* **1** (*wonderful, very good*) amazing, astonishing, astounding, brilliant, (*coll.*) fantastic, (*coll.*) magic, marvellous, (*coll.*) sensational, spectacular, superb, (*coll.*) terrific, very good, wonderful. ANTONYMS: commonplace. **2** (*beyond belief, incredible*) inconceivable, incredible, unbelievable. ANTONYMS: credible. **3** (*exaggerated, absurd*) absurd, exaggerated, ridiculous. **4** (*feigned, fictitious*) apocryphal, fantastic, feigned, fictitious, imaginary, invented, made-up, unreal. ANTONYMS: actual. **5** (*related or described in fables; unhistorical*) fabled, legendary, mythical, unhistorical.

facade *n.* **1** (*the front of a building*) face, front, frontage. **2** (*an outward appearance, esp. one put on for show or to deceive*) appearance, disguise, exterior, front, guise, illusion, mask, pretence, semblance, show, veneer.

face *n.* **1** (*the front part of the head, from the chin to the top of the forehead*) (*sl.*) clock, countenance, (*sl.*) dial, features, (*sl.*) kisser, lineaments, (*sl.*) mug, (*coll.*) phiz, physiognomy, (*sl.*) puss, visage. **2** (*a grimace*) frown, grimace, moue, pout, scowl. **3** (*that part of anything which presents itself to the view*) exterior, facade, facet, front, mask, surface, veneer. **4** (*the outward visible state of things*) air, appearance, aspect, look, semblance, show. **5** (*dignity, reputation*) authority, dignity, honour, image, name, prestige, reputation, repute, standing, status. **6** (*composure, coolness*) assurance, composure, confidence, coolness. **7** (*impudence, effrontery*) audacity, boldness, brashness, brass, cheek, effrontery, gall, impudence, (*coll.*) neck, nerve, presumption, (*coll.*) sauce. ANTONYMS: timidity.
~*v.t.* **1** (*to meet in front*) encounter, experience, meet. **2** (*to confront boldly*) beard, brave, confront, defy, oppose, resist, stand up to. **3** (*to acknowledge without evasion*) accept, acknowledge, admit, come to terms with, cope with, deal with, face up to, grasp the nettle, tackle. ANTONYMS: avoid. **4** (*to put a coating or covering on*) clad, coat, cover, dress, encrust, finish, level, line, overlay, sheathe, surface, veneer. ANTONYMS: strip.
~*v.i.* (*to be situated with a certain aspect*) front onto, look onto, overlook.

facetious *a.* **1** (*given to or characterized by levity; flippant*) flippant, frivolous, jesting, jocose, jocular, joking, playful, tongue-in-cheek, waggish, witty. ANTONYMS: earnest. **2** (*intended to be amusing*) amusing, comical, droll, funny, humorous. ANTONYMS: serious.

facile *a.* **1** (*easily done; easily surmountable*) easy, effortless, simple, uncomplicated. **2 a** (*ready, fluent*) adept, adroit, dexterous, fluent, proficient, quick, ready, skilful, smooth. **b** (*glib, superficial*) cursory, glib, hasty, light, shallow, slick, superficial. ANTONYMS: careful, deep. **3** (*easy-tempered, gentle*) affable, complaisant, docile, easygoing, gentle, mild, yielding. ANTONYMS: hostile, stubborn.

facilitate *v.t.* **1** (*to make easy or less difficult*) ease, simplify. ANTONYMS: complicate. **2** (*to further, to help forward*) advance, aid, assist, expedite, forward, further, help, promote, speed up. ANTONYMS: hinder, impede.

facility *n.* **1** (*easiness in performing or in being performed*) easiness, effortlessness, simplicity. ANTONYMS: difficulty. **2** (*ease, fluency* (*of speech etc.*)) ease, efficiency, fluency, readiness, smoothness. **3** (*quickness, dexterity*) ability, adroitness, alacrity, aptitude, craft, dexterity, expertise, gift, knack, mastery, proficiency, quickness, skilfulness, skill, talent. ANTONYMS: awkwardness, incompetence. **4** (*means or equipment provided to facilitate any activity*) advantage, aid, amenity, appliance, convenience, equipment, means, opportunity, resource. **5** (*a lavatory*) convenience, lavatory, (*coll.*) powder room, toilet.

facsimile *n.* (*an exact copy of printing, a picture etc.*) carbon, copy, duplicate, photocopy, print, replica, reproduction, transcript. ANTONYMS: original.

fact *n.* **1** (*something that has really occurred or is known to be true*) act, deed, episode, event, experience, happening, incident, occurrence, truth. **2** (*a piece of information that can be discovered*) circumstance, data, detail, element, factor, feature, information, item, (*coll.*) lowdown, particular, point, specific. **3** (*reality, the concrete basis of experience*) actuality, certainty, reality, truth. ANTONYMS: fiction.

faction *n.* **1** (*a body of persons combined or acting in union*) band, bloc, cabal, cadre, camp, caucus, circle, clique, confederacy, contingent, coterie, division, gang, junta, lobby, minority, party, ring, set, splinter group, wing. **2** (*partisanship, dissension*) conflict, contention, controversy, disagreement, discord, disharmony, dissension, disunity, division, divisiveness, friction, infighting, partisanship, rebellion, sedition, strife, tumult, turbulence, upheaval. ANTONYMS: harmony, unanimity.

factious *a.* (*given to faction or party; seditious*) argumentative, conflicting, contentious, disagreeing, discordant, disputatious, disruptive, dissident, divisive, insurrectionary, malcontent, mutinous, partisan, quarrelsome, rebellious, refractory, sectarian, seditious, turbulent, warring.

factor *n.* **1** (*any circumstance or influence which contributes to a result*) aspect, cause, circumstance, determinant, fact, influence. **2** (*each of the quantities that multiplied together make up a given number or expression*) component, constituent, detail, element, facet, ingredient, item, part, piece, point. **3** (*an agent, a deputy*) agent, deputy, go-between, intermediary, middleman, proxy, representative. **4** (*a steward or agent of an estate*) agent, estate manager, steward.

factory *n.* (*a building in which any manufacture is carried out*) foundry, mill, plant, shop, works, workshop.

factual *a.* (*concerned with or containing facts; actual*) accurate, actual, authentic, bona fide, correct, exact, faithful, genuine, literal, objective, precise, real, straightforward, true, unadorned, unbiased, undistorted, unvarnished, valid, veritable. ANTONYMS: false, fanciful.

faculty *n.* **1** (*a natural power of the mind; a capacity for any natural action, such as seeing, speaking*) capacity, reason, sense, will. **2** (*power or ability of any special kind*) ability, adroitness, aptitude, bent, capability, cleverness, dexterity, facility, flair, gift, knack, power, proficiency, propensity, readiness, skill, talent. ANTONYMS: inability, shortcoming. **3** (*the members collectively of any of the learned professions*) department, profession, school. **4** (*any one of the departments of instruction in a university*) department, discipline, profession, school, staff. **5** (*an authorization or licence to perform certain functions, esp. ecclesiastical*) authorization, dispensation, liberty, licence, permission, prerogative, privilege, right, sanction.

fad *n.* (*a passing fancy or fashion*) affectation, craze, fancy, fashion, mania, mode, rage, taste, trend, vogue, whim.

fade *v.i.* **1** (*to grow pale or indistinct*) blanch, bleach, blench, dim, discolour, dull, lighten, lose colour, pale, wash out, whiten. ANTONYMS: darken. **2** (*to lose freshness or vigour*) droop, flag, languish, perish, sag, shrivel, wilt, wither. **3** (*to disappear gradually*) die away, die out, diminish, disperse, dissolve, dwindle, ebb, evanesce, fall, melt away, peter out, vanish, wane, waste away. ANTONYMS: grow. **4** ((*of a person*) *to grow weaker*) decline, fail, weaken. **5** ((*of electronic signals*) *to decrease in strength or volume*) decrease, diminish, dwindle, weaken. ANTONYMS: increase.

fag *n.* **1** (*a cigarette*) (*coll.*) cig, cigarette, (*sl.*) smoke. **2** (*a boring, tiresome or unwelcome task*) (*coll.*) bind, bore, bother, chore, (*coll.*) drag, inconvenience, irritation, nuisance, pain, (*coll.*) pain in the neck. **3** (*a junior at a public school who has to perform certain duties for a senior boy*) drudge, flunkey, lackey, menial, servant, underling.
~*v.i.* (*to work till one is weary*) labour, toil, work.
~*v.t.* (*to weary* (*often with out*)) exhaust, fatigue, prostrate, tire, wear out, weary. ANTONYMS: refresh.

fail *v.i.* **1** (*not to succeed* (*in*)) fall, fall through, falter, (*coll.*) flop, founder, go wrong, miscarry, misfire. **2** (*not to succeed in the attainment* (*of*)) come to grief, come to nothing, fizzle out, miss. ANTONYMS: succeed. **3** (*not to pass an examination*) (*chiefly N Am., coll.*) flunk, not pass. ANTONYMS: pass, succeed. **4** (*to come short of the due amount or measure*) decline, diminish, dwindle, fall short, run out, run short. **5** (*to lose strength or spirit*) break down, collapse, crumble, decay, decline, flag, gutter, languish, peter out, wane. **6** (*to become bankrupt or insolvent*) close down, crash, fold, go bankrupt, (*coll.*) go broke, go bust, go to the wall, go under, smash. ANTONYMS: flourish, prosper.
~*v.t.* **1** (*to disappoint, to desert*) abandon, deceive, desert, disappoint, forsake, let down. **2** (*to neglect or omit* (*to do something*)) forget, neglect, omit.

failing *n.* **1** (*a deficiency, shortcoming*) deficiency, drawback, shortcoming. **2** (*an imperfection, a weakness*) blemish, defect, fault, flaw, foible, imperfection, lapse, weakness. ANTONYMS: strength.

failure *n.* **1** (*lack of success*) abortion, breakdown, collapse, defeat, disaster, downfall, fiasco, (*coll.*) flop, frustration, miscarriage, overthrow, (*coll.*) wash-out. ANTONYMS: success. **2** (*an unsuccessful person or thing*) (*coll.*) also-ran, damp squib, (*coll.*) dead duck, disappointment, (*sl.*) dud, incompetent, (*sl.*) lemon, loser, no-hoper, non-starter. **3** (*an omission, non-occurrence*) default, deficiency, dereliction, neglect, negligence, non-observance, non-occurrence, non-performance, omission, shortcoming. **4** (*decay, breaking down*) breakdown, decay, decline, deterioration, failing, loss. **5** (*insolvency, bankruptcy*) bankruptcy, collapse, crash, folding, insolvency, ruin.

faint *a.* **1** ((*of sound or brightness*) *dim, indistinct*) bleached, blurred, delicate, dim, dull, faded, faltering, feeble, hazy, ill-defined, indistinct, low, muffled, muted, pale, slight, soft, subdued, thin, vague. ANTONYMS: bright, strong. **2** (*weak, frail*) drooping, enervated, exhausted, feeble, languid, lethargic, weak, weary. ANTONYMS: energetic, vigorous. **3** (*giddy, inclined to faint*) dizzy, giddy, lightheaded, muzzy, vertiginous, (*coll.*) woozy. **4** (*slight, remote*) distant, imperceptible, little, remote, slight. **5** (*timid, fearful*) fearful, lilylivered, timid, timorous.
~*v.i.* (*to lose consciousness because of hunger, shock etc.*) black out, collapse, (*coll.*) keel over, pass out, swoon.
~*n.* (*a fainting fit*) blackout, collapse, swoon, unconsciousness.

faint-hearted *a.* (*cowardly, spiritless*) afraid, (*coll.*) chicken, cowardly, diffident, frightened, half-hearted, irresolute, reluctant, shy, spineless, spiritless, timid, timorous, unenthusiastic, (*coll.*) yellow. ANTONYMS: bold, brave.

fair[1] *a.* **1** (*just, reasonable*) dispassionate, equitable, even-handed, impartial, just, lawful, legitimate, objective, proper, reasonable, right, square, unbiased. ANTONYMS: biased, unfair. **2** (*light in colour or complexion; blond*) blond, blonde, flaxen, light, pale. ANTONYMS: dark. **3** (*passably good, of moderate quality*) adequate, all right, average, mediocre, middling, moderate, not bad, (*coll.*) OK, (*coll.*) okay, passable, reasonable, satisfactory, (*coll.*) so-so, tolerable. ANTONYMS: excellent, good. **4** (*attractive, pleasing to the eye*) attractive, beautiful, bonny, comely, good-looking, handsome, lovely, pleasing, pretty. ANTONYMS: ugly. **5** (*clear, pure*) clean, clear, pure. **6** (*not effected by unlawful or underhand means*) above-board, honest, honourable, trustworthy. **7** (*free from spot or blemish*) immaculate, serene, spotless, unblemished. **8** ((*of the weather*) *fine and sunny*) bright, clear, clement, cloudless, dry, favourable, fine, pleasant, sunny. ANTONYMS: stormy, unsettled. **9** (*favourable, promising*) auspicious, favourable, promising. **10** (*obliging, polite*) civil, courteous, obliging, polite, respectful, well-mannered. **11** (*legible, plain*) clear, distinct, intelligible, legible, plain, readable.

fair[2] *n.* **1** (*a funfair*) carnival, festival, fête, funfair, gala. **2** (*a market or gathering for trade in a particular town or place*) bazaar, market, mart. **3** (*a trade show*) exhibition, expo, exposition, trade show.

fairly *adv.* **1** (*in a fair or just manner*) deservedly, equitably, honestly, impartially, justly, objectively, properly. **2** (*moderately, passably*) adequately, (*coll.*) kind of, moderately, passably, pretty well, quite, rather, reasonably, somewhat, sort of, sufficiently, tolerably. **3** (*completely, absolutely*) absolutely, actually, completely, positively, really, totally, utterly, veritably.

fairy *n.* (*an imagined small supernatural being having magical powers*) brownie, elf, fay, goblin, imp, leprechaun, pixie, Robin Goodfellow, sprite.

fairy story *n.* **1** (*a tale about fairies*) folk tale, romance. **2** (*a fanciful or highly improbable story*) cock and bull story, fabrication, fantasy, fiction, invention, lie, (*rhyming sl.*) porky, tall story, untruth.

faith *n.* **1** (*firm and earnest belief, complete confidence*) assurance, belief, confidence, conviction, credence, dependence, reliance, trust. ANTONYMS: disbelief, doubt. **2** (*a system of religious belief*) church, communion, creed, denomination, doctrine, dogma, persuasion, religion, sect. **3** (*commitment to keep a promise etc., loyalty*) allegiance, constancy, faithfulness, fealty, fidelity, loyalty, steadfastness, truth, truthfulness. ANTONYMS: disloyalty, unfaithfulness. **4** (*a promise or engagement*) engagement, honour, pledge, promise, sincerity, vow, word. **5** (*reliability*) credibility, reliability, trustworthiness. **6** (*a philosophical or political creed or system of doctrines*) creed, doctrine, dogma, persuasion.

faithful *a.* **1** (*loyal to one's promises or engagements*) conscientious, constant, dedicated, dependable, devoted, dutiful, loyal, reliable, staunch, steadfast, unswerving, unwavering. ANTONYMS: disloyal, unfaithful. **2** (*upright, honest*) honest, righteous, scrupulous, true, upright, virtuous. **3** (*truthful, worthy of belief*) trusted, trustworthy, trusty, truthful. ANTONYMS: untruthful. **4** (*exact, accurate*) accurate, close, correct, exact, factual, just, literal, precise, strict, true. ANTONYMS: inaccurate.

faithless *a.* **1** (*lacking faith, unbelieving*) agnostic, atheistic, disbelieving, doubting, sceptical, unbelieving. **2** (*disloyal, not true to promises or duty*) dishonest, disloyal, false, fickle, inconstant, shifty, unfaithful, unreliable, untrue, untruthful. ANTONYMS: faithful. **3** (*treacherous*) crooked, hypocritical, insincere, perfidious, traitorous, treacherous, unscrupulous, untrustworthy.

fake *v.t.* **1** (*to pretend, to simulate*) affect, assume, copy, counterfeit, dissemble, falsify, feign, pretend, put on, sham, simulate. **2** (*to cover up defects and faults so as to give a more valuable appearance to, to contrive*) contrive, cover up, doctor, do up, fabricate, forge, make up. **3** (*to cheat*) cheat, deceive, defraud.
~*n.* **1** (*a thing, e.g. a manufactured antique, made to deceive*) copy, counterfeit, falsification, forgery, fraud, hoax, imitation, impostor, reproduction, sham. **2** (*a swindle*) cheat, dodge, swindle.
~*a.* (*sham, counterfeit*) bogus, counterfeit, ersatz, false, forged, fraudulent, imitation, (*coll.*) phoney, pseudo, sham, spurious, synthetic. ANTONYMS: authentic, genuine.

fall *v.i.* **1** (*to descend from a higher to a lower place or position by the force of gravity*) descend, go down. ANTONYMS: ascend, climb. **2** (*to descend suddenly, to drop*) dive, drop, nosedive, pitch, plummet, plunge. **3** (*to sink, to become lower in level of surface*) cascade, flow down, incline, lower, settle, sink, slide, slope. **4** (*to hang down*) droop, hang down. **5** (*to become prostrate*) (*coll.*) keel over, stumble,

topple, trip, tumble. **6** (*to be killed* (*esp. in battle*)) die, meet one's end, perish. ANTONYMS: survive. **7** (*to be overthrown, to lose power*) falter, lose power, slip. **8** (*to be taken by the enemy*) capitulate, give in, give way, resign, submit, succumb, surrender, yield. ANTONYMS: endure, hold out. **9** (*to decrease in amount, value etc.*) decrease, depreciate, diminish, fall off, lessen, reduce. ANTONYMS: escalate, increase. **10** (*to subside, to die away*) abate, die away, dwindle, ebb, flag, languish, slump, subside. **11** (*to sink into sin, to give way to temptation*) err, go astray, lapse, sin, transgress. **12** (*to turn out, to result*) become, befall, come about, come to pass, fall out, happen, occur, result, take place, turn out.
~*v.t.* (*to cut down, to fell*) cut down, drop, fell, let fall.
~*n.* **1** (*the act of falling*) descent, dive, drop, nosedive, plummet, plunge, slip, spill, tumble. **2** (*a decrease in amount, value etc.*) abatement, cut, decline, decrease, deterioration, diminution, dip, drop, dwindling, falling, lessening, lowering, reduction, slump. **3** (*a downward slope*) declivity, incline, slant, slope. **4** (*the distance through which anything falls*) descent, drop, gap. **5** (*a waterfall*) cascade, cataract, waterfall. **6** (*downfall from greatness or prosperity, ruin*) collapse, defeat, degradation, disgrace, downfall, failure, ruin. **7** (*death, overthrow*) death, destruction, overthrow, seizure. **8** (*the surrender or capture of a town*) capitulation, resignation, submission, surrender. **9** (*the act of cutting down*) cutting down, felling. **10** (*a yielding to temptation*) lapse, sin, transgression, trespass. **to fall apart** (*to collapse, to go to pieces*) break up, collapse, come apart, crumble, disintegrate, dissolve, fall to pieces, fragment, shatter. **to fall back** (*to recede, to give way*) draw back, give way, recede, recoil, retire, retreat, withdraw. **to fall behind** (*to be passed by, to lag behind*) drop back, get left behind, lag, trail. **to fall in** (*to give way inwards*) cave in, collapse, sink. **to fall on/upon 1** ((*of the eyes, glance etc.*) *to be directed towards*) alight on, be directed towards. **2** (*to attack*) assail, attack, belabour, descend on, lay into, pitch into, set upon, tear into. **3** (*to meet or discover by chance*) chance on, come across, happen on. **to fall out 1** (*to happen, to turn out*) chance, come to pass, happen, occur, pan out, result, take place, turn out. **2** (*to quarrel*) altercate, argue, clash, differ, disagree, dispute, fight, quarrel, squabble, wrangle. **to fall short 1** (*to be deficient*) be deficient, lack, want. **2** (*to drop before reaching the mark or target*) disappoint, drop short, fail, miss, prove inadequate. **to fall through** (*to fail, to come to nothing*) come to nothing, die, fail, fizzle out, (*coll.*) flop, miscarry.

fallacious *a.* (*based on unsound reasoning or incorrect information*) deceptive, delusive, delusory, erroneous, false, fictitious, illogical, illusory, incorrect, invalid, misleading, mistaken, sophistic, spurious, unsound, untrue, wrong. ANTONYMS: true.

fallacy *n.* 1 (*a prevalent but mistaken belief*) misapprehension, misconception, misjudgement, mistake. 2 (*an error, a sophism*) casuistry, deception, delusion, error, falsehood, fiction, illusion, sophism, untruth. ANTONYMS: truth.

fallible *a.* (*liable to make mistakes*) erring, frail, human, imperfect, mortal, uncertain, unreliable, weak. ANTONYMS: infallible, unerring.

fallow *a.* 1 ((*of land*) *ploughed and tilled but not sown*) uncultivated, unplanted, unsown. ANTONYMS: cultivated. 2 (*unused, neglected*) dormant, idle, inactive, inert, neglected, resting, undeveloped, unused.

false *a.* 1 (*not conformable to fact; incorrect*) concocted, deceptive, erroneous, fallacious, faulty, fictitious, flawed, improper, inaccurate, incorrect, invalid, misleading, mistaken, unfounded, unreliable, unsound, untrue, untruthful, wrong. ANTONYMS: correct, right, true. 2 (*deceiving; faithless*) deceitful, deceiving, delusive, dishonest, dishonourable, disloyal, double-dealing, duplicitous, faithless, fraudulent, hypocritical, lying, mendacious, perfidious, treacherous, two-faced, unfaithful, untrustworthy. ANTONYMS: faithful, honest. 3 (*feigned, counterfeit*) bogus, counterfeit, ersatz, fake, feigned, forged, imitation, mock, sham, spurious. ANTONYMS: authentic, genuine. 4 (*forced, unconvincing*) affected, false, unconvincing. 5 (*artificial, man-made*) artificial, fabricated, fake, man-made, simulated, synthetic, unreal.

falsehood *n.* 1 (*lying, lies*) falseness, lies, lying, mendacity, perjury, untruthfulness. ANTONYMS: truth. 2 (*a lie, an untruth*) distortion, fabrication, falsity, fib, fiction, lie, misstatement, (*rhyming sl.*) porky, prevarication, story, untruth. 3 (*deceitfulness, unfaithfulness*) deceit, deceitfulness, deception, dishonesty, unfaithfulness.

falsify *v.t.* 1 (*to make false*) alter, distort, fiddle. 2 (*to give a false or spurious appearance to* (*a document, statement etc.*)) doctor, fudge, (*N Am.*) put a spin on. 3 (*to misrepresent*) adulterate, belie, (*coll.*) cook, garble, massage, misrepresent, misstate, pervert, tamper with, twist. 4 (*to counterfeit, to forge*) counterfeit, fake, forge. 5 (*to disappoint* (*expectations*), *to disprove*) confute, disappoint, disprove, fall short of.

falter *v.i.* 1 (*to stumble, to be unsteady*) dodder, shake, stumble, totter, tremble, waver. 2 (*to stammer, to stutter*) halt, stammer, stutter. 3 (*to hesitate in action*) hesitate, vacillate. ANTONYMS: persevere, persist. 4 (*to tremble, to flinch*) flinch, quail, shake, tremble. ANTONYMS: stand firm.

fame *n.* 1 (*the state of being well-known, celebrity*) celebrity, renown, stardom. ANTONYMS: oblivion. 2 (*reputation, esp. good reputation*) acclaim, credit, eminence, esteem, glory, honour, illustriousness, name, prominence, reputation, repute, status. ANTONYMS: disgrace, disrepute.

famed *a.* (*much talked of; renowned*) acclaimed, celebrated, recognized, renowned, talked-of, widely-known.

familiar *a.* 1 (*of one's own acquaintance, well-known*) amicable, close, confidential, cordial, friendly, intimate, well-known. ANTONYMS: aloof, unfriendly. 2 (*knowing a thing well; intimate* (*with*)) acquainted (with), au fait (with), cognizant (of), conversant (with), intimate (with), well-versed (in). ANTONYMS: unacquainted (with). 3 (*easily understood, not obscure*) clear, recognizable, understandable. 4 (*usual, ordinary*) accustomed, common, conventional, customary, domestic, everyday, frequent, habitual, household, mundane, ordinary, routine, stock, usual. ANTONYMS: novel, unfamiliar. 5 (*too informal; presumptuous*) bold, cheeky, disrespectful, forward, impudent, insolent, intrusive, presuming, presumptuous. 6 (*unconstrained, free*) affable, casual, easy, free, friendly, informal, open, relaxed, sociable, unceremonious, unconstrained. ANTONYMS: formal, reserved.

familiarity *n.* 1 (*the state of being familiar*) acquaintance, awareness, cognizance, comprehension, conversance, experience, grasp, knowledge, understanding. ANTONYMS: ignorance, unfamiliarity. 2 (*close friendship, intimacy*) closeness, ease, fellowship, friendliness, friendship, intimacy, neighbourliness. 3 (*presumptuous behaviour*) boldness, disrespect, forwardness, impertinence, impropriety, impudence, insolence, liberty, presumption. ANTONYMS: constraint, respect.

familiarize *v.t.* (*to make well acquainted* (*with*), *to accustom* (*to*)) accustom (to), acquaint (with), break in, coach (in), educate (in), enlighten (in), habituate (to), inform (about), initiate (in), instruct (in), inure (to), prime (in), school (in), season (in), teach, train (in), tutor (in).

family *n.* 1 (*a group of people related to one another, esp. parents and their children*) household, kin, kinsfolk, ménage, nearest and dearest, next of kin, relations, relatives. **2** (*children, as distinguished from their parents*) brood, children, descendants, issue, (*coll.*) kids, offspring, progeny. **3** (*those people who can trace their descent from a common ancestor; lineage*) blood, descendants, extraction, house, kindred, line, lineage, stock. **4** (*a group of peoples from a common stock*) blood, people, race, stock, strain. **5** (*a group of persons or peoples united by bonds of civilization, religion etc.*) clan, group, tribe. **6** (*a group of related things or beings having common characteristics*) class, genre, genus, group, kind, species, subdivision, system, type. **7** (*honourable descent*) ancestry, descent, dynasty, forebears, forefathers, genealogy, lineage, nobility, parentage, pedigree, progenitors.

famine *n.* **1** (*an extreme scarcity of anything*) dearth, deficiency, destitution, exiguity, lack, paucity, scarcity, shortage, want. ANTONYMS: plenty. **2** (*starvation*) hunger, starvation.

famished *a.* (*feeling extremely hungry*) craving, empty, hungry, ravening, ravenous, starved, starving, voracious. ANTONYMS: full.

famous *a.* (*very well-known; renowned*) acclaimed, celebrated, conspicuous, distinguished, eminent, famed, glorious, honoured, illustrious, legendary, memorable, notable, praiseworthy, pre-eminent, prominent, remarkable, renowned, venerable, well-known. ANTONYMS: obscure, unknown.

fan[1] *n.* **1** (*an apparatus with revolving blades to give a current of air for ventilation*) air conditioner, blower, ventilator. **2** (*an implement or object shaped like an open fan*) propeller, vane. **~v.t. 1** (*to cool with a fan*) blow, cool, refresh. **2** (*to agitate (the air) with a fan*) air-condition, ventilate. **3** (*to stir up*) agitate, arouse, excite, impassion, inflame, provoke, rouse, stimulate, stir up, whip up, work up. ANTONYMS: quell. **4** (*to winnow*) sweep away, winnow. **~v.i.** (*to move or blow gently*) blow, waft.

fan[2] *n.* (*an enthusiastic admirer; a devotee*) addict, adherent, admirer, aficionado, (*coll.*) buff, (*coll.*) bug, devotee, enthusiast, fanatic, (*coll.*) fiend, follower, (*coll.*) freak, (*sl.*) groupie, (*coll.*) hound, (*sl.*) junkie, lover, (*sl.*) nut, supporter, zealot.

fanatic *n.* (*a person who has an extreme enthusiasm for something*) activist, addict, bigot, (*coll.*) buff, devotee, enthusiast, extremist, fan, (*coll.*) fiend, (*coll.*) freak, maniac, militant, radical, visionary, zealot. ANTONYMS: moderate.

fanatical *a.* (*extremely enthusiastic*) bigoted,

dogmatic, enthusiastic, excessive, extravagant, extreme, fervent, frantic, frenetic, frenzied, immoderate, keen, mad, maniacal, obsessive, passionate, rabid, radical, visionary, wild, zealous. ANTONYMS: restrained.

fanaticism *n.* (*extreme enthusiasm*) bigotry, dedication, devotion, dogmatism, enthusiasm, extravagance, extremism, fervour, immoderation, infatuation, madness, mania, monomania, obsessiveness, overenthusiasm, passion, radicalism, single-mindedness, zeal, zealotry.

fanciful *a.* **1** (*arising from the imagination; unreal*) baseless, imaginary, unreal. **2** (*indulging in fancies; whimsical*) capricious, chimerical, curious, fabulous, fairy-tale, fantastic, flighty, imaginative, impulsive, mythical, poetic, romantic, visionary, whimsical, wild. ANTONYMS: realistic. **3** (*highly ornamented*) elaborate, extravagant, ornamented. ANTONYMS: ordinary, sober.

fancy *v.t.* **1** (*to want to have or do*) crave, desire, feel like, hanker after, hope for, long for, pine for, relish, thirst for, want, wish for, yearn for. **2** (*to be attracted, esp. sexually, to*) be attracted to, be captivated by, desire, lust after, take to. **3** (*to choose (a person, team etc.) as the probable winner*) choose, favour, prefer, select. **4** (*to breed as a hobby or sport*) breed, raise, rear. **5** (*to imagine, to believe*) conceive, conceptualize, conjecture, conjure up, (*coll.*) dream up, envisage, guess, imagine, infer, picture, reckon, suppose, surmise, think, understand, visualize. **~n. 1** (*a personal inclination or liking*) attachment, craving, desire, fondness, hankering, inclination, liking, longing, partiality, penchant, predilection, preference, taste, tendency, urge, wish, yearning. ANTONYMS: aversion. **2** (*a liking that does not last long, a whim*) caprice, humour, impulse, liking, notion, thought, vagary, whim. **3** (*an imaginary or improbable idea*) delusion, improbability. **4** (*the power to conceive imagery*) creativity, imagination, inventiveness. **5** (*a mental image*) conception, dream, fantasy, idea, image, impression, vision. **6** (*a hobby*) craze, fad, hobby, whim. **~a. 1** (*elaborate, decorative*) baroque, decorated, elaborate, elegant, fanciful, luxurious, ornamental, ornate, ostentatious, showy. ANTONYMS: plain, undecorated. **2** (*extravagant or expensive*) capricious, embroidered, expensive, extravagant, fanciful, fantastic, fine, impressive, rococo. **3** (*needing skill to be performed*) complex, complicated, intricate.

fanfare *n.* **1** (*a short, loud sounding of trumpets, bugles etc.*) flourish, trump, trumpet blast. **2** (*fuss or publicity to accompany* *something such as an announcement*) ado, announcement, ballyhoo, commotion, fanfaronade, fuss, publicity, show, stir, (*coll.*) to-do, welcome.

fantasize *v.i.* **1** (*to conjure up and indulge in gratifying mental images*) conjure up, envisage, envision, imagine, invent, mull, muse, romance, speculate, stargaze. **2** (*to dream up fantastic* (*and usu. impracticable*) *schemes, ideas etc.*) build castles in the air, daydream, dream up, hallucinate.

fantastic *a.* **1** (*wonderful, very good*) (*coll.*) brill, (*sl.*) crucial, enjoyable, (*coll.*) fabulous, first-rate, good, marvellous, (*coll.*) mega, (*coll.*) sensational, splendid, superb, (*coll.*) terrific, tremendous, wonderful. ANTONYMS: ordinary. **2** (*very great; extravagant*) ambitious, extravagant, grandiose, great, wild. **3** (*fanciful, strange*) capricious, chimerical, fanciful, far-fetched, illusory, imaginary, strange, unreal, unrealistic, whimsical. ANTONYMS: realistic. **4** (*odd, grotesque*) absurd, alien, bizarre, comical, crazy, eccentric, exotic, freakish, grotesque, implausible, incredible, ludicrous, mad, nightmarish, odd, outlandish, peculiar, preposterous, ridiculous, weird.

fantasy *n.* **1** (*a fanciful mental image or daydream*) apparition, daydream, dream, nightmare, reverie. **2** (*an extravagant or bizarre idea*) fancy, idea, image. **3** (*the faculty of inventing or forming fanciful images*) creativity, fancy, imagination, invention, originality. **4** (*a fanciful or whimsical design*) fable, fabrication, fiction, flight of fancy, make-believe, masquerade, pretence, whimsy. **5** (*a hallucination*) delusion, hallucination, illusion, mirage, phantom, pipe dream, vision.

far *a.* **1** (*distant, a long way off*) distant, faraway, far-flung, far-off, outlying, way off. ANTONYMS: alongside, near. **2** (*extending or reaching a long way*) extensive, long-reaching. **3** (*more distant of two*) opposite, other. **4** (*remote from or contrary to one's purpose*) out of the way, remote, removed.
~*adv.* **1** (*at or to a great distance in space or time*) afar, deep, distant, removed. **2** (*to a great degree or extent*) clearly, considerably, decidedly, definitely, extremely, greatly, incomparably, much, undoubtedly.

faraway *a.* **1** (*remote in time or place*) distant, far, far-flung, far-off, far-removed, outlying, remote. **2** (*dreamy, absent-minded*) absent-minded, abstracted, detached, distant, dreamy, lost.

farce *n.* **1** (*a humorous play in which the actors are involved in ridiculously complex and improbable situations*) burlesque, comedy, satire, slapstick. ANTONYMS: tragedy. **2** (*a ridiculously futile or disorganized situation or action*) absurdity, joke, mockery, nonsense, parody, pretence, sham, travesty.

farcical *a.* **1** (*of or relating to farce; ludicrous*) amusing, comic, comical, diverting, droll, funny, humorous, ludicrous. ANTONYMS: tragic. **2** (*ridiculous, absurd*) absurd, contemptible, derisory, foolish, laughable, nonsensical, preposterous, ridiculous, risible, silly.

fare *n.* **1** (*the sum of money to be paid by a passenger for a journey by bus, train etc.*) charge, cost, fee, passage, price. **2** (*a passenger who pays to travel in a taxi etc.*) passenger, traveller. **3** (*food provided in a restaurant or café*) diet, eatables, food, meals, menu, nourishment, provisions, sustenance, victuals.
~*v.i.* **1** (*to get on, progress*) do, get along, get on, (*coll.*) make out, manage, progress, survive. **2** (*to happen, to turn out* (*well or badly*)) happen, pan out, turn out.

farewell *int.* (*goodbye, adieu*) adieu, (*coll.*) be seeing you, God speed, goodbye, (*coll.*) so long, take care.
~*n.* **1** (*words said at another person's leave-taking*) goodbye, valediction. **2** (*departure; leave-taking*) departure, leave-taking, parting, send-off.

far-fetched *a.* ((*of an explanation*) *improbable, unconvincing*) doubtful, dubious, fantastic, implausible, improbable, incredible, preposterous, questionable, unbelieving, unconvincing, unlikely, unrealistic. ANTONYMS: feasible, probable.

farm *n.* **1** (*an area of land together with its buildings, used for growing crops or rearing animals*) farmstead, holding, plantation, smallholding. **2** (*a farmhouse*) croft, farmhouse, homestead, ranch.
~*v.t.* **1** (*to use* (*land*) *for growing crops or rearing animals*) cultivate, plant, till, work. **2** (*to lease* (*taxes, offices etc.*) *at a fixed sum or rate per cent*) contract out, lease, let out, subcontract.

farmer *n.* (*a person who runs or owns a farm*) agriculturist, agronomist, husbandman, smallholder, yeoman.

farming *n.* (*the business of growing crops or rearing animals*) agriculture, agronomy, cultivation, husbandry.

far-reaching *a.* (*having broad influence or implications*) broad, extensive, important, influential, momentous, pervasive, significant, sweeping, thoroughgoing, widespread.

far-sighted *a.* (*considering what will happen in the future and so making wise judgements*) acute, astute, canny, cautious, discerning, far-seeing, foresighted, insightful, judicious, long-sighted, perceptive, politic, prescient, provident, prudent, sagacious, sage, sharp, shrewd, wise. ANTONYMS: short-sighted.

fascinate *v.t.* (*to exercise an irresistible influence over; to captivate*) absorb, allure, attract, beguile, bewitch, captivate, charm, delight, enamour, enchant, engross, enrapture, enthral, entrance, hypnotize, mesmerize, rivet, spellbind, transfix. ANTONYMS: bore.

fascination *n.* (*the state of exercising an irresistible influence over someone*) allure, appeal, attraction, captivation, charm, draw, enchantment, entrancement, glamour, hypnotism, lure, magic, magnetism, mesmerism, pull, sorcery, spell, witchcraft. ANTONYMS: repulsion.

fashion *n.* 1 (*the activity or business concerned with the style of clothes*) haute couture. 2 (*the current popular style of clothes or way of behaving*) craze, fad, latest, look, mania, mode, rage, style, taste, trend, vogue. 3 (*a way or style of doing something*) approach, attitude, convention, custom, manner, method, mode, pattern, sort, usage, way. 4 (*the form or style of anything*) appearance, cast, configuration, cut, design, figure, form, guise, kind, line, make, model, mould, pattern, shape, stamp, style, type. 5 (*fashionable or genteel society*) beau monde, high society, jet set.
~*v.t.* 1 (*to give shape and form to*) construct, contrive, create, design, forge, form, frame, make, manufacture, mould, shape, work. 2 (*to fit, to adapt*) accommodate, adapt, adjust, fit, suit, tailor.

fashionable *a.* 1 (*popular and favoured at a particular time*) current, favoured, (*esp. N Am.,* (*dated*) *sl.*) hip, in, in vogue, modern, popular, prevailing, up-to-date, up-to-the-minute. ANTONYMS: dated, unfashionable. 2 (*approved or patronized by people of fashion*) à la mode, chic, (*coll.*) cool, elegant, modish, smart, stylish, (*coll.*) trendy, (*coll.*) with it.

fast[1] *a.* 1 (*moving quickly*) accelerated, brisk, expeditious, express, fleet, flying, hasty, hurried, (*coll.*) nippy, quick, rapid, speedy, swift. ANTONYMS: slow. 2 (*taking a short time*) brief, quick, short. 3 (*firmly fixed*) bound, close, fastened, firm, fixed, immovable, secure, solid, stable, tight. ANTONYMS: loose, unstable. 4 (*faithful, close*) close, constant, faithful, loyal, sound, stalwart, staunch, steadfast, steady, unwavering. 5 ((*of a colour*) *permanent, not washing out*) durable, lasting, permanent, unfading. 6 ((*of a person*) *immoral, promiscuous*) dissipated, dissolute,

extravagant, giddy, immoral, intemperate, licentious, loose, pleasure-seeking, profligate, promiscuous, rakish, reckless, self-indulgent, wanton, wild. ANTONYMS: moral. 7 (*acquired with little effort or by shady means*) dubious, quick, shady, slick.
~*adv.* 1 (*quickly, without delay*) apace, briskly, expeditiously, hastily, hotfoot, hurriedly, post-haste, quickly, rapidly, speedily, swiftly. ANTONYMS: leisurely, slowly. 2 (*tightly, securely*) firmly, fixedly, immovably, securely, soundly, tightly. ANTONYMS: loosely. 3 (*completely, thoroughly*) completely, deeply, soundly, thoroughly. 4 (*in an immoral or promiscuous manner*) immorally, loosely, promiscuously, rakishly, self-indulgently, wantonly, wildly.

fast[2] *v.i.* (*to abstain from food*) abstain, diet, go hungry.
~*n.* 1 (*a (period of) total or partial abstinence from food*) abstention, abstinence, self-denial, self-deprivation. 2 (*a time set apart for fasting*) diet, fasting.

fasten *v.t.* 1 (*to fix firmly, to make secure*) affix, anchor, attach, bind, bond, clamp, connect, fix, fuse, grip, join, make fast, secure, stick, tether, unite. ANTONYMS: unfasten. 2 (*to secure, as by a bolt, knot etc.*) bolt, buckle, button, chain, hook, knot, lace, latch, lock, pin, strap, tie. ANTONYMS: unlock. 3 (*to fix or set firmly or earnestly*) concentrate, direct, fix, focus, point, rivet, set.

fastidious *a.* 1 (*extremely refined, esp. in matters of taste; fussy*) careful, (*coll.*) choosy, critical, delicate, discriminating, finicky, fussy, meticulous, nice, (*coll.*) nit-picking, particular, (*coll.*) pernickety, (*coll.*) picky, punctilious, refined. ANTONYMS: careless, easygoing. 2 (*difficult to please*) difficult, hard to please, implacable. 3 (*squeamish, easily disgusted*) dainty, disgusted, prurient, squeamish.

fastidiousness *n.* (*extreme refinement, esp. in matters of taste*) daintiness, discrimination, fastidiousness, fussiness, meticulousness, over-refinement, (*coll.*) pernicketiness, politeness, preciseness, punctiliousness, refinement, scrupulousness, ultrapoliteness. ANTONYMS: coarseness, roughness, vulgarity.

fat *a.* 1 (*having a lot of flesh and overweight*) beefy, big, chubby, corpulent, flabby, fleshy, gross, heavy, large, obese, overweight, paunchy, plump, podgy, portly, pot-bellied, rotund, stout, thick, tubby. ANTONYMS: lean, thin. 2 (*oily, greasy*) adipose, fatty, greasy, lipidic, oily, oleaginous, resinous, unctuous. 3 (*prosperous, rich*) affluent, flourishing, lucrative, profitable, prosperous, rich, thriving, wealthy, well off. ANTONYMS: poor.

4 (*fertile, fruitful*) abundant, fertile, fruitful, plentiful, productive, rich. ANTONYMS: unproductive. **5** ((*of a book*) *thick, substantial*) broad, solid, substantial, thick.

fatal *a.* **1** (*causing death or ruin*) damaging, deadly, death-dealing, destructive, final, harmful, incurable, killing, lethal, malignant, mortal, murderous, pernicious, ruinous, terminal, toxic. ANTONYMS: harmless, wholesome. **2** (*having very undesirable consequences*) baleful, baneful, calamitous, catastrophic, disastrous, dreadful, poisonous, undesirable. ANTONYMS: beneficial. **3** (*fateful, decisive*) critical, crucial, decisive, destined, determining, doomed, fateful. **4** (*decreed by fate, inevitable*) decreed, destined, fated, inevitable, ordained, predestined, predetermined, preordained.

fatality *n.* **1** (*a* (*person who suffers*) *death by accident or violence*) causality, loss, victim. **2** (*predetermination by fate, esp. to death or disaster*) destiny, fate, predetermination. **3** (*a fatal influence*) deadliness, death, mortality.

fate *n.* **1** (*a power considered to control and decide events unalterably*) chance, destiny, fortune, Lady Luck, providence. **2** (*one's ultimate condition as brought about by circumstances and events; the course of these events*) destiny, doom, fortune, issue, lot, luck, outcome, portion, stars, upshot. **3** (*death, destruction*) collapse, death, destruction, disaster, downfall, end, nemesis, ruin, undoing.

fated *a.* **1** (*doomed to destruction*) cursed, damned, doomed, marked down. **2** (*decreed by fate, predetermined*) certain, decreed, destined, foreordained, inescapable, inevitable, predestined, predetermined, preordained, sure, written.

fateful *a.* **1** (*having momentous, often catastrophic, consequences*) consequential, crucial, decisive, earth-shaking, important, momentous, pivotal, portentous, significant, weighty. ANTONYMS: inconsequential, insignificant. **2** (*bringing death or destruction*) cataclysmic, catastrophic, deadly, destructive, disastrous, fatal, lethal, ominous, ruinous.

father *n.* **1** (*a male parent*) (*coll.*) dad, (*coll.*) daddy, (*sl.*) governor, (*coll.*) old man, (*coll.*) pa, papa, parent, pater, paterfamilias, (*N Am., coll.*) pop. ANTONYMS: mother. **2** (*any male animal considered as regards its offspring*) begetter, progenitor, sire. ANTONYMS: offspring. **3** (*a male ancestor, a patriarch*) ancestor, forebear, forefather, patriarch, predecessor. **4** (*the first to practise any art; an early leader*) architect, author, contriver, creator, founder, framer, initiator, inventor, maker, originator,

prime mover. **5** (*a priest, a religious teacher etc.*) abbé, chaplain, confessor, curé, minister, padre, parson, pastor, priest. **6** (*pl.*) (*elders, senators, the leading men* (*of a city etc.*)) city father, elder, patron, senator.
~*v.t.* **1** (*to beget*) beget, engender, get, procreate, sire. **2** (*to originate*) author, create, establish, found, frame, generate, initiate, institute, invent, make, originate.

fatherly *a.* (*like a father; caring*) affectionate, amiable, benevolent, benign, caring, comforting, devoted, fond, forbearing, friendly, gentle, indulgent, kind, kindly, loving, nurturing, parental, paternal, patriarchal, protective, sheltering, supportive, sympathetic, tender, understanding, warm.

fathom *v.t.* **1** (*to penetrate, to comprehend; often with out*) ascertain, comprehend, divine, get to the bottom of, grasp, interpret, investigate, penetrate, probe, search, see, understand, work out. **2** (*to measure the depth of*) gauge, measure, plumb, sound.

fathomless *a.* (*not to be fathomed*) abysmal, bottomless, deep, immeasurable, impenetrable, incomprehensible, profound, unfathomable, unplumbed. ANTONYMS: shallow.

fatigue *n.* (*exhaustion from bodily or mental exertion*) debility, enervation, ennui, exhaustion, languor, lassitude, lethargy, listlessness, prostration, sluggishness, tiredness, weariness. ANTONYMS: energy, vigour.
~*v.t.* (*to exhaust the strength of by bodily or mental exertion*) debilitate, drain, enervate, exhaust, fag, jade, (*coll.*) knacker, (*esp. N Am., coll.*) poop, prostrate, tire, weaken, wear out, weary, (*coll.*) whack. ANTONYMS: refresh, revive.

fatness *n.* (*the state of being fat*) blubber, bulkiness, chubbiness, corpulence, fat, flab, flesh, girth, grossness, heaviness, obesity, paunchiness, plumpness, podginess, portliness, rotundity, size, stoutness, weight.

fatten *v.t.* (*to make* (*esp. animals*) *fat, to feed for the table*) bloat, broaden, build up, cram, distend, expand, feed, make fat, nourish, overfeed, put on weight, spread, stuff, swell, thicken. ANTONYMS: slim.

fatuous *a.* **1** (*idiotic, inane*) absurd, idiotic, inane, ludicrous, senseless, silly, vacuous. ANTONYMS: sensible. **2** (*stupid, foolish*) asinine, brainless, dense, dull, foolish, imbecile, lunatic, mindless, moronic, puerile, stupid, weak-minded, witless.

fault *n.* **1** (*a defect, imperfection*) blemish, defect, deficiency, drawback, flaw, foible, frailty, imperfection, infirmity, shortcoming, snag,

weakness. ANTONYMS: strength, virtue. **2** (*a mistake or blunder*) blunder, (*coll.*) boob, error, failing, failure, faux pas, gaffe, (*coll.*) howler, inaccuracy, indiscretion, lapse, mistake, negligence, omission, oversight, slip, slip-up. **3** (*a slight offence or deviation from right*) crime, delinquency, deviation, impropriety, misconduct, misdeed, misdemeanour, offence, peccadillo, sin, transgression, trespass, vice, wrong. **4** (*responsibility for a mistake or wrongdoing, blame*) accountability, answerability, blame, blameworthiness, culpability, liability, responsibility.
~*v.t.* (*to find fault in, to criticize*) accuse, blame, call to account, censure, criticize, find fault, hold accountable, impugn.

fault-finding *a.* (*constantly criticizing*) captious, carping, cavilling, censorious, complaining, contentious, critical, criticizing, fussy, hair-splitting, nagging, niggling, (*coll.*) nit-picking, pettifogging, querulous, quibbling. ANTONYMS: uncritical.
~*n.* (*constant criticism*) censoriousness, criticism, (*coll.*) nit-picking, (*coll.*) pickiness.

faultless *a.* (*perfect, flawless*) accurate, blameless, correct, exemplary, faithful, flawless, foolproof, guiltless, immaculate, impeccable, irreproachable, model, perfect, pure, sinless, spotless, stainless, unblemished, unspotted, without fault. ANTONYMS: flawed, imperfect.

faulty *a.* (*having faults; defective*) bad, blemished, broken, damaged, defective, erroneous, fallacious, flawed, impaired, imperfect, imprecise, inaccurate, invalid, malfunctioning, (*coll.*) on the blink, out of order, unsound, weak, wrong. ANTONYMS: perfect, working.

favour *n.* **1** (*a kind or indulgent act*) courtesy, good turn, indulgence, kindness, service. **2** (*friendly regard, approval*) approbation, approval, backing, championship, esteem, friendliness, goodwill, grace, kindness, patronage, regard, sanction. ANTONYMS: disapproval. **3** (*preference, excessive kindness*) bias, favouritism, partiality, preference, prejudice. **4** (*support, advantage (of)*) advantage, aid, behalf, convenience, facility, furtherance, promotion, support. **5** (*a token of love or affection, esp. something given by a woman to her lover*) gift, keepsake, memento, present, souvenir, token.
~*v.t.* **1** (*to approve, to prefer*) approve, choose, like, prefer, select. ANTONYMS: disapprove, dislike. **2** (*to befriend, to support*) abet, accommodate, advance, advocate, aid, assist, back, befriend, benefit, champion, commend, encourage, endorse, espouse, esteem, help, incline, recommend, sponsor, support. **3** (*to

facilitate) ease, expedite, facilitate. **4** (*to promote*) advance, forward, promote. **5** (*to oblige (with)*) assist, help, oblige, succour. **6** (*to resemble in features*) look like, resemble, take after. **7** (*to avoid using, to treat with special care (as an injured limb)*) guard, nurse, protect, spare.

favourable *a.* **1** (*approving, commending*) affirmative, approving, commending, consenting, enthusiastic, positive, sympathetic. ANTONYMS: disapproving. **2** (*friendly, encouraging*) agreeable, amicable, auspicious, benign, encouraging, friendly, kind, promising, propitious, reassuring, understanding, welcoming, well-disposed. ANTONYMS: inauspicious, unfavouring, unpromising. **3** (*convenient, advantageous*) advantageous, appropriate, beneficial, convenient, fit, helpful, opportune, suitable, timely. ANTONYMS: disadvantageous.

favoured *a.* **1** (*chosen*) choice, chosen, favourite, pet, preferred, recommended, selected, singled out. **2** (*receiving special attention*) advantaged, blessed, elite, lucky, privileged, rich, wealthy.

favourite *a.* **1** (*preferred before all others*) chosen, preferred, selected. **2** (*regarded with special favour*) favoured, pet. **3** (*beloved*) beloved, best-loved, darling, dearest.
~*n.* **1** (*a person or thing regarded with special affection or preference*) choice, pick, preference. **2** (*a person chosen as a companion and intimate by a superior and unduly favoured*) apple of one's eye, beloved, (*coll.*) blue-eyed boy, companion, confederate, creature, darling, dear, (*often facet.*) flavour of the month, friend, intimate, pet, (*coll.*) thing.

favouritism *n.* (*showing an unfair special preference for a person or group*) bias, nepotism, one-sidedness, partiality, partisanship, preference, preferment, prejudice. ANTONYMS: impartiality, neutrality.

fear *n.* **1** (*an unpleasant feeling caused by impending danger, pain etc.*) (*N Am.*) blue funk, fright, horror, panic, terror, timidity. **2** (*dread, a state of alarm*) alarm, apprehension, consternation, dismay, dread, qualm, trepidation. **3** (*a cause of fear*) bête noire, bogey, bugbear, nightmare, phobia. **4** (*anxiety, worry*) agitation, angst, anxiety, apprehension, concern, disquietude, distress, doubt, foreboding, misgiving, solicitude, suspicion, unease, uneasiness, worry. ANTONYMS: reassurance. **5** (*awe, reverence*) awe, respect, reverence, veneration, wonder. ANTONYMS: disrespect. **6** (*possibility (of something unpleasant happening)*) chance, possibility, risk.
~*v.t.* **1** (*to be afraid of*) be afraid of, be scared of, dread, take fright at. **2** (*to suspect, to doubt*) be

concerned about, doubt, have misgivings about, suspect. **3** (*to shrink from, to hesitate* (*to do*)) hesitate, shrink from, shudder at, tremble at. **4** (*to show reverence towards*) be in awe of, respect, revere, reverence, venerate.

~*v.i.* **1** (*to feel anxiety or worry*) apprehend, panic, take fright, worry. **2** (*to doubt, to mistrust*) doubt, mistrust, question, suspect.

fearful *a.* **1** (*apprehensive, afraid* (*lest*)) afraid, alarmed, anxious, apprehensive, frightened, scared, terrified, uneasy. **2** (*timid, timorous*) diffident, edgy, faint-hearted, hesitant, jittery, jumpy, nervous, panicky, pusillanimous, shy, timid, timorous. ANTONYMS: bold, intrepid. **3** (*terrible, frightful*) appalling, atrocious, awful, dire, dreadful, fearsome, formidable, frightful, ghastly, grim, grisly, gruesome, hideous, horrendous, horrific, loathsome, monstrous, repugnant, shocking, terrible. ANTONYMS: wonderful. **4** (*extraordinary, annoying*) annoying, bothersome, extraordinary, trying, unusual.

fearless *a.* (*not afraid; courageous*) bold, brave, confident, courageous, daring, dauntless, doughty, gallant, game, gutsy, heroic, indomitable, intrepid, plucky, unabashed, unafraid, undaunted, unflinching, valiant, valorous. ANTONYMS: fearful.

fearsome *a.* (*terrible, formidable*) alarming, appalling, awesome, awful, baleful, daunting, dismaying, dreadful, fearful, formidable, frightening, hair-raising, horrendous, horrifying, intimidating, menacing, terrible, terrifying, unnerving.

feasible *a.* **1** (*that may or can be done, practicable*) doable, practicable, practical, probable, realistic, viable, workable. ANTONYMS: impossible. **2** (*manageable*) achievable, attainable, manageable. **3** (*likely, plausible*) likely, plausible, reasonable, sensible.

feast *n.* **1** (*a large and sumptuous meal enjoyed by a great number of people*) banquet, (*coll.*) beanfeast, (*sl.*) blow-out, dinner, junket, meal, repast, (*coll.*) spread. **2** (*an anniversary or periodical celebration of some great event or person*) anniversary, celebration, commemoration, festival, fête, gala, holiday, holy day, rite, ritual, saint's day. **3** (*anything giving great enjoyment to body or mind*) delight, enjoyment, gratification, pleasure, treat.

~*v.t.* **1** (*to entertain sumptuously*) entertain, regale, wine and dine. **2** (*to gratify or please greatly, as with something delicious*) cheer, delight, gladden, gratify, please, thrill.

~*v.i.* **1** (*to eat and drink sumptuously*) banquet, dine, eat one's fill, gorge, gormandize, (*esp.N Am., sl.*) pig out, stuff. **2** (*to be highly gratified or pleased*) enjoy, indulge.

feat *n.* **1** (*a notable act, esp. one displaying great skill or daring*) achievement, act, coup, deed, performance, tour de force. **2** (*an exploit, an accomplishment*) accomplishment, achievement, attainment, coup, deed, exploit, stroke.

feathery *a.* **1** (*featherlike, resembling feathers*) downy, featherlike, fluffy, plumed, plumose, plumous. **2** (*flimsy, fickle*) fickle, flimsy, light, wispy.

feature *n.* **1** (*a distinctive or prominent part of anything*) aspect, attraction, attribute, characteristic, facet, hallmark, highlight, mark, peculiarity, point, property, quality, speciality, trait. **2** (*a part of the face, such as the eyes or mouth*) countenance, face, (*sl.*) kisser, looks, (*sl.*) mug, physiognomy, visage. **3** (*a special article in a newspaper or magazine on a particular topic*) article, column, comment, item, piece, report, story.

~*v.t.* (*to give prominence to, to make a feature of*) accentuate, call attention to, emphasize, give prominence to, headline, highlight, (*coll.*) hype, play up, promote, puff up, spotlight, star, stress. ANTONYMS: play down.

feckless *a.* **1** (*weak, ineffective*) aimless, feeble, futile, hopeless, ineffective, ineffectual, useless, weak, worthless. **2** (*incompetent, irresponsible*) incompetent, irresponsible, shiftless.

fecund *a.* (*fertile, productive*) abundant, fertile, fructiferous, fruitful, productive, prolific, rich, teeming. ANTONYMS: barren, infertile.

fecundity *n.* **1** (*the quality of being fruitful or prolific*) fructiferousness, fruitlessness. **2** (*the power or property of producing young or germinating*) fertility, productiveness.

federation *n.* **1** (*a federal government or group of states*) confederacy, entente, federacy, union. **2** (*a confederated body*) alliance, coalition, confederation, league, syndicate. **3** (*the act of uniting in a confederacy*) amalgamation, association, combination, confederation, union.

fee *n.* **1** (*payment or remuneration to a public officer, a professional person or an organization*) compensation, emolument, honorarium, pay, payment, recompense, remuneration, reward, salary, stipend, wage. **2** (*a charge paid for admission to a society, public building etc.*) charge, cost, fare, hire, subscription, tariff, toll. **3** (*charge, payment*) bill, charge, payment. **4** (*a gratuity*) baksheesh, gratuity, tip.

feeble *a.* **1** (*weak, destitute of physical strength*) ailing, debilitated, decrepit, delicate, doddering, frail, infirm, puny, sickly, weak, (*coll.*) weedy. ANTONYMS: robust, strong. **2** (*lacking in* *force or energy)* drained, drooping, enervated, enfeebled, exhausted, failing, imperceptible, indistinct, obscure, unclear, weak. ANTONYMS: forceful, strong. **3** *(ineffective, pointless)* inadequate, incompetent, indecisive, ineffective, ineffectual, inefficient, insignificant, insipid, pointless, powerless, unavailing. ANTONYMS: effective. **4** *(unconvincing, lame)* flimsy, half-baked, inadequate, lame, meagre, paltry, pathetic, poor, shoddy, thin, unconvincing.

feeble-minded *a.* **1** *(stupid, unintelligent)* *(sl.)* boneheaded, *(coll.)* brain-dead, dimwitted, *(coll.)* dozy, dull, *(coll.)* dumb, empty-headed, gormless, half-witted, idiotic, moronic, obtuse, stupid, *(coll.)* thick, unintelligent, vacant. ANTONYMS: clever, intelligent. **2** *(mentally deficient)* addled, imbecilic, mentally deficient, retarded, simple, slow, soft in the head, subnormal, weak-minded.

feed *v.t.* **1** *(to give food to)* nourish, victual, wine and dine. **2** *(to supply with that which is necessary to continuance or development)* cater for, maintain, provide for, provision, support, sustain. ANTONYMS: starve. **3** *(to cause to grow or develop)* nourish, nurture, rear. **4** *(to gratify)* gratify, indulge, pander to, satisfy.
~*v.i.* **1** *(to take food; to eat)* devour, dine, eat, fare, graze, partake of, take food. **2** *(to subsist (on or upon))* exist, live, subsist, survive.
~*n.* **1** *(food, fodder)* fodder, food, forage, pasturage, provender, silage. **2** *(a meal, a feast)* feast, meal, *(sl.)* nosh, *(coll.)* spread.

feel *v.t.* **1** *(to perceive by touch)* notice, perceive, sense. **2** *(to examine or explore by touch)* examine, explore, fumble, grope, sound, test, try. **3** *(to touch, to try by handling)* caress, finger, fondle, handle, manipulate, maul, *(coll.)* paw, pet, stroke, touch. **4** *(to have a sensation of, otherwise than by the senses of sight, hearing, taste or smell)* *(coll.)* feel in one's bones, have a hunch, sense. **5** *(to be conscious of)* be aware of, be conscious of, know. **6** *(to experience, to undergo)* bear, endure, enjoy, experience, go through, suffer, undergo, withstand. **7** *(to know in one's inner consciousness, think)* be convinced that, believe, consider, deem, discern, guess, hold, judge, think.
~*n.* **1** *(the sense of touch)* feeling, touch. **2** *(the characteristic sensation of something, esp. to the touch; general impression)* air, ambience, atmosphere, climate, feeling, impression, quality, sensation, sense, tone, *(coll.)* vibes. **to feel for 1** *(to feel after)* grope for, test for. **2** *(to have the emotions stirred by)* be moved by, be stirred by, bleed for, commiserate with, empathize with, pity, sympathize with.

feeling *n.* **1** *(the sense of touch; the sensation produced when a material body is touched)* feel, touch. **2** *(a physical sensation of any kind)* sensation, sense. **3** *(an emotional state or reaction)* emotion, sensibility, sensitivity, sentiment. **4** *(pl.)* *(susceptibilities, sympathies)* ego, emotions, self-esteem, sensibilities, susceptibilities, sympathies. **5** *(sympathy or love)* affection, ardour, compassion, fervour, love, passion, sympathy, tenderness. ANTONYMS: indifference. **6** *(an impression, an intuition)* apprehension, consciousness, hunch, idea, impression, inkling, intuition, notion, perception, premonition, presentiment, sense, suspicion. **7** *(a belief or conviction)* belief, conviction, inclination, instinct, opinion, sentiment, thought, viewpoint. **8** *(the emotional content of a work of art, or the emotional response it evokes)* air, ambience, atmosphere, aura, feel, mood, quality.
~*a.* **1** *(easily affected or moved, sensitive)* ardent, compassionate, emotional, fervent, passionate, sensitive, sympathetic, tender, warm. ANTONYMS: unfeeling. **2** *(expressive of or manifesting great sensibility)* sensible, sentient.

feign *v.t.* **1** *(to pretend, to simulate)* affect, counterfeit, devise, fabricate, fake, forge, imitate, invent, pretend, sham, simulate. **2** *(to imagine)* fictionalize, imagine.
~*v.i.* *(to make pretences; to dissimulate)* act, assume, dissemble, dissimulate, make pretences.

feint *n.* *(a pretence of aiming at one point while another is the real object)* artifice, blind, bluff, deception, distraction, dodge, dummy, manoeuvre, ploy, ruse, sham, stratagem, subterfuge, tactic, wile.

felicitate *v.t.* *(to congratulate)* compliment, congratulate, praise.

felicitous *a.* **1** *(well-suited, apt)* apposite, appropriate, apropos, apt, fitting, opportune, pertinent, suitable, timely, well-chosen, well-expressed, well-suited. ANTONYMS: inappropriate. **2** *(happy, prosperous)* delightful, fortunate, happy, inspired, lucky, propitious, prosperous, seasonable, successful.

felicity *n.* **1** *(happiness, blissfulness)* bliss, blissfulness, delectation, delight, ecstasy, happiness, joy, rapture. ANTONYMS: misery, unhappiness. **2** *(appropriateness, neatness)* applicability, appropriateness, aptness, neatness, pertinence, propitiousness, propriety, suitability. ANTONYMS: inappropriateness.

fell *v.t.* **1** *(to cut down)* cut down, hew. **2** *(to bring to the ground)* bring to the ground, demolish, flatten, floor, knock down, level, mow down, prostrate, raze, strike down.

fellow n. **1** (*a man, a boy*) boy, gentleman, man. **2** (*a person*) (*coll.*) bloke, (*coll.*) chap, character, (*coll.*) customer, (*coll.*) geezer, (*coll.*) guy, individual, person, (*coll.*) punter. **3** (*an associate, a partner*) ally, associate, colleague, companion, comrade, co-worker, friend, partner. **4** (*an equal in rank, a peer*) compeer, equal, peer. **5** (*a person or thing like or equal to another, a counterpart*) accessory, complement, counterpart, double, duplicate, equivalent, match, mate, twin.
~a. (*associated with oneself or of the same class or relationship*) affiliated, akin, allied, associated, auxiliary, like, related, similar.
~v.t. (*to pair with*) match, pair with, suit.

fellowship n. **1** (*companionship, community of interest*) affability, amity, association, brotherhood, camaraderie, closeness, communion, companionship, comradeship, cordiality, familiarity, fraternization, friendliness, friendship, intimacy, participation, sisterhood, sociability, togetherness, warmth. ANTONYMS: enmity. **2** (*a body of associates*) association, bloc, cartel, circle, clan, clique, club, lodge, order, organization, set, society, trust. **3** (*a fraternity*) brotherhood, fraternity, sisterhood, sorority. **4** (*a corporation, a guild*) company, consortium, corporation, guild, league, partnership, union. **5** (*an endowment for maintaining a graduate engaged in research*) endowment, grant.

felon n. (*a person who has committed a felony*) convict, criminal, culprit, lawbreaker, malefactor, miscreant, offender, outlaw, wrongdoer.

female a. (*relating to or characteristic of women or female animals*) feminine, gentle, tender, womanly. ANTONYMS: male.

feminine a. **1** (*relating to or characteristic of women or the female sex*) female. ANTONYMS: male, masculine. **2** (*womanly; effeminate*) affected, camp, effeminate, effete, girlish, ladylike, womanly. ANTONYMS: manly, masculine. **3** (*having qualities associated with women; gentle*) deferential, delicate, docile, gentle, graceful, modest, pretty, soft, submissive, tender.

fen n. (*low, flat and marshy land*) bog, marsh, morass, quagmire, slough, swamp.

fence n. **1** (*a structure, e.g. a line of posts, serving to enclose and protect a piece of ground*) barbed wire, barricade, barrier, defence, enclosure, hedge, paling, palisade, railing, rampart, stockade, wall. **2** (*an obstacle in steeplechasing or showjumping*) gate, hurdle, jump, obstacle. **3** (*a guardplate or gauge of various kinds in machinery etc.*) defence, gauge, guard, guardplate, guide.
~v.t. **1** (*to enclose or protect with or as with a fence*) bound, circumscribe, confine, coop, encircle, enclose, impound, pen, pound, protect, restrict, shut in, surround. **2** (*to defend or protect*) defend, guard, protect, shield. ANTONYMS: expose. **3** (*to parry, to ward off*) fend off, parry, ward off.
~v.i. (*to parry enquiries adroitly, to equivocate*) avoid, beat about the bush, cavil, dodge, equivocate, evade, fend off, (*coll.*) flannel, fudge, hedge, parry, prevaricate, quibble, shift, shilly-shally, sidestep, (*coll.*) waffle.

fend v.i. **to fend for** (*to provide or to get a living for*) get a living, look after, make do, make out, make provision for, provide for, (*coll.*) scrape along, shift for, support, sustain, take care of. **to fend off** (*to ward off*) avert, beat off, deflect, discourage, divert, drive back, fight off, forestall, hold at bay, keep off, parry, repel, repulse, resist, stave off, turn aside, ward off.

feral a. (*wild, savage*) bestial, brutal, cruel, ferocious, fierce, savage, unbroken, vicious, wild. ANTONYMS: domesticated, tamed.

ferment[1] n. **1** (*agitation, uproar*) agitation, commotion, disruption, excitement, fever, frenzy, furore, heat, hubbub, stew, stir, tumult, turbulence, turmoil, unrest, uproar. ANTONYMS: peace, tranquillity. **2** (*leaven*) leaven, yeast.

ferment[2] v.t. **1** (*to excite fermentation in*) brew, leaven, rise. **2** (*to rouse, to agitate*) agitate, excite, fester, foment, incite, inflame, provoke, rouse, seethe, smoulder, stir up. ANTONYMS: calm.
~v.i. (*to be in a state of fermentation*) boil, effervesce, foam, froth, seethe.

ferocious a. **1** (*fierce, cruel*) barbaric, barbarous, bestial, bloodthirsty, brutal, cruel, feral, fierce, harsh, inhuman, merciless, pitiless, predatory, rapacious, ruthless, savage, severe, vicious, violent, wild. ANTONYMS: docile, gentle. **2** (*intense, extreme*) extreme, fierce, intense, severe.

ferocity n. (*the quality of being ferocious; savageness*) barbarity, bloodthirstiness, brutality, cruelty, ferociousness, fierceness, fury, inhumanity, rapacity, ruthlessness, savageness, savagery, severity, viciousness, violence, wildness.

fertile a. **1** (*able to support abundant growth*) abundant, lush, luxuriant. **2** (*able to bear offspring, fruitful*) fecund, flowering, fruit-bearing, fruitful, plentiful, profuse, prolific, teeming. ANTONYMS: barren, infertile. **3** (*productive, fruitful*) fruitful, generative, productive, rich, yielding. **4** ((*of the mind*) resourceful) creative, inventive, resourceful.

fertilize *v.t.* **1** (*to make fertile or productive*) fecundate, fructify, impregnate, inseminate, pollinate. **2** (*to make* (*esp. soil*) *rich*) compost, dress, enrich, feed, manure, marl, mulch, nourish, top dress.

fervent *a.* **1** (*ardent, vehement*) animated, ardent, devout, eager, earnest, ecstatic, emotional, enthusiastic, excited, fervid, frantic, frenzied, heartfelt, impassioned, intense, keen, passionate, vehement, zealous. ANTONYMS: apathetic, frigid. **2** (*hot, glowing*) boiling, burning, fiery, flaming, glowing, hot, warm. ANTONYMS: cool.

fervour *n.* **1** (*ardour, intensity of feeling*) animation, ardour, eagerness, earnestness, ebullience, enthusiasm, fervency, gusto, intensity, keenness, passion, spirit, vehemence, verve, zeal. ANTONYMS: apathy. **2** (*heat, warmth*) fire, glow, heat, warmth.

fester *v.i.* **1** (*to become septic*) become infected, go septic. **2** (*to cause persistent annoyance or resentment*) aggravate, chafe, gall, inflame, intensify, irk, irritate, rankle, rile, smoulder. **3** (*to become rotten; to decay*) corrupt, decay, decompose, mortify, putrefy, rot, ulcerate. **4** (*to form pus*) ooze, run, suppurate.
~*n.* (*a tumour or sore containing pus*) abscess, boil, gathering, pustule, sore, tumour, ulcer.

festival *n.* **1** (*a day or period of celebration or holiday, often with religious significance*) anniversary, celebration, commemoration, feast, holiday, holy day, saint's day. **2** (*a series of concerts, plays etc., in a town*) gala, programme, series. **3** (*a merrymaking*) banquet, carnival, celebration, entertainment, festivities, fête, fiesta, gala, jubilee, merrymaking, treat.

festive *a.* **1** (*of, relating to or used for a feast or festival*) festal, gala, holiday. **2** (*joyous, celebratory*) celebratory, cheery, convivial, gay, happy, hearty, jolly, jovial, joyful, joyous, jubilant, light-hearted, merry, mirthful, sportive. ANTONYMS: gloomy, mournful.

festivity *n.* **1** (*mirth, joyfulness*) amusement, conviviality, frivolity, fun, gaiety, glee, hilarity, jollification, joviality, joyfulness, jubilation, merriment, mirth, pleasure, rejoicing. **2** (*a joyous celebration or entertainment*) carnival, carousal, celebration, entertainment, feast, festival, party. **3** (*pl.*) (*celebrations; merrymaking*) celebrations, merrymaking, revelry.

fetch *v.t.* **1** (*to go for and bring back*) bring back, carry, conduct, convey, deliver, get, go for, obtain, retrieve, transport. **2** (*to draw forth* (*breath*)) draw forth, heave, summon. **3** (*to bring in, to sell for* (*a price*)) bring in, earn, make, realize, sell for, yield. **4** (*to derive*) derive, elicit, produce.

fetching *a.* (*attractive, charming*) alluring, attractive, captivating, charming, cute, enchanting, enticing, fascinating, intriguing, sweet, taking, winning, winsome. ANTONYMS: repulsive.

fête *n.* **1** (*an outdoor event with stalls and entertainments*) bazaar, carnival, fair, gala, garden party, jamboree, street party. **2** (*a festival, an entertainment*) carnival, celebration, entertainment, festival, fiesta, gala. **3** (*the festival of the saint after whom a person is named*) feast day, festival, holiday, saint's day. ~*v.t.* (*to entertain, to honour lavishly*) entertain, feast, honour, lionize, wine and dine.

fetid *a.* (*having an offensive smell; stinking*) corrupt, foul, malodorous, mephitic, noisome, offensive, rancid, rank, reeking, smelly, stinking. ANTONYMS: fragrant, sweet-smelling.

fetish *n.* **1** (*any material object supposed to give special powers*) amulet, charm, talisman, totem. **2** (*an object of devotion*) compulsion, fixation, idol, mania, obsession, (*coll.*) thing.

fetter *n.* **1** (*a chain for the feet*) ball and chain, leg-iron. **2** (*a shackle, a bond*) bond, chain, manacle, shackle. ~*v.t.* **1** (*to bind with fetters*) bind, chain, manacle, shackle, tie. ANTONYMS: release. **2** (*to confine, restrain*) confine, curb, encumber, hamper, hobble, impede, restrain, restrict.

feud *n.* **1** (*hostility between two tribes or families in revenge for an injury*) blood feud, vendetta. **2** (*a long and bitter dispute or quarrel*) breach, disagreement, dispute, quarrel, row, rupture, squabble. ANTONYMS: agreement. **3** (*enmity, animosity*) animosity, antagonism, argument, bad blood, bickering, conflict, contention, discord, dissension, enmity, faction, hatred, hostility, quarrel, rivalry, strife. ~*v.i.* (*to carry on a feud*) bicker, brawl, clash, conflict, contend, disagree, dispute, duel, fall out, fight, quarrel, row, squabble, war.

fever *n.* **1** (*an abnormally high body temperature and quickened pulse, often accompanied by delirium*) delirium, feverishness, high temperature, pyrexia. **2** (*any one of a group of diseases, e.g. scarlet fever or yellow fever, characterized by this*) disease, illness, sickness. **3** (*a state of nervous excitement; agitation*) agitation, ecstasy, excitement, ferment, fervour, flush, frenzy, heat, intensity, nervousness, passion, restlessness, turmoil, unrest. ANTONYMS: composure.

feverish *a.* **1** (*indicating fever; resembling a*

fever) burning, febrile, flaming, flushed, hot, inflamed, pyretic. **2** (*excited, hectic*) agitated, ardent, desperate, distracted, excited, fervent, frantic, frenetic, frenzied, hectic, impatient, obsessive, overwrought, restless, zealous. ANTONYMS: calm, composed.

few *a.* **1** (*not many*) hardly any, infrequent, meagre, negligible, not many, occasional, rare, scanty, scarce, scattered, sporadic, thin. ANTONYMS: many, numerous. **2** (*restricted in number*) inconsiderable, limited, restricted, small.
~*pron.* (*a small number* (*of*)) handful, not many, scattering, small number, some.

fiasco *n.* (*a complete and humiliating failure*) (*taboo sl.*) balls-up, botch, breakdown, catastrophe, (*sl.*) cock-up, debacle, disaster, failure, (*coll.*) flop, (*taboo sl.*) fuck-up, ignominy, mess, muddle, (*coll.*) wash-out. ANTONYMS: triumph.

fib *n.* (*a harmless lie*) cock and bull story, fabrication, fairy tale, falsehood, fiction, invention, lie, misrepresentation, (*rhyming sl.*) porky, prevarication, story, untruth, white lie, (*sl.*) whopper. ANTONYMS: truth.
~*v.i.* (*to tell a fib*) falsify, lie, misrepresent, prevaricate.

fibre *n.* **1** (*a slender filament*) filament, strand, string, thread, wisp. **2** (*the substances composed of animal or vegetable tissue forming the raw material in textile manufacture*) cloth, fabric, material. **3** (*a structure composed of filaments*) pile, structure, texture, tissue. **4** (*essence, character*) character, composition, constitution, disposition, essence, material, mould, nature, nerve, quality, spirit, stamina, strength, substance, toughness.

fickle *a.* (*changeable, inconstant*) capricious, changeable, erratic, faithless, fitful, flighty, frivolous, inconstant, irresolute, mercurial, temperamental, unpredictable, unreliable, unstable, unsteady, vacillating, variable, volatile, wavering, whimsical. ANTONYMS: constant, reliable.

fiction *n.* **1** (*an invented narrative; a story*) fable, fantasy, legend, myth, novel, romance, story, tale, yarn. **2** (*literature, esp. in prose, describing imaginary people and events*) literature, prose. **3** (*a falsehood*) falsehood, fib, lie, (*rhyming sl.*) porky, tall story, untruth. ANTONYMS: truth. **4** (*the act or art of feigning or inventing*) dissembling, feigning, imagination, invention. **5** (*that which is feigned or imagined*) concoction, fabrication, fancy, fantasy, figment, invention.

fictitious *a.* (*imaginary, false*) apocryphal,

artificial, assumed, bogus, counterfeit, fabricated, false, fanciful, feigned, imaginary, invented, made-up, make-believe, mythical, spurious, unreal, untrue. ANTONYMS: actual, true.

fiddle *n.* **1** (*a violin or stringed instrument with a bow*) viola, violin. **2** (*a swindle, a dishonest practice*) cheat, diddle, fix, fraud, racket, (*N Am., sl.*) scam, (*sl.*) sting, swindle, (*coll.*) wangle.
~*v.i.* **1** (*to make restless movements with the hands or fingers*) fidget, finger. **2** (*to move aimlessly; to waste time in aimless activity*) (*sl.*) doss, idle, waste time. **3** (*to tinker* (*with*), *to tamper* (*with*)) fool, fuss, interfere, mess around, monkey, muck around, play, tamper, tinker, toy, trifle.
~*v.t.* **1** (*to falsify* (*accounts etc.*)) (*coll.*) cook, falsify, massage. **2** (*to contrive to do or obtain* (*something*) *by underhand means*) manoeuvre, (*coll.*) wangle.

fidelity *n.* **1** (*careful and loyal observance of duty*) devotion, dutifulness, faithfulness. **2** (*loyalty, faithfulness, esp. to one's husband or wife*) allegiance, constancy, faithfulness, fealty, loyalty, staunchness, steadfastness. ANTONYMS: disloyalty, infidelity. **3** (*honesty, veracity*) dependability, honesty, integrity, reliability, trustworthiness, veracity. **4** (*accurate correspondence* (*of a copy, description etc.*) *to the original*) accordance, accuracy, adherence, closeness, conformity, correspondence, exactitude, exactness, faithfulness, precision, scrupulousness. ANTONYMS: inaccuracy.

fidget *v.i.* **1** (*to move about restlessly*) bustle, chafe, fiddle, jitter, move about, shuffle, squirm, twiddle, twitch, wriggle. **2** (*to worry, to be uneasy*) fret, fuss, worry.
~*n.* (*pl.*) (*a state of nervous restlessness*) dither, fidgetiness, (*sl.*) jitters, nervousness, restlessness, unease, uneasiness.

fidgety *a.* (*tending to fidget a lot*) edgy, fretful, impatient, jerky, jittery, jumpy, nervous, on edge, restive, restless, twitchy, uneasy. ANTONYMS: composed, still.

field *n.* **1** (*a piece of land, esp. one enclosed for crops or pasture*) common, grassland, green, meadow, pasture. **2** (*the area of grass on which games are played*) ground, pitch. **3** (*all the entrants, candidates etc. in a contest*) applicants, candidates, competition, competitors, contestants, entrants, participants, players, possibilities, runners. **4** (*the place where a battle is fought*) battlefield, battleground. **5** (*a sphere of activity or knowledge; an interest*) area, (*coll., esp. facet.*) bailiwick, department, discipline, domain, environment, province, realm, speciality, sphere, territory. **6** (*the range of view or perception*) area, bounds, confines, extent, limits, range, scope.

~*v.t.* **1** (*in cricket etc., to catch or stop* (*the ball*) *and return it*) catch, pick up, retrieve, return, stop. **2** (*to assemble* (*a team, an army*) *ready for action*) assemble, present, put together, put up. **3** (*to deal with* (*questions etc.*), *esp. off the cuff*) answer, cope with, deal with, deflect, handle. **4** (*to retrieve* (*something or someone liable to go astray*)) retrieve, return.

fiend *n.* **1** (*an evil spirit*) demon, devil, evil spirit, imp. **2** (*a person of extreme wickedness or cruelty*) barbarian, beast, brute, degenerate, monster, ogre, savage. **3** (*an addict*) addict, devotee, enthusiast, fan, fanatic, (*coll.*) freak, maniac, (*sl.*) nut.

fiendish *a.* **1** (*cruel or unpleasant*) accursed, atrocious, black-hearted, cruel, demonic, devilish, diabolical, evil, ghoulish, hellish, infernal, inhuman, malevolent, malicious, malignant, monstrous, satanic, savage, unspeakable, wicked. ANTONYMS: angelic. **2** (*very difficult*) challenging, complex, complicated, difficult, intricate. ANTONYMS: easy, simple.

fierce *a.* **1** (*furiously aggressive; violent*) aggressive, baleful, barbarous, bloodthirsty, brutish, cruel, ferocious, fiery, furious, hostile, menacing, murderous, raging, ruthless, savage, stormy, tempestuous, threatening, violent, wild. ANTONYMS: benign, harmless. **2** (*vehement, impetuous*) ardent, blustery, boisterous, eager, frenzied, impetuous, passionate, vehement. ANTONYMS: gentle. **3** (*strong in an unpleasant way*) biting, bitter, dire, intense, keen, powerful, racking, relentless, severe, strong. ANTONYMS: mild.

fiery *a.* **1** (*on fire, flaming with fire*) ablaze, afire, aflame, blazing, burning, flaming. **2** (*producing a burning sensation*) heated, hot. **3** (*glowing or red, like fire*) aglow, brilliant, glaring, gleaming, glowing, incandescent, luminous, radiant, red. **4** ((*of skin*) *inflamed*) burning, fevered, flushed, heated, hot, inflamed. **5** ((*of curry etc.*) *hot-tasting*) hot, spicy. ANTONYMS: mild. **6** (*vehement, passionate*) ardent, choleric, eager, edgy, excitable, fervent, fierce, heated, hot-headed, hot-tempered, impetuous, irascible, irritable, passionate, peppery, spirited, temperamental, touchy, vehement, violent. ANTONYMS: cool. **7** (*pugnacious, untamed*) aggressive, mettlesome, pugnacious, untamed, wild.

fight *v.i.* **1** (*to contend in battle, or in single combat* (*with, against*)) brawl, clash, close, combat, come to blows, conflict, contend, dispute, feud, tussle. **2** (*to strive for victory or superiority*) assault, battle, combat, do battle, engage, war. **3** (*to strive in a determined way to achieve something*) campaign, strive, struggle, try. **4** (*to oppose*) confront, contest, defy, dispute, oppose, refute, resist, withstand. **5** (*to quarrel, to disagree*) argue, bicker, disagree, dispute, fall out, quarrel, squabble, wrangle.

~*v.t.* **1** (*to contend with, to struggle against*) conflict, contend, contest, grapple, struggle, wrestle. **2** (*to carry on* (*a contest, lawsuit etc.*)) carry on, conduct, engage in, prosecute, wage. **3** (*to take part in* (*a boxing match*)) box, spar.

~*n.* **1** (*a struggle between individuals, armies or animals, to injure each other or obtain the mastery*) affray, altercation, brawl, brush, clash, disturbance, fighting, fracas, fray, free-for-all, riot, (*coll.*) scrap, (*coll.*) set-to, struggle. **2** (*a battle, a combat*) action, battle, combat, conflict, duel, engagement, hostilities, skirmish, strife, war. **3** (*a contest of any kind*) competition, contention, contest, encounter, match. **4** (*a boxing match*) bout, boxing match. **5** (*a quarrel, a row*) altercation, argument, disagreement, dispute, dissension, feud, quarrel, row, (*coll.*) run-in, squabble. ANTONYMS: concord. **6** (*power of or inclination for fighting*) belligerence, mettle, militancy, spirit, truculence. **to fight back 1** (*to resist*) put up resistance, resist. **2** (*to counter-attack*) counter-attack, hit back, reply, retaliate. **3** (*to hold back* (*tears, an emotion*) *with an effort*) bottle up, contain, control, curb, hold back, hold in check, restrain. **to fight off** (*to repel*) beat off, hold at bay, repel, repress, repulse, resist, stave off, ward off.

figment *n.* (*an invented statement, something that exists only in the imagination*) creation, fable, fabrication, falsehood, fancy, fiction, illusion, improvisation, invention, notion, story. ANTONYMS: fact.

figurative *a.* **1** (*representing something by a figure or type*) illustrative, indicative, representative, typical. **2** (*symbolic, metaphorical*) allegorical, emblematic, illustrative, metaphorical, symbolic. ANTONYMS: literal. **3** (*flowery, ornate*) descriptive, fanciful, florid, flowery, ornate, poetical. ANTONYMS: prosaic.

figure *n.* **1** (*the external form of a person or thing*) body, configuration, form, frame, shape, structure. **2** (*bodily shape, esp. from the point of view of its attractiveness*) build, cast, cut, frame, physique, torso. **3** (*an unidentified person seen in outline*) outline, profile, shadow, silhouette. **4** (*a personage, a character*) celebrity, character, dignitary, notable, personage, personality, somebody, worthy. ANTONYMS: nobody. **5** (*the mental impression that a person makes*) appearance, distinction, impression.

6 (*the representation of any form, as by carving or modelling*) depiction, illustration, portrayal, representation. **7** (*a statue, an image*) bust, effigy, image, likeness, model, sculpture, statue. **8** (*a diagram, an illustrative drawing*) diagram, drawing, illustration, model, pattern, picture, sketch. **9** (*an emblem, a type*) device, emblem, motif. **10** (*a creation of the imagination*) creation, fancy, idea. **11** (*a symbol representing a number, esp. any one of the 10 Arabic numerals*) character, cipher, digit, number, numeral, symbol. **12** (*an amount*) amount, sum, total. **13** (*a value*) cost, price, value.
~*v.t.* **1** (*to form an image or representation of*) depict, illustrate, portray. **2** (*to represent, to imagine*) conceive, imagine, picture, represent, symbolize. **3** (*to cover or ornament a pattern with figures*) adorn, decorate, embellish, ornament. **4** (*to work out in figures*) add, calculate, compute, count, enumerate, reckon, sum, tally, tot up, work out. **5** (*to mark with numbers or prices*) mark, variegate. **6** (*to consider, to conclude*) assume, believe, conclude, consider, judge, presume, reckon, think.
~*v.i.* (*to be conspicuous*) act, appear, be conspicuous, feature, participate. **to figure out 1** (*to ascertain by computation*) calculate, compute, estimate, reckon, work out. **2** (*to understand*) (*coll.*) catch on, comprehend, decipher, fathom out, get the hang of, grasp, interpret, make out, perceive, resolve, see, solve, (*sl.*) suss, translate, (*coll.*) twig, understand.

filament *n.* (*a slender, threadlike fibre*) fibre, fibril, hair, strand, string, thread, wire, wisp.

filch *v.t.* (*to steal, to pilfer*) embezzle, (*rhyming sl.*) half-inch, (*coll.*) lift, misappropriate, (*sl.*) nick, pilfer, (*coll.*) pinch, purloin, (*coll.*) rip off, steal, (*coll.*) swipe, take, thieve. ANTONYMS: return.

file[1] *n.* **1** (*a box or folder etc. in which documents are kept in order*) box, case, dossier, folder, portfolio, string, wire. **2** (*the set of papers kept in this way*) documents, papers. **3** (*a row of people or things arranged one behind the other from front to back*) column, line, queue, rank, row, string. **4** (*a list*) catalogue, list, roll. **5** (*a series*) class, rank, series.
~*v.t.* **1** (*to arrange in order*) alphabetize, arrange, catalogue, categorize, classify, document, enter, order, organize, pigeon-hole, sort, systematize. **2** (*to initiate* (*charges, a lawsuit*)) initiate, place on record, register. **3** (*to send in* (*a story*) *to a newspaper*) complete, fill in, send in, submit.
~*v.i.* (*to walk in file or line*) march, parade, pass, queue, troop, walk in file.

file[2] *n.* (*a steel instrument with a ridged surface,*

used for cutting and smoothing metals, fingernails etc.*) rasp, scraper.
~*v.t.* **1** (*to smooth or polish with a file*) abrade, burnish, polish, rub down, smooth. **2** (*to cut* (*the surface*) *away with a file*) grind, rasp, scrape. **3** (*to polish, to elaborate*) elaborate, polish, refine, touch up.

fill *v.t.* **1** (*to put or pour into until all the space is occupied*) brim over, cram, fill up, jam, pack, stuff. ANTONYMS: empty, void. **2** (*to spread over or throughout*) cover, imbue, impregnate, infuse, occupy, overspread, pervade, saturate, suffuse. **3** (*to block up* (*a crack with putty, a hollow tooth with stopping etc.*)) block up, bung, caulk, close, cork, plug, seal, stop. **4** (*to appoint a person to discharge the duties of*) appoint, assign, engage. **5** (*to discharge the duties of*) carry out, discharge, do, execute, fulfil, hold, perform. **6** (*to satisfy, to glut*) content, glut, gorge, sate, satiate, satisfy. **7** (*to fulfil*) answer, fulfil, meet. **8** (*to stock or store abundantly*) furnish, replenish, stock, store, supply. **9** (*to distend* (*as sails*)) distend, fill out, inflate, swell.
~*n.* (*as much as will satisfy*) ample, enough, plenty, sufficient, surfeit. **to fill in 1** (*to complete* (*anything that is unfinished, such as an outline or a form*)) answer, complete, fill out, fill up, make out. **2** (*to provide with necessary or up-to-date information*) acquaint, apprise, bring up to date, inform, notify, tell. **3** (*to act as a temporary substitute* (*for*)) deputize (for), replace, stand in (for), sub (for), substitute (for), take the place (of).

filling *a.* ((*esp. of food*) *satisfying*) ample, heavy, satisfying, square, substantial.
~*n.* (*anything serving to fill up*) contents, innards, insides, padding, stuffing, wadding.

film *n.* **1** (*a series of connected moving images projected on a screen; a story represented in this way*) (*coll.*) flick, motion picture, movie, picture, video. **2** (*a thin coating or layer*) coat, coating, layer, membrane, sheet, skin. **3** (*a fine thread*) filament, thread. **4** (*a thin, slight covering or veil*) covering, dusting, overlay, screen, veil. **5** (*a dimness or opaqueness affecting the eyes*) blur, cloud, dimness, haze, haziness, mist, mistiness, murkiness, opacity, opaqueness.
~*v.t.* (*to record on a photographic film*) photograph, shoot, take, video.
~*v.i.* (*to become covered with or as with a film*) blear, blur, cloud, coat, dim, dull, glaze, haze, mist, obscure, veil.

filmy *a.* **1** (*thin and gauzy*) chiffon, cobwebby, delicate, diaphanous, fine, fine-spun, flimsy, floaty, fragile, gauzy, gossamer, insubstantial, light, peekaboo, see-through, sheer, thin, translucent, transparent. **2** (*covered with or as if with film; blurred*) bleary, blurred, blurry, cloudy, dim, hazy, milky, misty, murky, opalescent, opaque, pearly. ANTONYMS: clear, distinct.

filter *n.* (*an apparatus for straining liquids and freeing them from impurities*) colander, gauze, membrane, mesh, net, riddle, screen, sieve, strainer.
~*v.t.* (*to purify by passing through a filter*) clarify, filtrate, purify, refine, screen, sieve, sift, strain.
~*v.i.* **1** (*to pass through a filter*) percolate, strain. **2** (*to percolate*) drain, dribble, drip, escape, exude, leach, leak, ooze, percolate, seep, transude, trickle.

filth *n.* **1** (*anything dirty or foul*) contamination, corruption, (*sl.*) crap, (*sl.*) crud, dirt, dung, effluent, excrement, filthiness, foulness, garbage, grime, (*coll.*) grot, (*coll.*) gunge, muck, ordure, pollution, refuse, sewage, (*taboo sl.*) shit, slime. ANTONYMS: cleanness. **2** (*foul language, obscenity*) corruption, dirty-mindedness, foul language, grossness, impurity, indecency, obscenity, perversion, pornography, smut, vulgarity.

filthy *a.* **1** (*dirty, foul*) defiled, dirty, foul, grimy, grubby, (*coll.*) gungy, mucky, polluted, putrid, (*sl.*) scuzzy, slimy, soiled, sordid, squalid, tainted, unclean, unwashed, vile. ANTONYMS: clean, spotless. **2** (*morally impure; obscene*) bawdy, blue, coarse, corrupt, depraved, dirty-minded, foul, gross, immoral, impure, indecent, lewd, licentious, obscene, pornographic, ribald, smutty, vulgar. **3** ((*of weather*) *wet and windy*) inclement, stormy, wet, wild. **4** (*disgraceful, unpleasant*) base, despicable, disgraceful, low, offensive, unpleasant, vile.

final *a.* **1** (*occurring at or relating to the end or conclusion*) closing, concluding, ending, eventual, last, latest, terminal, ultimate. ANTONYMS: first, opening. **2** (*that cannot be changed or questioned; decisive*) absolute, certain, conclusive, decided, decisive, definite, definitive, finished, immutable, incontrovertible, indisputable, irrefutable, irreversible, irrevocable, settled.

finale *n.* (*the end, conclusion*) climax, close, conclusion, culmination, denouement, end, epilogue, finis, finish, termination. ANTONYMS: beginning, prologue.

finality *n.* (*the state of being finally and completely settled*) certitude, conclusiveness, decisiveness, definiteness, incontrovertibility, inevitability, irrefutability, irrevocability, resolution, unavoidability.

finally *adv.* **1** (*after a long time*) at last, eventually, in the end, in the long run, lastly,

ultimately. **2** (*in a finished state, decisively*) absolutely, completely, conclusively, convincingly, decisively, definitely, for ever, for good, irrevocably, once and for all, permanently.

finance *n.* **1** (*the system of management of (esp. public) revenue and expenditure*) accounting, banking, business, commerce, economics, financial affairs, investment. **2** (*money*) assets, capital, cash, funds, holdings, money, resources, wealth, wherewithal.
~*v.t.* (*to provide with capital*) back, bankroll, float, fund, guarantee, invest in, pay for, subsidize, support, underwrite.

financial *a.* (*monetary, fiscal*) budgetary, economic, fiscal, monetary, money, pecuniary.

find *v.t.* **1** (*to chance on, to meet with*) bump into, chance on, come across, come up with, encounter, happen upon, hit, light upon, meet with, stumble upon, upon. **2** (*to discover or acquire by search or study*) acquire, discover, ferret out, learn, locate, track down, turn up, uncover, unearth. **3** (*to rediscover (something lost)*) get back, recoup, recover, rediscover, regain, repossess, retrieve. **4** (*to ascertain by experience or experiment*) arrive at, ascertain, determine. **5** (*to perceive, to recognize*) descry, detect, discern, notice, observe, perceive, realize, recognize, spot. **6** (*to be of the opinion that*) consider, feel, regard, think. **7** (*to succeed in obtaining*) achieve, acquire, attain, earn, gain, get, obtain, procure, secure, win. ANTONYMS: lose. **8** (*to summon up*) call up, muster, rouse, summon up. **9** (*to supply, to provide*) contribute, furnish, provide, supply. **10** (*to decide, to declare by verdict*) decide, declare, determine, judge, pronounce.
~*n.* **1** (*the discovery of anything valuable*) discovery, strike. **2** (*the thing so found*) acquisition, asset, bargain, catch, discovery, finding, windfall. **to find out 1** (*to discover*) come to know, detect, discover, learn, perceive. **2** (*to get information*) ascertain, determine, glean, learn. **3** (*to unravel, to solve*) crack, decipher, resolve, solve, unravel, work out. **4** (*to detect, to discover the dishonesty of*) catch, detect, disclose, expose, reveal, (*sl.*) rumble, (*sl.*) suss, uncover, unmask.

finding *n.* **1** (*a discovery*) discovery, find. **2** (*the act of returning a verdict; a verdict*) award, conclusion, decision, declaration, decree, determination, judgement, pronouncement, recommendation, sentence, verdict.

fine[1] *a.* **1** (*excellent in quality or appearance*) choice, excellent, exceptional, first-class, first-rate, high quality, magnificent, outstanding, select, splendid, sterling, superior, supreme. ANTONYMS: inferior, poor. **2** (*good, enjoyable*) acceptable, all right, enjoyable, good, (*coll.*) OK, (*coll.*) okay, pleasant, satisfactory. **3** (*well, in good health*) fit, healthy, robust, sound, strong, well. **4** ((*of weather*) *bright and sunny*) balmy, bright, clear, clement, cloudless, dry, fair, nice, pleasant, sunny. ANTONYMS: cloudy, dull, rainy. **5** (*pure, free from extraneous matter*) clear, pure, refined, unadulterated, unalloyed, uncontaminated, untainted. **6** ((*of taste, differences etc.*) *delicate, subtle*) dainty, delicate, fastidious, minute, nice, subtle. **7** (*in small grains or particles*) powdered, powdery, pulverized. **8** (*thin, slender*) attenuated, little, slender, slight, small, tenuous, thin. **9** (*keen, sharp*) cutting, honed, keen, razor-sharp, sharp. ANTONYMS: blunt. **10** (*of delicate texture or material*) delicate, diaphanous, flimsy, fragile, frail, gauzy, gossamer, light, sheer. ANTONYMS: coarse. **11** (*accomplished, brilliant*) accomplished, acute, brilliant, consummate, critical, discriminating, finished, intelligent, precise, quick. **12** (*handsome, beautiful*) attractive, beautiful, elegant, exquisite, good-looking, handsome, lovely, pretty, striking. **13** (*showy, smart*) decorative, ornate, pretentious, showy, smart, stylish, tasteful. **14** (*dignified, impressive*) dignified, distinguished, impressive, noble. **15** (*complimentary; euphemistic*) appreciative, complimentary, euphemistic, favourable, flattering. **16** (*iron.*) (*unpleasant or unsatisfactory*) nasty, (*iron.*) nice, unpleasant, unsatisfactory.

fine² *n.* (*a sum of money imposed as a penalty for an offence*) damages, fee, forfeit, mulct, penalty, punishment.
~*v.t.* (*to impose a financial penalty upon*) charge, mulct, penalize, punish.

finery *n.* (*fine clothes, showy decorations*) decorations, frippery, (*coll.*) gear, (*coll.*) glad rags, ornaments, splendour, (*coll.*) Sunday best, trappings, trinkets.

finesse *n.* **1** (*elegance, refinement*) delicacy, diplomacy, discretion, elegance, grace, panache, polish, refinement, savoir faire, sophistication, style, subtlety, tact, taste. ANTONYMS: clumsiness. **2** (*artifice or artful manipulation*) artifice, bluff, contrivance, deceit, deception, device, expedient, feint, intrigue, machination, manipulation, manoeuvre, ruse, stratagem, trick, wile. **3** (*skill, dexterity, esp. in handling difficult situations*) adeptness, adroitness, artfulness, cleverness, craft, dexterity, expertise, facility, (*coll.*) know-how, mastery, proficiency, quickness, skill, talent. ANTONYMS: ineptitude.

finger *n.* (*anything resembling or serving the purpose of a finger, a catch*) catch, gripper, guide, pointer.

~*v.t.* **1** (*to touch with or turn about in the fingers*) feel, handle, maul, (*coll.*) paw, touch. **2** (*to meddle or interfere with*) fiddle with, interfere with, meddle with, play about with, toy with. **3** (*to pilfer*) (*sl.*) nick, pilfer, steal. **4** (*to identify* (*to the police*)) (*sl.*) grass up, identify, inform on, peach on, point out, (*sl.*) put the finger on.

finicky *a.* **1** (*affecting great precision or delicacy*) delicate, detailed, nice, precise. **2** (*fussy, fastidious*) (*coll.*) choosy, critical, dainty, difficult, fastidious, fussy, hard to please, (*coll.*) nit-picking, overnice, (*coll.*) pernickety, (*coll.*) picky, squeamish. **3** (*particular about details or trifles*) meticulous, particular, punctilious, scrupulous.

finish *v.t.* **1** (*to bring to an end*) close, conclude, end, finalize, stop, terminate. ANTONYMS: begin, start. **2** (*to complete*) accomplish, achieve, carry through, complete, deal with, discharge, execute, fulfil, get done, perform, round off, settle, wrap up. **3** (*to perfect*) cap, consummate, crown, perfect, round off. **4** (*to give the final touches to, to treat the surface of*) coat, dress, face, gild, perfect, polish, refine, smooth, texture, touch up, trim, varnish, veneer, wax. **5** (*to consume, to get through*) consume, deplete, dispose of, drain, empty, expend, get through, spend, use up. **6** (*to kill, to defeat*) annihilate, (*coll.*) bump off, defeat, destroy, dispose of, eliminate, exterminate, get rid of, kill, overcome, rout, (*N Am., sl.*) rub out, ruin, (*sl.*) waste, worst.
~*v.i.* **1** (*to come to the end, to expire*) cease, expire, reach the end, stop. **2** (*to end up*) culminate, end up, wind up.
~*n.* **1** (*the act of finishing*) ending, finishing, settling, stopping. **2** (*the final stage; the end of a race when the competitors reach the winning post*) cessation, close, completion, conclusion, consummation, culmination, denouement, end, finale, termination, winding up. ANTONYMS: beginning, start. **3** (*the appearance, texture etc. of the surface of wood, cloth etc.*) appearance, coating, grain, lustre, patina, polish, shine, surface, texture, varnish, veneer. **4** (*elegance, refinement*) culture, elegance, grace, perfection, polish, refinement, sophistication.

finished *a.* **1** (*completed*) achieved, complete, concluded, done, ended, finalized, fulfilled, over, terminated, through, wrapped up. ANTONYMS: incomplete, unfinished. **2** (*having a smooth or smart appearance*) elegant, flawless, impeccable, perfected, polished, refined, smooth, trim. **3** (*ruined or defeated*) bankrupt, dead, defeated, (*coll.*) done for, doomed, exhausted, gone, lost, played out, ruined, used-up, (*sl.*) washed up, wiped out, wrecked.

4 (*performed or endowed with great skill*) accomplished, consummate, cultivated, expert, masterly, professional, proficient, skilled. ANTONYMS: unskilled.

finite *a.* (*having limits or bounds*) bounded, circumscribed, demarcated, finite, limited, measurable, restricted, terminable. ANTONYMS: boundless, infinite.

fire *n.* **1** (*combustion, incandescence*) burning, combustion, flame, incandescence. **2** (*a conflagration*) blaze, conflagration, inferno. **3** (*a light or glow resembling fire*) glow, light, luminosity, lustre, radiance, sparkle. **4** (*the discharge of firearms*) barrage, bombardment, broadside, cannonade, flak, fusillade, hail, salvo, shelling, sniping, volley. **5** (*ardent emotion*) animation, ardour, brio, dash, eagerness, élan, emotion, energy, enthusiasm, excitement, fervour, force, impetuosity, intensity, life, passion, spirit, verve, vigour, vivacity. ANTONYMS: coldness. **6** (*liveliness of imagination*) fancy, imagination, inspiration. **7** (*a severe affliction*) affliction, anguish, persecution, suffering, torture.

~*v.t.* **1** (*to cause to explode; to propel from a gun*) detonate, discharge, explode, hurl, launch, let off, loose, propel, set off, shell, shoot, touch off. **2** (*to set on fire*) ignite, kindle, light, set ablaze, set alight, set on fire. ANTONYMS: extinguish. **3** (*to dismiss from employment*) axe, cashier, discharge, dismiss, downsize, give the boot, let go, make redundant, sack. ANTONYMS: appoint, hire. **4** (*to excite, to inspire*) animate, arouse, electrify, enliven, enthuse, excite, foment, galvanize, impassion, incite, inflame, inspire, invigorate, motivate, provoke, quicken, rouse, stimulate, stir, whip up.

firm[1] *a.* **1** (*stable, steady*) anchored, fast, fixed, immovable, rooted, secure, stable, steady, tight. ANTONYMS: unstable. **2** (*solid, compact*) compact, compressed, concentrated, congealed, dense, frozen, hard, inelastic, inflexible, rigid, set, solid, stiff, unyielding. ANTONYMS: soft, yielding. **3** (*securely established, unchanging*) definite, established, immutable, unchanging, undeviating. **4** (*steadfast, determined*) adamant, constant, determined, dogged, obdurate, obstinate, steadfast, strict, stubborn, tenacious. **5** (*enduring, resolute*) enduring, resolute, staunch, strong, sturdy. **6** ((*of prices etc.*) *not changing in level*) constant, unwavering.

firm[2] *n.* (*a business partnership*) association, business, company, concern, conglomerate, corporation, enterprise, establishment, house, organization, (*coll.*) outfit, partnership.

first *a.* **1** (*foremost in order or excellence*) foremost, highest. ANTONYMS: last, lowest. **2** (*earliest in occurrence*) earliest, initial, introductory, opening, original, primary. **3** (*coming next* (*to something specified or implied*)) nearest, next. **4** (*chief, highest*) chief, greatest, head, highest, leading, noblest, preeminent, prime, principal, ruling, supreme, top. **5** (*basic, fundamental*) basic, cardinal, elementary, essential, fundamental, key, primary, rudimentary.

~*adv.* **1** (*before all others in order or excellence*) before all else, firstly, initially, in the first place, to begin with. **2** (*before some time or event*) beforehand, in advance. **3** (*in preference*) in preference, rather, sooner.

~*n.* (*the beginning; the first day of a month*) beginning, commencement, inception, introduction, outset, start.

fishy *a.* **1** (*like or relating to fish*) fishlike, piscatorial, piscine. **2** (*of a doubtful character, questionable*) (*coll.*) dodgy, doubtful, dubious, funny, implausible, improbable, odd, peculiar, queer, questionable, (*sl.*) rum, shady, strange, suspect, suspicious, unlikely.

fissure *n.* **1** (*a cleft made by the splitting or parting of any substance*) breach, break, chasm, chink, cleavage, cleft, crack, cranny, crevice, division, fault, fracture, gap, hole, opening, parting, rent, rift, rupture, split. **2** (*a slit or narrow opening*) depression, opening, slit.

fit[1] *a.* **1** (*adapted, suitable*) adapted, apposite, appropriate, fitting, suitable, well-suited. ANTONYMS: ill-suited, inappropriate. **2** (*qualified, competent*) able, capable, competent, eligible, qualified. **3** (*in a suitable condition* (*to do or for*)) adequate, prepared, ready. **4** (*in good physical condition*) able-bodied, hale, healthy, hearty, in good shape, in training, robust, strapping, strong, sturdy, toned up, trim, vigorous, well. ANTONYMS: out of shape, unfit. **5** (*proper, right*) appropriate, apt, becoming, befitting, correct, deserving, expedient, proper, right, seemly. ANTONYMS: inappropriate.

~*v.t.* **1** (*to be of the right size and shape for*) accord, befit, satisfy, suit. **2** (*to adapt to any shape or size*) adapt, adjust, alter, arrange, change, fashion, modify, place, position, shape. **3** (*to make suitable, to find room for*) accommodate, find room for, make suitable. **4** (*to insert*) fix, insert, install. **5** (*to prepare*) make ready, prepare, qualify. **6** (*to supply, to equip*) arm, equip, furnish, kit out, outfit, provide, rig out, supply. **7** (*to be in harmony with*) belong, go with, harmonize with, meet. **8** (*to correspond to exactly*) agree, conform, correspond to, go together, match, tally.

fit[2] *n.* **1** (*a violent seizure or paroxysm*) attack, convulsion, paroxysm, seizure, spasm. **2** (*a sudden transitory attack of illness*) bout, period, spell, throe. **3** (*a short burst*) burst, eruption, explosion, outbreak, outburst, seizure, spasm. **4** (*a transient state of impulsive action*) caprice, fancy, humour, mood, whim.

fitful *a.* (*spasmodic, wavering*) broken, capricious, desultory, disturbed, erratic, flickering, fluctuating, haphazard, impulsive, inconstant, intermittent, irregular, occasional, periodic, spasmodic, sporadic, uneven, unstable, variable, wavering. ANTONYMS: regular, steady.

fitness *n.* **1** (*suitability*) adaptation, adequacy, applicability, appropriateness, aptness, competence, eligibility, pertinence, propriety, qualifications, readiness, seemliness, suitability. ANTONYMS: unsuitability. **2** (*good physical condition or health*) condition, fettle, good shape, health, robustness, strength, tone, vigour.

fitting *a.* (*suitable, proper*) apposite, appropriate, apt, becoming, befitting, correct, decent, decorous, desirable, fit, germane, meet, proper, right, seemly, suitable. ANTONYMS: ill-suited, unsuitable.

fix *v.t.* **1** (*to fasten, to secure firmly*) affix, anchor, attach, bind, cement, connect, couple, fasten, fuse, glue, link, make fast, nail, pin, rivet, secure, stabilize, stick, tie, weld. ANTONYMS: dislodge, move. **2** (*to determine, to decide* (*on*)) conclude, decide, define, determine, limit, resolve, set, settle, specify. **3** (*to establish, to implant*) embed, establish, implant. **4** (*to attract and hold* (*a person's eyes, attention etc.*)) attract, fascinate, freeze, hold, hypnotize, immobilize, mesmerize, rivet. **5** (*to direct steadily*) aim, concentrate, direct, focus, level. **6** (*to mend or repair*) mend, patch up, repair, restore. ANTONYMS: damage. **7** (*to identify a definite position for*) install, locate, place, position. **8** (*to adjust, to arrange properly*) adjust, arrange, correct, emend, rectify, regulate, remedy, set rights, straighten out. **9** (*to prepare* (*food or drink*)) organize, pour out, prepare. **10** (*to solidify*) congeal, consolidate, firm up, harden, set, solidify, stiffen, thicken. **11** (*to punish, to get even with*) even the score with, get even with, pay back, punish, repay, retaliate against, (*coll.*) sort out, wreak vengeance on. **12** (*to influence illicitly*) bribe, buy, corrupt, influence, manipulate, pull strings.
~*n.* **1** (*an awkward predicament*) bind, corner, difficulty, dilemma, embarrassment, (*coll.*) hole, (*coll.*) hot water, jam, mess, (*coll.*) pickle, pinch, plight, predicament, quandary, situation, spot, tight spot. **2** (*an act or instance of bribery*) bribery, fiddle, set-up. **to fix up 1** (*to arrange, to organize*) arrange, fix, organize, plan, settle, sort out. **2** (*to assemble or construct*) assemble, build, construct, erect. **3** (*to provide*) furnish, lay on, provide, supply.

fixation *n.* (*an obsession*) complex, compulsion, fetish, (*coll.*) hang-up, infatuation, mania, obsession, preoccupation, (*coll.*) thing.

fixed *a.* **1** (*fast, firm*) anchored, attached, fast, firm, immovable, permanent, rigid, rooted, secure, set, solid, stable, stationary, steady. ANTONYMS: unstable. **2** (*established, unalterable*) constant, established, settled, unalterable, unchanging, undeviating, unwavering.

fizz *v.i.* **1** (*to make a hissing or spluttering sound*) hiss, splutter. **2** ((*of a drink*) *to effervesce*) bubble, effervesce, ferment, fizzle, froth, sparkle.
~*n.* **1** (*a hissing, spluttering sound*) hiss, splutter. **2** (*effervescence*) effervescence, froth.

flabbergasted *a.* (*overwhelmed by wonder or horror*) abashed, amazed, astonished, astounded, (*coll.*) bowled over, confounded, dazed, disconcerted, dumbfounded, dumbstruck, (*sl.*) gobsmacked, nonplussed, overcome, overwhelmed, speechless, staggered, stunned. ANTONYMS: unimpressed.

flabby *a.* **1** (*hanging loosely*) drooping, flaccid, floppy, lax, limp, loose, pendulous, sagging, slack, soft, toneless, yielding. ANTONYMS: firm, rigid. **2** (*feeble, wasteful*) effete, enervated, feeble, impotent, ineffective, ineffectual, languid, nerveless, spineless, wasteful, weak, (*coll.*) wimpish.

flaccid *a.* **1** (*lacking firmness or vigour*) soft, weak, yielding. **2** (*limp, flabby*) drooping, flabby, floppy, limp, loose. **3** (*relaxed, feeble*) feeble, lax, nerveless, relaxed.

flag[1] *n.* (*a piece of cloth, usu. square or oblong, displayed as a banner or signal*) banner, colour, ensign, jack, pennant, standard.
~*v.t.* **1** (*to signal or communicate by means of a flag or flags*) hail, salute, signal, warn, wave. **2** (*to mark* (*a passage in a book or document etc.*) *for someone's attention*) indicate, label, mark up, notate, tab.

flag[2] *v.i.* **1** (*to lose strength or vigour*) fade, fail, faint, lag, languish, tire, weaken, weary, wilt. **2** (*to become spiritless or dejected*) dwindle, ebb, falter, lose interest. **3** (*to hang loosely*) dangle, droop, fall, hang down, sag, slump.

flagrant *a.* (*glaring, outrageous*) arrant, atrocious, audacious, barefaced, blatant, bold, brazen, conspicuous, glaring, immodest, infamous, notorious, open, ostentatious, outrageous, scandalous, shameless, shocking, undisguised. ANTONYMS: disguised, subtle.

flair *n.* **1** (*a natural aptitude or gift; talent*) ability, accomplishment, aptitude, bent, disposition, faculty, feel, genius, gift, knack, mastery, propensity, skill, talent. **2** (*stylishness; panache*) chic, dash, élan, elegance, panache, style, stylishness, verve. **3** (*keen perception*) discernment, perception, taste.

flake *n.* **1** (*a fleecy particle* (*as of snow*)) flock, particle, scrap, snowflake, tuft. **2** (*a thin piece peeled off*) layer, peeling, shaving, sliver, wafer. **3** (*a thin scalelike fragment*) bit, chip, piece, scale.

~*v.t.* (*to form into flakes or loose particles*) blister, chip, fragment.

~*v.i.* (*to peel or scale off in flakes*) exfoliate, peel, scale. **to flake out** (*to collapse or fall asleep from exhaustion*) collapse, faint, fall asleep, (*coll.*) keel over, pass out, swoon.

flamboyant *a.* **1** (*exuberant, showy*) brilliant, dazzling, extravagant, exuberant, flashy, (*coll.*) glitzy, ostentatious, over-the-top, resplendent, showy, theatrical. **2** (*florid, highly decorated*) baroque, decorated, elaborate, fancy, florid, ornate, rococo. ANTONYMS: plain. **3** (*gorgeously coloured*) bright, gaudy, highly coloured, rich, vivid.

flame *n.* **1** (*a blaze; fire*) blaze, conflagration, fire. **2** (*a bright light*) brightness, glow, light. **3** (*excitement, passion*) ardour, eagerness, enthusiasm, excitement, fervency, fervour, fire, heat, intensity, keenness, passion, warmth, zeal. ANTONYMS: coolness. **4** (*a boyfriend or girlfriend*) beau, beloved, boyfriend, girlfriend, heart-throb, lady-love, lover, sweetheart.

~*v.t.* (*to inflame, to excite*) arouse, excite, inflame, stimulate.

~*v.i.* **1** (*to burst into flames*) blaze, burn, burst into flames. **2** (*to break* (*out*) *or blaze* (*up*) *in violent passion*) blaze out, erupt, explode, flare up. **3** (*to shine, to glow*) flash, glow, shine.

flammable *a.* (*that can catch fire and burn easily*) combustible, ignitable, incendiary, inflammable. ANTONYMS: non-flammable.

flank *n.* **1** (*the fleshy or muscular part of the side between the hips and the ribs*) ham, haunch, hip, loin, quarter, side, thigh. **2** (*either side of a building, mountain etc.*) side, wing.

~*v.t.* (*to stand or be at the flank or side of*) border, bound, edge, fringe, limit, line, screen, skirt, touch, wall.

flannel *n.* **1** (*a piece of flannel used for washing the face etc.*) cloth, face cloth. **2** (*flattery*) flattery, (*coll.*) soft soap, (*coll.*) sweet talk. **3** (*evasive waffling, nonsense*) (*coll.*) baloney, blarney, (*taboo sl.*) bullshit, (*sl.*) crap, equivocation, evasion, hedging, humbug, nonsense, prevarication, rubbish, (*coll.*) waffle.

~*v.i.* **1** (*to speak in a flattering way*) flatter, (*coll.*) soft-soap, (*coll.*) sweet-talk. **2** (*to waffle*

on evasively) equivocate, hedge, mislead, prevaricate, pull the wool, (*coll.*) waffle.

flap *v.t.* **1** (*to move* (*wings, one's arms etc.*) *rapidly up and down or to and fro*) agitate, beat, flail, flutter, shake, thrash, thresh, vibrate, wag, waggle, wave. **2** (*to beat or drive away with anything broad and flexible*) beat, drive away, flail, slap, strike.

~*v.i.* **1** (*to be moved loosely to and fro*) flutter, oscillate, swing about, swish, vibrate. **2** (*to be in a state of anxiety or confusion*) fuss, panic, worry.

~*n.* **1** (*anything broad and flexible, hanging loosely, or attached by one side only*) apron, cover, fly, fold, overlap, skirt, tab, tail. **2** (*the motion or act of flapping*) beating, flapping, flutter, shaking, swinging, waving. **3** (*a state of anxiety or confusion*) ado, agitation, commotion, confusion, fluster, panic, (*coll.*) state, (*coll.*) stew, (*coll.*) sweat, (*coll.*) tizzy, (*coll.*) to-do, (*coll.*) twitter, upset.

flare *v.i.* **1** (*to open or spread outwards at one end*) broaden, enlarge, expand, increase, open, splay, spread outwards, widen. ANTONYMS: taper. **2** (*to flame up or to glow, esp. with an unsteady light*) blaze, dazzle, flame up, flash, flicker, flutter, glare, gleam, glimmer, glow, shimmer, sparkle, waver. **3** (*to burst into anger*) blaze, (*coll.*) blow one's top, (*coll.*) blow up, boil over, break out, burst out, chafe, erupt, explode, (*coll.*) fly off the handle, fume, lose control, lose one's temper, rage, seethe, throw a tantrum. **4** (*to bounce, to swagger*) bounce, (*esp. N Am.*) sashay, strut, swagger.

~*n.* **1** (*a large unsteady light*) dazzle, flame, flash, flicker, glare, light. **2** ((*a device producing*) *a blaze of light used for illumination or to attract attention*) blaze, brilliance, illumination, incandescence, luminosity.

flash *v.i.* **1** (*to send out a quick or regular gleam*) coruscate, flare, flicker, glare, gleam, scintillate, shimmer, sparkle, twinkle. **2** (*to reflect light, to glitter*) burst forth, glint, glisten, glitter. **3** (*to burst suddenly into flame or perception*) blaze, burn, burst, flame, flare, ignite, light. **4** (*to rush swiftly, to dash*) bolt, break, (*coll.*) burn rubber, dart, dash, fly, hasten, race, rush, scuttle, shoot, speed, splash, sprint, streak, sweep, whistle, zip, zoom. ANTONYMS: crawl.

~*v.t.* **1** (*to display or expose suddenly and briefly*) display, exhibit, expose, show. ANTONYMS: conceal, hide. **2** (*to display ostentatiously*) brandish, flaunt, flourish. **3** (*to convey or transmit instantaneously* (*as news by radio*)) broadcast, convey, transmit.

~*n.* **1** (*a sudden and transitory gleam of bright light*) beam, blaze, burst, coruscation, dazzle,

flame, flare, flicker, gleam, glimmer, glint, light, ray, scintillation, shaft, shimmer, spark, sparkle, streak, twinkle. **2** (*an instant*) instant, (*coll.*) jiffy, minute, moment, second, shake, split second, trice, twinkling. **3** (*a sudden occurrence or display of feeling or understanding*) outburst, revelation. **4** (*a sudden outburst, as of anger, wit etc.*) burst, demonstration, display, explosion, manifestation, outbreak, outburst, show, sign, touch. **5** (*vulgar show, ostentation*) gaudiness, ostentation, showiness. **6** (*a body of water driven along with violence*) deluge, flood, torrent. **7** (*a sticker on goods etc. advertising e.g. a reduction in price*) label, sticker, tag.
~*a.* (*gaudy, vulgarly showy*) cheap, dazzling, gaudy, glamorous, (*sl.*) naff, ostentatious, showy, (*sl.*) snazzy, (*coll.*) swish, (*coll.*) tacky, tasteless, vulgar.

flashy *a.* **1** (*cheap and showy*) brash, cheap, flamboyant, flash, garish, gaudy, glaring, (*coll.*) glitzy, jazzy, loud, (*sl.*) naff, ostentatious, pretentious, shallow, showy, (*sl.*) snazzy, (*coll.*) tacky, tasteless, tawdry, vulgar. ANTONYMS: plain, unaffected. **2** (*showy but empty*) cosmetic, empty, facile, glib, insubstantial, shallow, skin-deep, slick, superficial, surface, thin. ANTONYMS: profound.

flat¹ *a.* **1** (*having a level and even surface*) even, level, plane. **2** (*horizontal, level*) horizontal, level. **3** (*having few or no elevations or depressions*) even, smooth, unbroken. **4** (*lying prone, prostrate*) low, outstretched, prone, prostrate, reclining, recumbent, spread-eagled, supine. ANTONYMS: upright. **5** (*plain, absolute*) absolute, categorical, direct, downright, explicit, final, out-and-out, outright, plain, point blank, positive, unconditional, unequivocal, unqualified, utter. **6** (*monotonous, dull*) bland, boring, dry, dull, featureless, flavourless, insipid, lacklustre, lifeless, monotonous, pointless, prosaic, spiritless, tedious, uninteresting, vapid, weak. ANTONYMS: interesting, exciting. **7** (*having lost sparkle or freshness*) low, stale, still. ANTONYMS: fizzy, sparkling. **8** (*depressed, dejected*) dejected, depressed, low. **9** ((*of a tyre*) *deflated*) burst, collapsed, deflated, punctured. **10** (*without variety of contrast or shading*) uncontrasting, uniform, untinted, unvarying. **11** ((*of a rate or price*) *fixed*) fixed, standard. **12** ((*of paint*) *not glossy; matt*) dull, matt, non-reflective.
~*adv.* **1** (*flatly, positively*) baldly, directly, flatly, plainly, positively. **2** (*exactly, completely*) absolutely, categorically, completely, definitely, directly, exactly, irrevocably, positively, precisely, uncompromisingly, utterly, wholly.
~*n.* **1** (*a level plain or low tract of land*) bog, fen, heath, lowland, marsh, moor, mudflat,

pampas, plain, prairie, savannah, steppe, swamp. **2** (*a shallow, a low tract flooded at high tide*) sandbank, shallow, shoal.

flat² *n.* (*a set of rooms on one floor forming a separate residence*) apartment, chambers, penthouse, rooms, set, studio, suite.

flatten *v.t.* **1** (*to make flat, to level*) compress, crush, even out, iron out, level, make flat, press, roll, smooth, squash. **2** (*to knock down or out*) bowl over, demolish, fell, floor, knock down, prostrate, raze, subdue.

flatter *v.t.* **1** (*to praise falsely or unduly*) adulate, blandish, compliment, fawn, lay it on, puff. ANTONYMS: criticize, insult. **2** (*to display to advantage*) complement, enhance, set off, show to advantage, suit. **3** (*to cajole by adulation or acclaim*) beguile, butter up, cajole, coax, court, inveigle, pander to, (*coll.*) soft-soap, (*coll.*) suck up to, (*coll.*) sweet-talk, toady to, wheedle.

flattering *a.* **1** ((*of clothes, photographs etc.*) *making one appear attractive*) becoming, effective, enhancing, well-chosen. ANTONYMS: plain, unbecoming. **2** ((*of remarks*) *praising, esp. in a false or uncritical way*) adulatory, complimentary, fawning, fulsome, gratifying, honeyed, ingratiating, laudatory, (*coll.*) smarmy, sugary, unctuous. ANTONYMS: candid, uncomplimentary.

flattery *n.* (*false praise; adulation*) adulation, (*sl.*) arse-kissing, beguilement, blandishment, bootlicking, cajolery, compliments, fawning, (*coll.*) flannel, fulsomeness, obsequiousness, praise, servility, (*coll.*) soft soap, (*coll.*) sweet talk, sycophancy, toadyism. ANTONYMS: abuse.

flatulent *a.* **1** (*affected with or troubled by wind in the alimentary canal*) gassy, windy. **2** (*turgid*) bombastic, long-winded, pompous, tedious, turgid, verbose, wordy. ANTONYMS: terse. **3** (*pretentious, empty*) empty, inflated, pretentious, vain.

flaunt *v.t.* **1** (*to display ostentatiously or impudently*) boast, brandish, display, exhibit, flash about, flourish, parade, show off, sport, vaunt. **2** (*to flutter in the wind*) flap, flutter, wave.

flavour *n.* **1** (*that quality in any substance which affects the taste, or the taste and smell*) aroma, essence, odour, piquancy, relish, savour, scent, smack, smell, tang, taste, zest, zing. ANTONYMS: flatness, vapidity. **2** (*a characteristic or distinctive quality*) air, aspect, characteristic, distinction, essence, feel, feeling, mark, nature, property, quality, spirit, stamp, style, tone. **3** (*a faint mixture of a usu. unpleasant quality*) hint, soupçon, suggestion, tinge, touch, trace. **4** (*flavouring*) additive, flavouring, seasoning.

~*v.t.* (*to give a flavour to, to season*) ginger up, imbue, infuse, lace, leaven, season, spice.

flaw *n.* **1** (*a defect, an imperfection*) blemish, damage, defect, disfigurement, error, failing, imperfection, mark, mistake, scar, speck, spot, taint, weakness. **2** (*a crack, a slight fissure*) breach, break, chink, chip, cleft, crack, crevice, fissure, fracture, gash, rent, rift, rip, scission, slit, split, tear.

flawless *a.* (*perfect, with no defects*) clean, faultless, immaculate, impeccable, intact, perfect, pristine, pure, sound, spotless, unblemished, undamaged, unimpaired, unsullied, whole. ANTONYMS: flawed, imperfect.

flay *v.t.* **1** (*to strip the skin from*) excoriate, skin. **2** (*to peel*) pare, peel, skin. **3** (*to strip, to plunder*) plunder, ravage, spoil, strip. **4** (*to criticize severely*) attack, berate, castigate, criticize, execrate, (*coll.*) pan, pull to pieces, revile, (*coll.*) slam, tear into, tear to pieces, upbraid. ANTONYMS: praise, recommend.

fleck *n.* **1** (*a dot or patch of colour or light*) dot, mark, patch, stain. **2** (*a spot, a speck*) freckle, speck, spot, stain.

~*v.t.* (*to variegate with spots or flecks*) bespeckle, besprinkle, dapple, dot, mark, mottle, speckle, spot, stipple, streak, variegate.

flee *v.i.* **1** (*to run away, as from danger to a place of safety*) abscond, bail out, beat a retreat, bolt, (*sl.*) bugger off, (*coll.*) clear out, cut and run, decamp, depart, (*sl.*) do a runner, fly, (*sl.*) hook it, leave, make off, run away, (*sl.*) scarper, (*coll.*) skedaddle, (*coll.*) slope off, take flight, take off. ANTONYMS: stay. **2** (*to disappear*) disappear, fade, pass out of sight, vanish.

~*v.t.* **1** (*to run away from*) abscond from, depart from, escape from, leave, run away from. **2** (*to shun*) avoid, evade, shun.

fleece *v.t.* **1** (*to swindle, to overcharge*) (*coll.*) bleed, cheat, (*sl.*) con, defraud, diddle, milk, overcharge, plunder, rifle, (*coll.*) rip off, swindle, (*sl.*) take to the cleaners. **2** (*to rob, to plunder*) loot, pillage, plunder, ravage, rifle, rob, steal from. **3** (*to shear the wool from*) clip, shear, strip.

fleet[1] *n.* **1** (*a number of ships or smaller vessels with a common object*) armada, convoy, flotilla, squadron, task force. **2** (*the entire body of warships belonging to one government, a navy*) navy, sea power. **3** (*a collection of aircraft or road vehicles used for a common purpose and usu. under one ownership*) convoy, flotilla.

fleet[2] *a.* (*rapid, speedy*) agile, expeditious, fast,

flying, mercurial, nimble, pacy, quick, rapid, speedy, swift, winged. ANTONYMS: slow.

fleeting *a.* (*passing quickly, transient*) brief, ephemeral, evanescent, flitting, flying, fugitive, momentary, passing, short, short-lived, temporary, transient, transitory. ANTONYMS: lasting, permanent.

flesh *n.* **1** (*the soft part of an animal body, esp. the muscular tissue, between the bones and the skin*) meat, muscle, tissue. **2** (*excess weight; fat*) fat, spare, weight. **3** (*animal tissue used as food, as distinct from vegetable, fish, and sometimes from poultry*) beef, food, meat. **4** (*the soft pulpy part of a fruit or plant*) pith, pulp. **5** (*the body, as distinguished from the soul, esp. when considered to be sinful*) body, corporeality, flesh and blood, sinful nature. **6** (*carnal appetites*) animality, carnality, physicality, sensuality. **7** (*the human race*) Homo sapiens, humanity, human race, man, mankind, mortality, people, world. **8** (*kindred*) blood, family, kin, kindred, kinsfolk, kith and kin, relations, relatives, stock.

fleshly *a.* **1** (*of or relating to the flesh, sensual*) animal, carnal, erotic, lascivious, lecherous, lustful, sensual. **2** (*human, as distinct from spiritual*) bodily, corporeal, human, material, physical. ANTONYMS: spiritual. **3** (*mortal, material*) material, mortal, of this earth. ANTONYMS: divine, supernatural. **4** (*worldly*) earthly, mundane, terrestrial, worldly.

fleshy *a.* **1** (*like flesh*) fleshlike. **2** (*fat, plump*) ample, beefy, brawny, chubby, chunky, corpulent, fat, hefty, meaty, obese, overweight, plump, podgy, portly, rotund, stout, tubby, well-padded. ANTONYMS: lean, thin.

flexible *a.* **1** (*pliant, easily bent*) bendable, ductile, elastic, limber, lithe, malleable, plastic, pliable, pliant, springy, stretchy, supple, tensile, willowy, yielding. ANTONYMS: inflexible, rigid. **2** (*tractable, easily persuaded*) amenable, biddable, complaisant, compliant, docile, malleable, manageable, persuadable, responsive, submissive, tractable. ANTONYMS: hostile, stubborn. **3** (*adaptable, versatile*) adaptable, adjustable, variable, versatile. ANTONYMS: fixed.

flick *n.* **1** (*a smart, light blow or flip*) blow, flip, hit, jab, peck, rap, strike, tap, touch. **2** (*a light, sharp sound*) click, snap. **3** (*a film*) film, movie.

~*v.t.* **1** (*to strike or move with a flick*) dab, hit, jab, peck, rap, strike, tap, touch. **2** (*to flip (dust etc.) away*) flip, jerk, whisk.

flicker *v.i.* **1** (*to shine unsteadily*) blink, flare, flash, glimmer, glint, glitter, gutter, shimmer, sparkle, twinkle, waver. **2** (*to move quickly to and fro*) flap, fluctuate, flutter, oscillate, quiver, shake, shudder, tremble, twitter, vibrate. **3** ((*of hope etc.*) *to appear faintly and briefly*) rise up, spark.

~*n.* **1** (*an unsteady or dying light*) flare, flash, glare, gleam, glimmer, glint, sparkle, twinkle, twinkling. **2** (*a brief and faint feeling etc.*) atom, breath, drop, glimmer, hint, iota, scintilla, spark, suggestion, trace, vestige.

flight[1] *n.* **1** (*the act, manner or power of flying through the air*) aeronautics, aviation, flying, gliding, mounting, soaring, winging. **2** (*an air or space journey, esp. a scheduled trip made by a commercial airline*) journey, run, shuttle, trip, voyage. **3** (*the basic tactical unit of an air force*) formation, squadron, unit, wing. **4** (*a soaring, an excursion*) effort, excursion, sally, soaring. **5** (*a number of birds or insects moving together*) cloud, flock, swarm. **6** (*a migration*) exodus, migration. **7** (*a volley* (*of arrows, spears etc.*)) barrage, shower, volley.

flight[2] *n.* **1** (*the act of running away*) escape, fleeing, retreat, running away. **2** (*a hasty departure*) departure, escape, evasion, exit, getaway, retreat, rout, stampede.

flighty *a.* **1** (*capricious, fickle*) capricious, changeable, dizzy, erratic, fanciful, fickle, frivolous, giddy, impetuous, impulsive, inconstant, irresponsible, light-headed, mercurial, scatterbrained, skittish, thoughtless, unsteady, volatile, wild. ANTONYMS: constant, steady. **2** (*mentally unstable*) crazy, deranged, mad, (*sl.*) nutty, unbalanced, unstable.

flimsy *a.* **1** (*without strength or solidity*) delicate, fragile, insubstantial, light. ANTONYMS: solid, strong. **2** (*easily torn or damaged*) delicate, fragile, makeshift, ramshackle, rickety, shaky. ANTONYMS: robust, sturdy. **3** ((*of an excuse etc.*) *weak, unconvincing*) feeble, implausible, inadequate, ineffective, pathetic, poor, unconvincing, unsatisfactory, weak. **4** (*thin, slight*) filmy, frail, gauzy, gossamer, sheer, slight, thin, transparent. **5** (*trivial, superficial*) frivolous, paltry, shallow, superficial, trivial.

flinch *v.i.* **1** (*to shrink from* (*an undertaking, suffering etc.*)) baulk, blench, cower, cringe, draw back, quail, recoil, shrink. **2** (*to wince, to give way*) dodge, duck, fail, flee, give way, retreat, shirk, shy away, wince, withdraw.

fling *v.t.* (*to cast or throw with sudden force*) cast, catapult, (*coll.*) chuck, heave, hurl, jerk, let fly, lob, pitch, precipitate, propel, send, shy, sling, throw, toss.

~*n.* **1** (*a cast or throw from the hand*) cast, lob, pitch, shot, throw, toss. **2** (*a period of*

unrestrained behaviour or enjoyment*) bash, (*coll.*) binge, debauch, fun, good time, party, (*coll.*) rave-up, self-indulgence, spree.

flip *v.t.* **1** (*to flick or toss* (*e.g. a coin*) *quickly to make it spin in the air*) cast, flick, jerk, pitch, spin, throw, toss. **2** (*to strike lightly*) rap, strike, tap. **3** (*to turn over*) turn over, twist.

~*v.i.* **1** (*to lose control of oneself, to become very angry*) (*sl.*) go ballistic, go crazy, go off the deep end, (*coll.*) hit the roof, (*coll.*) lose one's cool. **2** (*to become wildly enthusiastic*) enthuse, (*coll.*) freak out, rave.

~*n.* **1** (*a quick, light blow*) flick, rap, tap. **2** (*a short, quick tour*) day out, excursion, trip.

~*a.* **1** (*flippant*) flippant, frivolous, offhand. **2** (*impertinent*) cheeky, disrespectful, impertinent.

flippancy *n.* (*the state of being flippant*) (*coll.*) cheek, disrespectfulness, facetiousness, frivolity, impertinence, impudence, insolence, irreverence, jocularity, levity, (*sl.*) lip, pertness, (*coll.*) sauce. ANTONYMS: respect, seriousness.

flippant *a.* **1** (*trifling, lacking in seriousness*) (*coll.*) flip, frivolous, glib, offhand, shallow, superficial, trifling. ANTONYMS: serious. **2** (*impertinent, disrespectful*) cheeky, disrespectful, impertinent, impudent, irreverent, pert, rude, saucy, supercilious. ANTONYMS: respectful.

flirt *v.i.* (*to make sexual advances for amusement or self-gratification*) (*sl.*) chat up, (*coll.*) come on to, dally, lead on, make advances, make eyes at, ogle, philander, tease, toy, trifle.

~*n.* (*a person who flirts a lot*) (*taboo sl.*) cockteaser, coquette, hussy, philanderer, playboy, tease, vamp, wanton.

flirtatious *a.* (*behaving as if making sexual advances, but not in a serious way*) alluring, amorous, arch, coquettish, coy, enticing, flirty, provocative, seductive, sportive, teasing, vampish.

flit *v.i.* **1** (*to pass from place to place*) go, move, pass. **2** (*to fly about lightly and rapidly*) dart, dash, flash, flitter, flutter, fly, hop, skim, skip, speed, whisk, wing. **3** (*to depart*) depart, flee, leave, retreat. **4** (*to move from one place of abode to another*) (*sl.*) do a runner, move, (*coll.*) up sticks.

float *v.i.* **1** (*to swim or get afloat on water*) bob, ride, sail, swim. ANTONYMS: drown, sink. **2** (*to hover in the air*) hang, hover, poise. **3** (*to move or glide without effort*) glide, slide, slip along. **4** (*to move aimlessly, e.g. in the mind*) drift, meander.

~*v.t.* **1** ((*of water*) *to bear up or bear along*) bear along, bear up, hold up, support. **2** (*to set* *afloat*) launch, push off, set afloat. **3** (*to flood with a liquid*) deluge, flood, inundate. **4** (*to form into a limited company with a view to making a public issue of shares*) establish, found, get going, launch, organize, set up, start. ANTONYMS: dissolve. **5** (*to suggest* (*an idea etc.*) *for consideration*) offer up, promote, put forward, suggest.

flock *n.* **1** (*a group of animals, esp. sheep or birds*) colony, drove, flight, gaggle, herd, pack, swarm. **2** (*a crowd, a large body*) assembly, band, bevy, body, collection, company, crowd, gathering, host, mass, multitude, throng, troop. **3** (*a group of children or pupils*) class, form, group, set.
~*v.i.* (*to congregate, to assemble*) assemble, cluster, collect, come together, congregate, converge, crowd, gather, group, herd, huddle, mass, swarm, throng, troop. ANTONYMS: disperse.

flog *v.t.* **1** (*to beat with a whip or stick as punishment*) beat, cane, castigate, chastise, flagellate, flay, horsewhip, lash, scourge, strap, thrash, trounce, whack, whip. **2** (*to repeat or labour to the point of tedium*) overdo, overtax, overwork, strain, tax. **3** (*to sell*) promote, publicize, push, sell.

flood *n.* **1** (*an abundant flow of water*) flow, outpouring, spate, stream. **2** (*a body of water rising and overflowing land, an inundation*) flash flood, inundation. **3** (*a downpour, a torrent*) cataract, deluge, downpour, torrent. ANTONYMS: drought. **4** (*a river, the sea*) (*poet.*) deep, (*also poet.*) †main, river, sea. **5** (*an overflowing abundance*) abundance, excess, glut, overflow, plethora, profusion, superfluity, surfeit, surplus.
~*v.t.* **1** (*to overflow, to deluge*) deluge, drown, engulf, immerse, inundate, overflow, submerge, swamp. ANTONYMS: drain. **2** (*to supply copiously* (*with*)) deluge, overrun, oversupply, overwhelm. **3** (*to supply too much petrol to* (*the carburettor*)) choke, saturate.
~*v.i.* (*to rise and overflow*) brim over, gush, overflow, pour forth, rush, surge.

floor *n.* **1** (*the bottom surface of a room, on which people walk*) bottom, ground. **2** (*the boards or other material of which this is made*) boarding, flooring, planking. **3** (*the bottom of the sea, a cave etc.*) bottom, depths. **4** (*a storey in a building*) deck, level, stage, storey, tier.
~*v.t.* **1** (*to knock down*) fell, knock down, prostrate. **2** (*to baffle, to put to silence* (*as in argument*)) astound, baffle, bewilder, (*coll.*) bowl over, bring up short, confound, disconcert, dumbfound, faze, nonplus, perplex, puzzle, stump, (*coll.*) throw. **3** (*to get the better of, to defeat*) beat, conquer, crush, defeat,

get the better of, overthrow, overwhelm, rout, worst.

flop *v.i.* **1** (*to tumble about or fall loosely*) dangle, droop, drop, fall, hang, sag, slump, topple, tumble. **2** (*to sway about heavily*) flap, sway, swing, wave. **3** (*to move or walk about* (*in an ungainly manner*)) move, stumble, walk about. **4** (*to move or sit suddenly*) collapse, flounce down, plump down. **5** (*to fail dismally*) (*coll.*) bomb, fail, fall flat, fold, founder, (*esp. N Am., coll.*) go belly up, misfire. ANTONYMS: flourish, succeed.
~*n.* **1** (*the act or motion of flopping*) flopping, slump, tumble. **2** (*a complete failure*) (*sl.*) cock-up, debacle, disaster, (*sl.*) dud, failure, fiasco, (*sl.*) lemon, loser, non-starter, (*coll.*) wash-out. ANTONYMS: success, triumph.

floppy *a.* (*soft and flexible*) baggy, droopy, flaccid, flapping, flexible, hanging, limp, loose, pendulous, sagging, soft.

florid *a.* **1** (*flushed with red, ruddy*) blowzy, flushed, rosy, rubicund, ruddy. ANTONYMS: pale, pallid. **2** (*bright in colour*) bright, colourful. **3** (*flowery, highly embellished*) baroque, busy, elaborate, embellished, euphuistic, fancy, figurative, flowery, fussy, ornate. ANTONYMS: bare, plain. **4** (*covered with or abounding in flowers; showy*) flamboyant, flowery, high-flown, showy.

flounce *v.i.* **1** (*to move abruptly or violently*) bounce, fling, jerk, spring, toss. **2** (*to exaggerate one's movements as a means of calling attention to oneself*) parade, preen, stamp, storm, strut.

flounder *v.i.* **1** (*to struggle or stumble about violently, as when stuck in mud*) plunge, stagger, struggle, stumble, thrash, toss, tumble, wallow. **2** (*to struggle along with difficulty*) muddle along, struggle along. **3** (*to blunder along, to do things badly*) blunder, fumble, grope.

flourish *v.i.* **1** (*to grow in a strong and healthy way*) bloom, blossom, boom, burgeon, flower, grow, increase, wax. ANTONYMS: decline, deteriorate. **2** (*to thrive, to prosper*) do well, get on, prosper, succeed, thrive.
~*v.t.* **1** (*to brandish or wave about*) brandish, fling, flutter, shake, sweep, swing, twirl, wield. **2** (*to show ostentatiously*) display, flaunt, show off, swagger, vaunt. **3** (*to embellish with ornamental or fantastic figures*) decorate, embellish, ornament.
~*n.* **1** (*a brandishing or waving of a weapon or other thing*) brandishing, twirl, wave. **2** (*a figure formed by strokes or lines fancifully drawn*) curlicue, decoration, embellishment, figure, ornament, plume, sweep. **3** (*rhetorical*

display) display, expression, gesture, ostentation, parade, show. **4** (*a fanfare of trumpets etc.*) blast, fanfare, salute.

flout *v.t.* **1** (*to mock, to insult*) belittle, decry, degrade, denigrate, denounce, deprecate, deride, disdain, gibe at, guy, insult, mock, put down, ridicule, taunt. ANTONYMS: honour, respect. **2** (*to treat with contempt*) defy, despise, disregard, scorn, spurn.
~*v.i.* **1** (*to sneer*) jeer, scoff, scorn, sneer. **2** (*to behave with contempt or mockery*) jeer, mock, ridicule, scorn, show contempt.

flow *v.i.* **1** ((*of a fluid*) *to move or spread*) course, drift, move, ooze, pour, purl, ripple, roll, run, seep, spill, spread, surge, sweep, swirl, trickle. **2** ((*of blood etc.*) *to circulate*) circulate, course. **3** (*to issue, to gush out*) cascade, emanate, gush out, issue, rush, spring, spurt, squirt, stream, well forth. **4** (*to move easily or freely*) float, glide, hang, sway, undulate. **5** (*to come or go in abundance or great numbers*) abound, pour out, teem. **6** (*to result, to be descended (from)*) issue, result, spring. **7** ((*of talk etc.*) *to proceed smoothly without hesitation*) continue, issue, proceed.
~*n.* **1** (*the act or motion of flowing*) circulation, drift, flowing, movement, outpouring, progression, rush, spate, surge. **2** (*a flowing liquid, a stream*) course, current, flood, flux, gush, issue, river, stream. **3** (*a plentiful supply*) abundance, deluge, plenty, plethora. **4** (*the rise of the tide*) current, surge, tide, undertow. **5** (*an overflowing*) deluge, discharge, flood, overflowing.

flower *n.* **1 a** (*the organ or growth comprising the organs of reproduction in a plant*) bud, flower-bud. **b** (*the blossom, the bloom*) bloom, blossom, efflorescence, floret, floweret, inflorescence. **2** (*the best individual, part etc.*) best, choice, cream, elite, finest, pick. **3** (*the period of youthful vigour*) height, peak, prime, vigour.
~*v.i.* **1** (*to produce flowers, to blossom*) bloom, blossom, blow, bud, burgeon, come out, effloresce, flourish, open, unfold. ANTONYMS: wither. **2** (*to be in the prime*) blossom, develop, mature.

flowery *a.* (*highly figurative or decorative*) affected, baroque, bombastic, decorative, elaborate, embellished, fancy, figurative, florid, grandiloquent, high-flown, ornamented, ornate, overwrought, pompous, rhetorical, rococo, showy. ANTONYMS: plain, unadorned.

flowing *a.* **1** (*moving as a stream*) falling, gushing, rolling, rushing, streaming, sweeping. **2** (*copious, fluent*) abounding, brimming over, copious, easy, fluent, graceful, mellifluous,

prolific, rich, teeming. ANTONYMS: lacking, stilted. **3** (*smooth, unbroken*) continuous, smooth, unbroken, uninterrupted. **4** (*hanging loose and waving*) flying, loose, waving.

fluctuate *v.i.* **1** (*to vary, to change irregularly in degree*) alter, change, shift, vary, veer. ANTONYMS: stabilize. **2** (*to rise and fall like waves*) ebb and flow, oscillate, rise and fall, see-saw, swing, undulate. **3** (*to hesitate*) hesitate, vacillate, waver.

fluctuation *n.* (*a variation, irregular change*) alternation, change, inconstancy, instability, oscillation, shift, swing, undulation, unsteadinesss, vacillation, variation, wave, wavering. ANTONYMS: stability.

fluency *n.* **1** (*fluent command of a foreign language*) command, control. **2** (*readiness and easy flow (of words or ideas)*) articulateness, eloquence, readiness, volubility. **3** (*the quality of being fluent*) assurance, ease, facility, flow, glibness, slickness, smoothness.

fluent *a.* **1** (*ready and natural in the use of words*) articulate, easy, eloquent. **2** (*eloquent, voluble*) eloquent, glib, ready, voluble. ANTONYMS: stilted. **3** (*moving or curving smoothly*) easy, effortless, facile, graceful, slick, smooth. **4** (*fluid, changeable*) changeable, flexible, fluid, mobile, movable, shifting. **5** (*flowing, liquid*) flowing, liquid, melted, running.

fluffy *a.* (*like or relating to fluff*) airy, downy, feathery, fleecy, flossy, furry, fuzzy, gossamer, insubstantial, light, puffy, silky, soft, wispy, woolly.

fluid *n.* (*a liquid or gas, not a solid*) gas, juice, liquid, solution, vapour. ANTONYMS: solid.
~*a.* **1** (*capable of flowing, as water*) aqueous, flowing, running, watery. **2** (*liquid, gaseous*) gaseous, liquid, melted, molten. **3** (*not rigid or stable*) adaptable, adjustable, changeable, flexible, floating, fluctuating, mercurial, mobile, shifting. ANTONYMS: firm, rigid. **4** (*smooth and graceful*) easy, elegant, feline, flowing, fluent, graceful, sinuous, smooth.

fluke *n.* (*an accidentally successful stroke; any lucky chance*) accident, blessing, chance, coincidence, fortuity, freak, lucky break, quirk, serendipity, stroke of luck, twist, windfall.

flurry *n.* **1** (*a squall*) gust, squall. **2** (*a short and intense period of activity*) burst, outbreak, spell, spurt. **3** (*commotion, bustle*) ado, agitation, bustle, commotion, confusion, disturbance, ferment, (*coll.*) flap, fluster, flutter, furore, fuss, haste, hubbub, hurry, stir, (*coll.*) to-do, tumult, whirl. ANTONYMS: calm. **4** (*nervous excitement*) agitation, excitement, jumpiness, nerviness.

~*v.t.* (*to fluster, to bewilder with noise or excitement*) agitate, bewilder, bother, bustle, confound, confuse, disconcert, disturb, excite, faze, fluster, fuss, (*coll.*) hassle, perturb, put out, rattle, ruffle, shake, unsettle, upset. ANTONYMS: compose.

flush[1] *v.i.* (*to colour as if with a rush of blood, to blush*) blush, colour, glow, go red, redden. ANTONYMS: blanch.

~*v.t.* **1** (*to cause to colour or become red*) colour, embarrass. **2** (*to redden*) burn, crimson, redden, suffuse. **3** (*to inflame*) burn, ignite, inflame, kindle. **4** (*to encourage, to excite, as with passion*) animate, arouse, cheer, delight, elate, elevate, encourage, excite, exhilarate, impassion, quicken, rouse, stir, thrill. ANTONYMS: damp.

~*n.* **1** (*a sudden flow or rush of blood to the face causing a redness*) blush, colour, redness, rosiness. **2** (*any warm colouring or glow*) bloom, glow, radiance. ANTONYMS: pallor. **3** (*a sudden rush of emotion, excitement*) animation, elation, excitement, exhilaration, thrill. **4** (*bloom, blossoming*) bloom, blossoming.

flush[2] *v.t.* **1** (*to cleanse by a rush of water*) cleanse, douche, douse, drain, hose down, rinse, swab, wash. **2** (*to remove* (*an object*)) eject, empty, expel, remove. **3** (*to flood*) deluge, drench, flood, inundate.

flush[3] *a.* **1** (*on the same plane* (*with*)) even, flat, level, plane, smooth, square, true. ANTONYMS: uneven. **2** (*plentifully supplied, esp. with money*) affluent, moneyed, rich, (*coll.*) rolling, wealthy, well-heeled, well-off. ANTONYMS: poor. **3** (*abundant; filled up*) abundant, filled up, replete. **4** (*copious, abounding*) abounding, copious, generous, lavish, liberal, prodigal. ANTONYMS: mean.

fluster *v.t.* **1** (*to flurry or confuse*) baffle, bewilder, confound, confuse, excite, flurry, (*coll.*) hassle. **2** (*to agitate, to make nervous*) agitate, bother, discommode, disconcert, disquiet, disturb, perturb, rattle, ruffle, throw off balance, unnerve, upset, worry. **3** (*to befuddle, to make tipsy*) befuddle, daze, dazzle, intoxicate.

~*n.* (*confusion of mind, agitation*) agitation, bewilderment, bustle, commotion, confusion, disquiet, disturbance, dither, (*coll.*) flap, flurry, flutter, furore, perturbation, ruffle, (*coll.*) state, turmoil. ANTONYMS: composure.

fluted *a.* (*channelled, furrowed*) channelled, corrugated, furrowed, grooved.

flutter *v.i.* **1** (*to flap the wings rapidly*) bat, beat, flap, wave. **2** (*to hover or move about in a fitful, restless way*) dance, flit, flitter, hover. **3** (*to move with quick, irregular motions*) flicker,

jerk. **4** (*to quiver, to vibrate*) fluctuate, oscillate, palpitate, quiver, ripple, shake, tremble, vibrate, waver.

~*v.t.* (*to agitate or alarm*) agitate, alarm, ruffle, shake.

~*n.* **1** (*the act of fluttering*) batting, flapping, fluttering, waving. **2** (*short and irregular vibration*) fluctuation, oscillation, palpitation, quiver, shiver, shudder, tremble, tremor, twitching, vibration. **3** (*a state of excitement or agitation*) agitation, anxiety, confusion, dither, excitement, flurry, fluster, perturbation, (*coll.*) state, tumult. **4** (*disorder, stir*) commotion, disorder, stir. **5** (*a gamble, a bet*) bet, gamble, speculation, wager. **6** (*a toss* (*as of a coin*)) spin, toss. **7** (*a venture*) risk, speculation, venture.

fly *v.i.* **1** (*to move through the air with wings*) flap, flit, float, glide, hover, mount, sail, soar, wing. **2** (*to pilot or ride in an aircraft*) aviate, control, operate, pilot. **3** (*to flutter or wave in the air*) flap, float, flutter, show, wave. **4** ((*of time*) *to pass very swiftly*) elapse, pass, roll on, run its course, rush, slip away. **5** (*to depart in haste*) bolt, career, dart, dash, hare, hasten, hurry, race, rush, shoot, speed, sprint, tear. ANTONYMS: amble. **6** (*to flee, to run away*) abscond, beat a retreat, (*coll.*) clear out, cut and run, decamp, (*sl.*) do a runner, escape, flee, run away, (*sl.*) scarper, (*coll.*) skedaddle, take flight, take off. ANTONYMS: remain, stay. **7** (*to pass suddenly or violently*) burst, hasten, pass, spring, start.

foam *n.* **1** (*a mass of bubbles produced in liquids by violent agitation or fermentation*) bubbles, head, lather, suds. **2** (*the similar formation produced by saliva in an animal's mouth*) saliva, spittle. **3** (*froth, spume*) bubbles, effervescence, froth, spray, spume, suds.

~*v.i.* (*to produce or emit foam*) boil, bubble, effervesce, fizz, froth, lather.

focus *n.* **1** (*a point at which rays of light, heat etc. meet after reflection or refraction*) centre, convergence, core, heart, meeting point, nucleus. **2** (*the point from which any activity* (*such as a disease or an earthquake wave*) *originates*) epicentre, source. **3** (*the point on which attention or activity is concentrated*) centre, centre of attention, core, crux, focal point, heart, nucleus, target.

~*v.t.* (*to bring* (*rays*) *to a focus or point*) aim, bring to bear, direct, fix, line up, pinpoint, spotlight, zero in, zoom in.

~*v.i.* **1** (*to concentrate*) aim, concentrate, direct, fix. **2** (*to converge to a focus*) converge, join, meet.

fodder *n.* **1** (*food such as straw or hay fed to cattle*) feed, forage, hay, silage. **2** (*food*) food, foodstuff, provender, rations, tuck, victuals.

foe n. (*a personal enemy; an opponent*) adversary, antagonist, competitor, enemy, opponent, rival. ANTONYMS: ally, friend.

fog n. **1** (*a dense watery vapour rising from land or water, reducing visibility*) haze, mist, (*coll.*) pea-souper, smog, vapour. **2** (*a dense cloud of smoke with similar effect*) cloud, gloom, miasma, murk, murkiness, smoke. **3** (*a state of uncertainty or perplexity*) bewilderment, blindness, confusion, daze, haziness, obscurity, perplexity, stupor, uncertainty, vagueness.
~v.t. **1** (*to surround or cover with or as if with a fog*) becloud, befog, cloud, darken, dim, obscure, shroud, stifle, veil. ANTONYMS: clarify. **2** (*to perplex, to bewilder*) befuddle, bewilder, blind, confuse, daze, muddle, mystify, nonplus, obfuscate, perplex, stupefy.
~v.i. (*to become foggy*) cloud, mist up.

foggy a. **1** (*thick, murky*) cloudy, dim, grey, hazy, misty, murky, nebulous, smoggy, soupy, thick, vaporous. **2** (*confused, vague*) befuddled, bewildered, blurred, clouded, cloudy, confused, dazed, indistinct, muddled, obscure, perplexed, stupefied, unclear, vague. ANTONYMS: clear, lucid.

foible n. (*a weak point in a person's character*) blemish, defect, eccentricity, failing, fault, flaw, (*coll.*) hang-up, idiosyncrasy, imperfection, infirmity, kink, peculiarity, preoccupation, quirk, shortcoming, weakness. ANTONYMS: strength.

foil[1] n. (*something that serves to set off something else to advantage*) antithesis, background, complement, contrast, setting.

foil[2] v.t. **1** (*to baffle, to frustrate*) baffle, baulk, check, disappoint, frustrate, nullify, offset, outwit, stop, thwart. **2** (*to defeat, to parry*) checkmate, circumvent, counter, defeat, hamper, impede, parry, repel, repulse.

foist v.t. **1** (*to impose (an unwelcome thing or person) (on)*) impose, thrust. **2** (*to palm off (on or upon) as genuine*) dump, fob off, get rid of, palm off, pass off, put over, unload. **3** (*to introduce surreptitiously or wrongfully*) insert, insinuate, interpolate, introduce, sneak in.

fold v.t. **1** (*to double or lay one part of (a flexible thing) over another*) bend, double over, overlap, turn under. **2** (*to entwine (e.g. arms, legs)*) bring together, entwine. **3** (*to clasp (arms etc.) round*) clasp, intertwine. **4** (*to enfold, to envelop*) do up, enclose, enfold, envelop, wrap. **5** (*to enswathe, to conceal*) conceal, enclose, enswathe, hide.
~v.i. **1** (*to shut in folds*) crease, crimp, gather, pleat, tuck. **2** (*to fail, to go bankrupt*) cease, close, collapse, fail, go bankrupt, go bust, go to the wall, go under, shut down. ANTONYMS: prosper, thrive.
~n. **1** (*a line made by folding*) crease, wrinkle. **2** (*a bend or doubling*) bend, doubling, layer, overlap, pleat, tuck, turn. **3** (*an embrace*) coil, embrace, folding.

folk n. **1** (*people collectively*) citizenry, people, populace, population, public, society. **2** (*members of one's own family*) family, kin, kindred, kinsfolk, relatives. **3** (*a nation or ethnic group*) clan, ethnic group, nation, people, race, tribe.
~a. **1** (*originating among the common people*) common. **2** (*based on or employing traditional or popular motifs*) popular, traditional.

follow v.t. **1** (*to go or come after*) come after, go after, succeed. ANTONYMS: precede. **2** (*to pursue (e.g. an enemy)*) chase, dog, hound, hunt, pursue, run after, shadow, stalk, tail, track, trail. **3** (*to come or happen after in point of time or importance*) come next, happen after. **4** (*to imitate, to pattern oneself upon*) adopt, copy, emulate, imitate, pattern oneself upon. **5** (*to engage in (as a profession)*) engage in, practise, pursue, undertake. **6** (*to act upon (a rule, policy etc.)*) act upon, comply with, conform to, obey. **7** (*to watch the course of*) observe, regard, watch. **8** (*to grasp the meaning of*) appreciate, comprehend, fathom, get, grasp, see, take in, understand. **9** (*to result (from)*) emanate, ensue, flow, issue, proceed, result, spring. **10** (*to try to attain*) aim for, aspire to, seek after. **11** (*to accompany, to attend upon*) accompany, attend upon, escort, go with, tag along. ANTONYMS: abandon, desert. **12** (*to support the cause of*) adhere to, favour, side with, support. **13** (*to follow up, to prosecute (an affair)*) execute, follow up, prosecute, pursue.

follower n. **1** (*a devotee, a disciple*) acolyte, adherent, admirer, apostle, backer, believer, convert, devotee, disciple, fan, hanger-on, imitator, proponent, protagonist, protégé, protégée, pupil, student, supporter. ANTONYMS: leader, teacher. **2** (*a companion*) colleague, companion, comrade. **3** (*a subordinate, a servant*) attendant, henchman, lackey, minion, retainer, servant, (*coll.*) sidekick, subordinate.

following a. (*coming next after, succeeding*) coming, consequent, ensuing, later, next, resulting, subsequent, succeeding, successive. ANTONYMS: preceding.
~n. (*a body of followers or adherents*) adherents, admirers, audience, circle, clientele, coterie, entourage, fans, followers, patronage, public, retinue, suite, support, supporters, train.

folly n. (*foolishness, lack of judgement*) absurdity, craziness, daftness, fatuity, foolishness, idiocy, imbecility, imprudence, indiscretion, insanity, irrationality, lunacy, madness, nonsense, preposterousness, rashness, recklessness, senselessness, silliness, stupidity. ANTONYMS: prudence, wisdom.

foment v.t. **1** (to cause (trouble or a riot) to develop) incite, provoke. **2** (to encourage, to promote) agitate, arouse, egg on, encourage, excite, foster, galvanize, goad, inspire, instigate, motivate, nourish, promote, prompt, raise, spur, stimulate, stir up, whip up. ANTONYMS: discourage, quell.

fond a. **1** (doting on, delighting in) adoring, caring, devoted, doting, indulgent. ANTONYMS: aloof, unforgiving. **2** (tender or loving) affectionate, amorous, loving, tender, warm. ANTONYMS: cold. **3** (foolishly naive) absurd, credulous, deluded, empty, foolish, naive, overoptimistic, vain. ANTONYMS: rational, sensible.

fondle v.t. (to caress) caress, cuddle, dandle, pat, pet, snuggle, stroke, touch.

fondness n. **1** (liking) attachment, fancy, liking, partiality, penchant, predilection, preference, susceptibility, taste, weakness. ANTONYMS: aversion, dislike. **2** (affection, love) affection, attachment, care, devotion, kindness, love, tenderness. ANTONYMS: hatred.

food n. **1** (any substance, esp. solid in form, which, taken into the body, assists in nourishing the living being) nourishment, sustenance. **2** (victuals, provisions) aliment, board, bread, comestibles, diet, (coll.) eats, fare, feed, fodder, foodstuffs, forage, (sl.) grub, meals, (sl.) nosh, nutriment, provender, provisions, rations, refreshment, victuals.

fool n. **1** (a person without common sense or judgement) ass, (sl.) berk, (sl.) clot, (coll.) dimwit, (sl.) dipstick, (sl.) dope, dunce, (sl.) jerk, (sl.) nerd, nincompoop, (coll.) nitwit, numbskull, (sl.) plonker, (sl.) prat, (sl.) prick, (sl.) twerp, (coll.) twit, (sl.) wally. ANTONYMS: genius, savant. **2** (a dupe) butt, dupe, (coll.) fall guy, (N Am., sl.) patsy, (coll.) sucker. **3** (a jester, a buffoon) buffoon, clown, harlequin, jester, pierrot. **4** (an idiot, an imbecile) dolt, halfwit, idiot, imbecile, moron, simpleton.
~v.t. (to cheat, to trick) bamboozle, beguile, cheat, (sl.) con, cozen, deceive, delude, dupe, hoax, hoodwink, impose upon, (coll.) kid, mislead, play tricks upon, swindle, take in, trick.
~v.i. **1** (to play the fool) cavort, frolic, jest, joke, lark about, (sl.) piss about, play the fool. **2** (to trifle, to idle) fiddle, idle, meddle, play, tamper, toy, trifle.

foolhardy a. (daring without sense or judgement) adventurous, audacious, bold, brash, daredevil, daring, desperate, hasty, hotheaded, impetuous, imprudent, incautious, irresponsible, madcap, precipitate, rash, reckless, venturesome, wild. ANTONYMS: cautious, prudent.

foolish a. **1** (silly, not sensible) brainless, crazy, daft, fatuous, (coll.) goofy, (sl.) half-baked, half-witted, hare-brained, idiotic, ill-advised, imbecilic, imprudent, injudicious, ludicrous, mad, nonsensical, silly, stupid, unintelligent, unwise. ANTONYMS: sensible, wise. **2** (absurd or ridiculous) absurd, illogical, irrational, ludicrous, preposterous, ridiculous, unreasonable, wild.

foolishness n. (lack of judgement, nonsense) absurdity, claptrap, craziness, folly, idiocy, imprudence, inanity, irresponsibility, madness, nonsense, senselessness, silliness, stupidity, tomfoolery. ANTONYMS: sense.

foolproof a. (secure against any ignorant mishandling) certain, guaranteed, infallible, never-failing, reliable, safe, secure, (coll.) sure-fire, trustworthy, unfailing, warranted.

footing n. **1** (a place for standing or putting the feet on) base, basis, establishment, foundation, groundwork, standpoint. **2** (foothold) foothold, purchase, support. **3** (relative position or condition) condition, grade, level, position, relationship, status, terms.

footstep n. **1** (the act of stepping or treading with the feet) step, tread. **2** (a footprint) footmark, footprint, trace, track. **3** (the sound of the step of a foot) footfall, tread.

fop n. (a man overfond of dress) beau, coxcomb, dandy, popinjay, (coll.) smoothie, †swell.

foppish a. (dressing in showy clothes) affected, conceited, dandified, dapper, dressy, (coll.) natty, spruce, vain.

forage n. (food for horses and cattle) feed, fodder, food, provender.
~v.i. **1** (to seek for or to collect forage) search, seek. **2** (to hunt for supplies) hunt, scavenge, (coll.) scrounge. **3** (to rummage (about)) rummage, scour, scratch about. **4** (to carry out a raid) pillage, plunder, raid, ransack.

foray n. (a sudden attacking expedition) assault, attack, descent, incursion, inroad, invasion, raid, sally, sortie, swoop. ANTONYMS: retreat, withdrawal.

forbear v.t. **1** (to refrain or abstain from) abstain, cease, desist, hold back, pause, refrain, stop, withhold. ANTONYMS: indulge. **2** (to bear with, to treat with patience) bear with, put up with, stand, tolerate.

forbearance n. (*patience, self-control*) abstinence, clemency, leniency, lenity, moderation, patience, resignation, restraint, self-control, temperance, tolerance. ANTONYMS: impatience, intolerance.

forbid v.t. 1 (*to interdict, to prohibit*) ban, debar, disallow, interdict, outlaw, preclude, prohibit, proscribe, taboo, veto. ANTONYMS: permit, sanction. 2 (*to exclude, to oppose*) exclude, hinder, impede, inhibit, oppose, prevent, rule out. ANTONYMS: allow.

forbidding a. 1 (*repulsive, disagreeable*) abhorrent, daunting, disagreeable, grim, odious, offensive, off-putting, repellent, repulsive, unpleasant. ANTONYMS: attractive, charming. 2 (*threatening, formidable*) formidable, harsh, hostile, menacing, ominous, sinister, stern, threatening, unforgiving, unfriendly. ANTONYMS: welcoming.

force n. 1 (*strength, active power*) energy, might, muscle, power, strength. ANTONYMS: feebleness, weakness. 2 (*coercion, compulsion*) coercion, compulsion, constraint, duress, pressure, violence. 3 (*an organized body of e.g. soldiers or police officers; an army or part of an army*) army, battalion, corps, detachment, division, host, legion, outfit, patrol, regiment, squad, squadron, team, troop, unit. 4 (*validity*) cogency, efficacy, operation, validity. 5 (*significance, full meaning*) emphasis, impact, import, meaning, significance, stress, weight. 6 (*persuasive or convincing power*) bite, impact, persuasiveness, punch. 7 (*power exerted on a person or object*) animation, drive, dynamism, energy, impulse, life, momentum, potency, vehemence, vigour, vividness.
~v.t. 1 (*to constrain (a person) by force or against their will*) bulldoze, coerce, compel, constrain, dragoon, drive, enforce, impel, make, necessitate, oblige, press, pressure, pressurize, require, urge. 2 (*to use violence on*) blast, break open, crack, prise, wrench, wrest. 3 (*to push violently or against resistance*) drive, propel, push, thrust.

forced a. 1 (*constrained, affected*) affected, contrived, laboured, mannered, stiff, stilted, strained, studied, wooden. 2 (*brought about by force*) compelled, compulsory, conscripted, constrained, enforced, involuntary, mandatory, obligatory, slave, unwilling. ANTONYMS: voluntary. 3 (*unnatural*) artificial, false, unnatural. ANTONYMS: natural.

forceful a. 1 (*full of or possessing force*) aggressive, dynamic, energetic, forcible, mighty, potent, powerful, strong, vigorous. 2 (*violent, impetuous*) impetuous, uncontrolled, violent, wild.

forcible a. 1 (*done or brought about by force*) aggressive, armed, coercive, compulsory, forced, obligatory, violent. 2 (*having force, powerful*) cogent, compelling, effective, efficacious, forceful, impressive, mighty, pithy, potent, powerful, strong, telling, valid, weighty. ANTONYMS: weak.

forebear n. (*an ancestor*) ancestor, forefather, foremother, forerunner, predecessor, progenitor. ANTONYMS: descendant.

foreboding n. (*prophecy or anticipation, esp. of evil*) anticipation, anxiety, apprehension, augury, dread, fear, feeling, intuition, misgiving, omen, portent, prediction, premonition, presage, presentiment, prophecy, sign, token, warning.

forecast v.t. 1 (*to foresee, to predict*) anticipate, augur, divine, foresee, foretell, predict, prognosticate, prophesy, speculate. 2 (*to calculate beforehand*) calculate, estimate, plan, predetermine, project.
~n. (*a statement or calculation of probable events, esp. regarding future weather*) anticipation, augury, conjecture, divination, outlook, prediction, prognosis, projection, prophecy, speculation.

forefather n. 1 (*an ancestor*) ancestor, foremother, forerunner, progenitor. 2 (*a member of a previous generation of a people or family*) father, forebear, mother, predecessor, procreator, progenitor. ANTONYMS: offspring.

foreign a. 1 (*belonging to or derived from a country or nation other than one's own*) alien, non-native. ANTONYMS: domestic, native. 2 (*dealing with other countries*) international, overseas. ANTONYMS: domestic, internal. 3 (*introduced from outside*) borrowed, exterior, external, imported. ANTONYMS: indigenous, native. 4 (*unfamiliar, strange*) alien, dissimilar, distant, exotic, extraneous, extrinsic, outlandish, remote, strange, unfamiliar, unknown, unusual. ANTONYMS: familiar, usual. 5 (*having no connection with, irrelevant*) impertinent, inappropriate, irrelevant, unconnected, unrelated. ANTONYMS: pertinent, relevant.

foreigner n. 1 (*a person born in or belonging to a foreign country*) alien, immigrant, non-native. ANTONYMS: native. 2 (*a stranger, an outsider*) newcomer, outsider, stranger, visitor.

foremost a. 1 (*first in time or importance*) first, front, highest, inaugural, initial, primary. 2 (*chief, most notable*) chief, head, leading, main, notable, paramount, prime, principal, supreme.

forerunner n. 1 (*a predecessor, an ancestor*)

ancestor, forebear, forefather, foremother, predecessor, progenitor. ANTONYMS: successor. **2** (*a precursor, herald*) harbinger, herald, precursor. **3** (*an omen*) augury, foretoken, forewarning, indication, omen, portent, premonition, prognostic, sign, token.

foresee *v.t.* (*to know beforehand*) anticipate, augur, divine, envisage, envision, expect, forebode, forecast, foretell, picture, predict, presage, prophesy.

foreshadow *v.t.* (*to show or be a sign or warning of beforehand*) augur, betoken, bode, forebode, indicate, portend, predict, presage, promise, prophesy, signal, signify.

foresight *n.* **1** (*consideration beforehand, forethought*) anticipation, foreknowledge, forethought, premeditation, prescience, vision. ANTONYMS: retrospection. **2** (*provident care for the future, prudence*) care, caution, circumspection, far-sightedness, precaution, preparedness, provision, prudence, sagacity, watchfulness. ANTONYMS: carelessness, improvidence.

forest *n.* **1** (*an extensive wood or area of wooded country*) wood, woodland. **2** (*a wild uncultivated tract of ground partly covered with trees and underwood*) copse, grove, plantation, thicket, wood.

forestall *v.t.* (*to act beforehand in order to prevent*) avert, baulk, delay, fend off, frustrate, head off, hinder, intercept, obstruct, obviate, parry, prevent, stop, thwart, ward off.

foretell *v.t.* **1** (*to predict, to prophesy*) augur, divine, forecast, predict, presage, prognosticate, prophesy. **2** (*to foreshadow*) betoken, forebode, foreshadow, prefigure.

forethought *n.* **1** (*consideration beforehand*) anticipation, premeditation. **2** (*foresight, provident care*) anticipation, far-sightedness, foresight, precaution, providence, provision, prudence. ANTONYMS: improvidence, inconsideration.

forever *adv.* **1** (*for all future time, eternally*) always, eternally, everlastingly, evermore, for good, for keeps, in perpetuity, till the end of time, world without end. ANTONYMS: temporarily. **2** (*continually, persistently*) all the time, constantly, continually, incessantly, interminably, perpetually, persistently, unceasingly, unremittingly.

forewarn *v.t.* **1** (*to warn or caution beforehand*) alert, caution, dissuade, put on guard, tip off, warn. **2** (*to give notice to beforehand*) admonish, advise, give notice.

foreword *n.* (*a short introduction at the beginning of a book, often written by someone other than the author*) introduction, preamble, preface, preliminary, prelude, prologue. ANTONYMS: epilogue.

forfeit *n.* (*a fine, esp. a stipulated sum to be paid in case of breach of contract*) charge, damages, fee, fine, forfeiture, mulct, penalty, sequestration. ANTONYMS: reward.
~*v.t.* (*to lose the right to or possession of by fault or neglect*) give up, lose, relinquish, renounce, surrender, waive, yield.

forge *v.t.* **1** (*to invent or imitate fraudulently*) coin, copy, counterfeit, fake, feign, reproduce. **2** (*to counterfeit or alter a signature or document with intent to defraud*) counterfeit, defraud, fabricate, falsify. **3** (*to make or construct*) construct, contrive, create, devise, fabricate, fashion, form, frame, make, mould, shape, work. **4** (*to form or fabricate by heating and hammering*) cast, hammer out, shape, work.
~*n.* (*the workshop of a smith*) foundry, smithy, works, workshop.

forgery *n.* **1** (*the act of forging or falsifying*) counterfeiting, falsifying, forging. **2** (*a fraudulent imitation*) counterfeit, fake, fraud. **3** (*a deception*) deception, falsification, imitation, (*coll.*) phoney, sham.

forget *v.t., v.i.* **1** (*to fail to remember or bring through inadvertence*) have no recollection of, lose sight of, overlook. ANTONYMS: recall, remember. **2** (*to neglect (to do something)*) let slip, neglect, omit, overlook, pass over. **3** (*to put out of mind purposely*) consign to oblivion, dismiss from one's mind, disregard, ignore, put out of one's mind.

forgetful *a.* **1** (*tending to be absent-minded*) absent-minded, abstracted, distracted, dreamy, inattentive, preoccupied. **2** (*neglectful, forgetting*) careless, forgetting, heedless, neglectful, negligent, oblivious, unmindful. ANTONYMS: mindful.

forgive *v.t.* **1** (*to pardon, not to punish (a person or offence)*) allow, condone, excuse, indulge, overlook, pardon. ANTONYMS: blame, reprove. **2** (*not to exact the penalty for*) let off, spare. ANTONYMS: punish. **3** (*to pardon or remit (an offence or debt)*) absolve, acquit, clear, exonerate, pardon, remit.

forgiveness *n.* **1** (*the act of forgiving*) forgiving, pardoning. **2** (*the tendency to forgive*) clemency, compassion, indulgence, leniency, mercy, tolerance. **3** (*remission, pardon*) absolution, acquittal, amnesty, exoneration, pardon, remission, reprieve, vindication. ANTONYMS: punishment.

forgo *v.t.* **1** (*to go without, to refrain from*) abjure, abstain from, eschew, go without, refrain from, shun, turn down. **2** (*to renounce, relinquish*) abandon, decline, deny oneself, forsake, forswear, give up, hand over, kick, omit, quit, relinquish, renounce, sacrifice, surrender, waive, yield.

fork *n.* **1** (*a forking or bifurcation*) bifurcation, division, forking, separation. **2** (*a tributary*) confluent, tributary.
~*v.t.* (*to dig or break up (ground) with a fork*) break up, dig, turn over.
~*v.i.* **1** (*to divide into two*) bifurcate, divide, part, separate, split. ANTONYMS: unite. **2** (*to send out branches*) branch, diverge.

forlorn *a.* **1** (*lonely and sad*) depressed, despondent, disconsolate, gloomy, joyless, lonely, melancholy, miserable, mournful, pathetic, pitiful, sad, unhappy, woebegone. ANTONYMS: happy. **2** (*deserted, uncared-for*) abandoned, deserted, forsaken, lost, outcast, uncared-for. **3** (*helpless, wretched*) cheerless, comfortless, desolate, friendless, helpless, homeless, hopeless, wretched. **4** (*deprived, bereft (of)*) bereft, deprived, destitute.

form *n.* **1** (*the shape or external appearance of anything apart from its colour*) appearance, cast, configuration, shape. **2** (*outline, esp. of the human body*) anatomy, being, body, build, contour, figure, frame, outline, person, physique, silhouette. **3** (*particular arrangement or organization*) arrangement, constitution, disposition, organization. **4** (*a document with blanks to be filled in*) application, document, paper, sheet. **5** (*established practice*) method, practice, procedure. **6** (*a rule of ceremony*) ceremony, procedure, protocol, ritual. **7** (*kind, specific state*) breed, character, description, design, genre, guise, kind, manner, sort, species, stamp, variation, variety, way. **8** (*a mould or model upon which a thing is fashioned*) cut, format, framework, model, mould, pattern, shape, structure. **9** (*a customary method or formula*) formula, method, practice, procedure. **10** (*mode of expression, as opposed to content*) appearance, design, format, look, mode, style. **11** (*orderly arrangement of parts*) harmony, order, symmetry. **12** (*behaviour according to accepted rules or conventions*) behaviour, ceremony, conduct, convention, custom, decorum, deportment, etiquette, formality, manners, procedure, propriety, protocol, ritual, rule. **13** (*good physical condition or fitness, general state*) condition, fettle, fitness, health, shape, state, training, trim. **14** (*in sport, the performance of a person or animal over a period of time*) performance, record. **15** (*a class in a school*

considered as a unit, all or a subdivision of the pupils in a particular year*) class, grade, group, rank, set, shell, stream, year.
~*v.t.* **1** (*to give form or shape to*) fashion, model, mould, shape. **2** (*to arrange in any particular manner*) arrange, contrive, dispose, draw up, organize, plan, set up. **3** (*to make or create*) assemble, build, construct, create, erect, fabricate, fashion, forge, make, manufacture, produce, put together. ANTONYMS: destroy. **4** (*to model or mould to a pattern*) fashion, model, mould, shape. **5** (*to train, to shape by discipline*) bring up, discipline, educate, instruct, mould, pattern, rear, school, shape, teach, train. **6** (*to conceive (ideas etc.)*) acquire, conceive, concoct, construct, contract, develop, devise, invent, think up. **7** (*to be the material for*) compose, comprise, constitute, make, make up. **8** (*to be or constitute (a part or one of)*) be, constitute, represent.
~*v.i.* (*to assume a form*) accumulate, appear, arise, crystallize, grow, materialize, take shape. ANTONYMS: vanish.

formal *a.* **1** (*observant of established form, serious*) affected, aloof, ceremonious, correct, dignified, pompous, precise, prim, proper, punctilious, reserved, serious, solemn, starched, stately, stiff, strait-laced, strict, stuffy, unbending. ANTONYMS: casual, informal. **2** (*conventional, perfunctory*) conventional, customary, established, perfunctory, prescribed, routine. ANTONYMS: conventional. **3** (*explicit, definite*) definite, exact, explicit, express. **4** (*orderly, regular*) approved, official, orderly, regular, standard. **5** (*in a set form*) established, fixed, rigid, set.

formality *n.* **1** (*conventionality, mere form*) convention, custom, form. **2** (*an established order or method, an observance required by custom or etiquette*) ceremony, correctness, custom, decorum, etiquette, form, gesture, practice, procedure, protocol, rite, ritual, usage.

format *n.* **1** (*the external form and size of a book, magazine etc.*) dimension, form, size. **2** (*a general arrangement and style*) appearance, arrangement, composition, design, layout, look, order, organization, plan, style, type.
~*v.t.* (*to arrange in a specific format*) arrange, configure, lay out, set.

formation *n.* **1** (*the act or process of forming or creating*) creating, forming, making. **2** (*the state of being formed or created*) accumulation, compilation, composition, constitution, construction, crystallization, development, establishment, evolution, generation, genesis, manufacture, production. ANTONYMS: destruction. **3** (*arrangement, structure*) arrangement, array, configuration, conformation, design, display, disposition, figure, grouping, layout, organization, pattern, structure.

former *a.* **1** (*preceding in time*) antecedent, anterior, foregoing, preceding, previous, prior. ANTONYMS: latter, subsequent. **2** (*mentioned before something else, the first-mentioned* (*of two*)) above, aforementioned, aforesaid, first-mentioned. **3** (*past, earlier*) ancient, bygone, departed, earlier, erstwhile, late, past. ANTONYMS: future.

formerly *adv.* (*of the past or earlier times*) before, heretofore, historically, hitherto, lately, once, previously, time was, (*coll.*) way back.

formidable *a.* **1** (*tending to excite fear or respect*) alarming, appalling, awesome, daunting, dismaying, dreadful, fearful, frightful, great, impressive, indomitable, intimidating, menacing, mighty, petrifying, powerful, shocking, terrifying, threatening. ANTONYMS: comforting, reassuring. **2** (*difficult to overcome or accomplish*) arduous, burdensome, challenging, difficult, onerous, overwhelming, staggering, toilsome. ANTONYMS: easy.

formless *a.* **1** (*without form, shapeless*) amorphous, indefinite, nebulous, shapeless, unformed, vague, without form. **2** (*having no regular form*) chaotic, disorganized, incoherent, irregular.

formula *n.* **1** (*the expression of a rule or principle in algebraic symbols*) equation, symbol. **2** (*a prescribed form of words*) formulary, rite, ritual, rubric. **3** (*a conventional usage*) convention, rule, set expression, usage. **4** (*a formal enunciation of doctrine, principle etc.*) doctrine, precept, principle. **5** (*a prescription, a recipe*) blueprint, prescription, procedure, recipe.

formulate *v.t.* **1** (*to express in a formula*) articulate, express, state. **2** (*to set forth in a precise and systematic form*) codify, define, detail, itemize, particularize, set forth, specify, systematize. **3** (*to devise*) coin, conceive, develop, devise, draw up, evolve, forge, invent, originate, plan, think up, work out.

forsake *v.t.* **1** (*to leave, to abandon*) abandon, desert, flee, leave, quit, withdraw from. **2** (*to renounce, to reject*) cast off, deny, disown, forgo, give up, jettison, jilt, kick, reject, relinquish, renounce, repudiate, surrender, swear off, yield.

forswear *v.t.* **1** (*to renounce upon oath or with protestations*) abandon, abjure, drop, forgo, give up, reject, relinquish, renounce. ANTONYMS: retain. **2** (*to swear falsely*) lie, perjure oneself, renege. **3** (*to break* (*an oath, allegiance,*

etc.)) deny, disavow, disclaim, disown, recant, reject, repudiate, retract. ANTONYMS: affirm.

fort *n.* (*a fortified place*) blockhouse, camp, castle, citadel, defence, fastness, fortification, fortress, garrison, hill fort, redoubt, stronghold.

forte *n.* (*a person's strong point*) gift, métier, speciality, strength, strong point, talent. ANTONYMS: shortcoming, weakness.

forth *adv.* **1** (*forward in place or order*) ahead, forward, onward. **2** (*out from home or another starting point*) abroad, away, on the way. **3** (*out of doors*) out of doors, outside.

forthcoming *a.* **1** (*ready to appear or to be produced etc.*) coming, future, prospective, (*esp. N Am.*) upcoming. **2** (*approaching, soon to take place*) approaching, awaited, expected, imminent, impending, nearing, (*esp. N Am.*) upcoming. **3** (*available*) accessible, at hand, available, obtainable, ready. **4** ((*of a person*) *communicative, responsive*) affable, chatty, communicative, expansive, free, informative, open, outgoing, responsive, sociable, talkative, unreserved. ANTONYMS: reserved, reticent.

forthright *a.* (*outspoken, direct*) blunt, candid, direct, downright, frank, open, outspoken, plain-spoken, straightforward, to the point, unequivocal, uninhibited, (*coll.*) upfront. ANTONYMS: evasive, furtive.

fortification *n.* **1 a** (*the act or science of fortifying a place or position against the attacks of an enemy*) fortifying, securing, strengthening. **b** (*a defensive work, a fort*) bastion, castle, citadel, defence, fastness, fort, fortress, keep, stronghold. **c** (*pl.*) (*works erected to defend a place against attack*) battlement, bulwarks, defences, ramparts. **2** (*an accession of strength, a strengthening*) consolidation, embattlement, reinforcement, strengthening.

fortify *v.t.* **1** (*to strengthen by forts, ramparts etc.*) secure, strengthen. **2** (*to make defensible against the attack of an enemy*) defend, garrison, protect, secure. **3** (*to give strength to, to encourage*) brace, cheer, encourage, hearten, inspire, invigorate, reassure, revive, sustain. ANTONYMS: demoralize, dishearten. **4** (*to strengthen the structure of*) augment, bolster, brace, buttress, consolidate, reinforce, shore up, stiffen, strengthen, support. ANTONYMS: undermine, weaken. **5** (*to enrich* (*a food*) *by adding vitamins etc.*) boost, enhance, enrich, supplement. **6** (*to confirm*) confirm, corroborate, verify.

fortitude *n.* (*the strength of mind which enables one to meet danger or endure pain with calmness*) backbone, bravery, composure,

courage, determination, endurance, fearlessness, firmness, forbearance, (*coll.*) guts,
hardihood, intrepidity, mettle, patience, perseverance, pluck, resolution, strength, tenacity,
valour. ANTONYMS: weakness.

fortuitous *a.* (*happening by chance*) accidental, arbitrary, casual, chance, contingent,
fluky, fortunate, lucky, providential, serendipitous, unforeseen, unplanned. ANTONYMS:
intentional, planned.

fortunate *a.* 1 (*lucky, prosperous*) golden,
happy, lucky, prosperous, successful. ANTO-
NYMS: unfortunate, unhappy. 2 (*happening by
good luck*) advantageous, blessed, favoured,
fortuitous, (*coll.*) jammy, lucky, providential.
ANTONYMS: ill-starred. 3 (*bringing or indicating
good fortune*) auspicious, convenient, encouraging, expedient, favourable, felicitous,
helpful, opportune, promising, timely. ANTO-
NYMS: discouraging, ominous.

fortune *n.* 1 (*wealth*) affluence, assets, holdings, opulence, possessions, property, prosperity, riches, treasure, wealth. ANTONYMS:
destitution, poverty. 2 (*a large property or sum
of money*) (*coll.*) bomb, (*sl.*) bundle, mint, nest
egg, (*coll.*) packet, (*coll.*) pile. 3 (*chance, luck*)
accident, chance, luck. 4 (*a supernatural
power supposed to control one's lot*) fate, Lady
Luck, providence. 5 (*good luck*) good luck,
luck, prosperity, success. 6 (*a person's future
destiny*) destiny, doom, expectation, fate,
future, lot, portion, prospect.

forward *a.* 1 (*at or near the forepart of anything*) anterior, first, fore, foremost, front,
head, leading. ANTONYMS: back. 2 (*onward*) on,
onward. ANTONYMS: backward. 3 (*in advance*)
advanced, in advance. 4 (*well-advanced, premature*) early, precocious, premature, progressing, well-advanced, well-developed.
5 (*eager, prompt*) eager, prompt, ready, willing.
6 (*pert, presumptuous*) assuming, audacious,
barefaced, bold, brash, brazen, cheeky, cocky,
confident, familiar, (*coll.*) fresh, impertinent,
impudent, insolent, pert, presuming, presumptuous, (*coll.*) pushy. ANTONYMS: diffident,
reserved.
~*n.* (*a mainly attacking player at football etc.
stationed at the front of a formation*) attacker,
striker.
~*v.t.* 1 (*to help onward, to promote*) accelerate,
advance, aid, assist, back, encourage, expedite, favour, foster, further, hasten, help, hurry,
nourish, promote, quicken, speed, support.
ANTONYMS: hinder, obstruct. 2 (*to send on or
ahead*) pass on, relay, send on. 3 (*to send*) convey, dispatch, freight, mail, post, send, ship,
transmit.

~*adv.* (*towards the front*) ahead, forth, frontally,
future, on, onward, out. ANTONYMS: backward.

foster *v.t.* 1 (*to promote the growth of*) advance,
cherish, cultivate, encourage, feed, foment,
maintain, nourish, nurture, promote, stimulate, succour, support, sustain, uphold. ANTO-
NYMS: oppose, resist. 2 (*to bring up or nurse
(esp. a child not one's own)*) bring up, mother,
nurse, raise, rear, take care of. 3 (*to harbour (an
ill feeling)*) accommodate, cherish, entertain,
harbour, nourish, sustain.

foul *a.* 1 (*dirty, filthy*) dirty, filthy, (*coll.*) grotty,
soiled, sullied, tainted, unclean. ANTONYMS:
clean. 2 (*loathsome, offensive to the senses*)
decayed, fetid, loathsome, malodorous,
nasty, noisome, obnoxious, offensive, putrid,
rank, rotten, sickening, squalid, stinking,
(*coll.*) yucky. ANTONYMS: attractive, fresh.
3 (*overgrown with weeds*) choked, clogged,
overgrown. 4 (*disgusting, revolting*) disgusting,
offensive, repellent, repulsive, revolting.
5 (*morally offensive, obscene*) base, blasphemous, coarse, despicable, disgusting, foul-
mouthed, gross, heinous, ignoble, indecent,
infamous, lewd, low, obscene, offensive,
profane, ribald, scurrilous, smutty, wicked.
ANTONYMS: noble. 6 (*polluted*) contaminated,
defiled, dirty, impure, polluted, soiled. 7 (*unfair, dishonest*) crooked, dirty, dishonest, dishonourable, fraudulent, inequitable, shady,
underhand, unfair, unjust, unlawful, unscrupulous, unsporting. ANTONYMS: fair. 8 (*stormy,
rainy*) bad, blustery, cloudy, foggy, gloomy,
murky, overcast, rainy, rough, stormy, wet,
wild. ANTONYMS: fine.
~*n.* (*in sport, a foul stroke*) breach, illegality,
infraction, infringement, violation.
~*v.t.* 1 (*to make foul or dirty*) befoul, begrime,
besmear, dirty, smear, smirch, soil, stain, sully,
taint. ANTONYMS: clean. 2 (*to soil, to pollute*)
contaminate, defile, pollute, soil. 3 (*to impede
or entangle*) block, catch, choke, clog, ensnare,
entangle, impede, jam, snarl, twist. ANTONYMS:
clear.

found *v.t.* 1 (*to set up or establish (an institution, organization etc.) by providing the
necessary money*) constitute, create, endow,
establish, inaugurate, institute, set up. ANTO-
NYMS: abolish. 2 (*to begin to erect or build*)
build, construct, erect, raise. 3 (*to originate*)
organize, originate, start. 4 (*to construct or base
(upon)*) base, construct, establish, ground,
root. 5 (*to fix firmly*) fix, secure, set.
~*v.i.* (*to rest (upon) as a foundation or basis*)
establish, place, rest.

foundation *n.* 1 (*the natural or artificial base
of a structure*) base, bottom. 2 (*the part of a
structure below the surface of the ground*)

footing, substructure, underpinning. ANTO-NYMS: superstructure. **3** (*the principles or basis on which anything stands*) basis, grounds, groundwork, principles, root. **4** (*the reasons on which an opinion etc. is founded*) rationale, reasoning, reasons. **5** (*the act of founding or establishing*) creation, endowment, establishment, founding, inauguration, institution, organization, origination. **6** (*that on which anything is established or by which it is sustained*) basis, bedrock, grounds, support. **7** (*the fund or endowment which supports an institution*) endowment, fund, settlement. **8** (*an endowed institution*) establishment, institution, organization. **9** (*a woman's undergarment that supports the figure, e.g. a corset*) corset, undergarment.

founder[1] *n.* (*a person who founds or originates anything*) architect, author, benefactor, builder, creator, designer, father, framer, generator, initiator, inventor, maker, mother, organizer, originator, parent, patriarch, progenitor.

founder[2] *v.i.* **1** ((*of a ship*) *to fill with water and sink*) go down, go under, sink. **2** (*to fail, to break down*) abort, break down, collapse, come to grief, fail, fall through, falter, miscarry, misfire. **3** (*to fall in, to give way*) collapse, fall in, fall through, give way.

fountain *n.* **1** (*an ornamental jet of water driven high into the air by pressure*) jet, spout, spray. **2** (*the structure for producing such a jet*) font, spout. **3** (*a spring of water*) fount, spring, well. **4** (*the source of a river or stream*) source, spring. **5** (*a first principle*) beginning, cause, fountainhead, genesis, origin, rise, source, well-head, wellspring.

foxy *a.* **1** (*tricky, crafty*) artful, astute, calculating, canny, clever, crafty, cunning, devious, foxlike, guileful, knowing, scheming, sharp, shrewd, sly, tricky, wily. ANTONYMS: artless. **2** (*physically attractive*) alluring, attractive, seductive, sexy, voluptuous.

fraction *n.* (*a very small amount or portion*) bit, division, fragment, part, piece, portion, scrap, section, segment. ANTONYMS: whole.

fractious *a.* **1** (*apt to quarrel*) argumentative, contentious, quarrelsome. **2** (*snappish, peevish*) captious, crabby, cross, fretful, grouchy, irritable, peevish, petulant, querulous, quibbling, (*sl.*) ratty, snappish, testy, tetchy, touchy, waspish. ANTONYMS: affable, genial. **3** (*unruly*) awkward, contrary, perverse, rebellious, recalcitrant, refractory, unruly.

fracture *n.* **1** (*the act of breaking by violence*) breaking, cracking. **2** (*a break, a breakage*) break, breakage. **3** (*the result of breaking*)

cleavage, cleft, crack, division, fissure, gap, opening, rent, rift, rupture, schism, split. ~*v.t.* (*to break across*) breach, break, crack, rupture, splinter, split, tear. ANTONYMS: mend.

fragile *a.* **1** (*brittle, easily broken*) breakable, brittle, frangible. ANTONYMS: durable, unbreakable. **2** (*weak, delicate*) dainty, delicate, feeble, fine, flimsy, frail, infirm, shaky, slight, thin, weak. ANTONYMS: strong.

fragment[1] *n.* **1** (*a piece broken off*) bit, chip, crumb, morsel, particle, piece, scrap, shard, shiver, shred, sliver, snatch, snippet, speck. **2** (*an incomplete or unfinished portion*) fraction, part, portion. **3** (*the surviving portion of a whole work of art etc. that has been destroyed*) relic, remnant, trace, vestige.

fragment[2] *v.i.* (*to break into fragments*) break, break up, come apart, crumble, disintegrate, disunite, divide, explode, fall apart, shatter, shiver, splinter, split, split up. ANTONYMS: bond, fuse. ~*v.t.* (*to cause to break into fragments*) break, break up, divide, shatter, split, split up. ANTONYMS: bond, bring together, fuse.

fragmentary *a.* (*made up of many different parts*) bitty, broken, disconnected, disjointed, fragmental, incoherent, incomplete, partial, piecemeal, scattered, scrappy, sketchy, unfinished.

fragrance *n.* **1** (*a sweet smell*) fragrancy. ANTONYMS: stink. **2** (*the particular scent of a perfume, toilet water etc.*) aroma, balm, bouquet, odour, perfume, redolence, scent, smell.

fragrant *a.* (*emitting a pleasant perfume, sweet-smelling*) ambrosial, aromatic, balmy, odoriferous, odorous, perfumed, pleasant, redolent, scented, sweet-smelling. ANTONYMS: fetid, smelly.

frail *a.* **1** (*fragile, delicate*) breakable, brittle, delicate, flimsy, fragile, frangible, insubstantial, slender, slight, thin, vulnerable. **2** (*infirm, in weak health*) ailing, feeble, ill, infirm, poorly, puny, sick, tender, unwell, weak. ANTONYMS: healthy, strong. **3** (*weak in character or resolution*) biddable, easily led, fallible, impressionable, suggestible, susceptible, weak.

frailty *n.* **1** (*the condition of being frail*) delicacy, feebleness, fragility, frailness, infirmity. ANTONYMS: sturdiness. **2** (*a weakness or fault*) blemish, defect, deficiency, failing, fault, flaw, foible, imperfection, shortcoming, weakness. ANTONYMS: strength. **3** (*a liability to be led astray*) fallibility, impressionability, liability, suggestibility, susceptibility.

frame n. **1** (*a case or border to enclose or surround a picture, a pane of glass etc.*) border, case, casing, mount, setting. **2** (*a structure that gives strength and shape to something*) chassis, framework, shell, skeleton, structure, substructure, support. **3** (*the structure of a human body*) anatomy, body, build, carcass, physique, skeleton. **4** (*the construction or constitution of anything*) build, constitution, construction, form, make-up, shape. **5** (*the established order or system (of society or the body politic)*) government, order, pattern, system. **6** (*disposition of mind*) attitude, bent, condition, disposition, humour, mood, state, temper.
~v.t. **1** (*to surround with a frame; to serve as a frame to*) box, case, enclose, mount, surround. **2** (*to form or construct by fitting parts together*) assemble, build, constitute, construct, fabricate, fashion, forge, form, institute, make, manufacture, model, mould, put together, set up. **3** (*to adapt*) adapt, adjust, fit. **4** (*to contrive*) concoct, contrive, (*coll.*) cook up, draw up, hatch. **5** (*to devise, to invent*) devise, formulate, invent. **6** (*to arrange, to express*) arrange, compose, express, map out, organize, outline, plan. **7** (*to form in the mind, to conceive*) conceive, imagine. **8** (*to articulate, to form with the lips*) articulate, mouth. **9** (*to (conspire to) incriminate*) entrap, (*sl.*) fit up, incriminate, (*coll.*) set up, trap.

franchise n. **1** (*the right to vote*) the vote, voting rights. **2** (*the qualification for this*) suffrage, vote. **3** (*a licence to market a company's goods or services in a specified area*) authorization, charter, licence. **4** (*a privilege or exemption granted to an individual or to a body*) exemption, freedom, immunity, prerogative, privilege, right.

frank a. **1** (*candid, sincere*) artless, blunt, candid, clear, direct, downright, forthright, genuine, guileless, honest, ingenuous, open, outright, outspoken, plain, sincere, straightforward, transparent, undisguised, (*coll.*) upfront. ANTONYMS: artful, devious. **2** (*generous, liberal*) free, generous, liberal, profuse, unrestrained.

frantic a. **1** (*wildly excited or desperately worried*) berserk, beside oneself, delirious, distracted, distraught, excited, fraught, frenzied, hysterical, mad, nervous, overwrought, raging, raving, (*coll.*) uptight, worried. ANTONYMS: composed, (*coll.*) laid-back. **2** (*marked by extreme haste or agitation*) agitated, confused, desperate, frenetic, furious, hasty, hectic, hurried, wild. ANTONYMS: calm. **3** (*intense, very great*) extreme, great, intense, severe.

fraternity n. **1** (*a brotherhood, a group of men associated for a common interest or for religious purposes*) brotherhood, fellowship. **2** (*a group of men associated or linked together by similarity of profession, interests etc.*) association, circle, clan, clique, club, community, company, coterie, group, guild, league, set, society, union. **3** (*the state of being a brother; brotherliness*) brotherliness, camaraderie, companionship, fellowship, friendship, kinship.

fraternize v.i. (*to associate with others of like occupation or tastes*) associate, consort, cooperate, fall in, go around, (*sl.*) hang out, hobnob, keep company, mingle, mix, rub shoulders, socialize, sympathize, unite. ANTONYMS: shun.

fraud n. **1** (*an act or course of deception deliberately practised to gain unlawful or unfair advantage*) deceit, deception, double-dealing, embezzlement, forgery, sharp practice. **2** (*a trick, trickery*) artifice, cheating, deception, duplicity, fraudulence, hoax, imposture, ruse, (*N Am., sl.*) scam, (*sl.*) sting, stratagem, swindle, treachery, trick, trickery, wile. ANTONYMS: honesty. **3** (*a deceitful person or thing*) charlatan, cheat, fake, fraudster, impostor, (*coll.*) phoney, quack, swindler.

fraudulent a. **1** (*practising fraud*) crafty, criminal, crooked, deceitful, dishonest, double-dealing, duplicitous, false, swindling, treacherous, tricky, wily. ANTONYMS: honest. **2** (*intended to defraud, deceitful*) counterfeit, fake, false, forged, imitation, (*coll.*) phoney, sham, spurious. ANTONYMS: genuine.

fraught a. **1** (*involving, filled (with)*) abounding (in), accompanied (by), attended (by), entailing, involving. ANTONYMS: devoid (of). **2** (*characterized by or inducing anxiety or stress*) agitated, anxious, difficult, distracted, distressful, emotional, fretful, nerve-racking, strained, stressful, strung-up, taut, trying, (*coll.*) uptight, (*sl.*) wired. **3** (*laden, stored (with)*) charged, filled, freighted, full, heavy, laden, loaded, packed, replete, stored, stuffed, teeming.

fray[1] v.t. **1** (*to wear away by rubbing*) abrade, chafe, rub, shred, tatter, unravel, wear. **2** (*to make strained or irritated*) chafe, fret, irritate, strain, stress, vex.

fray[2] n. **1** (*a noisy quarrel, fighting*) affray, argument, brawl, broil, disturbance, fight, fracas, mêlée, quarrel, riot, row, rumpus, (*coll.*) set-to, (*coll.*) shindig, wrangle. **2** (*a combat, a contest*) battle, clash, combat, competition, conflict, contest. **3** (*anxiety, fear*) alarm, anxiety, apprehension, concern, dread, fear.

freak n. **1** (*an abnormal or deformed person or*

thing) aberration, abnormality, anomaly, deformity, grotesque, malformation, monster, monstrosity, mutant, mutation. **2** (*an unconventional or eccentric person*) eccentric, (*coll.*) queer fish, (*coll.*) weirdo. **3** (*an unrestrained enthusiast for a certain thing*) aficionado, (*coll.*) buff, devotee, enthusiast, fan, (*coll.*) fiend, (*sl.*) nut. **4** (*a highly unusual or abnormal occurrence*) abnormality, anomaly, curiosity, oddity, phenomenon, rarity. **5** (*a sudden wanton whim or caprice*) caprice, crotchet, fad, fancy, folly, humour, idiosyncrasy, notion, peculiarity, quirk, turn, twist, vagary, whim, whimsy.
~*a.* (*highly unusual, abnormal*) aberrant, abnormal, anomalous, atypical, bizarre, erratic, exceptional, extraordinary, fluky, fortuitous, freakish, odd, queer, rare, strange, unaccountable, unexpected, unparalleled, unusual, weird.

free¹ *a.* **1** (*at liberty; not under restraint*) at large, at liberty, emancipated, footloose, independent, liberated, unrestrained. **2** ((*of a state*) *not under foreign domination*) autonomous, independent, self-governing, self-ruling, sovereign. ANTONYMS: autocratic, despotic. **3** (*released from authority or control*) clear, disengaged, emancipated, liberated, released. **4** (*not confined or impeded*) unchecked, unconfined, unfettered, unhampered, unimpeded, unobstructed, unregulated, unrestricted, untrammelled. ANTONYMS: fettered, restricted. **5** (*at liberty to choose or act*) able, allowed, permitted. **6** (*independent, unconnected with the State*) independent, self-reliant, unaided, unattached, unconnected. **7** (*available without payment or charge*) complimentary, free of charge, gratis, gratuitous, on the house, unpaid. **8** (*not subject to* (*duties, fees etc.*)) exempt from, immune to, unaffected by. **9** (*without restriction, open*) gratuitous, open, unrestricted. **10** (*liberal, generous*) (*coll., often iron.*) big, bounteous, bountiful, charitable, extravagant, generous, hospitable, lavish, liberal, munificent, open-handed, prodigal, unsparing, unstinting, willing. ANTONYMS: mean, ungenerous. **11** (*released, exempt* (*from*)) clear (of), exempt (from), released (from), safe (from), without. **12** (*not bound or limited* (*by rules, conventions etc.*)) unbound, unconstrained, unlimited. **13** (*spontaneous, unforced*) casual, easy, familiar, free and easy, informal, (*coll.*) laid-back, lax, relaxed, spontaneous, unforced, voluntary. **14** (*unoccupied, vacant*) empty, idle, leisure, spare, unemployed, unoccupied, unused, vacant. **15** (*clear, unobstructed*) clear, open, unimpeded, unobstructed. **16** (*not busy, having no obligations or commitments*) footloose, uncommitted,

unengaged. **17** ((*of a translation*) *not literal*) loose, rough, vague. ANTONYMS: close, exact, literal. **18** (*unconventional, reckless*) careless, reckless, unceremonious, unconventional. **19** (*forward, impudent*) forward, impudent, overfamiliar, presumptuous. **20** (*unreserved, frank*) candid, frank, ingenuous, unreserved.
~*adv.* **1** (*freely*) abundantly, copiously, freely, idly, loosely. **2** (*without cost or charge*) free of charge, gratis, without charge.

free² *v.t.* **1** (*to set at liberty, to emancipate*) deliver, discharge, emancipate, let go, liberate, loose, release, set at liberty, set free, turn loose, unbind, unbridle, uncage, unchain, unfetter, unleash, untie. **2** (*to rid or relieve* (*of or from*)) relieve, rescue, rid. **3** (*to clear, to disentangle*) clear, cut loose, disengage, disentangle, extricate, redeem, unburden, undo, unshackle.

freedom *n.* **1** (*the state of being free, liberty*) autonomy, deliverance, emancipation, independence, liberty. ANTONYMS: captivity, slavery. **2** (*liberty of action, free will*) free rein, free will, latitude, leeway, opportunity. **3** (*exemption, immunity* (*from*)) exemption, immunity, impunity. **4** (*frankness, excessive familiarity*) abandon, candour, directness, ease, familiarity, frankness, informality, ingenuousness, openness, unconstraint, unconventionality. **5** (*ease or facility in doing anything*) ability, discretion, ease, elbow room, facility, flexibility. **6** (*participation in certain privileges and immunities of citizenship of a city or membership of a company*) exception, exemption, immunity, licence, privilege. **7** (*boldness in form*) audacity, boldness, brazenness, disrespect, forwardness, gall, impertinence, impudence, laxity, licence, nerve, presumption, presumptuousness.

freely *adv.* **1** (*willingly*) spontaneously, voluntarily, willingly. **2** (*frankly, candidly*) candidly, frankly, openly, plainly, unreservedly. **3** (*in large quantities*) abundantly, amply, bountifully, copiously, extravagantly, lavishly, liberally, unstintingly.

freeze *v.i.* **1** (*to be turned from a fluid to a solid state by cold*) congeal, harden, solidify, stiffen. ANTONYMS: melt. **2** (*to become covered or clogged by ice*) ice over, ice up.
~*v.t.* **1** (*to form ice upon or convert into ice*) glaciate, ice over. **2** (*to preserve* (*food*) *by freezing and storing at a temperature below freezing point*) chill, refrigerate. **3** (*to anaesthetize* (*as if*) *by cold*) anaesthetize, chill, numb. **4** (*to render motionless or paralysed*) benumb, paralyse. **5** (*to stop at a particular stage or state*) stand still, stop, suspend. **6** (*to fix or stabilize* (*prices etc.*)) fix, hold, peg, set, stabilize.

freezing *a.* (*very cold*) arctic, biting, bitter, cold, frigid, frosty, glacial, icy, numbing, penetrating, perishing, raw, wintry. ANTONYMS: hot.

freight *n.* **1** (*the transportation of goods by road, railway, sea or air*) carriage, conveyance, shipment, transportation. **2** (*goods transported, a cargo*) bulk, cargo, consignment, goods, merchandise, shipment. **3** (*a burden or load*) burden, charge, haul, lading, load, payload, tonnage.

frenetic *a.* (*frantic, frenzied*) demented, distraught, frantic, frenzied, (*sl.*) hyped up, insane, mad, maniacal, obsessive, overwrought, unbalanced, wild. ANTONYMS: calm, composed.

frenzy *n.* **1** (*a violent bout of wild or unnatural agitation or fury*) agitation, excitement, fever, fury, passion, rage. ANTONYMS: calm, composure. **2** (*delirium, madness*) delirium, distraction, hysteria, insanity, lunacy, madness, mania. **3** (*a violent attack or seizure*) attack, bout, burst, convulsion, fit, outburst, paroxysm, seizure, spasm, transport.

frequent¹ *a.* **1** (*occurring often, common*) common, many, numerous. ANTONYMS: few, rare. **2** (*repeated at short intervals*) constant, continual, persistent, recurrent, recurring, reiterated, repeated. ANTONYMS: sporadic. **3** (*constant, habitual*) common, customary, everyday, familiar, habitual, usual. ANTONYMS: unusual.

frequent² *v.t.* (*to visit or resort to often or habitually*) attend, go to, haunt, patronize, resort, visit. ANTONYMS: avoid.

frequently *adv.* (*often, at frequent intervals*) again and again, commonly, constantly, customarily, habitually, much, often, over and over, regularly, repeatedly, thick and fast, time after time, usually. ANTONYMS: infrequently, seldom.

fresh *a.* **1** (*not known previously, recent*) latest, modern, new, newfangled, novel, original, recent, up-to-date. **2** (*other, additional*) added, additional, auxiliary, different, extra, further, more, other, renewed, supplementary. **3** (*newly produced, not faded*) new, unfaded, untainted, unwearied, unwithered, verdant. ANTONYMS: faded, stale. **4** (*pure, not salt*) drinkable, potable, pure. **5** (*not preserved with salt, or by pickling, freezing etc.*) natural, raw, uncured, undried, unprocessed, unsalted. ANTONYMS: processed, salted. **6** (*raw, inexperienced*) callow, crude, green, inexperienced, natural, raw, uncultivated, untrained, untried. **7** (*looking young or healthy*) blooming, florid, glowing, hardy, healthy, hearty, rosy, ruddy, wholesome, young, youthful. **8** (*bright and clean in appearance*) bright, clean, smart, tidy, trim. **9** (*distinctly retained in the mind*) clear, undimmed, unfaded, vivid. **10** (*refreshed, reinvigorated*) refreshed, reinvigorated, rested, restored, revived. ANTONYMS: exhausted, tired. **11** (*vigorous, fit*) active, alert, bouncing, brisk, energetic, fit, keen, lively, sprightly, spry, vigorous, vital. **12** ((*of air, a breeze etc.*) *refreshing, cool*) bracing, bright, clean, cool, crisp, invigorating, pure, refreshing, reviving, spanking, sparkling, stiff, sweet. ANTONYMS: musty, stale. **13** (*cheeky, amorously impudent*) bold, brassy, brazen, cheeky, disrespectful, familiar, (*coll.*) flip, forward, impertinent, impudent, insolent, overfamiliar, pert, presumptuous, rude, saucy. ANTONYMS: respectful.

freshen *v.t.* **1** (*to make fresh*) air, purify, ventilate. **2** (*to enliven, to revive*) enliven, invigorate, liven up, refresh, revitalize, revive, rouse, spruce up, stimulate.
~*v.i.* (*to become brisk, to gain strength*) fortify, increase, revive, strengthen.

fret¹ *v.i.* **1** (*to be worried or troubled*) agonize, anguish, be anxious, worry. **2** (*to grieve, to be discontented*) brood, grieve, mope, pine.
~*v.t.* **1** (*to irritate, annoy*) affront, annoy, bother, goad, harass, irk, irritate, nettle, provoke, rile, trouble, vex. ANTONYMS: soothe. **2** (*to make uneasy or distressed*) concern, discompose, distress, torment, upset. **3** (*to eat away, to corrode*) corrode, eat away, eat into, erode, gnaw into. **4** (*to wear away, to rub*) abrade, chafe, fray, rub, wear. **5** (*to make rough or disturb* (*as water*)) disturb, upset.

fret² *v.t.* (*to ornament, to decorate*) adorn, decorate, ornament.

fretful *a.* **1** (*worried, distressed*) anxious, distressed, disturbed, edgy, tense, uneasy, upset, worried. **2** (*captious*) angry, captious, cross, crotchety, fractious, irritable, peevish, petulant, querulous, splenetic, testy, touchy, waspish.

friction *n.* **1** (*the act of two bodies rubbing together*) abrasion, attrition, chafing, erosion, grating, grinding, rasping, rubbing, scraping. **2** (*conflict, disagreement*) animosity, antagonism, argument, bickering, conflict, contention, controversy, disagreement, discontent, discord, disharmony, dispute, dissension, dissent, hostility, incompatibility, opposition, resentment, rivalry, strife. ANTONYMS: agreement, harmony.

friend *n.* **1** (*a person known well to another and regarded with affection*) (*coll.*) buddy, (*coll.*) chum, companion, comrade, confidant, confidante, crony, familiar, intimate, mate, (*coll.*) pal, partner, playmate, soul mate. ANTONYMS:

adversary, enemy. **2** (*an acquaintance*) acquaintance, contact. **3** (*a person of the same nation or party, one who is not an enemy*) colleague, confederate, fellow. **4** (*a person on the same side, a patron* (*of a cause, institution etc.*)) adherent, advocate, ally, associate, backer, benefactor, partisan, patron, promoter, protagonist, supporter, sympathizer, well-wisher.

friendly *a.* **1** (*acting as a friend*) (*coll.*) chummy, companionable, comradely, familiar, friendlike, good-natured, (*coll.*) matey, neighbourly, (*coll.*) pally. **2** (*amicable, not hostile*) affable, affectionate, amiable, amicable, benevolent, benign, conciliatory, confiding, convivial, favourable, fond, genial, intimate, kind, kindly, peaceable, sociable, sympathetic, well-disposed. ANTONYMS: hostile, unfriendly. **3** (*favourable, propitious*) auspicious, favourable, propitious. **4** (*played for amusement or entertainment, not as part of a competition*) casual, informal, non-competitive. **5** (*useful, convenient*) advantageous, beneficial, convenient, helpful, opportune, useful.

friendship *n.* (*the state of being friends*) affection, amiability, amicability, amity, attachment, companionship, comradeship, concord, congeniality, cordiality, familiarity, fellowship, fondness, friendliness, harmony, intimacy, love, neighbourliness, rapport, regard. ANTONYMS: animosity, enmity.

fright *n.* **1** (*sudden and violent fear or alarm*) alarm, apprehension, consternation, dismay, fear, panic, scare, shock, trepidation. ANTONYMS: courage, reassurance. **2** (*a state of terror*) dread, horror, terror. **3** (*a person or thing that presents a ridiculous or grotesque appearance*) mess, monstrosity, sight, (*coll.*) state.

frighten *v.t.* (*to terrify, scare*) alarm, cow, daunt, dismay, horrify, intimidate, petrify, (*coll.*) put the wind up, scare, shock, startle, terrify, terrorize, unman, unnerve. ANTONYMS: comfort, reassure.

frightful *a.* **1** (*dreadful, shocking*) dreadful, fearful, fearsome, shocking, terrible. ANTONYMS: delightful, nice. **2** (*horrible, hideous*) awful, dire, disagreeable, distressing, ghastly, grim, grisly, gruesome, hideous, horrible, horrid, horrifying, nauseating, unspeakable. **3** (*causing fright*) alarming, frightening, scary, terrifying. **4** (*awful, extreme*) appalling, awful, extraordinary, extreme, monstrous, outrageous.

frigid *a.* **1** (*lacking warmth or feeling*) chilly, cool, frosty, glacial, icy, wintry. ANTONYMS: warm. **2** (*stiff, formal*) aloof, austere, forbidding, formal, prim, rigid, stiff, unapproachable, unbending, unfeeling, unfriendly.

3 (*without animation or spirit*) dull, flat, impassive, indifferent, lifeless, passionless, spiritless. ANTONYMS: ardent, lively, spirited.

frigidity *n.* (*the state of being frigid*) aloofness, apathy, austerity, chill, cold-heartedness, coldness, formality, frostiness, iciness, impassivity, indifference, lifelessness, passivity, stiffness, unapproachability, unfriendliness, unresponsiveness. ANTONYMS: warmth.

frill *n.* **1** (*a pleated or fluted strip of cloth sewn upon one edge only*) flute, pleat. **2** (*a ruffle, a flounce*) flounce, ruche, ruffle, tuck. **3** (*a ruff or frill-like fringe of hair, feather etc.*) border, fringe, ruff, trimming, valance. **4** (*pl.*) (*decorative non-essentials*) decorations, embellishments, fanciness, finery, frippery, ornamentation, superfluity, trimmings. **5** (*pl.*) (*airs, affectations*) affectation, airs, mannerisms, ostentation, showiness.

fringe *n.* **1** (*an ornamental border to dress or furniture, consisting of loose threads or tassels*) hem, tassel, trimming. **2** (*a border, an edging*) border, edge, edging, limits, margin, periphery. ANTONYMS: centre.
~*v.t.* (*to border with or as if with a fringe*) border, edge, enclose, skirt, surround, trim.
~*a.* **1** (*existing alongside mainstream or conventional forms, institutions etc.*) alternative, avant-garde, unconventional, unofficial, unorthodox. **2** (*marginal, secondary*) marginal, peripheral, secondary.

frisk *v.i.* (*to leap or gambol about*) bounce, caper, cavort, curvet, dance, frolic, gambol, hop, jump, leap, play, prance, rollick, romp, skip, sport, trip.
~*v.t.* (*to search* (*a person*) *for firearms etc.*) check, examine, go over, inspect, search.

frisky *a.* (*playful, lively*) active, animated, bouncy, coltish, frolicsome, full of beans, gay, high-spirited, kittenish, lively, playful, rollicking, romping, spirited, sportive. ANTONYMS: sedate, sombre.

fritter *v.t.* **to fritter away** (*to waste* (*esp. time or money*)) dissipate, fool away, idle, misspend, run through, spend, squander, waste. ANTONYMS: save.

frivolity *n.* (*the state of being frivolous*) childishness, flightiness, flippancy, folly, foolishness, frivolousness, fun, gaiety, giddiness, levity, light-heartedness, lightness, nonsense, silliness, superficiality, triviality. ANTONYMS: seriousness, sobriety.

frivolous *a.* **1** (*trifling, of little or no importance*) inconsequential, insignificant, minor, niggling, paltry, peripheral, petty, shallow, superficial, trifling, trivial, trumpery, unimportant, worthless. ANTONYMS: important, serious. **2** (*lacking seriousness, inclined to silly behaviour*) casual, childish, dizzy, feather-brained, flighty, (*sl.*) flip, flippant, foolish, giddy, idle, irresponsible, juvenile, puerile, scatterbrained, silly, slight, trifling.

frolic *v.i.* **1** (*to play pranks*) play jokes, play pranks. **2** (*to frisk*) caper, cavort, frisk, gambol, lark, play, rollick, romp, sport.
~*n.* **1** (*a wild prank*) antic, escapade, game, lark, prank. **2** (*an outburst of gaiety and mirth*) fun, gaiety, high jinks, jollity, mirth. **3** (*a merry-making*) merriment, merrymaking, revelry, sport. **4** (*a light-hearted entertainment*) amusement, drollery, entertainment.

frolicsome *a.* (*playful, lively*) animated, coltish, frisky, gay, kittenish, lively, merry, playful, rollicking, spirited, sportive, sprightly, wanton. ANTONYMS: sedate.

front *n.* **1** (*the forward part or side of anything*) anterior, forepart. ANTONYMS: back. **2** (*the beginning, the first part*) beginning, start. **3** (*a face of a building, esp. the principal face*) exterior, facade. **4** (*a frontage*) facing, frontage, obverse. **5** (*a seaside promenade*) prom, promenade, seafront. **6** (*a position directly ahead, or in the foremost part of something*) fore, forefront, foreground. **7** (*the position of leadership*) head, lead, top. **8** (*the vanguard*) front line, van, vanguard. ANTONYMS: rear. **9** (*a group of people or organizations who make common cause together*) bloc, faction, league, movement, organization, wing. **10** (*outward appearance or bearing*) air, appearance, aspect, bearing, countenance, demeanour, expression, manner, mien. **11** (*impudence, boldness*) boldness, cheek, effrontery, haughtiness, impudence. **12** (*something which serves as a cover or disguise for secret or illegal activities*) blind, cover, disguise, facade, mask, pretext, show.
~*a.* (*relating to or situated in or at the front*) advance, first, foremost, forward, frontal, head, leading, main, topmost. ANTONYMS: back.
~*v.t.* **1** (*to face, to look* (*to or towards*)) face, look on, overlook. **2** (*to confront, to meet face to face*) confront, encounter, meet, oppose. **3** (*to be the leader or head of*) direct, head, head up, lead. **4** (*to be the presenter of* (*a TV programme etc.*)) compère, present.

frontier *n.* **1** (*that part of a country which fronts or borders upon another*) border, boundary, marches, perimeter. **2** (*often pl.*) (*the current limit of knowledge or attainment in a particular sphere*) bounds, confines, edge, extremes, limits, reaches.

frosty *a.* **1** (*excessively cold*) chilly, cold, freezing, frigid, frozen, glacial, icy, wintry. ANTONYMS: hot. **2** (*cool, unfriendly*) aloof, cool,

discouraging, distant, frigid, indifferent, unenthusiastic, unfriendly, unwelcoming. ANTONYMS: encouraging, friendly, welcoming.

froth *n.* **1** (*the mass of small bubbles caused in liquors by shaking or fermentation*) bubbles, effervescence, foam, head, lather, spume, suds. **2** (*foamy excretion*) excretion, scum. **3** (*empty display of ideas or talk*) drivel, emptiness, gibberish, humbug, idle talk, nonsense, rubbish, trivia, triviality.
~*v.i.* (*to form or emit froth*) bubble, effervesce, fizz, foam, lather, salivate.

frown *v.i.* **1** (*to scowl, to lour*) glare, glower, grimace, look daggers, lour, lower, pout, scowl. ANTONYMS: smile. **2** (*to express displeasure* (*at or upon*)) disapprove of, discourage, dislike, look askance at, show displeasure at, (*coll.*) take a dim view of. ANTONYMS: approve of.
~*n.* (*a knitting of the brows in displeasure or mental absorption*) dirty look, glare, grimace, knitting of the brows, scowl.

frozen *a.* **1** (*very cold*) arctic, chilled, cold, freezing, frigid, frosted, glacial, icebound, icy. ANTONYMS: hot. **2** (*fixed, immobilized*) fixed, immobilized, petrified, rooted, stock-still. **3** ((*of prices etc.*) *pegged at a certain level*) held, pegged, stopped, suspended. **4** (*frigid, aloof*) aloof, disdainful, formal, frigid, stiff, unfriendly.

frugal *a.* **1** (*thrifty, sparing*) economical, prudent, sparing, thrifty. **2** (*not profuse or lavish*) abstemious, meagre, mean, niggardly, paltry, parsimonious, poor, scanty, stingy. ANTONYMS: lavish, profuse. **3** (*economical in the use or expenditure of food, money etc.*) careful, economical, penny wise, provident, prudent, saving, temperate.

frugality *n.* (*economy, thrift*) carefulness, conservation, economy, husbandry, meagreness, moderation, parsimony, temperance, thrift, thriftiness. ANTONYMS: extravagance.

fruit *n.* **1** (*the vegetable products yielded by the earth, serving for food to humans and animals*) crop, harvest, produce, yield. **2** (*result or consequence*) consequence, effect, issue, outcome, product, result. **3** (*benefit, profit*) advantage, benefit, profit, return, reward.
~*v.i.* (*to bear fruit*) bear fruit, crop, produce, yield.

fruitful *a.* **1** (*producing fruit in abundance*) fructiferous, fruit-bearing. ANTONYMS: barren, fruitless. **2** (*successful, productive*) advantageous, beneficial, effective, fertile, flourishing, gainful, productive, profitable, rewarding, successful, worthwhile. ANTONYMS: infertile.

3 (*bearing children, prolific*) abundant, copious, fecund, plentiful, profuse, prolific.

fruition *n*. **1** (*attainment, fulfilment*) achievement, attainment, completion, consummation, fulfilment, materialization, maturation, perfection, realization, ripeness, success. ANTONYMS: failure. **2** (*pleasure or satisfaction derived from attainment of a desire*) enjoyment, gratification, pleasure, satisfaction.

fruitless *a*. **1** (*not bearing fruit, unproductive*) barren, sterile, unfruitful, unprolific. ANTONYMS: fertile, fruitful. **2** (*unsuccessful, useless*) abortive, bootless, futile, idle, ineffectual, pointless, unavailing, unprofitable, unsuccessful, useless, vain, worthless. ANTONYMS: profitable, successful.

frustrate *v.t*. **1** (*to prevent from succeeding, to thwart*) baffle, baulk, block, check, circumvent, confound, confront, counter, dash, defeat, foil, forestall, hinder, inhibit, prevent, thwart, undo. ANTONYMS: promote. **2** (*to nullify, to disappoint*) disappoint, neutralize, nullify. **3** (*to cause feelings of dissatisfaction or discouragement*) depress, discourage, dishearten, exasperate, upset. ANTONYMS: encourage.

frustration *n*. **1** (*the fact of preventing something from succeeding*) baulking, blocking, circumvention, defeat, failure, hindrance, obstruction, prevention, thwarting. **2** (*the feeling of being dissatisfied or discouraged*) annoyance, disappointment, dissatisfaction, grievance, irritation, resentment, vexation.

fuel *n*. **1** (*combustible matter, such as wood or coal burnt to provide heat or power*) coal, combustible, gas, kindling, oil, peat, petrol, tinder, wood. **2** (*food considered as a source of energy*) fodder, food, nourishment, nutriment, nutrition, sustenance. **3** (*anything which serves to increase passion or excitement*) ammunition, encouragement, incitement, provocation, stimulus.
~*v.t*. **1** (*to supply or store with fuel*) store, supply. **2** (*to feed or sustain*) charge, feed, incite, increase, nourish, stoke up, sustain.

fugitive *a*. **1** (*fleeing, running away*) fleeing, runaway. **2** (*transient, not stable*) transient, unstable, volatile. ANTONYMS: durable. **3** (*fleeting, of only passing interest*) brief, ephemeral, evanescent, fleeing, fleeting, flitting, flying, fugacious, momentary, passing, short, short-lived, temporary, transitory. ANTONYMS: permanent.
~*n*. (*a runaway, a refugee*) deserter, escapee, refugee, runaway.

fulfil *v.t*. **1** (*to accomplish, to carry out*) accomplish, achieve, bring about, carry out, discharge, do, effect, effectuate, execute, perform. **2** (*to satisfy, to comply with*) abide by, answer, comply with, conform to, correspond to, keep, meet, obey, observe, satisfy. ANTONYMS: dissatisfy. **3** (*to finish, to complete (a term of office etc.*)) complete, conclude, consummate, finish, perfect.

fulfilment *n*. (*the act of fulfilling*) accomplishment, achievement, attainment, completion, compliance, consummation, discharge, effecting, end, execution, implementation, observance, perfection, performance, realization, satisfaction.

full *a*. **1** (*filled up, replete*) filled up, replete. ANTONYMS: empty. **2** (*having no space empty, containing as much as the limits will allow*) brimful, brimming, bursting, crammed, crowded, jammed, jam-packed, occupied, packed, stuffed, taken. **3** (*well supplied, having abundance (of)*) loaded, stocked, well-supplied. ANTONYMS: exhausted. **4** (*filled to repletion, satisfied with*) gorged, replete, sated, satiated, satisfied. **5** (*charged or overflowing (with feeling etc.*)) charged, overflowing, saturated. **6** (*preoccupied or engrossed with*) absorbed, engrossed, preoccupied, rapt. **7** (*plentiful, ample*) abundant, adequate, ample, comprehensive, copious, detailed, exhaustive, generous, plentiful, sufficient, thorough. **8** (*complete, at the height of development*) complete, developed, entire, intact, integral, perfect, unabridged, whole. ANTONYMS: partial. **9** (*ample or intense in volume or extent*) ample, baggy, buxom, capacious, curvaceous, extensive, intense, loose, plump, puffy, rounded, swelling, vast, voluminous, voluptuous, wide. **10** (*strong, sonorous*) deep, loud, resonant, rich, sonorous, strong. ANTONYMS: muted. **11** ((*of clothes etc.*) *made of a large amount of material*) baggy, big, broad, large, wide.
~*adv*. **1** (*quite, equally*) equally, quite. **2** (*completely, exactly*) altogether, completely, directly, entirely, fully, thoroughly, wholly. ANTONYMS: partly.

full-grown *a*. (*mature, fully developed*) adult, developed, fully-fledged, grown-up, mature, ripe. ANTONYMS: adolescent, immature.

fully *adv*. (*completely, entirely*) absolutely, abundantly, adequately, altogether, completely, comprehensively, enough, entirely, intimately, perfectly, plentifully, positively, quite, satisfactorily, sufficiently, thoroughly, totally, utterly, wholly. ANTONYMS: inadequately, partly, unsatisfactorily.

fulminate *v.i*. **1** (*to explode with a loud noise or* *report, to detonate*) blow up, burst, detonate, explode. **2** (*to express denunciations very loudly*) fume, inveigh, protest, rage, rail, remonstrate, roar, thunder, vituperate.

~*v.t.* (*to utter* (*threats, denunciations or censures*)) berate, blast, castigate, censure, condemn, criticize, curse, decry, denounce, execrate, lambast, put down, tear into, threaten, upbraid, vilify. ANTONYMS: extol, recommend.

fulmination *n.* **1** (*a loud denunciation or censure*) censure, condemnation, denunciation, diatribe, invective, obloquy, tirade. **2** (*an explosion*) blast, detonation, explosion.

fulsome *a.* **1** ((*esp. of compliments, flattery etc.*) *excessive, satiating*) adulatory, cloying, coarse, disgusting, excessive, extravagant, fawning, gross, immoderate, ingratiating, inordinate, insincere, nauseating, overdone, saccharine, satiating, sickening, sycophantic, unctuous. **2** (*abundant, copious*) abundant, ample, copious, plentiful. ANTONYMS: meagre, paltry.

fumble *v.i.* **1** (*to grope about*) feel around, grope about, (*coll.*) paw, scrabble, search. **2** (*to bungle in any business*) bungle, flounder, stumble.

~*v.t.* (*to handle or manage awkwardly*) botch, bungle, (*sl.*) cock up, (*taboo sl.*) fuck up, mess up, mishandle, mismanage, muff, spoil.

fume *n.* **1** (*a smoke, vapour or gas, esp. an unpleasant or toxic one*) effluvium, exhalation, exhaust, gas, haze, miasma, pollution, reek, smog, smoke, stench, vapour. **2** (*mental agitation, esp. an angry mood*) agitation, dither, fit, fret, fury, mood, passion, rage, (*coll.*) stew, storm. ANTONYMS: calm.

~*v.i.* **1** (*to emit smoke or vapour*) emit, exhale, reek, smoke. **2** (*to show irritation*) bluster, boil, chafe, champ at the bit, (*coll.*) get steamed up about, rage, rant, rave, seethe, smoulder, storm.

fun *n.* ((*a source of*) *amusement, enjoyment*) amusement, cheer, diversion, enjoyment, entertainment, festivity, frolic, gaiety, glee, high jinks, jollity, joy, merriment, merrymaking, mirth, play, pleasure, recreation, romp, sport. ANTONYMS: melancholy, misery.

function *n.* **1** (*a specific purpose*) part, purpose, role, use. **2** (*duty, occupation*) business, capacity, duty, employment, job, mission, occupation, office, position, post, province, responsibility, role, situation, task. **3** (*a social entertainment of some importance*) affair, dinner, (*coll.*) do, event, gathering, party, reception. **4** (*a specific activity or operation*) activity, execution, exercise, operation, performance.

~*v.i.* **1** (*to perform a function or duty*) act, behave, perform. **2** (*to operate*) go, operate, run, work.

functional *a.* **1** (*practical, utilitarian*) durable, practical, sensible, serviceable, useful, utilitarian. **2** (*able to perform* (*its function*)) functioning, going, operative, running, working.

fund *n.* **1** (*a sum of money or stock of anything available for use or enjoyment*) pool, reserve, stock, store, supply. **2** (*assets, capital*) assets, capital, savings. **3** (*a sum of money set apart for a specific purpose*) accumulation, cache, hoard, kitty, mine, pool, repository, reserve, reservoir, savings, store, treasury. **4** (*financial resources*) cash, finance(s), funding, means, money, resources, wealth, wherewithal.

~*v.t.* **1** (*to provide money for*) back, bankroll, capitalize, endow, finance, float, pay for, promote, stake, subsidize, support. **2** (*to collect, store*) accumulate, amass, collect, hoard, save, store.

fundamental *a.* (*basic, essential*) basic, cardinal, constitutional, critical, crucial, elementary, essential, first, important, indispensable, integral, intrinsic, key, necessary, primary, principal, quintessential, rudimentary, underlying, vital. ANTONYMS: secondary, subsidiary.

~*n.* (*a principle or rule forming the basis or groundwork*) axiom, basic, basis, cornerstone, essential, foundation, law, principle, rudiment, rule.

funeral *n.* (*the ceremony held at the burial or cremation of a dead person*) burial, cremation, entombment, exequies, inhumation, interment, obsequies.

funereal *a.* **1** (*relating to or suitable for a funeral*) funerary. **2** (*dismal, sad*) depressing, dirgeful, dismal, doleful, dreary, grave, grievous, lugubrious, melancholy, morose, mournful, sad, sepulchral, solemn, sombre, sorrowful, unhappy, woeful. ANTONYMS: joyful. **3** (*gloomy, dark*) dark, gloomy, sober, sombre.

funny *a.* **1** (*amusing, causing laughter*) amusing, diverting, hilarious, humorous, mirthful, side-splitting, witty. ANTONYMS: serious, sober. **2** (*comical, laughable*) absurd, comical, droll, facetious, farcical, laughable, ludicrous, ridiculous, risible. **3** (*strange, odd*) bizarre, curious, eccentric, mysterious, odd, peculiar, perplexing, puzzling, queer, remarkable, (*sl.*) rum, strange, unusual, weird. ANTONYMS: normal, ordinary. **4** (*suspicious; involving trickery*) devious, dubious, suspicious, underhand. **5** (*slightly unwell*) ill, peculiar, queasy, queer, unwell.

~*n.* (*a joke*) joke, pun, quip, wisecrack, witticism.

furious *a.* **1** (*extremely angry*) angry, cross, enraged, frantic, frenzied, fuming, incensed, infuriated, irate, livid, mad, maddened, (*sl.*) pissed off, raging, violent, wild, wrathful. ANTONYMS: calm, imperturbable. **2** (*rushing with vehemence or impetuosity*) agitated, boisterous, fierce, impetuous, savage, stormy, tempestuous, tumultuous, turbulent, vehement, wild. ANTONYMS: peaceful, tranquil. **3** (*vehement, eager*) eager, fervent, intense, vehement.

furnish *v.t.* **1** (*to equip, to fit up, esp.* (*a house or room*) *with movable furniture*) equip, fit up, kit out, outfit, rig. **2** (*to provide or supply* (*with*)) bestow, give, grant, offer, provide, provision, stock, store, supply. **3** (*to supply, to yield*) afford, give, supply, yield. **4** (*to decorate*) appoint, decorate, ornament, refurbish.

furniture *n.* **1** (*movable articles, e.g. beds, chairs, tables etc. with which a house or room is furnished*) appliances, appointments, belongings, chattels, effects, fittings, fixtures, furnishings, goods, movables, possessions, property, (*coll.*) things, trappings. **2** (*equipment, outfit*) apparatus, equipage, equipment, outfit.

furore *n.* **1** (*an outburst of public indignation*) commotion, disturbance, outburst, outcry, stir, (*coll.*) to-do, uproar. **2** (*great excitement or enthusiasm*) enthusiasm, excitement. ANTONYMS: apathy. **3** (*a craze, a rage*) craze, enthusiasm, fad, mania, obsession, rage, vogue.

furrow *n.* **1** (*a narrow trench or groove*) fissure, flute, groove, hollow, trench, trough. ANTONYMS: ridge. **2** (*a rut*) channel, gutter, rut, seam. **3** (*a wrinkle on the face*) crease, crow's foot, line, wrinkle.
~*v.t.* **1** (*to plough*) harrow, plough. **2** (*to make furrows or wrinkles in*) corrugate, crease, cut, flute, gash, groove, knit, pucker, score, seam, wrinkle.

further[1] *a.* (*more advanced*) additional, extra, fresh, more, new, other, supplementary.
~*adv.* **1** (*at or to a greater distance or degree*) beyond, farther, longer, more, past. ANTONYMS: nearer. **2** (*moreover, in addition*) also, as well as, besides, furthermore, in addition, moreover, on top, too, what is more, yet.

further[2] *v.t.* (*to help forward, to advance*) advance, aid, assist, champion, encourage, expedite, facilitate, favour, forward, foster, hasten, help, patronize, (*coll.*) plug, promote, push, speed, support, work for. ANTONYMS: hinder, retard.

furtherance *n.* (*help, advancement*) advancement, advocacy, aid, assistance, backing, boosting, championship, encouragement, help, patronage, promotion, prosecution, pursuit, support. ANTONYMS: hindrance.

furthermore *adv.* (*moreover, besides*) additionally, also, as well, besides, further, in addition, moreover, too, what is more, yet.

furthest *a.* (*most remote in time or place*) extreme, farthest, furthermost, most distant, outermost, outmost, remote, remotest, ultimate, utmost, uttermost. ANTONYMS: nearest.

furtive *a.* **1** (*stealthy, sly*) covert, crafty, cunning, foxy, shifty, skulking, sly, sneaky, stealthy, untrustworthy, wily. **2** (*surreptitious, designed to escape attention*) clandestine, cloaked, conspiratorial, hidden, private, secret, secretive, surreptitious, underhand. ANTONYMS: candid, open.

fury *n.* **1** (*vehement, uncontrollable anger*) anger, frenzy, indignation, ire, rage, temper, wrath. **2** (*impetuosity, uncontrolled violence*) ferocity, fierceness, impetuosity, savagery, tempestuousness, turbulence, violence, wildness. ANTONYMS: calm, tranquillity. **3** (*intense, ecstatic passion*) enthusiasm, inspiration, intensity, madness, passion, vehemence. **4** (*a furious woman, a virago*) (*sl., offensive*) bitch, hag, hell-cat, she-devil, shrew, spitfire, termagant, virago, vixen, witch.

fuse *v.t.* **1** (*to reduce to a liquid or fluid state by heat*) dissolve, liquefy. **2** (*to unite by or as if by melting together*) amalgamate, blend, coalesce, combine, commingle, compound, integrate, intermingle, intermix, join, merge, smelt, solder, unite, weld. ANTONYMS: separate.

fusion *n.* **1** (*the act of melting or rendering liquid by heat*) liquefaction, melting. **2** (*union by or as if by melting together*) amalgamation, blend, blending, commingling, integration, mixture, synthesis, union, welding. **3** (*a product of such melting or blending*) alloy, amalgam, meld. **4** (*coalescence or coalition* (*as of political parties*)) coalescence, coalition, federation, merger.

fuss *n.* **1** (*excessive activity or trouble, taken or exhibited*) agitation, bother, bustle, commotion, confusion, disturbance, excitement, fidget, flurry, fluster, flutter, hubbub, stir, (*coll.*) to-do, uproar, upset. ANTONYMS: peace, quiet. **2** (*unnecessary bustle or commotion*) ado, (*coll.*) flap, palaver. **3** (*a quarrel or protest*) altercation, argument, complaint, difficulty, dispute, objection, protest, quarrel, row, squabble, trouble, unrest, upset.
~*v.i.* **1** (*to make a fuss*) fume, gripe, kick up a fuss, make a scene. **2** (*to move fussily*) bustle, fidget, (*coll.*) flap, fluster. **3** (*to worry, to be restless*) chafe, fret, fume, (*coll.*) get in a stew, worry.

~*v.t.* (*to worry, to agitate*) agitate, bother, (*coll.*) hassle, pester, worry.

fussy *a.* **1** (*nervous, excitable*) crotchety, excitable, fidgety, fretful, nervous, restless. ANTONYMS: placid. **2** (*finicky, fastidious*) (*coll.*) choosy, dainty, demanding, difficult, discriminating, exacting, faddy, fastidious, finicky, hard to please, (*coll.*) nit-picking, particular, (*coll.*) pernickety, (*coll.*) picky. ANTONYMS: easygoing. **3** (*overelaborate*) busy, cluttered, elaborate, fancy, ornate, overworked, rococo. ANTONYMS: plain, simple.

fusty *a.* **1** (*mouldy, musty*) damp, mildewy, mouldy, musty. **2** (*rank, smelling unpleasant*) ill-smelling, malodorous, rank, smelly, stale. **3** (*close, stuffy*) airless, close, stuffy, unventilated. ANTONYMS: fresh. **4** (*old-fashioned*) antiquated, archaic, old-fashioned, out-of-date, passé. ANTONYMS: modern.

futile *a.* **1** (*useless, of no effect*) abortive, barren, bootless, empty, forlorn, fruitless, hollow, idle, impotent, ineffectual, pointless, profitless, sterile, unavailing, unproductive, unprofitable, unsuccessful, useless, vain. ANTONYMS: effective, fruitful. **2** (*trifling, worthless*) frivolous, insignificant, minor, trifling, trivial, unimportant, worthless. ANTONYMS: important.

futility *n.* (*a lack of purpose or importance*) emptiness, fruitlessness, idleness, ineffectiveness, insignificance, pointlessness, triviality, unimportance, uselessness, vanity, worthlessness. ANTONYMS: importance, purpose, usefulness.

future *a.* (*that is to come or happen after the present*) approaching, coming, destined, eventual, expected, forthcoming, impending, in the offing, later, prospective, subsequent, to come, ultimate. ANTONYMS: bygone, past.
~*n.* **1** (*time to come*) hereafter, time to come. **2** (*prospective condition, career, etc.*) expectation, outlook, prospect.

fuzzy *a.* **1** (*covered with fuzz, fluffy*) downy, fleecy, flossy, fluffy, furry, fuzzed, woolly. **2** (*blurred, indistinct*) bleary, blurred, dim, distorted, faint, foggy, hazy, ill-defined, indistinct, misty, muffled, obscure, out of focus, shadowy, unclear, unfocused, vague. ANTONYMS: clear, sharp.

G

gab *n*. **the gift of the gab** (*a talent for speaking, fluency*) articulacy, articulateness, eloquence, glibness, loquaciousness, loquacity, oratory, persuasiveness, rhetoric. ANTONYMS: inarticulacy, taciturnity.

gabble *v.i.* (*to talk rapidly and incoherently*) babble, cackle, chatter, gibber, gossip, jabber, prattle, (*coll.*) rabbit, (*coll.*) rabbit on, rattle on, (*sl.*) run off at the mouth, (*coll.*) witter, yabber, (*sl.*) yak. ANTONYMS: articulate.
~*n*. (*rapid, incoherent or inarticulate talk*) babble, babbling, cackle, cackling, chatter, chattering, chitter-chatter, gibbering, gibberish, gossip, jabbering, prattle, prattling, (*coll.*) rabbiting, (*coll.*) wittering, yabber, yabbering, (*sl.*) yackety-yak, (*sl.*) yakking.

gad *v.i.* (*to rove or wander idly* (*about, out etc.*)) gallivant, meander, ramble, range, roam, rove, run (around), stray, traipse (about), travel (about), wander.

gadabout *n*. (*a person who gads about habitually*) gadder, gallivanter, globe-trotter, rambler, rover, wanderer. ANTONYMS: stay-at-home.

gaffe *n*. (*a social blunder, esp. a tactless comment*) (*coll.*) bloomer, blunder, (*coll.*) boob, (*coll.*) booboo, (*coll.*) clanger, error, faux pas, indiscretion, mistake, slip, solecism. **to make a gaffe** (*to commit a social blunder*) (*coll.*) boob, commit an indiscretion, commit a solecism, (*coll.*) drop a clanger, make a faux pas, make a mistake, make a slip, put one's foot in it.

gag *v.t.* **1** (*to stop the mouth of* (*a person*) *so as to prevent speech*) apply a gag to, muffle, put a gag on, silence, stifle. **2** (*to silence, esp. to deprive of freedom of speech*) curb, muzzle, repress, restrain, silence, suppress.
~*v.i.* **1** (*to struggle for breath, choke, retch*) choke, gasp, heave, retch. **2** (*to crack jokes*) jest, joke, make jokes, quip.
~*n*. (*a joke, esp. a rehearsed one*) (*coll.*) crack, (*coll.*) funny, hoax, jest, joke, quip, (*coll.*) wisecrack, witticism.

gaiety *n*. **1** (*mirth, merriment*) blitheness, cheerfulness, exhilaration, gayness, gladness, glee, good humour, happiness, high spirits, hilarity, joie de vivre, joy, joyfulness, lightheartedness, liveliness, merriment, mirth,

vivacity. ANTONYMS: gloom, melancholy, misery. **2** (*brilliance in appearance; showiness*) brightness, brilliance, colourfulness, flamboyance, flashiness, garishness, glitter, showiness, sparkle. ANTONYMS: drabness, dullness.

gain *n*. **1** (*anything obtained as an advantage or in return for labour*) acquisition, advantage, benefit, dividend, earnings, emolument, income, pickings, proceeds, profit, return, revenue, reward, takings, winnings, yield. ANTONYMS: deficiency, disadvantage, loss. **2** (*increase, growth*) accession, accretion, augmentation, growth, increase, increment, rise. ANTONYMS: decrease, fall, loss. **3** (*profits, emoluments*) booty, earnings, emoluments, income, pickings, proceeds, profits, returns, revenue, rewards, takings, winnings, yield. ANTONYMS: losses.
~*v.t.* **1** (*to obtain through effort*) achieve, acquire, attain, (*coll.*) bag, build up, capture, collect, come to have, gather, get, glean, harvest, net, obtain, pick up, procure, reap, secure, win. ANTONYMS: forfeit, lose. **2** (*to earn, to acquire*) bring in, clear, earn, get, gross, make, net, produce, realize, yield. ANTONYMS: lose. **3** (*to reach, to attain to*) achieve, arrive at, attain, come to, get to, reach. ANTONYMS: miss.
~*v.i.* (*to gain ground, to encroach* (*upon*)) advance, gain ground, improve, make advances, make progress, make strides, progress. ANTONYMS: lose, lose ground, retrogress. **to gain ground** (*to make progress*) advance, gain, make advances, make progress, progress. ANTONYMS: lose ground, retrogress. **to gain on/ upon** (*to get nearer to* (*an object of pursuit*)) approach, catch up on, catch up with, close in on, come up to, get closer to, get nearer to, narrow the gap between, overtake. ANTONYMS: be left behind, get further from. **to gain the upper hand** (*to be victorious*) be successful, be superior, be the winner, be victorious, carry the day, come out on top, gain supremacy, gain victory, overcome, prevail, reign, succeed, supreme, triumph, win, win the day. ANTONYMS: be the loser, lose, lose the day. **to gain time** (*to obtain delay for any purpose*) dally, delay, procrastinate, stall, temporize, use delaying tactics, use Fabian tactics.

gainful *a*. (*profitable, remunerative*) advantageous, beneficial, financially rewarding, fruitful, lucrative, moneymaking, money-spinning, paying, productive, profitable, remunerative, rewarding, worthwhile.

gainsay *v.t.* (*to contradict, to deny*) challenge, contradict, controvert, deny, disagree with, disbelieve, dispute, oppose, rebut. ANTONYMS: confirm, support.

gait *n.* (*a manner of walking or going, carriage*) bearing, carriage, pace, step, stride, walk.

gala *n.* (*a festivity, a fête*) carnival, celebration, feast day, festivity, fête, holiday, jamboree, pageant, party, special occasion.
~*a.* (*festive*) carnival, celebratory, ceremonial, festive, glamorous, joyful, merry, showy, spectacular. ANTONYMS: everyday, ordinary, run-of-the-mill.

galaxy *n.* **1** (*a star system held together by gravitational attraction*) constellation, stars. **2** (*a brilliant assemblage of persons or things*) assemblage, assembly, dazzling assembly, gathering, glittering assembly.

gale *n.* **1** (*a wind stronger than a breeze but less violent than a storm*) blast, cyclone, hurricane, squall, storm, tornado, typhoon, wind. ANTONYMS: breeze, zephyr. **2** (*an outburst*) burst, eruption, explosion, fit, howl, outbreak, outburst, peal, ring, scream, shout, shriek, yell.

gall[1] *n.* **1** (*cheek, impudence*) assurance, audacity, boldness, (*coll.*) brashness, brass neck, brazenness, (*coll.*) cheek, chutzpah, effrontery, (*coll.*) face, impertinence, impudence, insolence, (*coll.*) nerve, (*N Am., coll.*) sassiness, (*coll.*) sauce, sauciness, self-assurance, temerity. ANTONYMS: diffidence, shyness, timidity. **2** (*rancour, bitterness of mind*) acrimony, animosity, animus, antipathy, asperity, bad blood, bad feeling, (*coll.*) bad vibes, bitterness, enmity, hostility, ill feeling, malevolence, malice, malignity, rancour, sourness, spite, venom.

gall[2] *v.t.* (*to annoy, to vex*) anger, annoy, bother, exasperate, fret, get on one's nerves, (*coll.*) get to, harass, (*coll.*) hassle, infuriate, irk, irritate, nettle, (*coll.*) peeve, pester, (*sl.*) piss off, plague, provoke, (*coll.*) put one's back up, rankle, (*coll.*) rattle one's cage, rile, rub up the wrong way, vex. ANTONYMS: delight, please.

gallant[1] *a.* (*brave, courageous*) bold, brave, brave as a lion, courageous, daring, doughty, fearless, (*coll.*) game, heroic, intrepid, knowing no fear, lion-hearted, manly, mettlesome, plucky, stout-hearted, valiant, valorous, with nerves of steel, without fear. ANTONYMS: cowardly, fearful, lily-livered, timorous.

gallant[2] *a.* (*specially attentive to women*) attentive, charming, chivalrous, considerate, courteous, courtly, gentlemanly, gracious, mannerly, noble, polite. ANTONYMS: boorish, discourteous, rude.

gallantry[1] *n.* (*courage of a bold, dashing, kind*) boldness, bravery, courage, daring, doughtiness, fearlessness, (*coll.*) gameness, heroism, intrepidity, manliness, mettle, nerve, nerves of steel, pluck, stout-heartedness, valour. ANTONYMS: cowardice, fearfulness, timorousness.

gallantry[2] *n.* (*politeness and deference to women*) attentiveness, charm, chivalry, consideration, courteousness, courtesy, gentlemanliness, gentlemanly behaviour, graciousness, mannerliness, manners, nobility, politeness. ANTONYMS: boorishness, discourtesy, rudeness.

gallery *n.* (*a room or building used for the exhibition of works of art; a collection of works of art*) art gallery, art museum, exhibition area, exhibition hall, salon.

galling *a.* (*vexing, irritating*) annoying, bothersome, exasperating, infuriating, irksome, irritating, provoking, troublesome, vexatious, vexing. ANTONYMS: delightful, pleasing.

gallivant *v.i.* (*to gad about, to go around seeking pleasure*) gad, gad about, meander, ramble, range, roam, rove, run around, stray, traipse about, travel about.

gallop *v.i.* **1** (*to run in a series of springs, as a horse at its fastest pace*) canter, career, frisk, prance. ANTONYMS: amble. **2** (*to go or do anything at a very rapid pace*) bolt, dart, dash, fire on all cylinders, fly, go at full speed, (*coll.*) go hell for leather, hasten, hurry, race, run, rush, scurry, shoot, speed, sprint, tear, zoom. ANTONYMS: crawl, drag one's feet, saunter.

gallows *n.sing.* (*a framework on which criminals are executed by hanging*) gibbet, scaffold.

galore *adv.* (*in plenty, abundantly*) and to spare, aplenty, in abundance, in numbers, in plenty, in profusion. ANTONYMS: in dribs and drabs.

galvanize *v.t.* (*to rouse into life or activity as by a galvanic shock*) animate, arouse, awaken, electrify, energize, excite, fire, inspire, invigorate, jolt, kick-start, prod, provoke, rouse, set in motion, shock, spur on, startle, stimulate, stir, urge, vitalize, wake up. ANTONYMS: dull, inhibit.

gamble *v.i.* **1** (*to play, esp. a game of chance, for money*) bet, (*coll.*) have a flutter, lay a bet, lay a wager, place a bet, (*coll.*) punt, wager. **2** (*to risk large sums or other possessions on some* *contingency*) (*coll.*) have a flutter, speculate, take a chance, (*sl.*) take a flyer, take a risk, venture.

~*n.* (*a gambling venture or speculation*) bet, (*coll.*) flutter, (*coll.*) punt, wager.

gambol *v.i.* (*to skip about; to frolic*) bounce, caper, cavort, dance, frisk, frolic, hop, jump, leap, prance, romp, skip.

game[1] *n.* **1** (*an exercise for diversion, usu. with other players, a pastime*) amusement, distraction, diversion, entertainment, leisure activity, pastime, playing, recreation, sport. ANTONYMS: work. **2** (*a contest played according to specified rules and decided by chance, strength or skill*) athletic event, athletic meeting, competition, contest, event, match, meeting, sports event, sports meeting, tournament. **3** (*a single round in a sporting or other contest*) bout, heat, round. **4** (*a plan or scheme designed to defeat others*) design, game plan, machinations, manoeuvre, plan, plot, ploy, policy, project, scheme, stratagem, strategy, tactics, trick. **5** (*jest, as opposed to being serious*) bit of fun, hoax, jest, joke, lark, prank, trick. **6** (*an object of pursuit*) prey, quarry. **7** (*an occupation or business*) business, calling, job, line, line of country, occupation, profession, trade.

~*a.* **1** (*plucky, spirited*) bold, brave, courageous, daring, fearless, gallant, heroic, intrepid, plucky, spirited, unafraid, valiant. **2** (*ready, willing (to do etc.*)) disposed (to), eager (to), enthusiastic (about), inclined (to), interested (in), prepared (to), ready (to), willing (to). ANTONYMS: uninterested (in), unwilling (to). **to give the game away** (*to reveal a secret or strategy*) blab, divulge a secret, give away a secret, let slip a secret, let the cat out of the bag, reveal all, tell tales. ANTONYMS: keep a secret, keep mum. **to make (a) game of** (*to turn into ridicule*) deride, make a fool of, make a laughing stock of, make fun of, mock, ridicule, scoff at, (*coll.*) send up. **to play the game** (*to abide by the rules*) be honourable, be sportsmanlike, play by the rules, play fair, play straight, stick to the rules. ANTONYMS: cheat, (*coll.*) play dirty.

game[2] *a.* (*lame, crippled*) bad, crippled, deformed, disabled, (*coll.*) gammy, injured, lame, maimed.

game plan *n.* (*any carefully planned strategy*) battle plan, campaign, course of action, grand plan, line of action, manoeuvres, plan, policy, scheme, strategy, tactics.

gamut *n.* (*the whole range or extent*) compass, extent, field, full sweep, range, scale, scope, series, spectrum.

gang *n.* **1** (*a number of persons associated for a*

particular purpose (*often in a bad sense*)) band, circle, clique, club, company, coterie, (*coll.*) crew, gathering, group, herd, horde, lot, mob, pack, party, ring, set, team. **2** (*a number of manual workers under a supervisor, or of convicts*) detachment, group, squad, team, troop, troupe. **to gang up** (*to join with others (in doing something*)) amalgamate, band together, combine, get together, join forces, join together, unite.

gangling *a.* (*loosely built, lanky*) angular, awkward, lanky, loose-limbed, rangy, raw-boned, skinny, spindly, stringy, tall. ANTONYMS: plump, small.

gangster *n.* (*a member of a criminal gang*) criminal, (*coll.*) crook, gang member, (*sl.*) heavy, (*N Am., sl.*) hood, mobster, thug.

gap *n.* **1** (*an opening, a breach, as in a hedge, a fence etc.*) aperture, breach, break, cavity, chink, cleft, crack, cranny, crevice, discontinuity, fissure, fracture, hole, opening, rent, rift, space. **2** (*a breach of continuity, an interruption*) blank, break, hiatus, interlude, intermission, interval, lull, pause. **3** (*a deficiency*) blank, deficiency, hiatus, lacuna, omission, void. **4** (*a wide divergence*) breach, difference, disagreement, disparity, divergence, inconsistency.

gape *v.i.* **1** (*to stare with open mouth in surprise or perplexity*) gawk, gawp, goggle, stare. **2** (*to split or stand open*) crack, open, open up, open wide, split, split open, yawn.

garb *n.* **1** (*dress, costume*) apparel, array, attire, clothes, clothing, costume, dress, (*sl.*) duds, garments, (*coll.*) gear, outfit, rig-out, (*coll.*) togs, wear. **2** (*distinctive style of dress*) costume, dress, habit, livery, trappings, uniform. **3** (*outward appearance*) appearance, exterior, guise, look, semblance.

~*v.t.* (*to put garments upon*) attire, clothe, cover, dress, kit out, rig out, robe.

garbage *n.* (*kitchen waste*) debris, detritus, junk, leftovers, litter, refuse, rubbish, scraps, slops, swill, (*N Am.*) trash, waste.

garble *v.t.* (*to distort or mutilate (an account, story etc.*) *deliberately, to convey a false impression*) change, confuse, distort, falsify, jumble, misrepresent, misstate, mix up, pervert, slant, twist. ANTONYMS: clarify, decipher.

gargantuan *a.* (*immense, incredibly big*) Brobdingnagian, colossal, elephantine, enormous, giant, gigantic, huge, hulking, immense, mammoth, massive, monumental, mountainous, prodigious, towering, tremendous, vast.

garish *a.* (*gaudy, flashy*) bold, brash, dazzling,

flamboyant, (*sl.*) flash, flashy, gaudy, glaring, harsh, loud, (*sl.*) naff, ostentatious, showy, tasteless, tawdry, vulgar. ANTONYMS: muted, subtle, tasteful.

garland *n.* (*a wreath or festoon of flowers, leaves etc. worn round the neck or hung up*) chaplet, crown, festoon, fillet, headband, lei, wreath.
~*v.t.* (*to deck with a garland*) adorn, deck, decorate, festoon, wreathe.

garment *n.* **1** (*an article of clothing, esp. one of the larger articles, such as a coat or gown*) article of clothing, item of clothing, piece of clothing. **2** (*pl.*) (*clothes*) apparel, attire, clothes, clothing, (*sl.*) duds, garb, (*coll.*) gear, outfit, (*coll.*) togs, wear.

garner *v.t.* (*to store in or as in a granary, to gather*) accumulate, amass, assemble, away, collect, gather, get together, heap up, hoard, lay by, pile up, put reserve, save, stockpile, store.

garnish *v.t.* (*to adorn; to embellish* (*as a dish of food*) *with something laid round it*) add the finishing touch to, adorn, beautify, decorate, dress, embellish, enhance, ornament, prettify, set off, trim.
~*n.* (*an ornament, a decoration, especially things put round a dish of food as embellishment*) adornment, decoration, embellishment, finishing touch, ornament, ornamentation, trim, trimming.

garret *n.* (*an upper room immediately under the roof, an attic*) attic, loft, roof-space.

garrison *n.* **1** (*a body of troops stationed in a fort or fortified place*) armed force, military detachment, occupying force, soldiers, troops. **2** (*a fortified place manned with soldiers, guns, etc., a stronghold*) blockade, camp, fort, fortification, fortress, post, station, stronghold.
~*v.t.* (*to furnish* (*a fortress*) *with soldiers*) defend, guard, protect, safeguard, secure. ANTONYMS: attack.

garrulous *a.* (*talkative, chattering*) babbling, chattering, chatty, effusive, eloquent, (*sl.*) gabby, gossiping, gossipy, gushing, long-winded, loquacious, (*coll.*) mouthy, talkative, verbose, voluble, wordy. ANTONYMS: silent, taciturn, uncommunicative.

gash *n.* (*a long deep cut, esp. in flesh; a flesh wound*) cut, gouge, incision, laceration, nick, rent, slash, slit, tear, wound.
~*v.t.* (*to make a long deep cut in*) cut, gouge, lacerate, nick, rend, slash, slit, tear, wound.

gasp *v.i.* (*to breathe in a convulsive manner, as from exhaustion or astonishment*) catch one's breath, choke, draw in one's breath, fight for breath, gulp, pant, puff, puff and pant.
~*v.t.* (*to emit or utter with gasps*) ejaculate, exclaim, gulp, pant.
~*n.* **1** (*a short, painful catching of the breath*) choke, choking, gulp, pant, panting, puff, puffing. **2** (*an utterance gasped out*) ejaculation, exclamation, gulp.

gastric *a.* (*of or relating to the stomach*) abdominal, intestinal, stomach.

gate *n.* (*an opening in a wall or fence affording entrance and exit to an enclosure*) access, barrier, door, doorway, entrance, exit, gateway, opening, passage, portal.

gather *v.t.* **1** (*to bring together, to cause to assemble*) assemble, bring together, call together, collect, congregate, convene, marshal, muster, round up, summon. ANTONYMS: disperse. **2** (*to accumulate, to acquire*) accumulate, amass, collect, garner, get together, heap up, hoard, pile up, put together, stack up, stockpile, store. **3** (*to cull, to pluck*) collect, crop, cull, garner, harvest, pluck, pull. **4** (*to deduce, to conclude*) assume, be given to understand, be led to believe, believe, be of the belief, be under the impression, come to the conclusion, conclude, deduce, draw the conclusion, infer, surmise, understand. **5** (*to draw together, to contract*) fold, pleat, pucker, ruffle, shirr, tuck. ANTONYMS: straighten out. **6** (*to take* (*someone*) *into one's arms in an embrace*) clasp, cuddle, embrace, enfold, hold, hug, pull towards one. ANTONYMS: push away, repel.
~*v.i.* **1** (*to come together, to assemble*) assemble, cluster together, collect, come together, congregate, convene, converge, flock together, foregather, get together, group together, meet, muster. ANTONYMS: break up, disperse. **2** (*to grow by addition, to increase*) build up, enlarge, expand, grow, increase, rise, swell, wax. **3** (*to concentrate, to generate pus or matter*) come to a head, draw to a head, fester, suppurate.

gathering *n.* **1** (*the act of collecting or assembling together*) accumulating, accumulation, aggregating, amassing, assembling, assembly, collecting, collection, garnering, marshalling, stockpiling. **2** (*people collected together; a meeting*) assemblage, assembly, conclave, convention, (*coll.*) get-together, meeting, party, rally. **3** (*an abscess, a boil*) abscess, boil, carbuncle, pimple, pustule, spot, (*sl.*) zit.

gauche *a.* **1** (*awkward, clumsy*) awkward, clumsy, graceless, inelegant, inept, lumbering, maladroit, ungainly. **2** (*tactless, uncouth*) boorish, insensitive, tactless, uncouth, uncultivated, uncultured, unsophisticated.

gaudy *a.* (*vulgarly and tastelessly brilliant and ornate*) bold, brash, dazzling, flamboyant, (*sl.*) flash, flashy, glaring, harsh, loud, (*sl.*) naff, ostentatious, overbright, showy, tasteless, tawdry, vulgar. ANTONYMS: muted, subtle, tasteful.

gauge *v.t.* **1** (*to ascertain the dimensions or capacity of*) calculate, check, compute, count, determine, measure. **2** (*to estimate or appraise* (*abilities, character etc.*) adjudge, appraise, assess, estimate, evaluate, guess, (*coll.*) guesstimate, judge, make an appraisal of, rate, reckon, value, weigh up.
~*n.* (*a standard of measurement*) basis, benchmark, criterion, example, exemplar, guide, guideline, indicator, litmus test, measure, model, norm, pattern, rule, standard, test, test case, touchstone, yardstick.

gaunt *a.* (*emaciated, haggard*) all skin and bone, angular, (*coll.*) anorexic, attenuated, bony, cadaverous, drawn, emaciated, haggard, hollow-cheeked, pinched, scraggy, scrawny, shrivelled, skeletal, skin and bone, skinny, starved-looking, thin, wasted. ANTONYMS: chubby, plump.

gauntlet[1] *n.* to throw down the gauntlet (*to challenge, to defy*) challenge, dare, defy, issue a challenge to, offer a challenge to.

gauntlet[2] *n.* to run the gauntlet (*to be exposed to an ordeal, severe criticism etc.*) get a lot of flak, meet with hostility, (*coll.*) receive brickbats, (*coll.*) take a knocking, take a lot of flak.

gawk *n.* (*a clumsy, awkward person*) blockhead, booby, dolt, (*coll.*) dope, fool, idiot, nincompoop, ninny, (*coll.*) nitwit, oaf, simpleton, (*coll.*) twit.
~*v.i.* (*to stare* (*at or about*) *stupidly*) gape, gawp, gaze, gaze open-mouthed, (*coll.*) gaze with eyes on stalks, gaze with open mouth, goggle, (*sl.*) rubberneck, stand and stare, stare.

gawky *a.* (*awkward, clownish*) awkward, blundering, clodhopping, clumsy, doltish, gauche, lanky, loutish, lumbering, maladroit, oafish, ungainly. ANTONYMS: adept, elegant, graceful.

gawp *v.i.* (*to gape, esp. in astonishment*) gape, gawk, gaze, gaze open-mouthed, (*coll.*) gaze with eyes on stalks, gaze with open mouth, goggle, (*sl.*) rubberneck, stand and stare, stare.

gay *a.* **1** (*full of mirth; cheerful*) animated, blithe, buoyant, carefree, cheerful, effervescent, exuberant, full of fun, glad, gleeful, happy, high-spirited, jolly, joyful, lighthearted, lively, merry, sparkling, sprightly, vivacious, without a care. ANTONYMS: gloomy, miserable, unhappy. **2** ((*of an occasion*) *very entertaining and enjoyable*) amusing, convivial, enjoyable, entertaining, festive, fun-filled, fun-packed, happy. ANTONYMS: dull, miserable. **3** (*showy, brilliant in appearance*) bright, bright and gay, brightly coloured, brilliant, colourful, flamboyant, flashy, garish, gaudy, multicoloured, richly coloured, showy, vivid. ANTONYMS: drab, dull, muted. **4** (*homosexual*) (*sl.*) bent, camp, homoerotic, homosexual, lesbian, (*offensive sl.*) poofy, (*sl.*) queer. ANTONYMS: heterosexual, (*sl.*) straight.
~*n.* (*a homosexual*) (*offensive sl.*) dyke, (*offensive sl.*) faggot, (*offensive sl.*) fairy, (*sl.*) homo, homosexual, lesbian, (*offensive sl.*) one of them, (*offensive sl.*) poof, (*offensive sl.*) poofter, (*sl.*) queer, (*offensive sl.*) shirt-lifter. ANTONYMS: heterosexual.

gayness *n.* (*the state of being homosexual*) homoeroticism, homosexualism, homosexuality, lesbianism. ANTONYMS: heterosexualism, heterosexuality.

gaze *v.i.* (*to fix the eye intently* (*at or upon*)) contemplate, (*sl.*) eyeball, gape, gawk, look fixedly, look in wonder, ogle, regard, (*sl.*) rubberneck, stare, stare in fascination, view, watch. ANTONYMS: glance.
~*n.* (*a fixed look*) fixed look, gape, intent look, look, stare, steady stare, watching. ANTONYMS: glance.

gear *n.* **1** (*apparatus, equipment*) accessories, accoutrements, apparatus, appliances, equipment, harness, implements, instruments, kit, outfit, paraphernalia, supplies, tackle, things, tools, tools of the trade. **2** (*clothes*) apparel, array, attire, clothes, clothing, costume, dress, (*sl.*) duds, garb, garments, outfit, rig-out, (*coll.*) togs, wear. **3** (*goods, movables*) accoutrements, bag and baggage, baggage, bags, belongings, effects, goods, goods and chattels, kit, luggage, paraphernalia, personal effects, personal possessions, possessions, (*coll.*) stuff, things, trappings.

gelatinous *a.* (*of the nature of or consisting of gelatin*) gluey, glutinous, (*coll.*) gooey, gummy, jelly-like, sticky, viscid, viscous.

geld *v.t.* (*to castrate* (*esp. a horse*), *to emasculate*) castrate, emasculate, neuter.

genealogy *n.* (*pedigree, lineage*) ancestry, birth, bloodline, descent, extraction, family, family history, family tree, heritage, line, lineage, line of descent, parentage, pedigree, roots, stemma, stirps, stock, strain.

general *a.* **1** (*usual, prevalent*) accepted, accustomed, common, conventional, customary, everyday, habitual, normal, ordinary, prevalent, regular, run-of-the-mill, standard, typical, unexceptional, usual. ANTONYMS: exceptional, irregular, unusual. **2** (*not special or local*) broad, broad-based, common, extensive, general, popular, prevalent, public, universal, widespread. ANTONYMS: local, narrow, particular. **3** (*not limited in scope or application*) across-the-board, all-inclusive, blanket, broad, broad-ranging, catholic, comprehensive, encyclopedic, generic, global, indiscriminate, non-discriminatory, sweeping, total, universal. ANTONYMS: limited, restricted. **4** (*indefinite, vague*) approximate, bare-bones, broad, ill-defined, imprecise, indefinite, inexact, loose, non-detailed, non-specific, rough, unspecific, vague, without detail. ANTONYMS: definite, exact, precise, well-defined. **5** (*not specialized or restricted*) diversified, miscellaneous, mixed, non-specialist, nonspecialized. ANTONYMS: restricted, specialist.

generality *n.* **1** (*the state of being general, as opposed to specific*) breadth, broadness, commonness, comprehensiveness, extensiveness, prevalence, universality, widespreadness. ANTONYMS: narrowness, restrictedness, specificity. **2** (*a general statement or principle*) general law, general principle, general rule, general statement. **3** (*a vague statement*) generalization, imprecise statement, loose statement, sweeping statement. **4** (*the main body, the majority*) bulk, greater part, majority, mass. ANTONYMS: minority. **5** (*vagueness*) approximateness, imprecision, indefiniteness, inexactness, lack of detail, lack of precision, looseness, roughness, vagueness. ANTONYMS: exactness, precision.

generally *adv.* **1** (*for the most part, in most cases*) almost always, as a general rule, as a rule, as often as not, by and large, commonly, for the most part, in general, in most cases, in the majority of cases, largely, mainly, normally, on average, on the whole, ordinarily, typically, usually. ANTONYMS: hardly ever, rarely, unusually. **2** (*commonly, usually*) by most people, extensively, universally, widely. ANTONYMS: individually, locally. **3** (*without minute detail, without specifying*) broadly, in general terms, loosely, non-specifically, without detail. ANTONYMS: in detail, in specific terms, specifically.

general practitioner *n.* (*a physician or surgeon treating all kinds of cases*) doctor, family doctor, GP.

generate *v.t.* (*to produce or bring into existence*) bring about, cause, create, form, give rise to, initiate, make, originate, produce, propagate, sow the seeds of, spawn. ANTONYMS: destroy, extinguish, kill.

generation *n.* **1** (*a single succession or step in natural descent or in development*) age, epoch, era, lifespan, lifetime. **2** (*the people of the same period or age*) age group, peer group. **3** (*creation, bringing into existence*) causing, creation, formation, inception, initiation, making, origination, production, propagation, spawning.

generic *a.* **1** (*of or relating to a class or kind, as opposed to specific*) blanket, collective, common, general, non-specific, wide. ANTONYMS: particular, specific. **2** (*comprehensive, applied to large classes of goods or drugs*) common, non-exclusive, non-trademarked. ANTONYMS: exclusive, special, trademarked.

generosity *n.* **1** (*the quality of being liberal or kind*) beneficence, benevolence, bounteousness, bountifulness, bounty, charitableness, charity, hospitableness, hospitality, kindness, largess, largesse, liberality, liberalness, magnanimity, munificence, open-handedness. ANTONYMS: meanness, miserliness, parsimony. **2** (*the quality of being magnanimous or high-spirited*) altruism, goodness, high-mindedness, honour, magnanimity, nobleness, unselfishness. ANTONYMS: meanness, selfishness. **3** (*abundance*) abundance, ampleness, copiousness, largeness, lavishness, plentifulness. ANTONYMS: meanness, paucity, sparseness.

generous *a.* **1** (*open-handed, liberal*) beneficent, benevolent, bounteous, bountiful, charitable, free, free-handed, giving, hospitable, kind, liberal, munificent, open-handed, princely, ungrudging, unstinting. ANTONYMS: mean, miserly, parsimonious. **2** (*magnanimous, high-spirited*) altruistic, good, high-minded, honourable, magnanimous, noble, unselfish. ANTONYMS: ignoble, mean, selfish. **3** (*overflowing, abundant*) abundant, ample, copious, large, lavish, overflowing, plentiful, rich, substantial, superabundant. ANTONYMS: mean, small, sparse.

genesis *n.* (*creation, beginning*) beginning, birth, commencement, creation, dawn, formation, generation, inception, making, origin, origination, outset, production, propagation, root, source, start. ANTONYMS: death, destruction, end.

genial *a.* (*of a cheerful and kindly disposition, cordial*) affable, agreeable, amiable, cheerful, cheery, companionable, congenial, convivial, cordial, easygoing, friendly, good-humoured, good-natured, gracious, happy, jolly, jovial, kind, merry, nice, pleasant, sociable, sympathetic, warm, well-disposed. ANTONYMS: nasty, sullen, unfriendly.

genitals *n.pl.* (*the external reproductive organ(s)*) genitalia, (*coll., facet.*) naughty bits, private parts, pudenda, reproductive organs, sex organs.

genius n. **1** (*a person of extraordinary intellectual or inventive ability*) adept, brain, (*coll.*) brainbox, (*coll.*) buff, (*coll.*) egghead, expert, gifted child, intellectual, maestro, master, mastermind, prodigy, virtuoso, (*coll.*) whiz, (*coll.*) wiz. ANTONYMS: dunce, dunderhead, fool. **2** (*an extraordinary endowment of ability*) ability, aptitude, bent, brains, brilliance, capability, cleverness, creativity, endowment, faculty, flair, gift, inclination, knack, talent.

genre n. **1** (*a kind, class, particularly in the field of the arts*) brand, category, class, genus, kind, sort, species, type, variety. **2** (*a style, manner, esp. artistic*) character, fashion, manner, stamp, style.

genteel a. **1** (*gentlemanly or ladylike*) aristocratic, blue-blooded, gentlemanly, ladylike, noble, patrician, well-born. **2** (*well-bred, refined, free from vulgarity*) affected, civil, courteous, courtly, cultivated, decorous, elegant, gentlemanly, gracious, ladylike, mannerly, polite, refined, respectable, stylish, well-bred, well-mannered. ANTONYMS: boorish, coarse, ill-bred, rude, unrefined.

gentility n. **1** (*social superiority, polite good breeding*) aristocracy, blue blood, gentry, good breeding, high birth, nobility, noble birth, refinement, upper class. **2** (*respectable manners and habits associated with good society*) affectation, civility, courtesy, cultivation, decorum, elegance, good manners, mannerliness, politeness, propriety, refinement, respectability, style, stylishness.

gentle a. **1** (*mild, kindly*) benign, compassionate, docile, humane, kind, kindly, lenient, meek, merciful, mild, peaceful, placid, quiet, serene, sweet-tempered, tender, tenderhearted, tranquil. ANTONYMS: cruel, hard, heartless. **2** (*not rough or stern*) light, smooth, soft, soothing, tender. ANTONYMS: coarse, rough, violent. **3** (*moderate, not severe*) balmy, calm, clement, light, mild, moderate, soft, temperate. ANTONYMS: extreme, harsh, rough, severe. **4** (*not steep*) easy, gradual, slight. ANTONYMS: abrupt, steep.

gentlemanly a. (*like a gentleman in appearance or behaviour*) chivalrous, civil, considerate, courteous, cultivated, cultured, debonair, gallant, genteel, gracious, honourable, mannerly, noble, polished, polite, refined, suave, thoughtful, urbane, well-behaved, well-bred, well-mannered. ANTONYMS: boorish, ill-bred, ill-mannered, rude.

genuine a. **1** (*not counterfeit or false*) actual, authentic, bona fide, honest-to-goodness, kosher, legal, (*coll.*) legit, legitimate, original, pukka, pure, real, sound, sterling, the real McCoy, true, unadulterated, valid, veritable. ANTONYMS: artificial, false, sham, spurious. **2** (*sincere, honest*) artless, candid, frank, honest, ingenuous, (*coll.*) kosher, open, sincere, straight, truthful. ANTONYMS: deceitful, dishonest, false.

genus n. (*a kind, group*) category, class, family, genre, group, kind, order, set, sort, species, type, variety.

germ n. **1** (*a micro-organism, esp. the type that is supposed to cause disease*) bacillus, bacterium, (*coll.*) bug, microbe, micro-organism. **2** (*the portion of living matter from which an organism develops*) bud, egg, embryo, nucleus, ovule, ovum, seed. **3** (*the origin or elementary principle*) beginning, commencement, embryo, fountainhead, inception, origin, rudiment, seed, source, start.

germane a. (*relevant (to), appropriate*) akin (to), allied (with), apposite (to), apropos (of), apt, connected (with), fitting, having relevance (to), material (to), pertaining (to), pertinent (to), relating (to), relevant (to), to the point. ANTONYMS: extraneous (to), immaterial (to), irrelevant (to).

germinate v.i. **1** (*to sprout, to bud*) bud, burgeon, develop, generate, grow, pullulate, shoot, spring up, sprout, start growing. **2** (*to develop*) begin, commence, develop, grow, originate, start, take root.

gestation n. (*the process of being carried in the uterus from the time of conception to that of birth*) development, growth, incubation, maturation, pregnancy.

gesticulate v.i. (*to make expressive gestures or motions*) gesture, indicate, make a sign, make signs, motion, sign, signal, use gestures, use sign language, wave.

gesture n. **1** (*a motion of the face, body or limbs, used to express emotion*) gesticulation, indication, motion, sign, signal, wave. **2** (*a significant move or act, usu. of a friendly nature*) act, action, deed, symbolic act.
~v.i. (*to gesticulate*) gesticulate, indicate, make a sign, make signs, motion, sign, signal, use gestures, use sign language.
~v.t. (*to accompany or represent with gestures or action*) gesticulate, indicate, motion, sign, signal.

get v.t. **1** (*to obtain, to gain possession of*) acquire, (*coll.*) bag, come by, come into possession of, gain possession of, get hold of, procure, secure. **2** (*to earn, to win*) be paid, bring home, bring in, clear, earn, gross, make, net, pocket, take home. **3** (*to receive, to obtain*) be given, be in receipt of, be sent, be the recipient of, obtain, receive. **4** (*to receive as one's penalty, to suffer*) be given, be handed out, be meted out, be subjected to, receive, suffer, sustain. **5** (*to understand, learn*) comprehend, fathom, follow, get the drift of, grasp, (*coll.*) have the faintest idea about, make head or tail of, perceive, take in, understand. **6** (*to succeed in obtaining, bringing etc.*) achieve, attain, (*coll.*) bag, find, gain, get hold of, procure, realize, secure, win. **7** (*to induce, to persuade (to)*) cajole, coax, induce, persuade, prevail upon, talk into, wheedle, win over. **8** (*to outwit, to nonplus*) baffle, catch out, confound, get the better of, mystify, outwit, perplex, puzzle, (*coll.*) stump. **9** (*to become infected with (an illness)*) be afflicted by, be infected with, be smitten with, catch, come down with, contract, suffer from, take. **10** (*to establish communication with*) communicate with, contact, get in contact with, get in touch with, reach. **11** (*to fetch*) bring, carry, collect, convey, fetch, go and get, go for, transport. **12** (*to arrest, to catch*) arrest, capture, (*coll.*) collar, get hold of, grab, (*sl.*) nab, seize, take. **13** (*to affect emotionally*) affect, arouse, excite, move, stimulate, stir, (*coll.*) turn on. **14** (*to prepare*) cook, (*coll.*) fix, get ready, make preparations for, make the necessary preparations for, prepare. **15** (*to annoy, to irritate*) annoy, (*sl.*) bug, enrage, exasperate, (*coll.*) get one's back up, get on one's nerves, (*coll.*) get to, (*sl.*) get up one's nose, incense, infuriate, irk, irritate.

~*v.i.* **1** (*to arrive at any place*) arrive at, come to, (*coll.*) make it, reach. **2** (*to succeed, to find the way (to)*) be able to (to), be successful (in), find an opportunity (to), get the chance (of), succeed (in). **3** (*to become*) become, come to be, grow, turn, turn into, wax. **4** (*to start doing something*) begin, commence, get to the point of, reach the stage of, start. **to get about 1** (*to become known, to be reported abroad*) be broadcast, be circulated, be communicated, be made known, be made public, be publicized, be reported, get around. **2** (*to travel from place to place*) get around, move, move about, move around, travel about. **to get across** (*to communicate, to make oneself understood*) communicate, convey, get over, get through, impart, make clear, make understood, pass on, put over, relay, transmit. **to get ahead** (*to prosper*) advance, be successful, do well, flourish, get on, get on in the world, (*coll.*) go places, make advances, make good, (*coll.*) make it, make one's way in the world, (*coll.*) make out, make progress, make something of oneself, progress, prosper, succeed. **to get along 1** (*to fare, to manage (well or badly)*)

advance, cope, fare, (*coll.*) get by, get on, (*coll.*) make out, manage, proceed, progress. **2** (*to have a friendly relationship*) agree, be compatible, be friendly, be on friendly terms, be on good terms, be on the same wavelength, get on, (*coll.*) hit it off, see eye to eye, talk the same language. **to get at 1** (*to be able to reach*) attain, come to grips with, gain access, get hold of, reach. **2** (*to criticize repeatedly, esp. in an annoying way*) attack, be on (someone's) back, blame, carp at, criticize, find fault with, (*coll.*) hassle, nag, pick on, taunt. **3** (*to corrupt, bribe (a jockey etc.)*) bribe, buy off, corrupt, influence, suborn. **4** (*to imply, to hint at*) hint, imply, lead up to, mean, suggest. **to get away** (*to escape*) abscond, break free, break out, clear out, decamp, depart, escape, make good one's escape, make one's escape, (*coll.*) slope off, sneak off, (*N Am., sl.*) vamoose. **to get away with 1** (*to make off with*) abscond with, appropriate, kidnap, make off with, (*sl.*) nick, purloin, run away with, steal, (*sl.*) swipe, (*coll.*) waltz off with. **2** (*to escape discovery in connection with (something wrong or illegal)*) escape detection, escape punishment, escape undetected, escape unpunished, get off, get off scot-free, get off with, not be found out. **to get back 1** (*to receive back, to recover*) recoup, recover, regain, repossess, retrieve. **2** (*to return, to come back*) arrive back, arrive home, come back, come home, return, return home. **to get back at** (*to retaliate against*) avenge oneself on, be avenged on, get even with, get vengeance, give as good as one gets, give tit for tat, hit back at, retaliate, revenge oneself on, settle a score with, take revenge, take vengeance. **to get by 1** (*to have enough money only for the things one needs, to survive*) cope, exist, get along, keep one's head above water, keep the wolf from the door, make (both) ends meet, (*coll.*) make out, manage, subsist, survive. **2** (*to be good enough*) be acceptable, be all right, be good enough, (*coll.*) be okay, be sufficient, come up to scratch, pass muster. **to get down to** (*to concentrate upon*) apply oneself to, (*coll.*) buckle to, concentrate on, give one's attention to, make an effort, pay attention to, put one's mind to, put one's shoulder to the wheel, start work on. **to get even** (*to revenge oneself*) avenge oneself on, be avenged on, get back at, get vengeance on, hit back at, retaliate, revenge oneself on, settle a score with, take revenge on, take vengeance on. **to get it into one's head** (*to become convinced (that)*) become obsessed (by), be convinced (of), begin to believe (that), be of the belief (that), be of the opinion (that), get it fixed in one's head (that), get the idea (that). **to get off 1** (*to dismount, to alight (from)*) alight, climb off, descend, disembark, dismount, exit, jump off, leave. **2** (*to be acquitted, to be let off* (*with or for*)) be absolved, be acquitted, be cleared, be exonerated, be let off, be pardoned, escape punishment, go scot-free, receive a pardon. **to get off with** (*to begin or have a sexual relationship with*) (*sl.*) get one's leg over, go to bed with, have an affair with, have sex with, (*sl.*) score with, start a relationship with. **to get on 1** (*to succeed or prosper*) (*coll.*) arrive, be successful, do well, flourish, (*coll.*) make it, (*coll.*) make out, prosper, succeed, thrive, triumph. **2** (*to have a friendly relationship*) agree, be compatible, be friendly, be on friendly terms, be on good terms, be on the same wavelength, get along, (*coll.*) hit it off, see eye to eye, talk the same language. **3** (*to fare or manage* (*with or without*)) advance, cope, fare, get along, (*coll.*) get by, (*coll.*) make out, manage, proceed, progress. **4** (*to mount*) ascend, board, climb on, embark, enter, jump on, mount. **to get on to 1** (*to make contact with*) be in communication with, be in touch with, communicate with, contact, get hold of, get in touch with, make contact with, reach. **2** (*to become aware of, discover*) become aware of, detect, discover, expose, find out, perceive, recognize, trace, uncover, unmask. **to get out 1** (*to escape from any place of confinement or restraint*) abscond, break free, clear out, decamp, depart, escape, get away, make good one's escape, make one's escape, (*coll.*) slope off, sneak off, (*N Am., sl.*) vamoose. **2** (*to be divulged*) be circulated, be communicated, be disclosed, be publicized, be reported, get around, leak out, spread. **to get out of** (*to avoid* (*doing something*)) avoid, dodge, duck, escape, evade, shirk. **to get over 1** (*to surmount, overcome* (*a difficulty etc.*)) conquer, defeat, get the better of, master, overcome, shake off, surmount, triumph over, vanquish. **2** (*to recover from* (*illness, disappointment etc.*)) (*coll.*) bounce back, get back on one's feet, get back to normal, get better, get well, live to fight another day, pull through, rally, recover, revive, survive. **3** (*to make intelligible*) communicate, convey, get across, make clear, make intelligible, make understood, put across, put over, transmit. **to get there 1** (*to succeed*) achieve one's aim, achieve success, be successful, realize one's goal, succeed. ANTONYMS: be unsuccessful, fail. **2** (*to understand*) comprehend, follow, (*coll.*) get the drift, get the hang of it, (*coll.*) latch on, (*coll.*) twig, understand. **to get through 1** (*to succeed in doing, to complete*) accomplish, bring to completion, complete, execute, finalize, finish, get to the end of, (*coll.*) wrap up. **2** (*to pass* (*an examination*)) be successful in, (*coll.*) come up to scratch in, pass, pass muster, succeed in. ANTONYMS: come a cropper, fail.

3 ((*of a bill*) *to be passed*) be accepted, be approved, be passed, be ratified, be sanctioned. **to get through to 1** (*to make a telephone connection with*) communicate with, contact, get in touch with, make contact with, phone, reach, speak to, telephone. **2** (*to make understand or pay attention*) communicate with, get a reaction from, get one's message across to, make understand. **to get to 1** (*to begin* (*a task etc.*)) address oneself to, begin, commence, concentrate on, get the show on the road, put one's shoulder to the wheel, set to, start, start the ball rolling. **2** (*to annoy or irritate*) annoy, (*sl.*) bug, enrage, exasperate, (*coll.*) get, (*coll.*) get one's back up, get on one's nerves, (*sl.*) get up one's nose, incense, infuriate, irk, irritate, rile, upset. **to get together 1** (*to meet, to assemble*) assemble, congregate, convene, converge, foregather, gather, have a meeting, join together, meet, rally. ANTONYMS: break up, separate. **2** (*to bring together, to amass*) accumulate, amass, assemble, collect, gather, put together. **to get under way** (*to cause to begin*) begin, come into being, come into existence, commence, start. ANTONYMS: come to an end, end, finish. **to get up** (*to rise* (*as from a bed etc.*)) arise, get out of bed, get to one's feet, rise, (*coll.*) rise and shine, stand up, (*coll.*) surface.

get-up *n.* (*a person's dress and other accessories*) attire, clothes, clothing, costume, dress, garb, outfit, rig-out.

get-up-and-go *n.* (*energy and enthusiasm*) ambition, drive, eagerness, energy, enterprise, initiative, keenness, passion, push, verve, vigour, zest, (*coll.*) zip. ANTONYMS: inertia, laziness, lethargy.

ghastly *a.* **1** (*horrible, shocking*) appalling, awful, dreadful, frightening, frightful, grim, grisly, gruesome, heinous, hideous, horrendous, horrible, shocking, terrible, terrifying. ANTONYMS: delightful, pleasing. **2** (*awful, unpleasant*) appalling, awful, base, contemptible, disagreeable, (*coll.*) dreadful, foul, hateful, loathsome, low, mean, nasty, odious, repellent. ANTONYMS: agreeable, nice, pleasant. **3** (*pale, haggard*) ashen, cadaverous, colourless, corpselike, deathlike, deathly pale, drawn, ghostlike, haggard, pale, pallid, spectral, wan, white, white as a sheet. ANTONYMS: flushed, red, ruddy. **4** (*very ill*) dreadful, ill, sick as a dog, terrible, unwell. ANTONYMS: fine, healthy, well.

ghost *n.* **1** (*the spirit or soul of a dead person appearing to the living*) apparition, phantom, revenant, shade, soul, spectre, spirit, (*coll.*) spook, wraith. **2** (*a mere shadow or semblance*) glimmer, hint, semblance, shadow, suggestion, trace. **3** (*the remotest likelihood*) chance, glimmer, likelihood, possibility, probability, prospect.

ghostly *a.* (*of or relating to ghosts or apparitions*) eerie, ghostlike, illusory, insubstantial, other-worldly, phantom, phantom-like, shadowy, spectral, spectre-like, (*coll.*) spooky, supernatural, uncanny, unearthly, unnatural, weird, wraithlike. ANTONYMS: earthly, mortal, substantial.

ghoulish *a.* (*like a ghoul*) grisly, gruesome, macabre, morbid, (*coll.*) sick, unhealthy, unwholesome. ANTONYMS: healthy, wholesome.

giant *n.* (*any person, animal etc. of abnormal size*) behemoth, colossus, leviathan, monster, ogre, titan. ANTONYMS: dwarf.
~*a.* (*gigantic*) colossal, elephantine, enormous, gargantuan, gigantic, huge, immense, (*coll.*) jumbo, mammoth, massive, monstrous, monumental, prodigious, stupendous, ultra-large, vast. ANTONYMS: dwarf, Lilliputian, midget, minute, tiny.

gibber *v.i.* (*to jabber, to talk rapidly and inarticulately*) babble, chatter, gabble, jabber, prattle, (*coll.*) rabbit, (*coll.*) witter. ANTONYMS: articulate.

gibberish *n.* **1** (*inarticulate sounds*) babble, chatter, chattering, gabbling, jabbering, prattle, prattling, (*coll.*) rabbiting, (*coll.*) wittering. **2** (*unmeaning or unintelligible language, jargon*) balderdash, (*sl.*) bilge, (*sl.*) bosh, (*sl.*) bullshit, (*coll.*) bunkum, gobbledegook, jargon, mumbo-jumbo, nonsense, piffle, (*sl.*) poppycock, (*coll.*) rot, rubbish, technobabble, (*coll.*) tommyrot, (*sl.*) tosh, (*coll.*) tripe, twaddle.

gibe *v.i.* (*to use sneering or taunting expressions*) deride, hold up to ridicule, jeer at, laugh at, make fun of, mock, poke fun at, rag, (*coll.*) rib, ridicule, scoff at, scorn, sneer at, (*sl.*) take the piss out of, taunt, tease, twit.
~*n.* (*a sneer, a taunt*) barb, derision, dig, jeer, jeering, mockery, scoff, scoffing, sneer, sneering, taunt.

giddy *a.* **1** (*having a swimming or dizziness in the head*) dizzy, faint, light-headed, reeling, staggering, suffering from vertigo, unsteady, vertiginous, (*coll.*) woozy. **2** (*changeable, flighty*) capricious, changeable, erratic, feather-brained, fickle, flighty, flippant, frivolous, heedless, inconstant, irresolute, irresponsible, light-minded, reckless, scatterbrained, silly, skittish, thoughtless, unstable, unsteady, vacillating, volatile. ANTONYMS: constant, serious, steady.

gift *n.* **1** (*a thing given, a present*) benefaction,

bequest, bonus, boon, bounty, contribution, donation, endowment, grant, gratuity, handout, largesse, legacy, offering, present, tip. ANTONYMS: loan, pay. **2** (*a natural quality or talent*) ability, aptitude, aptness, attribute, bent, capability, capacity, endowment, facility, faculty, flair, genius, knack, power, skill, talent.
~*v.t.* (*to give as a gift*) bequeath, bestow, confer, contribute, donate, endow, give, present.

gifted *a.* (*largely endowed with intellect, talented*) able, bright, brilliant, clever, intelligent, smart. ANTONYMS: slow, stupid.

gig *n.* (*a job, esp. a booking for a musician to perform*) appearance, booking, concert, engagement, job, performance, show.

gigantic *a.* (*enormous; extraordinary*) Brobdingnagian, colossal, elephantine, enormous, gargantuan, giant, huge, immense, (*coll.*) jumbo, mammoth, massive, monstrous, monumental, ultra-large, vast. ANTONYMS: dwarf, midget, tiny.

giggle *v.i.* (*to laugh in a nervous, catchy way*) cackle, chortle, chuckle, laugh, (*coll.*) laugh like a drain, snicker, snigger, (*coll.*) tee-hee, titter.

gild *v.t.* **1** (*to make brilliant, to brighten*) adorn, beautify, bedeck, brighten, brighten up, decorate, dress up, embellish, enhance, garnish, ornament, prettify. **2** (*to give a specious or agreeable appearance to*) add some windowdressing to, camouflage, disguise, dress up, embellish, embroider, sugar-coat, windowdress.

gimcrack *a.* (*showy but flimsy and worthless*) cheap, (*coll.*) flash, flashy, jerry-built, kitsch, shoddy, showy, (*coll.*) tacky, (*coll.*) tatty, tawdry, worthless. ANTONYMS: solid, substantial, valuable.

gimmick *n.* (*a trick or device used to attract extra attention or publicity*) advertising ploy, device, ploy, publicity stunt, scheme, stratagem, stunt, trick.

gingerly *adv.* (*cautiously, so as to move without noise*) as though treading on eggs, carefully, cautiously, charily, daintily, fastidiously, guardedly, hesitantly, judiciously, prudently, reluctantly, suspiciously, timidly, vigilantly, warily, with due care and attention. ANTONYMS: carelessly, confidently, recklessly.

gird *v.t.* **1** (*to secure (one's clothes) with a girdle, belt etc.*) belt, bind, fasten, secure. **2** (*to surround or encircle with or as with a girdle*) circle, confine, encircle, enclose, encompass, ring, surround. **to gird (up) one's loins** (*to* *prepare oneself for* (*vigorous*) *action*) brace oneself, (*coll.*) gear oneself up, get ready, make preparations, make provisions, prepare oneself, (*coll.*) psych oneself up, ready oneself, steel oneself, take the necessary steps.

girl *n.* **1** (*a female child, a young, unmarried woman*) (*dial.*) lass, (*arch*) maid, (*now chiefly facet.*) wench, young lady, young woman. ANTONYMS: boy, woman. **2** (*a girlfriend*) fiancée, girlfriend, lady love, lover, mistress, sweetheart.

girlfriend *n.* (*a regular female companion, esp. one with whom there is a romantic relationship*) fiancée, girl, lady love, lover, mistress, sweetheart.

girth *n.* (*the measurement round anything, the circumference*) circumference, perimeter.

gist *n.* (*the essence or main point of a question*) burden, core, crux, drift, essence, force, general meaning, import, kernel, main thrust, nub, nucleus, pith, quintessence, sense, significance, substance.

give *v.t.* **1** (*to hand over or transfer the possession of without compensation*) accord, award, bequeath, bestow, confer, consign, contribute, donate, entrust, gift, give a donation to, grant, leave, make a gift of, make a present of, make over, will. ANTONYMS: receive, take. **2** (*to bestow, to confer*) deliver, furnish, offer, provide, supply. **3** (*to grant, to concede*) accord, allow, concede, grant, offer, permit, yield. **4** (*to hand over, to deliver*) allocate, allot, apportion, deliver, (*coll.*) dish out, distribute, dole out, hand out, hand over, mete out. ANTONYMS: get, receive. **5** (*to surrender, to relinquish*) cede, give up, relinquish, surrender. **6** (*to yield as product*) afford, produce, yield. **7** (*to communicate, to impart*) announce, broadcast, circulate, communicate, convey, impart, publicize, transmit. **8** (*to occasion, to cause*) be the source of, cause, create, lead to, occasion, produce. **9** (*to show or exhibit*) demonstrate, display, evidence, exhibit, indicate, manifest, offer, proffer, set forth, show. **10** (*to utter, to emit*) emit, issue, let out, utter. **11** (*to perform*) carry out, do, effect, execute, make, perform. **12** (*to organize* (*a party*)) arrange, lay on, organize, put on, (*coll.*) throw.

~*v.i.* (*to yield to pressure, to collapse*) bend, break, buckle, cave in, collapse, come apart, fall apart, fall to pieces, give way, yield. ANTONYMS: resist. **to give away 1** (*to make over as a gift, to transfer*) donate, give, give without charge, hand over for free, make over, sign over, transfer. ANTONYMS: charge for, sell. **2** (*to let out or divulge inadvertently*) disclose, divulge, leak, let out, let slip, reveal. ANTONYMS: keep mum about, keep secret, keep

under wraps. **to give back** (*to restore, return something to someone*) restore, return, send back. ANTONYMS: keep, retain. **to give in** (*to yield*) acknowledge defeat, admit defeat, capitulate, concede, concede defeat, give up, submit, succumb, surrender, (*coll.*) throw in the towel, yield. ANTONYMS: fight on, resist. **to give off** (*to emit*) discharge, emit, exhale, exude, give out, pour out, produce, release, send out, throw out, vent. **to give out 1** (*to emit*) discharge, emit, exhale, exude, give off, pour out, produce, release, send out, throw out, vent. **2** (*to publish, to proclaim*) announce, broadcast, communicate, disseminate, impart, make known, proclaim, publish, utter. ANTONYMS: keep secret, keep under wraps. **3** (*to distribute*) allocate, allot, apportion, deal, dispense, distribute, dole out, give, hand out, issue, mete out, share out. **4** (*to break down*) (*sl.*) be kaput, break down, come to a halt, (*sl.*) conk out, seize up, stop working. **5** (*to run short*) be consumed, be depleted, be exhausted, be finished, be used up, come to an end, run out, run short. **to give over 1** (*to hand over, to transfer*) assign, give, hand over, make over, transfer. ANTONYMS: keep, retain. **2** (*to devote or addict*) abandon, dedicate, devote, give way to, surrender. **3** (*to cease* (*from*), *to desist*) cease, desist from, discontinue, leave off, quit, stop. ANTONYMS: keep on, persist in. **to give up 1** (*to surrender*) acknowledge defeat, admit defeat, capitulate, concede, concede defeat, give in, quit, submit, surrender, (*coll.*) throw in the sponge, (*coll.*) throw in the towel, yield. ANTONYMS: fight on, resist. **2** (*to resign*) quit, relinquish, resign from, retire from. **3** (*to commit*) commit, deliver, give, hand over. ANTONYMS: keep, retain. **4** (*to despair of*) abandon hope, be discouraged by, cease to help, despair of, give up hope for, lose hope for. **5** (*to stop doing*) abandon, (*sl.*) chuck, cut out, desist from, forswear, leave off, quit, renounce, stop. **to give way 1** (*to yield, to fail to resist*) acknowledge defeat, acquiesce, admit defeat, back down, cave in, concede, concede defeat, give in, give up, make concessions. ANTONYMS: fight on, resist. **2** (*to make room for*) be replaced by, be succeeded by, be superseded by, give place to, give precedence to, make room for. **3** (*to break down, to collapse*) bend, break, buckle, cave in, collapse, come apart, crumble, fall apart, fall to pieces, give. **4** (*to abandon* (*oneself to*)) abandon oneself to, devote oneself to, give oneself over to, surrender oneself to.

give-away *n.* **1** (*an unintentional revelation*) betrayal, disclosure, divulgence, exposure, revelation. **2** (*something given free*) (*coll.*) freebie, gift, present. ANTONYMS: purchase.

given name *n.* (*a forename, a baptismal name*) baptismal name, Christian name, first name, forename. ANTONYMS: surname.

giver *n.* (*a person that gives something, esp. money*) (*coll.*) angel, backer, benefactor, contributor, donator, donor, fairy godmother. ANTONYMS: recipient, taker.

gizmo *n.* (*a gadget*) apparatus, appliance, contraption, device, gadget, implement, instrument, mechanism, thing, tool, widget.

glacial *a.* (*due to or like ice*) arctic, bitter, freezing, freezing cold, frigid, frozen, gelid, icy, raw, Siberian, wintry. ANTONYMS: equatorial, sweltering.

glad *a.* **1** (*pleased, gratified*) cheerful, (*coll.*) chuffed, delightful, gratified, happy, joyful, overjoyed, pleased as Punch, thrilled. ANTONYMS: displeased, sad, unhappy. **2** (*indicating pleasure or satisfaction*) animated, bright, cheerful, gay, gleeful, happy, joyful, joyous, merry, pleased, satisfied. ANTONYMS: miserable, sad, unhappy. **3** (*affording pleasure or satisfaction*) cheerful, cheering, delightful, happy, joyful, pleasant, pleasing, satisfying, welcome. ANTONYMS: depressing, sad. **4** (*willing and eager*) eager, happy, keen, more than willing, pleased, prepared, ready, willing. ANTONYMS: disinclined, reluctant, unwilling.

gladden *v.t.* (*to make glad or joyful*) brighten up, (*coll.*) buck up, cheer, cheer up, delight, gift a lift to, give pleasure to, hearten, make happy, please, raise the spirits of, rejoice. ANTONYMS: depress, make miserable, make unhappy.

gladly *adv.* (*willingly and eagerly*) cheerfully, eagerly, happily, readily, willingly, with pleasure. ANTONYMS: grudgingly, reluctantly, unwillingly.

glamorous *a.* **1** (*fascinating and attractive due largely to grooming, expensive clothes or other artifice*) dazzling, exciting, fascinating, glittering, (*coll.*) glitzy, (*coll.*) ritzy, showy. ANTONYMS: dull, humdrum, pedestrian, unexciting. **2** (*charming and bewitching*) alluring, beautiful, bewitching, captivating, dazzling, elegant, entrancing, fascinating, showy. ANTONYMS: dull, ordinary, plain.

glamour *n.* (*fascinating attractiveness due largely to expensive clothes or other artifice*) allure, attraction, attractiveness, charm, enchantment, excitement, fascination, (*coll.*) glitz, (*coll.*) glitziness, magic, (*coll.*) pizazz, (*coll.*) ritziness. ANTONYMS: dullness, plainness, tedium.

glance *v.i.* **1** (*to give a quick or cursory look* (*at*))

flip through, have a quick look (at), leaf through, look briefly (at), look quickly (at), riffle through, scan, (*sl.*) take a butcher's (at), (*coll.*) take a dekko (at), (*coll.*) take a gander (at), take a hurried look (at), (*sl.*) take a shufti at, (*coll.*) take a squint at, thumb through. ANTONYMS: examine, gaze, peruse, study. **2** (*to glide off or from* (*as a blow*)) be deflected off, bounce off, brush, graze, ricochet off, skim, touch. **3** (*to dart or flash a gleam of light or brightness*) be reflected, flash, flicker, gleam, glint, glisten, glitter, shimmer, shine, sparkle, twinkle. **4** (*to allude, to hint* (*at*)) allude to, hint at, make an allusion to, make reference to, mention, mention in passing, refer to. ANTONYMS: dwell on.

~*n.* **1** (*a quick or transient look, a hurried glimpse* (*at*)) brief look, (*sl.*) butcher's, cursory look, (*coll.*) dekko, (*coll.*) gander, glimpse, quick look, rapid look, (*sl.*) shufti, (*coll.*) squint. ANTONYMS: gaze. **2** (*a flash, a gleam*) flash, flicker, gleam, glint, sparkle, twinkle.

glare *v.i.* **1** (*to shine with a dazzling or overpowering light*) beam, blaze, dazzle, flame, flare. ANTONYMS: flicker, glow. **2** (*to look with fierce, piercing eyes, to stare*) frown, give black looks, (*coll.*) give dirty looks, glower, look daggers, look stern, lour, lower, scowl, stare angrily, stare fiercely, stare menacingly, stare threateningly. ANTONYMS: smile.

~*n.* **1** (*an intense, fierce look or stare*) angry stare, black look, (*coll.*) dirty look, fierce stare, frown, glower, lour, lower, menacing stare, scowl, stare, threatening stare. ANTONYMS: smile. **2** (*a fierce, overpowering light, disagreeable brightness*) beam, blaze, dazzle, flame, flare. ANTONYMS: flicker, glow. **3** (*tawdry splendour*) conspicuousness, dazzle, garishness, gaudiness, loudness, overbrightness. ANTONYMS: subtlety.

glaring *a.* **1** (*shining with dazzling brightness*) blazing, blinding, bright, dazzling, flaming, flaring, ultra-bright. ANTONYMS: flickering, glowing. **2** (*staring*) fierce, glowering, louring, lowering, scowling, staring. ANTONYMS: smiling. **3** (*too conspicuous or overcoloured*) conspicuous, dazzling, garish, gaudy, loud, overbright, overcoloured, sticking out like a sore thumb. ANTONYMS: inconspicuous, muted, subtle.

glass *n.* **1** (*a drinking vessel*) beaker, goblet, tumbler. **2** (*a mirror, a looking-glass*) looking-glass, mirror, reflector, speculum. **3** (*pl.*) (*spectacles, pair of glasses*) binoculars, eyeglasses, field glasses, (*coll.*) specs, spectacles.

glassy *a.* **1** (*dull, fixed* (*of the eye*)) blank, deadpan, dull, empty, expressionless, fixed, glazed, lifeless, staring, vacant. **2** (*lustrous,* *smooth (of water))* clear, glass-like, glossy, lustrous, mirror-like, shining, shiny, slippery, smooth.

glaze *v.t.* **1** *(to overlay (pottery) with a vitreous substance)* coat, enamel, lacquer, varnish. **2** *(to cover (a surface) with a thin, glossy coating)* coat, ice, sugar-coat. **3** *(to make smooth and glossy)* burnish, furbish, polish.
~v.i. (to become glassy (as the eyes)) adopt a fixed expression, become blank, become expressionless, grow dull, look empty, seem vacant.
~n. **1** *(a smooth, lustrous coating)* coating, frosting, icing, topping. **2** *(a coating, formed of various substances, used to glaze earthenware, paper etc.)* coat, coating, enamel, finish, gloss, lacquer, lustre, polish, varnish.

gleam *n. (a flash, a beam, esp. one of a faint or transient kind)* beam, flare, flash, flicker, glimmer, glint, ray, shaft, shimmer, sparkle, twinkle.
~v.i. **1** *(to send out rays of a quick and transient kind)* blink, coruscate, flare, flash, flicker, glimmer, glint, shimmer, sparkle, twinkle, wink. **2** *(to shine, to glitter)* be highly polished, glitter, shimmer, shine. ANTONYMS: be dull.

glee *n. (joy, delight)* blitheness, cheerfulness, delight, elation, euphoria, exhilaration, exuberance, exultation, fun, gaiety, gladness, happiness, high spirits, hilarity, jollity, joy, joyfulness, merriment, mirth, pleasure, triumph, verve. ANTONYMS: depression, gloom, sadness.

gleeful *a. (merry, joyous)* cheerful, cheery, *(coll.)* chipper, chirpy, cock-a-hoop, delighted, elated, euphoric, exhilarated, exuberant, exultant, glad, happy, merry, mirthful, overjoyed, pleased as Punch, rapt, triumphant. ANTONYMS: depressed, gloomy, sad.

glib *a. (fluent, not sincere)* fluent, having kissed the Blarney Stone, insincere, loquacious, plausible, slick, smooth, smooth-spoken, suave, sweet-talking, talkative, voluble, with the gift of the gab. ANTONYMS: hesitant, inarticulate, insincere, tongue-tied.

glide *v.i.* **1** *(to slip or slide along, as on a smooth surface)* coast, drift, float, move effortlessly, sail, skate, skim, slide, slip. ANTONYMS: lumber, lurch, stumble. **2** *(to pass imperceptibly (away))* flow, fly, roll on, run, slip, steal.

glimmer *v.i. (to shine faintly)* blink, flicker, glint, glisten, glitter, glow, shimmer, sparkle, twinkle, wink.
~n. **1** *(a faint, unsteady light)* flicker, glint, glow, ray, shimmer, sparkle, twinkle. **2** *(a faint vestige, an uncertain sign)* flicker, gleam, grain, hint, inkling, ray, suggestion, trace.

glimpse *n. (a momentary look, a rapid and imperfect view (of))* brief view, peep, quick look, rapid sighting. ANTONYMS: examination.
~v.t. (to see for an instant) catch a glimpse of, catch sight of, see briefly, spot. ANTONYMS: examine, study.

glint *v.i. (to glitter, to sparkle)* blink, flash, gleam, glimmer, glitter, shimmer, shine, sparkle, twinkle, wink.
~n. (a gleam, a flash) blink, flash, gleam, glimmer, sparkle, twinkle.

glisten *v.i. (to gleam, to sparkle, usu. by reflection)* coruscate, gleam, glimmer, glint, shimmer, shine, sparkle, twinkle, wink.

glitter *v.i. (to shine with a succession of brilliant gleams or flashes)* coruscate, flash, gleam, glimmer, glint, glisten, scintillate, shimmer, shine, sparkle, twinkle, wink.
~n. **1** *(a bright, sparkling light)* gleam, glimmer, glint, shimmer, sparkle, twinkle. **2** *(speciousness, attractiveness)* attractiveness, flashiness, garishness, gaudiness, gilt, glamour, *(coll.)* glitz, ostentation, pageantry, *(coll.)* pizazz, razzle-dazzle, *(coll.)* ritziness, show, showiness, sparkle, speciousness, tinsel.

gloat *v.i. (to dwell (on) with exultant feelings of malignity, greed etc.)* be triumphant, crow (about), delight (in), drool (over), exult (in), glory (in), rejoice (in), relish, revel (in), *(coll.)* rub it in, take pleasure (in), triumph (in).

global *a.* **1** *(relating to the globe as an entirety)* international, pandemic, universal, world, worldwide. ANTONYMS: local. **2** *(taking in entire groups or classes)* across-the-board, all-encompassing, all-inclusive, comprehensive, encyclopedic, exhaustive, general, thorough, total, with no exceptions. ANTONYMS: limited, restricted.

globe *n.* **1** *(a sphere, a round or spherical body)* ball, orb, round, sphere. **2** *(the earth)* earth, planet, universe, world.

globule *n. (a particle of matter in the form of a small globe)* ball, bead, drop, droplet, particle, pearl, pellet.

gloom *n.* **1** *(obscurity, partial darkness)* blackness, cloudiness, dark, darkness, dimness, dullness, dusk, gloaming, gloominess, murkiness, obscurity, shade, shadow, twilight. ANTONYMS: brightness, daylight, light. **2** *(depression, melancholy)* dejection, depression, desolation, despair, despondency, downheartedness, grief, hopelessness, low spirits, melancholy, misery, pessimism, sadness, sorrow, the blues, the dumps, *(coll.)* the hump, unhappiness, woe. ANTONYMS: happiness, high spirits.

gloomy *a.* **1** (*dark, obscure*) black, cloudy, crepuscular, dark, dim, dismal, dreary, dull, dusky, murky, obscure, overcast, shadowy, shady, sombre, Stygian, sunless. ANTONYMS: bright, light, sunny. **2** (*sad, melancholy*) bad, black, bleak, cheerless, depressing, discouraging, disheartening, dismal, dispiriting, distressing, melancholy, miserable, pessimistic, sad, saddening, sombre. ANTONYMS: cheerful, happy. **3** (*sullen, morose*) blue, dejected, depressed, despondent, disconsolate, disheartened, distressed, down, downcast, downhearted, down in the mouth, glum, in low spirits, miserable, morose, sad, sorrowful, sullen, unhappy, woebegone. ANTONYMS: cheerful, happy, in high spirits, joyful.

glorify *v.t.* **1** (*to pay honour and glory to in worship, to praise*) adore, exalt, honour, magnify, pay homage to, revere, reverence, venerate, worship. **2** (*to magnify, to praise*) acclaim, applaud, eulogize, extol, hail, laud, lionize, magnify, praise, sing the praises of. ANTONYMS: condemn, decry, disparage.

glorious *a.* **1** (*entitling one to fame or honour*) celebrated, distinguished, eminent, excellent, famed, famous, grand, illustrious, magnificent, major, noble, noted, prestigious, renowned, splendid, supreme. ANTONYMS: ignoble, infamous, minor. **2** (*splendid, magnificent*) grand, impressive, magnificent, marvellous, splendid, (*coll.*) terrific, wonderful. ANTONYMS: mediocre, modest, unimpressive. **3** (*completely satisfactory*) delightful, enjoyable, excellent, (*coll.*) fab, (*coll.*) fabulous, (*coll.*) great, marvellous, perfect, pleasant, pleasurable, splendid, (*coll.*) terrific, wonderful. ANTONYMS: boring, dull.

glory *n.* **1** (*high honour, honourable distinction*) distinction, eminence, excellence, fame, grandness, honour, illustriousness, kudos, nobility, prestige, renown, splendour. ANTONYMS: infamy. **2** (*magnificence, grandeur*) excellence, grandeur, impressiveness, magnificence, majesty, splendour, wonder. ANTONYMS: mediocrity, modesty. **3** (*brilliance, splendour*) beauty, brightness, brilliance, effulgence, pomp, radiance, resplendence, splendour. ANTONYMS: dullness, ugliness. **to glory in** (*to be proud of*) be proud of, boast about, crow about, exult in, feel triumphant about, rejoice in, revel in, take pleasure in, take pride in. ANTONYMS: feel ashamed about.

gloss¹ *n.* **1** (*the brightness or lustre from a polished surface*) brightness, brilliance, burnish, gleam, lustre, polish, sheen, shimmer, shine, sparkle, varnish. ANTONYMS: dullness, mattness. **2** (*a specious or deceptive outward appearance*) camouflage, disguise, facade, false appearance, false front, front, mask, semblance, show, surface, veneer. ~*v.t.* **1** (*to make glossy or lustrous*) burnish, furbish, glaze, polish, put a sheen on, shine, varnish. **2** (*to render specious or plausible*) camouflage, conceal, cover up, disguise, draw a veil over, hide, mask, smooth over, veil, whitewash. ANTONYMS: reveal, uncover.

gloss² *n.* (*a glossary or commentary*) annotation, comment, commentary, elucidation, explanation, explication, footnote, interpretation, marginalia, margin note, note, translation. ~*v.t.* (*to explain by note or comment*) add footnotes to, add margin notes to, annotate, comment on, elucidate, explain, explicate, give a commentary on, give an explanation of, give an explication of, interpret, translate.

glossary *n.* (*a list or dictionary of explanations of technical or dialectal words*) dictionary, gloss, lexicon, vocabulary, wordlist.

glossy *a.* (*having a smooth, lustrous surface*) bright, brilliant, burnished, glassy, glazed, gleaming, like glass, lustrous, polished, shimmering, shining, shiny, smooth, sparkling. ANTONYMS: dull, matt.

glove *n.* (*a covering for the hand, usu. with a separate division for each finger*) gauntlet, mitt, mitten.

glow *v.i.* **1** (*to radiate light and heat, esp. without flame*) gleam, smoulder. **2** (*to be bright or red with heat, to show a warm colour*) blush, colour, flush, go crimson, go red, go scarlet, redden, turn pink. ANTONYMS: grow pale, pale. **3** (*to be warm or flushed with passion or fervour*) radiate, thrill, tingle. ~*n.* **1** (*incandescence, red or white heat*) gleam, incandescence, lambency, luminosity, phosphorescence, subdued light. **2** (*redness, warmth of colour*) bloom, blush, flush, pink, pinkness, red, reddening, redness, rosiness, scarlet. ANTONYMS: paleness, pallor. **3** (*vehemence, ardour*) ardour, earnestness, enthusiasm, fervour, intensity, passion, vehemence, warmth. ANTONYMS: coolness, indifference, lukewarmness. **4** (*a strong feeling of satisfaction or pleasure*) contentment, happiness, pleasure, satisfaction, warmth. ANTONYMS: discontent, dissatisfaction.

glower *v.i.* (*to scowl, to stare fiercely or angrily*) frown, give a black look, (*coll.*) give a dirty look, glare, look daggers, lour, lower, scowl. ANTONYMS: smile. ~*n.* (*a savage stare, a scowl*) black look, (*coll.*) dirty look, frown, glare, lour, lower, scowl. ANTONYMS: smile.

glowing *a.* **1** (*radiating light, heat etc.*) aglow, gleaming, incandescent, lambent, luminous, phosphorescent, smouldering, suffused. **2** (*enthusiastic, ardent*) acclamatory, adulatory, complimentary, ecstatic, enthusiastic, eulogistic, highly favourable, laudatory, panegyrical, (*coll.*) rave, rhapsodic. ANTONYMS: condemnatory, lukewarm, scathing. **3** (*red with heat, showing a warm colour*) blushing, crimson, flushed, pink, red, rosy, ruddy, scarlet. ANTONYMS: pale, wan.

glue *n.* (*an adhesive or sticky substance*) adhesive, epoxy resin, fixative, gum, mucilage, paste.
~*v.t.* (*to join or fasten with glue*) affix, cement, fix, gum, paste, stick.

glum *a.* (*sullen, dejected*) blue, crestfallen, dejected, depressed, despondent, disheartened, down, downcast, downhearted, down in the mouth, gloomy, in low spirits, in the dumps, low, melancholy, moody, morose, sad, sorrowful, sullen, unhappy, woebegone. ANTONYMS: cheerful, happy, in high spirits, joyful.

glut *n.* (*a surfeit*) excess, overabundance, oversupply, superabundance, superfluity, surfeit, surplus. ANTONYMS: dearth, scarcity, shortage.
~*v.t.* **1** (*to fill to excess, to stuff*) cram full, fill, fill up, gorge, overfeed, sate, satiate, stuff. **2** (*to fill with an oversupply (as a market)*) flood, inundate, overload, oversupply, saturate.

glutton *n.* (*a person who eats to excess*) (*sl.*) gannet, gorger, gourmand, gourmandizer, (*coll.*) greedy pig, guzzler, (*coll.*) pig.

gluttonous *a.* (*of or relating to a glutton, greedy*) (*sl.*) gannet-like, gourmandizing, greedy, gutsy, hoggish, insatiable, piggish, ravenous, voracious. ANTONYMS: (*coll.*) anorexic, faddy.

gluttony *n.* (*the act or habit of eating to excess*) gourmandism, gourmandizing, greed, greediness, gutsiness, voraciousness, voracity.

gnarled *a.* (*rugged, twisted*) arthritic, bumpy, contorted, crooked, knotted, knurled, leathery, lined, lumpy, nodular, rough, rugged, twisted, weather-beaten, wrinkled. ANTONYMS: level, smooth, straight.

gnash *v.t.* (*to strike or grind (the teeth) together*) grate, grind, grit, rasp, strike together.

gnaw *v.t.* **1** (*to bite or eat away by degrees*) bite, chew, crunch, munch, nibble, worry. **2** (*to consume or wear away by degrees*) consume, corrode, eat away, eat into, erode, fret, rub away, wear away, wear down. **3** (*to cause persistent distress to*) distress, fret, harry, nag, plague, torment, trouble, worry.

go *v.i.* **1** (*to move from one place or condition to another*) advance, journey, move, pass, proceed, progress, travel, walk. ANTONYMS: halt, stop. **2** (*to start to move from a place, to depart, as opposed to come*) (*sl.*) beat it, decamp, depart, leave, set off, set out, (*coll.*) slope off, travel, withdraw. ANTONYMS: arrive, come. **3** (*to be operating or working*) be in working order, be operative, be working, function, move, operate, perform, run, work. ANTONYMS: break down, stop. **4** (*to end, to turn out (well or ill)*) end, end up, fare, finish, (*coll.*) pan out, progress, result, turn out, work out. **5** (*to be circulated or current*) be current, be passed on, be spread around, circulate, go round. **6** (*to extend, to point in a certain direction*) extend to, lead to, reach, stretch to. **7** (*to tend, to conduce*) contribute, help, incline, serve, tend, work towards. **8** (*to be applicable, to fit (with)*) accord (with), agree (with), be compatible (with), be in line with (with), blend (with), complement, comply (with), correspond (to), fit (with), go together (with), harmonize (with), match, suit. **9** (*to be abandoned or abolished*) (*sl.*) be axed, be discarded, be disposed of, (*sl.*) be given the chop, be got rid of, be thrown away. **10** (*to fail, to give way*) break, cave in, collapse, crumble, disintegrate, fail, fall down, fall to pieces, give way. **11** (*to die*) be dead, decease, die, expire, give up the ghost, (*sl.*) kick the bucket, pass away. **12** (*to pass into a certain state, to become*) become, come to be, get, grow, wax. **13** (*to be spent*) be consumed, be exhausted, be finished, be spent, be used up. **14** (*to belong*) be located, belong, be situated, fit, fit in, have a place. **15** ((*of time*) *to elapse or pass*) elapse, go by, move on, pass, pass by, proceed, roll on, slip away, tick away. **to go about 1** (*to get to work at*) approach, begin, set about, start, tackle, undertake. **2** (*to go from place to place*) be current, be passed round, be spread, circulate, get around, get round, go around, pass. **to go against** (*to be in opposition to*) be against, be contrary to, be in opposition to, oppose, resist, withstand. **to go ahead 1** (*to proceed in advance*) go in front, go on in advance. **2** (*to start*) forge ahead, make a start on, make progress, proceed, progress. **to go astray** (*to wander from the right path*) get lost, go missing, go off course, lose one's way. **to go at 1** (*to attack*) attack, launch an attack on, set about, set upon. **2** (*to work at vigorously*) attack, be committed to, be engrossed in, concentrate on, set to, work hard at. **to go away** (*to depart*) (*sl.*) beat it, decamp, depart, exit, leave, make one's departure, make one's exit, (*coll.*) slope off, take one's leave, withdraw. ANTONYMS: arrive. **to go by 1** (*to pass by*) elapse, move on, pass, pass by, proceed. **2** (*to take as a criterion*) be guided by, take as a criterion, take as a guideline, take as a pattern, take as the basis, use as a guide. **to go down 1** (*to descend*) descend, fall, fall to the ground, make one's way down. **2** (*to fall, become lower*) become lower, be reduced, decrease, drop, fall, lower, plummet. ANTONYMS: go up, rise. **3** (*to set*) set, sink. **4** (*to founder* (*as a ship*)) capsize, founder, submerge. **5** (*to fall* (*before a conqueror*)) be beaten, be defeated, fail, go under, lose, submit, suffer defeat. **6** (*to be set down in writing*) be commemorated, be committed to posterity, be recorded, be set down in writing. **7** (*to be palatable or acceptable*) be acceptable, be palatable, be satisfactory, go down well. **to go far** (*to be very successful*) be a success, be successful, do well, do well for oneself, get ahead, get on, get on in the world, make a name for oneself, make good, (*coll.*) make it, make one's mark, make one's mark in the world, prosper, succeed. ANTONYMS: fail, not make the grade. **to go for 1** (*to go somewhere to obtain something*) collect, fetch, go and get, pick up. ANTONYMS: deliver. **2** (*to attack*) assail, assault, attack, begin to fight, launch an attack on, make an assault on, set upon. **3** (*to be true for, include*) apply to, be appropriate to, be relevant to, be true for, have relevance to, include, take in. ANTONYMS: exclude. **4** (*to be attracted by*) be attracted to, be fond of, (*coll.*) fancy, favour, find attractive, go in for, have a fondness for, have a liking for, have a preference for, have a weakness for, like, opt for, prefer. ANTONYMS: be put off by, dislike. **5** (*to be sold for*) bring in, fetch, net, realize, sell for. ANTONYMS: buy for. **to go in for 1** (*to be in favour of*) be in favour of, choose, favour, go for, have a liking for, have a preference for, have a weakness for, like, opt for, prefer. ANTONYMS: avoid, dislike. **2** (*to follow as a pursuit or occupation*) engage in, participate in, practise, pursue, take part in, take up. **3** (*to enter or take part in* (*an examination or competition*)) be a candidate in, be a competitor in, be an entrant in, compete in, enter, participate in, take part in. **to go into** (*to investigate or discuss*) analyse, check, consider, delve into, dig into, examine, inquire into, investigate, look into, make an analysis of, make an examination of, probe, research, review, scrutinize, study. **to go off 1** (*to depart*) depart, go away, leave, make one's departure, set off, take one's leave. ANTONYMS: arrive. **2** (*to be fired, explode* (*as a gun, firework etc.*)) be discharged, be fired, detonate, explode, (*coll.*) go bang. **3** (*to rot, putrefy*) be high, be past the sell-by-date, be rotten, decay, go bad, go sour, rot. ANTONYMS: be fresh. **4** (*to fall away*) decline, decrease, deteriorate, drop, fall off, slump, worsen. ANTONYMS: improve. **5** (*to fare,*

to succeed (*well or badly*)) fare, go, happen, occur, proceed, progress, take place, turn out. **to go on 1** (*to continue, to persevere*) continue, endure, last, persevere, persist, proceed. ANTONYMS: halt, stop. **2** (*to talk at length*) babble, blether, chatter, jabber, prattle, (*coll.*) rabbit on, ramble, (*coll.*) witter, yabber, (*sl.*) yak. **3** (*to happen*) happen, occur, take place, transpire. **to go out 1** (*to depart, to leave* (*a room etc.*)) depart, exit, leave. ANTONYMS: enter. **2** (*to be extinguished*) be doused, be extinguished, be quenched, be switched off, be turned off, fade. **3** (*to have a romantic or sexual relationship*) be a couple, (*coll.*) be an item, be in a relationship, court, (*esp. N Am.*) date, go steady, go together, have an affair, have a relationship. **to go out with** (*to have a romantic or sexual relationship with*) be in a relationship with, (*esp. N Am.*) date, go steady with, have an affair with, have a relationship with. **to go over 1** (*to cross, to pass over*) cross, go across, pass over, span. **2** (*to change one's party or opinions*) change one's mind, change sides, do a U-turn, go over to the other side, reverse one's opinions, tergiversate. ANTONYMS: stick to one's guns. **3** (*to read, to examine*) examine, inspect, look over, peruse, read over, review, run over, scan, scrutinize, study. **to go steady** (*to go about regularly with the same boyfriend or girlfriend*) be a couple, (*coll.*) be an item, be in a relationship, court, (*esp. N Am.*) date, go out, go together, have an affair, have a relationship. **to go through 1** (*to undergo*) bear, be subjected to, be the victim of, brave, endure, experience, stand, suffer, tolerate, undergo, weather, withstand. **2** (*to examine*) check, consider, examine, explore, inspect, look over, look through, scrutinize, search through. **3** (*to use or consume*) consume, exhaust, spend, squander, use, use up. **to go together 1** (*to be suitable to or match each other*) accord, agree, be compatible, be suited, blend, fit together, go with each other, harmonize, match. ANTONYMS: clash, jar. **2** (*to have a romantic or sexual relationship*) be a couple, (*coll.*) be an item, be in a relationship, court, (*esp. N Am.*) date, go out, go steady, have an affair, have a relationship. **to go under 1** (*to sink*) be submerged, founder, go down, sink. **2** (*to be submerged or ruined*) be ruined, fail, fold, founder, go bankrupt, (*sl.*) go bust, go into receivership, go to the wall. ANTONYMS: flourish, thrive. **to go with 1** (*to accompany*) accompany, escort, go along with, keep company. **2** (*to suit, to match*) be compatible with, blend with, complement, fit with, harmonize with, match, suit. ANTONYMS: clash with. **3** (*to have a romantic or sexual relationship with*) be in a relationship with, court, (*esp. N Am.*) date, go out with, go steady with, have an affair with, have a relationship with, woo. **to go without** (*to be or manage without, to put up with the want of*) be denied, be deprived of, be in need of, be in want of, do without, go short of.

goad *n.* **1** (*a pointed instrument to urge oxen to move faster*) prod, spike, staff, stick. **2** (*anything that spurs or incites*) encouragement, impetus, incentive, incitement, inducement, instigation, irritant, jolt, motivation, poke, pressure, prick, spur, stimulus.
~*v.t.* (*to stimulate, to incite*) drive, egg on, encourage, exhort, harass, (*coll.*) hassle, hound, incite, prod, prompt, propel, spur, stimulate, urge. ANTONYMS: deter, discourage, dissuade.

go-ahead *a.* (*characterized by energy and enterprise*) aggressive, ambitious, energetic, enterprising, go-getting, progressive, (*coll.*) pushy, thrusting, (*coll.*) up-and-coming. ANTONYMS: idle, (*coll.*) laid-back, unambitious.
~*n.* (*permission to go ahead*) agreement, approval, assent, authorization, confirmation, consent, (*coll.*) green light, leave, (*coll.*) OK, (*coll.*) okay, sanction, thumbs up. ANTONYMS: (*coll.*) red light, refusal, thumbs down.

goal *n.* (*the ultimate aim of a person's ambition*) aim, ambition, aspiration, design, destination, end, intention, object, objective, purpose, target. ANTONYMS: starting-point.

goalpost *n.* **to move the goalposts** (*to change the conditions, regulations etc. applying to a particular matter*) alter the regulations, change the rules, make alterations to the conditions, make changes to the rules, modify the guidelines, readjust the rules. ANTONYMS: keep the status quo, stick to the rules.

goat *n.* **1** (*a fool*) ass, (*coll.*) chump, dolt, fool, idiot, (*sl.*) nerd, ninny, (*coll.*) twit. **2** (*a lascivious person, a lecher*) dirty old man, (*sl.*) lech, lecher. **to get one's goat** (*to make one angry*) anger, exasperate, get one's back up, get on one's nerves, get up one's nose, incense, infuriate, irritate, make angry, provoke, rile, rub up the wrong way.

gobble *v.t.* (*to swallow down greedily or noisily*) bolt, devour, gorge oneself, guzzle, (*sl.*) pig out on, (*coll.*) scoff, wolf. ANTONYMS: nibble, peck at.

gobbledegook *n.* (*pretentious, unintelligible language*) cant, circumlocution, double talk, gibberish, jargon, mumbo-jumbo, nonsense, officialese, technobabble, twaddle, verbiage. ANTONYMS: plain English, plain language.

go-between *n.* (*a person who acts as an intermediary between two parties*) agent, broker, contact, dealer, factor, intermediary, liaison,

mediator, medium, middleman, negotiator, pander, peacemaker, pimp, third party.

goblin *n.* (*a mischievous spirit of ugly or grotesque shape*) dwarf, elf, gnome, hobgoblin, imp.

god *n.* **1** (*a supernatural being regarded as controlling natural forces and worshipped by humans*) deity, divine being, divinity, spirit. **2** (*in monotheistic religions, the Supreme Being*) Allah, God Almighty, God the Father, Jehovah, Our Maker, the Almighty, the Lord. **3** (*a person or thing greatly idolized*) golden boy, golden girl, hero, icon, idol.

godly *a.* (*pious, devout*) church-going, devout, God-fearing, good, holy, pious, religious, saintly, virtuous. ANTONYMS: atheistic, wicked.

godsend *n.* (*an unlooked-for acquisition, a piece of good fortune*) blessing, bonanza, boon, manna from heaven, stroke of luck, windfall. ANTONYMS: calamity, disaster.

goggle *v.i.* (*to stare*) gawk, gawp, gaze, ogle, (*sl.*) rubberneck, stare.

going *n.* (*the condition of ground, racecourse etc., as regards walking, riding, etc.*) course, ground, terrain, turf.

going concern *n.* (*a business etc., in actual operation*) active business, functioning business, profitable company. ANTONYMS: bankrupt firm.

goings-on *n.pl.* (*behaviour, conduct* (*usu. in a bad sense*)) behaviour, conduct, funny business, (*coll.*) hanky-panky, misbehaviour, mischief, misconduct, monkey business, pranks, shenanigans.

gold *n.* (*wealth, riches*) fortune, money, riches, treasure, wealth.
~*a.* (*coloured like gold*) gold-coloured, mustard, old gold, yellow.

gold dust *n.* **like gold dust** (*very rare*) at a premium, in short supply, rare, scarce, sparse. ANTONYMS: common, plentiful.

golden *a.* **1** (*of the colour or lustre of gold*) blond/blonde, bright, fair, flaxen, gleaming, gold-coloured, shining, tow-coloured, yellow. ANTONYMS: dark, dull. **2** (*precious, most valuable*) delightful, excellent, glorious, good, happy, joyful, precious, rich, treasured, valuable. ANTONYMS: unhappy, worthless. **3** (*most favourable*) advantageous, auspicious, excellent, favourable, fortunate, good, opportune, promising, propitious, providential, rosy. ANTONYMS: adverse, disadvantageous, unfavourable.

good *a.* **1** (*proper, suitable*) appropriate,

correct, decorous, expedient, fit, fitting, proper, right, seemly, suitable. ANTONYMS: inappropriate, unsuitable, wrong. **2** (*adequate, satisfactory*) A1, able, accomplished, adequate, capable, competent, dexterous, efficient, excellent, expert, first-class, first-rate, gifted, proficient, reliable, satisfactory, skilful, sound, talented, tip-top, top-notch. ANTONYMS: bad, incompetent, poor. **3** (*advantageous, beneficial*) advantageous, beneficial, convenient, favourable, fitting, fortunate, lucky, propitious, suitable. ANTONYMS: disadvantageous, inconvenient, unfavourable, unlucky. **4** (*genuine, sound*) authentic, bona fide, genuine, (*coll.*) legit, legitimate, sound, valid. ANTONYMS: bogus, fraudulent, illegitimate. **5** (*complete, thorough*) complete, entire, perfect, sound, thorough, whole. ANTONYMS: incomplete, part. **6** (*reliable, safe*) dependable, infallible, reliable, safe, sure, trustworthy. ANTONYMS: undependable, unreliable. **7** (*ample, considerable*) ample, considerable, goodly, large, sizeable, substantial, (*coll.*) tidy. ANTONYMS: insubstantial, paltry, small. **8** (*possessed of moral excellence, virtuous*) admirable, estimable, ethical, exemplary, full of integrity, honest, honourable, moral, noble, praiseworthy, righteous, right-minded, upright, virtuous, worthy. ANTONYMS: bad, dishonourable, immoral, wicked. **9** (*kind, benevolent*) altruistic, amiable, benevolent, charitable, courteous, friendly, generous, gracious, kind, kindly, magnanimous, obliging. ANTONYMS: discourteous, unfriendly, unkind. **10** (*pleasant, acceptable*) acceptable, admirable, agreeable, choice, enjoyable, excellent, fine, first-class, first-rate, great, marvellous, palatable, pleasant, satisfactory, splendid, tip-top, top-notch. ANTONYMS: bad, poor, unacceptable. **11** (*well-behaved*) malleable, manageable, obedient, tractable, well-behaved, well-mannered. ANTONYMS: bad, disobedient. **12** (*beneficial to one's health, wholesome*) beneficial, health-giving, healthy, nutritional, nutritious, salubrious, wholesome. ANTONYMS: (*coll.*) junk, unhealthy, unwholesome. **13** ((*of weather*) *dry and sunny*) bright, clear, clement, cloudless, dry, fair, fine, mild, sunny, warm. ANTONYMS: bad, cloudy, dull, wet.
~*n.* **1** (*benefit, advantage*) advantage, benefit, gain, interest, profit, prosperity, use, welfare, well-being. ANTONYMS: detriment, disadvantage, loss. **2** (*goodness, good qualities*) charity, ethics, goodness, honesty, honour, integrity, morality, moral rectitude, nobility, probity, rectitude, righteousness, uprightness, virtue, virtuousness, worthiness. ANTONYMS: badness, immorality, vice, wickedness. **for good (and all)** (*finally, definitely*) completely, definitely,

finally, for always, for ever, irrevocably, never to return, once and for all, permanently. ANTONYMS: for a short time, temporarily. **to make good 1** (*to perform, to become successful*) carry out, discharge, effect, fulfil, perform. ANTONYMS: fail. **2** (*to compensate (for)*) compensate (for), indemnify, make amends (for), make payment (for), make recompense (for), make restitution (for), make up (for), reimburse (for), replace, supply any deficiency (in). **3** (*to confirm*) authenticate, back up, confirm, demonstrate the truth of, prove, substantiate, validate. ANTONYMS: disprove, invalidate. **4** (*to prosper, to be successful*) achieve success, become rich, be successful, do well, flourish, get ahead, prosper, succeed. ANTONYMS: be unsuccessful, fail. **to the good** (*extra, as a balance or profit*) all to the good, as profit, for the best, on the credit side, to one's advantage.

goodbye *int.* (*farewell*) adieu, au revoir, (*coll.*) bye, (*coll.*) bye-bye, cheerio, cheers, farewell, see you, see you later, so long, (*coll.*) ta-ta. ANTONYMS: hello.
~*n.* (*a farewell*) adieu, au revoir, farewell, leave-taking, valediction. ANTONYMS: hello.

good-for-nothing *a.* (*of no value, worthless*) feckless, idle, lazy, no-good, useless, without value, worthless.
~*n.* (*an idle person, a vagabond*) black sheep, idler, layabout, loafer, ne'er-do-well, waster, wastrel.

good-humoured *a.* (*having a cheerful temperament, amiable*) affable, amiable, cheerful, cheery, congenial, genial, good-natured, good-tempered, happy, in a good mood, in a good temper, in good humour, pleasant. ANTONYMS: bad-tempered, churlish, cross, ill-natured.

good-looking *a.* (*handsome, attractive*) attractive, beautiful, comely, gorgeous, handsome, personable, pretty. ANTONYMS: plain, ugly, unattractive.

good luck *n.* (*good fortune, prosperity*) felicity, good fortune, happiness, prosperity, success. ANTONYMS: bad luck, misfortune.
~*int.* (*an expression wishing good fortune*) all the best, best wishes, break a leg, the best of British. ANTONYMS: bad luck.

goodly *a.* (*large, considerable*) ample, considerable, great, large, significant, sizeable, substantial, (*coll.*) tidy. ANTONYMS: insignificant, small.

good-natured *a.* (*kind and not getting angry easily*) accommodating, amiable, benevolent, charitable, friendly, generous, helpful, kind, kind-hearted, kindly, nice, warm-hearted, well-disposed. ANTONYMS: mean, nasty.

goodness *n.* **1** (*moral excellence, virtue*)

charity, ethics, good, honesty, honour, integrity, morality, moral rectitude, nobility, probity, rectitude, righteousness, uprightness, virtue, virtuousness, worthiness. ANTONYMS: badness, immorality, vice, wickedness. **2** (*kindness, generosity*) altruism, benevolence, charity, courtesy, friendliness, generosity, goodwill, graciousness, kind-heartedness, kindliness, kindness, magnanimity, obligingness, warm-heartedness. **3** (*the nutritious or wholesome part of something*) healthiness, nourishment, nutrition, nutritional value, salubriousness, wholesomeness. ANTONYMS: unwholesomeness.

goods *n.pl.* **1** (*merchandise*) commodities, merchandise, produce, stock, wares. **2** (*possessions that can be moved*) accoutrements, appurtenances, belongings, chattels, effects, furniture, gear, goods and chattels, movable property, paraphernalia, possessions, property, stuff, things, trappings.

good-tempered *a.* (*good-humoured*) affable, amiable, cheerful, cheery, congenial, genial, good-humoured, good-natured, happy, in a good humour, in a good mood, in a good temper, pleasant. ANTONYMS: bad-tempered, churlish, cross, ill-natured.

goodwill *n.* (*kindly feeling or disposition*) amiability, amity, benevolence, friendliness, friendship, generosity, kindness. ANTONYMS: enmity, hostility, ill feeling.

good word *n.* (*a recommendation or endorsement*) approbation, approval, commendation, praise, recommendation, reference. ANTONYMS: denigration, disapproval, disparagement.

goody-goody *a.* (*priggishly good*) Grundyish, holier-than-thou, priggish, prim, prudish, sanctimonious.

gooey *a.* **1** (*sticky*) gluey, glutinous, gummy, mucilaginous, sticky, tacky, viscous. **2** (*sentimental*) maudlin, mawkish, (*sl.*) mushy, over-emotional, sentimental, (*sl.*) slushy, soppy, syrupy.

gore *v.t.* (*to pierce, to stab*) impale, pierce, run through, stab, transfix.

gorge *n.* (*a narrow pass between cliffs or hills*) canyon, defile, pass, ravine.
~*v.t.* **1** (*to swallow, to devour greedily*) bolt, devour, gobble, gulp, guzzle, (*sl.*) pig out on, wolf. ANTONYMS: nibble, pick at. **2** (*to glut, to satiate*) glut, overeat, overfill, sate, satiate, stuff, surfeit.

gorgeous *a.* **1** (*splendid, magnificent*) beautiful, breathtaking, brilliant, dazzling, elegant, glittering, glorious, grand, imposing, impressive, luxurious, magnificent, marvellous, opulent, ornate, resplendent, showy, splendid, sumptuous, superb, wonderful. ANTONYMS: dull, plain, ugly. **2** (*very fine, beautiful etc.*) attractive, beautiful, delightful, enjoyable, excellent, fine, good-looking, handsome, marvellous, pleasing, pretty, (*coll.*) stunning, (*coll.*) terrific, wonderful. ANTONYMS: boring, dull, unattractive.

gory *a.* **1** (*covered with gore*) blood-covered, blood-soaked, blood-spattered, blood-stained, bloody. **2** (*bloody, involving bloodshed and killing*) (*sl.*) blood-and-guts, bloodthirsty, bloody, brutal, horror-filled, murderous, nasty, savage, unpleasant, vicious, violent.

gospel *n.* **1** (*the doctrine preached by Christ and the Apostles*) Christian doctrine, good news, New Testament, teaching of Christ, writings of the Apostles. **2** (*anything accepted as infallibly true*) absolute truth, certainty, fact, truth, whole truth. ANTONYMS: lie, untruth. **3** (*the principle that one adopts as a guide to life or action*) belief, credo, creed, ethic, guidelines, philosophy, principle, tenet.

gossip *n.* **1** (*idle talk, tittle-tattle*) chit-chat, (*sl.*) dirt, (*coll.*) gen, idle talk, news, report, scandal, talk, tittle-tattle. **2** (*mere rumour*) grapevine, hearsay, idle talk, report, rumour. **3** (*informal chat or writing, esp. about persons or incidents of the day*) blather, blether, chat, (*coll.*) chinwag, (*sl.*) jaw, small talk, (*sl.*) yak. **4** (*a person who regularly indulges in tittle-tattle*) babbler, blather, blether, busybody, chatterbox, gossipmonger, prattler, scandalmonger, tattler, tittle-tattler.

gouge *v.t.* (*to cut or scoop* (*out*) *with or as with a gouge*) cut (out), dig (out), hollow (out), scoop (out), scratch (out).

gourmet *n.* (*a connoisseur of good food, an epicure*) bon vivant, connoisseur, epicure, (*coll.*) foodie, gastronome.

govern *v.t.* **1** (*to rule with authority, esp. to administer the affairs of a state*) administer, be in charge of, command, conduct, control, direct, have power over, hold sway over, lead, manage, order, oversee, preside over, reign over, rule, superintend, supervise. **2** (*to influence, to determine*) be a factor in, decide, determine, guide, have an influence on, have a say in, influence, sway. **3** (*to restrain, to curb*) bridle, check, contain, control, curb, discipline, hold back, hold in check, inhibit, keep back, keep in check, rein in, restrain, subdue, tame. ANTONYMS: give freedom to, let loose.

government *n.* **1** (*control, exercise of authority*) administration, charge, command, conduct, control, direction, guidance, leadership, management, power, regulation, rule, superintendence, supervision. **2** (*the body of persons in charge of the government of a state, an administration*) administration, congress, executive, ministry, parliament, regime, the establishment, (*often facet.*) the powers that be. **3** (*self-control, manageableness*) control, discipline, restraint, self-control, self-discipline. ANTONYMS: indiscipline, lack of control.

governor *n.* (*a ruler, a head of the executive*) (*coll.*) boss, chief, director, head, (*sl.*) head honcho, (*sl.*) honcho, leader, manager.

gown *n.* **1** (*a dress, esp. a handsome or stylish one*) ballgown, dress, evening gown, formal dress, frock. **2** (*a long, loose robe worn by judges, lawyers etc.*) costume, habit, robe.

grab *v.t.* **1** (*to snatch or grasp suddenly*) appropriate, (*coll.*) bag, catch hold of, clutch at, (*sl.*) collar, grab hold of, grasp, grip, pluck, seize, snatch, take hold of. **2** (*to capture, to arrest*) apprehend, arrest, capture, catch, (*coll.*) collar, (*sl.*) nab, (*sl.*) nail, pick up, (*sl.*) pinch, seize. **3** (*to interest*) arouse interest in, attract, be of interest to, fascinate, grip, interest, intrigue. **up for grabs** (*on offer*) accessible, available, for sale, for the asking, for the taking, obtainable, on offer, to be had.

grace *n.* **1** (*the quality which makes form or manner elegant and refined*) charm, cultivation, elegance, finesse, good taste, gracefulness, poise, polish, refinement, smoothness, taste, tastefulness. ANTONYMS: awkwardness, clumsiness, coarseness. **2** (*a courteous or affable demeanour*) consideration, courteousness, courtesy, decency, decorum, good manners, goodness, kindness, manners, politeness, propriety, tact, tactfulness. ANTONYMS: discourtesy, rudeness. **3** (*clemency, mercy*) charity, clemency, compassion, forgiveness, indulgence, leniency, lenity, mercifulness, mercy, pardon, reprieve. ANTONYMS: cruelty, harshness. **4** (*a boon, a benefaction*) benefaction, boon, charity, favour, generosity, gift, goodwill, kindness, present. **5** (*a short prayer before a meal invoking a blessing or expressing thanks*) benediction, blessing, prayer, thanks, thanksgiving. **6** (*an indulgence, esp. an extension of time allowed after a payment falls due*) deferment, deferral, delay, extension, postponement.
~*v.t.* **1** (*to lend grace to, to dignify*) adorn, beautify, decorate, embellish, enhance, garnish, ornament, prettify. **2** (*to give honour to, to give dignity to*) add distinction to, dignify, distinguish, elevate, favour, glorify, honour.

graceful *a.* (*full of grace or elegance, esp. of*

form or movement) agile, attractive, beautiful, charming, cultivated, elegant, natural, nimble, pleasing, poised, polished, smooth, supple, tasteful. ANTONYMS: awkward, clumsy, coarse.

gracious *a.* **1** (*exhibiting grace or kindness*) accommodating, affable, benevolent, civil, considerate, cordial, courteous, friendly, kind, kindly, nice, obliging, polite. ANTONYMS: discourteous, rude, unfriendly, unkind. **2** (*benignant, merciful*) charitable, clement, compassionate, forgiving, gentle, humane, indulgent, lenient, merciful. ANTONYMS: cruel, harsh, unforgiving.

grade *n.* **1** (*a degree or step in rank, order etc.*) degree, degree of proficiency, echelon, level, notch, order, place, placing, position, rank, rung, stage, standing, step. **2** (*a class of people of similar rank, ability etc.*) category, class, classification, division, group, grouping, set, type. **3** (*gradient, the degree of slope in a road*) acclivity, declivity, gradient, hill, incline, rise, slope.
~*v.t.* (*to arrange in grades*) categorize, class, classify, evaluate, group, order, rank, sort, value. **to make the grade** (*to succeed*) be successful, come through with flying colours, come up to expectations, come up to scratch, come up to standard, get through, have success, (*coll.*) make it, measure up, meet with success, pass, pass muster, succeed, win through. ANTONYMS: be found wanting, be unsuccessful, fail.

gradient *n.* (*degree of slope, inclination*) acclivity, declivity, grade, hill, incline, rise, slope.

gradual *a.* (*regular and slow, as opposed to abrupt, steep*) continuous, degree by degree, even, gentle, measured, moderate, progressive, regular, slow, steady, step by step, systematic, unhurried. ANTONYMS: abrupt, rapid, steep, sudden.

gradually *adv.* (*in a gradual manner, slowly*) bit by bit, by degrees, continuously, evenly, gently, inch by inch, little by little, moderately, progressively, regularly, slowly, steadily, step by step. ANTONYMS: abruptly, steeply, suddenly.

graduate *v.i.* **1** (*to be awarded a first degree from a university*) become a graduate, have a degree conferred on one, receive a degree. **2** (*to change or pass by degrees*) advance, be promoted, move on, move up, progress.
~*v.t.* **1** (*to mark with degrees*) calibrate, grade, mark off, measure off. **2** (*to apportion (a tax etc.) according to a scale of grades*) band, categorize, class, classify, group, order, rank.

graft[1] *n.* **1** (*a small shoot of a tree or plant inserted into another tree*) bud, scion, shoot, slip, splice, sprout. **2** (*living tissue from a person or animal transplanted to another*) implant, transplant. **3** (*hard work, unremitting labour*) donkey work, effort, exertion, (*coll.*) grind, hard work, labour, slog, (*coll.*) sweat, toil. ANTONYMS: idleness, leisure.
~*v.t.* **1** (*to insert* (*a shoot*) *in or upon another plant or tree*) affix, engraft, insert, join, slip, splice. **2** (*to transplant* (*as living animal tissue*)) implant, transplant.

graft[2] *n.* (*acquisition of money etc. by taking advantage of an official position*) bribery, bribery and corruption, (*coll.*) palm-greasing, (*sl.*) payola, subornation.

grain *n.* **1** (*a single seed of a plant, particularly of food plants*) kernel, seed. **2** (*the fruit of cereal plants, such as wheat, barley etc.*) cereal crops, cereals, corn. **3** (*any small, hard particle*) crumb, granule, particle. **4** (*the smallest particle or amount*) atom, bit, crumb, fragment, granule, iota, jot, molecule, morsel, scrap, spark, speck, suspicion, trace, whit. ANTONYMS: dollop, hunk, mass, slab. **5** (*texture, arrangement of particles, esp. of the fibres of wood*) fabric, fibre, intertexture, nap, surface, texture, weave. **6** (*disposition, natural tendency*) character, disposition, humour, inclination, make-up, nature, temper, temperament. **against the grain** (*contrary to inclination, reluctantly*) against one's inclination, contrary to one's instincts, contrary to one's nature, not in line with one's feelings.

grand *a.* **1** (*great or imposing in size or appearance*) glorious, great, imposing, impressive, lavish, luxurious, magnificent, majestic, marvellous, noble, opulent, ostentatious, palatial, showy, splendid, stately, striking, stunning, sumptuous, superb, wonderful. **2** (*highly satisfactory, excellent*) enjoyable, excellent, fine, first-class, first-rate, (*coll.*) great, marvellous, outstanding, satisfactory, (*coll.*) smashing, splendid, (*coll.*) super, superb, (*coll.*) terrific, very good, wonderful. ANTONYMS: boring, run-of-the-mill, unsatisfactory. **3** (*distinguished, fashionable or aristocratic*) aristocratic, august, celebrated, dignified, distinguished, elevated, eminent, esteemed, exalted, famous, fashionable, great, highest, illustrious, important, leading, noble, notable, pre-eminent, principal, prominent, renowned. ANTONYMS: common, insignificant, lowly, unimportant, unknown. **4** (*comprehensive, complete*) all-in, all-inclusive, complete, comprehensive, exhaustive, final, inclusive, total. ANTONYMS: partial.

grandeur *n.* **1** (*the quality of being grand*) augustness, dignity, distinction, eminence, fame, greatness, illustriousness, importance, nobility, pre-eminence, prominence, renown. ANTONYMS: commonness, insignificance, lowliness. **2** (*splendid or magnificent appearance or effect*) glory, impressiveness, lavishness, luxuriousness, luxury, magnificence, majesty, nobility, opulence, ostentation, pomp, splendour, stateliness, sumptuousness.

grandiose *a.* (*affecting impressiveness, pompous*) affected, ambitious, extravagant, flamboyant, high-flown, (*coll.*) over-the-top, pompous, pretentious, showy. ANTONYMS: down-to-earth, unpretentious.

grant *v.t.* **1** (*to bestow or give, esp. in answer to a request*) allocate, allot, assign, award, bestow, confer, endow, give, hand out, impart, present, supply. ANTONYMS: deny, refuse, withhold. **2** (*to allow as a favour or indulgence*) accede to, accord, allow, assent to, consent to, give one's assent to, give permission for, permit, vouchsafe. ANTONYMS: refuse, turn down. **3** (*to admit as true, to concede*) acknowledge, admit, allow, cede, concede, go along with, yield. ANTONYMS: contradict, deny, repudiate.
~*n.* **1** (*a sum of money bestowed or allowed*) allocation, allowance, award, bequest, bounty, bursary, donation, endowment, handout, subsidy. **2** (*a gift, formal bestowal*) allocation, award, contribution, donation, gift, handout, present, supply. **to take for granted** (*to assume as admitted basis of an argument*) assume the truth of, assume to be true, take as read.

granular *a.* (*composed of or resembling granules*) grainy, granulated, gravelly, gritty, sandlike.

granule *n.* (*a small particle*) bit, crumb, fragment, grain, particle, speck. ANTONYMS: chunk, dollop, mass.

graph *n.* (*a diagram representing a mathematical or scientific relationship*) chart, diagram, grid.

graphic *a.* **1** (*vividly or forcibly descriptive*) clear, cogent, crystal-clear, descriptive, detailed, effective, explicit, expressive, forcible, illustrative, lucid, striking, telling, vivid, well-described. ANTONYMS: confused, imprecise, vague. **2** (*shown by means of diagrams etc. instead of statistics etc.*) delineative, diagrammatic, illustrative, pictorial, representational, visual.

grapple *v.i.* **1** (*to contend or struggle* (*with or together*) *in close fight*) battle, clash, close, combat, contend, engage, fight, struggle, tussle, wrestle. **2** (*to strive to accomplish*) address oneself to, come to grips with, confront, cope with, deal with, face, face up to, get down to, get to grips with, tackle. ANTONYMS: dodge, evade, shirk.

~*v.t.* (*to seize, to clutch*) catch hold of, clasp, clench, clutch, grab, grab hold of, grasp, hold, lay hold of, rip, seize, take hold of.

grasp *v.t.* **1** (*to seize and hold fast*) catch, catch hold of, clasp, clench, clutch, grab, grapple, grip, hold, seize, snatch, take hold of. **2** (*to comprehend with the mind*) apprehend, be aware of, catch on, comprehend, follow, get, get a grip of, (*coll.*) get it, get the drift of, latch onto, perceive, realize, see, take in, understand. ANTONYMS: fail to grasp, miss, misunderstand.
~*n.* **1** (*a fast grip or hold*) clasp, clench, clutch, grip, hold, possession. **2** (*forcible possession, mastery*) clutches, command, control, dominion, mastery, power, rule, sway. **3** (*intellectual comprehension*) apprehension, awareness, comprehension, grip, knowledge, mastery, perception, realization, understanding.

grasping *a.* (*greedy*) acquisitive, avaricious, close-fisted, covetous, greedy, mean, miserly, niggardly, parsimonious, penny-pinching, possessive, rapacious, stingy, (*N Am., sl.*) tight-assed, tight-fisted. ANTONYMS: generous, liberal.

grass *n.* **to let the grass grow under one's feet** (*to waste time and so lose an opportunity*) delay, lose an opportunity, miss a chance, procrastinate, waste time.

grate *v.t.* **1** (*to rub against a rough surface so as to reduce to small particles*) pulverize, shred. **2** (*to rub, as one thing against another, so as to cause a harsh sound*) creak, grind, jar, rasp, scrape, squeak. **3** (*to irritate, to vex*) annoy, exasperate, gall, get on one's nerves, infuriate, irk, irritate, jar on, nettle, rankle with, rile, rub up the wrong way, set one's teeth on edge. ANTONYMS: calm down, soothe, tranquillize.

grateful *a.* (*thankful, indicative of gratitude*) appreciative, indebted, obligated, obliged, thankful, under an obligation. ANTONYMS: unappreciative, ungrateful.

gratify *v.t.* **1** (*to please, to delight*) delight, give pleasure to, gladden, make happy, please, satisfy, warm the cockles of someone's heart. ANTONYMS: displease, dissatisfy. **2** (*to indulge, to give free rein to*) cater to, comply with, fulfil, give in to, humour, indulge, pacify, pander to, satisfy. ANTONYMS: disappoint.

grating *a.* (*harsh, irritating*) annoying, discordant, harsh, irksome, irritating, jarring, piercing, rasping, raucous, scraping, scratchy, screeching, shrill, squeaky, strident,

unpleasant. ANTONYMS: musical, pleasant, soothing.

gratis *adv.* (*without charge, free*) at no cost, (*sl.*) buckshee, for free, for nothing, free, free of charge, gratuitously, on the house, unpaid, without charge, without paying, without payment. ANTONYMS: at a cost, for payment.

gratitude *n.* (*grateful feeling towards a benefactor*) acknowledgement, appreciation, gratefulness, indebtedness, obligation, recognition, thankfulness, thanks. ANTONYMS: ingratitude, ungratefulness.

gratuitous *a.* **1** (*without cause or warrant*) groundless, motiveless, needless, superfluous, uncalled-for, unfounded, unjustified, unmerited, unnecessary, unprovoked, unwarranted, without cause, without reason. ANTONYMS: justifiable, provoked, well-founded. **2** (*granted without claim or charge*) at no cost, (*sl.*) buckshee, complimentary, for free, for nothing, free, free of charge, gratis, on the house, unpaid, voluntary, without charge, without payment. ANTONYMS: for payment, paid.

gratuity *n.* (*a present voluntarily given in return for a service, a tip*) baksheesh, bonus, bounty, donation, douceur, fringe benefit, gift, (*coll.*) perk, perquisite, pourboire, present, recompense, reward, tip.

grave[1] *n.* (*a hole in the earth for burying a dead body in*) burial chamber, burial place, burying place, crypt, mausoleum, sepulchre, tomb, vault.

grave[2] *a.* **1** (*important, serious*) acute, crucial, earnest, exigent, important, life-and-death, momentous, of consequence, pivotal, pressing, serious, significant, urgent, vital, weighty. ANTONYMS: insignificant, trifling, trivial, unimportant. **2** (*solemn, dignified*) dignified, dour, earnest, gloomy, grim, long-faced, preoccupied, serious, severe, sober, solemn, sombre, stony-faced, subdued, thoughtful, unsmiling. ANTONYMS: flippant, frivolous, undignified.

graveyard *n.* (*a burial ground*) burial ground, cemetery, charnel house, churchyard, necropolis, (*N Am.*) potter's field.

gravitate *v.i.* **1** (*to be powerfully drawn (towards)*) be attracted (to), be drawn (to), be pulled (towards), head (towards), incline (towards), lean (towards), move (towards), tend (towards). **2** (*to tend downwards, to sink*) be precipitated, descend, drop, fall, precipitate, settle, sink.

gravity *n.* (*importance, seriousness*) acuteness,

consequence, earnestness, exigence, exigency, importance, momentousness, seriousness, significance, urgency, vitalness, weightiness. ANTONYMS: insignificance, triviality, unimportance.

graze v.t. **1** (*to touch or brush slightly in passing*) brush, glance off, kiss, rub, scrape, shave, skim, touch. **2** (*to scrape or abrade in rubbing past*) abrade, bark, bruise, chafe, contuse, cut, scrape, scratch, skin.
~n. (*a slight abrasion*) abrasion, bruise, contusion, cut, scrape, scratch.

greasy a. **1** (*made of or like grease*) fat, fatty, oily, oleaginous. **2** (*slimy or slippery with something having the effect of grease*) oily, slimy, slippery, slippy. **3** (*gross, unpleasantly unctuous*) bootlicking, fawning, glib, grovelling, ingratiating, oily, slick, (*coll.*) smarmy, smooth, smooth-tongued, suave, sycophantic, toadying, unctuous, wheedling.

great a. **1** (*large in bulk or degree*) big, bulky, colossal, enormous, extensive, giant, gigantic, huge, immense, large, mammoth, monumental, prodigious, spacious, stupendous, tremendous, vast, voluminous. ANTONYMS: little, small, tiny. **2** (*beyond the ordinary, extreme*) considerable, decided, exceptional, excess, extravagant, inordinate, prodigious, pronounced, sizeable, strong, substantial. ANTONYMS: average, ordinary, usual. **3** (*important, critical*) consequential, critical, crucial, dominant, essential, grave, important, momentous, serious, significant, vital, weighty. ANTONYMS: insignificant, trivial, unimportant. **4** (*of the highest importance, pre-eminent*) chief, head, leading, main, major, primary, principal, prominent. ANTONYMS: lowly, minor, second-rate. **5** (*of exceptional ability, highly gifted*) celebrated, distinguished, eminent, excellent, famed, famous, first-class, first-rate, gifted, illustrious, incomparable, leading, notable, noted, noteworthy, outstanding, pre-eminent, prominent, renowned, superior, talented, top, top-notch. ANTONYMS: inferior, talentless, unknown. **6** (*very skilful, experienced or knowing (at)*) able, ace, adept, adroit, crack, excellent, experienced, expert, good, masterly, proficient, skilful, skilled, tip-top. ANTONYMS: bad, hopeless, poor. **7** (*having lofty moral qualities, noble*) heroic, high-minded, honourable, magnanimous, noble, noble-minded. **8** (*grand, majestic*) distinguished, grand, imposing, impressive, magnificent, majestic, splendid, stately, striking, superb. ANTONYMS: lowly, undistinguished, unimpressive. **9** (*excellent*) (*coll.*) brill, (*coll.*) brilliant, enjoyable, excellent, (*coll.*) fab, (*coll.*) fabulous, fine, first-class, first-rate,

marvellous, (*coll.*) super, (*coll.*) terrific, very good, wonderful. ANTONYMS: boring, dull, poor. **10** (*excessive, grievous*) burdensome, excessive, heavy, onerous, severe, taxing, troublesome, weighty. ANTONYMS: light, minor, slight. **11** (*high in rank etc.*) aristocratic, blue-blooded, high-born, noble, titled, well-born. ANTONYMS: humble, low-born, lowly. **12** (*marked by enthusiasm*) active, devoted, eager, enthusiastic, intense, keen, obsessed, zealous. ANTONYMS: apathetic, indifferent, unenthusiastic. **to be great at** (*to be skilful at*) (*coll.*) be a dab hand at, be adept at, be expert at, be good at, be skilful at, be skilled in, have a gift for, have a talent for, have the knack of. ANTONYMS: be hopeless at, be poor at.

greatly adv. (*to a great degree, exceedingly*) considerably, enormously, exceedingly, highly, hugely, immensely, in a major way, markedly, much, remarkably, to a great extent, to a marked extent, tremendously, vastly, very, very much. ANTONYMS: in a minor way, to a small extent, very little.

greed n. **1** (*avarice, covetousness*) acquisitiveness, avarice, covetousness, cupidity, graspingness, meanness, miserliness, parsimony, rapaciousness, rapacity, tight-fistedness. ANTONYMS: generosity, largesse, munificence. **2** (*an inordinate desire for food or drink*) edaciousness, edacity, gluttony, gourmandizing, greediness, gutsiness, hoggishness, insatiability, piggishness, ravenousness, voraciousness, voracity.

greedy a. **1** (*having an inordinate desire for food or drink, gluttonous*) edacious, gluttonous, gutsy, hoggish, insatiable, piggish, ravenous, voracious. **2** (*eager to obtain, desirous (of)*) anxious (for), avid (for), covetous (of), craving, desirous (of), eager (for), hungry (for), impatient (for). ANTONYMS: apathetic, disinclined (to), reluctant (to). **3** (*full of greed, grasping*) acquisitive, avaricious, covetous, grasping, mean, miserly, parsimonious, rapacious, tight-fisted. ANTONYMS: generous, munificent.

green a. **1** (*unripe, immature*) immature, not ripe, unripe. ANTONYMS: mature, ripe. **2** (*inexperienced, easily imposed on*) callow, credulous, gullible, ignorant, immature, inexperienced, inexpert, ingenuous, innocent, naive, raw, unpolished, unqualified, unsophisticated, untrained, unversed, wet behind the ears. ANTONYMS: experienced, mature, sophisticated, worldly-wise. **3** (*fresh, not dried, cured or tanned*) fresh, raw, unseasoned, unsmoked. ANTONYMS: cured, dried, seasoned, smoked, withered. **4** (*pale, sickly*) ashen, greenish, ill, nauseous, pale, pallid,

sick, sickly, unhealthy, wan, white. ANTONYMS: blooming, healthy, well. **5** (*feeling jealous*) covetous, envious, grudging, jealous, resentful. **6** (*concerned about the protection of the environment*) conservationist, ecological, environmental, preservationist.
~*n.* (*a grassy plot or piece of land*) common, grass, lawn, sward, turf, village green.

greenhorn *n.* (*an inexperienced or foolish person*) apprentice, beginner, ingénue, learner, newcomer, new recruit, novice, raw recruit, simpleton, tyro. ANTONYMS: expert, old hand.

greenhouse *n.* (*a glasshouse for cultivating and preserving tender plants*) conservatory, glasshouse, hothouse.

green light *n.* (*a signal to proceed*) approval, assent, authorization, blessing, clearance, confirmation, consent, go-ahead, imprimatur, leave, (*coll.*) OK, (*coll.*) okay, permission, sanction, thumbs up, warranty. ANTONYMS: (*coll.*) red light, refusal, thumbs down.

greet *v.t.* **1** (*to address with a salutation at meeting*) acknowledge, hail, nod to, salute, say hello to. ANTONYMS: say goodbye to. **2** (*to receive at meeting or on arrival* (*with speech, gesture etc.*)) bid welcome, receive, welcome. ANTONYMS: see out.

greeting *n.* **1** (*a salutation, a welcome*) address, hallo, hello, hullo, nod, salutation, welcome, words of greeting, words of welcome. ANTONYMS: farewell, goodbye. **2** (*an expression of good wishes*) best wishes, congratulations, good wishes, tidings.

gregarious *a.* (*tending to associate with others, sociable*) affable, companionable, convivial, cordial, friendly, outgoing, sociable, social. ANTONYMS: antisocial, solitary, unsociable.

grey *a.* **1** (*of a colour between white and black, ash-coloured*) anaemic, ashen, colourless, pallid, wan. ANTONYMS: red, rosy, ruddy. **2** (*dull, clouded*) cloudy, dark, dim, dull, gloomy, murky, overcast, sunless. ANTONYMS: bright, sunny. **3** (*dark, dismal*) cheerless, dark, depressing, dismal, drab, dreary, gloomy. ANTONYMS: bright, cheerful. **4** (*of or relating to old age, ancient*) aged, elderly, grey-haired, old. ANTONYMS: young, youthful. **5** (*nondescript, lacking in charisma*) anonymous, boring, characterless, colourless, dull, faceless, neutral, uninteresting, without character. ANTONYMS: characterful, colourful, individual.

grief *n.* **1** (*deep sorrow or mental distress due to loss or disappointment*) affliction, anguish, broken-heartedness, distress, heartache, heartbreak, lamenting, misery, mourning, pain,

regret, remorse, sadness, sorrow, suffering, tribulation, trouble, woe. ANTONYMS: happiness, joy. **2** (*something which causes sorrow or sadness*) burden, calamity, disaster, trial, trouble, woe, worry.

grief-stricken *a.* (*suffering great sorrow*) broken-hearted, grieving, heartbroken, mourning, sorrowful, sorrowing, wretched. ANTONYMS: elated, joyful.

grievance *n.* **1** (*a cause for complaint*) charge, complaint, gripe, (*coll.*) grouse, grumble, moan, protest. **2** (*a wrong, an injustice*) damage, injury, injustice, wrong.

grieve *v.t.* (*to cause pain or sorrow to*) break the heart of, bring sorrow to, cause suffering to, distress, hurt, pain, sadden, upset, wound. ANTONYMS: bring solace to, cheer, make happy.
~*v.i.* (*to feel grief, to mourn*) be broken-hearted, be heartbroken, be miserable, lament, mourn, sorrow, suffer, wail, weep, weep and wail. ANTONYMS: be joyful, rejoice.

grievous *a.* **1** (*causing grief or pain, hurtful*) agonizing, hurtful, injurious, painful, severe, wounding. **2** (*atrocious, heinous*) appalling, atrocious, dire, dreadful, flagrant, glaring, gross, heinous, horrible, horrific, iniquitous, monstrous, outrageous, shameful, shocking.

grim *a.* **1** (*stern, unyielding*) inflexible, intractable, obstinate, relentless, resolute, stern, tenacious, uncompromising, unrelenting, unyielding. ANTONYMS: irresolute, yielding. **2** (*of a forbidding aspect*) cross, fearsome, ferocious, fierce, forbidding, formidable, frightening, harsh, implacable, ruthless, severe, sombre, sour, stern, surly, threatening. ANTONYMS: cheerful, friendly, kind. **3** (*hideous, ghastly*) abhorrent, appalling, dire, dreadful, frightful, ghastly, grisly, gruesome, harrowing, heinous, hideous, horrendous, horrible, horrid, iniquitous, macabre, monstrous, nasty, outrageous, shameful, shocking, unspeakable. ANTONYMS: agreeable, delightful, pleasant. **like grim death** (*tenaciously*) determinedly, relentlessly, resolutely, tenaciously, unrelentingly, unyieldingly, with all one's might, with great determination, with tenacity.

grimace *n.* (*a distortion of the features, expressing disgust, contempt etc.*) face, frown, moue, scowl, sneer.
~*v.i.* (*to make grimaces*) frown, make a face, pull a face, scowl, sneer.

grime *n.* (*dirt, smut*) (*sl.*) crud, dirt, dust, filth, (*coll.*) gunge, muck, mud, smut, soot.

grimy *a.* (*covered with grime; dirty*) dirty, dusty, filthy, (*coll.*) gungy, mucky, muddy, smutty, sooty. ANTONYMS: clean, spotless.

grin *v.i.* (*to show the teeth as in laughter or pain*) grin from ear to ear, grin like a Cheshire cat, smile, smile broadly, smile from ear to ear.

grind *v.t.* **1** (*to reduce to powder or fine particles by crushing and friction*) comminute, crush, granulate, mash, mill, pound, powder, pulverize, smash, triturate. **2** (*to sharpen or polish by friction, esp. on a grindstone*) file, polish, sand, sharpen, smooth, whet. **3** (*to grate*) gnash, grate, grit, rasp, scrape. **4** (*to oppress with laws, taxes etc.*) afflict, harass, harry, hound, ill-treat, maltreat, molest, oppress, persecute, torment, torture, tyrannize.
~*v.i.* (*to toil hard and distastefully*) drudge, plod, slave, slog, sweat, toil.
~*n.* (*hard and monotonous work*) chore, drudgery, hard labour, slavery, slog, (*coll.*) sweat, toil. ANTONYMS: leisure.

grindstone *n.* **to keep one's nose to the grindstone** (*to stick to one's work*) concentrate, concentrate on one's work, exert oneself, focus on one's work, work hard.

grip *v.t.* **1** (*to grasp or hold tightly*) catch hold of, clasp, clench, clutch, grab, grasp, hold, seize, take hold of. ANTONYMS: let go of. **2** (*to hold the attention of*) absorb, engross, enthral, entrance, fascinate, hold, hold spellbound, mesmerize, rivet, spellbind. ANTONYMS: bore.
~*n.* **1** (*a firm grasp, a clutch*) clasp, clench, clutch, grasp, hold. **2** (*a suitcase, a hold-all*) bag, flight bag, hold-all, overnight bag, suitcase. **3** (*power, control*) clutches, command, control, dominance, domination, dominion, hold, influence, mastery, possession, power, rule. **4** (*understanding*) apprehension, comprehension, grasp, knowledge, mastery, perception, understanding. **to come to grips with** (*to deal with, tackle (a problem etc.*)) confront, contend with, cope with, deal with, encounter, face, face up to, grapple with, handle, meet head on, tackle, take on. ANTONYMS: dodge, evade, shirk.

gripe *v.i.* (*to complain, esp. in a persistent, peevish way*) (*sl.*) beef, (*coll.*) bellyache, (*sl.*) bitch, bleat, carp, complain, groan, grouch, grouse, grumble, (*N Am., sl.*) kvetch, moan, nag, whine.
~*n.* (*a complaint, esp. of a minor nature*) (*sl.*) beefing, (*coll.*) bellyaching, (*sl.*) bitching, complaint, groan, grousing, grumble, moan, objection, protest, whining.

gripping *a.* (*having the power of holding the attention, absorbing*) absorbing, compelling, compulsive, engrossing, enthralling, entrancing, fascinating, riveting, spellbinding, thrilling. ANTONYMS: boring.

grisly *a.* (*horrible, grim*) appalling, awful, disgusting, dreadful, frightful, ghastly, grim, gruesome, hideous, horrendous, horrible, horrid, horrifying, loathsome, macabre, nasty, odious, repellent, repugnant, repulsive, revolting, shocking, sickening, terrible. ANTONYMS: agreeable, delightful, pleasant.

grit *n.* **1** (*coarse rough particles such as sand or gravel*) dirt, gravel, pebbles, sand. **2** (*firmness, determination*) backbone, (*sl.*) balls, (*sl.*) bottle, bravery, courage, determination, doggedness, endurance, fortitude, gameness, (*coll.*) guts, mettle, nerve, perseverance, pluck, resolution, spirit, spunk, stamina, strength of character, tenacity, toughness, valour. ANTONYMS: cowardice, irresolution, spinelessness.
~*v.t.* (*to grind or grate (as the teeth*)) clench, gnash, grate, grind.

groan *v.i.* **1** (*to utter a deep moaning sound, as in pain or grief*) call out, cry, moan, sigh, wail, whimper. **2** (*to complain*) (*sl.*) beef, (*coll.*) bellyache, (*sl.*) bitch, bleat, carp, complain, gripe, grouch, grouse, grumble, (*N Am., sl.*) kvetch, moan, nag, object, protest, whine.
~*n.* **1** (*a low moaning sound, as of someone in pain or sorrow*) cry, moan, sigh, wail, whimper. **2** (*a complaint*) (*sl.*) beefing, (*coll.*) bellyaching, (*sl.*) bitching, complaint, gripe, grouse, grumble, moan, objection, protest, whine.

groggy *a.* (*dazed, unsteady through illness, drink etc.*) befuddled, bewildered, confused, dazed, dizzy, faint, in a stupor, muddled, muzzy, reeling, shaky, staggering, stunned, stupefied, unsteady, wobbly, (*coll.*) woolly-headed, (*coll.*) woozy. ANTONYMS: clear-headed.

groom *v.t.* **1** (*to prepare and train (a person*)) coach, drill, educate, instruct, make ready, prepare, prime, ready, school, teach, train, tutor. **2** (*to clean and brush (an animal*)) brush, clean, curry, rub down. **3** (*to make (oneself or one's hair) neater or smarter*) brush, comb, dress, fix, preen, primp, put in order, smarten up, spruce up, tidy. ANTONYMS: mess up, muss, untidy.

groove *n.* **1** (*a channel or long hollow, esp. cut with a tool for something to fit into*) canal, channel, cut, cutting, flute, furrow, gutter, hollow, rabbet, rebate, rut, score, trench, trough. **2** (*natural course or events of one's life, a rut*) habit, routine, rut, treadmill.

grope *v.i.* (*to feel one's way*) feel one's way, fumble one's way, move blindly, pick one's way, proceed blindly.
~*v.t.* **1** (*to fondle for sexual gratification*) caress sexually, fondle sexually, stroke sexually. **2** (*to seek out by feeling with the hands in the dark, or*

as a blind person) cast about for, feel for, fish for, fumble for, scrabble for.

gross *a.* **1** (*fat, bloated*) bloated, colossal, corpulent, fat, huge, hulking, massive, obese, overweight. ANTONYMS: skinny, tiny. **2** (*flagrant, glaring*) arrant, blatant, egregious, flagrant, glaring, manifest, obvious, outrageous, plain, rank, serious, shocking. ANTONYMS: hidden, slight, subtle. **3** (*total, not net*) aggregate, before deductions, entire, total, whole. ANTONYMS: net. **4** (*coarse, obscene*) bawdy, blue, coarse, crude, dirty, earthy, filthy, improper, impure, indecent, indelicate, lewd, obscene, offensive, pornographic, ribald, risqué, rude, smutty, vulgar. ANTONYMS: decent, proper, pure. **5** (*lacking fineness, dense*) boorish, coarse, crass, ignorant, insensitive, loutish, oafish, tasteless, thick, uncultivated, unrefined, unsophisticated, vulgar. ANTONYMS: refined, sensitive.
~*v.t.* (*to earn as total income*) bring in, earn, make. ANTONYMS: net, take home.

grotesque *a.* **1** (*distorted or irregular in appearance*) deformed, distorted, malformed, misshapen, twisted. ANTONYMS: normal, regular. **2** (*ludicrous through being distorted or irregular in appearance; bizarre*) absurd, bizarre, extravagant, fanciful, fantastic, freakish, incongruous, ludicrous, odd, outlandish, peculiar, preposterous, ridiculous, strange, unnatural, weird, whimsical. ANTONYMS: normal, ordinary.

ground *n.* **1** (*the surface of the earth as distinct from the air or the sea*) dry land, earth, land, terra firma. ANTONYMS: sea, sky. **2** (*a floor or other supporting surface*) (*coll.*) deck, floor. ANTONYMS: ceiling, roof. **3** (*a region or tract of land*) country, district, land, region, terrain, territory. **4** (*private enclosed land attached to a house*) acres, estate, gardens, land, park, parkland, property. **5** (*basis, the first or fundamental principles*) basis, call, cause, excuse, foundation, justification, motive, occasion, pretext, rationale, reason. **6** (*sediment, dregs, esp. of coffee*) deposit, dregs, lees, precipitate, sediment, settlings. ANTONYMS: froth, head.
~*v.t.* **1** (*to base or establish (on)*) establish, fix, found, settle. **2** (*to instruct thoroughly (in) the elementary principles of*) coach, drill, educate, familiarize with, initiate, instruct, teach, train, tutor. **down to the ground** (*thoroughly*) absolutely, completely, perfectly, thoroughly, totally, utterly. **to gain ground** (*to advance, to meet with success*) advance, get ahead, go forward, make headway, make progress, meet with success, progress, succeed. ANTONYMS: fail, fall back, lose ground. **to get off the ground** (*to make a start, esp. one that is*

successful) begin, commence, get going, get off to a good start, make a start, start. ANTONYMS: abort, come to an end, fail.

groundless *a.* (*without foundation or warrant, baseless*) baseless, empty, uncalled-for, uncorroborated, unfounded, unjustified, unsupported, unwarranted, without foundation. ANTONYMS: corroborated, justified, well-founded.

groundwork *n.* (*preliminary work necessary before further work can be undertaken, a foundation*) base, basis, cornerstone, footing, foundation, fundamentals, preliminaries, preparation, spadework. ANTONYMS: finishing touches.

group *n.* **1** (*a number of persons or things stationed near each other, an assemblage*) assemblage, assembly, band, body, bunch, cluster, collection, company, congregation, crowd, flock, gang, gathering, pack, party. **2** (*a number of persons or things classed together on account of certain resemblances*) association, batch, bracket, category, circle, class, classification, clique, club, coterie, faction, family, genus, league, lot, section, set, species.

grouse *v.i.* (*to grumble*) (*sl.*) beef, (*coll.*) bellyache, (*sl.*) bitch, complain, gripe, groan, grouch, grumble, (*N Am., sl.*) kvetch, moan, object, protest, whine, (*coll.*) whinge.
~*n.* (*a grievance*) complaint, grievance, gripe, groan, grumble, moan, objection, protest.

grovel *v.i.* (*to behave in an obsequious manner*) abase oneself, bootlick, bow and scrape, (*sl.*) brown-nose, crawl, cringe, fawn, humble oneself, kowtow, lick someone's boots, prostrate oneself, toady. ANTONYMS: be proud, hold one's head high.

grow *v.i.* **1** (*to increase in bulk by the assimilation of new matter into the living organism*) fill out, get bigger, get larger, get taller, grow bigger, grow up, stretch. ANTONYMS: get smaller. **2** (*to increase in number, degree etc.*) advance, develop, enlarge, escalate, expand, extend, flourish, get bigger, get larger, grow bigger, increase, intensify, multiply, mushroom, proliferate, snowball, thrive. ANTONYMS: decrease, get less, grow smaller. **3** (*to exist as a living thing*) burgeon, flourish, shoot up, spring up, sprout. **4** (*to be produced, to arise*) arise, issue, originate, spring up, stem. **5** (*to pass into a certain state*) become, come to be, develop into, get, get to be, turn.
~*v.t.* (*to cultivate, to raise by cultivation*) cultivate, produce, propagate. **to grow up** (*to arrive at manhood or womanhood*) become adult, become a man, become a woman, become mature, come of age, grow to manhood,

grow to womanhood, mature, reach manhood, reach womanhood.

growl *v.i.* (*to speak angrily or gruffly*) bark, grunt, snarl.

grown-up *a.* (*adult*) adult, fully-developed, fully-grown, mature, of age. ANTONYMS: childish, immature, undeveloped.
~*n.* (*an adult*) adult, grown man/ woman, man/ woman, mature person. ANTONYMS: child, minor.

growth *n.* **1** (*increase, development, in number, stature etc.*) advancement, augmentation, development, enlargement, escalation, expansion, extension, increase, intensification, multiplication, progress, proliferation, rise. ANTONYMS: decline, decrease, lessening. **2** (*cultivation of vegetable produce*) cultivation, production, propagation. **3** (*an abnormal formation, such as a tumour*) carcinoma, lump, tumour.

grubby *a.* (*dirty, grimy*) (*sl.*) cruddy, dirty, dusty, filthy, grimy, (*coll.*) grotty, (*coll.*) gungy, messy, mucky, soiled, sooty, unwashed. ANTONYMS: clean, spotless.

grudge *v.t.* **1** (*to feel discontent or envy at*) be jealous of, envy, feel envious of, feel resentful about, resent. **2** (*to give or take unwillingly or reluctantly*) begrudge, give reluctantly, give unwillingly. ANTONYMS: give generously, give unstintingly.
~*n.* (*ill will, a feeling of malice or malevolence*) animosity, antagonism, antipathy, bitterness, dislike, enmity, hate, hatred, ill will, loathing, malevolence, malice, pique, rancour, resentment, spite, spitefulness, umbrage. ANTONYMS: friendship, goodwill, love.

gruelling *a.* (*arduous, demanding*) arduous, demanding, difficult, exacting, exhausting, fatiguing, hard, harsh, inexorable, laborious, punishing, relentless, strenuous, taxing, tiring, unrelenting, wearying. ANTONYMS: easy, simple, undemanding.

gruesome *a.* (*frightful, horrible*) abhorrent, appalling, awful, disgusting, frightful, ghastly, grim, hideous, horrendous, horrible, horrid, horrific, horrifying, macabre, nasty, outrageous, repellent, repugnant, repulsive, revolting, shocking, sickening, terrible. ANTONYMS: agreeable, nice, pleasant.

gruff *a.* **1** (*rough, harsh*) angry, bad-tempered, blunt, brusque, crabbed, cross, crotchety, curt, discourteous, grumpy, harsh, ill-natured, impolite, rough, rude, sour, sullen, surly, tetchy, uncivil. ANTONYMS: civil, gentle, good-natured. **2** (*hoarse-voiced*) croaking, croaky, deep, guttural, harsh, hoarse, husky, rough, thick, throaty. ANTONYMS: high, musical.

grumble *v.i.* **1** (*to complain in a surly or muttering tone*) (*sl.*) beef, (*coll.*) bellyache, (*sl.*) bitch, carp, complain, gripe, groan, grouch, grouse, (*N Am., sl.*) kvetch, moan, object, protest, whine, (*coll.*) whinge. **2** (*to growl, to mutter*) growl, gurgle, murmur, mutter, rumble.
~*n.* (*a complaint*) gripe, groan, grouse, moan, objection, protest, (*coll.*) whingeing.

grumpy *a.* (*surly, ill-tempered*) bad-tempered, cantankerous, crabbed, crabby, cross, crotchety, crusty, grouchy, grumbling, ill-humoured, ill-tempered, irritable, petulant, querulous, sullen, surly, testy, tetchy. ANTONYMS: affable, even-tempered, good-natured.

guarantee *n.* (*a formal promise to see an agreement or liability fulfilled*) assurance, bond, guaranty, oath, pledge, promise, security, surety, undertaking, warranty, word, word of honour.
~*v.t.* **1** (*to pledge oneself or engage (that)*) give an assurance, give one's word, pledge, promise, swear. **2** (*to become guarantor or surety for*) provide security for, provide surety for, put up collateral for, underwrite.

guard *v.t.* **1** (*to watch over, to protect (from or against)*) conserve, defend, patrol, police, preserve, protect, safeguard, save, secure, shelter, shield, stand guard over, watch, watch over. ANTONYMS: attack, neglect. **2** (*to stand guard over, to prevent the escape of*) keep under guard, keep under surveillance, keep watch over, mind, oversee, stand guard over, supervise, watch. ANTONYMS: let go, set free.
~*v.i.* (*to be cautious or take precautions (against)*) be careful, be cautious, be on the alert, be on the lookout, be on the qui vive, be vigilant, beware, be wary, keep an eye out, (*coll.*) keep one's eyes peeled, (*coll.*) keep one's eyes skinned, keep one's wits about one, take care, take precautions. ANTONYMS: be careless, be negligent.
~*n.* **1** (*a state of vigilance, watch against attack, surprise etc.*) alertness, attention, attentiveness, care, caution, close watch, heed, heedfulness, vigilance, wariness, watchfulness. ANTONYMS: carelessness, negligence. **2** (*a person or body of people on guard*) bodyguard, custodian, defender, escort, lookout, patrol, picket, protector, security guard, sentinel, sentry, watch, watchman. **3** (*a contrivance to prevent injury or loss*) buffer, bulwark, bumper, cushion, fender, pad, safeguard, safety device, safety guard, screen, shield. **4** (*a prison warder*) gaoler, jailer, keeper, prison guard, (*sl.*) screw, warder. **off one's guard** (*unprepared for attack, surprise etc.*) napping, off guard, unprepared, with one's defences down. ANTONYMS: on one's

guard, on the alert. **on one's guard** (*prepared for attack, surprise etc.*) careful, cautious, keeping an eye out, (*coll.*) keeping one's eyes peeled, (*coll.*) keeping one's eyes skinned, keeping one's wits about one, on the alert, on the lookout, on the qui vive, prepared, ready, vigilant, wary. ANTONYMS: off guard, off one's guard. **to stand guard** ((*of a sentry*) *to keep watch*) act as sentry, defend, guard, keep watch, mount guard, patrol, police, protect, safeguard, watch.

guarded *a.* ((*of a comment, remark etc.*) *cautious, avoiding commitment*) (*coll.*) cagey, careful, cautious, chary, circumspect, non-committal, reserved, restrained, reticent, unspontaneous, wary. ANTONYMS: careless, spontaneous.

guardian *n.* (*a person who has the charge or custody of any person or thing*) caretaker, curator, custodian, defender, guard, keeper, protector, steward, trustee, warden.

guess *v.t.* **1** (*to judge or estimate on imperfect grounds*) estimate, (*coll.*) guesstimate, hazard a guess, hypothesize, judge, make a guess, reckon, speculate, surmise, theorize. ANTONYMS: ascertain, be sure of, confirm. **2** (*to suppose*) believe, conjecture, consider, deem, fancy, feel, imagine, judge, reckon, suppose, surmise, suspect, think.
~*n.* (*an estimate or supposition based on imperfect grounds*) conjecture, estimate, feeling, (*coll.*) guesstimate, guesswork, hypothesis, judgement, notion, reckoning, speculation, supposition, surmise, theory. ANTONYMS: certainty, fact.

guesswork *n.* (*the procedure of guessing*) conjecture, estimate, hypothesis, speculation, supposition, surmise, theory. ANTONYMS: certainty, fact.

guest *n.* **1** (*a person invited by another to a meal, party etc. or to stay at their house*) caller, company, visitor. ANTONYMS: host. **2** (*a person who stays temporarily at a hotel, guest house etc.*) boarder, lodger, visitor. ANTONYMS: landlord/ landlady.

guffaw *n.* (*a burst of loud or coarse laughter*) belly laugh, chortle, hearty laugh, horse laugh, roar of laughter, roar of mirth, shout of laughter.

guidance *n.* **1** (*direction*) auspices, charge, conduct, control, direction, government, handling, instruction, leadership, management, rule. **2** (*help and advice, as given to a young or inexperienced person by someone in authority*) advice, counsel, counselling, direction, help, information, recommendation.

guide *v.t.* **1** (*to direct or conduct*) accompany, attend, conduct, convoy, direct, escort, lead, pilot, shepherd, show, show (someone) the way, steer, usher. **2** (*to rule, to govern*) be in charge of, command, control, direct, govern, handle, manage, preside over, regulate, rule, superintend, supervise. **3** (*to give help and advice to*) advise, counsel, give advice to, give counselling to, give hints to, give information to, give pointers to, influence, inform, instruct, make recommendations to, supply with information.
~*n.* **1** (*a conductor, esp. a person employed to conduct a party of tourists etc.*) attendant, chaperon, chaperone, cicerone, conductor, courier, director, escort, leader, pilot, tour leader, usher. **2** (*an adviser*) adviser, confidant, confidante, counsellor, guru, mentor, therapist. **3** (*anything adopted as a sign or mark of direction*) beacon, guiding light, indicator, landmark, lodestar, marker, pointer, sign, signal, signpost. **4** (*a guidebook*) guidebook, handbook, tourist guide, travel guide. **5** (*anything adopted as a criterion of accuracy*) benchmark, criterion, example, exemplar, gauge, guiding principle, ideal, master, measure, model, norm, paradigm, pattern, standard, touchstone, yardstick. **6** (*a book giving information about something or about how to do something*) (*coll.*) book of the words, directory, handbook, instructions, key, manual.

guidebook *n.* (*a book for tourists, describing places of interest, means of transit etc.*) guide, handbook, tourist guide, travel guide.

guideline *n.* (*a statement setting out future policy, courses of action etc.*) bounds, indicator, limit, margin, parameter, restraint, stricture.

guiding light *n.* (*a person or thing used as a guide or model*) ideal, idol, model, paragon, trailblazer, trendsetter.

guild *n.* (*a society or corporation belonging to the same trade or pursuit*) association, brotherhood, club, company, consortium, corporation, federation, fraternity, league, lodge, order, organization, sisterhood, society, sorority, union.

guile *n.* (*deceit, cunning*) art, artfulness, artifice, chicanery, craft, craftiness, cunning, deceit, deceitfulness, deception, duplicity, foxiness, gamesmanship, skulduggery, slyness, treachery, trickery, underhandedness, wiles, wiliness.

guileless *a.* (*without guile; honest*) aboveboard, artless, candid, frank, genuine, honourable, ingenuous, innocent, naive, open, simple, sincere, straightforward, truthful, unsophisticated, unworldly, (*coll.*) upfront. ANTONYMS: cunning, deceitful, duplicitous.

guilt *n.* **1** (*the state of having committed a crime or offence*) blame, blameworthiness, criminality, culpability, delinquency, guiltiness, iniquity, misbehaviour, misconduct, responsibility, sin, sinfulness, unlawfulness, wickedness, wrong, wrongdoing. ANTONYMS: blamelessness, innocence, virtue. **2** (*the feeling that one is to blame*) bad conscience, compunction, conscience, contriteness, penitence, regret, remorse, repentance, self-condemnation, self-reproach, shame. ANTONYMS: clear conscience.

guiltless *a.* (*free from guilt*) above reproach, blameless, fault-free, faultless, good, guilt-free, impeccable, innocent, in the clear, irreproachable, pure, unimpeachable, unsullied, virtuous. ANTONYMS: blameworthy, guilty.

guilty *a.* **1** (*having committed a crime*) at fault, blameworthy, censurable, criminal, culpable, delinquent, erring, felonious, offending, responsible, to blame, wrongdoing. ANTONYMS: blameless, innocent. **2** (*characterized by or feeling guilt*) ashamed, conscience-stricken, contrite, penitent, regretful, remorseful, repentant, rueful, sheepish, sorry. ANTONYMS: impenitent, unashamed, unrepentant.

guise *n.* **1** (*external appearance*) appearance, costume, demeanour, dress, form, habit, likeness, style. **2** (*semblance, pretence*) blind, cover, disguise, facade, front, mask, pretence, semblance, show.

gulf *n.* **1** (*an inlet of the sea, deeper and narrower proportionately than a bay*) bay, bight, cove, inlet. **2** (*a deep chasm or abyss*) abyss, chasm, cleft, crevice, fissure, gorge, gully, hole, hollow, opening, pit, ravine, rent, rift, split. **3** (*an impassable difference between two opinions, negotiating positions etc.*) breach, chasm, difference, division, rift, separation, split.

gullet *n.* (*the oesophagus*) craw, crop, oesophagus, throat.

gullible *a.* (*credulous, easily deceived*) credulous, easily deceived, green, inexperienced, ingenuous, innocent, naive, overtrustful, simple, trustful, trusting, unsophisticated, unsuspecting, wet behind the ears. ANTONYMS: cynical, sceptical, suspicious.

gully *n.* **1** (*a channel or ravine worn by water*) canyon, channel, gorge, gulch, ravine, valley. **2** (*a drain or gutter*) ditch, drain, gutter.

gulp *v.t.* (*to swallow (down) eagerly or in large draughts*) bolt, devour, gobble, guzzle, knock back, quaff, (*coll.*) swig, swill, toss off, tuck into, wolf.

~*v.i.* (*to make a noise in swallowing or trying to swallow, to gasp*) choke, gasp, swallow.

~*n.* (*a large mouthful*) draught, quaff, swallow, (*coll.*) swig. **to gulp back** (*to keep back or suppress (esp. tears)*) choke back, fight back, repress, smother, stifle, suppress.

gum *n.* (*a sticky substance which exudes from certain trees, used for sticking things together*) adhesive, epoxy resin, fixative, glue, mucilage, paste, resin.

~*v.t.* (*to fasten or stick (down, in, together, up) with or as with gum*) affix, cement, glue, paste, stick. ANTONYMS: peel off, unstick. **to gum up the works** (*to interfere with, spoil something*) act as an impediment, bring things to a halt, cause a delay, hinder things, hold things back, impede progress, interfere with progress, throw a spanner in the works.

gummy *a.* (*sticky, adhesive*) adhesive, gluey, sticky, tacky, viscid, viscous.

gumption *n.* (*common sense, practical shrewdness*) acumen, astuteness, cleverness, common sense, enterprise, grit, horse sense, initiative, mettle, native wit, (*coll.*) nous, pluck, resourcefulness, (*sl.*) savvy, shrewdness, spirit, wits. ANTONYMS: spinelessness, stupidity.

gum tree *n.* **to be up a gum tree** (*to be cornered, in a fix*) be in a difficult situation, be in a fix, be in a jam, (*coll.*) be in a pickle, be in a predicament, be in a tight spot.

gun *n.* (*a tubular weapon from which projectiles are shot by means of gunpowder or other explosive force*) automatic, pistol, rifle, (*sl.*) shooter, shotgun. **to go great guns** (*to make vigorous and successful progress*) be highly successful, bloom, burgeon, flourish, get on like a house on fire, make great strides, make headway, make rapid progress, prosper, thrive. ANTONYMS: be a flop, fail miserably. **to gun for** (*to seek to harm or destroy*) aim to destroy, (*coll.*) have a down on, have a grudge against, have it in for, plot against, (*coll.*) put on a hit list, seek to harm, (*sl.*) take out a contract on. **to jump the gun** (*to begin prematurely*) act prematurely, act too soon, be ahead of time, be premature, be previous, take premature action. ANTONYMS: be behindhand, be too late. **to stick to one's guns** (*to maintain an opinion in the face of opposition*) (*sl.*) hang on in there, persevere, persist, see it through, soldier on, stand one's ground, stick at it, stick it out, (*sl.*) tough it out. ANTONYMS: capitulate, give in, give up.

gunman *n.* (*an armed gangster*) armed robber, assassin, hired gun, (*coll.*) hitman, sniper.

gurgle *v.i.* (*to make a bubbling sound, as water poured from a bottle*) bubble, burble, murmur, purl.

guru *n.* (*a mentor with particular expertise or knowledge*) guiding light, leader, maharishi, master, mentor, religious teacher, sage, spiritual teacher, swami, teacher.

gush *v.i.* **1** (*to flow or rush out copiously or with violence*) burst forth, cascade, emanate, flood, flow out, issue, jet, pour forth, run, rush forth, spout, spurt, stream, surge, well out. ANTONYMS: drip, trickle. **2** (*to be effusive or affectedly sentimental*) babble, be effusive, be emotional, (*coll.*) be over the top, bubble over, effervesce, effuse, enthuse, fuss, get carried away, overenthuse, overstate the case, wax lyrical. ANTONYMS: be restrained.
~*n.* (*a violent and copious issue of a fluid*) burst, cascade, flood, freshet, jet, outpouring, rush, spate, spout, spurt, stream, surge, torrent. ANTONYMS: drip, trickle.

gust *n.* **1** (*a short but violent rush of wind, a squall*) blast, flurry, gale, puff, rush, squall. **2** (*an outburst of passion*) burst, eruption, explosion, fit, outbreak, outburst, paroxysm, storm.

gusto *n.* (*zest, enjoyment*) appreciation, delight, enjoyment, fervour, joy, liking, pleasure, relish, savour, zest. ANTONYMS: apathy, dislike, distaste.

gut *n.* **1** (*pl.*) (*the intestines*) abdomen, belly, bowels, colon, entrails, (*coll.*) innards, (*coll.*) insides, intestines, stomach, viscera. **2** (*pl.*) (*the core or essential part of something*) basis, central part, centre, core, essential part, middle. **3** (*pl.*) (*courage, persistence*) audacity, boldness, (*sl.*) bottle, bravery, courage, daring, grit, gumption, mettle, nerve, pluck, spirit, valour.
~*v.t.* **1** (*to eviscerate, to draw the entrails out of*) clean, disembowel, draw, dress, eviscerate. **2** ((*of fire etc.*) *to remove or destroy the contents*

of) clear out, destroy, empty, lay waste, loot, pillage, plunder, ransack, ravage, rifle, rob, strip.
~*a.* (*of or relating to instinctive feelings, intuition*) basic, emotional, innate, instinctive, intuitive, involuntary, natural, spontaneous.

gutless *a.* (*cowardly*) (*coll.*) chicken, cowardly, craven, faint-hearted, fearful, lily-livered, pusillanimous, spineless, timid, weak-kneed, (*coll.*) yellow. ANTONYMS: bold, brave, courageous, gutsy.

gutsy *a.* **1** (*greedy*) edacious, gluttonous, hoggish, insatiable, piggish, ravenous, voracious. **2** (*plucky*) audacious, bold, brave, courageous, daring, determined, (*chiefly N Am.*) feisty, gallant, game, mettlesome, plucky, spirited, (*sl.*) with bottle. ANTONYMS: cowardly, gutless, spineless.

gutter *n.* (*a trench, conduit etc. for the passage of water or other fluid*) channel, conduit, culvert, ditch, drain, duct, pipe, sewer, sluice, trench, trough.

guttersnipe *n.* (*a street urchin*) ragamuffin, street arab, street urchin, waif.

guttural *a.* (*produced or formed in the throat*) croaking, croaky, deep, gravelly, gruff, harsh, hoarse, husky, low, rasping, rough, thick, throaty. ANTONYMS: clear, high-pitched, musical.

guy *n.* (*a man, a fellow*) (*coll.*) bloke, (*coll.*) chap, fellow, lad, man.

guzzle *v.i.* (*to drink or eat greedily*) bolt, devour, gobble, gulp, knock back, quaff, (*coll.*) swig, swill, toss off, tuck into, wolf.

gypsy *n.* (*a member of a nomad people* (*calling themselves Romany*)*, prob. of Hindu extraction*) diddicoy, didicoi, Romany, traveller, tzigane, tzigany.

gyrate *v.i.* (*to rotate, revolve, in either a circle or a spiral*) circle, pirouette, revolve, rotate, spin, spiral, swirl, turn round, twirl, wheel, whirl.

H

habit *n.* **1** (*a settled inclination, disposition or trend of mind*) character, constitution, disposition, frame of mind, humour, make-up, nature, temper, temperament. **2** (*a manner or custom, acquired by frequent repetition*) custom, mannerism, practice, proclivity, propensity, routine, tendency, wont. **3** (*an addiction*) addiction, dependence, fixation, obsession. **4** (*dress or costume, esp. of a religious order*) apparel, attire, clothes, clothing, costume, dress, garb, garment, (*coll.*) gear.

habitat *n.* **1** (*the natural home or locality of an animal or plant*) environment, home, natural element, natural environment, natural setting, natural surroundings. **2** (*the place where a person or group is at home or usually found*) abode, dwelling-place, habitation, home, home ground, location, residence, residency, territory.

habitation *n.* **1** (*the act of inhabiting*) inhabitance, inhabitancy, occupancy, occupation, tenancy. **2** (*a place of abode*) abode, accommodation, domicile, dwelling, home, house, living quarters, lodging, residence, residency, rooms.

habitual *a.* **1** (*according to habit, usual*) accustomed, customary, familiar, fixed, normal, ordinary, regular, routine, set, standard, traditional, usual, wonted. ANTONYMS: exceptional, infrequent, irregular, unusual. **2** (*customary, constant*) constant, continual, frequent, inveterate, non-stop, perpetual, persistent, recurrent. ANTONYMS: occasional. **3** (*given to a specified habit*) addicted, chronic, confirmed, hardened, ingrained, inveterate.

habituate *v.t.* (*to accustom (to)*) acclimatize (to), accustom (to), adapt (to), break in, condition (to), familiarize (with), harden (to), inure (to), make familiar (with), make used (to).

habitué *n.* (*a person who habitually frequents a place, esp. a place of amusement*) frequenter, (*coll.*) regular, regular customer, regular patron, regular visitor.

hack¹ *v.t.* **1** (*to cut irregularly or into small pieces*) chop, cut, dice, hew. **2** (*to cut unskilfully*) lacerate, mangle, mutilate, slash. **3** (*to tolerate*) abide, bear, endure, put up with, stand, stomach, suffer, take, tolerate.

~*v.i.* (*to emit a short dry cough*) bark, cough, rasp.

hack² *n.* **1** (*an inferior or worn-out horse*) jade, nag. **2** (*a person who earns money from routine literary or journalistic work*) journalist, (*sl.*) journo, literary drudge, literary hack, scribbler.
~*a.* (*trite and ineffective*) banal, commonplace, hackneyed, overused, pedestrian, stale, stereotyped, stock, tired, trite, unoriginal, worn-out. ANTONYMS: fresh, innovative, original.

hackle *n.* to make someone's hackles rise (*to make someone angry*) anger, annoy, enrage, exasperate, (*coll.*) get someone's dander up, infuriate, irritate, make (someone) see red. ANTONYMS: calm, placate, soothe.

hackneyed *a.* ((*of a phrase*) *used so often that it has become stale and ineffective*) banal, clichéd, commonplace, corny, hack, (*coll.*) old hat, overused, overworked, pedestrian, platitudinous, played out, stale, stereotyped, stock, threadbare, timeworn, tired, trite, unoriginal, worn-out. ANTONYMS: fresh, innovative, original.

hag *n.* (*a witch*) crone, witch.

haggard *a.* (*care-worn or gaunt from fatigue, trouble etc.*) cadaverous, care-worn, drained, drawn, emaciated, gaunt, ghastly, hollow-cheeked, hollow-eyed, ill-looking, peaked, pinched, wan. ANTONYMS: healthy, plump-cheeked.

haggle *v.i.* (*to wrangle, esp. over a bargain*) argue, bargain, chaffer, dispute, higgle, palter, wrangle.

hail¹ *n.* **1** (*frozen rain or particles of frozen vapour falling in showers*) frozen rain, hailstones, sleet. **2** (*a great number of violent or abusive words etc.*) barrage, bombardment, rain, shower, storm, volley.
~*v.t.* (*to pour down or out (abuse, blows etc.), as hail*) bombard, pelt, pour down, rain, shower.

hail² *v.t.* **1** (*to call or signal to (a person, taxi etc.) from a distance*) accost, call, flag down, make a sign to, shout to, signal, wave down. **2** (*to designate or acclaim (as)*) acclaim, acknowledge, announce, declare, designate, name, proclaim. **3** (*to welcome, to salute*) acknowledge, greet, salute. ANTONYMS: cut, ignore, snub.

~v.i. (to come (from a particular place) originally or as one's home) be a native (of), be (from), come (from), have one's roots (in).

hair n. **1** (the mass of filaments forming a covering for the human head) head of hair, locks, mane, mop, shock, tresses. **2** (the mass of filaments forming a covering for an animal) coat, fleece, fur, hide, mane, pelt, wool. **by a hair** (by a very small margin) by a fraction, by a hair's breadth, (coll.) by a whisker, by the narrowest of margins, by the skin of one's teeth, narrowly. ANTONYMS: by a mile. **not to turn a hair** (not to show any sign of fatigue or alarm) (coll.) keep one's cool, (coll.) keep one's hair on, not bat an eyelid, remain calm. ANTONYMS: become agitated, become hysterical, go into a frenzy. **to let one's hair down** (to forget ceremony, to behave uninhibitedly) (esp. N Am., coll.) chill out, (N Am., coll.) hang loose, (sl.) let it all hang out, relax, throw off one's inhibitions, (coll.) veg out. **to split hairs** (to quibble about trifles, to be overnice) cavil, find fault, niggle, (coll.) nit-pick, quibble.

hairdo n. (a (woman's) hairstyle when it has been curled or put up) coiffure, cut, haircut, hairstyle, style.

hairless a. (without hair) bald, bald-headed, beardless, clean-shaven, shorn. ANTONYMS: hairy, hirsute.

hair-raising a. (very frightening) alarming, blood-curdling, frightening, horrifying, petrifying, scary, shocking, spine-chilling, startling, terrifying.

hairy a. **1** (covered with hair) bearded, be-whiskered, bushy, fleecy, furry, fuzzy, hair-covered, hirsute, shaggy, unshaven, woolly. ANTONYMS: bald, hairless. **2** (exciting or dangerous) dangerous, difficult, hazardous, perilous, risky.

halcyon a. **1** (peaceful, calm) calm, mild, moderate, peaceful, placid, quiet, serene, still, temperate, tranquil, undisturbed, windless. ANTONYMS: rough, stormy, turbulent. **2** (happy, pleasant) carefree, flourishing, golden, happy, palmy, prosperous, thriving. ANTONYMS: failing, miserable, sad.

hale a. ((esp. of an elderly man) sound and vigorous, robust) blooming, fit, hale and hearty, healthy, in good health, in the pink, robust, sound, strong, sturdy, vigorous, well. ANTONYMS: unhealthy, unwell, weak.

half n. (a half part or share) equal part, equal share, fifty per cent.
~a. **1** (consisting of or forming a half) bisected, halved. ANTONYMS: whole. **2** (partial) incomplete, partial, slight. ANTONYMS: complete, full.

~adv. (partially, imperfectly (often in comb.)) all but, almost, barely, inadequately, incompletely, in part, insufficiently, partially, partly. ANTONYMS: completely, fully, wholly. **by half** (to a considerable degree) by far, considerably, excessively.

half-baked a. **1** (not thorough) ill-conceived, imperfect, incomplete, not thought through, poorly planned, undeveloped, unformed, unplanned. ANTONYMS: complete, developed, perfect, refined. **2** (half-witted, silly) brainless, (coll.) crackpot, crazy, foolish, hare-brained, inane, senseless, silly, stupid. ANTONYMS: clever, sensible.

half-hearted a. (lukewarm, indifferent) apathetic, cool, dispassionate, indifferent, lukewarm, unenthusiastic, uninterested. ANTONYMS: avid, enthusiastic, fervent, passionate, zealous.

halfway adv. **1** (in the middle) at the midpoint, in the middle, midway. **2** (more or less) in part, in some measure, more or less, partly, to a certain degree, to a certain extent, to some extent. ANTONYMS: fully, wholly.
~a. (situated in the middle; equidistant from two extremes) central, centre, equidistant, intermediate, medial, median, mid, middle, midway.

halfwit n. (a silly person) (sl.) airhead, (coll.) dimwit, dolt, dullard, dunce, fool, idiot, (coll.) nitwit, numskull, (sl.) nut, simpleton.

half-witted a. (silly) (sl.) barmy, (coll.) batty, (coll.) crackpot, crazy, doltish, feeble-minded, foolish, half-baked, idiotic, (coll.) nutty, silly, simple-minded, stupid. ANTONYMS: clever, sensible, wise.

hall n. **1** (a large room, esp. one in which public meetings or concerts are held, the large public room in a palace, castle etc.) assembly room, auditorium, chamber, church hall, concert hall, town hall. **2** (a room or passage forming the entry area of a house) entrance hall, entry, hallway, porch, vestibule.

hallmark n. **1** (an official stamp on gold and silver articles to guarantee the standard) assay mark, mark of authentication, official seal, official stamp. **2** (a distinctive feature) badge, indication, indicator, mark, sign, stamp, sure sign, tell-tale sign.

hallowed a. **1** (made holy) blessed, consecrated, holy, sacred, sanctified. **2** (respected, revered) honoured, respected, revered, sacrosanct. ANTONYMS: despised, reviled.

hallucinate v.i. (to have hallucinations) (coll.) be on a trip, fantasize, (coll.) freak out, have hallucinations, see things, see visions.

hallucination n. (*an apparent appearance of an external object that is not present in reality, an illusion*) fantasy, figment of one's/ the imagination, illusion, mirage, phantasmagoria, (*coll.*) trip, vision.

halo n. (*a nimbus or bright disc surrounding the heads of saints etc.*) aureola, aureole, gloriole, nimbus.

halt n. (*a stop or interruption in activity or motion*) break, cessation, close, end, finish, impasse, pause, rest, standstill, stop, stoppage, termination. ANTONYMS: beginning, commencement, opening, start.
~v.i. **1** (*to come to a stop*) come to a halt, come to a standstill, come to a stop, draw up, pull up, stop. ANTONYMS: drive off, set out, start out. **2** (*to stop an activity*) break off, call it a day, cease, come to an end, come to a stop, end, finish, knock off, stop. ANTONYMS: begin, commence, start.
~v.t. (*to cause to stop*) arrest, bring to a halt, bring to a stop, check, close, curb, cut short, end, finish, obstruct, put an end to, put a stop to, staunch, stem, stop, terminate. ANTONYMS: begin, commence, start.

halting a. **1** (*slow and hesitant in speech*) faltering, hesitant, hesitating, stammering, stumbling, stuttering, uncertain. ANTONYMS: confident, fluent. **2** (*slow and hesitant in movement*) faltering, hesitant, limping, stumbling, unsteady. ANTONYMS: steady.

halve v.t. (*to divide into two equal parts*) bisect, cut in half, divide in two, share equally, split in two.

hammer v.t. **1** (*to strike or drive with or as with a hammer*) bang, batter, beat, hit, knock, slap, strike, (*coll.*) wallop. **2** (*to forge or form with a hammer*) beat out, fashion, forge, form, make, shape. **3** (*to defeat easily, coll.*) beat hollow, (*sl.*) clobber, defeat utterly, drub, (*coll.*) lick, run rings round, (*sl.*) tank, thrash, trounce, (*coll.*) wipe the floor with, worst. **to hammer away** (*to work hard and persistently*) beaver away, keep on, labour away, peg away, persevere, persist, slog away. **to hammer home** (*to stress greatly*) accentuate, emphasize, lay emphasis on, lay stress on, stress, underline. **to hammer into** (*to repeat constantly to (someone) in order to instruct*) din into, drum into. **to hammer out** (*to produce (an agreement) after a lot of discussion and disagreement*) sort out, thrash out, work out.

hamper v.t. (*to obstruct or impede (movement etc.)*) cramp, curb, frustrate, handicap, hinder, hold up, impede, inhibit, interfere with, obstruct, restrain, restrict, retard, slow down, throw a spanner in the works of, thwart. ANTONYMS: aid, assist, help, promote.

hamstring v.t. (*to prevent (someone) from carrying out their plan*) baulk, foil, frustrate, hamper, prevent, ruin, stop, thwart. ANTONYMS: aid, assist, help, promote.

hand n. **1** (*the power of execution, skill*) ability, art, artistry, craftsmanship, handiwork, skill. **2** (*pl.*) (*possession, control*) authority, care, charge, command, control, custody, disposal, keeping, possession, power, supervision. **3** (*pl.*) (*labourers, the crew of a ship etc.*) crew-members, employees, hired hands, hired help, labourers, operatives, workers. **4** (*a part, a share*) agency, influence, part, participation, share. **5** (*an act of helping*) aid, assistance, help, helping hand, support. **6** (*a style of handwriting*) calligraphy, handwriting, penmanship, script, writing. **7** (*the pointer or index finger of a clock or counter*) indicator, marker, needle, pointer. **8** (*a round of applause*) applause, handclapping, ovation, round of applause.
~v.t. **1** (*to give or deliver with the hand*) deliver, give, hand over, pass, present. ANTONYMS: keep, retain. **2** (*to assist or conduct with the hand (into, out of etc.)*) aid, assist, give a helping hand to, guide, help. ANTONYMS: impede, obstruct. **at hand 1** (*close by*) close at hand, close by, imminent, in the vicinity, near, near at hand, to hand. ANTONYMS: at a distance, far away. **2** (*available*) accessible, available, close at hand, handy, (*coll.*) on tap, readily available, ready, to hand, within easy reach, within reach. ANTONYMS: inaccessible, out of reach, unavailable. **by hand** (*by a person, with the hands (as distinct from with instruments or machines)*) manually, with one's hands. ANTONYMS: by machine. **from hand to mouth** (*without provision for the future*) in poverty, on the breadline, precariously. ANTONYMS: affluently, in comfort. **hand and foot** (*completely, attending to every need*) completely, like a slave, thoroughly. **hand in glove** (*on most intimate terms (with)*) hand in hand, in association, (*sl.*) in cahoots, in collusion, in league, in partnership, together. **hand in hand** (*in union, unitedly*) (*sl.*) hand in glove, in association, (*sl.*) in cahoots, in collusion, in league, in partnership, together. **in hand 1** (*in a state of preparation or execution*) in preparation, in the pipeline, under way. **2** (*in possession*) available, in reserve, put by, ready. **3** (*under control*) under control. **on one's hands** (*(left) to one's responsibility*) in one's care, in one's charge, left to one's responsibility. **to hand 1** (*near*) at hand, close at hand, close by, imminent, in the vicinity, near, near at hand. ANTONYMS: at a distance, far away. **2** (*available*)

accessible, at hand, available, close at hand, handy, (*coll.*) on tap, readily available, ready, within easy reach, within reach. ANTONYMS: inaccessible, out of reach, unavailable. **to hand down 1** (*to bequeath*) bequeath, transfer, will. **2** (*to pass on after use*) hand on, pass on, transfer. **to hand out** (*to distribute*) allocate, apportion, deal out, dish out, dispense, distribute, dole out, give out, mete out, pass out. ANTONYMS: keep, retain. **to hand over** (*to deliver* (*to a person*)) deliver, give, hand, pass, present, surrender, transfer, yield. ANTONYMS: keep, retain.

handbag *n.* (*a small bag for carrying money and personal things*) bag, clutch bag, (*N Am.*) purse, shoulder bag.

handbill *n.* (*a small printed sheet for circulating information*) bulletin, circular, flyer, leaflet, notice, pamphlet.

handbook *n.* (*a small book or treatise on any subject, a manual*) (*coll.*) book of the words, guide, guidebook, instruction book, manual.

handful *n.* (*a small number or quantity*) few, scattering, smattering, sprinkling. ANTONYMS: (*coll.*) loads, (*coll.*) masses.

handicap *n.* (*a disadvantage*) barrier, block, check, constraint, curb, disadvantage, drawback, encumbrance, hindrance, impediment, limitation, millstone round one's neck, obstacle, obstruction, restraint, restriction, stumbling-block. ANTONYMS: advantage, aid, asset, benefit, help.
~*v.t.* (*to put at a disadvantage*) block, check, constrain, curb, disadvantage, hamper, hamstring, hinder, impede, limit, obstruct, place/put at a disadvantage, restrain, restrict, retard. ANTONYMS: aid, assist, be an advantage to, boost, help.

handiness *n.* **1** (*the state of being useful and easy to use*) convenience, helpfulness, manageability, practicality, serviceability, usefulness. ANTONYMS: impracticality, inconvenience, unwieldiness, uselessness. **2** (*the state of being close at hand*) accessibility, availability, closeness, convenience, nearness. ANTONYMS: inaccessibility, remoteness, unavailability. **3** (*the state of being skilful with the hands*) adeptness, adroitness, aptitude, deftness, dexterity, expertise, proficiency, skilfulness, skill. ANTONYMS: awkwardness, clumsiness, hamfistedness, incompetence, maladroitness.

handiwork *n.* **1** (*work done by the hands*) craft, craftsmanship, handicraft, handwork, workmanship. **2** (*the product of one's hands or effort*) act, action, doing, effort, labour, product, work.

handle *v.t.* **1** (*to touch, to feel with the hands*) feel, finger, fondle, grasp, hold, (*coll.*) paw, pick up, poke, stroke, touch. **2** (*to deal with, to manage*) cope with, deal with, manage, take care of. **3** (*to deal in*) deal in, market, sell, trade in, traffic in. **4** (*to treat of*) deal with, discourse on, discuss, treat. **5** (*to be in charge of*) administer, be in charge of, conduct, direct, manage, run, supervise, take care of. **6** (*to operate or control*) control, drive, manoeuvre, operate, steer.
~*n.* (*that part of a tool or instrument, by which it is grasped and held in the hand*) grip, handgrip, hilt, knob, shaft, stock.

handling *n.* **1** (*the action of touching, feeling etc. with the hand*) feeling, fingering, fondling, grasping, holding, (*coll.*) pawing, poking, stroking, touching. **2** (*the act of dealing with or coping with*) coping, dealing, management. **3** (*administration*) administration, care, charge, conduct, direction, management, running, supervision. **4** (*treatment*) discussion, treatment. **5** (*the act of dealing in*) dealing, marketing, selling, trading, trafficking.

handout *n.* **1** (*a statement handed out to the press*) bulletin, circular, leaflet, literature, notice, pamphlet, press release. **2** (*a gift of money etc. esp. to the poor*) alms, charity, dole, gift.

hand-picked *a.* (*carefully chosen*) choice, chosen, elite, select.

handsome *a.* **1** (*good-looking, finely featured*) attractive, comely, (*sl.*) dishy, good-looking, personable. ANTONYMS: ugly, unattractive, unprepossessing, unsightly. **2** (*ample, large*) abundant, ample, bountiful, considerable, generous, large, liberal, magnanimous, plentiful, sizeable. ANTONYMS: meagre, mean, miserly, small, stingy.

handwriting *n.* **1** (*writing done by hand*) longhand, script, writing. **2** (*the style of writing peculiar to a person*) fist, penmanship, script, writing.

handy *a.* **1** (*useful and easy to use*) convenient, easy to use, functional, helpful, manageable, practical, serviceable, useful, user-friendly. ANTONYMS: impractical, inconvenient, unwieldy, useless. **2** (*close at hand, near*) accessible, at hand, at one's fingertips, available, close, close at hand, convenient, near, near at hand, nearby, on hand, to hand, within reach. ANTONYMS: inaccessible, inconvenient, unavailable. **3** (*dexterous, skilful with the hands*) adept, adroit, competent, deft, dexterous, expert, good with one's hands, nimble-fingered, proficient, skilful, skilled. ANTONYMS: awkward, clumsy, ham-fisted, incompetent, maladroit.

hang *v.t.* **1** (*to attach to a point of support higher than its own height*) mount, suspend. **2** (*to suspend by the neck on a gallows as capital punishment*) gibbet, put the noose on, send to the gallows, send to the gibbet, (*coll.*) string up. **3** (*to attach* (*wallpaper*) *in vertical strips to a wall*) attach, fasten, fix, glue, paste, stick. **4** (*to cover or decorate with anything suspended*) adorn, cover, deck, decorate, drape, ornament.
~*v.i.* **1** (*to be hung or suspended*) be pendent, be suspended, dangle, hang down, swing. **2** ((*of clothing*) *to drape or fall*) droop, fall, sag, trail. **3** (*to be immobile in the air*) drift, float, flutter, hover. **4** (*to droop, to bend forward*) bend forward, incline, lean over. **to hang about/ around 1** (*to loiter, to loaf*) dally, linger, loaf, loiter, tarry, waste time. **2** (*to stay near, to frequent*) be a regular visitor to/ at, frequent, (*sl.*) hang out at, haunt. **3** (*to wait*) hang on, hold on, wait. **4** (*to associate* (*with*)) associate (with), be a companion (of), be a friend (of), (*sl.*) hang out (with), keep company (with). **to hang back 1** (*to act reluctantly, to hesitate*) be reluctant, demur, hesitate, show reluctance. **2** (*to stay behind*) hold back, recoil, shrink back, stay behind. **to hang down** (*to droop*) droop, sag, trail. **to hang on 1** (*to grasp or hold*) cling, clutch, grasp, grip hold, hold fast. ANTONYMS: let go. **2** (*to persist*) carry on, continue, endure, go on, hold on, hold out, persevere, persist. ANTONYMS: give up, stop. **3** (*to depend on*) be conditional on, be contingent on, be dependent on, be determined by, hinge on, rest on. **4** (*to wait*) hold on, wait. **5** (*to listen closely to*) (*coll.*) be all ears to, be rapt by, concentrate on, listen attentively to. ANTONYMS: be inattentive, ignore. **to hang over 1** (*to be hanging or immobile above*) bend over, bow over, droop over, lean over, overhang. **2** (*to be oppressively present to*) be imminent, (*coll.*) be just around the corner, draw near, loom over, menace, threaten.

hang-dog *a.* (*sullen, guilty-looking*) browbeaten, cowed, crestfallen, cringing, defeated, guilty-looking, shamefaced, sheepish, sullen. ANTONYMS: confident, triumphant.

hanger-on *n.* (*a person who hangs on or sticks to a person, place etc., a parasite*) camp follower, dependant, flunkey, follower, (*coll.*) freeloader, (*sl.*) groupie, henchman, lackey, leech, minion, parasite, (*sl.*) sponger, sycophant.

hanging *a.* (*suspended, dangling*) beetling, dangling, drooping, overhanging, pendent, suspended, swinging.

hang-out *n.* (*a haunt*) den, favourite place, haunt, resort.

hang-up *n.* (*a neurosis or anxiety*) difficulty, fixation, inhibition, obsession, phobia, preoccupation, problem, (*coll.*) thing.

hank *n.* (*a coil or skein*) coil, length, loop, skein, twist.

hanker *v.i.* (*to have strong desire or longing* (*after*)) (*fig.*) be dying (for), covet, crave, desire, have a longing (for), (*coll.*) have a yen (for), have one's heart set (on), hunger (for), itch (for), long (for), lust (after), pine (for), thirst (after), want, wish (for), yearn (for).

hankering *n.* (*a strong desire or longing*) craving, desire, hunger, itch, longing, lust, thirst, want, wish, yearning, (*coll.*) yen.

haphazard *a.* (*random*) aimless, chance, hit-and-miss, indiscriminate, irregular, random, undirected, unmethodical, unplanned, unsystematic. ANTONYMS: methodical, planned, systematic.

hapless *a.* (*unfortunate, luckless*) ill-fated, ill-starred, luckless, miserable, unfortunate, unhappy, unlucky, wretched. ANTONYMS: fortunate, happy, lucky.

happen *v.i.* **1** (*to occur*) arise, chance, come about, crop up, materialize, occur, pan out, take place, transpire. **2** (*to chance* (*to*)) chance, have the bad fortune (to), have the good fortune (to). **3** (*to light* (*upon*)) chance (upon), discover by chance, encounter, find, meet by chance, stumble (on). ANTONYMS: ferret out, search out.

happening *n.* (*something that happens, a chance occurrence*) affair, event, incident, occasion, occurrence, proceedings.

happily *adv.* **1** (*cheerfully*) blissfully, blithely, cheerfully, delightedly, ecstatically, elatedly, euphorically, exuberantly, gaily, merrily, raptly. ANTONYMS: miserably, sadly, unhappily, wretchedly. **2** (*willingly*) freely, gladly, willingly, with pleasure. ANTONYMS: reluctantly, unwillingly. **3** (*favourably*) advantageously, auspiciously, favourably, felicitously, fortunately, luckily, opportunely, propitiously, providentially. ANTONYMS: inopportunely, unfavourably, unfortunately, unluckily.

happiness *n.* (*the state of being happy*) bliss, blitheness, cheerfulness, contentment, delight, ecstasy, elation, euphoria, exuberance, gaiety, joy, joyfulness, light-heartedness, merriment, pleasure, raptness, satisfaction. ANTONYMS: depression, discontent, displeasure, dissatisfaction, misery, sadness, sorrow, wretchedness.

happy *a.* **1** (*enjoying pleasure from something good*) cheerful, cock-a-hoop, delighted, ecstatic, elated, euphoric, exuberant, glad, in good spirits, in seventh heaven, joyful, light-hearted, merry, (*coll.*) on cloud nine, on top of the world, overjoyed, over the moon, pleased, rapt, thrilled. ANTONYMS: depressed, miserable, sad, unhappy, wretched. **2** (*contented, satisfied*) content, contented, pleased, satisfied, untroubled, unworried, willing. ANTONYMS: discontented, displeased, dissatisfied. **3** (*lucky, fortunate*) advantageous, auspicious, favourable, felicitous, fortunate, lucky, opportune, propitious, providential, timely. ANTONYMS: disadvantageous, inauspicious, inopportune, unfortunate, unlucky. **4** (*apt, felicitous*) appropriate, apt, convenient, felicitous, fit, fitting, proper, right, seemly. ANTONYMS: inappropriate, inapt, infelicitous, unfit. **5** (*willing*) eager, enthusiastic, glad, willing. ANTONYMS: reluctant, unwilling.

happy-go-lucky *a.* (*careless, thoughtless*) blithe, carefree, careless, casual, devil-may-care, easygoing, free and easy, heedless, improvident, insouciant, irresponsible, light-hearted, unconcerned, untroubled, unworried. ANTONYMS: care-worn, concerned, formal, responsible, worried.

harangue *n.* **1** (*a declamatory address to a large assembly*) address, lecture, oration, speech, spiel, talk. **2** (*a noisy and vehement speech, a tirade*) denunciation, diatribe, philippic, stream of invective, tirade, verbal onslaught.

harass *v.t.* **1** (*to torment*) annoy, badger, bother, chivvy, disturb, exasperate, fret, (*coll.*) give (someone) a hard time, (*coll.*) hassle, hound, molest, nag, persecute, pester, plague, provoke, tease, torment, worry. **2** (*to tire out with care or worry*) agitate, exhaust, fatigue, fluster, pressurize, strain, stress, tire, wear out, worry. **3** (*to worry by repeated attacks*) beleaguer, harry, press hard, raid.

harassed *a.* (*anxious and strained because one has too much to do or too many problems*) agitated, anxious, care-worn, distraught, exhausted, fatigued, flustered, (*coll.*) hassled, strained, stressed, tired, under pressure, under strain, worn-out, worried.

harassment *n.* (*the state of being harassed*) molestation, persecution, pestering, tormenting.

harbinger *n.* **1** (*a person who announces the approach of another*) herald, usher. **2** (*a person who or thing which foretells what is coming*) augury, indicator, omen, portent, sign, signal. **3** (*a precursor*) forerunner, precursor.

harbour *n.* **1** (*a port or haven*) anchorage, dock, haven, port. **2** (*an asylum, a place of shelter*) asylum, haven, place of safety, refuge, retreat, sanctuary, shelter.

~*v.t.* **1** (*to shelter*) give shelter to, hide, house, protect, provide a refuge for, shelter, shield. **2** (*to keep in mind, esp. secretly*) brood over, cherish, cling to, entertain, foster, hold, maintain, nurse, nurture, retain. ANTONYMS: forget, put aside, put out of one's mind.

hard *a.* **1** (*firm, solid*) close-packed, compact, compressed, dense, firm, impenetrable, inflexible, rigid, stiff, strong, tough, unyielding. ANTONYMS: pliable, soft. **2** (*fatiguing, strenuous*) arduous, back-breaking, burdensome, difficult, exacting, fatiguing, formidable, heavy, Herculean, laborious, onerous, rigorous, strenuous, tiring, tough, uphill. ANTONYMS: easy, effortless. **3** (*intolerable, full of problems*) difficult, disagreeable, distressing, grievous, grim, harsh, insupportable, intolerable, painful, severe, uncomfortable, unendurable, unpleasant. ANTONYMS: agreeable, comfortable, pleasant. **4** (*intricate, perplexing*) baffling, complex, complicated, difficult, enigmatic, intricate, involved, knotty, perplexing, puzzling, thorny. ANTONYMS: easy, simple, straightforward, uncomplicated. **5** (*harsh, unfeeling*) callous, cold, cold-hearted, cruel, grim, hard-hearted, harsh, implacable, inflexible, merciful, oppressive, ruthless, severe, stern, strict, tyrannical, unfeeling, unjust, unkind, unrelenting, unsympathetic. ANTONYMS: compassionate, gentle, kind, lenient, sympathetic, warm-hearted. **6** (*hostile, resentful*) acrimonious, angry, antagonistic, bitter, hostile, rancorous, resentful, spiteful. ANTONYMS: affectionate, cordial, friendly. **7** (*not open to dispute, definite*) actual, definite, indisputable, straightforward, undeniable, verifiable, verified. ANTONYMS: disputable, doubtful, open to dispute. **8** (*high in alcohol*) alcoholic, spirituous, strong. **9** ((*of a drug*) *highly addictive and harmful*) addictive, habit-forming, harmful. ANTONYMS: soft. **10** (*using force*) fierce, forceful, heavy, powerful, strong, violent. ANTONYMS: gentle, light, slight.

~*adv.* **1** (*forcibly, violently*) energetically, forcefully, forcibly, heartily, heavily, strenuously, strongly, vigorously, violently, with all one's might, with force, with vigour. ANTONYMS: gently, lightly, weakly. **2** (*strenuously, using a lot of effort*) assiduously, conscientiously, diligently, doggedly, earnestly, indefatigably, industriously, persistently, sedulously, steadily, with application, zealously. ANTONYMS: idly, lazily. **3** (*severely, with hardship or pain*) badly, distressingly, harshly, intensely, painfully, severely. ANTONYMS: mildly, slightly. **4** (*with effort or difficulty*) laboriously, painfully, with difficulty, with effort. ANTONYMS:

easily, effortlessly. **5** (*close, near*) close, near. **6** (*closely, carefully*) carefully, closely, keenly, painstakingly, sharply. ANTONYMS: cursorily, rapidly. **7** ((*of rain*) *very heavily*) (*coll.*) cats and dogs, heavily, steadily. **hard by** (*close by*) close at hand, close by, near at hand, nearby, not far away. ANTONYMS: far away.

hard and fast *a.* (*strict; that must be strictly adhered to*) binding, fixed, immutable, inflexible, invariable, rigid, set, strict, stringent. ANTONYMS: adaptable, flexible, variable.

hardbitten *a.* (*tough and not easily shocked*) callous, case-hardened, cynical, (*coll.*) hard-boiled, hardened, hard-headed, (*coll.*) hard-nosed, inured, shrewd, tough, unsentimental. ANTONYMS: gentle, idealistic, romantic, sentimental.

hard-core *a.* **1** (*loyal to beliefs and resistant to change*) dedicated, diehard, dyed-in-the-wool, extreme, intransigent, loyal, rigid, staunch, steadfast. ANTONYMS: apathetic, moderate, wavering. **2** ((*of pornography*) *sexually explicit*) blatant, explicit, full-frontal, obscene. ANTONYMS: soft-core.

harden *v.t.* **1** (*to make hard or harder*) anneal, congeal, freeze, make hard, make harder, set, solidify, stiffen. ANTONYMS: melt, soften. **2** (*to confirm* (*in wickedness, obstinacy etc.*)) accustom, confirm, habituate, inure, season, train. **3** (*to make unfeeling or callous*) brutalize, case-harden, deprive of feeling, make callous, make hard, make insensitive, make tough, toughen. ANTONYMS: soften.
~*v.i.* (*to become hard or harder*) become hard, become harder, congeal, freeze, set, solidify, stiffen. ANTONYMS: melt, soften.

hardened *a.* (*seasoned, inveterate*) chronic, habitual, impenitent, incorrigible, inured, inveterate, reprobate, seasoned.

hard-headed *a.* (*practical, not sentimental*) astute, hardbitten, (*coll.*) hard-boiled, level-headed, matter-of-fact, practical, pragmatic, rational, realistic, sensible, sharp, shrewd, tough, unsentimental, with one's feet on the ground. ANTONYMS: idealistic, impractical, romantic, sentimental, unrealistic.

hard-hearted *a.* (*cruel, unfeeling*) callous, cold, cold-hearted, cruel, hard, heartless, indifferent, inhuman, insensitive, merciless, pitiless, stony-hearted, uncaring, unconcerned, unfeeling, unkind, unsympathetic. ANTONYMS: compassionate, kind-hearted, kindly, sympathetic, understanding, warm.

hard-hitting *a.* (*forceful, effective*) blunt, forceful, frank, pulling no punches, straight-talking, tough, uncompromising, unsparing,

vigorous. ANTONYMS: diplomatic, mild, restrained, tactful.

hardiness *n.* (*the state of being unaffected by fatigue; robustness*) fitness, healthiness, lustiness, robustness, strength, sturdiness, toughness, vigour.

hardline *a.* ((*of a policy*) *uncompromising, extreme*) extreme, inflexible, intransigent, tough, uncompromising, unyielding. ANTONYMS: flexible, yielding.

hardly *adv.* (*scarcely, not quite*) almost not, barely, just, not quite, only just, scarcely. ANTONYMS: by all means, certainly, easily.

hard-pressed *a.* **1** (*closely pursued*) closely pursued, harried, hotly pursued, hounded. **2** (*having difficulties; under strain*) overloaded, overworked, under pressure, under strain, with one's back to the wall.

hardship *n.* (*that which is hard to bear, as suffering, injustice*) adversity, affliction, deprivation, disaster, distress, misery, misfortune, need, pain, privation, suffering, torment, tribulation, trouble, want, worry, wretchedness. ANTONYMS: comfort, ease, good fortune, prosperity.

hard up *a.* (*in need, esp. of money, very poor*) (*coll.*) broke, impecunious, impoverished, in the red, (*coll.*) on one's beam ends, (*coll.*) on one's uppers, penniless, poor, short of money, (*coll.*) strapped for cash, (*coll.*) without two pennies to rub together. ANTONYMS: affluent, rich, wealthy, well off.

hard-wearing *a.* (*durable*) durable, resilient, stout, strong, tough. ANTONYMS: flimsy.

hard-working *a.* (*given to working hard and diligently*) assiduous, busy, conscientious, diligent, energetic, industrious, sedulous, with one's shoulder to the wheel, zealous. ANTONYMS: dilatory, idle, lazy.

hardy *a.* (*unaffected by fatigue; robust*) fit, fit as a fiddle, hale and hearty, healthy, lusty, robust, stalwart, strong, sturdy, tough, vigorous. ANTONYMS: delicate, feeble, frail, sickly, weak.

hare-brained *a.* **1** ((*of a plan*) *very silly; unlikely to be successful*) (*coll.*) crackpot, crazy, foolhardy, foolish, (*coll.*) half-baked, ill-conceived, madcap, rash, reckless, ridiculous, silly. ANTONYMS: rational, sensible, wise. **2** (*giddy, flighty*) dizzy, empty-headed, feather-brained, flighty, foolish, giddy, harum-scarum, silly. ANTONYMS: sensible, wise.

hark *v.i.* **to hark back to** (*to return to* (*some point or matter from which a temporary digression has been made*)) go back to, look back to, recall, recollect, remember, revert to, think back to.

†**harlot** n. (a prostitute; a promiscuous woman) call-girl, (sl.) hooker, loose woman, (sl.) pro, prostitute, (sl.) scrubber, streetwalker, strumpet, (sl.) tart, (sl.) tramp.

harm n. **1** (hurt, damage) abuse, damage, destruction, detriment, havoc, hurt, ill, impairment, injury, loss, mischief, ruin, suffering. ANTONYMS: assistance, benefit, gain, good, help, improvement, reparation. **2** (evil) badness, evil, immorality, iniquity, sin, vice, wickedness, wrongdoing. ANTONYMS: goodness, morality, virtue.
~v.t. (to hurt or damage) abuse, cause damage to, cause harm to, damage, do mischief to, hurt, ill-treat, ill-use, impair, inflict damage on, injure, maltreat, mar, ruin, spoil, wound. ANTONYMS: assist, benefit, do good to, help, improve, repair.

harmful a. (hurtful, detrimental) abusive, damaging, deleterious, destructive, detrimental, disadvantageous, evil, hurtful, injurious, mischievous, noxious, pernicious, toxic, wounding. ANTONYMS: advantageous, beneficial, harmless, helpful.

harmless a. **1** (not hurtful or injurious) innocuous, non-toxic, safe. ANTONYMS: dangerous, harmful, toxic. **2** (inoffensive) blameless, gentle, innocent, inoffensive. ANTONYMS: blameworthy, harmful, offensive.

harmonious a. **1** (musical, tuneful) dulcet, euphonious, harmonizing, mellifluous, melodious, musical, rhythmic, sweet-sounding, tuneful. ANTONYMS: cacophonous, discordant, grating, harsh, tuneless. **2** (concordant, having harmony) compatible, concordant, congruous, coordinated, in harmony, matching, well-matched. ANTONYMS: contrasting, incompatible, inharmonious. **3** (without discord or dissension) agreeable, amiable, amicable, compatible, congenial, cordial, en rapport, friendly, in accord, in harmony, in tune, peaceable, peaceful, sympathetic, tranquil. ANTONYMS: disagreeable, hostile, unfriendly.

harmonize v.i. **1** (to agree in sound or effect) be compatible, be congruous, be harmonious, be well-coordinated, blend, fit together, go together, match, mix well. ANTONYMS: be discordant, be inharmonious, clash. **2** (to correspond, to be congruous (with)) agree (with), be congruent (with), be in accord (with), be in agreement (with), coincide (with), correspond (to), tally (with). ANTONYMS: be incongruent (with), be in disagreement (with), disagree (with).

harmony n. **1** (the adaptation of parts to each other, so as to form a symmetrical or pleasing whole) balance, blending, compatibility, congruity, consonance, coordination, symmetry. ANTONYMS: discordance, incompatibility. **2** (the agreeable combination of simultaneous sounds, the production of musical chords) euphoniousness, euphony, melodiousness, melody, tune, tunefulness. ANTONYMS: cacophony, discord. **3** (concord or agreement in views, sentiments etc.) accord, accordance, agreement, amity, assent, compatibility, concord, congruity, consensus, like-mindedness, peace, rapport, sympathy, unison, unity.

harness n. (the working gear of a horse or other draught animal) equipment, gear, tack, tackle.
~v.t. **1** (to put a harness on (a horse etc.)) hitch up, saddle, yoke. **2** (to utilize (natural forces, e.g. water) for motive power) apply, channel, employ, exploit, make use of, put to use, turn to account, use, utilize.

harp v.i. (to dwell incessantly (on)) dwell (on), go on (about), go on and on (about), labour, press the point (about), reiterate, repeat.

harridan n. (an ill-tempered or bullying (old) woman) (coll.) battleaxe, fury, gorgon, hag, harpy, nag, scold, shrew, termagant, virago.

harrow v.t. (to torment, to cause suffering to) cause anguish to, cause suffering to, distress, rack, torment, torture, traumatize, wound.

harrowing a. (causing anguish or torment) agonizing, chilling, distressing, excruciating, heartbreaking, horrific, painful, racking, terrifying, traumatic, wounding.

harry v.t. **1** (to plunder, to pillage) despoil, devastate, lay waste, pillage, plunder, raid, rob, sack. **2** (to harass) annoy, badger, bother, chivvy, disturb, harass, (coll.) hassle, molest, persecute, pester, plague, tease, torment, trouble, vex, worry.

harsh a. **1** (discordant, irritating) croaking, discordant, dissonant, grating, gruff, guttural, hoarse, jangling, jarring, rasping, raucous, rough, strident. ANTONYMS: harmonious, mellifluous, soft, sweet-sounding. **2** (rigorous, inclement) austere, barren, bitter, bleak, desolate, grim, inclement, rigorous, rough, severe, Spartan, stark, stern, stringent. ANTONYMS: clement, gentle, mild. **3** (unfeeling) barbarous, brutal, cruel, despotic, merciless, pitiless, ruthless, savage, tyrannical, uncompassionate, unfeeling, unkind, unrelenting, unsympathetic. ANTONYMS: compassionate, kind, lenient, merciful, sympathetic. **4** (unpleasantly loud or bright) garish, gaudy, glaring, loud, overbold, strident, vulgar. ANTONYMS: muted, soft.

harum-scarum *a.* (*giddy, reckless*) dizzy, erratic, giddy, impetuous, irresponsible, madcap, rash, reckless, scatterbrained, wild.

harvest *n.* (*the product or result of any labour or effort*) fruition, fruits, produce, product, result, return, yield.
~*v.t.* **1** (*to reap and gather in* (*corn, grain etc.*)) collect, gather, gather in, glean, pick, pluck, reap. **2** (*to garner, to lay up*) accumulate, amass, collect, garner, hoard.

hash *n.* (*hashish*) cannabis, (*coll.*) grass, hashish, marihuana, marijuana, (*coll.*) pot.

hassle *n.* **1** (*something causing difficulty or problems*) bother, difficulty, inconvenience, problems, struggle, trials and tribulations, trouble. **2** (*an argument*) altercation, argument, disagreement, dispute, fight, quarrel, row, (*coll.*) set-to, squabble, tussle, wrangle.
~*v.t.* (*to harass*) annoy, badger, bother, (*sl.*) bug, (*coll.*) give (someone) a hard time, harass, hound, nag, pester, plague, torment.

haste *n.* **1** (*speed of movement; urgency*) alacrity, dispatch, expedition, expeditiousness, hurry, promptness, quickness, rapidity, rapidness, speed, swiftness, urgency. ANTONYMS: delay, deliberation, leisureliness, slowness. **2** (*excessive speed*) hastiness, impetuosity, impulsiveness, precipitateness, rashness, recklessness, rushing.

hasten *v.i.* (*to move with haste or speed*) (*N Am.*) barrel along, bolt, dash, fly, (*coll.*) get a move on, (*N Am., coll.*) hightail it, (*sl.*) hotfoot it, hurry, hurry up, make haste, race, run, rush, speed, sprint, (*coll.*) tear along. ANTONYMS: crawl, creep, dawdle.
~*v.t.* (*to expedite*) accelerate, advance, boost, expedite, facilitate, further, hurry, hurry up, precipitate, quicken, speed up, step up. ANTONYMS: decelerate, hinder, impede, slow down.

hasty *a.* **1** (*hurried, quick*) brief, cursory, expeditious, fast, fleeting, hurried, passing, perfunctory, quick, rapid, speedy, swift. ANTONYMS: leisurely, protracted, slow, superficial. **2** (*eager, precipitate*) foolhardy, headlong, heedless, hurried, impetuous, impulsive, precipitate, rash, reckless, rushed, thoughtless. ANTONYMS: deliberate, slow, thoughtful. **3** (*irritable*) choleric, excitable, fiery, hot-headed, hot-tempered, irascible, irritated, passionate, quick-tempered, snappy, volatile. ANTONYMS: calm, emotionless, (*coll.*) laid-back.

hat *n.* (*a covering for the head*) boater, bonnet, bowler, bowler hat, cap, panama, stetson, straw hat, top hat, trilby.

hatch *v.t.* **1** (*to produce* (*young*) *from eggs by incubation or artificial heat*) bring forth, incubate. **2** (*to produce young from* (*eggs*)) cover, incubate, sit on. **3** (*to evolve, to devise* (*a plan, plot etc.*)) conceive, concoct, contrive, (*coll.*) cook up, design, devise, (*coll.*) dream up, formulate, invent, manufacture, originate, plan, plot, think up, trump up.

hatchet *n.* (*a small axe with a short handle for use with one hand*) axe, chopper, cleaver, machete, tomahawk.

hate *n.* **1** (*extreme dislike, hatred*) abhorrence, animosity, antagonism, antipathy, aversion, detestation, dislike, enmity, hatred, hostility, ill will, loathing, odium, repugnance, revulsion. ANTONYMS: adoration, affection, devotion, fondness, liking, love. **2** (*a hated thing or person*) anathema, aversion, bane, bête noire, bugbear, pet hate. ANTONYMS: joy, love, pleasure.
~*v.t.* **1** (*to dislike exceedingly; to detest*) abhor, abominate, be repelled by, despise, detest, dislike, execrate, have an aversion to, loathe, recoil from. ANTONYMS: be fond of, like, love. **2** (*to be unwilling or reluctant* (*to do something*)) be loath (to), be reluctant (to), be sorry (to), be unwilling (to), dislike (to), flinch (from), regret, shrink (from), shy away (from).

hateful *a.* (*causing hate; detestable*) abhorrent, detestable, foul, heinous, horrible, loathsome, nasty, obnoxious, odious, repellent, repugnant, repulsive, revolting, vile. ANTONYMS: agreeable, attractive, desirable, likeable, lovable, pleasant.

hatred *n.* (*great dislike or aversion*) abhorrence, animosity, antagonism, antipathy, aversion, detestation, dislike, enmity, hate, hostility, ill will, loathing, odium, repugnance, revulsion. ANTONYMS: adoration, affection, devotion, fondness, liking, love.

haughtiness *n.* (*the state of being haughty*) airs, airs and graces, arrogance, assumption, conceit, condescension, contempt, disdain, egotism, high-handedness, imperiousness, presumption, pride, scorn, self-importance, snobbishness, (*coll.*) snootiness, superciliousness, vanity. ANTONYMS: modesty, self-effacement.

haughty *a.* (*proud, arrogant*) arrogant, conceited, condescending, contemptuous, disdainful, egotistical, (*coll.*) high and mighty, high-handed, hoity-toity, imperious, (*coll.*) on one's high horse, overbearing, overweening, patronizing, presumptuous, proud, scornful, self-important, snobbish, (*coll.*) snooty, stuck-up, supercilious, (*coll.*) swollen-headed, vain. ANTONYMS: modest, self-effacing, unassuming.

haul *v.t.* **1** (*to pull or drag with force*) drag, draw, pull, tow, trail, tug. **2** (*to transport by dragging or in a lorry etc.*) carry, cart, convey, move, transport.

~*n.* **1** (*a hauling, a pull*) hauling, pull, tug. **2** (*an amount that is taken or stolen at once*) booty, catch, find, harvest, loot, spoils, takings, yield.

haulage *n.* (*transporting of goods*) carriage, conveyance, transport.

haunt *v.t.* **1** (*to visit* (*a place or person*) *frequently as a ghost or spirit*) visit, walk. **2** (*to frequent; to frequent the company of*) be a regular visitor to, frequent, hang around, (*sl.*) hang out in, visit frequently, visit regularly. **3** (*to recur to the mind of* (*a person*) *frequently in an irritating way*) beset, come back to haunt, obsess, oppress, plague, prey on, prey on the mind of, torment, weigh on, worry.

~*n.* (*a place which one often visits or frequents*) favourite spot, (*coll.*) hang-out, resort, stamping ground.

haunting *a.* (*having a lasting effect on the emotions; poignant*) atmospheric, disturbing, evocative, indelible, poignant, unforgettable, wistful.

have *v.t.* **1** (*to possess, to hold as owner*) have possession of, hold, own, possess. **2** (*to hold at one's disposal*) hold, keep, retain. ANTONYMS: give, give away. **3** (*to enjoy, to experience*) be subjected to, endure, enjoy, experience, go through, put up with, suffer, tolerate, undergo. **4** (*to give birth to; to have given birth to*) bear, be delivered of, bring into the world, give birth to, produce. **5** (*to receive, to get*) acquire, gain, get, obtain, procure, receive, secure, take. ANTONYMS: give. **6** (*to take for consumption; to eat or drink*) consume, drink, eat, take. **7** (*to require, to claim*) ask, bid, direct, get, order, request, require, tell. **8** (*to hold mentally, to retain*) cherish, entertain, feel, foster, harbour, have in mind, nurse. ANTONYMS: forget, put out of one's mind. **9** (*to show as an action*) demonstrate, display, exhibit, express, manifest, show. ANTONYMS: conceal, hide. **10** (*usu. neg.*) (*to tolerate, to entertain*) accept, allow, brook, endure, entertain, permit, put up with, stand, support, tolerate. **11** (*to hold as part, quality etc., to contain*) comprise, contain, embody, embrace, include, incorporate, take in. **12** (*to cheat*) cheat, deceive, diddle, (*coll.*) do, dupe, fool, outwit, swindle, take in, trick. **to have had it 1** (*to have let one's opportunity or moment go by*) have failed, have no chance, have no chance of success, have no hope. ANTONYMS: achieve success. **2** (*to have done something that will have serious consequences for one*) be about to be finished, (*coll.*) be for it, (*coll.*) be for the high jump, be in for a scolding. **3** (*to have been killed or overcome*) be

defeated, (*coll.*) be finished, have lost. ANTONYMS: be victorious, win. **4** (*to be exhausted*) be drained, be exhausted, be fatigued, (*coll.*) be knackered, be ready to drop, be shattered. ANTONYMS: be energetic, be fresh as a daisy. **to have on 1** (*to be wearing* (*something*)) be clad in, be clothed in, be dressed in, be wearing, sport, wear. **2** (*to have* (*something*) *planned*) have arranged, have on the agenda, have planned. **3** (*to deceive* (*someone*), *to trick* (*someone*)) deceive, play a hoax on, play a joke on, play a trick on, tease, trick, (*sl.*) wind up. **to have to** (*to be obliged to*) be bound to, be compelled to, be forced to, be obliged to, be under an obligation to, must, ought to, should. ANTONYMS: choose to, volunteer to.

haven *n.* **1** (*a port, a harbour*) anchorage, dock, harbour, moorage, port. **2** (*a refuge, an asylum*) asylum, refuge, retreat, sanctuary, sanctum, shelter.

havoc *n.* **1** (*widespread destruction; devastation*) carnage, damage, desolation, destruction, devastation, ruin, waste, wreckage. **2** (*chaos*) chaos, confusion, disorder, disorganization, disruption, mayhem, shambles. ANTONYMS: order, orderliness. **to play havoc with** (*to upset*) disrupt, ruin, spoil, upset, wreck.

hawk *v.t.* (*to carry about for sale, to try to sell*) market, peddle, sell, tout, vend. ANTONYMS: buy, purchase.

hawker *n.* (*a person who travels around selling goods in the street or from house to house*) door-to-door salesman, door-to-door salesperson, door-to-door saleswoman, door-to-door seller, huckster, pedlar.

haywire *a.* **to go haywire** (*to become chaotic*) become chaotic, be thrown into confusion, be thrown into disarray, break down, go out of control, go wild, go wrong.

hazard *n.* **1** (*a danger, a risk*) danger, jeopardy, menace, peril, pitfall, risk, threat. **2** (*chance*) accident, chance, fortuitousness, fortuity, luck. ANTONYMS: certainty.

hazardous *a.* **1** (*full of danger or risk*) danger-filled, dangerous, (*coll.*) dicey, fraught with danger, (*coll.*) hairy, insecure, menacing, perilous, precarious, risky, threatening, unsafe. ANTONYMS: safe, secure. **2** (*depending on chance*) chancy, haphazard, precarious, risky, uncertain, unpredictable. ANTONYMS: certain, predictable, sure.

haze *n.* **1** (*a very thin mist or vapour, usu. due to heat*) cloud, film, fog, mist, smog, vapour. ANTONYMS: brightness, clearness, transparency. **2** (*obscurity or indistinctness of perception, understanding etc.*) befuddlement, bewilderment, confusion, indistinctness, muddle, obscurity, vagueness. ANTONYMS: clarity, clearness, lucidity.

hazy *a.* **1** (*misty; thick with haze*) blurry, cloudy, filmy, foggy, misty, smoggy, smoky, steamy. ANTONYMS: clear, transparent. **2** (*vague, indistinct*) dim, fuzzy, ill-defined, indistinct, muddled, muzzy, nebulous, uncertain, unclear, vague. ANTONYMS: bright, clear, distinct, well-defined.

head[1] *n.* **1** (*the foremost part of the body of an animal, the uppermost in a human*) (*sl.*) bonce, (*coll.*) conk, cranium, crown, (*sl.*) loaf, (*sl.*) nut, (*facet.*) pate, poll, sconce, skull. **2** (*the upper part of anything, the top*) apex, crest, summit, tip, top, upper end, vertex. ANTONYMS: base, bottom, lower part, nadir. **3** (*the front part of a procession, column of troops etc.*) forefront, front, van, vanguard. ANTONYMS: back, rear. **4** (*the first or most honourable place, the forefront, the place of command*) command, control(s), directorship, forefront, headship, leadership, top. ANTONYMS: background, bottom. **5** (*a ruler or leader*) boss, chairman, chief, commander, controller, director, governor, headman/ woman, (*N Am., sl.*) honcho, leader, manager, managing director, master, premier, president, principal, ruler, superintendent, supervisor. **6** (*a head teacher of a school*) headmaster/ headmistress, head teacher, principal. **7** (*froth on liquor*) foam, froth, lather. **8** (*a promontory*) cape, foreland, headland, point, promontory. **9** (*a main division, a category*) category, class, classification, division, heading, section, subject, topic. **10** (*a culmination, a crisis*) climax, conclusion, crisis, critical point, crux, culmination, turning-point. **11** (*an aptitude for something specified*) ability, aptitude, capacity, faculty, flair, gift, mind, talent. **12** (*the mind, the intellect, esp. as distinguished from the feelings*) brain(s), (*coll.*) grey matter, intellect, intelligence, (*sl.*) loaf, mind, reasoning, understanding, wits. **13** (*the origin, the source*) beginning, commencement, fountainhead, origin, rise, source, start, wellspring.
~*a.* (*chief, principal*) arch, chief, foremost, front, highest, leading, main, premier, prime, principal, topmost. **head over heels** (*completely (in love)*) completely, fervently, intensely, (*coll.*) madly, passionately, thoroughly, utterly, wholeheartedly. ANTONYMS: mildly, partially, slightly. **to go to one's head 1** ((*of alcoholic drink*) *to make one slightly drunk*) intoxicate, make drunk, make tipsy, (*coll.*) make woozy. **2** ((*of success etc.*) *to make one vain, arrogant etc.*) make arrogant, make boastful, make conceited, make vain. **to keep one's head** (*to remain calm*) keep calm, keep control of

oneself, (*coll.*) keep one's cool, (*coll.*) stay cool, calm and collected. ANTONYMS: get excited, get hysterical, lose one's head. **to lose one's head** (*to be carried away by excitement*) (*coll.*) blow one's top, (*coll.*) fly off the handle, (*coll.*) freak out, get carried away, get flustered, get hysterical, lose control, (*coll.*) lose one's cool, panic. ANTONYMS: keep calm, keep control of oneself, keep one's head.

head[2] *v.t.* (*to lead, to direct*) be at the head of, be in charge of, be in command of, be in control of, command, control, direct, govern, guide, head up, lead, manage, rule, run, supervise.
~*v.i.* (*to go or tend in a direction*) aim for, go to, go towards, make a beeline for, make for, set out for, steer towards, turn towards. **to head off 1** (*to intercept, to get ahead of and turn back or aside*) cut off, deflect, divert, intercept, turn aside. **2** (*to forestall*) avert, baulk, check, fend off, forestall, prevent, stop, ward off. **to head up** (*to be in charge of* (*a team of people etc.*)) be at the head of, be in charge of, be in command of, be in control of, command, control, direct, govern, guide, lead, manage, rule, run, supervise.

headache *n.* **1** (*a neuralgic or other persistent pain in the head*) (*formal*) cephalalgia, migraine, sore head. **2** (*a source of worry*) bane, bother, inconvenience, nuisance, pest, problem, trouble, worry.

head first *adv.* **1** (*with the head in front* (*of a plunge*)) head foremost, headlong, on one's head. **2** (*precipitately*) carelessly, hastily, heedlessly, hurriedly, impetuously, impulsively, in haste, pell-mell, precipitately, rashly, recklessly, wildly, without thinking. ANTONYMS: after due consideration, carefully, deliberately, slowly.

heading *n.* **1** (*an inscription at the head of an article, chapter etc.*) caption, headline, name, title. **2** (*a division of the topics of a discourse*) category, class, classification, division, head, section, subject, topic.

headland *n.* (*a point of land projecting into the sea, a promontory*) cape, foreland, head, point, promontory.

headlong *adv.* **1** (*head first*) head first, head foremost, on one's head. ANTONYMS: feet first. **2** (*hastily, rashly*) carelessly, hastily, heedlessly, hurriedly, impetuously, impulsively, in haste, pell-mell, precipitately, rashly, recklessly, wildly, without thinking. ANTONYMS: after due consideration, carefully, deliberately, slowly.

headquarters *n.* (*the main office of an organization*) head office, HQ, main branch, main office. ANTONYMS: area office, branch office, local office, regional office.

headstone n. (*a stone at the head of a grave*) gravestone, memorial, tombstone.

headstrong a. (*obstinate, self-willed*) inflexible, intractable, intransigent, mulish, obdurate, obstinate, perverse, pig-headed, recalcitrant, refractory, self-willed, stiff-necked, stubborn, ungovernable, unruly, unyielding, wayward, wilful. ANTONYMS: manageable, pliant, tractable.

headway n. (*motion ahead, rate of progress*) advance, improvement, progress, way forward. **to make headway** (*to advance, to make progress*) advance, gain ground, get ahead, get on, go forward by leaps and bounds, make progress, make strides, make way, proceed, progress. ANTONYMS: lose ground, retrogress.

heady a. 1 (*intoxicating*) inebriating, intoxicating, spirituous, strong. 2 (*exciting, exhilarating*) exciting, exhilarating, invigorating, rousing, stimulating, thrilling. ANTONYMS: depressing. 3 (*impetuous*) hasty, impetuous, impulsive, precipitate, rash, reckless, thoughtless, wild. ANTONYMS: careful, thoughtful.

heal v.t. 1 (*to restore to health; to cure of* (*disease etc.*)) cure, make better, make well, mend, remedy, restore. ANTONYMS: injure, make ill, make worse, wound. 2 (*to reconcile* (*differences etc.*)) conciliate, harmonize, patch up, reconcile, settle. ANTONYMS: aggravate, exacerbate. 3 (*to end the suffering caused by*) allay, alleviate, ameliorate, appease, assuage, mitigate, palliate, soothe. ANTONYMS: aggravate, distress, hurt, make worse.

healing a. 1 (*tending to heal*) curative, medicinal, remedial, restorative, therapeutic. 2 (*soothing, mollifying*) alleviating, assuaging, mitigative, palliative, soothing. ANTONYMS: aggravating, exacerbating.

health n. 1 (*freedom from bodily or mental disease or decay*) fine fettle, fitness, good condition, good health, healthiness, robustness, soundness, strength, vigour, well-being. ANTONYMS: debility, disease, illness. 2 (*physical condition (good, bad etc.)*) condition, constitution, physical condition, physical state, state of health.

healthy a. 1 (*enjoying good health*) blooming, fit, hale and hearty, healthy, in fine fettle, in good condition, in good health, in good shape, in the pink, robust, strong, sturdy, vigorous, well. ANTONYMS: ailing, ill, infirm, unhealthy. 2 (*hale, sound*) disease-free, in good condition, in good health, sound, strong. ANTONYMS: diseased, unsound, weak. 3 ((*of food*) *promoting health*) beneficial, good for one, healthful, health-giving, nourishing, nutritious, wholesome. ANTONYMS: bad for one, unhealthy,

unwholesome. 4 ((*of a climate*) *promoting health*) bracing, invigorating, refreshing, salubrious. ANTONYMS: insalubrious, unhealthy.

heap n. 1 (*a pile or accumulation of many things placed or thrown one on another*) accumulation, aggregation, collection, hoard, lot, mass, mound, mountain, pile, stack, stockpile, store. 2 (*esp. in pl., coll.*) (*a large number, a lot*) abundance, a great deal, a lot, (*coll.*) lashings, (*coll.*) loads, mass, mint, (*coll.*) oceans, (*coll.*) oodles, plenty, (*coll.*) pots, quantities, (*coll.*) stacks, (*coll.*) tons. ANTONYMS: a few, a little, very few, very little. 3 (*esp. in pl., coll.*) (*a good many times*) a lot, frequently, often, very often.

~v.t. 1 (*to throw* (*together*) *or pile* (*up*) *in a heap*) accumulate, amass, collect, gather, hoard, pile (up), stack, stockpile, store. 2 (*to pile* (*upon*)) bestow (on/upon), confer (on/upon), give, load (on), shower (upon).

hear v.t. 1 (*to perceive by the ear, to perceive the sound of*) catch, eavesdrop on, (*coll.*) get, listen to, overhear, take in. 2 (*to listen to, to attend to*) attend to, listen to. ANTONYMS: ignore. 3 (*to listen to as a judge etc.*) examine, inquire into, investigate, judge, pass judgement on, try. 4 (*to be informed of by report*) be given to understand, be informed of, be told of, discover, find out, gather, (*coll.*) get wind of, hear tell, learn, understand.

hearing n. 1 (*the sense by which sound is perceived*) faculty of hearing, sense of hearing. 2 (*audience, attention*) audience, chance to speak, interview, opportunity to speak. 3 (*a judicial trial or investigation*) examination, inquest, inquiry, investigation, review, trial, tribunal. 4 (*earshot*) auditory range, earshot, hearing distance, hearing range, range of hearing.

hearsay n. (*common talk, report or gossip*) (*coll.*) buzz, gossip, idle talk, report, rumour, talk, the grapevine, tittle-tattle.

heart n. 1 (*the muscular central organ of the circulation of the blood*) (*coll.*) ticker. 2 (*the emotions or affections, esp. the passion of love*) affection, emotion, love, passion. ANTONYMS: apathy, coldness, indifference. 3 (*sensibility, tenderness*) benevolence, compassion, concern, humanity, pity, sympathy, tender feelings, tenderness. ANTONYMS: callousness, indifference, inhumanity. 4 (*ardour, spirit*) eagerness, enthusiasm, inclination, keenness, spirit. ANTONYMS: aversion, disinclination, reluctance. 5 (*courage*) boldness, bravery, courage, gumption, (*coll.*) guts, intrepidity, mettle, nerve, pluck, spirit, spunk, valour.

ANTONYMS: cowardice, cowardliness. **6** (*the central or most important part*) centre, core, crux, essence, hub, kernel, marrow, middle, nucleus, pith, quintessence. **at heart** (*in reality, at bottom*) at bottom, basically, essentially, fundamentally, in essence, in reality, intrinsically, really, truly. ANTONYMS: perfunctorily, superficially. **by heart** (*by rote, from memory*) by rote, from memory, off pat, parrot-fashion, pat, word for word. **from (the bottom of) one's heart 1** (*with absolute sincerity*) absolutely, sincerely, thoroughly, utterly, with all one's heart. **2** (*fervently*) deeply, devoutly, fervently, heartily, passionately, profoundly. ANTONYMS: apathetically, coolly, with detachment. **heart and soul** (*with full commitment, devotedly*) absolutely, completely, enthusiastically, entirely, gladly, thoroughly, wholeheartedly, zealously. ANTONYMS: apathetically, reluctantly. **to take heart** (*to pluck up courage*) (*coll.*) be bucked up, be cheered, be encouraged, be heartened, cheer up, (*coll.*) perk up. ANTONYMS: be cast down, be depressed. **with all one's heart** (*completely, utterly*) absolutely, completely, deeply, fervently, from the bottom of one's heart, heartily, passionately, profoundly, sincerely, thoroughly, utterly, wholeheartedly. ANTONYMS: apathetically, coolly, with detachment.

heartache *n.* (*anguish of mind*) agony of mind, anguish, distress, grief, heartbreak, hurt, misery, pain, sadness, suffering, torment, wretchedness. ANTONYMS: happiness, joy.

heartbreaking *a.* (*making one feel very sad and distressed*) agonizing, distressing, harrowing, heart-rending, hurtful, painful, pitiful, poignant, sad, tragic. ANTONYMS: cheerful, happy, joyful.

heartbroken *a.* (*extremely sad or disappointed*) broken-hearted, crestfallen, dejected, desolate, despondent, disappointed, disconsolate, dismal, downcast, grieved, grieving, in low spirits, miserable, sad, sorrowful, suffering, unhappy, wretched. ANTONYMS: cheerful, exuberant, happy, joyful, pleased.

hearten *v.t.* (*to encourage, to inspire*) animate, buck up, buoy up, energize, inspire, (*coll.*) pep up, revitalize, stimulate, uplift. ANTONYMS: cast down, discourage, dispirit.

heartfelt *a.* (*deeply felt, sincere*) ardent, deep, devout, earnest, fervent, genuine, honest, passionate, profound, sincere, unfeigned, warm, wholehearted. ANTONYMS: apathetic, false, feigned, half-hearted, insincere.

heartily *adv.* **1** (*sincerely*) cordially, deeply, feelingly, from the bottom of one's heart, profoundly, sincerely, warmly, wholeheartedly,

with all one's heart, with feeling. ANTONYMS: apathetically, half-heartedly, insincerely. **2** (*eagerly, with enthusiasm*) eagerly, energetically, enthusiastically, vigorously, with eagerness, with enthusiasm, zealously. **3** (*thoroughly, very much*) absolutely, thoroughly, totally, utterly, very much.

heartless *a.* (*having or showing no feeling or affection; cruel*) brutal, callous, cold, cold-hearted, cruel, hard, hard-hearted, harsh, inhuman, inhumane, merciless, pitiless, ruthless, uncaring, unfeeling, unkind, unsympathetic. ANTONYMS: caring, compassionate, kind, sympathetic, warm-hearted.

heart-rending *a.* (*heartbreaking, intensely afflictive*) agonizing, distressing, harrowing, heartbreaking, hurtful, painful, pitiful, poignant, sad, tragic. ANTONYMS: cheerful, happy, joyful.

heart-to-heart *n.* (*a conversation of a searching and intimate nature*) confidential chat, cosy chat, tête-à-tête.

~*a.* (*of a searching and intimate nature*) confidential, frank, intimate, open, personal.

heart-warming *a.* (*inspiring emotional approval*) affecting, cheering, encouraging, heartening, moving, touching, warming. ANTONYMS: depressing, discouraging, disheartening.

hearty *a.* **1** (*proceeding from the heart, sincere*) cordial, eager, earnest, effusive, enthusiastic, heartfelt, sincere, unreserved, warm, wholehearted. ANTONYMS: half-hearted, unenthusiastic. **2** (*abundant, satisfying*) abundant, ample, filling, large, sizeable, solid, substantial.

heat *n.* **1** (*hotness, the sensation produced by a hot body*) hotness, warmness, warmth. ANTONYMS: cold, coolness. **2** (*hot weather*) dog days, heatwave, high temperatures, hot spell, sultriness, torridity, torridness. ANTONYMS: cold, low temperatures. **3** (*vehemence; anger*) anger, fury, irritation, violence, wrath. **4** (*warmth of temperament; animation*) ardour, excitement, fervour, fire, intensity, passion, vehemence, warmth. ANTONYMS: apathy, coldness, indifference.

~*v.t.* **1** (*to make hot*) heat up, reheat, warm, warm up. ANTONYMS: cool, cool down. **2** (*to inflame; to excite*) agitate, anger, arouse, enrage, excite, inflame, rouse, stir up.

~*v.i.* (*to become hot*) get hot, get warm, heat up, warm. ANTONYMS: cool, cool down.

heated *a.* (*passionate, angry*) angry, bitter, enraged, excited, fiery, furious, impassioned, inflamed, intense, passionate, raging, stormy, vehement, violent. ANTONYMS: calm, peaceful, reasoned.

heathen n. 1 (*a non-believer, a pagan*) infidel, non-believer, pagan, unbeliever. 2 (*an unenlightened or barbarous person*) barbarian, savage.

heave v.t. 1 (*to lift, to raise, with effort*) heft, hoist, lever up, lift, raise. 2 (*to utter or force from the breast*) breathe, give, let out, utter. 3 (*to throw, to cast (something heavy)*) cast, (*coll.*) chuck, fling, hurl, let fly, pitch, send, (*coll.*) sling, throw, toss.

heaven n. 1 (*the sky; the atmosphere enveloping the earth*) firmament, sky. ANTONYMS: earth. 2 (*the abode of God or the gods and the blessed*) kingdom of God, life hereafter, next world, nirvana, paradise. ANTONYMS: hell. 3 (*something extremely pleasing*) bliss, ecstasy, joy, paradise, rapture, seventh heaven, supreme happiness, utopia. ANTONYMS: hell, misery.

heavenly a. 1 (*relating to the heavens, celestial*) celestial, cosmic, extraterrestrial. ANTONYMS: earthly, terrestrial. 2 (*inhabiting heaven; divine*) angelic, beatific, blessed, blest, celestial, cherubic, divine, holy, immortal, seraphic. ANTONYMS: earthly, human. 3 (*highly pleasing, delicious*) beautiful, delightful, (*coll.*) divine, enchanting, exquisite, glorious, ideal, lovely, marvellous, perfect, superb, wonderful. ANTONYMS: appalling, dreadful, horrible, miserable.

heavily adv. 1 (*awkwardly*) awkwardly, clumsily, ponderously, weightily. 2 (*with difficulty*) laboriously, with difficulty. ANTONYMS: easily, lightly. 3 (*utterly*) absolutely, completely, thoroughly, totally, utterly. ANTONYMS: partially, slightly. 4 (*to a great extent, to excess*) a great deal, considerably, excessively, greatly, to a great extent, to excess, very much. ANTONYMS: slightly, to some extent. 5 (*densely*) closely, compactly, densely, thickly. 6 (*deeply*) deeply, soundly.

heaviness n. 1 (*the state of having great weight*) bigness, bulkiness, heftiness, largeness, massiveness, might, weightiness. ANTONYMS: lightness, smallness. 2 (*the state of being dense*) density, solidity, thickness. ANTONYMS: lightness. 3 (*the state of requiring great effort*) arduousness, difficulty, hardness, laboriousness. ANTONYMS: easiness, effortlessness. 4 (*force, powerfulness*) force, forcefulness, hardness, might, mightiness, power, powerfulness, severity, strength, violence. ANTONYMS: lightness, slightness, weakness. 5 (*the state of being difficult to bear*) difficulty, hardness, intolerability, oppressiveness. ANTONYMS: easiness, lightness. 6 (*abundance*) abundance, copiousness, plentifulness, profuseness. ANTONYMS:

lightness, sparseness. 7 (*the state of being serious*) earnestness, gravity, profundity, solemnity, weightiness. ANTONYMS: flippancy, frivolity, triviality. 8 (*tedium*) boredom, dryness, dullness, tedium. ANTONYMS: amusement, entertainment, interest. 9 (*severity*) extremity, greatness, intensity, seriousness, severity. ANTONYMS: lightness, slightness. 10 (*drowsiness, dullness*) apathy, drowsiness, dullness, inactivity, indolence, inertia, lassitude, listlessness, sleepiness, sluggishness, torpor. ANTONYMS: activity, energy, liveliness. 11 (*dejection*) dejection, depression, dolefulness, gloom, melancholy, misery, sadness, sorrow, unhappiness. ANTONYMS: happiness, joy, merriment. 12 (*sternness*) hardness, harshness, sternness, strictness. ANTONYMS: gentleness, lenience. 13 (*muddiness*) marshiness, muddiness, stickiness. 14 (*darkness, cloudiness*) cloudiness, darkness, dullness, gloominess, greyness. ANTONYMS: brightness, clearness. 15 ((*of the sea*) *roughness, storminess*) roughness, storminess, tempestuousness, turbulence, wildness. ANTONYMS: calm, calmness.

heavy a. 1 (*having great weight, weighty*) big, bulky, burdensome, cumbersome, enormous, heavyweight, hefty, large, massive, mighty, onerous, substantial, unwieldy, weighty. ANTONYMS: light, lightweight, small. 2 (*of great density, dense*) dense, solid, thick. ANTONYMS: light. 3 (*powerful, forcible*) forceful, forcible, great, hard, mighty, powerful, severe, strong, violent. ANTONYMS: light, slight, weak. 4 (*requiring great effort, difficult*) arduous, demanding, difficult, exacting, hard, laborious. ANTONYMS: easy, effortless. 5 (*plentiful; large in amount*) abundant, considerable, copious, large, plentiful, profuse. ANTONYMS: few, small, sparse. 6 (*weighed down, loaded (with)*) burdened, encumbered, laden, loaded, weighted. 7 (*not easily borne, oppressive*) burdensome, difficult, hard, intolerable, onerous, oppressive, unbearable. ANTONYMS: easy, light. 8 (*stern, strict*) exacting, hard, harsh, stern, strict, unrelenting. ANTONYMS: gentle, lenient, mild. 9 (*drowsy, sluggish*) apathetic, drowsy, dull, inactive, indolent, listless, sleepy, sluggish, torpid. ANTONYMS: active, energetic, lively. 10 (*tedious*) boring, dry, dull, heavyweight, tedious, wearisome. ANTONYMS: amusing, interesting, light, lightweight. 11 (*depressing, depressed*) dejected, depressed, disconsolate, doleful, downcast, gloomy, melancholy, miserable, sad, sorrowful, unhappy. ANTONYMS: happy, joyful, merry. 12 (*excessively serious, sombre*) deep, earnest, grave, heavyweight, profound, serious, solemn, weighty. ANTONYMS: flippant, frivolous, lightweight, trivial. **13** (*severe*) extreme, great, intense, major, serious, severe. ANTONYMS: light, minor. **14** ((*of the ground*) *soft and wet*) boggy, clayey, clogged, difficult, marshy, muddy, sticky. **15** ((*of the sky, clouds etc.*) *threatening, louring*) cloudy, dark, dull, gloomy, grey, leaden, louring, overcast, threatening. ANTONYMS: bright, clear. **16** ((*of the sea*) *rough*) rough, stormy, tempestuous, turbulent, wild. ANTONYMS: calm. **17** ((*of weather*) *sultry*) humid, muggy, oppressive, sticky, sultry. ANTONYMS: cool, fresh. **18** (*of food*) *indigestible*) filling, solid, stodgy, substantial. ANTONYMS: light.

heavy-duty *a.* (*designed to sustain more than usual wear*) durable, hard-wearing, strong, sturdy, tough. ANTONYMS: flimsy.

heavy-handed *a.* **1** (*clumsy, awkward*) awkward, blundering, bungling, clumsy, graceless, (*coll.*) ham-fisted, (*coll.*) ham-handed, maladroit. ANTONYMS: adept, dexterous, graceful. **2** (*tactless*) insensitive, tactless, thoughtless, undiplomatic. ANTONYMS: diplomatic, sensitive, tactful. **3** (*oppressive*) autocratic, despotic, domineering, hard, harsh, oppressive, overbearing, stern, tyrannical. ANTONYMS: gentle, indulgent, lenient.

heavy-hearted *a.* (*dejected*) cast down, dejected, depressed, despondent, disconsolate, discouraged, dismal, downcast, downhearted, forlorn, melancholy, miserable, morose, mournful, sad, sorrowful. ANTONYMS: cheerful, happy, joyful.

heckle *v.t.* (*to interrupt* (*a public speaker*) *by deliberately inconvenient questions etc.*) barrack, disrupt, harass, interrupt, shout down.

hectic *a.* (*full of excitement; very busy*) bustling, busy, chaotic, confused, excited, exciting, fast and furious, fevered, flurried, frantic, frenetic, frenzied, tumultuous, very busy. ANTONYMS: calm, peaceful, quiet, tranquil.

hector *v.t.* (*to bully, to treat with insolence*) badger, browbeat, (*coll.*) bulldoze, bully, coerce, cow, intimidate, ride roughshod over, threaten.
~*v.i.* (*to play the bully, to bluster*) bluster, boast, brag, (*coll.*) huff and puff, rant.

hedge *n.* **1** (*a fence of bushes or small trees*) hedgerow, quickset. **2** (*a barrier of any kind*) barrier, protection, screen, windbreak. **3** (*a means of securing oneself against loss*) cover, guard, insurance, protection, safeguard, shield.
~*v.t.* **1** (*to surround or enclose with a hedge*) circle, encircle, enclose, fence, surround. **2** (*to

surround or enclose as with a hedge*) confine, hem in, hinder, impede, limit, obstruct, restrict. **3** (*to secure oneself against loss* (*on a speculation etc.*)) cover, guard, insure, protect, safeguard, shield.
~*v.i.* (*to act in a shifty way, to avoid making a decisive statement*) be ambivalent, beat about the bush, be evasive, beg the question, dodge the issue, dodge the question, equivocate, (*coll.*) flannel, hum and haw, prevaricate, pussyfoot around, quibble, sidestep the issue, temporize, (*coll.*) waffle. ANTONYMS: be decisive.

hedonism *n.* **1** (*the doctrine or belief that pleasure is the chief good*) epicurism, sybaritism. **2** (*behaviour motivated by this*) pleasure-seeking, pursuit of pleasure, self-indulgence, sensualism.

hedonistic *a.* **1** (*of or relating to hedonism*) epicurean, sybaritic. **2** (*pleasure-seeking*) pleasure-seeking, self-indulgent, sensualist.

heed *v.t.* (*to pay attention to, to take notice of*) attend to, bear in mind, be heedful of, consider, follow, listen to, mind, note, obey, observe, pay attention to, take heed of, take into account, take into consideration, take note of, take notice of, turn a deaf ear to. ANTONYMS: disobey, disregard, ignore.
~*n.* (*care, attention*) attention, attentiveness, care, caution, consideration, heedfulness, mindfulness, note, notice, regard, watchfulness. ANTONYMS: carelessness, disregard, inattention, neglect.

heedful *a.* (*attentive, regardful* (*of*)) attentive, careful, cautious, chary, mindful, vigilant, wary. ANTONYMS: careless, heedless.

heedless *a.* **1** (*thoughtless*) careless, foolhardy, incautious, precipitate, rash, reckless, thoughtless, unthinking. ANTONYMS: careful, cautious, circumspect. **2** (*negligent* (*of*)) careless, inattentive, negligent, regardless, unmindful, unwary.

heel[1] *n.* **to take to one's heels** (*to run away*) escape, flee, (*sl.*) hotfoot it, run away, run off, show a clean pair of heels, (*coll.*) skedaddle, (*sl.*) split, take flight, (*N Am., sl.*) vamoose.

heel[2] *v.i.* ((*of a ship*) *to incline or cant over to one side*) cant, careen, incline, keel, lean, list, tilt, tip.

hefty *a.* **1** (*strong, muscular*) beefy, big, brawny, burly, heavy, hulking, large, powerful, powerfully-built, robust, stout, strapping, strong, sturdy. ANTONYMS: feeble, slight, thin, weak, (*coll.*) weedy. **2** (*forceful*) forceful, hard, heavy, mighty, powerful, violent. ANTONYMS: light, slight. **3** (*large and heavy*) big, bulky, cumbersome, heavy, large, unwieldy, weighty. ANTONYMS: light. **4** (*big*) big, considerable, large, sizeable, substantial. ANTONYMS: insignificant, small, tiny.

height *n.* **1** (*the distance of the top above the foot or foundation*) elevation, highness, stature, tallness. **2** (*an eminence, a summit*) cliff, eminence, hill, mountain, peak, rise, summit. **3** (*the fullest extent or degree*) acme, limit, ne plus ultra, utmost limit, uttermost, very limit. **4** (*the highest or most extreme point*) apex, climax, crowning point, culmination, high point, peak, top, zenith. ANTONYMS: bottom, low point, nadir.

heighten *v.t.* **1** (*to make high or higher, to raise*) elevate, lift, make higher, raise. ANTONYMS: lower. **2** (*to increase, to enhance*) elevate, enhance, exalt, improve, increase, magnify, raise. ANTONYMS: decrease, lower, reduce. **3** (*to intensify, to accentuate*) add to, aggravate, amplify, augment, increase, intensify, magnify, strengthen. ANTONYMS: detract from, lower, reduce.

heinous *a.* (*abominable; wicked in the highest degree*) abhorrent, abominable, atrocious, awful, despicable, detestable, evil, execrable, hateful, hideous, horrible, iniquitous, loathsome, monstrous, nefarious, odious, outrageous, reprehensible, revolting, shocking, unspeakable.

heir *n.* (*a person who succeeds another in the possession of property or rank*) beneficiary, inheritor, legatee, next in line, scion, successor.

heiress *n.* (*a woman who succeeds another in the possession of property or rank*) beneficiary, inheritor, inheritress, inheritrix, legatee, next in line, scion, successor.

hell *n.* **1** (*the place of punishment for the wicked after death in Christianity, Judaism and Islam*) abode of the damned, bottomless pit, Hades, hellfire, underworld. ANTONYMS: heaven. **2** (*a place of extreme suffering; torture*) affliction, agony, anguish, misery, suffering, torment, torture, tribulation, woe. ANTONYMS: bliss, heaven. **3** (*punishment, castigation*) castigation, censure, punishment, reprimand, scolding, upbraiding, vituperation. **hell for leather** (*very fast*) at the double, fast, hotfoot, hurriedly, (*coll.*) like a bat out of hell, pell-mell, post haste, rapidly, speedily, swiftly.

hellish *a.* **1** (*of or relating to hell*) damnable, damned, demonic, devilish, diabolical, fiendish, infernal, satanic. ANTONYMS: celestial, heavenly. **2** (*detestable*) abominable, accursed, atrocious, cruel, evil, execrable, hateful,

horrible, monstrous, nefarious, vicious, wicked. ANTONYMS: agreeable, pleasant.

helm *n.* **at the helm** (*in control, at the head*) at the head, at the wheel, in authority, in charge, in command, in control, in the driving seat.

help *v.t.* **1** (*to provide with something needed or wanted to achieve an end; to assist*) aid, assist, be of service to, be useful to, lend (someone) a hand, lend (someone) a helping hand, succour. ANTONYMS: hinder, impede, obstruct. **2** (*to contribute to*) aid, assist, back, boost, contribute to, support. **3** (*to improve* (*a situation etc.*)) alleviate, ameliorate, cure, ease, facilitate, heal, improve, mitigate, relieve, remedy, restore, soothe. ANTONYMS: aggravate, exacerbate, make worse. **4** (*to remedy, to prevent*) abstain from, avoid, hinder, keep from, prevent, stop. ~*n.* **1** (*the act of helping; the fact of being helped*) aid, assistance, guidance, helping hand, service, succour, support, use. ANTONYMS: hindrance, impediment, obstruction. **2** (*a person hired for a job, esp. a farm worker or domestic servant*) assistant, employee, hand, helper, worker. **3** (*succour, relief*) alleviation, amelioration, balm, cure, ease, improvement, mitigation, relief, remedy, restorative, salve, succour. ANTONYMS: aggravation, exacerbation.

helper *n.* (*a person who gives assistance*) aide, assistant, auxiliary, deputy, girl/ Man Friday, helpmate, henchman, right-hand man/ woman, (*coll.*) sidekick.

helpful *a.* **1** (*giving help, useful*) advantageous, beneficial, constructive, favourable, instrumental, of service, of use, practical, productive, profitable, useful, valuable. ANTONYMS: destructive, disadvantageous, unfavourable, unproductive, useless. **2** (*obliging*) accommodating, benevolent, caring, charitable, cooperative, friendly, kind, obliging, supportive. ANTONYMS: obstructive, unfriendly, unhelpful, unkind.

helping *n.* (*a portion of food given at table*) bowlful, piece, plateful, portion, ration, serving.

helpless *a.* **1** (*lacking power to help oneself*) bed-ridden, debilitated, defenceless, dependent, feeble, impotent, incapable, incompetent, infirm, invalid, powerless, unfit, vulnerable, weak. ANTONYMS: capable, competent, fit, strong. **2** (*without help*) abandoned, defenceless, destitute, exposed, forlorn, unprotected, vulnerable. ANTONYMS: protected, under protection.

hem *n.* (*the edge or border of a garment or piece of cloth, esp. when doubled and sewn in*) binding, border, edge, edging, flounce, frill, fringe, trim, trimming.

~v.t. **1** (*to double over and sew in the border of*) bind, edge, trim. **2** (*to enclose or shut* (*in, about or round*)) close in, confine, encircle, enclose, hedge in, pen in, restrain, shut in, surround.

henceforth *adv.* (*from this time on*) after this, from now on, from this day forward/ on, from this time forward/ on, hereafter, in future, in the future, subsequently.

henchman *n.* (*a faithful follower or supporter*) aide, assistant, flunkey, follower, girl/ Man Friday, lackey, minion, right-hand man/ woman, (*coll.*) sidekick, subordinate, supporter.

henpeck *v.t.* ((*of a woman*) *to harass* (*a man, esp. her husband*) *by constant nagging*) bully, carp at, domineer, go on at, harass, (*coll.*) hassle, nag, scold.

herald *n.* (*a harbinger, a precursor*) forerunner, harbinger, indication, indicator, omen, precursor, sign, signal, usher.
~v.t. **1** (*to announce publicly*) advertise, announce, broadcast, make known, make public, publicize, publish, trumpet. ANTONYMS: conceal, hush up, keep secret. **2** (*to introduce, to usher in*) augur, be the forerunner of, be the precursor of, foreshadow, harbinger, indicate, pave the way for, portend, precede, presage, show in, signal, usher in.

Herculean *a.* (*exceedingly difficult or dangerous* (*as the labours of Hercules*)) arduous, demanding, difficult, exacting, formidable, gruelling, hard, heavy, laborious, onerous, prodigious, strenuous, taxing, tough, uphill. ANTONYMS: easy, effortless, simple.

herd *n.* **1** (*a number of beasts or cattle, kept or driven together*) drove, flock, pack. **2** (*a crowd of people, a rabble*) crowd, drove, flock, horde, host, mass, mob, multitude, pack, swarm, throng. **3** (*a keeper of a herd*) cattle herder, cattle owner, cattle raiser, cowherd, drover, goatherd, herdsman, rancher, shepherd.
~v.i. (*to go in herds or companies*) assemble, collect, congregate, flock, gather, get together, huddle, muster, rally.
~v.t. **1** (*to tend or watch* (*cattle etc.*)) guard, keep watch over, look after, stand guard over, take care of, tend, watch. **2** (*to drive in a herd*) drive, force, guide, lead, round up, shepherd, urge. **the herd** (*the masses*) mob, populace, (*coll., derog.*) proles, rabble, riff-raff, (*coll.*) the great unwashed, the hoi polloi, the masses, the plebs. ANTONYMS: aristocracy, (*coll.*) the upper crust.

hereafter *adv.* (*for the future*) after this, from now on, from this day on, from this time on, henceforth, in future, in the future. ANTONYMS: thereafter.
~n. (*the future life*) afterlife, afterworld, heaven, life after death, next world.

hereditary *a.* **1** (*descending or passing by inheritance*) ancestral, bequeathed, family, handed down, inherited, willed. **2** (*transmitted by descent from generation to generation*) congenital, familial, family, genetic, inborn, inbred, transmissible.

heredity *n.* (*genetically transmitted characteristics*) congenital characteristics, genetic constitution, genetic make-up.

heresy *n.* (*departure from what is held to be true doctrine*) agnosticism, apostasy, atheism, dissension, dissent, dissidence, heterodoxy, idolatry, nonconformity, recusancy, revisionism, scepticism, schism, sectarianism, separatism, unbelief, unorthodoxy. ANTONYMS: belief, conformity, faith, orthodoxy.

heretic *n.* (*a person who holds unorthodox opinions, esp. in religious matters*) agnostic, apostate, atheist, dissenter, dissident, idolater, nonconformist, recusant, renegade, revisionist, sceptic, schismatic, separatist, unbeliever. ANTONYMS: believer, conformist.

heretical *a.* (*of or relating to heresy*) agnostic, atheistic, dissident, heterodox, idolatrous, nonconformist, recusant, renegade, revisionist, sceptical, schismatic, separatist, unorthodox. ANTONYMS: conformist, orthodox.

heritage *n.* **1** (*land or other property that passes by descent to an heir*) bequest, birthright, endowment, estate, inheritance, legacy, patrimony. **2** (*anything passed from one generation to another*) ancestry, inheritance, legacy, tradition.

hermetic *a.* (*having an airtight closure*) airtight, sealed, shut tight.

hermit *n.* (*any person living in solitary contemplation*) anchorite, ascetic, eremite, recluse, solitary, stylite.

hero *n.* **1** (*a person of extraordinary valour or fortitude*) champion, conqueror, exemplar, knight in shining armour, lion, role model, victor. **2** (*the principal male character in a novel, film etc.*) lead actor, leading man, male lead, principal male character. **3** (*a person who is greatly admired*) heart-throb, ideal man, idol.

heroic *a.* **1** (*having the qualities or attributes of a hero*) bold, brave, courageous, daring, dauntless, doughty, fearless, gallant, intrepid, lion-hearted, undaunted, valiant, valorous. ANTONYMS: cowardly, craven, timid. **2** (*relating to or describing the deeds of heroes*) epic, legendary. **3** ((*of language*) *high-flown or* *bombastic*) bombastic, exaggerated, extravagant, grandiloquent, grandiose, high-flown, high-sounding, orotund, pretentious, rhetorical, turgid. ANTONYMS: plain, simple.

heroine *n.* **1** (*a heroic woman*) amazon, champion, conqueror, exemplar, victor, virago. **2** (*the principal female character in a novel, film etc.*) female lead, leading lady, principal female character.

heroism *n.* (*extreme bravery*) boldness, courage, courageousness, daring, fearlessness, gallantry, intrepidity, mettle, valour. ANTONYMS: cowardice, timidity.

hero-worship *n.* (*excessive devotion shown to a person who is regarded as a hero*) admiration, adoration, adulation, idealization, idolization, putting on a pedestal, veneration, worship. ANTONYMS: contempt, scorn.

hesitance *n.* **1** (*doubt, vacillation in doing something*) diffidence, doubt, doubtfulness, dubiety, indecision, indecisiveness, irresolution, oscillation, reluctance, shyness, timidity, uncertainty, unsureness, vacillation, wavering. ANTONYMS: certainty, decisiveness, resolution. **2** (*stammering in speaking*) faltering, hesitation, slowness, stammering, stumbling, stuttering. ANTONYMS: articulacy, fluency.

hesitant *a.* **1** (*hesitating, undecided*) diffident, doubtful, dubious, indecisive, irresolute, reluctant, shy, timid, uncertain, unsure, vacillating, wavering. ANTONYMS: confident, decisive, enthusiastic, firm, positive, resolute, sure, unhesitating. **2** (*stammering in speech*) faltering, halting, hesitant, slow, stammering, stumbling, stuttering. ANTONYMS: articulate, confident, fluent.

hesitate¹ *v.i.* **1** (*to stop or pause in action*) dally, delay, (*coll.*) dilly-dally, hang back, pause, stall, stop, temporize, wait. ANTONYMS: act, proceed. **2** (*to be doubtful or undecided*) be doubtful, be indecisive, be irresolute, be uncertain, be undecided, dither, have doubts, oscillate, shilly-shally, vacillate, waver. ANTONYMS: be decisive, be positive, be resolute, have no doubts. **3** (*to be reluctant (to*)) baulk (at), be reluctant (to), be unwilling (to), demur (at), have misgivings (about), have qualms (about), have scruples (about). ANTONYMS: be certain (about), be enthusiastic (about), be willing (to). **4** (*to stammer*) be hesitant, falter, halt, stammer, stumble, stutter. ANTONYMS: be articulate, be fluent.

hesitation *n.* **1** (*delay*) delay, (*coll.*) dilly-dallying, pause, stalling, wait, waiting-period. **2** (*uncertainty or doubt*) dithering, doubt, doubtfulness, indecision, indecisiveness,

irresolution, oscillation, shilly-shallying, uncertainty, vacillation, wavering. ANTONYMS: decisiveness, resolution. **3** (*reluctance*) demurral, disinclination, misgivings, qualms, reluctance, scruples, unwillingness. ANTONYMS: certainty, enthusiasm, willingness. **4** (*hesitance, stammering*) faltering, slowness, stammering, stumbling, stuttering. ANTONYMS: articulacy, fluency.

hew *v.t.* **1** (*to cut (down, away etc.) with an axe etc.*) chop, cut, fell, hack, lop, saw. **2** (*to make or fashion with toil and exertion*) carve, fashion, form, model, sculpt, sculpture, shape.

heyday *n.* (*the time of greatest vigour, prosperity etc.*) bloom, crowning point, culmination, full flowering, peak, pinnacle, prime, prime of life.

hiatus *n.* **1** (*a gap, a break in a manuscript, connected series etc.*) aperture, breach, break, chasm, discontinuity, gap, hole, interruption, lacuna, opening, rift, space. **2** (*a break or interruption in an activity*) break, intermission, interruption, interval, lull, pause, rest.

hibernate *v.i.* **1** ((*of some animals) to pass the winter in sleep or torpor*) lie dormant, overwinter, sleep, winter. **2** (*to live in seclusion or remain inactive at a time of stress*) (*N Am., coll.*) hole up, lie low, stagnate, vegetate.

hidden *a.* **1** (*difficult to see or find; concealed*) concealed, covered, not on view, not visible, out of sight, secret, unrevealed, unseen. ANTONYMS: obvious, on view, visible. **2** (*not easily noticed; secret*) abstruse, arcane, concealed, covert, cryptic, indistinct, mysterious, obscure, occult, recondite, secret, ulterior, unclear, vague, veiled. ANTONYMS: clear, obvious, transparent.

hide¹ *v.t.* **1** (*to put out of or withhold from sight or observation*) conceal, secrete, stow away. ANTONYMS: display, exhibit, reveal, show. **2** (*to obscure from view, to cover up*) blot out, cloak, cloud, conceal, cover up, darken, eclipse, obscure, screen, shroud, veil. ANTONYMS: expose. **3** (*to keep secret, to withhold from knowledge*) conceal, hush up, keep dark, keep mum about, keep secret, (*coll.*) keep (something) under one's hat, mask, suppress, veil, withhold. ANTONYMS: disclose, divulge, reveal.
~*v.i.* (*to lie concealed, to conceal oneself*) go into hiding, go to ground, go underground, (*N Am., coll.*) hole up, keep out of sight, lie low, take cover.

hide² *n.* (*the skin of an animal, esp. when dressed*) coat, fur, pelt, skin.

hidebound *a.* (*narrow-minded, obstinate*) bigoted, inflexible, intolerant, narrow, narrow-minded, prejudiced, reactionary, rigid, set, set

in one's ways, ultra-conventional, uncompromising. ANTONYMS: broad-minded, flexible,
tolerant.

hideout n. (a place where someone can hide
or take refuge) den, hideaway, hiding place,
refuge, retreat, sanctuary, shelter.

hiding n. (a thrashing, a flogging) beating,
caning, flogging, (coll.) licking, spanking,
thrashing, (coll.) walloping, whipping.

†**hie** v.i., v.refl. (to hasten, to hurry) dash,
hasten, hurry, rush, speed.

hierarchy n. (a system of persons or things
arranged in a graded order) grading, pecking
order, ranking.

hieroglyphics n. (hieroglyphic writing; hiero-
glyphs) cipher, code, cryptogram, scrawl,
scribble.

high a. 1 (rising or extending upwards for or to
a great extent) elevated, lofty, soaring, tall,
towering. ANTONYMS: low, short. 2 (exalted in
rank or position) chief, distinguished, eminent, exalted, high-ranking, illustrious, important, influential, leading, main, major, notable,
powerful, principal, prominent, ruling, superior, top. ANTONYMS: low, lowly, low-ranking,
minor, undistinguished, unimportant. 3 (of
noble character or purpose; exalted in quality)
high-minded, lofty, moral, noble, virtuous.
ANTONYMS: base, ignoble. 4 (proud, lofty in tone
or temper) arrogant, boastful, haughty, lofty,
lordly, overbearing, proud. ANTONYMS: diffident, modest. 5 (extreme, intense) extreme,
forceful, great, intense, powerful, strong,
violent. ANTONYMS: mild, slight. 6 (expensive,
costly (in price)) costly, dear, excessive, exorbitant, expensive, extortionate, high-priced,
inflated, (coll.) steep. ANTONYMS: cheap, low,
low-priced. 7 ((of a sound) of a high frequency,
acute in pitch) acute, high-frequency, high-
pitched, penetrating, piercing, piping, sharp,
shrill, soprano, treble. ANTONYMS: alto, bass,
deep, gruff, low. 8 ((esp. of meat) tainted, approaching putrefaction) bad, (coll.) niffy, off,
(coll.) ponging, rotten, rotting, smelling,
tainted. 9 (intoxicated by alcohol or drugs,
coll.) delirious, drugged, (coll.) freaked out,
hallucinating, inebriated, intoxicated, (sl.)
loaded, (coll.) on a trip, (dated sl.) spaced-out,
(sl.) stoned, (coll.) tripping, (sl.) zonked. 10 (in
an animated or hysterical state, coll.) animated,
boisterous, bouncy, ebullient, elated, excited,
exhilarated, high-spirited, hysterical, in high
spirits, joyful, merry, overexcited. ANTONYMS:
depressed, in low spirits, melancholy. 11 ((of
an opinion of someone) favourable) admiring,
approving, favourable, good. ANTONYMS: poor,
unfavourable. 12 ((of a way of life) extravagant,

luxurious) extravagant, grand, lavish, luxurious, rich. ANTONYMS: mean, modest, poor.
~adv. (to a great altitude, aloft) aloft, far up, on
high, way up. ANTONYMS: low, low down.
~n. 1 (the highest level, the highest point) apex,
height, peak, pinnacle, summit, top, zenith.
2 (a state of euphoria, esp. one due to intoxication with drugs) delirium, (sl.) freak-out, state
of euphoria, state of intoxication, (coll.) trip.

high and dry adv. (left behind, stranded without resources) abandoned, helpless, marooned,
stranded.

high and low adv. (everywhere) all over,
everywhere, exhaustively, extensively, far and
wide, leaving no stone unturned.

high and mighty a. (arrogant) arrogant,
conceited, condescending, disdainful, egotistic, haughty, imperious, overbearing, proud,
self-important, stuck-up, supercilious, superior. ANTONYMS: modest, self-effacing.

high-born a. (of noble birth) aristocratic, blue-
blooded, born with a silver spoon in one's
mouth, noble, noble-born, of noble birth,
patrician, well-born. ANTONYMS: low-born,
lowly, of peasant stock.

highbrow n. (an intellectual or cultural
person) (coll.) egghead, intellectual, scholar.
ANTONYMS: idiot, lowbrow, philistine.
~a. (intellectual, cultural) bookish, cultivated,
cultured, intellectual, scholarly. ANTONYMS:
ignorant, lowbrow, philistine.

high-class a. (of high quality, refined) A1,
choice, (coll.) classy, de luxe, first-rate, high-
quality, (coll.) posh, select, superior, top-flight,
upmarket, upper-class. ANTONYMS: cheap, inferior, low-class, low-quality, mediocre.

high-coloured a. ((of the complexion) having
a strong deep colour, flushed) blushing, florid,
flushed, pale, red-faced, rosy-cheeked, rubicund, ruddy, wan.

highfalutin a. (bombastic, affected) affected,
grandiose, high-flown, high-sounding, pompous, pretentious, supercilious, (coll.) swanky.
ANTONYMS: plain, simple.

high-flown a. ((of language, style etc.) turgid,
bombastic) bombastic, elaborate, exaggerated,
extravagant, flowery, grandiloquent, grandiose, (coll.) highfalutin, high-sounding, inflated, lofty, ornate, pretentious, turgid.
ANTONYMS: down-to-earth, plain, simple,
straightforward, unpretentious.

high-handed a. (overbearing, domineering)
arbitrary, arrogant, autocratic, bossy, despotic,
dictatorial, domineering, imperious, oppressive, overbearing, peremptory, tyrannical.
ANTONYMS: democratic, unassuming.

highlight n. (*a moment or event of particular importance or interest*) best part, climax, feature, focal point, focus, high point, high spot. ANTONYMS: low point.
~*v.t.* (*to put emphasis on*) accent, accentuate, call attention to, emphasize, focus attention on, give emphasis to, give prominence to, place emphasis on, play up, point up, spotlight, stress, underline. ANTONYMS: ignore, neglect, play down.

highly adv. **1** (*in a high degree, extremely*) decidedly, eminently, exceptionally, extraordinarily, extremely, greatly, immensely, intensely, supremely, to a great extent, to a marked degree, (*coll.*) tremendously, vastly, very much. ANTONYMS: slightly. **2** (*honourably, favourably*) admiringly, appreciatively, approvingly, favouringly, warmly, well, with approbation. ANTONYMS: unfavourably, with disapprobation.

highly strung a. (*of a nervous and tense disposition*) edgy, excitable, nervous, nervy, neurotic, on edge, overwrought, stressed, temperamental, tense, (*sl.*) wired. ANTONYMS: calm, tranquil.

high-minded a. (*magnanimous, having high moral principles*) ethical, good, honourable, moral, noble, noble-minded, principled, righteous, upright, virtuous. ANTONYMS: bad, immoral, unethical.

high-powered a. (*important or influential*) aggressive, ambitious, assertive, driving, dynamic, effective, energetic, enterprising, forceful, go-ahead, go-getting, important, influential, vigorous. ANTONYMS: ineffective, lazy, unambitious.

high-pressure a. ((*of selling*) *persuasive in an aggressive and persistent manner*) aggressive, coercive, forceful, high-powered, importunate, insistent, persistent, persuasive, (*coll.*) pushy.

high-priced a. (*expensive, costly*) costly, dear, exorbitant, expensive, extortionate, pricey. ANTONYMS: cheap, low-cost.

high-sounding a. (*pompous, ostentatious*) affected, bombastic, elaborate, exaggerated, extravagant, flowery, grandiloquent, grandiose, (*coll.*) highfalutin, high-flown, inflated, ornate, ostentatious, pompous, pretentious, turgid. ANTONYMS: down-to-earth, plain, simple, straightforward, unpretentious.

high-speed a. (*moving or operating at a high speed*) express, fast, quick, rapid, souped-up, speedy, swift. ANTONYMS: slow.

high-spirited a. (*very lively*) animated, boisterous, bouncy, buoyant, ebullient, effervescent, energetic, exuberant, full of life, lively, sparky, spirited, vibrant, vivacious. ANTONYMS: depressed, in low spirits, listless.

high spirits n.pl. (*cheerfulness, liveliness*) animation, boisterousness, bounce, buoyancy, ebullience, effervescence, exhilaration, exuberance, hilarity, liveliness, vitality, vivacity. ANTONYMS: depression, melancholy.

hijack v.t. (*to take over (a vehicle, aircraft etc.) by force, esp. to divert it from its route*) commandeer, expropriate, seize, skyjack, take over.

hike n. **1** (*a ramble, a long country walk*) ramble, tramp, trek, walk. **2** (*an increase, e.g. in prices*) increase, rise. ANTONYMS: decrease, lowering, reduction.
~*v.i.* (*to go for a hike*) backpack, ramble, tramp, trek, walk.
~*v.t.* **1** (*to hoist; to hitch up*) hitch, hoist, lift, pull up, raise. **2** (*to increase (prices etc.)*) increase, jack up, put up, raise. ANTONYMS: decrease, lower, reduce.

hilarious a. **1** (*extremely funny*) amusing, comical, entertaining, funny, humorous, side-splitting, uproarious. ANTONYMS: grave, serious. **2** (*cheerful, merry*) cheerful, convivial, exhilarated, exuberant, happy, jolly, jovial, joyful, lively, merry, mirthful, noisy, uproarious. ANTONYMS: dull, quiet, sad, sedate.

hilariousness n. **1** (*extreme humorousness*) amusement, comicalness, entertainment, funniness, humorousness, humour, uproariousness. ANTONYMS: gravity, seriousness. **2** (*cheerfulness, merriness*) cheerfulness, conviviality, exhilaration, exuberance, gaiety, glee, happiness, high spirits, jollity, joviality, joy, joyfulness, laughter, levity, merriment, mirth, noisiness, uproariousness. ANTONYMS: dullness, quietness, sadness, sedateness.

hill n. **1** (*a noticeable natural elevation on the surface of the earth*) elevation, eminence, fell, height, hillock, hummock, knoll, mound, mount, prominence, ridge, rise, rising ground. **2** (*a heap, a mound*) heap, mound, mountain, pile, stack. **3** (*a sloping stretch of road, an incline*) acclivity, gradient, incline, rise, slope.

hilt n. (*the handle of a sword, dagger etc.*) grip, haft, handgrip, handle, shaft. **up to the hilt** (*to the fullest extent*) all the way, completely, entirely, fully, totally, wholly. ANTONYMS: partially, partly.

hind a. (*relating to or situated at the back or rear*) back, hinder, hindmost, posterior, rear. ANTONYMS: front.

hinder v.t. (*to impede, to prevent from proceeding or moving*) block, check, curb, delay, deter, foil, forestall, frustrate, hamper, hamstring, handicap, hold back, hold up, impede, inhibit, interfere with, interrupt, obstruct, prevent, retard, slow down, stop, stymie, thwart, trammel. ANTONYMS: accelerate, advance, facilitate, further, help, promote.

hindermost *a.* (*last in position, furthest back*) back, endmost, last, rear, rearmost, terminal. ANTONYMS: front.

hindrance *n.* (*that which hinders; an impediment*) bar, barrier, block, check, curb, deterrent, difficulty, drawback, encumbrance, handicap, hitch, impediment, inhibition, interference, interruption, obstacle, obstruction, stoppage, stumbling-block. ANTONYMS: aid, boost, encouragement, help.

hinge *v.i.* (*to depend* (*upon*)) be contingent (on), be subject (to), centre (on), depend (on), hang (on), pivot (on), rest (on), revolve (around), turn (on).

hint *n.* **1** (*a slight or distant allusion*) allusion, clue, indication, inkling, innuendo, insinuation, intimate, mention, suggestion, tip-off, whisper, word to the wise. **2** (*a small piece of helpful or practical information*) helpful suggestion, piece of advice, pointer, suggestion, tip. **3** (*a small amount* (*of*)*; a trace*) breath, dash, soupçon, speck, sprinkling, suggestion, suspicion, taste, tinge, touch, trace, whiff, whisper.
~*v.t.* (*to mention indirectly, to allude to*) allude to, give (someone) a clue about, give (someone) a tip-off about, imply, indicate, insinuate, intimate, let it be known that, make an allusion to, mention, suggest, tip (someone) off about.

hippy *n.* (*a member of the youth culture of the 1960s, which stressed universal love and brotherhood*) beatnik, bohemian, flower child, flower person.

hire *n.* **1** (*the act of hiring or the state of being hired*) charter, lease, rent, rental. **2** (*the price paid for labour or services or the use of things*) charge, fee, pay, price, salary, wage.
~*v.t.* **1** (*to procure the temporary use of for an agreed payment*) charter, engage, lease, rent. **2** (*to employ* (*a person*) *for a stipulated payment*) appoint, commission, employ, engage, sign on, sign up, take on.

hirsute *a.* (*rough or hairy*) bearded, bristly, hairy, rough, shaggy, unshaven. ANTONYMS: bald, clean-shaven, smooth.

hiss *v.i.* **1** ((*of a person or animal*) *to make a sound like that of the letter 's', to make a sibilant sound*) buzz, sibilate, whistle. **2** ((*esp. of a crowd or audience*) *to express disapproval by*

making such a sound) (*coll.*) blow raspberries, boo, hoot, jeer, utter catcalls. ANTONYMS: applaud, cheer, clap.
~*n.* **1** (*a hissing sound*) buzz, hissing, sibilance, sibilation, whistle. **2** (*an expression of derision or disapproval*) boo, catcall, hoot, jeer, (*coll.*) raspberry. ANTONYMS: applause, ovation.

historian *n.* (*a writer of history, esp. one who is an authority on it*) annalist, archivist, biographer, chronicler, historiographer, recorder.

historic *a.* **1** (*celebrated in history, associated with historical events*) celebrated, famed, famous, memorable, notable, noted, outstanding, remarkable, renowned, well-known. ANTONYMS: forgotten, unknown. **2** (*potentially important, momentous*) epoch-making, important, momentous, red-letter, significant. ANTONYMS: insignificant, unimportant.

historical *a.* **1** (*of the nature of history; not fictitious etc.*) actual, attested, authentic, authenticated, documented, factual, real, recorded, verified. ANTONYMS: fictitious, legendary, mythical. **2** (*belonging to the past; dealing with the past*) ancient, bygone, former, old, past. ANTONYMS: contemporary, current, future, present-day.

history *n.* **1** (*a systematic record of past events, esp. those of public importance*) annals, chronicle, historical account, memoirs, record, story. **2** (*a record, e.g. of someone's past medical treatment*) background, record. **3** (*the past considered as a whole*) ancient history, bygone days, days gone by, days of yore, former times, olden days, the good old days, the old days, the past, time gone by, yesteryear. ANTONYMS: the future, the present. **4** (*the past events in someone's life, esp. when recorded in a book*) adventures, background, life story, story.

histrionic *a.* ((*of behaviour*) *theatrical, affected*) affected, artificial, bogus, camp, dramatic, forced, insincere, melodramatic, sensational, stagey, theatrical, unnatural, unreal.
~*n.* (*in pl.*) (*an ostentatious display of usu. false emotion*) dramatics, hysterics, tantrums.

hit *v.t.* **1** (*to strike or touch with a blow or missile, esp. after taking aim*) bang, bash, batter, beat, (*coll.*) belt, box, buffet, (*coll.*) clip, (*sl.*) clobber, clout, cuff, flog, hammer, lambast, pound, pummel, punch, slap, smack, (*sl.*) sock, strike, swat, (*coll.*) swipe, thump, (*coll.*) wallop, whack. **2** (*to collide with*) bang into, bump into, collide with, crash into, knock into, meet head-on, run into, smash into. **3** (*to affect suddenly or adversely, to wound*) affect, damage, have an effect on, hurt, influence, knock for six, leave a mark on, leave an

impression on, make an impact on, make an impression on, move, overwhelm, touch, wound. **4** (*to arrive at; to guess*) accomplish, achieve, arrive at, attain, gain, reach, touch. **5** (*to encounter, meet*) be faced with, come up against, encounter, experience, meet.
~*n.* **1** (*a blow; a collision*) bang, (*coll.*) belt, blow, box, buffet, (*coll.*) clip, clout, cuff, knock, punch, slap, smack, (*sl.*) sock, (*coll.*) swipe, (*coll.*) wallop, whack. **2** (*a successful effort*) (*coll.*) sensation, smash hit, success, triumph, winner. **3** (*a stroke of sarcasm, wit etc.*) dig, gibe, jeer, taunt. **to hit it off with** (*to get along well together, to agree*) be on good terms with, be on the same wavelength as, (*coll.*) click, get on well with, get on with, have much in common with, take to. **to hit off** (*to represent or describe rapidly or cleverly*) capture, catch, impersonate, mimic, represent, (*coll.*) take off. **to hit on/ upon** (*to light or chance on*) chance on, come upon, come up with, discover, guess, light on, stumble on, think of. **to hit out at** (*to attack vigorously, either physically or verbally*) assail, attack, inveigh against, lash out at, launch an attack on, rail against, strike out at.

hit-and-miss *a.* (*succeeding and failing in a haphazard way*) aimless, disorganized, haphazard, indiscriminate, random, undirected, unplanned, unsystematic. ANTONYMS: organized, planned, systematic.

hitch *v.t.* **1** (*to fasten with a hook or knot, esp. temporarily*) attach, bind, couple, fasten, harness, join, tether, tie, yoke. ANTONYMS: disconnect, release, uncouple, unhitch. **2** (*to pull up with a jerk*) hike up, jerk up, pull up, tug up, yank up.
~*v.i.* (*to hitch-hike*) hitch a lift, hitch-hike, thumb a lift.
~*n.* **1** (*an impediment, a temporary difficulty*) catch, delay, difficulty, drawback, hindrance, hold-up, impediment, obstacle, obstruction, problem, snag, stumbling-block, trouble. **2** (*an abrupt pull or jerk up*) hike, jerk, pull, tug, yank.

hitherto *adv.* (*up to this time*) previously, so far, thus far, till now, until now, up till now, up to now.

hoar *n.* (*hoar frost*) frost, hoar frost, rime.

hoard *n.* (*an accumulated store* (*often of valuables*) *hidden away for future use*) accumulation, cache, collection, fund, heap, mass, pile, reserve, reservoir, (*coll.*) stash, stockpile, store.
~*v.t.* (*to collect and put away, to store*) accumulate, amass, collect, garner, gather, lay up, put away, put by, save, (*coll.*) stash away, stockpile, stock up, store, stow away. ANTONYMS: exhaust, spend, use.

hoarder *n.* (*a person who hoards*) collector, (*coll.*) magpie, miser, saver, (*coll.*) squirrel, stockpiler.

hoarse *a.* ((*of the voice*) *harsh or husky*) croaking, croaky, gravelly, gruff, guttural, harsh, husky, rasping, raucous, rough, throaty.

hoary *a.* **1** (*white- or grey-headed*) grey-haired, grizzled, silvery-haired, white-haired. **2** (*of great antiquity, venerable*) aged, ancient, antique, elderly, old, time-honoured, venerable. ANTONYMS: modern, new, young. **3** (*old and trite*) antiquated, hackneyed, old, trite. ANTONYMS: fresh, new, novel.

hoax *n.* (*a deception meant as a practical joke*) (*sl.*) con, deception, (*coll.*) fast one, jest, joke, practical joke, prank, ruse, (*N Am., sl.*) scam, spoof, trick.
~*v.t.* (*to play a practical joke upon, to take in for sport*) (*sl.*) con, hoodwink, play a practical joke on, play a prank on, play a trick on, trick, (*sl.*) wind up.

hoaxer *n.* (*a person who carries out a hoax*) (*sl.*) conman, conwoman, joker, prankster, trickster.

hobble *v.i.* (*to walk lamely or awkwardly*) falter, halt, limp, shuffle, stumble, totter.

hobby *n.* (*any recreation or pursuit*) amusement, diversion, entertainment, leisure activity, leisure interest, leisure pursuit, pastime, recreation, sport.

hobgoblin *n.* (*a kind of goblin or elf*) elf, fairy, goblin, imp, sprite.

hobnob *v.i.* (*to associate familiarly* (*with*)) associate, consort, fraternize, go around, (*sl.*) hang out, keep company, mix, socialize.

hoi polloi *n.* (*the common herd, the masses*) canaille, commonalty, populace, proletariat, the common herd, (*coll.*) the common people, (*coll.*) the great unwashed, the masses, the mob, the plebs, the rabble, the riff-raff. ANTONYMS: aristocracy, (*coll.*) the upper crust.

hoist *v.t.* (*to raise up*) elevate, erect, hike up, jack up, lift, raise. ANTONYMS: lower.
~*n.* **1** (*an apparatus for hoisting or raising*) crane, pulley, tackle, winch. **2** (*a lift or elevator*) elevator, lift.

hoity-toity *a.* (*haughty and petulant*) arrogant, conceited, disdainful, haughty, (*coll.*) high and mighty, proud, scornful, snobbish, (*coll.*) snooty, stuck-up, supercilious, (*sl.*) toffee-nosed, (*coll.*) uppity. ANTONYMS: humble, self-effacing.

hold¹ *v.t.* **1** (*to grasp and retain*) clasp, clench, cling to, clutch, grasp, grip, seize. ANTONYMS: let go, release. **2** (*to keep in, to confine*) confine,

detain, hold in custody, imprison, lock up, restrain. ANTONYMS: let go, release. **3** (*to enclose, to contain*) accommodate, contain, enclose, have the capacity of, take. **4** (*to keep back, to restrain*) check, hold back, impede, prevent, restrain, stop. **5** (*to keep in a certain manner or position*) continue, keep, remain, stay. **6** (*to retain possession or control of*) hang on to, have, hold on to, keep, retain. ANTONYMS: give up, surrender, yield. **7** (*to occupy, to possess* (*a house, qualifications etc.*)) have, have possession of, occupy, own, possess. **8** (*to regard, to believe*) assume, believe, consider, deem, judge, presume, reckon, regard, suppose, think, view. **9** (*to maintain* (*that*)) assert, declare, insist, maintain, state. **10** (*to conduct* (*a meeting etc.*)) assemble, call, carry on, conduct, convene, have, officiate at, preside over, run. **11** (*to occupy or fill* (*a job*)) be in, fill, have, hold down, occupy. **12** (*to have, to retain* (*a grudge etc.*)) harbour, have, retain. **13** (*to bear, to support the weight of*) bear, carry, hold up, keep up, shoulder, support, sustain, take. **14** (*to clasp, to embrace*) clasp, clutch, embrace, enfold, hug. **15** (*to keep, to occupy* (*one's attention*)) absorb, catch, engage, engross, keep, maintain, occupy. ANTONYMS: lose. **16** (*to give or host* (*a party*)) give, have, host.
~*v.i.* **1** (*to continue firm, not to break*) carry on, continue, go on, last, persist, remain, stay. ANTONYMS: break, stop. **2** (*to be valid or true, to stand*) apply, be in force, be in operation, be the case, be valid, exist, hold good, operate, remain, remain valid, stand. ANTONYMS: be invalid, be obsolete. **to hold back 1** (*to restrain, to prevent* (*something or someone*) *from progressing*) curb, hinder, impede, inhibit, obstruct, prevent, restrain. ANTONYMS: assist, encourage. **2** (*to retain in one's possession*) hang on to, keep back, suppress, withhold. ANTONYMS: disclose, reveal. **3** (*to keep oneself in check*) desist, forbear, keep from, restrain oneself, stop oneself. **4** (*to stop oneself from expressing* (*an emotion*)) keep back, repress, smother, stifle, suppress. ANTONYMS: give rein to. **to hold down 1** (*to repress, to restrain*) oppress, repress, restrain, tyrannize over. **2** (*to keep at a low level*) keep down, keep low. ANTONYMS: increase. **3** (*to be good enough at* (*one's job etc.*) *to retain it*) continue in, keep, retain, stay in. ANTONYMS: (*coll.*) be sacked from, lose. **to hold forth 1** (*to stretch or put forward*) extend, hold out, offer, proffer, stretch out. **2** (*to speak in public or for a long time*) declaim, discourse, go on, harangue, lecture, orate, sermonize, speak at length, spout. **to hold off 1** (*to keep* (*someone or something*) *at a distance*) fend off, keep at bay, keep off, repel, repulse, stave off, ward off. **2** (*to delay*) defer, delay, keep from, postpone, put

off. **3** (*to keep away, not to happen*) delay, keep away, keep off, not happen, not occur. ANTONYMS: happen, occur. **to hold on 1** (*to continue without interruption, to persist*) carry on, continue, endure, hang on, keep going, last, persist, survive. ANTONYMS: give in, give up. **2** (*to stop*) halt, pause, stop, wait. ANTONYMS: go on, proceed. **to hold one's own 1** (*to maintain one's position*) maintain one's position, stand fast, stand firm, stand one's ground, stay put, stick to one's guns. ANTONYMS: change one's ground, change one's stance. **2** (*to survive*) be on an even keel, not to get worse, stay alive, survive. ANTONYMS: deteriorate, get worse. **to hold on to 1** (*to keep holding, to clutch*) clasp, cling to, clutch, grasp, grip, hold. ANTONYMS: let go of, release. **2** (*to retain possession of*) keep, keep hold of, keep possession of, retain. ANTONYMS: give up, let go. **to hold out 1** (*to offer*) extend, hold forth, offer, proffer, stretch out. **2** (*to endure, not to yield*) endure, hang on, put up resistance, resist, stand fast, stand firm, withstand. **3** (*to persist, to last*) continue, last, persist, remain. ANTONYMS: come to an end, run out. **to hold over** (*to keep back, to defer*) adjourn, defer, delay, postpone, put off, suspend. **to hold to** (*to adhere to*) abide by, adhere to, comply with, stand by, stick to. ANTONYMS: give up. **to hold up 1** (*to raise or lift up*) brandish, display, exhibit, flaunt, lift, present, put on show, raise, show. **2** (*to sustain*) bear, carry, hold, prop up, shore up, support, sustain. **3** (*to stop and rob by violence or threats*) commit armed robbery on, hold to ransom, mug, rob, (*coll.*) stick up, waylay. **4** (*to arrest the progress of, to obstruct*) bring to a halt, delay, detain, hinder, impede, retard, set back, slow down. ANTONYMS: aid, boost, encourage. **to hold with** (*to approve of, to side with*) agree with, approve of, back, be in favour of, give support to, side with, subscribe to, support. ANTONYMS: disagree with, disapprove of.

hold² *n.* **1** (*a grasp, a clutch*) clasp, clutch, grasp, grip. **2** (*mental grasp*) awareness, comprehension, grasp, grip, mastery, perception, understanding. **3** (*a support, anything to hold by or support oneself by*) anchorage, foothold, footing, leverage, prop, purchase, support. **4** (*influence, sometimes when this is not honest or legal*) influence, power, (*coll.*) pull, sway. **5** (*control or power*) ascendancy, authority, control, dominion, power. **on hold** (*deferred until later*) deferred, delayed, on ice, on the back burner, postponed, put off. **to get hold of 1** (*to grasp*) clutch, grasp, grip, take hold of. ANTONYMS: let go, release. **2** (*to get in contact with*) communicate with, contact, get in contact with, get in touch with.

holder *n.* **1** (*a device or implement for holding something*) case, casing, container, cover, covering, housing, sheath. **2** (*a tenant or owner*) occupier, owner, proprietor, tenant. **3** (*a person who holds a title etc.*) bearer, owner, possessor.

hold-up *n.* **1** (*a robbery, esp. an armed one*) armed robbery, burglary, mugging, robbery, (*sl.*) stick-up, theft. **2** (*a delay, stoppage*) bottleneck, deferment, delay, difficulty, drawback, hitch, impediment, jam, obstruction, problem, setback, snag, stoppage, wait.

hole *n.* **1** (*a hollow place or cavity*) cavity, crater, depression, excavation, hollow, mine, pit, pothole, recess, shaft. **2** (*an aperture, an orifice*) aperture, breach, break, crack, fissure, gap, gash, incision, opening, orifice, perforation, puncture, rent, slit, space, tear. **3** (*a wild animal's burrow*) burrow, covert, den, earth, lair, set. **4** (*an awkward situation*) fix, (*coll.*) hot water, jam, mess, muddle, (*coll.*) pickle, predicament, (*coll.*) spot, tight corner, tight spot, trouble. **5** (*a dingy, disreputable place*) (*coll.*) dive, (*coll.*) dump, hovel, (*sl.*) joint, slum. **to pick holes in** (*to find fault with*) criticize, denigrate, disparage, find fault with, (*coll.*) knock, (*coll.*) nit-pick, pull to pieces, rubbish, (*sl.*) slag off, slate. ANTONYMS: applaud, praise.

hole-and-corner *a.* (*secret, clandestine*) clandestine, furtive, secret, stealthy, surreptitious, underhand. ANTONYMS: above-board, honest, open.

holiday *n.* **1** (*a period away from work or school; an extended period spent away from home for recreation*) break, leave, leave of absence, recess, time off, (*N Am.*) vacation. **2** (*a day of exemption from work by law or custom*) bank holiday, feast day, festival, public holiday. ANTONYMS: workday, working day.

holier-than-thou *a.* (*convinced of one's moral superiority, sanctimonious*) (*coll., usu. derog.*) goody-goody, pietistic, pietistical, priggish, religiose, sanctimonious, self-righteous, self-satisfied, smug, (*coll.*) squeaky-clean, unctuous.

holiness *n.* **1** (*the state of being holy, sanctity*) blessedness, divinity, godliness, sacredness, sanctity. ANTONYMS: profanity, sacrilege. **2** (*moral purity or integrity*) devoutness, goodness, piety, purity, religiousness, righteousness, saintliness, virtue, virtuousness. ANTONYMS: badness, evil, impiety.

hollow *a.* **1** (*containing a cavity or empty space*) empty, hollowed-out, unfilled, vacant, void. ANTONYMS: filled, solid. **2** (*sunken, concave*) cavernous, concave, deepset, dented, depressed, sunken. **3** (*without significance, meaningless*) empty, fruitless, futile, insignificant, meaningless, of no avail, of no use, pointless, Pyrrhic, useless, valueless, worthwhile. **4** ((*of sounds*) *low and clear*) deep, dull, echoing, flat, low, sepulchral. **5** (*insincere, not genuine*) artificial, deceitful, empty, false, feigned, hypocritical, insincere, spurious, vain. ANTONYMS: genuine, real, sincere. **6** (*hungry, empty*) empty, famished, hungry, ravenous, starved, starving. ANTONYMS: full.
~*n.* **1** (*a depression or unoccupied space*) basin, cavity, concavity, crater, dent, depression, dip, excavation, hole, niche, pit, recess. **2** (*a valley*) dale, dell, glen, valley.

holocaust *n.* (*a wholesale sacrifice of life, or general destruction*) annihilation, carnage, conflagration, destruction, ethnic cleansing, extermination, genocide, inferno, massacre, mass murder, slaughter, wholesale destruction.

holy *a.* **1** (*associated with God or a deity*) divine, godlike, godly, religious. **2** (*sacred, consecrated*) blessed, consecrated, hallowed, sacred, sacrosanct, sanctified, venerated. ANTONYMS: profane, sacrilegious. **3** (*morally pure, free from sin*) devout, God-fearing, godly, pious, pure, religious, righteous, saintly, virtuous. ANTONYMS: immoral, impious, irreligious, sinful, wicked.

homage *n.* (*obeisance, reverence*) admiration, adulation, deference, honour, respect, reverence, worship. ANTONYMS: contempt, disrespect, irreverence.

home[1] *n.* **1** (*the place where one lives*) abode, domicile, dwelling, dwelling-place, habitation, house, property, residence. **2** (*the members of a family collectively*) family, family background, family circle, household. **3** (*one's own country or that of one's ancestors*) birthplace, country of origin, fatherland, homeland, home town, mother country, motherland, native country, native land. **4** (*a charitable institution for orphans or the destitute*) centre, hostel, institution, refuge, residential home, retreat. **5** (*the environment or habitat of a person or animal*) abode, domain, environment, habitat, haunt, home ground, natural habitat, stamping ground, territory.
~*a.* **1** (*connected with or produced at home or in one's native country*) home-bred, home-grown, home-made. **2** (*domestic, as opposed to foreign*) domestic, interior, internal, local, national. ANTONYMS: foreign, international, overseas. **at home 1** (*at ease, comfortable*) at ease, comfortable, in one's element, on familiar territory, relaxed. ANTONYMS: ill at ease,

uncomfortable. **2** (*conversant* (*with*)) conversant (with), familiar (with), knowledgeable (about), proficient (in), skilled (in), well-versed (in). ANTONYMS: ignorant (about), unfamiliar (with). **3** (*accessible to visitors, esp. when entertaining*) available, in. ANTONYMS: away from home, out. **4** (*receiving guests*) entertaining, receiving guests.

home² *v.i.* (*to be directed onto a target, e.g. with a navigational device*) be aimed at, be directed at, focus on, move towards, zero in on, zoom in on.

homeland *n.* (*one's native land*) birthplace, country of origin, fatherland, mother country, motherland, native country, native land.

homeless *a.* (*without a home*) down-and-out, of no fixed abode, vagrant, without a roof over one's head.

homely *a.* **1** (*homelike, making one feel comfortable*) comfortable, (*coll.*) comfy, congenial, friendly, homelike, homey, homy, informal, relaxed, snug, welcoming. ANTONYMS: formal, uncomfortable, unfriendly, unwelcoming. **2** (*plain, without affectation*) modest, ordinary, plain, simple, unassuming, unpretentious, unsophisticated. ANTONYMS: elaborate, ostentatious, pretentious, sophisticated. **3** ((*of a person*) *plain or ugly in manner, looks etc.*) ill-favoured, plain, ugly, unattractive. ANTONYMS: attractive, beautiful, pretty.

homespun *a.* (*unaffected, unsophisticated*) artless, modest, plain, rough, simple, unpolished, unrefined, unsophisticated. ANTONYMS: elaborate, refined, sophisticated.

homicidal *a.* (*of or relating to homicide*) deadly, fatal, lethal, maniacal, murderous, violent.

homicide *n.* **1** (*the act of killing a human being*) killing, manslaughter, murder, slaughter, slaying. **2** (*a person who kills another*) killer, murderer, slayer.

homily *n.* **1** (*a discourse or sermon on a moral or religious topic*) discourse, lecture, lesson, oration, sermon, speech, talk. **2** (*a tedious moral exhortation*) lecture, sermon.

homogeneous *a.* (*of the same kind or nature throughout*) all of a piece, all the same, consistent, identical, uniform, unvarying. ANTONYMS: heterogeneous, mixed, varied, varying.

homosexual *a.* (*feeling sexual attraction to one's own sex*) (*sl., offensive*) bent, (*sl., derog.*) butch, camp, (*sl.*) dyke, (*coll.*) gay, homophile, lesbian, (*sl., derog.*) queer.

honest *a.* **1** (*truthful, trustworthy in business or conduct*) decent, ethical, fair, good, high-minded, honourable, just, law-abiding, moral, principled, reputable, righteous, trustworthy, truthful, upright, upstanding, virtuous, worthy. ANTONYMS: crooked, deceitful, dishonest, disreputable, lying. **2** (*frank, candid*) candid, direct, forthright, frank, open, outspoken, sincere, straight, straightforward, truthful. ANTONYMS: dishonest, false, insincere, untruthful. **3** (*just, equitable*) disinterested, equitable, even-handed, fair, impartial, just, objective, unbiased, unprejudiced. ANTONYMS: prejudiced, unfair, unjust. **4** (*genuine, authentic*) actual, authentic, bona fide, genuine, real. ANTONYMS: bogus, false, feigned, spurious.

honestly *adv.* **1** (*in an honest way*) by fair means, by just means, ethically, fairly, honourably, lawfully, legally, legitimately, morally, on the level, virtuously. ANTONYMS: dishonestly, dishonourably, illegally, unlawfully. **2** (*really*) candidly, frankly, in all honesty, in all sincerity, in plain language, really, speaking honestly, speaking truthfully, to be honest, truthfully.

honesty *n.* **1** (*the quality or state of being honest*) decency, fairness, goodness, high-mindedness, honour, integrity, justness, probity, righteousness, trustworthiness, truthfulness, uprightness, virtue. ANTONYMS: crookedness, deceitfulness, dishonesty. **2** (*truthfulness*) candidness, directness, forthrightness, frankness, openness, outspokenness, sincerity, straightforwardness, straightness, truthfulness. ANTONYMS: dishonesty, falseness, insincerity, untruthfulness. **3** (*justness, impartiality*) even-handedness, fairness, impartiality, justice, justness, lack of bias, lack of prejudice. ANTONYMS: bias, partiality, prejudice, unfairness. **4** (*authenticity*) authenticity, genuineness, reality. ANTONYMS: falseness, spuriousness.

honorarium *n.* (*a fee or payment for the services of a professional person*) emolument, fee, pay, recompense, remuneration, salary.

honorary *a.* (*holding a title or an office without payment or without undertaking the duties*) complimentary, ex officio, in name only, nominal, titular, unofficial, unpaid. ANTONYMS: official, paid.

honour *n.* **1** (*respect, esteem*) acclaim, admiration, adulation, deference, esteem, homage, praise, recognition, regard, respect, reverence, veneration, worship. ANTONYMS: contempt, disregard, scorn. **2** (*reputation, glory*) good name, high standing, integrity, name, reputation. **3** (*nobleness of mind,* uprightness) decency, fairness, goodness, honesty, integrity, justice, justness, morality, principles, probity, rectitude, righteousness, trustworthiness, truth, truthfulness, uprightness, virtue, worth, worthiness. ANTONYMS: dishonour, unscrupulousness, unworthiness. **4** (*something conferred as a mark or token of distinction for bravery, achievement etc.*) accolade, award, tribute. **5** (*high rank; exalted position*) eminence, esteem, high rank, prestige, rank. **6** ((*of a woman*) *chastity, reputation of chastity*) chastity, modesty, morality, purity, virginity, virtue. ANTONYMS: immorality, promiscuity. **7** (*a source of pride, pleasure etc.*) compliment, joy, privilege, source of pleasure, source of pride.

~*v.t.* **1** (*to treat with reverence or respect*) admire, esteem, hold in esteem, hold in high regard, prize, respect, revere, value, venerate, worship. ANTONYMS: despise, hold in contempt, scorn. **2** (*to confer honour upon*) acclaim, applaud, laud, lionize, pay homage to, pay tribute to, praise. ANTONYMS: censure, condemn, criticize, deprecate. **3** (*to accept or pay* (*a bill or cheque*) *when due*) accept, cash, pay, take. **4** (*to carry out or fulfil* (*an agreement etc.*)) carry out, discharge, execute, fulfil, keep, observe. ANTONYMS: break, go back on, ignore.

honourable *a.* **1** (*of distinguished rank, noble*) distinguished, eminent, high-ranking, illustrious, noble, notable, prestigious, venerable, worthy. **2** (*actuated by principles of honour; not base*) decent, ethical, fair, good, high-principled, honest, just, moral, of honour, of principle, principled, righteous, trustworthy, truthful, upright, upstanding, virtuous, worthy. ANTONYMS: dishonest, dishonourable, untrustworthy. **3** (*accompanied or performed with or as with marks of honour*) distinguished, famous, glorious, great, noble, renowned. ANTONYMS: mediocre, unknown.

hoodwink *v.t.* (*to deceive, to take in*) cheat, (*sl.*) con, deceive, delude, dupe, fool, lead (someone) up the garden path, mislead, outwit, (*coll.*) pull a fast one on, pull the wool over (someone's) eyes, (*coll.*) put one over on, swindle, (*coll.*) take (someone) for a ride, take (someone) in, trick.

hook *n.* **1** (*a curved piece of metal or other material by which an object is caught or suspended*) peg. **2** (*a curved instrument for cutting grass or corn, a sickle*) billhook, scythe, sickle. **3** (*a kind of fastener on a dress etc.*) catch, clasp, fastener.
~*v.t.* **1** (*to catch or hold with or as with a hook*) catch, ensnare, snare, trap. **2** (*to fasten with a hook or hooks*) clasp, fasten, fix, secure. **by hook or by crook** (*by fair means or foul*) by any

means whatsoever, by fair means or foul, no matter how, somehow or other. **hook, line and sinker** (*completely*) completely, entirely, thoroughly, totally, utterly, wholly. ANTONYMS: in part, partially, partly.

hooked *a.* (*bent; hook-shaped*) aquiline, beaky, bent, curved, hooklike, hook-shaped.

hooligan *n.* (*any of a gang of street ruffians given to violent attacks on people*) delinquent, rowdy, ruffian, thug, tough, vandal, yob, yobbo.

hoop *n.* (*a strip of wood or metal bent into a band or ring*) band, circle, circlet, ring.

hoot *v.i.* **1** ((*of an owl*) *to utter its hollow cry*) call, cry, screech, tu-whit-tu-whoo, whoop. **2** (*to shout or make loud cries in contempt, or in amusement*) (*coll.*) blow raspberries, boo, hiss, jeer, utter catcalls, whistle. ANTONYMS: applaud, cheer. **3** (*to make a loud, high-pitched sound in laughter*) (*coll.*) crack up, (*coll.*) fall about, laugh, scream with laughter, split one's sides.
~*n.* **1** (*the cry of an owl*) call, cry, screech, tu-whit-tu-whoo, whoop. **2** (*an inarticulate shout in contempt or dissatisfaction*) boo, catcall, hiss, jeer, (*coll.*) raspberry, whistle. ANTONYMS: cheer. **3** (*an extremely funny or enjoyable person or event*) good laugh, laugh, real laugh, (*coll.*) scream. **not to care two hoots** (*not to care at all*) not to care a bit, not to care a scrap, not to care at all, not to give a damn, not to give a jot.

hop *v.i.* (*to leap or skip on one foot*) bounce, bound, jump, leap, spring.
~*n.* **1** (*a jump or light leap on one foot or* (*of animals etc.*) *on both or all feet*) bound, jump, leap, spring. **2** (*a dance*) dance, disco, party. **3** (*a short trip by aircraft, a short run*) jaunt, quick trip, short flight.

hope *n.* **1** (*an expectant desire; confidence in a future event*) ambition, anticipation, aspiration, conviction, desire, dream, dreaming, expectancy, expectation, hopefulness, longing, optimism, wish, wishing. **2** (*a person or thing that is the cause for hope*) chance, possibility, prospect.
~*v.i.* (*to feel hope*) be hopeful, be optimistic, be sanguine, have confidence.
~*v.t.* **1** (*to expect with desire*) desire, dream of, long for, wish for, yearn for. **2** (*to look forward to with confidence*) anticipate, aspire to, be convinced of, count on, expect, foresee, look forward to, rely on.

hopeful *a.* **1** (*feeling hope*) assured, confident, expectant, optimistic, sanguine. ANTONYMS: despairing, hopeless, pessimistic. **2** (*giving rise* *to hope*) auspicious, bright, cheerful, encouraging, optimistic, promising, propitious, rosy. ANTONYMS: desperate, hopeless.

hopefully *adv.* **1** (*in a hopeful way*) confidently, expectantly, optimistically, sanguinely, with assurance. **2** (*it is hoped*) if all goes according to plan, if all goes well, it is hoped, with luck.

hopeless *a.* **1** (*destitute of hope, despairing*) dejected, demoralized, despairing, desperate, despondent, disconsolate, downhearted, in despair, pessimistic, suicidal, without hope, wretched. ANTONYMS: hopeful, optimistic, sanguine. **2** (*affording no hope, desperate*) beyond hope, beyond remedy, beyond repair, desperate, incurable, irreparable, irreversible, lost. ANTONYMS: auspicious, hopeful, optimistic, promising, rosy. **3** (*futile, pointless*) futile, impossible, impracticable, pointless, useless, vain. ANTONYMS: profitable, useful, valuable, worthwhile. **4** (*incompetent or showing incompetence*) bad, inadequate, incompetent, ineffective, ineffectual, inferior, no good, pathetic, poor, useless. ANTONYMS: competent, effective, expert.

horde *n.* (*a gang, a multitude*) band, crew, crowd, drove, gang, host, mob, multitude, pack, swarm, throng, troop.

horizon *n.* **1** (*the circular line where the sky and the earth seem to meet*) skyline, vista. **2** (*the boundary of one's mental vision, experience etc.*) ambit, area of knowledge, compass, ken, outlook, perception, perspective, scope, sphere. **on the horizon** ((*of an event etc.*) *imminent; likely to appear or happen soon*) brewing, imminent, impending, in the air, in the offing, likely, on the cards, to be expected. ANTONYMS: distant, unlikely.

horizontal *a.* (*parallel to the plane of the horizon, at right angles to the vertical*) flat, flush, level, plumb, prone, supine. ANTONYMS: upright, vertical.

horn *n.* **to pull in one's horns** (*to curtail one's expenses*) budget, curb expenditure, cut down, cut down on expenses, economize, make economies, reduce expenditure, retrench, tighten one's belt.

horny *a.* **1** (*callous*) callous, callused, hard, hardened, leathery, rough. ANTONYMS: silky, smooth. **2** (*sexually excited; lustful*) lustful, passionate, randy, sexually excited, sexy, (*coll.*) turned on.

horrendous *a.* (*awful; horrifying*) appalling, awful, dreadful, fearful, frightful, ghastly, horrible, horrid, nasty, shocking, terrible. ANTONYMS: agreeable, lovely, pleasant.

horrible *a.* **1** (*causing or tending to cause horror; dreadful*) abhorrent, abominable, appalling, awful, dreadful, fearful, frightful, ghastly, grim, hateful, heinous, hideous, horrid, loathsome, repulsive, revolting, shocking, terrible, terrifying. **2** (*unpleasant, excessive*) awful, disagreeable, (*coll.*) dreadful, ghastly, (*coll.*) horrid, nasty, obnoxious, (*coll.*) terrible, unpleasant. ANTONYMS: agreeable, lovely, nice, pleasant.

horrify *v.t.* **1** (*to strike with horror*) alarm, frighten, frighten (someone) out of their wits, intimidate, make (someone's) blood run cold, petrify, scare, scare stiff, startle, strike fear into, strike terror into, terrify, terrorize. **2** (*to scandalize*) appal, disgust, offend, outrage, revolt, scandalize, shock.

horror *n.* **1** (*dread or terror*) alarm, dread, fear, fear and trembling, fearfulness, fright, panic, terror, trepidation. **2** (*intense loathing; hatred*) abhorrence, antipathy, aversion, detestation, disgust, dislike, distaste, hatred, loathing, odium, repugnance, revulsion. ANTONYMS: attraction, liking, love. **3** (*intense dismay*) amazement, astonishment, consternation, dismay, perturbation, surprise. **4** (*that which excites terror or repulsion*) abomination, anathema, nightmare, terror. **5** (*a bad or ugly person or thing*) devil, rascal, rogue, terror.

horror-stricken *a.* (*overwhelmed with horror; shocked*) aghast, appalled, frightened out of one's wits, horrified, petrified, scared stiff, scared to death, shocked, terrified, terrorized.

horse *n.* (*a solid-hoofed quadruped, with mane and tail of long coarse hair*) hack, mount, nag, steed. **to get on one's high horse** (*to be arrogant or disdainfully aloof*) act in a superior way, become arrogant, become condescending, become disdainful, become supercilious. ANTONYMS: become humble, eat humble pie. **to hold one's horses** (*to stop*) desist, halt, slow down, stop, wait. ANTONYMS: (*coll.*) get a move on, take action.

horseplay *n.* (*rough, boisterous play*) buffoonery, clowning, fooling, fooling around, high jinks, practical jokes, pranks, (*sl.*) rough house, (*coll.*) skylarking, tomfoolery.

horse sense *n.* (*common sense*) common sense, judgement, native wit, (*coll.*) nous, the sense one was born with.

hose *n.* ((*a piece of*) *flexible tubing for water or other fluid*) pipe, syphon, tube, tubing.

hospitable *a.* (*entertaining or disposed to entertain strangers or guests with kindness*) convivial, cordial, friendly, generous, kind,

kind-hearted, liberal, open-handed, sociable, welcoming. ANTONYMS: inhospitable, mean, unkind, unsociable, unwelcoming.

hospitality n. (*liberal entertainment of strangers or guests*) conviviality, cordiality, generosity, kindness, liberality, open-handedness, sociability, welcome. ANTONYMS: meanness, unkindness.

host[1] n. **1** (*a person who entertains another*) entertainer, party-giver. **2** (*the landlord of an inn or hotel*) hotelier, innkeeper, landlord, proprietor. **3** (*the compère of a TV or radio show*) anchor, anchor man, anchor woman, announcer, compère, presenter.
~v.t. **1** ((*of a person*) *to act as host at* (*a social event, occasion etc.*)) be the host/ hostess of, give, play host to, throw. **2** (*to be the compère of* (*a show etc.*)) compère, front, present.

host[2] n. (*a great number, a multitude*) army, crowd, drove, flock, horde, legion, mass, mob, multitude, myriad, pack, swarm, throng, troop.

hostage n. (*a person given or seized in pledge for the performance of certain conditions or for the safety of others*) captive, gage, pawn, prisoner, surety.

hostile a. **1** (*of or relating to an enemy*) aggressive, antagonistic, bellicose, belligerent, malevolent, militant, unfriendly, warlike, warring. ANTONYMS: amiable, cordial, friendly, peaceful. **2** ((*of a place, situation etc.*) *inhospitable, harsh*) adverse, disadvantageous, harsh, inauspicious, inhospitable, unfavourable, unfriendly, unpropitious, unwelcoming. ANTONYMS: advantageous, favourable, friendly, hospitable, propitious. **3** (*resistant*) against, antagonistic, anti, averse, inimical, opposed, resistant. ANTONYMS: for, in favour of, pro.

hostility n. **1** (*enmity; antagonism*) aggression, antagonism, bellicosity, belligerency, enmity, malevolence, militancy, unfriendliness, warlikeness. ANTONYMS: amity, cordiality, friendliness, peace, peacefulness. **2** (*state of war*) conflict, militancy, state of war, strife, war, warfare. ANTONYMS: harmony, peace. **3** (*opposition* (*in thought etc.*) *or resistance* (*to change etc.*)) antagonism, aversion, inimicalness, opposition, resistance. ANTONYMS: approval (of), goodwill (towards), support (of). **4** (*inhospitableness, harshness*) adverseness, disadvantageousness, harshness, inauspiciousness, inhospitableness, unfavourableness, unfriendliness, unpropitiousness. ANTONYMS: advantageousness, favourableness, friendliness, hospitableness, propitiousness.

hot a. **1** (*having a high temperature*) (*coll.*)

baking, blazing hot, blistering, (*coll.*) boiling, (*coll.*) boiling hot, flaming, red-hot, (*coll.*) roasting, scalding, scorching, searing, sultry, sweltering, torrid, tropical, warm. ANTONYMS: arctic, chilly, cold, freezing. **2** ((*of food*) *made by heating and served before cooling*) boiling, heated, piping, piping hot, scalding, sizzling, steaming, warmed. ANTONYMS: chilled, cold, cool. **3** ((*of spices etc.*) *acrid, pungent*) acrid, biting, fiery, peppery, piquant, pungent, sharp, spicy. ANTONYMS: bland, mild. **4** (*ardent; passionate*) ardent, excited, fervent, fierce, fiery, intense, passionate, strong, tempestuous, vehement, violent. ANTONYMS: apathetic, indifferent, (*coll.*) laid-back, moderate. **5** (*knowledgeable* (*about*)) au fait (with), conversant (with), experienced (in), expert (in), familiar (with), knowledgeable (about). ANTONYMS: ignorant (of), inexperienced (in). **6** (*eager, enthusiastic*) avid, eager, enthusiastic, fervent, keen, passionate. ANTONYMS: apathetic, cool, unenthusiastic, uninterested. **7** (*sexually excited*) (*sl.*) horny, lustful, randy, (*coll.*) turned on. ANTONYMS: frigid. **8** ((*of a player*) *very skilful*) (*coll.*) A1, accomplished, (*sl.*) ace, adept, crack, excellent, expert, first-rate, good, skilful, skilled, (*coll.*) top-notch. ANTONYMS: bad, hopeless, poor. **9** (*much favoured*) favoured, favourite, in demand, in favour, in vogue, popular, sought-after. ANTONYMS: out of favour, unpopular. **10** ((*of news*) *fresh, recent*) fresh, hot from the press, just out, latest, new, recent, up-to-the-minute. ANTONYMS: dated, old, stale. **11** (*dangerous*) dangerous, difficult, hazardous, perilous, problematic, risky, troublesome. ANTONYMS: easy, safe, trouble-free. **the hots** (*strong sexual desire*) (*sl.*) horniness, randiness, sexual arousal, sexual attraction, sexual desire. **to hot up** (*to become more intense, exciting etc.*) accelerate, escalate, heighten, increase, intensify. ANTONYMS: decelerate, slow down.

hot air n. (*boastful, empty talk*) bombast, bunkum, claptrap, empty talk, (*coll.*) guff, nonsense.

hotbed n. (*any place which favours rapid growth of disease, vice etc.*) breeding ground, nest.

hot-blooded a. **1** (*passionate, in love*) ardent, fervent, impassioned, lustful, passionate, sensual, sexual. ANTONYMS: asexual, frigid, sexless, unimpassioned. **2** (*excitable, easily angered*) excitable, fiery, impetuous, impulsive, irritable, rash, temperamental, wild. ANTONYMS: calm, restrained.

hotchpotch n. (*a confused mixture, a jumble*) jumble, medley, miscellany, mishmash.

hotel n. (*a commercial establishment providing accommodation, meals etc.*) boarding house, guest house.

hotfoot adv. (*very hastily, swiftly*) fast, hastily, hurriedly, post-haste, quickly, rapidly, speedily, swiftly. ANTONYMS: at a snail's pace, slowly.

hot-headed a. (*fiery, impetuous*) fiery, foolhardy, hasty, impetuous, impulsive, precipitate, rash, reckless, volatile. ANTONYMS: cautious, slow, wary.

hothouse n. (*a plant house where a relatively high artificial temperature is maintained to facilitate growth*) glasshouse, greenhouse.
~a. (*too sensitive, delicate*) coddled, delicate, frail, overprotected, pampered, sensitive. ANTONYMS: ill-treated, tough.
~v.t. (*to encourage or force the development of (skills etc.)*) accelerate, develop, encourage, force, further, promote.

hotly adv. (*passionately*) ardently, excitedly, fervently, fiercely, passionately, strongly, vehemently. ANTONYMS: apathetically, calmly, half-heartedly.

hot spot n. (*a place or situation of potential trouble*) danger area, fix, mess, pickle, predicament, quandary, trouble spot.

hot-tempered a. (*quick to anger; irascible*) choleric, fiery, irascible, (*coll.*) on a short fuse, quick-tempered, splenetic, testy, touchy. ANTONYMS: easygoing, placid.

hound v.t. 1 (*to hunt or chase with or as with hounds*) chase, follow, give chase to, hunt, hunt down, pursue, stalk, track, trail. 2 (*to urge (on), to nag*) badger, browbeat, goad, harass, harry, nag, pester, pressure, pressurize, prod, urge (on).

house[1] n. 1 (*a building for shelter or residence, a dwelling*) abode, domicile, dwelling, habitation, home, (*coll.*) pad, residence. 2 (*a household*) family, family circle, household, ménage. 3 (*a family or stock, esp. a noble family*) clan, dynasty, family, line, lineage. 4 (*an assembly, esp. one of the legislative assemblies of a country*) assembly, chamber, congress, legislative assembly, legislative body, parliament. 5 (*the audience at a place of entertainment*) assembly, audience, gate, gathering, spectators. 6 (*a commercial establishment*) business, company, concern, corporation, establishment, firm, organization. 7 (*a pub*) inn, pub, public house, tavern. **on the house** ((*esp. of alcoholic drinks*) *given for no payment*) complimentary, for nothing, free, gratis.

house[2] v.t. 1 (*to lodge, contain*) accommodate, board, contain, have room for, have space for, lodge, put up, sleep, take. 2 (*to provide accommodation for*) billet, lodge, provide a home for, provide (someone) with accommodation, provide (someone) with a house, provide (someone) with housing. 3 (*to enclose, to cover*) contain, cover, enclose, protect, sheathe.

household n. (*those who live together under the same roof and compose a domestic unit*) family, family circle, home, house, ménage.
~a. (*of or relating to the house and family, domestic*) domestic, for the home, for the house.

householder n. (*the head of a household, the occupier of a house*) homeowner, occupant, occupier, resident, tenant.

housekeeping n. (*the care of a household*) home economics, household management, husbandry.

housing n. 1 (*lodging, accommodation*) accommodation, habitation, homes, houses, lodging, shelter. 2 (*a protective case for machinery*) capsule, case, casing, container, cover, covering, holder, jacket, sheath.

hovel n. (*a miserable dwelling*) cabin, hut, shack, shanty, shed.

hover v.i. 1 (*to hang or remain (over or about) fluttering in the air or on the wing*) be suspended, drift, float, flutter, hang. 2 (*to loiter (about)*) hang (about), linger, loiter, wait (around). 3 (*to be irresolute, to waver*) dither, fluctuate, oscillate, see-saw, shilly-shally, vacillate, waver.

however adv. (*nevertheless, notwithstanding*) after all, anyhow, anyway, be that as it may, nevertheless, nonetheless, notwithstanding, regardless, still, though, yet.

howl v.i. 1 (*to utter a protracted hollow cry, as a dog or wolf*) bay, quest, yowl. 2 (*to wail*) bawl, cry, lament, scream, shriek, ululate, wail, weep, yell. 3 (*to make a loud cry with laughter*) hoot, laugh heartily, roar, roar with laughter, shriek, shriek with mirth, split one's sides.
~n. 1 (*the cry of a wolf or dog*) bay, baying, yowl, yowling. 2 (*a protracted, hollow cry, esp. one of anguish or distress*) bawl, bawling, caterwauling, crying, lament, lamenting, scream, screaming, shriek, shrieking, ululation, wail, wailing, weeping, yelling. 3 (*a loud cry of laughter*) hoot, roar, shriek.

howler n. (*a ludicrous blunder*) blunder, (*sl.*) booboo, (*sl.*) clanger, error, gaffe, mistake.

hub n. (*a place of central importance*) centre, core, focal point, focus, heart, middle, nerve centre, pivot.

hubbub *n.* **1** (*a confused noise*) babel, noise. **2** (*a noisy disturbance*) brouhaha, commotion, disturbance, fracas, hullabaloo, riot, row, rumpus. **3** (*a tumult, an uproar*) bedlam, clamour, din, hurly-burly, pandemonium, racket, tumult, uproar.

huddle *v.i.* **1** (*to gather or crowd* (*up or together*) *closely*) cluster, congregate, crowd, gather, herd, pack, press. **2** (*to lie or sit with one's arms and legs close to one's body*) cuddle up, curl up, hunch up, nestle, snuggle up.
~*n.* **1** (*a secretive discussion between a group of people*) (*coll.*) confab, conference, consultation, discussion, powwow. **2** (*a confused crowd*) bunch, cluster, crowd, pack, press, throng. **3** (*disorder, confusion*) confusion, heap, jumble, mess, muddle, state of disorder, tangle.

hue *n.* **1** (*colour, tint*) colour, shade, tinge, tint, tone. **2** (*a kind or aspect*) aspect, cast, complexion, kind, sort, type, variety.

hue and cry *n.* **1** (*a clamour or outcry* (*against*)) objection(s), outcry, protest(s), series of complaints, storm of protest. **2** (*a great stir or alarm*) brouhaha, clamour, commotion, furore, hullabaloo, uproar.

huff *n.* **in a huff** (*annoyed, in a mood*) annoyed, in a bad mood, in a mood, in high dudgeon, miffed, offended, peeved, piqued, put out, sulking, sulky, vexed.

hug *v.t.* **1** (*to embrace closely*) clasp, cuddle, embrace, hold close, squeeze, take (someone) in one's arms. **2** (*to hold fast, to cherish*) cherish, cling to, foster, harbour, hold onto, keep, nurse, retain. ANTONYMS: abandon, give up. **3** (*to keep close to*) follow closely, keep close to, stay near to.
~*n.* (*a close embrace*) bear-hug, clasp, (*coll.*) clinch, cuddle, embrace, squeeze.

huge *a.* (*very large, enormous*) bulky, colossal, enormous, extensive, giant, (*coll.*) ginormous, great, hulking, immense, jumbo, massive, (*coll.*) mega, monstrous, monumental, mountainous, prodigious, stupendous, tremendous, vast. ANTONYMS: diminutive, microscopic, minuscule, minute, tiny.

hulk *n.* (*the hull or body of a ship, esp. an unseaworthy one*) derelict, frame, hull, ruin, shell, skeleton, wreck.

hulking *a.* (*bulky, unwieldy*) awkward, bulky, clumsy, cumbersome, lumbering, ungainly, unwieldy. ANTONYMS: dainty, elegant, graceful.

hull[1] *n.* (*the body of a ship*) body, frame, framework, shell, skeleton, structure.

hull[2] *n.* (*the outer covering of a nut or seed, the pod or shell*) husk, pod, shell, skin.

hullabaloo *n.* (*an uproar*) babel, bedlam, brouhaha, clamour, commotion, din, disturbance, furore, fuss, hue and cry, hurly-burly, noise, pandemonium, racket, rumpus, (*coll.*) to-do, tumult, uproar.

hum *v.i.* **1** (*to make a prolonged murmuring sound like a bee*) buzz, drone, murmur, purr, throb, vibrate, whir. **2** (*to make an inarticulate sound in speaking, from embarrassment or hesitation*) mumble, mutter, stammer.
~*n.* **1** (*a low droning or murmuring sound*) buzz, drone, murmur, purr, throb, vibration, whir. **2** (*an inarticulate expression of hesitation, disapproval etc.*) hesitation, stammer, stumble. **to hum and haw/ ha 1** (*to hesitate in speaking*) falter, hesitate, mumble, stammer, stumble. **2** (*to refrain from giving a decisive answer*) be hesitant, be indecisive, be irresolute, hesitate, shilly-shally, vacillate, waver. ANTONYMS: be decisive, be resolute.

human *a.* **1** (*of or relating to people or humankind*) anthropoid, manlike, mortal. ANTONYMS: animal, divine, mechanical. **2** (*having the nature or characteristics of people or humankind*) fallible, flesh and blood, frail, mortal, perishable, vulnerable, weak. ANTONYMS: divine, immortal, invulnerable. **3** (*having the good characteristics of humankind*) charitable, compassionate, humane, kind, kind-hearted, kindly, merciful, sympathetic, understanding. ANTONYMS: cruel, inhuman, unkind.

humane *a.* **1** (*tender, compassionate*) benevolent, charitable, compassionate, forbearing, generous, gentle, good, human, kind, kindly, lenient, magnanimous, merciful, sympathetic, tender, understanding. ANTONYMS: brutal, cruel, inhumane, merciless, unsympathetic. **2** (*relieving distress, aiding those in danger etc.*) compassionate, humanitarian, merciful. ANTONYMS: cruel, merciless.

humanitarian *a.* (*humane*) compassionate, humane, merciful. ANTONYMS: cruel, merciless, unkind.

humanity *n.* **1** (*human nature*) flesh and blood, human nature, humanness, mortality. ANTONYMS: divinity. **2** (*humankind, people*) Homo sapiens, human beings, humankind, human race, man, mankind, people. ANTONYMS: animals, God. **3** (*kindness, benevolence*) charitableness, charity, compassion, generosity, gentleness, goodness, humaneness, humanness, kindness, lenience, magnanimity, mercy, pity, sympathy, tenderness, understanding. ANTONYMS: brutality, cruelty, inhumanity, unkindness. **the humanities** (*the study of literature, music etc. as distinct from social or natural sciences*) arts, classical studies, classics, liberal arts.

humble *a.* **1** (*having or showing a sense of lowliness or inferiority, modest*) meek, modest, self-effacing, unassertive, unassuming, unpretentious. ANTONYMS: arrogant, conceited, haughty, pretentious, proud. **2** (*of lowly condition, dimensions etc.*) base, common, ignoble, inferior, low, lowly, low-ranking, mean, modest, plain, plebeian, simple, undistinguished, vulgar. ANTONYMS: aristocratic, distinguished, grand, high-ranking, noble, superior. **3** (*submissive, deferential*) deferential, obsequious, servile, submissive, subservient, sycophantic. ANTONYMS: arrogant, contemptuous, disdainful, proud.
~*v.t.* **1** (*to bring low, to abase*) abase, bring down, bring low, debase, degrade, demean, depreciate, disgrace, disparage, humiliate, mortify, put (someone) down, shame, take (someone) down a peg (or two). ANTONYMS: elevate, honour, praise, promote. **2** (*to bring to a state of subjection or inferiority*) bring (someone) to their knees, conquer, crush, defeat, subdue, vanquish.

humbug *n.* **1** (*a hoax*) deception, fraud, hoax, imposture, ruse, sham, swindle, trick. **2** (*nonsense, rubbish*) balderdash, bunkum, nonsense, (*coll.*) rot, rubbish, (*coll.*) tommyrot, twaddle. **3** (*an impostor*) charlatan, cheat, conman/ conwoman, deceiver, dissembler, fraud, fraudster, mountebank, (*coll.*) phoney, quack, sham, swindler, trickster.

humdrum *a.* (*dull, commonplace*) banal, boring, commonplace, dreary, dull, monotonous, mundane, ordinary, repetitious, repetitive, routine, run-of-the-mill, tedious, uneventful, uninteresting, unvaried, unvarying. ANTONYMS: eventful, exciting, extraordinary, interesting, stimulating.

humid *a.* (*moist, damp*) clammy, damp, dank, moist, muggy, soggy, sticky, sultry, watery, wet, wettish. ANTONYMS: arid, dry, torrid.

humidity *n.* (*the state of being humid*) clamminess, damp, dampness, dankness, humidness, moistness, moisture, mugginess, sogginess, stickiness, sultriness, wateriness, wetness. ANTONYMS: aridity, aridness, dryness, torridity.

humiliate *v.t.* (*to lower in self-esteem, to mortify*) abase, bring down, bring low, crush, debase, degrade, demean, discomfit, embarrass, humble, make (someone) eat humble pie, mortify, put (someone) down, put (someone) to shame, shame, subdue, take (someone) down a peg or two. ANTONYMS: elevate, honour, make proud.

humiliation *n.* (*shame, embarrassment*) degradation, discomfiture, disgrace, embarrassment, ignominy, indignity, loss of face, mortification, shame. ANTONYMS: honour, pride.

humility *n.* **1** (*modesty, a sense of unworthiness*) diffidence, humbleness, meekness, modesty, self-effacement. ANTONYMS: arrogance, pride, vanity. **2** (*self-abasement*) obsequiousness, servility, submissiveness, subservience, sycophancy. ANTONYMS: arrogance, assertiveness, forcefulness.

humorous *a.* **1** (*tending to excite laughter*) absurd, amusing, comic, comical, droll, entertaining, facetious, farcical, funny, hilarious, jocular, laughable, ludicrous, rib-tickling, ridiculous, side-splitting, whimsical, witty. ANTONYMS: sad, serious, solemn. **2** (*jocular*) amusing, entertaining, facetious, funny, jocular, playful, waggish, witty. ANTONYMS: earnest, grave, solemn.

humour *n.* **1** (*the quality of being amusing, witty etc.*) absurdity, amusement, comedy, comical aspect, drollness, entertainment, facetiousness, farce, farcicalness, funniness, funny side, hilarity, jocularity, laughableness, ludicrousness, ridiculousness, whimsy, wit, wittiness. ANTONYMS: sadness, seriousness, solemnity. **2** (*mental disposition, frame of mind*) disposition, frame of mind, mood, state of mind, temper. **3** (*caprice, whim*) bent, caprice, fancy, inclination, propensity, quirk, vagary, whim.
~*v.t.* (*to indulge, to give way to*) accommodate, give way to, go along with, indulge, make concessions to, pander to, spoil. ANTONYMS: oppose, stand up to.

hump *n.* **1** (*a swelling or protuberance, esp. on the back*) bulge, bump, intumescence, knob, lump, node, protrusion, protuberance, swelling. **2** (*a rounded hillock*) hillock, knoll, mound.
~*v.t.* (*to carry on the back*) carry, heave, hoist, lift, lug, transport.

hunch *n.* (*an intuitive feeling or premonition*) feeling, idea, impression, inkling, intuition, premonition, presentiment, sixth sense, suspicion.
~*v.t.* (*to crook, to arch (esp. the back)*) arch, crook, curve. ANTONYMS: straighten.
~*v.i.* (*to stoop*) bend, crouch, stoop. ANTONYMS: straighten.

hunger *n.* **1** (*a craving for food*) greed, voracity. **2** (*a painful sensation or weakened condition caused by lack of food*) emptiness, famishment, hungriness, lack of food, ravenousness, starvation. **3** (*any strong desire*) craving, desire, itch, longing, lust, need, thirst, yearning, (*coll.*) yen. ANTONYMS: disinclination, dislike, distaste, reluctance.

hungry *a.* **1** (*feeling a sensation of hunger*) empty, famished, famishing, ravenous, starving. ANTONYMS: full, satiated. **2** (*having a keen appetite*) greedy, voracious. **3** (*longing or craving eagerly*) avid, covetous, desirous, eager, greedy, keen, thirsty, voracious. ANTONYMS: apathetic, reluctant, unenthusiastic.

hunk *n.* (*a large piece*) block, chunk, lump, piece, slab, wedge.

hunt *v.t.* **1** (*to search for, to seek after*) ferret around for, forage for, look for, search for, seek, try to find. **2** (*to pursue or chase*) chase, follow, give chase to, hound, pursue, stalk, track, trail. ~*n.* **1** (*a search*) quest, search, searching. **2** (*pursuit*) chasing, following, pursuit, stalking, tracking, trailing.

hunted *a.* ((*of a facial expression etc.*) *showing distress, fatigue etc. as if being hunted*) careworn, distraught, distressed, haggard, harassed, tormented, worn.

hurdle *n.* **1** (*a movable framework of withes or split timber serving for gates, enclosures etc.*) barricade, barrier, fence, hedge, railing, wall. **2** (*a barrier for jumping over in racing*) bar, fence. **3** (*a barrier or obstacle*) bar, barrier, complication, difficulty, drawback, handicap, hindrance, impediment, obstacle, obstruction, snag, stumbling-block. ANTONYMS: aid, benefit, help.

hurl *v.t.* (*to throw with violence*) cast, (*coll.*) chuck, fire, fling, heave, launch, let fly, pitch, propel, shy, (*coll.*) sling, throw, toss.

hurricane *n.* (*an extremely violent gale*) cyclone, gale, squall, storm, tempest, tornado, typhoon.

hurried *a.* (*done in a hurry*) cursory, fast, fleeting, hasty, perfunctory, quick, rapid, rushed, speedy, superficial, swift. ANTONYMS: careful, leisurely, slow.

hurry *v.i.* (*to hasten*) be quick, dash, (*coll.*) get a move on, get cracking, hasten, hurry up, make haste, rush, scurry, shake a leg, speed up, step on it. ANTONYMS: crawl along, dawdle, hang back, slow down. ~*v.t.* **1** (*to impel to greater speed, to accelerate*) accelerate, expedite, hasten, hurry up, speed up. ANTONYMS: delay, retard, slow down. **2** (*to push forward*) drive on, goad, hustle, prod, push on, urge. ANTONYMS: impede, obstruct. ~*n.* **1** (*the act of hurrying*) celerity, expedition, fastness, haste, hurrying, promptness, quickness, rapidity, speed. ANTONYMS: slowness. **2** (*urgency, bustle, precipitation*) bustle, flurry, hubbub, hurry-scurry, rush. **to hurry up 1** (*to make haste*) be quick, (*coll.*) get a move on, get cracking, hasten, hurry up, make haste, rush,

scurry, shake a leg, speed up, step on it. ANTONYMS: dawdle, delay, hang back, slow down. **2** (*to cause or cajole* (*someone*) *to make haste*) drive on, goad, hustle, prod, urge on. ANTONYMS: impede, obstruct.

hurt *v.t.* **1** (*to cause pain or injury to*) bruise, cause injury to, cause pain to, injure, wound. ANTONYMS: alleviate, cure, heal, soothe. **2** (*to damage*) blight, damage, harm, impair, mar, spoil. ANTONYMS: repair, restore. **3** (*to grieve or distress* (*e.g. the feelings*)) cut to the quick, distress, give offence to, grieve, offend, pain, sadden, upset, wound. ANTONYMS: comfort, console, soothe. ~*v.i.* (*to be painful, to cause pain*) ache, be painful, be sore, be tender, heal, smart, sting, throb. ~*n.* **1** (*an injury, damage*) blight, damage, detriment, disadvantage, harm, injury, loss. ANTONYMS: improvement, reparation, restoration. **2** (*a wound*) bruise, injury, sore, wound. **3** (*pain*) ache, pain, smarting, soreness, stinging, throbbing. **4** (*distress*) anguish, distress, grief, misery, pain, sadness, sorrow, suffering.

hurtful *a.* **1** (*causing hurt, esp. to the feelings*) cutting, distressing, malicious, mean, mischievous, nasty, offensive, painful, unkind, unpleasant, upsetting, wounding. ANTONYMS: nice, palliative, pleasant, soothing. **2** (*damaging, injurious* (*to*)) damaging, deleterious, detrimental, disadvantageous, injurious, prejudicial, ruinous. ANTONYMS: advantageous, helpful, of service, valuable.

husband *n.* (*a married man in relation to his wife*) (*coll.*) hubby, (*dial., coll.*) man, (*coll.*) old man, partner, spouse. ANTONYMS: wife. ~*v.t.* (*to manage* (*resources*) *carefully, to economize*) be economical with, conserve, preserve, save, store, use sparingly. ANTONYMS: fritter away, squander, waste.

husbandry *n.* **1** (*the business of a farmer, agriculture*) agriculture, agronomics, agronomy, farming, farm management. **2** (*frugality, careful management*) budgeting, economy, frugality, good housekeeping, saving, thrift. ANTONYMS: extravagance.

hush *n.* (*silence, stillness*) calm, peace, peacefulness, quiet, quietness, silence, still, stillness, tranquillity. ANTONYMS: din, noise. **to hush up** (*to keep concealed, to suppress*) conceal, cover up, hide, keep dark, suppress. ANTONYMS: make known, make public, reveal.

hush-hush *a.* (*very secret*) classified, confidential, secret, top secret.

husky *a.* **1** (*hoarse or rough in sound*) coarse, croaking, croaky, gravelly, gruff, guttural, harsh, hoarse, rasping, raucous, rough, throaty.

2 (*strong, stalwart*) beefy, brawny, burly, hefty, muscular, powerful, powerfully-built, strapping, strong, thickset, well-built. ANTONYMS: frail, puny, skinny.

hut *n.* (*a small, simple house*) cabin, hovel, lean-to, shanty, shed.

hygiene *n.* (*practices that promote health*) cleanliness, sanitation.

hygienic *a.* (*clean, health-promoting*) clean, germ-free, sanitary, uncontaminated, unpolluted. ANTONYMS: dirty, filthy, insanitary, unhygienic.

hype *n.* (*exaggerated or false publicity used to sell or promote*) advertising, (*coll.*) plugging, promotion, publicity, puff, razzmatazz.

hypnotic *a.* **1** (*relating to or inducing hypnotism*) mesmeric, mesmerizing, spellbinding. **2** (*causing sleep*) narcotic, opiate, sedative, sleep-inducing, soporific. ANTONYMS: stimulating.

hypnotize *v.t.* **1** (*to affect with hypnosis*) mesmerize, put into a trance. **2** (*to capture the attention of completely*) bewitch, entrance, fascinate, rivet, spellbind.

hypocrisy *n.* (*pretence, a feigning to be what one is not*) deceit, deceitfulness, deception, dissembling, double-dealing, duplicity, imposture, insincerity, pietism, pretence, sanctimoniousness, sanctimony, speciousness. ANTONYMS: sincerity.

hypocrite *n.* (*a person who practises hypocrisy, a dissembler*) charlatan, deceiver, dissembler, fraud, impostor, pharisee, (*coll.*) phoney, pietist, sham, whited sepulchre.

hypocritical *a.* (*deceitful, pretending to be what one is not*) deceitful, dissembling, double-dealing, duplicitous, insincere, pharisaical, (*coll.*) phoney, pietistic, sanctimonious, specious, spurious, two-faced. ANTONYMS: sincere.

hypothesis *n.* (*a mere supposition or assumption*) assumption, presumption, supposition, theory.

hypothetic *a.* (*c#onjectural, conditional*) assumed, conjectural, imagined, notional, putative, speculative, supposed, theoretical. ANTONYMS: actual, proven, real.

hysterical *a.* **1** (*neurotically emotional or excitable*) agitated, berserk, beside oneself, distracted, distraught, frantic, frenzied, overwrought, uncontrolled, unrestrained. ANTONYMS: calm, composed, restrained. **2** (*very funny*) comical, farcical, funny, hilarious, rib-tickling, side-splitting, uproarious. ANTONYMS: grave, serious, solemn.

I

ice *v.t.* **1** (*to cool with ice*) chill, cool. ANTONYMS: warm. **2** (*to freeze* (*up, over*)) freeze, frost, glaze. **3** (*N Am., sl.*) (*to kill*) (*coll.*) bump off, (*sl.*) do in, kill, murder, (*sl.*) waste.

icy *a.* **1** (*like ice, frozen*) arctic, biting, bitter, chilly, cold, freezing, frosty, frozen, glacial, glassy, ice-cold, polar, raw, slippery, wintry. ANTONYMS: hot. **2** (*of a tone, look*) *cold and unfriendly*) aloof, cold, distant, flinty, forbidding, frigid, frosty, glacial, hostile, indifferent, remote, reserved, steely, stony, unfeeling, unfriendly, unwelcoming. ANTONYMS: cordial, friendly.

idea *n.* **1** (*a mental image or representation of anything*) form, image, representation. **2** (*a conception, a plan*) abstraction, concept, conception, plan, thought. **3** (*a more or less vague belief*) belief, clue, conviction, fancy, guess, hint, impression, inkling, intimation, notion, perception, suggestion, suspicion, theory, understanding. **4** (*an intention or design*) aim, design, end, goal, import, intention, meaning, object, objective, plan, point, purpose, reason, scheme, significance. **5** (*a way of thinking or conceiving* (*something*)) belief, feeling, hypothesis, interpretation, opinion, philosophy, sentiment, stance, viewpoint. **6** (*an archetype or pattern as distinct from an example of it*) archetype, essence, form, pattern.

ideal *a.* **1** (*reaching one's standard of perfection; perfect*) archetypal, classic, consummate, excellent, exemplary, idyllic, model, perfect, quintessential, supreme. ANTONYMS: flawed, imperfect. **2** (*visionary, fanciful*) fanciful, illusory, imaginary, unreal, visionary. ANTONYMS: actual, real. **3** (*consisting of or relating to ideas*) abstract, conceptual, hypothetical, intellectual, mental, theoretical, transcendental.
~*n.* **1** (*an imaginary standard of perfection*) aim, goal, objective, target. **2** (*an actual thing realizing this*) archetype, criterion, epitome, example, exemplar, last word, model, nonpareil, paradigm, paragon, pattern, prototype, standard.

idealistic *a.* (*having ideals that are impractical*) impracticable, impractical, optimistic, perfectionist, quixotic, romantic, starry-eyed, unrealistic, utopian, visionary. ANTONYMS: realistic.

identical *a.* **1** (*absolutely the same*) duplicate, indistinguishable, interchangeable, same, selfsame, twin. ANTONYMS: different. **2** ((*of different things*) *exactly alike*) alike, comparable, corresponding, equal, equivalent, like, matching, similar.

identification *n.* **1** (*the act of identifying*) cataloguing, classifying, designation, differentiation, (*sl.*) fingering, identifying, labelling, naming, perception, pinpointing, recognition. **2** (*a proof of identity*) credentials, ID, identity card, papers. **3** (*the assumption of the characteristics of another, esp. of an admired person*) association, empathy, involvement, rapport, sympathy.

identify *v.t.* **1** (*to determine or prove the identity of*) catalogue, classify, flag, label, name, recognize, tag. **2** (*to establish, to pinpoint* (*a problem*)) detect, diagnose, establish, make out, pick out, pinpoint, single out, specify, spot. **3** (*to unite or associate closely* (*with a party, interests etc.*)) ally (with), associate (with), empathize (with), feel (for), relate (to), sympathize (with).

identity *n.* **1** (*one's individuality*) distinctiveness, distinguishability, individuality, name, particularity, personality, self, singularity, uniqueness. **2** (*the state of being the same*) accord, agreement, correspondence, empathy, equality, likeness, oneness, rapport, sameness, unanimity, unity. ANTONYMS: difference.

ideology *n.* **1** (*the political or social philosophy of a nation, movement etc.*) credo, creed, doctrine, dogma, philosophy, principles, teachings, tenets. **2** (*an abstract or fanciful theory*) beliefs, ideas, philosophy, theory.

idiocy *n.* (*extreme stupidity*) absurdity, asininity, cretinism, fatuity, foolishness, imbecility, inanity, insanity, lunacy, senselessness, stupidity, tomfoolery. ANTONYMS: sense.

idiom *n.* **1** (*a phrase etc. whose meaning cannot be deduced simply from the meaning of each of its words*) expression, phrase, usage. **2** (*a mode of expression peculiar to a particular language*) expression, locution. **3** (*a dialect or language of a country*) argot, cant, dialect, jargon, language, parlance, patois, phraseology, speech, talk, tongue, vernacular. **4** (*a mode of artistic* *expression characteristic of a particular person or school*) mode, style.

idiosyncrasy *n.* **1** (*a characteristic or habit peculiar to an individual*) affectation, attitude, characteristic, habit, mannerism, speciality, trait, trick. **2** (*anything that is highly eccentric*) eccentricity, oddity, peculiarity, quirk, singularity.

idiosyncratic *a.* (*unusual, peculiar*) distinctive, individual, individualistic, peculiar, unusual.

idiot *n.* **1** (*a stupid, silly person*) ass, (*sl.*) berk, (*sl.*) dickhead, (*coll.*) dimwit, (*sl.*) dipstick, (*sl.*) divvy, dunce, fool, halfwit, (*sl.*) jerk, (*sl.*) nerd, nincompoop, (*coll.*) nitwit, numskull, (*sl.*) pillock, (*sl.*) plonker, (*sl.*) prat, (*sl.*) prick, (*coll.*) twit, (*sl.*) wally. **2** (*a person of very low intelligence*) cretin, imbecile, moron, simpleton.

idiotic *a.* (*foolish, silly*) absurd, asinine, (*coll.*) crackpot, crazy, daft, fatuous, foolhardy, foolish, half-witted, (*coll.*) hare-brained, imbecilic, inane, insane, (*coll.*) loopy, lunatic, moronic, senseless, stupid, unintelligent, witless. ANTONYMS: brilliant, wise.

idle *a.* **1** (*averse to work, lazy*) indolent, inert, lackadaisical, lazy, lethargic, listless, shiftless, slothful, sluggish. ANTONYMS: busy. **2** (*doing nothing, inactive*) dead, inactive, jobless, mothballed, redundant, stationary, unemployed. ANTONYMS: active. **3** (*not occupied, free*) empty, free, unoccupied, unused, vacant. **4** ((*of a machine*) *not in use*) inoperative, out of action. ANTONYMS: working. **5** ((*of a threat*) *useless, vain*) abortive, bootless, fruitless, futile, ineffectual, pointless, unavailing, unproductive, unprofitable, unsuccessful, useless, vain, worthless. ANTONYMS: fruitful, worthwhile. **6** ((*of a rumour*) *without foundation*) foolish, frivolous, insignificant, meaningless, shallow, superficial, trifling, trivial, unfounded, unimportant. ANTONYMS: meaningful, significant.
~*v.i.* (*to spend time in idleness*) coast, dally, dawdle, drift, fool, fritter, kill time, laze, loiter, loll, lounge, mark time, potter, slack, vegetate, (*coll.*) veg out, waste, while. ANTONYMS: work.

idler *n.* (*a person who spends their time in idleness*) (*sl.*) couch potato, dawdler, (*coll.*) deadbeat, dodger, drone, good-for-nothing, laggard, layabout, lazybones, loafer, lounger, malingerer, ne'er-do-well, shirker, (*coll.*) skiver, slacker, sloth, (*sl.*) slouch, sluggard, timewaster.

idol *n.* **1** (*an image, esp. one worshipped as a god*) effigy, icon, image. **2** (*a false god*) deity,

god, graven image. **3** (*a person or thing loved or honoured excessively*) beloved, celebratory, darling, favourite, god, hero, luminary, pet, pin-up, superstar.

idolize *v.t.* **1** (*to love or venerate to excess*) admire, adore, adulate, dote upon, exalt, glorify, lionize, look up to, love, put on a pedestal, revere, reverence, venerate, worship. **2** (*to make an idol of*) deify, glorify, immortalize, worship.

idyllic *a.* (*perfect, esp. because peaceful and beautiful*) Arcadian, beautiful, blissful, bucolic, charming, halcyon, heavenly, ideal, pastoral, peaceful, perfect, picturesque, rustic, unspoiled.

if *conj.* **1** (*providing that; in the case that*) in the case that, on condition that, providing that. **2** (*on the supposition that*) admitting that, allowing that, assuming that, granting that, supposing that. **3** (*although*) although, though.
~*n.* **1** (*an uncertain or doubtful factor*) doubt, hesitation, uncertainty. **2** (*a condition*) condition, proviso, stipulation.

ignite *v.t.* **1** (*to set on fire*) fire, kindle, light, set alight, set on fire, touch off. ANTONYMS: extinguish, put out. **2** (*to arouse or excite* (*interest, controversy*)) arouse, awake, excite, inflame, stimulate.
~*v.i.* (*to catch fire*) burn, burst into flames, catch fire, flare up, kindle, take fire.

ignominious *a.* **1** (*disgraceful*) base, contemptible, despicable, discreditable, disgraceful, dishonourable, disreputable, ignoble, indecorous, inglorious, low, mean, shabby, undignified, unworthy. ANTONYMS: creditable, honourable. **2** (*humiliating*) abject, humiliating, shameful, sorry.

ignorance *n.* (*the state of being ignorant, lack of knowledge* (*of*)) blindness, darkness, greenness, illiteracy, inexperience, innocence, oblivion, unawareness, unconsciousness, unfamiliarity, unintelligence. ANTONYMS: enlightenment, knowledge.

ignorant *a.* **1** (*lacking knowledge*) crass, dense, green, illiterate, inexperienced, innocent, (*coll.*) thick, uneducated, unenlightened, uninitiated, unknowledgeable, unlearned, unlettered, unread, unschooled. ANTONYMS: learned. **2** (*unaware* (*of a fact etc.*)) oblivious, unaware, unconscious, uninformed, unknowing, unwitting. ANTONYMS: aware.

ignore *v.t.* (*to pass over without notice, to disregard*) cold-shoulder, cut, discount, disregard, neglect, overlook, pass over, reject, skip, snub. ANTONYMS: acknowledge, heed.

ill *a.* **1** (*unwell, diseased*) ailing, (*sl.*) dicky, diseased, (*coll.*) funny, indisposed, infirm, laid up, off-colour, out of sorts, poorly, queasy, queer, (*coll.*) seedy, sick, under the weather, unhealthy, unsound, unwell. ANTONYMS: healthy, well. **2** (*malevolent, hostile*) acrimonious, adverse, antagonistic, belligerent, cantankerous, crabbed, cross, harsh, hateful, hostile, inimical, irritable, malevolent, malicious, sullen, surly, unfriendly, unkind. **3** (*mischievous, harmful*) bad, damaging, deleterious, detrimental, harmful, iniquitous, injurious, mischievous, noxious, pernicious, ruinous. **4** (*unfavourable, unlucky*) disturbing, foreboding, inauspicious, ominous, sinister, threatening, unfavourable, unfortunate, unlucky, unpromising, unpropitious, unwholesome. ANTONYMS: favourable, promising. **5** (*morally bad, evil*) bad, depraved, evil, foul, immoral, iniquitous, sinful, vile, wicked, wrong. ANTONYMS: good. **6** (*incorrect*) faulty, improper, incorrect.
~*adv.* **1** (*not well, badly*) adversely, badly, not well. ANTONYMS: well. **2** (*not easily*) barely, by no means, hardly. **3** (*imperfectly*) imperfectly, improperly, insufficiently, poorly, scantily. **4** (*unfavourably*) inauspiciously, unfavourably, unfortunately, unluckily.
~*n.* **1** (*evil*) abuse, badness, cruelty, damage, depravity, evil, malice, mischief, suffering, wickedness. ANTONYMS: good. **2** (*injury, harm*) affliction, calamity, disaster, hardship, harm, hurt, injury, mischief, misery, misfortune, pain, suffering, tribulation, trouble, unpleasantness, woe. **3** (*a disease*) ailment, complaint, disease, disorder, illness, indisposition, infirmity, malady, malaise, sickness.

ill-advised *a.* **1** (*imprudent*) foolhardy, foolish, hasty, impolitic, improvident, imprudent, inappropriate, incautious, indiscreet, injudicious, misguided, rash, short-sighted, unwise, wrong-headed. ANTONYMS: cautious, wise. **2** ((*of a plan*) *not well thought out*) ill-considered, ill-judged, reckless, thoughtless.

ill-bred *a.* (*brought up badly; rude*) bad-mannered, boorish, churlish, coarse, discourteous, ill-mannered, impolite, rude, uncivil, uncouth, ungallant, ungentlemanly, unladylike, unmannerly, unrefined, vulgar. ANTONYMS: polite, well-bred.

ill-defined *a.* (*lacking a clear outline*) blurred, dim, fuzzy, indistinct, nebulous, shadowy, unclear, vague, woolly. ANTONYMS: clear, distinct.

illegal *a.* (*contrary to the law, unlawful*) banned, contraband, criminal, felonious, forbidden, illegitimate, illicit, lawless, outlawed, prohibited, proscribed, unauthorized, unconstitutional, unlawful, unlicensed, unofficial, wrongful. ANTONYMS: lawful, legal.

illegible *a.* (*that cannot be read or deciphered*) crabbed, faint, incomprehensible, indecipherable, obscure, scrawled, scribbly, undecipherable, unreadable. ANTONYMS: legible, readable.

illegitimate *a.* **1** (*born of parents not married to each other*) base-born, bastard, fatherless, misbegotten, natural. ANTONYMS: legitimate. **2** (*contrary to law or recognized usage*) forbidden, illegal, illicit, unauthorized, unconstitutional, unlawful. ANTONYMS: lawful, legal. **3** (*irregular*) improper, incorrect, irregular. **4** (*contrary to logical rules*) illogical, incorrect, invalid, spurious, unsound.

ill-fated *a.* (*destined to end badly or in failure*) blighted, doomed, fated, hapless, ill-omened, ill-starred, luckless, star-crossed, unfortunate, unlucky. ANTONYMS: lucky.

ill-founded *a.* (*lacking any foundation in fact*) baseless, empty, erroneous, groundless, idle, mistaken, uncorroborated, unjustified, unproven, unreliable, unsubstantiated, unsupported.

ill-humoured *a.* (*bad-tempered*) bad-tempered, crabby, cross, disagreeable, grumpy, huffy, impatient, irascible, irritable, moody, morose, petulant, (*sl.*) ratty, sharp, snappy, sulky, sullen, testy, touchy, waspish. ANTONYMS: cheerful, genial.

illiberal *a.* **1** (*narrow-minded*) bigoted, hidebound, intolerant, narrow-minded, prejudiced, reactionary, small-minded. ANTONYMS: broad-minded, tolerant. **2** (*not characterized by wide views or by culture*) uncultivated, uncultured, uneducated. **3** (*not generous; niggardly*) close-fisted, mean, miserly, niggardly, parsimonious, selfish, stingy, tight, tight-fisted, uncharitable, ungenerous. ANTONYMS: generous.

illicit *a.* **1** (*not allowed or permitted*) banned, bootleg, clandestine, contraband, forbidden, furtive, guilty, immoral, improper, prohibited, sneaky, unallowed, unauthorized, underhand, unlicensed, unofficial, unpermitted, unsanctioned, wrong. ANTONYMS: allowed. **2** (*unlawful*) criminal, felonious, illegal, illegitimate, unlawful. ANTONYMS: lawful.

illiterate *a.* (*ignorant, uncultivated*) benighted, ignorant, uncultivated, uncultured, uneducated, unenlightened, unlearned, unlettered, unschooled, untaught, untutored. ANTONYMS: cultivated, literate.

ill-mannered *a.* (*rude, boorish*) bad-mannered, boorish, churlish, coarse, discourteous, disrespectful, ill-behaved, ill-bred, impolite, impudent, indecorous, insolent, insulting, rude, uncivil, uncouth, ungallant, unmannerly. ANTONYMS: polite, well-mannered.

ill-natured *a.* (*unkind, churlish*) bad-tempered, churlish, cross, disagreeable, malevolent, malicious, mean, nasty, perverse, petulant, spiteful, sulky, sullen, surly, unfriendly, unkind, unpleasant. ANTONYMS: amiable, good-natured.

illness *n.* (*sickness, a disease*) affliction, ailment, attack, complaint, disability, disease, disorder, ill health, indisposition, infirmity, malady, malaise, sickness.

illogical *a.* (*contrary to reason*) absurd, fallacious, faulty, illogical, inconclusive, inconsistent, incorrect, invalid, irrational, meaningless, senseless, sophistical, specious, spurious, unreasonable, unscientific, unsound. ANTONYMS: logical.

ill-tempered *a.* (*having a bad temper, peevish*) annoyed, bad-tempered, choleric, cross, curt, grumpy, ill-humoured, impatient, irascible, irritable, peevish, (*sl.*) ratty, sharp, sour, spiteful, testy, touchy. ANTONYMS: cheerful, good-tempered.

ill-treat *v.t.* (*to treat badly or cruelly*) abuse, batter, damage, harass, harm, harry, hurt, ill-use, injure, knock about, maltreat, mishandle, mistreat, misuse, oppress, persecute, wrong.

illuminate *v.t.* **1** (*to light up*) brighten, irradiate, light up. ANTONYMS: darken. **2** (*to throw light upon* (*a subject, problem*)) clarify, clear up, elucidate, enlighten, explain, explicate, inform, reveal, throw light upon. ANTONYMS: obscure, veil. **3** (*to decorate* (*a manuscript etc.*) *with coloured pictures, letters etc.*) adorn, decorate, embellish, illustrate, ornament.

illumination *n.* **1** (*the act of lighting up or state of being lit up*) brightening, fluorescence, incandescence, lighting, luminosity, phosphorescence, radiance. **2** (*enlightenment*) awareness, enlightenment, insight, inspiration, perception, revelation, understanding. **3** (*a source of light*) beam, brightness, light, ray. **4** (*the decoration of manuscripts etc. with ornamental coloured letters and pictures*) decoration, illustration. **5** (*clarification*) clarification, edification, explanation, instruction.

illusion *n.* **1** (*a mistaken belief or false perception*) chimera, daydream, delusion, error, fallacy, fancy, fantasy, figment, misapprehension, misconception. **2** (*a deceptive appearance or impression*) deception, false impression, mockery, semblance. **3** (*an unreal image presented to the vision*) hallucination, mirage, phantasm, phantom, spectre, vision.

illusory *a.* (*delusive, deceptive*) apparent, chimerical, deceptive, delusive, fallacious, fanciful, fictional, hallucinatory, illusive, imaginary, misleading, mistaken, sham, unreal. ANTONYMS: real, true.

illustrate *v.t.* **1** (*to embellish* (*a book, etc.*) *with pictures*) adorn, decorate, depict, draw, embellish, emblazon, illuminate, ornament, picture, sketch. **2** (*to make clear or explain by means of examples, figures etc.*) bring home, clarify, demonstrate, elucidate, emphasize, exemplify, exhibit, explain, explicate, illuminate, instance, interpret, show. ANTONYMS: obscure.

illustration *n.* **1** (*an engraving or drawing illustrating a book or article in a periodical*) depiction, diagram, drawing, engraving, figure, photograph, picture, plate, representation. **2** (*something which illustrates, a typical instance*) analogy, case, clarification, demonstration, elucidation, example, exemplar, exemplification, explanation, instance, interpretation, sample, specimen, typification.

illustrative *a.* (*serving as an illustration or example*) descriptive, diagrammatic, exemplary, explanatory, explicatory, expository, graphic, interpretative, pictorial, representative, sample, typical.

illustrious *a.* **1** (*distinguished, famous*) acclaimed, admired, brilliant, celebrated, distinguished, eminent, esteemed, exalted, famed, famous, great, noble, notable, noted, prominent, renowned, respected, venerable, well-known. ANTONYMS: infamous, obscure. **2** (*glorious*) glorious, magnificent, resplendent, splendid.

ill will *n.* (*malevolence; enmity*) acrimony, animosity, antagonism, antipathy, aversion, bad blood, bitterness, dislike, enmity, envy, grudge, hatred, hostility, malevolence, malice, rancour, resentment, spite, unfriendliness, venom. ANTONYMS: friendliness, goodwill.

image *n.* **1** (*a visible representation or likeness of a person or thing, esp. in sculpture*) appearance, effigy, figure, icon, idol, likeness, picture, portrait, representation, sculpture, statue. **2** (*the impression given to others of a person's character etc.*) impression, perception, vision. **3** (*a copy, a counterpart*) clone, copy, counterpart, double, duplicate, facsimile, match, replica, reproduction, (*coll.*) spit, (*coll.*) spitting image, twin. **4** (*the living embodiment of a particular quality*) archetype, embodiment, epitome, essence, example, incarnation, materialization, model, personification, representative. **5** (*an idea, a conception*) conceit, concept, conception, idea, notion. **6** (*an expanded metaphor or simile*) allusion, metaphor, simile, symbol.

imaginary *a.* (*existing only in the imagination*) abstract, chimerical, fancied, fanciful, fictional, fictitious, hypothetical, ideal, illusive, illusory, imagined, invented, legendary, made-up, mythical, shadowy, supposed, unreal, unsubstantial, visionary. ANTONYMS: actual, real.

imagination *n.* **1** (*the constructive or creative faculty of the mind*) creativity, enterprise, imaginativeness, ingenuity, insight, inspiration, invention, inventiveness, mind's eye, originality, perception, resourcefulness, vision, wit. **2** (*fancy, fantasy*) chimera, conception, dream, fancy, fantasy, idea, illusion, impression, notion, supposition. ANTONYMS: reality.

imaginative *a.* **1** (*endowed with imagination*) clever, creative, dreamy, enterprising, fanciful, fantastic, ingenious, innovative, inspired, inventive, original, resourceful. ANTONYMS: unimaginative. **2** (*produced or characterized by imagination*) contrived, fanciful, fantastic, fictional, poetical, visionary, vivid, whimsical.

imagine *v.t.* **1** (*to form an image of in the mind*) conceive, conceptualize, conjure up, contemplate, (*coll.*) dream up, envisage, fantasize, frame, invent, picture, plan, project, scheme, think up, visualize. **2** (*to suppose, to think*) apprehend, believe, fancy, presume, suppose, surmise, suspect, think. ANTONYMS: know. **3** (*to conjecture, to guess*) assume, conjecture, deduce, gather, guess, infer. **4** (*to plot, to devise*) create, devise, plot, realize.

imbecile *a.* **1** (*mentally weak, half-witted*) feeble-minded, half-witted, imbecilic, moronic, simple, witless. **2** (*stupid, fatuous*) absurd, asinine, foolish, idiotic, inane, ludicrous, ridiculous, silly, stupid, thick. ANTONYMS: clever.
~*n.* **1** (*a person of abnormally low intelligence*) cretin, dolt, halfwit, idiot, moron, simpleton. **2** (*a stupid or foolish person*) (*sl.*) berk, coot, (*sl.*) dipstick, (*sl.*) divvy, fool, (*sl.*) jerk, (*sl.*) nerd, numskull, (*sl.*) pillock, (*sl.*) plonker, (*sl.*) prat, (*sl.*) prick, (*coll.*) thickhead, (*taboo sl.*) tosser, (*coll.*) twit, (*sl.*) wally.

imbibe *v.t.* **1** (*to drink*) consume, drink, (*coll.*) knock back, quaff, (*coll.*) sink, suck, swallow, (*coll.*) swig, tipple. **2** (*to absorb* (*liquid etc.*)) absorb, soak up, take in. **3** (*to assimilate* (*ideas etc.*)) acquire, assimilate, gain, gather, incorporate, take in. **4** (*to draw in* (*air*)) draw in, ingest, take in.

imbue *v.t.* **1** (*to inspire, to impregnate* (*with*)) impregnate, inculcate, infuse, inspire, instil,

permeate, pervade. ANTONYMS: purge. **2** (*to saturate* (*with*)) bathe, saturate, soak, steep. **3** (*to dye* (*with*)) colour, dye, stain, suffuse, tinge, tint.

imitate *v.t.* **1** (*to follow the example of*) copy, duplicate, echo, emulate, follow, repeat, reproduce. **2** (*to mimic, to ape*) affect, ape, burlesque, caricature, (*coll.*) do, impersonate, mimic, mock, parody, parrot, satirize, send up, spoof, (*coll.*) take off, travesty. **3** (*to produce a likeness or copy of*) counterfeit, fake, forge. **4** (*to be like; to resemble*) mirror, resemble, simulate.

imitation *n.* **1** (*the act of imitating; an instance of this*) burlesque, emulation, impersonation, impression, mimicry. **2** (*a copy or likeness*) copy, duplication, echo, likeness, reflection, replica, reproduction, resemblance, simulation. ANTONYMS: original. **3** (*something that is not genuine*) counterfeit, fake, forgery, mockery, parody, replica, reproduction, simulation, substitution, (*coll.*) take-off, travesty.

immaculate *a.* **1** (*spotlessly clean or tidy*) clean, dapper, neat, pristine, spick-and-span, spotless, spruce, tidy, trim. **2** (*pure; free from blemish*) chaste, guiltless, incorrupt, innocent, irreproachable, pure, sinless, stainless, unblemished, uncontaminated, undefiled, unpolluted, unsoiled, unsullied, untarnished, virginal, virtuous. ANTONYMS: corrupt, impure. **3** ((*of a performance etc.*) *absolutely faultless*) faultless, flawless, impeccable, perfect.

immaterial *a.* **1** (*irrelevant, unimportant*) extraneous, inconsequential, insignificant, irrelevant, minor, petty, trifling, trivial, unimportant, unnecessary. ANTONYMS: important, material. **2** (*not consisting of matter; incorporeal*) airy, bodiless, disembodied, ephemeral, ethereal, evanescent, incorporeal, insubstantial, intangible. ANTONYMS: physical. **3** (*spiritual*) metaphysical, spiritual, supernatural. ANTONYMS: earthly.

immature *a.* **1** (*not fully developed*) crude, imperfect, incomplete, premature, rudimentary, undeveloped, unfinished, unfledged, unformed, unseasonable. ANTONYMS: developed, fully-fledged, mature. **2** (*lacking the appropriate maturity of character etc.*) adolescent, babyish, callow, childish, inexperienced, infantile, juvenile, puerile, raw, unsophisticated, young, youthful. ANTONYMS: adult, mature. **3** (*not ripe*) green, unripe. ANTONYMS: ripe.

immatureness *n.* **1** (*the state of not being fully developed*) crudity, imperfection, incompleteness. **2** (*a lack of maturity of character*) adolescence, childishness, inexperience, puerility, rawness, unsophistication, youth. ANTONYMS: adulthood, maturity. **3** (*a lack of ripeness*) greenness, unripeness. ANTONYMS: ripeness.

immeasurable *a.* **1** (*that cannot be measured*) bottomless, boundless, endless, illimitable, incalculable, inestimable, inexhaustible, infinite, limitless, measureless, unbounded, unfathomable, unlimited, unmeasurable. ANTONYMS: calculable, measurable. **2** (*immense*) colossal, enormous, huge, immense, massive, tremendous, vast.

immediate *a.* **1** (*done or occurring at once, instant*) abrupt, automatic, instant, instantaneous, prompt, spontaneous, swift, unhesitating. ANTONYMS: delayed, tardy. **2** (*situated in the closest relation; nearest*) adjacent, closest, direct, nearby, nearest. ANTONYMS: distant. **3** (*nearest in time*) close, near, next. **4** (*present; of most concern*) actual, current, existing, latest, present, pressing, primary, urgent. ANTONYMS: future.

immediately *adv.* **1** (*without delay, at once*) at once, directly, forthwith, (*coll.*) in a jiffy, instantly, now, post-haste, promptly, (*coll.*) pronto, right away, straight away, this minute, unhesitatingly, without delay. ANTONYMS: later. **2** (*closely or directly*) at first hand, closely, directly, intimately.

immense *a.* (*huge, vast*) colossal, elephantine, enormous, giant, gigantic, (*coll.*) ginormous, huge, immeasurable, infinite, interminable, jumbo, mammoth, massive, monstrous, monumental, prodigious, stupendous, tremendous, vast, voluminous. ANTONYMS: infinitesimal, small.

immerse *v.t.* **1** (*to plunge, to dip* (*into or under water or other fluid*)) baptize, bathe, dip, douse, duck, dunk, inundate, plunge, sink, souse, submerge, submerse. **2** (*to involve or absorb deeply* (*in difficulty, debt etc.*)) absorb, busy, engage, engross, involve, occupy, take up.

immigrant *n.* (*a person who immigrates*) alien, arrival, foreigner, incomer, migrant, newcomer, settler.

imminent *a.* (*impending; close at hand*) approaching, brewing, close at hand, coming, fast-approaching, forthcoming, gathering, immediate, impending, in the offing, looming, menacing, near, nigh, threatening, upcoming. ANTONYMS: past, remote.

immobile *a.* **1** (*not moving*) at rest, frozen, immobilized, motionless, rigid, riveted, stable, stationary, stiff, still, stock-still, unmoving. ANTONYMS: mobile. **2** (*not mobile, immovable*) fixed, immovable, rooted, set, static.

immobilize *v.t.* (*to render* (*a vehicle, an attacker etc.*) *immobile*) cripple, disable, lay up, paralyse, put out of action, render inoperative, sabotage, stop.

immoderate *a.* **1** (*excessive*) enormous, exaggerated, excessive, extreme, (*coll.*) steep. ANTONYMS: controlled, moderate. **2** (*unreasonable*) exorbitant, extravagant, inordinate, intemperate, outrageous, over the top, preposterous, profligate, uncalled-for, unconscionable, undue, unreasonable, unwarranted, wanton. ANTONYMS: reasonable, temperate.

immodest *a.* **1** (*not modest, forward*) arrogant, audacious, bold, brash, brazen, cheeky, disrespectful, forward, (*coll.*) fresh, impertinent, impudent, pert, presumptuous, (*coll.*) pushy, shameless, unblushing. ANTONYMS: bashful, modest. **2** (*improper, indecent*) bawdy, coarse, depraved, gross, immoral, improper, impure, indecent, indecorous, indelicate, lewd, obscene, provocative, revealing, rude, titillating, unchaste, wanton. ANTONYMS: decorous.

immodesty *n.* **1** (*a lack of modesty, forwardness*) arrogance, audacity, (*sl.*) balls, boldness, brashness, (*coll.*) cheek, disrespectfulness, forwardness, gall, impertinence, impudence, pertness, presumption, (*coll.*) pushiness, shamelessness. ANTONYMS: modesty. **2** (*indecency*) bawdiness, coarseness, depravity, grossness, immorality, impropriety, impurity, indecency, indecorousness, indelicacy, lewdness, obscenity, provocativeness, rudeness, wantonness. ANTONYMS: decency, decorousness.

immoral *a.* **1** (*not moral*) bad, corrupt, degenerate, depraved, dishonest, dissolute, evil, impure, iniquitous, nefarious, profligate, sinful, treacherous, unethical, unprincipled, unregenerate, unscrupulous, vile, wicked, wrong. ANTONYMS: good, moral. **2** (*licentious, vicious*) carnal, concupiscent, debauched, dirty, filthy, immodest, lascivious, lecherous, lewd, libertine, libidinous, licentious, lustful, obscene, pornographic, salacious, smutty, wanton. ANTONYMS: virtuous.

immorality *n.* **1** (*the state of not being moral*) corruption, degeneracy, depravity, dishonesty, dissoluteness, evil, impurity, iniquity, nefariousness, profligacy, sin, unscrupulous, vice, vileness, wickedness. ANTONYMS: morality. **2** (*licentiousness*) carnality, concupiscence, debauchery, dirt, filth, immodesty, indecency, lasciviousness, lecherousness, lewdness, licentiousness, lustfulness, obscenity, pornography, salaciousness, wantonness. ANTONYMS: virtue.

immortal *a.* **1** (*not mortal, not subject to death*) deathless, undying. ANTONYMS: mortal. **2** (*imperishable*) imperishable, incorruptible, indestructible. ANTONYMS: perishable. **3** (*everlasting*) abiding, ceaseless, constant, endless, enduring, eternal, everlasting, lasting, perennial, perpetual, timeless, unfading. ANTONYMS: ephemeral, passing. **4** (*eternally famous*) celebrated, classic, famous, honoured, lauded, praised, remembered, renowned.
~*n.* (*a being who is immortal, esp. one of the ancient gods*) god, goddess.

immortality *n.* **1** (*the state of not being mortal*) deathlessness. ANTONYMS: death, mortality. **2** (*the state of being imperishable*) imperishability, incorruptibility, indestructibility. **3** (*endlessness*) ceaselessness, constancy, endlessness, eternity, perpetuity, timelessness. **4** (*eternal fame*) celebrity, fame, glory, greatness, renown.

immovable *a.* **1** (*that cannot be moved*) immobile, stationary. **2** (*firmly fixed*) anchored, fast, firm, fixed, jammed, rigid, riveted, rooted, secure, set, stable, stiff, stuck. **3** (*steadfast*) adamant, constant, determined, dogged, obdurate, resolute, staunch, steadfast, unflinching, unswerving, unwavering. **4** (*unchanging, unalterable*) immutable, inflexible, unalterable, unchangeable, unchanging, unshakeable, unyielding. ANTONYMS: changeable, flexible. **5** (*unfeeling*) emotionless, impassive, stony-hearted, unbending, unfeeling, unmoved.

immune *a.* **1** (*protected against a particular disease, infection etc.*) inoculated, vaccinated. **2** (*unaffected; exempt* (*from*)) clear (of), exempt (from), free (of), insusceptible (to), invulnerable (to), not liable (to), proof (against), protected (from), resistant (to), safe (from), unaffected (by), untouched (by). ANTONYMS: liable (to), susceptible (to).

immunity *n.* **1** (*freedom from liability to infection*) immunization, protection, resistance. ANTONYMS: susceptibility. **2** (*freedom or exemption from an obligation or penalty*) amnesty, exclusion, exemption, exoneration, freedom, indemnity, invulnerability, liberty, licence, prerogative, privilege, protection, resistance. ANTONYMS: liability.

immunize *v.t.* (*to give protection against a disease to, usu. by inoculation*) inoculate, protect, vaccinate.

imp *n.* **1** (*a mischievous child*) brat, rascal, rogue, scamp, urchin. **2** (*a little devil or malignant spirit*) demon, devil, elf, fairy, familiar, goblin, pixie, spirit, sprite.

impact[1] *n.* **1** (*a forcible striking* (*upon or against*)) bang, bash, blow, bump, collision, contact, crash, force, jolt, knock, shock, smash, stroke, thump. **2** (*an effect or influence*) bearing, brunt, burden, consequences, effect, import, impression, influence, meaning, power, repercussions, results, significance, thrust, weight.

impact[2] *v.t.* **1** (*to press or drive firmly together*) compact, drive together, pack, press together. **2** (*to have an effect on*) affect, impinge, influence. **3** (*to collide*) bump, clash, collide, crush, hit, jolt, knock, strike.

impair *v.t.* (*to damage or weaken in quality, strength etc.*) blunt, cripple, damage, debilitate, decrease, deteriorate, diminish, enervate, enfeeble, harm, hinder, injure, lessen, mar, reduce, spoil, undermine, vitiate, weaken, worsen. ANTONYMS: improve, strengthen.

impale *v.t.* (*to transfix, esp. to put to death by transfixing with a sharp stake*) lance, pierce, run through, skewer, spear, spike, spit, stick, transfix.

impalpable *a.* **1** (*not able to be readily apprehended by the mind*) airy, delicate, disembodied, fine, incorporeal, indistinct, insubstantial, intangible, shadowy, tenuous, thin. **2** (*not perceptible to the touch*) imperceptible, undetectable.

impart *v.t.* **1** (*to communicate* (*knowledge, information*)) communicate, confide, convey, disclose, discover, divulge, intimate, make known, pass on, relate, reveal, tell, transmit. ANTONYMS: suppress. **2** (*to give, to bestow* (*a quality, feeling*)) accord, afford, assign, bestow, cede, confer, contribute, give, grant, lend, offer, yield. ANTONYMS: withhold.

impartial *a.* (*not favouring one party or one side more than another*) balanced, detached, disinterested, dispassionate, equal, equitable, even-handed, fair, just, neutral, non-partisan, objective, open-minded, unbiased, unprejudiced. ANTONYMS: biased, partial.

impartiality *n.* (*the state of being impartial*) balance, detachment, disinterest, dispassion, equality, equity, even-handedness, fairness, neutrality, non-partisanship, objectivity, open-mindedness. ANTONYMS: bias, prejudice.

impassable *a.* (*that cannot be passed or travelled through*) blocked, closed, impenetrable, impermeable, impervious, obstructed, pathless, trackless, unnavigable. ANTONYMS: passable, penetrable.

impasse *n.* (*an insurmountable obstacle; deadlock*) blind alley, block, dead end, deadlock, obstacle, stalemate, stand-off.

impassioned *a.* (*charged with passion*) animated, ardent, charged, eager, emotional, enthusiastic, excited, fervent, fiery, forceful, furious, glowing, heated, inflamed, intense, passionate, rousing, spirited, vehement, zealous. ANTONYMS: cool, indifferent.

impassive *a.* **1** (*not showing or affected by feeling or passion*) apathetic, dispassionate, emotionless, unemotional, unfeeling. ANTONYMS: emotional. **2** (*unmoved, serene*) aloof, calm, cold-blooded, collected, composed, cool, imperturbable, indifferent, inscrutable, phlegmatic, reserved, serene, stoical, stolid, taciturn, (*coll.*) unfazed, unmoved, unperturbed, unruffled. ANTONYMS: excitable.

impatience *n.* **1** (*agitation, restlessness*) agitation, anxiety, avidity, eagerness, fretfulness, nervousness, restiveness, restlessness, uneasiness. **2** (*a lack of patience, intolerance*) haste, heat, impetuosity, intolerance, irritability, rashness, shortness, snappiness, vehemence. ANTONYMS: patience, tolerance.

impatient *a.* **1** (*eager (for or to)*) agitated, anxious, chafing, eager, excitable, fidgety, fretful, hasty, headlong, impetuous, jumpy, nervous, precipitate, reckless, restive, restless, uneasy, unquiet, vehement, violent. ANTONYMS: patient. **2** (*not patient or tolerant*) abrupt, brusque, curt, demanding, edgy, indignant, intolerant, irascible, irritable, short-tempered, testy, waspish. ANTONYMS: tolerant.

impeach *v.t.* **1** (*to charge with a crime, esp. treason*) accuse, arraign, blame, censure, charge, denounce, incriminate, indict. ANTONYMS: exonerate, vindicate. **2** (*to call in question (a person's honesty etc.)*) challenge, deprecate, discredit, disparage, impugn, malign, question.

impeccable *a.* ((*of manners, behaviour etc.*) *faultless*) above suspicion, blameless, exact, exemplary, exquisite, faultless, flawless, immaculate, incorrupt, innocent, irreproachable, perfect, precise, pure, sinless, spotless, stainless, unblemished, unerring, unimpeachable. ANTONYMS: flawed, imperfect.

impecunious *a.* **1** (*having no money*) (*coll.*) broke, (*sl.*) cleaned out, destitute, insolvent, penniless, poverty-stricken, (*sl.*) skint, (*sl.*) stony. ANTONYMS: affluent, wealthy. **2** (*short of money*) indigent, poor, (*coll.*) short, (*coll.*) strapped.

impede *v.t.* (*to hinder, to obstruct*) bar, block, brake, check, clog, curb, delay, disrupt, encumber, foil, hamper, hinder, hold up, obstruct, prevent, restrain, retard, slow, stop, thwart. ANTONYMS: assist, further.

impediment *n.* **1** (*something which impedes; a hindrance*) bar, barrier, block, check, clog, curb, defect, difficulty, encumbrance, hindrance, hitch, obstacle, obstruction, restraint, snag, stumbling-block. ANTONYMS: aid. **2** (*a speech defect*) lisp, stammer, stutter.

impel *v.t.* **1** (*to drive or urge (to an action or to do)*) compel, constrain, drive, force, goad, incite, inspire, instigate, motivate, move, oblige, persuade, power, press, prod, prompt, spur, stimulate, urge. ANTONYMS: deter, dissuade. **2** (*to drive or push forward*) propel, push.

impending *a.* (*imminent*) approaching, brewing, close, coming, forthcoming, gathering, hovering, imminent, in the offing, looming, menacing, nearing, threatening, upcoming.

impenetrable *a.* **1** (*that cannot be penetrated or pierced*) dense, impassable, impermeable, impervious, inviolable, solid, thick. ANTONYMS: penetrable. **2** (*inscrutable, incomprehensible*) abstruse, arcane, baffling, dark, enigmatic, hidden, incomprehensible, inexplicable, inscrutable, mysterious, obscure, recondite, unfathomable, unintelligible. ANTONYMS: accessible, intelligible.

impenitent *a.* (*not penitent, not contrite*) defiant, hardened, incorrigible, obdurate, remorseless, unabashed, unashamed, uncontrite, unreformed, unrepentant. ANTONYMS: contrite, penitent.

imperative *a.* **1** (*urgent*) exigent, pressing, urgent. ANTONYMS: unimportant. **2** (*obligatory*) binding, compulsory, crucial, essential, indispensable, mandatory, necessary, obligatory, required, vital. ANTONYMS: discretionary, nonessential. **3** (*authoritative, peremptory*) authoritative, autocratic, commanding, dictatorial, domineering, high-handed, imperious, lordly, magisterial, peremptory, tyrannical.

imperceptible *a.* **1** (*not able to be perceived*) impalpable, inaudible, indiscernible, indistinguishable, invisible, undetectable, unnoticeable. ANTONYMS: discernible, noticeable. **2** (*extremely slight or small*) faint, fine, gradual, infinitesimal, microscopic, minute, shadowy, slight, small, subtle, tiny.

imperfect *a.* **1** (*not perfect, defective*) broken, damaged, defective, faulty, flawed, impaired. ANTONYMS: perfect. **2** (*incomplete, not fully made, done etc.*) deficient, incomplete, inexact, limited, partial, rudimentary, sketchy, undeveloped, unfinished, wanting. ANTONYMS: complete.

imperfection *n.* **1** (*a defect*) blemish, crack, defect, error, fault, flaw, scar, scratch, stain, taint, tear. ANTONYMS: perfection. 2 (*deficiency*) deficiency, failing, fallibility, foible, frailty, inadequacy, infirmity, insufficiency, shortcoming, weakness. ANTONYMS: sufficiency.

imperial *a.* 1 (*suitable to or like an emperor; majestic*) kingly, lordly, majestic, princely, queenly, regal, royal, sovereign. 2 ((*of commodities and products*) *of a superior size, quality etc.*) august, grand, great, high, imperious, imposing, lofty, magisterial, magnificent, noble, stately, superior, supreme. ANTONYMS: lowly.

imperious *a.* 1 (*dictatorial, overbearing*) arrogant, authoritative, autocratic, bossy, commanding, despotic, dictatorial, domineering, haughty, high-handed, imperative, lordly, magisterial, overbearing, proud, tyrannical. ANTONYMS: humble. 2 (*urgent, pressing*) exigent, imperative, pressing, urgent.

imperishable *a.* 1 (*enduring permanently*) abiding, enduring, eternal, everlasting, immortal, lasting, perennial, permanent, perpetual, unfading, unforgettable. ANTONYMS: mortal. 2 (*not subject to decay*) incorruptible, indestructible, undecaying, undying. ANTONYMS: perishable.

impersonal *a.* 1 (*without personality*) characterless, faceless. 2 (*lacking in human warmth*) aloof, bureaucratic, businesslike, cold, detached, disinterested, dispassionate, formal, inhuman, neutral, objective, prim, remote, stiff, stuffy. ANTONYMS: friendly, personal.

impersonate *v.t.* 1 (*to pretend to be* (*someone*) *in order to entertain or deceive*) masquerade as, pass oneself off as, pose as. 2 (*to play the part of* (*a character*)) act, ape, burlesque, caricature, copy, (*coll.*) do, imitate, mimic, mock, parody, play, (*coll.*) take off.

impertinence *n.* 1 (*impudence, insolence*) audacity, boldness, (*coll.*) cheek, discourtesy, disrespect, effrontery, flippancy, forwardness, front, gall, impoliteness, impudence, incivility, insolence, (*coll.*) nerve, pertness, presumption, presumptuousness, rudeness, (*coll.*) sauce. ANTONYMS: politeness. 2 (*inappropriateness*) inapplicability, inappositeness, inappropriateness, irrelevance. ANTONYMS: pertinence.

impertinent *a.* 1 (*impudent, insolent*) audacious, bold, brash, brassy, brazen, cheeky, discourteous, disrespectful, (*coll.*) flip, forward, (*coll.*) fresh, impolite, insolent, pert, presumptuous, rude, saucy, uncivil. ANTONYMS: polite. 2 (*inappropriate*) inapplicable, inapposite, inappropriate, irrelevant. ANTONYMS: pertinent, relevant.

imperturbable *a.* (*not easily disturbed or excited*) calm, collected, complacent, composed, cool, equanimous, impassive, placid, sedate, self-possessed, serene, stoical, tranquil, undisturbed, unexcitable, (*coll.*) unfazed, (*coll.*) unflappable, unmoved, unruffled. ANTONYMS: disturbed, excitable.

impervious *a.* 1 (*not receptive or open* (*to*)) blind (to), immune (to), insensitive (to), invulnerable (to), resistant (to), thick-skinned, unaffected (by), unmoved (by), unreceptive (to), untouched (by). ANTONYMS: open (to), receptive (to). 2 (*not allowing passage of a liquid*) hermetic, impassable, impenetrable, impermeable, proof, sealed, tight. ANTONYMS: permeable.

impetuous *a.* (*acting hastily or suddenly*) ardent, eager, fierce, hasty, headlong, heedless, impassioned, impulsive, precipitate, rash, reckless, spontaneous, spur-of-the-moment, thoughtless, unbridled, unplanned, unpremeditated, unrestrained, vehement, volatile. ANTONYMS: cautious, wary.

impetus *n.* 1 (*an impulse or driving force*) catalyst, driving force, encouragement, goad, impulse, incentive, motivation, push, spur, stimulus. 2 (*the force with which a body moves or is impelled*) energy, force, momentum, power, thrust.

impious *a.* 1 (*lacking reverence, esp. towards God*) blasphemous, godless, iniquitous, irreligious, profane, sacrilegious, sinful, ungodly, unholy, unrighteous, wicked. ANTONYMS: devout, pious. 2 (*irreverent, lacking respect*) disrespectful, irreverent. ANTONYMS: respectful, reverent.

implacable *a.* 1 (*not to be appeased*) intractable, unappeasable, uncompromising, unyielding. 2 (*inexorable, unrelenting*) adamant, cruel, harsh, inexorable, inflexible, merciless, pitiless, relentless, ruthless, unbending, unrelenting. ANTONYMS: merciful.

implant *v.t.* 1 (*to plant for the purpose of growth*) embed, graft, plant, root. 2 (*to set or fix* (*in*)) fix, insert, place, set. 3 (*to inculcate, to instil* (*ideas etc.*)) imbue, impress, imprint, inculcate, insinuate, instil, introduce, sow.

implausible *a.* (*not having an appearance of truth and credibility*) debatable, doubtful, dubious, far-fetched, flimsy, improbable, incredible, questionable, suspect, unbelievable, unconvincing, unlikely, unreasonable, weak. ANTONYMS: plausible.

implement *n.* 1 (*a tool, a utensil*) appliance, contraption, contrivance, device, gadget, tool, utensil. 2 (*pl.*) (*things that serve for equipment,* *furniture, etc.*) apparatus, equipment, furniture. **3** (*fig.*) (*an agent, an instrument*) agency, agent, instrument, vehicle.

~*v.t.* **1** (*to carry* (*a policy, law etc.*) *into effect*) bring about, carry out, effect, enforce, execute, perform, put into effect. **2** (*to fulfil*) accomplish, fulfil, perform, realize.

implicate *v.t.* **1** (*to show* (*a person*) *to be involved* (*in*)) compromise, incriminate, inculpate. ANTONYMS: acquit. **2** (*to involve*) associate, concern, embroil, enmesh, ensnare, entangle, involve, mire, tie up with. ANTONYMS: disentangle. **3** (*to imply*) imply, include, involve. **4** (*to enfold*) encircle, enfold, entwine.

implication *n.* **1** (*something that is implied or suggested*) conclusion, connotation, drift, hint, inference, innuendo, insinuation, intimation, meaning, overtone, presumption, ramification, significance, substance, suggestion. **2** (*the act of implicating; the state of being implicated*) association, connection, entanglement, incrimination, inculpation, involvement.

implicit *a.* **1** (*implied rather than directly stated*) implied, indirect, inferred, inherent, latent, understood. ANTONYMS: direct, explicit. **2** (*tacitly contained* (*in*) *but not expressed*) tacit, unexpressed, unspoken. **3** (*unquestioning, unreserved*) absolute, complete, constant, entire, firm, fixed, full, sheer, steadfast, total, unconditional, undiluted, unhesitating, unmitigated, unqualified, unquestioning, unreserved, unshakeable, utter, wholehearted. ANTONYMS: reserved.

imply *v.t.* **1** (*to indicate strongly the truth or existence of* (*something*) *in an indirect way*) indicate, suggest. **2** (*to mean indirectly, to hint*) hint, infer, insinuate, intimate, suggest. ANTONYMS: declare. **3** (*to signify*) betoken, connote, denote, entail, evidence, import, mean, point to, signify.

impolite *a.* (*not polite, ill-mannered*) bad-mannered, boorish, churlish, discourteous, disrespectful, ill-bred, ill-mannered, impertinent, impudent, indecorous, indelicate, insolent, rude, uncivil, uncouth, ungentlemanly, ungracious, unladylike, unmannerly. ANTONYMS: polite, refined.

importance *n.* **1** (*the quality of being important*) import, significance. ANTONYMS: unimportance. **2** (*authority, consequence*) authority, concern, consequence, moment, substance, value, weight, worth. **3** (*personal consideration, self-esteem*) distinction, eminence, esteem, influence, mark, power, pre-eminence, prestige, prominence, rank, regard, standing, status.

important *a.* **1** (*of great moment or consequence*) consequential, considerable, critical, essential, far-reaching, grave, material, meaningful, momentous, portentous, primary, salient, serious, significant, substantial, urgent, valuable, vital, weighty. ANTONYMS: inconsequential, unimportant. **2** (*notable, eminent*) distinguished, eminent, esteemed, influential, leading, notable, noteworthy, outstanding, powerful, pre-eminent, prestigious, prominent.

impose *v.t.* **1** (*to lay* (*e.g. a burden, tax, toll etc.*) *upon*) burden, charge, decree, establish, exact, lay upon, levy, place, put, saddle. ANTONYMS: lift. **2** (*to force* (*one's beliefs, views etc.*) *upon*) dictate, enforce, enjoin, force upon, inflict, prescribe, require.

~*v.i.* **1** (*to cause inconvenience*) bother, butt in, encroach, foist, force oneself, (*sl.*) horn in, inconvenience, intrude, obtrude, presume, take liberties, trespass. **2** (*to take advantage of someone's good nature or kindness*) abuse, (*sl.*) con, deceive, dupe, exploit, hoodwink, play on, take advantage of, trick, use.

imposing *a.* (*commanding; impressive*) august, commanding, dignified, effective, grand, impressive, magnificent, majestic, stately, striking. ANTONYMS: modest, unimposing.

imposition *n.* **1** (*the act of imposing or placing upon*) enforcement, infliction, injunction, prescription. **2** (*an unfair and excessive burden*) encroachment, intrusion, liberty, presumption. **3** (*a duty or tax*) burden, charge, duty, levy, tax.

impossible *a.* **1** (*impracticable, not feasible*) impracticable, inconceivable, unattainable, unfeasible, unobtainable, unthinkable, unworkable. ANTONYMS: feasible, possible. **2** (*that cannot be done, thought etc.*) illogical, inadmissible, intolerable, unacceptable, unimaginable, unreasonable. **3** (*coll.*) (*outrageous*) absurd, crazy, farcical, ludicrous, outlandish, out of the question, outrageous, preposterous, ridiculous, weird.

impostor *n.* **1** (*a person who falsely assumes a character*) fake, impersonator, (*coll.*) phoney, pretender, sham. **2** (*a deceiver by false pretences*) charlatan, cheat, (*sl.*) conman, deceiver, fraud, mountebank, quack, swindler, trickster.

imposture *n.* **1** (*deception by the assumption of a false character*) artifice, cheat, deception, hoax, imposition, pretence, ruse, trick, wile. **2** (*a fraud*) deception, fraud, swindle.

impotent *a.* **1** (*powerless; helpless*) debilitated, disabled, enervated, feeble, frail, helpless, inadequate, incapable, incapacitated, incompetent, ineffective, inept, infirm, power-less, unable, unmanned, weak. ANTONYMS: potent, powerful. **2** ((*of a male*) *unable to have sexual intercourse because of an inability to achieve an erection*) barren, infertile, sterile.

impoverish *v.t.* **1** (*to make poor*) bankrupt, beggar, break, pauperize, ruin. **2** (*to exhaust the strength or resources of*) deplete, diminish, drain, exhaust, reduce, sap, use up, wear out. ANTONYMS: enrich.

impoverished *a.* **1** (*poor*) bankrupt, (*coll.*) broke, destitute, distressed, hard up, im-pecunious, indigent, insolvent, necessitous, needy, penniless, penurious, poor, poverty-stricken, ruined, (*coll.*) short, (*sl.*) skint. ANTO-NYMS: rich, wealthy. **2** (*having exhausted one's resources or fertility*) barren, denuded, depleted, desolate, diminished, drained, empty, exhausted, played out, reduced, sapped, spent, sterile, stripped, used up, wasted, worn out.

impracticable *a.* **1** (*not able to be carried out in practice*) impossible, out of the question, unachievable, unattainable, unfeasible, un-workable. ANTONYMS: possible. **2** (*unsuitable for a particular purpose*) awkward, imprac-tical, inapplicable, inconvenient, unfit, un-serviceable, unsuitable, useless. ANTONYMS: practicable, serviceable.

impractical *a.* (*not practical*) idealistic, impossible, impracticable, inapplicable, in-effective, inoperable, non-viable, unrealistic, unserviceable, unworkable, visionary, wild. ANTONYMS: practical, viable.

imprecise *a.* (*not precise*) ambiguous, blurred, careless, cloudy, equivocal, fuzzy, hazy, ill-defined, inaccurate, indefinite, indeterminate, indistinct, inexact, inexplicit, loose, rough, sloppy, vague, woolly. ANTONYMS: exact, precise.

impregnable *a.* **1** ((*of a castle or defences*) *that cannot be taken by assault*) unassailable, well-fortified. **2** (*able to resist all attacks*) immovable, impenetrable, indestructible, in-domitable, invincible, inviolable, invulner-able, irrefutable, resistant, secure, strong, unassailable, unbeatable, unshakeable. ANTO-NYMS: vulnerable, weak.

impregnate *v.t.* **1** (*to make pregnant*) fecun-date, fertilize, inseminate, make pregnant. **2** (*to saturate* (*with*)) drench, fill, saturate, seep, soak, steep, suffuse. **3** (*to imbue, to in-spire* (*with*)) imbue, infuse, inspire, penetrate, permeate, pervade.

impress *v.t.* **1** (*to produce a favourable effect on*) encourage, hearten, inspire. **2** (*to affect*

strongly) affect, excite, (*coll.*) grab, influence, move, reach, stir, strike, sway, touch. **3** (*to press or stamp* (*a mark etc., in or upon*)) imprint, press, print, stamp. **4** (*to make a mark etc. on* (*something*) *with a stamp or seal*) brand, emboss, engrave, indent, mark. **to impress on/upon** (*to emphasize to* (*someone*)) bring home, emphasize, fix, inculcate, instil, stress, underline, urge.

impression *n.* **1** (*an effect produced upon the senses, feelings etc.*) effect, feeling, impact, influence, sensation, sense. **2** (*a vague notion or belief*) awareness, belief, concept, con-viction, fancy, feeling, hunch, idea, memory, notion, opinion, perception, recollection, sense, suspicion. **3** (*an imitation or imper-sonation*) imitation, impersonation, parody, satire, (*coll.*) send-up, (*coll.*) take-off. **4** (*the mark made by impressing*) brand, dent, hollow, impress, imprint, indentation, mark, outline, stamp. **5** (*a reprint from standing type, as distinct from an edition*) edition, imprinting, issue, printing, reprint, run.

impressionable *a.* (*easily impressed*) gul-lible, ingenuous, open, receptive, responsive, sensitive, suggestible, susceptible, vulnerable. ANTONYMS: hardened, unreceptive.

impressive *a.* (*making an impression on the mind; inspiring*) awe-inspiring, commanding, exciting, forcible, formidable, grand, impos-ing, inspiring, moving, portentous, powerful, redoubtable, stirring, striking. ANTONYMS: unimpressive.

imprint[1] *v.t.* **1** (*to impress, to stamp*) imprint, stamp. **2** (*to print*) engrave, etch, print.

imprint[2] *n.* (*a mark or impression*) impression, indentation, mark, print, sign, stamp.

imprison *v.t.* **1** (*to put into prison*) incarcerate, jail, put behind bars, remand, send down. ANTONYMS: discharge. **2** (*to hold in custody or captivity*) confine, constrain, detain, hold in captivity, immure, intern, lock up, put away. ANTONYMS: free, release.

imprisonment *n.* (*the state of being held in custody or captivity*) captivity, confinement, custody, detention, incarceration, internment, (*sl.*) porridge, remand. ANTONYMS: freedom.

improbable *a.* **1** (*not likely to be true*) doubtful, dubious, fanciful, far-fetched, im-plausible, inconceivable, incredible, question-able, unbelievable, uncertain, unconvincing. ANTONYMS: certain. **2** (*not likely to happen*) remote, unlikely. ANTONYMS: likely, probable.

improper *a.* **1** (*unbecoming, indecent*) corrupt, immodest, immoral, impolite, indecent, indecorous, indelicate, lewd, obscene, off colour, offensive, risqué, smutty, suggestive, unbecoming, unfitting, unseemly, untoward, vulgar, wicked. ANTONYMS: becoming, proper. **2** (*unsuitable*) ill-timed, impractical, inapplicable, inapposite, inappropriate, inapt, incompatible, incongruous, inopportune, uncalled-for, unfit, unseasonable, unsuitable, untimely, unwarranted. ANTONYMS: appropriate, suitable. **3** (*not accurate, wrong*) abnormal, amiss, erroneous, false, faulty, imprecise, inaccurate, incorrect, inexact, irregular, mistaken, untrue, wrong. ANTONYMS: accurate, correct.

improve *v.t.* **1** (*to make better*) amend, better, correct, enhance, help, improve, mend, polish, put right, rectify, reform, restore, touch up, upgrade. ANTONYMS: damage, impair. **2** (*to increase the value of* (*land etc.*) *by cultivating or building*) advance, augment, develop, increase, perk up, pick up, rally, recover, rise.
~*v.i.* (*to become better*) ameliorate, convalesce, get better, mend, rally, recover, recuperate, revive. ANTONYMS: worsen.

improvement *n.* **1** (*the act of improving or the state of being improved*) advance, advancement, amelioration, amendment, betterment, correction, development, enhancement, furtherance, rectification, repair. **2** (*something which is added or done to something in order to improve it*) addition, alteration, amendment, correction, enhancement, rectification, repair.

improvident *a.* **1** (*neglecting to make provision for the future*) reckless, short-sighted. ANTONYMS: provident. **2** (*thriftless*) extravagant, lavish, prodigal, profligate, spendthrift, thriftless, uneconomical, unthrifty, wasteful. **3** (*careless, heedless*) careless, heedless, impetuous, imprudent, incautious, negligent, rash, reckless, shiftless, thoughtless, unthinking, unwary. ANTONYMS: careful, prudent.

improvise *v.t.*, *v.i.* **1** (*to play or perform, composing as one goes along*) ad-lib, extemporize, fake it, play by ear, (*coll.*) wing it. **2** (*to do or make without prior preparation, using the materials to hand*) concoct, contrive, devise, invent, make do, throw together.

imprudent *a.* (*rash, incautious*) careless, foolhardy, foolish, hasty, heedless, ill-advised, ill-considered, ill-judged, impolitic, improvident, impulsive, incautious, indiscreet, inexpedient, injudicious, irresponsible, rash, reckless, thoughtless, unwise. ANTONYMS: careful, prudent.

impudence *n.* **1** (*rudeness and disrespect*) (*coll.*) cheek, disrespect, effrontery, impertinence, insolence, (*sl.*) lip, rudeness, uncivility. ANTONYMS: respect. **2** (*a lack of shame or modesty, forwardness*) assurance, audacity,

boldness, brazenness, bumptiousness, (*coll.*) face, forwardness, front, immodesty, (*coll.*) nerve, presumption, (*coll.*) sauce, shamelessness. ANTONYMS: politeness, shame.

impudent *a.* **1** (*rude and disrespectful*) cheeky, cocky, disrespectful, (*coll.*) fresh, impertinent, insolent, (*sl.*) lippy, rude, uncivil. ANTONYMS: respectful. **2** (*lacking in shame or modesty, forward*) assured, audacious, bold, brazen, bumptious, forward, immodest, pert, presumptuous, saucy, shameless. ANTONYMS: polite, shameful.

impulse *n.* **1** (*a sudden desire or whim*) caprice, desire, drive, feeling, inclination, instinct, notion, passion, urge, whim, wish, (*coll.*) yen. **2** (*the application or effect of an impelling force*) boost, surge, thrust. **3** (*a stimulus, an inspiration*) catalyst, incitement, inspiration, motive, push, spur, stimulus. **4** (*a large force acting for an extremely short time*) force, impetus, momentum, thrust.

impulsive *a.* (*resulting from or liable to be actuated by impulse rather than reflection*) emotional, hasty, headlong, heedless, impetuous, instinctive, intuitive, natural, passionate, precipitate, quick, rash, reckless, snap, spontaneous, unconsidered, unplanned, unpredictable, unpremeditated, wild. ANTONYMS: cautious, deliberate.

impure *a.* **1** (*not pure; mixed with other substances*) adulterated, alloyed, debased, mixed, unrefined. ANTONYMS: pure. **2** (*defiled, unclean*) contaminated, defiled, dirty, filthy, foul, infected, polluted, rotten, soiled, sullied, tainted, unclean, unwholesome. ANTONYMS: clean, undefiled. **3** (*unchaste*) carnal, corrupt, depraved, gross, immodest, immoral, indecent, indelicate, lewd, licentious, lustful, obscene, ribald, salacious, smutty, unchaste, wanton. ANTONYMS: chaste, moral.

impurity *n.* **1** (*the state or quality of being impure*) adulteration, contamination, defilement, dirtiness, filth, foulness, infection, mixture, pollution, taint. **2** (*something that is impure*) contaminant, dirt, dross, filth, foreign body, grime, pollutant, scum, smut, spot, stain. **3** (*immorality*) carnality, corruption, depravity, grossness, immodesty, immorality, indecency, indelicacy, lewdness, licentiousness, lust, obscenity, ribaldry, salaciousness, smuttiness, wantonness. ANTONYMS: chastity.

imputation *n.* **1** (*the act of imputing*) ascription, attribution. **2** (*something which is imputed as a charge or fault*) accusation, challenge, charge, indictment. **3** (*reproach, censure*) allegation, aspersion, blame, calumny, censure, defamation, implication, insinuation, reproach, slander, slur.

impute v.t. (to ascribe or attribute (esp. something dishonourable) to a person) accredit, ascribe, assign, attribute, blame, charge, credit, hint at, imply, insinuate, put down, refer, set down to, suggest.

inability n. (the state of being unable (to do, understand etc.)) disability, impotence, inadequacy, incapability, incompetence, ineptitude, powerlessness. ANTONYMS: ability, competence.

inaccessible a. **1** (that cannot be reached or approached) impassable, impenetrable, out of reach, unapproachable, unattainable, unavailable, (coll.) unget-at-able, unreachable. ANTONYMS: accessible, approachable. **2** ((of a person) not affable) aloof, cold, remote. ANTONYMS: affable, friendly.

inaccurate a. (not accurate) amiss, defective, erroneous, false, faulty, imperfect, imprecise, incorrect, inexact, mistaken, out, unreliable, unsound, wrong. ANTONYMS: accurate, exact.

inactive a. **1** (not active) placid, quiet, still. ANTONYMS: active. **2** (sluggish, inert) abeyant, dormant, dull, immobile, inert, latent, lethargic, passive, quiescent, slow, sluggish, somnolent, torpid. **3** (idle, indolent) idle, indolent, languid, lazy, listless, slothful, unemployed, unoccupied. ANTONYMS: busy, diligent.

inadequate a. **1** (not adequate; insufficient) defective, deficient, faulty, flawed, imperfect, inadequate, incomplete, insubstantial, insufficient, lacking, meagre, scant, scarce, short, skimpy, sparse, unsatisfactory, unsuitable, wanting. ANTONYMS: adequate, satisfactory. **2** (unable to cope) inapt, incapable, incompetent, inept, unequal, unfit, unqualified. ANTONYMS: capable, competent.

inadmissible a. ((of evidence) that cannot be allowed or received) disallowed, exceptionable, forbidden, immaterial, improper, inapplicable, inappropriate, incompetent, irrelevant, objectionable, prohibited, unacceptable, unallowable, unqualified, unreasonable, unsuitable.

inadvertence n. **1** (the art or state of being unintentional, error) accident, blunder, chance, error, involuntariness, mistake, omission, oversight, slip. **2** (carelessness) carelessness, heedlessness, neglect, thoughtlessness.

inadvertent a. **1** ((of an action) unintentional, accidental) accidental, chance, involuntary, unintended, unintentional, unplanned, unpremeditated, unthinking. ANTONYMS: intentional, planned. **2** (not paying attention) inattentive, unobservant. ANTONYMS: attentive. **3** (careless, negligent) careless, heedless, negligent, thoughtless, unheeding, unmindful. ANTONYMS: careful.

inane a. **1** (silly, fatuous) absurd, asinine, daft, dumb, fatuous, foolish, frivolous, futile, idiotic, imbecilic, mindless, nonsensical, senseless, silly, stupid, trifling, unintelligent, unreasonable. ANTONYMS: profound, sensible. **2** (empty, void) devoid, empty, vacant, vacuous, void.

inanimate a. **1** (not living; lacking any sign of life) dead, defunct, extinct, lifeless. ANTONYMS: alive, living. **2** (void of animation, lifeless) dormant, dull, immobile, inactive, inert, insensate, lifeless, quiescent, sluggish, soulless, spiritless, vapid. ANTONYMS: animated, lively.

inapplicable a. (irrelevant) extraneous, inapposite, inappropriate, inapt, irrelevant, unconnected, unfit, unrelated, unsuitable. ANTONYMS: applicable, relevant.

inappropriate a. (not appropriate, unsuitable) ill-suited, improper, inapplicable, inapposite, inapt, incompatible, incongruous, infelicitous, inopportune, irrelevant, out of place, unbecoming, unbefitting, unfit, unfitting, unseemly, unsuitable, untimely. ANTONYMS: appropriate, suitable.

inarticulate a. **1** (unable to express oneself clearly) faltering, halting, hesitant, poorly spoken. ANTONYMS: articulate, well-spoken. **2** (not uttered with distinct articulation) blurred, confused, garbled, incoherent, incomprehensible, indistinct, jumbled, muddled, muffled, mumbled, rambling, scrambled, unclear, unintelligible. ANTONYMS: clear, distinct. **3** (dumb) dumb, mute, silent, speechless, tongue-tied, unspoken, unuttered, unvoiced, voiceless, wordless. **4** (not articulated, not jointed) disjointed, unconnected.

inattention n. (lack of attention; negligence) absent-mindedness, carelessness, daydreaming, disregard, forgetfulness, heedlessness, inadvertence, inattentiveness, indifference, neglect, negligence, oversight, preoccupation, thoughtlessness, unconcern, wool-gathering. ANTONYMS: care.

inattentive a. (not attentive) absent-minded, careless, distracted, dreamy, forgetful, heedless, inadvertent, neglectful, negligent, oblivious, preoccupied, regardless, slack, slapdash, thoughtless, uncaring, unmindful, vague. ANTONYMS: attentive, careful.

inaudible a. (that cannot be heard) faint, imperceptible, indistinct, low, muffled, mumbling, muted, noiseless, quiet, silent, soft, soundless, stifled, unheard. ANTONYMS: audible.

inaugurate *v.t.* **1** (*to install or induct into office solemnly or with appropriate ceremonies*) induct, install, invest, ordain. **2** (*to commence, introduce, or celebrate the opening of, esp. in a formal ceremony*) begin, commence, initiate, institute, introduce, (*coll.*) kick off, launch, open, originate, start. ANTONYMS: close, terminate.

inauguration *n.* **1** (*the art of installing someone into office*) induction, installation, investiture, ordination. **2** (*a commencement or opening, esp. with a formal ceremony*) beginning, commencement, initiation, institution, introduction, (*coll.*) kick-off, launch, opening, origination, start. ANTONYMS: close, termination.

inauspicious *a.* **1** (*unlucky, unfortunate*) unfortunate, unlucky, untoward. **2** (*unfavourable*) discouraging, doomed, ill-omened, ill-starred, ominous, portentous, unfavourable, unpromising, unpropitious. ANTONYMS: auspicious, encouraging.

inborn *a.* (*innate, naturally inherent*) congenital, hereditary, inbred, ingrained, inherent, inherited, innate, instinctive, intuitive, native, natural. ANTONYMS: acquired.

incalculable *a.* **1** (*that cannot be reckoned or estimated in advance*) inestimable, unpredictable. **2** (*too vast or numerous to be calculated*) boundless, countless, enormous, immeasurable, immense, infinite, innumerable, limitless, measureless, numberless, uncountable, unfathomable, untold, vast. **3** (*not to be reckoned upon, uncertain*) uncertain, unpredictable, unreliable.

incandescent *a.* **1** (*glowing with heat*) burning, fiery, flaming, glowing, heated, luminous, phosphorescent, red-hot. **2** (*strikingly radiant or bright*) bright, brilliant, radiant, shining. ANTONYMS: dull.

incantation *n.* (*a formula, said or sung, supposed to add force to magical ceremonies*) chant, charm, conjuration, formula, invocation, magic, sorcery, spell, witchcraft.

incapable *a.* **1** (*not physically, intellectually, or morally capable (of)*) incompetent, inept, unable. ANTONYMS: capable. **2** (*lacking ability or fitness (of doing, committing etc.)*) feeble, helpless, impotent, inadequate, ineffective, insufficient, powerless, unequal, unfit, weak. ANTONYMS: adequate, fit.

incapacitate *v.t.* (*to render incapable; to disable*) cripple, deactivate, debilitate, disable, enervate, immobilize, indispose, lame, lay up, paralyse, render incapable.

incarcerate *v.t.* (*to imprison*) cage, commit, confine, coop up, detain, immure, impound, imprison, intern, jail, lock up, put away, send down, shut up. ANTONYMS: release, set free.

incarnation *n.* **1** (*embodiment, esp. in human form*) embodiment, manifestation. **2** (*a vivid exemplification or personification (of)*) archetype, epitome, exemplification, personification, type.

incautious *a.* (*lacking in caution; rash*) careless, hasty, headlong, heedless, ill-advised, ill-judged, impolitic, improvident, imprudent, impulsive, indiscreet, injudicious, negligent, precipitate, rash, reckless, thoughtless, unguarded, unthinking, unwary. ANTONYMS: cautious, wary.

incendiary *a.* **1** (*exciting or tending to excite seditions or quarrels*) inflammatory, provocative, quarrelsome, rabble-rousing, seditious, subversive. **2** ((*of a device, substance*) *capable of causing fires or igniting readily*) combustible, flammable.
~*n.* **1** (*a person who maliciously sets fire to property etc.*) arsonist, (*coll.*) firebug, fire-raiser, pyromaniac. **2** (*a person who excites factions, seditions etc.*) agitator, demagogue, firebrand, insurgent, rabble-rouser, rebel, revolutionary, troublemaker.

incense[1] *n.* **1** (*the smoke of a mixture of fragrant gums, spices etc.*) fumes, smoke. **2** (*any agreeable perfume*) aroma, balm, bouquet, fragrance, perfume, redolence, scent.

incense[2] *v.t.* (*to inflame, to enrage*) anger, annoy, enrage, exasperate, excite, gall, inflame, infuriate, irk, irritate, madden, (*sl.*) nark, provoke, (*coll.*) rile, rouse. ANTONYMS: pacify.

incentive *n.* **1** (*something which acts as a motive or spur (to action)*) bait, carrot, cause, encouragement, enticement, goad, impetus, impulse, incitement, inducement, lure, motivation, motive, persuasion, prod, spur, stimulant, stimulus. ANTONYMS: deterrent. **2** (*a payment or benefit offered to workers to encourage greater output*) benefit, bonus, payment, (*coll.*) perk.

inception *n.* (*a beginning*) beginning, birth, commencement, dawn, inauguration, initiation, (*coll.*) kick-off, launch, origin, outset, rise, start. ANTONYMS: end, finish.

incessant *a.* (*unceasing, continual*) ceaseless, constant, continual, endless, eternal, everlasting, interminable, never-ending, perpetual, persistent, relentless, unbroken, unceasing, unending, unrelenting, unremitting. ANTONYMS: intermittent, periodic.

incident n. 1 (an event or occurrence) adventure, circumstance, event, experience, fact, happening, occasion, occurrence, proceeding. 2 (a relatively minor conflict between two countries) brush, clash, confrontation, skirmish. 3 ((a minor event causing a) public disturbance) affair, commotion, contretemps, disturbance, encounter, fracas, mishap, scene, upset. 4 (a distinct episode in a narrative) chapter, episode.

incidental a. 1 (happening in connection with something that is more important; casual) accidental, casual, chance, fortuitous, haphazard, odd, random, serendipitous, unplanned. 2 (naturally connected with or related to) accompanying, attendant on, concomitant with, connected with, contingent on, contributory to, related to. 3 (occasional) ancillary, inconsequential, insignificant, lesser, minor, negligible, non-essential, occasional, paltry, petty, secondary, subordinate, subsidiary, trivial, unimportant. ANTONYMS: essential, important.

incipient a. (beginning; in the first stages) beginning, commencing, developing, embryonic, inceptive, inchoate, initial, nascent, originating, rudimentary, starting. ANTONYMS: complete.

incision n. (a cut; a gash) cut, gash, notch, opening, slash, slit.

incisive a. 1 (sharp, acute) acute, keen, piercing, sharp. 2 (trenchant, penetrating) acerbic, acid, acrid, biting, caustic, cutting, mordant, penetrating, sarcastic, sardonic, satirical, severe, stinging, tart, trenchant, vitriolic. ANTONYMS: mild. 3 (clear and direct) clear, clear-cut, direct, sharp. 4 (having a sharp cutting edge) edged, sharp. ANTONYMS: blunt, dull.

incite v.t. (to stir up; to prompt (to action)) agitate, encourage, excite, foment, goad, impel, inflame, inspire, instigate, prick, prod, prompt, provoke, rouse, spur, stimulate, stir up, urge, whip up. ANTONYMS: deter, dissuade.

incitement n. (a stimulus, an incentive) agitation, arousal, encouragement, exhortation, fomentation, goad, impetus, impulse, incentive, inducement, instigation, motivation, motive, prompting, provocation, spur, stimulation, stimulus.

incivility n. (rudeness, impoliteness) boorishness, discourtesy, disrespect, ill-breeding, impoliteness, indecorousness, rudeness, unmannerliness. ANTONYMS: civility, politeness.

inclement a. 1 ((of weather) rough, stormy) bad, bitter, extreme, foul, harsh, intemperate, rainy, raw, rough, severe, squally, stormy, tempestuous, windy. ANTONYMS: clement, mild. 2 (without clemency, merciless) callous, cruel, hard-hearted, harsh, merciless, pitiless, rigorous, severe, tyrannical, unfeeling, unmerciful. ANTONYMS: kind, merciful.

inclination n. 1 (a disposition or tendency (to, towards)) aptitude, bent, bias, disposition, leaning, predisposition, prejudice, proclivity, propensity, tendency. ANTONYMS: antipathy. 2 (a liking or preference (for)) affection, appetite, craving, desire, fancy, fondness, liking, longing, partiality, penchant, predilection, preference, stomach, taste, thirst, wish. ANTONYMS: aversion, dislike. 3 (the act of inclining or bending) bending, bow, incline, nod. 4 (a deviation from any direction regarded as the normal one) bend, deviation, distortion. 5 (the angle that a plane makes with another, esp. a horizontal or vertical plane) angle, gradient, incline, pitch, slant, slope, tilt.

incline[1] v.i. 1 (to be disposed (to)) be disposed, be in the vein, be likely, be prepared. 2 (to have a tendency (to)) gravitate, lean, tend. 3 (to bend down or forward) angle, bank, bend, cant, lean, slant, slope, tilt, tip.
~v.t. 1 (to give a leaning or tendency to) be predisposed, tend. 2 (to cause (the head or body) to bend down) bend down, bow, lower, nod, stoop. 3 (to cause to deviate from a line or direction) bias, deflect, influence, lead, persuade, prejudice, sway, turn.

incline[2] n. (a slope, a gradient) acclivity, ascent, declivity, descent, dip, gradient, inclination, pitch, plane, ramp, rise, slant, slope.

inclined a. (tending or likely (to do something)) apt, disposed, given, keen, liable, likely, minded, predisposed, prone, tending, willing. ANTONYMS: unlikely.

include v.t. 1 (to contain as a part, member etc.) comprise, contain, cover, embody, embrace, encompass, incorporate, involve, subsume, take in. ANTONYMS: exclude. 2 (to put in or classify as part of a set etc.) catalogue, categorize, classify, file, group, list, register, tabulate.

inclusive a. 1 (including, containing) containing, covering, embracing, including, incorporating, taking in. 2 (including everything) all-embracing, all together, comprehensive, full, general, total, umbrella. ANTONYMS: exclusive.

incognito a., adv. (with one's real name or identity disguised or kept secret) concealed, disguised, in secret, undercover, unknown, unrecognized.

incoherent *a.* **1** (*inarticulate, unable to express oneself intelligibly*) inarticulate, rambling, stammering, stuttering, unintelligible, wandering. ANTONYMS: coherent. **2** (*lacking cohesion; disconnected*) confused, disconnected, discursive, disjointed, disordered, garbled, illogical, incohesive, inconsistent, jumbled, loose, mixed up, muddled, scrambled, unconnected, uncoordinated. ANTONYMS: connected, ordered.

income *n.* (*the amount of money accruing as payment, interest etc. from work or property*) earnings, gains, interest, means, pay, payment, proceeds, profits, receipts, return, revenue, salary, takings, wages, yield. ANTONYMS: expenditure.

incomparable *a.* **1** (*not to be compared (to or with*)) different, other, unlike. **2** (*unequalled, peerless*) beyond compare, inimitable, matchless, paramount, peerless, superior, superlative, supreme, surpassing, transcendent, unequalled, unique, unmatched, unparalleled, unrivalled, unsurpassed. ANTONYMS: ordinary.

incompatible *a.* **1** (*opposed in nature; discordant*) clashing, conflicting, contrary, discordant, jarring, opposed. ANTONYMS: alike, compatible. **2** (*inconsistent (with*)) contradictory, incongruous, inconsistent. ANTONYMS: consistent, harmonious. **3** ((*of two people*) *unable to live or work together*) antagonistic, antipathetic, hostile, irreconcilable, mismatched, uncongenial, unsuited.

incompetent *a.* **1** (*lacking in ability or fitness for a task*) inadequate, incapable, ineffectual, inefficient, inept, unable, unequal, unfit, useless. ANTONYMS: capable, competent. **2** (*showing a lack of skill or ability*) awkward, bungling, clumsy, floundering, gauche, inexpert, maladroit, unskilled.

incomplete *a.* (*not complete; not perfect*) abridged, broken, defective, deficient, fragmentary, imperfect, insufficient, lacking, partial, short, unaccomplished, undeveloped, undone, unexecuted, unfinished, wanting. ANTONYMS: complete, perfect.

incomprehensible *a.* (*that cannot be conceived or understood*) abstruse, baffling, cryptic, enigmatic, impenetrable, incoherent, inconceivable, indecipherable, inexplicable, inscrutable, mysterious, obscure, opaque, perplexing, puzzling, unfathomable, unintelligible, unthinkable. ANTONYMS: plain, understandable.

inconceivable *a.* **1** (*not conceivable; incomprehensible*) impossible, incomprehensible, unimaginable, unknowable, unthinkable.

ANTONYMS: conceivable, possible. **2** (*incredible, most extraordinary*) absurd, extraordinary, incredible, mind-boggling, out-of-the-question, overwhelming, preposterous, staggering, unbelievable, undreamt of, unheard-of.

inconclusive *a.* ((*of evidence, a discussion etc.*) *not decisive*) ambiguous, indecisive, indefinite, indeterminate, open, uncertain, unconvincing, undecided, unresolved, unsettled, vague. ANTONYMS: conclusive, decisive.

incongruous *a.* **1** (*improper, out of place*) improper, inappropriate, inapt, inconsistent, out of keeping, out of place, unbecoming, unfitting, unsuitable. ANTONYMS: appropriate, becoming. **2** (*not agreeing or harmonizing (with*)) conflicting, contradictory, discordant, dissonant, incompatible, unharmonious. ANTONYMS: harmonious.

inconsequential *a.* **1** (*of no consequence, trivial*) inconsiderable, insignificant, meaningless, minor, negligible, paltry, petty, slight, trifling, trivial, unimportant, worthless. ANTONYMS: meaningful, significant. **2** (*not consequential, inconsequent*) disconnected, illogical, immaterial, incongruous, inconsequent, inconsistent, irrelevant.

inconsiderable *a.* **1** (*small*) slight, small. ANTONYMS: considerable. **2** (*not deserving consideration; insignificant*) immaterial, inconsequential, insignificant, light, minor, negligible, petty, trifling, trivial, unimportant. ANTONYMS: important, serious, weighty.

inconsiderate *a.* **1** (*hasty, incautious*) careless, hasty, incautious. **2** (*having no consideration for the feelings of others*) heedless, insensitive, rude, self-centred, selfish, tactless, thoughtless, uncaring, uncharitable, ungracious, unkind, unsympathetic, unthinking. ANTONYMS: considerate, thoughtful.

inconsistent *a.* **1** (*not in keeping; incompatible (with*)) at odds, conflicting, contradictory, contrary, discordant, discrepant, incoherent, incompatible, incongruous, irreconcilable, out of keeping, out of step. ANTONYMS: compatible. **2** ((*of behaviour etc.*) *changeable*) capricious, changeable, erratic, fickle, inconstant, irregular, uneven, unpredictable, unreliable, unstable, unsteady, variable. ANTONYMS: constant, uniform.

inconsolable *a.* ((*of a person, grief etc.*) *not to be consoled*) broken-hearted, comfortless, desolate, despairing, disconsolate, forlorn, grief-stricken, grieving, heartbroken, hopeless, miserable, prostrate, wretched. ANTONYMS: cheerful.

inconspicuous *a.* (*not conspicuous; not easy to see*) camouflaged, concealed, discreet, hidden, insignificant, modest, muted, ordinary, plain, quiet, retiring, unassuming, undistinguished, unnoticeable, unobtrusive, unostentatious. ANTONYMS: conspicuous, obtrusive.

inconstant *a.* **1** (*not constant, changeable*) capricious, changeable, fickle, flighty, irresolute, mercurial, temperamental, undependable, vacillating, volatile, wayward. ANTONYMS: constant, reliable. **2** (*variable, unsteady*) erratic, fitful, fluctuating, inconsistent, irregular, mutable, uncertain, unreliable, unsettled, unstable, unsteady, variable, wavering. ANTONYMS: steady.

incontestable *a.* (*indisputable, unquestionable*) certain, incontrovertible, indisputable, indubitable, irrefutable, self-evident, sure, unarguable, unassailable, undeniable, unquestionable. ANTONYMS: arguable, uncertain.

incontinent *a.* **1** (*unable to restrain one's desires, esp. sexual desires*) debauched, dissolute, impure, lascivious, lecherous, lewd, libertine, libidinous, licentious, loose, lustful, profane, profligate, promiscuous, salacious, unchaste, wanton. ANTONYMS: chaste. **2** (*not able to control the passing of waste from the body*) bedwetting, self-soiling. **3** (*lacking control* (*of*)) unbridled, unchecked, unconstrained, uncontrollable, uncontrolled, uncurbed, ungovernable, unrestrained. ANTONYMS: controlled.

incontrovertible *a.* (*incontestable, indisputable*) certain, definitive, established, incontestable, indisputable, indubitable, irrefutable, positive, sure, unarguable, undeniable, unquestionable, unshakeable. ANTONYMS: dubious.

inconvenience *n.* **1** (*the quality or state of being inconvenient*) awkwardness, cumbersomeness, inopportuneness, troublesomeness, untimeliness, unwieldiness. ANTONYMS: convenience. **2** (*something which inconveniences, a cause of difficulty*) annoyance, bother, difficulty, disadvantage, disruption, disturbance, drawback, fuss, (*coll.*) hassle, hindrance, impediment, nuisance, pain, problem, upset, vexation. ANTONYMS: help.
~*v.t.* (*to put to inconvenience; to trouble*) annoy, bother, discommode, disrupt, disturb, hinder, incommode, irk, irritate, put out, trouble, upset. ANTONYMS: assist.

inconvenient *a.* **1** (*not convenient*) awkward, cumbersome, inopportune, troublesome, unmanageable, untimely, unwieldy. ANTONYMS: convenient. **2** (*causing or tending to cause trouble*) annoying, awkward, bothersome, difficult, disadvantageous, disruptive, disturbing, problematic, tiresome, troublesome, upsetting, vexing.

incorporate *v.t.* (*to unite or combine into one body* (*with*)) absorb, amalgamate, assimilate, blend, coalesce, combine, comprise, consolidate, embody, embrace, fuse, include, integrate, meld, merge, mix, subsume, unify, unite. ANTONYMS: sever, split.

incorrect *a.* **1** (*wrong, inaccurate*) erroneous, fallacious, false, faulty, flawed, inaccurate, inexact, mistaken, unsound, untrue, wrong. ANTONYMS: accurate, correct. **2** (*improper, unbecoming*) improper, inappropriate, unbecoming, unfitting, unseemly, unsuitable. ANTONYMS: fitting, proper.

incorrigible *a.* (*bad beyond hope of amendment*) bad, hardened, hopeless, incurable, intractable, inveterate, irredeemable, irremediable, lost, obdurate, sinful, stubborn, unreformed, wicked. ANTONYMS: reformable.

incorruptible *a.* **1** (*not to be bribed; high-principled*) above suspicion, high-principled, honest, honourable, just, moral, straight, trustworthy, unbribable, unimpeachable, upright, virtuous. ANTONYMS: crooked, dishonest. **2** (*incapable of corruption; eternal*) abiding, deathless, eternal, everlasting, immortal, imperishable, indestructible, lasting, undecaying, undying. ANTONYMS: perishable.

increase[1] *v.i.* (*to become greater in quantity, degree etc.*) accrue, augment, build up, develop, dilate, enlarge, escalate, expand, grow, heighten, inflate, magnify, mount, multiply, proliferate, rise, snowball, swell. ANTONYMS: abate, diminish.
~*v.t.* **1** (*to make greater in quantity, value etc.*) add to, advance, enhance, enlarge, extend, lengthen, prolong, spread. ANTONYMS: curtail, reduce. **2** (*to intensify*) amplify, boost, intensify, raise.

increase[2] *n.* **1** (*the act or process of increasing; growth*) augmentation, boost, enlargement, escalation, expansion, extension, growth, intensification, multiplication, rise, upsurge. ANTONYMS: reduction. **2** (*the amount by which something increases*) addition, extra, increment, supplement.

incredible *a.* **1** (*not credible; difficult to believe*) absurd, beyond belief, far-fetched, implausible, impossible, improbable, inconceivable, preposterous, unbelievable, unimaginable, unlikely, unthinkable. ANTONYMS: credible, likely. **2** (*very great, amazing*) (*sl.*) ace, amazing, astonishing, astounding, brilliant, extraordinary, fabulous, fantastic, great, marvellous, (*coll.*) mega, prodigious, sensational, stupendous, tremendous, wonderful.

incredulity *n.* (*disbelief, scepticism*) disbelief, distrust, doubt, incredulousness, mistrust, scepticism, unbelief. ANTONYMS: belief.

incredulous *a.* (*indisposed to believe, sceptical* (*of*)) disbelieving, distrustful, doubtful, dubious, mistrustful, sceptical, suspicious, unbelieving, unconvinced. ANTONYMS: credulous.

increment *n.* (*an increase, esp. one of a series*) accrual, accruement, addition, augmentation, enlargement, gain, growth, increase, rise, supplement. ANTONYMS: decrease.

incriminate *v.i.* **1** (*to make seem guilty*) blame, point the finger at. ANTONYMS: vindicate. **2** (*to charge with a crime*) accuse, arraign, charge, impeach, inculpate, indict. **3** (*to involve* (*a person*) *in a charge*) implicate, involve.

incumbent *a.* **1** (*imposed* (*upon*) *as a duty or obligation*) binding, compulsory, mandatory, necessary, obligatory, required. ANTONYMS: optional. **2** (*lying or resting* (*on*); *pressing or weighing* (*upon*)) leaning, lying, pressing, reclining, resting, weighing.

incur *v.t.* (*to bring upon oneself* (*risk, injury etc.*)) arouse, attract, bring, contract, draw, earn, expose oneself to, gain, induce, invite, meet with, provoke, risk. ANTONYMS: avoid.

incurable *a.* (*that cannot be cured or healed*) fatal, hopeless, inoperable, irrecoverable, irremediable, terminal. ANTONYMS: curable.

incursion *n.* (*a sudden raid*) attack, encroachment, foray, infiltration, inroad, invasion, penetration, raid, sally. ANTONYMS: retreat.

indebted *a.* (*being under a debt or obligation* (*to or for*)) beholden, bound, grateful, indebted, liable, obligated, obliged, owing, responsible.

indecent *a.* **1** (*offensive to modesty or propriety*) blue, coarse, crude, degenerate, dirty, filthy, foul, gross, immodest, improper, impure, indelicate, lewd, licentious, obscene, pornographic, prurient, salacious, smutty. ANTONYMS: clean, pure. **2** (*unbecoming, unseemly*) ill-bred, improper, indecorous, offensive, outrageous, shameful, shocking, tasteless, unbecoming, unseemly, vulgar. ANTONYMS: proper, tasteful.

indecipherable *a.* (*not decipherable, illegible*) crabbed, illegible, indistinguishable, undecipherable, unintelligible, unreadable. ANTONYMS: decipherable, legible.

indecision *n.* (*lack of decision; irresolution*) ambivalence, dithering, doubt, hesitancy, hesitation, indecisiveness, irresolution, uncertainty, vacillation, wavering. ANTONYMS: resolution.

indecisive *a.* **1** (*not decisive, not final*) inconclusive, indefinite, indeterminate, open, unfinished, unresolved, unsettled. ANTONYMS: conclusive, final. **2** (*irresolute, hesitating*) dithering, doubtful, faltering, hesitating, irresolute, tentative, uncertain, undecided, undetermined, vacillating, wavering, wishy-washy. ANTONYMS: resolute, sure.

indecorous *a.* (*violating propriety or good manners*) boorish, churlish, coarse, ill-bred, immodest, impolite, improper, indecent, rude, tasteless, unbecoming, uncivil, uncouth, undignified, unmannerly, unseemly, untoward, vulgar. ANTONYMS: decorous.

indeed *adv.* (*in reality, in truth*) absolutely, actually, certainly, definitely, doubtlessly, exactly, in reality, in truth, positively, really, strictly, surely, truly, undeniably, veritably.

indefatigable *a.* (*not yielding to fatigue; unwearied*) assiduous, diligent, dogged, indomitable, inexhaustible, patient, persevering, persistent, relentless, tireless, unfatigued, unflagging, unremitting, untiring, unwearied, unwearying. ANTONYMS: indolent, lazy.

indefensible *a.* (*incapable of being defended or justified*) faulty, inexcusable, insupportable, unforgiving, unjustifiable, unpardonable, untenable, unwarrantable, wrong. ANTONYMS: excusable, justifiable.

indefinite *a.* (*not limited or defined*) ambiguous, confused, doubtful, equivocal, evasive, hazy, ill-defined, imprecise, indecisive, indeterminate, indistinct, inexact, loose, obscure, uncertain, unclear, undefined, unlimited, unsettled, vague. ANTONYMS: clear, definite.

indelible *a.* (*that cannot be blotted out or effaced*) enduring, fixed, indestructible, ineffaceable, ineradicable, ingrained, lasting, permanent. ANTONYMS: erasable.

indelicate *a.* **1** (*lacking delicacy or tact*) immodest, improper, tactless. ANTONYMS: diplomatic, tactful. **2** (*coarse, unrefined*) coarse, crude, rough, unrefined. **3** (*offensive to modesty or propriety*) blue, embarrassing, gross, immodest, improper, indecent, low, obscene, offensive, risqué, rude, suggestive, tasteless, unbecoming, unseemly. ANTONYMS: becoming, decorous.

indemnify *v.t.* **1** (*to secure from damage or penalty*) endorse, guarantee, insure, protect, secure, underwrite. **2** (*to compensate* (*a* _person_) _for loss, damage etc._) compensate, pay, reimburse, remunerate, repair, requite, satisfy.

indemnity _n._ **1** (_security against damage or penalty_) assurance, guarantee, insurance, protection, security. **2** (_compensation for damage or penalties incurred_) compensation, recompense, redress, reimbursement, remuneration, reparation, repayment, restitution, restoration, satisfaction. **3** (_legal exemption from liabilities or penalties incurred_) exemption, immunity, impunity, privilege.

indentation _n._ (_a notch or incision, esp. in a margin_) bash, cut, dent, depression, dimple, dip, hollow, incision, jag, mark, nick, notch, pit, score.

independence _n._ (_the quality or state of being independent_ (_from, of_)) autarchy, autonomy, freedom, home rule, liberty, self-determination, self-government, self-reliance, self-rule, self-sufficiency, sovereignty. ANTONYMS: bondage, dependence.

independent _a._ **1** (_not dependent upon or subject to the control or authority of another_) autocratic, autonomous, free, liberated, self-determining, self-governing, sovereign. **2** (_confident and capable of acting by oneself_) bold, confident, self-assured, self-confident. **3** (_unwilling to accept help from others_) self-contained, self-reliant, self-sufficient, self-supporting, unaided. ANTONYMS: dependent. **4** (_not affiliated with or part of a larger organization_) separate, unaffiliated, unconnected. ANTONYMS: subsidiary.

indescribable _a._ **1** (_too fine, bad etc. to be described_) beyond description, ineffable, inexpressible, unutterable. ANTONYMS: commonplace. **2** (_vague, imprecise_) imprecise, indefinable, inexact, vague.

indestructible _a._ (_incapable of being destroyed_) abiding, durable, enduring, everlasting, immortal, immutable, imperishable, incorruptible, indelible, indissoluble, lasting, long-lasting, non-perishable, perennial, permanent, unalterable, unbreakable, undying, unfading. ANTONYMS: impermanent, perishable.

indeterminate _a._ **1** (_not fixed or limited in scope, nature etc._) uncertain, undetermined, unfixed, unknown, unlimited, unsettled. ANTONYMS: fixed, limited. **2** (_indefinite, not precise_) confused, imprecise, indefinite, inexact, obscure, undefined, vague. ANTONYMS: definite, precise.

index _n._ **1** (_a list of names, subjects etc. in alphabetical order_) catalogue, directory, file, guide, key, list, listing, table. **2** (_a pointer on a dial_,

watch etc.) hand, needle, pointer. **3** (_a sign or indicator_) clue, hint, indication, indicator, mark, pointer, sign, symptom, token.

indicate _v.t._ **1** (_to show, to point out_) designate, mark, point out, point to, show, specify. **2** (_to be a sign or token of_) bespeak, betoken, denote, evince, signify. **3** (_to require; to call for_) call for, demand, need, recommend, require. **4** (_to state briefly, to suggest_) hint, imply, intimate, suggest. **5** ((_of an instrument_) _to show a reading of_) disclose, display, express, read, record, show, state, tell.

indication _n._ **1** (_something which indicates or suggests_) clue, evidence, explanation, forewarning, hint, index, inkling, intimation, manifestation, mark, note, omen, portent, sign, signal, suggestion, symbol, symptom, token, warning. **2** (_a reading shown by a gauge etc._) degree, measure, reading.

indict _v.t._ (_to charge_ (_a person_) _with a crime or misdemeanour_) accuse, arraign, charge, impeach, incriminate, inculpate, prosecute, summon. ANTONYMS: acquit.

indictment _n._ (_a formal accusation of a crime or misdemeanour_) accusation, allegation, arraignment, charge, impeachment, prosecution, summons. ANTONYMS: acquittal.

indifference _n._ **1** (_lack of interest or attention_ (_to or towards_)) aloofness, apathy, carelessness, coolness, detachment, disinterest, disregard, heedlessness, impassivity, inattention, insensibility, listlessness, negligence, nonchalance, unconcern. ANTONYMS: concern, enthusiasm. **2** (_impartiality, neutrality_) dispassion, evenhandedness, fairness, impartiality, neutrality, objectivity. ANTONYMS: bias, partiality. **3** (_unimportance, insignificance_) inconsequence, insignificance, irrelevance, triviality, unimportance. ANTONYMS: importance.

indifferent _a._ **1** (_unconcerned, apathetic_) aloof, apathetic, careless, cool, detached, distant, heedless, impassive, impervious, inattentive, insensitive, nonchalant, regardless, uncaring, unconcerned, uninterested, unmoved, unresponsive. ANTONYMS: concerned, interested. **2** (_having no inclination or disinclination_ (_to_); _impartial_) disinclined, disinterested, dispassionate, equitable, impartial, neutral, non-partisan, objective, unbiased, unprejudiced. ANTONYMS: partial, prejudiced. **3** (_neither good nor bad_) average, middling, (_coll._) so so. **4** (_of no importance, of little moment_ (_to_)) immaterial, inconsequential, insignificant, irrelevant, unimportant. ANTONYMS: important. **5** (_of a barely passable quality, not good_) fair, inferior, mediocre, moderate, ordinary, passable, poor. ANTONYMS: excellent.

indigenous *a.* 1 ((*of people*) *not immigrant or descended from immigrants, native*) aboriginal, endemic, local, native. ANTONYMS: exotic, immigrant. 2 (*natural, innate* (*to*)) congenital, inborn, inbred, inherent, innate, natural. ANTONYMS: acquired.

indignant *a.* (*feeling or showing indignation, esp. at meanness, injustice etc.*) angry, annoyed, disgruntled, enraged, exasperated, fuming, furious, incensed, irate, livid, (*coll.*) mad, miffed, (*sl.*) narked, outraged, (*sl.*) peeved, (*taboo sl.*) pissed off, provoked, riled, (*coll.*) sore, wrathful. ANTONYMS: calm.

indignation *n.* (*a feeling of anger and scorn provoked by supposed injustice or unfairness*) anger, annoyance, disgruntlement, exasperation, fury, irritation, outrage, pique, rage, resentment, scorn, umbrage, vexation, wrath.

indignity *n.* 1 (*undeserved contemptuous treatment*) embarrassment, humiliation, outrage, shame. 2 (*a slight, an insult*) abuse, affront, aspersion, disrespect, injury, insult, obloquy, reproach, slight, snub. ANTONYMS: respect.

indirect *a.* 1 (*not direct, deviating from a direct line*) circuitous, circumlocutory, crooked, deviating, erratic, meandering, oblique, rambling, roundabout, roving, tortuous, wandering, winding. ANTONYMS: direct, undeviating. 2 (*not resulting directly or immediately from a cause*) accidental, ancillary, collateral, contingent, incidental, secondary, unintended. ANTONYMS: intended, primary. 3 (*not open or straightforward*) devious, evasive. ANTONYMS: straightforward.

indiscernible *a.* (*not discernible, not distinguishable*) hidden, impalpable, imperceptible, inconsiderable, indistinct, indistinguishable, invisible, slight, subtle, unapparent. ANTONYMS: discernible, visible.

indiscreet *a.* 1 (*not discreet*) tactless, undiplomatic. ANTONYMS: discreet. 2 (*injudicious, rash*) foolish, hasty, heedless, ill-advised, ill-considered, ill-judged, impetuous, impolitic, improvident, imprudent, impulsive, incautious, inconsiderate, injudicious, naive, precipitate, rash, reckless, unthinking, unwise. ANTONYMS: cautious, prudent.

indiscretion *n.* 1 (*lack of discretion*) lack of diplomacy, tactlessness. ANTONYMS: discretion, tact. 2 (*imprudence, rashness*) folly, foolishness, heedlessness, impetuosity, improvidence, imprudence, injudiciousness, insensitivity, rashness, recklessness, thoughtlessness. ANTONYMS: caution. 3 (*an indiscreet act*) (*sl.*) bloomer, blunder, (*coll.*) boob, error, faux pas, gaffe, lapse, mistake, slip.

indiscriminate *a.* 1 (*not discriminating or making distinctions*) aimless, careless, desultory, general, random, sweeping, uncritical, undiscriminating, unmethodical, unselective, unsystematic, wholesale. ANTONYMS: discriminating. 2 (*confused*) chaotic, confused, disordered, disorganized, erratic, haphazard, jumbled, mingled, miscellaneous, mixed, mongrel, motley, undistinguishable.

indispensable *a.* (*that cannot be dispensed with; absolutely necessary*) basic, compulsory, crucial, essential, fundamental, imperative, key, necessary, needed, needful, required, requisite, unavoidable, urgent, vital. ANTONYMS: superfluous, unnecessary.

indisposed *a.* 1 (*disinclined, unwilling*) averse, disinclined, hesitant, loath, reluctant, resistant, unwilling. ANTONYMS: eager, willing. 2 (*slightly ill*) ailing, ill, laid up, out of sorts, poorly, sick, unsound, unwell. ANTONYMS: healthy, well.

indisputable *a.* (*that cannot be disputed or doubted*) absolute, certain, definitive, evident, fixed, incontestable, incontrovertible, indubitable, irrefutable, positive, sure, unarguable, unassailable, undeniable, unquestionable. ANTONYMS: dubious, questionable.

indissoluble *a.* 1 (*that cannot be dissolved or disintegrated*) enduring, eternal, imperishable, incorruptible, indestructible, indivisible, inseparable, lasting, permanent. ANTONYMS: perishable. 2 ((*of a bond etc.*) *stable and binding*) binding, fixed, stable.

indistinct *a.* 1 (*not distinct, obscure*) ambiguous, equivocal, ill-defined, indistinguishable, inseparable, obscure, unclear, vague. ANTONYMS: distinct, well-defined. 2 (*confused, faint*) bleary, blurred, confused, dim, faint, filmy, foggy, fuzzy, hazy, indefinite, indiscernible, muddy, muffled, murky, obscure, shadowy, vague, weak. ANTONYMS: clear.

indistinguishable *a.* (*not distinguishable* (*from*)) alike, identical, imperceptible, indefinite, indiscernible, indistinct, inseparable, invisible, like, obscure, same, similar, twin, unclear, undifferentiated. ANTONYMS: distinguishable.

individual *a.* 1 (*existing as a single indivisible entity*) sole, solitary, unique. 2 (*single, particular as opposed to general*) particular, peculiar, single. ANTONYMS: general. 3 (*separate or distinct*) distinct, separate, specific. 4 (*characteristic of a particular person or thing, distinctive*) characteristic, distinctive, special. 5 (*designed for one person*) exclusive, own, personal, personalized, single, singular.

~n. (*a single person, esp. when regarded as distinct or separate from a group*) being, body, character, child, creature, head, human, human being, man, mortal, one, party, person, personage, soul, woman. ANTONYMS: group.

indoctrinate *v.t.* **1** (*to teach* (*someone*) *to accept, esp. without questioning, a set of beliefs*) brainwash, imbue, implant, inculcate, infuse, instil, propagandize. **2** (*to instruct*) discipline, drill, ground, initiate, instruct, school, teach, train.

indolent *a.* (*habitually idle or lazy*) apathetic, idle, inactive, inert, lackadaisical, languid, lazy, lethargic, listless, lumpish, shiftless, slack, slothful, slow, sluggish, torpid, workshy. ANTONYMS: diligent, industrious.

indomitable *a.* **1** (*untameable, unconquerable*) invincible, unbeatable, unconquerable, untameable. **2** (*stubbornly determined*) bold, determined, indefatigable, irrepressible, persistent, resolute, staunch, steadfast, stubborn, tireless, unflagging, unflinching, unwavering, unyielding. ANTONYMS: cowardly, yielding.

induce *v.t.* **1** (*to lead by persuasion or reasoning* (*to do something*)) convince, draw, egg on, encourage, entice, goad, impel, incite, influence, instigate, move, persuade, press, prevail on, prod, prompt, spur, sway, talk into, urge. ANTONYMS: curb, deter. **2** (*to bring about, to cause*) bring about, cause, create, effect, engender, generate, lead to, occasion, produce, set in motion, set off. ANTONYMS: prevent.

inducement *n.* **1** (*the act of inducing*) convincing, encouraging, enticing, inciting, inducing, persuading, prompting. **2** (*something which induces*) attraction, bait, carrot, (*sl.*) come-on, encouragement, influence, lure, persuasion. ANTONYMS: deterrent. **3** (*a motive, an incitement* (*to*)) enticement, impulse, incentive, incitement, motive, reason, spur, stimulus, urge.

indulge *v.t.* **1** (*to yield to* (*a desire, whim etc.*)) feed, give in to, succumb to, yield to. **2** (*to favour; to gratify the wishes of*) baby, cater to, coddle, cosset, favour, foster, gratify, humour, minister to, mollycoddle, oblige, pamper, pander to, pet, regale, satisfy, spoil, treat. ANTONYMS: deny.
~*v.i.* (*to yield to one's desires* (*in*)) bask (in), luxuriate (in), revel (in), wallow (in), yield (to).

indulgence *n.* **1** (*the act or practice of indulging or complying to a desire etc.*) appeasement, fulfilment, gratification, satiation, satisfaction. **2** (*an indulgent act, a favour granted*) extravagance, favour, kindness, luxury, privilege, treat. **3** (*a pleasurable thing or habit indulged in*) excess, fondness, intemperance, weakness. **4** (*kindness, patience*) clemency, forbearance, leniency, patience, suffering, tolerance, understanding.

indulgent *a.* (*indulging or disposed to indulge the wishes of others*) clement, compliant, easygoing, favourable, fond, forbearing, gentle, gratifying, kind, kindly, lenient, liberal, mild, obliging, patient, permissive, tender, tolerant, understanding. ANTONYMS: intolerant, strict.

industrious *a.* (*diligent and assiduous*) active, assiduous, busy, conscientious, diligent, dogged, energetic, hard-working, laborious, persevering, persistent, productive, sedulous, tireless, zealous. ANTONYMS: idle, lazy.

industry *n.* **1** (*mechanical and manufacturing work as distinct from agriculture and commerce*) manufacture, production, trade. **2** (*any branch of these*) business, commerce, trade. **3** (*steady application to a pursuit*) application, assiduity, diligence, effort, labour, perseverance, persistence, sedulity, tirelessness, toil, vigour, work, zeal. ANTONYMS: idleness.

inebriated *a.* (*drunk*) (*sl.*) blitzed, (*sl.*) blotto, drunk, (*sl.*) half-cut, intoxicated, (*coll.*) legless, (*coll.*) merry, (*sl.*) paralytic, (*taboo sl.*) pissed, (*sl.*) plastered, (*sl.*) smashed, (*coll.*) sozzled, (*sl.*) stoned, (*sl.*) tight, (*coll.*) under the influence, (*sl.*) wasted, (*coll.*) well-oiled. ANTONYMS: sober.

ineffable *a.* (*unutterable, beyond expression*) beyond words, indefinable, indescribable, inexpressible, unmentionable, unspeakable, unutterable. ANTONYMS: commonplace.

ineffective *a.* **1** (*not having an effect*) barren, bootless, feeble, fruitless, futile, idle, impotent, inadequate, ineffectual, inefficacious, unavailing, unfruitful, unproductive, useless, vain, weak, worthless. ANTONYMS: effective, worthwhile. **2** ((*of a person*) *inefficient*) incapable, incompetent, ineffectual, inefficient, inept, lame, unskilled. ANTONYMS: able, competent.

ineffectual *a.* **1** (*not producing any effect or the desired effect*) abortive, barren, bootless, feeble, fruitless, futile, idle, impotent, inadequate, ineffective, inefficacious, powerless, sterile, unavailing, unproductive, useless, vain, weak. ANTONYMS: effectual. **2** ((*of a person*) *not able to achieve results*) incapable, incompetent, ineffective, inefficient, inept, lame, unskilled.

inelegant *a.* (*lacking grace, refinement etc.*) awkward, clumsy, coarse, crass, crude, gauche, graceless, indelicate, laboured, rough, rude, uncourtly, uncouth, uncultivated, ungainly, ungraceful, unpolished, unrefined. ANTONYMS: elegant, graceful.

ineligible *a.* 1 (*not eligible*) disqualified, unfit, unqualified. ANTONYMS: eligible. 2 (*not suitable*) improper, inappropriate, objectionable, unacceptable, undesirable, unsuitable, unsuited. ANTONYMS: suitable.

inept *a.* 1 (*clumsy, incompetent*) awkward, bumbling, bungling, (*sl.*) cack-handed, clumsy, gauche, incompetent, ineffectual, inexpert, unskilful. ANTONYMS: competent. 2 (*silly, absurd*) absurd, foolish, meaningless, nonsensical, pointless, silly. 3 (*not apt or suitable*) improper, inappropriate, inapt, inexpedient, unfit, unseemly, unsuitable, unsuited. ANTONYMS: apt, suitable.

inequality *n.* 1 (*a lack of equality*) bias, discrimination, inequity, injustice, partiality, preferentiality, prejudice, unfairness. ANTONYMS: equality. 2 (*variability*) difference, diversity, variability. 3 (*irregularity, unevenness*) discrepancy, disparity, disproportion, imbalance, imparity, irregularity, unevenness. ANTONYMS: evenness, uniformity.

inert *a.* 1 (*lacking inherent power of motion*) dead, dormant, immobile, inactive, inanimate, lifeless, motionless, powerless, static, still, unmoving, unresponsive. ANTONYMS: active, mobile. 2 (*slow, sluggish*) dull, idle, indolent, lazy, leaden, lethargic, passive, slack, slothful, slow, sluggish, torpid. 3 (*not chemically reactive*) inactive, unreactive.

inertia *n.* (*reluctance to move or act*) apathy, drowsiness, dullness, idleness, immobility, inactivity, indolence, languor, lassitude, laziness, lethargy, listlessness, passivity, sloth, sluggishness, stillness, stupor, torpor, unresponsiveness. ANTONYMS: activity, animation.

inessential *a.* 1 (*not essential or necessary*) needless, optional, unnecessary. ANTONYMS: essential, necessary. 2 (*dispensable*) dispensable, extraneous, extrinsic, spare, superfluous, surplus.

inevitable *a.* 1 (*that cannot be avoided or prevented*) ineluctable, inescapable, inexorable, irrevocable, unavoidable, unchangeable, unpreventable. ANTONYMS: avoidable, preventable. 2 (*that is sure to happen or predictable*) assured, certain, destined, fated, ordained, predictable, sure.

inexact *a.* (*not exact, not precisely accurate*) erroneous, imprecise, inaccurate, incorrect, indefinite, indeterminate, loose, muddled, off, rough, wrong. ANTONYMS: accurate, exact, precise.

inexcusable *a.* (*that cannot be excused or justified*) indefensible, intolerable, outrageous, unforgivable, unjustifiable, unpardonable, unwarrantable. ANTONYMS: excusable, pardonable.

inexhaustible *a.* 1 (*that cannot be exhausted*) bottomless, boundless, endless, illimitable, infinite, limitless, measureless, never-ending, unbounded, unlimited, unrestricted. ANTONYMS: finite, limited. 2 (*unfailing, unceasing*) indefatigable, tireless, unceasing, undaunted, unfailing, unflagging, unwearying. ANTONYMS: flagging, tiring.

inexorable *a.* 1 (*relentless*) cruel, hard, harsh, implacable, inescapable, merciless, pitiless, relentless, remorseless, severe, unrelenting. 2 (*incapable of being persuaded or moved by entreaty*) adamant, immovable, inflexible, obdurate, unbending, unmovable, unpersuadable, unswervable, unyielding. ANTONYMS: flexible, persuadable.

inexpensive *a.* (*not expensive, cheap*) bargain, budget, cheap, economical, low-cost, low-priced, modest, reasonable. ANTONYMS: dear, expensive.

inexperienced *a.* (*lacking experience*) callow, fresh, green, ignorant, inexpert, innocent, new, raw, unaccustomed, unacquainted, unfamiliar, unfledged, unpractised, unschooled, unseasoned, unskilled, untrained, untried, unversed, wet behind the ears. ANTONYMS: experienced, practised.

inexplicable *a.* (*that cannot be explained*) baffling, bewildering, confounding, enigmatic, incomprehensible, inscrutable, insoluble, mysterious, mystifying, perplexing, puzzling, strange, unaccountable, unexplainable, unfathomable, unintelligible. ANTONYMS: explicable.

inexpressible *a.* (*incapable of being expressed or described*) beyond words, incommunicable, indefinable, indescribable, ineffable, unspeakable, unutterable. ANTONYMS: commonplace.

infallible *a.* (*exempt from liability to error or to failure*) certain, dependable, faultless, foolproof, impeccable, perfect, reliable, sure, (*coll.*) sure-fire, trustworthy, unerring, unfailing. ANTONYMS: fallible, unreliable.

infamous *a.* 1 (*having a very bad reputation*) dishonourable, disreputable, ill-famed, notorious. ANTONYMS: esteemed, respected. 2 (*detestable, scandalous*) abominable, atrocious, base, despicable, detestable, disgraceful, heinous, ignominious, iniquitous, loathsome, monstrous, nefarious, odious, opprobrious, outrageous, scandalous, shameful, shocking, vile, wicked.

infamy n. 1 (*total loss of reputation or character*) discredit, disgrace, dishonour, disrepute, ignominy, ill fame, notoriety, obloquy, odium, opprobrium, shame. ANTONYMS: honour. 2 (*an infamous act*) abomination, atrocity, evil, iniquity, misdeed, outrage, scandal, villainy, wickedness.

infant n. (*a child during the earliest years of its life*) babe, baby, child, suckling, toddler. ANTONYMS: adult.
~a. (*at an early stage of development*) baby, dawning, early, emergent, fledgling, growing, immature, initial, newborn, young.

infantile a. (*characteristic of infancy, childish*) babyish, childish, immature, newborn, puerile, young. ANTONYMS: adult, mature.

infatuated a. (*inspired with an extravagant passion, usu. for a person*) beguiled, besotted, bewitched, captivated, carried away, charmed, (*coll.*) crazy, enamoured, enchanted, enraptured, fascinated, mesmerized, obsessed, possessed, (*coll.*) smitten.

infatuation n. (*an extravagant passion*) beguilement, captivation, (*coll.*) crush, fascination, fixation, folly, foolishness, madness, obsession, passion, possession, (*coll.*) thing.

infect v.t. 1 (*to contaminate (water, food etc.) with a bacterium, virus etc., and so cause disease*) contaminate, poison, pollute, taint. ANTONYMS: sterilize. 2 (*to imbue with noxious opinions etc.*) blight, corrupt, defile.

infection n. 1 (*the act or process of infecting*) contamination, pollution, taint. 2 (*an infectious disease*) contagion, disease, germ, plague, virus. 3 (*moral contamination*) corruption, defilement.

infectious a. 1 ((*of a disease*) *liable to be communicated by the atmosphere, water etc.*) catching, communicable, contagious, contaminating, infective, pestilent, spreading, transmittable, virulent, vitiating. 2 ((*of feelings etc.*) *apt to spread, catching*) catching, corrupting, defiling.

infelicitous a. 1 (*unfortunate*) inauspicious, miserable, unfavourable, unfortunate, unhappy, unlucky, woeful, wretched. ANTONYMS: felicitous. 2 (*inappropriate, inapt*) inappropriate, inapt, incongruous, unfitting, unsuitable, wrong. ANTONYMS: appropriate.

infer v.t. (*to deduce as a fact, consequence or result*) assume, conclude, deduce, derive, gather, guess, presume, surmise, understand.

inferior a. 1 (*lower in rank, value etc.*) humble, insignificant, junior, lesser, lower, menial, minor, secondary, subordinate, subservient, subsidiary, unimportant. ANTONYMS: higher, superior. 2 (*of mediocre or poor quality*) bad, defective, (*coll.*) grotty, imperfect, indifferent, low-grade, mean, mediocre, poor, second-class, second-rate, shoddy. ANTONYMS: excellent, fine.
~n. (*a person who is inferior to another in ability, rank etc.*) junior, menial, subordinate, underling.

infernal a. 1 (*worthy of hell; diabolic*) demoniacal, demonic, devilish, diabolic, fiendish, satanic. ANTONYMS: celestial, heavenly. 2 (*coll.*) (*abominable, detestable*) abominable, accursed, (*coll.*) confounded, damnable, damned, detestable, dire, dreadful, evil, execrable, iniquitous, malevolent, malicious, sinister, villainous, wicked.

infertile a. (*not fertile; unfruitful*) barren, fruitless, infecund, sterile, unfruitful, unproductive. ANTONYMS: fertile.

infest v.t. ((*of vermin, parasites*) *to swarm over in large numbers*) beset, crawl, flood, infiltrate, inundate, invade, overrun, overspread, penetrate, permeate, pervade, plague, ravage, swarm, throng.

infidelity n. 1 (*breach of trust, disloyalty, esp. unfaithfulness to the marriage vow*) adultery, betrayal, (*coll.*) cheating, cuckoldry, disloyalty, duplicity, faithlessness, falseness, perfidy, treachery, unfaithfulness. ANTONYMS: faithfulness. 2 (*disbelief in a religion such as Christianity*) apostasy, disbelief, heresy, irreligion, scepticism, unbelief. ANTONYMS: belief.

infiltrate v.i. 1 (*to secretly gain or cause someone to gain access to an enemy organization*) creep in, enter, gain access, insinuate oneself, penetrate, sneak in. 2 (*to permeate by infiltration*) percolate, permeate, pervade.

infinite a. 1 (*having no bounds or limits*) bottomless, boundless, endless, illimitable, immeasurable, indeterminable, indeterminate, inexhaustible, limitless, measureless, unbounded, unfathomable, unlimited. ANTONYMS: bounded, limited. 2 (*very great*) eternal, everlasting, great, inexhaustible, never-ending, perpetual, undying, unending. 3 (*numerous, very many*) incalculable, innumerable, many, multitudinous, numberless, numerous, uncounted, untold.

infinitesimal a. (*infinitely or extremely small*) imperceptible, inappreciable, insignificant, little, microscopic, minuscule, minute, negligible, small, (*coll.*) teeny, tiny. ANTONYMS: huge, vast.

infirm a. 1 (*lacking bodily strength or health, esp. through age or disease*) ailing, debilitated, decrepit, doddering, doddery, enfeebled, failing, feeble, fragile, frail, ill, indisposed, lame, sickly, unhealthy, unwell, weak. ANTONYMS: healthy, strong. 2 (*weak-minded, irresolute*) faltering, inconstant, indecisive, irresolute, vacillating, wavering, weak-minded. ANTONYMS: resolute. 3 (*uncertain, unstable*) flimsy, insecure, shaky, uncertain, unsound, unstable, unsteady, weak, wobbly. ANTONYMS: certain.

infirmity n. (*an illness, bad health*) affliction, ailment, debility, decrepitude, defect, deficiency, disability, disorder, failing, feebleness, frailty, ill health, illness, imperfection, malady, sickness, weakness. ANTONYMS: health, strength.

inflame v.t. 1 (*to stir up strong feelings in (someone)*) anger, animate, arouse, embitter, enrage, exasperate, excite, fire, impassion, incense, incite, infuriate, intoxicate, madden, prod, provoke, (*coll.*) rile, rouse, stimulate, stir up. ANTONYMS: calm, pacify. 2 (*to intensify, to aggravate*) aggravate, augment, deepen, exacerbate, fan, fuel, heighten, increase, worsen. ANTONYMS: allay, mitigate. 3 (*to cause to blaze, to kindle*) ignite, kindle, light, set alight.

inflammable a. 1 (*that may be easily set on fire*) combustible, flammable, ignitable, incendiary. ANTONYMS: non-flammable. 2 (*easily excited*) excitable, fiery, temperamental, volatile. ANTONYMS: placid.

inflammation n. (*an abnormal physical condition characterized by heat, redness, swelling and pain*) burning, heat, irritation, pain, rash, redness, sore, soreness, swelling, tenderness.

inflate v.t. 1 (*to cause (a balloon, mattress etc.) to expand by filling with air*) blow up, pump up. ANTONYMS: deflate. 2 (*to make greater than normal or appropriate*) amplify, balloon, bloat, blow up, boost, dilate, distend, enlarge, escalate, increase, swell. ANTONYMS: diminish, shrink. 3 (*to raise (prices, reputation etc.) excessively*) bump up, exaggerate, puff up.

inflated a. 1 (*distended with air*) blown up, pumped up. 2 (*bombastic, turgid*) bombastic, grandiloquent, grandiose, high-flown, orotund, ostentatious, pompous, pretentious, puffed up, turgid. 3 (*greater than normal or appropriate*) bloated, conceited, distended, exaggerated, overblown, swollen.

inflect v.t. 1 (*to modulate (the voice)*) intonate, intone, modulate. 2 (*to change the form, esp.

the ending of a word in order to express gender, tense, mood etc.*) conjugate, decline. 3 (*to bend, to curve*) arch, bend, bow, crook, curve, flex, round. ANTONYMS: straighten.

inflexible a. 1 (*incapable of being bent or curved*) firm, hard, inelastic, rigid, stiff, taut, unbending, unyielding. ANTONYMS: elastic, flexible. 2 (*firm; obstinate*) adamant, dogged, firm, immovable, implacable, intractable, obdurate, obstinate, persevering, relentless, resolute, steadfast, strict, stubborn. 3 (*unalterable; inexorable*) fixed, inexorable, set, unalterable, unchangeable.

inflict v.t. (*sometimes facet.*) 1 (*to impose (suffering, a penalty) on*) apply, impose. 2 (*to deal out (defeat, a blow etc.)*) administer, deal out, deliver, mete out, visit, wreak. ANTONYMS: spare. 3 †(*to afflict*) afflict, oppress, torment, trouble.

influence n. 1 (*power to direct or control, ascendancy (over)*) ascendancy, authority, (*coll.*) clout, connections, control, hold, leverage, power, prestige, pull, sway. 2 (*the effect of such power*) direction, effect, guidance, mastery, pressure, rule, weight.
~v.t. 1 (*to exercise influence upon; to affect*) affect, alter, modify. 2 (*to bias, to sway*) bias, control, direct, guide, impel, impress, incite, incline, induce, instigate, lead, manipulate, move, persuade, prompt, sway.

influential a. (*having great influence*) authoritative, cogent, controlling, effective, efficacious, forceful, forcible, guiding, important, instrumental, leading, meaningful, moving, persuasive, potent, powerful, prestigious, significant, telling, weighty. ANTONYMS: insignificant, powerless, weak.

inform v.t. 1 (*to communicate knowledge to, to tell (of, about)*) acquaint, advise, apprise, brief, communicate, disclose, divulge, enlighten, impart, leak, notify, report, reveal, tell, tip off. 2 (*to impart some essential quality to*) characterize, imbue, permeate, suffuse, typify. 3 (*to educate*) educate, instruct, teach.
~v.i. (*to make an accusation (against)*) betray, blab, denounce, (*sl.*) finger, (*sl.*) grass, incriminate, peach, (*coll.*) rat, (*sl.*) shop, (*sl.*) sing, (*sl.*) snitch, (*sl.*) split, (*sl.*) squeal, tell on.

informal a. 1 (*without formality; relaxed*) casual, easy, familiar, natural, relaxed, simple, unceremonious, unofficial, unstilted. ANTONYMS: formal, stiff. 2 (*ordinary; everyday*) common or garden, commonplace, everyday, ordinary. 3 ((*of writing, language*) *containing everyday conventional vocabulary*) colloquial, everyday, vernacular.

information n. 1 (*something communicated; knowledge*) advice, blurb, counsel, data, (*sl.*) dope, facts, (*coll.*) gen, (*coll.*) info, instruction, intelligence, knowledge, (*coll.*) lowdown. 2 (*news (on, about)*) (*coll.*) latest, message, news, notice, report, tidings, word.

informer n. 1 (*a person who informs against someone else*) (*sl.*) grass, (*sl.*) nark, sneak, stool pigeon, traitor. 2 (*a person who provides information or advice*) adviser, announcer, informant, reporter, source.

infrequent a. (*rare, uncommon*) few, occasional, rare, scarce, sporadic, uncommon, unusual. ANTONYMS: common, frequent.

infringe v.t. (*to break or violate (a law, contract etc.)*) break, contravene, disobey, infract, overstep, transgress, violate. ANTONYMS: obey, observe.
~v.i. (*to encroach, to intrude (on, upon)*) encroach, impinge, intrude, invade, trespass.

infringement n. (*a breaking or violation of a law etc.*) breach, contravention, disobedience, infraction, intrusion, invasion, transgression, trespass, violation. ANTONYMS: compliance, observance.

infuriate v.t. (*to provoke to fury*) anger, annoy, enrage, exasperate, fire up, gall, incense, inflame, irk, irritate, madden, (*sl.*) nark, nettle, (*taboo sl.*) piss off, provoke, (*coll.*) rile, stir up, vex. ANTONYMS: appease, pacify.

infuse v.t. 1 (*to pervade or fill (with)*) charge, fill, imbue, pervade. 2 (*to inculcate, to instil (vitality, life etc. into something)*) engraft, implant, inculcate, infix, ingrain, inspire, instil, introduce. 3 (*to steep (tea, herbs) in liquid so as to extract the flavour*) brew, imbue, macerate, permeate, saturate, soak, steep.

ingenious a. 1 (*skilful, clever, esp. at inventing*) adroit, clever, deft, dexterous, handy, skilful. ANTONYMS: clumsy, unskilful. 2 (*having great intelligence or talent*) acute, bright, brilliant, crafty, creative, cunning, gifted, intelligent, inventive, masterly, original, resourceful, shrewd, subtle, talented. ANTONYMS: stupid.

ingenuity n. (*skill, cleverness*) adroitness, brilliance, cleverness, craft, creativity, cunning, deftness, dexterity, faculty, flair, genius, imagination, ingeniousness, inventiveness, originality, resourcefulness, sharpness, shrewdness, skill, talent. ANTONYMS: ineptitude.

ingenuous a. 1 (*innocent or artless*) artless, childlike, guileless, innocent, naive, simple, unsophisticated, unstudied. ANTONYMS: artful,

sly. 2 (*candid, frank*) candid, direct, forthright, frank, honest, open, plain, sincere, straightforward, trustworthy, unreserved. ANTONYMS: insincere.

ingenuousness n. (*the state of being ingenuous*) artlessness, candour, frankness, guilelessness, honesty, innocence, naivety, openness, simplicity, sincerity. ANTONYMS: insincerity, subtlety.

inglorious a. 1 (*shameful, ignominious*) base, despicable, discreditable, dishonourable, disreputable, humiliating, ignoble, ignominious, infamous, low, shameful. ANTONYMS: glorious. 2 (*unknown, not famous*) humble, lowly, obscure, unknown, unrenowned, unsung. ANTONYMS: famous.

ingrain v.t. (*to cause (a dye etc.) to permeate something*) embed, engraft, entrench, fix, imbue, implant, impregnate, impress, imprint, infuse, instil, permeate, root.

ingrained a. 1 (*(of a habit, belief etc.) deeply imprinted*) deep-rooted, deep-seated, fixed, imprinted. 2 (*(of dirt etc.) worked into the fibres, pores etc.*) deep-rooted, deep-seated, hereditary, inbred, inbuilt, inherent, innate, intrinsic, inveterate, organic, rooted, worked in.

ingratiate v.t. (*to insinuate (oneself) into goodwill or favour (with) another*) blandish, crawl, curry favour, fawn, flatter, get in with, grovel, insinuate, pander to, play up to, rub up to, (*coll.*) suck up to, toady.

ingratitude n. (*lack of gratitude*) nonrecognition, thanklessness, unappreciativeness, ungratefulness. ANTONYMS: appreciation, gratitude.

ingredient n. (*an element or a component part in a recipe, mixture etc.*) component, constituent, element, factor, part. ANTONYMS: whole.

inhabit v.t. (*to live or dwell in (a house, town etc.)*) abide in, dwell in, live in, lodge in, occupy, people, populate, reside in, tenant. ANTONYMS: vacate.

inhabitant n. (*a person who lives in a particular place*) aborigine, citizen, denizen, dweller, inmate, native, occupant, occupier, resident, tenant.

inhale v.t. (*to breathe in*) breathe in, draw in, gasp, gulp, inspire, puff, respire, sniff, suck in, take in. ANTONYMS: exhale, expire.

inharmonious a. (*not harmonious; unmusical*) atonal, cacophonous, clashing, discordant, dissonant, grating, harsh, jangling, jarring, strident, tuneless, unharmonious, unmelodious, unmusical. ANTONYMS: harmonious.

inherent *a.* **1** (*inseparable from and permanently existing* (*in*)) basic, built-in, essential, fundamental, immanent, ingrained, intrinsic, native, natural. ANTONYMS: extraneous. **2** (*innate, inborn*) congenital, hereditary, inborn, inbred, innate.

inherit *v.t.* **1** (*to receive* (*property, a title etc.*) *by legal succession upon the death of a former possessor*) acquire, come into, get, receive. ANTONYMS: bequeath. **2** (*to take over* (*a position etc.*) *from a predecessor*) accede to, succeed to, take over.

inheritance *n.* **1** (*something which is inherited*) bequest, legacy. **2** (*the right of an heir to succeed*) birthright, heritage, patrimony.

inhibit *v.t.* **1** (*to restrain, to hinder*) arrest, block, bridle, check, constrain, curb, discourage, frustrate, hinder, hold back, impede, obstruct, prevent, repress, restrain, stop, suppress. ANTONYMS: encourage, promote. **2** (*to prohibit, to forbid* (*from doing something*)) ban, bar, forbid, prohibit.

inhibition *n.* **1** (*the unconscious restraining of an impulse or instinct*) repression, retention. **2** (*an inability to express a thought, action etc. because of feelings of embarrassment, shyness etc.*) constraint, (*coll.*) hang-up, reserve, reticence, self-consciousness, shyness. **3** (*the act of inhibiting; the state of being inhibited*) prohibition, repression, restraint. **4** (*something that prohibits or hinders*) arrest, ban, bar, barrier, check, embargo, hindrance, impediment, obstacle.

inhospitable *a.* **1** (*not inclined to show hospitality to strangers*) aloof, antisocial, cool, uncongenial, unfriendly, ungenerous, ungracious, unkind, unsociable, unwelcoming. ANTONYMS: friendly, hospitable. **2** ((*of a landscape, region etc.*) *affording no shelter, desolate*) barren, bleak, desolate, empty, forbidding, God-forsaken, hostile, lonely, unfavourable, uninhabitable, uninviting, wild.

inhuman *a.* (*brutal; savage*) barbaric, bestial, brutal, callous, cold-blooded, cruel, fiendish, hardhearted, heartless, implacable, inhumane, insensitive, merciless, pitiless, remorseless, ruthless, savage, unfeeling, unkind, vicious. ANTONYMS: compassionate, humane.

inimical *a.* **1** (*hostile*) antagonistic, destructive, harmful, hostile, ill-disposed, pernicious, unfriendly. ANTONYMS: friendly. **2** (*adverse, unfavourable* (*to*)) adverse, contrary, opposed, unfavourable. ANTONYMS: favourable.

inimitable *a.* **1** (*that cannot be imitated; unique*) sui generis, unique. **2** (*superb*) consummate, incomparable, matchless, peerless, superb, unequalled, unexampled, unmatched, unparalleled, unrivalled, unsurpassable.

iniquity *n.* **1** (*a lack of equity, gross injustice*) inequity, injustice, unfairness. ANTONYMS: equity, fairness. **2** (*unrighteousness, wickedness*) abomination, crime, evil, infamy, misdeed, offence, sin, sinfulness, unrighteousness, vice, wickedness, wrong, wrongdoing. ANTONYMS: righteousness.

initial *a.* (*of or relating to the beginning*) beginning, commencing, early, first, inaugural, inceptive, incipient, introductory, opening, original, primary. ANTONYMS: closing, final.

initiate[1] *v.t.* **1** (*to begin or originate*) begin, break the ice, commence, enter upon, found, get under way, inaugurate, institute, (*coll.*) kick off, launch, open, originate, pioneer, set in motion, set up, start, trigger. ANTONYMS: close. **2** (*to instruct* (*a person*) *in the rudiments or principles of something*) break in, coach, drill, ground, indoctrinate, instruct, introduce, prime, teach, train, tutor. **3** (*to admit* (*a person*) *into a society, usu. with ceremonial rites*) admit, enrol, induct, invest.

initiate[2] *n.* (*a person who has been newly initiated; a novice*) apprentice, beginner, convert, member, novice, probationer, recruit.

initiative *n.* **1** (*the energy and resourcefulness typical of those able to initiate new projects etc.*) ambition, drive, dynamism, energy, enterprise, get-up-and-go, inventiveness, leadership, originality, (*coll.*) pep, push, resourcefulness, vigour. **2** (*a first step*) advantage, beginning, commencement, first move, lead, opening.

inject *v.t.* **1** (*to introduce* (*a fluid*) *into the body by or as if by a syringe*) inoculate, (*coll.*) jab, vaccinate. **2** (*to introduce or insert*) bring in, imbue, infuse, insert, instil, introduce.

injection *n.* **1** (*the act of injecting*) inoculation, (*coll.*) jab, (*coll.*) shot, vaccination. **2** (*something which is injected, esp. a fluid injected into the body*) dose, (*coll.*) shot, vaccine.

injudicious *a.* (*done without judgement*) foolish, hasty, ill-advised, ill-judged, ill-timed, impolitic, imprudent, incautious, inconsiderate, indiscreet, inexpedient, rash, unthinking, unwise. ANTONYMS: cautious, judicious.

injunction *n.* **1** (*a writ or process whereby a party is required to refrain from doing certain acts*) process, writ. **2** (*a direction or order*) admonition, behest, command, dictate, direction, directive, exhortation, instruction, interdict, mandate, order, precept, prohibition, restraint, restriction, ruling, warning.

injure *v.t.* **1** (*to hurt, to damage*) damage, hurt, wound. **2** (*to do wrong or harm to*) abuse, harm, ill-treat, maltreat, offend, wrong. **3** (*to impair or diminish*) deface, diminish, disable, disfigure, impair, maltreat, mar, spoil, weaken.

injurious *a.* **1** (*wrongful*) unjust, wrongful. **2** (*hurtful; detrimental (to)*) adverse, bad, baneful, corrupting, damaging, deleterious, destructive, detrimental, disadvantageous, harmful, hurtful, iniquitous, mischievous, pernicious, ruinous, unfavourable, unhealthy. ANTONYMS: beneficial. **3** (*insulting, abusive*) abusive, defamatory, denigrating, derogatory, disparaging, insulting, libellous, offensive, scornful, slanderous.

injury *n.* **1** (*damage, harm*) damage, detriment, harm, hurt, ill, impairment, wound. **2** (*a wrong*) evil, grievance, injustice, mischief, wrong. **3** (*an insult, an affront*) abuse, affront, insult, offence.

injustice *n.* **1** (*the quality of being unjust; unfairness*) bias, bigotry, discrimination, favouritism, inequality, inequity, iniquity, partiality, partisanship, prejudice, unfairness. ANTONYMS: fairness, justice. **2** (*a violation of justice, a wrong*) grievance, injury, violation, wrong.

inland *a.* **1** (*situated in the interior of a country away from the sea*) interior, up-country. **2** (*carried on within a country; domestic*) domestic, home, internal. ANTONYMS: foreign.

inlet *n.* **1** (*a small arm of the sea; a creek*) arm, bay, bight, cove, creek, firth. **2** (*a means of entrance*) entrance, ingress, opening, passage.

innate *a.* (*inborn, natural*) congenital, connate, immanent, inborn, inbred, indigenous, ingrained, inherent, inherited, instinctive, intrinsic, intuitive, native, natural. ANTONYMS: acquired, cultivated.

inner *a.* **1** (*interior; nearer the centre*) innermost, inside, interior, internal, inward. ANTONYMS: outer. **2** (*spiritual; relating to the mind, soul etc.*) emotional, mental, psychological, spiritual. **3** (*more obscure or hidden*) central, hidden, intimate, obscure, personal, private, repressed, secret, unrevealed. ANTONYMS: exposed, revealed.

innocent *a.* **1** (*free from moral guilt; blameless*) blameless, chaste, clean, faultless, immaculate, impeccable, irreproachable, pristine, pure, sinless, spotless, unblemished, unsullied, untainted, upright, virginal, virtuous. ANTONYMS: corrupt, impure. **2** (*guiltless (of a*

crime etc.)) clear, guiltless, inculpable. ANTONYMS: guilty. **3** (*naive or credulous*) artless, childlike, credulous, frank, guileless, gullible, ingenuous, naive, simple, unsophisticated, unworldly. ANTONYMS: worldly. **4** (*harmless*) benign, harmless, innocuous, innoxious, inoffensive, safe. ANTONYMS: malignant.
~*n.* (*an innocent person, esp. a child*) babe, child, infant, ingénue.

innocuous *a.* (*having no injurious qualities, harmless*) harmless, innocent, innoxious, inoffensive, safe, unobjectionable. ANTONYMS: harmful, injurious.

innovation *n.* (*a new idea, method etc.*) alteration, change, departure, introduction, invention, modernism, modernization, newness, novelty, variation.

innuendo *n.* (*an indirect or oblique hint, esp. one that is disapproving*) allusion, aspersion, hint, implication, imputation, insinuation, intimation, overtone, suggestion, whisper.

innumerable *a.* (*countless, numberless*) countless, incalculable, infinite, many, multitudinous, myriad, numberless, numerous, unnumbered, untold. ANTONYMS: few, finite.

inoffensive *a.* (*giving no offence; harmless*) harmless, humble, innocent, innocuous, innoxious, mild, neutral, peaceable, quiet, retiring, tame, unobjectionable, unobtrusive, unoffending. ANTONYMS: offensive.

inoperative *a.* **1** (*not in operation*) broken, defective, invalid, null and void, out of action, out of commission, out of order, unserviceable. ANTONYMS: operative, working. **2** (*producing no result; ineffective*) ineffective, ineffectual, inefficacious, inefficient, unproductive, useless, worthless.

inopportune *a.* (*not opportune; unseasonable*) ill-chosen, ill-timed, inappropriate, inauspicious, inconvenient, unfavourable, unfortunate, unpropitious, unseasonable, unsuitable, untimely, untoward. ANTONYMS: opportune, timely.

inordinate *a.* **1** (*excessive, immoderate*) disproportionate, excessive, exorbitant, extravagant, extreme, immoderate, uncalled-for, undue, unreasonable, unwarranted. ANTONYMS: moderate. **2** (*unrestrained*) intemperate, unrestrained. ANTONYMS: restrained. **3** (*irregular, disorderly*) disorderly, erratic, irregular, uncontrolled.

inquire *v.i.* **1** (*to ask questions (of)*) ask, enquire, interrogate, query, question. **2** (*to investigate (into)*) examine, explore, inspect, investigate, look into, probe, research, scrutinize, search, study, survey.

inquiry n. 1 (*an official investigation*) hearing, inquest, investigation. 2 (*the act of inquiring*) inquisition, interrogation, questioning. 3 (*a question*) enquiry, query, question. 4 (*a searching for information or knowledge*) exploration, probe, research. 5 (*examination of facts or principles*) examination, inspection, scrutiny, study, survey.

inquisitive a. (*unduly given to asking questions; prying*) curious, inquiring, intrusive, meddlesome, (*coll.*) nosy, probing, prying, questioning. ANTONYMS: indifferent, uninterested.

insalubrious a. (*unhealthy*) dirty, injurious, insanitary, noxious, unclean, unhealthful, unhealthy, unhygienic, unwholesome. ANTONYMS: salubrious.

insane a. 1 (*deranged in mind; mad*) (*sl.*) barmy, (*coll.*) batty, (*sl.*) bonkers, (*sl.*) crackers, crazy, demented, deranged, (*coll.*) dotty, (*sl.*) loony, (*coll.*) loopy, lunatic, mad, (*coll.*) mental, (*sl.*) nuts, (*coll.*) out to lunch, (*coll.*) round the bend, unbalanced, unhinged. ANTONYMS: lucid, sane. 2 (*exceedingly rash or foolish*) absurd, daft, foolish, (*coll.*) harebrained, idiotic, irrational, irresponsible, ludicrous, preposterous, rash, reckless, ridiculous, senseless, silly, stupid, wild. ANTONYMS: reasonable, sensible.

insanity n. 1 (*derangement in mind; madness*) aberration, craziness, delirium, dementia, derangement, frenzy, lunacy, madness, mania, mental illness, psychosis, schizophrenia. ANTONYMS: sanity. 2 (*extreme folly*) absurdity, daftness, folly, foolishness, idiocy, irresponsibility, lunacy, nonsense, recklessness, senselessness, stupidity. ANTONYMS: sense.

insatiable a. 1 (*that cannot be satisfied or appeased*) insatiate, unappeasable, unquenchable. ANTONYMS: appeasable, satiable. 2 (*very greedy (of)*) gluttonous, greedy, omnivorous, rapacious, ravenous, voracious.

inscribe v.t. 1 (*to write or engrave (words, a design etc.) on a stone, paper or some other surface*) carve, cut, engrave, etch, impress, mark, pen, write. ANTONYMS: erase. 2 (*to address or dedicate (a book to someone)*) address, autograph, dedicate, sign. 3 (*to enter (a name) in or on a book, list etc.*) enlist, enrol, enter, record, register.

inscription n. (*something which is inscribed, e.g. a dedicatory address, the words on the reverse of some coins*) address, autograph, dedication, engraving, epitaph, label, legend, lettering, saying, words.

inscrutable a. (*unfathomable, mysterious*) blank, deadpan, enigmatic, hidden, impenetrable, incomprehensible, inexplicable, mysterious, poker-faced, sphinxlike, unfathomable, unintelligible, unreadable. ANTONYMS: evident, obvious.

insecure a. 1 (*lacking in self-confidence; apprehensive*) afraid, anxious, apprehensive, disconcerted, hesitant, jumpy, nervous, uncertain, unconfident, unsure, worried. ANTONYMS: confident. 2 (*not secure; not strongly fixed*) dangerous, flimsy, frail, hazardous, insubstantial, loose, perilous, precarious, rickety, risky, rocky, shaky, unreliable, unsafe, unsound, unstable, unsteady, unsupported, weak, wobbly. ANTONYMS: safe, secure. 3 (*not effectually guarded*) defenceless, exposed, open, unguarded, unprotected, unshielded, vulnerable. ANTONYMS: guarded, protected.

insensible a. 1 (*not having the power of feeling or perceiving, unconscious*) anaesthetized, inert, insensate, insentient, numb, senseless, unconscious, unfeeling. ANTONYMS: sentient. 2 (*unaware (of); indifferent (to)*) indifferent (to), oblivious (to), unaware (of). 3 (*not susceptible of feeling or passion; callous*) apathetic, callous, cold, deaf, dispassionate, impassive, impervious, insensitive, thick-skinned, unaffected, unemotional, unfeeling, unmoved, unsusceptible, untouched. ANTONYMS: susceptible. 4 (*that cannot be perceived or felt; imperceptible*) imperceptible, negligible, unnoticeable.

insensitive a. 1 (*unfeeling, unsympathetic (to)*) callous, hard, indifferent, insensate, insensible, uncaring, unfeeling, unresponsive, unsympathetic. ANTONYMS: caring. 2 (*not sensitive (to)*) immune (to), impervious (to), proof (against), unaffected (by), unsusceptible (to). ANTONYMS: sensitive (to).

inseparable a. (*incapable of being separated*) inalienable, indissoluble, indivisible, inseverable.

insert v.t. 1 (*to set or place (a thing) into another*) embed, enter, implant, introduce, put, set. 2 (*to introduce (text, an article etc.) into something, such as a newspaper*) interpolate, interpose.

inside[1] a. 1 (*situated within; interior*) inner, innermost, interior, internal, inward. ANTONYMS: exterior. 2 (*confidential*) classified, confidential, exclusive, private, restricted, secret.
~n. 1 (*the inner or interior part*) contents, interior. 2 (*the bowels*) belly, bowels, entrails, guts, (*coll.*) innards, stomach, vitals.

inside[2] adv. 1 (*in or into the interior; indoors*)

indoors, under cover, within. ANTONYMS: outside. **2** (*in or into prison*) confined, imprisoned, incarcerated, (*sl.*) in clink.

insidious *a.* **1** (*treacherous, sly*) artful, crafty, crooked, cunning, deceitful, deceptive, designing, duplicitous, guileful, intriguing, slick, sly, smooth, stealthy, subtle, surreptitious, treacherous, tricky, wily. ANTONYMS: artless, ingenuous. **2** (*developing subtly but dangerously*) creeping, invasive.

insight *n.* **1** (*the capacity to discern the real character of things*) acuity, acumen, discernment, intuition, intuitiveness, judgement, observation, penetration, perception, perspicacity, sharpness. **2** (*a clear and often sudden understanding of something*) comprehension, understanding, vision.

insignificant *a.* **1** (*unimportant, trivial*) inconsequential, inconsiderable, irrelevant, paltry, petty, scanty, trifling, trivial, unimportant. ANTONYMS: important, significant. **2** ((*of a person*) *of little distinction*) undistinguished, unremarkable. ANTONYMS: distinguished. **3** (*small*) diminutive, meagre, measly, minor, negligible, puny, small.

insincere *a.* **1** (*not sincere; false*) false, hollow, untrue. ANTONYMS: sincere. **2** (*hypocritical*) deceitful, deceptive, devious, dishonest, disingenuous, dissembling, double-dealing, duplicitous, evasive, faithless, hypocritical, lying, mendacious, perfidious, slippery, treacherous, two-faced, unfaithful, untruthful. ANTONYMS: honest, truthful.

insinuate *v.t.* **1** (*to indicate indirectly or obliquely*) allude, hint, imply, impute, indicate, intimate, suggest. **2** (*to introduce* (*oneself, a person etc.*) *into favour, a place etc. by gradual and artful means*) curry favour, infiltrate, ingratiate, inveigle oneself, worm one's way in.

insinuation *n.* **1** (*the art or power of insinuating*) infiltration, infusion, ingratiating, injection, instillation, introduction. **2** (*an indirect suggestion*) allusion, aspersion, hint, implication, imputation, innuendo, slur, suggestion.

insipid *a.* **1** (*tasteless, savourless*) bland, flavourless, savourless, tasteless, unappetizing, watery, wishy-washy. ANTONYMS: appetizing, tasty. **2** (*lacking in life or animation*) anaemic, banal, bland, characterless, drab, dry, dull, flat, lifeless, limp, prosaic, spiritless, stale, tame, tedious, trite, unimaginative, uninteresting, vapid, weak. ANTONYMS: animated, vivid.

insist *v.t.* **1** (*to maintain emphatically*) assert, asseverate, aver, claim, contend, declare, emphasize, hold, maintain, persist, reiterate, repeat, state, stress, swear, urge, vow. **2** (*to demand strongly or without accepting any refusal*) call for, command, demand, importune, press, require, stand firm.

insistent *a.* (*insisting; demanding strongly and continually*) assertive, demanding, dogged, emphatic, exigent, firm, forceful, inexorable, insisting, peremptory, persevering, persistent, pressing, resolute, stubborn, tenacious, unrelenting, urgent.

insolent *a.* **1** (*showing overbearing contempt; impudent*) bold, brazen, cheeky, contemptuous, (*coll.*) fresh, impertinent, impudent, insubordinate, pert, presumptuous, saucy. ANTONYMS: deferential, respectful. **2** (*insulting*) abusive, insulting, offensive, rude.

insoluble *a.* (*that cannot be solved*) baffling, impenetrable, indecipherable, inexplicable, mysterious, mystifying, obscure, unaccountable, unfathomable, unsolvable. ANTONYMS: fathomable, soluble.

insolvent *a.* (*not able to discharge all debts or liabilities*) bankrupt, (*coll.*) broke, bust, destitute, penniless, ruined.

inspect *v.t.* **1** (*to look closely into or at; to scrutinize carefully*) check out, examine, go over, investigate, look into, look over, oversee, peruse, pore over, probe, research, scan, scrutinize, search, study, survey. **2** (*to view and examine officially*) audit, check, superintend, supervise, vet.

inspection *n.* (*a careful, close or critical examination or survey*) check-up, examination, investigation, review, scan, scrutiny, search, supervision, surveillance, survey.

inspector *n.* (*an overseer, a superintendent*) censor, critic, examiner, investigator, overseer, scrutineer, superintendent, supervisor.

inspiration *n.* **1** (*an act of inspiring or infusing feelings, ideas etc.*) arousal, awakening, encouragement, influence, provocation, stimulation. ANTONYMS: deterrent. **2** (*a person, idea etc. that inspires others*) genius, incentive, muse, spur, stimulus. **3** (*feelings, ideas, creativity etc. imparted by or as by divine agency*) creativity, enthusiasm, genius, passion, vigour, zeal. **4** (*a sudden and brilliant idea*) illumination, insight, revelation.

inspire *v.t.* **1** (*to stimulate* (*a person*) *to some activity, esp. creative activity*) encourage, fire, influence, move, persuade, spur, stimulate. ANTONYMS: discourage. **2** (*to imbue or animate* (*a person with a feeling*)) animate, arouse, enkindle, enliven, excite, galvanize, hearten, imbue, inspirit, quicken, rouse, stir. ANTONYMS: dishearten. **3** (*to infuse or instil* (*an emotion in or into*)) infuse, instil.

install *v.t.* **1** (*to put* (*apparatus, equipment etc.*) *in position for use*) place, position, put, set up. **2** (*to settle or establish* (*a person, oneself*) *somewhere*) ensconce, establish, fix, lodge, settle. **3** (*to place* (*a person*) *in an official position with customary ceremonies*) inaugurate, induct, instate, institute, invest.

installation *n.* **1** (*the act of installing or the process of being installed*) connection, establishment, fitting, instalment, placing, positioning, setting up. **2** (*a piece of machinery, equipment etc. installed for use*) equipment, machinery, plant. **3** (*a military base etc.*) base, camp, depot, establishment, post, station. **4** (*the placing of a person in an official position*) consecration, inauguration, induction, initiation, instatement, institution, investiture.

instance *n.* **1** (*an example, illustrative case*) example, exemplar, exemplification, illustration, precedent. **2** (*a particular situation or case*) case, occasion, occurrence, situation, time. **3** (*a process or suit*) process, suit. **4** (*a request or demand*) behest, demand, entreaty, insistence, instigation, pressure, prompting, request, solicitation, urging. ~*v.t.* (*to bring forward as an instance or example*) adduce, bring up, cite, mention, name, quote.

instant *a.* **1** (*immediate*) direct, immediate, instantaneous, overnight, prompt, quick. **2** ((*esp. of food*) *processed so as to be quickly and easily prepared*) convenience, fast, pre-cooked, ready-made, ready-mixed. **3** (*pressing; urgent*) burning, crying, imperative, pressing, urgent. **4** (*present, current*) current, present. ~*n.* **1** (*a particular point of time*) juncture, moment, point, time. **2** (*a moment, a very brief space of time*) flash, (*coll.*) jiffy, moment, second, (*coll.*) tick, trice, twinkling.

instantaneous *a.* (*happening or done in an instant or immediately*) at once, direct, forthwith, immediate, prompt, simultaneous.

instead *adv.* (*in the place* (*of*)) alternatively, in lieu, in place, in preference, opposed to, rather.

instigate *v.t.* **1** (*to provoke or bring about* (*an action*)) actuate, bring about, get going, impel, (*coll.*) kick-start, prod, prompt, provoke, set off, start, trigger. **2** (*to incite, to urge on* (*to an action esp. of an evil kind*)) encourage, foment, incite, move, persuade, rouse, spur, stimulate, stir up, urge, whip up. ANTONYMS: discourage, put off.

instil *v.t.* (*to introduce slowly and gradually* (*into the mind of a person*)) engender, engraft, imbue, impart, implant, impress, inculcate, infuse, ingrain, insinuate, introduce.

instinct *n.* **1** (*a natural impulse present in most animals, leading them to perform certain actions*) impulse, reflex. **2** (*a similar innate or intuitive impulse in human beings*) aptitude, bent, capacity, faculty, gift, knack, leaning, predisposition, proclivity, propensity, talent, tendency. **3** (*unreasoning perception of rightness, beauty etc.*) feeling, intuition, sixth sense, subconscious.

instinctive *a.* **1** (*prompted by instinct*) congenital, inborn, inbred, inherent, innate, instinctual, intrinsic, intuitional, intuitive, native. ANTONYMS: acquired. **2** (*spontaneous, impulsive*) automatic, impulsive, involuntary, mechanical, natural, reflex, spontaneous, subconscious, unpremeditated, unthinking. ANTONYMS: deliberate.

institute *v.t.* **1** (*to set up, to establish*) constitute, enact, establish, fix, found, launch, organize, set up. ANTONYMS: abolish. **2** (*to start, to begin*) begin, commence, originate, pioneer, set in motion, start. ANTONYMS: end, stop. **3** (*to appoint* (*to or into*), *esp. an ecclesiastical benefice*) appoint, induct, initiate, install, introduce, invest, nominate, ordain.

institution *n.* **1** (*the act of instituting*) constitution, creation, enactment, establishment, formation, foundation, initiation, introduction, organization, origination. **2** (*a society or association established esp. for charitable or educational purposes*) academy, association, asylum, college, establishment, foundation, home, hospital, institute, school, society, university. **3** (*an established law or custom*) convention, custom, law, order, regulation, rule, tradition. **4** (*the act or ceremony of investing a member of the clergy with the spiritual part of a benefice*) inauguration, induction, installation, investiture, investment, ordination.

instruct *v.t.* **1** (*to teach, to educate* (*in a subject*)) coach, discipline, drill, educate, enlighten, ground, guide, school, teach, train, tutor. **2** (*to order or direct* (*someone to do something*)) bid, charge, command, direct, enjoin, order, tell. **3** (*to inform* (*someone of, that*)) acquaint, advise, apprise, counsel, inform, notify, tell. **4** (*to authorize* (*a barrister or solicitor*) *to act for one*) authorize, brief.

instruction *n.* **1** (*a direction or order*) command, demand, direction, directive, injunction, mandate, order, ruling. **2** (*the act of instructing; teaching*) coaching, discipline, drill, education, enlightenment, grounding, guidance, indoctrination, information, preparation, schooling, teaching, training, tuition, tutelage.

instructor n. (a person who instructs) adviser, coach, demonstrator, educator, guide, lecturer, master, mentor, pedagogue, professor, teacher, trainer, tutor.

instrument n. **1** (a tool or implement) apparatus, appliance, contraption, device, gadget, implement, mechanism, tool, utensil. **2** (something by means of which work is done or any purpose effected) agency, agent, catalyst, channel, force, means, medium, organ, vehicle. **3** (an agent, a person used as a means by another) agent, dupe, factor, medium, pawn, puppet, tool. **4** (Law) (a document giving formal expression to an act) agreement, compact, contract, covenant, document, pact, paper.

instrumental a. (serving as an instrument or means (to some end or in some act)) active, assisting, auxiliary, catalytic, conducive, contributory, helpful, influential, significant, subsidiary, supportive, useful, utilitarian.

insubordinate a. (not submissive to authority; disobedient) defiant, disobedient, disorderly, fractious, insurgent, insurrectionist, mutinous, obstreperous, quarrelsome, rebellious, recalcitrant, refractory, riotous, seditious, turbulent, undisciplined, unruly. ANTONYMS: obedient, submissive.

insubordination n. (disobedience, a lack of submission to authority) defiance, disobedience, disorder, indiscipline, insurgency, insurrection, mutinousness, rebelliousness, recalcitrance, revolt, riotousness, sedition, turbulence, unruliness. ANTONYMS: compliance, obedience.

insufferable a. (not able to be borne or endured) detestable, dreadful, impossible, insupportable, intolerable, outrageous, unbearable, unendurable, unspeakable. ANTONYMS: bearable, tolerable.

insufficient a. (not sufficient; inadequate) deficient, inadequate, incapable, incompetent, lacking, meagre, scant, scarce, short, unfitted, unsatisfactory. ANTONYMS: ample, sufficient.

insular a. **1** (of the nature of an island; remote) circumscribed, cut off, isolated, remote. **2** (narrow in outlook) blinkered, illiberal, inward-looking, narrow-minded, petty, prejudiced, provincial. ANTONYMS: broad-minded, tolerant.

insulate v.t. **1** (to separate from other bodies by a non-conductor, so as to prevent the passage of electricity or heat) cover, cushion, lag, protect, shield, wrap. **2** (to place in a detached situation or position) cut off, detach, isolate, segregate, separate.

insult¹ v.t. **1** (to treat or speak to rudely or contemptuously) abuse, call names, defame, libel, put down, revile, (sl.) slag off, slight, snub. ANTONYMS: compliment, praise. **2** (to offend) affront, hurt, injure, offend.

insult² n. **1** (an insulting act or remark) abuse, aspersion, barb, dig, discourtesy, indignity, insolence, put-down, slap in the face, slight, slur, snub. **2** (an affront; something that is offensive) affront, offence, rudeness.

insuperable a. (impossible to overcome) impassable, insurmountable, invincible, unconquerable. ANTONYMS: surmountable.

insurance n. (the act of insuring against damage or loss) assurance, bond, cover, coverage, guarantee, indemnification, indemnity, protection, safeguard, security, surety, warranty.

insure v.t. **1** (to secure compensation in the event of loss or injury by paying a periodical premium) cover, protect. **2** ((of the owner or the insurance company) to secure the payment of (a specified sum) in the event of loss, injury etc.) assure, guarantee, indemnify, protect, secure, underwrite, warrant.

insurgent a. (rising up in revolt; rebellious) disobedient, insubordinate, insurrectionary, mutinous, rebellious, revolting, revolutionary, riotous, seditious.
~n. (a person who rises up against established government or authority) insurrectionist, mutineer, rebel, revolutionary, rioter.

insurmountable a. (that cannot be surmounted or overcome) impassable, impossible, insuperable, invincible, overwhelming, unconquerable. ANTONYMS: surmountable.

insurrection n. (the act of rising in open opposition to established authority) coup, insurgency, mutiny, rebellion, revolt, revolution, riot, rising, sedition, uprising.

insusceptible a. (not susceptible (of, to); incapable of being moved by any feeling or impression) immovable, immune, indifferent, insensible, insensitive, unfeeling, unimpressionable, unmovable, unresponsive. ANTONYMS: susceptible.

intact a. **1** (untouched) undefiled, untainted, untouched, unviolated, virgin. **2** (unimpaired; uninjured) perfect, sound, unblemished, unbroken, undamaged, unharmed, unhurt, unimpaired, uninjured, unscathed. ANTONYMS: broken, imperfect. **3** (*entire*) complete, entire, integral, total, whole. ANTONYMS: partial.

intangible *a.* (*not tangible; imperceptible to the touch*) airy, elusive, ethereal, evanescent, immaterial, impalpable, imperceptible, incorporeal, indefinite, invisible, shadowy, unreal, unsubstantial, vague. ANTONYMS: tangible.

integral *a.* **1** (*whole, complete*) complete, entire, full, whole. **2** (*forming an essential part of a whole*) basic, elemental, essential, fundamental, indispensable, intrinsic, necessary, requisite. ANTONYMS: inessential. **3** (*forming a whole*) component, constituent.

integrate *v.t.* (*to combine into a whole*) amalgamate, assimilate, blend, coalesce, combine, consolidate, fuse, incorporate, intermix, join, knit, meld, merge, mesh, unite. ANTONYMS: disperse, separate.

integrity *n.* **1** (*honesty; high principle*) candour, decency, goodness, honesty, honour, incorruptibility, morality, principle, probity, purity, rectitude, righteousness, uprightness, veracity, virtue. ANTONYMS: corruption, dishonesty. **2** (*entireness, completeness*) completeness, entireness, unity, wholeness. **3** (*soundness*) coherence, cohesion, soundness.

intellect *n.* **1** (*the faculty of understanding, thinking and reasoning*) comprehension, mind, rationality, reasonableness, sense, understanding. **2** (*the understanding; intelligence*) (*coll.*) brains, intelligence, understanding. **3** (*an intelligent or clever person*) (*coll.*) brain, (*coll.*) egghead, genius, highbrow, scholar, thinker. **4** (*intellectual people collectively*) academe, cognoscenti, intelligentsia.

intellectual *a.* **1** (*possessing intellect in a high degree*) brainy, bright, intelligent, learned, studious, thoughtful. ANTONYMS: dim, ignorant. **2** (*relating to or performed by the intellect*) bookish, cerebral, highbrow, mental, rational, scholarly.
~*n.* **1** (*an intellectual person*) academic, (*coll.*) egghead, genius, highbrow, scholar, thinker. **2** (*the most enlightened people* (*in a country etc.*)) academe, cognoscenti, intelligentsia.

intelligence *n.* **1** (*the exercise of the understanding; intellectual power*) comprehension, insight, reason, understanding, wit. **2** (*quickness or sharpness of intellect*) acuteness, alertness, aptitude, (*coll.*) brains, brightness, capacity, discernment, keenness, penetration, perception, perspicaciousness, quickness, sagacity, sharpness. **3** (*news, information*) data, (*sl.*) dope, facts, findings, (*coll.*) gen, (*coll.*)

info, information, (*coll.*) low-down, news, notice, notification, report, tidings, word. ANTONYMS: misinformation.

intelligent *a.* (*clever, quick*) acute, alert, apt, astute, brainy, bright, clever, discerning, enlightened, erudite, keen, knowing, penetrating, perspicacious, quick, rational, sharp, shrewd, smart. ANTONYMS: foolish, stupid.

intelligible *a.* (*capable of being understood, comprehensible*) clear, comprehensible, decipherable, distinct, fathomable, legible, lucid, open, plain, understandable. ANTONYMS: unintelligible.

intemperate *a.* **1** (*not exercising due moderation or self-restraint; immoderate*) excessive, extravagant, immoderate, inordinate, prodigal, profligate, unbridled, uncontrollable, unrestrained. ANTONYMS: moderate, restrained. **2** (*indulging any appetite or passion in excess*) immoderate, incontinent, self-indulgent. ANTONYMS: self-disciplined. **3** (*addicted to excessive indulgence in alcoholic drink*) alcoholic, dipsomaniac, intoxicated. ANTONYMS: teetotal. **4** ((*of a climate etc.*) *extreme; inclement*) extreme, inclement, rough, severe, tempestuous, violent, wild. ANTONYMS: clement.

intend *v.t.* **1** (*to propose, to plan*) aim, design, plan, project, propose. **2** (*to mean, to have in mind*) contemplate, have in mind, mean. **3** (*to destine* (*for*)) destine, earmark, mark out.

intense *a.* **1** (*extreme in degree*) acute, close, deep, drastic, excessive, extreme, fierce, forceful, great, harsh, intensive, powerful, profound, severe, strong, unqualified. ANTONYMS: mild. **2** (*strongly or deeply emotional*) ardent, burning, consuming, eager, earnest, emotional, fervent, fervid, fierce, flaming, frenzied, impassioned, passionate, serious, sincere, vehement, zealous. ANTONYMS: cool.

intensify *v.t.* (*to render more intense*) aggravate, augment, boost, concentrate, deepen, double, emphasize, enhance, escalate, exacerbate, focus, heighten, increase, magnify, quicken, reinforce, sharpen, step up, strengthen. ANTONYMS: dull, weaken.

intensity *n.* (*the condition or quality of being intense*) ardour, concentration, earnestness, emotion, energy, excess, fanaticism, fervency, fervour, fierceness, fire, focus, passion, potency, power, strength, tension, vehemence, vigour.

intent *n.* **1** (*purpose, intention*) aim, design, end, goal, intention, object, objective, plan, purpose, target. **2** (*meaning, drift*) drift, meaning, significance.
~*a.* **1** (*bent or determined* (*on*)) bent, committed,

determined, eager, industrious, resolute, resolved, set, steadfast, zealous. ANTONYMS:
casual, indifferent. **2** (*giving complete attention to something*) absorbed, concentrated,
engrossed, focused, preoccupied, rapt,
wrapped up. **3** (*fixed; earnest*) earnest, fixed,
intense, piercing, steady, watchful.

intention *n.* (*purpose, intent*) aim, ambition,
design, end, goal, idea, intent, object, objective, plan, purpose, target.

intentional *a.* (*done with design or purpose*)
calculated, contrived, deliberate, designed,
intended, meant, planned, preconceived,
premeditated, purposeful, studied, wilful.
ANTONYMS: accidental, unplanned.

intercept *v.t.* **1** (*to stop or seize on the way from
one place to another*) catch, grab, seize, stop,
take, trap. **2** (*to obstruct; to stop*) arrest, block,
check, cut off, deflect, head off, impede, interrupt, obstruct, shut off, stop.

intercourse *n.* **1** (*association, communication
etc., between people, nations etc.*) association,
commerce, communication, communion, contact, conversation, converse, correspondence,
dealing, exchange, fellowship, interaction,
trade, traffic. **2** (*sexual intercourse*) carnal
knowledge, coitus, congress, copulation, going
to bed with someone, lovemaking, mating, sex,
sexual intercourse, sexual relations, sleeping
with someone.

interdict[1] *n.* (*an official prohibition*) ban, bar,
disallowance, interdiction, prohibition, taboo,
veto.

interdict[2] *v.t.* (*to forbid; to prohibit*) ban, bar,
debar, disallow, forbid, outlaw, prevent, prohibit, proscribe, veto.

interest[1] *n.* **1** (*lively or curious attention*) affection, attention, attentiveness, concern, curi-
osity, notice, regard, scrutiny, sympathy.
ANTONYMS: apathy, disinterest. **2** (*the power of
eliciting attention or concern*) attraction,
fascination. ANTONYMS: boredom. **3** (*something, such as a hobby or subject, in which one
has a personal concern*) activity, diversion,
hobby, pastime, preoccupation, pursuit,
relaxation, speciality. **4** (*benefit, advantage*)
advantage, benefit, gain, good, profit. **5** (*proprietary right or concern; a share (in)*) claim,
cut, involvement, participation, percentage,
portion, right, share, stake. **6** (*a business etc. in
which a group or party has a concern*) affair,
business, care, concern, matter.

interest[2] *v.t.* **1** (*to arouse or hold the attention
or curiosity of*) absorb, affect, amuse, arouse,
attract, captivate, divert, engross, excite, fascinate, hold, intrigue, move, provoke, touch.

ANTONYMS: bore. **2** (*to cause to participate (in)*)
engage, induce, involve, persuade, talk, tempt.

interested *a.* **1** (*having one's interest excited*)
absorbed, affected, attentive, attracted, curious, drawn, engaged, excited, fascinated, intent, intrigued, keen, responsive, stimulated.
ANTONYMS: unaffected. **2** (*having an interest or
share in*) concerned, involved. **3** (*liable to be
biased through personal interest*) biased, implicated, partial, partisan, prejudiced. ANTO-
NYMS: disinterested.

interesting *a.* (*arousing interest or curiosity*)
absorbing, amusing, appealing, arousing, attractive, captivating, compelling, curious, enchanting, engaging, engrossing, entertaining,
exciting, gripping, intriguing, inviting, pleasing, provocative, riveting, stimulating. ANTO-
NYMS: boring, uninteresting.

interfere *v.i.* **1** (*to hinder or obstruct a process,
activity etc.*) block, clash, collide, conflict,
cramp, encumber, frustrate, hamper, handicap,
hinder, impede, inhibit, obstruct, retard, slow,
subvert. **2** (*to meddle (with)*) butt in, interpose
(in), interrupt (in), intervene (in), intrude (on),
meddle (with), tamper (with).

interim *n.* (*the intervening time or period*)
interregnum, interval, meantime, meanwhile.
~*a.* (*temporary, provisional*) acting, improvised,
intervening, makeshift, provisional, stopgap,
temporary.

interior *a.* **1** (*internal, inner*) inner, inside,
internal, inward. ANTONYMS: external. **2** (*remote from the coast, frontier or exterior*)
central, inland, up-country, upland. **3** (*domestic, as distinct from foreign*) domestic, home,
internal. ANTONYMS: exterior, foreign, international. **4** (*of or relating to the inner consciousness or spiritual matters*) hidden, inner,
innermost, intimate, personal, private, secret,
spiritual.
~*n.* **1** (*the internal part of anything; the inside*)
centre, core, heart, (*coll.*) innards, inside.
ANTONYMS: exterior. **2** (*the central or inland
part of a country*) centre, heartland, hinterland,
uplands. **3** (*the inward nature; the soul*) bosom,
soul.

interject *v.t.* (*to insert (a remark etc.) abruptly*)
insert, interpolate, interpose, introduce, put
in, throw in.

interjection *n.* **1** (*the act of interjecting*) interpolation, interposition. **2** (*a word which
expresses sudden feeling*) cry, ejaculation,
exclamation, utterance.

interloper *n.* **1** (*an intruder*) gatecrasher,
intruder, trespasser. **2** (*a person who interferes
in someone else's affairs*) busybody, meddler,
(*coll.*) Nosy Parker.

interlude n. **1** (*a pause between the acts of a play*) entr'acte, pause, relief. **2** (*an intervening period or event that contrasts with what comes before and after*) break, delay, episode, gap, halt, hiatus, intermission, interval, (*coll.*) let-up, lull, pause, respite, rest, spell, stop, stoppage, wait.

intermediary a. (*being, coming or acting between; intermediate*) between, halfway, (*coll.*) in-between, intermediate, intervening, mean, middle, midway.
~n. (*an intermediate agent, a go-between*) agent, arbitrator, broker, go-between, intermediate, mediator, middleman, referee, representative, third party.

intermediate a. (*coming between two things, extremes etc.*) between, halfway, (*coll.*) in-between, intermediary, intervening, mean, middle, midway, transitional.

interminable a. **1** (*endless or seeming to have no end*) boundless, endless, immeasurable, infinite, limitless, unbounded, unlimited. ANTONYMS: finite, limited. **2** (*tediously protracted*) ceaseless, dragging, everlasting, long, long-winded, never-ending, perpetual, protracted, wearisome. ANTONYMS: brief, succinct.

intermittent a. (*occurring at intervals*) broken, disconnected, discontinuous, fitful, irregular, occasional, periodic, punctuated, random, recurrent, recurring, spasmodic, sporadic. ANTONYMS: continuous, steady.

internal a. **1** (*relating to or situated in the inside*) inner, inside, interior. ANTONYMS: exterior. **2** (*domestic as opposed to foreign*) civil, domestic, home. ANTONYMS: external, foreign. **3** (*inherent, intrinsic*) built-in, inborn, inbred, inherent, innate, intrinsic. **4** (*relating to the inner being, inward*) innermost, inward, personal, private, spiritual.

international a. (*recognized or used by many countries*) cosmopolitan, global, intercontinental, supranational, universal, worldwide. ANTONYMS: national.

internecine a. (*deadly, destructive*) bloody, deadly, destructive, fatal, mortal, murderous, ruinous.

interpolate v.t. (*to insert* (*esp. a word or passage*) *in* (*a book or document*)) add, insert, interpose, introduce.

interpose v.i. **1** (*to intervene; to mediate* (*between*)) intercede, interfere, intermediate, intervene, intrude, mediate, step in. **2** (*to remark by way of interruption, to interrupt*) interject, interrupt.

interpret v.t. **1** (*to explain the meaning of*) analyse, clarify, clear up, decipher, decode, define, elucidate, explain, explicate, expound, illuminate, paraphrase, read, render, spell out, translate. **2** (*to find out the meaning of, to understand in a particular way*) adapt, construe, understand.

interpretation n. (*an explanation, rendering*) analysis, clarification, construction, diagnosis, elucidation, explanation, explication, exposition, inference, meaning, performance, portrayal, reading, rendering, sense, solution, translation, understanding, version.

interrogate v.t. (*to put questions to, esp. in a formal or thorough way*) ask, cross-examine, cross-question, examine, (*coll.*) grill, pump, question, quiz.

interrupt v.t. **1** (*to stop or obstruct by breaking in upon*) barge in, break in, butt in, check, chime in, cut, cut in, cut off, cut short, interfere in, intrude on. **2** (*to break the continuity of*) break off, disconnect, discontinue, punctuate, suspend. **3** (*to obstruct* (*a view etc.*)) cease, end, halt, hinder, hold up, obstruct, stop, terminate.

interruption n. **1** (*an instance of stopping someone from speaking*) disruption, disturbance, hindrance, hitch, impediment, intrusion, obstacle, obstruction. **2** (*a break in the continuity of something*) break, cessation, check, gap, halt, hiatus, intermission, interval, pause, punctuation, respite, suspension.

intersperse v.t. **1** (*to scatter here and there* (*among etc.*)) bestrew, intermix, pepper, scatter, sprinkle. **2** (*to variegate* (*with scattered objects, colours etc.*)) diversify, variegate.

intertwine v.t. (*to entwine or twist together*) braid, convolute, cross, entwine, interlace, interweave, link, reticulate, twist.

interval n. **1** (*an intervening space or time*) distance, space, time. **2** (*a gap or pause*) break, delay, gap, hiatus, interim, interlude, intermission, lapse, meantime, pause, period, recess, respite, rest, spell, wait.

intervene v.i. **1** (*to happen or break in so as to interrupt or disturb*) break in, butt in, intercede, interfere, interpose, interrupt, intrude, meddle, step in. **2** (*to occur between points of time or events*) befall, come to pass, ensue, happen, occur, take place.

interview n. **1** (*a meeting in which an employer questions a candidate for a job etc. in order to test the candidate's suitability*) appraisal, assessment, evaluation, vetting. **2** (*a meeting between a person of public interest and a press representative for publication*) audience, conference, press conference. **3** (*a meeting between two persons face to face*) conversation, dialogue, discussion, encounter, meeting, talk.

~*v.t.* (*to hold an interview with*) appraise, evaluate, examine, interrogate, question, sound out, talk to, vet.

interweave *v.t.* **1** (*to weave together (with)*) braid, interlace, intertwine, splice, weave together. **2** (*to mingle closely together*) blend, mingle.

intimate[1] *a.* **1** (*close in friendship; familiar*) affectionate, bosom, cherished, close, dear, familiar, friendly, loving, near, (*coll.*) thick, warm. **2** (*private, personal*) confidential, personal, private, secret. **3** (*having an atmosphere conducive to close personal relationships*) comfortable, (*coll.*) comfy, confidential, cosy, friendly, informal, private, snug. **4** (*thorough*) deep, detailed, exhaustive, experienced, first-hand, immediate, penetrating, thorough.

~*n.* (*a close friend*) associate, (*coll.*) buddy, (*coll.*) chum, colleague, companion, comrade, confidant, confidante, crony, familiar, friend, mate, (*coll.*) pal, (*coll.*) sidekick. ANTONYMS: stranger.

intimate[2] *v.t.* **1** (*to make known, to announce*) announce, caution, communicate, declare, impart, make known, state, tip off, warn. **2** (*to indicate, to hint*) hint, imply, indicate, insinuate, suggest.

intimation *n.* (*an indication, hint*) allusion, clue, hint, idea, indication, inkling, insinuation, reminder, suggestion, warning.

intimidate *v.t.* (*to frighten or to influence with aggressive behaviour*) alarm, awe, browbeat, bully, coerce, cow, daunt, dishearten, dismay, dispirit, frighten, (*coll.*) lean on, menace, overawe, scare, terrify, terrorize, threaten.

intolerable *a.* (*not tolerable, unendurable*) impossible, insufferable, insupportable, unacceptable, unbearable, unendurable. ANTONYMS: bearable, tolerable.

intolerant *a.* (*not enduring or allowing difference of opinion, teaching etc.*) biased, bigoted, chauvinistic, dictatorial, dogmatic, fanatical, illiberal, impatient, narrow, narrow-minded, one-sided, opinionated, prejudiced, small-minded, uncharitable, unsympathetic, warped. ANTONYMS: broad-minded, tolerant.

intonation *n.* (*modulation of the voice; accent*) accent, accentuation, articulation, cadence, delivery, inflection, modulation, pronunciation, tone, vocalization.

intoxicate *v.t.* **1** (*to make drunk*) addle,

inebriate, stupefy. **2** (*to excite; to make delirious, as with joy*) animate, elate, electrify, enliven, enrapture, entrance, excite, exhilarate, galvanize, inflame, invigorate, overwhelm, stimulate, thrill.

intoxication *n.* **1** (*the state of being drunk*) drunkenness, inebriation, insobriety, tipsiness. **2** (*the state of being excited with joy*) delirium, elation, euphoria, exaltation, excitement, exhilaration, infatuation, rapture, stimulation.

intractable *a.* **1** (*unmanageable*) awkward, difficult, incurable, insoluble, ungovernable, unmanageable. ANTONYMS: soluble. **2** (*difficult, obstinate*) cantankerous, contrary, difficult, fractious, headstrong, intransigent, obdurate, obstinate, perverse, pig-headed, refractory, self-willed, stubborn, unbending, uncooperative, undisciplined, unyielding, wayward, wild, wilful. ANTONYMS: malleable.

intransigent *a.* (*uncompromising, inflexible*) immovable, inflexible, intractable, obdurate, obstinate, stubborn, tenacious, unbending, uncompromising, unyielding. ANTONYMS: compliant, flexible.

intrepid *a.* (*fearless, bold*) adventurous, audacious, bold, brave, courageous, daring, dashing, dauntless, doughty, fearless, heroic, plucky, resolute, stalwart, unafraid, undaunted, unflinching, valiant. ANTONYMS: cowardly, irresolute.

intricate *a.* (*involved, complicated*) complex, complicated, convoluted, elaborate, entangled, fancy, involved, labyrinthine, perplexing, sophisticated, tangled, tortuous, winding. ANTONYMS: plain, simple.

intrigue[1] *v.i.* (*to carry on a plot to effect some object by underhand means*) connive, conspire, machinate, manoeuvre, plot, scheme.

~*v.t.* (*to make curious or to fascinate*) attract, beguile, captivate, charm, fascinate, interest, rivet, titillate.

intrigue[2] *n.* **1** (*a plot to effect some object by underhand means*) collusion, conspiracy, deception, machination, manipulation, manoeuvre, plot, ruse, scheme, stratagem, subterfuge, trickery, wile. **2** (*a secret love affair*) affair, amour, attachment, intimacy, liaison, romance.

intrinsic *a.* (*inherent; belonging to the nature of a thing*) basic, built-in, congenital, elemental, fundamental, genuine, inborn, inbred, inherent, innate, native, natural, organic, underlying. ANTONYMS: extraneous, extrinsic.

introduce *v.t.* **1** (*to make (a person, oneself)*)

known in a formal way to another) acquaint, do the honours, familiarize, make known, present. **2** *(to bring into use or notice)* advance, air, bring up, broach, moot, offer, propose, put forward, recommend, set forth, submit, suggest, ventilate. **3** *(to present (a programme etc.) to an audience)* anchor, front, present. **4** *(to bring or lead in)* begin, bring in, commence, establish, found, inaugurate, initiate, institute, launch, lead in, organize, originate, pioneer, set up, start, usher in. **5** *(to insert)* add, inject, insert, interpolate, interpose, put in, throw in. **6** *(to preface)* lead into, open, preface.

introduction *n.* **1** *(the act of introducing)* establishment, inauguration, induction, initiation, institution. **2** *(a formal presentation of new product etc.)* debut, launch, presentation. **3** *(a preface or preliminary discourse in a book etc.)* foreword, preamble, preface, preliminary. **4** *(an opening section in a piece of music) (coll.)* intro, lead-in, opening, overture, prelude, prologue. ANTONYMS: conclusion, epilogue. **5** *(something that is introduced)* addition, insertion, interpolation.

introspective *a.* *(tending to examine one's own thoughts and feelings)* brooding, contemplative, introverted, inward-looking, meditative, pensive, self-centred, subjective, withdrawn.

intrude *v.i.* *(to force oneself upon others; to enter without invitation)* barge in, butt in, encroach, infringe, interfere, interrupt, intervene, meddle, obtrude, push in, trespass, violate.

intruder *n.* *(someone who enters a place illegally or without invitation)* burglar, gatecrasher, housebreaker, infiltrator, interloper, invader, prowler, raider, snooper, spy, squatter, thief, trespasser.

intrusion *n.* *(an unwelcome visit, interruption etc.)* encroachment, infringement, interference, interruption, invasion, trespass, violation.

intuition *n.* *(immediate perception by the mind without reasoning)* discernment, foreboding, hunch, insight, instinct, perception, percipience, perspicacity, premonition, presentiment, sixth sense, wit.

inundate *v.t.* **1** *(to overflow, to flood)* deluge, flood, glut, immerse, overflow, submerge. **2** *(to overwhelm)* deluge, drown, engulf, overrun, overwhelm, submerge, swamp.

invade *v.t.* **1** *(to enter (a country) by force, as an enemy)* assail, assault, attack, burst in, descend upon, occupy, raid. **2** *(to overrun)* overrun, swamp, swarm over. **3** *((of bacteria*

etc.) to assail (a body etc.)) infect, penetrate, pervade. **4** *(to violate (someone's privacy, rights etc.))* encroach on, infringe, violate.

invalid[1] *a.* *(having no force or cogency)* baseless, false, faulty, ill-founded, illogical, impaired, incorrect, inoperative, irrational, nugatory, null, spurious, unfounded, unsound, untenable, untrue, void, worthless, wrong. ANTONYMS: cogent, logical.

invalid[2] *a.* *(infirm or disabled through ill health or injury)* ailing, bedridden, disabled, feeble, frail, ill, infirm, poorly, sick, sickly, weak. ~*n.* *(an infirm or disabled person)* convalescent, cripple, incurable, patient.

invalidate *v.t.* *(to render not valid)* abrogate, annul, cancel, disqualify, nullify, overrule, overthrow, quash, rescind, rule out, undermine, undo, weaken. ANTONYMS: ratify, validate.

invaluable *a.* *(precious above estimation; priceless)* costly, dear, expensive, inestimable, precious, priceless, valuable. ANTONYMS: cheap, worthless.

invariable *a.* *(uniform; not liable to change)* changeless, consistent, constant, fixed, immutable, regular, rigid, set, stable, unalterable, unchangeable, unchanging, unfailing, uniform, unvarying, unwavering. ANTONYMS: changing, variable.

invariably *adv.* *(always)* always, consistently, constantly, customarily, ever, habitually, inevitably, perpetually, regularly, unfailingly, without exception.

invasion *n.* **1** *(the act of invading)* attacking, invading, occupation, raiding. **2** *(a hostile attack upon or entrance into the territory of others)* aggression, assault, attack, drive, foray, incursion, inroad, offensive, onslaught, raid. **3** *(an infringement or violation)* breach, encroachment, infiltration, infraction, infringement, intrusion, transgression, trespass, usurpation, violation. **4** *(the approach or onset of anything dangerous or harmful, esp. of a disease)* approach, incidence, onset.

invective *n.* *(a violent expression of censure or abuse)* abuse, berating, castigation, censure, condemnation, criticism, denunciation, obloquy, reproach, revilement, sarcasm, scorning, tirade, tongue-lashing, vilification, vituperation.

inveigh *v.i.* *(to speak censoriously and abusively (against))* abuse, berate, castigate, censure, condemn, criticize, denounce, lambast, reproach, revile, scorn, upbraid, vilify, vituperate. ANTONYMS: praise.

inveigle *v.t.* (*to entice; to entrap* (*into*)) allure, beguile, cajole, coax, (*sl.*) con, decoy, ensnare, entice, entrap, lead on, lure, manipulate, manoeuvre, persuade, (*coll.*) sweet-talk, talk into, wheedle.

invent *v.t.* **1** (*to devise or contrive* (*a new means, instrument etc.*)) coin, come up with, conceive, conjure up, contrive, create, design, devise, discover, (*coll.*) dream up, formulate, hit upon, imagine, improvise, originate, think up. **2** (*to concoct, to fabricate*) concoct, (*coll.*) cook up, fabricate, feign, forge, make up, manufacture, trump up.

invention *n.* **1** (*the act of inventing*) conception, creation, designing, origination. **2** (*the faculty or power of inventing*) creativity, genius, imagination, ingenuity, inspiration, inventiveness, originality, resourcefulness. **3** (*something which is invented; a contrivance*) contraption, contrivance, creation, design, development, device, discovery, gadget, (*coll.*) gizmo, innovation, instrument. **4** (*a fabrication, a fiction*) deceit, fabrication, fake, falsehood, fantasy, fib, fiction, figment, lie, prevarication, sham, story, tale, tall story, yarn.

inventive *a.* (*ingenious; imaginative*) creative, fertile, gifted, imaginative, ingenious, innovative, inspired, original, resourceful. ANTONYMS: uninventive, unoriginal.

inventory *n.* (*a detailed list or catalogue of goods, possessions etc.*) account, catalogue, file, list, log, manifest, record, register, roll, roster, schedule.

inverse *a.* **1** (*opposite in order or relation*) contrary, converse, opposite, reverse. **2** (*inverted*) inverted, upside down.

invert *v.t.* **1** (*to turn upside down*) capsize, overset, overturn, turn upside down, upset, upturn. **2** (*to place in a reverse position or order*) reverse, transpose.

invest *v.t.* **1** (*to employ* (*money*) *in business, stocks etc.*) advance, lay out, put in, sink, spend, venture. **2** (*to devote* (*effort, time etc.*) *to a project etc. for future rewards*) allot, contribute, devote, provide, spend, supply. **3** (*to provide or endue* (*with office, authority etc.*)) adopt, consecrate, establish, inaugurate, induct, initiate, install, ordain, swear in.

investigate *v.t.* (*to examine or inquire into closely*) analyse, consider, examine, explore, go into, inquire into, inspect, look into, make inquiries, probe, research, scrutinize, search, sift, study, turn over.

investigation *n.* (*the act or an instance of investigation*) analysis, examination,

exploration, hearing, inquest, inquiry, inquisition, inspection, probe, quest, questioning, research, review, scrutiny, search, study, survey.

investiture *n.* (*the ceremony of investing with office, rank etc.*) admission, adoption, consecration, enthronement, establishment, inauguration, induction, initiation, installation, instatement, investment, ordination, swearing-in.

investment *n.* **1** (*the act of investing money*) investing, speculation, venture. **2** (*money invested*) asset, capital, cash, finance, funds, interest, money, nest egg, principal, savings, stake. **3** (*something in which money is invested*) property, share(s), stock(s).

inveterate *a.* **1** (*determinedly settled in a habit*) chronic, confirmed, habitual, hardened, incorrigible, incurable, ineradicable, ingrained, obstinate. **2** (*long-established, deeply-rooted*) deep-rooted, deep-seated, entrenched, established, long-standing.

invigorate *v.t.* **1** (*to give vigour or strength to*) brace, energize, fortify, harden, strengthen. **2** (*to animate; to encourage*) animate, encourage, enliven, exhilarate, freshen up, galvanize, lift, nerve, pep up, perk up, quicken, refresh, rejuvenate, revitalize, stimulate.

invincible *a.* (*that cannot be conquered*) impregnable, indestructible, indomitable, infallible, insuperable, invulnerable, unassailable, unbeatable, unconquerable, unstoppable, unsurmountable. ANTONYMS: surmountable.

inviolate *a.* (*not violated or profaned*) entire, intact, pure, sacred, stainless, unbroken, undefiled, undisturbed, unpolluted, unsullied, untouched, virgin, whole. ANTONYMS: broken, violated.

invisible *a.* **1** (*not visible; imperceptible to the eye*) imperceptible, indiscernible, undetectable, unperceivable, unseen. ANTONYMS: discernible, visible. **2** (*too small, distant etc. to be seen*) inappreciable, inconspicuous, infinitesimal, microscopic. **3** (*not in sight; hidden*) camouflaged, concealed, covered, disguised, hidden, masked, veiled.

invitation *n.* **1** (*the act of inviting or the fact of being invited*) asking, bidding, call, inviting, request, solicitation, supplication. **2** (*a card, letter etc. inviting someone*) (*coll.*) invite, summons. **3** (*allurement; attraction*) advance, allure, allurement, attraction, bait, challenge, (*sl.*) come-on, draw, enticement, incitement, inducement, overture, provocation, pull, temptation.

invite v.t. **1** (*to ask* (*someone*) *courteously to do something, come to an event etc.*) ask, beg, bid, call, summon. **2** (*to request formally and courteously*) request, solicit. **3** (*to allure, to attract*) allure, attract, draw, encourage, entice, lead, provoke, tempt, welcome. **4** (*to draw upon one, esp. unintentionally*) ask for, court, risk.

inviting a. **1** (*attractive*) appealing, attractive, delightful, fascinating, intriguing, welcoming, winning, winsome. ANTONYMS: uninviting. **2** (*seductive; enticing*) alluring, beguiling, bewitching, captivating, engaging, enticing, entrancing, magnetic, seductive, tantalizing, tempting. ANTONYMS: repellent.

invocation n. **1** (*the act of invoking*) beseeching, invoking. **2** (*a supplication or call to God, a god etc.*) appeal, call, entreaty, petition, prayer, supplication.

invoke v.t. **1** (*to address in prayer*) call upon, petition, pray to. **2** (*to solicit earnestly for* (*assistance, protection etc.*)) beg, beseech, entreat, implore, petition, plead, solicit, supplicate. **3** (*to appeal to as an authority*) appeal to, call on, have recourse to, resort to, turn to. **4** (*to summon by magical means*) call up, conjure up, raise, summon.

involuntary a. **1** (*done unintentionally, not from choice*) accidental, compulsory, forced, obligatory, reluctant, unintended, unintentional, unwilling. ANTONYMS: intentional, willing. **2** ((*of a movement*) *performed independently of will or volition*) automatic, blind, conditioned, instinctive, instinctual, reflex, spontaneous, unconscious, uncontrolled, unthinking, unwilling. ANTONYMS: deliberate.

involve v.t. **1** (*to cause to take part* (*in*)*; to include* (*in*)) comprise, contain, cover, embrace, encompass, include, incorporate, subsume, take in. **2** (*to comprise as a logical or necessary consequence; to imply*) entail, imply, mean, necessitate, presuppose, require. **3** (*to implicate* (*in a crime etc.*)) affect, associate, compromise, concern, connect, draw in, implicate, incriminate, inculpate, mix up. **4** (*to enwrap, to enfold* (*in*)) complicate, embroil, enfold, enmesh, entangle, enwrap, mire, snarl up, tangle.

involved a. **1** (*concerned or associated*) affected, associated, caught up, concerned, embroiled, enmeshed, implicated, interested, mixed up, participating. **2** ((*of a story, explanation etc.*) *complicated*) Byzantine, complex, complicated, confusing, convoluted, difficult, elaborate, intricate, knotty, labyrinthine, snarled, sophisticated, tangled, tortuous, twisted. ANTONYMS: straightforward, uncomplicated.

involvement n. **1** (*the act of involving*) association, commitment, concern, connection, interest, participation, responsibility. **2** (*a complicated affair*) complexity, complication, confusion, difficulty, embarrassment, entanglement, imbroglio, intricacy, problem.

invulnerable a. (*incapable of being wounded or injured*) impenetrable, impervious, indestructible, insusceptible, invincible, safe, secure, unassailable. ANTONYMS: vulnerable.

inward a. **1** (*internal; situated or being within*) inner, interior, internal, within. ANTONYMS: external, outer. **2** (*towards the interior*) arriving, entering, inbound, incoming, inflowing, ingoing. **3** (*connected with the mind or soul*) inner, personal, spiritual.

iota n. (*usu. with neg.*) (*a very small quantity*) atom, bit, glimmer, grain, hint, jot, mite, particle, scrap, shadow, speck, tittle, trace, whit.

irascible a. (*easily excited to anger; irritable*) angry, cantankerous, choleric, crabby, cross, hasty, hot-tempered, irritable, petulant, quick-tempered, (*sl.*) ratty, short-tempered, snappy, testy, tetchy, touchy, waspish.

irate a. (*angry, enraged*) angry, annoyed, cross, enraged, exasperated, fuming, furious, incensed, indignant, infuriated, irritated, livid, (*coll.*) mad, (*taboo sl.*) pissed off, provoked, riled, worked up, wrathful. ANTONYMS: good-humoured, placid.

irk v.t. (*to annoy or irritate*) aggravate, annoy, bore, (*sl.*) bug, exasperate, gall, infuriate, irritate, miff, nettle, (*sl.*) peeve, pester, provoke, put out, (*coll.*) rile, ruffle, vex.

irksome a. (*annoying, tedious*) aggravating, annoying, boring, bothersome, burdensome, disagreeable, exasperating, galling, infuriating, irritating, monotonous, tedious, tiring, troublesome, uninteresting, unwelcome, vexatious, vexing, wearisome. ANTONYMS: pleasing.

ironic a. **1** (*sarcastic*) derisive, double-edged, ironical, mocking, mordacious, sarcastic, sardonic, satirical, scoffing, sneering, wry. **2** (*incongruous, inconsistent*) contrary, incongruous, inconsistent, paradoxical, perverse.

irony n. **1** (*an expression, often humorous or slightly sarcastic, intended to convey the opposite of its usual meaning*) derision, mockery, ridicule, sarcasm, satire. **2** (*incongruity between what is expected and what happens*) contrariness, incongruity, paradox, perversity.

irrational a. **1** (*without reason or understanding*) aberrant, crazy, demented, foolish, insane, ludicrous, mindless, preposterous, raving, ridiculous, senseless, unstable, wild. **2** (*illogical, contrary to reason*) absurd, illogical, unreasonable. ANTONYMS: logical, reasonable.

irreconcilable *a.* **1** (*incapable of being reconciled; implacably hostile*) hostile, implacable, inexorable, inflexible, intransigent, unappeasable, uncompromising, unpersuadable, unyielding. ANTONYMS: reconcilable. **2** (*incompatible*) at variance, clashing, incompatible, incongruous, inconsistent, opposed. ANTONYMS: compatible.

irrecoverable *a.* (*that cannot be recovered; irreparable*) irreclaimable, irredeemable, irremediable, irreparable, irretrievable, lost, unsalvageable. ANTONYMS: salvageable.

irrefutable *a.* (*incapable of being refuted*) beyond question, certain, incontestable, incontrovertible, indisputable, indubitable, irresistible, sure, unanswerable, unarguable, unassailable, undeniable, unquestionable. ANTONYMS: arguable, questionable.

irregular *a.* **1** (*not according to rule or established principles*) abnormal, anomalous, capricious, exceptional, extraordinary, immoderate, improper, inappropriate, inordinate, nonconformist, odd, offbeat, peculiar, queer, quirky, unconventional, unofficial, unorthodox, unusual. ANTONYMS: conventional, orthodox. **2** (*not uniform or even*) asymmetrical, crooked, eccentric, erratic, fluctuating, fragmentary, haphazard, inconstant, lopsided, patchy, random, shifting, uncertain, unequal, uneven, unmethodical, unsteady, unsystematic, variable, wavering. ANTONYMS: symmetrical, uniform. **3** (*not occurring at regular times*) desultory, fitful, intermittent, occasional, periodic, spasmodic, sporadic. **4** (*lawless; disorderly*) deceitful, dishonest, disorderly, lawless.

irrelevant *a.* (*not applicable or pertinent*) alien, extraneous, foreign, immaterial, impertinent, inapplicable, inapposite, inappropriate, inapt, inconsequent, unconnected, unrelated, unsuitable. ANTONYMS: applicable, relevant.

irreligious *a.* **1** (*hostile or indifferent to religion*) blasphemous, impious, irreverent, profane, sacrilegious, sinful, ungodly, unholy, wicked. **2** (*not having a religion*) agnostic, atheistic, godless, heathen, pagan, sceptical, unbelieving.

irremediable *a.* (*incapable of being remedied or corrected*) deadly, fatal, final, hopeless, incurable, irreclaimable, irrecoverable, irredeemable, irreparable, irreversible, lost, mortal, terminal, uncurable, unsalvageable.

irreparable *a.* (*incapable of being repaired or restored*) beyond repair, incurable, irreclaimable, irrecoverable, irremediable, irreplaceable, irretrievable, irreversible, uncurable, unsalvageable. ANTONYMS: reparable, salvageable.

irrepressible *a.* (*that cannot be repressed*) boisterous, bubbling, buoyant, ebullient, effervescent, insuppressible, lively, uncontainable, uncontrollable, unmanageable, unquenchable, unrestrainable, unstoppable. ANTONYMS: repressible.

irreproachable *a.* (*blameless, faultless*) beyond reproach, blameless, faultless, guiltless, honest, immaculate, impeccable, inculpable, innocent, irreprehensible, irreprovable, perfect, pure, spotless, unblemished, unimpeachable.

irresistible *a.* **1** (*that cannot be resisted or withstood*) inescapable, inevitable, inexorable, unavoidable. **2** (*extremely attractive or alluring*) alluring, attractive, compelling, enchanting, enticing, fascinating, overwhelming, ravishing, seductive, tempting. ANTONYMS: repulsive.

irresolute *a.* (*undecided, hesitating*) doubtful, faltering, fickle, half-hearted, hesitant, indecisive, infirm, shifting, tentative, undecided, undetermined, unresolved, unsettled, unstable, unsure, vacillating, wavering, weak. ANTONYMS: determined, resolute.

irresponsible *a.* **1** (*performed or acting without a proper sense of responsibility*) careless, ill-considered, rash, reckless, wild. ANTONYMS: responsible. **2** (*lacking the capacity to bear responsibility*) feckless, flighty, giddy, immature, scatterbrained, shiftless, thoughtless, undependable, unreliable, unruly, untrustworthy. ANTONYMS: reliable, sensible.

irreverent *a.* (*lacking in reverence; disrespectful*) cheeky, contemptuous, derisive, discourteous, disrespectful, (*coll.*) flip, flippant, (*coll.*) fresh, impertinent, impious, impudent, insolent, insulting, mocking, rude, saucy. ANTONYMS: respectful, reverent.

irreversible *a.* (*not reversible; irrevocable*) final, fixed, incurable, irremediable, irreparable, irrevocable, permanent, terminal, unalterable, unchangeable. ANTONYMS: reversible.

irrevocable *a.* (*incapable of being revoked or altered*) changeless, enduring, fated, fixed, immutable, invariable, irremediable, irretrievable, irreversible, permanent, predestined, predetermined, settled, unalterable, unchangeable. ANTONYMS: retrievable.

irritable *a.* **1** (*easily provoked or angered*) bad-tempered, cantankerous, crabby, cross, crotchety, grouchy, ill-humoured, impatient, irascible, moody, peevish, petulant, prickly, quarrelsome, (*sl.*) ratty, snappy, temperamental, testy, tetchy, touchy. ANTONYMS: even-tempered, imperturbable. **2** (*easily inflamed or made painful*) sensitive, sore, tender.

irritate *v.t.* **1** (*to annoy; to exasperate*) aggravate, anger, annoy, bother, enrage, exasperate, fret, gall, harass, incense, infuriate, nag, (*coll.*) needle, offend, pester, (*taboo sl.*) piss off, provoke, ruffle, vex. **2** (*to stir up, to excite*) arouse, excite, rouse, stimulate, stir up. ANTONYMS: calm, placate. **3** (*to cause discomfort in* (*the skin, an organ etc.*)) aggravate, chafe, exacerbate, inflame, rub. ANTONYMS: soothe.

isolate *v.t.* **1** (*to place apart; to detach*) cut off, detach, disconnect, divorce, place apart, separate, set apart. **2** (*to quarantine* (*a person thought to be contagious*)) quarantine, segregate, separate.

isolated *a.* (*cut off from society or contact; remote*) cut-off, hidden, lonely, outlying, out-of-the-way, remote, secluded, solitary, unfrequented.

issue *n.* **1** (*the act of giving out or putting into circulation*) circulation, delivery, dispersion, dissemination, distribution, issuing, promulgation, publication, sending out, supply. **2** (*something which is published at a particular time as part of a regular series*) copy, edition, instalment, number, version. **3** (*the whole quantity or number of stamps, copies of a newspaper etc. sent out or put on sale at one time*) impression, printing, print run, run. **4** (*an outgoing, outflow*) discharge, outflow, outgoing. **5** (*progeny, offspring*) children, descendants, heirs, offspring, progeny, young. ANTONYMS: parent, progenitor. **6** (*a result; a consequence*) conclusion, consequence, culmination, effect, end, finale, outcome, (*coll.*) pay-off, result, upshot. ANTONYMS: beginning. **7** (*an important point or subject of debate*)

affair, argument, matter, point, problem, question, subject, topic.
~*v.i.* **1** (*to go or come out*) come out, emit, exit, go out. **2** (*to emerge* (*from*)) discharge, emanate, emerge. **3** (*to be descended*) arise, derive, flow, originate, proceed, rise, spring, stem. **4** (*to proceed, to be derived* (*from*)) end, flow, result, spring.
~*v.t.* **1** (*to publish; to put into circulation*) circulate, deliver, disseminate, distribute, promulgate, publish, put out, release, send out. ANTONYMS: withdraw. **2** (*to provide or supply officially* (*with*)) equip, give, kit out, provide, supply. **3** (*to announce officially* (*a warning etc.*)) announce, broadcast, declare, put out.

itch *v.i.* **1** (*to have an uncomfortable and irritating sensation in the skin*) crawl, irritate, prickle, tickle, tingle. **2** (*to feel a constant teasing desire* (*to do something*)) ache, burn, crave, desire, hanker, hunger, long, lust, pant, pine, thirst, want, wish, yearn.
~*n.* **1** (*a sensation of uneasiness in the skin causing a desire to scratch*) irritation, itchiness, prickling, tickle, tingling. **2** (*an impatient desire or craving*) craving, desire, hankering, hunger, longing, lust, passion, restlessness, thirst, wish, yearning, (*coll.*) yen.

item *n.* **1** (*any of a series of things listed or enumerated*) article, aspect, component, consideration, detail, element, ingredient, matter, particular, point, thing. **2** (*an article, esp. one of a number*) account, article, bulletin, dispatch, feature, mention, note, notice, paragraph, piece, report. **3** (*two people who are in a romantic or sexual relationship*) couple, match.

itinerant *a.* (*passing or moving from place to place*) ambulatory, gypsy, migrant, migratory, nomadic, peripatetic, roaming, roving, strolling, travelling, vagrant, wandering, wayfaring. ANTONYMS: resident, settled.

itinerary *n.* **1** (*a route taken or to be taken*) circuit, journey, line, programme, route, schedule, timetable, tour. **2** (*an account of places and their distances on a road*) guide, guidebook.

J

jab v.t. **1** (*to poke violently*) dig, elbow, nudge, poke, prod, punch, stab. **2** (*to thrust* (*something*) *roughly* (*into*)) drive, force, press, push, ram, shove, stick, thrust.

jabber v.i. (*to talk volubly and incoherently*) babble, blather, blether, chatter, gabble, prattle, (*coll.*) rabbit on, ramble, rattle, (*sl.*) run off at the mouth, (*coll.*) waffle, (*coll.*) witter, (*sl.*) yak, (*coll.*) yap.

jack v.t. **1** (*to lift or move with a jack*) elevate, hoist, lift, lift up, raise. ANTONYMS: lower, put down. **2** (*to resign, to give* (*up*)) give up, leave, quit, resign, vacate. **3** (*to raise* (*prices etc.*)) hike up, increase, inflate, push up, put up, raise. ANTONYMS: decrease, lower, put down.

jacket n. **1** (*a short coat or sleeved outer garment*) blazer, sports coat, sports jacket. **2** (*an outer covering of paper put on a book bound in cloth or leather*) cover, dust jacket, paper cover, wrapper. **3** (*an exterior covering, esp. a covering round a boiler, steam pipe etc., to prevent radiation of heat*) case, casing, cover, covering, sheath, sheathing, skin, wrapper, wrapping.

jackpot n. (*a fund of prize money*) bank, kitty, pool, prize, winnings. **to hit the jackpot 1** (*to win a large prize*) (*coll.*) make a killing, strike it rich. **2** (*to have a big success*) be very successful, have great success, (*coll.*) hit the big time.

jaded a. (*tired and bored, esp. having had too much of something*) bored, cloyed, glutted, satiated, surfeited, tired, wearied, weary, worn out. ANTONYMS: (*coll.*) bright-eyed and bushy-tailed, eager, enthusiastic, fresh, keen.

jagged a. (*ragged, sharply uneven*) barbed, denticulate, indented, notched, pointed, ragged, rough, serrated, spiked, toothed, uneven. ANTONYMS: level, regular, smooth.

jail n. (*a prison, a public place of confinement for persons charged with or convicted of crime*) (*sl., esp. N Am.*) can, (*sl.*) choky, (*sl.*) cooler, detention centre, gaol, (*sl.*) inside, (*N Am.*) jailhouse, (*sl.*) jug, lock-up, (*sl.*) nick, (*N Am.*) penitentiary, prison, (*sl.*) quod, (*sl.*) slammer, (*sl.*) stir.
~v.t. (*to put in jail*) confine, detain, immure, impound, imprison, incarcerate, intern, lock up, put in prison, (*coll.*) send down, send to prison. ANTONYMS: free, liberate, set free.

jailer n. (*the keeper of a prison*) captor, gaoler, guard, keeper, prison warden, prison warder, (*sl.*) screw, warden, warder.

jam v.t. **1** (*to wedge or squeeze* (*in or into*)) cram, force, insert, press, push, ram, sandwich, squeeze, stick, stuff, thrust, wedge. **2** (*to squeeze together*) cram, crowd, crush, pack, squeeze. **3** (*to block up by crowding into*) block, clog, congest, obstruct.
~v.i. ((*of a machine etc.*) *to become immovable or unworkable by rough handling*) become stuck, break down, halt, stall, stick, stop.
~n. **1** (*a crush, a squeeze*) congestion, crush, overcrowding, squeeze. **2** (*a stoppage in a machine due to jamming*) breakdown, halting, jamming, stalling, sticking, stoppage. **3** (*a crowd, a press*) crowd, crush, herd, horde, mass, mob, multitude, pack, press, swarm, throng. **4** (*congestion*) bottleneck, congestion, (*N Am.*) gridlock, hold-up, obstruction. **to be in a jam** (*to be in a predicament*) (*coll.*) be in a fix, (*sl.*) be in a hole, (*coll.*) be in a pickle, be in a predicament, (*coll.*) be in a tight corner, (*coll.*) be in a tight spot, be in difficulties, be in dire straits, be in trouble.

jamb n. (*any one of the upright sides of a doorway or window*) door-jamb, doorpost, pillar, post, upright.

jangle v.i. (*to sound harshly or discordantly*) clang, clank, clash, clatter, clink, rattle, vibrate.
~n. (*discordant sound, as of bells out of tune*) cacophony, clang, clangour, clank, clash, clatter, clink, din, dissonance, rattle, reverberation, stridency, stridor. ANTONYMS: mellifluousness.

jar[1] v.i. **1** (*to emit a harsh or discordant sound*) grate, rasp, scrape, scratch, screech, squeak. **2** (*to clash, to be inconsistent* (*with*)) be at odds (with), be at variance (with), be dissimilar (to), be in conflict (with), be inconsistent (with), clash (with), conflict (with), differ (from), disagree (with), diverge (from), vary (from). ANTONYMS: accord (with), agree (with), be consistent (with), be in accord (with), concur (with).
~v.t. **1** (*to cause to shake or tremble*) jerk, jolt, shake, vibrate. **2** (*to offend, to displease*)

agitate, annoy, disturb, get on (someone's) nerves, grate on, irritate, jangle, nettle, upset.

jar² n. (a vessel of glass or earthenware, used for various domestic purposes) carafe, container, flagon, pot, receptacle, urn, vase, vessel.

jargon n. (any technical or specialized language) cant, gobbledegook, (coll.) lingo, mumbo-jumbo, specialized language, technobabble.

jarring a. **1** ((of a sound) harsh or discordant) grating, harsh, rasping, raucous, scraping, scratching, squeaking, strident. **2** (disagreeing, esp. in an unpleasant way) disagreeable, discordant, grating, harsh, quarrelsome, unpleasant. ANTONYMS: agreeable, harmonious, pleasant.

jaundiced a. (affected by jealousy, prejudice etc.) biased, bigoted, bitter, cynical, distorted, distrustful, envious, hostile, jealous, misanthropic, partisan, pessimistic, prejudiced, resentful, sceptical, spiteful, suspicious. ANTONYMS: open-minded, optimistic, trusting, unbiased, unprejudiced.

jaunt n. (an excursion, a short journey) airing, drive, excursion, expedition, journey, outing, tour, trip.

jaunty a. **1** (sprightly, perky) airy, blithe, bouncy, breezy, buoyant, carefree, cheerful, frisky, lively, merry, nonchalant, (coll.) perky, self-confident, self-satisfied, (coll.) sparky, sprightly. ANTONYMS: depressed, lifeless, miserable. **2** (smart) dapper, fancy, fashionable, flashy, (coll.) natty, smart, spruce, stylish, trim. ANTONYMS: conservative, (coll.) fuddy-duddy.

jazz v.i. **to jazz up** (to make more attractive, livelier etc.) add colour to, animate, brighten, cheer up, enhance, enliven, liven up.

jealous a. **1** (apprehensive of being supplanted in the love or favour (of a wife, husband, lover or friend)) anxious, apprehensive, distrustful, doubting, insecure, mistrustful, possessive, suspicious. ANTONYMS: secure, trusting. **2** (solicitous or anxiously watchful (of one's honour, rights etc.)) attentive, careful, heedful, protective, solicitous, vigilant, wary, watchful. ANTONYMS: careless, heedless. **3** (envious (of another or another's advantages etc.)) covetous, desirous, emulous, envious, (coll.) green, green-eyed, grudging, resentful.

jealousy n. **1** (apprehension of being supplanted in the love or favour (of a wife, husband, lover or friend)) anxiety, apprehension, apprehensiveness, distrust, doubt, insecurity, mistrust, possessiveness, suspicion.

ANTONYMS: security, trust. **2** (the state of being jealous, envy) covetousness, enviousness, envy, grudge, grudgingness, ill will, resentment. **3** (solicitousness (of one's honour, rights etc.)) attentiveness, care, carefulness, heedfulness, protectiveness, solicitousness, vigilance, wariness, watchfulness. ANTONYMS: carelessness.

jeer v.i. (to scoff, to mock (at)) boo, deride, flout, hiss, jibe (at), laugh (at), mock, ridicule, scoff (at), sneer (at), taunt, tease. ANTONYMS: acclaim, applaud, praise.
~n. (a scoff, a taunt) boo, catcall, hiss, jibe, sneer, taunt. ANTONYMS: applause, praise.

jejune a. **1** (devoid of interest or life) banal, boring, colourless, dry, dull, flat, insipid, prosaic, tedious, trite, uninteresting, vapid, (coll.) wishy-washy. **2** (puerile, childish) childish, immature, inexperienced, juvenile, naive, puerile, silly, simple, uninformed, unsophisticated. ANTONYMS: adult, experienced, mature.

jell v.i. **1** (to turn into jelly) congeal, harden, set, solidify, thicken. ANTONYMS: melt. **2** ((of ideas etc.) to come together) come together, crystallize, form, materialize, take form, take shape.

jeopardize v.t. (to put in jeopardy) endanger, expose to danger, expose to risk, gamble with, imperil, lay (someone/ something) open to danger, menace, put at risk, put in jeopardy, risk, take a chance with, threaten. ANTONYMS: protect, secure.

jeopardy n. (risk, danger) danger, hazard, insecurity, menace, peril, precariousness, risk, threat, vulnerability. ANTONYMS: protection, safety, security.

jerk v.t. (to pull or thrust sharply) pull, throw, thrust, tug, wrench, (coll.) yank.
~v.i. (to move with jerks) jolt, lurch, shake, tremble, twitch.
~n. **1** (a sharp, sudden push or tug) pull, thrust, tug, wrench, (coll.) yank. **2** (sl.) (a stupid or contemptible person) (sl.) creep, fool, (sl.) heel, idiot, (sl.) nerd, (coll.) nitwit, scoundrel, (coll.) twit. **3** (a quick, sudden movement, twitch) bump, jolt, lurch, shake, start, tremble, twitch.

jerky a. (making irregular movements) bouncing, bumpy, convulsive, fitful, irregular, jolting, jumpy, lurching, rough, shaky, spasmodic, tremulous, twitchy, uncontrolled, uneven. ANTONYMS: even, regular, smooth.

jerry-built a. (cheaply and badly built) badly built, cheapjack, cheaply built, flimsy, gimcrack, improvised, insubstantial, ramshackle, rickety, shoddy, slipshod, thrown together, unstable. ANTONYMS: solidly built, sturdy, substantial, well-built.

jersey *n.* (*a knitted garment worn on the upper part of the body*) jumper, pullover, sweater, top, (*coll.*) woolly.

jest *n.* (*a joke, something ludicrous said or done to provoke mirth*) banter, bon mot, (*coll.*) funny, gag, hoax, jape, joke, pleasantry, practical joke, prank, quip, trick, witticism.
~*v.i.* **1** (*to joke*) crack a joke, quip, tell jokes. **2** (*to provoke mirth by ludicrous actions or words*) be funny, have fun, (*coll.*) have (someone) on, joke, (*coll.*) kid, play a hoax, play a practical joke, pull (someone's) leg, tease. **in jest** (*not seriously or in earnest*) as a jest, as a joke, for a laugh, for fun, in fun, teasingly. ANTONYMS: in earnest, seriously.

jester *n.* **1** (*a person who jests or jokes*) comedian, comic, hoaxer, humorist, joker, practical joker, prankster, wag, wit. **2** (*a buffoon, esp. one formerly retained by persons of high rank to make sport*) buffoon, clown, court fool, fool, harlequin, (*Hist.*) zany.

jet *v.i.* **1** (*to spurt, to come out in a jet or jets*) flow, gush, issue, rush, shoot, spew, spray, spurt, squirt, stream, surge, well. **2** (*to travel by jet plane*) fly, travel by air, zoom.
~*n.* **1** (*a sudden spurt or shooting out of water or flame, esp. from a small orifice*) flow, fountain, gush, rush, spout, spray, spring, spurt, stream. **2** (*a spout or nozzle for the discharge of water etc.*) atomizer, nozzle, rose, spout, spray, sprinkler.

jettison *v.t.* (*to cast aside; to rid oneself of*) abandon, cast aside, discard, (*coll.*) dump, get rid of, rid oneself of, scrap, throw away, throw out, toss out.

jetty *n.* (*a landing pier*) breakwater, dock, harbour, mole, pier, quay, wharf.

jewel *n.* **1** (*a precious stone, a gem*) brilliant, gem, gemstone, precious stone, (*sl.*) rock, (*sl.*) sparkler, stone. **2** (*a personal ornament containing a precious stone or stones*) piece of jewellery, trinket. **3** (*a person or thing of very great value or excellence*) gem, one in a million, (*coll.*) one of a kind, pearl, treasure, wonder. **4** (*the best or most valuable part of something*) cream, crème de la crème, flower, jewel in the crown, pearl, plum, pride.

jewellery *n.* (*jewels in general*) costume jewellery, gems, precious stones, regalia, trinkets.

jib *v.i.* **to jib at** ((*of a person*) *to refuse to do* (*something*)) baulk at, recoil from, refuse, shrink from, stop short of.

jiff *n.* (*a moment, an extremely short time*) flash, instant, minute, second, trice, twinkling, twinkling of an eye, (*coll.*) two shakes of a lamb's tail.

jig *v.i.* (*to skip about*) bob up and down, bounce, caper, hop, jiggle, jump, leap about, leap up and down, prance, skip.

jiggle *v.t.* (*to jerk or rock lightly to and fro*) agitate, jerk, shake, wiggle.
~*v.i.* (*to fidget*) bounce, fidget, jig, jog, shake.

jilt *v.t.* (*to throw over or discard* (*one's lover*)) abandon, break with, desert, discard, (*sl.*) ditch, (*coll.*) drop, forsake, leave, reject, throw over.

jingle *v.i.* (*to make a clinking or tinkling sound like that of small bells, bits of metal etc.*) chime, chink, clink, jangle, ring, tinkle.
~*v.t.* (*to cause to make a clinking or tinkling sound*) clink, jangle, tinkle.
~*n.* **1** (*a tinkling metallic sound*) clink, clinking, jangle, jangling, ring, ringing, tinkling. **2** (*a simply rhythmical verse, esp. one used in advertising*) chorus, ditty, doggerel, limerick.

jingoism *n.* ((*excessive*) *belligerent patriotism*) blind patriotism, chauvinism, (*coll.*) flag-waving, nationalism.

jinx *n.* (*a person or thing that brings ill luck*) curse, evil eye, hex, (*esp. N Am., coll.*) hoodoo, voodoo.

jitters *n.pl.* (*nervous apprehension*) agitation, anxiety, apprehension, apprehensiveness, fearfulness, (*coll.*) heebie-jeebies, (*coll.*) jumpiness, nerves, nervousness, tenseness, trembling, (*coll.*) willies.

jittery *a.* (*nervous or apprehensive*) agitated, anxious, apprehensive, fearful, frightened, (*coll.*) jumpy, nervous, nervy, tense, trembling, twitchy, (*sl.*) wired. ANTONYMS: calm, confident, (*coll.*) laid-back, relaxed.

job *n.* **1** (*a piece of work, esp. one done for a stated price*) assignment, chore, contract, enterprise, piece of work, task, undertaking, venture, work. **2** (*an occupation*) business, calling, career, craft, employment, (*coll.*) line, line of work, métier, occupation, profession, pursuit, trade, vocation, work. **3** (*a responsibility or duty*) assignment, capacity, charge, chore, concern, duty, function, responsibility, role, task. **4** (*a difficult task*) difficulty, hard time, problem, trial, trouble. **5** (*a situation in paid employment*) employment, occupation, position, post, situation.

jobber *n.* (*a person who deals in stocks and shares on the Stock Exchange*) agent, broker, dealer, stockbroker.

jobless *a.* (*having no paid work*) idle, out of work, unemployed, without work. ANTONYMS: employed, in work, working.

jockey *n.* (*a professional rider in horse races*) horseman/ woman, rider.
~*v.t.* **1** (*to deceive in a bargain*) cheat, deceive, dupe, exploit, fool, hoodwink, swindle, take in, trick. **2** (*to outwit, outmanoeuvre etc.*) engineer, manipulate, manoeuvre, out-manoeuvre, outwit.

jocular *a.* (*facetious, amusing*) amusing, comic, comical, diverting, droll, entertaining, facetious, funny, hilarious, humorous, jesting, jocose, jocund, joking, jolly, jovial, merry, playful, roguish, sportive, waggish, whimsical, witty. ANTONYMS: grave, serious, solemn.

jocund *a.* (*sportive, merry*) blithe, buoyant, carefree, cheerful, cheery, gay, happy, jolly, jovial, light-hearted, merry. ANTONYMS: miserable, sad, unhappy.

jog *v.t.* **1** (*to nudge, esp. to excite attention*) elbow, knock, nudge, prod, push. **2** (*to stimulate* (*one's memory or attention*)) activate, arouse, prompt, remind, stimulate, stir.
~*v.i.* **1** (*to run at a steady, slow pace for exercise*) dogtrot, jogtrot, lope, trot. **2** (*to move with an up-and-down leisurely pace*) bob, bounce, jerk, jiggle, jolt, shake. **3** (*to walk or trudge heavily or slowly* (*on, along etc.*)) lumber, pad, plod, stump, tramp, trudge.

joie de vivre *n.* (*joy of living; exuberance*) ebullience, enthusiasm, (*coll.*) gusto, joy, joyfulness, merriment, pleasure, relish, zest. ANTONYMS: apathy, dejection, depression.

join *v.t.* **1** (*to connect, to fasten together*) attach, bind, cement, combine, connect, couple, fasten, fuse, glue, knit, link, marry, splice, stick together, tie, unite, weld, yoke. ANTONYMS: detach, disconnect, separate, sever, unfasten, untie. **2** (*to become a member of* (*a club etc.*)) become a member of, enlist in, enrol in, sign up for. ANTONYMS: leave, resign from.
~*v.i.* **1** (*to be contiguous or in contact*) abut (on), adjoin, border, butt, conjoin, extend (to), meet, reach, touch, verge (on). **2** (*to become associated or combined* (*with etc.*) *in partnership, action etc.*) affiliate, ally, amalgamate, associate, band together, collaborate, cooperate, join forces, merge, team up. ANTONYMS: break up, dissociate, divide, separate.
~*n.* (*a point or mark of junction*) coupling, intersection, joint, juncture, seam, union. **to join up** (*to enlist*) enlist, join the army, join the forces.

joint *n.* **1** (*the place where two things are joined together*) coupling, intersection, join, junction, seam, union. **2** (*sl.*) (*a marijuana cigarette*) (*sl.*) reefer, (*sl.*) spliff. **3** (*a place, building etc.*) (*coll.*) dump, (*coll.*) hole, place. **4** (*a bar or nightclub*) bar, club, nightclub, pub.

~*a.* (*performed or produced by different persons in conjunction*) allied, collective, combined, common, communal, concerted, cooperative, joined, mutual, shared, united. ANTONYMS: individual, single, sole.
~*v.t.* (*to connect by joints*) connect, couple, fasten, join, unite. **to put someone's nose out of joint** (*to upset or supplant a person*) annoy, disconcert, hurt, pique, upset.

jointly *adv.* (*together or in conjunction with others*) as a group, as one, collectively, cooperatively, in partnership, in unison, mutually, together, unitedly. ANTONYMS: by oneself, individually, separately.

joke *n.* **1** (*something said or done to excite laughter or merriment*) (*coll.*) funny, gag, hoax, jape, jest, (*coll.*) lark, leg-pull, practical joke, prank, quip, sally, trick, (*coll.*) wisecrack, witticism. **2** (*a ridiculous incident, person etc.*) laughing stock, mockery, parody, travesty.
~*v.i.* (*to make jokes, to jest*) banter, be funny, crack jokes, fool, have (someone) on, (*coll.*) kid, make jokes, pull (someone's) leg, tease, (*coll.*) wisecrack. ANTONYMS: be serious.

joker *n.* **1** (*a person who jokes, a jester*) buffoon, clown, comedian, comic, humorist, jester, practical joker, prankster, trickster, wag, wit. ANTONYMS: sobersides. **2** (*a fellow*) (*coll.*) bloke, (*coll.*) chap, (*sl.*) cove, fellow, (*coll.*) guy. **3** (*an unforeseen factor*) catch, drawback, hindrance, hitch, pitfall, snag, snare, trap, unknown factor.

jolly *a.* **1** ((*of a person*) *happy and cheerful*) bright, buoyant, carefree, cheerful, cheery, (*coll.*) chirpy, gay, genial, glad, gleeful, happy, jovial, joyful, light-hearted, lively, merry, mirthful, playful, sociable, (*sl.*) upbeat. ANTONYMS: dejected, depressed, miserable, unsociable. **2** ((*of an occasion*) *pleasant, agreeable*) agreeable, charming, delightful, enjoyable, entertaining, nice, pleasant. ANTONYMS: boring, disagreeable, unpleasant.

jolt *v.t.* **1** (*to shake with sharp, sudden jerks, as in a vehicle along a rough road*) bang, bump, jar, jerk, jog, jostle, shake. **2** (*to disturb, to shock*) amaze, astonish, discompose, disturb, perturb, shake, shake up, shock, (*coll.*) stagger, startle, stun, surprise, upset.
~*v.i.* ((*of a vehicle*) *to move with sharp, sudden jerks*) bounce, bump, jerk, lurch.
~*n.* **1** (*a sudden shock or jerk, esp. physical*) bang, bump, jar, jerk, knock, lurch, shake, start. **2** (*sudden, unexpected news*) blow, bolt from the blue, bombshell, shock, surprise, thunderbolt, upset.

jostle *v.t.* **1** (*to push against, to hustle*) bump, jog, jolt, press, push, shove, thrust. **2** (*to elbow*) elbow, push, shove, squeeze, thrust.

~*v.i.* (*to hustle, to crowd*) crowd, hustle, push, squeeze, throng.

jot *n.* (*a tittle, an iota*) atom, bit, grain, iota, morsel, particle, scrap, (*coll.*) smidgeon, speck, trifle, whit. ANTONYMS: a great deal, a lot.

~*v.t.* (*to write* (*down a brief note or memorandum of*)) chronicle, list, make a list of, make a note of, mark down, note, note down, put down, record, register, scribble down, take down, write down.

journal *n.* **1** (*a record of events or news; any newspaper or other periodical published at regular intervals*) magazine, newspaper, paper, periodical, publication. **2** (*an account of daily transactions*) chronicle, commonplace book, daybook, diary, log, logbook, record. **3** (*the transactions of a learned society etc.*) magazine, periodical, proceedings, records, transactions.

journalism *n.* (*the work of collecting, writing and publishing news and information*) Fleet Street, newspapers, print media, (*facet.*) the fourth estate, the press.

journalist *n.* (*an editor of or contributor to a newspaper or other journal*) contributor, correspondent, hack, (*sl.*) journo, (*coll.*) news hound, newsman/ woman, newspaperman/ woman, pressman/ woman, reporter, the press, writer.

journey *n.* (*travel from one place to another, esp. at a long distance*) excursion, expedition, odyssey, outing, tour, trip, voyage.

~*v.i.* (*to make a journey*) go, go on a journey, go on an expedition, go on a trip, tour, travel, voyage.

jovial *a.* (*merry, cheerful*) blithe, cheerful, cheery, convivial, cordial, friendly, gay, genial, glad, good-natured, happy, jocose, jocular, jocund, jolly, merry, mirthful, sociable. ANTONYMS: antisocial, lugubrious, miserable, morose, unsociable.

joy *n.* **1** (*the emotion produced by gratified desire, success etc.; happiness*) bliss, delight, ecstasy, elation, enjoyment, euphoria, exultation, gaiety, gladness, glee, happiness, hilarity, joyfulness, jubilation, pleasure, rapture, rejoicing, transports, triumph. ANTONYMS: disappointment, misery, sorrow, unhappiness. **2** (*a cause of joy or happiness*) delight, gem, jewel, pride, pride and joy, prize, treasure. **3** (*success or satisfaction*) gratification, luck, satisfaction, success. ANTONYMS: bad luck, dissatisfaction.

joyful *a.* **1** (*very happy*) delighted, ecstatic, elated, enraptured, euphoric, exultant, gay,

glad, gleeful, happy, in seventh heaven, in transports, jolly, jovial, joyous, jubilant, merry, (*coll.*) on cloud nine, overjoyed, (*coll.*) over the moon, pleased, pleased as Punch, rapt, (*coll.*) tickled pink. ANTONYMS: disappointed, miserable, unhappy. **2** (*causing great happiness*) cheerful, delightful, exciting, glad, happy, joyous, (*coll.*) out of this world, pleasing, thrilling. ANTONYMS: distressing, sad.

joyless *a.* **1** ((*of a person*) *very sad*) dejected, depressed, despondent, melancholy, miserable, morose, mournful, sad, unhappy. ANTONYMS: delighted, euphoric, joyful. **2** (*causing no joy*) bleak, cheerless, depressing, desolate, dismal, drab, dreary, gloomy. ANTONYMS: bright, cheerful.

joyous *a.* **1** (*joyful*) delighted, ecstatic, elated, enraptured, euphoric, exultant, gay, glad, gleeful, happy, in seventh heaven, in transports, jolly, jovial, joyful, jubilant, merry, (*coll.*) on cloud nine, overjoyed, (*coll.*) over the moon, pleased, pleased as Punch, rapt, (*coll.*) tickled pink. ANTONYMS: disappointed, miserable, unhappy. **2** (*causing joy*) celebratory, cheerful, festive, gay, happy, jolly, merry. ANTONYMS: melancholy, miserable, mournful.

jubilant *a.* (*exultant, rejoicing*) cock-a-hoop, elated, enraptured, euphoric, exuberant, exultant, in seventh heaven, in transports, joyful, (*coll.*) on cloud nine, overjoyed, (*coll.*) over the moon, pleased as Punch, rejoicing, thrilled, (*coll.*) tickled pink, triumphant. ANTONYMS: dejected, despondent, disappointed, downcast, sad, unhappy.

jubilee *n.* (*a season of great public rejoicing or festivity*) anniversary, carnival, celebration, commemoration, feast day, festival, festivity, fête, gala, holiday, revelry.

Judas *n.* (*a traitor*) betrayer, traitor, turncoat.

judge *n.* **1** (*a civil officer invested with power to hear and determine causes in a court of justice*) (*sl.*) beak, high-court judge, magistrate. **2** (*a person authorized to decide a dispute or contest*) adjudicator, arbiter, arbitrator, mediator, referee, umpire. **3** (*a person skilled in deciding on relative merits, a connoisseur*) appraiser, arbiter, assessor, authority, connoisseur, critic, evaluator, expert.

~*v.t.* **1** (*to hear or try* (*a cause*)) hear evidence, pass sentence, pronounce sentence, rule, sit, try. **2** (*to examine and form an opinion upon*) appraise, assess, criticize, evaluate, examine, gauge, review, (*coll.*) size up, weigh up. **3** (*to consider, to estimate*) believe, conclude, consider, deduce, deem, estimate, guess, reckon, think. **4** (*to decide the winner in a competition, dispute etc.*) adjudge, adjudicate, arbitrate, mediate, referee, umpire.

judgement n. 1 (a judicial decision, a sentence of a court of justice) decree, finding, ruling, sentence, verdict. 2 (discernment, discrimination) acumen, common sense, discernment, discrimination, good sense, good taste, intelligence, judiciousness, penetration, perception, percipience, perspicacity, prudence, sagacity, sense, shrewdness, taste, understanding, wisdom. ANTONYMS: folly, lack of judgement, poor taste, stupidity. 3 (criticism) appraisal, assessment, criticism, evaluation, gauging, review, (coll.) sizing up, weighing up. 4 (opinion, estimate) belief, conclusion, consideration, deduction, estimate, evaluation, opinion, point of view, reckoning, thinking, view. 5 (a misfortune regarded as sent by God) damnation, doom, fate, punishment, retribution.

judicial a. (relating to or proper to courts of law or the administration of justice) judiciary, juridical, legal.

judicious a. (sagacious, discerning) acute, astute, careful, cautious, circumspect, common-sense, considered, discerning, discreet, discriminating, informed, politic, prudent, rational, reasonable, sagacious, sensible, shrewd, sound, thoughtful, well-advised, well-judged, wise. ANTONYMS: careless, ill-advised, indiscreet, stupid.

jug n. (a vessel, usu. with a swelling body, narrow neck, and handle, for holding liquids) ewer, pitcher.

juggle v.t. (to manipulate (facts, figures etc.) in order to deceive) alter, change, (coll.) cook, (coll.) doctor, fake, falsify, (coll.) fix, manipulate, manoeuvre, (coll.) massage, modify, rig.

juice n. (the watery part of fruits etc. or the fluid part of animal bodies) extract, liquor, sap.

juicy a. 1 (abounding in juice, succulent) lush, moist, succulent, watery. ANTONYMS: dried out, dry. 2 (interesting, esp. in a titillating or scandalous way) colourful, exciting, provocative, racy, risqué, sensational, spicy, (coll.) suggestive. ANTONYMS: boring, tame.

jumble v.t. (to mix confusedly) confuse, disarrange, dishevel, disorder, disorganize, mix, mix up, muddle, put into disarray, tangle, throw into disorder. ANTONYMS: disentangle, straighten out, tidy up.
~n. (a muddle, disorder) chaos, clutter, confusion, disarray, disorder, hotchpotch, litter, medley, mess, miscellany, mishmash, mixture, motley collection, muddle.

jumbo a. (huge or oversized) elephantine, extra-large, giant, gigantic, (sl.) ginormous, huge, immense, (sl.) mega, oversized, vast. ANTONYMS: dwarf, minuscule, minute, tiny.

jump v.i. 1 (to leap, to bound) bounce, bound, caper, cavort, frolic, gambol, hop, leap, skip, spring. 2 (to start or rise (up) abruptly) flinch, jerk, (coll.) jump out of one's skin, recoil, rise suddenly, start, wince. 3 (to rise or increase suddenly by a significant amount) be hiked up, escalate, go up, increase, mount, rise, soar. ANTONYMS: fall, plummet.
~v.t. 1 (to pass over or cross by leaping) clear, go over, hurdle, jump over, leap, sail over, vault. 2 (to skip (a chapter, pages etc.)) cut out, disregard, ignore, leave out, miss out, omit, pass over. 3 (to pounce on or attack) assault, attack, (coll.) mug, pounce upon, set upon.
~n. 1 (the act of jumping) bound, hop, leap, skip, spring. 2 (a start, an involuntary nervous movement) flinch, jerk, jolt, shake, start, twitch, wince. 3 (a sudden rise (in price, value etc.)) escalation, (sl.) hike, increase, leap, rise, upturn. 4 (an obstacle to be jumped) barrier, fence, gate, hedge, hurdle, rail. 5 (a break, a gap) breach, break, gap, hiatus, interruption, lacuna, space. **to jump at** (to accept eagerly) (coll.) go for, grab, seize, snatch, welcome, welcome with open arms. ANTONYMS: refuse, reject, turn down.

jumper n. (a knitted upper garment) jersey, knit, sweater, top, (coll.) woolly.

jumpy a. (nervous, easily startled) agitated, alarmed, anxious, apprehensive, edgy, fearful, fidgety, frightened, (coll.) jittery, nervous, nervy, on edge, panicky, restive, restless, tense, twitchy, uneasy, (sl.) wired. ANTONYMS: calm, composed, confident, (coll.) laid-back.

junction n. 1 (a joint, a point of union) coupling, join, joint, seam, union. 2 (the point where roads or railway lines meet) crossing, crossroads, interchange, intersection.

juncture n. 1 (the place or point at which two things are joined, a joint) coupling, join, joint, junction, seam, union. 2 (a point of time marked by the occurrence of critical events or circumstances) critical moment, crux, moment, moment of truth, period, point, stage, time, turning point.

jungle n. 1 (land covered with forest trees or dense, matted vegetation) forest, rainforest, tropical forest. 2 (a confusing mass) confusion, disarray, hotchpotch, jumble, mishmash, motley collection, tangle.

junior a. 1 (the younger (esp. as distinguishing a son from his father of the same name)) younger. ANTONYMS: elder, older, senior. 2 (lower in standing) inferior, lesser, lower, minor, secondary, subordinate. ANTONYMS: senior, superior.

junk n. (*rubbish, valueless odds and ends*) cast-offs, debris, (*esp. N Am.*) garbage, litter, odds and ends, refuse, rubbish, scrap, (*esp. N Am.*) trash, waste.

junket n. (*a feast, an entertainment*) (*sl.*) bash, (*coll.*) beanfeast, celebration, (*coll.*) do, feast, festivity, party, revelry, spree, (*sl.*) thrash.

jurisdiction n. **1** (*the legal power or right of making and enforcing laws or exercising other authority*) administration, authority, command, control, dominion, influence, leadership, mastery, power, rule, sovereignty, sway. **2** (*the district or extent within which such power may be exercised*) area, district, domain, dominion, province, scope, territory.

just a. **1** (*acting according to what is right and fair*) decent, equitable, ethical, even-handed, fair, fair-minded, good, honest, honourable, impartial, moral, objective, open-minded, principled, right, righteous, straight, truthful, unbiased, unprejudiced, upright, upstanding, virtuous. ANTONYMS: biased, (*coll.*) crooked, dishonourable, partisan, prejudiced, unjust. **2** (*exact, accurate*) accurate, close, correct, exact, faithful, precise, proper, strict, true. ANTONYMS: imprecise, inaccurate, inexact. **3** (*merited, deserved*) appropriate, apt, deserved, due, fitting, justified, merited, rightful, suitable, valid, well-deserved. **4** (*lawful, legal*) genuine, lawful, legal, legitimate, rightful, sound, valid. ANTONYMS: illegal, unlawful.
~adv. **1** (*exactly, precisely*) absolutely, completely, entirely, exactly, perfectly, precisely, totally. **2** (*barely, with nothing to spare*) barely, by a hair's breadth, (*coll.*) by the skin of one's teeth, hardly, only just, scarcely. **3** (*only a moment ago, a very little time ago*) a minute ago, a moment ago, a second ago, just now, lately, not long ago, recently. ANTONYMS: ages ago, a long time ago. **4** (*simply, merely*) at most, merely, no more than, nothing but, only. **just about** (*more or less*) all but, almost, more or less, nearly, practically.

justice n. **1** (*the quality of being just*) equity, even-handedness, fairness, fair play, impartiality, justness, lack of bias, lack of prejudice, objectivity. **2** (*uprightness, honesty*) decency, goodness, honesty, honour, integrity, morality, principle, rectitude, righteousness,

uprightness, virtue. **3** (*just requital of deserts*) amends, compensation, penalty, punishment, recompense, redress, reparation, requital, retribution. **4** (*a person legally commissioned to hold courts and administer justice between individuals*) judge, magistrate. **5** (*lawfulness, legality*) lawfulness, legality, legitimacy, rightfulness, soundness, validity. ANTONYMS: illegality, unlawfulness. **to do justice to 1** (*to treat fairly*) be fair to, be just to, treat fairly, treat justly. **2** (*to treat appreciatively*) appreciate, deal with appreciatively, deal with as well as one should, treat with appreciation. **to do oneself justice** (*to acquit oneself worthily of one's ability*) do as well as one can, do one's best, reach one's full potential.

justifiable a. (*acceptable because there is a good reason for it*) acceptable, defensible, excusable, lawful, legal, legitimate, proper, reasonable, right, sound, supportable, sustainable, tenable, understandable, valid, within reason. ANTONYMS: indefensible, inexcusable, unjustifiable, untenable.

justification n. **1** (*an acceptable reason for doing something*) defence, grounds, reason, vindication. **2** (*proof*) certification, confirmation, proof, substantiation, validation, verification.

justify v.t. **1** (*to prove or show to be just or right*) certify, confirm, establish, legitimize, prove, substantiate, validate, verify. **2** (*to vindicate, to show grounds for*) explain, give reasons for, show just cause for, show to be reasonable. **3** (*to exonerate*) absolve, acquit, clear, excuse, pardon.

justly adv. **1** (*in a just or fair manner*) equitably, fairly, impartially, objectively, without bias, without prejudice. ANTONYMS: unfairly, unjustly. **2** (*deservedly*) deservedly, rightfully, rightly, with good reason, with reason. ANTONYMS: undeservedly, unjustly, wrongly.

jut v.i. (*to project, to stick (out)*) bulge out, extend, overhang, poke out, project, protrude, stick out.

juvenile a. **1** (*young, youthful*) child, junior, young. ANTONYMS: adult, grown-up, senior. **2** (*immature*) callow, childish, immature, infantile, jejune, puerile, unsophisticated. ANTONYMS: adult, grown-up, mature, sophisticated.

keel *v.i.* **to keel over 1** (*to capsize, to turn over*) capsize, overturn, topple over, turn over, turn turtle, turn upside down, upset. **2** (*to fall over*) become unconscious, (*coll.*) black out, collapse, faint, fall down, fall over, lose consciousness, pass out.

keen *a.* **1** (*enthusiastic, eager*) assiduous, avid, conscientious, diligent, eager, earnest, enthusiastic, fervent, fervid, impassioned, impatient, intense, interested, passionate, willing, zealous. ANTONYMS: apathetic, indifferent, uninterested. **2** (*acute, penetrating*) acute, discerning, perceptive, sensitive, sharp. ANTONYMS: dull, insensitive. **3** (*having a sharp edge or point*) razor-sharp, sharp, sharp-edged, sharpened. ANTONYMS: blunt. **4** ((*of cold etc.*) *biting, intense*) biting, bitter, chilly, cold, freezing, icy, raw. ANTONYMS: warm. **5** (*bitter, acrimonious*) acerbic, acrimonious, biting, bitter, caustic, cutting, incisive, mordant, razor-like, sarcastic, sardonic, sharp, trenchant, virulent, vitriolic. ANTONYMS: mild. **6** (*strong, intense*) acute, deep, great, intense, powerful, profound, strong. ANTONYMS: faint, mild. **7** (*clever, quick to understand*) astute, brainy, bright, clever, intelligent, quick, quick-witted, sharp, sharp-witted, shrewd, smart. ANTONYMS: dull-witted, stupid, unintelligent. **keen on** (*enthusiastic about, interested in*) conscientious about, devoted to, diligent about, fond of, interested in. ANTONYMS: averse to.

keenness *n.* **1** (*sharpness*) razor-sharpness, sharpness. ANTONYMS: bluntness. **2** (*enthusiasm, eagerness*) assiduousness, avidity, avidness, conscientiousness, diligence, eagerness, earnestness, enthusiasm, fervidness, fervour, impatience, intensity, passion, zeal, zest. **3** (*sensitivity, acuteness*) acuteness, discernment, perception, sensitivity. **4** (*cleverness*) brightness, cleverness, intelligence, perception, perceptiveness, quickness, quickness of wit, quick-wittedness, sharp, sharpness of wit, sharp-wittedness, shrewdness. ANTONYMS: dull-wittedness, lack of intelligence, stupidity. **5** (*strength, intensity*) depth, intensity, powerfulness, profundity, strength. ANTONYMS: faintness, mildness. **6** (*bitterness, coldness*) bitterness, chill, chilliness, coldness, iciness, rawness. **7** (*acrimony*) acerbity, acrimoniousness, acrimony, bitterness, incisiveness,

mordancy, sarcasm, sharpness, trenchancy, virulence. ANTONYMS: mildness.

keep[1] *v.t.* **1** (*to hold for a significant length of time, to retain*) (*coll.*) hang on to, hold, hold on to, keep hold of, keep in one's possession, retain. ANTONYMS: discard, give up, lose. **2** (*to guard, preserve*) conserve, keep alive, keep fresh, preserve. ANTONYMS: neglect. **3** (*to maintain in a given state, position etc.*) conserve, keep in good order, keep up, look after, maintain, manage, mind, supervise. ANTONYMS: neglect. **4** (*to supply with the necessaries of life*) feed, maintain, provide for, support, sustain. **5** (*to own and tend, to look after out of interest or for profit*) care for, defend, guard, look after, mind, preserve, protect, safeguard, shelter, shield, take care of, tend, watch over. ANTONYMS: abuse, neglect. **6** (*to observe, to pay proper regard to*) celebrate, commemorate, hold, honour, mark, observe, respect. ANTONYMS: ignore, neglect. **7** (*to fulfil*) abide by, carry out, comply with, fulfil, honour, keep faith with, keep to, obey, observe, stand by. ANTONYMS: break, ignore. **8** (*to have regularly on sale; to stock*) carry, deal in, have in stock, have on sale, sell, stock. **9** (*to restrain* (*from*), *to cause to abstain* (*from*)) deter, hinder, hold back, impede, keep (someone) back, obstruct, prevent, prohibit, restrain. ANTONYMS: assist, enable, encourage. **10** (*to detain* (*in custody etc.*), *to cause to wait or be late*) check, delay, detain, hold up, make (someone) late, retard, slow. ANTONYMS: accelerate, speed up. **11** (*to refrain from divulging*) conceal, hide, hush up, keep hidden, keep quiet about, keep secret, keep (something) dark, (*coll.*) keep (something) under one's hat, not breathe a word of, suppress, withhold. ANTONYMS: disclose, divulge, reveal, tell.

~*v.i.* **1** (*to continue to be* (*in a specified condition etc.*)) continue to be, remain, stay. **2** (*to continue* (*doing*)) carry on, continue, keep on, persevere, persist. **3** (*to remain unspoiled, untainted etc.*) be edible, stay fresh. ANTONYMS: rot. **to keep at** (*to persist with*) carry on, continue, (*coll.*) hang on in there, keep going, keep on, keep one's nose to the grindstone, (*coll.*) peg away, persevere, persist, (*coll.*) stick at it, work on. ANTONYMS: give up, stop. **to keep back 1** (*to restrain, to hold back*) curb, delay, detain, deter, hinder, hold back, impede, keep (someone) from, obstruct, prevent, prohibit. ANTONYMS: accelerate, assist, enable, encourage, speed up. **2** (*to keep secret*) conceal, hide, hush up, keep hidden, keep quiet about, keep secret, keep (something) dark, keep (something) under one's hat, not breathe a word about, suppress, withhold. ANTONYMS: disclose, divulge, make known, reveal, tell. **to keep down 1** (*to repress, to subdue*) control, crush, hold in check, keep under control, quash, quell, repress, subdue, subjugate. **2** (*to keep (expenses etc.) low*) curb, cut, cut back on, economize on, reduce, retrench. **to keep from 1** (*to abstain or refrain from*) abstain from, give up, keep off, quit, refrain from, renounce, stop, turn aside from. ANTONYMS: continue, indulge in, take up. **2** (*not to tell (someone about something)*) conceal, hide, keep hidden, keep secret, withhold. **3** (*to stop or prevent*) prevent, restrain, stop. ANTONYMS: assist. **4** (*to protect or preserve*) guard, keep safe, preserve, protect, safeguard, shelter, shield. ANTONYMS: expose to danger, expose to harm. **to keep in** (*to repress, to restrain*) bottle up, check, curb, muffle, repress, restrain, smother, stifle, suppress. ANTONYMS: express, give expression to. **to keep in with** (*to remain on friendly terms with*) keep friendly with, keep on good terms with, maintain a friendship with, stay close to. ANTONYMS: fall out with, quarrel with. **to keep off 1** (*to hinder from approach*) avert, drive back, repel, ward off. **2** (*to remain at a distance*) keep at a distance, keep away, not go near, stay away from, stay off. **3** (*to abstain from*) abstain from, give up, quit, refrain from, renounce, stop, turn aside from. ANTONYMS: continue, indulge, take up. **4** (*to avoid mentioning or discussing*) avoid, dodge, eschew, evade, not mention, steer clear of. ANTONYMS: introduce, mention. **to keep on 1** (*to continue (doing etc.), to persist*) carry on, continue, keep, persevere, persist. ANTONYMS: discontinue, give up. **2** (*to talk continuously, esp. in an annoying way; to nag*) go on, go on and on, nag, (*coll.*) rabbit on, ramble, rant on. **to keep oneself to oneself** (*to avoid other people*) avoid company, be a private person, be a recluse, be unsociable, shun company. ANTONYMS: be gregarious, be sociable. **to keep out** (*to hinder from entering or taking possession (of)*) avert, drive back, keep at bay, repel, ward off. ANTONYMS: let in. **to keep to 1** (*to adhere strictly to*) abide by, adhere to, comply with, honour, keep, obey, stand by, stick to. ANTONYMS: break, ignore. **2** (*not to stray from*) not stray from, not wander from, stay on, stick to. ANTONYMS: leave, stray from. **to keep under** (*to hold down, to repress*) control, crush, keep down, keep in check, keep under control, keep under one's thumb, oppress, quash, quell, repress, subdue, subjugate,

tyrannize. **to keep up 1** (*to keep in repair or good condition*) keep in good repair, look after, maintain, preserve. **2** (*to prevent from falling or diminishing*) bolster up, maintain, prop up, support, sustain. **3** (*to carry on*) carry on, continue, go on with, keep going, maintain. ANTONYMS: cancel, give up, stop. **4** (*to go on at the same pace (with)*) keep abreast, keep pace, not lag behind. **to keep up with 1** (*to stay informed about*) be au fait with, be aware of, have one's ear to the ground, keep abreast of, keep informed about, keep pace with. **2** (*to maintain contact with*) be in communication with, be in contact with, communicate with, keep in contact with, keep in touch with, maintain contact with, stay in contact with, stay in touch with. ANTONYMS: lose contact with, lose touch with.

keep² *n.* **1** (*subsistence, maintenance*) board, board and lodging, food, livelihood, living, maintenance, subsistence, support, upkeep. **2** (*a donjon, the main tower or stronghold of a medieval castle*) castle, donjon, fastness, fortress, stronghold, tower. **for keeps** (*permanently*) for always, for ever, for good, permanently. ANTONYMS: temporarily.

keeper *n.* **1** (*a person who has the care or superintendence of anything, esp. of a park, art gallery etc.*) attendant, caretaker, curator, steward, superintendent. **2** (*a person who retains others in custody or charge*) custodian, gaoler, guard, jailer, (*sl.*) screw, sentry, warden, warder.

keeping *n.* **1** (*custody, guardianship*) aegis, care, charge, custody, guardianship, protection, safe keeping, supervision. **2** (*consistency, congruity*) accord, accordance, agreement, compliance, concurrence, conformity, congruity, consistency, harmony. ANTONYMS: conflict, contradiction, disagreement.

keepsake *n.* (*anything kept as a reminder of the giver*) favour, memento, remembrance, souvenir, token.

keg *n.* (*a small cask or barrel*) barrel, butt, cask, drum, vat.

kernel *n.* (*the gist or essence*) (*coll.*) brass tacks, centre, core, essence, gist, heart, keynote, (*coll.*) nitty-gritty, nub, nucleus, (*coll.*) nuts and bolts, pith, quintessence, substance.

key *n.* **1** (*a portable instrument, usu. of metal, for working the bolt of a lock to and fro*) latchkey, master key, pass-key. **2** (*that which explains anything difficult, a solution*) annotation, answer, clarification, clue, cue, explanation, exposition, gloss, guide, indicator, interpretation, lead, pointer, solution, translation. **3** (*one of several systems of musical* notes having definite tonic relations among themselves) pitch, timbre, tone. **4** (the general tone or style (of a picture, literary composition etc.)) character, humour, mood, spirit, style, theme, tone, vein.

keynote n. (the general tone or spirit (of a picture, poem etc.)) centre, core, essence, gist, heart, marrow, nub, nucleus, pith, policy line, salient point, spirit, substance, theme, tone, vein.

keystone n. **1** (the central stone of an arch locking the others together) central stone, cornerstone, quoin. **2** (the fundamental element, principle etc.) basis, cornerstone, foundation, linchpin, mainspring.

kibosh n. to put the kibosh on (to put an end to) bring to an end, bring to a stop, check, crack down on, curb, nip in the bud, put an end to, put a stop to, quash, ruin.

kick v.t. **1** (to strike with the foot or hoof etc.) boot, punt. **2** (to abandon, give up, esp. an addiction) abandon, desist from, give up, leave off, quit, refrain from, stop.
~v.i. (to show opposition, dislike etc. (against, at etc.)) (sl.) beef, (sl.) bitch, complain, (coll.) gripe, (coll.) grouse, grumble, object, oppose, protest, rebel, resist.
~n. **1** (a blow with the foot or hoof etc.) boot, punt. **2** (a sudden thrill of excitement) amusement, (sl.) buzz, enjoyment, entertainment, excitement, fun, pleasure, stimulation, thrill. **3** (an enthusiastic, short-lived interest) burst of enthusiasm, craze, enthusiasm, fad, (sl.) jag, mania, (coll.) spree. **4** (energy, strong effect) potency, punch, strength, zing, (coll.) zip. **to kick about/ around 1** (to go from place to place aimlessly) drift, meander, ramble, roam, wander. **2** (to treat harshly) abuse, maltreat, mistreat, (coll.) push around. **3** (to discuss informally, to raise but not consider seriously) debate, discuss, talk over, thrash out. **to kick off** (to begin) begin, commence, get going, get under way, initiate, open, start. ANTONYMS: close, end, wind up. **to kick out** (to eject or dismiss unceremoniously or with violence) (sl.) boot out, (sl.) chuck out, dismiss, eject, evict, expel, get rid of, (sl.) give (someone) the boot, (sl.) give (someone) the bum's rush, (coll.) give (someone) their marching orders, oust, remove, (coll.) sack, (coll.) show (someone) the door, throw out, turn out.

kickback n. (a sum paid to another person, confidentially, for favours past or future) bribe, (sl.) bung, (sl.) cut, gift, (sl.) graft, pay-off, reward, sop, (coll.) sweetener, tip.

kick-off n. (a start) beginning, commencement, initiation, opening, outset, start. ANTONYMS: close, end.

kid[1] n. (a child, a young person) baby, boy, child, girl, infant, little one, (sl.) sprog, teenager, toddler, (coll.) tot, young one, young person, youngster, youth. ANTONYMS: adult, grown-up.

kid[2] v.t. (to deceive for fun, to tease) fool, (coll.) have (someone) on, play a joke on, play a trick on, pull (someone's) leg, tease, trick, (sl.) wind (someone) up.
~v.i. (to joke, to deceive someone for fun) fool around, jest, joke, pretend, tease, trick. ANTONYMS: be in earnest, be serious.

kidnap v.t. (to carry off (a person) by force or illegally, to abduct) abduct, carry off, hold to ransom, seize, snatch, take hostage.

kill v.t. **1** (to deprive of life, to put to death) assassinate, (sl.) bump off, (sl.) do in, do to death, murder, slaughter, slay, (sl.) take out, take (someone's) life, wipe out. **2** (to put an end to, to destroy) destroy, extinguish, put an end to, quash, quell, ruin, scotch, stop, suppress, veto. ANTONYMS: begin, initiate. **3** (to deaden, to still (pain etc.)) deaden, dull, smother, stifle, still. ANTONYMS: exacerbate. **4** (to cause pain or discomfort to) ache, be agonizing, be painful, be sore, be uncomfortable (for), cause pain (to), hurt, throb. **5** (to cause great amusement to) amuse greatly, (coll.) have (someone) rolling in the aisles, (coll.) have (someone) splitting their sides, (sl.) make (someone) crack up. **6** (to pass or consume (time) idly) fill up, pass, use up, while away. **7** (to discard, to cancel) cancel, cut out, delete, discard, eradicate, erase, expunge, obliterate, remove, (sl.) zap.

killer n. (a person that kills) assassin, executioner, gunman, hit man, homicide, murderer, slaughterer, slayer.

killing a. **1** (that kills) deadly, death-dealing, fatal, homicidal, lethal, mortal, murderous. **2** (excruciatingly funny) hilarious, hysterical, ludicrous, rib-tickling, side-splitting, uproarious.
~n. (the act of causing death or a death, slaughter) assassination, bloodshed, carnage, execution, extermination, homicide, liquidation, manslaughter, massacre, murder, slaughter, slaying. **to make a killing** (to make a large profit) be financially successful, (sl.) make a bomb, make a lot of money, make huge profits, (coll.) make oodles of money.

killjoy n. (a person who sheds a general depression on company, a wet blanket) damper, (sl.) party-pooper, spoilsport, wet blanket.

kin n. (one's blood relations or family connections collectively, kindred) connections, family, (coll.) folks, kindred, kinsfolk, kinsmen, kinswomen, kith and kin, people, relations, relatives.

kind *n.* **1** (*a species, a natural group*) breed, class, family, genus, group, race, species. **2** (*sort, variety*) brand, category, class, sort, type, variety. **3** (*essential nature*) character, disposition, nature.
~*a.* (*disposed to do good to others*) accommodating, altruistic, amiable, amicable, benevolent, big-hearted, caring, charitable, compassionate, congenial, considerate, decent, forbearing, friendly, generous, genial, giving, good, good-natured, gracious, helpful, hospitable, humanitarian, indulgent, kind-hearted, kindly, lenient, loving, magnanimous, merciful, neighbourly, nice, obliging, philanthropic, pleasant, soft-hearted, sympathetic, tender-hearted, thoughtful, tolerant, understanding, warm. ANTONYMS: hard-hearted, heartless, mean, merciless, nasty, unkind.

kindle *v.t.* **1** (*to set fire to, to light*) ignite, light, set alight, set fire to, set on fire, (*sl.*) torch. **2** (*to excite, to stir up* (*to action or feeling*)) arouse, awaken, excite, foment, incite, induce, inflame, inspire, provoke, rouse, stimulate, stir up, touch off.

kindly *a.* (*kind, benevolent*) accommodating, altruistic, amiable, amicable, benevolent, caring, charitable, compassionate, considerate, cordial, decent, generous, giving, good-natured, helpful, kind, kind-hearted, magnanimous, nice, philanthropic, pleasant, sympathetic, thoughtful, understanding, warm-hearted. ANTONYMS: cruel, harsh, mean, nasty, unkind, unsympathetic.

kindness *n.* (*the fact or condition of being kind, kind behaviour*) affection, altruism, amiability, amicability, benevolence, big-heartedness, charity, compassion, consideration, cordiality, decency, friendliness, generosity, geniality, goodness, goodwill, hospitality, indulgence, kind-heartedness, leniency, magnanimity, mercy, neighbourliness, niceness, philanthropy, pleasantness, soft-heartedness, sympathy, tender-heartedness, thoughtfulness, tolerance, understanding, warmth. ANTONYMS: hard-heartedness, harshness, meanness, mercilessness, nastiness, unkindness.

kindred *n.* **1** (*relatives, kin*) connections, family, (*coll.*) folks, kin, kinsfolk, kinsmen, kinswomen, kith and kin, people, relations, relatives. **2** (*relationship by blood or marriage*) blood ties, family ties, kinship, relationship, ties.
~*a.* **1** (*related by blood or marriage*) cognate, connected, related. **2** (*of like nature or qualities, sympathetic*) allied, corresponding, like, similar. ANTONYMS: different, dissimilar.

king *n.* **1** (*the male sovereign of a nation, esp. a hereditary sovereign of an independent state*) monarch, ruler. **2** (*a person who or thing which is pre-eminent in any sphere*) (*sl.*) big shot, (*sl.*) big wheel, kingpin, leading light, luminary, star, (*coll.*) superstar.

kingdom *n.* **1** (*the territory under the rule of a king or queen*) country, land, monarchy, nation, realm, state. **2** (*a domain, a territory*) area, domain, field, province, sphere, territory. **3** (*the position or attributes of a king*) kingship, sovereignty.

kink *n.* **1** (*a twist or abrupt bend in a rope, thread etc.*) bend, coil, crimp, curl, twist. **2** (*a prejudice, a whim*) deviation, eccentricity, fetish, foible, idiosyncrasy, perversion, quirk, vagary. **3** (*an imperfection*) complication, defect, difficulty, fault, flaw, hitch, imperfection. **4** (*a cramp in part of the body*) cramp, crick, pain, spasm, stab of pain, twinge.

kinky *a.* **1** (*given to abnormal sexual practices*) abnormal, depraved, deviant, perverted, unnatural, warped. ANTONYMS: normal. **2** (*eccentric, odd*) bizarre, eccentric, odd, (*sl.*) off-the-wall, outlandish, outré, peculiar, queer, quirky, strange, unconventional, (*sl.*) wacko. ANTONYMS: conventional, normal, usual. **3** (*twisted, curly*) bent, coiled, crimped, curled, curly, twisted. ANTONYMS: straight.

kinship *n.* (*relationship by blood*) family ties, kindred, relationship, ties.

kiosk *n.* (*an open-fronted structure for the sale of newspapers etc.*) booth, news-stand, stall, stand.

kismet *n.* (*fate, destiny*) destiny, fate, fortune, predestination, preordination, providence.

kiss *n.* (*a touch with the lips, esp. in affection or as a salutation*) embrace, French kiss, (*formal*) osculation, peck, peck on the cheek, (*sl.*) smacker, smack on the lips, (*sl.*) smooch, (*coll.*) snog.
~*v.t.* **1** (*to press or touch with the lips, esp. in affection or as a salutation*) (*coll.*) canoodle, embrace, (*coll.*) neck, (*formal*) osculate, peck, (*sl.*) smooch, (*coll.*) snog. **2** ((*of a ball or balls*) *in snooker, billiards etc., to touch lightly in passing*) brush, glance off, graze, touch.

kit *n.* **1** (*the equipment needed for a particular job, sport etc.*) accoutrements, apparatus, equipment, gear, implements, instruments, outfit, paraphernalia, supplies, tackle, things, tools, trappings, utensils. **2** (*the clothes needed for a particular activity, e.g. playing football*) clothes, clothing, colours, dress, gear, outfit, rig-out, strip, uniform.
~*v.t.* (*to fit out with the necessary clothes or*

equipment) arm, deck out, equip, fit out, (*coll.*) fix up with, furnish with, provide with, rig out, supply with.

knack *n.* (*a trick or an adroit way of doing a thing*) aptitude, bent, capacity, dexterity, expertise, expertness, facility, flair, forte, genius, gift, skill, talent, trick.

knead *v.t.* **1** (*to work up* (*flour, clay etc.*) *into a plastic mass by pressing and folding it with the hands*) blend, form, manipulate, press, shape, squeeze, work. **2** (*to pummel and press with the heel of the hand in massage*) manipulate, massage, rub.

kneel *v.i.* (*to bend or incline the knees*) bend the knees, fall to one's knees, genuflect, get down on one's knees.

knell *n.* **1** (*the sound of a bell when struck, esp. for a death or funeral*) peal, pealing, ring, ringing, sound, toll, tolling. **2** (*an evil omen, a death blow*) beginning of the end, death-knell, end.

knickers *n.pl.* (*women's underpants*) bloomers, briefs, drawers, (*coll.*) panties, pants.

knick-knack *n.* (*any little ornamental article*) bauble, bibelot, gewgaw, ornament, piece of bric-a-brac, trifle, trinket.

knife *v.t.* (*to stab or cut with a knife*) cut, impale, pierce, run through, slash, stab, transfix.

knit *v.t.* **1** (*to join closely together, to unite*) ally, bind, connect, draw together, intertwine, join, link, tie, unite. ANTONYMS: divide, separate. **2** (*to contract into folds or wrinkles*) crease, furrow, pucker, wrinkle.
~*n.* (*a knitted garment, knitted fabric*) (*coll.*) cardie, cardigan, jersey, jumper, pullover, sweater, (*coll.*) woolly.

knob *n.* **1** (*a rounded protuberance, usu. at the end of something*) boss, bump, knot, knur, lump, protrusion, swelling. **2** (*a rounded handle of a door, drawer etc.*) door handle, doorknob, handle, switch. **3** (*a small lump* (*of coal, sugar etc.*)) lump, nub.

knock *v.t.* **1** (*to strike so as to make a sound, to hit*) bang, batter, (*coll.*) belt, box, buffet, (*coll.*) clip, (*coll.*) clout, cuff, hit, punch, rap, slap, smack, strike, thump, thwack, (*coll.*) wallop. **2** (*coll.*) (*to criticize*) censure, condemn, criticize, deprecate, disparage, find fault with, (*coll.*) lambast, (*coll.*) pan, pick holes in, run down, (*sl.*) slag off, (*coll.*) slam, (*coll.*) slate. ANTONYMS: admire, praise, rave about.
~*v.i.* **1** (*to strike hard or smartly* (*at, against, together etc.*)) bang, hammer, pound, rap, strike, tap. **2** (*to collide* (*with*)) bang (into),

bump (into), collide (with), crash (into), dash (against), knock (into), smash (into).
~*n.* **1** (*a blow*) bang, (*coll.*) belt, blow, box, buffet, (*coll.*) clip, (*coll.*) clout, cuff, punch, rap, slap, smack, thump, thwack, (*coll.*) wallop. **2** (*a rap, esp. on a door for admittance or attention*) bang, rap, rat-tat, tap. **3** (*an unpleasant experience, a setback*) bad luck, blow, misfortune, reversal, setback. **to knock about/ around 1** (*to strike with repeated blows*) abuse, batter, beat, beat up, (*coll.*) belt, hit, ill-treat, maltreat, mistreat, punch, strike. **2** (*to wander about, to lead an irregular life*) gallivant, ramble, range, roam, rove, travel around, wander. **to knock against 1** (*to collide with*) bang into, bump into, crash against, dash against, knock into, smash into. **2** (*to encounter casually*) (*coll.*) bump into, come across, encounter, meet, meet by chance, run into, stumble upon. **to knock back 1** (*to drink quickly, to eat up*) down, drain, gulp down, quaff, swallow, toss off. **2** (*to shock*) amaze, appal, astonish, astound, dumbfound, horrify, shock, (*coll.*) stagger. **3** (*to reject, to rebuff*) decline, give the thumbs down to, rebuff, refuse, reject, say no to, turn down. ANTONYMS: accept, give the thumbs up to, say yes to. **to knock down 1** (*to fell with a blow*) (*sl.*) deck, fell, floor, throw to the floor. **2** (*to demolish*) demolish, level, pull down, raze, raze to the ground. **3** (*to lower in price, quality etc.*) bring down, cut, decrease, lower, put down, reduce, slash. ANTONYMS: increase, put up, raise. **to knock off 1** (*to cease work*) call it a day, (*coll.*) clock off, finish, finish work, (*coll.*) shut up shop, stop work. ANTONYMS: (*coll.*) clock on, start work. **2** (*to deduct* (*from a price etc.*)) deduct, subtract, take off. ANTONYMS: add on. **3** (*to steal*) filch, (*sl.*) nick, pilfer, (*coll.*) pinch, purloin, steal, thieve. **to knock out 1** (*to make unconscious by a blow to the head*) floor, (*coll.*) kayo, knock cold, knock unconscious, (*coll.*) KO, prostrate. **2** (*to eliminate from a contest by defeating*) beat, defeat, eliminate, put out. **3** (*to astonish or impress*) amaze, astound, (*coll.*) bowl over, dazzle, impress, overwhelm. **to knock up 1** (*to arouse by knocking*) awaken, call, get (someone) out of bed, rouse, wake, wake up. **2** (*to fatigue, to exhaust*) debilitate, enervate, exhaust, fatigue, tire out, wear out, weary. ANTONYMS: refresh. **3** (*to put together or make up hastily*) improvise, (*coll.*) knock together, prepare hastily, (*coll.*) throw together. **4** (*to make* (*someone*) *pregnant*) (*coll.*) get (someone) in the family way, (*sl.*) give (someone) a bun in the oven, impregnate, make (someone) pregnant, (*sl.*) put (someone) in the club, (*sl.*) put (someone) up the spout. **5** (*to practise before starting to play a ball game*) have a practice game, practise, warm up.

knockout *n.* **1** (*a blow that knocks the opponent out*) coup de grâce, (*coll.*) kayo, (*coll.*) KO. **2** (*a marvel, a wonder*) (*coll.*) hit, marvel, sensation, (*coll.*) smash hit, triumph, (*coll.*) winner, wonder. ANTONYMS: failure, (*coll.*) flop.

knoll *n.* (*a rounded hill, a mound*) barrow, hillock, mound.

knot *n.* **1** (*the interlacement or intertwining of a rope or ropes, cords etc.*) join, ligature, loop, twist. **2** (*a group, a cluster*) bunch, clump, cluster, collection, group. **3** (*a protuberance or excrescence*) excrescence, gnarl, knob, knur, knurl, lump, node, protuberance.
~*v.t.* (*to tie in a knot or knots*) bind, loop, secure, tether, tie.

knotty *a.* **1** (*full of knots*) bumpy, gnarled, knotted, knurled, lumpy, nodular. ANTONYMS: smooth. **2** (*perplexing, difficult to solve*) baffling, Byzantine, complex, complicated, difficult, hard, intricate, mystifying, perplexing, puzzling, thorny, tricky, troublesome. ANTONYMS: easy, simple.

know *v.t.* **1** (*to have a clear and certain perception of*) be aware of, be cognizant of, be conscious of, perceive, realize, recognize, sense. ANTONYMS: be unaware of, be unconscious of. **2** (*to recognize from memory or description, to identify*) differentiate, distinguish, identify, recognize, tell, tell which is which. **3** (*to be acquainted with*) associate with, be acquainted with, be friendly with, have dealings with, have met. **4** (*to have personal experience of*) be acquainted with, be familiar with, have experienced, have experience of, have undergone. **5** (*to be familiar with*) be acquainted with, be conversant with, be familiar with, comprehend, have grasped, have knowledge of, have learned, have studied, understand. ANTONYMS: be ignorant of, have no knowledge of.

know-how *n.* (*specialized skill, expertise*) ability, adroitness, aptitude, capability, dexterity, expertise, faculty, flair, knack, knowledge, proficiency, savoir faire, skilfulness, skill, talent.

knowing *a.* **1** (*conscious, deliberate*) aware, conscious, deliberate, intended, intentional, on purpose. ANTONYMS: accidental, unconscious. **2** (*sharp, cunning*) alert, astute, canny, clever, (*sl.*) clued up, discerning, perceptive, sharp, well-informed, worldly. **3** (*showing that one understands something*) aware, eloquent, expressive, meaningful, significant.

knowingly *adv.* (*consciously, deliberately*) by design, calculatedly, consciously, deliberately, intentionally, on purpose, purposefully, willingly. ANTONYMS: accidentally, unconsciously, unwillingly.

knowledge *n.* **1** (*familiarity or understanding gained by experience or study; an instance of this*) acquaintanceship, conversance, experience, familiarity. ANTONYMS: inexperience, lack of familiarity. **2** (*learning, the sum of what is known*) edification, education, enlightenment, erudition, instruction, learning, letters, scholarship, schooling, wisdom. **3** (*certain or clear apprehension of truth or fact*) apprehension, awareness, cognition, comprehension, consciousness, discernment, grasp, judgement, recognition, savoir faire, understanding. ANTONYMS: ignorance, unawareness. **4** (*information, notice*) data, facts, (*coll.*) gen, information, notice.

knowledgeable *a.* **1** (*intelligent; well informed*) educated, informed, intelligent, learned, scholarly, well-informed, well-read. ANTONYMS: ill-informed, uneducated. **2** (*having knowledge of*) acquainted with, conversant with, experienced in, expert in, familiar with, having knowledge of, well-informed about. ANTONYMS: inexperienced in, unacquainted with.

known *a.* (*publicly acknowledged*) acknowledged, admitted, avowed, confessed, declared, proclaimed, published, recognized. ANTONYMS: unacknowledged, undeclared, unknown.

knuckle *v.i.* **to knuckle under** (*to bow to the pressure of authority*) accede, capitulate, give in, give way, submit, surrender, yield. ANTONYMS: resist.

kowtow *v.i.* (*to act obsequiously*) bow and scrape, (*sl.*) brown-nose, curry favour, fawn, grovel, humble oneself, toady.

kudos *n.* (*glory, credit*) acclaim, credit, distinction, esteem, fame, glory, honour, praise, prestige, renown, repute, tribute. ANTONYMS: discredit, disrepute, ignominy, infamy.

L

label n. 1 (*a piece of paper, plastic or other material attached to an object to indicate contents or other particulars*) docket, flag, ID, identifier, mark, marker, stamp, sticker, tag, tally, ticket. 2 (*a descriptive phrase associated with a person, group etc.*) characterization, classification, description, designation, epithet, identification, sobriquet. 3 (*a firm's trade name or logo*) brand, company, hallmark, logo, mark, trade mark, trade name.
~v.t. 1 (*to affix a label to*) earmark, flag, imprint, mark, stamp, tag, tally, ticket. 2 (*to describe, to categorize*) brand, call, categorize, characterize, class, classify, define, describe, designate, identify, name, pigeon-hole.

laborious a. 1 (*difficult, arduous*) arduous, backbreaking, burdensome, difficult, exhausting, fatiguing, gruelling, hard, Herculean, onerous, strenuous, taxing, tiresome, toilsome, tough, uphill, wearing, wearisome. ANTONYMS: easy, effortless. 2 (*forced, laboured*) forced, laboured, overworked, ponderous, strained, unnatural. ANTONYMS: fluent, natural. 3 (*industrious, assiduous*) assiduous, determined, diligent, dogged, hardworking, indefatigable, industrious, obdurate, obstinate, painstaking, persevering, persistent, relentless, scrupulous, sedulous, steadfast, thorough, tireless, unflagging, untiring. ANTONYMS: indolent, lazy.

labour n. 1 (*physical or mental exertion, the performance of work*) donkey work, drudgery, effort, elbow grease, exertion, grind, industry, laboriousness, pains, slavery, strain, (*coll.*) sweat, toil, travail, work. ANTONYMS: idleness. 2 (*workers, esp. manual workers, usu. as opposed to management*) employees, hands, labourers, workers, workforce. ANTONYMS: management. 3 (*a task, esp. a task requiring great effort*) challenge, chore, job, task, undertaking. 4 (*the process of childbirth from the start of frequent uterine contractions to delivery*) childbirth, confinement, delivery, parturition, travail.
~v.i. 1 (*to work hard, to exert oneself*) drudge, exert oneself, grind, slave, sweat, toil, travail, work hard. ANTONYMS: relax, rest. 2 (*to strive, to work (for, to do)*) endeavour, strain, strive, work. 3 (*to be burdened or handicapped (by)*) be burdened (by), be deceived (by), be deluded (by), be disadvantaged (by), be handicapped (by), endure, suffer. 4 ((*of ships) to pitch heavily*) heave, pitch, roll, toss.

~v.t. (*to overelaborate, to deal with at too great length*) belabour, dwell on, harp on, (*coll.*) make a production of, overdo, overelaborate, overemphasize, strain.

laboured a. 1 (*showing signs of strain, effort or contrivance*) affected, artificial, contrived, elaborate, excessive, ornate, overdone, overembellished, overworked, overwrought, ponderous, studied, unnatural, unspontaneous. ANTONYMS: fluent, natural, spontaneous. 2 ((*of breathing) performed with difficulty*) awkward, difficult, forced, heavy, laborious, stiff, strained.

labourer n. (*a person who performs work requiring manual labour but little skill*) blue-collar worker, drudge, hand, manual worker, navvy, unskilled worker, worker, working man, working woman.

labyrinth n. 1 (*a structure composed of intricate winding passages, paths etc., a maze*) coil, maze. 2 (*an intricate combination, arrangement etc.*) complexity, complication, convolution, entanglement, intricacy, jungle, perplexity, puzzle, riddle, snarl, tangle, windings.

labyrinthine a. 1 (*like a labyrinth or maze*) Byzantine, circuitous, convoluted, Daedalian, gnarled, Gordian, knotted, knotty, mazelike, mazy, sinuous, snarled, tangled, tortuous, twisting, winding. 2 (*complex, very difficult to understand*) baffling, complex, complicated, confounding, confused, confusing, enigmatic, intricate, involved, perplexing, puzzling. ANTONYMS: simple, straightforward.

lace n. 1 (*a kind of ornamental network of threads forming a fabric of open texture*) filigree, lacework, mesh, net, netting, openwork, tatting, web, webbing. 2 (*a cord or string used to bind or fasten*) bootlace, cord, lacing, shoelace, shoestring, string, thong, tie.
~v.t. 1 (*to fasten by means of a lace or string*) attach, bind, close, do up, fasten, tie. ANTONYMS: undo. 2 (*to add a small quantity of spirits, a drug to*) fortify, spike, strengthen. 3 (*to introduce into or intermingle with*) intermingle with, introduce into, mix in. 4 (*to intertwist or interweave (with thread etc.)*) interlace, intertwine, intertwist, interweave, string, thread, twine, weave. ANTONYMS: unravel.

lacerate v.t. 1 (*to tear, to mangle*) claw, cut, gash,

jag, maim, mangle, mutilate, rip, slash, tear. ANTONYMS: mend. **2** (*to distress or afflict severely*) afflict, distress, harrow, hurt, pain, rend, torment, torture, wound.

lack *n.* (*deficiency, need (of)*) absence, dearth, deficiency, deficit, deprivation, destitution, inadequacy, insufficiency, need, paucity, privation, scantiness, scarcity, shortage, shortcoming, shortness, want. ANTONYMS: abundance, plenty.
~*v.t.* (*to be in need of, to be deficient in*) be deficient in, be in need of, be short of, be without, miss, need, require, want. ANTONYMS: have, possess.

lackey *n.* **1** (*a servile political follower or hanger-on*) (*coll.*) arselicker, creature, fawner, flatterer, follower, hanger-on, minion, parasite, pawn, puppet, sycophant, toady, tool, (*coll.*) yes-man. **2** (*a menial attendant*) attendant, flunkey, footman, manservant, menial, servant, underling, valet. ANTONYMS: master.

lacklustre *a.* (*dull, without brightness*) bland, boring, colourless, dismal, drab, dreary, dry, dull, flat, insipid, leaden, lifeless, muted, slow, two-dimensional, unimaginative, uninspired, uninteresting, vapid. ANTONYMS: brilliant, exciting.

laconic *a.* (*using few words, concise*) brief, compact, concise, crisp, curt, pithy, sententious, short, succinct, terse, to the point. ANTONYMS: verbose, wordy.

lad *n.* **1** (*a boy, a youth*) boy, juvenile, kid, stripling, young man, youngster, youth. **2** (*a man; a fellow*) (*coll.*) chap, companion, fellow, guy, man, mate. **3** (*an extrovert, audacious or roguish man*) extrovert, rogue.

lady *n.* **1** (*a woman regarded as being of refinement or social standing*) baroness, noble, noblewoman, peeress. ANTONYMS: commoner. **2** (*a polite term for a woman*) (*sl., esp. N.Am.*) dame, female, woman.

ladylike *a.* (*refined, graceful*) courtly, cultured, decorous, elegant, genteel, graceful, gracious, modest, polished, polite, proper, refined, respectable, well-bred. ANTONYMS: discourteous, unseemly.

lag *v.i.* (*to fall behind*) dally, dawdle, delay, (*coll.*) drag one's feet, fall behind, hang behind, idle, linger, loiter, saunter, straggle, tarry, trail. ANTONYMS: hurry.

laggard *n.* (*a loiterer*) dawdler, idler, lingerer, loafer, loiterer, lounger, saunterer, (*coll.*) skiver, slouch, slowcoach, sluggard, snail, straggler.

laid-back *a.* (*relaxed, casual*) casual, (*coll.*) cool, easygoing, free and easy, relaxed, unflappable. ANTONYMS: tense, (*coll.*) uptight.

laid up *a.* (*ill; confined to bed or the house*) bedridden, confined to bed, housebound, ill, immobilized, incapacitated, injured, (*coll.*) out of action, (*coll.*) out of commission, sick. ANTONYMS: recovered, up and about, well.

lair *n.* **1** (*the den or retreat of a wild animal*) burrow, cave, covert, den, earth, hole, hollow, nest, retreat, tunnel. **2** (*a person's private room or place, a den*) den, hideaway, hideout, (*coll.*) hidey-hole, refuge, retreat, sanctuary.

lambent *a.* **1** ((*of flame or light*) *playing or moving about, touching slightly without burning*) dancing, flickering, fluttering, licking, playing, touching, twinkling. ANTONYMS: steady. **2** (*softly radiant*) gleaming, glistening, glowing, luminous, lustrous, radiant, refulgent, shimmering. ANTONYMS: dull. **3** ((*of wit*) *light, sparkling*) brilliant, light, sparkling, vivacious.

lame *a.* **1** (*disabled in the foot or leg*) crippled, disabled, handicapped. **2** (*limping, halting*) defective, halting, hobbling, impaired, incapacitated, limping. **3** ((*of an excuse, argument*) *unsatisfactory, unconvincing*) awkward, clumsy, feeble, flimsy, half-baked, implausible, inadequate, ineffective, insufficient, pathetic, poor, thin, unconvincing, unpersuasive, unsatisfactory, weak. ANTONYMS: convincing, strong.
~*v.t.* (*to cripple, to disable*) cripple, disable, hobble, incapacitate.

lament *v.i.* (*to mourn, to wail*) cry, grieve, mourn, wail.
~*v.t.* **1** (*to bewail, to mourn over*) bemoan, bewail, keen over, mourn over, sorrow over, weep over. **2** (*to deplore, to express regret or remorse for*) complain about, deplore, regret, rue. ANTONYMS: rejoice in.
~*n.* **1** (*a passionate expression of sorrow in cries or complaints*) complaint, keening, lamentation, moaning, mourning, ululation, wail. **2** (*an elegy, a dirge*) dirge, elegy, knell. **3** (*a mournful song or melody*) monody, requiem, threnody.

lamentable *a.* **1** (*very unfortunate, deplorable*) awful, deplorable, despicable, intolerable, regrettable, terrible, unfortunate, unsatisfactory. ANTONYMS: excellent, satisfactory. **2** (*wretched*) desperate, low, meagre, mean, miserable, pitiful, poor, sorry, woeful, wretched. **3** (*mournful, sad*) distressing, grievous, harrowing, mournful, sad, sorrowful, tragic. ANTONYMS: cheerful, happy, rejoicing.

lamentation *n.* **1** (*an audible expression of grief*) dirge, grief, grieving, keening, lament, moan, mourning, plaint. ANTONYMS: rejoicing. **2** (*a wail*) crying, sobbing, ululation, wailing, weeping.

lampoon *n.* (*a satire, often a scurrilous personal one*) burlesque, caricature, mockery, parody, pasquinade, satire, (*coll.*) send-up, skit, squib, (*coll.*) take-off.

~v.t. (*to write lampoons about; to satirize*) burlesque, caricature, mock, parody, pasquinade, put down, ridicule, run down, satirize, (*coll.*) send up, squib, (*coll.*) take off.

lance n. (*a thrusting weapon consisting of a long shaft with a sharp point*) assegai, javelin, pike, spear.
~v.t. (*to pierce with or as with a lance*) cut, incise, open, pierce, prick, puncture, slit, stab.

land n. **1** (*the solid portion of the earth's surface, as distinct from the oceans and seas*) dry land, earth, ground, landmass, terra firma. **2** (*this solid surface considered as a usable commodity, ground*) dirt, earth, loam, mould, sod, soil, turf. **3** (*a country or nation*) country, fatherland, homeland, motherland, nation, native land, state. **4** (*a district, a region*) area, district, empire, province, realm, region, territory. **5** (*landed property, real estate*) acreage, demesne, grounds, property, real estate, realty.
~v.t. (*to win or secure* (*a prize, business deal*)) acquire, attain, bag, capture, catch, get, obtain, secure, win.
~v.i. **1** (*to come or go on shore*) berth, disembark, dock, go ashore. **2** (*to return to the ground after a flight, leap etc.*) alight, come down, come to earth, come to rest, ground, settle on, splash down, touch down.

landing n. **1** (*the act or an instance of returning to earth after a flight, leap etc.*) docking, landfall, splashdown, touchdown. **2** (*the act or an instance of going or setting on land from a vessel*) alighting, deplaning, disembarkation. **3** (*a place for disembarking or alighting*) dock, jetty, pier, quay, stage, strip, wharf.

landlady n. **1** (*a woman who lets a building, lodgings etc. to a tenant*) freeholder, lessor, owner, proprietor. **2** (*a woman who keeps a public house or a boarding house*) host, hostess, hotelier, hotel-keeper, innkeeper, licensee, manager, publican, restaurateur.

landlord n. **1** (*a man who lets a building, lodgings etc. to a tenant*) freeholder, lessor, owner, proprietor. **2** (*a man who keeps a public house or a boarding house*) host, hotelier, hotel-keeper, innkeeper, licensee, manager, publican, restaurateur.

landmark n. **1** (*a prominent object on land serving as a guide*) feature, monument. **2** (*an important event in history etc.*) crisis, milestone, monument, turning point, watershed. **3** (*anything set up to mark the boundaries of land*) benchmark, boundary, cairn, guide-post, milepost, signpost.

landscape n. (*an extensive area of ground, esp. in the country, regarded as a setting or scenery*) aspect, countryside, outlook, panorama, prospect, scene, scenery, view, vista.

landslide n. (*a landslip*) avalanche, landslip, rockfall.
~a. ((*of a victory or majority in an election*) *receiving many more votes than others*) decisive, overwhelming, runaway.

language n. **1** (*the communication of ideas by articulate sounds or words of agreed meaning*) communication, conversation, discourse, expression, interaction, interchange, parlance, speech, talk, utterance, verbalization, vocalization. **2** (*the vocabulary peculiar to a nation or people*) argot, cant, dialect, idiom, jargon, (*coll.*) lingo, lingua franca, patois, speech, terminology, tongue, vernacular, vocabulary. **3** (*the phraseology or wording* (*of a book, speech etc.*)) diction, phraseology, phrasing, style, wording, words.

languid a. **1** (*lacking energy; indisposed to exertion*) apathetic, indifferent, lackadaisical, languorous, lazy, listless, slothful, spiritless, unenthusiastic, uninterested. ANTONYMS: enthusiastic, spirited. **2** (*limp, slack*) drooping, exhausted, faint, feeble, flagging, languishing, limp, pining, sickly, slack, tired, weak, weary. **3** (*lacking animation, slow-moving*) dull, heavy, inactive, inert, lethargic, slow-moving, sluggish, torpid. ANTONYMS: energetic, vigorous.

languish v.i. **1** (*to become weak or sluggish*) decline, fail, faint, flag, sicken, waste, weaken, wilt, wither. ANTONYMS: prosper, thrive. **2** (*to suffer hardship or deprivation*) rot, suffer, waste away. **3** (*to fall off, to fade*) fade, fall off, slacken. **4** (*to droop, to pine* (*for*)) desire, hanker (after), long (for), pine (for), sigh (for), want, yearn (for).

languor n. **1** (*lack of energy*) apathy, ennui, indolence, inertia, languidness, lassitude, laziness, lethargy, listlessness, sluggishness, torpor. ANTONYMS: enthusiasm. **2** (*faintness, weakness*) debility, enervation, exhaustion, faintness, fatigue, feebleness, frailty, heaviness, tiredness, weakness, weariness. ANTONYMS: energy. **3** (*a pleasantly relaxed or sleepy state*) doziness, dreaminess, drowsiness, sleepiness, sloth. **4** (*oppressive stillness* (*of the air etc.*)) calm, hush, lull, oppressiveness, silence, stillness, tranquillity.

lank a. **1** (*lean, long and thin*) angular, attenuated, bony, emaciated, gangling, gaunt, lanky, lean, long, raw-boned, scraggy, scrawny, shrunken-looking, skinny, slender, slim, spare, tall, thin. ANTONYMS: dumpy, stunted. **2** (*of hair*) *long, straight and falling limply*) dull, lifeless, limp, long, lustreless, straggling, straight.

lanky a. ((*of a person, limb*) *tall or long, thin and rather ungainly*) angular, bony, gangling, gaunt, long, loose-jointed, loose-limbed, rangy, raw-boned, scraggy, scrawny, spare, tall, thin, ungainly, (*coll.*) weedy. ANTONYMS: portly, stocky.

lap¹ *n.* **1** (*one circuit of a racecourse, running track etc.*) circle, circuit, course, orbit, round, tour. **2** (*a stage of a journey or similar undertaking*) leg, part, stage, stretch.

~*v.t.* **1** (*to twist, to roll* (*around, about etc.*)) roll, turn, twist, wrap. **2** (*to enfold, to enwrap*) enfold, enwrap, fold, swaddle, swathe.

lap² *v.t.* **1** (*to drink or consume by lapping*) drink, lick, sip, sup. **2** ((*of water*) *to strike against* (*the shore, the side of a boat*) *with a rippling sound*) gurgle, plash, purl, ripple, slap, splash, swish, wash.

lapse *v.i.* **1** (*to glide, to pass insensibly or by degrees*) drift, glide, slide, slip. **2** (*to decline into or revert to a worse or inferior state*) decline, degenerate, deteriorate, drop, fail, fall, revert, sink. **3** (*to discontinue one's membership of or support for an organization*) discontinue, end, finish, stop, terminate. **4** (*to become void*) become obsolete, expire, run out, void. ANTONYMS: continue.

~*n.* **1** (*a mistake, an error*) deviation, error, failing, indiscretion, mistake, negligence, omission, oversight, slip. **2** (*a falling into disuse or decay*) backsliding, decline, descent, deterioration, drop, fall, relapse. ANTONYMS: improvement. **3** (*an interval of time, esp. a break in the occurrence of something; the imperceptible passage of time*) break, gap, intermission, interruption, interval, lull, passage, pause. ANTONYMS: continuation.

larceny *n.* (*the unlawful taking away of another's personal goods with intent to convert them for one's own use*) burglary, misappropriation, pilfering, robbery, stealing, theft.

large *a.* **1** (*great in size, number, quantity, extent or capacity*) great, numerous. **2** (*big, bulky*) big, bulky, colossal, considerable, elephantine, enormous, giant, gigantic, (*coll.*) ginormous, huge, immense, jumbo, massive, (*coll.*) mega, monumental, sizeable, stout, substantial, vast. ANTONYMS: slight, small. **3** (*wide, extensive*) broad, extensive, wide. ANTONYMS: narrow. **4** (*wide in range or scope*) comprehensive, far-reaching. **5** (*operating on a large scale*) large-scale, roomy, spacious, sweeping, wide. **6** (*having breadth of understanding or sympathy*) sympathetic, understanding. **7** (*liberal, generous*) generous, grand, grandiose, lavish, liberal, prodigal. ANTONYMS: mean, petty. **8** (*free, unrestrained*) free, licentious, roaming, unconfined, unrestrained.

largely *adv.* (*to a large extent*) as a whole, by and large, chiefly, considerably, extensively, generally, greatly, in general, mainly, mostly, predominantly, primarily, principally, to a great extent, widely. ANTONYMS: partly.

lark *n.* **1** (*a prank*) antic, caper, escapade, fling,

frolic, fun, gambol, game, jape, mischief, prank, revel, romp, skylark, spree. **2** (*any activity or undertaking*) activity, business, undertaking.

~*v.i.* (*to behave in a carefree or mischievous way*) caper, cavort, cut capers, frolic, gambol, have fun, make mischief, misbehave, play, rollick, romp, sport.

lascivious *a.* **1** (*lewd, wanton*) concupiscent, (*sl.*) horny, lecherous, lewd, libidinous, licentious, lustful, prurient, randy, salacious, sensual, unchaste, voluptuous, wanton. ANTONYMS: chaste. **2** (*exciting or provoking lust*) bawdy, (*sl.*) blue, coarse, crude, dirty, exciting, indecent, lust-provoking, obscene, offensive, pornographic, ribald, scurrilous, smutty, stimulating, suggestive, vulgar.

lash *n.* **1** (*a stroke with a whip*) blow, hit, stripe, (*coll.*) swipe, whiplash. **2** (*a whip, a scourge*) cat-o'-nine-tails, horsewhip, scourge, whip.

~*v.t.* **1** (*to whisk or flick* (*e.g. a tail*) *suddenly or with a jerk in a menacing fashion*) flick, jerk, whisk. **2** (*to strike or flog with anything pliant and tough*) beat, birch, chastise, flagellate, flog, horsewhip, (*coll.*) lam, lambast, scourge, thrash, whip. ANTONYMS: caress, soothe. **3** (*to assail fiercely with satire, reproach etc.*) attack, belabour, berate, blast, castigate, censure, criticize, flay, lambast, lampoon, put down, reproach, ridicule, satirize, scold, tear into, upbraid. ANTONYMS: commend, praise. **4** ((*of rain, waves*) *to beat or dash against*) beat, buffet, dash, drum, hammer, hit, knock, lambast, pound, punch, smack, strike. **5** (*to fasten or bind with a rope or cord*) bind, make fast, rope, secure, strap, tie. ANTONYMS: untie.

lass *n.* (*a young woman, a girl*) (*sl.*) bird, (*sl.*) chick, (*Ir.*) colleen, damsel, girl, maid, maiden, miss, schoolgirl, (*now esp. facet.*) wench, young woman.

lassitude *n.* **1** (*weariness*) exhaustion, fatigue, tiredness, weariness. **2** (*lack of energy or animation*) apathy, drowsiness, dullness, enervation, ennui, heaviness, inertia, languor, lethargy, listlessness, prostration, sluggishness, torpor. ANTONYMS: animation.

last¹ *a.* **1** (*coming after all others or at the end, final*) closing, concluding, final, terminal, ultimate. ANTONYMS: first, foremost. **2** (*conclusive, definitive*) authoritative, conclusive, decisive, definitive. **3** (*utmost, extreme*) extreme, furthest, remotest, utmost. **4** (*next before the present, most recent*) aftermost, at the end, hindmost, latest, most recent, rearmost.

~*n.* (*the end, the conclusion*) close, completion, conclusion, end, ending, finale, finish, termination. ANTONYMS: beginning.

~*adv.* (*after all the others*) after, at the end, behind, in the rear.

last² *v.i.* **1** (*to continue in existence, to go on*) abide, carry on, continue, go on, keep, keep on, persist, remain, stay. ANTONYMS: cease, stop. **2** (*to continue unexhausted or unimpaired, to endure*) endure, hold on, hold out, stand up, survive, wear. ANTONYMS: capitulate, give in.

lasting *a.* **1** (*continuing in existence*) abiding, constant, continuing, eternal, everlasting, long-term, perennial, perpetual, persisting, unceasing, undying, unending. ANTONYMS: ephemeral, transient. **2** (*permanent, durable*) durable, enduring, indelible, permanent, strong. ANTONYMS: flimsy.

latch *n.* (*a fastening for a door, gate etc., consisting of a bolt and catch*) bar, bolt, catch, clamp, fastening, hasp, hook, lock, (*dial.*) sneck.
~*v.t., v.i.* (*to fasten with a latch*) bar, bolt, fasten, lock, make fast, secure.

late *a.* **1** (*tardy, long delayed*) backward, behind, behindhand, belated, delayed, last-minute, overdue, slow, tardy, unpunctual. ANTONYMS: early, punctual. **2** (*far advanced, far on in development*) advanced, developed. **3** (*deceased, departed* (*esp. recently*)) dead, deceased, defunct, departed. **4** (*former; recently in office etc.*) ex-, former, old, past, preceding, previous. **5** (*recent in date*) current, fresh, latest, modern, new, recent, up-to-the-minute.
~*adv.* **1** (*after the proper or usual time*) at the last minute, behindhand, behind time, belatedly, dilatorily, slowly, tardily, unpunctually. ANTONYMS: early, in advance. **2** (*formerly, of old*) formerly, of old.

lately *adv.* (*a short time ago, recently*) just now, latterly, of late, recently.

latent *a.* **1** (*hidden or concealed*) concealed, hidden, veiled. ANTONYMS: visible. **2** (*not seen, not apparent*) implicit, inherent, invisible, lurking, secret, tacit, undeveloped, unexpressed, unrealized, unseen. ANTONYMS: apparent, evident, visible. **3** (*dormant, potential*) dormant, inactive, potential, quiescent.

later *adv.* (*at a later time*) after, afterwards, by and by, in a while, in time, next, subsequently, thereafter. ANTONYMS: earlier.

lateral *a.* (*relating to, at, from or towards the side*) edgeways, flanking, indirect, oblique, side, sideward, sideways.

lather *n.* **1** (*froth or foam made by soap moistened with water*) bubbles, foam, froth, soap, suds. **2** (*a flustered or excited state*) bother, (*coll.*) dither, fever, (*coll.*) flap, fluster, fuss, (*coll.*) state, (*coll.*) stew, (*coll.*) sweat, (*coll.*) tizzy, (*coll.*) twitter.
~*v.i.* (*to form a lather, e.g. by using soap and water*) foam, froth.

~*v.t.* (*to thrash, to flog*) beat, cane, drub, flog, lambast, strike, thrash, whip.

latitude *n.* **1** (*freedom of action; freedom to deviate from a standard or rule*) elbow room, freedom, leeway, liberty. **2** (*absence of strictness, tolerance*) breadth, compass, extent, indulgence, laxity, licence, range, room, scope, space, span, spread, sweep, tolerance, width. ANTONYMS: restriction.

latter *a.* **1** ((*of two*) second, second-mentioned) second. ANTONYMS: former, preceding. **2** ((*of more than two*) last-mentioned) last, last-mentioned, latest. **3** (*coming or happening after something else, later*) later, subsequent. ANTONYMS: antecedent, earlier. **4** (*recent, modern*) modern, present, recent. **5** (*of or relating to the end of a period, life, the world etc.*) closing, concluding, ending, ultimate.

latterly *adv.* (*recently*) hitherto, lately, of late, recently.

lattice *n.* (*a structure of laths or strips of metal or wood crossing and forming openwork*) fretwork, grating, grid, grille, mesh, network, openwork, reticulation, trellis, web.

laud *v.t.* (*to praise, to extol*) acclaim, approve, celebrate, extol, glorify, honour, praise, sing the praises of. ANTONYMS: criticize.

laudable *a.* (*praiseworthy, commendable*) admirable, commendable, creditable, estimable, excellent, meritorious, praiseworthy, worthy. ANTONYMS: blameworthy, contemptible.

laugh *v.i.* **1** (*to express amusement or scorn by inarticulate sounds and the convulsive movements of the face and body*) (*coll.*) bust a gut, chortle, chuckle, crack up, (*coll.*) crease up, giggle, guffaw, howl with laughter, roar with laughter, snigger, split one's sides, titter. ANTONYMS: cry, weep. **2** (*to jeer or scoff* (*at*)) belittle, deride, jeer, lampoon, make fun of, mock, ridicule, scoff, (*sl.*) take the mickey, taunt.
~*n.* **1** (*an act or explosion of laughter*) belly laugh, chortle, chuckle, giggle, guffaw, shriek of laughter, snigger, titter. ANTONYMS: cry, sob. **2** (*someone that causes laughter*) (*sl.*) card, (*coll.*) caution, clown, comedian, (*coll.*) hoot, one, scream, wag, wit. **3** (*something that causes laughter; a bit of fun*) escapade, fun, (*coll.*) hoot, joke, lark.

laughable *a.* **1** (*ludicrous, ridiculous*) absurd, derisory, laughable, ludicrous, nonsensical, preposterous, ridiculous. ANTONYMS: reasonable, sensible. **2** (*exciting laughter, comical*) amusing, comical, diverting, droll, farcical, funny, hilarious, humorous, mirthful, risible. ANTONYMS: serious.

laughter *n.* **1** (*the act or sound of laughing*)

chortling, chuckling, giggling, guffawing, laughing, tittering. ANTONYMS: crying. **2** (*fun*) amusement, fun, glee, hilarity, merriment, mirth. ANTONYMS: gloom.

launch *v.t.* **1** (*to cause to glide into the water* (*e.g. a vessel*), *or take off from land* (*e.g. a space rocket*)) float, send off, set afloat, take off. **2** (*to throw, to propel*) cast, discharge, dispatch, fire, hurl, project, propel, throw. **3** (*to start or set* (*a person etc.*) *going*) begin, commence, initiate, instigate, move, set going, set in motion, start. ANTONYMS: stop, terminate. **4** (*to introduce a new product or publication onto the market*) establish, found, inaugurate, open.

lavatory *n.* (*a room with a toilet and usu. a basin*) (*esp. N Am.*) bathroom, (*sl.*) bog, cloakroom, convenience, gents, (*sl.*) head, (*sl.*) john, ladies, ladies' room, latrine, (*coll.*) little boys' room, little girls' room, (*coll.*) loo, men's room, powder room, privy, public convenience, toilet, urinal, washroom, water closet, WC.

lavish *a.* **1** (*spending or giving with profusion*) bountiful, effusive, free, generous, liberal, munificent, open-handed, unstinting. ANTONYMS: frugal, mean. **2** (*extravagant, unrestrained*) extravagant, prodigal, spendthrift, unrestrained, wild. **3** (*existing or produced in profusion*) abundant, copious, exuberant, fulsome, lush, luxuriant, opulent, plentiful, profuse, prolific, sumptuous. ANTONYMS: scant. **4** (*excessive, superabundant*) exuberant, immoderate, improvident, intemperate, superabundant, thriftless, wasteful. ANTONYMS: thrifty.
~*v.t.* **1** (*to expend or bestow profusely*) deluge, dissipate, expend, heap, pour, shower, spend. ANTONYMS: stint. **2** (*to be excessively free or liberal with*) squander, waste.

law *n.* **1** (*a rule of conduct imposed by authority or accepted by the community as binding*) act, canon, charter, command, commandment, decree, demand, edict, enactment, order, ordinance, regulation, rule, statute. **2** (*a system of such rules regulating the dealings of people within a state, or of states with one another*) code, constitution. **3** (*the practical application of these rules, esp. by trial in courts of justice; litigation*) judicial process, justice, legislation, litigation. **4** (*the interpretation of these rules, the science of legal principles*) jurisprudence. **5** (*a generalized statement of such conditions and their consequences*) axiom, canon, criterion, formula, precept, principle, standard.

lawbreaker *n.* (*a person who violates the law*) criminal, (*coll.*) crook, culprit, felon, offender, sinner, transgressor, villain, wrongdoer.

lawful *a.* **1** (*conformable with law*) constitutional, legal, legalized, licit. ANTONYMS: illegal,

unlawful. **2** (*legitimate, valid*) allowable, authorized, just, legitimate, permissible, proper, right, rightful, valid, warranted. ANTONYMS: forbidden, prohibited.

lawless *a.* **1** (*not subject to or governed by law*) anarchic, chaotic, disorderly, ungoverned, unruly. ANTONYMS: civilized, orderly. **2** (*regardless of or unrestrained by the law*) insubordinate, insurgent, mutinous, rebellious, riotous, seditious. ANTONYMS: law-abiding. **3** (*unbridled, licentious*) licentious, reckless, unbridled, unrestrained, wild. ANTONYMS: restrained.

lawlessness *n.* (*the state of being lawless*) anarchy, chaos, disorder, mob rule, rebelliousness, unruliness.

lawsuit *n.* (*an action in a court of law*) action, argument, case, cause, contest, dispute, litigation, proceedings, prosecution, suit, trial, tribunal.

lawyer *n.* (*a person who practises law, esp. an attorney or solicitor*) advocate, attorney, barrister, (*coll.*) brief, counsel, counsellor, legal adviser, solicitor.

lax *a.* **1** (*not strict; careless*) careless, casual, easygoing, indulgent, lenient, neglectful, negligent, permissive, remiss, slapdash, slipshod, tolerant. ANTONYMS: scrupulous, strict. **2** (*ambiguous, vague*) ambiguous, broad, equivocal, general, imprecise, inaccurate, indefinite, inexact, non-specific, shapeless, vague. ANTONYMS: exact, precise. **3** (*not tight or firm*) flabby, flaccid, loose, slack, soft, yielding.

laxative *n.* (*a laxative medicine*) aperient, cathartic, purgative, purge, salts.

lay¹ *v.t.* **1** (*to cause to lie, to place in a horizontal position*) lay down, rest. ANTONYMS: pick up. **2** (*to put or bring into a certain state or position*) locate, organize, place, position, put. **3** (*to put in proper position*) arrange, dispose, lay out, put in position, set out. **4** (*to put down, to deposit*) deposit, establish, place, plant, posit, put down, set, set down. **5** ((*of a bird*) *to produce* (*eggs*)) bear, deposit, produce. **6** (*to spread on a surface*) apply, spread. **7** (*to cause to be still, to calm*) allay, alleviate, appease, assuage, calm, pacify, quiet, relieve, soothe, still, suppress. ANTONYMS: arouse, disturb. **8** (*to put forward, to present*) advance, bring forward, lodge, offer, present, put forward, submit. ANTONYMS: withdraw. **9** (*to attribute, to impute*) allocate, allot, ascribe, assign, attribute, charge, impute. **10** (*to impose, to inflict*) apply, burden, charge, encumber, enjoin, impose, inflict, saddle, tax. **11** (*to stake, to wager*) bet, gamble, hazard, risk, stake, wager. **12** (*to devise, to prepare*) concoct, contrive, design, devise, hatch, plan, plot, prepare, think out, work out.

13 (*to have sexual intercourse with*) bed, (*taboo sl.*) fuck, (*sl.*) have, (*taboo sl.*) screw, seduce, (*taboo sl.*) shag.
~*n.* **1** (*the way or position in which a region or object is situated*) direction, position, way. **2** (*an act of sexual intercourse*) (*taboo sl.*) fuck, (*taboo sl.*) screw, (*taboo sl.*) shag. **to lay aside 1** (*to give up, to abandon*) abandon, cast aside, dismiss, give up, postpone, put aside, put off, reject, shelve, sideline. **2** (*to store for future use*) lay up, stockpile, store, warehouse. **to lay bare 1** (*to reveal*) disclose, divulge, explain, expose, reveal, show, unveil. **2** (*to strip*) strip, undress. **to lay down 1** (*to put down*) discard, drop, put down, rest. **2** (*to resign, to surrender*) give up, relinquish, resign, surrender, yield. **3** (*to declare; to stipulate*) affirm, assert, assume, declare, establish, ordain, postulate, prescribe, stipulate. **4** (*to formulate, to draw up*) draw up, formulate. **5** (*to record on paper*) commit to paper, set down, write. **to lay in** (*to acquire a store of*) accumulate, acquire, amass, collect, gather, hoard, stockpile, stock up, store, warehouse. **to lay into** (*to assault physically or verbally*) assail, assault, belabour, fight, hit, lambast, let fly at, pitch into, set about, take to task. **to lay off 1** (*to discharge* (*workers*) *permanently*) discharge, dismiss, drop, (*coll.*) fire, let go, make redundant, pay off, (*coll.*) sack. **2** (*to stop*) cease, desist, give up, quit, refrain from, stop. **to lay on 1** (*to provide* (*facility, entertainment*)) cater for, furnish, give, provide. **2** (*to install and supply* (*water, gas*)) install, purvey, supply. **3** (*to impose, to inflict*) impose, inflict. **4** (*to apply*) apply, spread on. **to lay out 1** (*to arrange according to a plan*) arrange, design, plan. **2** (*to spread out*) display, exhibit, spread out. **3** (*to expound, to explain*) argue, explain, expound. **4** (*to expend*) disburse, expend, (*coll.*) fork out, invest, pay, (*coll.*) shell out, spend. **5** (*to knock to the ground or render unconscious*) (*coll.*) knock for six, knock out, knock to the ground, render unconscious. **to lay up 1** (*to store, to save*) accumulate, amass, garner, hoard, keep, preserve, put away, save, store, treasure. **2** ((*of illness*) *to confine* (*someone*) *to their bed or room*) confine, hospitalize, incapacitate. **3** (*to decommission a ship or take out of service*) decommission, retire, take out of commission.

lay[2] *a.* **1** (*of or relating to the people as distinct from the clergy*) laic, non-clerical, secular. ANTONYMS: clerical, ecclesiastical. **2** (*non-professional, lacking specialized knowledge*) amateur, inexpert, non-professional, non-specialist. ANTONYMS: expert, professional, specialist.

lay[3] *n.* (*a lyric song or ballad*) ballad, lyric song, ode, poem, song.

layabout *n.* (*an idle person, a lounger*) (*esp. N Am., coll.*) bum, (*sl.*) couch potato, good-for-

nothing, idler, laggard, loafer, lounger, ne'er-do-well, shirker, (*coll.*) skiver, wastrel.

layer *n.* (*a thickness or anything spread out* (*usu. one of several*)*, a stratum*) bed, film, mantle, ply, row, seam, sheet, stratum, thickness, tier.

layout *n.* **1** (*a planned arrangement of buildings etc.*) arrangement, design, disposition, formation, geography. **2** (*the way in which text, illustrations etc. are arranged on a printed page*) draft, outline, plan.

laze *v.i.* (*to live in idleness*) fritter away, hang around, idle, loaf, lounge around, relax, (*coll.*) veg out, waste time, while away the time. ANTONYMS: work.

laziness *n.* (*the state of being lazy*) dilatoriness, idleness, inactivity, indolence, sloth, slothfulness, sluggishness, tardiness. ANTONYMS: industry.

lazy *a.* **1** (*idle, disinclined to labour or exertion*) dilatory, idle, inactive, indolent, inert, lackadaisical, slack, slothful, workshy. ANTONYMS: active, energetic. **2** ((*of movement*) *slow; languorous*) drowsy, languid, languorous, lethargic, sleepy, slow, sluggish, somnolent, torpid.

lazybones *n.* (*a lazy person, an idler*) idler, loafer, lounger, shirker, (*coll.*) skiver, sleepyhead, sluggard, wastrel.

leach *v.t.* **1** (*to wash out or separate* (*a soluble constituent*) *by percolation*) percolate, seep. **2** (*to strain or drain* (*liquid*) *from some material* (*usu. out or away*)) drain, extract, filter, filtrate, strain.

lead *v.t.* **1** (*to conduct, to guide by taking by the hand or by showing the way*) conduct, convoy, escort, guide, pilot, precede, show the way, steer, usher. **2** (*to direct the actions, opinions etc. of*) direct, marshal. **3** (*to be in command of*) command, control, direct, govern, head, manage, preside over, rule, supervise. **4** (*to direct or induce by persuasion or advice*) bring on, cause, dispose, draw, incline, induce, influence, persuade, prevail, prompt, tend. **5** (*to be ahead of in a race, competition etc.*) exceed, excel, outdo, outstrip, surpass, transcend. **6** (*to live or cause to live* (*a certain kind of life*)) experience, have, live, pass, spend, undergo.
~*n.* **1** (*guidance, direction, esp. by going in front*) direction, guidance. **2** (*command, leadership*) command, leadership, precedence. **3** (*a position ahead of all the others*) first place, pole position, precedence, priority, supremacy, vanguard. **4** (*the distance or amount by which one is ahead*) advantage, edge, margin. **5** (*a cord or strap for leading a dog*) leash, strap. **6** (*an example for others to follow*) example, model. **7** (*a clue*) clue, guide, hint, indication, pointer, suggestion, tip, trace. **8** (*the principal role in a play, film etc.; the*

person playing this role) leading role, principal, protagonist, star part, title role.
~a. (*principal, main*) chief, first, foremost, head, leading, main, premier, primary, prime, principal. **to lead on 1** (*to entice, to draw further towards some end*) attract, beguile, draw, entice, inveigle, lure, seduce, (*coll.*) string along, tempt. **2** (*to fool or trick*) deceive, delude, fool, trick. **to lead up to** (*to pave the way for*) approach, intimate, introduce, make advances, make overtures, pave the way, prepare for, prepare the way.

leaden *a.* **1** (*of the colour of lead, dark*) dark, dingy, grey, greyish, lacklustre, lead-coloured, lowering, lustreless, overcast, sombre. **2** (*heavy, burdensome*) burdensome, crushing, cumbersome, heavy, laboured, onerous, oppressive, plodding, slow, sluggish. **3** (*inert, indisposed to action or exertion*) dismal, dreary, dull, gloomy, inactive, inert, languid, lifeless, listless, spiritless, stiff, stilted, wooden.

leader *n.* (*a chief, a commander*) boss, captain, chief, commander, director, guide, head, pioneer, ringleader, ruler, superior. ANTONYMS: follower, supporter.

leadership *n.* **1** (*the authority, firmness etc. expected of a leader; the ability to lead*) authority, control, direction, directorship, domination, firmness, guidance, initiative, management, sway. **2** (*the leaders of an organization as a group*) administration, management.

leading *a.* **1** (*main, principal*) chief, dominant, main, outstanding, pre-eminent, primary, principal. **2** (*in first position*) best, first, foremost, greatest, highest, superior, supreme. ANTONYMS: lesser, subsidiary. **3** (*guiding, influential*) guiding, influential.

leaf *n.* **1** (*any of the usu. flat, green, lateral organs of plants*) blade, bract, flag, foliole, frond, needle. **2** (*a sheet of paper in a book or manuscript, usu. comprising two pages*) folio, page, sheet.
~v.i. (*to shoot out or produce leaves or foliage*) bud, shoot. **to leaf through** (*to turn the pages of a book, magazine etc., in a casual way*) browse through, dip into, flick through, glance through, riffle, skim, thumb through.

leaflet *n.* (*a handbill, circular*) (*coll.*) advert, bill, booklet, brochure, circular, flyer, handbill, handout, mailshot, pamphlet.

leafy *a.* ((*of a place*) *pleasantly shaded with or abounding in foliage*) green, shaded, shady, verdant, wooded.

league *n.* **1** (*a combination or union for mutual help or the pursuit of common interests*) coalition, combination, consortium, partnership, union. **2** (*a treaty or compact of alliance*) alliance, compact, confederacy, confederation, treaty. **3** (*a category or group*) ability, band, category, class, group, level, order. **4** (*an association of clubs that play matches against one another*) association, fellowship, fraternity, guild, table.

leak *v.i.* **1** (*to let liquid, gas etc. pass in or out through a hole or fissure*) discharge, dribble, drip, pass. **2** ((*of a liquid, gas etc.*) *to pass in or out through a hole or fissure*) escape, exude, ooze, percolate, seep, spill, trickle. **3** (*to urinate*) (*coll.*) piddle, (*taboo sl.*) piss, urinate, (*sl.*) wee.
~v.t. (*to divulge* (*confidential information*)) disclose, divulge, expose, give away, let slip, let the cat out of the bag, make known, pass on, reveal, spill the beans, tell. ANTONYMS: conceal.
~n. **1** (*a crack, hole etc. which accidentally lets water, gas etc. in or out*) aperture, chink, crack, crevice, fissure, hole, opening, puncture, split. **2** (*the oozing of water, gas etc. through such an opening*) drip, escape, leakage, leaking, oozing, percolation, seepage. **3** (*a disclosure of confidential information*) disclosure, divulgence.

leaky *a.* (*having a leak or leaks*) cracked, (*coll.*) holey, leaking, porous, punctured, split, waterlogged.

lean[1] *v.i.* **1** (*to incline one's body from an erect attitude*) bend, incline, list, slant, slope, tilt, tip. **2** (*to incline one's body so as to rest* (*against or upon*)) recline, repose, rest. **3** (*to deviate from a straight or perpendicular line or direction*) deviate, diverge. **4** (*to depend* (*upon*) *as for support*) confide (in), count (on), depend (on), have faith (in), rely (on), trust (in). **5** (*to have a tendency or propensity* (*to or towards*)) be disposed (to), be inclined (to), gravitate (towards), incline (towards), prefer, tend (towards).
~v.t. **1** (*to cause to incline*) incline, prop, tilt. **2** (*to support, to rest* (*upon or against*)) rest, support.

lean[2] *a.* **1** (*thin, without surplus fat or flesh*) angular, bony, emaciated, gaunt, lank, rangy, scraggy, scrawny, sinewy, skinny, slender, slight, slim, spare, thin, wiry. ANTONYMS: chubby, fat. **2** ((*of foodstuffs*) *low in calories or fat*) light, low-calorie, low-fat, non-fattening. ANTONYMS: fattening, fatty. **3** (*meagre, of poor quality*) bare, inadequate, meagre, pitiful, poor, scanty, sparse. ANTONYMS: abundant, rich. **4** (*unproductive, unrewarding*) barren, infertile, unfruitful, unproductive, unremunerative, unrewarding. ANTONYMS: fertile, productive.

leaning *n.* (*inclination, partiality* (*towards or to*)) aptitude (for), bent (for), bias (towards), disposition (to), inclination (towards), liking (for), partiality (for), penchant (for), predilection (for), prejudice (towards), proclivity (to), propensity (to), taste (for), tendency (towards).

leap *v.i.* **1** (*to jump, to spring upwards or forward*) bounce, bound, caper, cavort, clear, frisk, frolic, gambol, hop, jump, skip, spring, vault. **2** (*to act or react swiftly; to rush*) dart, fly, react, rush. **3** ((*of prices*) *to increase suddenly by a large amount*) escalate, increase, rise, rocket, soar, surge. ANTONYMS: drop.

~*v.t.* (*to jump or spring over or across*) clear, jump across, spring over.

~*n.* **1** (*the act of leaping, a jump*) bound, caper, frolic, hop, jump, skip, spring, vault. **2** (*a space or interval*) gap, interval, space. **3** (*a sudden transition*) change, jump, transition. **4** (*a sudden increase*) escalation, increase, rise, surge, upsurge, upswing. ANTONYMS: decrease, drop.

learn *v.t.* **1** (*to acquire knowledge of or skill in by study or instruction*) acquire, attain, comprehend, gather, glean, grasp, imbibe, master, pick up. **2** (*to fix in the memory*) commit to memory, memorize. ANTONYMS: forget. **3** (*to find out, to be informed of*) ascertain, be informed of, detect, determine, discern, discover, find out, hear, (*sl.*) suss out, understand.

learned *a.* **1** (*having acquired learning by study, erudite*) educated, erudite, experienced, expert, lettered, literate, versed, well-informed, well-read. ANTONYMS: ignorant, uneducated. **2** (*skilled, skilful (in)*) skilful, skilled. **3** (*characterized by great learning or scholarship*) academic, bluestocking, cultured, highbrow, intellectual, scholarly.

learner *n.* (*a person who learns*) apprentice, beginner, disciple, neophyte, novice, pupil, scholar, student, trainee. ANTONYMS: expert, master, teacher.

learning *n.* (*knowledge acquired by study, scholarship*) attainment, culture, education, erudition, information, instruction, knowledge, letters, lore, research, scholarship, schooling, study, tuition, wisdom. ANTONYMS: ignorance.

lease *v.t.* (*to grant or to take under lease*) charter, hire, let, loan, rent.

leash *n.* **1** (*a lead for a dog or other animal*) lead, rein, strap, tether. **2** (*something which controls or restrains as if by a leash*) check, curb, hold, restraint.

~*v.t.* **1** (*to bind or fasten by a leash*) bind, fasten, secure, tether, tie up. **2** (*to hold back, to restrain*) check, control, curb, hold back, restrain, suppress.

least *a.* (*less than all others in size, amount etc.*) feeblest, fewest, last, lowest, meanest, minimum, minutest, poorest, slightest, smallest, tiniest. ANTONYMS: greatest, highest, maximum, most.

leave[1] *v.t.* **1** (*to go or depart from*) depart from, go, quit, retire, set out, take off. ANTONYMS: arrive, come, stay. **2** (*to allow to remain when one departs, to go without taking*) forget, lay down, leave behind, mislay. **3** (*to cease to live or work at*) decamp, evacuate, pull out of, relinquish, vacate. ANTONYMS: keep. **4** (*to forsake, to abandon*) abandon, abscond, depart, desert, disappear, exit, flit, forsake, give up, renounce, withdraw from. **5** (*to bequeath*) bequeath, demise, devise, hand down, transmit, will. **6** (*to refrain from removing or interfering with*) forbear, give up, refrain from. **7** (*to cease, to discontinue*) cease, desist from, discontinue, drop, relinquish, stop, surrender. **8** (*to commit, to refer for consideration, approval etc.*) allot, assign, cede, commit, consign, entrust, give over, refer. **to leave off 1** (*to stop, to cease*) cease, end, halt, stop. **2** (*to desist from, to discontinue*) abstain from, break off, desist from, discontinue, (*coll.*) give over, kick, (*coll.*) knock off, refrain. ANTONYMS: continue. **to leave out** (*to omit*) bar, cast aside, count out, disregard, except, exclude, ignore, neglect, omit, overlook, pass over, reject. ANTONYMS: include.

leave[2] *n.* **1** (*permission*) allowance, authorization, concession, consent, dispensation, freedom, liberty, licence, permission, sanction. ANTONYMS: prohibition. **2** (*permission to be absent from duty*) furlough, leave of absence. **3** (*the period of this*) sabbatical, time off. **4** (*the act of departing, a farewell*) adieu, departure, farewell, goodbye, leave-taking, parting, retirement, withdrawal. ANTONYMS: greeting. **5** (*a holiday*) holiday, vacation.

leavings *n.pl.* (*residue, remnant*) bits, dregs, fragments, leftovers, refuse, remains, remnants, residue, scraps, spoil, sweepings, waste.

lecherous *a.* (*feeling or motivated by strong sexual desire*) carnal, concupiscent, lascivious, lewd, libidinous, licentious, lustful, prurient, randy, salacious, unchaste, wanton. ANTONYMS: chaste, virtuous.

lecture *n.* **1** (*a formal expository or instructive discourse on any subject, before an audience or a class*) address, discourse, disquisition, harangue, homily, instruction, lesson, sermon, speech, talk. **2** (*a reproof, a reprimand*) castigation, censure, chiding, (*coll.*) dressing down, (*N Am., coll.*) going-over, rebuke, reprimand, reproof, scolding, (*coll.*) talking-to, (*coll.*) telling-off, (*coll.*) wigging. ~*v.i.* (*to deliver a lecture or lectures*) address, discourse, expound, harangue, hold forth, speak, spout, talk, teach. ~*v.t.* (*to reprimand, to talk seriously to*) admonish, berate, (*coll.*) carpet, castigate, censure, chide, criticize, (*coll.*) give a talking-to, rebuke, reprimand, reprove, scold, (*coll.*) tear off a strip, (*coll.*) tell off, upbraid. ANTONYMS: commend, praise.

ledge *n.* **1** (*a shelf or shelflike projection*) mantle, projection, shelf, sill, step. **2** (*a shelflike ridge or outcrop of rock on a cliff or mountain*) outcrop, ridge.

lee *n.* (*shelter, protection*) cover, protection, refuge, screen, shade, shadow, shelter, shield.

leer *n.* **1** (*an oblique or sly look*) eye, goggle, squint, stare, wink. **2** (*a look expressing a feeling of lasciviousness or triumph*) drool, gloat, grin, ogle, smirk.

lees *n.pl.* **1** (*the sediment of liquor which settles to the bottom*) deposit, grounds, precipitate, sediment, settlings. **2** (*dregs, refuse*) dregs, refuse, remains, residue.

leeway *n.* (*allowable scope, toleration inside defined limits*) (*coll.*) air, elbow room, latitude, margin, play, scope, space.

left *a.* **1** (*relating to or situated on the side that is to the west when a person faces south, as opposed to right*) larboard, left-hand, port, sinistral. **2** (*radical, politically innovative*) leftist, left-wing, radical. ANTONYMS: conservative, right-wing. **3** (*of or relating to socialism or communism*) communist, socialist.

left-handed *a.* **1** (*turning from right to left; turning anticlockwise*) anticlockwise, counter-clockwise, widdershins. **2** (*awkward, clumsy*) (*dial.*) cack-handed, careless, clumsy, fumbling, stupid. **3** (*insincere, malicious*) insincere, malicious, sinister. **4** (*ambiguous, equivocal*) ambiguous, backhanded, double-edged, equivocal, sardonic.

leftover *n.* (*usu. pl.*) (*a remainder, esp. of uneaten food*) leavings, oddments, odds and ends, remainder, remains, remnants, residue, scraps, surplus.

leg *n.* **1** (*each of the limbs by which humans and other mammals walk*) limb, member, (*coll.*) pin, (*facet.*) stump. **2** (*each of a set of posts or rods supporting a table, chair etc.*) brace, post, prop, rod, support, upright. **3** (*a stage in a long-distance flight, race etc.*) lap, part, section, segment, stage, stretch.

legacy *n.* **1** (*a bequest, money or property bequeathed by will*) bequest, devise, estate, gift, heirloom, inheritance. **2** (*anything left or handed on by a predecessor*) birthright, endowment, estate, heritage, patrimony.

legal *a.* **1** (*lawful, recognized or sanctioned by the law*) allowable, allowed, authorized, constitutional, lawful, legitimate, licit, permissible, proper, rightful, sanctioned, valid. ANTONYMS: illegal, unlawful. **2** (*concerned with the law; characteristic of lawyers*) forensic, judicial, juridical.

legality *n.* (*lawfulness*) lawfulness, legitimacy, permissibility, rightfulness, validity. ANTONYMS: illegality, unlawfulness.

legalize *v.t.* **1** (*to make lawful*) allow, approve, authorize, license, permit, sanction, validate, warrant. ANTONYMS: forbid, prohibit, veto. **2** (*to bring into harmony with the law*) decriminalize, legitimate, legitimatize, legitimize. ANTONYMS: outlaw.

legate *n.* **1** (*a papal emissary*) emissary, nuncio. **2** (*an ambassador, an envoy*) ambassador, delegate, deputy, envoy, lieutenant, plenipotentiary.

legation *n.* **1** (*a diplomatic mission headed by a minister*) delegation, diplomatic mission, embassy. **2** (*the official residence or office of a diplomatic minister*) consulate, embassy, ministry, residence. **3** (*a body of delegates*) delegates, deputies, envoys.

legend *n.* **1** (*a traditional story, esp. one popularly accepted as true*) fiction, narrative, story, tale. **2** (*a myth, a fable*) fable, folk tale, myth, saga, urban myth. **3** (*a person who is renowned for outstanding deeds or qualities*) celebrity, champion, hero, luminary. **4** (*an inscription on a coat of arms or round the field of a medal or coin*) device, inscription, motto. **5** (*a caption to an illustration; a key to a map, table etc.*) caption, code, heading, key.

legendary *a.* **1** (*of or relating to legend*) apocryphal, fabled, fabulous, fanciful, make-believe, mythical. ANTONYMS: factual. **2** (*famous or notorious enough to be a subject of legend*) celebrated, famed, famous, great, illustrious, immortal, notorious, renowned, well-known. ANTONYMS: unknown.

legible *a.* **1** (*clear enough to be read*) easy to read, readable. ANTONYMS: illegible. **2** (*clear, plain*) clear, distinct, evident, neat, plain, tidy. ANTONYMS: obscure, unclear.

legion *n.* **1** (*a military force*) army, brigade, company, division, force, troop, unit. **2** (*a multitude*) army, drove, horde, host, mass, multitude, myriad, number, throng.

legislation *n.* **1** (*the act or process of making laws*) codification, enactment, law-making, prescription, regulation. **2** (*laws or prospective laws*) act, bill, charter, law, measure, ordinance, regulation, ruling, statute.

legislature *n.* (*a body of people in which is vested the power or right to enact or suspend laws*) assembly, congress, council, diet, government, house, parliament, senate.

legitimate *a.* **1** (*lawful, properly authorized*) authorized, constitutional, genuine, lawful, legal, licit. ANTONYMS: illegitimate. **2** (*proper, natural*)

natural, proper, regular, right. **3** (*conformable to accepted standards or usage*) acceptable, admissible, allowable, conforming, permissible. **4** (*following by logical sequence*) just, logical, reasonable, sensible, valid. **5** (*of or relating to formal or serious theatre rather than television, cinema etc.*) formal, mainstream, serious, traditional.

legitimize v.t. (*to render legitimate*) approve, authorize, decriminalize, legalize, legitimate, legitimatize, permit, sanction, validate.

leisure n. **1** (*freedom from business or hurry*) break, freedom, holiday, liberty, peace and quiet, recreation, relaxation, respite, rest, retirement, time off, vacation. ANTONYMS: obligation, work. **2** (*time at one's own disposal, unoccupied time*) breathing space, free time, pause, spare time. **3** (*opportunity, convenience*) convenience, ease, opportunity.
~a. (*unoccupied, free*) free, idle, unoccupied.

leisurely a. (*done at a slow, unhurried pace*) comfortable, easy, gentle, (*coll.*) laid-back, lazy, relaxed, restful, slow, unhurried. ANTONYMS: hasty, rushed.
~adv. (*without haste*) comfortably, deliberately, easily, gently, lazily, restfully, slowly, unhurriedly, without haste. ANTONYMS: hastily, hurriedly.

lend v.t. **1** (*to grant the use of on condition of repayment or compensation*) charter, hire, rent. **2** (*to let out* (*money*) *at interest*) advance, loan. ANTONYMS: borrow. **3** (*to furnish, to contribute, esp. for temporary service*) afford, bestow, confer, contribute, furnish, give, grant, impart, present, provide, supply.

length n. **1** (*measure or extent from end to end, as distinct from breadth or thickness*) extent, measure. ANTONYMS: breadth, width. **2** (*the longest line that can be drawn from one extremity of anything to the other*) extent, reach, span, stretch. **3** (*extent of time, duration*) duration, period, space, span, stretch, term. **4** (*the distance anything extends*) distance, extent, longitude. **5** (*a definite portion of the linear extent of anything*) piece, portion, section, segment.

lengthen v.t. **1** (*to draw out, to extend*) continue, draw out, elongate, expand, extend, increase, stretch. ANTONYMS: cut, shorten. **2** (*to protract*) prolong, protract, spin out, stretch.

lengthy a. **1** (*long and usu. tedious*) diffuse, drawn-out, extended, interminable, lengthened, long, long-drawn-out, long-winded, overlong, prolonged, protracted, tedious. ANTONYMS: concise, short. **2** (*wordy*) prolix, verbose, wordy. ANTONYMS: brief, concise, succinct.

lenience n. (*the state of being lenient*) clemency, compassion, forbearance, forgiveness, gentleness, indulgence, kindness, lenity, mercy,

mildness, moderation, pity, quarter, tenderness, tolerance. ANTONYMS: mercilessness, pitilessness.

lenient a. **1** (*merciful, tending not to be strict or punish severely*) compassionate, forbearing, forgiving, indulgent, kind, merciful, sparing, tolerant. ANTONYMS: severe, strict. **2** ((*of a punishment*) *mild, gentle*) clement, gentle, mild, moderate, soft, tender. ANTONYMS: harsh. **3** (*soothing, emollient*) emollient, mitigating, soothing.

lenitive a. **1** (*soothing, palliative*) alleviating, assuaging, balmy, calming, easing, palliative, relieving, soothing. ANTONYMS: irritant. **2** (*having the power or quality of softening or mitigating*) emollient, mitigating, mollifying, softening.

lesbian n. (*a female homosexual*) (*sl.*) dyke, homosexual, sapphist.
~a. (*of or relating to lesbians or homosexuality in women*) (*sl.*) butch, (*sl.*) femme, (*coll.*) gay, homosexual, sapphic.

lesion n. (*a hurt, an injury*) abrasion, bruise, contusion, cut, hurt, impairment, injury, scratch, sore, trauma, wound.

less a. **1** (*of smaller size, amount, degree etc.*) shorter, slighter, smaller. ANTONYMS: bigger, greater. **2** (*fewer*) fewer, inferior, lower, minor, secondary, subordinate. ANTONYMS: more.
~prep. (*minus, with deduction of*) excepting, lacking, minus, subtracting, without. ANTONYMS: plus.
~adv. (*in a smaller or lower degree*) barely, little, lower, smaller.

lessen v.t. **1** (*to make less in size, quantity or degree*) abridge, curtail. **2** (*to reduce, to degrade*) degrade, depreciate, impair, minimize, moderate, narrow, reduce.
~v.i. **1** (*to become less in size, degree or quantity*) abate, contract, de-escalate, die down, dwindle, ease, erode, lighten, lower, relax, slacken, slow, weaken, wind down. ANTONYMS: escalate, intensify. **2** (*to decrease, to shrink*) contract, decrease, diminish, shrink. ANTONYMS: increase.

lesser a. **1** (*less, smaller*) less, slighter, smaller. ANTONYMS: greater. **2** (*inferior*) inferior, less important, lower, minor, secondary, subordinate. ANTONYMS: superior.

lesson n. **1** (*the time allocated for a period of instruction in a timetable*) class, lecture, period, seminar, tutorial. **2** (*a course of instruction (in any subject)*) coaching, course, instruction, teaching. **3** (*an assignment or exercise set for a pupil by a teacher*) assignment, drill, exercise, homework, practice, task. **4** (*an occurrence or example taken as a warning or caution*) caution, deterrent, example, exemplar, message, model, moral, warning. **5** (*a reprimand, admonition*) admonition, censure, chiding, lecture, punishment, rebuke, reprimand, reproof, scolding.

let¹ *v.t.* **1** (*to permit, to allow* (*to be or do*)) allow, authorize, enable, entitle, grant, permit, sanction, tolerate, warrant. **2** (*to cause to*) allow, cause, enable, grant, make, permit. **3** (*to grant the use or possession of for a stipulated sum, to lease*) charter, hire, lease, rent. **to let down 1** (*to allow to sink or fall*) let fall, lower. **2** (*to fail or disappoint* (*someone*)) disappoint, disenchant, disillusion, dissatisfy, fail, fall short, leave in the lurch. **to let off 1** (*to refrain from punishing or to punish lightly*) absolve, acquit, exempt, exonerate, forgive, pardon, spare. ANTONYMS: condemn, punish. **2** (*to discharge* (*an arrow, gun etc.*); *to detonate* (*a bomb, firework*)) detonate, discharge, explode, fire off. **3** (*to allow or cause* (*air, liquid*) *to escape from*) emit, exude, give off, leak, release. **to let on 1** (*to divulge, to let out*) admit, disclose, divulge, give away, let out, let the cat out of the bag, reveal, say, (*sl.*) split. **2** (*to pretend*) act, counterfeit, dissemble, feign, pretend, profess, simulate. **to let out 1** (*to free from restraint*) free, let go, liberate, release. **2** (*to divulge*) betray, disclose, divulge, leak, let fall, let slip, reveal. **3** (*to utter, give vent to*) emit, give vent to, produce, utter, voice. **4** (*to enlarge or make less tight-fitting*) adjust, enlarge, loosen. **5** (*to lease or let on hire*) hire, lease, let, rent out. **6** (*to disqualify, rule out*) discount, dispense from, disqualify, rule out. **to let up** (*to become less* (*severe*), *to abate*) abate, cease, decrease, diminish, ease, improve, lessen, moderate, relax, slacken, stop, subside. ANTONYMS: increase.

let² *n.* (*a hindrance, an obstacle*) constraint, hindrance, impediment, interference, obstacle, obstruction, prohibition, restriction.

let-down *n.* (*a disappointment*) anticlimax, blow, (*esp. N Am., sl.*) bummer, comedown, disappointment, disillusionment, frustration, setback, (*coll.*) wash-out.

lethal *a.* (*deadly, fatal*) dangerous, deadly, deathly, destructive, fatal, mortal, murderous, noxious, poisonous, virulent. ANTONYMS: harmless, safe.

lethargic *a.* **1** (*feeling that one has no energy and no interest in doing anything*) apathetic, debilitated, dull, enervated, heavy, idle, inactive, indifferent, inert, languid, lazy, listless, slothful, slow, sluggish, stupefied, torpid. ANTONYMS: energetic, lively. **2** (*unnaturally sleepy*) comatose, drowsy, sleepy, somnolent.

lethargy *n.* **1** (*a state of apathy or inactivity*) apathy, dullness, heaviness, idleness, inaction, inactivity, indifference, inertia, languor, lassitude, laziness, listlessness, sloth, slowness, sluggishness, stupor, torpidity, torpor. ANTONYMS: vitality. **2** (*unnatural sleepiness*) drowsiness, sleepiness.

letter *n.* **1** (*a mark or character employed to represent a sound in speech*) character, sign, symbol. **2** (*a written, typed or printed message or communication usually sent by post*) acknowledgement, answer, communication, dispatch, epistle, line, message, missive, note, reply.

lettered *a.* (*learned, erudite*) accomplished, cultivated, cultured, educated, erudite, learned, literate, scholarly, versed, well-read. ANTONYMS: ignorant, uneducated.

level *n.* **1** (*a horizontal line or plane*) horizontal, plane. **2** (*the altitude of any point or surface*) altitude, elevation, height. **3** (*a stage or degree of progress or rank*) degree, grade, position, rank, stage, standard, standing, status. **4** (*level country*) flat, plain, steppe. ANTONYMS: hill.
~*a.* **1** (*horizontal*) horizontal, plane. ANTONYMS: slanted, tilted. **2** (*even, not higher or lower at any part*) consistent, even, flat, smooth. ANTONYMS: uneven. **3** (*at the same height as or horizontal with something else*) aligned, balanced, commensurate, flush, in line. **4** ((*of runners, competitors*) *equal in position, score etc.*) equal, even, neck and neck, on a par. ANTONYMS: unequal. **5** (*equable, well-balanced*) equable, even-tempered, proportionate, stable, steady, uniform, well-balanced.
~*v.t.* **1** (*to make smooth or even*) equalize, even, flatten, plane, smooth. **2** (*to make level* (*with the ground etc.*), *to knock down*) bulldoze, demolish, destroy, devastate, flatten, knock down, overthrow, pull down, raze, tear down. ANTONYMS: build. **3** (*to point* (*a gun*) *in taking aim*) direct, point, take aim. **4** (*to aim, to direct* (*an attack, satire etc.*)) aim, beam, direct, focus, train.

level-headed *a.* (*sensible, untemperamental*) balanced, calm, collected, composed, cool, even-tempered, reasonable, self-possessed, sensible, shrewd, steady, unflappable, untemperamental. ANTONYMS: excitable, temperamental, unbalanced.

lever *n.* **1** (*a bar of metal or other rigid substance resting on a fixed point of support, used to lift a certain weight*) bar, crowbar, jemmy. **2** (*a projecting handle that can be moved to operate a machine*) handle, rod, switch.
~*v.t.* (*to move or lift with or as with a lever*) force, jemmy, lift, move, prise, raise.

leverage *n.* (*means of accomplishing, influencing etc.*) advantage, authority, (*coll.*) clout, influence, power, (*coll.*) pull, rank, weight.

leviathan *n.* (*a huge sea monster*) behemoth, colossus, giant, monster, whale.

levity *n.* **1** (*lack of seriousness or earnestness, frivolity*) facetiousness, flightiness, flippancy, frivolity, giddiness, light-heartedness, silliness, skittishness, triviality. ANTONYMS: earnestness, seriousness. **2** (*fickleness, inconstancy*) fickleness, inconstancy, unreliability.

levy *n.* **1** (*the act of raising or collecting* (*e.g. a tax, a fee*)) charge, collection, due, duty, exaction, excise, fee, imposition, tariff, tax, toll. **2** (*the calling out of troops for military service*) call to arms, call-up, mobilization, muster.
~*v.t.* **1** (*to impose and collect* (*as a tax or forced contribution*)) charge, collect, demand, exact, gather, impose, tax. **2** (*to collect together, to enlist* (*as an army*)) call up, collect together, conscript, enlist, gather, mobilize, muster, press, raise, summon.

lewd *a.* **1** (*lascivious, indecent*) bawdy, (*sl.*) blue, coarse, dirty, indecent, lascivious, lecherous, libidinous, licentious, loose, lustful, obscene, pornographic, profligate, ribald, salacious, smutty, unchaste, vulgar. ANTONYMS: chaste, decent. **2** (*depraved, wicked*) depraved, wanton, wicked, worthless.

lexicon *n.* (*a dictionary*) dictionary, glossary, thesaurus, vocabulary, wordbook.

liability *n.* **1** (*the state of being liable*) accountability, answerability, culpability, duty, obligation, onus, responsibility. **2** (*debts, pecuniary obligations*) arrears, debit, debt, indebtedness, obligation. **3** (*a person or thing that hinders or causes trouble*) burden, disadvantage, drag, drawback, encumbrance, handicap, hindrance, impediment, inconvenience, millstone, nuisance, obstacle.

liable *a.* **1** (*tending or likely* (*to*)) apt, disposed, inclined, likely, probable, prone, tending. ANTONYMS: improbable, unlikely. **2** (*bound or obliged in law or equity*) bound, obligated, obliged. **3** (*responsible* (*for*)) accountable, amenable, answerable, responsible. **4** (*subject* (*to*)) subject, susceptible. **5** (*exposed or open* (*to*)) exposed, open, vulnerable. ANTONYMS: secure.

liaison *n.* **1** (*communication and contact between units, groups etc.*) communication, contact, interchange, intercourse. **2** (*an illicit intimacy between a man and woman*) affair, amour, entanglement, intrigue, relationship, romance. **3** (*a bond, a connection*) alliance, bond, connection, link, tie.

liar *n.* (*a person who knowingly utters a falsehood*) fabricator, falsifier, fibber, perjurer, prevaricator, (*coll.*) storyteller.

libel *n.* (*an unfair representation or defamatory statement*) aspersion, calumny, defamation, denigration, misrepresentation, obloquy, slander, slur, smear, vilification, vituperation. ANTONYMS: eulogy, praise.
~*v.t.* (*to defame, to misrepresent*) blacken, calumniate, defame, denigrate, drag through the mud, malign, misrepresent, revile, slander, smear, traduce, vilify.

libellous *a.* (*being or containing a libel*) aspersive, calumniatory, defamatory, denigratory, derogatory, false, injurious, malicious, maligning, scurrilous, slanderous, traducing, untrue, vilifying, vituperative.

liberal *a.* **1** (*favourable to individual freedom, democratic government and moderate reform*) advanced, democratic, enlightened, humanistic, latitudinarian, libertarian, progressive, radical, reformist. ANTONYMS: reactionary. **2** (*abundant, profuse*) abundant, ample, copious, handsome, lavish, plentiful, profuse, rich. **3** (*generous, openhanded*) altruistic, beneficent, benevolent, bounteous, bountiful, charitable, generous, munificent, open-handed, philanthropic, unstinting. ANTONYMS: mean. **4** (*broad-minded, unprejudiced*) broad-minded, catholic, flexible, indulgent, lenient, permissive, tolerant, unbiased, unprejudiced. ANTONYMS: bigoted, narrow-minded, prejudiced. **5** (*free, candid*) candid, free, open.

liberality *n.* **1** (*munificence, generosity*) altruism, beneficence, benevolence, bounty, charity, generosity, kindness, largesse, munificence, open-handedness, philanthropy, unselfishness. ANTONYMS: stinginess. **2** (*largeness or breadth of views*) breadth, broad-mindedness, candour, catholicity, impartiality, indulgence, latitude, liberalism, libertarianism, open-mindedness, permissiveness, tolerance, toleration. ANTONYMS: narrow-mindedness, prejudice.

liberalize *v.t.* (*to make more liberal*) ameliorate, broaden, democratize, ease, expand, loosen, make liberal, mitigate, moderate, modify, reform, relax, slacken, soften, stretch.

liberate *v.t.* (*to release from injustice or confinement*) deliver, discharge, disenthral, emancipate, free, let out, loose, manumit, redeem, release, rescue, set at liberty, set free, set loose. ANTONYMS: confine, imprison.

liberation *n.* (*the act of setting free*) deliverance, emancipation, freedom, liberty, manumission, redemption, release, unfettering, unshackling.

libertine *n.* (*a licentious or dissolute person*) debauchee, lecher, philanderer, playboy, profligate, rake, reprobate, roué, seducer, voluptuary, womanizer.
~*a.* (*licentious, dissolute*) abandoned, corrupt, debauched, decadent, degenerate, depraved, dissolute, immoral, licentious, loose, profligate, rakish, reprobate, unprincipled, wanton. ANTONYMS: chaste.

liberty *n.* **1** (*the quality or state of being free from captivity or despotic control*) autonomy, emancipation, freedom, independence, liberation, release, self-determination, sovereignty. ANTONYMS: captivity, slavery. **2** (*any instance of a* *person treating someone or something with too little respect*) disrespect, familiarity, forwardness, impertinence, impudence, presumptuousness. ANTONYMS: respect. **3** (*privileges or exemptions, enjoyed by grant or prescription*) authorization, carte blanche, dispensation, exemption, franchise, immunity, latitude, leave, licence, permission, prerogative, privilege, right, sanction.

libidinous *a.* (*characterized by lewdness or lust*) bawdy, (*sl.*) blue, carnal, concupiscent, debauched, dirty, indecent, lascivious, lecherous, lewd, loose, lustful, obscene, pornographic, prurient, ribald, salacious, smutty, vulgar, wanton. ANTONYMS: chaste, pure.

licence *n.* **1** (*a document certifying consent or permission (to marry, drive a motor vehicle etc.)*) authority, authorization, certificate, permit, warrant. **2** (*authority, permission*) authority, carte blanche, charter, consent, dispensation, entitlement, exemption, immunity, leave, liberty, permission, privilege, right. ANTONYMS: constraint, prohibition. **3** (*permitted freedom of thought or action*) freedom, independence, latitude, liberty, self-determination. **4** (*unrestrained liberty of action, disregard of law or propriety*) abandon, anarchy, disorder, immoderation, impropriety, indulgence, irresponsibility, lawlessness, laxity, unrestraint, unruliness. ANTONYMS: restraint. **5** (*abuse of freedom, licentiousness*) abuse, debauchery, dissipation, excess, licentiousness, profligacy.

license *v.t.* **1** (*to authorize by a legal permit*) authorize, certify, charter, warrant. **2** (*to allow, to permit, esp. to allow entire freedom of action, comment etc.*) accredit, allow, commission, empower, permit, sanction. ANTONYMS: prohibit, veto.

licentious *a.* (*immoral, dissolute*) abandoned, debauched, disorderly, dissolute, immoral, impure, lascivious, lax, lecherous, lewd, libertine, libidinous, loose, lubricious, lustful, profligate, promiscuous, sensual, unchaste, wanton. ANTONYMS: chaste, virtuous.

licentiousness *n.* (*the state of being licentious*) abandon, debauchery, dissipation, dissoluteness, immorality, lechery, lewdness, libertinism, libidinousness, lubricity, lust, profligacy, promiscuity, prurience, salaciousness, wantonness. ANTONYMS: chastity.

lick *v.t.* **1** (*to draw or pass the tongue over*) lap, taste, tongue. **2** ((*of flames etc.*) *to stroke or pass lightly over*) brush, flicker at, play over, ripple over, stroke, touch. **3** (*to overcome, to defeat*) beat, (*sl.*) clobber, conquer, defeat, overcome, rout, (*coll.*) run rings round. **4** (*to thrash*) beat, flog, slap, spank, thrash, (*coll.*) wallop.

~*n.* **1** (*a slight smear or coat (as of paint); a small amount*) bit, brush, dab, smear, speck, touch. **2** (*a smart blow or slap*) blow, cuff, slap. **3** (*great exertion or pace*) (*sl.*) clip, effort, exertion, pace, rate, speed.

licking *n.* (*a beating, a defeat*) beating, defeat, drubbing, flogging, (*coll.*) hiding, (*coll.*) pasting, spanking, thrashing, whipping.

lid *n.* **1** (*a hinged or detachable cover or cap, usu. for shutting a vessel or container*) cap, cover, top. **2** (*a curb, a restraint*) block, check, curb, restraint.

lie[1] *v.i.* **1** (*to say or write anything with the deliberate intention of deceiving*) dissimulate, equivocate, fabricate, fib, invent, prevaricate. ANTONYMS: tell the truth. **2** (*to convey a false impression, to deceive*) deceive, falsify, misrepresent, perjure.
~*n.* **1** (*a false statement deliberately made for the purpose of deception*) equivocation, fabrication, falsehood, falsification, fib, fiction, invention, mendacity, (*sl.*) porky, prevarication, untruth. ANTONYMS: truth. **2** (*a deception, an imposture*) deceit, deception, imposture.

lie[2] *v.i.* **1** (*to rest or place oneself in a reclining or horizontal posture*) couch, loll, lounge, recline, repose, rest, sprawl, stretch out. **2** (*to rest on or over a horizontal surface*) deposit, rest. **3** (*to be situated in a specified location or direction*) be found, be located, be situated. **4** (*to stretch or extend*) extend, reach, stretch. **5** (*to exist, to be in a specified state, position etc.*) be, consist, dwell, exist, remain. **6** (*to be buried*) be buried, be interred, be laid to rest. **7** (*to seem to weigh heavily on*) burden, oppress, press, rest, weigh.
~*n.* **1** (*position, arrangement*) arrangement, direction, position. **2** (*the retiring-place or lair (of an animal)*) den, hole, lair. **to lie in wait (for)** (*to wait in ambush or concealment (in order to waylay)*) ambush, attack, hold up, waylay. **to lie low** (*to remain in hiding*) conceal oneself, go to earth, go underground, hide, hide out, hole up, keep a low profile, lurk, skulk, take cover.

liege *n.* (*a feudal superior, a lord*) chief, leader, lord, master, overlord, sovereign, superior. ANTONYMS: servant, vassal.

life *n.* **1** (*the state or condition which distinguishes animate beings from dead ones and from inorganic matter*) animation, being, breath, existence, sentience, viability, vigour, vitality. ANTONYMS: death. **2** (*the period from birth to death*) lifespan, lifetime. **3** (*the period of time for which an object functions or operates*) career, continuance, course, days, duration, span, time. **4** (*living things collectively, animated existence*) creatures, living world, organisms, wildlife. **5** (*a person's individual existence*) essence, heart, lifeblood, soul, spirit, vital spark. **6** (*a person's* *manner or course of living; any particular aspect of this*) behaviour, conduct, lifestyle, way of life. **7** (*human affairs*) human affairs, human condition. **8** (*animation, vivacity*) animation, enthusiasm, get-up-and-go, high spirits, liveliness, (*sl.*) oomph, pep, (*sl*) pizazz, sparkle, spirit, verve, vigour, vitality, vivacity, zest. ANTONYMS: lethargy. **9** (*the average period which a person of a given age may expect to live*) life expectancy, lifespan, threescore years and ten. **10** (*a narrative of one's existence, a biography*) autobiography, biography, confessions, history, life story, memoirs.

lifeless *a.* **1** (*deprived of life; dead, inorganic*) cold, dead, deceased, defunct, extinct, inanimate, inert, inorganic. ANTONYMS: alive, living. **2** (*unconscious*) comatose, (*coll.*) dead to the world, insensate, insensible, (*coll.*) out cold, unconscious. ANTONYMS: conscious. **3** (*lacking vitality or interest, dull*) bland, colourless, dull, flat, heavy, hollow, inactive, insipid, lacklustre, lethargic, listless, sluggish, spiritless, static, torpid, uninteresting, vapid. ANTONYMS: exciting, lively.

lifelike *a.* ((*of a portrait*) *like the original*) accurate, authentic, exact, faithful, photographic, real, realistic, true-to-life, vivid.

lift *v.t.* **1** (*to raise to a higher position, to elevate*) bear aloft, buoy up, draw up, elevate, hoist, hold up, jack, raise, support. **2** (*to raise or take up from the ground, to pick up*) pick up, pull up, raise, take up. ANTONYMS: drop. **3** (*to take hold of in order to move or remove, e.g. from a hook or shelf*) remove, take hold of. **4** (*to remove* (*a restriction, ban*)) annul, cancel, countermand, raise, relax, remove, rescind, revoke, stop, terminate. ANTONYMS: impose, put on. **5** (*to give* (*one's confidence or spirits*) *a boost*) boost, raise, uplift. **6** (*to improve the quality of, esp. to make more interesting and lively*) advance, ameliorate, enhance, exalt, improve, promote, upgrade. **7** (*to make audible; to make louder*) heighten, make louder, raise in pitch. **8** (*to steal, to appropriate*) appropriate, (*sl.*) blag, carry off, (*sl.*) half-inch, (*sl.*) nick, pilfer, pinch, plagiarize, pocket, purloin, steal, take, thieve.

~*v.i.* **1** (*to rise, to move upwards*) ascend, climb, mount, rise. ANTONYMS: fall. **2** (*to rise and disperse, as a mist*) disappear, disperse, dissipate, thin, vanish.

~*n.* **1** (*a compartment or platform for people or goods travelling between different floors of a building, levels in a mine etc.*) elevator. **2** (*a ride in a vehicle as a passenger*) drive, ride, run. **3** (*a rise in spirits*) boost, encouragement, pick-me-up, reassurance, uplift. **4** (*a rise in condition, status etc.*) climb, improvement, rise.

ligature *n.* (*anything that unites, a bond*) band, binding, bond, connection, ligament, link, tie.

light¹ *n.* **1** (*the brightness from a light, the sun etc. that allows one to see things*) blaze, brightness, brilliance, effulgence, flash, glare, gleam, glint, glow, illumination, incandescence, lambency, luminescence, luminosity, lustre, phosphorescence, radiance, ray, shine, sparkle. ANTONYMS: darkness. **2** (*a source of light, the sun etc.*) beacon, bulb, candle, flare, lamp, lantern, lighthouse, star, sun, taper, torch. **3** (*daylight*) dawn, daybreak, daylight, daytime, morning, sun, sunrise, sunshine. ANTONYMS: night. **4** (*something that kindles or ignites; a device which produces this*) flame, lighter, match, spark. **5** (*exposure, publicity*) exposure, general knowledge, publicity, the open. **6** (*point of view, aspect*) angle, approach, aspect, attitude, context, interpretation, point of view, slant, vantage point, viewpoint. **7** (*mental illumination, enlightenment*) awareness, comprehension, elucidation, enlightenment, explanation, illustration, information, insight, knowledge, understanding. ANTONYMS: mystification, obscurity. **8** (*a person who or something which enlightens, an example*) example, exemplar, model, paragon.

~*a.* **1** ((*of a room, space*) *well provided with* (*natural*) *light*) aglow, bright, brilliant, glowing, illuminated, lit, luminous, shining, sunny. ANTONYMS: dark. **2** ((*of colours*) *reflecting a lot of light, pale*) bleached, faded, pale, pastel, reflective. ANTONYMS: dark. **3** ((*of hair, complexion*) *pale-coloured, fair*) bleached, blond, fair, pale. ANTONYMS: black, dark.

~*v.t.* **1** (*to kindle, to set fire to*) fire, ignite, kindle, put a match to, set fire to. ANTONYMS: extinguish. **2** (*to fill* (*up*) *with light*) floodlight, illuminate, illumine, irradiate, lighten, light up. ANTONYMS: darken. **3** (*to conduct with a light*) escort, guide, show. **4** (*to brighten*) animate, brighten, cheer, irradiate, lighten.

~*v.i.* (*to begin to burn*) burn, ignite, smoulder, take fire.

light² *a.* **1** (*of little weight, not heavy*) insubstantial, lightweight, portable, small, unsubstantial, weightless. ANTONYMS: heavy. **2** (*having relatively low density*) airy, buoyant. **3** (*short in weight, below the standard weight*) short, underweight. **4** (*not great in degree, number, intensity etc.*) scanty, sparse, thin. **5** ((*of a task, duties etc.*) *easy to perform*) (*coll.*) cushy, easy, effortless, manageable, simple, undemanding, unexacting, untaxing. ANTONYMS: arduous, difficult, hard. **6** ((*of a meal*) *small in quantity and consisting of easily digestible food*) digestible, frugal, modest, small. **7** ((*of food*) *not rich, low in fat, sugar etc.; easily digested*) digestible, low-fat, not rich, sugar-free. ANTONYMS: heavy, rich. **8** ((*of reading, entertainment*) *intended for amusement, not serious*) amusing, diverting, entertaining, frivolous, funny, gay, humorous, light-hearted, superficial, trifling, trivial, witty. ANTONYMS: serious, weighty. **9** (*of a remark*) *of little consequence, unimportant*) inconsequential, inconsiderable, insignificant, trivial, unimportant. ANTONYMS: important, serious. **10** ((*of movement*) *active, quick*) active, agile, airy, deft, dexterous, graceful, light-footed, lithe, mobile, nimble, quick, sprightly, supple, sylphlike. **11** ((*of fabrics*) *thin, delicate*) delicate, flimsy, thin. ANTONYMS: thick. **12** ((*of a blow, impact*) *gentle, slight*) delicate, faint, gentle, mild, moderate, slight, soft, weak. ANTONYMS: forcible, harsh. **13** ((*of a mood*) *cheerful, merry*) airy, animated, blithe, carefree, cheerful, cheery, gay, jolly, lively, merry, sunny. **14** (*dizzy, giddy*) delirious, dizzy, giddy, light-headed, mercurial, volatile. **15** ((*of soil*) *loose, porous*) crumbly, friable, loose, porous, sandy.

light³ *v.i.* **1** ((*of a bird*) *to descend as from flight, to settle*) descend, land, perch, settle. **2** (*to alight, to dismount*) alight, dismount. **to light on/ upon** (*to happen on, to find by chance*) chance upon, discover, encounter, find, happen on, hit on, stumble on.

lighten¹ *v.i.* (*to become light, to brighten*) become light, brighten, illuminate, irradiate, light, light up. ANTONYMS: darken.
~*v.t.* (*to illuminate, to enlighten*) enlighten, illuminate.

lighten² *v.t.* **1** (*to reduce the weight or load of*) disburden, disencumber, unload. ANTONYMS: burden, encumber. **2** (*to relieve, to alleviate*) allay, alleviate, ameliorate, assuage, ease, facilitate, lessen, mitigate, reduce, relieve. ANTONYMS: aggravate. **3** (*to cheer*) brighten, buoy up, cheer, elate, encourage, gladden, hearten, inspire, lift, perk up, revive, uplift. ANTONYMS: depress, oppress.

light-fingered *a.* (*given to thieving*) (*coll.*) crooked, dishonest, pilfering, shifty, sly, stealing, thieving.

light-headed *a.* **1** (*delirious*) confused, delirious. **2** (*giddy*) dizzy, faint, hazy, (*coll.*) woozy. **3** (*frivolous, thoughtless*) birdbrained, feather-brained, fickle, flighty, flippant, foolish, frivolous, happy-go-lucky, inane, scatterbrained, shallow, silly, superficial, thoughtless, trivial. ANTONYMS: deep, sober.

light-hearted *a.* (*free from care or anxiety, cheerful*) blithe, bright, carefree, cheerful, chirpy, effervescent, frolicsome, gay, genial, glad, gleeful, jolly, jovial, joyful, merry, playful. ANTONYMS: dejected, gloomy.

lightweight *a.* (*trivial*) frivolous, inconsequential, insignificant, paltry, petty, slight, trifling, trivial, unimportant, worthless. ANTONYMS: deep, profound, serious.

like¹ *prep.* **1** (*similar to, resembling*) resembling, similar to. **2** (*for example*) for example, such as, viz.
~*a.* (*similar, having the same qualities as*) akin, alike, allied, analogous, approximate, corresponding, equivalent, identical, parallel, relating, resembling, same, similar. ANTONYMS: different, opposite.
~*adv.* **1** (*likely*) likely, probable. **2** (*as it were, so to speak*) as it were, in a certain way, so to speak, to some extent.
~*n.* **1** (*a counterpart*) counterpart, parallel. ANTONYMS: opposite. **2** (*a similar or equal thing, person or event*) equal, equivalent, fellow, match, peer, twin.

like² *v.t.* **1** (*to find pleasure or satisfaction in, to enjoy*) delight in, (*dated sl.*) dig, enjoy, pleasure in, relish, revel in. **2** (*to be pleased with*) admire, appreciate, approve. **3** (*to be inclined towards or attracted by*) be attracted by, fancy, feel inclined towards, go for. **4** (*to be fond of*) adore, be fond of, cherish, esteem, hold dear, love, prize, take a shine to, take to. ANTONYMS: dislike, hate. **5** (*to wish, prefer*) care to, choose, desire, prefer, select, want, wish.
~*n.* (*things that one likes*) favour, liking, partiality, predilection, preference.

likeable *a.* (*pleasant, easy to like*) agreeable, amiable, appealing, attractive, charming, engaging, friendly, genial, lovable, nice, pleasant, pleasing, sympathetic, winning, winsome. ANTONYMS: disagreeable, unpleasant.

likelihood *n.* (*probability*) chance, liability, likeliness, possibility, probability, prospect.

likely *a.* **1** (*probable, plausible*) believable, conceivable, credible, feasible, imaginable, plausible, possible, probable, reasonable. ANTONYMS: improbable, incredible. **2** (*liable, expected* (*to*)) anticipated, expected, inclined, liable, prone, tending. ANTONYMS: unlikely. **3** (*suitable, well-adapted*) appropriate, apt, befitting, disposed, fair, fit, promising, proper, qualified, suitable, well-adapted. ANTONYMS: inappropriate, unsuitable.

like-minded *a.* (*having similar opinions, purpose etc.*) agreeing, compatible, harmonious, in accord, of one mind, unanimous.

liken *v.t.* (*to compare, to represent as similar* (*to*)) compare (to), equate (with), juxtapose (with), match (with), parallel (to), relate (to), set (alongside).

likeness *n.* **1** (*similarity, resemblance*) affinity, correspondence, resemblance, sameness, similarity, similitude. ANTONYMS: difference, dissimilarity. **2** (*a picture or other representation of a person or thing*) copy, counterpart, depiction, effigy, facsimile, image, model, photograph, picture, portrait, replica, representation, reproduction, study. **3** (*form, appearance*) appearance, form, guise, semblance.

likewise *adv.* **1** (*also, moreover*) also, besides, further, furthermore, in addition, moreover, too. **2** (*in like manner*) in like manner, in the same way, similarly, the same. ANTONYMS: otherwise.

liking *n.* (*fondness, fancy (for)*) affection (for), affinity (with), appreciation (of), attraction (towards), bent (for), bias (towards), desire (for), fancy (for), fondness (for), inclination (towards), love (of), partiality (for), penchant (for), predilection (for), preference (for), propensity (for), stomach (for), taste (for), thirst (for), weakness (for). ANTONYMS: aversion (to), dislike (of).

lilt *n.* (*a jaunty, springing rhythm or movement*) beat, cadence, jauntiness, rhythm, spring, sway, swing.

limb *n.* **1** (*each of the articulated extremities of an animal, an arm, leg or wing*) appendage, arm, extremity, leg, wing. **2** (*a main branch of a tree*) bough, branch. **3** (*a projecting part*) extension, offshoot, part, projection, spur. **4** (*a member, branch or arm of a larger group or institution*) arm, branch, chapel, division, member.

limber *a.* **1** (*lithe, agile*) agile, graceful, lissom, lithe, loose-limbed, supple. **2** (*flexible*) elastic, flexible, plastic, pliable, supple. **to limber up 1** (*to stretch and flex the muscles in preparation for physical exercise*) exercise, flex, get ready, prepare, stretch, warm up. ANTONYMS: relax, wind down. **2** (*to make (something) flexible, to loosen up*) flex, loosen up. ANTONYMS: stiffen.

limelight *n.* (*the glare of publicity*) celebrity, fame, prominence, public eye, publicity, spotlight.

limit *n.* **1** (*a line or edge marking termination or utmost extent*) boundary, edge, extremity, far point, termination, ultimate, utmost. **2** (*the boundary of an area or district*) border, boundary, confines, district, frontier, pale, perimeter, periphery, precinct. **3** (*the maximum or minimum amount permissible or possible*) ceiling, cut-off point, deadline, end point, limitation, maximum. **4** (*a restraint, a check*) check, curb, limitation, obstruction, restraint, restriction.
~*v.t.* **1** (*to set a limit or boundary to*) bound, circumscribe, delimit, demarcate. **2** (*to confine within certain bounds*) confine, hem in, keep within bounds. **3** (*to restrict (to)*) check, curb, hinder, ration, restrain, restrict.

limitation *n.* **1** (*something which limits a person's achievements, competence etc.*) disadvantage, drawback, impediment, weakness. **2** (*a restriction*) block, check, condition, control, curb,

obstruction, qualification, restraint, restriction, snag.

limited *a.* **1** (*not universal or general, confined within limits*) bounded, checked, circumscribed, confined, constrained, controlled, curbed, defined, finite, fixed, hampered. ANTONYMS: boundless, unlimited. **2** (*restricted, narrow*) cramped, hemmed in, narrow, restricted. **3** (*few, sparse*) few, inadequate, insufficient, minimal, reduced, scant, scanty, short, sparse. **4** (*not very clever or well-read*) dim, mediocre, slow. ANTONYMS: bright, clever, intelligent.

limitless *a.* (*without limit, unending*) boundless, countless, endless, illimitable, immeasurable, immense, incalculable, inexhaustible, infinite, measureless, never-ending, numberless, unbounded, undefined, unending, unlimited, untold, vast. ANTONYMS: limited.

limp[1] *v.i.* (*to proceed slowly and with difficulty*) falter, halt, hobble, shamble, shuffle, stagger.
~*n.* (*a limping step or walk*) hobble, lameness.

limp[2] *a.* **1** (*not stiff, flexible*) drooping, flabby, flaccid, flexible, floppy, lax, pliable, relaxed, slack, soft. ANTONYMS: firm, stiff. **2** (*lacking in energy or impact*) debilitated, drained, enervated, exhausted, feeble, inert, lethargic, spent, tired, weak, worn out. ANTONYMS: dynamic, energetic.

limpid *a.* **1** (*clear, transparent*) bright, clear, crystalline, pellucid, translucent, transparent. ANTONYMS: opaque. **2** (*lucid, perspicuous*) clear, comprehensible, intelligible, lucid, perspicuous, unambiguous, understandable. ANTONYMS: incomprehensible. **3** (*calm, peaceful*) calm, peaceful, placid, quiet, serene, still, tranquil, unruffled, untroubled. ANTONYMS: agitated, troubled.

line[1] *n.* **1** (*a long thin mark or a streak, wrinkle etc. resembling the mark of a pencil etc.*) band, bar, crease, dash, furrow, groove, mark, rule, score, scratch, seam, streak, strip, stripe, stroke, underline, wrinkle. **2** (*the edge or contour of a shape, outline*) configuration, contour, edge, features, figure, lineament, outline, profile, silhouette. **3** (*pl.*) (*the general appearance or outline of a thing*) appearance, configuration, contour, cut, outline, shape, style. **4** (*a limit, a boundary*) border, borderline, boundary, demarcation, edge, frontier, limit, mark. **5** (*a row or continuous series of words, people or other objects*) column, crocodile, file, procession, queue, rank, row, sequence, series. **6** (*a short letter, a note*) card, communication, letter, message, note, postcard, report, word. **7** (*pl.*) (*the words of an actor's part*) libretto, part, script, text, words. **8** (*a length of rope or string*) cord, rope, strand, string, thread, wire. **9** (*a rope, string etc. used for a specific purpose*) clothes line, fishing line, plumb line.

10 (*a wire or cable for telegraph or telephone*) cable, filament, wire. **11** (*the course or direction taken by a moving object*) axis, course, direction, path, route, track, trajectory, way. **12** (*a series of persons related in direct descent or succession, lineage*) ancestry, breed, descent, extraction, family, house, lineage, race, stock, strain, succession. **13** (*a branch of business, particular interest*) activity, area, business, calling, employment, field, forte, interest, job, occupation, profession, province, pursuit, trade, vocation. **14** (*mode of procedure, conduct*) approach, avenue, belief, course, course of action, ideology, method, policy, position, practice, procedure, scheme, system. **15** (*a series of trenches, ramparts etc.*) defences, firing line, front, front line, position, trenches. **16** (*a useful hint or tip*) angle, clue, hint, indication, information, lead, tip.
~*v.t.* **1** (*to draw lines upon, to cover with lines*) draw, inscribe, trace, underline. **2** (*to mark* (*in, off etc.*) *with lines*) crease, cut, furrow, mark, rule, score. **to line up 1** (*to align*) align, arrange, array, marshal, order, range, regiment, straighten. **2** (*to queue*) fall in, form ranks, queue. **3** (*to prepare*) arrange, assemble, come up with, lay on, obtain, organize, prepare, secure.

line² *v.t.* **1** (*to put a covering of different material on the inside of* (*a garment, box etc.*)) cover, face. **2** (*to fill the inside of*) fill, stuff.

lineage *n.* (*descendants in a direct line from a common progenitor, ancestry*) ancestors, ancestry, birth, breed, descendants, descent, extraction, family, forebears, forefathers, genealogy, heredity, house, line, offspring, pedigree, progeny, stock, succession.

lineament *n.* **1** (*characteristic lines or features*) characteristics, countenance, face, features, lines, physiognomy, trait, visage. **2** (*outline, contour*) configuration, contour, outline, profile.

lined *a.* **1** ((*of paper*) *having straight lines printed across it*) feint, ruled. **2** ((*of skin*) *having wrinkles, old*) furrowed, wizened, worn, wrinkled.

line-up *n.* (*a row or group of persons assembled for a particular purpose*) arrangement, array, group, row, selection, side, team.

linger *v.i.* **1** (*to delay going, to be slow to leave*) dally, dawdle, delay, hang around, idle, lag. ANTONYMS: leave. **2** (*to remain in or around a place*) haunt, remain, stay, stop, tarry. **3** (*not to dissipate or disappear*) abide, continue, endure, persist. **4** (*to remain alive, though slowly dying*) cling on, hang on, last, survive. **5** (*to loiter; to be slow in doing something*) loiter, prevaricate, procrastinate, wait.

lingering *a.* (*slow to finish*) drawn-out, prolonged, protracted, slow.

liniment *n.* (*a liquid preparation, usu. with oil, for rubbing on bruised or inflamed parts*) balm, balsam, cream, embrocation, emollient, lotion, ointment, salve, unguent.

link *n.* **1** (*a ring or loop of a chain*) hoop, loop, ring. **2** (*a connecting part in machinery etc. or in a series, argument etc.*) component, connection, constituent, coupling, division, element, member, part, piece. **3** (*a logical relationship*) affiliation, affinity, association, attachment, bond, connection, joint, liaison, relationship, tie.
~*v.t.* **1** (*to connect or attach* (*to, together etc.*) *by or as by a link or links*) attach, bind, connect, couple, fasten, join, tie, unite, yoke. ANTONYMS: detach, separate. **2** (*to connect by association*) associate, bracket, connect, identify, relate. **3** (*to clasp* (*hands*) *or intertwine* (*arms*)) clasp, entwine, intertwine.

lionize *v.t.* (*to treat as an object of interest or curiosity*) acclaim, adulate, aggrandize, celebrate, crack up, eulogize, exalt, fête, glorify, honour, idolize, sing the praises of.

lip *n.* **1** (*the edge of a container etc., rim*) border, brim, brink, edge, flange, margin, rim. **2** (*impudence, cheek*) (*coll.*) backchat, cheek, effrontery, impertinence, impudence, insolence, rudeness, (*coll.*) sauce. ANTONYMS: politeness, respect.

liquid *a.* **1** (*flowing or capable of flowing, like water or oil*) aqueous, flowing, fluid, liquefied, melted, molten, running, runny, thawed, watery, wet. ANTONYMS: solid. **2** (*transparent, clear*) bright, brilliant, clear, limpid, shining, translucent, transparent. **3** ((*of sounds*) *not guttural, easily pronounced*) dulcet, fluent, mellifluent, mellifluous, melting, pure, smooth, soft, sweet.
~*n.* (*a substance that is able to flow*) fluid, juice, liquor, solution.

liquidate *v.t.* **1** (*to pay off* (*a debt etc.*)) clear, discharge, honour, pay, pay off, settle, square. **2** (*to wind up* (*a bankrupt estate etc.*)) settle, wind up. **3** (*to convert* (*assets*) *into cash*) cash, convert, realize, sell off, sell up. **4** (*to assassinate; to destroy*) abolish, annihilate, annul, assassinate, (*sl.*) blow away, (*coll.*) bump off, cancel, destroy, dispatch, dissolve, (*sl.*) do in, eliminate, eradicate, exterminate, finish off, get rid of, kill, murder, remove, (*NAm, sl.*) rub out, (*sl.*) take out, terminate, (*sl.*) wipe out.

liquor *n.* **1** (*an alcoholic drink, usu. not including wine or beer; such drinks collectively*) alcohol, (*coll.*) booze, drink, grog, (*coll.*) hard stuff, (*N Am., coll.*) hooch, intoxicant, spirits. **2** (*a liquid or fluid substance, e.g. the water used for cooking*) broth, extract, fluid, infusion, secretion, solution, stock.

list¹ *n.* (*a record or catalogue of items, names etc.*)

which are related in some way) catalogue, directory, file, index, inventory, listing, record, register, roll, schedule, tally.

~*v.t.* (*to make a list of*) book, catalogue, enumerate, file, index, itemize, note, record, register, schedule, tabulate.

list² *n.* (*the fact of leaning over to one side* (*of a ship, building etc.*)) cant, leaning, slant, tilt.

~*v.i.* (*to lean over*) careen, heel, incline, lean over, tilt, tip.

listen *v.i.* **1** (*to make an effort to hear*) hear, overhear. **2** (*to pay attention* (*to*)) attend, be attentive, hark, pay attention. **3** (*to heed, to obey*) concentrate, follow, heed, mind, obey, observe, take notice. ANTONYMS: ignore. **4** (*to wait in the hope or expectation of hearing*) eavesdrop, (*coll.*) pin back one's ears, prick up one's ears.

listless *a.* (*lacking the will or energy to do anything*) apathetic, bored, dissatisfied, enervated, heavy, impassive, inactive, inattentive, indifferent, inert, languid, lethargic, lifeless, limp, sluggish, spiritless, torpid, uneasy, weary. ANTONYMS: alert, energetic.

listlessness *n.* (*the state of being listless*) apathy, dissatisfaction, enervation, ennui, inactivity, inattention, indifference, inertia, languor, lethargy, lifelessness, limpness, sluggishness, spiritlessness, torpidity, uneasiness, weariness. ANTONYMS: energy, liveliness.

literacy *n.* **1** (*the ability to read and write*) ability to read, ability to write. ANTONYMS: illiteracy. **2** (*the state of being educated*) articulacy, articulateness, cultivation, education, erudition, knowledge, learning, proficiency, scholarship.

literal *a.* **1** (*following the exact words* (*as a translation*)) accurate, close, exact, faithful, precise, strict, verbatim, word-for-word. ANTONYMS: loose. **2** (*unimaginative, matter-of-fact*) boring, colourless, down-to-earth, dull, factual, matter-of-fact, prosaic, prosy, unimaginative, uninspired. ANTONYMS: exciting, imaginative. **3** (*without exaggeration; so called without exaggeration*) actual, bona fide, genuine, gospel, plain, real, simple, true, unexaggerated, unvarnished.

literary *a.* **1** (*versed or engaged in literature*) bookish, lettered, literate. ANTONYMS: illiterate. **2** (*well-read*) erudite, learned, scholarly, well-read. ANTONYMS: ignorant. **3** (*consisting of written or printed compositions*) printed, written.

literate *a.* **1** (*able to read and write*) able to read, able to write. ANTONYMS: illiterate. **2** (*educated*) cultivated, cultured, educated, erudite, learned, lettered, scholarly, schooled, well-informed, well-read. **3** (*having knowledge or competence in*) competent at, expert at, informed about, knowledgeable about.

literature *n.* **1** (*the class of writings distinguished for beauty of form or expression, as poetry, novels etc.*) belles-lettres, letters. **2** (*printed matter, usu. of an informative kind*) books, brochures, leaflets, mailshots, pamphlets, publications, texts, writings, written works.

lithe *a.* (*flexible, supple*) agile, elastic, flexible, graceful, limber, lissom, nimble, pliable, pliant, supple.

litigation *n.* **1** (*the process of bringing or contesting a lawsuit*) contending, dispute, disputing. **2** (*judicial proceedings*) action, case, contest, dispute, lawsuit, proceedings, process, prosecution.

litigious *a.* (*quarrelsome, contentious*) argumentative, belligerent, combative, contentious, disputatious, pugnacious, quarrelsome.

litter *n.* **1** (*rubbish, esp. waste paper, scattered about in a public place*) garbage, refuse, rubbish, trash, waste. **2** (*a scattered, disorderly collection of odds and ends*) debris, detritus, fragments, odds and ends. **3** (*a state of disorder or untidiness*) clutter, confusion, disarray, disorder, jumble, mess, untidiness. ANTONYMS: tidiness. **4** (*the young brought forth by a sow, cat etc. at one birth*) brood, family, offspring, progeny, young. **5** (*straw, hay or other soft material used as a bed for horses, cattle etc.*) bedding, mulch.

~*v.t.* **1** (*to scatter* (*things*) *about carelessly*) scatter, strew. **2** (*to make* (*a place*) *untidy with articles scattered about*) clutter, derange, disarrange, disorder, mess up, untidy. ANTONYMS: tidy.

little *a.* **1** (*small, not great in size, amount or quantity*) infinitesimal, insufficient, meagre, miniature, minute, scant, small, (*coll.*) teeny-weeny, tiny. ANTONYMS: great, large. **2** (*not tall, short in stature*) diminutive, dwarf, elfin, petite, pygmy, short, slender. ANTONYMS: tall. **3** (*short in duration or distance*) brief, fleeting, hasty, limited, passing, short, short-lived. ANTONYMS: lengthy. **4** (*trifling, petty*) inconsiderable, insignificant, minor, negligible, paltry, petty, slight, trifling, trivial, unimportant. ANTONYMS: considerable, important. **5** (*young or younger*) babyish, childish, immature, infant, junior, undeveloped, young, younger.

~*adv.* **1** (*to only a small extent, not much*) barely, hardly, not much, not quite, only just. ANTONYMS: much. **2** (*not at all*) hardly ever, not at all, not often, rarely, scarcely, seldom.

~*n.* (*a small amount, space etc.*) bit, dash, drop, fragment, hint, jot, modicum, particle, pinch, snippet, speck, spot, touch, trace, trifle. ANTONYMS: lot.

liturgy *n.* **1** (*a form of public worship laid down by a Church*) devotion, worship. **2** (*a Church's entire ritual for public worship*) celebration, ceremony, rite, ritual, service.

live[1] *v.i.* **1** (*to have life, to be alive*) be alive, breathe, draw breath, exist. ANTONYMS: die. **2** (*to reside, to dwell* (*at, in etc.*)) abide, dwell, (*sl.*) hang out, inhabit, lodge, reside, settle. **3** (*to be nourished, to subsist* (*on or upon*)) feed, subsist, survive. **4** (*to receive or gain a livelihood* (*by*)) earn a living, support oneself. **5** (*to pass or conduct one's life in a particular condition, manner etc.*) abide, continue, endure, get along, make ends meet. **6** (*to live strenuously, to enjoy life intensely*) enjoy life, flourish, (*coll.*) have a ball, (*coll.*) live it up, luxuriate, make the most of life, (*coll.*) make whoopee, paint the town red, prosper, revel, thrive. **7** (*to continue alive, to survive*) endure, last, persist, prevail, survive.

live[2] *a.* **1** (*alive, living*) alive, animate, breathing, existent, living, quick, vital. ANTONYMS: dead. **2** (*charged with energy, esp. with electrical energy*) charged, potent. **3** ((*of coals*) *burning, ignited*) alight, blazing, burning, glowing, ignited, smouldering. **4** ((*of an issue*) *of current interest and concern*) burning, controversial, current, hot, pertinent, pressing, prevalent, topical, unsettled, vital. **5** (*lively, energetic*) active, alert, brisk, dynamic, earnest, energetic, lively, sparky, spirited, vigorous, vivid.

livelihood *n.* (*means of subsistence; occupation*) employment, income, job, living, maintenance, means, occupation, subsistence, support, sustenance, work.

liveliness *n.* (*the state of being lively*) activity, animation, boisterousness, bounciness, brio, briskness, dynamism, energy, gaiety, life, quickness, smartness, spirit, sprightliness, vigour, vitality, vivacity.

livelong *a.* **1** (*long-lasting*) everlasting, longdrawn-out, long-lasting. **2** (*the whole, entire, the whole length of*) complete, entire, full, unbroken, whole.

lively *a.* **1** (*full of life, active*) active, agile, alert, brisk, (*esp. N Am., coll.*) chipper, chirpy, energetic, keen, nimble, perky, quick, sprightly, spry, vigorous. ANTONYMS: apathetic, lethargic. **2** (*vivacious, cheerful*) animated, blithe, blithesome, cheerful, frisky, frolicsome, gay, merry, sociable, sparky, spirited, (*coll.*) upbeat, vivacious. **3** (*animated, stimulating*) animated, bustling, busy, buzzing, exciting, invigorating, moving, refreshing, stimulating, stirring. **4** ((*of a description*) *lifelike*) actual, graphic, lifelike, realistic, vivid. **5** ((*of an impression*) *striking*) forceful, forcible, remarkable, striking. **6** ((*of a colour*) *bright*) bright, colourful, intense, rich, strong, vivid. ANTONYMS: dull. **7** (*exciting, dangerous*) dangerous, exciting, fast-moving, racy.

liven *v.t.* (*to make lively, to enliven*) animate, brighten, enliven, hot up, pep up, put life into, rouse, stir, vitalize, vivify.
~*v.i.* (*to cheer* (*up*)) brighten up, buck up, cheer up, perk up, rouse, stir up.

livery *n.* (*a distinctive dress worn by the servants of a particular person or the members of a city company*) attire, clothing, costume, dress, garb, regalia, (*coll.*) rig-out, suit, uniform, vestments.

livid *a.* **1** (*furious, very angry*) angry, boiling, cross, enraged, exasperated, fuming, furious, incensed, indignant, infuriated, (*coll.*) mad, outraged. ANTONYMS: calm, content, happy. **2** (*of a leaden colour*) ashen, blanched, bloodless, greyish, leaden, pale, pallid, pasty, wan, waxen. **3** (*black and blue, discoloured* (*as by a bruise*)) black and blue, bruised, contused, discoloured, purple.

living *a.* **1** (*alive, having life*) active, alive, animated, breathing, existent, existing, in the land of the living, live, lively, quick, strong, vigorous, vital. ANTONYMS: dead. **2** (*alive now, existing*) active, contemporary, continuing, current, existing, extant, ongoing, operative, persisting.
~*n.* **1** (*the state of being alive, existence*) animation, being, existence, life. ANTONYMS: death. **2** (*livelihood, means of subsistence*) income, job, livelihood, maintenance, means of support, occupation, profession, subsistence, sustenance, work. **3** (*the benefice of a member of the clergy*) benefice, incumbency, stipend. **4** (*manner of life*) lifestyle, manner of life, mode of living, way of life, way of living.

load *n.* **1** (*something which is laid on or put in anything for conveyance*) bale, cargo, consignment, freight, lading, shipment. **2** (*something which is borne with difficulty; a mental burden*) affliction, anxiety, burden, commitment, encumbrance, millstone, onus, oppression, pressure, trouble, weight, worry. **3** (*pl., coll.*) (*heaps, lots*) a large amount, heaps, lots. **4** (*something which obstructs or resists*) obstruction, pressure.
~*v.t.* **1** (*to put a load upon or in*) burden, pile. ANTONYMS: unload. **2** (*to put* (*a load or cargo*) *on or in a ship, vehicle etc.*) lade, pack. **3** (*to add weight to, to make heavy or heavier*) weigh down, weight. **4** (*to encumber, to oppress*) encumber, hamper, oppress, saddle with, trouble, weigh down, worry. **5** (*to charge* (*a gun etc.*)) charge, make ready, prime. **6** (*to fill to overflowing*) cram, fill, stuff. **7** (*to heap or overwhelm* (*with abuse, honours etc.*)) cover, heap, overwhelm, pile. **8** (*to bias, esp. with something to increase strength or weight*) bias, distort, prejudice, twist.

loaded *a.* **1** (*carrying a* (*heavy*) *load*) burdened, full, laden. **2** ((*of a gun*) *charged with ammunition*) charged, primed, ready. **3** (*wealthy*) affluent, flush, rich, wealthy, well off. **4** (*drunk or drugged*) drugged, drunk. **5** (*biased, weighted in a* *certain direction*) biased, distorted, prejudiced, twisted, weighted. **6** (*likely to cause argument*) contentious, manipulative, provocative, tricky.

loaf[1] *n.* **1** (*a moulded mass of any material, esp. a conical mass of refined sugar*) block, cake, cube, lump, slab. **2** (*the head or brains*) brains, head, intelligence, sense.

loaf[2] *v.i.* (*to lounge or idle about*) fritter away, idle, kill time, laze about, loiter, loll around, lounge about, pass time, relax, take it easy, (*coll.*) veg out, waste time.

loafer *n.* (*a person who loafs, an idler*) (*sl.*) couch potato, good-for-nothing, idler, layabout, (*coll.*) lazybones, lounger, ne'er-do-well, shirker, (*coll.*) skiver, sluggard, wastrel.

loan *n.* (*something which is lent, esp. a sum of money lent at interest*) accommodation, advance, allowance, credit, mortgage. ANTONYMS: debt.
~*v.t.* (*to grant the loan of*) accommodate, advance, allow, credit, lend. ANTONYMS: borrow.

loath *a.* (*unwilling, reluctant*) against, averse, backward, disinclined, indisposed, opposed, reluctant, unwilling. ANTONYMS: enthusiastic, keen.

loathe *v.t.* (*to abhor, to detest*) abhor, abominate, be repulsed by, despise, detest, dislike, execrate, feel revulsion for, hate, have an aversion to. ANTONYMS: adore, love.

loathing *n.* (*disgust, abhorrence*) abhorrence, abomination, antipathy, aversion, detestation, disgust, execration, hatred, horror, odium, repugnance, repulsion, revulsion. ANTONYMS: love.

loathsome *a.* (*causing loathing or disgust, detestable*) abhorrent, abominable, detestable, disgusting, execrable, hateful, horrible, nasty, nauseating, obnoxious, obscene, odious, repugnant, repulsive, revolting, vile, (*sl.*) yucky. ANTONYMS: attractive, lovely.

lob *v.t.* (*to hit or throw* (*a ball*) *in a high arc*) loft, pitch, shy, throw, toss.

lobby *n.* **1** (*a passage or vestibule, usu. opening into several apartments*) corridor, passage, passageway, vestibule. **2** (*a small hall or anteroom*) anteroom, atrium, entrance hall, foyer, hall, hallway, porch. **3** (*a group of people who try to influence legislators on behalf of special interests*) campaign, pressure group, special interest group.
~*v.i.* (*to seek to gain support, esp. from legislators,* (*for*)) campaign (for), promote, push (for), seek support (for), solicit.
~*v.t.* (*to attempt to influence or persuade* (*legislators*) *to support something*) bring pressure to bear on, exert influence on, influence, persuade, press, pressure, urge.

local *a.* **1** (*existing in or peculiar to a particular place*) district, home, parochial, provincial, regional, small-town. **2** (*of or relating to a neighbourhood*) community, neighbourhood. **3** (*of or relating to a part, not the whole* (*as a disease etc.*)) confined, limited, narrow, restricted. ANTONYMS: general.
~*n.* **1** (*an inhabitant of a particular place*) inhabitant, native, resident. **2** (*a public house in one's neighbourhood*) bar, inn, pub, public house, tavern.

locality *n.* **1** (*a particular place or neighbourhood*) area, district, neck of the woods, neighbourhood, region, vicinity. **2** (*the site or scene of something*) locale, location, place, position, scene, setting, site, spot.

localize *v.t.* **1** (*to ascertain or indicate the exact place or locality of*) ascribe, pinpoint, specify. **2** (*to restrict to a particular place*) circumscribe, concentrate, confine, contain, limit, restrain, restrict. **3** (*to decentralize*) decentralize, devolve.

locate *v.t.* **1** (*to discover or determine the site of*) come across, detect, determine, discover, ferret out, find, lay one's hands on, pin down, pinpoint, run to earth, track down, unearth. **2** (*to set or place in a particular locality*) establish, fix, place, put, seat, set. ANTONYMS: remove. **3** (*to situate*) settle, situate.
~*v.i.* (*to settle, to take up residence*) reside, settle.

location *n.* **1** (*situation or position*) bearings, locale, locality, locus, place, point, position, site, situation, spot, venue, whereabouts. **2** (*the act of locating*) detection, discovery, finding, pinpointing, unearthing.

lock[1] *n.* **1** (*a device for fastening doors etc., usu. having a bolt moved by a key of a particular shape*) bolt, clasp, fastening, padlock, (*dial.*) sneck. **2** (*a mechanical device for checking or preventing movement, as of a wheel*) catch, check, restraint. **3** (*a hug or grapple in wrestling that prevents an opponent from moving a limb*) bear-hug, grapple, hold, hug.
~*v.t.* **1** (*to fasten* (*a door, window etc.*) *by means of a lock*) bolt, clasp, fasten, latch, shut, (*dial.*) sneck. ANTONYMS: unfasten, unlock. **2** (*to secure* (*a building, car etc.*) *by locking its doors etc.*) close up, seal, secure. **3** (*to fix together* (*a coupling, interlocking parts*) *so as to make secure or immovable*) entangle, immobilize, interlock, join, link, unite. **4** (*to hold closely and firmly* (*in an embrace*)) clasp, clench, clutch, embrace, entwine, hold, hug. **5** (*to engage in a contest, struggle etc.*) contend, engage, grapple, struggle. **to lock away 1** (*to hide, keep in a secure place*) hide, keep safe, safeguard. **2** (*to imprison*) confine, imprison, incarcerate, jail. **to lock out** (*to prevent from entering by locking doors etc.*) ban, bar, debar,

exclude, keep out, refuse admittance, shut out. **to lock up 1** (*to fasten or secure with lock and key*) close, fasten, secure. **2** (*to hide, keep in a secure place*) hide, hoard, keep safely. **3** (*to imprison*) cage, confine, detain, imprison, incarcerate, jail, put away, put behind bars, shut up. ANTONYMS: release, set free.

lock² *n.* **1** (*a number of strands of hair curled or hanging together, a tress*) curl, ringlet, strand, tress. **2** (*a tuft of wool or similar substance*) bunch, strand, tuft, wisp.

locomotion *n.* **1** (*the act or power of moving from place to place*) motion, movement, moving. **2** (*moving about, travelling*) headway, progress, travel, travelling.

locution *n.* **1** (*a phrase or expression considered with regard to style or idiom*) expression, idiom, phrase, term, turn of speech, wording. **2** (*style of speech, mode of delivery*) accent, diction, inflection, intonation, phrasing, style of speech.

lodge *n.* **1** (*a small house at the entrance to or in a park, esp. for a gatekeeper or gardener*) gatehouse. **2** (*a cottage, a cabin for seasonal use*) cabin, chalet, cottage, hunting lodge, hut. **3** (*a local branch or place of meeting of certain societies*) branch, chapel, chapter.
~*v.t.* **1** (*to supply with temporary quarters, esp. for sleeping*) accommodate, board, entertain, harbour, put up, shelter, take in. **2** (*to find accommodation for*) billet, house, quarter. **3** (*to deposit, to leave for security (in, with etc.)*) deposit, file, leave, place, put, put on record, register, submit. **4** (*to implant, to fix*) embed, fix, imbed, implant, lay, place, put, set, stick.
~*v.i.* **1** (*to reside temporarily, esp. to have sleeping quarters*) dwell, live, reside, room, sojourn, stay, stop. **2** (*to stay or become fixed (in)*) become fixed, catch, come to rest, imbed, implant.

lodger *n.* (*a person who rents and occupies furnished rooms*) boarder, guest, paying guest, resident, tenant. ANTONYMS: landlady, landlord.

lodging *n.* **1** (*a temporary residence*) abode, accommodation, quarters, residence. **2** (*usu. pl.*) (*a room or rooms hired in another's house*) (*coll.*) digs, rooms. **3** (*formal*) (*a dwelling-place*) apartment, dwelling-place, habitation, shelter.

lofty *a.* **1** (*very high, towering*) high, raised, sky-high, soaring, tall, towering. **2** (*elevated in character, style etc.*) august, dignified, distinguished, elevated, eminent, exalted, grand, illustrious, imposing, magnificent, majestic, noble, renowned, stately, sublime, superior. ANTONYMS: lowly. **3** (*high-flown, grandiose*) grandiose, high-flown, rich. **4** (*haughty, arrogant*) arrogant, condescending, contemptuous, disdainful, haughty, (*coll.*) high and mighty, lordly, overbearing,

patronizing, proud, scornful, snobbish, (*coll.*) snooty, (*sl.*) snotty, supercilious, superior, (*sl.*) toffee-nosed. ANTONYMS: humble, unassuming.

log *n.* **1** (*a bulky piece of unhewn timber*) stump, timber, trunk. **2** (*a block*) block, chunk. **3** (*a logbook*) daybook, journal, logbook. **4** (*any record of events, transmissions made etc. or of the work done by a computer*) account, chart, journal, listing, note, record, register, report, tally.
~*v.t.* **1** (*to enter in the logbook or other regular record*) book, chart, enter, note, record, register, report, set down, tally. **2** (*to fell (trees) for timber*) chop, fell, hew.

logic *n.* **1** (*the science of reasoning, correct thinking*) deduction, proving, reasoning. **2** (*reasoning, argument etc. considered with regard to correctness or incorrectness*) argument, dialectics, reasoning. **3** (*reasoned argument*) good sense, judiciousness, rationality, sound judgement, wisdom.

logical *a.* **1** (*used in or according to the rules of logic*) clear, cogent, coherent, consistent, deducible, pertinent, rational, reasonable, relevant, sound, valid, well-organized. ANTONYMS: illogical. **2** (*reasonable*) judicious, necessary, obvious, plausible, reasonable, sensible, wise.

loiter *v.i.* **1** (*to linger, to dawdle*) dally, dawdle, delay, (*coll.*) dilly-dally, hang around, lag, linger, loaf, loll, tarry. ANTONYMS: hurry. **2** (*to move or travel with frequent halts*) meander, saunter, stroll, wander.
~*v.t.* (*to waste or consume (time) in trifles, to idle (time) away*) idle, waste.

loll *v.i.* **1** (*to sit or lie in a lazy attitude*) flop, lean, lie, loaf, lounge, recline, relax, repose, rest, slouch, sprawl. **2** ((*of the tongue*) *to hang from the mouth*) dangle, droop, drop, flap, flop, hang, sag.

lone *a.* **1** (*solitary, without company or a comrade*) by oneself, lonesome, on one's own, single, solitary, unaccompanied. **2** (*unmarried, widowed*) unattached, unmarried, widowed. **3** (*uninhabited, deserted*) deserted, isolated, lonely, retired, separate, sole, solitary, uninhabited.

lonely *a.* **1** (*sad through lacking company or companionship*) abandoned, bereft, destitute, estranged, forlorn, forsaken, friendless, lonesome, outcast. **2** (*solitary, companionless*) alone, apart, by oneself, companionless, isolated, lone, on one's own, reclusive, single, solitary, withdrawn. **3** ((*of a place*) *unfrequented, causing feelings of loneliness*) deserted, desolate, God-forsaken, isolated, out-of-the-way, remote, secluded, sequestered, solitary, unfrequented, uninhabited. ANTONYMS: bustling, populous. **4** ((*of an object*) *standing alone*) single, solitary.

long¹ *a.* **1** (*of considerable or relatively great linear* *extent*) elongated, expanded, extensive. **2** (*of great or relatively great extent in time*) drawn-out, extended, lengthy, prolonged, stretched. ANTO-NYMS: abbreviated, brief. **3** (*seeming to be of greater duration than it actually is*) dragging, interminable, lingering, long-winded, protracted, slow, sustained, tardy. **4** (*lengthy, verbose*) lengthy, prolix, tedious, verbose. ANTONYMS: brief, concise, succinct.

long² *v.i.* **1** (*to have an earnest desire (for)*) covet, desire, dream (of), hanker (after), itch (for), lust (for), thirst (for), want, wish. **2** (*to yearn (to or for)*) crave, pine, yearn.

longing *n.* (*an intense desire (for)*) ambition, aspiration, craving (for), desire (for), fancy (for), hankering (after), hunger (for), itch (for), thirst (for), urge (for), wish, yearning (for), (*coll.*) yen (for). ANTONYMS: antipathy (towards), loathing (of).

long-suffering *a.* (*patient, enduring*) easygoing, enduring, forbearing, forgiving, patient, resigned, stoical, tolerant, uncomplaining.

long-winded *a.* (*wordy, tiresome*) diffuse, discursive, drawn-out, garrulous, interminable, lengthy, long-drawn-out, overlong, prolix, pro-longed, rambling, repetitious, tedious, tiresome, verbose, wordy. ANTONYMS: concise, succinct.

look *v.i.* **1** (*to direct the eyes (towards, at etc.) in order to see an object*) glance, glimpse, peep, see. **2** (*to watch*) observe, watch. **3** (*to gaze, to stare*) gaze, ogle, peer, stare. **4** (*to stare in astonishment, wonder etc.*) gape, gawk, gawp, goggle, (*coll.*) rubberneck. **5** (*to direct the mind or under-standing*) consider, contemplate. **6** (*to face, to be turned or have a particular direction (towards, to, into etc.)*) face, front, give onto, overlook. **7** (*to seem, to appear*) appear, manifest, seem, show. **8** (*to make a physical or mental search*) forage, hunt, search, seek.
~*v.t.* **1** (*to view, to inspect*) behold, (*sl.*) clock, examine, eye, (*esp. N Am., sl.*) eyeball, (*sl.*) get a load of, inspect, notice, regard, scan, scrutinize, study, survey, view. **2** (*to ascertain, to determine*) ascertain, check, check out, determine. **3** (*to expect, to hope (to do something)*) anticipate, await, expect, hope.
~*n.* **1** (*the act of looking or seeing*) (*sl.*) butcher's, (*coll.*) dekko, examination, eyeful, (*coll.*) gander, gaze, glance, glimpse, inspection, (*coll.*) look-see, observation, (*coll.*) once-over, peek, scrutiny, (*sl.*) shufti, sight, stare, survey, view. **2** (*pl.*) (*personal appearance, esp. of the face, attractiveness*) air, appearance, aspect, attractiveness, bearing, beauty, cast, complexion, countenance, demean-our. **3** (*fashion (for clothes or general design)*) fashion, guise, line, manner, semblance, style. **to look after 1** (*to take care of*) care for, guard, keep

an eye on, mind, nurse, protect, safeguard, take care of. ANTONYMS: neglect. **2** (*to attend to*) attend to, supervise, tend to, watch. **to look down on/upon** (*to despise*) contemn, despise, disdain, disparage, hold in contempt, look down one's nose at, scorn, sneer, spurn, turn up one's nose at. ANTONYMS: respect, revere. **to look forward to** (*to anticipate or hope for with pleasure*) anticipate, await, count on, expect, hope for, long for, look for, wait for. **to look into** (*to inspect carefully, to investigate*) check out, delve into, dissect, examine, explore, follow up, go into, inquire about, inspect, look over, make inquiries, probe, research, scrutinize, study. **to look out** (*to be on the watch, to be prepared (for)*) be alert, be aware, be in readiness, be prepared, keep an eye out, keep one's eyes open, pay attention, watch out. **to look over 1** (*to inspect by making a tour of*) check, examine, inspect, view. **2** (*to read or examine cursorily*) cast an eye over, flick through, glance at, look through, peruse, scan, skim through. **to look up 1** (*to search for, esp. in a book*) find, hunt for, research, search for, seek out, track down. **2** (*to pay a visit to*) call in on, drop in on, look in on, visit. **3** (*to improve, to become more pros-perous*) ameliorate, come along, improve, perk up, pick up, progress, shape up. **to look up to** (*to admire and respect*) admire, defer to, esteem, have a high opinion of, hold in high regard, honour, respect, revere. ANTONYMS: despise.

lookout *n.* **1** (*watch*) alertness, guard, heed, vigil, vigilance, watch, watchfulness. **2** (*a person engaged in watching or looking out*) guard, guard-ian, patrol, sentinel, sentry, watch, watchman. **3** (*a place from which watch or observation is kept*) beacon, citadel, crow's nest, observation post, post, tower, watchtower. **4** (*a view, a prospect*) panorama, prospect, view. **5** (*future prospect*) chances, future, likelihood, outlook, prospect, view. **6** (*a person's personal affair or concern*) business, concern, (*coll.*) funeral, (*coll.*) headache, problem, responsibility, worry.

loom *v.i.* **1** (*to appear indistinctly or faintly in the distance*) appear, become visible, emerge, hover, manifest, materialize, surface, take shape. ANTONYMS: recede. **2** (*to appear larger than the real size, as in a mist, and often threatening*) bulk, rise, soar, tower. **3** ((*of an event) to be imminent, esp. ominously so*) dominate, hang over, impend, menace, mount, overhang, overshadow, threaten.

loop *n.* **1** (*a folding or doubling of a string, thread etc. across itself to form a curve*) bight, fold, noose. **2** (*anything resembling this, e.g. a pattern in a fingerprint*) circle, coil, convolution, curl, curve, eyelet, hoop, noose, ring, spiral, twirl, twist, whorl. **3** (*a ring or curved piece by which anything is hung up, fastened etc.*) circlet, eye, ring.
~*v.t.* **1** (*to form into a loop or loops*) bend, coil, curl, curve round, fold, knot, spiral, twist, wind

round. **2** (*to encircle with a loop*) circle, curve round, encircle, ring, wind round.

loose *a.* **1** (*not tied or fastened*) released, unbound, unchained, unconfined, undone, unfastened, unfettered, unrestricted, unsecured, untied. ANTONYMS: secured, tied. **2** (*unfastened; hanging partly free*) baggy, detachable, drooping, floating, free, hanging, insecure, movable, unattached, unfastened, wobbly. ANTONYMS: secure, tight. **3** (*not fixed or tight*) unfixed, untightened. **4** (*relaxed, slack*) flexible, relaxed, slack. **5** (*careless, slovenly*) careless, casual, heedless, imprudent, lax, negligent, rash, sloppy, slovenly, thoughtless, unmindful. ANTONYMS: careful, prudent. **6** (*vague, indefinite*) broad, diffuse, disordered, ill-defined, imprecise, inaccurate, indefinite, indistinct, inexact, rambling, random, vague. ANTONYMS: exact, precise, strict. **7** (*incorrect; ungrammatical*) incorrect, sloppy, ungrammatical. **8** (*dissolute, wanton*) abandoned, debauched, disreputable, dissipated, dissolute, fast, immoral, lewd, libertine, licentious, profligate, promiscuous, unchaste, wanton. ANTONYMS: chaste, virtuous.

~*v.t.* **1** (*to release, to set at liberty*) deliver, free, let go, liberate, release, set free, unbind, unbridle. ANTONYMS: imprison, restrain. **2** (*to untie, to unfasten*) detach, disconnect, disengage, undo, unfasten, unleash, unloose, untie. ANTONYMS: fasten, secure. **3** (*to free from obligation or burden*) ease, relieve. **4** (*to relax*) loosen, relax, slacken. **5** (*to discharge (a projectile, volley etc.)*) discharge, fire, unwind.

loosen *v.t.* **1** (*to make less tight, fixed etc.*) detach, separate, unbind, unbuckle, undo, unloose, unstick, untie, work free, work loose. ANTONYMS: tighten. **2** (*to make less strict or severe*) ease up, go easy, lessen, let out, let up, mitigate, moderate, relax, slacken, soften, weaken. **3** (*to free, to set loose*) deliver, free, let go, liberate, release, set free.

loot *n.* **1** (*booty, plunder, esp. from a conquered city*) booty, goods, haul, plunder, prize, takings. **2** (*stolen money, jewellery etc.*) contraband, spoils, (*sl.*) swag. **3** (*money*) cash, money, (*coll.*) readies, (*sl.*) spondulicks.

~*v.t.* **1** (*to steal (unprotected goods) or to steal from (unprotected premises), e.g. during a riot*) rob, sack, steal from. **2** (*to plunder, to pillage, esp. a city*) despoil, maraud, pillage, plunder, raid, ransack, ravage, rifle, sack.

lop *v.t.* **1** (*to cut off the top or extremities of (a tree, body etc.)*) cut off. **2** (*to trim (trees, shrubs etc.) by cutting*) clip, cut, prune, snip, top, trim. **3** (*to omit or remove as superfluous*) chop, crop, curtail, cut, dock, hack, omit, prune, remove, trim, truncate.

lopsided *a.* **1** (*heavier on one side than the other*) one-sided. **2** (*not symmetrical*) askew, asymmetrical, awry, cock-eyed, crooked, out of shape, out of true, (*coll.*) skew-whiff, tilted, unequal, uneven, unsymmetrical, warped. **3** (*ill-balanced*) disproportionate, ill-balanced, off-balance, unbalanced.

loquacious *a.* (*talkative, chattering*) babbling, blathering, chattering, chatty, (*coll.*) gabby, garrulous, gossipy, talkative, verbose, voluble, wordy. ANTONYMS: taciturn, tongue-tied.

lord *n.* **1** (*a ruler, a master*) chief, commander, governor, king, leader, liege, master, monarch, overlord, potentate, prince, ruler, sovereign. **2** (*God*) God, Jehovah, the Almighty. **3** (*Jesus Christ*) Christ, Jesus Christ. **4** (*a nobleman, a peer of the realm*) baron, noble, nobleman, peer. ANTONYMS: commoner.

lordly *a.* **1** (*proud, haughty*) arrogant, despotic, dictatorial, domineering, haughty, (*coll.*) high and mighty, high-handed, hoity-toity, imperious, lofty, overbearing, patronizing, proud, snobbish, (*coll.*) snooty, stuck-up, supercilious, tyrannical. ANTONYMS: humble. **2** (*becoming or befitting a lord, noble*) aristocratic, dignified, exalted, gracious, grand, imperial, kingly, lofty, magnificent, majestic, noble, princely, regal, stately. ANTONYMS: lowly.

lore *n.* **1** (*the collective traditions and knowledge relating to a given subject*) beliefs, culture, doctrine, experience, folklore, knowledge, traditions, wisdom. **2** (*learning*) erudition, (*coll.*) know-how, learning, letters, scholarship. **3** (*teaching or something that is taught*) sayings, teaching.

lose *v.t.* **1** (*to be deprived of*) be deprived of. **2** (*to be unable to find; to stray from*) confuse, displace, mislay, misplace, miss, stray from, wander from. **3** (*to fail to gain or enjoy*) be defeated, capitulate, (*coll.*) come a cropper, come to grief, default, fail, fall short, forfeit, get the worst of, lose out, miss, yield. ANTONYMS: gain. **4** (*to fail to hold or grasp*) drop, forget, let slip. **5** (*to spend uselessly, to waste*) consume, deplete, dissipate, drain, exhaust, expend, fritter away, lavish, let slip, misspend, squander, use up, waste. ANTONYMS: keep. **6** (*coll.*) (*to outdistance (a pursuer)*) dodge, elude, escape, evade, leave behind, outdistance, outrun, outstrip, overtake, pass, shake off, throw off.

loser *n.* **1** (*a person who loses, esp. a race*) also, also-ran. **2** (*a person who seems destined to be unfortunate or to lose*) dud, failure, (*coll.*) flop, (*sl.*) lemon, misfit, (*sl.*) no-hoper, underdog.

loss *n.* **1** (*the act of losing or the state of being deprived of something*) bereavement, denial, deprivation, mislaying, privation. ANTONYMS:

acquisition, gain. **2** (*failure to win or gain*) defeat, failure. **3** (*something which is lost or the cost of this*) cost, damage, debit, debt, deficit, drain, forfeiture, harm, hurt, injury, losings, sacrifice. **4** (*pl.*) (*casualties and those taken prisoner in war*) casualties, dead, fatalities. **5** (*detriment, disadvantage*) depletion, detriment, disadvantage, impairment, misfortune, ruin. **6** (*wasted expenditure, effort etc.*) squandering, waste.

lost *a.* **1** (*unable to find the way or determine one's position or whereabouts*) adrift, all at sea, astray, disorientated, off-course, off-track, way off-beam. **2** (*missing, unable to be found*) disappeared, forfeited, irrecoverable, irretrievable, mislaid, misplaced, missed, missing, strayed, vanished, wayward. ANTONYMS: found. **3** (*confused, bewildered*) baffled, bewildered, clueless, confounded, confused, helpless, mystified, perplexed, puzzled. **4** (*ruined, destroyed*) abolished, annihilated, dead, demolished, destroyed, devastated, eradicated, exterminated, misused, obliterated, perished, ruined, wasted, wiped out, wrecked. **5** (*no longer possessed or known*) consumed, dissipated, extinct, forgotten, frittered away, gone, lapsed, misspent, obsolete, past, squandered, wasted. **6** (*engrossed*) absorbed, abstracted, distracted, engrossed, entranced, preoccupied, rapt, spellbound. **7** (*morally fallen or corrupted*) abandoned, corrupted, depraved, dissolute, fallen, incorrigible, licentious, loose, profligate, unchaste, wanton. ANTONYMS: virtuous.

lot *n.* **1** (*often in pl.*) (*a considerable quantity or amount, a great deal*) abundance, a great deal, heap, large amount, (*coll.*) loads, masses, oceans, (*coll.*) oodles, (*coll.*) pile, plenty, quantities, (*coll.*) stacks. **2** (*the share or fortune falling to anyone*) accident, chance, doom, end, fate, fortune, hazard, luck, portion, share. **3** (*one's fortune, destiny or condition in life*) condition, destiny, doom, fate, fortune. **4** (*a distinct portion, collection of things offered for sale, esp. at auction*) allowance, collection, (*coll.*) cut, parcel, part, piece, portion, quota, ration, share. **5** (*a number or quantity of things or persons*) assortment, batch, bunch, collection, consignment, crowd, group, number, quantity, set.

lotion *n.* (*a medicinal or cosmetic liquid application for external use*) balm, cream, embrocation, liniment, ointment, salve, unguent.

loud *a.* **1** (*powerful in sound, sonorous*) sonorous, sounding. ANTONYMS: inaudible. **2** (*noisy, clamorous*) blaring, booming, clamorous, deafening, ear-piercing, ear-splitting, forte, noisy, piercing, resounding, shrill, stentorian, strident, strong, thundering. ANTONYMS: quiet, soft. **3** ((*of attire, manners etc.*) *ostentatious, flashy*) blatant, brash, brassy, conspicuous, flamboyant, flashy, garish,

gaudy, glaring, lurid, ostentatious, showy, (*sl.*) snazzy, tasteless, tawdry, vulgar. ANTONYMS: subdued. **4** ((*of behaviour*) *aggressive*) aggressive, boisterous, brash, brazen, bumptious, coarse, crass, crude, loudmouthed, obstreperous, offensive, raucous, rowdy, tumultuous, turbulent, vehement, vociferous. ANTONYMS: reserved, shy.

lounge *v.i.* **1** (*to loll or recline*) loll, recline, relax, sprawl, take it easy. **2** (*to move lazily, to saunter*) dawdle, saunter. **3** (*to idle about*) hang around, (*sl.*) hang out, idle, kill time, laze around, loaf about, loiter, potter about, vegetate, (*coll.*) veg out, waste time.
~*n.* (*the sitting room in a house*) front room, living room, sitting room.

lour *v.i.* **1** ((*of clouds, weather etc.*) *to appear dark or gloomy*) blacken, cloud up, darken, impend, loom, lower, menace, threaten. ANTONYMS: brighten. **2** (*to frown, to scowl*) frown, glare, glower, pout, scowl. ANTONYMS: smile.

louring *a.* **1** ((*of clouds, weather etc.*) *dark or gloomy*) black, clouded, cloudy, dark, darkening, forbidding, foreboding, gloomy, grey, heavy, impending, looming, menacing, murky, ominous, overcast, threatening. ANTONYMS: bright, clear. **2** (*frowning, scowling*) brooding, forbidding, frowning, glowering, grim, scowling, sullen, surly.

lousy *a.* **1** (*infested with lice*) lice-infested, lice-ridden, pedicular. **2** (*bad, inferior*) awful, bad, contemptible, dirty, disgraceful, disgusting, inferior, low, mean, miserable, poor, rotten, second-rate, terrible, unkind, unsatisfactory, vile.

lout *n.* (*a rough, ill-mannered person*) bear, boor, brute, bumpkin, churl, clod, dolt, layabout, (*coll.*) lummox, ne'er-do-well, oaf, yahoo, yob.

lovable *a.* **1** (*worthy of love*) worthy of love. **2** (*amiable*) adorable, attractive, captivating, charming, cherished, cuddly, cute, delightful, desirable, enchanting, endearing, engaging, fetching, gorgeous, likeable, lovely, pleasing, sweet, winning, winsome. ANTONYMS: hateful, repellent.

love *n.* **1** (*a feeling of deep fondness and devotion (for, towards etc.*)) delight, devotion, enjoyment, fondness, friendship, inclination, liking, partiality, regard, relish, weakness. **2** (*deep affection, usu. accompanied by yearning or desire for*) adoration, adulation, affection, amity, ardour, attachment, desire, infatuation, passion, rapture, tenderness, warmth, yearning. ANTONYMS: hatred. **3** (*sexual desire or passion*) desire, lust, passion. **4** (*a beloved one, a sweetheart (as a term of endearment*)) angel, beloved, darling, dear, dearest, intended, loved one, lover, sweetheart. **5** (*in games, no points scored, nil*) nil, no points, nothing, zero.

~*v.t.* **1** (*to have strong affection for, to be fond of*) adore, adulate, be attached to, be fond of, be in love with, cherish, dote on, feel affection for, hold dear, idolize, prize, think the world of, treasure, worship. ANTONYMS: detest, hate. **2** (*to desire passionately, to be in love with*) desire, (*coll.*) fancy, (*sl.*) have the hots for. **3** (*to have a strong partiality or liking for*) appreciate, delight in, (*dated sl.*) dig, enjoy, have a weakness for, like, relish, savour, take pleasure in.

love affair *n.* **1** (*a romantic or sexual attachment between two people*) affair, amour, attachment, (*coll.*) fling, intrigue, liaison, relationship, romance. **2** (*an enthusiasm for or fascination with (an object, activity etc.)*) appreciation, devotion, enthusiasm, fascination, mania, passion.

loveless *a.* **1** (*destitute of love*) without love. **2** (*not loving*) cold, cold-hearted, formal, frigid, hard, heartless, icy, indifferent, insensitive, unfeeling, unfriendly, unloving, unresponsive, unsympathetic. **3** (*not loved*) despised, disliked, forsaken, friendless, hated, lovelorn, rejected, unappreciated, uncherished, unloved, unvalued. ANTONYMS: adored, appreciated.

lovely *a.* **1** (*beautiful and attractive*) alluring, attractive, beautiful, charming, comely, exquisite, fair, fetching, graceful, handsome, pretty, ravishing. ANTONYMS: ugly, unattractive. **2** (*delightful, enjoyable*) agreeable, captivating, delightful, enchanting, engaging, enjoyable, gratifying, nice, pleasant, pleasing, satisfactory. ANTONYMS: horrible, unpleasant. **3** (*lovable, amiable*) admirable, adorable, amiable, lovable, sweet, winning.

lovemaking *n.* **1** (*sexual play or intercourse between partners*) carnal knowledge, coition, coitus, congress, copulation, coupling, going to bed with someone, (*coll., facet.*) how's your father, intercourse, intimacy, mating, (*sl.*) nooky, sex, sexual intercourse, sexual relations, sleeping with someone, (*sl.*) the other. **2** (*courtship, amorous attentions*) courtship, seduction, wooing.

lover *n.* **1** (*a person with whom one is having a sexual relationship*) admirer, beau, beloved, boyfriend, (*sl., derog.*) fancy man, (*sl., derog.*) fancy woman, (*coll.*) flame, girlfriend, mate, mistress, paramour, sexual partner, suitor, sweetheart, (*coll.*) toyboy. **2** (*a person who is fond of anything*) devotee, enthusiast, fan.

loving *a.* (*feeling or showing affection*) affectionate, amorous, ardent, attentive, caring, concerned, cordial, dear, demonstrative, devoted, doting, fond, friendly, kind, solicitous, tender, warm-hearted. ANTONYMS: cold, indifferent.

low *a.* **1** (*below the usual or normal height*) little, short, small, squat, stubby, stunted. ANTONYMS: high, tall. **2** (*below or little above a given surface or*

level) below, deep, depressed, low-lying, sunken. ANTONYMS: elevated, raised. **3** (*small or below the norm in amount, intensity etc.*) deficient, inadequate, inferior, insufficient, mediocre, pathetic, poor, puny, second-rate, shoddy, substandard. **4** (*reduced in amount, nearly exhausted*) depleted, meagre, paltry, reduced, scant, scanty, sparse. **5** (*humble in rank or position*) humble, low-born, lowly, mean, meek, obscure, plain, plebeian, poor, simple, unpretentious. **6** (*dejected, depressed*) (*coll.*) blue, crestfallen, dejected, depressed, despondent, disheartened, dismal, down, downcast, fed up, forlorn, gloomy, glum, melancholy, miserable, morose, unhappy, wretched. ANTONYMS: cheerful, happy. **7** (*lacking in vigour, weak*) debilitated, drained, enervated, exhausted, feeble, frail, infirm, prostrate, reduced, sickly, stricken, weak. **8** ((*of sounds*) *not raised in pitch, not loud*) deep, gentle, hushed, muffled, muted, quiet, soft, subdued. ANTONYMS: loud. **9** (*not exalted, commonplace*) commonplace, ordinary, worldly. **10** (*coarse, vulgar*) coarse, common, crude, disgraceful, dishonourable, disreputable, gross, ill-bred, improper, obscene, risqué, rough, rude, scurrilous, unbecoming, undignified, unrefined, unseemly, vulgar. **11** (*base, dishonourable*) abject, base, contemptible, degraded, depraved, despicable, dishonourable, ignoble, malicious, mean, menial, nasty, servile, sordid, unworthy, vile, vulgar. ANTONYMS: honourable. **12** (*inexpensive*) cheap, economical, good value, inexpensive, moderate, modest, reasonable. ANTONYMS: expensive.

lower *a.* **1** (*situated at a less high level than, or below, another thing*) below, inferior, junior, lesser, minor, secondary, smaller, subordinate, under. ANTONYMS: superior. **2** (*smaller in quantity, number etc.*) curtailed, cut, decreased, diminished, lessened, moderated, pared down, reduced, softened. ANTONYMS: enlarged, increased.

~*v.t.* **1** (*to bring down in height, intensity, price etc.*) abate, bring down, curtail, decline, die down, dwindle, moderate, prune, reduce, slash, soften, subside, tone down. ANTONYMS: augment. **2** (*to haul or let down*) haul down, let down. **3** (*to degrade, to demean*) abase, belittle, condescend, debase, degrade, demean, devalue, discredit, disgrace, downgrade, humble, humiliate, shame. **4** (*to diminish*) decrease, diminish, lessen, minimize. ANTONYMS: increase.

~*v.i.* (*to sink, to fall*) depress, descend, drop, sink, submerge. ANTONYMS: rise.

lowly *a.* **1** (*humble, modest*) average, common, humble, low-born, meek, modest, obscure, ordinary, plain, plebeian, proletarian, simple, unassuming, unpretentious. ANTONYMS: lofty, pretentious. **2** (*low in rank or condition*) junior, subordinate. **3** (*mean, inferior*) ignoble, inferior, low, mean. **4** (*comparatively undeveloped or unevolved*) undeveloped, unevolved.

loyal *a.* (*faithful in a trust or obligation* (*to*)) constant, dedicated, dependable, devoted, dutiful, faithful, reliable, staunch, steadfast, true, true-blue, trustworthy, trusty. ANTONYMS: disloyal, treacherous.

loyalty *n.* (*the state of being loyal*) allegiance, constancy, dedication, dependability, devotion, dutifulness, faithfulness, fealty, fidelity, reliability, staunchness, steadfastness, trustworthiness. ANTONYMS: infidelity.

lubricate *v.t.* **1** (*to cover or treat with grease, oil or similar substance, in order to reduce friction*) grease, oil. **2** (*to make smooth or slippery*) make slippery, smear, smooth.

lucid *a.* **1** (*clear, easily understood*) clear, comprehensible, distinct, evident, intelligible, limpid, pellucid, perspicuous, transparent, understandable. ANTONYMS: incomprehensible, vague. **2** (*sane; denoting an interval of sanity occurring during insanity or dementia*) (*coll.*) all there, clear-headed, rational, reasonable, sane, sensible, sober, sound. ANTONYMS: confused, muddled. **3** (*shining, radiant*) beaming, bright, brilliant, effulgent, gleaming, luminous, radiant, resplendent, shining.

luck *n.* **1** (*chance, as bringer of fortune, whether good or bad*) accident, chance, fortuity, hazard. **2** (*what happens to one, fortune*) destiny, fate, fortune, hap, lot. **3** (*good fortune, success*) blessing, (*coll.*) break, fluke, godsend, good luck, prosperity, serendipity, stroke, success, windfall. ANTONYMS: misfortune.

luckily *adv.* (*fortunately*) advantageously, conveniently, favourably, fortunately, happily, opportunely, propitiously, providentially.

luckless *a.* (*unfortunate*) cursed, disastrous, doomed, hapless, hopeless, ill-fated, ill-starred, jinxed, unfortunate, unhappy, unlucky, unpropitious, unsuccessful. ANTONYMS: fortunate, lucky.

lucky *a.* **1** (*characterized or usu. attended by good luck, favoured by fortune*) adventitious, fortuitous, fortunate, opportune, propitious, providential, serendipitous, timely. ANTONYMS: unfortunate. **2** (*successful, esp. by a fluke or more than is deserved*) blessed, charmed, fluky, (*coll.*) jammy, successful. **3** (*bringing luck, auspicious*) auspicious, luck-bringing. ANTONYMS: cursed.

lucrative *a.* (*producing gain, profitable*) fruitful, gainful, high-income, money-making, paying, productive, profitable, remunerative, rewarding, well-paid. ANTONYMS: unprofitable.

lucre *n.* (*pecuniary gain or advantage, usu. as an object of greed*) gain, money, profit, riches, spoils, wealth.

ludicrous *a.* (*liable to excite laughter or derision; ridiculous*) absurd, comic, comical, crazy, derisible, farcical, incongruous, laughable, nonsensical, outlandish, preposterous, ridiculous, risible, silly. ANTONYMS: logical, sensible.

lug *v.t.* **1** (*to pull, esp. roughly or with exertion*) drag, haul, heave, pull, tow, tug, yank. **2** (*to carry with effort and difficulty*) carry, (*coll.*) hump.

luggage *n.* (*a traveller's suitcases, trunks etc.*) baggage, bags, belongings, cases, effects, gear, impedimenta, paraphernalia, suitcases, (*coll.*) things, trunks.

lugubrious *a.* (*mournful, dismal*) depressing, dismal, doleful, dreary, funereal, gloomy, melancholy, morose, mournful, sad, serious, sombre, sorrowful, woeful. ANTONYMS: cheerful, jolly.

lukewarm *a.* **1** (*moderately warm, tepid*) room-temperature, tepid. **2** (*indifferent, lacking enthusiasm or conviction*) apathetic, chill, chilly, cold, cool, half-baked, half-hearted, indifferent, unenthusiastic, uninterested, unmoved, unresponsive. ANTONYMS: enthusiastic, keen.

lull *v.t.* **1** (*to soothe to sleep, to calm*) calm, compose, hush, mollify, pacify, quell, quiet, quieten, soothe, still, subdue. ANTONYMS: disturb. **2** (*to allay the fears, anxieties etc. of, usu. in order to deceive*) allay, appease, assuage, reassure.

~*v.i.* (*to subside, to become quiet*) abate, cease, decrease, diminish, dwindle, ease off, lessen, let up, moderate, quieten down, slacken, subside, wane. ANTONYMS: increase.

~*n.* **1** (*a temporary calm*) calm, hush, pause, peace, quiet, respite, silence, stillness, tranquillity. **2** (*an intermission or abatement*) abatement, break, delay, hiatus, interlude, intermission, interruption, interval, lapse, (*coll.*) let-up.

lumber[1] *v.i.* (*to move heavily or clumsily*) clump, plod, shamble, shuffle, stagger, stump, trudge, trundle, waddle.

lumber[2] *n.* **1** (*discarded articles of furniture and other rubbish taking up room*) bits and pieces, cast-offs, discards, jumble, junk, odds and ends, rejects. **2** (*useless and cumbersome things*) clutter, encumbrances, (*coll.*) rubble. **3** (*rubbish, refuse*) litter, refuse, rubbish, trash. **4** (*timber sawn into marketable shape*) beams, boards, planks, timber, wood.

~*v.t.* **1** (*to burden* (*with*), *to leave to deal with* (*something unwanted or unpleasant*)) burden (with), impose upon, land (with), load (with), saddle (with). **2** (*to encumber, to obstruct*) black, encumber, hamper, obstruct.

lumbering *a.* (*heavy or clumsy*) awkward, blundering, bovine, clumsy, heavy, heavy-footed, hulking, lubberly, lumpish, oafish, overgrown, ponderous, ungainly, unwieldy. ANTONYMS: dainty, nimble.

luminary *n.* **1** (*a famous person*) big name, celebrity, dignitary, lion, notable, (*coll.*) somebody, VIP. **2** (*a person who enlightens people or is a brilliant exponent of a subject*) expert, genius, guru, inspiration, sage.

luminous *a.* **1** (*emitting light*) alight, effulgent, illuminated, lit, radiant, resplendent. ANTONYMS: dark. **2** (*shining brightly*) bright, brilliant, lustrous, shining, vivid. **3** (*visible in darkness; phosphorescent*) aglow, fluorescent, glowing, incandescent, luminescent, phosphorescent. **4** (*shedding light* (*on a subject etc.*)) clear, comprehensible, evident, explicit, illuminating, intelligible, lucid, obvious, penetrating, perspicuous, plain, revelatory, transparent. ANTONYMS: obscure, unintelligible.

lump[1] *n.* **1** (*a small mass of matter of no definite shape*) ball, cake, chunk, clod, dab, gob, gobbet, hunk, nugget, piece, spot, wedge. **2** (*a quantity, a lot*) bunch, cluster, group, heap, lot, mass, quantity, wad. **3** (*a swelling*) boss, bulge, bump, excrescence, growth, hump, nodule, prominence, protrusion, protuberance, swelling, tumescence, tumour. **4** (*a heavy, stupid person*) dolt, hulk, idiot, (*coll.*) lummox.
~*v.t.* (*to put together in a lump, to form into a mass*) accumulate, batch, blend, bunch, collect, combine, conglomerate, consolidate, group, mass, pool, put together.
~*v.i.* (*to form or collect into lumps*) agglutinate, aggregate, cluster, coagulate, coalesce, collect, combine, group, mass, unite.

lump[2] *v.t.* (*to put up with*) accept, bear, brook, endure, put up with, stand, suffer, take, tolerate.

lumpish *a.* **1** (*like a lump*) lump-like. **2** (*heavy*) awkward, bovine, bungling, clumsy, gawky, heavy, lethargic, lumbering, ungainly. **3** (*lazy, inert*) idle, inert, lazy. **4** (*stupid*) doltish, dull, oafish, obtuse, stolid, stupid.

lumpy *a.* (*full of lumps*) bumpy, chunky, clotted, curdled, knobbly, uneven.

lunacy *n.* **1** (*unsoundness of mind, insanity*) dementia, derangement, idiocy, imbecility, insanity, madness, mania, psychosis, unsoundness. ANTONYMS: sanity. **2** (*gross folly, a senseless action*) absurdity, craziness, folly, foolhardiness, idiocy, illogicality, imbecility, madness, senselessness, stupidity.

lunatic *a.* **1** (*insane*) (*sl.*) barking, (*sl.*) barmy, (*sl.*) bonkers, crazy, demented, deranged, insane, (*coll.*) loopy, mad, manic, (*sl.*) nuts, off one's head, (*esp. N Am., coll.*) out to lunch, psychotic, unhinged. ANTONYMS: sane. **2** (*extremely foolish*)

absurd, (*coll.*) crackpot, crazy, daft, foolhardy, foolish, frantic, idiotic, irrational, mad, senseless, stupid. ANTONYMS: sensible.
~*n.* (*an insane person*) (*coll.*) head case, idiot, imbecile, (*sl.*) loony, madman, madwoman, maniac, (*sl.*) nut, (*sl.*) nutcase, (*sl.*) nutter, psychopath.

lunge *n.* **1** (*a sudden thrust with a sword etc.*) cut, jab, poke, strike, swing, (*coll.*) swipe, thrust. **2** (*a sudden forward movement, a plunge*) charge, plunge, pounce, spring.
~*v.i.* **1** (*to make a lunge*) charge, fall upon, launch oneself, set upon. **2** (*to plunge or rush forward suddenly*) bound, dash, dive, launch oneself, leap, plunge, pounce, rush forward.
~*v.t.* (*to thrust* (*a weapon*) *forward*) cut, jab, strike, thrust.

lurch *v.i.* **1** ((*of a ship*) *to roll suddenly to one side*) heave, heel, lean, list, pitch, rock, roll, tilt. **2** (*to stagger*) reel, stagger, stumble, sway, totter, weave.
~*n.* **1** (*a sudden roll sideways, as of a ship*) heel, lean, list, roll, tilt. **2** (*a stagger*) stagger, sway.

lure *n.* **1** (*an enticement, an allurement*) allurement, attraction, carrot, (*sl.*) come-on, enticement, inducement, temptation. ANTONYMS: repulsion. **2** (*an object resembling a fowl, used to recall a hawk*) bait, decoy.
~*v.t.* **1** (*to attract or bring back by a lure*) allure, attract, beckon, bring back, decoy, draw, ensnare, inveigle, invite, lead on. ANTONYMS: repel. **2** (*to entice*) entice, seduce, tempt.

lurid *a.* **1** (*shockingly or glaringly bright*) bright, dazzling, flaming, glaring, intense, livid. ANTONYMS: pale. **2** (*gaudy, in bright colours*) bright, gaudy, showy, vivid. ANTONYMS: pale. **3** ((*of a story etc.*) *shocking, horrifying*) appalling, disgusting, exaggerated, explicit, gory, graphic, grim, grisly, gruesome, horrid, horrifying, intense, macabre, melodramatic, revolting, sensational, shocking, violent, vivid. **4** (*ghastly, unearthly*) baleful, ghastly, unearthly. **5** (*of a pale yellow colour, wan*) ashen, pale, pallid, sallow, wan, yellow.

lurk *v.i.* (*to move about furtively*) crouch, prowl, skulk, slink, sneak, snoop, steal.

luscious *a.* **1** (*very sweet, delicious*) ambrosial, appetizing, delectable, delicious, juicy, lip-smacking, mouth-watering, palatable, rich, savoury, succulent, sweet, tasty, toothsome. ANTONYMS: revolting. **2** (*extremely attractive, voluptuous*) attractive, gorgeous, voluptuous. **3** ((*of music, poetry etc.*) *over-rich in imagery, sensuousness etc.*) cloying, fulsome, over-rich.

lush *a.* **1** (*luxuriant in growth*) abundant, dense, flourishing, green, lavish, luxuriant, overgrown, prolific, rank, verdant. ANTONYMS: sparse, stunted. **2** (*succulent, juicy*) fleshy, fresh, juicy, moist, ripe, succulent, tender. **3** ((*of sound, colour*) *rich and voluptuous*) elaborate, extravagant, grand, lavish, luxurious, opulent, ornate, palatial, (*coll.*) plushy, rich, sumptuous, voluptuous.

lust *n.* **1** (*a powerful desire for sexual pleasure*) carnality, concupiscence, desire, lasciviousness, mlechery, lewdness, libido, licentiousness, prurience, randiness, salaciousness, sensuality, sexuality, wantonness. ANTONYMS: frigidity. **2** (*sensual appetite*) appetite, hunger, thirst. **3** (*passionate desire* (*for*)) avidity, covetousness, craving, cupidity, greed, longing, passion, voracity, yearning. ANTONYMS: disinterest, indifference. **4** (*passionate enjoyment, relish*) enjoyment, relish.
~*v.i.* (*to have powerful or inordinate desire* (*for or after*)) covet, crave (for), desire, hunger (for), (*sl.*) lech (after), long (for), thirst (for), want, yearn (for).

lustful *a.* (*feeling or showing a powerful sexual desire*) carnal, concupiscent, craving, (*sl.*) horny, lascivious, lecherous, lewd, libidinous, licentious, passionate, prurient, randy, (*coll.*) raunchy, salacious, sensual, sexy, unchaste, wanton. ANTONYMS: chaste.

lustily *adv.* (*in a powerful way*) energetically, enthusiastically, forcefully, hard, healthily, loudly, mightily, powerfully, robustly, stoutly, strappingly, strongly, sturdily, vigorously.

lustre *n.* **1** (*bright light, reflected light*) brightness, burnish, gleam, glint, glitter, gloss, reflectiveness, sheen, shimmer, shine, sparkle. ANTONYMS: dullness. **2** (*radiant or brilliant light*) brightness, brilliance, dazzle, effulgence, lambency, luminousness, radiance, resplendence. **3** (*illustriousness, glory* (*of an achievement etc.*)) distinction, fame, glory, honour, illustriousness, prestige, renown, splendour.

lusty *a.* (*full of health and vigour*) brawny, energetic, enthusiastic, forceful, hale, healthy, hearty, loud, mighty, powerful, red-blooded, robust, rugged, stalwart, stout, strapping, strong, sturdy, vigorous, virile. ANTONYMS: feeble, weak.

luxuriant *a.* **1** ((*of vegetation*) *abundant in growth*) abundant, dense, exuberant, flourishing, fruitful, lush, productive, prolific, rank, rife, teeming, thriving. ANTONYMS: barren, thin. **2** (*fertile, prolific*) ample, bounteous, copious, excessive, exuberant, full, lavish, plenteous, plentiful, prodigal, profuse, prolific, superabundant. ANTONYMS: meagre. **3** ((*of style*) *ornate, extravagant*) baroque, decorated, elaborate, extravagant, fancy, flamboyant, florid, flowery,

ornate, ostentatious, rococo, sumptuous. ANTONYMS: plain, unadorned.

luxuriate *v.i.* **1** (*to revel, to indulge oneself voluptuously*) bask, delight, enjoy, indulge, relish, revel, savour, swim, wallow. **2** (*to grow abundantly or profusely*) bloom, burgeon, flourish, grow, mushroom, prosper, thrive. ANTONYMS: wither. **3** (*to live luxuriously*) (*coll.*) be in the lap of luxury, enjoy the good life, (*coll.*) live the life of Riley, take it easy.

luxurious *a.* **1** (*characterized by luxury, provided with an ample supply of comforts and pleasures*) pampered, well provided for. **2** (*extremely comfortable*) comfortable, costly, de luxe, expensive, extravagant, grand, lavish, magnificent, opulent, palatial, plush, (*coll.*) plushy, (*coll.*) posh, rich, splendid, sumptuous, (*coll.*) swanky, well-appointed. ANTONYMS: austere, economical. **3** (*self-indulgent*) epicurean, gourmet, pleasure-loving, self-indulgent, sensual, sybaritic, voluptuous. ANTONYMS: ascetic.

luxury *n.* **1** (*great comfort with abundant provision of pleasant and delightful things*) abundance, bliss, comfort, delight, enjoyment, indulgence, pleasure, satisfaction, well-being. **2** (*something which is not a necessity, esp. something particularly delightful and expensive*) expendable, extra, extravagance, frill, indulgence, non-essential, treat. **3** (*luxuriousness*) affluence, grandeur, hedonism, luxuriousness, magnificence, opulence, richness, splendour, sumptuousness, voluptuousness. ANTONYMS: austerity, privation.

lying *a.* (*telling lies; deceitful*) deceitful, dishonest, dissembling, duplicitous, (*coll.*) economical with the truth, false, hypocritical, mendacious, perfidious, treacherous, untruthful. ANTONYMS: honest, truthful.
~*n.* (*an act of telling lies*) deceit, dishonesty, dissimulation, duplicity, fabrication, falsity, fibbing, mendacity, perjury, untruthfulness. ANTONYMS: honesty.

lyric *a.* **1** ((*of a poem*) *expressing the individual emotions of the poet*) expressive, lyrical, rhapsodic, sentimental. **2** (*intended to be sung or fitted for expression in song*) melodic, melodious, musical. **3** ((*of singing*) *having a light quality and tone*) bright, clear, delicate, dulcet, flowing, graceful, light, lilting, mellow, silvery, sweet, tinkling.
~*n.* **1** (*a lyric poem*) ode, poem. **2** (*the words of a popular song*) libretto, text, words.

lyrical *a.* **1** (*lyric*) lyric, poetic. **2** (*extremely enthusiastic and effusive*) ecstatic, effusive, emotional, enthusiastic, expressive, exuberant, impassioned, inspired, rapturous, rhapsodic.

M

macabre *a.* (*gruesome*) cadaverous, chilling, deathly, dreadful, eerie, frightful, ghastly, ghostly, ghoulish, gory, grim, grisly, grotesque, gruesome, hideous, horrible, horrid, morbid, unearthly, weird. ANTONYMS: delightful, pleasant.

macerate *v.t.* **1** (*to soften by steeping*) soak, soften, steep. **2** (*to separate the parts of* (*food*) *by a digestive process*) chew, mash, pulp.

machiavellian *a.* (*unscrupulous, scheming*) amoral, artful, astute, crafty, cunning, deceitful, designing, devious, foxy, intriguing, opportunist, scheming, shrewd, sly, tricky, underhand, unscrupulous, wily.

machinate *v.i.* (*to plot, to intrigue*) conspire, contrive, design, devise, engineer, hatch, intrigue, invent, manoeuvre, plan, plot, scheme.

machination *n.* (*a secret and clever plot*) artifice, cabal, conspiracy, design, device, dodge, gambit, intrigue, manipulation, manoeuvre, move, plan, plot, ploy, ruse, scheme, stratagem, tactic, trick, wile.

machine *n.* **1** (*a mechanical apparatus by which motive power is applied*) apparatus, appliance, contraption, contrivance, device, engine, gadget, instrument, mechanism, tool. **2** (*any organization of a complex character designed to apply power of any kind*) agency, machinery, organization, system. **3** (*a person who acts mechanically and without intelligence*) agent, automaton, puppet, robot, (*coll.*) thing, zombie. **4** (*any intricate structure or system of control*) cabal, clique, faction, gang, party, ring, set-up, structure, system. ~*v.t.* (*to produce by means of machinery*) make, manufacture, shape.

machinery *n.* **1** (*the parts or mechanism of a machine*) apparatus, equipment, gear, instruments, mechanism, tackle, tools, workings, works. **2** (*any combination to keep anything in action or to effect a purpose*) agency, channels, machine, organization, procedure, structure, system.

macho *a.* (*masculine, virile, esp. in an ostentatious or exaggerated way*) arrogant, manly, masculine, muscle-bound, proud, virile. ANTONYMS: effeminate.

mad *a.* **1** (*disordered in mind, insane*) (*sl.*) bananas, (*sl.*) barmy, (*coll*) batty, (*sl.*) bonkers, (*sl.*) crackers, crazy, daft, demented, deranged, (*coll.*) dotty, insane, (*sl.*) loony, (*coll.*) loopy, lunatic, (*coll.*) mental, (*sl.*) nutty, raving, unbalanced, unhinged. ANTONYMS: sane. **2** (*frantic, wildly excited*) abandoned, agitated, boisterous, delirious, ebullient, energetic, excited, frantic, frenetic, frenzied, furious, hysterical, riotous, uncontrolled, unrestrained, wild. ANTONYMS: calm. **3** (*infatuated, fanatical*) ardent, avid, crazy, daft, devoted, enamoured, enthusiastic, extravagant, fanatical, fervent, fond, frolicsome, hooked, impassioned, infatuated, inflamed, in love with, keen, wild, zealous. ANTONYMS: indifferent. **4** (*exceedingly foolish, very unwise*) absurd, asinine, daft, foolhardy, foolish, idiotic, imprudent, inane, irrational, ludicrous, nonsensical, preposterous, reckless, senseless, silly, unreasonable, unsafe, unsound, unwise. ANTONYMS: sensible. **5** (*coll.*) (*enraged, annoyed*) angry, annoyed, (*N Am.*) ape, berserk, cross, enraged, exasperated, fuming, furious, incensed, infuriated, irate, irritated, livid, provoked, raging, resentful, vexed, wild, wrathful. ANTONYMS: pleased.

madden *v.t.* (*to make* (*someone*) *very angry*) aggravate, annoy, (*sl.*) bug, derange, drive crazy, enrage, exasperate, gall, incense, infuriate, irritate, provoke, torment, unhinge, upset, vex. ANTONYMS: calm, mollify.

madly *adv.* **1** (*in an insane manner*) crazily, deliriously, dementedly, distractedly, feverishly, frantically, frenziedly, hysterically, insanely, rabidly. **2** (*coll.*) (*extremely*) ardently, desperately, devotedly, exceedingly, excessively, extremely, fanatically, furiously, intensely, passionately, vehemently, violently, wildly. **3** (*very foolishly*) absurdly, foolishly, idiotically, inanely, irrationally, ludicrously, nonsensically, senselessly, stupidly, unreasonably, wildly.

madman *n.* (*a man who is insane*) (*coll.*) crackpot, (*coll.*) head case, idiot, (*sl.*) loony, lunatic, maniac, (*coll.*) mental case, (*sl.*) nut, (*sl.*) nutcase, (*sl.*) nutter, psycho, psychopath, psychotic, (*esp. N Am., coll.*) screwball.

madness *n.* **1** (*insane behaviour*) aberration, craziness, delirium, delusion, dementia, derangement, distraction, insanity, lunacy, mania, mental illness, psychopathy, psychosis. ANTONYMS: sanity. **2** (*wild excitement*) abandon, agitation, excitement, frenzy, furore, intoxication, riot, unrestraint, uproar. **3** (*fanaticism*) ardour, craze, enthusiasm, fanaticism, keenness, passion, rage, zeal. **4** (*extreme folly or nonsense*) absurdity, daftness, folly, foolhardiness, futility, idiocy, illogicality, impracticality, nonsense, pointlessness, preposterousness, recklessness, ridiculousness, senselessness, stupidity, wildness. ANTONYMS: sense. **5** (*extreme anger*) anger, exasperation, frenzy, fury, ire, rage, raving, wildness, wrath. ANTONYMS: calm, composure.

madwoman n. (*a woman who is insane*) (*coll.*) crackpot, (*coll.*) head case, idiot, (*sl.*) loony, lunatic, maniac, (*coll.*) mental case, (*sl.*) nut, (*sl.*) nutcase, (*sl.*) nutter, psycho, psychopath, psychotic, (*esp N Am., coll.*) screwball.

magazine n. **1** (*a periodical publication containing miscellaneous articles by different people*) brochure, journal, pamphlet, paper, periodical, publication, review. **2** (*a building or apartment for military stores, esp. ammunition*) ammunition dump, armoury, arsenal, munitions dump, powder room. **3** (*a place for storage, a warehouse*) depot, store, warehouse.

magic n. **1** (*the supposed art of employing supernatural power to influence or control events*) enchantment, spell. **2** (*sorcery, witchcraft*) black art, diabolism, necromancy, occultism, sorcery, witchcraft, wizardry. **3** (*any agency or action that has astonishing results*) conjuring, hocus-pocus, illusion, jiggery-pokery, legerdemain, sleight of hand, trickery.

magical a. **1** (*of or relating to magic*) mystical, necromantic, occult, supernatural. **2** (*exciting, charming*) bewitching, charming, enchanting, entrancing, excellent, fascinating, hypnotic, magnetic, marvellous, mesmerizing, miraculous, spellbinding, wonderful.

magician n. **1** (*a person supposedly employing magic*) enchanter, enchantress, necromancer, sorcerer, sorceress, warlock, witch, wizard. **2** (*a conjuror*) conjuror, illusionist, prestidigitator. **3** (*a person who produces astonishing results*) genius, maestro, marvel, master, miracle-worker, virtuoso, wizard.

magisterial a. **1** (*authoritative, commanding*) authoritative, commanding, imperative, lordly, masterful. **2** (*dictatorial, domineering*) arrogant, bossy, dictatorial, haughty, highhanded, imperious, lofty, overbearing, peremptory. ANTONYMS: diffident, humble.

magistrate n. (*a public officer commissioned to administer the law*) (*sl.*) beak, JP, justice of the peace.

magnanimity n. (*generosity, great-mindedness*) beneficence, benevolence, big-heartedness, bounty, charity, clemency, generosity, kindness, largesse, liberality, munificence, nobility, open-handedness, philanthropy, selflessness, tolerance, unselfishness. ANTONYMS: meanness.

magnanimous a. (*generous, great-minded*) beneficent, benevolent, (*coll.*) big, big-hearted, bountiful, charitable, clement, generous, great-minded, handsome, kind, liberal, munificent, noble, open-handed, philanthropic, selfless, ungrudging, unstinting. ANTONYMS: mean, petty.

magnate n. (*a person of great wealth and influence, esp. in business*) baron, (*sl.*) big cheese, (*coll.*) big noise, (*coll.*) big shot, (*N Am., sl.*) big wheel, (*coll.*) bigwig, entrepreneur, (*esp. N Am., coll.*) fat cat, industrialist, mogul, notable, personage, plutocrat, tycoon, VIP. ANTONYMS: nobody.

magnetic a. (*attractive, mesmeric*) alluring, attractive, captivating, charismatic, charming, compelling, enchanting, enthralling, entrancing, fascinating, hypnotic, inviting, irresistible, mesmeric, seductive, spellbinding, winning, winsome. ANTONYMS: offensive, repulsive.

magnetism n. (*personal attractiveness, charm*) allure, appeal, attraction, attractiveness, charisma, charm, draw, enchantment, fascination, hypnotism, irresistibility, lure, magic, mesmerism, power, pull, seductiveness, spell.

magnificence n. **1** (*grandness in appearance*) elegance, grandness, impressiveness, majesty, nobility, stateliness. **2** (*luxury, generous profusion*) brilliance, glory, gorgeousness, grandeur, luxuriousness, luxury, opulence, pomp, profusion, resplendence, splendour, sumptuousness. **3** (*excellence*) excellence, splendour, sublimity, transcendence.

magnificent a. **1** (*grand in appearance, splendid*) august, elegant, elevated, exalted, grand, imposing, impressive, majestic, noble, princely, regal, stately. ANTONYMS: humble, modest. **2** (*characterized by luxury or generous profusion*) brilliant, glorious, gorgeous, lavish, luxurious, opulent, profuse, resplendent, rich, splendid, sumptuous. ANTONYMS: poor. **3** (*first-rate, excellent*) excellent, exquisite, fine, first-rate, outstanding, sublime, superb, superior, transcendent. ANTONYMS: undistinguished.

magnify *v.t.* **1** (*to make greater, to increase*) amplify, augment, boost, build up, deepen, dilate, enlarge, expand, heighten, increase, intensify. ANTONYMS: diminish, reduce. **2** (*to exaggerate*) aggrandize, (*coll.*) blow up, dramatize, exaggerate, inflate, overdo, over-emphasize, overestimate, overplay, overrate, overstate. ANTONYMS: belittle, deflate. **3** (*to extol, to glorify*) adore, extol, glorify, praise, worship. ANTONYMS: criticize, disparage.

magniloquent *a.* (*using high-flown or bombastic language*) bombastic, declamatory, elevated, exalted, grandiloquent, high-flown, high-sounding, inflated, lofty, orotund, over-blown, pompous, pretentious, rhetorical, sonorous, stilted, tumid, turgid. ANTONYMS: plain.

magnitude *n.* **1** (*size, extent*) amount, amplitude, bigness, bulk, capacity, dimensions, enormity, expanse, extent, greatness, huge-ness, immensity, largeness, mass, measure, proportions, quantity, size, strength, vastness, volume. **2** (*importance*) consequence, import-ance, mark, moment, note, significance, weight. ANTONYMS: insignificance, unimport-ance. **3** (*the degree of brightness of a star etc.*) brightness, luminosity.

maid *n.* **1** (*a female servant*) chambermaid, daily, domestic, housemaid, maidservant, servant-girl, servant maid, serving-maid. **2** (*also poet.*)† (*a girl, a young unmarried woman*) damsel, girl, (*esp. Sc., North.*) lass, (*esp. Sc., North.*) lassie, maiden, miss, nymph, virgin, wench.

maiden *n.* (*also poet.*)† (*a girl, an unmarried woman*) damsel, girl, (*esp. Sc., North.*) lass, (*esp. Sc., North.*) lassie, maid, miss, nymph, virgin, wench. ANTONYMS: lad.
~*a.* **1** (*of or relating to a maid*) girl-like, maidlike. **2** (*unmarried*) chaste, intact, pure, undefiled, unmarried, unwed, virgin, virginal. **3** (*first, un-used*) first, fresh, inaugural, initial, initiatory, introductory, new, untapped, untried, unused.

maidenly *a.* (*of or like a maiden*) chaste, decent, decorous, demure, gentle, girlish, modest, pure, reserved, undefiled, unsullied, vestal, virginal, virtuous. ANTONYMS: impure, wanton.

mail *n.* **1** (*the letters etc. conveyed by the post*) correspondence, letters, packages, parcels, post. **2** (*the system of conveying letters etc., the postal system*) post, postal service, postal system.
~*v.t.* (*to send by mail, to post*) dispatch, forward, post, send.

maim *v.t.* **1** (*to cripple, to mutilate*) cripple, dis-able, incapacitate, lame, mangle, mutilate. **2** (*to damage emotionally etc.*) damage, harm, hurt, impair, injure, mar, wing, wound.

main[1] *a.* **1** (*chief, most important*) basic, capital, cardinal, central, chief, crucial, essen-tial, foremost, indispensable, leading, neces-sary, outstanding, paramount, particular, predominant, pre-eminent, primary, prime, principal, supreme. ANTONYMS: minor, second-ary. **2** ((*of force*) *concentrated or fully exerted*) absolute, brute, concentrated, direct, down-right, entire, out-and-out, pure, sheer, undis-guised, utmost, utter. **3** (*mighty, powerful*) biggest, greatest, largest, mighty, powerful, strongest.

main[2] *n.* **1** (*a chief conduit, electric cable etc.*) cable, channel, conductor, conduit, duct, line, pipe, sewer. **2** (*also poet.*)† (*the high sea, the ocean*) high sea, ocean, the deep. **3**† (*strength, violent effort*) effort, energy, force, might, potency, power, puissance, strength, vigour.

mainly *adv.* (*principally, chiefly*) above all, at bottom, by and large, chiefly, essentially, first and foremost, for the most part, generally, in general, in the main, largely, mostly, on the whole, predominantly, primarily, principally, substantially, usually. ANTONYMS: partly.

maintain *v.t.* **1** (*to keep in order, proper con-dition or repair*) care for, keep in order, keep up, look after, preserve. ANTONYMS: abandon, neglect. **2** (*to support, to provide with the means of living*) finance, nurture, provide for, supply, support. **3** (*to sustain, to keep up*) continue, keep going, keep up, sustain. **4** (*to preserve or carry on in any state*) carry on, conserve, hold, keep, perpetuate, preserve, retain. **5** (*to assert, to support by reasoning, argument etc.*) affirm, allege, assert, avow, claim, contend, declare, hold, insist, profess, state, support. ANTONYMS: deny, disavow. **6**† (*to represent*) advocate, back, champion, defend, justify, represent, stand by, uphold, vindicate. ANTONYMS: attack.

maintenance *n.* **1** (*the act of maintaining or the state of being maintained*) care, con-servation, continuance, continuation, nurture, perpetuation, persistence, preservation, pro-longation, repairs, upkeep. ANTONYMS: neglect. **2** (*means of support*) alimony, allowance, contribution, food, keep, livelihood, living, stipend, subsistence, support, sustenance, upkeep.

majestic *a.* (*impressive, grand*) august, digni-fied, elevated, exalted, glorious, grand, im-perial, imposing, kingly, lordly, magnificent, monumental, noble, princely, queenly, regal, royal, splendid, stately, sublime. ANTONYMS: lowly, unassuming.

majesty *n.* **1** (*impressive dignity, grandeur*) dignity, glory, grandeur, kingliness, loftiness, magnificence, nobility, pomp, queenliness, royalty, splendour, stateliness, sublimity. ANTONYMS: humility. **2** (*sovereign power and dignity*) regality, sovereignty.

major *a.* **1** (*of considerable importance*) considerable, critical, crucial, grave, great, important, (*coll.*) mega, notable, outstanding, pre-eminent, serious, significant, vital, weighty. ANTONYMS: inconsequential, minor. **2** (*main, principal*) chief, dominant, elder, foremost, head, higher, leading, main, most, paramount, primary, prime, principal, senior, superior, supreme, uppermost. ANTONYMS: junior, secondary. **3** (*greater in quantity, extent or importance*) better, bigger, greater, higher, larger. **4** (*denoting the older of two siblings*) elder, older, senior, superior. ANTONYMS: junior, younger.

majority *n.* **1** (*the greater part, more than half*) best part, bulk, greater part, mass, preponderance. ANTONYMS: minority. **2** (*the amount of the difference between the greater and the lesser number, esp. of votes in an election*) advantage, difference, margin. **3** (*the greater number*) greater number, lion's share, more, most, plurality. **4** (*full legal age*) adulthood, manhood, maturity, seniority, womanhood. ANTONYMS: infancy.

make *v.t.* **1** (*to construct, to produce*) assemble, build, construct, fabricate, fashion, forge, form, frame, manufacture, mould, produce, put together, shape. ANTONYMS: dismantle. **2** (*to bring into existence, to create*) bring into existence, contrive, create, devise, invent, originate. ANTONYMS: destroy. **3** (*to give rise to, to bring about*) bring about, cause, effect, engender, generate, give rise to, occasion, result in. **4** (*to perform, to accomplish*) accomplish, act, carry out, execute, perform, practise, prosecute. ANTONYMS: undo. **5** (*to compose* (*a book, verses etc.*)) author, compile, compose, devise, prepare, write. **6** (*to prepare for consumption; to infuse* (*tea*)) brew, infuse, prepare. **7** (*to establish, to enact*) draw up, enact, establish, fix, form, frame, pass. **8** (*to appoint to a rank or dignity*) appoint, assign, create, designate, elect, install, invest, nominate, ordain, raise. **9** (*to constitute, to become*) add up to, amount to, become, compose, comprise, constitute, embody, form, turn out to be. **10** (*to gain, to achieve*) achieve, acquire, clear, earn, gain, get, net, obtain, realize, secure, win. ANTONYMS: spend. **11** (*to proceed* (*towards etc.*)) head, move, proceed. **12** (*to cause, to compel* (*to do*)) cause, coerce, compel, constrain, dragoon, drive, force, impel, induce,

oblige, press, require, urge. ANTONYMS: prevent. **13** (*to cause to appear, to represent to be*) cause, imagine, produce, represent. **14** (*to calculate or decide to be*) calculate, decide, estimate, gauge, judge, reckon. **15** (*to conclude, to think*) conclude, suppose, think. **16** (*to arrive in time for*) arrive at, attain, catch. ~*n.* (*the brand, type etc. of manufacture*) brand, marque, model, type. **to make do** (*to cope or be satisfied* (*with*) *though the resources etc. are not completely adequate*) cope, get by, improvise, manage, muddle through, scrape by, survive. **to make for 1** (*to conduce to*) conduce to, contribute to, encourage, facilitate, favour, promote. **2** (*to move towards*) aim for, be bound for, head for, move towards, steer for, try for. **3** (*to attack*) assail, assault, attack, fall on, fly at, go for, (*coll.*) have a go at, set upon, storm. **to make off 1** (*to hurry away*) beat a retreat, bolt, clear out, cut and run, decamp, flee, fly, hasten away, hurry away, make away, run off, (*coll.*) skedaddle, take to one's heels. **2** (*to abscond*) abscond, (*sl.*) do a runner, slink off, slope off. **to make off with** (*to take away wrongfully*) abduct, carry off, filch, kidnap, (*sl.*) knock off, (*coll.*) lift, make away with, (*sl.*) nab, (*sl.*) nick, pilfer, (*coll.*) pinch, purloin, run off with, steal, (*coll.*) swipe, take away. **to make out 1** (*to identify or distinguish with the eyes or ears*) descry, detect, discern, distinguish, espy, identify, perceive, recognize, see. **2** (*to understand*) ascertain, comprehend, decipher, fathom, follow, grasp, perceive, realize, see, (*sl.*) suss, understand, work out. **3** (*to prove, to establish*) demonstrate, describe, establish, prove, represent, show. **4** (*to claim or allege*) assert, claim, hint, imply, impute, insinuate, intimate, let on, pretend. **5** (*to draw up, to write out*) complete, draw up, fill in, fill up, write out. **6** (*to be successful, to get on*) be successful, fare, get on, make good, manage, prosper, succeed, thrive. **7** (*to engage in necking or petting*) (*coll.*) get off, neck, pet. **to make up 1** (*to compose*) compose, comprise, constitute, form. **2** (*to fabricate, to concoct*) coin, compose, concoct, construct, (*coll.*) cook up, create, devise, dream up, fabricate, formulate, frame, hatch, invent, manufacture, originate, trump up, write. **3** (*to complete, to supply* (*what is lacking*)) complete, fill, finish, flesh out, meet, supply. **4** (*to compensate*) atone, balance, compensate, make amends, make good, offset, recompense, redeem, redress, requite. **5** (*to be reconciled, to stop quarrelling*) bury the hatchet, come to terms, make peace, reconcile, settle, shake hands. **6** (*to settle, to adjust*) adjust, arrange, resolve, settle.

make-believe *n.* (*pretending, a sham*) charade, dream, fairy tale, fancy, fantasy, imagination, imagining, play-acting, pretence, pretending, sham, unreality. ANTONYMS: reality.

~*a.* (*unreal*) dream, fairy tale, fantasized, fantasy, imaginary, imagined, made-up, mock, pretend, sham, unreal. ANTONYMS: real.

~*v.t., v.i.* (*to pretend* (*that*)) dream, fancy, fantasize, imagine, play-act, pretend.

maker *n.* (*a person who makes something*) author, builder, constructor, creator, fabricator, manufacturer, producer.

makeshift *a.* (*used as a temporary expedient*) emergency, expedient, improvised, make-do, provisional, replacement, rough-and-ready, slapdash, stopgap, substitute, temporary.

maladjusted *a.* (*unable to adjust oneself to the physical or social environment*) alienated, disturbed, estranged, (*sl.*) hung up, neurotic, unbalanced, unstable.

maladministration *n.* (*defective or dishonest management, esp. of public affairs*) blundering, bungling, corruption, dishonesty, incompetence, inefficiency, malpractice, misgovernment, mismanagement, misrule.

maladroit *a.* (*awkward, clumsy*) awkward, bungling, (*sl.*) cack-handed, clumsy, gauche, (*coll.*) ham-fisted, incompetent, inelegant, inept, inexpert, tactless, unskilful. ANTONYMS: dexterous.

malady *n.* (*a disease, esp. a lingering or deep-seated disorder*) affliction, ailment, complaint, disease, disorder, illness, indisposition, infirmity, sickness.

malcontent *n.* (*a person who is discontented, esp. with the government*) agitator, complainer, fault-finder, grouch, grumbler, mischief-maker, rebel, troublemaker.

~*a.* (*discontented, esp. with the government or its administration*) disaffected, discontented, disgruntled, displeased, dissatisfied, dissenting, factious, ill-disposed, rebellious, resentful, restive, uneasy, unhappy, unsatisfied. ANTONYMS: content.

male *a.* (*of, relating to or characteristic of men or male animals*) manful, manly, masculine, virile. ANTONYMS: female.

malefactor *n.* (*an evildoer, a criminal*) convict, criminal, (*coll.*) crook, culprit, delinquent, evildoer, felon, lawbreaker, miscreant, offender, outlaw, sinner, transgressor, villain, wrongdoer.

malevolent *a.* (*malicious, wishing evil on others*) baleful, envious, evil-minded, hostile, ill-disposed, ill-natured, malicious, malign, malignant, pernicious, rancorous, resentful,

revengeful, spiteful, vengeful, vicious, vindictive. ANTONYMS: benevolent, kind.

malformed *a.* (*irregularly or badly formed*) abnormal, contorted, crippled, crooked, deformed, distorted, irregular, misshapen, twisted. ANTONYMS: regular, well-formed.

malfunction *n.* **1** (*a failure to function*) breakdown, failure. **2** (*defective function or operation*) defect, fault, (*sl.*) glitch, impairment.

~*v.i.* (*to operate defectively*) break down, fail, go down, go wrong.

malice *n.* (*the desire to harm others deliberately*) animosity, bitterness, enmity, evil intent, hate, hatred, hostility, ill will, malevolence, maliciousness, malignity, rancour, spite, spitefulness, spleen, vengefulness, venom, vindictiveness. ANTONYMS: benevolence.

malicious *a.* (*characterized by malice*) baleful, (*sl., derog.*) bitchy, bitter, cruel, evil-minded, hateful, hostile, ill-disposed, ill-natured, malevolent, malign, malignant, mischievous, pernicious, rancorous, resentful, spiteful, vengeful, vicious. ANTONYMS: friendly, kind.

malign *a.* **1** (*unfavourable, hurtful*) harmful, hostile, hurtful, malignant, pernicious, unfavourable. ANTONYMS: benign. **2** (*malevolent*) bad, baleful, baneful, evil, malevolent, wicked. ANTONYMS: good.

~*v.t.* (*to speak evil of, to slander*) abuse, (*coll.*) bad-mouth, blacken, calumniate, damn, defame, denigrate, disparage, (*coll.*) knock, libel, revile, rubbish, run down, (*sl.*) slag off, slander, smear, traduce, vilify. ANTONYMS: commend, praise.

malignant *a.* **1** ((*of a disease, tumour etc.*) *threatening life*) cancerous, dangerous, deadly, fatal, incurable, irremediable, life-threatening, uncontrollable. ANTONYMS: benign. **2** (*exercising a pernicious influence*) destructive, harmful, injurious, pernicious, virulent. **3** (*motivated by malice*) baleful, bitter, hostile, invidious, malevolent, malicious, malign, rancorous, spiteful, venomous, vicious, vindictive.

~*n.* (*a malevolent person*) agitator, complainer, fault-finder, grouch, grumbler, malcontent, mischief-maker, rebel, troublemaker.

malleable *a.* **1** (*capable of being rolled out or shaped by hammering without being broken*) ductile, flexible, plastic, soft, tensile, workable. **2** (*easily influenced by outside forces, pliant*) adaptable, biddable, compliant, flexible, governable, impressionable, manageable, pliable, tractable.

malpractice *n.* (*illegal or immoral conduct,*

esp. improper treatment of a case by a physician, lawyer etc.) abuse, dereliction, illegality, immorality, misbehaviour, misconduct, misdeed, mismanagement, negligence, offence, transgression.

maltreat *v.t.* (*to ill-treat, to abuse*) abuse, damage, harm, hurt, ill-treat, injure, mistreat.

maltreatment *n.* (*an instance of maltreating someone*) abuse, damage, harm, hurt, ill treatment, injury, mistreatment.

mammoth *a.* (*gigantic, huge*) colossal, elephantine, enormous, gargantuan, giant, gigantic, huge, immense, jumbo, massive, (*coll.*) mega, mighty, monumental, mountainous, prodigious, stupendous, titanic, vast. ANTONYMS: minute, tiny.

man *n.* **1** (*an adult male of the human race*) (*coll.*) bloke, (*coll.*) chap, fellow, gentleman, (*coll.*) guy, male. ANTONYMS: female, woman. **2** (*a human being, a person*) adult, Homo sapiens, human, human being, individual, mortal, person, personage, somebody, soul. **3** (*collect.*) (*humankind, the human race*) human beings, humanity, humankind, human race, mankind, mortals, people. **4** (*dial., coll.*) (*a husband, a male lover*) beau, boyfriend, husband, lover, partner, spouse. **5** (*a manservant, a valet*) attendant, manservant, retainer, valet, workman. ANTONYMS: master. **6** (*pl.*) (*soldiers, esp. privates*) privates, soldiers, troops. **7** (*a person under one's control*) employee, hand, hireling, worker. **8** (*a vassal, a tenant*) liegeman, subject, tenant, vassal.
~*v.t.* (*to furnish with* (*a person or persons*)*, esp. for defence, a period of duty etc.*) cover, crew, fill, garrison, occupy, operate, people, staff, work.

manacle *n.* (*usu. pl.*) (*a handcuff, shackle*) (*sl.*) bracelet, cuff, fetter, handcuff, iron, shackle.
~*v.t.* (*to put manacles on*) chain, clap in irons, cuff, fetter, handcuff, put in chains, shackle.

manage *v.t.* **1** (*to direct, to carry on*) carry on, conduct, control, direct, run. **2** (*to conduct the affairs of*) administer, command, conduct, direct, govern, organize, oversee, preside over, rule, run, superintend, supervise, watch over. ANTONYMS: mismanage. **3** (*to handle, to wield*) handle, manipulate, operate, use, wield. **4** (*to bring or keep under control*) control, dominate, guide, handle, influence, manipulate, pilot, ply, steer.
~*v.i.* **1** (*to contrive* (*to do etc.*)) accomplish, achieve, arrange, bring about, contrive, effect, engineer, manoeuvre, succeed. **2** (*to get on* (*with or without*)) cope, fare, get by, get on, make do, muddle through, survive.

manageable *a.* (*easy to control or deal with*) amenable, compliant, controllable, convenient, docile, easy, governable, handy, submissive, tameable, tractable. ANTONYMS: unmanageable.

management *n.* **1** (*the act of managing*) administration, care, charge, command, conduct, control, direction, government, guidance, handling, operation, organization, regulation, rule, running, stewardship, supervision. **2** (*those who manage, a board of directors etc.*) administration, board, bosses, (*coll.*) brass, directorate, directors, employers, executive, managers, proprietors. ANTONYMS: workforce.

manager *n.* (*a person who manages, esp. a business, institution etc.*) administrator, boss, chief, controller, director, employer, executive, (*coll.*) gaffer, (*sl.*) governor, head, overseer, proprietor, superintendent, supervisor.

mandate *n.* (*an authoritative charge or order*) authority, authorization, charge, command, commission, decree, directive, edict, injunction, instruction, order, precept, sanction, warrant.

mandatory *a.* (*obligatory, compulsory*) binding, compulsory, essential, necessary, obligatory, required, requisite. ANTONYMS: discretionary, optional.

manful *a.* (*brave, courageous*) bold, brave, courageous, daring, determined, gallant, heroic, intrepid, manly, noble, resolute, stalwart, valiant, vigorous.

mangle *v.t.* **1** (*to mutilate, to disfigure by hacking*) butcher, cut, disfigure, hack, lacerate, mutilate, rend, tear. **2** (*to mar, to ruin*) cripple, deform, destroy, maim, mar, ruin, spoil, (*esp. N Am., coll.*) trash, wreck.

mangy *a.* (*infected with mange*) dingy, dirty, (*sl.*) grungy, mean, miserable, moth-eaten, poor, ragged, (*coll.*) scabby, (*coll.*) scruffy, (*sl.*) scuzzy, seedy, shabby, shoddy, sorry, squalid, tatty, unkempt. ANTONYMS: spotless, well-kept.

manhandle *v.t.* **1** (*to move by manpower alone*) carry, haul, heave, (*coll.*) hump, lift, manoeuvre, move, pull, push, shove, tug. **2** (*coll.*) (*to handle roughly*) abuse, batter, ill-treat, knock about, maltreat, maul, mistreat, (*coll.*) paw, rough up.

manhood *n.* **1** (*the state of being a male person of full age*) adulthood, masculinity, maturity, virility. ANTONYMS: womanhood. **2** (*manliness, courage*) boldness, bravery, courage, determination, firmness, force, fortitude, grit, hardihood, manfulness, manliness, mettle, pluck, resolution, spirit, stamina, strength, valour.

mania n. **1** (*a form of mental disorder charac-terized by emotional excitement and violence*) aberration, craziness, delirium, dementia, derangement, disorder, frenzy, hysteria, insanity, lunacy, madness. ANTONYMS: sanity. **2** (*an infatuation, a craze*) compulsion, craving, craze, desire, enthusiasm, fad, fetish, fixation, infatuation, obsession, partiality, passion, preoccupation, rage, (*coll.*) thing, urge, yearning, (*coll.*) yen. ANTONYMS: phobia.

maniac n. **1** (*a person who suffers from mania*) (*coll.*) crackpot, (*coll.*) head case, (*sl.*) loony, lunatic, madman, madwoman, (*sl.*) nutcase, (*sl.*) nutter, psycho, psychopath. **2** (*a person with an obsessive enthusiasm for a hobby, craze etc.*) enthusiast, fan, fanatic, (*coll.*) fiend, (*coll.*) freak, (*sl.*) nut.

maniacal a. (*crazy*) berserk, crazed, crazy, delirious, demented, deranged, frenzied, hysterical, insane, (*sl.*) loony, lunatic, mad, manic, (*sl.*) nutty, psychotic, raving, unbalanced, wild. ANTONYMS: calm, sane.

manifest a. (*plainly apparent, obvious*) apparent, blatant, clear, conspicuous, distinct, evident, explicit, glaring, noticeable, obvious, open, overt, palpable, patent, plain, unambiguous, unconcealed, unmistakable, visible. ANTONYMS: concealed, disguised, hidden.
~v.t. **1** (*to make manifest, to show clearly*) set forth, show. **2** (*to display, to exhibit*) declare, disclose, display, evince, exhibit, expose, express, make known, make plain, reveal. ANTONYMS: conceal, obscure. **3** (*to be evidence of*) corroborate, demonstrate, prove, substantiate.

manifestation n. **1** (*manifesting or being manifested*) appearance, materialization. **2** (*a public demonstration*) declaration, demonstration, disclosure, display, exhibition, exposure, expression, indication, proof, revelation, show, sign, symptom, token.

manifold a. **1** (*of various forms or kinds*) assorted, diverse, diversified, miscellaneous, multifarious, sundry, varied. **2** (*many and various*) abundant, copious, many, multiple, multitudinous, numerous, various. ANTONYMS: few.

manipulate v.t. **1** (*to operate on with the hands, to handle*) employ, handle, operate, ply, use, wield, work. **2** (*to influence or tamper with by artful or sly means*) choreograph, conduct, control, direct, engineer, exploit, guide, influence, manage, manoeuvre, negotiate, orchestrate, play on, steer, subvert, tamper with.

mankind n. **1** (*the human species*) Homo sapiens, humanity, humankind, human race, man, people. **2** (*male people as distinct from females*) males, men.

manly a. **1** (*having qualities such as courage and resoluteness*) bold, brave, chivalrous, courageous, daring, firm, gallant, hardy, heroic, intrepid, macho, magnanimous, mighty, muscular, powerful, resolute, robust, vigorous. ANTONYMS: effeminate, weak. **2** (*befitting a man, mannish*) male, manful, mannish, masculine, virile. ANTONYMS: womanly.

man-made a. (*made by humans, artificial*) artificial, ersatz, manufactured, synthetic. ANTONYMS: natural.

manner n. **1** (*the way in which something is done or happens, method*) approach, fashion, means, method, procedure, style, way. **2** (*practice, habit*) custom, habit, practice, procedure, routine, tack, use, wont. **3** (*demeanour, bearing*) air, appearance, bearing, carriage, demeanour, guise, look, mien. **4** (*pl.*) (*conduct in social interaction, behaviour*) behaviour, conduct, decorum, deportment, etiquette, niceties, social graces. **5** (*pl.*) (*habits showing good breeding*) breeding, courtesy, politeness. **6**† (*sort, kind*) brand, breed, category, form, genre, kind, line, make, nature, sort, type, variety.

mannered a. (*betraying mannerisms, affected*) affected, artificial, hoity-toity, idiosyncratic, insincere, (*coll.*) la-di-da, pretentious, pseudo-, put-on, stilted, unnatural. ANTONYMS: natural.

mannerism n. (*an idiosyncrasy, the excessive adherence to the same manner*) characteristic, foible, gesture, habit, idiosyncrasy, peculiarity, quirk, trait.

manoeuvre n. **1** (*a tactical movement or change of position by troops or warships*) deployment, move, movement, tactic. **2** (*tactical exercises in imitation of war*) drill, exercises, training, war game. **3** (*a contrived plan or action*) action, artifice, device, dodge, intrigue, machination, operation, plan, plot, ruse, scheme, stratagem, subterfuge, trick.
~v.i. (*to employ a stratagem*) intrigue, machinate, manipulate, plan, plot, scheme.
~v.t. (*to move or effect by means of strategy or skilful management*) contrive, devise, engineer, manage, (*coll.*) wangle.

mansion n. (*a residence of considerable size and pretensions*) castle, country seat, hall, palace, stately home, villa. ANTONYMS: hovel.

mantle n. **1** (*a sleeveless cloak or loose outer garment*) cape, cloak, hood, pelisse, shawl, wrap. **2** (*a covering*) blanket, canopy, cloud, cover, covering, curtain, envelope, pall, screen, sheet, shroud, veil. **3** (*leadership or*

authority, esp. as handed on) authority, control, leadership, power, supremacy.
~*v.t.* 1 (*to clothe in or as a mantle*) blanket, cloak, clothe. 2 (*to cover, to conceal*) cloud, conceal, cover, disguise, envelop, hide, mask, obscure, screen, shroud, veil, wrap.

manual *a.* 1 (*of or performed with the hands*) by hand, hand-operated. 2 (*involving physical exertion*) blue-collar, physical.
~*n.* (*a book of instructions*) directions, guide, guidebook, handbook, instructions.

manufacture *n.* (*the making of articles by means of labour or machinery, esp. on a large scale*) assembly, building, construction, creation, fabrication, making, mass production, production.
~*v.t.* 1 (*to produce or fashion by labour or machinery, esp. on a large scale*) assemble, build, compose, construct, create, fabricate, fashion, forge, form, mass-produce, mould, process, produce, put together, shape, turn out. 2 (*to fabricate, to invent* (*a story, evidence etc.*)) concoct, (*coll.*) cook up, devise, dream up, fabricate, hatch, invent, make up, originate, think up.

manufacturer *n.* (*a person, company etc. that manufactures goods*) builder, constructor, creator, fabricator, industrialist, maker, producer.

manure *n.* 1 (*animal dung used to fertilize land for cultivation*) droppings, dung, excrement, muck, ordure. 2 (*any substance, including compost or chemical preparations, used to fertilize land*) compost, dressing, fertilizer.

manuscript *n.* 1 (*an author's text in its original state, as submitted for publication*) script, text. 2 (*handwritten copy or form*) handwriting, script, writing.

many *a.* (*numerous, comprising a great number*) abundant, copious, countless, †divers, frequent, great, innumerable, manifold, multifarious, multitudinous, myriad, numberless, numerous, profuse, several, sundry, umpteen, uncountable, varied, various. ANTONYMS: few.
~*n.* 1 (*a multitude*) crowd, majority, multitude, people. 2 (*a great number*) drove, flock, flood, (*esp. in pl., coll.*) heap, horde, hundreds, lot, mass, multitude, (*esp. in pl., coll.*) pile, plenty, profusion, scores, shoal, swarm, thousand and one, thousands, throng, (*usu. pl., coll.*) ton.

map *n.* 1 (*a representation of a portion of the earth's surface etc. on a two-dimensional surface*) atlas, chart, gazetteer, plan. 2 (*any delineation or diagram of a route etc.*) chart, diagram, graph, plan.
~*v.t.* (*to represent or set down in a map*) chart, plan, plot. **to map out** (*to plan in detail, to lay out a plan of*) draft, outline, plan, sketch.

mar *v.t.* (*to spoil, to disfigure*) blight, blot, damage, deface, disfigure, harm, hurt, impair, injure, maim, mangle, mutilate, ruin, scar, spoil, stain, sully, taint, tarnish. ANTONYMS: improve.

marauder *n.* (*a person who steals or kills*) bandit, brigand, buccaneer, corsair, freebooter, looter, (*Hist.*) mosstrooper, outlaw, pillager, pirate, plunderer, raider, ravager, robber.

march *v.i.* 1 (*to move with regular steps like a soldier*) file, footslog, parade, stalk, step, stride, strut, tramp, tread, trek. 2 (*to walk in a deliberate or determined manner*) pace, plod, stride, tread, walk. 3 (*to continue steadily*) advance, forward, make headway, proceed. ANTONYMS: halt. 4 (*to participate in a protest march*) demonstrate, protest, rally.
~*n.* 1 (*the act of marching*) gait, hike, pace, step, stride, tramp, trek, walk. 2 (*a deliberate or measured movement, esp. of soldiers*) column, file, parade, procession. 3 (*progress, advance*) advance, development, evolution, headway, progress, progression.

margin *n.* 1 (*an edge, a border*) border, bound, boundary, brim, brink, confine, edge, frontier, limit, line, lip, perimeter, periphery, rim, side, verge. 2 (*the space of time or the range of conditions within which a thing is just possible*) compass, elbow room, freedom, latitude, leeway, play, range, room, scope, space. 3 (*an allowance of time, money etc. for contingencies, growth etc.*) allowance, extra, surplus.

marginal *a.* 1 (*of or relating to a margin, near the limit*) borderline, on the edge, peripheral. 2 (*small, slight*) infinitesimal, low, minimal, minor, negligible, slight, small, tiny.

marine *a.* 1 (*found in or produced by the sea*) aquatic, maritime, oceanic, pelagic, saltwater, sea. ANTONYMS: land. 2 (*used at sea or in navigation*) nautical, naval, ocean-going, seafaring.
~*n.* (*the shipping, fleet or navy of a country*) fleet, merchant marine, merchant navy, navy, shipping.

mariner *n.* (*a sailor*) Jack tar, (*coll.*) matelot, navigator, sailor, sea dog, seafarer, seaman, (*coll.*) tar.

marital *a.* (*of or relating to marriage*) conjugal, connubial, married, matrimonial, nuptial, spousal, wedded. ANTONYMS: celibate.

maritime *a.* (*of or relating to the sea*) aquatic, coastal, marine, nautical, naval, ocean-going, oceanic, pelagic, salt-water, sea, seafaring, seaside.

mark *n.* 1 (*a visible sign or impression, such as a stroke or dot*) blemish, blot, blotch, bruise, dent, impression, incision, line, nick, scar, scratch, sign, smirch, smudge, splotch, spot, stain, streak. **2** (*a symbol, character*) badge, character, device, emblem, flag, indication, label, proof, symbol, token. **3** (*a model or type*) brand, model, stamp, type. **4** (*a distinguishing feature*) characteristic, distinction, earmark, feature, hallmark, symptom. **5** (*a limit, a standard*) criterion, level, limit, measure, norm, par, standard, yardstick. **6** (*the point to be reached*) aim, end, goal, object, objective, purpose. **7** (*a distinguishing sign, a seal etc.*) brand, seal, signet. **8** (*a victim, esp. of fraud*) dupe, (*N Am., sl.*) patsy, sucker, victim.

~*v.t.* **1** (*to make a mark on*) blemish, blot, blotch, bruise, dent, impress, imprint, nick, scar, scratch, smirch, smudge, splotch, stain, streak. **2** (*to distinguish or indicate by a mark or marks*) brand, flag, identify, label, stamp. **3** (*to award marks to* (*a student's work etc.*)) appraise, assess, correct, evaluate, grade, score. **4** (*to indicate or serve as a mark to*) designate, indicate, register. **5** (*to be a feature of*) betoken, characterize, denote, distinguish, exemplify, illustrate, show. **6** (*to select, to single out*) mark out, select, single out. **7** (*to pay heed to*) attend, heed, mind, note, notice, observe, pay attention, pay heed, regard, remark, watch. **8** (*to celebrate a particular event or occasion*) celebrate, commemorate, honour, keep, observe, recognize.

marked *a.* **1** (*noticeable, definite*) apparent, clear, considerable, conspicuous, definite, distinct, evident, manifest, notable, noticeable, obvious, outstanding, patent, prominent, pronounced, significant, striking. ANTONYMS: imperceptible, unnoticeable. **2** ((*of a person*) *destined to suffer attack, suspicion etc.*) destined, doomed, ill-fated.

market *n.* **1** (*an open space or large building in which commodities are offered for sale*) bazaar, exchange, fair, mart. **2** (*demand for a commodity*) call, demand, requirement.

~*v.t.* (*to sell in a market*) deal in, hawk, merchandise, peddle, retail, sell, vend.

maroon *v.t.* **1** (*to put ashore and abandon on a desolate island*) cast ashore, cast away. **2** (*to leave isolated or unable to leave*) abandon, cut off, desert, forsake, isolate, leave, seclude, strand.

marriage *n.* **1** (*the legal union of a man and woman*) espousal, matrimony, union, wedlock. ANTONYMS: divorce. **2** (*the act or ceremony of marrying, a wedding*) marriage ceremony, nuptials, wedding. **3** (*close conjunction or union*) affiliation, alliance, amalgamation, association, confederation, coupling, fusion, integration, link, merger, union. ANTONYMS: separation.

marrow *n.* (*the essence, the pith*) core, essence, gist, heart, kernel, pith, quick, quintessence, soul, spirit, substance.

marry *v.t.* **1** (*to take as one's husband or wife*) espouse, take as husband, take as wife. **2** (*to join closely together*) affiliate, ally, amalgamate, associate, bond, combine, connect, couple, fuse, join, knit, link, merge, splice, tie, unite, weld, yoke. ANTONYMS: separate, split.

~*v.i.* (*to enter into the state of wedlock*) (*sl.*) get hitched, (*coll.*) take the plunge, (*coll.*) tie the knot, wed.

marsh *n.* (*a tract of low land covered with water*) bog, fen, lowland, morass, quagmire, slough, swamp.

marshal *v.t.* **1** (*to arrange or rank in order*) align, arrange, array, collect, deploy, dispose, group, line up, order, organize, rank. ANTONYMS: disorder. **2** (*to conduct in a ceremonious manner*) conduct, escort, guide, lead, shepherd, usher.

~*v.i.* ((*of armies, processions etc.*) *to take up a position*) assemble, deploy, draw up, gather, muster.

marshy *a.* ((*of land*) *covered with water*) boggy, fenny, low-lying, miry, spongy, swampy, waterlogged, wet.

martial *a.* **1** (*of or suited to war*) armed, fighting, military, soldierly. **2** (*warlike, courageous*) bellicose, belligerent, brave, courageous, militant, pugnacious, warlike.

marvel *n.* **1** (*a wonderful or astonishing thing*) miracle, phenomenon, wonder. **2** (*a prodigy*) genius, phenomenon, prodigy. **3** (*wonder, astonishment*) amazement, astonishment, surprise, wonder.

~*v.i.* (*to be astonished* (*at or that*)) be amazed at, be astonished at, gape, goggle, wonder.

marvellous *a.* **1** (*astonishing, prodigious*) amazing, astonishing, astounding, breathtaking, extraordinary, miraculous, phenomenal, prodigious, remarkable, singular, spectacular, stupendous, wondrous. ANTONYMS: ordinary. **2** (*excellent*) (*sl.*) ace, (*N Am., sl.*) bad, (*coll.*) brill, (*coll.*) cool, (*sl.*) crucial, excellent, fabulous, (*coll.*) fantastic, great, magnificent, (*coll.*) mean, (*coll.*) mega, (*coll.*) sensational, (*coll.*) smashing, splendid, (*coll.*) super, superb, (*coll.*) terrific, (*sl.*) wicked, wonderful. ANTONYMS: awful, disappointing.

masculine *a.* **1** (*belonging to or having the characteristic qualities of the male sex*) male. ANTONYMS: female, feminine. **2** (*strong, vigorous*) bold, brave, (*sl.*) butch, gallant, hardy, macho, mighty, muscular, resolute, robust, strapping, strong, vigorous, virile. **3** (*manly*) male, manful, manly, spirited, virile. **4** (*mannish*) manlike, mannish. ANTONYMS: feminine.

mash *v.t.* (*to crush into a pulpy mass*) beat, bruise, crush, pound, pulp.

mask *n.* **1** (*a covering for the face, for protection or to conceal one's identity*) domino, visor. **2** (*a disguise, a subterfuge*) blind, camouflage, cloak, cover, disguise, facade, front, guise, pretence, protection, screen, shield, subterfuge, veil.
~*v.t.* **1** (*to conceal or disguise*) camouflage, cloak, conceal, disguise, hide, obscure, screen, shroud, veil. ANTONYMS: reveal. **2** (*to screen during a process*) protect, screen, shield. ANTONYMS: expose.

masquerade *n.* **1** (*a ball or assembly at which people wear masks*) ball, costume ball, dance, fancy-dress party, masked ball, revel. **2** (*a disguise, a pretence*) bluff, cloak, cover, deception, disguise, dissimulation, front, guise, imposture, pose, pretence, put-on, screen, subterfuge.
~*v.i.* (*to wear a mask or disguise*) disguise, dissemble, dissimulate, impersonate, mimic, pass oneself off, pose, pretend.

mass *n.* **1** (*a body of matter formed into a coherent whole of indefinite shape*) block, chunk, concretion, hunk, lump, nugget, piece. **2** (*a compact aggregation of things*) accumulation, aggregation, batch, body, bunch, collection, combination, conglomeration, crowd, group, heap, horde, host, load, pile, sum, totality, whole. **3** (*a great quantity or amount*) abundance, heap, horde, host, load, mountain, pile, profusion, quantity, stack. **4** (*the greater proportion, the principal part or the majority* (*of*)) body, bulk, lion's share, majority. **5** (*volume, magnitude*) bulk, dimension, magnitude, size, volume.
~*v.i.* (*to gather into a mass*) accumulate, aggregate, amass, cluster, collect, congregate, flock together, gather, muster, rally, swarm, throng. ANTONYMS: disperse.
~*a.* (*affecting or involving a very large number of people*) extensive, general, large-scale, popular, wholesale, widespread. ANTONYMS: limited.

massacre *n.* (*indiscriminate slaughter, wholesale murder*) annihilation, bloodbath, butchery, carnage, extermination, genocide, holocaust, killing, mass slaughter, murder, pogrom, slaughter.
~*v.t.* **1** (*to kill or slaughter indiscriminately*) butcher, execute, exterminate, kill, mow down, murder, slaughter, slay, wipe out. **2** (*to defeat emphatically*) annihilate, (*sl.*) blow

away, cut to pieces, decimate, defeat, destroy, eliminate, eradicate, exterminate, liquidate, mow down, murder, obliterate, slaughter, (*sl.*) take out, wipe out.

massage *n.* (*treatment by rubbing or kneading the muscles and body, usu. with the hands*) acupressure, kneading, manipulation, reflexology, rubbing, rub-down.
~*v.t.* **1** (*to subject to massage*) knead, manipulate, rub, rub down. **2** (*to manipulate or misrepresent* (*esp. statistics*)) (*coll.*) fiddle, manipulate, misrepresent.

massive *a.* **1** (*heavy, bulky*) bulky, great, heavy, hefty, imposing, ponderous, prodigious, weighty. **2** (*very large*) big, colossal, elephantine, enormous, extensive, gargantuan, gigantic, (*coll.*) ginormous, huge, hulking, immense, large, mammoth, (*coll.*) mega, monster, monumental, titanic, vast, (*sl.*) whopping. ANTONYMS: minuscule, tiny. **3** (*substantial, solid*) solid, substantial, weighty. ANTONYMS: frail.

master *n.* **1** (*a person thoroughly acquainted with or skilled in an art, craft etc.*) ace, adept, craftsman, craftswoman, doyen, doyenne, expert, genius, grand master, maestro, past master, (*coll.*) pro, virtuoso, wizard. ANTONYMS: amateur, novice. **2** (*a person who has secured the control or upper hand*) boss, chief, commander, controller, director, (*sl.*) governor, head, manager, principal. **3** (*a person who has control or authority over others*) lord, overlord, overseer, superintendent. ANTONYMS: servant, slave. **4** (*a schoolmaster, a teacher*) guide, guru, instructor, pedagogue, preceptor, schoolmaster, swami, teacher, tutor. **5** (*the captain of a merchant vessel*) captain, skipper.
~*a.* **1** (*having control or authority*) adept, controlling, crack, expert, masterly, proficient, skilful, skilled. ANTONYMS: amateurish, inept. **2** (*principal, largest*) chief, controlling, foremost, grand, great, largest, leading, main, major, predominant, prime, principal. ANTONYMS: minor.
~*v.t.* **1** (*to become thoroughly conversant with or skilled in using*) acquire, get the hang of, grasp, learn. **2** (*to overpower, to defeat*) conquer, defeat, (*coll.*) lick, overcome, overpower, triumph over, vanquish. ANTONYMS: surrender. **3** (*to subdue, to bring under control*) bridle, bring under control, check, curb, quash, quell, repress, subdue, subjugate, suppress, tame. **4** (*to be the master of, to rule as a master*) command, control, direct, dominate, govern, manage, regulate, rule.

masterful *a.* **1** (*expressing mastery, masterly*) accomplished, adept, adroit, clever, consummate, crack, deft, dexterous, excellent, expert, exquisite, fine, first-rate, masterly, matchless, peerless, proficient, skilful, skilled, superlative. ANTONYMS: amateurish, unskilled. **2** (*domineering, self-willed*) arrogant, authoritarian, authoritative, autocratic, bossy, despotic, dictatorial, domineering, high-handed, imperious, magisterial, overbearing, overweening, peremptory, self-willed, tyrannical. ANTONYMS: weak.

masterly *a.* ((*of a performance, display etc.*) *showing great skill*) ace, adept, adroit, clever, consummate, crack, dexterous, excellent, expert, exquisite, fine, first-rate, masterful, polished, proficient, skilful, skilled, superior, superlative. ANTONYMS: inept.

masterpiece *n.* (*an achievement showing surpassing skill*) classic, magnum opus, masterwork, pièce de résistance, tour de force.

mastery *n.* **1** (*control, authority*) ascendancy, authority, command, conquest, control, domination, dominion, power, rule, superiority, supremacy, sway, upper hand, victory, whip hand. **2** (*the skill of a master*) ability, attainment, deftness, dexterity, expertise, finesse, proficiency, prowess, skill, talent, virtuosity. **3** (*complete competence, thorough knowledge* (*of*)) command, competence, comprehension, familiarity, grasp, knowledge, understanding. ANTONYMS: ignorance, incompetence.

match *n.* **1** (*a person or thing like or corresponding to another*) copy, double, duplicate, equal, fellow, like, lookalike, mate, parallel, peer, replica, (*coll.*) spitting image, twin. **2** (*a counterpart, a facsimile*) competitor, counterpart, equivalent, facsimile, replica. **3** (*a person able to cope with another*) equal, rival. **4** (*a contest of skill, strength etc.*) bout, competition, contest, duel, game, test, trial. **5** (*a pairing or alliance by marriage*) affiliation, alliance, betrothal, combination, compact, marriage, pair, pairing, partnership, union.
~*v.t.* **1** (*to be a match for, to compare as equal*) compare, emulate, equal, resemble. **2** (*to find a match for*) couple, link, link up, pair. ANTONYMS: separate. **3** (*to oppose as a rival, opponent etc.*) compete, contend, oppose, pit, rival, vie. **4** (*to be the equal of, to correspond to*) be equivalent to, correspond to, equal. **5** (*to join in marriage*) join, marry, unite.
~*v.i.* ((*of different things or persons*) *to agree, to correspond*) accompany, accord, adapt, agree, blend, coordinate, correspond, equal, fit, go with, harmonize, suit, tally.

matching *a.* (*like, corresponding*) analogous, comparable, complementary, coordinating, corresponding, double, duplicate, equal, equivalent, identical, like, paired, parallel,

same, similar, toning, twin. ANTONYMS: contrasting, dissimilar.

matchless *a.* (*without equal, incomparable*) beyond compare, consummate, ideal, incomparable, inimitable, peerless, perfect, superlative, supreme, unequalled, unique, unmatched, unparalleled, unrivalled, unsurpassed, without equal. ANTONYMS: average, ordinary.

mate *n.* **1** (*a companion, an equal*) associate, (*coll.*) buddy, (*coll.*) chum, colleague, companion, comrade, crony, equal, fellow worker, friend, match, (*coll.*) pal. **2** (*a suitable partner, esp. in marriage, a spouse*) other half, partner, (*N Am., coll.*) significant other, spouse. **3** (*an assistant*) apprentice, assistant, helper, subordinate.
~*v.t.* **1** (*to pair* (*birds, animals etc.*) *for breeding*) breed, copulate, couple, pair. **2** (*to match, to couple*) couple, join, synchronize, yoke. ANTONYMS: separate. **3** (*to join together in marriage*) marry, wed.

material *n.* **1** (*the substance or matter from which anything is made*) matter, stuff, substance. **2** (*stuff, fabric*) cloth, fabric, stuff, textile. **3** (*elements or component parts* (*of*)) components, constituents, elements. **4** (*notes, ideas etc. for a written or oral composition*) data, documents, evidence, facts, ideas, information, notes, papers, resources, work. **5** (*a person or persons suitable to fulfil a specified function after training etc.*) personnel, staff, worker, workforce.
~*a.* **1** (*corporeal, substantial*) bodily, concrete, corporeal, earthly, palpable, physical, solid, substantial, tangible, unspiritual, worldly. ANTONYMS: abstract, spiritual. **2** (*of or relating to the essence of a thing, not to the form*) basic, essential, fundamental, inherent, innate, intrinsic. **3** (*important, essential*) consequent, crucial, essential, grave, important, key, meaningful, momentous, relevant, serious, significant, vital, weighty. ANTONYMS: irrelevant, trivial.

materialize *v.i.* **1** (*to become actual fact*) come about, come to pass, happen, occur, take place. **2** ((*of a spirit*) *to appear*) appear, emerge, manifest, take shape. **3** (*to arrive on the scene*) arrive, show, turn up.

materially *adv.* (*to a significant extent*) basically, considerably, essentially, gravely, greatly, much, palpably, seriously, significantly, substantially. ANTONYMS: barely, hardly.

maternal *a.* (*motherly*) caring, devoted, doting, fond, kindly, maternalistic, motherly, nurturing, protective, tender.

mathematical *a.* **1** (*of or relating to mathematics*) algebraic, arithmetic, geometric. **2** (*rigidly precise or accurate*) accurate, exact, precise, rigid, rigorous, strict.

matrimonial *a.* (*of or relating to marriage*) conjugal, connubial, marital, married, nuptial, spousal, wedded.

matrimony *n.* (*the act of marrying*) marital rites, marriage, nuptials, wedding.

matter *n.* **1** (*that which constitutes the substance of physical things, as distinguished from thought, mind etc.*) body, material, stuff, substance. **2** (*a subject for thought or feeling*) issue, question, subject, topic. **3** (*meaning or sense (of a book, discourse etc.)*) argument, context, meaning, purport, sense, substance, thesis. **4** (*an affair, a business*) affair, business, circumstance, concern, episode, event, occurrence, situation. **5** (*the cause or occasion of or for difficulty, regret etc.*) complication, difficulty, dilemma, distress, problem, trouble, upset, worry. **6** (*importance, moment*) consequence, importance, moment, note, significance, weight. **7** (*an indefinite amount or quantity*) amount, portion, quantity, sum. **8** (*pus*) discharge, purulence, pus, secretion.
~*v.i.* (*to be important, to signify*) be important, count, mean something, signify.

matter-of-fact *a.* **1** (*treating of or adhering to facts or realities*) factual, realistic. **2** (*not fanciful or imaginary*) emotionless, sober, straightforward, unfanciful, unimaginative, unsentimental. **3** (*plain, ordinary*) commonplace, deadpan, down-to-earth, dry, dull, everyday, flat, lifeless, mundane, ordinary, plain, prosaic, unvarnished.

mature *a.* **1** (*ripe, ripened*) aged, blooming, mellow, ripe, ripened, seasoned. **2** (*fully grown*) adult, complete, consummated, developed, full-grown, fully developed, fully fledged, grown-up, prepared, ready. ANTONYMS: immature, undeveloped. **3** (*fully elaborated, considered etc.*) considered, elaborated, full, sober, well-thought-out.
~*v.i.* (*to become ripened or fully developed*) age, bloom, develop, grow up, mellow, ripen, season.

maudlin *a.* (*characterized by sickly sentimentality*) emotional, gushy, mawkish, (*sl.*) mushy, pathetic, (*esp. N Am., coll.*) schmaltzy, sentimental, sickly, (*sl.*) slushy, (*coll.*) soppy.

maul *v.t.* **1** (*to handle roughly*) knock about, manhandle, rough up. **2** (*to beat, to bruise*) assault, batter, beat, beat up, bruise, do over. **3** (*to damage*) abuse, damage, harm, hurt, illtreat, injure. **4** ((*of an animal*) *to paw and mutilate*) claw, lacerate, mutilate, paw.

mawkish *a.* **1** (*falsely or feebly sentimental*) emotional, gushy, maudlin, (*sl.*) mushy, pathetic, (*esp. N Am., coll.*) schmaltzy, sentimental, (*sl.*) slushy, (*coll.*) soppy. **2** (*nauseating or insipid in flavour, smell etc.*) disgusting, feeble, flat, foul, insipid, loathsome, nauseating, nauseous, offensive, sickly, stale, tasteless, vapid, weak.

maxim *n.* **1** (*a general principle of a practical kind*) adage, aphorism, axiom, byword, dictum, epigram, motto, proverb, saw, saying, slogan. **2** (*a rule derived from experience*) principle, rule, rule of thumb.

maximum *n.* (*the greatest quantity or degree attainable in any given case*) apex, apogee, ceiling, climax, crest, extreme, height, limit, peak, pinnacle, summit, top, utmost, zenith. ANTONYMS: minimum.
~*a.* (*at the greatest or highest degree*) climactic, crowning, extreme, greatest, highest, maximal, most, paramount, supreme, top, topmost, utmost, uttermost. ANTONYMS: least, minimal.

maybe *adv.* (*perhaps, possibly*) conceivably, peradventure, perchance, perhaps, possibly. ANTONYMS: definitely.

mayhem *n.* **1** (*a state of disorder or confusion*) chaos, commotion, confusion, disorder, fracas, havoc, trouble, violence. **2** (*wilful damage*) damage, destruction, devastation.

maze *n.* **1** (*a network of paths and hedges etc. designed as a puzzle*) convolutions, network, tangle, web. **2** (*a confusing network of winding and turning passages*) complex, labyrinth. **3** (*a state of bewilderment, perplexity*) bewilderment, confusion, perplexity, uncertainty.

meadow *n.* (*a tract of land under grass, esp. if grown for hay*) field, grassland, lea, pasture.

meagre *a.* **1** (*thin, lacking flesh*) bony, emaciated, gaunt, hungry, lank, lean, scraggy, scrawny, skinny, slight, starved, thin, underfed, undernourished. ANTONYMS: fat, plump. **2** (*destitute of fertility or productiveness*) barren, destitute, infertile, sterile, unfruitful, unproductive. ANTONYMS: rich. **3** (*poor, scanty*) deficient, inadequate, insubstantial, insufficient, little, measly, paltry, pathetic, poor, puny, scant, scanty, short, skimpy, slender, slight, small, spare, sparse, trifling. ANTONYMS: ample.

meal *n.* (*food taken at one of the customary times of eating*) banquet, collation, feast, nourishment, repast, snack, (*coll.*) spread, victuals.

mean[1] *v.t.* **1** (*to intend, to have in mind*) aim, aspire, contemplate, have in mind, intend, plan, propose, purpose. **2** (*to denote, to signify*) betoken, connote, denote, drive at, express, hint at, imply, portend, presage, purport, refer to, represent, signify, stand for, suggest, symbolize. **3** (*to entail, to involve*) bring about, cause, engender, entail, involve, lead to, necessitate, produce, result in. **4** (*to design, to destine (for)*) design, destine, make, predestine, preordain.

mean[2] *a.* **1** (*occupying a middle position*) halfway, median, medium, middle, middling. **2** (*moderate, not excessive*) average, medium, moderate, normal, standard. **3** (*intervening*) intermediate, intervening.
~*n.* **1** (*the middle point, course or degree between two extremes*) compromise, middle, midpoint. ANTONYMS: extreme. **2** (*an average*) average, median, norm.

mean[3] *a.* **1** (*low in quality, rank etc.*) base, low, lowly. **2** (*inferior, poor*) feeble, inefficient, inferior, poor, weak. **3** (*stingy, miserly*) beggarly, close, low-minded, mercenary, miserly, money-grubbing, niggardly, parsimonious, penny-pinching, penurious, petty, selfish, stingy, tight, tight-fisted, ungenerous. ANTONYMS: generous. **4** (*shabby, lowly*) common, down-at-heel, humble, lowly, miserable, ordinary, paltry, run-down, scruffy, seedy, shabby, sordid, squalid, tawdry, vulgar, wretched. ANTONYMS: magnificent. **5** (*disreputable, despicable*) abject, base, contemptible, degenerate, degraded, despicable, disgraceful, dishonourable, disreputable, ignoble, low, narrow-minded, petty, shabby, shameful, small-minded, sordid. ANTONYMS: big-hearted, noble. **6** (*esp. N Am.*) (*bad-tempered, aggressive*) aggressive, bad-tempered, callous, cantankerous, churlish, cruel, disagreeable, hostile, ill-tempered, malicious, nasty, rude, sour, unfriendly, unkind, unpleasant, vicious. **7** (*coll.*) (*having or showing great skill*) ace, excellent, skilful, wonderful.

meander *v.i.* (*to wind or flow in a tortuous course*) amble, bend, curve, drift, loop, ramble, snake, stray, turn, twist, wander, wind, zigzag.

meandering *a.* (*winding or flowing in a tortuous course*) circuitous, convoluted, curvy, indirect, labyrinthine, roundabout, serpentine, sinuous, snaking, tortuous, wandering, winding. ANTONYMS: direct, undeviating.

meaning *n.* (*that which is meant, significance*) connotation, content, drift, explanation, gist, implication, import, interpretation, message, purport, sense, significance, substance, upshot.

meaningful *a.* **1** (*significant*) consequential, important, material, pithy, purposeful, relevant, serious, significant, useful, valid, weighty,

worthwhile. ANTONYMS: meaningless, trivial. **2** (*clearly expressing someone's thoughts or feelings*) eloquent, expressive, meaning, pointed, pregnant, sententious, speaking, suggestive, telling.

meaningless *a.* (*having no purpose or meaning*) aimless, empty, futile, hollow, inconsequential, insignificant, insubstantial, irrelevant, nonsensical, pointless, purposeless, senseless, trivial, unimportant, useless, vacuous, worthless. ANTONYMS: meaningful, portentous.

means *n.pl.* **1** (*that by which anything is done or a result attained*) agency, avenue, channel, course, expedient, instrument, measure, medium, method, mode, process, vehicle, way. **2** (*available resources, income*) affluence, capital, estate, fortune, funds, income, money, property, resources, revenue, riches, substance, wealth. ANTONYMS: poverty.

meantime *adv.* **1** (*in the intervening time*) for now, for the moment, in the interim, in the interval. **2** (*while this was happening etc.*) at the same time, concurrently, simultaneously.

measly *a.* (*coll.*) (*paltry, meagre*) beggarly, contemptible, meagre, mean, miserable, niggardly, paltry, pathetic, petty, pitiful, poor, puny, scanty, skimpy, sparse, stingy, ungenerous, worthless.

measure *n.* **1** (*the extent or dimensions of a thing as determined by measuring*) amount, amplitude, breadth, bulk, capacity, degree, dimension, extent, height, length, magnitude, mass, proportions, quantity, range, reach, size, volume, weight, width. **2** (*a standard of measurement*) criterion, example, model, norm, par, standard, test, touchstone, yardstick. **3** (*a system of measuring*) method, standard, system. **4** (*a prescribed or allotted length or quantity*) allotment, allowance, division, part, piece, portion, proportion, quota, ration, share. ANTONYMS: whole. **5** (*limit, moderation*) bound, constraint, control, end, extent, extreme, limit, limitation, moderation, restraint. **6** (*metre, poetical rhythm*) beat, cadence, foot, melody, rhythm, verse. **7** (*an action to achieve a purpose*) act, action, course, deed, expedient, manoeuvre, means, procedure, proceeding, step. **8** (*a law, a statute*) act, bill, enactment, law, legislation, proposal, resolution, statute.
~*v.t.* **1** (*to determine the extent or quantity of by comparison with a definite standard*) calculate, calibrate, compute, determine, mark out, quantify, sound, work out. **2** (*to weigh, to estimate by comparison with a rule or standard*) appraise, assess, estimate, evaluate, gauge,

judge, rate, value, weigh. **3** (*to allot or apportion by measure*) allot, apportion, share. **4** (*to survey, look up and down*) look up and down, size up, survey. **5** (*to regulate, to keep within bounds*) adapt, adjust, calculate, choose, fit, judge, keep within bounds, regulate, tailor.

measured *a.* **1** (*well-considered, carefully weighed*) calculated, careful, cautious, considered, planned, premeditated, prudent, reasoned, sober, studied, systematic, weighed, well-considered, well-thought-out. **2** (*of definite measure*) definite, exact, modulated, precise. **3** (*deliberate and uniform*) deliberate, dignified, even, leisurely, regular, regulated, sedate, slow, solemn, stately, steady, unhurried, uniform. **4** (*rhythmical*) regular, rhythmical, steady.

measurement *n.* **1** (*the act of measuring*) appraisal, assessment, calculation, calibration, computation, estimation, evaluation, judgement, mensuration, survey, valuation. **2** (*an extent or dimension determined by measurement*) amount, amplitude, area, breadth, capacity, depth, dimension, extent, height, length, magnitude, size, volume, weight, width. **3** (*pl.*) (*detailed dimensions*) dimensions, size, statistics, vital statistics.

meat *n.* **1** (*the flesh of animals, usu. excluding fish and fowl, used as food*) flesh, viands. **2** (*the substance of something, the pith*) basics, core, crux, essence, essentials, gist, heart, kernel, marrow, nub, nucleus, pith, point, substance. **3** (*solid food of any kind*) aliment, (*coll.*) chow, comestibles, eatables, (*coll.*) eats, edibles, fare, food, (*sl.*) grub, (*sl.*) nosh, nourishment, nutriment, provender, provisions, rations, subsistence, sustenance, victuals.

mechanical *a.* **1** (*of or relating to machinery or mechanisms*) automated, automatic, machine-powered, power-driven. **2** (*done from force of habit, slavish*) automatic, cold, emotionless, habitual, impersonal, insensible, instinctive, involuntary, lacklustre, lifeless, machine-like, perfunctory, reflex, robotic, routine, slavish, spiritless, unconscious, unfeeling, unthinking. ANTONYMS: conscious, wholehearted.

mechanism *n.* **1** (*the structure or correlation of parts of a machine*) action, components, gears, (*coll.*) innards, machinery, motor, workings, works. **2** (*a piece of machinery*) apparatus, appliance, contrivance, device, engine, instrument, machine, motor. **3** (*a means*) agency, means, medium, method, operation, performance, procedure, process, system, technique, way.

meddle *v.i.* (*to interfere (in) officiously*) butt in, interfere, interlope, intermeddle, interpose,

intervene, intrude, poke one's nose in, pry, snoop, tamper (with).

mediate *v.t.* (*to interpose between (parties) in order to reconcile them*) arbitrate, bring to terms, conciliate, reconcile, referee, umpire. ~*v.i.* (*to interpose (between) in order to reconcile parties etc.*) intercede, interpose, intervene.

mediation *n.* (*the act of mediating*) arbitration, conciliation, good offices, intercessions, interposition, intervention, reconciliation.

mediator *n.* (*a person who tries to reconcile two parties*) advocate, appeaser, arbiter, arbitrator, go-between, honest broker, interceder, intercessor, intermediary, judge, middleman, moderator, negotiator, peace-maker, referee, umpire.

medical *a.* (*healing, medicinal*) curative, healing, medicinal.

medicinal *a.* (*curing an illness*) analeptic, curative, healing, medical, remedial, restorative, therapeutic.

medicine *n.* (*a substance, usu. taken internally, used for the alleviation or removal of disease*) cure, draught, drug, medicament, medication, nostrum, panacea, pharmaceutical, physic, prescription, remedy.

mediocre *a.* **1** (*of middling quality*) average, commonplace, everyday, indifferent, insignificant, medium, middling, ordinary, passable, run-of-the-mill, so so, tolerable, undistinguished, unimaginative, uninspired. ANTONYMS: distinctive, excellent. **2** (*of inferior quality*) inferior, second-rate, substandard.

meditate *v.i.* **1** (*to engage in contemplation, esp. on religious or spiritual matters*) consider, contemplate, deliberate, reflect. **2** (*to ponder, to engage in thought (upon)*) cogitate, concentrate, engage in thought, muse, ponder, ruminate, think. ~*v.t.* **1** (*to dwell upon mentally*) chew over, dwell upon, mull over, study, think over. **2** (*to plan, to intend*) design, intend, plan, purpose, scheme.

meditation *n.* (*the act of meditating*) brown study, cerebration, cogitation, concentration, contemplation, deliberation, musing, pondering, reflection, reverie, rumination, study, thought.

medium *n.* **1** (*anything serving as an agent or instrument*) agent, instrument, intermediary. **2** (*a means of communication*) agency, avenue, channel, instrument, means, mode, organ, vehicle, way. **3** (*an intervening substance or element, such as the air or ether*) atmosphere, conditions, element, environment, habitat,

milieu, surroundings. **4** (*a middle or inter-mediate object, quality etc.*) average, centre, compromise, mean, middle, midpoint. **5** (*a person claiming to receive communications from the spirit world*) psychic, spiritualist.
~*a.* **1** (*intermediate in quantity or quality*) inter-mediate, mean, medial, median, midway. ANTONYMS: extreme. **2** (*average, middling*) average, fair, mediocre, middle, middling, moderate. ANTONYMS: extraordinary.

medley *n.* **1** (*a musical or literary miscellany*) anthology, collection, miscellany. **2** (*a mixed or confused mass, esp. of incongruous objects, persons etc.*) agglomeration, assortment, blend, confusion, conglomeration, farrago, gal-limaufry, hotchpotch, jumble, mélange, mish-mash, mixture, patchwork, pot-pourri, ragbag, stew.

meek *a.* (*mild, forbearing*) acquiescent, com-pliant, deferential, docile, forbearing, gentle, humble, long-suffering, lowly, mild, modest, patient, resigned, shy, soft, submissive, tame, timid, unassuming, yielding. ANTONYMS: arrog-ant, proud.

meet *v.t.* **1** (*to come face to face with*) bump into, chance on, come across, contact, en-counter, face, happen upon, run into, stumble into. ANTONYMS: miss. **2** ((*of a road, railway, etc.*) *to unite with*) abut, adjoin, come together, connect, converge, cross, intersect, join, link up, reach, touch, unite. **3** (*to confront, to oppose*) confront, counter, encounter, oppose. **4** (*to experience*) bear, encounter, endure, experience, face, go through, gratify, handle, match, measure up, perform, satisfy, settle, take charge of. **5** (*to pay, to discharge*) defray, discharge, liquidate, pay, settle.
~*v.i.* (*to assemble*) assemble, collect, congregate, convene, gather, get together, muster, rally, rendezvous. ANTONYMS: disperse, scatter.

meeting *n.* **1** (*an assembly*) assembly, assignation, conclave, concourse, conference, confrontation, congress, convention, convoca-tion, encounter, engagement, gathering, (*coll.*) get-together, introduction, meet, rally, rendez-vous, reunion, session, tryst. **2** (*the persons assembled*) audience, company, congregation. **3** (*a confluence, intersection*) concourse, confluence, conjunction, convergence, cross-ing, intersection, junction. ANTONYMS: diver-gence. **4** (*a contest, duel etc.*) competition, contest, duel, head-to-head.

melancholy *n.* **1** (*Med.*) (*a gloomy, dejected state of mind*) blues, dejection, depression, despondency, gloom, low spirits, melancho-lia, misery, moodiness, sadness, sorrow, un-happiness, woe. ANTONYMS: cheerfulness,

happiness. **2** (*poet.*) (*pensive contemplation*) contemplation, pensiveness, thoughtfulness.
~*a.* **1** (*sad, depressed in spirits*) (*coll.*) blue, dejected, depressed, despondent, discon-solate, dismal, dispirited, doleful, down, downcast, downhearted, gloomy, glum, heavy-hearted, low, melancholic, miserable, morose, sad, unhappy. ANTONYMS: elated. **2** (*mournful, saddening*) mournful, saddening, sorrowful. **3** (*pensive*) distracted, pensive, thoughtful.

mellifluous *a.* (*flowing smoothly and sweetly* (*usu. of a voice, words etc.*)) dulcet, euphon-ious, flowing, fluent, harmonious, honeyed, mellow, melodious, musical, pleasant, silvery, smooth, soft, soothing, sweet. ANTONYMS: discordant, harsh.

mellow *a.* **1** (*of fruit*) *fully ripe*) juicy, luscious, mature, pulpy, ripe, sweet, tender. ANTONYMS: immature, unripe. **2** (*ripened or softened by age and experience*) affable, amiable, cheerful, cordial, easygoing, expansive, felicitous, genial, jovial, kindly, pleasant, relaxed, warm. **3** (*jolly, half tipsy*) happy, jolly, merry, tipsy. ANTONYMS: sober. **4** ((*of tones and colours*) *soft and rich*) muted, pastel, rich, soft, subtle. **5** ((*of sounds*) *pleasant and smooth*) dulcet, full, mellifluous, melodious, musical, rich, rounded, smooth, soft, sweet, tuneful.
~*v.i.* (*to become mature or softened, by age etc.*) age, develop, improve, mature, ripen, season, soften, sweeten.

melodious *a.* (*agreeably tuneful, melodic*) con-cordant, dulcet, euphonious, golden, harmon-ious, lyrical, mellifluous, melodic, musical, silvery, sweet, tuneful. ANTONYMS: cacophon-ous, discordant.

melodramatic *a.* (*sensational and ex-travagant*) blood-and-thunder, exaggerated, extravagant, (*sl.*) hammy, histrionic, overdone, overdramatic, over-emotional, overwrought, sensational, sentimental, stagy, theatrical.

melody *n.* **1** (*an agreeable succession of sounds, esp. of simple tones in the same key*) air, descant, measure, refrain, song, strain, tune. **2** (*the chief part in harmonic music*) air, theme, tune. **3** (*tunefulness*) euphony, har-mony, melodiousness, music, musicality, song, tunefulness. ANTONYMS: discord.

melt *v.i.* **1** (*to pass from a solid to a liquid state by heat*) liquefy, thaw. **2** (*to dissolve*) deli-quesce, diffuse, dissolve, evaporate, fuse. **3** (*to be dissipated, to vanish* (*away*)) decline, decrease, diminish, disappear, disperse, dissipate, dissolve, dwindle, evanesce, evaporate, fade, go away, pass, shrink, vanish. **4** (*to be softened to kindly influences, to give way*) assuage, disarm, give way, mellow, mollify, move, soften, touch, yield. **5** (*to merge or blend* (*into*)) be assimilated (into), become lost (in), blend (into), merge (into). **6** (*to be uncomfortably hot*) faint, perspire, stifle, sweat.

member *n.* **1** (*a person belonging to a society or body*) adherent, associate, fellow, subscriber. **2** (*a branch or division of a society or organization*) arm, branch, division, part. **3** (*a component part or element of an organism or complex whole*) component, constituent, element, part. **4** (*a limb, a part or organ of the body*) appendage, arm, extremity, leg, limb, organ, part.

memento *n.* (*a souvenir*) keepsake, memorial, relic, remembrance, reminder, souvenir, token, trophy.

memoir *n.* **1** (*an account of events or transactions in which the narrator took part*) account, narrative, recollection, reminiscence. **2** (*an autobiography or a biography*) autobiography, biography, confession, diary, history, journal, life. **3** (*a communication to some learned society on a special subject*) dissertation, essay, monograph, paper, treatise. **4** (*pl.*) (*the published proceedings of a learned society*) annals, chronicle, proceedings, record, register, transactions.

memorable *a.* **1** (*worthy to be remembered*) catchy, never-to-be-forgotten, unforgettable. ANTONYMS: unmemorable. **2** (*notable, remarkable*) celebrated, distinguished, eventful, extraordinary, famous, great, historic, illustrious, important, impressive, momentous, notable, noteworthy, remarkable, signal, significant, striking, worthy. ANTONYMS: insignificant, ordinary.

memorandum *n.* **1** (*a note to help the memory*) aide-mémoire, memo, reminder. **2** (*a short, informal letter, often sent internally within a company etc.*) letter, message, note. **3** (*a brief record or note*) chit, chitty, minute, note, record, slip, statement. **4** (*Law*) (*a summary or draft of an agreement etc.*) abstract, draft, outline, sketch, summary, synopsis.

memorial *a.* (*intended to preserve the memory of a past event, person etc.*) commemorative, monumental.
~*n.* **1** (*a monument, festival etc. commemorating a person, event etc.*) cenotaph, commemoration, festival, inscription, marker, memento, monument, plaque, remembrance, reminder, souvenir, statue. **2** (*a chronicle or record*) chronicle, history, memorandum, record, statement.

memorize *v.t.* (*to learn by heart*) commit to

memory, learn, learn by heart, learn by rote, remember, retain. ANTONYMS: forget.

memory *n.* **1** (*the exercise of the faculty of retaining and recalling previous ideas and impressions*) recall, recollection, remembrance, retention, retrospection. ANTONYMS: forgetfulness. **2** (*something that is remembered*) recollection, remembrance, reminiscence. **3** (*posthumous reputation*) celebration, commemoration, fame, glory, homage, honour, regard, renown, reputation, repute, respect, tribute. ANTONYMS: oblivion.

menace *n.* **1** (*a threat*) danger, hazard, intimidation, jeopardy, peril, risk, scare, threat, warning. **2** (*a nuisance*) annoyance, nuisance, (*coll.*) pain, pest, plague, vexation.
~*v.t.* (*to threaten*) alarm, bully, cow, daunt, frighten, intimidate, scare, terrify, terrorize, threaten, warn. ANTONYMS: reassure.

menacing *a.* (*making one expect something harmful or unpleasant*) alarming, baleful, dangerous, daunting, forbidding, frightening, hazardous, impending, intimidating, looming, louring, minatory, ominous, perilous, risky, scary, terrifying, threatening. ANTONYMS: auspicious, promising.

mend *v.t.* **1** (*to repair, to restore*) darn, fix, make good, patch, remedy, renew, renovate, repair, restore. **2** (*to improve, to make better*) ameliorate, cure, improve, make better. ANTONYMS: deteriorate. **3** (*to correct, to amend*) amend, correct, emend, rectify, reform, revise.
~*v.i.* **1** (*to grow better, to improve*) ameliorate, grow better, improve. ANTONYMS: deteriorate. **2** (*to recover health*) convalesce, get better, recover, recuperate.
~*n.* (*a repaired part* (*in a garment etc.*)) darn, patch, repair, stitch.

mendacious *a.* (*given to lying, untruthful*) deceitful, deceptive, dishonest, duplicitous, fallacious, false, fraudulent, insincere, lying, perfidious, perjured, untrue, untruthful. ANTONYMS: honest, truthful.

mendacity *n.* (*lying, untruthfulness*) deceit, deceitfulness, deception, dishonesty, distortion, duplicity, falsehood, falsification, falsity, fraudulence, insincerity, lie, lying, misrepresentation, perfidy, perjury, untruthfulness. ANTONYMS: honesty.

menial *a.* (*servile, degrading*) base, boring, degrading, demeaning, dull, humble, humdrum, ignoble, low, lowly, mean, routine, servile, unskilled. ANTONYMS: dignified, noble.
~*n.* (*a person doing servile work*) attendant, (*coll.*) dogsbody, domestic, drudge, flunkey, labourer, lackey, minion, serf, servant, (*sl.*)

skivvy, slave, underling, vassal. ANTONYMS: master.

mensuration n. (*the act or practice of measuring*) assessment, calculation, calibration, computation, estimation, measurement, measuring, survey, surveying.

mental a. 1 (*of or relating to the mind*) cerebral, cognitive, intellectual, psychological. 2 (*slightly deranged in mind*) (*sl.*) bananas, (*sl.*) bonkers, (*sl.*) crackers, crazy, demented, deranged, disordered, disturbed, insane, (*sl.*) loony, lunatic, mad, mentally ill, (*sl.*) nuts, (*sl.*) nutty, psychotic, unbalanced, unstable. ANTONYMS: sane. 3 (*very enthusiastic, fanatical*) enthusiastic, fanatical, keen, mad.

mention n. 1 (*a concise notice (of), an allusion*) allusion, announcement, indication, notification, observation, reference, referral, remark. 2 (*a referring to by name*) acknowledgement, citation, praise, recognition, tribute.
~v.t. 1 (*to refer to, to allude to*) allude to, bring up, broach, call attention to, cite, hint at, introduce, name, quote, refer to, touch on. 2 (*to reveal by speaking of*) disclose, divulge, hint, impart, imply, insinuate, intimate, make known, point out, speak of, suggest.

mentor n. (*an experienced adviser*) adviser, coach, confidant, confidante, counsellor, guide, guru, instructor, master, teacher, tutor.

mercantile a. (*of or relating to buying and selling*) commercial, marketable, saleable, trade, trading.

mercenary a. 1 (*done from or actuated by motives of gain*) acquisitive, avaricious, covetous, grasping, greedy, money-grubbing, predatory, selfish, sordid. ANTONYMS: generous, philanthropic. 2 (*bribable, venal*) bribable, brought, hired, paid, venal.
~n. (*a person who is hired, esp. a soldier hired in foreign service*) hireling, soldier of fortune.

merchandise n. (*goods for sale and purchase*) commodities, goods, produce, products, stock, vendibles, ware.
~v.t. 1 (*to trade in (a commodity)*) buy and sell, deal in, trade in, traffic in. 2 (*to put (a product) on the market*) market, put on the market, retail, sell, vend. 3 (*to promote, advertise etc.*) advertise, promote, push.

merchant n. 1 (*a person who carries on trade on a large scale, esp. with foreign countries*) broker, dealer, trader. 2 (*esp. N Am., Sc.*) (*a retailer, a shopkeeper*) purveyor, retailer, salesman, seller, shopkeeper, supplier, trader, tradesman, tradeswoman, trafficker, vendor, wholesaler.

merciful a. (*showing mercy, kind*) beneficent, charitable, clement, compassionate, considerate, forbearing, forgiving, generous, humane, indulgent, kind, lenient, liberal, magnanimous, pitying, soft, sparing, sympathetic, tender-hearted. ANTONYMS: cruel, merciless.

merciless a. (*showing no mercy, cruel*) barbarous, callous, cruel, hard, harsh, heartless, implacable, inhuman, pitiless, ruthless, savage, severe, stony-hearted, unfeeling, unforgiving, unkind, unmerciful, unrelenting, unsparing, unsympathetic. ANTONYMS: kind, merciful.

mercurial a. (*volatile, fickle*) active, capricious, changeable, energetic, erratic, fickle, flighty, impulsive, inconstant, irrepressible, light-hearted, lively, spirited, sprightly, temperamental, unpredictable, unstable, variable, vivacious, volatile. ANTONYMS: consistent, unchanging.

mercy n. 1 (*a disposition to temper justice with mildness*) clemency, forbearance, leniency, mildness, pity. 2 (*forbearance, compassion*) benevolence, charity, clemency, compassion, favour, forbearance, humanity, indulgence, kindness, magnanimity, passion, pity, tolerance. ANTONYMS: brutality, severity. 3 (*pardon, forgiveness*) forgiveness, grace, pardon, quarter. 4 (*liberty to punish or spare*) control, discretion, power, will.

mere a. (*such and no more*) absolute, bare, complete, entire, plain, pure, sheer, simple, stark, unadulterated, undiluted, unmitigated, utter.

merely adv. (*only, solely*) barely, basically, entirely, essentially, fundamentally, just, only, purely, scarcely, simply, solely, utterly.

meretricious a. 1 (*alluring by false or empty show*) cheap, flashy, garish, showy, trashy. 2 (*seeming attractive but unreal*) bogus, counterfeit, deceitful, false, hollow, insincere, (*coll.*) phoney, sham, specious, spurious, unreal. ANTONYMS: genuine.

merge v.i. (*to be absorbed or swallowed up (with)*) blend (with), coalesce (with), combine (with), converge (with), fuse (with), join (with), meet (with), melt (into), mingle (with), mix (with). ANTONYMS: diverge (from).
~v.t. (*to cause to be swallowed up or absorbed in*) amalgamate, combine, consolidate, incorporate, join, pool, sink, unite. ANTONYMS: separate.

merger n. 1 (*the merging of a company etc. into another*) amalgamation, blending, coalescence, coalition, combination, consolidation, fusion, merging, mingling, mixing, pooling, union. ANTONYMS: separation. 2 (*absorption*) absorption, assimilation, incorporation.

meridian n. (*point of highest splendour or vigour*) acme, apex, apogee, climax, crest, culmination, height, high point, peak, pinnacle, summit, zenith. ANTONYMS: nadir.

merit n. 1 (*the quality of deserving*) advantage, asset, claim, credit, desert, due, right. 2 (*excellence deserving honour or reward, worth*) excellence, good, integrity, quality, strong point, talent, value, virtue, worth, worthiness. ANTONYMS: fault. 3 (*a mark or award of merit*) award, recompense, reward. ANTONYMS: demerit.
~v.t. 1 (*to deserve, to earn*) be worthy of, deserve, earn, incur, rate, warrant. 2 (*to be entitled to receive as a reward*) be entitled to, have a claim to, have a right to.

meritorious a. (*deserving reward, praiseworthy*) commendable, creditable, deserving, estimable, excellent, exemplary, good, honourable, laudable, outstanding, praiseworthy, right, righteous, virtuous, worthy. ANTONYMS: discreditable, undeserving.

merriment n. (*laughter and fun*) amusement, cheerfulness, conviviality, exuberance, festivity, fun, gaiety, glee, happiness, hilarity, jocularity, jollity, joy, jubilation, laughter, levity, mirth, revelry, sport. ANTONYMS: depression, gloom.

merry a. 1 (*cheerful, happy*) blithe, buoyant, cheerful, cheery, chirpy, convivial, exuberant, festive, gleeful, happy, hilarious, jocund, jolly, jovial, joyful, jubilant, mirthful, rejoicing, vivacious. ANTONYMS: dejected, gloomy. 2 (*coll.*) (*slightly tipsy*) (*sl.*) half-cut, mellow, (*coll.*) squiffy, (*coll.*) tiddly, tipsy. ANTONYMS: sober.

mesh n. 1 (*a fabric or structure of network*) lattice, net, netting, network, reticulation, screen, tracery, web. 2 (*the engagement of gear teeth etc.*) bite, engagement, interlocking. 3 (*a trap, a snare*) entanglement, snare, tangle, trap.
~v.t. 1 (*to cause to engage (gear teeth etc.)*) bring together, engage, interlock. 2 (*to catch in a net, to ensnare*) catch, enmesh, ensnare, entangle, net, snare, tangle, trap. ANTONYMS: free.
~v.i. 1 (*to coordinate (with)*) combine, connect, coordinate, dovetail, harmonize. 2 ((*of gear teeth etc.*) *to engage (with)*) bite, engage, interlock.

mesmerize v.t. 1 (*to hypnotize*) entrance, hypnotize, magnetize. 2 (*to occupy (someone's attention) totally*) absorb, captivate, enthral, entrance, fascinate, grip, magnetize, occupy, spellbind.

mess n. 1 (*a state of dirt and disorder*) botch, chaos, clutter, (*sl.*) cock-up, confusion,

dirtiness, disarray, disorder, disorganization, hash, hotchpotch, jumble, litter, mishmash, muddle, shambles, state, turmoil. ANTONYMS: order. 2 (*a muddle, a difficulty*) difficulty, dilemma, fine kettle of fish, fix, (*coll.*) hot water, imbroglio, jam, mix-up, muddle, perplexity, (*coll.*) pickle, pinch, plight, predicament, quandary, spot, (*coll.*) stew, (*coll.*) tight spot, trouble.
~v.t. 1 (*to mix together, to muddle*) botch, bungle, clutter, (*sl.*) cock up, confuse, disarrange, dishevel, jumble, litter, mess up, mix together, muck up, muddle, scramble, untidy. ANTONYMS: clear. 2 (*to dirty, to soil*) befoul, besmirch, dirty, foul, pollute, soil. **to mess about 1** (*to tumble or fool about*) dabble, dally, fool about, muck about, (*taboo sl.*) piss about, play about, trifle, tumble about. **2** (*to treat improperly or inconsiderately*) exploit, illtreat, mistreat, neglect. **3** (*to potter about*) fiddle, meddle, play, potter about, tamper, tinker, toy. **4** (*to flirt*) flirt, fool around, philander, run around, seduce, sleep around, toy, trifle.

message n. 1 (*a communication, oral or written, from one person to another*) bulletin, communication, communiqué, dispatch, information, intelligence, intimation, letter, memorandum, missive, note, notice, report, tidings, word. 2 (*the chief theme of a play, novel etc.*) essence, idea, implication, import, meaning, moral, point, purport, theme. 3 (*an errand, a mission*) commission, errand, job, mission, task.

messenger n. (*a person who carries a message*) agent, bearer, carrier, courier, delivery boy, delivery girl, emissary, envoy, errand boy, errand girl, go-between, (*coll.*) gofer, harbinger, herald, intermediary, legate, nuncio, page, runner.

messy a. 1 (*dirty, muddled*) chaotic, cluttered, confused, dirty, dishevelled, disordered, disorganized, grubby, littered, muddled, (*coll.*) shambolic, sloppy, slovenly, unkempt, untidy. ANTONYMS: neat, tidy. 2 (*complicated and difficult to handle*) awkward, complex, complicated, tricky, troublesome.

metamorphosis n. 1 (*a change of form*) alteration, change, changeover, conversion, modification. 2 (*transformation, such as that of a chrysalis into a winged insect*) mutation, rebirth, regeneration, transfiguration, transformation, translation, transmutation, transubstantiation.

metaphor n. (*a figure of speech by which a word is transferred in application from one object to another, so as to imply comparison*) allegory, allusion, analogy, emblem, figure of speech, image, simile, symbol.

metaphysical *a.* **1** (*transcendental, dealing with abstractions*) abstract, ideal, immaterial, intellectual, intelligible, philosophical, profound, speculative, theoretical, transcendental. ANTONYMS: material. **2** (*abstruse, oversubtle*) abstruse, esoteric, oversubtle, recondite. **3** (*imaginary, fantastic*) fantastic, imaginary, spiritual, supernatural.

meteoric *a.* **1** (*rapid, like a meteor*) fast, overnight, rapid, speedy, sudden, swift. **2** (*brilliant but fading quickly*) brief, brilliant, dazzling, ephemeral, evanescent, flashing, fleeting, impermanent, momentary, short-lived, spectacular, temporary, transient, transitory. ANTONYMS: prolonged.

method *n.* **1** (*a mode of procedure, way or order of doing*) approach, course, form, manner, means, mode, modus operandi, order, plan, practice, procedure, process, programme, route, routine, rule, scheme, style, technique, way. **2** (*a systematic or logical arrangement*) arrangement, design, logic, order. **3** (*orderliness, system*) design, form, order, orderliness, organization, pattern, structure, system. ANTONYMS: disorder.

methodical *a.* (*habitually proceeding in a systematic way*) businesslike, deliberate, disciplined, efficient, exact, laborious, meticulous, neat, ordered, orderly, organized, painstaking, planned, precise, regular, routine, structured, systematic, tidy, well-regulated. ANTONYMS: casual, haphazard.

meticulous *a.* **1** (*very careful*) accurate, careful, detailed, exact, painstaking, particular, perfectionist, precise, punctilious, scrupulous, strict, thorough. ANTONYMS: careless, slapdash. **2** (*cautious or overscrupulous about trivial details*) cautious, fastidious, finicky, fussy, overscrupulous.

metropolis *n.* **1** (*the chief town or capital of a country*) administrative centre, capital, chief town. **2** (*a large town or city*) city, conurbation, municipality, town.

mettle *n.* **1** (*quality of temperament or disposition*) calibre, character, disposition, humour, kidney, make-up, nature, quality, stamp, temper, temperament. **2** (*constitutional ardour*) animation, ardour, (*sl.*) balls, energy, fervour, fire, indomitability, life, vigour. **3** (*spirit, courage*) boldness, (*sl.*) bottle, bravery, courage, daring, fortitude, grit, (*coll.*) guts, nerve, pluck, resolution, resolve, spirit, valour.

microscopic *a.* (*very small*) imperceptible,

infinitesimal, invisible, minuscule, minute, negligible, tiny, very small. ANTONYMS: enormous, huge.

midday *n.* (*noon, the middle of the day*) noon, noonday, noontide, noontime, twelve noon.

middle *a.* **1** (*placed equally distant from the extremes*) central, halfway, mid. ANTONYMS: extreme. **2** (*intervening, intermediate*) inner, inside, intermediate, intervening. **3** (*average*) average, mean, medial, medium. ~*n.* **1** (*the waist*) midriff, stomach, (*coll.*) tummy, waist. **2** (*the midst, the centre*) centre, core, heart, mean, midpoint, mid section, midst. ANTONYMS: edge.

middling *a.* **1** (*of middle size, quality or condition*) average, medium. **2** (*moderately good*) adequate, all right, fair, moderate, modest, (*coll.*) OK, (*coll.*) okay, passable, so so, tolerable. **3** (*mediocre, second-rate*) indifferent, mediocre, ordinary, run-of-the-mill, second-rate, unexceptional, unremarkable. ANTONYMS: exceptional.

midst *n.* (*the middle*) bosom, centre, core, depths, halfway point, heart, hub, middle, midpoint, thick. ANTONYMS: edge.

might *n.* **1** (*strength, force*) ability, capability, capacity, (*coll.*) clout, efficacy, efficiency, energy, force, muscle, potency, prowess, puissance, strength, valour, vigour. ANTONYMS: weakness. **2** (*power, esp. to enforce arbitrary authority*) ascendancy, authority, dominion, influence, power, superiority, sway, weight.

mighty *a.* **1** (*strong, powerful*) brawny, burly, doughty, forceful, hardy, hearty, indomitable, lusty, manful, muscular, potent, powerful, puissant, robust, stalwart, stout, strapping, strong, sturdy, vigorous. ANTONYMS: feeble, weak. **2** (*huge, immense*) bulky, colossal, elephantine, enormous, gigantic, great, huge, immense, large, massive, (*coll.*) mega, monumental, prodigious, stupendous, titanic, towering, tremendous, vast. ANTONYMS: tiny, unimposing. **3** (*coll.*) (*great, considerable*) considerable, great, impressive, massive, tremendous.

migrant *n.* (*a person who moves permanently from one place to another*) drifter, emigrant, gypsy, immigrant, itinerant, nomad, rover, transient, traveller, vagrant, wanderer. ~*a.* (*moving permanently from one place to another*) displaced, drifting, floating, gypsy, immigrant, itinerant, migratory, nomadic, peripatetic, roaming, rootless, roving, shifting, transient, travelling, unsettled, vagrant, wandering. ANTONYMS: permanent, settled.

migrate *v.i.* (*to move permanently from one*

place to another) drift, emigrate, go, immigrate, journey, move, range, relocate, resettle, roam, rove, shift, transmigrate, travel, trek, voyage, wander. ANTONYMS: remain, stay.

migratory *a. (moving permanently from one place to another)* displaced, drifting, floating, gypsy, immigrant, itinerant, migrant, nomadic, peripatetic, roaming, rootless, roving, shifting, transient, travelling, unsettled, vagrant, wandering.

mild *a.* **1** *(gentle in manners or disposition)* affable, amiable, compassionate, docile, easy, easygoing, forbearing, forgiving, genial, gentle, indulgent, inoffensive, kind, lenient, lenitive, meek, merciful, placid, pleasant, serene, soothing, tender, tranquil, unassuming. **2** *((of weather) not cold or wet; pleasant)* balmy, bland, calm, clement, equable, pacific, pleasant. **3** *((of fruit, liquor etc.) soft, not sharp or strong)* mellow, soft. ANTONYMS: harsh, sharp. **4** *(moderate, not extreme)* moderate, tame, temperate. ANTONYMS: extreme.

mildness *n.* **1** *(gentleness in manner or disposition)* affability, amiableness, compassion, docility, forbearance, forgiveness, geniality, gentleness, indulgence, kindness, leniency, lenity, meekness, mercy, placidity, serenity, tenderness, tranquillity. **2** *((of weather) pleasantness)* balminess, blandness, calmness, clemency, equableness, pleasantness. **3** *((of fruit, liquor etc.) softness, in contrast to sharpness)* mellowness, softness. **4** *(moderation)* moderation, temperateness.

milieu *n. (environment, surroundings)* background, element, environment, environs, locale, location, medium, setting, sphere, surroundings.

militant *a.* **1** *(combative, aggressive)* aggressive, assertive, bellicose, belligerent, combatant, hawkish, pugnacious, truculent, warlike. ANTONYMS: appeasing, pacific. **2** *(actively engaged in fighting)* contending, fighting, warring.
~*n. (a militant person)* activist, aggressor, belligerent, combatant, fighter, gladiator, partisan, soldier, warrior.

military *a. (soldierly, martial)* armed, fighting, martial, soldierly, warlike. ANTONYMS: civilian.
~*n.* **1** *(soldiers generally)* soldiers, soldiery. **2** *(the army)* armed forces, army, services.

militate *v.i.* **1** *(to have weight or influence)* influence, tell, weigh. **2** *(to be or stand opposed)* cancel, conflict (with), contend (with), counter, counteract, countervail, discourage, foil, go against, hinder, oppose, prevent, reduce, resist, war.

militia *n. (a supplementary military force consisting of citizens not enrolled in the regular army)* reserve, trainband, yeomanry.

milk *v.t.* **1** *(to draw milk from)* drain, draw off, express, extract, let out, press, syphon, tap, withdraw. **2** *(to exploit to the full) (coll.)* bleed, capitalize on, drain, exploit, extract, impose on, pump, take advantage of, use, wring.

milky *a. ((of liquids) white, clouded)* alabaster, clouded, cloudy, opaque, white.

mill *n.* **1** *(a building with machinery for grinding corn to a fine powder)* watermill, windmill. **2** *(a machine for reducing solid substances of any kind to a finer consistency)* crusher, grater, grinder, roller. **3** *(a building fitted up with machinery for any industrial purpose)* factory, foundry, plant, shop, works.
~*v.t. (to grind (as corn) in a mill)* comminute, crush, granulate, grate, grind, pound, powder, press, pulverize, triturate.
~*v.i. (to move slowly (around))* crowd, seethe, swarm, throng.

mimic *n. (a person who mimics)* caricaturist, *(coll.)* copycat, imitator, impersonator, impressionist, mimicker, parodist.
~*a.* **1** *(imitative)* imitation, imitative, mimetic. **2** *(counterfeit)* counterfeit, fake, make-believe, mock, pretend, sham, simulated. ANTONYMS: authentic, genuine.
~*v.t.* **1** *(to imitate, esp. in order to ridicule)* caricature, *(coll.)* do, imitate, impersonate, lampoon, mock, parody, ridicule, satirize, *(coll.)* take off. **2** *(to ape, to copy)* ape, copy, duplicate, echo, mirror, reproduce, simulate. **3** *((of animals, plants etc.) to resemble closely)* imitate, look like, resemble.

minatory *a. (threatening, menacing)* baleful, dangerous, hostile, menacing, minacious, threatening.

mince *v.t.* **1** *(to cut or chop into very small pieces)* chop, crumble, cut up, dice, grind, hash. **2** *(to restrain (one's words) for politeness' sake)* euphemize, hold back, moderate, play down, tone down. **3** *(to minimize, to gloss over)* diminish, extenuate, gloss over, hold back, minimize, moderate, palliate, play down, soften, spare, tone down, weaken.
~*v.i. (to walk in a prim and affected manner)* attitudinize, *(sl.)* ponce, pose, posture, put on airs.

mincing *a. (affectedly elegant)* affected, camp, dainty, dandyish, delicate, effeminate, foppish, *(coll.)* la-di-da, *(sl.)* poncey, posey, posturing, precious, pretentious, twee.

mind *n.* **1** *(the intellectual powers of a human being, the understanding)* brains, *(coll.)* grey

matter, intellect, intelligence, mentality, perception, reason, sagacity, sense, shrewdness, understanding, wisdom, wits. **2** (*one's candid opinion*) attitude, belief, feeling, idea, judgement, opinion, outlook, point of view, sentiment, view, viewpoint. **3** (*recollection, memory*) memory, recollection, remembrance. **4** (*sanity*) judgement, rationality, reason, sanity, senses, wits. **5** (*way of feeling or thinking*) disposition, fancy, leaning, liking. **6** (*intention, inclination*) bent, desire, inclination, intention, notion, purpose, tendency, urge, will, wish. **7** (*mental concentration*) attention, concentration, thoughts. **8** (*a person regarded as an intellect*) (*coll.*) brainbox, genius, intellect, intellectual, sage, thinker.
~*v.t.* **1** (*to heed, to notice*) heed, mark, note, notice, regard, watch. **2** (*to pay attention to, to concern oneself with*) apply oneself (to), attend, concentrate (on), concern oneself (with), pay attention (to). ANTONYMS: ignore. **3** (*to object to*) disapprove of, dislike, object to, take offence at. **4** (*to look after*) care for, guard, look after, take care of, tend, watch over. ANTONYMS: neglect.
~*v.i.* (*to take care, to be on the watch*) be careful, beware, observe, take care, take heed, watch for.

mindful *a.* (*attentive, heedful* (*of*)) alert (to), attentive (to), aware (of), careful (of), chary (of), cognizant (of), conscientious, conscious (of), heedful (of), regardful (of), sensible (of), thoughtful, vigilant, wary (of), watchful. ANTONYMS: inattentive, thoughtless.

mindless *a.* **1** (*done without need for thought*) automatic, brainless, mechanical, thoughtless, unthinking. **2** (*heedless, stupid*) asinine, careless, foolish, forgetful, gratuitous, heedless, idiotic, imbecilic, inane, moronic, neglectful, negligent, oblivious, obtuse, regardless, senseless, stupid, thoughtless, witless. ANTONYMS: attentive, mindful.

mine *v.t.* **1** (*to dig into or burrow in*) bore, burrow, delve, dig, excavate, tunnel. **2** (*to obtain by excavating in the earth*) excavate, extract, hew, quarry, unearth. **3** (*to undermine, to sap*) sap, subvert, undermine, weaken. ANTONYMS: support.
~*n.* **1** (*an excavation in the earth for the purpose of obtaining minerals*) coalfield, colliery, excavation, pit, shaft. **2** (*a receptacle filled with explosive, floating in the sea or buried in the ground*) bomb, depth-charge, explosive, landmine. **3** (*a rich source of wealth, or of information etc.*) abundance, fund, hoard, reserve, source, stock, store, supply, treasury, wealth. **4** (*a rich deposit of minerals suitable for mining*) deposit, lode, seam, vein.

mingle *v.t.* **1** (*to mix up together*) alloy, amalgamate, blend, coalesce, combine, commingle, compound, intermingle, intermix, interweave, join, marry, meld, merge, mix, unite. ANTONYMS: detach, separate. **2** (*to come into close association* (*with*)) associate, circulate, consort, fraternize, hang about, (*sl.*) hang out, hobnob, rub shoulders, socialize.
~*v.i.* (*to be blended or united* (*with*)) blend, mix, unite.

miniature *a.* **1** (*smaller than the norm*) baby, diminutive, dwarf, mini, pocket, reduced, scaled down, small, undersized. **2** (*represented on a very small scale*) baby, bantam, diminutive, dwarf, Lilliputian, little, microscopic, midget, mini, minuscule, minute, pocket, pygmy, reduced, scaled down, small, (*coll.*) teeny-weeny, tiny, toy, wee. ANTONYMS: giant, large.

minimal *a.* **1** (*least possible*) least, least possible. **2** (*smallest, very small*) littlest, slightest, smallest, tiniest. **3** (*relating to or being a minimum*) minimal, nominal, token.

minimize *v.t.* **1** (*to reduce to the smallest possible amount or degree*) abbreviate, abridge, attenuate, curtail, cut, decrease, diminish, lessen, miniaturize, pare, reduce, shorten, shrink. ANTONYMS: increase. **2** (*to belittle, to underestimate*) belittle, decry, deprecate, depreciate, devalue, discount, disparage, downplay, play down, underestimate, underrate, undervalue. ANTONYMS: praise.

minimum *n.* (*the smallest amount or degree possible or usual*) bottom, depth, least, lowest, nadir. ANTONYMS: maximum.
~*a.* (*least possible*) least, littlest, minimal, slightest, smallest. ANTONYMS: greatest, maximal.

minion *n.* **1** (*a servile dependant*) bootlicker, creature, dependant, flatterer, flunkey, follower, hanger-on, henchman, lackey, lickspittle, parasite, subordinate, sycophant, toady, underling, yes-man. ANTONYMS: master. **2** (*a darling, a favourite*) darling, favourite, pet.

minister *n.* **1** (*the pastor of a church, esp. a nonconformist one*) chaplain, churchman, churchwoman, clergyman, clergywoman, cleric, curate, divine, ecclesiastic, evangelist, father, padre, parson, pastor, preacher, priest, rector, reverend, vicar. ANTONYMS: layman, laywoman. **2** (*a person representing their government with another state, an ambassador*) ambassador, consul, delegate, dignitary, diplomat, emissary, envoy, legate, plenipotentiary. **3** (*a person charged with the performance of a duty, or the execution of a will etc.*) administrator, delegate, executive, official. **4** (*a person who acts under the authority of* *another*) agent, aide, assistant, instrument, lieutenant, subordinate.

~*v.i.* (*to render service or attendance*) accommodate, administer, aid, assist, attend on, cater, help, oblige, pander, serve, take care of, tend, wait on.

~†*v.t.* (*to furnish, to supply*) furnish, supply.

ministry *n.* 1 (*a government department*) administration, bureau, cabinet, council, department, government, office. 2 (*the occupation or calling of a minister of religion*) church, clergy, cloth, holy orders, priesthood, religion. 3 (*the act of ministering*) administration, attention, caring, ministering, serving.

minor *a.* 1 (*less, smaller*) lesser, secondary, smaller, subordinate, subsidiary. ANTONYMS: major. 2 (*petty, comparatively unimportant*) inconsequential, inconsiderable, insignificant, negligible, paltry, petty, small, trifling, trivial, unimportant. ANTONYMS: important, significant.

~*n.* (*a person under legal age*) adolescent, boy, child, girl, infant, stripling, teenager, young person, youngster, youth.

minstrel *n.* (*a travelling musician or entertainer*) balladeer, entertainer, gleeman, jongleur, musician, performer, player, singer, troubadour.

mint *n.* (*a great quantity or amount*) billion, (*coll.*) bomb, (*sl.*) bundle, fortune, (*coll.*) heap, king's ransom, (*coll.*) load, lot, million, (*coll.*) packet, (*coll.*) pile, (*coll.*) pot, (*coll.*) ton, (*coll.*) wad.

~*v.t.* 1 (*to make* (*coin by stamping metal*)) cast, coin, fabricate, forge, make, produce, punch, stamp, strike. 2 (*to invent, to coin* (*a phrase etc.*)) coin, construct, create, devise, fashion, formulate, invent, think up.

~*a.* ((*of a book, coin etc.*) *in its unused state, as new*) brand-new, excellent, fine, first-class, fresh, new, perfect, pristine, unblemished, undamaged, untarnished, unused.

minute[1] *n.* 1 (*the 60th part of an hour*) sixtieth of an hour, sixty seconds. 2 (*a very small portion of time*) blink, flash, instant, (*coll.*) jiffy, moment, second, shake, (*coll.*) tick, trice, twinkling, two shakes of a lamb's tail. 3 (*pl.*) (*official records of proceedings of a committee etc.*) journal, log, note, proceedings, record, transcript.

~*v.t.* (*to take a note of*) document, log, note, take down, transcribe.

minute[2] *a.* 1 (*very small*) diminutive, fine, infinitesimal, little, microscopic, miniature, minuscule, pint-sized, slender, small, tiny, wee. ANTONYMS: enormous, huge. 2 (*petty, trifling*) inconsiderable, meagre, minor,

negligible, paltry, petty, puny, slight, trivial, unimportant. ANTONYMS: important. 3 (*particular, exact*) close, critical, detailed, exact, exhaustive, meticulous, painstaking, particular, precise, punctilious, scrupulous. ANTONYMS: cursory, superficial.

miracle *n.* 1 (*a marvellous event or act attributed to a supernatural agency*) marvel, prodigy, wonder. 2 (*an extraordinary occurrence*) phenomenon, sensation.

miraculous *a.* 1 (*of the nature of a miracle*) amazing, astonishing, astounding, extraordinary, fabulous, fantastic, incredible, inexplicable, marvellous, phenomenal, preternatural, prodigious, remarkable, spectacular, superhuman, unaccountable, unbelievable, wonderful, wondrous. ANTONYMS: commonplace, ordinary. 2 (*supernatural*) divine, supernatural.

mirage *n.* (*an illusory thing, a delusion*) delusion, hallucination, illusion, optical illusion, phantasm.

mire *n.* 1 (*swampy ground, a bog*) bog, fen, marsh, morass, quagmire, slough, swamp. 2 (*mud, dirt*) dirt, muck, mud, ooze, slime.

~*v.t.* 1 (*to soil with mire*) befoul, begrime, besmirch, bespatter, blacken, cake, defile, dirty, muddy, smear, smudge, soil, sully, tarnish. 2 (*to involve in difficulties*) enmesh, entangle, involve.

~*v.i.* (*to sink in a mire*) bog down, flounder, sink.

mirror *n.* 1 (*a looking-glass; reflector*) glass, looking-glass, reflector, speculum. 2 (*a pattern, a model*) copy, double, exemplar, image, likeness, model, paragon, pattern, picture, reflection, replica, representation, reproduction, twin.

~*v.t.* (*to reflect in or as in a mirror*) copy, depict, echo, emulate, follow, imitate, reflect, repeat, represent, reproduce, show.

mirth *n.* (*merriment, jollity*) amusement, cheerfulness, festivity, fun, gaiety, gladness, happiness, hilarity, jocularity, jollity, joviality, joy, laughter, levity, merriment, merrymaking, pleasure, revelry, sport. ANTONYMS: melancholy, sadness.

mirthful *a.* (*merry, jolly*) amused, blithe, cheerful, festive, frolicsome, funny, glad, gleeful, happy, hilarious, jocund, jolly, jovial, joyful, laughable, light-hearted, merry, playful, sportive. ANTONYMS: dismal, gloomy.

misadventure *n.* 1 (*an unlucky chance or accident*) accident, calamity, catastrophe, debacle, disaster, failure, mischance, mishap, reverse, setback. 2 (*bad luck*) bad luck, hard luck, ill fortune, ill luck, misfortune.

misanthropic *a.* (*disliking and avoiding other poeple*) antisocial, cynical, egocentric, egoistic, egotistical, inhumane, malevolent, selfish, unfriendly, unsociable. ANTONYMS: philanthropic.

misanthropy *n.* (*dislike and avoidance of other people*) cynicism, egoism, inhumanity, malevolence, selfishness, unfriendliness, unsociability. ANTONYMS: philanthropy.

misapprehend *v.t.* (*to misunderstand*) misconceive, misconstrue, misinterpret, misread, mistake, misunderstand.

misapprehension *n.* (*misunderstanding*) delusion, error, fallacy, false impression, misconception, misconstruction, misinterpretation, misreading, mistake, misunderstanding, wrong idea.

misappropriate *v.t.* (*to apply to a wrong use or purpose* (*esp. funds to one's own use*)) defalcate, embezzle, expropriate, misapply, misspend, misuse, peculate, pervert, pocket, steal, swindle.

misbehave *v.i.* (*to behave badly or improperly*) (*coll.*) act up, carry on, muck about. ANTONYMS: behave.

misbehaviour *n.* (*bad or improper behaviour*) delinquency, disobedience, impropriety, incivility, indiscipline, insubordination, mischief, misconduct, misdeeds, misdemeanour, naughtiness, rudeness.

miscalculate *v.t.* (*to calculate wrongly*) blunder, err, go wrong, make a mistake, miscompute, miscount, misjudge, misread, misreckon, overestimate, overrate, slip up, underestimate, underrate, undervalue.

miscarriage *n.* **1** (*the spontaneous premature expulsion of a foetus before it can survive outside the womb*) abortion. **2** (*an act or instance of miscarrying*) mismanagement, perversion, thwarting, undoing. **3** (*failure*) botch, breakdown, collapse, defeat, error, failure, frustration, misadventure, mischance, misfire, mishap. ANTONYMS: success.

miscarry *v.i.* **1** (*to have a miscarriage*) abort, have a miscarriage. **2** (*to fail, to be unsuccessful*) come to grief, fail, fall through, founder, go astray, go awry, go wrong, misfire, perish. ANTONYMS: succeed.

miscellaneous *a.* **1** (*consisting of several kinds, mixed*) assorted, confused, diverse, diversified, heterogeneous, indiscriminate, jumbled, mingled, mixed, motley, several, sundry, varied. **2** (*various, many-sided*) manifold, many-sided, multifarious, multiform, various.

miscellany *n.* (*a mixture of various kinds, a medley*) anthology, assortment, collection, diversity, farrago, gallimaufry, hash, hotchpotch, jumble, medley, mélange, mess, mixed bag, mixture, odds and ends, pot-pourri, ragbag, variety.

mischance *n.* (*misfortune, bad luck*) accident, bad luck, calamity, disaster, ill luck, misadventure, misfortune, mishap.

mischief *n.* **1** (*irritating behaviour that is non-malicious, esp. practical jokes*) devilment, devilry, impishness, misbehaviour, misconduct, (*coll.*) monkey business, naughtiness, playfulness, rascality, roguery, roguishness. **2** (*harm, injury*) damage, detriment, disadvantage, disruption, evil, harm, hurt, ill, injury, nuisance, trouble. ANTONYMS: good. **3** (*a person who is mischievous*) devil, imp, monkey, nuisance, pest, prankster, rascal, rogue, scallywag, scamp, trickster, villain.

mischievous *a.* **1** ((*of a child*) *full of pranks, continually in mischief*) annoying, bad, devilish, elfish, exasperating, frolicsome, impish, naughty, playful, rascally, roguish, sportive, teasing, troublesome, vexatious, wayward. ANTONYMS: good, well-behaved. **2** (*causing or intending to cause harm*) baleful, damaging, deleterious, destructive, detrimental, evil, harmful, injurious, malevolent, malicious, malignant, pernicious, spiteful, vicious, wicked. ANTONYMS: beneficial.

misconceive *v.t.* (*to have a wrong idea of*) get the wrong idea, misapprehend, miscalculate, misconstrue, misinterpret, misjudge, misread, mistake, misunderstand.

misconception *n.* (*a wrong idea*) delusion, error, fallacy, misapprehension, miscalculation, misconstruction, misunderstanding, wrong idea.

misconduct *n.* **1** (*improper conduct, e.g. adultery*) delinquency, dereliction, impropriety, malpractice, misbehaviour, misdeed, misdemeanour, transgression, wrongdoing. **2** (*mismanagement*) mismanagement, negligence.

misconstrue *v.t.* **1** (*to put a wrong interpretation or construction upon*) misread, (*coll.*) take the wrong way. **2** (*to mistake the meaning of*) misapprehend, misconceive, misjudge, mistake, mistranslate, misunderstand.

miscreant *n.* **1** (*a vile wretch, a scoundrel*) blackguard, criminal, evildoer, good-for-nothing, knave, malefactor, mischief-maker, ne'er-do-well, rascal, reprobate, rogue, ruffian, scamp, scoundrel, sinner, vagabond, villain, wretch, wrongdoer. **2†** (*an unbeliever*) heretic, infidel, unbeliever.

~*a.* **1** (*depraved, villainous*) base, corrupt, criminal, depraved, evil, felonious, iniquitous, malevolent, mischievous, nefarious, rascally, reprehensible, reprobate, scoundrelly, unprincipled, vicious, vile, villainous, wicked, wretched. **2** (*unbelieving*) heretic, infidel, unbelieving.

misdeed *n.* (*a crime*) crime, fault, felony, misconduct, misdemeanour, misdoing, offence, sin, transgression, trespass, villainy, wrong.

misdemeanour *n.* (*misbehaviour, misconduct*) fault, infringement, misbehaviour, misconduct, misdeed, offence, peccadillo, transgression, trespass, violation.

miser *n.* (*a person who denies themselves the comforts of life for the sake of hoarding*) (*coll.*) cheapskate, cheese-parer, curmudgeon, hoarder, niggard, penny-pincher, Scrooge, skinflint, (*sl.*) tight-arse. ANTONYMS: spendthrift.

miserable *a.* **1** (*very wretched or unhappy*) broken-hearted, crestfallen, dejected, depressed, desolate, despondent, disconsolate, distressed, doleful, downcast, forlorn, gloomy, glum, heartbroken, melancholy, sad, sorrowful, unhappy, woeful, wretched. ANTONYMS: cheerful, happy. **2** (*causing misery, distressing*) depressing, dismal, distressing, disturbing, gloomy, sad, upsetting. **3** (*despicable, worthless*) abject, bad, base, contemptible, deplorable, despicable, detestable, disgraceful, inadequate, lamentable, pathetic, pitiful, shabby, sordid, sorry, squalid, vile, worthless, wretched. ANTONYMS: admirable. **4** (*very poor or mean*) destitute, down and out, impoverished, indigent, low, meagre, mean, needy, penniless, poor, poverty-stricken, short. ANTONYMS: rich.

miserly *a.* (*like a miser*) avaricious, beggarly, cheese-paring, close, covetous, grasping, mean, money-grubbing, niggardly, parsimonious, penny-pinching, penurious, selfish, stingy, tight, tight-fisted, ungenerous. ANTONYMS: generous, prodigal.

misery *n.* **1** (*great unhappiness or wretchedness of mind or body*) dejection, depression, desolation, despair, despondency, gloom, grief, melancholy, sadness, sorrow, unhappiness, woe, wretchedness. **2** (*affliction, poverty*) affliction, anguish, burden, curse, distress, hardship, load, need, poverty, privation, suffering, torment, trial, tribulation, want. ANTONYMS: comfort. **3** (*coll.*) (*an ill-tempered, gloomy person*) grouch, killjoy, moaner, (*esp. N Am., sl.*) party-pooper, pessimist, (*coll.*) sourpuss, spoilsport, (*coll.*) wet blanket. **4** (*miserliness, avarice*) avarice, greed, miserliness.

misfire *v.i.* (*to fail to achieve the intended effect*) abort, fail, fall through, (*coll.*) flop, (*coll.*) go phut, go wrong, miscarry.

misfit *n.* (*an awkward person*) eccentric, fish out of water, individual, maverick, nonconformist, oddball, square peg.

misfortune *n.* **1** (*bad luck, calamity*) bad luck, hard luck, ill fortune, ill luck, infelicity. ANTONYMS: fortune. **2** (*a mishap, a disaster*) accident, adversity, affliction, blow, calamity, disaster, failure, hardship, loss, misadventure, mischance, mishap, reverse, setback, tragedy, trial, tribulation, trouble.

misgiving *n.* (*a doubt, a suspicion*) anxiety, apprehension, concern, disquiet, distrust, doubt, foreboding, hesitation, mistrust, qualm, question, reservation, scruple, suspicion, trepidation, uncertainty, unease, worry. ANTONYMS: assurance.

misguided *a.* (*mistaken in thought, foolish*) deluded, erroneous, fallacious, foolish, ill-advised, imprudent, injudicious, misdirected, misinformed, misled, misplaced, unwarranted, unwise, wrong. ANTONYMS: judicious.

mishandle *v.t.* **1** (*to deal with* (*a matter etc.*) *ineffectively or incorrectly*) botch, (*sl.*) bugger up, bungle, (*coll.*) make a hash of, make a mess of, mangle, mess up, mismanage, muddle, muff, ruin, (*sl.*) screw up, wreck. **2** (*to handle roughly, to ill-treat*) abuse, harm, hurt, ill-treat, injure, maltreat, manhandle, maul, mistreat, molest.

mishap *n.* **1** (*an unfortunate accident, a mischance*) accident, adversity, calamity, contretemps, disaster, infelicity, misadventure, mischance. **2** (*bad luck*) bad luck, ill fortune, misfortune.

misinform *v.t.* (*to give erroneous information to*) (*sl.*) con, deceive, delude, dupe, fool, lead astray, misdirect, misguide, mislead.

misinterpret *v.t.* **1** (*to interpret wrongly*) distort, garble, get wrong, misapprehend, misconceive, misread, misrepresent, misunderstand. **2** (*to draw a wrong conclusion from*) get wrong, misapprehend, misconstrue, misjudge, misread, misrepresent, mistake, misunderstand.

misjudge *v.t.* (*to form an erroneous opinion of*) get the wrong idea about, miscalculate, misconstrue, misinterpret, misunderstand, overestimate, overrate, underestimate, underrate.

mislay *v.t.* (*to put in a wrong place or in a place that cannot be remembered*) lose, misplace, miss. ANTONYMS: find, locate.

mislead *v.t.* (*to deceive, to delude*) bamboozle, beguile, bluff, deceive, delude, dupe, fool, hoodwink, humbug, lead astray, misdirect, misguide, misinform, take in, throw off the track, trick.

mismanage *v.t., v.i.* (*to manage badly or wrongly*) botch, bungle, make a mess of, maladminister, mess up, misconduct, misdirect, misgovern, mishandle.

misplace *v.t.* (*to mislay*) lose, mislay, miss.

misprint *n.* (*a mistake in printing*) corrigendum, erratum, error, literal, mistake, (*coll.*) typo.

misrepresent *v.t.* (*to represent falsely or incorrectly*) belie, colour, disguise, distort, falsify, garble, mangle, misinterpret, misstate, pervert, (*N Am.*) put a spin on.

misrule *n.* **1** (*bad government*) maladministration, misgovernment, mismanagement. **2** (*disorder, confusion*) anarchy, chaos, confusion, disorder, lawlessness, riot, tumult, turmoil. ANTONYMS: order.

miss[1] *v.t.* **1** (*to fail to reach, hit or meet*) be absent from, fail, lose, miscarry, mistake. **2** (*to fall short of, to overlook*) disregard, fall short of, let slip, lose, neglect, overlook, pass over, skip, slip, trip. **3** (*to fail to understand*) misapprehend, miscomprehend, mistake, misunderstand. **4** (*to omit*) forgo, leave out, omit. **5** (*to escape, to dispense with*) avoid, dispense with, dodge, escape, evade. **6** (*to feel the lack or absence of*) hunger for, long for, need, pine for, want, wish, yearn for.
~*v.i.* **1** (*to fail to hit the mark*) go astray, go wide. **2** (*to go astray, to err*) blunder, err, go astray.
~*n.* **1** (*a failure to hit, reach, obtain etc.*) blunder, error, failure, fault, mistake, omission, oversight, slip. **2** (*loss, feeling of loss*) hunger, loss, want.

miss[2] *n.* (*a girl*) damsel, girl, lass, maid, maiden, schoolgirl, spinster, virgin, young lady.

misshapen *a.* (*abnormally or irregularly shaped*) awry, contorted, crippled, crooked, deformed, distorted, gnarled, grotesque, ill-made, ill-proportioned, malformed, monstrous, twisted, ugly, ungainly, unshapely, unsightly, warped. ANTONYMS: shapely.

missile *n.* (*a weapon or other object projected or propelled through the air*) arrow, brickbat, projectile, rocket, shot, weapon.

missing *a.* **1** (*absent, lost*) absent, astray, gone, left out, lost, mislaid, misplaced. ANTONYMS: available, found. **2** (*lacking*) lacking, needed, wanted.

mission *n.* **1** (*the commission or charge of a messenger, agent etc.*) charge, commission, duty, office. **2** (*a person's appointed or chosen vocation*) calling, métier, occupation, profession, trade, vocation, work. **3** (*a body of persons sent on a diplomatic errand, an embassy*) commission, delegation, deputation, embassy, legation, ministry. **4** (*a task, goal etc. assigned to a person, group etc.*) aim, assignment, business, errand, goal, job, objective, purpose, quest, task, undertaking.

missionary *n.* (*a person sent to teach people about a religion*) apostle, converter, evangelist, preacher, propagandist, proselytizer.

missive *n.* (*a message, a letter*) communication, dispatch, epistle, letter, line, memorandum, message, note, report.

misspend *v.t.* (*to spend wastefully or inadvisedly*) dissipate, idle away, misapply, misuse, squander, throw away, waste.

misstate *v.t.* (*to state wrongly*) distort, falsify, garble, misquote, misreport, misrepresent, pervert, twist.

mist *n.* **1** (*visible water vapour in the atmosphere at or near the surface of the earth*) cloud, fog, haze, smog. **2** (*a watery condensation dimming a surface*) condensation, dew. **3** (*a suspension of a liquid in a gas*) drizzle, spray, steam, vapour.
~*v.t.* (*to cover as with mist*) becloud, befog, blur, cloud, dim, film, fog, obscure, steam up.

mistake *v.t.* **1** (*to understand wrongly*) misapprehend, misconceive, misconstrue, misinterpret, misjudge, misread, misunderstand. **2** (*to take (one person or thing) for another*) confuse, mix up, take for.
~*v.i.* (*to be in error, to err in judgement*) be wrong, blunder, err, miscalculate, misjudge, put one's foot in it, slip up.
~*n.* **1** (*an error of judgement or opinion*) error, fault, faux pas, gaffe, inaccuracy, miscalculation, misjudgement, oversight, slip, solecism. **2** (*a misunderstanding*) misapprehension, misconception, misunderstanding. **3** (*a thing done incorrectly, a blunder*) (*sl.*) bloomer, blunder, (*coll.*) boob, (*sl.*) clanger, (*coll.*) howler.

mistaken *a.* (*wrong in judgement, opinion etc.*) amiss, erroneous, fallacious, false, faulty, imprecise, inaccurate, incorrect, inexact, misguided, misled, off target, unfounded, unsound, untrue, wide of the mark, wrong. ANTONYMS: correct, true.

mistreat *v.t.* (*to ill-treat*) abuse, batter, brutalize, damage, harm, ill-treat, ill-use, injure, knock about, maltreat, manhandle, maul, misuse, molest, wrong.

mistreatment *n.* (*ill treatment*) abuse, battery, brutalization, cruelty, damage, harm, ill treatment, ill-usage, injury, maltreatment, manhandling, mauling, misuse, molestation, unkindness, wrong.

mistress *n.* **1** (*a woman with whom a man has a long-term extramarital relationship*) (*sl.*) bit on the side, concubine, courtesan, (*sl., derog.*) fancy woman, (*derog.*) floozie, girlfriend, kept woman, lover, mate, partner, (*N Am., coll.*) significant other. **2** (*a female teacher*) governess, headmistress, instructress, schoolteacher, teacher. **3** (*a woman who has authority or control*) head, owner, proprietor. **4** (*a woman beloved and courted, a sweetheart*) beloved, inamorata, lady-love, paramour, sweetheart.

mistrust *v.t.* (*to regard with doubt or suspicion*) apprehend, beware, be wary of, disbelieve, distrust, doubt, fear, suspect. ANTONYMS: trust.
~*n.* (*distrust, suspicion*) apprehension, distrust, doubt, dubiety, fear, misgiving, qualm, reservation, scepticism, suspicion, uncertainty, wariness. ANTONYMS: confidence.

misty *a.* **1** (*characterized by or overspread with mist*) cloudy, foggy, hazy, mist-laden, mist-shrouded. **2** (*indistinct, obscure*) bleary, blurred, dark, dim, fuzzy, indistinct, murky, nebulous, obscure, opaque, shadowy, unclear, vague. ANTONYMS: clear, distinct.

misunderstand *v.t.* (*to mistake the meaning or sense of*) get wrong, misapprehend, miscalculate, misconceive, misconstrue, mishear, misinterpret, misjudge, misread, miss the point, mistake. ANTONYMS: understand.

misunderstanding *n.* **1** (*a failure of understanding*) error, false impression, misapprehension, miscalculation, misconception, misconstruction, misinterpretation, misjudgement, mistake, mix-up, wrong idea. **2** (*a slight disagreement or argument*) argument, breach, clash, conflict, controversy, difference, difficulty, disagreement, discord, dispute, dissension, falling-out, quarrel, rift, rupture, squabble, variance. ANTONYMS: agreement.

misuse[1] *v.t.* **1** (*to use or treat improperly*) abuse, corrupt, desecrate, dissipate, exploit, mistreat, pervert, profane, prostitute, squander, waste. ANTONYMS: respect. **2** (*to apply to a wrong purpose*) misapply, misemploy. **3** (*to ill-treat*) abuse, brutalize, exploit, harm, ill-treat, ill-use, injure, maltreat, manhandle, maul, mistreat, molest, wrong.

misuse[2] *n.* **1** (*improper use*) misapplication, misemployment, perversion, profanation, solecism, squandering, waste. **2** (*abuse*) abuse,

corruption, desecration, dissipation, exploitation, harm, ill treatment, ill-usage, injury, maltreatment, manhandling, mistreatment, rough handling.

mitigate *v.t.* **1** (*to make less rigorous or harsh*) allay, assuage, ease, relax. **2** (*to alleviate* (*pain, violence etc.*)) alleviate, appease, lighten, relieve. ANTONYMS: aggravate, intensify. **3** (*to diminish, to moderate*) abate, blunt, calm, check, diminish, dull, extenuate, lessen, moderate, modify, mollify, pacify, placate, reduce, remit, soften, soothe, subdue, temper, tone down.

mix *v.i.* **1** (*to become united*) blend, merge, unite. **2** (*to be sociable*) mingle, socialize. **3** (*to be associated or be regularly sociable* (*with*)) associate, consort, fraternize, hang around, hobnob, socialize.
~*n.* **1** (*mixed ingredients for a cake etc.*) constituents, ingredients, mixture. **2** (*a mixture, a combination*) alloy, amalgam, assortment, blend, combination, compound, fusion, medley, meld, mixture.

mixed *a.* **1** (*consisting of various kinds or constituents*) alloyed, amalgamated, blended, combined, composite, compound, fused, incorporated, joint, mingled, united. ANTONYMS: unmixed. **2** (*consisting of various different types of people*) cross-bred, hybrid, interbred, interdenominational, mongrel, multiracial. **3** (*not of consistent quality*) ambivalent, confused, diverse, equivocal, inconsistent, indifferent, motley, muddled, uncertain, varied.

mixed-up *a.* **1** (*confused, muddled*) at sea, bewildered, chaotic, confounded, confused, disordered, disorientated, entangled, garbled, involved, jumbled, maladjusted, messed up, mistaken, muddled, perplexed, puzzled, scrambled, tangled up. **2** (*in emotional turmoil*) distraught, distressed, disturbed, upset.

mixture *n.* **1** (*something which is being or has been mixed*) admixture, alloy, assortment, blend, brew, combination, conglomeration, fusion, hotchpotch, jumble, medley, mélange, mess, mingling, miscellany, mix. **2** (*a combination of different qualities and characteristics*) alloy, amalgam, amalgamation, association, blend, combination, composite, compound, cross, fusion, merger, synthesis.

moan *n.* **1** (*a low, prolonged sound expressing pain or sorrow*) cry, groan, lament, sigh, sob, wail. **2** (*a complaint*) (*sl.*) bitch, complaint, gripe, grouch, grumble, protest, whine.
~*v.i.* **1** (*to utter a moan or moans*) bawl, bemoan, bewail, cry, groan, keen, lament, sigh, sob, wail, weep, whimper, whine. **2** (*to complain,

grumble) bemoan, bewail, (*sl.*) bitch, bleat, carp, complain, deplore, grieve, gripe, grouch, grouse, grumble, mourn, sorrow, whine, (*coll.*) whinge. ANTONYMS: rejoice.

mob *n.* **1** (*a gang of criminals engaged in organized crime*) gang, syndicate. **2** (*a disorderly or riotous crowd*) crowd, crush, drove, horde, press, rabble, swarm, throng. **3** (*coll., derog.*) (*a group or class (of people of a specified kind)*) body, class, company, crew, group, lot, set, troop. **4** (*derog.*) (*the masses*) commonalty, (*coll.*) great unwashed, herd, hoi polloi, hosts, masses, multitude, pack, people, populace, proletariat, public, riff-raff, scum.
~*v.t.* **1** (*to attack in a mob*) attack, overrun, set upon. **2** (*to crowd roughly round and annoy*) beset, crowd around, jostle, surround, swarm around, throng.

mobile *a.* **1** (*movable, free to move*) free, movable. ANTONYMS: immobile. **2** (*easily moved*) manoeuvrable, motile, portable, transportable. **3** (*easily changing*) animated, changeable, ever-changing, expressive, flexible, plastic, variable. **4** (*able to be moved from place to place*) ambulant, ambulatory, itinerant, migrant, peripatetic, travelling, wandering.

mock *v.t.* **1** (*to deride, to laugh at*) chaff, deride, disparage, guy, insult, jeer, laugh at, make fun of, poke fun at, rag, ridicule, scoff, scorn, sneer, (*sl.*) take the mickey, (*taboo sl.*) take the piss, tantalize, taunt, tease, wind up. ANTONYMS: praise, respect. **2** (*to mimic, esp. in derision*) ape, burlesque, caricature, counterfeit, imitate, impersonate, lampoon, mimic, parody, satirize, send up, simulate, spoof, (*coll.*) take off, travesty. **3** (*to defy contemptuously*) defeat, defy, disappoint, flout, foil, frustrate, thwart. **4** (*to delude, to take in*) belie, cheat, deceive, delude, dupe, elude, fool, let down, mislead, take in.
~*a.* (*false, counterfeit*) artificial, bogus, counterfeit, dummy, ersatz, fake, false, feigned, forged, fraudulent, imitation, (*coll.*) phoney, pretended, (*coll.*) pseudo, sham, simulated, spurious, substitute, synthetic. ANTONYMS: authentic, genuine.
~*n.* **1** (*something which is derided or deserves derision*) butt, dupe, fool, jest, laughing stock, sport, travesty. **2** (*an imitation*) counterfeit, fake, forgery, fraud, imitation, (*coll.*) phoney, sham, substitute. **3** (*a derisive action, a sneer*) banter, derision, gibe, jeering, mockery, ridicule, scorn, sneer.

mockery *n.* **1** (*the act of mocking, ridicule*) abuse, contempt, contumely, derision, disdain, disparagement, disrespect, gibe, insult, jeering, mocking, ridicule, scoffing, scorn, taunt. ANTONYMS: respect. **2** (*a delusive*

imitation) burlesque, caricature, deception, farce, imitation, impersonation, lampoon, laughing stock, mimicry, parody, pretence, satire, semblance, (*coll.*) send-up, sham, spoof, (*coll.*) take-off, travesty.

mode *n.* **1** (*method, way of doing, existing etc.*) approach, condition, course, manner, method, methodology, plan, system, technique, vein, way, wise. **2** (*style*) form, quality, style. **3** (*common fashion, prevailing custom*) craze, custom, fad, fashion, look, practice, procedure, process, rage, trend, vogue.

model *n.* **1** (*a representation or pattern in miniature of something made on a larger scale*) copy, dummy, facsimile, image, imitation, likeness, maquette, miniature, mock-up, replica, representation, scale model. **2** (*a particular style or type, e.g. of a car*) brand, configuration, design, form, kind, mark, sort, stamp, style, type, variety, version. **3** (*a person employed to pose as subject to an artist*) poser, sitter, subject. **4** (*a standard, an example to be imitated*) archetype, epitome, example, exemplar, ideal, mould, norm, original, par, paradigm, pattern, prototype, standard, template.
~*a.* **1** (*serving as a model or example*) archetypal, exemplary, illustrative, standard, typical. **2** (*worthy of imitation, perfect*) ideal, paradigmatic, perfect. ANTONYMS: impaired, imperfect.
~*v.t.* **1** (*to display (clothes) by wearing them*) display, parade, show, sport, wear. **2** (*to mould or fashion in clay etc.*) base, carve, cast, fabricate, fashion, form, make, mould, produce, sculpt, shape, stamp. **3** (*to give a plan or shape to (a document, book etc.)*) design, plan.
~*v.i.* (*to act as a mannequin*) pose, sit.

moderate[1] *a.* **1** (*temperate, reasonable*) calm, cool, deliberate, equable, gentle, judicious, mild, modest, reasonable, sober, steady, temperate. **2** (*not extreme or excessive*) controlled, limited, restrained. ANTONYMS: extreme, unrestrained. **3** (*of medium quantity or quality*) average, fair, indifferent, mediocre, medium, middle-of-the-road, middling, modest, ordinary, passable, so so, unexceptional.

moderate[2] *v.t.* **1** (*to reduce to a calmer or less intense condition*) allay, appease, assuage, calm, pacify, reduce. ANTONYMS: intensify. **2** (*to restrain from excess*) curb, regulate, repress, restrain, subdue, tame. **3** (*to temper, to mitigate*) allay, alleviate, mitigate, temper.
~*v.i.* **1** (*to become less violent*) abate, ameliorate, calm, ease, lessen, relax, soften, temper. **2** (*to quieten or settle down*) diminish, quieten, settle down. **3** (*to preside as a moderator*)

arbitrate, chair, judge, mediate, preside, referee, take the chair, umpire.

moderation n. **1** (*the act of moderating or reducing to a less intense condition*) appeasement, mitigation, reduction. **2** (*the quality or state of being moderate*) calm, composure, coolness, equanimity, fairness, judiciousness, justice, mildness, reasonableness. ANTONYMS: immoderation. **3** (*temperance, self-restraint*) control, regulation, self-restraint, temperance.

modern a. **1** (*of or relating to the present or recent time*) contemporary, current, late, latest, present, recent. **2** (*not old-fashioned or obsolete*) à la mode, chic, contemporary, faddish, fashionable, fresh, ((*esp. N Am., (dated) sl.*)) hip, (*coll.*) hot, modish, new, newfangled, novel, present-day, stylish, trendy, up to date, up-to-the-minute, (*coll.*) with it. ANTONYMS: obsolete, old-fashioned.

modernize v.t., v.i. (*change (something) by bringing it up to date*) bring up to date, do over, make over, refashion, refurbish, rejuvenate, remodel, renew, renovate, revamp, update.

modest a. **1** (*humble, unassuming in regard to one's merits or importance*) diffident, humble, self-conscious, self-effacing, unassuming, unpresuming. ANTONYMS: proud. **2** (*not presumptuous, retiring*) bashful, blushing, coy, meek, quiet, reluctant, reserved, reticent, retiring, shy, timid, unostentatious, unpretentious. ANTONYMS: arrogant, forward. **3** (*restrained by a sense of propriety*) proper, restrained. **4** (*decorous, chaste*) chaste, decent, decorous, demure, discreet. **5** (*moderate, not extreme*) fair, limited, medium, middling, moderate, ordinary, simple, small, understated, unexceptional. ANTONYMS: excessive.

modesty n. **1** (*the quality of being modest*) bashfulness, coyness, diffidence, humility, meekness, reticence, self-consciousness, self-effacement, shyness, timidity, unpretentiousness. ANTONYMS: arrogance, immodesty. **2** (*a sense of propriety*) propriety, restraint. **3** (*chastity*) chastity, decency, demureness, discreetness.

modification n. (*alteration*) adjustment, alteration, change, limitation, modulation, mutation, qualification, refinement, reformation, restriction, revision, variation.

modify v.t. **1** (*to alter, to make different*) adapt, adjust, alter, amend, convert, recast, reconstruct, redo, refashion, reform, remake, remodel, remould, reorganize, reshape, revamp, revise, rework, transform, vary. **2** (*to reduce in degree or extent*) abate, decrease,

diminish, ease, lessen, limit, lower, moderate, modulate, qualify, reduce, relax, restrain, restrict, soften, temper, tone down.

modulate v.t. **1** (*to adjust, to regulate*) adjust, balance, change, moderate, modify, regulate, soften, vary. **2** (*to vary or inflect the sound or tone of*) attune, harmonize, inflect, tune.

mogul n. (*a powerful and influential entrepreneur*) baron, (*sl.*) big cheese, (*sl.*) big gun, (*coll.*) big noise, (*coll.*) big shot, (*N Am., sl.*) big wheel, (*coll.*) bigwig, entrepreneur, (*esp. N Am., coll.*) hotshot, magnate, mandarin, potentate, tycoon, VIP.

moist a. **1** (*moderately wet, damp*) clammy, damp, dank, dewy, dripping, foggy, humid, misty, muggy, soggy, steamy, wet. **2** (*rainy*) drizzly, (*dial.*) mizzly, rainy, showery.

moisture n. (*liquid throughout or on the surface of something, or in a vapour*) condensation, damp, dampness, dankness, dew, humidity, liquid, perspiration, sweat, vapour, water, wetness. ANTONYMS: dryness.

mole n. (*a pile of masonry, such as a breakwater or jetty by a port*) breakwater, dyke, embankment, groyne, jetty, pier, sea wall.

molest v.t. **1** (*to trouble, to harm*) annoy, badger, beset, bother, (*sl.*) bug, disturb, harass, harm, harry, hector, irritate, persecute, pester, plague, tease, torment, trouble, upset, vex, worry. **2** (*to attack, esp. for sexual purposes*) abuse, accost, assail, assault, attack, harm, hurt, ill-use, injure, interfere with, maltreat, manhandle, mistreat, (*coll.*) paw, rape.

mollify v.t. **1** (*to soften, to assuage*) abate, allay, alleviate, assuage, blunt, curb, cushion, ease, lessen, lull, mitigate, moderate, modify, reduce, relieve, soften, temper, tone down. ANTONYMS: aggravate, provoke. **2** (*to pacify, to appease*) appease, calm, compose, conciliate, pacify, placate, propitiate, quell, quiet, soothe, still, sweeten, tranquillize. ANTONYMS: disturb.

moment n. **1** (*a very brief portion of time*) (*coll.*) blink of an eye, flash, instant, (*coll.*) jiffy, minute, second, shake, split second, (*coll.*) tick, trice, twinkling, two shakes. **2** (*a particular point in time*) hour, instant, juncture, point, stage, time. **3** (*importance, consequence*) concern, consequence, gravity, import, importance, note, seriousness, significance, substance, value, weight, worth. ANTONYMS: insignificance.

momentary a. (*transient, ephemeral*) brief, ephemeral, evanescent, fleeting, flying, fugitive, hasty, passing, quick, short, short-lived, temporary, transient, transitory. ANTONYMS: lasting, lengthy.

momentous *a.* (*weighty, important*) consequential, critical, crucial, decisive, fraught, grave, historic, important, major, pivotal, portentous, serious, significant, vital, weighty. ANTONYMS: trivial, unimportant.

momentum *n.* (*impetus, power of overcoming resistance to motion*) drive, energy, force, impetus, impulse, inertia, power, propulsion, push, strength, thrust.

monarch *n.* **1** (*a sole ruler*) lord, master, potentate, ruler. **2** (*a hereditary sovereign, such as a king or queen*) crowned head, emperor, empress, king, prince, princess, queen, sovereign, tsar, tsarina. ANTONYMS: subject. **3** (*the chief of its class*) boss, chief, leader, (*coll.*) number one.

monarchy *n.* **1** (*government in which the supreme power is vested in a monarch*) absolutism, autocracy, despotism, kingship, monocracy, queenship, royalism, sovereignty, totalitarianism, tyranny. **2** (*a state under this system, a kingdom*) domain, dominion, empire, kingdom, principality, realm.

monastery *n.* (*a residence for a community, esp. of monks*) abbey, cloister, convent, friary, nunnery, priory.

monastic *a.* (*resembling the way of life of a monastic community*) ascetic, austere, celibate, cloistered, coenobitic, contemplative, eremitic, hermit-like, monkish, reclusive, secluded, sequestered, solitary, withdrawn. ANTONYMS: secular.

monetary *a.* (*of or relating to money or coinage*) budgetary, capital, cash, financial, fiscal, numismatic, pecuniary.

money *n.* **1** (*coin or other material used as medium of exchange*) (*sl.*) brass, (*sl.*) bread, cash, coin, (*sl.*) dosh, (*sl.*) dough, (*sl.*) lolly, (*coll.*) loot, (*derog. or facet.*) lucre, silver, small change, (*pl., sl.*) spondulicks, (*coll.*) the necessary, (*coll.*) the needful. **2** (*banknotes, bills*) banknotes, bills, folding money, paper money, (*pl., coll.*) readies. **3** (*wealth, property*) assets, capital, fortune, funds, means, property, resources, riches, wealth, wherewithal. **4** (*coins of a particular country or denomination*) currency, legal tender, medium of exchange.

moneyed *a.* (*rich*) affluent, flush, (*coll.*) loaded, prosperous, rich, wealthy, (*coll.*) well-heeled, well off, well-to-do. ANTONYMS: impoverished, poor.

mongrel *n.* (*anything, esp. a dog, of mixed breed*) cross, cur, half-breed, hybrid, mutt. ~*a.* (*of mixed breed, arising from the crossing of*

two varieties) bastard, cross-bred, hybrid, mixed.

monitor *n.* **1** (*a television screen used e.g. with a computer*) screen, VDU, visual display unit. **2** (*a person who warns or admonishes*) guardian, guide, invigilator, overseer, supervisor, watchdog. ~*v.t., v.i.* **1** (*to maintain regular surveillance on (a situation)*) check, examine, keep an eye on, observe, scan, spy on, study, supervise, survey, watch. **2** (*to listen to (radio broadcasts) in order to glean information*) audit, listen to, record.

monkey *n.* **1** (*a long-tailed mammal of various species*) ape, primate, simian. **2** (*coll.*) (*a rogue, a mischievous child*) devil, imp, mischief, (*coll.*) pickle, rascal, rogue, scamp. **3** (*an ape, a mimic*) ape, copier, impersonator, mimic. ~*v.i.* (*to meddle or interfere (with)*) fiddle, fool, interfere, meddle, mess, play, (*sl.*) screw, tamper, tinker, trifle. ~*v.t.* (*to mimic, to ape*) ape, copy, duplicate, imitate, impersonate, mimic.

monopolize *v.t.* (*to engross the whole of (attention, conversation etc.)*) absorb, appropriate, control, corner, dominate, engross, (*sl.*) hog, take over.

monotonous *a.* (*wearisome through sameness, tedious*) boring, colourless, droning, dull, everyday, flat, humdrum, plodding, repetitive, routine, (*coll.*) samey, soporific, tedious, tiresome, unchanging, unexciting, uniform, uninteresting, unvaried, wearisome. ANTONYMS: interesting, varied.

monotony *n.* (*lack of variety, sameness*) boredom, colourlessness, dreariness, dullness, flatness, repetitiousness, repetitiveness, routine, sameness, tedium, tiresomeness, uniformity, wearisomeness.

monster *n.* **1** (*something misshapen, a deformed creature*) abortion, deformity, freak, horror, miscreation, monstrosity, mutant, mutation. **2** (*an imaginary animal, usually compounded of incongruous parts*) centaur, gorgon, griffin, mermaid. **3** (*an abominably cruel or depraved person*) barbarian, beast, brute, demon, devil, fiend, ghoul, ogre, sadist, savage, villain. **4** (*a person, animal or thing of extraordinary size*) behemoth, colossus, giant, leviathan, mammoth, titan. ANTONYMS: midget. ~*a.* (*of extraordinary size, huge*) colossal, elephantine, enormous, gargantuan, gigantic, (*coll.*) ginormous, huge, (*sl.*) humongous, immense, jumbo, mammoth, massive, (*coll.*) mega, monstrous, stupendous, titanic, tremendous.

monstrous *a.* **1** (*unnatural in form*) abnormal,

deformed, freakish, grotesque, hideous, horrendous, miscreated, misshapen, nightmarish, obscene, terrible, unnatural. ANTONYMS: beautiful, natural. **2** (*enormous, huge*) colossal, elephantine, enormous, gargantuan, gigantic, (*coll.*) ginormous, huge, (*sl.*) humongous, immense, jumbo, mammoth, massive, (*coll.*) mega, monster, prodigious, stupendous, titanic, tremendous. ANTONYMS: insignificant, small. **3** (*shocking, outrageous*) appalling, atrocious, cruel, devilish, diabolical, disgraceful, evil, fiendish, foul, heinous, horrifying, loathsome, outrageous, scandalous, shocking, vicious, vile, villainous. ANTONYMS: good, kind. **4** (*absurd, incredible*) absurd, incredible, ludicrous, ridiculous, unbelievable.

monument *n.* **1** (*anything by which the memory of persons or things is preserved, esp. a building or permanent structure*) cairn, cenotaph, marker, memorial, obelisk, pillar, shrine. **2** (*anything that serves as a memorial of a person or of past times*) memento, memorial, reminder. **3** (*a document, a record*) commemoration, document, memorial, record, remembrance, testament, token, witness. **4** (*a tomb*) gravestone, headstone, mausoleum, tablet, tomb, tombstone. **5** (*a statue, an effigy*) effigy, statue.

monumental *a.* **1** (*of or serving as a monument*) commemorative, funerary, memorial. **2** (*stupendous, colossal*) awe-inspiring, awesome, classic, colossal, enormous, gigantic, great, immense, important, impressive, majestic, massive, outstanding, prodigious, significant, staggering, striking, stupendous, tremendous, vast. ANTONYMS: trivial. **3** (*lasting*) enduring, immortal, lasting, memorable, unforgettable. ANTONYMS: ephemeral.

mood *n.* **1** (*a state of mind, disposition*) disposition, frame of mind, humour, state of mind, temper. **2** (*the expression of mood in art, literature etc.*) atmosphere, feeling, spirit, tenor, vein.

moody *a.* **1** (*indulging in unpredictable moods*) capricious, changeable, erratic, faddish, fickle, fitful, flighty, impulsive, mercurial, temperamental, unpredictable, unstable, volatile. ANTONYMS: constant, stable. **2** (*peevish, sullen*) angry, broody, cantankerous, crabby, cross, fretful, gloomy, glum, huffish, irascible, irritable, melancholy, morose, offended, out of sorts, peevish, petulant, sulky, sullen, testy. ANTONYMS: content, happy.

moor[1] *v.t.* (*to secure (a ship, boat etc.) with cable and anchor*) fasten, fix, lash, make fast, secure, tie up. ANTONYMS: untie.

~*v.i.* (*to secure a ship in this way*) anchor, berth, dock.

moor[2] *n.* (*a tract of wild open land*) common, fell, heath, moorland, wasteland.

mop *n.* **1** (*a bundle of rags fastened to a long handle, and used for cleaning floors etc.*) sponge, squeegee, swab. **2** (*a thick mass, as of hair*) mane, shock, tangle, thatch.

~*v.t.* (*to wipe or soak up moisture from with a mop etc.*) clean, soak up, sponge, swab, wash, wipe out.

moral *a.* **1** (*of or relating to conduct in terms of the distinction between right and wrong*) ethical. ANTONYMS: amoral. **2** (*conforming to or regulated by what is right, esp. in sexual relations*) blameless, chaste, ethical, fair, good, high-minded, honest, honourable, incorruptible, innocent, just, noble, principled, proper, pure, right, upright, upstanding, virtuous. ANTONYMS: immoral, unethical. **3** (*practical, virtual*) practical, purist, virtual.

~*n.* (*the moral lesson taught by a story, incident etc.*) adage, aphorism, lesson, maxim, meaning, message, point, proverb, saw, saying, significance.

morale *n.* **1** (*mental or moral condition*) attitude, disposition, humour, mood, spirit, temper, will. **2** (*courage and endurance in supporting threats to one's mental well-being*) courage, dedication, endurance, heart, mettle, spirit.

morality *n.* **1** (*the principles or practice of moral duties, ethics*) behaviour, conduct, ethics, habits, ideals, integrity, manners, morals, mores, principles, scruples, standards. **2** (*moral conduct, esp. in sexual relations*) chastity, decency, ethicality, ethics, goodness, honesty, integrity, justice, principle, rectitude, righteousness, rightness, uprightness, virtue.

morass *n.* **1** (*anything that is confused or complicated, esp. when it impedes progress*) chaos, confusion, entanglement, jam, mess, mix-up, muddle, quicksand, tangle. **2** (*a swamp, a bog*) bog, fen, marsh, quagmire, slough, swamp.

morbid *a.* **1** (*unhealthily preoccupied with unpleasant matters, esp. with death*) funereal, ghastly, ghoulish, gloomy, grim, grisly, grotesque, gruesome, hideous, horrid, macabre, monstrous, morose, pessimistic, sombre, unhealthy, unwholesome. ANTONYMS: cheerful, wholesome. **2** (*Med.*) (*unhealthy, diseased*) ailing, diseased, infected, malignant, sick, sickly, unhealthy, unsound. ANTONYMS: healthy.

mordant *a.* (*caustic, pungent*) acerbic, acid,

acrimonious, astringent, biting, bitter, caustic, corrosive, cutting, edged, incisive, pungent, sarcastic, scathing, sharp, stinging, trenchant, venomous, vitriolic, waspish. ANTONYMS: soothing.

more *a.* **1** (*greater in quantity, extent, importance etc.*) expanded, extended, greater. ANTONYMS: less. **2** (*additional, extra*) added, additional, extra, fresh, further, new, other, spare, supplementary.
~adv. (*further, besides*) again, besides, better, further, longer.

moreover *adv.* (*besides, in addition*) additionally, also, as well, besides, further, furthermore, in addition, likewise, to boot, too, what is more.

morning *n.* (*the first part of the day, esp. from dawn to midday*) dawn, daybreak, forenoon, morn, sunrise.

moron *n.* (*coll.*) (*a very stupid or foolish person*) ass, (*sl.*) dickhead, (*coll.*) dimwit, (*sl.*) divvy, dolt, (*sl.*) dope, dunce, fool, halfwit, idiot, ignoramus, imbecile, (*sl.*) jerk, (*sl.*) nerd, (*coll.*) nitwit, numskull, (*sl.*) plonker, (*sl.*) prat, simpleton, (*sl.*) wally. ANTONYMS: genius.

morose *a.* (*sullen, gloomy*) brooding, churlish, crabby, crotchety, depressed, dour, gloomy, glum, grouchy, ill-humoured, ill-tempered, melancholy, moody, peevish, saturnine, sour, sulky, sullen, surly, taciturn. ANTONYMS: genial, jolly.

morsel *n.* **1** (*a bite, a small piece of food*) bite, crumb, drop, mouthful, nibble, snack, taste. **2** (*a small quantity, a piece*) bit, fraction, fragment, grain, part, piece, pinch, scrap, segment, shred, (*coll.*) smidgen, (*N Am., coll.*) tad, titbit.

mortal *a.* **1** (*liable to die; human*) corporeal, earthly, ephemeral, human, physical, temporal, transient, worldly. ANTONYMS: immortal. **2** (*causing death, fatal*) deadly, destructive, fatal, killing, lethal, murderous, terminal. **3** (*inveterate, implacable*) implacable, inveterate, irreconcilable, remorseless, sworn, unrelenting. **4** (*extreme, excessive*) awful, dire, excessive, extreme, grave, great, intense, severe, terrible.
~n. **1** (*a being subject to death; a human being*) human, human being, individual, man, person, woman. **2** (*a person*) body, individual, person.

mortality *n.* **1** (*the quality of being mortal*) ephemerality, impermanence, temporality, transience. ANTONYMS: immortality. **2** (*loss of life, esp. on a large scale*) bloodshed, carnage, death, destruction, fatality, killing, loss of life.

mortification *n.* (*embarrassment, humiliation*) abasement, abashment, annoyance, chagrin, chastening, confusion, discomfiture, discomposure, displeasure, dissatisfaction, embarrassment, humiliation, loss of face, shame, vexation. ANTONYMS: delight.

mortify *v.t.* **1** (*to humiliate, to wound*) abase, abash, affront, annoy, chagrin, chasten, confound, deflate, discomfit, discompose, displease, embarrass, humble, humiliate, put down, rebuff, shame, vex, wound. **2** (*to subdue* (*the passions etc.*) *by abstinence or self-discipline*) control, crush, deny, discipline, subdue, subjugate. ANTONYMS: indulge.
~v.i. (*to decay, to go gangrenous*) corrupt, decay, decompose, die, fester, putrefy, rot.

mortuary *n.* (*a building for the temporary reception of the dead*) chapel of rest, funeral parlour, morgue.

mostly *adv.* **1** (*chiefly, mainly*) chiefly, generally, in the main, largely, mainly, on the whole, particularly, primarily, principally. **2** (*on most occasions, usually*) as a rule, customarily, for the most part, ordinarily, usually.

mother *n.* **1** (*a female parent*) dam, (*coll.*) ma, (*coll.*) mam, mama, (*sl.*) mater, (*coll.*) mum, (*coll.*) mummy, (*coll.*) old lady, parent. ANTONYMS: father. **2** (*the source or origin of anything*) fount, genesis, origin, source.
~v.t. **1** (*to act as mother towards*) baby, care for, cherish, coddle, fuss over, indulge, nourish, nurse, nurture, pamper, protect, raise, rear, spoil, tend. **2** (*to give birth to*) bear, bring forth, drop, give birth to. **3** (*to give rise to*) bring about, give rise to, produce.
~a. (*natural, inborn*) connate, inborn, innate, native, natural, vernacular.

motherly *a.* (*like a mother; nurturing, loving*) affectionate, caring, comforting, devoted, fond, gentle, kind, loving, maternal, matriarchal, nurturing, parental, protective, sheltering, supportive, tender, understanding, warm.

motif *n.* **1** (*the dominant feature or idea in a literary, musical or other artistic composition*) concept, design, form, idea, shape, subject, topic. **2** (*a theme in music*) device, leitmotiv, refrain, theme.

motion *n.* **1** (*the act, process or state of moving*) action, activity, change, drift, flow, locomotion, mobility, movement, shift. ANTONYMS: rest. **2** (*passage of a body from place to place*) passage, passing, progress, transit, travel. **3** (*a gesture*) gesticulation, gesture, sign, signal, wave. **4** (*a proposal, esp. in a deliberative assembly*) offering, proposal, proposition,

recommendation, submission, suggestion. **5** (*impulse, instigation*) impulse, instigation, motivation.
~*v.t.* (*to propose*) offer, propose, recommend, submit, suggest.
~*v.i.* (*to make significant gestures*) beckon, gesticulate, gesture, nod, signal, wave.

motionless *a.* (*not moving, stationary*) fixed, frozen, halted, immobile, immovable, inanimate, inert, lifeless, paralysed, standing, static, stationary, still, stock-still, transfixed, unmoving. ANTONYMS: animated, moving.

motivate *v.t.* **1** (*to provide an incentive or motive to*) galvanize, goad, incite, inspire, inspirit, persuade, prod, prompt, provoke, stimulate. ANTONYMS: deter. **2** (*to instigate*) actuate, cause, instigate, set off. **3** (*to rouse to interest or effort*) arouse, drive, impel, induce, move, rouse, spur, stir, trigger.

motive *n.* (*that which incites to action, or determines the will*) cause, design, drive, ground, impulse, incentive, incitement, inducement, inspiration, intention, mainspring, motivation, object, occasion, purpose, rationale, reason, spur, stimulus, thinking.
~*a.* (*causing or initiating motion*) activating, driving, impelling, motivating, moving, operative, prompting, propulsive.

motley *a.* **1** (*of varied character, heterogeneous*) assorted, disparate, dissimilar, diverse, diversified, heterogeneous, mingled, miscellaneous, mixed, varied. ANTONYMS: homogeneous, uniform. **2** (*variegated in colour*) chequered, multicoloured, particoloured, polychromatic, rainbow, variegated.

mottled *a.* (*having spots of different colours, blotched*) blotchy, brindled, chequered, dappled, flecked, freckled, marbled, motley, piebald, pied, speckled, spotted, stippled, streaked, tabby, variegated.

motto *n.* **1** (*a short, pithy sentence or phrase expressing a sentiment*) adage, aphorism, byword, maxim, proverb, saw, saying, slogan. **2** (*a principle or maxim adopted as a rule of conduct*) maxim, precept, principle, rule, watchword. **3** (*a joke or maxim contained in a paper cracker*) joke, rhyme, verse. **4** (*a word or sentence used with a crest or coat of arms*) caption, inscription, legend.

mould[1] *n.* **1** (*a hollow shape into which molten metal etc. is poured in a fluid state to cool into a permanent shape*) cast, die, form, matrix, pattern, shape, stamp. **2** (*physical form, shape*) brand, build, configuration, construction, cut, design, fashion, form, format, frame, kind, line, make, pattern, shape, stamp, structure,

style. **3** (*character, nature*) calibre, character, ilk, kidney, kind, nature, quality, sort, stamp, type.
~*v.t.* **1** (*to form into a particular shape*) carve, cast, form, model, sculpt, shape. **2** (*to make, to produce*) construct, create, fashion, forge, form, make, produce, stamp, work.

mould[2] *n.* (*a minute fungoid growth forming a furry coating on matter left in the damp*) blight, fungus, mildew, mouldiness, mustiness.

moulder *v.i.* **1** (*to turn to dust by natural decay*) decay, decompose, rot. **2** (*to crumble*) crumble, disintegrate. **3** (*to waste away gradually*) dwindle, perish, waste away.

mouldy *a.* **1** (*covered with mould*) blighted, decaying, decomposed, fusty, mildewed, mould-covered, musty, putrescent, putrid, rancid, rank, rotten, spoiled, stale. ANTONYMS: fresh. **2** (*coll.*) (*bad, nasty*) bad, feeble, nasty, poor, weak. ANTONYMS: good. **3** (*coll.*) (*mean, shabby*) mean, rotten, shabby.

mound *n.* **1** (*an artificial elevation of earth, stones etc.*) bank, bulwark, drift, heap, pile, rampart, stack. **2** (*a hillock, a knoll*) dune, embankment, hillock, hummock, knoll, rise. **3** (*a barrow, a tumulus*) barrow, earthwork, tumulus.

mount *v.t.* **1** (*to ascend, to climb*) ascend, clamber up, climb, escalade, go up, scale. ANTONYMS: descend. **2** (*to ascend upon, to get up on to*) bestraddle, bestride, board, climb onto, get astride, get up on, jump on. ANTONYMS: dismount. **3** (*to prepare for use*) launch, prepare, ready. **4** (*to put (a picture etc.) on a mount*) display, frame. **5** (*to affix (a stamp, photograph etc.) with mounts*) affix, install, place, position, put in place, set up. **6** (*to stage (a play etc.); to present (an exhibition etc.) for public view*) exhibit, get up, present, produce, put on, stage.
~*v.i.* **1** (*to rise, to ascend*) ascend, go up, move upwards, rise. **2** (*to rise in amount*) accumulate, build, escalate, expand, grow, increase, intensify, multiply, pile up, rise, swell, wax. ANTONYMS: decrease, dwindle. **3** (*to soar*) balloon, rocket, soar, tower.
~*n.* **1** (*something on which anything is mounted*) backing, base, fixture, frame, mounting, setting. **2** (*the parts by which various objects are strengthened or ornamented*) base, stand, support. **3** (*a horse with the appurtenances necessary for riding*) charger, horse, ride, steed.

mountain *n.* **1** (*a natural elevation of the earth's surface rising high above the surrounding land*) alp, elevation, fell, height, hill, mount, peak, summit. **2** (*a large heap or pile*) abundance, accumulation, heap, mass, mound, pile, stack, ton.

mountainous *a.* **1** (*full of mountains*) alpine, craggy, high, rocky, soaring, steep, towering, upland. **2** (*exceedingly large*) enormous, formidable, gigantic, great, huge, hulking, immense, large, mammoth, mighty, monumental, overwhelming, prodigious, staggering. ANTONYMS: puny, tiny.

mourn *v.i.* (*to express or feel sorrow or grief*) bemoan, bewail, cry, deplore, keen, lament, wail, weep.
~*v.t.* (*to grieve or sorrow for*) grieve, regret, rue, sorrow. ANTONYMS: rejoice.

mournful *a.* (*very sad*) broken-hearted, depressed, disconsolate, distressed, doleful, downcast, funereal, gloomy, grief-stricken, heartbroken, heavy-hearted, lugubrious, melancholy, piteous, plaintive, sad, sombre, sorrowful, unhappy, woeful. ANTONYMS: happy, joyful.

mourning *n.* **1** (*grief, sorrow*) bereavement, grief, grieving, keening, lamentation, sorrow, wailing, weeping, woe. **2** (*the customary dress, usu. black, worn by mourners*) black, weeds.

mouth *n.* **1** (*the opening through which food is taken into the body*) chops, gob, jaws, (*sl.*) kisser, lips, maw, (*sl.*) trap. **2** (*the opening of a cave or the like*) access, aperture, cavity, crevice, door, entrance, gateway, inlet, opening, orifice. **3** (*impudent talk, cheek*) (*coll.*) backchat, cheek, (*sl.*) chutzpah, disrespect, impertinence, impudence, insolence, (*sl.*) lip, presumptuousness, rudeness, (*N Am., coll.*) sass, (*coll.*) sauce.

mouthful *n.* (*a small quantity of food etc.*) bit, bite, drop, forkful, gob, hunk, morsel, sample, sip, snack, spoonful, sup, swallow, taste.

movable *a.* **1** (*capable of being moved*) detachable, mobile, portable, transferable, transportable, unfixed. ANTONYMS: fixed. **2†** (*changeable, inconstant*) changeable, fluctuating, inconstant, unsettled, variable.

move *v.t.* **1** (*to cause to change position or posture*) budge, change position, reposition. **2** (*to carry, draw or push from one place to another*) carry, draw, push, shift, shove, switch, transfer, transport, transpose. **3** (*to put in motion, to stir*) actuate, drive, instigate, prod, propel, put in motion, set going, start, stir. **4** (*to incite, to rouse* (*to action*)) impel, impress, incite, incline, inspire, motivate, persuade, prompt, rouse, spur, stimulate. ANTONYMS: deter, discourage. **5** (*to excite, to provoke* (*laughter etc.*)) cause, excite, give rise to, induce, provoke. **6** (*to prevail upon*) influence, persuade, prevail upon, sway, win over. **7** (*to affect with feelings, usu. of tenderness, to touch*) affect, agitate, disquiet, disturb, ruffle, stir, touch. **8** (*to propose, to submit for discussion*) advocate, propose, put forward, recommend, submit, suggest, urge.
~*v.i.* **1** (*to go from one place to another*) depart, go, leave, pass, proceed, travel. **2** (*to advance, to progress*) advance, proceed, progress, shift, stir, walk. **3** (*to change one's place of residence*) decamp, flit, leave, migrate, quit, relocate, remove, (*coll.*) up sticks. ANTONYMS: stay. **4** (*to make an application, appeal etc.*) appeal, apply, call, petition, request. **5** (*to take action, to proceed*) proceed, take action, take steps.
~*n.* **1** (*the act of moving*) motion, movement. **2** (*the right to move* (*in chess etc.*)) go, time, turn. **3** (*action, line of conduct*) act, action, deed, line of conduct, measure, proceeding. **4** (*a step, a device to obtain an object*) artifice, caper, device, manoeuvre, ploy, ruse, shift, step, stratagem, stroke, trick, turn. **5** (*a change of abode*) change of address, migration, relocation, removal.

movement *n.* **1** (*the act of changing position or posture*) act, action, advance, change, development, displacement, exercise, gesture, migration, motion, move, progress, repositioning, shift, transfer. **2** (*the working mechanism of a clock, machine etc.*) action, (*coll.*) innards, machinery, mechanism, moving parts, workings, works. **3** (*a connected series of efforts and actions, directed to a special end*) campaign, crusade, drive, fight, struggle. **4** (*a tendency in art, politics etc.*) current, drift, flow, tendency, trend. **5** (*the people involved in a political etc. movement*) camp, clique, faction, front, group, grouping, organization, party, wing. **6** (*the mode or rate of a piece of music*) beat, cadence, measure, metre, pace, rhythm, swing, tempo.

movie *n.* (*a cinema film*) feature, film, (*coll.*) flick, motion picture, picture.

moving *a.* **1** (*in motion*) active, going, in motion, operative, running, working. **2** (*impelling, persuading*) compelling, dynamic, exciting, impelling, impressive, inspiring, motivating, persuasive, propelling, stimulating. **3** (*pathetic, affecting*) affecting, arousing, emotional, emotive, heart-rending, pathetic, poignant, stirring, touching. ANTONYMS: unemotional, unmoving.

mow *v.t.* (*to cut down* (*grass, corn etc.*) *with a mower, scythe etc.*) clip, crop, cut, prune, scythe, shear, trim. **to mow down 1** (*to kill in great numbers*) annihilate, decimate, massacre, slaughter, wipe out. **2** (*to destroy indiscriminately*) (*sl.*) blow away, butcher, cut down, cut to pieces, eradicate, exterminate, kill, liquidate.

much *a.* **1** (*great in quantity or amount*) considerable, copious, great, lot, sizeable, substantial. ANTONYMS: little. **2** (*long in duration*) lengthy, long, prolonged. **3†** (*numerous, many*) abundant, ample, many, numerous, plenteous, plentiful. ANTONYMS: inadequate, scant.

~*adv.* **1** (*in or to a great degree or extent*) considerably, exceedingly, frequently, greatly, indeed, often, regularly. ANTONYMS: barely, hardly. **2** (*almost, nearly*) about, almost, nearly, practically.

~*n.* (*a great quantity, a great deal*) a great deal, (*coll.*) heaps, (*coll.*) loads, (*coll.*) lots, plenty. ANTONYMS: little.

muck *n.* **1** (*dung or manure*) (*taboo*) crap, droppings, dung, excrement, faeces, manure, ordure, sewage, (*taboo sl.*) shit. **2** (*refuse, filth*) (*sl.*) crap, (*sl.*) crud, detritus, dirt, filth, (*coll.*) grot, (*coll.*) gunge, (*coll.*) gunk, mire, mud, ooze, refuse, scum, slime, sludge, waste. **3** (*coll.*) (*untidiness*) disarray, disorder, mess, untidiness.

~*v.t.* **1** (*to make dirty or untidy*) dirty, soil, stain. **2** (*to bungle, to make a mess of*) blunder, bodge, bungle, mess, mess up. **3** (*to manure*) manure, muckspread.

mucky *a.* (*dirty*) begrimed, bespattered, dirty, filthy, grimy, grubby, messy, muddy, soiled, sticky. ANTONYMS: clean, spotless.

mud *n.* **1** (*moist, soft earth, or earthy matter*) clay, dirt, earth, soil. **2** (*mire*) mire, ooze, silt, slime, sludge.

muddle *v.t.* **1** (*to confuse, to bewilder*) befuddle, bewilder, confound, confuse, disorient, perplex, stupefy. **2** (*to mix* (*up*)*, to jumble* (*together*) *confusedly*) disarrange, disorder, disorganize, jumble, mess up, mix up, scramble, tangle. **3** (*to make a mess of, to squander*) bungle, mess up, spoil, squander, waste.

~*n.* **1** (*a mess*) chaos, clutter, disarray, disorder, disorganization, (*sl.*) dog's dinner, hotchpotch, jumble, mess, mix-up, (*sl.*) pig's breakfast. ANTONYMS: order. **2** (*a state of confusion or bewilderment*) bewilderment, confusion, disorientation, perplexity, stupefaction.

muddy *a.* **1** (*covered with mud*) befouled, bespattered, boggy, dirty, grimy, grubby, marshy, miry, mucky, mud-caked, oozy, slimy, soiled, swampy. ANTONYMS: clean. **2** (*turbid, cloudy*) blurred, cloudy, dingy, dull, murky, opaque, turbid. ANTONYMS: clear. **3** (*confused, obscure*) addled, confused, dim, fuzzy, hazy, indistinct, muddled, obscure, unclear, vague, woolly. ANTONYMS: clear.

~*v.t.* **1** (*to make muddy or foul*) befog, befoul, begrime, besmirch, bespatter, dirty, smear, smirch, soil. **2** (*to confuse*) cloud, confuse, muddle.

muffle *v.t.* **1** (*to wrap or cover* (*up*) *closely and warmly*) cloak, conceal, cover, disguise, enfold, envelop, hood, mask, protect, shroud, swaddle, swathe, wrap. ANTONYMS: expose, reveal. **2** (*to wrap up the head of so as to silence*) gag, hush, mute, muzzle, quieten, silence, soften, stifle, suppress. **3** (*to dull, to deaden*) damp, deaden, dull.

muffled *a.* ((*of sound*) *not heard clearly*) dull, faint, hushed, indistinct, muted, soft, stifled, strangled, subdued, suppressed. ANTONYMS: clear, loud.

mug[1] *n.* **1** (*a drinking vessel, used without a saucer*) beaker, cup, flagon, jug, pot, tankard. **2** (*the contents of this*) cupful, jugful, mugful. **3** (*a dupe, a gullible person*) dupe, fool, gull, (*sl.*) soft touch, (*coll.*) sucker. **4** (*the face or mouth*) face, (*sl.*) kisser, mouth.

mug[2] *v.t.* (*to rob* (*someone*) *violently, esp. in the street*) assail, assault, attack, beat up, (*sl.*) do over, (*sl.*) duff up, hold up, rob, set upon, (*sl.*) steam.

muggy *a.* (*damp and close*) clammy, close, damp, dank, humid, moist, oppressive, soggy, steamy, sticky, stifling, stuffy, sultry. ANTONYMS: fresh.

mull *v.t.* (*to ponder, consider* (*usu. followed by over*)) chew (over), cogitate, consider, contemplate, deliberate, evaluate, examine, meditate, muse (on), ponder, reflect (on), review, ruminate (on), study, think (over), turn over, weigh (up).

multifarious *a.* (*having great multiplicity or diversity*) different, diverse, diversified, legion, manifold, many, miscellaneous, motley, multiform, multiple, multitudinous, numerous, sundry, varied, variegated.

multiply *v.i.* (*to increase in number or extent*) accumulate, augment, breed, build up, expand, extend, grow, increase, intensify, proliferate, propagate, reproduce, spread. ANTONYMS: decrease, reduce.

multitude *n.* **1** (*a great number*) army, collection, concourse, flock, host, legion, lot, mass, myriad, sea, swarm. ANTONYMS: few. **2** (*a very large crowd or throng of people*) assemblage, assembly, congregation, crowd, horde, mob, throng.

mumble *v.i.* (*to speak indistinctly, to mutter*) murmur, mutter, speak unclearly.

~*n.* (*an indistinct utterance*) murmur, mutter.

munch *v.t.* (*to chew audibly*) champ, chew, chomp, crunch, masticate, scrunch.

mundane *a.* **1** (*everyday, banal*) banal, commonplace, everyday, humdrum, ordinary, prosaic, routine, workaday. **2** (*belonging to this* *world, earthly*) earthly, fleshly, material, mortal, physical, secular, temporal, terrestrial, worldly. ANTONYMS: ethereal, heavenly, spiritual.

municipal *a.* (*of or relating to local government*) borough, city, civic, community, council, government, local, metropolitan, parish, public, town, urban, village.

municipality *n.* **1** (*a town, city or district enjoying local self-government*) borough, burgh, city, district, metropolis, suburb, town, township, urban area. **2** (*the local government of such an area*) council, local government.

munificent *a.* (*generous, bountiful*) beneficent, benevolent, big-hearted, bounteous, bountiful, charitable, free-handed, generous, lavish, liberal, magnanimous, open-handed, philanthropic, princely, rich, unstinting. ANTONYMS: mean, stingy.

murder *n.* **1** (*Law*) (*a premeditated killing of another person*) assassination, bloodshed, butchery, carnage, destruction, homicide, killing, manslaughter, massacre, slaughter, slaying. **2** (*coll.*) (*an extremely unpleasant or dangerous experience*) agony, danger, difficulty, hell, misery, ordeal, trouble, unpleasantness.
~*v.t.* **1** (*coll.*) (*to kill* (*a human being*) *with malice aforethought*) assassinate, (*sl.*) blow away, (*coll.*) bump off, butcher, dispatch, (*sl.*) do in, (*sl.*) eliminate, eradicate, exterminate, (*esp. N Am., sl.*) hit, kill, liquidate, massacre, (*coll.*) polish off, (*N Am., sl.*) rub out, slaughter, slay, (*sl.*) take out, (*sl.*) waste. **2** (*to spoil, by blundering or clumsiness*) mar, mutilate, ruin, spoil. **3** (*to defeat severely*) (*sl.*) cream, defeat, drub, (*coll.*) hammer, (*coll.*) lick, mangle, ruin, slaughter, thrash, (*coll.*) wipe the floor with.

murderer *n.* (*a person who murders another*) assassin, butcher, executioner, (*sl.*) hitman, killer, slaughterer, slayer, terrorist.

murderous *a.* **1** ((*apparently*) *intent on murder*) barbarous, bloodthirsty, bloody, brutal, cruel, deadly, destructive, ferocious, homicidal, lethal, sanguinary, savage, slaughterous. **2** (*extremely unpleasant or difficult*) arduous, dangerous, demanding, difficult, exhausting, perilous, rigorous, sapping, unpleasant. ANTONYMS: easy.

murky *a.* **1** (*dark, gloomy*) cheerless, dark, dim, dismal, dreary, dull, dusky, funereal, gloomy, sombre. ANTONYMS: bright, cheerful. **2** (*unclear, hazy*) cloudy, foggy, grey, hazy, misty, nebulous, obscure, overcast, unclear. ANTONYMS: clear. **3** (*turbid, muddy*) cloudy, muddy, turbid. **4** (*dubiously respectable*) dubious, shady, suspicious, unrespectable.

murmur *n.* **1** (*a low, continuous sound*) babble, buzzing, drone, hum, purr, rumble, susurration, susurrus, undercurrent. **2** (*a half-suppressed protest or complaint, a grumble*) (*sl.*) beef, complaint, gripe, grouse, grumble, moan, mutter, protest. **3** (*a subdued speech*) mumble, mutter, undertone, whisper.
~*v.i.* **1** (*to make a low, continued noise, like that of running water*) babble, buzz, drone, hum, purr, rumble. **2** (*to mutter in discontent*) cavil, complain, gripe, grouse, grumble, moan, mutter. **3** (*to find fault*) carp, criticize, find fault.
~*v.t.* (*to utter in a low voice*) mumble, mutter, whisper.

muscular *a.* (*having well-developed muscles, brawny*) athletic, beefy, brawny, broad-shouldered, burly, (*esp. N Am., coll.*) husky, lusty, muscly, powerful, robust, rugged, sinewy, stalwart, strapping, strong, sturdy, thickset, vigorous, well-built, well-developed. ANTONYMS: puny, wiry.

muse *v.i.* **1** (*to ponder, to meditate* (*upon*)) brood (over), chew (over), cogitate (on), deliberate (on), meditate (on), mull (over), ponder (on), ruminate (on), speculate (on), think (over), weigh (up). **2** (*to study or reflect* (*upon*) *in silence*) consider, contemplate, reflect, study. **3** (*to dream, to engage in reverie*) daydream, dream.

mushroom *v.i.* **1** (*to grow or increase quickly*) boom, burgeon, flourish, grow, increase, luxuriate, multiply, proliferate, prosper, shoot up, spread, spring up, sprout, thrive. ANTONYMS: contract, decline. **2** ((*of bullets*) *to expand and flatten out*) expand, flatten out, spread out.

musical *a.* (*harmonious, melodious*) dulcet, euphonious, harmonious, lilting, lyrical, mellifluous, melodic, melodious, tuneful. ANTONYMS: discordant, unmusical.

musician *n.* (*a person skilled in music, esp. in playing an instrument*) artiste, composer, instrumentalist, minstrel, performer, player.

muster *v.t.* **1** (*to summon* (*up*) (*strength, courage etc.*)) call together, call up, call upon, summon. **2** (*to bring together*) bring together, enrol, gather, group, marshal, mobilize, round up. **3** (*to collect or assemble for review, roll-call etc.*) assemble, collect, congregate, convene, gather, group, levy, meet, rally. ANTONYMS: disperse.
~*n.* **1** (*the assembling of troops for parade or review*) levy, parade, review. **2** (*a register of forces mustered*) register, roll-call. **3** (*a collection, a gathering*) assemblage, assembly, collection, concourse, congregation, convention, convocation, gathering, meeting, rally, round-up.

musty *a.* **1** (*mouldy*) mildewed, mouldy. ANTONYMS: fresh. **2** (*sour, stale*) airless, damp, dank, decayed, fusty, ill-smelling, putrid, rancid, rank, rotten, smelly, sour, spoilt, stale. **3** (*vapid, antiquated*) ancient, antediluvian, antiquated, clichéd, hackneyed, hoary, obsolete, old, old-fashioned, (*coll.*) old hat, spiritless, stuffy, vapid. ANTONYMS: new, original.

mutation *n.* (*the act or process of changing*) alteration, change, deviation, evolution, metamorphosis, modification, transfiguration, transformation, translation, variation.

mute *a.* **1** (*uttering no sound, speechless*) mum, quiet, silent, speechless, taciturn, tight-lipped, uncommunicative. ANTONYMS: talkative. **2** (*not having the power of speech, dumb*) aphasic, dumb, voiceless. **3** (*not spoken*) implied, tacit, unexpressed, unsaid, unspoken, wordless. **4** (*not sounded*) unpronounced, unsounded.
~*v.t.* **1** (*to deaden or muffle the sound of*) dampen, deaden, hush, lower, muffle, soften, stifle. **2** (*to make more subdued*) moderate, restrain, subdue, tone down.

mutilate *v.t.* **1** (*to maim, to mangle*) cripple, disable, lame, maim, mangle. **2** (*to disfigure*) damage, deface, disfigure, hack, injure, lacerate, mar. ANTONYMS: mend, repair. **3** (*to cut off a limb or an essential part of*) amputate, butcher, dismember, lop off. **4** (*to damage* (*literary and other work*) *by excision*) adulterate, bowdlerize, butcher, censor, cut, expurgate, hack.

mutinous *a.* (*ready or inclined to mutiny; rebellious*) defiant, disobedient, insubordinate, insurgent, obstinate, rebellious, recalcitrant, refractory, revolutionary, riotous, seditious, subversive, turbulent, ungovernable, unruly. ANTONYMS: dutiful, obedient.

mutiny *n.* ((*an instance of*) *open resistance to or a revolt against constituted authority*) defiance, disobedience, insubordination, insurrection, rebellion, resistance, revolt, revolution, riot, rising, sedition, uprising. ANTONYMS: obedience.
~*v.i.* (*to rise or rebel against authority*) disobey, rebel, resist, revolt, rise up, subvert. ANTONYMS: obey.

mutter *v.i.* **1** (*to speak, in a low voice or with compressed lips*) grunt, mumble, murmur. **2** (*to grumble, to murmur* (*at or against*)) complain, grouch, grouse, grumble, murmur.

mutual *a.* **1** (*reciprocally given and received*) complementary, correlative, interactive, interchangeable, reciprocal, requited, returned, two-sided. **2** (*shared by or common to two or more persons*) common, communal, joint, shared.

myriad *a.* (*innumerable, countless*) countless, immeasurable, incalculable, innumerable, many, multitudinous, numerous, untold. ANTONYMS: few.
~*n.* (*a very great number*) army, flood, horde, host, mass, millions, mountain, multitude, scores, sea, swarm, thousands.

mysterious *a.* **1** (*incomprehensible, not easily understood*) baffling, bewildering, cryptic, curious, enigmatic, incomprehensible, inexplicable, inscrutable, insoluble, mystifying, obscure, perplexing, puzzling, recondite, secret, strange, uncanny, unfathomable, weird. ANTONYMS: clear, manifest. **2** (*mystic, occult*) arcane, metaphysical, mystic, occult, paranormal, preternatural, supernatural.

mystery *n.* **1** (*a secret or obscure matter*) conundrum, enigma, problem, puzzle, question, riddle, secret, (*coll.*) teaser. **2** (*secrecy, obscurity*) inscrutability, obscurity, secrecy.

mystical *a.* (*occult, esoteric*) abstruse, allegorical, arcane, cabalistic, cryptic, enigmatic, esoteric, hidden, inscrutable, metaphysical, mysterious, occult, otherworldly, paranormal, preternatural, supernatural, symbolic, transcendental.

mystify *v.t.* (*to bewilder, to puzzle*) baffle, bamboozle, beat, befog, bewilder, confound, confuse, flummox, hoax, humbug, nonplus, perplex, puzzle, stump. ANTONYMS: enlighten.

myth *n.* **1** (*a fictitious legend or tradition*) epic, fable, legend, saga, superstition, tradition. **2** (*the body of such legends or traditions*) folklore, lore. **3** (*a parable, an allegorical story*) allegory, epic, fairy tale, parable, story, tale. **4** (*a fictitious event, person etc.*) fancy, fantasy, fiction, figment, illusion, imagination. **5** (*a thing widely believed in but not true*) fabrication, falsehood, fib, lie, untruth, (*sl.*) whopper. ANTONYMS: fact.

mythical *a.* **1** (*of or relating to myths*) allegorical, folkloric, mythic, mythological. **2** (*legendary*) fabled, fabulous, fairy-tale, legendary, traditional. ANTONYMS: historical. **3** (*imaginary, untrue*) fabricated, false, fanciful, fantastic, fictitious, imaginary, invented, made-up, unreal, untrue. ANTONYMS: real, true.

mythology *n.* (*a system of myths in which are embodied the beliefs of a people concerning their origin, deities etc.*) folklore, folk tales, legend, lore, myths, tradition.

N

nadir n. (*the lowest point or stage* (*of decline, degradation etc.*)) all-time low, bottom, depths, lowest level, lowest point, minimum, rock bottom, (*sl.*) the pits, zero. ANTONYMS: high point, peak, top, zenith.

nag v.t. **1** (*to find fault with or scold continually*) (*sl.*) be on (someone's) back, berate, carp at, chivvy, criticize, find fault with, (*coll.*) go on at, henpeck, (*coll.*) keep on at, pick on, scold, upbraid. **2** (*to be continually pestering with complaints or fault-finding*) annoy, badger, harass, (*coll.*) hassle, pester, plague, torment, worry.

nagging a. **1** (*continually pestering with complaints or fault-finding*) carping, chivvying, critical, fault-finding, scolding. **2** (*causing constant slight pain or discomfort*) aching, chronic, continuous, distressing, painful, persistent. ANTONYMS: acute, severe.

nail n. (*a small, pointed spike, usu. of metal, with a head*) brad, pin, rivet, tack.
~v.t. **1** (*to fasten or secure with nails*) attach, fasten, fix, hammer, pin, secure, tack. **2** (*to seize, to catch*) apprehend, arrest, capture, catch, (*sl.*) collar, grab, (*sl.*) nab, seize. **3** (*to engage* (*attention*)) get hold of, get the attention of, (*coll.*) pin (someone) down.

naive a. **1** (*artless, ingenuous*) artless, childlike, confiding, frank, guileless, ingenuous, innocent, jejune, natural, open, simple, trusting, unaffected, unpretentious, unsophisticated, unworldly. ANTONYMS: artful, sophisticated, urbane, worldly. **2** (*gullible, credulous*) callow, credulous, green, gullible, immature, inexperienced, jejune, overtrustful, raw, unsuspecting, unsuspicious, (*coll.*) wet behind the ears. ANTONYMS: disingenuous, experienced, incredulous, mature, suspicious.

naivety n. **1** (*unaffected simplicity, artlessness*) artlessness, frankness, guilelessness, ingenuousness, innocence, jejuneness, lack of sophistication, naturalness, openness, simpleness, simplicity, unworldliness. ANTONYMS: artfulness, sophistication, urbanity, worldliness. **2** (*gullibility, inexperience*) callowness, credulity, credulousness, greenness, gullibility, immaturity, inexperience, jejuneness, lack of suspicion, rawness. ANTONYMS: experience, incredulity, maturity, suspicion.

naked a. **1** (*without clothing, nude*) bare, (*esp. N Am., sl.*) buck naked, disrobed, exposed, (*coll.*) in one's birthday suit, (*coll.*) in the altogether, (*coll.*) in the buff, in the nude, (*coll.*) in the raw, nude, (*sl.*) starkers, stark naked, stripped, unclothed, uncovered, undressed, (*coll.*) without a stitch on. ANTONYMS: clothed, dressed, fully clothed. **2** (*not sheathed*) exposed, uncovered, unguarded, unprotected, unsheathed. ANTONYMS: covered. **3** (*exposed, defenceless*) defenceless, exposed, helpless, insecure, unarmed, unguarded, unprotected, unsheltered, unshielded, vulnerable, weak. ANTONYMS: invulnerable, powerful, protected, secure. **4** (*plain, undisguised*) apparent, bald, bare, blatant, evident, flagrant, glaring, manifest, open, overt, patent, plain, simple, stark, unadorned, undisguised, unexaggerated, unmistakable, unqualified, unvarnished. ANTONYMS: concealed, disguised, exaggerated, qualified.

nakedness n. **1** (*nudity*) bareness, nudity, state of undress, undress. **2** (*bareness, plainness*) baldness, bareness, blatancy, flagrancy, openness, overtness, plainness, simplicity, starkness. ANTONYMS: adornment, disguise, ornamentation. **3** (*exposure, defencelessness*) defencelessness, exposure, helplessness, insecurity, lack of protection, vulnerability, weakness. ANTONYMS: invulnerability, powerfulness, protection, security.

namby-pamby a. **1** (*weakly and insipidly sentimental*) insipid, maudlin, mawkish, oversentimental, sentimental. ANTONYMS: down-to-earth, realistic, sensible. **2** (*lacking strength or vigour*) anaemic, colourless, effeminate, effete, feeble, insipid, prissy, unmanly, vapid, weak, (*coll.*) weedy, (*coll.*) wet, (*coll.*) wimpish, wishy-washy. ANTONYMS: manly, strong, vigorous, vivid.

name n. **1** (*a word by which a person, animal, place or thing is known*) appellation, denomination, designation, epithet, (*sl.*) handle, label, (*sl.*) moniker, sobriquet, style, tag, title. **2** (*a famous person*) big name, (*sl.*) big noise, (*sl.*) big shot, (*coll.*) celeb, celebrity, dignitary, luminary, star, VIP. **3** (*reputation, honourable character, fame, glory*) distinction, eminence, esteem, fame, glory, honour, importance, note, prestige, prominence, renown, reputation, repute. ANTONYMS: insignificance, obscurity.

~v.t. **1** (*to give a name to, to call*) baptize, call, christen, denominate, dub, entitle, give a name to, label, style, term. **2** (*to nominate, to appoint*) appoint, choose, designate, nominate, pick, select. **3** (*to mention, to cite*) cite, give, identify, mention, specify. **in the name of** (*with the authority of*) as a representative of, in place of, on behalf of, representing, with the authority of.

nameless *a.* **1** (*anonymous*) anonymous, unlabelled, unnamed, untagged, untitled. **2** (*inexpressible, indefinable*) indefinable, inexpressible, silent, unspoken. **3** (*unfit to be named, abominable*) abominable, horrible, indescribable, ineffable, inexpressible, unmentionable, unspeakable, unutterable.

namely *adv.* (*that is to say*) specifically, that is to say, to wit, viz.

nap[1] *v.i.* (*to sleep lightly or briefly, to doze*) catnap, doze, get one's head down, (*sl.*) get some shut-eye, (*sl.*) get some zizz, (*sl.*) have a kip, (*coll.*) have a lie-down, (*coll.*) have a snooze, rest, (*coll.*) snatch forty winks, take a nap.
~n. (*a short sleep, a doze, esp. in the daytime*) catnap, doze, (*coll.*) forty winks, (*sl.*) kip, (*coll.*) lie-down, rest, (*sl.*) shut-eye, siesta, sleep, (*coll.*) snooze, (*sl.*) zizz.

nap[2] *n.* (*the smooth and even surface produced on cloth by cutting and smoothing the fibre or pile*) down, fibre, grain, pile, shag, surface, weave.

narcissism *n.* (*a state of self-love*) conceit, egotism, self-admiration, self-conceit, self-love, vanity. ANTONYMS: humility, modesty, self-loathing.

narcissistic *a.* (*full of self-love*) conceited, egotistic, in love with oneself, self-admiring, vain. ANTONYMS: humble, low in self-esteem, modest.

narcotic *a.* (*allaying pain and causing sleep or dullness*) anaesthetic, dulling, hypnotic, numbing, opiate, painkilling, sedative, sleep-inducing, somnolent, soporific, stupefacient, stupefying.
~n. (*a substance that allays pain by inducing sleep or torpor*) anaesthetic, drug, opiate, painkiller, sedative, sleeping pill, soporific.

narrate *v.t.* (*to tell, to relate*) chronicle, describe, detail, give an account of, give a report of, portray, recite, recount, relate, report, set forth, tell, unfold.

narrative *n.* (*a recital of a series of events, a story*) account, chronicle, description, portrayal, recital, report, statement, story, tale.
~a. (*in the form of narration*) storytelling.

narrator *n.* **1** (*the person who narrates events or tells the story*) author, chronicler, describer, recounter, relater, reporter, writer. **2** (*a person who tells stories, a raconteur*) anecdotist, raconteur, storyteller, tale-teller.

narrow *a.* **1** (*of little breadth or extent from side to side*) attenuated, slender, slim, tapering, thin. ANTONYMS: broad, wide. **2** (*restricted, of limited scope*) close, confined, constricted, cramped, limited, restricted, tight. ANTONYMS: capacious, roomy, spacious. **3** (*illiberal in views or sentiments; bigoted*) biased, bigoted, discriminatory, dogmatic, illiberal, insular, intolerant, narrow-minded, parochial, partial, partisan, prejudiced, provincial, prudish, reactionary. ANTONYMS: broad-minded, liberal, tolerant, unbiased. **4** (*precise, accurate*) close, exact, literal, precise. ANTONYMS: imprecise, loose.
~v.i. (*to become narrow or narrower*) attenuate, become narrow/ narrower, become thin/ thinner, get narrow/ narrower, get thin/ thinner, taper. ANTONYMS: broaden, get broad/ broader, get wide/ wider, widen.
~v.t. (*to contract in range or sentiments*) constrict, contract, diminish, limit, reduce. ANTONYMS: expand, extend, increase.
~n. (*a strait*) channel, passage, sound, strait.

narrowly *adv.* (*by only a small amount*) barely, by a hair's breadth, by a narrow margin, by a whisker, just, just and no more, only just, scarcely. ANTONYMS: by a wide margin, easily.

narrow-minded *a.* (*illiberal, bigoted*) biased, bigoted, discriminatory, dogmatic, illiberal, insular, intolerant, narrow, parochial, partial, partisan, prejudiced, provincial, prudish, reactionary. ANTONYMS: broad-minded, liberal, tolerant, unbiased.

nascent *a.* (*coming into being; beginning to develop*) beginning, budding, developing, embryonic, evolving, growing, immature, incipient, young. ANTONYMS: developed, fully developed, mature.

nasty *a.* **1** (*awkward, trying*) alarming, awkward, critical, dangerous, difficult, serious, trying, uncomfortable. ANTONYMS: comfortable, safe. **2** (*spiteful, vicious*) bad-tempered, disagreeable, hateful, horrible, loathsome, malicious, mean, objectionable, obnoxious, odious, offensive, spiteful, unpleasant, vicious, vile. ANTONYMS: agreeable, kindly, likeable, pleasant. **3** (*foul, filthy to a repulsive degree*) dirty, filthy, foul, (*sl.*) grotty, impure, polluted, repugnant, revolting, squalid, tainted, (*coll.*)

yucky. ANTONYMS: clean, pure. **4** (*indecent, obscene*) bawdy, (*sl.*) blue, dirty, filthy, foul, gross, impure, indecent, lascivious, lewd, licentious, obscene, pornographic, ribald, risqué, smutty, vile, vulgar. ANTONYMS: decent, pure. **5** (*repellent to taste, smell etc., nauseous*) disgusting, evil-smelling, fetid, foul-smelling, malodorous, mephitic, nauseating, nauseous, rank, repugnant, repulsive, revolting, sickening, smelly, stinking, unappetizing, unpalatable, vile. ANTONYMS: appetizing, delicious, sweet-smelling. **6** ((*of weather*) *unpleasantly wet*) disagreeable, foul, miserable, rainy, unpleasant, wet. ANTONYMS: fine, pleasant, sunny.

nation *n.* (*a people under the same government and inhabiting the same country*) community, people, population.

national *a.* **1** (*peculiar to a nation*) domestic, indigenous, internal. ANTONYMS: international. **2** (*public, general, as distinct from local*) countrywide, general, nationwide, public, state, widespread. ANTONYMS: local. ~*n.* (*a member or subject of a particular nation*) citizen, inhabitant, native, resident, subject.

nationalism *n.* (*extreme devotion to one's nation*) chauvinism, jingoism, love of one's country, patriotism, xenophobia.

nationalistic *a.* (*extremely devoted to one's nation*) chauvinistic, jingoistic, patriotic, xenophobic.

nationality *n.* (*a national group, esp. one of several, forming a political state*) ethnic group, nation, race.

nationwide *a., adv.* (*covering the whole nation*) coast-to-coast, countrywide, general, national, state, widespread. ANTONYMS: local.

native *n.* **1** (*a person born in a specified place*) citizen, inhabitant, national, resident. **2** (*offensive*) (*a member of a non-white indigenous people of a country*) aborigine, autochthon. ~*a.* **1** (*relating to a place or country by birth, indigenous*) aboriginal, autochthonous, indigenous, original. ANTONYMS: exotic, foreign. **2** (*belonging to a person, animal or thing, by nature; natural*) built-in, congenital, inborn, inbred, ingrained, inherent, innate, instinctive, in the blood, intrinsic, intuitive, natural, natural-born. ANTONYMS: acquired, extrinsic. **3** (*of or relating to the natives of a place or region*) domestic, indigenous, local, vernacular. ANTONYMS: foreign, international.

natter *v.i.* (*to chatter idly; to exchange gossip*) (*coll.*) blather, (*coll.*) blether, chat, chatter, gabble, gossip, jabber, (*sl.*) jaw, prattle, (*coll.*) rabbit on, (*coll.*) witter.

~*n.* (*a chat, gossip*) (*coll.*) blather, (*coll.*) blether, chat, (*coll.*) chinwag, conversation, gossip, (*sl.*) jaw, talk, tête-à-tête.

natty *a.* (*neat, tidy*) chic, dapper, elegant, fashionable, neat, smart, (*sl.*) snazzy, spruce, stylish, tidy, (*coll.*) trendy, trim, well-dressed, well-turned-out. ANTONYMS: dowdy, untidy.

natural *a.* **1** (*not artificial; (of food) with nothing added*) additive-free, organic, pure, unbleached, unpolished, unprocessed, unrefined, whole. ANTONYMS: processed, synthetic. **2** (*inborn, instinctive*) built-in, congenital, inborn, inbred, ingrained, inherent, innate, instinctive, in the blood, intrinsic, intuitive, native, natural-born. ANTONYMS: acquired, extrinsic. **3** (*in conformity with the ordinary course of nature, normal*) common, everyday, normal, ordinary, regular, routine, run-of-the-mill, typical, usual. ANTONYMS: abnormal, exceptional, unnatural. **4** (*unaffected, not forced or exaggerated*) artless, candid, frank, genuine, ingenuous, open, real, relaxed, simple, sincere, spontaneous, unaffected, unpretentious, unstudied. ANTONYMS: affected, artificial, (*coll.*) phoney, pretentious, unnatural.

naturalist *n.* (*a person who is versed in natural history*) biologist, botanist, ecologist, zoologist.

naturalistic *a.* (*realistic, not conventional or ideal*) factual, factualistic, lifelike, realistic, real-life, representational, true-to-life, (*coll.*) warts and all. ANTONYMS: fantasy, idealistic.

naturalize *v.t.* **1** (*to adopt (a foreign expression or custom)*) absorb, accept, adopt, assimilate, take in. **2** (*to acclimatize*) acclimatize, domesticate. **3** (*to confer the rights and privileges of a natural-born subject on*) confer citizenship on, enfranchise, grant citizenship to.

naturally *adv.* **1** (*spontaneously*) artlessly, candidly, frankly, ingenuously, openly, simply, sincerely, spontaneously, unaffectedly, unpretentiously. ANTONYMS: affectedly, pretentiously, unnaturally. **2** (*as might be expected, of course*) as a matter of course, as was expected, as you would expect, certainly, of course, predictably. ANTONYMS: unexpectedly.

nature *n.* **1** (*the essential qualities of anything*) attributes, character, characteristic, complexion, constitution, essence, features, identity, make-up, personality, quality, stamp, traits. **2** (*natural character or disposition*) disposition, humour, mood, temper, temperament. **3** (*kind, sort*) category, class, description, kind, sort, species, style, type, variety. **4** (*the whole sum of forces and laws constituting the physical universe*) cosmos, creation, earth, environment, mother nature, natural forces, universe, world.

naught *n.* (*nothing*) nil, nothing, nought, zero, (*sl.*) zilch.

naughty *a.* **1** (*mischievous; badly behaved*) bad, badly-behaved, delinquent, disobedient, errant, evil, impish, misbehaved, mischievous, perverse, refractory, roguish, ungovernable, unmanageable, unruly, wayward, wicked, wrongdoing. ANTONYMS: good, virtuous, well-behaved. **2** (*mildly indecent*) bawdy, (*sl.*) blue, dirty, improper, lewd, obscene, off-colour, ribald, risqué, smutty, vulgar. ANTONYMS: decent, proper.

nausea *n.* **1** (*a feeling of sickness, with a propensity to vomit*) biliousness, gagging, queasiness, retching, sickness, (*sl.*) throwing up, vomiting. **2** (*loathing*) abhorrence, aversion, detestation, disgust, distaste, hatred, loathing, odium, repugnance, revulsion.

nauseate *v.t.* **1** (*to cause to feel nausea*) make one's gorge rise, make sick, sicken, turn one's stomach. **2** (*to fill with loathing*) disgust, repel, repulse, revolt.

nauseating *a.* **1** (*causing nausea*) nauseous, sickening, (*coll.*) sick-making. **2** (*very unpleasant, disgusting*) disgusting, repellent, repugnant, repulsive, revolting.

nauseous *a.* **1** (*feeling sick*) (*coll.*) green about the gills, nauseated, off-colour, queasy, sick, (*N Am.*) sick to one's stomach, unwell. **2** (*causing nausea*) disgusting, nauseating, repellent, repulsive, revolting.

nautical *a.* (*relating to ships or sailors; naval*) marine, maritime, nautical, naval, oceanic, seafaring, seagoing.

navigable *a.* (*deep and wide enough for a ship etc. to travel through*) clear, negotiable, passable, unobstructed.

navigate *v.t.* **1** (*to pass over or across, in a ship etc.*) cross, cruise, sail, voyage. **2** (*to manage the course, to conduct* (*a ship, aircraft etc.*)) conduct, direct, guide, manoeuvre, pilot, sail, steer.

navigation *n.* (*the art or science of navigating*) pilotage, sailing, seamanship, steering.

navigator *n.* (*a person who navigates*) guide, helmsman, pilot, steerer, steersman.

navvy *n.* (*a labourer in any kind of excavating work*) labourer, manual worker, workman.

navy *n.* (*the warships of a nation*) armada, fleet, flotilla, ships, warships.

near *adv.* (*at or to a short distance; not remote in place, time or degree*) at close quarters, at close range, at hand, close by, in the neighbourhood, near at hand, nearby, not far away, not far off, within a stone's throw, within close range, (*coll.*) within spitting distance. ANTONYMS: far away, far off.

~*prep.* (*close to in place, time etc.*) adjacent to, alongside, close to, in the neighbourhood of, next to, not far from, within close range of, within spitting distance of. ANTONYMS: far away from, far from.

~*a.* **1** (*close at hand, not distant in place or degree*) accessible, adjacent, adjoining, alongside, bordering, close, close by, contiguous, handy, nearby, neighbouring, nigh, within a hair's breadth of, (*coll.*) within spitting distance of. ANTONYMS: distant, far-off, remote. **2** (*close in time, imminent*) approaching, close, close at hand, coming, in the offing, looming, near at hand. ANTONYMS: far away, far off. **3** (*closely related*) closely related, connected, intimate, related.

~*v.t.* (*to approach, to draw near to*) approach, come/ get close to, come/ get near to, come/ go towards, draw near to. ANTONYMS: keep one's distance from.

nearby[1] *a.* (*situated close at hand*) adjacent, adjoining, close, contiguous, handy, near, neighbouring. ANTONYMS: far-off.

nearby[2] *adv.* (*close at hand*) close by, in the neighbourhood, near at hand, within a stone's throw, within close range. ANTONYMS: far away, far off.

nearly *adv.* (*almost*) about, all but, approximately, as good as, close to, just about, next to, not quite, practically, (*coll.*) pretty well, roughly, virtually.

nearness *n.* **1** (*the state of being near in place*) accessibility, closeness, contiguity, handiness, propinquity, proximity. ANTONYMS: distance, remoteness. **2** (*the state of being near in time*) closeness, immediacy, imminence.

near-sighted *a.* (*short-sighted*) myopic, short-sighted.

near thing *n.* (*a situation in which danger or trouble is only just avoided*) (*coll.*) close shave, close thing, narrow escape, near miss.

neat *a.* **1** (*tidy, trim*) dapper, in apple-pie order, in good order, (*coll.*) natty, neat and tidy, neat as a new pin, orderly, shipshape, shipshape and Bristol fashion, spick and span, spruce, tidy, trim. ANTONYMS: messy, untidy. **2** (*elegantly and concisely phrased*) apt, elegant, felicitous, pithy, well-expressed, well-turned, witty. ANTONYMS: inapt, inelegant. **3** (*adroit, dexterous, clever*) adept, adroit, apt, clever, deft, dexterous, efficient, effortless, expert, nimble, practised, skilful, stylish. ANTONYMS: awkward, clumsy.

neatness *n.* **1** (*tidiness*) good order, (*coll.*) nattiness, order, orderliness, spruceness, tidiness, trimness. ANTONYMS: messiness, untidiness. **2** (*elegance or aptness*) aptness, elegance, felicity, pithiness, wit, wittiness. ANTONYMS: inaptness, inelegance. **3** (*adroitness, dexterity*) adeptness, adroitness, aptness, cleverness, deftness, dexterity, efficiency, effortlessness, expertness, nimbleness, precision, skilfulness, skill, style, stylishness. ANTONYMS: awkwardness, clumsiness.

nebulous *a.* (*vague, indistinct*) amorphous, hazy, imprecise, indefinite, indeterminate, indistinct, obscure, uncertain, unclear, unformed, vague. ANTONYMS: certain, clearcut, definite.

necessarily *adv.* **1** (*automatically*) automatically, like it or not, naturally, of course, of necessity, perforce, willy-nilly. **2** (*of necessity; inevitably*) certainly, inescapably, inevitably, inexorably, unavoidably, undoubtedly.

necessary *a.* **1** (*requisite, requiring to be done*) compulsory, de rigueur, essential, imperative, indispensable, mandatory, needed, needful, obligatory, required, requisite, vital. ANTONYMS: dispensable, expendable, non-essential, unnecessary, unneeded. **2** (*such as cannot be avoided, inevitable*) certain, fated, inescapable, inevitable, inexorable, unavoidable. ANTONYMS: avoidable.

necessitate *v.t.* (*pl.*) (*to make necessary or unavoidable*) call for, compel, demand, entail, force, involve, leave one no choice but to, make necessary, oblige, require.

necessity *n.* **1** (*pl.*) (*something which is necessary, an essential requisite*) basic requirement, desideratum, essential, fundamental, prerequisite, requirement, requisite, sine qua non. ANTONYMS: extra, inessential, non-essential. **2** (*the quality of being necessary; inevitableness*) certainty, inescapability, inevitableness, inexorability, unavoidableness. ANTONYMS: uncertainty. **3** (*absolute need, indispensability*) demand, exigency, indispensability, need, needfulness, requirement. **4** (*want, poverty*) deprivation, destitution, distress, indigence, need, penury, poverty, privation, want. ANTONYMS: affluence, wealth. **5** (*pl.*) (*basic things that are necessary*) bare essentials, basic requirements, essentials, exigencies, needs, requirements, requisites. ANTONYMS: inessentials.

necromancy *n.* (*enchantment, magic*) black art, black magic, demonology, enchantment, magic, sorcery, spell-casting, thaumaturgy, voodooism, witchcraft, witchery, wizardry.

necropolis *n.* (*a cemetery, esp. one on a large scale*) burial ground, cemetery, churchyard, graveyard.

need *v.t.* **1** (*to be in want of, to require*) be in want of, be without, call for, demand, have need of, lack, miss, necessitate, require, want. **2** (*to require, to be under obligation* (*to do something*)) be compelled (to), be forced (to), be obliged (to), be under an obligation (to), have (to).
~*n.* **1** (*a state of urgently requiring something; lack of something*) inadequacy, insufficiency, lack, paucity, requirement, shortage, want, wish. ANTONYMS: abundance, superfluity. **2** (*something which is wanted, a requirement*) call, demand, essential, requirement, requisite. ANTONYMS: inessential, non-essential. **3** (*indigence, destitution*) deprivation, destitution, distress, indigence, penury, poverty, want. ANTONYMS: affluence, wealth. **4** (*a difficult or perilous situation; an emergency*) crisis, distress, emergency, trouble. ANTONYMS: comfort, ease, peace.

needful *a.* (*necessary*) essential, indispensable, necessary, needed, required, requisite, stipulated, vital. ANTONYMS: inessential, unnecessary.

needless *a.* (*unnecessary, not required*) dispensable, excessive, expendable, gratuitous, inessential, non-essential, pointless, redundant, superfluous, uncalled-for, unnecessary, unwanted, useless. ANTONYMS: necessary, needed.

needy *a.* (*in need*) deprived, destitute, disadvantaged, distressed, impecunious, impoverished, indigent, in straitened circumstances, necessitous, penniless, poor, poverty-stricken. ANTONYMS: affluent, privileged.

ne'er-do-well *n.* (*a lazy, useless person*) good-for-nothing, idler, layabout, loafer, shirker, (*sl.*) skiver, wastrel.

nefarious *a.* (*wicked, infamous*) abominable, atrocious, base, criminal, depraved, detestable, dreadful, evil, foul, heinous, horrendous, horrible, infamous, iniquitous, loathsome, odious, outrageous, shameful, shocking, sinful, vicious, vile, wicked. ANTONYMS: honourable, upright, virtuous.

negate *v.t.* **1** (*to render negative, to nullify*) abrogate, annul, cancel, countermand, invalidate, nullify, overrule, render null and void, repeal, rescind, retract, reverse, revoke, void. ANTONYMS: confirm, ratify. **2** (*to deny, to affirm* the non-existence of) call into question, contradict, deny, disclaim, disprove, dispute, gainsay, oppose, refute, renounce, repudiate. ANTONYMS: affirm, testify to.

negation n. 1 (denial) contradiction, denial, disproving, refutal, refutation, renunciation, repudiation. ANTONYMS: affirmation. 2 (the act of cancelling or nullifying) abrogation, cancellation, countermanding, invalidation, nullification, repeal, rescinding, retraction, reversal, revocation, voiding. ANTONYMS: confirmation, ratification. 3 (the absence or the opposite of certain qualities) absence, antithesis, contrary, converse, deficiency, lack, opposite, reverse, want. ANTONYMS: presence. 4 (nullity, voidness) blankness, non-existence, nothingness, nullity, vacuity, void, voidness. ANTONYMS: fullness.

negative a. 1 (declaring or implying negation) countermanding, invalidating, nullifying, repealing, revoking. ANTONYMS: affirming, ratifying. 2 (denying, contradicting) contradictory, denying, dissenting, gainsaying, opposing, refusing, rejecting, resisting. ANTONYMS: accepting, approving, concurring. 3 (lacking positive qualities such as optimism or enthusiasm) cynical, defeatist, gloomy, jaundiced, pessimistic, unenthusiastic, uninterested. ANTONYMS: hopeful, optimistic, positive.
~n. (a reply, word etc., expressing negation) contradiction, denial, dissension, refusal, rejection. ANTONYMS: affirmation.
~v.t. 1 (to reject, to refuse to accept or enact) forbid, (coll.) give the red light to, give the thumbs down to, negate, nullify, prohibit, reject, turn down, veto. ANTONYMS: accept, (coll.) give the green light to, give the thumbs up to, sanction. 2 (to disprove) belie, contradict, deny, discredit, disprove, explode, gainsay, give the lie to, invalidate, refute. ANTONYMS: give credence to, prove, validate.

neglect v.t. 1 (to treat carelessly) be lax about, be remiss about, let slide, not attend to, not take care of, pay no attention to, pay no heed to, shirk, slight. ANTONYMS: look after, pay attention to. 2 (to slight, to disregard) disregard, ignore, overlook, pass by, pay no heed to, scorn, slight, spurn, take for granted. ANTONYMS: appreciate, notice, pay heed to, take note of. 3 (to omit (to do or doing)) fail, forget, not remember, omit. ANTONYMS: do, remember.
~n. 1 (disregard (of)) disregard (of), heedlessness (of), ignoring, inattention (to), indifference (to), rebuff (to), scorn (for), slighting, spurning. ANTONYMS: attention (to), regard (of). 2 (carelessness, negligence) carelessness, dereliction, inattention, lack of proper care and attention, laxity, slovenliness. ANTONYMS: attention, care.

neglected a. 1 (not looked after properly) mistreated, uncared-for, unkempt, untended. 2 (disregarded) disregarded, ignored, scorned, slighted, spurned, unheeded. ANTONYMS: appreciated, heeded.

neglectful a. (not giving something sufficient attention; failing to look after someone properly) careless, forgetful, heedless, inattentive, inconsiderate, indifferent, lax, negligent, offhand, remiss, slack, slapdash, slipshod, thoughtless, uncaring, unmindful. ANTONYMS: attentive, careful, caring.

negligence n. (failure to exercise the proper care) carelessness, forgetfulness, heedlessness, inattention, inattentiveness, inconsideration, indifference, laxity, laxness, neglect, omission, oversight, remissness, slackness, slapdashness, slipshodness, thoughtlessness. ANTONYMS: attention, attentiveness, care, carefulness.

negligent a. (careless, neglectful) careless, derelict, disregardful, forgetful, heedless, inattentive, inconsiderate, indifferent, lax, offhand, remiss, slack, slapdash, slipshod, thoughtless, unmindful. ANTONYMS: attentive, careful, caring, considerate, painstaking.

negligible a. (so small or unimportant that it is not worth considering) imperceptible, inappreciable, inconsequential, insignificant, minor, minute, of no account, paltry, petty, small, tiny, trifling, trivial, unimportant. ANTONYMS: important, major, significant, vital.

negotiable a. 1 (capable of being negotiated or discussed) debatable, discussable, discussible, open to discussion, subject to bargaining. 2 (able to be transferred in exchange for money) exchangeable, transferable. 3 (that can be travelled along) clear, navigable, passable, unblocked, unobstructed. ANTONYMS: blocked, obstructed, unpassable.

negotiate v.i. (to discuss a matter with other people in order to make a bargain, agreement etc.) bargain, confer, consult together, debate, discuss, discuss terms, haggle, hold discussions, hold talks, parley, (coll.) wheel and deal.
~v.t. 1 (to arrange, bring about or procure by negotiating) agree on, arrange, bring about, bring off, come to terms about, complete, conclude, contract, engineer, execute, fulfil, orchestrate, pull off, reach an agreement about, settle, thrash out, transact, work out. 2 (to accomplish, to get over successfully) clear, cross, get across, get over, get past, get round, get through, navigate, pass over, pass through, surmount.

negotiation n. **1** (*the arrangement of an agreement etc. by discussion or bargaining*) arrangement, completion, conclusion, contracting, engineering, execution, settlement, settling, thrashing out, transaction, working out. **2** (*bargaining, discussion*) arbitration, bargaining, debate, discussion, haggling, parleying, talks, transaction, wheeler-dealing.

negotiator n. (*a person who negotiates*) arbitrator, bargainer, broker, diplomat, haggler, intermediary, mediator, wheeler-dealer.

neighbourhood n. **1** (*the locality round or near; the vicinity*) district, environs, locality, surrounding district, vicinity. **2** (*the part of a town etc. in which people live*) area, community, district, locality, neck of the woods, part. **in the neighbourhood of** (*approximately*) about, almost, approximately, around, close to, just about, nearly, roughly. ANTONYMS: exactly, precisely.

neighbouring a. (*situated or living near*) abutting, adjacent, adjoining, bordering, close, close at hand, closest, connecting, contiguous, in the vicinity, near, near at hand, nearby, nearest, next. ANTONYMS: distant, far-off, remote.

neighbourly a. (*friendly and helpful*) affable, amiable, amicable, civil, companionable, cordial, friendly, generous, genial, helpful, hospitable, kind, kindly, obliging, sociable, social. ANTONYMS: unfriendly, unhelpful, unkind, unsociable.

neither a. (*not either*) not either, not the one or the other.

nemesis n. (*retributive justice*) destiny, fate, retribution, retributive justice, vengeance.

neologism n. (*a new word or phrase, or a new sense for an old one*) (*coll.*) buzzword, coinage, new word/ phrase, vogue word.

neophyte n. (*a beginner, a novice*) apprentice, beginner, greenhorn, learner, newcomer, novice, probationer, proselyte, recruit, (*sl.*) rookie, student, trainee, tyro.

ne plus ultra n. (*the most perfect or uttermost point*) acme, culmination, extreme, last word, peak, perfection, ultimate, uttermost point, zenith. ANTONYMS: nadir, (*sl.*) the pits.

nepotism n. (*favouritism towards one's relations, for example in business*) favouritism, partiality, partisanship, patronage, preferential treatment, (*coll.*) the old boy network.

nerve n. **1** (*strength, coolness*) (*sl.*) bottle, braveness, bravery, coolness, courage, courageousness, daring, determination, fearlessness, fortitude, gameness, grit, (*sl.*) guts, intrepidity, mettle, pluck, resolution, spirit, (*sl.*) spunk, strength. ANTONYMS: cowardice, fear, weakness. **2** (*an excited or disordered condition of the nerves, nervousness*) anxiety, apprehension, apprehensiveness, butterflies in the stomach, nervousness, nervous tension, strain, tenseness, tension, (*coll.*) the collywobbles, (*sl.*) the jitters, worry. ANTONYMS: calmness, tranquillity. **3** (*impudence, cheek*) audacity, boldness, (*sl.*) brass neck, brazenness, cheek, (*coll.*) chutzpah, effrontery, (*sl.*) face, gall, impertinence, impudence, insolence, (*sl.*) neck, presumption, temerity. **to get on someone's nerves** (*to irritate someone*) anger, annoy, enrage, exasperate, incense, infuriate, irritate, provoke, rub (someone) up the wrong way, try one's patience.

nerve-racking a. (*frightening, worrying*) distressing, frightening, harassing, harrowing, stressful, tense, trying, worrying.

nervous a. (*having weak or sensitive nerves, timid*) agitated, anxious, apprehensive, edgy, excitable, fidgety, flustered, fretful, highly strung, hysterical, (*coll.*) in a state, (*coll.*) jittery, (*coll.*) jumpy, (*coll.*) nervy, neurotic, on edge, on tenterhooks, quaking, restless, ruffled, shaking in one's shoes, strained, tense, timid, (*coll.*) twitchy, uneasy, (*coll.*) uptight, (*sl.*) wired, with one's heart in one's mouth, worried. ANTONYMS: calm, calm and collected, confident, cool, (*coll.*) laid-back, relaxed, tranquil.

nervous breakdown n. (*an attack or period of mental illness which prevents a person from functioning normally*) breakdown, clinical depression, collapse, nervous disorder.

nervousness n. (*the state of being nervous*) agitation, anxiety, apprehension, disquiet, edginess, excitability, restlessness, strain, tension, timidity, timorousness, twitchiness, uptightness, worry. ANTONYMS: calmness, coolness, relaxation, tranquillity.

nervy a. (*nervous jumpy*) agitated, anxious, apprehensive, edgy, excitable, fearful, fidgety, flustered, fretful, highly strung, hysterical, (*coll.*) in a state, (*coll.*) jittery, (*coll.*) jumpy, nervous, neurotic, on edge, on tenterhooks, quaking, restless, ruffled, shaking, (*coll.*) twitchy, uneasy, (*coll.*) uptight, with one's heart in one's mouth, worried. ANTONYMS: calm, calm and collected, confident, cool, (*coll.*) laid-back, relaxed, tranquil.

nest egg n. (*a sum of money laid by as savings for the future*) cache, life savings, reserve, savings, (*coll.*) something for a rainy day.

nestle v.i. **1** (*to settle oneself* (*down, in etc.*))

(*coll., esp. N Am.*) cosy up, curl up, settle. **2** (*to press closely up to someone*) cuddle up, huddle, nuzzle, press up, snuggle up.

net[1] *n.* **1** (*a fabric of twine, cord etc., knotted into meshes for protecting, carrying etc.*) lattice-work, mesh, meshwork, netting. **2** (*a snare*) mesh, snare, trap.
~*v.t.* (*to catch in a net*) bag, capture, catch, (*sl.*) collar, ensnare, (*sl.*) nab, snare, take captive, trap.

net[2] *a.* **1** (*obtained or left after all deductions*) after-tax, clear, post-deductions, take-home. **2** ((*of a result etc.*) *final, ultimate*) closing, concluding, conclusive, end, final. ANTONYMS: beginning, opening.
~*v.t.* (*to yield or realize as clear profit*) bring in, clear, earn, gain, get, give, make, pocket, realize, receive, yield.

†**nether** *a.* **1** (*lower*) bottom, low, lower, low-level, underneath. ANTONYMS: high, higher. **2** (*belonging to the region below the heavens or the earth*) hellish, infernal, Stygian, under-world.

nettle *v.t.* (*to irritate, to provoke*) anger, annoy, exasperate, fret, gall, (*coll.*) get in (someone's hair), (*coll.*) get on one's nerves, harass, (*coll.*) hassle, incense, infuriate, irk, irritate, provoke, (*coll.*) rub (someone) up the wrong way, ruffle, try one's patience, vex.

network *n.* **1** (*an open-work fabric, netting*) fretwork, latticework, meshwork, netting, openwork. **2** (*a system of intersecting lines, a reticulation*) circuitry, grid, grill, labyrinth, maze, mesh, web. **3** (*a system of units related in some way, e.g. part of a business organization*) complex, nexus, organization, structure, system, web.

neurotic *a.* **1** (*suffering from neurosis*) mentally disturbed, mentally ill, mentally unstable. **2** (*unreasonably anxious, oversensitive*) anxious, compulsive, disturbed, hysterical, irrational, maladjusted, nervous, obsessive, oversensitive, overwrought, phobic, unstable. ANTONYMS: (*coll.*) laid-back, rational, stable, well-adjusted.

neuter *a.* (*neither masculine nor feminine*) asexual, sexless, unsexed.
~*v.t.* (*to remove the reproductive organs of (an animal)*) castrate, (*coll.*) doctor, dress, (*coll.*) fix, geld, spay.

neutral *a.* **1** (*taking no part with either side, esp. not assisting either of two belligerents*) detached, disinterested, dispassionate, impartial, non-aligned, non-partisan, objective, open-minded, unaligned, unbiased, uninvolved, unprejudiced. ANTONYMS: biased,

interested, partisan, prejudiced. **2** (*belonging to a state that takes no part in hostilities*) non-belligerent, non-combatant, non-interventionist. ANTONYMS: belligerent, combatant. **3** (*having no distinct or determinate character, colour etc.*) average, bland, colourless, commonplace, dull, indeterminate, indistinct, insipid, ordinary, run-of-the-mill, uninteresting, unremarkable. ANTONYMS: distinctive, interesting, remarkable, special. **4** (*having a pale or light colour, e.g. grey or light brown*) beige, natural, stone, stone-coloured. ANTONYMS: bright, vivid.

neutrality *n.* (*the state of being neutral or non-biased*) detachment, disinterest, disinterestedness, impartiality, lack of bias, lack of prejudice, non-alignment, non-involvement, non-partisanship, objectivity, open-mindedness. ANTONYMS: bias, partiality, partisanship, prejudice.

neutralize *v.t.* (*to render inoperative or ineffective, to counteract*) cancel, counteract, counterbalance, frustrate, invalidate, negate, nullify, offset, undo.

never *adv.* **1** (*not ever, at no time*) at no time, not at any time, not once. **2** (*not at all*) certainly not, not at all, not in any circumstances, (*coll.*) not on your life, (*sl.*) not on your nellie, on no account, under no circumstances.

never-ending *a.* (*seeming to last for ever*) ceaseless, continual, continuous, endless, eternal, everlasting, incessant, infinite, interminable, non-stop, perpetual, relentless, unceasing, unending, unfaltering, uninterrupted, unremitting, without end.

never-never *n.* (*the hire-purchase system*) hire purchase, HP, payment by instalment.

nevertheless *conj.* (*notwithstanding; all the same*) all the same, be that as it may, even so, for all that, however, in any event, just the same, nonetheless, notwithstanding, regardless, still, yet.

new *a.* **1** (*lately made or introduced*) advanced, contemporary, current, fresh, latest, modern, modernistic, modish, newfangled, new-fashioned, novel, original, present-day, recent, state-of-the-art, topical, up-to-date, up-to-the-minute. ANTONYMS: antiquated, old, old-fashioned. **2** (*never before used, not worn or exhausted*) brand-new, in mint condition, mint, pristine, unused, virgin. ANTONYMS: old, used, worn. **3** (*fresh, unfamiliar*) different, fresh, strange, unaccustomed, unfamiliar, unknown. ANTONYMS: accustomed, familiar, old.

newcomer *n.* **1** (*a person who has recently arrived in a place*) immigrant, incomer, intruder, (*coll.*) johnny-come-lately, new arrival, outsider, parvenu, settler, stranger. ANTONYMS: oldest resident. **2** (*a person who has just begun to take part in something*) beginner, greenhorn, initiate, learner, neophyte, new recruit, novice, probationer, trainee, tyro. ANTONYMS: expert, veteran.

newfangled *a.* (*new-fashioned; different from the accepted fashion*) contemporary, fashionable, gimmicky, modern, new-fashioned, state-of-the-art, ultra-modern. ANTONYMS: antiquated, dated, old-fashioned, outmoded, passé.

newly *adv.* (*recently*) freshly, just, lately, recently.

news *n.* (*recent or fresh information*) bulletin, communication, communiqué, data, disclosure, dispatch, exposé, facts, (*coll.*) gen, gossip, (*coll.*) info, information, intelligence, newsflash, news item, news release, news report, press release, release, report, revelation, tidings.

newsletter *n.* (*a printed report of news sent out regularly to a particular group*) bulletin, leaflet, magazine, newspaper.

newspaper *n.* (*a printed publication, usu. issued daily or weekly, containing news*) broadsheet, daily, paper, tabloid, weekly.

newsworthy *a.* (*interesting enough to be reported as news*) important, interesting, noteworthy, of interest, remarkable, significant.

next *a.* **1** (*nearest in place, time or degree*) abutting, adjacent, adjoining, bordering, closest, contiguous, nearest, neighbouring. **2** (*nearest in order or succession, immediately following*) consequent, ensuing, following, later, subsequent, succeeding, successive.
~*adv.* **1** (*nearest or immediately after*) after that, afterwards, later, subsequently, then, thereafter. **2** (*in the next place or degree*) closest, following.

nibble *v.t.* (*to bite little bits off*) bite, gnaw, munch, peck at, pick at.
~*n.* **1** (*pl.*) (*party snacks, such as crisps and nuts*) canapés, snacks, titbits. **2** (*a little bite*) bite, gnaw, munch, peck. **3** (*a bit which is nibbled off*) bite, crumb, morsel, taste.

nice *a.* **1** (*pleasing or agreeable*) agreeable, amusing, delightful, diverting, enjoyable, entertaining, good, interesting, marvellous, pleasant, pleasurable, satisfying, wonderful. ANTONYMS: boring, dreary, uninteresting. **2** (*delightful, kind*) agreeable, amiable, attractive, charming, civil, compassionate, courteous, delightful, friendly, generous, good, good-natured, gracious, kind, kindly, likeable,

pleasant, polite, sympathetic, tolerant, understanding. ANTONYMS: nasty, unfriendly, unkind, unpleasant. **3** (*fastidious, overparticular*) dainty, discriminating, exacting, fastidious, finicky, fussy, hard to please, meticulous, overparticular, over-refined, particular, (*coll.*) pernickety, polite, precise, punctilious, refined, scrupulous, ultra-polite. ANTONYMS: coarse, rough, unrefined, vulgar. **4** (*requiring delicate discrimination or tact, subtle*) delicate, fine, minute, precise, subtle, tiny, ultra-fine. ANTONYMS: large, massive. **5** ((*of weather*) *warm and pleasant*) fine, pleasant, sunny, warm. ANTONYMS: nasty, wet.

nicely *adv.* **1** (*in a pleasant or friendly way*) agreeably, amiably, attractively, charmingly, compassionately, courteously, delightfully, generously, good-naturedly, graciously, pleasantly, politely, sympathetically, tolerantly, well. ANTONYMS: badly, nastily, unattractively, unpleasantly. **2** (*in a satisfactory or pleasing way*) all right, fine, satisfactorily, very well.

niceness *n.* **1** (*friendliness and pleasantness*) amiableness, charm, civility, compassion, courteousness, delightfulness, friendliness, generosity, good-naturedness, goodness, graciousness, kindliness, kindness, pleasantness, politeness, sympathy, tolerance, understanding. ANTONYMS: nastiness, unfriendliness, unkindness, unpleasantness. **2** (*delicacy or minuteness*) delicacy, fineness, minuteness, preciseness, precision, tininess, ultra-fineness.

nicety *n.* **1** (*exactness, precision*) accuracy, exactness, meticulousness, precision, rigour. ANTONYMS: inaccuracy, inexactness, roughness. **2** (*a minute point, a delicate distinction*) detail, fine distinction, nuance, subtlety.

niche *n.* **1** (*a recess in a wall for a statue, vase etc.*) alcove, corner, hollow, nook, recess. **2** (*one's proper place or natural position*) calling, place, position, (*sl.*) slot, vocation.

nick *n.* (*a small notch or dent, esp. used as a tally or score for keeping account*) chip, cut, dent, mark, notch, score, scratch.

nickname *n.* (*a name given in derision or familiarity*) epithet, family name, pet name, sobriquet.

nifty *a.* **1** (*quick, slick*) adroit, agile, clever, deft, neat, nimble, quick, skilful. ANTONYMS: awkward, clumsy. **2** (*smart, stylish*) attractive, chic, fashionable, neat, sharp, smart, spruce, stylish. ANTONYMS: dowdy, unfashionable.

niggard *n.* (*a stingy person; a person who is grudging*) (*sl.*) cheapskate, miser, (*coll.*) penny-pincher, Scrooge, skinflint. ANTONYMS: spendthrift, squanderer.

niggardly *a.* **1** (*miserly, mean*) avaricious, greedy, mean, mercenary, miserly, (*coll.*) near, parsimonious, penny-pinching, stingy, tight-fisted. ANTONYMS: generous, liberal, prodigal. **2** (*worth very little*) beggarly, inadequate, insubstantial, insufficient, meagre, mean, measly, miserable, paltry, (*coll.*) piddling, scant, scanty, skimpy, small, wretched. ANTONYMS: abundant, copious, lavish, plentiful.

niggle *v.i.* (*to busy oneself with petty details*) carp, cavil, criticize, fuss, nag, nit-pick.
~*v.t.* (*to worry, to annoy*) annoy, irritate, rankle, trouble, worry.

night *n.* (*the time of darkness from sunset to sunrise*) dark, darkness, dead of night, hours of darkness, night-time. ANTONYMS: day, daylight hours, daytime.

nightfall *n.* (*the beginning of night; dusk*) dusk, evening, sundown, sunset, twilight. ANTONYMS: dawn, daybreak, sunrise.

nightly *a.* (*occurring at night or every night*) at night, night-time, nocturnal. ANTONYMS: daytime.
~*adv.* (*every night*) each night, every night, night after night. ANTONYMS: daily.

nightmare *n.* **1** (*a terrifying dream*) bad dream, incubus. **2** (*anything inspiring such a feeling; a terrifying experience*) horror, ordeal, torment, torture, trial.

nil *n.* (*nothing; zero*) duck, love, naught, none, nothing, nought, zero, (*sl.*) zilch.

nimble *a.* **1** (*light and quick in motion; agile*) active, agile, brisk, deft, dexterous, fast, graceful, lively, (*coll.*) nippy, (*sl.*) p.d.q., proficient, prompt, quick, quick-moving, skilful, smart, sprightly, spry, swift. ANTONYMS: awkward, clumsy, lumbering, slow, slow-moving. **2** (*alert, clever*) alert, bright, clever, quick-thinking, quick-witted, ready. ANTONYMS: dull, dull-witted, slow-witted.

nip *v.t.* **1** (*to pinch, to squeeze*) bite, grip, pinch, squeeze, tweak. **2** (*to cut or pinch off the end or point of*) clip, cut, dock, lop, pinch, snip. **3** (*to sting, to pain*) bite, hurt, pain, sting.
~*v.i.* (*to move or go quickly (in, out, etc.)*) dart, dash, hasten, hurry, race, run, rush, sprint. ANTONYMS: amble, stroll.

nipple *n.* (*the small prominence in the breast of female mammals, by which milk is sucked*) dug, mamilla, pap, papilla, teat, (*sl.*) tit, udder.

nippy *a.* **1** (*cold*) biting, chilly, cold, freezing, icy, piercing, raw, sharp, stinging. **2** (*active; agile*) agile, fast, nimble, quick, rapid, swift. ANTONYMS: lumbering, slow.

nirvana *n.* (*bliss, heaven*) bliss, ecstasy, heaven, paradise.

nit-picking *n.* (*petty criticism of minor details*) carping, cavilling, fault-finding, hair-splitting, pedantry, petty criticism, quibbling.

nitty-gritty *n.* (*the basic facts, the realities of a situation*) basics, (*coll.*) brass tacks, centre, core, crux, essence, essentials, facts, fundamentals, gist, heart, heart of the matter, kernel, nucleus, nuts and bolts, reality, substance.

nitwit *n.* (*a foolish or stupid person*) (*coll.*) chump, (*coll.*) dimwit, (*sl.*) dock, dolt, donkey, (*coll.*) dope, (*sl.*) dummy, dunce, fool, (*sl.*) geek, ignoramus, (*sl.*) nerd, nincompoop, ninny, oaf, simpleton, (*coll.*) twit, (*sl.*) wally.

no *adv.* (*a word of denial or refusal, the categorical negative*) absolutely not, by no means, never, no indeed, (*coll.*) not on your life, (*sl.*) not on your nellie, (*coll.*) no way, under no circumstances. ANTONYMS: certainly, yes, yes indeed.

nobble *v.t.* **1** (*to dose or otherwise tamper with (a horse) to prevent its winning a race*) disable, handicap, incapacitate, interfere with, tamper with, weaken. **2** (*to persuade or win over by dishonest means, to influence (a member of a jury etc.), esp. by bribery or threats*) bribe, (*coll.*) get at, influence, intimidate, threaten, win over. **3** (*to catch, to nab*) catch, catch hold of, (*sl.*) collar, get hold of, grab, (*sl.*) nab, seize, take, take hold of.

nobility *n.* **1** (*magnanimity, greatness*) dignity, eminence, esteem, excellence, grandness, greatness, high-mindedness, honour, illustriousness, loftiness, magnanimity, magnificence, majesty, stateliness, superiority, worthiness. ANTONYMS: dishonour, humbleness, inferiority, lowliness. **2** (*nobles, the peerage*) aristocracy, high society, lords, lords and ladies, nobles, (*sl.*) nobs, peerage, peers, peers of the realm, ruling class, upper class. ANTONYMS: lower class, peasants.

noble *a.* **1** (*lofty or illustrious in character or dignity; magnanimous*) august, dignified, distinguished, eminent, grand, great, high-minded, honourable, illustrious, lofty, magnanimous, magnificent, majestic, superior, worthy. ANTONYMS: dishonourable, ignoble, inferior. **2** (*of high rank, belonging to the nobility*) aristocratic, blue-blooded, born with a silver spoon in one's mouth, high-born, landed, patrician, titled. ANTONYMS: base, humble, low-born, lowly. **3** (*magnificent, stately*) grand, imposing, impressive, majestic, splendid, stately, striking, superb. ANTONYMS: humble, insignificant, mean, ordinary.

~n. (a nobleman or noblewoman, a peer) aristocrat, lady, lord, member of the nobility, (sl.) nob, nobleman, noblewoman, peer, peer of the realm.

nobody pron. (no one, no person) no one, not a single person. ANTONYMS: everyone.
~n. (a person of no importance) cipher, nonentity, non-person.

nocturnal a. (occurring in the night, performed or active by night) night, nightly, night-time, of the night. ANTONYMS: daytime.

nod v.i. 1 (to incline the head with a slight, quick motion in token of assent) agree, assent, show agreement. 2 (to incline the head with a slight, quick motion in token of salutation) greet, salute. 3 (to incline the head with a slight, quick motion in token of command or indication) indicate, show, sign, signal. 4 (to let the head fall forward; to be drowsy) be sleepy, doze, go to sleep, nap, nod off, sleep, take a nap. 5 (to make a careless mistake) blunder, (sl.) boob, commit an error, make a mistake, slip up.
~v.t. 1 (to bend or incline (the head)) bend, bob, bow, dip, duck, incline. 2 (to signify by a nod) gesture, indicate, motion, sign, signal.
~n. (a quick bend of the head) bend, bob, bow, dip, ducking, inclination, incline.

node n. (a knot, a knob) bud, bulge, bump, excrescence, growth, knob, knot, lump, nodule, protuberance, swelling.

noise n. (a sound of any kind, esp. a loud or disagreeable one) babble, blare, clamour, commotion, din, hubbub, pandemonium, racket, row, rumpus, sound, tumult, uproar.

noisome a. ((esp. of a smell) offensive, disgusting) disagreeable, disgusting, fetid, foul, horrible, malodorous, mephitic, nauseating, offensive, repugnant, repulsive, revolting, smelly, stinking, unpleasant. ANTONYMS: agreeable, nice, pleasant, sweet-smelling.

noisy a. 1 (causing noise) blaring, cacophonous, deafening, ear-splitting, loud, piercing, strident. ANTONYMS: muted, silent, soft. 2 (making a lot of noise) boisterous, chattering, clamorous, obstreperous, (coll.) rackety, riotous, turbulent, vociferous. ANTONYMS: peaceful, quiet.

nomad n. (a wanderer) drifter, itinerant, migrant, rambler, rover, transient, traveller, vagabond, vagrant, wanderer.

nomadic a. (wandering) itinerant, migrant, migratory, peripatetic, roaming, roving, transient, travelling, wandering.

nom de plume n. (a pen-name) alias, assumed name, pen-name, pseudonym.

nomenclature n. (a system of terminology) classification, phraseology, taxonomy, terminology, vocabulary.

nominal a. 1 (existing in name only, as distinct from real) in name only, ostensible, professed, purported, self-styled, so-called, supposed, theoretical, titular. ANTONYMS: actual. 2 (trivial, inconsiderable) inconsiderable, insignificant, minimal, small, tiny, token, trifling, trivial. ANTONYMS: large, significant.

nominate v.t. 1 (to propose as a candidate) present, propose, put forward, recommend, submit, suggest. 2 (to appoint to an office or duty) appoint, choose, designate, elect, name, select. 3 (to name, to designate) designate, name.

nomination n. 1 (the act of proposing someone as a candidate) presentation, proposal, recommendation, suggestion. 2 (the act of appointing someone to an office or duty) appointment, choice, designation, election, naming, selection.

nominee n. (a person named or appointed by name) candidate, contestant, entrant.

nonchalance n. (the state of being nonchalant) apathy, calmness, carelessness, casualness, composure, coolness, detachment, dispassion, indifference, insouciance, lack of concern. ANTONYMS: concern, emotion, worry.

nonchalant a. (cool, indifferent) airy, apathetic, blasé, calm, careless, casual, collected, composed, cool, detached, dispassionate, indifferent, insouciant, (coll.) laid-back, offhand, unconcerned, unemotional, (coll.) unfazed, unmoved, unperturbed. ANTONYMS: anxious, concerned, emotional, worried.

non-combatant n. (a civilian, esp. a surgeon, chaplain etc. attached to troops) civilian.
~a. (being a member of the armed forces but not actually fighting) civilian, neutral, non-belligerent, non-combative, pacifist. ANTONYMS: belligerent, combatant, fighting.

non-committal a. (not committing oneself, impartial) careful, cautious, circumspect, diplomatic, discreet, equivocal, evasive, giving nothing away, guarded, indefinite, neutral, playing one's cards close to one's chest, politic, prudent, reticent, sitting on the fence, tactful, temporizing, tentative, vague, wary. ANTONYMS: committed, definite.

nonconformist n. (a person who does not conform to usual or normal ways of behaving or thinking) dissenter, dissentient, iconoclast, individualist, maverick, protester, radical, rebel, seceder. ANTONYMS: conformist, traditionalist.

nonconformity *n.* (*behaviour or thinking that does not conform to what is considered usual or normal*) dissent, eccentricity, heterodoxy, unconventionality. ANTONYMS: conformity, conventionality.

nondescript *a.* (*not easily described or classified; neither one thing nor another*) bland, characterless, colourless, common-or-garden, commonplace, dull, featureless, indefinite, indeterminate, insipid, mediocre, ordinary, run-of-the-mill, undistinguished, unexceptional, uninspiring, uninteresting, vague. ANTONYMS: distinctive, extraordinary, memorable, remarkable.

none *pron.* **1** (*no one, no person*) never a one, nobody, no one, not a single person, not a soul, not one. ANTONYMS: all, everyone, someone. **2** (*not any, not any portion*) nil, not a bit, not any, not a part, not a single thing, not a thing, nothing, nothing at all, (*sl.*) sweet FA, (*sl.*) sweet Fanny Adams, zero, (*sl.*) zilch. ANTONYMS: all, everything, something.

nonentity *n.* (*an unimportant person or thing*) cipher, (*coll.*) lightweight, nobody, nonperson, person of no account, small beer, (*coll.*) small fry. ANTONYMS: celebrity, dignitary, notable, someone.

nonetheless *adv.* (*nevertheless*) be that as it may, despite that, even so, in any event, in spite of that, just the same, nevertheless, notwithstanding, regardless.

non-existent *a.* (*not existing, not real*) fancied, fantasy, fictional, fictitious, hypothetical, illusory, imaginary, imagined, legendary, mythical, unreal. ANTONYMS: existent, real.

non-intervention *n.* (*the principle or policy of not becoming involved in the disputes of other nations*) inaction, laissez-faire, neutrality, non-interference, non-involvement, non-participation, passivity. ANTONYMS: intervention, involvement.

nonplus *v.t.* (*to confound, to bewilder*) astonish, astound, baffle, bewilder, confound, discomfit, disconcert, discountenance, dismay, dumbfound, embarrass, (*coll.*) faze, (*coll.*) floor, (*coll.*) flummox, make one halt in one's tracks, mystify, perplex, puzzle, stump, stun, surprise, take aback.

nonsense *n.* **1** (*unmeaning words, ideas etc.*) balderdash, bilge, (*sl.*) bosh, (*sl.*) bull, (*sl.*) bullshit, bunkum, (*coll.*) claptrap, (*sl.*) crap, double Dutch, drivel, (*coll.*) flannel, garbage, gibberish, gobbledegook, (*coll.*) piffle, (*coll.*) poppycock, rot, rub, (*coll.*) tommyrot, (*coll.*) tripe, twaddle, (*coll.*) waffle. ANTONYMS: common sense, reason, sense, wisdom. **2** (*foolery,*

absurdity) absurdity, buffoonery, clowning, folly, foolishness, idiocy, inanity, ludicrousness, ridiculousness, senselessness, stupidity. ANTONYMS: common sense, sense.

nonsensical *a.* (*foolish, absurd*) absurd, asinine, fatuous, foolish, idiotic, inane, irrational, ludicrous, ridiculous, senseless, silly, stupid. ANTONYMS: rational, sensible, wise.

non-stop *a.* (*without a pause*) ceaseless, constant, continual, continuous, endless, incessant, interminable, never-ending, persistent, relentless, steady, unbroken, unceasing, unending, unfaltering, uninterrupted, unremitting. ANTONYMS: discontinuous, intermittent, irregular, sporadic.

nook *n.* **1** (*a corner*) alcove, corner, cranny, niche, opening, recess. **2** (*a secluded retreat*) den, hideaway, hideout, refuge, retreat.

noon *n.* (*the middle of the day, twelve o'clock*) midday, twelve hundred hours, twelve midday, twelve noon. ANTONYMS: midnight.

no one *pron.* (*nobody, no person*) never a one, nobody, not anyone, not a one, not a person, not a single one, not a single person, not a soul. ANTONYMS: someone.

norm *n.* (*a standard or model*) average, benchmark, criterion, gauge, mean, measure, model, pattern, rule, touchstone, type, yardstick.

normal *a.* **1** (*according to rule or established law; regular, typical*) accepted, acknowledged, average, common, (*coll.*) common or garden, commonplace, conventional, general, habitual, natural, ordinary, regular, routine, run-of-the-mill, standard, typical, usual. ANTONYMS: atypical, irregular, uncommon, unnatural, unusual. **2** (*mentally healthy, not suffering from any mental disorder*) rational, sane, well-adjusted, well-balanced.

normality *n.* **1** (*the state of being normal or usual*) commonness, conventionality, habitualness, naturalness, ordinariness, regularity, usualness. ANTONYMS: abnormality, unusualness. **2** (*the state of being mentally healthy, not suffering from any mental disorder*) balance, rationality, sanity. ANTONYMS: abnormality, imbalance, insanity, irrationality.

normally *adv.* **1** (*usually*) as a general rule, as a rule, commonly, generally, ordinarily, regularly, typically, usually. ANTONYMS: uncommonly, unusually. **2** (*in the conventional way*) as usual, naturally, ordinarily, regularly, typically. ANTONYMS: abnormally, atypically.

nose *n.* **1** (*the projecting part of the face between the forehead and mouth*) (*sl.*) beak, (*sl.*) conk, (*sl.*) hooter, (*sl.*) neb, proboscis, (*esp. N Am.,* *sl.*) schnozzle, (*sl.*) snitch, (*sl.*) snout. **2** (*odour; aroma, esp. the bouquet of wine*) aroma, bouquet, fragrance, perfume, scent. **3** (*an instinctive ability to find something*) insight, instinct, intuition, sixth sense.

~*v.t.* **1** (*to perceive or detect by smelling*) run to earth, run to ground, scent out, smell out, sniff out. **2** (*to find out*) detect, discover, expose, ferret out, find, reveal, search out. **3** (*to rub or push with the nose*) nudge, nuzzle, push. **4** (*to push (one's way*)) ease, edge, inch, move.

~*v.i.* (*to search, to pry*) meddle, (*sl.*) poke one's nose in, pry, search, (*sl.*) snoop.

nosedive *n.* **1** (*a sudden plunge towards the earth made by an aircraft*) dive, drop, plummeting, plunge, swoop. **2** (*any sudden plunge*) decline, drop, fall, plummeting, plunge.

nostalgia *n.* (*a yearning for the past*) pining, regret, regretfulness, reminiscence, wistfulness, yearning for the past.

nosy *a.* (*very inquisitive*) curious, inquisitive, interfering, meddlesome, prying, (*coll.*) snooping.

notable *a.* (*worthy of note; memorable*) extraordinary, important, impressive, marked, memorable, momentous, noteworthy, of note, outstanding, particular, pronounced, rare, remarkable, signal, significant, striking, unforgettable, unusual. ANTONYMS: insignificant, ordinary, run-of-the-mill.

~*n.* (*a notable person*) (*sl.*) big noise, (*sl.*) big shot, (*coll.*) celeb, celebrity, dignitary, leading light, luminary, notability, personage, star, VIP, worthy. ANTONYMS: unknown.

notably *adv.* (*particularly*) conspicuously, distinctly, especially, extraordinarily, markedly, particularly, remarkably, signally, singularly, uncommonly, unusually.

notch *n.* **1** (*a nick, a cut*) cut, dent, gash, gouge, groove, incision, indentation, mark, nick, score, scratch. **2** (*a step on a scale, a degree*) gradation, grade, level, rung, stage, step.

~*v.t.* (*to cut a notch or notches in*) cut, dent, gain, gash, indent, nick, register, score, scratch. **to notch up** (*to score, to achieve*) achieve, attain, gain, make, record, register, score.

note *n.* **1** (*a brief record, a memorandum*) account, memo, memorandum, message, minute, record. **2** (*a short or informal letter*) letter, missive, notelet, short letter. **3** (*a bank note or piece of paper money*) bank note, bill. **4** (*a comment or gloss, appended to a passage in a book etc.*) annotation, comment, explanation, explication, exposition, footnote, gloss, jotting, (*pl.*) marginalia. **5** (*distinction, repute*) consequence, distinction, eminence, fame,

importance, prestige, renown, report, reputation. ANTONYMS: obscurity, unimportance. **6** (*a significant tone or mode of expression*) inflection, intonation, sound, tone. **7** (*a sign or mark*) mark, sign, symbol, token.

~*v.t.* **1** (*to take notice of; to show respect to; to pay attention to*) observe, pay attention to, pay heed to, perceive, see, take heed of, take note of, take notice of. **2** (*to make a memorandum of; to record as worth remembering*) enter, jot down, mark down, put down, record, register, set down, write down. **of note 1** (*important, distinguished*) acclaimed, celebrated, conspicuous, distinguished, eminent, famed, famous, illustrious, notable, noted, noteworthy, pre-eminent, prominent, renowned, well-known. ANTONYMS: obscure, unknown. **2** (*worthy of attention*) exceptional, extraordinary, important, impressive, marked, memorable, momentous, notable, outstanding, particular, rare, remarkable, significant, striking, unforgettable, unusual. ANTONYMS: insignificant, ordinary, run-of-the-mill, unremarkable.

notebook *n.* (*a book for writing notes in*) exercise book, Filofax®, jotter, memo pad, notepad, personal organizer.

noted *a.* (*eminent, remarkable*) acclaimed, celebrated, conspicuous, distinguished, eminent, famed, famous, illustrious, notable, of note, pre-eminent, prominent.

noteworthy *a.* **1** (*worth attention*) exceptional, extraordinary, important, impressive, marked, memorable, momentous, notable, of note, outstanding, particular, pronounced, rare, remarkable, significant, striking, unforgettable, unusual. ANTONYMS: insignificant, ordinary, run-of-the-mill, unremarkable. **2** (*outstanding, famous*) acclaimed, celebrated, conspicuous, distinguished, eminent, famed, famous, illustrious, notable, noted, of note, pre-eminent, prominent, renowned, well-known. ANTONYMS: obscure, unknown.

nothing *n.* **1** (*not anything, nought*) duck, love, naught, nil, none, nought, zero, (*sl.*) zilch. ANTONYMS: something. **2** (*no amount, zero*) cipher, nought, zero. **3** (*nothingness, non-existence*) emptiness, nihility, non-being, non-existence, nothingness, nullity, oblivion, vacuum, void. **4** (*an insignificant or unimportant thing, a trifle*) bagatelle, (*coll.*) no big deal, trifle. **5** (*a person of no importance*) cipher, (*coll.*) lightweight, nobody, nonentity, non-person, person of no account, small beer. ANTONYMS: (*coll.*) big shot, celebrity, dignitary, luminary. **for nothing 1** (*free, without paying*) for free, free, gratis, gratuitously, without charge, without payment. ANTONYMS: for payment. **2** (*to no purpose*) futilely, in vain, needlessly, to no avail, to no purpose, unsuccessfully. ANTONYMS: successfully. **to come to nothing** (*to turn out a failure*) be in vain, be unsuccessful, (*coll.*) bite the dust, (*coll.*) come a cropper, fail, fall through, miscarry, misfire. ANTONYMS: be successful, succeed. **to think nothing of** (*not to pay much attention to something; not to consider important or unusual*) have no hesitation about, regard (something) as normal, regard (something) as routine, take (something) in one's stride.

nothingness *n.* (*the state of not being; non-existence*) emptiness, nihility, non-being, non-existence, nothing, nullity, oblivion, vacuum, void.

notice *n.* **1** (*regard, attention*) attention, cognizance, consideration, heed, observation, regard, vigilance. **2** (*information, warning*) advice, announcement, information, instructions, intimation, news, notification, order, warning. **3** (*a written or printed paper giving information or directions*) bill, bulletin, circular, communication, information sheet, leaflet, pamphlet, poster. **4** (*intimation of the termination of an agreement, contract of employment etc., at a specified date*) (*coll.*) marching orders, notice to quit, redundancy notice. **5** (*an account of something in a newspaper etc., esp. a review*) criticism, review, write-up.

~*v.t.* (*to take notice of, to perceive*) detect, discern, distinguish, heed, mark, note, observe, perceive, see, spot, take note of. ANTONYMS: be unaware of, ignore, miss, overlook. **to take no notice of** (*to pay no attention to; to ignore*) brush aside, disregard, ignore, pay no attention to, shut one's eyes to, take no heed of, turn a blind eye to. ANTONYMS: pay attention to, take note of.

noticeable *a.* (*easy to see or recognize*) apparent, blatant, clear, conspicuous, detectable, discernible, distinct, evident, manifest, obvious, patent, perceptible, plain, pronounced, striking, unmistakable, visible. ANTONYMS: inconspicuous, indistinct.

notification *n.* **1** (*the act of making known information*) announcement, broadcasting, communication, declaration, disclosure, divulgence, publication, publishing, revealing, revelation. ANTONYMS: concealment. **2** (*the act of informing someone of something*) acquainting, advising, apprising, informing, notifying, telling, warning. **3** (*a notice informing someone of something*) advice, announcement, communication, declaration, information, intelligence, intimation, notice, statement.

notify *v.t.* **1** (*to give notice to, to inform* (*of or that*)) acquaint, advise, apprise, inform, let know, tell, warn. **2** (*to make known, to announce*) announce, broadcast, communicate, declare, disclose, divulge, make known, publish, reveal. ANTONYMS: conceal, hush up, keep secret.

notion *n.* **1** (*an idea, a conception*) belief, concept, conception, conviction, hypothesis, idea, impression, opinion, theory, thought, understanding, view. **2** (*an inclination or whim*) caprice, desire, fancy, impulse, inclination, whim, wish.

notional *a.* (*abstract, hypothetical*) abstract, conceptual, fanciful, hypothetical, ideal, illusory, imaginary, speculative, suppositional, theoretical, unreal, unsubstantiated, visionary. ANTONYMS: actual, real.

notoriety *n.* (*the state of being notorious*) bad name, bad reputation, dishonour, disrepute, ill repute, infamy, obloquy, opprobrium.

notorious *a.* (*widely or commonly known for something bad*) dishonourable, disreputable, ill-famed, infamous, of ill repute. ANTONYMS: eminent, famous.

notwithstanding *prep.* (*in spite of, despite*) despite, in spite of, regardless of.
~*adv.* (*nevertheless; in spite of this*) be that as it may, even so, for all that, however, in any event, in spite of that, just the same, nevertheless, nonetheless, still, yet.

nought *n.* (*zero*) love, naught, nil, nothing, zero, (*sl.*) zilch. ANTONYMS: something.

nourish *v.t.* **1** (*to feed, to sustain*) feed, nurture, provide for, support, sustain. **2** (*to cherish, to nurse*) cherish, encourage, foster, nurse, promote.

nourishing *a.* (*providing nourishment*) beneficial, good for one, health-giving, healthy, nutritious, nutritive, wholesome.

nourishment *n.* (*food, sustenance*) aliment, food, nutriment, nutrition, provisions, subsistence, sustenance.

nouveau riche *n.* (*a person who has recently acquired wealth but who has not acquired good taste or manners*) arriviste, parvenu(e).

novel *n.* (*a long written story about imaginary people and events*) book, narrative, romance, story, tale, work of fiction.
~*a.* **1** (*new, fresh*) fresh, ground-breaking, innovative, new, original, trailblazing. ANTONYMS: ancient, old, stale. **2** (*unusual, strange*) different, rare, singular, strange, uncommon, unfamiliar, unusual. ANTONYMS: common, ordinary, run-of-the-mill.

novelist n. (*a writer of novels*) author, creative writer, writer.

novelty n. 1 (*newness, freshness*) freshness, innovation, innovativeness, newness, originality. ANTONYMS: age, oldness, staleness. 2 (*something new*) new event, new experience, novel event, something new, strange experience. 3 (*a cheap, unusual object, sold as a gift or souvenir*) bauble, curiosity, knick-knack, memento, souvenir, trifle, trinket.

novice n. (*an inexperienced person, a beginner*) apprentice, beginner, greenhorn, learner, neophyte, newcomer, novitiate, probationer, proselyte, raw recruit, (*sl.*) rookie, trainee, tyro.

now adv. 1 (*at the present time*) at present, at the moment, at the present time, at this moment in time, at this time, just now, right now. ANTONYMS: at that time, then. 2 (*at once, immediately*) at once, forthwith, immediately, instantly, right away, right now, straight away, without delay. **now and again** (*from time to time, now and then*) every once in a while, from time to time, occasionally, once in a while, periodically, sometimes. ANTONYMS: all the time, frequently.

nowadays adv. (*at the present time; in these days*) at the present time, in this day and age, now, these days, today. ANTONYMS: then.

noxious a. (*harmful, unwholesome*) damaging, deadly, deleterious, destructive, detrimental, harmful, hurtful, injurious, insalubrious, malignant, noisome, pernicious, poisonous, ruinous, toxic, unhealthy, unwholesome. ANTONYMS: harmless, healthy, safe, wholesome.

nuance n. (*a fine distinction between feelings, opinions etc.*) degree, fine distinction, gradation, hint, shade, shading, slight difference, subtlety, suggestion, suspicion.

nub n. (*a tangle, a knot*) bulge, bump, knob, knot, lump, node.

nucleus n. (*a central part about which aggregation or growth goes on*) centre, core, focus, gist, heart, kernel, marrow, meat, nub, pith, pivot.

nude a. (*naked, unclothed*) bare, (*esp. N Am., sl.*) buck naked, disrobed, exposed, (*coll.*) in one's birthday suit, (*coll.*) in the altogether, (*coll.*) in the buff, in the nude, (*coll.*) in the raw, naked, (*sl.*) starkers, stark naked, stripped, unclothed, undressed, (*coll.*) without a stitch on. ANTONYMS: clothed, dressed, fully clothed.

nudge v.t. (*to push gently, esp. with the elbow*) bump, dig, elbow, jab, jog, poke, prod, push, shove.

nudity n. (*the state of being nude*) bareness, nakedness, state of undress.

nugget n. (*a lump of metal, esp. of gold*) chunk, hunk, lump, mass, piece.

nuisance n. (*anything that annoys or troubles*) annoyance, bother, disadvantage, (*sl.*) drag, handicap, (*coll.*) hassle, inconvenience, irritant, irritation, pest, plague, problem, thorn in the flesh, thorn in the side, trial, tribulation, trouble, vexation, worry.

null a. (*having no legal force or validity*) annulled, cancelled, invalid, null and void, nullified, repealed, rescinded, void. ANTONYMS: in force.

nullify v.t. 1 (*to make void*) countermand, negate, neutralize, reverse. 2 (*to annul, to invalidate*) abolish, abrogate, annul, cancel, countermand, declare null and void, invalidate, negate, quash, render null and void, renounce, repeal, rescind, reverse, revoke, set aside, terminate, veto, void. ANTONYMS: ratify.

numb a. (*deprived of sensation and motion*) anaesthetized, benumbed, dead, deadened, devoid of feelings, frozen, immobilized, insentient, paralysed, torpid, unresponsive, without feeling, without sensation. ANTONYMS: responsive, sentient.

~v.t. (*to benumb, to paralyse*) anaesthetize, benumb, chill, deaden, dull, freeze, immobilize, paralyse.

number n. 1 (*a word or symbol representing a quantity, a numeral*) character, cipher, digit, figure, integer, numeral, symbol, unit. 2 (*a sum or aggregate of people, things or abstract units*) aggregate, sum, tally, total. 3 (*one of a numbered series, for example a single issue of a periodical*) copy, edition, imprint, issue, printing. 4 (*multitude, numerical preponderance*) amount, collection, crowd, group, many, quantity, several. 5 (*a song or piece of music forming part of a popular musician's act or repertoire*) item, piece, piece of music, song, tune, turn.

~v.t. 1 (*to count; to ascertain the number of*) add, add up, assess, calculate, compute, count, enumerate, reckon, tell, total, tot up. 2 (*to assign a number to, to distinguish with a number*) assign a number to, categorize by number, give a number to, specify a number for. 3 (*to include, to comprise (among etc.)*) count, include, reckon. **without number** (*too many to be counted*) countless, endless, infinite, innumerable, many, multitudinous, myriad, numberless, numerous, untold. ANTONYMS: few.

numbness n. (*a lack of feeling; state of being*

numb) chill, deadness, immobility, lack of feeling, lack of responsiveness, lack of sensation, paralysis, sentience, torpor. ANTONYMS: insentience, responsiveness.

numeral *n.* (*a word, symbol or group of symbols denoting number*) character, cipher, digit, integer, number, symbol, unit.

numerous *a.* (*many in number*) a great deal of, (*coll.*) a lot of, innumerable, (*coll.*) lots of, many, quite a few, several. ANTONYMS: few.

nunnery *n.* (*a religious home for nuns*) cloister, convent.

nuptial *a.* (*of or relating to a wedding*) bridal, conjugal, connubial, marital, marriage, matrimonial, wedding.

nuptials *n.pl.* (*a wedding*) marriage, marriage ceremony, wedding ceremony.

nurse *n.* (*a person employed to look after young children*) children's nurse, nanny, nursemaid, nursery nurse.
~*v.t.* **1** (*to look after* (*a sick person*)) attend to, care for, look after, minister to, take care of, tend, treat. **2** (*to suckle; to feed* (*an infant*)) breast-feed, feed, suckle. **3** (*to foster, to promote growth in*) advance, aid, assist, boost, contribute to, cultivate, develop, encourage, forward, foster, further, help, nurture, promote, stimulate, support. ANTONYMS: discourage, hinder, impede. **4** (*to cherish, to brood over*) cherish, entertain, foster, harbour, have, hold, keep alive, sustain.

nursery *n.* **1** (*a room set apart for young children*) baby's room, children's room, playroom. **2** (*a day nursery or nursery school*) crèche, day-care centre, kindergarten, nursery school, playgroup, play school.

nurture *n.* **1** (*the act of bringing up, training*) bringing up, education, rearing, training, upbringing. **2** (*nourishment*) food, nourishment, nutriment, nutrition, subsistence, sustenance. **3** (*active encouragement to help the development of something*) advancement, assistance, boosting, cultivation, development, encouragement, forwarding, fostering, furthering, helping, nursing, promotion, stimulation, support. ANTONYMS: discouragement, hindering, hindrance, impediment, impeding, obstructing, obstruction.
~*v.t.* **1** (*to nourish*) feed, give nourishment to, nourish, provide for, sustain. **2** (*to rear, to train*) bring up, care for, educate, rear, train. **3** (*to help the development of*) advance, aid, assist, boost, contribute to, cultivate, develop, encourage, forward, foster, further, help, nurse, promote, stimulate, support. ANTONYMS: discourage, hinder, impede.

nut *n.* **1** (*the fruit of certain trees, containing a kernel in a hard shell*) kernel, stone. **2 a** (*a crazy or eccentric person*) (*sl.*) crackpot, (*coll.*) head case, (*sl.*) loony, lunatic, madman, maniac, (*sl.*) nutcase, (*sl.*) nutter, psycho, psychopath, (*sl.*) weirdo. **b** (*a fanatic*) aficionado, (*sl.*) buff, devotee, enthusiast, fan, (*sl.*) follower, freak. **nuts and bolts** (*the basic essential facts*) basics, details, essentials, fundamentals, (*coll.*) nitty-gritty, practicalities.

nutrition *n.* (*nourishment, food*) aliment, food, nourishment, nutriment, subsistence, sustenance.

nutritious *a.* (*affording nourishment, efficient as food*) beneficial, good for one, healthful, health-giving, healthy, nourishing, nutritive, strengthening, wholesome. ANTONYMS: unhealthy, unwholesome.

nuzzle *v.t.* **1** (*to rub or press the nose against*) nose, nudge, prod, push. **2** (*to fondle*) cuddle, fondle, pet.
~*v.i.* (*to nestle, to hide the head, as a child in its mother's bosom*) burrow, (*coll., esp. N Am.*) cosy up, nestle, snuggle.

nymph *n.* (*any one of a class of mythological youthful female divinities inhabiting groves, the sea etc.*) dryad, naiad, oread, sprite, sylph.

O

oaf *n.* (*a silly, stupid person*) (*sl.*) airhead, (*sl.*) berk, clod, (*sl.*) dickhead, (*sl.*) dipstick, dolt, dunce, fool, halfwit, idiot, imbecile, (*sl.*) jerk, lout, moron, (*sl.*) nerd, (*coll.*) nitwit, (*sl.*) plonker, (*sl.*) prat, (*coll.*) twit, (*sl.*) wally.

oath *n.* **1** (*a solemn appeal to God or some revered person or thing, in witness of the truth of a statement or of the binding nature of a promise*) affirmation, avowal, bond, pledge, plight, promise, vow, word. **2** (*a profane imprecation or expletive*) blasphemy, curse, expletive, imprecation, malediction, obscenity, profanity, swear word.

obdurate *a.* **1** (*stubborn*) adamant, dogged, firm, fixed, headstrong, immovable, inexorable, inflexible, iron, obstinate, perverse, pigheaded, relentless, stiff-necked, stubborn, unbending, unimpressible, unrelenting, unshakeable, unyielding. ANTONYMS: flexible, tractable. **2** (*hardened in heart, esp. against moral influence*) callous, cold, hardened, hard-hearted, harsh, insensitive, unfeeling.

obedient *a.* (*doing what one is told to do*) acquiescent, agreeable, amenable, biddable, compliant, deferential, docile, dutiful, lawabiding, observant, passive, pliant, regardful, respectful, submissive, subservient, timid, tractable, well-trained, yielding. ANTONYMS: disobedient, disrespectful.

obeisance *n.* **1** (*a bow or any gesture signifying submission, respect or salutation*) bow, curtsy, genuflection. **2** (*homage*) deference, homage, honour, respect, reverence, salutation, submission, worship. ANTONYMS: disrespect.

obese *a.* (*excessively fat, corpulent*) chubby, corpulent, fat, fleshy, gross, heavy, outsize, overweight, paunchy, plump, podgy, portly, pot-bellied, rotund, stout, tubby, (*facet.*) wellupholstered. ANTONYMS: lean, thin.

obey *v.t.* **1** (*to perform or carry out (a command or direction)*) act upon, carry out, discharge, do, effect, execute, fulfil, meet, perform, satisfy, serve. **2** (*to yield to the direction or control of*) bend to, bow to, give in to, give way to, knuckle under, submit to, succumb to, surrender to, toe the line, yield to. ANTONYMS: defy, disobey. **3** (*to act according to*) abide by, adhere to, comply with, conform to, embrace,

follow, heed, mind, observe. ANTONYMS: disregard, ignore.

object[1] *v.t.* (*to oppose*) argue against, demur, expostulate, oppose, protest, remonstrate, take exception to. ANTONYMS: accept, concur with.

object[2] *n.* **1** (*a material thing*) article, body, entity, fact, item, thing. **2** (*an aim, ultimate purpose*) aim, design, end, goal, idea, intent, motive, objective, point, purpose, reason.

objection *n.* **1** (*the act of objecting*) censure, dissent, opposition. ANTONYMS: agreement, endorsement. **2** (*an adverse reason or statement*) argument, challenge, demur, doubt, exception, expostulation, grievance, protest, remonstrance, scruple. **3** (*disapproval, dislike*) antipathy, disapproval, dislike.

objectionable *a.* **1** (*liable to objection, reprehensible*) blamable, regrettable, reprehensible. **2** (*offensive, unpleasant*) abhorrent, abominable, deplorable, detestable, disagreeable, displeasing, distasteful, exceptionable, intolerable, loathsome, obnoxious, odious, offensive, repugnant, repulsive, shameful, unacceptable, undesirable, unpleasant, unseemly, unsufferable. ANTONYMS: agreeable, pleasant.

objective *a.* **1** (*real, self-existent*) actual, existent, external, real, self-existent, substantive, true. ANTONYMS: abstract, theoretical. **2** (*uninfluenced by emotion, prejudice etc.*) detached, disinterested, dispassionate, equitable, even-handed, external, fair, impartial, impersonal, just, neutral, open-minded, unbiased, uncoloured, unemotional, uninvolved, unprejudiced. ANTONYMS: biased, prejudiced, subjective.
~*n.* (*an aim or target*) aim, ambition, aspiration, design, end, goal, hope, intention, mark, object, purpose, target.

obligation *n.* **1** (*a duty, responsibility*) accountability, burden, charge, commitment, compulsion, debt, demand, duty, liability, onus, requirement, responsibility, trust. **2** (*Law*) (*a binding agreement*) agreement, bond, contract, covenant, engagement, promise, understanding.

obligatory *a.* (*compulsory*) binding, coercive, compulsory, demanded, enforced, essential, imperative, incumbent, indispensable, mandatory, necessary, required, unavoidable. ANTONYMS: optional, voluntary.

oblige *v.t.* **1** (*to constrain by legal, moral or physical force*) bind, coerce, compel, constrain, demand, dragoon, force, impel, make, necessitate, obligate, require. **2** (*to do a favour to, to gratify*) accommodate, benefit, cater to, do (someone) a favour, gratify, help, indulge, please, serve. ANTONYMS: disoblige, put out.

obliging *a.* **1** (*kind, complaisant*) agreeable, amenable, amiable, amicable, civil, complaisant, considerate, courteous, friendly, good-natured, gracious, indulgent, kind, polite, willing. ANTONYMS: disagreeable, unfriendly. **2** (*helpful, accommodating*) accommodating, cooperative, helpful, supportive. ANTONYMS: unhelpful, unobliging.

oblique *a.* **1** (*deviating from the vertical or horizontal*) angled, askew, aslant, banked, canted, crooked, diagonal, divergent, inclined, sidelong, slanted, sloped, tilted. **2** (*evasive, not to the point*) circuitous, circumlocutory, evasive, indirect, roundabout. ANTONYMS: direct, straightforward.

obliterate *v.t.* **1** (*to efface, to erase*) cancel, delete, efface, eliminate, eradicate, erase, expunge, rub out, rule out, strike out, wipe out, write off. ANTONYMS: create, restore. **2** (*to wear out, to destroy*) annihilate, blot out, destroy, eliminate, eradicate, exterminate, extirpate, kill, wear out, wipe out.

oblivion *n.* **1** (*forgetfulness, unawareness*) abeyance, disregard, forgetfulness, heedlessness, insensibility, neglect, obliviousness, unawareness, unconsciousness. ANTONYMS: awareness, sensibility. **2** (*the state of being forgotten*) anonymity, darkness, eclipse, extinction, limbo, obscurity, void. **3** (*an amnesty*) amnesty, pardon.

oblivious *a.* **1** (*forgetful* (*of*)) forgetful, forgetting. **2** (*unaware* (*of*), *paying no heed* (*to*)) blind (to), careless (of), deaf (to), disregardful (of), heedless (of), ignorant (of), inattentive (to), insensible (of), neglectful (of), negligent (of), unaware (of), unconcerned (about), unconscious (of), unmindful (of), unobservant (of). ANTONYMS: attentive (to), mindful (of). **3** (*lost in thought or abstraction*) absent-minded, abstracted, lost in thought, removed.

obloquy *n.* **1** (*censorious language*) abuse, aspersion, attack, blame, calumny, censure, criticism, defamation, detraction, invective, opprobrium, reproach, slander, vilification. ANTONYMS: praise. **2** (*discredit, disgrace*) discredit, disgrace, dishonour, humiliation,

ignominy, ill repute, infamy, odium, shame. ANTONYMS: glory, honour.

obnoxious *a.* (*offensive, objectionable*) abhorrent, abominable, detestable, disgusting, distasteful, execrable, foul, hateful, loathsome, nasty, nauseating, objectionable, odious, offensive, repellent, repugnant, repulsive, revolting, sickening, vile. ANTONYMS: agreeable, pleasant.

obscene *a.* (*indecent, disgusting*) (*sl.*) blue, coarse, degenerate, dirty, disgusting, filthy, foul, immoral, improper, impure, indecent, lewd, licentious, offensive, pornographic, prurient, rude, salacious, smutty, suggestive. ANTONYMS: decent, respectable.

obscure *a.* **1** (*dark, dim*) dark, dim, dingy, dismal, dull, gloomy, sombre. ANTONYMS: bright. **2** (*not clear, indistinct*) blurred, cloudy, dusky, hazy, indefinite, indistinct, murky, nebulous, obfuscated, opaque, shadowy, shady, tenebrous, unclear, vague. ANTONYMS: clear, distinct. **3** (*abstruse*) abstruse, ambiguous, arcane, deep, esoteric, intricate, involved, recondite. **4** (*difficult to understand*) impenetrable, incomprehensible, unfathomable. ANTONYMS: comprehensible, intelligible. **5** (*unexplained, doubtful*) baffling, confusing, cryptic, doubtful, enigmatic, mysterious, mystifying, occult, perplexing, puzzling, unexplained. **6** (*hidden, remote from public observation*) hidden, remote, secluded, veiled. ANTONYMS: conspicuous. **7** (*unknown, lowly*) anonymous, humble, inconsequential, inconspicuous, inglorious, insignificant, lowly, mean, minor, nameless, undistinguished, unheard-of, unimportant, unknown, unseen, unsung. ANTONYMS: famous, well-known.

~*v.t.* **1** (*to make dark, to cloud*) cloud, darken. **2** (*to make less intelligible or visible*) blur, confuse, muddy, obfuscate. ANTONYMS: clarify. **3** (*to dim, to throw into the shade*) block out, dim, dull, eclipse, mask, outshine, overshadow, shade, shroud. **4** (*to conceal*) cloak, conceal, cover, disguise, hide, screen, veil.

obsequious *a.* (*fawning, over-ready to comply with the desires of others*) abject, crawling, cringing, deferential, fawning, flattering, grovelling, ingratiating, menial, servile, slavish, slimy, smarmy, submissive, subservient, sycophantic, toadying, unctuous. ANTONYMS: critical, independent.

observance *n.* **1** (*the act of observing, complying with etc.*) adherence, attention, carrying out, discharge, examination, execution, fulfilment, heeding, honouring, inspection, observation, performance, regard, respect, scrutiny. ANTONYMS: disregard, non-observance. **2** (*a* *customary rite or ceremony*) celebration, cere-monial, ceremony, rite, ritual, service. **3** (*a rule or practice*) convention, custom, fashion, form, practice, rule, tradition, usage. **4** (*respectful submission, deference*) attention, compliance, deference, obedience, submission.

observant *a.* (*watchful, attentive*) alert, attent-ive, aware, eagle-eyed, heedful, keen, mindful, obedient, perceptive, quick, sharp-eyed, sub-missive, vigilant, watchful. ANTONYMS: in-attentive, unobservant.

observation *n.* **1** (*the act or faculty of ob-serving*) attention, cognition, consideration, inspection, monitoring, notice, review, scrutiny, surveillance, survey, viewing, watch-ing. ANTONYMS: inattention. **2** (*scientific watch-ing and noting of phenomena as they occur*) analysis, examination, study. **3** (*a fact scientif-ically noted or taken from an instrument*) finding, result. **4** (*experience and knowledge gained by systematic observing*) experience, information, knowledge. **5** (*a remark, an in-cidental comment or reflection*) comment, declaration, expression, note, opinion, pro-nouncement, reflection, remark, statement, thought, utterance.

observe *v.t.* **1** (*to regard attentively, to take notice of*) detect, discern, discover, espy, mark, note, notice, perceive, regard, see, spot, wit-ness. **2** (*to watch, to scrutinize*) check, check out, contemplate, examine, (*esp. N Am., sl.*) eyeball, keep an eye on, look at, monitor, pay attention to, scrutinize, study, survey, view, watch. **3** (*to follow attentively, to heed*) follow, heed, mind. **4** (*to perform duly*) accomplish, fulfil, perform. **5** (*to comply with*) abide by, adhere to, comply, conform to, honour, keep, obey, respect. ANTONYMS: disregard, ignore. **6** (*to celebrate*) celebrate, commemorate, hon-our, keep, mark, remember, solemnize. **7** (*to remark, to express as an opinion*) comment, de-clare, express, mention, note, reflect, remark, say, state, utter.

observer *n.* (*a person who observes*) beholder, bystander, commentator, eyewitness, looker-on, onlooker, spectator, spotter, viewer, watcher, witness.

obsess *v.t.* **1** (*to beset, to trouble* (*as an evil spirit*)) bedevil, beset, harass, haunt, plague, torment, trouble. **2** (*to preoccupy the mind of* (*as a fixed idea*)) consume, dominate, engross, grip, hold, monopolize, possess, preoccupy, rule.

obsession *n.* ((*the condition of having*) *an unhealthily deep-rooted or persistent fixa-tion*) complex, compulsion, conviction, enthusiasm, fetish, fixation, (*coll.*) hang-up,

infatuation, mania, passion, phobia, pre-occupation, (*coll.*) thing.

obsolete *a.* **1** (*passed out of use, no longer current*) anachronistic, defunct, discontinued, disused, extinct, superseded. ANTONYMS: cur-rent. **2** (*discarded, out of date*) ancient, an-tiquated, antique, archaic, bygone, dated, dead, discarded, old, old-fashioned, out-moded, out of date, outworn, passé, super-annuated. ANTONYMS: contemporary, up to date.

obstacle *n.* (*an impediment, an obstruction*) bar, barrier, block, blockage, catch, check, dif-ficulty, hindrance, hitch, hurdle, impediment, interference, interruption, obstruction, snag, stumbling-block. ANTONYMS: assistance, help.

obstinate *a.* (*stubbornly adhering to one's opinion or purpose*) adamant, contrary, deter-mined, dogged, immovable, inflexible, in-tractable, intransigent, obdurate, persistent, pertinacious, pig-headed, recalcitrant, refract-ory, self-willed, single-minded, steadfast, strong-minded, stubborn, tenacious. ANTO-NYMS: amenable, compliant.

obstreperous *a.* **1** (*noisy, clamorous*) clamorous, loud, noisy, rackety, raucous. **2** (*boisterous, unruly*) boisterous, disorderly, irrepressible, out of control, riotous, roister-ous, rowdy, rumbustious, tempestuous, tumul-tuous, turbulent, uncontrolled, undisciplined, unmanageable, unrestrained, unruly, up-roarious, vociferous, wild. ANTONYMS: calm, orderly.

obstruct *v.t.* **1** (*to block up, to close by means of obstacles*) block, bung, choke, close. **2** (*to hinder, to impede*) delay, hinder, hold up, im-pede, stall, stay. **3** (*to hamper, to stop*) arrest, bar, barricade, check, clog, curb, forbid, frus-trate, halt, hamper, inhibit, interrupt, prevent, prohibit, restrict, retard, shut off, slow, stop, thwart. ANTONYMS: advance, further.

obstruction *n.* (*something that blocks or hinders progress*) bar, barricade, barrier, block, blockage, catch, check, constraint, difficulty, hindrance, hitch, hurdle, impediment, ob-stacle, restriction, snag, stop, stoppage. ANTO-NYMS: assistance, help.

obtain *v.t.* **1** (*to gain, to acquire*) achieve, ac-quire, capture, come by, earn, gain, get, grasp, secure, seize. ANTONYMS: give up, lose. **2** (*to procure, to get*) buy, get, procure, purchase. ~*v.i.* (*to be prevalent or accepted*) be prevalent, exist, hold sway, prevail.

obtrusive *a.* **1** (*thrusting oneself forward*) forceful, forward, importunate, interfer-ing, intrusive, meddlesome, nosy, officious, presumptuous, prying, (*coll.*) pushy. ANTO-NYMS: diffident, retiring. **2** (*noticeable, esp. in an unpleasant way*) blatant, conspicuous, noticeable, obvious, prominent, protuberant, sticking out. ANTONYMS: inconspicuous, unobtrusive.

obtuse *a.* **1** (*blunt*) blunt, rounded. ANTONYMS: acute, pointed. **2** (*stupid, slow of apprehension*) (*sl.*) boneheaded, dense, dimwitted, dull, (*coll.*) dumb, insensitive, loutish, oafish, retarded, slow, stolid, stupid, thick, uncomprehending, unintelligent. ANTONYMS: astute, shrewd.

obvious *a.* **1** (*plain to the eye, immediately evident*) apparent, clear, conspicuous, distinct, evident, indisputable, manifest, noticeable, open, ostensible, palpable, patent, perceptible, plain, self-evident, straightforward, transparent, undisguised, unmistakable, visible. ANTONYMS: ambiguous, obscure. **2** (*unsubtle*) blatant, glaring, overt, unsubtle. ANTONYMS: understated.

occasion *n.* **1** (*an event, circumstance or position of affairs*) circumstance, event, incident, moment, occurrence, time. **2** (*reason, need*) call, cause, excuse, ground, incitement, inducement, influence, justification, motive, need, provocation, reason. **3** (*an opportunity*) chance, opening, opportunity, window. **4** (*an incidental or immediate cause*) cause, condition. **5** (*an event, esp. of special importance*) affair, celebration, ceremony, event, experience, function, happening, occurrence, party.
~*v.t.* (*to cause directly or indirectly*) bring about, bring on, call forth, cause, create, effect, elicit, engender, evoke, generate, give rise to, impel, induce, inspire, lead to, move, originate, produce, prompt, provoke. ANTONYMS: prevent.

occasional *a.* **1** (*happening or done as opportunity arises*) chance, opportunistic. **2** (*irregular, infrequent*) casual, desultory, incidental, infrequent, intermittent, irregular, odd, periodic, random, rare, sporadic, uncommon. ANTONYMS: frequent, regular. **3** (*of or made for a special occasion*) ceremonial, particular, ritual, special.

occasionally *adv.* (*sometimes, not regularly*) at intervals, at times, every so often, from time to time, infrequently, intermittently, irregularly, now and again, now and then, off and on, on and off, once in a while, periodically, rarely, seldom, sometimes, sporadically, uncommonly. ANTONYMS: often, regularly.

occult *a.* **1** (*supernatural, mystical*) alchemical, cabbalistic, magical, mystical, supernatural. **2** (*kept secret, esoteric*) arcane, concealed, esoteric, hidden, invisible, obscure, private,

secret, shrouded, unrevealed, veiled. ANTO-NYMS: evident, plain. **3** (*mysterious, beyond the range of ordinary knowledge or perception*) inexplicable, mysterious, perplexing, puzzling, recondite, unexplained, unfathomable, unknown.
~*n.* (*the supernatural*) black arts, black magic, cabbalism, mysticism, sorcery, supernatural, unknown, witchcraft.

occupant *n.* **1** (*a person who resides or is in a place*) addressee, denizen, dweller, householder, incumbent, inhabitant, inmate, occupier, resident. **2** (*a tenant in possession as distinct from an owner*) boarder, leaseholder, lessee, lodger, roomer, tenant. **3** (*a person who establishes a claim by taking possession*) holder, owner.

occupation *n.* **1** (*the act of occupying or taking possession (e.g. of a country by a foreign army)*) appropriation, bondage, conquest, invasion, oppression, rule, seizure, subjection, subjugation. **2** (*occupancy, tenure*) control, holding, occupancy, possession, residence, tenancy, tenure, use. **3** (*employment, job*) activity, appointment, business, calling, career, craft, employment, field, job, line, position, post, profession, pursuit, situation, trade, vocation, work.

occupy *v.t.* **1** (*to take possession of*) capture, conquer, garrison, grab, invade, overrun, seize, take over, take possession of. ANTONYMS: abandon, desert. **2** (*to hold in possession, to be the tenant of*) hold, own, possess, tenant. **3** (*to reside in, to be in*) be in, dwell in, inhabit, live in, reside in. **4** (*to take up, to fill*) cover, fill, permeate, pervade, take up, use, utilize. **5** (*to employ, to engage (oneself)*) absorb, amuse, beguile, busy, distract, divert, employ, engage, engross, immerse, interest, involve, preoccupy, tie up.

occur *v.i.* **1** (*to happen, to take place*) arise, befall, betide, chance, come about, come to pass, crop up, develop, happen, materialize, result, surface, take place, transpire, turn up. **2** (*to be found, to exist*) appear, exist, manifest. **3** (*to present itself to the mind*) come to mind, dawn on, enter one's head, hit, spring to mind, strike one, suggest itself.

occurrence *n.* **1** (*an event, an incident*) adventure, affair, circumstance, episode, event, experience, happening, incident, instance, matter, occasion, phenomenon, proceeding, transaction. **2** (*the happening or taking place of anything*) appearance, development, existence, happening, manifestation, materialization.

ocean *n.* (*the sea*) (*coll.*) briny, (*sl.*) Davy

Jones's locker, deep, depths, (*coll.*) drink, main, sea.

odd *a.* **1** (*not even, not divisible by two*) uneven. ANTONYMS: even. **2** (*lacking a match or pair*) lone, remaining, single, solitary, spare, surplus, unmatched, unpaired. **3** (*strange, eccentric*) abnormal, anomalous, atypical, bizarre, curious, eccentric, exceptional, extraordinary, fantastic, freakish, funny, irregular, peculiar, queer, singular, strange, uncanny, uncommon, unusual, weird. ANTONYMS: normal, usual. **4** (*occasional, casual*) casual, fragmentary, incidental, irregular, miscellaneous, occasional, periodic, random, seasonal, sporadic, sundry, varied, various. **5** (*ellipt.*) (*approximately* (*used after a number, as two hundred odd*)) approximately, give or take, or more, roughly.

odds and ends *n.pl.* (*miscellaneous remnants, scraps etc.*) bits, bits and pieces, fragments, (*coll.*) odds and sods, remnants, scraps, snippets.

odious *a.* (*hateful, repulsive*) abhorrent, abominable, detestable, disgusting, execrable, foul, hateful, horrible, horrid, loathsome, objectionable, obnoxious, obscene, offensive, repugnant, repulsive, revolting, unpleasant, vile. ANTONYMS: pleasant.

odour *n.* **1** (*a smell, whether pleasant or unpleasant*) aroma, smell. **2** (*scent, fragrance*) bouquet, essence, fragrance, perfume, redolence, scent. **3** (*a bad smell*) fetor, (*coll.*) niff, reek, smell, stench, stink. **4** (*repute, esteem*) esteem, favour, repute.

off *adv.* **1** (*away, at a distance or to a distance in space or time*) afar, apart, aside, away, elsewhere, out. **2** (*to the end, completely*) completely, to the end.
~*a.* **1** (*more distant, further*) distant, further, remote. ANTONYMS: near. **2** (*beginning to decay*) bad, mouldy, rancid, rotten, sour. **3** (*right, as opposed to left*) driver's side, right. **4** (*removed or aside from the main street etc., divergent*) aside, divergent, removed, subsidiary. **5** (*unacceptable, unfair*) unacceptable, unfair, unjust.

offence *n.* **1** (*the act of offending, an aggressive act*) assault, attack, offensive. ANTONYMS: defence. **2** (*an affront, an insult*) affront, harm, hurt, indignity, injury, injustice, insult, outrage, put-down, slight, snub. **3** (*the state or a sense of being hurt or annoyed*) anger, annoyance, displeasure, indignation, irritation, resentment, umbrage, wrath. **4** (*a transgression, an illegal act*) breach, crime, delinquency, dereliction, error, fault, felony, infringement, lapse, misdeed, misdemeanour, sin, slip, transgression, trespass, violation, wrong.

offend *v.t.* **1** (*to wound the feelings of, to hurt*) hurt, insult, pain, slight, snub, upset, wound. **2** (*to make angry, to cause displeasure in*) affront, aggravate, anger, annoy, disgruntle, disgust, displease, gall, irritate, outrage, (*taboo sl.*) piss off, provoke, put down, rile, vex. ANTONYMS: appease, pacify.
~*v.i.* **1** (*to transgress or violate a law*) break the law, transgress, violate. **2** (*to cause anger, disgust etc.*) anger, disgust, nauseate, repel, repulse, scandalize, sicken.

offender *n.* (*a person who does wrong or is guilty of a crime*) criminal, (*coll.*) crook, culprit, delinquent, lawbreaker, malefactor, miscreant, outlaw, sinner, transgressor, villain, wrongdoer.

offensive *a.* **1** (*relating to or used for attack, aggressive*) aggressive, attacking, hostile, invading. ANTONYMS: inoffensive. **2** (*causing or meant to cause offence*) abusive, antagonistic, combative, contentious, detestable, discourteous, impertinent, insolent, insulting, objectionable, provocative, quarrelsome, rude, uncivil, unmannerly. ANTONYMS: respectful. **3** (*annoying*) annoying, irritating, vexing. **4** (*disagreeable, repulsive*) abominable, detestable, disagreeable, disgusting, grisly, loathsome, nasty, nauseating, noisome, obnoxious, odious, repellent, repulsive, revolting, sickening, unpalatable, unpleasant, unsavoury, vile, (*coll.*) yucky. ANTONYMS: agreeable, pleasant.
~*n.* (*a strategic attack*) assault, attack, drive, incursion, invasion, offence, onslaught, (*Mil.*) push.

offer *v.t.* **1** (*to present, to tender for acceptance or refusal*) extend, give, hold out, present, put forward, tender. ANTONYMS: retract, revoke. **2** (*to sacrifice, to immolate*) dedicate, immolate, present, sacrifice. **3** (*to propose*) advance, propose, put forward, submit, suggest. **4** (*to attempt*) attempt, essay, try. **5** (*to make available for sale*) proffer, put on the market, put up for sale, tender.
~*v.i.* (*to present or show itself*) appear, occur, present itself, show itself.
~*n.* **1** (*an act of offering*) offering, proffering. **2** (*a proposal, to be accepted or refused*) proffer, proposal, proposition, submission, suggestion, tender. **3** (*an attempt*) attempt, endeavour, essay, overture.

offering *n.* **1** (*a gift*) contribution, donation, gift, present. **2** (*a sacrifice*) oblation, sacrifice.

offhand *adv.* **1** (*without preparation or warning*) ad lib, extempore, impromptu, off the cuff, without warning. **2** (*casually, brusquely*) brusquely, casually, cursorily, curtly, incidentally, informally, summarily, superficially.

~*a.* **1** (*impromptu*) impromptu, informal. **2** (*casual*) careless, casual, cavalier, glib, nonchalant, superficial, unconcerned, uninterested. ANTONYMS: premeditated, responsible. **3** (*curt or brusque*) abrupt, aloof, brusque, cool, cursory, curt, distant, perfunctory, summary, unceremonious.

office *n.* **1** (*a room or other place where business is carried on*) area, bureau, room, workplace, workroom. **2** (*collect.*) (*the persons charged with business at a particular place*) organization, staff. **3** (*the duties or service attached to a particular post*) business, charge, chore, commission, duty, function, obligation, responsibility, service, task. **4** (*a post of trust or authority, esp. under a public body*) appointment, assignment, berth, capacity, job, place, position, post, role, situation. **5** (*a government department or agency*) agency, branch, department, division, section. **6** (*an act of worship of prescribed form, an act of kindness or duty*) duty, kindness, worship.

official *a.* **1** (*of or relating to an office or public duty*) ceremonial, conventional, established, formal, ritual. **2** (*duly authorized*) accredited, authorized, bona fide, certified, endorsed, formal, legitimate, licensed, proper, sanctioned. ANTONYMS: unauthorized, unofficial.
~*n.* (*a person who holds a public office*) agent, bureaucrat, dignitary, executive, functionary, officer, representative.

officious *a.* **1** (*aggressively interfering*) aggressive, demanding, dictatorial, interfering. **2** (*forward in doing or offering unwanted kindness*) bold, bustling, forward, impertinent, inquisitive, insistent, intrusive, meddling, mischievous, obtrusive, opinionated, overzealous, persistent, (*coll.*) pushy, self-important. ANTONYMS: reserved, shy.

offset *v.t.* **1** (*to balance by an equivalent*) balance out, cancel out. **2** (*to counterbalance, to compensate*) compensate, counteract, counterbalance, counterpoise, countervail, even out, make good, make up for, neutralize, recompense, redress, square.

offspring *n.* **1** (*issue, progeny*) brood, issue, progeny, scion, seed, spawn, young. **2** (*children, descendants*) children, descendants, family, fry, heirs, successors. ANTONYMS: ancestors, parents. **3** (*a result of any kind*) production, result.

often *adv.* (*frequently, many times*) again and again, day in day out, frequently, generally, many times, much, oft, oftentimes, over and over again, regularly, repeatedly, time after time, time and again, usually. ANTONYMS: infrequently, rarely, seldom.

oily *a.* **1** (*consisting of, covered with or like oil*) fatty, greasy, oiled, oleaginous, slimy, slippery, smeary, swimming. **2** (*smooth, insinuating*) flattering, fulsome, glib, hypocritical, insinuating, obsequious, servile, smarmy, smooth, sycophantic, unctuous, urbane.

ointment *n.* (*a soft unctuous preparation applied to diseased or injured parts or used as a cosmetic*) balm, cream, embrocation, emollient, liniment, lotion, salve, unguent.

OK *a.* (*quite correct, all right*) acceptable, adequate, agreed, all right, approved, convenient, correct, fine, good, mediocre, (*coll.*) okay, passable, permitted, satisfactory, (*coll.*) so so, tolerable. ANTONYMS: incorrect, unsatisfactory.
~*int.* (*all right*) all right, (*coll.*) okay, right, very well, yes.
~*v.t.* (*to authorize, to approve*) agree to, allow, approve, authorize, consent to, endorse, give the go-ahead to, pass, ratify, rubber stamp, sanction, support.
~*n.* (*approval, agreement*) agreement, approbation, approval, assent, authorization, consent, endorsement, go-ahead, (*coll.*) green light, permission, ratification, sanction, say-so, seal of approval.

old *a.* **1** (*advanced in years or long in existence*) advanced in years, aged, ancient, elderly, getting on, grey, grizzled, hoary, mature, (*coll.*) over the hill, (*coll.*) past it, senescent, senile, venerable. ANTONYMS: juvenile, young. **2** (*like an old person, experienced*) experienced, hardened, practised, thoughtful, veteran, vintage. ANTONYMS: inexperienced. **3** (*crafty, practised (at)*) adept (at), confirmed (in), crafty, cunning, expert (at), practised (at), proficient (in), skilled (in), versed (in). **4** (*decayed by process of time, dilapidated*) broken-down, crumbling, decayed, decrepit, dilapidated, disintegrated, ramshackle, timeworn, worn. **5** (*stale, trite*) done, hackneyed, stale, trite, unoriginal. **6** (*customary, wonted*) customary, habitual, usual, wonted. **7** (*obsolete, out of date*) antiquated, antique, dated, effete, obsolete, old-fashioned, outmoded, out of date, passé, superannuated, unfashionable. ANTONYMS: up to date. **8** (*made or established long ago, ancient*) aboriginal, ancient, archaic, bygone, immemorial, prehistoric, primeval, primitive, primordial, remote. **9** (*previous, former*) early, erstwhile, former, olden, onetime, previous.

old-fashioned *a.* (*out of date, outmoded*) ancient, antiquated, antique, archaic, corny, dated, fusty, obsolescent, obsolete, old hat, old-time, outdated, outmoded, out of date, passé, past, (*coll.*) square, stale, superannuated, unfashionable. ANTONYMS: contemporary, up to date.

omen *n.* **1** (*a sign taken as indicating a good or evil event or outcome*) augury, foreboding, foretoken, harbinger, indication, portent, premonition, sign, token, warning. **2** (*prophetic signification*) forecast, prediction, prognostication.

ominous *a.* **1** (*threatening, portending evil*) baleful, black, dark, fateful, forbidding, foreboding, gloomy, louring, menacing, portentous, sinister, threatening, unpromising. ANTONYMS: promising, reassuring. **2** (*inauspicious*) ill-starred, inauspicious, unlucky, unpropitious. ANTONYMS: auspicious.

omission *n.* **1** (*the act of omitting or fact of being omitted*) exception, exclusion, forgetfulness, neglect. ANTONYMS: inclusion. **2** (*something omitted*) default, failure, gap, lack, oversight, shortcoming.

omit *v.t.* **1** (*to leave out, not to include*) except, exclude, leave out, pass over, skip. ANTONYMS: include. **2** (*to neglect, to leave undone*) disregard, fail, forget, ignore, leave undone, let slide, neglect, overlook.

once *adv.* (*at some past time*) at one time, before, formerly, in the past, in times gone by, long ago, previously. ANTONYMS: now.

onerous *a.* (*heavy, troublesome*) arduous, burdensome, crushing, demanding, difficult, exacting, exhausting, formidable, grave, hard, heavy, laborious, oppressive, responsible, taxing, toilsome, troublesome, weighty. ANTONYMS: easy, undemanding.

one-sided *a.* (*favouring one side of an argument, topic etc.*) biased, bigoted, coloured, inequitable, lopsided, partial, partisan, prejudiced, unbalanced, unfair. ANTONYMS: even-handed, impartial.

onlooker *n.* (*a spectator, a person who looks on*) bystander, eyewitness, looker-on, observer, passer-by, spectator, viewer, watcher, witness.

only *a.* (*single or alone in its or their kind*) alone, exclusive, individual, lone, single, sole, solitary, unique.
~*adv.* (*solely, merely*) alone, barely, exclusively, just, merely, purely, simply, solely.

onset *n.* **1** (*an attack, an onslaught*) assault, attack, charge, onrush, onslaught, sortie, strike. **2** (*the beginning*) beginning, birth, commencement, genesis, inception, (*coll.*) kick-off, outbreak, outset, start. ANTONYMS: end, finish.

onus *n.* (*a duty or obligation*) burden, duty, liability, load, obligation, responsibility, task.

onward *adv.* (*towards the front or a point in advance*) ahead, beyond, forth, forward, in front, on.
~*a.* **1** (*moving or directed forward*) forward, ongoing, outward. **2** (*advancing*) advancing, progressing, progressive.

ooze *n.* **1** (*wet mud, slime*) mire, muck, mud, slime, sludge. **2** (*a gentle, sluggish flow, an exudation*) exudation, flow, seeping.
~*v.i.* **1** (*to flow or pass gently*) bleed, drain, dribble, drip, drop, flow, seep, trickle, weep. **2** (*to percolate* (*through the pores of a body etc.*)) drip, filter, leak, percolate, secrete, seep, sweat, trickle.
~*v.t.* (*to exude*) discharge, emit, exude.

opalescent *a.* (*characterized by a play of iridescent colours*) iridescent, lustrous, nacreous, opaline, pearly.

opaque *a.* **1** (*impervious to rays of light, not transparent*) blurred, clouded, cloudy, dark, dim, filmy, hazy, impenetrable, impermeable, lustreless, muddied, muddy, murky, obfuscated, smoky, turbid. ANTONYMS: clear, transparent. **2** (*obscure, unintelligible*) abstruse, ambiguous, baffling, cryptic, difficult, elusive, enigmatic, equivocal, incomprehensible, indefinite, mysterious, mystifying, obscure, perplexing, puzzling, unclear, unfathomable, unintelligible, vague. **3** (*obtuse, unintelligent*) backward, dense, dull, obtuse, slow, stupid, thick, unintelligent.

open *a.* **1** (*not closed, not obstructed*) unblocked, unenclosed, unobstructed. ANTONYMS: closed, obstructed. **2** (*affording passage or access*) accessible, available, free, general, public. **3** (*having any barrier, cover etc. removed or unfastened*) agape, ajar, gaping, unbarred, unbolted, unclosed, unfastened, unlatched, unlocked, unsealed, unshut, withdrawn, yawning. **4** (*uncovered, exposed*) airy, bare, exposed, uncovered, unsheltered. **5** (*unconcealed, manifest*) apparent, barefaced, blatant, downright, evident, flagrant, frank, manifest, noticeable, obvious, overt, plain, revealed, unconcealed, undisguised, visible. ANTONYMS: disguised, hidden. **6** (*unrestricted, not limited*) unlimited, unregulated, unrestrained, unrestricted. ANTONYMS: exclusive, limited. **7** (*liable, subject* (*to*)) exposed, liable, prone, subject, susceptible, vulnerable. ANTONYMS: invulnerable. **8** (*unoccupied, vacant*) empty, unfilled, unoccupied, vacant. **9** (*disengaged, free*) disengaged, free, uncommitted. **10** (*affording wide views*) expansive, rolling, spacious, sweeping, wide. **11** (*generous, *liberal*) bountiful, generous, liberal, magnanimous, munificent, prodigal. **12** (*frank, candid*) artless, candid, fair, frank, guileless, honest, ingenuous, innocent, natural, sincere, straightforward, transparent, unreserved. ANTONYMS: cunning, sly. **13** (*spread out, unfolded*) outspread, outstretched, spread out, unfolded, unfurled. **14** (*not decided; debatable*) arguable, debatable, moot, problematic, undecided, unresolved, unsettled. ANTONYMS: settled.

~*v.t.* **1** (*to make open*) break open, broach, push open. ANTONYMS: close, shut. **2** (*to unfasten, unlock*) undo, unfasten, unlock, unseal, untie. **3** (*to remove the covering from*) uncover, unwrap. **4** (*to unfold, spread out*) expand, spread out, unfold, unfurl, unroll. **5** (*to free from obstruction or restriction*) clear, crack, free, unbar, unblock, unclog, uncork, unobstruct. ANTONYMS: block, obstruct. **6** (*to reveal, to make public*) disclose, display, divulge, exhibit, expose, lay bare, publicize, reveal, show, uncover, unveil. **7** (*to widen, to enlarge*) develop, enlarge, widen. **8** (*to make a start in*) begin, commence, inaugurate, initiate, (*coll.*) kick off, launch, start. ANTONYMS: close, end.

~*v.i.* (*to crack, to gape*) come apart, crack, fissure, gape, rupture, separate, split.

opening *a.* (*beginning, first in order*) beginning, commencing, early, first, inaugural, initial, initiatory, introductory, maiden, primary. ANTONYMS: closing.

~*n.* **1** (*a gap, an aperture*) aperture, breach, break, chink, cleft, crack, crevice, fissure, gap, hole, orifice, perforation, pit, rent, rift, rupture, slot, space, split, vent. ANTONYMS: blockage, obstruction. **2** (*a beginning, the first part*) beginning, birth, commencement, dawn, inauguration, inception, initiation, (*coll.*) kick-off, launch, launching, onset, origin, outset, overture, preface, prelude, start. ANTONYMS: close, finish. **3** (*an opportunity*) (*coll.*) break, chance, foothold, (*coll.*) look-in, opportunity, place, vacancy, window.

open-minded *a.* (*accessible to ideas, unprejudiced*) broad-minded, candid, catholic, dispassionate, enlightened, fair, free, impartial, just, liberal, reasonable, receptive, tolerant, unbiased, undogmatic, unprejudiced, unreserved. ANTONYMS: bigoted, intolerant, narrow-minded.

operate *v.t.* **1** (*to work or control the working of*) control, use, work. **2** (*to manage, run (a business, an organization etc.*)) carry on, conduct, control, direct, handle, manage, manipulate, manoeuvre, ply, run.

~*v.i.* (*to work, to act*) act, function, go, perform, run, serve, work. ANTONYMS: break down, fail.

operation *n.* **1** (*the act or process of operating*) functioning, performance. **2** (*working, action*) action, exercise, motion, movement, procedure, process, use, working. **3** (*activity, performance of a function*) activity, function, handling, manipulation. **4** (*a planned campaign or series of military movements*) assault, campaign, exercise, manoeuvre, mission. **5** (*a commercial or financial transaction*) affair, business, deal, enterprise, proceeding, project, transaction, undertaking, venture. **6** (*a process*) exercise, procedure, process.

operative *a.* **1** (*acting, exerting force*) acting, active, current, functional, operational, serviceable, working. ANTONYMS: inoperative. **2** (*effective*) effective, efficacious, efficient. ANTONYMS: ineffective. **3** (*relevant, significant*) crucial, important, indicative, influential, key, relevant, significant. **4** (*practical*) feasible, practical, viable, workable. ANTONYMS: contemplative, theoretical.

~*n.* **1** (*a (skilled) worker, an operator*) artisan, craftsman, employee, hand, labourer, mechanic, operator, worker. **2** (*a private detective or secret agent*) agent, detective, secret agent, spy, undercover agent.

opinion *n.* **1** (*a judgement or belief*) assessment, belief, conception, conjecture, conviction, fancy, feeling, idea, impression, judgement, notion, sentiment, theory, thought. **2** (*estimation, reputation*) appraisal, assessment, estimate, estimation, evaluation, impression, judgement.

opinionated *a.* **1** (*obstinate in one's opinions*) independent, opinionative, resolute, strong-minded. **2** (*dogmatic, stubborn*) adamant, arrogant, biased, bigoted, dictatorial, doctrinaire, dogged, dogmatic, inflexible, obdurate, obstinate, overbearing, partisan, pig-headed, prejudiced, single-minded, stubborn, uncompromising. ANTONYMS: open-minded, receptive.

opponent *n.* **1** (*a person who opposes, esp. in a debate or contest*) challenger, competitor, contender, contestant, disputant, rival. **2** (*an adversary, an antagonist*) adversary, enemy, foe. ANTONYMS: ally, friend.

opportune *a.* **1** (*occurring, done etc. at a favourable moment*) advantageous, auspicious, favourable, felicitous, fortunate, happy, lucky, propitious. **2** (*seasonable, well-timed*) seasonable, timely, well-timed. ANTONYMS: inopportune. **3** (*fit, suitable*) appropriate, apt, becoming, convenient, fit, fitting, germane, pertinent, suitable. ANTONYMS: inappropriate, unsuitable.

opportunity *n.* **1** (*a chance, an opening*) (*coll.*)

break, chance, opening, possibility, scope, window. **2** (*an opportune or convenient time or occasion*) convenience, moment, occasion, time.

oppose *v.t.* **1** (*to set against as an obstacle or contrast* (*to*)) compare, contrast, counterbalance, match, offset, play off, refute, set against, set off. **2** (*to resist, withstand*) bar, block, check, combat, confront, contest, contradict, counter, defy, fight, foil, frustrate, hinder, impede, inhibit, obstruct, prevent, resist, take issue with, withstand. ANTONYMS: back, promote.

opposite *a.* **1** (*fronting, facing*) corresponding, facing, fronting. **2** (*antagonistic, diametrically different* (*to or from*)) adverse, antagonistic, antithetical, conflicting, contradictory, contrary, contrasted, different, divergent, diverse, hostile, incompatible, inconsistent, inimical, irreconcilable, opposed, reverse, unlike. ANTONYMS: alike, matching.
~*n.* **1** (*a person who or something which is opposite*) antithesis, contradiction, converse, inverse, reverse. **2** (*an opponent, an adversary*) adversary, opponent, rival.

opposition *n.* **1** (*antagonism, hostility*) antagonism, antipathy, conflict, confrontation, contrast, defiance, disapproval, hostility, obstructiveness, resistance, unfriendliness. ANTONYMS: approval, friendliness. **2** (*antithesis, contrast*) antithesis, contrariety, contrast, reversal. **3** (*an obstacle, a hindrance*) hindrance, †let, obstacle, obstruction.

oppress *v.t.* **1** (*to tyrannize over, to keep subservient*) crush, overpower, put down, repress, subdue, subjugate, suppress, trample underfoot, tyrannize. ANTONYMS: liberate, set free. **2** (*to inflict hardships or cruelties upon, to govern cruelly or unjustly*) abuse, afflict, burden, harass, harry, maltreat, mistreat, persecute, torment, trouble, vex. **3** (*to lie heavy on the mind of*) depress, press, sadden, weigh down. ANTONYMS: relieve. **4** (*to overburden*) encumber, overburden, overload.

oppression *n.* (*cruel or unjust treatment*) abuse, anguish, brutality, calamity, cruelty, despotism, enslavement, hardship, harshness, injury, injustice, maltreatment, misery, persecution, repression, subjection, subjugation, suffering, tyranny. ANTONYMS: benevolence, liberty.

oppressive *a.* **1** (*overbearing, tyrannous*) brutal, burdensome, cruel, depressing, despotic, exacting, grinding, harsh, heavy, inhuman, onerous, overbearing, overwhelming, repressive, severe, tyrannical, unjust. ANTONYMS: gentle, merciful. **2** (*hard to tolerate*)

intolerable, unbearable, unendurable. **3** ((*of the weather*) *close, muggy*) airless, close, heavy, muggy, overpowering, stifling, stuffy, suffocating, sultry, torrid, uncomfortable.

opprobrious *a.* (*abusive, scornful*) abusive, calumniatory, contemptuous, damaging, defamatory, derogatory, hateful, insolent, insulting, invective, offensive, reproachful, scandalous, scornful, scurrilous, slanderous, vitriolic, vituperative. ANTONYMS: laudatory.

opt *v.i.* (*to make a choice* (*for, between*)) choose, decide, elect, go for, make a choice, plump for, prefer, select. ANTONYMS: reject.

optimistic *a.* (*hopeful about the future*) assured, bright, buoyant, cheerful, confident, encouraged, expectant, hopeful, idealistic, positive, sanguine, utopian. ANTONYMS: pessimistic, realistic.

option *n.* (*a choice, a preference*) choice, election, preference, selection.

optional *a.* (*open to choice*) discretionary, elective, non-compulsory, unforced, voluntary. ANTONYMS: compulsory, mandatory.

opulent *a.* **1** (*rich, wealthy*) affluent, comfortable, flush, lavish, (*coll.*) loaded, luxurious, moneyed, prosperous, rich, sumptuous, wealthy, (*coll.*) well-heeled, well off, well-to-do. ANTONYMS: destitute, penniless. **2** (*abundant, profuse*) abundant, bountiful, copious, exuberant, lavish, luxuriant, plentiful, profuse, prolific. ANTONYMS: meagre, sparse.

oral *a.* (*spoken; by word of mouth*) articulated, enunciated, pronounced, said, spoken, uttered, verbal, vocal, voiced. ANTONYMS: written.

oration *n.* (*a formal speech*) address, declamation, declaration, discourse, eulogy, harangue, homily, lecture, monologue, panegyric, recitation, speech.

orb *n.* **1** (*a sphere, a globe*) ball, globe, sphere. **2** (*a circle or ring*) circle, orbit, ring, round.

orbit *n.* **1** (*the path of a celestial body around another*) circle, circuit, course, cycle, ellipse, path, revolution, rotation, track, trajectory. **2** (*a course or sphere of action*) ambit, career, compass, domain, influence, range, reach, scope, sphere, sweep.
~*v.t.* (*to move in a curved path around*) circle, encircle, go round, revolve around.

ordain *v.t.* **1** (*to set apart for religious office or duty*) anoint, appoint, call, consecrate, induct, invest, nominate. ANTONYMS: unfrock. **2** (*to decree, to destine*) bid, command, decree, demand, destine, dictate, enact, enjoin, establish, fix, lay down, legislate, order, prescribe, pronounce, rule, set, will.

ordeal n. (*an experience testing endurance, patience etc.*) adversity, affliction, agony, anguish, disaster, distress, grief, hardship, misery, misfortune, nightmare, suffering, test, torture, trial, tribulation, trouble. ANTONYMS: pleasure.

order n. **1** (*regular or methodical disposition or arrangement*) arrangement, array, categorization, classification, codification, disposal, disposition, grouping, line-up, organization, placement. **2** (*sequence, esp. as regulated by a system*) pattern, plan, progression, sequence, series, succession. **3** (*a state of efficiency, tidiness*) calm, discipline, neatness, orderliness, tidiness. ANTONYMS: chaos, disorder. **4** (*a rule, regulation*) law, regulation, rule. **5** (*an authoritative direction, a command*) behest, canon, command, decree, dictate, direction, directive, edict, injunction, instruction, mandate, ordinance, precept, stipulation. **6** (*a direction to supply specified commodities or to carry out specified work*) application, booking, commission, request, requisition, reservation. **7** (*a social class or degree*) class, degree, grade, hierarchy, position, rank, status. **8** (*kind, sort*) breed, cast, genre, (*coll.*) ilk, kind, quality, sort, type. **9** (*a class or body of persons united by some common purpose*) association, community, company, guild, league, lodge, organization, sect, society, union. **10** (*a society of monks or nuns, bound by the same rule of life*) brotherhood, fraternity, sisterhood, sorority. ~v.t. **1** (*to direct, to command*) adjure, bid, charge, decree, demand, direct, enact, enjoin, instruct, ordain, prescribe, require. **2** (*to instruct (a person, firm etc.) to supply goods or perform work*) apply for, ask for, authorize, book, call for, commission, contract for, engage, prescribe, request, requisition, reserve, send for. **3** (*to regulate, organize*) adjust, arrange, catalogue, categorize, class, classify, codify, control, dispose, group, lay out, manage, marshal, organize, regulate, set in order, sort out, straighten, systematize, tidy. ANTONYMS: disarrange, muddle. **4** (*to direct the supplying or making of*) administer, direct, oversee, supervise.

orderly a. **1** (*in order*) in order, well-organized. **2** (*methodical, regular*) businesslike, harmonious, methodical, neat, regular, ship-shape, systematic, tidy, trim. ANTONYMS: untidy. **3** (*free from disorder or confusion*) civilized, controlled, decorous, disciplined, law-abiding, peaceable, quiet, restrained, well-behaved. ANTONYMS: disorderly, undisciplined.

ordinance n. **1** (*an order or regulation laid down by a constituted authority*) canon, command, decree, edict, enactment, law, order, precept, regulation, rule, ruling, statute. **2** (*an established rule or ceremony etc.*) ceremony, observance, rite, ritual, rule, sacrament.

ordinarily adv. (*usually, normally*) as a rule, by and large, commonly, customarily, generally, habitually, in general, normally, routinely, typically, usually. ANTONYMS: rarely, unusually.

ordinary a. **1** (*normal, not exceptional or unusual*) accustomed, banal, common, conventional, customary, habitual, humdrum, mundane, normal, regular, routine, standard, stock, typical, undistinguished, unexceptional, uninspired, unoriginal, unremarkable, usual. ANTONYMS: exceptional, unusual. **2** (*commonplace*) commonplace, everyday, run-of-the-mill, workaday. **3** (*mediocre*) average, fair, indifferent, inferior, mean, mediocre, middling, pedestrian, second-rate, (*coll.*) so so.

organic a. **1** (*of or relating to the nature of organisms, plants or animals*) animate, biological, live, living, natural. ANTONYMS: inorganic. **2** (*structural, inherent*) basic, constitutional, elementary, essential, fundamental, inherent, integral, primary, structural. ANTONYMS: extraneous. **3** (*organized, systematic*) coherent, coordinated, integrated, methodical, ordered, organized, structured, systematic. ANTONYMS: unsystematic.

organization n. **1** (*the act of organizing*) assembling, categorization, classification, codification, coordination, organizing, systematization. **2** (*the state of being organized*) arrangement, composition, configuration, conformation, constitution, design, format, framework, grouping, method, organism, pattern, plan, shape, structure, system, unity, whole. **3** (*an organized body or society*) association, body, combine, company, concern, confederation, consortium, corporation, federation, group, institution, league, (*coll.*) outfit, society, syndicate, system. **4** (*tidiness, method*) method, orderliness, tidiness.

organize v.t. **1** (*to make the necessary arrangements for (an event or activity)*) arrange, be in charge of, be responsible for, coordinate, manage, prepare, set up. **2** (*to arrange or dispose (things or a body of people) in order to carry out some purpose effectively*) arrange, catalogue, categorize, classify, codify, constitute, construct, coordinate, dispose, frame, group, marshal, order, set up, shape, sort, straighten out, structure, systematize, tabulate. ANTONYMS: disorganize, upset.

orgy n. **1** (*a wild revel, esp. involving indiscriminate sexual activity*) (*pl.*) bacchanalia, carousal, revel. **2** (*a bout of indulgence*) (*sl.*) bender, (*coll.*) binge, bout, excess, fling, indulgence, splurge, spree, surfeit. **3** (*pl.*) (*revelry*) debauchery, revelry.

orifice *n.* (*an opening or aperture, esp. of the body*) aperture, cleft, hole, mouth, opening, perforation, pore, rent, vent.

origin *n.* **1** (*the beginning, commencement* (*of anything*)) beginning, birth, commencement, creation, dawn, emergence, genesis, inauguration, inception, launch, origination, outset, rise, start. ANTONYMS: conclusion, end. **2** (*derivation, a source*) derivation, fount, root, source, spring, wellspring. **3** (*extraction, a person's ancestry*) ancestry, beginnings, birth, descent, extraction, family, genealogy, heritage, lineage, parentage, pedigree, stock. **4** (*ground, foundation*) base, basis, cause, foundation, ground, occasion.

original *a.* **1** (*first, initial*) beginning, commencing, earliest, early, first, initial, introductory, opening, primary, primitive, primordial, starting. ANTONYMS: closing, latest. **2** (*not copied; fresh*) fresh, genuine, ground-breaking, innovative, innovatory, new, novel, unconventional, unprecedented, untried. ANTONYMS: derivative, derived, unoriginal. **3** (*able to think for oneself; creative*) creative, fertile, imaginative, ingenious, inventive, resourceful. ~*n.* **1** (*the pattern, the archetype*) archetype, master, model, paradigm, pattern, precedent, prototype, standard, type. ANTONYMS: copy, imitation. **2** (*an eccentric person*) (*sl.*) case, character, eccentric, individualist, nonconformist, (*sl.*) nut, oddball, oddity, (*coll.*) weirdo. **3** (*origin, ancestry*) ancestry, cause, derivation, stock.

originate *v.t.* (*to bring into existence*) beget, begin, bring about, conceive, concoct, contrive, create, engender, formulate, found, generate, give birth to, inaugurate, initiate, institute, introduce, invent, launch, set up, start. ANTONYMS: abolish, terminate. ~*v.i.* (*to have origin* (*in, from or with*)) arise, begin, come, derive, develop, emanate, emerge, evolve, flow, grow, issue, proceed, result, rise, spring, start, stem.

ornament[1] *n.* **1** (*a thing or part that adorns; a decoration*) accessory, adornment, bauble, decoration, embellishment, festoon, frill, frippery, garnish, gewgaw, knick-knack, trimming, trinket. **2** (*ornamentation*) decoration, embellishment, ornamentation. **3** (*a person or quality that reflects honour*) flower, gem, hero, honour, jewel, leading light, pride, treasure.

ornament[2] *v.t.* (*to decorate, to embellish*) accessorize, adorn, beautify, brighten, deck,

decorate, dress up, elaborate, embellish, enhance, festoon, garnish, gild, grace, prettify, trim. ANTONYMS: strip.

ornate *a.* **1** (*ornamented, richly decorated*) adorned, baroque, bedecked, busy, convoluted, decorated, elaborate, elegant, embellished, fancy, flamboyant, frilly, fussy, lavish, ornamented, rococo. ANTONYMS: bare, spartan. **2** ((*of literary style etc.*) *florid*) bombastic, elaborate, florid, flowery, grandiose, highflown, laboured, pompous.

orthodox *a.* (*accepted, conventional*) accepted, approved, authorized, conformist, conservative, conventional, doctrinal, established, official, popular, prevailing, received, standard, traditionalist. ANTONYMS: heretical, unorthodox.

oscillate *v.i.* **1** (*to swing, to move like a pendulum*) sway, swing. **2** (*to vibrate*) vibrate, wobble. **3** (*to fluctuate, to vary*) equivocate, falter, fluctuate, hesitate, see-saw, shilly-shally, vacillate, vary, waver. ANTONYMS: decide, settle.

ostensible *a.* **1** (*put forward for show or to hide the reality*) apparent, manifest, outward, superficial. **2** (*professed, seeming*) alleged, avowed, pretended, professed, purported, seeming, supposed. ANTONYMS: real.

ostentation *n.* **1** (*pretentious or ambitious display*) affectation, boasting, exhibitionist, flamboyance, flashiness, flaunting, pretentiousness, showiness, (*coll.*) showing off, (*coll.*) swank, vaunting. ANTONYMS: modesty, reserve. **2** (*parade, pomp*) display, flourish, pageantry, parade, pomp, show.

ostentatious *a.* (*showy, pretentious*) affected, boastful, brash, conspicuous, exhibitionist, extravagant, flamboyant, flashy, flaunting, gaudy, mannered, obtrusive, pompous, pretentious, showy, (*coll.*) swanky, vain, vulgar. ANTONYMS: modest, subdued.

other *a.* **1** (*different, distinct in kind*) different, dissimilar, distinct, diverse, separate. ANTONYMS: same. **2** (*alternative, additional*) added, additional, alternative, auxiliary, extra, further, more, spare, supplementary. **3** (*opposite, contrary*) contrary, contrasting, opposite.

out *adv.* **1** (*not in, not within*) outdoors, out of doors, outside. ANTONYMS: in, inside. **2** (*forth or away*) abroad, absent, away, elsewhere, forth, gone. **3** (*no longer in prison*) at liberty, free, loose, released. **4** (*not in fashion*) antiquated, behind the times, dated, dead, obsolete, old-fashioned, outdated, outmoded, passé, unfashionable. ANTONYMS: fashionable, trendy. **5** (*in error, wrong*) erroneous, faulty, inaccurate, incorrect, mistaken, wrong. ANTO-NYMS: correct. **6** (*not to be thought of*) forbidden, impossible, prohibited, ruled out, unacceptable, unthinkable. **7** (*so as to be visible, published etc.*) broadcast, declared, disclosed, exposed, published, revealed. **8** (*exhausted or extinguished*) cold, dead, ended, expired, extinguished, finished, gone, over, used up. **9** (*coll.*) (*no longer conscious*) insensible, senseless, unconscious. ANTONYMS: conscious. **10** (*completely, thoroughly*) completely, effectively, entirely, thoroughly.

outbreak n. **1** (*a sudden bursting forth*) bursting forth, eruption, explosion, flare-up, flash, outburst, rash, spasm, upsurge. **2** (*a riot*) insurrection, revolt, riot, uprising.

outburst n. (*an outbreak, an explosion*) attack, blow-up, discharge, eruption, explosion, fit, flare-up, gush, outbreak, outpouring, paroxysm, seizure, spasm, storm, surge, tantrum, upsurge.

outcast n. **1** (*a castaway, a vagabond*) castaway, derelict, reprobate, untouchable, vagabond, wanderer, wretch. **2** (*an exile*) evacuee, exile, expatriate, pariah, refugee.

outcome n. (*result, consequence*) aftermath, conclusion, consequence, culmination, effect, end, issue, result, sequel, upshot.

outcry n. **1** (*a vehement or loud cry*) cry, exclamation, howl, scream, screech, shout, yell. **2** (*noise, clamour*) clamour, commotion, hue and cry, hullabaloo, noise, outburst, protest, uproar, vociferation.

outdo v.t. (*to excel, to surpass*) beat, best, defeat, eclipse, exceed, excel, outclass, outfox, outmanoeuvre, outrun, outshine, (*coll.*) outsmart, outstrip, outweigh, outwit, overcome, surpass, top, transcend, trump.

outer a. **1** (*being on the exterior side, external*) exposed, exterior, external, outside. ANTO-NYMS: internal. **2** (*farther from the centre or the inside*) outlying, peripheral, remote. **3** (*objective, material*) material, objective, substantive. ANTONYMS: subjective.

outfit n. **1** (*the act of equipping for a journey, expedition etc.*) equipping, preparation, rigging out. **2** (*the tools and equipment required for a trade, profession etc.*) accoutrements, equipment, gear, paraphernalia, tackle, tools. **3** (*a set of* (*esp. selected*) *clothes*) attire, costume, ensemble, garb, (*coll.*) gear, get-up, kit, set of clothes, suit, (*coll.*) things, (*coll.*) togs, trappings. **4** (*a set or group of people who work as a team*) clique, company, concern, crew, firm, group, organization, set, squad, team, unit.

~v.t. (*to fit out, to provide with an outfit*) accoutre, appoint, equip, fit out, furnish, kit out, provide, provision, rig out, stock, supply, turn out.

outing n. (*an excursion*) airing, excursion, expedition, jaunt, junket, pleasure trip, ride, (*coll.*) spin, tour, trip.

outlandish a. **1** (*strange, extraordinary*) exotic, extraordinary, fantastic, foreign-looking, freakish, grotesque, odd, queer, strange, unfamiliar, weird. ANTONYMS: commonplace, ordinary. **2** (*foreign, alien*) alien, exotic, foreign. **3** (*bizarre, unconventional*) bizarre, eccentric, unconventional. ANTONYMS: conventional.

outlaw n. **1** (*a lawless person*) bandit, brigand, criminal, desperado, footpad, gangster, (*Hist.*) highwayman, (*Hist.*) highwaywoman, marauder, renegade, robber, villain. **2†** (*a fugitive*) exile, fugitive, outcast.

~v.t. (*to make illegal*) ban, banish, bar, condemn, disallow, embargo, exclude, forbid, interdict, prohibit, proscribe. ANTONYMS: allow, permit.

outlay n. (*expenditure*) cost, disbursement, expenditure, expenses, investment, outgoings, payment, spending. ANTONYMS: income.

outlet n. **1** (*a passage outwards*) avenue, channel, duct. **2** (*a vent*) opening, vent. **3** (*a means of egress*) egress, escape, exit, loophole, way out. **4** (*an agency or market for goods*) agency, market, mart, shop, store.

outline n. **1** (*a drawing of lines enclosing a figure*) configuration, contour, delineation, figure, form, profile, shape, silhouette. **2** (*the first general sketch, rough draft*) draft, drawing, frame, framework, layout, plan, rough, sketch, summary. **3** (*pl.*) (*general features, principles etc.*) abstract, digest, overview, précis, recapitulation, résumé, rough idea, rundown, summary, synopsis.

~v.t. (*to sketch*) delineate, draft, profile, rough out, sketch, summarize, trace.

outlook n. **1** (*the prospect, general appearance of things, esp. as regards the future*) expectations, forecast, future, prospect. **2** (*a view, a prospect*) aspect, panorama, prospect, scene, view, vista. **3** (*a general attitude, perspective*) attitude, opinion, perspective, slant, standpoint, viewpoint.

outlying a. (*situated at a distance, or on the exterior frontier*) backwoods, distant, far-flung, far-off, furthest, outer, out-of-the-way, peripheral, provincial, remote. ANTONYMS: central, inner.

outpouring n. (*an uncontrolled flow*) cascade,

cataract, deluge, effluence, efflux, effusion, emanation, flood, flow, flux, gush, issue, outflow, spate, spurt, stream, torrent.

output *n.* (*the produce of a factory, mine etc.*) crop, harvest, manufacture, produce, product, production, result, yield.

outrage *n.* **1** (*wanton injury to or violation of the rights of others*) injury, violation. **2** (*a gross offence against order or decency*) atrocity, barbarism, desecration, enormity, evil, inhumanity, offence, profanation, rape, shock. **3** (*a flagrant insult*) abuse, affront, insult, slight. **4** (*fierce anger or indignation*) anger, bitterness, fury, hurt, indignation, resentment, shock, wrath.
~*v.t.* **1** (*to injure or insult in a flagrant manner*) affront, injure, insult. **2** (*to violate, to commit a rape upon*) abuse, defile, desecrate, maltreat, rape, ravage, ravish, violate. **3** (*to shock and anger*) anger, displease, enrage, incense, infuriate, madden, offend, scandalize, shock, vex.

outrageous *a.* **1** (*flagrant, atrocious*) abominable, atrocious, barbaric, beastly, cruel, extravagant, flagrant, grisly, heinous, hideous, horrible, infamous, inhuman, iniquitous, nefarious, unspeakable, unthinkable, vicious, vile, wicked. **2** (*excessive, shocking*) exaggerated, excessive, exorbitant, immoderate, over-the-top, preposterous, scandalous, shocking, (*coll.*) steep, unreasonable, unwarranted. ANTONYMS: reasonable. **3** (*violent, furious*) brutish, furious, violent. **4** (*grossly offensive or abusive*) abusive, dirty, filthy, immoral, indecent, indecorous, lewd, obscene, offensive, profane, rude, salacious, smutty.

outright *adv.* **1** (*completely, entirely*) absolutely, completely, entirely, totally, unreservedly, utterly. **2** (*at once, once for all*) at once, directly, immediately, instantaneously, instantly, on the spot, straight away, there and then. **3** (*openly*) openly, overtly, plainly, straightforwardly.
~*a.* **1** (*downright, positive*) absolute, bald, consummate, direct, downright, out-and-out, positive, pure, sheer, stark, thorough, undisguised, unmistakable, unmitigated, utter. **2** (*unrestrained, thorough*) clear, complete, definite, direct, full, thorough, total, unconditional, unequivocal, unmistakable, unqualified, unreserved, unrestrained, unrestricted.

outrun *v.t.* **1** (*to run faster or farther than*) beat, excel, outdistance, outdo, outstrip, overtake, surpass. **2** (*to escape by running*) escape, get away, leave behind, lose, shake off. **3** (*to go beyond* (*a specified point*)) exceed, go beyond.

outset *n.* (*beginning, start*) beginning, commencement, inauguration, inception, (*coll.*)

kick-off, onset, opening, start. ANTONYMS: end, finish.

outshine *v.t.* (*to surpass in ability, excellence etc.*) eclipse, excel, outclass, outdo, outstrip, overshadow, put in the shade, surpass, top, transcend, upstage.

outside *n.* **1** (*the external part or surface, the exterior*) casing, exterior, shell. **2** (*the external appearance*) appearance, aspect, facade, face, front, skin, surface. **3** (*the utmost limit*) border, edge, extreme, limit, utmost.
~*a.* **1** (*situated on or near the outside*) exterior, outdoor, outer, outermost, outward. ANTONYMS: inner, inside. **2** (*external, superficial*) external, extraneous, peripheral, superficial, surface. **3** (*highest or greatest possible*) extreme, greatest, highest, maximum, most. **4** (*remote, most unlikely*) distant, faint, marginal, negligible, remote, slight, slim, small, unlikely.

outsider *n.* **1** (*a person who is not a member of a profession, circle etc.*) alien, foreigner, gatecrasher, incomer, interloper, intruder, invader, newcomer, non-member, stranger, trespasser. **2** (*a person not admissible to decent society*) outcast, pariah.

outskirt *n.* (*usu. pl.*) (*the outer border*) border, boundary, edge, environs, fringe, periphery, suburbia, vicinity. ANTONYMS: centre.

outspoken *a.* (*candid, frank in speech*) abrupt, blunt, brusque, candid, direct, downright, explicit, forthright, frank, free, open, plainspoken, straightforward, unceremonious, unequivocal, unreserved. ANTONYMS: reserved, reticent.

outspread[1] *v.t.* (*to spread out*) expand, extend, fan out, outstretch, spread out, unfold, unfurl.

outspread[2] *a.* (*spread out*) expanded, extended, fanlike, flared, open, outstretched, spread out, unfolded, unfurled. ANTONYMS: closed.

outstanding *a.* **1** (*remaining unpaid*) due, ongoing, owing, payable, pending, remaining, unpaid, unresolved, unsettled. ANTONYMS: met, paid. **2** (*conspicuous, prominent*) arresting, conspicuous, eye-catching, marked, memorable, notable, noteworthy, prominent, salient, signal, striking. **3** (*superior, excellent*) celebrated, distinguished, eminent, excellent, exceptional, famous, great, important, impressive, marvellous, pre-eminent, renowned, special, superb, superior, superlative, wellknown. ANTONYMS: ordinary, unexceptional.

outstrip *v.t.* **1** (*to outrun, to leave behind*) leave behind, outdistance, outpace, outrun. **2** (*to escape by running*) escape, lose, shake off. **3** (*to* *surpass in progress*) beat, better, eclipse, exceed, excel, outclass, outdo, outperform, outshine, overcome, overtake, surpass, top, transcend.

outward *a.* 1 (*exterior, outer*) exterior, outer, outside. ANTONYMS: inner, inside. 2 (*external, visible*) apparent, evident, external, manifest, noticeable, obvious, ostensible, perceptible, superficial, surface, visible. 3 (*material, worldly*) corporeal, material, secular, terrestrial, worldly. ANTONYMS: spiritual. 4 (*extraneous, extrinsic*) exterior, extraneous, extrinsic, peripheral.

outweigh *v.t.* 1 (*to weigh more than*) tip the scales, top. 2 (*to be of more value, importance etc. than*) cancel, compensate for, eclipse, exceed, make up for, outbalance, overbalance, overcome, override, preponderate, prevail over, surpass.

outwit *v.t.* 1 (*to defeat by superior ingenuity and cunning*) beat, defeat, overcome. 2 (*to overreach, to cheat*) cheat, circumvent, deceive, defraud, dupe, fool, get the better of, hoax, hoodwink, outfox, outmanoeuvre, (*coll.*) outsmart, overreach, (*coll.*) put one over on, swindle, take in, trick.

ovation *n.* (*enthusiastic applause*) acclaim, acclamation, applause, cheering, cheers, clapping, laudation, plaudits, praise, tribute. ANTONYMS: abuse, derision.

over *prep.* 1 (*above, in a higher position than*) above, higher than. 2 (*above or superior to in excellence or value*) better, improved, superior. 3 (*more than, in excess of*) exceeding, in excess of, more than. 4 (*in charge of, concerned with*) concerned with, engaged with, in charge of.
~*adv.* 1 (*so as to pass from side to side or across some space, barrier etc.*) across, beyond. 2 (*at an end*) accomplished, at an end, bygone, closed, completed, concluded, done, ended, finished, gone, past, settled, up. 3 (*in addition*) in addition, in excess. 4 (*excessively, with repetition, again*) again, excessively, once more.
~*a.* 1 (*upper*) outer, upper. 2 (*extra*) beyond, extra, in addition, in excess, left over, outstanding, remaining, superfluous, surplus, unused, unwanted.

overall[1] *a.* (*from end to end, total*) all-embracing, all-inclusive, blanket, complete, comprehensive, entire, general, global, inclusive, long-range, long-term, sweeping, total, umbrella, universal, whole.

overall[2] *adv.* (*everywhere, in all parts or directions*) broadly, everywhere, generally

speaking, in general, in large, in the long term, on the whole.

overawe *v.t.* (*to keep in awe*) abash, awe, browbeat, bully, cow, daunt, disconcert, dominate, frighten, hector, intimidate, overwhelm, scare, terrify, upset. ANTONYMS: reassure.

overbearing *a.* (*arrogant, haughty*) arrogant, autocratic, bossy, bullying, despotic, dictatorial, domineering, haughty, high-handed, imperious, lordly, magisterial, officious, oppressive, peremptory, (*coll.*) pushy, repressive, supercilious, tyrannical. ANTONYMS: humble, unassertive.

overcast *a.* (*clouded all over (of the sky)*) clouded, cloudy, darkened, dismal, dreary, dull, gloomy, grey, hazy, leaden, louring, menacing, murky, sombre, sunless, threatening. ANTONYMS: bright, cloudless.

overcome *v.t.* (*to overpower, to conquer*) beat, conquer, crush, defeat, get the better of, (*coll.*) lick, master, overpower, overthrow, overwhelm, prevail, quell, rise above, subdue, subjugate, surmount, survive, triumph over, vanquish, worst. ANTONYMS: submit.
~*a.* (*helpless, affected by emotion etc.*) affected, beaten, (*coll.*) bowled over, exhausted, helpless, influenced, moved, overwhelmed, speechless, subdued, worsted.

overdo *v.t.* 1 (*to do to excess*) belabour, do to death, gild the lily, go off the deep end, go overboard, go too far, lay it on thick, over-indulge, overreach, overstate, overwork. ANTONYMS: belittle. 2 (*to exaggerate*) enhance, exaggerate, overplay. ANTONYMS: underplay. 3 (*to fatigue, to wear out*) exhaust, fatigue, overburden, overload, overtax, overwork, tire, wear out.

overdue *a.* 1 (*remaining unpaid after the date on which it is due*) due, in arrears, owing, payable, unpaid. 2 (*not arrived at the time it was due*) behind, behindhand, behind schedule, behind time, belated, delayed, late, tardy, unpunctual. ANTONYMS: early, punctual.

overflow[1] *v.t.* (*to flow over, to flood*) deluge, drown, flood, flow over, inundate, pour forth, submerge, swamp. ANTONYMS: subside.
~*v.i.* 1 (*to run over*) brim over, bubble over, overrun, overspill, run over, shower, slop over, spill, surge, well over. 2 (*to abound*) abound, teem.

overflow[2] *n.* 1 (*a flood, an inundation*) discharge, flood, inundation, spill. 2 (*a profusion*) profusion, superabundance, surplus.

overhaul[1] *v.t.* 1 (*to examine thoroughly*) check, examine, fix up, inspect, recondition, re-examine, refurbish, renovate, repair, re-store, service, survey. **2** (*to overtake, to gain upon*) catch up with, draw level with, gain upon, get ahead of, lap, leave behind, outdistance, outstrip, overtake, pass.

overhaul[2] *n.* (*inspection, thorough examination*) check, check-up, examination, (*coll.*) going-over, inspection, rebuilding, reconditioning, service.

overhead[1] *adv.* (*above the head, aloft*) above, aloft, atop, high up, on high, skywards, upwards. ANTONYMS: below, underneath.
~*a.* (*situated overhead*) above, aerial, elevated, overhanging, raised, upper.

overhead[2] *n.* (*pl., N Am. sing.*) (*expenses of administration etc.*) fixed costs, operating costs, regular costs, running costs.

overjoyed *a.* (*extremely happy*) delighted, delirious, ecstatic, elated, enraptured, euphoric, happy, joyful, jubilant, over the moon, pleased, rapt, rapturous, thrilled, (*coll.*) tickled pink, transported. ANTONYMS: dejected, unhappy.

overload *v.t.* (*to load too heavily*) burden, encumber, handicap, load, oppress, overburden, overcharge, overtax, saddle, strain, weigh down. ANTONYMS: relieve.

overlook *v.t.* **1** (*to pass over, to disregard*) condone, disregard, excuse, forget, forgive, gloss over, ignore, look over, miss, neglect, omit, pardon, pass over, slight, turn a blind eye to, wink at. ANTONYMS: condemn, spot. **2** (*to be situated so as to command a view of from above*) command a view of, front onto, look onto, look over. **3** (*to superintend, to oversee*) oversee, superintend, supervise. **4** (*to peruse, esp. in a cursory way*) glance at, inspect, look over, peruse.

overpower *v.t.* **1** (*to overcome, conquer*) beat, best, conquer, crush, defeat, knock out, (*coll.*) lick, master, overcome, overthrow, put down, quell, subdue, subjugate, vanquish, worst. **2** (*to overcome the feelings or judgement of*) amaze, daze, (*coll.*) floor, nonplus, overcome, overwhelm, stagger, stun, stupefy.

overpowering *a.* (*very strong, intense*) amazing, compelling, crushing, dazzling, extreme, forceful, intense, invincible, irrefutable, irresistible, nauseating, oppressive, overcoming, overwhelming, powerful, sickening, staggering, strong, stunning, stupefying, unbearable. ANTONYMS: weak.

overrate *v.t.* (*to rate too highly*) exaggerate, make too much of, overestimate, overpraise, overprize, oversell, overvalue. ANTONYMS: underrate.

overreach *v.t.* **1** (*to reach beyond*) extend beyond, reach beyond. **2** (*to get the better of, to cheat*) cheat, circumvent, deceive, defraud, dupe, get the better of, (*coll.*) outsmart, outwit, swindle, trick, victimize.

override *v.t.* **1** (*to trample as if underfoot, to supersede*) annul, cancel, countermand, discount, disregard, ignore, nullify, outweigh, overrule, quash, reverse, set aside, supersede, trample underfoot, upset, vanquish. **2** (*to fatigue or exhaust by excessive riding*) exhaust, fatigue, ride into the ground. **3** (*to overtake*) outride, overtake, ride past.

overrule *v.t.* **1** (*to control by superior power or authority*) control, direct, dominate, govern, influence, prevail over, rule, sway. **2** (*to set aside*) alter, annul, cancel, countermand, disallow, invalidate, nullify, outvote, override, overturn, recall, repeal, rescind, reverse, revoke, rule against, set aside, supersede, veto. **3** (*to reject*) disallow, reject. ANTONYMS: allow, permit.

overrun *v.t.* **1** (*to run over*) run over, spread over. **2** (*to grow over*) choke, grow over, infest, overgrow. **3** (*to invade or harass by hostile incursions*) attack, conquer, defeat, despoil, destroy, devastate, harass, invade, maraud, massacre, occupy, overwhelm, pillage, put to flight, ravage, rout, sack, scourge, storm, swamp.
~*v.i.* **1** (*to overflow*) inundate, overflow. **2** (*to extend beyond the proper limits*) exceed, go beyond, overreach, overshoot.

overseer *n.* (*a superintendent, an inspector*) boss, foreman, (*coll.*) gaffer, inspector, manager, master, superintendent, superior, supervisor.

overshadow *v.t.* **1** (*to obscure with or as with a shadow*) bedim, cloud, darken, dim, obfuscate, obscure, shade, shadow, veil. **2** (*to protect*) defend, guard, protect, shelter. **3** (*to tower high above, to exceed in importance*) dominate, dwarf, eclipse, excel, outshine, outweigh, rise above, surpass, take precedence over, tower above. **4** (*to make something seem less important*) blight, mar, ruin, spoil, take the edge off, temper.

oversight *n.* **1** (*superintendence, supervision*) administration, care, charge, control, custody, direction, guidance, handling, inspection, keeping, superintendence, supervision, surveillance. **2** (*an unintentional error or omission*) blunder, carelessness, delinquency, error, failure, inadvertence, inattention, lapse, laxity, mistake, neglect, omission, slip.

overt *a.* (*plain, apparent*) apparent, blatant,

clear, deliberate, evident, manifest, observable, obvious, open, patent, plain, public, unconcealed, undisguised, visible. ANTONYMS: covert, disguised.

overtake v.t. **1** (*to come up with, to catch*) catch, catch up with, come up with, draw level with, leave behind, outdistance, outdo, outstrip, overhaul, pass. **2** (*to reach*) attain to, reach. **3** (*to take by surprise, to come upon suddenly*) befall, catch unprepared, come upon, engulf, happen, hit, surprise.

overthrow[1] v.t. **1** (*to overturn, demolish*) abolish, demolish, depose, destroy, dethrone, do away with, oust, overturn, raze, ruin, subvert, throw down, topple, unseat, upset. ANTONYMS: maintain. **2** (*to overcome, conquer*) beat, conquer, crush, defeat, master, overcome, overpower, overwhelm, rout, subdue, subjugate, vanquish.

overthrow[2] n. **1** (*defeat, discomfiture*) conquest, defeat, discomfiture, displacement, downfall, end, fall, ousting, overturn, subversion, suppression, undoing. **2** (*ruin, destruction*) demolition, destruction, ruin. ANTONYMS: restoration.

overture n. **1** (*Mus.*) (*a prelude to an opera, oratorio etc.*) introduction, opening, preface, prelude, prologue. ANTONYMS: closing, finale. **2** (*usu. pl.*) (*a preliminary proposal*) advance, approach, invitation, offer, proposal, proposition, suggestion, tender. ANTONYMS: rejection.

overturn v.t. (*to turn over*) capsize, depose, invert, keel over, knock over, overbalance, overthrow, overturn, reverse, spill, tip over, topple, tumble, turn over, turn turtle, upend, upset, upturn.

overweight a. (*exceeding the normal or accepted weight*) ample, bulky, chubby, chunky, corpulent, fat, flabby, fleshy, gross, heavy, hefty, huge, obese, outsize, plump, podgy, portly, rotund, stout, tubby. ANTONYMS: skinny, underweight.

overwhelm v.t. **1** (*to cover completely*) cover, submerge. **2** (*to crush, to engulf*) bury, deluge, engulf, flood, inundate, snow under, submerge, swamp. **3** (*to destroy utterly*) crush, destroy, devastate, massacre. **4** (*to overcome, to overpower*) bear down, overcome, overpower, overrun, prostrate, quell, rout. ANTONYMS: submit.

overwrought a. **1** (*overworked*) overdone, overworked. **2** (*agitated, nervous*) agitated, beside oneself, edgy, excited, frantic, frenetic, frenzied, (*coll.*) in a state, (*coll.*) jittery, (*coll.*) jumpy, keyed up, nervous, on edge, overexcited, stirred, (*coll.*) strung up, tense, touchy, (*coll.*) uptight, (*sl.*) wired, (*coll.*) wound up. ANTONYMS: calm, collected. **3** (*elaborately decorated*) baroque, busy, contrived, elaborate, florid, flowery, fussy, garish, gaudy, ostentatious, overdone, over-elaborate, overembellished, over-ornate, rococo. ANTONYMS: plain.

owing a. **1** (*due as a debt*) due, in arrears, outstanding, overdue, payable, unpaid, unsettled. **2** (*resulting from, on account of*) ascribable, attributable, on account of, resulting from.

own[1] a. (*belonging to, individual*) individual, particular, personal, private. **to get one's own back** (*to be even with*) avenge oneself, be avenged, get even, get vengeance, give as good as one gets, give tit for tat, hit back, retaliate, revenge oneself, settle a score, take revenge, take vengeance.

own[2] v.t. **1** (*to possess*) have, possess. **2** (*to have as property by right*) enjoy, have, hold, keep, possess, retain. **3** (*to recognize the authorship etc. of*) acknowledge, avow, grant, recognize. **4** (*to concede as true or existent*) admit, allow, concede. **to own up** (*to confess (to)*) admit, (*coll.*) come clean, confess, make a clean breast, tell the truth. ANTONYMS: deny.

owner n. (*a lawful proprietor*) holder, landlady, landlord, lord, master, mistress, possessor, proprietor, proprietress.

P

pace *n.* **1** (*a step, the space between the feet in stepping*) measure, step, stride, tread. **2** (*gait, manner of walking or running*) gait, step, walk. **3** (*the action of a horse etc.*) action, carriage. **4** (*rate of speed or progress*) (*sl.*) clip, (*coll.*) lick, momentum, motion, movement, progress, rate, velocity. **5** (*Mus.*) (*speed*) speed, tempo, time.
~*v.i.* **1** (*to walk with slow or regular steps*) march, pound, step, stride, tread, walk. **2** (*to amble*) amble, saunter, stroll.
~*v.t.* (*to measure by carefully regulated steps*) count, determine, estimate, figure, gauge, judge, mark out, measure, reckon, step.

pacific *a.* **1** (*inclined or tending to peace*) appeasing, conciliatory, diplomatic, non-belligerent, pacifist, peace-loving, peace-making, placatory, propitiatory. ANTONYMS: antagonistic, argumentative. **2** (*quiet, peaceful*) calm, halcyon, peaceable, peaceful, placid, quiet, serene, smooth, still, tranquil, unruffled. ANTONYMS: troubled.

pacify *v.t.* (*to appease, to calm*) allay, appease, assuage, calm, compose, conciliate, lull, moderate, mollify, placate, propitiate, quell, quiet, smooth over, soften, soothe, still, subdue, tranquillize. ANTONYMS: aggravate, provoke.

pack *n.* **1** (*a bundle of things tied or wrapped together for carrying*) bale, bundle. **2** (*a backpack*) backpack, duffel bag, haversack, kitbag, knapsack, rucksack. **3** (*a burden, a load*) burden, load, parcel. **4** (*a small packet, e.g. of cigarettes*) package, packet. **5** (*usu. derog.*) (*a crew, a gang*) band, bunch, company, coterie, crew, crowd, gang, group, lot, mob, set, troop.
~*v.t.* **1** (*to put together into a pack or packs*) batch, bundle, package, packet, put together. ANTONYMS: unpack. **2** (*to stow into a bag, suitcase etc. for transporting or storing*) store, stow. **3** (*to crowd closely together*) compact, compress, crowd, throng. **4** (*to cram (with)*) cram, jam, press, ram, squeeze, stuff, tamp, wedge. **5** (*to cover with some material to prevent leakage, loss of heat etc.*) lag, surround, wrap. **6** (*coll.*) (*to carry (e.g. a gun)*) carry, tote. **7** (*to load with a pack*) burden, lade, load.

package *n.* **1** (*a parcel, a bundle*) bundle, pack, parcel. **2** (*the container, wrapper etc. in which a thing is packed*) box, carton, case, container,

packet, wrapper, wrapping. **3** (*a number of items offered together*) amalgamation, bundle, collection, combination, deal, entity, unit, whole.
~*v.t.* (*to place in a pack*) batch, box, case, containerize, enclose, pack, packet, parcel, wrap.

packet *n.* **1** (*a small package*) bag, carton, container, package, parcel, wrapper. **2** (*a large sum of money*) (*coll.*) bomb, (*sl.*) bundle, fortune, (*coll.*) loads, (*coll.*) megabucks, mint, (*coll.*) pile, (*usu. pl., coll.*) pot, (*coll.*) tidy sum, (*coll.*) wad.

pact *n.* (*an agreement, a compact*) agreement, alliance, arrangement, bargain, bond, compact, concord, contract, convention, covenant, deal, entente, league, protocol, treaty, understanding.

pad *n.* **1** (*a soft cushion*) buffer, cushion, pillow, wad. **2** (*a bundle or mass of soft stuff of the nature of a cushion*) filling, padding, stuffing, wadding. **3** (*a number of sheets of paper fastened together at the edge for writing upon*) block, jotter, memo pad, notepad, tablet, writing pad. **4** (*a rocket-launching platform*) launching pad, launch pad, platform. **5** (*the cushion-like sole of the foot, or the soft cushion-like paw of certain animals*) foot, paw, sole. **6** (*one's home or room, esp. a flat*) apartment, (*coll.*) digs, flat, home, quarters, room.
~*v.t.* **1** (*to stuff or line with padding*) cushion, fill, line, pack, stuff, upholster, wad. **2** (*to fill out (a sentence, article etc.) with unnecessary words*) amplify, eke, elaborate, expand, fill out, flesh out, inflate, protract, puff up, spin out, stretch. ANTONYMS: condense.

pagan *n.* **1** (*a heathen*) heathen, infidel. **2** (*a person who has no religion or disregards Christian beliefs*) agnostic, atheist, polytheist, unbeliever. ANTONYMS: believer.
~*a.* (*heathen, irreligious*) agnostic, atheistic, godless, heathen, idolatrous, infidel, irreligious, polytheistic, unenlightened.

page[1] *n.* **1** (*a leaf or either side of a leaf of a book etc.*) folio, leaf, sheet, side. **2** (*an episode*) age, chapter, episode, epoch, era, event, incident, period, phase, point, stage, time.

page[2] *n.* **1** (*a young male attendant on people of rank*) attendant, boy, servant. **2** (*a boy in livery* employed to go on errands, attend to the door etc.) (*N Am.*) bellboy, (*N Am.*) bellhop, footman, page-boy.

~*v.t.* (*to summon* (*a person in a hotel etc.*) *by calling their name aloud*) announce, call, send for, summon.

pageant *n.* **1** (*a brilliant display or spectacle, esp. a parade*) display, extravaganza, gala, parade, procession, show, spectacle. **2** (*a theatrical exhibition, usu. representing well-known historical events*) exhibition, re-enactment, tableau.

pageantry *n.* (*the colour and splendour of official celebrations and ceremonies*) ceremony, display, drama, extravagance, glamour, glitter, grandeur, magnificence, ostentation, parade, pomp, show, showiness, spectacle, splash, splendour, state, theatricality.

pain *n.* **1** (*bodily or mental suffering*) affliction, agony, anguish, discomfort, distress, grief, hardship, heartache, hurt, misery, suffering, torment, torture, travail, tribulation, woe. ANTONYMS: relief. **2** (*an instance of bodily or mental suffering*) ache, cramp, irritation, pang, smarting, soreness, spasm, tenderness, throb, twinge. **3** (*pl.*) (*effort, trouble*) bother, effort, exertion, labour, toil, trouble. **4** (*coll.*) (*a nuisance*) aggravation, annoyance, bore, bother, (*coll.*) drag, gall, (*coll.*) headache, irritation, nuisance, (*coll.*) pain in the neck, pest, vexation.

~*v.t.* **1** (*to distress bodily or mentally*) ache, afflict, agonize, ail, chafe, discomfort, distress, harm, hurt, inflame, injure, smart, sting, throb, torment, torture, trouble, vex, worry, wound. **2** (*to annoy or upset*) annoy, exasperate, gall, harass, irritate, rile, upset, vex.

painful *a.* **1** ((*of a part of the body*) *hurting, sore*) aching, agonizing, bitter, burning, excruciating, harrowing, hurting, inflamed, raw, sensitive, sharp, smarting, sore, stabbing, stinging, tender, throbbing. ANTONYMS: comforting, painless. **2** (*causing mental or physical pain*) afflictive, aggravating, annoying, disagreeable, distasteful, distressing, disturbing, grievous, irksome, troubling, unpleasant, worrying. ANTONYMS: pleasant. **3** (*laborious, difficult*) arduous, demanding, difficult, diligent, earnest, exacting, hard, laborious, rigorous, severe, tedious, toilsome, troublesome, trying, vexatious. ANTONYMS: effortless, undemanding.

painstaking *a.* (*extremely thorough*) assiduous, careful, conscientious, diligent, earnest, exacting, hard-working, industrious, methodical, meticulous, persevering, punctilious, scrupulous, sedulous, strenuous, thorough, thoroughgoing. ANTONYMS: careless, negligent.

paint *n.* **1** (*a solid colouring pigment, used to give a coloured coating to surfaces*) colour, colouring, dye, emulsion, enamel, pigment, stain, tint. **2** (*facet.*) (*colouring matter used as a cosmetic, esp. rouge*) cosmetics, greasepaint, make-up, rouge, (*coll.*) warpaint.

~*v.t.* **1** (*to cover or coat with paint*) apply, brush, coat, cover, daub, (*coll.*) slap on. **2** (*to give a specified colour to with paint*) colour, dye, stain, tint. **3** (*to portray or represent in colours*) delineate, depict, picture, portray, render, represent, sketch. **4** (*to adorn*) adorn, decorate, embellish.

pair *n.* **1** (*a set of two, a couple, usu. corresponding to each other*) brace, couple, duo, tandem, twins, twosome. **2** (*an engaged or married couple*) couple, (*coll.*) item, match.

~*v.t.* **1** (*to make or arrange in pairs or couples*) bracket, couple, double, match, pair off, twin. ANTONYMS: separate. **2** (*to join in marriage*) join, marry, unite, wed, yoke.

palatable *a.* **1** (*pleasing to taste*) appetizing, delectable, delicious, luscious, mouth-watering, savoury, tasty, toothsome. ANTONYMS: bland, tasteless. **2** (*agreeable, acceptable*) acceptable, agreeable, attractive, enjoyable, fair, pleasant, satisfactory. ANTONYMS: unpleasant.

palatial *a.* (*magnificent or splendid like a palace*) (*coll.*) classy, de luxe, elegant, gorgeous, grand, illustrious, imposing, luxurious, magnificent, majestic, opulent, (*coll.*) plushy, regal, (*coll.*) ritzy, spacious, splendid, stately, sumptuous, (*coll.*) swanky.

pale[1] *a.* **1** (*ashen, lacking in colour*) anaemic, ashen, bleached, bloodless, colourless, drained, light, livid, pallid, pasty, sallow, wan, washed-out, waxen, white, whitish. ANTONYMS: florid, ruddy. **2** ((*of a colour or light*) *faint*) dim, faint, light. **3** (*poor, feeble*) feeble, flimsy, half-baked, inadequate, lifeless, meagre, poor, puny, spiritless, thin, weak. ANTONYMS: strong.

~*v.i.* **1** (*to turn pale*) blanch, blench, go white, lose colour, whiten. **2** (*to be pale or poor in comparison*) abate, decrease, dim, diminish, dull, fade, lessen, lose lustre.

pale[2] *n.* **1** (*a pointed stake*) spike, stake. **2** (*a narrow board used in fencing*) fencing, paling, palisade, picket, post, slat, upright. **3** (*a limit or boundary*) border, boundary, limit, restriction. **4** (*a region, a district*) confines, district, region, sphere, territory. **beyond the pale** (*unacceptable*) inappropriate, intolerable, unacceptable, unsuitable.

pall[1] *n.* **1** (*a large cloth, thrown over a coffin*) cloth, drape. **2** (*anything that covers or* *shrouds*) cover, mantle, shroud, veil. **3** (*an oppressive atmosphere*) cloud, cold water, damper, dismay, gloom, melancholy, shadow, (*coll.*) wet blanket.

pall[2] *v.i.* (*to become insipid; to become boring*) bore, cloy, glut, gorge, irk, irritate, jade, satiate, sicken, surfeit, tire, weary.

palliative *n.* (*a substance serving to alleviate a disease etc. without curing it*) analgesic, anodyne, drug, painkiller, sedative, tranquillizer.
~*a.* (*serving to alleviate a disease etc. without curing it*) alleviative, anodyne, calming, demulcent, lenitive, mitigatory, mollifying, soothing.

pallid *a.* **1** (*pale, wan*) anaemic, ashen, colourless, pale, pasty, sallow, wan, waxen, whey-faced, white, whitish. **2** (*feeble, insipid*) anaemic, bloodless, feeble, insipid, lifeless, spiritless, sterile, tame, tired, uninspired, vapid. ANTONYMS: lively, strong.

pallor *n.* (*paleness, lack of healthy colour*) bloodlessness, colourfulness, paleness, pallidity, wanness, whiteness.

palpable *a.* **1** (*easily perceived, obvious*) apparent, blatant, clear, conspicuous, evident, manifest, obvious, open, overt, patent, perceptible, plain, unmistakable, visible. **2** (*perceptible to the touch*) concrete, corporeal, material, physical, real, solid, substantial, tangible, touchable. ANTONYMS: impalpable.

palpitate *v.i.* **1** ((*of the heart*) *to beat rapidly*) beat, pound, pulsate, throb. **2** (*to throb, to flutter*) flutter, pulsate, pulse, quiver, shiver, throb, tremble, vibrate.

paltry *a.* (*petty, trivial*) base, beggarly, contemptible, derisory, despicable, inconsiderable, insignificant, little, meagre, mean, miserable, pathetic, petty, pitiful, poor, slight, sorry, trivial, unimportant, wretched. ANTONYMS: impressive, substantial.

pamper *v.t.* **1** (*to indulge* (*a person, oneself*), *often excessively*) baby, cater to, coddle, cosset, fondle, humour, indulge, mollycoddle, over-indulge, pander to, pet, spoil. ANTONYMS: discipline. **2** (*to gratify* (*tastes etc.*) *to excess*) glut, gratify, satiate.

pamphlet *n.* (*a small unbound booklet of a few sheets*) booklet, brochure, circular, folder, handbill, handout, leaflet, tract, treatise.

pandemonium *n.* (*confusion, uproar*) bedlam, chaos, clamour, commotion, confusion, din, disorder, frenzy, furore, hubbub, hue and cry, hullabaloo, racket, (*esp. N Am.*) ruckus, (*coll.*) ruction, rumpus, tumult, turmoil, uproar. ANTONYMS: calm, tranquillity.

pander *v.i.* (*to do something that someone wants*) bow (to), cater (to), fulfil, gratify, humour, indulge, pamper, play up (to), please, satisfy, yield (to).

pang *n.* (*a sudden paroxysm of extreme pain, either physical or mental*) ache, agony, anguish, discomfort, distress, gripe, pain, paroxysm, pinch, prick, spasm, stab, sting, stitch, throe, twinge, wrench.

panic *n.* (*sudden, overpowering fear*) agitation, alarm, consternation, dismay, dread, fright, horror, hysteria, scare, terror. ANTONYMS: composure.
~*v.t., v.i.* (*to affect or be affected with panic*) alarm, dismay, fall apart, fear, go to pieces, lose one's nerve, scare, startle, terrify, unnerve. ANTONYMS: reassure.

panoramic *a.* ((*of a view*) *wide-ranging, complete*) all-embracing, all-encompassing, bird's-eye, commanding, comprehensive, extensive, far-reaching, general, inclusive, overall, scenic, sweeping, wide, wide-ranging.

pant *v.i.* **1** (*to breathe quickly, to gasp for breath*) blow, breathe, gasp, heave, huff, puff, wheeze. **2** (*to throb, to palpitate*) palpitate, pulsate, throb. **3** (*to long, to yearn for*) ache, covet, crave, desire, die for, hanker after, hunger for, long for, pine for, sigh for, thirst for, want, yearn for.
~*n.* **1** (*a gasp*) breath, gasp, huff, puff, wheeze. **2** (*a throb, a palpitation*) palpitation, pulse, throb.

paper *n.* **1** (*a piece of the material used for writing and printing on, wrapping etc.*) leaf, sheet. **2** (*a newspaper*) daily, gazette, journal, newspaper, periodical, (*derog.*) rag, (*derog.*) sheet, tabloid, weekly. **3** (*a written or printed document*) certificate, deed, docket, document, form, instrument, letter, record. **4** (*an essay, a dissertation*) analysis, article, assignment, composition, critique, dissertation, essay, manuscript, monograph, report, study, thesis, tract, treatise. **5** (*pl.*) (*documents establishing identity etc.*) credentials, ID, identification.
~*a.* (*like paper*) cardboard, disposable, flimsy, insubstantial, papery, thin.
~*v.t.* (*to cover with or decorate with paper*) hang, line, paste up, wallpaper.

par *n.* **1** (*average or normal condition, rate etc.*) average, level, mean, median, norm, rank, standard, usual. **2** (*a state of equality*) balance, equality, equilibrium, equivalence, parity.

parable *n.* (*an allegory, esp. of a religious kind*) allegory, fable, lesson, morality tale, story.

parade *n.* **1** (*a muster of troops for inspection*

etc.) cavalcade, column, march, muster, review. **2** (*a parade ground*) drill ground, parade ground. **3** (*show, ostentatious display*) array, display, exhibition, flaunting, ostentation, pomp, show, spectacle, vaunting. ANTONYMS: modesty. **4** (*a procession, esp. in celebration of an important event*) ceremony, pageant, procession, train. **5** (*a public promenade*) esplanade, promenade, seafront. **6** (*a row of shops*) arcade, mall, precinct.
~*v.t.* **1** (*to march through (streets) in a parade*) file, march, process, promenade, walk. **2** (*to display, esp. ostentatiously*) air, brandish, display, exhibit, flaunt, show, (*coll.*) show off, strut, swagger, vaunt.

paradise *n.* **1** (*heaven*) City of God, Elysian Fields, heaven, heavenly kingdom, promised land, Shangri-La, Utopia, Valhalla. ANTONYMS: hell, purgatory. **2** (*a place or condition of perfect bliss*) bliss, delight, ecstasy, felicity, joy, rapture, seventh heaven, utopia. **3** (*the garden of Eden*) Eden, Garden of Eden.

paradox *n.* (*a self-contradictory statement*) absurdity, ambiguity, anomaly, contradiction, dilemma, enigma, incongruity, inconsistency, mystery, oddity, puzzle, quandary, riddle, self-contradiction. ANTONYMS: truism.

paragon *n.* (*a model, an exemplar*) apotheosis, archetype, criterion, epitome, exemplar, ideal, model, nonpareil, norm, paradigm, pattern, prototype, quintessence, standard.

paragraph *n.* (*a distinct portion of a discourse or writing marked by a break in the lines*) clause, item, notice, part, passage, portion, section, subdivision.

parallel *a.* **1** ((*of lines etc.*) *having the same direction and equidistant everywhere*) aligned, alongside, equidistant. **2** (*having the same tendency, corresponding*) akin, analogous, complementary, congruent, corresponding, equivalent, like, matching, resembling, similar, uniform. ANTONYMS: different.
~*n.* **1** (*a comparison*) analogy, comparison, correlation, correspondence, kinship, likeness, parallelism, resemblance, similarity. ANTONYMS: difference. **2** (*a person or thing corresponding to or analogous with another*) analogue, complement, corollary, correspondent, counterpart, duplicate, equal, equivalent, likeness, match, opposite number, twin.
~*v.t.* **1** (*to be parallel to, to match*) equal, match, rival. **2** (*to find a match for*) agree, complement, conform, correlate, correspond, match. ANTONYMS: differ, diverge.

paralyse *v.t.* **1** (*to affect with paralysis*) cripple, debilitate, disable, incapacitate, lame. **2** (*to render powerless or ineffective*) arrest, halt, stop dead, stun, stupefy. **3** (*to render immobile or unable to function*) cripple, disable, freeze, immobilize, inactivate.

paramount *a.* (*pre-eminent, most important*) cardinal, chief, dominant, eminent, first, foremost, main, outstanding, predominant, pre-eminent, primary, principal, superior, supreme. ANTONYMS: inferior, subordinate.

paraphernalia *n.pl.* (*miscellaneous belongings, equipment*) accoutrements, apparatus, appurtenances, baggage, belongings, bits and pieces, chattels, (*sl.*) clobber, effects, equipment, gear, impedimenta, junk, material, possessions, rubbish, stuff, tackle, things, trappings.

paraphrase *n.* **1** (*a free translation or rendering of a passage*) explanation, interpretation, rendering, rendition, rephrasing, rewording, rewrite, translation, version. **2** (*a restatement of a passage in different terms*) rehash, rephrasing, restatement.
~*v.t.* (*to express or interpret in other words*) explain, interpret, render, rephrase, restate, reword, translate.

parasite *n.* (*a person who lives off other people*) bloodsucker, cadger, drone, freeloader, hanger-on, leech, (*coll.*) scrounger, sponge, sponger, sycophant.

parcel *n.* **1** (*a bundle, a package*) box, bundle, carton, case, pack, package, packet. **2** (*a distinct portion, for example of land*) patch, plot, property, tract. **3** (*a number or quantity of things dealt with as a separate lot*) band, batch, bunch, collection, gang, group, lot, pack, set.
~*v.t.* **1** (*to make into a parcel*) bundle up, do up, pack, package, tie up, wrap. ANTONYMS: undo. **2** (*to divide (out) into parts or lots*) allocate, allot, apportion, carve up, deal out, dispense, distribute, divide, dole out, hand out, mete out, portion, share out, split up.

parched *a.* **1** (*dried up*) arid, baked, dehydrated, desiccated, dried up, dry, roasted, scorched, shrivelled, torrid, waterless, withered. ANTONYMS: flooded. **2** (*very thirsty*) dry, (*coll.*) gasping, thirsty.

pardon *n.* **1** (*the act of excusing or forgiving*) absolution, acquittal, allowance, condonation, excuse, exoneration, forgiving, indulgence. ANTONYMS: punishment, retribution. **2** (*a complete or partial remission of the legal consequences of crime*) absolution, acquittal, amnesty, discharge, exoneration, remission, reprieve.
~*v.t.* **1** (*to forgive, to absolve from*) absolve, acquit, condone, exculpate, exonerate, forgive, overlook, release. ANTONYMS: blame, punish.

2 (*to remit the penalty of*) remit, reprieve, spare. **3** (*to refrain from exacting*) excuse, let off, (*coll.*) let off the hook. **4** (*to make allowances for*) allow for, excuse.

pare *v.t.* **1** (*to cut or shave (away or off)*) clip, cut, shave. **2** (*to cut away or remove the rind etc. of (fruit etc.)*) peel, skin. **3** (*to diminish by degrees*) crop, curtail, cut back, decrease, diminish, dock, lessen, lop, lower, prune, reduce, shear, slash.

parent *n.* **1** (*a father or mother*) begetter, father, mother, procreator, progenitor, sire. **2** (*a source, origin*) architect, author, cause, creator, fount, occasion, origin, originator, prototype, root, source, wellspring.

parentage *n.* (*birth, lineage*) ancestry, birth, bloodline, derivation, descent, extraction, family, heritage, line, lineage, origin, paternity, pedigree, race, roots, stock, strain.

parity *n.* **1** (*equality of rank, value etc.*) consistency, equality, equivalence, evenness, par, uniformity, unity. **2** (*parallelism, analogy*) affinity, agreement, analogy, conformity, congruity, correspondence, likeness, parallelism, resemblance, sameness, similarity, similitude. ANTONYMS: disparity.

parliament *n.* **1** (*a deliberative assembly*) assembly, congress, convocation, council, diet. **2** (*a legislative body*) congress, government, House of Commons, House of Lords, House of Representatives, legislative, legislature, senate.

parochial *a.* (*petty, narrow in outlook*) bigoted, close-minded, conservative, dogmatic, insular, intolerant, inward-looking, limited, local, narrow, narrow-minded, opinionated, petty, provincial, regional, restricted, small-minded. ANTONYMS: broad-minded, liberal.

parody *n.* **1** (*a literary composition imitating an author's work for the purpose of humour*) burlesque, caricature, lampoon, satire, (*coll.*) send-up, skit, spoof, (*coll.*) take-off. **2** (*a poor imitation, a mere travesty*) apology, corruption, debasement, distortion, imitation, mockery, perversion, travesty.
~*v.t.* (*to turn into a parody*) ape, burlesque, caricature, deride, guy, imitate, lampoon, mimic, mock, poke fun at, ridicule, satirize, send up, spoof, (*coll.*) take off, travesty.

paroxysm *n.* (*a sudden and violent fit*) attack, convulsion, eruption, explosion, fit, outburst, seizure, spasm, throe.

parry *v.t.* **1** (*to ward off (a blow or thrust)*) block, deflect, fend off, hold at bay, rebuff, repel, repulse, stave off, ward off. **2** (*to evade cleverly,*

to shirk) avert, avoid, circumvent, dodge, (*coll.*) duck, evade, shirk, shun, sidestep.

parsimonious *a.* **1** (*careful in the expenditure of money*) careful, economical, thrifty. **2** (*niggardly, stingy*) close, frugal, grasping, mean, (*coll.*) mingy, miserly, niggardly, penny-pinching, penurious, sparing, stingy, stinting, tightfisted. ANTONYMS: extravagant, spendthrift.

part *n.* **1** (*a piece or amount of a thing or number of things*) bit, fraction, particle, piece, portion, scrap, shard. ANTONYMS: whole. **2** (*a portion separate from the rest or considered as separate*) branch, department, division, ingredient. **3** (*a small component of a machine, vehicle etc.*) component, constituent, element, module, unit. **4** (*a member, an organ*) limb, member, organ. **5** (*any of several equal portions or numbers into which a thing is divided*) allotment, lot, percentage, segment, share, slice. **6** (*interest, concern*) concern, interest, participation. **7** (*side, party*) behalf, cause, concern, faction, interest, party, side. **8** (*the role allotted to an actor*) character, role, words. **9** (*a copy of the words so allotted*) lines, script. **10** (*a person's allotted duty or responsibility*) bit, capacity, charge, duty, function, office, place, responsibility, role, say, share, task, work. **11** (*pl.*) (*accomplishments, talents*) accomplishments, qualities, skills, talents. **12** (*pl.*) (*region, district*) area, corner, district, neighbourhood, quarter, region, territory, vicinity.
~*v.t.* **1** (*to divide into portions, pieces etc.*) break, cleave, detach, disconnect, disjoin, divide, rend, separate, sever, share, split, sunder, tear. ANTONYMS: join, stick, unite. **2** (*to separate*) break up, separate, split up.
~*v.i.* (*to separate from another person or other people*) break up, depart, go, leave, part company, quit, retire, say goodbye, separate, split up, withdraw. ANTONYMS: arrive, stay.

partial *a.* **1** (*affecting a part only, incomplete*) fragmentary, imperfect, incomplete, limited, restricted, uncompleted, unfinished. ANTONYMS: complete, whole. **2** (*biased in favour of one side or party*) biased, discriminatory, influenced, interested, one-sided, partisan, predisposed, prejudiced, tendentious, unfair, unjust. ANTONYMS: impartial, unprejudiced. **3** (*having a preference for something*) fond of, keen on, taken with.

participate *v.i.* (*to have or enjoy a share, to partake (in)*) contribute (to), engage (in), enter (into), get in on the act, help (in), join (in), partake (of), perform, share (in), take part (in). ANTONYMS: abstain (from), opt out (of).

particle *n.* **1** (*an atom*) atom, molecule. **2** (*a* minute *part or portion*) bit, crumb, fragment, grain, hint, iota, jot, mite, morsel, mote, piece, scintilla, scrap, shred, sliver, speck, spot, suggestion, tittle, whit.

particular *a.* **1** (*of or relating to a single person or thing as distinct from others*) distinct, singular, specific. **2** (*special, characteristic*) certain, characteristic, peculiar, special. ANTONYMS: general. **3** (*single, individual*) individual, separate, single. **4** (*minute, circumstantial*) circumstantial, detailed, itemized, minute, painstaking, precise, selective, strict, thorough. **5** (*fastidious, precise*) (*coll.*) choosy, critical, dainty, demanding, difficult, discriminatory, exact, fastidious, finicky, fussy, meticulous, (*coll.*) pernickety, (*coll.*) picky, precise. ANTONYMS: casual, uncritical. **6** (*remarkable, noteworthy*) exceptional, marked, notable, noteworthy, remarkable, singular, uncommon, unusual. ANTONYMS: ordinary.
~*n.* (*an item, a detail*) circumstance, detail, fact, feature, information, instance, item, particularity, point.

parting *n.* **1** (*a departure, leave-taking*) adieu, departure, farewell, going, goodbye, leave-taking, valediction. **2** (*separation, division*) breaking, cleavage, detachment, divergence, division, partition, rift, rupture, separation, severance, split.
~*a.* (*given or bestowed on departure or separation*) closing, concluding, departing, dying, farewell, final, last, valedictory. ANTONYMS: opening.

partisan *n.* **1** (*an adherent of a party, cause etc., esp. one showing unreasoning devotion*) adherent, backer, champion, devotee, disciple, enthusiast, fan, follower, party member, stalwart, supporter, zealot. ANTONYMS: opponent, rival. **2** (*a member of a body of irregular troops carrying out special enterprises, such as raids*) freedom fighter, guerrilla, irregular, resistance fighter, underground member.
~*a.* (*relating or attached to a party*) biased, bigoted, factional, interested, limited, one-sided, partial, prejudiced, sectarian, tendentious. ANTONYMS: bipartisan, impartial.

partition *n.* **1** (*division into parts, distribution*) allotment, apportionment, distribution, dividing, division, portion, rationing out, segmentation, segregation, separation, severance, splitting. **2** (*something which separates into parts, esp. a wall or screen*) barrier, divider, screen, wall.
~*v.t.* **1** (*to divide into parts or shares*) apportion, cut up, divide, parcel out, portion, section, segment, separate, share, split up, subdivide. **2** (*to separate* (*off*)) divide, fence off, screen, separate, wall off.

partner *n.* **1** (*a person who shares with another, esp. one associated with others in business; an associate*) accessory, accomplice, ally, associate, collaborator, colleague, companion, comrade, confederate, co-partner, helper, mate, (*coll.*) pal, participant, (*coll.*) sidekick. ANTONYMS: rival. **2** (*either party in a marriage or a romantic relationship*) boyfriend, companion, consort, girlfriend, husband, lover, mate, other half, (*N Am., coll.*) significant other, spouse, wife.

partnership *n.* **1** (*the state of being a partner or partners*) collaboration, companionship, connection, cooperation, fellowship. **2** (*a contractual relationship between a number of people involved in a business enterprise*) alliance, association, combine, company, conglomeration, cooperative, corporation, firm, house, society, union.

party *n.* **1** (*a social gathering, often to celebrate a special occasion*) (*sl.*) bash, celebration, (*coll.*) do, festivity, function, gathering, (*coll.*) get-together, (*coll.*) knees-up, (*coll.*) rave, reception, (*coll.*) shindig, social, soirée. **2** (*a number of persons united together for a particular purpose, esp. a national political group*) alliance, association, band, bloc, body, camp, circle, clique, coalition, combination, confederacy, coterie, denomination, faction, group, grouping, junta, league, set, side. **3** (*accessory, a person concerned in any affair*) accessory, accomplice, defendant, litigant, participant, plaintiff. **4** (*a person*) individual, person.
~*v.i.* (*to attend parties, go out drinking etc.*) carouse, celebrate, revel.

pass *v.i.* **1** (*to move from one place to another, to go* (*along, on, quickly etc.*)) course, go, make one's way, move, proceed, roll, run, travel. ANTONYMS: halt, stop. **2** (*to be changed from one state to another*) change, transform. **3** (*to change hands, to be transferred*) change hands, transfer. **4** (*to disappear, to vanish*) disappear, dissolve, evaporate, fade, melt away, vanish. **5** (*to die*) cease, die, dwindle, ebb, end, expire, succumb, terminate, wane. **6** (*to go by, to elapse*) depart, elapse, flow, go by, lapse, leave. **7** (*to be successful in a test or examination*) answer, get through, graduate, qualify, succeed. ANTONYMS: fail, lose. **8** (*to happen, to occur*) arise, befall, come about, develop, fall out, happen, occur, take place. **9** (*in team games, to kick or hit the ball to a team-mate*) convey, deliver, exchange, give, hand, kick, send, throw, transfer, transmit. **10** (*to choose not to do something, esp. to answer a question*) decline, reject, turn down.
~*v.t.* **1** (*to go by, through etc.*) go beyond, go by, go over, go through, move through, proceed

through. **2** (*to transfer, to hand round*) distribute, hand round, transfer. **3** (*to spend* (*time etc.*)) devote, dissipate, employ, expend, experience, fill, fritter away, kill, occupy, spend, while away. **4** (*to endure*) endure, go through, suffer, undergo. **5** (*to approve, to enact*) admit, adopt, allow, approve, authorize, decree, enact, endorse, establish, legislate, ordain, ratify, sanction, tolerate, validate. ANTONYMS: prohibit, veto. **6** (*to outstrip, to surpass*) beat, exceed, go beyond, outdistance, outdo, outstrip, overtake, surmount, surpass, transcend. **7** (*to pronounce, to utter*) declare, deliver, express, pronounce, utter. **8** (*to void, to discharge*) defecate, discharge, empty, evacuate, excrete, expel, void. **9** (*to overlook, to disregard*) disregard, ignore, miss, neglect, overlook, reject, renounce, skip, waive. ANTONYMS: acknowledge, notice. **10** (*to omit*) exclude, leave out, omit.
~*n.* **1** (*the act of passing*) going by, passing. **2** (*a passage, esp. a narrow way*) avenue, opening, passage. **3** (*a narrow passage through mountains*) canyon, defile, gap, gorge, gully, ravine. **4** (*a written or printed permission to pass*) authorization, passport, permit, safe conduct, warrant. **5** (*a critical state or condition of things*) condition, crisis, juncture, pinch, plight, predicament, situation, stage, straits. **6** (*in fencing, a thrust*) feint, jab, lunge, push, swing, thrust. **7** (*a sexual advance*) advance, approach, overture, (*coll.*) play, proposal, proposition, suggestion. **8** (*in team games, the act of passing the ball*) handover, throw, toss, transfer. **to pass out 1** (*to faint*) blackout, collapse, faint, (*coll.*) keel over, swoon. **2** ((*of an officer cadet*) *to complete training at a military academy*) graduate, qualify. **3** (*to hand out, to distribute*) deal out, distribute, dole out, hand out.

passable *a.* **1** (*acceptable, fairly good*) acceptable, adequate, admissible, allowable, all right, average, fair, indifferent, mediocre, middling, moderate, not bad, (*coll.*) OK, (*coll.*) okay, ordinary, presentable, satisfactory, (*coll.*) so so, tolerable, unexceptional. ANTONYMS: exceptional, outstanding. **2** (*able to be passed*) clear, crossable, navigable, open, traversable, unblocked, unobstructed. ANTONYMS: blocked, impassable.

passage *n.* **1** (*movement from one place to another, transit*) flow, going, migration, motion, movement, progress, transit. **2** (*transition from one state to another*) change, conversion, metamorphosis, mutation, progression, shift, transition. **3** (*a voyage, a crossing*) crossing, journey, tour, travel, trek, trip, voyage. **4** (*a way by which one passes*) alley, avenue, channel, course, lane, opening, path, road, route, thoroughfare, way. **5** (*a corridor or gallery giving admission to different rooms in a building*) corridor, entrance, entrance hall, exit, foyer, gallery, hall, hallway, lobby, passageway, vestibule. **6** (*right or liberty of passing*) authorization, freedom, permission, right of way, safe conduct, warrant. **7** (*a separate portion of a book, piece of music etc.*) citation, clause, excerpt, extract, paragraph, piece, portion, quotation, reading, section, selection, sentence, text, verse. **8** (*the passing of a bill etc. into law*) approval, enactment, endorsement, establishment, legalization, legislation, legitimization, passing, ratification, sanction. **9** (*pl.*) (*events etc. that pass between people*) episodes, events, incidents. **10** (*a duct in the body*) aperture, duct, hole, orifice.

passenger *n.* **1** (*a person who travels on a public conveyance*) commuter, fare, rider, traveller. **2** (*a person, esp. a member of a team who benefits from something without contributing to it*) hanger-on, parasite, sponger.

passing *a.* **1** (*going by, occurring*) elapsing, going by, happening, occurring. **2** (*incidental, casual*) casual, cursory, dismissive, glancing, hasty, incidental, quick, shallow, short, slight, summary, superficial. **3** (*transient, fleeting*) brief, ephemeral, fleeting, momentary, short, short-lived, temporary, transient, transitory. ANTONYMS: permanent.
~*n.* **1** (*passage*) lapse, passage, transit. **2** (*death*) death, decease, demise, disappearance, dying, end, expiration, extinction, finish, loss, termination.

passion *n.* **1** (*a deep and overpowering affection of the mind*) emotion, feeling, intensity. ANTONYMS: apathy, indifference. **2** (*an outburst of violent anger*) anger, fit, flare-up, frenzy, fury, indignation, ire, outburst, paroxysm, rage, resentment, storm, vehemence, wrath. ANTONYMS: composure. **3** (*strong sexual love*) adoration, affection, ardour, attachment, desire, fondness, infatuation, love, lust, yearning. **4** (*ardent enthusiasm* (*for*)) animation, craving, eagerness, enthusiasm, excitement, fascination, fervour, fire, gusto, heat, mania, obsession, rapture, spirit, transport, verve, vivacity, warmth, zeal, zest.

passionate *a.* (*easily moved to strong feeling, esp. love or anger*) amorous, animated, ardent, eager, emotional, enthusiastic, excited, fervent, fiery, frenzied, hot, impassioned, intense, sensual, sexy, stormy, strong, tempestuous, vehement, warm, wild. ANTONYMS: frigid, unemotional.

passive *a.* **1** (*suffering, acted upon*) acted upon, enduring, suffering. ANTONYMS: active.

2 (*inactive, submissive*) acquiescent, compliant, dispassionate, docile, inactive, inert, lifeless, meek, placid, pliable, quiescent, resigned, submissive, tractable, unassertive, uninvolved, unresisting, unresponsive. ANTONYMS: lively, spirited.

past *a.* **1** (*just elapsed*) accomplished, completed, dead, defunct, done, elapsed, ended, extinct, finished, forgotten, gone, gone by, over, spent. **2** (*former*) ancient, bygone, early, erstwhile, former, last, late, obsolete, olden, preceding, previous, prior, recent.
~*n.* **1** (*past times*) antiquity, days gone by, days of old, former times, good old days, history, long ago, olden days, times past, yesterday, yesteryear. ANTONYMS: future, present. **2** (*one's past career*) background, career, experience, history, life, past life.
~*prep.* (*beyond in time or place*) after, beyond, outside, over, subsequent to.
~*adv.* (*so as to go by*) across, ago, beyond, further, nearby, on, over.

paste *n.* **1** (*a spread made of ground meat or fish*) pâté, spread, topping. **2** (*any doughy or plastic mixture, esp. of solid substances with liquid*) adhesive, cement, glue, gum.
~*v.t.* **1** (*to fasten or stick with paste*) cement, fasten, fix, glue, stick. **2** (*to thrash, to beat*) beat, (*N Am., coll.*) cream, flog, (*coll.*) lick, thrash.

pastime *n.* (*something that makes time pass agreeably, a hobby*) activity, amusement, distraction, diversion, entertainment, game, hobby, leisure, pursuit, recreation, relaxation, sport. ANTONYMS: work.

pastoral *a.* **1** ((*of poetry etc.*) *portraying country life*) Arcadian, bucolic, country, idyllic, provincial, rural, rustic. **2** (*befitting a pastor*) church, clerical, ecclesiastical, ministerial, priestly.

pasture *n.* (*grass suitable for the grazing of cattle etc.*) grass, grassland, grazing, lea, meadow.

pat *v.t.* **1** (*to strike gently and quickly with something flat, esp. the hand*) dab, slap, tap. **2** (*to tap, to stroke gently*) caress, fondle, pet, stroke, touch.
~*n.* **1** (*a light, quick blow with the hand*) blow, caress, clap, dab, slap, stroke, tap, touch. **2** (*a small mass or lump (of butter etc.) moulded by patting*) dab, lump, patty, portion.

patch *n.* **1** (*a piece of cloth or other material put on to mend anything*) cloth, cover, covering, material. **2** (*a small piece of ground, a plot*) area, field, ground, land, lot, plot, tract. **3** (*coll.*) (*the district for which a police officer,*

social worker etc. has responsibility*) area, bailiwick, responsibility, territory. **4** (*coll.*) (*a period of time*) period, phase, spell, stretch, time. **5** (*a scrap, a shred*) bit, scrap, shred, snippet, spot.
~*v.t.* (*to mend with a patch or patches (usu. with up)*) fix, mend, repair, sew, stitch.

patent *n.* (*the official exclusive right to make or sell a new invention*) copyright, licence, mark, trade mark.
~*a.* **1** (*plain, obvious*) apparent, blatant, clear, conspicuous, evident, explicit, flagrant, glaring, manifest, obvious, plain, self-evident, tangible, transparent, unequivocal, unmistakable. **2** (*protected or conferred by letters patent*) protected, registered.

paternal *a.* **1** (*fatherly*) benevolent, caring, concerned, devoted, fatherly, fond, kindly, protective, solicitous, vigilant. **2** (*connected or related through the father*) patrilineal, patrimonial.

path *n.* **1** (*a footway, esp. one beaten only by feet*) footpath, footway, pathway, towpath. **2** (*a course or track*) course, passage, road, route, track, trail, walk, way. **3** (*a course of life, action etc.*) approach, avenue, course of action, direction, means, plan, procedure, route, scheme, strategy.

pathetic *a.* **1** (*affecting the feelings, esp. those of pity and sorrow*) affecting, distressing, doleful, emotional, harrowing, heartbreaking, heart-rending, moving, pitiable, plaintive, poignant, sad, sentimental, stirring, tender, touching. **2** (*coll.*) (*poor or contemptible*) contemptible, deplorable, feeble, inadequate, lamentable, meagre, measly, miserable, paltry, petty, pitiful, poor, puny, sorry, trashy, useless, weak, (*coll.*) wet, woeful, worthless.

patience *n.* **1** (*the quality of being patient*) calmness, composure, (*coll.*) cool, equanimity, forbearance, imperturbability, leniency, resignation, restraint, self-control, serenity, sufferance, tolerance, toleration. ANTONYMS: exasperation, impatience. **2** (*calm endurance of pain, provocation etc.*) constancy, diligence, endurance, fortitude, indefatigability, long-suffering, perseverance, persistence, pertinacity, resignation, steadfastness, stoicism, submission, tenacity.

patient *a.* **1** (*capable of bearing pain, suffering etc. without fretfulness*) calm, composed, enduring, imperturbable, long-suffering, passive, philosophical, quiet, resigned, self-possessed, serene, stoical, submissive, uncomplaining. ANTONYMS: impatient. **2** (*not easily provoked, indulgent*) accommodating, compliant, even-tempered, forbearing, forgiving, indulgent,

lenient, mild, tolerant, understanding. **3** (*persevering, diligent*) assiduous, determined, diligent, dogged, firm, indefatigable, persevering, persistent, pertinacious, resolute, resolved, sedulous, tenacious, untiring, unyielding.
~*n.* (*a person under medical treatment*) case, inmate, invalid, sufferer.

patriotic *a.* (*loving one's country and devoted to its interests*) chauvinistic, flag-waving, jingoistic, loyal, nationalistic, true-blue.

patrol *n.* **1** (*the action of moving around an area, esp. at night, for security*) beat, defending, guarding, policing, protection, round, safeguarding, vigilance, watchfulness. **2** (*the detachment of soldiers, police etc., doing this*) garrison, guard, lookout, police, sentinel, sentry, watch. **3** (*a routine operational voyage or flight*) flight, milk run, voyage.
~*v.i.* (*to go on a patrol*) defend, guard, inspect, keep guard, keep vigil, keep watch, police, pound, protect, range, safeguard, walk the beat, watch over.

patron *n.* **1** (*a person who supports or fosters a person, cause etc.*) advocate, (*coll.*) angel, backer, benefactor, champion, defender, friend, guardian, philanthropist, promoter, protector, sponsor, supporter, sympathizer. **2** (*a regular customer (at a shop etc.*)) buyer, client, customer, frequenter, habitué, regular, shopper.

patronize *v.t.* **1** (*to treat in a condescending way*) condescend towards, demean, disdain, humiliate, look down on, put down, scorn, talk down to. **2** (*to act as a patron towards*) aid, back, champion, encourage, foster, help, maintain, promote, sponsor, subscribe to, support, underwrite. **3** (*to frequent as a customer*) buy from, deal with, favour, frequent, shop at, trade with.

pattern *n.* **1** (*a decorative design for a carpet, fabric etc.*) arrangement, decoration, design, device, figure, motif, ornament. **2** (*a type, style*) kind, shape, sort, style, type, variety. **3** (*a model or original to be copied or serving as a guide in making something*) blueprint, diagram, guide, instructions, layout, model, original, plan, stencil, template. **4** (*a model, an exemplar*) archetype, criterion, exemplar, guide, ideal, model, norm, original, par, paragon, prototype, standard. **5** (*a sample or specimen (of cloth etc.*)) example, instance, representation, sample, specimen, swatch.
~*v.t.* **1** (*to copy, to model (after, from or upon*)) copy, emulate, follow, imitate, mimic, model, mould, order, shape, simulate, style. **2** (*to decorate with a pattern*) decorate, design, ornament, trim.

pause *n.* **1** (*a cessation or intermission of action, speaking etc.*) abeyance, cessation, discontinuance, intermission, interruption. **2** (*a break in reading, speaking etc., esp. for the sake of emphasis*) break, delay, gap, halt, hesitation, hiatus, interlude, interval, lacuna, lapse, (*coll.*) let-up, lull, respite, rest, stay, stoppage, wait.
~*v.i.* (*to make a pause or short stop*) break, cease, delay, desist, discontinue, falter, halt, hesitate, hold up, interrupt, mark time, rest, stop, suspend, wait, waver. ANTONYMS: continue, proceed.

pave *v.t.* (*to make a hard, level surface upon, with stone, bricks etc.*) cobble, concrete, cover, flag, floor, surface, tarmac, tile.

pay *v.t.* **1** (*to hand over to (someone) what is due in discharge of a debt or for services or goods*) recompense, reimburse, remunerate. ANTONYMS: owe. **2** (*to give (money) to someone in discharge of a debt or for services or goods*) (*sl.*) cough up, extend, (*coll.*) fork out, give, hand over, lay out, offer, present, proffer, refund, render, spend. ANTONYMS: withhold. **3** (*to discharge (a bill, claim etc.*)) clear, defray, discharge, foot, honour, liquidate, meet, satisfy, settle, square up. ANTONYMS: owe. **4** (*to deliver as due*) bestow, deliver, give, pass on, transmit. **5** (*to reward or punish*) get even, hit back, pay back, punish, reciprocate, repay, requite, retaliate, reward. **6** (*to compensate, to recompense*) answer, atone, compensate, make amends, recompense, requite. **7** (*to bestow, to tender (a compliment, visit etc.*)) bestow, tender.
~*v.i.* (*to make an adequate return (to*)) benefit, bring in, produce, profit, return, yield.
~*n.* **1** (*wages, salary*) earnings, emolument, fee, income, salary, stipend, takings, wages. **2** (*payment, compensation*) compensation, consideration, gain, payment, profit, recompense, reimbursement, remittance, remuneration, reward, settlement.

payment *n.* (*an amount of money paid*) amount, contribution, earnings, fee, pay, remittance, remuneration, settlement.

pay-off *n.* **1** (*the final payment of a bill etc.*) defrayal, discharge, outlay, paying, remittance, settlement. **2** (*a return on an investment etc.*) fee, outlay, pay, recompense, remuneration, return, yield. **3** (*a conclusion, final result*) conclusion, consequence, outcome, result, upshot.

peace *n.* **1** (*a state of quiet or tranquillity*) calm, hush, peacefulness, quiet, repose, silence, stillness, tranquillity. **2** (*calmness of mind*) calm, composure, contentment, placidity, relaxation, repose, serenity. **3** (*freedom from or cessation of war*) armistice, ceasefire, pacification, peacetime, truce. ANTONYMS: war. **4** (*a treaty reconciling two hostile nations*) pact, reconciliation, settlement, treaty. **5** (*absence of civil disturbance or agitation*) accord, agreement, amity, concord, harmony. ANTONYMS: dissent, disturbance.

peaceable *a.* **1** (*disposed to peace*) amiable, amicable, conciliatory, congenial, friendly, gentle, inoffensive, mild, pacific, peaceful, peace-loving, placatory, placid, temperate. ANTONYMS: belligerent. **2** (*peaceful, quiet*) balmy, calm, peaceful, quiet, restful, serene, still, tranquil, undisturbed. ANTONYMS: troubled.

peaceful *a.* **1** (*quiet, peace-loving*) amicable, conciliatory, friendly, mild, peaceable, peace-loving, placatory, quiescent, quiet, unwarlike. ANTONYMS: antagonistic, hostile. **2** (*free from noise or disturbance*) calm, gentle, placid, quiet, restful, serene, still, undisturbed, unruffled, untroubled. ANTONYMS: agitated. **3** (*in a state of peace*) at peace, free from strife, harmonious. ANTONYMS: warring.

peak *n.* **1** (*a sharp point or top, esp. of a mountain*) apex, brow, crest, pinnacle, point, ridge, summit, tip, top. ANTONYMS: foot. **2** (*a mountain with a peak*) elevation, eminence, height, hill, mountain. **3** (*the projecting brim in front of a cap*) brim, shade, visor. **4** (*the point of greatest activity, demand etc.*) acme, apogee, climax, consummation, crown, culmination, high point, zenith.
~*v.i.* (*to reach a peak*) climax, come to a head, crest, culminate, reach one's zenith, rise, top.

peasant *n.* **1** (*a rustic labourer*) farm worker, labourer. **2** (*coll.*) (*a country person*) bumpkin, churl, countryman, countrywoman, (*coll.*) hick, provincial, rustic, yokel. **3** (*a rough, uncouth person*) boor, lout, oaf.
~*a.* (*rustic, rural*) agricultural, rural, rustic.

peck *v.t.* **1** (*to strike with a beak or pointed instrument*) bite, dig, hit, jab, pick, poke, prick, rap, strike, tap. **2** (*to eat, esp. in small amounts*) eat, nibble, play with.
~*n.* (*a sharp stroke with or as with a beak*) bite, dig, hit, jab, pick, poke, prick, rap, stroke, tap.

peculiar *a.* **1** (*strange, odd*) aberrant, abnormal, bizarre, curious, eccentric, exceptional, extraordinary, freakish, funny, odd, (*coll.*) offbeat, off the wall, outlandish, queer, quirky, singular, strange, uncommon, unusual, weird. ANTONYMS: commonplace, ordinary. **2** (*belonging particularly and exclusively (to)*) characteristic (of), exclusive (to), particular (to), specific (to). **3** (*of or relating to the individual*)

individual, individualistic, personal. **4** (*particular, special*) distinctive, idiosyncratic, particular, special, unique. **5** (*one's own, private*) own, private. ANTONYMS: general. **6** (*feeling unwell*) ill, out of sorts, sick, unwell.

peculiarity *n.* **1** (*the quality of being peculiar*) oddity, singularity, strangeness. **2** (*an idiosyncrasy*) abnormality, curiosity, eccentricity, foible, idiosyncrasy, irregularity, kink, mannerism, oddity, quirk. **3** (*a characteristic*) attribute, characteristic, feature, hallmark, mark, property, quality, singularity, speciality, trait.

pecuniary *a.* (*relating to or consisting of money*) commercial, financial, fiscal, monetary.

pedantic *a.* (*giving too much attention to rules and small details*) didactic, fastidious, finicky, formal, fussy, hair-splitting, meticulous, (*coll.*) nit-picking, particular, (*coll.*) picky, pompous, precise, pretentious, priggish, punctilious, quibbling, sententious, stiff, stilted, stuffy.

peel *v.t.* (*to strip (rind etc.) off a fruit etc.*) flay, pare, shuck, skin, strip.
~*v.i.* **1** (*to lose the skin or rind, to become bare*) flake off, scale. **2** (*to undress*) disrobe, doff, strip, undress.
~*n.* (*skin, rind*) coating, peeling, rind, skin.

peep *v.i.* **1** (*to look through a crevice or narrow opening*) peek, peer, squint. **2** (*to look slyly or furtively*) sneak a look, spy, steal a look. **3** (*to appear partially or cautiously*) appear, come out, emerge, show.
~*n.* (*a furtive look, a hasty glance*) (*coll.*) gander, glance, glimpse, look, peek, (*sl.*) shufti.

peer[1] *v.i.* (*to look very closely (at, into etc.)*) examine, gaze, inspect, pore over, scan, scrutinize, snoop, spy, squint.

peer[2] *n.* **1** (*a noble, esp. a member of a hereditary legislative body*) aristocrat, baron, count, duke, earl, lady, lord, marquess, marquis, noble, nobleman, noblewoman, viscount. ANTONYMS: commoner. **2** (*an equal in any respect*) associate, co-equal, colleague, compeer, equal, fellow, like, match, mate. ANTONYMS: inferior, superior.

peerless *a.* (*without an equal*) beyond compare, excellent, incomparable, inimitable, matchless, nonpareil, pre-eminent, second to none, superlative, supreme, unequalled, unique, unmatched, unparalleled, unrivalled, unsurpassed, without equal. ANTONYMS: average, standard.

peevish *a.* (*irritable, expressing discontent*) cantankerous, captious, churlish, crotchety, crusty, discontent, fractious, fretful, grumpy, irritable, petulant, querulous, (*sl.*) ratty, snappy, sour, splenetic, sullen, surly, testy, waspish. ANTONYMS: affable, genial.

pelt *v.t.* **1** (*to strike or assail by throwing missiles*) assail, batter, beat, belabour, bomb, (*sl.*) clobber, pound, strafe, strike, thrash. **2** (*to throw*) cast, hurl, sling, throw. **3** (*to strike repeatedly*) bombard, pepper, pummel, rain down, shower. **4** (*to assail with insults or abuse*) abuse, insult, pillory.
~*v.i.* **1** ((*of rain etc.*) *to beat down heavily*) beat, (*coll.*) bucket down, dash, (*Sc., North.*) hozzle, pound, pour, (*coll.*) rain cats and dogs, teem. **2** (*to hurry* (*along*)) (*sl.*) belt, (*coll.*) burn rubber, career, charge, dash, hurry, run, rush, scurry, shoot, speed, tear, whiz. ANTONYMS: amble.

pen[1] *n.* (*an instrument for writing with ink*) ballpoint, felt tip, fountain pen, quill.
~*v.t.* (*to compose and write*) commit to paper, compose, draft, jot down, note, scratch, scrawl, scribble, write.

pen[2] *n.* **1** (*a small enclosure for cattle, sheep etc.*) cage, coop, corral, enclosure, fold, hutch, pound, stall, sty. **2** (*N Am., sl.*) (*a penitentiary, a prison*) gaol, jail, penitentiary, prison.
~*v.t.* (*to shut or coop* (*up or in*)) cage, confine, coop up, detain, enclose, fence in, hedge, hem in, impound, incarcerate, round up, shut up. ANTONYMS: free, release.

penalize *v.t.* (*to subject to a penalty or handicap*) correct, discipline, fine, handicap, punish, sentence. ANTONYMS: reward.

penalty *n.* **1** (*legal punishment for a crime or misdemeanour*) discipline, penance, punishment, retribution, sentence. ANTONYMS: reward. **2** (*a fine, a forfeit*) fine, forfeit, mulct, price. **3** (*a handicap imposed for a breach of rules or on the winner in a previous contest*) disadvantage, handicap.

penance *n.* **1** (*sorrow for sin evinced by acts of self-mortification etc.*) contrition, penitence, regret, repentance, sorrow. **2** (*an act of self-mortification undertaken as a satisfaction for sin, esp. one imposed by a priest before giving absolution*) amends, atonement, humiliation, mortification, penalty, punishment, reparation, sackcloth and ashes.

penchant *n.* (*a strong inclination or liking*) affinity, bent, bias, disposition, fondness, inclination, leaning, liking, partiality, predilection, predisposition, preference, proclivity, proneness, propensity, taste, tendency, weakness. ANTONYMS: aversion.

pending *a.* (*awaiting settlement, undecided*) depending, forthcoming, imminent, impending, in abeyance, inconclusive, on hold, undecided, undetermined, unresolved, unsettled. ANTONYMS: decided.

penetrable *a.* **1** (*that can be penetrated or entered*) accessible, clear, open, passable, permeable, pervious, porous, vulnerable. ANTONYMS: impenetrable. **2** (*that can be penetrated or understood*) accessible, clear, comprehensible, fathomable, intelligible. ANTONYMS: impenetrable.

penetrate *v.t.* **1** (*to pass into or through*) enter, go through, pass into. **2** (*to saturate or imbue* (*with*)) diffuse, filter, imbue, impregnate, infiltrate, invade, percolate, permeate, pervade, saturate, seep, suffuse. **3** (*to reach or discern by the senses or intellect*) comprehend, decipher, discern, discover, fathom, figure out, get, grasp, perceive, sense, (*sl.*) suss, understand, unravel, work out. **4** (*to move or affect the feelings of*) affect, come across, impress, move, reach, register, touch. **5** (*to pierce*) bore, drill, impale, lance, perforate, pierce, prick, probe, puncture, spear, stab.

penetrating *a.* **1** (*subtle, discerning*) acute, astute, critical, deep, discerning, discriminating, incisive, intelligent, keen, perceptive, perspicacious, profound, quick, sagacious, searching, sensitive, shallow, sharp-witted, shrewd, smart, subtle, unperceptive. **2** (*sharp, piercing*) biting, carrying, harsh, intrusive, mordant, pervasive, piercing, pungent, sharp, shrill, stinging, strident, strong, trenchant.

penitence *n.* (*repentance*) compunction, contrition, grief, penance, regret, remorse, repentance, ruefulness, self-reproach, shame, sorrow. ANTONYMS: impenitence.

penitent *a.* (*repentant, sorry*) abject, apologetic, atoning, conscience-stricken, contrite, grief-stricken, regretful, remorseful, repentant, shamefaced, sorrowful, sorry. ANTONYMS: impenitent, unrepentant.

penniless *a.* (*without money, destitute*) bankrupt, (*coll.*) broke, (*sl.*) cleaned out, destitute, (*coll.*) flat broke, impecunious, indigent, necessitous, needy, penurious, poor, poverty-stricken, short, (*sl.*) skint, (*sl.*) stony-broke, (*coll.*) strapped. ANTONYMS: rich, wealthy.

pensive *a.* **1** (*thoughtful*) brooding, cogitative, contemplative, distracted, dreamy, meditative, musing, preoccupied, reflective, ruminative, thoughtful. ANTONYMS: carefree. **2** (*anxious, melancholy*) anxious, (*coll.*) blue, grave, melancholy, mournful, sad, serious, sober, solemn, sorrowful, wistful. ANTONYMS: happy, light-hearted.

penurious *a.* **1** (*poor, penniless*) (*coll.*) broke, destitute, hard up, impecunious, impoverished, indigent, needy, penniless, poor, poverty-stricken. ANTONYMS: rich. 2 (*niggardly, stingy*) begrudging, close, frugal, grudging, mean, miserly, niggardly, parsimonious, penny-pinching, stingy, thrifty, tight-fisted. ANTONYMS: generous.

people *n.* 1 (*usu. as pl.*) (*the persons composing a nation, community or race*) bodies, commonalty, human beings, humanity, humans, individuals, mankind, masses, mortals, multitude, persons. 2 (*usu. as pl.*) (*any body of persons, such as those belonging to a place*) citizens, clan, class, community, company, congregation, folk, inhabitants, nation, populace, population, public, race, society, tribe. 3 (*as pl.*) (*one's family, kindred*) family, kin, kindred, relations, relatives. 4 (*as pl., N Am.*) (*one's ancestors*) ancestors, forebears. 5 (*as pl.*) (*followers, servants etc.*) followers, retinue, servants.
~*v.t.* 1 (*to stock with inhabitants*) colonize, populate, settle, stock. 2 (*to occupy, to inhabit*) dwell in, inhabit, live in, occupy, reside in.

peppery *a.* 1 (*tasting of or like pepper*) fiery, highly seasoned, hot, piquant, pungent, spicy. ANTONYMS: bland, mild. 2 (*hot-tempered, irascible*) choleric, hasty, hot-tempered, irascible, irritable, quick-tempered, snappish, testy, touchy, vitriolic, waspish. 3 (*pungent, sharp*) biting, caustic, incisive, pungent, sarcastic, sharp, stinging, trenchant, vitriolic.

perceive *v.t.* 1 (*to observe, to see*) behold, descry, discern, espy, glimpse, make out, notice, observe, see, spot. 2 (*to apprehend with the mind, to discern*) appreciate, apprehend, catch on, comprehend, conclude, deduce, discern, fathom, feel, gather, get, grasp, infer, realize, (*sl.*) suss, understand.

perceptible *a.* (*able to be perceived by the senses or intellect*) apparent, appreciable, clear, conspicuous, detectable, discernible, distinct, distinguishable, evident, noticeable, observable, obvious, palpable, perceivable, recognizable, tangible, visible. ANTONYMS: imperceptible, invisible.

perception *n.* 1 (*intuitive apprehension, discernment*) appreciation, apprehension, awareness, comprehension, conception, consciousness, discernment, feeling, grasp, insight, intuition, knowledge, observation, percipience, recognition, sensation, sense, taste, understanding. 2 (*an impression based on one's perception of something*) awareness, conception, idea, impression, notion.

perceptive *a.* (*discerning, astute*) acute, alert, aware, discerning, insightful, intuitive, observant, penetrating, percipient, perspicacious, quick, responsive, sensitive, sharp, shrewd. ANTONYMS: insensitive, obtuse.

perch *n.* 1 (*a pole or bar used as a rest or roost for birds*) bar, branch, pole, post, rest, roost. 2 (*a high seat or position*) location, perspective, position, spot, vantage point.
~*v.i.* 1 ((*of a bird*) *to alight or rest*) alight, rest, roost. 2 (*to alight or settle on or as if on a perch*) alight, balance, land, settle on, sit on.

percolate *v.i.* (*to pass through small interstices*) drain, drip, exude, filter (through), leach, ooze, penetrate, permeate, pervade, seep, transfuse, trickle.
~*v.t.* (*to strain*) filter, filtrate, strain.

perdition *n.* (*the loss of the soul or of happiness in a future state*) condemnation, damnation, destruction, doom, downfall, hell, hellfire, ruin, ruination. ANTONYMS: salvation.

peremptory *a.* 1 (*imperious, dictatorial*) arbitrary, assertive, authoritative, autocratic, bossy, despotic, dictatorial, dogmatic, domineering, high-handed, imperious, insistent, intolerant, overbearing, tyrannical. 2 (*absolute, decisive*) absolute, binding, categorical, commanding, compelling, decisive, determined, final, imperative, incontrovertible, irrefutable, mandatory, obligatory, positive, undeniable.

perennial *a.* 1 (*lasting throughout the year*) all-year-round, year-round. 2 (*lasting long, never ceasing*) abiding, ceaseless, constant, continuing, endless, enduring, everlasting, imperishable, incessant, inveterate, lasting, lifelong, never-ending, perpetual, persistent, recurrent, unceasing, unchanging, unfailing, uninterrupted. ANTONYMS: ephemeral.

perfect[1] *a.* 1 (*complete in all its parts, qualities etc.*) complete, finished. ANTONYMS: imperfect. 2 (*thoroughly trained, skilled etc.*) accomplished, adept, deft, experienced, expert, finished, masterly, polished, practised, proficient, skilful, skilled, versed. 3 (*precise, exact*) accurate, authentic, close, correct, exact, faithful, precise, right, (*coll.*) spot-on, strict, true, unerring. ANTONYMS: imprecise, inaccurate. 4 (*of the best kind*) best, consummate, highest. 5 (*entire, complete*) absolute, complete, entire, full, unadulterated, unalloyed, unmitigated, unqualified, utter, whole. 6 (*without defect or fault*) blameless, clean, excellent, exemplary, exquisite, faultless, flawless, ideal, immaculate, impeccable, mint, pure, spotless, sublime, superb, superlative, supreme, unblemished, unmarred, untarnished. ANTONYMS: damaged, defective.

perfect[2] *v.t.* 1 (*to finish or complete*) accomplish, achieve, carry out, complete, consummate, effect, execute, finish, fulfil, perform, realize. 2 (*to render thoroughly versed or* *skilled* (*in*)) ameliorate, correct, cultivate, develop, elaborate, hone, improve, polish, rectify, refine. ANTONYMS: spoil.

perfection *n.* **1** (*supreme excellence*) excellence, superiority. **2** (*complete development*) accomplishment, achievement, completeness, consummation, fulfilment, realization. **3** (*faultlessness*) faultlessness, flawlessness, integrity, purity. ANTONYMS: imperfection. **4** (*a perfect person or thing*) acme, archetype, crown, essence, ideal, model, paragon, pattern, pinnacle, quintessence, standard, summit.

perfectly *adv.* **1** (*completely, totally*) absolutely, altogether, completely, consummately, entirely, fully, positively, purely, quite, thoroughly, totally, truly, utterly, very, wholly. ANTONYMS: incompletely, partly. **2** (*in a perfect way, without faults*) admirably, exquisitely, faultlessly, flawlessly, ideally, impeccably, incomparably, marvellously, superbly, superlatively, supremely, to perfection, wonderfully. ANTONYMS: badly, imperfectly.

perfidious *a.* (*treacherous, deceitful*) corrupt, deceitful, dishonest, disloyal, double-dealing, faithless, false, hypocritical, treacherous, two-faced, unfaithful, untrustworthy. ANTONYMS: faithful, loyal.

perforate *v.t.* (*to bore through, to pierce*) bore, drill, hole, penetrate, pierce, prick, punch, puncture, riddle.

perform *v.t.* **1** (*to carry through, to accomplish*) accomplish, achieve, bring about, carry through, do, effect, execute, knock off, pull off. **2** (*to discharge, fulfil*) complete, discharge, fulfil, satisfy. **3** (*to represent on the stage*) enact, mount, play, present, produce, put on, stage. **4** (*to play* (*music*)) play, render. *~v.i.* **1** (*to act a part*) act, depict, interpret. **2** (*to play a musical instrument, sing etc.*) play, sing. **3** (*to function* (*well*)) function, go, operate, respond, run, work.

performance *n.* **1** (*carrying out, completion*) accomplishment, achievement, carrying out, completion, consummation, discharge, execution, fulfilment. **2** (*a thing done, an action*) act, action. **3** (*a feat, a notable deed*) accomplishment, deed, exploit, feat. **4** (*the performing of a play, display of feats etc.*) acting, display, enactment, exhibition, interpretation, play, portrayal, presentation, production, show, staging. **5** (*an entertainment*) entertainment, (*coll.*) gig. **6** ((*of a vehicle etc.*) *the capacity to function* (*well*)) action, conduct, efficiency, functioning, operation, practice, running, working. **7** (*an elaborate or laborious action, a fuss*) bother, business, (*coll.*) carry-on, fuss,

(*coll.*) palaver, rigmarole, (*coll.*) to-do. **8** (*a return on an investment*) income, profit, return, yield.

performer *n.* (*a person who performs, esp. an actor, musician etc.*) actor, actress, artist, artiste, dancer, entertainer, musician, player, singer, thespian, trouper.

perfume *n.* **1** (*a sweet smell*) aroma, bouquet, fragrance, redolence, scent, smell, sweetness. ANTONYMS: stench, stink. **2** (*a substance emitting a sweet odour, scent*) eau-de-Cologne, essence, extract, fragrance, incense, scent, toilet water.

perfunctory *a.* (*done merely as a duty or in a careless manner*) automatic, careless, cursory, dismissive, half-hearted, heedless, inattentive, indifferent, mechanical, negligent, offhand, routine, sketchy, slipshod, slovenly, superficial, thoughtless, unconcerned, uninterested. ANTONYMS: conscientious, thorough.

perhaps *adv.* (*possibly*) conceivably, feasibly, maybe, †perchance, possibly. ANTONYMS: definitely.

peril *n.* (*danger, exposure to injury or destruction*) danger, exposure, hazard, insecurity, jeopardy, menace, risk, susceptibility, threat, uncertainty, vulnerability. ANTONYMS: safety, security.

perilous *a.* (*dangerous*) chancy, dangerous, exposed, fraught, (*coll.*) hairy, hazardous, insecure, menacing, precarious, risky, threatening, uncertain, unsafe, vulnerable. ANTONYMS: safe.

perimeter *n.* **1** (*the bounding line of a plane figure*) circuit, circumference. **2** (*the boundary of a camp etc.*) ambit, border, borderline, boundary, bounds, confines, edge, fringe, limit, margin, periphery, verge. ANTONYMS: centre, middle.

period *n.* **1** (*any specified portion of time*) duration, interval, space, span, spell, stretch, term, time, while. **2** (*a definite or indefinite portion of time, an age*) aeon, age, course, cycle, date, days, epoch, era, generation, season, stage, term, time, years. **3** (*a length of time allotted to a school lesson*) class, lesson, seminar, tutorial.

periodic *a.* (*happening or appearing at fixed intervals*) cyclic, episodic, intermittent, occasional, periodical, recurrent, regular, repeated, seasonal, spasmodic, sporadic. ANTONYMS: continuous.

periodical *n.* (*a magazine or other publication published at regular intervals, e.g. monthly*) journal, magazine, monthly, organ, paper, publication, quarterly, review, serial, weekly.

peripatetic *a.* (*walking about, itinerant*) ambulant, itinerant, migrant, mobile, nomadic, roaming, roving, travelling, wandering.

peripheral *a.* **1** (*of relatively little importance*) beside the point, incidental, inessential, irrelevant, marginal, minor, secondary, superficial, tangential, unimportant. **2** (*of or relating to a periphery*) external, outer, surface. **3** (*being an additional device, esp. in computing*) additional, auxiliary, supplementary, supporting.

perish *v.i.* **1** (*to be destroyed, to come to nothing*) break down, collapse, decline, disappear, fade, fail, fall, vanish. ANTONYMS: last. **2** (*to die*) decease, die, expire, pass away. **3** (*to decay, to wither*) decay, decompose, disintegrate, moulder, rot, waste, wither.

perishable *a.* (*liable to perish, subject to rapid decay*) decaying, decomposable, destructible, short-lived, unstable, vulnerable. ANTONYMS: lasting, non-perishable.

perk *v.t., v.i.* **to perk up** (*coll.*) ((*to cause*) *to be more cheerful or lively*) brighten, buck up, cheer up, invigorate, liven up, (*coll.*) pep up, quicken, rally, recover, recuperate, revive, take heart.

perky *a.* **1** (*lively*) animated, bouncy, effervescent, frisky, lively, spirited, sprightly, vigorous. **2** (*cheerful, jaunty*) bright, bubbly, buoyant, cheerful, cheery, chirpy, gay, genial, jaunty, jolly, sparkling, sunny, vivacious. ANTONYMS: depressed, lethargic.

permanent *a.* (*lasting, remaining or intended to remain in the same state, place or condition*) abiding, constant, durable, endless, enduring, eternal, everlasting, fixed, immovable, immutable, imperishable, indestructible, invariable, lasting, perennial, perpetual, persistent, stable, unchanging, unending. ANTONYMS: ephemeral, temporary.

permeable *a.* (*yielding passage to fluids, penetrable*) absorbent, absorptive, penetrable, pervious, porous, spongy, yielding. ANTONYMS: impermeable.

permeate *v.t.* **1** (*to penetrate and pass through*) enter, filter through, infiltrate, pass through, penetrate. **2** (*to pervade, to saturate*) charge, diffuse, fill, imbue, impregnate, percolate, pervade, saturate, seep through, soak through, spread through.

permissible *a.* (*allowed by the law or by rules*) acceptable, admissible, allowable, all right, authorized, excusable, lawful, legal, legitimate, licit, (*coll.*) OK, (*coll.*) okay, permitted, proper, sanctioned, tolerable. ANTONYMS: forbidden, unauthorized.

permission *n.* (*consent or authorization given*) acquiescence, allowance, approval, assent, authorization, consent, dispensation, freedom, go-ahead, indulgence, laxity, leave, lenience, liberty, licence, permit, right, sanction, sufferance, tolerance. ANTONYMS: prohibition.

permit[1] *v.t.* **1** (*to give permission to, to authorize*) authorize, empower, enable, entitle, franchise, give permission to, grant, license, sanction, warrant. ANTONYMS: forbid, prohibit. **2** (*to allow by consent*) admit, agree, allow, assent, consent to, countenance, endorse, endure, tolerate.

permit[2] *n.* (*an order to permit something, a warrant*) authority, franchise, liberty, licence, order, pass, passport, permission, sanction, warrant.

permutation *n.* **1** (*each of the different arrangements in which a number of things can be ordered*) arrangement, configuration, order, variation. **2** (*alteration, transmutation*) alteration, change, rearrangement, shift, transformation, transmutation, transposition.

pernicious *a.* **1** (*destructive, very harmful*) damaging, dangerous, deadly, deleterious, destructive, detrimental, fatal, harmful, hurtful, injurious, lethal, malignant, mortal, noxious, offensive, pestilent, poisonous, ruinous. **2** (*malicious, wicked*) bad, baleful, evil, maleficent, malevolent, malicious, malign, malignant, wicked. ANTONYMS: benign.

perpendicular *a.* **1** (*at right angles to the plane of the horizon*) erect, on end, plumb, standing, straight, upright, vertical. ANTONYMS: horizontal. **2** ((*of a hill, road etc.*) *nearly vertical, extremely steep*) sheer, steep, vertical.

perpetrate *v.t.* (*to perform, to commit (a wrong)*) accomplish, be guilty of, bring about, carry out, commit, do, effect, enact, execute, inflict, perform, practise, wreak.

perpetual *a.* **1** (*unending, eternal*) ageless, endless, eternal, everlasting, immortal, infinite, timeless, undying, unending. ANTONYMS: temporary, transitory. **2** (*persistent, constant*) abiding, ceaseless, constant, continual, enduring, incessant, lasting, perennial, persistent, recurrent, repeated, unceasing, unchanging, unfailing, uninterrupted, unremitting. **3** (*for a lifetime*) lifelong, permanent.

perpetuate *v.t.* (*to cause to continue for a long time*) continue, eternalize, extend, immortalize, keep alive, keep going, keep up, maintain, preserve, sustain. ANTONYMS: destroy, end.

perplex *v.t.* **1** (*to puzzle, to bewilder*) baffle,

bamboozle, befuddle, bewilder, confound, confuse, daze, disconcert, distract, dumbfound, flabbergast, flummox, mix up, muddle, mystify, nonplus, puzzle, stump, stupefy. **2** (*to complicate; to make difficult to understand*) complicate, confuse, embroil, encumber, entangle, involve, jumble, mix up, snarl up, tangle, thicken. ANTONYMS: simplify, unravel.

perplexity *n.* **1** (*the state of being perplexed or puzzled*) bafflement, bewilderment, confusion, doubt, incomprehension, mystification, puzzlement, stupefaction. ANTONYMS: enlightenment. **2** (*something complicated and difficult to understand*) complexity, difficulty, impenetrability, inextricability, intricacy, involvement, obscurity, unfathomability.

persecute *v.t.* **1** (*to afflict with suffering, esp. for adherence to a particular opinion or creed*) abuse, afflict, distress, hound, hunt, ill-treat, injure, maltreat, martyr, molest, oppress, punish, pursue, suppress, torment, torture, victimize. ANTONYMS: humour, indulge. **2** (*to harass, to importune*) annoy, badger, bait, bother, bully, harass, harry, (*coll.*) hassle, importune, irritate, pester, plague, tease, trouble, vex, worry.

perseverance *n.* (*persistence in any plan or undertaking*) constancy, decisiveness, dedication, determination, diligence, doggedness, endeavour, endurance, firmness, indefatigability, inflexibility, obstinacy, patience, persistence, pertinacity, purposefulness, resolution, resolve, stamina, steadfastness, tenacity, tirelessness.

persevere *v.i.* (*to persist in or with any undertaking*) carry on, cling to, continue, endure, go on, hang on, hold fast, hold on, keep going, keep on, maintain, persist, plug away, pursue, remain, stand firm, stick with, sustain. ANTONYMS: give up, stop.

persist *v.i.* **1** (*to continue steadfastly, in the pursuit of any plan*) carry on, cling to, continue, endure, hang on, hold fast, hold on, keep going, keep on, maintain, plug away, pursue, remain, stand firm, stick with, sustain. ANTONYMS: give up, stop. **2** (*to remain, to continue*) abide, carry on, continue, endure, hold on, insist, keep up, last, linger, persevere, remain, stand firm, strive, toil. ANTONYMS: cease, desist.

persistent *a.* **1** (*persisting, persevering*) assiduous, determined, dogged, firm, indefatigable, inflexible, obdurate, obstinate, persevering, persisting, pertinacious, resolute, resolved, steadfast, stiff-necked, stubborn, tenacious, tireless, unflagging, unwavering. ANTONYMS: wavering. **2** (*constantly repeated*) constant,

continual, incessant, interminable, never-ending, perpetual, relentless, repeated, steady, unceasing, unrelenting, unremitting. ANTONYMS: intermittent, occasional.

person *n.* (*a human being, an individual*) being, body, child, human, human being, individual, man, mortal, soul, woman.

personal *a.* **1** (*individual, private*) confidential, exclusive, individual, intimate, own, particular, peculiar, private, secret, special. ANTONYMS: public. **2** ((*of criticism etc.*) *reflecting on an individual, esp. disparaging*) adverse, critical, deprecating, derogatory, disparaging, hostile, insulting, nasty, offensive, pejorative, slighting, unfriendly. **3** (*of or relating to the physical person, bodily*) bodily, corporeal, material, physical.

personality *n.* **1** (*individual existence or identity*) existence, identity, individuality. **2** (*a distinctive personal character*) character, disposition, make-up, nature, psyche, temper, temperament, traits. **3** (*a strong or attractive character*) attraction, attractiveness, charisma, charm, dynamism, likeableness, magnetism. **4** (*an important or famous person*) (*coll.*) celeb, celebrity, luminary, megastar, name, notable, personage, star, VIP.

personify *v.t.* (*to exemplify, to typify*) embody, epitomize, exemplify, incarnate, represent, stand for, symbolize, typify.

perspective *n.* **1** (*the relation of facts or other matters as viewed by the mind*) balance, equilibrium, proportion, relation. **2** (*a view, a prospect*) outlook, panorama, prospect, scene, view, vista. **3** (*a point of view from which something is considered*) angle, attitude, point of view, position, standpoint, vantage point, viewpoint.

perspicacious *a.* (*mentally penetrating or discerning*) acute, alert, astute, aware, clear-sighted, clever, discerning, intelligent, keen, observant, penetrating, perceptive, percipient, quick-sighted, sagacious, sharp, shrewd, wise. ANTONYMS: dull, slow.

perspiration *n.* (*sweat*) dampness, exudation, moisture, secretion, sweat, wetness.

perspire *v.i.* (*to sweat*) sweat, swelter. ~*v.t.* (*to give out* (*the excretions of the body*) *through the pores of the skin, to sweat*) exude, secrete, sweat.

persuade *v.t.* **1** (*to influence or convince by argument, entreaty etc.*) bring round, convert, convince, influence, win over. ANTONYMS: deter, dissuade. **2** (*to induce*) allure, entice, impel, incite, induce, inveigle, prevail upon, prompt, sway, talk into, urge.

persuasion n. **1** (*the act of persuading*) blandishment, cajolery, conversion, enticement, exhortation, inducement, influence, inveiglement, persuading, temptation, wheedling. ANTONYMS: dissuasion. **2** (*power to persuade, persuasiveness*) cogency, force, persuasiveness, potency, power, pull. **3** (*creed, belief, esp. in religious matters*) affiliation, belief, credo, creed, faith, opinion. **4** (*a religious sect or denomination*) cult, denomination, faction, party, school, sect, side. **5** (*coll. or facet.*) (*a sort, a kind*) kind, sort, type, variety.

persuasive a. (*able or tending to persuade, winning*) authoritative, cogent, compelling, convincing, credible, effective, efficacious, eloquent, forceful, impelling, impressive, inducing, influential, plausible, sound, telling, touching, valid, weighty, winning. ANTONYMS: unconvincing, unpersuasive.

pert a. **1** (*saucy, forward*) audacious, bold, brash, brazen, cheeky, disrespectful, (*coll.*) flip, flippant, forward, (*coll.*) fresh, impertinent, impudent, insolent, presumptuous, (*coll.*) pushy, rude, (*N Am., coll.*) sassy, saucy, smart. ANTONYMS: bashful. **2** (*sprightly, lively*) animated, bright, brisk, cheerful, dapper, daring, dashing, ebullient, gay, jaunty, lively, nimble, perky, smart, spirited, sprightly, vivacious.

pertinent a. **1** (*relevant, apposite*) apposite, germane, relevant. ANTONYMS: irrelevant. **2** (*fit, suitable*) applicable, appropriate, apropos, apt, fit, fitting, proper, seemly, suitable. ANTONYMS: unfitting, unsuitable.

perturb v.t. **1** (*to throw into confusion or physical disorder*) addle, confuse, disarrange, disorder, disorganize, muddle, unsettle. **2** (*to disturb, to agitate*) agitate, alarm, bother, discomfit, discompose, disconcert, discountenance, disquiet, disturb, faze, fluster, ruffle, shake up, trouble, unnerve, unsettle, upset, vex, worry. ANTONYMS: compose, reassure.

pervade v.t. (*to permeate, to saturate*) diffuse, fill, imbue, impregnate, infuse, overspread, penetrate, percolate, permeate, saturate, spread through, suffuse.

perverse a. **1** (*wilfully or obstinately wrong*) abnormal, awry, contrary, incorrect, irregular, wayward, wrong. **2** (*turned against what is reasonable or fitting*) awkward, contrary, contumacious, delinquent, difficult, disobedient, headstrong, intractable, miscreant, rebellious, refractory, troublesome, unmanageable, unreasonable, wayward, wilful. ANTONYMS: complaisant, malleable. **3** (*petulant, peevish*) bad-tempered, cantankerous, crabby, cross, crusty, fractious, grouchy, ill-tempered, intractable, irascible, obstinate, obstreperous,

peevish, petulant, snappish, splenetic, (*coll.*) stroppy, stubborn, unreasonable, waspish. ANTONYMS: affable, amiable. **4** (*perverted*) depraved, deviant, improper, (*coll.*) kinky, perverted, unhealthy. **5†** (*unlucky, unpropitious*) inauspicious, unfortunate, unlucky, unpropitious.

perversion n. **1** (*a misinterpretation or misapplication*) corruption, deviation, distortion, falsification, misapplication, misinterpretation, misrepresentation, misuse, subversion, twisting. **2** (*abnormal sexual behaviour*) debauchery, depravity, deviancy, immorality, (*coll.*) kinkiness, vice. **3** (*an act of perversion*) aberration, abnormality, irregularity, unnaturalness.

pervert[1] v.t. **1** (*to put to improper use*) abuse, deflect, distort, divert, falsify, garble, misuse, twist, warp. **2** (*to misapply, to misinterpret*) misapply, misconstrue, misinterpret, misunderstand. **3** (*to lead astray, to corrupt*) corrupt, debase, degrade, deprave, desecrate, initiate, lead astray, mislead, seduce, subvert.

pervert[2] n. **1** (*a person who has been perverted*) deviant, (*coll.*) weirdo. **2** (*a person with abnormal sexual behaviour*) debauchee, degenerate, (*sl.*) perve, (*coll.*) weirdo.

pessimistic a. (*gloomy and despondent about the future*) bleak, cynical, dark, defeatist, dejected, depressed, despairing, despondent, distrustful, downhearted, fatalistic, foreboding, gloomy, glum, inauspicious, melancholy, morose, negative, resigned, sad. ANTONYMS: buoyant, optimistic.

pest n. **1** (*a person who or something which is extremely destructive or annoying*) annoyance, bane, bore, bother, (*coll.*) drag, gall, irritant, irritation, nuisance, (*coll.*) pain, trial, vexation. ANTONYMS: blessing. **2** (*any plant or animal that harms crops, livestock or humans*) blight, bug, curse, infection. **3** (*plague, pestilence*) epidemic, pestilence, plague, scourge.

pester v.t. (*to bother, to annoy*) aggravate, annoy, badger, bother, (*sl.*) bug, disturb, exasperate, get at, harass, (*coll.*) hassle, heckle, hound, irk, nag, provoke, (*N Am.*) ride, torment, trouble, vex, worry.

pestilence n. (*any contagious disease that is epidemic and deadly, esp. bubonic plague*) affliction, bane, blight, cancer, canker, disease, epidemic, pandemic, plague, scourge.

pestilent a. **1** (*noxious to health or life, deadly*) contagious, contaminated, dangerous, deadly, deleterious, destructive, detrimental, diseased, fatal, harmful, infectious, injurious, insalubrious, lethal, noxious, pernicious, pestilential, poisonous, ruinous, unhealthy. ANTONYMS: beneficial, pure. **2** (*vexatious, troublesome*) annoying, bothersome, galling, irksome, irritating, mischievous, (*esp. N Am., coll.*) pesky, tiresome, troublesome, vexatious, vexing.

pet *n.* **1** (*an animal kept in the house as a companion*) animal, domestic animal, four-legged friend, pet animal. **2** (*a darling, a favourite*) (*coll., usu. derog.*) blue-eyed boy, (*coll., usu. derog.*) blue-eyed girl, darling, favourite, idol, jewel, treasure.
~*a.* **1** (*kept as a pet*) domesticated, household, house-trained, tame, trained. ANTONYMS: wild. **2** (*often facet.*) (*favourite*) adored, beloved, cherished, dearest, favoured, favourite, indulged, particular, precious, preferred, prized, special, treasured.
~*v.t.* **1** (*to pamper*) baby, coddle, cosset, dote on, humour, mollycoddle, pamper, spoil. ANTONYMS: discipline. **2** (*to fondle*) caress, fondle, nuzzle, pat, stroke.
~*v.i.* (*to engage in amorous fondling*) (*coll.*) canoodle, cuddle, kiss, (*coll.*) neck, (*coll.*) smooch, (*coll.*) snog.

petition *n.* (*an entreaty, a request*) address, appeal, application, entreaty, invocation, memorial, plea, prayer, request, solicitation, suit, supplication.
~*v.t.* (*to solicit, to ask humbly for etc.*) ask for, beg, beseech, crave, entreat, implore, importune, plead, pray, request, solicit, sue, supplicate.

petrify *v.t.* **1** (*to convert into stone or a stony substance*) calcify, fossilize, harden, ossify, set, solidify, turn to stone. **2** (*to stupefy with fear, astonishment etc.*) amaze, appal, astonish, astound, confound, disconcert, dumbfound, flabbergast, horrify, immobilize, numb, paralyse, scare, shock, stagger, stun, stupefy, terrify, transfix. ANTONYMS: reassure.

petty *a.* **1** (*trifling, insignificant*) contemptible, inconsiderable, inessential, inferior, insignificant, little, (*coll.*) measly, negligible, paltry, puny, slight, small, trifling, trivial, unimportant. ANTONYMS: considerable, important. **2** (*small-minded, mean*) cheap, close, grudging, mean, miserly, niggardly, parsimonious, shabby, small-minded, spiteful, stingy, tight, ungenerous. ANTONYMS: generous, magnanimous. **3** (*minor, subordinate*) inferior, junior, lesser, lower, minor, secondary, subordinate.

petulant *a.* (*given to fits of bad temper*) bad-tempered, cantankerous, crabby, crotchety, fretful, grouchy, ill-humoured, impatient, irascible, irritable, moody, peevish, perverse, querulous, (*sl.*) ratty, snappish, sour, splenetic, sullen, waspish. ANTONYMS: affable, congenial.

phantom *n.* **1** (*an apparition, a ghost*) apparition, ghost, phantasm, shade, spectre, spirit, (*coll.*) spook, wraith. **2** (*an illusion, an imaginary appearance*) chimera, delusion, figment, hallucination, illusion, mirage, vision.

phase *n.* **1** (*a stage of change or development*) chapter, development, juncture, occasion, period, point, stage, state, step, time. **2** (*a particular aspect or appearance*) angle, appearance, aspect, configuration, form, look, shape.

phenomenal *a.* (*extraordinary, prodigious*) amazing, astonishing, exceptional, extraordinary, (*coll.*) fantastic, marvellous, mind-blowing, miraculous, notable, outstanding, prodigious, remarkable, sensational, singular, staggering, unbelievable, uncommon, unparalleled, unusual, wonderful. ANTONYMS: common, unremarkable.

phenomenon *n.* **1** (*something which appears or is perceived by observation or experiment*) circumstance, episode, event, experience, fact, happening, incident, occasion, occurrence. **2** (*coll.*) (*a remarkable or unusual person or thing*) curiosity, exception, marvel, nonpareil, prodigy, rarity, sensation, sight, spectacle, wonder.

philanderer *n.* (*a man who has casual affairs with women*) Casanova, Don Juan, flirt, gallant, ladies' man, lady-killer, Lothario, playboy, rake, Romeo, roué, (*sl.*) stud, trifler, (*coll.*) wolf, womanizer.

philanthropic *a.* (*actively benevolent towards one's fellow humans*) altruistic, beneficent, benevolent, benignant, charitable, generous, humane, humanitarian, kind, kind-hearted, liberal, magnanimous, munificent, open-handed, public-spirited, ungrudging, unstinting. ANTONYMS: mean, ungenerous.

Philistine *n.* (*a person of narrow ideas; a person deficient in liberal culture*) barbarian, boor, bourgeois, ignoramus, lout, lowbrow, vulgarian, yahoo. ANTONYMS: aesthete, intellectual.
~*a.* (*uncultured, prosaic*) boorish, bourgeois, commonplace, crass, ignorant, lowbrow, materialistic, narrow-minded, prosaic, tasteless, uncultivated, uncultured, uneducated, unlettered, unread, unrefined. ANTONYMS: cultured, intellectual.

philosopher *n.* (*a person who studies philosophy*) dialectician, logician, metaphysician, sage, scholar, theorist, thinker, wise man.

philosophical *a.* **1** (*devoted to or skilled in philosophy*) abstract, erudite, esoteric, impractical, learned, logical, rational, sagacious, scholarly, theoretical, thoughtful, wise. **2** (*wise, calm*) calm, cogitative, collected, composed, contemplative, cool, detached, impassive, imperturbable, meditative, patient, pragmatic, reflective, resigned, sedate, serene, serious, stoical, thoughtful, tranquil, wise. ANTONYMS: emotional, impulsive.

philosophy *n.* **1** (*the investigation of ultimate reality or of general principles of existence*) knowledge, logic, metaphysics, rationalism, reasoning, thinking, thought, wisdom. **2** (*a particular system of philosophic principles*) ideology, opinion, outlook, viewpoint, world-view. **3** (*the fundamental principles of a science etc.*) aesthetics, beliefs, convictions, doctrine, ethics, principles, tenets, values. **4** (*practical wisdom, calmness of temper*) aplomb, calmness, composure, coolness, dispassion, equanimity, patience, resignation, restraint, self-possession, serenity, serious-ness, stoicism.

phlegmatic *a.* (*calm, unemotional*) apathetic, cold, cool, dull, heavy, impassive, indifferent, indolent, lethargic, listless, passive, placid, sluggish, stoical, stolid, undemonstrative, unemotional, unenthusiastic, unresponsive. ANTONYMS: animated, emotional.

phobia *n.* (*an irrational fear or hatred*) abhorrence, antipathy, anxiety, detestation, dislike, distaste, dread, execration, fear, hatred, horror, loathing, obsession, repugnance, repulsion, revulsion, terror, (*coll.*) thing, version. ANTONYMS: fondness, partiality.

phone *v.t., v.i.* (*to telephone*) buzz, call, call up, give (someone) a bell, (*sl.*) give (someone) a buzz, give (someone) a ring, (*coll.*) give (someone) a tinkle, ring, telephone. ~*n.* (*a telephone*) (*coll.*) blower, (*N Am., sl.*) horn, telephone.

phoney *a.* (*false, counterfeit*) bogus, counterfeit, fake, false, feigned, forged, fraudulent, sham, spurious. ANTONYMS: genuine, real.

photograph *n.* (*a picture taken by means of photography*) image, likeness, photo, picture, print, shot, slide, snap, snapshot, transparency. ~*v.t.* (*to take a photograph*) film, photo, picture, shoot, snap, take.

phrase *n.* **1** (*an expression denoting a single idea or forming a distinct part of a sentence*) clause, expression, remark, utterance. **2** (*a style of expression, diction*) diction, locution, parlance. **3** (*an idiomatic expression*) adage, axiom, colloquialism, idiom, motto, proverb, saw, saying, slogan, tag. ~*v.t.* (*to express in words or phrases*) articulate, express, formulate, frame, present, put, say, term, utter, voice, word.

physical *a.* **1** (*bodily, corporeal*) bodily, carnal, corporeal, earthly, fleshly, incarnate, mortal, unspiritual. ANTONYMS: spiritual. **2** (*obvious to or cognizable by the senses*) actual, concrete, manifest, palpable, real, solid, substantial, tangible, true, visible.

pick *v.t.* **1** (*to choose, to select carefully*) choose, decide upon, elect, fix upon, hand-pick, mark out, opt for, select, settle upon, sift out, single out, sort out. ANTONYMS: reject, turn down. **2** (*to pluck, to gather*) collect, cull, cut, gather, glean, harvest, pluck, pull. **3** (*to strike at with something pointed*) peck, prick, strike at. **4** (*to eat in little bits*) bite, nibble, peck, play with, toy with. **5** (*to find an occasion for* (*a quarrel etc.*)) foment, incite, initiate, instigate, provoke, start, stir up. **6** (*to open* (*a lock*) *with an implement other than the key*) break into, break open, crack, force, jemmy, open, prise open. **7** (*to pluck*) extract, pluck, pull apart, remove. **8** (*to pierce with a pointed instrument*) break, indent, pierce, prick. ~*n.* **1** (*choice, selection*) choice, decision, option, preference, selection. **2** (*the best* (*of*)) best, choicest, cream, elect, elite, flower, pride, prize, tops. **to pick up 1** (*to take up with the fingers, beak etc.*) gather, grasp, hoist, lift, raise, take up. ANTONYMS: drop. **2** (*to gather or acquire little by little*) acquire, come by, gather, glean, happen upon, learn, master, obtain, scrape. **3** (*to collect and take away*) call for, collect, fetch, get. **4** (*to accept and pay* (*a bill*)) foot, pay, settle. **5** (*to arrest and detain* (*a suspect etc.*)) apprehend, arrest, (*sl.*) bust, (*coll.*) collar, detain, (*coll.*) lift, (*sl.*) nab, (*sl.*) nick, (*sl.*) pinch, (*sl.*) pull in. **6** (*to recover one's health*) advance, get better, improve, mend, (*coll.*) perk up, rally, recoup, recover.

pictorial *a.* **1** (*relating to or illustrated by pictures*) expressive, graphic, illustrated, representational. **2** (*picturesque*) picturesque, scenic, striking, vivid.

picture *n.* **1** (*a painting or drawing representing a person, natural scenery or other objects*) delineation, depiction, drawing, effigy, illustration, image, likeness, painting, portrait, portrayal, print, representation, sketch. **2** (*a photograph, engraving or other representation on a plane surface*) engraving, photo, photograph, print. **3** (*coll.*) (*an image, a copy*) copy, double, duplicate, image, twin. **4** (*a perfect example*) archetype, embodiment, epitome, essence, incarnation, model, personification, prototype. **5** (*a film*) film, (*coll.*) flick, motion picture, movie.

~*v.t.* **1** (*to represent in a painting, photograph etc.*) delineate, depict, draw, illustrate, paint, portray, render, represent, show, sketch. **2** (*to form a mental likeness of*) conceive, envisage, envision, fancy, image, imagine, see, visualize.

piece *n.* **1** (*a distinct part of anything*) component, limb, section. **2** (*a detached portion, a fragment (of)*) bit, chunk, fraction, fragment, hunk, length, morsel, mouthful, part, portion, quantity, remnant, scrap, shard, shred, sliver. ANTONYMS: whole. **3** (*a division, a section*) division, section, segment, slice, wedge. **4** (*a plot (of land)*) allotment, plot, portion. **5** (*an example, an instance*) case, example, instance, occurrence, sample, specimen, stroke. **6** (*an artistic or literary composition or performance, usu. short*) article, composition, creation, item, number, performance, production, study, work.
~*v.t.* **1** (*to mend, to patch*) fix, mend, patch, repair, restore. **2** (*to form (a theory) by putting facts together*) put together, work out. **3** (*to put together so as to form a whole*) assemble, join together, unite. ANTONYMS: separate.

pierce *v.t.* **1** (*to penetrate or transfix with a pointed instrument*) bore, drill, fix, impale, lance, penetrate, poke, prick, run through, skewer, spear, spike, spit, stab, stick, transfix. **2** (*to make a hole in*) hole, perforate, puncture. **3** (*to affect or penetrate keenly*) affect, cut, excite, hurt, melt, move, pain, penetrate, rouse, sting, stir, strike, thrill, touch, wound. **4** ((*of sound) to break (a silence etc.)*) break, bring to an end, destroy, interrupt, shatter.

piercing *a.* **1** (*penetrating*) ear-splitting, harsh, high-pitched, loud, penetrating, sharp, shattering, shrill, strident. ANTONYMS: inaudible, muted. **2** (*very cold*) biting, bitter, cold, freezing, keen, nippy, raw, wintry. **3** (*intense, penetrating*) acute, agonizing, excruciating, exquisite, fierce, intense, keen, painful, powerful, racking, severe, sharp, shooting, stabbing. ANTONYMS: dull, soft.

piety *n.* **1** (*the quality of being pious*) dedication, devotion, dutifulness, loyalty, respect. **2** (*reverence towards God*) devoutness, duty, faith, godliness, grace, holiness, piousness, religion, reverence, sanctity, veneration. ANTONYMS: impiety.

pile *n.* **1** (*a heap, a mass of things heaped together*) heap, mass, mound, mountain, stack. **2** (*a very large building or group of buildings*) mansion, palace. **3** (*an accumulation*) accumulation, agglomeration, aggregation, assemblage, assortment, batch, collection, hoard, stockpile. **4** (*a great quantity or sum*) (*coll.*) lots, (*coll.*) oodles, (*coll.*) stacks, (*coll.*) tons.

5 (*a fortune*) (*coll.*) bomb, (*sl.*) bundle, fortune, (*coll.*) megabucks, mint, money, (*coll.*) packet, (*usu. pl., coll.*) pot, pretty penny, (*coll.*) tidy sum, (*coll.*) wad, wealth.
~*v.t.* (*to collect or heap up or together*) accumulate, amass, assemble, collect, gather, heap, hoard, mass, stack, store. ANTONYMS: disperse, scatter.
~*v.i.* (*to move in a crowd*) charge, crowd, crush, flock, jam, pack, rush, stream.

pill *n.* **1** (*a little ball of some medicinal substance to be swallowed whole*) capsule, pellet, pilule, tablet. **2** (*something unpleasant which has to be accepted or put up with*) annoyance, bore, (*coll.*) drag, nuisance, (*coll.*) pain, pest, trial.

pillage *n.* **1** (*the act of plundering*) defilement, depredation, despoliation, destruction, devastation, levelling, marauding, plunder, rapine, robbery, sack, spoliation. **2** (*plunder, esp. the property of enemies taken in war*) booty, loot, plunder, spoils.
~*v.t.* (*to lay waste*) despoil, devastate, lay waste, level, maraud, raid, ransack, raze, sack, strip.
~*v.i.* (*to ravage, to plunder*) loot, plunder, ravage, rifle, rob.

pillar *n.* **1** (*an upright structure used for support; a column*) column, pedestal, pier, pilaster, post, prop, shaft, stanchion, support, upright. **2** (*a person or group of people acting as chief support of an institution, movement etc.*) backbone, leading light, mainstay, rock, worthy.

pilot *n.* **1** (*a person directing the course of an aeroplane, spacecraft etc.*) aeronaut, airman, aviator, captain, co-pilot, coxswain, flier, helmsman, navigator, steerer. **2** (*a guide or director, esp. in difficult or dangerous circumstances*) conductor, director, guide, leader.
~*a.* (*serving as a preliminary test or trial*) experimental, model, test, trial.
~*v.t.* **1** (*to direct the course of (a ship, aircraft etc.)*) conduct, control, direct, drive, fly, guide, handle, lead, manage, navigate, operate, run, shepherd, steer, usher. **2** (*to introduce or test (a new scheme etc.)*) introduce, sample, test, try out.

pin *n.* **1** (*a slender, pointed piece of metal etc., used for fastening parts of clothing, papers etc., together*) bolt, dowel, fastener, hairpin, nail, ninepin, peg, rivet, spike, tack, thole. **2** (*an ornamental device with a pin used as a fastening etc., or as a decoration*) brooch, clip.
~*v.t.* **1** (*to fasten (to, on, up etc.) with or as if with a pin*) affix, attach, clip, fasten, fix, join, secure, staple. **2** (*to pierce, to transfix*) drill, pierce, spike, transfix. **3** (*to secure*) fix, hold

fast, immobilize, make fast, pinion, press, restrain, secure, seize.

pinch *v.t.* **1** (*to press so as to cause pain or inconvenience*) chafe, compress, confine, cramp, crush, hurt, nip, pain, press, squeeze, tweak. **2** (*to distress, esp. with cold, hunger etc.*) afflict, distress, oppress, press. **3** (*to straiten, to stint*) economize, skimp, spare, stint. ANTONYMS: squander. **4** (*to steal*) (*sl.*) blag, filch, (*sl.*) knock off, (*coll.*) lift, (*sl.*) nick, pilfer, purloin, rob, (*coll.*) snaffle, snatch, (*sl.*) snitch, steal, (*coll.*) swipe. **5** (*to arrest, to take into custody*) apprehend, arrest, (*sl.*) bust, (*coll.*) collar, (*coll.*) do, (*coll.*) lift, (*sl.*) nab, (*sl.*) nick, (*sl.*) pull in, take into custody.

~*n.* **1** (*a sharp nip or squeeze, as with the ends of the fingers*) nip, squeeze, tweak, twinge. **2** (*as much as can be taken up between the finger and thumb*) bit, dash, jot, mite, speck, taste, touch. **3** (*a pain, a pang*) pain, pang, twinge. **4** (*distress, a dilemma*) crisis, difficulty, dilemma, distress, emergency, hardship, jam, necessity, oppression, pass, (*coll.*) pickle, plight, predicament, pressure, (*coll.*) scrape, strait, stress.

pine *v.i.* **1** (*to languish, waste away*) decay, decline, droop, dwindle, fade, flag, languish, sicken, sink, waste, weaken, wilt, wither. ANTONYMS: revive. **2** (*to long or yearn* (*for, after or to*)) ache (for), covet, crave, desire, hanker (after), hunger (for), long (for), lust (after), sigh (for), thirst (for), wish, yearn (for).

pinnacle *n.* **1** (*the apex, the culmination* (*of*)) acme, apex, apogee, cap, climax, crown, culmination, extreme, maximum, meridian, top, utmost, zenith. **2** (*a pointed summit*) crest, eminence, height, peak, summit. ANTONYMS: base, foot. **3** (*a turret, usu. pointed, placed as an ornament on the top of a buttress etc.*) belfry, spire, steeple, turret.

pioneer *n.* **1** (*an early leader or developer of an enterprise*) developer, forerunner, founder, founding father, innovator, leader, pacemaker, precursor, trailblazer, trendsetter. **2** (*an explorer*) colonist, colonizer, explorer, frontiersman, groundbreaker, pathfinder, settler.

~*v.t.* **1** (*to initiate or develop* (*a new enterprise*)) begin, create, develop, discover, establish, inaugurate, initiate, instigate, institute, introduce, invent, (*coll.*) kick off, launch, open up, originate, prepare, set off, start. **2** (*to lead, to conduct*) conduct, direct, lead.

pious *a.* **1** (*reverencing God, devout*) dedicated, devout, faithful, God-fearing, godly, holy, religious, reverent, reverential, righteous, saintly, spiritual, worshipful. ANTONYMS: impious, irreverent. **2** (*sanctimonious*) (*coll., usu. derog.*) goody-goody, (*coll.*) holier-than-thou,

hypocritical, mealy-mouthed, oily, pietistic, sanctimonious, self-righteous, (*coll.*) smarmy, unctuous.

pipe *n.* **1** (*a long hollow tube or line of tubes, esp. for conveying liquids, gas etc.*) channel, conduit, duct, hose, line, main, passage, pipeline, tube. **2** (*a wind instrument consisting of a tube*) fife, whistle, wind instrument.

~*v.t.* **1** (*to play or execute on a pipe*) blow, play, sound, toot. **2** (*to whistle*) cheep, peep, tootle, trill, tweet, warble, whistle. **3** (*to convey or transmit along a pipe or wire*) channel, conduct, convey, deliver, supply, syphon, transmit.

piquant *a.* **1** (*having an agreeably pungent taste*) acerbic, biting, hot, peppery, pungent, savoury, sharp, spicy, stinging, tangy, tart, zesty. ANTONYMS: bland, insipid. **2** (*stimulating, lively*) interesting, intriguing, lively, provocative, racy, salty, scintillating, sparkling, spirited, stimulating, titillating. ANTONYMS: dull, uninteresting.

pique *v.t.* **1** (*to irritate*) affront, annoy, displease, gall, get, hurt, incense, irk, irritate, (*coll.*) miff, mortify, nettle, offend, (*coll.*) peeve, put out, rile, sting, upset, vex, wound. ANTONYMS: please. **2** (*to stimulate or excite* (*curiosity etc.*)) arouse, excite, galvanize, goad, kindle, provoke, rouse, spur, stimulate, stir, whet.

~*n.* (*ill feeling, resentment*) annoyance, displeasure, grudge, huff, ill feeling, indignation, irritation, (*coll.*) miff, offence, resentment, umbrage, vexation.

pirate *n.* **1** (*a robber on the high seas, a marauder*) buccaneer, corsair, freebooter, marauder, privateer, raider, rover, sea-rover. **2** (*a person who infringes the copyright of another*) infringer, plagiarist, plagiarizer.

~*v.t.* **1** (*to publish* (*literary or other matter belonging to others*) *without permission*) copy, crib, infringe, plagiarize, reproduce. **2** (*to plunder*) appropriate, plunder, poach, rob, steal.

pit *n.* **1** (*a natural or artificial hole in the ground*) cavity, hole, pothole, shaft, trench. **2** (*a pit made in order to obtain minerals or for industrial or agricultural operations*) excavation, mine, quarry, working. **3** (*hell*) abyss, hell, perdition, purgatory. **4** (*a depression in the surface of the ground, of the body etc.*) dent, depression, dimple, hollow, indentation. **5** (*a hollow scar, esp. one left by smallpox*) pockmark, scar. **6** (*an abyss*) abyss, chasm, crater, crevasse, gulf, well.

~*v.t.* **1** (*to match, to set in competition against*) contend, match, oppose, set against. **2** (*to mark with hollow scars, as with smallpox) dent, dig, dint, gouge, hole, indent, mark, nick, notch, scar.

pitch v.t. **1** (*to fix or plant in the ground*) erect, fix, locate, place, plant, put up, raise, settle, set up, station. **2** (*to set in orderly arrangement, to fix in position*) arrange, fix, order. **3** (*to throw, to fling*) (*sl.*) bung, (*coll.*) chuck, fire, fling, heave, hurl, launch, let fly, lob, send, shoot, sling, throw, toss.
~v.i. **1** (*to encamp*) encamp, make camp. **2** (*to settle*) light, settle. **3** (*to plunge, to fall*) drive, drop, fall, plummet, plunge. **4** ((*of a ship*) *to plunge at the bow or stern*) flounder, lurch, plunge, reel, roll, toss, wallow.
~n. **1** (*the delivery of the ball in various games*) ball, delivery, throw, toss. **2** (*height, intensity*) degree, depth, height, intensity. **3** (*extreme point*) extremity, height, point, summit. **4** (*degree of steepness*) angle, cant, dip, gradient, inclination, incline, slant, slope, steepness, tilt. **5** (*the place or position taken up by a person for buying and selling, a stall*) barrow, booth, stall. **6** (*coll.*) (*an attempt at persuasion, usu. to induce someone to buy something*) line, patter, spiel. **7** (*any area marked out for playing sports, e.g. football*) area, field, ground, sports field. **8** (*Mus.*) (*the degree of acuteness or gravity of a musical tone*) harmonic, modulation, sound, timbre, tone.

piteous a. (*exciting or deserving pity, lamentable*) affecting, distressing, grievous, harrowing, heartbreaking, heart-rending, lamentable, miserable, mournful, moving, pathetic, pitiable, pitiful, plaintive, poignant, regrettable, sad, sorry, woeful, wretched.

pithy a. **1** (*condensed*) brief, cogent, compact, concise, condensed, laconic, meaningful, pointed, sententious, short, succinct, terse, trenchant, weighty. ANTONYMS: long-winded, verbose. **2** (*forcible, energetic*) energetic, forceful, forcible.

pitiable a. (*deserving or calling for pity*) deplorable, dismal, distressing, doleful, grievous, harrowing, lamentable, miserable, pathetic, piteous, pitiful, poor, regrettable, sad, sorry, woeful, wretched. ANTONYMS: enviable.

pitiful a. **1** (*calling for pity*) deplorable, distressing, grievous, harrowing, heartbreaking, heart-rending, lamentable, miserable, pathetic, piteous, pitiable, sad, woeful, wretched. ANTONYMS: cheering, happy. **2** (*contemptible*) abject, base, contemptible, despicable, dismal, inadequate, insignificant, low, meagre, mean, measly, miserable, paltry, scurvy, shabby, sorry, trifling, unimportant, vile, worthless. ANTONYMS: admirable. **3** (*full of pity,*

compassionate) compassionate, merciful, sympathetic.

pitiless a. (*feeling no pity, hard-hearted*) brutal, callous, cold-blooded, cruel, flinty, hard-hearted, harsh, heartless, implacable, inexorable, inhuman, merciless, relentless, ruthless, uncaring, unfeeling, unkind, unmerciful, unsparing, unsympathetic. ANTONYMS: compassionate, merciful.

pity n. **1** (*a feeling of tenderness aroused by the distress of others*) charity, clemency, commiseration, compassion, condolence, fellow feeling, forbearance, grace, grief, humanity, kindness, mercy, quarter, sorrow, sympathy, tenderness, understanding. ANTONYMS: mercilessness, ruthlessness. **2** (*a cause of regret, an unfortunate fact*) (*coll.*) crime, disappointment, disgrace, misfortune, regret, sacrilege, shame, (*dated, coll.*) sin.
~v.t. (*to feel pity for*) bleed for, commiserate with, condole with, feel for, feel sorry for, grieve for, sympathize with, weep for.

pivot n. **1** (*a shaft or bearing on which anything turns*) axis, axle, bearing, fulcrum, pin, shaft, spindle, swivel. **2** (*a thing or event on which an important issue depends*) centre, crux, focal point, heart, hinge, hub, kingpin, linchpin.
~v.i. **1** (*to turn on or as if on a pivot*) revolve, rotate, spin, swivel, turn, twirl, whirl. **2** (*to hinge (on)*) depend (on), hang (on), hinge (on), rely (on), revolve (round), turn (on).

placard n. (*a written or printed paper posted up in a public place*) advertisement, bill, (*N Am.*) billboard, notice, poster, sign, sticker.

placate v.t. (*to appease, to pacify*) appease, assuage, calm, conciliate, humour, mollify, pacify, propitiate, satisfy, soothe, win over.

place n. **1** (*a particular portion of space*) area, position, spot. **2** (*a spot, a locality*) area, locale, locality, location, point, position, quarter, site, situation, spot, station, venue, vicinity, whereabouts. **3** (*a city, a town*) city, district, hamlet, neighbourhood, town, village. **4** (*a residence*) abode, apartment, domicile, dwelling, flat, home, house, lodgings, manor, mansion, (*coll.*) pad, property, residence, seat. **5** (*stead*) lieu, stead. **6** (*space, room for a person*) accommodation, berth, billet, room, space, stead. **7** (*rank, official position*) grade, position, rank, standing, station, status. **8** (*situation, employment*) appointment, (*coll.*) billet, employment, job, livelihood, occupation, position, post, situation. **9** (*duty*) charge, concern, duty, function, prerogative, province, responsibility, right, role, sphere.
~v.t. **1** (*to put or set in a particular place*) deposit, dispose, establish, lay, locate, plant, position,

put, rest, set in place, settle, situate, stand, station. ANTONYMS: remove. **2** (*to set, to fix*) fix, install, put, set. **3** (*to arrange in proper places*) arrange, order, organize, sort. ANTONYMS: disarrange. **4** (*to identify*) associate, identify, pinpoint, recognize. **5** (*to assign a class to*) categorize, class, classify, grade, group, rank. **6** (*to appoint to a post*) appoint, put in office. ANTONYMS: dismiss. **7** (*to put in someone's care*) commit, entrust, give. **8** (*to make* (*an order for goods*)) charge, commission. **to give place to** (*to be succeeded by*) be replaced by, be succeeded by, make room for, make way for. ANTONYMS: precede.

placid *a.* **1** (*gentle, quiet*) gentle, halcyon, quiet, still, tranquil. ANTONYMS: tempestuous. **2** (*calm, peaceful*) calm, collected, composed, cool, equable, even, even-tempered, imperturbable, mild, peaceful, self-possessed, serene, undisturbed, unexcitable, (*coll.*) unfazed, unflappable, unmoved, unruffled, untroubled. ANTONYMS: disturbed, troubled.

plagiarize *v.t., v.i.* (*to appropriate and give out as one's own* (*the writings or ideas of another*)) appropriate, borrow, copy, crib, infringe, (*coll.*) lift, pirate, poach, steal, thieve, usurp.

plague *n.* **1** (*a pestilence, an intensely malignant epidemic*) contagion, disease, epidemic, infection, pandemic, pestilence, visitation. **2** (*an infestation*) blight, infestation. **3** (*a calamity, an affliction*) affliction, blow, calamity, cancer, curse, evil, scourge, torment, trial, trouble. **4** (*a nuisance, a trouble*) aggravation, annoyance, (*sl.*) bitch, bother, (*coll.*) drag, (*coll.*) hassle, (*coll.*) headache, irritant, irritation, nuisance, (*coll.*) pain, pest, problem, vexation. ANTONYMS: blessing.
~*v.t.* **1** (*to afflict with any calamity or evil*) afflict, badger, bedevil, disturb, harass, harry, (*coll.*) hassle, hound, molest, pain, persecute, pester, torment, torture, trouble. **2** (*to tease, to annoy*) annoy, bother, fret, gall, irk, irritate, tease, vex.

plain *a.* **1** (*clear, evident*) apparent, blatant, clear, distinct, evident, manifest, palpable, patent, transparent, unambiguous, unequivocal, unmistakable. ANTONYMS: ambiguous, obscure. **2** (*without difficulties, easy to understand*) comprehensible, easy, graphic, intelligible, legible, lucid, simple, understandable. ANTONYMS: incomprehensible, unintelligible. **3** (*easily seen*) clear, evident, obvious, visible. **4** (*without ornament*) unadorned, unembellished, unornamented, unpatterned, unvarnished. ANTONYMS: elaborate, fancy, ornate. **5** (*unvariegated, uncoloured*) colourless, flat, uncoloured, unvariegated. **6** (*unaffected, unsophisticated*) common, commonplace, everyday, frugal, homely, lowly, modest, ordinary,

simple, unaffected, unpretentious, unsophisticated, workaday. **7** (*straightforward, frank*) frank, guileless, honest, ingenuous, open, sincere, straightforward. ANTONYMS: devious. **8** (*direct, outspoken*) artless, blunt, candid, direct, downright, forthright, outspoken, (*coll.*) upfront. **9** (*not luxurious*) austere, bare, basic, discreet, modest, muted, pure, restrained, severe, simple, Spartan, stark. ANTONYMS: luxurious. **10** (*ugly*) (*N Am.*) homely, ill-favoured, ugly, unattractive, unprepossessing. ANTONYMS: attractive, good-looking.
~*adv.* **1** (*plainly, clearly*) clearly, directly, plainly, straightforwardly. **2** (*totally*) absolutely, totally, utterly.
~*n.* (*a tract of level country*) downland, flat, grassland, level, lowland, pampas, plateau, prairie, savannah, steppe, tableland.

plaintive *a.* **1** (*expressive of sorrow or grief*) disconsolate, doleful, grief-stricken, grieving, heart-rending, melancholy, mournful, mourning, pathetic, pitiful, sad, sorrowful, wistful, woebegone, woeful. ANTONYMS: joyful. **2** (*having a mournful sound*) doleful, funereal, melancholy, mournful.

plan *n.* **1** (*a drawing of a building, machine etc., by projection on a plane surface, showing the positions of the parts*) blueprint, chart, delineation, diagram, illustration, layout, map, representation, scale drawing, sketch. **2** (*a scheme, a design*) arrangement, contrivance, design, device, idea, plot, programme, project, proposal, proposition, scenario, scheme, suggestion. **3** (*an outline of a discourse, sermon etc.*) draft, gist, main points, outline, skeleton. **4** (*method of procedure*) method, procedure, strategy, system, technique.
~*v.t.* (*to design, to devise*) arrange, concoct, contrive, design, devise, draft, formulate, frame, invent, organize, outline, plot, prepare, represent, scheme, think out, work out.
~*v.i.* (*to make plans*) aim, contemplate, envisage, expect, foresee, intend, mean, propose, purpose.

plane[1] *n.* **1** (*a surface such that a straight line joining any two points in it lies wholly within it*) flat, flat surface, level. **2** (*a level* (*of thought, existence etc.*)) condition, degree, footing, level, position, status, stratum.
~*a.* (*level, without depressions or elevations*) even, flat, flush, horizontal, level, plain, regular, smooth, unbroken, uniform, uninterrupted. ANTONYMS: uneven.
~*v.i.* (*to skim across water*) sail, skate, skid, skim, slide, slip.

plane[2] *n.* (*an aeroplane*) aeroplane, aircraft, airliner, (*N Am.*) airplane, jet.

plant n. 1 (*any vegetable organism that grows in the earth and has a stem, roots and leaves*) bush, flower, herb, shrub, tree, vegetable, weed. 2 (*a shoot*) cutting, scion, shoot, slip. 3 (*the tools, machinery and fixtures used in an industrial concern*) apparatus, equipment, fixtures, gear, machinery, tools. 4 (*a factory*) factory, foundry, mill, shop, works, yard. 5 (*coll.*) (*a person used to entrap another*) agent, decoy, informant, informer, spy.
~v.t. 1 (*to set in the ground for growth*) bed, set. 2 (*to furnish or lay out with plants*) lay out, transplant. 3 (*to fix firmly*) embed, fix, root, station. 4 (*to settle, to found*) establish, found, insert, institute, introduce, lodge, root, settle. 5 (*to implant (an idea etc.)*) embed, implant, ingrain, insinuate, instil.
~v.i. (*to sow seed*) scatter, seed, sow. ANTONYMS: uproot.

plaster n. 1 (*a mixture of lime, sand etc., for coating walls etc.*) mortar, stucco. 2 (*a sticking plaster*) adhesive plaster, bandage, Band-Aid ®, dressing, Elastoplast ®, sticking plaster.
~v.t. (*to daub, to smear over*) coat, daub, overlay, smear, spread.

plastic a. 1 (*made of plastic, any of a group of continuously pliable synthetic substances*) artificial, man-made, plasticky. 2 (*outwardly and conventionally attractive but lacking substance or reality*) insubstantial, superficial, unreal. 3 (*synthetic, insincere*) artificial, bogus, counterfeit, fake, false, insincere, meretricious, (*coll.*) phoney, (*coll.*) pseudo, sham, specious, spurious, superficial, synthetic. 4 (*capable of being modelled or moulded*) compliant, docile, impressionable, malleable, pliable, receptive, responsive, susceptible, tractable. ANTONYMS: intractable, stubborn. 5 (*continuously pliable without rupturing*) ductile, extensible, flexible, mouldable, pliable, pliant, soft, supple, tensile. ANTONYMS: rigid, stiff.

plate n. 1 (*a small shallow dish for eating from*) dish, platter, vessel. 2 (*a portion served on a plate*) helping, plateful, portion, serving. 3 (*N Am.*) (*a main course of a meal*) course, dish, (*orig. N Am.*) entrée. 4 (*a flat, thin piece of metal etc.*) layer, leaf, pane, panel, sheet, slab. 5 (*a very thin coating of one metal upon another*) coat, coating, lamination, layer, plating. 6 (*a print taken from a plate*) illustration, lithograph, print. 7 (*an illustration in a book, often on different paper from the text*) illustration, picture.
~v.t. (*to coat with a layer of metal, esp. gold, silver or tin*) coat, cover, electroplate, face, gild, laminate, overlay, silver, veneer.

platform n. 1 (*a stage or raised flooring in a hall*

etc., for speaking from*) dais, podium, rostrum, stage, stand. 2 (*a raised metal structure moored to the seabed and used for offshore drilling etc.*) oil rig, rig. 3 (*a political programme*) manifesto, party line, plan, policy, principle, programme, tenet.

platitude n. 1 (*a trite remark*) banality, (*coll.*) bromide, cliché, commonplace, inanity, stereotype, truism. 2 (*flatness, triteness*) banality, commonplaceness, dullness, flatness, inanity, insipidity, triteness, triviality, vapidity.

plausible a. 1 (*apparently reasonable, but specious*) believable, conceivable, credible, glib, likely, persuasive, possible, probable, reasonable, specious, verisimilar. ANTONYMS: implausible, unlikely. 2 (*apparently trustworthy, but insincere*) ingratiating, insincere, smooth, smooth-talking, untrustworthy.

play n. 1 (*sport, amusement*) amusement, caper, diversion, entertainment, exercise, foolery, frolic, fun, gambol, game, jest, lark, pastime, pleasure, prank, recreation, romp, sport. ANTONYMS: work. 2 (*a manoeuvre, esp. in a game*) action, drive, manoeuvre, move, routine. 3 (*free, aimless movement*) action, activity, motion, movement. 4 (*space or scope for freedom of action*) elbow room, flexibility, latitude, leeway, margin, scope, space. 5 (*gambling*) betting, gambling, gaming. 6 (*a drama*) comedy, drama, entertainment, farce, masque, melodrama, performance, piece, show, tragedy. 7 (*conduct or dealing towards others*) behaviour, conduct, demeanour, deportment.
~v.i. 1 (*to sport, to frolic*) caper, carouse, cavort, fool, frisk, gambol, revel, romp, sport. 2 (*to toy, to trifle (with)*) fiddle (with), toy (with), trifle (with). 3 (*coll.*) (*to participate, to cooperate*) cooperate, join in, participate, take part. 4 (*to move about in a lively or aimless manner*) dance, flicker, frisk, shimmer. 5 (*to take part in a game of chance*) bet, chance, gamble, hazard, risk, speculate, take, wager. 6 (*to behave in regard to others*) act, behave, conduct oneself. 7 (*to play a part, esp. on stage*) act, interpret, perform, present.
~v.t. 1 (*to give a performance or performances of*) present, produce, put on, stage. 2 (*to act the role of*) act, depict, perform, portray, represent. 3 (*to pretend to be*) impersonate, pretend. 4 (*to deal with*) deal with, handle, regard (as). 5 (*to oppose, to compete against*) challenge, compete with, contend with, oppose, rival, take on, vie with. **to play down** (*to treat as unimportant*) belittle, deprecate, diminish, gloss over, make light of, minimize, (*coll.*) soft-pedal, underestimate, underplay, underrate. ANTONYMS: emphasize, play up, stress. **to play up 1** (*to cause trouble or suffering (to)*) bother,

hurt, irritate, pain, trouble. **2** (*to misbehave*) (*coll.*) act up, give trouble, misbehave. **3** (*to malfunction*) (*coll.*) go on the blink, go wrong, malfunction, misfire. **4** (*to give prominence to*) accentuate, bring to the fore, build up, call attention to, dramatize, emphasize, highlight, magnify, point up, stress, underline, underscore. ANTONYMS: play down.

player *n.* **1** (*a person who plays*) competitor, contender, contestant, participant. **2** (*an actor*) actor, actress, artiste, entertainer, performer, thespian, trouper. **3** (*a performer on a musical instrument*) instrumentalist, musician, performer, virtuoso.

playful *a.* **1** (*frolicsome, sportive*) arch, cheerful, coy, flirtatious, frisky, frolicsome, gay, impish, jocular, jolly, joyous, lively, merry, mischievous, roguish, spirited, sportive, sprightly, teasing, waggish. ANTONYMS: gloomy, serious. **2** (*humorous, amusing*) amusing, funny, humorous, jocular.

plea *n.* **1** (*an urgent entreaty*) appeal, entreaty, overture, petition, prayer, request, suit, supplication. **2** (*Law*) (*the accused's answer to an indictment*) answer, argument, defence. ANTONYMS: accusation. **3** (*Law*) (*something alleged by a party to legal proceedings in support of a claim*) action, allegation, cause, suit. **4** (*an excuse*) apology, claim, defence, excuse, explanation, extenuation, justification, pretext, vindication.

plead *v.i.* **1** (*to speak or argue in support of a claim or in defence against a claim*) argue, claim, maintain. **2** (*to supplicate earnestly*) appeal, ask, beg, beseech, crave, demand, entreat, implore, importune, petition, request, solicit, supplicate. **3** (*to urge arguments for or against something*) adduce, argue, assert, declare, maintain, put forward, reason, swear.

pleasant *a.* **1** (*pleasing, agreeable*) acceptable, agreeable, amusing, delightful, enjoyable, fair, fine, gratifying, lovely, nice, pleasing, pleasurable, satisfying, welcome. ANTONYMS: horrible, unpleasant. **2** (*affable, friendly*) affable, amiable, charming, cheerful, congenial, engaging, friendly, genial, good-humoured, gracious, likeable, nice, sociable. ANTONYMS: disagreeable, unfriendly.

please *v.t.* (*to give pleasure to, to be agreeable to*) amuse, charm, cheer, content, delight, divert, entertain, give pleasure to, gladden, humour, satisfy, tickle. ANTONYMS: displease, offend.
~*v.i.* (*to like, to prefer*) choose, desire, elect, like, opt, prefer, think fit, want, will, wish.

pleased *a.* **1** (*gratified, satisfied*) (*sl.*) chuffed, contented, gratified, satisfied. **2** (*delighted, happy*) delighted, elated, euphoric, glad, happy, overjoyed, over the moon, rapt, thrilled, tickled. ANTONYMS: upset.

pleasing *a.* (*giving pleasure or enjoyment*) agreeable, amiable, amusing, attractive, charming, delightful, engaging, enjoyable, entertaining, gratifying, likeable, lovely, nice, pleasant, pleasurable, polite, satisfying, winning. ANTONYMS: displeasing, unpleasant.

pleasure *n.* **1** (*enjoyment, delight*) amusement, bliss, comfort, contentment, delectation, delight, diversion, ease, enjoyment, fulfilment, gladness, gratification, happiness, joy, recreation, satisfaction, solace. ANTONYMS: displeasure, misery. **2** (*formal*) (*choice, desire*) choice, command, desire, fancy, inclination, mind, option, preference, purpose, will, wish.

plebeian *n.* (*one of the common people*) average person, commoner, man in the street, member of the rank and file, ordinary person, peasant, (*derog.*) pleb, (*coll., derog.*) prole, proletarian.
~*a.* **1** (*of or relating to the common people*) blue-collar, low-born, lower class, proletarian, working-class. ANTONYMS: aristocratic, upper-class. **2** (*ignorant, uncultured*) ignorant, uncultivated, uncultured, unrefined. ANTONYMS: cultivated, cultured. **3** (*common, vulgar*) base, brutish, coarse, common, crass, ignoble, mean, uncouth, vulgar. ANTONYMS: elevated.

pledge *n.* **1** (*anything given as a guarantee of security for the repayment of money borrowed*) bail, bond, collateral, deposit, guarantee, security, surety. **2** (*a token*) earnest, proof, token. **3** (*an agreement, promise*) agreement, assurance, covenant, engagement, oath, promise, undertaking, vow, warrant, word. **4** (*a health, a toast*) cheer, health, toast.
~*v.t.* **1** (*to give as a pledge or security*) bind, engage, guarantee. **2** (*to deposit in pawn*) deposit, mortgage, pawn. **3** (*to promise solemnly*) contract, engage, promise, swear, undertake, vouchsafe, vow. **4** (*to drink a toast to*) drink the health of, drink to, toast.

plentiful *a.* **1** (*existing in abundance, copious*) abundant, ample, bountiful, complete, copious, full, generous, inexhaustible, infinite, lavish, liberal, overflowing, profuse, replete. ANTONYMS: inadequate, sparse. **2** (*yielding abundance*) fertile, fruitful, luxuriant, productive, prolific, thriving. ANTONYMS: sterile.

plenty *n.* **1** (*a large quantity or number, lots*) enough, excess, glut, great deal, (*coll.*) heaps, (*coll.*) loads, (*coll.*) lots, masses, mountains, multitude, (*coll.*) oodles, (*coll.*) piles, plethora, quantity, (*coll.*) stacks, sufficiency, superfluity,

(*coll.*) tons. **2** (*abundance, copiousness*) abundance, affluence, amplitude, bounty, copiousness, exuberance, fullness, lavishness, luxury, opulence, plenitude, plentifulness, prodigality, profusion, prosperity, wealth. ANTONYMS: lack. **3** (*fruitfulness*) fertility, fruitfulness, productiveness.
~*adv.* (*coll.*) (*very*) abundantly, extremely, very.

pliable *a.* **1** (*easily bent, flexible*) bendable, bendy, ductile, elastic, flexible, malleable, plastic, pliant, tensile. ANTONYMS: inflexible, rigid. **2** (*supple, limber*) limber, lissom, lithe, supple. **3** (*yielding readily to influence or arguments*) adaptable, compliant, docile, impressionable, manageable, persuadable, pliant, receptive, responsive, susceptible, tractable, yielding. ANTONYMS: intractable, unyielding.

plight *n.* (*condition, esp. one of distress*) (*coll.*) bind, case, circumstances, condition, difficulty, dilemma, fix, (*coll.*) hole, jam, mess, (*coll.*) pickle, position, predicament, quandary, (*coll.*) scrape, situation, spot, state, straits, trouble.

plod *v.i.* **1** (*to walk slowly and laboriously*) clump, drag, lumber, slog, stomp, stumble, stump, tramp, tread, trudge. **2** (*to toil, to drudge*) drudge, grind, grub, labour, peg away, persevere, plough through, plug away, slave, slog, soldier on, toil.

plot *n.* **1** (*a small piece of ground*) allotment, area, ground, lot, parcel, patch, tract. **2** (*a conspiracy, a plan*) conspiracy, intrigue, machination, plan, scheme, stratagem. **3** (*the plan of the story in a play, novel etc.*) action, narrative, outline, scenario, skeleton, story, subject, theme, thread.
~*v.t.* **1** (*to make a plan or diagram of*) chart, map, plan. **2** (*to mark (e.g. the course of a ship or aircraft on a map etc.)*) calculate, chart, locate, log, mark, outline. **3** (*to contrive, esp. secretly, to devise*) brew, conceive, concoct, contrive, (*coll.*) cook up, design, devise, frame, hatch, imagine, intrigue, machinate, manoeuvre, plan, scheme.
~*v.i.* (*to form plots against another, to conspire*) collude, conspire, intrigue, scheme.

pluck *v.t.* **1** (*to pull out, to pick*) draw, extract, gather, pick, pull off, remove, withdraw. **2** (*to pull*) catch, clutch, jerk, pull, snatch, tug, tweak, twitch, yank. **3** (*to pull the strings of (a guitar etc.) with the fingers or a plectrum*) finger, pick, plunk, strum.
~*n.* **1** (*courage, spirit*) backbone, (*sl.*) balls, boldness, (*sl.*) bottle, bravery, courage, determination, fortitude, grit, (*coll.*) guts, heart, intrepidity, mettle, nerve, resolution, spirit,

steadfastness, valour. ANTONYMS: cowardice. **2** (*a pull, a twitch*) pull, tug, tweak, twitch, yank.

plucky *a.* (*having pluck or courage*) (*sl.*) ballsy, bold, brave, courageous, daring, determined, fearless, game, gritty, (*coll.*) gutsy, heroic, intrepid, mettlesome, resolute, spirited, steadfast, valiant. ANTONYMS: cowardly, spineless.

plug *n.* **1** (*a piece of wood or other substance used to stop a hole*) bung, cork, peg, stopper, wedge. **2** (*a small piece of compressed tobacco*) cake, chew, quid, stick, twist, wad. **3** (*a piece of favourable publicity, esp. one inserted into other material*) advertisement, blurb, (*coll.*) hype, mention, promotion, publicity, puff, recommendation.
~*v.t.* **1** (*to stop with a plug*) close, cork, seal, stop up. **2** (*to insert as a plug*) block, bung, choke, clog, dam, jam, obstruct, pack, stuff. ANTONYMS: unblock. **3** (*to shoot*) (*sl.*) blow away, gun down, pick off, pot, shoot. **4** (*to give favourable publicity to (something), esp. by alluding to it repeatedly*) advertise, build up, commend, (*coll.*) hype, mention, promote, publicize, puff, push, write up.

plump *a.* (*well-rounded, fat*) ample, burly, buxom, chubby, corpulent, dumpy, fat, fleshy, full-bodied, obese, overweight, podgy, portly, rotund, squat, stout, tubby, well-covered, well-rounded, (*facet.*) well-upholstered. ANTONYMS: lean, thin.

plunder *v.t.* **1** (*to pillage, to rob*) desolate, despoil, devastate, lay waste, loot, maraud, pillage, raid, ransack, ravage, rifle, sack, spoil, strip, vandalize. **2** (*to steal from*) rob, steal.
~*n.* **1** (*forcible or systematic robbery*) depredation, despoliation, looting, pillage, robbery, sack, vandalism. **2** (*spoil, booty*) booty, loot, prey, prize, spoils, (*sl.*) swag.

plunge *v.t.* **1** (*to immerse*) dip, douse, duck, engulf, immerse, submerge. **2** (*to force, to drive (into a condition, action etc.)*) drive, force, push, thrust.
~*v.i.* **1** (*to throw oneself, to dive (into)*) dive, immerse oneself, throw oneself. **2** (*to rush or enter impetuously (into a place, condition, etc.)*) burst, career, charge, dash, hasten, hurry, hurtle, lurch, precipitate, race, rush, tear. ANTONYMS: amble. **3** (*to fall or descend very steeply or suddenly*) cast, descend, drop, fall, pitch, plummet, tumble.
~*n.* **1** (*the act of plunging, a dive*) descent, dive, drop, fall, immersion, jump, nosedive, pitch, plummet, submersion, swoop. **2** (*a risky or critical step*) bet, gamble, risk, wager.

ply *v.t.* **1** (*to use (a tool) vigorously or busily*) employ, handle, manipulate, swing, use, utilize, wield. **2** (*to work at, to employ oneself in*) carry on, exercise, follow, practise, pursue, work at. **3** (*to pursue, to persist in questioning*) assail, beset, besiege, bombard, harass, importune, persist, press, pursue, urge. **4** (*to supply* (*with*) *or subject* (*to*) *repeatedly*) lavish, provide, subject, supply.

pocket *n.* **1** (*a small bag, esp. inserted in the clothing, to contain articles carried about the person*) bag, pouch, purse, sack. **2** (*a pouchlike compartment in a car door etc.*) compartment, cubby hole, receptacle. **3** (*an isolated area*) area, patch. **4** (*a cavity in rock, containing foreign matter*) cavity, crater, hollow, pit.
~*a.* (*small*) abridged, compact, concise, little, miniature, (*coll.*) pint-sized, portable, potted, small.
~*v.t.* **1** (*to appropriate, esp. illegitimately*) appropriate, embezzle, filch, (*coll.*) lift, (*sl.*) nick, palm, pilfer, (*coll.*) pinch, purloin, (*coll.*) rip off, (*coll.*) snaffle, steal, (*coll.*) swipe, take, thieve. ANTONYMS: return. **2** (*to put up with*) accept, bear, brook, endure, put up with, stomach, swallow, take, tolerate.

poetic *a.* (*of or relating to poetry*) elegiac, lyric, lyrical, melodic, metrical, musical, rhapsodic, rhythmical, songlike. ANTONYMS: prosaic.

poignant *a.* **1** (*painful to the emotions, moving*) affecting, distressing, emotional, grievous, harrowing, heartbreaking, heart-rending, intense, melancholy, moving, pathetic, piteous, pitiable, pitiful, plaintive, sad, sharp, stirring, touching, upsetting. **2** (*stimulating to the palate, pungent*) acrid, piquant, pungent, stinging, tangy, tasty. **3** (*keen, piercing*) acerbic, acid, acute, barbed, biting, caustic, cutting, incisive, keen, penetrating, piercing, pointed, sarcastic, severe. ANTONYMS: dull. **4** (*bitter, painful*) agonizing, bitter, excruciating, painful.

point *n.* **1** (*a mark made by the end of anything sharp*) dot, mark, speck. **2** (*Print.*) (*a full stop*) full stop, period, stop. **3** (*a particular item, a detail*) aspect, detail, facet, feature, instance, item, particular. **4** (*a particular place or position*) locale, location, place, position, site, spot, station. **5** (*a state or condition*) circumstance, condition, degree, extent, position, state. **6** (*a particular moment*) instant, juncture, moment, time. **7** (*a step or stage in an argument, discourse etc.*) argument, stage, step. **8** (*a unit used in measuring or counting, e.g. scoring in games*) goal, hit, mark, run, score, tally, unit. **9** (*a salient quality, a characteristic*) aspect, attribute, characteristic, feature, peculiarity, property, quality, respect, trait. **10** (*the essential element, the exact object* (*of a discussion, joke etc.*)) burden, crux, drift,

essence, focus, gist, heart, import, matter, meaning, nub, object, pith, proposition, purport, question, subject, substance, theme, thrust. **11** (*the aim, the purpose*) aim, design, end, goal, intent, intention, motive, object, objective, purpose, reason, use, usefulness, utility. **12** (*a conclusion*) conclusion, culmination, end, finish. **13** (*a suggestion, a tip*) hint, suggestion, tip. **14** (*the sharp end of a tool, weapon etc.*) apex, end, nib, prong, tip, top. **15** (*a promontory*) cape, headland, promontory. **16** (*effectiveness, force*) effectiveness, efficacy, force, power, pungency.
~*v.t.* **1** (*to sharpen*) barb, edge, sharpen, taper, whet. ANTONYMS: blunt, dull. **2** (*to indicate, to show*) bespeak, call attention to, denote, designate, direct, indicate, point up, show, signify. **3** (*to turn in a particular direction, to aim*) aim, bring to bear, direct, level, train.

pointed *a.* **1** (*having a sharp point*) sharp, sharpened, tapering. ANTONYMS: blunt. **2** (*having a point, penetrating*) acute, barbed, biting, cogent, cutting, edged, incisive, keen, penetrating, pertinent, piercing, telling, trenchant.

pointless *a.* **1** (*having no point*) blunt, endless, tipless. **2** (*purposeless, futile*) absurd, aimless, empty, fruitless, futile, inane, ineffective, irrelevant, meaningless, nonsensical, purposeless, senseless, unproductive, unprofitable, useless, vain, worthless. ANTONYMS: meaningful, worthwhile.

poise *v.t.* (*to balance to hold or carry in equilibrium*) balance, hold, suspend.
~*v.i.* (*to hang* (*in the air*) *over*) float, hang, hover.
~*n.* **1** (*composure, self-assurance*) aplomb, assurance, calmness, composure, confidence, (*coll.*) cool, dignity, equanimity, imperturbability, presence, reserve, sang-froid, self-assurance, self-possession, tranquillity. **2** (*equipoise, equilibrium*) equilibrium, equipoise, parity, stability. ANTONYMS: imbalance, instability.

poison *n.* **1** (*a substance that injures or kills an organism into which it is absorbed*) toxin, venom. **2** (*anything destructive or corrupting*) blight, cancer, canker, contagion, contamination, corruption, disease, malignancy, pestilence, plague, virus.
~*v.t.* **1** (*to put poison in or upon*) adulterate, contaminate, envenom, infect, pollute. ANTONYMS: cleanse, purify. **2** (*to kill or injure by this means*) destroy, dispatch, kill, murder. **3** (*to corrupt, to pervert*) corrupt, debase, defile, deprave, pervert, subvert, taint, undermine, vitiate, warp.

poisonous *a.* **1** (*that injures or kills an organism into which it is absorbed*) deadly, fatal, lethal, miasmic, mortal, noxious, toxic, venomous, virulent. ANTONYMS: harmless. **2** (*destructive or corrupting*) baleful, corrupting, corruptive, dangerous, destructive, evil, foul, malevolent, malicious, malignant, pernicious, pestilential, vicious.

poke *v.t.* **1** (*to push* (*in, out, through etc.*) *with the end of something*) push, shove, stab, stick, thrust. **2** (*to prod* (*with a finger, a stick etc.*)) butt, dig, elbow, hit, jab, jostle, nudge, prod. **3** (*to stir* (*a fire*) *with a poker*) stir, stoke. **4** (*to punch*) cuff, hit, punch, strike.
~*v.i.* **1** (*to thrust, to jab*) jab, prod, push, thrust. **2** (*to protrude*) protrude, stick out. **3** (*coll.*) (*to pry, to search*) butt in, interfere, intrude, investigate, meddle, nose, peek, probe, pry, snoop, tamper.
~*n.* **1** (*a push, a thrust*) butt, dig, jostle, nudge, prod, push, shove, stab, thrust. **2** (*a punch*) blow, box, cuff, hit, punch, smack.

police *n.* **1** (*a civil force organized by a state for the detection of crime and the apprehension of offenders*) boys in blue, constabulary, (*coll.*) cops, (*sl.*) fuzz, police officers, (*coll.*) the law, (*sl.*) the Old Bill. **2** (*as pl.*) (*constables etc. belonging to this force*) (*coll.*) bobbies, constables, (*coll.*) coppers, (*coll.*) cops, (*derog.*) flatfoots, law-enforcement officers, officers, patrolmen, (*sl., offensive*) pigs, policemen, police officers, policewomen, (*sl.*) rozzers, (*sl., offensive*) the filth, (*sl.*) the fuzz.
~*v.t.* **1** (*to control by the use of police*) control, guard, keep in order, keep the peace in, patrol, protect, watch. **2** (*to supervise, to regulate*) administer, check, discipline, enforce, monitor, observe, oversee, regulate, supervise.

policy *n.* **1** (*a course of action or administration adopted by a government, organization etc.*) action, approach, code, course, custom, design, line, method, party line, plan, practice, principle, procedure, programme, protocol, rule, stratagem, system, tactic, theory. **2** (*prudence in conducting, esp. state affairs*) discretion, foresight, prudence, sagacity, sense, shrewdness, wisdom. ANTONYMS: folly.

polish *v.t.* **1** (*to make smooth or glossy, usu. by friction*) brighten, buff, burnish, gloss, rub, shine, smooth, wax. ANTONYMS: tarnish. **2** (*to refine, to free from roughness*) brush up, correct, cultivate, emend, enhance, improve, perfect, refine, touch up.
~*n.* **1** (*a smooth, glossy surface, esp. produced by friction*) brightness, brilliance, finish, gleam, gloss, lustre, radiance, sheen, shine, smoothness, sparkle, veneer. ANTONYMS: dullness. **2** (*a substance applied to impart a polish*) oil, varnish, wax. **3** (*refinement, elegance of manners*) breeding, (*coll.*) class, elegance, finesse,

finish, grace, refinement, sophistication, style, suavity, urbanity.

polished *a.* **1** (*accomplished*) accomplished, adept, expert, faultless, fine, flawless, impeccable, masterly, outstanding, perfect, professional, proficient, skilful, superlative, virtuoso. ANTONYMS: inept, unskilled. **2** (*polite and graceful*) civilized, cultivated, debonair, elegant, finished, genteel, graceful, polite, refined, sophisticated, urbane, well-bred. ANTONYMS: coarse, unrefined. **3** (*smooth and glossy*) bright, brilliant, burnished, glassy, gleaming, glossy, lustrous, shiny, slick, slippery, smooth. ANTONYMS: dull, tarnished.

polite *a.* **1** (*refined in manners; courteous*) affable, civil, cordial, courteous, deferential, formal, gracious, obliging, respectful, tactful, well-behaved, well-mannered. ANTONYMS: ill-mannered, rude. **2** (*cultivated*) civilized, cultivated, cultured. **3** ((*of literature*) *elegant*) elegant, genteel, polished, refined, urbane. ANTONYMS: crude, unrefined.

politic *a.* **1** (*prudent and sagacious*) astute, far-sighted, ingenious, intelligent, prudent, sagacious, shrewd, subtle, wise. **2** (*prudently devised, judicious*) advisable, cautious, diplomatic, discreet, expedient, judicious, sensible, tactful, wary. ANTONYMS: rash. **3** (*crafty, scheming*) artful, canny, crafty, cunning, designing, evasive, foxy, intriguing, scheming, shifty, sly, unscrupulous, wily.

poll *n.* **1** (*the voting at an election, the number of votes polled*) election, figures, returns, tally, vote. **2** (*an attempt to ascertain public opinion by questioning a few individuals*) ballot, canvass, census, count, opinion poll, sampling, survey. **3** (*an enumeration of people entitled to vote at elections*) enumeration, head count, register.
~*v.t.* **1** (*to take the votes of*) count, enumerate, record, register, tally. **2** (*to ascertain the opinion of, in a poll*) ask, ballot, canvass, interview, question, sample, survey.

pollute *v.t.* **1** (*to make foul or unclean*) befoul, besmirch, dirty, foul, mar, smirch, soil, stain, taint. ANTONYMS: clean. **2** (*to contaminate* (*an environment*)*, esp. with man-made waste*) adulterate, contaminate, infect, poison. ANTONYMS: decontaminate, sterilize. **3** (*to corrupt the moral purity of*) corrupt, debase, debauch, defile, deprive. **4** (*to profane*) desecrate, profane, sully.

pomp *n.* **1** (*a pageant*) ceremony, pageant, pageantry. **2** (*ceremonial display*) display, extravaganza, flourish, grandeur, magnificence, splendour, state. ANTONYMS: simplicity. **3** (*ostentatious display*) display, ostentation,

parade, pomposity, show, vainglory. ANTO-
NYMS: humility.

pompous *a.* **1** (*exaggeratedly solemn, self-
important*) affected, arrogant, bloated, conceited, grandiose, haughty, imperious, lofty,
magisterial, overbearing, portentous, puffed
up, self-important, showy, snobbish, supercilious, vain. ANTONYMS: humble. **2** (*ostentatious, pretentious*) boastful, bombastic, flatulent, flowery, grandiloquent, high-flown,
inflated, magniloquent, orotund, ostentatious,
overblown, pedantic, pretentious, stuffy,
turgid, windy. ANTONYMS: plain-spoken, unpretentious. **3** (*grand, magnificent*) grand,
magnificent, splendid, stately.

ponder *v.t.* (*to consider deeply, to reflect upon*)
chew over, consider, examine, mull over, puzzle over, reflect upon, think over, weigh.
~*v.i.* (*to think deeply, to muse* (*on, over etc.*))
brood, cogitate, contemplate, deliberate,
meditate, muse, ruminate, study, think.

ponderous *a.* **1** (*very heavy or weighty*) heavy,
hefty, huge, massive, weighty. ANTONYMS: light,
weightless. **2** (*bulky, unwieldy*) awkward,
bulky, clumsy, cumbersome, heavy-footed,
laborious, lumbering, unwieldy. **3** (*dull, tedious*) dreary, dull, heavy, inflated, laboured,
lifeless, long-winded, pedantic, pedestrian,
plodding, stilted, stodgy, tedious, tiresome,
turgid, verbose, wordy. **4** (*pompous, self-
important*) pompous, pretentious, self-
important.

pool¹ *n.* **1** (*a small body of water*) lagoon, lake,
mere, pond, tarn. **2** (*a puddle*) puddle, splash.
3 (*a swimming pool*) leisure pool, lido,
paddling pool, swimming bath, swimming
pool.

pool² *n.* **1** (*a group of people, vehicles etc.
available for use when required*) cartel,
collective, combine, consortium, group, syndicate, team. **2** (*a group of people who share
duties or routine work*) team, trust. **3** (*the
collective stakes in a betting arrangement*)
bank, funds, jackpot, kitty, pot, purse, stakes.
~*v.t.* (*to put* (*funds, risks etc.*) *into a common fund
or pool*) accumulate, amalgamate, collect,
consolidate, gather, join forces, league, merge,
put together. ANTONYMS: distribute.

poor *a.* **1** (*lacking enough money to live on,
needy*) badly off, bankrupt, (*coll.*) broke,
destitute, (*coll.*) dirt-poor, (*coll.*) flat broke,
hard up, impecunious, impoverished, indigent, insolvent, necessitous, needy, penniless,
penurious, poverty-stricken, ruined, short,
(*sl.*) skint, (*sl.*) stony-broke. ANTONYMS: rich,
wealthy. **2** (*badly supplied, lacking* (*in*))
deficient, depleted, exhausted, lacking. **3** ((*of

land) *barren, unproductive*) bad, bare, barren,
depleted, exhausted, fruitless, impoverished,
infertile, sterile, unfruitful, unproductive.
ANTONYMS: fertile, productive. **4** (*inadequate in
quantity or quality*) inadequate, incomplete,
insufficient, meagre, measly, miserable,
niggardly, reduced, scanty, skimpy, slight,
sparse, unsatisfactory. ANTONYMS: adequate,
plentiful. **5** (*thin, unhealthy*) lean, thin,
unhealthy, wasted. **6** (*paltry, contemptible*)
contemptible, faulty, inferior, (*coll.*) lousy,
mediocre, miserable, paltry, (*coll.*) rotten,
second-rate, shabby, shoddy, sorry, weak,
worthless. ANTONYMS: excellent, first-rate.
7 (*often iron.*) (*humble, meek*) humble, inconsequential, insignificant, lowly, mean,
meek, modest, paltry, plain, slight, trifling,
trivial. **8** (*unfortunate, used as a term of pity*)
hapless, ill-fated, ill-starred, luckless, miserable, pathetic, pitiable, pitiful, †star-crossed,
unfortunate, unhappy, unlucky, wretched.
ANTONYMS: fortunate, lucky.

pop *v.i.* **1** (*to make a short, explosive noise*)
bang, burst, crack, explode, go off, report,
snap. **2** ((*esp. of the eyes*) *to protrude as with
amazement*) bulge, protrude, stick out.
~*v.t.* (*to push* (*in, out, up*) *suddenly*) insert, push,
shove, slip, stick, thrust, tuck.
~*n.* **1** (*a short, explosive noise*) bang, burst,
crack, explosion, report. **2** (*an effervescing
drink*) (*coll.*) bubbly, fizzy drink, lemonade,
soft drink.

populace *n.* (*the common people*) commonalty, commoners, crowd, general public,
hoi polloi, inhabitants, masses, mob, multitude, people, population, rabble, throng.

popular *a.* **1** (*pleasing to or esteemed by the
general public or a specific group*) accepted,
approved, celebrated, esteemed, famous,
fashionable, favoured, favourite, (*coll.*) hot, in,
in vogue, liked, sought-after, stylish, (*coll.*)
trendy, well-liked. ANTONYMS: hated, unpopular. **2** (*suitable to or easy to be understood by
ordinary people*) average, common, commonplace, conventional, current, everyday,
general, ordinary, prevailing, prevalent, public, standard, stock, ubiquitous, universal,
widespread. ANTONYMS: exclusive.

populate *v.t.* **1** (*to furnish with inhabitants*)
colonize, people, settle. **2** (*to form the population of*) dwell in, inhabit, occupy, reside in.

population *n.* (*the inhabitants of a country
etc.*) citizenry, citizens, community, denizens,
inhabitants, natives, people, populace, resid-
ents, society.

populous *a.* (*densely populated*) crawling,
crowded, jammed, jam-packed, overpopu-

lated, packed, peopled, populated, swarming, teeming, thronged. ANTONYMS: deserted.

pore[1] *n.* (*a minute opening, esp. a hole in the skin*) aperture, hole, opening, orifice, outlet, perforation, vent.

pore[2] *v.i.* **1** (*to gaze at or study with steady attention*) examine, gaze at, go over, peruse, ponder, read, scrutinize, study, work over. **2** (*to meditate or study patiently and persistently (over, upon etc.)*) brood, contemplate, dwell on, meditate, study.

pornographic *a.* (*showing erotic acts in an obscene manner*) (*sl.*) blue, dirty, filthy, indecent, lewd, licentious, obscene, offensive, prurient, raunchy, salacious, smutty.

porous *a.* (*permeable to liquids etc.*) absorbent, absorptive, penetrable, permeable, pervious, spongelike, spongy. ANTONYMS: impermeable, non-porous.

port *n.* (*Naut.*) (*a sheltered piece of water into which vessels can enter and remain in safety*) anchorage, harbour, haven, mooring, roads, roadstead, seaport.

portable *a.* **1** (*capable of being easily carried, esp. about the person*) carriable, compact, convenient, handy, little, manageable, movable, pocket, small, transportable. **2** (*not bulky or heavy*) light, lightweight. ANTONYMS: bulky, heavy.

portentous *a.* **1** (*ominous*) alarming, crucial, fateful, forbidding, foreboding, ill-fated, ill-omened, important, inauspicious, louring, menacing, momentous, ominous, significant, sinister, threatening, unfavourable, unpropitious. **2** (*impressive*) amazing, astounding, awe-inspiring, awesome, crucial, extraordinary, fabulous, impressive, miraculous, phenomenal, prodigious, remarkable, significant, wonderful. ANTONYMS: insignificant, ordinary. **3** (*solemn*) heavy, ponderous, solemn, weighty. **4** (*self-consciously solemn*) bloated, pompous, pretentious, self-important.

portion *n.* **1** (*a share, a part assigned*) allocation, allotment, bit, division, fraction, fragment, lot, measure, morsel, parcel, part, piece, quantity, ration, scrap, section, segment, share, slice. **2** (*a helping*) helping, piece, ration, serving. **3** (*one's destiny in life*) cup, destiny, fate, fortune, lot, luck. ~*v.t.* **1** (*to divide into portions, to distribute*) carve up, distribute, divide, dole out, parcel out, partition, split up. **2** (*to allot, to assign*) allocate, allot, apportion, assign.

portly *a.* (*stout, corpulent*) ample, beefy, bulky, burly, corpulent, fat, fleshy, heavy, large,

obese, overweight, plump, rotund, stout, tubby. ANTONYMS: lean, slim.

portrait *n.* **1** (*a likeness or representation of a person or animal*) drawing, image, likeness, painting, photograph, picture, portraiture, representation, sketch. **2** (*a vivid description*) account, characterization, depiction, description, portrayal, profile, rendering, sketch, study, vignette.

portray *v.t.* **1** (*to make a portrait of*) delineate, depict, draw, figure, illustrate, †limn, paint, render, represent, sketch. **2** (*to describe*) characterize, depict, describe. **3** (*to play the role of*) act, impersonate, perform, play, pose as, represent.

pose *v.t.* **1** (*to cause (an artist's model etc.) to take a certain attitude*) arrange, model, place, position, sit, stand. **2** (*to ask (a question etc.)*) advance, ask, broach, posit, postulate, predicate, present, propound, put, set, state, submit. **3** (*to present, to be the cause of*) cause, create, present, produce, result in. ~*v.i.* **1** (*to assume an attitude or character*) feign, imitate, impersonate, masquerade as, mimic, pass oneself off as, portray, represent, sham. **2** (*to behave affectedly*) affect, attitudinize, posture, put on airs, (*coll.*) show off, strike an attitude. ~*n.* (*a bodily or mental position, esp. one put on for effect*) act, affectation, air, attitude, attitudinizing, bearing, display, facade, front, mannerism, masquerade, position, posture, posturing, pretence, role, show, stance.

posh *a.* **1** (*coll.*) (*smart, fashionable*) elegant, exclusive, fashionable, grand, high-class, high-toned, lavish, luxurious, rich, (*coll.*) ritzy, royal, smart, (*sl.*) snazzy, stylish, sumptuous, (*coll.*) swanky, (*coll.*) swish, up-market. ANTONYMS: vulgar. **2** (*sometimes derog.*) (*genteel, upper-class*) genteel, (*coll.*) la-di-da, upper-class.

position *n.* **1** (*the place occupied by a person or thing*) area, locale, location, place, point, site, situation, spot, station, whereabouts. **2** (*a posture*) attitude, pose, posture. **3** (*arrangement, disposition*) arrangement, attitude, disposition, placement. **4** (*a point of view, a stance*) angle, belief, opinion, outlook, point of view, slant, stance, standpoint, viewpoint. **5** (*a situation, a state of affairs*) circumstances, condition, pass, plight, predicament, situation, state of affairs, strait. **6** (*status, condition*) caste, class, condition, consequence, eminence, importance, place, prestige, rank, reputation, standing, station, stature, status. **7** (*a post, an appointment*) appointment, (*coll.*) billet, capacity, duty, employment, function, job, occupation, office, place, post, role, situation. **8** (*Logic*) (*a principle laid down*) assertion, belief, contention, hypothesis, principle, proposition, thesis.

~*v.t.* (*to place in position; to locate*) arrange, array, determine, dispose, establish, fix, lay out, locate, place, put, set, settle, site, situate, stand, (*coll.*) stick.

positive *a.* **1** (*definitely affirmed*) affirmative, in agreement. ANTONYMS: negative. **2** (*explicit, definite*) categorical, clear, definite, explicit, express, precise. ANTONYMS: vague. **3** (*inherent, absolute*) absolute, inherent, intrinsic. ANTONYMS: relative. **4** (*real, actual*) actual, concrete, existing, real, substantial. **5** (*authoritatively laid down*) laid down, prescribed. **6** (*incontestable, certain*) certain, conclusive, decisive, incontestable, indisputable, unambiguous, undoubted, unequivocal, unmistakable. ANTONYMS: doubted. **7** (*fully convinced*) assured, certain, confident, convinced, satisfied, sure. ANTONYMS: uncertain, unconvinced. **8** (*confident, dogmatic*) arrogant, assertive, cocksure, confident, decided, dogmatic, emphatic, firm, forceful, obstinate, opinionated, peremptory, resolute, stubborn. ANTONYMS: diffident, unassertive. **9** (*downright, thorough*) absolute, complete, consummate, downright, out-and-out, perfect, rank, thorough, thoroughgoing, total, unmitigated, utter. **10** (*constructive, helpful*) beneficial, constructive, effective, efficacious, favourable, helpful, productive, progressive, useful. ANTONYMS: impractical, unhelpful.

possess *v.t.* **1** (*to own as property, to have full power over*) control, dominate, govern, have, hold, occupy, own. ANTONYMS: lose. **2** (*to occupy, to dominate the mind of*) bewitch, charm, consume, control, dominate, enchant, enthral, fixate, influence, mesmerize, obsess, preoccupy, spellbind. **3** (*to acquire*) acquire, come by, gain, get, obtain, procure, secure, seize, take.

possession *n.* **1** (*the act or state of possessing*) care, control, custody, guardianship, keeping, ownership, proprietorship, tenure, title. **2** (*a person or thing which is possessed*) asset, belonging, chattel, effect, estate, property. **3** (*holding as owner*) holding, occupancy, occupation. **4** (*territory, esp. a subject dependency*) colony, dominion, protectorate, province, territory. **5** (*pl.*) (*property, goods*) goods, property, wealth, worldly goods.

possibility *n.* **1** (*the state, or the fact, of being possible*) chance, conceivability, feasibility, hope, likelihood, practicability, probability. ANTONYMS: impossibility. **2** (*a possible thing*) alternative, choice, option, preference. **3** (*usu.*

pl.) (*potential*) advantages, opportunities, potential, promise, prospects.

possible *a.* **1** (*that may happen or be done*) conceivable, credible, hypothetical, imaginable, likely, plausible, potential. ANTONYMS: inconceivable, unimaginable. **2** (*feasible, practicable*) attainable, doable, feasible, on, practicable, realizable, viable, workable. ANTONYMS: impossible. **3** (*that may be dealt with or put up with*) bearable, reasonable, tolerable.

possibly *adv.* **1** (*by any possible means*) at all, by any means, in any way, under any circumstances. **2** (*perhaps*) God willing, maybe, †perchance, perhaps. ANTONYMS: certainly.

post[1] *n.* (*a piece of timber, metal etc., set upright, and intended as a support to something, or to mark a boundary*) brace, column, pale, picket, pier, pile, pillar, prop, shaft, stake, stanchion, stock, support, timber, upright.

~*v.t.* **1** (*to fix* (*usu. up*) *on a post or in a public place*) affix, display, fix, hang up, pin up, put up, stick up, tack up. **2** (*to advertise, to make known*) advertise, announce, circulate, make known, proclaim, promulgate, propagate, publicize, publish.

post[2] *n.* **1** (*a fixed place or position*) place, position, station. **2** (*a military station*) outpost, station. **3** (*a situation, an appointment*) appointment, assignment, (*coll.*) billet, employment, job, office, place, position, situation.

~*v.t.* (*to place* (*an employee, soldiers etc.*) *in a particular position*) appoint, assign, establish, locate, place, position, put, set, situate, station.

post[3] *n.* **1** (*an established system of conveyance and delivery of letters and parcels*) mail, mail service, mail system, postal service, postal system. **2** (*the letters etc. delivered at a house at one time*) correspondence, letters, mail, packages, parcels.

~*v.t.* (*to send by post*) dispatch, forward, mail, send.

poster *n.* (*a large placard or advertising bill*) advertisement, announcement, bill, flyer, notice, placard, public notice, sticker.

posterior *a.* **1** (*later*) ensuing, following, later, latter, subsequent, succeeding. **2** (*situated behind or at the back*) back, behind, hind, rear. ANTONYMS: front.

posterity *n.* **1** (*descendants*) children, descendants, family, heirs, issue, offspring, progeny, scions, seed, successors. ANTONYMS: ancestry. **2** (*succeeding generations*) future, succeeding generations. ANTONYMS: past, present.

postpone *v.t.* (*to put off, to delay*) adjourn, defer, delay, hold over, lay aside, put back, put off, shelve, suspend. ANTONYMS: advance, bring forward.

postscript *n.* **1** (*a paragraph added to a letter after the writer's signature*) afterword, epilogue. **2** (*any supplement added on to the end of a book, talk etc.*) addition, afterthought, appendix, supplement. ANTONYMS: foreword, preface.

postulate *v.t.* (*to suggest, to claim*) advance, assume, claim, demand, hypothesize, posit, predicate, presuppose, propose, put forward, suggest, suppose, take for granted, theorize. ANTONYMS: prove.

posture *n.* **1** (*the manner of holding the body*) attitude, bearing, carriage, deportment, pose, position, stance. **2** (*a mental attitude*) attitude, disposition, feeling, frame of mind, inclination, mood, opinion, outlook, point of view, sentiment, stance, standpoint. **3** (*a situation, state (of affairs etc.)*) circumstance, condition, mode, phase, position, situation, state.
~*v.i.* **1** (*to assume a posture, to pose*) pose, set oneself. **2** (*to endeavour to look or sound impressive*) affect, attitudinize, do for effect, put on airs, (*coll.*) show off.

potent *a.* **1** (*powerful, mighty*) forceful, formidable, mighty, powerful, strong, vigorous. ANTONYMS: impotent, weak. **2** (*having great influence*) authoritative, commanding, dominant, dynamic, influential, powerful. **3** (*cogent*) cogent, compelling, convincing, effective, efficacious, forceful, impressive, persuasive, telling. ANTONYMS: unconvincing. **4** (*intoxicating*) intoxicating, strong.

potential *a.* **1** ((*of energy*) *existing but not in action*) covert, dormant, hidden, inherent, latent, unrealized. **2** (*existing in possibility, not yet in actuality*) budding, embryonic, likely, possible, prospective, undeveloped, unrealized.
~*n.* **1** (*a possibility*) likelihood, possibility, potency. **2** (*as yet undeveloped value or ability*) ability, aptitude, capability, capacity, potentiality, power, promise, talent, wherewithal.

potion *n.* **1** (*a liquid mixture intended as a medicine or a magic charm*) dose, elixir, philtre. **2** (*a drink*) beverage, brew, concoction, cup, draught, drink, mixture, tonic.

pounce *n.* (*an abrupt swoop, spring etc.*) assault, attack, bound, jump, leap, spring, swoop.
~*v.i.* **1** (*to sweep down and seize prey with the claws*) ambush, attack, mug, seize, snatch, strike. **2** (*to seize (upon)*) dart upon, dash

upon, descend on, drop, fall upon, jump upon, leap upon, spring upon, swoop upon, take by surprise, take unawares.

pound *v.t.* **1** (*to crush, to pulverize*) bruise, crush, mash, powder, pulverize. **2** (*to strike heavily*) batter, beat, strike. **3** (*to thump, to pommel*) bang, beat, bludgeon, (*sl.*) clobber, cudgel, pelt, pommel, thrash, thump. ANTONYMS: stroke.
~*v.i.* **1** (*to walk or go heavily (along)*) clomp, march, stomp, stump, tramp. **2** ((*of the heart, a drum etc.*) *to beat heavily or very fast*) beat, drum, hammer, palpitate, pulsate, pulse, throb, thump.

pour *v.t.* **1** (*to serve (a drink) by pouring*) decant, serve. **2** (*to discharge*) discharge, emit, empty. **3** (*to utter, to give vent to*) express, give vent to, utter, voice.
~*v.i.* **1** (*to flow in a stream of rain, to fall copiously*) (*coll.*) bucket down, (*Sc., North.*) hozzle, pelt, rain, sheet, teem. **2** (*to rush in great numbers*) crowd, stream, swarm, teem, throng. **3** (*to come in a constant stream*) cascade, course, flood, flow, gush, spew, spill, splash, spout, spurt, stream.

pout *v.i.* (*to thrust out the lips in displeasure or contempt*) brood, frown, glower, grimace, lour, mope, pull a face, scowl, sulk. ANTONYMS: smile.

poverty *n.* **1** (*the state of being poor*) beggary, destitution, distress, hardship, impoverishment, indigence, insolvency, necessity, need, pauperism, pennilessness, penury, privation, want. ANTONYMS: affluence, wealth. **2** (*scarcity, dearth (of)*) barrenness, dearth, meagreness, scarcity. ANTONYMS: fertility. **3** (*deficiency (in)*) deficiency (in), insufficiency (of), lack (of), paucity (of), shortage (of). ANTONYMS: abundance (of), plenty.

powder *n.* **1** (*any dry, dustlike substance or fine particles*) dust, grains, particles. **2** (*a cosmetic in the form of fine dust*) cosmetic, talc, talcum.
~*v.t.* **1** (*to reduce to powder*) crush, granulate, grind, pestle, pound, pulverize. **2** (*to sprinkle or cover with powder*) coat, cover, dredge, dust, scatter, sprinkle, strew.

power *n.* **1** (*the ability to do or act so as to effect something*) ability, capability, capacity. ANTONYMS: inability. **2** (*a mental or bodily faculty*) aptitude, capability, capacity, competence, competency, faculty, genius, gift, knack, potential, skill, talent. ANTONYMS: incapacity, incompetence. **3** (*strength, force*) (*coll.*) clout, energy, force, intensity, might, muscle, potency, strength, vigour, weight. **4** (*influence, authority (over)*) ascendancy, authority, command, control, dominance, domination, dominion, influence, mastery, rule, sovereignty, supremacy, sway. ANTONYMS: impotence, weakness. **5** (*right or ability to control*) prerogative, privilege, right. **6** (*legal authority or authorization*) authority, authorization, licence, warrant. **7** (*the capacity* (*of a machine etc.*) *for performing mechanical work*) drive, energy, force, impetus, inertia, momentum.

powerful *a.* **1** (*having great strength or energy*) energetic, robust, stalwart, strapping, strong, sturdy, tough, vigorous. **2** (*mighty, potent*) forceful, formidable, mighty, potent, vigorous. **3** (*influential, forcible*) authoritative, cogent, compelling, convincing, efficacious, forceful, forcible, impressive, influential, persuasive, striking, substantial, telling, weighty. **4** (*producing great effects*) effective, effectual, productive, useful. ANTONYMS: ineffective. **5** (*coll.*) (*great, numerous*) extreme, great, high, intense, numerous.

powerless *a.* **1** (*without strength or power*) debilitated, disabled, feeble, frail, helpless, impotent, incapable, incapacitated, ineffective, ineffectual, infirm, paralysed, prostrate, strengthless, unfit, vulnerable, weak. ANTONYMS: powerful, strong. **2** (*unable* (*to*)) incapable, incompetent, unable.

practicable *a.* **1** (*capable of being done, feasible*) achievable, attainable, doable, feasible, possible, viable, workable. ANTONYMS: impracticable, unfeasible. **2** ((*of roads etc.*) *usable, passable*) navigable, passable, usable, viable.

practical *a.* **1** (*realistic, down-to-earth*) businesslike, commonsense, down-to-earth, everyday, expedient, matter-of-fact, mundane, ordinary, realistic, reasonable, sensible, workaday. ANTONYMS: impractical, unrealistic. **2** (*capable of being used, available*) applicable, doable, feasible, functional, practicable, pragmatic, serviceable, sound, suitable, useful, workable. **3** (*derived from practice, experienced*) accomplished, competent, efficient, experienced, practised, proficient, qualified, seasoned, skilled, trained, versed, veteran, working. ANTONYMS: inexperienced, unskilled.

practical joke *n.* (*a joke or trick intended to make the victim look foolish*) hoax, lark, prank, trick.

practically *adv.* **1** (*in a practical manner*) clearly, matter-of-factly, rationally, realistically, reasonably, sensibly, simply, unsentimentally. **2** (*virtually, in effect*) all but, almost, at bottom, basically, close to, essentially, fundamentally, in effect, just about, nearly, to all intents and purposes, very nearly, virtually, well-nigh.

practice *n.* **1** (*habitual or customary action or procedure*) action, method, mode, procedure, routine, rule, system, way. **2** (*a habit, a custom*) convention, custom, habit, tradition, usage, use, wont. **3** (*professional work*) business, career, office, profession, pursuit, vocation, work. **4** (*actual performance or doing*) action, application, doing, effect, execution, operation, performance. ANTONYMS: intention, theory. **5** (*conduct, dealings*) actions, behaviour, conduct, dealings. **6** (*regular, repeated exercise in order to gain proficiency in something*) discipline, drill, exercise, preparation, rehearsal, repetition, study, training.

practise *v.t.* **1** (*to perform habitually; to carry out*) carry out, do, engage in, perform. **2** (*to exercise as a profession etc.*) carry on, engage in, ply, pursue, specialize in, undertake, work at. **3** (*to exercise oneself in or on* (*to improve or maintain a skill etc.*)) go over, go through, polish, prepare, rehearse, repeat, run through. **4** (*to instruct, to drill* (*in a subject, art etc.*)) drill, exercise, instruct, train.

practised *a.* (*experienced, expert*) able, accomplished, adept, capable, consummate, experienced, expert, gifted, proficient, qualified, rehearsed, schooled, seasoned, skilled, talented, trained, versed. ANTONYMS: inexperienced.

pragmatic *a.* (*concerned with practicalities rather than principles*) businesslike, down-to-earth, efficient, expedient, hard-headed, matter-of-fact, practicable, practical, realistic, sensible, utilitarian. ANTONYMS: impractical, unrealistic.

praise *v.t.* **1** (*to express approval and commendation of*) acclaim, admire, applaud, approve, commend, compliment, congratulate, cry up, eulogize, honour, laud. ANTONYMS: criticize, damn. **2** (*to extol, to glorify*) adore, bless, exalt, extol, glorify, hallow, magnify, revere, venerate, worship.
~*n.* **1** (*the act, or an instance, of praising*) acclaim, acclamation, accolade, applause, approbation, approval, commendation, compliment, congratulation, encomium, endorsement, eulogy, laudation, ovation, panegyric, plaudit, tribute. ANTONYMS: criticism. **2** (*glorifying, extolling*) adoration, adulation, devotion, exaltation, glorification, homage, reverence, veneration, worship.

praiseworthy *a.* (*laudable, commendable*) admirable, commendable, creditable, deserving, estimable, excellent, exemplary, fine, honourable, laudable, meritorious, worthy. ANTONYMS: deplorable, reprehensible.

prance *v.i.* **1** (*to spring or caper on the hind legs,* *as a horse)* bound, caper, cavort, curvet, dance, frisk, gambol, jump, leap, romp, skip, spring, trip. **2** *(to walk or strut in a swaggering style)* parade, preen, *(coll.)* show off, strut, swagger, *(coll.)* swank.

prank *n.* **1** *(a wild frolic)* antic, caper, escapade, frolic, jape, lark, stunt. **2** *(a trick, a practical joke)* jest, practical joke, *(coll.)* skylarking, trick.

pray *v.t.* *(to speak (to God), to beseech)* appeal to, beg, beseech, call upon, crave, entreat, implore, importune, invoke, petition, plead, request, solicit, sue, supplicate, urge.

prayer *n.* **1** *(a solemn petition or a thanksgiving addressed to God or any object of worship)* collect, doxology, invocation, litany, petition, request. **2** *(the practice of praying)* communion, devotion, intercession, invocation, supplication. **3** *(an entreaty)* appeal, entreaty, petition, plea, request, suit, supplication.

preach *v.i.* **1** *(to deliver a sermon or public discourse on some religious subject)* address, catechize, declare, deliver a sermon, evangelize, exhort, orate, proclaim, promulgate, speak, teach. **2** *(to give earnest religious or moral advice, esp. in an obtrusive way)* admonish, advise, advocate, harangue, lecture, moralize, pontificate, sermonize, urge.

preacher *n.* *(a person who preaches a sermon)* cleric, divine, ecclesiastic, evangelist, member of the clergy, minister, missionary, parson, revivalist, speaker.

precarious *a.* **1** *(not well-established, unstable)* insecure, shaky, unreliable, unsafe, unsettled, unstable, unsteady, unsure. ANTONYMS: reliable, secure. **2** *(uncertain, hazardous)* chancy, dangerous, *(coll.)* dicey, difficult, *(coll.)* dodgy, doubtful, dubious, *(coll.)* hairy, hazardous, *(coll.)* iffy, perilous, risky, slippery, treacherous, tricky, uncertain. ANTONYMS: certain.

precaution *n.* **1** *(a measure taken beforehand to guard against something)* cover, insurance, protection, provision, safeguard. **2** *(prudent foresight)* alertness, anticipation, apprehension, care, caution, circumspection, foresight, forethought, providence, prudence, vigilance, wariness.

precede *v.t.* **1** *(to go before in time or order)* antecede, antedate, come first, forerun, foreshadow, go before, lead, predate, take precedence. ANTONYMS: follow. **2** *(to cause to come before)* preface, prelude.

precedent *n.* *(something done or said which may serve as an example to be followed in a*

similar case) antecedent, authority, criterion, example, exemplar, instance, lead, model, paradigm, pattern, prototype, standard, yardstick.

preceding *a.* *(going before in time, order etc.)* above, aforementioned, antecedent, anterior, earlier, foregoing, former, past, previous, prior. ANTONYMS: following, subsequent.

precept *n.* **1** *(a command, a mandate)* behest, canon, charge, command, decree, direction, edict, injunction, instruction, law, mandate, order, ordinance, regulation, statute. **2** *(a rule of conduct)* guideline, principle, rule. **3** *(a maxim)* adage, aphorism, axiom, byword, dictum, maxim, motto, proverb, saying, slogan. **4** *(a writ, a warrant)* warrant, writ.

precious *a.* **1** *(of great price or value)* choice, exquisite, fine, high-priced, inestimable, invaluable, priceless, prized, rare, valuable. **2** *(very costly)* costly, dear, expensive. **3** *(highly esteemed, beloved)* adored, beloved, cherished, darling, dear, dearest, esteemed, favourite, idolized, loved, prized, revered, treasured, valued. **4** *(affected, over-refined in manner etc.)* affected, artificial, fastidious, flowery, mannered, overdone, overnice, over-refined, pretentious, studied, *(usu. derog.)* twee. ANTONYMS: natural.

precipitate[1] *v.t.* **1** *(to throw headlong)* cast, discharge, fling, hurl, launch, let fly, propel, send forth, throw. **2** *(to urge on with eager haste or violence)* incite, instigate, provoke, urge on. ANTONYMS: hold back. **3** *(to hasten; to bring on, esp. prematurely)* accelerate, advance, bring on, dispatch, expedite, further, hasten, hurry, press, push forward, quicken, speed up. ANTONYMS: retard.

precipitate[2] *a.* **1** *(headlong)* breakneck, headlong, plunging. **2** *(flowing or rushing with haste and violence)* fast, meteoric, rapid, rushing, speedy, swift, violent. **3** *(hasty, rash)* careless, foolhardy, frantic, hasty, heedless, hot-headed, hurried, ill-advised, impetuous, impulsive, inconsiderate, indiscreet, madcap, precipitous, rash, reckless, thoughtless, volatile. ANTONYMS: careful, cautious.

precipitous *a.* **1** *(like or of the nature of a precipice)* abrupt, bluff, dizzy, high, perpendicular, sheer, steep, vertical. **2** *(hasty, rash)* abrupt, careless, foolhardy, hasty, headlong, heedless, hurried, ill-advised, impulsive, precipitate, rash, reckless, sudden, volatile. ANTONYMS: careful, cautious.

precise *a.* **1** *(definite, well-defined)* absolute, clearcut, definite, explicit, sharp, specific, well-defined. ANTONYMS: indefinite, vague.

2 (*accurate, exact*) accurate, authentic, correct, exact, literal, perfect, strict, true. ANTONYMS: inaccurate, inexact. **3** (*strictly observant of rule, punctilious*) fastidious, finicky, formal, meticulous, nice, overnice, over-scrupulous, prim, punctilious, puritanical, rigid, scrupulous, severe, stiff, strict.

precision *n.* (*accuracy, exactness*) accuracy, care, correctness, definiteness, exactitude, exactness, faithfulness, fastidiousness, faultlessness, fidelity, flawlessness, meticulousness, nicety, particularity, perfection, preciseness, rigour, scrupulousness, strictness. ANTONYMS: vagueness.

preclude *v.t.* **1** (*to shut out, to exclude*) exclude, shut out. **2** (*to hinder, to prevent*) avert, avoid, bar, block, check, debar, forestall, frustrate, hinder, impede, inhibit, obstruct, obviate, prevent, prohibit, put a stop to, restrain, rule out, stop, thwart. ANTONYMS: encourage, promote.

precocious *a.* **1** (*prematurely developed intellectually*) advanced, ahead, bright, clever, developed, early, gifted, intelligent, premature, quick, smart. ANTONYMS: backward, retarded. **2** (*forward, pert*) cheeky, forward, impertinent, pert, (*coll.*) pushy, saucy.

preconception *n.* (*an opinion that is formed beforehand*) assumption, bias, notion, predisposition, prejudice, prepossession, presumption, presupposition.

precursor *n.* **1** (*a forerunner, a harbinger*) forerunner, harbinger, herald, messenger, usher, vanguard. **2** (*a predecessor in office etc.*) ancestor, antecedent, forebear, forefather, foremother, forerunner, originator, pioneer, predecessor.

predatory *a.* **1** (*habitually hunting and killing other animals for food*) carnivorous, hunting, predacious, ravening. **2** (*of or relating to plunder or pillage*) despoiling, greedy, looting, marauding, pillaging, piratical, plundering, ravaging, robbing, thieving. **3** (*rapacious, exploitive*) avaricious, exploitive, extortionate, greedy, rapacious, usurious, voracious.

predecessor *n.* **1** (*a person or thing preceding another*) antecedent, forerunner, precursor. **2** (*an ancestor*) ancestor, antecedent, forebear, forefather, foremother. ANTONYMS: successor.

predicament *n.* (*a particular state, esp. a difficult one*) (*coll.*) bind, condition, corner, crisis, dilemma, fix, (*coll.*) hole, (*coll.*) hot water, impasse, jam, mess, (*coll.*) pickle, pinch, plight, position, quandary, (*coll.*) scrape, situation, spot, state.

predict *v.t.* (*to forecast, to foretell*) augur, divine, forebode, forecast, foresee, foreshadow, foretell, forewarn, portend, presage, prognosticate, prophesy, soothsay.

prediction *n.* **1** (*something predicted*) augury, divination, forecast, prognosis, prognostication, prophecy. **2** (*the act, or the art, of predicting*) divination, prognostication, soothsaying.

predisposition *n.* (*a tendency to behave in a particular way*) bent, bias, disposition, inclination, likelihood, penchant, potentiality, predilection, preference, proclivity, proneness, propensity, susceptibility, tendency, vulnerability, willingness.

predominant *a.* **1** (*predominating (over)*) dominant, predominating. **2** (*superior, controlling*) ascendant, capital, chief, controlling, leading, main, overruling, paramount, prevailing, prevalent, primary, prime, principal, prominent, ruling, sovereign, superior, supreme, transcendent. ANTONYMS: subordinate, unimportant.

predominate *v.i.* **1** (*to be superior in strength or authority*) dominate, take precedence. **2** (*to prevail, to have the ascendancy (over)*) have the ascendancy, hold sway, outweigh, override, overrule, overshadow, prevail, rule.

pre-eminent *a.* (*superior to or surpassing all others*) chief, consummate, distinguished, excellent, foremost, incomparable, inimitable, matchless, outstanding, paramount, predominant, prevailing, renowned, superb, superior, supreme, transcendent, unequalled, unrivalled, unsurpassed.

preen *v.t., v.i.* **1** (*to clean and arrange (feathers) using the beak*) clean, groom, plume. **2** (*to take great trouble with (one's appearance)*) array, deck out, (*coll.*) doll up, dress up, prettify, primp, spruce up, (*sl.*) tart up, titivate, trim. **3** (*to congratulate oneself (on)*) congratulate oneself, pride oneself.

preface *n.* (*something spoken or written as introductory to a discourse or book*) foreword, introduction, preamble, preliminary, prelude, prologue. ANTONYMS: epilogue. ~*v.t.* (*to introduce (with preliminary remarks etc.)*) begin, introduce, open, precede, prefix. ANTONYMS: close.

prefer *v.t.* **1** (*to like better*) adopt, choose, desire, elect, embrace, fancy, favour, go for, incline towards, lean towards, like better, opt for, pick, plump for, select, single out, wish. ANTONYMS: reject. **2** (*to bring forward, to submit*) bring forward, enter, file, lodge, place, present, press, proffer, propose, put forward, submit, tender. ANTONYMS: withdraw. **3** (*to recommend, to favour*) advance, commend, elevate, favour, move up, promote, raise, recommend, upgrade. ANTONYMS: downgrade, pass over.

preferable *a.* (*more desirable*) best, better, choice, chosen, favoured, superior, worthier. ANTONYMS: inferior, undesirable.

preference *n.* **1** (*liking for one thing more than another*) advantage, bent, bias, fancy, favouritism, inclination, leaning, liking, partiality, predilection, predisposition, prejudice, proclivity. **2** (*something which is preferred*) choice, desire, favourite, option, pick, selection.

pregnant *a.* **1** (*having a child or young developing in the womb*) expectant, expecting, gravid, (*sl.*) in the club, parturient, with child. **2** (*full of meaning, significant*) eloquent, expressive, meaningful, pointed, significant, suggestive, telling. **3** (*inventive, imaginative*) creative, imaginative, inventive, original, seminal. **4** (*fruitful*) abundant, fecund, fertile, fruitful, full, productive, prolific, replete, rich, teeming. ANTONYMS: barren, infertile. **5** (*portentous, fraught*) charged, fraught, loaded, portentous, weighty.

prejudice *n.* **1** (*opinion or bias formed without due consideration of facts*) bias, favouritism, jaundice, leaning, opinion, partiality, preconception, predilection, predisposition, prejudgement, twist, warp. ANTONYMS: impartiality. **2** (*intolerance or hostility towards a particular group, race etc.*) apartheid, bigotry, chauvinism, discrimination, hostility, inequality, injustice, intolerance, narrowmindedness, racism, sexism, unfairness. **3** (*damage or detriment arising from unfair judgement*) damage, detriment, disadvantage, harm, hurt, impairment, loss, mischief.
~*v.t.* **1** (*to prepossess with prejudice, to bias*) bias, colour, distort, incline, influence, jaundice, poison, predispose, prepossess, slant, sway, warp. **2** (*to impair the validity of a right etc.*) damage, harm, hinder, hurt, impair, injure, invalidate, mar, spoil, undermine.

prejudicial *a.* (*causing prejudice or injury*) damaging, deleterious, detrimental, harmful, hurtful, inimical, injurious, pernicious, undermining, unfavourable.

preliminary *a.* (*introductory*) advance, antecedent, beginning, exploratory, first, initiatory, introductory, opening, pilot, preceding, precursory, prefatory, preparatory, prior, qualifying, test, trial. ANTONYMS: final.
~*n.* (*something introductory*) beginning, foreword, foundation, groundwork, initiation,

introduction, overture, preamble, preface, prelims, prelude, prologue, start.

prelude *n.* **1** (*something done, happening etc., introductory to that which follows*) beginning, commencement, curtainraiser, foreword, introduction, overture, preamble, preface, preliminary, preparation, prologue, start. ANTONYMS: finale. **2** (*a harbinger, a precursor*) forerunner, harbinger, herald, messenger, precursor.

premature *a.* **1** (*ripe or mature too soon*) embryonic, green, immature, incomplete, raw, undeveloped, unfledged, unready, unripe, unseasonable, untimely. **2** (*happening or performed before the proper time*) beforehand, early, forward. ANTONYMS: late. **3** (*overhasty*) hasty, ill-considered, ill-timed, impulsive, inopportune, overhasty, precipitate, (*coll.*) previous, rash, reckless.

premise *n.* **1** (*Logic*) (*a statement from which another is inferred*) argument, assertion, assumption, conjecture, hypothesis, premiss, presupposition, proposal, proposition, statement, supposition, surmise, theorem. **2** (*pl.*) (*a piece of land and the buildings upon it, esp. considered as a place of business*) building, establishment, land, lot, place, plot, property, site.

premium *n.* **1** (*a payment* (*usu. periodical*) *made for insurance*) instalment, investment, payment. **2** (*a sum paid in addition to interest, wages etc., a bonus*) bonus, boon, bounty, commission, dividend, extra, incentive, (*coll.*) percentage, (*coll.*) perk, tip. **3** (*the rate at which shares, money etc. are selling above their nominal value*) appreciation, margin, profit, value. **4** (*a reward, a recompense*) prize, recompense, remuneration, reward.

premonition *n.* **1** (*a foreboding, a presentiment*) apprehension, feeling, foreboding, hunch, idea, intuition, misgiving, omen, portent, presentiment, sign, suspicion. **2** (*previous warning or notice*) advance notice, forewarning, warning.

preoccupied *a.* (*thinking about one thing to the exclusion of all others*) absent-minded, absorbed, brooding, cogitative, distracted, engrossed, faraway, heedless, immersed, inattentive, intent, lost in thought, oblivious, pensive, rapt, reflective, thoughtful, unaware, vague, wrapped up. ANTONYMS: alert, attentive.

preparation *n.* **1** (*the act, or an instance, of preparing*) development, foundation, groundwork, spadework. **2** (*the state of being prepared*) alertness, anticipation, expectation, fitness, preparedness, readiness. **3** (*a preparatory act or measure*) arrangement, measure, plan, precaution, provision, safeguard. **4** (*anything prepared by a special process, such as food, a medicine etc.*) composition, compound, concoction, food, medicine, mixture, tincture. **5** (*the preparing of lessons or schoolwork*) homework, (*sl.*) prep, revision, schoolwork.

preparatory *a.* (*introductory* (*to*)) before, in advance of, in anticipation of, initial, introductory, opening, precursory, prefatory, preliminary, preparative, previous to, prior to.

prepare *v.t.* **1** (*to make ready*) arrange, dispose, make ready, order, organize, plan, prime, ready. **2** (*to make ready* (*food, a meal etc.*)) (*esp. NAm.*) fix, make, produce, put together, (*coll.*) rustle up. **3** (*to make ready or fit* (*to do, to receive etc.*)) adapt, brace, equip, fortify, make fit, outfit, ready, steel, strengthen. **4** (*to produce*) concoct, contrive, fabricate, fashion, make, manufacture, produce. **5** (*to construct, to put together*) assemble, construct, draw up, put together. **6** (*to get* (*a speech, a part etc.*) *ready by practice, study etc.*) brief, cram, practise, study, (*coll.*) swot, train.

prepossessing *a.* (*tending to win favour, attractive*) alluring, appealing, attractive, beautiful, bewitching, captivating, charming, enchanting, engaging, fair, fascinating, fetching, glamorous, good-looking, handsome, likeable, lovely, pleasing, striking, winsome. ANTONYMS: displeasing, unattractive.

preposterous *a.* **1** (*contrary to reason or common sense*) illogical, irrational, nonsensical, senseless, unnatural, unreasonable. ANTONYMS: natural, sensible. **2** (*obviously wrong, absurd*) absurd, (*sl.*) barmy, crazy, exorbitant, extravagant, extreme, farcical, fatuous, foolish, impossible, incredible, insane, laughable, ludicrous, mad, monstrous, outrageous, ridiculous, shocking.

prerogative *n.* (*any peculiar right or privilege etc.*) advantage, authority, birthright, choice, claim, franchise, liberty, option, power, privilege, right, sanction, title.

prescribe *v.t.* **1** (*to direct* (*a medicine etc.*) *to be used as a remedy*) dose, treat. **2** (*to recommend* (*some course of action*)) advise, advocate, counsel, recommend, urge. **3** (*to state with authority*) appoint, bid, command, decree, define, demand, dictate, enjoin, impose, instruct, lay down, ordain, order, require, rule, set, specify, stipulate.

prescription *n.* **1** (*something which is prescribed, esp. a written direction for the preparation of medical remedies*) direction, formula, instruction, recipe, recommendation. **2** (*the medication etc. prescribed*) drug,

medication, medicine, mixture, preparation, remedy.

presence *n.* **1** (*the quality or state of being present*) attendance, being, companionship, company, existence. **2** (*the immediate vicinity of a person*) closeness, nearness, proximity, vicinity. **3** (*an imposing or dignified bearing*) carriage, comportment, demeanour, dignity. **4** (*the ability to grasp and hold an audience's attention*) air, aura, bearing, character, charisma, confidence, ease, magnetism, personality, poise, self-assurance, self-possession. **5** (*an influence as of a being invisibly present*) apparition, ghost, manifestation, spectre, spirit, wraith.

present[1] *a.* **1** (*being here or in a place referred to*) attendant, here, in attendance. ANTONYMS: absent. **2** (*being in view or at hand*) at hand, available, close, in view, near, nearby, ready, there, to hand. **3** (*now existing or occurring*) contemporary, current, existent, existing, immediate, instant.
~*n.* (*the present time*) here and now, now, today. ANTONYMS: future, past.

present[2] *v.t.* **1** (*to introduce to the acquaintance of, esp. to introduce formally*) acquaint with, introduce, make known. **2** (*to exhibit, to show*) demonstrate, display, exhibit, give, mount, produce, put on, show, stage. **3** (*to hold in position or point* (*a gun etc.*)) display, hold in position, point. **4** (*to offer for consideration, to submit*) advance, hold out, offer, pose, proffer, put forward, raise, submit, suggest, tender. **5** (*to act as the presenter of* (*as a television programme*)) compère, front, host, introduce. **6** (*to portray, to represent*) characterize, depict, describe, portray, represent. **7** (*to give, esp. in a ceremonious way*) award, bestow, confer, donate, give, grant, hand over, offer, proffer. ANTONYMS: withhold. **8** (*to invest or endow* (*with a gift*)) endow, give, invest. **9** (*to tender, to deliver*) deliver, extend, offer, tender.

present[3] *n.* (*something which is presented, a gift*) benefaction, bounty, donation, endowment, favour, gift, grant, gratuity, handout, offering, (*coll.*) prezzie.

presentation *n.* **1** (*a formal offering or proffering*) award, bestowal, conferral, delivery, giving, grant, investiture, offering, proffering. **2** (*a present, a gift*) donation, gift, offering, present. **3** (*an exhibition, a theatrical representation*) demonstration, display, exhibition, performance, production, rendition, representation, show, staging. **4** (*a verbal report on, or exposé of, a subject, often with illustrative material*) address, exposé, lecture, report, speech, talk. **5** (*a formal introduction,* *esp. to a superior personage*) coming out, debut, introduction, launch, reception, unveiling.

presently *adv.* (*soon, shortly*) before long, by and by, in a minute, in due course, later, shortly, soon.

preservation *n.* (*the act, or an instance, of preserving*) care, conservation, continuation, defence, keeping, maintenance, perpetuation, protection, retention, safeguarding, safe keeping, safety, salvation, security, support, upholding. ANTONYMS: destruction.

preserve *v.t.* **1** (*to keep safe, to protect*) care for, conserve, defend, guard, keep, protect, safeguard, secure, shelter, shield, spare, store, watch over. ANTONYMS: destroy. **2** (*to rescue*) rescue, save. **3** (*to maintain in a good or the same condition*) conserve, keep up, maintain, sustain, uphold. **4** (*to retain, to keep intact*) continue, keep intact, perpetuate, retain. **5** (*to keep (food) from decay or decomposition by pickling, freezing etc.*) boil, can, conserve, cure, dry, freeze, pickle, smoke, store.
~*n.* **1** (*fruit boiled with sugar or preservative substances, jam*) confection, confiture, conserve, jam, jelly. **2** (*a place where game is preserved*) game reserve, park, reserve, sanctuary. **3** (*something reserved for certain people only*) area, domain, field, realm, sphere.

preside *v.i.* **1** (*to be set in authority over others, esp. in charge of a meeting, ceremony etc.*) chair, control, direct, govern, head, officiate, rule. **2** (*to lead, to superintend*) administer, administrate, conduct, handle, lead, manage, oversee, regulate, run, superintend, supervise.

press *v.t.* **1** (*to push (something up, down, against etc.) with steady force*) force, push. **2** (*to squeeze, to compress*) bear down on, compress, condense, crush, depress, force down, jam, mash, reduce, squeeze, stuff. **3** (*to make smooth by pressure (as cloth or paper)*) flatten, iron, mangle, smooth, steam. ANTONYMS: crumple. **4** (*to embrace, to hug*) clasp, cram, crush, embrace, encircle, enfold, hold close, hug, squeeze. **5** (*to invite with persistent warmth*) insist, invite, urge. **6** (*to put forward vigorously and persistently*) beg, entreat, exhort, implore, importune, petition, plead, pressurize, sue, supplicate, urge. **7** (*to weigh down, to distress*) afflict, assail, beset, besiege, disquiet, distress, harass, plague, torment, trouble, vex, weigh down, worry. **8** (*to straiten, to constrain*) compel, constrain, enjoin, straiten. **9** (*to enforce strictly, to impress*) demand, enforce, impress.
~*v.i.* **1** (*to exert pressure; to weigh heavily (on)*) bear heavily, exert pressure, weigh heavily.

2 (*to make demands (for)*) demand, enjoin, urge. **3** (*to throng, to crowd*) cluster, congregate, converge, crowd, encroach, flock, gather, herd, huddle, intrude, mill, seethe, swarm, throng. **4** (*to strive eagerly, to push one's way*) hasten, strain, strive.
~*n.* **1** (*a crowd, a throng*) bunch, crowd, crush, flock, herd, horde, huddle, mob, multitude, (*usu. derog.*) pack, push, swarm, throng. **2** (*urgency, hurry*) bustle, demand, (*coll.*) hassle, haste, hurry, hustle, pressure, strain, stress, urgency. **3** (*the news media collectively, esp. newspapers; journalists*) fourth estate, journalists, media, newspapers, paparazzi, reporters.

pressing *a.* (*urgent, insistent*) burning, compelling, constraining, critical, crucial, grave, imperative, important, importunate, insistent, major, momentous, pivotal, portentous, profound, serious, significant, urgent, vital. ANTONYMS: trivial, unimportant.

pressure *n.* **1** (*the act of pressing*) compression, crushing. **2** (*a force steadily exerted upon or against a body by another in contact with it*) force, influence, power, sway. **3** (*the amount of this, usu. measured in units of weight upon a unit of area*) heaviness, weight. **4** (*constraining force, compulsion*) coercion, compulsion, constraint, obligation. **5** (*stress, urgency*) strain, stress, tension, urgency. **6** (*trouble, oppression*) adversity, affliction, burden, demands, difficulty, distress, harassment, (*coll.*) hassle, hurry, load, oppression, trouble, vexation.

pressurize *v.t.* (*to seek to coerce*) bully, compel, constrain, force, oblige, press, put pressure on, (*coll.*) put the screws on.

prestige *n.* (*influence derived from excellence, achievements etc.*) authority, cachet, celebrity, credit, distinction, eminence, esteem, fame, honour, importance, influence, rank, regard, renown, significance, standing, stature, status, weight.

presume *v.t.* **1** (*to assume without previous inquiry*) assume, believe, conclude, conjecture, fancy, gather, (*N Am., coll.*) guess, imagine, infer, postulate, presuppose, speculate, suppose, surmise, suspect, take for granted, take it, theorize, think, understand. ANTONYMS: know. **2** (*to venture*) dare, make bold, undertake, venture.
~*v.i.* (*to take liberties*) be so bold, encroach, impose, make so bold, take liberties, venture.

presumption *n.* **1** (*assumption of the truth or existence of something without direct proof*) anticipation, assumption, belief, conjecture, guess, hypothesis, opinion, preconception, premise, presupposition, proposition, supposition, surmise. **2** (*a ground for presuming*) basis, feasibility, grounds, likelihood, plausibility, probability, reason. **3** (*arrogance, impudence*) arrogance, audacity, boldness, brass, brazenness, (*coll.*) cheek, effrontery, forwardness, front, gall, immodesty, impertinence, impudence, insolence, (*coll.*) neck, (*coll.*) nerve, overconfidence, presumptuousness, pride, temerity. ANTONYMS: modesty.

presumptuous *a.* **1** (*arrogant, forward*) arrogant, audacious, (*coll.*) big-headed, bold, brash, brazen, (*coll.*) cheeky, cocksure, disrespectful, forward, (*coll.*) fresh, immodest, impertinent, impudent, insolent, overconfident, proud, (*coll.*) pushy, saucy, (*coll.*) uppish. ANTONYMS: bashful, shy. **2** (*rash, venturesome*) foolhardy, hasty, rash, reckless, venturesome.

pretence *n.* **1** ((*an act of*) *pretending or feigning*) acting, charade, deceit, deception, fabrication, falsehood, feigning, invention, make-believe, pretending, sham, simulation, subterfuge, trickery. ANTONYMS: reality. **2** (*an excuse, a pretext*) artifice, camouflage, cloak, cover, excuse, guise, mask, masquerade, pretext, ruse, wile. **3** (*show, ostentation*) affectation, appearance, display, facade, ostentation, pretentiousness, semblance, show, veneer.

pretend *v.t.* **1** (*to assume the appearance of; to feign to be*) feign, make believe, put on. **2** (*to simulate, to counterfeit in order to deceive*) counterfeit, fake, sham, simulate. **3** (*to make believe in play, to imagine*) act, imagine, make believe, make up, play, suppose. **4** (*to allege or put forward falsely*) affect, allege, dissemble, dissimulate, fake, falsify, feign. **5** (*to assert, to claim*) assert, claim, put forward. **6** (*to aspire to*) aim at, aspire to, hope for.

pretentious *a.* **1** (*full of pretension; making specious claims to excellence etc.*) deceptive, empty, false, misleading, specious. **2** (*arrogant, conceited*) affected, arrogant, assuming, bombastic, conceited, exaggerated, extravagant, flamboyant, grandiloquent, high-flown, hollow, inflated, mannered, ostentatious, pompous, showy, snobbish, superficial, vainglorious. ANTONYMS: modest, unassuming.

pretext *n.* **1** (*an excuse*) camouflage, cloak, cover, device, excuse, guise, mask, ploy, pretence, ruse, show, simulation, veil. **2** (*an ostensible reason or motive*) explanation, motive, reason.

pretty *a.* **1** (*good-looking, attractive*) appealing, attractive, beautiful, charming, comely, fair, fetching, good-looking, graceful, lovely,

personable, winsome. ANTONYMS: plain, ugly, unattractive. **2** (*aesthetically pleasing*) bijou, dainty, delicate, elegant, fine, pleasant, pleasing, tasteful, trim. **3** (*large*) big, considerable, large.

~*adv.* **1** (*moderately, fairly*) fairly, moderately, quite, rather, reasonably, somewhat, tolerably. **2** (*very*) completely, extremely, utterly, very.

prevail *v.i.* **1** (*to have the mastery or victory (over, against etc.*)) carry the day, gain mastery, hold sway, overcome, overrule, prove, reign, rule, succeed, triumph, win. **2** (*to predominate*) abound, be current, obtain, predominate, preponderate.

prevailing *a.* **1** (*predominant, most frequent*) chief, dominant, influential, main, powerful, predominant, preponderant, principal, ruling, superior. ANTONYMS: subordinate. **2** (*generally accepted*) accepted, common, current, customary, established, fashionable, general, ordinary, popular, prevalent, set, universal, usual, widespread.

prevent *v.t.* **1** (*to keep from happening, to stop*) baulk, block, check, counteract, foil, forbid, forestall, frustrate, halt, hamper, hinder, impede, inhibit, intercept, obstruct, preclude, prohibit, stop, thwart. ANTONYMS: encourage, support. **2†** (*to precede*) anticipate, go before, precede.

prevention *n.* **1** (*the act of preventing*) anticipation, avoidance, baulking, deterrence, elimination, forestalling, impedance, mitigation, obviation, precaution, prohibition, retardation, safeguard, thwarting. **2** (*hindrance, obstruction*) bar, block, check, deterrence, frustration, hindrance, impediment, interruption, obstacle, obstruction, stoppage.

previous *a.* **1** (*going before in time or order*) aforementioned, aforesaid, antecedent, anterior, earlier, erstwhile, foregoing, former, going before, past, preceding, prior, sometime. ANTONYMS: following, subsequent. **2** (*premature, hasty*) hasty, precipitate, premature, untimely.

prey *n.* **1** (*an animal which is or may be seized to be devoured by carnivorous animals*) game, kill, quarry. **2** (*booty, plunder*) booty, plunder, prize, spoil. **3** (*a person who becomes a victim of an unscrupulous person*) dupe, fall guy, (*coll.*) mark, (*coll.*) mug, (*N Am., sl.*) patsy, target, victim.

~*v.i.* **1** (*to take booty or plunder*) bully, cheat, destroy, exploit, intimidate, plunder, rob, stalk, terrorize, victimize. **2** (*to take food by violence*) consume, devour, eat, feed upon, hunt, live off, seize.

price *n.* **1** (*the amount asked for a thing or for which it is sold*) amount, asking price. **2** (*the cost of a thing*) bill, charge, cost, (*sl.*) damage, estimate, expenditure, expense, fee, figure, outlay, payment. **3** (*that which must be expended, sacrificed etc., to secure a thing*) consequence, cost, penalty, sacrifice, toll. **4** (*value, preciousness*) estimation, preciousness, value, worth.
~*v.t.* (*to fix the price of, to value*) appraise, assess, cost, estimate, evaluate, fix the price of, put a price on, rate, value.

priceless *a.* **1** (*invaluable, inestimable*) beyond price, costly, dear, expensive, incalculable, incomparable, inestimable, invaluable, irreplaceable, precious, unique, valuable, without price. ANTONYMS: cheap, inexpensive. **2** (*very funny*) amusing, comic, droll, hilarious, (*coll.*) killing, rib-tickling, ridiculous, riotous, side-splitting.

prick *n.* **1** (*a point or small hole made by or as by pricking*) cut, gash, hole, perforation, pinhole, pinprick, puncture, wound. **2** (*a sharp, stinging pain*) pain, pang, pinch, prickle, smart, spasm, sting, tingle, twinge.
~*v.t.* (*to pierce slightly, to puncture*) barb, needle, point, prong, spike.

prickle *n.* **1** (*a small, sharp point*) barb, needle, point, prong, spike. **2** (*a small thorn, spine etc.*) bristle, burr, spine, spur, thorn. **3** (*a prickling sensation*) itch, pins and needles, smart, tickle, tingle, tingling.
~*v.t.* **1** (*to prick slightly*) jab, nick, prick, stick. **2** (*to give a pricking or tingling sensation to*) itch, smart, sting, tickle, tingle, twitch.

pride *n.* **1** (*satisfaction arising out of some accomplishment or relationship*) delight, elation, gratification, joy, pleasure, satisfaction. **2** (*unreasonable conceit of one's own superiority*) arrogance, (*coll.*) big-headedness, conceit, egotism, haughtiness, insolence, loftiness, presumption, pretension, pretentiousness, self-esteem, self-importance, self-love, smugness, snobbery, superciliousness, vainglory, vanity. ANTONYMS: humility, modesty. **3** (*sense of dignity, self-respect*) dignity, honour, self-esteem, self-respect, self-worth. **4** (*the highest point, the best condition*) acme, best, boast, choice, elite, flower, gem, glory, high point, jewel, pick, prize, treasure.

priest *n.* (*a minister in the Roman Catholic, Orthodox or Anglican Church*) churchman, churchwoman, clergyman, cleric, curate, divine, ecclesiastic, evangelist, father, man of God, man of the cloth, minister, padre, parson, pastor, preacher, rector, vicar. ANTONYMS: layman.

prim *a.* (*affectedly proper, demure*) demure, fastidious, formal, fussy, (*derog.*) old-maidish, particular, precise, priggish, prissy, proper, prudish, puritanical, staid, starchy, stiff, strait-laced. ANTONYMS: casual, relaxed.

primary *a.* **1** (*first in time or order; original*) earliest, first, first-hand, initial, original, radical. ANTONYMS: last. **2** (*primitive, fundamental*) aboriginal, basic, elementary, fundamental, primal, primeval, primitive, primordial. **3** (*first in rank or importance*) best, capital, cardinal, chief, dominant, foremost, greatest, highest, leading, main, paramount, prime, principal, top. ANTONYMS: inferior, minor. **4** (*first in development, elementary*) basic, elementary, introductory, preparatory, rudimentary, simple. ANTONYMS: secondary, succeeding.

prime[1] *a.* **1** (*first in time or importance*) first, initial. **2** ((*esp. of meat and provisions*) *excellent*) best, capital, chief, choice, excellent, first-rate, foremost, highest, leading, outstanding, predominant, pre-eminent, quality, select, superior, supreme, top. ANTONYMS: inferior. **3** (*original, primary*) basic, earliest, elemental, elementary, fundamental, original, primary, underlying. **4** (*in the vigour of maturity, blooming*) blooming, mature, vigorous.
~*n.* **1** (*the period or state of highest perfection*) acme, height, maturity, peak, perfection, pinnacle, zenith. **2** (*the best part (of anything)*) best, bloom, cream, flower. **3** (*the first stage (of anything*)) beginning, commencement, opening, start. **4** (*dawn, youth*) dawn, morning, spring, youth.

prime[2] *v.t.* **1** (*to prepare something, esp. a gun, for use*) charge, load, prepare, ready. **2** (*to supply (with information*)) advise, apprise, brief, (*coll.*) clue up, (*coll.*) fill in, (*coll.*) gen up, inform, notify, tell. **3** (*to coach*) break in, coach, drill, groom, instruct, prepare, train, tutor.

primeval *a.* (*belonging to the earliest ages, ancient*) aboriginal, ancient, earliest, early, first, old, original, prehistoric, primal, primitive, primordial. ANTONYMS: modern.

primitive *a.* **1** (*of or relating to the beginning or the earliest periods, ancient*) ancient, earliest, early, first, original, primal, primeval, primordial. **2** (*simple, plain*) old-fashioned, plain, rude, simple. **3** (*crude, uncivilized*) barbarian, barbaric, coarse, crude, rough, rude, rudimentary, savage, uncivilized, uncultivated, uncultured, unrefined, unsophisticated. ANTONYMS: civilized, refined. **4** ((*of a culture or society*) *lacking a written language and all but basic technical skills*) backward, undeveloped.

ANTONYMS: advanced, developed. **5** (*Hist.*) (*behaving in a naive or apparently untaught manner*) childlike, naive, native, simple, simplistic, untrained, untutored.

princely *a.* **1** (*of or relating to a prince*) noble, regal, royal, sovereign. **2** (*stately, dignified*) august, dignified, grand, high-born, imperial, imposing, lofty, luxurious, magnificent, majestic, noble, plush, (*coll.*) ritzy, royal, sovereign, stately, sumptuous. **3** (*generous, lavish*) bountiful, generous, gracious, lavish, liberal, magnanimous, munificent, open-handed, rich. ANTONYMS: mean, stingy.

principal *a.* (*main, first in importance*) capital, cardinal, chief, controlling, dominant, essential, first, foremost, highest, key, leading, main, paramount, pre-eminent, prevailing, primary, prime, strongest. ANTONYMS: auxiliary.
~*n.* **1** (*a chief or head*) boss, chief, director, head, leader, manager, master, owner, proprietor, ruler, superintendent. **2** (*the head of a college etc.*) chancellor, dean, director, governor, head, head teacher, master, president, rector. **3** (*a performer who takes a leading role*) lead, star. **4** (*a capital sum invested or lent, as distinguished from income*) assets, capital, investment, money, resources.

principle *n.* **1** (*a fundamental cause or element*) cause, ground, origin, source. **2** (*a comprehensive truth or proposition from which others are derived*) assumption, axiom, canon, criterion, doctrine, dogma, ethic, formula, law, maxim, postulate, precept, proposition, rule, standard, truth, verity. **3** (*a fundamental doctrine or tenet*) belief, code, credo, creed, doctrine, ethic, morality, opinion, philosophy, tenet. **4** (*the habitual regulation of conduct by moral law*) conscience, duty, honour, integrity, morals, probity, rectitude, scruples, uprightness.

print *n.* **1** (*an indentation or other mark made by pressure*) impression, imprint, indentation, mark. **2** (*printed lettering*) characters, face, font, lettering, letters, type, typeface. **3** (*a printed publication, esp. a newspaper*) book, magazine, newspaper, periodical, publication, typescript. **4** (*an engraving, a lithograph etc.*) engraving, etching, linocut, lithograph, woodcut. **5** (*a reproduction of a work of art made by a photographic process*) copy, duplicate, facsimile, replica, reproduction. **6** (*a positive photographic image produced from a negative*) photo, photograph, picture. **7** (*a fingerprint*) (*often pl., sl.*) dab, fingerprint.
~*v.t.* (*to impress, to mark by pressure*) engrave, impress, imprint, mark.

~*v.i.* (*to publish books etc.*) go to press, issue, publish, put out, run off.

prior *a.* (*former, earlier*) aforementioned, antecedent, anterior, earlier, erstwhile, foregoing, former, preceding, previous. ANTONYMS: subsequent.

priority *n.* **1** (*precedence, a superior claim*) antecedence, precedence, pre-eminence, preference, primacy, rank, seniority, superiority, supremacy. **2** (*something given or meriting special attention*) essential, main issue, primary concern, requirement. **3** (*the right to proceed while other vehicles wait*) prerogative, right of way.

prison *n.* **1** (*a place of confinement, esp. a public building for the confinement of criminals*) (*sl.*) can, (*sl.*) choky, (*sl.*) clink, (*sl.*) cooler, detention centre, dungeon, gaol, (*sl.*) glasshouse, (*sl.*) inside, jail, (*sl.*) jug, lock-up, (*sl.*) nick, penitentiary, pound, reformatory, remand centre, (*sl.*) slammer, (*sl.*) stir. **2** (*confinement, captivity*) captivity, confinement.

pristine *a.* **1** (*of or relating to an early or original state or time*) earliest, first, former, initial, primary. **2** (*ancient, primitive*) ancient, primal, primeval, primitive, primordial. **3** (*pure, unadulterated*) as new, chaste, immaculate, new, perfect, pure, spotless, unadulterated, uncorrupted, undefiled, unspoiled, unsullied, untarnished, untouched, virgin, virginal.

privacy *n.* **1** (*the state of being private*) isolation, reclusiveness, retirement, retreat, seclusion, separateness, sequestration, solitude. **2** (*secrecy*) concealment, confidentiality, covertness, secrecy.

private *a.* **1** (*kept or withdrawn from publicity or observation*) concealed, hidden, inaccessible, isolated, retired, secluded, sequestered, solitary, unobserved, withdrawn. ANTONYMS: public. **2** (*secret, confidential*) clandestine, closet, confidential, covert, (*coll.*) hush-hush, off the record, secret, unofficial. ANTONYMS: known, open. **3** (*not administered or provided by the state*) denationalized, independent, non-public, privatized. ANTONYMS: state. **4** (*personal, not of or relating to the community*) exclusive, individual, intimate, own, particular, personal, reserved, special. ANTONYMS: communal, general. **5** (*secretive, reticent*) reclusive, reserved, reticent, retiring, secretive, solitary, unsocial, withdrawn. ANTONYMS: gregarious, sociable.

privation *n.* **1** (*deprivation or lack of what is necessary to a comfortable life*) beggary, deprivation, destitution, distress, hardship, indigence, lack, misery, necessity, need, pauperism, penury, poverty, suffering, want. **2** (*loss, negation (of)*) absence, loss, negation.

privilege *n.* **1** (*a right or advantage belonging to a person, class etc.*) advantage, authority, benefit, birthright, claim, concession, dispensation, due, entitlement, exemption, favour, freedom, immunity, indulgence, leave, liberty, permission, prerogative, right, sanction. **2** (*a right of precedence*) precedence, priority. **3** (*a franchise, patent etc. granted to an individual or a company*) franchise, licence, monopoly, patent.

prize[1] *n.* **1** (*something which is offered or won as the reward of merit or superiority in a competition*) accolade, award, honour, premium, recompense, reward, trophy. **2** (*a sum of money or other object offered for competition in a lottery etc.*) haul, jackpot, purse, receipts, stakes, windfall, winnings. **3** (*a desirable object of perseverance, enterprise etc.*) aim, ambition, conquest, desire, gain, goal, hope.
~*a.* (*gaining or worthy of a prize*) award-winning, best, champion, choice, first-class, first-rate, outstanding, select, superior, superlative, top, winning.
~*v.t.* (*to value highly, to esteem*) appreciate, cherish, esteem, hold dear, (*coll.*) rate, treasure, value. ANTONYMS: underrate.

prize[2] *n.* **1** (*something which is taken from an enemy in war, esp. a ship*) booty, loot, pickings, plunder, spoils, trophy. **2** (*a find, a windfall*) find, haul, jackpot, windfall.

probable *a.* (*likely to happen or prove true*) apparent, believable, credible, feasible, likely, on the cards, ostensible, plausible, possible, reasonable. ANTONYMS: improbable, unlikely.

probably *adv.* (*being likely to happen or prove true*) as likely as not, doubtlessly, in all probability, likely, maybe, perhaps, possibly, presumably, quite, undoubtedly. ANTONYMS: doubtfully, improbably.

probe *n.* **1** (*a surgical instrument, for exploring cavities of the body, wounds etc.*) rod. **2** (*a thorough investigation, as by a newspaper of e.g. alleged corruption*) detection, examination, exploration, inquiry, investigation, research, scrutiny, study. **3** (*an unmanned spacecraft carrying equipment for collecting scientific measurements of conditions*) satellite, spacecraft.
~*v.t.* **1** (*to examine (a wound, ulcer etc.) with, or as with, a probe*) delve into, examine, explore, feel around, poke about, search. **2** (*to scrutinize or inquire into thoroughly*) go into, inquire into, investigate, look into, query, research, scrutinize, study. **3** (*to pierce with or

as if with a probe*) penetrate, pierce, poke, prod.

problem *n.* **1** (*a question proposed for solution*) conundrum, enigma, poser, puzzle, question, riddle. ANTONYMS: solution. **2** (*a matter or situation that is difficult to understand*) (*coll.*) can of worms, complication, difficulty, dilemma, disagreement, dispute, mess, muddle, obstacle, (*coll.*) pickle, predicament, trouble. **3** (*a source of perplexity or distress*) anxiety, confusion, worry.
~*a.* ((*esp. of children*) *hard to deal with*) delinquent, difficult, disturbed, intractable, obstreperous, uncontrollable, ungovernable, unmanageable, unruly.

problematic *a.* (*difficult to deal with*) controversial, debatable, difficult, enigmatic, moot, open to question, puzzling, questionable, sensitive, tricky, uncertain, unsettled. ANTONYMS: easy, simple.

procedure *n.* **1** (*an act, or a manner, of proceeding*) approach, conduct, form, formula, method, mode, operation, performance, process, system, transaction, way. **2** (*the established mode of conducting business etc., e.g. at a meeting*) custom, drill, practice, routine, standard operating procedure, tradition, wont. **3** (*a course of action*) course of action, plan of action, policy, scheme, strategy. **4** (*a step in a sequence of actions*) action, measure, step.

proceed *v.i.* **1** (*to go* (*in a specified direction or to a specified place*)) advance, go, move. **2** (*to advance, to continue to progress*) advance, forge ahead, get going with, get under way, go ahead, go forward, go on, make headway, move on, press on, progress. ANTONYMS: retreat. **3** (*to carry on a series of actions, to go on* (*with or in*)) carry on, continue, pick up, resume. ANTONYMS: break off, discontinue. **4** (*to originate (from)*) arise, begin, come forth, derive, descend, develop, emanate, emerge, ensue, flow, follow, grow, issue, originate, result, spring, start, stem.

process *n.* **1** (*a course or method of proceeding or doing*) approach, course, manner, means, method, mode, operation, practice, procedure, proceeding, system, technique. **2** (*a natural series of continuous actions, changes etc.*) action, measure, stage, step. **3** (*a progressive movement; course*) advance, course, development, evolution, movement, progress, progression. **4** (*the course of proceedings in an action at law*) action, case, suit, trial. **5** (*a writ or order commencing this*) order, writ. **6** (*Anat., Zool., Bot.*) (*an outgrowth, a protuberance of a bone etc.*) enlargement, formation, growth, outgrowth, protuberance.

~*v.t.* **1** (*to subject to routine procedure, to deal with*) answer, deal with, dispose of, fulfil, handle, organize, sort out, take care of. **2** (*to treat* (*food etc.*) *by a preservative or other process*) alter, change, convert, modify, prepare, refine, transform, treat.

procession *n.* **1** (*a group of persons, vehicles etc. proceeding in regular order for a ceremony, demonstration etc.*) cavalcade, column, cortege, file, line, march, motorcade, parade, queue, train. **2** (*a series of people or things appearing one after the other*) chain, course, cycle, progression, run, sequence, series, string, succession, train.

proclaim *v.t.* **1** (*to announce publicly*) advertise, affirm, announce, blaze, broadcast, circulate, declare, denunciate, enunciate, give out, herald, make known, promulgate, pronounce, publish, trumpet. ANTONYMS: hush up, suppress. **2** (*to reveal or indicate*) indicate, reveal, show.

proclamation *n.* (*a public announcement*) announcement, declaration, decree, edict, manifesto, notice, promulgation, pronouncement, publication, release, statement.

proclivity *n.* (*a tendency, bent*) bent, bias, disposition, facility, fondness, inclination, leaning, liking, partiality, penchant, predilection, predisposition, propensity, tendency, weakness. ANTONYMS: aversion, dislike.

procrastinate *v.i.* **1** (*to put off action*) adjourn, dally, defer, delay, postpone, protract, put off, retard, shelve, stall, temporize. ANTONYMS: expedite, hasten. **2** (*to be dilatory*) equivocate, hesitate, pause, shilly-shally, vacillate, waver.

procure *v.t.* **1** (*to obtain, to get by some means or effort*) acquire, appropriate, buy, come by, earn, effect, find, gain, lay hands on, obtain, pick up, purchase, secure, win. ANTONYMS: lose. **2** (*to bring about*) accomplish, bring about, cause, contrive, effect, manage, produce.

prod *n.* **1** (*a pointed instrument, a goad*) goad, needle, poker, spur, stick. **2** (*a poke with or as with this*) dig, elbow, jab, nudge, poke, push, shove. **3** (*a stimulus to action*) boost, cue, prompt, push, reminder, signal, stimulus.
~*v.t.* **1** (*to poke with or as with the finger or a pointed instrument*) dig, elbow, jab, nudge, poke, prick, push, shove. **2** (*to goad, to incite*) egg on, encourage, goad, impel, incite, motivate, move, prompt, provoke, rouse, spur, stimulate, stir up, urge.

prodigal *a.* **1** (*given to extravagant expenditure*) excessive, extravagant, immoderate, improvident, intemperate, profligate, reckless,

spendthrift, squandering, wanton, wasteful. ANTONYMS: frugal, thrifty. **2** (*wasteful, lavish* (*of*)) abundant, copious, exuberant, lavish, luxuriant, profuse, sumptuous, teeming.

prodigious *a.* **1** (*wonderful, astounding*) amazing, astonishing, astounding, extraordinary, fabulous, (*coll.*) fantastic, impressive, marvellous, miraculous, phenomenal, remarkable, sensational, spectacular, staggering, startling, striking, stupendous, wonderful. ANTONYMS: normal, unexceptional. **2** (*enormous in size, extent etc.*) colossal, enormous, gargantuan, giant, gigantic, huge, immeasurable, immense, inordinate, mammoth, massive, monstrous, monumental, stupendous, titanic, tremendous, vast. ANTONYMS: minute, small.

prodigy *n.* **1** (*something wonderful or extraordinary*) marvel, miracle, phenomenon, sensation, wonder. **2** (*a person, esp. a child, with extraordinary gifts or qualities*) genius, mastermind, talent, virtuoso, wizard, wonder child. **3** (*a monstrosity*) abnormality, curiosity, freak, grotesque, monster, monstrosity, mutation.

produce[1] *v.t.* **1** (*to bring into view, to bring forward*) advance, bring forward, bring into view, bring to light. **2** (*to publish, to exhibit*) demonstrate, exhibit, present, publish, set forth, show. **3** (*to bear, to yield*) afford, bear, beget, breed, bring forth, deliver, furnish, give birth to, hatch, provide, render, supply, yield. ANTONYMS: withhold. **4** (*to manufacture, to make*) assemble, compose, construct, create, develop, fabricate, invent, make, manufacture, originate, put together, turn out. ANTONYMS: destroy. **5** (*to bring about, to cause*) bring about, cause, effect, generate, give rise to, make for, occasion, provoke, set off. **6** (*to extend, to continue* (*a line*) *in the same direction*) continue, extend, lengthen, prolong, protract. **7** (*to act as producer of* (*a play or film*)) direct, do, mount, present, put on, show, stage.

produce[2] *n.* **1** (*goods produced or yielded*) commodities, goods, products. **2** (*the natural or agricultural products of a country etc. collectively*) crop, fruit, harvest, vegetables, yield.

product *n.* **1** (*that which is produced by a manufacturing process*) artefact, commodity, creation, goods, merchandise, output, produce, production, work. **2** (*an effect, a result*) consequence, effect, fruit, issue, offshoot, outcome, result, returns, spin-off, upshot, yield. ANTONYMS: cause.

production *n.* **1** (*the act, or an instance, of producing*) creation, productivity. ANTONYMS: consumption. **2** (*the process of being manufactured*) assembly, building, construction, creation, fabrication, formation, making, manufacture, origination, preparation, producing. ANTONYMS: destruction. **3** (*a thing produced, a product*) product, result, work. **4** (*the amount produced, the output*) fruits, harvest, output, return, yield. **5** (*the work of a film etc. producer*) direction, management, presentation, staging.

productive *a.* (*yielding in abundance, fertile*) abundant, bountiful, creative, fecund, fertile, fruitful, generative, inventive, plentiful, prolific, rich, teeming, vigorous. ANTONYMS: barren, unproductive.

profane *a.* **1** (*not sacred; secular*) lay, mundane, secular, temporal, unholy, worldly. ANTONYMS: holy. **2** ((*of a person*) *irreverent towards holy things*) disrespectful, impious, irreligious, irreverent, sacrilegious, sinful, wicked. **3** ((*of language*) *irreverent, blasphemous*) abusive, bad, bawdy, blasphemous, coarse, crude, dirty, filthy, foul, improper, indelicate, obscene, ribald, scurrilous, smutty, taboo. ANTONYMS: clean, decorous. **4** (*heathenish*) godless, heathenish, idolatrous, infidel, pagan, ungodly. **5** (*common, vulgar*) common, uncouth, vulgar.
~*v.t.* **1** (*to treat with irreverence*) debase, defile, desecrate, dishonour. ANTONYMS: honour, revere. **2** (*to violate, to pollute*) abuse, contaminate, corrupt, debase, defile, desecrate, pervert, pollute, prostitute, violate.

profess *v.t.* **1** (*to make open or public declaration of*) acknowledge, announce, avow, declare, proclaim, pronounce, say, state, utter. **2** (*to affirm one's belief in or allegiance to*) admit, affirm, assert, asseverate, confess, confirm, own. **3** (*to pretend* (*to be or do*)) allege, claim, dissemble, fake, feign, let on, make out, pretend, purport, sham, simulate.

profession *n.* **1** (*the act of professing; a declaration*) avowal, declaration. **2** (*an open acknowledgement of sentiments, religious belief etc.*) acknowledgement, admission, affirmation, assertion, attestation, claim, confession, statement, testimony. ANTONYMS: denial, repudiation. **3** (*a vow binding oneself to, or the state of being a member of, a religious order*) oath, vow. **4** (*a calling, esp. an occupation involving high qualifications*) business, calling, career, craft, employment, field, job, line, métier, occupation, office, sphere, trade, vocation, work.

professional *a.* **1** (*characterized by, or conforming to, the technical or ethical standards of a profession*) excellent, finished, high-quality, polished. **2** (*competent, conscientious*) adept, efficient, experienced, expert, masterly, paid,

practised, proficient, qualified, skilled, slick, thorough, trained. ANTONYMS: amateurish, incompetent.
~*n.* (*a person who shows great skill and competence in any activity*) adept, authority, (*coll.*) dab hand, expert, maestro, master, (*coll.*) pro, specialist. ANTONYMS: amateur.

proficient *a.* ((*of a person*) *well versed or skilled in any art, science etc.*) able, accomplished, adept, capable, clever, competent, conversant, dexterous, efficient, experienced, expert, gifted, masterly, polished, practised, qualified, skilful, talented, trained, versed. ANTONYMS: incompetent, inept.

profile *n.* **1** (*an outline, a contour*) contour, outline. **2** (*a drawing, silhouette or other representation of the human face*) drawing, figure, portrait, side view, silhouette, sketch. **3** (*a set of statistical data showing the salient features of some organization*) analysis, breakdown, examination, graph, review, statistics, study, survey, table. **4** (*a short biographical or character sketch*) biography, characterization, life, portrait, sketch, vignette.

profit *n.* **1** (*an advantage or benefit*) advancement, advantage, avail, benefit, gain, good, improvement, use, value. **2** (*often pl.*) (*excess of receipts over outlay*) earnings, emoluments, excess, gain, margin, proceeds, receipts, return, revenue, surplus, takings, winnings, yield. ANTONYMS: loss.
~*v.t.* (*to benefit, to be of advantage to*) advance, aid, avail, benefit, be of advantage to, better, contribute, further, gain, help, improve, promote, serve.
~*v.i.* **1** (*to make a profit*) clean up, clear, earn, gain, (*coll.*) make a killing, (*coll.*) make a packet, make money, rake in, realize. **2** (*to receive benefit or advantage* (*by or from*)) capitalize on, (*coll.*) cash in on, exploit, learn from, make the most of, maximize, put to good use, take advantage of, use.

profitable *a.* **1** (*yielding or bringing profit or gain*) commercial, cost-effective, fruitful, gainful, lucrative, paying, remunerative, rewarding, well-paid, worthwhile. ANTONYMS: unprofitable, unrewarding. **2** (*advantageous, useful*) advantageous, beneficial, fruitful, helpful, productive, rewarding, serviceable, useful, valuable, worthwhile. ANTONYMS: disadvantageous, useless.

profligate *a.* **1** (*licentious, dissolute*) abandoned, corrupt, debauched, degenerate, depraved, dissipated, dissolute, immoral, iniquitous, lascivious, lewd, libertine, licentious, loose, promiscuous, unprincipled, unrestrained, vicious, wanton, wild. ANTONYMS:

chaste, upright. **2** (*wildly extravagant*) excessive, extravagant, immoderate, improvident, prodigal, reckless, spendthrift, squandering, wasteful. ANTONYMS: thrifty.

~*n.* (*a profligate person*) debauchee, degenerate, libertine, pervert, prodigal, rake, reprobate, roué, sinner, spendthrift, squanderer, wastrel.

profound *a.* **1** (*having great intellectual penetration or insight*) acute, analytical, discerning, erudite, insightful, keen, penetrating, sharp, subtle, thoughtful. **2** (*having great knowledge*) knowledgeable, learned, philosophical, sagacious, sage, scholarly, well-read, wise. **3** (*requiring great research, abstruse*) abstruse, deep, esoteric, inscrutable, involved, obscure, recondite, unfathomable. ANTONYMS: obvious, superficial. **4** ((*of a quality etc.*) *deep, intense*) deep, extreme, great, heartfelt, heart-rending, hearty, intense, keen, sincere. **5** (*reaching to or extending from a great depth*) abysmal, bottomless, cavernous, deep, fathomless, yawning. ANTONYMS: shallow. **6** (*thoroughgoing, extensive*) absolute, complete, consummate, downright, exhaustive, extensive, out-and-out, pronounced, thoroughgoing, total, unqualified, utter.

profuse *a.* **1** (*poured out lavishly, exuberant*) abundant, ample, bountiful, bursting, copious, exuberant, fruitful, lavish, lush, luxuriant, overflowing, plentiful, prolific, superabundant, teeming, thriving. ANTONYMS: inadequate, sparse. **2** (*liberal to excess, extravagant*) excessive, extravagant, free, generous, liberal, magnanimous, open-handed, prodigal, unsparing, unstinting. ANTONYMS: frugal, moderate.

prognosis *n.* **1** (*a forecast of the probable course or result of an illness*) diagnosis, forecast. **2** (*a prediction*) expectation, forecast, prediction, prognostication, projection, speculation, surmise.

programme *n.* **1** ((*a paper, booklet etc. giving*) *a list of the successive items of any entertainment, course of study etc.*) agenda, bill of fare, line-up, list, listing, menu, plan, schedule. **2** (*a broadcast presented at a scheduled time*) broadcast, performance, presentation, production, show, transmission. **3** (*a curriculum or syllabus*) curriculum, syllabus, timetable. **4** (*a plan of actions to be carried out*) abstract, design, outline, plan, procedure, project, scheme.

~*v.t.* **1** (*to arrange a programme for*) arrange, book, design, engage, lay on, line up, map out, organize, plan, prearrange, schedule, set, work out. **2** (*to enter in a programme*) bill, itemize, list.

progress[1] *n.* **1** (*movement onward, advance*) advance, course, movement, passage, progression, way. **2** (*advance towards completion or a more developed state*) advance, advancement, amelioration, betterment, breakthrough, development, elevation, evolution, furtherance, gain, growth, headway, improvement, increase, progression, promotion, rise. ANTONYMS: decline, retrogression.

progress[2] *v.i.* **1** (*to move forward, to advance*) advance, come on, continue, forge ahead, gain ground, gather way, get on, go forward, make headway, make strides, move forward, press on, proceed, push on, travel. **2** (*to improve, to develop*) advance, ameliorate, better, blossom, burgeon, develop, gain, grow, improve, increase, mature, ripen, rise.

prohibit *v.t.* **1** (*to forbid authoritatively*) ban, bar, debar, disallow, forbid, interdict, outlaw, proscribe, veto. ANTONYMS: allow, permit. **2** (*to hinder, to prevent*) block, check, constrain, foil, frustrate, hamper, hinder, impede, inhibit, obstruct, preclude, prevent, restrain, restrict, rule out, stop, thwart.

prohibitive *a.* **1** (*tending to prohibit*) discouraging, forbidding, inhibitory, preventive, prohibiting, prohibitory, proscriptive, repressive, restraining, restrictive, suppressive. **2** ((*of costs, prices etc.*) *such as to debar purchase, use etc.*) costly, dear, excessive, exorbitant, expensive, extortionate, high-priced, outlandish, outrageous, preposterous, (*coll.*) steep. ANTONYMS: cheap, inexpensive.

project[1] *n.* **1** (*a plan, a scheme*) design, layout, plan, programme, proposal, scheme. **2** (*an esp. large-scale planned undertaking*) activity, enterprise, job, occupation, task, undertaking, venture, work. **3** (*a piece of work undertaken by a pupil to supplement and apply classroom studies*) assignment, study.

project[2] *v.t.* **1** (*to throw or shoot forward*) cast, discharge, eject, fling, hurl, launch, propel, shoot, throw, toss. **2** (*to cause to jut out*) beetle, bulge, extend, jut, overhang, protrude, stand out, stick out. **3** (*to predict or expect (something) based on known data*) calculate, estimate, expect, extrapolate, forecast, gauge, predict, reckon. **4** (*to plan (a course of action etc.*)) concoct, conjure up, contrive, design, devise, draft, frame, map out, outline, plan, prepare, propose, purpose, scheme.

projection *n.* **1** (*a part or thing that projects, a prominence*) bulge, crag, extension, jut, ledge, overhang, prominence, protrusion, protuberance, ridge, shelf, sill. **2** (*the act of planning*) blueprint, diagram, map, outline, plan, proposal, representation, scheme. **3** (*a prediction* *based on known data*) calculation, computation, estimate, estimation, extrapolation, forecast, prediction, prognostication, reckoning.

proliferate *v.i.* **1** (*to grow by budding or multiplication of parts*) breed, grow, multiply, reproduce. **2** (*to grow or increase rapidly*) burgeon, escalate, expand, grow, increase, mushroom, snowball.

prolific *a.* **1** (*producing offspring, esp. abundantly*) abundant, bountiful, copious, lush, luxuriant, plentiful, profuse, rank, rich, rife, teeming. **2** (*fruitful, productive*) creative, fecund, fertile, fruitful, generative, productive. ANTONYMS: sterile, unproductive.

prolong *v.t.* **1** (*to extend in duration*) delay, drag out, draw out, extend, keep up, perpetuate, protract, spin out, string out. ANTONYMS: abbreviate, shorten. **2** (*to extend in space or distance*) carry on, continue, elongate, extend, lengthen, stretch.

prominent *a.* **1** (*standing out, protuberant*) bulging, elevated, hanging over, jutting, projecting, protruding, protuberant, standing out. ANTONYMS: indented. **2** (*conspicuous*) apparent, blatant, conspicuous, evident, eye-catching, flagrant, glaring, marked, noticeable, obtrusive, obvious, outstanding, patent, pronounced, remarkable, salient, striking, unmistakable. ANTONYMS: inconspicuous, unnoticeable. **3** (*distinguished*) acclaimed, celebrated, chief, distinguished, eminent, famous, foremost, illustrious, important, leading, notable, noteworthy, outstanding, popular, pre-eminent, prestigious, renowned, respected, top, well-known. ANTONYMS: obscure, unknown.

promiscuous *a.* **1** (*indulging in casual indiscriminate sexual intercourse*) abandoned, debauched, depraved, dissipated, dissolute, fast, immoral, lax, libertine, licentious, loose, profligate, unbridled, unchaste, unfaithful, wanton, wild. ANTONYMS: chaste, virtuous. **2** (*mixed together in a disorderly manner*) chaotic, confused, disordered, disorganized, scrambled. ANTONYMS: ordered. **3** (*of different kinds mingled confusedly together*) diverse, heterogeneous, ill-assorted, indiscriminate, intermingled, intermixed, jumbled, mingled, miscellaneous, mixed, motley. ANTONYMS: homogeneous. **4** (*coll.*) (*accidental, casual*) accidental, careless, casual, fortuitous, haphazard, heedless, indifferent, indiscriminate, irresponsible, negligent, random, slipshod, slovenly, thoughtless, uncontrolled, uncritical, undiscriminating, unfussy, unselective. ANTONYMS: careful, responsible.

promise *n.* **1** (*a verbal or written engagement to do some specific act*) agreement, assurance, bond, commitment, compact, contract, covenant, engagement, guarantee, oath, pledge, undertaking, vow, warranty, word. **2** (*a ground or basis of expectation, esp. of success or excellence*) ability, aptitude, capability, capacity, expectation, flair, potential, talent. ~*v.t.* **1** (*to engage to do* (*something*)) assure, contract, engage, guarantee, pledge, swear, undertake, vow, warrant. **2** (*to give good grounds for expecting*) augur, bespeak, betoken, bid fair, denote, foretell, hint at, indicate, look alike, suggest.

promising *a.* **1** (*likely to be successful*) able, capable, gifted, likely, rising, talented, (*coll.*) up-and-coming. **2** (*hopeful, favourable*) auspicious, bright, cheering, encouraging, favourable, heartening, hopeful, optimistic, positive, propitious, reassuring, rosy. ANTONYMS: discouraging, ominous.

promote *v.t.* **1** (*to raise to a higher rank or position*) aggrandize, dignify, elevate, exalt, honour, (*coll.*) kick upstairs, prefer, raise, upgrade. ANTONYMS: demote. **2** (*to contribute to the increase or advancement of*) advance, aid, assist, back, boost, contribute, develop, forward, further, help, stimulate. **3** (*to support, to encourage*) advocate, champion, commend, encourage, endorse, foster, nurture, patronize, popularize, push for, recommend, sponsor, support, urge, work for. ANTONYMS: discourage, oppose. **4** (*to encourage the sale of* (*a product*) *by advertising*) advertise, (*coll.*) hype, (*coll.*) plug, publicize, puff, push, sell.

promotion *n.* **1** (*advancement in position*) advancement, aggrandizement, elevation, exaltation, honour, preferment, upgrading. ANTONYMS: demotion. **2** (*furtherance, encouragement*) advancement, advocacy, aiding, backing, boosting, cultivation, development, encouragement, espousal, furtherance, improvement, inspiration, nurturing, progress, stimulation, support. ANTONYMS: hindrance. **3** ((*an advertising campaign etc., intended as a means of*) *bringing a product to public notice*) advertising, campaign, (*coll.*) hype, (*coll.*) plugging, propaganda, publicity, special offer.

prompt *a.* **1** (*acting quickly*) alert, brisk, eager, efficient, expeditious, keen, quick, ready, responsive, smart, willing. **2** (*done or said at once*) brisk, direct, early, fast, immediate, instant, instantaneous, on time, punctual, quick, rapid, speedy, swift, timely, unhesitating. ANTONYMS: hesitating, slow. ~*adv.* (*punctually*) at once, directly, exactly, immediately, instantly, on the dot, post-haste, promptly, punctually, sharp, speedily, swiftly.

~*n.* (*the act of prompting, or the thing said to prompt an actor etc.*) cue, help, hint, jog, jolt, prod, reminder, spur, stimulus.

~*v.t.* **1** (*to urge or incite* (*to action or to do*)) coax, egg on, encourage, exhort, goad, impel, incite, induce, inspire, instigate, motivate, move, nudge, persuade, prod, provoke, rouse, spur, stimulate, urge. ANTONYMS: deter, put off. **2** (*to suggest* (*thoughts, feelings etc.*) *to the mind*) awake, bring about, call forth, cause, elicit, evoke, excite, occasion, provoke, stimulate, suggest. **3** (*to assist* (*a speaker, actor etc.*) *when at a loss, by suggesting the words forgotten*) assist, cue, help, hint, jog the memory of, prod, remind.

prone *a.* **1** (*lying flat*) flat, horizontal, lying flat, prostrate, reclining, recumbent, supine. ANTONYMS: perpendicular, upright. **2** (*disposed, inclined*) apt, bent, disposed, given, inclined, liable, likely, predisposed, subject, susceptible, tending. ANTONYMS: averse, unlikely.

pronounce *v.t.* **1** (*to utter articulately, to say correctly*) articulate, enunciate, express, say, sound, speak, stress, utter, vocalize, voice. **2** (*to declare, to affirm*) affirm, announce, assert, aver, broadcast, declaim, declare, decree, deliver, judge, proclaim, promulgate, publicize, publish, state. ANTONYMS: suppress.

pronounced *a.* **1** (*strongly marked, emphatic*) clear, decided, definite, downright, emphatic, marked, outright, strong, utter. **2** (*conspicuous, obvious*) clear, conspicuous, decided, definite, distinct, noticeable, obvious, plain, prominent, recognizable, striking, strong, unmistakable, well-defined. ANTONYMS: vague.

proof *n.* **1** (*the act of proving*) test, trial. **2** (*testing, experiment*) assay, examination, experiment, scrutiny, testing. **3** (*convincing evidence of the truth or falsity of a statement, charge etc., esp. as submitted in a trial*) attestation, authentication, certification, confirmation, corroboration, evidence, substantiation, testimony, validation, verification. ANTONYMS: conjecture, speculation. **4** (*a trial impression from type for correction*) galley, impression, page proof.

~*a.* **1** (*tested as to strength, firmness etc.*) proved, tested. **2** (*impenetrable*) impenetrable, impervious, impregnable, repellent, tight, treated. **3** (*able to resist physically or morally*) immune, resistant.

~*v.t.* (*to make proof, esp. waterproof*) seal, waterproof.

prop *n.* (*a rigid support, esp. a loose or temporary one*) brace, buttress, mainstay, pillar, stanchion, stay, support, truss, upright, vertical.

~*v.t.* (*to support or hold* (*up*) *with or as with a prop*) bear, bolster, brace, buttress, hold up, maintain, shore, stay, support, sustain, truss, uphold.

propagate *v.t.* **1** (*to cause to multiply by natural generation or other means*) beget, breed, engender, generate, increase, multiply, procreate, produce, proliferate, reproduce. **2** (*to hand down* (*a characteristic*) *to the next generation*) bequeath, hand down, pass on. **3** (*to cause to spread or extend*) develop, extend, grow, spread. **4** (*to make known, to disseminate*) advertise, broadcast, circulate, diffuse, disperse, disseminate, make known, proclaim, promote, promulgate, publicize, publish. ANTONYMS: stifle, suppress.

propel *v.t.* **1** (*to cause to move forward or onwards*) drive, force, impel, launch, move, project, push, send, set in motion, shoot, shove, start, thrust. ANTONYMS: check, stop. **2** (*to urge on*) encourage, spur, urge on.

proper *a.* **1** (*correct, accurate*) accepted, accurate, conventional, correct, customary, established, exact, formal, orthodox, precise, right, usual. ANTONYMS: wrong. **2** (*suitable, appropriate*) apposite, appropriate, apt, becoming, befitting, fit, fitting, right, suitable, suited. ANTONYMS: inappropriate, unsuitable. **3** (*decent, respectable*) decent, decorous, dignified, genteel, polite, punctilious, refined, respectable, seemly. ANTONYMS: improper, rude. **4** (*usu. following its noun*) (*according to strict definition*) actual, genuine, real. **5** own) characteristic, individual, own, particular, peculiar, personal. ANTONYMS: common. **6** (*thorough, complete*) complete, perfect, thorough, unmitigated, utter.

property *n.* **1** (*a possession, possessions*) assets, belongings, building, capital, chattels, effects, estate, fortune, goods, holdings, house, means, possessions, real estate, realty, resources, riches, wealth. **2** (*an inherent quality*) attribute, characteristic, feature, hallmark, idiosyncrasy, mark, oddity, peculiarity, quality, quirk, trait, virtue. **3** (*character, nature*) character, disposition, make-up, nature. **4** (*articles required for the production of a play on the stage*) prop, stage property.

prophecy *n.* **1** (*a prediction, esp. one divinely inspired*) augury, forecast, prediction, prognosis, revelation. **2** (*the prediction of future events*) clairvoyance, crystal-gazing, divination, forecasting, foretelling, prediction, prognostication, soothsaying.

prophetic *a.* **1** (*of or relating to prophecy*) augural, divinatory, sibylline. **2** (*predictive, anticipative*) anticipative, oracular, portentous, predictive, prescient, prognostic.

propitiate v.t. (to appease, to conciliate) appease, conciliate, make peace, mollify, pacify, placate, reconcile, satisfy. ANTONYMS: offend.

propitious a. **1** ((of an omen) favourable) advantageous, auspicious, favourable. ANTONYMS: unfavourable. **2** (disposed to be kind or gracious) benevolent, benign, friendly, gracious, kind, well-disposed. ANTONYMS: hostile. **3** (auspicious, suitable) auspicious, bright, encouraging, fortunate, happy, lucky, opportune, promising, providential, rosy, suitable.

proportion n. **1** (the comparative relation of one part or thing to another with respect to magnitude or number) correlation, ratio, relation, relationship. **2** (suitable or pleasing adaptation of one part or thing to others) agreement, balance, concord, congruity, correspondence, harmony, symmetry, uniformity. ANTONYMS: disproportion. **3** (a share) allotment, cut, division, fraction, lot, measure, part, percentage, quota, segment, share. ANTONYMS: whole. **4** (pl.) (dimensions) amplitude, area, breadth, bulk, capacity, dimensions, expanse, extent, magnitude, measurements, range, scope, size, volume.
~v.t. **1** (to adjust in suitable proportion) adjust, arrange, change, modify, modulate, regulate. **2** (to make proportionate (to)) balance, conform, equate, fit, harmonize, match.

proportional a. (having due proportion) analogous, balanced, commensurate, comparable, compatible, consistent, correspondent, corresponding, equitable, equivalent, even, harmonious, in proportion, just, proportionate, symmetrical. ANTONYMS: disproportionate, incompatible.

proposal n. (something proposed) bid, design, draft, idea, offer, outline, overture, plan, presentation, project, proposition, recommendation, scheme, suggestion, tender.

propose v.t. **1** (to present for consideration) advance, offer, present, proffer, propound, put forward, set forth, submit, suggest, table, tender. **2** (to nominate for election) introduce, invite, name, nominate, present, put up, recommend. ANTONYMS: scratch, withdraw. **3** (to put forward as a plan) aim, design, intend, mean, plan, purpose, scheme.

propriety n. **1** (fitness, correctness of behaviour) appropriateness, aptness, correctness, fitness, properness, rightness, seemliness, suitability. ANTONYMS: impropriety. **2** (pl.) (the rules of correct or polite behaviour) courtesy, decorum, delicacy, etiquette, gentility, good manners, niceties, politeness, protocol, rectitude, refinement, respectability, social graces. ANTONYMS: bad manners, impoliteness.

prosaic a. **1** (unpoetic, unimaginative) unimaginative, unpoetic, unromantic. **2** (dull, commonplace) banal, bland, boring, clichéd, commonplace, dry, dull, everyday, flat, humdrum, matter-of-fact, mundane, ordinary, pedestrian, routine, stale, stereotyped, trite, vapid. ANTONYMS: exciting, interesting.

proscribe v.t. **1** (to forbid) ban, boycott, forbid, interdict, prohibit, reject. ANTONYMS: allow, permit. **2** (to denounce as dangerous) censure, condemn, damn, denounce. **3** (to banish, to exile) banish, deport, exclude, excommunicate, exile, expatriate, expel, ostracize.

prosecute v.t. **1** (to take legal proceedings against) accuse, arraign, bring to trial, charge, impeach, indict, litigate, prefer charges, proceed against, put on trial, sue, summon, try. ANTONYMS: defend. **2** (to pursue with a view to accomplishing) carry through, follow up, persevere, persist, pursue, see through. ANTONYMS: give up. **3** (to carry on (work, trade etc.)) carry on, conduct, continue, direct, discharge, engage in, manage, perform, practise, work at.

prospect[1] n. **1** (an extensive view of a landscape etc.) landscape, panorama, view, vista. **2** (a scene) aspect, outlook, perspective, scene, sight, spectacle, vision. **3** (expectation, ground of expectation) anticipation, chance, contemplation, expectancy, expectation, future, hope, likelihood, odds, opening, outlook, plan, possibility, presumption, probability, promise, proposal, thought.

prospect[2] v.i. (to explore a place, esp. for minerals) explore, go after, look for, search, seek, survey.

prospective a. **1** (of or relating to the future) approaching, coming, forthcoming, future, impending, nearing, pending. **2** (anticipated, expected) anticipated, awaited, destined, eventual, expected, hoped-for, likely, looked-for, planned, possible, potential, probable, (esp. N Am.) upcoming, would-be.

prosperous a. **1** (successful, thriving) affluent, blooming, booming, flourishing, flush, lucky, opulent, prospering, rich, successful, thriving, wealthy. ANTONYMS: poor, unsuccessful. **2** (favourable, fortunate) advantageous, auspicious, bright, favourable, fortunate, good, profitable, promising, propitious, timely. ANTONYMS: unpromising.

prostitute n. (a person (esp. a woman or girl) who engages in sexual activity for money) call-girl, camp follower, courtesan, fallen woman, harlot, (sl.) hooker, lady of the night, (sl., offensive) scrubber, streetwalker, †strumpet, (sl.) tart, trollop, whore, (sl.) working girl.

~*v.t.* **1** (*to hire* (*oneself, another*) *out for sexual purposes*) pander, pimp, sell. **2** (*to offer or sell for unworthy purposes*) abuse, cheapen, debase, defile, degrade, demean, desecrate, devalue, lower, misapply, misuse, pervert, profane.

prostrate¹ *a.* **1** (*lying flat or prone*) abject, flat, low, prone. **2** (*lying in a horizontal position*) horizontal, procumbent, recumbent, stretched out, supine. **3** (*overcome* (*by grief etc.*), *exhausted*) bowled over, brought low, (*sl.*) bushed, crushed, dejected, depressed, desolate, drained, exhausted, (*coll.*) fagged out, (*coll.*) knackered, overcome, overwhelmed, paralysed, (*sl.*) shagged out, (*coll.*) slaughtered, spent, (*coll.*) wiped out, worn out.

prostrate² *v.t.* **1** (*to lay* (*a person etc.*) *flat*) lay flat, lay out. **2** (*to throw* (*oneself*) *down, esp. in reverence* (*before*)) abase, bow and scrape, crawl, cringe, fall to one's knees, grovel, kneel, submit, throw down. **3** (*to overthrow, to overcome*) bowl over, bring low, crush, demolish, depress, disarm, floor, humble, lay low, overcome, overpower, overthrow, overwhelm, paralyse, reduce, ruin, throw down. **4** (*to reduce to physical exhaustion*) drain, exhaust, (*coll.*) fag out, fatigue, sap, tire, wear out, weary.

protect *v.t.* (*to defend or keep safe* (*from or against injury, danger etc.*)) care for, cover, defend, foster, guard, harbour, keep safe, look after, mind, nurture, preserve, safeguard, save, screen, secure, shelter, shield, support, tend, watch over. ANTONYMS: endanger, expose.

protection *n.* **1** (*the act, or an instance, of protecting*) care, charge, custody, defence, guardianship, preservation, protecting, safe keeping, safety, security. **2** (*something which protects, a covering*) armour, barrier, buffer, bulwark, covering, defence, guard, haven, refuge, safeguard, screen, shelter, shield. **3** (*protection money*) blackmail, extortion, protection money.

protective *a.* **1** (*intended to protect*) defensive, insulating, preservative, protecting, safeguarding, sheltering, shielding. **2** ((*of a person*) *desirous of shielding another from harm or distress*) attentive, careful, caring, fatherly, heedful, jealous, maternal, motherly, paternal, possessive, vigilant, watchful.

protest¹ *v.i.* **1** (*to express dissent or objection*) complain, cry out, demonstrate, demur, deny, disagree, disapprove, disclaim, dissent, expostulate, grumble, object, oppose, remonstrate, scruple, take exception. ANTONYMS: agree. **2** (*to make a solemn affirmation*) affirm, argue, assert, asseverate, attest, avow, contend, declare, insist, maintain, profess, testify, vow.

protest² *n.* (*a solemn or formal declaration of opinion, usu. of dissent*) complaint, declaration, demonstration, demur, denial, disagreement, disapproval, dissent, exception, grievance, grumble, objection, opposition, outcry, protestation, remonstrance.

protract *v.t.* (*to extend in duration*) continue, drag out, draw out, elongate, extend, keep going, lengthen, prolong, spin out, stretch out. ANTONYMS: abridge, curtail.

protrude *v.i.* (*to be thrust forward, or above a surface*) bulge, come through, jut, obtrude, point, poke, project, shoot out, stand out, start, stick out, thrust forward.

protuberance *n.* (*a swelling, a prominence*) bulge, bump, excrescence, hump, knob, lump, outcrop, outgrowth, process, projection, prominence, protrusion, swelling, tumour. ANTONYMS: cavity, hole.

proud *a.* **1** (*haughty, arrogant*) arrogant, (*coll.*) big-headed, boastful, conceited, disdainful, egotistical, haughty, (*coll.*) high and mighty, imperious, lofty, lordly, overbearing, presumptuous, self-important, self-satisfied, smug, snobbish, (*coll.*) snooty, stuck-up, vain. ANTONYMS: humble, modest. **2** (*having a due sense of dignity*) dignified, self-respecting. **3** (*feeling honoured, pleased*) content, delighted, elated, exultant, glad, gratified, honoured, pleased, satisfied, well-pleased. ANTONYMS: dissatisfied. **4** (*grand, imposing*) august, distinguished, eminent, grand, great, illustrious, imposing, magnificent, majestic, noble, splendid, stately. **5** ((*of deeds etc.*) *inspiring pride, noble*) exalted, glorious, grand, gratifying, illustrious, memorable, noble, notable, noteworthy, pleasing, rewarding, satisfying, worthy. **6** (*standing out from a plane surface*) bulging, jutting, projecting, prominent, protruding, protuberant, standing out, sticking out, swollen.

prove *v.t.* **1** (*to establish or demonstrate the truth of by argument or testimony*) ascertain, attest, bear out, confirm, corroborate, demonstrate, determine, establish, evidence, justify, substantiate, sustain, uphold. ANTONYMS: disprove, refute. **2** (*to test, to try by experiment*) analyse, assay, check, experiment, test, try. **3** (*to show to be true*) demonstrate, determine, evince, show, substantiate. **4** (*to have experience of, to undergo*) experience, undergo. **5** (*to establish the validity of, esp. to obtain probate of* (*a will*)) authenticate, certify, validate, verify.
~*v.i.* (*to turn out* (*to be*)) end up, result, turn out.

proverb *n.* (*a short, pithy sentence, containing some truth or wise reflection*) adage, aphorism, apophthegm, axiom, dictum, epigram, homily, maxim, moral, saw, saying.

provide *v.t.* **1** (*to procure or prepare beforehand*) anticipate, arrange for, forearm, get ready, plan ahead, plan for, prepare for, take precautions. ANTONYMS: neglect, overlook. **2** (*to furnish, to supply*) accommodate, cater, contribute, furnish, give, provender, provision, purvey, stock, supply. ANTONYMS: keep back. **3** (*to equip* (*with*)) equip, fit out, fix up, outfit. **4** (*to lay down as a preliminary condition*) determine, lay down, require, specify, state, stipulate.

providence *n.* **1** (*the beneficent care or control of God or nature*) beneficence, care, concern, guidance, protection. **2** (*a manifestation of such care*) destiny, fate, fortune, God's will, lot, predestination. **3** (*timely care or preparation*) anticipation, far-sightedness, foresight, forethought, preparation. **4** (*frugality, prudence*) conservation, discretion, economy, frugality, prudence, thrift.

provident *a.* **1** (*making provision for the future*) economical, frugal, thrifty. ANTONYMS: improvident, profligate. **2** (*showing foresight, prudent*) careful, cautious, discreet, farsighted, forearmed, judicious, prudent, sagacious, shrewd, thoughtful, vigilant, wary, wise. ANTONYMS: careless, reckless.

province *n.* **1** (*a large administrative division of a kingdom, country or state*) colony, county, department, dependency, district, division, domain, dominion, patch, quarter, realm, region, section, state, territory, tract, zone. **2** (*a proper sphere of business, knowledge etc.*) area, bailiwick, business, capacity, concern, discipline, field, function, line, orbit, responsibility, role, sphere, (*coll.*) turf.

provincial *a.* **1** (*of or relating to a province*) local, regional. **2** (*of or characteristic of the provinces*) country, (*coll.*) hick, home-grown, homespun, rural, rustic. ANTONYMS: cosmopolitan, urban. **3** (*narrow, uncultured*) boorish, ingenuous, insular, inward-looking, limited, loutish, naive, narrow, narrow-minded, oafish, parochial, rude, small-minded, small-town, uncultured, unpolished, unsophisticated. ANTONYMS: refined, sophisticated.
~*n.* (*a narrow-minded or unsophisticated person*) bumpkin, (*N Am., Austral., New Zeal.*) hayseed, (*coll.*) hick, yokel.

provision *n.* **1** (*the act, or an instance, of providing*) accoutrement, catering, equipping, fitting out, furnishing, providing, supplying, victualling. **2** (*something provided, or prepared beforehand*) arrangement, measure, plan, prearrangement, preparation. **3** (*a stipulation or condition providing for something*) catch, condition, demand, prerequisite, proviso, qualification, requirement, reservation, restriction, rider, stipulation. **4** (*a clause in a law or a deed*) clause, term. **5** (*pl.*) (*food and drink prepared for an expedition*) comestibles, drinkables, food, groceries, stocks, stores, supplies.

provisional *a.* **1** (*provided for present need; temporary*) interim, limited, pro tem, stopgap, temporary, transitional. ANTONYMS: permanent. **2** (*requiring future confirmation*) conditional, contingent, provisory, qualified.

provocation *n.* **1** (*the act, or an instance, of provoking*) agitation, cause, grounds, incitement, inducement, instigation, irritation, motivation, provoking, reason, stimulus. ANTONYMS: appeasement. **2** (*something that provokes or irritates*) affront, annoyance, challenge, dare, grievance, indignity, injury, insult, irritation, offence, taunt, vexation.

provocative *a.* **1** (*tending to provoke, esp. sexual desire*) alluring, arousing, bewitching, erotic, exciting, fascinating, inviting, seductive, sensual, (*coll.*) sexy, stimulating, suggestive, tantalizing, teasing, tempting, voluptuous. ANTONYMS: repulsive. **2** (*annoying, esp. with the intention to excite anger*) (*coll.*) aggravating, annoying, challenging, disquieting, distressing, disturbing, enraging, exasperating, galling, infuriating, insulting, irksome, irritating, maddening, offensive, outrageous, provoking, stinging, upsetting, vexing. ANTONYMS: soothing.

provoke *v.t.* **1** (*to incite to action, anger etc.*) arouse, call forth, egg on, elicit, encourage, evoke, excite, generate, incite, induce, inflame, inspire, kindle, motivate, move, prompt, rouse, spur, stimulate, stir. ANTONYMS: deter. **2** (*to irritate, to exasperate*) affront, (*coll.*) aggravate, anger, annoy, enrage, exasperate, frustrate, gall, (*coll.*) hassle, incense, infuriate, insult, irk, irritate, madden, (*sl.*) nark, offend, put out, rile, vex. ANTONYMS: appease, soothe. **3** (*to instigate, to cause*) bring about, bring on, cause, instigate, lead to, occasion, precipitate, produce, promote, start.

prowess *n.* **1** (*outstanding ability or skill*) ability, accomplishment, adeptness, adroitness, aptitude, attainment, capability, command, dexterity, excellence, expertise, facility, finesse, genius, know-how, mastery, proficiency, skill, talent. ANTONYMS: incompetence, ineptitude. **2** (*valour, bravery*) boldness, bravery, courage, daring, dauntlessness, fearlessness, fortitude, gallantry, hardihood, heroism, intrepidity, mettle, might, strength, valour. ANTONYMS: cowardice, timidity.

prowl *v.i.* (*to rove* (*about*) *stealthily as if in search of prey*) hunt, lurk, nose around, rove, skulk, slink, sneak, stalk, steal.

proximity *n.* (*immediate nearness in place, time etc.*) adjacency, closeness, contiguity, juxtaposition, nearness, neighbourhood, propinquity, vicinity. ANTONYMS: distance, remoteness.

prudent *a.* **1** (*cautious, discreet*) alert, attentive, careful, cautious, circumspect, discerning, discreet, discriminating, judicious, politic, reasonable, sagacious, sensible, shrewd, thoughtful, vigilant, wary, watchful. ANTONYMS: careless, imprudent. **2** (*showing good judgement or foresight*) economical, farsighted, frugal, provident, sparing, thrifty. ANTONYMS: improvident.

prune *v.t.* **1** (*to cut or lop off the superfluous branches etc. from* (*a shrub or tree*)) clip, cut, dock, lop off, snip, trim. **2** (*to reduce* (*costs, administration etc.*)) cut back, pare down, reduce.

pry *v.i.* **1** (*to look closely or inquisitively*) examine, inquire, investigate, peep, peer, spy. **2** (*to inquire impertinently* (*into*)) interfere (in), intrude (in), meddle (in), nose (into), poke (into), snoop (into).

psychic *a.* **1** (*of or relating to the human spirit or mind*) cerebral, mental, metaphysical, psychological, spiritual. **2** (*of or relating to phenomena that appear to be outside the domain of physical law*) extrasensory, mystic, occult, paranormal, psychical, supernatural, telepathic, unearthly.
~*n.* (*a person believed to have psychic powers*) clairvoyant, medium, spiritualist.

psychological *a.* **1** (*relating to or affecting the mind*) cerebral, cognitive, intellectual, mental. ANTONYMS: physical. **2** (*existing only in the mind*) emotional, imaginary, irrational, subconscious, subjective, unconscious, unreal.

public *a.* **1** (*of, relating to or affecting the people as a whole*) common, general, national, popular, social, universal. ANTONYMS: personal, private. **2** (*open to the use or enjoyment of all*) accessible, communal, free, open, unrestricted. ANTONYMS: exclusive, restricted. **3** (*done, existing or such as may be observed by all*) acknowledged, apparent, conspicuous, exposed, known, manifest, obvious, overt, patent, plain, published, recognized, unconcealed, visible. ANTONYMS: clandestine, secret. **4** (*well-known, prominent*) celebrated, disreputable, eminent, famous, illustrious, important, infamous, influential, notable, noted, notorious, prominent, renowned, respected, well-known. **5** (*of or provided by local or central government*) civic, civil, governmental, national, official, state.
~*n.* **1** (*the people in general*) bourgeoisie, citizens, commonalty, community, country, electorate, everyone, hoi polloi, masses, mob, multitude, nation, ordinary people, people, people in the street, populace, population, rank and file, society, (*coll.*) the great unwashed, voters. **2** (*any particular section of the people; a group of people with a particular interest*) business, buyers, class, clientele, consumers, customers, group, patrons, portion, purchasers, sector, segment, special-interest group, trade.

publication *n.* **1** (*the act, or an instance, of making publicly known*) advertisement, airing, announcement, appearance, broadcasting, communication, declaration, disclosure, dissemination, notification, proclamation, promulgation, pronouncement, publishing, putting out, reporting, revelation. ANTONYMS: suppression. **2** (*a work printed and published*) book, booklet, brochure, edition, hardback, issue, journal, leaflet, magazine, newspaper, pamphlet, paper, paperback, periodical, title, work.

publish *v.t.* **1** (*to make public, to announce publicly*) advertise, announce, broadcast, circulate, communicate, declare, disclose, disseminate, divulge, expose, impart, leak, make public, proclaim, promulgate, publicize, report, reveal, spread, tell. ANTONYMS: suppress. **2** (*to issue or print and offer for sale* (*a book, newspaper etc.*) *to the public*) bring out, issue, print, produce, put out.

puerile *a.* (*childish, inane*) babyish, childish, frivolous, immature, inane, infantile, irresponsible, juvenile, silly, trivial. ANTONYMS: adult, mature.

puff *v.i.* **1** (*to emit or expel air, steam etc. in short, sudden blasts*) blow, breathe, exhale. **2** (*to breathe hard*) gasp, gulp, huff, pant, wheeze.
~*v.t.* **1** (*to emit, with a short sudden blast or blasts*) blow out, breathe out, emit, exhale. **2** (*to draw at* (*a cigarette, pipe*)) (*coll.*) drag, draw at, inhale, pull at, smoke, suck. **3** (*to inflate*) balloon, bloat, dilate, distend, expand, inflate, swell. ANTONYMS: deflate. **4** (*to praise or advertise in an exaggerated way*) advertise, crack up, flatter, (*coll.*) hype, overpraise, (*coll.*) plug, praise, promote, publicize, push. ANTONYMS: criticize, disparage.
~*n.* **1** (*a short, sudden blast of breath, smoke etc.*) blast, breath, draught, emanation, gust, whiff, wind. **2** (*a small amount of breath, smoke etc., emitted at one puff*) (*coll.*) drag, draught, pull, smoke. **3** (*an exaggerated or misleading adver-*

tisement, review etc.) advertisement, blurb, commendation, (*coll.*) hype, mention, notice, (*coll.*) plug, praise, publicity.

pugnacious *a.* (*inclined to fight; quarrelsome*) aggressive, antagonistic, argumentative, bellicose, belligerent, choleric, combative, contentious, disputatious, fractious, hot-tempered, irascible, irritable, petulant, quarrelsome, short-tempered, testy. ANTONYMS: conciliatory, peaceable.

pull *v.t.* **1** (*to draw towards one by force*) draw, tug. ANTONYMS: push, shove. **2** (*to drag, to haul*) drag, haul, jerk, lug, trail, tug, yank. **3** (*to remove by plucking*) detach, draw, draw out, extract, gather, pick, pluck, remove, take out. **4** (*to draw (beer etc.) from a barrel etc.*) draw, pour. **5** (*to strip (a fowl) of feathers*) draw, pluck, strip. **6** (*to attract (a crowd, support etc.)*) attract, draw, interest, prompt. **7** (*to succeed in attracting sexually*) attract, captivate, entice, fascinate, lure, magnetize, seduce. ANTONYMS: deter, repel.
~*v.i.* **1** (*to haul*) haul, tug. **2** (*to suck (at a pipe)*) (*coll.*) drag, draw, suck. **3** (*to pluck, to tear (at)*) dislocate, pluck, rend, rip, sprain, strain, stretch, tear, wrench.
~*n.* **1** (*the act of pulling, a tug*) force, jerk, tug, twitch, yank. **2** (*a draught, a swig*) draught, mouthful, (*coll.*) swig. **3** (*influence or advantage*) advantage, clout, influence, leverage, muscle, weight. **4** (*a spell of hard exertion*) effort, exertion. **5** (*something which draws one's attention*) appeal, attraction, drawing power, influence, lure, magnetism, power, seductiveness. **6** (*a draw at a cigarette*) (*coll.*) drag, draw, inhalation, puff. **to pull apart 1** (*to pull into pieces*) pick apart, pull asunder. **2** (*to become separated*) fall apart, separate, sever. **3** (*to criticize severely*) attack, blast, criticize, damn, find fault, flay, (*coll.*) knock, lambast, (*coll.*) lay into, (*coll.*) pan, put down, run down, (*sl.*) slam, slate, tear into. **to pull off 1** (*to remove by pulling*) detach, remove, rip off, separate, tear off, wrench off. **2** (*to accomplish (something difficult or risky)*) accomplish, achieve, bring off, carry out, complete, do, manage, perform, succeed. ANTONYMS: fail. **to pull out 1** (*to remove by pulling*) extract, remove, uproot, withdraw. **2** (*to leave, to depart*) abandon, depart, evacuate, leave, quit, take off. **3** (*to withdraw*) draw back, recede, retreat, withdraw. **to pull through** (*to (cause to) survive or recover*) come through, get better, get over, improve, live, pull round, rally, recover, survive, weather.

pulpy *a.* (*of the consistency of pulp*) fleshy, mushy, soft, squashy, succulent. ANTONYMS: hard.

pulse *n.* **1** (*the rhythmic beating of the arteries caused by the propulsion of blood along them from the heart*) beating, rhythm. **2** (*a pulsation, a vibration*) oscillation, palpitation, pulsation, quiver, throbbing, vibration. **3** (*a throb, a thrill*) excitement, thrill, throb. **4** (*bustle, excitement*) bustle, commotion, excitement, stir.
~*v.i.* (*to pulsate*) beat, hammer, oscillate, palpitate, pound, pulsate, quiver, reverberate, throb, thud, thump, tick, vibrate.

pulverize *v.t.* **1** (*to reduce to fine powder or dust*) comminute, crumble, crush, granulate, grind, mill, pestle, pound, powder, reduce to dust, triturate. **2** (*coll.*) (*to demolish, to defeat utterly*) annihilate, crush, defeat, demolish, destroy, devastate, flatten, (*coll.*) lick, ruin, shatter, smash, vanquish, wreck.

pump *v.t.* **1** (*to free from water or make dry with a pump*) bail out, drain, draw off, drive out, empty, evacuate, force out, siphon. **2** (*to propel with or as with a pump*) drive, force, pour, propel, push, send. **3** (*to elicit information from by persistent interrogation*) cross-examine, examine, (*coll.*) grill, interrogate, probe, question, quiz. **to pump up** (*to inflate (a tyre)*) bloat, blow up, dilate, expand, inflate, puff up, swell. ANTONYMS: deflate.

punch *n.* **1** (*a tool for making holes*) auger, awl, bodkin, drill. **2** (*a blow with the fist*) bash, (*coll.*) biff, blow, bop, clip, clout, hit, jab, knock, (*sl.*) plug, smack, (*sl.*) sock, (*coll.*) wallop, whack. **3** (*vigour, forcefulness*) forcefulness, gusto, life, verve, vigour, vim, vitality, zest. **4** (*striking power*) bite, drive, effect, effectiveness, force, impact, point, power.
~*v.t.* **1** (*to stamp or perforate with a punch*) bore, cut, drill, perforate, pierce, prick, puncture, stamp. **2** (*to strike, esp. with the fist*) bash, (*coll.*) belt, (*coll.*) biff, bop, box, clip, clout, cuff, hit, jab, (*sl.*) plug, pummel, slug, smash, (*sl.*) sock, strike, (*coll.*) wallop, whack.

punctilious *a.* **1** (*precise or exact*) careful, conscientious, exacting, finicky, fussy, meticulous, minute, nice, particular, precise, scrupulous, strict. **2** (*strictly observant of ceremony or etiquette*) ceremonious, formal, proper.

punctual *a.* **1** (*exact in matters of time*) exact, precise, punctilious, strict. **2** (*done or occurring exactly at the proper time*) early, in good time, on the dot, prompt, seasonable, timely. ANTONYMS: late.

puncture *n.* **1** (*a small hole made with something pointed*) hole, leak, opening, perforation, prick, rupture. **2** (*the perforation of a pneumatic tyre and the consequent loss of pressure*) (*sl.*) blow-out, flat, flat tyre.

~*v.t.* **1** (*to make a puncture in*) bore, hole, impale, perforate. **2** (*to pierce or prick with something pointed*) penetrate, pierce, prick, stab. **3** (*to deflate* (*a person's self-esteem*)) deflate, discourage, disillusion, humble, take down a peg.

~*v.i.* ((*of a tyre, balloon etc.*) *to sustain a puncture*) deflate, go down, go flat.

pungent *a.* **1** (*sharply affecting the senses, esp. those of smell or taste*) aromatic, flavoursome, hot, peppery, seasoned, sharp, smelly, sour, spicy, strong, tangy, tart, tasty. ANTONYMS: bland, tasteless. **2** (*caustic, biting*) acid, acrid, acrimonious, acute, barbed, biting, bitter, caustic, cutting, incisive, keen, penetrating, piercing, pointed, scathing, stern, stringent, telling, trenchant, vitriolic. ANTONYMS: mild. **3** (*piquant, stimulating*) interesting, lively, piquant, sparkling, stimulating. ANTONYMS: dull, uninteresting.

punish *v.t.* **1** (*to inflict a penalty on* (*a person*) *for an offence*) admonish, beat, castigate, chasten, chastise, correct, discipline, flog, lash, penalize, rebuke, reprove, scold, scourge, sentence, whip. ANTONYMS: reward. **2** (*to inflict pain or injury on*) abuse, batter, damage, harm, hurt, injure, knock about, maltreat, manhandle, maul, misuse, oppress, rough up. **3** (*to give great trouble to* (*opponents in a game, race etc.*)) put to the sword, thrash, trounce.

puny *a.* **1** (*small and feeble, tiny*) delicate, diminutive, dwarfish, feeble, frail, little, minute, (*coll.*) pint-sized, pygmy, sickly, small, stunted, tiny, underfed, undersized, undeveloped, weak. ANTONYMS: robust, sturdy. **2** (*petty, trivial*) inconsequential, inferior, insignificant, minor, negligible, paltry, petty, trifling, trivial, unimportant, useless, worthless.

pupil *n.* (*a young person under the care of a teacher*) apprentice, disciple, follower, learner, neophyte, novice, scholar, schoolboy, schoolchild, schoolgirl, student, trainee. ANTONYMS: coach, teacher.

purchase *v.t.* **1** (*to obtain by payment*) acquire, buy, get, pay for, procure, secure. ANTONYMS: sell. **2** (*to acquire at the expense of some sacrifice, danger etc.*) achieve, attain, earn, gain, realize, win.

~*n.* **1** (*the act, or an instance, of purchasing or buying*) acquisition, buying, procurement, purchasing. **2** (*a thing which is purchased*) acquisition, asset, buy, gain, investment, possession, property. ANTONYMS: sale. **3** (*advantage gained by the application of any mechanical power*) advantage, edge, leverage. **4** (*an effective position for leverage, a foothold*) foothold, footing, grasp, grip, hold, toehold.

pure *a.* **1** (*unmixed, unadulterated*) flawless, neat, perfect, unadulterated, unalloyed, undiluted, unmixed. ANTONYMS: adulterated, impure. **2** (*free from anything foul or polluting*) antiseptic, clean, clear, disinfected, germ-free, pasteurized, sanitary, spotless, sterile, unblemished, uncontaminated, unpolluted, untainted, wholesome. ANTONYMS: foul, polluted. **3** (*free from moral defilement, innocent*) blameless, guiltless, honest, innocent, true. ANTONYMS: guilty. **4** (*unsullied, chaste*) chaste, guileless, immaculate, impeccable, intact, modest, uncorrupted, undefiled, unspotted, unstained, unsullied, upright, virginal, virtuous. ANTONYMS: corrupt, depraved. **5** (*mere, absolute*) absolute, complete, downright, mere, outright, sheer, thorough, total, unmitigated, unqualified, utter. **6** ((*of sciences*) *entirely theoretical*) abstract, academic, conceptual, hypothetical, philosophical, speculative, theoretical. ANTONYMS: applied.

purge *v.t.* **1** (*to cleanse or purify*) cleanse, purify, scour, wash. **2** (*to clear* (*of an accusation, suspicion etc.*)) absolve, clear, exculpate, exonerate, forgive, pardon. **3** (*to rid* (*a state or a party*) *of persons actively in opposition*) axe, clean out, dismiss, eject, eradicate, expel, exterminate, kill, liquidate, oust, remove, root out, sweep away, weed out, wipe out. **4** (*to expiate* (*guilt, spiritual defilement etc.*)) annul, atone for, expiate.

~*n.* **1** (*the act, or an instance, of purging*) cleanup, ejection, elimination, eradication, expulsion, liquidation, ousting, removal, suppression, witch-hunt. **2** (*a purgative medicine*) cathartic, emetic, enema, laxative, purgative.

purify *v.t.* **1** (*to make pure, to cleanse*) clarify, clean, cleanse, decontaminate, disinfect, distil, filter, freshen, fumigate, refine, sanitize, wash. ANTONYMS: contaminate, foul. **2** (*to free from sin, guilt etc.*) absolve, cleanse, clear, exculpate, exonerate, redeem, sanctify.

puritanical *a.* (*extremely strict in conduct*) ascetic, austere, bigoted, disapproving, fanatical, forbidding, intolerant, moralistic, narrow-minded, prim, proper, puritan, rigid, severe, stern, stiff, strait-laced, strict, uncompromising. ANTONYMS: indulgent, liberal.

purity *n.* **1** (*the state of being pure, cleanness*) brilliance, clarity, cleanliness, cleanness, clearness, correctness, faultlessness, fineness, flawlessness, perfection, pureness, simplicity, spotlessness, wholesomeness. ANTONYMS: impurity. **2** (*moral cleanness, innocence*) blamelessness, chastity, decency, guilelessness, honesty, innocence, integrity, modesty, morality, piety, propriety, rectitude, sincerity, virginity, virtue, virtuousness. ANTONYMS: immorality, vice.

purport[1] *v.t.* **1** (*to convey as the meaning, to signify*) convey, denote, express, imply, import, indicate, intend, mean, signify, suggest. **2** (*to profess, to be meant to appear* (*to*)) allege, assert, claim, declare, maintain, pretend, proclaim, profess.

purport[2] *n.* **1** (*meaning, sense*) bearing, drift, gist, idea, implication, import, meaning, sense, significance, spirit, tendency, tenor. **2** (*object, purpose*) aim, design, intent, intention, object, plan, purpose.

purpose *n.* **1** (*an end in view, an aim*) aim, ambition, aspiration, design, desire, end, goal, hope, intention, object, objective, plan, point, scheme, target, wish. **2** (*an effect, result*) consequence, effect, gain, outcome, profit, result, return, use. **3** (*determination, resolution*) constancy, deliberation, determination, doggedness, drive, firmness, perseverance, persistence, resolution, resolve, single-mindedness, steadfastness, stubbornness, tenacity, will.
~*v.t.* (*to intend, to design*) aim, aspire, consider, contemplate, decide, design, determine, intend, mean, meditate, plan, propose, resolve, work towards.

purposeful *a.* (*determined, resolute*) decided, decisive, deliberate, determined, firm, fixed, immovable, persistent, pertinacious, positive, resolute, resolved, settled, single-minded, staunch, steadfast, strong-willed, sure, tenacious, unfaltering. ANTONYMS: irresolute, undecided.

pursue *v.t.* **1** (*to follow with intent to seize, kill etc.*) chase, dog, follow, go after, hound, hunt, shadow, stalk, tail, track. **2** (*to try persistently to gain or obtain*) aim for, aspire to, desire, purpose, seek, strive for, try for, work towards. **3** (*to continue with, to be engaged in* (*a course of action, studies*)) carry on, continue, cultivate, keep on, maintain, persevere, persist, proceed, see through, stick with. **4** (*to apply oneself to, to practise continuously*) apply oneself, conduct, engage in, perform, ply, practise, prosecute, tackle, work at. **5** ((*of misfortune, consequences etc.*) *to attend persistently*) attend, harass, harry, haunt, plague, run after. ANTONYMS: shun, steer clear of. **6** (*to try persistently to make the acquaintance of*) chase after, court, make up to, pay suit, set one's cap at, woo.

pursuit *n.* **1** (*the act, or an instance, of pursuing*) chase, following, hunt, pursuing, quest, search. **2** (*an endeavour to attain some end*) endeavour, prosecution, pursuance. **3** (*an employment or recreation that one follows*)

activity, area, business, calling, career, employment, field, hobby, interest, line, occupation, pastime, pleasure, profession, (*sl.*) racket, recreation, speciality, trade, vocation.

purvey *v.t.* **1** (*to supply, esp. provisions*) cater, deal in, furnish, provide, provision, retail, sell, supply, trade in, victual. **2** (*to procure*) get, make available, obtain, procure.

push *v.t.* **1** (*to press against with force, tending to urge forward or away*) depress, drive, poke, press, ram, shove, thrust. ANTONYMS: pull. **2** (*to move* (*a body along, up, down etc.*) *thus*) impel, move, propel, send. **3** (*to make* (*one's way*) *vigorously*) elbow, force, jostle, make one's way, nudge, shoulder, shove, squeeze, thrust. **4** (*to impel, to drive*) compel, drive, egg on, encourage, expedite, hurry, impel, incite, motivate, persuade, press, prod, prompt, rouse, spur, stimulate, urge. ANTONYMS: discourage, dissuade. **5** (*to put pressure on* (*a person*)) browbeat, coerce, constrain, dragoon, influence, oblige, pressurize. **6** (*to seek to promote, esp. to promote the sale or use of*) advertise, boost, cry up, (*coll.*) hype, (*coll.*) plug, promote, propagandize, publicize, puff. **7** (*to peddle* (*drugs*)) deal in, peddle.
~*v.i.* (*to exert pressure or butt* (*against*)) butt, jolt, nudge, poke, prod, shove, thrust.
~*n.* **1** (*the act, or an instance, of pushing*) press, shove, thrust. **2** (*a vigorous effort*) attempt, effort, onset. **3** (*a crisis, an extremity*) crisis, exigency, extremity. **4** (*persevering energy, self-assertion*) ambition, determination, drive, dynamism, energy, enterprise, enthusiasm, go, initiative, (*coll.*) pep, verve, vigour, vitality, zeal. **5** (*an offensive*) advance, assault, attack, campaign, charge, foray, incursion, offensive, onslaught, raid, sally, sortie, strike, thrust. **to get the push** (*sl.*) (*to be dismissed from a job*) be dismissed, be made redundant, (*coll.*) get one's marching orders, get one's notice, (*sl.*) get the boot, (*coll.*) get the heave-ho, (*coll.*) get the sack. **to give the push** (*sl.*) (*to dismiss from a job*) dismiss, give notice, (*sl.*) give (someone) the boot, (*coll.*) give (someone) the heave-ho, (*coll.*) give (someone) their marching orders, (*coll.*) give the sack, make redundant.

pushy *a.* (*coll.*) (*forceful*) aggressive, ambitious, arrogant, bold, brash, brassy, bullying, bumptious, cocky, demanding, forceful, impertinent, obnoxious, obtrusive, offensive, officious, presumptuous, pushing, self-assertive. ANTONYMS: meek, unassertive.

pusillanimous *a.* (*lacking courage, faint-hearted*) abject, afraid, chicken-hearted, cowardly, craven, faint-hearted, fearful, feeble, (*coll.*) gutless, spineless, timid, weak, (*coll.*) yellow. ANTONYMS: courageous, intrepid.

put *v.t.* **1** (*to move so as to place in some position*) locate, move, position, stand, station. **2** (*to set or deposit*) deposit, establish, lay, place, rest, set, settle, situate. **3** (*to append, to affix*) affix, append, attach, fix. **4** (*to connect, to add*) add, combine, connect, link. **5** (*to express, to state*) express, phrase, pose, say, state, utter, word. **6** (*to render, to translate* (*into*)) render, reword, translate, turn. **7** (*to apply, to impose*) apply, impose, inflict, levy, set. **8** (*to stake* (*money on*)) bet, chance, gamble, hazard, risk, stake, wager. **9** (*to subject, to commit* (*to or upon*)) commit, condemn, consign, subject. **10** (*to propose* (*for consideration etc.*), *to submit* (*to a vote*)) advance, bring forward, forward, offer, posit, present, propose, submit, tender. **11** (*to force, to make* (*a person do etc.*)) constrain, force, incite, induce, make, oblige, require. **12** (*to throw* (*a weight etc.*) *as a sport*) bowl, cast, fling, heave, lob, pitch, send, shoot, throw, toss. **to put away 1** (*to return to its proper place*) put back, replace, tidy up. ANTONYMS: get out. **2** (*to lay by*) keep, lay by, put by, save, set aside, store away. **3** (*to shut up* (*in a prison, mental institution etc.*)) certify, commit, confine, imprison, incarcerate, institutionalize, lock up, send down, shut up. ANTONYMS: release. **4** (*to consume* (*food or drink*)) bolt, consume, devour, eat, gobble, gulp down, wolf down. **to put down 1** (*to suppress, to crush*) crush, quash, quell, repress, silence, stamp out, suppress. **2** (*to snub, to degrade*) belittle, condemn, deflate, degrade, deprecate, dismiss, disparage, humiliate, mortify, reject, shame, slight, snub, take down. **3** (*to reduce, to diminish*) diminish, lower, reduce. **4** (*to write down, to enter*) enter, inscribe, jot down, list, log, record, register, set down, subscribe, take down, transcribe, write down. **5** (*to reckon, to attribute*) attribute, consider, reckon. **6** (*to kill, esp. an old or ill animal*) destroy, kill, put to sleep. **7** ((*of an aircraft*) *to land*) land, set down, touch down. **8** (*to preserve, to store*) pickle, preserve, store. **to put off 1** (*to lay aside, to discard*) discard, lay aside, take off. **2** (*to postpone* (*an appointment*)) adjourn, defer, delay, hold over, postpone, put back, shelve, stay. **3** (*to disappoint, to evade* (*a person*)) disappoint, elude, evade. **4** (*to hinder, to distract the attention of*) confuse, disconcert, distract, faze, hinder, (*coll.*) throw. **5** (*to dissuade* (*from*)) discourage, dishearten, dissuade. ANTONYMS: encourage. **6** (*to foist, to palm off* (*with*)) foist, palm off. **to put on 1** (*to clothe oneself with*) attire oneself in, change into, clothe oneself in, don, dress in, slip into, wear. ANTONYMS: shed, take off. **2** (*to pretend to feel* (*an emotion*)) affect, assume, bluff, fake, feign, make believe, pretend, sham, simulate. **3** (*to*

add, *to apply*) add, affix, apply, attach. **4** (*to bring into play, to exert*) apply, bring into play, bring to bear, exert. **5** (*to cause to operate* (*a light etc.*)) switch on, turn on. **6** (*to stage, to produce* (*a play etc.*)) do, mount, perform, present, produce, show, stage. **to put out 1** (*to eject*) discharge, eject, release. **2** (*to extinguish* (*a light*)) blow out, douse, extinguish, quench, smother, snuff out, stamp out. ANTONYMS: ignite. **3** (*to disconcert; to annoy*) anger, annoy, confound, disturb, exasperate, harass, irk, irritate, nettle, perturb, provoke, vex. **4** (*to inconvenience*) bother, discommode, impose upon, incommode, inconvenience, trouble, upset. **5** (*to publish, to broadcast*) bring out, broadcast, circulate, issue, make public, publish, release. **to put up 1** (*to raise* (*a hand etc.*)) elevate, lift, raise. **2** (*to erect, to build*) build, construct, erect, fabricate, raise. ANTONYMS: demolish, knock down. **3** (*to offer for sale*) auction, make available, offer, present. **4** (*to show, as a fight, resistance etc.*) display, give, show. **5** (*to lodge and entertain*) accommodate, board, entertain, house, lodge, quarter, take in. **6** (*to provide* (*money, a prize*)) advance, contribute, donate, give, invest, pay, pledge, provide, supply. **7** (*to present as a candidate*) nominate, offer, present, propose, recommend, submit. **to put up with** (*to tolerate*) abide, accept, bear, brook, endure, (*coll.*) lump, pocket, stand, stomach, submit to, suffer, swallow, take, tolerate. ANTONYMS: reject, resist.

putrefy *v.t.* **1** (*to cause to rot or decay*) decay, decompose, deteriorate, go bad, go off, moulder, rot, spoil. **2** (*to make carious or gangrenous*) fester, suppurate.

puzzle *n.* **1** (*a perplexing problem or question*) conundrum, enigma, labyrinth, maze, mystery, paradox, poser, problem, question. ANTONYMS: solution. **2** (*a toy, riddle etc. for exercising ingenuity or patience*) brain-teaser, jigsaw, riddle, toy. **3** (*a state of bewilderment*) bafflement, bewilderment, confusion, difficulty, dilemma, perplexity, quandary, uncertainty. ~*v.t.* (*to perplex, to mystify*) baffle, beat, bewilder, confound, confuse, flummox, mystify, nonplus, perplex, stump. **to puzzle out** (*to work out by mental labour*) clear up, crack, decipher, discover, figure out, resolve, see, solve, sort out, (*sl.*) suss out, think through, unlock, unravel, work out.

pygmy *n.* **1** (*a dwarf, a small person*) dwarf, homunculus, midget, (*coll.*) shrimp. ANTONYMS: giant. **2** (*an insignificant person*) cipher, mediocrity, nobody, nonentity. ~*a.* (*of or relating to pygmies; diminutive*) baby, diminutive, dwarf, midget, miniature, minuscule, pocket, small, stunted, tiny, undersized.

Q

quaff *v.t.* (*to drink in large draughts*) (*coll.*) down, drink, gulp, guzzle, imbibe, sup, swallow, (*coll.*) swig.

quagmire *n.* **1** (*an area of soft marshy ground that sinks under the feet*) bog, fen, marsh, mire, morass, quicksand, slough, swamp. **2** (*an awkward or difficult predicament*) difficulty, dilemma, fix, impasse, jam, mess, muddle, pass, (*coll.*) pickle, plight, predicament, quandary, (*coll.*) scrape.

quail *v.i.* (*to shrink back with fear*) blench, cower, cringe, droop, falter, flinch, lose heart, quake, recoil, shake, shrink, shudder, tremble.

quaint *a.* **1** (*old-fashioned*) antiquated, archaic, old-fashioned, old-world, picturesque. ANTONYMS: fashionable, new. **2** (*odd, whimsical*) bizarre, curious, droll, eccentric, extraordinary, fanciful, fantastic, odd, offbeat, outlandish, peculiar, queer, (*sl.*) rum, singular, strange, uncommon, unusual, whimsical. ANTONYMS: ordinary.

quake *v.i.* (*to shake, to tremble*) convulse, pulsate, quiver, rock, shake, shiver, shudder, stagger, throb, totter, tremble, vibrate, waver, wobble.

qualification *n.* **1** (*modification or limitation of meaning*) allowance, caveat, condition, criterion, exception, exemption, limitation, modification, objection, prerequisite, proviso, requirement, reservation, restriction, rider, stipulation. **2** (*any quality fitting a person (for an office, employment etc.)*) ability, accomplishment, aptitude, attainment, attribute, capability, capacity, competence, eligibility, endowment, experience, fitness, gift, (*coll.*) know-how, quality, skill, suitability, talent. ANTONYMS: disqualification.

qualify *v.t.* **1** (*to provide with the requisite qualities*) capacitate, condition, empower, endow, equip, fit, ground, prepare, ready, train. **2** (*to make competent or capable (for any action or occupation)*) certify, commission, license, permit, sanction. ANTONYMS: disqualify, forbid. **3** (*to narrow the scope, force etc. of (a statement or word)*) circumscribe, limit, modify, narrow, reduce, restrain, restrict. **4** (*to moderate, to mitigate*) abate, adapt, assuage, diminish, ease, lessen, mitigate, moderate, modify, modulate, regulate, soften, temper,

vary. **5** (*to reduce the strength or flavour of (spirit etc.) with water*) dilute, temper, water down. **6** (*esp. Gram.*) (*to describe or characterize as*) characterize, describe, designate, distinguish, name.

quality *n.* **1** (*a distinctive property or attribute*) aspect, attribute, condition, feature, mark, peculiarity, property. **2** (*distinguishing character*) character, constitution, description, essence, kind, make, nature, sort. **3** (*a mental or moral characteristic*) characteristic, distinction, idiosyncrasy, peculiarity, trait. **4** (*a particular function*) capacity, function, value. **5** (*degree of excellence*) calibre, grade, position, rank, standing, status, worth. **6** (*a high standard of excellence*) distinction, excellence, grandeur, merit, nobility, pre-eminence, superiority.

qualm *n.* **1** (*a sensation of fear or uneasiness*) anxiety, apprehension, concern, disinclination, disquiet, doubt, fear, funny feeling, hesitation, trepidation, uncertainty, uneasiness. **2** (*a misgiving, a scruple*) compunction, contrition, misgiving, regret, reluctance, remorse, scruple, second thought, twinge. **3** (*a feeling of sickness*) agony, attack, nausea, pang, queasiness, sickness, spasm, throe, twinge.

quantity *n.* **1** (*extent, amount or number*) amount, bulk, capacity, expanse, extent, greatness, length, magnitude, mass, measure, number, size, volume, weight. **2** (*a sum, a number*) aggregate, number, quota, sum, total. **3** (*a certain or a large number or amount*) amount, lot, part, portion.

quarrel *n.* **1** (*a noisy or violent contention or dispute*) altercation, argument, (*coll.*) barney, brawl, contention, controversy, debate, difference, disagreement, disputation, feud, fight, misunderstanding, row, (*chiefly N Am.*) spat, squabble, tiff, vendetta, wrangle. ANTONYMS: agreement, concord. **2** (*a breach of friendship*) breach, falling-out. **3** (*a ground or cause of complaint or dispute*) (*sl.*) beef, bone to pick, complaint, gripe, grouse.

~*v.i.* **1** (*to dispute violently*) altercate, argue, bicker, brawl, clash, differ, disagree, dispute, fight, row, spar, squabble, wrangle. ANTONYMS: agree. **2** (*to break off friendly relations (with)*) fall out, part company. **3** (*to find fault (with)*) carp (at), cavil (at), complain (about), decry, disapprove (of), find fault (with), object (to), take exception (to).

quarrelsome *a.* **1** (*inclined or apt to quarrel*) antagonistic, argumentative, belligerent, combative, contentious, contrary, disputatious, dissentious. **2** (*easily provoked*) choleric, cranky, cross, fractious, grouchy, ill-tempered, irascible, irritable, peevish, petulant, pugnacious, querulous, quick-tempered, testy, touchy. ANTONYMS: equable, placid.

quarter *n.* **1** (*a fourth part*) fourth, quadrant. **2** (*a particular region or locality*) area, direction, district, locality, location, neighbourhood, part, province, region, section, territory, zone. **3 a** (*pl.*) (*a place of lodging that is occupied by troops etc.*) abode, accommodation, barracks, billet, cantonment, chambers, (*coll.*) digs, domicile, dwelling, habitation, home, lodging, post, residence, rooms, shelter, station. **b** (*usu. pl.*) (*allotted position, esp. for troops*) place, point, position, spot, station. **4** (*mercy, clemency*) clemency, compassion, favour, forgiveness, leniency, mercy, pity.
~*v.i.* (*to be stationed or lodged*) accommodate, billet, board, house, install, lodge, place, post, put up, station.

quash *v.t.* **1** (*to annul or make void*) abolish, annul, cancel, declare null and void, invalidate, nullify, overrule, reject, repeal, rescind, reverse, revoke, set aside, throw out, void. **2** (*to suppress, to crush*) beat, crush, destroy, extinguish, extirpate, overthrow, put down, quench, repress, squash, subdue, suppress.

quaver *v.i.* **1** (*to tremble, to vibrate*) flicker, flutter, oscillate, pulsate, quake, shake, shiver, shudder, thrill, tremble, vibrate, waver. **2** (*to sing or play with tremulous modulations or trills*) trill, twitter, warble.

queer *a.* **1** (*strange, odd*) abnormal, anomalous, bizarre, curious, disquieting, eerie, erratic, extraordinary, funny, odd, outlandish, peculiar, singular, strange, uncanny, unconventional, unnatural, unorthodox, unusual, weird. ANTONYMS: normal, ordinary. **2** (*questionable, suspicious*) doubtful, dubious, (*coll.*) fishy, irregular, mysterious, puzzling, questionable, shady, suspect, suspicious. **3** (*slightly unwell, faint*) dizzy, faint, giddy, ill, light-headed, out of sorts, poorly, queasy, reeling, sick, unwell. **4** (*sl., offensive*) (*homosexual*) (*sl., offensive*) bent, (*coll.*) gay, homosexual, lesbian. **5** (*coll.*) (*mentally unbalanced*) (*coll.*) cracked, crazy, daft, demented, deranged, (*coll.*) dotty, eccentric, idiosyncratic, insane, irrational, (*sl.*) loony, mad, (*sl.*) nutty, odd, (*coll.*) touched, unbalanced, unhinged.

~*n.* (*sl., offensive*) (*a homosexual*) (*coll.*) gay, homosexual, lesbian.

quell *v.t.* **1** (*to suppress, to subdue*) extinguish, put down, quash, repress, stamp out, stifle, subdue, suppress. **2** (*to crush*) conquer, crush, defeat, overcome, overpower, vanquish. **3** (*to cause to subside, to calm*) allay, alleviate, appease, assuage, blunt, calm, compose, deaden, dull, mitigate, moderate, mollify, pacify, quiet, silence, soothe. ANTONYMS: aggravate.

querulous *a.* **1** (*complaining*) carping, censorious, complaining, critical, fault-finding, finicky, fussy, grumbling. ANTONYMS: uncomplaining. **2** (*discontented, fretful*) bad-tempered, cantankerous, crabby, cross, crotchety, discontented, fretful, grouchy, grumpy, ill-humoured, irascible, irritable, peevish, petulant, plaintive, sour, testy, tetchy, touchy, waspish. ANTONYMS: content, placid.

query *n.* **1** (*a question*) demand, inquiry, question. ANTONYMS: answer, solution. **2** (*a point or objection to be answered, a doubt*) doubt, hesitation, objection, problem, reservation, scepticism, suspicion, uncertainty.
~*v.t.* **1** (*to express as a question*) ask, inquire, question. **2** (*to express doubt concerning*) challenge, disbelieve, dispute, distrust, doubt, mistrust, suspect. ANTONYMS: accept.

question *n.* **1** (*a sentence requiring an answer*) interrogative, query. **2** (*the act of asking or enquiring*) examination, inquiry, interrogation, investigation. **3** (*doubt, uncertainty*) argument, confusion, contention, controversy, debate, difficulty, dispute, doubt, misgiving, objection, problem, uncertainty. **4** (*a problem requiring solution*) issue, matter, problem. **5** (*a subject to be discussed*) subject, theme, topic. **6** (*a proposition or subject to be debated and voted on, esp. in a deliberative assembly*) motion, proposition, subject.
~*v.t.* **1** (*to ask a question or questions of*) ask, cross-examine, examine, (*coll.*) grill, inquire, interrogate, interview, pump, query, quiz. ANTONYMS: answer, reply. **2** (*to study (phenomena etc.) with a view to acquiring information*) examine, investigate, probe, study. **3** (*to treat as doubtful or unreliable*) call into question, challenge, controvert, disbelieve, dispute, distrust, doubt, impugn, mistrust, object to, oppose, query, refute, suspect. ANTONYMS: accept.

questionable *a.* **1** (*open to suspicion, esp. with regard to honesty, morality etc.*) borderline, (*coll.*) dodgy, doubtful, dubious, (*coll.*) fishy, (*coll.*) iffy, shady, suspect, suspicious. **2** (*disputable*) ambiguous, arguable, controversial, debatable, disputable, equivocal, moot, paradoxical, problematical, uncertain. ANTONYMS: incontrovertible, unequivocal.

queue *n.* **1** (*a line of people, vehicles etc. waiting their turn*) column, file, line, row, string, tailback. **2** (*a sequence of items to be dealt with in order*) chain, order, progression, sequence, series, succession, train.

quick *a.* **1** (*rapid in movement*) brisk, fast, fleet, nimble, rapid, swift. ANTONYMS: slow. **2** (*done or happening in a short time*) brief, cursory, perfunctory. **3** (*speedy, prompt*) expeditious, express, hasty, hurried, prompt, speedy, timely. **4** (*alert, acutely responsive*) able, acute, adroit, alert, astute, bright, clever, deft, dexterous, discerning, intelligent, perceptive, quick-witted, receptive, responsive, sensitive, sharp, shrewd, skilful, smart. **5** ((*of a temper*) *irritable*) choleric, irascible, irritable, peppery, petulant, temperamental, testy, touchy, waspish. **6** (*rash, hasty*) abrupt, curt, excitable, hasty, impatient, passionate, precipitate, rash. **7** (*ready* (*to act or respond*)) eager, prepared, ready, willing. ANTONYMS: reluctant. **8†** (*alive, living*) alive, animate, live, living. ANTONYMS: dead.

quicken *v.t.* **1** (*to make faster*) accelerate, dispatch, expedite, hasten, hurry, impel, precipitate, speed. ANTONYMS: slow down. **2** (*to give or restore life to*) activate, animate, energize, enliven. **3** (*to stimulate, to rouse*) arouse, excite, galvanize, incite, inspire, invigorate, kindle, rouse, stimulate, whet. **4** (*to cheer, to refresh*) cheer, refresh, reinvigorate, resuscitate, revitalize, revive, strengthen, vitalize, vivify.

quickly *adv.* (*fast, promptly*) abruptly, apace, briskly, expeditiously, fast, forthwith, hastily, hurriedly, immediately, instantly, post-haste, promptly, (*coll.*) pronto, quick, rapidly, shortly, soon, speedily, straight away, swiftly. ANTONYMS: slowly.

quiet *a.* **1** (*making little or no noise*) dumb, hushed, inaudible, low, noiseless, silent, soft, soundless. ANTONYMS: loud, noisy. **2** (*in a state of rest, motionless*) motionless, resting, stationary, still. **3** (*peaceful, undisturbed*) calm, peaceful, placid, restful, serene, tranquil, undisturbed, unruffled, untroubled. ANTONYMS: agitated, turbulent. **4** (*gentle, mild*) calm, collected, contented, docile, even-tempered, gentle, imperturbable, meek, mild, pacific, peaceable, phlegmatic, placid, reserved, retiring, sedate, shy, unexcitable. ANTONYMS: excitable, passionate. **5** (*unobtrusive*) conservative, modest, plain, restrained, simple, sober, subdued, unassuming, unobtrusive, unpretentious. ANTONYMS: glaring, showy. **6** (*retired,*

secluded) isolated, private, secluded, secret, sequestered, undisturbed, unfrequented, withdrawn. ANTONYMS: public.

~n. 1 (*silence, peace*) calm, calmness, hush, peace, silence, stillness. **2** (*a state of rest or repose*) repose, rest, still, stillness. **3** (*tranquillity*) calm, peacefulness, serenity, tranquillity. ANTONYMS: disturbance. **4** (*peace of mind*) calm, patience, peace of mind, placidness.

quieten *v.t.* **1** (*to make quiet*) hush, muffle, mute, quiet, shush, silence. **2** (*to soothe, to calm*) allay, alleviate, appease, assuage, calm, compose, deaden, dull, lull, mitigate, mollify, palliate, quell, soothe, stifle, still, stop, subdue, tranquillize. ANTONYMS: (*coll.*) aggravate, provoke.

quirk *n.* **1** (*a mannerism*) aberration, caprice, characteristic, eccentricity, fancy, foible, habit, idiosyncrasy, kink, mannerism, oddity, peculiarity, singularity, trait, vagary, whim. **2** (*an artful trick*) artifice, evasion, shift, subterfuge, trick.

quit *v.t.* **1** (*to give up, to abandon*) abandon, abdicate, give up, relinquish, renounce, resign, rid oneself of, surrender. **2** (*to leave, to depart from*) decamp, depart, desert, exit, forsake, go, leave, pull out, retire, withdraw. ANTONYMS: enter. **3** (*to cease, to desist from*) cease, desist, discontinue, drop, end, halt, stop, suspend. ANTONYMS: continue.

quite *adv.* **1** (*completely, to the fullest extent*) absolutely, altogether, completely, considerably, entirely, fully, largely, perfectly, positively, thoroughly, totally, unequivocally, unreservedly, utterly, very, wholly. ANTONYMS: partly. **2** (*to some extent, fairly*) fairly, moderately, pretty, rather, reasonably, relatively, somewhat. **3** (*yes* (*used to indicate agreement*)) certainly, indeed, yes.

quiver *v.i.* **1** (*to tremble or be agitated with a rapid tremulous motion*) agitate, fluctuate, oscillate, palpitate, vibrate, wobble. **2** (*to shake, to shiver*) quake, quaver, shake, shiver, shudder, tremble, tremor.

quizzical *a.* **1** (*questioning, mocking*) arch, derisive, inquiring, mocking, puzzled, questioning, sardonic, supercilious, teasing. **2** (*amusingly odd*) curious, eccentric, odd, queer.

quotation *n.* **1** (*a passage or phrase quoted*) allusion, citation, cutting, excerpt, extract, line, passage, quote, reference, selection. **2** (*an estimate supplied by a contractor for a job of work*) charge, cost, estimate, figure, price, quote, rate, tender.

rabble *n.* **1** (*a noisy crowd of people*) crowd, gang, herd, horde, mob, swarm, throng. **2** (*the common people*) commonalty, commoners, hoi polloi, lower orders, masses, mob, peasantry, populace, proletariat, riff-raff, scum, (*coll.*) the great unwashed. ANTONYMS: aristocracy, gentry.

race[1] *n.* **1** (*a contest of speed between runners, motor vehicles etc.*) chase, dash, marathon, pursuit, rally, sprint. **2** (*fig.*) (*any competitive contest, esp. one depending chiefly on speed*) competition, contention, contest, rivalry. **3** (*a rapid current of water, esp. in the sea or a tidal river*) current, flow, rush, tide.
~*v.i.* (*to run or move swiftly*) career, dart, dash, fly, gallop, hare, hasten, hurry, run, rush, scramble, speed, sprint, (*coll.*) tear. ANTONYMS: amble.
~*v.t.* (*to contend against in speed or in a race*) compete against, contend with, contest, rival, vie with.

race[2] *n.* **1** (*a particular ethnic stock*) ethnic group, folk, nation, people, stock, tribe. **2** (*a genus, species etc. of plants or animals*) genus, species, stock, strain, variety. **3** (*fig.*) (*lineage, pedigree*) ancestry, blood, breed, descent, issue, line, lineage, pedigree. **4** (*a clan*) clan, family, house, kin.

racket *n.* **1** (*a clamour, a confused noise*) clamour, din, noise. ANTONYMS: quiet, silence. **2** (*a commotion*) ado, ballyhoo, brouhaha, commotion, disturbance, fuss, hubbub, hue and cry, outcry, pandemonium, row, rumpus, tumult, turmoil, uproar. ANTONYMS: peace. **3** (*uproarious excitement or dissipation*) excitement, frolic, gaiety, spree. **4** (*sl.*) (*an underhand plan*) artifice, (*sl.*) caper, dodge, ruse, scheme, stratagem, trick. **5** (*an organized illegal or unethical activity*) crime, fraud, swindle. **6** (*a line of business*) business, game, line, occupation, profession, trade.

racy *a.* **1** (*lively, spirited*) animated, buoyant, energetic, entertaining, exciting, exhilarating, fresh, heady, interesting, lively, sparkling, spirited, sprightly, stimulating, vigorous, zestful. **2** (*suggestive, bordering on the indecent*) adult, bawdy, (*sl.*) blue, broad, dirty, filthy, immodest, indecent, indelicate, lewd, naughty, pornographic, (*coll.*) raunchy, ribald, risqué, salty, sexy, smutty, suggestive, vulgar. **3** (*strongly flavoured, piquant*) distinctive, flavourful, hot, piquant, pungent, rich, savoury, sharp, spicy, strong, tangy, tart, tasty, zesty.

radiant *a.* **1** (*emitting rays of light or heat*) blazing, glowing, incandescent, luminous. **2** (*fig.*) (*beaming* (*with joy, love etc.*)) beaming, beatific, blissful, blithe, delighted, ecstatic, elated, exultant, gay, glad, gleeful, glowing, happy, joyful, joyous, jubilant, overjoyed, rapt, rapturous, shining. ANTONYMS: depressed, gloomy. **3** (*splendid, brilliant*) beaming, bright, brilliant, effulgent, gleaming, glittering, glorious, glossy, lustrous, resplendent, shining, sparkling, splendid, sunny. ANTONYMS: dark, sombre.

radiate *v.i.* **1** (*to emit rays of light, heat or other electromagnetic radiation*) beam, blaze, burn, diffuse, disseminate, emanate, emit, give off, gleam, glitter, glow, pour, scatter, send out, shed, shimmer, shine, sparkle, spread. **2** (*to issue or be emitted in rays from or as from a centre*) branch out, diverge, issue, spread out.

radical *a.* **1** (*inherent, fundamental*) constitutional, deep-seated, essential, ingrained, inherent, innate, native, natural, organic, profound. ANTONYMS: superficial. **2** (*going to the root, extreme*) complete, comprehensive, drastic, entire, excessive, exhaustive, extreme, fanatical, severe, sweeping, thoroughgoing. **3** (*in politics, favouring extreme action or changes*) anarchist, extreme, extremist, fanatical, militant, revolutionary. ANTONYMS: conservative, moderate. **4** (*original, basic*) basic, cardinal, elemental, elementary, original, primary, rudimentary. **5** (*sl.*) (*excellent, very good*) (*sl.*) ace, (*N Am., sl.*) bad, (*coll.*) cool, excellent, outstanding, (*sl.*) wicked.
~*n.* (*a person promoting extreme measures*) anarchist, extremist, fanatic, militant, revolutionary, zealot. ANTONYMS: conservative, moderate.

rage *n.* **1** (*violent anger, fury*) agitation, anger, fury, ire, madness, wrath. ANTONYMS: contentment, equanimity. **2** (*a fit of passionate anger*) frenzy, outburst, passion, rampage, raving, tantrum, temper. **3** (*fig.*) (*extreme vehemence or intensity* (*of*)) intensity, vehemence, violence. **4** (*a violent desire or enthusiasm (for)*) desire (for), enthusiasm (for), mania (for), obsession (with). **5** (*coll.*) (*an object of temporary enthusiasm or devotion*) craze, fad, fashion, mode, style, vogue. **6** (*intense emotion*) ardour, emotion, passion.

~*v.i.* **1** (*to be furious with anger*) blow a fuse, (*coll.*) blow up, boil, explode, (*coll.*) fly off the handle, fret, fume, (*coll.*) hit the roof, rant, rave, see red, seethe, storm, (*coll.*) throw a wobbly. **2** (*to be at the highest state of vehemence or activity*) rampage, storm, surge.

ragged *a.* **1** (*worn into rags, tattered*) frayed, holed, patched, rent, tattered, threadbare, torn, worn. **2** (*rough, shaggy*) dishevelled, rough, shaggy, unkempt. **3** (*uneven in outline or surface*) broken, fragmented, jagged, nicked, notched, rough, saw-toothed, serrated, uneven. ANTONYMS: smooth. **4** (*irregular, imperfect*) desultory, disjointed, imperfect, irregular. **5** (*lacking in uniformity, finish etc.*) crude, unfinished. **6** (*harsh, dissonant*) discordant, dissonant, grating, harsh, hoarse, rasping, scratchy. **7** (*shabby, miserable in appearance*) broken-down, contemptible, dilapidated, dishevelled, down at heel, mean, messy, miserable, poor, run-down, scraggy, seedy, shabby, tatty, unkempt. ANTONYMS: smart.

raid *n.* **1** (*a sudden hostile incursion as of armed troops, criminals etc.*) assault, attack, foray, incursion, inroad, invasion, onset, onslaught, sally, sortie. **2** (*esp. facet.*) (*a foray to obtain something*) excursion, foray, mission.

~*v.t.* (*to make a raid upon*) assault, attack, descend on, fall upon, invade, maraud, pillage, plunder, pounce upon, ransack, rifle, sack, sally forth, set upon, storm, swoop down upon.

rain *n.* **1** (*the condensed moisture of the atmosphere falling in drops*) precipitation, rainfall. **2** (*a fall of such drops*) cloudburst, deluge, downpour, drizzle, shower, squall. **3** (*a large quantity of anything falling quickly*) deluge, flood, hail, outpouring, shower, spate, sprinkling, stream, torrent, volley.

~*v.i.* **1** (*to fall in drops of water from the clouds*) (*coll.*) bucket down, come down, drizzle, pelt, pour, shower, spit, teem. **2** (*to fall in showers like rain*) pour, run, shower, sprinkle, trickle.

raise *v.t.* **1** (*to move or put into a higher position*) move up, put up. ANTONYMS: lower. **2** (*to cause to rise, to elevate*) elevate, haul up, hoist, uplift. **3** (*to cause to stand up*) set upright, stand up. ANTONYMS: lie down. **4** (*to increase the amount or value of*) escalate, increase, inflate, jack up. **5** (*to increase the strength or intensity of*) amplify, augment, boost, enhance, enlarge, exaggerate, intensify, magnify, reinforce,

strengthen. ANTONYMS: decrease. **6** (*to build, to construct*) build, construct, erect, put up. ANTONYMS: demolish, raze. **7** (*to rouse, to stir up*) aggravate, animate, arouse, awaken, evoke, excite, foment, foster, incite, instigate, invigorate, kindle, motivate, provoke, rouse, stimulate, stir up, summon up, whip up. ANTONYMS: calm, quell. **8** (*to create, to cause*) bring about, cause, create, engender, give rise to, institute, occasion, originate, produce, prompt. **9** (*to cause to be known, to suggest* (*a point etc.*)) advance, bring up, broach, introduce, open, present, put forward, suggest. **10** (*to bring up, to rear*) bring up, educate, foster, nurture, rear, train. **11** (*to grow or breed*) breed, cultivate, farm, grow, plant, propagate. **12** (*to collect, to levy* (*money etc.*)) assemble, collect, convene, form, gather, get, levy, mass, mobilize, muster, rally, recruit, round up. **13** (*to advance, to make higher or nobler*) advance, exalt, heighten, prefer, promote, upgrade. ANTONYMS: demote. **14** (*to bring to an end* (*a ban, blockade etc.*)) abandon, eliminate, end, give up, lift, relieve, remove, terminate. ANTONYMS: begin.

rake[1] *v.t.* **1** (*to collect or gather* (*up or together*) *with a rake*) assemble, collect, gather, scrape together. **2** (*to scrape, smooth etc.* (*soil*) *with a rake*) clean, harrow, hoe, scrape, scratch, smooth. **3** (*to search with or as with a rake, to ransack*) comb, examine, hunt, pick through, probe, ransack, rummage, scan, scour, scrutinize, search, sift. **4** (*to fire along the length of*) enfilade, pepper, sweep.

rake[2] *n.* (*a dissolute or immoral man*) cad, debauchee, ladies' man, lecher, libertine, playboy, prodigal, profligate, roué, sensualist, voluptuary, womanizer.

rally *v.t.* **1** (*to reunite, to bring* (*disordered troops etc.*) *together again*) bring together, bring to order, marshal, mobilize, muster, organize, reunite, round up. ANTONYMS: disband, disperse. **2** (*to gather or bring together for a common purpose*) assemble, bond together, bring together, gather. **3** (*to restore, to revive*) pull together, reanimate, restore, revive.

~*v.i.* **1** (*to come together again after a reverse or rout*) come together, reassemble, regroup. **2** (*to come together for a cause or purpose*) come together, convene, gather. **3** (*to return to a state of health or courage*) come round, get better, improve, mend, perk up, pick up, pull through, recover, recuperate, revive. ANTONYMS: deteriorate, worsen.

~*n.* **1** (*the act of rallying or recovering health, energy etc.*) improvement, recovery, recuperation, regrouping, renewal, reorganization, resurgence, revival. ANTONYMS: deterioration, relapse. **2** (*an assembly, a reunion*) assembly, conference, congregation, congress, convention, convocation, gathering, meeting, muster, reunion.

ram *v.t.* **1** (*to drive or force* (*down, in, into etc.*) *by heavy blows*) beat, dash, drive, drum, force, hammer, hit, pound, press, slam, smash, strike. **2** (*to compress, to force* (*into*) *with pressure*) compress, cram, crowd, force, jam, pack, squeeze, stuff, tamp, thrust.
~*v.i.* (*to crash or collide violently*) bump, butt, collide, crash, impact, run into.

ramble *v.i.* **1** (*to walk or move about freely, as for recreation*) amble, drift, perambulate, range, roam, rove, saunter, straggle, stray, stroll, trek, walk, wander. **2** (*to wander or be incoherent in speech, writing etc.*) babble, chatter, digress, gibber, maunder, (*coll.*) rabbit, rattle on, (*coll.*) waffle, (*coll.*) witter on. **3** ((*of a plant*) *to grow in a straggling manner*) meander, snake, twist, wander, wind.
~*n.* (*a walk for pleasure or without a definite object*) excursion, hike, perambulation, peregrination, roam, saunter, stroll, tour, tramp, trek, trip, walk, wander.

ramification *n.* **1** (*a subdivision in a complex system, structure etc.*) branch, development, division, excrescence, extension, forking, offshoot, outgrowth, subdivision. **2** (*a consequence, esp. one that causes complications*) complication, consequence, effect, implication, result, upshot.

rampage[1] *v.i.* (*to rage, to behave violently*) dash about, go berserk, rage, rant, rave, run amok, run riot, rush, storm, tear.

rampage[2] *n.* (*boisterous, violent behaviour*) excitement, frenzy, fury, rage, spree, storm, tempest, tumult, turmoil, uproar, violence.

rampant *a.* **1** (*wild, violent*) aggressive, dominant, excessive, flagrant, outrageous, raging, rampaging, riotous, unbridled, uncontrolled, ungovernable, unrestrained, vehement, violent, wanton, wild. ANTONYMS: controlled, restrained. **2** ((*of weeds etc.*) *rank, luxuriant*) epidemic, exuberant, flourishing, luxuriant, prevalent, profuse, rank, rife, unchecked, uncontrolled, uninhibited, unrestrained, widespread.

ramshackle *a.* ((*of a building, vehicle etc.*) *tumbledown, rickety*) broken-down, crumbling, decrepit, derelict, dilapidated, flimsy, jerry-built, rickety, ruinous, run-down, shaky, tottering, tumbledown, unsafe, unstable, unsteady. ANTONYMS: steady, sturdy.

rancid *a.* (*rank, stale*) bad, decayed, fetid, foul, fusty, musty, off, putrid, rank, rotten, sour, spoiled, stale, tainted. ANTONYMS: fresh.

rancour *n.* (*deep-seated malice*) animosity, antagonism, antipathy, bad blood, bitterness, enmity, grudge, hate, hatred, hostility, ill feeling, ill will, malevolence, malice, malignity, resentment, spite, spleen, venom, vindictiveness. ANTONYMS: benevolence.

random *a.* (*done, made etc. without calculation or method; occurring by chance*) accidental, arbitrary, casual, chance, fortuitous, haphazard, incidental, indefinite, indiscriminate, purposeless, serendipitous, spot, stray, uncalculated, unplanned, unpremeditated. ANTONYMS: calculated, premeditated.

range *n.* **1** (*the extent of variation in something*) diversity, extent, variation. **2** (*the limits between which such variation occurs*) bounds, confines, limits, parameters. **3** (*the area or extent of power, variation etc.*) ambit, amplitude, area, compass, domain, extent, field, gamut, latitude, orbit, pale, province, purview, radius, reach, scope, span, sphere, sweep. **4** (*the entire collection of products of a designer, manufacturer, stockist etc.*) assortment, collection, selection, stock. **5** (*a row or line* (*e.g. of mountains*)) chain, file, line, rank, row, sequence, series, string, tier.
~*v.t.* **1** (*to set in a row or rows*) align, arrange, line up. **2** (*to arrange in definite order, place etc.*) arrange, array, classify, dispose, draw up, order, rank. **3** (*to pass over, along or through*) migrate, pass over, roam. **4** (*to make level or flush*) align, level, straighten.
~*v.i.* **1** (*to extend or reach*) extend, lie, reach, stretch. **2** (*to vary*) fluctuate, vary. **3** (*to roam, to sail* (*along etc.*)) cruise, explore, ramble, roam, rove, sail, straggle, stray, stroll, sweep, traverse, wander. **4** (*to rank, to be in place* (*among, with etc.*)) be bracketed, be classed, be classified, be filed, be graded, be pigeon-holed, be sorted, rank.

rank[1] *n.* **1** (*relative degree of excellence etc.*) classification, degree, division. **2** (*high position, eminence*) aristocracy, ascendancy, dignity, eminence, influence, nobility, prestige, priority, quality, seniority, superiority, title, weight. **3** (*relative degree, class*) caste, class, degree, echelon, grade, level, place, position, standing, station, status, stratum. **4** (*a row, a line*) column, file, line, queue, row, series, string, tier. **5** (*order, array*) arrangement, array, order.
~*v.t.* **1** (*to classify, to give a* (*specified*) *rank to*) arrange, array, assort, class, classify, dispose, estimate, grade, graduate, locate, marshal, order, organize, position, range, rate, sort. **2** (*to draw up or arrange in rank or ranks*) align, line up.

rank[2] *a.* **1** (*excessively luxuriant in growth*)

abundant, dense, exuberant, fertile, flourishing, lush, luxuriant, over-abundant, productive, profuse, prolific, rampant, superabundant, vigorous. ANTONYMS: sparse. **2** (*rancid, evil-smelling*) bad, disagreeable, disgusting, evil-smelling, fetid, foul, musty, noisome, noxious, off, offensive, pungent, putrid, rancid, revolting, stale, stinking, strong-smelling, (*coll.*) yucky. **3** (*indecent, obscene*) corrupt, dirty, filthy, indecent, obscene, scurrilous, smutty. **4** (*strongly marked, flagrant*) arrant, blatant, excessive, extravagant, flagrant, glaring, gross, rampant, thorough, unalloyed, undisguised, unmitigated. **5** (*coarse, gross*) abusive, atrocious, base, coarse, crass, gross, low, nasty, vulgar. **6** (*complete, total*) absolute, complete, downright, sheer, total, utter.

ransack *v.t.* **1** (*to pillage, to plunder*) despoil, loot, pillage, plunder, ravage, rifle, rob, sack, strip. **2** (*to search thoroughly*) comb, examine, explore, go through, rake, rummage, scour, scrutinize, search.

ransom *n.* **1** (*a sum of money demanded or paid for the release of a person from captivity*) demands, money, pay-off, pay-out, price. **2** (*release from captivity in return for such a payment*) deliverance, liberation, redemption, release, rescue.
~*v.t.* **1** (*to redeem from captivity by paying a sum of money*) buy out, redeem. **2** (*to release in return for a ransom*) deliver, free, liberate, release. **3** (*to redeem from sin, to atone for*) atone for, deliver, redeem, save.

rant *v.i.* **1** (*to use loud or violent language*) bellow, bluster, cry, rave, roar, shout, vociferate, yell. **2** (*to declaim in a theatrical or noisy fashion*) declaim, expound, harangue, hold forth, lecture, pontificate, preach, speak.
~*n.* **1** (*bombastic or violent declamation*) bombast, grandiloquence, raving. **2** (*a noisy declamation*) bluster, declamation, diatribe, harangue, rhetoric, tirade, vociferation.

rap *v.t.* **1** (*to strike with a slight, sharp blow*) crack, cuff, hit, knock, strike, tap. **2** (*to rebuke*) blast, (*coll.*) carpet, castigate, censure, (*N Am., coll.*) chew out, criticize, lambast, (*coll.*) pan, rebuke, scold, (*coll.*) tick off. **3** (*usu. with out*) (*to utter in a quick, abrupt way*) bark, spit.
~*v.i.* **1** (*to strike a sharp blow, esp. at a door*) knock, tap. **2** (*to talk*) chat, chew the fat, converse, discourse, gossip, talk.
~*n.* **1** (*a slight, sharp blow*) blow, clout, crack, knock, tap. **2** (*a sharp rebuke*) censure, chiding, rebuke. **3** (*blame, punishment*) blame, punishment, (*coll.*) the can. **4** (*an informal talk, chat*) chat, conversation, dialogue, discourse, discussion, talk.

rapacious *a.* **1** (*grasping, extortionate*) acquisitive, avaricious, covetous, extortionate, grasping, greedy, insatiable, mercenary, ravenous, voracious, wolfish. **2** (*given to plundering or seizing by force, predatory*) marauding, plundering, predacious, predatory, preying.

rape *v.t.* **1** (*to force to have sexual intercourse*) deflower, ravish, sexually assault, violate. **2** (*to despoil, to violate*) despoil, loot, pillage, plunder, ransack, sack.
~*n.* **1** (*sexual intercourse with someone, usu. a woman, against the person's will*) ravishment, sexual assault, violation. **2** (*violation, despoiling* (*e.g. of the countryside*)) abuse, defilement, desecration, despoliation, perversion, pillage, plundering, sack, violation.

rapid *a.* (*very swift, quick*) brisk, expeditious, express, fast, fleet, flying, hasty, hurried, instant, precipitate, prompt, quick, speedy, sudden, swift. ANTONYMS: slow.

rapidity *n.* (*speed*) alacrity, briskness, celerity, dispatch, expedition, fleetness, haste, hurry, immediateness, precipitateness, promptitude, quickness, rush, speed, swiftness, velocity. ANTONYMS: slowness.

rapport *n.* (*sympathetic relationship, harmony*) accord, affinity, agreement, bond, correspondence, empathy, harmony, identification, interrelationship, link, relationship, sympathy, tie, understanding.

rapt *a.* **1** (*carried away by one's thoughts or emotions*) bewitched, blissful, captivated, carried away, charmed, delighted, ecstatic, enchanted, enraptured, happy, overjoyed, rapturous, ravished, transported. **2** (*absorbed, engrossed*) absorbed, engrossed, enthralled, entranced, fascinated, gripped, held, hypnotized, intent, mesmerized, preoccupied, spellbound. ANTONYMS: bored.

rapture *n.* (*ecstatic joy*) bliss, delight, ecstasy, elation, enchantment, enthusiasm, euphoria, exaltation, felicity, happiness, joy, pleasure, ravishment, rhapsody, seventh heaven, spell, thrill, transport. ANTONYMS: sorrow.

rapturous *a.* (*extremely happy, ecstatic*) blissful, delighted, ecstatic, elated, enchanted, enthusiastic, euphoric, exalted, happy, in seventh heaven, joyful, joyous, overjoyed, over the moon, rapt, ravished, rhapsodic, thrilled, transported. ANTONYMS: disappointed, sad.

rare *a.* **1** (*seldom existing or occurring, unusual*) exceptional, extraordinary, few, infrequent, scant, scarce, singular, sparse, sporadic, uncommon, unfamiliar, unusual. ANTONYMS: common. **2** (*especially excellent, first-rate*) admirable, choice, excellent, exquisite, fine, first-rate, great, incomparable, matchless, outstanding, precious, priceless, select, superb, superlative, valuable.

rarely *adv.* **1** (*seldom*) hardly ever, infrequently, little, once in a blue moon, once in a while, scarcely ever, seldom. ANTONYMS: frequently, often. **2** (*exceptionally*) exceptionally, extraordinarily, notably, remarkably, singularly, uncommonly, unusually.

rascal *n.* **1** (*a mischievous person, esp. a child*) scallywag, (*coll.*) scamp. **2** (*a dishonest or contemptible fellow*) cad, devil, good-for-nothing, imp, knave, miscreant, ne'er-do-well, (*dated or facet.*) rapscallion, reprobate, rogue, (*coll.*) scamp, scoundrel, villain.

rash[1] *a.* **1** (*hasty, impetuous*) adventurous, bold, brash, hasty, headlong, headstrong, hot-headed, impetuous, impulsive, madcap, precipitate, premature, venturesome, wild. **2** (*acting or done without reflection*) careless, devil-may-care, foolhardy, hare-brained, heedless, ill-advised, ill-considered, imprudent, incautious, indiscreet, injudicious, reckless, thoughtless, unthinking, unwary. ANTONYMS: careful, cautious.

rash[2] *n.* **1** (*an eruption of spots or patches on the skin*) eruption, outbreak. **2** (*a series of unwelcome, unexpected events*) deluge, epidemic, flood, multitude, outbreak, plague, profusion, series, spate, succession, wave.

rasp *v.t.* **1** (*to scrape or grate with a rough implement*) abrade, excoriate, grate, rub down, scrape. **2** (*to file with a rasp*) file, grind, rub, sand, scour. **3** (*to utter in harsh tones*) croak, grate, screech. **4** (*to irritate, to grate upon (feelings etc.*)) annoy, get, get on someone's nerves, grate upon, irk, irritate, jar, nettle, rub up the wrong way, vex, wear on.
~*n.* **1** (*an instrument like a coarse file with projections for scraping away surface material*) file, grater. **2** (*a harsh, grating noise*) grating, grinding, scraping, scratching, stridulation.

rate *n.* **1** (*the proportional measure of something in relation to some other thing*) degree, percentage, proportion, ratio, relation, scale. **2** (*a cost, charge etc.*) amount, charge, cost, dues, duty, fee, figure, hire, price, tariff, tax, toll, value. **3** (*relative speed of movement, change etc.*) (*sl.*) clip, gait, measure, pace, speed, tempo, time, velocity. **4** (*rank or class*) class, classification, degree, grade, kind, place, position, quality, rank, rating, sort, standing, status, type, value, worth.
~*v.t.* **1** (*to estimate the value or relative worth of*) adjudge, appraise, assess, calculate, class, classify, compute, count, estimate, evaluate, gauge, grade, judge, measure, rank, reckon,

value, weigh. **2** (*to consider, to regard as*) consider, reckon, regard. **3** (*to merit, to deserve*) deserve, earn, merit. **4** (*to think highly of*) admire, esteem, respect, think highly of, value.

rather *adv.* **1** (*preferably*) for choice, instead, preferably, sooner. **2** (*more properly or accurately*) accurately, properly, rightly, truly. **3** (*slightly, somewhat*) a bit, a little, fairly, (*coll.*) kind of, moderately, pretty, quite, relatively, slightly, somewhat, (*coll.*) sort of. ANTONYMS: very. **4** (*coll.*) (*very much, certainly*) assuredly, certainly, indeed, very much, yes.

ratify *v.t.* (*to establish or make valid (by formal approval)*) affirm, approve, authenticate, authorize, bind, certify, confirm, consent to, corroborate, endorse, establish, guarantee, sanction, sign, support, uphold, validate, verify, warrant. ANTONYMS: repudiate, revoke.

ratio *n.* (*the relation of one quantity or magnitude to another of a similar kind*) correlation, correspondence, equation, fraction, percentage, proportion, rate, relation, relationship.

ration *n.* **1** (*a fixed statutory allowance of provisions in a time of shortage*) allowance, quota. **2** (*usu. pl.*) (*a portion allotted to an individual*) allotment, helping, measure, part, portion, share. **3** (*pl.*) (*provisions, esp. food*) eatables, food, provender, provisions, stores, supplies, victuals.
~*v.t.* **1** (*to supply with rations*) allocate, allot, apportion, deal, distribute, divide, dole, give out, hand out, issue, measure out, mete, parcel out, supply. **2** (*to limit to a fixed allowance*) budget, conserve, control, limit, restrict, save. ANTONYMS: squander.

rational *a.* **1** (*having the faculty of reasoning*) lucid, sane, well-balanced. ANTONYMS: insane. **2** (*agreeable to reasoning, sensible*) enlightened, intelligent, judicious, logical, practical, pragmatic, realistic, reasonable, sagacious, sane, sensible, sound, wise. ANTONYMS: foolish, irrational. **3** (*based on what can be tested by reason*) cerebral, cognitive, reasoning, thinking.

rattle *v.i.* **1** (*to make a rapid succession of sharp noises, as of things clattered together*) bang, clatter, jangle, knock, tinkle. **2** (*to talk rapidly or foolishly*) babble, blather, cackle, chatter, gabble, gibber, jabber, natter, prate, prattle, (*coll.*) rabbit, ramble, run on, (*coll.*) witter, (*coll.*) yak. **3** (*to move or act with a rattling noise*) bounce, bump, jar, jiggle, joggle, jolt, shake, vibrate.
~*v.t.* **1** (*to cause to make a rattling noise*) bump, clatter, shake, vibrate. **2** (*to utter rapidly*) enumerate, list, recite, reel off, rehearse, run through, spiel off, utter. **3** (*to disconcert, to*

frighten) agitate, alarm, discomfit, discompose, disconcert, discountenance, disturb, faze, fluster, frighten, perturb, put off, scare, shake, stir up, unnerve, upset. ANTONYMS: reassure.

raucous *a.* (*hoarse or harsh in sound*) discordant, dissonant, grating, harsh, hoarse, husky, jarring, loud, noisy, piercing, rasping, rough, scratching, shrill, strident. ANTONYMS: quiet, soft.

ravage *n.* (*devastation, ruin*) damage, demolition, depredation, desolation, destruction, devastation, havoc, pillage, plunder, rape, ruin, ruination, spoliation, waste.
~*v.t.* (*to devastate, to pillage*) damage, demolish, desolate, destroy, devastate, gut, lay waste, loot, mar, pillage, plunder, ransack, raze, ruin, sack, shatter, spoil, wreak havoc, wreck.

rave *v.i.* **1** (*to wander in mind, to talk wildly*) babble, ramble. **2** (*to speak in a furious way* (*against, at etc.*)) bellow, fulminate, fume, (*coll.*) raise hell, rant, roar, splutter, storm, thunder. **3** (*to be excited, to go into raptures* (*about etc.*)) applaud, enthuse, extol, gush, praise, rhapsodize. **4** (*to move or dash furiously*) go berserk, rage, run amok.

ravenous *a.* **1** (*hungry, famished*) famished, hungry, starved, starving. ANTONYMS: full, satiated. **2** (*eager for gratification*) avaricious, covetous, devouring, ferocious, gluttonous, grasping, greedy, insatiable, predatory, rapacious, voracious, wolfish.

raving *a.* **1** (*frenzied*) berserk, crazed, crazy, frantic, frenzied, furious, hysterical, insane, irrational, mad, maniacal, manic, rabid, raging, wild. ANTONYMS: composed, sane. **2** (*marked*) extraordinary, great, marked, outstanding, phenomenal, pronounced, rare, ravishing, striking, (*sl.*) stunning, uncommon, unusual.

ravish *v.t.* **1** (*to violate, to rape*) abuse, defile, deflower, molest, outrage, sexually assault, violate. **2** (*to enrapture, to transport* (*with pleasure etc.*)) bewitch, bowl over, captivate, carry away, charm, enchant, enrapture, enthral, entrance, fascinate, overjoy, spellbind, transport. ANTONYMS: repel.

ravishing *a.* (*enchanting, filling one with rapture*) alluring, attractive, beautiful, bewitching, captivating, charming, dazzling, delightful, enchanting, enthralling, entrancing, fascinating, gorgeous, lovely, radiant, rapturous, spellbinding, (*sl.*) stunning, transporting. ANTONYMS: repulsive.

raw *a.* **1** (*uncooked*) bloody, fresh, uncooked, unprepared. ANTONYMS: cooked. **2** (*in the natural state*) green, natural. **3** (*not manufactured or refined; requiring further treatment*) natural, organic, unprocessed, unrefined, untreated. ANTONYMS: processed, refined. **4** ((*of spirits*) *not blended or diluted*) neat, straight, undiluted. **5** (*crude, untempered*) basic, coarse, crude, rough, unfinished, untempered. ANTONYMS: finished. **6** (*inexperienced, fresh*) callow, fresh, green, ignorant, immature, inexperienced, naive, new, undisciplined, unpractised, unripe, unseasoned, unskilled, untrained, untried. ANTONYMS: experienced, trained. **7** (*having the skin off, chafed*) abraded, chafed, exposed, galled, grazed, inflamed, scratched, skinned. **8** (*sore or sensitive as if from chafing*) painful, sensitive, sore, tender. **9** ((*of weather*) *cold and damp*) biting, bitter, bleak, chill, chilly, cold, damp, freezing, harsh, keen, (*coll.*) nippy, penetrating, piercing, sharp, unpleasant, wet.

ray *n.* **1** (*a beam of light proceeding from a radiant point*) bar, beam, flash, gleam, shaft, streak. **2** (*fig.*) (*a gleam or slight manifestation* (*of hope, enlightenment etc.*)) flicker, gleam, glimmer, hint, indication, scintilla, spark, trace, vestige.

raze *v.t.* **1** (*to demolish, to level to the ground*) bulldoze, demolish, destroy, flatten, knock down, level, pull down, tear down, throw down. ANTONYMS: build. **2** (*to erase, to obliterate*) delete, efface, erase, excise, expunge, extirpate, obliterate, rub out, strike out, wipe out.

reach *v.t.* **1** (*to stretch out, to extend*) extend, hold out, outstretch, stretch out. **2** (*to extend towards so as to touch, to extend as far as*) amount to, arrive at, attain, extend to, get to, land at, make, stretch to, touch. **3** (*to communicate with*) communicate with, contact, find, get, get hold of, get in touch with, get through to, make contact with. **4** (*to affect, to influence*) affect, impress, influence, move, sway. **5** (*to deliver, to pass*) deliver, hand, pass.
~*n.* (*extent, power*) ambit, capacity, command, compass, control, extension, extent, grasp, influence, jurisdiction, orbit, power, range, scope, sphere, spread, sweep, territory.

react *v.i.* **1** (*to act in response* (*to a stimulus etc.*)) acknowledge, answer, reply, respond, retort. **2** (*to act in an opposite manner, direction etc.*) counteract, counterbalance, rebound, recoil.

read *v.t.* **1** (*to perceive and understand the meaning of* (*printed, written or other characters, signs etc.*)) glance at, look at, peruse, pore over, refer to, review, scan, skim, study. **2** (*to discover the meaning of by observation*) construe, decipher, explain, interpret. **3** (*to assume as implied in a statement etc.*) assume,

conclude, impute, infer, presume. **4** (*to accurately deduce or comprehend*) comprehend, deduce, see, understand. **5** (*to learn or ascertain by reading*) ascertain, discover, learn. **6** ((*of a meteorological instrument etc.*) *to indicate*) display, indicate, record, register, show.
~*v.i.* (*to pronounce written or printed matter aloud*) announce, articulate, declaim, deliver, present, pronounce, recite, speak, utter.

readable *a.* **1** (*worth reading, interesting*) absorbing, engaging, enjoyable, entertaining, enthralling, gripping, interesting, pleasant, rewarding, stimulating, worthwhile. ANTONYMS: boring, tedious. **2** (*legible*) clear, comprehensible, decipherable, distinct, intelligible, legible, plain, understandable. ANTONYMS: illegible, unreadable.

readily *adv.* **1** (*willingly, without reluctance*) cheerfully, eagerly, freely, gladly, graciously, happily, promptly, quickly, ungrudgingly, unhesitatingly, voluntarily, willingly. ANTONYMS: reluctantly. **2** (*without difficulty, easily*) easily, effortlessly, smoothly, without difficulty. ANTONYMS: hesitatingly.

ready *a.* **1** (*fit for use or action*) all set, arranged, completed, fit, in condition, in shape, organized, prepared, primed, ripe, set. **2** (*willing, disposed*) acquiescent, agreeable, apt, consenting, content, disposed, eager, enthusiastic, game, given, glad, happy, inclined, keen, minded, predisposed, prone, willing. ANTONYMS: disinclined, reluctant. **3** (*on the point (of), about (to)*) about (to), close (to), liable (to), likely (to), on the point (of), on the verge (of). **4** (*quick, prompt*) prompt, quick, rapid, speedy, swift, timely. **5** (*able, expert*) able, adroit, agile, alert, astute, clever, deft, dexterous, expert, facile, handy, nimble, skilful. ANTONYMS: clumsy, inexpert. **6** (*at hand, within reach*) accessible, at hand, at the ready, available, close to hand, convenient, handy, near, on call, present, within reach. ANTONYMS: inaccessible, inconvenient.
~*v.t.* (*to make ready, to prepare*) arrange, equip, fit out, get ready, make ready, order, organize, prepare, prime, set.

real *a.* **1** (*actually existing; not imaginary*) actual, existing, factual. ANTONYMS: fictitious, imaginary. **2** (*genuine, not counterfeit*) authentic, bona fide, genuine, honest, legitimate, natural, right, sincere, true, unaffected, valid, verifiable. ANTONYMS: counterfeit, fake. **3** (*Law*) (*consisting of fixed or permanent things, such as lands or houses*) corporeal, material, permanent, physical, tangible. **4** (*complete, utter*) absolute, certain, complete, essential, intrinsic, utter.

realistic *a.* **1** (*of or relating to realism*) actual, real. **2** (*matter-of-fact, common-sense*) businesslike, common-sense, down-to-earth, hardheaded, level-headed, matter-of-fact, practical, pragmatic, rational, sensible, sober, unromantic, unsentimental. ANTONYMS: idealistic, unrealistic. **3** (*true to life*) authentic, convincing, faithful, graphic, lifelike, natural, naturalistic, representational, true to life, vivid.

realize *v.t.* **1** (*to apprehend clearly, to become aware of*) appreciate, apprehend, become aware of, catch on, comprehend, conceive, cotton on, discern, grasp, imagine, perceive, recognize, see, take in, (*coll.*) twig, understand. ANTONYMS: misunderstand. **2** (*to bring into actual existence, to achieve*) accomplish, achieve, bring about, bring off, bring to fruition, carry out, complete, consummate, do, effect, effectuate, fulfil, incarnate, perform. **3** (*to bring in, as a price*) bring in, clear, earn, fetch, gain, get, make, net, produce, return, sell for.

really *adv.* **1** (*in fact, in reality*) actually, in actuality, in fact, in reality. **2** (*positively, truly*) absolutely, assuredly, categorically, certainly, definitely, extremely, genuinely, honestly, indeed, positively, surely, truly, undoubtedly, unquestionably, verily, very.

rear[1] *n.* **1** (*the back or hindmost part*) back, stern, tail. ANTONYMS: front. **2** (*Mil.*) (*the hindmost division of a military force*) rearguard, support. ANTONYMS: vanguard. **3** (*euphem.*) (*the buttocks*) backside, behind, bottom, (*sl.*) bum, (*N Am., sl.*) buns, (*N Am., sl.*) butt, buttocks, posterior, rump.
~*a.* (*of or at the rear*) aft, back, hind, hindmost, last, rearmost, trailing.

rear[2] *v.t.* **1** (*to bring up, to educate*) breed, bring up, care for, educate, foster, instruct, nurse, nurture, raise, train. **2** (*to elevate to an upright position*) elevate, hoist, hold up, lift, raise, set up. ANTONYMS: lower. **3** (*to cultivate*) cultivate, grow, raise. **4** (*to build, to uplift*) build, construct, erect, fabricate, put up, uplift. ANTONYMS: demolish.
~*v.i.* (*to rise to a great height, to tower*) loom, rise, soar, tower.

reason *n.* **1** (*that which serves as a ground or motive for an act, opinion etc.*) argument, basis, end, excuse, ground, intention, justification, motive, object, occasion, pretext, purpose, rationale, rationalization, support, vindication. **2** (*the intellectual faculties*) apprehension, brains, comprehension, intellect, logic, mentality, mind, rationality. **3** (*good sense, judgement*) common sense, good sense, insight, intelligence, judgement, sanity, understanding. ANTONYMS: folly. **4** (*sensible conduct, moderation*) bounds, limits, moderation, propriety, reasonableness, sense, sensibleness, wisdom.

~*v.i.* **1** (*to use the faculty of reason*) analyse, calculate, ponder, reckon, think. **2** (*to employ argument* (*with*) *as a means of persuasion*) argue, debate, dispute, dissuade, expostulate, move, persuade, prevail upon, remonstrate, urge, win over. **3** (*to reach conclusions by way of inferences from premises*) conclude, deduce, infer, resolve, solve, work out.

reasonable *a.* **1** (*rational, governed by reason*) intelligent, rational, reasoning, sagacious, sane. ANTONYMS: irrational. **2** (*conformable to reason, sensible*) advisable, appropriate, judicious, logical, practical, proper, sensible, sober, sound, suitable, well-advised, wise. ANTONYMS: unreasonable. **3** (*moderate, esp. in price*) acceptable, average, cheap, conservative, economical, fair, inexpensive, low-priced, moderate, modest, tolerable. ANTONYMS: expensive. **4** (*average, quite good*) average, moderate, (*coll.*) OK, (*coll.*) okay, passable, quite good.

reassure *v.t.* (*to encourage, to restore to confidence*) bolster, brace, buoy up, cheer up, comfort, embolden, encourage, hearten, inspire, support, uplift. ANTONYMS: perturb, worry.

rebel[1] *n.* **1** (*a person who forcibly resists the established government*) freedom fighter, insurgent, revolutionary, revolutionist, secessionist, traitor. **2** (*a person who resists authority or control*) insurrectionary, mutineer. **3** (*a person who refuses to conform to the accepted social norms or conventions*) dissenter, heretic, nonconformist.

~*a.* (*rebellious*) insubordinate, insurgent, insurrectionary, mutinous, rebellious, revolutionary.

rebel[2] *v.i.* **1** (*to act in rebellion* (*against*)) challenge, defy, disobey, dissent, flout, resist. ANTONYMS: conform (to). **2** (*to revolt against any authority, control etc.*)) mutiny, revolt, rise up. **3** (*to feel or show repugnance*) flinch, recoil, shrink, shy away.

rebellion *n.* **1** (*organized, esp. armed, resistance to the established government*) insurgence, insurgency, insurrection, resistance, revolution, sedition. **2** (*opposition to any authority*) mutiny, opposition, revolt, rising, uprising. **3** (*refusal to conform to accepted social norms or conventions*) apostasy, defiance, disobedience, dissent, heresy, insubordination, nonconformity, schism.

rebellious *a.* **1** (*disposed to rebel, insubordinate*) disloyal, disobedient, insubordinate, uncontrollable, unmanageable, unruly. ANTONYMS: obedient. **2** (*defying or opposing lawful authority*) defiant, insurgent, insurrectionary, mutinous, rebel, revolutionary, seditious. **3** (*resisting treatment, refractory*) difficult, incorrigible, intractable, obstinate, recalcitrant, refractory, resistant, stubborn, unyielding. ANTONYMS: compliant.

rebuff *n.* **1** (*a rejection*) (*coll.*) brush-off, check, cold shoulder, discouragement, dismissal, refusal, rejection, repudiation, thumbs down. ANTONYMS: acceptance. **2** (*a curt denial, a snub*) denial, slight, snub. **3** (*a defeat, an unexpected repulse*) defeat, failure, repulse, reverse.

~*v.t.* (*to give a rebuff to, to repel*) brush off, check, cold-shoulder, cut, decline, deny, discourage, drive away, ignore, put off, refuse, reject, repel, repudiate, repulse, slight, snub, spurn, turn down. ANTONYMS: accept, encourage.

rebuke *v.t.* (*to reprove, to reprimand*) admonish, (*coll.*) bawl out, berate, castigate, censure, (*N Am., coll.*) chew out, chide, criticize, (*coll.*) dress down, haul over the coals, lecture, reprehend, reprimand, reproach, reprove, scold, take to task, (*coll.*) tell off, (*coll.*) tick off, upbraid. ANTONYMS: approve, praise.

~*n.* (*a reproof*) admonition, blame, castigation, censure, (*coll.*) dressing-down, lecture, reprimand, reproach, reproof, reproval, row, (*coll.*) telling-off, (*coll.*) ticking-off, tongue-lashing, (*coll.*) wigging. ANTONYMS: commendation, praise.

recall[1] *v.t.* **1** (*to call back, to summon to return*) call back, order back, summon. **2** (*to bring back to mind, to recollect*) look back to, recollect, remember, reminisce. ANTONYMS: forget. **3** (*to remind one of*) bring to mind, call to mind, evoke, remind one of, summon up. **4** (*to revoke, to take back*) annul, call in, cancel, countermand, nullify, overrule, recant, repeal, rescind, retract, revoke, take back, withdraw.

recall[2] *n.* **1** (*a summons to return*) calling back, recalling, summons. **2** (*the act or power of remembering*) memory, recollection, remembrance, reminiscence. **3** (*the possibility of revoking or cancelling*) annulment, cancellation, denial, disavowal, nullification, recision, repeal, rescindment, rescission, retraction, revocation, withdrawal.

recede *v.i.* **1** (*to go back or away* (*from*)) go back, leave. ANTONYMS: advance. **2** (*to slope backwards or away*) incline, slope, tend. **3** (*to retreat, to withdraw* (*from*)) fall back, retire, retreat, withdraw. **4** (*to decline*) abate, decline, diminish, dwindle, ebb, lessen, retrograde, shrink, sink, subside, wane. **5** (*to draw back, e.g. from a promise*) draw back, go back on, renege on.

receive *v.t.* **1** (*to obtain or take as a thing offered or given*) acquire, collect, come by, gain, get, inherit, obtain, pick up. ANTONYMS: give. **2** (*to encounter, to experience*) encounter, experience, go through, meet with, suffer, undergo. **3** (*to take or stand the onset of*) endure, stand, sustain, take. **4** (*to understand, to regard* (*in a particular light*)) apprehend, ascertain, gather, hear, learn, perceive, regard, understand. **5** (*to support the weight of*) bear, support. **6** (*to welcome, to entertain as a guest*) admit, entertain, greet, take in, welcome.

recent *a.* **1** (*of or relating to time not long past*) contemporary, current, present. ANTONYMS: ancient, past. **2** (*that happened or came into existence lately*) late, latter. ANTONYMS: former. **3** (*newly begun or established*) fresh, modern, new, novel, up to date. ANTONYMS: old.

reception *n.* **1** (*the act of receiving something*) acknowledgement, greeting, reaction, response, treatment, welcome. **2** (*receipt, acceptance*) acceptance, admission, receipt. **3** (*an occasion of formal receiving of visitors*) (*coll.*) do, entertainment, function, party. **4** (*an area of a hotel, office etc. where people report on arrival*) entrance-hall, foyer, lobby.

recess *n.* **1** (*a part that recedes, a niche*) alcove, bay, corner, cranny, depression, hollow, indentation, niche. ANTONYMS: projection. **2 a** (*a suspension of business*) break, closure, holiday, interlude, intermission, interval, pause, respite, rest, vacation. **b** (*N Am.*) (*a short break* (*e.g. between school classes*)) break, interlude, intermission, interval, pause, rest. **3** (*often pl.*) (*a secluded or secret place, a nook*) nook, retreat. **4** (*Anat.*) (*a depression or fold*) cavity, depression, fold, indentation.

reciprocal *a.* **1** (*acting, done or given in return*) mutual, reciprocative, requited, returned. ANTONYMS: unreciprocated. **2** (*inversely correspondent, complementary*) complementary, correlative, corresponding, equivalent, interdependent.

recite *v.t.* **1** (*to repeat aloud from memory, esp. before an audience*) declaim, deliver, give, quote, render, speak, tell. **2** (*to give details of*) chronicle, describe, detail, narrate, recount, relate, report. **3** (*to enumerate*) enumerate, itemize, list.

reckless *a.* **1** (*heedless of the consequences or danger*) dangerous, devil-may-care, foolhardy, hasty, ill-advised, imprudent, impulsive, incautious, injudicious, irresponsible, precipitate, rash, unwise, wild. ANTONYMS: cautious, responsible. **2** (*careless, heedless*) careless, hare-brained, heedless, inattentive, mindless, neglectful, negligent, regardless, thoughtless. ANTONYMS: careful, wary.

reckon *v.t.* **1** (*to add* (*up*), *calculate*) add, calculate, compute, count, enumerate, figure, number, sum up, tally, total, work out. **2** (*to regard* (*as*), *to consider* (*to be*)) account, appraise, consider, deem, esteem, estimate, evaluate, gauge, hold, judge, look upon, rate, regard. **3** (*to be of the opinion, to guess* (*that*)) calculate, guess, judge. **4** (*sl.*) (*to think highly of*) regard favourably, think highly of, value.
~*v.i.* **1** (*to compute, to calculate*) calculate, compute, work out. **2** (*to settle accounts* (*with*)) attend to, cope, deal, face, handle, look after, see to, settle accounts, take care of, treat. **3** (*to rely, to place dependence* (*upon*)) bank (on), calculate (on), count (on), depend (on), hope (for), lean (on), rely (on), take for granted, trust (in). **4** (*to suppose, to believe*) assume, believe, calculate, conjecture, expect, fancy, (*N Am., coll.*) guess, imagine, presume, suppose, surmise, think, venture.

recluse *n.* (*a person who lives retired from the world, a hermit*) anchoress, anchorite, ascetic, hermit, monk, nun.

recognize *v.t.* **1** (*to to recall the identity of*) identify, know, place, recall, recollect, remember. **2** (*to realize or perceive the nature of*) detect, identify, make out, notice, perceive, ratify, realize, see, spot, understand. ANTONYMS: ignore, overlook. **3** (*to acknowledge, to admit the truth of*) accept, acknowledge, admit, allow, concede, confess, grant, own. **4** (*to reward, to thank*) remunerate, reward, thank. **5** (*to show appreciation of*) acknowledge, appreciate, approve. **6** (*to give a sign of knowing* (*a person*)) acknowledge, greet, honour, salute.

recoil *v.i.* **1** (*to shrink back, as in fear or disgust*) baulk at, draw back, falter, flinch, quail, shrink, shy away, wince. **2** (*to start or spring back*) bounce back, jump back, spring back, start back. **3** (*to rebound*) react, rebound, ricochet. **4** (*to go wrong and harm the perpetrator*) backfire, blow up in one's face, boomerang, misfire. **5** ((*of a firearm*) *to be driven back when fired*) jerk, kick.

recollect *v.t.* (*to recall to memory, to remember*) call to mind, place, recall, remember, reminisce, summon up.

recommend *v.t.* **1** (*to commend to another's favour, esp. to represent as suitable for employment*) approve, back, commend, endorse, favour, (*coll.*) plug, praise, promote, push, second, support, vouch for. **2** (*to advise* (*a* *certain course of action etc.*)) advise, advocate, counsel, enjoin, exhort, guide, prescribe, propose, put forward, suggest, urge. **3** ((*of qualities etc.*) *to make acceptable or desirable*) make acceptable, make desirable, make interesting, make serviceable.

reconcile *v.t.* **1** (*to restore to friendship after an estrangement*) appease, conciliate, make peace with, make up, pacify, placate, propitiate, reunite. **2** (*to make content or submissive* (*to*)) accept, resign, submit, yield. ANTONYMS: oppose. **3** (*to make consistent or compatible* (*with*)) compose, harmonize, make consistent. **4** (*to settle* (*differences etc.*)) adjust, mend, patch, put to rights, rectify, resolve, settle, square.

reconnoitre *v.t.* (*to make a reconnaissance of*) (*sl.*) case, check out, explore, inspect, investigate, make a reconnaissance of, observe, patrol, (*coll.*) recce, scan, scout, scrutinize, spy out, survey, view.

record[1] *v.t.* **1** (*to write an account of, to set down permanent evidence of*) chronicle, document, enrol, enter, inscribe, log, minute, note, put down, register, report, set down, take down, transcribe, write down. **2** (*to transfer* (*sound, a programme etc.*) *by electronic means on to a storage medium for later reproduction*) cut, lay down, tape, video. **3** (*to indicate, to register*) indicate, read, register, show.

record[2] *n.* **1** (*a written or other permanent account of a fact, event etc.*) account, statement. **2** (*a report of proceedings*) annals, archive, chronicle, diary, document, entry, file, journal, log, memoir, memorandum, minute, register, report, transactions. **3** (*a thin plastic disc on to which sound is recorded*) album, disc, EP, forty-five, gramophone record, LP, (*sl.*) platter, recording, seventy-eight, single, vinyl. **4** (*an official report of proceedings, judgement etc.*) documentation, evidence, memorial, testimony, witness. **5** (*the past history of a person's career, achievements etc.*) background, career, curriculum vitae, CV, history, track record. **6** (*something that bears witness, testimony*) attestation, testimony. **7** (*a portrait or other memento of a person, event etc.*) memento, monument, portrait, souvenir.

recount *v.t.* (*to relate in detail, to narrate*) delineate, depict, describe, detail, enumerate, impart, narrate, portray, recite, rehearse, relate, repeat, report, tell.

recover *v.t.* **1** (*to regain, to win back*) get back, make good, recapture, reclaim, recoup, redeem, regain, repair, repossess, restore, take back, win back. ANTONYMS: lose. **2** (*to save* (*the reusable by-products of an industrial process*)) reclaim, recycle, rescue, salvage, save.

~*v.i.* (*to regain a former state, esp. after sickness, misfortune etc.*) bounce back, come round, convalesce, get better, get well, heal, improve, mend, pick up, pull through, rally, recuperate, revive. ANTONYMS: deteriorate, relapse.

recovery *n.* **1** (*the act of recovering or the state of having recovered*) advance, amelioration, betterment, gain, improvement, increase, rally, rehabilitation, restoration, revival, upturn. ANTONYMS: loss. **2** (*restoration to health after sickness etc.*) convalescence, cure, healing, improvement, mending, rally, recuperation, revival. ANTONYMS: relapse. **3** (*the retrieval of by-products from an industrial process*) reclamation, recycling, rescue, retrieval, salvage.

recreation *n.* **1** (*the act or process of renewing one's strength after toil*) enjoyment, entertainment, fun, play, pleasure, refreshment, relaxation, relief. **2** (*a pleasurable exercise or activity*) activity, diversion, exercise, hobby, pastime, pursuit, sport.

recruit *v.t.* **1** (*to enlist* (*people*) *to join the armed forces*) call up, conscript, draft, enlist, impress, levy, mobilize, muster, sign up. **2** (*to raise or increase the strength of* (*an army, crew etc.*) *by enlisting recruits*) raise, reinforce, strengthen. **3** (*to enrol* (*members*)) engage, enrol, induct, take on. ANTONYMS: dismiss, fire. **4** (*to replenish with fresh supplies*) furnish, renew, replenish, supply.

~*n.* **1** (*a serviceman or servicewoman newly enlisted*) conscript, greenhorn, (*sl.*) rookie. **2** (*a person who has newly joined a society etc.*) apprentice, beginner, convert, initiate, learner, novice, trainee. ANTONYMS: veteran.

rectify *v.t.* **1** (*to set right, to correct*) adjust, amend, correct, cure, emend, fix, improve, make good, mend, put right, redress, reform, regulate, remedy, repair, revise, right, set right, square, straighten. **2** (*to purify* (*spirit etc.*) *by repeated distillations*) distil, purify, refine, separate.

recuperate *v.i.* (*to recover from sickness, exhaustion etc.*) convalesce, get better, get well, heal, improve, mend, pick up, pull through, rally, recover, revive, survive. ANTONYMS: relapse.

red *a.* **1** (*of the colour of blood*) cardinal, carmine, cherry, coral, crimson, maroon, rose, ruby, scarlet, vermilion, wine. **2** ((*of hair*) *reddish-brown*) auburn, copper, ginger, reddish-brown, ruddy, russet, sandy, tawny. **3** (*flushed, esp. as a sign of anger or shame*) bloodshot, blooming, blushing, embarrassed, florid, flushed, inflamed, rosy, rubicund, suffused. ANTONYMS: pallid, white. **4** (*involving bloodshed or violence*) blood-soaked, bloodstained, bloody, gory, sanguine, violent. **5** (*revolutionary, anarchistic*) anarchistic, revolutionary. **6** (*coll. or derog.*) (*left-wing, communist*) communist, left-wing, socialist.

redeem *v.t.* **1** (*to buy back*) buy back, reclaim, recover, regain, repurchase, retrieve, win back. **2** (*to discharge* (*a mortgage*), *to buy off* (*an obligation etc.*)) buy off, clear, discharge, pay off, recover, repossess. **3** (*to exchange* (*tokens etc.*) *for goods or cash*) cash, change, exchange, trade in. **4** (*to rescue, to reclaim*) deliver, reclaim, rescue, save. **5** (*to atone for, to make amends for*) atone for, compensate for, defray, make amends for, make good, make up for, offset, outweigh, redress, save. **6** (*to recover from captivity by purchase*) deliver, emancipate, free, liberate, ransom, set free. **7** ((*of Christ*) *to deliver from sin and its penalty*) absolve, deliver, ransom. **8** (*to perform* (*a promise*)) abide by, acquit, adhere to, be faithful to, carry out, discharge, fulfil, hold to, keep, make good, perform, satisfy.

redolent *a.* **1** (*suggestive, reminding one* (*of*)) characteristic, evocative, remindful, reminiscent, suggestive. **2** (*fragrant*) aromatic, fragrant, perfumed, scented, sweet-smelling. **3** (*giving out a strong, esp. bad, smell*) odorous, reeking, smelly.

redoubtable *a.* **1** (*formidable*) awe-inspiring, awful, dreadful, fearful, fearsome, formidable, mighty, powerful, strong, terrible. **2** (*valiant*) courageous, doughty, indomitable, resolute, undaunted, valiant.

redress *v.t.* **1** (*to amend, to make reparation for*) amend, compensate for, make amends for, make up for, put right, recompense, remedy. **2** (*to set straight or right again*) adjust, amend, correct, even up, mend, put right, readjust, rectify, reform, regulate, remedy, repair, set right, set straight, square.
~*n.* **1** (*reparation*) amends, atonement, compensation, payment, recompense, reparation, restitution. **2** (*rectification*) aid, assistance, correction, cure, ease, help, justice, rectification, relief, remedy, satisfaction.

reduce *v.t.* **1** (*to make smaller or less in size, extent etc.*) abbreviate, abridge, curtail, cut, cut down, diminish, shorten, trim, truncate. **2** (*to convert from one form into another, esp. simpler, form*) break down, cancel out, convert. **3** (*to simplify so as to conform* (*to a formula, fundamental classification etc.*)) modify, simplify, systematize. **4** (*to bring down, to diminish*) bring down, degrade, demote, dilute, diminish, downgrade, humble, humiliate, impair, lessen, lower, minimize, moderate, take down a peg or two, tone down,

turn down, weaken, wind down. ANTONYMS: elevate, promote. **5** (*to lower the price of*) cheapen, cut, discount, lower, mark down, slash. ANTONYMS: raise. **6** (*to impoverish*) bankrupt, break, impoverish, pauperize, ruin. **7** (*to subdue, to conquer*) conquer, crush, master, overcome, overpower, quell, subdue, subjugate, vanquish.
~*v.i.* **1** (*to become smaller or less*) abate, contract, decrease, diminish. **2** (*to lose weight*) diet, lose weight, slim.

redundant *a.* **1** (*superfluous, unnecessary*) excessive, inessential, inordinate, superabundant, superfluous, surplus, unnecessary, unwanted. ANTONYMS: essential, necessary. **2** (*deprived of one's job as no longer necessary*) (*coll.*) on the dole, out of work, unemployed, with one's services no longer required. **3** (*using more words than are necessary*) circumlocutory, long-winded, padded, prolix, tautological, verbose, wordy. ANTONYMS: succinct, terse.

reek *v.i.* **1** (*to give off a strong disagreeable odour*) (*coll.*) pong, smell, stink. **2** (*to give a strong impression* (*of something offensive or undesirable*)) evoke, suggest, (*coll.*) whiff of. **3** (*to emit smoke or vapour*) fume, smoke, steam.
~*n.* **1** (*a stale or disagreeable odour*) effluvium, fetor, (*coll.*) niff, odour, (*coll.*) pong, smell, stench, stink. **2** (*vapour, fume*) exhalation, fumes, smoke, steam, vapour.

reel *v.i.* **1** (*to stagger, to sway*) falter, flounder, lurch, pitch, rock, roll, stagger, stumble, sway, totter, waver, wobble. **2** (*to whirl, to rock*) revolve, spin, swim, twirl, whirl.

refer *v.t.* **1** (*to assign* (*to a certain cause, place etc.*)) accredit, ascribe, assign, attribute, credit, impute, put down to, trace back. **2** (*to hand over* (*for consideration and decision*)) commit, consign, deliver, hand over, pass on, submit, transfer, turn over. **3** (*to direct* (*a person*) *for information, treatment etc.*) direct, guide, point, send.
~*v.i.* **1** (*to apply for information*) apply, consult, look up, turn to. **2** (*to appeal, to have recourse*) appeal, have recourse to, invoke. **3** (*to cite, to direct attention* (*to*)) allude (to), bring up, cite, make mention (of), mention, quote, speak (of), touch (on). **4** (*to have relation* (*to*)) apply, belong, concern, pertain, relate.

reference *n.* **1** (*the act of referring*) referral. **2** (*relation, correspondence*) applicability, bearing, concern, connection, consideration, correspondence, pertinence, regard, relation, relevance, respect. **3** (*allusion, directing of attention*) allusion, citation, direction, hint, insinuation, intimation, mention, note, quotation, remark, suggestion. **4** (*a testimonial, esp. one not seen by the person described within it*) certification, character, credentials, endorsement, good word, recommendation, testimonial.

refine *v.t.* **1** (*to clear from impurities, defects etc.*) clarify, cleanse, clear, decontaminate, distil, filter, process, purify, rarefy, sift. ANTONYMS: contaminate, pollute. **2** (*to educate, to cultivate the manners etc. of*) civilize, cultivate, educate, hone, improve, perfect, polish, sharpen, temper.

refined *a.* **1** (*freed from impurities*) clarified, clean, distilled, filtered, processed, pure, purified. ANTONYMS: impure. **2** (*highly cultivated, elegant*) civil, civilized, courteous, courtly, cultivated, cultured, dignified, elegant, genteel, gentlemanly, gracious, ladylike, noble, polished, polite, sophisticated, urbane, wellbred, well-mannered. ANTONYMS: inelegant, unrefined.

reflect *v.t.* **1** (*to turn or throw back* (*light, heat etc.*)) return, send back, throw back, turn back. **2** (*to reproduce exactly, to correspond in features*) copy, correspond to, echo, imitate, mirror, reproduce. **3** (*to show, to give an idea of*) bear out, bespeak, betray, bring to light, communicate, demonstrate, disclose, display, exemplify, exhibit, illustrate, indicate, lay bare, manifest, reveal, show, uncover. **4** (*to cast* (*honour, disgrace etc.*) *upon*) bring, cast, throw.

~*v.i.* (*to turn the thoughts back, to ponder*) cogitate, consider, contemplate, deliberate, evaluate, meditate, mull over, muse, ponder, ruminate, think, weigh, wonder.

reflection *n.* **1** (*rays of light, heat etc. or an image thrown back from a reflecting surface*) echo, image, likeness, profile, shadow. **2** (*continued thought, meditation*) cerebration, cogitation, consideration, contemplation, deliberation, meditation, musing, perusal, pondering, rumination, study, thinking, thought. **3** (*a thought or opinion resulting from deliberation*) comment, feeling, idea, impression, observation, opinion, thought, view. **4** (*discredit, reproach* (*cast upon a person etc.*)) aspersion, censure, criticism, derogation, discredit, imputation, reproach, slur.

reform *v.t.* **1** (*to change from worse to better by removing faults*) better, correct, rectify, straighten out. **2** (*to improve, to remedy*) ameliorate, amend, better, cure, emend, improve, mend, rebuild, redress, remedy, renovate, reorganize, repair, restore, revise.

~*v.i.* (*to amend one's habits, conduct etc.*) clean

up one's act, go straight, pull up one's socks, shape up, turn over a new leaf.

~*n.* **1** (*the act of reforming, esp. the correction of political abuses*) correction, emendation, rectification. **2** (*an alteration for the better, an improvement*) amelioration, amendment, betterment, change, improvement, progress. ANTONYMS: corruption.

refrain *v.i.* (*to abstain* (*from an act or doing*)) abstain, avoid, cease, desist, discontinue, do without, eschew, forbear, forgo, give up, (*coll.*) kick, leave off, renounce, stop. ANTONYMS: indulge.

~†*v.t.* (*to restrain* (*oneself, one's tears etc.*)) curb, hold back, restrain.

refresh *v.t.* **1** (*to make fresh again, to reinvigorate*) reanimate, reinvigorate, rejuvenate, resuscitate. **2** (*to revive after depression, fatigue etc.*) brace, cheer, enliven, exhilarate, fortify, inspire, inspirit, restore, revive. **3** (*to stimulate* (*one's memory*)) arouse, awaken, brush up, freshen up, jog, prod, prompt, stimulate. **4** (*to repair, to renovate*) fix up, overhaul, recondition, refurbish, renew, renovate, repair, restore. **5** (*to replenish*) fill up, refill, reload, replenish, restock, top up.

refuge *n.* **1** (*shelter from danger or distress*) protection, security, shelter. **2** (*a retreat, a sanctuary*) asylum, bolt-hole, harbour, haven, hideaway, hideout, retreat, safe house, sanctuary, stronghold. **3** (*an expedient, a subterfuge*) dodge, evasion, excuse, expedient, pretext, resort, ruse, stratagem, subterfuge, trick.

refund[1] *v.t.* (*to pay back, to repay*) give back, make good, pay back, recompense, reimburse, repay, restore, return. ANTONYMS: withhold.

refund[2] *n.* **1** (*an act of refunding money*) reimbursement, repayment. **2** (*an amount refunded*) rebate, repayment, return.

refuse[1] *v.t.* **1** (*to decline to accept or consent to*) decline, pass by, rebuff, repudiate, withhold. ANTONYMS: accept, agree. **2** (*to deny the request of*) deny, disallow, reject, repel, spurn, turn down.

refuse[2] *n.* (*something which is rejected as waste or useless matter*) debris, detritus, dregs, dross, dust, garbage, junk, litter, rubbish, scraps, trash, waste.

regain *v.t.* **1** (*to recover possession of*) get back, recapture, recoup, recover, repossess, retake, retrieve, take back, win back. ANTONYMS: lose. **2** (*to reach again*) get back to, reach again, reattain, return to.

regal *a.* (*relating to or fit for a king or queen*)

august, grand, imperial, kingly, lordly, majestic, noble, princely, proud, queenly, royal, sovereign, stately, superior.

regard *v.t.* **1** (*to view in a specified way, to consider* (*as*)) believe, consider, contemplate, hold, look upon, perceive, view. **2** (*to look at, to notice*) behold, check out, (*sl.*) clock, eye, gaze at, look at, mark, notice, observe, remark, scrutinize, view, watch. ANTONYMS: ignore. **3** (*to pay honour to, to esteem*) deem, esteem, honour, rate, value. **4** (*to relate to, to concern*) affect, apply to, bear upon, concern, interest, involve, pertain to, refer to, relate to. **5** (*to pay attention to, to take into account*) attend, heed, listen to, mind, note, respect, take into account.

~*n.* **1** (*observant attention, care*) attention, care, consideration, heed, interest, mind, notice. **2** (*kindly or respectful feeling*) admiration, affection, approval, care, concern, consideration, deference, esteem, fondness, honour, liking, love, note, reputation, repute, respect, reverence, store, sympathy, thought. ANTONYMS: contempt. **3** (*a look, a gaze*) gaze, glance, look, scrutiny, stare. **4** (*reference*) application, association, bearing, concern, connection, link, pertinence, reference, relation, relevance. **5** (*relation*) aspect, detail, feature, item, matter, particular, point, relation, respect.

regardless *a.* (*careless, negligent* (*of*)) careless, disregarding, heedless, inattentive, inconsiderate, indifferent, neglectful, negligent, rash, reckless, remiss, thoughtless, unconcerned, unmindful. ANTONYMS: heedful, mindful.

~*adv.* (*without concern for the consequences, drawbacks etc.*) anyhow, anyway, come what may, despite everything, for all that, in any case, in any event, in spite of everything, nevertheless, no matter what, nonetheless, notwithstanding.

regime *n.* (*a prevailing system of government or management*) administration, establishment, government, leadership, management, reign, rule, system.

region *n.* **1** (*a tract of land, sea etc. of large but indefinite extent*) area, expanse, locality, neighbourhood, part, patch, place, range, spot, territory, tract, vicinity. **2** (*a part of the world or the physical or spiritual universe*) country, land, nation, state. **3** (*a district, a realm*) district, domain, dominion, field, orbit, province, realm, scope, sphere, world. **4** (*a civil division of a town, district or country*) area, bailiwick, department, district, division, parish, precinct, quarter, sector, ward, zone.

register *n.* **1** (*an official list of names, facts etc.,*

as of births, marriages etc.*) catalogue, index, inventory, list, rota, tally. **2** (*an official written record*) memorandum, record. **3** (*a book or other document in which such a record is kept*) annals, archives, chronicle, daybook, diary, file, journal, ledger, log, roll, roster, schedule. **4** (*a cash register*) cash register, checkout, till. **5** (*the range or compass of a voice or instrument*) compass, range, spread.

~*v.t.* **1** (*to enter or cause to be entered in a register*) catalogue, enlist, enrol, enter, inscribe, list, log, sign up. **2** (*to record or note as if in a register*) chronicle, jot down, note, record, set down, take down. **3** (*to express* (*an emotion*) *facially or by one's bearing*) bespeak, betray, display, divulge, exhibit, express, manifest, reflect, reveal, say, show. **4** ((*of an instrument*) *to indicate*) indicate, mark, measure, point to, read, record, represent, specify.

~*v.i.* **1** (*to enter one's name in or as in a register*) apply, enlist, poll, sign up. **2** (*to make an impression*) become apparent, come home, dawn on, get through, have an effect, impress, make an impression, sink in, tell.

regret *n.* **1** (*distress or sorrow for a disappointment or loss*) bitterness, disappointment, distress, lamentation, ruefulness, sorrow. **2** (*grief or remorse for a wrongdoing or omission*) compunction, conscience, contrition, grief, guilt, penitence, qualm, regretfulness, remorse, repentance, self-reproach. ANTONYMS: contentment, satisfaction.

~*v.t.* (*to be distressed for* (*a disappointment, loss etc.*)) bemoan, bewail, cry over, deplore, deprecate, grieve, lament, miss, mourn, repent, rue, sorrow, weep over. ANTONYMS: rejoice.

regular *a.* **1** (*methodical; conforming to rule*) consistent, dependable, efficient, methodical, systematic. ANTONYMS: inconsistent, irregular. **2** (*done or happening in an orderly or habitual manner*) accustomed, common, commonplace, constant, customary, established, everyday, habitual, normal, orderly, ordinary, periodic, rhythmic, routine, set, steady, typical, uniform, usual, wonted. ANTONYMS: casual, disorderly, erratic. **3** (*symmetrical, harmonious*) balanced, even, flat, harmonious, level, normal, plane, smooth, straight, symmetrical, unvarying. **4** (*conforming to custom, etiquette etc.*) approved, bona fide, classic, comfortable, conventional, correct, established, formal, official, orthodox, prevailing, proper, sanctioned, standard, time-honoured, traditional. ANTONYMS: unconventional. **5** (*duly authorized*) authorized, qualified. **6** (*complete, unmistakable*) absolute, complete, out-and-out, thorough, unmistakable, unmitigated, utter.

regulate *v.t.* **1** (*to adjust or control by rule*) adjust, administer, balance, control, direct, govern, handle, maintain, manage, modify, monitor, order, organize, oversee, run, settle, superintend, supervise, tune. **2** (*to subject to restrictions*) moderate, modulate, restrain, restrict.

regulation *n.* **1** (*the act of regulating*) adjustment, administration, arrangement, balance, control, direction, government, maintenance, management, modification, modulation, organization, supervision, tuning. **2** (*a prescribed order or direction*) commandment, decree, dictate, direction, directive, edict, law, order, ordinance, precept, procedure, requirement, rule, standing order, statute.
~*a.* **1** (*prescribed by regulation*) mandatory, obligatory, prescribed, required. **2** (*formal, accepted*) accepted, formal, normal, official, standard. **3** (*ordinary, usual*) customary, ordinary, orthodox, typical, usual. ANTONYMS: unorthodox.

rehearse *v.t.* **1** (*to practise* (*a play, musical performance etc.*) *before public performance*) act, drill, go over, practise, prepare, ready, recite, run through. **2** (*to train for a public performance by rehearsal*) study, train. **3** (*to repeat, to recite*) go over, recite, repeat. **4** (*to relate, to enumerate*) delineate, depict, describe, detail, enumerate, go over, list, narrate, recapitulate, recite, recount, relate, report, review, run through, spell out, tell.

reign *n.* **1** (*the period during which a sovereign reigns*) monarchy, regime, rule. **2** (*supreme power, sovereignty*) ascendancy, dominion, empire, hegemony, leadership, power, sovereignty. **3** (*rule, influence*) command, control, direction, domination, influence, jurisdiction, mastery, rule, sway.
~*v.i.* **1** (*to exercise sovereign authority*) administer, command, control, direct, govern, hold sway, influence, lead, rule. **2** (*to predominate, to prevail*) hold sway, obtain, predominate, prevail. ANTONYMS: submit.

rein *n.* **1** (*a long narrow strip, usu. of leather, attached at each end to a bit for guiding and controlling a horse*) bridle, harness. **2** (*a means of restraint*) brake, check, constraint, control, curb, harness, hold, limitation, restraint, restriction.
~*v.t.* (*to curb, to restrain*) bridle, check, control, curb, govern, halt, hold, hold back, limit, pull back, restrain, restrict, slow. ANTONYMS: indulge.

reinforce *v.t.* **1** (*to add new strength or support to*) emphasize, increase, stiffen, strengthen, stress, supplement, support, toughen, underline. ANTONYMS: undermine. **2** (*to strengthen or*

support with additional troops, ships etc.*) augment, fortify, strengthen, support. **3** (*to strengthen by adding to the size, thickness etc.*) bolster, brace, buttress, prop, shore up. ANTONYMS: weaken.

reject[1] *v.t.* **1** (*to put aside, to discard*) cast off, discard, eliminate, exclude, jettison, put aside. **2** (*to refuse to accept, grant etc.*) decline, deny, disallow, refuse. ANTONYMS: accept, permit. **3** (*to rebuff* (*a person*)) drop, jilt, rebuff, renounce, repudiate, repulse, shun, spurn, turn down, veto. **4** (*to repel, to vomit*) cast up, repel, vomit.

reject[2] *n.* (*someone who or something which has been rejected*) cast-off, discard, failure, second.

rejoice *v.i.* **1** (*to delight or exult* (*in*)) delight, exult, glory, triumph. ANTONYMS: lament, mourn. **2** (*to express joy, to celebrate*) celebrate, express joy, make merry, revel.

relapse *v.i.* **1** (*to fall or slip back* (*into a former bad state or practice*)) backslide, decline, degenerate, fail, fall, go back, lapse, regress, retreat, retrogress, revert, slip back, weaken. **2** (*to become ill again after partial recovery*) deteriorate, fade, fail, sicken, weaken, worsen. ANTONYMS: improve, recover.
~*n.* (*a falling back into a former bad state, esp. in a patient's state of health after partial recovery*) backsliding, deterioration, lapse, regression, return, reversion, setback, weakening, worsening. ANTONYMS: recovery.

relate *v.t.* **1** (*to tell, to narrate*) chronicle, communicate, describe, detail, divulge, impart, make known, narrate, present, recite, recount, rehearse, report, reveal, set forth, tell. ANTONYMS: suppress. **2** (*to bring into relation or connection* (*with*)) ally, associate, connect, coordinate, correlate, couple, join, link, relate, tie. ANTONYMS: disconnect, divorce. **3** (*to ascribe to as source or cause*) ascribe, attribute, show.
~*v.i.* (*to have relation, to refer* (*to*)) appertain (to), apply (to), bear (upon), concern, pertain (to), refer (to).

relation *n.* **1** (*the condition of being related or connected*) affiliation, affinity, association, connection, relationship. **2** (*the way in which a thing or person is conceived in regard to another, as similarity, difference etc.*) contrast, correspondence, dependence, difference, independence, similarity. **3** (*connection by blood or marriage, kinship*) blood tie, consanguinity, kindred, kinship. **4** (*a person so connected, a relative*) kin, kinsman, kinswoman, member of one's family, relative. **5** (*respect, reference*) application, bearing, bond, comparison, connection, correlation, link, reference, regard, respect, tie-in. **6** (*pl.*) (*dealings, affairs* (*with*)) affairs, business, dealings. **7** (*a narrative, a story*) account, delineation, description, narration, portrayal, recapitulation, recital, recitation, recounting, report, story, tale.

relative *a.* **1** (*depending on relation to something else*) contingent, dependent. **2** (*considered or being in relation to something else*) correlative, reciprocal. **3** (*proportionate to something else*) comparable, comparative, proportionate. **4** (*relevant, closely related* (*to*)) applicable, apposite, appropriate, appurtenant, apropos, germane, pertinent, relevant. **5** (*having mutual relation, corresponding*) affiliated, allied, analogous, associated, connected, corresponding, related, respective.
~*n.* (*a person connected by blood or marriage, a relation*) family, kin, kinsman, kinswoman, member of one's family, relation.

relax *v.i.* **1** (*to become less tense or severe*) ease, mellow, soften. ANTONYMS: tense, tighten. **2** (*to take relaxation*) calm down, (*esp. N Am., coll.*) chill out, (*sl.*) cool it, laze, (*coll.*) let one's hair down, loosen up, rest, slow down, take it easy, unbend, unwind. ANTONYMS: work. **3** (*to become less energetic*) abate, curb, decrease, diminish, ease, ebb, lessen, let up, loosen, lower, mitigate, moderate, modify, modulate, reduce, relieve, slacken, temper, tone down, weaken. ANTONYMS: intensify.

release *v.t.* **1** (*to set free from restraint or confinement*) deliver, discharge, emancipate, extricate, free, let go, let out, liberate, loose, set free, turn loose, unchain, undo, unfasten, unfetter, unloose, untie. ANTONYMS: imprison, incarcerate. **2** (*to free from obligation or penalty*) absolve, acquit, clear, dispense, excuse, exempt, exonerate, let go, let off. **3** (*to issue* (*a recording, film etc.*) *for general sale, exhibition etc.*) issue, publish, put out. **4** (*to make* (*information, news etc.*) *public*) break, circulate, disseminate, distribute, make known, make public, present. ANTONYMS: suppress. **5** (*Law*) (*to surrender, to remit* (*a right, claim etc.*)) quit, remit, surrender, waive.
~*n.* **1** (*liberation from restraint, pain etc.*) acquittal, deliverance, delivery, discharge, emancipation, freedom, liberation, liberty, relief, remission. ANTONYMS: imprisonment, incarceration. **2** (*a discharge from liability, responsibility etc.*) absolution, acquittal, dispensation, exemption, exoneration, (*coll.*) let-off. **3** (*anything newly issued for sale or to the public*) announcement, issue, proclamation, publication, report, story.

relent *v.i.* **1** (*to give way to compassion*) acquiesce, bend, capitulate, comply, compromise, forbear, give in, give way, melt, soften,

succumb, unbend, yield. ANTONYMS: harden, resist. **2** (*to let up, to slacken*) die down, drop, ease, fall, let up, relax, slacken, slow, weaken. ANTONYMS: increase, strengthen.

relentless *a.* **1** (*unyielding, inexorable*) adamant, determined, dogged, implacable, inexorable, inflexible, intransigent, obdurate, obstinate, persevering, rigid, stiff, unbending, uncompromising, undeviating, unforgiving, unrelenting, unstoppable, unswerving, unyielding. ANTONYMS: submissive, yielding. **2** (*merciless, pitiless*) cruel, fierce, grim, hard, harsh, merciless, pitiless, remorseless, ruthless, unmerciful, unsparing. ANTONYMS: compassionate, merciful. **3** (*incessant, unremitting*) ceaseless, continual, continuous, incessant, non-stop, perpetual, persistent, punishing, steady, sustained, unabated, unbroken, unceasing, unfailing, unfaltering, unflagging, unrelenting, unrelieved, unremitting, unstoppable.

relevant *a.* (*bearing on the matter in hand, apposite*) admissible, akin, allied, applicable, apposite, appurtenant, apt, associated, fitting, germane, material, pertinent, proper, related, relative, significant, suited, to the point. ANTONYMS: immaterial, irrelevant.

reliable *a.* **1** (*that may be relied on*) certain, dependable, infallible, predictable, regular, safe, secure, sound, stable, sure, unfailing. ANTONYMS: unreliable. **2** (*trustworthy*) conscientious, faithful, honest, punctilious, reputable, responsible, staunch, trustworthy, trusty, upright. ANTONYMS: untrustworthy.

relic *n.* **1** (*any ancient object of historical interest*) artefact, find, object. **2** (*a keepsake, a memento*) heirloom, keepsake, memento, memorial, remembrance, souvenir, token. **3** (*usu. pl.*) (*some part or thing remaining after the loss or decay of the rest*) fragment, remnant, scrap, survival, trace, vestige.

relief *n.* **1** (*alleviation of pain, discomfort etc.*) abatement, alleviation, assuagement, balm, comfort, cure, deliverance, ease, easement, liberation, mitigation, palliation, release, remedy, solace. ANTONYMS: aggravation. **2** (*anything that breaks monotony or relaxes tension*) break, (*coll.*) breather, diversion, (*coll.*) let-up, lull, refreshment, relaxation, remission, respite, rest. **3** (*assistance given to people in need or distress*) aid, assistance, comfort, help, succour, support, sustenance. **4** (*a person acting as a substitute*) locum, replacement, stand-in, substitute, surrogate.

relieve *v.t.* **1** (*to alleviate, to lighten*) abate, allay, alleviate, appease, assuage, calm, comfort, diminish, dull, ease, lessen, lighten, mitigate, mollify, reduce, relax, salve, soften, solace, soothe. ANTONYMS: aggravate, exacerbate. **2** (*to provide aid to*) aid, assist, help, succour, support, sustain. **3** (*to release from a post, responsibility etc., esp. to take turn on guard or at a post*) stand in for, substitute, take over from, take the place of. **4** (*to remove a burden or responsibility from*) deliver, disburden, discharge, disembarrass, disencumber, exempt, free, liberate, release, rescue, unburden. **5** (*to break the monotony, dullness etc. of*) break, brighten, interrupt, slacken, vary. **6** (*coll.*) (*to take or steal from*) deprive, steal from, take from. **7** (*to bring out or make conspicuous by contrast*) be a foil to, contrast, highlight.

religious *a.* **1** (*of or relating to religion*) devotional, divine, doctrinal, holy, sacred, scriptural, spiritual, theological. ANTONYMS: irreligious, secular. **2** (*pious, devout*) churchgoing, devout, faithful, God-fearing, godly, good, holy, pious, pure, reverent, righteous, saintly. ANTONYMS: godless, impious. **3** (*conscientious, strict*) conscientious, exact, faithful, fastidious, meticulous, precise, punctilious, rigid, rigorous, scrupulous, strict, undeviating, unerring, unswerving. ANTONYMS: lax.

relish *n.* **1** (*great enjoyment, gusto*) appetite, appreciation, enjoyment, fancy, fondness, gusto, liking, love, partiality, penchant, pleasure, predilection, preference, stomach, taste, zest. ANTONYMS: aversion, distaste. **2** (*pleasing anticipation*) anticipation, avidity, eagerness. **3** (*something taken with food to give a flavour, a condiment*) appetizer, condiment, flavouring, sauce, seasoning. **4** (*the effect of anything on the palate, distinctive flavour*) flavour, piquancy, savour, spice, tang, taste. **5** (*a slight flavouring, a trace (of)*) flavouring, smack, trace.
~*v.t.* **1** (*to be gratified by, to enjoy*) delight in, enjoy, savour. **2** (*to look forward to with pleasure*) anticipate, get excited about, look forward to. **3** (*to partake of with pleasure, to like*) appreciate, fancy, like, luxuriate in, prefer, revel in. ANTONYMS: dislike. **4** (*to give agreeable flavour to*) flavour, season.

reluctant *a.* (*unwilling, disinclined (to)*) antagonistic, averse, backward, cautious, chary, circumspect, disinclined, grudging, hesitant, indisposed, loath, recalcitrant, slow, unenthusiastic, unwilling, wary. ANTONYMS: eager, willing.

rely *v.i.* (*to trust or depend (on or upon) with confidence*) bank (on), bet (on), count (on), depend (on), lean (on), reckon (on), swear (by), trust (in). ANTONYMS: distrust (in).

remain *v.i.* **1** (*to stay behind or be left after use, separation etc.*) linger, stay, tarry, wait. ANTONYMS: depart, go. **2** (*to survive*) endure, stand, survive. **3** (*to continue in a place or state*) carry on, continue, go on, persist. **4** (*to last, to endure*) abide, cling, continue, dwell, endure, last, persevere, prevail.

remains *n.pl.* **1** (*that which remains behind*) balance, leavings, remainder, remnants, residue, rest. **2** (*ruins, relics*) crumbs, debris, detritus, dregs, fragments, pieces, relics, ruins, scraps, traces, vestiges. **3** (*a dead body, a corpse*) body, cadaver, carcass, corpse.

remark *v.t.* **1** (*to comment (that)*) assert, comment, declare, mention, observe, reflect, say, state, utter. **2** (*to observe with particular attention*) espy, heed, look at, make out, mark, note, notice, observe, perceive, regard, see, take note of.
~*n.* (*an observation, a comment*) assertion, attention, comment, declaration, heed, mention, notice, observation, opinion, reflection, regard, statement, thought, utterance, word.

remarkable *a.* **1** (*worthy of special observation or notice*) astounding, conspicuous, distinguished, famous, impressive, marvellous, miraculous, notable, noteworthy, outstanding, phenomenal, pre-eminent, prominent, signal, significant, singular, special, uncommon, unique, wonderful. ANTONYMS: commonplace. **2** (*unusual, extraordinary*) bizarre, curious, extraordinary, odd, peculiar, rare, strange, striking, surprising, unusual, weird. ANTONYMS: unexceptional.

remedy *n.* **1** (*something which cures a disease*) antidote, cure, nostrum, panacea, restorative. **2** (*medicine, healing treatment*) drug, medicament, medication, medicine, prescription, †specific, therapy, treatment. **3** (*something which serves to remove or counteract any evil*) answer, antidote, corrective, countermeasure, panacea, relief, solution. **4** (*redress, reparation*) amends, compensation, redress, reparation.
~*v.t.* **1** (*to cure, to heal*) alleviate, assuage, control, cure, ease, heal, help, mitigate, palliate, relieve, restore, soothe, treat. ANTONYMS: aggravate. **2** (*to repair, to rectify*) ameliorate, correct, fix, improve, mend, put right, rectify, redress, reform, relieve, set to rights, solve, straighten out.

remember *v.t.* **1** (*to keep in mind, not to forget*) bear in mind, keep in mind, retain. ANTONYMS: forget. **2** (*to recall to mind*) call to mind, look back on, recall, recognize, reminisce, summon up. **3** (*to hold in the memory, to know by heart*) have, know, memorize. **4** (*to keep in mind with *gratitude, respect etc.*) cherish, honour, revere. **5** (*to commemorate* (*e.g. the dead*)) commemorate, honour, memorialize, pay tribute to, recognize.

remind *v.t.* **1** (*to put in mind* (*of*)) bring to mind, call to mind, call up, put in mind. **2** (*to cause to remember* (*to do etc.*)) cue, jog one's memory, prompt, refresh one's mind.

reminiscence *n.* **1** (*the act or power of remembering or recalling past knowledge*) recollection, reflection, remembrance, retrospection, review. **2** (*an account of a past event, experience etc.*) anecdote, memory, retrospective. **3** (*a collection of personal recollections of past events etc.*) biography, memoir.

remnant *n.* **1** (*that which is left after a larger part has been separated, used or destroyed*) balance, butt, end, leftovers, relic, remains, residue, rest, rump, stub. **2** (*a fragment, a surviving trace*) bit, fragment, oddment, piece, scrap, shred, trace, vestige.

remorse *n.* **1** (*the pain caused by a sense of guilt or bitter regret*) anguish, anxiety, bitterness, compassion, contrition, grief, guilt, humiliation, mortification, penitence, pity, regret, repentance, ruefulness, self-reproach, shame, sorrow, woe. ANTONYMS: satisfaction. **2** (*compunction, reluctance to commit a wrong*) compunction, hesitation, qualm, reluctance.

remorseless *a.* **1** (*without compassion, cruel*) callous, cruel, hard, hard-hearted, harsh, implacable, inhumane, merciless, pitiless, ruthless, savage, stony-hearted, uncompassionate, unforgiving, unmerciful. ANTONYMS: compassionate, merciful. **2** (*unrelenting*) inexorable, relentless, unrelenting, unremitting, unstoppable.

remote *a.* **1** (*distant in time or space*) distant, faraway, far off. ANTONYMS: nearby, neighbouring. **2** (*far away from a centre of population, isolated*) God-forsaken, inaccessible, isolated, lonely, outlying, out of the way, removed, secluded, sequestered. **3** (*not closely connected*) alien, extraneous, extrinsic, foreign, immaterial, inappropriate, irrelevant, obscure, outside, removed, subtle, unconnected, unfamiliar, unrelated, unusual. ANTONYMS: related, relevant. **4** (*removed in likeness or relation*) different, distinct, removed, separated. **5** (*usu. superl.*) (*slight, inconsiderable*) doubtful, dubious, faint, implausible, inconsiderable, insignificant, least, meagre, negligible, outside, poor, slender, slight, slim, small, unlikely. ANTONYMS: good, strong. **6** ((*of a person*) *aloof, cold*) abstracted, aloof, cold, detached, distant, faraway, indifferent, introspective, introverted, removed, reserved,

stand-offish, unapproachable, uncommunicative, uninterested, uninvolved, withdrawn. ANTONYMS: friendly, sociable.

removal *n.* **1** (*the act of removing or displacing*) dislodgement, displacement, ejection, expulsion, extraction, purging, stripping, subtraction, uprooting, withdrawal. **2** (*change of place or site*) departure, move, relocation, transfer, translocation. **3** (*dismissal*) deposition, discharge, dismissal, (*coll.*) sack. **4** (*murder*) assassination, elimination, eradication, execution, extermination, killing, liquidation, murder, slaughter, (*sl.*) wasting.

remove *v.t.* **1** (*to move or take from a place or position*) amputate, carry off, cast off, detach, doff, extract, take away. ANTONYMS: put back, replace. **2** (*to move to another place*) dislodge, displace, move, shift, translocate. **3** (*to take away, to get rid of*) abolish, delete, eject, erase, excise, expel, expunge, get rid of, obliterate, strike out, take away. **4** (*to transfer to another post or office*) move, transfer, transport. **5** (*to dismiss*) depose, dismiss, displace, (*coll.*) fire, oust, purge, relegate, (*coll.*) sack, shed, throw out, unseat. ANTONYMS: appoint, install. **6** (*to kill, to murder*) assassinate, (*coll.*) bump off, dispose of, (*coll.*) do away with, (*sl.*) do in, eliminate, execute, kill, liquidate, murder, (*sl.*) take out, (*sl.*) wipe out.

~*v.i.* (*to go away* (*from*), *esp. to change one's place or abode*) depart, go, leave, move, quit, shift, transfer, vacate.

remuneration *n.* (*payment for a service*) compensation, consideration, earnings, emolument, fee, income, indemnity, payment, profit, recompense, redress, reimbursement, reparation, repayment, restitution, return, reward, salary, stipend, wages.

render *v.t.* **1** (*to make, to cause to be*) cause, make, produce. **2** (*to give, to furnish*) bestow, contribute, deliver, furnish, give, hand out, make available, pay. ANTONYMS: withhold. **3** (*to give in return*) exchange, give, return, swap, trade. **4** (*to pay or give back*) give back, make restitution, pay back, repay, restore, return. **5** (*to present, to submit*) hand in, offer, present, proffer, provide, show, submit, supply, tender, turn over, yield. **6** (*to express, to represent*) act, construe, create, decipher, depict, do, execute, explain, express, give, interpret, perform, picture, play, portray, present, put, reproduce, transcribe, translate. **7** (*to melt and clarify* (*fat*)) boil down, clarify, extract, melt. **8** (*to give up, to surrender*) cede, deliver, give, give up, hand over, relinquish, resign, surrender, turn over, yield.

rendition *n.* **1** (*surrender, giving up*) giving up, surrender. **2** (*translation, interpretation*) construction, explanation, interpretation, reading, transcription, translation, version. **3** (*performance, rendering (of music etc.*)) arrangement, delivery, depiction, execution, performance, portrayal, presentation, reading, rendering, version.

renegade *n.* **1** (*a deserter*) deserter, mutineer, runaway. **2** (*a turncoat*) defector, dissident, traitor, turncoat. **3** (*a rebel, an outlaw*) fugitive, outlaw, rebel. **4** (*an apostate*) apostate, heretic.
~*a.* **1** (*having deserted or turned against a cause, faith etc.*) disloyal, dissident, perfidious, traitorous, treacherous, unfaithful. **2** (*rebellious*) mutinous, rebel, rebellious.

renew *v.t.* **1** (*to make new again or as good as new*) refresh, renovate, restore. **2** (*to restore to the original or a sound condition*) do over, fix up, mend, modernize, overhaul, recondition, re-establish, refit, refurbish, repair, restore, revamp. **3** (*to make fresh or vigorous again*) reanimate, regenerate, reinvigorate, rejuvenate, resuscitate, revitalize, revivify, transform. **4** (*to replenish*) fill up, refill, replace, replenish, restock. **5** (*to make, say etc. over again*) begin again, reaffirm, recommence, recreate, redo, reiterate, reopen, repeat, restart, resume. **6** (*to grant or be granted a further period of validity or effectiveness of (a lease, licence etc.*)) continue, extend, prolong.

renounce *v.t.* **1** (*to surrender or give up (a claim, right etc.), esp. by formal declaration*) abdicate, abjure, abnegate, cede, decline, discard, give up, relinquish, resign, surrender, waive, yield. ANTONYMS: retain. **2** (*to declare against, to reject formally*) cast off, deny, disclaim, disown, reject, repudiate, spurn, throw off. ANTONYMS: acknowledge. **3** (*to give up, to withdraw from*) abandon, abstain from, eschew, forgo, forsake, forswear, give up, leave off, quit, (*coll.*) swear off, withdraw from.

renown *n.* (*exalted reputation, fame*) acclaim, celebrity, distinction, eminence, esteem, fame, glory, honour, illustriousness, lustre, mark, note, prestige, prominence, reputation, repute, stardom. ANTONYMS: notoriety.

repair *v.t.* **1** (*to restore to a sound state after dilapidation or wear*) fix, mend, restore. ANTONYMS: damage, ruin. **2** (*to make good the damaged or dilapidated parts of*) make good, mend, patch, renew, renovate. **3** (*to remedy, to set right*) compensate for, correct, make amends, make up for, put right, rectify, redress, remedy, set right.
~*n.* **1** (*restoration to a sound state*) adjustment, improvement, overhaul, renewal, renovation, restoration, service. **2** (*a part that has been*

mended or repaired*) darn, mend, patch. **3** (*good or comparative condition*) condition, fettle, form, (*coll.*) nick, shape, state.

repay *v.t.* **1** (*to pay back, to refund*) pay back, refund, reimburse. **2** (*to deal (a blow etc.) in retaliation or recompense*) avenge, deal, even the score with, get back at, get even with, hit back, reciprocate, retaliate, return, revenge, reward. **3** (*to pay (a creditor etc.*)) pay, remunerate, settle up with, square. **4** (*to make recompense for, to requite*) compensate, make restitution, recompense, requite, restore.

repeal *v.t.* (*to revoke, to annul (a law etc.*)) abolish, abrogate, annul, cancel, countermand, invalidate, nullify, obviate, overrule, recall, rescind, reverse, revoke, set aside, void, withdraw. ANTONYMS: confirm, ratify.
~*n.* (*abrogation, annulment*) abolition, abrogation, annulment, cancellation, invalidation, nullification, rescinding, rescission, reversal, revocation, withdrawal.

repeat *v.t.* **1** (*to do or say over again*) recapitulate, redo, retell. **2** (*to reiterate*) emphasize, reiterate, restate. **3** (*to recite from memory, to rehearse*) quote, recite, rehearse. **4** (*to reproduce, to imitate*) copy, duplicate, echo, imitate, replicate, reproduce.
~*n.* **1** (*the act of repeating, repetition*) encore, recapitulation, reiteration, repetition, replay, reprise, reproduction, rerun, reshowing. **2** (*something repeated*) copy, duplicate, echo, replica, reproduction.

repel *v.t.* **1** (*to drive or force back*) drive back, force back. **2** (*to ward off, to keep at a distance*) beat off, confront, decline, drive off, fend off, fight, hold off, oppose, parry, put to flight, rebuff, refuse, reject, repulse, resist, spurn, ward off, withstand. ANTONYMS: welcome. **3** (*to produce aversion or disgust in*) disgust, give one the creeps, nauseate, offend, revolt, sicken, turn one's stomach. ANTONYMS: delight, please.

repent *v.i.* (*to feel sorrow for something done or left undone*) atone, be contrite, bemoan, be penitent, deplore, feel contrition, feel remorse, lament, regret, relent, reproach oneself, rue, show penitence, sorrow.

repetition *n.* **1** (*the act of repeating, reiteration*) duplication, recapitulation, recurrence, reiteration, replication, restatement. **2** (*recital from memory*) recital, rehearsal, reprise. **3** (*a copy, a reproduction*) copy, duplicate, repeat, replica, reproduction.

replace *v.t.* **1** (*to put back again in place*) put back, reinstate, restore, return. ANTONYMS: remove. **2** (*to take the place of, to succeed*)

replete 559 repress

substitute, succeed, supplant, take the place of. **3** (*to supersede, to displace*) displace, oust, supersede.

replete *a.* **1** (*abundantly supplied or stocked* (*with*)) abundant, brimming, bursting, charged, filled, jam-packed, loaded, overflowing, packed, teeming, well-provided, well-stocked, well-supplied. ANTONYMS: bare, empty. **2** (*filled to excess, gorged* (*with*)) crammed, full up, glutted, gorged, jammed, sated, satiated, stuffed. ANTONYMS: hungry, starving.

reply *v.i.* (*to answer, to respond*) acknowledge, answer, counter, react, reciprocate, rejoin, respond, riposte, write back. ANTONYMS: ask.
~*n.* (*that which is said or done in answer*) acknowledgement, answer, (*sl.*) comeback, counter, reaction, reciprocation, rejoinder, response, retaliation, retort, return, riposte. ANTONYMS: question.

report *v.t.* **1** (*to give an account of*) describe, detail, narrate, recite, recount, relate, state, tell. **2** (*to prepare a record of, esp. for official use or for publication*) document, record. **3** (*to take down in full or to summarize* (*a speech, sermon etc.*)) note, summarize, take down. **4** (*to make a formal or official statement about*) announce, broadcast, certify, circulate, communicate, declare, disclose, divulge, make public, mention, pass on, proclaim, promulgate, publicize, publish, put out, relay, reveal, set forth. ANTONYMS: suppress. **5** (*to give information against*) (*sl.*) grass up, inform against, peach on, (*coll.*) rat on, tell on.
~*v.i.* **1** (*to act as a reporter*) cover, inquire into, investigate, probe, research, study. **2** (*to present oneself* (*at a certain place etc.*)) appear, arrive, check in, clock in, present oneself, show up, sign in, surface, turn up.
~*n.* **1** (*the formal statement of the result of an investigation, trial etc.*) announcement, declaration, statement. **2** (*a detailed account of a speech, meeting etc., esp. for publication in a newspaper*) account, article, bulletin, communication, communiqué, description, dispatch, message, minute, narrative, note, piece, record, relation, statement, story, summary, tale, write-up. **3** (*common talk, popular rumour*) gossip, hearsay, rumour, talk. **4** (*a loud noise, esp. of an explosive kind*) bang, blast, boom, crack, crash, detonation, discharge, explosion, noise, reverberation, shot, sound. **5** (*fame, repute*) character, eminence, esteem, fame, regard, renown, reputation, repute.

repose *n.* **1** (*cessation of activity, excitement etc.*) cessation, inactivity, inertia, respite, rest, restfulness. ANTONYMS: activity. **2** (*sleep*) doze, relaxation, siesta, sleep, slumber, snooze.

3 (*quiet, calmness*) calmness, peace, quiet, stillness, tranquillity. **4** (*composure, ease of manner etc.*) aplomb, composure, dignity, ease, equanimity, peace of mind, poise, self-possession, serenity, tranquillity.
~*v.i.* **1** (*to lie at rest*) lie, lie down, recline, relax, rest. **2** (*to rest*) drowse, rest, sleep, slumber.

reprehensible *a.* (*open to censure or blame*) appalling, bad, blameworthy, censurable, condemnable, culpable, delinquent, discreditable, disgraceful, errant, erring, guilty, ignoble, objectionable, opprobrious, regrettable, remiss, shameful, unforgivable, unworthy. ANTONYMS: commendable, praiseworthy.

represent *v.t.* **1** (*to stand for, to correspond to*) correspond to, equal, equate with, serve as, speak for, stand for. **2** (*to be an example or specimen of*) embody, epitomize, exemplify, personify, typify. **3** (*to serve as symbol for*) betoken, symbolize. **4** ((*of a picture etc.*) *to serve as a likeness of*) delineate, denote, depict, illustrate, outline, picture, portray, render, reproduce, sketch. **5** (*to present to the mind by describing, imitating etc.*) present, produce, put on, show, stage. **6** (*to take the place of as deputy, substitute etc.*) act for, deputize for, replace, stand in for, substitute for. **7** (*to describe* (*as*), *to make out* (*to be*)) describe (as), make out (to be), masquerade (as), pass off (as), pose (as), pretend (to be). **8** (*to enact* (*a play etc.*) *on the stage, to play the part of*) act, appear as, enact, imitate, impersonate, mimic, perform, personate, play the part of.

representative *a.* **1** (*able or fitted to represent, typical*) archetypal, emblematic, exemplary, illustrative, symbolic, typical. ANTONYMS: untypical. **2** (*acting as delegate, deputy etc.*) chosen, delegated, elected, elective.
~*n.* **1** (*a typical instance or embodiment*) archetype, embodiment, epitome, example, exemplar, instance, personification, specimen, type. **2** (*a deputy or substitute, esp. a person chosen by a body of electors*) agent, councillor, delegate, deputy, member, stand-in, substitute. **3** (*a travelling salesperson, a sales representative*) commercial traveller, door-to-door seller, rep, salesperson, seller, traveller.

repress *v.t.* **1** (*to keep under restraint*) check, constrain, control, curb, deter, disallow, discourage, frustrate, hamper, hinder, hold back, inhibit, limit, restrain. ANTONYMS: encourage, free. **2** (*to suppress, to quell*) crush, master, overcome, overpower, put down, quash, quell, subdue, subjugate, suppress. **3** (*to prevent from breaking out etc.*) muffle, silence, smother, stifle. ANTONYMS: let out. **4** (*to banish* (*unpleasant thoughts etc.*) *to the unconscious*) banish, bottle up.

reprieve *v.t.* **1** (*to suspend the execution of* (*someone*) *for a time*) let off, pardon, postpone, remit, spare, suspend. **2** (*to grant a respite to*) abate, allay, alleviate, mitigate, palliate, relieve, respite. **3** (*to rescue, to save* (*from*)) deliver, rescue, save, set free.

~*n.* **1** (*the temporary suspension of a sentence on a prisoner*) stay of execution, suspension. **2** (*a respite*) abeyance, alleviation, amnesty, deferment, delay, (*coll.*) let-up, mitigation, pardon, postponement, relief, remission, respite.

reprimand¹ *n.* (*a severe reproof, a rebuke*) admonition, blame, castigation, censure, criticism, (*coll.*) dressing-down, lecture, rebuke, reproach, scolding, slap on the wrist, (*coll.*) talking-to, (*coll.*) telling-off, (*coll.*) ticking-off, tongue-lashing, upbraiding, (*coll.*) wigging. ANTONYMS: praise.

reprimand² *v.t.* (*to reprove severely, to rebuke*) admonish, (*coll.*) bawl out, berate, castigate, censure, chide, (*coll.*) dress down, haul over the coals, lecture, rap over the knuckles, rebuke, reproach, reprove, scold, slate, take to task, (*coll.*) tear off a strip, (*coll.*) tell off, (*coll.*) tick off, upbraid. ANTONYMS: applaud, congratulate.

reproach *v.t.* **1** (*to censure, to upbraid*) abuse, blame, blast, censure, chide, condemn, defame, lambast, rebuke, reprehend, reprimand, reprove, scold, (*coll.*) tear off a strip, upbraid. ANTONYMS: approve. **2** (*to find fault with* (*something done*)) criticize, disparage, find fault with. **3** (*to disgrace*) discredit, disgrace, dishonour.

~*n.* **1** (*a rebuke, a censure*) abuse, admonition, blame, censure, condemnation, disapproval, rebuke, reprimand, reproof, scorn. ANTONYMS: approval. **2** (*shame, disgrace*) discredit, disgrace, disrepute, ignominy, indignity, infamy, obloquy, odium, opprobrium, shame, slight, slur, stain, stigma. ANTONYMS: honour.

reprobate *n.* **1** (*a wicked, depraved wretch*) degenerate, evildoer, miscreant, ne'er-do-well, outcast, profligate, rake, (*esp. N Am.*) ratfink, scoundrel, (*taboo sl.*) shit, sinner, (*derog.*) son of a bitch, villain, wastrel, wretch, wrongdoer. **2** (*facet.*) (*a rogue, a rascal*) rascal, rogue, scallywag, (*coll.*) scamp, scoundrel.

~*a.* (*depraved*) abandoned, amoral, bad, base, corrupt, degenerate, depraved, despicable, dissolute, evil, immoral, incorrigible, iniquitous, low, profligate, shameless, sinful, unprincipled, vile, wicked. ANTONYMS: virtuous.

reproduce *v.t.* **1** (*to copy*) copy, duplicate, echo, emulate, imitate, match, mirror, parallel, print, recreate, repeat, replicate, represent, simulate, transcribe. **2** (*to produce* (*new life*)

through sexual or asexual processes*) beget, young, breed, bring forth, generate, multiply, procreate, produce, proliferate, propagate, regenerate, spawn.

reproduction *n.* **1** (*the act of reproducing*) breeding, generation, increase, multiplication, procreation, proliferation, propagation. **2** (*any of the sexual or asexual processes by which animals or plants produce offspring*) copulation, mating, sex. **3** (*a copy, an imitation*) clone, copy, duplicate, facsimile, imitation, picture, print, replica, twin. **4** (*the quality of the sound of a recording*) faithfulness, fidelity.

reprove *v.t.* (*to rebuke, to censure*) admonish, (*coll.*) bawl out, berate, blame, castigate, censure, chide, criticize, (*coll.*) dress down, rebuke, reprehend, reprimand, reproach, scold, take to task, (*coll.*) tear off a strip, (*coll.*) tell off, (*coll.*) tick off, upbraid. ANTONYMS: commend, praise.

repudiate *v.t.* **1** (*to refuse to acknowledge, to disown*) deny, disclaim, disown, wash one's hands of. ANTONYMS: acknowledge. **2** (*to reject, to refuse to accept*) abandon, cast off, desert, disavow, discard, forsake, refuse, reject, renounce, rescind, retract, reverse, revoke, scorn, turn down. ANTONYMS: admit, recognize.

repugnant *a.* **1** (*conflicting, incompatible*) adverse, antagonistic, antipathetic, averse, conflicting, contradictory, contrary, hostile, incompatible, inconsistent, inimical, opposed. **2** (*unpleasant and offensive*) abhorrent, disgusting, distasteful, execrable, foul, horrid, intolerable, loathsome, nauseating, objectionable, obnoxious, odious, offensive, off-putting, repellent, repulsive, revolting, sickening, unpleasant, vile. ANTONYMS: agreeable, pleasant.

repulse *v.t.* **1** (*to beat or drive back*) beat back, check, drive back, fend off, fight off, repel, resist, throw back, ward off. **2** (*to reject, esp. in a rude manner*) disdain, disregard, rebuff, refuse, reject, snub, spurn, turn down. ANTONYMS: welcome. **3** (*to disgust, to be repulsive to*) disgust, nauseate, offend, repel, revolt, sicken. ANTONYMS: delight, please.

~*n.* **1** (*the act of repulsing*) rejection, repulsion. **2** (*a rebuff, a refusal*) check, defeat, denial, disappointment, failure, rebuff, refusal, reverse, snub.

repulsive *a.* **1** (*loathsome, disgusting*) abhorrent, abominable, detestable, disagreeable, disgusting, displeasing, foul, gross, hideous, horrible, loathsome, nauseating, objectionable, obnoxious, offensive, repellent, repugnant, revolting, sickening, unpleasant. ANTONYMS: appealing, lovely. **2**† (*acting so as to repel,* *forbidding*) forbidding, menacing, uninviting, unsympathetic.

reputation *n.* **1** (*the estimation in which one is generally held*) character, repute. **2** (*good estimation, esteem*) credit, distinction, eminence, esteem, estimation, fame, good name, honour, name, opinion, position, renown, respectability, standing, stature, status.

request *n.* (*the act of asking for something to be granted or done*) appeal, application, asking, begging, call, demand, desire, entreaty, petition, plea, prayer, requisition, solicitation, suit, supplication. ~*v.t.* **1** (*to ask for*) appeal for, apply for, ask for, demand, desire, insist on, plead for, put in for, seek, sue for. **2** (*to address a request to*) appeal to, beg, beseech, entreat, importune, petition, pray, solicit, supplicate.

require *v.t.* **1** (*to have need of*) ask for, call for, depend upon, entail, have need of, involve, lack, miss, necessitate, need. **2** (*to command, to instruct*) bid, call upon, command, enjoin, instruct, order. **3** (*to demand* (*something of a person*)) coerce, compel, demand, exact, force, insist, make, oblige, press. **4** (*to want to have*) crave, desire, want, wish.

requisite *a.* (*necessary for completion etc.*) called-for, compulsory, crucial, essential, imperative, indispensable, mandatory, necessary, needed, needful, obligatory, prerequisite, required, vital. ANTONYMS: dispensable, nonessential. ~*n.* (*a necessary part or quality*) condition, essential, must, necessary, necessity, need, precondition, prerequisite, requirement, stipulation.

rescue *v.t.* **1** (*to save from danger or injury*) deliver, extricate, free, get out, let go, liberate, loose, release, salvage, save, set free. **2** (*to liberate by unlawful means from custody*) break out, (*coll.*) bust, liberate. **3** (*to recover* (*property etc.*)) recover, redeem. ANTONYMS: abandon, lose. ~*n.* (*the act of saving from danger or injury*) deliverance, extrication, freeing, liberation, ransom, recovery, redemption, release, relief, salvage, salvation, saving.

research *n.* **1** (*a course of critical investigation*) analysis, examination, inquiry, investigation, probe, study. **2** (*diligent and careful inquiry or investigation*) delving, examination, exploration, fact-finding, inquiry, investigation, probing, scrutiny. ~*v.t.* (*to make careful and systematic investigation into*) analyse, check out, delve into, examine, explore, inquire into, inspect, investigate, look into, scrutinize, study, work over.

resemblance *n.* (*similarity, likeness*) accord, affinity, agreement, analogy, closeness, comparability, conformity, congruity, correspondence, equivalence, kinship, likeness, parity, sameness, semblance, similarity, similitude. ANTONYMS: difference, dissimilarity.

resent *v.t.* (*to regard as an injury or insult*) begrudge, dislike, harbour a grudge, object to, take amiss, take exception to, take offence at. ANTONYMS: accept, welcome.

resentful *a.* (*bitter and indignant*) aggrieved, angry, antagonistic, begrudging, bitter, disgruntled, displeased, envious, exasperated, hurt, incensed, indignant, irritated, (*coll.*) miffed, offended, (*coll.*) peeved, piqued, put out, unhappy, wounded. ANTONYMS: content, satisfied.

reserve *v.t.* **1** (*to keep back for future use, enjoyment etc.*) conserve, defer, delay, hoard, hold, husband, keep back, lay up, postpone, preserve, put by, put off, retain, save, set aside, stockpile, store, withhold. ANTONYMS: use. **2** (*to book*) book, charter, contract, engage, hire, retain, secure. **3** (*in p.p.*) (*to set apart for a certain fate*) destine, preordain, set apart. ~*n.* **1** (*something which is reserved*) cache, hoard, nest egg, reservoir, savings, stock, stockpile, supply. **2** (*a sum of money reserved*) capital, contingency fund. **3** (*a reservation of land for a special use*) park, preserve, reservation, sanctuary, tract. **4** (*a part of the military or naval forces not embodied in the regular army and navy, but liable to be called up in case of emergency*) auxiliary, reinforcements. **5** (*mental reservation*) exception, qualification, reservation. **6** (*caution in speaking or action*) aloofness, aplomb, caution, constraint, coolness, detachment, formality, modesty, reluctance, reservation, restraint, reticence, secretiveness, self-restraint, shyness, silence, taciturnity.

reserved *a.* **1** (*backward in communicating one's thoughts or feelings*) aloof, backward, cautious, close, constrained, cool, demure, detached, distant, guarded, remote, restrained, reticent, retiring, secretive, shy, stand-offish, taciturn, undemonstrative, unemotional, withdrawn. ANTONYMS: frank, uninhibited. **2** (*retained for a particular use, person etc.*) booked, engaged, held, kept, ordered, restricted, retained, set aside, set by, spoken for, taken. ANTONYMS: available, free.

resident *n.* **1** (*a person who dwells permanently in a place*) citizen, denizen, dweller, householder, inhabitant, local, lodger, occupant, occupier, tenant. ANTONYMS: visitor. **2** (*a hotel guest*) guest, inmate, patron.

resign *v.i.* (*to give up office, to retire (from)*) give in one's notice, hand in one's notice, quit, stand down, step down.

~*v.t.* **1** (*to surrender, to relinquish*) abdicate, cede, give up, quit, relinquish, surrender. **2** (*to give up, to abandon*) abandon, forgo, forsake, give up, renounce. **3** (*to submit, to reconcile (oneself, one's mind etc. to)*) accept, acquiesce (in), bow (to), give in (to), give up, reconcile, submit (to), succumb (to), yield (to).

resignation *n.* **1** (*the act of resigning, esp. an office*) abandonment, abdication, capitulation, departure, notice, relinquishment, renunciation, retirement, surrender. **2** (*the state of being resigned, submission*) acceptance, acquiescence, compliance, endurance, forbearance, fortitude, non-resistance, passivity, patience, reconciliation, submission, sufferance. ANTONYMS: defiance, resistance.

resilient *a.* **1** (*resuming its original shape after compression or stretching*) bouncy, elastic, flexible, plastic, pliable, rubbery, springy, stretchable, supple. ANTONYMS: inflexible, rigid. **2** (*able to recover quickly from illness or misfortune*) buoyant, hardy, impervious, irrepressible, self-reliant, strong, tough. ANTONYMS: delicate, weak.

resist *v.t.* **1** (*to strive against, to act in opposition to*) battle, combat, confront, contend with, counteract, countervail, defy, dispute, fight back, oppose, refuse, stand against, strive against, struggle against. ANTONYMS: accept, give in. **2** (*to oppose successfully, to withstand*) block, check, curb, frustrate, hinder, hold out against, impede, inhibit, keep at bay, obstruct, preclude, prevent, repel, restrain, stand firm, stem, stop, thwart, weather, withstand. **3** (*not to yield to (temptation or pleasure)*) abstain from, avoid, desist, forbear, forgo, keep from, leave alone, refrain from, refuse, turn down. ANTONYMS: give in, succumb, yield.

resolute *a.* (*having a fixed purpose, determined*) bold, constant, decided, determined, dogged, firm, indefatigable, inflexible, intent, obstinate, purposeful, relentless, set, stalwart, staunch, steadfast, stubborn, tenacious, undaunted, unwavering. ANTONYMS: irresolute, unsteady.

resolution *n.* **1** (*firmness and boldness in adhering to one's purpose*) boldness, constancy, courage, dedication, determination, doggedness, earnestness, firmness, fortitude, indefatigability, obstinacy, perseverance, persistence, purposefulness, relentlessness, resolve, steadfastness, stubbornness, tenacity, zeal. ANTONYMS: irresolution. **2** (*a settled purpose*) aim, intent, intention, purpose, resolve.

3 (*a formal decision by a public meeting*) decision, declaration, determination, judgement, proposition, resolve, statement, verdict. **4** (*a proposition put forward for discussion and approval*) motion, proposal, proposition, suggestion. **5** (*a solution to a problem etc.*) answer, end, finding, issue, outcome, result, solution, upshot, working out. **6** (*the act or process of resolving or separating anything into its component parts*) analysis, breakdown, decomposition. **7** (*the definition of a television or film image*) definition, focus, sharpness.

resolve *v.t.* **1** (*to cause (someone) to decide*) decide, motivate, push. **2** (*to separate into its component parts*) analyse, anatomize, break down, dissect, dissolve, reduce, separate, split up. **3** (*to solve, to explain*) answer, clear up, crack, elucidate, explain, fathom, figure out, solve, (*sl.*) suss, work out.

~*v.i.* **1** (*to make one's mind up, to decide*) conclude, decide, determine, fix, make up one's mind, settle. **2** (*to separate into the component parts*) break up, dissolve, separate.

~*n.* **1** (*a resolution, a firm decision*) conclusion, decision, design, determination, intention, objective, project, purpose, resolution, undertaking. **2** (*firmness of purpose*) boldness, constancy, courage, determination, doggedness, earnestness, firmness, fortitude, perseverance, persistence, purposefulness, resoluteness, resolution, steadfastness, tenacity, will-power. ANTONYMS: cowardice, irresolution.

resort *n.* **1** (*a place frequented by holidaymakers*) haunt, holiday centre, refuge, rendezvous, retreat, spa, spot, tourist centre, watering place. **2** (*something to which one has recourse*) alternative, chance, course, expedient, hope, possibility, remedy.

~*v.i.* **1** (*to go*) attend, betake oneself, frequent, go, haunt, head for, patronize, repair, visit. **2** (*to have recourse, to turn to (for aid etc.)*) apply to, avail oneself of, turn to, utilize.

resource *n.* **1** (*an expedient, a device*) appliance, contrivance, course, device, expedient. **2** (*a means of support or safety*) backup, escape route, means, resort. **3** (*stocks or supply available*) hoard, reserve, source, stockpile, stocks, store, supply. **4** (*assets available*) assets, property. **5** (*capacity for devising means*) ability, aptitude, capability, capacity, forte, gumption, imagination, quick-wittedness, resourcefulness, skill, talent. **6** (*practical ingenuity*) creativity, ingenuity, initiative, inventiveness.

respect *n.* **1** (*esteem, deferential regard*) admiration, appreciation, approbation, consideration, deference, esteem, estimation, honour, recognition, regard, reverence, veneration. ANTONYMS: contempt, disrespect. **2** (*attention*

(to), heed (to)) attention, attentiveness, heed, regard. **3** *(a particular, an aspect)* aspect, attribute, characteristic, detail, element, facet, feature, matter, particular, point, property, quality, sense, trait, way. **4** *(relation, reference)* bearing, comparison, connection, reference, regard, relation.
~*v.t.* **1** *(to esteem, to regard with deference)* admire, adore, appreciate, defer to, esteem, honour, look up to, pay homage to, prize, recognize, regard, revere, reverence, set store by, think highly of, value, venerate. ANTONYMS: despise, scorn. **2** *(to treat with consideration)* abide by, adhere to, attend, comply with, consider, follow, heed, honour, notice, obey, observe, pay attention to, regard, show consideration, spare. ANTONYMS: disobey, ignore.

respectable *a.* **1** *(worthy of respect, of good repute)* admirable, commendable, dignified, estimable, laudable, praiseworthy, reputable, respected, venerable. ANTONYMS: disreputable. **2** *(honest, decent)* decent, decorous, demure, genteel, good, honest, honourable, presentable, proper, refined, seemly, upright, worthy. ANTONYMS: dishonest, improper. **3** *(above the average in number, merit etc.)* above average, ample, appreciable, considerable, decent, fair, goodly, good-sized, reasonable, significant, sizeable, substantial, *(coll.)* tidy. ANTONYMS: inconsiderable, paltry. **4** *(fairly good)* fairly good, passable, tolerable. **5** *(prim and conventional)* conventional, demure, prim, proper.

respite *n.* **1** *(an interval of rest or relief)* break, *(coll.)* breather, breathing-space, holiday, intermission, interruption, interval, *(coll.)* let-up, lull, recess, relaxation, relief, reprieve, rest. **2** *(a temporary intermission of suffering etc., esp. a delay in the execution of a sentence)* adjournment, delay, extension, hiatus, moratorium, pause, postponement, reprieve, stay, suspension.

respond *v.i.* **1** *(to answer, to reply)* acknowledge, answer, come back, rejoin, reply, retort. ANTONYMS: ignore. **2** *(to perform an act in answer or correspondence to something)* act in response, answer, reciprocate. **3** *(to react (to an external irritation or stimulus))* counter, react, return. **4** *(to show sympathy or sensitiveness (to))* commiserate (with), empathize (with), feel (for), pity, sympathize (with).

response *n.* **1** *(the act of answering)* rejoinder, replying, retort. **2** *(an answer, a reply)* acknowledgement, answer, *(sl.)* comeback, counterattack, counterblast, effect, feedback, reaction, rejoinder, reply, retort, return, riposte.

responsibility *n.* **1** *(the state of being responsible)* accountability, answerability, blame, chargeability, dependability, fault, guilt, liability, obligation. **2** *(the ability to act according to the laws of right and wrong)* conscientiousness, dependability, level-headedness, maturity, rationality, reliability, sensibleness, soberness, stability, trustworthiness. **3** *(something for which one is responsible)* burden, care, charge, duty, onus, role, task, trust.

responsible *a.* **1** *(answerable, accountable (to or for))* accountable, answerable, bound, chargeable, culpable, duty-bound, guilty, liable, subject. ANTONYMS: unaccountable. **2** *(able to discriminate between right and wrong)* discriminating, ethical, moral. **3** *(respectable, trustworthy)* adult, conscientious, dependable, level-headed, mature, rational, reliable, respectable, sensible, sober, sound, stable, trustworthy. ANTONYMS: irresponsible, unreliable.

rest[1] *v.i.* **1** *(to cease from motion or activity)* break off, cease, desist, discontinue, halt, have a break, knock off, stay, stop, *(coll.)* take a breather. ANTONYMS: continue. **2** *(to be relieved from work or exertion)* calm down, laze, lounge about, relax, repose, unwind. ANTONYMS: work. **3** *(to lie in sleep or death)* doze, drowse, idle, *(sl.)* kip, lie down, nap, sit down, sleep, slumber, snooze, take it easy. **4** *(to be supported (by), to stand (on))* lay, lean, lie, place, position, prop, put, recline, repose, set, sit, stand. **5** *(to depend, to rely (on))* depend, hang, hinge, rely. **6** *(to put one's confidence (in))* put one's confidence in, trust.
~*n.* **1** *(cessation from bodily or mental exertion or activity)* doze, forty winks, idleness, inactivity, indolence, inertia, *(sl.)* kip, leisure, lie-down, nap, relaxation, relief, repose, siesta, sleep, slumber, snooze, somnolence, standstill. ANTONYMS: activity, tumult. **2** *(freedom from disturbance, peace)* calm, peace, stillness, tranquillity. **3** *(a brief pause or interval)* break, *(coll.)* breather, breathing-space, cessation, halt, holiday, interlude, intermission, interval, lull, pause, recess, respite, stop, time off, vacation. **4** *(a place for lodging)* haven, lodging, refuge, retreat, shelter, stopping place. **5** *(something on which anything stands or is supported)* base, brace, bracket, holder, prop, shelf, stand, support, trestle.

rest[2] *n.* *(the remaining part or parts)* excess, leftovers, others, remainder, remains, remnants, residue, rump, surplus.
~*v.i.* *(to remain, to continue (in a specified state))* continue, go on, keep, remain, stay.

restful *a.* **1** *(inducing rest, soothing)* calming, comforting, relaxing, sedative, soothing, soporific, tranquillizing. ANTONYMS: disturbing. **2** *(at rest, quiet)* at rest, calm, comfortable, languid, pacific, peaceful, placid, quiet, relaxed, serene, sleepy, tranquil, undisturbed, unhurried. ANTONYMS: agitated, troubled.

restless *a.* (*not resting, fidgety*) agitated, anxious, disturbed, edgy, excitable, fidgety, fitful, fretful, ill at ease, jittery, (*coll.*) jumpy, nervous, restive, skittish, troubled, turbulent, uneasy, unsettled, (*coll.*) uptight, worried. ANTONYMS: calm.

restoration *n.* (*the act of restoring*) reconstruction, recovery, re-establishment, refurbishment, rehabilitation, reinstallation, reinstalment, rejuvenation, renewal, renovation, repair, replacement, restitution, return, revival.

restore *v.t.* 1 (*to bring back to a former state, to repair*) fix, mend, rebuild, recondition, reconstruct, recover, refurbish, rehabilitate, repair, retouch, set to rights, touch up. ANTONYMS: demolish, ruin. 2 (*to put back, to replace*) put back, replace, return, take back. 3 (*to bring back to health*) build up, cure, heal, reanimate, refresh, reinvigorate, rejuvenate, resuscitate, revitalize, revive, revivify, strengthen. ANTONYMS: decline, sicken. 4 (*to bring back to a former position*) bring back, reconstitute, reinstate, reintroduce. 5 (*to bring into existence or use again*) re-establish, renew, renovate. 6 (*to make restitution of*) give back, hand back, make restitution of, reimburse, repay.

restrain *v.t.* 1 (*to hold back, to check*) bridle, check, curb, hold back. ANTONYMS: encourage. 2 (*to keep under control, to restrict*) contain, curtail, debar, hamper, handicap, harness, hinder, hold in check, inhibit, interfere with, keep under control, limit, muzzle, regulate, rein in, repress, restrict, stifle, subdue, suppress. 3 (*to confine, to imprison*) arrest, bind, chain, confine, detain, gaol, hold, imprison, incarcerate, jail, lock up, shut up, tie up. ANTONYMS: free, release.

restraint *n.* 1 (*the act of restraining*) coercion, command, compulsion, curtailment, hindrance, inhibition, moderation, prevention, proscription, suppression. 2 (*control, self-repression*) check, control, repression, self-control, self-discipline, self-repression, self-restraint. 3 (*restriction, limitation*) bridle, check, curb, limit, limitation, restriction. 4 (*deprivation of liberty, confinement*) arrest, bondage, captivity, confinement, detention, imprisonment. ANTONYMS: freedom. 5 (*something used to retain a person or animal physically*) bridle, harness, leash, rein.

restrict *v.t.* 1 (*to confine, to keep within certain bounds*) bound, circumscribe, confine, contain, cramp, demarcate, hamper, handicap,

hem in, impede, inhibit, keep within bounds, limit, mark off, qualify, regulate, restrain. ANTONYMS: broaden, free. 2 (*to withhold from disclosure*) hold back, suppress, withhold.

restriction *n.* 1 (*something that restricts*) check, confinement, constraint, containment, control, curb, demarcation, handicap, inhibition, limitation, restraint. ANTONYMS: freedom. 2 (*a restrictive law or regulation*) condition, law, provision, proviso, qualification, regulation, rule, stipulation.

result *v.i.* 1 (*to terminate or end* (*in*)) conclude, culminate, end, finish, terminate, wind up. ANTONYMS: begin, start. 2 (*to follow as the logical consequence*) appear, arise, come about, come to pass, derive, develop, emanate, emerge, ensue, evolve, flow, follow, happen, issue, occur, proceed, spring, stem, turn out. ~*n.* (*consequence, effect*) aftermath, conclusion, consequence, decision, denouement, development, effect, end, event, follow-up, fruit, issue, outcome, product, reaction, sequel, termination, upshot. ANTONYMS: cause.

resume *v.t.* 1 (*to begin again, to go on with after interruption*) begin again, carry on, continue, go on, pick up, proceed, recommence, reinstitute, renew, reopen, restart, take up. ANTONYMS: cease, stop. 2 (*to take back, to reoccupy*) recover, reoccupy, take back. 3† (*to sum up*) recapitulate, sum up.

resurrection *n.* 1 (*a rising again from the dead*) raising from the dead, rising from the dead. 2 (*a springing again into life or prosperity*) reappearance, rebirth, regeneration, renaissance, renascence, renewal, restoration, resurgence, resuscitation, return, revival.

resuscitate *v.t.* 1 (*to restore from apparent death*) breathe new life into, bring round, quicken, restore to life, revive, revivify, save. 2 (*to restore to vigour, usage etc.*) reanimate, reinvigorate, renew, restore, resurrect, revitalize.

retain *v.t.* 1 (*to hold or keep possession of*) grasp, grip, hang onto, hold, keep. ANTONYMS: let go, release. 2 (*to continue to have*) maintain, preserve. 3 (*to remember*) bear in mind, have, keep in mind, memorize, recall, recollect, remember. ANTONYMS: forget. 4 (*to keep in place*) detain, hold back, keep in place, reserve. 5 (*to engage the services of* (*someone*) *by paying a preliminary fee*) commission, employ, engage, hire, pay, reserve, take on.

retaliate *v.i.* (*to repay an injury or result*) avenge, counter, even the score, exact retribution, get back (at), get even (with), get one's own back, hit back, make reprisal, pay back, reciprocate, repay, requite, return, revenge, strike back. ANTONYMS: accept, forgive.

retire *v.i.* **1** (*to withdraw, to retreat*) decamp, depart, ebb, exit, fall back, give ground, give way, go away, leave, pull back, pull out, recede, remove, retreat, withdraw. **2** (*to withdraw from business to a private life*) cease work, stop work. **3** (*to resign one's office or appointment*) quit, resign, stand down, step down. **4** (*to go to bed*) go to bed, go to sleep, (*coll.*) hit the hay, (*coll.*) hit the sack, (*sl.*) kip down, lie down, nap, snooze, take it easy, (*coll.*) turn in. **5** (*to go into privacy or seclusion*) hibernate, sequester oneself, withdraw.

retiring *a.* (*shy, not forward*) bashful, coy, demure, diffident, distant, humble, meek, modest, quiet, reclusive, removed, reserved, reticent, self-effacing, shrinking, shy, timid, unassertive, unassuming, unsociable. ANTONYMS: brash, forward.

retreat *v.i.* **1** (*to move back, esp. before an enemy*) back away, decamp, draw back, evacuate, flee, give ground, go back, move back, pull back, recoil, retire, take flight, turn tail, withdraw. ANTONYMS: advance. **2** (*to recede*) ebb, fall back, recede, shrink.
~*n.* **1** (*the act of withdrawing, esp. of an army before an enemy*) departure, ebb, evacuation, flight, retirement, withdrawal. **2** (*a state of retirement or seclusion*) isolation, privacy, retirement, seclusion, solitude. **3** (*a place of privacy or seclusion*) asylum, den, haunt, haven, hideaway, refuge, resort, sanctuary, shelter. **4** (*an institution for the care of old or mentally ill people*) asylum, home, rest home, shelter.

retribution *n.* (*a suitable return, esp. for evil*) compensation, justice, punishment, reckoning, recompense, redress, repayment, reprisal, requital, retaliation, return, revenge, satisfaction, vengeance. ANTONYMS: pardon.

retrieve *v.t.* **1** ((*of a dog*) *to find and bring in* (*a stick, a ball etc.*)) bring in, fetch, find, get back. **2** (*to recover by searching or recollecting*) find, recall, recover. **3** (*to regain* (*something which has been lost, impaired etc.*)) recapture, recoup, recover, redeem, regain, repossess, win back. ANTONYMS: lose. **4** (*to rescue* (*from*)) redeem, rescue, salvage, save. **5** (*to restore* (*one's fortunes etc.*)) re-establish, restore. **6** (*to remedy, to repair*) make amends, make good, remedy, repair.

return *v.i.* **1** (*to come or go back, esp. to the same place or state*) come back, go back, rebound, recoil, retreat, turn back. **2** (*to happen again*) recur, revert.
~*v.t.* **1** (*to carry or convey back*) bring back, carry back, convey. **2** (*to give or send back*) give back,

put back, re-establish, reinstate, remit, render, replace, restore, send back, take back. ANTONYMS: remove. **3** (*to repay, to send in return*) pay back, reciprocate, recompense, refund, reimburse, repay, requite. **4** (*to yield* (*a profit*)) benefit, bring in, earn, gain, make, net, profit, repay, yield. **5** (*to say in reply*) answer, come back, communicate, rejoin, reply, respond, retort. **6** (*to report* (*a verdict*) *officially*) announce, arrive at, bring in, deliver, give, offer, proffer, render, report, submit. **7** (*to elect*) choose, elect, pick, vote in.
~*n.* **1** (*the act of coming or going back*) homecoming, rebound, retreat, reversion. **2** (*the act of paying or putting back*) compensation, reciprocation, recompense, reimbursement, reparation, repayment, replacement, requital, restitution, restoration, retaliation, reward. **3** (*a reply*) answer, (*sl.*) comeback, rejoinder, reply, response, retort, riposte. **4** (*an official account or report*) account, form, list, report, statement, summary. **5** (*often pl.*) (*the proceeds or profits on labour, investments etc.*) advantage, benefit, earnings, income, interest, proceeds, profit, results, revenue, takings, yield. ANTONYMS: loss.

reveal *v.t.* **1** (*to allow to appear*) bring to light, display, exhibit, expose, manifest, show, uncover, unveil. ANTONYMS: conceal. **2** (*to disclose, to divulge* (*something private or unknown*)) announce, betray, broadcast, communicate, disclose, divulge, give away, impart, leak, let on, let slip, make known, make public, proclaim, publish, tell.

revel *v.i.* **1** (*to make merry*) carouse, celebrate, cut loose, (*coll.*) live it up, make merry, (*coll.*) make whoopee, party, (*coll.*) push the boat out, (*coll.*) rave, (*coll.*) whoop it up. ANTONYMS: mourn. **2** (*to take great enjoyment* (*in*)) bask (in), delight (in), enjoy, gloat (over), indulge (in), luxuriate (in), rejoice (in), relish, savour, take pleasure (in), thrive (on), wallow (in). ANTONYMS: dislike, hate.
~*n.* (*an act of revelling*) bacchanal, carnival, carousal, celebration, debauch, festivity, fling, gala, jamboree, jollification, merrymaking, orgy, party, (*coll.*) rave, revelry, romp, spree.

revelation *n.* **1** (*the act of revealing, a disclosing of knowledge*) announcement, betrayal, broadcasting, communication, declaration, disclosure, discovery, exposé, exposition, exposure, manifestation, proclamation, pronouncement, publication, unearthing, unmasking. **2** (*knowledge or information which is revealed*) bulletin, communication, information, knowledge, leak, message, news, sign, statement.

revenge *n.* **1** (*retaliation or spiteful return for* *an injury)* reprisal, requital, retaliation, retribution, satisfaction, vengeance. ANTONYMS: forgiveness. **2** *(the desire to inflict revenge)* spitefulness, vindictiveness.

~*v.t.* *(to take retribution for, to retaliate)* even the score, exact retribution, get even, pay back, repay, requite, retaliate, return, settle the score.

revenue *n.* *(income, esp. of a considerable amount)* gain, income, interest, proceeds, profits, receipts, returns, rewards, takings, yield. ANTONYMS: expenditure.

revere *v.t.* *(to regard with awe mingled with affection)* admire, adore, adulate, defer to, esteem, exalt, honour, idolize, look up to, respect, reverence, sanctify, think highly of, venerate, worship. ANTONYMS: despise, scorn.

reverent *a.* **1** *(feeling or expressing reverence)* adoring, awed, decorous, devout, loving, pious, respectful, reverential, solemn. ANTONYMS: disrespectful. **2** *(submissive, humble)* deferential, humble, meek, submissive.

reverse *v.t.* **1** *(to turn in the contrary direction)* overturn, turn inside out, turn over, turn round, turn upside down, upend, upset. ANTONYMS: right. **2** *(to invert, to transpose)* exchange, interchange, invert, transpose. **3** *(to cause to go backwards)* back, backtrack, back up, retreat, turn back. ANTONYMS: advance. **4** *(to annul, to nullify)* abandon, alter, annul, cancel, countermand, invalidate, negate, nullify, obviate, overrule, quash, repeal, rescind, retract, revoke, set aside, undo, veto.

~*a.* **1** *(having an opposite direction)* contrary, converse, opposite. **2** *(turned backwards, upside down)* back to front, backwards, inverse, inverted, mirror, reversed, upside down.

~*n.* **1** *(the opposite)* antithesis, contradiction, contrary, converse, inverse, opposite. **2** *(the back surface (of a coin etc.))* back, flip side, other side, rear, underside, verso. ANTONYMS: front, obverse. **3** *(a complete change of affairs for the worse)* affliction, blow, catastrophe, check, defeat, difficulty, disappointment, disaster, failure, hardship, misadventure, misfortune, mishap, problem, reversal, setback, trial, trouble, vicissitude.

review *n.* **1** *(an examination, esp. by people in authority)* analysis, examination, perusal, report, scrutiny, study, survey. **2** *(a reconsideration, a second view)* fresh look, reassessment, recapitulation, reconsideration, re-evaluation, re-examination, rethink, retrospect, revision, second look. **3** *(a critical account of a book etc.)* criticism, critique, evaluation, judgement, notice. **4** *(a periodical publication containing essays and criticisms)*

journal, magazine, periodical. **5** *(a formal inspection of military forces)* cavalcade, display, inspection, march past, parade, procession.

~*v.t.* **1** *(to go over in memory, to revise)* call to mind, go over, look back on, reassess, recall, recapitulate, recollect, reconsider, re-evaluate, re-examine, reflect on, remember, rethink, revise, summon up. **2** *(to look over carefully and critically)* assess, consider, discuss, evaluate, examine, judge, look over, regard, run over, scrutinize, study, survey, weigh. **3** *(to write a critical review of)* criticize, write a critique of.

revise *v.t.* **1** *(to re-examine for correction or emendation)* look over, reconsider, re-examine, review, rework. **2** *(to correct or amend)* alter, amend, change, correct, edit, emend, improve, modify, overhaul, rectify, redo, revamp, rewrite, update. **3** *(to reread (course notes etc.) for an examination)* go over, learn, memorize, reread, run through, study, (*coll.*) swot up.

revive *v.i.* **1** *(to return to life or consciousness)* awaken, come round, come to, quicken, recover, regain consciousness, wake. **2** *(to become encouraged again)* cheer, perk up, rally, recover, recuperate, restore, take heart.

~*v.t.* **1** *(to bring back to life or consciousness)* animate, awaken, bring round, bring to, quicken, resuscitate, rouse. **2** *(to make encouraged again)* cheer, comfort, encourage, hearten, refresh, rekindle, restore. **3** *(to make popular or successful again)* breathe new life into, reanimate, reawaken, re-establish, regenerate, rejuvenate, renew, revitalize.

revoke *v.t.* *(to annul, to cancel (a law etc.))* abolish, annul, cancel, countermand, deny, disclaim, invalidate, negate, nullify, recall, renounce, repeal, repudiate, rescind, retract, reverse, set aside, take back, void, withdraw. ANTONYMS: endorse, uphold.

revolt *v.i.* *(to rise in rebellion)* defect, dissent, mutiny, rebel, resist, rise. ANTONYMS: submit.

~*v.t.* *(to nauseate, to disgust)* appal, disgust, nauseate, offend, repel, repulse, shock, sicken, (*coll.*) turn off. ANTONYMS: attract.

~*n.* **1** *(a rebellion)* insurgency, insurrection, mutiny, putsch, rebellion, rising, sedition, uprising. **2** *(revulsion)* disgust, nausea, revulsion, sickening.

revolting *a.* *(horrible, disgusting)* abhorrent, abominable, disagreeable, disgusting, distasteful, foul, gross, hideous, horrid, loathsome, nasty, nauseating, obnoxious, offensive, repellent, repulsive, shocking, sickening, unpleasant, vile. ANTONYMS: agreeable, pleasant.

revolution *n.* **1** *(a fundamental change in government, esp. by the forcible overthrow of* *the existing system*) coup, coup d'état, insurgency, insurrection, mutiny, overthrow, putsch, rebellion, revolt, rising, sedition, uprising. **2** (*a radical change of circumstances*) alteration, change, innovation, metamorphosis, reformation, sea change, shift, transformation, upheaval. **3** (*a cycle or regular recurrence*) circle, circuit, cycle, gyration, lap, orbit, rotation, round, spin, turn, wheel, whirl.

revolve *v.i.* **1** (*to turn round*) move round, turn round. **2** (*to move round a centre, to rotate*) circle, cycle, go round, gyrate, move round, orbit, pivot, reel, rotate, spin, swivel, turn, twist, wheel, whirl.
~*v.t.* **1** (*to cause to revolve or rotate*) rotate, spin, turn. **2** (*to meditate on, to ponder*) chew over, consider, contemplate, deliberate, meditate, mull over, ponder, reflect, ruminate, study, think about, think over, turn over, weigh.

revulsion *n.* (*a strong feeling of disgust*) abhorrence, abomination, antipathy, aversion, detestation, disgust, distaste, execration, hatred, loathing, nausea, odium, recoil, repugnance, repulsion. ANTONYMS: attraction, liking.

reward *n.* **1** (*something which is given in return usu. for good done or received*) award, benefit, bonus, compensation, gain, payment, premium, prize, profit, recompense, remuneration, repayment, requital, return, wages. ANTONYMS: fine, penalty. **2** (*a requital, retribution*) (*coll.*) come-uppance, recompense, requital, retribution. **3** (*a sum of money offered for the detection of a criminal or for the restoration of anything lost*) award, bounty, payment, price, recompense.
~*v.t.* (*to repay, to recompense* (*a service or a doer*)) compensate, pay, recompense, redress, remunerate, repay, requite. ANTONYMS: punish.

ribald *a.* ((*of language*) *coarse, lewd*) bawdy, (*sl.*) blue, broad, coarse, dirty, earthy, filthy, gross, indecent, lewd, licentious, obscene, racy, (*coll.*) raunchy, risqué, rude, salacious, scurrilous, smutty, vulgar. ANTONYMS: decent, pure.

rich *a.* **1** (*wealthy, having a lot of valuable possessions*) affluent, flush, (*coll.*) loaded, moneyed, opulent, prosperous, (*coll.*) rolling, wealthy, (*coll.*) well-heeled, well-off, well-to-do. ANTONYMS: penniless, poor. **2** (*abundantly supplied (in or with)*) abounding (in), full (of), profuse, replete (with), rife (with), well-endowed (with), well-provided (with), well-stocked (with), well-supplied (with). **3** (*fertile, abundant*) abounding, abundant, ample, bountiful, copious, fecund, fertile, fruitful, full, plenteous, plentiful, productive, prolific. ANTONYMS: barren, infertile. **4** (*valuable,*

precious) costly, dear, expensive, exquisite, fine, invaluable, precious, priceless, valuable. ANTONYMS: cheap. **5** (*elaborate, splendid*) elaborate, gorgeous, lavish, lush, luxurious, magnificent, opulent, splendid, sumptuous, superb. **6** (*containing a lot of fat, sugar, spices etc.*) creamy, delicious, flavoursome, juicy, luscious, mouth-watering, piquant, savoury, spicy, succulent, sweet, tasty. ANTONYMS: bland, tasteless. **7** (*vivid, bright*) bright, deep, gay, intense, lustrous, strong, vibrant, vivid, warm. ANTONYMS: dull. **8** ((*of a sound*) *mellow, deep*) deep, dulcet, full, mellifluous, mellow, musical, resonant, sonorous. **9** (*comical, full of humorous suggestion*) absurd, amusing, comical, funny, hilarious, humorous, laughable, ludicrous, ridiculous, risible, side-splitting.

rickety *a.* **1** (*shaky, tumbledown*) broken, broken-down, derelict, dilapidated, flimsy, insecure, precarious, ramshackle, shaky, teetering, tottering, tumbledown, unsafe, unsound, unsteady, weak, wobbly. **2** (*feeble in the joints*) decrepit, feeble, frail, infirm. ANTONYMS: sturdy.

rid *v.t.* (*to clear, to disencumber* (*of*)) clear, deliver, disburden, disembarrass, free, lighten, make free, purge, release, relieve, rescue, save, unburden.

ride *v.t.* **1** (*to sit on and be carried along by* (*a horse etc.*)) go, journey, move, proceed, progress, sit on, travel. **2** (*to sit on and control the movement of* (*a cycle etc.*)) control, handle, manage, propel, sit on. **3** (*to tyrannize, to domineer* (*over*)) dominate, enslave, grip, haunt, intimidate, oppress, terrorize, tyrannize. **4** (*to annoy, to pester*) annoy, badger, bully, harass, (*coll.*) hassle, heckle, hector, irritate, nag, pester, plague, provoke.
~*n.* **1** (*a journey on horseback or in a public conveyance*) drive, excursion, expedition, jaunt, journey, lift, outing, (*coll.*) spin, tour, trip. **2** (*a path for riding on, esp. through a wood*) bridleway, path.

ridicule *n.* **1** (*derision, mockery*) derision, irony, jeering, laughter, mocking, raillery, ribbing, sarcasm, satire, scorn, taunting. **2** (*words or actions intended to express contempt and excite laughter*) banter, gibe, jeer, mockery, sneer, taunt.
~*v.t.* (*to laugh at, to make fun of*) burlesque, caricature, deride, guy, humiliate, jeer, lampoon, laugh at, laugh to scorn, make fun of, mock, parody, poke fun at, satirize, scoff, send up, sneer, (*taboo sl.*) take the piss out of, taunt, tease.

ridiculous *a.* **1** (*meriting or exciting ridicule*)

amusing, comical, droll, farcical, funny, hilarious, humorous, laughable, mirthful, risible. **2** (*absurd, foolish*) absurd, bizarre, contemptible, crazy, derisory, fantastic, foolish, grotesque, inane, incredible, insane, ludicrous, nonsensical, outlandish, outrageous, preposterous, silly, stupid, unbelievable, weird. ANTONYMS: sensible, serious.

rift *n.* **1** (*a cleft, a fissure*) chink, cleft, cranny, crevice, fault, fissure, flaw. **2** (*a wide opening made by splitting*) breach, break, cleavage, crack, fracture, gap, gulf, hole, opening, rent, space, split, tear. **3** (*a serious quarrel causing a split between people*) alienation, breach, conflict, difference, disagreement, distance, division, estrangement, falling out, quarrel, schism, separation, split. ANTONYMS: reconciliation.

right *a.* **1** (*being or done in accordance with justice*) equitable, ethical, fair, good, honest, honourable, just, lawful, moral, proper, righteous, true, upright, virtuous. ANTONYMS: bad, wrong. **2** (*correct, true*) accurate, admissible, authentic, correct, exact, factual, genuine, precise, satisfactory, sound, (*coll.*) spot-on, true, unerring, valid, veracious. ANTONYMS: inaccurate, unsatisfactory. **3** (*fit, most suitable*) advantageous, appropriate, becoming, convenient, deserved, desirable, due, favourable, fit, fitting, opportune, preferable, proper, propitious, rightful, seemly, strategic, suitable. ANTONYMS: inappropriate, unfitting. **4** (*sound, sane*) balanced, fine, fit, healthy, lucid, normal, rational, reasonable, sane, sound, unimpaired, well. ANTONYMS: insane, unsound. **5** (*real, genuine*) absolute, complete, genuine, out-and-out, outright, pure, real, thorough, unmitigated, utter, veritable. **6** (*on or towards the side of the body which is to the south when the face is to the sunrise, as opposed to left*) right-hand, starboard. **7** (*direct*) direct, straight. **8** (*politically conservative, right-wing*) conservative, reactionary, right-wing. ANTONYMS: left-wing, socialist.

~*adv.* **1** (*justly, equitably*) equitably, fairly, justly, rightly. **2** (*correctly, properly*) accurately, correctly, ethically, exactly, factually, fairly, genuinely, justly, precisely, properly, righteously, truly. ANTONYMS: inaccurately. **3** (*satisfactorily, well*) appropriately, aptly, befittingly, fittingly, properly, satisfactorily, suitably, well. **4** (*coll.*) (*immediately*) at once, directly, forthwith, immediately, instantly, promptly, quickly, straight away, swiftly. **5** (*completely*) absolutely, altogether, completely, entirely, perfectly, quite, thoroughly, totally, utterly, wholly. ANTONYMS: incompletely. **6**† (*very, to the full*) most, quite, very.

~*n.* **1** (*what is right or just*) justice, rightness.

2 (*fair or equitable treatment*) equity, fairness, good, honour, integrity, lawfulness, legality, morality, propriety, reason, rectitude, righteousness, truth, uprightness, virtue. ANTONYMS: immorality, inequity. **3** (*just claim or title*) authority, claim, due, freedom, interest, justification, liberty, licence, permission, prerogative, privilege, title.

~*v.t.* **1** (*to restore to an upright position; to correct*) amend, correct, fix, put right, rectify, repair, settle, set upright, sort out, straighten. **2** (*to do justice to*) rehabilitate, repay, vindicate. **3** (*to relieve from injustice*) compensate, redress.

righteous *a.* **1** (*upright, morally good*) blameless, ethical, fair, good, holy, honest, honourable, innocent, just, law-abiding, moral, pure, reputable, saintly, trustworthy, upright, upstanding, virtuous. ANTONYMS: unjust, wicked. **2** (*equitable, fitting*) appropriate, apt, correct, deserved, equitable, fitting, justifiable, justified, right. ANTONYMS: unjustifiable.

rightful *a.* **1** (*entitled or held by legitimate claim*) authorized, bona fide, correct, entitled, genuine, lawful, legitimate, right, true, valid. ANTONYMS: wrongful. **2** (*equitable, fair*) equitable, fair, just, proper, real, suitable.

rigid *a.* **1** (*stiff, not easily bent*) firm, hard, inelastic, inflexible, stiff, unbending, unyielding. ANTONYMS: elastic, pliant. **2** (*strict, inflexible*) adamant, austere, exact, fixed, hard, inflexible, intransigent, rigorous, severe, steely, stern, strict, stringent, uncompromising, undeviating, unrelenting, unswerving, unyielding.

rigorous *a.* **1** (*strict, severe*) austere, challenging, demanding, exacting, firm, hard, harsh, inflexible, precise, rigid, severe, strict, stringent, tough. ANTONYMS: flexible, indulgent. **2** (*logically accurate, precise*) accurate, conscientious, exact, meticulous, nice, painstaking, precise, punctilious, scrupulous, thorough. ANTONYMS: lax, negligent. **3** (*inclement, harsh*) bad, bleak, extreme, harsh, inclement, inhospitable, severe. ANTONYMS: clement, pleasant.

rigour *n.* **1** (*exactness in enforcing rules*) accuracy, conscientiousness, exactitude, exactness, meticulousness, precision, punctiliousness, scrupulousness, strictness, thoroughness. ANTONYMS: laxity. **2** (*inflexibility of opinion, observance etc.*) austerity, firmness, hardness, inflexibility, rigidity, severity, stiffness. **3** (*sternness, harshness*) harshness, sternness, stringency. **4** (*inclemency of the weather etc.*) distress, hardship, inclemency. **5** (*harsh conditions*) ordeal, privation, suffering, trial.

rim *n.* (*an outer edge or margin*) border, brim, brink, circumference, edge, flange, lip, margin, perimeter, periphery, verge. ANTONYMS: centre, middle.

ring[1] *n.* **1** (*a circlet*) circlet, ringlet. **2** (*anything in the form of a circle*) band, circle, circuit, girdle, halo, hoop, loop, round. **3** (*a group of people, things etc.*) association, bloc, circle, clan, concourse, coterie, crew, federation, group, league, organization, pack, set, team. **4** (*a circular enclosure for circus performances etc.*) arena, circus, enclosure, rink. **5** (*a combination of people acting together, often illegally*) band, cabal, cartel, cell, clique, faction, gang, junta, mob, syndicate.
~*v.t.* (*to encircle, to enclose*) circle, circumscribe, compass, embrace, enclose, encompass, gird, girdle, hem in, loop, seal off, surround.

ring[2] *v.i.* **1** (*to give a clear vibrating sound, like a sonorous metallic body when struck*) chime, clang, peal, sound, strike, tinkle, toll. **2** (*to resound, to reverberate*) re-echo, resound, reverberate. **3** ((*of the ears*) *to have a sensation as of vibrating metal*) buzz, tingle. **4** (*to give a summons or signal by ringing*) call, signal, summon. **5** (*to telephone someone*) (*sl.*) buzz, call, phone, telephone.
~*n.* **1** (*the sound of a bell or other resonant body*) chime, knell, peal, toll. **2** (*coll.*) (*a telephone call*) (*coll.*) bell, (*sl.*) buzz, call, telephone call, (*coll.*) tinkle. **3** (*the characteristic sound of a voice*) timbre, tone.

riot *n.* **1** (*an outbreak of lawlessness*) affray, bother, commotion, disorder, disruption, disturbance, fracas, fray, hubbub, quarrel, row, rumpus, strife, (*coll.*) to-do, tumult, turbulence, turmoil, unrest, upheaval, uproar. ANTONYMS: order. **2** (*wanton or unrestrained conduct*) boisterousness, carousal, excess, festivity, frolic, high jinks, jollification, merrymaking, revelry, romp, wantonness. ANTONYMS: sobriety. **3** (*lavish display*) display, extravaganza, flourish, show, (*sl.*) splash.
~*v.i.* **1** (*to take part in a riot*) brawl, cut loose, (*coll.*) raise hell, rampage, rebel, revolt, run riot, storm, take to the streets. **2** (*to revel, to behave or live licentiously*) carouse, frolic, make merry, paint the town red, revel, roister, romp.

rip *v.t.* **1** (*to tear or cut forcibly* (*out, off, up etc.*)) claw, cut, gash, hack, lacerate, score, slash, slit, tear. **2** (*to rend, to split*) burst, rend, split. ANTONYMS: mend.
~*n.* (*a rent made by ripping*) cleavage, cleft, gash, hole, laceration, rent, rift, rupture, slash, slit, split, tear.

ripe *a.* **1** (*ready for reaping or gathering*) grown, mature, mellow, ripened. ANTONYMS: unripe. **2** (*fully developed, in a fit state* (*for*)) advanced, aged, complete, developed, finished, fit, grown, mature, mellow, perfect, prepared, ready, seasoned. ANTONYMS: immature. **3** (*resembling ripe fruit*) luscious, rosy, rounded.

rise *v.i.* **1** (*to move upwards, to soar*) arise, ascend, climb, go up, levitate, lift, mount, move up, soar. **2** (*to get up from a lying or sitting position*) arise, get up, stand up, surface. ANTONYMS: descend. **3** (*to end a session*) adjourn, end. ANTONYMS: open. **4** (*to come to life again*) reawaken, resuscitate, revive. **5** (*to become high or tall*) enlarge, flood, grow, heighten, improve, increase, swell, wax. **6** (*to be promoted, to thrive*) advance, get on, (*coll.*) go places, progress, prosper, thrive. **7** (*to increase in energy, intensity etc.*) escalate, increase, intensify. ANTONYMS: abate, decline. **8** (*to come into existence*) arise, come about, emanate, flow, issue, occur, originate, spring. **9** (*to come to the surface, to come into sight*) appear, emerge, surface. **10** (*to revolt, to rebel* (*against*)) mutiny, rebel, resist, revolt, take up arms. **11** ((*of the wind*) *to start to blow*) blow up, get up, pick up. ANTONYMS: abate, die down.
~*n.* **1** (*the act of rising*) advance, rising. **2** (*ascent, elevation*) ascent, climb, elevation. **3** (*an upward slope*) incline, slope. **4** (*a hill, a knoll*) acclivity, eminence, hill, hillock, knoll, prominence. **5** (*source, origin*) origin, source, start. **6** (*an increase in price, value etc.*) gain, increase, increment, pay rise, rise, upsurge, upturn. ANTONYMS: drop, fall. **7** (*upward progress in social position*) advancement, progress, promotion. **to give rise to** (*to cause*) begin, be the cause of, be the origin of, bring about, cause, create, engender, generate, lead to, occasion, originate, produce, result in.

risk *n.* (*a chance of injury, loss etc.*) chance, danger, gamble, hazard, jeopardy, peril, pitfall, possibility, speculation, uncertainty, venture.
~*v.t.* **1** (*to expose to risk or hazard*) dare, endanger, expose to danger, hazard, imperil, jeopardize. **2** (*to take the chance of*) chance, gamble on, take a chance on, venture on.

risky *a.* (*dangerous, hazardous*) chancy, dangerous, daring, (*coll.*) dicey, (*coll.*) dodgy, hazardous, (*coll.*) iffy, perilous, precarious, touch-and-go, tricky, uncertain, unsafe, venturesome. ANTONYMS: certain, safe.

rival *n.* **1** (*one's competitor for something*) adversary, antagonist, challenger, competitor, contender, contestant, opponent, opposition. ANTONYMS: ally. **2** (*a person or thing considered as equal to another*) equal, equivalent, fellow, match, peer.

~*a.* (*in competition*) competing, competitive, conflicting, emulating, opposed, opposing.

~*v.t.* (*to strive to equal or surpass*) challenge, combat, come up to, compare with, compete, contend, contest, equal, measure up, measure up to, oppose, struggle, surpass, vie. ANTO-NYMS: back, support.

roam *v.i.* (*to wander about without any definite purpose*) amble, cruise, dally, dawdle, drift, meander, perambulate, ramble, range, rove, saunter, stray, stroll, wander.

roar *n.* **1** (*a loud, deep sound, as of a lion etc.*) bellow, howl, snarl. **2** (*a confused din resembling this*) boom, clamour, crash, cry, din, hullabaloo, noise, outburst, outcry, racket, rumble, shout, thunder, yell. **3** (*a burst of mirth or laughter*) guffaw, hoot, laugh.

~*v.i.* **1** ((*of a lion etc.*) *to make a loud, deep sound*) bay, bellow, howl, snarl. **2** ((*of a person laughing, of the sea etc.*) *to make a confused din like this*) bawl, clamour, crash, cry, rumble, shout, squall, thunder, yell, yowl.

rob *v.t.* **1** (*to take something by secret theft from*) burgle, cheat, defraud, fleece, hold up, (*coll.*) mug, (*coll.*) rip off, steal from, swindle, take from. **2** (*to plunder, to pillage*) deprive, despoil, loot, pillage, plunder, raid, ransack, rifle, sack, strip.

robber *n.* (*a person who steals something from someone*) bandit, brigand, burglar, cheat, (*sl.*) conman, fraud, highwayman, highwaywoman, housebreaker, looter, (*coll.*) mugger, pickpocket, shoplifter, swindler, thief.

robbery *n.* **1** (*the act or practice of robbing*) burglary, embezzlement, filching, fraud, larceny, pilfering, piracy, stealing, theft, thieving. **2** (*an instance of robbing*) break-in, burglary, fraud, heist, hold-up, (*coll.*) mugging, raid, (*coll.*) rip-off, (*sl.*) stick-up, swindle, theft. **3** (*extortion, overpricing*) (*coll.*) daylight robbery, extortion, overpricing.

robust *a.* **1** (*strong, capable of endurance*) able-bodied, enduring, fit, hale, hardy, healthy, hearty, lusty, rude, rugged, sound, staunch, stout, strapping, strong, sturdy, vigorous, well. ANTONYMS: unfit, unhealthy. **2** ((*of wine*) *full-bodied*) fruity, full-bodied, pungent, rich, strong, well-rounded. **3** (*sinewy, muscular*) athletic, brawny, (*esp. N Am., coll.*) husky, muscular, powerful, sinewy, thickset, well-knit. ANTONYMS: delicate, frail. **4** ((*of an opinion*) *strongly held*) direct, forceful, no-nonsense, straightforward, strong.

rock *v.t.* **1** (*to cause (a cradle) to move to and fro*) sway, swing. **2** (*to lull to sleep*) lull, soothe. **3** (*to shock, to distress*) amaze, astonish,

astound, daze, disconcert, distress, dumb-found, jar, overwhelm, (*coll.*) rattle, shake, shock, stagger, stun, stupefy, surprise, (*coll.*) throw, unnerve.

~*v.i.* **1** (*to move backwards and forwards*) oscillate, swing. **2** (*to sway, to reel*) lurch, pitch, reel, roll, sway, wobble.

rod *n.* **1** (*a straight, slender piece of wood*) birch, cane, dowel, pole, shaft, stick, wand. **2** (*punishment*) chastisement, discipline, punishment. **3** (*a baton, a sceptre*) baton, mace, sceptre, staff. **4** (*a slender bar of metal, esp. forming part of machinery etc.*) bar, shaft.

rogue *n.* **1** (*a dishonest person, a criminal*) blackguard, charlatan, cheat, (*sl.*) conman, criminal, (*coll.*) crook, cur, fraud, good-for-nothing, knave, (*Hist.*) mountebank, ne'er-do-well, reprobate, scoundrel, swindler, trickster, villain, wastrel, wretch. **2** (*coll.*) (*a mischievous person, esp. a child*) (*dated or facet.*) rapscallion, rascal, (*coll.*) scamp.

role *n.* **1** (*a part or character taken by an actor*) character, impersonation, lines, part, portrayal, representation. **2** (*any part or function one is called upon to perform*) capacity, duty, function, job, part, place, position, post, responsibility, situation, task.

roll *n.* **1** (*a small individual loaf of bread*) bap, bun. **2** (*a pastry or cake rolled round a filling*) cake, pastry. **3** (*an official record, a list of names*) annals, catalogue, census, chronicle, directory, document, index, inventory, list, muster, record, register, roster, rota, schedule, scroll, table. **4** (*a cylindrical or semicylindrical mass of anything*) bale, bobbin, bolt, cylinder, drum, reel, scroll, spool, tube. **5** (*Archit.*) (*a fold, a turned-back edge*) fold, swell, tossing, undulation, volute, wave. **6** (*the act of rolling*) coil, curl, gyration, revolution, spin, twirl. **7** (*a gymnastic exercise in which the body is curled up and rolled over*) somersault, tumble. **8** (*a resounding peal of thunder etc.*) boom, growl, grumble, peal, resonance, reverberation, roar, rumble, thunder. **9** (*a wad of money*) bankroll, bundle, wad.

~*v.t.* **1** (*to cause to move along by turning over and over on its axis*) push, send. **2** (*to press or level with or as with a roller*) even, flatten, level, press, smooth, spread. **3** (*to wrap (up in)*) bind, coil, curl, enfold, entwine, envelop, enwrap, furl, swathe, twist, wind, wrap. **4** (*to carry or impel forward with a sweeping motion*) carry forward, impel. **5** (*to utter with a prolonged, deep sound*) boom, drum, echo, grumble, resound, reverberate, roar, rumble, thunder.

~*v.i.* **1** (*to revolve*) go round, gyrate, orbit, pivot, revolve, rotate, spin, swivel, twirl, wheel, whirl. **2** (*to operate or cause to operate*) operate, work. **3** (*to progress*) elapse, flit, flow, glide, go, pass, progress, run, slip. **4** (*to go from side to side; to move along with such a motion*) lumber, lurch, reel, rock, stagger, swagger, sway, swing, toss, tumble, waddle.

romance *n.* **1** (*the spirit or atmosphere of imaginary adventure, chivalrous or idealized love*) adventure, charm, chivalry, colour, excitement, fascination, glamour, love, mystery, nostalgia, sentiment. **2** (*a love affair*) affair, amour, attachment, dalliance, intrigue, involvement, liaison, love affair, passion, relationship. **3** (*a work of sentimental love stories*) love story, tear-jerker. **4** (*a story, usu. in prose, with characters and incidents remote from ordinary life*) epic, fable, fairy tale, fantasy, fiction, idyll, legend, melodrama, myth, narrative, novel, story, tale. **5** (*a fabrication, a falsehood*) absurdity, concoction, exaggeration, fabrication, fairy tale, falsehood, fib, fiction, flight of fancy, invention, lie, nonsense, tall story. ANTONYMS: fact.
~*v.i.* (*to make false or exaggerated statements*) exaggerate, fabricate, fib, lie, tell stories.
~*v.t.* (*to have a love affair with*) court, make love to, woo.

romantic *a.* **1** (*relating to or given to romance*) affectionate, amorous, fond, loving, passionate, sentimental, (*coll.*) soppy, sugary, tender. ANTONYMS: unromantic. **2** (*extravagant, fanciful*) dreamy, emotional, extravagant, fanciful, high-flown, idealistic, imaginary, impractical, poetic, sensitive, unrealistic, utopian, visionary, whimsical. ANTONYMS: practical, realistic. **3** ((*of conduct etc.*) *fantastic, unpractical*) exaggerated, extravagant, fabulous, fairytale, fancied, fanciful, fantastic, fictitious, idyllic, illusory, imaginary, imagined, improbable, legendary, sentimental, unpractical, unrealistic. **4** ((*of scenery etc.*) *picturesque, suggestive of romance*) charming, colourful, exciting, exotic, picturesque, wild.
~*n.* (*a person given to sentimental thoughts or acts of love*) dreamer, idealist, romancer, sentimentalist, utopian, visionary.

room *n.* **1** (*space regarded as available for occupation, accommodation etc.*) allowance, area, capacity, compass, elbow room, expanse, extent, latitude, leeway, margin, play, range, space, territory, volume. **2** (*opportunity, scope*) chance, occasion, opportunity, scope. **3** (*a portion of space in a building enclosed by walls, floor and ceiling*) apartment, cell, chamber, compartment, office.

root[1] *n.* **1** (*the descending part of a plant which fixes itself in the earth and draws nourishment from it*) rhizome, stem, tuber. **2** (*the cause or source*) beginnings, cause, derivation, fount, germ, mainspring, occasion, origin, seat, seed, source, start, wellspring. **3** (*the basis, the fundamental part*) base, basis, bottom, foundation, sustenance. **4** (*pl.*) (*one's ancestry, origins*) ancestry, birthplace, cradle, descent, family, heritage, house, lineage, origin, pedigree, stock.
~*v.t.* (*to fix or implant firmly* (*to the spot*)) anchor, embed, entrench, establish, fasten, fix, found, ground, implant, set, stick, take root. ANTONYMS: uproot.

root[2] *v.t.* (*to dig or grub* (*up*) *with the snout, beak etc.*) dig, grub up, turn up.
~*v.i.* **1** (*to turn up the ground in this manner in search of food*) burrow. **2** (*to rummage* (*about, in etc.*)) delve, ferret, forage, hunt, nose, poke, pry, ransack, rummage, search.

rope *n.* **1** (*a stout cord of twisted fibres of cotton, nylon etc., or wire*) cable, cord, hawser, line, string. **2** (*a series of things strung together in a line*) chain, row, series, string.
~*v.t.* (*to secure with a rope*) attach, bind, fasten, hitch, lash, moor, secure, tether, tie.

rosy *a.* **1** (*of the colour of a pink or red rose*) cerise, cherry, pink, red, roseate, rose-coloured. **2** (*healthy, blooming*) blooming, blushing, florid, flushed, fresh, glowing, healthy, radiant, rubicund, ruddy. ANTONYMS: pallid, wan. **3** (*favourable, auspicious*) auspicious, bright, cheerful, cheering, encouraging, favourable, hopeful, optimistic, promising, reassuring, sunny. ANTONYMS: discouraging, ominous.

rot *v.i.* **1** (*to decompose through natural change*) decay, decompose, fester, go bad, moulder, perish, putrefy, spoil, taint. ANTONYMS: keep, preserve. **2** (*to crumble* (*away*) *through decomposition*) corrode, crumble, deteriorate, disintegrate, fall to bits, rust. **3** (*to pine away*) languish, pine away, waste away, wither away. **4** (*to die out gradually*) decline, die, peter out. **5** (*to become morally corrupt*) corrupt, degenerate.
~*n.* **1** (*putrefaction, rottenness*) blight, canker, corrosion, corruption, decay, decomposition, mildew, mould, putrefaction, putrescence, rottenness. **2** (*dry rot, wet rot*) dry rot, wet rot. **3** (*nonsense, rubbish*) (*sl.*) balls, bosh, (*taboo sl.*) bullshit, bunkum, claptrap, (*sl.*) cobblers, (*sl.*) codswallop, (*sl.*) crap, drivel, garbage, (*coll.*) guff, nonsense, rubbish, (*taboo sl.*) shit, (*sl.*) tosh, (*coll.*) tripe, twaddle. ANTONYMS: sense. **4** (*a rapid deterioration*) decline, deterioration, disintegration.

rotate *v.i.* **1** (*to revolve round an axis or centre*) go round, gyrate, pirouette, pivot, revolve, spin, swivel, turn, wheel, whirl. **2** (*to act in rotation*) alternate, exchange, interchange, swap, switch, take turns.

rotten *a.* **1** (*decomposed, decayed*) bad, corroded, crumbling, decayed, decomposed, disintegrating, festering, fetid, foul, mildewed, mouldering, mouldy, perished, putrescent, putrid, rancid, rank, sour, stinking, tainted. ANTONYMS: fresh, wholesome. **2** (*unsound, liable to break, tear etc.*) brittle, fragile, unsound. **3** (*morally corrupt, untrustworthy*) amoral, (*sl.*) bent, corrupt, crooked, deceitful, degenerate, dishonest, dishonourable, disloyal, evil, faithless, immoral, iniquitous, mercenary, perfidious, perverted, treacherous, untrustworthy, vicious, wicked. ANTONYMS: honest, moral. **4** (*coll.*) (*poor or contemptible in quality*) bad, base, contemptible, deplorable, despicable, disappointing, (*sl.*) duff, inadequate, inferior, (*coll.*) lousy, low, poor, sorry, substandard, unacceptable, unsatisfactory. **5** (*coll.*) (*unpleasant*) annoying, disagreeable, unpleasant. **6** (*coll.*) (*unwell*) awful, bad, ill, nauseous, off colour, poorly, (*coll.*) ropy, rough, sick, unwell.

rotund *a.* **1** (*circular or spherical*) bulbous, circular, globular, rounded, spherical. ANTONYMS: angular. **2** ((*of language*) *sonorous*) deep, full, grandiloquent, magniloquent, mellow, orotund, resonant, reverberant, rich, round, sonorous. **3** (*plump, well-rounded*) chubby, corpulent, fat, fleshy, heavy, obese, overweight, paunchy, plump, podgy, portly, rolypoly, rounded, stout, tubby, well-covered, well-rounded. ANTONYMS: gaunt, lean.

rough *a.* **1** (*having an uneven or irregular surface*) broken, bumpy, irregular, jagged, lumpy, uneven. ANTONYMS: even, smooth. **2** (*shaggy, hairy*) bristly, bushy, fuzzy, shaggy, tangled, tousled, uncut, unkempt, unshaven, unshorn. **3** (*rugged, hilly*) hilly, rocky, rugged. **4** (*harsh to the senses, discordant*) astringent, cacophonous, discordant, grating, gruff, harsh, husky, inharmonious, jarring, rasping, raucous, severe, unmusical. **5** (*boisterous, tempestuous*) boisterous, forceful, noisy, tempestuous, violent. **6** ((*of language*) *crude*) coarse, crude, earthy, gross, unpolished. **7** (*turbulent*) agitated, choppy, inclement, squally, stormy, tempestuous, turbulent, wild. ANTONYMS: calm. **8** (*disorderly*) dishevelled, disorderly, messy, ruffled, unkempt, untidy. ANTONYMS: neat, tidy. **9** (*harsh in temper or manners*) bearish, blunt, brusque, churlish, curt, harsh, ill-bred, ill-mannered, impolite, loutish, rude, rugged, unceremonious, uncivil, uncouth, uncultured, ungracious, unmannerly, unpolished, unrefined. ANTONYMS:

refined, well-mannered. **10** (*cruel, unfeeling*) brutal, cruel, nasty, severe, sharp, tough, unfeeling, unjust, violent. ANTONYMS: gentle, kind. **11** (*lacking finish, not completely wrought*) basic, crude, imperfect, incomplete, raw, rudimentary, sketchy, unfinished, unpolished, unprocessed, unrefined, unwrought. ANTONYMS: complete, finished. **12** (*approximate, not exact*) amorphous, approximate, estimated, foggy, general, hazy, imprecise, inexact, sketchy, vague. ANTONYMS: exact, precise. **13** (*difficult, hard* (*to bear*)) arduous, austere, difficult, hard, laborious, rugged, spartan, tough, uncomfortable, unpleasant. **14** (*unwell or low in spirits*) below par, ill, low, out of sorts, poorly, (*coll.*) ropy, (*coll.*) rotten, sick, under the weather, upset.

~*n.* **1** (*a rough person, a rowdy*) (*coll.*) bruiser, bully, hooligan, lout, rowdy, ruffian, thug, tough. **2** (*a draft, a rough drawing*) draft, mock-up, outline, preliminary sketch, suggestion.

round *a.* **1** (*spherical, circular or approximately so*) circular, cylindrical, discoid, spherical. **2** (*convexly curved, plump*) ample, bowed, bulbous, convex, corpulent, curved, fleshy, full, globular, plump, rotund, rounded. ANTONYMS: concave. **3** (*continuous, unbroken*) complete, continuous, entire, full, solid, unbroken, undivided, whole. **4** (*frank, candid*) blunt, candid, direct, fair, frank, honest, open, outspoken, plain, straightforward, truthful, unvarnished, (*coll.*) upfront. ANTONYMS: evasive. **5** ((*of pace etc.*) *quick, brisk*) brisk, quick, smart. **6** (*full-toned, resonant*) full-toned, mellifluous, mellow, orotund, resonant, reverberant, rich, sonorous, vibrant. **7** (*ample, considerable*) ample, bounteous, bountiful, considerable, generous, great, large, liberal, substantial. **8** (*approximate, without fractions*) approximate, rough. ANTONYMS: exact.

~*n.* **1** (*a round object, piece etc.*) circle, disc. **2** (*a circle, sphere*) ball, circle, coil, globe, orb, ring, sphere. **3** (*something which surrounds, extent*) circumference, extent, surround. **4** (*a circular course*) circuit, course, orbit. **5** (*a heat, a cycle*) heat, lap, level, stage, turn. **6** (*a bout, a session*) bout, period, session, spate, spell. **7** (*a series of actions*) cycle, sequence, series, succession. **8** (*a burst of applause*) burst, outbreak, outburst. **9** (*a single shot fired from a firearm*) burst, salvo, volley. **10** (*ammunition for this*) bullet, cartridge, charge, shell, shot. **11** (*a circuit of inspection, the route taken*) ambit, beat, circuit, route, tour.

~*v.t.* **1** (*to make round or curved*) curve, level, smooth. **2** (*to go or travel round*) bypass, circle, circumnavigate, flank, go round, pass, skirt. **to get round 1** (*to coax by flattery or deception*) cajole, coax, convert, persuade, prevail upon, sway, talk round, wheedle, win over. **2** (*to evade* (*a law or rule*)) bypass, circumvent, evade, find a loophole in, find a way round, outmanoeuvre, skirt round. **to round up** (*to gather* (*horse, cattle etc.*) *together*) assemble, bring together, collect, corral, draw together, drive, gather together, group, herd, marshal, muster, rally. ANTONYMS: disperse.

rouse *v.t.* **1** (*to wake*) arise, arouse, awaken, call, get up, rise, wake. **2** (*to excite to thought or action*) animate, enkindle, galvanize, incite, inspire, inspirit, instigate, stimulate. **3** (*to provoke, to stir* (*up*)) agitate, anger, arouse, bestir, disturb, electrify, excite, exhilarate, fire up, foment, goad, inflame, invigorate, move, prod, provoke, startle, stir, whip up. ANTONYMS: soothe.

rout *n.* **1** (*an utter defeat and overthrow*) conquest, debacle, defeat, drubbing, (*coll.*) hiding, (*coll.*) licking, overthrow, (*sl.*) pasting, ruin, shambles, subjugation, thrashing, trouncing. ANTONYMS: victory. **2** (*a disorderly retreat of a defeated army etc.*) flight, retreat, withdrawal. **3** (*a disorderly gathering*) crowd, mob, rabble. **4** (*a riot, a brawl*) brawl, disturbance, riot, uproar.
~*v.t.* (*to defeat utterly and put to flight*) beat, best, (*sl.*) clobber, conquer, crush, cut to pieces, defeat, destroy, devastate, dispel, drive off, (*coll.*) lick, overrun, overthrow, overwhelm, put to flight, scatter, thrash, trample, trounce.

route *n.* (*the way or road*(*s*) *travelled or to be travelled*) avenue, circuit, course, itinerary, journey, passage, path, road, round, run, way.
~*v.t.* (*to send by a certain route*) carry, convey, direct, dispatch, send, steer.

routine *n.* **1** (*a course of procedure or official duties etc., regularly pursued*) method, order, pattern, procedure, way. **2** (*any regular or mechanical practice*) custom, (*coll.*) drill, formula, grind, groove, habit, practice, usage, wont. **3** (*a sequence of jokes, movements etc. regularly performed by a comedian, dancer etc.*) act, performance, piece, sequence.
~*a.* **1** (*repetitive, commonplace*) automatic, boring, clichéd, commonplace, dull, hackneyed, humdrum, mechanical, mind-numbing, monotonous, perfunctory, predictable, repetitive, stereotypical, tedious, tiresome, trite, unimaginative, uninteresting, unoriginal. **2** (*of or relating to a set procedure*) accustomed, conventional, customary, everyday, familiar, habitual, normal, ordinary, regular, standard, typical, usual, wonted. ANTONYMS: exceptional, unusual.

row[1] *n.* (*a series of persons or things in a straight or nearly straight line*) bank, column, file, line, queue, range, rank, sequence, string, succession, tier.

row[2] *n.* **1** (*a noisy disturbance, a commotion*) bedlam, clamour, commotion, din, disturbance, fracas, fuss, hubbub, noise, pandemonium, racket, (*esp. N Am., coll.*) ruckus, rumpus, (*coll.*) scrap, stir, trouble, tumult, turmoil, uproar. ANTONYMS: quiet. **2** (*a quarrel*) altercation, argument, brawl, conflict, controversy, disagreement, dispute, falling-out, fight, quarrel, (*coll.*) shouting match, spat, squabble, tiff. ANTONYMS: agreement, harmony. **3** (*a scolding*) castigation, (*coll.*) dressing-down, lecture, reprimand, reproof, (*coll.*) rollicking, scolding, (*coll.*) talking-to, (*coll.*) telling-off, (*coll.*) ticking-off, tongue-lashing.
~*v.i.* (*to make a row, to quarrel*) argue, bicker, brawl, disagree, dispute, fall out, fight, quarrel, (*coll.*) scrap, spar, squabble, tiff, wrangle.

rowdy *a.* (*rough, riotous*) boisterous, disorderly, loud, loutish, noisy, obstreperous, riotous, rough, rowdy, unruly, uproarious, wild. ANTONYMS: orderly, peaceful.

royal *a.* **1** (*of or relating to a king or queen*) kingly, queenly. **2** (*regal*) imperial, kingly, monarchical, princely, queenly, regal, sovereign. **3** (*noble, majestic*) august, awesome, dignified, grand, imposing, impressive, magnificent, majestic, noble, stately. **4** (*extremely fine, splendid*) fine, first-rate, great, splendid, superb, superior.

rub *v.t.* **1** (*to apply friction to, to move one's hand or other object over the surface of*) caress, massage, pat, press against, stroke. **2** (*to polish, to scrape*) brush, buff, burnish, clean, graze, polish, scour, scrape, scrub, shine, stroke, wipe. **3** (*to slide or pass* (*a hand or other object*) *along, over or against something*) knead, press, smooth, work. **4** (*to irritate*) aggravate, anger, annoy, (*sl.*) bug, (*coll.*) get on one's nerves, irk, irritate, (*sl.*) nark, (*coll.*) peeve, (*taboo sl.*) piss off, provoke, vex. **5** (*to spread on or mix into something by rubbing*) apply, mix into, put, smear, spread.
~*v.i.* **1** (*to move or slide along a surface, to chafe* (*against, on etc.*)) abrade, chafe, grate, graze. **2** (*to cause pain or fraying by rubbing*) chafe, fray.
~*n.* **1** (*the act or a spell of rubbing*) caress, kneading, massage, polish, shine, stroke, wipe. **2** (*a hindrance, a difficulty*) catch, difficulty, drawback, hindrance, hitch, impediment, obstacle, obstruction, problem, setback, snag, trouble. **to rub out 1** (*to remove or erase*) cancel, delete, efface, erase, excise, expunge, obliterate, remove, wipe out. **2** (*to kill*) assassinate, (*sl.*) blow away, (*coll.*) bump off, butcher, dispatch, (*sl.*) do in, eliminate,

execute, (*esp. N Am., sl.*) hit, kill, (*coll.*) knock off, murder, slaughter, slay, (*sl.*) take out, (*sl.*) waste.

rubbish *n.* **1** (*waste matter, refuse*) (*sl.*) crap, debris, detritus, dregs, dross, flotsam, garbage, jetsam, junk, litter, lumber, offal, refuse, remnants, residue, rubble, scourings, scrap, trash, waste. **2** (*nonsense*) balderdash, (*sl.*) balls, bosh, (*taboo sl.*) bullshit, bunkum, claptrap, (*sl.*) cobblers, codswallop, (*sl.*) crap, drivel, gibberish, (*sl.*) hogwash, moonshine, nonsense, (*coll.*) piffle, (*taboo sl.*) shit, (*sl.*) tosh, (*coll.*) tripe, twaddle. ANTONYMS: sense.

rude *a.* **1** (*impolite, insulting*) abusive, bad-mannered, blunt, brusque, cheeky, curt, discourteous, disrespectful, gruff, ill-mannered, impertinent, impolite, impudent, insolent, insulting, offensive, peremptory, tactless, uncivil, unmannerly. ANTONYMS: civil, polite. **2** (*unformed, unfinished*) artless, awkward, basic, clumsy, crude, inartistic, inelegant, makeshift, primitive, raw, rough, simple, unfinished, unformed, unskilled. ANTONYMS: finished. **3** (*primitive, uncivilized*) barbarous, boorish, brutish, crude, graceless, loutish, low, oafish, primitive, rough, rugged, savage, uncivilized, uncultivated, uncultured, ungracious, unpolished, unrefined, unsophisticated. ANTONYMS: civilized, refined. **4** (*violent, boisterous*) abrupt, boisterous, harsh, sharp, startling, sudden, tempestuous, unpleasant, violent. **5** (*coarse, indecent*) coarse, crude, dirty, gross, indecent, lewd, obscene, scurrilous, smutty, uncouth, vulgar. **6** (*robust, strong*) hearty, robust, strong. **7** (*uneducated*) ignorant, illiterate, uneducated, untutored.

rudimentary *a.* (*elementary, not advanced*) basic, early, elementary, embryonic, first, fundamental, immature, initial, introductory, primary, primitive, undeveloped, vestigial. ANTONYMS: developed, sophisticated.

ruffle *v.t.* **1** (*to disturb the smoothness or order of*) crease, derange, disarrange, discompose, dishevel, disorder, disturb, mess up, mix up, rumple, tousle, wrinkle. ANTONYMS: order, smooth. **2** (*to disturb, to discompose*) agitate, confuse, discompose, disconcert, disquiet, disturb, faze, fluster, harass, (*coll.*) hassle, perturb, put out, rattle, (*coll.*) shake up, stir, (*coll.*) throw, trouble, unnerve, upset. ANTONYMS: calm, soothe.

rugged *a.* **1** (*having an extremely uneven surface full of inequalities*) broken, bumpy, irregular, jagged, pitted, ragged, rough, uneven. ANTONYMS: even, smooth. **2** (*rocky, of abrupt contour*) abrupt, craggy, rocky. **3** ((*of a man*) *having strong, virile features*) beefy, brawny,

burly, hale, muscular, robust, strong, sturdy, tough, vigorous, virile. ANTONYMS: delicate, weak. **4** ((*of a sound*) *harsh, grating*) grating, harsh, jarring, rough. **5** (*rough in temper, stern*) austere, crabbed, dour, gruff, hard, harsh, rough, rude, severe, sour, stern, surly, unbending. ANTONYMS: forgiving, pleasant. **6** (*rude, unpolished*) blunt, crude, graceless, rude, uncouth, uncultured, unpolished, unrefined. **7** (*N Am.*) ((*of weather, waves etc.*) *tempestuous*) stormy, tempestuous, turbulent, wild. **8** (*strenuous, hard*) arduous, demanding, difficult, exacting, hard, harsh, laborious, rigorous, rough, stern, strenuous, taxing, tough, trying, uncompromising. **9** (*hardy, sturdy*) durable, hardy, stalwart, sturdy.

ruin *n.* **1** (*a state of wreck, a downfall*) breakdown, collapse, crash, damage, decay, defeat, destruction, devastation, disaster, disintegration, disrepair, dissolution, downfall, failure, fall, overthrow, ruination, subversion, undoing, wreck. ANTONYMS: preservation, success. **2** (*bankruptcy*) bankruptcy, destitution, insolvency, liquidation. **3** (*often in pl.*) (*the remains of a building etc. that has been demolished*) debris, rubble, shell, wreckage.
~*v.t.* **1** (*to bring to ruin*) annihilate, break, crush, defeat, devastate, lay waste, shatter, smash, (*esp. N Am., coll.*) trash, wreck. ANTONYMS: mend, restore. **2** (*to reduce to ruins, to dilapidate*) demolish, dilapidate, flatten, raze, reduce. ANTONYMS: build. **3** (*to destroy, to overthrow*) bring down, destroy, overthrow, overturn, overwhelm, subvert. **4** (*to harm, to disfigure*) botch, (*sl.*) cock up, damage, disfigure, harm, impair, injure, mangle, mar, mess up, nullify, (*sl.*) screw up, spoil, undo. **5** (*to bankrupt*) bankrupt, impoverish, pauperize.

ruinous *a.* **1** (*causing ruin, destructive*) baleful, calamitous, catastrophic, crippling, deadly, destructive, devastating, dire, disastrous, extravagant, fatal, harmful, immoderate, injurious, murderous, nasty, noxious, pernicious, poisonous, shattering. ANTONYMS: beneficial. **2** (*fallen into ruin, dilapidated*) broken-down, decrepit, derelict, dilapidated, ramshackle, ruined.

rule *n.* **1** (*something which is established as a principle or guide of action*) axiom, canon, criterion, decree, direction, directive, guide, guideline, law, maxim, order, ordinance, precept, principle, regulation, standard, tenet. **2** (*a regular practice, an established custom*) convention, custom, form, habit, practice. **3** (*the act of ruling or the state of being ruled, government*) administration, ascendancy, authority, command, control, direction, domination, dominion, government, jurisdiction,

leadership, mastery, power, regime, reign, sovereignty, supremacy, sway. **4** (*a strip of wood, plastic etc., used for measurement*) measure, ruler, yardstick. **5** (*a prescribed formula etc. for solving a mathematical problem of a given kind*) course, formula, method, procedure, way. **6** (*Law*) (*a decision by a judge or court, usu. with reference to a particular case only*) decision, dictum, direction, order, ruling. **7** (*the general way of things*) routine, tradition, way of things, wont.
~*v.t.* **1** (*to govern, to control*) administer, command, control, curb, direct, dominate, govern, manage, oversee, preside over, regulate, restrain, run, supervise. **2** (*to be the ruler of*) govern, hold sway (over), reign (over).
~*v.i.* **1** (*to decide, to make a decision*) adjudge, adjudicate, decide, declare, decree, determine, establish, find, judge, lay down, pronounce, resolve, settle. **2** (*to dominate, to be prevalent*) dominate, predominate, preponderate, prevail.

ruler *n.* **1** (*a person who rules or governs*) administrator, chief, commander, controller, crowned head, emperor, empress, governor, head of state, king, leader, lord, monarch, potentate, president, prince, princess, queen, sovereign. ANTONYMS: subject. **2** (*an instrument with straight edges, used as a guide in drawing straight lines*) measure, rule, yardstick.

rumour *n.* **1** (*popular report, hearsay*) chat, gossip, grapevine, hearsay, report, talk, tittle-tattle. **2** (*a current story without any known authority*) canard, report, story, whisper, word.
~*v.t.* (*to report or circulate as a rumour*) circulate, communicate, gossip, intimate, leak, noise abroad, pass around, publish, put about, report, reveal, say, suggest, tell, whisper.

rumple *v.t.* (*to make uneven, to crease*) crease, crinkle, crumple, crush, derange, dishevel, disorder, mess up, pucker, ruffle, screw up, scrunch, tousle, untidy, wrinkle. ANTONYMS: smooth, straighten out.

run *v.i.* **1** (*to move or pass over the ground by using the legs with a springing motion*) jog, lope, sprint, trot. ANTONYMS: walk. **2** (*to hasten*) bolt, career, dart, dash, hare, hasten, hurry, race, rush, scamper, scramble, scud, scurry, scuttle, speed, tear. ANTONYMS: saunter. **3** ((*of a horse etc.*) *to move quickly*) canter, gallop, trot. **4** (*to flee, to try to escape*) abscond, beat a retreat, (*sl.*) beat it, bolt, clear out, cut and run, decamp, depart, (*sl.*) do a bunk, (*sl.*) do a runner, escape, flee, (*coll.*) fly the coop, (*coll.*) leg it, make off, (*sl.*) scarper, (*coll.*) skedaddle, slope off, take flight, take off. **5** (*to seek election etc.*) challenge, compete, contend, put up for, stand. **6** (*to be in action or operation*) function, go, operate, perform, work. ANTONYMS:

cease, stop. **7** (*to glide, to elapse*) course, elapse, glide, move, pass, roll, skim, slide. **8** (*to flow*) cascade, discharge, flow, gush, issue, pour, spill, spout, stream. **9** (*to melt, to dissolve and spread*) dissolve, fuse, liquefy, melt, spread. **10** (*to drip, to emit liquid*) bleed, drip, flow, leak. **11** (*to extend, to continue (for a certain distance or duration)*) continue, extend, go on, last, lie, proceed, range, reach, stretch. **12** (*to be allowed to grow (wild)*) climb, creep, spread, trail. **13** ((*of stockings, tights etc.*) *to ladder*) come apart, come undone, ladder, tear, unravel.
~*v.t.* **1** (*to cause to run or go*) activate, set in motion, set off, start up. **2** (*to cause or allow to pass, penetrate etc.*) impale, pierce, run through, spit, stab, stick, thrust, transfix. **3** (*to drive, to propel*) control, direct, drive, guide, propel, steer. **4** (*to pursue, to chase*) chase, follow, hunt, pursue, track. **5** (*to perform (a race, an errand etc.)*) complete, do, execute, perform. **6** (*to follow (a course etc.)*) follow, pursue. **7** (*to manage, to work*) administer, carry on, conduct, control, coordinate, direct, handle, keep going, look after, manage, operate, oversee, regulate, superintend, supervise, take care of. **8** (*to enrol (as a contender)*) enrol, enter. **9** (*to get past or through (e.g. a blockade)*) break, get past, get through. **10** (*to discharge*) discharge, exude, flow with, release. **11** (*to convey in a motor vehicle, to give a lift to*) bear, carry, convey, drive, give a lift to, take, transport. **12** (*to publish*) carry, display, feature, print, publish. **13** (*to mould*) cast, found, mould. **14** (*to deal in, to smuggle*) bootleg, deal in, ship, smuggle, traffic in, transport. **15** (*to incur, to expose oneself to*) expose oneself, hazard, incur.
~*n.* **1** (*an act or spell of running*) dash, gallop, jog, race, rush, sprint, spurt. **2** (*the distance or duration of a run or journey*) distance, duration, (*coll.*) joyride, junket, outing, ride, (*coll.*) spin, trek, trip, visit. **3** (*a continuous course, a period of operation*) chain, course, cycle, passage, period, round, season, spate. **4** (*a sequence or series (e.g. of cards, luck etc.)*) progression, sequence, series, spell, stretch, string, succession. **5** (*a pipe or course for flowing liquid*) conduit, course, duct, pipe. **6** (*the general direction, the way things tend to move*) course, current, direction, drift, flow, motion, movement, passage, path, progress, stream, tendency, tenor, tide, trend, way of things. **7** (*a ladder or rip in a stocking etc.*) ladder, rip, snag, tear. **8** (*general nature, character*) category, character, class, kind, order, sort, type, variety. **9** (*a group of animals, fish etc.*) batch, drove, flock, shoal. **10** (*a regular track (of certain animals), a burrow*) burrow, track. **11** (*an enclosure for fowls*) cage, coop, enclosure, pen.

12 (*free use or access*) access, freedom, liberty. **to run down 1** (*to stop through not being wound up, recharged etc.*) expire, peter out, wind down. **2** (*to make enfeebled by overwork etc.*) (*coll.*) burn out, debilitate, enfeeble, exhaust, sap, tire, undermine, weaken. **3** (*to pursue and overtake*) overhaul, overtake, pursue. **4** (*to search for and discover*) discover, find, hunt, locate, pursue, search for, shadow, stalk, trace, track down. **5** (*to disparage, to abuse*) abuse, belittle, criticize, decry, defame, denigrate, deprecate, depreciate, disparage, (*coll.*) knock, (*coll.*) pan, put down, revile, rubbish, (*sl.*) slag off, speak ill of, vilify. ANTONYMS: praise. **6** (*to collide with*) collide with, hit, knock down, run into, run over, slam into, strike. **7** (*to reduce in size or amount*) curtail, cut back, decrease, downsize, pare down, reduce, trim. **to run out** (*to come to an end*) cease, close, come to an end, consume, dry up, end, exhaust, expire, fail, finish, give out, peter out, terminate, use up.

rupture *n.* **1** (*the act of breaking or the state of being broken or violently parted*) breach, break, breakage, burst, cleavage, cleft, crack, fissure, fracture, parting, rend, rift, split, tear. **2** (*a breach of friendly relations*) altercation, breach, bust-up, contention, disagreement, disruption, dissolution, division, estrangement, falling-out, feud, hostility, quarrel, rift, schism, split.
~*v.t.* **1** (*to break, to separate by violence*) break, burst, cleave, crack, fracture, part, puncture, rend, separate, sever, split, sunder, tear. ANTONYMS: mend. **2** (*to sever* (*a friendship etc.*)) break off, come between, disrupt, dissever, divide, sever, split. ANTONYMS: reconcile.

rural *a.* **1** (*of or relating to the country*) countrified, country. ANTONYMS: urban. **2** (*pastoral, agricultural*) agrarian, agricultural, pastoral. **3** (*suiting or resembling the country*) bucolic, rustic.

rush *v.t.* **1** (*to move or push with haste*) accelerate, dispatch, drive, expedite, force, hurry, move, press, push, quicken, speed up, urge. ANTONYMS: procrastinate, slow down. **2** (*to perform or complete quickly*) dash off, hurry. **3** (*to take by sudden assault*) assault, attack, capture, charge, overcome, storm, take by storm. **4** (*to seize and occupy*) occupy, pass, seize, surmount. **5** (*coll.*) (*to cheat, to swindle by overcharging*) cheat, diddle, fleece, swindle.
~*v.i.* **1** (*to move or run precipitately*) bolt, bustle,

career, dart, dash, fly, hasten, hurry, hustle, lose no time, make haste, race, run, scramble, scurry, shoot, speed, sprint, tear. ANTONYMS: dally. **2** (*to flow with violence and impetuosity*) flow, roll, run.
~*n.* **1** (*the act of rushing*) charge, dash, dispatch, expedition, haste, hurry, race, scramble, speed, stampede, swiftness, urgency. **2** (*a violent or impetuous movement*) assault, charge, dash, onslaught, push, storm. **3** (*a sudden onset of activity or movement*) onrush, onset, thronging. **4** (*a surge of euphoria induced by or as if by a drug*) charge, sensation, surge, thrill.
~*a.* (*characterized by or requiring much speed or urgency*) brisk, cursory, emergency, expeditious, fast, hasty, hurried, prompt, quick, rapid, speedy, swift, urgent. ANTONYMS: slow, unhurried.

rustic *a.* **1** (*of or relating to the country, rural*) Arcadian, bucolic, countrified, country, pastoral, peasant, provincial, rural, sylvan, upcountry. ANTONYMS: urban. **2** (*like or characteristic of country life or people*) artless, guileless, homespun, ingenuous, naive, plain, simple, unsophisticated. ANTONYMS: sophisticated. **3** (*rude, unpolished*) rude, unpolished, unrefined, unsophisticated. ANTONYMS: sophisticated. **4** (*awkward, uncouth*) awkward, boorish, churlish, cloddish, loutish, lumpish, plodding, uncouth, uncultured, ungainly, unmannerly. **5** (*of rough workmanship, plain*) coarse, crude, plain, rough.
~*n.* **1** (*a country person or dweller*) countryman, countrywoman, (*N Am., Austral., New Zeal.*) hayseed, (*coll.*) hick, (*N Am., usu. derog.*) hillbilly, peasant, yokel. **2** (*an unsophisticated or uncouth person*) boor, bumpkin, clod, clown.

rustle *v.i.* (*to make a quick succession of small sounds like the rubbing of dry leaves*) crackle, crinkle, sibilate, swish, whisper.
~*n.* (*a rustling*) crackle, crinkling, rustling, sibilance, susurration, swish, whisper.

rut *n.* **1** (*a sunken track made by wheels, a groove*) furrow, gouge, groove, hollow, indentation, pothole, score, track, trough, wheelmark. **2** (*a settled habit or course*) course, grind, groove, habit, pattern, routine, system.
~*v.t.* (*to make ruts in*) cut, furrow, gouge, groove, hole, routine, score.

ruthless *a.* (*merciless, cruel*) adamant, brutal, callous, cruel, ferocious, fierce, hard-hearted, harsh, heartless, inexorable, merciless, pitiless, remorseless, savage, severe, stern, unfeeling, unmerciful, unrelenting, vicious. ANTONYMS: gentle, merciful.

sabbatical *n.* (*an extended period of leave from one's work*) furlough, holiday, leave of absence, leisure, rest, study leave, time off, vacation.

sabotage *n.* (*malicious damage to industrial plant etc., as a protest by discontented workers, or as a non-military act of warfare*) damage, destruction, disablement, disruption, hindrance, impairment, insurrection, Luddism, sedition, spoiling, subversion, undermining, vandalism, wrecking.
~*v.t.* (*to commit sabotage on*) cripple, damage, deactivate, derail, destroy, disable, dislocate, disrupt, hinder, incapacitate, knock out, make useless, paralyse, put out of action, ruin, spoil, subvert, (*sl.*) take out, undermine, vandalize, wreck.

saboteur *n.* (*a person who commits sabotage*) anarchist, destroyer, fifth columnist, (*esp. N Am.*) filibuster, hinderer, insurrectionist, meddler, rebel, revolutionary, secret agent, spoiler, subversive, vandal, wrecker.

saccharine *a.* (*ingratiatingly pleasant or polite*) cloying, honeyed, ingratiating, mawkish, sentimental, sickly sweet, sugary, sycophantic, syrupy, treacly, unctuous, wheedling.

sack¹ *n.* **1** (*a large, usu. oblong bag of strong coarse material, for holding coal etc.*) bag, pouch. **2** (*dismissal from employment*) (*sl.*) axe, (*sl.*) boot, (*sl.*) bum's rush, (*sl.*) chop, discharge, dismissal, firing, (*coll.*) heave-ho, (*coll.*) marching orders, (*sl.*) push, redundancy. **3** (*bed*) bed, (*coll.*) the hay.
~*v.t.* (*to give the sack to*) discharge, dismiss, fire, give (someone) notice, (*sl.*) give (someone) the axe, (*sl.*) give (someone) the boot, give (someone) their cards, (*sl.*) give (someone) the push, (*coll.*) give (someone) the sack, lay off, let go, make redundant. ANTONYMS: appoint, employ.
to hit the sack (*to go to bed*) (*sl.*) crash out, go to bed, go to sleep, (*coll.*) hit the hay, retire, turn in.

sack² *v.t.* **1** (*to plunder or pillage* (*a place taken by storm*)) despoil, lay waste, maraud, pillage, plunder, raid, ravage. **2** (*to ransack, to loot*) loot, ransack, rifle, rustle.
~*n.* (*the pillaging of a captured place*) despoliation, marauding, pillaging, plunder.

sacrament *n.* (*a religious rite*) liturgy, observance, office, ordinance, rite.

sacramental *a.* **1** (*relating to or constituting a sacrament*) liturgical, ritual. **2** (*bound by oath, consecrated*) consecrated.

sacred *a.* **1** (*dedicated to religious use*) ceremonial, churchly, consecrated, divine, ecclesiastical, heavenly, hieratic, holy, liturgical, priestly, religious, ritual, sacramental, solemn, spiritual. ANTONYMS: secular. **2** (*consecrated*) blessed, blest, consecrated, dedicated, hallowed, heavenly, holy, revered, sainted, sanctified, venerated. **3** (*sanctified by religion, reverence etc.*) inviolable, inviolate, protected, sacrosanct, untouchable. ANTONYMS: blasphemous, profane.

sacrifice *n.* **1** (*the giving up of anything for the sake of another person, object or interest*) forfeiture, forgoing, giving up, loss, offer, relinquishment, renunciation, surrender, yielding up. **2** (*the act of offering an animal, person etc., esp. by ritual slaughter, or the surrender of a valued possession to a deity*) immolation, oblation, offering. ANTONYMS: acquisition, gain.
~*v.t.* **1** (*to surrender for the sake of another person, object etc.*) abnegate, devote, forbear, forfeit, forgo, forswear, give up, let go, lose, refrain from, relinquish, renounce, surrender, yield. **2** (*to offer to a deity as a sacrifice*) immolate, offer.

sacrificial *a.* (*offered as or relating to a sacrifice*) atoning, conciliatory, expiatory, given up, immolated, offered, propitiatory, sacrificed, surrendered, votive, yielded.

sacrilege *n.* **1** (*the violation or profanation of sacred things*) profanation, violation. **2** (*irreverence towards something or someone* (*considered*) *sacred*) abuse, blasphemy, contamination, debasement, defilement, desecration, dishonouring, disrespect, heresy, impiety, irreverence, maltreatment, misuse, mockery, offence, outrage, perversion, profanity, prostitution, secularization, vitiation. ANTONYMS: honour, respect, reverence.

sacrilegious *a.* (*of or relating to sacrilege*) blasphemous, disrespectful, godless, heretical, impious, irreligious, irreverent, mocking, profane, sinful, unholy.

sad *a.* **1** (*sorrowful, mournful*) (*coll.*) blue, broken-hearted, cast down, chap-fallen, cheerless, crestfallen, dejected, depressed, despondent, disconsolate, disheartened, dispirited, heartsick, lamenting, low, lugubrious, melancholy, miserable, morose, mournful, sorrowful, unhappy, woebegone, wretched. ANTONYMS: cheerful, delighted, glad, happy, joyful. **2** (*bad, shocking*) appalling, awful, bad, bleak, calamitous, deplorable, desperate, disappointing, disheartening, dismal, distressing, grievous, lamentable, (*coll.*) lousy, miserable, pathetic, pitiable, pitiful, regrettable, (*coll.*) rotten, saddening, shocking, sombre, sorry, terrible, tragic, unfortunate, wretched. ANTONYMS: fortunate, heartening, pleasing.

sadden *v.t.* (*to make sad*) aggrieve, cast down, deject, depress, disappoint, discourage, dishearten, dispirit, distress, grieve, make unhappy, sorrow. ANTONYMS: cheer up, encourage, hearten, please.

sadistic *a.* (*cruel and deriving pleasure from inflicting pain*) beastly, brutal, brutish, callous, cruel, inhuman, malevolent, malicious, merciless, monstrous, perverse, pitiless, ruthless.

sadly *adv.* **1** (*in a sad way*) dejectedly, despondently, dismally, gloomily, lugubriously, miserably, morosely, mournfully, sombrely, unhappily, wretchedly. ANTONYMS: cheerfully, happily. **2** (*unfortunately*) alas, deplorably, depressingly, disappointingly, dispiritingly, grievously, lamentably, regrettably, sad to relate, tragically, unfortunately, unhappily, unluckily. ANTONYMS: fortunately, happily, luckily.

sadness *n.* (*the state of being sad*) cheerlessness, dejection, depression, despondency, disappointment, dispiritedness, dolour, downheartedness, gloom, grief, melancholy, misery, moroseness, mourning, regret, sorrow, sorrowfulness, unhappiness, wretchedness. ANTONYMS: cheerfulness, happiness.

safe *a.* **1** (*free or secure from danger or damage*) impregnable, invulnerable, out of harm's way, protected, safeguarded, secure, sheltered, shielded. ANTONYMS: exposed, vulnerable. **2** (*uninjured, unharmed*) all right, intact, (*coll.*) OK, (*coll.*) okay, sound, undamaged, unharmed, unhurt, uninjured, unscathed, whole. **3** (*not dangerous or risky*) harmless, innocuous, non-poisonous, non-toxic, risk-free, riskless, unpolluted. ANTONYMS: dangerous, endangering, harmful, risky. **4** (*cautious, prudent*) careful, cautious, conservative, prudent, trusty. ANTONYMS: reckless. **5** (*certain, sure*) certain, certified, conservative, dependable, reliable, solid, sure, tried and tested,

trustworthy, unfailing. ANTONYMS: undependable, unreliable.
~*n.* (*a steel fireproof and burglarproof receptacle for valuables*) chest, coffer, repository, safe deposit, strongbox.

safeguard *n.* **1** (*a person who or thing which protects*) defence, protection, security. **2** (*a precaution, circumstance etc. that tends to save loss, trouble etc.*) insurance, precaution, provision, proviso.
~*v.t.* (*to make safe or secure by precaution, stipulation etc.*) care for, conserve, defend, guard, keep, keep safe, look after, preserve, protect, save, secure, shelter, shield. ANTONYMS: endanger, imperil, threaten.

safe keeping *n.* **1** (*the act of keeping or preserving in safety*) keeping, preservation. **2** (*secure guardianship*) care, charge, custody, guardianship.

safety *n.* **1** (*freedom from injury, danger or risk*) safeness, security. **2** (*safe keeping or custody*) cover, custody, preservation, protection, refuge, safe keeping, sanctuary, shelter.

sag *v.i.* **1** (*to droop or give way esp. in the middle, under weight or pressure*) bend, curve, dip, droop, falter, flag, give way, sink, slump, wilt, yield. **2** (*to lose vigour*) droop, slump, weaken, wilt. **3** ((*of prices, esp. of stocks*) *to decline*) come down, decline, decrease, descend, diminish, drop, fall, go down, lessen, slide, slip, subside. ANTONYMS: rise, stiffen, strengthen.
~*n.* (*the act or state of sagging or giving way*) bend, curve, decline, decrease, dip, droop, drop, fall, faltering, flagging, giving way, lessening, sagging, sinkage, sinking, slide, slump, subsidence, weakening, wilting, yielding.

saga *n.* (*a story of heroic adventure*) adventure, chronicle, cycle, epic, history, legend, narrative, romance, story, tale.

sagacious *a.* (*quick to understand or discern*) astute, clever, comprehending, discerning, intelligent, knowing, penetrating, perceptive, perspicacious, sage, sapient, sensible, shrewd, understanding, wise. ANTONYMS: dim, dull, stupid.

sagacity *n.* (*the state of being sagacious*) cleverness, discernment, intelligence, knowledge, perceptiveness, perspicacity, sense, shrewdness, understanding, wisdom. ANTONYMS: dimness, dullness, stupidity.

sage *a.* (*wise, prudent*) astute, clever, commonsensical, comprehending, discerning, discreet, intelligent, judicious, knowing, perceptive, perspicacious, profound, prudent, reasonable, sagacious, sapient, sensible, shrewd, understanding, wise. ANTONYMS: foolish, stupid.

~n. (a person of great wisdom) authority, doyen, doyenne, elder, expert, guru, master, oracle, philosopher, savant(e), wise man, wise woman. ANTONYMS: fool, idiot.

sail n. (a piece of fabric spread on rigging to catch the wind, and cause a ship or boat to move) canvas, sheet.
~v.i. **1** (to be conveyed in a vessel by water) coast, cruise, float. **2** (to set sail) embark, put to sea, set sail. **3** (to pass gently (along), to float (as a bird)) flit, float, flow, fly, glide, plane, scud, skim, slide, slip, waft. **4** (to go along in a stately manner) (coll.) breeze, drift.
~v.t. (to cause to sail, to set afloat) direct, navigate, pilot, set afloat, steer.

sailing ship n. (a ship with sails) boat, clipper, dinghy, frigate, galleon, Indiaman, ketch, man-of-war, sailboat, schooner, sloop, smack, vessel, yacht, yawl.

sailor n. (a member of the crew of a boat or ship, as distinguished from an officer) (sl.) bluejacket, boatman, boatwoman, deckhand, Jack tar, mariner, (coll.) matelot, rating, (coll.) salt, (coll.) sea dog, seafarer, seagoer, seaman, (N Am., sl.) swab, (coll.) tar.

saintly a. (very holy, very good) angelic, beatific, blameless, blessed, blest, devout, godly, good, holy, innocent, kind, pious, pure, reverent, righteous, sainted, seraphic, stainless, unstained, unsullied, virtuous. ANTONYMS: demonic, evil, godless, wicked.

sake n. **1** (purpose) end, objective, purpose, result. **2** (reason, cause) account, advantage, behalf, benefit, cause, consideration, gain, good, motive, profit, reason, regard, well-being.

salacious a. **1** (lustful, lecherous) lascivious, lecherous, libidinous, licentious, lustful, prurient. **2** (arousing lust, erotic) arousing, bawdy, dirty, erotic, indecent, lewd, lusty, obscene, pornographic, sensual, sexy, smutty. ANTONYMS: innocent, pure.

salary n. (a fixed payment given periodically, usu. monthly, esp. for work not of a manual kind) compensation, earnings, emolument, fee, income, pay, remuneration, stipend, wage.

sale n. **1** (the act of selling) selling, vending. **2** (the exchange of a commodity for money or other equivalent) bargain, barter, deal, exchange, transaction. **3** (an event at which goods are sold) car boot sale, garage sale, jumble sale, rummage sale, (N Am.) yard sale. **4** (a disposal of a shop's remaining goods at reduced prices) clearance, discount, markdown, reduction, sell-off. **on/ for/ up for sale** (offered for purchase) available, in stock, offered for

purchase, on offer, on sale, on the market, on the shelves, (coll.) up for grabs.

salesperson n. (a salesman or saleswoman) clerk, counter assistant, (N Am.) sales clerk, sales executive, salesgirl, salesman, sales representative, saleswoman, shop assistant, shopgirl, shop staff.

salient a. **1** (conspicuous, prominent) chief, conspicuous, distinctive, distinguishing, eminent, important, impressive, marked, notable, noteworthy, noticeable, outstanding, primary, principal, prominent, pronounced, remarkable, significant, striking, unique. ANTONYMS: inconspicuous. **2** (pointing or projecting outwards) jutting, projecting, protruding. ANTONYMS: flat.

sallow a. (of a sickly yellowish or pale brown colour) anaemic, brownish, pallid, pasty, wan, yellowish. ANTONYMS: florid, ruddy.

salt n. **1** (chloride of sodium, used for seasoning and preserving food, obtained from sea water or brine) rock salt, sodium chloride, table salt. **2** (wit, repartee in talk etc.) acuteness, bite, liveliness, pep, pepper, piquancy, (sl.) pizazz, punch, pungency, relish, repartee, spice, vigour, vitality, wit, zest. **3** (that which gives flavour) flavour, flavouring, savour, seasoning, taste. **4** (a sailor) mariner, sailor, seafarer, seaman.
~a. **1** (impregnated or flavoured with or tasting of salt) brackish, briny, saline, salted, salty. **2** (cured with salt) corned, cured, kippered, marinated, pickled, soused. **3** ((of wit etc.) pungent) acerbic, biting, pungent. **4** ((of grief) bitter) bitter, piercing, sharp. **5** (indecent, salacious) indecent, lewd, obscene, pornographic, salacious, sexy, smutty.
~v.t. **1** (to season with salt) flavour, marinate, season, souse. **2** (to cure or preserve with salt) corn, cure, pickle, preserve. **3** (to add liveliness to (a story etc.)) enliven, pepper, spice up. **to salt away/ down** (to save or hoard (money etc.)) accumulate, amass, hoard, lay by, pile up, put by, reserve, save, secrete, set aside, set by, squirrel away, (coll.) stash away, stockpile, store up, warehouse.

salubrious a. **1** ((of climate etc.) promoting health, wholesome) health-giving, healthy, wholesome. **2** (spiritually wholesome, respectable) beneficial, improving, respectable, salutary, upright. **3** ((of surroundings etc.) agreeable) agreeable, pleasant.

salute v.t. **1** (to show respect to (a military superior) by a salute) honour, pay tribute, show respect. **2** (to greet with a gesture or words of welcome or recognition) address, greet, hail, wave. **3** (to accost or welcome (as with a bow, *kiss etc.*)) accost, embrace, welcome. **4** (*to praise, acknowledge*) acknowledge, mark, praise, recognize. ANTONYMS: deride, ignore.

~*n.* (*gesture of welcome, recognition etc.*) acknowledgement, address, greeting, recognition, salutation, tribute, welcome.

salvage *n.* (*the saving and recycling of waste or scrap material*) reclamation, recovery, recycling, redemption, rescue, retrieval, salvation.

~*v.t.* (*to save or recover from wreck, fire etc.*) reclaim, recover, recycle, redeem, rescue, retrieve, save. ANTONYMS: give up, let go, surrender.

salvation *n.* (*deliverance, preservation from danger, evil etc.*) deliverance, liberation, preservation, redemption, rescue, saving. ANTONYMS: damnation.

salve *n.* **1** (*a healing ointment*) cream, demulcent, dressing, embrocation, liniment, lotion, ointment, unguent. **2** (*anything that soothes or palliates*) anodyne, balm, cure, emollient, narcotic, opiate, palliative, relief, tranquillizer.

~*v.t.* **1** (*to soothe, to ease*) alleviate, appease, assuage, comfort, ease, heal, make good, mitigate, mollify, palliate, relieve, soothe. ANTONYMS: exacerbate, irritate. **2** (*to dress with a salve*) anoint.

same *a.* **1** (*identical*) duplicate, exact, identical, selfsame, very. **2** (*identical or similar in kind, quality etc.*) alike, equivalent, similar. ANTONYMS: at variance, different. **3** (*just mentioned, aforesaid*) aforementioned, aforesaid. **4** (*unchanged, uniform*) constant, monotonous, unaltered, unchanged, unchanging, uniform, unmodified, unvaried, unvarying, word-for-word. **all the same** (*nevertheless*) anyhow, anyway, at any rate, at the same time, but, even so, for all that, having said that, in any case, in any event, just the same, nevertheless, nonetheless, notwithstanding, regardless, still, yet.

sample *n.* **1** (*a part taken or used as illustrating the whole, an example*) bite, cross-section, example, exemplar, illustration, model, pattern, representation, representative, sampler, sampling, specimen, taste, tester. **2** (*in electronics, a sound created by sampling*) excerpt, extract, snatch.

~*v.t.* (*to take samples of, to test*) experience, taste, test, try.

~*a.* (*representative, illustrative*) illustrative, representational, representative, specimen, test, trial.

sanatorium *n.* **1** (*an institution for the treatment of chronic diseases*) clinic. **2** (*a place to*

which people resort for the sake of their health) health farm, spa. **3** (*an institution for invalids, esp. convalescents*) convalescent home, rest home. **4** (*a sickroom, esp. in a boarding school*) sickbay, sickroom.

sanctify *v.t.* **1** (*to make holy, to consecrate*) beatify, bless, canonize, consecrate, enshrine, exalt, glorify, hallow, make holy, make sacred. ANTONYMS: desecrate. **2** (*to purify from sin*) cleanse, purify. **3** (*to give a sacred character to, to sanction*) confirm, justify, legalize, legitimize, license, ratify, sanction.

sanctimonious *a.* (*making a show of piety or saintliness*) (*coll., usu. derog.*) goody-goody, holier-than-thou, hypocritical, mealy-mouthed, Pharisaical, pietistic, self-righteous, smug, unctuous.

sanction *n.* **1** (*the act of ratifying, confirmation by superior authority*) approval, authorization, certification, confirmation, endorsement, imprimatur, legalization, legitimization, licence, permission, ratification, seal, stamp, validation. **2** (*support, encouragement conferred by usage etc.*) acquiescence, affirmation, agreement, aid, assent, backing, compliance, concurrence, countenance, encouragement, favour, help, (*coll.*) OK, (*coll.*) okay, sponsorship, support. **3** (*a coercive measure taken by one state against another to force compliance with international law etc.*) ban, boycott, embargo, penalty, punishment, redress, restriction, retaliation, retribution.

~*v.t.* **1** (*to authorize, to ratify*) advocate, allow, authorize, back, confirm, encourage, endorse, legalize, legitimize, license, ratify, second, sponsor, support, validate. ANTONYMS: forbid, prohibit. **2** (*to approve*) approve, commission, consent to, countenance, favour, permit, subscribe to. **3** (*to enforce by penalty etc.*) boycott, coerce, penalize, restrict.

sanctity *n.* **1** (*the state of being holy, holiness*) divinity, godliness, grace, holiness. **2** (*spiritual purity, saintliness*) piety, purity, righteousness, saintliness. **3** (*sacredness, inviolability*) inviolability, sacredness, sacrosanctity. ANTONYMS: profanity.

sanctuary *n.* **1** (*a church, temple or other building devoted to sacred uses*) altar, chapel, church, house of God, house of worship, mosque, pagoda, sanctum, shrine, synagogue, temple. **2** (*a place where deer, birds etc. are left undisturbed*) conservation area, national park, reservation, wildlife preserve, wildlife reserve. **3** (*a place of immunity, a refuge*) asylum, haven, refuge, retreat, shelter. **4** (*immunity, protection*) immunity, protection, safety.

sanctum *n.* **1** (*a sacred or private place*) holy of holies, most holy place, sanctuary, shrine, temple. **2** (*a private room, retreat*) cubby hole, den, hideaway, hideout, hiding place, retreat, study.

sane *a.* **1** (*sound in mind, not deranged*) (*coll.*) all there, compos mentis, level-headed, lucid, mentally sound, normal, of sound mind, rational, well-balanced. ANTONYMS: deranged, insane, mad. **2** ((*of views etc.*) *sensible, reasonable*) judicious, reasonable, right-minded, sensible.

sang-froid *n.* (*calmness, composure in danger etc.*) aplomb, calmness, cold-bloodedness, composure, cool, coolness, equanimity, imperturbability, phlegm, poise, self-possession, (*coll.*) unflappability. ANTONYMS: hot-headedness, passion.

sanguinary *a.* **1** (*accompanied by bloodshed or carnage*) bloody, brutal, gory, grim. **2** (*delighting in bloodshed, murderous*) barbarous, bloodthirsty, brutish, cruel, homicidal, merciless, murderous, ruthless, sanguineous, savage, slaughterous.

sanguine *a.* **1** (*cheerful, confident*) ardent, buoyant, cheerful, confident, enthusiastic, expectant, fervid, forward-looking, hopeful, keen, optimistic, rosy. ANTONYMS: discouraged, pessimistic. **2** ((*of the complexion*) *ruddy, florid*) florid, flushed, rosy, ruddy. ANTONYMS: anaemic, pale, sallow. **3** (*sanguinary*) bloody, sanguinary.

sanitary *a.* **1** (*relating to or concerned with the preservation of health, relating to hygiene*) healthy, hygienic, wholesome. **2** (*free from dirt, disease-causing organisms etc., hygienic*) antiseptic, aseptic, clean, disinfected, germ-free, hygienic, salubrious, sterile, unpolluted. ANTONYMS: dirty, insanitary, unhygienic.

sanity *n.* **1** (*saneness, mental soundness*) balance, lucidity, mental health, normality, rationality, reason, sense, stability. ANTONYMS: insanity, madness. **2** (*reasonableness, moderation*) moderation, reasonableness, temperance.

sap¹ *n.* **1** (*the watery juice or circulating fluid of living plants*) essence, fluid, juice. **2** (*the sapwood of a tree*) alburnum, sapwood. **3** (*vital fluid, strength*) lifeblood, strength, vigour. **4** (*a gullible person*) (*sl.*) charlie, (*sl.*) chump, dimwit, dunce, dupe, fall guy, fool, idiot, (*coll.*) ninny, nitwit, (*N Am., sl.*) patsy, pushover, (*sl.*) saphead, (*chiefly N Am., coll.*) schlemiel, simpleton, softhead, (*coll.*) sucker, twit.
~*v.t.* **1** (*to draw off sap*) draw off, milk, tap. **2** (*to exhaust the strength or vitality of*) drain, draw, exhaust, weaken. ANTONYMS: strengthen, support.

sap² *v.t.* **1** (*to undermine*) cripple, sabotage, undermine, weaken. **2** (*to subvert or destroy insidiously*) debilitate, deplete, devitalize, drain, enervate, erode, subvert.
~*n.* (*a deep trench or mine for approach to or attack on a fortification*) ditch, mine, trench.

sarcasm *n.* **1** (*an ironical or wounding remark*) gibe, taunt. **2** (*bitter or contemptuous irony*) acerbity, acridity, acrimony, asperity, bitterness, contempt, cynicism, derision, disdain, invective, irony, malevolence, poison, sardonism, satire, scorn, spite, trenchancy, venom.

sarcastic *a.* (*containing or characterized by sarcasm*) acerbic, acid, acrid, acrimonious, biting, bitter, caustic, contemptuous, cutting, cynical, derisive, disdainful, ironical, malevolent, nasty, poisonous, sardonic, satirical, scathing, scornful, spiteful, trenchant, venomous, virulent.

sardonic *a.* **1** (*forced, insincere*) affected, forced, insincere, unnatural. **2** ((*of laughter etc.*) *sneering, bitterly ironical*) cynical, derisive, ironical, malevolent, malignant, mocking, sarcastic, scornful, sneering. ANTONYMS: sincere, sympathetic.

satanic *a.* (*emanating from or having the qualities of Satan*) abominable, black, damnable, dark, devilish, diabolical, evil, fiendish, ghoulish, godless, heinous, hellish, impious, infernal, malevolent, monstrous, ungodly, unholy, unspeakable, vile, wicked. ANTONYMS: angelic, godlike.

satellite *n.* **1** (*a secondary planet revolving round a primary one*) moon. **2** (*a man-made device projected into space to orbit the earth, moon etc.*) probe, spacecraft. **3** (*something dependent on another*) dependant, subordinate. ANTONYMS: leader. **4** (*an obsequious follower, dependant*) acolyte, attendant, dependant, disciple, hanger-on, helper, henchman, lieutenant, minion, parasite, retainer, shadow, (*coll.*) sidekick, sycophant, vassal.
~*a.* (*on the periphery*) peripheral, secondary. ANTONYMS: central.

satiate *v.t.* **1** (*to satisfy (as a desire or appetite) fully*) quench, satisfy, slake. **2** (*to sate, to surfeit*) bore, choke, cloy, deluge, fill, flood, glut, gorge, jade, overfill, over-indulge, pall, sate, saturate, stuff, suffocate, surfeit, weary. ANTONYMS: deprive, starve.

satiety *n.* **1** (*the state of being sated or glutted*) gratification, saturation. **2** (*excess of gratification producing disgust*) excess, glut, over-indulgence, superfluity, surfeit.

satire *n.* **1** (*ridicule, sarcasm*) invective, irony, mockery, ridicule, sarcasm. **2** (*a composition in* *which wickedness or folly or individual persons are held up to ridicule*) burlesque, caricature, lampoon, parody, pasquinade, (*coll.*) send-up, skit, spoof, (*coll.*) take-off, travesty.

satirical *a.* (*using or relating to satire*) burlesque, chaffing, derisive, disparaging, flippant, ironical, irreverent, mocking, ridiculing, sarcastic, sardonic, scornful, trenchant.

satirize *v.t.* (*to ridicule by means of satire*) burlesque, caricature, deride, lampoon, make fun of, mock, parody, pillory, poke fun at, ridicule, (*coll.*) send up, (*coll.*) take off, travesty.

satisfaction *n.* **1** (*gratification, contentment*) contentment, enjoyment, gratification, happiness, joy, pleasure. ANTONYMS: dissatisfaction. **2** (*payment of a debt, fulfilment of an obligation*) fulfilment, indemnification, indemnity, payment, remuneration, repayment, requital, restitution, settlement. **3** (*compensation, amends*) amends, compensation, damages, expiation, recompense, redress, reparation, vindication. **4** (*atonement, esp. the atonement for sin achieved by Christ's death*) atonement, expiation, propitiation.

satisfactory *a.* **1** (*meeting all needs, desires or expectations*) acceptable, adequate, all right, fair, good enough, not bad, (*coll.*) OK, (*coll.*) okay, passable, sufficient. ANTONYMS: not good enough, unsatisfactory. **2** (*relieving the mind from doubt*) reassuring.

satisfy *v.t.* **1** (*to supply or gratify to the full*) answer, fill, gratify, indulge, look after, meet, provide for, quench, sate, satiate, serve, slake. **2** (*to gratify, to please*) appease, comfort, content, gratify, pacify, placate, please. ANTONYMS: dissatisfy. **3** (*to pay (a debt etc.)*) discharge, indemnify, liquidate, make good, pay, redress, repay, settle, write off. **4** (*to fulfil*) comply with, discharge, fulfil, meet. **5** (*to free from doubt*) assure, content, reassure, resolve, solve. **6** (*to convince*) convince, persuade, win over.
~*v.i.* **1** (*to give satisfaction*) answer, give satisfaction, serve. **2** (*to make payment or reparation*) atone, compensate, make amends, make reparation, pay, recompense, redress, requite.

satisfying *a.* **1** (*meeting all needs, desires or expectations*) adequate, filling, fulfilling, satiating, satisfactory, sufficient. **2** (*pleasing*) comforting, gratifying, pleasing, pleasurable, satisfactory.

saturate *v.t.* **1** (*to soak or imbue thoroughly*) drench, imbue, impregnate, permeate, soak, souse, steep, suffuse, waterlog, wet. ANTONYMS: drain, dry out. **2** (*to fill or charge (a body, substance etc.) with another substance, fluid*

etc. to the point where no more can be held) charge, fill, suffuse. **3** (*to supply (a market) with more than is necessary*) flood, overfill, oversupply.

sauce *n.* **1** (*a preparation, usu. liquid, taken with foods as an accompaniment or to enhance the taste*) condiment, dressing, gravy, ketchup, relish. **2** (*impertinence, impudence*) audacity, backchat, brazenness, cheek, cheekiness, disrespect, gall, impertinence, impudence, insolence, (*sl.*) lip, (*coll.*) nerve, pertness, (*N Am., coll.*) sass, sauciness, temerity.

saucy *a.* **1** (*impudent, cheeky*) cheeky, (*coll.*) fresh, impertinent, impudent, insolent, pert, presumptuous, (*N Am., coll.*) sassy. ANTONYMS: respectful. **2** (*smutty, suggestive*) dirty, lewd, smutty, suggestive.

saunter *v.i.* **1** (*to wander about idly and leisurely*) amble, dawdle, idle, meander, (*esp. N Am., coll.*) mosey, ramble, (*coll.*) traipse, wander. ANTONYMS: hurry, stride. **2** (*to walk leisurely (along)*) stroll, walk.
~*n.* (*a leisurely ramble or stroll*) meander, ramble, stroll, walk.

savage *a.* **1** (*fierce, cruel*) barbaric, bestial, bloodthirsty, bloody, brutal, brutish, cruel, ferocious, fierce, harsh, inhuman, merciless, murderous, sadistic, vicious, violent. ANTONYMS: gentle, kind. **2** (*uncivilized, in a primitive condition*) primitive, uncivilized, uncultivated, wild. **3** (*untamed, wild*) feral, unbroken, uncultivated, undomesticated, untamed, wild. ANTONYMS: cultivated, tame. **4** (*extremely angry, enraged*) angry, enraged, (*coll.*) wild.
~*n.* **1** (*a person of extreme brutality*) barbarian, brute, Caliban. **2** (*offensive*)† (*a human being in a primitive state, esp. a member of a nomadic tribe living by hunting and fishing*) aborigine, native, primitive, wild man, wild woman.
~*v.t.* **1** ((*esp. of an animal*) *to attack violently*) attack, bite, brutalize, tear, trample. **2** (*to attack or criticize*) attack, criticize, destroy, pull to pieces, (*sl.*) put the boot in.

savagery *n.* (*very cruel behaviour*) barbarism, brutalism, brutishness, cruelty, ferocity, fierceness, mercilessness, murderousness, viciousness, violence, wildness.

save *v.t.* **1** (*to preserve, rescue or deliver as from danger or harm*) deliver, free, liberate, preserve, recover, release, rescue, retrieve, salvage. ANTONYMS: abandon, give up. **2** (*to deliver from sin*) deliver, ransom, redeem, release. **3** (*to keep from being spent, used or lost*) conserve, guard, hoard, hold, keep back, keep untouched, preserve, protect, safeguard, secure, shelter, shield, store. **4** (*to refrain from* spending or using) husband, keep, lay aside, lay by, put aside, put away, put by, refrain, reserve, retain, scrape, scrimp, set apart, set by. **5** (*to spare*) avoid, exempt, spare. **6** (*to prevent*) obviate, preclude, prevent. **7** (*to preserve an opponent from scoring (a goal etc.)*) block, prevent, stop.

~*v.i.* **1** (*to avoid waste or undue expenditure*) avoid waste, be economical, be thrifty, economize. **2** (*to set aside money for future use*) lay up, put by, set aside. ANTONYMS: spend, squander, waste.

~*prep.* **1** (*except, saving*) but for, except, saving. **2** (*leaving out, not including*) excluding, leaving out, not including, omitting.

~*conj.* (*unless*) if not, unless.

~*n.* **1** (*the act of preventing an opponent from scoring a goal*) block, parry, stop, take. **2** (*an economy*) economy, saving.

saving *a.* **1** (*preserving from danger, loss etc.*) compensating, extenuating, preserving, qualifying, redeeming, redemptive, safeguarding. **2** (*economical, frugal*) economical, frugal, parsimonious, provident, prudent, sparing, thrifty. ANTONYMS: wasteful.

~*n.* **1** (*the act of economizing*) economizing, frugality, prudence, scrimping, sparingness, thrift. **2** (*an exception, a reservation*) exception, proviso, reservation.

~*prep.* **1** (*save, except*) apart from, except, save. **2** (*with due respect to*) with all due respect, with due respect to.

saviour *n.* (*a person who rescues or redeems*) champion, deliverer, emancipator, friend in need, good Samaritan, knight in shining armour, liberator, preserver, redeemer, rescuer. **Our/ the Saviour** (*Christ, as the redeemer of humankind*) Christ, Jesus, Our Lord, the King of Kings, the Lamb of God, the Messiah, the Prince of Peace, the Son of God.

savoir faire *n.* (*quickness to do the right thing, esp. in social situations*) adroitness, diplomacy, discretion, finesse, grace, knowledge, poise, polish, presence of mind, (*sl.*) savvy, skill, sophistication, style, suaveness, tact, urbanity.

savour *n.* **1** ((*characteristic*) *flavour, taste*) flavour, piquancy, relish, smack, tang, taste, zest. **2** (*suggestive quality*) breath, dash, hint, quality, soupçon, suggestion, trace. **3** (*smell, perfume*) bouquet, fragrance, odour, perfume, redolence, scent, smell.

~*v.t.* **1** (*to relish, to enjoy the savour of*) appreciate, delight in, enjoy, lick one's chops/ lips, luxuriate in, relish, revel in, smack one's lips/ chops, wallow in. **2** (*to perceive, to discern*) descry, detect, discern, identify, mark, note, notice, observe, perceive, sense, taste.

~*v.i.* (*to have a particular smell or flavour*) smack (of).

savoury *a.* **1** (*palatable, appetizing*) appetizing, delectable, delicious, flavoursome, luscious, palatable, tasteful, tasty, toothsome. ANTONYMS: bland, insipid, tasteless. **2** (*salty, spicy etc.* (*as opposed to sweet*)) piquant, salty, spicy, tangy. ANTONYMS: mild. **3** (*respectable, wholesome*) creditable, decent, honest, honourable, proper, reputable, respectable, seemly, upright, wholesome.

~*n.* (*a savoury dish, esp. as served as an appetizer or digestive*) appetizer, dainty, dessert, hors d'oeuvre, morsel, starter, titbit.

saw[1] *v.t.* (*to cut with a saw*) cut, divide, sever.

saw[2] *n.* (*a saying, a proverb*) adage, aphorism, apophthegm, (*N Am.*) apothegm, axiom, byword, catchphrase, catchword, cliché, commonplace, dictum, epigram, maxim, motto, platitude, proverb, saying, slogan, truism.

say *v.t.* **1** (*to utter in or as words, to speak*) articulate, deliver, phrase, pronounce, rephrase, speak, translate, utter, voice. ANTONYMS: stifle, suppress. **2** (*to repeat*) recite, rehearse, repeat. **3** (*to tell, to state*) affirm, announce, assert, asseverate, aver, declare, express, foretell, hold, maintain, put, remark, state, tell, verbalize. **4** (*to allege, to report*) allege, bring to light, bring up, claim, disclose, divulge, hint, impart, mention, noise abroad, put about, report, reveal, rumour, suggest, whisper. **5** (*to promise*) pledge, promise, swear, vow. **6** (*to suppose, to assume*) assume, believe, conjecture, estimate, guess, imagine, judge, suppose, think, venture. **7** (*to give as an opinion or answer, to decide*) answer, decide, opine, reply, respond. **8** (*to convey (meaning or intention)*) communicate, convey, denote, imply, indicate, intend, mean, signify, suggest, symbolize.

~*v.i.* (*to speak, to answer*) answer, reply, respond, speak, talk.

~*n.* **1** (*what one says or has to say, a statement*) affirmation, declaration, expression, statement, utterance, voice. **2** (*one's turn to speak*) chance, opportunity, turn, vote. **3** (*authority, influence*) authority, (*coll.*) clout, influence, power, sway, weight.

~*adv.* **1** (*approximately, about*) about, approximately, around, circa, nearly, roughly. **2** (*for example*) for example, for instance.

saying *n.* (*a maxim, an adage*) adage, aphorism, axiom, dictum, maxim, proverb, saw, superstition.

say-so *n.* **1** (*a dictum*) dictum, maxim. **2** (*an unfounded assertion*) assertion, hypothesis, theory. **3** (*right of decision, authority*) authority, authorization, order, permission, say, word.

scald *v.t.* (*to burn with or as with a hot liquid or vapour*) brand, burn, scorch, sear.
~*n.* (*an injury to the skin from hot liquid or vapour*) burn, scorch.

scale¹ *n.* **1** (*each of the thin, horny plates forming a protective covering on the skin of fishes, reptiles etc.*) imbrication, plate, skin, squama. **2** (*a modified leaf, hair or other structure resembling this*) lamella, lamina, scute, scutum. **3** (*a thin flake of dry skin*) dandruff, flake, scurf. **4** (*an incrustation*) cake, caking, crust, encrustation, incrustation, overlay. **5** (*a coating deposited on the insides of pipes, kettles etc. by hard water*) coating, deposit, layer. **6** (*plaque formed on teeth*) plaque, tartar.
~*v.t.* (*to strip the scales off*) descale.

scale² *n.* (*a simple balance*) balance, pair of scales.

scale³ *n.* (*anything graduated or marked with lines or degrees at regular intervals*) calibration, classification, gradation, graduation, hierarchy, ladder, order, progression, range, ranking, ratio, register, scope, sequence, series, spectrum.
~*v.t.* **1** (*to climb by or as by a ladder*) ascend, clamber up, climb, escalade, go up, mount, surmount. ANTONYMS: come down, descend, dismount. **2** (*to adjust according to a standard*) adjust, proportion, regulate. **in scale** (*in proportion to the surroundings etc.*) in proportion, proportionate, pro rata. **to scale down** (*to make smaller proportionately*) decrease, diminish, downsize, lower, reduce. **to scale up** (*to make larger proportionately*) enlarge, increase, raise.

scaly *a.* (*covered wtih small, flat pieces of hard skin, rough*) imbricated, rough, scabby, scabrous, scaled, scruffy, scurfy, shingly, uneven. ANTONYMS: even, smooth.

scan *v.t.* **1** (*to examine closely or intently*) examine, explore, inspect, investigate, pore over, research, scrutinize, search, study. **2** (*to examine and produce an image of* (*a body part*) *using X-rays etc.*) X-ray. **3** (*to glance at or read through hastily*) browse, flip over/ through, glance at/ through, leaf through, look over, read hastily, read over, skim, thumb over/ through.
~*n.* (*an act of scanning*) check, examination, inspection, look, overview, survey, X-ray.

scandal *n.* **1** (*a disgraceful action, person etc.*) affront, outrage, sin. **2** (*offence or censure at some act or conduct, esp. as expressed in common talk*) censure, indignation, offence. **3** (*damage to reputation, shame*) calumny, damage, degradation, discredit, disgrace, dishonour, disrepute, embarrassment, ignominy, infamy, obloquy, opprobrium, reproach,

shame. ANTONYMS: honour, respect. **4** (*malicious gossip*) abuse, aspersion, blemish, blot, defamation, defilement, dirt, innuendo, insinuation, libel, slander, slur, spot, stigma, taint.

scandalize *v.t.* (*to offend by improper or outrageous conduct*) affront, appal, disturb, gall, horrify, offend, outrage, rankle, shock, upset.

scandalous *a.* **1** ((*of behaviour*) *disgraceful, shocking*) appalling, atrocious, calumniatory, despicable, discreditable, disgraceful, dishonourable, disreputable, evil, heinous, ignominious, indecent, indecorous, infamous, iniquitous, lewd, licentious, offensive, outrageous, shameful, shocking, sordid, unseemly, wicked. ANTONYMS: creditable, respectable. **2** (*damaging someone's reputation*) abusive, aspersive, calumniatory, defamatory, injurious, libellous, opprobrious, scurrilous, slanderous.

scanty *a.* **1** (*deficient, insufficient*) deficient, inadequate, insufficient, lacking, little, meagre, not enough, paltry, scant, scarce, short, small, sparse, thin on the ground. ANTONYMS: ample, enough, sufficient. **2** (*scarcely adequate in extent, size or quantity*) barely adequate, barely sufficient, limited, (*coll.*) measly, minimal, miserly, restricted, scarce, skimpy.

scapegoat *n.* (*a person made to bear blame due to another*) Aunt Sally, dupe, fall guy, gull, (*coll.*) sucker, victim, whipping boy.

scar *n.* **1** (*a mark left by a wound, burn etc.*) blemish, brand, burn, cicatrice, cut, damage, dent, disfigurement, mar, mark, scratch, wound. **2** (*the after-effects of emotional distress*) injury, trauma.
~*v.t.* **1** (*to mark with a scar or scars*) blemish, brand, burn, cut, damage, dent, disfigure, mar, mark, scratch. **2** (*to leave with lasting adverse effects*) injure, traumatize, wound.

scarce *a.* **1** (*infrequent, uncommon*) at a premium, hard to come by, infrequent, in short supply, rare, seldom encountered, thin on the ground, uncommon. ANTONYMS: common, frequent. **2** (*insufficient, not plentiful*) deficient, few, inadequate, insufficient, lacking, meagre, not plentiful, rare, scant, scanty, short, wanting. ANTONYMS: adequate, plentiful.
~*adv.* (*hardly, scarcely*) barely, hardly, scarcely.

scarcely *adv.* **1** (*hardly, barely*) barely, hardly, just, only just. **2** (*only with difficulty*) only with difficulty. **3** (*certainly not*) by no means, certainly not, definitely not, in no way, not at all, not in the least, nowise, on no account, under no circumstances.

scarcity *n.* (*a deficiency or dearth* (*of*)) dearth, deficiency, inadequacy, insufficiency, lack, need, paucity, shortage, want. ANTONYMS: abundance, plenty.

scare *v.t.* **1** (*to frighten, to alarm*) affright, alarm, cow, daunt, dismay, frighten, horrify, intimidate, make one's hair stand on end, scare the hell out of, scare the (living) daylights out of, (*coll.*) scare the pants off, shock, (*chiefly N Am., coll.*) spook, startle, strike with fear, terrify, terrorize. ANTONYMS: comfort, reassure. **2** (*to drive* (*away*) *through fear*) frighten away, scare off.
~*n.* (*a sudden fright, a panic*) fright, panic, shock, start, surprise, terror.

scared *a.* (*frightened*) afraid, alarmed, daunted, frightened, horrified, intimidated, shocked, (*chiefly N Am., coll.*) spooked, startled, terrified, terrorized.

scary *a.* (*frightening*) alarming, blood-curdling, creepy, daunting, eerie, frightening, hair-raising, horrifying, intimidating, spine-chilling, (*coll.*) spooky, terrifying.

scathing *a.* **1** (*hurtful, harmful*) damaging, harmful, hurtful. **2** ((*of sarcasm etc.*) *very bitter or severe*) biting, bitter, caustic, critical, cutting, ferocious, incisive, merciless, mocking, mordant, sarcastic, savage, scornful, searing, severe, sharp, trenchant, vicious, vitriolic, withering. ANTONYMS: approving, sympathetic.

scatter *v.t.* **1** (*to throw loosely about, to fling in all directions*) fling, sow, throw around, toss about. **2** (*to strew*) bestrew, litter, shower, sprinkle, strew. **3** (*to cause to separate in various directions, to disperse*) break up, disband, disperse, go off, separate, spread. ANTONYMS: collect, concentrate, gather, unify. **4** (*to dissipate*) dispel, dissipate, dissolve, evaporate, melt away. **5** (*to diffuse* (*radiation etc.*) *or cause to spread out*) broadcast, circulate, diffuse, disseminate, distribute.
~*v.i.* (*to disperse*) disperse, go separate ways.

scatterbrained *a.* (*not able to think seriously or to concentrate*) (*sl.*) dippy, disorganized, dizzy, flighty, giddy, (*coll.*) hare-brained, (*coll.*) rattle-brained, (*coll.*) rattle-headed, slap-happy, wool-gathering.

scattering *n.* (*a small amount or number irregularly strewn*) bit, hint, litter, shower, smattering, soupçon, sprinkling, suggestion.

scenario *n.* **1** (*a sketch or outline of the scenes and main points of a play etc.*) outline, précis, résumé, summary, synopsis. **2** (*the script of a film with dialogue and directions for the producer*) film script, screenplay. **3** (*an account or outline of projected or imagined future events*) design, framework, layout, outline, plan, programme, scheme.

scene *n.* **1** (*the place where anything occurs or is exhibited as on a stage*) area, background, locale, location, place, site, sphere, spot, whereabouts. **2** (*the place in which the action of a play or story is supposed to take place*) scene, setting. **3** (*a single event or incident in a play or film*) action, episode, event, happening, incident, scenario, section, situation. **4** (*a striking incident, esp. an exhibition of feeling or passion*) altercation, brouhaha, commotion, display, disturbance, exhibition, furore, fuss, outburst, passion, row, tantrum, upset. **5** (*a film or television sequence*) episode, incident, sequence, unit. **6** (*a landscape, regarded as a piece of scenery*) landscape, panorama, picture, prospect, scenery, sight, tableau, view, vista.

scenic *a.* **1** (*characterized by beautiful natural scenery*) attractive, beautiful, breathtaking, grand, impressive, picturesque, pretty, spectacular, striking. **2** (*arranged for effect*) dramatic, exaggerated, histrionic, theatrical.

scent *v.t.* **1** (*to perceive by smell*) smell, sniff, whiff. **2** (*to begin to suspect*) discern, sense, suspect. **3** (*to trace or hunt* (*out*) *by or as by smelling*) detect, discern, distinguish, find out, get wind of, perceive, recognize, sense, sniff out, trace.
~*v.i.* **1** (*to exercise the sense of smell*) aromatize, smell. **2** (*to give forth a smell*) reek, stink, whiff.
~*n.* **1** (*odour, esp. of a pleasant kind*) aroma, bouquet, odour, redolence, smell, trace, whiff. **2** (*the odour left by an animal forming a trail by which it can be followed*) spoor, track, trail. **3** (*a trail to be pursued*) track, trail. **4** (*a clue*) clue, hint, trace. **5** (*a liquid essence containing fragrant extracts from flowers etc.*) fragrance, perfume.

sceptic *n.* **1** (*a person of a questioning habit of mind*) critic, disbeliever, doubter, Doubting Thomas, questioner. **2** (*a person who casts doubt on any statement, theory etc., esp. in a cynical manner*) cynic, doubter, scoffer. **3** (*an agnostic*) agnostic, doubter. **4** (*an atheist*) atheist, humanist, non-believer.

sceptical *a.* (*given to doubting or questioning*) agnostic, cynical, disbelieving, distrustful, doubting, dubious, incredulous, questioning, scoffing, suspicious, unbelieving, unconvinced, unpersuaded. ANTONYMS: convinced, persuaded.

scepticism *n.* (*a sceptical attitude*) agnosticism, cynicism, disbelief, distrust, doubt, doubtfulness, incredulity, mistrust, questioning, suspicion. ANTONYMS: belief, conviction, faith, trust.

schedule *n.* **1** (*a timetable*) calendar, itinerary, outline, plan, scheme, timetable. **2** (*a planned programme of events, tasks etc.*) agenda, plan, programme, to-do list. **3** (*a written or printed list or inventory* (*appended to a document*)) catalogue, inventory, list, listing, record, register, table.
~*v.t.* **1** (*to enter in a schedule*) allot, appoint, arrange, assign, book, earmark, organize, outline, plan, time, timetable. **2** (*to make a list of*) catalogue, list, programme. **3** (*to include a building*) *in a list for preservation or protection*) designate, list, protect, record, register.

schematic *a.* (*having, or in the nature of, a plan or schema*) charted, diagrammatic, diagrammatical, graphic, representational.
~*n.* (*a schematic diagram, esp. of an electrical circuit*) blueprint, chart, design, diagram, graph, layout, plan, representation, scheme.

scheme *n.* **1** (*a proposed method of doing something*) approach, blueprint, chart, design, draft, game plan, layout, manoeuvre, map, method, order, outline, pattern, plan, project, proposal, scenario, schematic. **2** (*a plot, a conspiracy*) conspiracy, contrivance, device, dodge, (*coll.*) game, intrigue, machination, plot, ploy, ruse, stratagem, subterfuge, tactic, trick. **3** (*a table or schedule of proposed acts, events etc.*) course, programme, schedule, syllabus, table. **4** (*a systematic arrangement of facts, principles etc.*) diagram, graphic, system.
~*v.t.* (*to plan, to plot*) concoct, conspire, contrive, (*coll.*) cook up, design, devise, frame, hatch, intrigue, organize, plan, plot, project.
~*v.i.* **1** (*to form plans*) form plans, plan. **2** (*to plot*) connive, conspire, intrigue, machinate, plot.

scheming *a.* (*given to forming schemes*) artful, calculating, conniving, conspiratorial, cunning, designing, devious, intriguing, machiavellian, machinating, manipulative, plotting, sly, treacherous, tricky, underhanded, wily. ANTONYMS: guileless, honest, trustworthy.

schism *n.* (*a split or division in a community*) breach, disunion, division, rift, rupture, separation, split. ANTONYMS: solidarity, unity.

schismatic *a.* (*of or relating to a schism*) breakaway, dissident, divisive, heretical, schismatical, separatist.

scholar *n.* **1** (*a learned person*) academic, authority, bookman, bookwoman, (*coll.*) brain, (*coll.*) brainbox, (*coll.*) egghead, expert, highbrow, intellectual, man of letters, philosopher, professor, pundit, sage, savant(e), teacher, woman of letters. ANTONYMS: fool, ignoramus. **2** (*a pupil, a student*) pupil, schoolboy, schoolgirl, student, undergraduate.

scholarly *a.* (*learned*) academic, (*coll.*) brainy, deep, erudite, (*coll., often derog.*) highbrowed, intellectual, learned, lettered, profound, scholastic.

scholarship *n.* **1** (*education, instruction*) education, erudition, instruction, knowledge, learning, letters, preparation, schooling, training. ANTONYMS: ignorance. **2** (*education, usu. with maintenance, free or at reduced fees*) award, bursary, endowment, exhibition, grant.

school[1] *n.* **1** (*an institution for the education of children*) boarding school, college, day school, high school, junior school, kindergarten, middle school, night school, nursery school, primary school, secondary school, senior school, special school. **2** (*a faculty of a university*) academy, college, department, faculty, institute, institution. **3** (*the body of disciples or followers of a philosopher, artist etc.*) adherents, devotees, disciples, faction, followers, persuasion, votaries. **4** (*a group of people assembled for a common purpose, such as playing poker*) circle, class, clique, coterie, group, sect, set.
~*v.t.* **1** (*to instruct, to educate*) coach, educate, equip, inculcate, indoctrinate, instil, instruct, mould, prepare, prime, ready, shape, teach, train, tutor. **2** (*to discipline, to bring under control*) bring under control, discipline, tame, train.

school[2] *n.* (*a shoal of fish, porpoises etc.*) shoal.

schoolbook *n.* (*a book for use in schools*) copybook, exercise book, grammar, notebook, primer, reader, textbook.

schoolchild *n.* (*a child attending a school*) pupil, schoolboy, schoolgirl, student.

schooling *n.* **1** (*education at school*) education, instruction, learning, teaching, training, tuition. **2** (*training, tuition*) coaching, guidance, indoctrination, learning, preparation, study, teaching, training, tuition, tutelage. **3** (*discipline*) discipline, training.

schoolteacher *n.* (*a person who teaches in a school*) headmaster, headmistress, head teacher, instructor, pedagogue, professor, (*N Am., coll.*) school-ma'am, schoolmaster, schoolmistress, teacher, tutor.

science *n.* **1** (*systematized knowledge about the physical world, developed by observation and experiment*) discipline, laws, principles, study. **2** (*exceptional skill due to knowledge and training, as distinguished from natural ability*) art, expertise, method, proficiency, skill, system, technique. **3** (*knowledge*) data, facts, information, knowledge.

scientific *a.* **1** (*made or done according to the principles of science*) detailed, exact, logical, methodical, meticulous, painstaking, precise, systematic, thorough, well-organized, well-regulated. ANTONYMS: illogical, imprecise, unscientific, vague. **2** ((*of boxing etc.*) *skilful, expert*) expert, skilful.

scintillating *a.* **1** (*witty and interesting*) brilliant, coruscating, fascinating, glittering, interesting, lively, shining, sparkling, stimulating, thrilling, witty. ANTONYMS: boring, dull, unexceptional. **2** (*sparkling*) brilliant, coruscating, dazzling, effervescent, effulgent, flashing, gleaming, glistening, glittering, lustrous, radiant, shimmering, shining, sparkling, twinkling. ANTONYMS: dull.

scoff[1] *v.i.* (*to mock or jeer* (*at*)) deride, disparage, gibe at, jeer at, lampoon, laugh at, make fun of, mock, poke fun at, put down, sneer at, taunt, tease. ANTONYMS: admire, respect.

scoff[2] *v.t.* (*to eat ravenously*) bolt, cram, devour, eat ravenously, gobble, gorge, gulp, guzzle, put away, stuff, wolf.

scold *v.i.* (*to find fault noisily or angrily*) censure, chide, find fault, remonstrate.
~*v.t.* (*to chide or find fault with noisily or angrily*) berate, castigate, censure, chide, criticize, (*coll.*) dress down, find fault with, give (someone) a hard time, give (someone) hell, haul over the coals, jump on, lecture, rebuke, reprimand, reproach, reprove, rip into, take to task, tear into, (*coll.*) tell off, (*coll.*) tick off, upbraid. ANTONYMS: approve, praise.
~*n.* (*a noisy, nagging woman*) amazon, battleaxe, beldam, fishwife, fury, harridan, hell-cat, nag, shrew, termagant, tigress, virago.

scoop *n.* **1** (*a short-handled shovel-like implement for lifting and moving loose material*) shovel, spade. **2** (*a large ladle or dipping-vessel*) bailer, bucket, dipper, ladle, spoon. **3** (*a large profit made in a speculation or competitive transaction*) gain, profit, return, surplus. **4** (*the publication or broadcasting of a piece of sensational news in advance of rival newspapers etc.*) (*sl.*) dope, exclusive, (*coll.*) gen, (*coll.*) info, inside story, (*coll.*) latest, (*coll.*) low-down, revelation, sensation.
~*v.t.* **1** (*to ladle or to hollow* (*out*) *with a scoop*) bail, dig, dip, hollow, ladle, spoon. **2** (*to lift* (*up*) *with a scoop*) gather up, lift, pick up, remove, sweep up, take up. **3** (*to scrape or hollow* (*out*)) cut, dig, excavate, gouge, hollow out, scrape, spoon out. **4** (*to gain* (*a large profit*) *by a deal etc.*) gain, profit. **5** (*to forestall* (*rival newspapers etc.*) *with a piece of sensational news*) anticipate, forestall, pre-empt.

scope *n.* **1** (*range of action or observation*) area,

breadth, compass, expanse, extent, field, orbit, outlook, reach, span, sphere, view. **2** (*extent of or room for activity, development etc.*) capacity, elbow room, freedom, latitude, leeway, liberty, range, room, space, spread, stretch. **3** (*outlet, opportunity*) opportunity, outlet, vent.

scorch *v.t.* **1** (*to burn the outside of so as to injure or discolour without consuming*) bake, blacken, blister, char, dry, fry, parch, roast, scald, sear, shrivel, singe. **2** (*to criticize or censure severely*) censure, criticize, denounce, find fault with.
~*v.i.* **1** (*to be singed or dried up with or as with heat*) blister, dry up, fry, parch, shrivel. **2** (*coll.*) (*to go at an excessive rate of speed*) (*coll.*) burn, hurtle, speed.
~*n.* (*a mark caused by scorching*) burn, mark.

scorching *a.* **1** (*extremely hot*) boiling, broiling, hellish, hot, parching, searing, shrivelling, torrid. **2** (*very critical*) acrimonious, biting, bitter, caustic, critical, cutting, excoriating, mordant, scathing, vituperative, wounding.

score *n.* **1** (*the points made by a player or side at any moment in, or in total in certain games and contests*) mark, points, tally, total. **2** (*the record of this*) amount, grade, mark, number, record, register, result, sum, tally, total. **3** (*pl.*) (*large numbers*) army, crowd(s), dozens, herd(s), horde(s), host(s), hundreds, legion(s), many, mass(es), multitude(s), myriad(s), pack(s), swarm(s), thousands. **4** (*account, reason*) account, basis, category, cause, count, grounds, motive, provocation, rationale, reason. **5 a** (*a copy of a musical work in which all the component parts are shown, either fully or in a compressed form*) copy, music, notation. **b** (*the music for a film, play etc.*) accompaniment, film score, incidental music. **6** (*sl.*) (*a remark etc. in which one scores off another person*) rebuff, retort. **7** (*coll.*) (*the situation, the facts*) condition, facts, (*coll.*) latest, news, position, situation, state of affairs, story, word. **8** (*a scratch, incision*) cut, groove, incision, line, mark, nick, notch, scratch, stroke. **9** (*an account, a debt*) account, bill, debt, obligation. **10** (*a reckoning, esp. a running account for liquor marked up against a customer's name at a tavern*) reckoning, running account, slate, tab, tally, (*coll.*) tick. **11** (*anything laid up or recorded against one*) count, grievance, grudge, injury, resentment, wrong.
~*v.t.* **1** (*to gain* (*a point, a win etc.*) *in a game or contest*) achieve, earn, gain, get, make, notch up, win. **2** (*to count for a score of* (*points etc.*)) count, reckon. **3** (*to mark* (*up*) *or enter in a score*) enter, mark up, record, register, tally. **4** (*to mark with notches, lines etc.*) cut, deface, gouge, incise, line, mar, mark, nick, notch,

scrape, scratch, slash. **5** (*to orchestrate*) adapt, arrange, orchestrate, set. **6** (*to groove, to furrow*) furrow, gash, gouge, groove.

~*v.i.* **1** (*to win points, advantages etc.*) make a hit, succeed, win points. **2** (*to keep a score*) keep score, tally. **3** (*to successfully seduce someone into having sexual intercourse*) (*sl.*) get laid, (*coll.*) get off, (*N Am., coll.*) make out.

scorn *n.* **1** (*contempt, disdain*) contempt, contemptuousness, deprecation, disdain, dismissal, rejection. **2** (*mockery, derision*) derision, derisiveness, jeering, mockery, ridicule, scoffing, sneering, taunting.

~*v.t.* (*to hold in extreme contempt or disdain*) despise, disdain, disregard, flout, hold in contempt, jeer at, laugh at, look down on, look down one's nose at, mock, pooh-pooh, put down, rebuff, reject, scoff at, shun, slight, sneer at, snub, spurn, taunt, turn up one's nose at. ANTONYMS: respect, revere.

scornful *a.* (*showing or feeling scorn*) contemptuous, derisive, disdainful, dismissive, disparaging, haughty, mocking, scoffing, sneering, snide, (*coll.*) snooty, supercilious, superior. ANTONYMS: respectful, reverential.

scoundrel *n.* (*an unprincipled person, a rogue*) blackguard, bounder, cad, cur, good-for-nothing, (*coll.*) heel, knave, mischief-maker, ne'er-do-well, rascal, reprobate, rogue, (*coll.*) rotter, villain. ANTONYMS: gentleman, good sort.

scour[1] *v.t.* **1** (*to clean or polish by friction*) buff, burnish, clean, cleanse, polish, shine, wash. ANTONYMS: dirty, soil, tarnish. **2** (*to remove or clean (away, off etc.) by rubbing*) abrade, rub, scrub. **3** (*to flush or clear out*) cleanse, clear out, empty, flush.

scour[2] *v.i.* **1** (*to rove, to range*) drift, range, roam, rove. **2** (*to skim, to scurry*) fly, scud, scurry, skim. **3** (*to search about*) hunt, scrape about, scrape around, search about.

~*v.t.* **1** (*to move rapidly over, esp. in search*) move rapidly over, sweep over. **2** (*to search thoroughly*) comb, ransack, search thoroughly, turn upside down.

scourge *n.* **1** (*a whip with thongs used as an instrument of punishment*) cat-o'-nine-tails, horsewhip, lash, quirt, strap, switch, whip. **2** (*any means of inflicting punishment or suffering*) misery, penalty, punishment, suffering, torment, torture, vengeance, woe. **3** (*a pestilence or plague*) adversity, affliction, bane, curse, evil, misfortune, pestilence, plague, visitation. ANTONYMS: blessing, favour.

~*v.t.* **1** (*to whip with or as with a scourge*) beat, belt, flagellate, flog, horsewhip, lash, thrash, whip. **2** (*to afflict, to chastise*) afflict, castigate,

chastise, discipline, harass, punish, torment, torture. ANTONYMS: favour, indulge.

scout *n.* **1** (*a person sent out to bring in information*) lookout, outrider, spy, vanguard. **2** (*a person employed to search for people with talent in a particular field*) headhunter, talent spotter. **3** (*a scouting expedition*) exploration, reconnoitre. **4** (*a member of a worldwide organization, intended to train and develop qualities of leadership, responsibility etc.*) boy scout, girl scout.

~*v.t.* (*to explore to get information about*) cast around for, examine, get information about, glean, hunt for, observe, spy, watch.

~*v.i.* (*to make a search*) explore, investigate, look, reconnoitre, research, search, seek, study.

scowl *v.i.* (*to look sullen or ill-tempered*) frown, glare, glower, grimace, look daggers at, look sullen, lower. ANTONYMS: beam, grin, smile.

~*n.* (*an angry frown*) dirty look, frown, glare, glower, grimace.

scrabble *v.i.* (*to scratch or grope (about) as if to obtain something*) cast about, grope about, scrape, scratch.

scraggy *a.* (*thin and bony*) angular, bony, gaunt, haggard, lean, scrawny, skinny, spare, thin. ANTONYMS: ample, well-covered.

scramble *v.i.* **1** (*to climb or move along by clambering*) clamber, crawl, wriggle. **2** (*to move with urgent or disorderly haste*) dash, hasten, hurry, hustle, race, rush, scamper, scurry, scuttle. ANTONYMS: dawdle, idle. **3** (*to seek or struggle (for, after etc.) in a rough-and-tumble or eager manner*) bustle, compete, contest, fight, scrabble, strive, struggle.

~*v.t.* **1** (*to put together hurriedly or haphazardly*) collect, gather, put together. **2** (*to mix or jumble up*) blend, combine, commingle, confuse, intermingle, jumble, mingle, mix up. **3** (*to make (a radiotelephonic conversation) unintelligible without a decoding receiver by altering the frequencies*) code, encode.

~*n.* **1** (*a climb over rocks etc., or in a rough-and-tumble manner*) climb, walk. **2** (*a rough or unceremonious struggle for something*) clash, commotion, conflict, disorder, fight, free-for-all, mêlée, muddle, riot, rough-and-tumble, rush, scrimmage, scrum, scrummage, struggle, tussle.

scrap[1] *n.* **1** (*a small detached piece, a bit*) atom, bit, crumb, fragment, grain, iota, jot, molecule, morsel, particle, piece, shard, sherd, shred, sliver, snatch, snippet, speck, tittle. ANTONYMS: entirety, whole. **2** (*a picture, paragraph etc., cut from a newspaper etc., for preservation*) clip, clipping, cutting, extract, snipping. **3** (*waste, *esp. old pieces of discarded metal collected for melting down etc.*) debris, junk, refuse, rubbish, spoil, waste. **4** (*pl.*) (*bits, odds and ends*) bits, discards, leavings, odds and ends, rejects, residue, scrapings, traces, vestiges. **5** (*pl.*) (*leftover fragments of food*) leftovers, remains, remnants, scrapings.

~*v.t.* **1** (*to consign to the scrap heap*) consign to the scrap heap, make scrap of, reject. **2** (*to discard as worn out, obsolete etc.*) abandon, condemn, discard, dispose of, forsake, get rid of, give up, junk, reject, throw away. ANTONYMS: keep, preserve.

scrap² *n.* (*coll.*) (*a fight, a scuffle*) affray, argument, battle, battle royal, brawl, contest, disagreement, dispute, dust-up, fight, fracas, quarrel, row, (*chiefly N Am.*) ruckus, scuffle, set-to, spat, wrangle.

~*v.i.* (*to engage in a fight*) argue, battle, bicker, brawl, disagree, fight, quarrel, row, scuffle, spar, squabble, wrangle.

scrapbook *n.* (*a blank book into which pictures, cuttings from newspapers etc. are pasted for preservation*) album, archive, collection, cuttings, portfolio.

scrape *v.t.* **1** (*to rub the surface of with something rough or sharp*) grate, grind, rub, scratch, scuff. **2** (*to abrade or smooth (a surface) with something rough or sharp*) abrade, clean, scour, scratch, shave, smooth. **3** (*to excavate or hollow (out) by scraping*) claw, dig away at, dig out, excavate, gouge out, hollow out. **4** (*to rub against with a rasping or grating noise*) file, rasp. **5** (*to damage or graze by rubbing on a rough surface*) bark, bruise, damage, graze, injure, skin, wound. **6** (*to collect or get together by scraping*) accumulate, aggregate, amass, assemble, collect, dredge up, gather, get together, glean, marshal, muster, scrabble together, (*coll.*) scrounge. **7** (*to save or amass with difficulty or by small amounts*) be frugal, be thrifty, economize, save, scrimp, scrimp and save, skimp.

~*v.i.* **1** (*to rub the surface of something with a rough or sharp instrument*) grate, grind, rub, scuff. **2** (*to abrade, to smooth something with a rough or sharp instrument*) abrade, clean, smooth. **3** (*to rub (against something) with a scraping or rasping noise*) file, rasp. **4** (*to get through with difficulty or by a close shave*) cope, get by, make it, manage, scrabble, (*coll.*) squeak by, struggle, survive. **5** (*to be parsimonious*) economize, save. **6** (*to pass an examination etc. with difficulty*) pass narrowly, (*coll.*) squeak through.

~*n.* **1** (*a scraped place (on the skin etc.)*) abrasion, bark, bruise, damage, graze, injury, scratch, scuff, wound. **2** (*an awkward predicament*)

difficulty, dilemma, fix, pinch, plight, position, predicament, quandary, situation, (*coll.*) stew, tight spot, trouble.

scratch *v.t.* **1** (*to tear or mark the surface of lightly with something sharp*) cut, mar, mark, tear. **2** (*to wound slightly*) bark, bruise, damage, graze, injure, wound. **3** (*to rub or scrape with the nails*) abrade, grate against, rub, scrape, scuff. **4** (*to hollow out with the nails or claws*) claw, gash, gouge out, hollow out. **5** (*to erase, to score (out, through etc.)*) cross out, delete, eliminate, erase, exclude, obliterate, rub off, rub out, score out, strike off, strike out. **6** (*to scrape (up or together)*) glean, scrape together.

~*v.i.* **1** (*to use the nails or claws in tearing, scraping etc.*) hollow out, mark, scrape, tear. **2** (*to scrape one's skin with the nails*) rub, scrape. **3** (*to manage with difficulty*) get by, manage, scrape.

~*n.* **1** (*a mark made by scratching*) cut, damage, gash, gouge, laceration, line, mark, scuff, tear. **2** (*a slight wound*) abrasion, bruise, graze, injury, scar, scrape, wound.

~*a.* **1** (*improvised*) casual, extempore, hasty, hurried, impromptu, rough, unplanned, unprepared. **2** (*put together hastily or haphazardly*) cobbled together, makeshift, multifarious, nondescript, off the cuff. **up to scratch** (*fulfilling the desired standard or requirements*) acceptable, adequate, competent, competitive, good enough, satisfactory, sufficient, up to par, (*coll.*) up to snuff, up to standard. ANTONYMS: inadequate, sub-standard, unacceptable.

scratchy *a.* **1** (*tending to scratch or rub*) irritating, itchy, prickly, rough. **2** (*uneven, irregular*) grating, heterogeneous, hoarse, irregular, raspy, raw, rough, uneven. ANTONYMS: even, regular, smooth.

scrawl *v.t.* (*to draw or write clumsily or illegibly*) doodle, draw, mark, scribble, write.

~*v.i.* (*to mark with illegible writing etc.*) mark, scribble.

~*n.* (*a piece of clumsy or illegible writing*) scribble, squiggle.

scrawny *a.* (*excessively lean, bony*) angular, (*coll.*) anorexic, bony, cadaverous, drawn, emaciated, gaunt, lean, reedy, scraggy, skinny, spare, thin. ANTONYMS: bulky, fleshy.

scream *v.i.* **1** (*to make a piercing, prolonged cry as if in extreme pain or terror*) bawl, caterwaul, cry, howl, screech, shout, shriek, wail, yell, yowl. **2** (*to give out a shrill sound*) guffaw, hoot, howl, laugh, roar, whistle.

~*v.t.* (*to utter or say in a screaming tone*) bawl, cry, screech, shout, shriek, squeal, wail, yell.

~*n.* **1** (*a loud, shrill cry, as of one in extreme pain* *or terror*) bawl, caterwaul, cry, howl, screech, shout, shriek, squeal, wail, yell, yowl. **2** (*something or someone excruciatingly funny*) (*sl.*) card, (*coll.*) killer, (*coll.*) riot.

screen *n.* **1** (*a partition separating a portion of a room from the remainder*) blind, curtain, divider, partition, wall. **2** (*anything serving to protect or conceal*) camouflage, cloak, concealment, cover, guard, protection, shelter. **3** (*the film industry, moving pictures collectively*) big screen, cinema, Hollywood, motion pictures, movies, silver screen. **4** (*a coarse sieve or riddle*) colander, filter, mesh, riddle, sieve, strainer.

~*v.t.* **1** (*to shelter or protect from inconvenience or pain*) guard, protect, shade, shelter, shield. **2** (*to hide, to conceal wholly or partly*) camouflage, cloak, conceal, cover, hide, mask, veil. ANTONYMS: expose, reveal. **3** (*to separate with a screen*) divide, partition, separate, wall off. **4** (*to test for the presence of disease, weapons etc.*) frisk, test, vet. **5** (*to examine or check thoroughly in order to assess suitability, sort into categories etc.*) categorize, check, cull, evaluate, examine, gauge, grade, interview, process, scan, select, separate, sort, vet. **6** (*to project* (*a film*) *on a screen*) project, show. **7** (*to sift*) filter, riddle, sieve, sift.

screw *n.* **1** (*a piece in spiral form*) corkscrew, helix, spiral. **2** (*a turn of a screw*) turn, twist. **3** (*sl., offensive*) (*a prison warder*) guard, prison officer, warder. **4** (*sl.*) (*an act of sexual intercourse*) (*sl.*) bonk, (*taboo sl.*) fuck, (*taboo sl.*) lay, (*taboo sl.*) ride. **5** (*sl.*) (*a partner in sexual intercourse*) (*taboo sl.*) fuck, (*taboo sl.*) lay, (*sl.*) mate, (*taboo sl.*) ride.

~*v.t.* **1** (*to fasten, join etc. with a screw or screws*) fasten, join, secure, tighten. **2** (*to turn* (*a screw*)) rotate, turn. **3** (*to oppress, esp. by exactions*) grind down, oppress, press hard. **4** (*to extort* (*money etc.*) *out of*) coerce, extort, squeeze. **5** (*to cheat*) bilk, cheat, clip, defraud, do out of, fleece, gull, swindle, (*coll.*) take. **6** (*to contort* (*as the face*)) contort, distort, twist. **7** (*taboo sl.*) (*to have sexual intercourse with*) (*sl.*) bonk, (*taboo sl.*) fuck, have sex with, (*taboo sl.*) lay. **8** (*to bungle*) bungle, mess up.

~*v.i.* **1** (*to turn as a screw*) rotate, turn. **2** (*to move obliquely or spirally*) swerve, twist. **to screw up 1** (*to twist*) contort, deform, twist, warp. **2** (*sl.*) (*to bungle, mess up*) botch, bungle, (*taboo sl.*) fuck up, louse up, (*coll.*) make a hash of, mishandle, muddle, ruin, spoil. **3** (*sl.*) (*to make confused or neurotic*) confuse, disturb. **4** (*to summon* (*one's courage*)) call up, call upon, draw on, summon, tap.

scribble *v.i.* (*to write hastily or illegibly*) doodle, jot, scratch, scrawl, write hastily.

~*n.* (*hasty or careless writing*) doodle, jottings, scratchings.

scribe *n.* **1** (*a writer*) author, columnist, dramatist, editor, essayist, hack, journalist, newspaperman, newspaperwoman, newswriter, novelist, playwright, poet, scribbler, wordsmith, writer. **2** (*a secretary, a copyist*) amanuensis, clerk, copier, copyist, (*Hist.*) scrivener, secretary, transcriber.

scrimp *v.t.* (*to limit, to skimp*) economize, limit, restrict, skimp, stint, straiten. ANTONYMS: lavish, squander.

~*v.i.* (*to be niggardly*) be niggardly, restrict, skimp, stint.

script *n.* **1** (*a piece of writing*) manuscript, writing. **2** (*handwriting as distinct from print*) calligraphy, hand, handwriting, penmanship, writing. **3** (*an alphabet or system of writing*) alphabet, writing system. **4** (*the written text or draft of a film, play or radio or television broadcast*) film script, libretto, lines, play, scenario, screenplay, teleplay, text.

~*v.t.* (*to write the script for*) create, pen, prepare, write.

scripture *n.* **1** (*a sacred writing or book*) sacred writing, scriptures. **2** (*usu.* **Scripture**) (*the Bible, esp. the books of the Old and New Testament without the Apocrypha*) Bible, Good Book, Gospel, Holy Bible, Holy Scripture, Holy Writ, Word of God.

scrounge *v.t.* **1** (*to pilfer*) (*sl.*) nick, pilfer, (*coll.*) pinch. **2** (*to cadge*) beg, borrow, cadge.

~*v.i.* **1** (*to hunt around*) ferret out, forage, hunt around, nose around, scrape together, seek out, smell out. **2** (*to cadge things*) beg, borrow, (*esp. N Am., coll.*) bum, cadge, freeload, importune, sponge, steal.

scrounger *n.* (*a person who cadges food or money from others*) beggar, cadger, (*N Am.*) freeloader, parasite, sponger.

scrub[1] *v.t.* **1** (*to rub hard with something coarse and rough*) abrade, buff, burnish, clean, cleanse, polish, rub, scour, shine, wash. **2** (*to get rid of, cancel*) abort, call off, cancel, delete, discontinue, drop, erase, expunge, forget, get rid of, give up, scratch, terminate.

~*v.i.* **1** (*to clean or brighten things by rubbing hard*) clean, cleanse, rub, scour, wash. **2** (*to work hard*) drudge, labour, toil, work hard.

scrub[2] *n.* **1** ((*a tract of*) *undergrowth or stunted trees*) brushwood, bush, undergrowth. **2** (*a stunted tree, bush etc.*) bush, stunted tree.

scruffy *a.* (*untidy, dirty*) dirty, disreputable, down-at-heel, messy, seedy, shabby, slovenly, unkempt, untidy. ANTONYMS: neat, tidy, well-groomed.

scruple *n.* **1** (*a doubt or hesitation from conscientious or moral motives*) compunction, conscience, doubt, hesitation, misgiving, objection, qualm, reluctance, squeamishness, uneasiness. **2** (*a small quantity, a particle*) fraction, particle.
~*v.i.* (*to hesitate, to be reluctant* (*to do etc.*)) baulk at, be loath to, be reluctant to, be uneasy about, demur, have compunction about, have doubts about, have misgivings about, have scruples about, hesitate, shrink from, think twice, waver.

scrupulous *a.* **1** (*influenced by scruples*) ethical, honourable, moral, principled, upstanding. ANTONYMS: immoral, lax, unprincipled. **2** (*careful, cautious*) careful, cautious, conscientious, critical, exact, fastidious, fussy, meticulous, neat, nice, painstaking, precise, punctilious, rigorous, strict.

scrutinize *v.t.* (*to examine minutely*) analyse, check, dissect, examine, go over/ through, inspect, investigate, peruse, pore over, probe, sift, study.

scrutiny *n.* **1** (*close observation or investigation*) inspection, investigation, observation, perusal, probing, sifting, study, verification. **2** (*critical examination*) analysis, check, examination, exploration, inquiry. **3** (*a searching look*) searching look, stare.

scud *v.i.* (*to run or fly swiftly*) fly, race, run, scoot, shoot, speed.
~*v.t.* (*to move swiftly over*) move swiftly over, skim.

scuff *v.i.* **1** (*to drag or scrape with the feet in walking*) drag, scrape, shuffle. **2** (*to become abraded or roughened, esp. by use*) abrade, roughen, wear.
~*v.t.* **1** (*to scrape or shuffle* (*the feet*)) scrape, shuffle. **2** (*to touch lightly*) brush, graze, kiss, touch lightly. **3** (*to roughen the surface of*) abrade, roughen, scratch.
~*n.* (*a mark or roughened place caused by scuffing*) abrasion, mark, scratch.

scuffle *v.i.* **1** (*to fight or struggle in a rough-and-tumble way*) brawl, fight, struggle, tussle. **2** (*to scrape with the feet*) scrape, shuffle.
~*n.* (*a confused and disorderly fight or struggle*) affray, brawl, fight, rumpus, set-to, struggle, tussle.

sculpture *n.* (*a piece of work carved or cast from wood, stone etc.*) bronze, bust, carving, cast, figure, figurine, marble, objet d'art, relief, statue, statuette.

scum *n.* **1** (*impurities that rise to the surface of liquid, esp. in fermentation or boiling*) impurities, residue, sediment. **2** (*froth or any film*

of floating matter) film, foam, froth. **3** (*the vile and worthless part*) dregs, dross, refuse.

scurrilous *a.* (*using or expressed in grossly abusive or indecent language*) abusive, coarse, defamatory, derogatory, disparaging, foulmouthed, gross, indecent, insulting, low, obscene, offensive, profane, rude, scabrous, vilifying, vituperative, vulgar. ANTONYMS: respectable.

scurry *v.i.* (*to go with great haste, to hurry*) bolt, bustle, dart, dash, fly, hasten, hurry, race, rush, scamper, scramble, scuttle, speed, sprint, tear, zip. ANTONYMS: amble, idle.

scurvy *a.* (*mean, contemptible*) abject, base, contemptible, despicable, ignoble, low, mean, paltry, rotten, shabby, sorry, vile, worthless. ANTONYMS: admirable.

sea *n.* **1** (*the body of salt water covering the greater part of the earth's surface*) (*coll.*) briny, Davy Jones's locker, deep, (*coll.*) drink, high seas, main, Neptune's kingdom, ocean, (*facet.*) pond. ANTONYMS: land, shore. **2** (*a great wave, a billow*) billow, breaker, wave. **3** (*the set or direction of the waves*) current, surge, tide. **4** (*a vast quantity or expanse, a flood* (*of people, troubles etc.*)) abundance, flood, heaps, legion, mass, mountains, multitude, plethora, profusion, spate.
~*a.* (*relating to or used in, on or near the sea*) marine, maritime, oceanic. **all at sea** (*perplexed, uncertain*) adrift, at a loss, at sixes and sevens, bewildered, confused, disoriented, flummoxed, lost, mystified, perplexed.

seafaring *a.* (*travelling by sea*) marine, maritime, nautical, naval, navigational, sailing.

seal *n.* **1** (*a die or stamp having a device for making an impression on wax*) die, stamp. **2** (*a special official mark or design; the impression made with a stamp on wax*) badge, coat of arms, crest, design, emblem, escutcheon, imprint, insignia, monogram, sign, signet, stamp. **3** (*any act or event regarded as authenticating or guaranteeing*) assurance, attestation, authentication, confirmation, corroboration, endorsement, guarantee, notification, pledge, ratification, verification. **4** (*a symbolic or characteristic mark or impress*) impress, mark, symbol, token. **5** (*anything used to close a gap, prevent the escape of gas etc.*) bung, cork.
~*v.t.* **1** (*to stamp with a seal or stamp, esp. as a mark of correctness or authenticity*) rubber stamp, stamp. **2** (*to fasten with a seal*) batten down, bolt, fasten, secure. **3** (*to close hermetically, to shut up*) close, cork, make airtight, make waterproof, shut, zip up. **4** (*to confine securely*) confine, lock up. **5** (*to secure against leaks, draughts etc.*) bung, cork. **6** (*to confirm*)

clinch, confirm, settle. **7** (*to ratify, to certify*) affirm, attest, authenticate, certify, confirm, corroborate, endorse, guarantee, ratify, sanction, verify. **8** (*to set a mark on*) designate, destine, set a mark on.

seam *n.* **1** (*a ridge between two parts or things, esp. two pieces of cloth etc. sewn together*) joint, junction, juncture, ridge. **2** (*a crack, a fissure*) crack, fissure, line of separation. **3** (*a line on the surface of anything, esp. the face*) cicatrix, line, scar, wrinkle. **4** (*a thin layer separating two strata of rock*) bed, layer, thickness, vein. **5** (*a thin stratum of coal*) layer, lode, stratum.
~*v.t.* **1** (*to join together with or as with a seam*) join together, rivet. **2** (*to mark with a seam, scar etc.*) furrow, mark, scar.

seaman *n.* **1** (*a mariner, a sailor, esp. one below the rank of officer*) Jack tar, mariner, (*coll.*) matelot, sailor, seafarer, (*coll.*) tar. **2** (*a person able to navigate a ship*) navigator, steerer.

seamy *a.* (*disreputable, unpleasant*) degenerate, depraved, disreputable, distasteful, low, repellent, scurvy, shameful, sordid, squalid, ugly, unattractive, unsavoury, unseemly, unwholesome, vile. ANTONYMS: pleasant, respectable.

search *v.t.* **1** (*to go over and examine for what may be found or to find something*) check, examine, inspect, look at/ into, scrutinize. **2** (*to explore, to probe*) explore, investigate, probe, pry into, scour, sift through. **3** (*to look for, to seek* (*out*)) hunt for, leave no stone unturned, look for, rummage through, scour, scout out, seek. ANTONYMS: ignore.
~*v.i.* (*to make a search or investigation*) inquire, investigate, make a search.
~*n.* (*investigation, examination*) analysis, examination, exploration, hunt, inquiry, investigation, probe, pursuit, quest, scouring, scrutiny, study.

searching *a.* **1** (*making search or inquiry*) inquiring, probing. **2** (*penetrating, thorough*) close, concentrated, deep, intent, keen, minute, penetrating, piercing, sharp, thorough. ANTONYMS: superficial, vague.

searing *a.* (*feeling like a burn, severe*) agonizing, burning, painful, scorching. ANTONYMS: soothing.

seashore *n.* (*the shore, coast or margin of the sea*) beach, coast, coastline, littoral, sand(s), seaboard, seaside, shore, shoreline, strand.

season *n.* **1** (*any one of the four divisions of the year*) autumn, spring, summer, winter. **2** (*a favourable time*) chance, occasion, opportunity.
~*v.t.* **1** (*to render palatable or give a higher relish to by the addition of condiments etc.*) flavour, relish, salt, spice. **2** (*to make more piquant or pleasant*) add zest to, enliven, pep up, salt, spice. **3** (*to make sound or fit for use by preparation, esp. by tempering, maturing*) acclimatize, age, condition, harden, inure, mature, ripen, temper. **4** (*to moderate* (*justice with mercy etc.*)) mitigate, moderate, qualify.

seasonable *a.* **1** (*occurring or done at the proper time*) expedient, opportune, providential, timely, well-timed. ANTONYMS: untimely. **2** (*suitable to the season*) appropriate, apt, auspicious, fit, fitting, happy, proper, propitious, suitable, well-suited. ANTONYMS: inappropriate.

seasoning *n.* **1** (*anything added to food to make it more palatable*) condiment, garnish, herb, pepper, relish, salt, spice. **2** (*anything that increases enjoyment*) flavour, relish, sauce, spice, zest.

seat *n.* **1** (*something on which a person sits or may sit*) bench, chair, pew, settee, settle, sofa, stall, stool, throne. **2** (*the part of a machine or other structure on which another part is supported*) base, foundation, mounting. **3** (*the buttocks or the part of trousers etc. covering them*) (*taboo sl.*) arse, (*coll.*) backside, behind, bottom, (*sl.*) bum, (*N Am., sl.*) butt, buttocks, derrière, fundament, posterior, rear, rump. **4** (*the place where anything is, location*) locale, location, site, situation. **5** (*a place in which authority is vested*) capital, centre, cradle, headquarters, hub. **6** (*a country residence*) abode, domicile, estate, home, house, mansion, residence. **7** (*the right of sitting, esp. in a legislative body*) incumbency, membership, position.
~*v.t.* **1** (*to cause to sit down*) accommodate, contain, hold, sit. **2** (*to settle, to establish*) ensconce, enthrone, establish, fix, install, instate, invest, locate, place, settle.

seating *n.* (*the provision of seats*) accommodation, capacity, room, space.

secluded *a.* **1** (*hidden from view, private*) cloistered, hidden, monastic, private, retired, screened, sequestered, sheltered, withdrawn. ANTONYMS: exposed, public. **2** (*away from others, solitary*) detached, far-off, isolated, lonely, off the beaten track, out-of-the-way, remote, segregated, separate, solitary.

second *a.* **1** (*next in value, rank or position*) following, later, next, subsequent. ANTONYMS: first. **2** (*secondary, inferior*) inferior, secondary, second-best. ANTONYMS: principal, superior. **3** (*additional*) additional, another, duplicate, extra, further, supplementary.

~*n*. **1** (*a person who supports another*) aide, aide-de-camp, assistant, attendant, backer, lieutenant, number two, right-hand man, subordinate, supporter, understudy. ANTONYMS: opponent. **2** (*a very short time*) flash, instant, (*coll.*) jiffy, minute, moment, (*coll.*) sec, split second, (*coll.*) tick, trice, twinkling, (*coll.*) two shakes (of a lamb's/ dog's tail).

~*v.t.* (*to support*) advance, approve, back, encourage, endorse, favour, forward, further, go along with, promote, sponsor, subscribe to, support. ANTONYMS: oppose.

secondary *a*. **1** (*not primary, subordinate*) alternative, auxiliary, derivative, derived, extra, indirect, minor, reserve, second-hand, spare, subordinate, subsidiary, supplementary, supporting, unoriginal. ANTONYMS: original, primary. **2** (*of the second or of inferior rank, importance etc.*) inessential, inferior, lesser, less important, lower, non-essential.

~*n*. **1** (*a delegate or deputy*) delegate, deputy. **2** (*a secondary planet, a satellite*) moon, satellite.

second-hand *a*. **1** (*not primary or original*) derivative, derived, indirect, secondary, unoriginal. **2** (*sold or for sale after having been used or worn*) (*coll.*) hand-me-down, old, recycled, resold, used, worn.

secrecy *n*. **1** (*the state of being secret*) concealment, hiding. **2** (*the quality of being secretive*) confidentiality, covertness, furtiveness, mystery, secretiveness, stealth, surreptitiousness. ANTONYMS: openness, transparency. **3** (*solitude*) retirement, seclusion, solitude.

secret *a*. **1** (*concealed from notice, kept or meant to be kept private*) clandestine, concealed, confidential, covert, hidden, (*coll.*) hush-hush, private, quiet, surreptitious, undercover, undisclosed, unpublished, unrevealed. ANTONYMS: open, revealed. **2** (*occult, mysterious*) abstruse, arcane, cryptic, encoded, mysterious, occult, recondite, unseen. **3** (*given to secrecy, secretive*) close, reserved, reticent, secretive. **4** (*secluded*) isolated, private, secluded. ANTONYMS: public.

~*n*. **1** (*a thing kept back from general knowledge*) confidence, private matter. **2** (*a mystery, something that cannot be explained*) enigma, mystery, riddle.

secrete *v.t.* **1** (*to conceal, to hide*) bury, cache, camouflage, cloak, conceal, hide, mask, screen, (*coll.*) stash away, veil. ANTONYMS: expose, reveal. **2** (*to separate from the blood, sap etc. by the process of secretion*) discharge, drain, drip, emanate, emit, excrete, exude, leak, ooze, pass, release, seep, trickle.

secretion *n*. **1** (*the process of separating materials from the blood, sap etc. for the service*

of the body or for rejection as excreta*) discharging, draining, dripping, emanation, excretion, exudation, leakage, oozing, release, secreting, seepage, trickling. **2** (*any matter thus secreted, such as mucus, gastric juice etc.*) discharge, drip, emanation, emission, excreta, exudation, fluid, gastric juices, leakage, mucus, release, sap, seepage, semen, trickle, urine.

secretive *a*. (*given to secrecy, uncommunicative*) close, close-mouthed, reserved, reticent, taciturn, tight-lipped, uncommunicative. ANTONYMS: communicative, open.

secretly *adv*. (*in a secret manner*) clandestinely, confidentially, covertly, furtively, mysteriously, (*coll.*) on the qt., on the sly, quietly, stealthily, sub rosa, surreptitiously.

sect *n*. **1** (*a religious denomination, a nonconformist Church*) cult, denomination, order. **2** (*a party, a faction*) body, cabal, clique, faction, group, (*usu. derog.*) ism, party, persuasion, set, splinter group.

sectarian *a*. (*of or resulting from strong feelings of different religious or political groups*) clannish, cultish, denominational, factional, fanatical, indoctrinated, intolerant, narrow-minded, parochial, partial, partisan, prejudiced. ANTONYMS: open-minded, tolerant.

~*n*. (*a person with sectarian opinions*) adherent, believer, cultist, extremist, fanatic, (*coll.*) fiend, member, (*sl.*) nut, partisan, votary, zealot.

section *n*. **1** (*separation by cutting*) division, separation. **2** (*that which is cut off or separated*) fraction, fragment, part, piece, portion, segment, stage. ANTONYMS: entirety, whole. **3** (*each of a series of parts into which anything naturally separates or is constructed*) component, element, module, segment. **4** (*a division or subdivision of a book, chapter etc.*) chapter, division, leg, paragraph, statute, subdivision. **5** (*a thin slice of any substance prepared for microscopic examination*) cross-section, sample, slice.

~*v.t.* (*to divide or arrange in sections*) allocate, allot, apportion, cleave, cut, divide, measure out, segment, split.

sector *n*. (*a distinct part, a section*) area, block, district, field, precinct, quarter, region, section, zone.

secular *a*. **1** (*of or relating to the present world or to things not spiritual or sacred*) civil, lay, non-clerical, non-religious, non-spiritual, state. ANTONYMS: religious, sacred. **2** (*worldly, profane*) material, mundane, profane, temporal, terrestrial, worldly.

secure *a*. **1** (*free from danger or risk*) free from danger, risk-free, safe, unexposed, unimperilled, unthreatened. **2** (*safe from attack, impregnable*) defended, immune, impregnable, invulnerable, protected, safe, safeguarded, sheltered, shielded. ANTONYMS: endangered, vulnerable. **3** (*certain, sure* (*of*)) assured, certain, confident, definite, ensured, established, fastened, firm, healthy, reliable, settled, stable, steady, sturdy, sure, tight, unquestionable. ANTONYMS: insecure, unreliable, unsettled. **4** (*firmly fixed or held*) anchored, fast, fixed, held, immovable, moored. **5** (*trustworthy*) dependable, reliable, solid, sound, trustworthy.
~*v.t*. **1** (*to make safe or secure*) defend, guard, make safe, preserve, protect, safeguard, shelter, shield. **2** (*to close or confine securely*) anchor, bind, close, confine, enclose, fasten, fix, lock, make fast, tie. ANTONYMS: release, set free. **3** (*to make safe against loss, to guarantee payment of*) assure, collateralize, guarantee, insure, underwrite. **4** (*to gain possession of*) acquire, come by, gain, gain possession of, get, obtain, procure, take possession of, win. ANTONYMS: lose.

security *n*. **1** (*freedom from danger or risk, safety*) asylum, care, custody, immunity, protection, refuge, safe keeping, safety, sanctuary, shelter. ANTONYMS: danger, insecurity, risk. **2** (*certainty, assurance*) assuredness, certainty, confidence, conviction, overconfidence, sureness. **3** (*a pledge, a guarantee*) collateral, deposit, gage, guarantee, pledge, promise, warranty. **4** (*a document constituting evidence of debt or of property*) bond, certificate, document.

sedate *a*. (*calm, staid*) calm, collected, composed, conventional, cool, dignified, eventempered, imperturbable, peaceful, placid, proper, quiet, serene, sober, staid, stiff, straitlaced, tranquil, (*coll*.) unflappable, unruffled. ANTONYMS: impulsive, ruffled.
~*v.t*. (*to administer a sedative to*) calm, quieten, relax, soothe, still, suppress, tranquillize.

sedative *a*. (*allaying nervous irritability, soothing*) anodyne, assuaging, calming, lenitive, narcotic, relaxing, soothing, soporific, tranquillizing.
~*n*. (*a sedative medicine, influence etc*.) anodyne, barbiturate, calmative, (*sl*.) knockout drops, (*esp. N Am*.) Mickey Finn, narcotic, opiate, sleeping pill, tranquillizer.

sedentary *a*. **1** (*sitting*) seated, sitting. ANTONYMS: standing. **2** (*accustomed or obliged by occupation, to sit a great deal*) desk-bound, housebound, immobile, inactive, rooted, set. ANTONYMS: active, mobile.

sediment *n*. (*lees, dregs*) deposit, detritus, dregs, grounds, lees, precipitate, remains, residue, settlings.

sedition *n*. **1** (*disorder or commotion in a state, not amounting to insurrection*) agitation, commotion, disorder, insubordination. ANTONYMS: calm, obedience. **2** (*conduct tending to promote treason or rebellion*) incitement, insurgency, insurrection, mutiny, rebellion, revolution, subversion, treason.

seditious *a*. ((*of actions, writings etc*.) encouraging rebellion) dissident, inflammatory, insurgent, insurrectionist, mutinous, rabble-rousing, rebellious, refractory, revolutionary, subversive.

seduce *v.t*. **1** (*to lead astray, esp. to induce* (*someone*) *to sexual intercourse*) corrupt, debauch, defile, deflower, dishonour, lead astray, ravish, violate. **2** (*to entice or lure, esp. by offering rewards*) allure, attract, charm, corrupt, deprave, draw on, entice, inveigle, lure, (*coll*.) sweet-talk, tempt, vamp. ANTONYMS: alienate, repel.

seducer *n*. (*a man who seduces someone*) Casanova, charmer, Don Juan, lady-killer, lecher, Lothario, lover, playboy, ravisher, (*coll*.) sweet-talker, (*coll*.) wolf.

seductive *a*. (*very attractive, esp. sexually*) alluring, attractive, beguiling, bewitching, captivating, enchanting, enticing, fascinating, inviting, provocative, sexy, siren, tantalizing, tempting, winning. ANTONYMS: off-putting, repellent.

seductress *n*. (*a female seducer*) enchantress, femme fatale, lover, man-eater, siren, temptress, vamp.

see[1] *v.t*. **1** (*to discern, to look at*) catch a glimpse of, catch sight of, descry, discern, glimpse, look at/ upon, make out, mark, note, notice, observe, perceive, regard, sight, spot, spy. ANTONYMS: ignore, miss. **2** (*to perceive mentally, to understand*) appreciate, apprehend, be aware, be conscious of, comprehend, get, grasp, perceive, realize, recognize, take in, understand. **3** (*to experience, to go through*) endure, experience, go through, have knowledge of, know, survive, undergo. **4** (*to be a spectator of*) behold, spectate, watch, witness. **5** (*to imagine, to picture to oneself*) conceive, conjure up, divine, dream of, envisage, foresee, imagine, picture, visualize. **6** (*to ascertain or establish*) ascertain, determine, discover, establish, find out, investigate, learn. **7** (*to call on, to pay a visit to*) call on, grant an interview to, have a word with, meet, pay a visit, receive, sit down with, talk with, visit with. **8** (*to escort, to conduct* (*a person home etc.*)) accompany, attend, bring, conduct, convoy, drive, escort, lead, show, take, usher, walk. **9** (*to ensure*) be vigilant, ensure, make certain, make sure, mind. **10** (*to consider; to deduce*) consider, contemplate, deduce, deliberate, give some thought to, make up one's mind, meditate on, mull over, ponder, reflect on, ruminate on, think about/ over. **11** (*to meet socially, esp. regularly as a boyfriend or girlfriend*) associate with, consort with, consult with, court, (*esp. N Am.*) date, go out with, go steady with, woo. **12** (*to consult*) consult, seek advice from, turn to. **13** (*to supervise* (*an action etc.*)) attend to, look after, look to, manage, organize, see to, sort out, supervise, take care of, take charge of.

~*v.i.* **1** (*to have or exercise the power of sight*) discern, glimpse, look, observe, perceive. **2** (*to discern*) comprehend, discern, distinguish. **3** (*to inquire*) inquire, investigate, study. **4** (*to reflect, to consider carefully*) consider, ponder, reflect, think. **5** (*to take care* (*that*)) ensure, make certain, make sure, take care. **to see about 1** (*to give attention to*) attend to, consider, give some thought to, look after, manage, organize, oversee, pay attention to, see to, sort out, supervise, take care of, think about. **2** (*to make preparations for etc.*) inquire about, investigate, look into, make inquiries about, make preparations for, probe, study. **to see off 1** (*to escort on departure*) bid adieu, bid bon voyage, bid farewell, escort, say goodbye to, usher out. **2** (*to get rid of*) chase away, frighten off, get rid of, repel, repulse, scare off, warn off. **to see through 1** (*to penetrate, not to be deceived by*) be wise to, detect, penetrate, perceive, understand. **2** (*to persist* (*in a task etc.*) *until it is finished*) last, persevere, persist, ride out, see out, see to the end, stick out, survive. ANTONYMS: abandon, give up. **3** (*to help through a difficulty, danger etc.*) aid, assist, help.

see[2] *n.* (*the diocese or jurisdiction of a bishop or archbishop*) bishopric, diocese, episcopate.

seed *n.* **1** (*the mature fertilized ovule of a flowering plant, consisting of the embryo germ or reproductive body and its covering*) bulb, corm, embryo, germ, grain, kernel, ovule, pit, spore. **2** (*the germ from which anything springs, beginning*) basis, beginning, cause, first principle, germ, grounds, motivation, motive, origin, reason, root, source. **3** (*offspring, descendants*) children, descendants, heirs, issue, offspring, progeny, successors, young.

~*v.t.* **1** (*to sow or sprinkle with seed*) distribute, scatter, sow, sprinkle. **2** (*to classify* (*a good player*) *for a tournament, in a system whereby*

the best players do not meet in the early rounds*) classify, rank.

seedy *a.* **1** (*shabby, down at heel*) deteriorated, dilapidated, down-at-heel, grubby, mangy, run-down, shabby, sleazy, squalid, tatty, unkempt, worn out. ANTONYMS: elegant, smart. **2** (*off colour, as after a debauch*) ailing, (*coll.*) grotty, ill, lousy, off colour, out of sorts, poorly, shaky, sick, sickly, (*coll.*) under the weather, unwell, worn out. ANTONYMS: vital, well.

seek *v.t.* **1** (*to try to find, to look for*) be after, go after, hunt, look for, quest after, search for. ANTONYMS: find, locate. **2** (*to ask, to solicit* (*a thing of a person*)) ask for, beg, demand, entreat, invite, request, solicit. **3** (*to aim at*) aim at, aspire to, desire, essay, hope for, pursue, undertake, want.

~*v.i.* **1** (*to make search or inquiry* (*after or for*)) make inquiry. **2** (*to try* (*to do*)) attempt, endeavour, try.

seem *v.i.* **1** (*to appear* (*to do or to be the fact that*)) appear, feel, give every appearance of, give every indication of, look as if, look like, sound. ANTONYMS: be. **2** (*to be evident*) be apparent, be evident.

seemingly *adv.* (*apparently*) allegedly, apparently, evidently, feasibly, ostensibly, outwardly, plausibly, professedly, purportedly, superficially. ANTONYMS: actually, in fact.

seemly *a.* **1** (*becoming, decent*) becoming, befitting, decent, dignified, genteel, gentlemanly, ladylike, meet, proper, right. ANTONYMS: improper, unseemly. **2** (*suited to the occasion, purpose etc.*) apposite, appropriate, apropos, apt, comme il faut, fitting, sensible, suitable. ANTONYMS: unsuitable.

seep *v.i.* (*to percolate, to ooze*) bleed, drip, leach, leak, ooze, percolate, run, soak, trickle, weep.

seer *n.* (*a person who foresees, a prophet*) augur, clairvoyant, crystal-gazer, fortune-teller, oracle, prophet, prophetess, psychic, sage, soothsayer.

see-saw *v.i.* (*to move up and down or backwards and forwards*) alternate, fluctuate, oscillate, swing, switch, totter, vacillate, waver.

seethe *v.t.* (*to boil*) boil, bubble, burn, ferment, foam, froth, simmer, smoulder, stew.

~*v.i.* (*to be agitated, to bubble over*) be feverish, be furious, be incensed, be in ferment, bubble over, foam at the mouth, fume, (*coll.*) get all steamed up, rage, simmer, smoulder.

see-through *a.* ((*esp. of clothing*) (*semi-*) *transparent*) diaphanous, filmy, gauzy, gossamer, revealing, sheer, transparent.

segment *n.* (*a portion cut or marked off as*

separable, *a division*) component, division, element, fraction, length, part, piece, portion, section, slice. ANTONYMS: entirety, whole.

~*v.i.* (*to divide or be divided into segments*) divide, fragment, part, separate, split, subdivide.

~*v.t.* (*to divide into segments*) divide, fragment, part, partition, section, separate, split, subdivide.

segregate *v.t.* **1** (*to separate from others*) compartmentalize, dissociate, exclude, isolate, ostracize, partition, seclude, separate, sequester, set apart. ANTONYMS: join, unite. **2** (*to place in a separate class*) categorize, classify, group.

segregation *n.* **1** (*the act of segregating*) compartmentalization, discrimination, exclusion, isolation, ostracism, partition, seclusion, segmentation, separation, setting apart. **2** (*separation of a community on racial grounds*) apartheid, discrimination, racism.

seize *v.t.* **1** (*to grasp or lay hold of suddenly*) clasp, clutch, grab, grasp, grip, lay hold of, possess, snatch, take hold of, take possession of. ANTONYMS: let go, release. **2** (*to grasp mentally, to comprehend*) comprehend, grasp, master, understand. **3** (*to affect suddenly and forcibly*) affect, come upon, overcome. **4** (*to confiscate*) apprehend, appropriate, arrest, capture, commandeer, confiscate, impound, (*sl.*) nab, pick up, round up, sequestrate, take. ~*v.i.* (*to become stuck*) become stuck, bind, freeze, jam, lock, stick, stop.

seizure *n.* **1** (*the act of seizing*) annexation, appropriation, commandeering, confiscation, impounding, sequestration, usurpation. ANTONYMS: release. **2** (*a sudden attack, as of a disease*) attack, convulsion, fit, paroxysm, spasm.

seldom *adv.* (*rarely, not often*) hardly ever, infrequently, not often, rarely, very occasionally. ANTONYMS: frequently, often.

select *a.* **1** (*chosen, picked out*) choice, chosen, favoured, hand-picked, picked out, preferred, selected. **2** (*taken as superior to or more suitable than the rest*) best, exceptional, finest, first-class, prime, special, superior, supreme. ANTONYMS: inferior. **3** (*strict in selecting new members etc., exclusive*) closed, elite, exclusive, privileged, restricted, valuable. ANTONYMS: common, open.

~*v.t.* (*to choose, to pick out* (*the best etc.*)) choose, hand-pick, opt for, pick, pick out, prefer, single out.

selection *n.* **1** (*the right or opportunity of selecting, choice*) choice, election, opting for, pick, preference, settling on, singling out, voting for. **2** (*that which is selected*) abstract,

excerpt, extract, number, passage, piece, quotation. **3** (*a range of goods* (*as in a shop*) *from which to choose*) assortment, collection, range, series, set, variety.

selective *a.* (*given to selecting only what suits*) choosy, demanding, discriminating, exacting, fussy, particular, (*coll.*) picky.

self-centred *a.* (*interested solely in oneself and one's own affairs, egotistic*) egocentric, egotistic, narcissistic, self-interested, selfish, self-regarding, self-seeking. ANTONYMS: selfless.

self-confidence *n.* (*self-assurance*) assertiveness, confidence, independence, self-assurance, self-esteem, self-reliance, self-respect. ANTONYMS: diffidence, shyness.

self-confident *a.* (*self-assured*) assertive, confident, independent, positive, self-assured, self-reliant, sure of oneself. ANTONYMS: self-conscious, shy.

self-conscious *a.* (*conscious of one's actions, situation etc., esp. as observed by others*) affected, awkward, bashful, coy, diffident, modest, nervous, reserved, self-aware, sheepish, shy, timid, uncomfortable. ANTONYMS: unabashed.

self-contained *a.* **1** (*reserved, not communicative*) aloof, collected, detached, distant, formal, imperturbable, in control, independent, placid, reserved, reticent, self-possessed, self-reliant, serene, stand-offish, uncommunicative, unemotional, (*coll.*) unflappable, unruffled, withdrawn. ANTONYMS: dependent. **2** (*complete in itself*) complete, entire, standalone, unitary, whole.

self-control *n.* (*power of controlling one's feelings, impulses etc.*) calmness, control, coolheadedness, discipline, equanimity, even temper, forbearance, level-headedness, mettle, moral fibre, patience, poise, restraint, self-discipline, self-possession, serenity, strength of character, will-power.

self-denial *n.* (*refusal to gratify one's own appetites or desires*) abstemiousness, abstinence, altruism, giving up, renunciation, self-abnegation, self-deprivation, selflessness, self-sacrifice, unselfishness. ANTONYMS: self-indulgence.

self-esteem *n.* (*a good opinion of oneself*) amour propre, confidence, egotism, pride, self-approbation, self-confidence, self-importance, self-regard, self-respect, self-satisfaction, vanity.

self-evident *a.* (*obvious in itself, not requiring proof or demonstration*) apparent, axiomatic, clear, distinct, evident, express, incontestable, manifest, obvious, palpable, patent, plain, tangible, unmistakable.

self-important *a.* (*conceited, pompous*) arrogant, conceited, egotistic, haughty, overbearing, pompous, self-aggrandizing, self-centred, self-regarding, self-satisfied, (*coll.*) snooty, vain, vainglorious. ANTONYMS: self-denigrating.

self-indulgent *a.* (*gratifying one's inclinations etc.*) dissipated, dissolute, epicurean, greedy, hedonistic, immoderate, intemperate, licentious, sybaritic. ANTONYMS: self-denying.

selfish *a.* **1** (*attentive only to one's own interests*) egocentric, egotistic, grasping, greedy, self-absorbed, self-centred, self-seeking, self-serving. ANTONYMS: altruistic, selfless. **2** (*not regarding the interests or feelings of others*) inconsiderate, mean, possessive, tight, tight-fisted, uncharitable. ANTONYMS: considerate, generous.

selfless *a.* (*having no regard for self, unselfish*) altruistic, charitable, considerate, giving, magnanimous, self-denying, self-sacrificing, ungrudging, unselfish. ANTONYMS: selfish.

self-possessed *a.* (*calm, having presence of mind*) calm, collected, controlled, even-tempered, imperturbable, poised, self-assured, serene, (*coll.*) unflappable, unruffled. ANTONYMS: flustered, nervous.

self-respect *n.* (*due regard for one's character and position*) dignity, honour, integrity, pride, self-esteem, self-regard.

self-righteous *a.* (*pharisaical*) holier-than-thou, mealy-mouthed, pharisaical, pietistic, priggish, sanctimonious, self-satisfied, superior.

self-sufficient *a.* (*capable of fulfilling one's own requirements, needs etc. without aid*) independent, self-reliant, self-supporting, self-sustaining.

self-willed *a.* (*determined to do what one wants, even when this is unreasonable*) contrary, determined, difficult, incorrigible, intractable, obstinate, perverse, pig-headed, recalcitrant, stubborn, uncooperative, wilful.

sell *v.t.* **1** (*to transfer or dispose of* (*property*) *to another for an equivalent in money*) barter, dispose of, exchange, (*sl.*) flog, hawk, peddle, retail, trade, vend. ANTONYMS: buy, purchase. **2** (*to be a regular dealer in*) deal in, market, merchandise, trade in, traffic in. **3** (*to surrender for a reward or bribe*) betray, deliver up, double-cross, inform against, prostitute, (*coll.*) rat on, (*coll.*) sell down the river, (*sl.*) shop,

surrender. **4** (*sl.*) (*to cheat*) cheat, disappoint, play a trick upon.

seller *n.* (*a person who sells*) chandler, dealer, merchant, peddler, representative, retailer, (*N Am.*) sales clerk, salesperson, shopkeeper, vendor.

semblance *n.* **1** (*external appearance, seeming*) air, appearance, exterior, facade, face, figure, form, front, look, mask, mien, seeming. **2** (*a mere show*) cloak, facade, pretence, show, veneer. **3** (*a likeness, an image*) image, likeness, resemblance, similarity.

seminal *a.* **1** (*formative*) creative, embryonic, formative, germinal, incipient, potential, primary, propagative. **2** (*important to the future development of anything*) important, influential, landmark, telling. **3** (*containing new ideas, original*) innovative, new, original, unprecedented.

seminary *n.* (*a place of education, a college*) academy, college, institute, institution, school, training ground, university.

send *v.t.* **1** (*to arrange for* (*a letter, message etc.*) *to go or be taken to some destination*) address, consign, convey, deliver, direct, dispatch, e-mail, fax, forward, mail, post, redirect, remit. **2** (*to cause* (*a signal*) *to be broadcast or transmitted*) broadcast, communicate, radio, relay, telegraph, transmit. **3** (*to propel, to hurl*) cast, deliver, discharge, fire, fling, hurl, impart, let fly, project, propel, release, shoot, throw, toss. **4** (*to bestow, to inflict*) bestow, grant, inflict. **5** (*to cause to be, to bring about*) assign, bring about, cause, charge, commission, depute, direct, order. **6** (*to affect emotionally; to move to rapture*) charm, delight, electrify, enrapture, move, stir, thrill.

~*v.i.* (*to dispatch a messenger or letter*) consign, dispatch, forward, mail, post. **to send down 1** (*to suspend from university*) disbar, disqualify, suspend. **2** (*to send to prison*) gaol, imprison, incarcerate, jail, put away, sentence. **to send for** (*to summon*) ask for, call for, order, request, summon. **to send forth** (*to emit*) discharge, emit, exude, give off, grow, radiate. **to send up 1** (*to parody*) burlesque, lampoon, parody, satirize, (*coll.*) take off. **2** (*to ridicule*) make fun of, ridicule, take the mickey out of.

senile *a.* (*suffering from the* (*mental*) *infirmities associated with old age*) aged, decrepit, doddering, (*coll.*) dotty, incapable, infirm, old, senescent. ANTONYMS: capable, young.

senior *a.* **1** (*elder*) elder, older. **2** (*older or higher in rank or service*) chief, higher, superior. ANTONYMS: junior, lower.

~*n.* (*an aged person*) aged person, OAP, old-age pensioner, pensioner, senior citizen.

sensation n. 1 (*the mental state or affection resulting from the excitation of an organ of sense*) awareness, excitation, feeling, impression, perception, sense. 2 (*a state of excited feeling or interest*) agitation, commotion, excitement, furore, fuss, scandal, shock, stir, thrill.

sensational a. 1 (*causing or relating to sensation*) astounding, breathtaking, electrifying, (*coll.*) mind-blowing, spectacular, spine-tingling, staggering, stimulating, stirring, superb, thrilling. ANTONYMS: boring, commonplace. 2 (*intending to shock or excite people*) incredible, lurid, melodramatic, scandalous, shocking, unbelievable, vivid. 3 (*coll.*) (*very good*) (*coll.*) brilliant, excellent, (*coll.*) fantastic, (*coll.*) great, phenomenal, stupendous, (*coll.*) superb, (*coll.*) terrific, very good, wonderful.

sense n. 1 (*any one of the five faculties by which sensation is received through special bodily organs*) ability, capacity, faculty, power. 2 (*the faculty of sensation, perception*) feeling, perception, sensation, sensitiveness. 3 (*intuitive perception*) appreciation, comprehension, discernment, discrimination, intuition, understanding. 4 (*sound judgement, good mental capacity*) common sense, intelligence, judgement, (*coll.*) nous, quick-wittedness, reason, sagacity, wisdom, wit. ANTONYMS: foolishness, incapacity. 5 (*meaning, signification*) coherence, drift, gist, implication, import, intelligibility, meaning, message, nuance, signification.
~v.t. (*to perceive by the senses*) appreciate, be aware of, detect, discern, divine, feel, get the impression that, have a hunch about, perceive, pick up, suspect.

senseless a. 1 (*incapable of sensation*) anaesthetized, benumbed, comatose, deadened, insensate, insensible, knocked out, numb, unconscious, unfeeling. ANTONYMS: sensitive. 2 (*contrary to reason, foolish*) absurd, against reason, (*coll.*) batty, crazy, daft, empty-headed, fatuous, foolish, idiotic, illogical, incongruous, insane, irrational, ludicrous, mad, mindless, nonsensical, pointless, silly, stupid, witless. ANTONYMS: rational, sensible.

sensible a. 1 (*acting with or characterized by good sense or judgement*) commonsensical, discreet, intelligent, judicious, logical, practical, prudent, rational, realistic, reasonable, sagacious, sane, shrewd, sound, well-advised, wise. ANTONYMS: foolish, ill-advised, stupid. 2 (*perceptible by the senses*) apprehensible, detectable, discernible, evident, manifest, material, observable, palpable, perceptible, recognizable, substantive, tangible, visible. ANTONYMS: imperceptible.

sensitive a. 1 (*impressible, delicately susceptible*) attuned, conscious, excitable, fragile, impressionable, irritable, quick-tempered, reactive, receptive, responsive, susceptible, temperamental, tender, testy, thin-skinned, touchy, volatile, vulnerable. ANTONYMS: insensitive, unresponsive. 2 (*of or depending on the senses, sensory*) sensory, sentient. 3 ((*of information*) *secret*) classified, (*coll.*) hush-hush, restricted, secret.

sensitivity n. 1 (*the quality of being sensitive, esp. being easily upset*) delicacy, hypersensitivity, irritability, oversensitivity, sensitiveness, soreness, touchiness. 2 (*compassion and understanding*) compassion, concern, empathy, feeling, sympathy, tender-heartedness, tenderness, understanding, warmth. 3 (*the state of being sensitive or impressible*) acuteness, appreciation, awareness, consciousness, feeling, perception, receptiveness, sensitiveness, susceptibility, understanding.

sensual a. 1 (*relating to or affecting the senses, carnal*) bodily, carnal, fleshly, physical. ANTONYMS: intellectual, spiritual. 2 (*relating to or devoted to the indulgence of the appetites or passions, esp. those of sex*) debauched, dissipated, dissolute, erotic, goatish, lascivious, lecherous, lewd, libidinous, licentious, (*formal*) lubricious, lustful, passionate, salacious, sexual, voluptuous, wanton.

sensuous a. (*abounding in or suggesting sensible images*) aesthetic, epicurean, gorgeous, hedonistic, lavish, luxurious, pleasant, pleasurable, sumptuous, sybaritic.

sentence n. 1 (*Law*) **a** (*a penalty or declaration of penalty upon a condemned person*) condemnation, judgement, penalty, punishment, (*coll.*) rap. **b** (*a judicial decision, verdict*) decree, judgement, judicial decision, verdict. 2† (*a decision or opinion*) decision, determination, opinion, ruling.
~v.t. 1 (*to pronounce judgement on*) doom, pronounce judgement on. 2 (*to condemn to punishment*) condemn, doom, penalize, punish. ANTONYMS: acquit, pardon.

sentiment n. 1 (*an opinion or attitude*) attitude, belief, judgement, opinion, position. 2 (*a thought or mental tendency derived from or characterized by emotion*) belief, idea, notion, outlook, thought, view. 3 (*mental feeling excited by aesthetic, moral or spiritual ideas*) emotion, feeling, sensibility. 4 (*susceptibility to emotion*) sensibility, sentimentality, susceptibility, tender-heartedness, tenderness. ANTONYMS: realism.

sentimental a. 1 (*swayed by emotion*) emotional, nostalgic, romantic. ANTONYMS: realistic. 2 (*showing too much emotion, mawkish*) corny, gushy, maudlin, mawkish, nauseating, over-emotional, pathetic, (*esp. N Am., coll.*) schmaltzy, sickening, (*coll.*) soppy, tear-jerking, weepy. **3** (*susceptible to emotion*) compassionate, sympathetic, tender, tender-hearted, warm-hearted.

sentimentality *n.* (*the quality of showing too much emotion*) corniness, emotionalism, mawkishness, (*sl.*) mushiness, nostalgia, romanticism, (*esp. N Am., coll.*) schmaltz, (*sl.*) slushiness, (*coll.*) soppiness, tearfulness, weepiness.

separate[1] *v.t.* **1** (*to set or keep apart*) break up, cleave, detach, disassemble, disconnect, disengage, disentangle, dissociate, disunite, divide, divorce, isolate, part, partition, segregate, set apart, single out, split (up), sunder, take apart, uncouple. ANTONYMS: combine, join, unite. **2** (*to come or be between*) be between, be the boundary of, come between, divide, part, split.
~*v.i.* **1** (*to withdraw (from)*) be disconnected, part, withdraw. **2** (*to disperse*) disintegrate, disperse, fall apart. **3** ((*of a married couple*) *to agree to live apart*) divorce, live apart.

separate[2] *a.* (*disconnected, considered apart*) apart, detached, disconnected, discrete, distinct, divorced, independent, isolated, removed, secluded, separated, unattached, unrelated. ANTONYMS: connected, joined.

separately *adv.* (*on one's own*) alone, by oneself, independently, individually, in turn, one by one, severally, singly. ANTONYMS: together.

separation *n.* (*the act of separating or the state of being separated, esp. cessation of cohabitation between married persons*) break-up, cleavage, detachment, disconnection, disintegration, dissociation, division, divorce, estrangement, fragmentation, isolation, partition, schism, segmentation, segregation, split, taking apart. ANTONYMS: connection, union.

sequel *n.* **1** (*a succeeding part, a continuation (of a story etc.)*) continuation, development, follow-up, supplement. ANTONYMS: prequel. **2** (*the consequence or result (of an event etc.)*) consequence, issue, outcome, result, upshot.

sequence *n.* **1** (*succession, the process of coming after in space, time etc.*) arrangement, concatenation, order, organization, progression, succession, system, train. ANTONYMS: disorder. **2** (*a series of things following one another consecutively*) chain, course, cycle, line, run, serial, series, set, string. **3** (*a scene in a film*) episode, scene, set.
~*v.t.* (*to arrange in definite order*) arrange, dispose, marshal, order, organize.

serene *a.* **1** (*placid, tranquil*) calm, collected, cool, even-tempered, imperturbable, peaceful, placid, poised, self-possessed, still, tranquil, (*coll.*) unflappable, unruffled, untroubled. ANTONYMS: agitated, upset. **2** ((*of the sky, atmosphere etc.*) *calm and clear*) calm, clear, cloudless, fair, halcyon, idyllic. ANTONYMS: overcast, unsettled.

series *n.* (*a number, set or continued succession of things similar to each other*) chain, course, cycle, line, number, progression, row, run, sequence, set, string, succession, train.

serious *a.* **1** (*grave, thoughtful*) dour, grave, grim, humourless, sedate, severe, sober, solemn, sombre, stern, unsmiling. ANTONYMS: jokey, light-hearted. **2** (*in earnest, not pretended*) genuine, honest, in earnest, resolute, sincere. ANTONYMS: hypocritical, insincere. **3** (*of great importance, momentous*) consequential, crucial, important, life-and-death, momentous, of consequence, portentous, pressing, significant, urgent, vital. ANTONYMS: slight, trivial. **4** (*having serious consequences, dangerous*) acute, alarming, bad, critical, dangerous, life-threatening, perilous, precarious, severe. **5** (*coll.*) (*significantly costly*) costly, dear, expensive, valuable. ANTONYMS: cheap.

seriously *adv.* **1** (*in a serious manner*) candidly, earnestly, intently, joking aside, no kidding, sincerely, soberly, truly, without a doubt. **2** (*to a serious extent*) badly, critically, extremely, gravely, honestly, really, severely, very.

sermon *n.* **1** (*a discourse founded on a text of Scripture delivered in church*) address, homily, message, talk. **2** (*a similar discourse delivered elsewhere*) address, discourse, lecture, lesson, message, speech, talk. **3** (*a serious exhortation or reproof*) (*coll.*) dressing-down, exhortation, harangue, reprimand, reproof, scolding, (*coll.*) talking-to.

serrated *a.* (*notched on the edge*) denticulate, jagged, notched, sawtoothed, serrate, serrulate, toothed, zigag. ANTONYMS: smooth, unbroken.

servant *n.* **1** (*a person employed by another person to work for wages, esp. in the house of the employer and undertaking domestic tasks*) attendant, butler, charlady, cleaner, daily, dogsbody, domestic, drudge, factotum, footman, help, houseboy, housekeeper, maidservant, manservant, menial, page, retainer, slave, valet. ANTONYMS: master, mistress. **2** (*a devoted follower, a person willing to perform the will of another*) devotee, disciple, follower.

serve *v.t.* **1** (*to act as servant to, to be in the employment of*) answer to, attend, work for. ANTONYMS: command, employ. **2** (*to be useful to, to render service to*) accommodate, assist, oblige, render service to. **3** (*to attend to as a shop assistant*) attend to, look after, minister to. **4** (*to satisfy, to suffice*) avail, be sufficient, measure up, satisfy, suffice. **5** (*to supply, to perform* (*a purpose, function etc.*)) discharge, fulfil, function, perform, supply. **6** (*to undergo the punishment prescribed by* (*a sentence*) *or for* (*a specified time*)) complete, endure, go through, last, spend, survive, undergo. **7** (*to treat* (*well, badly etc.*)) behave towards, deal with, treat. **8** (*to dish* (*up*) *for eating, to bring to and set on the table*) dish out, dish up. **9** (*to distribute to those at table*) deal out, distribute, dole out, give out, pass round, set out. **10** (*to supply* (*a person with*)) furnish, offer, provide, supply.
~*v.i.* **1** (*to be employed, to perform the duties of or to hold an office etc.*) be employed, perform, work. **2** (*to be used* (*as*), *to be a satisfactory substitute* (*for*)) answer, avail, be sufficient, be used as, measure up, substitute, suffice, suit, take the place of.

service *n.* **1** (*work done for an employer or for the benefit of another*) employment, labour, work. **2** (*a benefit or advantage conferred on someone*) advantage, benefit, favour. **3** (*a department of state or public work, the organization performing this*) agency, bureau, department. **4** (*use, assistance*) aid, assistance, help, use, usefulness, utility. ANTONYMS: uselessness. **5** (*a liturgical form for worship*) ceremony, observance, office, ordinance, rite, ritual, sacrament, worship. **6** (*maintenance work undertaken by the vendor after a sale*) checking, maintenance, mending, overhaul, repair, servicing.
~*v.t.* (*to repair or maintain* (*a car etc.*) *after sale*) check, maintain, overhaul, repair.

serviceable *a.* **1** (*able or willing to render service*) functional, functioning, operating, operative, usable, workable, working. **2** (*durable, fit for service*) durable, fit for service, hard-wearing, long-lasting, resilient, resistant, tough, utilitarian.

servile *a.* (*cringing, fawning*) abject, (*taboo sl.*) arse-licking, base, bootlicking, craven, cringing, deferential, dependent, fawning, grovelling, low, mean, menial, obsequious, slavish, subservient, sycophantic, unctuous. ANTONYMS: proud.

session *n.* **1** (*a sitting or meeting of a court, council etc. for the transaction of business*) assembly, conference, gathering, hearing, meeting, seating, sitting. **2** (*a period devoted to* an activity) period, term. **3** (*coll.*) (*a period of heavy drinking*) (*sl.*) bender, (*coll.*) binge.

set[1] *v.t.* **1** (*to place, to put*) deposit, install, locate, lodge, mount, park, place, position, put, set down, site, stand, station. ANTONYMS: move, relocate. **2** (*to fix*) establish, fasten on, fix, secure. **3** (*to bring or put in a specified or right position or state*) deposit, lay, place, put, site. **4** (*to arrange for use, display etc.*) adjust, arrange, concoct, dispose, prepare, put right, set up. **5** (*to attach, to fasten*) attach, fasten, join, stick. **6** (*to determine, to appoint*) appoint, decide, define, delineate, designate, determine, establish, lay down, ordain, propound, schedule, set forth, settle, specify, stipulate. ANTONYMS: alter, change. **7** (*to arrange, to compose* (*type*)) arrange, compose, typeset. **8** (*to adapt or fit* (*words etc.*) *to music usu. composed for the purpose*) adapt to music, arrange, orchestrate, put to music, score. **9** (*Naut.*) (*to spread* (*sail*)) hoist, raise, spread.
~*v.i.* **1** (*to become solid or firm from a fluid condition, to congeal*) cake, clot, congeal, freeze, gel, harden, solidify, stiffen, thicken. ANTONYMS: melt, soften. **2** (*to take shape*) become fixed, gel, take shape. **3** (*to move or incline in a definite or specified direction*) go, incline, move, tend. **4** ((*of flowers or fruit*) *to mature, to develop*) burgeon, develop, grow, mature, thrive. **5** (*to decline, to pass away*) decline, disappear, go down, pass away, sink, subside. ANTONYMS: grow, rise.
~*a.* **1** (*fixed, immovable*) defined, definite, firm, fixed, immovable, settled, unchanging, unvaried, unyielding. **2** (*determined, intent* (*on or upon*)) bent, determined, intent. **3** (*motionless*) motionless, rigid, stationary. **4** (*established, prescribed*) conventional, customary, decided, established, habitual, normal, prearranged, predetermined, prescribed, scheduled, standard, traditional, usual. **to set about 1** (*to begin*) begin, break the ice, get to work, get under way, set in motion, start the ball rolling. **2** (*to prepare or take steps* (*to do etc.*)) address oneself to, enter upon, get cracking, get ready, launch, make ready, prepare, tackle, take steps, undertake. ANTONYMS: complete, finish. **3** (*to attack*) assail, assault, attack, beat up, fight. **to set against 1** (*to oppose*) contrast, estrange, oppose. **2** (*to balance* (*one thing*) *against another*) balance, compare, contrast, evaluate, rate, weigh. **3** (*to make* (*a person*) *unfriendly to or prejudiced against*) alienate, antagonize, disunite, divide, prejudice, set at odds. **to set apart** (*to separate, to reserve* (*for some special purpose*)) differentiate, distinguish, earmark, keep back, put aside, put away, reserve, save, separate, set aside, set by, store. **to set aside 1** (*to reserve*) earmark, keep

back, put aside, put away, reserve, save, set apart, set by, store. **2** (*to reject*) discard, reject, throw out. **3** (*to annul, to quash*) abrogate, annul, cancel, declare null and void, nullify, overrule, overturn, quash, repudiate. **to set back 1** (*to turn backwards*) move back, reverse, turn backwards. **2** (*to hinder the progress of, to impede*) delay, frustrate, hinder, hold up, impede, inhibit, obstruct, put back, retard, slow, stay, thwart. ANTONYMS: advance, progress. **to set down 1** (*to put on the ground*) deposit, ground, land, put down. **2** (*to put in writing, to note*) jot down, list, mark down, note, put down, put in writing, record, register, write. **3** (*to attribute*) ascribe, assign, attribute, charge, impute. **4** (*to snub, to rebuke*) put down, rebuke, snub. **to set forth 1** (*to start (on a journey etc.*)) begin, depart, embark, get under way, go, leave, push off, set off, set out, start. **2** (*to demonstrate, to make known*) articulate, broach, declare, demonstrate, describe, enunciate, explain, expound, express, make known, move, present, propose, propound, set out, show, state, submit, suggest. **to set in** (*to begin in a steady manner*) arrive, begin, commence, start. **to set off 1** (*to make more attractive or brilliant by contrast*) contrast, display, enhance, highlight, make attractive, show off, throw into relief. **2** (*to beautify, to adorn*) adorn, beautify, decorate. **3** (*to start (laughing etc.*)) activate, begin, commence, start. **4** (*to set out*) depart, embark, get under way, go, leave, push off, sally forth, set forth, set out, start out. ANTONYMS: arrive, return. **5** (*to detonate*) blow up, detonate, explode, ignite, kindle, light, touch off, trigger, trip. **to set on 1** (*to incite, to urge (to attack*)) encourage, incite, instigate, urge. **2** (*to employ (on a task*)) employ, use, utilize. **3** (*to make an attack on*) assault, attack, fall on, fly at, pounce on, set upon. **to set out 1** (*to start (upon a journey etc.*)) begin, embark, leave, set off, start out. **2** (*to intend*) aim, intend, purpose. **3** (*to display, to state at length*) display, explain, expound, publish, show, state at length. **4** (*to assign, to allot*) allot, ascribe, assign, attribute, charge, impute. **5** (*to plant out*) arrange, display, dispose, lay out, plant out, put out. **to set up 1** (*to erect, to display*) assemble, build, construct, display, erect, fix up, put together, put up. **2** (*to raise, to exalt*) elevate, exalt, raise up. **3** (*to establish*) establish, found, inaugurate, institute. **4** (*to start a business (as*)) begin, establish, found, inaugurate, initiate, organize, start. ANTONYMS: close. **5** (*coll.*) (*to arrange for (someone else) to be blamed, to frame*) (*sl.*) fit up, (*coll.*) frame, incriminate. **6** (*to prepare*) arrange, get ready, make ready, organize, prepare. **to set upon** (*to set on*) ambush, assault, attack, beat up, fall

upon, fly at, mug, pounce on, set about, set on.

set² *n.* **1** (*a number of similar, related or complementary things or persons, a group*) band, batch, circle, clique, collection, combination, company, coterie, crowd, faction, gang, group, grouping, number, party, sect. **2** (*a number of things intended to be used together or required to form a whole*) kit, outfit, rig. **3** (*a clutch of eggs*) clutch, sitting. **4** (*the direction of a current, opinion etc., drift*) direction, drift, tendency, trend. **5** (*posture*) bearing, carriage, pose, position, posture. **6** (*permanent inclination, bias*) bend, bias, displacement, inclination. **7** (*a set theatre scene*) backdrop, background, (theatre) scene, (theatre) setting. **8** (*an apparatus for radio or television receiving*) radio, television, TV, wireless. **9** (*a class of pupils of the same or similar ability*) class, form, shell. **10** (*a sequence of songs or pieces of music to be performed*) programme, sequence, series.

setback *n.* **1** (*a check, an arrest*) arrest, block, blow, check, defeat, delay, (*coll.*) hiccup, hindrance, hitch, hold-up, reversal, reverse, upset. **2** (*a relapse*) deterioration, lapse, regression, relapse, worsening.

setting *n.* **1** (*hardening*) concretion, hardening, solidification. **2** (*the framing etc. in which something (such as a jewel) is set*) background, frame, framework, mount, mounting. **3** (*the surroundings or environment of a thing, event etc.*) background, context, environment, environs, frame, habitat, home, locale, location, milieu, placement, site, surroundings. **4** (*the scenery and other stage accessories of a play*) backdrop, mise en scene, scene, scenery, set, stage set. **5** (*the music to which words, a song etc. are fitted*) arrangement, music, orchestration, score, tune.

settle *v.t.* **1** (*to place firmly, to put in a permanent or fixed position*) affirm, appoint, confirm, establish, fix, place, position, set. **2** (*to put in order*) dispose, organize, set to rights, sort out, straighten out. ANTONYMS: confuse, disorder. **3** (*to determine, to decide*) agree, choose, decide, determine, fix on, pick, select. **4** (*to plant with inhabitants, to colonize*) colonize, inhabit, people, populate. ANTONYMS: desert, migrate. **5** (*to cause to sink or subside*) abate, drop, precipitate, sink. ANTONYMS: raise, stir up. **6** (*to clear of dregs*) clarify, clear. ANTONYMS: muddy. **7** (*to deal with, to finish with*) deal with, discharge, dispose of, do for, finish with, put an end to. **8** (*to adjust and liquidate (a disputed account*)) clear, liquidate. ANTONYMS: owe. **9** (*to pay (an account*)) clear, discharge, pay, pay up. **10** (*to adjust, to* *accommodate (a quarrel, dispute etc.))* accommodate, adjust, arrange, classify, compose, coordinate, patch up, reconcile, resolve.

~*v.i.* **1** (*to sit down, to alight*) alight, land, light, put down, sit down. **2** (*to cease from movement, agitation etc.*) lodge, perch, repose, rest, roost. **3** (*to take up a permanent abode, mode of life etc.*) dwell, inhabit, live, reside. **4** (*to become established, to become a colonist* (*in*)) colonize, live, people, populate. **5** (*to subside, to sink to the bottom*) descend, drop, fall, sink, subside. **6** (*to determine, to resolve* (*upon*)) conclude, determine, reconcile, resolve. **to settle down 1** (*to become regular in one's mode of life*) abide, dwell, live, put down roots, remain, reside, set up home, stay. **2** (*to begin to apply oneself* (*to a task etc.*)) concentrate, persevere. **3** (*to stop being excited, to calm down*) calm down, quieten down, relax, soothe, subside, tranquillize.

settlement *n.* **1** (*the act of settling an agreement; an official agreement*) accommodation, adjustment, affirmation, agreement, arbitration, arrangement, choice, clearing, conclusion, confirmation, decision, determination, establishment, rapprochement, reconciliation, regulation, resolution, selection, setting, settling, stabilization, working-out. ANTONYMS: disagreement. **2** (*the act of paying back money*) clearance, defrayal, discharge, liquidation, payment, quittance. **3** (*a subsidence*) slippage, subsidence. **4** (*a community or group of persons living together, esp. in order to carry out social work among the poor*) camp, colony, community, encampment, hamlet, kibbutz, outpost, village.

settler *n.* (*a person who settles, esp. a colonist*) colonial, colonist, frontiersman, frontierswoman, immigrant, pioneer.

set-up *n.* **1** (*an arrangement*) arrangement, composition, construction, format, frame, framework, layout, make-up, organization, pre-arrangement, regime, structure, system. **2** (*a situation*) circumstances, conditions, situation. **3** (*a situation in which someone is tricked or framed*) (*sl.*) con, deception, (*sl.*) double-cross, (*coll.*) put-up job, trap, trick.

sever *v.t.* **1** (*to part, to separate*) break off, break up, cease, detach, disconnect, discontinue, disjoin, dissociate, dissolve, disunite, divide, part, separate, stop, suspend, terminate. ANTONYMS: combine, join, unite. **2** (*to divide, to cleave*) bob, chop, cleave, cut off, dock, hack off, lop, shear off, slice, split, sunder.

several *a.* **1** (*consisting of a number, more than two but not many*) a few, a handful, a number of, a sprinkling, not many, some, sundry,

various. ANTONYMS: many, numerous. **2** (*separate, distinct*) assorted, different, disparate, dissimilar, distinct, individual, own, particular, respective, separate. **3** (*not common, not shared with others*) uncommon, unique.

severe *a.* **1** (*rigorous, strict*) austere, autocratic, cold, demanding, despotic, dictatorial, dour, exacting, flinty, forbidding, grave, grim, hard, hard-hearted, harsh, inexorable, inflexible, mean, merciless, oppressive, rigid, rigorous, ruthless, serious, stern, stiff, stony, strait-laced, strict, taxing, tough, tyrannical, uncompromising, unrelenting, unsympathetic. ANTONYMS: compromising, indulgent, mild. **2** (*trying, hard to endure or sustain*) burdensome, Draconian, grievous, hard to endure, harsh, onerous, punishing, punitive, stringent, tough, trying. **3** (*distressing, bitter*) acute, bitter, distressing, extreme, fierce, harsh, inclement, intense, keen, painful, penetrating, piercing, stormy, turbulent, violent, wicked. **4** (*grave, serious*) acute, awful, critical, dangerous, dire, dreadful, fatal, grave, grievous, life-threatening, mortal, serious, sombre, terminal. **5** (*rigidly conforming to rule, unadorned*) ascetic, austere, bare, basic, conformist, crude, modest, monastic, plain, restrained, self-denying, simple, spare, Spartan, stark, unadorned, undecorated, unembellished, unembroidered. ANTONYMS: adorned, decorated.

severely *adv.* **1** (*in a rigorous or strict manner*) acutely, awfully, badly, coldly, coolly, critically, dreadfully, forbiddingly, fully, gravely, grievously, grimly, harshly, mercilessly, mortally, oppressively, painfully, relentlessly, rigorously, seriously, sternly, strictly, stringently, terminally, tyrannically, very. **2** (*in an unadorned manner*) ascetically, austerely, barely, crudely, dourly, modestly, monastically, plainly, primitively, simply, sparely, sparsely, starkly.

severity *n.* **1** (*the state of being rigorous or strict*) austerity, brutality, coldness, cruelty, despotism, gravity, grimness, hardness, harshness, inexorability, inflexibility, meanness, mercilessness, oppressiveness, pitilessness, rigidity, rigour, ruthlessness, savagery, sternness, strictness, stringency, tyranny. ANTONYMS: kindness, sympathy. **2** (*the state of being serious, e.g. of illness*) acuteness, dangerousness, gravity, intensity, seriousness, violence, virulence. **3** (*the state of being hard to endure or sustain*) burdensomeness, grievousness, harshness, onerousness, oppressiveness, painfulness, punishment, punitiveness, stringency. ANTONYMS: leniency. **4** (*the state of being fierce or intense, e.g. of storms*) ferocity, fierceness, furiousness, fury, harshness, inclemency, intensity, storminess, tempestuousness, violence. **5** (*the state of being unadorned*) asceticism, austerity, bareness, crudeness, modesty, monasticism, plainness, primitiveness, simplicity, spareness, sparseness, starkness.

sew *v.t.* (*to make, mend etc. by sewing*) attach, darn, fasten, hem, mend, repair, sew on, sew up, stitch, tack, thread.

sex *n.* **1** (*the sum total of the physiological, anatomical and functional characteristics which distinguish male and female*) gender, sexuality. **2** (*coll.*) (*sexual intercourse*) (*sl.*) bonking, coition, coitus, congress, consummation, copulation, coupling, (*taboo sl.*) fucking, going to bed with someone, intercourse, intimacy, lovemaking, mating, (*sl.*) screwing, sexual intercourse, sexual relations, (*taboo sl.*) shagging, sleeping with someone, union.

sexual *a.* (*of or relating to generation or copulation, venereal*) animal, bodily, carnal, copulative, erotic, genital, libidinous, lustful, physical, procreant, reproductive, sensual, sensuous, sexy, venereal.

sexy *a.* **1** (*sexually stimulating*) arousing, attractive, coarse, dirty, erotic, filthy, (*coll.*) hot, lascivious, lewd, lusty, naughty, obscene, pornographic, provocative, (*coll.*) raunchy, risqué, seductive, sensual, sensuous, stimulating, titillating, voluptuous. **2** (*interesting, in fashion*) alluring, appealing, captivating, enchanting, exciting, fascinating, fashionable, impressive, interesting, inviting, pleasing, striking, stunning, tempting.

shabby *a.* **1** (*ragged, threadbare*) battered, broken-down, dilapidated, dingy, dirty, down-at-heel, faded, frayed, (*coll.*) grotty, grubby, mangy, neglected, ragged, ramshackle, run-down, scruffy, seedy, squalid, (*coll.*) tacky, tatty, threadbare, tumbledown, worn, worn out. ANTONYMS: elegant, smart. **2** (*mean, despicable*) contemptible, despicable, discreditable, dishonourable, disreputable, ignominious, impolite, low, mean, niggardly, odious, paltry, rude, stingy, uncouth, unfair, unworthy, vile. ANTONYMS: honourable, noble. **3** (*of poor quality*) cheap, inferior, poor, shoddy.

shack *n.* (*a rude cabin, esp. one built of logs*) cabin, hovel, hut, lean-to, shanty, shed.

shackle *n.* **1** (*a fetter or handcuff*) bond, (*pl., sl.*) bracelet, chain, (*pl., coll.*) cuff, fetter, gyve, handcuff, iron, leg-iron, manacle, restraint. **2** (*pl.*) (*restraints, impediments*) barriers, bars, blocks, checks, encumbrances, hindrances, impediments, obstacles, obstructions, restraints, restrictions. ~*v.t.* **1** (*to chain, to fetter*) bind, chain, fetter,

handcuff, manacle, pinion, restrain, secure, tether, tie, truss. ANTONYMS: loose, release. **2** (*to impede, to hamper*) bridle, check, control, curb, deter, hamper, handicap, hinder, hobble, hold back, impede, inhibit, limit, obstruct, rein, restrain, restrict. ANTONYMS: free, release.

shade *n.* **1** (*obscurity or partial darkness caused by the interception of the rays of light*) dimness, murk, murkiness, obscurity, semi-darkness, shadiness, shadow. **2** (*gloom, darkness*) darkness, dusk, duskiness, gloom. ANTONYMS: brightness, light, sunshine. **3** (*a place sheltered from the sun*) cover, shelter. **4** (*a screen for protecting from or moderating light*) awning, canopy, covering, parasol, protection, screen, shield, shutter, veil. **5** (*N Am.*) (*a window blind*) blind, venetian blind, window blind. **6** (*a colour*) colour, hue, intensity, tinge, tint, tone. **7** (*a scarcely perceptible degree, a small amount*) atom, bit, dash, degree, fraction, grain, hair's breadth, hint, intimation, iota, jot, modicum, nuance, overtone, scintilla, (*coll.*) smidgen, soupçon, speck, sprinkling, suggestion, suspicion, tinge, tittle, touch, trace, undertone, vestige. **8** (*the soul after its separation from the body, a spectre*) apparition, ghost, phantasm, phantom, spectre, spirit, (*coll.*) spook, wraith. ~*v.t.* **1** (*to shelter or screen from light or heat*) conceal, cover, mask, protect, screen, shelter, shield, shroud, veil. ANTONYMS: expose, reveal, unveil. **2** (*to obscure, to darken* (*an object in a picture*) *so as to show gradations of colour*) blacken, black out, blot out, cloud, darken, dim, eclipse, obscure, shadow. **3** (*to graduate as to light and shade or colour*) colour, graduate, tint.

shadow *n.* **1** (*shade*) darkness, dimness, dusk, gloom, murk, shade. ANTONYMS: brightness, light. **2** (*the dark figure of a body projected on the ground etc. by the interception of light*) outline, profile, silhouette. **3** (*an inseparable companion*) alter ego, boon companion, (*coll.*) buddy, (*coll.*) chum, companion, comrade, (*sometimes derog.*) crony, (*coll.*) pal, (*coll.*) sidekick. **4** (*darkness, obscurity*) darkness, inconspicuousness, obscurity, privacy. **5** (*protection, shelter*) concealment, cover, covering, curtain, protection, screen, shelter, shield, veil. **6** (*an imperfect or faint representation*) adumbration, outline, representation, type. **7** (*a dim foreshadowing, a premonition*) foreshadowing, premonition, sense. **8** (*a faint trace, the slightest degree*) hint, intimation, remnant, suggestion, suspicion, trace, vestige. **9** (*a phantom, a ghost*) apparition, ghost, phantasm, phantom, spectre, spirit, wraith. **10** (*gloom or sadness*) blight, gloom, pall, sadness.

~v.t. **1** (*to darken, to cloud*) cloud, darken, eclipse, obscure, shade. **2** (*to set* (*forth*) *dimly or in outline, to typify*) adumbrate, outline, represent, typify. **3** (*to watch secretly, to spy upon*) dog, follow, hound, pursue, spy upon, stalk, tail, trace, track, trail, watch.

shadowy *a.* **1** (*dark*) dark, dim, dusky, gloomy, murky, tenebrous. ANTONYMS: bright, clear. **2** (*vague, unclear*) dreamlike, ethereal, faint, ghostly, hazy, ill-defined, illusory, imaginary, impalpable, indistinct, insubstantial, obscure, shady, spectral, unclear, unreal, vague, wraith-like. ANTONYMS: clear, real.

shady *a.* **1** (*sheltered from the light and heat of the sun*) protected, screened, shaded, sheltered, umbral. **2** (*casting shade*) dark, gloomy, shaded, shadowed, shadowy, umbrageous. ANTONYMS: bright, light. **3** (*disreputable, of equivocal honesty*) (*sl.*) bent, devious, dishonest, disreputable, doubtful, dubious, (*coll.*) fishy, questionable, shifty, slippery, suspect, suspicious, tricky, underhand, unethical, unscrupulous. ANTONYMS: honest, respectable.

shaft *n.* **1** (*the slender stem of a spear, arrow etc.*) stalk, stem, stock. **2** (*anything more or less resembling this, such as a ray* (*of light*) *or a bolt of lightning*) barb, beam, bolt, dart, gibe, gleam, knock, pencil, ray, retort, sting, streak, thrust. **3** (*a column between the base and the capital*) column, pillar, post, stanchion, upright. **4** (*the handle of a tool*) handle, heft, shank, trunk. **5** (*a large axle or long, cylindrical bar, esp. rotating and transferring motion*) axle, bar, pole, rod, staff, stick. **6** (*a well-like excavation, usu. vertical, giving access to a mine*) mine shaft, pit, well shaft. **7** (*an upward vent to a mine, tunnel etc.*) duct, flue, passage, tunnel, vent.
~v.t. **1** (*to cheat, to treat unfairly*) cheat, defeat, outwit, trick. **2** (*to have sexual intercourse with*) (*taboo sl.*) fuck, have sex with, (*sl.*) screw, seduce.

shake *v.t.* **1** (*to cause to tremble or quiver*) churn, jar, jiggle, jolt, oscillate, pulsate, rattle, roll, sway, swing, tremble, twitch, vibrate, waggle, wiggle, wobble. **2** (*to shock, to disturb*) agitate, convulse, disturb, shock. **3** (*to brandish*) brandish, display, exhibit, flap, flourish, flutter, parade, show off, vaunt, waggle, wave. **4** (*to weaken the stability of*) damage, disaffect, disappoint, discourage, disenchant, harm, impair, shatter, undermine, weaken.
~v.i. **1** (*to move quickly to and fro or up and down*) shiver, shudder, totter, tremble. **2** (*to quiver*) quiver, rock, sway.
~n. **1** (*a jerk, a shock*) concussion, convulsion, jar, jarring, jerk, jolt, jolting, shock. **2** (*the state of being shaken, agitation*) agitation, gyration,

jiggle, quaking, quivering, roll, shaking, shudder, sway, swing, tremble, trembling, twitch, vibration, wavering, wiggle, wobble. **to shake off 1** (*to get rid of by shaking, to cast off*) cast off, discard, dislodge, drop, get rid of, rid oneself of. **2** (*to get rid of* (*someone who is following one*)) brush off, elude, evade, give the slip to, lose, throw off. **to shake up 1** (*to mix, disturb etc. by shaking*) agitate, disturb, mix. **2** (*coll.*) (*to reorganize drastically*) rearrange, reorganize, reshuffle. **3** (*to rouse or shock*) confound, discomfit, disconcert, disquiet, distress, fluster, frighten, rattle, rouse, scare, shock, startle, surprise, unnerve, unsettle, upset.

shaky *a.* **1** (*liable to shake, unsteady*) decrepit, dilapidated, doddering, feeble, flimsy, insecure, precarious, ramshackle, rickety, shivery, tenuous, tottering, tremulous, unsound, unstable, unsteady, unsubstantiated, wobbly. ANTONYMS: firm, sound. **2** (*of doubtful integrity, ability etc.*) doubtful, dubious, (*coll.*) iffy, insolvent, questionable, uncertain, undependable, unreliable, weak. ANTONYMS: firm, sound, strong.

shallow *a.* **1** (*not having much depth*) skin-deep, superficial, surface, thin. ANTONYMS: deep. **2** (*trivial, silly*) empty, flimsy, foolish, frivolous, idle, meaningless, petty, silly, slight, superficial, trifling, trivial, unimportant.
~n. (*a shallow place, a shoal*) bank, bar, sandbank, sandbar, shelf, shoal.

sham *v.t.* (*to feign, to make a pretence of*) counterfeit, fake, feign, pretend, put on, simulate.
~n. **1** (*an imposture, a pretence*) copy, imposture, pretence. **2** (*a fraud, a person who or thing which pretends to be someone or something else*) counterfeit, fake, feint, forgery, fraud, hoax, humbug, imitation, (*coll.*) phoney.
~a. (*feigned, pretended*) artificial, bogus, counterfeit, fake, false, feigned, imitation, make-believe, mock, (*coll.*) phoney, pretended, simulated, spurious. ANTONYMS: genuine.

shambles *n.* (*utter confusion, a disorganized mess*) chaos, confusion, disaster, disorder, disorganization, mess, muddle.

shame *n.* **1** (*a painful feeling due to consciousness of guilt, humiliation etc.*) abashment, chagrin, embarrassment, guilt, humiliation, mortification. ANTONYMS: pride. **2** (*the instinct to avoid this, modesty*) coyness, decency, decorum, diffidence, humility, modesty, pride, propriety, prudishness, respectability, shyness, timidity. **3** (*a state of disgrace*) calumniation, contempt, defamation, degradation, denigration, discredit, disgrace, dishonour, disrepute, ignominy, infamy, loss of face, obloquy, odium, scandal, vilification. ANTO-NYMS: honour. **4** (*anything that brings disappointment*) bad luck, calamity, disappointment, misfortune, pity.

~*v.t.* (*to bring shame on, to cause to feel disgraced*) besmirch, chagrin, chasten, confound, degrade, discredit, disgrace, dishonour, embarrass, humble, humiliate, mortify, put down.

shamefaced *a.* (*bashful, easily abashed*) bashful, coy, diffident, embarrassed, guilty, meek, modest, retiring, self-effacing, shamed, sheepish, shy, timid, timorous. ANTONYMS: unabashed.

shameful *a.* **1** (*causing shame*) chastening, degrading, humbling, humiliating, ignominious, inglorious, mortifying, shaming. ANTO-NYMS: glorious, honourable. **2** ((*of behaviour*) *very bad, shocking*) atrocious, base, deplorable, despicable, disgraceful, dishonouring, embarrassing, guilty, heinous, immoral, indecent, low, mean, scandalous, shocking, unethical, unprincipled, vile.

shameless *a.* (*immodest*) abandoned, barefaced, brazen, depraved, flagrant, forward, hardened, immodest, impudent, indecent, outrageous, unabashed, unashamed, unprincipled, unreserved, wanton, wild. ANTONYMS: ashamed, coy.

shape *v.t.* **1** (*to form, to create*) build, construct, create, devise, form, make, produce. **2** (*to make into a particular form, to fashion*) cast, fashion, forge, model, mould, sculpt. **3** (*to adapt, to make conform (to)*) accommodate, adapt, adjust, change, conform to, fit, modify, remodel, suit. **4** (*to regulate, to direct*) control, decree, define, determine, direct, frame, give form to, govern, influence, regulate.

~*v.i.* **1** (*to take shape, to develop (well, ill etc.)*) develop, evolve, form, grow. **2** (*to become fit or adapted (to)*) adapt, fit, match.

~*n.* **1** (*the outward form or figure*) body, build, configuration, contour, figure, form, lines, outline, physique, profile, silhouette. **2** (*outward aspect, appearance*) appearance, aspect, cut, form, guise, image, likeness, semblance. **3** (*fit or orderly form or condition*) condition, fettle, health, order, state, status. **4** (*an image, an apparition*) apparition, appearance, image, phantom. **5** (*a pattern, a mould*) cast, model, mould, pattern.

shapeless *a.* **1** (*having no regular form*) amorphous, bent, deformed, distorted, formless, indefinite, irregular, misshapen, nebulous, twisted, unformed, unshapely, unstructured, vague. **2** (*lacking in symmetry*) asymmetrical, unsymmetrical. ANTONYMS: symmetrical.

shapely *a.* **1** (*well-formed, well-proportioned*) well-formed, well-proportioned. **2** (*having beauty or regularity*) attractive, beautiful, comely, curvaceous, elegant, graceful, neat, pleasing, regular, sexy, streamlined, trim, voluptuous. ANTONYMS: ill-proportioned, ugly, unattractive.

share *n.* **1** (*a part or portion detached from a common amount or stock*) allocation, allotment, allowance, apportionment, cut, division, due, helping, interest, part, piece, portion, quota, ration, serving, slice, stake. ANTONYMS: entirety, whole. **2** (*an allotted part, esp. any one of the equal parts into which the capital of a company is divided*) dividend, equity, lot.

~*v.t.* **1** (*to divide into portions, to distribute among a number*) allocate, allot, apportion, appropriate, deal out, distribute, divide, dole out, parcel out, partition, pay out, ration, share out, split. **2** (*to have or endure with others, to participate in*) join in, partake of, participate in, share in.

sharp *a.* **1** (*having a keen edge or fine point*) cutting, keen, knifelike, razor-sharp, sharpened. ANTONYMS: blunt, dull. **2** (*pointed, edged*) edged, peaked, pointed, serrated. **3** (*angular, abrupt*) abrupt, angular, marked, precipitous, sheer, sudden, vertical. **4** (*clearly outlined or defined*) clean-cut, crisp, distinct, focused, well-defined. **5** (*pungent, sour*) acid, acrid, hot, piquant, pungent, sour, spicy, tangy, tart. ANTONYMS: bland, sweet. **6** (*shrill, piercing*) biting, cutting, deafening, ear-splitting, harsh, high-pitched, loud, penetrating, piercing, shrill, strident. **7** (*harsh, sarcastic*) acerbic, acrimonious, bitter, caustic, cutting, excruciating, fierce, harsh, hurtful, intense, malicious, painful, sarcastic, sardonic, scathing, severe, spiteful, stabbing, trenchant, unkind, violent, virulent, vitriolic. ANTONYMS: mild. **8** (*acute, keen-witted*) acute, astute, clever, discerning, intelligent, keen-witted, knowing, perspicacious, quick-witted, sharp-witted, shrewd, smart. **9** (*attentive, alert*) agile, alert, attentive, bright, observant, penetrating, vigilant. ANTONYMS: stupid. **10** (*alive to one's interests, dishonest*) artful, calculating, crafty, cunning, dishonest, foxy, sly, (*coll.*) sneaky, subtle, tricky, underhand, unscrupulous. ANTONYMS: honest, straight-dealing. **11** (*quick, energetic*) brisk, energetic, impetuous, quick, speedy, vigorous. **12** (*stylish*) chic, dapper, dressy, fashionable, (*coll.*) natty, (*coll.*) nifty, smart, snappy, spruce, stylish, (*coll.*) swanky, †swell.

~*adv.* **1** (*punctually, exactly*) exactly, (*esp. N Am., sl.*) on the button, (*coll.*) on the dot, (*coll.*) on the nose, precisely, punctually. **2** (*suddenly, abruptly*) abruptly, markedly, suddenly.

sharpen *v.t., v.i.* (*to make sharp*) edge, grind, hone, make sharp, point, strop, whet.

shatter *v.t.* **1** (*to break up at once into many pieces*) break, pulverize. **2** (*to smash, to shiver*) burst, crack, dash to pieces, disintegrate, fracture, fragment, pulverize, shiver, smash, splinter, split. ANTONYMS: mend, preserve, save. **3** (*to destroy, to ruin*) blast, crush, dash, demolish, destroy, devastate, dissipate, overthrow, ruin, torpedo, undermine, wreck. ANTONYMS: restore. **4** (*to upset, distress*) confound, daze, deject, depress, distress, overcome, overwhelm, perturb, shake up, stun, stupefy, trouble, unnerve, upset. **5** (*to tire out*) exhaust, tire out, wear out.
~*v.i.* (*to break into fragments*) break, disintegrate, smash.

shave *v.t.* **1** (*to remove hair from* (*the face, a person etc.*) *with a razor*) clip, crop, cut, shear, snip off, trim. **2** (*to pare or cut thin slices off the surface of* (*leather, wood etc.*)) cut, pare, plane, remove, scrape, whittle. **3** (*to pass by closely with or without touching, to brush past*) brush past, graze, skim, touch.
~*n.* (*a narrow escape or miss*) narrow escape, near miss, (*coll.*) near squeak, scrape.

shed[1] *v.t.* **1** (*to let fall, to drop*) discharge, drop, effuse, emanate, exude, flow out, let fall, ooze, pour forth, pour out, radiate, spill, stream out, surge forth, weep. **2** (*to throw off*) abandon, cast off, diffuse, discard, doff, emit, flake, peel, scatter, spread around, throw off. ANTONYMS: keep, retain. **3** (*to take off* (*clothes*)) remove, strip off, take off. **4** (*to reduce one's number of* (*employees*)) axe, cut, get rid of, reduce.

shed[2] *n.* **1** (*a slight, simple building, usu. a roofed structure with the ends or ends and sides open*) outhouse, shelter. **2** (*a hut*) hovel, hut, lean-to, shack, shanty.

sheepish *a.* **1** (*bashful, timid*) abashed, bashful, coy, diffident, docile, meek, modest, passive, self-conscious, self-effacing, shy, timid, timorous, withdrawn. **2** (*ashamed*) ashamed, chastened, embarrassed, mortified, remorseful, shamefaced.

sheer *a.* **1** (*pure, absolute*) absolute, arrant, bitter, complete, downright, out-and-out, plain, pure, rank, simple, thorough, total, unadulterated, unmitigated, unmixed, unqualified, utter. ANTONYMS: incomplete, partial. **2** (*perpendicular*) abrupt, bluff, perpendicular, precipitous, steep, vertical. ANTONYMS: gentle. **3** ((*of a fabric*) *very thin, diaphanous*) diaphanous, filmy, fine, gauzy, gossamer, see-through, thin, translucent, transparent. ANTONYMS: dense, heavy, thick.

~*adv.* **1** (*vertically*) perpendicularly, plumb, vertically. **2** (*entirely, outright*) entirely, outright.

sheet *n.* **1** (*a rectangular piece of linen, cotton or nylon used in a bed*) bed-sheet, blanket, covering, fitted sheet, flat sheet. **2** (*a piece of metal etc., rolled out, hammered etc. into a thin sheet*) pane, panel, plate, slab. **3** (*a piece of paper*) folio, leaf, page. **4** (*a newspaper*) broadsheet, daily, gazette, journal, monthly, newspaper, paper, (*derog.*) rag, tabloid, weekly. **5** (*a broad expanse or surface*) area, expanse, layer, membrane, stratum, stretch, surface, veneer.

shell *n.* **1** (*a hard outside covering etc.*) carapace, case, casing. **2** (*the hard outside covering of a seed etc., a pod*) capsule, crust, husk, pod, rind. **3** (*the framework or walls of a house, ship etc., with the interior removed or not yet built*) chassis, exterior, externals, facade, frame, framework, hull, outside, skeleton, walls. **4** (*a hollow projectile containing a bursting-charge, missiles etc., exploded by a time or percussion fuse*) cartridge, explosive, grenade, missile, pellet, projectile, shot.
~*v.t.* **1** (*to strip or break off the shell from*) hull, husk, peel. **2** (*to throw shells at, to bombard*) barrage, blitz, bomb, bombard, cannonade, fire upon, strafe.

shelter *n.* **1** (*anything that covers or shields from injury, danger etc.*) cover, defence, guard, screen, shield, umbrella. **2** (*being sheltered, security*) protection, safety, security. **3** (*a place of safety*) accommodation, asylum, concealment, covert, harbour, haven, home, refuge, retreat, sanctuary. **4** (*an air-raid shelter*) air-raid shelter, (*Hist.*) Anderson shelter, (*Hist.*) Morrison shelter.
~*v.t.* **1** (*to protect, to cover*) cover, defend, guard, protect, safeguard, secure, shield. **2** (*to conceal, to screen*) conceal, harbour, hide, (*N Am., coll.*) hole up, keep, screen. ANTONYMS: expose.

shelve *v.t.* (*to defer indefinitely*) defer, hold in abeyance, lay aside, mothball, postpone, put aside, put off, put on ice, put on the back burner.

shield *n.* (*defence, a protection*) bulwark, defence, defender, guard, protection, rampart, safeguard, shelter.
~*v.t.* (*to screen or protect with or as with a shield*) cover, defend, guard, hide, keep, mask, protect, safeguard, screen, shelter. ANTONYMS: expose.

shift *v.t.* **1** (*to change the position of*) rearrange, relocate, reposition. **2** (*to remove, esp. with an effort*) budge, edge, remove. **3** (*to change* (*one thing*) *for another*) alter, change, exchange, interchange, swap, switch, transfer, transpose, vary. **4** (*to dispose of, sell*) dispose of, market, sell.

~*v.i.* **1** (*to change place or position*) change place, change position. **2** (*to resort to expedients, to do the best one can*) contrive, devise, fend, get along, get by, make do, manage, scrape by. **3** (*sl.*) (*to move quickly*) (*coll.*) move, race, speed.

~*n.* **1** (*a change of place, form or character*) change, movement, shifting. **2** (*a substitution of one thing for another*) substitution, vicissitude. **3** (*a relay of workers*) watch, workers, workforce. **4** (*the period of time for which a shift works*) hours, period, stint, watch. **5** (*a device, an expedient*) contrivance, device, expedient, resort. **6** (*a trick, an artifice*) artifice, dodge, evasion, ruse, scheme, stratagem, subterfuge, trick, wile.

shifty *a.* (*furtive, sly*) artful, calculating, crafty, (*coll.*) crooked, cunning, deceitful, devious, dishonest, evasive, foxy, furtive, scheming, slick, slippery, sly, smooth, treacherous, tricky, two-faced, underhand, unreliable, untrustworthy. ANTONYMS: honest, straightforward.

shimmer *v.i.* (*to beam or glisten faintly*) flash, flicker, glimmer, glint, glitter, glow, phosphoresce, ripple, scintillate, shine, sparkle, twinkle.

~*n.* (*a faint or tremulous light*) flash, flicker, gleam, glimmer, glint, gloss, glow, iridescence, light, phosphorescence, shimmering, shine, sparkle, twinkle. ANTONYMS: dullness.

shine *v.i.* **1** (*to be bright, to beam*) beam, coruscate, gleam, glimmer, glisten, glitter, gloss, glow, lustre, radiate, shimmer, twinkle. **2** (*to be brilliant or conspicuous*) excel, outshine, sparkle, stand out, surpass.

~*v.t.* (*to cause to shine, to polish*) brighten, brush, buff, burnish, polish, rub.

~*n.* (*fair weather, brightness*) brightness, brilliance, glaze, gleam, gloss, glow, iridescence, lustre, patina, phosphorescence, radiance, sheen, shimmer, sparkle, sunshine.

shiny *a.* (*bright and reflecting light*) beaming, bright, brilliant, burnished, coruscating, dazzling, gleaming, glistening, glittering, glossy, glowing, iridescent, lustrous, phosphorescent, polished, radiant, scintillating, shining, sparkling, twinkling. ANTONYMS: dull.

ship *n.* (*a large seagoing vessel*) clipper, craft, cutter, galleon, liner, steamer, vessel, warship, windjammer.

~*v.t.* **1** (*to send or carry in a ship*) carry by sea, transport by sea. **2** (*to send* (*goods*) *by any recognized means of conveyance*) airfreight, cart, convey, deliver, ferry, freight, haul, send, transport, truck.

shipshape *a.* (*well arranged, neat*) in good order, neat, orderly, spick and span, spotless, tidy, trim, well arranged. ANTONYMS: disordered, untidy.

shirk *v.t.* (*to avoid or get out of unfairly*) avoid, dodge, (*coll.*) duck, evade, get out of, shrink from, shun, sidestep, (*coll.*) skive off. ANTONYMS: volunteer.

~*v.i.* (*to avoid the performance of work or duty*) avoid, malinger.

shiver *v.i.* (*to tremble or shake, as with fear, cold or excitement*) flutter, palpitate, quake, quiver, shake, shudder, tremble, vibrate.

~*n.* (*a shivering movement*) flutter, quake, quiver, shake, shudder, thrill, tremble, trembling, tremor, vibration.

shock *n.* **1** (*an impact, a blow*) blow, collision, concussion, impact, jolt. **2** (*prostration brought about by a violent and sudden disturbance of the system*) breakdown, collapse, nervous exhaustion, paralysis, prostration. **3** (*a sudden mental agitation, a violent disturbance* (*of belief, trust etc.*)) agitation, bolt from the blue, bombshell, disturbance, eyeopener, horror, revelation, shocker, stupefaction, surprise, thunderbolt, trauma, upset.

~*v.t.* (*to give a violent sensation of horror or indignation to*) appal, astound, disgust, disturb, flabbergast, frighten, horrify, jar, jolt, nauseate, numb, offend, outrage, paralyse, repel, revolt, scandalize, shake, sicken, stagger, startle, stun, stupefy, surprise, traumatize. ANTONYMS: delight, please.

shocking *a.* **1** (*disgraceful*) disgraceful, offensive, outrageous, scandalous, shameful. **2** (*dreadful*) abhorrent, abominable, appalling, astounding, atrocious, disgusting, dreadful, ghastly, hideous, horrific, monstrous, nauseating, numbing, repulsive, revolting, sickening, terrible, unspeakable. ANTONYMS: delightful, pleasing.

shoddy *a.* **1** (*inferior*) cheap, (*sl.*) crappy, inferior, poor, rubbishy, second-rate, shabby, (*coll.*) tacky, tatty, tawdry, trashy. **2** (*not genuine, sham*) adulterated, counterfeit, fake, pretend, sham.

~*n.* (*anything of an inferior or adulterated kind*) counterfeit, fake, imitation, sham.

shoot *v.i.* **1** (*to go or come* (*out, along, up etc.*) *swiftly*) bolt, bound, dart, dash, flash, fly, hurtle, leap, race, rush, speed, spring, streak, tear, zip. **2** (*to put out buds etc. to extend in growth*) bud, germinate, grow, mushroom, spring up, sprout. **3** (*to protrude, to jut out*) jut out, project, protrude. **4** (*to discharge a missile, esp. from a firearm*) detonate, discharge, fire, let off.

~v.t. **1** (*to discharge or send with sudden force*) discharge, eject, fling, hurl, launch, let fly, propel, send, throw, toss. **2** (*to wound or kill with a missile from a firearm*) bag, blast, hit, hurt, injure, kill, (*sl.*) knock off, slay, wound. ANTONYMS: miss.

~n. (*a young branch or sprout*) branch, offshoot, scion, sprout, stem, sucker, twig.

shop n. **1** (*a building in which goods are sold by retail*) boutique, department store, retail outlet, store, supermarket, superstore. **2** (*a building in which a manufacture, craft or repairing is carried on*) craftshop, factory, machine shop, works, workshop.

~v.i. (*to visit shops for the purpose of purchasing goods*) buy, purchase.

~v.t. **1** (*to inform against to the police*) betray, (*coll.*) blow the whistle on, inform against, peach on, (*coll.*) rat on, (*sl.*) snitch on, tell on. **2** (*to discharge from employment*) discharge, dismiss, sack.

short a. **1** (*not extended in time or duration*) brief, ephemeral, fleeting, limited, momentary, quick, short-lived, temporary, transient, transitory. ANTONYMS: long-lived. **2** (*below the average in stature, not tall*) diminutive, dumpy, dwarfish, midget, minuscule, petite, (*coll.*) pint-sized, slight, small, squat, stubby, stunted, tiny, (*coll.*) wee. ANTONYMS: tall. **3** (*deficient, in want (of)*) deficient (in), insufficient, in want (of), lacking, low (on), meagre, needful (of), scant, scanty, sparse, wanting. ANTONYMS: ample, enough. **4** (*brief, curt*) abbreviated, abridged, abrupt, blunt, brief, brusque, compact, compressed, concise, condensed, curt, curtailed, cut, direct, laconic, offhand, pithy, sharp, shortened, straightforward, succinct, terse. ANTONYMS: affable, extended. **5** (*crumbling or breaking easily*) breakable, brittle, crumbly, friable.

~adv. **1** (*abruptly, at once*) abruptly, at once, hastily, hurriedly, immediately, instantly, out of the blue, peremptorily, suddenly, unexpectedly, without warning. **2** (*without having stocks etc. in hand*) deficient, impecunious, penniless, pinched, poor, straitened, underfunded.

shortage n. (*a deficiency*) dearth, deficiency, deficit, inadequacy, insufficiency, lack, need, paucity, scarcity, shortfall, want. ANTONYMS: glut.

shorten v.t. **1** (*to make short in time, extent etc.*) abbreviate, abridge, compress, condense, diminish, lessen, make short, reduce. ANTONYMS: extend, lengthen. **2** (*to curtail*) curtail, cut, dock, lop off, prune, trim.

~v.i. (*to become short*) contract, lessen, shrink.

shot n. **1** (*a missile for a firearm, esp. a solid or non-explosive projectile*) ball, buckshot, bullet, cannonball, missile, projectile, slug. **2** (*the discharge of a missile from a firearm or other weapon*) discharge, firing, report, shooting. **3** (*a photographic exposure*) photo, photograph, picture, snap, snapshot. **4** (*the film taken between the starting and stopping of a cine-camera*) scene, take. **5** (*an injection by hypodermic needle*) injection, inoculation, (*coll.*) jab, vaccination. **6** (*a stroke at various games*) hit, strike, stroke. **7** (*an attempt to guess etc.*) attempt, chance, (*coll.*) crack, effort, endeavour, essay, go, guess, opportunity, (*coll.*) stab, try, (*sl.*) whack. **8** (*a marksman*) aim, eye, marksman, markswoman, rifleman, sharpshooter, sniper. **9** (*a remark aimed at someone*) barb, dig, remark, retort. **10** (*a drink of esp. spirits*) dram, drink, finger, nip, (*coll.*) slug, (*coll.*) snort, swallow, (*coll.*) swig, tot.

shout n. (*a loud, vehement call or expression of a strong emotion such as anger or joy*) bawl, call, cry, exclamation, howl, outcry, roar, scream, vociferation, whoop, yell, yelp.

~v.i. (*to utter a loud cry or call*) bawl, bellow, call, cry, exclaim, (*esp. N Am., coll.*) holler, howl, roar, scream, vociferate, whoop, yell, yelp. ANTONYMS: murmur, whisper.

shove v.t. **1** (*to push, to move forcibly along*) drive, move along, propel, push, thrust. ANTONYMS: pull. **2** (*to push against*) elbow, jostle, push against.

~v.i. (*to push*) drive, propel, push, thrust.

~n. (*an act of prompting into action*) nudge, prod, prompt.

show v.t. **1** (*to cause or allow to be seen, to reveal*) disclose, display, divulge, exhibit, expose, express, indicate, lay bare, offer to view, play, present, put on, register, represent, reveal, screen, stage. ANTONYMS: conceal, hide. **2** (*to give, to offer*) accord, bestow, give, grant, offer. **3** (*to make clear, to explain*) bear out, clarify, confirm, corroborate, demonstrate, elucidate, explain, illustrate, inform, instruct, make clear, make known, point out, portray, prove, substantiate, teach, tell, verify. **4** (*to conduct (round or over a house etc.)*) accompany, conduct, direct, escort, guide, lead, steer, usher.

~v.i. (*to become visible or noticeable*) appear, become visible, manifest, stand out.

~n. **1** (*outward appearance, semblance*) appearance, facade, front, impression, pretence, semblance. **2** (*ostentation, pomp*) affectation, display, illusion, ostentation, parade, pomp, pretension, pretentiousness. **3** (*a spectacle, an entertainment*) demonstration, display, drama, entertainment, exhibition, Expo, fair, musical, pageant, play, presentation, production, spectacle. **4** (*an opportunity, a concern*) affair, business, chance, concern, opportunity, undertaking. **to show off 1** (*to set off, to show to advantage*) display, enhance, make attractive, set off, show to advantage. **2** (*coll.*) (*to make a display of oneself, one's talents etc.*) advertise, boast, brag, display, exhibit, flaunt, parade, pose, posture, preen, swagger. **to show up 1** (*to expose*) contrast, expose, give away, highlight, reveal, unmask. **2** (*to be clearly visible*) appear, be visible, stand out. **3** (*to be present*) appear, arrive, come, turn up. ANTONYMS: depart, leave. **4** (*to embarrass or humiliate*) eclipse, embarrass, humiliate, mortify, outshine, overshadow, shame, upstage.

shower *n*. **1** (*a fall of rain, hail or snow of short duration*) cloudburst, deluge, drizzle. **2** (*a brief fall of arrows, bullets etc.*) barrage, stream, volley. **3** (*a copious supply* (*of*)) abundance, barrage, deluge, flood, overflow, profusion, stream, torrent. **4** (*a collection of* (*inferior etc.*) *people*) crew, crowd, group, party.
~*v.t.* (*to discharge or deliver in a shower*) bombard, drench, drop, fall, heap, inundate, lavish, load, overwhelm, pour, spray.
~*v.i.* (*to fall in a shower*) precipitate, rain, sprinkle.

showy *a*. (*ostentatious, gaudy*) bravura, conspicuous, elaborate, fancy, flamboyant, flashy, florid, garish, gaudy, loud, ornate, ostentatious, pretentious, rococo. ANTONYMS: modest, subdued.

shred *n*. (*a strip, a fragment*) atom, bit, chip, fragment, grain, hint, iota, jot, particle, piece, rag, remnant, scintilla, scrap, sliver, snippet, speck, strip, suggestion, tatter, tittle, trace, whit. ANTONYMS: whole.
~*v.t.* (*to tear or cut into shreds*) cut, demolish, destroy, dispose of, fragment, rip, scrap, tatter, tear, throw away, (*esp. N Am., coll.*) trash.

shrewd *a*. (*astute, discerning*) acute, artful, astute, calculated, canny, clever, crafty, cunning, discerning, discriminating, intelligent, knowing, perceptive, percipient, quick-witted, resourceful, sage, sly, smart, wily, wise. ANTONYMS: slow, stupid.

shriek *v.i.* **1** (*to utter a sharp, shrill cry*) cry, scream, screech, shout, squawk, squeal, yell. **2** (*to laugh wildly*) hoot, howl, laugh wildly.
~*n*. (*a sharp, shrill cry*) cry, scream, screech, shout, squall, squawk, squeal, yell.

shrill *a*. **1** (*high-pitched and piercing in tone*) acute, ear-splitting, high, high-pitched, penetrating, piercing, piping, screeching, sharp. ANTONYMS: low, soft. **2** (*noisy, importunate*) importunate, loud, noisy. ANTONYMS: quiet.

shrink *v.i.* **1** (*to grow smaller*) contract, decrease, diminish, dwindle, grow smaller, narrow, reduce, shorten, shrivel, wither. ANTONYMS: expand, grow. **2** (*to draw back, to recoil*) baulk at, cower, cringe, draw back, give way, recoil, retire, retreat, shy away from, withdraw. ANTONYMS: stand. **3** (*to flinch*) flinch, quail, wince.
~*n*. (*a psychiatrist*) psychiatrist, therapist, (*sl.*) trick cyclist.

shrivel *v.i.* (*to contract, to wither*) contract, curl up, desiccate, dry up, shrink, wilt, wither, wizen, wrinkle. ANTONYMS: swell.

shudder *v.i.* (*to shiver suddenly as with fear; to quake*) convulse, jerk, quake, quaver, quiver, shake, shiver, shrink, tremble, twitch.
~*n*. (*a sudden shiver or trembling*) convulsion, frisson, paroxysm, quake, quaver, quiver, rattle, shake, shiver, spasm, tremble, tremor, twitch, vibration.

shuffle *v.t.* **1** (*to shift to and fro or from one to another*) scuffle, scuff the feet, shift to and fro. **2** (*to mix* (*up*), *to throw into disorder*) confuse, disarrange, disorder, disorganize, intermingle, jumble, mess up, mix up, muddle, rearrange, scatter, turn topsy-turvy. ANTONYMS: order, sort.
~*v.i.* **1** (*to prevaricate*) bumble, dodge, equivocate, evade, falter, hedge, hem and haw, prevaricate, quibble. **2** (*to move* (*along*) *with a dragging gait*) drag, falter, hobble, limp, scuffle, shamble.
~*n*. **1** (*a shuffling movement of the feet etc.*) scraping, scuffling, shamble, shambling. **2** (*an evasive or prevaricating piece of conduct*) dodge, evasion, prevarication, quibble, shift, shuffling, sidestep, subterfuge, trick.

shun *v.t.* (*to avoid, to keep clear of*) avoid, cold-shoulder, disdain, eschew, evade, fight shy of, forgo, give up, ignore, keep clear of, rebuff, reject, send to Coventry, shrink from, shy away from, spurn, steer clear of, turn from. ANTONYMS: court.

shut *v.t.* **1** (*to close by means of a door, lid etc.*) close, do up, secure. ANTONYMS: open. **2** (*to cause* (*a door, lid etc.*) *to close an aperture*) bolt, fasten, lock, seal, secure. **to shut in 1** (*to confine*) bottle up, box in, cage in, confine, coop up, enclose, entrap, fence in, immure, imprison, incarcerate, intern, jail, keep in, pen, seclude, secure. ANTONYMS: free, release. **2** (*to encircle*) encircle, encompass, surround. **3** (*to prevent egress or prospect from*) block in, close in, wall up. **to shut out 1** (*to exclude, to bar*) ban, bar, block out, cut out, debar, disallow, eliminate, exclude, keep away, keep out, lock out, ostracize. ANTONYMS: admit, allow. **2** (*to prevent the possibility of*) exclude, prevent, prohibit. **3** (*to block from the memory*) deny, forget, stifle. **to shut up 1** (*to close and fasten up* (*a box etc.*)) close up, do up, fasten up. **2** (*to put away in a box etc.*) pack away, put away, secrete, wrap up. **3** (*to confine*) bottle up, box in, cage, confine, coop up, immure, imprison, incarcerate, intern, jail, lock up, shut in. ANTONYMS: liberate, release. **4** (*to confute, to silence*) confute, gag, hush, keep mum, keep quiet, mute, quieten, shush, silence, stifle.

shy *a.* **1** (*fearful, timid*) afraid, anxious, fearful, frightened, timid, timorous, uncourageous, worried. ANTONYMS: bold. **2** (*bashful, shrinking from approach or familiarity*) apprehensive, backward, bashful, cowardly, coy, craven, diffident, introverted, meek, modest, nervous, reserved, reticent, retiring, self-conscious, sheepish, shrinking, unconfident, withdrawn. **3** (*wary, suspicious*) cautious, chary, distrustful, guarded, suspicious, wary. **4** (*careful, watchful* (*of*)) careful, circumspect, vigilant, watchful.
~*v.i.* ((*of a horse*) *to start or turn aside suddenly*) start, turn aside.

sick *a.* **1** (*ill, in bad health*) afflicted, ailing, diseased, ill, indisposed, infirm, laid up, out of sorts, poorly, sickly, under the weather, unhealthy, unwell, weak. ANTONYMS: healthy, well. **2** (*affected with nausea, inclined to vomit*) airsick, carsick, nauseated, nauseous, queasy, seasick. **3** (*feeling disturbed, upset*) annoyed, chagrined, depressed, disgusted, disturbed, heartsick, irritated, miserable, put out, repelled, revolted, sickened, troubled, upset, wretched. **4** (*mentally ill, or having a warped personality*) backward, crazy, deranged, disturbed, insane, mad, (*coll.*) mental, neurotic, perverse, psychotic, retarded, unbalanced, warped. **5** (*tired* (*of*)) bored (with), fed up (with), jaded, satiated, tired (of), weary (of). **6** ((*of humour*) *macabre, referring to subjects not usu. considered suitable for jokes*) bizarre, black, cruel, ghoulish, grotesque, gruesome, macabre, morbid, peculiar, sadistic, shocking, weird.

sicken *v.i.* **1** (*to grow ill*) fail, fall ill, take sick, weaken. **2** (*to develop the symptoms* (*for a particular illness*)) catch, come down with, contract, succumb.
~*v.t.* **1** (*to make sick*) affect, afflict, make sick. ANTONYMS: delight, please. **2** (*to affect with nausea*) nauseate, turn the stomach. **3** (*to disgust*) appal, disgust, offend, put out, repel, repulse, revolt, shock, upset.

sickly *a.* **1** (*weak in health, affected by illness*) afflicted, ailing, diseased, ill, indisposed,

infirm, laid up, poorly, sick, under the weather, unhealthy, unwell, weak. ANTONYMS: healthy, well. **2** (*ill-looking*) delicate, drawn, faint, feeble, ill-looking, languid, pale, pallid, peakish, peaky, wan. **3** (*sentimental*) cloying, insipid, maudlin, mawkish, (*sl.*) mushy, sentimental, watery, weak.

side *n.* **1** (*any of the bounding surfaces* (*or lines*) *of a material object*) end, face, facet, surface. **2** (*such a surface as distinct from the top and bottom, back and front, or the two ends*) bank, border, boundary, brim, brink, edge, end, face, facet, flank, limit, margin, perimeter, periphery, plane, rim, verge. **3** (*an aspect or partial view of a thing*) angle, aspect, attitude, opinion, position, standpoint, view, viewpoint. **4** (*either of two opposing parties or teams*) body, camp, faction, interest, party, philosophy, school, sect, squad, string, team, wing. **5** (*either of the opposing views or causes represented*) argument, cause, interest, view. **6** (*a television channel*) channel, programme, station.
~*v.i.* (*to align oneself* (*with one of two opposing parties*)) align oneself (with), ally (with), favour, go along (with), identify (with), join, prefer, support, take sides (with), team up (with). ANTONYMS: oppose.
~*a.* **1** (*situated at or on the side*) flanking, lateral. **2** (*being from or towards the side, oblique*) ancillary, auxiliary, incidental, inconsequential, inconsiderable, indirect, insignificant, lesser, marginal, minor, oblique, secondary, subordinate, subsidiary, tangential, unimportant.

siege *n.* (*the military operation of surrounding a town or fortified place with troops and subjecting it to constant bombardment, in order to force its surrender*) beleaguerment, besiegement, blockade, encirclement.

sift *v.t.* **1** (*to separate into finer and coarser particles by means of a sieve*) choose, filter, pick, riddle, screen, select, separate, sieve, sort, strain, weed out, winnow. **2** (*to examine minutely*) analyse, examine, investigate, probe, scrutinize, study.
~*v.i.* ((*of snow etc.*) *to fall or be sprinkled sparsely or lightly*) be sprinkled, dust, fall.

sigh *v.i.* **1** (*to inhale and exhale deeply and audibly, as an involuntary expression of grief, fatigue etc.*) breathe, exhale. **2** (*to yearn* (*for*)) grieve (for), lament, long (for), mourn (for), pine (for), regret, weep (for), yearn (for). **3** (*to make a sound like sighing*) groan, moan.
~*n.* (*an act or sound of sighing*) breath, exhalation, groan, murmur.

sight *n.* **1** (*the faculty of seeing*) eyes, eyesight, seeing. **2** (*view, range of vision*) eyeshot, field of view, gaze, ken, perception, range of vision, view, visibility, vision, vista. ANTONYMS: blindness. **3** (*that which is seen, a scene, esp. a delightful or shocking one*) atrocity, (*coll.*) bomb-site, catastrophe, disaster, display, eyesore, fright, mess, monstrosity, muddle, pageant, scene, show, spectacle. **4** (*something interesting, or worth going to see*) attraction, curiosity, marvel, monument, phenomenon, place of interest, rarity, tourist attraction, wonder.

~*v.t.* (*to see, catch sight of*) behold, catch a glimpse of, catch sight of, descry, discern, distinguish, espy, glimpse, mark, note, notice, observe, peek, peep, perceive, remark, see, spot, spy, view. ANTONYMS: miss.

sign *n.* **1** (*a mark expressing a particular meaning*) icon, indicator, mark, symbol, token. **2** (*a symptom or proof* (*of*), *esp. a miracle as evidence of a supernatural power*) augury, evidence, foreshadowing, forewarning, hint, indication, indicator, omen, portent, presage, proof, prophecy, representation, suggestion, symbol, symptom, token, trace, vestige, warning. **3** (*a password, a secret formula or gesture by which confederates etc. recognize each other*) countersign, formula, password. **4** (*a motion or gesture used to convey information, commands etc., e.g. one used in a sign language*) action, gesticulation, gesture, motion, movement, signal. **5** (*a board or panel giving information or indicating directions etc.*) board, notice, panel, placard, poster, signboard. **6** (*a device, usu. painted on a board, displayed as a token or advertisement of a trade*) advertisement, badge, brand, cipher, design, device, emblem, logo, monogram, seal, stamp, trademark.

~*v.t.* **1** (*to mark with a sign, esp. with one's signature or initials as an acknowledgement, ratification etc.*) autograph, countersign, endorse, initial, inscribe, mark, witness, write. **2** (*to order or make known by a gesture*) beckon, gesticulate, gesture, signal, wave.

signal *n.* **1** (*a sign in the form of an action, light or sound, agreed upon or understood as conveying information*) indication, pointer, sign, token. **2** (*an event that is the occasion or cue for some action*) cue, goad, impetus, incitement, prick, prompt, spur, stimulus, token, trigger. **3** (*the apparatus used for conveying information*) beacon, flag, gesture, indication, siren. **4** (*a set of transmitted electrical impulses received as a sound or image on radio or television*) image, impulse, picture, reception.

~*v.t.* **1** (*to convey, announce etc. by signals*) announce, beckon, communicate, convey, gesticulate, gesture, indicate, mime, motion,

nod, notify, order, sign, wave, whistle, wink. **2** ((*of an event*) *to signify or indicate* (*a certain change or development*)) express, herald, indicate, mark, mean, show, signify.

~*a.* (*conspicuous, notable*) conspicuous, exceptional, extraordinary, important, memorable, momentous, notable, noteworthy, outstanding, remarkable, significant, singular, special, striking, unique, unparalleled, unusual, weighty. ANTONYMS: mundane, ordinary.

significance *n.* **1** (*importance, consequence*) consequence, importance, moment, relevance, seriousness, weight. **2** (*meaning, real import*) force, implication, import, meaning, message.

significant *a.* **1** (*meaning something*) eloquent, expressive, indicative, informative, meaningful, pithy, pregnant, suggestive, telling. ANTONYMS: insignificant, meaningless. **2** (*meaning something important, and relevant*) consequential, critical, crucial, historic, important, impressive, momentous, notable, noteworthy, relevant, signal, substantial, valuable, vital, weighty. ANTONYMS: trite, trivial.

signify *v.t.* **1** (*to make known by signs or words*) gesticulate, indicate, make known, signal. **2** (*to communicate, to announce*) announce, communicate, convey, declare, express, proclaim, tell. **3** (*to mean or denote, to have as its meaning*) augur, betoken, connote, denote, disclose, impart, imply, intimate, mean, portend, represent, reveal, say, show, sign, signal, specify, suggest, symbolize.

~*v.i.* (*to be of consequence, to matter*) be of consequence, be significant, carry weight, count, impress, matter, stand out.

silence *n.* **1** (*the absence of noise, stillness*) calm, calmness, hush, noiselessness, peace, peacefulness, quiet, quietness, quietude, serenity, soundlessness, stillness, tranquillity. ANTONYMS: noise. **2** (*avoidance of comment, or withholding of information, secrecy*) blackout, secrecy. **3** (*uncommunicativeness, taciturnity*) dumbness, muteness, reticence, speechlessness, taciturnity, uncommunicativeness. ANTONYMS: garrulity, talkativeness.

~*v.t.* (*to reduce to silence with an unanswerable argument*) damp, deaden, emasculate, gag, hush, inhibit, muffle, muzzle, pacify, put down, quash, quell, quiet, repress, restrain, shut off, smother, soothe, stifle, still, subdue, suppress.

silent *a.* **1** (*not speaking, not making any sound*) calm, hushed, inaudible, noiseless, pacific, passive, peaceful, placid, quiescent, quiet, serene, soundless, still, tranquil, undisturbed, unruffled, untroubled. ANTONYMS: loud, noisy. **2** ((*of a letter*) *written but not pronounced, as* *the unpronounced k in knee*) mute, unpronounced, unuttered. **3** (*uncommunicative, taciturn*) close-mouthed, dumb, mum, mute, reserved, reticent, secretive, speechless, taciturn, tight-lipped, uncommunicative, unspeaking, voiceless. ANTONYMS: chatty, talkative. **4** (*saying nothing (about or on a topic), making no mention*) implicit, implied, tacit, understood, unexpressed, unsaid, unspoken, unstated. ANTONYMS: explicit, expressed.

silly *a.* **1** (*foolish, weak-minded*) absurd, asinine, childish, fatuous, foolish, idiotic, inane, indiscreet, irrational, irresponsible, nonsensical, puerile, ridiculous, risible, weak-minded. ANTONYMS: sensible. **2** (*showing poor judgement, unwise*) brainless, foolhardy, imprudent, stupid, unintelligent, unwise, witless. **3** (*mentally weak, imbecile*) crazy, imbecilic, insane, mad. **4** (*senseless as a result of a blow*) benumbed, dazed, dizzy, giddy, muzzy, numbed, senseless, stunned, stupefied.

silvery *a.* **1** (*having the appearance of silver*) bright, burnished, gleaming, lustrous, pearly, polished, shining, shiny, silver. **2** (*having a soft, clear sound*) clear, delicate, dulcet, euphonious, mellifluous, melodious, musical, sweet.

similar *a.* (*resembling each other, alike*) akin, alike, allied, analogous, close, comparable, corresponding, equivalent, like, much the same, resembling, uniform. ANTONYMS: different.

simmer *v.i.* **1** (*to boil gently*) boil gently, bubble, cook. **2** (*to be in a state of suppressed emotion, esp. rage*) burn, chafe, fume, rage, seethe, smoulder, steam, stew.

simple *a.* **1** (*clear, easy to understand*) clear, comprehensible, intelligible, lucid, understandable. ANTONYMS: obscure. **2** (*not difficult, easy to do*) easy, effortless. **3** (*not complicated, straightforward*) easy, straightforward, uncomplicated, uninvolved, unsophisticated. ANTONYMS: complex. **4** (*not elaborate, not adorned*) austere, bare, basic, clean, fundamental, plain, severe, Spartan, stark, unadorned, uncluttered, unembellished. ANTONYMS: elaborate. **5** (*all of one kind or consisting of only one thing, not analysable*) elementary, pure, single, uncompounded, undivided, unmingled. **6** (*absolute, nothing but*) absolute, mere, nothing but, sheer. **7** (*weak in intellect*) backward, bovine, brainless, cretinous, dense, dull, dumb, feeble-minded, foolish, half-witted, ignorant, imbecilic, inexperienced, moronic, retarded, silly, slow-witted, stupid, (*coll.*) thick, unintelligent, witless. ANTONYMS: clever, intelligent. **8** (*unsophisticated, artless*) artless,

candid, childlike, credulous, direct, forthright, four-square, frank, guileless, ingenuous, innocent, natural, open, sincere, unaffected, uncontrived, unsophisticated. **9** (*humble, of low degree*) common, homely, honest, humble, inferior, lowly, mean, modest, naked, plain, subordinate, subservient, unassuming, unostentatious, unpretentious, unvarnished.

simply *adv.* **1** (*in a clear, straightforward manner*) clearly, comprehensibly, distinctly, lucidly, obviously, unambiguously. ANTONYMS: obscurely. **2** (*in a simple or plain manner*) ascetically, austerely, plainly, severely, starkly. **3** (*in an unsophisticated, artless manner*) artlessly, guilelessly, ingenuously, innocently, modestly, naturally, openly, unaffectedly, unpretentiously. **4** (*absolutely, without qualification*) absolutely, altogether, artlessly, ascetically, austerely, barely, clearly, completely, distinctly, entirely, fully, guilelessly, ingenuously, innocently, just, merely, modestly, naturally, obviously, openly, plainly, purely, really, severely, solely, sparsely, starkly, totally, unaffectedly, unambiguously, unpretentiously, unqualifiedly, unreservedly, utterly, very, wholly. **5** (*merely, only*) barely, just, merely, purely, solely.

sin *n.* **1** (*wickedness, moral depravity*) badness, corruption, depravity, evil, immorality, impiety, impiousness, iniquity, irreverence, sacrilege, sinfulness, ungodliness, vice, wickedness, wrongfulness. **2** (*a transgression, an offence*) crime, dereliction, evil, fault, infraction, infringement, iniquity, misdeed, misdemeanour, offence, peccadillo, profanation, sacrilege, transgression, trespass, vice, violation, wrong. ANTONYMS: virtue. **3** (*a breach of etiquette, social standards etc.*) breach of etiquette, faux pas, gaffe.

~*v.i.* (*to commit a sin*) err, fall, go astray, go wrong, lapse, offend, stray, transgress, trespass.

sincere *a.* (*not feigned or put on, genuine*) artless, candid, direct, earnest, forthright, frank, genuine, guileless, honest, on the level, open, plain, straightforward, truthful, unaffected, undissembling, (*coll.*) upfront, veracious. ANTONYMS: insincere.

sinful *a.* **1** (*(of a person) frequently or habitually sinning*) corrupt, depraved, sinning. **2** (*(of an act) reprehensible, or entailing sin*) bad, base, corrupt, criminal, culpable, depraved, evil, guilty, immoral, impious, iniquitous, irreverent, profane, reprehensible, sacrilegious, ungodly, unholy, vile, wicked, wrong, wrongful. ANTONYMS: virtuous.

sing *v.i.* **1** (*to utter words in a tuneful manner, to* render a song vocally) carol, chorus, croon, vocalize, yodel. **2** ((of birds, or certain insects) to emit sweet or melodious sounds) chirp, peep, pipe, trill, warble. **3** ((of a kettle, the wind etc.) to make a murmuring or whistling sound) howl, moan, murmur, whistle. **4** ((of the ears) to ring) buzz, ring, throb. **5** (sl.) (to confess, to inform) blow the whistle, confess, (sl.) grass, name names, peach, (coll.) rat, (sl.) snitch, spill the beans, (sl.) squeal.

~v.t. (to utter (words, a song etc.) in a tuneful or melodious manner) chant, trill, voice.

singe v.t. (to burn slightly, to burn the surface of) blacken, burn, char, scorch, sear.

~n. (a slight or superficial burn) burn, scald, scorch.

single a. **1** (consisting of one only, sole) one, only, sole. **2** (individual, solitary) alone, distinct, individual, isolated, lone, particular, separate, singular, solitary, unaccompanied, unaided, unique. ANTONYMS: numerous. **3** (unmarried, or without a current partner) by oneself, free, on one's own, unattached, unmarried, unwed. ANTONYMS: married. **to single out** (to choose from a group) choose, cull, distinguish, fasten on, fix on, pick, prefer, segregate, select, separate, set apart, set aside, sort out. ANTONYMS: reject.

singular a. **1** (out of the usual, remarkable) atypical, conspicuous, different, distinct, distinguished, eminent, exceptional, extraordinary, notable, outstanding, prominent, rare, remarkable, signal, significant, uncommon, unique, unparalleled, unusual. ANTONYMS: ordinary. **2** (peculiar, odd) bizarre, curious, eccentric, (sl.) far out, odd, offbeat, outlandish, outré, peculiar, queer, strange. **3** (single, individual) individual, isolated, lone, particular, separate, single, sole.

sinister a. **1** (malevolent) baleful, corrupt, dark, diabolical, evil, furtive, gloomy, harmful, ill-looking, insidious, malevolent, malign, pernicious, sneaky, treacherous, underhand, villainous, wicked. **2** (ill-omened, inauspicious) fateful, foreboding, ill-omened, inauspicious, menacing, ominous, portentous, threatening, unfavourable, unpropitious.

sink v.i. **1** (to go downwards, to fall gradually) decline, descend, drop, fall, go downwards. ANTONYMS: rise. **2** (to drop below the surface of a liquid) go down, go under, immerse, plunge, submerge. **3** (to deteriorate) degenerate, deteriorate, fail, flag, weaken. **4** (to subside or decline) abate, cave in, collapse, ebb, settle, slip away, subside. **5** (to expire or come to an end by degrees) die, expire, (col.) go downhill, languish. **6** (to become lower in intensity, price

etc.) decrease, diminish, drop, reduce, slump. **7** (to become shrunken or hollow, to slope downwards) dip, hollow, recede, shrink, slope.

~v.t. **1** (to submerge (as) in a fluid, to send below the surface) dip, dunk, submerge. **2** (to excavate, to make by excavating) bore, dig, drill, excavate. **3** (to put out of sight, to conceal) conceal, lose sight of, put out of sight, suppress. **4** (to lower, to ruin) degrade, demolish, destroy, lower, ruin. **5** (to invest (money in an enterprise)) invest, lose, risk, spend, squander, venture, waste. **6** (to drink, to quaff) drink, quaff, (coll.) swig.

~n. **1** (a plastic, porcelain or metal basin, usu. fitted to a water supply and drainage system in a kitchen) basin, washbasin, washbowl. **2** (a cesspool or sewer) cesspit, cesspool, sewer. **3** (a place of iniquity) den, (coll.) dive, hell-hole, pit. **to sink in** (to become absorbed, to penetrate) become absorbed, get through to, impress, penetrate, register.

sinner n. (someone who habitually sins, a sinful person) criminal, delinquent, evildoer, malefactor, miscreant, offender, reprobate, sinful person, transgressor, trespasser, wrongdoer. ANTONYMS: saint.

sip v.t., v.i. (to drink or imbibe in small quantities using the lips) drink, imbibe, sample, sup, taste.

~n. (a very small draught of liquid) bit, dram, draught, drop, mouthful, nip, sample, soupçon, spoonful, swallow, swig, taste, thimbleful.

sit v.i. **1** (to set oneself or be in a resting posture with the body nearly vertical supported on the buttocks) be seated, rest, seat, settle, sit down, squat, take a seat. ANTONYMS: stand. **2** (to perch) perch, roost, settle. **3** (to rest or weigh (on)) burden, press, rest, weigh. **4** (to meet, to hold a session) assemble, convene, gather, get together, hold a session, meet, officiate, preside. **5** (to hold or occupy a seat (on a deliberative body or in a specified capacity)) be a member of, hold a seat, occupy a seat, participate in. **6** (to remain, to abide) abide, dwell, lie, mark time, remain, rest, stay.

~v.t. (to cause to sit, to set) place, position, set.

site n. (the ground on which anything, esp. a building, stands) area, centre, ground, locale, locality, location, neighbourhood, place, plot, position, situation, spot.

~v.t. (to position, locate) install, locate, place, position, put, situate.

situation n. **1** (the place in which something is situated, position) locale, locality, location, place, position, scene, setting, site, spot. **2** (a state of affairs or set of circumstances) background, (*coll.*) ballgame, case, circumstances, conditions, lie of the land, picture, plight, predicament, state of affairs, status quo. **3** (*a paid office or post*) employment, job, office, place, position, post, rank.

size *n.* (*extent, dimensions*) amount, area, bigness, bulk, dimensions, expanse, extent, immensity, magnitude, mass, measurement, proportions, range, scope, vastness, volume. ~*v.t.* (*to sort or arrange according to size*) arrange, grade, rank, sort.

skilful *a.* **1** (*having or showing skill* (*at or in something*)) masterly, skilled, talented. **2** (*expert, adroit*) able, accomplished, adept, adroit, apt, clever, competent, deft, dexterous, experienced, expert, gifted, handy, masterful, practised, professional, proficient, qualified, quick, trained, versed. ANTONYMS: incompetent, inept.

skill *n.* **1** (*familiar knowledge of any art or science combined with dexterity*) art, knowledge, mastery. **2** (*practical mastery of a craft, sport etc., often attained by training*) ability, adeptness, adroitness, aptitude, artistry, capability, craftsmanship, deftness, dexterity, experience, expertise, facility, faculty, finesse, gift, handiness, ingenuity, knack, know-how, proficiency, strength, talent, technique, training. ANTONYMS: incompetence, ineptitude. **3** (*tact, diplomacy*) diplomacy, discretion, tact.

skim *v.t.* **1** (*to take* (*cream etc.*) *from the surface of a liquid*) cream off, ladle off, remove, scoop off, take off. **2** (*to touch lightly or nearly touch the surface of, to graze*) brush, glance, graze, touch. ANTONYMS: penetrate. **3** (*to glance over or read superficially*) dip into, flick through, glance over, leaf through, read, scan, thumb through. ~*v.i.* (*to pass lightly and rapidly* (*over or along a surface*)) coast, fly, glide, pass over, sail, skate, slide, soar.

skin *n.* **1** (*the hide of an animal removed from the body*) fleece, fur, hide, integument, pelt. **2** (*one's colouring or complexion*) colour, colouring, complexion. **3** (*the outer layer or covering of a plant, fruit etc.*) husk, peel, rind. **4** (*a film, e.g. the skinlike film that forms on certain liquids*) crust, film, incrustation. **5** (*the outer layer or covering of an object, structure etc.*) coating, covering, lamina, outer layer, outside, overlay, shell, veneer. ~*v.t.* **1** (*to strip the skin from, to peel*) excoriate, flay, hull, husk, pare, peel, shell, strip. **2** (*to graze* (*e.g. one's knee*)) abrade, bark, graze, scrape. **3** (*to cheat, to swindle*) cheat, fleece, (*coll.*) rip off, (*sl.*) sting, swindle.

skinny *a.* **1** (*very lean or thin*) bony, emaciated, gangling, gaunt, half-starved, hollow-cheeked, lanky, lean, pinched, scraggy, scrawny, spare, thin, undernourished, underweight, wasted. ANTONYMS: fat, plump. **2** ((*of garments, esp. knitted ones*) *tight-fitting*) skintight, tight-fitting. ANTONYMS: baggy, loose.

skip *v.i.* **1** (*to frisk, to gambol*) bounce, bound, caper, cavort, dance, frisk, gambol, hop, prance, romp. **2** (*to jump repeatedly over a skipping rope*) jump, leap, spring. **3** (*to pass rapidly* (*from one thing to another*)) avoid, cut, disregard, exclude, ignore, leave out, miss out, neglect, omit, overlook, pass over, steer clear of. ~*v.t.* **1** (*to miss deliberately, to absent oneself from* (*a meal, a class etc.*)) absent oneself, miss, (*coll.*) skive, (*sl.*) wag. **2** (*esp. N Am.*) (*to leave* (*town*) *quickly and quietly, to abscond from*) abscond from, bolt, make off from. ~*n.* **1** (*a step and a hop on one foot, or a type of forward movement hopping on each foot in turn*) hop, step. **2** (*a light leap or spring*) bounce, leap, spring. **3** (*an act of omitting or leaving out*) avoidance, disregard, gap, miss, omission.

skirmish *n.* **1** (*a slight or irregular fight, esp. between small parties or scattered troops*) battle, fight, (*coll.*) scrap. **2** (*a struggle, esp. of a preliminary or minor nature*) affray, brawl, brush, clash, combat, confrontation, contest, (*coll.*) dust-up, encounter, engagement, fracas, fray, mêlée, scrimmage, scrum, set-to, showdown, struggle, tussle. **3** (*an altercation or clash of wit*) altercation, argument, banter, exchange, sparring.

sky *n.* **1** (*the apparent vault of heaven, the firmament*) firmament, heaven, vault. **2** (*the upper region of the atmosphere, the region of clouds*) azure, clouds, ether, upper atmosphere. ANTONYMS: earth, ground.

slab *n.* **1** (*a thin, flat, regularly shaped piece of anything, esp. of stone, concrete etc.*) block, chunk, hunk, lump, piece. **2** (*a large slice of bread, cake etc.*) (*sl.*) doorstep, slice, wedge.

slack *a.* **1** (*not drawn tight, loose*) baggy, loose. **2** (*limp, relaxed*) drooping, droopy, flabby, flaccid, limp, relaxed, sagging. ANTONYMS: taut. **3** (*careless, negligent*) careless, dilatory, idle, inactive, inattentive, indolent, laggardly, lax, lazy, lethargic, negligent, quiet, remiss, slothful. ANTONYMS: active, busy. **4** ((*of trade or the market*) *sluggish, slow*) dull, slow, sluggish, tardy.

slacken *v.i., v.t.* (*to become or make slack or slacker*) abate, decline, decrease, diminish, ease, lessen, let go, let up, loose, loosen, moderate, reduce, relax, release, slow, tire, weaken. ANTONYMS: intensify, tighten.

slam *v.t.* **1** (*to shut* (*a door, lid etc.*) *suddenly with a loud noise*) bang, close, crash, dash, fling, hurl, shut, slap, smash. **2** (*to thrash, to defeat completely*) (*sl.*) clobber, defeat, hit, thrash, trounce. **3** (*to criticize severely*) attack, condemn, criticize, damn, denounce, flay, (*coll.*) pan, pillory, pounce on, put down, run down, shoot down, slate, vilify.
~*v.i.* ((*of a door*) *to shut violently or noisily*) bang, close, crash, dash, fling, hurl, shut, slap, smash.

slander *n.* **1** (*a false statement maliciously uttered to injure a person*) blackening, false statement, slur. **2** (*the making of malicious and untrue statements, defamation*) abuse, aspersion, calumny, defamation, detraction, disparagement, libel, misrepresentation, obloquy, scandal, slur, smear, vilification.
~*v.t.* (*to injure by the malicious utterance of a false report*) abuse, backbite, calumniate, decry, defame, disparage, libel, malign, misrepresent, smear, traduce, vilify. ANTONYMS: admire, praise.

slant *v.i.* (*to incline from or be oblique to a vertical or horizontal line*) angle, bend, cant, incline, lean, list, pitch, tilt, tip.
~*v.t.* (*to present in a biased or unfair way*) angle, bend, bias, colour, deviate, distort, twist, warp, weight.
~*n.* **1** (*a slope*) angle, camber, cant, deflection, gradient, inclination, incline, lean, leaning, pitch, rake, ramp, slope. **2** (*an angle of approach, a point of view*) angle, approach, aspect, attitude, idea, standpoint, viewpoint. **3** (*a bias or unfair emphasis*) bent, bias, one-sidedness, partiality, prejudice, turn.

slap *v.t.* **1** (*to strike with the open hand, to smack*) bat, beat, clip, clout, cuff, hit, rap, smack, spank, strike, whack, whip. **2** (*to lay or throw forcefully or quickly*) fling, hurl, slam down, sling, splash, throw down, toss. **3** (*to put* (*on*) *or apply hastily*) apply hastily, daub, plaster.
~*n.* (*a blow, esp. with the open hand*) blow, clout, cuff, hit, rap, smack, spank, (*coll.*) wallop, whack.

slash *v.t.* **1** (*to cut by striking violently at random*) cut, hack, knife, lacerate, slit. **2** (*to make long incisions or narrow gashes in*) gash, hack, rip, scar, score, slit, wound. **3** (*to reduce* (*prices etc.*) *drastically*) cut, decrease, drop, lower, mark down, reduce, trim. ANTONYMS: increase, raise. **4** (*to lash* (*with a whip etc.*)) beat, flagellate, flail, flay, flog, horsewhip, lash, scourge, thrash, whip.
~*v.i.* (*to strike* (*at etc.*) *violently and at random with a knife, sword etc.*) cut, gash, hack, lacerate, rip, scar, score, slit, wound.

~*n.* **1** (*a long cut or incision*) cut, gash, gouge, incision, laceration, rent, rip, score, slice, slit. **2** (*an act of urinating*) (*sl.*) leak, (*coll.*) piddle, (*taboo sl.*) piss, urination.

slaughter *n.* (*wholesale or indiscriminate killing*) assassination, bloodbath, bloodletting, bloodshed, butchery, carnage, execution, extermination, genocide, killing, liquidation, manslaughter, (*coll.*) massacre, mass murder, murder, sacrifice, slaying.
~*v.t.* **1** (*to kill wantonly or ruthlessly, to massacre*) assassinate, butcher, destroy, execute, exterminate, kill, liquidate, massacre, murder, put to death, put to the sword, slay. **2** (*to defeat decisively*) (*coll.*) annihilate, (*sl.*) clobber, crush, defeat, destroy, (*coll.*) massacre, murder, overcome, overwhelm, rout, smash, thrash, trounce, vanquish.

slave *n.* **1** (*a person who is the property of and bound in obedience to another*) bondservant, serf, servant, vassal. ANTONYMS: master, owner. **2** (*a person who is entirely under the domination of another person, the influence* (*of e.g. fashion*) *or a helpless victim* (*to drugs etc.*)) addict, fag, lackey. **3** (*a person who works like a slave, esp. for low wages, a drudge*) dogsbody, drudge, hack, labourer, (*sl.*) skivvy, workhorse.
~*v.i.* (*to toil like a slave, to drudge*) drudge, grind, grub, labour, (*sl.*) skivvy, sweat, toil, work.

slavery *n.* (*the condition of being a slave*) bondage, captivity, drudgery, enslavement, enthralment, grind, serfdom, servitude, subjugation, thraldom, thrall, toil, travail, vassalage, yoke. ANTONYMS: freedom.

sleazy *a.* **1** (*squalid or seedy*) cheap, (*sl.*) crummy, dirty, disreputable, low-grade, mean, ramshackle, run-down, seedy, shabby, slipshod, sordid, squalid, tatty, tawdry, trashy. **2** (*slatternly*) base, bent, corrupt, disreputable, distasteful, immoral, seedy, shabby, sordid, squalid.

sleek *a.* **1** ((*of fur, skin etc.*) *smooth, glossy*) glossy, lustrous, shining, shiny, silken, silky, smooth, velvety. ANTONYMS: rough. **2** (*well-groomed and well-fed, prosperous-looking*) graceful, prosperous-looking, streamlined, trim, well-fed, well-groomed. **3** (*unctuous, smooth-spoken*) fawning, insincere, oily, slick, slimy, smarmy, smooth-spoken, specious, suave, unctuous.

sleep *n.* **1** (*a state of rest in which consciousness is almost entirely suspended*) beauty sleep, repose, slumber. ANTONYMS: wakefulness. **2** (*a period or spell of this*) catnap, doze, drowse, forty winks, nap, siesta, snooze. **3** (*a state with the characteristics of sleep, such as death or the hibernating state of certain animals*) death, hibernation, quiet, repose, rest, torpor.

~v.i. **1** (*to take rest in sleep*) be asleep, catnap, doze, drowse, nap, repose, rest, slumber, snooze. ANTONYMS: wake. **2** (*to be or lie dormant or in abeyance*) hibernate, lie dormant, lie low. **3** (*to fall asleep*) (*coll.*) drop off, fall asleep, (*coll.*) nod off.

~v.t. (*to provide with accommodation for sleeping, to lodge (a certain number*)) accommodate, lodge, put up.

sleepless *a.* **1** ((*of a night*) *during which one cannot get to sleep*) disturbed, insomniac, unsleeping, wakeful. ANTONYMS: sleepy. **2** (*constantly watchful and active*) active, alert, awake, restless, vigilant, watchful.

sleepy *a.* **1** (*inclined to sleep, drowsy*) (*esp. N Am., coll.*) beat, (*coll.*) dead on one's feet, dozy, drowsy, exhausted, fatigued, knocked out, nodding, (*esp. N Am., coll.*) pooped, slumberous, somnolent, tired, weary. ANTONYMS: wakeful. **2** (*lazy, habitually inactive*) boring, dormant, dull, inactive, indolent, lazy, lethargic, quiet, slow, sluggish, torpid. ANTONYMS: alert. **3** (*tending to induce sleep*) hypnotic, sleep-inducing, soporific.

slender *a.* **1** (*small in circumference or width as compared with length*) narrow, small. **2** (*attractively or gracefully thin*) frail, graceful, lanky, lean, lissom, lithe, slight, slim, snake-hipped, spare, svelte, sylphlike, thin, willowy. ANTONYMS: plump. **3** (*slight, inadequate*) faint, flimsy, inadequate, inconsiderable, insignificant, insufficient, little, meagre, poor, scanty, slight, small, trifling, trivial. ANTONYMS: ample. **4** ((*of hopes etc.*) *not strong or well-founded*) feeble, ill-founded, remote, unlikely.

slice *n.* **1** (*a broad, thin piece cut off, esp. from bread etc., or a wedge cut from a circular cake etc.*) helping, layer, piece, portion, rasher, shaving, slab, sliver, wedge. **2** (*a part, share etc., separated or allotted from a larger quantity*) allotment, part, share.

~v.t. (*to cut, to divide*) carve, cut, divide, split.

slide *v.i.* **1** (*to move smoothly along a surface with continuous contact*) coast, glide, glissade, move smoothly, plane, skate, skid, skim, slip, slither, toboggan. **2** (*to pass (away, into etc.) gradually or imperceptibly*) decline, decrease, drift, drop, fall, pass, take its course. **3** (*to move secretly or unobtrusively*) creep, move, slink, slip, steal. **4** (*to glide or gloss (over a subject best avoided*)) forget, glide over, gloss over, ignore, let ride, neglect, pass over, pay no heed to.

~n. **1** (*a downward turn (e.g. in value), a rapid deterioration*) deterioration, sliding, slip, slippage. **2** (*a landslip*) avalanche, earth-slip, landslide, landslip, mud-slide, subsidence.

3 (*a clasp for the hair*) clasp, hairgrip, hairslide.

slight *a.* **1** (*inconsiderable, insignificant*) inconsequential, inconsiderable, insignificant, minor, unimportant. ANTONYMS: considerable. **2** (*small in amount, intensity etc.*) imperceptible, light, minor, negligible. **3** (*inadequate, negligible*) bantam, inadequate, inconsequential, infinitesimal, insubstantial, miniature, minute, negligible, paltry, petty, pocket-sized, superficial, tiny, trifling, trivial, (*coll.*) wee. **4** (*frail, weak*) faint, feeble, flimsy, fragile, frail, precarious, unstable, weak. **5** ((*of a person's figure*) *small and slender*) dainty, delicate, diminutive, lightly built, little, petite, (*coll.*) pint-sized, short, slender, slim, small, thin, tiny.

~n. (*an act of disregard or neglect, a snub*) affront, cold shoulder, contempt, disparagement, disregard, disrespect, ill-treatment, indifference, insult, neglect, offence, rebuff, scorn, snub. ANTONYMS: respect.

~v.t. (*to treat disrespectfully, to snub*) affront, cold-shoulder, cut, depreciate, diminish, disdain, disparage, disrespect, ignore, insult, minimize, mortify, offend, rebuff, scorn, snub. ANTONYMS: acknowledge.

slim *a.* **1** (*tall and narrow in shape*) narrow, slender, tall. **2** (*gracefully thin, of slight shape or build*) graceful, lanky, lean, lissom, lithe, slender, slight, spare, svelte, thin, willowy. ANTONYMS: fat, plump. **3** (*poor, inadequate*) feeble, inadequate, insignificant, insufficient, little, meagre, poor, remote, scanty, slight, small, trifling, unlikely, weak. **4** (*economically streamlined*) economical, efficient, modernized, rationalized, streamlined.

~v.i. (*to diet and exercise in order to become slimmer*) diet, exercise, lose weight, shed weight.

slimy *a.* **1** (*slippery, difficult to grasp*) clammy, difficult to grasp, (*coll.*) gooey, (*coll.*) gunky, miry, mucilaginous, mucous, muddy, oozy, slippery, squishy, viscous. **2** (*repulsively mean or cringing*) abject, creeping, cringing, dishonest, grovelling, mean, obsequious, servile, slippery, smarmy, sycophantic, toadying, unctuous.

sling *n.* **1** (*a band or other arrangement of rope, chains etc., for suspending, hoisting or transferring anything*) band, belt, loop, strap, support. **2** (*a throw*) cast, slingshot, throw.

~v.t. **1** (*to throw, to hurl*) (*coll.*) chuck, fire, fling, heave, hurl, launch, let fly, lob, pitch, propel, shoot, shy, throw, toss. **2** (*to cast (out*)) bin, cast out, reject, throw away, throw out. **3** (*to hang loosely so as to swing*) dangle, hang, suspend, swing.

slink *v.i.* (*to steal or sneak* (*away etc.*) *in a furtive or cowardly manner*) creep, prowl, skulk, sneak, steal.

slip¹ *v.i.* **1** (*to slide unintentionally and miss one's footing*) fall, lose one's balance, lose one's footing, miss one's footing, stumble, trip, tumble. **2** (*to slide, to glide*) glide, skid, slide, slither. **3** (*to move or pass unnoticed or quickly*) creep, go unnoticed, sneak. **4** (*to go* (*along*) *swiftly*) slide, zip, zoom. **5** (*to get* (*out, through etc.*), *become free, or escape thus*) drop, escape, evade, get out, get through. **6** (*to commit a small mistake or oversight*) blunder, botch, err, go wrong, miscalculate, (*sl.*) screw up, slip up. **7** (*to decline*) decline, deteriorate, drop, fall, lapse.
~*v.t.* **1** (*to cause to move in a sliding manner*) run, slide. **2** (*to put* (*on or off*) *or to insert* (*into*) *with a hasty or careless motion*) insert into, put off, put on. **3** (*to let loose*) let loose, undo, unleash. **4** (*to put* (*a garment on*) *or take* (*a garment off*) *speedily or easily*) pull off, pull on, put on, take off. **5** (*to escape or free oneself from*) escape from, free oneself from.
~*n.* **1** (*an unintentional error, a lapse*) (*sl.*) bloomer, blunder, (*coll.*) boob, error, fault, faux pas, impropriety, inadvertence, indiscretion, lapse, mistake, offence, oversight, peccadillo, slip of the tongue, slip-up, transgression. **2** (*a garment that a woman wears under her dress or skirt*) jupon, †kirtle, petticoat, underskirt. **3** (*a landslide*) landslide, landslip, subsidence.

slip² *n.* **1** (*a small piece of paper for writing messages etc. on*) chit, memo, note, paper. **2** (*a small form for filling in*) chit, chitty, document, form, pass, permit. **3** (*a long, narrow strip of paper, wood or other material*) scrap, sliver, strip. **4** (*a slight young person, a stripling*) child, infant, stripling, youth.

slippery *a.* **1** (*so smooth, wet or slimy as to be difficult to hold*) glassy, greasy, icy, lubricated, oily, sleek, slick, slimy, smooth, wet. **2** (*so wet, muddy etc. as to cause slipping*) hazardous, perilous, treacherous, unsafe. **3** (*shifty, dishonest*) crafty, devious, dishonest, foxy, perfidious, questionable, shady, shifty, slick, sly, sneaky, treacherous, tricky, undependable, unreliable, untrustworthy. ANTONYMS: trustworthy.

slipshod *a.* (*careless, slovenly*) careless, disorderly, disorganized, haphazard, lax, messy, negligent, slapdash, slatternly, sloppy, slovenly, unorganized, untidy. ANTONYMS: attentive, careful.

slit *n.* (*a long cut or narrow opening*) aperture, cleft, cut, fissure, gash, groove, incision, opening, rip, slash, slice, split, tear. ANTONYMS: joint, seam.

~*v.t.* **1** (*to make a long cut in*) cut, gash, knife, slice, split. **2** (*to cut or tear lengthways*) rip, tear.

slope *n.* (*a piece of ground whose surface makes an angle with the horizon*) acclivity, angle, bank, camber, cant, decline, declivity, dip, gradient, hill, inclination, incline, mount, pitch, rake, ramp, rise, slant, tilt, tip. ANTONYMS: level.
~*v.i.* (*to be inclined at an angle to the horizon*) angle, decline, dip, incline, lean, list, rake, shelve, slant, tilt, tip.

sloping *a.* (*inclining at an angle to the horizon, slanting*) angled, inclined, inclining, leaning, listing, oblique, pitched, shelving, slanted, slanting, tilted, tipped. ANTONYMS: level.

sloppy *a.* **1** (*wet, covered with spilt water or puddles*) rainy, sloshy, sodden, soggy, sopping, soppy, splashed, watered, wet. ANTONYMS: dry. **2** ((*of food*) *watery and insipid*) insipid, tasteless, watery. **3** ((*of work*) *done carelessly*) careless, dishevelled, disordered, disorderly, messy, scruffy, shabby, slapdash, slipshod, slovenly, unkempt. **4** ((*of clothes*) *untidy, badly fitting*) badly fitting, loose, raggy, untidy. **5** (*weakly sentimental or maudlin*) effusive, emotional, gushing, gushy, maudlin, mawkish, (*sl.*) mushy, over-emotional, pathetic, sentimental, (*sl.*) slushy, (*coll.*) soppy, (*coll.*) wet.

slot *n.* **1** (*a groove or opening, esp. in a machine for some part to fit into*) aperture, channel, crack, depression, fissure, groove, hole, hollow, notch, opening, slit. **2** (*a place or niche* (*e.g. in an organization*)) assignment, job, niche, opening, place, position, post, vacancy. **3** (*a* (*usu. regular*) *position in a sequence or schedule* (*e.g. of a television programme*)) appointment, pigeon-hole, space, spot, window.
~*v.t.* **1** (*to fit or place* (*as*) *into a slot*) assign, fit, pigeon-hole, place into, position, schedule. **2** (*to make a slot in*) fissure, groove, hollow out, notch, slit.
~*v.i.* (*to fit* (*together or into*) *by means of a slot or slots*) dovetail, fit into, fit together.

slouch *n.* **1** (*an ungainly or negligent drooping or stooping gait, or movement*) droop, hunch, lumber, sag, shamble, shuffle, slump, stoop. **2** (*a slovenly or incapable person*) idler, laggard, lazybones, loafer, malingerer, sluggard.
~*v.i.* **1** (*to stand or move in a drooping or ungainly attitude*) lumber, shamble, shuffle, stoop. **2** (*to droop or hang down*) droop, hang down, hunch, loll, sag, slump.

slow *a.* **1** (*taking a long time in acting or doing something*) easy, lax, leisurely, lingering, plodding, ponderous, protracted, relaxed,

slow-moving, slow-paced, snail-like, tortoise-like, unhurried. ANTONYMS: fast, speedy. **2** (*deliberate* (*of speech etc.*)) deliberate, measured. **3** (*gradual, e.g. in growth or development*) gradual, imperceptible, measurable, moderate, progressive. **4** (*not prompt or willing* (*to do something*)) averse, crawling, creeping, dawdling, disinclined, hesitant, laggardly, lagging, lazy, leaden, leaden-footed, loath, reluctant, sluggish, torpid, unwilling. **5** (*not hasty, not precipitate*) considered, not hasty, thoughtful. **6** (*tardy, backward*) backward, delayed, dilatory, tardy. ANTONYMS: prompt. **7** (*stupid, dull*) backward, bovine, dense, dim, dimwitted, doltish, dull, dumb, obtuse, simple, slow on the uptake, slow-witted, stupid, (*coll.*) thick, unimaginative, unintelligent, unresponsive. ANTONYMS: quick, smart. **8** ((*of a party or similar event*) *lifeless*) boring, dull, humdrum, lifeless, monotonous, tame, tedious, tiresome, uneventful, uninteresting, wearisome. ANTONYMS: exhilarating, lively. **9** ((*of business, trade etc.*) *slack*) inactive, quiet, slack, sluggish, unproductive.
~*v.i.* (*to slacken or moderate speed* (*up or down*)) brake, check, decelerate, delay, go slower, hold back, hold up, retard, slacken off. ANTONYMS: accelerate, speed.

sluggish *a.* **1** (*habitually lazy, inactive*) drowsy, dull, heavy, idle, inactive, indolent, languid, lazy, lethargic, sleepy, slothful. ANTONYMS: quick. **2** (*slow in movement or response, inert*) inert, lifeless, phlegmatic, shiftless, slow, stagnant, torpid, unresponsive. ANTONYMS: alert.

slump *v.i.* **1** (*to fall or sink* (*down*) *heavily*) drop, fall, sink. **2** ((*of prices, prosperity etc.*) *to fall, to collapse*) collapse, crash, descend, dive, drop, fall, go into a tailspin, plummet, plunge, sag, slip. ANTONYMS: rise. **3** (*to decline quickly or drastically*) decline, decrease.
~*n.* (*a heavy fall or decline, a collapse* (*of prices etc.*)) collapse, crash, decline, depression, descent, dip, downslide, drop, failure, fall, falling-off, fall-off, nosedive, plunge, recession, tailspin. ANTONYMS: boom.

slur *v.t.* **1** (*to pronounce indistinctly*) garble, lisp, misarticulate, mispronounce, mumble, stutter. **2** (*to speak slightingly of*) brand, calumniate, disgrace, insult, slander, slight, stigmatize. **3** (*to pass lightly over*) disregard, gloss over, ignore, pass over.
~*n.* (*a reproach or disparagement*) affront, aspersion, brand, calumny, discredit, disparagement, imputation, insinuation, insult, libel, mark, put-down, reproach, slander, slight, smear, snub, spot, stain, stigma.

sly *a.* **1** (*crafty, cunning*) artful, astute, canny, clever, conniving, crafty, cunning, deceitful, designing, devious, disingenuous, foxy, guileful, insidious, plotting, scheming, sharp, shifty, shrewd, subtle, treacherous, tricky, wily. ANTONYMS: artless, guileless. **2** (*furtive, not open or frank*) clandestine, close, furtive, secretive, shady, sneaky, stealthy, underhand. ANTONYMS: frank, open. **3** (*playfully roguish*) arch, devilish, elfin, impish, knowing, mischievous, naughty, puckish, roguish, scampish, waggish.

small *a.* **1** (*deficient or relatively little in size, stature, amount etc.*) deficient, diminutive, elfin, immature, inadequate, insufficient, Lilliputian, little, (*coll.*) measly, microscopic, midget, miniature, minuscule, minute, petite, (*coll.*) piddling, (*coll.*) pint-sized, pocket-sized, short, (*coll.*) teeny, tiny, undersized, (*coll.*) wee, young. ANTONYMS: ample, big. **2** (*of less dimensions than the standard kind*) lesser, smaller. **3** (*of minor importance, slight, trifling, petty*) inconsequential, insignificant, negligible, petty, puny, secondary, skimpy, slight, trifling, trivial, unimportant. **4** (*of low degree, humble*) base, humble, low, lowly, plebeian, poor. **5** (*unpretentious*) modest, simple, unpretentious. ANTONYMS: elaborate, grand. **6** (*ignoble, narrow-minded*) ignoble, matter-of-fact, meagre, mean, mundane, narrow-minded, paltry, scanty, shallow, small-minded, two-dimensional, unimaginative, uninspired, unoriginal, unprofound.
~*adv.* **1** (*into small pieces*) finely, little, thinly. **2** (*quietly, in a low voice*) gently, quietly, softly.

smart *a.* **1** (*spruce, well-groomed*) à la mode, chic, dapper, elegant, fashionable, modish, (*coll.*) natty, neat, (*coll.*) posh, snappy, spruce, stylish, tidy, trim, well-groomed, well-turned-out. ANTONYMS: casual, slovenly, untidy. **2** (*astute, intelligent*) adept, astute, aware, bright, brilliant, canny, capable, clever, erudite, ingenious, intelligent, knowledgeable, learned, perspicacious, well-educated, well-read. **3** (*shrewd, quick to spot a chance and take advantage of it*) active, acute, agile, alive, discerning, perceptive, percipient, prompt, quick, quick-witted, ready, sharp, shrewd, wide awake. **4** (*witty, esp. impertinently so*) nimble-witted, pert, poignant, saucy, trenchant, witty. **5** ((*of equipment etc.*) *clean, bright and in good repair*) bright, clean. **6** ((*of a resort, rendezvous etc.*) *stylish, fashionable*) chic, elegant, fashionable, select, stylish. **7** ((*of people in society*) *sophisticated*) admired, chic, elegant, sophisticated. **8** (*vigorous, lively*) active, alert, animated, breezy, brisk, energetic, jaunty, lively, perky, quick, spirited, vigorous. ANTONYMS: slow. **9** (*stinging, severe*) keen, painful, pungent, quick, severe, sharp, smarting, stiff, stinging, swift. ANTONYMS: dull.

10 (*computer-controlled, electronically operated or technologically advanced*) computer-controlled, technologically advanced.
~v.i. **1** (*to feel or give or cause sharp pain or mental distress*) ache, burn, hurt, pain, pierce, pinch, prick, prickle, stab, sting, throb, tingle, wound. **2** ((*of a rebuff or injustice*) *to rankle*) gall, rankle.
~n. **1** (*a sharp pain, a stinging sensation*) affliction, harm, injury, pain, pang, prick, sting, twinge. **2** (*a feeling of resentment*) gall, rancour, resentment. **3** (*distress, anguish*) anguish, distress, smarting, suffering.

smash *v.t.* **1** (*to break to pieces by violence, to shatter*) break, crash, dash, demolish, destroy, pulverize, ruin, shatter, shiver, splinter, wreck. **2** (*to hit with a crushing blow*) hit, whack. **3** (*to overthrow completely, to rout*) crush, defeat, demolish, destroy, overthrow, rout.
~v.i. **1** (*to break to pieces*) break up, disintegrate, shatter. **2** (*to crash* (*into*)) collide, crash.
~n. **1** (*an act or instance of smashing*) breakage, crash. **2** (*a smash-up, a crash between vehicles*) collision, crash, destruction, ruin, smash-up, wreck. **3** (*a smash hit*) (*coll.*) hit, winner. **4** (*a violent blow with the fist*) blow, punch. **5** (*a collapse; the bankruptcy or ruin of a person or concern*) bankruptcy, break-up, collapse, defeat, disaster, failure.

smear *v.t.* **1** (*to rub or daub with anything greasy or sticky*) anoint, bedaub, besmear, daub, rub, spread, wipe. **2** (*to apply thickly*) apply thickly, cake, coat, cover, daub, plaster. **3** (*to stain or dirty*) begrime, besmirch, dirty, smudge, soil, stain, sully, tarnish. ANTONYMS: clean, scour. **4** (*to malign* (*someone*) *or blacken* (*their name*) *publicly*) blacken, calumniate, defame, defile, discredit, libel, malign, muddy, scandalize, slander, slur, stigmatize, sully, tarnish, vilify.
~v.i. (*to become blurred, smudged etc.*) blur, smudge.
~n. **1** (*a stain or mark made by smearing*) blot, daub, mark, patch, smear, smudge, splodge, spot, stain, taint. **2** (*an attack on a person's reputation*) aspersion, calumny, criticism, defamation, libel, mud-slinging, reflection, scandal, slander, slur, vilification.

smell *n.* **1** (*the sensation or the act of smelling*) sniff, whiff. **2** (*that which affects the organs of smell*) aroma, bouquet, breath, fragrance, odour, perfume, redolence, scent, whiff. **3** (*a bad odour*) effluvium, fetor, (*coll.*) pong, reek, stench, stink.
~v.t. **1** (*to notice or perceive through the sense of smell*) inhale, scent, sniff. **2** (*to scent or detect*) detect, notice, perceive, scent.
~v.i. **1** (*to suggest, to indicate* (*of*)) indicate, smack (of), suggest. **2** (*to stink*) (*sl.*) hum, (*coll.*) pong, reek, stench, stink.

smile *v.i.* **1** (*to express amusement or pleasure by an instinctive lateral movement of the lips with an upward turn at the corners*) beam, grin, simper, smirk. ANTONYMS: frown, grimace. **2** ((*of the weather, fortune etc.*) *to look favourably* (*on or upon someone*)) favour, help.
~n. (*a cheerful or favourable expression*) beam, grin, simper, smirk. ANTONYMS: scowl.

smirk *v.i.* (*to smile affectedly or smugly*) grimace, grin, leer, simper, smile, sneer.

smoke *n.* **1** (*volatile products of combustion in the form of visible vapour or fine particles escaping from a burning substance*) fog, fumes, gas, mist, smog, vapour. **2** (*a cigarette*) cheroot, cigar, cigarette, pipe, (*coll.*) roll-up.
~v.i. **1** (*to draw into the mouth or inhale and exhale the smoke of tobacco etc.*) draw, exhale, inhale, puff. **2** (*to emit smoke*) fume, smoulder.
~v.t. **1** (*to blacken, flavour etc., with smoke*) blacken, colour, cure, flavour. **2** (*to cleanse* (*a place*) *of infestation, e.g. by insects, with smoke*) cleanse, disinfect, fumigate.

smooth *a.* **1** (*having a continuously even surface, free from roughness*) even, flat, flush, level, plane, regular, unbroken, uniform, unwrinkled. ANTONYMS: uneven. **2** (*not hairy*) bald, bare, clean-shaven, depilated, glabrous, hairless, naked, smooth-shaven, unhaired. **3** ((*of water*) *unruffled*) calm, glassy, mirror-like, peaceful, polished, satiny, serene, shiny, silken, silky, sleek, slick, still, tranquil, undisturbed, unruffled, velvety. **4** ((*of liquids or semi-liquids*) *without lumps*) lump-free, mixed. **5** (*free from obstructions or impediments*) effortless, even, free, orderly, uncluttered, unconstrained, uneventful, unimpeded, uninterrupted, unobstructed, well-ordered. **6** ((*of sound, taste etc.*) *not harsh*) harmonious, mellifluous, silky. **7** ((*of e.g. breathing or movement*) *flowing rhythmically or evenly*) easy, even, flowing, fluent, regular, rhythmic, well-modulated. **8** (*calm, pleasant*) agreeable, believable, calm, credible, equable, mellow, mild, nonchalant, pleasant, polite, soft. ANTONYMS: rough. **9** (*suave, flattering*) bland, conniving, crafty, cunning, eloquent, facile, flattering, foxy, glib, honey-tongued, machiavellian, oily, persuasive, plausible, scheming, shifty, shrewd, silver-tongued, slick, slimy, slippery, sly, smarmy, smooth-spoken, suave, tricky, unctuous, urbane. **10** ((*of wine*) *not harsh-tasting or astringent*) dulcet, mellow, sweet.
~v.t. **1** (*to make smooth, to even* (*out*)) even out, level. **2** (*to flatten* (*lumps or projections out*) *or ease* (*difficulties or problems away*)) buff, burnish, ease, flatten, iron, level, plane, polish, press, sand. **3** (*to free from obstructions,*

irregularities etc.) calm, clear, ease, facilitate, free, lubricate, open, prepare, prime, ready. **4** (*to extenuate, to alleviate*) allay, alleviate, ameliorate, appease, assuage, calm, dispel, extenuate, gloss over, lay, lessen, minimize, mitigate, mollify, pacify, palliate, reduce, soften, soothe, temper.

smother *v.t.* **1** (*to suffocate, to stifle*) asphyxiate, choke, stifle, strangle, suffocate, throttle. **2** (*to keep (a fire) down by covering it with ashes etc.*) damp down, extinguish, put out, snuff out. **3** (*to hide, to conceal (the truth etc.)*) blanket, blank out, check, choke back, conceal, cover up, hide, hold back, keep back, keep secret, mask, muffle, repress, stifle, subdue, suppress. **4** (*to overcome, to overwhelm*) overcome, overwhelm. **5** (*to cover thickly, to enclose*) blanket, cover, enclose, enshroud, envelop, heap, inundate, shower, shroud, surround, wrap.

smoulder *v.i.* **1** (*to burn in a smothered way without flames*) boil, burn, foam, fume, smoke, stew. **2** (*to feel or show strong repressed emotions (such as anger, jealousy)*) boil, chafe, fester, fume, (*coll.*) get all steamed up, rage, see red, seethe, simmer.

smug *a.* (*self-satisfied, complacent*) complacent, conceited, content, holier-than-thou, overconfident, proud, self-important, self-righteous, self-satisfied, vain.

smutty *a.* (*obscene*) bawdy, (*coll.*) blue, coarse, crude, dirty, earthy, filthy, indecent, obscene, pornographic, racy, ribald, risqué, vulgar. ANTONYMS: clean, respectable.

snag *n.* **1** (*an unexpected or concealed difficulty*) catch, complication, difficulty, disadvantage, drawback, hindrance, hitch, impediment, obstacle, obstruction, problem, stricture, stumbling-block. **2** (*a jagged projection, as the stumpy base of a branch left in pruning*) knot, projection, stump. **3** (*a tear, a flaw in fabric*) flaw, pull, rip, tear.
~*v.t.* (*to catch or damage on a snag*) catch, damage, rip, tear.

snap *v.i.* **1** (*to break with a sharp report*) break, crack. **2** (*to close or fit into place suddenly with a sharp click*) click into place, part, pop. **3** ((*of a dog*) *to make a biting movement (at)*) bark, bite, growl, nip. **4** (*to snatch or grasp (at an opportunity, chance etc.)*) grasp, seize, snatch. **5** (*to speak or shout sharply or irritably (at someone)*) shout, speak sharply. **6** (*to collapse (under pressure, strain of work etc.)*) break down, collapse, come apart.
~*v.t.* **1** (*to break (something) with a sharp report*) break, fracture. **2** (*to cause to click (shut, open etc.)*) click open, click shut. **3** (*to cause a*

whip, one's fingers etc.) *to make a sharp crack or report*) click, crack, lash, whip. **4** (*to seize suddenly, to take advantage of eagerly*) capture, get, grab, make off with, (*sl.*) nab, pluck, pounce on, secure, seize, snatch, take.
~*n.* **1** (*the act or an instance or the sound of snapping*) cracking, snapping. **2** (*a crisp ginger-flavoured biscuit*) biscuit, cracker. **3** (*a snapshot*) (*coll.*) click, photo, photograph, shoot, snapshot. **4** (*a sudden spell of severe weather*) interval, period, spell, wave. **5** (*vigour, briskness*) alertness, animation, bounce, briskness, dash, élan, energy, get-up-and-go, go, liveliness, (*coll.*) pep, (*sl.*) pizazz, sparkle, sprightliness, verve, vigour, vitality, (*coll.*) zip. **6** (*an abrupt reply or retort*) crack, lash, retort, riposte.
~*a.* (*done, taken etc., suddenly or on the spur of the moment*) abrupt, hasty, hurried, incautious, instant, instantaneous, not well-thought-out, precipitate, quick, rash, sudden, unplanned, unpremeditated.

snappy *a.* **1** (*snappish*) sharp, snappish. **2** (*irritable, cross*) cross, crusty, grumpy, illtempered, irascible, irritable, peevish, peppery, petulant, testy, touchy, waspish. ANTONYMS: affable, cheerful. **3** (*sharp, lively*) abrupt, brisk, brusque, crisp, curt, lively, quick, rapid, sharp, speedy. **4** (*smart, stylish*) chic, dapper, elegant, fashionable, modish, (*coll.*) natty, smart, stylish, (*coll., sometimes derog.*) trendy, up to date. ANTONYMS: dowdy.

snatch *v.t.* **1** (*to seize suddenly or without permission or ceremony*) abduct, kidnap, seize. **2** (*to steal, grab*) capture, catch, clasp, clutch, grab, grasp, grip, latch on to, lay hold of, pluck, pull, snap up, steal, take, wrest. ANTONYMS: release. **3** (*to remove or rescue (from, away etc.) suddenly or hurriedly*) deliver, remove, rescue, save. **4** (*to win or gain narrowly*) gain, get, lay one's hands on, win.
~*n.* **1** (*an act of snatching, a grab (at)*) catch, grab, grasp, grip. **2** (*that which is snatched; a short spell e.g. of rest, work*) haul, shift, spell, stint. **3** (*a fragment of talk, song etc.*) bit, extract, fragment, morsel, sample, scrap, snippet, specimen. **4** (*a robbery, a kidnapping*) abduction, grab, kidnapping, robbery.

sneak *v.i.* **1** (*to creep (about, away, off etc.), as if afraid or ashamed to be seen*) cower, creep, lurk, pad, prowl, sidle, skulk, slink, slip, steal. **2** (*to tell tales*) (*sl.*) grass (on), inform (on), tell tales.
~*v.t.* (*to steal*) (*sl.*) nab, pilfer, (*coll.*) pinch, steal.
~*n.* (*a person who sneaks*) (*sl.*) grass, informer, (*sl.*) nark, stool-pigeon, tell-tale.

sneer *n.* (*a smile or verbal expression of contempt*) gibe, insult, jeer, scorn, taunt. ANTONYMS: respect.

~*v.i.* **1** (*to show contempt by a smile or laugh*) scoff, show contempt. **2** (*to scoff, to express derision or contempt* (*at*)) deride, disdain, gibe, jeer, mock, put down, scoff, scorn. ANTONYMS: admire.

sniff *v.i.* (*to draw air audibly up the nose in order to smell, clear the nasal passages etc.*) breathe in, inhale, smell, snort, snuff, snuffle.
~*n.* **1** (*an act or the sound of sniffing*) sniffing, snort, snuffle. **2** (*that which is sniffed in* (e.g. *a scent*)) breath, feeling, hint, odour, scent, suggestion, whiff.

snigger *v.i.* (*to laugh in a half-suppressed or discourteous manner*) chuckle, giggle, laugh, smirk, sneer, titter.

snip *v.t.* (*to cut or clip* (*off*) *sharply or quickly with shears or scissors*) clip, crop, cut, dock, lop, nick, prune, slit, trim.
~*n.* **1** (*a cut with scissors or shears*) cut, gash, incision, nick, slash, slit. **2** (*a small piece snipped off*) bit, clipping, cutting, fragment, morsel, piece, remnant, scrap, shred, snippet. **3** (*a bargain*) bargain, certainty, (*coll.*) cinch.

snivel *v.i.* **1** (*to weep with nose running, to be tearful*) blubber, cry, mewl, sob, weep, whimper, whine, (*coll.*) whinge. **2** (*to run at the nose, sniffing continually*) sniff, sniffle, snuffle.
~*n.* **1** (*mucus running from the nose*) mucus, (*sl.*) snot. **2** (*audible or affected weeping*) sniffing, sobbing, whimpering. **3** (*hypocrisy*) cant, hypocrisy, insincerity.

snobbish *a.* (*behaving as if one is better, of a higher social class etc. than other people*) aristocratic, conceited, condescending, disdainful, egotistic, haughty, high and mighty, (*coll.*) highfalutin, hoity-toity, lofty, patronizing, pompous, self-important, self-satisfied, smug, (*coll.*) snooty, (*sl.*) snotty, stuck-up, supercilious, superior, (*sl.*) toffee-nosed, (*coll.*) uppity, vain. ANTONYMS: humble, self-deprecating.

snug *a.* **1** (*sheltered and comfortable*) casual, close, comfortable, (*coll.*) comfy, easy, friendly, homely, intimate, protected, relaxing, restful, safe, sheltered. ANTONYMS: exposed. **2** (*cosy, comfortable*) comforting, cosy, warm. **3** (*compact, trim, well secured*) close-fitting, compact, neat, secure, small, tight, trim. **4** (*not exposed to view*) concealed, private, secluded.

snuggle *v.i.* (*to move or lie close* (*up to*) *for warmth*) lie close, nestle.
~*v.t.* (*to draw close to one*) cuddle, curl up, draw close, nestle, nuzzle.

soak *v.t.* **1** (*to put* (*something*) *in liquid to become permeated*) immerse, saturate, souse,

steep. **2** (*to wet thoroughly*) bathe, damp, douse, drench, inundate, moisten, wet. ANTONYMS: dry. **3** (*to suck* (*in or up*), *to absorb* (*liquid*)) absorb, assimilate, sponge up, suck in, suck up. **4** (*coll.*) (*to tax heavily*) overcharge, overtax.
~*v.i.* **1** (*to lie in liquid so as to become permeated*) immerse, saturate, souse, steep. **2** (*to permeate* (*into, through etc.*)) infuse, penetrate, permeate. **3** (*coll.*) (*to drink excessively*) (*coll.*) booze, (*sl.*) hit the bottle, tipple.
~*n.* (*a heavy drinker*) alcoholic, (*coll.*) boozer, dipsomaniac, drinker, drunk, drunkard, sot, (*sl.*) souse, (*coll.*) sponge, tippler, toper.

soar *v.i.* **1** (*to fly into the air, to rise*) ascend, climb, fly, rise, rocket, shoot up, skyrocket, spiral. ANTONYMS: descend, sink. **2** (*of a bird, aircraft etc.*) *to sail, float at a great height*) float, hang, hover, sail. **3** (*to rise intellectually or in spirit, status etc.*) climb, mount, rise. **4** (*to increase or rise rapidly in amount, degree etc.*) balloon, escalate, increase, rise.

sob *v.i.* **1** (*to weep violently, catching one's breath in a convulsive manner*) bawl, blubber, cry, howl, mewl, moan, pule, shed tears, snivel, wail, weep, whimper, yowl. ANTONYMS: laugh. **2** (*to gasp convulsively from physical exhaustion or distress*) gasp, sniff, snuffle.
~*v.t.* (*to say with a sob or sobs*) moan, stammer out, wail, weep.
~*n.* (*a convulsive catching of the breath, as in weeping*) catch, cry, howl, wail, whimper.

sober *a.* **1** (*not drunk; temperate in the use of alcoholic liquors etc.*) abstemious, abstinent, (*coll.*) straight, teetotal, temperate, (*coll.*) with it. ANTONYMS: drunk. **2** (*well-balanced, sane*) balanced, clear-headed, level-headed, moderate, rational, reasonable, sane, well-balanced. **3** (*self-possessed, calm*) calm, composed, cool, dignified, dispassionate, earnest, grave, sedate, self-possessed, serene, serious, solemn, sombre, staid, steady, tranquil, unexcited, unflustered, unperturbed, unruffled. **4** ((*of a view, facts, the truth etc.*) *objective, not exaggerated*) dispassionate, impartial, neutral, objective, unbiased, unexaggerated. **5** ((*of colours etc.*) *subdued, quiet*) cold, colourless, drab, dreary, neutral, plain, quiet, repressed, simple, sound, subdued.
~*v.t., v.i.* (*to make or become calm or grave*) calm, cool down, quieten.

sociable *a.* **1** (*fit or inclined to associate or be friendly, companionable*) accessible, affable, amiable, amicable, approachable, (*coll.*) chummy, communicative, companionable, congenial, convivial, cordial, extrovert, friendly, genial, gregarious, neighbourly, outgoing, social, warm. ANTONYMS: unsociable. **2** ((*of a* party etc.) *of a friendly, not formal, character)* casual, easygoing, informal, relaxed. ANTONYMS: formal, stiff.

social *a.* **1** (*living in communities, tending to associate with others*) associative, communal, community, gregarious, group, societal. **2** (*practising the division of labour, cooperative*) collective, cooperative. **3** (*of or relating to the social services*) civic, civil, public. **4** (*sociable, companionable*) affable, amiable, companionable, convivial, friendly, genial, gregarious, sociable. ANTONYMS: reserved, unfriendly.
~*n.* (*a social gathering*) gathering, (*coll.*) get-together, party.

society *n.* **1** (*the general body of persons or nations constituting the human race regarded as a community*) civilization, community, humanity, human race, mankind, people, public, world. **2** (*social organization*) culture, system. **3** (*the privileged and fashionable classes of a community or some subdivision*) aristocracy, elite, gentry, high society, nobility, polite society, upper classes, (*coll.*) upper crust. ANTONYMS: working class. **4** (*a club or an association*) alliance, association, body, brotherhood, circle, club, fraternity, group, guild, institute, league, organization, sisterhood, sorority, union. **5** (*the company of other people, companionship*) camaraderie, companionship, company, fellowship, friendship, intercourse.

soft *a.* **1** (*yielding easily to pressure, easily moulded or worked*) elastic, flexible, malleable, mushy, plastic, pliable, pliant, pulpy, spongy, squashable, squashy, squeezeable, supple. ANTONYMS: hard. **2** (*smooth to the touch*) downy, feathery, fleecy, fluffy, furry, fuzzy, satiny, silken, smooth, velvety. ANTONYMS: coarse, rough. **3** (*not loud or harsh*) faint, light, low, melodious, quiet. **4** (*affecting the senses in a mild or delicate manner*) bland, delicate, dulcet, gentle, mellifluous, mellow, mild, moderate, softened, soothing, sweet, temperate. ANTONYMS: harsh. **5** ((*of a day, a breeze etc.*) *balmy, gentle*) balmy, clement, fair, gentle, halcyon, lazy, pleasant, relaxing, restful, springlike, summery, tranquil. **6 a** ((*of light colours*) *not brilliant, not glaring*) delicate, diffuse, muted, pale, pastel, soothing, subdued, toned down. **b** ((*of an image*) *blurred*) blurred, blurry, dim, foggy, fuzzy, woolly. **7** ((*of a drug*) *relatively harmless or non-addictive*) harmless, non-addictive. ANTONYMS: hard. **8** ((*of pornography*) *titillating but not explicit*) inexplicit. ANTONYMS: hardcore. **9** ((*of prices etc.*) *likely to drop*) declining, depressed, slow, unprofitable. **10** (*gentle or mild in disposition, yielding*) conciliatory,

gentle, mild, yielding. **11** (*impressionable, sympathetic*) benign, compassionate, impressionable, indulgent, kind, merciful, sensitive, sympathetic. **12** (*easily imposed on, lenient*) docile, easygoing, lax, lenient, liberal, permissive, tolerant. ANTONYMS: severe, unforgiving. **13** (*weak, effeminate*) deferential, delicate, effeminate, effete, feeble, frail, namby-pamby, puny, sissy, submissive, tame, timorous, unmanful, unmanly, weak. **14** (*silly, simple*) daft, foolish, silly, simple. **15** (*amorous, sentimental*) amorous, sentimental, soft-hearted, tender-hearted. **16** (*out of condition, pampered*) cosseted, flabby, flaccid, non-physical, out of training, pampered, unfit. **17** ((*of a job*) *easy*) comfortable, (*coll.*) cushy, easy, luxurious, opulent, pampered, plush, (*coll.*) posh, rich, (*coll.*) ritzy, (*coll.*) swanky, undemanding.

soften *v.t.* **1** (*to make soft or softer*) make soft, melt. **2** (*to palliate, to tone down*) abate, allay, appease, assuage, calm, cushion, deaden, diminish, ease, lessen, lighten, mellow, mitigate, moderate, mollify, muffle, mute, pacify, palliate, quell, quieten, relieve, soothe, subdue, temper, tone down.

soil[1] *n.* **1** (*the ground, esp. the top stratum of the earth's crust*) clay, dirt, earth, ground, loam. **2** (*territory, region*) country, land, region, territory.

soil[2] *v.t.* **1** (*to make dirty*) begrime, besmirch, blot, dirty, mark, spot, stain. **2** (*to tarnish, to pollute*) befoul, blacken, contaminate, defile, disgrace, foul, muddy, pollute, smear, sully, taint, tarnish.
~*n.* **1** (*a dirty spot or defilement*) contamination, defilement, smear, spot, stain, taint. **2** (*any foul matter, filth*) dirt, dregs, dung, dust, excrement, filth, mire, muck, mud, refuse, sludge, waste.

solace *n.* (*comfort in grief, trouble etc.*) balm, comfort, compensation, condolence, consolation, reassurance, relief.
~*v.t.* **1** (*to comfort or console in trouble etc.*) cheer, comfort, condole, console. ANTONYMS: distress. **2** (*to alleviate, to allay*) allay, alleviate, ameliorate, assuage, mitigate, reassure, relieve, soothe.

soldier *n.* **1** (*a person engaged in military service, esp. a private or non-commissioned officer*) enlisted man, enlisted woman, fighter, foot soldier, (*N Am., coll.*) GI, infantryman, man-at-arms, military man, military woman, private, recruit, serviceman, servicewoman, Tommy, trooper, warrior. **2** (*a person of military skill or experience, esp. a tried and successful commander*) commander, officer. **3** (*a*

person who works diligently for a cause) fighter, hard worker, militant, stalwart, supporter.
~*v.i.* (*to serve as a soldier*) campaign, serve.

sole *a.* **1** (*single, only*) alone, exclusive, individual, lone, one, only, particular, personal, single, unique. ANTONYMS: numerous. **2†** (*solitary, alone*) alone, by oneself, on one's own, solitary.

solemn *a.* **1** (*performed with or accompanied by ceremonies or due formality*) ceremonial, ceremonious, devotional, formal, holy, religious, ritual, sacred. ANTONYMS: informal, profane. **2** (*awe-inspiring, impressive*) august, awe-inspiring, dignified, grand, imposing, impressive, majestic, stately. **3** (*serious, momentous*) grave, momentous, sedate, serious. **4** (*formal, pompous*) affected, earnest, formal, grave, pompous, self-important, sincere, sober, staid. **5** (*dull, sombre*) dull, gloomy, glum, sombre. ANTONYMS: carefree, frivolous.

solicit *v.t.* **1** (*to make earnest or importunate requests for*) ask, beg, crave, request, seek. **2** (*to make earnest or persistent requests or appeals to*) accost, appeal to, approach, beseech, call upon, canvass, entreat, implore, importune, petition, pray to, supplicate. **3** (*to entice or incite (someone) to do something illegal or immoral*) entice, (*sl.*) hustle, incite, lure, urge. **4** ((*of a prostitute*) *openly to offer sexual relations to in exchange for money*) approach, proposition.
~*v.i.* **1** (*to make earnest or importunate appeals*) appeal, ask (for), beg, request. **2** ((*of a prostitute*) *to proposition someone as a potential client*) approach, proposition.

solid *a.* **1** (*firm, unyielding*) concrete, congealed, firm, frozen, rigid, set, solidified, stable, unshakeable, unyielding. **2** (*composed of particles closely cohering; not hollow*) (*coll.*) chock-a-block, chock-full, compact, compressed, concentrated, congested, crammed, crowded, dense, filled, firm, hard, jammed, jam-packed, packed, swarming, teeming. **3** (*uniform, the same throughout*) complete, consistent, continuous, entire, homogeneous, pure, unalloyed, unbroken, undivided, uniform, uninterrupted, unmixed, whole. **4** (*substantial, not flimsy*) cogent, durable, forceful, powerful, rugged, sound, steady, stout, strong, sturdy, substantial, tough, weighty, well-built, well-constructed, well-made. **5** (*of or in three dimensions*) cubic, prismatic, three-dimensional. **6** (*reliable, well-grounded*) authentic, decent, dependable, genuine, level-headed, logical, real, reasonable, regular, reliable, sensible, sober, stalwart, steadfast, steady, straight, sure, true, trustworthy, trusty, upright, valid, well-grounded, worthy.

solidify *v.t., v.i.* (*to make or become solid*) cake, clot, coagulate, compact, compress, congeal, consolidate, crystallize, draw together, freeze, gel, harden, jell, make solid, pull together, set, thicken, unify, unite. ANTONYMS: melt.

solitary *a.* **1** (*living or being alone*) alone, lonely, lonesome, separate. **2** (*passed or spent alone*) cloistered, companionless, friendless, hermitical, reclusive, solo, unsociable, unsocial. **3** ((*of a place*) *unfrequented, secluded*) cut off, deserted, desolate, distant, isolated, out-of-the-way, private, remote, secluded, sequestered, unfrequented, withdrawn. **4** (*single, individual*) individual, lone, one, only, single, sole.

solitude *n.* **1** (*seclusion, loneliness*) aloneness, isolation, loneliness, privacy, remoteness, retirement, seclusion, solitariness. ANTONYMS: society. **2** (*somewhere isolated and empty of people*) desert, emptiness, wilderness.

solo *a., adv.* (*unaccompanied, alone*) alone, individual, solitary, unaccompanied.

solution *n.* **1** (*the resolution or act or process of solving a problem, difficulty etc.*) conclusion, denouement, outcome, resolution, result, settlement, settling, solving. **2** (*the correct answer to a problem, puzzle etc. or the means of solving it*) answer, clarification, deciphering, discovery, elucidation, explanation, explication, figuring out, finding out, key, revelation, unravelling, working out. ANTONYMS: problem. **3** (*the liquefaction of a solid or gaseous body by mixture with a liquid*) dissolution, dissolving, liquefaction. **4** (*the liquid combination so produced*) blend, emulsion, suspension.

solve *v.t.* (*to resolve or find an answer to (a problem etc.*)) answer, clear up, crack, decipher, disentangle, elucidate, explain, explicate, fathom, interpret, make clear, make plain, put an end to, resolve, settle, unfold, unravel, untangle, work out. ANTONYMS: complicate, obscure.

sombre *a.* **1** (*dark, gloomy*) black, bleak, dark, darkling, dim, dingy, dismal, drab, dull, dusky, foreboding, gloomy, grey, leaden, murky, overcast, shadowy. **2** (*solemn, melancholy*) cheerless, depressed, depressing, dismal, doleful, dolorous, dreary, funereal, gloomy, joyless, lowering, melancholy, morbid, morose, mournful, sad, serious, solemn, unhappy. ANTONYMS: cheerful, jolly. **3** (*grave, worrying*) grave, grim, grim-faced, grim-visaged, sober, worrying.

somebody *pron.* (*some person*) one, someone, some person.
~*n.* (*a person of consequence*) (*sl.*) big cheese, (*sl.*) big gun, (*coll.*) big noise, (*coll.*) big-timer,

(*N Am., coll.*) big wheel, (*coll.*) bigwig, celebrity, dignitary, (*esp. N Am., coll.*) hotshot, household name, luminary, notable, personage, public figure, star, superstar, VIP. ANTONYMS: nobody.

sometimes *adv.* (*occasionally, now and then*) at times, every so often, from time to time, now and again, now and then, occasionally, off and on, on and off, once in a while, on occasion, periodically. ANTONYMS: never.

song *n.* **1** (*a short poem intended or suitable for singing, esp. one set to music*) lyric, ode, sonnet. **2** (*a musical composition accompanied by words for singing*) air, anthem, ballad, carol, composition, ditty, hymn, lay, melody, number, psalm, tune. **3** (*a melodious utterance, as the musical cry of a bird*) chirrup, cry. **4** (*poetry*) poems, poetry, verse.

soon *adv.* **1** (*in a short time from now*) anon, any minute now, any time now, at the double, before long, before you know it, directly, early, ere long, forthwith, (*coll.*) in a jiffy, in a minute, in a second, in a short time, in the near future, momentarily, presently, (*coll.*) pronto, quickly, shortly, speedily, straight away, without delay. ANTONYMS: later. **2** (*readily, willingly*) gladly, happily, †lief, quickly, readily, willingly.

soothe *v.t.* **1** (*to calm, to tranquillize*) calm, compose, pacify, quiet, relax, tranquillize. **2** (*to mitigate, to assuage*) allay, alleviate, appease, assuage, comfort, ease, mitigate, moderate, palliate, relieve, soften, temper. ANTONYMS: distress, irritate. **3** (*to gratify*) flatter, gratify, humour, mollify.

sophisticated *a.* **1** (*worldly-wise; refined*) (*coll.*) cool, cosmopolitan, cultivated, cultured, educated, elegant, experienced, jet-set, knowledgeable, polished, refined, seasoned, self-assured, soigné, suave, urbane, worldly-wise. ANTONYMS: raw, uncouth, uncultured. **2** (*complex, highly developed*) advanced, complex, complicated, elaborate, highly developed, intricate, multifaceted. ANTONYMS: primitive, unsophisticated.

sorcery *n.* (*magic, witchcraft*) black art, black magic, charm, diabolism, enchantment, magic, necromancy, shamanism, spell-making, white magic, witchcraft, wizardry.

sordid *a.* **1** (*foul, dirty*) defiled, deteriorated, dingy, dirty, fetid, filthy, flyblown, foul, hovel-like, insanitary, mucky, polluted, poor, putrid, ramshackle, seamy, seedy, shabby, sleazy, slimy, squalid, tumbledown, unclean, unsanitary, untidy. **2** (*mean, ignoble*) abased, base, corrupt, debased, degraded, despicable,

disgraceful, dishonourable, disreputable, execrable, ignoble, ignominious, low, mean, rotten, scurvy, shameful, vile. ANTONYMS: honourable, respectable. **3** (*avaricious, niggardly*) avaricious, grasping, greedy, mercenary, miserly, money-grubbing, niggardly, parsimonious, rapacious, selfish, stingy, ungenerous, venal. ANTONYMS: generous, unselfish.

sore *a.* **1** ((*of a part of the body*) *tender and painful to the touch*) agonizing, angry, bitter, burning, chafing, fierce, hurt, hurting, inflamed, injured, painful, raw, smarting, stinging, tender. **2** (*mentally distressed, vexed* (*at*)) aggrieved, distressed, irked, (*sl.*) peeved, upset, vexed. ANTONYMS: pleased. **3** (*coll.*) (*annoyed*) angered, angry, annoyed, bitter, cross, irritated, resentful. **4** (*causing annoyance or distress, exasperating*) afflictive, annoying, burdensome, distressing, exasperating, harrowing, heavy, irksome, irritating, onerous, oppressive, thorny, ticklish, troublesome. **5** (*grievous, grave*) acute, critical, desperate, dire, extreme, grave, grievous, pressing, severe, sharp, urgent. **6** (*easily annoyed; touchy*) delicate, prickly, sensitive, tender, touchy.
~†*adv.* (*severely, intensely*) grievously, intensely, severely, sorely.
~*n.* (*a sore place on the body where the surface is broken or inflamed by a boil, ulcer etc.*) abrasion, abscess, boil, bruise, burn, canker, cut, damage, gathering, infection, inflammation, injury, laceration, rawness, scrape, swelling, ulcer, wound.

sorrow *n.* **1** (*mental pain or distress from loss, disappointment etc.*) agony, anguish, desolation, disappointment, distress, dolour, grief, heartache, heartbreak, misery, pain, sadness, torment, unhappiness, woe, wretchedness. ANTONYMS: happiness, joy. **2** (*an event, thing or person causing this, a misfortune*) adversity, affliction, bad luck, cares, hardship, misfortune, pressure, strain, suffering, travail, trial, tribulation, trouble, worry. **3** (*mourning, lamentation*) lamentation, mourning, regret.
~*v.i.* **1** (*to grieve*) agonize, grieve, weep. ANTONYMS: rejoice. **2** (*to lament*) bemoan, bewail, despair, keen, lament, moan, mourn, regret.

sorrowful *a.* (*very sad*) (*coll.*) blue, brokenhearted, crestfallen, dejected, depressed, disconsolate, doleful, downcast, (*coll.*) down in the mouth, gloomy, grief-stricken, heartbroken, heartsick, heavy-hearted, melancholy, miserable, mournful, piteous, regretful, rueful, sad, sorry, tearful, unhappy, weeping, woeful, wretched. ANTONYMS: happy, joyful.

sorry *a.* **1** (*penitent, apologetic*) apologetic,

conscience-stricken, contrite, guilt-ridden, penitent, remorseful, repentant, shamefaced, sheepish. ANTONYMS: impenitent, unabashed. **2** (*feeling or showing grief, regretful* (*that*)) distressed, grieving, regretful, sad, sorrowful, unhappy. ANTONYMS: happy. **3** (*feeling pity* (*for*)) moved, pitying, sympathetic. **4** (*paltry, pitiful*) abject, base, deplorable, depressing, despicable, dismal, grim, ill-starred, mean, miserable, paltry, pathetic, piteous, pitiable, pitiful, poor, shabby, sordid, stark, wretched.

sort *n.* **1** (*a group of instances of a certain thing identifiable, by having the same set of characteristics, a kind*) brand, breed, category, character, class, denomination, description, family, genus, group, ilk, kind, make, manner, nature, order, phylum, race, species, stock, strain, style, subdivision, subgroup, type, variety. **2** (*a more or less adequate example or instance of a kind*) case, example, instance. **3** (*a person, a type* (*of person*)) individual, lot, person, thing, type.
~*v.t.* **1** (*to separate into sorts, classes etc.*) arrange, assort, catalogue, categorize, characterize, choose, class, classify, combine, describe, divide, file, grade, group, merge, mould, order, organize, rank, select, separate, sort out, systematize, type. ANTONYMS: confuse, muddle. **2** (*esp. Sc.*) (*to fix or punish*) deal with, fix, punish, resolve, sort out.

soul *n.* **1** (*the spiritual part of a person*) psyche, spirit. **2** (*the moral and emotional part of a person*) emotion, feeling, morality, sentiment. **3** (*the rational part of a person*) consciousness, intellect, mind, rationality. **4** (*the essential or animating force or principle, the energy in anything*) anima, animation, ardour, dynamism, energy, fervour, force, inspiration, life, vitality, vivacity, warmth. **5** (*a person regarded as providing this, a leader*) centre, driving force, leader, moving spirit. **6** (*spirit, courage*) courage, nobility, sincerity, spirit. **7** (*a disembodied spirit*) ghost, spectre, spirit. **8** (*a human being, a person*) being, body, creature, human being, individual, man, mortal, person, woman. **9** (*an embodiment or exemplification*) embodiment, epitome, essence, exemplification, incarnation, personification, quintessence, typification.

sound[1] *n.* **1** (*the sensation produced through the organs of hearing*) hearing. **2** (*that which causes this sensation, the vibrations affecting the ear*) cacophony, din, noise, racket, report. ANTONYMS: quiet, silence. **3** (*vibration*) oscillation, resonance, resounding, reverberation, vibration. **4** (*a specific tone or note*) note, ring, timbre, tone. **5** (*an articulate utterance corresponding to a particular vowel or consonant*) phoneme, utterance. **6** (*an impression given by words*) aspect, characteristic, effect, impression, look, quality. **7** (*mere talk*) chatter, hearsay, rumour, talk. **8** (*hearing distance, earshot*) earshot, hearing, range.
~*v.i.* **1** (*to convey a particular impression by sound or word*) appear, look, resemble, seem. **2** (*to resonate*) echo, resonate, resound, reverberate, ring.
~*v.t.* **1** (*to utter* (*a letter etc.*) *audibly*) articulate, cry, enunciate, pronounce, shout, utter, vocalize, voice, yell. **2** (*to make known, to proclaim*) announce, declare, make known, proclaim.

sound[2] *a.* **1** (*free from injury, defect or decay*) flawless, in good condition, in good shape, intact, perfect, unbroken, undamaged, unhurt, unimpaired, uninjured, unmarred, unscathed, whole. ANTONYMS: faulty. **2** (*not diseased or impaired*) blooming, fit, hale, healthy, hearty, robust, rosy, ruddy, undiseased, unimpaired, vigorous, wholesome. **3** (*well-grounded, wise*) well-established, well-grounded, wise. **4** (*orthodox*) accepted, established, orthodox, traditional, true. **5** (*based on truth or reason*) balanced, commonsensical, correct, fair, good, judicious, level-headed, logical, lucid, normal, perceptive, politic, practical, proper, prudent, rational, reasonable, responsible, right, sane, sensible, true, valid. **6** (*thorough, complete*) complete, good, thorough. **7** (*stable, firm*) durable, firm, rugged, safe, secure, solid, stable, strong, sturdy, substantial, tough, well-built, well-constructed. **8** (*trustworthy, honest*) dependable, honest, reliable, trustworthy. ANTONYMS: unreliable. **9** (*solvent*) non-speculative, profitable, riskless, solvent. **10** ((*of sleep*) *deep, unbroken*) deep, peaceful, restful, unbroken, undisturbed, uninterrupted, untroubled.

sound[3] *v.t.* **1** (*to measure the depth of* (*a sea, channel etc.*) *or test the quality of* (*its bed*) *with a sounding line*) fathom, measure, plumb, test. **2** (*to find the depth of water in* (*the hold of a ship*)) fathom, measure, plumb. **3** (*to test or examine by means of a probe etc.*) canvass, check, examine, inquire into, investigate, poll, probe, question, survey.
~*v.i.* **1** (*to take soundings, to ascertain the depth of water*) fathom, plumb, take soundings. **2** ((*of a whale etc.*) *to dive deeply*) dive, plunge, submerge.

sound[4] *n.* (*a narrow passage of water, such as a strait connecting two seas*) bay, bight, channel, cove, fjord, inlet, loch, narrow, passage, strait.

sour *a.* **1** (*sharp or acid to the taste, tart*) acerbic, acid, acidic, acidulous, bitter, lemony, pungent, sharp, tart, vinegary. **2** (*tasting sharp through fermentation, rancid*) bad, curdled,

fermented, off, rancid, spoiled, spoilt, turned. ANTONYMS: sweet. **3** (*bad-tempered, morose*) bad-tempered, brusque, caustic, churlish, (*coll.*) crabby, (*esp. N Am.*) cranky, cross, crusty, curmudgeonly, curt, embittered, grouchy, ill-tempered, nasty, peevish, petulant, snappy, sullen, surly, testy, touchy, waspish. ANTONYMS: genial, good-humoured. **4** (*disagreeable, inharmonious*) acrimonious, disagreeable, distasteful, inharmonious, jarring, offensive, terrible, unpleasant.
~*v.t.* **1** (*to cause to have a sour taste*) acidify, curdle, ferment, go bad, go off, sharpen, spoil, turn. **2** (*to cause* (*a relationship*) *to become unfriendly*) disenchant, disillusion, embitter, exasperate, (*coll.*) peeve, vex.

source *n.* **1** (*the spring or fountainhead from which a stream of water proceeds; cause*) cause, fountainhead, rise, spring, wellspring. **2** (*an origin, a beginning*) beginning, commencement, derivation, inception, origin, outset, root, start. **3** (*a person who or something that initiates or creates something*) author, creator, initiator, originator. **4** (*a person or thing that provides inspiration or information*) authority, documentation, (*coll.*) horse's mouth, informer, inspiration, inspirer.

sovereign *a.* **1** (*supreme*) all-powerful, chief, dominant, foremost, governing, greatest, highest, leading, paramount, predominant, pre-eminent, principal, ranking, regnant, reigning, ruling, superior, supreme. **2** (*royal*) aristocratic, imperial, kingly, lordly, majestic, noble, queenly, regal, royal. **3** ((*of a remedy*) *effectual*) effective, effectual, efficacious, excellent. **4** (*utter, absolute*) absolute, unlimited, utter.
~*n.* (*a supreme ruler, a monarch*) autocrat, chief, emperor, empress, king, lord, master, mistress, monarch, potentate, prince, princess, queen, ruler, shah, sheik, sultan, supremo, tsar, tsarina. ANTONYMS: subject, underling.

sow *v.t.* **1** (*to scatter seed over* (*ground etc.*)) plant, seed. ANTONYMS: harvest, reap. **2** (*to scatter over, to cover thickly with*) cover, scatter, strew. **3** (*to disseminate, to spread*) broadcast, disseminate, propagate, spread.
~*v.i.* (*to scatter seed for growth*) plant, seed.

space *n.* **1** (*continuous extension in three dimensions or any quantity or portion of this*) area, distance, expanse, extension, latitude, margin, range, scope, spaciousness, span, volume. **2** (*the universe beyond the earth's atmosphere, outer space*) cosmos, infinity, outer space, sky, universe. **3** (*an interval between points etc.*) blank, break, elbow room, gap, interruption, interval, latitude, leeway, play. **4** (*emptiness*) emptiness, vacancy.

5 (*room*) capacity, room, volume. **6** (*an unoccupied seat*) berth, place, room, seat. **7** (*an interval of time*) duration, extent, hiatus, intermission, interval, lapse, pause, period, span, spell, stretch, time, wait, while. **8** (*advertising slots in newspapers etc., or on radio or television*) slot, window. **9** (*an area sold or rented as business premises*) accommodation, premises.
~*v.t.* (*to set so that there will be spaces between*) align, arrange, array, lay out, measure, order, organize, range, rank, set out, spread out.

spacious *a.* **1** (*having ample room*) ample, copious, generous, plentiful. **2** (*roomy, extensive*) big, broad, capacious, commodious, enormous, expansive, extensive, great, huge, immense, large, outsized, oversize, roomy, sizeable, vast, voluminous, wide. ANTONYMS: small.

span *n.* **1** (*the space from end to end of a bridge etc.*) course, distance, extent, interval, stretch. **2** (*an entire stretch of distance or time*) distance, duration, interval, lifespan, lifetime, period, reach, spell, spread, stretch, term, time.
~*v.t.* **1** ((*of a bridge etc.*) *to extend from side to side of* (*a river etc.*)) bridge, extend from, reach across. **2** ((*of an engineer etc.*) *to build a bridge across* (*a river etc.*)) bridge, cross, extend across, reach across, stretch over, traverse. **3** (*to cover* (*a range, a period of time*)) cover, encompass, extend across.

spank *v.t.* (*to strike with the open hand, to slap, esp. on the buttocks*) beat, (*coll.*) give a good hiding to, put over one's knee, slap, smack, strike, (*coll.*) tan (someone's) hide, thrash, (*coll.*) wallop, whack.
~*n.* (*a resounding blow with the open hand, a slap, esp. on the buttocks*) beating, blow, (*coll.*) hiding, slap, smack, (*coll.*) tanning, thrashing, (*coll.*) wallop, whack.

spare *a.* **1** (*not needed for routine purposes, able to be spared*) additional, extra, leftover, leisure, not needed, odd, over, superfluous, supernumerary, surplus. **2** (*available for use in emergency etc.*) auxiliary, (*coll.*) backup, emergency, kept in reserve, supplementary. **3** (*unoccupied, not in use*) free, not in use, unoccupied, unwanted. **4** ((*of someone's figure*) *thin, lean*) cadaverous, gangling, gaunt, lanky, lean, meagre, raw-boned, scrawny, skin and bone, skinny, slender, slim, thin, wiry. ANTONYMS: plump. **5** ((*of style*) *concise, not wasting words*) brief, concise, precise, succinct, terse. **6** ((*of diet etc.*) *meagre, frugal*) frugal, meagre, modest, scanty, skimpy, small, sparing, sparse. ANTONYMS: ample.

~*v.t.* **1** (*to be able to afford*) afford, allow, bestow, donate, give, let go, let have, part with, relinquish, yield. ANTONYMS: keep. **2** (*to dispense with or do without*) avoid, dispense with, do without, forgo, forsake, give up, manage without, sacrifice, surrender. **3** (*to relieve, to release*) protect, release, relieve, save. **4** (*to refrain from punishing, destroying etc.*) be merciful, deliver, free, have mercy on, let go, let off, liberate, pardon, redeem, rescue, save, show lenience to. ANTONYMS: punish. **5** (*to refrain from inflicting*) hold back, refrain from, withhold. **6** (*to use frugally*) economize on, husband, use frugally.

~*n.* (*that which is surplus to immediate requirements and available for use*) addition, copy, duplicate, extra, supplement.

sparing *a.* **1** (*using only a very small quantity*) careful, chary, cheap, close, close-fisted, economical, frugal, mean, (*coll.*) mingy, miserly, niggardly, parsimonious, penny-pinching, penurious, prudent, saving, stingy, thrifty, (*coll.*) tight, tight-fisted. ANTONYMS: profligate. **2** (*little, meagre*) inappreciable, insignificant, limited, little, meagre, not much, scant, sparse.

spark *n.* **1** (*an incandescent particle thrown off from a burning substance, or produced from a match etc.*) flash, flicker, gleam, glimmer, glint, incandescence, scintilla, sparkle. **2** (*a trace, a hint* (*of kindled interest etc.*)) atom, hint, iota, jot, soupçon, suggestion, trace, vestige, whit. **3** (*a vivacious and witty person*) pundit, wag, wit. **4** (*a brilliant point, facet etc.*) facet, gleam, point, speck.

~*v.t.* (*to cause or start*) activate, animate, electrify, energize, excite, galvanize, ignite, initiate, inspire, kindle, precipitate, provoke, set in motion, set off, start, stimulate, stir, touch off, trigger.

sparkle *n.* **1** (*a gleam, glitter*) brightness, brilliance, coruscation, dazzle, flash, flicker, gleam, glimmer, glint, glitter, radiance, scintillation, shine, spark, twinkle. ANTONYMS: dullness. **2** (*vivacity, wit*) animation, brightness, cheer, cheerfulness, dash, effervescence, élan, energy, excitement, fire, get-up-and-go, life, liveliness, (*sl.*) oomph, (*sl.*) pizazz, spirit, vigour, (*coll.*) vim, vivacity, wit, wittiness, zeal, zing, (*coll.*) zip. **3** (*effervescence*) effervescence, fizz.

~*v.i.* **1** (*to emit sparks*) spark. **2** (*to glisten, to twinkle*) beam, blaze, blink, burn, coruscate, flame, flash, flicker, gleam, glimmer, glint, glisten, glitter, scintillate, shimmer, shine, twinkle, wink. **3** ((*of some wines, mineral waters etc.*) *to emit carbon dioxide in little bubbles*) bubble, effervesce, fizz. **4** (*to be vivacious or witty*) be bubbly, be lively, be vivacious, scintillate, shine.

sparse *a.* (*thinly scattered, not dense*) dispersed, few, inappreciable, in short supply, insignificant, limited, little, meagre, not much, occasional, scant, scanty, scarce, scattered, sparing, spread out, thin, thinly scattered. ANTONYMS: dense, plentiful.

Spartan *a.* **1** (*hardy, strict etc.*) brave, courageous, fearless, hard, hardy, heroic, intrepid, valiant. ANTONYMS: cowardly, timorous. **2** (*austere, rigorous*) abstemious, abstinent, ascetic, austere, controlled, disciplined, frugal, harsh, rigid, rigorous, self-denying, severe, stern, strict, stringent. ANTONYMS: indulgent, soft.

spasm *n.* **1** (*a convulsive and involuntary muscular contraction*) attack, contraction, convulsion, cramp, fit, paroxysm, seizure, throe, tic, twitch. **2** (*a sudden or convulsive act, movement etc.*) convulsion. **3** (*a burst of emotion or effort*) burst, eruption, outburst.

spasmodic *a.* **1** (*caused or affected by a spasm or spasms*) convulsive, paroxysmal, spasmodical. **2** (*happening at irregular intervals*) arrhythmic, broken, cyclical, discontinuous, erratic, fitful, impulsive, intermittent, interrupted, irregular, jerking, jerky, occasional, periodic, pulsating, random, sporadic, sudden, unpredictable, unsustained. ANTONYMS: regular.

spatter *v.t.* **1** (*to scatter or splash* (*water etc.*) *about*) bespatter, scatter about, splash about, splatter, strew. **2** (*to sprinkle or splash* (*someone etc.*) *with water, mud etc.*) shower, spot, spray, sprinkle. **3** (*to slander, to defame*) defame, disparage, slander, smear, vilify.

~*v.i.* **1** (*to sprinkle drops about*) bespatter, splatter, spray, sprinkle. **2** (*to be scattered about in drops*) scatter about, strew.

~*n.* (*a shower, a sprinkling*) pattering, scattering, shower, sprinkling.

speak *v.i.* **1** (*to utter articulate sounds or words in the ordinary tone as distinct from singing*) articulate, enunciate, pronounce, say, state, tell, utter, voice. **2** (*to talk, to converse*) chat, converse, discuss, talk. **3** (*to deliver a speech or address*) address, deliver a speech, discourse, harangue, hold forth, lecture. **4** (*to communicate by other means*) betoken, communicate, convey, indicate, signify, symbolize.

~*v.t.* **1** (*to utter articulately*) articulate, enunciate, pronounce, say, state, tell, utter, voice. **2** (*to declare* (*one's thoughts, opinions etc.*)) affirm, communicate, declare, make known, proclaim, say, state, tell. **3** (*to talk or converse in* (*a language*)) converse in, express oneself in, get by in, have, talk. **4** ((*of behaviour*) *to reveal* (*someone*) *as*) prove, reveal.

special *a.* **1** (*exceptionally good or important*) good, important, memorable, momentous, red-letter, remarkable, significant. **2** (*particular, not ordinary or general*) definite, different, distinct, distinctive, distinguished, especial, exceptional, express, extraordinary, individual, noteworthy, out of the ordinary, particular, peculiar, precise, rare, singular, specialized, specific, uncommon, unique, unusual, weird. ANTONYMS: ordinary. **3** (*close, intimate*) best, bosom, close, dear, devoted, esteemed, faithful, good, intimate, loyal, particular, staunch, steadfast, valued. **4** (*additional, extra*) additional, auxiliary, extra, supplementary.

specialist *n.* (*a person who is trained in a particular branch of a profession etc.*) adept, artist, artiste, authority, connoisseur, consultant, expert, maestro, master, professional.

species *n.* **1** (*a class of things with certain characteristics in common*) category, class, genus. **2** (*a kind, a sort*) description, kind, sort, type, variety.

specific *a.* **1** (*clearly specified or particularized, precise*) certain, circumscribed, clear, clearcut, definite, definitive, delineated, exact, explicit, express, fixed, particular, precise, set, specified, unambiguous. ANTONYMS: ambiguous, general. **2** (*special, peculiar (to)*) characteristic, distinct, distinctive, especial, peculiar, special, unique.
~*n.* **1** (*a medicine, remedy etc. for a particular part of the body*) agent, medicine, remedy. **2** (*that which is particular or specific*) detail, factor, item, particular.

specify *v.t.* (*to mention expressly*) cite, define, delineate, denominate, describe, designate, detail, enumerate, establish, identify, indicate, itemize, list, name, particularize, set forth, set out, spell out, state, stipulate.

specimen *n.* (*a part or an individual intended to illustrate or typify the nature of a whole or a class*) case, example, exemplar, illustration, instance, model, pattern, representative, sample, type.

speck *n.* **1** (*a small spot or blemish*) atom, bit, blemish, crumb, dot, flaw, fleck, grain, hint, iota, jot, mite, modicum, (*coll.*) smidgen, speckle, spot, stain, suggestion, suspicion, tinge, tittle, touch, whit. **2** (*a minute particle*) atom, mite, molecule, particle.
~*v.t.* (*to mark with a speck or specks*) blemish, fleck, mark, speckle.

spectacle *n.* **1** (*something exhibited to the view, a show*) demonstration, display, event, exhibit, exhibition, exposition, extravaganza, marvel, pageant, parade, performance, phenomenon, picture, presentation, scene, sensation, show, sight, vision, wonder. **2** (*a sight attracting ridicule, laughter etc.*) curiosity, fool, laughing stock.

spectator *n.* (*a person who looks on, esp. at a show or spectacle*) audience, beholder, bystander, eyewitness, looker-on, observer, onlooker, viewer, watcher, witness.

spectre *n.* **1** (*an apparition, a ghost*) apparition, ghost, phantom, shade, spirit, (*coll.*) spook, wraith. **2** (*an unpleasant thought or image that haunts one*) image, picture, thought, vision.

speculate *v.i.* **1** (*to guess or conjecture*) conjecture, contemplate, deliberate, guess, hypothesize, judge, mull over, muse, ponder, postulate, reflect, ruminate, suppose, surmise, theorize, wonder. ANTONYMS: know. **2** (*to make purchases, investments etc. on the chance of profit*) buy, invest, play the market, purchase. **3** (*to gamble recklessly*) gamble, risk, wager.

speculation *n.* **1** (*a mental inquiry or series of conjectures about a subject*) conjecture, contemplation, deliberation, guess, guesswork, hypothesis, inquiry, opinion, pondering, postulation, reflection, rumination, supposition, surmise, theory, thought, view, wondering. ANTONYMS: certainty. **2** (*a speculative business transaction or investment*) gamble, gambling, investment, transaction, undertaking, wager.

speech *n.* **1** (*the faculty or act of uttering articulate sounds or words*) articulation, elocution, enunciation, speaking, utterance. **2** (*a public address, an oration*) address, conversation, dialogue, discourse, disquisition, harangue, homily, lecture, oration, sermon, talk, tirade. **3** (*an individual's characteristic manner of speech*) accent, lilt, manner of speech. **4** (*that which is spoken, an utterance*) communication, expression, remark, utterance. **5** (*the language or dialect of a nation, region etc.*) dialect, diction, idiolect, idiom, jargon, language, (*coll.*) lingo, parlance, tongue.

speechless *a.* **1** (*unable to speak, silent, esp. through emotion*) dumb, inarticulate, mute, silent, tongue-tied, unable to speak, voiceless, wordless. **2** (*dumbfounded*) amazed, astounded, dazed, dumbfounded, dumbstruck, (*sl.*) gobsmacked, nonplussed, shocked, thunderstruck.

speed *n.* **1** (*rapidity, swiftness*) abruptness, alacrity, briskness, celerity, dispatch, expedition, fleetness, haste, hastiness, hurriedness, hurry, precipitateness, promptness, quickness, rapidity, speediness, suddenness, swiftness, timeliness. ANTONYMS: slowness. **2** (*rate of* *motion*) acceleration, pace, rate, velocity. **3** (*success or good fortune*) good fortune, prosperity, success.

~*v.i.* (*to move rapidly, to hasten*) accelerate, belt along, bolt, (*coll.*) burn rubber, career, charge, dart, fly, (*coll.*) go like greased lightning, hasten, (*N Am., coll.*) hightail it, hurry, hustle, put one's foot down, race, rush, scamper, scurry, shoot, sprint, (*coll.*) step on it, streak, tear, zip, zoom.

~*v.t.* (*to make prosperous, to cause to succeed*) advance, aid, assist, expedite, facilitate, forward, further, help, promote.

speedy *a.* (*very fast*) brisk, early, expeditious, fast, hasty, hurried, immediate, nimble, precipitate, precipitous, prompt, quick, rapid, summary, swift, winged. ANTONYMS: slow.

spell[1] *n.* **1** (*a series of words used as a charm, an incantation*) charm, formula, incantation. **2** (*the power of an occult force*) bewitchment, captivation, enchantment, enthralment, magic, sorcery, witchcraft. **3** (*a powerful attraction or fascination*) allure, appeal, attraction, draw, fascination, influence, lure, magnetism, pull.

spell[2] *n.* **1** (*a shift or turn of work*) bout, course, round, run, shift, stint, stretch, tour, turn, watch. **2** (*a* (*usu. short*) *period of time*) interval, period, season, term, time.

spend *v.t.* **1** (*to pay out* (*money etc. on something or someone*)) disburse, (*coll.*) fork out, lay out, pay out, (*coll.*) shell out, splash out. **2** (*to use up, to expend* (*time, energy etc.*)) consume, dissipate, expend, fritter away, go through, lavish, splurge, squander, throw away, use up, waste. ANTONYMS: preserve, save. **3** (*to pass* (*time*)) allot, apply, assign, devote, employ, invest, occupy, pass, put in, while away. **4** (*to wear out*) exhaust, tire, wear out.

spendthrift *n.* (*a prodigal or wasteful person*) prodigal, profligate, spender, squanderer, wastrel. ANTONYMS: miser.

~*a.* (*prodigal, wasteful*) extravagant, improvident, prodigal, thriftless, wasteful. ANTONYMS: thrifty.

spent *a.* (*exhausted, tired out*) (*coll.*) all in, burnt out, consumed, depleted, dog-tired, (*coll.*) done in, drained, emptied, exhausted, expended, fatigued, finished, gone, (*coll.*) knackered, played out, (*esp. N Am., coll.*) pooped, prostrate, shattered, tired, used up, wearied, worn out.

sphere *n.* **1** (*a ball, a globe, esp. one of the heavenly bodies*) ball, globe, globule, orb, spherule. **2** (*the sky, the heavens*) celestial sphere, heavens, sky. **3** (*an area of knowledge or a discipline*) (*coll.*) bag, forte, speciality,

(*coll.*) thing. **4** (*field of action, influence etc.*) area, beat, department, discipline, domain, field, order, place, position, province, range, realm, scope, subject, territory.

spice *n.* **1** (*any aromatic and pungent vegetable substance used for seasoning food*) condiment, flavouring, herb, relish, seasoning. **2** (*a touch, a trace*) flavour, savour, touch, trace. **3** (*zest or interest*) bite, colour, dash, excitement, interest, kick, life, piquancy, (*sl.*) pizazz, poignancy, punch, pungency, sharpness, spiciness, spirit, stimulation, tang, vigour, (*coll.*) vim, zest, (*coll.*) zip.

~*v.t.* **1** (*to season with spice*) flavour, season. **2** (*to add interest to*) inspire, inspirit, invigorate, liven up, pep up, stimulate.

spicy *a.* **1** (*flavoured with spice*) seasoned, spiced. **2** (*pungent, piquant*) aromatic, biting, flavourful, flavoursome, fragrant, full-blooded, hot, peppery, piquant, pungent, savoury, sharp, snappy, tangy, zestful, zesty. ANTONYMS: insipid, tasteless. **3** (*suggestive of scandal*) bawdy, (*coll.*) hot, indecent, notorious, racy, revealing, ribald, risqué, salacious, scandalous, sensational, sexy, suggestive, titillating.

spike *n.* (*a pointed piece of metal, e.g. one of a number fixed on the top of a railing or fence*) nail, needle, peg, picket, pike, pin, point, prong, skewer, stake.

~*v.t.* **1** (*to pierce with or impale on a spike*) impale, lance, pierce, reject, skewer, spear, spit, stab, stick. **2** (*to lace* (*a drink*) *with spirits*) drug, poison, strengthen. **3** (*to render useless*) annul, baulk, block, cancel, check, disable, disarm, foil, frustrate, nullify, thwart, void.

spill *v.t.* **1** (*to cause* (*liquid, powder etc.*) *to fall or run out of a vessel, esp. accidentally*) disgorge, overflow, overturn, pour out, slop, upset. **2** (*to shed*) discharge, scatter, shed. **3** (*to throw out of a vehicle or from a saddle*) throw, unseat. **4** (*to give away, disclose* (*information*)) blab, (*sl.*) blow the gaff, confess, disclose, divulge, give away, (*coll.*) let out of the bag, reveal, tattle, tell.

~*v.i.* **1** ((*of liquid*) *to run or fall out of a vessel*) brim over, fall out, run out, run over. **2** ((*of a crowd*) *to pour* (*out of a place*)) disgorge, pour out, run out.

~*n.* **1** (*an instance of spilling, or the amount spilt*) flood, leak, leakage, outpouring, spilling. **2** (*a fall, esp. from a vehicle or saddle*) accident, (*coll.*) cropper, fall, header, tumble.

spin *v.t.* **1** (*to make* (*something or someone*) *rotate or whirl round rapidly*) gyrate, pirouette, pivot, reel, revolve, rotate, turn, twirl, wheel, whirl round. **2** (*to draw out and twist* (*wool, cotton etc.*) *into threads*) draw out, twist. **3** (*to* tell, compose etc. (a tale), at great length) compose, concoct, develop, devise, fabricate, invent, make up, narrate, produce, recount, relate, retail, tell, unfold, weave. **4** (to toss (a coin)) flick, flip, toss.

~v.i. **1** (to turn round quickly) rotate, swing round, turn round, twist, wheel round, whirl round. **2** ((of one's head) to be dizzy with amazement or excitement) be dizzy, be giddy, suffer vertigo, swim, whirl.

~n. **1** (the act or motion of spinning, a whirl) pirouette, reel, revolution, revolving, rotating, rotation, spinning, turn, turning, twirl, twist, whirl, whirling. **2** (a rapid diving descent by an aircraft accompanied by a continued gyration) dive, gyration. **3** (a brief run in a car, aircraft etc.) excursion, jaunt, joyride, outing, ride, run, tour, whirl. **4** (a cosmetic twist given to information in presentation) distortion, manipulation, massage. **to spin out 1** (to compose or tell (a yarn etc.) at great length) compose, narrate, tell. **2** (to prolong, to protract) amplify, continue, drag out, draw out, extend, keep alive, keep going, lengthen, make last, pad out, perpetuate, prolong, protract, stretch out. ANTONYMS: abridge, cut short.

spine n. **1** (the spinal column, the backbone) backbone, spinal column, vertebrae, vertebral column. **2** (Bot.) (a thorn) barb, point, spike, thorn. **3** (esp. Zool.) (a sharp projection, outgrowth etc.) barbel, bristle, needle, prickle, projection, prong, quill, ray, ridge, spur.

spineless a. (of weak character, lacking decision) (coll.) chicken, cowardly, craven, faint-hearted, fearful, feeble, impotent, indecisive, ineffectual, irresolute, lily-livered, pusillanimous, spiritless, squeamish, timorous, weak, weak-willed, wimpish, (coll.) yellow. ANTONYMS: brave, courageous.

spiral a. **1** (forming a spire or coil) coiled, corkscrew, helical, screw, scrolled, voluted, whorled. **2** (continually winding, as the thread of a screw) twisting, winding. ANTONYMS: straight.

~n. (a helix) coil, corkscrew, curl, helix, screw, scroll, turn, volute, whorl.

~v.i. **1** (to move upwards in a spiral) corkscrew, spin. **2** ((esp. of prices and wages) to rise or fall rapidly) plummet, plunge, rocket, soar.

spirit n. **1** (the vital principle animating a person or animal) anima, breath, consciousness, essence, heart, life, psyche, self, soul, vitality, vital spirit. **2** (a disembodied soul; an incorporeal or supernatural being) angel, apparition, demon, elf, fairy, phantom, spectre, sprite. **3** (a person considered with regard to their individual qualities of mind or temperament) character, nature, persona. **4** (vigour

of mind or intellect) intelligence, mind, will, will-power, wit. ANTONYMS: body. **5** (vivacity, enthusiasm) animation, ardour, courage, dash, drive, eagerness, élan, energy, enthusiasm, fervour, fire, get-up-and-go, grit, (pl., coll.) gut, liveliness, mettle, motivation, passion, pluck, resolution, resolve, stout-heartedness, vigour, vivacity, zeal, zest. ANTONYMS: apathy. **6** (mental attitude) attitude, bent, disposition, feeling, humour, inclination, mood, morale, outlook, sentiment, temper, temperament. **7** (characteristic quality or tendency) aim, core, drift, essence, gist, heart, implication, intention, marrow, meaning, meat, message, pith, purpose, quintessence, sense, significance, substance, tenor. **8** (distilled alcoholic liquors, such as brandy, whisky etc.) alcohol, (coll.) booze, (coll.) firewater, (N Am., coll.) hooch, liquor.

~v.t. **1** (to convey (away, off etc.) secretly and rapidly) abduct, abscond with, convey, make off with, take away, transport, whisk away. **2** (to animate, to inspirit) animate, encourage, inspire, inspirit.

spirited a. (full of spirit or life, lively) active, animated, ardent, brave, buoyant, courageous, dynamic, effervescent, energetic, enthusiastic, fervent, lively, sprightly, vigorous, vivacious. ANTONYMS: apathetic.

spiritual a. **1** (immaterial, incorporeal) ethereal, ghostly, immaterial, incorporeal, inner, intangible, mental, psychic, psychological, supernatural. ANTONYMS: physical. **2** (derived from or relating to God, holy) churchly, devotional, divine, ecclesiastic, holy, inspired, pious, pure, religious, sacerdotal, sacred. ANTONYMS: profane, secular, temporal.

spit v.t. **1** (to eject (saliva etc.), throw (out) from the mouth) dribble, drool, expectorate, salivate, slaver. **2** (to utter or throw (out) in a violent or spiteful way) discharge, eject, spew forth.

~v.i. **1** (to eject saliva from the mouth) dribble, drool, expectorate, salivate, slaver. **2** ((of a frying pan, fire etc.) to throw out hot fat, sparks etc.) spark, splutter, sputter. **3** (to drizzle with rain) drizzle, (dial.) mizzle.

~n. (spittle, saliva) drool, saliva, spittle, sputum.

spite n. (ill will, malice) animosity, antagonism, bitchiness, bitterness, gall, grudge, hate, hatred, hostility, ill will, malevolence, malice, pique, rancour, resentment, spleen, venom. ANTONYMS: benevolence.

~v.t. **1** (to thwart maliciously) be a dog in the manger about, be bloody-minded about, thwart. **2** (to vex or annoy) annoy, discomfit, hurt, injure, irritate, offend, (coll.) peeve, pique, provoke, put out, upset, vex, wound. ANTONYMS: please. **in spite of** (*notwithstanding, despite*) despite, ignoring, in defiance of, in the face of, notwithstanding, regardless of.

spiteful *a.* (*malicious*) acrimonious, antagonistic, bitter, cruel, hateful, hostile, malevolent, malicious, rancorous, retaliatory, retributive, venomous, vindictive. ANTONYMS: kindly.

splash *v.t.* **1** (*to bespatter with water, mud etc.*) bespatter, besprinkle, mottle, shower, spatter, splatter, splodge, spot, spray, sprinkle. **2** (*to dash* (*liquid etc., about, over, etc.*)) dash, strew, wash. **3** (*to spend recklessly*) spend, spend like water, squander, throw about, waste. **4** (*to display prominently in a newspaper*) blazon, display, plaster, spread.
~*n.* **1** (*a spot or patch of liquid, colour etc.*) patch, smear, smudge, spatter, splatter, splodge, splotch, spot, spray, sprinkle, stain, touch. **2** (*a vivid display*) brouhaha, commotion, display, excitement, furore, impression, sensation, show, spectacle, (*coll.*) to-do, uproar.

splendid *a.* **1** (*magnificent, sumptuous*) gorgeous, grand, lavish, lush, luxurious, magnificent, majestic, ornate, plush, (*coll.*) posh, resplendent, rich, sumptuous. **2** (*glorious, illustrious*) celebrated, dashing, famous, glorious, illustrious, meritorious. **3** (*brilliant, dazzling*) (*coll.*) brill, brilliant, dazzling, lustrous. **4** (*fine, excellent*) awesome, excellent, exceptional, exemplary, fabulous, (*coll.*) fantastic, fine, first-class, first-rate, great, marvellous, outstanding, remarkable, stupendous, sublime, (*coll.*) super, superb, superlative, wonderful. ANTONYMS: poor.

splendour *n.* (*magnificence, brilliance*) beauty, brightness, brilliance, exquisiteness, glitter, glory, grandeur, lavishness, lustre, luxuriousness, magnificence, majesty, parade, pomp, (*coll.*) poshness, radiance, resplendence, richness, shine, sumptuousness.

splinter *n.* (*a thin piece of wood, glass etc. broken or shivered off*) chip, fragment, needle, piece, scrap, shard, shred.
~*v.t.* (*to split or rend into splinters or fragments*) break up, disintegrate, fragment, rend, shatter, shiver, smash, split.

split *v.t.* (*to break or divide*) bisect, break, chop in two, cleave, crack, cut, divide, divorce, part, partition, pull apart, rend, rupture, section, sever, tear. ANTONYMS: join, unite.
~*v.i.* **1** (*to be broken or divided*) be broken, be divided, burst, diverge, fork. **2** (*to come to pieces*) break up, come apart, come to pieces. **3** (*to betray the secrets of, to inform* (*on*)) betray, (*sl.*) grass (on), inform (on), peach, (*coll.*) rat, sneak (on). **4** (*to depart*) depart, (*coll.*) disappear, go, leave, run.

~*n.* **1** (*an instance, or the resultant state, of splitting*) channel, chink, cleft, cranny, crevice, fissure, fracture, furrow, gap, gash, groove, hiatus, opening, rent, rip, slash, slit, slot, tear. **2** (*a separation, a division into opposing parties*) breach, break, chasm, dichotomy, discord, disunion, division, partition, rift, rupture, schism, separation. ANTONYMS: reunion, union.
~*a.* (*fractured*) bisected, broken, cleft, cut, divided, fractured, halved, separated.

spoil *v.t.* **1** (*to impair the goodness, usefulness etc., of*) blemish, damage, deface, despoil, destroy, disfigure, harm, hurt, impair, injure, mar, mess up, ruin, scar, upset, vitiate, wreck. ANTONYMS: improve, restore. **2** (*to detract from one's enjoyment of, to mar*) detract from, impair, mar, ruin. **3** (*to impair the character of by over-indulgence*) baby, coddle, cosset, dote on, indulge, mollycoddle, over-indulge, pamper, spoon-feed.
~*v.i.* **1** ((*of perishable food*) *to decay, to deteriorate through keeping*) addle, curdle, decay, decompose, deteriorate, go bad, go off, mildew, moulder, putrefy, rot, turn. **2** (*to be eager or only too ready* (*for a fight*)) be eager for, crave, desire, itch for, lust for, thirst for, yearn for.
~*n.* **1** (*plunder, booty*) booty, goods, loot, pickings, plunder, (*sl.*) swag, take. **2** (*offices or emoluments acquired as the result of a victory*) emolument, honour, office, prize. **3** (*pillage, spoliation*) pillage, plunder, rape, rapine, spoliation.

spontaneous *a.* **1** (*not due to external constraint, voluntary*) free, gratuitous, natural, unbidden, unforced, unprompted, voluntary, willing. ANTONYMS: forced. **2** (*not due to conscious volition or motive*) automatic, involuntary, (*coll.*) knee-jerk, mechanical, reflex, unconscious, unthinking, unwitting. **3** (*instinctive, automatic*) ad-lib, extemporaneous, extempore, immediate, impetuous, impromptu, impulsive, instinctive, offhand, off the cuff, spur-of-the-moment, unannounced, unplanned, unpremeditated, unprepared, unrehearsed. ANTONYMS: prepared.

sporadic *a.* (*occurring here and there or irregularly*) chance, dispersed, erratic, fitful, infrequent, intermittent, irregular, isolated, occasional, periodic, random, scattered, separate, spasmodic, uneven. ANTONYMS: regular.

sport *n.* **1** (*a competitive pastime, esp. an athletic or outdoor pastime*) exercise, game, pastime. **2** (*amusement, fun*) amusement, badinage, banter, distraction, diversion, divertissement, enjoyment, entertainment, fun, humour, jest, joke, mirth, mockery, play, pleasantry, pleasure, raillery, recreation, relaxation. **3** (*a fair or obliging person*) fair player, good loser, good sport, sportsman.

~*v.i.* **1** (*to play, to divert oneself*) amuse oneself, caper, cavort, disport, divert oneself, frisk, frolic, gambol, lark, play, rollick, romp, skip about. **2** (*to trifle (with a person's feelings etc.)*) jest, play, toy, trifle.

~*v.t.* (*to wear or display in an ostentatious manner*) display, exhibit, flaunt, show off, wear.

spot *n.* **1** (*a small mark or stain*) blot, blotch, discoloration, dot, flaw, mark, patch, smudge, speck, speckle, splodge, splotch, stain, taint. **2** (*a pimple or blemish on the skin*) acne, blackhead, blemish, boil, eruption, pimple, pustule. **3** (*a stain on one's character or reputation*) blemish, blot, disgrace, scandal, stain. **4** (*a small extent of space*) area, neighbourhood, quarter, scene, section. **5** (*a particular place*) locale, locality, location, place, setting, site, situation. **6** (*a place used for a certain activity*) place, site, venue. **7** (*a small amount (of anything)*) bit, bite, morsel, (*coll.*) smidgen, trace.

~*v.t.* **1** (*to pick out beforehand (e.g. the winner of a race)*) pick out, predict. **2** (*to recognize, to detect*) descry, detect, espy, identify, make out, recognize, see. **3** (*to catch sight of*) catch sight of, discern, glimpse, sight. **4** (*to pinpoint (the enemy's position), esp. from the air*) discern, pinpoint, single out. **5** (*to mark or discolour with a spot or spots*) bespatter, discolour, fleck, mark, smudge, spatter, speckle, splash, spray. **6** (*to sully, to blemish (someone's reputation)*) besmirch, blemish, blot, dirty, soil, stain, sully, taint, tarnish. **7** (*impers.*) (*to rain slightly*) drizzle, (*dial.*) mizzle, spit.

spotless *a.* **1** (*very clean*) clean, gleaming, immaculate, perfect, polished, pure, shiny, spick and span, stainless. ANTONYMS: dirty, soiled. **2** (*completely honest in character*) blameless, faultless, flawless, immaculate, irreproachable, pure, stainless, unassailable, unblemished, unspotted, unsullied, untarnished.

spout *n.* **1** (*a short pipe or channelled projection for carrying off water from a gutter, conducting liquid from a vessel etc.*) channel, conduit, downspout, drain, duct, outlet, pipe. **2** (*a continuous stream of water etc.*) column, jet, stream.

~*v.t.* (*to pour out or discharge with force or in large volume*) discharge, disgorge, eject, emit, erupt, flow, gush, jet, pour, shoot, spew, spit, spray, spurt, squirt, stream, surge, vomit.

~*v.i.* (*to declaim, to hold forth*) carry on, declaim, expatiate, go on, hold forth, maunder on,

orate, pontificate, ramble on, rant, rave, (*often derog.*) speechify, (*coll.*) witter on.

sprawl *v.i.* **1** (*to lie or stretch out the body and limbs in a careless or awkward posture*) lie about, lie around, loll, lounge, recline, slouch, slump, straddle, stretch out. **2** (*(of a town, plant etc.) to straggle, to be spread out in an irregular or ungraceful form*) branch out, spread out, straggle.

~*n.* (*an area of land, esp. one on which buildings are spread out in an unplanned way*) expanse, expansion, spread, stretch.

spray[1] *n.* **1** (*water or other liquid flying in small, fine drops*) drizzle, foam, mist, shower, spindrift, sprinkle, spume. **2** (*an appliance for spraying*) aerosol, atomizer, hairspray, sprayer, sprinkler, vaporizer.

~*v.t.* (*to throw or apply (liquid) in the form of spray*) atomize, diffuse, disperse, scatter, shower, spatter, splash, spread.

spray[2] *n.* **1** (*a small branch or sprig, esp. with leaves, flowers etc.*) bough, branch, shoot, sprig. **2** (*a decorative bouquet of this shape*) bouquet, corsage, floral arrangement, nosegay, posy.

spread *v.t.* **1** (*to extend in length and breadth by opening (out), unfolding etc.*) broaden, develop, dilate, draw out, expand, extend, flatten out, increase, open, prolong, separate, stretch, swell, unfold, unfurl, unroll, widen. ANTONYMS: contract, shrink. **2** (*to scatter, to smooth into a thin, wide layer*) circulate, diffuse, disperse, layer, propagate, radiate, scatter, shed, sow, strew. **3** (*to disseminate, to publish*) advertise, air, announce, broadcast, disseminate, distribute, herald, make known, make public, promulgate, pronounce, propagate, publicize, publish, repeat, televise, tell the world. ANTONYMS: suppress. **4** (*to cover the surface of*) blanket, cloak, coat, cover, daub, glaze, lay, layer, paint, plaster, plate, smear, varnish, wash. **5** (*to display, lay (out) before the eye or mind*) display, fan out, lay out.

~*n.* **1** (*breadth, extent*) area, bounds, breadth, compass, depth, development, dimensions, expanse, extent, limits, range, reach, scope, size, span, stretch, sweep, vastness. **2** (*diffusion, dissemination*) diffusion, dispensing, dispersal, dispersion, dissemination, distribution, radiation, transmission. **3** (*a meal set out, a feast*) banquet, dinner, feast, (*coll.*) feed, meal, repast. **4** (*a sweet or savoury paste for spreading over bread etc.*) butter, confiture, conserve, jam, jelly, margarine, paste, preserve. **5** (*a bedspread*) bedspread, counterpane, cover, coverlet, duvet, quilt, throw. **6** (*an extensive ranch*) farm, holding, homestead, landholding, plantation, ranch.

spree *n.* (*a lively frolic, esp. with drinking*) (*sl.*) bender, (*coll.*) binge, debauch, drinking-bout, escapade, fling, frolic, lark, orgy, outing, party, revel, romp.

sprightly *a.* (*lively, spirited*) active, agile, airy, alert, animated, blithe, brisk, buoyant, cheerful, (*esp. N Am., coll.*) chipper, energetic, gay, jaunty, lively, nimble, perky, spirited, sportive, spry, vivacious. ANTONYMS: dull, lifeless.

spring *v.i.* **1** (*to leap, to jump*) bounce, bound, dart, fly, hop, jump, leap, skip, vault. **2** (*to move suddenly by or as by the action of a spring*) rebound, recoil. **3** (*to come* (*up*) *from or as from a source, to appear, esp. unexpectedly*) appear, arise, burst forth, derive from, emanate, emerge, evolve, flow, grow, issue, originate, proceed from, rise, shoot up, sprout, start, stem from. ANTONYMS: disappear, end.
~*v.t.* **1** (*to cause to move, act etc., suddenly by or as by releasing a spring*) activate, trigger. **2** (*to bring about the escape from prison of*) free, liberate, rescue.
~*n.* **1** (*a leap, jump*) bound, hop, jump, leap, skip, vault. **2** (*a backward movement as from release from tension*) rebound, recoil. **3** (*elasticity, resilience*) bounce, buoyancy, elasticity, flexibility, give, resilience, springiness. **4** (*a source, an origin*) beginning, fount, fountainhead, origin, root, source, well, wellspring. **5** (*an escape by prisoners*) breakout, escape.

sprout *v.i.* (*to develop shoots, to germinate*) arise, bloom, blossom, bud, burgeon, come up, flower, germinate, shoot forth, spring. ANTONYMS: die, wither.
~*v.t.* (*to put forth or produce* (*shoots etc.*)) develop, produce, put forth.
~*n.* (*a new shoot on a plant*) bud, scion, shoot.

spruce *a.* (*neat, smart*) dapper, elegant, (*coll.*) natty, neat, smart, tidy, trim, well-groomed, well-turned-out. ANTONYMS: unkempt, untidy.
~*v.t.* (*to smarten* (*up*)) clean, neaten, primp, smarten, straighten, tidy, titivate.

spur *n.* **1** (*incentive, stimulus*) encouragement, goad, impulse, incentive, incitement, inducement, instigation, motivation, pressure, prick, prod, prompting, provocation, stimulus, urging. ANTONYMS: deterrent. **2** (*a spur-shaped projection or part*) barb, barbel, barbule, gaff, point, process, projection, prong, quill, spike, spine, tine. **3** (*a ridge projecting from a mountain range*) buttress, ridge.
~*v.t.* **1** (*to prick with spurs*) goad, prick, prod. **2** (*to urge* (*on*), *to incite*) drive, egg on, encourage, impel, incite, induce, motivate, prompt, provoke, urge. ANTONYMS: deter. **3** (*to stimulate* (*interest, enthusiasm etc.*)) animate, excite, stimulate.

~*v.i.* (*to ride hard, to press* (*on or forward*)) drive, press, pressure, push, ride hard.

spurn *v.t.* (*to reject with disdain; to treat with scorn*) cold-shoulder, contemn, despise, disdain, disregard, look down on, rebuff, refuse, reject, repudiate, scorn, sneer at, snub, turn down. ANTONYMS: accept, respect.

spurt *v.i.* (*to gush out in a jet or sudden stream*) burst, erupt, gush, jet, shoot, spew, squirt, surge.
~*n.* **1** (*a forcible gush or jet of liquid*) burst, gush, jet, outbreak, spate, spout, squirt, surge. **2** (*a short burst of intense effort or speed*) acceleration, advance, effort, improvement, increase, rise.

spy *n.* **1** (*a person employed by a government or business to obtain information about the operations of an enemy, business rival etc.*) agent, double agent, fifth columnist, foreign agent, intelligence agent, mole, secret agent. **2** (*a person who keeps a constant secret or surreptitious watch on the actions, movements etc., of others*) detective, (*chiefly N Am., sl.*) fink, informant, informer, scout, stool-pigeon, undercover agent.
~*v.t.* (*to detect, to discover, esp. by close observation*) catch sight of, descry, detect, discern, discover, espy, glimpse, make out, note, notice, observe, see, spot, watch.
~*v.i.* (*to act as a spy, to keep a surreptitious watch* (*on*)) (*sl.*) case, check out, follow, keep under surveillance, reconnoitre, shadow, tail, trail, watch.

squabble *n.* (*a petty or noisy quarrel, a wrangle*) altercation, argument, bickering, brawl, contention, disputation, dispute, fight, quarrel, row, tiff, wrangle. ANTONYMS: agreement, concord.
~*v.i.* (*to engage in a petty or noisy quarrel, to wrangle*) altercate, argue, bicker, brawl, contend, dispute, fight, quarrel, row, wrangle. ANTONYMS: agree.

squad *n.* **1** (*a small party of people, e.g. engaged in a task together*) band, crew, force, gang, group, party, section, squadron, unit. **2** (*a small number of soldiers assembled for drill or inspection*) cadre, company, platoon, troop. **3** (*a sports team*) side, team.

square *n.* **1** (*a rectangle with equal sides*) rectangle. **2** (*any surface, object etc., of this shape*) cube, quadrilateral. **3** (*an open quadrilateral area surrounded by buildings, usu. laid out with trees etc.*) court, courtyard, green, market place, market square, piazza, place, plaza, quad, quadrangle. **4** (*a conventional, old-fashioned person*) conservative, fogey, (*coll., usu. derog.*) goody-goody, stick-in-the-mud, (*coll.*) stuffed shirt.

~*a.* **1** (*having four equal sides and four right angles*) four-sided, quadrilateral, rectilinear. **2** ((*of corners or angles*) *of right-angled shape, measuring 90°*) cubic, equilateral, quadrangular, quadrate, rectangular, right-angled. **3** (*at right angles* (*to*)) at right angles, perpendicular. **4** (*level or parallel* (*with*)) accurate, correct, even, exact, level, parallel, precise, straight, true. **5** (*even* (*with*), *quits* (*with*)) even, level, quits, straight. ANTONYMS: uneven. **6** (*just, honest*) above board, decent, equitable, ethical, fair, honest, just, on the level, proper, right, straightforward, upright. ANTONYMS: dishonest, unjust. **7** ((*of scores*) *equal*) balanced, equal, even, on a par, tied. **8** (*coll.*) ((*of a person or their tastes*) *conventional, old-fashioned*) antediluvian, behind the times, conformist, conservative, fogeyish, (*coll.*) fuddy-duddy, naive, not with it, old-fashioned, strait-laced, traditionalist. ANTONYMS: avant-garde, (*coll., sometimes derog.*) trendy. **9** ((*of a meal*) *full and satisfying*) filling, generous, healthy, nutritious, satisfying, solid, substantial.
~*adv.* (*evenly*) evenly, flush.
~*v.t.* **1** (*to make square or rectangular*) make rectangular, make square. **2** (*to adjust, to bring into conformity* (*with or to*)) accommodate, accord, adjust, align, arrange, balance, fit, harmonize, match, meet, modify, reconcile, regulate, suit, tailor. **3** (*to settle, to pay* (*a bill*)) clear up, discharge, fix, liquidate, pay, satisfy, settle. **4** (*to hold* (*one's shoulders*) *back, and at an even height*) stiffen, straighten, tense, throw back. **5** (*to bribe, to win over with gifts, money etc.*) bribe, (*coll.*) grease someone's palm, pay off, sort. **6** (*to even the scores in* (*a match etc.*)) equal, even the score, level, match, tie.
~*v.i.* (*to conform precisely, to harmonize* (*with*)) agree, conform, correspond, harmonize, tally.

squeamish *a.* **1** (*easily nauseated or disgusted*) delicate, easily disgusted, qualmish, queasy. **2** (*finicky, unduly scrupulous*) dainty, difficult, exacting, fastidious, finicky, (*coll.*) fuddy-duddy, fussy, hypercritical, meticulous, nice, (*coll.*) pernickety, prudish, punctilious.

squeeze *v.t.* **1** (*to press closely, esp. between two bodies or with the hand*) compact, compress, press. **2** (*to crush* (*out*), *to extract* (*moisture etc.*) *thus*) clasp, clench, clutch, constrict, crush, extract, wring. **3** (*to force* (*oneself etc., or one's way, into, out of etc. a narrow space etc.*)) cram, crowd, force, jam, pack, press, ram, stuff, wedge. **4** (*to exact* (*money etc.*) *by extortion etc.*) bleed, exact, extort, milk, pry, tear, wrench, wrest. **5** (*to constrain by arbitrary or illegitimate means*) bring pressure to bear on, influence, lean on, oppress, pressurize, put pressure on, (*coll.*) put the screws on, (*coll.*) put the squeeze on, twist someone's arm.

~*v.i.* (*to press, to force one's way* (*into, through etc.*)) force one's way, get by, get through, pass, press, push, (*coll.*) squeak by.
~*n.* **1** (*pressure*) burden, grip, oppression, pressure. **2** (*a close embrace*) clasp, (*coll.*) clinch, clutch, embrace, hug. **3** (*a throng, a crush*) crowd, crush, jam, press, squash, throng.

squirm *v.i.* **1** (*to wriggle, to move* (*up, through etc.*) *by wriggling*) fidget, flounder, move, shift, turn, twist, wriggle, writhe about. **2** (*to display discomfort, embarrassment etc.*) agonize, display discomfort, shift, sweat.

stab *v.t.* (*to pierce or wound with a pointed, usu. short, weapon*) bayonet, cut, gore, impale, jab, knife, lance, pierce, pin, poke, prick, puncture, run through, skewer, spear, spit, stick, transfix.
~*v.i.* (*to aim a blow with or as with a pointed weapon* (*at*)) aim a blow at, lunge at, thrust at.
~*n.* **1** (*a blow or thrust with a pointed weapon*) blow, cut, gash, jab, puncture, thrust, wound. **2** (*a secret, malicious injury*) ache, hurt, injury, pain, pang, twinge. **to have/ make a stab at** (*to attempt, to have a go at* (*doing something*)) attempt, essay, guess, (*coll.*) have a go, have a try, make an effort, (*coll.*) take a shot.

stable *a.* **1** (*firmly fixed, established*) deep-rooted, established, fast, fixed. **2** (*firm, unwavering*) abiding, constant, enduring, firm, immutable, lasting, long-standing, permanent, reliable, resolute, secure, solid, sound, steadfast, stout, sure, unchanging, unwavering. ANTONYMS: unstable. **3** (*mentally and emotionally steady*) balanced, responsible, sane, sensible, steady, well-balanced.

stack *n.* **1** (*a pile, a heap, esp. of an orderly kind*) accumulation, bale, bank, deposit, heap, hill, hoard, load, mass, mound, mountain, pile, store, supply. **2** (*a round or rectangular pile of corn in the sheaf, or of hay, straw etc.*) cock, haycock, hayrick, haystack, rick. **3** (*a great quantity*) abundance, accumulation, amount, array, collection, host, load, mass, multitude, number, profusion, quantity, sea, swarm, throng, volume.
~*v.t.* (*to pile in a stack or stacks*) accumulate, agglomerate, aggregate, amass, collect, heap, hoard, load, pile, (*coll.*) squirrel away, (*coll.*) stash, stock, stockpile, store.

staff *n.* **1** (*a stick carried for help in walking, climbing etc., or as a weapon*) cane, club, crook, pike, pikestaff, stake, stave, stick, truncheon, wand. **2** (*a rod carried as a symbol of authority*) baton, crosier, rod, sceptre. **3** (*a thing or person that affords support or sustenance*) prop, support. **4** (*a body of employees, e.g. in a firm under a manager*) crew, employees, organization,

personnel, team, workers, workforce. **5** (*the body of those in authority in an organization, esp. the teachers of a school collectively*) authorities, managers, officers, teachers.
~*v.t.* (*to supply* (*a firm, hospital etc.*) *with staff*) equip, man, provide, supply.

stage *n.* **1** (*a point in a progressive movement, a definite period or phase in development*) echelon, grade, juncture, level, period, phase, point, position, spot, station, stratum, tier. **2** (*a raised platform on which theatrical or other performances take place before an audience*) dais, platform, podium, rostrum, scaffold, shelf, staging. **3** (*the profession of an actor, actors collectively*) acting, (*coll.*) boards, drama, (*coll.*) showbiz, (*coll.*) show business, theatre. **4** (*the scene of action*) scene, setting, situation. **5** (*any one of a series of regular stopping places on a route*) post, station, stop, stopping place.
~*v.t.* **1** (*to put* (*a play etc.*) *on the stage*) concoct, contrive, devise, exhibit, make up, originate, perform, present, produce, put on. **2** (*to plan and execute* (*an event*)) mastermind, mount, organize, plan.

stagger *v.i.* **1** (*to move unsteadily in walking, to totter*) lurch, pitch, reel, rock, sway, teeter, totter, wobble. **2** (*to begin to give way*) falter, give way, hesitate, vacillate, waver.
~*v.t.* **1** (*to amaze or shock*) amaze, astonish, astound, bewilder, (*sl.*) blow one's mind, dumbfound, flabbergast, jolt, shake up, shock, startle, stun, stupefy, surprise, take aback, take one's breath away, throw off balance. **2** (*to overlap, to place zigzag*) alternate, overlap, vary, zigzag.

stagnant *a.* **1** ((*of water*) *without current, motionless*) brackish, contaminated, dirty, filthy, foul, inert, motionless, polluted, putrescent, putrid, quiet, standing, static, still. ANTONYMS: flowing. **2** ((*of people or their lives, of business etc.*) *dull, sluggish*) dull, flat, sluggish, stale, unfruitful, unoriginal.

staid *a.* (*sober, steady*) calm, composed, demure, dignified, grave, prim, quiet, reserved, rigid, sedate, serious, settled, sober, solemn, steady, stiff. ANTONYMS: frivolous.

stain *v.t.* **1** (*to discolour, to soil*) blacken, blemish, blot, blotch, contaminate, defile, dirty, discolour, mark, smudge, soil, spatter, speckle, splash, splatter, spot, sully, taint, tarnish, tinge. **2** (*to tarnish, to blemish* (*a reputation etc.*)) besmirch, contaminate, corrupt, defile, disgrace, ruin, shame, soil, spoil, stigmatize, sully, taint, tarnish. **3** (*to colour by means of dye or another agent acting chemically or by absorption*) colour, dye, tinge, tint. **4** (*to*

impregnate (*an object for microscopic examination*) *with a colouring matter affecting certain parts more powerfully than others*) impregnate, mark.
~*n.* **1** (*a discoloration*) colour, colouring, discoloration, dye, pigment, tinge, tint. **2** (*a spot of a distinct colour*) blotch, mark, splodge, splotch, spot. **3** (*a blot, a blemish*) blemish, blot, disgrace, shame, slur, stigma, taint.

stake[1] *n.* **1** (*a stick or post pointed at one end and set in the ground, as a support, part of a railing etc.*) pale, paling, palisade, picket, pike, pole, post, spike, stave, stick. **2** (*a prop or upright part or fitting for supporting a machine etc.*) column, pillar, prop, upright.
~*v.t.* (*to fasten or protect with a stake or stakes*) chain, fasten, hitch, lash, leash, picket, protect, secure, support, tether, tie up.

stake[2] *n.* **1** (*anything, esp. a sum of money, wagered on a competition or contingent event, esp. deposited with a stakeholder*) ante, bet, chance, gamble, hazard, pledge, risk, venture, wager. **2** (*an interest or involvement* (*in some concern*)) concern, interest, investment, involvement, share.
~*v.t.* **1** (*to wager, to venture* (*something, esp. a sum of money, on an event etc.*)) bet, gamble, hazard, venture, wager. **2** (*to risk*) imperil, jeopardize, risk, venture.

stale *a.* **1** (*dry, musty*) dried-out, dry, flat, fusty, hard, hardened, limp, musty, not fresh, wilted, withered. ANTONYMS: fresh. **2** (*insipid or tasteless from being kept too long*) insipid, mouldy, musty, off, rotten, sour, spoiled, tasteless, turned, unfresh. ANTONYMS: fresh. **3** ((*of jokes etc.*) *trite;* (*of news*) *old*) antiquated, boring, clichéd, commonplace, dull, familiar, hackneyed, old, old-fashioned, overused, stereotyped, stock, tired, trite, unoriginal. **4** ((*of e.g. an athlete or person studying*) *in a debilitated condition from overtraining or overexertion*) debilitated, exhausted, tired, unenthusiastic, unfit, weary.

stalk[1] *n.* (*the stem or axis of a plant*) axis, cane, spike, stem, trunk.

stalk[2] *v.t.* **1** (*to pursue* (*game or other prey, or an enemy*) *stealthily by the use of cover*) hound, pursue, tail, track, trail. **2** (*to follow* (*a person, esp. a public figure*) *persistently and with a sinister or unwelcome purpose*) dog, follow, haunt, shadow, tail.
~*v.i.* (*to walk with a stately stride*) flounce, march, pace, stride, strut. ANTONYMS: slink.

stall[1] *n.* **1** (*a booth or shed in a market, street etc., or a bench, table etc. in a building for the sale of goods*) bench, booth, shed, stand, table. **2** (*a cowshed or stable*) barn, byre, coop, corral, cote, cowshed, enclosure, fold, pen, stable, sty. **3** (*a division or compartment for a horse, ox etc., in a stable or byre*) compartment, cubicle, horsebox. **4** (*a seat in the choir of a large church*) bench, pew, seat.

~*v.i.* ((*of a vehicle or its engine*) *to cease working suddenly, e.g. when the fuel supply is inadequate*) cease, come to a standstill, (*coll.*) conk out, die, fail, (*coll.*) pack up, quit, shut down, stop.

stall[2] *v.i.* (*to play for time; to be evasive*) dally, dawdle, dilly-dally, dither, drag one's feet, equivocate, hedge, hesitate, linger, play for time, prevaricate, procrastinate, temporize, vacillate.

~*v.t.* (*to obstruct or delay*) delay, hinder, obstruct, put off, stonewall.

~*n.* (*an act of stalling*) beating about the bush, delay, evasion, hedging, manoeuvre, obstructionism, playing for time, prevarication, procrastination, ruse, stonewalling, stratagem.

stalwart *a.* **1** (*strong in build, sturdy*) beefy, brawny, fit, hale, hardy, healthy, hearty, hefty, lusty, muscular, powerful, robust, rugged, solid, strong, sturdy. ANTONYMS: weak. **2** (*determined, resolute*) courageous, determined, fearless, firm, game, heroic, indefatigable, indomitable, manful, persistent, plucky, redoubtable, resolute, staunch, steadfast, stout, tenacious, unwavering, unyielding, valiant. ANTONYMS: irresolute, wavering.

~*n.* (*a valiant supporter or partisan*) faithful, hero, heroine, loyalist, partisan, supporter, trouper, trusty, upholder.

stammer *v.i.* (*to speak with nervous hesitation or repetitions of the same sound*) falter, hesitate, hum and haw, pause, stumble, stutter.

~*n.* (*this kind of speech disorder; a tendency to stammer or stutter*) speech impediment, stutter.

stamp *v.t.* **1** (*to bring* (*one's foot*) *down heavily*) step, stomp, tramp, trample, tread. **2** (*to crush or flatten with one's foot thus*) beat, crush, flatten, pound. **3** (*to extinguish* (*e.g. the remains of a fire*) *thus, to put* (*out*)) extinguish, put out. **4** (*to impress* (*a mark, pattern etc.*) *on a surface with a die or similar implement*) brand, categorize, characterize, classify, designate, emboss, engrave, identify, impress, imprint, initial, inscribe, label, mark, name, print, sign, style, tag.

~*v.i.* (*to bring one's foot down heavily or forcibly on the ground*) step, stomp, tread.

~*n.* **1** (*an instrument for stamping marks, designs etc.*) block, cast, die, plate, punch. **2** (*the mark made by this*) impression, insignia. **3** (*a small piece of adhesive paper for affixing to letters, receipts etc., to show that the required charge*

has been paid) postage stamp. **4** (*a distinguishing mark or impress*) brand, coat of arms, colophon, crest, emblem, escutcheon, hallmark, impress, imprint, initials, insignia, logo, mark, monogram, print, seal, sign, signature, symbol. **5** (*a kind or type*) cast, character, class, classification, cut, description, fashion, genre, genus, grade, kind, level, make, mould, sort, species, style, type, variety. **to stamp out 1** (*to extinguish* (*a fire*) *by stamping*) extinguish, put out. **2** (*to suppress*) abolish, annihilate, crush, destroy, eliminate, end, eradicate, exterminate, extirpate, get rid of, kill, put an end to, put down, quell, repress, snuff out, subdue, suppress.

stampede *n.* (*a sudden rush of people, esp. in panic*) charge, dash, flight, panic, rout, rush, scattering.

~*v.i.* (*to take part in a stampede*) charge, dash, flee, fly, run, rush, take flight, take to one's heels.

~*v.t.* (*to cause to do this*) frighten, panic, rout, scatter.

stand *v.i.* **1** (*to be in, take or keep an upright position, esp. on the feet, or on a base*) arise, be upstanding, get up, rise. **2** (*to remain firm or constant, to persist*) abide, accept, bear up, continue, cope with, endure, hold, last through, persist, remain, resist, stay, survive. **3** ((*of rules, laws etc.*) *to remain valid*) apply, continue, exist, hold good, obtain, persist, prevail, remain. **4** (*to act or serve in a specified role or capacity*) act, function, serve.

~*v.t.* **1** (*to set in an erect or a specified position*) move, place, position, put, set, upend. **2** (*to endure without giving way or complaining*) bear, brook, endure, face, handle, put up with, stand for, stomach, suffer, sustain, take, tolerate, wear, weather, withstand.

~*n.* **1** (*a cessation of motion or progress, a stop*) cessation, halt, rest, standstill, stay, stop, stoppage. ANTONYMS: motion, progress. **2** (*a show of resistance, defensive effort etc.*) defence, defiance, effort, opposition, resistance. ANTONYMS: submission, surrender. **3** (*someone's attitude or standpoint in regard to an issue*) attitude, belief, feeling, line, opinion, philosophy, point of view, policy, position, posture, sentiment, stance, standpoint, viewpoint. **4** (*a small frame or piece of furniture for supporting anything, a base or holder*) base, bracket, coat-rack, frame, hat stand, holder, rack. **5** (*a trading stall in a street or market, or a commercial company's information booth at a conference etc.*) barrow, booth, cart, counter, kiosk, stall, table. **6** (*an erection with banks of seats or steps for spectators to stand or sit on*) bandstand, dais, grandstand, platform, stage, staging. **7** (*a clump of plants or trees*) brake, clump, coppice, copse, grove, spinney, thicket, wood. **to stand by 1** (*to uphold, to support firmly*) back, defend, side with, stand behind, stand up for, stick up for, support, sympathize with, uphold. ANTONYMS: abandon, desert. **2** (*to abide by* (*one's decision etc.*)) abide by, adhere to, affirm, confirm, maintain, persist in, reaffirm, stick to, support. **3** (*to stand near in readiness to act promptly as directed*) stand in readiness, wait on the sidelines. **to stand down** (*to withdraw or resign from a body, competition etc.*) abdicate, bow out, resign, retire, step down, withdraw. **to stand for 1** (*to represent, to imply*) allude to, betoken, denote, epitomize, exemplify, illustrate, imply, mean, refer to, represent, signify, symbolize, typify. **2** (*usu. with neg.*) (*to tolerate, to endure*) allow, brook, countenance, endure, permit, put up with, tolerate. ANTONYMS: oppose, prohibit. **3** (*to support the cause of*) advocate, back, champion, espouse, favour, lend one's name to, lend support to, promote, second, sponsor, subscribe to, support. **to stand one's ground** (*to remain resolute, to stay fixed in position*) defy, fight on, hold out against, resist, withstand. ANTONYMS: give in, yield. **to stand out 1** (*to be conspicuous or outstanding*) be conspicuous, beetle, be noticeable, be prominent, bulge, extend, jut out, obtrude, overhang, project, protrude, stick out. **2** (*to persist in opposition or support, to hold out* (*for or against*)) hold out against, hold out for. **to stand up for** (*to support, to take the side of*) champion, defend, fight for, maintain, rally behind, stick up for, uphold. ANTONYMS: oppose.

standard *n.* **1** (*a measure of extent, quantity etc. established by law or custom as an example or criterion for others*) average, benchmark, canon, criterion, exemplar, gauge, guide, guideline, law, mean, measure, norm, par, principle, requirement, rule, scale, yardstick. **2** (*any particular level of quality or competence*) grade, level, rating. **3** (*a flag as the distinctive emblem of an army, government etc.*) banner, colours, emblem, ensign, flag, pennant, pennon. **4** (*an upright pillar or other support*) column, footing, lamp-post, pedestal, pier, pillar, pole, post, stanchion, support. **5** (*something taken as a model to imitate*) archetype, example, ideal, model, paragon, pattern, sample, touchstone, type. ~*a.* (*being of the normal or regulation quality, size etc.*) accepted, basic, conventional, customary, definitive, established, familiar, habitual, normal, ordinary, orthodox, prevailing, recognized, regular, staple, stock, textbook, typical, universal, usual. ANTONYMS: irregular, unorthodox.

standpoint *n.* (*a point of view or viewpoint*) perspective, point of view, position, stance, viewpoint.

standstill *n.* (*a stoppage, a cessation of progress*) cessation, deadlock, halt, hold-up, jam, rest, stalemate, stop, stoppage. ANTONYMS: progress.

staple *n.* (*the main elements of diet etc.*) basics, essentials, fundamentals, necessities.
~*a.* (*chief, principal*) basic, chief, customary, elementary, essential, fundamental, habitual, indispensable, main, necessary, normal, ordinary, prevailing, primary, principal, requisite, standard, universal, usual, vital. ANTONYMS: minor.

star *n.* **1** (*any celestial body appearing as a luminous point*) asteroid, celestial body, heavenly body. **2** (*a brilliant or prominent person, esp. an actor or singer*) big name, bigwig, celebrity, leading light, luminary, superstar. ~*a.* (*outstanding, brilliant*) brilliant, famous, illustrious, major, outstanding, prominent, talented.

stare *v.i.* (*to look with eyes fixed and wide open, as in admiration, surprise etc.*) gape, gawk, gawp, goggle, look, (*coll.*) rubberneck, watch. ANTONYMS: ignore.
~*n.* (*a staring gaze*) gaze, goggle, look.

stark *a.* **1** (*of a landscape etc.*) bare, desolate) bare, barren, bleak, depressing, desolate, dreary, empty, grim, hard, harsh, ravaged, vacant. **2** (*plain, simple, esp. harshly so*) austere, bald, blunt, cold, plain, severe, simple, Spartan, unadorned, unembellished. **3** (*stubborn, inflexible*) fixed, inflexible, stubborn. **4** (*complete, downright*) absolute, arrant, clear, complete, downright, flagrant, gross, mere, out-and-out, outright, patent, plain, pure, rank, sheer, thorough, unmitigated, unqualified, utter. ~*adv.* (*wholly, absolutely*) absolutely, altogether, certifiably, clearly, completely, entirely, fully, obviously, plainly, quite, totally, utterly, wholly. ANTONYMS: partially.

start *v.i.* **1** (*to commence, to come into existence*) arise, begin, come into being, come into existence, come up, commence, crop up, develop, emerge. **2** (*to set out, to begin a journey*) depart, get going, (*coll.*) get the show on the road, get under way, go, (*sl.*) hit the road, leave, move off, set forth, set off, set out. **3** ((*of a machine, engine etc.*) *to begin operating*) crank up, ignite, kick off, switch on, turn on. **4** (*to begin complaining*) complain, fuss, play up. **5** (*to make a sudden involuntary movement, as from fear, surprise etc.*) blench, draw back, flinch, jerk, jump, quail, recoil, shrink, shy, twitch, wince. **6** (*to appear or well up suddenly*) appear, arise, issue, well up.

~*v.t.* **1** (*to begin*) begin, commence, initiate, undertake. **2** (*to set going, to set in motion*) activate, actuate, get going, get off the ground, set in motion, set off. **3** (*to set* (*someone*) *up* (*in business etc.*)) establish, form, found, institute, set up. **4** (*to originate, to set going*) activate, beget, create, establish, father, found, give birth to, inaugurate, initiate, institute, launch, open, originate, pioneer, set going. ANTONYMS: close, end.

~*n.* **1** (*the beginning of a journey, enterprise etc., a setting-out*) beginning, birth, commencement, creation, dawn, emergence, establishment, foundation, genesis, inauguration, inception, initiation, (*coll.*) kick-off, onset, opening, origin, outset, rise. ANTONYMS: end. **2** (*a starting-place*) fountainhead, origin, source, starting-place. **3** (*an advantageous initial position in life, in business etc.*) advantage, edge, head start, lead. **4** (*a sudden involuntary movement, as of fear, surprise etc.*) jump, spasm, surprise, twitch.

startle *v.t.* (*to cause to start in surprise etc.*) alarm, amaze, astonish, astound, discompose, dismay, disturb, frighten, give (someone) a turn, jolt, make jump, perturb, scare, shock, stun, surprise, take aback, upset. ANTONYMS: compose, reassure.

starve *v.i.* **1** (*to die of hunger*) die, perish. **2** (*to suffer severely from hunger or malnourishment*) be famished, be ravenous, fast, hunger. ANTONYMS: gorge. **3** (*to long* (*for e.g. affection, stimulation*)) ache (for), burn (for), crave, desire, hanker (after), hunger (for), long (for), pine (for), thirst (for), want, yearn (for).

~*v.t.* (*to deprive* (*of affection etc.*)) deny, deprive.

state *n.* **1** (*the situation, or relation to circumstances, of a person or thing*) case, circumstances, condition, form, mode of existence, phase, shape, situation, stage, state of affairs. **2** (*coll.*) (*an untidy or confused condition*) fix, jam, mess, (*coll.*) pickle, plight, predicament. **3** (*a political community organized under a government, a nation*) body politic, commonwealth, constitution, country, government, kingdom, land, nation, realm, republic, structure. **4** (*dignity, rank*) brilliance, ceremony, dignity, glory, grandeur, magnificence, majesty, pomp, position, rank, splendour, status, style.

~*a.* (*of or relating to the state or body politic*) ceremonial, dignified, federal, formal, governmental, imperial, majestic, national, official, political, regal, royal, solemn, stately.

~*v.t.* **1** (*to set forth in speech or writing, esp. with explicitness and formality*) assert, aver, avow,

proclaim, set forth, write. **2** (*to declare*) announce, articulate, assert, declare, express, proclaim, profess, report, say, testify, utter, voice. ANTONYMS: suppress. **3** (*to determine, to specify*) affirm, confirm, determine, fix, have, hold, maintain, specify.

stately *a.* (*grand, dignified*) august, awesome, dignified, distinguished, elevated, grand, imperial, imposing, lofty, magnificent, majestic, noble, pompous, regal, royal, solemn, splendid, striking. ANTONYMS: humble, unimposing.

statement *n.* **1** (*that which is stated; a declaration*) affirmation, allegation, announcement, annunciation, assertion, asseveration, averment, avowal, communication, communiqué, declaration, disclosure, expression, proclamation, testimony, utterance. **2** (*a formal account or narration*) account, narration, recital, report. **3** (*an itemized record of additions to and withdrawals from a bank account*) bank statement, record. **4** (*a formal presentation of money owed for goods, services etc.*) account, bill, invoice.

station *n.* **1** (*a place where trains stop to set down or take up passengers or goods*) passenger station, railway station, terminus, train station. **2** (*a similarly equipped terminus or assembly point for coaches or buses*) bus station, coach station, depot, terminus. **3** (*the place where a person or thing stands, esp. an appointed or established place*) location, place, position, post, site, situation, spot, stand. **4** (*a place where a particular service or operation is based*) base, headquarters, office. **5** (*a particular broadcasting establishment, or the radio or television channel it serves*) channel, programme. **6** (*position, rank, esp. high rank*) caste, class, condition, degree, level, occupation, position, rank, standing, status.

~*v.t.* (*to assign to or place in a particular station*) appoint, assign, (*coll.*) billet, establish, fix, garrison, install, locate, place, position, post, site, spot. ANTONYMS: move.

stationary *a.* (*remaining in one place, not moving*) constant, fixed, motionless, resting, still, unmoving.

statue *n.* (*a representation of a person or animal sculptured or cast, e.g. in marble or bronze*) bust, carving, effigy, figure, figurine, head, image, sculpture, statuette.

stature *n.* **1** (*the natural height of a body, esp. of a person*) height, size, tallness. **2** (*eminence or social standing*) eminence, fame, importance, renown, reputation, standing.

status *n.* **1** (*relative standing or position in*

society) degree, eminence, grade, importance, position, pre-eminence, prestige, prominence, rank, reputation, significance, standing, station, stature. **2** (*the current situation or state of affairs*) condition, situation, state of affairs.

staunch *a.* (*loyal, trustworthy*) constant, dependable, devoted, faithful, firm, loyal, reliable, resolute, steadfast, true, true-blue, trusted, trustworthy, trusty, unswerving, unwavering. ANTONYMS: uncertain, wavering.

stay *v.i.* **1** (*to continue in a specified place or state, not to move or change*) continue, linger, persist, remain. **2** (*to remain* (*e.g. calm, cheerful*)) continue, keep, remain. **3** (*to reside temporarily* (*at, with etc.*)) abide, live, lodge at, reside at, settle, sojourn, stop at. **4** (*to keep going or last out in a race etc., or till some other conclusion*) endure, keep going, last out, persist. **5†** (*to wait*) delay, linger, loiter, rest, tarry, wait.
~*v.t.* **1** (*to spend* (*a period of time*) *somewhere*) pass, spend. **2** (*to hinder, to stop the progress etc. of* (*e.g. a disease*)) arrest, block, check, curb, deter, discontinue, discourage, foil, halt, hamper, hinder, impede, obstruct, prevent, retard, slow, stop. **3** (*temporarily to satisfy* (*someone's hunger*)) mollify, satiate, satisfy. **4** (*to postpone, to suspend* (*judgement, a decision etc.*)) adjourn, defer, delay, postpone, put off, suspend. ANTONYMS: hasten.
~*n.* **1** (*continuance in a place etc.*) delay, halt, holiday, pause, postponement, prevention, rest, sojourn, stop, visit, wait. **2** (*a suspension of judicial proceedings*) reprieve, suspension. **3** (*a check, a restraint*) check, deterrent, halt, restraint.

steadfast *a.* (*resolute, unwavering*) constant, dedicated, determined, enduring, faithful, firm, indefatigable, intent, loyal, resolute, single-minded, staunch, unfaltering, unflinching, unwavering. ANTONYMS: irresolute.

steady *a.* **1** (*firmly fixed, not wavering*) firm, fixed, safe, solid, sound, stable, stout, strong, substantial, undeviating, unwavering. ANTONYMS: unsteady. **2** (*moving or acting in a regular way, constant*) balanced, changeless, constant, continual, even, habitual, incessant, regular, relentless, rhythmic, uniform, uninterrupted, unrelieved, unremitting, unvarying. ANTONYMS: irregular, uneven. **3** (*persistent, tenacious*) consistent, devoted, faithful, firm, inveterate, long-standing, loyal, persistent, staunch, steadfast, tenacious. **4** (*serious and conscientious*) calm, conscientious, cool, equable, imperturbable, level-headed, rational, reliable, sensible, serious, (*coll.*) unflappable. **5** (*well controlled*) controlled, well controlled.

~*v.t.* (*to make steady*) brace, hold fast, secure, stabilize, strengthen, support.
~*n.* **1** (*coll.*) (*a regular boyfriend or girlfriend*) boyfriend, girlfriend, partner, sweetheart. **2** (*a rest or support for keeping the hand etc. steady*) prop, rest, support.

steal *v.t.* (*to take* (*someone else's property*) *away without right or permission or intention of returning it*) appropriate, embezzle, filch, hijack, (*coll.*) lift, misappropriate, (*sl.*) nick, pilfer, (*coll.*) pinch, pirate, poach, purloin, rob, (*coll.*) swipe, thieve, (*coll.*) usurp, walk off with. ANTONYMS: restore, return.
~*v.i.* **1** (*to take anything feloniously*) burgle, rob, thieve. **2** (*to go or come furtively or silently*) creep, lurk, prowl, pussyfoot, skulk, slink, slip, sneak, tiptoe.

stealthy *a.* (*secret and quiet*) clandestine, closet, covert, furtive, secret, secretive, skulking, sly, sneaking, sneaky, stealthful, surreptitious, undercover, underhand. ANTONYMS: open.

steamy *a.* **1** (*emitting or covered with steam*) befogged, blurred, boiling, clouded, damp, dank, dripping, fogged up, humid, misted, moist, muggy, sticky, sultry, sweaty, sweltering. **2** (*erotic*) arousing, erotic, exciting, (*sl.*) horny, (*coll.*) hot, passionate, pornographic, sexy.

steel *n.* (*weaponry consisting of a sword or swords*) blade, dagger, dirk, knife, stiletto, sword.
~*v.t.* (*to harden* (*one's heart etc. against*), *to brace* (*oneself for*)) bite the bullet, brace, fortify, grit one's teeth, harden, insulate, inure, nerve, stiffen, toughen. ANTONYMS: weaken.

steep *a.* **1** (*sharply inclined, sloping at a high angle*) bluff, inclined, precipitous, sharp, sheer, sloping. ANTONYMS: flat, level. **2** ((*of a rise or fall*) *swift, sudden*) abrupt, sudden, swift. ANTONYMS: gradual. **3** ((*of a price, demand etc.*) *excessive, unreasonable*) dear, excessive, exorbitant, expensive, extortionate, extravagant, extreme, high, overpriced, stiff, unreasonable. ANTONYMS: moderate, reasonable.

steer *v.t.* (*to guide* (*a ship, aeroplane, vehicle etc.*) *by a rudder, wheel, handle etc.*) channel, conduct, control, direct, guide, lead, manage, pilot. **to steer clear of** (*to avoid*) avoid, circumvent, dodge, eschew, evade, give a wide berth to, keep away from, shun.

stem[1] *n.* **1** (*the stalk, or ascending part of a tree, shrub, or other plant*) axis, shaft, stalk, stock, trunk. **2** (*the slender stalk of a flower, leaf etc.*) peduncle, shoot, stalk. **to stem from** (*to spring* *from*) arise from, come from, derive from, descend from, develop from, emanate from, flow from, generate from, grow out of, issue from, originate in, proceed from, result from, spring from, sprout from.

stem² *v.t.* **1** (*to check, to hold back*) arrest, check, control, curb, cut, diminish, draw up, halt, hold back, lessen, quell, reduce, restrain, retard, slow, stay, stop, suppress. **2** (*to dam up* (*a stream etc.*)) block, dam up, plug, staunch.

stench *n.* (*a foul or offensive smell*) effluvium, fetor, odour, (*coll.*) pong, reek, smell, stink. ANTONYMS: perfume.

step *v.i.* (*to walk or dance slowly or with dignity*) move, pace, stride, tread, walk.
~*n.* **1** (*a single complete movement of one leg in the act of walking, dancing etc.*) pace, stride, tread. **2** (*an action or measure taken in a series directed to some end*) act, action, deed, degree, gradation, initiative, measure, motion, move, movement, phase, proceeding, progression, stage. **3** (*a single stair in a flight of stairs*) rung, stair, tread. **4** (*a footprint*) footprint, impression, imprint, mark, spoor, trace, track. **5** (*the noise made by a foot in walking etc.*) footfall, footstep. **to step down 1** (*to resign, relinquish one's position etc.*) abdicate, bow out, relinquish, resign, retire, stand down, withdraw. **2** (*to decrease the voltage etc. of*) decrease, diminish, reduce. ANTONYMS: step up. **to step up 1** (*to advance by one or more stages*) accelerate, advance, progress, speed up. **2** (*to increase the power, voltage etc. of*) augment, boost, escalate, improve, increase, intensify, raise. ANTONYMS: reduce, step down. **3** (*to come forward*) come forward, volunteer.

sterile *a.* **1** (*not producing crops, young etc.*) bare, barren, childless, empty, fruitless, infecund, infertile, stale, unfruitful, unproductive, unprolific. ANTONYMS: fruitful. **2** ((*of arguments etc.*) *unproductive, pointless*) abortive, futile, pointless, senseless, useless. **3** (*containing no living bacteria, microbes etc.*) antiseptic, aseptic, disinfected, germ-free, pure, sanitary, sterilized, uncontaminated, uninfected, unpolluted.

sterling *a.* **1** ((*of coins and precious metals*) *of standard value, genuine*) authentic, fine, first-class, genuine, pure, real, standard, true. ANTONYMS: fake. **2** ((*of work, efforts etc.*) *sound, not showy*) admirable, estimable, excellent, good, solid, sound, true, worthy.
~*n.* (*British* (*as distinct from foreign*) *money*) L.S.D., pounds sterling.

stern *a.* **1** (*severe, forbidding*) austere, authoritarian, crabby, crusty, dour, flinty, forbidding, frowning, gloomy, grave, grim, gruff, lugubrious, rigorous, saturnine, serious, severe, sombre, sour, steely. ANTONYMS: lenient. **2** (*harsh, strict*) critical, demanding, firm, hard, harsh, rigid, strict, stringent, tough. **3** (*ruthless, unyielding*) adamant, determined, hard-hearted, immovable, inexorable, inflexible, obdurate, relentless, resolute, ruthless, uncompromising, unyielding.

stew *v.t., v.i.* (*to cook by boiling slowly or simmering in a closed dish or pan*) boil slowly, seethe, simmer.
~*v.i.* **1** (*to be stifled or oppressed by a close atmosphere*) be oppressed, be stifled, suffocate. **2** (*coll.*) (*to fret or agonize* (*over*)) agonize, be agitated, be anxious, burn, chafe, dither, fret, (*coll.*) get steamed up about, seethe, smoulder.
~*n.* **1** (*a meat dish etc. cooked by stewing*) goulash, hash, hotpot, mess. **2** (*a state of mental agitation or worry*) agitation, anxiety, bother, dither, excitement, lather, (*coll.*) state, sweat, tizzy, worry.

stick¹ *n.* **1** (*a shoot or branch of a tree or shrub broken or cut off*) branch, shoot, twig. **2** (*a slender piece of wood or other material used as a rod, walking cane etc.*) baton, birch, cane, club, pole, rod, staff, stake, switch, walking stick, wand. **3** (*coll.*) (*hostile criticism*) blame, censure, criticism, hostility. **4** (*a person, esp. someone elderly and old-fashioned*) bloke, chap, fogey, man, woman.

stick² *v.t.* **1** (*to pierce, to stab*) bore, drill, gore, jab, penetrate, perforate, pierce, prick, punch, puncture, riddle, stab. **2** (*to fix or insert* (*in, into*)) fix, insert, install, penetrate. **3** (*to fix or impale on or as on, by or as by, a point*) fix, impale, pin, run through, spear, spike, spit, transfix. **4** (*to cause to adhere*) affix, bind, cement, cleave, cling, cohere, fasten, fix, fuse, glue, gum, hold, join, nail, paste, set, solder, tack, tape. ANTONYMS: separate. **5** (*to put* (*something somewhere*)) deposit, drop, lay, place, plant, plonk, put, (*coll.*) shove. **6** (*to tolerate, endure*) abide, bear, endure, stand, tolerate.
~*v.i.* **1** (*to be inserted or thrust*) dig, insert, poke, prod, push, put, thrust. **2** (*to protrude, project*) beetle, bulge, extend, jut out, obtrude, overhang, project, protrude, stand out. **3** (*to become fixed, to adhere*) adhere, bond, fix, fuse. **4** (*to endure or persist*) endure, last, persist. **5** (*to stay, remain*) abide, continue, dwell, linger, lodge, remain, stay, stop. **6** (*to persist, to persevere* (*at*)) continue, keep (at), persevere, persist. **7** (*to have scruples or misgivings*) baulk, hesitate, scruple. **to stick up for** (*to take the part of, to defend*) champion, defend, rally behind, stand by, stand up for, support, take the part of, take up the cudgels for. ANTONYMS: oppose.

sticky *a.* **1** (*tending to stick, adhesive*) adhesive, tacky. **2** (*viscous, glutinous*) gluey, glutinous, (*coll.*) gooey, gummy, viscid, viscous. **3** (*coll.*) (*difficult, painful*) awkward, delicate, difficult, discomfiting, embarrassing, (*coll.*) hairy, painful, sensitive, ticklish, tricky, uncomfortable, unpleasant. **4** ((*of the weather*) *unpleasantly hot and damp*) clammy, close, damp, dank, humid, muggy, oppressive, sultry, sweltering. ANTONYMS: fresh.

stiff *a.* **1** (*rigid, not easily bent or moved*) hard, inelastic, rigid, unbendable, unmoved. ANTONYMS: limp. **2** (*not flexible, not yielding*) brittle, compact, dense, firm, hard, inflexible, solid, stiffened, thick, tough, unyielding. **3** (*hard to accomplish; difficult*) arduous, challenging, difficult, exacting, exhausting, fatiguing, hard, harrowing, laborious, rigorous, rough, steep, strenuous, tiring, toilsome, tough, trying, uphill. ANTONYMS: easy. **4** ((*of a person or their manner*) *constrained, awkward*) affected, artificial, austere, awkward, clumsy, cold, constrained, forced, formal, haughty, laboured, mannered, prim, reserved, rigid, stand-offish, stuffy, tense, (*coll.*) uptight, wooden. **5** (*stubborn, persistent*) determined, dogged, firm, indomitable, obstinate, persistent, relentless, resolute, resolved, staunch, stubborn, tenacious, unyielding. **6** (*severe, harsh*) brisk, cruel, excessive, extreme, forceful, fresh, gusty, harsh, keen, merciless, powerful, severe, steady, stringent, strong, unsparing, vigorous. ANTONYMS: lenient, light. **7** ((*of liquor*) *strong*) alcoholic, intoxicating, strong. **8** ((*of prices*) *high*) dear, excessive, exorbitant, expensive, high, steep. **9** ((*of a mixture etc.*) *not fluid, viscous*) thick, viscous.
~*n.* (*a corpse*) body, cadaver, corpse.

stifle *v.t., v.i.* (*to smother, to suffocate*) asphyxiate, choke, smother, strangle, suffocate, throttle.
~*v.t.* **1** (*to suppress*) check, choke back, control, cover up, curb, hold in, hush, keep back, prevent, quell, repress, restrain, silence, suppress, withhold. **2** (*to stamp out, quash*) choke, crush, demolish, destroy, extinguish, kill, quash, stamp out.

still *a., adv.* **1** (*at rest, motionless*) at rest, immobile, inert, motionless, stagnant, static, stationary, unmoving. **2** ((*of sea, weather etc.*) *calm*) calm, quiet, tranquil. **3** (*silent, hushed*) calm, flat, hushed, noiseless, pacific, peaceful, placid, quiescent, quiet, restful, sedate, serene, silent, smooth, soundless, tranquil, undisturbed, unruffled. ANTONYMS: agitated, troubled.
~*n.* (*calm, quiet*) calm, hush, noiselessness, peace, peacefulness, quiet, silence, stillness, tranquillity. ANTONYMS: noise.

~*adv.* **1** (*without moving*) motionless, quiet, silent, stock-still, unmoving. **2** (*even to this or that time, yet*) even, yet. **3** (*nevertheless, in spite of that*) all the same, but, even then, however, in spite of, nevertheless, notwithstanding, yet.
~*v.t.* **1** (*to quiet, to calm*) calm, compose, hush, lull, quiet, quieten, tranquillize. **2** (*to appease*) allay, alleviate, appease, assuage, check, mollify, pacify, relieve, settle, soothe, stop, subdue. ANTONYMS: disturb.

stimulate *v.t.* **1** (*to rouse to action or greater exertion*) activate, animate, arouse, awaken, encourage, excite, fire, galvanize, impel, inflame, inspire, invigorate, kindle, nourish, quicken, rouse, stir up, (*coll.*) turn on, wake up. **2** (*to spur on, to incite*) foment, goad, incite, instigate, motivate, prick, prompt, provoke, spur, urge. ANTONYMS: deter, dissuade.

sting *n.* **1** (*any acute pain, ache etc.*) ache, bite, burn, distress, hurt, injury, pain, prick, smart, tingle, wound. **2** (*a swindle*) con, deception, ruse, swindle, trick.
~*v.t.* **1** (*to pierce or wound with a sting*) afflict, bite, burn, hurt, injure, nettle, pain, pierce, prick, stick, wound. ANTONYMS: soothe. **2** (*to goad* (*into*)) goad, prick, spur. **3** (*to cheat, to overcharge*) cheat, defraud, fleece, overcharge, (*coll.*) rip off, rob, (*coll.*) soak, swindle, (*coll.*) take for a ride.

stint *v.t.* (*to give or allow* (*someone*) *money, food etc. scantily or grudgingly*) begrudge.
~*v.i.* (*to be too sparing or parsimonious* (*of a certain commodity*)) confine, control, curb, cut corners, economize, hold back, limit, pinch, restrain, restrict, save, scrimp, skimp, withhold. ANTONYMS: lavish.
~*n.* **1** (*limit, restriction*) bound, check, condition, constraint, control, curb, limit, limitation, qualification, reservation, restraint, restriction. **2** (*an allotted quantity, turn of work etc.*) allotment, amount, assignment, bit, charge, chore, duty, job, obligation, part, quantity, quota, ration, responsibility, share, shift, spell, stretch, task, term, time, tour, turn.

stipulate *v.t.* (*to lay down or specify as an essential condition to an agreement or bargain*) insist, lay down, set forth, specify.
~*v.i.* **1** (*to make a specific demand* (*for*)) call for, demand, require. **2** (*to settle terms*) agree, contract, covenant, engage, guarantee, pledge, promise, provide for, settle terms, warrant.

stipulation *n.* (*an essential condition that is part of an agreement*) agreement, clause, condition, contract, covenant, demand, essential, obligation, prerequisite, promise, provision, proviso, qualification, requirement, requisite, specification, term, undertaking, warranty.

stir *v.t.* **1** (*to move a spoon etc. round and round in* (*a liquid or liquid mixture*) *to blend the ingredients*) amalgamate, beat, blend, churn, fold, intermingle, merge, mingle, mix, whip. **2** (*to cause to move, to disturb*) affect, agitate, disturb, mix, move, rustle, scramble, shake, trouble, upset. **3** (*to move vigorously, to bestir* (*oneself etc.*)) bestir oneself, exert oneself, (*coll.*) get a move on, look lively, (*often int.*) shake a leg. **4** (*to rouse* (*up*), *to animate*) affect, animate, arouse, awaken, energize, excite, galvanize, goad, incite, inflame, inspire, motivate, move, prod, prompt, provoke, rouse, spur, stimulate, touch, urge.
~*v.i.* **1** (*to move*) budge, go, move, shift. ANTONYMS: remain, stay. **2** (*to wake up, or get up after sleep*) arise, get up, rise, wake up.
~*n.* **1** (*commotion, bustle*) action, activity, ado, agitation, bother, bustle, commotion, confusion, disorder, disturbance, excitement, flurry, fuss, hubbub, hustle, movement, stirring, tumult, uproar. ANTONYMS: tranquillity. **2** (*a movement*) movement, whisper.

stirring *a.* (*exciting, stimulating*) animated, awe-inspiring, dramatic, emotional, emotive, evocative, exciting, exhilarating, gripping, heady, impassioned, inspiring, intoxicating, lively, melodramatic, rousing, spirited, stimulating, thrilling. ANTONYMS: dull.

stock *n.* **1** (*the aggregate of goods ready for sale or distribution*) goods, merchandise, wares. **2** (*a supply of anything, available for use*) accumulation, array, assortment, cache, collection, fund, hoard, inventory, range, reserve, reservoir, selection, stockpile, store, supply, variety. **3** (*livestock*) animals, beasts, cattle, goats, horses, livestock, oxen, pigs, sheep. **4** (*the capital of a corporate company divided into shares*) assets, capital, commodities, funds, property, shares. **5** (*one's reputation or standing*) name, reputation, standing. **6** (*the trunk or main stem of a tree or other plant*) stalk, stem, trunk. **7** (*a family, a line of descent*) ancestry, bloodline, breed, breeding, descent, dynasty, extraction, family, genealogy, heritage, house, lineage, line of descent, parentage, pedigree, race, roots, species, type. **8** (*the principal supporting or holding part of anything, the handle, base etc.*) base, block, body, butt, handle, shaft.
~*a.* (*habitually used, permanent*) banal, basic, clichéd, commonplace, customary, everyday, hackneyed, normal, ordinary, regular, routine, run-of-the-mill, set, stale, standard, staple, stereotyped, tired, traditional, trite, usual, worn out. ANTONYMS: unusual.
~*v.t.* **1** (*to provide* (*e.g. shops*) *with goods*, (*farms*) *with livestock etc.*) carry, deal in, equip, furnish, have, make available, market, offer,

provide, provision, sell, supply, trade in. **2** (*to keep* (*goods*) *in stock*) accumulate, amass, cache, hoard, keep in stock, lay in, pile up, reserve, save, stockpile, store.

stoical *a.* (*resigned, impassive*) calm, controlled, cool, disciplined, dispassionate, emotionless, frigid, impassive, imperturbable, long-suffering, patient, philosophical, phlegmatic, resigned, self-possessed, stoic, stolid, unemotional. ANTONYMS: excitable.

stomach *n.* **1** (*the belly, the abdomen*) abdomen, belly, (*sl.*) breadbasket, gut, paunch, pot, pot belly, (*coll.*) spare tyre, (*coll.*) tummy. **2** (*appetite* (*for food*) *or an inclination or liking* (*for some enterprise*)) appetite (for), craving (for), desire (for), hankering (after), hunger (for), inclination (to), leaning (towards), liking (for), longing (for), need (for), relish (for), taste (for), thirst (for), yearning (for). ANTONYMS: dislike.
~*v.t.* **1** (*to accept as palatable*) accept, countenance. **2** (*to put up with, to brook*) abide, bear, brook, endure, put up with, reconcile oneself to, resign oneself to, stand, (*coll.*) stick, suffer, swallow, take, tolerate.

stony *a.* **1** (*relating to or consisting of stone*) pebbly, rocky, shingled, shingly. **2** (*hard, incapable of feeling or emotion*) adamantine, callous, cold, cruel, flinty, hard, heartless, icy, impenetrable, implacable, intractable, pitiless, rigid, steely, unresponsive, unsentimental, unsympathetic. **3** (*obdurate, perverse*) inflexible, obdurate, perverse, stubborn.

stoop *v.i.* **1** (*to bend the body downwards and forward*) bend, crouch, squat. **2** (*to have a habitual forward inclination of the head and shoulders*) bow, droop, duck, hunch, incline, lean, slouch. **3** (*to lower or bring oneself down* (*to some demeaning act*)) abase oneself, acquiesce, condescend, degrade oneself, deign, demean oneself, descend, humble oneself, lower oneself, sink, submit, yield. **4** ((*of a hawk etc.*) *to swoop towards a prey*) dive at, pounce, swoop.
~*n.* (*a habitual inclination of the shoulders etc.*) crouch, hunch, inclination, slouch.

stop *v.t.* **1** (*to cause to cease moving, working etc.*) break off, bring to an end, cease, discontinue, finish, halt, quit, terminate. **2** (*to hinder; to prevent* (*from doing something*)) block, check, curb, delay, hamper, hinder, impede, obstruct, prevent, repress, restrain, stall, suppress, thwart. **3** (*to cause to cease action*) defeat, foil, prevent, thwart. **4** (*to close by filling or obstructing*) bar, block, choke, clog up, close, dam, hold back, jam up, obstruct, plug, seal, staunch, stem, stuff. **5** (*to keep back,* *to suspend* (*wages etc.*)) cut off, keep back, suspend, withhold.

~*v.i.* **1** (*to come to an end*) arrest, cease, come to an end, complete, conclude, desist, discontinue, end, finish, leave off, quit, terminate. **2** (*to halt; to come to rest*) halt, pause, rest. **3** (*to stay, to remain temporarily*) linger, lodge, remain, rest, sojourn, stay, tarry, visit, wait. ANTONYMS: move on.

~*n.* **1** (*an act of stopping or state of being stopped*) arrest, break, cessation, conclusion, end, finish, intermission, interruption, pause, standstill, stoppage, termination. ANTONYMS: continuation. **2** (*a regular halt for a bus or train, a place where passengers get on or off*) halt, station, stopping-place, terminus. **3** (*a punctuation mark indicating a pause, esp. a full point; in telegrams etc., a full point*) full stop, period, point. **4** (*a block, peg etc. used to stop the movement of something at a particular point*) bar, block, hindrance, impediment, obstacle, peg, pin, plug, stopper.

store *n.* **1** (*a stock laid up for drawing upon*) cache, fund, hoard, inventory, reserve, reservoir, stock, stockpile. **2** (*an abundant supply, plenty*) abundance, accumulation, collection, mass, plenty, supply. **3** (*a place where things are laid up or kept for sale, a warehouse*) depository, depot, repository, storehouse, warehouse. **4** (*sometimes in pl.*) (*a shop selling basic commodities*) emporium, grocery, market, mart, outlet, retail outlet, shop, supermarket.

~*v.t.* **1** (*to deposit* (*furniture etc.*) *in a warehouse etc. for safe keeping*) hold, husband, keep, preserve, stow away, warehouse. ANTONYMS: consume, discard. **2** (*to accumulate or lay* (*usu. up or away*) *for future use*) accumulate, aggregate, amass, assemble, collect, cumulate, garner, hoard, hold, lay up, pile up, put aside, reserve, save, set aside, stockpile. **3** (*to stock or supply* (*with*)) carry, deal in, keep, sell, stock, supply. **4** (*to have a capacity for holding a reserve, e.g. of water*) hoard, hold, put aside, reserve, save, set aside.

storm *n.* **1** (*a violent disturbance of the atmosphere accompanied by wind, rain, snow, hail, or thunder and lightning*) blizzard, dust storm, hailstorm, ice storm, monsoon, rainstorm, sandstorm, snowstorm, tempest, thunderstorm, turbulence. **2** (*a wind of force 10 or 11, between a gale and a hurricane*) cyclone, gale, hurricane, squall, tornado, typhoon, whirlwind, windstorm. **3** (*a violent disturbance or agitation of society, the mind etc., a tumult*) agitation, commotion, disorder, disturbance, furore, outbreak, riot, rumpus, stir, tumult, turbulence, turmoil. ANTONYMS: calm. **4** (*a hail or shower* (*of blows or missiles*)) blitz, fusillade,

hail, shower, volley. **5** (*a violent outburst* (*of cheers etc.*)) eruption, explosion, outburst, outcry, outpouring, tantrum. **6** (*a direct assault on, or the capture of, a fortified place*) assault, attack, capture, charge, onset, onslaught, raid, rush.

~*v.i.* **1** (*to rage* (*at etc.*)*, to behave violently*) (*N Am., coll.*) blow one's stack, (*coll.*) blow one's top, bluster, explode, fly off the handle, fume, (*sl.*) raise Cain, raise hell, raise the roof, rant, rave, roar, thunder. **2** ((*of wind, rain etc.*) *to rage*) blow, bluster, hail, howl, rage, rain, sleet, snow, squall, thunder.

~*v.t.* (*to take* (*a stronghold etc.*) *by storm*) assail, assault, attack, barrage, besiege, blitz, bombard, capture, charge, fire upon, lay siege to, raid, rush, shell, take by storm.

stormy *a.* **1** ((*of winds*) *tempestuous*) bad, blustery, foul, gusty, howling, inclement, nasty, raging, roaring, squally, tempestuous, windy. ANTONYMS: calm, fair. **2** (*vehement, passionate*) feverish, fierce, fiery, frantic, frenetic, frenzied, furious, nerve-racking, passionate, raging, raving, rough, tempestuous, turbulent, vehement, violent, wild. ANTONYMS: peaceful.

story *n.* **1** (*a narrative or recital in prose or verse, of actual or fictitious events, a tale*) account, allegory, anecdote, chronicle, epic, fable, fairy tale, fiction, †gest, history, legend, myth, narrative, novel, novella, parable, recital, romance, saga, tale, yarn. **2** (*the plot or incidents of a novel or play; a storyline*) outline, plot, scenario, storyline, summary. **3** (*an account of an incident, experience etc.*) allegation, assertion, contention, representation, statement, testimony, version. **4** (*a descriptive article in a newspaper*) article, copy, dispatch, exclusive, feature, information, item, news, piece, release, report, tidings. **5** (*a falsehood, a fib*) alibi, confabulation, excuse, falsehood, fib, lie, untruth. ANTONYMS: truth.

stout *a.* **1** (*corpulent, bulky*) big, bulky, burly, corpulent, fat, fleshy, heavy, heavy-set, large, obese, overweight, plump, portly, rotund, thickset, tubby. ANTONYMS: lean, thin. **2** (*strong, sturdy*) sound, strong, sturdy, substantial, well-built. **3** (*brave, resolute*) bold, brave, courageous, dauntless, doughty, durable, fearless, firm, hardy, intrepid, lusty, plucky, resolute, robust, rugged, stalwart, staunch, tough, valiant, vigorous. ANTONYMS: weak.

~*n.* (*a type of strong beer made from roasted malt or barley*) malt, porter.

straggle *v.i.* **1** (*to lose tightness or compactness*) loosen, spread. **2** (*to become sporadic or irregular*) disperse, separate, thin out. **3** (*to wander away from or trail behind the main* *body*) deviate, digress, drift, lag, loiter, meander, prowl, ramble, range, roam, rove, stray, trail behind, wander away.

straight *a.* **1** (*not bent or crooked*) regular, unbending, unbent, uncurved, uniform. **2** (*Geom.*) ((*of a line*) *lying along the shortest path between any two of its points*) direct, linear. **3** (*successive, in an unbroken run*) back-to-back, consecutive, successive, unbroken. **4** (*uninterrupted; coming direct from its source*) direct, undeviating, uninterrupted, unswerving, uobstructed. **5** (*level, even*) even, flat, horizontal, level, perpendicular, plumb, right, smooth, square, true, upright, vertical. ANTONYMS: crooked. **6** (*in proper order or condition; arranged to one's satisfaction*) arranged, in condition, in order, neat, orderly, organized, satisfactory, shipshape, sorted out, spruce, straightened out, tidy. ANTONYMS: disordered, untidy. **7** (*clear*) agreed, clear, even, settled, square, staightened out, understood. **8 a** (*honest, not deviating from truth or fairness*) above-board, accurate, authoritative, correct, decent, equitable, explicit, fair, honest, just, legitimate, plain, right, square, straightforward, true, unqualified, upright. ANTONYMS: dishonest. **b** (*not evasive or ambiguous*) blunt, candid, dependable, direct, forthright, frank, honourable, no-nonsense, point-blank, reliable, respectable, trustworthy, unambiguous, unequivocal, (*coll.*) upfront. **9 a** (*unmodified, unmitigated*) pure, unadulterated, unalloyed, unaltered, unmitigated, unmixed, unmodified. **b** ((*of a drink*) *undiluted*) neat, pure, undiluted, unmixed. **10** ((*of a person*) *conventional, not outrageous*) composed, conventional, emotionless, impassive, sedate, sober, staid, taciturn, unemotional.
~*adv.* **1** (*directly*) directly, head-on. **2** (*without ambiguity or circumlocution*) candidly, explicitly, forthrightly, frankly, honestly, outright, plainly, point-blank, right, simply, straightforwardly, unambiguously, undeviatingly, unequivocally, unswervingly. **3** (*with an accurate aim*) accurately, directly. **4** (*immediately, at once*) at once, directly, forthwith, immediately, instantly, promptly, right away, straight away, without delay. **straight away** (*at once, without delay*) at once, directly, forthwith, immediately, instantly, now, promptly, right away, summarily, without delay. ANTONYMS: later.

strain¹ *v.t.* **1** (*to stretch tight; to make taut*) extend, stretch, tauten, tighten. ANTONYMS: relax. **2** (*to exert* (*e.g. oneself, one's senses, one's eyes etc.*) *to the utmost*) exert, press, push, stress. **3** (*to force beyond due limits*) exceed, force, overexert, overtax, overwork, push, surpass. **4** (*to weaken or injure by excessive effort*) damage, distort, harm, impair, injure, sprain, tax, tire, weaken. **5** (*to purify from extraneous matter by passing through a colander or other strainer*) drain, draw off, purify, screen, separate, sieve, sift, winnow. **6** (*to remove* (*solid matter*) *by filtering* (*out*)) filter, percolate, remove, seep.
~*v.i.* **1** (*to become fully stretched*) stretch, tauten, tense. **2** (*to exert oneself*) exert oneself, tax oneself. **3** (*to pull or tug* (*at*)) crane, heave, pull, tug, twist, wrench. **4** (*to toil or labour* (*under a burden etc.*)) labour, strive, struggle, toil. **5** (*to be filtered, to percolate*) drip through, filter, percolate, trickle.
~*n.* **1** (*an act of straining, a violent effort*) effort, exertion, pull, straining, stretch, struggle. ANTONYMS: relaxation. **2** (*the force thus exerted; tension*) force, pressure, stress, tension. **3** (*an injury, distortion caused by excessive effort or tension*) distortion, harm, injury, sprain, wrench. **4** (*mental tension, fatigue from overwork etc.*) anxiety, exhaustion, fatigue, worry. **5** (*a song, a piece of poetry*) air, lay, melody, music, poem, song, sound, theme, tune. **6** (*tone, style*) cast, character, complexion, drift, humour, impression, inclination, manner, mood, pitch, quality, spirit, style, tendency, tenor, theme, tone, vein.

strain² *n.* **1** (*family, breed*) ancestry, background, bloodline, derivation, descendants, descent, extraction, family, heritage, line, lineage, parentage, pedigree, race, roots, stock. **2** (*natural tendency or disposition*) disposition, evidence, hint, indication, mark, sign, soupçon, streak, suggestion, suspicion, tendency, trace, trait, vein, vestige.

strange *a.* **1** (*unusual, surprising*) abnormal, bizarre, curious, eccentric, extraordinary, fantastic, grotesque, inexplicable, irregular, odd, offbeat, outlandish, peculiar, quaint, queer, singular, surprising, uncanny, unusual, weird. ANTONYMS: normal, ordinary. **2** (*not well known, unfamiliar*) inexperienced, little known, new, novel, unaccustomed, unfamiliar, unheard-of, unknown, untried. ANTONYMS: familiar. **3** (*alien, foreign*) alien, exotic, foreign. **4** (*fresh or unused* (*to*), *unacquainted*) fresh, unaccustomed, unacquainted, unused.

stranger *n.* **1** (*a person from another place*) newcomer, outlander, outsider. ANTONYMS: local. **2** (*a foreigner*) alien, foreigner. ANTONYMS: native, resident. **3** (*a guest, a visitor*) guest, visitor.

strategy *n.* **1** (*the art of war*) generalship, tactics. **2** (*a long-term plan aimed at achieving a specific goal*) action plan, blueprint, design, game plan, master plan, plan, plan of action, procedure, programme, scenario, scheme. **3** (*a* *political or economic plan of action*) approach, plan, policy, procedure.

stray *v.i.* **1** (*to wander from the direct or proper course*) deviate, digress, diverge, drift, get sidetracked, go off at a tangent, go off track, go wrong, lose one's way, meander, ramble, range, roam, rove, straggle, swerve, wander. **2** (*to err or sin*) err, go astray, sin, wander.
~*n.* (*a straggler, a waif*) (*esp. N Am.*) hobo, straggler, vagrant, waif.
~*a.* **1** (*gone astray*) abandoned, derelict, gone astray, homeless, lost, roaming, roving, vagrant, wandering. **2** (*occasional, sporadic*) accidental, casual, chance, freak, haphazard, isolated, lone, occasional, odd, random, scattered, separate, single, singular, sporadic, straggling, unexpected.

streak *n.* **1** (*an esp. irregular line or long narrow mark of a distinct colour from the background*) band, bar, dash, daub, fleck, line, mark, slash, smear, striation, strip, stripe, stroke. **2** (*a vein or element*) element, layer, seam, strain, touch, trace, vein. **3** (*a run or stretch, esp. of good or bad luck*) period, run, spate, spell, stretch.
~*v.t.* (*to mark with streaks*) bar, daub, line, mark, slash, smear, striate, stripe.
~*v.i.* (*to move in a straight line at speed*) bolt, dart, flash, fly, hasten, hurry, hurtle, race, run, rush, scoot, speed, sprint, tear, whistle, whiz, zip, zoom.

stream *n.* **1** (*a small river*) beck, brook, brooklet, burn, channel, creek, river, rivulet, streamlet, tributary, watercourse. **2** (*a steady flow, a current*) barrage, cascade, deluge, drift, effusion, flood, flow, fountain, line, outpouring, row, rush, series, spurt, string, succession, surge, swarm, tide, torrent. **3** (*a band of schoolchildren of the same general academic ability, taught as a group*) class, group, remove, set, shell.
~*v.i.* **1** (*to flow or move in or as a stream*) cascade, course, file, flow, glide, gush, march, move, proceed, run, slide, slip, surge, walk. **2** (*to pour out or emit liquid abundantly*) emanate, emit, flood, issue, pour out. **3** (*to hang or wave in the wind etc.*) billow, flap, float, hang, wave.

street *n.* **1** (*a road in a city or town with houses on one side or on both*) alley, avenue, boulevard, byway, circle, concourse, drive, high road, lane, passage, road, roadway, row, terrace. **2** (*the part of the road used by vehicles*) thoroughfare, way.

strength *n.* **1** (*muscular force*) brawn, energy, force, hardiness, might, muscle, robustness, sinew, sturdiness, toughness, vigour. ANTONYMS: weakness. **2** (*firmness, solidity*) backbone, determination, durability, endurance,

firmness, fortitude, grit, (*coll.*) guts, nerve, perseverance, persistence, resoluteness, solidity, stamina, stoutness, tenacity, will-power. **3** (*power, potency*) cogency, efficacy, incisiveness, persuasiveness, potency, power, soundness, validity, weight. **4** (*intensity*) concentration, intensity, vehemence. **5** (*an attribute or quality seen as a character asset*) ability, aptitude, asset, attribute, gift, quality, talent. **6** (*the full number or complement*) complement, number, total.

strengthen *v.t.* (*to make strong or stronger*) back up, bolster, build up, buttress, confirm, corroborate, encourage, fortify, harden, heighten, intensify, nourish, reinforce, renew, steel, step up, stiffen, substantiate, support, toughen. ANTONYMS: undermine, weaken.

strenuous *a.* **1** (*energetic, vigorous*) active, ardent, dynamic, eager, earnest, energetic, enthusiastic, forceful, intense, resolute, sincere, vigorous, zealous. ANTONYMS: feeble, weak. **2** (*requiring effort*) arduous, burdensome, demanding, difficult, exhausting, hard, laborious, taxing, tiring, toilsome, tough, uphill. **3** (*eagerly persistent*) determined, dogged, indefatigable, persistent, tenacious, tireless.

stress *n.* **1** (*tension, pressure or strain exerted on an object*) pressure, strain, tension. **2** (*constraining or impelling force*) force, forcefulness. **3** (*demands made on one physically, mentally or emotionally*) burden, demands, load. **4** (*physical, mental or emotional strain resulting from this*) anguish, anxiety, distress, grief, pain, strain, suffering, tension, worry. **5** (*importance, emphasis*) emphasis, force, importance, insistence, prominence, significance, urgency, weight. **6** (*emphasis on a word or syllable*) accent, accentuation, emphasis, ictus.
~*v.t.* **1** (*to emphasize*) bring home, dwell on, emphasize, feature, focus on, harp on, highlight, make a point of, mark, note, point up, repeat, spotlight, underline, underscore. **2** (*to put the stress or accent on*) accent, accentuate, lay stress on. **3** (*to subject to physical or mental stress or mechanical force*) burden, distress, disturb, pressure, pressurize, put under strain, strain, upset, worry.

stretch *v.t.* **1** (*to extend in any direction or to full length*) balloon, blow up, dilate, draw out, enlarge, expand, extend, increase, inflate, pull out. ANTONYMS: contract. **2** (*to tighten, to make longer or wider by tension*) broaden, elongate, lengthen, tauten, tighten, widen. **3** (*to extend lengthwise, to straighten (a limb etc.)*) straighten, straighten out. **4** (*to hit so as to prostrate*) flatten, floor, prostrate. **5** (*to distend*) distend, strain, swell. **6** (*to exaggerate (e.g. the* *truth*)) distort, do violence to, exaggerate, twist. **7** (*to utilize fully or challenge sufficiently*) challenge, do justice to, push, tax.

~*v.i.* **1** (*to have a specified extension in space or time, to reach or last*) cover, extend, last, reach, span, spread. **2** (*to be drawn out or admit of being drawn out*) draw out, give. **3** (*to extend or straighten one's body or limbs*) extend, straighten.

~*n.* **1** (*a reach or tract* (*of land, water etc.*)) area, reach, sweep, tract. **2** (*an act of stretching or state of being stretched*) elasticity, give, resilience, stretchability, stretchiness. **3** (*extent or reach*) compass, expanse, extent, range, reach, scope, space. **4** (*a period of service*) period, shift, spell, stint, term, time, tour.

strict *a.* **1** (*defined or applied exactly, accurate*) accurate, careful, close, confining, conscientious, constrictive, defined, exact, exacting, faithful, meticulous, narrow, particular, precise, scrupulous, undeviating. ANTONYMS: inexact, loose. **2** (*rigorous, severe*) austere, authoritarian, autocratic, firm, hard, harsh, inflexible, iron-fisted, pitiless, rigid, rigorous, ruthless, severe, stern, stringent, tough, tyrannical, uncompromising, unsympathetic. ANTONYMS: lenient.

strident *a.* (*sounding harsh, grating*) cacophonous, clamorous, creaking, croaking, discordant, grating, gravelly, grinding, guttural, harsh, jarring, loud, rasping, raucous, rough, scraping, scratchy, shrill, vociferous. ANTONYMS: soft.

strife *n.* (*conflict, hostile struggle*) animosity, antagonism, arguing, bad blood, battle, bickering, conflict, contention, disagreement, discord, dispute, dissension, enmity, fight, friction, hatred, hostility, ill will, rivalry, trouble. ANTONYMS: accord, peace.

strike *v.t.* **1** (*to hit, to inflict* (*a blow etc.*)) bash, batter, belabour, clout, crown, cuff, flog, hammer, hit, knock, pound, pummel, punch, slap, smack, smite, tap, thump, (*coll.*) wallop, whack. ANTONYMS: stroke. **2** (*to come into violent contact with*) bump into, collide with, come into contact with, crash into, hit. **3** (*to drive, to send* (*a ball etc.*) *with force*) club, drive with force, hit, smack. **4** (*to attack* (*an enemy craft, location etc.*)) assail, assault, attack, raid, set upon. **5 a** (*to produce or bring into a particular state by a stroke, e.g. to ignite* (*a match*), *to stamp or mint* (*a coin*)) effect, form, ignite, impress, light, make, mint, print, produce, punch, render, stamp. **b** (*to afflict*) afflict, cripple, disable, incapacitate, invalid. **6** (*to impress strongly, to occur suddenly to the mind of*) affect, come to, dawn on, happen upon, hit upon, implant, impress, induce, influence,

instil, occur to, reach, register with, stumble on. **7** (*to make* (*a bargain*)) agree, attain, conclude, make, reach. **8** (*to lower* (*sails, a flag etc.*)) dismantle, haul down, knock. **9** (*to assume* (*an attitude*)) adopt, affect, assume, display, put on, take on.

~*v.i.* **1** (*to deliver a blow or blows* (*at, upon*); *to dash* (*against, upon etc.*)) bang, bump, collide, crash, dash, deliver a blow, hit, impact, land on, run into, smash, touch. **2** (*to sound the time;* (*of time*) *to be sounded*) chime, ring, sound. **3** (*to leave off work to enforce a demand for higher wages etc.*) down tools, leave off, mutiny, rebel, revolt, walk off the job, walk out. **4** (*to arrive suddenly, to happen* (*upon*)) arrive, happen upon. **5** (*to enter or turn* (*in a certain direction*)) enter, head, steer, turn.

~*n.* **1** (*an act of striking*) blow, impact, striking. **2** (*an act of striking for an increase of wages etc.*) go-slow, sit-down strike, walkout, work-to-rule. **3** (*an attack upon an enemy location, craft etc.; an attack on a target from the air*) assault, attack, blitz. **to strike out 1** (*to hit from the shoulder* (*e.g. in boxing*)) hit, lash out. **2** (*to delete, to expunge*) blot out, cancel, cross out, delete, efface, eliminate, eradicate, erase, expunge, obliterate, rub out, scratch, wipe out. **3** (*to set off*) leave, move out, set off, set out.

striking *a.* (*surprising, noticeable*) amazing, astonishing, astounding, awe-inspiring, conspicuous, exceptional, extraordinary, forcible, imposing, impressive, noticeable, out of the ordinary, remarkable, stunning, surprising, unusual, wondrous. ANTONYMS: commonplace, ordinary.

string *n.* **1** (*twine, usu. thicker than thread and thinner than cord*) cable, cord, filament, line, rope, strand, thread, twine. **2** (*a length of this or strip of other material, used for tying, fastening or as a decoration etc.*) chain, chaplet, choker, lead, leash, loop, necklace. **3** (*a stringlike fibre, tendon, nerve etc.*) fibre, ligament, nerve, tendon. **4** (*conditions, complications*) catch, complication, condition, limitation, obligation, prerequisite, provision, proviso, qualification, requirement, stipulation, term. **5** (*a sequence of alphabetic or numeric characters in a computer program*) chain, file, line, procession, queue, row, sequence, series, stream, succession, train.

~*v.t.* **1** (*to tie with string*) array, chain together, drape, festoon, hang, join, link, sling, suspend, tie. **2** (*to thread* (*beads etc.*) *on a string*) sling, thread. **to string along 1** (*to accompany*) accompany, come along, follow, tag along. **2** (*to agree with, go along with*) agree with, collaborate, concur, follow, go along with. **3** (*to fool, deceive*) bluff, cheat, deceive, dupe, fool, hoax, keep waiting, play fast and loose with, take (someone) for a ride, trick. **to string out** (*to prolong, esp. unnecessarily*) delay, drag out, extend, lengthen, postpone, prolong, protract, reach, space out, spin out, spread out, straggle, stretch.

strip[1] *v.t.* **1** (*to pull the clothes or covering from, to skin*) bare, clean, decorticate, denude, excoriate, flay, husk, lay bare, peel, skin, uncover. **2** (*to deprive (of e.g. titles or property), to plunder*) deprive, despoil, gut, loot, pillage, plunder, ransack, rob, sack. **3** (*to remove (clothes, bark etc.)*) confiscate, expropriate, remove, seize, take away.

~*v.i.* (*to take (off) one's clothes, to undress*) disrobe, divest oneself, get undressed, peel off, shed one's clothes, take off one's clothes, undress. ANTONYMS: cover.

~*n.* (*a striptease*) streak, striptease.

strip[2] *n.* (*a long narrow piece*) band, belt, fillet, piece, ribbon, shred, swath.

stripe *n.* **1** (*a long, narrow band of a distinctive colour or texture*) band, bar, length, line, slash, streak, striation, strip, stroke. **2** (*a chevron on the sleeve of a uniform indicating rank*) chevron, tab. **3** (*a cast of character or opinion*) cast, character, class, complexion, description, feather, kidney, kind, nature, persuasion, sort, style, type. **4** (*a stroke with a whip, scourge etc.*) lash, scourge, stroke, whip.

strive *v.i.* **1** (*to try hard, to make a great effort (for something, to do something etc.)*) aim, aspire, attempt, do, do one's utmost, endeavour, exert oneself, make every effort, try, work at. **2** (*to struggle or contend (against)*) compete, contend, fight, labour, strain, struggle, toil.

stroke[1] *n.* **1** (*an act of striking, the impact, noise etc., of this*) blow, cuff, hit, knock, rap, slam, slap, smack, strike, swipe, tap, thump, (*coll.*) wallop, whack. **2** (*a sudden attack of illness etc., esp. a thrombosis in the brain, sometimes causing unconsciousness or paralysis*) aneurysm, apoplexy, attack, collapse, embolism, fit, paralysis, seizure, spasm, thrombosis. **3** (*a single movement of something, esp. any one of a series of recurring movements*) beat, pulsation, pulse, throb, thump. **4** (*the slightest movement or action*) bit, hint, iota, jot, scrap, stitch, suggestion, tittle, touch. **5** (*a mark made by a single movement of a pen, pencil etc.; a detail*) dash, detail, mark, touch. **6** (*a move or happening*) accomplishment, achievement, act, action, feat, flourish, gesture, go, happening, matter, motion, move, movement, work.

stroke[2] *v.t.* (*to pass the hand over the surface of (fur, hair, an animal etc.) caressingly*) caress, fondle, massage, pat, pet, rub, soothe, touch.

stroll *v.i.* **1** (*to walk in a leisurely way, to saunter*) amble, meander, (*esp. N Am., coll.*) mosey, saunter, stray, wander. ANTONYMS: stride. **2** (*to achieve the desired result easily*) coast, walk.

~*v.t.* (*to saunter or ramble along on foot*) ramble, saunter.

~*n.* **1** (*a leisurely ramble*) airing, amble, breath of fresh air, constitutional, excursion, meander, (*esp. N Am., coll.*) mosey, promenade, ramble, saunter, walk, wander. **2** (*an easy success*) (*coll.*) cinch, piece of cake.

strong *a.* **1** (*able to withstand force; not easily damaged*) impenetrable, resistant, sturdy. **2** ((*of a person or their constitution*) *able to fight off illness, or not prone to suffer from it*) active, dynamic, energetic, hale, hardy, healthy, hearty, indefatigable, lusty, tough, vigorous. **3** ((*of people's nerves*) *not easily shattered*) defensive, hard-headed, obstinate, recalcitrant, self-willed, strong-minded, stubborn, wilful. **4** ((*of a market*) *maintaining high or rising prices*) balanced, stable, steady. **5** (*muscular; capable of sustained effort*) athletic, beefy, brawny, burly, craggy, hefty, husky, mighty, muscular, powerful, robust, rugged, sinewy, stalwart, stout, strapping, sturdy, wiry. **6** (*effective, forceful*) durable, effective, effectual, efficacious, forceful, formidable, hard-wearing, heavy-duty, mighty, powerful, redoubtable, reinforced, solid, sound, sturdy, substantial, tough, well-built, well-established, well-founded. **7** (*firm, not wavering*) ardent, assiduous, dedicated, determined, enthusiastic, fervent, firm, persistent, regular, resolute, staunch, steadfast, tenacious, uncompromising, unswerving, unwavering, vehement, zealous. ANTONYMS: weak. **8** ((*of a position or argument*) *difficult to attack, convincing*) cogent, compelling, conclusive, convincing, forceful, influential, invulnerable, irrefutable, persuasive, potent, profound, substantial, telling, well-substantiated, well-supported. **9** (*having a powerful impact on the senses or emotions*) blinding, bright, dazzling, deep, deep-felt, earnest, emotional, fierce, graphic, hot, intense, keen, passionate, potent, sharp, stunning, violent, vivid. **10** ((*of e.g. a military force, team etc.*) *powerful, well-trained*) able, capable, competent, considerable, efficient, experienced, great, high-quality, large, numerous, powerful, qualified, skilled, talented, well-equipped, well-trained. **11** ((*of a beverage or a solution*) *concentrated*) concentrated, intensified, potent, undiluted. **12** (*used (following the number) to specify numbers present, the size of a gathering etc.*) in number, in strength, numerically. **13** ((*of someone's voice*) *loud*) carrying, loud, powerful, stentorian, strident. **14** ((*of food, its flavour or smell*) *pungent*) acrid, aromatic, foul, fragrant, heady, hot, miasmic, noisome, odoriferous, penetrating, piquant, potent, pungent, putrid, rotten, sharp, smelly, spicy, stinking, tasty. **15** ((*of written style*) *telling; forceful or compact*) cogent, compact, forceful, succinct, telling. **16** ((*of moves or measures*) *forceful, drastic*) aggressive, draconian, drastic, effective, extreme, forceful, harsh, high-handed, rigorous, severe, stiff, strenuous, stringent, tough.

structure *n.* **1** (*a combination of parts, as a building, machine etc., esp. the supporting framework*) building, construction, edifice, erection, fabric, machine, organism. **2** (*the arrangement of parts, organs, atoms etc., in a complex whole*) arrangement, character, composition, configuration, design, form, formation, framework, make-up, nature, order, organization, shape, system.
~*v.t.* (*to give a structure to*) arrange, build, construct, design, form, organize, shape, systematize.

struggle *v.i.* **1** (*to make violent movements in trying to break free from restraint etc.*) squirm, twist, wiggle, worm, wrestle, wriggle, writhe. **2** (*to strive* (*for something, or to do something*)) attempt, endeavour, exert oneself, labour, strain, strive, try, work. **3** (*to contend* (*with or against*)) battle, compete, contend, fight. ANTONYMS: give up, yield.
~*n.* **1** (*a strenuous effort*) drudgery, effort, endeavour, exertion, labour, strain, striving, struggling, toil, travail, trouble, work. **2** (*a fight or contest, esp. of a confused character*) battle, clash, competition, conflict, contention, contest, encounter, fight, match, skirmish, strife, tussle. ANTONYMS: harmony, peace.

strut *v.i.* (*to walk with a pompous, conceited gait*) flounce, parade, prance, promenade, stalk, swagger.

stub *n.* **1** (*a stump or remnant of anything, e.g. of a cigarette or a pencil*) butt, end, (*coll.*) fag end, remnant, stump, tail. **2** (*a counterfoil, esp. of a cheque or receipt*) counterfoil, receipt.

stubborn *a.* **1** (*unreasonably obstinate, refractory*) adamant, contrary, determined, dogged, headstrong, inflexible, intransigent, mulish, obdurate, obstinate, persistent, pertinacious, perverse, pig-headed, recalcitrant, refractory, tenacious, unbending, unmanageable, unrelenting, wilful. ANTONYMS: amenable. **2** (*unyielding, immovable*) immovable, stiff, unyielding.

student *n.* **1** (*a person engaged in study, esp. someone receiving instruction at a university or college*) learner, postgraduate, pupil, undergraduate. ANTONYMS: master, teacher. **2** (*a schoolboy or schoolgirl*) pupil, schoolboy, schoolchild, schoolgirl. **3** (*a person at the trainee or apprentice stage*) apprentice, learner, probationer, trainee.

studied *a.* (*deliberate; contrived*) calculated, conscious, considered, contrived, deliberate, feigned, forced, intentional, laboured, planned, premeditated, well-thought-out, wilful. ANTONYMS: spontaneous, unconscious.

study *n.* **1** (*mental application to books, art, science etc., the pursuit of knowledge*) analysis, application, consideration, contemplation, examination, meditation, pursuit of knowledge, thought. **2** (*a subject that is studied or worth studying; the pursuit of such subjects*) analysis, attention, bookwork, consideration, contemplation, cramming, examination, exploration, inquiry, investigation, lessons, meditation, reading, reflection, research, scrutiny, thought, work. **3** (*a room devoted to study, literary work etc.*) den, library, office, reading-room, retreat, sanctum, workroom. **4** (*a sketch or other piece of work done for practice or as a preliminary design for a picture etc.*) design, sketch.
~*v.t.* **1** (*to apply the mind to for the purpose of learning*) analyse, apply the mind to, attend to, contemplate, ponder. **2** (*to inquire into, to investigate*) (*sl.*) bone up on, inquire into, investigate, learn about, look at, look into, research. **3** (*to contemplate, to consider attentively*) chew over, cogitate, consider, contemplate, deliberate over, meditate over, mull over, muse about, ponder, reflect on, ruminate on, think over, turn over, weigh. ANTONYMS: ignore. **4** (*to commit* (*the words of one's role etc.*) *to memory*) commit to memory, (*coll.*) cram, learn, memorize, (*coll.*) mug up, (*coll.*) swot. **5** (*to read* (*a book etc.*) *carefully and analytically*) analyse, examine, inspect, observe, peruse, pore over, read, scan, scrutinize, survey.
~*v.i.* (*to meditate, to rack one's brains*) cogitate, meditate, muse, rack one's brains, think deeply.

stuff *n.* **1** (*the material of which anything is made or may be made*) material, matter. **2** (*the fundamental substance, essence of anything*) attributes, building blocks, essence, essentials, fundamentals, grit, ingredients, makings, qualities, spirit, substance. **3** (*household goods, furniture etc.*) effects, furniture, lumber, property, things, utensils. **4** (*clothes, belongings etc.*) accessories, accoutrements, baggage, belongings, bits and pieces, chattels, (*sl.*) clobber, clothes, effects, equipment, gear,

goods, impedimenta, kit, paraphernalia, possessions, property, tackle, things, trappings. **5** (*a textile fabric, esp. woollen, as opposed to silk or linen*) cloth, fabric, material, textile, wool. **6** (*worthless matter, nonsense, trash*) balderdash, bosh, (*sl.*) bull, bunkum, claptrap, (*sl.*) codswallop, (*sl.*) crap, garbage, (*sl.*) hogwash, hot air, humbug, junk, (*coll.*) malarkey, nonsense, (*coll.*) rot, rubbish, trash, (*coll.*) tripe, twaddle.
~*v.t.* **1** (*to cram, to stop (up)*) bung, cram, fill, pack, stop. **2** (*to crowd into a confined space etc.; to push roughly*) compress, cram, crowd, force, jam, press, push, ram, shove, squash, squeeze, thrust. **3** (*to fill (a fowl etc.) with stuffing or seasoning for cooking*) fill, line, pack. **4** (*to fill with food*) gluttonize, gorge, gormandize, make a pig of, over-indulge, (*esp. N Am., sl.*) pig out.

stuffy *a.* **1** (*ill-ventilated, close*) airless, close, fetid, frowzy, fusty, ill-ventilated, mildewed, mouldy, muggy, musty, oppressive, stale, stifling, suffocating, sultry, unventilated. ANTONYMS: airy, fresh. **2** (*boring, uninspiring*) boring, dreary, tedious, uninspiring, uninteresting. ANTONYMS: exciting. **3** (*strait-laced, conventional*) conservative, conventional, dull, (*coll.*) fuddy-duddy, old-fashioned, pompous, priggish, prim, rigid, (*coll.*) square, staid, stiff, stodgy, strait-laced, uninteresting, (*coll.*) uptight.

stumble *v.i.* **1** (*to trip in walking or to strike the foot against something without falling*) fall, miss one's footing, slip, trip. **2** (*to move (along) unsteadily*) flounder, lurch, stagger, waver. **3** (*to read or speak blunderingly*) blunder, err, falter, hesitate, pause, slip, trip. **4** (*to come (upon) by chance*) bump into, chance upon, come across, discover, encounter, find, happen upon, hit upon, run across. ANTONYMS: miss.
~*n.* (*an act of stumbling*) fall, slip, trip.

stump *n.* **1** (*the part left in the earth after a tree has fallen or been cut down*) root, trunk. **2** (*any part left when the rest of a branch, limb etc., has been cut away or worn out*) butt, end, remnant, stub.
~*v.i.* (*to walk awkwardly or noisily*) clomp, clump, lumber, plod, stamp, stomp, trudge.
~*v.t.* ((*of a question or problem*) *to be too difficult for*) baffle, bewilder, confound, confuse, dumbfound, flummox, foil, mystify, nonplus, perplex, puzzle, stop, stymie.

stun *v.t.* **1** (*to render senseless with a blow*) knock out, render senseless. **2** (*to shock or overwhelm*) amaze, astonish, astound, bowl over, dumbfound, flabbergast, jar, jolt, overcome, overwhelm, paralyse, shake up, shock, stagger, strike dumb, stupefy, take someone's breath away. **3** (*to daze or deafen with noise*) benumb, daze, deafen, numb.

stunning *a.* **1** (*stupefying*) benumbing, knockout, numbing, paralysing, staggering, stupefying. **2** (*wonderfully good, fine etc.*) amazing, astounding, beautiful, brilliant, dazzling, extraordinary, fabulous, glorious, lovely, magnificent, marvellous, ravishing, remarkable, sensational, splendid, staggering, stupendous, sublime, superb, wonderful.

stupid *a.* **1** (*slow in understanding, unintelligent*) asinine, birdbrained, brainless, cretinous, dense, dim, dozy, dumb, feeble-minded, foolish, half-witted, idiotic, imprudent, moronic, obtuse, silly, simple, slow, (*coll.*) thick, unintelligent. ANTONYMS: intelligent, quick. **2** (*senseless, nonsensical*) absurd, (*sl.*) barmy, (*coll.*) cock-eyed, crazy, daft, foolhardy, foolish, frivolous, idiotic, inane, insane, irrational, irresponsible, ludicrous, mad, nonsensical, ridiculous, risible, senseless, silly. **3** (*in a state of stupor, stupefied*) dazed, groggy, sluggish, stunned, stupefied, torpid. ANTONYMS: alert.

style *n.* **1** (*a sort, pattern, esp. with reference to appearance*) category, character, configuration, cut, design, form, genre, kind, line, make, pattern, quality, shape, sort, spirit, tenor, tone, type, variety, vein. **2** (*manner of writing, expressing ideas, behaving etc., as distinct from the matter expressed or done*) approach, manner, method, mode, technique, treatment, way. **3** (*the general characteristics of literary diction or artistic expression distinguishing a particular people, period etc.*) diction, language, phraseology, phrasing, vocabulary, wording. **4** (*a manner or form of a superior or fashionable kind*) chic, craze, culture, dash, design, élan, elegance, fashion, flair, look, panache, period, rage, refinement, sophistication, stylishness, taste, trend, urbanity, vogue.
~*v.t.* **1** (*to design or shape*) arrange, cut, design, do, fashion, form, set, shape, tailor. **2** (*to designate, to describe formally by name and title*) brand, call, characterize, denominate, describe, designate, dub, label, name, tag, term.

stylish *a.* (*fashionable in style, showy*) à la mode, chic, (*coll.*) classy, (*coll.*) cool, elegant, fashionable, in, in vogue, modish, neat, (*coll.*) sharp, showy, smart, (*sl.*) snazzy, sophisticated, suave, trendy, urbane. ANTONYMS: dowdy, mundane.

suave *a.* (*agreeable, polite*) affable, agreeable, bland, charming, civil, cosmopolitan, courteous, cultivated, debonair, diplomatic, gracious, nonchalant, pleasant, polite, smooth, sophisticated, urbane, worldly. ANTONYMS: blunt, rough.

subdue *v.t.* **1** (*to conquer, to overcome*) beat down, conquer, crush, defeat, discipline, dominate, get the better of, hold in check, humble, master, overcome, overpower, overwhelm, put down, quell, rout, subjugate, triumph over, vanquish. **2** (*to check, to curb*) check, control, curb, quash, reduce, repress, restrain, suppress. **3** (*to render gentle or mild*) break, bridle, tame, train. **4** (*to tone down, to make less glaring*) mellow, moderate, mute, quieten, soften, soft-pedal, temper, tone down.

subject¹ *n.* **1** (*the topic under consideration*) affair, issue, matter, question, topic. **2** (*the theme of discussion or description*) gist, theme, thesis. **3** (*the cause or occasion (for)*) basis, cause, excuse, ground, motive, object, occasion, rationale, reason, source. **4** (*a branch of learning or study*) area, branch of knowledge, course of study, discipline, field. **5** (*Gram.*) (*the noun or its equivalent about which something is affirmed*) nominative, noun. **6** (*someone under the dominion or political rule of a person or state; a member of a state as related to the sovereign or government*) citizen, dependent, liegeman, national, subordinate, taxpayer, vassal, voter. ANTONYMS: ruler. **7** (*a person regarded as subject to any specific disease, mental tendency etc.*) case, client, guinea pig, participant, patient, victim.
~*a.* **1** (*being under the authority of another, owing obedience (to)*) inferior, obedient, subjugated, subordinate, subservient. **2** (*exposed, disposed (to)*) at the mercy (of), disposed (to), exposed (to), liable (to), open (to), prone (to), susceptible (to), vulnerable (to). ANTONYMS: invulnerable. **3** (*dependent, conditional*) conditional, contingent, dependent, depending.

subject² *v.t.* **1** (*to expose, to make liable (to)*) expose (to), lay open (to), make liable (to). **2** (*to cause to undergo*) cause to undergo, impose on, put through, submit, treat. **3** (*to subdue, to reduce to subjection (to)*) conquer, crush, enslave, humble, master, quell, subdue, subjugate, subordinate, vanquish.

sublime *a.* **1** (*of the most lofty or exalted nature*) elevated, exalted, heavenly, high, lofty, magnificent, superb, supreme. ANTONYMS: ridiculous. **2** (*characterized by nobility or majesty*) august, beatified, canonized, dignified, eminent, ennobled, glorified, glorious, good, grand, great, high-minded, honourable, majestic, noble, sanctified, stately. **3** (*inspiring awe*) awe-inspiring, awesome, humbling, imposing, inspiring, mind-boggling, overpowering, overwhelming, splendid. **4** ((*of e.g. ignorance, impudence*) *unparalleled*) complete, outstanding, unparalleled, utter.

submerge *v.t.* **1** (*to put under water etc., to*

flood) deluge, dip, douse, drench, duck, dunk, flood, immerse, plunge, put under water, saturate, submerse, wash, wet. **2** (*to inundate, to overwhelm*) bury, camouflage, cloak, conceal, deluge, drown, engulf, hide, inundate, obscure, overwhelm, shroud, swamp, veil.
~*v.i.* (*to sink or dive under water etc.*) descend, dive, go down, plummet, plunge, sink, sound.

submit *v.t.* **1** (*to yield or surrender (oneself) to the domination of someone else*) accede, acquiesce, agree, bend, bow, capitulate, comply, concede, conform, consent, defer, knuckle under, obey, stoop, succumb, surrender, yield. ANTONYMS: resist. **2** (*to present or refer for consideration, decision etc.*) enter, hand in, offer, present, proffer, refer, tender. **3** (*to put forward (a theory etc.) deferentially*) advance, propose, put forward, suggest. ANTONYMS: withdraw.
~*v.i.* (*to yield, to surrender*) give in, give way, resign oneself, surrender, yield.

subordinate *a.* **1** (*inferior (to) in rank, importance etc.*) inferior, junior, lesser, lower, minor. **2** (*subsidiary (to)*) ancillary, auxiliary, dependent, secondary, subject, subservient, subsidiary.
~*n.* (*a person working under another or inferior in official standing*) aide, assistant, dependant, hireling, inferior, junior, lackey, servant, slave, subaltern, subject, subsidiary, underling, vassal. ANTONYMS: superior.

subscribe *v.t.* **1** (*to contribute or pledge to contribute (an annual or other specified sum) to or for a fund etc.*) contribute, pledge, promise. **2** (*to sign (a document, promise etc.)*) endorse, sign.
~*v.i.* **1** (*to engage to pay a contribution, to allow one's name to be entered in a list of contributors*) (*coll.*) chip in, contribute, donate, give, pay. **2** (*to assent or give support (to an opinion etc.)*) accept, advocate, agree, approve, assent, back, consent, countenance, endorse, support, tolerate, underwrite. ANTONYMS: oppose. **3** (*to write one's name at the end of a document*) endorse, sign.

subsequent *a.* (*coming immediately after in time or order; following*) after, consequent, ensuing, following, future, later, next, posterior, resultant, resulting, succeeding, successive. ANTONYMS: previous.

subside *v.i.* **1** (*to settle down, to become tranquil*) abate, calm down, decrease, die, diminish, dwindle, ebb, lessen, let up, lull, moderate, pass, peter out, quieten, recede, settle down, wane, wear off. ANTONYMS: increase. **2** (*to sink, to fall in level*) decline, descend, drop, fall, go down, settle, sink. **3** (*to* *collapse*) cave in, collapse, sink in. ANTONYMS: rise.

subsidiary *a.* **1** (*auxiliary, supplemental*) accessory, additional, aiding, assistant, auxiliary, complementary, helpful, instrumental, supplemental, supplementary. **2** (*subordinate or secondary in importance*) ancillary, inferior, lesser, secondary, subordinate, subservient. ANTONYMS: primary.
~*n.* (*a subsidiary person or thing, an auxiliary*) accessory, auxiliary, supporter.

subsistence *n.* **1** (*the state or means of subsisting*) being, existence, living, subsisting, survival. **2** (*the minimum required to support life*) aliment, board, food, keep, maintenance, nourishment, nutriment, provision, rations, support, sustenance, upkeep, victuals.

substance *n.* **1** (*matter as opposed to form*) body, element, fabric, material, matter, stuff. **2** (*the essential part, gist*) burden, core, crux, drift, essence, gist, gravamen, heart, kernel, meat, nub, pith, point, quiddity, quintessence, significance, subject, sum and substance, sum total, theme. **3** (*firmness, solid foundation*) actuality, corporeality, reality, solidity, substantiality. **4** (*property, wealth*) affluence, assets, estate, means, possessions, property, resources, riches, wealth. **5** (*a narcotic or intoxicating drug or chemical, esp. an illegal one*) chemical, drug, narcotic.

substantial *a.* **1** (*of considerable importance, amount etc.*) abundant, ample, big, considerable, generous, goodly, great, healthy, important, impressive, large, major, massive, numerous, respectable, significant, sizeable, (*coll.*) tidy, valuable, worthwhile. ANTONYMS: insignificant. **2** (*material, practical*) material, practical, real. **3** (*solid, strongly constructed*) durable, firm, solid, sound, stout, strong, sturdy, weighty, well-built, well-established, well-founded. ANTONYMS: flimsy, weak. **4** (*having sufficient means, well-to-do*) affluent, influential, landed, powerful, profitable, propertied, prosperous, rich, sound, successful, wealthy, well-to-do. ANTONYMS: indigent, poor. **5** (*real, actually existing*) actual, corporeal, existing, genuine, material, physical, positive, real, true, valid. ANTONYMS: illusory, imaginary.

substantiate *v.t.* **1** (*to establish, to prove*) affirm, authenticate, back up, bear out, certify, confirm, corroborate, document, establish, make good, prove, show, support, sustain, validate, verify. ANTONYMS: refute. **2** (*to make real*) actualize, make real, realize.

substitute *n.* **1** (*a person or thing put in the place of or serving for another*) alternative, equivalent, locum, relief, replacement, representative, stand-in, substitution, surrogate, understudy. **2** (*Sc. Law*) (*a deputy*) agent, delegate, deputy, proxy.
~*v.t.* **1** (*to put or use in exchange* (*for*) *another person or thing*) change, exchange, interchange, swap, switch. **2** (*to replace* (*a person or thing by or with another*)) displace, relieve, replace, supplant.
~*v.i.* (*to act as a substitute* (*for*)) cover for, deputize for, double for, relieve, stand in for, sub for, take the place of, understudy.

subtle *a.* **1** (*delicate, elusive*) attenuated, delicate, elusive, faint, fine, imperceptible, implied, indirect, insubstantial, nice, rarefied, refined, slight, sophisticated, thin. **2** (*difficult to comprehend, not obvious*) abstruse, arcane, concealed, deep, hidden, incomprehensible, nebulous, obscure, profound, recondite, remote, shadowy, unclear, vague, veiled. ANTONYMS: obvious. **3** (*making fine distinctions, discerning*) acute, astute, deep, discerning, discriminating, keen, penetrating, perspicacious, shrewd. ANTONYMS: stupid. **4** (*ingenious, skilful*) clever, ingenious, skilful, smart. **5** (*crafty, insidious*) artful, casuistic, crafty, cunning, deceptive, designing, devious, foxy, insidious, machiavellian, scheming, shifty, slick, slimy, sly, smarmy, strategic, tricky, underhand, wily. ANTONYMS: artless, guileless.

subtract *v.t.* (*to take away* (*a part, quantity etc.*) *from the rest*) deduct, detract from, diminish, remove, take away, take from, take off, withdraw. ANTONYMS: add.

subversive *a.* (*intending to weaken or destroy a government etc.*) destructive, disruptive, insurrectionary, radical, revolutionary, riotous, seditionary, seditious, subversionary, traitorous, treacherous, treasonous, weakening.
~*n.* (*a subversive person*) collaborator, defector, dissident, fifth columnist, insurgent, insurrectionary, insurrectionist, quisling, radical, rebel, revolutionary, rioter, saboteur, seditionary, traitor.

succeed *v.i.* **1** (*to be successful, to end well or prosperously*) achieve success, advance, arrive, be successful, end well, flourish, gain success, get ahead, (*coll.*) get to the top, make good, (*coll.*) make it, prevail, progress, prosper, thrive, triumph, win, work. ANTONYMS: fail. **2** (*to follow in time or order*) ensue, follow, supervene. **3** (*to be the heir or successor* (*to an office, estate etc.*)) be heir to, be successor to, inherit.
~*v.t.* **1** (*to follow, to come after* (*in time or order*)) come after, come next, follow. ANTONYMS: precede. **2** (*to be heir or successor to*) replace, take the place of.

success n. 1 (*the act of succeeding, favourable result*) accomplishment, achievement, ascendancy, attainment, fame, fortune, (*coll.*) hit, luck, prosperity, triumph, victory. ANTONYMS: failure. 2 (*attainment of prosperity or high position*) celebrity, name, sensation, star. 3 (*the issue or result of an undertaking*) issue, outcome, result.

successful a. 1 (*having the desired or intended result*) fruitful, productive, profitable, rewarding. ANTONYMS: unsuccessful. 2 ((*e.g. of a business or film*) *popular and profitable*) acclaimed, best-selling, booming, flourishing, leading, lucrative, popular, profitable, thriving. ANTONYMS: failing. 3 ((*of a person*) *famous or earning a lot of money*) acclaimed, affluent, celebrated, eminent, famous, flush, fortunate, leading, lucky, prominent, prosperous, renowned, wealthy, well-known, well-to-do. ANTONYMS: unsuccessful.

succession n. 1 (*a series of things following in order*) chain, concatenation, course, cycle, flow, order, procession, progression, run, sequence, series, train, turn. 2 (*the act or right of succeeding to an office or inheritance*) accession, heredity, inheritance. 3 (*the line of persons so succeeding*) descendants, lineage, posterity.

succinct a. (*compressed into few words, concise*) brief, compact, compressed, concise, condensed, curt, epigrammatic, laconic, pithy, short, summary, terse. ANTONYMS: long-winded.

succumb v.i. (*to yield, to submit* (*to*)) accede, capitulate, give in, give way, submit, surrender, yield. ANTONYMS: resist.

suck v.t. (*to draw liquid from with or as with the mouth*) absorb, draw in, imbibe, soak up. **to suck up** (*to act in an obsequious manner, toady*) curry favour, fawn, flatter, ingratiate, toady.

sudden a. 1 (*happening unexpectedly, without warning*) startling, surprising, unannounced, unanticipated, unexpected, unforeseen, unwonted, without warning. 2 (*instantaneous, abrupt*) abrupt, brief, brisk, hasty, immediate, impetuous, impulsive, instantaneous, momentary, precipitate, quick, rapid, rash, swift. ANTONYMS: gradual.

sue v.t. 1 (*to prosecute or to pursue a claim* (*for*) *by legal process*) accuse, bring suit, charge, indict, prefer charges, prosecute, summon, take to court. ANTONYMS: defend. 2 (*to entreat, to petition*) appeal, apply, beg, beseech, entreat, implore, petition, plead, pray, request, solicit, supplicate.
~v.i. (*to petition* (*to or for*)) beg, beseech, entreat, implore, make entreaty, petition, plead.

suffer v.i. 1 (*to undergo or endure pain, grief etc.*) ache, agonize, be in pain, endure, feel, grieve, hurt, smart, sweat, writhe. 2 (*to be at a disadvantage*) be at a disadvantage, decline, deteriorate, diminish, fall off, go down.
~v.t. 1 (*to experience or undergo* (*something painful or unjust*)) experience, feel, go through, live through, undergo. 2 (*to endure, to sustain* (*unflinchingly etc.*)) bear, endure, submit to, support, sustain, take, undergo. 3 (*to tolerate, to put up with*) abide, brook, (*coll.*) put up with, stand, support, tolerate, withstand. 4 (*to permit, to allow* (*of*)) admit, allow, humour, indulge, let, permit.

suffering n. (*pain or agony*) affliction, agony, discomfort, distress, grief, hardship, misery, ordeal, pain, torment, torture, trial, tribulation. ANTONYMS: comfort, ease.

sufficiency n. (*an adequate supply* (*of*)) abundance, enough, plenty.

sufficient a. (*enough, adequate*) abundant, adequate, ample, enough, plentiful, satisfactory, sufficing. ANTONYMS: deficient.

suggest v.t. 1 (*to propose* (*a plan, idea etc.*) *for consideration*) advance, advise, advocate, introduce, mention, offer, present, proffer, propose, put forward, recommend, set forward, submit, support, urge. 2 (*to cause* (*an idea etc.*) *to arise in the mind*) bring up, call to mind, evoke, provoke. 3 (*to hint at, indicate*) hint at, imply, indicate, insinuate, intimate.

suggestion n. 1 (*something which is suggested*) advice, counsel, idea, notion, opinion, plan, prompting, proposal, proposition, recommendation, urging. 2 (*a hint, an insinuation*) breath, hint, implication, indication, innuendo, insinuation, intimation, iota, jot, soupçon, suspicion, tinge, tittle, touch, trace, whisper.

suggestive a. 1 (*containing or conveying* (*a*) *suggestion*) evocative, indicative, redolent, reminiscent. 2 (*tending to suggest thoughts of a rude and sexual nature*) (*coll.*) blue, crude, dirty, earthy, indecent, lewd, naughty, obscene, pornographic, provocative, prurient, racy, (*coll.*) raunchy, risqué, rude, salacious, sexy, smutty, spicy, vulgar.

suit n. 1 (*a set of outer clothes* (*usu. a jacket and trousers or a skirt*), *esp. when made of the same cloth*) business suit, lounge suit, outfit. 2 (*a set of clothes or an article of clothing for a particular purpose*) clothes, clothing, costume, ensemble, garb, habit, livery, outfit, uniform. 3 (*a legal prosecution or action for the recovery of a right etc.*) action, case, cause, lawsuit, litigation, proceeding, process, prosecution,

trial. **4** (*the act of suing, a request*) appeal, application, entreaty, petition, plea, prayer, request, solicitation, supplication. **5** (*courtship*) addresses, courtship, wooing. **6** (*sl.*) (*a person who wears a business suit, esp. a bureaucrat without character or individuality*) bureaucrat, businessman, businesswoman, mandarin.
~*v.t.* **1** (*to be appropriate to, to make* (*one*) *look attractive*) agree with, be appropriate for, become, befit, harmonize with, look attractive on, match. **2** (*to satisfy, to meet the desires etc. of*) fill someone's needs, gratify, please, satisfy. **3** (*to adapt, to make fitting* (*to*)) accommodate, adapt, adjust, conform, fashion, fit, make appropriate, proportion, tailor.
~*v.i.* (*to correspond; to be convenient*) accord, agree, correspond, match, satisfy.

suitable *a.* (*fitting, convenient*) acceptable, agreeable, applicable, apposite, appropriate, apt, becoming, befitting, convenient, correct, fitting, meet, opportune, pertinent, proper, relevant, right, satisfactory, seemly, timely. ANTONYMS: unsuitable.

suite *n.* **1** (*a set* (*of connecting rooms, matching furniture etc.*)) apartment, collection, number, set. **2** (*Mus.*) (*a series of instrumental compositions*) album, book, series, set. **3** (*a company, a retinue*) attendants, bodyguard, company, convoy, cortege, entourage, escort, followers, retinue, train.

sulk *v.i.* (*to be silent and bad-tempered*) be put out, brood, mope, pout, scowl.

sulky *a.* (*morose, bad-tempered*) bad-tempered, brooding, moody, morose, put out, resentful, sullen.

sullen *a.* **1** (*persistently morose, cross*) bad-tempered, bitter, brooding, churlish, crotchety, crusty, dour, dyspeptic, funereal, glowering, grumpy, lugubrious, moody, morose, peevish, petulant, resentful, sour, sulky, surly. ANTONYMS: cheerful. **2** (*dismal, forbidding*) depressing, dismal, forbidding, gloomy.

sultry *a.* **1** (*very hot, close and heavy*) close, damp, heavy, hot, humid, moist, muggy, oppressive, steaming, steamy, sticky, stifling, stuffy, suffocating, sweltering. ANTONYMS: cool. **2** (*passionate, sensual*) erotic, hot, lustful, passionate, provocative, seductive, sensual, sexy, voluptuous.

sum *n.* **1** (*the aggregate of two or more numbers, the total*) aggregate, amount, entirety, grand total, quantity, score, tally, total, totality, whole. ANTONYMS: part. **2** (*essence, summary*) essence, substance, summary.
~*v.t.* (*to add or combine into one total*) add, add up, calculate, collect, combine, count, measure, reckon, tally, total up, tot up. **to sum up 1**

(*to recapitulate*) recapitulate, review, summarize. **2** (*to form a rapid opinion or estimate of*) assess, estimate, evaluate, size up. **3** (*to put in a few words*) abridge, condense, consolidate, digest, encapsulate, epitomize, synopsize.

summit *n.* (*the highest point, the top*) acme, apex, apogee, cap, climax, crown, culmination, height, highest point, peak, pinnacle, top, vertex, zenith. ANTONYMS: base.

summon *v.t.* **1** (*to call or command to meet or attend*) bid, call, cite, command, invite, order, send for. **2** (*to order by a summons to appear in court*) arraign, subpoena, summons. **3** (*to call upon to do something*) assemble, call together, convene, convoke, mobilize, muster. ANTONYMS: dismiss. **4** (*to call* (*up*) (*courage etc.*)) arouse, call up, draw up, rouse.

sumptuous *a.* **1** (*costly, expensive*) costly, dear, exorbitant, expensive. ANTONYMS: cheap. **2** (*showing lavish expenditure*) extravagant, lavish, luxurious. **3** (*splendid, magnificent*) dazzling, de luxe, gorgeous, grand, magnificent, majestic, opulent, palatial, (*coll.*) plushy, (*coll.*) posh, regal, rich, (*coll.*) ritzy, royal, showy, splendid, superb.

sundry *a.* (*various, miscellaneous*) assorted, different, †divers, diverse, diversified, miscellaneous, mixed, several, varied, various.

sunless *a.* (*having no light from the sun*) black, bleak, cheerless, cloudy, dark, depressing, dismal, dreary, dusky, funereal, gloomy, grey, grim, inky, murky, pitchy, shadowy, sombre, tenebrous, unlit. ANTONYMS: sunny.

sunny *a.* **1** (*bright with or warmed by sunlight*) bright, clear, cloudless, fine, radiant, shining, summery, sunlit, sunshiny. ANTONYMS: dull, overcast. **2** (*bright, cheerful*) beaming, blithe, bubbly, buoyant, cheerful, cheery, ebullient, friendly, gay, genial, happy, jolly, joyful, joyous, light-hearted, mirthful, outgoing, smiling, warm.

superb *a.* **1** (*grand, magnificent*) brilliant, classic, dazzling, exquisite, fabulous, fantastic, glorious, grand, great, imposing, magnificent, majestic, marvellous, sensational, splendid, staggering, stately, stupendous, sumptuous, wonderful. **2** (*excellent, first-rate*) admirable, exceptional, fine, first-rate, (*coll.*) magic, matchless, outstanding, perfect, (*coll.*) smashing, (*coll.*) super, superior, superlative, (*coll.*) terrific.

superficial *a.* **1** (*of or relating to or lying on the surface*) exterior, external, outer, surface. **2** (*not penetrating deep*) cursory, hasty, nominal, perfunctory, slapdash. ANTONYMS: thorough. **3** (*apparent, but not in reality*) apparent, empty, illusory, ostensible, outward, seeming. ANTONYMS: actual, real. **4** (*not deep or profound in character*) cosmetic, frivolous, insignificant, insubstantial, passing, shallow, skin-deep, slight, trivial, unimportant, unprofound. ANTONYMS: deep.

superfluous *a.* (*more than is necessary or sufficient, excessive*) dispensable, excess, excessive, extra, gratuitous, needless, overabundant, redundant, superabundant, surplus, uncalled-for, unnecessary, unneeded. ANTONYMS: deficient.

superior *a.* **1** (*of higher position, rank etc.*) higher, loftier, nobler, upper. **2** (*better or greater relatively* (*to*)) better, greater, over. **3** (*of a quality above the average*) above average, choice, distinguished, estimable, excellent, exceptional, fine, first-rate, high-class, matchless, nonpareil, noteworthy, outstanding, peerless, preferred, select, sterling, superlative, supreme, unequalled. ANTONYMS: inferior. **4** (*situated near the top, in the higher part or above*) elevated, near the top, raised, upper. **5** (*supercilious*) arrogant, condescending, contemptuous, disdainful, haughty, high and mighty, (*coll.*) highfalutin, hoity-toity, (*coll.*) la-di-da, lofty, lordly, overbearing, patronizing, pompous, pretentious, scornful, snobbish, stuffy, supercilious, (*coll.*) uppity.
~*n.* (*a person superior to another or others*) better, boss, chief, director, manager, senior, supervisor.

supernatural *a.* (*due to or exercising powers above the usual forces of nature*) abnormal, ghostly, miraculous, mysterious, mystical, occult, other-worldly, paranormal, preternatural, psychic, spectral, spiritual, unearthly, unnatural. ANTONYMS: normal.

supersede *v.t.* **1** (*to set aside, to annul*) annul, discard, override, overrule, set aside. **2** (*to take the place of, to displace*) displace, oust, replace, substitute, succeed, supplant, take the place of, usurp.

supervise *v.t.* (*to have oversight of, to oversee*) administer, control, direct, govern, handle, keep an eye on, manage, overlook, oversee, run, superintend, watch over.

supple *a.* **1** (*pliant, easily bent*) bendable, elastic, flexible, plastic, pliable, pliant, tractile. ANTONYMS: rigid, stiff. **2** (*able to move and bend easily*) graceful, limber, lissom, lithe, nimble, willowy. **3** (*submissive, obsequious*) accommodating, acquiescent, complaisant, compliant, fawning, ingratiating, obliging, obsequious, servile, soft, submissive, toadying, tractable, unresistant, unresisting, yielding.

supplement[1] *n.* **1** (*an addition, esp. one that supplies a deficiency*) accessory, addition, adjunct, annexe, complement, continuation, extension. **2** (*an addition or update to a book, newspaper or periodical*) addendum, appendage, appendix, codicil, end-piece, epilogue, insert, postscript, sequel, update. **3** (*an additional charge for additional facilities or services*) extra, surcharge.

supplement[2] *v.t.* (*to make additions to*) add to, augment, extend, top up.

supplementary *a.* (*serving as a supplement, additional*) added, additional, ancillary, annexed, appended, attached, auxiliary, complementary, contributory, excess, extra, extraneous, new, secondary, subordinate, subsidiary, supplemental, supportive.

supplication *n.* (*earnest asking or begging, e.g. in prayer*) appeal, entreaty, invocation, petition, pleading, request, solicitation.

supply *v.t.* **1** (*to furnish with what is wanted, to provide* (*with*)) bestow, cater to, come up with, contribute, deliver, distribute, endow, equip, fit, furnish, grant, kit out, outfit, present, provide, provision, stock, victual, yield. ANTONYMS: withhold. **2** (*to fill* (*the place of*), *to make up for* (*a deficiency etc.*)) fill, make up for, replace, replenish. **3** (*to satisfy*) accommodate, fulfil, satisfy.
~*n.* **1** (*the act of supplying things needed*) delivery, distribution, equipping, furnishing, outfitting, providing, provision, provisioning, purveying, stocking, stockpiling, supplying. **2** (*a store of things available for use*) accumulation, cache, fund, hoard, inventory, quantity, reserve, reservoir, stock, stockpile, store. **3** (*necessary stores or provisions*) essentials, provisions, stores. **4** (*a person who fills a position temporarily, a substitute*) dep, locum, relief, stand-in, substitute.

support *v.t.* **1** (*to bear the weight of, to sustain*) bear, carry, hold up, sustain, uphold. ANTONYMS: drop. **2** (*to keep from yielding or giving way*) bolster, brace, buttress, prop, shore up. **3** (*to give strength or endurance to*) fortify, reinforce, strengthen. **4** (*to furnish with necessaries, to provide for*) furnish, keep, maintain, provide for, sustain. **5** (*to give assistance to*) abet, aid, assist, help, second. **6** (*to advocate, to back*) advocate, back, boost, champion, defend, finance, foster, fund, nurture, second, stand by, stand up for, stick up for, subsidize, take up (the) cudgels for. ANTONYMS: oppose. **7** (*to promote, to encourage*) advance, encourage, forward, further, promote. **8** (*to substantiate, to corroborate*) bear out, confirm, corroborate, endorse, substantiate, verify.

ANTONYMS: refute. **9** (*to take a keen interest in* (*a sports team etc.*); *to want* (*a team etc.*) *to win*) cheer for, favour, follow, take interest in. **10** (*to endure, to put up with*) abide, bear, brook, countenance, endure, face, put up with, stand for, (*coll.*) stick, stomach, submit to, suffer, tolerate, undergo.
~*n.* **1** (*a person who or something which supports*) base, brace, foundation, prop, stanchion, stay, supporter, upright. **2** (*subsistence, livelihood*) keep, livelihood, maintenance, subsistence, sustenance, upkeep. **3** (*aid, assistance*) aid, assistance, backing, encouragement, friendship, furtherance, help, patronage, protection, sponsorship. ANTONYMS: opposition.

supporter *n.* (*a person who or something which supports or maintains*) adherent, admirer, advocate, aficionado, ally, assistant, backer, champion, colleague, devotee, enthusiast, exponent, fan, follower, helper, patron, promoter, sponsor, well-wisher.

suppose *v.t.* **1** (*to take to be the case, to accept as probable*) accept, believe, conjecture, fancy, guess, hypothesize, imagine, posit, postulate, surmise, suspect, theorize. ANTONYMS: know. **2** (*to lay down without proof, to assume by way of argument*) assume, presume, presuppose, take as read, take for granted. **3** (*to involve or require as a condition, to imply*) imply, involve, presuppose, require. **4** (*to require or expect*) expect, oblige, require. **5** (*to believe* (*to*)) believe, conclude, opine, think.

supposed *a.* (*believed to be so*) accepted, alleged, assumed, believed, expected, hypothetical, imagined, intended, meant, obliged, presumed, putative, reputed, required, so-called, suppositious, theoretical, theorized.

suppress *v.t.* **1** (*to overpower, to quell*) cease, conquer, crack down on, crush, cut off, discontinue, end, extinguish, halt, overpower, put an end to, put down, quell, quench, snuff out, stamp out, stop, subdue, terminate. **2** (*to keep in or back, to stifle*) block, check, curb, forbid, hinder, hold in, inhibit, interdict, keep back, muffle, mute, obstruct, prevent, prohibit, repress, restrain, silence, smother, stifle, withhold. **3** (*to keep back from disclosure or circulation*) censor, conceal, cover up, hide, keep back, keep quiet.

supreme *a.* **1** (*highest in authority or power*) highest, sovereign. ANTONYMS: lowest. **2** (*highest in degree or importance, utmost*) best, chief, consummate, crowning, first, foremost, greatest, leading, main, maximum, paramount, peerless, pre-eminent, primary, principal, superlative, top, transcendent, unparalleled, utmost. **3** (*last, final*) final, last, ultimate.

sure *a.* **1** (*certain, undoubting*) assured, certain, confident, undoubting. ANTONYMS: uncertain. **2** (*free from doubts* (*of*)) convinced, decided, free from doubt, persuaded, satisfied. ANTONYMS: doubtful. **3** (*believing, confidently trusting* (*that*)) believing, certain, definite, positive. **4** (*infallible, certain* (*to*)) certain, foolproof, indisputable, infallible, unquestionable. **5** (*trustworthy, unfailing*) dependable, established, firm, guaranteed, reliable, safe, secure, solid, steadfast, steady, tried and tested, trustworthy, trusty, unfailing, unfaltering, unflinching, unshakeable. **6** (*unquestionably true*) accurate, beyond question, incontrovertible, indisputable, true. **7** (*certain* (*of finding, gaining etc.*)) bound, definite, destined, inescapable, inevitable, unavoidable.

surface *n.* **1** (*the exterior part of anything, the outside*) exterior, face, outside. ANTONYMS: interior. **2** (*something which has length and breadth but no thickness*) face, plane, side. **3** (*something which is apparent at first view or on slight consideration*) appearance, coating, covering, facade, skin, top, veneer.
~*v.t.* (*to put a surface on*) coat, concrete, pave, tarmac.
~*v.i.* **1** (*to rise to the surface*) appear, arise, come up, crop up, emerge, pop up, rise. **2** (*to become known*) appear, materialize, show up. **3** (*to wake up or get out of bed*) arise, get up, stir, wake up.

surfeit *n.* **1** (*excess, esp. in eating or drinking*) deluge, excess, flood, glut. **2** (*oppression resulting from this, nausea*) nausea, oppression, over-indulgence, satiety. **3** (*an excessive supply or amount*) excess, over-abundance, overdose, overflow, oversupply, plethora, superabundance, superfluity, surplus. ANTONYMS: deficiency.
~*v.t.* **1** (*to fill or feed to excess*) overfeed, overfill, stuff. **2** (*to overload, to cloy*) cloy, overload.
~*v.i.* (*to overeat*) cram, glut, gorge, overeat, sate, satiate, stuff.

surge *n.* **1** (*a sudden onset*) flood, flow, gush, onset, outpouring, rush, stream. **2** (*a large wave, a swell*) billow, breaker, comber, eddy, roller, swell, wave, whitecap, white horse. **3** (*a heaving and rolling motion*) heave, roll, upsurge. **4** (*a sudden increase or rise*) acceleration, increase, rise, rocket, shoot.
~*v.i.* **1** ((*of waves*) *to swell, to move up and down*) billow, bulge, ebb and flow, heave, pulsate, rise, rise and fall, roll, swell, undulate, wave. **2** (*to well up, to move with a sudden swelling motion*) flood, flow, gush, rush, stream, well up. **3** (*to increase or rise suddenly*) increase, rise, rocket, shoot up.

surly *a.* (*rude and bad-tempered*) argumentative, bad-tempered, brusque, cantankerous, choleric, churlish, cross, curmudgeonly, curt, gruff, grumpy, ill-humoured, obstreperous, peevish, rude, short-tempered, splenetic, sullen, uncivil. ANTONYMS: affable.

surpass *v.t.* (*to excel, to go beyond in amount, degree etc.*) beat, better, cap, eclipse, exceed, excel, go beyond, leave behind, outclass, outdistance, outdo, outperform, outshine, outstrip, overshadow, pass, top, transcend.

surplus *n.* **1** (*an amount which remains over, excess beyond what is used or required*) excess, glut, over-abundance, overdose, oversupply, plethora, superabundance, surfeit. **2** (*the balance in hand after all liabilities are paid*) balance, leftover, remainder, rest.
~*a.* (*being more than is needed*) excess, extra, leftover, over-abundant, redundant, remaining, spare, superfluous, unused.

surprise *n.* **1** (*an unexpected event*) blow, bolt from the blue, bombshell, eye-opener, jolt, shocker. **2** (*emotion excited by something sudden or unexpected, astonishment*) amazement, astonishment, incredulity, shock, start, stupefaction, wonder. **3** (*the act of taking someone unawares or unprepared*) ambush, secret, trap, waylaying.
~*a.* (*unexpected*) astonishing, shocking, startling, unexpected.
~*v.t.* **1** (*to strike with astonishment*) amaze, astonish, astound, (*coll.*) bowl over, disconcert, dumbfound, flabbergast, (*coll.*) floor, knock for six, nonplus, rock, stagger, startle, take aback. **2** (*to shock, to scandalize*) scandalize, shock, stun. **3** (*to come or fall upon suddenly, esp. to attack unawares*) catch napping, catch off guard, catch red-handed, catch unawares, come upon, fall upon, take unawares.

surrender *v.t.* **1** (*to give up possession of, esp. upon compulsion or demand*) deliver up, forgo, forsake, give up, hand over, let go, part with, renounce, resign, turn over, yield. ANTONYMS: retain. **2** (*to yield up to the power or control of another*) abdicate, acquiesce, capitulate, cede, concede, give in, quit, (*coll.*) raise the white flag, submit, succumb, (*coll.*) throw in the towel, yield.
~*v.i.* **1** (*to give oneself up into the power of another, esp. to an enemy in war*) give oneself up. **2** (*to yield, to submit*) give in, give way, submit, yield.
~*n.* (*the act of surrendering or the state of being surrendered*) abdication, capitulation, relinquishment, renunciation, resignation, submission, transfer, yielding.

surreptitious *a.* **1** (*done by stealth or fraud*) furtive, sly, sneaky, stealthy, underhand. **2** (*secret, clandestine*) clandestine, covert, hidden, private, secret, secretive, veiled.

surround *v.t.* (*to lie or be situated all round, to encompass*) besiege, circle, encircle, enclose, encompass, envelop, environ, fence in, gird, girdle, hem in, ring.
~*n.* (*an edging, a border*) border, edging, frame, setting, verge.

surroundings *n.pl.* (*things around a person or thing, environment*) background, circumstances, environment, environs, locality, milieu, neighbourhood, setting.

survey[1] *v.t.* **1** (*to look over, to take a general view of*) look over, observe, scan, view. **2** (*to examine closely*) contemplate, examine, inspect, reconnoitre, review, scrutinize, study. **3** (*to examine and ascertain the condition, value etc. of* (*a building etc.*)) appraise, assess, calculate, estimate, evaluate, size up, take stock of, value. **4** (*to determine by accurate observation and measurement the boundaries, extent etc. of* (*an area of land*)) map, measure, plot.

survey[2] *n.* **1** (*a careful examination*) appraisal, assessment, evaluation, examination, inquiry, inspection, investigation, measure, measurement, review, scan, scanning, scrutiny, study. **2** (*a map, plan etc. recording the results of this*) graph, map, plan, report, study.

survive *v.i.* (*to be still alive or in existence*) exist, live, remain.
~*v.t.* **1** (*to live longer than, to outlive*) outlast, outlive. **2** (*to be alive after, to live through* (*an event, period etc.*)) endure, last, live through, pull through, remain, subsist.

suspect[1] *v.t.* **1** (*to have an impression of the existence of without proof, to surmise*) assume, believe, conjecture, expect, fancy, feel, guess, imagine, presume, sense, suppose, surmise, theorize, think. ANTONYMS: know. **2** (*to be inclined to believe to be guilty but upon slight evidence*) doubt, think badly of, think the worst of. **3** (*to believe to be uncertain, to doubt*) be wary of, disbelieve, distrust, doubt, have doubts about, mistrust. ANTONYMS: trust.

suspect[2] *a.* **1** (*suspicious*) suspected, suspicious, under suspicion. **2** (*doubtful, uncertain*) doubtful, dubious, questionable, shadowy, shady, uncertain.

suspend *v.t.* **1** (*to hang up, to hang from something above*) attach, dangle, fasten, hang, sling, swing. **2** (*to render temporarily inoperative or cause to cease for a time*) adjourn, arrest, cease, check, defer, delay, discontinue, hold up, intermit, interrupt, keep in abeyance, postpone, put off, shelve, stay, stop, withhold. **3** (*to debar temporarily from a privilege, office etc.*) debar, eject, eliminate, evict, exclude, expel, reject, relieve.

suspense *n.* (*a state of uncertainty or apprehensive waiting*) agitation, anticipation, anxiety, apprehension, doubt, excitement, expectancy, expectation, hesitation, indecision, insecurity, irresolution, nervousness, tension, uncertainty, vacillation.

suspicion *n.* **1** (*belief in the existence of wrong or guilt on inadequate proof, doubt*) apprehension, apprehensiveness, distrust, doubt, dubiousness, funny feeling, hesitation, misgiving, mistrust, qualm, scepticism, second thoughts, uncertainty, wariness. ANTONYMS: trust. **2** (*a very slight amount; a trace*) dash, flavour, glimmer, scintilla, shadow, soupçon, suggestion, tad, taste, tinge, touch, trace. **3** (*a feeling that something is probably true*) conjecture, feeling, guess, idea, inkling, notion, supposition, thought.

suspicious *a.* **1** (*inclined to suspect*) apprehensive, disbelieving, distrustful, doubtful, leery, mistrustful, sceptical, suspecting, unbelieving, uncertain, uneasy, wary. ANTONYMS: trusting. **2** (*exciting or likely to excite suspicion*) debatable, doubtful, dubious, (*coll.*) fishy, open to doubt, queer, questionable, shady, strange, suspect.

sustain *v.t.* **1** (*to bear the weight of, to keep from falling*) bear, carry, hold up, keep from falling, support. ANTONYMS: drop. **2** (*to stand, to undergo without yielding*) endure, stand, undergo, withstand. **3** (*to experience, to suffer*) brave, experience, put up with, suffer, tolerate, weather. **4** (*to nourish, to provide sustenance for*) feed, foster, nourish, nurture, provide for. **5** (*to enable to bear something, to strengthen*) aid, assist, bolster, buoy up, buttress, carry, comfort, encourage, help, keep up, prop up, reinforce, relieve, shore up, strengthen, support, underpin. **6** (*to support, to confirm*) approve, bear out, confirm, endorse, justify, ratify, sanction, substantiate, support, validate, verify.

swagger *v.i.* **1** (*to strut or go* (*about etc.*) *with an air of self-confidence or superiority*) parade, prance, (*chiefly N Am., sl.*) sashay, strut. **2** (*to talk or behave in a blustering or boastful manner*) bluster, boast, brag, hector, show off, (*coll.*) swank, vaunt.
~*n.* **1** (*a swaggering walk or manner*) prance, strut, strutting, swaggering. **2** (*bluster, conceit*) arrogance, bluster, boastfulness, braggadocio, conceit, dash, display, ostentation, show, showing off. **3** (*smartness*) display, smartness, style.

swallow *v.t.* **1** (*to take through the mouth and throat into the stomach*) (*coll.*) down, drink, eat, gulp, guzzle, ingest, (*coll.*) put away, (*coll.*) swig, swill. **2** (*to absorb, to overwhelm*) absorb, assimilate, consume, devour, dispatch, engulf, overcome, overwhelm. **3** (*to accept with credulity*) accept, allow, believe, (*sl.*) buy, credit, (*coll.*) fall for, take. **4** (*to accept without resentment, to put up with*) accept, endure, put up with, stomach, suffer, take, tolerate. **5** (*to refrain from showing or expressing*) choke back, control, repress, smother, stifle, suppress.
~*n.* (*the amount swallowed at once*) bite, drink, gulp, guzzle, morsel, mouthful, nibble, (*coll.*) swig.

swamp *n.* (*a tract of wet, spongy land*) bog, fen, marsh, morass, quagmire, slough.
~*v.t.* (*to render helpless with difficulties, numbers etc.*) deluge, engulf, flood, immerse, inundate, overburden, overcome, overload, overtax, overwhelm, saturate, snow under, submerge, swallow up.
~*v.i.* (*to fill with water*) founder, scuttle, sink.

swarm *n.* (*a large number of small animals, insects, people etc., esp. when moving in a confused mass*) army, bevy, bunch, cloud, concourse, crowd, drove, flock, flood, herd, horde, host, mass, mob, multitude, pack, shoal, stream, throng.
~*v.i.* (*to throng, to be very numerous*) abound, bristle (with), burst (with), cluster, congregate, crawl, crowd, flock, flood, flow, gather, infest, mass, overrun, stream, teem (with), throng. ANTONYMS: scatter.

swarthy *a.* (*dark or dusky in complexion*) black, brown, coal-black, dark, dark-complexioned, dark-skinned, dusky, ebony, jet-black, pitch-black, raven, sable. ANTONYMS: pale.

sway *v.i.* **1** (*to move backwards and forward, to oscillate irregularly*) oscillate, sweep, swing, undulate. **2** (*to be unsteady, to waver*) fluctuate, reel, totter, vacillate, wave, waver, wobble. **3** (*to lean or incline to one side or in different directions*) bend, divert, incline, lean, move, slant, tend, tilt, veer.
~*v.t.* **1** (*to cause to oscillate, waver*) oscillate, rock, swing, wave. **2** (*to bias; to influence*) bias, bring round, control, convince, direct, govern, guide, impress, influence, persuade, rule, talk into, win over.
~*n.* **1** (*rule, control*) ascendancy, authority, command, control, dominion, influence, leadership, mastery, power, rule, sovereignty. ANTONYMS: subjection. **2** (*the act of swaying, a swing*) oscillation, swaying, sweep, swing, wave.

swear *v.i.* **1** (*to affirm solemnly invoking God or some other sacred person or object as witness or pledge*) affirm, agree, assert, asseverate, aver, avow, pledge, state, take an oath, undertake, vouchsafe, vow, warrant. ANTONYMS: deny. **2** (*to use profane or obscene language*) blaspheme, curse, (*coll.*) cuss. **3** (*to make a promise on oath*) give one's word, promise, vow.
~*v.t.* **1** (*to utter or affirm with an oath*) affirm, depose. **2** (*coll.*) (*to declare, to vow*) declare, insist, promise, vow. **3** (*to promise or testify upon oath*) bear witness, promise, testify.

sweat *n.* **1** (*the moisture exuded from the skin of a person or animal*) perspiration. **2** (*the act or state of sweating*) glowing, perspiring, sweating. **3** (*coll.*) (*a state of anxiety, a flurry*) agitation, anguish, anxiety, confusion, distraction, distress, (*coll.*) dither, flurry, (*coll.*) lather, pother, (*coll.*) tizzy. **4** (*coll.*) (*drudgery, hard labour*) drudgery, exertion, grind, hard labour, laboriousness, slavery, slogging, sweating, (*coll.*) swotting, toil, work. **5** (*moisture exuded from or deposited in drops on any surface*) condensation, exudation, secretion.
~*v.i.* **1** (*to exude sweat, to perspire*) glow, perspire. **2** ((*of moisture*) *to exude*) exude, ooze, secrete, squeeze out, transude. **3** (*to be in a flurry or state of anxiety, panic etc.*) agonize, fret, fuss, panic, stew, torment oneself, torture oneself, worry. **4** (*to toil, to drudge*) drudge, grind, labour, slave, slog, (*coll.*) swot, toil.
~*v.t.* (*to subject to extortion, to bleed*) (*coll.*) bleed, extort, squeeze.

sweep *v.t.* **1** (*to clear dirt etc. from or clean with or as with a broom*) brush, clean, clear, vacuum, whisk. **2** (*to collect or gather (up) with or as with a broom*) collect, gather up. **3** (*to carry (along, away etc.) with powerful or unchecked force*) carry along, carry away. **4** (*to wipe out, destroy*) blot away, demolish, destroy, remove, wash away, wipe out. **5** (*to move swiftly and powerfully over, across or along*) dash, march, move, range, scour, swoop, tear, zoom. **6** ((*esp. of the eyes*) *to pass over in swift survey*) glance over, pass over, skim.
~*v.i.* **1** (*to clear or clean a place with a broom*) brush, clean, clear, whisk. **2** (*to glide or pass along with a strong, swift continuous motion*) glide, pass along, sail, skim.
~*n.* **1** (*the act of sweeping*) brushing, sweeping. **2** (*a clearance, a riddance*) clearance, emptying, riddance. **3** (*a sweeping curve, direction etc.*) arc, arch, bend, bow, curvature, curve, direction. **4** (*the range, reach or compass of a sweeping motion or of an instrument, weapon etc. having this motion*) compass, expanse, extent, range, reach, scope, span, spread, stretch, swing.

sweeping *a.* **1** (*wide-ranging, comprehensive*) all-embracing, all-inclusive, blanket, broad, catholic, comprehensive, exhaustive, extensive, general, global, thorough, total, umbrella, universal, wide, wide-ranging. ANTONYMS: specific. **2** (*without discrimination or qualification*) indiscriminate, undiscriminating, unqualified, wholesale.

sweet *a.* **1** (*having a taste like the taste of honey or sugar*) honeyed, honey-like, sugary. **2** (*containing sugar or a sweetening ingredient*) sugared, sweetened. **3** (*pleasing to the senses*) nice, pleasing, satisfying. **4** (*fragrant*) ambrosial, balmy, fragrant, perfumed, redolent, scented, sweet-scented, sweet-smelling. **5** (*pleasant or melodious in sound*) dulcet, euphonious, harmonious, mellifluous, mellow, melodious, musical, pleasant-sounding, silvery, soft, tuneful. ANTONYMS: discordant, harsh. **6** (*fresh, not salt or salted*) fresh, prime, ripe. ANTONYMS: bitter, sour, stale. **7** (*pleasant to the mind, delightful*) agreeable, appealing, attractive, charming, dear, delightful, lovable, nice, pleasant. ANTONYMS: nasty. **8** (*charming, amiable*) amiable, charming, easygoing, friendly, genial, gentle, kind, lovely, nice, pleasant, warm, winning.
~*n.* **1** (*a piece of confectionery, such as a toffee or a chocolate*) bon-bon, candy, chocolate, confection, sweetmeat, toffee. **2** (*a sweet dish, such as a tart or ice cream; this served as a course of a meal, after the main course*) (*coll.*) afters, dessert, pudding. **3** (*dear one, darling*) darling, love, sweetheart.

swell *v.i.* **1** (*to increase in bulk or extent, to expand*) dilate, distend, enlarge, expand, extend, grow, increase, spread, wax. ANTONYMS: shrink. **2** (*to bulge, to belly (out)*) balloon, belly, billow, bloat, bulge, fatten, mushroom. **3** (*to become greater in volume or intensity*) accumulate, amplify, augment, boost, grow louder, intensify, snowball, strengthen.
~*v.t.* **1** (*to increase the size or bulk of*) enlarge, increase. **2** (*to inflate, to puff up*) blow up, inflate, puff up.
~*n.* **1** (*the act or effect of swelling*) augmentation, broadening, enlargement, expansion, extension, increase, inflation, rise, spread, surge. **2** (*a succession of long, unbroken waves in one direction, for example after a storm*) billow, surge, wave. **3** (*a bulge, a bulging part*) bulge, swelling. **4** (*dated coll.*) (*a dashing or fashionable person*) beau, dandy, fop, (*sl.*) toff.
~*a.* **1** (*esp. N Am., coll.*) (*excellent, fine*) excellent, fine, (*coll.*) great, marvellous, spectacular, splendid, (*coll.*) super, (*coll.*) terrific, thrilling. **2** (*smart, foppish*) chic, dandified, de luxe, elegant, fashionable, foppish, grand,

luxurious, modish, (*coll.*) posh, smart, stylish, (*coll.*) swanky.

swelling *n.* **1** (*an unnatural enlargement or protuberance of a body part*) bulge, bump, distension, enlargement, excrescence, lump, node, nodule, prominence, protrusion, protuberance, tumefaction, tumescence, tumour. **2** (*the act of expanding, or the state of being swollen*) augmentation, dilation, enlargement, expansion, inflation, tumefaction.

swerve *v.i.* (*to turn to one side, to diverge from the direct or regular course*) career, deviate, diverge, drift, sheer off, skew, stray, swing, turn aside, veer, wander.
~*n.* (*a sudden divergence or deflection*) deflection, divergence.

swift *a.* **1** (*moving or able to move with great rapidity, quick*) abrupt, brisk, fast, fleet, hasty, hurried, lively, nimble, quick, rapid, speedy, sudden. ANTONYMS: slow. **2** (*ready, prompt*) alert, diligent, expeditious, prompt, ready.

swindle *v.t., v.i.* (*to cheat*) bilk, cheat, (*sl.*) con, cozen, deceive, defraud, diddle, (*coll.*) do, dupe, exploit, fleece, gull, hoodwink, mulct, rip off, rook, screw, (*coll.*) take for a ride, take in.
~*n.* (*a thing that is not what it pretends to be, a deception*) cheat, (*sl.*) con, confidence trick, deception, (*coll.*) fiddle, fraud, (*sl.*) racket, (*coll.*) rip-off, (*N Am., sl.*) scam, sharp practice, (*coll.*) swizzle, trickery.

swing *v.i.* **1** (*to move to and fro, like an object suspended by a point or one side, hang freely*) move to and fro, oscillate, rock, sway. **2** (*to move or wheel (round etc.) through an arc*) pivot, rotate, spin, wheel, whirl. **3** (*to fluctuate between emotions, decisions etc.*) dither, fluctuate, vacillate, waver.
~*v.t.* **1** (*to cause to move to and fro*) oscillate, rock, sway. **2** (*to wave to and fro*) brandish, wave, wield. **3** (*to cause to turn or move around, as on a pivot or through an arc*) arc, move around, pivot, turn around. **4** (*to manipulate, to influence*) convince, influence, manipulate, persuade.
~*n.* **1** (*a swinging or oscillating motion*) flapping, flourish, fluctuation, oscillation, rock, sway, swinging, vacillation, vibration, waggle, waver, wavering, wobble, zigzag. **2** (*the compass or sweep of a moving body*) compass, range, scope, sweep. **3** (*a curving or sweeping movement*) arc, curve, sweep. **4** (*a shift in opinion, condition etc.*) change, shift, switch.

swirl *v.i.* (*to form eddies, to whirl about*) boil, churn, circulate, curl, eddy, furl, gyrate, roll, seethe, spin, spiral, surge, turn, twirl, twist, whirl, whorl, wind.

~*n.* (*a whirling motion, an eddy*) curl, eddy, roll, spiral, twirl, twist, whirl.

switch *n.* **1** (*a mechanism for diverting trains from one line to another, or for completing or interrupting an electric circuit etc.*) on-off button, points. **2** (*a shift, change*) about-turn, alteration, change, reversal, shift. **3** (*an exchange*) exchange, swap, trade. **4** (*a small flexible twig or rod*) birch, cane, lash, rod, scourge, stick, twig, whip.
~*v.t.* **1** (*to turn (on or off) with a switch*) turn off, turn on. **2** (*to move, to whisk or snatch (away etc.) with a jerk*) move, snatch, whisk. **3** (*to lash or beat with a switch*) beat, birch, cane, flog, lash, strike, thrash, whip. **4** (*to change, to divert*) change, deviate, divert, exchange, shift.
~*v.i.* **1** (*to turn an electrical device (on or off) with a switch*) turn off, turn on. **2** (*to make a change, to shift*) change, exchange, replace, shift, substitute, swap, trade.

swivel *n.* (*a link or connection comprising a ring and pivot allowing the two parts to revolve independently*) ball-and-socket joint, elbow-joint, gimbals, pivot, revolve, spin, turn.
~*v.i., v.t.* (*to turn on a swivel or pivot*) pirouette, pivot, revolve, rotate, spin, turn.

swoop *v.i.* **1** ((*of a bird of prey*) *to descend upon prey etc. suddenly*) descend, dive, plunge, rush, stoop, sweep down. **2** (*to come (down upon), to attack suddenly*) attack, fall upon, pounce.
~*v.t.* (*to snatch (up)*) grab, seize, snatch, swipe.
~*n.* **1** (*a sudden plunge of or as of a bird of prey on its quarry*) dive, plunge, stoop. **2** (*a sudden descent or seizing*) attack, blow, descent, pounce, rush, snatch, stroke, sweep.

symbol *n.* **1** (*an object typifying or representing something by resemblance, association etc., an emblem*) allegory, arms, badge, banner, bearing, brand, coat of arms, crest, emblem, escutcheon, flag, image, insignia, logo, monogram, pennant, shield, standard, token, trademark. **2** (*a mark or letter accepted as representing or signifying some idea, process etc.*) abbreviation, acronym, character, code, codeword, cryptogram, figure, letter, mark, password, representation, sign, watchword.

symbolic *a.* (*serving as or using symbols*) allegorical, allusive, betokening, characteristic, connotative, denotative, emblematic, figurative, metaphorical, representative, symbolical, symptomatic, typical.

symbolize *v.t.* **1** (*to be the symbol of, to typify*) embody, represent, suggest, typify. **2** (*to represent by symbols*) betoken, connote, denote, epitomize, express, illustrate, imply, personify, represent, signify, stand for.

sympathetic *a.* **1** (*having sympathy or common feeling with another, sympathizing*) affectionate, caring, comforting, compassionate, concerned, considerate, consoling, good-natured, kind, kindly, responsive, solicitous, supportive, tender, understanding, warm, well-intentioned, well-meaning. ANTONYMS: unsympathetic. **2** (*being or acting in sympathy or agreement*) concordant, in agreement, in sympathy with. **3** (*in accord with one's mood or disposition, congenial*) agreeable, congenial, encouraging, friendly, like-minded, pleasant, well-disposed.

sympathize *v.i.* **1** (*to have or express sympathy with another, in pain, pleasure etc.*) comfort, commiserate, condole, console, empathize with, feel for, feel sorry for, grieve with, have sympathy for, mourn with, pity, suffer with. **2** (*to be of the same disposition, opinion etc.*) accord with, agree, back, (*dated sl.*) dig, feel rapport with, get along, harmonize with, identify, relate, see eye to eye with, side with, support, understand.

sympathy *n.* **1** (*fellow feeling, agreement, harmony*) agreement, compatibility, fellow feeling, fellowship, harmony. **2** (*a feeling of accord* (*with*)) accord, affinity, closeness, concord, congeniality, rapport. ANTONYMS: antipathy. **3** (*loyalty or support*) favour, loyalty, support. **4** (*compassion* (*for*)) commiseration, compassion, concern, condolence, empathy,

pity, solicitousness, tender-heartedness, tenderness, thoughtfulness, understanding, warm-heartedness, warmth. ANTONYMS: indifference. **5** (*unity or correlation of action*) correlation, unity.

symptom *n.* (*a sign, an indication*) characteristic, clue, cue, earmark, evidence, feature, indication, manifestation, mark, marker, sign, symbol, syndrome, token, trait, warning.

synthetic *a.* **1** (*artificially produced, man-made*) artificial, man-made, manufactured. **2** (*false, sham*) bogus, counterfeit, ersatz, fake, false, imitation, mock, pseudo, sham, spurious.

system *n.* **1** (*coordinated arrangement, organization*) arrangement, combination, method, organization, set-up, structure. **2** (*an established method or procedure*) approach, method, modus operandi, practice, procedure, process, protocol, routine, technique, way. **3** (*a logical grouping, a method of classification*) order, pattern, plan, scheme. **4** (*a group of related or linked natural objects, such as mountains*) chain, group, set.

systematic *a.* **1** (*methodical*) businesslike, methodical, meticulous. **2** (*done or arranged on a regular plan*) orderly, organized, planned, regular, routine, standard, standardized, systematized, well-ordered, well-organized. ANTONYMS: haphazard, unsystematic.

tab *n.* **1** (*a small flap, tag etc., as the flap of a shoe, the tip of lace etc.*) flap, tag, tongue. **2** (*a small paper flap attached to a file for identification purposes*) flag, label, marker, sticker, ticket. **3** (*a strap, a loop*) flap, loop, strap.

table *n.* **1** (*an article of furniture consisting of a flat surface resting on one or more supports, used for serving meals, writing etc.*) bar, bench, board, buffet, counter, stand. **2** (*the food served on a table*) board, cuisine, diet, fare, food, (*sl.*) grub, meals, (*sl.*) nosh, victuals. **3** (*a list of numbers, references, or other items arranged systematically, esp. in columns*) catalogue, chart, diagram, figure, graph, index, inventory, list, plan, tabulation.
~*v.t.* (*to put forward* (*a motion*) *for debate at a meeting*) enter, move, propose, put forward, submit, suggest. ANTONYMS: retract, withdraw.

tableau *n.* (*a striking or vivid representation or effect*) illustration, picture, portrayal, presentation, representation, scene, sight, spectacle.

tablet *n.* **1** (*a small solid measure of medicine or other substance*) capsule, lozenge, pill. **2** (*a shaped slab* (*of soap*)) bar, cake, piece, slab.

taboo *n.* (*ban, prohibition*) ban, interdict, prohibition, proscription, restriction.
~*a.* (*banned, prohibited, by religious or moral convention*) banned, beyond the pale, forbidden, frowned upon, outlawed, prohibited, proscribed, ruled out, unacceptable, vetoed. ANTONYMS: acceptable, allowed, permitted, sanctioned.

tabulate *v.t.* (*to reduce to or arrange* (*figures etc.*) *in tabular form*) arrange, catalogue, categorize, chart, class, classify, codify, grade, group, lay out, list, order, organize, range, set out, systematize.

tacit *a.* (*implied but not actually expressed*) assumed, implicit, implied, inferred, silent, taken for granted, undeclared, understood, unexpressed, unspoken, unvoiced, wordless. ANTONYMS: declared, explicit, stated, voiced.

taciturn *a.* (*habitually silent or uncommunicative*) aloof, antisocial, detached, distant, dour, dumb, mute, quiet, reserved, reticent, silent, tight-lipped, uncommunicative, unforthcoming, unsociable, withdrawn. ANTONYMS: chatty, communicative, garrulous, loquacious, talkative, verbose, voluble.

tack *n.* **1** (*a small flat-headed nail*) drawing pin, nail, rivet, staple, (*N Am.*) thumbtack. **2** (*a course of action, a policy*) approach, course of action, line of action, line of attack, method, plan, procedure, process, strategy, system, tactic, way.
~*v.t.* **1** (*to fasten with tacks*) affix, attach, fasten, fix, nail, pin, staple. **2** (*to stitch* (*fabric*) *temporarily or together in a hasty manner*) baste, do a running repair on, sew, stitch. **3** (*to annex, to append* (*to or onto*)) add, annex, append, attach (to), tag (on). ANTONYMS: detach (from), remove (from).

tackle *v.t.* **1** (*to grapple with*) intercept, seize, struggle with, take hold of. **2** (*to confront, to collar*) accost, challenge, confront, waylay. **3** (*to set to work vigorously upon*) apply oneself to, attempt, embark on, engage in, get to grips with, (*coll.*) have a go at, put one's shoulder to the wheel, set about, turn one's hand to, undertake. ANTONYMS: give up, renege on.

tacky *a.* **1** (*sticky*) gluey, (*coll.*) gooey, gummy, wet. **2** (*cheap, vulgar and ostentatious*) cheap, cheap and nasty, flash, flashy, garish, gaudy, kitsch, (*sl.*) naff, ostentatious, seedy, shabby, shoddy, tasteless, tatty, vulgar. ANTONYMS: aesthetic, artistic, elegant, tasteful.

tact *n.* (*adroitness in doing or saying the proper thing*) adroitness, delicacy, diplomacy, discernment, discretion, finesse, judgement, perception, savoir faire, sensitivity, subtlety, tactfulness, thoughtfulness, understanding. ANTONYMS: clumsiness, gaucheness, ineptness, insensitivity, tactlessness.

tactful *a.* (*having or using tact*) adroit, delicate, diplomatic, discerning, discreet, judicious, politic, sensitive, subtle, thoughtful, understanding. ANTONYMS: clumsy, indiscreet, insensitive, tactless, undiplomatic.

tactic *n.* (*a way of doing or achieving something*) approach, course of action, device, expedient, line of action, line of attack, manoeuvre, means, method, move, plan, ploy, policy, procedure, process, scheme, stratagem, tack, trick, way.

tactical *a.* (*skilful, diplomatic*) adroit, artful, clever, cunning, diplomatic, judicious, politic, skilful, smart, strategic. ANTONYMS: clumsy, gauche, inept, stupid.

tactics *n.* (*the art of manoeuvring military or naval forces, esp. in actual contact with the enemy*) battle plans, campaign, manoeuvres, strategy.

tactless *a.* (*lacking tact, showing a lack of tact*) blundering, clumsy, gauche, impolitic, indiscreet, inept, injudicious, insensitive, maladroit, thoughtless, undiplomatic, unsubtle. ANTONYMS: diplomatic, discreet, politic, tactful.

tag *n.* (*a label*) docket, flag, identification, label, marker, sticker, tab, ticket.
~*v.t.* **1** (*to fit or mark with a tag, to attach a tag to*) flag, identify, label, mark. **2** (*to attach* (*to, onto or together*)) add, affix, annex, append, attach, tack. **to tag along with** (*to go along with* (*someone*), *to follow*) accompany, dog, follow, go along with, shadow, tail, trail.

tail *n.* **1** (*the part of an animal, bird, fish or insect that extends from the end or the back of the body*) brush, dock, scut. **2** (*the rear or last part or parts of something*) close, conclusion, end, rear, tail-end. **3** (*the buttocks*) (*taboo sl.*) arse, (*coll.*) backside, behind, bottom, (*sl.*) bum, posterior, (*euphem.*) rear, (*coll.*) rear-end, rump. **4** (*the route that someone or something travelling or running away takes*) scent, track, trail. **5** (*a person who follows and watches another person or people*) detective, (*N Am., coll.*) gumshoe, investigator, (*coll.*) private eye, private investigator, shadow, (*coll.*) sleuth.
~*v.t.* (*to follow and keep under surveillance*) dog, dog the footsteps of, follow, keep a watch on, keep under surveillance, shadow, stalk, track, trail. **to tail off** (*to come to and end, or almost to an end*) decrease, die away, die out, drop off, dwindle, fade, fall away, fall off, peter out, wane. ANTONYMS: gather momentum, increase. **to turn tail** (*to run away*) cut and run, flee, retreat, run off, (*coll.*) skedaddle, take to one's heels, (*N Am., sl.*) vamoose.

tailor *n.* (*a person whose occupation is to cut out and make clothes, esp. outer clothes for men*) clothier, couturier, dressmaker, outfitter.
~*v.t.* (*to adapt for a particular purpose or need*) accommodate, adapt, adjust, convert, custom-build, custom-make, fit, modify, suit.

tailor-made *a.* (*perfectly suited or adapted*) custom-built, custom-made, fitting, ideal, just right, perfect, suitable.

taint *n.* **1** (*a blemish, a disgrace*) black mark, blemish, blot, defect, disgrace, dishonour, fault, flaw, shame, smear, smirch, stain, stigma. **2** (*a trace of decay, unsoundness etc.*) hint, suggestion, touch, trace.
~*v.t.* **1** (*to imbue or infect with a poisonous or corrupting element*) adulterate, befoul, contaminate, dirty, infect, poison, pollute, soil, spoil. ANTONYMS: clean, cleanse, disinfect, purify. **2** (*to dirty or tarnish*) besmirch, blacken, blemish, blot, damage, defile, dirty, disgrace, dishonour, harm, injure, muddy, ruin, smear, spoil, stain, stigmatize, sully, tarnish, vitiate.

take *v.t.* **1** (*to lay hold of, seize etc.*) abduct, acquire, arrest, capture, catch, clutch, earn, gain possession of, get, grasp, grip, lay hold of, obtain, receive, secure, seize, take hold of, take possession of, win. **2** (*to remove, carry away etc.*) carry, convey, escort, fetch, transport. **3** (*to remove without permission*) abstract, appropriate, carry off, filch, make off with, misappropriate, (*sl.*) nick, (*coll.*) pinch, (*coll.*) pocket, purloin, remove, run off with, steal, (*coll.*) swipe, walk off with. **4** (*to consume or swallow*) consume, devour, eat, imbibe, swallow. **5** (*to choose to go along* (*a specified road, direction etc.*)) drive along, follow, go along, travel along, use. **6** (*to put up with, endure etc.*) abide, accept, bear, brave, brook, endure, go through, put up with, stand, stomach, swallow, tolerate, undergo, weather, withstand. **7** (*to ascertain and record by weighing, measuring etc.*) ascertain, determine, find out, measure. **8** (*to understand, conclude etc.*) apprehend, assume, believe, comprehend, conclude, consider, deem, gather, grasp, hold, interpret, presume, understand. ANTONYMS: misunderstand. **9** (*to feel or show* (*a specified response, esp. an emotional one*)) deal with, handle, react to, respond to. **10** (*to need* (*a specified person or thing, esp. to ensure the desired outcome or action*)) call for, demand, have need of, necessitate, need, require. **11** (*to accommodate or have room for*) accommodate, contain, have room for, hold. **12** (*to note down or write up*) make a note of, note down, record, register, write down. **13** (*to choose to pursue* (*a specified course of action etc.*)) choose, opt for, pick, select. **14** (*to follow or teach* (*a specified subject, course of study etc.*)) follow, major in, pursue, read, study. **15** (*to buy or subscribe to* (*a specified newspaper or other publication*), *esp. on a regular basis*) buy, purchase, subscribe to. **16** (*to use or cite as a prime or illustrative example*) cite, consider, look at, quote. **17** (*to use* (*text written by someone else*) *as a quote etc.*) cite, mention, quote, refer to.
~*v.i.* (*to be successful or have the desired effect*) be effective, be efficacious, be successful, (*coll.*) do the trick, succeed, take effect, work. ANTONYMS: be ineffective, be unsuccessful, fail. **to be taken with** (*to be charmed by or very pleased with*) be attracted to, be captivated by, be charmed by, be delighted by, be enchanted with, be fascinated by, be pleased with, like, love. ANTONYMS: dislike, hate. **to take after** (*to*

resemble physically, mentally etc.) be a chip off the old block, be like, favour, look like, resemble. **to take against** (*to form a dislike for*) dislike, feel hostile to, hate, take a dislike to, view with disfavour. ANTONYMS: like, love, take a liking to. **to take back 1** (*to withdraw, to retract*) disclaim, renounce, retract, withdraw. **2** (*to stimulate memories of, esp. nostalgically*) evoke memories of, put in mind of, remind. **to take down 1** (*to write down*) commit to paper, document, jot down, make a note of, minute, note, note down, put in black and white, record, register, set down. **2** (*to lower* (*a garment*) *to one's knees or ankles, esp. temporarily*) drop, haul down, let down, lower, pull down. **3** (*to take apart, to pull to pieces*) demolish, disassemble, dismantle, level, pull down, raze, take apart, take to pieces, tear down. ANTONYMS: assemble. **4** (*to humiliate, to humble*) deflate, humble, humiliate, mortify, put down, take down a peg or two. **to take in 1** (*to admit, to receive*) accommodate, admit, let in, receive, welcome. ANTONYMS: eject, reject. **2** (*to include, to comprise*) comprise, contain, cover, embrace, encompass, include. ANTONYMS: exclude. **3** (*to understand, to accept as true*) absorb, assimilate, comprehend, digest, grasp, understand. ANTONYMS: misunderstand. **4** (*to deceive, to cheat*) cheat, (*sl.*) con, deceive, defraud, delude, (*coll.*) do, dupe, fool, hoodwink, mislead, pull the wool over someone's eyes, swindle, trick. **to take off 1** (*to remove, to withdraw*) detach, discard, divest oneself of, doff, pull off, remove, retract. ANTONYMS: don, put on. **2** (*to begin flight*) become airborne, lift off, take to the air. ANTONYMS: land. **3** (*to become popular*) be successful, catch on, do well, succeed. ANTONYMS: be unsuccessful, fail, fall off. **4** (*to deduct* (*from*)) subtract, take away. **5** (*to leave suddenly or hastily*) abscond, (*sl.*) beat it, decamp, depart, flee, go, leave, run away, (*coll.*) skedaddle, (*sl.*) split, take to one's heels, (*N Am., sl.*) vamoose. **6** (*to mimic, to ridicule*) caricature, imitate, impersonate, lampoon, mimic, mock, parody, ridicule, satirize, send up. **to take on 1** (*to engage for work etc.*) employ, engage, enlist, enrol, hire, sign on. ANTONYMS: declare redundant, (*coll.*) sack. **2** (*to undertake to do* (*work etc.*)) address oneself to, embark on, (*coll.*) have a go at, tackle, undertake. **3** (*to accept a challenge from, to engage in a contest with*) challenge, compete against, contend with, face, fight, oppose, pit oneself against, vie with. **4** (*to acquire, to adopt*) acquire, adopt, assume, come to have. **5** (*to be violently affected, to be upset*) get excited, (*coll.*) get in a tizz, get upset, (*coll.*) lose one's cool, make a fuss, overreact. ANTONYMS: keep calm, (*coll.*) keep one's cool. **to take out 1** (*to remove, to*

extract) extract, pull out, remove, yank out. **2** (*to invite and accompany on an outing etc.*) (*esp. N Am.*) date, escort, go out with. **to take over** (*to assume control of*) assume control of, gain control of, take charge of, take command of, take control of, take responsibility for. **to take to 1** (*to form a habit of*) begin, commence, make a habit of, start, take up. ANTONYMS: give up, kick, stop. **2** (*to form a liking for*) be attracted to, become friendly with, develop a liking for, get on with. **to take up 1** (*to lift* (*up*)) raise. ANTONYMS: lower, put down. **2** (*to begin to engage or take an interest in*) become involved in, begin, commence, engage in, interest oneself in, start. ANTONYMS: abstain from, give up. **3** (*to resume, to pursue*) carry on, continue with, pick up, recommence, restart, resume. **4** (*of an object*) *to occupy or fill physically*) absorb, consume, fill, occupy, use, use up. **5** (*to accept as an office*) accede to, accept, agree to, say yes to. ANTONYMS: reject, turn down.

take-off *n.* **1** (*the rising of an aircraft into the air*) ascent, departure, lift-off. ANTONYMS: descent, landing. **2** (*an act of mimicking, a caricature*) caricature, imitation, impersonation, lampoon, mimicking, mocking, parody, satire, (*coll.*) send-up, spoof.

taking *a.* (*pleasing, attractive*) attractive, beguiling, captivating, charming, delightful, enchanting, engaging, fascinating, (*coll.*) fetching, likeable, lovable, pleasant, pleasing, winning, winsome. ANTONYMS: boring, hateful, repulsive, unengaging, unpleasant.
~n. (*pl.*) (*money taken*) earnings, gain, income, pickings, proceeds, profits, receipts, returns, revenue, yield.

tale *n.* **1** (*a narrative, a story*) account, anecdote, fable, fiction, legend, myth, narrative, novel, parable, report, saga, story, (*coll.*) yarn. **2** (*an idle or malicious report*) allegation, gossip, hearsay, report, rumour, talk.

talent *n.* (*a particular aptitude or faculty*) ability, aptitude, aptness, bent, capacity, endowment, facility, faculty, flair, forte, genius, gift, knack, strength, strong point. ANTONYMS: weakness, weak point.

talented *a.* (*endowed with talents or ability*) able, accomplished, adept, apt, clever, deft, expert, gifted, proficient. ANTONYMS: incapable, talentless.

talisman *n.* (*a charm or an amulet that is believed to have magical powers*) amulet, charm, lucky charm, mascot.

talk *v.i.* **1** (*to communicate ideas or thoughts in spoken words*) articulate, babble, chat, chatter,

communicate, gabble, give utterance, give voice, gossip, jabber, prate, prattle, (*coll.*) rabbit on, rattle on, speak, spout, verbalize, (*coll.*) witter, yak. ANTONYMS: be silent, shut up. **2** (*to exchange thoughts in spoken words*) chat, (*sl.*) chew the fat, communicate, confer, consult, converse, gossip, have a conference, have a conversation, have a discussion, have a natter, have a powwow, have a tête-à-tête, (*coll.*) jaw, negotiate, parley, speak. **3** (*to have the power of speech*) articulate, speak, verbalize. ANTONYMS: be dumb, be mute. **4** (*to reveal secret or confidential information*) blab, give the game away, (*sl.*) grass, inform, let the cat out of the bag, reveal all, (*sl.*) sing, speak out, spill the beans, (*sl.*) squeal, tell, tell all, tell tales. ANTONYMS: keep a secret, keep quiet, keep (something) under one's hat, keep under wraps. **5** (*to gossip*) gossip, spread rumours, spread stories.
~*v.t.* **1** (*to express in speech*) articulate, enunciate, express, say, speak, state, utter, verbalize, voice. **2** (*to converse about, to discuss*) converse about, debate, discuss, speak about.
~*n.* **1** (*talking, speaking*) babbling, chatter, chattering, gabbling, gossiping, jabbering, nattering, prating, prattling, (*coll.*) rabbiting on, rattling on, (*coll.*) wittering, yakking. **2** (*conversation, chat*) chat, conclave, (*coll.*) confab, conference, consultation, conversation, debate, dialogue, gossip, negotiation, parley, powwow, tête-à-tête. **3** (*gossip, rumour*) gossip, hearsay, report, rumour, tittle-tattle. **4** (*a short speech or address*) address, discourse, disquisition, lecture, oration, sermon, speech. **5** (*a specified form of speaking*) cant, dialect, idiolect, idiom, jargon, language, (*coll.*) lingo, patois, slang, speech. **to talk down to** (*to speak to in a patronizing or condescending way*) condescend to, patronize, talk to like a child, treat condescendingly, treat patronizingly. **to talk into** (*to persuade to do by argument*) cajole into, coax into, convince, influence, persuade, prevail on, sway, win over. ANTONYMS: dissuade, talk out of. **to talk out of** (*to dissuade from doing by argument*) deter, discourage, dissuade, persuade against, stop. ANTONYMS: persuade, talk into. **to talk over** (*to discuss at length*) confer about, converse about, discuss, go into, have talks about, talk about, talk through, thrash out.

talkative *a.* (*given to talking a lot*) chatty, (*coll.*) gabby, garrulous, gossipy, long-winded, loquacious, (*coll.*) mouthy, prolix, verbose, voluble, wordy. ANTONYMS: quiet, reserved, taciturn, uncommunicative, unforthcoming.

talking-to *n.* (*a telling-off, a reproof*) (*coll.*) carpeting, (*coll.*) dressing-down, lecture,

rebuke, reprimand, reproof, scolding, telling-off, (*coll.*) ticking-off.

tall *a.* **1** (*high in stature, above the average height*) big, high, huge, lanky, lofty, ranging, soaring, towering. ANTONYMS: low, small, tiny. **2** (*having a specified height*) high, in height. **3** (*extravagant, boastful*) absurd, exaggerated, far-fetched, implausible, incredible, preposterous, unbelievable, unlikely, unrealistic. ANTONYMS: plausible, realistic, understated, unexaggerated. **4** (*exorbitant, excessive*) demanding, exorbitant, unreasonable. ANTONYMS: reasonable.

tally *n.* **1** (*a reckoning, an account*) account, count, reckoning, record, register, running total. **2** (*a number reckoned or registered, a score*) count, result, score, sum, total.
~*v.i.* (*to agree, to correspond* (*with*)) accord (with), agree (with), coincide (with), concur (with), correspond (to), fit, harmonize (with), match, square (with). ANTONYMS: clash (with), contradict, differ (from), disagree (with).

tame *a.* **1** ((*of an animal*) *having lost its native wildness, domesticated*) domestic, domesticated, house-trained, tamed. ANTONYMS: feral, savage, untamed, wild. **2** (*tractable, docile*) amenable, compliant, docile, manageable, meek, obedient, subdued, submissive, tractable, unresisting, yielding. ANTONYMS: disobedient, obdurate, recalcitrant, strong-willed, stubborn, unmanageable, wild. **3** (*dull, insipid*) boring, dull, flat, humdrum, insipid, monotonous, prosaic, run-of-the-mill, tedious, unexciting, uninspired, uninspiring, uninteresting, vapid, wearisome. ANTONYMS: exciting, interesting, spellbinding.
~*v.t.* **1** (*to domesticate, to make docile*) break in, domesticate, house-train, make tame, train. **2** (*to subdue, to humble*) bring to heel, conquer, control, discipline, humble, master, overcome, repress, subdue, suppress.

tamper *v.i.* **1** (*to interfere illegitimately* (*with*), *esp. to alter documents etc., to adulterate*) adulterate, interfere with, meddle with, monkey around with. **2** (*to employ blackmail*) blackmail, bribe, corrupt, (*sl.*) fix, get at, influence, interfere with, manipulate, rig.

tan *a.* (*yellowish-brown*) brownish-yellow, light brown, pale brown, tawny, yellowish-brown.
~*v.t.* **1** (*to make brown by exposure to the sun or to artificial ultraviolet rays*) brown, darken, make brown, suntan, turn brown. **2** (*to flog, to thrash*) beat, flog, lash, leather, thrash, (*coll.*) wallop, whip.

tang *n.* **1** (*a strong taste or flavour*) flavour, savour, smack, taste. **2** (*a distinctive quality*) hint, suggestion, tinge, touch, trace, whiff. **3** (*a* smell) aroma, odour, smell. **4** (*piquancy; an exciting quality*) bite, piquancy, punch, relish, sharpness, spice, spiciness, zest, zip.

tangible *a.* **1** (*perceptible by touch*) palpable, tactile, touchable, visible. ANTONYMS: impalpable, intangible. **2** (*definite, capable of realization*) actual, clear, clearcut, concrete, corporal, definite, discernible, evident, hard, manifest, material, perceptible, physical, positive, real, solid, substantial, unmistakable, well-defined. ANTONYMS: abstract, ethereal, immaterial, intangible, theoretical, unreal.

tangle *v.t.* (*to knot together or intertwine in a confused mass*) interlace, interlock, intertwine, knot, mat, ravel, snarl, tousle, twist. ANTONYMS: disentangle, straighten, unravel, untangle.
~*v.i.* (*to come into conflict with*) argue with, come into conflict with, come up against, cross swords with, fight with, have a dispute with, lock horns with, quarrrel with, squabble with, wrangle with.

tangled *a.* **1** (*entangled*) entangled, jumbled, knotted, matted, ravelled, scrambled, snarled, tousled, twisted. ANTONYMS: smooth, straightened. **2** (*complicated, convoluted*) chaotic, complex, complicated, convoluted, involved, jumbled, knotty, mixed-up. ANTONYMS: simple, straightforward, uncomplicated.

tangy *a.* (*sharp, piquant*) biting, piquant, pungent, salty, sharp, spicy, tart. ANTONYMS: bland, sweet.

tank *n.* **1** (*a cistern or vessel of large size for holding liquid, gas etc.*) cistern, container, receptacle, vat. **2** (*a heavily-armoured motor vehicle running on caterpillar tractors*) armoured car, combat vehicle.

tantalize *v.t.* (*to torment or tease by seeming to offer something badly wanted but continually withholding it*) baulk, disappoint, frustrate, lead (someone) on, make (someone's) mouth water, tease, thwart, torment.

tantamount *a.* (*equivalent* (*to*) *in value or effect*) as good (as), corresponding (to), equal (to), equivalent (to), synonymous (with).

tantrum *n.* (*a burst of ill temper, a fit of passion*) fit of anger, fit of rage, fit of temper, flare-up, outburst, (*coll.*) paddy, paroxysm, pet.

tap[1] *v.t.* (*to strike lightly or gently*) beat, drum, pat, rap, slap, strike, touch.
~*n.* (*a light or gentle blow, a rap*) blow, pat, rap, slap, touch.

tap[2] *n.* **1** (*a device that allows water or other fluid to be drawn out at a controlled rate; a faucet*) (*N Am.*) faucet, spigot, stopcock, valve. **2** (*a*

device connected secretly to a telephone and allowing someone other than the user to listen in to calls) bug, bugging device. **3** (*a plug or bung for closing a hole in a cask etc.*) bung, plug, stopper.
~*v.t.* **1** (*to pierce* (*a cask etc.*) *so as to let out a liquid*) broach, open, pierce. **2** (*to let out or draw off* (*a liquid*) *in this way*) bleed, drain, draw off, syphon off. **3** (*to draw upon* (*a source of supply*) *usually for the first time*) draw on, exploit, make use of, milk, put to use, turn to account, use, utilize. **4** (*to attach a device to* (*a telephone*) *in order to listen in to other people's conversations*) attach a bug to, bug, eavesdrop on, put a tap on. **on tap** (*freely available for use*) at hand, available, in reserve, on hand, ready, standing by, to hand.

tape *n.* **1** (*a continuous strip of paper or magnetized flexible material on which sound, pictures or other data can be recorded*) audiotape, videotape. **2** (*a unit containing a roll of tape for recording*) audio cassette, audiotape, cassette, video, video cassette, videotape. **3** (*a narrow strip of woven linen, cotton etc., used for tying things together*) band, ribbon, string, strip. **4** (*a narrow strip of adhesive material, used for sticking things down or together*) adhesive tape, insulating tape, Scotch tape®, Sellotape®.
~*v.t.* **1** (*to record* (*sound, pictures or other data*) *on magnetic tape*) record, tape-record, video, video-record. **2** (*to fasten or tie up with tapes*) bind, fasten, seal, secure, sellotape, stick.

taper *v.i.* **1** (*to become gradually smaller or narrower towards one end*) attenuate, come to a point, get narrower, narrow, thin. ANTONYMS: broaden, widen. **2** (*to become gradually smaller or less important*) decrease, die away, diminish, dwindle, fade, lessen, subside, tail off, wane. ANTONYMS: grow, increase, step up.

tardiness *n.* (*the state of being late*) belatedness, delay, dilatoriness, lateness, procrastination, slowness, unpunctuality. ANTONYMS: prematureness, punctuality, quickness, speed.

tardy *a.* (*late, after the expected or proper time*) behindhand, belated, delayed, dilatory, late, slow, unpunctual. ANTONYMS: on time, premature, punctual, quick, speedy.

target *n.* **1** (*an object set up as a mark to be fired at in archery etc.*) bull's eye, mark. **2** (*any person or thing made the object of attack, criticism etc., a butt*) butt, prey, quarry, scapegoat, victim. **3** (*the specific objective or aim of any* (*concerted*) *effort*) aim, ambition, end, goal, intention, object, objective.

tariff *n.* **1** (*a table of charges*) list of charges, menu, price list, prices, rates. **2** (*a duty on any* *particular kind of goods*) duty, excise, levy, tax, toll.

tarnish *v.t.* **1** (*to diminish or destroy the lustre of*) dim, discolour, dull. ANTONYMS: brighten, polish, shine. **2** (*to sully, to stain*) besmirch, blacken, blemish, blot, detract from, stain, sully, taint. ANTONYMS: enhance, improve.

~*v.i.* (*to lose lustre*) dim, discolour, dull, lose lustre.

tart¹ *n.* (*a pie containing fruit or some other sweet filling*) pastry, pie, quiche, tartlet.

tart² *n.* (*sl.*) (*a prostitute, a promiscuous woman*) call-girl, †harlot, (*sl.*) hooker, prostitute, streetwalker, †strumpet, whore.

tart³ *a.* **1** (*sharp to the taste, acid*) acid, bitter, piquant, sharp, sour, tangy. ANTONYMS: sugary, sweet. **2** (*biting, piercing*) acerbic, acid, astringent, barbed, biting, caustic, cutting, harsh, mordant, sharp, short, trenchant, vitriolic. ANTONYMS: gentle, pleasant.

task *n.* (*a piece of work*) assignment, charge, chore, commission, duty, engagement, errand, exercise, job, mission, piece of work, undertaking. **to take to task** (*to reprove, to reprimand*) berate, censure, criticize, lecture, read the riot act to, reprimand, reproach, reprove, scold, (*coll.*) tear (someone) off a strip, tell off. ANTONYMS: commend, compliment, praise.

taste *n.* **1** (*the sensation excited by the contact of various soluble substances with certain organs in the mouth, flavour*) flavour, relish, savour, tang. **2** (*a small quantity tasted or experienced, a bit taken as a sample*) bit, bite, dash, drop, morsel, mouthful, nip, sample, sip, soupçon, spoonful, swallow, touch. **3** (*the mental faculty or power of apprehending and enjoying the beautiful and the sublime in nature and art*) cultivation, discernment, discrimination, elegance, finesse, judgement, polish, refinement, style, stylishness. ANTONYMS: lack of discernment, lack of taste, (*coll.*) tackiness, tastelessness. **4** (*an inclination, a predilection (for)*) bent (for), desire (for), fancy (for), fondness (for), hankering (after), inclination (towards), leaning (towards), liking (for), love (for), partiality (for), penchant (for), predilection (for), preference (for), relish (for), (*coll.*) yen (for). ANTONYMS: aversion, disinclination, dislike, hatred.

~*v.t.* **1** (*to try the flavour of by taking into the mouth*) sample, sip, test, try. **2** (*to perceive the flavour of*) differentiate, discern, distinguish, make out, perceive. **3** (*to experience*) come face to face with, come up against, encounter, experience, have experience of, know, meet with, undergo.

~*v.i.* (*to have a specified taste, to have a smack or flavour (of)*) have a flavour (of), savour (of), smack (of).

tasteful *a.* **1** (*having or showing aesthetic taste*) aesthetic, artistic, beautiful, cultivated, elegant, graceful, harmonious, in good taste, pleasing, polished, refined, restrained, smart, stylish. ANTONYMS: flashy, showy, (*coll.*) tacky, tawdry, vulgar. **2** (*having or done with good taste*) appropriate, decorous, delicate, diplomatic, fitting, in good taste, proper, seemly, tactful. ANTONYMS: crude, inappropriate, indecorous, tactless.

tasteless *a.* **1** (*having no flavour, insipid*) bland, flavourless, insipid, thin, unappetizing, unflavoured, watery, weak. ANTONYMS: appetizing, delectable, delicious, flavoursome, tasty. **2** (*vapid, dull*) boring, uninspired, uninteresting, vapid. **3** (*having or done with bad taste*) crude, flash, flashy, garish, inartistic, in bad taste, inelegant, inharmonious, showy, (*coll.*) tacky, tawdry, ugly, vulgar. ANTONYMS: aesthetic, beautiful, harmonious, tasteful. **4** (*inappropriate, tactless*) crass, crude, improper, inappropriate, in bad taste, indecorous, indiscreet, tactless, unseemly, vulgar. ANTONYMS: appropriate, decorous, delicate, fitting, tactful.

tasty *a.* (*noticeably pleasant to the taste*) appetizing, delectable, delicious, flavoursome, luscious, mouth-watering, palatable, (*coll.*) scrumptious, toothsome, (*coll.*) yummy. ANTONYMS: bland, flavourless, insipid, tasteless, unappetizing.

tatter *n.* **in tatters 1** (*torn to pieces*) in bits, in rags, in shreds, ragged, ripped to pieces, tattered, threadbare, torn. **2** (*in a state of ruin or irretrievable breakdown*) destroyed, finished, in ruins, ruined.

tattle *v.i.* (*to chatter, to gossip*) babble, blather, blether, chat, chatter, gossip, jabber, natter, prattle, (*coll.*) rabbit, rattle on, yak.

taunt *v.t.* (*to reproach or upbraid sarcastically or contemptuously*) deride, gibe at, insult, jeer at, mock, poke fun at, provoke, ridicule, sneer at, (*taboo sl.*) take the piss out of, tease, torment.

~*n.* (*a bitter or sarcastic reproach*) barb, dig, gibe, insult, jeer, sarcasm, sneer, teasing.

taut *a.* **1** (*tight, not slack*) rigid, stretched, tensed, tight. ANTONYMS: loose, slack. **2** ((*of nerves*) *tense*) drawn, strained, stressed, tense. ANTONYMS: relaxed.

tautological *a.* (*repetitive*) pleonastic, prolix, redundant, reiterative, repetitious, repetitive.

tautology *n.* (*repetition of the same thing in different words*) pleonasm, prolixity, redundancy, reiteration, repetition, repetitiveness.

tawdry *a.* (*gaudy and of little or no value*) cheap, cheapjack, flash, flashy, garish, gaudy, gimcrack, in bad taste, kitsch, meretricious, (*sl.*) naff, shoddy, showy, (*coll.*) tacky, tasteless, tatty, tinsel, vulgar. ANTONYMS: elegant, in good taste, refined, tasteful.

tax *n.* **1** (*a compulsory contribution levied on a person, property or business to meet the expenses of government or other public services*) duty, excise, levy, tariff, toll. **2** (*a heavy demand, strain etc.*) burden, demand, drain, encumbrance, load, pressure, requirement, strain, stress, weight.
~*v.t.* **1** (*to impose a tax on*) charge duty on, impose a levy on, impose a tax on. **2** (*to deduct tax from* (*someone's income, etc.*)) charge tax on, deduct tax from. **3** (*to lay a heavy burden or strain upon, to make demands upon*) be a burden on, be an encumbrance on, burden, drain, encumber, enervate, exhaust, load, make demands on, overburden, push, put a strain on, put pressure on, sap, strain, stretch, tire, weaken, wear out, weary, weigh down, weigh heavily on. **4** (*to accuse* (*of*)) accuse, blame, call to account, charge, impeach, impugn, indict, lay at (someone's) door.

taxing *a.* (*demanding, difficult*) burdensome, draining, enervating, exacting, exhausting, hard, heavy, onerous, punishing, stressful, tiring, tough, troublesome, trying, wearing, wearisome. ANTONYMS: easy, effortless, light, trouble-free, undemanding.

teach *v.t.* **1** (*to cause* (*a person etc.*) *to learn* (*to do*) *or acquire knowledge or skill in, to instruct in*) coach, drill, edify, educate, give lessons to, ground, instruct, school, train, tutor. **2** (*to impart knowledge or information concerning* (*a subject etc.*), *to give lessons in*) give instruction in, give lessons in, give tuition in, inculcate, instil.

teacher *n.* (*a person who teaches others, esp. a schoolteacher*) coach, don, educationalist, educator, guru, instructor, lecturer, mentor, pedagogue, schoolmaster, schoolmistress, schoolteacher, trainer, tutor.

team *n.* **1** (*a group of people who form a side in a game or sport*) line-up, side, squad. **2** (*a group of people who work together etc.*) band, bunch, company, crew, gang, party, set, squad, troupe. **3** (*two or more horses, oxen etc., harnessed together*) pair, span, yoke.
~*v.t.* (*to join* (*with others*) *in a common bond or for the same purpose*) band together (with), cooperate (with), form an alliance (with), get together (with), join (with), unite (with), work together (with).

teamwork *n.* (*effective cooperation with other members of a team or group*) collaboration, cooperation, joint action, unity.

tear¹ *v.t.* **1** (*to pull forcibly apart*) pull apart, pull to pieces, rend, rip apart, rive, split, sunder. **2** (*to make a hole in, to rip*) gash, hole, lacerate, make a hole in, mutilate, rip, scratch, slash, wound. **3** (*to pull violently* (*away, out etc.*)) grab, pluck, pull, rip, seize, snatch, wrench, wrest, yank.
~*v.i.* (*to rush or act with speed or violence*) (*sl.*) belt, bolt, career, dart, dash, fly, gallop, hasten, hurry, race, run, shoot, speed, sprint, whiz, (*coll.*) zip, zoom. ANTONYMS: amble, stroll.
~*n.* (*a hole or rip*) hole, laceration, rent, rip, run, scratch, slash, split, wound.

tear² *n.* **1** (*a drop of the saline liquid secreted by the lachrymal glands, moistening the eyes or flowing down in strong emotion etc.*) teardrop. **2** (*a drop of liquid*) bead, drop, droplet, globule. **in tears** (*crying, weeping*) blubbering, crying, sobbing, tearful, weeping.

tearful *a.* **1** (*shedding or about to shed tears*) blubbering, crying, in tears, sobbing, weeping. ANTONYMS: dry-eyed, happy. **2** (*causing or characterized by sadness*) distressing, miserable, pathetic, sad, upsetting, woeful, wretched. ANTONYMS: happy, joyful.

tease *v.t.* (*to annoy or irritate with petty requests or jesting*) annoy, badger, bait, bother, chaff, gibe, goad, irritate, mock, needle, pester, poke fun at, provoke, rag, ridicule, taunt, torment, (*coll.*) wind up.

technical *a.* **1** (*of or relating to the mechanical arts and applied sciences*) mechanical, practical, scientific, technological. **2** (*using or requiring specialist knowledge, language etc.*) expert, scientific, specialist, specialized.

technique *n.* **1** (*a mode of artistic performance or execution*) delivery, execution, performance. **2** (*proficiency in some skill*) ability, adroitness, capability, dexterity, expertise, gift, knack, (*coll.*) know-how, proficiency, skilfulness, skill, talent. ANTONYMS: clumsiness, inability. **3** (*a particular way of carrying out or performing something*) approach, course of action, fashion, manner, means, method, mode, modus operandi, procedure, style, system, way.

tedious *a.* (*boring and continuing for a long time*) boring, drab, dreary, dull, fatiguing, flat, humdrum, laborious, monotonous, prosaic, tiresome, tiring, unexciting, uninteresting, vapid, wearisome. ANTONYMS: enthralling, exciting, interesting, stimulating.

tedium *n.* (*monotony, boredom*) boredom, drabness, dreariness, dullness, flatness, laboriousness, monotony, prosaicness, sameness, vapidity. ANTONYMS: excitement, interest, stimulation.

teem *v.i.* **1** (*to be prolific or abundant*) abound, be abundant, be copious, be plentiful. ANTONYMS: be scarce, be sparse. **2** (*to be abundantly stocked* (*with*)) be brim-full (of), be brimming (with), be crawling (with), be full (of), be seething (with), be swarming (with), burst at the seams (with), swarm (with).

teeny *a.* (*tiny*) diminutive, microscopic, miniature, minuscule, minute, (*coll.*) teeny-weeny, (*coll.*) wee. ANTONYMS: colossal, giant, huge.

teeter *v.i.* **1** (*to move to and fro unsteadily, to sway*) balance, rock, seesaw, stagger, sway, totter, wobble. **2** (*to hesitate or waver*) dither, hesitate, shilly-shally, vacillate, waver. ANTONYMS: be decisive.

telepathy *n.* (*the supposed communication between minds at a distance without using any of the five recognized senses, thought-transference*) ESP, extrasensory perception, mind-reading, sixth sense, thought-transference.

telephone *v.t.* (*to speak to* (*a person*) *by means of a telephone*) buzz, call, call up, give (someone) a bell, (*sl.*) give (someone) a buzz, give (someone) a ring, (*coll.*) give (someone) a tinkle, phone, ring.

telescope *v.t.* **1** (*to drive or force* (*sections etc.*) *into each other, like the sliding sections of a telescope*) concertina. **2** (*to condense* (*something*) *so that it takes up less space or time*) abbreviate, abridge, compress, condense, contract, cut, reduce, shorten, truncate. ANTONYMS: elongate, extend, lengthen, protract.

television *n.* (*a device designed to receive and decode incoming electrical television signals*) (*coll.*) goggle-box, television set, (*coll.*) telly, the box, (*N Am., coll.*) tube, TV, TV set.

tell *v.t.* **1** (*to relate, to recount*) chronicle, depict, describe, narrate, portray, recite, recount, relate, report. **2** (*to make known, to express in words*) announce, broadcast, communicate, declare, disclose, divulge, express, impart, make known, mention, proclaim, reveal, say, speak, state, utter, voice. **3** (*to inform, to assure*) acquaint, apprise, communicate, inform, let know, make aware, notify. **4** (*to give an order to, to direct*) bid, call upon, charge, command, direct, enjoin, give orders to, instruct, order. **5** (*to distinguish*) differentiate, discriminate, distinguish. **6** (*to ascertain by observing*) deduce, discern, discover, make

out, perceive, recognize, see, understand. **7** (*to assure emphatically*) assure, declare, give one's word, guarantee, promise, warrant.

~*v.i.* **1** (*to give information or an account* (*of*)) deal (with), describe, discuss, give details (of), talk (about), treat. **2** (*to inform*) blab, (*coll.*) blow the whistle, give the game away, (*sl.*) grass, inform, let the cat out of the bag, (*sl.*) rat, (*sl.*) sing, spill the beans, (*sl.*) squeal. **3** (*to produce a marked effect*) affect, have an effect (on), take its toll (on). **4** (*to have an effect*) carry weight, count, have an effect, have influence. **to tell off** (*to scold*) berate, chide, (*coll.*) give a dressing-down to, lecture, read the riot act to, rebuke, reprimand, reprove, scold, take to task, (*coll.*) tear (someone) off a strip, (*coll.*) tick off, upbraid. **to tell on** (*to report* (*someone*)) (*coll.*) blow the whistle on, (*sl.*) grass on, inform on, report, (*sl.*) squeal on.

telling *a.* (*producing a striking effect*) decisive, effective, effectual, forceful, forcible, impressive, influential, marked, potent, powerful, significant, striking, substantial, weighty. ANTONYMS: ineffective, ineffectual, powerless.

telling-off *n.* (*a rebuke, a mild scolding*) chiding, (*coll.*) dressing-down, lecture, rebuke, reprimand, scolding, talking-to, (*coll.*) ticking-off.

tell-tale *n.* (*a person who tells tales, esp. about the private affairs of others*) (*coll.*) blabbermouth, (*sl.*) grass, (*sl.*) squealer, talebearer.
~*a.* (*revealing, implicating*) (*coll.*) give-away, implicatory, indicative, revealing, revelatory, significant.

temerity *n.* (*impertinence, audacity*) audacity, boldness, (*coll.*) brass neck, brazenness, cheek, (*sl.*) chutzpah, effrontery, front, gall, impudence, nerve, presumption, presumptiveness. ANTONYMS: shyness, timidity.

temper *n.* **1** (*a disposition of mind, esp. with regard to emotional stability*) attitude, bent, character, complexion, constitution, disposition, frame of mind, humour, make-up, mind, mood, nature, personality, spirit, stamp, temperament. **2** (*composure, self-command*) calm, calmness, composure, (*coll.*) cool, coolness, equanimity, good humour, self-control. **3** (*anger, irritation*) anger, annoyance, bad mood, fury, ill humour, irascibility, irritation, passion, rage, tantrum. ANTONYMS: good mood.

temperament *n.* **1** (*a person's individual character, natural disposition*) bent, cast of mind, character, complexion, constitution, disposition, frame of mind, humour, make-up, mind, mood, nature, personality, spirit, stamp, temperament. **2** (*manifest sensitivity or emotionality*) emotionalism, excitability, hypersensitivity, mercurialism, moodiness, moods, oversensitivity, sensitivity, volatility. ANTONYMS: calm, even temper, self-control, stability.

temperamental *a. (having an erratic or neurotic temperament)* emotional, erratic, excitable, explosive, highly-strung, hypersensitive, mercurial, moody, neurotic, oversensitive, sensitive, touchy, volatile. ANTONYMS: calm, even-tempered, stable, unexcitable.

temperance *n.* **1** *(moderation, self-restraint, esp. where indulgence in food, alcohol etc. is concerned)* abstemiousness, austerity, moderation, restraint, self-control, self-denial, self-discipline, self-restraint. ANTONYMS: excess, immoderation, indulgence, licence, over-indulgence. **2** *(moderation or abstinence in the use of intoxicants)* abstemiousness, prohibition, sobriety, teetotalism. ANTONYMS: alcoholism, drunkenness.

temperate *a.* **1** *(self-restrained)* calm, composed, equable, even-tempered, moderate, reasonable, self-controlled, self-disciplined, self-restrained, stable. **2** *((of climate) not liable to excess of heat or cold, mild)* clement, equable, mild, moderate. ANTONYMS: cold, extreme, hot. **3** *(abstemious)* abstemious, austere, moderate, restrained, self-denying, self-disciplined, self-restrained. ANTONYMS: excessive, immoderate, indulgent, licentious, self-indulgent. **4** *(abstemious or abstinent in the use of intoxicants)* abstemious, abstinent, sober, teetotal. ANTONYMS: alcoholic, drunk.

tempest *n.* **1** *(a violent storm of wind, esp. with heavy rain)* cyclone, gale, hurricane, squall, storm, tornado, typhoon. **2** *(violent tumult or agitation)* commotion, disturbance, furore, storm, tumult, uproar.

tempestuous *a.* **1** *((of the weather) very stormy)* blustery, gusty, squally, stormy, turbulent, windy. ANTONYMS: calm. **2** *((of a person, relationship etc.) turbulent, passionate)* boisterous, emotional, impassioned, intense, passionate, stormy, turbulent, violent, wild. ANTONYMS: calm, peaceful, tranquil.

temple *n.* *(an edifice dedicated to the service of some deity or deities)* *(poet.)* fane, holy place, place of worship, shrine.

tempo *n.* **1** *(the specified speed at which a piece of music is or should be played)* beat, pulse, rhythm, time. **2** *(pace or rate)* pace, rate, space, speed.

temporal *a.* *(secular, as opposed to spiritual)* carnal, earthly, material, non-spiritual, secular, worldly. ANTONYMS: spiritual.

temporarily *adv.* **1** *(briefly, for a short time)* briefly, fleetingly, for a short time, for a short while, transiently. ANTONYMS: forever, permanently. **2** *(for the moment, for now)* briefly, for a short time, for now, for the moment, for the time being, pro tem. ANTONYMS: permanently.

temporary *a.* **1** *(lasting or intended only for a limited length of time)* impermanent, interim, pro tem, provisional, short-term. ANTONYMS: long-term, permanent. **2** *(transient or provisional)* brief, ephemeral, evanescent, fleeting, fugitive, momentary, passing, short-lived, transient, transitory. ANTONYMS: enduring, eternal, long-lasting, permanent.

temporize *v.i.* *(to pursue a procrastinating or time-serving policy)* delay, equivocate, play a waiting game, play for time, procrastinate, stall.

tempt *v.t.* **1** *(to incite or entice (to or to do something wrong or forbidden))* cajole, coax, egg on, entice, goad, incite, induce, influence, lead on, persuade, prompt, seduce, sway, urge. ANTONYMS: deter, discourage, dissuade, put off. **2** *(to attract, to invite)* allure, appeal to, attract, beguile, entice, invite, lure, seduce, tantalize, woo. ANTONYMS: deter, inhibit, repel.

temptation *n.* **1** *(the act or an instance of tempting, enticement to do something, esp. something wrong)* cajoling, coaxing, enticement, goading, incitement, inducement, influencing, persuasion, prompting, seduction, swaying, urging. ANTONYMS: determent, discouragement, dissuasion. **2** *(an inviting prospect or thing)* bait, *(sl.)* come-on, draw, enticement, inducement, invitation, lure, pull, snare. ANTONYMS: deterrent, *(coll.)* turn-off.

tenable *a.* **1** *(capable of being held or maintained against attack)* arguable, believable, credible, defensible, justifiable, plausible, reasonable, sound, supportable, viable. ANTONYMS: indefensible, unjustifiable, untenable. **2** *((of a position, office etc.) intended to be held (for a specified period or by a particular person))* available, holdable, occupiable.

tenacious *a.* **1** *(holding fast)* clinging, fast, firm, immovable, iron, powerful, strong, tight, unshakeable. ANTONYMS: slack, weak. **2** *(persistent, determined)* adamant, determined, dogged, firm, immovable, inexorable, inflexible, intransigent, obdurate, obstinate, persistent, pertinacious, resolute, staunch, steadfast, strong-willed, stubborn, sure, unswerving, unyielding. ANTONYMS: flexible, irresolute, vacillating, yielding. **3** *(adhesive, sticky)* adhesive, clinging, gluey, sticky.

tenacity *n.* **1** *(firmness, tightness)* fastness,

firmness, force, immovability, power, strength, tightness. ANTONYMS: slackness, weakness. **2** (*persistence, determination*) determination, doggedness, firmness, immovability, inexorability, inflexibility, intransigence, obdurateness, persistence, pertinacity, resoluteness, staunchness, steadfastness, strong-willedness, stubbornness, sureness. ANTONYMS: flexibility, irresolution, vacillation, yielding. **3** (*stickiness*) adhesiveness, glueyness, stickiness.

tenancy *n.* (*the holding of land, property etc. under a lease*) holding, lease, occupancy, occupation, tenure.

tenant *n.* (*a person who rents land or property from a landlord*) holder, leaseholder, lessee, occupant, occupier, renter.

tend¹ *v.i.* **1** (*to have a bent or attitude, to be inclined* (*to*)) be apt (to), be disposed (to), be inclined (to), be liable (to), be likely (to), gravitate (towards), have a tendency (to), incline (to), lean (towards), show a tendency (to). ANTONYMS: be averse (to), be unlikely (to). **2** (*to move, hold a course or be directed* (*in a certain direction etc.*)) aim (for), go (towards), head (for), make (for), move (towards), point (to).

tend² *v.t.* (*to attend, to look after*) attend, care for, cater for, guard, keep an eye on, look after, mind, minister to, nurse, nurture, protect, see to, take care of, wait on, watch over. ANTONYMS: neglect.

tendency *n.* **1** (*bent, inclination*) bent, disposition, drift, inclination, leaning, partiality, penchant, predilection, predisposition, proneness, propensity, readiness, susceptibility. ANTONYMS: aversion, disinclination. **2** (*a direction in which something moves*) bias, course, direction, drift, heading, movement, trend, turning.

tender¹ *a.* **1** ((*of food*) *easily chewed*) juicy, soft, succulent. ANTONYMS: dry, tough. **2** (*caring and gentle*) caring, compassionate, gentle, humane, kind, kind-hearted, merciful, sensitive, sentimental, soft-hearted, sympathetic, tenderhearted. ANTONYMS: cold-hearted, cruel, hard, unsympathetic. **3** (*easily broken, bruised etc., fragile*) breakable, delicate, feeble, fragile, frail, slight, soft, weak. ANTONYMS: robust, strong, tough. **4** (*painful when touched*) aching, bruised, inflamed, irritated, painful, raw, smarting, sore. **5** (*loving, affectionate*) affectionate, amorous, caring, devoted, emotional, fond, loving, warm. ANTONYMS: hostile, uncaring. **6** (*requiring to be treated delicately or cautiously, ticklish*) delicate, difficult, sensitive, ticklish, touchy, tricky. **7** (*young, early*) callow, green, immature, inexperienced, raw,

young, youthful. ANTONYMS: experienced, mature, old.

tender² *v.t.* (*to offer, to present for acceptance*) advance, extend, give, hand in, offer, present, proffer, put forward, submit, suggest, volunteer. ANTONYMS: retract, withdraw.

~*v.i.* (*to make a tender* (*to do certain work or supply goods etc.*)) bid, put in a bid, put in an estimate.

~*n.* (*an offer in writing to do certain work or supply certain articles, at a certain sum or rate*) bid, estimate, offer.

tenderness *n.* **1** (*the state of being easily chewed*) juiciness, softness, succulence. ANTONYMS: dryness, toughness. **2** (*care and gentleness*) compassion, compassionateness, gentleness, humaneness, humanity, kind, kind-heartedness, kindness, mercy, pity, sensitivity, sentimentality, soft-heartedness, sympathy, tender-heartedness, warm-heartedness. ANTONYMS: cold-heartedness, cruelty, hardness, insensitivity, lack of sympathy. **3** (*the state of being painful when touched*) ache, bruising, inflammation, irritation, pain, rawness, smarting, soreness. **4** (*affection, fondness*) affection, amorousness, caring, devotion, emotion, fondness, liking, loving, warmness, warmth. ANTONYMS: dislike, hatred, hostility. **5** (*the state of having to be treated delicately or cautiously*) delicacy, difficulty, sensitivity, ticklishness, touchiness, trickiness. **6** (*youth, inexperience*) callowness, greenness, immaturity, inexperience, rawness, youth, youthfulness.

tenet *n.* (*an opinion or dogma held by a person or organization*) belief, canon, conviction, credo, creed, doctrine, dogma, maxim, opinion, persuasion, precept, principle, rule, teaching, theory, thesis, view.

tenor *n.* **1** (*a settled course or direction*) course, direction, drift, flow, path, way. **2** (*general purport or drift* (*of thought etc.*)) burden, drift, essence, gist, import, meaning, purport, sense, substance, vein.

tense *a.* **1** (*stretched tight, strained to stiffness*) rigid, strained, stretched, taut, tight. ANTONYMS: flaccid, loose, relaxed, slack. **2** (*suffering from emotional stress*) agitated, anxious, apprehensive, distraught, edgy, fidgety, jittery, (*coll.*) jumpy, (*coll.*) keyed up, nervous, on edge, overwrought, strained, (*coll.*) twitchy, under a strain, under pressure, (*coll.*) uptight, (*sl.*) wired, worked up, worried, (*coll.*) wound up. ANTONYMS: at ease, calm, relaxed, serene. **3** (*producing emotional stress*) exciting, fraught, nerve-racking, stressful, worrying. ANTONYMS: calm, relaxing, tranquil.

tension *n.* **1** (*the act of stretching*) straining, stretching, tightening. ANTONYMS: loosening, relaxation. **2** (*the state of being stretched*) rigidity, stiffness, strain, stress, tautness, tightness. ANTONYMS: looseness, slackness. **3** (*mental strain or excitement*) anxiety, apprehension, disquiet, edginess, nerves, nervousness, pressure, strain, stress, suspense, (*sl.*) the jitters, unease, worry. **4** (*a state of hostility or anxiety*) enmity, hostility, ill feeling, strain.

tentative *a.* **1** (*consisting or done as a trial, experimental*) conjectural, experimental, pilot, provisional, speculative, test, trial. **2** (*hesitant, uncertain*) cautious, diffident, doubtful, faltering, hesitant, hesitating, timid, uncertain, unsure, wavering. ANTONYMS: bold, decisive, sure.

tenterhook *n.* **on tenterhooks** (*in a state of suspense and anxiety, usu. because of uncertainty or awaiting an outcome or result*) anxious, apprehensive, edgy, in suspense, jittery, (*coll.*) jumpy, (*coll.*) keyed up, nervous, nervy, on edge, restless, tense, under a strain, uneasy, (*sl.*) wired, worked up, worried, (*coll.*) wound up. ANTONYMS: calm, relaxed, unworried.

tenuous *a.* **1** (*insignificant, not able to stand up to much scrutiny*) flimsy, hazy, indefinite, insignificant, insubstantial, nebulous, shaky, slight, vague, weak. ANTONYMS: definite, strong, substantial. **2** (*thin, slender*) fine, slender, thin. ANTONYMS: fat, thick.

tepid *a.* **1** (*moderately warm, lukewarm*) lukewarm, warmish. ANTONYMS: cool. **2** (*unenthusiastic*) apathetic, cool, half-hearted, indifferent, unenthusiastic, uninterested. ANTONYMS: enthusiastic, passionate.

term *n.* **1** (*a word or expression that has a precise meaning and is used in a particular, often specialized, field*) appellation, designation, expression, name, phrase, title, word. **2** (*pl.*) (*conditions, stipulations*) clauses, conditions, premises, provisos, specifications, stipulations. **3** (*pl.*) (*prices, rates of payment*) charges, costs, fees, prices, rates. **4** (*pl.*) (*relative position, relation*) basis, footing, relations, relationship, standing. **5** (*a limited period of time during which a specified state pertains or a particular activity is carried out*) period, season, span, spell, time, while. **6** (*the end of the normal length of a pregnancy*) close, conclusion, culmination, end, fruition, limit. ANTONYMS: beginning, start. ~*v.t.* (*to designate, to call*) call, denominate, designate, dub, entitle, label, name, style. **in terms of** (*in relation to, with reference to*) as regards, in relation to, in respect of, regarding,

with reference to, with regard to. **to come to terms with 1** (*to find a way of coping and living with* (*some difficulty*)) accept, become reconciled to, learn to live with, reach an acceptance of, resign oneself to. **2** (*to make an agreement with*) come to an understanding with, conclude an agreement with, make an agreement with, reach an agreement with.

terminal *a.* **1** ((*of a disease*) *ending in death*) deadly, fatal, incurable, lethal, mortal. ANTONYMS: curable, mild, minor. **2** ((*of someone suffering from a disease*) *about to die*) at death's door, dying, on one's deathbed. **3** (*extreme, incurable*) acute, critical, deadly, extreme, incurable, intense, severe, utmost. ANTONYMS: mild, minor. **4** (*later, last*) concluding, final, last, later, ultimate. ANTONYMS: beginning, early, opening.

terminate *v.t.* (*to put an end to*) abort, axe, bring to an end, close, complete, conclude, discontinue, end, finish, put an end to, stop, wind up. ANTONYMS: begin, commence, start. ~*v.i.* (*to stop, to end* (*in etc.*)) cease, come to an end, conclude, end, expire, finish, stop. ANTONYMS: begin, commence, start.

termination *n.* **1** (*the act or state of terminating*) aborting, axing, cessation, closing, closure, concluding, discontinuation, ending, finishing, stopping, winding up. ANTONYMS: beginning, commencement, start. **2** (*the state of being terminated*) close, conclusion, end, expiry, finale, finish, wind-up. ANTONYMS: beginning, commencement, start.

terminology *n.* (*the set of terms used in any art, science etc.*) cant, jargon, language, (*coll.*) lingo, nomenclature, phraseology, terms, vocabulary, words.

terminus *n.* (*the point where a railway or bus route ends*) depot, garage, last stop, station.

terrain *n.* (*a region, an extent of land of a definite geological character or as thought of in terms of military operations*) country, going, ground, land, landscape, topography.

terrible *a.* **1** (*dreadful, appalling*) awful, disagreeable, dreadful, foul, frightful, horrible, horrid, loathsome, nasty, odious, repulsive, revolting, shocking, unpleasant. ANTONYMS: agreeable, attractive, pleasant. **2** (*very great or bad, extreme*) awful, bad, extreme, great, insufferable, intense, intolerable, severe, unbearable. ANTONYMS: mild, minor. **3** (*completely useless or incompetent*) bad, (*sl.*) duff, hopeless, incompetent, pathetic, poor, useless. ANTONYMS: brilliant, expert, talented, (*coll.*) terrific. **4** (*ill or unwell*) ailing, below par, poorly, sick, sickly, under the weather, unwell.

ANTONYMS: hale and hearty, healthy, well. **5** (*remorseful, regretful*) apologetic, conscience-stricken, contrite, guilty, penitent, regretful, remorseful, repentant, sorry. ANTONYMS: impenitent, unrepentant. **6** (*causing real terror or dread*) appalling, awful, dreadful, fearsome, frightful, grim, gruesome, hideous, horrible, horrific, horrifying, monstrous, shocking, terrifying, unspeakable.

terribly *adv.* (*very, extremely*) (*coll.*) awfully, decidedly, (*coll.*) dreadfully, exceedingly, extremely, (*coll.*) frightfully, thoroughly, very. ANTONYMS: slightly.

terrific *a.* **1** (*excellent, wonderful*) (*sl.*) ace, brilliant, excellent, (*coll.*) fabulous, (*coll.*) fantastic, (*coll.*) great, (*coll.*) magnificent, marvellous, outstanding, remarkable, (*coll.*) sensational, (*coll.*) smashing, (*coll.*) super, superb, very good, wonderful. ANTONYMS: appalling, dreadful, hopeless. **2** (*huge*) considerable, extraordinary, great, significant, sizeable, substantial, tremendous, very great. ANTONYMS: insignificant, little, minimal, trifling.

terrified *a.* (*extremely frightened*) alarmed, frightened, frightened out of one's wits, panic-stricken, petrified, scared, scared stiff, scared to death.

terrify *v.t.* (*to strike with terror, to frighten*) alarm, fill with terror, frighten, frighten (someone) out of their wits, frighten (someone) to death, intimidate, make one's blood run cold, make one's flesh creep, make one's hair stand on end, petrify, scare, scare stiff, scare to death, strike terror into, terrorize.

territory *n.* **1** (*the extent of land within the jurisdiction of a particular sovereign, state or other power*) country, district, domain, realm, state. **2** (*a field of action, interest etc.*) area, area of concern, area of interest, department, domain, field, province, realm. **3** (*an assigned area of a commercial traveller, goods distributor etc.*) ambit, beat, route, section. **4** (*land of a specified nature*) area, land, region, terrain, zone.

terror *n.* **1** (*extreme fear*) alarm, dread, fear, fear and trembling, fright, horror, intimidation, shock. **2** (*a person or thing that causes fear*) bogeyman, bugbear, demon, devil, fiend, monster. **3** (*an exasperating nuisance, troublesome child etc.*) bore, bugbear, (*coll.*) holy terror, horror, nuisance, rascal, rogue.

terrorize *v.t.* **1** (*to terrify*) alarm, fill with terror, frighten, frighten (someone) out of their wits, frighten to death, intimidate, make one's blood run cold, make one's flesh creep, make one's hair stand on end, petrify, scare, scare

stiff, scare to death, strike terror into, terrify. **2** (*to coerce with threats of violence etc.*) browbeat, bulldoze, bully, coerce, intimidate, menace, oppress, threaten, use strong-arm tactics on.

terse *a.* **1** ((*of style, language etc.*) *neat and compact*) brief, compact, concise, condensed, crisp, epigrammatic, incisive, short, succinct, to the point. ANTONYMS: discursive, long-winded, loquacious, verbose, wordy. **2** (*concise, abrupt, often to the point of being rude*) abrupt, blunt, brusque, concise, curt, short. ANTONYMS: chatty, long-winded, loquacious.

test *n.* **1** (*a critical trial or examination*) analysis, appraisal, assessment, check, evaluation, examination, exploration, inspection, investigation, probe, research, scrutiny, trial. **2** (*a means of trial, a standard*) criterion, measure, standard, touchstone, yardstick. **3** (*a minor examination in a school etc.*) exam, examination.

~*v.t.* **1** (*to put to the test, to prove by experiment*) analyse, appraise, check, conduct trials on, evaluate, examine, explore, inspect, investigate, probe, put to the test, research, scrutinize, try out. **2** (*to try severely, to tax* (*someone's endurance etc.*)) put a strain on, strain, tax, †tempt, try.

testament *n.* **1** (*a solemn instrument in writing by which a person disposes of their personal estate after death, a will*) last will and testament, will. **2** (*something which testifies proof, attestation*) attestation, evidence, proof, testimony, witness.

testify *v.i.* (*to bear witness* (*to, against etc.*)) attest, bear witness to, give evidence against, give evidence for, swear to.

~*v.t.* **1** (*to affirm or declare*) affirm, assert, declare, state. **2** (*to be evidence of, to serve as proof of*) bear out, be evidence of, be proof of, confirm, corroborate, demonstrate, establish, indicate, prove, show, verify. ANTONYMS: contradict, disprove, dispute.

testimonial *n.* (*a certificate of character, services etc., of a person*) character reference, credential, letter of recommendation, recommendation, reference.

testimony *n.* **1** (*a solemn declaration or statement*) affidavit, affirmation, attestation, avowal, declaration, deposition, statement, submission. **2** (*evidence, proof*) confirmation, corroboration, demonstration, evidence, indication, proof, support, verification.

testy *a.* (*irritable, petulant*) bad-tempered, cantankerous, captious, crabbed, cross, fractious, grumpy, ill-tempered, irascible, irritable, peevish, pettish, petulant, quarrelsome, querulous, (*sl.*) ratty, short-tempered, snappy, tetchy, touchy. ANTONYMS: even-tempered, good-tempered.

tetchy *a.* (*irritable, touchy*) bad-tempered, cantankerous, captious, crabbed, cross, grumpy, ill-tempered, irascible, irritable, peevish, petulant, quarrelsome, querulous, (*sl.*) ratty, short-tempered, snappy, touchy. ANTONYMS: even-tempered, good-tempered.

tête-à-tête *n.* (*a private interview, a close or confidential conversation*) chat, (*coll.*) confab, dialogue, private conversation, talk.

tether *n.* (*a rope or halter by which an animal is prevented from moving too far*) bond, chain, fetter, halter, lead, leash, manacle, restraint, rope, shackle.
~*v.t.* (*to confine with or as with a tether*) bind, chain, fasten, fetter, leash, manacle, restrain, rope, secure, shackle, tie. **at the end of one's tether** at the limit of one's endurance, at the limit of one's patience, at the limit of one's strength, not coping, not knowing how to cope with, not knowing how to deal with, not knowing what to do.

text *n.* **1** (*the words of something as printed, written or displayed on a video display unit*) wording, words. ANTONYMS: illustrations, pictures. **2** (*the actual words of a book or poem, as opposed to notes, appendices etc.*) body of the book, main matter. ANTONYMS: appendices, back matter, front matter. **3** (*a verse or passage of Scripture, esp. one selected as the theme of a discourse*) paragraph, passage, verse. **4** (*a subject, a topic*) argument, subject, subject matter, theme, topic. **5** (*any book or novel which is studied as part of an educational course*) reader, set book, set text.

texture *n.* **1** (*the quality of something as perceived by touch*) consistency, feel, grain, surface, touch. **2** (*the particular arrangement or disposition of threads, filaments etc., in a textile fabric*) composition, fabric, structure, weave.

thank *v.t.* (*to express gratitude (to or for)*) extend thanks, give thanks, offer thanks, say thank you, show one's appreciation, show one's gratitude.
~*n.* (*an expression of gratitude*) acknowledgement, appreciation, gratefulness, gratitude, recognition. **thanks to** (*because of, owing to*) as a result of, because of, by reason of, due to, owing to.

thankful *a.* **1** (*grateful, appreciative*) appreciative, glad, grateful, relieved. ANTONYMS: ungrateful, without gratitude. **2** (*indebted (to)*)

beholden, grateful, indebted, obliged, under an obligation.

thankless *a.* (*not appreciated or profitable*) fruitless, unappreciated, unpleasant, unprofitable, unrewarded, unrewarding. ANTONYMS: fruitful, profitable, worthwhile.

thaw *v.i.* **1** ((*of ice, snow etc.*) *to melt or become liquid*) defrost, dissolve, liquefy, melt. ANTONYMS: freeze, harden, solidify. **2** (*to relax one's stiffness, to become genial*) become friendly, become genial, become sociable, loosen up, relax. ANTONYMS: be aloof, be stand-offish, (*coll.*) be uptight.

theatrical *a.* **1** (*of or relating to the theatre*) dramatic, dramaturgic, stage, Thespian. **2** (*befitting or characteristic of actors, affected*) affected, artificial, dramatic, emotional, exaggerated, forced, histrionic, mannered, melodramatic, ostentatious, overdone, pretentious, showy, stagy, stilted, unreal. ANTONYMS: natural, unaffected, unexaggerated, unpretentious.

theft *n.* (*the act or an instance of stealing*) burglary, embezzlement, fraud, larceny, misappropriation, (*sl.*) nicking, pilfering, purloining, (*coll.*) ripping-off, robbery, stealing, swindling, (*coll.*) swiping, thievery, thieving.

theme *n.* **1** (*a subject on which a person thinks, writes or speaks*) argument, burden, idea, keynote, matter, subject, subject matter, substance, text, thesis, topic. **2** (*a short dissertation or essay by a student, school pupil etc. on a certain subject*) composition, dissertation, essay. **3** (*a melodic subject usu. developed with variations*) leitmotif, motif, recurrent image, recurrent theme, unifying idea.

theological *a.* (*religious*) doctrinal, ecclesiastical, holy, religious, scriptural.

theoretical *a.* (*relating to or founded on theory not facts or knowledge, speculative*) abstract, academic, conceptual, conjectural, hypothetical, ideal, impractical, notional, postulatory, speculative. ANTONYMS: factual, practical, realistic.

theorize *v.i.* (*to form a theory or theories (about)*) conjecture, formulate, guess, hypothesize, speculate, suppose.

theory *n.* **1** (*a speculative idea of something*) assumption, conjecture, hypothesis, notion, postulation, presumption, speculation, supposition, thesis. **2** (*mere hypothesis, abstract knowledge*) abstract knowledge, hypothesis, speculation. **3** (*an exposition of the general principles of a science etc.*) philosophy, scheme, system.

therapeutic *a.* **1** (*of or relating to healing or curing disease*) ameliorative, curative, healing, medicinal, remedial, restorative. **2** (*contributing to well-being*) beneficial, health-giving, salubrious. ANTONYMS: adverse, damaging, detrimental, harmful.

therapy *n.* **1** (*the treatment of disease or physical and mental disorders from a curative and preventive point of view, therapeutics*) cure, healing, remedy, therapeutics, treatment. **2** (*psychiatric or psychological therapy*) analysis, psychoanalysis, psychotherapy.

therefore *adv.* (*for that reason, accordingly*) accordingly, and so, as a result, consequently, ergo, for that reason, hence, so, then, thus.

thesis *n.* **1** (*a proposition advanced or maintained*) argument, contention, hypothesis, postulation, premiss, proposal, proposition, theory. **2** (*an essay or dissertation, esp. one submitted by a candidate for a degree etc.*) composition, disquisition, dissertation, essay, monograph, paper, treatise.

thick *a.* **1** (*having great or specified extent or depth from one surface to the opposite*) big, broad, bulky, deep, fat, large, solid, substantial, wide. ANTONYMS: narrow, thin. **2** (*arranged or planted closely, close packed*) close, close packed, concentrated, crowded, dense, impenetrable. ANTONYMS: sparse, thin, widely spaced. **3** (*abounding* (*with*), *following in quick succession*) brimming (with), bristling (with), bursting (with), chock-full (of), crawling (with), full (of), packed (with), swarming (with), teeming (with). **4** (*dense, foggy*) cloudy, dense, foggy, murky, opaque, smoggy, soupy. ANTONYMS: clear. **5** (*not very intelligent, stupid*) brainless, dense, dim, dim-witted, dull-witted, slow, slow-witted, stupid, unintelligent. ANTONYMS: clever, intelligent, sharp-witted. **6** ((*of articulation etc.*) *indistinct, muffled*) guttural, hoarse, husky, indistinct, muffled, rough, throaty. ANTONYMS: clear, distinct. **7** (*very friendly, familiar*) (*coll.*) buddy-buddy, (*coll.*) chummy, close, devoted, familiar, friendly, inseparable, intimate, (*coll.*) matey, on good terms, (*coll.*) pally, (*coll.*) palsy-walsy. ANTONYMS: hostile, on bad terms, unfriendly. **8** (*stiff, not flowing easily*) clotted, coagulated, firm, heavy. ANTONYMS: light, thin. **9** ((*of an accent*) *clearly belonging to a particular place; marked, pronounced*) broad, decided, distinct, marked, obvious, pronounced, strong. ANTONYMS: slight, subtle.

thicken *v.t., v.i.* (*to make or become thick or thicker*) cake, clot, coagulate, congeal, gel, jell, set. ANTONYMS: thin down.

thicket *n.* (*a thick growth of small trees, bushes etc.*) coppice, copse, grove, spinney, wood.

thickness *n.* **1** (*the extent from the upper surface to the lower*) depth, diameter, width. **2** (*the state of being thick*) breadth, broadness, bulkiness, fatness, largeness, solidness, width. ANTONYMS: narrowness, thinness. **3** (*the state of being arranged or planted closely, crowded together*) closeness, close-packedness, concentration, crowdedness, denseness, impenetrability. ANTONYMS: sparseness, thinness. **4** (*stiffness, the state of not flowing easily*) coagulation, heaviness, stiffness. ANTONYMS: lightness, thinness. **5** (*murkiness, fogginess*) cloudiness, denseness, fog, murkiness, opaqueness, smog, soupiness. ANTONYMS: clearness. **6** (*a lack of intelligence, stupidity*) brainlessness, denseness, dimness, dim-wittedness, dullness, lack of intelligence, slowness, slow-wittedness, stupidity. ANTONYMS: cleverness, intelligence, sharp-wittedness. **7** (*indistinct or muffled articulation*) hoarseness, huskiness, indistinctness, roughness, throatiness. ANTONYMS: clearness, distinctness. **8** (*an accent or pronunciation that clearly belongs to a particular place*) broadness, distinctness, markedness, obviousness, pronouncedness. ANTONYMS: slightness, subtlety. **9** (*the state of being friendly or familiar*) (*coll.*) chumminess, closeness, friendliness, friendship, intimacy, (*coll.*) mateyness, (*coll.*) palliness. ANTONYMS: hostility, unfriendliness.

thickset *a.* (*solidly built, stout*) (*coll.*) beefy, brawny, bulky, burly, heavy, muscular, powerfully-built, stocky, strong, stubby, sturdy, well-built. ANTONYMS: gaunt, scraggy, scrawny, (*coll.*) weedy.

thick-skinned *a.* (*insensitive to taunts, criticism etc.*) callous, case-hardened, hardened, impervious, insensitive, tough, unfeeling, unsusceptible, unsympathetic. ANTONYMS: oversensitive, sensitive, thin-skinned.

thief *n.* (*a person who steals, esp. furtively and without violence*) burglar, (*coll.*) crook, embezzler, filcher, fraudster, housebreaker, larcenist, pickpocket, pilferer, purloiner, robber, shoplifter, swindler.

thieve *v.t.* (*to take by theft*) burgle, embezzle, filch, (*sl.*) knock off, misappropriate, (*sl.*) nick, pilfer, (*coll.*) pinch, purloin, (*coll.*) rip off, rob, shoplift, (*sl.*) snitch, steal, swindle, (*coll.*) swipe.

thin *a.* **1** (*having the opposite surfaces close together, slender*) attenuated, narrow, slender. ANTONYMS: broad, fat, thick. **2** (*not close-packed, not dense*) scanty, scarce, scattered, sparse. ANTONYMS: close-packed, dense. **3** (*lean, not plump*) emaciated, gaunt, lean,

overweight, scrawny, skeletal, skinny, slender, slight, slim, spare, thin as a rake. ANTONYMS: fat, obese, overweight. **4** (*not full, scant*) bare, meagre, scant, sparse, wispy. ANTONYMS: thick. **5** (*flimsy, easily seen through*) delicate, diaphanous, fine, flimsy, gauzy, gossamer, light, see-through, sheer, translucent, transparent. ANTONYMS: heavy, opaque, thick. **6** (*of a watery consistency*) dilute, diluted, runny, watered-down, watery, weak. ANTONYMS: strong, thick, viscous. **7** (*weak in sound, not full-toned*) faint, feeble, low, soft, weak. ANTONYMS: loud, strong. **8** ((*of an excuse, reason etc.*) *unconvincing, weak*) feeble, flimsy, implausible, inadequate, insufficient, lame, poor, shallow, unconvincing. ANTONYMS: convincing, plausible, strong.
~*v.t.* **1** (*to make thin or thinner*) emaciate, reduce, slim (someone) down, take weight off. ANTONYMS: fatten, put weight on, thicken. **2** (*to make less crowded*) clear. ANTONYMS: crowd. **3** (*to thin out*) cut back, prune, trim, weed out. **4** (*to dilute*) dilute, water down, weaken. ANTONYMS: strengthen, thicken.
~*v.i.* **1** (*to become thin or thinner*) get slimmer, get thinner, lose weight, slim down. ANTONYMS: get fatter, put on weight, thicken. **2** (*to become less dense*) decrease, diminish, dwindle, get less dense, thin out.

thing *n.* **1** (*any thought*) concept, idea, notion, theory, thought. **2** (*whatever exists or is conceived to exist as a separate entity, esp. an inanimate object*) article, item, object, something. **3** (*an act, a fact etc.*) act, affair, circumstance, deed, episode, event, eventuality, exploit, feat, happening, incident, occurrence, phenomenon. **4** (*a quality, a feature*) attribute, characteristic, feature, property, quality, trait. **5** (*a person or other animate object regarded with commiseration, disparagement etc.*) creature, soul, wretch. **6** (*a specimen, a style*) example, fashion, specimen, style. **7** (*pl.*) (*belongings, luggage etc.*) apparatus, baggage, belongings, (*coll.*) bits and pieces, (*sl.*) clobber, equipment, gear, goods, implements, luggage, odds and ends, paraphernalia, possessions, stuff, tackle, tools. **8** (*pl.*) (*clothes*) apparel, attire, (*sl.*) clobber, clothing, garments, (*coll.*) gear, (*coll.*) togs. **9** (*pl.*) (*the current or usual state of affairs*) affairs, circumstances, conditions, matters, situation, state of affairs. **10** (*a fact, point*) aspect, detail, fact, particular, point. **11** (*a statement*) comment, declaration, pronouncement, remark, statement, utterance. **to have a thing about 1** (*to have an unaccountable prejudice or fear about*) have a dislike of, have a fear of, (*coll.*) have a hang-up about, have an aversion to, have a phobia about. **2** (*to have a strong liking for or preoccupation with*)

have a bee in one's bonnet about, (*coll.*) have a hang-up about, have a mania about, have an idée fixe about, have an obsession with, have a preoccupation with.

think *v.t.* **1** (*to believe* (*that*), *to judge* (*to be*)) believe, be of the opinion, be of the view, consider, deem, hold, imagine, judge, reckon, regard, suppose, surmise. **2** (*to expect*) anticipate, expect, imagine, surmise.
~*v.i.* **1** (*to exercise the mind actively, to reason*) be in a brown study, be lost in thought, brood, cerebrate, cogitate, concentrate, deliberate, meditate, muse, ponder, rack one's brains, reflect, ruminate. **2** (*to meditate, to consider* (*on, about etc.*)) consider, contemplate, mull (over), muse (on), ponder, reflect (on), review, weigh up.
~*n.* (*an act of thinking*) assessment, consideration, contemplation, reflection. **to think better of** (*to change one's mind, to decide not to pursue* (*a course of action*)) change one's mind, decide against, have a change of heart, have second thoughts, reconsider, think again. **to think highly of** (*to hold in high regard*) admire, esteem, have a high opinion of, have a high regard for, hold in high esteem, hold in high regard, respect, set store by, think much of, value. ANTONYMS: despise, have a low opinion of, hold in contempt, think little of. **to think over** (*to consider* (*a proposition etc.*)) consider, consider the pros and cons of, give consideration to, give thought to, mull over, reflect on, turn over (something) in one's mind, weigh up. **to think up** (*to devise, to invent*) come up with, concoct, devise, dream up, hatch, improvise, invent, manufacture, trump up.

thinker *n.* (*a person who thinks deeply, an intellectual person*) (*coll.*) brain, (*coll.*) egghead, intellectual, philosopher, sage, scholar, theorist.

thinking *n.* (*the opinion, received viewpoint etc. at a given time*) conclusions, ideas, opinion, outlook, philosophy, point of view, position, reasoning, theory, thoughts, view, viewpoint.
~*a.* (*given to thinking deeply*) contemplative, intellectual, intelligent, philosophical, rational, reasoning, reflective, thoughtful.

thin-skinned *a.* (*sensitive, easily offended*) easily hurt, easily offended, hypersensitive, oversensitive, sensitive, soft, touchy, vulnerable. ANTONYMS: callous, case-hardened, insensitive, thick-skinned.

third-rate *a.* (*of very bad quality*) indifferent, inferior, low-grade, mediocre, poor, shoddy, worthless. ANTONYMS: excellent, high-grade, superior.

thirst n. **1** (*a desire to drink liquid*) dehydration, dryness, thirstiness. **2** (*eager longing or desire*) appetite, avidity, craving, desire, eagerness, hankering, hunger, longing, love, lust, passion, yearning, (*coll.*) yen. ANTONYMS: aversion, dislike, distaste, repugnance.

~v.i. (*to feel eager longing or desire* (*for or after*)) covet, crave, desire, hanker (after), (*coll.*) have a yen (for), hunger (for), long (for), love, lust (after), yearn (for), (*coll.*) yen (for).

thirsty a. **1** (*feeling thirst, parched*) dehydrated, dry, parched. **2** (*eager* (*for*)) covetous (of), desirous (of), eager (for), greedy (for), hungry (for). ANTONYMS: averse (to).

thong n. (*a strip of leather used as a whiplash or for fastening anything*) belt, cord, rope, strap, strip.

thorn n. (*a sharp-pointed projection on a plant, a prickle*) barb, prickle, spike, spine.

thorn in one's side n. (*a constant source of trouble*) annoyance, bane, bête noire, bother, irritant, nuisance, pest, scourge, source of annoyance, torment, trouble.

thorny a. **1** (*having many thorns*) barbed, bristling, pointed, prickly, sharp, spiky, spined, spinous, spiny. ANTONYMS: smooth. **2** (*difficult to resolve, problematical*) awkward, bothersome, complicated, difficult, hard, irksome, problematic, sticky, ticklish, tough, tricky, troublesome, trying, worrying. ANTONYMS: easy, effortless, trouble-free.

thorough a. **1** (*complete, not superficial*) all-embracing, complete, comprehensive, exhaustive, extensive, full, in-depth, intensive, sweeping, total. ANTONYMS: incomplete, qualified, superficial. **2** (*very careful, meticulous*) assiduous, careful, conscientious, methodical, meticulous, painstaking, punctilious, scrupulous. ANTONYMS: careless, negligent, slapdash, sloppy. **3** (*absolute, utter*) absolute, complete, downright, out-and-out, perfect, sheer, total, unmitigated, unqualified.

thoroughbred a. (*of pure breed*) pedigree, pure-blooded, pure-bred. ANTONYMS: crossbred, half-breed, hybrid, mongrel.

thoroughfare n. **1** (*a road or street for public traffic*) highway, road, roadway, street. **2** (*a passage through from one street etc., to another, an unobstructed road or street*) access, passage, passageway, way.

thoroughly adv. **1** (*completely, not superficially*) completely, comprehensively, exhaustively, extensively, from top to toe, fully, inside out, intensively, leaving no stone unturned, totally. ANTONYMS: superficially. **2** (*very carefully, meticulously*) assiduously, carefully,

conscientiously, in detail, methodically, meticulously, painstakingly, punctiliously, scrupulously, with care. ANTONYMS: carelessly, sloppily. **3** (*absolutely, utterly*) absolutely, completely, (*coll.*) dead, downright, entirely, perfectly, positively, quite, totally, to the full, unreservedly, utterly, without qualification, without reservation.

though conj. **1** (*notwithstanding that, despite the fact that*) although, despite the fact that, in spite of the fact that, notwithstanding that. **2** (*even if, granting or supposing that*) even if, even supposing, even though.

~adv. (*however, all the same*) all the same, be that as it may, for all that, however, nevertheless, nonetheless, notwithstanding, still, yet.

thought n. **1** (*the act or process of thinking*) powers of reasoning, powers of thought, thinking. **2** (*reflection, serious consideration*) cogitation, consideration, contemplation, deliberation, introspection, meditation, musing, reasoning, reflection, rumination, thinking. **3** (*an idea, a conclusion etc.*) assessment, belief, conclusion, estimation, idea, judgement, line of thinking, notion, point of view, position, sentiment, stance, viewpoint. **4** (*deep concern or solicitude*) attentiveness, care, compassion, concern, consideration, kindness, regard, solicitude, sympathy, thoughtfulness. ANTONYMS: disregard, inattentiveness, lack of compassion, unkindness. **5** (*expectation, hope*) anticipation, aspiration, expectation, hope, prospect. **6** (*an aim, intention*) aim, design, idea, intention, object, objective, plan, purpose.

thoughtful a. **1** (*engaged in thinking*) absorbed, cogitative, contemplative, in a brown study, lost in thought, meditative, musing, pensive, rapt in thought, reflective, ruminative, serious, studious. **2** (*reflecting serious consideration*) careful, circumspect, considered, deep, profound, serious, studious, weighty, well-thought-out. ANTONYMS: light, shallow, superficial. **3** (*considerate, careful*) attentive, caring, charitable, compassionate, considerate, helpful, kind, kindly, polite, solicitous, sympathetic. ANTONYMS: inconsiderate, thoughtless, uncaring, unsympathetic.

thoughtless a. **1** (*inconsiderate, careless*) impolite, inattentive, inconsiderate, insensitive, rude, selfish, uncaring, unhelpful, unkind, unsympathetic. ANTONYMS: caring, considerate, impolite, thoughtful. **2** (*reflecting absence of serious consideration*) careless, foolish, heedless, ill-considered, imprudent, injudicious, rash, reckless, slapdash, unthinking, unwise. ANTONYMS: considered, thoughtful.

thrash *v.t.* **1** (*to beat severely, esp. with a stick etc.*) beat, (*coll.*) belt, birch, cane, chastise, flog, (*coll.*) give a hiding to, hide, lambast, leather, punish, spank, (*coll.*) tan (someone's) hide, (*coll.*) wallop, whip. **2** (*to defeat, beat convincingly*) beat, beat hollow, (*sl.*) clobber, conquer, crush, defeat, (*coll.*) lick, overwhelm, run rings round, trounce, vanquish, (*coll.*) wipe the floor with.
~*v.i.* (*to strike out wildly and repeatedly*) flail, jerk, squirm, thresh, toss and turn, twitch, writhe. **to thrash out** (*to discuss thoroughly in order to find a solution*) air thoroughly, argue out, debate, discuss, have (something) out, resolve, settle, talk over.

thread *n.* **1** (*a slender cord consisting of two or more yarns doubled or twisted, for sewing or weaving*) cotton, filament, yarn. **2** (*the continuing theme or linking element in an argument or story*) motif, plot, storyline, strain, theme, train of thought. **3** (*a fine line of colour etc.*) line, seam, strand, streak, strip. **4** (*a continuous course (of life etc.)*) course, direction, tenor.
~*v.t.* **1** (*to pass a thread through the eye or aperture of (a needle etc.)*) ease, pass. **2** (*to string (beads etc.) on a thread*) connect, link, loop, string. **3** (*to pick (one's way) or to go through an intricate or crowded place etc.*) ease, elbow, inch, pick, push, shoulder, squeeze.

threadbare *a.* **1** (*so worn that the thread is visible, having the nap worn off*) frayed, ragged, shabby, tattered, (*coll.*) tatty, worn. ANTONYMS: new, well-preserved. **2** ((*of an excuse, phrase etc.*) *trite, hackneyed*) banal, clichéd, cliché-ridden, hackneyed, overused, platitudinous, stale, stereotyped, stock, tired, trite, well-worn, worn. ANTONYMS: fresh, novel, original.

threat *n.* **1** (*a declaration of an intention to inflict punishment, injury etc.*) intimidating remark, threatening remark, warning. **2** (*a menace*) danger, hazard, menace, peril, risk. **3** (*an indication of an imminent danger*) foreboding, foreshadowing, omen, portent, presage, the writing on the wall, warning.

threaten *v.t.* **1** (*to use threats to*) browbeat, bully, intimidate, (*coll.*) lean on, make threats to, menace, pressurize, use threats to. **2** (*to indicate an imminent danger of*) forebode, foreshadow, give warning of, portend, presage, warn of. **3** (*to be a threat to, to endanger*) be a threat to, endanger, imperil, jeopardize, menace, place in peril, put at risk, put in danger, put in jeopardy.
~*v.i.* (*to be imminent, to loom*) be imminent, be in the air, be in the offing, impend, loom.

threatening *a.* **1** (*serving as a threat,*

menacing) bullying, intimidating, menacing, minatory, warning. **2** (*ominous*) inauspicious, ominous, sinister, unfavourable. ANTONYMS: auspicious, favourable, propitious.

threesome *n.* (*a group of three*) triad, trinity, trio, triplets, triumvirate, triune, troika.

threshold *n.* **1** (*the stone or plank at the bottom of a doorway*) doorsill, doorstep. **2** (*an entrance, a doorway*) doorway, entrance, entry. **3** (*a beginning*) beginning, brink, commencement, dawn, inception, opening, outset, start, starting-point, verge. ANTONYMS: close, conclusion, end, finish.

thrift *n.* (*good husbandry, economical management*) carefulness, economicalness, economizing, economy, frugality, frugalness, good husbandry, parsimony, saving, scrimping, thriftiness. ANTONYMS: extravagance, profligacy, squandering, waste.

thriftless *a.* (*extravagant*) extravagant, improvident, lavish, prodigal, profligate, spendthrift, wasteful.

thrifty *a.* (*frugal, economical*) careful, economical, economizing, frugal, parsimonious, saving, scrimping, sparing. ANTONYMS: extravagant, improvident, lavish, thriftless, wasteful.

thrill *v.t.* (*to affect with emotion so as to give a sense as of vibrating or tingling*) arouse, delight, excite, (*sl.*) give a buzz to, (*sl.*) give a charge to, give a kick to, stimulate, stir, titillate. ANTONYMS: bore, depress.
~*v.i.* (*to have a vibrating or tingling sense of emotion*) flutter, quiver, shiver, shudder, throb, tingle, tremble, vibrate.
~*n.* **1** (*an intense vibration, shiver*) flutter, quiver, shiver, shudder, throb, tingle, tremble, tremor, vibration. **2** (*a wave of strong emotion, such as joy or excitement*) (*sl.*) buzz, (*sl.*) charge, frisson, glow, kick, sensation, tingle, wave of pleasure. ANTONYMS: boredom, tedium. **3** (*anything exciting*) adventure, delight, joy, pleasure. ANTONYMS: bore, disappointment.

thrilling *a.* **1** (*exciting, stirring*) electrifying, exciting, gripping, joyful, pleasing, riveting, rousing, sensational, stimulating, stirring. ANTONYMS: boring, dull, monotonous, tedious. **2** (*vibrating, throbbing*) quivering, shivering, shuddering, throbbing, tingling, trembling, tremulous.

thrive *v.i.* **1** (*to prosper, to be successful*) advance, be successful, bloom, boom, flourish, get on, get on well, prosper, succeed. ANTONYMS: be unsuccessful, do badly, fail. **2** (*to grow vigorously*) bloom, burgeon, do well, flourish, grow well, shoot up. ANTONYMS: die, droop, shrivel, wilt, wither.

thriving *a.* **1** (*successful*) blooming, booming, burgeoning, flourishing, prospering, prosperous, successful, wealthy. ANTONYMS: bankrupt, failing, unsuccessful. **2** (*flourishing*) burgeoning, flourishing, healthy, lush, luxuriant, prolific, vigorous. ANTONYMS: drooping, wilting, withering.

throaty *a.* (*hoarse*) deep, gruff, guttural, hoarse, husky, low, thick. ANTONYMS: clear, high, light.

throb *v.i.* **1** (*to vibrate, to quiver*) quiver, shudder, vibrate. **2** ((*of the heart or pulse*) *to beat rapidly or forcibly*) beat, pulsate, pulse, thump. **3** (*to beat with pain*) be painful, be sore.

throe *n.* (*pl.*) (*the pains of childbirth or death*) agony, pain, suffering. **in the throes of** (*struggling with* (*a task etc.*)) in the midst of, in the process of, stuggling with, wrestling with.

throng *n.* (*a multitude of people or living things pressed close together, a crowd*) crowd, drove, flock, horde, host, mass, mob, multitude, pack. ~*v.i.* (*to crowd or press together*) crowd, flock, mill, press, swarm, troop. ~*v.t.* (*to crowd, to fill to excess*) cram, crowd, fill, jam, pack.

throttle *v.t.* (*to choke, to strangle*) choke, garrotte, strangle, strangulate.

through *prep.* (*by means or fault of, on account of*) as a consequence of, as a result of, because of, by means of, by virtue of, with the help of. **through and through** (*completely, in every way*) altogether, completely, entirely, fully, thoroughly, totally, to the core, utterly, wholly.

throughout *adv.* (*right through, from beginning to end*) all over, all through, everywhere, in every part.

throw *v.t.* **1** (*to fling, to hurl, esp. to a distance with some force*) cast, (*coll.*) chuck, fling, heave, hurl, lob, pitch, propel, send, shy, sling, toss. **2** (*to cast down, to cause to fall*) fell, floor, hurl to the ground, prostrate, throw to the ground. **3** (*to turn or direct* (*the eyes etc.*) *quickly or suddenly*) cast, dart, give, send. **4** (*to put on* (*clothes etc.*) *hastily or carelessly*) pull on, slip into. **5** (*to shape on a potter's wheel*) fashion, form, mould, shape, turn. **6** (*to move so as to operate* (*a lever etc.*)) move, operate, switch on. **7** (*coll.*) (*to hold* (*a party*)) give, hold, host, organize, put on. **8** (*coll.*) (*to puzzle or astonish*) astonish, baffle, confound, confuse, discomfit, disconcert, dumbfound, faze, put (someone) off their stroke. **9** (*to unseat* (*a rider*)) dislodge, throw to the ground, unseat. **to throw away 1** (*to cast from one, to discard*)

bin, cast off, (*coll.*) chuck out, discard, dispense with, dispose of, (*coll.*) ditch, dump, get rid of, jettison, (*coll.*) junk, reject, scrap, throw out. ANTONYMS: conserve, keep, preserve, retain, salvage, save. **2** (*to lose through carelessness or neglect*) (*sl.*) blow, fritter away, lose, pass up, squander, waste. ANTONYMS: exploit, make full use of, take advantage of. **to throw off 1** (*to get rid of, to discard*) abandon, cast off, discard, free oneself of, get rid of, rid oneself of, shake off. **2** (*to evade* (*pursuit*)) elude, escape from, evade, get away from, give (someone) the slip, leave behind, lose, outdistance, outrun, shake off, show a clean pair of heels to. **to throw out 1** (*to cast out, to reject*) bin, cast off, cast out, (*coll.*) chuck out, discard, dispense with, dispose of, (*coll.*) ditch, dump, get rid of, jettison, (*coll.*) junk, reject, scrap, throw away. ANTONYMS: conserve, keep, preserve, retain, save. **2** (*to expel*) (*coll.*) axe, cast out, dismiss, (*coll.*) ditch, dump, eject, evict, expel, get rid of, (*sl.*) give (someone) the bum's rush, (*coll.*) kick out, oust, put out, reject, (*coll.*) sack, show (someone) the door, (*coll.*) turf out. ANTONYMS: admit, employ, take on, welcome. **3** (*to emit*) diffuse, disseminate, emit, give off, give out, put forth, radiate. **to throw up 1** (*to abandon, to resign from*) abandon, (*coll.*) chuck in, give up, (*sl.*) jack in, leave, quit, relinquish, renounce, resign from, step down from. ANTONYMS: begin, take up. **2** (*to vomit*) be sick, (*esp. N Am., sl.*) chuck up, (*sl.*) puke, vomit.

thrust *v.t.* **1** (*to push suddenly or forcibly*) drive, elbow, force, push, ram, shove. **2** (*to stab*) jab, pierce, stab, stick. **3** (*to impose forcibly* (*on*)) force, impose, press, push. ~*n.* **1** (*a sudden or violent push or lunge*) lunge, poke, prod, shove. **2** (*an attack as with a pointed weapon, a stab*) jab, lunge, stab. **3** (*a pointed remark*) barb, censure, criticism, verbal attack. **4** (*force exerted by one body against another*) force, motive force, motive power, pressure. **5** (*the forceful part, or gist, of an argument etc.*) drift, essence, gist, message, point, tenor, theme. **6** (*a strong attack or onslaught*) advance, assault, attack, charge, drive, incursion, offensive, onslaught, push, raid. **7** (*drive, determination*) aggression, assertiveness, drive, energy, force, get-up-and-go, push.

thud *n.* (*a dull sound as of a blow on something soft*) clunk, thump, (*coll.*) wallop. ~*v.i.* (*to make a thud*) clunk, thump, (*coll.*) wallop.

thug *n.* (*a violent or brutal ruffian*) (*coll.*) crook, gangster, (*coll.*) heavy, hoodlum, hooligan, ruffian, tough, villain.

thumb *v.t.* (*to turn* (*the pages of a book*) *with the thumb*) flick through, flip through, glance through, leaf through, skim through. **to be all thumbs** (*to be clumsy and fumbling with one's hands*) be awkward, (*coll.*) be butter-fingered, (*coll.*) be cack-handed, be clumsy, (*coll.*) be ham-handed, be inept, be maladroit.

thumbs down *n.* (*an indication of failure or disapproval*) disapproval, negation, no, rebuff, (*coll.*) red light, refusal, rejection. ANTONYMS: acceptance, approval, (*coll.*) green light, thumbs up, yes.

thumbs up *n.* (*an indication of success or approval*) acceptance, affirmation, approval, go-ahead, (*coll.*) green light, (*coll.*) OK, (*coll.*) okay, yes. ANTONYMS: disapproval, no, (*coll.*) red light, refusal.

thump *v.t.* (*to strike with something giving a dull sound, esp. with the fist*) bang, batter, beat, clout, hit, knock, punch, smack, strike, (*coll.*) wallop, whack.
~*v.i.* (*to throb or pulsate violently*) pulsate, pulse, throb, thud.
~*n.* **1** (*a blow giving a dull sound*) bang, blow, knock, punch, smack, (*coll.*) wallop, whack. **2** (*the sound of this*) clunk, thud, (*coll.*) wallop, wham.

thumping *a.* (*very large*) colossal, enormous, gigantic, great, huge, mammoth, massive, monumental, tremendous, vast, (*sl.*) whopping. ANTONYMS: insignificant, minute, negligible, tiny.

thunder *n.* **1** (*a thunderbolt*) thunder clap, thundercrack. **2** (*a loud noise resembling atmospheric thunder*) boom, crash, rumble.
~*v.i.* **1** (*to make a loud noise*) boom, resound, reverberate, rumble. **2** (*to make loud denunciations etc.*) curse, fulminate, rail. **3** (*to shout very loudly*) bark, bellow, roar, shout, yell. ANTONYMS: whisper.

thundering *a.* (*extreme, remarkable*) colossal, enormous, gigantic, great, huge, immense, mammoth, massive, tremendous, vast, (*sl.*) whopping. ANTONYMS: insignificant, minute, negligible, tiny.

thunderous *a.* (*very loud*) booming, deafening, ear-splitting, loud, noisy, resounding, reverberating, roaring, tumultuous. ANTONYMS: muted, quiet, soft.

thunderstruck *a.* (*amazed, astounded*) aghast, amazed, astonished, astounded, (*coll.*) bowled over, dazed, disconcerted, dumbfounded, flabbergasted, (*coll.*) flummoxed, (*sl.*) gobsmacked, knocked for six, nonplussed, open-mouthed, speechless, staggered, struck dumb, stunned, taken aback.

thus *adv.* **1** (*in this manner*) in this manner, in this way, like so, like this, so. **2** (*accordingly*) accordingly, as a result, consequently, for that reason, hence, so, that being so, then, therefore.

thwack *v.t.* (*to hit with a loud heavy blow, esp. with something flat*) bash, beat, clout, flog, hit, lambast, slap, smack, strike, thump, (*coll.*) wallop, whack.

thwart *v.t.* (*to cross, to frustrate*) baulk, block, check, cross, foil, frustrate, hinder, obstruct, prevent, stop, stymie. ANTONYMS: aid, assist, encourage, facilitate.

tic *n.* (*a habitual convulsive twitching of muscles, esp. of the face*) jerk, spasm, twitch.

tick *v.i.* (*to make a small regularly recurring sound like that of a watch or clock*) click, tick-tock.
~*v.t.* (*to mark* (*off*) *with a tick*) check off, mark, mark off, put a tick by.
~*n.* **1** (*the sound made by a going watch or clock*) click, tick-tock. **2** (*coll.*) (*a moment*) flash, instant, (*coll.*) jiffy, minute, moment, no time at all, second, (*coll.*) shake, trice, twinkling of an eye, (*coll.*) two shakes of a lamb's tail. **to tick off 1** (*to mark off* (*a series*) *by ticks*) check off, mark off, put a tick by. **2** (*to reprimand, to tell off*) berate, chide, (*coll.*) give a dressing-down to, haul (someone) over the coals, lecture, read the riot act to, rebuke, reproach, reprove, scold, (*coll.*) tear (someone) off a strip, upbraid.

ticket *n.* **1** (*a card or paper with written or printed contents entitling the holder to admission to a concert etc., conveyance by train etc., or other privilege*) card, coupon, pass, slip, token, voucher. **2** (*a tag or label giving the price etc. of a thing it is attached to*) docket, label, sticker, tab, tag.

tickle *v.t.* (*to please, to amuse*) amuse, cheer, delight, divert, entertain, gladden, gratify, please. ANTONYMS: bore, irritate, weary.

ticklish *a.* (*difficult, needing tact or caution*) awkward, critical, delicate, difficult, nice, sensitive, thorny, touchy, tricky. ANTONYMS: simple, straightforward.

tide *n.* **1** (*a rush of water, a torrent*) current, flood, flow, rush, stream, torrent. **2** (*the course or tendency of events*) course, current, direction, drift, movement, run, tendency, tenor, trend. **to tide over** ((*to help*) *to surmount difficulties in a small way or temporarily*) bridge the gap, help, keep one going, keep one's head above water, see one through.

tidings *n.pl.* (*news, a report*) (*coll.*) gen, information, intelligence, news, report.

tidy *a.* **1** (*in good order, neat*) clean, in good order, in order, methodical, neat, ordered, orderly, shipshape, spick and span, spruce, systematic, trim, well-kept, well-ordered. ANTONYMS: disordered, messy, unsystematic, untidy. **2** (*considerable, fairly large*) ample, considerable, decent, fair, generous, goodly, handsome, hefty, large, largish, respectable, sizeable, substantial. ANTONYMS: insignificant, insubstantial, minute, small, trivial.

~*v.t.* (*to make tidy, to put in order*) clean, groom, make shipshape, neaten, order, put in order, put to rights, spruce, straighten. ANTONYMS: dirty, mess up, throw into confusion, untidy.

tie *v.t.* **1** (*to fasten with a cord etc., to bind*) attach, bind, chain, connect, fasten, fix, join, lash, secure, tether. ANTONYMS: loosen, undo, unfasten. **2** (*to confine, to restrict*) confine, constrain, cramp, curb, hamper, hinder, impede, limit, restrain, restrict. ANTONYMS: free, release.

~*v.i.* (*to be exactly equal* (*with*) *in a score*) be equal, be even, be neck and neck, draw. **to tie down** (*to restrict, to constrain*) constrain, cramp, curb, hamper, hinder, impede, limit, restrain, restrict. ANTONYMS: free, release. **to tie in 1** (*to agree or coordinate* (*with*)) agree (with), concur (with), correspond (to), dovetail (with), fit in (with). ANTONYMS: be at variance (with), disagree (with). **2** (*to be associated or linked* (*with*)) be associated (with), be connected (with), be linked (with), be relevant (to), relate (to). **to tie up 1** (*to fasten securely to a post etc.*) attach, bind, chain, connect, fasten, fix, join, lash, secure, tether. ANTONYMS: loosen, undo, unfasten. **2** (*to keep occupied to the exclusion of other activities*) busy, engage, engross, occupy. **3** (*to truss up*) bind, truss up. ANTONYMS: free, release. **4** (*to invest*) commit, invest, put in. **5** (*to bring to a close*) bring to a close, bring to a conclusion, close, conclude, end, terminate, wind up, (*coll.*) wrap up. ANTONYMS: begin, open, start.

tie-in *n.* (*a connection*) association, connection, link, relationship.

tier *n.* (*a row, a rank, esp. one of several rows placed one above another*) bank, layer, level, rank, row.

tiff *n.* (*a slight quarrel*) difference, disagreement, dispute, falling-out, quarrel, row, squabble, words.

tight *a.* **1** (*drawn or fitting closely*) close-fitting, fast, firm, fixed, secure, snug. ANTONYMS: loose, loose-fitting, slack. **2** (*compactly built or put together*) compact, compressed. ANTONYMS: loose. **3** (*impervious, not leaky* (*often in comb. as watertight*)) airtight, hermetic, impenetrable, impermeable, impervious, proof, sealed, sound, watertight. ANTONYMS: leaking, loose, open. **4** (*tense, stretched to the full*) rigid, stiff, strained, stretched, taut, tense. ANTONYMS: loose, slack. **5** (*mean, tight-fisted*) grasping, mean, miserly, niggardly, parsimonious, penurious, stingy, tight-fisted. ANTONYMS: extravagant, generous, liberal, spendthrift. **6** (*under strict control*) rigid, rigorous, stern, strict, stringent, tough. ANTONYMS: lax, relaxed. **7** ((*of money etc.*) *not easily obtainable*) inadequate, in short supply, insufficient, limited, scanty, scarce, sparse. ANTONYMS: abundant, copious, plentiful. **8** (*awkward, difficult*) awkward, dangerous, difficult, hazardous, perilous, precarious, problematic, risky, ticklish, tricky, troublesome. ANTONYMS: easy, safe, trouble-free. **9** (*drunk*) drunk, (*sl.*) half-cut, (*Naut., sl.*) half seas over, inebriated, in one's cups, intoxicated, (*coll.*) legless, (*sl.*) paralytic, (*taboo sl.*) pissed, (*coll.*) sozzled, (*Naut., sl.*) three sheets in the wind, (*coll.*) tiddly, tipsy, under the influence, (*sl.*) wasted. ANTONYMS: sober. **10** (*limited, restricted*) constricted, cramped, limited, restricted. ANTONYMS: unlimited, unrestricted. **11** (*close, even*) close, even, evenly-matched, near, neck and neck. **12** (*concise, succinct*) compact, concise, succinct, terse. ANTONYMS: discursive, verbose, wordy.

tighten *v.t.* **1** (*to make tight or tighter*) make fast, make tight, make tighter, secure. ANTONYMS: loosen, relax, slacken. **2** (*to make impermeable*) close, make airtight, make fast, make watertight, screw on. **3** (*to make taut*) make rigid, make taut, make tense, make tight, make tighter, stiffen, strain, stretch, tauten. ANTONYMS: loose, relax, slacken.

~*v.i.* (*to become tight or tighter*) constrict, contract, narrow, tauten. ANTONYMS: relax, slacken.

tight-fisted *a.* (*mean, stingy*) grasping, mean, miserly, niggardly, parsimonious, penurious, stingy, tight. ANTONYMS: extravagant, generous, liberal, spendthrift.

tight-lipped *a.* (*taciturn*) discreet, mute, quiet, reserved, reticent, secretive, silent, taciturn, uncommunicative, unforthcoming. ANTONYMS: communicative, open, talkative.

till¹ *n.* (*a cash register*) cash box, cash drawer, cash register, strong box.

till² *v.t.* (*to cultivate for crops*) cultivate, dig, farm, plough, work.

tilt *v.i.* **1** (*to tip, to be in a slanting position*) cant, heel, incline, lean, list, slant, slope, tip. **2** (*to charge with a lance, to joust, as in a tournament*) attack, charge, fight, joust.

~*n.* (*an inclination from the vertical, a slanting*

position) angle, cant, inclination, incline, slant, slope. **at full tilt** (*at full speed or force*) at breakneck speed, at full force, at full pelt, at full speed, like a bat out of hell, (*sl.*) like the clappers. ANTONYMS: at a snail's pace, unhurriedly.

timbre *n.* (*the quality of tone distinguishing particular voices, instruments etc.*) quality of sound, resonance, tonality, tone, tone colour.

time *n.* **1** (*a period characterized by certain events, persons etc., an era*) age, epoch, era, period, stage. **2** (*a portion of time allotted to a specified purpose*) period, span, spell, stretch, term, while. **3** (*the time available at one's disposal*) free time, leisure time, spare time. **4** (*a portion of time allotted to one*) allotted span, life, lifetime, span. **5** (*a portion of time as characterized by circumstances, conditions of existence etc.*) circumstances, conditions, situation. **6** (*a point in time, a particular moment or hour*) instant, juncture, occasion, point. **7** (*rate of movement, tempo*) beat, measure, metre, pace, rhythm, tempo.
~*v.t.* **1** (*to ascertain or mark the time, duration or rate of*) calculate, clock, count, measure. **2** (*to regulate as to time*) adjust, control, regulate, set, synchronize. **3** (*to arrange the time of, to schedule*) arrange, fix, programme, schedule, set, synchronize. **all the time** (*continuously*) always, at all times, constantly, continually, continuously, forever, perpetually. ANTONYMS: at intervals, at times, intermittently. **at one time 1** (*once, in the past* (*referring to an unspecified time*)) at one point, formerly, hitherto, in the past, once, previously. **2** (*simultaneously*) at once, at the same time, concurrently, simultaneously, together. ANTONYMS: separately. **at times** (*at intervals, now and then*) at intervals, every now and then, from time to time, intermittently, now and then, occasionally, on occasions, periodically. ANTONYMS: all the time, always, constantly. **for the time being** (*for the present*) for now, for the moment, for the present, in the meantime, meantime, meanwhile, temporarily. ANTONYMS: permanently. **in good time** (*early*) ahead of time, early, punctually, with time to spare. ANTONYMS: late. **in no time** (*very quickly*) at great speed, before you can say Jack Robinson, before you know it, in a flash, in a trice, (*coll.*) in two shakes of a lamb's tail, speedily, swiftly. **in time 1** (*not too late, early enough*) at the right time, early enough, on schedule, punctually, with time to spare. ANTONYMS: too late, unpunctually. **2** (*in the course of time, eventually*) as time goes by, by and by, eventually, in due course, one day, some day, sooner or later, ultimately. **on time** (*punctually*) early enough, in good time, (*coll.*) on the dot, punctually,

sharp. ANTONYMS: late, unpunctually. **time after time** (*repeatedly*) again and again, frequently, often, on many occasions, recurrently, repeatedly, time and again, time and time again. ANTONYMS: infrequently, rarely.

timeless *a.* (*without end, ageless*) abiding, ageless, changeless, deathless, endless, enduring, eternal, everlasting, immortal, immutable, lasting, permanent, undying, unending. ANTONYMS: fleeting, transient, transitory.

timely *a.* (*opportune, occurring at the right time*) appropriate, at the right time, convenient, felicitous, opportune, propitious, suitable, well-timed. ANTONYMS: inconvenient, inopportune, untimely.

timetable *v.t.* (*to put* (*an event etc.*) *on a timetable*) fix, programme, schedule, set.

timid *a.* (*easily frightened, shy*) afraid, apprehensive, bashful, coy, diffident, faint-hearted, fearful, frightened, nervous, nervy, retiring, shrinking, shy, timorous. ANTONYMS: bold, brave, daring, fearless.

timorous *a.* (*fearful, timid*) afraid, apprehensive, audacious, bashful, coy, diffident, faint-hearted, fearful, frightened, nervous, nervy, retiring, shrinking, shy, timid. ANTONYMS: assertive, bold, brave, daring.

tincture *n.* **1** (*a tinge or shade* (*of colour*), *a tint*) colour, dye, shade, stain, tinge, tint. **2** (*an alcoholic or other solution of some principle, usu. vegetable, used in medicine*) infusion, solution.

tinge *v.t.* (*to colour slightly, to stain* (*with*)) colour, dye, imbue, stain, suffuse, tint.
~*n.* **1** (*a slight admixture of colour, a tint*) colour, shade, tincture, tint, tone. **2** (*a smack, flavour*) bit, dash, drop, flavour, hint, pinch, smack, smattering, soupçon, sprinkling, suggestion, touch, trace.

tingle *v.i.* (*to feel a stinging, prickly sensation*) have pins and needles, prick, prickle, sting, tickle.
~*n.* (*a tingling sensation*) pins and needles, pricking, prickling, stinging, tingling.

tinker *v.t.* (*to mend or patch up in a rough-and-ready way, or in a clumsy or ineffective manner* (*with*)) fiddle with, mess about with, monkey about with, patch up, play about with, toy with.

tinkle *v.i.* (*to make a succession of sharp, metallic sounds as of a bell*) chime, jingle, peal, ring.
~*n.* **1** (*a tinkling sound*) chime, jingle, peal, ring. **2** (*a telephone call*) (*coll.*) bell, (*sl.*) buzz, call, phone, phone call, ring, telephone call.

tinsel n. (superficial brilliance, gaudy display) flamboyance, flashiness, garishness, gaudiness, glitter, ornateness, ostentation, showiness, tawdriness, trashiness.
~a. (gaudy, superficially fine) flamboyant, flash, flashy, garish, gaudy, glittering, glittery, ornate, showy, tasteless, tawdry, trashy. ANTONYMS: plain, simple, tasteful.

tint n. 1 (a variety of colour, esp. one produced by admixture with another colour, esp. white) colour, hue, shade, tone. 2 (a faint or pale colour spread over a surface) pale colour, pastel colour, soft colour. 3 (a dye or wash) colorant, dye, stain, wash.
~v.t. (to give a tint or tints to) colour, dye, stain.

tiny a. (very small) diminutive, dwarfish, infinitesimal, insignificant, little, microscopic, midget, miniature, minuscule, minute, negligible, petite, (coll.) pint-sized, slight, small, (coll.) teensy-weensy, (coll.) teeny-weeny. ANTONYMS: colossal, enormous, huge, large, vast.

tip[1] n. (the point or extremity, esp. of a small or tapering thing) apex, cap, crown, end, extremity, peak, point, summit, top.
~v.t. (to put a tip on) cap, cover, crown, surmount, top.

tip[2] v.t. 1 (to overturn, to upset) capsize, overturn, topple, upend, upset. 2 (to discharge (the contents of a cart, vessel etc.) thus) empty, pour out, spill, unload. 3 (to strike lightly, to tap) strike, tap, touch. 4 (to give a small gratuity to) give a tip to, remunerate, reward.
~v.i. 1 (to lean over, to tilt) cant, incline, lean, list, tilt. 2 (to upset) capsize, fall over, overturn, topple.
~n. 1 (a small present in money, a gratuity) baksheesh, gratuity, pourboire. 2 (a piece of private information, esp. for betting or investment purposes) forecast, information, inside information, recommendation. 3 (a place where rubbish is dumped) dump, midden, refuse dump, refuse heap, rubbish dump, rubbish heap. 4 (a small piece of practical advice) handy hint, hint, piece of advice, pointer, recommendation, suggestion, word of advice.
to tip off (to give a warning hint) advise, caution, forewarn, (coll.) tip (someone) the wink, warn.

tip-off n. (a piece of confidential information, warning etc.) advice, clue, forewarning, hint, information, notification, warning.

tipple v.i. (to drink alcoholic liquors habitually) be an alcoholic, (coll.) booze, drink, have a drink problem. ANTONYMS: (coll.) be on the wagon, be teetotal, be TT.
~v.t. (to sip repeatedly) drink, imbibe, quaff, sip, (coll.) swig.

~n. 1 (one's favourite (alcoholic) drink) drink, favourite drink, (coll.) poison. 2 (strong drink) (coll.) booze, drink, liquor, spirits, strong drink.

tippler n. (a person who tipples, a habitual drinker) (coll.) boozer, drinker, drunk, drunkard, hard drinker, problem drinker, (sl.) soak, toper.

tipsy a. (fuddled, partially intoxicated) fuddled, (coll.) merry, slightly drunk, slightly intoxicated, (coll.) tiddly, (sl.) tight, under the influence. ANTONYMS: sober.

tirade n. (a long, vehement speech or harangue, esp. of censure or reproof) diatribe, harangue, lecture, philippic, stream of abuse, stream of invective, verbal onslaught.

tire v.t. 1 (to exhaust the strength of by toil or labour, to fatigue) debilitate, drain, enervate, exhaust, fag out, fatigue, (coll.) knacker, (coll.) take it out of, tire out, wear out, weary. ANTONYMS: enliven, invigorate, refresh, revive. 2 (to exhaust the patience or attention of) annoy, bore, exasperate, (coll.) get on one's nerves, harass, (coll.) hassle, irk, irritate, (taboo sl.) piss off, weary.
~v.i. 1 (to become weary or exhausted) become exhausted, become tired, become weary, droop, flag, grow tired, grow weary. 2 (to become bored) become bored, become tired, get bored, (coll.) get fed up, get sick, grow weary.

tired a. 1 (fatigued) (coll.) all in, dead beat, (coll.) dead on one's feet, dog-tired, (coll.) done in, drained, drooping, drowsy, enervated, exhausted, fagged out, fatigued, flagging, (coll.) knackered, ready to drop, sleepy, spent, weary, (coll.) whacked, worn, (sl.) zonked. ANTONYMS: energetic, fresh, full of beans, lively, refreshed. 2 (bored, irritated) bored, exasperated, (coll.) fed up, impatient, irked, irritated, jaded, (taboo sl.) pissed off, sick, sick and tired, wearied, weary. ANTONYMS: enthusiastic, interested, keen. 3 (stale, hackneyed) banal, clichéd, conventional, (coll.) corny, familiar, hackneyed, outworn, platitudinous, stale, stock, trite, well-worn, worn out. ANTONYMS: fresh, innovative, original.

tireless a. (unwearied, endlessly energetic) determined, dogged, energetic, indefatigable, industrious, resolute, unflagging, untiring, unwearied, vigorous. ANTONYMS: flagging, half-hearted, weak, weary.

tiresome a. 1 (wearisome, tedious) boring, dull, humdrum, laborious, monotonous, routine, tedious, unexciting, uninteresting, wearing, wearisome, wearying. ANTONYMS: exciting, interesting, stimulating. **2** (*annoying*) annoying, exasperating, irksome, irritating, troublesome, trying, vexatious, wearing. ANTONYMS: attractive, charming, endearing.

tiring *a.* (*causing tiredness*) arduous, demanding, draining, enervating, exacting, exhausting, fatiguing, hard, laborious, strenuous, taxing, tiring, tough, wearing, wearying. ANTONYMS: easy, effortless, undemanding, unexacting.

tissue *n.* **1** (*a paper handkerchief*) paper handkerchief, (*coll.*) paper hankie. **2** (*a fabrication, a connected series* (*of lies, accidents etc.*)) accumulation, chain, mass, network, series, web.

titanic *a.* (*huge, colossal*) colossal, enormous, gigantic, herculean, huge, immense, mammoth, massive, mighty, prodigious, stupendous, vast. ANTONYMS: minute, tiny.

titbit *n.* **1** (*a delicate or dainty morsel of food*) dainty, delicacy, (*coll.*) goody, snack, tasty morsel, treat. **2** (*an interesting piece of gossip*) juicy bit of scandal, juicy piece of gossip.

titillate *v.t.* (*to excite or stimulate pleasurably*) arouse, excite, fascinate, interest, provoke, stimulate, tantalize, tease, thrill, (*coll.*) turn on.

titillating *a.* (*exciting, often in an erotic way*) erotic, exciting, seductive, stimulating, suggestive, teasing, thrilling.

titivate *v.t., v.i.* (*to dress up, to make smart*) (*coll.*) doll up, (*coll.*) do up, groom, make smart, primp, prink, smarten up, spruce up, (*coll.*) tart up, touch up.

title *n.* **1** (*an inscription serving as a name or designation, esp. of a book, chapter etc.*) caption, heading, inscription, legend, name, style. **2** (*a personal appellation denoting office, nobility or other qualification*) appellation, denomination, designation, epithet, form of address, (*sl.*) handle, label, (*sl.*) moniker, name, nickname, sobriquet, tag, term. **3** (*the right to ownership of property*) claim, entitlement, holding, ownership, prerogative, proprietorship, right. **4** (*the legal evidence of this, a title deed*) deed, ownership of document, proof of ownership, title deed. **5** (*a book or publication*) book, publication, volume, work. **6** (*in a sport, a championship*) championship, crown, first place, laurels.

titter *v.i.* (*to laugh in a restrained manner, to snigger*) chortle, chuckle, giggle, laugh, snicker, snigger, tee-hee.

tittle-tattle *n.* (*gossip*) chit-chat, gossip, hearsay, idle talk, rumour.

titular *a.* (*existing in name or in title only, nominal*) in name only, nominal, putative, self-styled, so-called, soi-disant, token. ANTONYMS: actual, functioning, real.

toady *n.* (*an obsequious person, a sycophant*) (*taboo sl.*) arselicker, (*esp. N Am., sl.*) asskisser, (*esp. N Am., sl.*) asslicker, bootlicker, (*N Am., sl.*) brown-nose, (*coll.*) crawler, fawner, flatterer, flunkey, groveller, hanger-on, jackal, kowtower, lackey, leech, minion, parasite, spaniel, sycophant, truckler, yes-man.
~*v.t.* (*to fawn upon, to be obsequious to*) (*taboo sl.*) arselick, (*esp. N Am., sl.*) ass-kiss, (*N Am., sl.*) asslick, be obsequious, bootlick, bow and scrape, (*N Am., sl.*) brown-nose, crawl to, curry favour with, fawn upon, flatter, grovel, (*taboo sl.*) kiss the arse of, (*esp. N Am., sl.*) kiss the ass of, kowtow to, lick the boots of, pander to, (*coll.*) suck up to.

toast *n.* **1** (*a drinking or a call for drinking to the health of some person, cause etc.*) compliments, drink, health, salutation, salute, tribute. **2** (*a celebrity* (*of a place*), *a person thought to be toasted often*) celebrity, darling, favourite, hero, heroine, pet.
~*v.t.* **1** (*to brown* (*bread*), *cook* (*bacon etc.*) *by radiant heat*) brown, crisp, grill. **2** (*to warm* (*the feet etc.*) *at a fire*) heat, heat up, warm, warm up. **3** (*to drink to the health or in honour of*) drink a toast to, drink to, drink to the health of, salute.

today *adv.* **1** (*on or during this or the present day*) this day, this very day. ANTONYMS: tomorrow, yesterday. **2** (*at the present day, nowadays*) now, nowadays, the present, the present day, the present time, this age, this era, this period, this time. ANTONYMS: the future, the past, tomorrow, yesterday.

toddle *v.i.* (*to walk with short unsteady steps, as a child does*) dodder, falter, teeter, totter, wobble.

to-do *n.* (*a fuss, a commotion*) brouhaha, commotion, disturbance, furore, fuss, rumpus, tumult.

together *adv.* **1** (*in company or union, unitedly*) as a group, as one, cheek by jowl, collectively, hand in glove, hand in hand, in a body, in a group, in conjunction, in cooperation, in unison, jointly, mutually, shoulder to shoulder, side by side. ANTONYMS: alone, independently, individually, separately, singly. **2** (*at the same time*) all at once, at the same time, concurrently, contemporaneously, in unison, simultaneously, synchronously, with one accord. ANTONYMS: one at a time, separately. **3** (*without cessation or intermission*) consecutively, continuously, in a row, in

succession, one after the other, on end, successively, uninterruptedly, without a break, without interruption. **4** (*in a well-organized way*) arranged, fixed, organized, settled, sorted out, straight, to rights, well-organized. ANTONYMS: confused, disorganized, unorganized.
~*a.* (*composed, well-organized*) assured, calm, competent, composed, cool, cool, calm and collected, efficient, stable, well-adjusted, well-balanced, well-organized. ANTONYMS: agitated, confused, disorganized, incompetent, (*coll.*) scatty.

toil *v.i.* **1** (*to labour with pain and fatigue of body or mind*) drive oneself, drudge, (*coll.*) graft, labour, push oneself, slave away, slog, (*coll.*) slog one's guts out, strive, struggle, (*coll.*) sweat, work, work like a Trojan, work one's fingers to the bone. **2** (*to move or progress painfully or laboriously*) drag oneself, labour, make heavy weather, struggle, (*coll.*) sweat.
~*n.* (*hard and unremitting work, labour*) donkey work, drudgery, effort, elbow grease, exertion, (*coll.*) graft, (*coll.*) grind, hard work, labour, slog, striving, travail, work. ANTONYMS: idleness, inactivity, inertia, sloth.

toilet *n.* **1** (*a lavatory*) (*esp. N Am.*) bathroom, (*sl.*) bog, (*sl.*) can, (*sl.*) carzey, convenience, (*coll.*) gents, (*sl.*) john, (*sl.*) kazi, (*coll.*) ladies, ladies' room, latrine, lavatory, little boys' room, little girls' room, (*coll.*) loo, men's, men's room, outhouse, powder room, privy, urinal, (*N Am.*) washroom, water closet, WC. **2** (*the act or process of washing oneself, dressing etc.*) ablutions, bathing, dressing, grooming, toilette.

token *n.* **1** (*a sign, a symbol*) badge, demonstration, emblem, evidence, expression, indication, manifestation, mark, proof, representation, sign, symbol. **2** (*a memorial of love or friendship, a keepsake*) keepsake, memento, memorial, remembrance, reminder, souvenir.
~*a.* (*nominal, done, given etc. for form's sake only*) for form's sake, hollow, minimal, nominal, perfunctory, superficial.

tolerable *a.* **1** (*endurable, supportable*) acceptable, allowable, bearable, endurable, sufferable, supportable. ANTONYMS: intolerable, unacceptable, unbearable. **2** (*passable, fairly good*) acceptable, adequate, all right, average, fair, fairly good, good enough, mediocre, middling, not bad, nothing to write home about, (*coll.*) OK, (*coll.*) okay, ordinary, passable, run-of-the-mill, satisfactory, so so, unexceptional. ANTONYMS: bad, dreadful, poor, unacceptable.

tolerance *n.* **1** (*the ability to endure pain, toil etc.*) acceptance, endurance, fortitude, stamina, staying power, toleration, toughness.

ANTONYMS: softness, weakness, yielding. **2** (*permitting other people to say and do as they like*) broad-mindedness, charity, forbearance, indulgence, lenience, liberalism, open-mindedness, patience, permissiveness, understanding. ANTONYMS: bias, bigotry, intolerance, narrow-mindedness, prejudice.

tolerant *a.* (*showing toleration*) broad-minded, catholic, charitable, forbearing, indulgent, lenient, liberal, open-minded, patient, permissive, unbiased, understanding, unprejudiced. ANTONYMS: bigoted, intolerant, narrow-minded, prejudiced.

tolerate *v.t.* **1** (*to endure, to permit by not preventing or forbidding*) abide, accept, admit, allow, bear, brook, condone, countenance, endure, permit, put up with, sanction, stand, stomach, swallow, take, (*Sc.*) thole, warrant. ANTONYMS: disallow, forbid, prohibit, veto. **2** (*to sustain, to endure* (*pain, toil etc.*)) bear, endure, put up with, stand, suffer, sustain. ANTONYMS: give in to, yield.

toleration *n.* **1** (*the act of tolerating*) broad-mindedness, charity, forbearance, indulgence, lenience, liberalism, open-mindedness, permissiveness, understanding. ANTONYMS: bias, bigotry, intolerance, narrow-mindedness, prejudice. **2** (*the spirit of tolerance*) acceptance, endurance, fortitude, stamina, staying power, tolerance, toughness. ANTONYMS: softness, weakness, yielding.

toll[1] *n.* **1** (*a tax or duty charged for some privilege, service etc., esp. for the use of a road, bridge etc.*) charge, duty, fee, levy, payment, tariff, tax. **2** (*damage, deaths etc., suffered in an accident, natural disaster etc.*) cost, damage, loss, penalty.

toll[2] *v.i.* ((*of a bell*) *to sound or ring with slow, regular strokes*) chime, knell, peal, ring, sound.

tomb *n.* (*a vault for the dead*) burial chamber, catacomb, crypt, grave, mausoleum, sarcophagus, sepulchre, vault.

tombstone *n.* (*a stone placed as a memorial over a grave*) gravestone, headstone, stone.

tome *n.* (*a volume, esp. a ponderous one*) book, title, volume, work.

tomfool *a.* (*very foolish*) asinine, foolish, idiotic, insane, irresponsible, mad, senseless, silly, stupid.

tomfoolery *n.* (*foolish or stupid behaviour*) buffoonery, foolery, foolishness, horseplay, idiocy, insanity, irresponsibility, (*coll.*) larking about, madness, senselessness, silliness, stupidity.

tone *n.* **1** (*sound, with reference to pitch, quality and volume*) pitch, sound, timbre. **2** (*modulation or inflection of the voice to express emotion etc.*) accentuation, expression, inflection, intonation, modulation, tone of voice. **3** (*general disposition, prevailing sentiment*) air, attitude, character, disposition, drift, feel, manner, mood, quality, spirit, style, temper, tenor, vein. **4** (*degree of luminosity of a colour*) colour, hue, shade, tincture, tinge, tint.
~*v.i.* (*to harmonize* (*with*) *in colour, tint etc.*) blend (with), go well (with), go (with), harmonize (with), match, suit. ANTONYMS: clash (with). **to tone down 1** (*to subdue, to soften* (*the tint, tone etc. of*)) lighten, mute, soften, subdue, temper. ANTONYMS: brighten, heighten. **2** (*to modify, to soften* (*a statement, demands etc.*)) decrease, moderate, modify, modulate, play down, reduce, restrain, soften, temper. ANTONYMS: increase, intensify.

tongue *n.* **1** (*speech, the voice*) articulation, speech, utterance, verbal expression, voice. **2** (*manner of speech*) dialect, idiom, language, (*coll.*) lingo, parlance, patois, speech.

tongue-tied *a.* (*afraid of or prevented from speaking freely*) at a loss for words, bereft of speech, dumb, inarticulate, mute, silent, speechless, struck dumb, wordless. ANTONYMS: garrulous, loquacious, voluble.

tonic *n.* **1** (*a restorative medicine*) cordial, pick-me-up, restorative, stimulant. **2** (*something that makes someone feel better, a boost*) boost, fillip, pick-me-up, (*coll.*) shot in the arm, stimulant. ANTONYMS: depressant, (*sl.*) downer.

too *adv.* **1** (*as well, in addition*) also, as well, besides, in addition, into the bargain, to boot. **2** (*moreover*) further, furthermore, in addition, moreover. **3** (*extremely, superlatively*) excessively, extremely, immoderately, inordinately, overly, unduly, unreasonably, very.

tool *n.* **1** (*a simple implement, esp. one used in manual work*) apparatus, appliance, contraption, contrivance, device, gadget, implement, instrument, machine, utensil. **2** (*anything used as a means to an end*) agency, aid, means, medium, vehicle. **3** (*a person employed as an instrument or agent*) cat's paw, creature, flunkey, henchman, lackey, minion, pawn, puppet.

toothsome *a.* (*palatable, pleasing to the taste*) appetizing, delectable, delicious, luscious, mouth-watering, palatable, (*coll.*) scrumptious, tasty, (*coll.*) yummy. ANTONYMS: disgusting, foul-tasting, horrible.

top *n.* **1** (*the highest part or point of anything, the summit*) apex, apogee, crest, crown, peak, pinnacle, summit, tip, vertex. ANTONYMS: base,
bottom, foot. **2** (*the upper side or surface*) upper layer, upper part, upper surface. ANTONYMS: underside. **3** (*the part of a plant above ground*) leaves, shoots, stalk, stem. ANTONYMS: root. **4** (*a garment for the upper body or the upper part of a two-piece garment*) blouse, jersey, jumper, shirt, sweater, T-shirt. **5** (*something which covers or closes something, a lid*) cap, cork, cover, lid, stopper. **6** (*the highest position, place etc.*) first place, head, highest rank, lead. ANTONYMS: bottom, last place, lowest rank. **7** (*the highest degree, the culmination*) acme, climax, crowning point, culmination, height, high point, meridian, peak, pinnacle, prime, zenith. ANTONYMS: low, nadir.
~*v.t.* **1** (*to rise to the top of, to surmount*) ascend, climb, crest, mount, reach the top of, scale. ANTONYMS: descend. **2** (*to surpass, to be higher than*) beat, best, better, eclipse, exceed, excel, go beyond, outdo, outshine, outstrip, surpass, transcend. ANTONYMS: fall short of. **3** (*to cover the top of*) cap, cover, crown, finish, garnish. **4** (*to be at the head of*) be at the head of, be first in, head, lead. ANTONYMS: be at the bottom of, be last in.
~*a.* **1** (*being on or at the top or summit*) highest, topmost, upper. ANTONYMS: bottom, lowest. **2** (*highest in position, degree etc.*) best, chief, commanding, crack, dominant, elite, finest, first, foremost, greatest, head, highest, lead, leading, main, pre-eminent, principal, superior, top-notch. ANTONYMS: inferior, lowest, worst. **3** (*maximum*) greatest, highest, maximum, utmost. ANTONYMS: least, lowest, minimum. **from top to toe** (*completely, from head to foot*) all over, completely, entirely, from head to foot, wholly. ANTONYMS: partially, partly. **off the top of one's head** (*without preparation, impromptu*) ad lib, extempore, impromptu, off the cuff, spontaneously, without preparation. **on top of the world** (*very happy indeed, exuberant*) ecstatic, elated, euphoric, exuberant, happy as a sandboy, happy as Larry, in seventh heaven, (*coll.*) on cloud nine, over the moon, walking on air. ANTONYMS: in the depths, miserable. **over the top** (*to excess*) (*coll.*) a bit much, exaggerated, excessive, going too far, immoderate, inordinate, (*coll.*) OTT, to excess, too much, uncalled for. ANTONYMS: minimal, too little, understated.

topic *n.* (*the subject of a discourse, argument or conversation*) issue, matter, point, point at issue, question, subject, subject matter, text, theme, thesis.

topical *a.* (*of or relating to news and current affairs*) contemporary, current, in the news, newsworthy, popular, up to date, up-to-the-minute. ANTONYMS: in the past, (*coll.*) old hat, out of date.

topmost a. 1 (*highest, uppermost*) highest, top, uppermost. ANTONYMS: base, bottom, lowest. 2 (*leading, foremost*) eminent, foremost, head, important, leading, main, major, paramount, principal, supreme, top. ANTONYMS: insignificant, minor, unimportant.

top-notch a. (*first-rate, excellent*) (*sl.*) ace, crack, excellent, first-rate, superb, superior, tiptop, top-grade, (*dated sl.*) wizard.

topple v.i. (*to totter and fall*) capsize, fall, keel over, overbalance, overturn, tip over, totter.
~v.t. 1 (*to cause to topple, to overturn*) capsize, knock over, overturn, push over, tip over, upset. ANTONYMS: set upright. 2 (*to overthrow* (*a government or leader*)) bring down, bring low, oust, overthrow, overturn, unseat. ANTONYMS: instate, reinstate.

topsy-turvy a. 1 (*upside down*) head over heels, upside down, wrong side up. 2 (*in an upset or disordered condition*) chaotic, confused, disarranged, disorderly, disorganized, jumbled, mixed-up, muddled, untidy, upside down. ANTONYMS: neat, orderly, organized, tidy.
~adv. (*in a confused manner*) in a jumble, in a mess, in a muddle, in chaos, in confusion, in disarray, in disorder, upside down.

torment[1] n. 1 (*extreme pain or anguish of body or mind*) affliction, agony, anguish, distress, hell, misery, pain, suffering, torture, wretchedness. ANTONYMS: ecstasy, joy. 2 (*a source or cause of this*) affliction, bane, bother, curse, (*coll.*) hassle, irritant, irritation, nuisance, (*coll.*) pain in the neck, pest, plague, scourge, thorn in one's side, trouble, vexation, worry. ANTONYMS: comfort, delight.

torment[2] v.t. 1 (*to subject to torment, to afflict*) afflict, distress, harrow, inflict pain on, rack, torture. ANTONYMS: comfort, soothe. 2 (*to annoy, to irritate*) annoy, badger, bother, harass, (*coll.*) hassle, irritate, pester, plague, tease, trouble, vex.

torn a. 1 (*having been cut or ripped*) cut, in tatters, lacerated, ragged, rent, ripped, slit, split, tattered. ANTONYMS: undamaged, whole. 2 (*having difficulty in choosing*) in two minds, irresolute, on the horns of a dilemma, uncertain, undecided, unsure, vacillating, wavering. ANTONYMS: certain, decisive, with one's mind made up.

tornado n. (*a very strong wind, a hurricane*) cyclone, gale, hurricane, squall, storm, tempest, (*esp. N Am.*) twister, typhoon, whirlwind.

torpid a. (*dull, sluggish*) apathetic, drowsy, dull, inactive, indolent, inert, lackadaisical, languid, lazy, lethargic, listless, sleepy, slothful, slow, slow-moving, sluggish, somnolent. ANTONYMS: active, energetic, lively, vigorous.

torpor n. (*the state of being torpid*) apathy, drowsiness, dullness, inaction, inactivity, indolence, inertia, languidness, languor, laziness, lethargy, listlessness, sleepiness, sloth, slowness, sluggishness, somnolence, torpidity. ANTONYMS: activity, energy, liveliness, vigour.

torrent n. 1 (*a violent rushing stream* (*of water, lava etc.*)) cascade, deluge, flood, gush, inundation, rush, spate, stream. 2 (*a flood* (*of abuse, passion etc.*)) barrage, flood, outburst, outpouring, stream, volley.

torrid a. 1 (*scorching, very hot*) arid, dried up, dry, parched, parching, scorched, scorching, sizzling, stifling, sultry, sweltering, tropical. ANTONYMS: arctic, cold, cool, freezing, frozen. 2 (*intense, passionate*) amorous, ardent, erotic, fervent, impassioned, intense, passionate, sexy, (*sl.*) steamy. ANTONYMS: apathetic, cool, passionless.

tortuous a. 1 (*twisting, winding*) bent, circuitous, crooked, curved, curving, meandering, serpentine, sinuous, twisting, winding, zigzag. ANTONYMS: straight. 2 (*roundabout, not direct*) ambiguous, circuitous, complicated, convoluted, indirect, involved. ANTONYMS: direct, simple, straightforward. 3 (*devious, not open and straightforward*) cunning, deceitful, deceptive, devious, tricky. ANTONYMS: honest, open, straightforward.

torture n. 1 (*the infliction of extreme physical pain as a punishment or to extort confession etc.*) pain, persecution, suffering, torment. 2 (*excruciating pain or anguish*) agony, anguish, distress, hell, misery, pain, suffering, torment. ANTONYMS: bliss, delight.
~v.t. 1 (*to subject to torture*) inflict pain on, inflict suffering on, persecute, put on the rack, torment. 2 (*to cause great suffering to*) afflict, cause anguish to, cause suffering to, distress, plague, put (someone) through hell, subject to misery, subject to pain, torment. ANTONYMS: comfort, solace, soothe.

toss v.t. 1 (*to throw, to fling, with an easy or careless motion*) cast, (*coll.*) chuck, fling, flip, lob, pitch, shy, sling, throw. 2 (*to throw back* (*the head*) *with a jerk*) jerk, throw back. 3 (*to throw about or from side to side, to cause to rise and fall*) agitate, jiggle, jolt, rock, roll, shake, tumble.
~v.i. 1 (*to roll and tumble about, to be agitated*) heave, lurch, pitch, rock, roll, sway, thrash, tumble. 2 (*to throw oneself from side to side*) roll, thrash around, toss and turn, writhe.
~n. (*the act of tossing*) fling, flip, lob, pitch, shy, sling, throw.

tot[1] *n.* **1** (*a small child*) baby, child, little one, mite, toddler. **2** (*a dram of liquor*) dram, drink, finger, measure, nip, (*coll.*) shot, slug, snifter.

tot[2] *v.t.* (*to add* (*up*)) add up, calculate, count, count up, reckon, tally, total. **to tot up to** (*to total, to amount to*) add up to, amount to, come to, total.

total *a.* **1** (*complete, comprising everything or constituting the whole*) aggregate, complete, comprehensive, entire, full, gross, integral, whole. ANTONYMS: incomplete, part, partial. **2** (*absolute, entire*) absolute, complete, downright, entire, out-and-out, outright, rank, sheer, thorough, thoroughgoing, unmitigated, unqualified, utter. ANTONYMS: partial.
~*n.* (*the total sum or amount*) aggregate, sum, totality.
~*v.t.* **1** (*to ascertain the total of*) calculate, count up, reckon, tot up. **2** (*to amount to as a total*) add up to, amount to, come to, tot up to. **3** (*to wreck* (*a vehicle*) *completely in a crash*) crash, demolish, wreck, write off.

totalitarian *a.* (*permitting no rival parties or policies*) absolute, authoritarian, despotic, dictatorial, monocratic, oppressive, tyrannical, undemocratic. ANTONYMS: democratic, egalitarian.

totality *n.* **1** (*the total sum or amount*) aggregate, sum, total. **2** (*the whole of something, the entirety*) completeness, entireness, entirety, fullness, wholeness. ANTONYMS: incompleteness.

totally *adv.* (*completely, wholly*) absolutely, completely, comprehensively, entirely, fully, perfectly, quite, thoroughly, utterly, wholly. ANTONYMS: in part, partially, partly, somewhat.

totter *v.i.* **1** (*to walk or stand unsteadily, to stagger*) lurch, reel, roll, stagger, stumble, sway, teeter, wobble. **2** (*to be on the point of falling*) be on the point of collapse, be shaky, be unstable, be unsteady, falter, teeter.

touch *v.t.* **1** (*to meet the surface of, to be in contact with*) abut, adjoin, be in contact with, border, brush, come into contact with, converge, graze, impinge on, meet. ANTONYMS: avoid, diverge. **2** (*to bring or put the hand or other part of the body or a stick etc., into contact with*) brush, caress, feel, finger, fondle, handle, lay a finger on, palpate, pat, stroke, tap. **3** (*to reach, to attain*) attain, get down to, get up to, reach. **4** (*to meddle, to interfere with*) fiddle with, handle, interfere with, play with, toy with. **5** (*to affect with tender feeling, to soften*) affect, arouse sympathy in, disturb, (*coll.*) get to, have an effect on, have an impact on,

influence, make an impression on, melt, move, soften, stir, upset. **6** (*to approach, to compare with*) approach, be a match for, be in the same league as, be on a par with, come near, compare with, equal, hold a candle to, match, parallel, rival. **7** (*to beg or borrow money from*) ask, beg from, borrow from. **8** (*to concern, to relate to*) affect, be relevant to, concern, have a bearing on, have relevance to, involve, relate to. ANTONYMS: be irrelevant to, have no relevance to. **9** (*to mention hastily or lightly*) allude to, make mention of, make reference to, mention, refer to. ANTONYMS: ignore, make no mention of. **10** (*to be associated with*) be associated with, be involved in/ with, be party to, have dealings with, have to do with. ANTONYMS: have nothing to do with. **11** (*to eat or drink, to consume*) consume, drink, eat, partake of, take. ANTONYMS: abstain from, refuse.
to touch down ((*of an aircraft or spacecraft*) *to make contact with the ground after a flight*) alight, land. ANTONYMS: take off. **to touch off 1** (*to cause to begin, to trigger*) arouse, begin, cause, foment, give rise to, launch, provoke, set in motion, set off, spark off, start, trigger. ANTONYMS: bring an end to, end, finish. **2** (*to set alight*) detonate, fire, ignite, put a match to, set alight, set fire to. ANTONYMS: extinguish. **to touch on/ upon** (*to allude to*) allude to, comment on, make mention of, make reference to, mention, refer to, speak of, talk of. ANTONYMS: ignore, make no mention of. **to touch up** (*to correct or improve by slight touches, to retouch*) (*coll.*) fix up, give a facelift to, patch up, renovate, retouch, revamp, titivate.

touch-and-go *a.* (*highly uncertain, very risky or hazardous*) close, close-run, critical, dangerous, (*coll.*) hairy, hazardous, near, perilous, precarious, risky, (*coll.*) sticky, uncertain. ANTONYMS: certain, safe.

touched *a.* **1** (*moved by some emotion, e.g. pity or gratitude*) affected, moved, stirred, upset. ANTONYMS: unaffected, unmoved. **2** (*slightly insane*) (*sl.*) barmy, (*coll.*) batty, (*sl.*) bonkers, crazed, daft, demented, deranged, (*coll.*) dotty, insane, irrational, (*coll.*) loopy, mad, not all there, not right in the head, (*coll.*) nuts, (*sl.*) off one's trolley, (*sl.*) out to lunch, soft in the head, unbalanced, unhinged. ANTONYMS: rational, sane, sensible.

touching *a.* (*moving, arousing pathos*) affecting, disturbing, emotive, heartbreaking, heartrending, moving, pathetic, piteous, pitiable, pitiful, poignant, sad, stirring, upsetting.

touchstone *n.* (*a standard, a criterion*) benchmark, criterion, gauge, guide, model, norm, par, pattern, standard, yardstick.

touchy *a.* (*apt to take offence, irritable*) bad-tempered, crabbed, cross, grumpy, hyper-sensitive, irascible, irritable, oversensitive, peevish, querulous, sensitive, testy, tetchy, thin-skinned. ANTONYMS: easygoing, good-humoured, thick-skinned.

tough *a.* **1** (*strong, not easily broken*) durable, firm, hard, resilient, resistant, solid, strong, sturdy. ANTONYMS: flimsy, fragile, soft. **2** (*able to endure hardship*) brawny, fit, hardy, robust, rugged, stalwart, stout, strapping, strong, sturdy, vigorous. ANTONYMS: puny, unfit, weak. **3** (*stubborn, unyielding*) adamant, firm, (*coll.*) hard-nosed, inflexible, intractable, obdurate, obstinate, resolute, ruthless, stern, stubborn, unbending, unyielding. ANTONYMS: accommodating, flexible, tractable, yielding. **4** (*aggressive, violent*) aggressive, disorderly, lawless, pugnacious, rough, rowdy, trouble-making, unruly, vicious, violent, wild. ANTONYMS: gentle, law-abiding, peaceable. **5** (*laborious*) arduous, demanding, difficult, exacting, hard, heavy, laborious, onerous, strenuous, taxing, uphill. ANTONYMS: easy, effortless, unexacting. **6** (*difficult*) awkward, baffling, difficult, knotty, perplexing, puzzling, thorny, ticklish, tricky. ANTONYMS: easy, simple, straightforward. **7** ((*of meat etc.*) *hard to cut or chew*) chewy, fibrous, gristly, leathery, sinewy, stringy. ANTONYMS: soft, tender.
~*n.* (*a burly lout, a bully*) (*coll.*) bruiser, brute, bully, (*coll.*) hard man, (*coll.*) heavy, hoodlum, hooligan, (*coll.*) roughneck, rowdy, ruffian, thug.

toughen *v.t.* **1** (*to make tougher*) fortify, harden, reinforce, strengthen. ANTONYMS: weaken. **2** (*to make more strict*) make stricter, stiffen, tighten. ANTONYMS: relax.
~*v.i.* (*to become tougher*) harden, stiffen, strengthen. ANTONYMS: weaken.

tough luck *int.* (*hard luck* (*used esp. where no sympathy is being offered*)) bad luck, (*coll.*) hard cheese, (*coll.*) hard lines, hard luck, too bad, unlucky. ANTONYMS: good luck, lucky.

tour *n.* **1** (*a journeying round from place to place in a district, country etc.*) excursion, expedition, jaunt, journey, outing, trip. **2** (*a circuit*) ambit, circuit, course, round. **3** (*a shift or turn of work or duty, esp. a period of service abroad*) shift, stint, stretch, tour of duty. **4** (*a brief visit to a place to look round it*) guided tour, tour of inspection, visit, walk-round.

tourist *n.* (*a person making a tour, esp. a holidaymaker*) holidaymaker, sightseer, traveller, tripper, visitor.

tournament *n.* **1** (*any contest of skill in which a number of people take part*) competition, contest, event, match, meeting, series. **2** (*a contest or pageant in which mounted knights contested*) joust, jousting, lists, tourney.

tousle *v.t.* (*to dishevel, to put into disorder*) disarrange, dishevel, disorder, mess up, ruffle, rumple, tangle. ANTONYMS: arrange, comb, groom.

tousled *a.* ((*esp. of hair*) *disarranged, untidy*) disarranged, dishevelled, in disarray, in disorder, messed up, (*N Am.*) mussed, rumpled, uncombed, unkempt, untidy. ANTONYMS: neat, tidy.

tout *v.i.* (*to solicit custom in an obtrusive way*) ask for, petition for, seek, solicit.
~*v.t.* (*to try persistently to persuade someone to buy*) hawk, offer for sale, peddle, sell.

tow *v.t.* (*to pull* (*a vehicle*) *behind another*) drag, draw, haul, lug, pull, trail, tug. **in tow** (*following*) accompanying, by one's side, following, in one's charge.

towards *prep.* **1** (*in the direction of*) en route for, in the direction of, on the road to, on the way to. **2** (*as regards, with respect to*) apropos, as regards, concerning, in relation to, regarding, respecting, with regard to, with respect to. **3** (*for, for the purpose of*) for, for the purpose of, in order to achieve, in order to get, in order to obtain, with the aim of. **4** (*near, about*) about, around, close to, coming up for, getting on for, just before, near, nearing, nearly, shortly before.

tower *n.* **1** (*a structure lofty in proportion to the area of its base, and circular, square or polygonal in plan*) belfry, bell tower, column, minaret, steeple, turret. **2** (*a place of defence, a protection*) castle, citadel, fort, fortification, fortress, keep, stronghold.
~*v.i.* (*to rise to a great height, to soar*) ascend, loom, mount, rear, rise, soar. **to tower above/over 1** (*to be much taller or higher than*) be head and shoulders above, loom, top. **2** (*to be much greater than in ability, quality etc.*) be head and shoulders above, cap, eclipse, excel, outclass, outshine, overshadow, put (someone) in the shade, run circles round, surpass, top, transcend.

towering *a.* **1** (*very high, lofty*) high, lofty, sky-high, tall. ANTONYMS: low. **2** ((*of passion etc.*) *violent, outrageous*) burning, extreme, fierce, frantic, frenzied, immoderate, intense, passionate, vehement, violent, wild. ANTONYMS: apathetic, low-key, moderate, restrained. **3** (*very great*) extraordinary, great, impressive, outstanding, pre-eminent, superior, surpassing. ANTONYMS: inferior, lesser.

toxic *a.* (*poisonous*) noxious, poisonous, venomous. ANTONYMS: harmless, non-toxic.

toy *n.* 1 (*a plaything, esp. for a child*) game, plaything. 2 (*something of an amusing or trifling kind, not serious or for actual use*) bauble, gewgaw, knick-knack, trifle, trinket.
~*a.* 1 (*replica*) copy, model, replica. 2 (*of a small variety*) diminutive, miniature, small, tiny. **to toy with** 1 (*to trifle with*) amuse oneself with, dally with, flirt with, play around with, trifle with. 2 (*to touch or move idly*) fiddle with, mess about with. 3 (*to consider casually*) have thoughts about, play with, think about.

trace *n.* 1 (*a token or sign of something that has existed or taken place*) evidence, indication, mark, record, relic, remains, remnant, sign, token, vestige. 2 (*a minute quantity*) bit, dash, drop, hint, iota, jot, shadow, soupçon, suggestion, suspicion, tinge, touch, whiff. 3 (*a mark left by a person or animal walking or thing moving, a track*) footmark(s), footprint(s), marks, print(s), scent, spoor, track, trail.
~*v.t.* 1 (*to follow the traces or track of*) dog, follow, pursue, shadow, stalk, tail, track, trail. 2 (*to ascertain the position or course of*) detect, dig up, discover, ferret out, find, hunt down, track down, turn up, uncover, unearth. 3 (*to delineate, to mark out*) chart, delineate, depict, draw, indicate, map, mark out, record, show. 4 (*to sketch out* (*a plan, scheme etc.*)) draft, draw up, outline, plan, rough out, sketch.

track *n.* 1 (*a series of marks left by the passage of a person, animal or thing, a trail*) footmark(s), footprint(s), marks, scent, slipstream, spoor, track, trail, wake. 2 (*a path, esp. one not constructed but beaten by use*) path, pathway, trail. 3 (*a racecourse, a route for racing*) racecourse, racetrack. 4 (*a course of action*) course, course of action, line of action, lines, procedure. 5 (*a set of rails, a monorail or a continuous line of railway*) line, rail, rails, railway line, railway track. 6 (*a course, the route followed by spaceships, ships etc.*) course, line, orbit, path, route, trajectory.
~*v.t.* (*to follow the track or traces of*) chase, dog, follow, pursue, shadow, stalk, tail, trace, trail. **to keep track of** (*to remain aware of* (*events, developments etc.*)) be aware of, follow, keep in contact with, keep in touch with, keep up to date with, keep up with, monitor, record. ANTONYMS: lose contact with, lose track of. **to lose track of** (*to cease to be aware of* (*events, developments etc.*)) be unaware of, forget, lose, lose contact with, lose touch with, misplace. ANTONYMS: keep in contact with, keep track of. **to make tracks** (*to run away, to leave*) depart, go, go away, (*sl.*) hit the road, leave, make one's departure, retire, run away, (*sl.*) split,

take off, take one's leave, (*N Am., sl.*) vamoose. **to make tracks for** (*to head for*) aim for, go towards, head for, make for, make one's way towards, steer a course towards. **to track down** (*to discover by tracking*) bring to light, detect, dig up, discover, expose, ferret out, find, get hold of, hunt down, (*coll.*) nose out, run to earth, sniff out, trace, uncover, unearth.

tract¹ *n.* (*a region or area of land or water of a considerable but undefined extent*) area, expanse, extent, plot, region, stretch, zone.

tract² *n.* (*a short treatise or pamphlet, esp. on religion or morals*) booklet, brochure, dissertation, essay, homily, leaflet, lecture, monograph, pamphlet, sermon, thesis, treatise.

tractable *a.* (*easily led or controlled, docile*) amenable, biddable, compliant, controllable, docile, manageable, obedient, submissive, tame, yielding. ANTONYMS: disobedient, intractable, refractory, unmanageable, wilful.

trade *n.* 1 (*the exchange of commodities, commerce*) barter, buying and selling, commerce, dealing, marketing, merchandising, trafficking, transacting. 2 (*a business, handicraft etc. carried out for profit, as distinct from agriculture, unskilled labour etc.*) area of commerce, business, line of business. 3 (*a business, handicraft etc., requiring training or an apprenticeship*) business, calling, career, craft, employment, job, line, line of business, line of work, occupation, profession. 4 (*an exchange of one thing for another*) barter, deal, exchange, swap, switch.
~*v.i.* 1 (*to buy and sell, to deal* (*in*)) barter, buy and sell, deal, peddle, traffic. 2 (*to carry on commerce or business* (*with*)) carry out transactions, deal, do business, run a business.
~*v.t.* (*to swap*) barter, exchange, swap, switch. **to trade on** (*to take advantage of*) capitalize on, exploit, make use of, profit from, take advantage of.

trader *n.* (*a person engaged in trade, a merchant*) broker, buyer and seller, dealer, hawker, marketer, merchant, peddler, tradesman.

tradesman *n.* 1 (*a retail dealer, a shopkeeper*) dealer, merchant, retailer, seller, shopkeeper, vendor. 2 (*a craftsperson*) artisan, craftsman, craftswoman, journeyman, skilled worker, tradeswoman, worker.

tradition *n.* 1 (*the handing down of practices, customs etc., from ancestors to posterity, esp. by oral communication*) folklore, oral history, oral tradition. 2 (*a belief, custom etc. so handed down*) belief, convention, custom, institution, practice, praxis, ritual. 3 (*a regular practice, a custom*) custom, habit, practice, routine, wont.

traditional *a.* **1** (*of or relating to tradition, based on tradition*) ancestral, folk, handed-down, historic, old, oral, time-honoured. ANTONYMS: avant-garde, contemporary, modern, new. **2** (*of or relating to a regular practice or custom*) accustomed, conventional, customary, established, fixed, habitual, routine, set, usual, wonted. ANTONYMS: innovative, novel, revolutionary, unusual.

traduce *v.t.* (*to defame, to speak ill of*) (*coll.*) bad-mouth, blacken the name of, calumniate, cast aspersions on, defame, denigrate, deprecate, disparage, malign, misrepresent, revile, run down, slander, smear, speak ill of, vilify. ANTONYMS: compliment, praise.

traffic *n.* **1** (*the vehicles etc. passing on a road etc.*) cars, lorries, vehicles. **2** (*the transportation of people, animals or goods by road, rail, sea or air*) conveyancing, freight, movement of goods, movement of passengers, transport, transportation. **3** (*the trade in a particular commodity etc., esp. the illegal trade*) bootlegging, dealing, peddling, smuggling. **4** (*the exchange of goods by barter or by the medium of money, trade*) barter, business, buying and selling, commerce, dealing, trade. **5** (*communication or dealing (with)*) communication, contact, dealings, relations, truck.
~*v.i.* **1** (*to deal (in) certain goods*) deal (in), do business (in), trade (in). **2** (*to deal (in) illegally*) bootleg, deal (in), peddle, smuggle.

tragedy *n.* **1** (*a fatal or calamitous event, esp. a murder or fatal accident*) calamity, disaster, fatality. **2** (*a serious event, a misfortune*) adversity, affliction, blow, calamity, catastrophe, disaster, misadventure, misfortune. ANTONYMS: good thing, joy, piece of good luck, stroke of luck.

tragic *a.* **1** (*lamentable, sad*) calamitous, catastrophic, disastrous, distressing, dreadful, lamentable, sad, sorrowful, terrible, unfortunate, unhappy, unlucky, woeful, wretched. ANTONYMS: cheerful, fortunate, happy, lucky. **2** (*characterized by loss of life*) deadly, fatal.

trail *v.t.* **1** (*to drag along behind, esp. along the ground*) drag, draw, haul, pull, tow. **2** (*to follow by the track or trail*) chase, follow, pursue, shadow, stalk, tail, track.
~*v.i.* **1** (*to be dragged along behind, to hang down loosely*) dangle, droop, sweep. **2** (*to lag behind*) bring up the rear, dawdle, fall behind, lag behind, linger, loiter, straggle. **3** (*to be losing in a contest etc.*) be behind, be down, be losing, lose. ANTONYMS: be ahead, be winning. **4** (*to tail (off), to fall (away)*) decrease, die away, disappear, dwindle, fade, fall away, grow faint, grow weak, melt away, peter out, vanish.

train *n.* **1** (*a line or long series or succession of people or things*) caravan, column, convoy, cortege, file, procession. **2** (*process, orderly succession*) chain, concatenation, progression, sequence, series, set, string, succession. **3** (*a retinue, a suite*) atttendants, cortege, court, entourage, followers, following, retinue, suite.
~*v.t.* **1** (*to bring to a state of proficiency by prolonged instruction, practice etc.*) coach, drill, educate, ground, guide, instruct, prepare, school, teach, tutor. **2** (*to prepare by diet and exercise (for a race etc.)*) coach, drill. **3** (*to bring to bear, to point or aim (a cannon, camera etc. on)*) aim, bring to bear, direct, focus, level, line up, point.
~*v.i.* **1** (*to prepare oneself or come into a state of efficiency (for a race, match etc.)*) do exercises, exercise, practise, work out. **2** (*to prepare oneself for a career, to study*) learn, study, take a course of study.

trainer *n.* (*a person who trains, esp. one who prepares athletes, horses etc.*) coach, handler, instructor.

training *n.* **1** (*the preparation of a person or animal for a particular activity, occupation etc.*) coaching, drill, education, grounding, guidance, guiding, instruction, preparation, schooling, teaching, tuition, tutoring. **2** (*the state of making oneself physically fit*) body-building, exercise, physical exercise, working out.

traipse *v.i.* (*to trudge, to drag along wearily*) drag oneself along, trail, trudge.

trait *n.* (*a distinguishing or peculiar feature*) attribute, characteristic, feature, idiosyncrasy, lineament, mannerism, peculiarity, quality, quirk.

traitor *n.* (*a person guilty of disloyalty or treachery, esp. to their country*) apostate, backstabber, betrayer, defector, deserter, (*coll.*) double-crosser, double-dealer, fifth columnist, Judas, renegade, snake in the grass, turncoat. ANTONYMS: loyalist, patriot.

traitorous *a.* (*of or like a traitor*) apostate, back-stabbing, disloyal, (*coll.*) double-crossing, double-dealing, faithless, false, false-hearted, perfidious, renegade, seditious, treacherous, unfaithful, untrue. ANTONYMS: constant, faithful, loyal, patriotic, true.

trajectory *n.* (*the path taken by a comet, projectile etc., under the action of given forces*) course, flight path, line, orbit, path, route, track.

trammel *n.* (*anything restraining freedom or activity*) bar, barrier, block, bonds, check, constraint, curb, fetters, handicap, hindrance,

impediment, obstacle, rein, restraint, shackles, stumbling-block.
~*v.t.* (*to confine, to hamper*) bar, block, check, confine, constrain, fetter, frustrate, hamper, handicap, hinder, impede, obstruct, restrain, restrict, shackle.

tramp *v.i.* **1** (*to walk, to go on foot, esp. for a considerable distance*) go on shanks's pony, hike, march, ramble, roam, slog, trek, walk, yomp. **2** (*to walk or tread heavily*) plod, stamp, stump, trudge, walk heavily.
~*v.t.* (*to tread heavily on, to trample*) crush, flatten, squash, stamp, trample, tread, walk over.
~*n.* **1** (*an itinerant beggar, a vagrant*) beggar, (*esp. N Am., coll.*) bum, derelict, (*sl.*) dosser, down-and-out, itinerant, vagabond, vagrant. **2** (*the sound of the tread of people etc. walking or marching, or of horses' hooves*) footfall, footsteps, stamping, tread. **3** (*a walk, a journey on foot*) hike, march, ramble, roam, trek, walk, yomp. **4** (*a promiscuous girl or woman*) (*sl.*) hooker, loose woman, prostitute, (*offensive*) slut, (*sl.*) tart, trollop, whore.

trample *v.t.* (*to tread down, to crush in this way*) crush, flatten, squash, stamp on, tread. **to trample on** (*to tread on with contempt*) disregard, encroach upon, infringe, ride roughshod over, set at naught, treat with contempt.

trance *n.* (*a state of mental abstraction, with no response to external surroundings or stimuli*) brown study, daze, dream, hypnotic state, muse, reverie, state of abstraction, stupor.

tranquil *a.* **1** ((*of a person*) *calm and not showing any worry or strong feeling*) at peace, at rest, calm, composed, cool, cool, calm and collected, even-tempered, peaceable, placid, serene, unexcitable, (*coll.*) unflappable, unperturbed, unruffled. ANTONYMS: agitated, excitable, (*coll.*) in a flap, ruffled. **2** ((*of a place*) *peaceful, serene*) peaceful, quiet, restful, still, undisturbed. ANTONYMS: busy, hectic, noisy.

tranquillity *n.* **1** (*the quality of calmness in a person's manner*) calm, composure, cool, coolness, equanimity, even-temperedness, placidity, repose, serenity, (*coll.*) unflappability. ANTONYMS: agitation, excitement. **2** (*the quality of peacefulness and quiet in a place*) hush, peace, peacefulness, quietness, restfulness, stillness. ANTONYMS: disturbance, noise, turmoil.

tranquillize *v.t.* (*to make calm, to reduce anxiety in, esp. with a sedative drug*) calm, calm down, pacify, quiet, relax, sedate, soothe. ANTONYMS: agitate, disturb, ruffle, upset.

tranquillizer *n.* (*a sedative drug, a drug to*

reduce anxiety) barbiturate, bromide, (*coll.*) downer, opiate, sedative.

transact *v.t.* (*to do, to carry out*) accomplish, carry out, conclude, conduct, discharge, do, enact, execute, handle, manage, negotiate, perform, prosecute, settle.

transaction *n.* **1** (*the management or carrying out of a piece of business etc.*) accomplishment, conclusion, conducting, discharge, enactment, execution, handling, management, negotiation, performance, prosecution, settlement. **2** (*something transacted, a piece of business*) action, affair, bargain, business, deal, matter, proceedings, undertaking. **3** (*the reports of the proceedings of a learned society*) affairs, dealings, minutes, proceedings, records.

transcend *v.t., v.i.* **1** (*to surpass, to exceed*) eclipse, exceed, excel, outdo, outrival, outshine, outstrip, outvie, overshadow, put in the shade, surpass. **2** (*to pass or be beyond the sphere or power* (*of human understanding etc.*)) exceed, go beyond.

transcendence *n.* (*the state of being transcendent*) ascendency, excellence, greatness, incomparability, magnificence, predominance, pre-eminence, superiority, supremacy.

transcendent *a.* (*excelling, supremely excellent*) consummate, excellent, extraordinary, great, incomparable, magnificent, matchless, paramount, predominant, pre-eminent, second to none, superior, supreme, unequalled, unparalleled, unrivalled, unsurpassed.

transcendental *a.* (*transcending ordinary ideas*) mysterious, mystic, mystical, otherworldly, preternatural, supernatural. ANTONYMS: natural, normal, ordinary.

transcribe *v.t.* **1** (*to copy in writing, to write out in full* (*shorthand notes etc.*)) copy in full, copy out, type out, write out. **2** (*to translate, to transliterate*) interpret, render, translate, transliterate. **3** (*to transfer* (*data*) *from one recording medium to another*) record, re-record, tape, tape-record, transfer.

transcript *n.* (*a written or recorded copy*) carbon copy, copy, documentation, printed copy, printed version, record, transcription, written copy, written version.

transfer[1] *v.t.* **1** (*to convey or shift from one place or person to another*) carry, convey, move, remove, shift, take, transport. **2** (*to make over the possession of*) assign, bequeath, convey, hand down, hand on, hand over, make over, sign over, transmit, turn over. **3** (*to remove to another club, department etc.*) move, relocate, shift.

transfer[2] *n*. **1** (*the removal or conveyance of a thing from one person or place to another*) carrying, conveyance, conveying, moving, removal, shifting, transport, transporting. **2** (*the act of conveying a right, property etc. from one person to another*) conveyance, handing over, handover, making over, passing on, transference, transmission. **3** (*the deed by which this is effected*) deed, deeds, papers, transfer document. **4** (*the removal of someone to another club, department etc.*) moving, relocation, shifting.

transfigure *v.t.* (*to change the outward appearance of, esp. so as to elevate and glorify*) alter, change, metamorphose, transform.

transfix *v.t.* **1** (*to pierce through, to impale*) impale, pierce, run through, skewer, spear, spike, stab, transpierce. **2** (*to render motionless with shock, fear etc.*) fascinate, halt (someone) in their tracks, hypnotize, mesmerize, paralyse, petrify, rivet, root to the spot, spellbind, stop (someone) dead, stop (someone) in their tracks, stun.

transform *v.t.* (*to change the form or appearance of, to metamorphose*) alter, change, convert, make over, metamorphose, rebuild, reconstruct, remodel, renew, revolutionize, transfigure, (*esp. facet.*) transmogrify.

transformation *n.* (*the act of transforming*) alteration, change, conversion, make-over, metamorphosis, radical change, rebuilding, reconstruction, remodelling, renewal, revolutionizing, sea change, transfiguration, transmogrification.

transgress *v.t.* (*to break (a rule or rules), to infringe*) breach, break, contravene, defy, disobey, encroach, go beyond, infringe, overstep, violate. ANTONYMS: keep, obey, observe.
~*v.i.* (*to offend by violating a law or rule, to sin*) break the law, do wrong, err, misbehave, offend, sin, trespass.

transgression *n.* **1** (*an offence, wrongdoing*) crime, error, evil, lapse, lawbreaking, misbehaviour, misconduct, misdemeanour, offence, peccadillo, sin, trespass, wrong, wrongdoing. **2** (*the breaking or violation of a rule or rules*) breaching, breaking, contravention, defiance, disobeying, encroachment, infringement, overstepping, violation. ANTONYMS: keeping, obeying, observance.

transgressor *n.* (*a person who transgresses*) criminal, culprit, evildoer, lawbreaker, miscreant, offender, sinner, trespasser, villain, wrongdoer.

transience *n.* (*the state of being momentary or brief*) brevity, briefness, ephemerality,

evanescence, fleetingness, fugacity, fugitiveness, impermanence, momentariness, mutability, short-livedness, shortness, temporariness, transitoriness. ANTONYMS: constancy, durability, permanence.

transient *a.* (*momentary, brief*) brief, ephemeral, evanescent, fleeting, flying, fugacious, fugitive, here today and gone tomorrow, impermanent, momentary, mutable, passing, short, short-lived, temporary, transitory. ANTONYMS: enduring, long-lasting, permanent, perpetual.

transit *n.* **in transit** (*being conveyed*) during transport, en route, on the journey, on the move, on the road, on the way, while travelling.

transition *n.* (*passage or change from one place, state or action to another*) change, changeover, conversion, development, evolution, jump, leap, metamorphosis, move, passage, passing, progression, shift, switch, transformation.

transitional *a.* **1** ((*of a period of time*) *involving change*) change-over, changing, conversion, developmental, evolutionary, intermediate, transition, unsettled. **2** (*temporary*) provisional, temporary. ANTONYMS: established, permanent.

transitory *a.* (*lasting only a short time, transient*) brief, ephemeral, evanescent, fleeting, flying, fugacious, fugitive, here today and gone tomorrow, impermanent, momentary, mutable, passing, short, short-lived, short-term, temporary, transient. ANTONYMS: constant, durable, long-lasting, permanent, perpetual.

translate *v.t.* **1** (*to render or express the sense of (a word, passage or work) into or in another language*) construe, convert, interpret, render, transcribe, transliterate. **2** (*to express in clearer terms*) decipher, decode, elucidate, explain, make clear, paraphrase, put in plain English, rephrase, reword, simplify, spell out. **3** (*to interpret (as)*) construe, interpret, read, understand. **4** (*to transform, to change*) alter, change, convert, metamorphose, transfigure, transform, transmute.

translation *n.* **1** (*the act or process of translating*) construction, conversion, interpretation, rendering, rendition, transcription, transliteration. **2** (*the product of translating; a rendition of the sense of a passage etc. in another language*) interpretation, rendition, transcription, transliteration. **3** (*the act of expressing in clearer terms*) deciphering, decoding, elucidation, explanation, paraphrasing, rephrasing, rewording, simplification, spelling out. **4** (*the act of transforming or changing*) change, conversion, metamorphosis, transfiguration, transformation, transmutation.

translucent *a.* (*allowing light to pass through but not transparent*) clear, diaphanous, limpid, lucent, pellucid, semi-transparent. ANTONYMS: opaque.

transmission *n.* **1** (*the act of sending something from one person or place to another*) carriage, conveying, dispatch, sending, shipment, transport. **2** (*the act of communicating something from one person or place to another*) communication, dissemination, imparting, spreading, transfer, transference. **3** (*the act of broadcasting a TV or radio programme*) broadcasting, relay, sending out. **4** (*a radio or TV broadcast*) broadcast, programme, show.

transmit *v.t.* **1** (*to send or convey from one person or place to another*) carry, convey, dispatch, send, transport. **2** (*to communicate from one person or place to another*) communicate, disseminate, hand on, impart, pass on, spread, transfer. **3** (*to broadcast* (*a TV or radio programme*)) broadcast, put on air, relay, send out.

transmute *v.t.* (*to change from one form, nature or substance into another; to transform* (*into*)) alter, change, convert, metamorphose, transfigure, transform.

transparency *n.* **1** (*the state of being easily seen through, clearness*) clarity, clearness, diaphaneity, diaphanousness, filminess, gauziness, glassiness, limpidity, limpidness, pellucidity, pellucidness, sheerness, translucence, translucency, transparence. ANTONYMS: darkness, murkiness, opaqueness. **2** (*the state of being obvious or evident*) discernibility, distinctness, obviousness, patentness, perceptibility, plainness, unmistakableness, visibleness. ANTONYMS: imperceptibility, indistinctness, vagueness. **3** (*frankness, sincerity*) artlessness, candidness, directness, forthrightness, frankness, ingenuousness, openness, plainness, plain-spokenness, sincerity, straightforwardness, straightness.

transparent *a.* **1** (*easily seen through*) clear, crystal-clear, crystalline, diaphanous, filmy, gauzy, glassy, limpid, lucent, pellucid, see-through, sheer, translucent. ANTONYMS: dark, murky, opaque. **2** (*plain, evident*) apparent, clear, crystal-clear, discernible, distinct, evident, manifest, noticeable, obvious, perceptible, plain, (*coll.*) plain as the nose on your face, plain to see, recognizable, undisguised, unmistakable, visible. ANTONYMS: imperceptible, indistinct, unclear, vague. **3** (*frank, sincere*) artless, candid, direct, forthright,

frank, ingenuous, open, plain-spoken, sincere, straight, straightforward. ANTONYMS: disingenuous, dissembling, insincere.

transpire *v.i.* **1** (*to leak out, become known*) become known, be disclosed, be revealed, come out, come to light, emerge. ANTONYMS: be concealed, remain secret. **2** (*to happen*) arise, befall, chance, come about, happen, occur, take place.

transport[1] *v.t.* **1** (*to carry or convey from one place to another*) bear, bring, carry, cart, convey, fetch, move, remove, shift, ship, take, transfer. **2** (*to remove* (*a criminal*) *to a penal colony*) banish, deport, exile, expatriate. **3** (*to carry away by powerful emotion, to entrance*) bewitch, captivate, carry away, charm, delight, enchant, enrapture, enthral, entrance, move, overjoy, ravish, spellbind, thrill. ANTONYMS: bore, depress.

transport[2] *n.* **1** (*transportation, conveyance from one place to another*) carriage, conveyance, transference, transportation. **2** (*a vehicle, aircraft etc. used for transporting people or goods*) car, conveyance, lorry, ship, transportation, truck, van, vehicle. **3** (*ecstasy*) bliss, delight, ecstasy, elation, euphoria, exhilaration, intense feeling, joy, passion, rapture, strong emotion. **in transports** (*extremely joyful*) delighted, ecstatic, elated, euphoric, exhilarated, in raptures, in seventh heaven, joyful, (*coll.*) on cloud nine, over the moon. ANTONYMS: depressed, in the doldrums, in the dumps, melancholy.

transpose *v.t.* (*to cause to change places*) exchange, interchange, rearrange, reorder, reverse, swap, switch, transfer.

transverse *a.* (*lying or being across or in a cross direction*) athwart, cross, crossways, crosswise, diagonal, oblique.

trap *n.* **1** (*a contrivance for catching an animal*) ambush, booby trap, gin, net, pitfall, snare, springe. **2** (*a trick or artifice for misleading or betraying a person, a stratagem*) ambush, artifice, deception, device, ploy, ruse, stratagem, subterfuge, trick, wile.
~*v.t.* **1** (*to catch in or as in a trap*) catch, corner, enmesh, ensnare, entrap, snare. ANTONYMS: release, set free. **2** (*to retain, to hold back*) confine, cut off, hold back, imprison. **3** (*to deceive, to ensnare*) ambush, beguile, deceive, dupe, ensnare, entrap, inveigle, trick.

trappings *n.pl.* (*decorations, adornments, esp. those of or relating to an office etc.*) accoutrements, adornments, appointments, appurtenances, decorations, equipment, finery, fittings,

furnishings, gear, livery, ornamentation, ornaments, paraphernalia, (*coll.*) things, trimmings.

trash *n.* **1** (*nonsense*) balderdash, (*sl.*) bilge,
drivel, garbage, nonsense, rubbish, (*coll.*)
tripe, twaddle. **2** (*domestic refuse*) garbage,
junk, litter, refuse, (*coll.*) rot, rubbish, waste.
3 (*a poor or worthless person or group of
people*) rabble, riff-raff, scum.

trashy *a.* (*of poor quality, worthless*) cheap,
cheapjack, inferior, meretricious, rubbishy,
shoddy, tawdry, worthless. ANTONYMS: first-
rate, valuable, worthwhile.

trauma *n.* **1** (*a psychological shock having a
lasting effect on the subconscious*) damage,
disorder, shock. **2** (*a distressing experience*)
disturbance, jolt, ordeal, shock, upheaval,
upset. **3** (*a wound or external injury*) injury,
lesion, wound. **4** (*distress, anguish*) agony,
anguish, distress, hurt, pain, strain, suffering,
torture.

traumatic *a.* **1** (*of or causing trauma*) agonizing, distressing, hurtful, painful, upsetting,
wounding. ANTONYMS: healing, soothing.
2 (*distressing*) disagreeable, distressing, irksome, troublesome, unpleasant. ANTONYMS:
agreeable, pleasant.

travel *v.i.* **1** (*to make a journey, esp. to distant or
foreign lands*) commute, journey, make a
journey, roam, take a trip, tour. **2** (*to move, to
go*) advance, be transmitted, go, move, proceed, progress. **3** (*to move quickly*) go at breakneck speed, go flat out, (*coll.*) go hell for
leather, (*coll.*) go like a bat out of hell, speed,
(*coll.*) tear up the miles. ANTONYMS: crawl,
creep.
~*v.t.* (*to journey over*) cross, journey, make one's
way over, range, roam, rove, traverse, wander.
~*n.* **1** (*the act of travelling*) journeying, touring,
travelling. **2** (*a journey or trip*) excursion, expedition, exploration, globe-trotting, journey,
journeying, sightseeing, tour, trip, voyage,
wandering.

traveller *n.* **1** (*a person who travels*) explorer,
globe-trotter, holidaymaker, journeyer, tourist,
tripper, wanderer. **2** (*a commercial traveller*)
agent, commercial traveller, (*coll.*) rep, representative, travelling salesman. **3** (*a gypsy*)
gypsy, itinerant, nomad.

traverse *v.t.* **1** (*to travel across*) cross, cut
across, go across, go over, make one's way
across, make one's way over, pass across, pass
over, travel across, travel over. **2** (*to lie across
or through*) cross, extend across, go across, lie
across, stretch across.

travesty *n.* (*a parody or ridiculous misrepresentation*) burlesque, caricature, distortion,

lampoon, misrepresentation, mockery, parody,
perversion, satire, (*coll.*) send-up, sham, spoof,
(*coll.*) take-off.
~*v.t.* (*to make a travesty of, to burlesque*)
burlesque, caricature, distort, lampoon, make
fun of, misrepresent, mock, satirize, (*coll.*)
send up, spoof, (*coll.*) take off.

treacherous *a.* **1** (*violating allegiance, disloyal*) back-stabbing, deceitful, disloyal, (*coll.*)
double-crossing, double-dealing, duplicitous,
faithless, false, false-hearted, perfidious, traitorous, (*coll.*) two-timing, untrue, untrustworthy. ANTONYMS: faithful, loyal, true.
2 (*unreliable, unsafe*) dangerous, deceptive,
(*coll.*) dicey, hazardous, perilous, precarious,
risky, unreliable, unsafe, unstable. ANTONYMS:
reliable, safe.

treachery *n.* (*the state of being treacherous*)
back-stabbing, betrayal, deceit, deceitfulness,
deception, disloyalty, (*coll.*) double-crossing,
double-dealing, duplicitousness, duplicity,
faithlessness, false-heartedness, falseness, infidelity, perfidiousness, perfidy, stab in the
back, traitorousness, treason, (*coll.*) two-
timing, unfaithfulness, untrustworthiness.
ANTONYMS: allegiance, faithfulness, loyalty,
trustworthiness.

tread *v.i.* (*to walk, to go*) go, step, tramp, walk.
~*v.t.* **1** (*to step or walk on*) put one's foot on, set
one's foot on, stamp on, step on, tramp on,
walk on. **2** (*to crush with the feet*) crush, flatten, squash, trample.
~*n.* **1** (*the act or manner of walking*) gait, step,
walk. **2** (*the sound of walking, a footstep*) footfall, footstep. **to tread on someone's toes** (*to
offend someone's susceptibilities*) hurt, hurt
the feelings of, offend, upset, vex.

treason *n.* (*a violation of allegiance by a subject
against the sovereign or government*) disaffection, disloyalty, high treason, lese-majesty,
mutiny, perfidy, rebellion, sedition, subversion, traitorousness, treachery. ANTONYMS:
allegiance, loyalty, patriotism.

treasonable *a.* (*consisting of or involving
treason*) disloyal, mutinous, perfidious, rebellious, seditious, subversive, traitorous, treacherous. ANTONYMS: faithful, loyal, patriotic.

treasure *n.* **1** (*precious metals in any form, or
gems*) cash, coins, fortune, gems, gold, jewels,
money, riches, valuables, wealth. **2** (*anything
highly valued, a precious or highly-prized
thing, esp. if portable*) prized possession. **3** (*a
person greatly valued, a beloved person*) apple
of one's eye, darling, gem, jewel, jewel in the
crown, pearl, pride and joy, prize.
~*v.t.* **1** (*to lay* (*up*) *as valuable, to hoard*) accumulate, collect, garner, hoard, lay up, salt

away, save, squirrel away, stash away, store up. ANTONYMS: discard, get rid of, spend, throw away. **2** (*to prize, to lay* (*up*) *in the memory as valuable*) cherish, hold dear, prize, revere, set great store by, think highly of, value, venerate. ANTONYMS: despise, hold in contempt, think little of.

treat *v.t.* **1** (*to act or behave to or towards*) act towards, behave towards, cope with, deal with, handle, look upon, manage, regard, use, view. **2** (*to deal with or manipulate for a particular result, to apply a particular process to*) apply to, put on, use on. **3** (*to apply medical care to*) apply treatment to, cure, give medication to, give treatment to, medicate. **4** (*to handle or express* (*a subject etc.*) *in a particular way*) deal with, discuss, express, handle, present, talk about, write about. **5** (*to supply with food, drink or entertainment at one's expense*) entertain, foot the bill for, pay for, pay the bill for, stand, take out, wine and dine.
~*v.i.* (*to arrange terms* (*with*)*, to negotiate*) bargain, confer, discuss terms, have talks, hold talks, negotiate, parley, talk.

treatise *n.* (*a literary composition expounding, discussing and illustrating some particular subject in a thorough way*) disquisition, dissertation, essay, exposition, monograph, pamphlet, paper, study, thesis, tract, work.

treatment *n.* **1** (*any medical procedure intended to bring about a cure*) care, cure, first aid, healing, medical care, medication, remedy, therapy. **2** (*the act or manner of treating*) action, behaviour, conduct, dealing, management, use.

treaty *n.* (*an agreement formally concluded and ratified between different states*) agreement, alliance, bargain, compact, concordat, contract, covenant, deal, entente, pact.

trek *v.i.* (*to journey, esp. with difficulty on foot*) hike, journey, march, plod, range, roam, rove, slog, (*coll.*) traipse, tramp, travel, trudge, walk, yomp.
~*n.* (*any long, arduous journey, esp. on foot*) expedition, hike, journey, march, roam, slog, tramp, trip, trudge, walk, yomp.

trellis *n.* (*a lattice, a grating*) fretwork, grating, grid, grille, lattice, mesh, network.

tremble *v.i.* **1** (*to shake involuntarily, as with fear, cold etc.*) quiver, shake, shiver, twitch, wiggle. **2** (*to be in a state of fear or agitation*) be anxious, be apprehensive, be fearful, be frightened, quake, shake in one's shoes, shiver with fear. **3** (*to totter, to quaver*) oscillate, quaver, quiver, rock, shake, teeter, totter, vibrate, wobble. ANTONYMS: be stable, be steady.

~*n.* **1** (*the act or state of trembling*) quivering, shaking, shivering, tremor, twitching, wiggling. **2** (*the act or state of quavering or oscillating*) oscillation, quavering, quivering, rocking, shaking, vibration, wobbling. **all of a tremble** (*very agitated*) agitated, anxious, flustered, (*coll.*) in a flap, nervous, nervy, on edge, on tenterhooks, worked up. ANTONYMS: calm, cool, calm and collected.

tremendous *a.* **1** (*of overpowering magnitude, violence etc.*) colossal, enormous, gargantuan, gigantic, great, huge, immense, large, mammoth, massive, prodigious, stupendous, terrific, vast, (*sl.*) whopping. ANTONYMS: diminutive, minuscule, small, tiny. **2** (*extraordinary, considerable*) brilliant, excellent, exceptional, extraordinary, (*coll.*) fabulous, (*coll.*) fantastic, (*coll.*) great, incredible, (*coll.*) magnificent, marvellous, outstanding, (*coll.*) sensational, (*coll.*) super, (*coll.*) terrific, very good, wonderful. ANTONYMS: dreadful, ordinary, poor, run-of-the-mill.

tremor *n.* **1** (*a trembling or quivering*) judder, paroxysm, quaver, shake, shaking, shiver, spasm, tremble, trembling, twitch. **2** (*a thrill*) (*sl.*) buzz, (*sl.*) charge, glow, thrill, tingle.

tremulous *a.* **1** (*trembling, quivering*) quivering, quivery, shaking, shaky, trembling, vibrating, weak. ANTONYMS: steady, strong. **2** (*timid, irresolute*) anxious, diffident, fearful, hesitant, irresolute, nervous, timid, uncertain, wavering. ANTONYMS: certain, confident, resolute.

trench *n.* (*a long narrow cut or deep furrow in the earth, a ditch*) channel, conduit, cut, ditch, drain, duct, earthwork, furrow, gutter, trough, waterway.

trenchant *a.* (*cutting, incisive*) acerbic, acid, astringent, biting, caustic, cutting, harsh, incisive, keen, mordant, penetrating, piercing, pointed, sarcastic, scathing, sharp, tart. ANTONYMS: mellow, soft, soothing.

trend *n.* **1** (*a general tendency or inclination*) bent, bias, course, current, drift, inclination, leaning, tendency. **2** (*a mode, fashion*) craze, fad, fashion, look, mode, (*coll.*) rage, style, vogue.

trendsetter *n.* (*a person who originates or dictates fashions*) arbiter of taste, fashion leader, leader of fashion, pace-setter.

trendy *a.* (*following the latest trends, fashionable*) fashionable, in fashion, in vogue, latest, modish, stylish, (*coll.*) up-to-the-minute, (*coll.*) with it.

trepidation *n.* (*a state of alarm or agitation*) agitation, alarm, anxiety, apprehension, (*coll.*)

butterflies in the stomach, (*coll.*) cold feet, cold sweat, consternation, dismay, disquiet, dread, fear, fright, (*sl.*) jitters, nerves, nervousness, palpitations, panic, trembling, uneasiness, unrest, worry. ANTONYMS: calm, calmness, composure, confidence, coolness.

trespass *n.* (*a wrongful act involving injury to the person or property of another, esp. unauthorized entry into another's land*) encroachment, illegal entry, infringement, intrusion, invasion, unlawful entry, wrongful entry.

~*v.i.* (*to commit an illegal intrusion* (*upon the property or personal rights of another*)) encroach on, infringe on, intrude on, invade.

trespasser *n.* (*a person who trespasses*) encroacher, gatecrasher, infringer, interloper, intruder, invader.

tress *n.* (*hair*) curls, hair, locks.

triad *n.* (*a collection of three*) threesome, trinity, trio, triplets, triumvirate, troika.

trial *n.* **1** (*the judicial examination and determination of the issues in a cause between parties before a judge, judge and jury or a referee*) case, court case, court hearing, inquiry, judicial investigation, legal investigation, litigation, tribunal. **2** (*experimental treatment*) probation, testing period, trial period. **3** (*a test, an experiment*) assay, check, (*coll.*) dry run, dummy run, examination, experiment, test, testing, test run, trial run, try-out. **4** (*a person who or thing which tries or tests strength, endurance, and other qualities*) affliction, annoyance, bane, bother, burden, cross to bear, (*coll.*) drag, (*coll.*) hassle, irritant, nuisance, (*coll.*) pain in the neck, pest, thorn in one's side, worry. ANTONYMS: comfort, delight, joy. **5** (*hardship, suffering etc.*) adversity, affliction, anxiety, burden, cross to bear, distress, grief, hardship, hard times, misery, ordeal, pain, suffering, trials and tribulations, tribulation, trouble, unhappiness, woe, worry, wretchedness. ANTONYMS: comfort, ease, happiness, joy.

~*v.t.* (*to subject to a performance test*) give a trial to, put through one's paces, put to the test, test, try out.

~*a.* (*experimental*) experimental, exploratory, pilot, probationary, testing.

tribe *n.* **1** (*a group of people ethnologically related and forming a community or a political division*) clan, dynasty, ethnic group, family, people. **2** (*a number of persons of the same character, profession etc.*) band, collection, company, crowd, gang, group, horde, number, party.

tribulation *n.* **1** (*severe affliction, suffering*) adversity, affliction, bad luck, distress, grief,

hardship, hard times, (*coll.*) hassle, misery, ordeal, pain, sadness, suffering, trials and tribulations, trouble, unhappiness, woe, worry, wretchedness. ANTONYMS: comfort, ease, happiness, joy. **2** (*a cause of this*) blow, burden, cross to bear, nuisance, pest, thorn in one's side.

tribunal *n.* **1** (*a court of justice*) court, hearing, industrial tribunal, judicial examination. **2** (*a board of arbitrators etc.*) arbitration board, court, forum, industrial tribunal.

tribute *n.* **1** (*a contribution or offering* (*of praise etc.*)) accolade, acknowledgement, applause, commendation, compliment, congratulations, contribution, encomium, eulogy, gratitude, homage, honour, laudation, paean, panegyric, praise, present, recognition, testimonial. **2** (*a praiseworthy thing attributable* (*to*)) evidence, indication, manifestation, proof, testimonial.

trick *n.* **1** (*an artifice, an artful device or stratagem*) artifice, (*sl.*) con, deceit, deception, device, dodge, fraud, ploy, (*sl.*) scam, sting, stratagem, subterfuge, swindle, wile. **2** (*an optical illusion*) mirage, trick of the light. **3** (*an ingenious or peculiar way of doing something, a knack*) ability, art, expertise, gift, (*coll.*) hang, knack, (*coll.*) know-how, skill, talent, technique. **4** (*a feat of dexterity, esp. of legerdemain or sleight of hand*) juggling, legerdemain, prestidigitation, sleight of hand. **5** (*a foolish or malicious act, a prank*) caper, hoax, jape, joke, lark. **6** (*a particular habit or practice, a mannerism*) characteristic, eccentricity, foible, habit, idiosyncrasy, mannerism, peculiarity, practice, quirk, trait.

~*v.t.* (*to cheat, to deceive* (*into, out of etc.*)) bamboozle, cheat, (*sl.*) con, cozen, deceive, defraud, delude, dupe, fool, gull, have (someone) on, hoax, hoodwink, mislead, outwit, (*N Am., coll.*) pull a fast one on, pull the wool over (someone's) eyes, (*coll.*) put one over on, (*N Am., coll.*) shaft, (*sl.*) sting, swindle, (*coll.*) take in, trap. **to do the trick** (*to achieve the required effect*) be effective, be effectual, be successful, have effect, produce the desired result, succeed, work. ANTONYMS: fail. **to trick out** (*to decorate, to dress up*) adorn, array, bedeck, deck out, decorate, (*coll.*) doll up, dress up, embellish, ornament, prink.

trickery *n.* (*duplicity, guile*) artifice, cheating, chicanery, (*sl.*) con, craft, craftiness, cunning, deceit, deception, dishonesty, double-dealing, duplicity, fraud, (*coll.*) funny business, guile, (*coll.*) hanky-panky, (*coll.*) jiggery-pokery, (*coll.*) monkey business, pretence, (*coll.*) skulduggery, swindling, wiles, wiliness. ANTONYMS: artlessness, honesty, openness.

trickle *v.i.* (*to flow in drops or in a small stream*) come out gradually, come out in dribbles, dribble, drip, drop, exude, leak, ooze, percolate, seep. ANTONYMS: pour, rush, stream.

trickster *n.* **1** (*a person who plays tricks*) hoaxer, joker, practical joker, prankster. **2** (*a person who deceives or cheats someone*) charlatan, cheat, (*sl.*) con artist, confidence man, (*sl.*) conman, deceiver, dissembler, fraud, fraudster, hoodwinker, impostor, mountebank, swindler.

tricky *a.* **1** (*difficult, awkward*) awkward, complex, complicated, delicate, difficult, knotty, precarious, problematic, risky, sensitive, sticky, thorny, ticklish, touchy. ANTONYMS: simple, straightforward, uncomplicated. **2** (*deceitful*) artful, crafty, cunning, deceitful, deceptive, devious, dishonest, foxy, scheming, slippery, sly, wily. ANTONYMS: above board, artless, honest, sincere, truthful.

trifle *n.* **1** (*a thing, matter etc. of no value or importance*) bagatelle, inessential, nothing, piece of trivia, something of no consequence, something of no import, something of no importance, thing of no consequence, thing of no importance. **2** (*a small amount of money etc.*) hardly anything, next to nothing, (*coll.*) piddling amount, (*coll.*) piddling sum, pittance. ANTONYMS: fortune, king's ransom, mint, (*coll.*) packet. **3** (*something of little value, bauble*) bauble, gewgaw, knick-knack, toy, trinket, whatnot. **4** (*a small amount of something*) bit, dash, drop, jot, little, pinch, spot, touch, trace. ANTONYMS: a great deal, a lot, (*coll.*) tons.
~*v.i.* (*to act or talk with levity*) amuse oneself, fool about, fritter away one's time, idle, mess about, potter about, waste time. **to trifle with 1** (*to treat with levity or lack of proper seriousness*) deal with casually, dismiss, fail to take seriously, treat in a cavalier fashion, treat lightly. ANTONYMS: take seriously, treat seriously. **2** (*to flirt with*) amuse oneself with, dally with, flirt with, play around with, toy with.

trifling *a.* **1** (*insignificant, trivial*) inconsequential, insignificant, petty, trivial, unimportant. ANTONYMS: crucial, important, significant, vital. **2** ((*of a sum of money*) *very small*) minuscule, negligible, paltry, (*coll.*) piddling, small, tiny, valueless, worthless. ANTONYMS: huge, large, valuable.

trigger *v.t.* **1** (*to cause to happen, to set off*) bring about, cause, give rise to, prompt, provoke, set in motion, set off, spark off, start. ANTONYMS: bring to an end, end, obstruct, put a stop to. **2** (*to activate, to put into operation*) activate, start, switch on, turn on. ANTONYMS: switch off, turn off.

trim *v.t.* **1** (*to remove irregularities, excrescences or superfluous or unsightly parts from*) clip, crop, cut, even up, neaten, pare, prune, shave, shear, snip, tidy up. **2** (*to cut or clip* (*those*) *away or off*) chop, clip, cut off, hack off, lop, remove, take off. **3** (*to reduce* (*e.g. costs*)) curtail, cut back on, decrease, diminish, dock, reduce, retrench. ANTONYMS: increase. **4** (*to decorate, to ornament* (*with trimmings etc.*)) adorn, bedeck, deck out, decorate, dress, embellish, festoon, ornament, trick out. **5** (*to decorate* (*e.g. a piece of clothing*) *esp. round the edges*) border, decorate, edge, embellish, embroider, fringe, ornament, pipe.
~*a.* **1** (*properly adjusted, in good order*) in good order, neat, neat and tidy, orderly, shipshape and Bristol fashion, spick and span, tidy, well-cared-for, well-looked-after, well-maintained. ANTONYMS: neglected, untidy. **2** (*well-equipped, smart*) groomed, neat, neat and tidy, smart, soigné(e), spruce, tidy, well-groomed, well-turned-out. ANTONYMS: sloppy, unkempt, untidy. **3** (*slim, in good condition*) fit, in good condition, in good shape, lean, slender, slim, svelte, willowy. ANTONYMS: fat, out of condition, unfit.
~*n.* **1** (*material used to trim clothes etc.*) adornment, border, decoration, edging, embellishment, embroidery, frills, fringe, fringing, ornamentation, piping, trimming. **2** (*an act of trimming, esp. hair*) clip, clipping, cropping, cut, cutting, haircut, neatening, paring, pruning, shave, shaving, shearing, snipping, tidyup. **3** (*good condition*) condition, fettle, fitness, good condition, good health, good order, good repair, good shape, shape.

trimming *n.* **1** (*material sewn on a garment for ornament*) adornment, border, decoration, edging, embellishment, embroidery, frills, fringe, fringing, ornamentation, piping, trim. **2** (*pl., coll.*) (*accessories to a dish*) accompaniments, extras, (*coll.*) frills, garnish, garnishings. **3** (*pl.*) (*anything additional to the main item*) accessories, accoutrements, appurtenances, extras, (*coll.*) frills, trappings. **4** (*pl.*) (*pieces trimmed off*) clippings, cuttings, parings, shavings.

trinket *n.* **1** (*a small personal ornament of no great value as a jewel, esp. a ring*) piece of costume jewellery. **2** (*any small ornament or fancy article*) bauble, gewgaw, knick-knack, ornament, piece of bric-a-brac, trifle, whatnot.

trio *n.* (*a set of three*) threesome, triad, trilogy, trine, trinity, triplets, triptych, triumvirate, triune, troika.

trip *v.i.* **1** (*to walk or run lightly or nimbly*) cavort, dance, frisk, hop, leap, prance, skip, spring, waltz. **2** (*to catch the foot* (*over* *something*) *so as nearly to fall, to stumble*) fall, lose one's balance, lose one's footing, slip, stumble. **3** (*to err, to go wrong*) be wrong, blunder, (*coll.*) boob, bungle, err, fail, lapse, make a botch of something, make a mistake, slip up.

~*v.t.* **1** (*to catch or detect in a mistake or offence*) catch out, (*coll.*) outsmart, outwit, (*coll.*) wrong-foot. **2** (*to activate, to set off*) activate, release, set off, switch on, throw, trigger, turn on. ANTONYMS: switch off, turn off.

~*n.* **1** (*a short excursion or journey*) excursion, expedition, foray, jaunt, journey, outing, run, tour, voyage. **2** (*a stumble, a false step*) false step, misstep, slip, stumble. **3** (*a failure, a mistake*) blunder, (*coll.*) boob, botch, bungle, error, failure, faux pas, lapse, mistake, oversight, slip, slip-up, wrongdoing.

tripe *n.* (*silly stuff, nonsense*) balderdash, (*sl.*) bilge, (*sl.*) bosh, (*taboo sl.*) bullshit, bunkum, (*sl.*) crap, drivel, garbage, (*coll.*) guff, nonsense, (*coll.*) piffle, (*sl.*) poppycock, (*coll.*) rot, rubbish, (*coll.*) tommyrot, twaddle.

triple *a.* **1** (*consisting of three parts or three things united, threefold*) threefold, three-way, tripartite. **2** (*multiplied by three*) three times the usual, treble.

~*v.t.* (*to treble, to make threefold*) increase threefold, treble.

tripper *n.* (*a person who goes on a trip, an excursionist*) excursionist, holidaymaker, sightseer, tourist, traveller.

trite *a.* (*commonplace, hackneyed*) banal, clichéd, commonplace, (*coll.*) corny, dull, hackneyed, humdrum, ordinary, overused, pedestrian, platitudinous, routine, run-of-the-mill, stale, stereotyped, stock, tired, unimaginative, uninspired, unoriginal, worn out. ANTONYMS: exciting, fresh, imaginative, novel, original.

triumph *n.* **1** (*victory, success*) ascendancy, conquest, success, victory, win. ANTONYMS: defeat, failure, loss. **2** (*joy or exultation at a success*) elation, exultation, happiness, joy, jubilation, pride, rejoicing. ANTONYMS: disappointment, misery, sadness. **3** (*a great example*) coup, feat, great achievement, hit, master stroke, supreme example, tour de force. ANTONYMS: failure, fiasco, (*coll.*) flop.

~*v.i.* **1** (*to gain a victory, to prevail* (*over*)) achieve success, be successful, be the victor, be victorious, carry the day, come first, come out on top, gain a victory, prevail, succeed, take the honours, take the prize, win, win the day. ANTONYMS: be defeated, be the vanquished, be unsuccessful, lose. **2** (*to boast or exult* (*over*)) be elated, be jubilant, boast, brag, celebrate,

crow, exult, gloat, glory, rejoice, revel, swagger. ANTONYMS: be modest, hold one's head in shame, show one's disappointment.

triumphant *a.* **1** (*victorious, successful*) conquering, dominant, successful, undefeated, victorious, winning. ANTONYMS: losing, unsuccessful, vanquished. **2** (*exultant*) boastful, bragging, celebratory, cock-a-hoop, elated, exultant, gloating, joyful, jubilant, proud, rejoicing, swaggering, triumphal. ANTONYMS: disappointed, modest.

trivia *n.pl.* (*trifles, inessentials*) inessentials, minutiae, petty details, trifles, trivialities. ANTONYMS: basics, essentials, fundamentals.

trivial *a.* **1** (*of little value or importance, trifling*) inconsequential, inessential, insignificant, insubstantial, minor, negligible, of no account, of no matter, paltry, petty, (*coll.*) piddling, slight, trifling, unimportant, valueless, worthless. ANTONYMS: crucial, important, major, significant, valuable, vital. **2** (*concerned with trivia*) feather-brained, frivolous, giddy, silly. ANTONYMS: earnest, grave, serious, solemn.

triviality *n.* **1** (*the state of being trivial*) inconsequence, insignificance, negligibility, paltriness, pettiness, unimportance, worthlessness. ANTONYMS: consequence, importance, significance, value, worth. **2** (*something unimportant*) detail, mere detail, nothing of consequence, nothing of importance, petty detail, trifle.

trivialize *v.t.* (*to cause to seem trivial, to minimize*) belittle, deprecate, make light of, minimize, play down, underestimate, underplay, undervalue. ANTONYMS: make much of, maximize, overestimate, overvalue.

trollop *n.* **1** (*a careless, slovenly woman, a slattern*) slattern, slovenly woman, slut. **2** (*a woman of bad character; a prostitute*) fallen woman, †harlot, (*sl.*) hooker, loose woman, (*sl.*) scrubber, (*sl.*) slag, slut, streetwalker, †strumpet, (*sl.*) tart, whore.

troop *n.* **1** (*an assemblage of persons or animals, a crowd*) assemblage, band, body, bunch, company, contingent, crew, crowd, drove, flock, gang, gathering, group, herd, horde, host, mob, multitude, pack, squad, stream, swarm, team, throng, unit. **2** (*pl.*) (*soldiers*) armed forces, armed services, army, fighting men and women, military, soldiers.

~*v.i.* (*to move* (*along a way etc.*) *in a troop*) crowd, flock, mill, stream, surge, swarm, throng.

trophy *n.* (*anything, esp. a cup, preserved as a memorial of victory or success*) award, booty, cup, laurels, prize, spoils.

tropical *a.* ((*of the weather*) *very hot*) hot, humid, steamy, stifling, sultry, sweltering, torrid. ANTONYMS: arctic, chilly, cold, freezing, icy.

trot *v.i.* (*to run with short brisk strides*) canter, jog, run, scamper. **on the trot** (*one after the other, successively*) consecutively, in a row, in succession, one after the other, without a break, without interruption. ANTONYMS: intermittently, occasionally. **to trot out** (*to utter* (*esp. something familiar or trite*)) come out with, recite, reiterate, repeat, utter.

trouble *v.t.* **1** (*to agitate, to disturb*) agitate, bother, distress, disturb, harass, (*coll.*) hassle, perturb, pester, plague, torment, upset, worry. ANTONYMS: calm, calm down. **2** (*to distress, to afflict*) afflict, burden, incapacitate, oppress, weigh down. **3** (*to inconvenience, to put to some exertion or pains*) bother, disturb, impose upon, incommode, inconvenience, put (someone) out, put to trouble. ANTONYMS: accommodate, assist, help.
~*v.i.* (*to take trouble or pains*) bother, exert oneself, go out of one's way, go to the effort, go to the trouble, take pains, take the time, take the trouble.
~*n.* **1** (*distress, worry*) adversity, affliction, agitation, anxiety, bother, difficulty, disquiet, distress, grief, harassment, hardship, (*coll.*) hassle, heartache, inconvenience, irritation, misery, misfortune, pain, problems, sadness, sorrow, suffering, torment, trials and tribulations, tribulation, vexation, woe, worry. ANTONYMS: ease, good fortune, happiness, peace. **2** (*exertion, inconvenience*) bother, effort, exertion, fuss, (*coll.*) hassle, inconvenience, labour, pains, work. **3** (*a cause of this*) bother, (*coll.*) hassle, inconvenience, nuisance, pest, problem. **4** (*a fault; something amiss*) blemish, defect, difficulty, disadvantage, failing, fault, imperfection, problem, shortcoming, weakness. ANTONYMS: advantage, asset, benefit. **5** (*fighting or unrest*) conflict, disorder, disturbance, fighting, rowing, strife, tumult, unrest, war. ANTONYMS: harmony, peace. **6** (*an illness*) affliction, ailment, complaint, disease, dysfunction, illness, upset. **in trouble 1** (*liable to suffer punishment or misfortune*) in a jam, in a mess, (*coll.*) in a pickle, in a predicament, in a spot, in a tight corner, in difficulty, in dire straits, (*coll.*) in hot water. **2** (*pregnant when not married*) (*coll.*) expecting, having a baby, (*sl.*) having a bun in the oven, (*sl.*) in the club, (*sl.*) up the spout.

troublemaker *n.* (*a person who stirs up discontent, strife etc.*) agent provocateur, agitator, inciter, instigator, mischief-maker, rabble-rouser, stormy petrel. ANTONYMS: arbitrator, conciliator, peace-maker.

troublesome *a.* (*annoying, vexatious*) annoying, arduous, bothersome, burdensome, demanding, difficult, disturbing, hard, irksome, irritating, problematic, taxing, tricky, trying, upsetting, vexatious, worrisome, worrying. ANTONYMS: easy, simple, undemanding.

trough *n.* **1** (*a long, narrow receptacle for holding water, fodder etc., for domestic animals*) crib, manger, rack. **2** (*a deep narrow channel or depression* (*in land, the sea etc.*)) channel, conduit, culvert, depression, ditch, drain, duct, furrow, groove, gully, gutter, trench.

trounce *v.t.* **1** (*to beat severely*) beat, chastise, flog, (*coll.*) give a hiding to, leather, spank, (*coll.*) tan the hide of, thrash, (*coll.*) wallop. **2** (*to inflict a decisive defeat upon*) (*coll.*) blow out of the water, defeat utterly, drub, (*coll.*) give a hiding to, (*coll.*) hammer, (*coll.*) lick, rout, run rings round, (*coll.*) slaughter, (*sl.*) tank, thrash, (*coll.*) walk all over, (*coll.*) wipe the floor with.

troupe *n.* (*a company of actors, performers etc.*) band, cast, company.

trouper *n.* (*a member of such a company*) actor, artiste, entertainer, performer, player, thespian.

trousers *n.pl.* (*a two-legged outer garment reaching from the waist to the ankles*) flannels, jeans, pair of trousers, (*N Am.*) pants, slacks.

truancy *n.* (*the act or practice of playing truant*) absence, absence without leave, malingering, shirking, (*coll.*) skiving.

truant *n.* **1** (*a child who stays away from school without leave*) absentee, chronic absentee, (*coll.*) skiver. **2** (*a person who shirks or neglects duty*) absentee, deserter, dodger, malingerer, shirker, (*coll.*) skiver.
~*a.* (*shirking, idle*) absent, absentee, deserting, malingering, shirking, (*coll.*) skiving, truanting.

truce *n.* (*a temporary cessation of hostilities*) armistice, ceasefire, cessation of hostilities, (*coll.*) let-up, lull in the fighting, moratorium, respite, suspension of hostilities, treaty.

truck[1] *n.* (*a strong, usu. four-wheeled vehicle for conveying heavy goods; a lorry*) articulated lorry, container lorry, heavy goods vehicle, HGV, juggernaut, lorry.

truck[2] *n.* (*dealings*) association, business, communication, connection, contact, dealings, intercourse, relations.

truculent *a.* (*aggressive*) aggressive, antagonistic, bad-tempered, bellicose, belligerent, combative, cross, defiant, fierce, hostile, ill-natured, ill-tempered, obstreperous, pugnacious, sullen, surly, violent. ANTONYMS: agreeable, amiable, civil, peaceable, peace-loving.

trudge *v.i.* (*to travel on foot, esp. with labour and fatigue*) clump, drag oneself along, lumber, plod, slog, stump, tramp, trek, yomp.

true *a.* **1** (*conformable to fact or reality, not false or erroneous*) accurate, correct, factual, reliable, right, truthful, valid, veracious. ANTONYMS: erroneous, false, incorrect, untrue, wrong. **2** (*in accordance with appearance, genuine*) actual, authentic, bona fide, genuine, honest-to-goodness, legitimate, real, valid. ANTONYMS: bogus, counterfeit, fake, (*coll.*) phoney, spurious. **3** (*in accordance with right or law, legitimate*) lawful, (*coll.*) legit, legitimate, rightful. ANTONYMS: illegitimate, unlawful. **4** (*accurate; exact*) accurate, close, correct, exact, faithful, precise, (*coll.*) spot-on, unerring. ANTONYMS: imprecise, inaccurate, inexact, loose. **5** (*faithful, loyal*) constant, dependable, devoted, dutiful, faithful, loyal, reliable, sincere, staunch, steady, trustworthy, trusty, unswerving. ANTONYMS: disloyal, inconstant, treacherous, unfaithful, unreliable, untrustworthy.
~*adv.* **1** (*truly*) candidly, honestly, sincerely, truly, truthfully, with truth. ANTONYMS: dishonestly, insincerely, untruthfully. **2** (*accurately*) accurately, on target, (*coll.*) spot on, unerringly, unswervingly, without deviating.

true-blue *a.* (*staunch, faithful*) confirmed, constant, dedicated, devoted, dyed-in-the-wool, faithful, loyal, staunch, trusty, uncompromising, unwavering. ANTONYMS: disloyal, faithless, inconstant.

truism *n.* (*a self-evident or unquestionable truth*) axiom, cliché, platitude, stock phrase.

truly *adv.* **1** (*sincerely*) candidly, frankly, honestly, openly, pulling no punches, sincerely, truthfully, with sincerity. ANTONYMS: dishonestly, falsely, insincerely. **2** (*genuinely*) genuinely, honestly, indeed, really, truthfully. ANTONYMS: dishonestly, untruthfully. **3** (*in reality*) absolutely, actually, beyond doubt, certainly, decidedly, definitely, indubitably, in fact, in reality, in truth, positively, really, surely, undoubtedly, unquestionably, without question. **4** (*faithfully, honestly*) constantly, dependably, devotedly, dutifully, faithfully, loyally, reliably, sincerely, staunchly, steadfastly, steadily, unswervingly, with all one's heart, with dedication, with devotion. ANTONYMS: half-heartedly, unreliably. **5** (*really, indeed*) extremely, greatly, indeed, really, sincerely, to be sure, very. ANTONYMS: not at all. **6** (*in accordance with truth, accurately*)

accurately, closely, correctly, exactly, faithfully, precisely, unerringly. ANTONYMS: inaccurately, incorrectly, inexactly, loosely.

trump *v.t.* (*to outdo*) outdo, outperform, surpass. **to trump up** (*to invent or fabricate (a charge etc.)*) concoct, contrive, (*coll.*) cook up, devise, fabricate, hatch, invent, make up.

trumpery *n.* (*worthless finery*) baubles, gewgaws, trinkets.

trumpet *v.t.* (*to proclaim by or as by a trumpet*) advertise, announce, broadcast, herald, noise abroad, proclaim, publish.
~*v.i.* ((*esp. of the elephant*) *to make a loud sound like a trumpet*) bellow, roar, shout. ANTONYMS: murmur, whisper.

truncate *v.t.* (*to cut the top or end from*) abbreviate, curtail, cut, cut short, decrease, diminish, dock, lop, pare, prune, reduce, shorten, trim. ANTONYMS: increase, lengthen, prolong, protract, stretch out.

truncheon *n.* (*a short club or cudgel, esp. one carried by a police officer in Britain*) baton, club, cudgel, staff.

trunk *n.* **1** (*the main stem of a tree, as opposed to the branches or roots*) bole, stem, stock. **2** (*the body of an animal apart from the limbs, head and tail*) body, torso. **3** (*a box or chest with a hinged lid for packing clothes etc. in for travel*) box, case, chest, cist, coffer, crate, kist, portmanteau. **4** (*the proboscis of an elephant or any analogous organ*) proboscis, snout.

truss *v.t.* (*to tie up securely, to bind*) bind, fasten, secure, tie up.
~*n.* **1** (*a supporting and strengthening structure in a roof, bridge etc.*) beam, brace, buttress, joist, prop, stay, strut, support. **2** (*a padded belt or other apparatus worn round the body for preventing or compressing a hernia*) support. **3** (*a bundle of hay or straw*) bale, bundle, roll.

trust *n.* **1** (*confident reliance on or belief in the integrity, veracity etc. of a person or thing*) belief, confidence, faith, reliance. ANTONYMS: distrust, doubt, mistrust, scepticism. **2** (*the obligation of a person who has received such a charge*) commitment, duty, obligation, responsibility. **3** (*care, safe keeping*) care, charge, custody, guardianship, protection, safe keeping, trusteeship.
~*v.t.* **1** (*to place confidence in, to believe in*) bank on, believe in, count on, depend on, have confidence in, have faith in, have trust in, pin one's faith on, place confidence in, rely on, swear by. ANTONYMS: distrust, have no confidence in, lack faith in, mistrust. **2** (*to believe, to have a confident hope or expectation*) assume, believe, expect, hope, presume,

suppose, surmise, think likely. **3** (*to commit to the care of a person, to entrust*) assign, commit, consign, delegate, entrust, put into the hands of, sign over, turn over to.

trustful *a.* (*full of trust, esp. when this is naïve*) credulous, gullible, ingenuous, innocent, naïve, simple, trusting, unsuspecting, unsuspicious, unwary. ANTONYMS: cautious, distrustful, suspicious, wary.

trusting *a.* (*full of trust, esp. when this is naïve*) credulous, gullible, ingenuous, innocent, naïve, simple, trustful, unsuspecting, unsuspicious, unwary. ANTONYMS: cautious, distrustful, suspicious, wary.

trustworthy *a.* (*deserving of trust or confidence*) dependable, ethical, faithful, honest, honourable, loyal, principled, reliable, reputable, responsible, sensible, stable, staunch, to be trusted, true, trusty, truthful, upright. ANTONYMS: deceitful, disloyal, unfaithful, unreliable.

trusty *a.* (*trustworthy, not liable to fail in time of need*) dependable, faithful, reliable, responsible, solid, staunch, steadfast, steady, true, trustworthy. ANTONYMS: irresponsible, undependable, unreliable.

truth *n.* **1** (*conformity to fact or reality*) accuracy, actuality, correctness, exactness, fact, factualness, genuineness, legitimacy, precision, reality, rightness, truthfulness, validity, veracity. ANTONYMS: falseness, inaccuracy, incorrectness, invalidity, unreality. **2** (*that which is true, a fact*) certainty, fact. **3** (*honesty, sincerity*) candour, frankness, honesty, honour, integrity, righteousness, sincerity, uprightness. **4** (*a principle or statement that is generally considered true*) adage, aphorism, axiom, maxim, proverb, saw, truism.

truthful *a.* **1** (*habitually speaking the truth*) candid, forthright, frank, honest, open, plainspoken, sincere, straight, straightforward, trustworthy. ANTONYMS: dishonest, insincere, lying, untruthful. **2** (*reliable, conformable to truth*) accurate, correct, exact, factual, honest, literal, precise, reliable, right, true, valid, veracious. ANTONYMS: fictitious, incorrect, inexact, untrue, untruthful.

try *v.t.* **1** (*to test, to examine by experiment*) check out, conduct trials on, essay, examine, experiment with, inspect, investigate, put to the test, sample, taste, test. **2** (*to determine the qualities etc. of by reference to a standard*) appraise, assay, assess, evaluate. **3** (*to subject to a severe or undue test, to strain*) make undue demands on, strain, stress, tax. **4** (*to subject to hardship, suffering etc., as if for a test, to afflict*) afflict, annoy, bother, harass, irk, irritate, nag, plague, torment, trouble, upset, vex. **5** (*to investigate* (*a charge, issue etc.*) *judicially, to subject* (*a person*) *to judicial trial*) adjudge, examine, hear.

~*v.i.* (*to endeavour, to make an attempt*) aim, attempt, do one's best, endeavour, exert oneself, (*coll.*) have a crack at, (*coll.*) have a go at, have a shot at, (*coll.*) have a stab at, make an attempt, make an effort, seek, strive, struggle, undertake.

~*n.* (*an attempt*) attempt, (*coll.*) crack, effort, endeavour, (*coll.*) go, shot, (*coll.*) stab. **to try out** (*to test*) conduct trials on, experiment with, put to the test, sample, test.

trying *a.* **1** (*irritating, annoying*) annoying, exasperating, irksome, irritating, tiresome, vexing. ANTONYMS: agreeable, delightful, pleasant. **2** (*difficult, demanding*) arduous, demanding, difficult, exhausting, fatiguing, hard, stressful, taxing, tiring. ANTONYMS: easy, straightforward, undemanding.

tubby *a.* (*tub-shaped, corpulent*) chubby, corpulent, fat, obese, overweight, plump, podgy, portly, stout. ANTONYMS: skinny, slender, thin.

tuck *v.t.* **1** (*to wrap or cover* (*up or in*) *closely or snugly*) bed down, cover up, make comfortable, put to bed, wrap up. **2** (*to gather up, to fold or draw together or into a small area*) fold, gather, pleat, ruck, ruffle. **3** (*to cram, to stow* (*away, into, etc.*)) cram, insert, push, stuff.

~*n.* **1** (*a horizontal fold in a dress etc., esp. one of a series*) fold, gather, pleat, ruck, ruffle. **2** (*food, esp. sweets, pastry etc.*) (*coll.*) eats, food, (*sl.*) grub, (*sl.*) nosh, (*coll.*) scoff, (*dial. or sl.*) scran. **to tuck in** (*to eat heartily*) eat up, (*coll.*) get stuck into, gobble up, wolf down.

tuft *n.* (*a cluster, a bunch of hairs, grass etc. held or fastened together at one end*) bunch, clump, cluster, collection, knot, tussock.

tug *v.t.* **1** (*to pull or draw with great effort or with violence*) haul, heave, jerk, pull, wrench, wrest, yank. **2** (*to haul, to tow*) drag, draw, haul, pull, tow, trail.

tuition *n.* (*teaching, instruction, esp. in a particular subject and separately paid for*) coaching, instruction, schooling, teaching, training, tutoring.

tumble *v.i.* **1** (*to fall* (*down etc.*) *suddenly or violently*) fall down, fall headlong, fall over, lose one's balance, lose one's footing, topple, trip up. **2** (*to roll or toss about*) heave, pitch, roll about, toss about. **3** (*to run or move about in a careless or headlong manner*) blunder, rush headlong, stumble. **4** (*to perform acrobatic feats, esp. without special apparatus*) somersault, turn head over heels, turn somersaults. **5** (*to decrease quickly*) collapse, drop, fall, plummet, plunge, slide, slump, (*coll.*) take a dive. ANTONYMS: go sky-high, soar. **6** (*to begin to*) *comprehend* (*often with to*)) comprehend, grasp, latch on, realize, (*sl.*) suss, understand. ANTONYMS: be in the dark, fail to grasp, misunderstand.

~*v.t.* (*to throw into disorder, to rumple*) disarrange, dishevel, disorder, mess up, (*N Am.*) muss up, ruffle, rumple, tousle. ANTONYMS: arrange, tidy up.

~*n.* **1** (*a fall*) fall, nosedive, spill, trip. **2** (*a state of disorder*) chaos, clutter, confusion, disarray, disorder, jumble, mess. ANTONYMS: good order, neatness, orderliness, tidiness. **3** (*an acrobatic feat, esp. a somersault*) acrobatic feat, somersault. **4** (*a sudden sharp decrease*) collapse, (*coll.*) dive, drop, fall, plummeting, plunge, slide, slump.

tumbledown *a.* (*dilapidated*) crumbling, dilapidated, disintegrating, falling down, falling to pieces, in ruins, ramshackle, rickety, ruined, shaky, tottering. ANTONYMS: sound, sturdy, well-kept.

tumour *n.* (*a swelling on some part of the body, esp. if due to an abnormal growth of tissue*) cancer, carcinoma, growth, lump, malignancy, neoplasm, sarcoma, swelling.

tumult *n.* **1** (*the commotion or agitation of a multitude, esp. with a confusion of sounds*) agitation, babble, bedlam, clamour, commotion, din, disturbance, hubbub, hullabaloo, pandemonium, racket, uproar. **2** (*a confused outbreak or insurrection*) affray, altercation, brawl, brouhaha, disturbance, fight, fracas, free-for-all, insurrection, mêlée, outbreak, quarrel, rebellion, riot, row. **3** (*uproar, riot*) chaos, confusion, disarray, disorder, disturbance, upheaval, uproar. **4** (*agitation or confusion of mind*) agitation, excitement, ferment, turmoil, upheaval.

tumultuous *a.* **1** (*extremely loud*) blaring, boisterous, clamorous, deafening, ear-shattering, noisy, unrestrained, uproarious. ANTONYMS: muted, quiet, restrained. **2** (*unruly, disorderly*) agitated, boisterous, disorderly, excited, lawless, noisy, restless, rioting, rowdy, unruly, violent, vociferous, wild. ANTONYMS: calm, orderly, peaceable, peaceful, serene. **3** (*passionate, vehement*) fervent, frenzied, passionate, raging, turbulent, uncontrolled, unrestrained, vehement, violent, wild. ANTONYMS: controlled, passionless, restrained.

tune *n.* (*a melodious succession of musical tones forming a coherent whole, a melody*) air, melody, song, strain, theme.

~*v.t.* (*to adjust, to adapt*) adapt, adjust, attune, regulate. **in tune** (*in harmony, agreement* (*with*)) in accord, in accordance, in agreement, in harmony, in sympathy. ANTONYMS: clashing, in conflict. **to change one's tune** (*to alter one's attitude or tone*) change one's mind, do an about-face, have a change of heart, have second thoughts, reconsider, take a different tack, think again.

tuneful *a.* (*melodious, musical*) catchy, dulcet, easy on the ear, euphonic, euphonious, (*coll.*) foot-tapping, harmonious, lyrical, mellifluous, melodic, melodious, musical, pleasant-sounding, sweet-sounding. ANTONYMS: cacophonous, discordant.

tunnel *n.* **1** (*an artificial underground passage or gallery*) subway, underground channel, underground passage, underpass. **2** (*a passage dug by a burrowing animal*) burrow, hole, underground passage.

~*v.t.* (*to make a tunnel through* (*a hill etc.*)) cut, dig, excavate, scoop out.

~*v.i.* (*to cut or make a tunnel*) burrow, dig, mine.

turbulent *a.* **1** (*disturbed, tumultuous*) agitated, confused, disturbed, in turmoil, troubled, unsettled. ANTONYMS: at peace, calm, tranquil. **2** ((*of a flow of air*) *causing disturbance*) choppy, rough, stormy, tempestuous. ANTONYMS: calm, still. **3** (*insubordinate, disorderly*) agitated, boisterous, disorderly, excited, noisy, obstreperous, restless, rioting, rowdy, tumultuous, unruly, violent, vociferous, wild. ANTONYMS: calm, peaceable, peaceful.

turf *n.* **1** (*surface earth filled with the matted roots of grass and other small plants*) grass, green, lawn, (*poet.*) sward. **2** (*a piece of this, a sod*) clod, divot, sod.

turgid *a.* **1** (*swollen, morbidly distended*) bloated, bulging, congested, distended, oedematose, puffed up, puffy, swollen, tumescent, tumid. **2** ((*esp. of writing*) *pompous and difficult to understand*) bombastic, flowery, fulsome, fustian, grandiloquent, grandiose, high-flown, high-sounding, inflated, magniloquent, oratorical, orotund, pompous, pretentious, rhetorical. ANTONYMS: basic, plain, simple.

turmoil *n.* (*a commotion, tumult*) agitation, bedlam, bustle, chaos, commotion, confusion, disarray, disorder, disturbance, ferment, flurry, pandemonium, tumult, upheaval, uproar. ANTONYMS: calm, peace, tranquillity.

turn *v.t.* **1** (*to cause to move round on or as on an axis, to give a rotary motion to*) revolve, rotate, spin, twirl, whirl. **2** (*to cause to go, look etc. in* *a different direction*) aim, direct, focus, point, train. **3** (*to expose the other side of, to invert*) flip over, invert, reverse, turn over, turn round, turn topsy-turvy. **4** (*to perform* (*a somersault*)) carry out, do, execute, perform. **5** (*to apply or devote to a different purpose or object, to give a new direction to*) apply, devote, employ, put to use, utilize. **6** (*to adapt, to change in form, condition, nature etc.*) adapt, alter, change, convert, metamorphose, mutate, transform. **7** (*to translate, to paraphrase*) change, paraphrase, render, translate. **8** (*to go or move to the other side of, to go round*) go round, negotiate, round. **9** (*to reach or pass beyond* (*a certain age, time*)) become, get to, pass, reach. **10** (*to cause to ferment, to make sour*) curdle, make rancid, sour, spoil, taint, turn sour. **11** (*to nauseate*) nauseate, sicken, upset. **12** (*to shape in a lathe or on a potter's wheel*) fashion, form, mould, shape.

~*v.i.* **1** (*to have a circular or revolving motion, to rotate*) circle, go round, gyrate, pirouette, pivot, revolve, rotate, spin, swivel, twirl, twist, wheel, whirl. **2** (*to move the body, face or head in a different direction, to change front from right to left etc.*) swing round, turn round, veer, wheel round, whirl round. **3** (*to reverse direction*) change course, change direction, do a three-point turn, do a U-turn, go back, go into reverse, make a U-turn, retrace one's footsteps, reverse direction, turn round, veer. **4** (*to give one's attention to, set about*) address oneself to, apply oneself to, devote oneself to, set about, turn one's attention to, undertake. **5** (*to be changed in nature, condition etc.*) alter, change, metamorphose, mutate, suffer a sea change, transform. **6** (*to become sour or spoiled*) become rancid, curdle, go bad, go off, go sour. **7** (*to become nauseated*) be nauseated, be unsettled, be upset. **8** (*to become*) become, come to be, get, go, grow. **9** (*to change sides*) apostatize, become a deserter, break faith, change sides, defect, desert, go over to the other side, renege, tergiversate, turn renegade, welsh.

~*n.* **1** (*the act of turning, rotary motion*) circle, cycle, gyration, revolution, rotation, spin, twirl, whirl. **2** (*a change of direction or tendency, a deflection*) change of course, change of direction, deflection, deviation, veer. **3** (*a bend, a curve*) bend, corner, curve, turning, twist, winding. **4** (*a change, a vicissitude*) alteration, change, difference, variation. **5** (*a short walk, a stroll*) airing, constitutional, promenade, saunter, stroll. **6** (*a bout or spell* (*of doing something*)) act, performance, routine, show. **7** (*an opportunity or time* (*for doing something*) *coming in succession to each of a number of persons*) chance, (*coll.*) go, opportunity, shot, spell, stint, time. **8** (*a purpose*) aim, end, object, objective, purpose.

9 (*a nervous shock*) fright, scare, shock, start. **10** (*character or disposition*) affinity, bent, cast, character, disposition, inclination, leaning, temper, tendency. **11** (*an action or deed*) act, action, deed, gesture, service. **to turn away** (*to send away, dismiss*) cold-shoulder, (*coll.*) give the brush-off to, rebuff, refuse admittance to, reject, repel, send away. ANTONYMS: admit, welcome. **to turn back** (*to begin to go back*) go back, retrace one's steps, retreat, return. ANTONYMS: go on, proceed. **to turn down 1** (*to lower* (*a light, the volume on a radio etc.*)) decrease, lessen, lower, lower the volume of, make softer, muffle, reduce, reduce the volume of. ANTONYMS: amplify, increase, turn up. **2** (*to reject*) decline, (*coll.*) give the red light to, give the thumbs down to, rebuff, reject, repudiate, spurn, veto. ANTONYMS: accept, take. **to turn in 1** (*to hand over, to surrender*) give up, hand over, surrender, turn over, yield. ANTONYMS: keep, retain. **2** (*to go to bed*) go to bed, go to sleep, (*coll.*) hit the hay, (*coll.*) hit the sack, retire. ANTONYMS: get up, rise. **3** (*to achieve* (*a score*)) achieve, attain, gain, reach, record, register. **4** (*to hand in*) deliver, give in, hand in, submit, tender. ANTONYMS: keep, retain. **to turn off 1** (*to deviate*) branch off, depart from, deviate from, leave, quit. **2** (*to shut or switch off*) deactivate, put out, switch off, turn out. ANTONYMS: put on, switch on, turn on. **3** (*to cause to lose interest in, esp. sexually*) alienate, disenchant, put off, repel, turn against. ANTONYMS: arouse, attract, excite, stimulate, turn on. **to turn on 1** (*to switch on*) activate, ignite, put on, start up, switch on. ANTONYMS: put out, switch off, turn off. **2** (*to hinge or depend upon*) be contingent on, depend on, hang on, hinge on, pivot on, rest on. **3** (*to attack*) assault, attack, (*coll.*) lay into, round on, set upon. **4** (*to excite, to arouse the interest of, esp. sexually*) arouse, attract, excite, stimulate, thrill, titillate, work up. ANTONYMS: put off, turn off. **to turn out 1** (*to drive out, to expel*) banish, (*sl.*) boot out, cast out, (*coll.*) chuck out, discharge, dismiss, drive out, drum out, eject, expel, (*coll.*) fire, kick out, oust, put out, (*coll.*) sack, throw out, (*coll.*) turf out. ANTONYMS: admit, let in, take in, welcome. **2** (*to clean* (*a room*) *thoroughly*) clean, clear out, (*coll.*) do out. **3** (*to produce, as the result of labour*) bring out, make, manufacture, process, produce, put out. **4** (*to prove to be*) come about, emerge, evolve, happen, pan out, prove to be the case, result, transpire. **5** (*to switch off*) deactivate, put out, switch off, turn off. ANTONYMS: start up, switch on, turn on. **6** (*to gather, to assemble*) appear, arrive, assemble, be present, come, gather, go, put in an appearance, show, show up, turn up. **7** (*to become*) become, come to be, develop into, end up, grow to be.

to turn over 1 (*to surrender, to hand over*) give up, hand over, surrender, yield. ANTONYMS: keep, retain. **2** (*to transfer* (*to*), *to put under other control*) assign, commit, consign, hand over, pass on, transfer. **3** (*to cause to turn over, to upset*) capsize, overturn, tip over, upend, upset. ANTONYMS: set upright. **4** (*to consider, to ponder*) consider, contemplate, deliberate, give thought to, mull over, ponder, reflect on, think about, think over. **to turn to 1** (*to have recourse to*) have recourse to, resort to, take to. **2** (*to seek the help of*) appeal to, apply to, approach, have recourse to, look to. **to turn up 1** (*to unearth, to bring to light*) bring to light, expose, ferret out, find, hit upon, root out, uncover, unearth. ANTONYMS: conceal, hide. **2** (*to come to light*) appear, be found, be located, come to light. ANTONYMS: be lost, be missing. **3** (*to happen*) arise, crop up, happen, occur, present oneself, transpire. **4** (*to make one's appearance*) appear, arrive, be present, make one's appearance, present oneself, put in an appearance, show, show up. ANTONYMS: be absent, stay away. **5** (*to increase* (*the brightness of a light, the volume of a radio etc.*)) amplify, increase, increase the volume of, make louder, raise the volume of. ANTONYMS: reduce, turn down.

turncoat *n.* (*a person who deserts their party or principles*) apostate, backslider, defector, deserter, renegade, seceder, tergiversator, traitor.

turning *n.* (*a bend, the point where a road meets another*) bend, corner, curve, turn.

turning point *n.* (*the point in place, time etc. on or at which a change takes place, the decisive point*) crisis, critical point, crossroads, crucial point, crux, moment of truth.

turn-off *n.* (*a turning off a main road*) exit, side road.

turnout *n.* **1** (*dress, get-up*) costume, dress, ensemble, get-up, outfit, (*coll.*) rig-out. **2** (*the number of people attending something*) attendance, audience, crowd, gate.

turnover *n.* **1** (*the amount of money turned over in a business in a given time*) financial flow, gross revenue, volume of business. **2** (*the rate at which employees leave and have to be replaced*) change, coming and going, movement, rate of change, replacement rate.

tussle *n.* **1** (*a difficult struggle*) arduous task, difficulty, effort, exertion, hard task, labour, strain, struggle, toil. **2** (*a fight, a scuffle*) battle, brawl, conflict, contest, fight, fracas, fray, (*coll.*) punch-up, (*coll.*) scrap, scrimmage, scuffle, (*coll.*) set-to, struggle.

tutor *n.* **1** (*a private teacher*) coach, instructor, mentor, teacher. **2** (*a college or university teacher who teaches and holds discussions with students in small groups*) instructor, lecturer, teacher.
~*v.t.* (*to act as a tutor to*) coach, cram, instruct, teach, train.

twaddle *n.* (*meaningless talk, nonsense*) balderdash, (*sl.*) bosh, (*taboo sl.*) bullshit, bunkum, claptrap, (*sl.*) crap, drivel, garbage, (*coll.*) gobbledegook, (*coll.*) guff, nonsense, (*coll.*) piffle, (*sl.*) poppycock, (*coll.*) rot, rubbish, (*coll.*) tommyrot, (*sl.*) tosh, trash, (*coll.*) tripe.

tweak *v.t.* (*to pinch and twist or pull with a sudden jerk, to twitch*) jerk, nip, pinch, pull, squeeze, twist, twitch.

twig *n.* (*a small shoot or branch of a tree, bush, etc., a branchlet*) branch, branchlet, offshoot, shoot, spray, stem, stick, twiglet.

twilight *n.* **1** (*the diffused light from the sky appearing a little before sunrise and after sunset*) dusk, (*poet.*) gloaming, half-light. **2** (*a period of decay, decline etc.*) decline, ebb, waning.

twin *n.* **1** (*a person or thing very closely resembling or related to another*) clone, (*coll.*) dead ringer, (*coll.*) dead spit, double, image, lookalike, (*coll.*) spit, (*coll.*) spitting image. **2** (*an exact counterpart*) complement, counterpart, fellow, match, mate.

twine *v.t.* (*to form by interweaving*) braid, interlace, interweave, knit, plait, twist, weave.
~*v.i.* **1** (*to entwine, to coil* (*about, round etc.*)) coil, entwine, twist, weave, wind, wrap. **2** (*to wind, to meander*) coil, curl, curve, loop, meander, snake, spiral, twist, twist and turn, wind, zigzag.
~*n.* **1** (*strong string made of two or three strands twisted together*) cord, string, thread, yarn. **2** (*a twist, a coil*) coil, convolution, spiral, twist, whorl.

twinge *n.* (*a sharp, shooting pain*) ache, pang, sharp pain, spasm, stab of pain, throb.

twinkle *v.i.* (*to shine with a broken quivering light, to sparkle*) blink, coruscate, flash, flicker, glimmer, glint, glitter, shimmer, sparkle, wink.
~*n.* (*a tremulous gleam, a sparkle*) blink, flash, flicker, glimmer, glint, glitter, shimmer, sparkle, wink.

twirl *v.t.* **1** (*to cause to rotate rapidly, esp. with the fingers, to spin*) spin, twist, whirl. **2** (*to twiddle, to curl* (*the moustache etc.*)) coil, curl, twist, wind.
~*v.i.* (*to revolve or rotate rapidly, to whirl* (*round*)) gyrate, pirouette, pivot, revolve, rotate, spin

around, turn, turn on one's heel, wheel, whirl around.

twist *v.t.* **1** (*to turn round*) bend, rotate, screw, turn round. **2** (*to wrench, to distort*) bend, contort, deform, distort, misshape, warp, wrench. ANTONYMS: straighten. **3** (*to pervert, to misrepresent*) falsify, garble, misquote, misreport, misrepresent, pervert. **4** (*to twine, to wreathe*) braid, coil, curl, twine, weave, wind, wrap, wreathe. **5** (*to sprain, to wrench*) rick, sprain, turn, wrench, wrest.
~*v.i.* **1** (*to move in a curving or irregular path*) bend, coil, curve, meander, snake, spiral, wind, zigzag. **2** (*to turn round*) rotate, swivel round, turn, turn round. **3** (*to writhe, to squirm*) squirm, wriggle, writhe. **4** (*to be distorted*) become distorted, contort, kink, screw up.
~*n.* **1** (*an act or the manner of twisting*) contortion, rotation, screw, turn, wrench, wrest. **2** (*the state of being twisted*) bend, contortion, deformation, distortion, kink, warp. **3** (*a sharp bend*) bend, coil, curve, spiral, turn, winding. **4** (*a peculiar tendency, an idiosyncrasy*) aberration, bent, characteristic, eccentricity, foible, idiosyncrasy, oddity, peculiarity, quirk. **5** (*an unexpected development in, or conclusion to, the plot of a story*) change, development, sea change, slant, turn. **6** (*a twisting strain*) rick, strain, turn, wrench. **to twist someone's arm** (*to use force or psychological pressure to persuade someone*) bully, coerce, force, pressurize, strong-arm, use bully-boy tactics.

twit *n.* (*a fool*) blockhead, (*sl.*) chump, clown, (*sl.*) dope, fool, idiot, (*sl.*) nerd, nincompoop, (*coll.*) ninny, (*coll.*) nitwit, numskull, oaf, (*sl.*) wally.

twitch *v.t.* (*to pull with a sudden or sharp jerk*) jerk, pull, tug, wrench, yank.
~*v.i.* (*to move with a spasmodic jerk or contraction*) blink, flutter, jerk, jump.
~*n.* **1** (*a sudden pull or jerk*) jerk, pull, tug, wrench, yank. **2** (*a sudden involuntary contraction of a muscle etc.*) blink, flutter, jerk, jump, spasm, tic, tremor.

twitter *v.i.* **1** (*to utter a succession of short, tremulous notes*) cheep, chirp, chirrup, trill, warble. **2** (*to talk idly*) chatter, jabber, prattle.
~*n.* **1** (*a state of excitement or nervous agitation*) dither, fluster, (*coll.*) state, state of agitation, state of excitement, (*coll.*) tizzy. **2** (*a chirping*) cheep, chirp, chirrup, trill, warble.

tycoon *n.* (*a financial or political magnate*) baron, captain of industry, (*chiefly N Am., coll.*) fat cat, financier, magnate, mogul.

type *n.* **1** (*a kind, a category*) category, class, classification, form, genre, genus, group, kind, order, set, sort, species, strain, variety. **2** (*any person or thing that stands as a characteristic example or representative specimen of another thing or class of things*) archetype, epitome, essence, example, exemplar, model, pattern, perfect, personification, quintessence, specimen. **3** (*a person (of a specified kind)*) character, individual, specimen.

typical *a.* **1** (*of the nature of or serving as a type*) archetypal, classic, quintessential, representative, standard, stock, true to type. ANTONYMS: anomalous, atypical, idiosyncratic, unrepresentative. **2** (*characteristic (of)*) characteristic (of), in character (with), in keeping (with), to be expected, true to type. ANTONYMS: out of character (with), out of keeping (with), uncharacteristic (of). **3** (*usual, average*) average, customary, normal, ordinary, routine, usual. ANTONYMS: out of the ordinary, unusual.

typify *v.t.* (*to be a type of, to exemplify*) characterize, embody, epitomize, exemplify, personify, represent, sum up, symbolize.

tyrannical *a.* (*acting like or characteristic of a tyrant, despotic*) absolute, arbitrary, autocratic, brutal, coercive, despotic, dictatorial, domineering, harsh, high-handed, imperious, oppressive, overbearing, overweening, peremptory, strict, unjust. ANTONYMS: democratic, lenient, liberal, tolerant.

tyrannize *v.i.* (*to behave tyrannically, to rule despotically (over)*) browbeat, bully, coerce, crush, dominate, domineer, enslave, have (someone) under one's thumb, intimidate, lord it over, oppress, repress, rule with a rod of iron, subjugate, terrorize.

tyranny *n.* (*arbitrary or oppressive exercise of power*) absolutism, arbitrariness, authoritarianism, autocracy, bullying, coercion, despotism, dictatorship, harshness, high-handedness, imperiousness, oppression, severity, strictness. ANTONYMS: democracy, liberality, tolerance.

tyrant *n.* **1** (*an arbitrary or despotic ruler*) absolute ruler, autocrat, despot, dictator. **2** (*a person who uses authority oppressively or cruelly*) authoritarian, bully, dictator, Hitler, martinet, slave-driver.

U

ugly *a.* **1** (*unpleasing to the sight*) hideous, ill-favoured, misshapen, plain, unattractive, unlovely, unprepossessing, unsightly. ANTONYMS: beautiful, lovely. **2** (*morally repulsive*) degenerate, depraved, disgusting, distasteful, filthy, frightful, grotesque, horrid, immoral, loathsome, monstrous, objectionable, obscene, offensive, perverted, repugnant, repulsive, unpleasant, vile. ANTONYMS: pleasant. **3** (*threatening, unpleasant*) baleful, dangerous, dark, forbidding, hostile, malevolent, menacing, nasty, ominous, sinister, spiteful, threatening, unpleasant. ANTONYMS: promising.

ultimate *a.* **1** (*last, final*) conclusive, decisive, end, eventual, final, last, terminal. ANTONYMS: first. **2** (*beyond which there is nothing existing or possible*) extreme, furthest, greatest, highest, maximum, paramount, superlative, supreme, topmost, utmost. **3** (*fundamental, primary*) basic, elementary, essential, fundamental, primary, radical, underlying.
~*n.* **1** (*the best achievable or conceivable*) best, epitome, extreme, greatest, height, peak, perfection, summit. **2** (*something final or fundamental*) culmination, last word.

unabashed *a.* (*not abashed; shameless*) blatant, bold, brazen, confident, shameless, unashamed, unawed, unblushing, unconcerned, undaunted, undismayed, unembarrassed. ANTONYMS: embarrassed, sheepish.

unable *a.* **1** (*not having sufficient power or ability*) impotent, ineffectual, powerless. ANTONYMS: able, potent. **2** (*incapable, incompetent*) inadequate, incapable, incompetent, unfit, unqualified.

unacceptable *a.* (*so wrong that it should not be allowed*) bad, disagreeable, displeasing, distasteful, improper, inadmissible, inappropriate, insupportable, objectionable, offensive, tasteless, undesirable, unpleasant, unpopular, unsatisfactory, unsuitable, unwelcome, wrong. ANTONYMS: acceptable.

unaccountable *a.* **1** (*not accountable or responsible*) free, independent, not answerable, not responsible. ANTONYMS: accountable, responsible. **2** (*inexplicable*) baffling, incomprehensible, inexplicable, inscrutable, unexplainable, unfathomable, unintelligible. ANTONYMS: explainable, explicable. **3** (*puzzling and strange*) bizarre, extraordinary, mysterious, odd, peculiar, puzzling, strange, unheard-of, unusual, weird.

unaccustomed *a.* **1** (*not usual or familiar*) curious, new, out of the ordinary, peculiar, rare, remarkable, special, strange, surprising, uncommon, unexpected, unfamiliar, unprecedented, unusual, unwonted. ANTONYMS: familiar, usual. **2** (*not used (to)*) green, inexperienced (in), not used (to), unfamiliar (with), uninitiated (in), unpractised (at), unused (to), unversed (in). ANTONYMS: experienced (in), used (to).

unaffected *a.* **1** (*not influenced or affected*) aloof, cool, immune, impervious, proof, remote, unaltered, unchanged, unimpressed, uninfluenced, unmoved, unresponsive, unstirred, untouched. ANTONYMS: affected, influenced. **2** (*without affectation, sincere*) artless, genuine, guileless, honest, ingenuous, naive, natural, plain, real, simple, sincere, straightforward, unartificial, unassuming, unfeigned, unpretentious, unsophisticated, unspoilt, unstudied, without airs.

unanimous *a.* (*being all of one mind*) agreed, agreeing, at one, common, concerted, concordant, harmonious, in accord, in agreement, like-minded, of one mind, united. ANTONYMS: differing, divided.

unanswerable *a.* (*that cannot be satisfactorily answered or refuted*) absolute, conclusive, incontestable, incontrovertible, indisputable, irrefutable, unarguable, unassailable, uncontestable, undeniable. ANTONYMS: inconclusive, unconvincing.

unappetizing *a.* (*unpleasant to eat*) disgusting, distasteful, insipid, off-putting, tasteless, unappealing, unattractive, unenticing, uninteresting, uninviting, unpalatable, unpleasant, unsavoury, vapid. ANTONYMS: appetizing, palatable.

unapproachable *a.* **1** (*that cannot be approached, inaccessible*) beyond reach, inaccessible, out-of-the-way, remote, unreachable. **2** (*reserved, distant in manner*) aloof, austere, cool, distant, forbidding, frigid, (*coll.*) offish, remote, reserved, stand-offish, unfriendly, unsociable, withdrawn. ANTONYMS: friendly, sociable.

unassailable *a.* 1 (*incapable of being assailed*) impregnable, invincible, invulnerable, secure, strong, well-defended. ANTONYMS: vulnerable. 2 (*incontestable*) absolute, certain, conclusive, incontestable, incontrovertible, indisputable, irrefutable, sure, unanswerable, unarguable, uncontestable, undeniable. ANTONYMS: arguable, disputable.

unassuming *a.* (*not arrogant; modest*) diffident, humble, meek, modest, quiet, reserved, retiring, self-effacing, shy, simple, unassertive, unobtrusive, unostentatious, unpretentious. ANTONYMS: arrogant, presumptuous.

unattached *a.* 1 (*not attached* (*to a club, organization etc.*)) autonomous, detached, free, independent, non-aligned, self-sustained, separate, unaffiliated, uncommitted. ANTONYMS: attached. 2 (*not married or having a partner*) available, single, unaccompanied, unmarried, unspoken for.

unattractive *a.* (*plain or unpleasant in appearance*) hideous, plain, ugly, unappealing, unappetizing, undesirable, uninviting, unlovely, unprepossessing. ANTONYMS: attractive, pretty.

unavoidable *a.* (*inevitable*) certain, compulsory, destined, fated, fixed, ineluctable, inescapable, inevitable, inexorable, irresistible, necessary, obligatory, predetermined, settled, sure, unalterable, unchangeable. ANTONYMS: avoidable.

unaware *a.* 1 (*not aware, ignorant* (*of*)) heedless (of), ignorant (of), insensible (to), oblivious (to), unacquainted (with), unenlightened, uninformed (about), unknowing, unmindful (of), unprepared, unsuspecting. ANTONYMS: aware (of), conscious (of). 2 (*careless, inattentive*) careless, inattentive.

unawares *adv.* 1 (*without warning; by surprise*) aback, abruptly, by surprise, off guard, (*coll.*) on the hop, suddenly, unexpectedly, unprepared, without warning. 2 (*undesignedly*) accidentally, by mistake, inadvertently, mistakenly, unconsciously, unintentionally, unknowingly, unwittingly, without warning. ANTONYMS: deliberately, knowingly.

unbalanced *a.* 1 (*not balanced*) asymmetrical, disproportionate, irregular, lopsided, overbalanced, shaky, unequal, uneven, unstable, unsteady, unsymmetrical, wobbly. ANTONYMS: balanced, symmetrical. 2 (*not mentally balanced*) (*sl.*) barking, (*coll.*) batty, (*sl.*) bonkers, crazy, demented, deranged, disturbed, eccentric, erratic, insane, irrational, (*coll.*) loopy, lunatic, mad, (*sl.*) nuts, (*coll.*) out to lunch, touched, unhinged, unsound, unstable. ANTONYMS: sane.

unbecoming *a.* 1 (*not becoming, not suited* (*to*)) ill-suited, inappropriate, inapt, incongruous, out of character, unattractive, unfit, unflattering, unsightly, unsuitable. ANTONYMS: becoming. 2 (*not befitting; improper*) discreditable, improper, indecorous, indelicate, offensive, tasteless, unseemly. ANTONYMS: befitting.

unbending *a.* (*unyielding, resolute*) aloof, distant, firm, formal, hardline, inflexible, intractable, reserved, resolute, rigid, severe, stiff, stubborn, tough, uncompromising, unyielding. ANTONYMS: approachable, flexible.

unbiased *a.* (*impartial*) disinterested, dispassionate, equitable, even-handed, fair, impartial, just, neutral, objective, open-minded, unbigoted, unprejudiced. ANTONYMS: biased, prejudiced.

unblemished *a.* (*not spoiled, without imperfections*) clean, faultless, flawless, immaculate, impeccable, perfect, pure, spotless, stainless, unflawed, unspotted, unstained, unsullied, untarnished. ANTONYMS: blemished, imperfect.

unbounded *a.* 1 (*boundless, not bounded* (*by*)) absolute, boundless, endless, illimitable, immeasurable, immense, interminable, limitless, unlimited, vast. 2 (*infinite, not subject to control*) immoderate, infinite, unbridled, unchecked, unconfined, unconstrained, uncontrolled, unrestrained. ANTONYMS: restrained.

unbridled *a.* (*unrestrained; unruly*) excessive, immoderate, intemperate, licentious, rampant, riotous, unchecked, unconstrained, uncontrolled, uncurbed, ungovernable, uninhibited, unrestrained, unruly, violent, wanton, wild. ANTONYMS: restrained.

unbroken *a.* 1 (*not broken*) complete, entire, intact, integral, solid, sound, total, unimpaired, whole. ANTONYMS: broken. 2 (*not subdued*) defiant, unbowed, untamed, wild. ANTONYMS: subdued, tamed. 3 (*uninterrupted, regular*) ceaseless, constant, continuous, endless, incessant, regular, uninterrupted, unremitting.

uncalled *a.* **uncalled for** (*not necessary; gratuitous*) gratuitous, inappropriate, needless, undeserved, unfair, unjust, unjustified, unnecessary, unprovoked, unsolicited, unwanted, unwarranted, unwelcome. ANTONYMS: appropriate, necessary.

uncanny *a.* 1 (*weird, mysterious*) creepy, eerie, ghostly, mysterious, odd, queer, (*coll.*) spooky, strange, supernatural, unearthly, unnatural, weird. 2 (*amazing*) amazing, astonishing, exceptional, extraordinary, fantastic, incredible, miraculous, prodigious, remarkable, singular, unheard-of, unusual. ANTONYMS: ordinary.

unceasing *a.* (*not ceasing; continual*) ceaseless, constant, continual, endless, eternal, everlasting, incessant, never-ending, non-stop, perpetual, persistent, regular, unending, unfailing, uninterrupted, unremitting. ANTONYMS: intermittent, irregular.

uncertain *a.* **1** (*not certain; doubtful*) ambiguous, conjectural, doubtful, haphazard, hazy, incalculable, indefinite, indeterminate, indistinct, unclear, unconfirmed, undetermined, unforeseeable, unresolved, unsettled. ANTONYMS: certain, definite. **2** (*not to be relied on*) dubious, (*coll.*) iffy, insecure, irregular, precarious, questionable, risky, touch-and-go, unpredictable, unreliable, variable. **3** (*changeable; capricious*) ambivalent, capricious, changeable, doubtful, erratic, fickle, fitful, hesitant, inconstant, irresolute, undecided, unsure, vacillating, vague, wavering. ANTONYMS: sure, unwavering.

unchanging *a.* (*remaining the same*) abiding, changeless, constant, enduring, eternal, immutable, imperishable, lasting, permanent, perpetual, unchanged, unvarying. ANTONYMS: temporary, transitory.

uncivilized *a.* (*cruel or uneducated*) barbaric, barbarous, boorish, brutish, churlish, coarse, crude, gross, illiterate, philistine, primitive, rough, rude, savage, uncouth, uncultivated, uneducated, vulgar, wild. ANTONYMS: civilized.

uncomfortable *a.* **1** (*making one feel discomfort*) cramped, disagreeable, hard, ill-fitting, incommodious, irritating, painful, rough, troublesome, unpleasant. ANTONYMS: comfortable. **2** (*making one feel embarrassed and not relaxed*) anxious, awkward, confused, discomfited, disquieted, distressed, disturbed, embarrassed, ill at ease, nervous, out of place, restless, self-conscious, troubled, uneasy, upset. ANTONYMS: comfortable, relaxed.

uncommon *a.* (*not common, remarkable*) bizarre, curious, distinctive, exceptional, extraordinary, incomparable, infrequent, inimitable, notable, noteworthy, novel, odd, peculiar, rare, remarkable, scarce, singular, strange, unfamiliar, unusual. ANTONYMS: common, mundane.

uncommunicative *a.* (*reserved, taciturn*) close, guarded, quiet, reserved, reticent, retiring, secretive, short, silent, taciturn, tight-lipped, unforthcoming, unresponsive, unsociable, withdrawn. ANTONYMS: communicative, talkative.

uncompromising *a.* (*not compromising; inflexible*) decided, determined, dogged, firm, implacable, inexorable, inflexible, intransigent, obdurate, obstinate, rigid, steadfast, strict, stubborn, unbending, unyielding. ANTONYMS: pliant, yielding.

unconcerned *a.* **1** (*not concerned (in or with)*) aloof, apathetic, cool, detached, dispassionate, distant, incurious, indifferent, oblivious, remote, uninterested, uninvolved, unsympathetic. ANTONYMS: interested, sympathetic. **2** (*free from anxiety*) blithe, callous, carefree, easy, insouciant, nonchalant, relaxed, serene, unaffected, unbothered, unperturbed, unruffled, untroubled, unworried. ANTONYMS: anxious, perturbed.

unconditional *a.* (*not conditional; absolute*) absolute, categorical, complete, downright, entire, explicit, full, out-and-out, outright, positive, total, unlimited, unqualified, unreserved, unrestricted, utter. ANTONYMS: conditional, reserved.

uncongenial *a.* (*unfriendly*) antagonistic, antipathetic, disagreeable, discordant, displeasing, distasteful, incompatible, uninviting, unpleasant, unsuited, unsympathetic. ANTONYMS: affable, congenial.

unconscious *a.* **1** (*ignorant, unaware (of)*) blind (to), deaf (to), heedless (of), ignorant (of), insensitive (to), lost (to), oblivious (to), unaware (of), unknowing, unmindful (of), unsuspecting. ANTONYMS: aware (of). **2** (*temporarily deprived of consciousness*) comatose, faint, insensible, knocked out, numb, out cold, senseless, stunned. ANTONYMS: conscious, sensible. **3** (*not perceived by the mind*) automatic, innate, instinctive, involuntary, latent, reflex, repressed, subconscious, subliminal, suppressed, unpremeditated, unthinking. ANTONYMS: deliberate, wilful.

unconventional *a.* (*not fettered by convention; unusual*) abnormal, atypical, bizarre, eccentric, freakish, idiosyncratic, individual, informal, irregular, nonconformist, odd, offbeat, (*coll.*) off the wall, peculiar, uncustomary, unfamiliar, unorthodox, unusual, (*coll.*) way-out. ANTONYMS: conventional, orthodox.

unconvincing *a.* ((*of an explanation, excuse etc.*) *not believable*) dubious, feeble, (*coll.*) fishy, flimsy, implausible, improbable, inconclusive, incredible, lame, questionable, specious, suspect, thin, unbelievable, unlikely, unpersuasive, weak. ANTONYMS: convincing, persuasive.

uncouth *a.* (*lacking in refinement or manners*) awkward, churlish, clumsy, coarse, crude, graceless, gross, ill-bred, ill-mannered, loutish, rough, rude, uncivilized, uncultivated, uncultured, ungainly, unrefined, unseemly, vulgar. ANTONYMS: elegant, well-mannered.

uncover *v.t.* **1** (*to remove a covering from*) bare, lay open, open, show, strip, unveil, unwrap. ANTONYMS: cover, wrap. **2** (*to make known, to disclose*) bring to light, disclose, divulge, expose, lay bare, make known, reveal, unearth, unmask. ANTONYMS: conceal, suppress.

undecided *a.* **1** (*not decided or settled*) debatable, (*coll.*) iffy, indefinite, moot, open, pending, tentative, unconcluded, undetermined, unresolved, unsettled, vague. ANTONYMS: decided, settled. **2** (*irresolute, wavering*) ambivalent, dithering, doubtful, dubious, hesitant, indecisive, irresolute, torn, uncertain, uncommitted, unsure, wavering. ANTONYMS: resolute, sure.

undemonstrative *a.* (*not demonstrative; reserved*) aloof, contained, distant, formal, impassive, reserved, restrained, reticent, sedate, shy, stiff, stolid, unaffectionate, uncommunicative, unemotional, unexcitable, unresponsive, withdrawn. ANTONYMS: affectionate, demonstrative.

undeniable *a.* **1** (*not capable of being denied*) beyond doubt, certain, definite, evident, incontestable, incontrovertible, indisputable, indubitable, irrefutable, manifest, obvious, patent, positive, proven, sound, sure, unassailable, undoubted, unquestionable. ANTONYMS: doubtful, questionable. **2** (*decidedly good, excellent*) excellent, good.

under *prep.* **1** (*in or to a place or position lower than*) below, lower than. ANTONYMS: above. **2** (*covered by, on the inside of*) beneath, inside, underneath. **3** (*less than in quality, rank, number etc.*) inferior to, less than. **4** (*subject or subordinate*) answerable, junior, secondary, subject, subordinate, subservient. **5** (*liable to; in accordance with*) in accordance with, liable to, on condition of, on pain of.
~*adv.* **1** (*in or into a lower or subordinate place or degree*) below, beneath, down, downward, lower, underneath. **2** (*in or into a state of unconsciousness*) cold, comatose, (*coll.*) out, unconscious.

undercover *a.* (*done in secret*) clandestine, concealed, confidential, covert, hidden, (*coll.*) hush-hush, private, secret, surreptitious, underground. ANTONYMS: open, public.

underestimate *v.t.* (*to estimate at too low a level*) belittle, disparage, hold cheap, minimize, miscalculate, misjudge, misprize, sell short, underrate, undervalue. ANTONYMS: exaggerate, overestimate.

undergo *v.t.* (*to endure; to bear up against*) bear, endure, experience, go through, live through, stand, submit to, suffer, sustain, weather, withstand.

underhand *a.* **1** (*secret, clandestine*) clandestine, covert, secret, secretive, undercover. ANTONYMS: frank, open. **2** (*sly; fraudulent*) crafty, (*coll.*) crooked, deceitful, deceptive, devious, dishonest, dishonourable, fraudulent, furtive, sly, sneaky, stealthy, surreptitious, treacherous, underhanded, unethical, unfair, unscrupulous. ANTONYMS: honest.

undermine *v.t.* **1** (*to harm by secret or underhand means*) impair, ruin, sabotage, subvert. ANTONYMS: strengthen. **2** (*to weaken (one's health etc.) by imperceptible degrees*) debilitate, drain, exhaust, sap, weaken. **3** ((*of the wind, a river etc.) to wear away the bottom of (a bank, cliff etc.)*) eat away at, erode, wear away. **4** (*to dig an excavation under*) burrow, dig, excavate, mine, sap, tunnel, undercut. ANTONYMS: buttress, underpin.

understand *v.t.* **1** (*to know or perceive the meaning of*) apprehend, assimilate, catch on, comprehend, cotton on, (*dated sl.*) dig, discern, fathom, follow, get the hang of, grasp, know, make out, penetrate, perceive, realize, recognize, see, take in. **2** (*to be sympathetic to*) commiserate with, empathize with, feel for, pity, show compassion to, sympathize with, tolerate. **3** (*to take as meant or implied*) assume, believe, conclude, construe, gather, hear, infer, interpret, learn, presume, suppose, take it, think, view.

understanding *a.* **1** (*intelligent and perceptive*) discerning, intelligent, perceptive, sensitive. **2** (*sympathetic, tolerant*) accepting, compassionate, considerate, forbearing, forgiving, kind, kindly, patient, responsive, sympathetic, tender, tolerant. ANTONYMS: inconsiderate, unforgiving.
~*n.* **1** (*the act of understanding; comprehension*) appreciation, awareness, comprehension, discernment, grasp, sensitivity. ANTONYMS: ignorance, incomprehension. **2** (*the power or faculty of apprehension*) apprehension, thinking. **3** (*clear insight and intelligence in practical matters*) brains, insight, intellect, intelligence, kind, knowledge, penetration, reason, sense, wisdom. **4** (*a personal perception of a situation etc.*) belief, conclusion, estimation, idea, interpretation, judgement, notion, opinion, perception, view, viewpoint. **5** (*union of minds or sentiments*) accord, meeting of minds, treaty. ANTONYMS: disagreement. **6** (*an informal agreement or compact*) agreement, alliance, arrangement, bargain, compact, concordat, contract, covenant, entente, pact, settlement.

7 (*sympathy, compassion*) acceptance, comfort, compassion, consideration, consolation, empathy, forbearance, forgiveness, patience, support, sympathy, tenderness, tolerance.

undertake *v.t.* **1** (*to take upon oneself* (*a task, enterprise etc.*)) accept, assume, attempt, begin, embark on, endeavour, engage in, enter upon, set about, start, tackle, take upon oneself, try, venture. **2** (*to promise* (*to do*)) agree, contract, covenant, engage oneself, pledge, promise, swear, vow. **3** (*to guarantee* (*that*)) affirm, guarantee, warrant.

undertaking *n.* **1** (*the act of undertaking any business*) handling, implementing, tackling. **2** (*something which is undertaken, a task*) affair, endeavour, enterprise, feat, initiative, project, task, venture, work. **3** (*an agreement; a promise*) agreement, assurance, commitment, contract, guarantee, pledge, promise, stipulation, vow, warranty, word.

underwrite *v.t.* **1** (*to accept* (*liability*) *in an insurance policy*) assure, guarantee, insure. **2** (*to undertake the financing of*) back, finance, fund, invest in, sponsor, subsidize, support, uphold. **3** (*to write beneath, to subscribe*) countersign, endorse, initial, sign, subscribe.

undesirable *a.* (*not desirable; unpleasant*) disagreeable, distasteful, inconvenient, objectionable, obnoxious, offensive, repugnant, unacceptable, unattractive, unfit, uninviting, unpleasant, unpopular, unsavoury, unsuitable, unwanted, unwelcome. ANTONYMS: desirable, pleasant.

undisciplined *a.* (*misbehaving, showing a lack of self-control*) disobedient, erratic, fitful, naughty, obstreperous, uncontrolled, uneducated, unreliable, unrestrained, unruly, unschooled, unsteady, untrained, untutored, wayward, wild, wilful. ANTONYMS: disciplined, restrained.

undisguised *a.* (*shown openly*) blatant, clear, complete, evident, explicit, genuine, manifest, obvious, open, overt, patent, thoroughgoing, transparent, unconcealed, unfeigned, unmistakable, unmitigated, unreserved, utter, wholehearted. ANTONYMS: disguised, veiled.

undisputed *a.* (*accepted as true*) accepted, acknowledged, admitted, beyond question, certain, clear, conclusive, definite, incontrovertible, indisputable, irrefutable, recognized, sure, unchallenged, uncontested, undeniable, undoubted, unquestioned. ANTONYMS: debatable, uncertain.

undistinguished *a.* (*not interesting or successful*) commonplace, everyday, homespun, indifferent, mediocre, middling,

ordinary, pedestrian, plain, prosaic, run-of-the-mill, (*coll.*) so so, unexceptional, unexciting, unimpressive, unremarkable. ANTONYMS: exceptional, remarkable.

undisturbed *a.* (*not affected or troubled*) calm, collected, composed, equable, even, motionless, placid, sedate, serene, tranquil, unagitated, unconcerned, (*coll.*) unfazed, uninterrupted, unperturbed, unruffled, untroubled. ANTONYMS: agitated, flustered.

undo *v.t.* **1** (*to reverse* (*something that has been done*)) annul, cancel, counteract, invalidate, neutralize, nullify, rescind, reverse, void. **2** (*to unfasten, to untie*) disengage, disentangle, loose, loosen, open, unbind, unbolt, unbutton, unfasten, unhook, unlace, unlock, unpin, unsnap, untie, unwrap, unzip. ANTONYMS: fasten. **3** (*to bring ruin to; to destroy*) crush, defeat, destroy, impoverish, invalidate, mar, overturn, quash, ruin, shatter, subvert, undermine, upset, wreck.

undress *v.t.* (*to remove the clothes from*) strip, unclothe.
~*v.i.* (*to undress oneself*) disrobe, divest oneself, (*coll.*) peel off, shed, strip. ANTONYMS: dress.
~*n.* (*the state of being partly or completely undressed*) deshabille, disarray, nakedness, nudity.

undue *a.* (*excessive, disproportionate*) disproportionate, excessive, extravagant, extreme, immoderate, inordinate, intemperate, needless, overmuch, too great, too much, uncalled for, undeserved, unjustified, unnecessary, unwarranted. ANTONYMS: appropriate, due.

unduly *adv.* (*to an excessive degree*) disproportionately, excessively, extravagantly, immoderately, improperly, inappropriately, inordinately, irrationally, out of all proportion, overly, overmuch, unjustifiably, unnecessarily, unreasonably. ANTONYMS: duly, reasonably.

undying *a.* **1** (*unceasing*) constant, continuing, endless, eternal, everlasting, infinite, lasting, perennial, permanent, perpetual, unceasing, undiminishing, unending. ANTONYMS: temporary, transient. **2** (*immortal*) deathless, immortal, imperishable, indestructible, inextinguishable. ANTONYMS: mortal, perishable.

unearthly *a.* **1** (*not earthly*) ethereal, preternatural, sublime, supernatural, unnatural, unworldly. **2** (*not of this world, supernatural*) creepy, eerie, ghostly, haunted, nightmarish, phantom, spectral, (*coll.*) spooky, supernatural, weird. **3** (*ridiculous and unreasonable*) absurd, extraordinary, outrageous, ridiculous, (*coll.*) ungodly, (*coll.*) unholy, unreasonable. ANTONYMS: reasonable.

uneasy *a.* **1** (*troubled, anxious*) agitated, alarmed, anxious, apprehensive, discomposed, disturbed, edgy, ill at ease, impatient, jittery, nervous, nervy, perturbed, restive, restless, troubled, uncomfortable, unsettled, upset, worried. ANTONYMS: relaxed, unperturbed. **2** (*disturbing, disquieting*) bothering, dismaying, disquieting, disturbing, troubling, upsetting, worrying. **3** (*awkward, constrained*) awkward, constrained, insecure, precarious, shaky, stiff, strained, tense, uncomfortable, unstable. ANTONYMS: comfortable, relaxed.

uneducated *a.* (*not educated, not well-educated*) ignorant, illiterate, unenlightened, unlettered, unread, unschooled, untaught. ANTONYMS: educated, literate.

unemotional *a.* (*not showing one's feelings*) aloof, apathetic, cold, cool, frigid, icy, impassive, indifferent, listless, passionless, phlegmatic, reserved, undemonstrative, unexcitable, unfeeling, unimpressionable, unmoved, unresponsive. ANTONYMS: emotional, excitable.

unemployed *a.* (*having no paid work; not in work*) idle, jobless, laid off, (*coll.*) on the dole, out of work, redundant, workless. ANTONYMS: employed.

unequal *a.* **1** (*not equal (to)*) found wanting, inadequate, incapable, insufficient, not up (to), unable. **2** (*uneven; varying*) asymmetrical, different, differing, disparate, disproportionate, dissimilar, irregular, unbalanced, uneven, unlike, unmatched, variable, varying. ANTONYMS: balanced, equal. **3** ((*of a contest etc.*) *not evenly balanced*) ill-matched, one-sided, unfair.

unequivocal *a.* (*not ambiguous; plain*) absolute, categorical, certain, clear, definite, evident, explicit, incontrovertible, indisputable, manifest, obvious, plain, positive, sure, unambiguous, uncontestable, undeniable, unmistakable, unquestionable. ANTONYMS: ambiguous, equivocal.

unethical *a.* (*wrong, immoral*) (*coll.*) crooked, dirty, dishonest, dishonourable, disreputable, illegal, immoral, improper, inequitable, shady, unconscionable, underhand, unfair, unprincipled, unprofessional, unscrupulous, wrong.

uneven *a.* **1** (*not even or smooth*) bumpy, lumpy, rough, rugged. ANTONYMS: even, level. **2** (*not uniform or regular*) broken, changeable, fitful, fluctuating, intermittent, irregular, jerky, patchy, spasmodic, unsteady, variable. ANTONYMS: regular, uniform. **3** ((*of a contest etc.*) *not equal*) ill-matched, one-sided, unequal, unfair.

unfair *a.* **1** (*not equitable; not impartial*) arbitrary, biased, bigoted, discriminatory, inequitable, one-sided, partial, partisan, prejudiced, uneven, unjust. ANTONYMS: fair, impartial. **2** (*dishonourable, fraudulent*) (*coll.*) crooked, dishonest, dishonourable, fraudulent, undue, unethical, unprincipled, unreasonable, unscrupulous, unsporting, unwarranted, wrongful. ANTONYMS: ethical, principled.

unfaithful *a.* **1** (*not faithful to a promise, vow etc.*) deceitful, disloyal, faithless, false, †false-hearted, perfidious, treacherous, treasonable, unreliable, untrustworthy. ANTONYMS: faithful, loyal. **2** (*adulterous*) adulterous, faithless, fickle, inconstant, (*coll.*) two-timing, unchaste, untrue.

unfamiliar *a.* **1** (*unknown*) alien, bizarre, curious, different, new, novel, odd, peculiar, strange, unaccustomed, uncommon, unconventional, unknown, unusual. ANTONYMS: familiar. **2** (*unacquainted* (*with*), *inexperienced* (*in*)) inexperienced (in), unaccustomed (to), unacquainted (with), uninformed (about), uninitiated (in), unpractised (in), unskilled (in), unused (to), unversed (in). ANTONYMS: experienced (in), used (to), versed (in).

unfashionable *a.* (*unpopular, not fashionable*) antiquated, behind the times, dated, obsolete, old-fashioned, (*coll.*) old hat, out, outmoded, out of date, out of fashion, passé, (*coll.*) square, unpopular. ANTONYMS: fashionable, modern.

unfavourable *a.* **1** (*not good*) adverse, bad, contrary, detrimental, disadvantageous, hostile, infelicitous, inimical, low, negative, poor, unfortunate, unfriendly, unsuited. **2** (*inconvenient*) inauspicious, inconvenient, inopportune, ominous, threatening, unlucky, unpromising, unpropitious, unseasonable, untimely, untoward. ANTONYMS: favourable, promising.

unfinished *a.* **1** (*not finished, incomplete*) deficient, imperfect, incomplete, lacking, uncompleted, undone, unfulfilled, wanting. ANTONYMS: finished. **2** (*not having been through a finishing process*) bare, crude, natural, raw, rough, unpolished, unrefined, unvarnished. ANTONYMS: perfected, refined.

unfit *a.* **1** (*not fit* (*to do, for etc.*)) ill-equipped, inadequate, incapable, incompetent, ineffectual, ineligible, inept, no good, unequal (to), unprepared, unqualified, untrained, useless. ANTONYMS: able, competent. **2** (*unsuitable* (*for*)) ill-adapted, inadequate, inappropriate, ineffective, unsuitable, useless. **3** (*not in good physical condition*) debilitated, decrepit, delicate, feeble, flabby, frail, in poor condition, out of condition, out of shape, out of trim, unhealthy, weak. ANTONYMS: fit, healthy.

unfledged *a.* (*inexperienced and immature*) callow, green, immature, inexperienced, raw, undeveloped, untried, young. ANTONYMS: experienced.

unfold *v.t.* **1** (*to open the folds of*) open out, spread out, unfurl. **2** (*to discover; to reveal*) clarify, describe, disclose, discover, divulge, explain, illustrate, make known, present, reveal, show, uncover.

~*v.i.* **1** (*to spread open; to expand*) expand, spread open, stretch out, uncoil, unfurl. **2** (*to develop*) blossom, develop, evolve, grow, mature.

unforeseen *a.* (*not expected*) abrupt, accidental, startling, sudden, surprise, unanticipated, undreamt of, unexpected, unlooked for, unpredicted, unsought. ANTONYMS: expected, foretold.

unforgivable *a.* (*so bad or cruel that it cannot be forgiven*) deplorable, disgraceful, indefensible, inexcusable, reprehensible, unjustifiable, unpardonable, unwarrantable. ANTONYMS: excusable, forgivable.

unfortunate *a.* **1** (*not fortunate, unlucky*) cursed, luckless, out of luck, unlucky. ANTONYMS: fortunate. **2** (*unhappy*) dismal, doomed, forlorn, hapless, hopeless, miserable, pathetic, poor, unhappy, unprosperous, wretched. ANTONYMS: happy. **3** (*regrettable*) deplorable, ill-advised, inappropriate, infelicitous, lamentable, regrettable, unsuitable. **4** (*unsuccessful; disastrous*) awful, calamitous, catastrophic, disastrous, ill-fated, ill-starred, inauspicious, inopportune, ruinous, terrible, tragic, unfavourable, unsuccessful, untoward. ANTONYMS: successful.

unfriendly *a.* **1** (*not friendly*) aloof, antagonistic, chilly, cold, cruel, disagreeable, distant, hostile, ill-disposed, inhospitable, quarrelsome, sour, surly, uncongenial, unsociable. ANTONYMS: amiable, friendly. **2** ((*of a climate or atmosphere*) *unfavourable*) alien, bleak, hostile, inhospitable, inimical, unfavourable, unpropitious.

ungainly *a.* (*clumsy, awkward*) awkward, clumsy, gangling, gawky, inelegant, loutish, lumbering, slouching, ugly, uncoordinated, uncouth, ungraceful, unwieldy. ANTONYMS: elegant, graceful.

ungodly *a.* **1** (*not godly; wicked*) atheist, bad, blasphemous, corrupt, depraved, diabolical, evil, godless, heretical, immoral, impious, iniquitous, irreligious, irreverent, profane, sacrilegious, sinful, vile, villainous, wicked. ANTONYMS: pious, religious. **2** (*outrageous*) appalling, awful, dreadful, frightful, horrendous, indecent, intolerable, nasty, outrageous, shocking, terrible, unearthly, (*coll.*) unholy, unreasonable, unseemly.

ungrateful *a.* (*not thankful*) heedless, †ingrate, selfish, unappreciative, unmindful, unthankful. ANTONYMS: appreciative, grateful.

unguarded *a.* **1** (*not guarded*) defenceless, exposed, open to attack, uncovered, undefended, unfortified, unpatrolled, unprotected, vulnerable. ANTONYMS: defended, protected. **2** (*careless, incautious*) careless, foolhardy, guileless, hasty, heedless, ill-considered, imprudent, inadvertent, inattentive, incautious, indiscreet, rash, thoughtless, undiplomatic, unmindful, unthinking, unwary, unwise. ANTONYMS: cautious, prudent.

unhappy *a.* **1** (*not happy, miserable*) (*coll.*) blue, crestfallen, dejected, depressed, despondent, disconsolate, dispirited, down, downhearted, forlorn, gloomy, glum, heavy-hearted, melancholy, miserable, mournful, sad, sorrowful, wretched. ANTONYMS: cheerful, happy. **2** (*unlucky, unfortunate*) cursed, doomed, hapless, ill-fated, ill-omened, ill-starred, inauspicious, luckless, unfortunate, unlucky, unpropitious. ANTONYMS: fortunate, lucky. **3** (*inappropriate*) awkward, clumsy, ill-advised, ill-timed, inappropriate, inept, inexpedient, infelicitous, injudicious, tactless, unsuitable, wrong. ANTONYMS: appropriate, suitable.

unhealthy *a.* **1** (*not enjoying good health*) ailing, debilitated, delicate, feeble, frail, ill, indisposed, infirm, in poor health, invalid, poorly, sick, sickly, unfit, unsound, unwell, weak. ANTONYMS: fit, healthy. **2** (*dangerous*) damaging, dangerous, deleterious, destructive, detrimental, harmful, injurious, insalubrious, insanitary, malign, noisome, noxious, unwholesome.

unheard-of *a.* **1** (*not heard of*) nameless, obscure, undiscovered, unfamiliar, unidentified, unknown, unremarked, unsung. ANTONYMS: famous, well-known. **2** (*unprecedented*) inconceivable, new, novel, singular, unbelievable, undreamt of, unimaginable, unique, unprecedented, unusual. ANTONYMS: conventional. **3** (*shocking, unthinkable*) disgraceful, extreme, offensive, outlandish, outrageous, preposterous, shocking, unacceptable, unthinkable.

unhesitating *a.* **1** (*firm, without hesitation*) implicit, resolute, staunch, steadfast, undeviating, unfaltering, unqualified, unquestioning, unreserved, unswerving, unwavering, wholehearted. ANTONYMS: hesitant, irresolute. **2** (*immediate*) immediate, instant, instantaneous, prompt, quick, rapid, ready, swift, without delay.

unhurried *a.* (*relaxed, not rushed*) calm, casual, deliberate, easy, easygoing, gradual, leisurely, sedate, slow, slow and steady, slow-paced, steady, unrushed. ANTONYMS: hectic, rushed.

unidentified *a.* (*unknown, unnamed*) anonymous, mysterious, nameless, strange, unclassified, unfamiliar, unknown, unmarked, unnamed, unrecognized, unrevealed. ANTONYMS: identified, known.

uniform *a.* (*the same, not changing*) alike, consistent, constant, even, homogeneous, identical, regular, similar, unaltering, unchanging, undeviating, unvarying. ANTONYMS: changeable, irregular.

unimaginative *a.* (*not creative*) banal, barren, commonplace, derivative, dry, dull, everyday, hackneyed, lifeless, ordinary, pedestrian, predictable, prosaic, routine, tame, trite, uncreative, uninspired, unoriginal, usual. ANTONYMS: creative, imaginative.

unimportant *a.* (*not important*) immaterial, inconsequential, inconsiderable, insignificant, irrelevant, minor, paltry, petty, slight, small, trifling, trivial, worthless. ANTONYMS: important, significant.

uninhabited *a.* (*in which no one lives*) abandoned, barren, depopulated, deserted, desolate, empty, trackless, unfrequented, unoccupied, unpopulated, unsettled, untenanted, vacant. ANTONYMS: inhabited.

uninhibited *a.* **1** (*expressing one's feelings openly*) candid, casual, easygoing, frank, free, free and easy, informal, instinctive, liberated, natural, open, outspoken, relaxed, spontaneous, unrepressed, unreserved, unselfconscious, (*coll.*) upfront. ANTONYMS: bashful, self-conscious. **2** (*unrestrained*) boisterous, free, intemperate, unbridled, unchecked, unconstrained, uncontrolled, uncurbed, unrestrained, unrestricted, wild. ANTONYMS: curbed, restrained.

uninteresting *a.* (*boring, dull*) boring, commonplace, drab, dreary, dry, dull, flat, humdrum, mind-numbing, monotonous, stale, tedious, tiresome, uneventful, unexciting, uninspiring, wearisome. ANTONYMS: interesting, intriguing.

uninviting *a.* (*not attractive, repellent*) disagreeable, disgusting, distasteful, nasty, obnoxious, offensive, off-putting, repellent, repulsive, revolting, sickening, unappealing, unappetizing, unattractive, undesirable, unpleasant, unsavoury, untempting, unwelcoming. ANTONYMS: attractive, inviting.

union *n.* **1** (*the act of uniting; the state of being united*) amalgamation, unification, uniting. **2** (*a combination of parts or members forming a whole*) amalgam, amalgamation, blend, combination, confederation, conjunction, fusion, junction, league, marriage, mixture, synthesis, uniting. ANTONYMS: separation. **3** (*a political unit formed by such a combination*) alliance, association, bloc, cartel, circle, club, coalition, confederacy, consortium, federation, fellowship, fraternity, guild, league, organization, party, ring, society, syndicate. **4** (*a trade union*) combination, guild, trade association, trade union. **5** (*agreement of mind, will or affection*) accord, agreement, concert, concord, concurrence, congruity, harmony, unanimity, unison, unity. ANTONYMS: discord. **6** (*marriage*) coupling, marriage, matrimony, wedlock.

unique *a.* **1** (*having no like or equal*) incomparable, inimitable, matchless, nonpareil, peerless, second to none, unequalled, unexampled, unmatched, unparalleled, unrivalled, unsurpassed, without equal. **2** (*very unusual or remarkable*) exceptional, extraordinary, peculiar, rare, remarkable, singular, unusual. ANTONYMS: commonplace.

unit *n.* **1** (*a single person, thing, or group, regarded as complete*) assembly, detachment, entity, group, section, system, whole. **2** (*each one of a number of things, persons etc., forming a plurality*) component, constituent, element, item, member, module, part, piece, portion, section, segment. **3** (*a quantity adopted as the standard of measurement or calculation*) measure, measurement, module, quantity. **4** (*a part of a larger military formation*) squad, task force, team.

unite *v.t.* **1** (*to join together so as to make one*) ally, associate, band, club together, cooperate, join together, pool, pull together. **2** (*to combine, to amalgamate*) amalgamate, blend, combine, consolidate, couple, fuse, incorporate, join, link, marry, meld, merge, mingle, mix, unify, wed. ANTONYMS: part, separate. **3** (*to cause to adhere*) bond, connect, fix, fuse, glue, join, stick, weld.

unity *n.* **1** (*the state or condition of being one or individual*) individuality, integrity, oneness, singularity. ANTONYMS: plurality. **2** (*the state of being united, union*) solidarity, unanimity, union, unison. **3** (*an agreement of parts or elements, structural coherence*) agreement, coherence, consistency, constancy, continuity, sameness, uniformity. **4** (*concord, agreement*) accord, agreement, assent, concord, concurrence, consensus, harmony, peace, rapport, sympathy. ANTONYMS: disagreement, discord. **5** (*a thing forming a coherent whole*) entity, unit, whole.

universal *a.* (*of or relating to the whole world or all persons or things in the world*) all-embracing, all-encompassing, all-inclusive, catholic, common, comprehensive, entire, general, limitless, omnipresent, prevalent, total, ubiquitous, unlimited, whole, wide-ranging, widespread, worldwide. ANTONYMS: limited, narrow.

unjustifiable *a.* (*wrong, having no good reason to justify it*) indefensible, inexcusable, outrageous, unacceptable, unforgivable, unpardonable, unwarrantable, wrong. ANTONYMS: justifiable.

unkempt *a.* 1 ((*of hair*) *uncombed*) tousled, uncombed, ungroomed. 2 (*scruffy and untidy*) bedraggled, disarranged, disarrayed, dishevelled, disordered, down-at-heel, messy, rumpled, scruffy, shabby, shaggy, sloppy, slovenly, sluttish, untidy. ANTONYMS: tidy, trim.

unkind *a.* 1 (*not kind, cruel*) callous, cruel, hard, harsh, heartless, inconsiderate, inhuman, insensitive, malicious, mean, nasty, pitiless, severe, spiteful, stern, unbending, unfeeling, unfriendly, unpitying, unsympathetic. ANTONYMS: kind, sympathetic. 2 (*not pleasant*) inclement, rough, unfavourable, unpleasant.

unknown *a.* 1 (*not known*) anonymous, nameless, uncharted, undiscovered, unexplored, unidentified, unnamed. 2 (*secret, hidden*) concealed, dark, hidden, mysterious, new, novel, secret, strange, unrecognized, unrevealed, untold. 3 (*not famous*) humble, little-known, obscure, undistinguished, unfamiliar, unheard-of, unsung. ANTONYMS: famous.

unlike *a.* (*dissimilar*) contrasted, different, disparate, dissimilar, distinct, distinguishable, divergent, diverse, ill-matched, incompatible, opposite, separate, unalike, unequal, unrelated. ANTONYMS: alike, similar.

unlikely *a.* 1 (*improbable*) doubtful, dubious, faint, improbable, remote, slight, unimaginable, unthinkable. ANTONYMS: likely. 2 (*unpromising*) implausible, inconceivable, incredible, questionable, unbelievable, unconvincing, unpromising.

unlimited *a.* 1 (*not limited; having no bounds*) boundless, countless, endless, extensive, great, illimitable, immeasurable, immense, incalculable, indefinite, inexhaustible, infinite, innumerable, interminable, limitless, measureless, never-ending, unbounded, unnumbered, vast. ANTONYMS: finite, limited. 2 (*unconfined, unrestrained*) absolute, all-encompassing, complete, full, total, unchecked, unconditional, unconfined, unconstrained, uncontrolled, unfettered, unqualified, unrestrained, unrestricted. ANTONYMS: confined, restricted.

unlucky *a.* 1 (*not lucky or fortunate*) adverse, luckless, miserable, poor, unfortunate, unhappy, unsuccessful, wretched. ANTONYMS: fortunate, lucky. 2 (*inauspicious, ill-omened*) cursed, doomed, hapless, ill-fated, ill-omened, ill-starred, inauspicious, ominous, unfavourable. 3 (*not well considered*) ill-considered, ill-judged.

unmanageable *a.* 1 (*not manageable; not easily controlled*) awkward, bulky, cumbersome, inconvenient, unwieldy. ANTONYMS: handy. 2 ((*esp. of young people*) *difficult to control*) difficult, intractable, obstreperous, out of hand, recalcitrant, refractory, (*coll.*) stroppy, uncontrollable, ungovernable, unruly, wild. ANTONYMS: compliant, manageable.

unmentionable *a.* (*not fit to be mentioned*) appalling, disgraceful, disreputable, forbidden, frowned on, immodest, indecent, indescribable, inexpressible, obscene, scandalous, shameful, shocking, taboo, unrepeatable, unspeakable, unutterable.

unmerciful *a.* (*showing no mercy*) brutal, cruel, hard, heartless, implacable, inexorable, mean, merciless, pitiless, relentless, remorseless, ruthless, stony-hearted, uncaring, unfeeling, unforgiving, unkind, unrelenting, unsparing, vicious. ANTONYMS: pitying, sparing.

unmistakable *a.* (*that cannot be mistaken; plain*) blatant, clear, conspicuous, decided, distinct, evident, glaring, indisputable, manifest, obvious, palpable, patent, plain, pronounced, sure, unambiguous, unequivocal, unquestionable. ANTONYMS: ambiguous, obscure.

unmitigated *a.* 1 (*not mitigated*) absolute, arrant, categorical, complete, consummate, downright, out-and-out, outright, plain, rank, sheer, thorough, thoroughgoing, total, utter. 2 (*unqualified*) grim, harsh, intense, oppressive, persistent, relentless, unabated, unalleviated, unalloyed, unbroken, undiluted, undiminished, unmixed, unmoderated, unmodified, unqualified, unredeemed, unrelieved, untempered.

unmoved *a.* 1 (*not changed in purpose, firm*) calm, collected, determined, firm, inflexible, resolute, resolved, steadfast, undeviating, unshaken, unwavering. ANTONYMS: irresolute, wavering. 2 (*not moved*) fast, firm, in place, in position, steady, unchanged, unshaken, untouched. **3** (*not affected emotionally*) adamant, aloof, cold, cool, dispassionate, dry-eyed, impassive, indifferent, stolid, stony, unaffected, uncaring, unemotional, unfeeling, unimpressed, unresponsive, unstirred, unsympathetic, untouched. ANTONYMS: affected, touched.

unnatural *a.* **1** (*not natural; contrary to nature*) aberrant, abnormal, anomalous, irregular, odd, perverse, perverted, unusual. ANTONYMS: natural, normal. **2** (*odd, not in accordance with accepted standards of behaviour*) bizarre, eccentric, extraordinary, freakish, grotesque, odd, outlandish, peculiar, queer, strange, supernatural, unaccountable, uncanny, unconventional, unexpected, weird. **3** (*monstrous, inhuman*) brutal, callous, cold-blooded, cruel, evil, fiendish, heartless, inhuman, monstrous, ruthless, savage, unfeeling, wicked. ANTONYMS: humane. **4** (*artificial*) artificial, false, feigned. ANTONYMS: genuine, honest. **5** (*forced, affected*) affected, assumed, contrived, forced, insincere, laboured, mannered, (*coll.*) phoney, restrained, self-conscious, stagy, stiff, stilted, strained, studied, theatrical.

unnecessary *a.* (*needless, superfluous*) dispensable, expendable, inessential, needless, non-essential, redundant, superfluous, surplus, uncalled for, unneeded, useless. ANTONYMS: essential, necessary.

unobtrusive *a.* (*not attracting attention*) humble, inconspicuous, low-key, meek, modest, quiet, reserved, restrained, reticent, retiring, self-effacing, subdued, suppressed, unassuming, unnoticeable, unostentatious, unpretentious. ANTONYMS: conspicuous, noticeable.

unorthodox *a.* (*different from what is generally accepted*) aberrant, abnormal, deviant, heretical, heterodox, irregular, nonconformist, (*coll.*) off the wall, unconventional, uncustomary, unusual, unwonted. ANTONYMS: conventional, orthodox.

unpalatable *a.* **1** (*tasting unpleasant*) bitter, disgusting, distasteful, horrid, inedible, nasty, sour, unappetizing, unattractive, uneatable, unpleasant, unsavoury. ANTONYMS: appetizing, palatable. **2** (*unpleasant and difficult to accept*) disagreeable, distasteful, offensive, repugnant, repulsive, unpleasant, unsavoury. ANTONYMS: pleasant.

unparalleled *a.* (*unequalled, unprecedented*) beyond compare, consummate, exceptional, incomparable, inimitable, matchless, peerless, rare, singular, special, superior, superlative, unequalled, unheard-of, unique, unmatched,

unprecedented, unrivalled, unsurpassed, unusual.

unpleasant *a.* (*not pleasant; disagreeable*) abhorrent, annoying, bad, detestable, displeasing, distasteful, horrid, ill-natured, irksome, nasty, objectionable, obnoxious, offensive, repulsive, troublesome, unattractive, unlikeable, unlovely, unpalatable. ANTONYMS: agreeable, pleasant.

unpopular *a.* (*not liked by most people*) avoided, detested, disliked, friendless, hated, ignored, objectionable, out of favour, rejected, shunned, snubbed, spurned, unattractive, undesirable, unloved, unwanted, unwelcome. ANTONYMS: liked, popular.

unpredictable *a.* **1** (*that cannot be predicted*) unforseeable. ANTONYMS: predictable. **2** (*whose behaviour cannot be predicted or relied on*) capricious, chance, changeable, doubtful, erratic, fickle, questionable, random, uncertain, unreliable, unstable, unsure, variable. ANTONYMS: dependable, reliable.

unprejudiced *a.* (*willing to consider different opinions*) balanced, detached, disinterested, even-handed, fair, fair-minded, impartial, indifferent, just, neutral, non-partisan, objective, open-minded, unbiased, unbigoted, uninfluenced. ANTONYMS: biased, prejudiced.

unpremeditated *a.* (*not planned beforehand; unintentional*) ad lib, automatic, casual, extemporaneous, extempore, impromptu, impulsive, natural, offhand, off the cuff, spontaneous, spur-of-the-moment, unarranged, uncontrived, unintentional, unplanned, unprepared, unstudied. ANTONYMS: deliberate, premeditated.

unpretentious *a.* (*simple, not (pretending to be) sophisticated*) honest, humble, modest, plain, simple, straightforward, unaffected, unassuming, unobtrusive, unostentatious. ANTONYMS: conceited, ostentatious.

unpromising *a.* (*not likely to be successful*) adverse, baleful, discouraging, doubtful, gloomy, hopeless, inauspicious, infelicitous, ominous, portentous, threatening, unfavourable, unpropitious. ANTONYMS: promising.

unqualified *a.* **1** (*not qualified; not competent*) ill-equipped, incapable, incompetent, ineligible, unfit, unprepared, unsuited, untrained. ANTONYMS: qualified. **2** (*not limited by conditions or exceptions*) absolute, categorical, complete, consummate, downright, outright, perfect, pure, thorough, thoroughgoing, total, true, unconditional, unlimited, unmitigated, unreserved, unrestricted, utter, wholehearted. ANTONYMS: half-hearted, partial.

unquestionable *a.* (*not to be questioned or doubted*) absolute, certain, clear, conclusive, definite, incontestable, incontrovertible, indisputable, indubitable, irrefutable, manifest, obvious, patent, self-evident, sure, undeniable, undoubted, unmistakable. ANTONYMS: dubious, questionable.

unravel *v.t.* **1** (*to separate the threads of; to disentangle*) disentangle, extricate, free, separate, straighten out, unknot, untangle, untwist, unwind. **2** (*to clear up* (*a mystery, the plot of a play etc.*)) clear up, decipher, explain, figure out, get straight, interpret, make out, puzzle out, resolve, solve, (*sl.*) suss out, work out.

unreal *a.* **1** (*not real*) artificial, counterfeit, fake, false, fraudulent, insincere, mock, ostensible, pretended, seeming, sham, spurious, synthetic. ANTONYMS: authentic, genuine. **2** (*visionary, imaginary*) dreamlike, fabulous, fanciful, fantastic, hypothetical, illusory, imaginary, immaterial, impalpable, insubstantial, intangible, make-believe, mythical, nebulous, non-existent, spectral, unrealistic, unsubstantial, visionary. **3** (*amazing*) amazing, (*coll.*) cool, impressive, stupendous, (*sl.*) wicked.

unreasonable *a.* **1** (*exorbitant, extravagant*) excessive, exorbitant, extortionate, extravagant, immoderate, improper, inordinate, outrageous, (*coll.*) steep, uncalled for, unconscionable, undue, unfair, unjust, unjustifiable, unwarranted. ANTONYMS: moderate, reasonable. **2** (*not sensible*) absurd, capricious, crazy, erratic, far-fetched, foolish, headstrong, idiotic, illogical, inconsistent, insane, irrational, ludicrous, mad, nonsensical, preposterous, quirky, senseless, silly, stupid. ANTONYMS: rational, sensible.

unrelenting *a.* (*continuing without stopping*) ceaseless, constant, continual, continuous, endless, incessant, inexorable, perpetual, relentless, remorseless, steady, unabated, unbroken, unremitting, unwavering. ANTONYMS: intermittent.

unreliable *a.* **1** (*not able to be trusted*) capricious, changeable, disreputable, erratic, irresponsible, treacherous, undependable, unstable, untrustworthy, weak. ANTONYMS: dependable, reliable. **2** (*likely to be wrong*) deceptive, delusive, erroneous, fake, fallible, false, implausible, inaccurate, mistaken, specious, uncertain, unconvincing, unsound. ANTONYMS: infallible.

unrepentant *a.* (*not ashamed of one's behaviour*) impenitent, incorrigible, inveterate, obdurate, shameless, unapologetic, unashamed, unembarrassed, unregenerate, unremorseful. ANTONYMS: contrite, repentant.

unreserved *a.* **1** (*not reserved*) available, free, unbooked. **2** (*open, frank*) demonstrative, extrovert, forthright, frank, free, open, outgoing, outspoken, uninhibited, unrestrained. ANTONYMS: demure, shy. **3** (*given or done without reservation*) absolute, complete, entire, full, total, unconditional, unlimited, unqualified, wholehearted. ANTONYMS: conditional.

unrest *n.* **1** (*restlessness, uneasiness*) agitation, agony, anguish, anxiety, concern, discontent, disquiet, dissatisfaction, distress, disturbance, nervousness, perturbation, restlessness, strife, trepidation, trouble, uneasiness, worry. **2** (*lack of rest*) agitation, discord, dissension, protest, rebellion, sedition, strife, tumult, turmoil, upheaval. ANTONYMS: peace, tranquillity.

unrestrained *a.* (*not controlled*) abandoned, free, immoderate, inordinate, intemperate, natural, unbridled, unchecked, unconstrained, uncontrolled, unhindered, uninhabited, unrepressed, wild. ANTONYMS: inhibited, restrained.

unruly *a.* (*not submitting to restraint; disorderly*) defiant, disobedient, disorderly, fractious, headstrong, insubordinate, obstreperous, rebellious, refractory, stubborn, tempestuous, tumultuous, turbulent, uncontrollable, undisciplined, ungovernable, unmanageable, wayward, wilful. ANTONYMS: obedient, orderly.

unsatisfactory *a.* (*not satisfactory; unacceptable*) defective, deficient, disappointing, displeasing, faulty, flawed, imperfect, inadequate, inappropriate, inferior, insufficient, lacking, mediocre, (*coll.*) pathetic, poor, unacceptable, unsuitable, wanting. ANTONYMS: excellent, satisfactory.

unsavoury *a.* **1** (*repellent, disgusting*) disagreeable, disgusting, distasteful, nasty, nauseating, objectionable, obnoxious, offensive, repellent, repugnant, repulsive, revolting, sickening, unattractive, unpleasant. **2** (*of unpleasant taste or smell*) flat, insipid, smelly, tasteless, unappetizing, unpalatable, vapid. ANTONYMS: appetizing, palatable. **3** (*morally offensive*) dubious, immoral, seamy, sordid.

unscrupulous *a.* (*having no scruples of conscience*) amoral, corrupt, (*coll.*) crooked, cunning, dishonest, dishonourable, faithless, immoral, roguish, ruthless, shameless, shifty, sly, sneaky, unconscientious, unethical, unprincipled. ANTONYMS: ethical, principled.

unseemly *a.* **1** (*inappropriate*) imprudent,

inappropriate, inexpedient, inopportune, out of place, unfortunate, unsuitable, untimely. ANTONYMS: appropriate, opportune. **2** (*not polite, rude*) coarse, discreditable, disreputable, improper, indecent, indecorous, indelicate, lewd, obscene, offensive, risqué, rude, shameful, unbecoming, unbefitting, undignified, ungentlemanly, unladylike, unrefined. ANTONYMS: becoming, dignified, polite.

unselfish *a.* (*concerned for the interests of others rather than one's own*) altruistic, charitable, devoted, disinterested, generous, giving, humanitarian, kind, liberal, magnanimous, noble, open-handed, philanthropic, self-denying, selfless, self-sacrificing, ungrudging, unsparing, unstinting. ANTONYMS: selfish.

unsettled *a.* **1** (*not fixed or determined*) changeable, debatable, disorderly, disorganized, doubtful, fluid, inconstant, insecure, moot, shaky, uncertain, undecided, undetermined, unpredictable, unresolved, unstable, unsteady, variable. ANTONYMS: determined, fixed. **2** (*undecided, hesitating*) agitated, anxious, changeable, confused, disturbed, flustered, hesitating, on edge, perturbed, restive, restless, ruffled, shaken, tense, troubled, turbulent, undecided, uneasy, unnerved, upset. ANTONYMS: calm, composed. **3** (*unpaid*) due, in arrears, outstanding, owing, payable, pending, unpaid. **4** (*not settled, uncolonized*) uncolonized, uninhabited, unoccupied, unpeopled, unpopulated.

unsightly *a.* (*unpleasing to the sight, ugly*) disagreeable, hideous, horrible, horrid, plain, repulsive, revolting, ugly, unattractive, unlovely, unpleasant, unprepossessing. ANTONYMS: attractive, pleasing.

unskilful *a.* (*not skilful, inept*) amateurish, awkward, bungling, clumsy, (*sl.*) cowboy, fumbling, (*coll.*) ham-fisted, incompetent, inept, inexpert, maladroit, plodding, unhandy, unpractised, unprofessional, untalented, unworkmanlike. ANTONYMS: skilful.

unsociable *a.* (*not sociable, solitary*) aloof, chilly, cold, cool, distant, hostile, inhospitable, introverted, reclusive, reticent, retiring, solitary, stand-offish, uncommunicative, uncongenial, unforthcoming, unfriendly, unsocial, withdrawn. ANTONYMS: gregarious, sociable.

unsolicited *a.* (*given without being asked for*) gratuitous, spontaneous, unasked for, uncalled for, uninvited, unrequested, unsought, unwelcome, voluntary. ANTONYMS: requested.

unsophisticated *a.* **1** (*simple, artless*) artless, childlike, guileless, inexperienced, ingenuous, innocent, naive, natural, plain, simple, straightforward, unaffected, uncomplicated, uninvolved, unpolished, unrefined, unspecialized, untutored, unworldly. ANTONYMS: sophisticated, worldly-wise. **2** (*pure, genuine*) genuine, pure, unadulterated, uncorrupted. ANTONYMS: artificial.

unsound *a.* **1** (*diseased*) afflicted, ailing, defective, delicate, demented, deranged, diseased, frail, ill, impaired, infirm, injured, insane, mad, sickly, unbalanced, unhealthy, unhinged, unstable, unwell. **2** (*weak, decayed*) decayed, dilapidated, rotten, weak. ANTONYMS: sound. **3** (*unreliable*) defective, faulty, flawed, flimsy, insecure, ramshackle, rickety, shaky, tottering, unreliable, unsafe, unstable, unsteady, wobbly. ANTONYMS: reliable, stable. **4** (*ill-founded, fallacious*) erroneous, fallacious, false, ill-founded, illogical, invalid, specious. ANTONYMS: valid. **5** (*unorthodox*) unconventional, unorthodox.

unspoiled *a.* (*not spoiled*) intact, natural, perfect, preserved, pristine, pure, simple, spotless, unaffected, unblemished, unchanged, undamaged, unharmed, unimpaired, unstained, unsullied, untainted, untouched, virgin, whole. ANTONYMS: damaged, spoiled.

unspoken *a.* **1** (*understood without being spoken*) assumed, implicit, implied, tacit, taken for granted, undeclared, understood, unexpressed, unstated. ANTONYMS: declared, explicit. **2** (*not uttered*) mute, silent, unsaid, unuttered, voiceless, wordless.

unstable *a.* **1** (*not stable, not firm*) insecure, precarious, rickety, risky, shaky, tottering, unsettled, unsteady, wobbly. ANTONYMS: firm, stable. **2** (*liable to sudden shifts of mood*) capricious, fickle, flighty, inconstant, indecisive, irrational, irresolute, mercurial, temperamental, vacillating, volatile. **3** (*changeable*) changeable, erratic, fitful, fluctuating, inconsistent, unpredictable, untrustworthy, variable. ANTONYMS: consistent, predictable.

unsuccessful *a.* **1** (*ineffective, unfruitful*) abortive, failed, fruitless, futile, ineffective, ineffectual, sterile, unavailing, unfruitful, unproductive, unprofitable, useless, vain, worthless. ANTONYMS: fruitful, successful. **2** (*defeated, unlucky*) beaten, cursed, defeated, foiled, frustrated, hapless, ill-fated, ill-starred, jinxed, losing, luckless, unfortunate, unlucky. ANTONYMS: victorious.

unsuitable *a.* (*not suitable, not appropriate*) impractical, improper, inapposite, inappropriate, inapt, incompatible, incongruous, infelicitous, out of keeping, out of place, unacceptable, unbecoming, unfitting, unseasonable, unseemly, unsuited. ANTONYMS: appropriate, suitable.

unsure *a.* (*uncertain*) distrustful, doubtful, dubious, hesitant, irresolute, mistrustful, sceptical, suspicious, uncertain, unconvinced, undecided. ANTONYMS: convinced, resolute.

unsuspecting *a.* (*not aware of what is happening*) confiding, credulous, gullible, ignorant, inexperienced, ingenuous, innocent, naive, off guard, trustful, trusting, unaware, unconscious, unknowing, unsuspicious, unwary.

unsympathetic *a.* (*uncaring, unkind*) aloof, apathetic, callous, cold, cruel, heartless, inconsiderate, indifferent, insensitive, pitiless, stony-hearted, uncaring, uncompassionate, unconcerned, unkind, unmoved, unpitying, unresponsive, untouched. ANTONYMS: compassionate, sympathetic.

untarnished *a.* (*not spoilt, clean*) bright, burnished, chaste, clean, immaculate, polished, pure, shining, spotless, stainless, unblemished, uncorrupted, unsoiled, unspotted, unstained, unsullied, untainted, virginal. ANTONYMS: tarnished.

unthinkable *a.* **1** (*incapable of being thought of*) beyond belief, extraordinary, implausible, incomprehensible, inconceivable, incredible, insupportable, (*coll.*) mind-boggling, unbelievable, unimaginable. ANTONYMS: conceivable, imaginable. **2** (*highly improbable*) absurd, illogical, impossible, improbable, laughable, ludicrous, out of the question, preposterous, ridiculous, unacceptable, unlikely. ANTONYMS: reasonable.

unthinking *a.* **1** (*heedless, careless*) automatic, careless, hasty, heedless, impulsive, inadvertent, instinctive, mechanical, mindless, moronic, negligent, oblivious, rash, regardless, senseless, unconscious, unmindful, unreasonable, vacant, witless. ANTONYMS: careful, thoughtful. **2** (*rude*) blundering, discourteous, impolite, imprudent, inconsiderate, indiscreet, insensitive, rude, selfish, tactless, thoughtless, uncivil, undiplomatic.

untidy *a.* (*not tidy, messy*) bedraggled, chaotic, cluttered, disarrayed, dishevelled, disorderly, jumbled, littered, messy, muddled, rumpled, scruffy, shambolic, slipshod, sloppy, slovenly, topsy-turvy, unkempt. ANTONYMS: neat, tidy.

untie *v.t.* **1** (*to undo* (*a knot*), *to unfasten*) unbind, undo, unfasten, unknot, unlace. ANTONYMS: tie. **2** (*to loose from bonds*) free, let go, loosen, release, set free, unbridle.

untiring *a.* (*never tiring; indefatigable*) constant, dedicated, determined, devoted, dogged, incessant, indefatigable, patient, persevering, persistent, staunch, steady, tireless, unfaltering, unflagging, unremitting, unwavering, unwearying. ANTONYMS: wavering.

untold *a.* **1** (*not told or communicated*) hidden, private, secret, uncommunicated, undisclosed, undivulged, unpublished, unrecounted, unrelated, unreported, unrevealed. **2** (*not able to be measured*) countless, immeasurable, incalculable, innumerable, measureless, myriad, uncounted, unnumbered. ANTONYMS: countable. **3** (*incapable of being thought of*) inconceivable, indescribable, inexpressible, undreamt of, unimaginable, unspeakable, unthinkable, unutterable.

untroubled *a.* (*not disturbed by care, sorrow etc.*) calm, collected, composed, peaceful, placid, poised, sedate, self-possessed, serene, steady, tranquil, unconcerned, undisturbed, (*coll.*) unfazed, (*coll.*) unflappable, unflustered, unperturbed, unruffled, unstirred, unworried. ANTONYMS: flustered, troubled.

untrue *a.* **1** (*not in accordance with facts, false*) deceptive, erroneous, fallacious, false, inaccurate, incorrect, lying, mistaken, untruthful, wrong. ANTONYMS: accurate, true. **2** (*not faithful, disloyal* (*to*)) capricious, deceitful, disloyal, faithless, false, fickle, inconstant, perfidious, treacherous, undependable, unfaithful, unreliable, untrustworthy. ANTONYMS: faithful, loyal. **3** (*not conforming to a rule or standard*) imperfect, imprecise, inexact, nonstandard, substandard.

untrustworthy *a.* (*that cannot be trusted*) capricious, deceitful, devious, dishonest, disloyal, faithless, false, fickle, treacherous, two-faced, undependable, unfaithful, unreliable. ANTONYMS: reliable, trustworthy.

untruthful *a.* (*dishonest*) (*coll.*) crooked, deceitful, deceptive, dishonest, dissembling, false, fibbing, hypocritical, insincere, lying, mendacious. ANTONYMS: honest, truthful.

unused[1] *a.* (*not having been or not being used*) fresh, intact, new, original, pristine, untouched.

unused[2] *a.* (*not accustomed* (*to*)) inexperienced (in), unaccustomed (to), unfamiliar (with), unhabituated (to), uninitiated (in), unpractised (in).

unusual *a.* **1** (*not usual*) atypical, exceptional, rare, unique, unprecedented. ANTONYMS: commonplace, usual. **2** (*remarkable*) abnormal, bizarre, curious, extraordinary, notable, odd, peculiar, phenomenal, queer, remarkable, singular, strange, surprising, un-conventional, unexpected, unfamiliar. ANTO-NYMS: ordinary, unremarkable.

unveil *v.t.* **1** (*to remove a covering from* (*a statue etc.*) *with public ceremony*) display, inaug-urate, launch, reveal. **2** (*to reveal, to disclose*) bare, bring to light, disclose, divulge, expose, lay bare, make known, reveal, throw light on, uncover, unmask. ANTONYMS: mask, obscure.

unwary *a.* (*not cautious*) careless, foolhardy, hasty, heedless, imprudent, incautious, indis-creet, mindless, rash, reckless, thoughtless, uncircumspect, unguarded, unthinking, unwatchful, unwise. ANTONYMS: circumspect, wary.

unwavering *a.* (*steadfast, firm*) certain, constant, dedicated, determined, firm, immovable, remorseless, resolute, single-minded, staunch, steadfast, steady, sure, un-blinking, undeviating, unfaltering, unflagging, unshakeable, unswerving, untiring. ANTONYMS: irresolute, wavering.

unwelcome *a.* **1** (*unwanted*) unacceptable, undesirable, uninvited, unpopular, unwanted, unwished for. ANTONYMS: desirable, welcome. **2** (*unpleasant*) disagreeable, displeasing, dis-tasteful, thankless, undesirable, unpleasant. ANTONYMS: agreeable, pleasant.

unwell *a.* **1** (*not well; sick*) ill, off-colour, out of sorts, poorly, sick, sickly, unhealthy. ANTO-NYMS: healthy, well. **2** (*indisposed*) ailing, indisposed, under the weather.

unwholesome *a.* **1** (*having a harmful physical or moral effect*) bad, corrupting, degrading, deleterious, demoralizing, depraving, detri-mental, evil, harmful, immoral, injurious, insalubrious, maleficent, noxious, pernicious, perverting, poisonous, tainted, unhealthy, wicked. ANTONYMS: beneficial, wholesome. **2** (*of unhealthy appearance*) anaemic, pale, pallid, pasty, sickly, wan.

unwieldy *a.* **1** (*that cannot be easily handled owing to size or weight*) awkward, burden-some, cumbersome, inconvenient, oversized, unmanageable, unmanoeuvrable. **2** (*bulky, ponderous*) bulky, clumsy, hefty, massive, ponderous, ungainly, weighty.

unworthy *a.* **1** (*not worthy, not deserving* (*of*)) ineligible, undeserving, unfit. ANTONYMS: de-serving, worthy. **2** (*not becoming, not seemly*) improper, inappropriate, incongruous, out of place, unbecoming, unbefitting, unseemly, unsuitable. ANTONYMS: appropriate, suitable. **3** (*contemptible*) base, contemptible, degrad-ing, despicable, discreditable, disgraceful, dishonourable, disreputable, ignoble, paltry, shameful, worthless.

unyielding *a.* **1** (*unbending, stiff*) inflexible, rigid, stiff, unbending. ANTONYMS: bending, flexible. **2** (*firm, obstinate*) adamant, deter-mined, firm, immovable, inexorable, intract-able, obdurate, obstinate, relentless, resolute, staunch, steadfast, steady, stubborn, uncom-promising, unwavering. ANTONYMS: irresolute.

upbraid *v.t.* (*to reproach; to reprove with severity*) admonish, berate, blame, (*coll.*) car-pet, castigate, chastise, chide, condemn, (*coll.*) dress down, lecture, rebuke, reprimand, reproach, reprove, scold, tear into, (*coll.*) tell off, (*coll.*) tick off. ANTONYMS: praise.

upheaval *n.* (*a violent disturbance, revolution etc.*) cataclysm, change, chaos, commotion, confusion, disorder, disruption, disturbance, eruption, furore, overthrow, revolution, tur-moil, unrest, upset.

uphold *v.t.* **1** (*to hold up*) hold up, support, sustain, take the weight of. **2** (*to support, to maintain*) advocate, aid, back, champion, defend, embrace, encourage, endorse, espouse, justify, maintain, preserve, promote, stand by, stick up for, support, sustain, vindicate. ANTO-NYMS: oppose. **3** (*to approve*) allow, approve, countenance, permit.

upkeep *n.* **1** (*maintenance*) conservation, keep, maintenance, operation, preservation, repair, running, subsistence, support, sustenance. **2** (*the cost of maintenance*) cost, expenditure, expenses, outlay, overheads.

upper *a.* **1** (*higher in place*) high, higher, top, topmost. ANTONYMS: lower. **2** (*superior in rank or status*) elevated, greater, important, superior. ANTONYMS: inferior, junior.

upright *a.* **1** (*erect, perpendicular*) erect, on end, perpendicular, plumb, straight, vertical. ANTONYMS: flat, prostrate. **2** (*righteous, honest*) conscientious, decent, ethical, faithful, good, high-minded, honest, honourable, incor-ruptible, just, moral, principled, righteous, straightforward, trustworthy, unimpeachable, upstanding, virtuous. ANTONYMS: corrupt, wicked.

uprising *n.* (*an insurrection, a riot*) coup, disturbance, insurgence, insurrection, mutiny, outbreak, rebellion, revolt, revolution, riot, rising, upheaval.

uproar *n.* (*a noisy or violent disturbance*) bedlam, brouhaha, clamour, commotion, confusion, din, disorder, disturbance, fracas, furore, fuss, hubbub, mayhem, outcry, pande-monium, racket, riot, (*esp. N Am.*) ruckus, (*coll.*) to-do, tumult. ANTONYMS: peace.

uproarious *a.* **1** (*noisy and disorderly*)

boisterous, clamorous, confused, deafening, disorderly, excited, frenzied, loud, noisy, riotous, rollicking, rowdy, tempestuous, tumultuous, turbulent, unrestrained, wild. ANTONYMS: quiet, still. **2** (*extremely funny*) (*coll.*) convulsive, funny, hilarious, hysterical, (*coll.*) killing, rib-tickling, (*coll.*) rip-roaring, side-splitting. ANTONYMS: sad, serious.

upset¹ *v.t.* **1** (*to overturn*) capsize, invert, knock over, overturn, spill, tip over, topple, upend. **2** (*to put out of one's normal state, to distress*) agitate, discompose, disconcert, dismay, disrupt, distress, disturb, faze, fluster, (*coll.*) hassle, perturb, put out, ruffle, sadden, throw, trouble, unnerve, unsettle, worry. **3** (*to disrupt*) change, disarrange, disorder, disorganize, disrupt, jumble, mess up, mix up, muddle, spoil.

upset² *n.* **1** (*the act of upsetting*) agitation, bother, discomposure, disquiet, distress, disturbance, (*coll.*) hassle, shock, trouble, worry. **2** (*an unexpected reversal in a game etc.*) defeat, reverse, rout, setback, (*coll.*) thrashing. ~*a.* **1** (*overturned*) capsized, inverted, overturned, tipped over, toppled, topsy-turvy, tumbled, upside down. **2** (*distressed*) agitated, apprehensive, bothered, confused, disconcerted, dismayed, disquieted, distracted, distressed, disturbed, frantic, (*coll.*) hassled, hurt, overwrought, perturbed, put out, ruffled, troubled, unnerved, worried. ANTONYMS: calm. **3** (*physically disturbed*) chaotic, confused, disarrayed, disordered, disturbed, jumbled, messed up, muddled. **4** (*feeling ill in one's stomach*) ill, poorly, queasy, sick.

up to date *a.* (*recent, modern*) abreast of the times, contemporary, current, fashionable, in, latest, modern, new, (*coll.*) now, recent, stylish, (*coll., sometimes derog.*) trendy, up-to-the-minute, voguish, (*coll.*) with it. ANTONYMS: old-fashioned, outdated.

urban *a.* (*of or relating to a city or town*) city, civic, metropolitan, municipal, town. ANTONYMS: rural.

urbane *a.* (*polite; suave*) civil, civilized, cosmopolitan, courteous, cultivated, cultured, debonair, elegant, mannerly, polished, polite, refined, smooth, sophisticated, suave, well-bred, well-mannered. ANTONYMS: gauche, uncouth.

urge *v.t.* **1** (*to drive or force onwards*) compel, constrain, drive, egg on, encourage, force, goad, hasten, impel, incite, induce, instigate, persuade, press, prod, prompt, propel, push, speed, spur, stimulate. ANTONYMS: deter, discourage. **2** (*to press earnestly with argument, entreaty etc.*) appeal to, beg, beseech, entreat, exhort, implore, importune, plead, press, solicit, supplicate. **3** (*to press the acceptance or adoption of*) advocate, champion, promote, push, recommend, support. ~*n.* **1** (*a strong impulse*) impetus, impulse, instinct. **2** (*an inner drive or compulsion*) compulsion, craving, desire, drive, fancy, hunger, itch, longing, thirst, wish, yearning, (*coll.*) yen. ANTONYMS: aversion, reluctance.

urgent *a.* **1** (*pressing, demanding early attention*) compelling, critical, crucial, immediate, imperative, important, instant, necessary, pressing, serious, top-priority, vital. ANTONYMS: unimportant. **2** (*demanding or soliciting with importunity*) clamorous, earnest, energetic, firm, forceful, importunate, insistent, intense, persistent, persuasive, pertinacious, solicitous, tenacious. ANTONYMS: apathetic, casual.

use¹ *n.* **1** (*the act of using*) exercise, handling, operation, practice, service, treatment, usage. **2** (*employment in or application to a purpose*) advantage, application, avail, benefit, employment, good, help, point, profit, service, usefulness, utility, value, worth. **3** (*the quality of serving a purpose*) basis, call, cause, end, necessity, object, occasion, point, purpose, reason. **4** (*practice, usage*) custom, habit, practice, usage, way, wont.

use² *v.t.* **1** (*to employ, to apply to a purpose*) apply, bring into play, employ, exercise, exert, find a use for, make use of, operate, ply, practise, press into service, profit by, put into operation, put to use, resort to, utilize, wield, work. **2** (*to exploit for one's own purposes*) abuse, act towards, behave towards, capitalize on, deal with, exploit, handle, manipulate, misuse, take advantage of, treat. **3** (*to use up, to wear out*) consume, deplete, eat, exhaust, expend, fritter away, run through, spend, squander, throw away, use up, waste, wear out. ANTONYMS: conserve, save. **4** (*to accustom, to habituate*) acclimatize, accustom, habituate. **to use up** (*to finish; to consume completely*) consume, deplete, drain, exhaust, finish.

used *a.* (*second-hand*) cast-off, dog-eared, pre-enjoyed, (*esp. N Am.*) pre-owned, second-hand, worn. ANTONYMS: fresh, new, unused.

useful *a.* **1** (*of use, serving a purpose*) functional, handy, helpful, of use, practical, serviceable, usable, utilitarian. ANTONYMS: unhelpful, useless. **2** (*good, advantageous*) advantageous, beneficial, effective, fruitful, gainful, good, productive, profitable, salutary, valuable, worthwhile. **3** (*competent or highly* *satisfactory*) competent, crack, satisfactory, skilled.

useless *a.* **1** (*serving no useful purpose*) abortive, barren, fruitless, futile, idle, impotent, impracticable, impractical, ineffective, pointless, profitless, purposeless, sterile, unavailing, unproductive, unserviceable, unsuccessful, unworkable, vain, worthless. ANTONYMS: productive, useful. **2** (*ineffectual, weak*) hopeless, incompetent, ineffectual, inefficient, inept, no good, stupid, weak. ANTONYMS: competent.

usual *a.* (*such as ordinarily occurs*) accustomed, common, conventional, customary, established, everyday, expected, familiar, general, habitual, normal, ordinary, regular, routine, run-of-the-mill, standard, stock, time-honoured, traditional, typical. ANTONYMS: extraordinary, unusual.

utilize *v.t.* (*to make use of*) employ, make use of, put to use, resort to, use.

utter[1] *a.* (*total, absolute*) absolute, arrant, complete, consummate, downright, entire, outright, perfect, sheer, stark, thorough, thoroughgoing, total, unmitigated, unqualified. ANTONYMS: partial.

utter[2] *v.t.* **1** (*to emit audibly*) articulate, enunciate, express, pronounce, put into words, say, speak, verbalize, vocalize, voice. **2** (*to give expression to*) announce, declare, divulge, express, make known, proclaim, promulgate, publish, reveal, state. ANTONYMS: suppress.

utterly *adv.* (*completely*) absolutely, altogether, categorically, completely, definitely, entirely, extremely, fully, overwhelmingly, perfectly, quite, thoroughly, totally, unequivocally, unreservedly, very, wholly.

V

vacancy n. **1** (an unfilled or vacant post or office) job, opening, position, post, situation, situation vacant. **2** (empty space, a gap) empty space, gap, space, vacuum, void. **3** (a lack of thought or interest) blankness, denseness, inaneness, inanity, silliness, stupidity, vacuity, vacuousness. ANTONYMS: cleverness, intelligence.

vacant a. **1** (unfilled, empty) available, empty, free, not in use, not taken, unfilled, uninhabited, unoccupied. ANTONYMS: in use, occupied, taken. **2** (unintelligent, empty-headed) blank, brainless, dense, empty-headed, expressionless, inane, silly, stupid, vacuous. ANTONYMS: clever, intelligent. **3** ((of time) not being used) free, idle, leisure, unoccupied. ANTONYMS: occupied, working.

vacate v.t. (to make vacant, to give up occupation or possession of (a room, property)) depart from, evacuate, give up, go away from, leave, move out of, quit, relinquish, withdraw from. ANTONYMS: move into, occupy, take up possession of.

vacation n. (a period of cessation of legal or other business, or of studies at university etc.) break, holiday, leave, recess, time out. ANTONYMS: term, work.

vaccinate v.t. (to inoculate with the modified virus of any disease so as to produce a mild form of the disease and prevent a serious attack) (coll.) give a jab to, inoculate.

vacillate v.i. (to oscillate from one opinion or resolution to another, to be irresolute) beat about the bush, be hesitant, be indecisive, be irresolute, blow hot and cold, dither, equivocate, fluctuate, hesitate, oscillate, shilly-shally, waver. ANTONYMS: be resolute.

vacuous a. **1** (showing no signs of feeling or intelligence) blank, dense, foolish, inane, silly, stupid, vacant. ANTONYMS: clever, intelligent. **2** (empty, unfilled) empty, unfilled, unoccupied, vacant, void. ANTONYMS: filled, full.

vacuum n. **1** (a space completely devoid of matter) emptiness, empty space, nothingness, space, vacuity, void. **2** (an emptiness or void caused by the removal or absence of a person or thing; a feeling of emptiness) empty space, gap, hollowness, lack, nothingness, vacuity, void.

vagabond n. (a person who wanders about without any settled home, a vagrant) beggar, (esp. N Am., coll.) bum, down-and-out, (esp. N Am.) hobo, knight of the road, person of no fixed address, rover, tramp, traveller, vagrant, wanderer.
~a. (wandering about, having no settled habitation) drifting, homeless, itinerant, nomadic, peripatetic, roaming, roving, transient, travelling, unsettled, vagrant, wandering. ANTONYMS: established, settled.

vagary n. (a whimsical idea, an extravagant notion) caprice, fancy, notion, whim, whimsy.

vagrant n. (a person wandering about without a settled home or visible means of subsistence, a tramp) beggar, (esp. N Am., coll.) bum, down-and-out, (esp. N Am.) hobo, person of no fixed address, rover, tramp, traveller, vagabond, wanderer.
~a. (wandering about without a settled home) drifting, homeless, itinerant, nomadic, peripatetic, roaming, roving, transient, travelling, unsettled, vagabond, wandering. ANTONYMS: established, settled.

vague a. **1** (of doubtful meaning or application; not expressed or understood clearly) doubtful, generalized, hazy, ill-defined, indefinite, indeterminate, indistinct, loose, nebulous, obscure, uncertain, unclear, unspecified, woolly. ANTONYMS: clear, definite, distinct, precise, specific. **2** ((of a shape or outline) not clear) blurred, dim, fuzzy, hazy, ill-defined, indistinct, nebulous, shadowy. ANTONYMS: clear, distinct, in focus. **3** (uncertain about what to do) hesitant, indecisive, indeterminate, irresolute, nebulous, non-specific, shilly-shallying, speculative, uncertain, unsure, wavering. ANTONYMS: decisive, resolute.

vaguely adv. **1** (to a small degree) in a way, not very well, slightly. ANTONYMS: very well. **2** (not exactly) approximately, imprecisely, roughly. ANTONYMS: exactly, precisely. **3** (not thinking clearly) absent-mindedly, inattentively, vacantly.

vain a. **1** (excessively proud of one's appearance or attainments, conceited) arrogant, (coll.) big-headed, cocky, conceited, egotistical, narcissistic, overweening, pleased with oneself, proud, proud as a peacock, self-admiring, self-important, stuck-up, swaggering, (*coll.*) swollen-headed. ANTONYMS: humble, modest. **2** (*empty, worthless*) empty, futile, hollow, idle, insignificant, insubstantial, unreal, worthless. ANTONYMS: significant, substantial. **3** (*not achieving the desired result*) abortive, fruitless, futile, ineffective, ineffectual, to no avail, unavailing, unproductive, unprofitable, unsuccessful, useless. ANTONYMS: effective, effectual, productive, successful. **in vain** (*unsuccessfully, without result*) futilely, ineffectively, ineffectually, to no avail, to no purpose, unsuccessfully, without success. ANTONYMS: successfully, with success.

valiant *a.* (*brave, daring*) audacious, bold, brave, brave as a lion, courageous, daring, fearless, gallant, gutsy, heroic, indomitable, intrepid, lion-hearted, plucky, redoubtable, stalwart, staunch, stout-hearted. ANTONYMS: cowardly, fearful, timid.

valid *a.* **1** (*based on sound reasoning*) cogent, convincing, effectual, efficacious, forceful, powerful, relevant, sound, telling, weighty, well-founded, well-grounded. ANTONYMS: ineffectual, unconvincing, weak. **2** (*legally sound and effective; legally binding*) binding, bona fide, effective, in effect, in force, lawful, legal, legally sound, legitimate, licit, official, operative. ANTONYMS: illegal, inoperative, invalid, unlawful.

validate *v.t.* **1** (*to make valid, to ratify*) authorize, certify, confirm, endorse, legalize, legitimize, license, make binding, ratify, sanction, set one's seal on, warrant. **2** (*to prove that something is true*) authenticate, confirm, corroborate, prove, substantiate, verify. ANTONYMS: disprove.

validity *n.* **1** (*the state of being legally sound*) lawfulness, legality, legitimacy. ANTONYMS: illegality, invalidity, unlawfulness. **2** (*the state of being based on sound reasoning*) cogency, effectiveness, effectualness, force, forcefulness, power, powerfulness, relevance, soundness, strength, weight, weightiness. ANTONYMS: ineffectualness, weakness.

valour *n.* (*personal bravery, courage esp. as displayed in fighting*) boldness, bravery, courage, daring, fearlessness, fortitude, gallantry, heroism, intrepidity. ANTONYMS: cowardice, fear, trepidation.

valuable *a.* **1** (*having great value, precious*) costly, dear, expensive, precious. ANTONYMS: cheap, low-cost, worthless. **2** (*very useful or important*) advantageous, beneficial, helpful, of service, of value, profitable, useful, worthwhile. ANTONYMS: useless, valueless,

worthless. **3** (*considered special or important*) cherished, esteemed, estimable, held dear, prized, treasured, valued, worthy. ANTONYMS: despised, underrated, undervalued.
~*n.* (*an object of high value, esp. a valuable piece of personal property*) heirlooms, treasures.

value *n.* **1** (*worth, the desirability of a thing, esp. as compared with other things*) advantage, benefit, desirability, gain, good, help, helpfulness, importance, merit, profit, significance, use, usefulness, worth. **2** (*worth estimated in money or other equivalent, the market price*) cost, market price, market value, monetary value, price. **3** (*moral principles, standards*) code of behaviour, ethics, morals, moral standards, principles, standards, standards of behaviour.
~*v.t.* **1** (*to estimate the value of, to appraise*) appraise, assess, evaluate, price, put a monetary value on, put a price on, set a value on. **2** (*to consider special or important*) appreciate, cherish, esteem, hold dear, hold in high esteem, hold in high regard, prize, respect, set great store by, think highly of, treasure. ANTONYMS: despise, disregard, underestimate, underrate, undervalue.

valued *a.* (*considered special or important*) cherished, dear, esteemed, loved, prized, respected, treasured.

valueless *a.* (*of no value, worthless*) of no financial value, of no monetary value, of no value, worthless. ANTONYMS: valuable.

vamp[1] *v.t.* (*to give a new appearance to, to renovate*) do up, gentrify, recondition, renovate, repair, restore.

vamp[2] *n.* (*an adventuress, a woman who exploits her sexual attractiveness to take advantage of men*) adventuress, enchantress, seductress, siren, temptress.
~*v.t.* (*to fascinate or exploit* (*men*)) flirt with, lure, make up to, seduce, tempt.

vanguard *n.* (*the leaders or leading position in a movement etc.*) advance guard, cutting edge, forefront, forerunners, front, front line, leaders, leading position, trailblazers, trendsetters, van. ANTONYMS: back, end, rear, tail-end.

vanish *v.i.* **1** (*to disappear suddenly*) become invisible, be lost to sight, be lost to view, depart, disappear, disappear from sight, evanesce, exit, go away, leave, melt away, recede from view, withdraw. ANTONYMS: appear, become visible, come into view. **2** (*to pass away, to pass out of existence*) become extinct, be no more, cease to be, come to an end, die out, disappear, end, fade, fade away, go, pass, pass away. ANTONYMS: begin, come into being.

vanity *n.* **1** (*empty pride, conceit about one's personal attainments or attractions*) airs, airs and graces, arrogance, (*coll.*) big-headedness, cockiness, conceit, conceitedness, egotism, narcissism, pretensions, pride, self-admiration, self-conceit, self-importance, self-love, (*coll.*) showing-off, (*coll.*) swollen-headedness. ANTONYMS: humility, modesty. **2** (*emptiness, futility*) emptiness, fruitlessness, futility, hollowness, insignificance, insubstantiality, pointlessness, triviality, unimportance, unreality, uselessness, worthlessness. ANTONYMS: importance, worth.

vanquish *v.t.* (*to conquer, to overcome*) beat, best, clobber, conquer, crush, defeat, get the better of, get the upper hand of, give a drubbing to, inflict a defeat on, (*coll.*) lick, master, overcome, overpower, overwhelm, put to rout, quash, quell, rout, (*coll.*) run rings round, subdue, subjugate, triumph, trounce, (*coll.*) wipe the floor with.

vapid *a.* (*lacking interest or excitement*) bland, boring, colourless, dull, flat, insipid, lifeless, spiritless, trite, uninspiring, uninteresting, wishy-washy. ANTONYMS: interesting, lively, spirited.

variable *a.* (*capable of varying, liable to change*) blowing hot and cold, capricious, chameleon-like, changeable, chopping and changing, fickle, fitful, fluctuating, inconsistent, inconstant, mercurial, mutable, protean, shifting, uneven, unstable, unsteady, vacillating, varying, volatile, wavering. ANTONYMS: constant, invariable, stable, steady, unchanging.

variance *n.* (*the fact of varying, difference of opinion*) difference, discrepancy, divergence, variation. ANTONYMS: sameness, similarity. **at variance 1** (*conflicting, not in accord* (*with one another*)) at odds (with), conflicting (with), different (from), inconsistent (with), out of line (with). **2** ((*of people*) *in disagreement or dispute*) at loggerheads, at odds, disagreeing, in conflict, in disagreement, quarrelling.

variant *a.* (*showing variation, differing in form or details*) alternative, different, divergent, modified, non-standard, varying. ANTONYMS: same, standard.
~*n.* (*a variant form, type etc.*) alternative, development, modification, mutant, variation.

variation *n.* **1** (*alteration, change*) alteration, change, departure, deviation, difference, divergence, diversification, modification, mutation, variety. ANTONYMS: sameness, uniformity.

2 (*the act or state of varying*) alteration, change, diversification, modification. ANTONYMS: uniformity. **3** (*the extent to which something varies*) departure, deviation, difference, discrepancy, divergence, fluctuation. ANTONYMS: sameness, similarity. **4** (*something that differs from a norm, standard etc.*) departure, deviation, fluctuation.

varied *a.* **1** (*possessing or showing variety, diverse*) diversified, varying. ANTONYMS: repetitive, uniform, unvarying. **2** (*consisting of many different kinds of things or people*) assorted, heterogeneous, miscellaneous, mixed, motley, sundry, various. ANTONYMS: same, similar.

variegated *a.* ((*of foliage, flowers*) *having pale patches*) dappled, flecked, many-coloured, marbled, motley, mottled, parti-coloured, pied, prismatic, rainbow-like, speckled, streaked, striated, varicoloured.

variety *n.* **1** (*the quality or state of being various; diversity*) change, difference, diversification, diversity, many-sidedness, multifariousness, variation. **2** (*a collection of diverse things*) array, assortment, collection, medley, miscellany, mixture, mulitplicity, range. **3** (*a kind, a sort; a thing of a particular sort or kind*) brand, breed, category, class, classification, kind, make, sort, species, strain, type.

various *a.* **1** (*differing from each other, diverse*) assorted, different, differing, disparate, diverse, miscellaneous, sundry, varied, variegated. ANTONYMS: alike, same, similar. **2** (*several*) many, numerous, several, sundry. ANTONYMS: one, single.

varnish *n.* (*a thin resinous solution for applying to the surface of wood, metal etc., to give it a hard, transparent, shiny coating*) coating, enamel, glaze, lacquer, shellac, veneer.
~*v.t.* **1** (*to cover with varnish*) coat, enamel, glaze, japan, lacquer, shellac, veneer. **2** (*to give an improved appearance to, to gloss over*) embellish, gild, gloss over, whitewash.

vary *v.t.* (*to change, to alter in appearance or substance*) alter, change, diversify, make changes to, modify, permutate, transform.
~*v.i.* **1** (*to undergo change*) alter, be transformed, change, metamorphose, suffer a sea change. **2** (*to be different or diverse, to be of different kinds*) be different, be dissimilar, be unlike, differ.

vast *a.* (*of great extent, immense*) astronomical, boundless, Brobdingnagian, bulky, colossal, elephantine, enormous, extensive, gigantic, (*coll.*) ginormous, great, huge, (*coll.*) hulking, immeasurable, immense, jumbo-sized, limitless, mammoth, massive, (*coll.*) mega, monstrous, monumental, prodigious, tremendous, unlimited, voluminous. ANTONYMS: limited, microscopic, tiny.

vault[1] *n.* **1** (*an arched roof; a continuous arch or semi-cylindrical roof*) arch, arched ceiling, arched roof. **2** (*an arched chamber, esp. underground; a cellar*) catacomb, cellar, crypt, tomb. **3** (*a strongroom for the deposit and storage of valuables*) depository, repository, strongroom.

vault[2] *v.t.* (*to leap over* (*a gate, obstacle etc.*)) clear, hurdle, jump, leap over, spring over.

vaunt *v.t.* (*to boast of*) boast about, brag about, crow about, exult in, give oneself airs about, (*coll.*) show off about.

veer *v.i.* (*to change direction esp. suddenly*) change course, change direction, sheer, swerve, tack, turn.

vegetate *v.i.* (*to live an idle, passive life*) be inert, idle, languish, loaf around, moulder, stagnate, (*coll.*) veg out.

vehemence *n.* (*the expression of very strong feelings or opinions*) ardour, eagerness, earnestness, emphasis, enthusiasm, fervour, fierceness, fire, force, forcefulness, impetuosity, intensity, passion, power, strength, verve, vigour, violence, zeal. ANTONYMS: apathy, half-heartedness, indifference.

vehement *a.* (*proceeding from or exhibiting intense fervour or passion, ardent*) ardent, eager, earnest, emphatic, enthusiastic, fervent, fervid, fierce, forceful, impassioned, impetuous, intense, passionate, powerful, strong, violent, zealous. ANTONYMS: apathetic, dispassionate, half-hearted, indifferent.

vehicle *n.* **1** (*any kind of carriage or conveyance for use on land, having wheels or runners*) conveyance, means of transport, transport, transportation. **2** (*any person or thing employed as a medium for the transmission of thought, feeling etc.*) agency, channel, means, medium, organ.

veil *n.* **1** (*a piece of cloth used to conceal, cover or protect something*) blanket, cloak, cover, covering, curtain, film, mantle, screen, shroud. **2** (*a mask, a disguise*) blind, cloak, cover, covering, curtain, disguise, mask, pretext, screen.
~*v.t.* **1** (*to cover with a veil*) blanket, cover, mantle, shroud. **2** (*to hide, to conceal*) camouflage, cloak, conceal, cover, hide, mask, obscure, screen.

veiled *a.* (*hidden or disguised*) camouflaged, concealed, covered up, covert, disguised,

hidden, masked, obscured. ANTONYMS: direct, obvious, transparent.

vein *n.* **1** (*a seam of any substance*) lode, seam, stratum. **2** (*a streak or wavy stripe of different colour, in wood, marble or stone*) line, streak, strip, thread. **3** (*a distinctive trait or quality*) character, strain, streak, trait. **4** (*a particular mood or humour*) disposition, frame of mind, humour, mood, temper, tenor.

velocity *n.* (*swiftness, rapidity*) fleetness, quickness, rapidity, speed, swiftness. ANTONYMS: slowness.

velvety *a.* (*feeling or looking smooth and soft like velvet*) downy, smooth, soft, velvet-like. ANTONYMS: rough.

venal *a.* (*ready to be bribed or to sacrifice honour or principle for sordid considerations*) (*sl.*) bent, bribable, corrupt, corruptible, crooked, grasping, mercenary, open to bribery, rapacious, unprincipled. ANTONYMS: honest, incorruptible, principled.

vendetta *n.* (*a feud, private warfare*) blood feud, conflict, feud, quarrel.

vendor *n.* (*a person who sells something, esp. property*) dealer, hawker, pedlar, salesman, salesperson, saleswoman, seller, trader.

veneer *n.* **1** (*a thin layer of superior wood for veneering*) covering, facing, finish. **2** (*superficial polish, a superficial appearance*) appearance, facade, front, gloss, guise, mask, pretence, semblance, show.

venerable *a.* (*worthy of reverence, esp. on account of old age and good character*) esteemed, honoured, respected, revered, reverenced, venerated, worshipped. ANTONYMS: despised, disdained, disreputable.

venerate *v.t.* (*to regard or treat with profound deference and respect, to revere*) esteem, hold in high regard, honour, look up to, respect, revere, reverence, worship. ANTONYMS: despise, disdain, scorn.

venereal *a.* (*relating to or produced by sexual intercourse*) sexual, sexually-transmitted.

vengeance *n.* (*punishment inflicted in return for an injury or wrong, retribution*) an eye for an eye, avenging, reprisal, requital, retaliation, retribution, tit for tat. ANTONYMS: exoneration, forgiveness, pardon, turning the other cheek.
with a vengeance (*to a greater degree than was anticipated or wished; emphatically*) emphatically, extremely, forcefully, furiously, to the utmost, vehemently, violently.

vengeful *a.* (*vindictive, revengeful*) avenging, implacable, retaliatory, revengeful, spiteful, unforgiving, vindictive. ANTONYMS: forgiving.

venial *a.* (*that may be pardoned or excused*) allowable, excusable, forgivable, insignificant, minor, pardonable, slight, tolerable, trivial, unimportant.

venom *n.* **1** (*a poisonous fluid secreted by snakes, scorpions etc., and injected by biting or stinging*) poison, toxicant, toxin. **2** (*extreme anger or hatred*) acrimony, animosity, bitterness, enmity, gall, hate, hostility, ill will, malevolence, malice, malignity, rancour, resentment, spite, spitefulness, spleen, viciousness, vindictiveness, virulence. ANTONYMS: benevolence, compassion, goodwill, kindness.

venomous *a.* **1** (*containing poison*) poisonous, toxic. **2** (*full of extreme anger or hatred*) acrimonious, bitter, hostile, malevolent, malicious, malignant, rancorous, resentful, spiteful, vicious, vindictive, virulent. ANTONYMS: benevolent, compassionate, kind.

vent *n.* (*a hole or aperture, esp. for the passage of air, water etc. into or out of a confined place*) aperture, duct, flue, gap, opening, orifice, outlet.
~*v.t.* (*to give vent to; to utter*) air, emit, express, give expression to, give vent to, let out, pour forth, pour out, release, utter, voice. ANTONYMS: bottle up, curb, suppress. **to give vent to** (*to give* (*often angry or violent*) *expression to, to express freely*) air, express, give expression to, pour out. ANTONYMS: bottle up, curb, suppress.

venture *n.* **1** (*an undertaking of a risky nature*) adventure, endeavour, enterprise, exploit, mission, project, undertaking. **2** (*a commercial speculation*) enterprise, gamble, risk, speculation.
~*v.t.* (*to* (*dare to*) *express* (*an opinion, guess*)) advance, chance, hazard, put forward, risk, volunteer.
~*v.i.* (*to dare; to have the courage or presumption* (*to do etc.*)) dare (to), make so bold as (to), presume (to), take the liberty (of).

veracious *a.* **1** (*habitually speaking or disposed to speak the truth*) candid, frank, honest, moral, reliable, sincere, trustworthy, truthful. ANTONYMS: dishonest, lying, untrustworthy. **2** (*characterized by truth and accuracy*) accurate, exact, factual, literal, precise, true, truthful. ANTONYMS: inaccurate, untrue.

veracity *n.* **1** (*truthfulness, honesty*) facts, truth, truthfulness. ANTONYMS: lies, lying. **2** (*accuracy*) accuracy, exactness, precision. ANTONYMS: imprecision, inaccuracy.

verbal *a.* **1** (*oral, spoken*) oral, said, spoken, unwritten, uttered, word-of-mouth. ANTONYMS: written. **2** (*literal, word for word*) close, exact, faithful, literal, precise, verbatim, word for word. ANTONYMS: free, loose, rough.

verbatim *adv.* (*word for word*) exactly, precisely, to the letter. ANTONYMS: loosely, roughly.

verbose *a.* (*using or containing more words than are necessary, prolix*) circumlocutory, garrulous, long-winded, loquacious, periphrastic, prolix, wordy. ANTONYMS: concise, succinct, terse.

verbosity *n.* (*the use of more words than are necessary*) circumlocution, garrulity, garrulousness, logorrhoea, long-windedness, loquaciousness, loquacity, periphrasis, prolixity, verbiage, verboseness, wordiness. ANTONYMS: conciseness, succinctness, terseness.

verdant *a.* (*covered with growing plants or grass*) flourishing, green, lush, luxuriant.

verdict *n.* (*an official decision*) adjudication, conclusion, decision, finding, judgement, ruling, sentence.

verge[1] *n.* **1** (*the extreme edge or margin*) boundary, brim, brink, edge, extreme, limit, lip, margin. **2** (*the grass edging of a bed or border or alongside a road*) edge, edging, roadside. **on the verge of** (*on the brink of*) about to, close to, near to, on the brink of, on the edge of, on the point of, on the threshold of.

verge[2] *v.i.* (*to move or incline in a particular direction, esp. downwards*) approach, border on, come near, incline to, incline towards, tend towards.

verification *n.* (*confirmation of the truth of something*) accreditation, attestation, authentication, confirmation, corroboration, endorsement, proof, substantiation, validation.

verify *v.t.* (*to confirm the truth of*) accredit, attest to, authenticate, bear out, corroborate, endorse, prove, substantiate, testify to, validate. ANTONYMS: deny, disprove, dispute, invalidate.

verminous *a.* (*infested with vermin*) flea-bitten, lousy, rat-infested.

vernacular *n.* **1** (*the native language or dialect of a particular place or country*) common parlance, dialect, idiom, native language, ordinary speech, patois, vulgar tongue. **2** (*the language or idiom of a particular group of people*) argot, cant, jargon, slang.

versatile *a.* (*readily adapting or applying oneself to new tasks, occupations etc., many-sided*) adaptable, adjustable, all-round, flexible, ingenious, many-sided, multifaceted, protean, resourceful. ANTONYMS: inflexible, limited, restricted.

verse *n.* **1** (*metrical composition as distinct from prose*) poetry. **2** (*a particular type of metrical composition*) ballad, ditty, lay, lyric, ode, poem, sonnet. **3** (*a group of metrical lines, a stanza*) canto, couplet, stanza, strophe.

versed *a.* (*skilled, proficient* (*in*)) accomplished (in), competent (in), conversant (with), experienced (in), familiar (with), knowledgeable (about), practised (at), proficient (in), qualified (in), skilled (at), well-informed (about). ANTONYMS: ignorant (of), incompetent (in), inexperienced (in), unskilled (at).

version *n.* **1** (*a statement or description of something from a person's particular point of view*) account, impression, interpretation, reading, rendering, report, side, story, understanding. **2** (*a variant form of something*) copy, design, form, kind, model, reproduction, style, type, variant, variation. **3** (*a translation of a work from one language into another*) interpretation, rendering, rendition, translation. **4** (*the adaptation of a work of art into another medium*) adaptation, translation.

vertex *n.* (*the highest point, the top*) acme, apex, apogee, crest, crown, culmination, height, pinnacle, summit, top, zenith. ANTONYMS: bottom, nadir.

vertical *a.* (*perpendicular to the plane of the horizon*) erect, on end, perpendicular, stand-up, upright. ANTONYMS: flat, horizontal, prone.

vertigo *n.* (*dizziness, a feeling as if one were whirling round*) dizziness, giddiness, light-headedness, (*coll.*) wooziness.

verve *n.* (*enthusiasm, energy*) animation, brio, élan, energy, enthusiasm, feeling, fervency, fire, get-up-and-go, gusto, life, liveliness, passion, pep, (*sl.*) pizazz, sparkle, spirit, vigour, (*coll.*) vim, vitality, vivacity, zing, (*coll.*) zip. ANTONYMS: apathy, inertia, lethargy, listlessness, torpor.

very *adv.* ((*used as an intensifier*) *in a high degree, extremely*) acutely, (*coll.*) awfully, decidedly, deeply, eminently, exceedingly, extremely, greatly, highly, noticeably, particularly, profoundly, really, remarkably, (*coll.*) terribly, to a great extent, truly, uncommonly, unusually, wonderfully. ANTONYMS: scarcely, slightly.
~*a.* **1** (*actual, precise*) exact, genuine, identical, real, same, self-same, true. **2** (*absolute*) pure, sheer, utter.

vessel *n.* **1** (*a hollow receptacle, esp. for holding liquids*) container, receptacle. **2** (*a ship or craft*) boat, craft, ship.

vest *v.t.* (*to invest or endow* (*with authority, etc.*)) confer, endow, entrust, invest, lodge, place, put in the hands of, settle.

vestibule *n.* (*a small hall or antechamber next to the outer door of a house*) anteroom, entrance, foyer, hall, lobby, porch, portico.

vestige *n.* **1** (*a sign or trace of something no longer present or in existence*) evidence, indication, relic, remainder, remains, remnant, residue, scrap, sign, trace, track. **2** (*a small piece, a particle*) atom, dash, drop, hint, iota, jot, particle, scrap, soupçon, suggestion, suspicion, tinge, touch, trace.

vestigial *a.* **1** (*of or being a vestige, very small or slight*) remaining, surviving. **2** ((*of an organ*) *having degenerated and nearly or entirely lost its function in the course of evolution*) imperfect, incomplete, non-functional, rudimentary, undeveloped.

vet *v.t.* (*to subject to careful scrutiny and appraisal*) appraise, check, check out, examine, (*coll.*) give (a person or thing) the once-over, investigate, look over, review, scan, scrutinize, size up.

veto *n.* (*any authoritative prohibition or interdict*) ban, boycott, embargo, interdict, refusal, rejection. ANTONYMS: approval, endorsement, go-ahead.
~*v.t.* (*to prohibit, to forbid*) ban, boycott, disallow, embargo, forbid, (*coll.*) give the red light to, give the thumbs down to, interdict, knock on the head, preclude, (*sl.*) put the kibosh on, refuse, reject, rule out, turn down. ANTONYMS: approve, endorse, give the go-ahead to, (*coll.*) give the green light to, give the thumbs up to.

vex *v.t.* (*to cause trouble or annoyance to, to irritate*) agitate, anger, annoy, bother, (*sl.*) bug, discompose, displease, distress, disturb, exasperate, fret, gall, get on one's nerves, grate on, harass, (*coll.*) hassle, irk, irritate, (*sl.*) needle, offend, (*coll.*) peeve, pique, put out, (*coll.*) rile, trouble, try the patience of, upset, worry. ANTONYMS: calm down, gratify, please, soothe.

vexation *n.* **1** (*the act of vexing or the state of being vexed, irritation*) agitation, anger, annoyance, discomposure, displeasure, distress, disturbance, exasperation, fury, gall, harassment, irritation, offence, perturbation, trouble, upset, worry. ANTONYMS: calm, gratification, pleasure. **2** (*that which causes irritation, an annoyance*) bother, (*coll.*) hassle, (*coll.*) headache, irritant, nuisance, (*coll.*) pain, (*coll.*) pain in the neck, pest, problem, thorn in one's side, trouble, worry.

vexatious *a.* (*making one feel annoyed*) annoying, bothersome, distressing, disturbing, exasperating, galling, infuriating, irksome, irritating, offensive, troublesome, trying, upsetting, worrisome, worrying. ANTONYMS: agreeable, calming, gratifying, pleasing.

vexed *a.* **1** (*annoyed, filled with vexation*) agitated, annoyed, bothered, displeased, distressed, disturbed, exasperated, fretting, (*sl.*) hacked off, harassed, (*coll.*) hassled, irked, irritated, offended, perturbed, troubled, upset, worried. ANTONYMS: calm, gratified, pleased. **2** ((*of a question or doctrine*) *much debated or contested*) contentious, contested, controversial, debated, disputed, in contention, in dispute, moot.

viable *a.* (*likely to become actual or to succeed, feasible*) feasible, operable, practicable, sound, workable. ANTONYMS: impracticable, unworkable.

vibrant *a.* **1** (*vibrating, tremulous*) oscillating, palpitating, quivering, shivering, trembling, tremulous. **2** (*thrilling, exciting*) animated, dynamic, electrifying, energetic, lively, sparkling, spirited, vigorous, vivacious. ANTONYMS: dull, lifeless. **3** (*resonant*) echoing, pulsating, resonant, reverberating, ringing, throbbing. **4** ((*of colour*) *very bright and eye-catching*) bright, colourful, striking, strong, vivid.

vibrate *v.i.* **1** (*to move to and fro rapidly, to swing*) move to and fro, oscillate, sway, swing. **2** (*to thrill, to quiver*) (*coll.*) judder, quiver, shake, shiver, shudder, tremble. **3** ((*of a sound*) *to resound, to ring*) echo, pulsate, resonate, reverberate, ring, throb.

vibration *n.* **1** (*oscillation*) swaying, swinging. **2** (*a trembling movement*) juddering, quiver, quivering, shaking, shivering, shuddering, trembling, tremor. **3** (*the resounding or ringing of a sound*) echoing, pulsating, pulse, resonating, reverberation, ringing, throb, throbbing.

vicar *n.* (*in the Church of England, the priest in charge of a parish*) clergyman, clergywoman, member of the clergy, minister, pastor, priest.

vicarious *a.* (*done or suffered for or instead of another*) at one remove, indirect, second-hand, surrogate. ANTONYMS: direct, first-hand.

vice *n.* **1** (*an evil or immoral practice or habit*) sin, transgression, wrongdoing. ANTONYMS: virtue. **2** (*evil conduct, gross immorality, depravity*) badness, degeneracy, depravity, evil, evildoing, immorality, iniquity, sin, sinfulness, turpitude, wickedness, wrong, wrongdoing. ANTONYMS: good, morality, righteousness, virtue. **3** (*a fault, a defect*) bad habit, blemish, defect, failing, fault, flaw, imperfection, shortcoming, weakness. ANTONYMS: good point, strength, strong point, virtue.

vice versa *adv.* (*the order or relation being inverted, the other way round*) contrariwise, conversely, inversely, the other way round.

vicinity *n.* **1** (*the neighbourhood, the adjoining or surrounding district*) area, district, environs, locality, neighbourhood, precincts, proximity, purlieus. **2** (*the state of being near, proximity*) closeness, nearness, propinquity, proximity.

vicious *a.* **1** (*bad-tempered, spiteful*) (*sl.*) bitchy, malevolent, malicious, malignant, mean, rancorous, spiteful, venomous, vindictive. ANTONYMS: compassionate, friendly, kindly. **2** (*ferocious, violent*) aggressive, brutal, dangerous, ferocious, fierce, savage, violent. ANTONYMS: docile, timid. **3** (*addicted to vice, depraved*) bad, barbarous, corrupt, cruel, degenerate, depraved, dishonourable, evil, foul, immoral, infamous, notorious, profligate, sinful, unprincipled, unscrupulous, vile, wicked. ANTONYMS: good, honourable, virtuous.

vicissitude *n.* (*a change of condition or fortune, a mutation*) alteration, change, shift, variation.

victim *n.* **1** (*a person killed or injured as a result of an event such as an accident or epidemic*) casualty, fatality, sufferer. ANTONYMS: survivor. **2** (*a dupe, a prey*) dupe, easy prey, easy target, fair game, fall guy, gull, innocent, (*sl.*) sap, scapegoat, sitting duck, sitting target, (*coll.*) sucker. ANTONYMS: aggressor, assailant, guilty party. **3** (*a living creature sacrificed to some deity or in the performance of some religious rite*) offering, sacrifice.

victimize *v.t.* (*to make a victim of*) (*coll.*) have a down on, have it in for, have one's knife in, persecute, pick on.

victor *n.* (*a person, nation etc. that conquers in battle or wins in a contest*) (*coll.*) champ, champion, conquering hero, conqueror, prizewinner, vanquisher, winner. ANTONYMS: loser, the vanquished.

victorious *a.* (*having conquered in a battle or any contest, triumphant*) champion, conquering, prizewinning, successful, top, vanquishing, winning. ANTONYMS: beaten, conquered, defeated, vanquished.

victory *n.* (*the defeat of an enemy in battle or war, or of an opponent in a contest*) conquest, success, triumph, win. ANTONYMS: defeat, failure, loss.

victual *n.* (*food, provisions*) comestibles, eats, food, foodstuffs, (*sl.*) grub, (*sl.*) nosh, provisions, rations, stores, supplies, viands.

vie *v.i.* (*to strive for superiority, to compete*

(*with*)) be rivals, compete, contend, contest, strive, struggle.

view n. **1** (*sight, range of vision*) field of vision, range of vision, sight, vision. **2** (*that which is seen, a scene*) aspect, outlook, panorama, perspective, prospect, scene, spectacle, vista. **3** (*a picture or drawing of this*) drawing, landscape, picture. **4** (*survey or examination by the eye*) contemplation, examination, inspection, look, observation, scan, scrutiny, study. **5** (*the manner or mode of looking at things, considering a matter etc.*) attitude, belief, conviction, feeling, idea, impression, judgement, notion, opinion, point of view, sentiment, theory, thought, viewpoint, way of thinking.
~v.t. **1** (*to examine with the eye, look over*) behold, contemplate, examine, eye, inspect, look at, observe, regard, scan, scrutinize, study, survey, (*coll.*) take a dekko at, watch. **2** (*to survey mentally or intellectually*) consider, contemplate, look on, ponder, reflect on, regard, think about. **3** (*to consider, to form a mental impression or judgement of*) consider, deem, judge, regard, see. **in view of** (*considering, having regard to*) bearing in mind, considering, in the light of, taking into account, taking into consideration. **on view** (*open to public inspection*) displayed, exhibited, on display, on exhibition, on show. **with a view to** (*with the intention of*) in the hope of, with the aim of, with the intention of, with the purpose of.

viewer n. **1** (*a person who views something*) observer, onlooker, spectator, watcher. **2** (*a person who watches television; a member of a particular television audience*) television watcher, TV watcher.

viewpoint n. (*a point of view*) angle, perspective, point of view, slant, stance, standpoint, way of thinking.

vigilance n. (*the state of being vigilant*) alertness, attention, attentiveness, carefulness, caution, circumspection, observation, surveillance, wariness, watchfulness. ANTONYMS: carelessness, inattention, inattentiveness.

vigilant a. (*awake and on the alert*) alert, attentive, awake, careful, cautious, circumspect, eagle-eyed, heedful, keeping one's eyes peeled, keeping one's eyes skinned, keeping one's wits about one, observant, on one's guard, on one's toes, on the alert, on the lookout, on the qui vive, wary, watchful, (*coll.*) wide awake. ANTONYMS: careless, inattentive.

vigorous a. **1** (*vital and strong*) active, animated, (*coll.*) bright-eyed and bushy-tailed, dynamic, energetic, full of energy, full of life, lively, sparkling, spirited, vivacious. ANTONYMS: apathetic, enervated, lethargic, listless, sluggish. **2** (*healthy, robust*) fit, fit as a fiddle, flourishing, hale and hearty, hardy, healthy, in good condition, in good health, in good shape, red-blooded, robust, strong, strong as an ox, sturdy, tough, virile. ANTONYMS: feeble, frail, unhealthy, weak. **3** (*energetic and enthusiastic in undertaking an activity*) aggressive, determined, dynamic, energetic, enthusiastic, fervent, forceful, forcible, intense, passionate, potent, powerful, resolute, spirited, strenuous, strong, vehement, zealous. ANTONYMS: apathetic, feeble, weak. **4** ((*of an activity*) undertaken with great energy and enthusiasm) cogent, effective, forceful, potent, powerful, robust, strong, to the point, trenchant. ANTONYMS: ineffective, weak, wishy-washy.

vigorously adv. (*with great energy; forcefully*) aggressively, all out, energetically, forcefully, hammer and tongs, powerfully, strenuously, strongly, with no holds barred. ANTONYMS: apathetically, weakly.

vigour n. **1** (*active physical or mental strength or energy*) fitness, hardiness, healthiness, robustness, strength, sturdiness, toughness, virility. ANTONYMS: feebleness, frailness, unhealthiness, weakness. **2** (*healthy condition or growth, robustness*) activeness, activity, animation, dynamism, energy, liveliness, (*sl.*) oomph, pep, sparkle, sprightliness, spryness, verve, (*coll.*) vim, vitality, vivacity, zest, zing, (*coll.*) zip. ANTONYMS: apathy, inertia, lethargy, listlessness, sluggishness. **3** (*power, intensity*) activity, aggression, determination, energy, enthusiasm, fervour, force, forcefulness, intensity, passion, potency, power, powerfulness, strength, strenuousness, vehemence, zeal. ANTONYMS: apathy, feebleness, inaction, weakness. **4** (*forcefulness, trenchancy*) cogency, effectiveness, force, forcefulness, potency, power, robustness, strength, trenchancy. ANTONYMS: ineffectiveness, weakness, wishy-washiness.

vile a. **1** (*foul, disgusting*) abominable, disgusting, foul, nauseating, noxious, repellent, repulsive, sickening. ANTONYMS: attractive, lovely. **2** (*depraved, abominably wicked*) abject, appalling, bad, base, contemptible, corrupt, debauched, degenerate, depraved, despicable, dissolute, evil, foul, hateful, heinous, horrible, ignoble, immoral, impure, iniquitous, loathsome, low, mean, monstrous, nasty, nefarious, odious, outrageous, perverted, reprehensible, reprobate, shocking, sinful, ugly, vicious, villainous, wicked, wretched. ANTONYMS: good, moral, righteous, virtuous, worthy. **3** (*very bad or unpleasant,* *abominable*) abominable, disagreeable, disgusting, foul, horrible, horrid, loathsome, nasty, nauseating, noxious, obnoxious, offensive, repellent, repugnant, repulsive, revolting, sickening, unpleasant, (*coll.*) yucky. ANTONYMS: agreeable, lovely, nice, pleasant.

vilify *v.t.* (*to say unpleasant things about*) abuse, (*coll.*) bad-mouth, blacken the reputation of, calumniate, cast aspersions on, conduct a smear campaign against, criticize, decry, defame, denigrate, disparage, (*coll.*) do a hatchet job on, drag through the mud, impugn, libel, malign, (*coll.*) pull to bits, revile, rubbish, run down, (*sl.*) slag off, slander, speak ill of, traduce. ANTONYMS: compliment, praise.

villain *n.* **1** (*a person guilty or capable of crime or great wickedness*) (*coll.*) baddy, blackguard, cad, criminal, (*coll.*) crook, evildoer, hoodlum, knave, miscreant, (*coll.*) rat, reprobate, rogue, ruffian, scoundrel, wretch, wrongdoer. ANTONYMS: angel, (*coll.*) goody, hero, heroine. **2** (*a rogue, a rascal*) brat, devil, imp, rascal, rogue, scallywag, scamp.

villainous *a.* **1** (*worthy or characteristic of a villain, depraved*) abominable, atrocious, bad, base, corrupt, criminal, (*coll.*) crooked, cruel, degenerate, depraved, diabolical, dissolute, evil, fiendish, foul, hateful, heinous, horrible, inhuman, iniquitous, lawless, mean, monstrous, nefarious, sinful, unprincipled, unscrupulous, vicious, vile, wicked. ANTONYMS: good, righteous, saintly, virtuous. **2** (*very bad*) awful, disagreeable, foul, horrible, horrid, nasty, objectionable, terrible, unpleasant. ANTONYMS: lovely, nice.

villainy *n.* **1** (*villainous behaviour*) badness, criminality, delinquency, evil, evildoing, iniquity, rascality, roguery, sin, sinfulness, turpitude, vice, viciousness, wickedness, wrongdoing. ANTONYMS: goodness, virtue. **2** (*a villainous act*) crime, misdeed, offence, sin, vice. ANTONYMS: good deed.

vindicate *v.t.* **1** (*to prove to be true or valid, to justify*) confirm, corroborate, justify, prove, substantiate, support, testify to, verify, warrant. ANTONYMS: disprove, refute. **2** (*to maintain* (*a claim, statement etc.*) *against attack or denial*) assert, defend, establish, maintain, support, uphold. ANTONYMS: deny, relinquish. **3** (*to defend* (*a person*) *against reproach, accusation etc.*) absolve, acquit, clear, defend, exculpate, excuse, exonerate, free from blame. ANTONYMS: accuse, blame, convict.

vindictive *a.* (*characterized or prompted by a desire for revenge*) grudge-bearing, implacable, malevolent, malicious, malignant, rancorous, relentless, resentful, revengeful, spiteful,

unforgiving, unrelenting, vengeful, venomous, vicious. ANTONYMS: forgiving, magnanimous, relenting.

vintage *n.* **1** (*the yield of grapes or wine from a vineyard or vine district for a particular season*) crop, crop gathering, grape harvest, harvest. **2** (*the season of gathering grapes*) year. **3** (*a time of origin*) epoch, era, period, time. ~*a.* **1** (*representative of what is best and most typical, esp. in a person's work*) best, choice, classic, prime, select, superior, typical. ANTONYMS: inferior, poor-quality, worst. **2** (*of an earlier period but of continuing interest*) antique, old, venerable. ANTONYMS: brand new, new.

violate *v.t.* **1** (*to infringe, to break* (*a law, obligation, duty etc.*)) breach, break, contravene, disobey, disregard, ignore, infringe, transgress. ANTONYMS: obey, observe, uphold. **2** (*to treat irreverently, to desecrate*) defile, desecrate, profane. ANTONYMS: honour, respect, worship. **3** (*to rape, to subject to sexual assault*) rape, ravish, sexually assault.

violence *n.* **1** (*the state or quality of being violent*) brutality, destructiveness, ferocity, frenzy, murderousness, savagery, thuggery. ANTONYMS: gentleness, mildness, restraint. **2** (*vehemence or intensity of feeling*) acuteness, fervour, force, forcefulness, intensity, passion, strength, vehemence. ANTONYMS: apathy, nonchalance, restraint. **3** (*violent exercise of power*) brutality, brute force, force, savagery, strong-arm tactics, thuggery. **4** (*stormy or windy weather*) tempestuousness, turbulence, wildness. ANTONYMS: calmness, mildness.

violent *a.* **1** (*acting with, or characterized by, the exertion of great physical force*) brutal, destructive, ferocious, forceful, murderous, powerful, savage, strong, vicious. ANTONYMS: gentle, mild. **2** (*vehement, impetuous*) frantic, furious, headstrong, hot-headed, impetuous, maniacal, tempestuous, unbridled, uncontrollable, uncontrolled, unrestrained, vehement, wild. ANTONYMS: controlled, restrained. **3** (*intense, immoderate*) excessive, extreme, great, immoderate, inordinate, intense, strong, vehement. ANTONYMS: moderate, restrained. **4** ((*of weather*) *stormy or windy*) tempestuous, turbulent, wild. ANTONYMS: calm, mild.

VIP *abbr.* (*a very important person*) big name, (*coll.*) big noise, (*coll.*) big shot, celebrity, leading light, luminary, notable, public figure, somebody, star.

virago *n.* (*a bad-tempered or scolding woman, a termagant*) harridan, scold, shrew, termagant, vixen.

virginal *a.* (*pure, chaste*) celibate, chaste, maidenly, pristine, pure, snow-white, un-defiled, unsullied, untouched, virgin, white. ANTONYMS: defiled, impure, sullied.

virginity *n.* (*the state of being a virgin, purity*) chastity, innocence, maidenhead, purity.

virile *a.* **1** (*characteristic of a man, manly; vigorous*) macho, manly, masculine, red-blooded. ANTONYMS: effeminate, unmanly. **2** ((*of a male*) *sexually potent*) potent. ANTONYMS: impotent.

virtual *a.* (*being such in effect or for practical purposes, though not in name or by strict definition; practical*) effective, essential, for all practical purposes, implicit, in all but name, indirect, in effect, practical, tacit, unacknowledged. ANTONYMS: actual, in reality.

virtually *adv.* (*almost, practically*) almost, as good as, in all but name, in effect, in essence, nearly, practically, to all intents and purposes. ANTONYMS: actually.

virtue *n.* **1** (*moral excellence, goodness*) blamelessness, decency, ethicalness, ethics, goodness, honour, honourableness, integrity, moral excellence, morality, rectitude, right-eousness, uprightness, worth, worthiness. ANTONYMS: badness, immorality, sin, vice. **2** (*a good quality or feature*) advantage, asset, attribute, benefit, good point, good quality, merit, plus, strength, strong point. ANTONYMS: bad point, disadvantage, failing, weakness. **3** (*sexual purity, chastity, esp. in women*) celibacy, chastity, innocence, purity, virginity. ANTONYMS: promiscuity. **4** (*inherent power or efficacy*) advantage, benefit, efficacy, merit, potency, power, usefulness, worth. ANTONYMS: disadvantage, worthlessness. **by virtue of** (*by or through the efficacy or authority of, on the strength of*) as a result of, by dint of, by reason of, in view of, on account of, owing to, thanks to.

virtuosity *n.* (*great skill*) brilliance, craftsmanship, excellence, expertise, finish, flair, mastery, panache, polish, prowess, skilfulness, skill, wizardry.

virtuoso *n.* (*a skilled performer in some fine art, esp. music*) artist, craftsman, craftsperson, craftswoman, genius, maestro, master, wizard. ~*a.* (*showing great skill*) bravura, brilliant, dazzling, expert, impressive, masterly, outstanding, skilful. ANTONYMS: ordinary, poor, run-of-the-mill, weak.

virtuous *a.* **1** (*characterized by virtue, morally good*) blameless, decent, ethical, exemplary, good, (*coll.*) goody-goody, honest, honourable, moral, pure, righteous, (*coll.*) squeaky-clean, upright, upstanding, worthy. ANTONYMS: bad, immoral, sinful, unethical, wicked. **2** (*chaste*) celibate, chaste, clean-living, innocent, pure, virgin, virginal. ANTONYMS: loose, promiscuous.

virulent *a.* **1** (*extremely poisonous*) deadly, lethal, poisonous, toxic. ANTONYMS: harmless, innocuous. **2** ((*of a micro-organism*) *highly infectious*) contagious, infectious, infective. **3** ((*of a disease*) *having a rapid course and severe effects*) extreme, harmful, injurious, lethal, pernicious, serious, severe. ANTONYMS: harmless, innocuous, mild. **4** (*extremely bitter or malignant*) acrimonious, bitter, hostile, malevolent, malicious, malignant, rancorous, resentful, spiteful, venomous, vicious, vindictive. ANTONYMS: benign, friendly, kind.

viscous *a.* ((*of liquids*) *thick and sticky*) adhesive, gelatinous, gluey, glutinous, (*coll.*) gooey, gummy, mucilaginous, syrupy, thick, treacly, viscid.

visible *a.* **1** (*capable of being seen, perceptible by the eye*) detectable, discernible, perceivable, perceptible. ANTONYMS: indiscernible, invisible, undetectable. **2** (*evident, obvious*) apparent, clear, conspicuous, detectable, distinct, evident, in sight, in view, manifest, noticeable, observable, obvious, palpable, patent, plain, to be seen, undisguised, unmistakable. ANTONYMS: invisible, unnoticeable, unseen.

vision *n.* **1** (*the act or faculty of seeing, sight*) eyesight, power of sight, seeing, sight. **2** (*a supernatural or prophetic apparition*) apparition, chimera, ghost, illusion, phantasm, phantom, spectre, wraith. **3** (*something vividly perceived by the imagination or fancy*) castle in Spain, castle in the air, daydream, dream, fantasy, figment of the imagination, hallucination, image, mental picture, pipe dream. **4** (*foresight, wise or imaginative planning for the future*) breadth of view, discernment, far-sightedness, foresight, imagination, insight, intuition, penetration. **5** (*a person or thing of great beauty*) beauty, dream, feast for the eyes, perfect picture, (*coll.*) sight for sore eyes. ANTONYMS: fright.

visionary *a.* **1** (*unreal and existing only in the mind*) fanciful, fantastic, hypothetical, idealistic, idealized, illusory, imaginary, impractical, speculative, theoretical, unreal, unworkable, Utopian. ANTONYMS: actual, practical, real. **2** (*given to daydreaming, fanciful theories etc.*) dreamy, idealistic, romantic, unrealistic, with one's head in the clouds. ANTONYMS: down-to-earth, practical.

visit *v.t.* **1** (*to go or come to see, as an act of friendship, civility etc.*) call on, come and see, drop in on, go and see, look in on, look (someone) up, pay a call on, pay a visit to, (*coll.*) stop by. **2** (*to come or go to for the purpose of inspection, supervision etc.*) call on, inspect, pay a call on, survey. **3** (*to reside temporarily with or in*) be the guest of, stay with. **4** ((*of diseases etc.*) *to overtake, to afflict*) afflict, assail, attack, befall, descend on, trouble.

~*v.i.* (*to call on or visit people*) be a guest, drop in, pay a call, pay a visit, pop in.

~*n.* **1** (*the act of visiting or going to see a person, place or thing; a call*) call, social call. **2** (*a stay or sojourn (with or at)*) sojourn, stay, stopoff, stopover.

visitation *n.* **1** (*a formal or official visit for the purpose of inspection, correction etc.*) examination, inspection, official visit, survey, tour of inspection, visit. **2** (*a divine dispensation, esp. a chastisement or affliction; any catastrophic occurrence*) affliction, calamity, cataclysm, catastrophe, chastisement, disaster, ordeal, pestilence, plague, punishment, scourge, tragedy, trial.

visitor *n.* **1** (*a person who makes a call*) caller, guest. **2** (*a person who visits a place*) tourist, traveller.

vista *n.* (*a long view*) perspective, prospect, view.

visual *a.* **1** (*relating to or used in sight or seeing*) ocular, optic, optical. **2** (*capable of being seen, visible*) discernible, observable, perceivable, perceptible, visible.

visualize *v.t.* (*to picture in the mind, to call up a visual image of*) conceive of, conjure up, envisage, imagine, picture, picture in one's mind's eye, see in the mind's eye.

vital *a.* **1** (*very important and necessary*) critical, crucial, essential, imperative, important, indispensable, key, life-and-death, necessary, needed, requisite, urgent. ANTONYMS: dispensable, inessential, unimportant, unnecessary. **2** (*relating to or supporting organic life*) cardinal, essential, fundamental, life-giving, life-sustaining. **3** (*full of life and activity, dynamic*) animated, dynamic, energetic, exuberant, lively, spirited, vibrant, vigorous, vivacious, zestful. ANTONYMS: apathetic, lethargic, listless, sluggish.

vitality *n.* (*physical or mental energy; liveliness*) animation, dynamism, energy, exuberance, life, liveliness, pep, sparkle, spirit, vibrancy, vigour, (*coll.*) vim, vivacity, zest, zestfulness, zing, (*coll.*) zip. ANTONYMS: apathy, lethargy, listlessness, sluggishness.

vitiate *v.t.* (*to impair the quality of; to render*

faulty or imperfect) blight, debase, devalue, impair, mar, spoil, sully, taint. ANTONYMS: improve.

vitriolic *a.* ((*of language*) *very cruel and hurtful*) acerbic, acid, acrimonious, astringent, bitter, caustic, malicious, mordant, sarcastic, sardonic, scathing, spiteful, trenchant, venomous, vicious, virulent.

vituperate *v.t.* (*to upbraid, to abuse*) abuse, berate, cast aspersions on, castigate, censure, chide, denounce, find fault with, fulminate against, inveigh against, (*coll.*) knock, rail against, revile, run down, scold, (*sl.*) slag off, slate, tear into, upbraid, vilify.

vituperative *a.* ((*of criticism*) *angry and cruel*) abusive, censorious, condemnatory, denunciatory, insulting, (*coll.*) knocking, sarcastic, sardonic, scurrilous, withering. ANTONYMS: admiring, commendatory, complimentary, laudatory.

vivacious *a.* (*lively, animated*) animated, bright, bubbly, dynamic, ebullient, effervescent, exuberant, gay, high-spirited, jolly, light-hearted, lively, merry, scintillating, sparkling, spirited, sprightly, vibrant, vital. ANTONYMS: dull, languid, listless, low-key.

vivacity *n.* (*liveliness; great energy*) animation, brightness, dynamism, ebullience, effervescence, exuberance, gaiety, high spirits, jollity, life, light-heartedness, liveliness, merriment, pep, sparkle, spirit, sprightliness, vibrancy, (*coll.*) vim, vitality, zing, (*coll.*) zip. ANTONYMS: dullness, inertia, languor, listlessness.

vivid *a.* **1** ((*of colour, light*) *very bright, intense*) bright, brilliant, clear, flamboyant, glowing, intense, rich. ANTONYMS: drab, muted, pale, sombre. **2** ((*of a person etc.*) *vigorous, lively*) animated, colourful, dramatic, graphic, impressive, lively, powerful, striking, vibrant, vigorous. ANTONYMS: boring, colourless, drab, dull. **3** (*clear and detailed*) clear, distinct, memorable, sharp, sharply-etched, well-defined. ANTONYMS: unmemorable, unremarkable, vague.

vocabulary *n.* (*a list or collection of words used in a language, science, book etc., usu. arranged in alphabetical order, and explained*) dictionary, glossary, lexicon, wordbook.

vocal *a.* **1** (*of or relating to the voice or oral utterance*) articulated, oral, said, spoken, uttered, voiced. ANTONYMS: tacit, written. **2** (*outspoken, freely expressing an opinion*) articulate, forthright, frank, loud, noisy, outspoken, plain-spoken, vociferous, voluble. ANTONYMS: quiet, reticent.

vocation n. (*a person's calling or occupation*) business, calling, career, employment, job, line of work, métier, occupation, profession, trade, walk of life, work.

vociferous a. (*making an outcry, expressing oneself loudly and insistently*) clamorous, insistent, loud, noisy, outspoken, strident, vehement, vocal. ANTONYMS: muted, quiet, reticent.

vogue n. **1** (*a fashion prevalent at any particular time*) craze, fad, fashion, mode, style, trend. **2** (*currency, popular acceptance or usage*) acceptance, currency, fashionableness, favour, modishness, popularity, prevalence. **in vogue** (*fashionable, currently popular*) fashionable, in, modish, popular, prevalent, (*coll., sometimes derog.*) trendy, up-to-the-minute. ANTONYMS: old-fashioned, outdated, outmoded, unfashionable.

voice n. **1** (*the faculty or power of vocal utterance*) language, power of speech, speech, utterance. **2** (*expression of the mind or will in words, whether spoken or written etc.*) comment, decision, opinion, say, view, viewpoint, vote, will, wish. **3** (*someone who expresses the will or judgement of others, a spokesperson*) agency, medium, mouthpiece, organ, spokesman, spokesperson, spokeswoman, vehicle.
~v.t. (*to give utterance to, to express*) air, articulate, assert, declare, divulge, enunciate, express, give expression to, give utterance to, mention, pronounce, put into words, say, speak of, talk of, utter. ANTONYMS: conceal, keep quiet about.

void a. **1** (*empty, unfilled*) bare, empty, unfilled, unoccupied, vacant. ANTONYMS: filled, full, occupied. **2** (*lacking, destitute (of)*) devoid of, free from, lacking, wanting, without. **3** (*having no legal force, invalid*) cancelled, ineffective, inoperative, invalid, not binding, not in force, null and void, nullified. ANTONYMS: in force, valid.
~n. (*an empty space*) blank, emptiness, empty space, space, vacuum.
~v.t. **1** (*to invalidate, to nullify*) cancel, invalidate, nullify, rescind. ANTONYMS: enforce, validate. **2** (*to discharge, to emit from the bowels*) discharge, drain, eject, eliminate, emit, empty, evacuate.

volatile a. **1** (*readily evaporating*) evaporative, unstable, vaporous. **2** ((*of a person*) *liable to change their mind quickly or to become angry suddenly*) changeable, erratic, fickle, flighty, inconstant, mercurial, moody, temperamental, unstable, unsteady, (*coll.*) up and down. ANTONYMS: calm, consistent, stable, steady.

3 ((*of a situation*) *unpredictable, liable to sudden violent change*) changeable, explosive, unsettled, unstable, unsteady. ANTONYMS: settled, stable, steady.

volition n. (*exercise of the will*) choice, free will, option, preference, will.

volley n. **1** (*a simultaneous discharge of missiles*) barrage, burst, cannonade, fusillade, hail, salvo, shower. **2** (*a noisy outburst or emission of many things at once*) battery, burst, deluge, shower, stream.

voluble a. (*producing or characterized by a flow of words, garrulous*) articulate, chatty, eloquent, fluent, (*coll.*) gabby, garrulous, glib, gossipy, loquacious, talkative, with the gift of the gab. ANTONYMS: inarticulate, taciturn, tongue-tied.

volume n. **1** (*a book, a tome*) book, publication, tome. **2** (*mass, bulk*) amount, bulk, capacity, cubic content, mass, quantity.

voluminous a. (*of great volume or size*) ample, big, billowing, bulky, capacious, cavernous, full, large, vast. ANTONYMS: skimpy, small, tiny.

voluntarily adv. (*acting, performed etc. of one's own free will or choice, not under external constraint*) by choice, by preference, freely, of one's own accord, of one's own choice, of one's own free will, willingly. ANTONYMS: under compulsion, unwillingly.

voluntary a. **1** (*acting, performed etc. of one's own free will or choice, not under external constraint*) at one's discretion, discretionary, elective, of one's own accord, optional, volitional. ANTONYMS: compulsory, mandatory, obligatory. **2** (*unpaid*) gratuitous, volunteer, without payment. ANTONYMS: paid.

volunteer v.t. (*to offer or undertake voluntarily*) advance, offer, present, proffer, put forward, tender.
~v.i. (*to offer one's services voluntarily*) offer one's service, put oneself at (someone's) disposal, step forward.

voluptuous a. **1** (*relating to or producing sensuous or sensual gratification*) carnal, epicurean, hedonistic, licentious, pleasure-loving, self-indulgent, sensual, sybaritic. **2** ((*of a woman*) *sexually alluring because of shapeliness or fullness of figure*) ample, buxom, (*coll.*) curvaceous, curvy, full-bosomed.

vomit v.t. **1** (*to eject from the stomach by the mouth*) bring up, eject, regurgitate, spew up, spit up. **2** (*to eject or discharge violently, to belch out*) belch forth, belch out, discharge, eject, emit, send forth.
~v.i. (*to eject the contents of the stomach by the*

mouth, *to be sick*) be sick, (*sl.*) puke, retch, spew, (*coll.*) throw up.

voracious *a.* **1** (*ravenous, gluttonous*) gluttonous, greedy, hungry, insatiable, omnivorous, ravening, unquenchable. **2** (*insatiable, very eager*) avid, compulsive, eager, enthusiastic, keen. ANTONYMS: reluctant, unenthusiastic.

vortex *n.* (*a whirling or rotating mass of fluid, esp. a whirlpool*) eddy, maelstrom, whirlpool.

vote *n.* **1** (*a formal expression of opinion or choice, usu. signified by voice or ballot*) ballot, election, plebiscite, poll, referendum. **2** (*the right to vote, the suffrage*) franchise, right to vote, suffrage.
~*v.i.* (*to give one's vote* (*for or against*)) cast one's vote.
~*v.t.* **1** (*to give one's vote for*) choose, elect, nominate, opt for, return. **2** (*to declare by general consent*) advocate, propose, recommend, suggest.

vouch *v.i.* (*to be a surety or guarantee, to answer* (*for*)) answer for, attest to, bear witness to, guarantee, testify to.

voucher *n.* (*a document etc. serving to confirm or establish something, as a payment, the correctness of an account etc.*) chit, slip, ticket, token.

vow *n.* (*a solemn promise or pledge, esp. made to God*) oath, pledge, promise.
~*v.t.* (*to promise solemnly*) give one's word of honour, pledge, promise, state under oath, swear, take an oath.

voyage *v.i.* (*to make a journey by water or air or through space*) cruise, journey, sail, take a trip, travel.

vulgar *a.* **1** (*common, coarse*) cheap, coarse, common, crass, flash, flashy, gaudy, gross, low, showy, tasteless, tawdry, unrefined, unsophisticated. ANTONYMS: refined, sophisticated, tasteful. **2** (*rude, boorish*) boorish, coarse, common, ill-bred, ill-mannered, impolite, rough, rude, unmannerly. ANTONYMS: mannerly, polite, well-mannered. **3** (*ordinary, in common use*) general, ordinary. **4** (*referring to sex in a rude or offensive way*) bawdy, (*sl.*) blue, coarse, crude, dirty, filthy, indelicate, lewd, off-colour, offensive, ribald, risqué, salacious, smutty, suggestive. ANTONYMS: clean, delicate.

vulnerable *a.* (*susceptible or liable to injury, attack etc.*) assailable, defenceless, exposed, open to attack, powerless, sensitive, tender, unguarded, unprotected, weak, wide open. ANTONYMS: invulnerable, strong, well-protected.

wad *n.* **1** (*a small, compact mass of some soft material*) ball, block, chunk, hunk, lump, mass, plug, roll. **2** (*a bundle of currency notes, documents etc.*) bundle, roll.

wadding *n.* (*a soft spongy material, used for stuffing garments, cushions etc.*) filler, lining, packing, padding, stuffing.

waddle *v.i.* (*to walk with an ungainly rocking or swaying motion and with short, quick steps*) sway, toddle, totter, wobble.

wade *v.i.* **1** (*to walk through water or a semi-fluid medium, such as snow, mud etc.*) paddle, splash. **2** (*to make one's way with difficulty and labour*) labour, plough, toil, trudge.
~*v.t.* (*to ford (a stream) on foot*) cross, ford, traverse. **to wade in/ into** (*to tackle or attack vigorously*) assail, attack, get stuck in (to), launch oneself at, (*sl.*) light into, (*coll.*) pitch in (to), set about, tackle, tear into.

waffle *v.i.* (*to talk or write aimlessly and at length*) babble, blather, jabber, prate, prattle, (*coll.*) rabbit on, ramble, (*coll.*) witter.
~*n.* (*vague or inconsequential talk or writing*) babble, blather, (*coll.*) gobbledegook, jabbering, logorrhoea, padding, prating, prattle, prolixity, (*coll.*) rabbiting, verbiage, verbosity, (*coll.*) wittering.

waft *v.t.* (*to carry or convey through the air*) bear, carry, convey, transmit, transport.
~*v.i.* (*to float or be borne on the air*) be carried, drift, float, glide, ride.

wag[1] *v.t.* (*to shake up and down or backwards and forward lightly and quickly*) shake, waggle, wiggle.
~*v.i.* (*to move up and down or to and fro, to oscillate*) bob, flutter, nod, oscillate, quiver, rock, shake, sway, swing, twitch, vibrate, waggle, wave, wiggle.
~*n.* (*an act or a motion of wagging, a shake*) bob, flutter, nod, oscillation, quiver, shake, sway, swing, waggle, wave, wiggle.

wag[2] *n.* (*a facetious person, a wit*) (*sl.*) card, clown, comedian, comic, humorist, jester, joker, (*coll.*) wisecracker, wit.

wage *n.* **1** (*payment for work done or services rendered, esp. for labour of a manual kind*) earnings, emolument, fee, pay, payment, remuneration, salary, stipend. **2** (*recompense, reward*) compensation, deserts, recompense, requital, returns, reward.
~*v.t.* (*to engage in, to carry on (a battle, war etc.*)) carry on, conduct, devote oneself, engage in, practise, prosecute, pursue, undertake.

wager *n.* (*something staked or hazarded on the outcome of a contest etc., a bet*) bet, (*coll.*) flutter, gamble, pledge, (*coll.*) punt, stake.
~*v.t., v.i.* (*to bet*) bet, gamble, (*coll.*) have a flutter on, hazard, lay a bet on, lay odds, pledge, put money on, speculate, stake, venture.

waggish *a.* (*amusing and clever*) amusing, comic, comical, droll, entertaining, facetious, funny, impish, jesting, jocose, jocular, joking, merry, mischievous, playful, puckish, roguish, sportive, whimsical, witty. ANTONYMS: serious, solemn.

waggle *v.t., v.i.* (*to wag or swing to and fro, esp. quickly and frequently*) flutter, oscillate, quiver, shake, sway, wag, wave, wiggle.

waif *n.* (*a homeless wanderer, esp. a forsaken child*) foundling, orphan, stray.

wail *v.i.* **1** (*to lament*) cry, grieve, groan, howl, lament, moan, mourn, sob, ululate, weep, whine. ANTONYMS: laugh, rejoice. **2** (*to utter wails*) bay, howl, ululate, yowl.
~*n.* (*a loud, high-pitched lamentation, a plaintive cry*) bay, complaint, crying, grieving, groan, howl, lament, lamentation, moan, mourning, sob, sobbing, ululation, weeping, whine, yowl. ANTONYMS: laughter, rejoicing.

wait *v.i.* **1** (*to remain inactive or in the same place until some event or time for action, to stay*) bide one's time, (*coll.*) cool one's heels, dally, delay, hang fire, hold on, (*coll.*) hold one's horses, linger, mark time, remain, sit tight, stand by, stay. ANTONYMS: depart, go away, leave. **2** (*to wait at table*) act a waiter/ waitress, be a waiter/ waitress, be employed as a waiter/ waitress, serve, wait at table.
~*v.t.* (*to postpone, to defer*) defer, delay, hold back, postpone, put back. ANTONYMS: bring forward.
~*n.* (*a period of waiting*) delay, halt, hold-up, interval, pause, stay. **to wait on/ upon** (*to attend on as a waiter or servant*) act as maid to, act as servant to, attend to, minister to, serve.

to wait up (*to remain out of bed waiting* (*for*)) keep awake, keep vigil, stay awake, stay up.

waive *v.t.* **1** (*to decide officially that something can be ignored*) abandon, abdicate, cede, disclaim, dispense with, disregard, forgo, give up, ignore, refrain from, relinquish, renounce, resign, set aside, surrender, yield. ANTONYMS: insist on, keep, keep to, uphold. **2** (*to defer, to postpone*) defer, delay, postpone, put off, (*coll.*) put on the back burner, shelve.

waiver *n.* (*the act of waiving a claim, a right etc.*) abandonment, abdication, disclaimer, relinquishment, renunciation, resignation, surrender.

wake *v.i.* **1** (*to be aroused from sleep, to cease to sleep*) arise, awake, awaken, bestir oneself, get up, rise, rouse oneself, wake up. ANTONYMS: go to bed, go to sleep, sleep, slumber, take a nap. **2** (*to revive from a trance, death etc.*) come round, come to. **3** (*to be roused or to rouse oneself from inaction, inattention etc.*) become alert, become aware, become conscious, become heedful, become mindful.
~*v.t.* **1** (*to rouse from sleep, to awake*) get (someone) up, rouse, waken, wake up. **2** (*to revive, to resuscitate*) bring round, bring to, call up, resuscitate, revive. **3** (*to arouse, to stir* (*up*)) activate, animate, arouse, awaken, excite, fire, galvanize, prod, provoke, spur, stimulate, stir up. ANTONYMS: assuage, calm, quell, quench.
~*n.* (*a vigil*) vigil, watch.

wakeful *a.* **1** (*not disposed or unable to sleep, restless*) insomniac, restless, tossing and turning. ANTONYMS: asleep, sleeping. **2** ((*of a night*) *passed without sleep*) broken, disturbed, restless, sleepless, unsleeping. ANTONYMS: restful, sleeping. **3** (*watchful, alert*) alert, attentive, heedful, observant, on guard, on the alert, on the lookout, on the qui vive, vigilant, wary, watchful. ANTONYMS: attentive, careless, heedless, off guard.

waken *v.t.* **1** (*to rouse from sleep*) get (someone) up, rouse, wake, wake up. **2** (*to rouse to action etc.*) activate, animate, arouse, awaken, excite, fire, galvanize, prod, provoke, spur, stimulate, stir up. ANTONYMS: assuage, calm, quell, quench. **3** (*to call forth*) call forth, conjure up, evoke, rouse, stir up.
~*v.i.* (*to wake, to cease from sleeping*) arise, awake, awaken, bestir oneself, get up, rise, rouse oneself, wake, wake up. ANTONYMS: go to bed, go to sleep, sleep, slumber.

walk *v.i.* **1** (*to go at the ordinary pace, not to run, not to go or proceed rapidly*) amble, hike, march, plod, saunter, step out, stride, stroll, tramp, trudge. ANTONYMS: dash, hurry, run, rush. **2** (*to go or travel on foot*) foot it, go by

shanks's pony, go on foot, (*sl.*) hoof it, travel on foot.
~*v.t.* (*to accompany on foot*) accompany, convoy, escort, take.
~*n.* **1** (*the pace or step of a person or animal that walks*) gait, pace, step, stride. **2** (*an act of walking for pleasure, exercise etc.*) airing, amble, constitutional, hike, march, promenade, ramble, saunter, stroll, tramp. **3** (*a piece of ground laid out for walking, a footpath etc.*) esplanade, footpath, lane, path, pathway, pavement, promenade, (*N Am.*) sidewalk, track, walkway. **4** (*the district or round of a hawker, postman etc.*) beat, circuit, round, route, run. **5** (*one's profession, occupation etc.*) area of work, calling, career, employment, field, job, line, line of work, métier, occupation, profession, social rank, social status, sphere, trade, vocation, work. **to walk away with** (*to win or gain easily*) have a walkover, walk off with, win an easy victory, win easily, win hands down. ANTONYMS: be trounced, lose badly. **to walk off with 1** (*to carry off, to steal*) carry off, embezzle, filch, make off with, pilfer, run off with, snatch, steal. **2** (*to walk away with*) have a walkover, walk away with, win an easy victory, win easily, win hands down. ANTONYMS: be trounced, lose badly. **to walk out 1** (*to depart suddenly, esp. in anger*) flounce out, get up and go, leave suddenly, make a sudden departure, storm out, take off, up and go, up and leave. **2** (*to stop work as a protest*) call a strike, down tools, go on strike, stage a strike, stop work, strike, take industrial action, withdraw one's labour. **to walk out on** (*to abandon*) abandon, (*coll.*) chuck, desert, (*coll.*) dump, forsake, leave, leave high and dry, leave in the lurch, run away from, throw over.

walker *n.* (*a person who walks, esp. for pleasure, exercise etc.*) hiker, pedestrian, rambler, wayfarer.

walking stick *n.* (*a stick carried in walking, esp. for support*) cane, crook, staff, stick.

walkout *n.* (*a sudden departure in anger, esp. of workers*) industrial action, protest, stoppage, strike.

walkover *n.* (*an easy victory*) (*coll.*) breeze, child's play, (*coll.*) doddle, easy victory, (*coll.*) picnic, piece of cake, (*coll.*) pushover. ANTONYMS: ordeal, strain, struggle.

wall *n.* **1** (*a continuous structure of stone, brick etc. forming an enclosure, a side or internal partition of a building etc.*) divider, enclosure, partition, room divider, screen. **2** (*a rampart, a fortification*) barricade, breastwork, bulwark, embankment, fortification, palisade, parapet, rampart, stockade. **3** (*a defence or obstacle*) barrier, block, impediment, obstacle, obstruction. **to go to the wall** (*to fail*) be ruined, collapse, fail, fall, go bankrupt, go bust, go under. **to have one's back to the wall** (*to be in a desperate position*) be in a fix, (*coll.*) be in a hole, be in a jam, be in a tight corner, be in deep trouble, be in dire straits, be in distress. **up the wall** (*in or into a state of distraction or exasperation*) angry, annoyed, crazy, demented, deranged, distraught, exasperated, furious, infuriated, insane, irritated, mad, maddened. ANTONYMS: calm, calm and collected, composed, cool.

wallet *n.* (*a small case for carrying paper money, credit cards etc.*) (*N Am.*) billfold, case, holder, notecase, pocketbook, purse.

wallop *v.t.* (*to thrash, to flog*) batter, beat, belt, (*sl.*) clobber, flog, hit, lambast, pound, pummel, punch, slug, smack, thrash, thump, whack.

wallow *v.i.* **1** (*to roll or tumble about in mud, water etc.*) flounder, lie around, roll around, splash around, tumble about. **2** (*to revel grossly or self-indulgently* (*in*)) bask (in), delight (in), get satisfaction (from), glory (in), indulge oneself (in), luxuriate (in), relish, revel (in), take pleasure (in).

wan *a.* **1** (*pale or sickly in hue, pallid*) anaemic, ashen, bloodless, colourless, ghastly, pale, pallid, pasty, peaky, sickly, washed out, waxen, white, white as a ghost, white as a sheet. ANTONYMS: healthy, rosy-cheeked, ruddy. **2** ((*of light etc.*) *dim, faint*) dim, faint, feeble, pale, weak. ANTONYMS: bright, strong.

wand *n.* (*a long, slender rod, esp. one used by conjurors or as a staff of office*) baton, rod, sprig, staff, stick, twig.

wander *v.i.* **1** (*to travel or go here and there without any definite route or object, to roam*) amble, cruise, drift, meander, (*coll.*) mooch around, ramble, range, roam, rove, saunter, (*Sc.*) stravaig, stray, stroll, traipse. **2** (*to follow an irregular or winding course*) bend, curve, meander, wind, zigzag. **3** (*to lose one's way, to go astray*) get lost, go astray, go off course, lose one's way. **4** (*to deviate from the right or proper course*) depart, deviate, digress, go off at a tangent, go off course, lose one's train of thought, stray, swerve, veer. ANTONYMS: be focused, stick to the point. **5** (*to talk or think in a confused or unclear way, to be delirious*) babble, be delirious, be incoherent, ramble, rave, talk nonsense.

~*n.* (*a short relaxed walk*) amble, cruise, meander, (*coll.*) mooch, ramble, saunter, stroll, traipse.

wanderer *n.* (*a person who travels around rather than settling in one place*) bird of passage, drifter, gypsy, itinerant, nomad, rambler, roamer, rolling stone, rover, tramp, traveller, vagabond.

wandering *a.* **1** ((*of people*) *travelling around rather than settling in one place*) drifting, itinerant, meandering, migrant, nomadic, peripatetic, rambling, roaming, roving, strolling, transient, travelling, vagabond, wayfaring. **2** (*following an irregular or winding course*) bending, curving, meandering, winding, zigzagging. **3** ((*of someone's speech*) *confused and unclear*) babbling, delirious, incoherent, rambling, raving.

wanderlust *n.* (*the desire to travel*) itchy feet, restlessness, (*coll.*) the travel bug.

wane *v.i.* (*to decrease in power, strength etc., to decline*) abate, be on the way out, contract, decline, decrease, degenerate, deteriorate, die out, dim, diminish, dwindle, ebb, fade away, fail, fall away, lessen, peter out, sink, subside, taper off, vanish, weaken, wither. ANTONYMS: develop, expand, flourish, grow, increase, wax.

~*n.* (*the act or process of waning, diminution*) abatement, contraction, decline, decrease, degeneration, deterioration, diminution, dimming, drop, dwindling, dying out, ebb, fading, failure, fall, lessening, petering out, sinking, subsiding, tapering off, vanishing, weakening. ANTONYMS: developing, expansion, flourishing, growth, increase, waxing.

wangle *v.t.* (*to achieve or gain by devious means*) bring off, contrive, engineer, (*coll.*) fiddle, (*sl.*) fix, manipulate, manoeuvre, pull off.

want *n.* **1** (*the state or condition of not having, lack* (*of*)) absence (of), dearth (of), deficiency (in), famine (of), inadequacy (of), insufficiency (of), lack (of), need (of), paucity (of), shortage (of). ANTONYMS: abundance (of), excess (of), glut (of), plenty (of), sufficiency (of). **2** (*need, poverty*) deprivation, destitution, indigence, need, neediness, pauperism, penury, poverty, privation. ANTONYMS: affluence, comfort, riches, wealth. **3** (*a longing or desire for something that is necessary or required for happiness etc.*) covetousness, craving, demand, desire, fancy, hankering, hunger, longing, lust, need, requirement, thirst, wish, yearning, (*coll.*) yen.

~*v.t.* **1** (*to feel a desire or longing for, to crave*) call for, covet, crave, demand, desire, fancy, feel a need for, hanker after, have a fancy for, (*coll.*) have a yen for, hope for, hunger for, long for, lust after, need, pine for, thirst after, wish for, yearn for. ANTONYMS: be sated by, hate, shun, spurn. **2** (*to be without, to lack*) be bereft of, be deficient in, be devoid of, be in need of, be lacking in, be short of, be without, have need of, lack, need, require. ANTONYMS: have an abundance of, have a surfeit of, have enough.

wanting *a.* **1** (*absent, missing*) absent, lacking, missing, not there, short. ANTONYMS: complete. **2** (*not meeting the required or expected standard*) defective, deficient, disappointing, faulty, imperfect, inadequate, inferior, lacking, not good enough, not up to par, not up to scratch, not up to standard, poor, substandard, unsatisfactory, unsound. ANTONYMS: acceptable, excellent, perfect, satisfactory.
~*prep.* (*without*) in need of, lacking, less, (*coll.*) minus, missing, requiring, short of.

wanton *a.* **1** ((*of a woman*) *immoral*) abandoned, bad, degenerate, dissipated, dissolute, fast, immodest, immoral, lascivious, lecherous, libidinous, licentious, loose, lustful, of easy virtue, promiscuous, shameless. ANTONYMS: modest, pure, puritanical, virtuous. **2** (*random, purposeless*) arbitrary, gratuitous, groundless, heedless, motiveless, needless, pointless, random, reckless, senseless, spiteful, uncalled-for, unjustifiable, unjustified, unmotivated, unnecessary, unprovoked, wilful. ANTONYMS: excusable, justified, motivated, provoked, warranted. **3** (*uncontrolled, wild*) extravagant, immoderate, lavish, uncontrolled, unrestrained, unruly, wild. ANTONYMS: controlled, restrained, subdued. **4** (*frolicsome, playful*) capricious, devil-may-care, frolicsome, impulsive, playful, sportive. ANTONYMS: serious, staid.
~*n.* (*an immoral person, esp. a woman*) harlot, (*sl.*) hooker, loose woman, prostitute, slut, trollop, whore.

war *n.* **1** (*a contest carried on by force of arms between nations, or between parties in the same state*) armed conflict, battle, combat, conflict, confrontation, contest, engagement, fight, fighting, skirmish, struggle. ANTONYMS: ceasefire, truce. **2** (*a state of armed hostilities with suspension of ordinary international relations*) animosity, bad blood, conflict, enmity, fighting, hostility, ill will, strife, warfare. ANTONYMS: harmony, peace. **3** (*a struggle or campaign*) battle, campaign, crusade, feud, fight, struggle.
~*v.i.* (*to make or carry on war*) be at war, conduct a war, cross swords, do battle, fight, make war, quarrel, take up arms, wrangle. **at war** (*engaged in hostilities* (*with*)) battling, feuding, fighting, in conflict, quarrelling, wrangling. ANTONYMS: at peace, harmonious, in harmony.

warble *v.i.* ((*esp. of birds*) *to sing in a continuous quavering or trilling manner*) chirp, chirrup, quaver, sing, trill, twitter.

ward *n.* **1** (*an administrative or electoral division of a town or city*) area, district, division, zone. **2** (*a separate division of a hospital, prison etc.*) compartment, cubicle, room. **3** (*a minor or other person under the care of a guardian*) charge, dependant, minor, protégé. **4** (*guardianship, protection*) care, charge, custody, guardianship, keeping, protection, safe keeping. **to ward off** (*to parry, to keep off*) avert, avoid, beat off, block, checkmate, deflect, fend off, foil, forestall, frustrate, keep at arm's length, keep at bay, parry, rebuff, repel, repulse, stave off, thwart, turn aside, turn away.

warden *n.* **1** (*a keeper, a guardian*) caretaker, curator, custodian, guard, guardian, janitor, keeper, steward, watch, watchman. **2** (*the head of a college, school or hostel*) overseer, superintendent, supervisor.

warder *n.* (*a jailer, a prison officer*) gaoler, guard, jailer, keeper, prison guard, prison officer, (*sl.*) screw, †turnkey.

wardrobe *n.* **1** (*a tall cupboard with rails, shelves etc. where clothes are hung up*) (*esp. N Am.*) closet, clothes cupboard, cupboard. **2** (*a person's stock of clothes*) apparel, attire, clothes, collection of stories, garments, outfit, set of clothes.

ware *n.* (*articles for sale, goods*) commodities, goods, goods for sale, merchandise, products, stock.

warehouse *n.* (*a building in which goods are stored, kept for sale or in bond*) depository, depot, stockroom, store, storehouse.

warfare *n.* (*a state of war, hostilities*) armed conflict, battle, combat, conflict, discord, fighting, hostilities, strife, war. ANTONYMS: armistice, harmony, peace, truce.

warily *adv.* (*in a cautious or watchful manner*) attentively, carefully, cautiously, circumspectly, discreetly, distrustfully, gingerly, guardedly, heedfully, mistrustfully, on one's guard, on the alert, on the qui vive, suspiciously, vigilantly, watchfully, with care, with caution. ANTONYMS: carelessly, inattentively, rashly, recklessly.

wariness *n.* (*the state of being cautious or watchful*) alertness, attention, attentiveness, care, carefulness, caution, circumspection, discretion, distrust, heedfulness, mistrust, prudence, suspicion, vigilance, watchfulness. ANTONYMS: carelessness, inattention, negligence, rashness, recklessness.

warlike *a.* (*threatening war, hostile*) aggressive, bellicose, belligerent, combative, hawkish, hostile, martial, militant, militaristic, pugnacious, unfriendly, warmongering. ANTONYMS: amicable, friendly, peaceful, peace-loving.

†**warlock** *n.* (*a wizard, a sorcerer*) enchanter, magician, male witch, necromancer, sorcerer, wizard.

warm *a.* **1** (*having heat in a moderate degree*) lukewarm, tepid, warmish. ANTONYMS: chilly, cold, cool. **2** (*ardent, enthusiastic*) affable, ardent, cordial, effusive, enthusiastic, fervent, friendly, genial, heartfelt, hearty, hospitable, kind, kindly, sincere, vehement, zealous. ANTONYMS: apathetic, cool, lukewarm, unenthusiastic, unwelcoming. **3** (*emotional, affectionate*) affectionate, amiable, caring, charitable, compassionate, friendly, genial, kind, kindly, loving, nice, pleasant, sympathetic, tender. ANTONYMS: aloof, cold, distant, hostile, nasty, stand-offish, unfriendly. **4** (*animated, heated*) animated, emotional, excitable, excited, heated, intense, passionate, stormy, vehement, violent. ANTONYMS: apathetic, calm, low-key. **5** (*near to finding an object, guessing a secret etc.* (*esp. in children's games*)) close, near. **6** (*unpleasant, uncomfortable*) dangerous, difficult, disagreeable, explosive, hazardous, heated, hostile, hot, nasty, perilous, risky, strained, tense, tricky, uncomfortable, unpleasant. ANTONYMS: comfortable, friendly, peaceful, pleasant, safe.
~*v.t.* **1** (*to make warm*) heat, heat up, make warm, reheat, warm up. ANTONYMS: chill, cool, freeze. **2** (*to make ardent or enthusiastic, to excite*) animate, cheer up, enliven, excite, (*coll.*) get going, liven up, put some life into, rouse, stimulate, wake up. ANTONYMS: bore, depress.
~*v.i.* **1** (*to become warm*) get hotter, get warmer, heat up, warm up. ANTONYMS: cool down, get colder, get cooler. **2** (*to become enthusiastic or sympathetic* (*to or towards*)) become fond of, begin to like, develop a liking for, grow enthusiastic about, grow to like. ANTONYMS: go off, lose one's enthusiasm for, take a dislike to.
to warm up 1 (*to make or become warm*) heat, heat up, melt, thaw, warm. ANTONYMS: cool down. **2** (*to reheat* (*cooked food*)) heat, heat up, make warm, reheat, warm. ANTONYMS: chill, cool, freeze. **3** (*to prepare for a contest, performance etc., esp. by exercising or practising*) exercise, limber up, loosen up, practise, prepare.

warm-blooded *a.* (*emotional, passionate*) ardent, emotional, enthusiastic, excitable, fervent, impetuous, impulsive, passionate, rash, spirited. ANTONYMS: apathetic, cold, emotionless, frigid, passionless.

warm-hearted *a.* (*having warm or kindly feelings*) affectionate, caring, compassionate, cordial, friendly, generous, kind, kind-hearted, kindly, loving, sympathetic, tender-hearted. ANTONYMS: callous, cold, cold-hearted, hardhearted, harsh, unfriendly, unkind.

warmly *adv.* (*in a friendly way*) affably, ardently, cordially, effusively, enthusiastically, fervently, genially, heartily, kindly, sincerely, vehemently, zealously. ANTONYMS: apathetically, coolly, unenthusiastically.

warmth *n.* **1** (*the state of being warm*) heat, hotness, warmness. **2** (*the state of having a moderate degree of heat*) lukewarmness, tepidity, tepidness, warmness. ANTONYMS: chilliness, coldness, coolness. **3** (*enthusiasm and friendliness*) affability, ardour, cordiality, effusiveness, enthusiasm, fervour, friendliness, geniality, heartiness, kindliness, kindness, sincerity, vehemence, zeal. ANTONYMS: apathy, coolness, lack of enthusiasm, lukewarmness. **4** (*sympathy and affection*) affection, amiability, charity, compassion, friendliness, geniality, kindliness, kindness, love, niceness, pleasantness, sympathy, tenderness. ANTONYMS: aloofness, coldness, coolness, hostility, nastiness, stand-offishness, unfriendliness. **5** (*excitement or vehemence*) animation, emotion, excitability, excitement, heat, intensity, passion, storminess, vehemence, violence. ANTONYMS: apathy, calmness, lack of emotion. **6** (*the state of being unpleasant or uncomfortable*) danger, difficulty, disagreeableness, explosiveness, hazard, hazardousness, heat, nastiness, peril, risk, riskiness, strain, tension, uncomfortableness, unpleasantness. ANTONYMS: comfort, friendliness, peacefulness, pleasantness, safety.

warn *v.t.* **1** (*to give notice to, to inform beforehand*) acquaint, advise, apprise, inform, let (someone) know, make aware, notify, tell. **2** (*to caution, to make aware of danger*) advise, alert, caution, counsel, forewarn, prewarn, tip (someone) off. **3** (*to expostulate with, to admonish*) admonish, give (someone) a warning, remonstrate.

warning *n.* **1** (*the act of cautioning or making aware of danger etc.*) advice, alert, alerting, caution, cautioning, counselling, forewarning, prewarning, tip-off. **2** (*previous notice*) advice, apprisal, notice, notification, word. **3** (*something serving to warn*) alarm, signal, alert, augury, caveat, omen, premonition, sign, signal, threat, token. **4** (*the act of admonish-ing*) admonishing, admonition, remonstration.
~*a.* (*serving to warn*) admonitory, cautionary, ominous, threatening.

warp *n.* **1** (*the state of being twisted or distorted, a twist or distortion in timber etc.*) bend, contortion, deformation, distortion, kink, twist. **2** (*a perversion or aberration of mind or disposition*) aberration, deviation, link, perversion, quirk.
~*v.t.* **1** (*to turn or twist out of shape, to distort*) bend, contort, deform, distort, make crooked, misshape, twist. ANTONYMS: straighten, straighten out. **2** (*to pervert, to bias*) corrupt, deprave, pervert.

warrant *v.t.* **1** (*to answer or give an assurance for, to guarantee*) affirm, answer for, bear witness to, certify, endorse, guarantee, pledge, swear to, testify to, underwrite, vouch for. **2** (*to give authority to, to sanction*) allow, approve, authorize, empower, license, permit, sanction, validate. **3** (*to serve as grounds or justification for*) be a defence of, be an excuse for, be a reason for, be grounds for, excuse, justify, vindicate.
~*n.* **1** (*anything that authorizes a person to do something*) approval, authority, authorization, licence, permission, permit, sanction, validation. **2** (*grounds, justification*) defence, excuse, grounds, justification, reason, vindication. **3** (*a document authorizing a person to receive money etc.*) chit, slip, voucher.

warrantable *a.* (*justifiable, defensible*) defensible, excusable, justifiable, reasonable. ANTONYMS: indefensible, inexcusable, unjustifiable, unwarrantable.

warring *a.* (*at war, fighting*) at daggers drawn, at each other's throats, at war, clashing, combatant, embattled, fighting, hostile, in conflict, opposing, rival. ANTONYMS: friendly, in harmony.

warrior *n.* (*a person experienced or distinguished in war, a distinguished soldier*) combatant, fighter, gladiator, soldier.

wary *a.* (*cautious, watchful against deception, danger etc.*) alert, attentive, careful, cautious, chary, circumspect, discreet, distrustful, guarded, heedful, leery, mistrustful, observant, on one's guard, on the qui vive, suspicious, vigilant, watchful, wide awake. ANTONYMS: careless, heedless, inattentive, negligent, rash, reckless.

wash *v.t.* **1** (*to cleanse with water or other liquid*) bathe, clean, cleanse, launder, scrub, shampoo, shower, wipe. **2** ((*of waves, the sea etc.*) *to fall upon or dash against*) beat against, break against, dash against, splash against. **3** (*to carry along, to sweep away etc.*) bear away, bear off, carry away, carry off, erode, sweep away, wear away.
~*v.i.* **1** (*to cleanse oneself, one's hands etc. with*

water etc.) bath, have a bath, have a shower, have a wash, shower, wash oneself. **2** ((*of a story etc.*) *to stand examination, to be accepted or believed*) be acceptable, bear examination, be plausible, hold up, hold water, stand examination, stand scrutiny, stand up. ANTONYMS: be unacceptable, be unconvincing. **3** ((*of water etc.*) *to move or splash or sweep along*) flow, splash, stream, sweep, swell.
~*n.* **1** (*the act or process of washing*) bath, bathe, bathing, clean, cleaning, cleansing, laundering, scrub, scrubbing, shampoo, shampooing, shower, showering, washing. **2** (*a quantity of clothes etc. washed at one time*) dirty washing, laundry, washing. **3** (*the motion of a body of water or air, esp. that caused by the passage of a ship or aircraft*) flow, roll, surge, swell. **4** (*a liquid used for healing or cosmetic purposes, a lotion*) lotion, salve. **5** (*a thin liquid for coating a wall etc.*) coating, film, overlay, paint, stain, varnish.

washed out *a.* **1** (*exhausted, worn out*) (*coll.*) all in, (*coll.*) done in, drained, exhausted, fatigued, (*coll.*) knackered, pale, tired out, wan, weary, worn out, zonked. ANTONYMS: energetic, lively, sprightly. **2** (*faded, colourless*) bleached, colourless, faded. ANTONYMS: bright, vivid.

washed up *a.* (*no longer successful or effective, finished*) failed, finished, ruined.

washing *n.* (*clothes etc. washed or to be washed together*) dirty clothes, dirty washing, laundry, soiled clothes, soiled linen.

wash-out *n.* (*a failure, a fiasco*) disaster, failure, fiasco, (*coll.*) flop. ANTONYMS: hit, success, triumph.

waspish *a.* (*bad-tempered and critical*) bad-tempered, cantankerous, captious, crabbed, cross, crotchety, grumpy, ill-tempered, irascible, irritable, peevish, petulant, querulous, short-tempered, snappish, splenetic, testy, tetchy, touchy. ANTONYMS: affable, genial, good-tempered.

waste *v.t.* **1** (*to spend, to use up carelessly or lavishly, to squander*) (*sl.*) blow, dissipate, fritter, go through, misspend, misuse, run through, squander, throw away. ANTONYMS: conserve, preserve, save. **2** (*to fail to use to advantage*) bungle, lose, miss, pass over, throw away. **3** (*to cause to lose weight, strength and health*) atrophy, debilitate, disable, emaciate, enfeeble, make weak, sap the strength of, shrivel, weaken, wither. ANTONYMS: make strong, strengthen. **4** (*to devastate, to lay waste*) despoil, destroy, devastate, lay waste, loot, maraud, pillage, ravage, ruin, sack, spoil, (*esp. N Am., coll.*) trash, wreak havoc on.

~*v.i.* (*to lose weight, strength and health*) atrophy, become emaciated, grow weak, wither. ANTONYMS: gain strength, grow strong.

~*a.* **1** (*superfluous, left over as useless or value-less*) left over, superfluous, supernumerary, unused, unwanted, useless, valueless, worthless. **2** (*sl.*) (*desolate, desert*) bare, barren, desert, desolate, devastated, dismal, empty, uncultivated, untilled. ANTONYMS: fruitful, habitable, productive.

~*n.* **1** (*the act or an instance of wasting or squandering*) (*sl.*) blowing, dissipating, dissipation, frittering, misapplication, misspending, misuse, squandering, throwing away, wastefulness. ANTONYMS: conservation, frugality, preservation, saving. **2** (*material, food etc. rejected as superfluous, useless or valueless; refuse*) debris, dregs, dross, garbage, trash, waste products. **3** (*a desolate or desert region, a wilderness*) barrenness, desert, emptiness, void, wasteland.

wasted *a.* **1** (*exhausted*) (*coll.*) all in, (*coll.*) done in, drained, exhausted, fatigued, (*coll.*) knackered, tired out, worn out, zonked. ANTONYMS: energetic, fresh. **2** (*showing the effects of alcohol or drug abuse*) (*sl.*) bombed, intoxicated, (*sl.*) smashed, (*sl.*) stoned. **3** (*used up unnecessarily or carelessly*) dissipated, frittered, misapplied, misspent, misused, squandered. **4** (*not used to advantage*) bungled, lost, missed, past, thrown away.

wasteful *a.* (*extravagant, spending or using recklessly or too lavishly*) extravagant, improvident, overlavish, prodigal, profligate, spendthrift, thriftless, uneconomical. ANTONYMS: economical, frugal, provident.

wastrel *n.* **1** (*a wasteful person*) profligate, spendthrift, squanderer. **2** (*a good-for-nothing*) good-for-nothing, idler, layabout, loafer, ne'er-do-well, shirker, (*coll.*) skiver.

watch *n.* **1** (*a state of alertness or vigilance*) lookout, observation, surveillance, vigil. **2** (*a watchman or body of watchmen, a guard*) caretaker, guard, night watchman, security guard, watchman. **3** (*a small timepiece activated by a spring or battery, for carrying on the person*) chronometer, pocket watch, timepiece, wristwatch.

~*v.i.* (*to be vigilant or expectant*) be attentive, be careful, be cautious, be observant, be on the alert, be on the lookout, be on the qui vive, be vigilant, be wary, be watchful, keep one's eye open, keep one's eyes peeled, keep one's eyes skinned, look out, mind out, pay attention, take heed. ANTONYMS: be careless, be inattentive.

~*v.t.* **1** (*to observe closely, to keep one's eye or eyes on*) behold, contemplate, examine, eye,

gaze at, (*sl.*) get a load of, inspect, look at, mark, note, observe, pay attention to, regard, scan, scrutinize, see, spectate at, stare at, survey, (*coll.*) take a dekko at, take a look at, view. ANTONYMS: ignore. **2** (*to monitor or keep under observation*) follow, keep an eye on, keep tabs on, keep under observation, observe, spy on, trail. **3** (*to tend, to look after*) guard, keep an eye on, keep safe, look after, mind, protect, shield, superintend, supervise, take care of, tend, watch over. ANTONYMS: neglect. **to keep watch** (*to be on guard in order to warn of danger while others are asleep*) act as a guard, be on guard, be on the alert, guard, keep a lookout. **to watch out 1** (*to be on the lookout (for)*) be on the alert for, be on the lookout for, be on the watch for, keep a lookout for, keep an eye open for, keep a sharp lookout for, keep a weather eye open for, keep one's eyes peeled for, keep one's eyes skinned for. **2** (*to take care*) be attentive, be careful, be cautious, be observant, be on the alert, be on the lookout, be on the qui vive, be vigilant, be wary, be watchful, keep one's eyes peeled, keep one's eyes skinned, look out, mind out, pay attention, take heed. ANTONYMS: be careless, be inattentive. **to watch over** (*to look after (someone), making sure no harm comes to them*) defend, guard, keep an eye on, keep safe, look after, mind, protect, shield, stand guard over, superintend, supervise, take care of, tend, watch. ANTONYMS: neglect.

watchdog *n.* (*a person or group that monitors the activities of an organization etc. to guard against illegal or undesirable practices*) custodian, guardian, inspector, monitor, protector, scrutineer.

watcher *n.* (*a person who watches or observes something*) looker-on, observer, onlooker, spectator, spy, viewer, witness.

watchful *a.* **1** (*careful to notice what is happening*) alert, attentive, careful, eagle-eyed, guarded, observant, vigilant. ANTONYMS: careless, inattentive, negligent. **2** (*cautious, wary*) cautious, chary, circumspect, distrustful, heedful, suspicious, wary. ANTONYMS: heedless, rash, unwary.

watchfulness *n.* (*care in noticing what is happening*) alertness, attention, care, carefulness, caution, cautiousness, circumspection, heed, heedfulness, vigilance, wariness. ANTONYMS: carelessness, inattention, negligence, unwariness.

watchman *n.* (*a person who guards a large building etc. at night*) caretaker, custodian, guard, lookout, night watch, patrol, security guard, security officer.

watchword n. 1 (a word or phrase symbolizing or epitomizing the principles of a party etc.) battle-cry, byword, catchphrase, catchword, maxim, motto, rallying-cry, slogan. **2** (a word given to sentinels etc. as a signal that one has the right of admission etc., a password) magic word, password, shibboleth, sign.

water n. **1** (a colourless, transparent liquid, without taste or smell) Adam's ale, bottled water, mineral water, tap water. **2** (a (natural) body of water, such as a sea, a lake) lake, loch, river, sea.
~v.t. **1** (to apply water to, to moisten or supply with water) damp, dampen, douse, drench, flood, hose down, irrigate, moisten, saturate, soak, souse, spray, sprinkle, wet. **2** (to dilute or adulterate with water) add water to, adulterate, dilute, put water in, thin down, water down, weaken. ANTONYMS: strengthen. **in hot water** (in trouble or disgrace) in a fix, in difficulty, in disgrace, in trouble. **to hold water** (to be sound or valid, to stand scrutiny) be acceptable, bear examination, bear scrutiny, be convincing, be plausible, be sound, be valid, hold up, stand examination, stand scrutiny, stand up, (coll.) wash. ANTONYMS: be unacceptable, be unconvincing, be unsound. **to water down 1** (to dilute with water) add water to, adulterate, dilute, put water in, thin down, water, weaken. **2** (to make less forceful, harsh etc.) downplay, minimize, play down, soft-pedal, tone down, underemphasize, understate. ANTONYMS: exaggerate, overemphasize.

waterfall n. (a steep or perpendicular descent of a river etc., a cataract) cascade, cataract, falls, linn.

waterlogged a. (saturated with water) flooded, saturated, sodden, submerged, swamped, water-filled.

watertight a. **1** (so tightly fastened or fitted as to prevent the passage of water in or out) sound, waterproof. **2** ((of an argument etc.) unable to be attacked or refuted) faultless, flawless, foolproof, impregnable, incontrovertible, indisputable, irrefutable, strong, unassailable, unquestionable. ANTONYMS: shaky, tenuous, unsound, weak.

watery a. **1** (containing too much water) boggy, damp, humid, marshy, moist, saturated, sodden, soggy, swampy, waterlogged, wet. ANTONYMS: arid, dried out, dry, parched. **2** (suffused or running with water) lachrymose, rheumy, tear-filled, tearful, weeping, weepy. **3** (thin or pale, like water) pale, pallid, transparent. **4** (of or consisting of water) aqueous, fluid, hydrous, liquefied, liquid. ANTONYMS: solid. **5** (taste-less, insipid) adulterated, dilute,

diluted, flavourless, insipid, runny, tasteless, thin, watered-down, weak, wishy-washy. ANTONYMS: concentrated, condensed, strong, thick.

wave v.i. **1** (to move to and fro with a sinuous or sweeping motion, to flutter) flap, flutter, oscillate, quiver, ripple, shake, stir, sway, swing, undulate, wag. **2** (to have an undulating shape or conformation, to be wavy) be curly, be wavy, curl, have a kink, kink, undulate. ANTONYMS: be straight. **3** (to greet or signal (to) by waving the hand etc.) beckon, gesture, indicate, sign, signal.
~v.t. **1** (to brandish (a weapon etc.)) flap, flourish, flutter, shake, swing, wag. **2** (to give an undulating surface or appearance to, to make wavy) curl, put a curl in, put a kink in, put a wave in. **3** (to indicate or command by a waving signal) beckon, gesture, indicate to, signal to, sign to.
~n. **1** (a moving ridge or long curved body of water or other liquid) billow, breaker, comber, ripple, roller, surf, swell, undulation, white cap, white horse. **2** (a waviness of the hair) curl, kink, undulation. **3** (the act or gesture of waving, as a greeting, signal etc.) gesture, sign, signal. **4** (a heightened volume or intensity of some force, emotion etc.) flood, groundswell, outbreak, rash, surge, upsurge, welling-up. **5** (a widespread advance or influx) flood, flow, rush, stream, surge. **to wave aside** (to dismiss with or as with a wave of the hand) dismiss, disregard, ignore, reject, set aside.

waver v.i. **1** (to be in a state of indecision, to vacillate) beat about the bush, be indecisive, be irresolute, blow hot and cold, dither, equivocate, hum and haw, pussyfoot around, shilly-shally, vacillate. ANTONYMS: be decisive, be firm, be resolute. **2** (to become less certain) begin to give way, falter. ANTONYMS: be resolute, stand firm. **3** (to reel, to be unsteady) reel, stagger, sway, teeter, totter, weave, wobble. **4** (to play or move to and fro) flicker, quiver, tremble. ANTONYMS: be resolute, stand firm.

wavy a. (having an alternately concave and convex outline, undulating) curling, curving, curvy, rippling, squiggly, undulating, winding. ANTONYMS: straight.

wax v.i. **1** (to increase gradually in size and brilliance, as the illuminated portion of the moon between new and full) become larger, develop, enlarge, expand, extend, get bigger, grow, grow stronger, increase, mount, mushroom, rise, spread, strengthen, swell. ANTONYMS: decrease, grow smaller, grow weaker, wane. **2** (to pass into a specified condition, to become gradually) become, get, grow.

way *n.* **1** (*a road, path or other place of passage*) highway, lane, path, pathway, road, roadway, street, thoroughfare, track, trail. **2** (*a length of space passed over, a distance to be traversed*) distance, extent, journey, space, stretch. **3** (*the course or route followed or to be followed between two places or to reach a place*) course, direction, road, route. **4** (*the method or manner of doing something, or proceeding to carry out some purpose*) approach, course of action, fashion, manner, means, method, mode, modus operandi, plan, practice, procedure, process, scheme, system, technique. **5** (*a usual or habitual mode of action or conduct, an idiosyncrasy*) characteristic, custom, disposition, habit, manner, mannerism, nature, peculiarity, personality, practice, style, temperament, trait, wont. **6** (*condition, state*) circumstance, condition, shape, situation, state. **7** (*relation, respect*) aspect, detail, feature, particular, point, respect, sense. **8** (*onward movement, progress*) advance, headway, progress. **9** (*room for passage or advance, ground over which one would proceed*) elbow room, room, space. **by the way** (*in passing, parenthetically*) by the by, by the bye, en passant, incidentally, in passing, parenthetically. **by way of 1** (*by the route of, via*) by a route through, through, via. **2** (*as a form of or substitute for, to serve as*) as a form of, as a means of, as a way of, to serve as. **in the way** (*in a position or of a nature to obstruct or hinder*) blocking the way, causing an obstruction, hindering, impeding, obstructing. **on one's way** (*travelling, moving on*) coming, going, journeying, proceeding, travelling. **on the way** (*in progress*) about to arrive, coming, coming soon. **to make one's way** (*to proceed*) advance, go, go forward, go on, move on, press on, proceed. **under way** ((*of a ship etc.*) *in motion*) afoot, begun, going, in motion, in operation, in progress, started.

wayfarer *n.* (*a traveller, esp. on foot*) hiker, journeyer, nomad, rambler, rover, traveller, vagabond, walker, wanderer.

waylay *v.t.* (*to wait for and stop or intercept*) accost, ambush, hold up, intercept, launch a surprise attack on, lay an ambush for, lie in wait for, pounce on, set upon, swoop down on.

way-out *a.* (*out of the ordinary, unconventional*) abnormal, avant-garde, bizarre, eccentric, experimental, (*sl.*) far-out, (*coll.*) offbeat, off-the-wall, outlandish, out-of-the-ordinary, queer, strange, unconventional, unorthodox, weird. ANTONYMS: conventional, normal, ordinary, orthodox.

wayward *a.* (*stubborn and difficult to control*) capricious, changeable, contrary, difficult, disobedient, erratic, fickle, fractious, headstrong, inconstant, insubordinate, mulish, obdurate, obstinate, perverse, rebellious, recalcitrant, refractory, self-willed, stubborn, unmanageable, unpredictable, unruly, wild, wilful. ANTONYMS: compliant, malleable, manageable, obedient, pliant, tractable.

weak *a.* **1** (*deficient in physical strength, not robust*) delicate, effete, feeble, frail, puny, slight, weakly. ANTONYMS: hefty, robust, strong, vigorous. **2** (*sickly, easily exhausted or fatigued*) ailing, debilitated, decrepit, feeble, frail, incapacitated, indisposed, infirm, sickly, spent, worn out. ANTONYMS: hale and hearty, healthy, strong. **3** (*characterized by or showing lack of resolution or will-power*) cowardly, impotent, indecisive, irresolute, powerless, shilly-shallying, spineless, submissive, timid, timorous, unreliable, weak-kneed, yielding. ANTONYMS: brave, powerful, resolute, valiant. **4** (*unreliable, ineffective*) feeble, ineffective, inefficacious, inefficient, useless, worthless. ANTONYMS: effective, efficient, strong, useful. **5** (*deficient in number, quantity etc.*) defective, deficient, faulty, imperfect, inadequate, poor, substandard. ANTONYMS: excellent, faultless, flawless, perfect. **6** (*lacking in flavour, watery*) adulterated, dilute, diluted, flavourless, insipid, tasteless, thinned down, watered-down, watery. ANTONYMS: concentrated, strong. **7** (*unsustained, unconvincing*) feeble, flimsy, lame, unconvincing, unsound, untenable. **8** ((*of light*) *difficult to see; dim or faint*) dim, faint, feeble, pale, wan. ANTONYMS: bright, strong. **9** ((*of sound*) *difficult to hear*) faint, feeble, low, muffled, muted, scarcely audible, stifled. ANTONYMS: loud, strong.

weaken *v.t.* **1** (*to make weak or weaker*) debilitate, enervate, enfeeble, impair, incapacitate, sap one's strength, tire. ANTONYMS: invigorate, refresh, revitalize, strengthen, undermine. **2** (*to reduce the force of*) decrease, diminish, impair, lessen, lower, moderate, reduce, temper. ANTONYMS: boost, heighten, increase, strengthen. **3** (*to add water or another liquid to*) adulterate, dilute, make weaker, thin, water down. ANTONYMS: make stronger, strengthen.

~*v.i.* **1** (*to become weak or weaker*) abate, decrease, diminish, dwindle, ease up, lessen, let up, wane. ANTONYMS: grow stronger, increase. **2** (*to become less determined, to change one's opinion and accept that of someone else*) accede, acquiesce, come round, give way, relent, yield. ANTONYMS: be resolute, be unyielding, stand firm.

weak-kneed *a.* (*giving way easily, lacking in resolution*) cowardly, indecisive, irresolute, powerless, submissive, tentative, timid, timorous, unsure, yielding. ANTONYMS: brave, powerful, resolute, valiant.

weakling *n.* (*a feeble person*) coward, (*coll.*) doormat, milksop, namby-pamby, (*coll.*) wimp.

weakly *a.* (*not strong in constitution; feeble, infirm*) ailing, debilitated, delicate, feeble, frail, infirm, puny, sickly. ANTONYMS: robust, strong, vigorous.

weakness *n.* **1** (*the state or condition of being deficient in physical strength*) delicateness, effeteness, feebleness, fragility, frailty, puniness, slightness. ANTONYMS: robustness, strength, vigorousness, vigour. **2** (*the state or condition of being infirm or sickly*) debilitation, decrepitude, feebleness, frailty, indisposition, infirmity, sickliness. **3** (*the state or quality of being unreliable or ineffective*) feebleness, ineffectiveness, inefficacy, uselessness, worthlessness. ANTONYMS: effectiveness, efficacy, strength. **4** (*the state or quality of being deficient in number, quantity etc.*) defectiveness, deficiency, faultiness, imperfection, inadequacy. ANTONYMS: excellence, faultlessness, flawlessness, perfection. **5** (*the state or quality of being unconvincing*) feebleness, flimsiness, lameness, unsoundness, untenability. ANTONYMS: plausibleness, soundness. **6** (*dimness or faintness of light*) dimness, faintness, feebleness, paleness, pallor, wanness. **7** (*a particular defect or fault, a weak point*) Achilles heel, blemish, chink in one's armour, defect, deficiency, failing, fault, flaw, foible, imperfection, lack, shortcoming, weak point. **8** (*a lack of resisting power*) cowardice, cowardliness, impotence, indecision, indecisiveness, irresolution, powerlessness, shilly-shallying, spinelessness, submissiveness, timidity, timorousness, unreliability. ANTONYMS: bravery, power, powerfulness, resoluteness, valour. **9** (*a self-indulgent fondness*) fondness, inclination, leaning, liking, love, partiality, passion, penchant, predilection, predisposition, preference, proclivity, soft spot. ANTONYMS: disinclination, dislike, hate.

wealth *n.* **1** (*riches, large possessions of money or lands*) affluence, assets, (*coll.*) big bucks, (*sl.*) bread, capital, cash, (*sl.*) dough, (*facet.*) filthy lucre, finance, fortune, funds, goods, (*derog. or facet.*) lucre, (*coll.*) megabucks, money, riches, substance, treasure, (*coll.*) wherewithal. ANTONYMS: deprivation, destitution, indigence, penury, poverty. **2** (*an abundance, a profusion (of)*) abundance, copiousness, cornucopia, plenitude, plenty, profusion. ANTONYMS: dearth, lack, paucity, scarcity, shortage, want.

wealthy *a.* (*rich, having many possessions*) affluent, comfortable, comfortably off, (*sl.*) filthy rich, in the money, (*coll.*) loaded, (*coll.*) made of money, moneyed, of means, of

substance, opulent, prosperous, rich, (*coll.*) rolling in it, (*coll.*) stinking rich, (*coll.*) well-heeled, well off, well-to-do. ANTONYMS: (*coll.*) broke, destitute, impoverished, penniless, poor, poverty-stricken.

wear *v.t.* **1** (*to be dressed in, esp. habitually*) be clothed in, be dressed in, have on, sport. **2** (*to exhibit, to display*) assume, display, exhibit, have, present, show. **3** (*to diminish or alter by rubbing or use*) abrade, corrode, erode, grind down, rub away, wash away, wear away, wear down. **4** (*to make thinner or weaker because of continuous use*) fray, make holes in, make thin, make threadbare, make worn, put holes in. **5** (*to exhaust or weary*) drain, enervate, exhaust, fatigue, (*coll.*) knacker, (*esp N Am., coll.*) poop, prostrate, put a strain on, stress, tire, wear out, wear to a frazzle, weary. **6** (*to stand for, to tolerate*) accept, allow, brook, countenance, permit, put up with, stand for, stomach, tolerate.

~*v.i.* **1** (*to become thinner or weaker because of continuous use*) become threadbare, become worn, fray, go into holes, show signs of wear, wear thin. **2** (*to stand continual use (well, badly etc.)*) endure, last, stand up to wear, survive.

~*n.* **1** (*the act of wearing*) employment, service, use. **2** (*something worn or to be worn, clothing*) apparel, attire, (*sl.*) clobber, clothes, clothing, dress, garb, garments, (*coll.*) gear, outfit, wardrobe. **3** (*damage or diminution by rubbing, use etc.*) abrasion, attrition, corrosion, damage, degeneration, depreciation, deterioration, erosion, friction, use, wear and tear. **to wear away** (*to efface or diminish by rubbing, use etc.*) abrade, corrode, erode, grind down, rub away, wash away, wear, wear down. **to wear down 1** (*to overcome gradually by persistent pressure*) chip away at, erode, overcome gradually, undermine. **2** (*to efface or diminish by rubbing, use etc.*) abrade, corrode, erode, grind down, rub away, wash away, wear, wear away. **to wear off 1** (*to efface or diminish by attrition; to rub off*) efface, rub off. **2** (*to be effaced or diminished by attrition*) be effaced, fade, rub off. **3** (*to decline or pass away gradually*) decrease, diminish, dwindle, fade, fade away, pass, peter out, subside, wane. ANTONYMS: increase, intensify. **to wear out 1** (*to use until no longer of use, to consume or render worthless by use*) fray, make thin, make threadbare, make worn, put holes in, use up. **2** (*to exhaust, to tire out*) drain, enervate, exhaust, fatigue, (*coll.*) knacker, (*esp. N Am., coll.*) poop, prostrate, put a strain on, sap the strength of, stress, tire, tire out, wear, wear to a frazzle, weary. ANTONYMS: invigorate, refresh, revitalize. **3** (*to be used up or rendered worthless by attrition and use*) become useless, become worn, fray.

weariness *n.* **1** (*the state of being tired or exhausted*) drowsiness, enervation, exhaustion, fatigue, languor, lassitude, lethargy, listlessness, prostration, sleepiness, tiredness. ANTONYMS: energy, freshness, liveliness, vigour. **2** (*the state of being bored*) boredom, discontent, indifference, lack of interest. ANTONYMS: enthusiasm, interest.

wearing *a.* (*tiresome*) draining, enervating, exhausting, fatiguing, irksome, stressful, taxing, tiring, trying, wearying. ANTONYMS: invigorating, refreshing, stimulating, undemanding.

wearisome *a.* (*tedious, causing weariness*) boring, draining, dull, enervating, exhausting, fatiguing, humdrum, irksome, monotonous, tedious, tiresome, tiring, trying, uninteresting, wearing. ANTONYMS: entertaining, exhilarating, interesting, stimulating.

weary *a.* **1** (*tired, exhausted*) (*coll.*) all in, (*sl.*) bushed, dead beat, (*coll.*) dead on one's feet, dog-tired, (*coll.*) done in, drained, drowsy, enervated, exhausted, fagged out, fatigued, flagging, (*coll.*) knackered, (*esp. N Am., coll.*) pooped, sleepy, spent, tired, (*coll.*) whacked, worn out, zonked. ANTONYMS: energetic, lively, refreshed, wide awake. **2** (*impatient or sick* (*of*)) bored (with), (*sl.*) browned off (with), (*coll.*) cheesed off (with), discontented (with), (*coll.*) fed up (with), indifferent (to), sick and tired (of), sick (of), uninterested (in). **3** (*tiresome, tedious*) boring, draining, dull, enervating, exhausting, fatiguing, humdrum, laborious, monotonous, taxing, tedious, tiresome, tiring, uninteresting, wearing, wearisome. ANTONYMS: entertaining, exhilarating, interesting, stimulating. **4** (*exhausting, irksome*) burdensome, exhausting, irksome, tedious, troublesome, trying, wearisome. ANTONYMS: invigorating, pleasing, stimulating. ~*v.t.* **1** (*to tire, to fatigue*) bore, drain, enervate, exhaust, fatigue, sap the strength of, (*coll.*) take it out of, tax, tire, tire out, try, wear out. ANTONYMS: enliven, invigorate, refresh, stimulate. **2** (*to make impatient or sick* (*of*)) bore (with), make discontented (with), (*coll.*) make fed up (with), make weary (of). ANTONYMS: fascinate, interest, stimulate. ~*v.i.* (*to become tired or fatigued*) become bored, become enthusiastic, become interested, become jaded, grow discontented, grow weary, have enough, tire.

weather *n.* (*the state of the atmosphere, esp. at a given time or place*) atmospheric conditions, climate. ~*v.t.* **1** (*to endure and come through* (*a crisis etc.*) *in safety*) come through, endure, get through, overcome, resist, ride out, stick out, surmount, survive, withstand. ANTONYMS: cave in, collapse, go under. **2** (*to expose to the action of the weather*) expose, season. **3** (*to wear or discolour* (*rock, masonry etc.*) *by this*) bleach, colour, discolour, wear. **under the weather** (*poorly, unwell*) ailing, below par, ill, indisposed, in poor health, not well, off-colour, out of sorts, poorly, (*coll.*) seedy, sick, unwell. ANTONYMS: healthy, in good health, well.

weave¹ *v.t.* **1** (*to form* (*threads, yarns etc.*) *into fabric by interlacing*) braid, entwine, interlace, intertwine, intertwist, knit, plait, twist together. **2** (*to interweave* (*facts, details etc.*) *into a story, theory etc.*) construct, contrive, create, fabricate, make, make up, put together, spin.

weave² *v.i.* (*to take a zigzag course, esp. to avoid obstructions*) criss-cross, weave one's way, wind, zigzag.

web *n.* **1** (*a network of threads constructed by spiders to catch their prey, a cobweb*) cobweb, spider's web. **2** (*any complex network or similar structure*) lattice, mesh, network, tangle, tissue.

wed *v.t.* **1** (*to marry*) marry, take as one's husband, take as one's wife. ANTONYMS: break up with, divorce, separate from. **2** (*to join in marriage*) (*sl.*) hitch, join in holy matrimony, join in matrimony, make one, marry, perform a wedding ceremony. **3** (*to unite, to attach firmly*) ally, amalgamate, combine, fuse, get together, join together, merge, unite. ANTONYMS: go their separate ways, separate, split up. ~*v.i.* (*to marry*) become husband and wife, become man and wife, (*sl.*) get hitched, get married, (*coll.*) get spliced, marry, tie the knot. ANTONYMS: break up, divorce, separate, split up.

wedded *a.* (*married, relating to matrimony*) conjugal, connubial, marital, married, matrimonial, nuptial.

wedding *n.* (*a marriage ceremony, usu. with the accompanying festivities*) marriage, marriage ceremony, nuptials, wedding ceremony. ANTONYMS: divorce.

wedge *n.* (*an object or portion of anything that is thick at one end and tapers to a thin edge at the other*) block, chunk, hunk, wodge. ~*v.t.* **1** (*to fix or fasten with a wedge or wedges*) fasten, secure. **2** (*to squeeze or push, esp. in or into a narrow space*) cram, crowd, force, jam, pack, ram, squeeze, stuff, thrust.

wedlock *n.* (*matrimony, the married state*) marriage, matrimony.

weed *v.t.* (*to sort* (*out*) (*useless or inferior elements, members etc.*) *for removal or elimination*) dispense with, eliminate, eradicate, extirpate, get rid of, remove, root out, separate out, shed, uproot.

weedy *a.* (*thin, weak*) feeble, frail, puny, skinny, thin, undersized, weak.

weekly *a.* (*happening or done once a week or every week*) by the week, every week, hebdomadal, once a week.

weep *v.i.* (*to shed tears*) (*sl.*) blub, blubber, cry, (*esp. Sc.*) greet, howl, lament, mourn, shed tears, snivel, sob, wail, whimper. ANTONYMS: laugh, rejoice, smile.

weepy *a.* (*tearful*) blubbering, (*sl.*) blubbing, crying, mournful, sad, snivelling, sobbing, tearful, teary, weeping, whimpering. ANTONYMS: cheerful, happy, laughing, smiling.

weigh *v.t.* **1** (*to find the weight of by means of scales etc.*) measure the weight of. **2** (*to be equivalent to in weight*) be equal to, be equivalent to, have a weight of. **3** (*to ponder, to consider carefully*) consider, contemplate, deliberate upon, evaluate, examine, give thought to, meditate upon, mull over, muse on, ponder, reflect upon, study, think over. **4** (*to estimate the relative value, advantages etc. of, to compare*) balance, compare, evaluate.
~*v.i.* **1** (*to have weight*) have a weight of, tip the scales at. **2** (*to be considered important, to have influence*) be important, be influential, carry weight, count, have influence, matter. ANTONYMS: be unimportant, have no influence, not count. **3** (*to be burdensome or oppressive* (*on or upon*)) be a burden (to), bear down (on or upon), be burdensome (to), be oppressive (to), burden, oppress, press down on, prey on, trouble, worry. **to weigh down** (*to oppress*) be a burden to, bear down, be burdensome, burden, oppress, press down on, trouble, weigh upon, worry.

weight *n.* **1** (*the relative mass or quantity of matter contained in a body, heaviness*) heaviness, mass. **2** (*a heavy load, a burden*) albatross, burden, cross to bear, load, millstone, millstone round one's neck, onus. **3** (*pressure, oppressiveness*) oppression, oppressiveness, strain, trouble, worry. **4** (*importance, influence*) (*coll.*) clout, consequence, import, importance, influence, power, significance, strength, substance, value. ANTONYMS: insignificance, unimportance. **5** (*preponderance*) force, main force, onus, preponderance.

weighty *a.* **1** (*having great weight, heavy*) heavy, hefty, massive, ponderous. ANTONYMS: light. **2** (*important, serious*) consequential, crucial, grave, important, momentous, of consequence, of great import, of importance, of moment, serious, significant, solemn,

substantial, vital. ANTONYMS: inconsequential, insignificant, trivial, unimportant. **3** (*convincing, influential*) authoritative, cogent, convincing, effective, forceful, persuasive, potent, powerful. ANTONYMS: feeble, unconvincing, weak. **4** (*difficult to deal with; worrying*) burdensome, demanding, exacting, onerous, oppressive, stressful, taxing, troublesome, worrisome, worrying.

weird *a.* **1** (*supernatural, unearthly*) creepy, (*Sc., N Am.*) eldritch, ghostly, mysterious, preternatural, (*coll.*) spooky, strange, supernatural, uncanny, unearthly, unnatural. ANTONYMS: natural, normal. **2** (*strange, peculiar*) bizarre, eccentric, (*sl.*) far-out, freakish, odd, (*coll.*) offbeat, outlandish, out on a limb, peculiar, queer, strange, (*coll.*) way-out. ANTONYMS: normal, ordinary, routine, run-of-the-mill.

welcome *a.* **1** (*admitted or received with pleasure and cordiality*) desirable, gladly received, wanted. ANTONYMS: unwanted, unwelcome. **2** (*producing satisfaction or gladness*) agreeable, cheerful, cheering, gladly received, happy, pleasant, pleasing. ANTONYMS: disagreeable, sad, unpleasant, unwelcome. **3** (*gladly permitted* (*to*)) allowed, free, permitted.
~*n.* (*a salutation or act of saying 'welcome' to a newcomer etc.*) greeting, hospitality, reception, salutation, warm reception.
~*v.t.* **1** (*to receive or entertain with kindness or cordiality*) bid welcome, greet, meet, offer hospitality to, receive, receive with open arms, roll out the red carpet for. ANTONYMS: slight, snub, turn away. **2** (*to receive or accept with pleasure*) be cheered by, be pleased by, receive gladly, take pleasure in. ANTONYMS: be saddened by, be upset by.

weld *v.t.* **1** (*to unite or join* (*pieces of metal*) *together by heat or by compressing, esp. after they have been softened by heat*) bond, fuse, solder. **2** (*to unite into a coherent mass, body etc.*) bind, bond, cement, connect, fuse, join, link, unite. ANTONYMS: disconnect, separate, sever.

welfare *n.* **1** (*health, well-being*) advantage, benefit, comfort, good fortune, good health, happiness, health, profit, prosperity, success, well-being. ANTONYMS: detriment, disadvantage, loss, misfortune. **2** (*financial and other aid given to those in need*) benefit, social security, state aid.

well[1] *adv.* **1** (*in a good or right manner, properly*) correctly, fittingly, in the right way, nicely, properly, satisfactorily, suitably. ANTONYMS: badly, improperly, unsuitably. **2** (*skilfully*) ably, adeptly, competently, effectively, efficiently, excellently, expertly, proficiently,

skilfully, with expertise. ANTONYMS: badly, incompetently, ineptly, inexpertly. **3** (*prosperously, successfully*) flourishingly, prosperously, successfully. ANTONYMS: badly, unsuccessfully. **4** (*happily, fortunately*) agreeably, (*coll.*) capitally, (*coll.*) famously, fortunately, happily, pleasantly, satisfactorily. ANTONYMS: unhappily, unpleasantly, unsatisfactorily. **5** (*adequately, sufficiently*) adequately, amply, sufficiently, thoroughly. ANTONYMS: imperfectly, inadequately, insufficiently, sketchily. **6** (*fully, perfectly*) completely, fully, perfectly, thoroughly, totally, wholly. ANTONYMS: partially. **7** (*to a considerable extent*) considerably, markedly, substantially, very much. **8** (*closely, intimately*) closely, deeply, intimately, personally, profoundly. ANTONYMS: distantly, vaguely. **9** (*heartily, cordially*) affably, civilly, cordially, generously, genially, graciously, heartily, hospitably, in a kindly way, in a kind way, politely, warmly. ANTONYMS: coldly, impolitely, rudely. **10** (*favourably, with approval*) admiringly, approvingly, favourably, generously, glowingly, graciously, highly, kindly, warmly, with admiration, with approval, with kindness. ANTONYMS: slightingly, unfavourably, unkindly. **11** (*justly, fairly*) fairly, justly, properly, reasonably. ANTONYMS: unfairly, unjustly. **12** (*very possibly, indeed*) indeed, likely, possibly, probably.
~*a.* **1** (*in good health*) fit, hale and hearty, healthy, in good health, robust, strong, up to par. ANTONYMS: ill, in poor health, poorly. **2** (*in a satisfactory state or circumstances*) all right, fine, (*coll.*) fine and dandy, (*coll.*) OK, (*coll.*) okay, satisfactory. ANTONYMS: unsatisfactory, wrong. **3** (*sensible, advisable*) advisable, fitting, proper, prudent, sensible, wise. ANTONYMS: foolish, imprudent, inadvisable. **as well** (*in addition*) besides, in addition, into the bargain, to boot.

well² *n.* **1** (*a shaft bored in the ground to obtain water, oil etc.*) bore, hole, pit, shaft. **2** (*a source*) fount, mine, repository, reservoir, source, wellspring. **3** (*a spring, a fountain*) fountain, pool, source, spring, waterhole.
~*v.i.* (*to spring or issue* (*forth etc.*) *as from a fountain*) exude, flow, gush, issue, jet, ooze, pour, rise, run, seep, spout, spring, spurt, stream, surge, trickle.

well advised *a.* (*prudent, wise*) advisable, circumspect, far-sighted, judicious, prudent, sensible, wise. ANTONYMS: foolish, imprudent, inadvisable.

well-balanced *a.* **1** (*sensible, sane*) level-headed, logical, practical, rational, reasonable, sane, sensible, sound, (*coll.*) together,

well-adjusted. ANTONYMS: foolish, illogical, insane, irrational. **2** (*having the parts well-matched*) balanced, proportional, symmetrical, well-ordered, well-proportioned.

well-behaved *a.* (*having or displaying good behaviour or manners*) courteous, good, manageable, obedient, polite, tractable, well-mannered. ANTONYMS: disobedient, unruly, wild.

well-being *n.* (*the state of being healthy, happy etc.*) comfort, good fortune, good health, happiness, health, prosperity, welfare.

well-bred *a.* (*having good breeding or manners*) civil, courteous, cultivated, genteel, mannerly, polished, polite, refined, urbane, well-brought-up, well-mannered. ANTONYMS: coarse, ill-mannered, rude.

well-built *a.* (*sturdy, muscular*) big, brawny, burly, hefty, hulking, muscular, robust, strapping, strong, sturdy. ANTONYMS: puny, slender, slight, small.

well disposed *a.* (*of favourable and kindly feeling* (*to or towards*)) amenable, benevolent, friendly, kindly, sympathetic, warm. ANTONYMS: hostile, unsympathetic.

well-dressed *a.* (*dressed in fashionable or elegant clothes*) chic, dapper, elegant, fashionable, (*coll.*) natty, neat, smart, soigné(e), spruce, stylish, well-turned-out. ANTONYMS: badly dressed, dowdy, frumpish, unfashionable, untidy.

well-founded *a.* (*based on certain or well-authenticated grounds*) authenticated, confirmed, justified, reasonable, substantiated, valid, verified, warranted. ANTONYMS: invalid, unjustified, unsubstantiated, unwarranted.

well-groomed *a.* (*neat and elegant in dress and appearance*) neat, neat and tidy, smart, soigné(e), spruce, tidy, trim, well-turned-out. ANTONYMS: messy, rumpled, unkempt, untidy.

well-grounded *a.* (*having all the basic knowledge of a subject etc.*) experienced, informed, instructed, knowledgeable, trained, well-informed, well-schooled, well-taught, well-trained, well-versed. ANTONYMS: ignorant, uninformed.

well-informed *a.* **1** (*having ample information*) informed, knowledgeable, well-grounded. ANTONYMS: ignorant, uninformed. **2** (*having knowledge of numerous subjects*) cultivated, educated, erudite, knowledgeable, learned, well-read. ANTONYMS: ignorant, illiterate, uneducated.

well-known *a.* **1** (*known to many people, familiar*) celebrated, eminent, familiar, famous, illustrious, notable, noted, notorious, popular, renowned. ANTONYMS: little-known, minor, obscure, undistinguished, unknown. **2** (*thoroughly known*) familiar, known, widely known. ANTONYMS: abstruse, little-known, obscure, unknown.

well-mannered *a.* (*well-bred, polite*) civil, courteous, genteel, mannerly, polite, refined, well-bred. ANTONYMS: ill-mannered, impolite, rude.

well-nigh *adv.* (*almost, nearly*) all but, almost, just about, more or less, nearly, practically, virtually.

well off *a.* **1** (*in good circumstances*) comfortable, flourishing, fortunate, lucky, thriving. ANTONYMS: unfortunate, unlucky. **2** (*wealthy, prosperous*) affluent, comfortable, comfortably off, flush, in the money, (*coll.*) loaded, (*coll.*) made of money, moneyed, of means, of substance, prosperous, rich, wealthy, (*coll.*) well-heeled, well-to-do. ANTONYMS: badly off, (*coll.*) broke, hard up, impoverished, penniless, poor, poverty-stricken. **3** (*having plenty of*) having an abundance of, having plenty of, well-equipped with, well-stocked with, well-supplied with. ANTONYMS: deficient in, lacking, short of.

well-read *a.* (*having read extensively, having wide knowledge gained from books*) educated, erudite, knowledgeable, learned, lettered, literate, well-educated, well-informed. ANTONYMS: ignorant, illiterate, uneducated.

well-spoken *a.* (*speaking well, eloquent*) articulate, eloquent, fluent, having kissed the blarney stone, lucid, silver-tongued, smooth-talking, (*coll.*) with the gift of the gab. ANTONYMS: faltering, hesitant, inarticulate, stumbling.

wellspring *n.* (*a source of continual supply*) fount, fund, mine, repository, reserve, reservoir, source, supply, well.

well-thought-of *a.* (*respected, esteemed*) acclaimed, admired, esteemed, held in high regard, highly regarded, looked up to, of repute, respected, revered, venerated. ANTONYMS: derided, despised, reviled, scorned.

well-timed *a.* (*opportune*) apposite, appropriate, at the right time, convenient, fitting, opportune, pertinent, propitious, suitable, timely. ANTONYMS: at the wrong time, inapposite, inappropriate, inopportune.

well-to-do *a.* (*well off*) affluent, comfortable, comfortably off, flush, in the money, (*coll.*) loaded, (*coll.*) made of money, moneyed, of means, of substance, prosperous, rich, wealthy, (*coll.*) well-heeled, well off. ANTONYMS: badly off, (*coll.*) broke, hard up, impoverished, penniless, poor, poverty-stricken.

well-worn *a.* **1** (*worn out*) frayed, shabby, used, worn out. ANTONYMS: fresh, new. **2** (*trite, hackneyed*) banal, clichéd, commonplace, hackneyed, overused, stale, stereotyped, threadbare, timeworn, tired, trite, worn out. ANTONYMS: fresh, innovative, original.

welter *n.* (*a turmoil, a confusion*) confusion, hotchpotch, jumble, mess, muddle, tangle, web.

wet *a.* **1** (*moistened or covered with water or other liquid*) aqueous, damp, dampened, dank, drenched, dripping, humid, moist, moistened, saturated, soaked, soaking, sodden, soggy, sopping, sopping wet, waterlogged, watery, wringing wet. ANTONYMS: arid, dried, dry, parched. **2** (*rainy*) damp, drizzly, pouring, raining, rainy, showery. ANTONYMS: dry, fine, sunny. **3** (*feeble, characterless*) characterless, effete, feeble, ineffective, ineffectual, inept, namby-pamby, sentimental, sloppy, spineless, weak, weedy. ANTONYMS: effective, strong, virile.
~*n.* **1** (*wetness, moisture*) condensation, damp, dampness, humidity, liquid, moistness, moisture, water, wetness. ANTONYMS: dry, dryness. **2** (*anything that wets, esp. rain*) damp, drizzle, rain. **3** (*a feeble or foolish person*) (*coll.*) drip, milksop, namby-pamby, weakling, (*coll.*) weed, (*coll.*) wimp.
~*v.t.* (*to make wet; to moisten or soak with liquid*) damp, dampen, dip, douse, drench, humidify, irrigate, moisten, saturate, soak, splash, spray, sprinkle, steep, water. ANTONYMS: dehydrate, dry.

whack *v.t.* (*to strike heavily*) bang, bash, batter, beat, belabour, belt, (*sl.*) clobber, clout, cuff, hit, lambast, slap, slug, thump, thwack, (*coll.*) wallop.

wharf *n.* (*a landing place for cargo beside a river, harbour etc.*) dock, jetty, landing stage, pier, quay.

wheedle *v.t.* (*to win over, to persuade by coaxing or flattery*) (*coll.*) butter up, cajole, charm, coax, entice, flatter, induce, inveigle, persuade, talk (someone) into.

wheel *v.t.* (*to move or push (a wheeled vehicle etc.) in some direction*) push, shove, trundle.
~*v.i.* **1** (*to turn or swing round as on a pivot*) spin round, swing round, turn round, whirl round. **2** (*to go round, to circle*) circle, go round, gyrate, revolve, rotate.

wheeze *v.i.* (*to breathe hard and with an audible sound, as in asthma*) breathe noisily, breathe roughly, gasp, hiss, rasp, whistle.
~*n.* (*a design, a scheme*) design, expedient, idea, plan, plot, ploy, ruse, scheme, stunt, trick.

whereabouts *n.* (*the approximate location of a person or thing*) locality, location, place, position, site, situation.

wherewithal *n.* (*the necessary means or resources, esp. money*) (*sl.*) bread, capital, cash, (*sl.*) dough, finance, funds, means, money, ready money, reserves, resources, (*coll.*) the readies.

whet *v.t.* **1** (*to sharpen by rubbing on a stone or similar substance*) edge, hone, put an edge on, sharpen, strop. **2** (*to excite, to stimulate*) arouse, excite, kindle, rouse, stimulate, stir, titillate.

whiff *n.* **1** (*a sudden expulsion of smoke etc., a light gust, esp. one carrying an odour*) blast, draught, gust, puff. **2** (*a small amount, a trace*) hint, soupçon, suggestion, suspicion, trace.

while *n.* (*a space of time, esp. the time during which something happens or is done*) period, spell, time. **to while away** (*to pass (time etc.) pleasantly or in a leisurely manner*) idle away, laze away, lounge away, pass.

whim *n.* (*a sudden fancy, a caprice*) caprice, craze, fad, fancy, idea, impulse, inclination, passing fancy, passion, quirk, sudden notion, urge, vagary.

whimper *v.i.* (*to cry with a soft, whining voice*) bleat, cry, grizzle, groan, moan, snivel, wail, whine, (*coll.*) whinge.

whimsical *a.* **1** (*oddly humorous*) bizarre, droll, fanciful, fantastic, fantastical, funny, playful, quaint, waggish. ANTONYMS: grave, serious, solemn. **2** (*odd-looking, curious*) bizarre, curious, eccentric, freakish, odd, odd-looking, peculiar, quaint, queer, singular, strange, unusual, weird. ANTONYMS: conventional, ordinary, run-of-the-mill, usual.

whimsy *n.* **1** (*a whim, a fancy*) caprice, craze, crotchet, fad, fancy, idea, impulse, inclination, passing fancy, passion, quirk, sudden notion, urge, vagary. **2** (*whimsical humour*) drollness, fancifulness, fantasy, quaintness, waggishness.

whine *v.i.* **1** (*to make a plaintive, long-drawn cry*) bleat, cry, grizzle, groan, moan, snivel, wail, whimper, (*coll.*) whinge. **2** (*to complain or find fault in a peevish way*) beef, (*coll.*) bellyache, carp, complain, fuss, go on, gripe, grizzle, grouse, grumble, (*N Am., sl.*) kvetch, moan, (*coll.*) whinge.

whip *v.t.* **1** (*to lash, to flog*) birch, cane, flagellate, flog, lash, scourge, strap, switch, tan (someone's) hide. **2** (*to strike forcefully as if with a whip*) beat, beat the living daylights out of, (*coll.*) give (someone) a hiding, (*coll.*) give (someone) a licking, hit, lambast, lay into, leather, smack, strike, thrash. **3** (*to beat (eggs, cream etc.) into a froth*) beat, whisk. **4** (*to move suddenly and quickly, to jerk (out, away etc.)*) jerk, pull, snatch, whisk, yank. **5** (*to beat, to defeat*) beat, clobber, conquer, crush, defeat, drub, give a drubbing to, (*coll.*) hammer, (*coll.*) lick, outdo, overcome, overpower, overwhelm, rout, (*coll.*) run rings round, thrash, trounce, (*coll.*) wipe the floor with. ANTONYMS: be the loser, lose to, suffer defeat. **6** (*to stir up the emotions of*) agitate, drive, goad, incite, prod, provoke, rouse, spur on, stir up, urge, work up.
~*v.i.* (*to move or start suddenly, to dart (out, in etc.)*) dart, dash, dive, dodge, fly, rush, shoot, tear, whisk. ANTONYMS: amble, stroll.
~*n.* (*an instrument for driving horses, punishing people etc., consisting of a lash tied to a handle*) birch, cat-o'-nine-tails, horsewhip, (*Hist.*) knout, lash, riding crop, scourge, switch, thong. **to whip up** (*to excite, arouse*) arouse, excite, foment, incite, inflame, instigate, kindle, rouse, stir up.

whipping *n.* **1** (*a lashing or flogging with a whip*) birching, caning, flagellation, flogging, scourging, strapping, switching, (*coll.*) tanning. **2** (*a beating*) beating, (*coll.*) hiding, lambasting, leathering, (*coll.*) licking, smacking, thrashing. **3** (*a severe defeat*) clobbering, defeat, drubbing, (*coll.*) hammering, (*coll.*) licking, routing, thrashing, trouncing.

whirl *v.t.* (*to swing round and round rapidly*) rotate, spin, twirl.
~*v.i.* **1** (*to turn round and round rapidly, to spin*) (*Sc.*) birl, circle, gyrate, pirouette, pivot, revolve, rotate, swirl, turn, twirl, wheel. **2** (*to move along swiftly*) fly, race, rush, shoot, speed, tear, whip. ANTONYMS: amble, stroll. **3** ((*of the brain etc.*) *to be giddy or confused, to seem to spin round*) be dizzy, be giddy, go round, reel, spin.
~*n.* **1** (*a whirling motion*) (*Sc.*) birl, circling, gyration, pirouette, revolution, rotation, spin, swirl, turn, twirl. **2** (*a confused state, giddiness*) daze, dither, dizziness, giddiness, muddle, spin, state of confusion. **3** (*commotion, bustle*) agitation, bustle, commotion, flurry, hurly-burly, stir, tumult. **4** (*an attempt, a trial*) attempt, (*sl.*) bash, (*coll.*) crack, (*coll.*) go, (*coll.*) shot, (*coll.*) stab, trial, try, try-out.

whirlpool *n.* (*an eddy or vortex*) eddy, maelstrom, vortex.

whirlwind *n.* (*a funnel-shaped column of air moving spirally round an axis*) tornado.

~*a.* (*developing or moving very rapidly*) hasty, headlong, impetuous, lightning, quick, rapid, speedy, swift. ANTONYMS: leisurely, slow, slow-moving, snail-like.

whisk *v.t.* **1** (*to sweep or flap* (*away or off*)) brush, sweep, wipe. **2** (*to carry* (*off*) *or take* (*away*) *swiftly or suddenly*) jerk, pull, snatch, whip, yank. **3** (*to shake or wave with a quick movement*) brandish, flick, flourish, shake, wave. **4** (*to beat up* (*eggs etc.*)) beat, whip.

~*v.i.* (*to move or go swiftly or suddenly*) dart, dash, dive, dodge, fly, rush, shoot, tear, whip.

whisper *v.i.* **1** (*to speak in a low voice so as not to be overheard*) murmur, mutter, speak in hushed tones, speak softly, talk in muted tones. ANTONYMS: roar, shout, yell. **2** (*to plot, to gossip*) gossip, spread rumours. **3** (*to make a soft rustling sound*) murmur, rustle, sigh, sough, swish.

~*v.t.* **1** (*to tell or utter in a whisper or privately*) murmur, mutter, say in hushed tones, say softly, utter in muted tones. **2** (*to hint or suggest privately or secretly*) gossip, hint, insinuate, suggest.

~*n.* **1** (*a whispering tone or voice*) hushed tones, low voice, murmur, mutter, soft voice, undertone. ANTONYMS: roar, shout, yell. **2** (*a hint, a rumour*) gossip, hint, innuendo, insinuation, rumour, suggestion. **3** (*a soft rustling sound*) murmur, rustle, sigh, sough, swish. **4** (*a very small amount of something*) hint, suggestion, suspicion, tinge, trace, whiff.

whit *n.* (*a jot, the least amount*) atom, bit, crumb, iota, jot, least bit, little, particle, scrap.

white *a.* **1** (*the colour of pure snow; pale, colourless*) ashen, bloodless, chalk-white, colourless, pale, pallid, pasty, peaky, wan, waxen, white as a ghost, white as a sheet. ANTONYMS: crimson, flushed, red, rosy-cheeked, ruddy. **2** (*silvery, whitish-grey*) grey, grizzled, hoary, silver, silvery, snow-white. **3** (*pure, clean*) clean, immaculate, snow-white, spick and span, spotless, ultra-clean. ANTONYMS: dirty, filthy, soiled. **4** (*spotless, innocent*) innocent, pure, squeaky-clean, unblemished, unsullied. ANTONYMS: corrupt, guilty, immodest, impure.

white-collar *a.* (*of or relating to non-manual employees, esp. administrative and clerical workers*) clerical, executive, non-manual, professional, salaried. ANTONYMS: blue-collar, manual, waged.

whiten *v.t.* (*to make white or whiter*) blanch, bleach, etiolate, make white, make whiter.

~*v.i.* (*to become white or whiter*) blanch, go white, grow pale, pale.

whitewash *n.* (*a false colouring given to the reputation of a person or institution to counteract allegations of disreputableness*) camouflage, concealment, cover-up, extenuation, mask, suppression.

~*v.t.* (*to cover up or conceal* (*a misdemeanour etc.*)) camouflage, conceal, downplay, extenuate, gloss over, hide, make light of, suppress. ANTONYMS: disclose, expose, reveal, uncover, unmask.

whittle *v.t.* **1** (*to shave or cut pieces or slices from with a knife*) cut, pare, shave, trim. **2** (*to shape thus*) carve, model, shape. **3** (*to reduce or bring down in amount etc., gradually or by degrees*) cut back, decrease, diminish, lessen, reduce. ANTONYMS: expand, increase.

whole *a.* **1** (*complete or entire*) complete, entire, full, in one piece, integral, solid, total, unabridged, undivided. ANTONYMS: abridged, divided, fragmented, in pieces. **2** (*not broken, intact*) flawless, in one piece, intact, perfect, sound, unbroken, undamaged, unimpaired, uninjured, unmutilated. ANTONYMS: broken, damaged, flawed, impaired.

~*n.* **1** (*all that there is of a thing, the entirety*) all, entirety, every part, everything, the lot. ANTONYMS: bit, part, portion. **2** (*a complete system, a complete combination of parts*) ensemble, entirety, entity, totality, unit. ANTONYMS: bit, component, fragment, part, piece, portion. **on the whole 1** (*all things considered*) all in all, all things considered, by and large, taking all things into consideration. **2** (*in most cases*) as a general rule, as a rule, for the most part, generally, in general, in most cases, in the main, mostly, predominantly.

wholehearted *a.* (*done or intended with all one's heart, sincere*) committed, complete, dedicated, devoted, earnest, emphatic, enthusiastic, genuine, heartfelt, hearty, sincere, true, unqualified, unreserved, unstinting, warm, zealous. ANTONYMS: apathetic, half-hearted, insincere.

wholesale *a.* (*done on a large scale, indiscriminate*) all-inclusive, broad, comprehensive, extensive, far-reaching, indiscriminate, mass, sweeping, wide-ranging. ANTONYMS: limited, partial, restricted, selective.

~*adv.* (*by the mass, on a large scale*) all at once, comprehensively, extensively, in a mass, indiscriminately, on a large scale.

wholesome *a.* **1** (*tending to promote physical health, salutary*) beneficial, good, good for one, health-giving, healthy, invigorating, nourishing, nutritious, refreshing, salubrious, salutary, strengthening. ANTONYMS: bad, poor, unhealthy, unhygienic, unwholesome. **2** (*promoting moral or mental health*) beneficial, edifying, ethical, good, improving, moral, pure, righteous, uplifting, virtuous, worthy. ANTONYMS: bad, corrupt, immoral, unethical, unwholesome, unworthy.

wholly *adv.* **1** (*entirely, completely*) completely, enthusiastically, entirely, fully, in every respect, in every way, one hundred per cent, perfectly, thoroughly, totally, unreservedly, utterly, zealously. ANTONYMS: in part, partially, partly, somewhat. **2** (*totally, exclusively*) exclusively, only, purely, solely.

whoop *n.* (*a loud shout of excitement, encouragement etc.*) call, cheer, cry, (*esp. N Am., coll. or dial.*) holler, hoot, scream, shout, shriek, yell.

whore *n.* (*a prostitute*) call-girl, courtesan, fallen woman, fille de joie, †harlot, (*sl.*) hooker, (*esp. N Am., sl.*) hustler, lady of the night, loose woman, prostitute, streetwalker, †strumpet, (*sl.*) tart, woman of easy virtue, woman of ill repute, woman of the streets.

wicked *a.* **1** (*sinful, depraved*) amoral, bad, base, black-hearted, corrupt, criminal, debased, degenerate, depraved, devilish, dissipated, dissolute, godless, immoral, impious, irreligious, lawless, nasty, nefarious, perverted, reprobate, sinful, ungodly, unprincipled, vicious, vile, villainous. ANTONYMS: good, moral, virtuous, well-behaved. **2** (*mischievous, roguish*) arch, impish, mischievous, naughty, rascally, roguish. **3** (*harmful, injurious*) dangerous, destructive, ferocious, fierce, harmful, injurious, perilous, terrible. ANTONYMS: harmless, innocuous. **4** (*very good*) excellent, expert, first-rate, great, outstanding, proficient, skilful, superior, superlative, very good. ANTONYMS: inferior, poor, very bad.

wide *a.* **1** (*having a great relative extent from side to side, broad*) broad. ANTONYMS: narrow. **2** (*vast, extensive*) extensive, large, spacious, vast. ANTONYMS: cramped, narrow. **3** (*not limited or restricted, comprehensive*) all-embracing, ample, broad, broad-ranging, catholic, comprehensive, encyclopedic, extensive, general, vast, wide-ranging. ANTONYMS: limited, narrow, restricted, small. **4** (*distant or deviating by a considerable extent or amount from a mark, point etc.*) nowhere near, off course, off target, off the mark, remote. ANTONYMS: close, near, (*coll.*) spot-on. **5** (*fully open or expanded*) dilated, fully open, wide open. ANTONYMS: closed, narrow. **6** ((*of clothes*) *hanging losely*) baggy, capacious, full, loose, roomy. ANTONYMS: narrow, tight, tight-fitting.

~*adv.* **1** (*to a great distance, extensively*) a great distance, extensively, far, far and wide. ANTONYMS: close by, near. **2** (*far from the mark or purpose*) nowhere near, off course, off target, off the mark, remote. **3** (*to the fullest extent, fully*) as far as possible, completely, fully, to the furthest extent. ANTONYMS: partially, partly.

wide awake *a.* **1** (*fully awake*) completely awake, fully awake, not asleep, unsleeping. ANTONYMS: asleep, drowsy, sleeping. **2** (*alert, wary*) alert, attentive, aware, chary, heedful, (*coll.*) keeping a weather eye open, keeping one's eyes peeled, keeping one's eyes skinned, keeping one's wits about one, observant, on one's toes, on the alert, on the ball, on the qui vive, vigilant, wary, watchful. ANTONYMS: heedless, inattentive, oblivious, unaware, unobservant.

wide-eyed *a.* **1** (*surprised, astonished*) amazed, astonished, astounded, surprised. **2** (*naive*) credulous, green, impressionable, inexperienced, ingenuous, innocent, naive, simple, trusting, unsophisticated, wet behind the ears. ANTONYMS: experienced, sophisticated, worldly-wise.

widen *v.t.* **1** (*to make wider*) broaden, make wider, stretch. ANTONYMS: make narrower, narrow. **2** (*to make more extensive or comprehensive*) add to, amplify, augment, broaden, enlarge, expand, extend, increase. ANTONYMS: decrease, narrow, reduce.
~*v.i.* **1** (*to become wider*) broaden, dilate, open wide. ANTONYMS: narrow. **2** (*to become more extensive or comprehensive*) broaden, enlarge, expand, extend, increase, intensify. ANTONYMS: contract, narrow.

wide open *a.* **1** (*fully open*) dilated, opened wide, open wide. ANTONYMS: closed tight. **2** (*open to attack*) at risk, defenceless, exposed, in danger, in peril, unprotected, vulnerable. ANTONYMS: invulnerable, protected, safe, secure. **3** (*of indeterminate or unpredictable outcome*) anyone's guess, indeterminate, in the balance, uncertain, unsettled, unsure, up in the air. ANTONYMS: certain, predictable, settled, sure. **4** (*spread out completely*) open wide, outspread, outstretched, spread open. ANTONYMS: closed tight.

widespread *a.* (*widely disseminated*) common, epidemic, extensive, far-reaching, general, pervasive, prevalent, rife, sweeping, universal, wholesale, wide-ranging. ANTONYMS: limited, local, restricted, uncommon.

width *n.* **1** (*the extent of a thing from side to side, breadth*) breadth, broadness, diameter, girth, reach, span, thickness, wideness.

ANTONYMS: narrowness, thinness. **2** (*comprehensiveness of mind, liberality*) ampleness, broadness, catholicity, compass, comprehensiveness, extensiveness, range, scope, span, vastness. ANTONYMS: limitation, narrowness, restriction.

wield *v.t.* **1** (*to handle or employ*) employ, handle, ply, put to use, use. **2** (*to exert or maintain (power etc.*)) bring to bear, exercise, exert, have, have at one's disposal, maintain, possess. **3** (*to brandish or wave*) brandish, flourish, shake, swing, wave.

wife *n.* (*a married woman, esp. in relation to her husband*) better half, consort, lady of the house, lawful wedded wife, (*facet.*) little woman, mate, (*coll.*) missis, (*coll.*) missus, (*coll.*) old lady, partner, spouse, woman. ANTONYMS: husband, man.

wig *n.* (*a covering for the head composed of false hair*) fall, hairpiece, periwig, (*Hist.*) peruke, (*coll.*) rug, switch, toupee.

wiggle *v.i.* (*to move (oneself) jerkily, esp. from side to side*) jiggle, shake, shimmy, squirm, waggle, wriggle.

wild *a.* **1** ((*esp. of animals*) *not tamed or domesticated*) feral, ferocious, fierce, undomesticated, untamed. ANTONYMS: domesticated, tamed. **2** ((*esp. of plants*) *growing naturally; uncultivated*) indigenous, native, uncultivated. **3** (*not civilized, savage*) barbaric, barbarous, brutish, ferocious, fierce, ignorant, primitive, savage, uncivilized. ANTONYMS: civilized. **4** ((*of land etc.*) *uncultivated, uninhabited*) barren, desert, God-forsaken, uncultivated, unfrequented, uninhabited, unpopulated, unsettled, waste. ANTONYMS: fertile, inhabited, populated, urban. **5** (*wayward, disorderly*) boisterous, disorderly, lawless, noisy, out of control, riotous, rough, rowdy, tempestuous, turbulent, uncontrolled, undisciplined, ungovernable, unmanageable, violent. ANTONYMS: cautious, orderly, quiet, well-behaved. **6** (*imprudent, extravagant*) extravagant, fanciful, fantastical, foolhardy, foolish, ill-advised, ill-considered, impracticable, impractical, imprudent, impulsive, irrational, madcap, rash, reckless, unwise. ANTONYMS: prudent, rational, reasoned, sensible, wise. **7** (*ungoverned, unrestrained*) unbridled, unconstrained, uncontrolled, uncurbed, undisciplined, unrestrained. ANTONYMS: controlled, restrained. **8** (*turbulent, stormy*) blustery, rough, stormy, turbulent. ANTONYMS: calm. **9** (*expressing very strong uncontrolled feelings, e.g. anger or excitement*) berserk, beside oneself, crazed, (*sl.*) crazy, demented, deranged, distracted, distraught,

excited, frantic, frenzied, hysterical, in a frenzy, insane, irrational, mad, maniacal, raving. ANTONYMS: calm, composed, rational, sane, tranquil. **10** (*excited, enthusiastic (about)*) avid, (*coll.*) crazy, eager, enthusiastic, excited, mad, (*sl.*) nuts. **11** (*very untidy*) disarranged, dishevelled, tousled, unkempt, untidy. ANTONYMS: neat, tidy. **12** ((*of a guess*) *made without much thought*) approximate, haphazard, hit-and-miss, hit-or-miss, random, rough, uninformed.

~*n.* (*an uninhabited and uncultivated tract*) back of beyond, desert, (*coll.*) middle of nowhere, wasteland, wilderness. **to run wild 1** (*to grow unchecked*) grow unchecked, ramble, spread like wildfire, straggle. **2** (*to behave in an uncontrolled way*) get out of control, go on the rampage, rampage, riot, run riot.

wilderness *n.* (*an uninhabited or uncultivated land, a desert*) desert, waste, wasteland, wilds.

wile *n.* (*usu. pl.*) (*a trick, deception*) artifice, deception, device, dodge, ploy, ruse, stratagem, subterfuge, trick.

wilful *a.* **1** (*intentional, deliberate*) calculated, conscious, deliberate, intended, intentional, malicious, on purpose, planned, premeditated, purposeful. ANTONYMS: accidental, purposeless, unintentional, unplanned, unpremeditated. **2** (*self-willed, headstrong*) adamant, determined, headstrong, inflexible, intractable, mulish, obdurate, obstinate, perverse, pig-headed, refractory, self-willed, strong-willed, stubborn, stubborn as a mule, uncompromising, unyielding, wayward. ANTONYMS: biddable, flexible, pliant, tractable.

will[1] *n.* **1** (*the mental power or faculty by which one initiates or controls one's activities*) choice, decision, preference, prerogative, volition. **2** (*the exercise of this power, an intention*) decree, desire, dictate, inclination, wish. **3** (*determination, the power of carrying out one's intentions or dominating others*) commitment, determination, firmness, grit, moral fibre, purpose, purposefulness, resolution, resolve, sense of purpose, single-mindedness, will-power. ANTONYMS: irresolution, lack of will-power. **at will** (*at one's pleasure or discretion*) as one pleases, as one thinks fit, as one wishes, at one's discretion, to suit oneself.

will[2] *v.t.* **1** (*to intend or bring about by the exercise of one's will, to resolve*) bid, command, decree, desire, determine, direct, ordain, order, wish. **2** (*to control or cause to act in a specified way by the exercise of one's will-power*) try to bring about, try to cause, try to effect, try to make. **3** (*to bequeath or devise by will*) bequeath, hand down, leave, pass on.

willing *a.* **1** (*ready, not averse or reluctant (to)*) agreeable (to), amenable (to), content (to), disposed (to), game (for), happy (to), inclined (to), in favour (of), in the mood (for), pleased (to), prepared (to), ready (to), so-minded (to). ANTONYMS: averse (to), disinclined (to), loath (to), reluctant (to), unwilling (to). **2** (*cheerfully acting, done etc.*) accommodating, cheerful, cooperative, enthusiastic, keen, obliging, ready. ANTONYMS: reluctant, uncooperative, unenthusiastic, unwilling.

willingly *adv.* **1** (*undertaken because of one's own choice, not because one is forced to*) by choice, by preference, by volition, freely, from choice, from preference, of one's own accord, of one's own free will, spontaneously, voluntarily. ANTONYMS: by force, involuntarily, unwillingly. **2** (*done, given etc. cheerfully*) cheerfully, eagerly, happily, readily, ungrudgingly, with all one's heart, without hesitation, with pleasure. ANTONYMS: grudgingly, reluctantly, unwillingly.

willingness *n.* **1** (*readiness or inclination*) agreeableness, agreement, amenability, compliance, consent, disposition, happiness, inclination, preparedness, readiness. ANTONYMS: aversion, disinclination, reluctance, unwillingness. **2** (*eagerness or enthusiasm*) cheerfulness, cooperation, cooperativeness, eagerness, keenness, readiness. ANTONYMS: lack of enthusiasm, reluctance, unwillingness.

willowy *a.* (*slender or graceful, like a willow*) graceful, lissom, lithe, pencil-slim, slender, slim, svelte, sylphlike. ANTONYMS: chubby, clumsy, graceless.

will-power *n.* (*control exercised deliberately over impulse or inclinations*) commitment, determination, doggedness, drive, firmness of purpose, firmness of will, force of will, grit, moral fibre, resolution, resolve, self-control, self-discipline, single-mindedness, strength of purpose, will. ANTONYMS: indecision, irresolution, weakness.

willy-nilly *adv.* (*willingly or unwillingly*) nolens volens, of necessity, whether desired or not, whether one likes it or not, whether one wants to or not.

wilt *v.i.* **1** (*to wither, to droop*) droop, sag, shrivel, wither. ANTONYMS: burgeon, flourish, revive, thrive. **2** (*to lose freshness or vigour*) ebb, fade, fail, flag, flop, languish, lose heart, sag, sink, wane, weaken, wither. ANTONYMS: (*coll.*) perk up, strengthen.

wily *a.* (*using or full of wiles, cunning*) artful, astute, cheating, crafty, (*coll.*) crooked, cunning, deceitful, designing, (*sl.*) fly, foxy,

fraudulent, scheming, shifty, shrewd, sly, tricky, underhand. ANTONYMS: artless, honest, ingenuous, naive, simple.

wimp *n.* (*a feeble, ineffectual person*) (*coll.*) drip, milksop, namby-pamby, sissy, weakling, (*coll.*) wet.

win *v.t.* **1** (*to gain or attain by fighting or superiority in a contest, wager etc.*) accomplish, achieve, acquire, attain, bag, catch, collect, come away with, gain, get, net, obtain, pick up, procure, receive, secure. ANTONYMS: fail to get, lose, miss. **2** (*to be victorious*) achieve victory, be the conqueror, be the victor, be victorious, carry the day, gain victory, triumph. ANTONYMS: be vanquished, suffer defeat. **3** (*to win over*) bring round, convert, convince, induce, influence, persuade, prevail upon, sway, talk round, win over. ANTONYMS: dissuade, put off. **4** (*to attract or charm*) attract, charm, disarm, gain, lure.
~*v.i.* (*to be successful or victorious in a fight, contest etc.*) be victorious, carry all before one, carry the day, come first, come out on top, come top, conquer, finish first, gain victory, prevail, succeed, take first prize, triumph. ANTONYMS: be the loser, lose, suffer defeat.
~*n.* (*a success, a victory*) conquest, success, triumph, victory. ANTONYMS: beating, defeat, failure, loss. **to win over** (*to persuade, to secure the support or assent of*) bring round, convert, convince, induce, influence, persuade, prevail upon, sway, talk round, win, win round.

wince *v.i.* (*to shrink or flinch, as from pain or a blow*) blench, cringe, draw back, flinch, grimace, recoil, shrink, squirm, start.

wind[1] *n.* **1** (*a natural air current, a breeze*) air current, breeze, draught, gale, gust, hurricane, tornado, zephyr. **2** (*the power of breathing in exertion etc., lung power*) breath, lung power, puff. **3** (*breath expended in words, meaningless talk or rhetoric*) (*sl.*) baloney, blather, blether, bluster, boasting, bragging, empty talk, (*coll.*) hot air, talk, twaddle. ANTONYMS: common sense, sense. **4** (*scent or odour carried on the wind*) odour, scent, smell. **5** (*a hint or indication*) gossip, hint, indication, information, inkling, intelligence, news, report, rumour, suggestion. **in the wind** (*showing signs of occurring*) about to happen, approaching, close at hand, coming, imminent, impending, in the offing, looming, near, on the cards, on the way. **to get the wind up** (*to get nervous, to become frightened*) become afraid, become alarmed, get frightened, get scared, take fright. **to put the wind up** (*to frighten*) alarm, frighten, make afraid, put fear into, scare, scare off.

wind[2] *v.i.* (*to turn or be twisted in a spiral or*

tortuous course or shape) bend, curve, loop, meander, snake, spiral, turn, twine, twist, twist and turn, wreathe, zigzag.
~v.t. (to coil round, to entwine) coil, roll, twine, twist, wrap.
~n. (a bend or curve) bend, coil, convolution, curve, loop, meander, turn, twist, undulation, whorl, zigzag. **to wind down 1** (to reduce gradually) decrease, diminish, dwindle, ease up, lessen, reduce, subside, taper off. ANTONYMS: expand, increase. **2** (to relax) calm down, ease up, (N Am., coll.) hang loose, relax, unwind. ANTONYMS: limber up, tense up. **3** (gradually to reduce the amount of work in (something), before it stops completely) bring to a close, bring to an end, make less active. **to wind up 1** (to coil up) coil, roll, twine, twist, wrap. **2** (to put into a state of tension or readiness for activity) agitate, discompose, disconcert, excite, fluster, make nervous, make tense, put on edge, strain, work up. ANTONYMS: calm down, make calm. **3** (to irritate, to annoy) annoy, irritate. **4** (to tease) have (someone) on, (coll.) kid, make fun of, pull (someone's) leg, tease. **5** (to bring to a conclusion, to conclude) bring to a close, bring to a conclusion, bring to an end, close, conclude, end, finalize, finish, terminate, wrap up. ANTONYMS: begin, commence, start. **6** (to come to a conclusion) close, come to a conclusion, come to an end, conclude, finish, wrap up. ANTONYMS: begin, start. **7** (to arrange the final settlement of the affairs of (a business etc.)) close down, declare bankrupt, dissolve, liquidate, put into liquidation. **8** (to go into liquidation) become bankrupt, close down, go bankrupt, go into liquidation, go to the wall. **9** (to end up in a certain state or situation) end up, find oneself, finish up.

winded a. (unable to breathe easily) breathless, gasping for breath, out of breath, out of puff, panting, (coll.) puffed, (coll.) puffed out.

windfall n. (a piece of unexpected good fortune, esp. a sum of money) bonanza, godsend, jackpot, manna from heaven, piece of good fortune, piece of luck, stroke of luck. ANTONYMS: disaster, piece of bad luck, setback.

winding n. (an instance of coiling etc.; bend or curve) bend, convolution, curve, meander, spiral, turn, twist, undulation, whorl, wind.
~a. (that winds) bending, circuitous, crooked, curving, deviating, looping, meandering, serpentine, sinuous, snaking, spiralling, tortuous, turning, twisting, twisting and turning, undulating, zigzagging. ANTONYMS: direct, straight, undeviating, unswerving.

wind-up n. **1** (an end or conclusion) close, end, finish, termination. ANTONYMS: beginning,

start, start-up. **2** (an instance of annoying or teasing someone) annoyance, irritation, legpull, provocation, teasing.

windy a. (stormy, boisterous) blowy, blustery, boisterous, breezy, gusting, gusty, squally, stormy, tempestuous, turbulent, wild. ANTONYMS: calm, still.

wing n. **1** (a part of a building that extends from the main part) adjunct, annexe, extension, side. **2** (an extreme faction of a party, group etc.) arm, branch, cabal, circle, clique, coterie, faction, group, grouping, section, segment, set.
~v.t. (to wound in the wing or the arm) clip, hit, injure, wound. **in the wings** (waiting in readiness) prepared, ready, ready to take over, standing by, waiting. **to take under one's wing** (to take under one's protection) act as guardian, act as mentor, adopt, protect, safeguard, shelter, shield, take as one's protégé(e).

wink v.i. (to close and open both eyes quickly, to blink) blink, nictate, nictitate.
~v.t. (to close and open (an eye or the eyes)) bat, blink, flutter, nictate, nictitate. **to wink at** (to pretend not to see) close one's eyes to, condone, connive at, disregard, ignore, overlook, shut one's eyes to, tolerate, turn a blind eye to. ANTONYMS: censure, condemn, criticize.

winkle v.i. **to winkle out 1** (to extract with difficulty) dig out, dislodge, extract, extricate, remove, smoke out. **2** (to elicit (information etc.) with difficulty) draw out, elicit, extract, extricate, prise out.

winner n. (a person or thing that wins) champion, conquering hero, conqueror, prizewinner, trophy winner, vanquisher, victor. ANTONYMS: loser.

winning a. **1** (that wins) conquering, successful, triumphant, vanquishing, victorious. ANTONYMS: defeated, losing. **2** (attractive, charming) alluring, appealing, attractive, bewitching, captivating, charming, cute, delightful, disarming, enchanting, endearing, engaging, fascinating, fetching, lovely, pleasing, sweet, taking, winsome. ANTONYMS: repellent, unappealing, unattractive.
~n. (the amount won in betting, gambling etc.) earnings, gains, proceeds, profits, spoils, takings.

winnow v.t. **1** (to separate and drive the chaff from (grain)) divide, get rid of, remove, separate, sort out. **2** (to sort, to examine thoroughly) analyse, comb, examine, go through, sift, sort.

wintry a. **1** (of or like winter) arctic, biting, chilly, cold, freezing, frosty, glacial, harsh, hibernal, hiemal, icy, (coll.) nippy, piercing, snowy. ANTONYMS: hot, summer, sunny, warm. **2** ((*of a smile, look etc.*) *cold and cheerless*) bleak, cheerless, chilly, cold, cool, distant, frosty, remote, unfriendly. ANTONYMS: friendly, warm.

wipe *v.t.* **1** (*to rub with something soft in order to clean or dry*) brush, clean, dry, dust, mop, rub, sponge, swab. **2** (*to remove* (*dirt etc.*) *by wiping*) brush off, clean off, efface, erase, get rid of, remove, rub off, sponge off, take off. ~*n.* (*an act of wiping*) brush, clean, dust, mop, rub, sponge. **to wipe out 1** (*to clean out by wiping*) brush, clean, dust, mop, rub, sponge, swab. **2** (*to efface, to obliterate*) blot out, efface, eradicate, expunge, extirpate, get rid of, obliterate, remove. **3** (*to destroy, to annihilate*) annihilate, destroy, eliminate, exterminate, massacre.

wiry *a.* **1** (*made of or resembling wire*) bristly, rigid, stiff. **2** ((*of a person*) *lean but sinewy*) lean, sinewy, spare, strong, tough.

wisdom *n.* (*practical discernment, judgement*) astuteness, circumspection, common sense, comprehension, discernment, enlightenment, erudition, forethought, insight, intelligence, judgement, judiciousness, knowledge, learning, logic, penetration, prudence, rationality, reason, sagacity, sense, shrewdness, understanding. ANTONYMS: folly, foolishness, stupidity.

wise *a.* **1** (*having or showing the power or faculty of discerning or judging rightly; sagacious*) astute, circumspect, discerning, enlightened, erudite, intelligent, judicious, learned, logical, penetrating, percipient, prudent, rational, sage, sapient, sensible, shrewd, understanding. ANTONYMS: foolish, injudicious, stupid, unwise. **2** (*informed, aware*) aware, (*coll.*) clued-up, conscious, informed, in the know. **to put someone wise** (*to inform someone*) alert, appraise, (*sl.*) clue (someone) in, (*sl.*) clue (someone) up, inform, notify, tell, tip (someone) off, warn.

wisecrack *n.* (*a witty comment*) (*coll.*) funny, gag, jest, joke, quip, witticism.

wish *v.t.* **1** (*to have a desire or craving* (*for*)) aspire to, covet, crave, desire, hanker after, (*coll.*) have a yen for, hope for, hunger for, long for, lust after, need, set one's heart on, sigh for, thirst after, want, yearn for. **2** (*to frame or express a desire or wish concerning*) ask, bid, command, demand, desire, direct, instruct, order, require. ~*n.* **1** (*a desire, a longing*) aspiration, craving, desire, fancy, hankering, hope, hunger, inclination, liking, love, lust, urge, want, whim, (*coll.*) yen. ANTONYMS: aversion, disinclination,

dislike, loathing, revulsion. **2** (*an expression of this, a request*) bidding, command, demand, desire, direction, instruction, order, request, requirement, want, will.

wishy-washy *a.* **1** (*lacking strength, forcefulness etc.*) bland, effete, feeble, ineffectual, puny, spineless, weak. **2** (*watery, insipid*) diluted, flavourless, tasteless, watery, weak. ANTONYMS: flavoursome, strong, tasty. **3** ((*of colours*) *pale, not bright or dark*) pale, pallid, sickly, wan. ANTONYMS: bold, brightly-coloured, vivid.

wisp *n.* (*a small bunch or handful of straw, hay etc.*) piece, shred, strand, thread, twist.

wispy *a.* (*like a wisp, fine*) delicate, ethereal, fine, flimsy, fragile, frail, insubstantial, thin, wisplike. ANTONYMS: strong, substantial, thick.

wistful *a.* (*full of vague yearnings, esp. for unattainable things, sadly longing*) contemplative, disconsolate, dreamy, forlorn, in a reverie, longing, melancholy, mournful, musing, pensive, reflective, sad, thoughtful, yearning.

wit *n.* **1** (*intelligence, understanding*) acumen, astuteness, brains, cleverness, common sense, comprehension, discernment, ingenuity, intellect, intelligence, judgement, mind, (*coll.*) nous, perception, reason, sagacity, sageness, sense, understanding, wisdom. ANTONYMS: dimness, stupidity, unintelligence. **2** (*the power of perceiving analogies and other relations between apparently incongruous ideas*) banter, facetiousness, fun, humour, jocularity, levity, raillery, repartee, waggishness, wordplay. ANTONYMS: gravity, seriousness, solemnity. **3** (*a person distinguished for this power, a witty person*) (*sl.*) card, comedian, comic, humorist, jester, joker, punster, wag. **at one's wits' end** (*at a complete loss as to what further steps to take, in a state of despair*) at the end of one's tether, baffled, bewildered, confused, despairing, desperate, stumped. **to have/ keep one's wits about one** (*to be alert*) be alert, be attentive, be circumspect, be on one's guard, be on the qui vive, be vigilant, be wary. ANTONYMS: be careless, be inattentive, be negligent.

witch *n.* (*a woman having dealings with evil spirits or practising sorcery*) enchantress, hex, magician, necromancer, sorceress.

witchcraft *n.* (*sorcery, magic*) black art, black magic, enchantment, magic, necromancy, occult, sorcery, sortilege, thaumaturgy, voodoo, witchery, wizardry.

withdraw *v.t.* **1** (*to take away, to remove*) extract, pull out, remove, take away, take out. ANTONYMS: insert, put in. **2** (*to state officially that something which one said previously is not* *true*) recall, rescind, retract, revoke, take back, unsay. ANTONYMS: introduce, present, put forward, submit.

~*v.i.* (*to retire, to go away*) depart, detach oneself, fall back, go away, go off, leave, make oneself scarce, retire, retreat. ANTONYMS: advance, go forward, proceed.

withdrawal *n.* **1** (*the act or an instance of withdrawing*) extraction, removal. ANTONYMS: insertion. **2** (*the act of offically stating that something which one said previously is not true*) recall, rescinding, retraction, revocation. ANTONYMS: introduction, presentation, submitting. **3** (*the act of leaving a place*) departure, exit, exodus, falling back, going away, leaving, retiral, retirement, retreat. ANTONYMS: advancing. **4** (*the act of no longer doing something*) abstention, cessation, giving up.

withdrawn *a.* (*very shy or reserved, socially isolated*) aloof, detached, diffident, distant, introverted, private, quiet, reserved, retiring, self-contained, shrinking, shy, silent, taciturn, uncommunicative, unforthcoming, unsociable. ANTONYMS: extrovert, forthcoming, gregarious, outgoing, sociable.

wither *v.t.* **1** (*to cause to shrivel or dry, to shrivel and dry* (*up*)) blast, blight, desiccate, dry out, dry up, kill, shrivel. ANTONYMS: invigorate. **2** (*to cause to lose freshness or vigour*) destroy, kill off, ruin, shrivel. ANTONYMS: boost, give new life to, invigorate. **3** (*to make abashed*) abash, crush, discomfit, humiliate, mortify, put down.

~*v.i.* **1** (*to become dry and shrivelled, to dry and shrivel* (*up*)) die, droop, dry out, dry up, fade, go limp, shrivel, wilt. ANTONYMS: be fresh, bloom, flourish, thrive. **2** (*to lose freshness, vigour etc.*) decline, die away, fade, shrink, wane, wilt. ANTONYMS: flourish, increase, thrive.

withering *a.* (*scornful*) contemptuous, snubbing.

withhold *v.t.* **1** (*to keep back; to deduct*) decline, refuse. ANTONYMS: allow, give. **2** (*to keep from action, to hold back*) check, curb, hold back, keep back, keep in check, restrain, suppress. ANTONYMS: give rein to, let out.

withstand *v.t.* (*to stand up against, to resist*) battle with, bear, confront, defy, endure, face, face up to, fight, hold out against, oppose, put up with, remain firm against, resist, stand up to, survive, take on, tolerate, weather. ANTONYMS: capitulate to, give in to, succumb to, yield to.

witness *n.* **1** (*a person who has seen an incident etc., a spectator*) bystander, eyewitness, looker-on, observer, onlooker, spectator, watcher. **2** (*a person who gives evidence in a law court or for judicial purposes, esp. on oath*) attestant, (*Law*) deponent, testifier. **3** (*attestation of a fact etc., evidence*) confirmation, corroboration, evidence, proof, testimony.

~*v.t.* **1** (*to see or know by personal presence, to be a spectator of*) be a witness to, be present at, look on, observe, see, view, watch. **2** (*to attest* (*a signature*), *to sign* (*a document*) *as witness*) countersign, endorse, sign. **3** (*to indicate, to show*) attest to, bear out, bear witness to, be evidence of, be proof of, confirm, corroborate, demonstrate, evince, indicate, prove, show, testify to, vouch for. ANTONYMS: disprove, give the lie to. **to bear witness 1** (*to give testimony*) give evidence, give testimony, testify. **2** (*to be a sign of*) attest to, bear out, be evidence of, be proof of, betoken, confirm, corroborate, demonstrate, evince, indicate, prove, show, testify to, vouch for. ANTONYMS: disprove, give the lie to.

witticism *n.* (*a witty phrase or saying, a jest*) bon mot, clever saying, epigram, jest, joke, play on words, pun, quip, sally, (*coll.*) wisecrack, witty remark.

witty *a.* (*showing or characterized by wit or humour*) amusing, clever, comic, droll, epigrammatic, facetious, funny, humorous, jocular, original, scintillating, sparkling, waggish. ANTONYMS: boring, serious, solemn.

wizard *n.* **1** (*a sorcerer, a magician*) enchanter, magician, male witch, necromancer, sorcerer, warlock. **2** (*a person who works wonders, a genius*) ace, adept, (*coll.*) dab hand, expert, genius, (*esp. N Am., coll.*) hotshot, maestro, master, star, virtuoso, (*coll.*) whiz, (*coll.*) wiz.

wizardry *n.* (*magic, sorcery*) black art, black magic, enchantment, magic, necromancy, occultism, sorcery, voodoo, witchcraft.

wizened *a.* (*withered or shrivelled, esp. with age*) dried up, gnarled, lined, shrivelled, withered, worn, wrinkled. ANTONYMS: fresh, smooth, wrinkle-free.

wobble *v.i.* **1** (*to incline to one side and then the other alternately, as when not properly balanced*) rock, seesaw, shake, sway, teeter, tremble, vibrate. **2** (*to go unsteadily, to stagger*) stagger, teeter, totter. **3** (*to waver, to be inconsistent or inconstant*) be uncertain, be undecided, dither, hesitate, shilly-shally, (*Sc.*) swither, vacillate. **4** (*to quaver or tremble*) quaver, quiver, shake, tremble.

wobbly *a.* **1** (*inclined to wobble*) rickety, shaky, unstable, unsteady, (*sl.*) wonky. **2** (*unsteady*) quivering, shaky, trembling, tremulous, unsteady.

woe *n.* **1** (*sorrow, overwhelming grief*) adversity, affliction, agony, anguish, depression, distress, gloom, hardship, heartache, heartbreak, misery, misfortune, pain, sadness, sorrow, suffering, torment, tribulation, wretchedness. ANTONYMS: good fortune, happiness, joy, pleasure, prosperity. **2** (*calamity, misfortune*) affliction, burden, disaster, grief, hardship, misfortune, pain, sorrow, trial, trouble. ANTONYMS: joy, pleasure.

woebegone *a.* (*overcome with woe, sorrowful-looking*) crestfallen, dejected, disconsolate, doleful, downcast, down in the mouth, forlorn, gloomy, grief-stricken, lugubrious, miserable, mournful, sad, sorrowful, troubled, wretched. ANTONYMS: happy, joyful, merry.

woeful *a.* **1** (*sorrowful, miserable*) distressed, gloomy, miserable, painful, sad, sorrowful, unhappy, wretched. ANTONYMS: carefree, cheerful, glad, happy, joyful. **2** (*inadequate, very poor*) abysmal, awful, bad, deplorable, disgraceful, dreadful, feeble, hopeless, inadequate, (*coll.*) lousy, pathetic, pitiable, pitiful, poor, rotten, shocking, sorry, terrible, wretched.

wolf *v.t.* (*to devour ravenously, to gulp or swallow* (*down*) *greedily*) bolt, devour, gobble, gorge oneself, gulp down, (*esp. N Am., sl.*) pig out on, (*coll.*) scoff, stuff.

woman *n.* (*an adult human female*) (*sl.*) bird, (*sl.*) chick, (*esp. N Am., sl.*) dame, female, girl, lady, lass, member of the opposite sex, she. ANTONYMS: (*coll.*) bloke, lad, male, man.

womanhood *n.* **1** (*the state of being a woman*) maturity. ANTONYMS: manhood. **2** (*the collective qualities associated with being a woman*) femininity, womanliness. ANTONYMS: maleness, manhood, masculinity. **3** (*women generally*) the female sex, womankind, women, womenfolk. ANTONYMS: men, menfolk, the male sex.

womanish *a.* (*having the characteristics or qualities of a woman, effeminate*) effeminate, effete, sissy, unmanly. ANTONYMS: mannish.

womanizer *n.* (*a man who has casual sexual relationships with many women*) Casanova, Don Juan, ladies' man, lady-killer, lecher, Lothario, philanderer, seducer, (*coll.*) wolf.

womankind *n.* (*women collectively, the female sex*) females, the female sex, womanhood, women, womenfolk. ANTONYMS: males, mankind, men, menfolk, the male sex.

womanly *a.* (*having the qualities associated with a woman, feminine*) female, feminine, gentle, matronly, motherly, soft, warm. ANTONYMS: harsh, masculine, unwomanly.

wonder *n.* **1** (*a remarkable or marvellous thing, person etc., a miracle*) curiosity, marvel, miracle, nonpareil, phenomenon, prodigy, rarity, sight, spectacle. **2** (*the emotion excited by that which is unexpected or inexplicable*) admiration, amazement, astonishment, awe, bewilderment, fascination, stupefaction, surprise, wonderment.
~*v.i.* **1** (*to be struck with wonder or surprise*) be amazed, be astonished, be flabbergasted, be surprised, feel surprise, find it surprising. **2** (*to look with wonder or admiration* (*at*)) be amazed (at), express wonder (at), gape (at), gawk (at), marvel (at), stand in awe (of), stare (at).
~*v.t.* (*to speculate about*) ask questions about, be curious about, be inquisitive about, be puzzled by, deliberate on, have one's doubts about, meditate about, muse about, ponder, puzzle over, speculate about, think about.

wonderful *a.* **1** (*remarkable, marvellous*) (*sl.*) ace, brilliant, excellent, (*coll.*) fab, (*coll.*) fabulous, (*coll.*) fantastic, fine, good, (*coll.*) great, (*coll.*) magnificent, marvellous, nice, outstanding, (*coll.*) smashing, (*coll.*) super, (*coll.*) terrific, very good. ANTONYMS: awful, bad, boring, dreadful, grim, miserable, unpleasant. **2** (*exciting wonder or astonishment*) amazing, astonishing, astounding, awe-inspiring, awesome, extraordinary, fantastic, incredible, miraculous, phenomenal, prodigious, remarkable, spectacular, staggering, startling, surprising, unprecedented. ANTONYMS: ordinary, run-of-the-mill, unremarkable, usual.

wonky *a.* (*unsteady, shaky*) rickety, shaky, unstable, unsteady, weak, wobbly. ANTONYMS: stable, steady, strong.

wont *a.* (*used, accustomed* (*to*)) accustomed (to), given (to), in the habit (of), used (to). ANTONYMS: unaccustomed (to), unused (to).
~*n.* (*custom, habit*) custom, habit, practice, routine, rule, way.

wonted *a.* (*customary, habitual*) accustomed, common, customary, habitual, normal, regular, routine, usual. ANTONYMS: unaccustomed, uncommon, unusual.

woo *v.t.* **1** (*to court, esp. with a view to marriage*) chase after, court, go out with, pay court to, pay one's addresses to, pay suit to, press one's suit with, pursue, seek the hand of, set one's cap at. **2** (*to seek to gain or attain*) chase after, go in search of, pursue, seek, set out to get, try to attain. **3** (*to solicit, to coax*) beg, coax, entreat, implore, importune, press, solicit, urge, wheedle.

wood *n.* **1** (*the fibrous substance of a tree between the bark and the pith*) timber.

2 (*timber*) firewood, fuel, kindling. **3** (*a large and thick collection of growing trees, a forest*) coppice, copse, forest, grove, thicket, trees, woodland, woods. **out of the wood** (*out of danger or difficulty*) free from danger, free from harm, out of danger, safe. ANTONYMS: in danger, in peril.

wooded *a.* (*covered with trees or woods*) forested, timbered, tree-clad, tree-covered, woody.

wooden *a.* **1** (*made of wood*) made of wood, of wood, timber, wood. **2** (*stiff, stilted*) awkward, clumsy, gauche, gawky, graceless, inelegant, maladroit, rigid, stiff, ungainly, unnatural. ANTONYMS: agile, graceful, natural, nimble. **3** (*spiritless, expressionless*) blank, deadpan, dull, emotionless, empty, expressionless, lifeless, spiritless, unemotional, unresponsive, vacant. ANTONYMS: emotional, expressive, responsive.

woodland *n.* (*land covered with woods, wooded country*) forest, trees, wood, woods.

wool *n.* **1** (*the fine, soft, curly hair forming the fleece of sheep, goats and some other animals*) fleece, hair. **2** (*yarn, fabric or clothing made from this*) worsted, yarn. **to pull the wool over someone's eyes** (*to deceive someone*) (*sl.*) con, deceive, delude, dupe, fool, hoodwink, (*coll.*) pull a fast one on, (*coll.*) put one over on, take in, trick.

wool-gathering *n.* (*absent-mindedness, inattention*) absent-mindedness, abstraction, building castles in the air, daydreaming, dreaming, inattention, musing, preoccupation, reverie. ANTONYMS: alertness, attention, concentration, observation.

woolly *a.* **1** (*bearing or naturally covered with wool, or with hair resembling wool*) fleecy, flocculent, fluffy, furry, hairy, shaggy, woollen. **2** (*lacking clear definition or incisiveness*) blurred, cloudy, foggy, fuzzy, hazy, ill-defined, indistinct, unclear. ANTONYMS: clear, distinct, sharp, well-defined. **3** (*with hazy ideas, muddled*) confused, disorganized, hazy, indefinite, muddled, nebulous, unclear, vague. ANTONYMS: clear, clearcut, definite, organized, precise.

woozy *a.* (*suffering from giddiness, nausea etc.*) befuddled, confused, dazed, dizzy, fuddled, giddy, muddled, unsteady, wobbly. ANTONYMS: clear-headed.

word *n.* **1** (*an articulate sound or combination of sounds*) expression, term. **2** (*speech, talk*) a few words, chat, (*coll.*) confab, consultation, conversation, discourse, discussion, powwow, talk, tête-à-tête. **3** (*something said, a remark*) comment, remark, statement, utterance.

4 (*news, a message*) advice, bulletin, communication, communiqué, dispatch, (*coll.*) gen, information, intelligence, intimation, message, news, notice, report, tidings. **5** (*a command, an order*) command, decree, edict, injunction, order, signal. **6** (*a password, a motto*) catchword, password, slogan, watchword. **7** (*one's assurance or definite affirmation*) affirmation, assurance, declaration, guarantee, oath, pledge, promise, solemn promise, undertaking, vow, word of honour. **8** (*the text of a song, speech etc.*) book, libretto, lyrics, text. **9** (*talk or remarks exchanged expressive of anger or reproach*) altercation, angry exchange, angry words, argument, disagreement, dispute, quarrel, row, (*coll.*) run-in, squabble. **10** (*a rumour*) gossip, hearsay, rumour, talk, (*coll.*) the grapevine.

~*v.t.* (*to express in words, to phrase*) couch, express, phrase, put, say, state, utter. **in a/ one word** (*briefly, in short*) briefly, concisely, in a nutshell, in brief, in short, not to mince words, succinctly, to put it briefly, to sum up. **word for word** (*in exactly the same words, verbatim*) accurately, exactly, faithfully, in the same words, precisely, verbatim. ANTONYMS: loosely.

wording *n.* (*choice of words, phrasing etc.*) language, phraseology, phrasing, terminology, vocabulary, words.

wordy *a.* (*using more words than necessary to express oneself, verbose*) diffuse, digressive, discursive, garrulous, long-winded, loquacious, prolix, protracted, rambling, tautological, verbose, voluble, wandering. ANTONYMS: brief, concise, terse, to the point.

work *n.* **1** (*the exertion of physical or mental energy or activity directed to some purpose*) effort, elbow grease, exertion, grind, labour, slog, (*coll.*) sweat, toil. ANTONYMS: leisure, relaxation, rest. **2** (*an undertaking, a task*) assignment, charge, chore, commission, duty, job, mission, task, undertaking. **3** (*employment as a means of livelihood, occupation*) business, calling, career, employment, field, job, line, line of work, métier, occupation, trade, vocation. ANTONYMS: hobby, leisure, recreation, retirement. **4** (*an action or achievement*) achievement, act, action, deed, feat, handiwork, performance, production. **5** (*a book or other literary composition, a musical or other artistic production*) composition, creation, oeuvre, opus, performance, piece, production. **6** (*an industrial establishment, a factory*) factory, mill, plant, shop, workshop. **7** (*the working part or mechanism (of a watch etc.)*) guts, (*coll.*) innards, (*coll.*) insides, mechanism, parts, working parts, workings. **8** (*moral duties or the performance of meritorious acts*) actions, acts, deeds. **9** (*skill in making things*) art, craft, craftsmanship, skill, workmanship.

~*v.i.* **1** (*to exert physical or mental energy for some purpose, to do work*) drudge, exert oneself, grind away, labour, make an effort, slave, slog, sweat, toil. ANTONYMS: relax, rest, take one's ease. **2** (*to be employed or occupied*) be employed, be in work, earn a living, have a job. **3** (*to operate, to function*) function, go, operate, perform, run. ANTONYMS: be out of order, break down, malfunction, stop. **4** (*to take effect, to be effective*) be effective, be effectual, be successful, succeed, take effect. **5** (*to be in a state of motion or agitation, to ferment*) become agitated, convulse, twist, twitch, writhe. **6** (*to reach a certain condition gradually*) become, come.

~*v.t.* **1** (*to run, to operate*) control, drive, handle, manage, operate, ply, use, wield. **2** (*to cultivate* (*land*)) cultivate, dig, farm, till. **3** (*to bring about, to produce as a result*) accomplish, achieve, bring about, carry out, cause, contrive, create, effect, execute, implement, produce. ANTONYMS: fail. **4** (*to prepare or alter the condition, shape or consistency of by some process, to fashion*) fashion, form, knead, model, mould, shape. **5** (*to arrange something in a clever and skilful way so that one benefits from it*) arrange, direct, edge, engineer, fix, guide, manipulate, manoeuvre, negotiate. **out of work** (*not in paid employment, unemployed*) jobless, (*coll.*) on the dole, out of a job, unemployed. ANTONYMS: employed, in work. **to work out 1** (*to solve, to understand*) calculate, figure out, find out, puzzle out, resolve, solve, (*sl.*) suss out. **2** (*to accomplish, to effect*) accomplish, achieve, attain, bring about, effect. **3** (*to devise, to formulate*) arrange, construct, contrive, develop, devise, evolve, form, formulate, organize, plan, put together. **4** (*to have a result*) come out, develop, evolve, go, happen, occur, pan out, turn out. **5** (*to undertake a series of exercises to get fit*) do exercises, exercise, follow an exercise programme, keep fit, train. **6** (*to be successful*) be effective, be successful, go as planned, go well, prove satisfactory, succeed. ANTONYMS: be ineffective, be unsuccessful, fail. **7** (*to add up to* (*a certain amount*)) add up to, amount to, come to, make, total. **to work over** (*to beat severely, to mug*) attack, beat up, (*coll.*) give (someone) a hiding, lay into, mug, (*sl.*) rough up. **to work up 1** (*to elaborate, to bring gradually into shape or efficiency*) develop, elaborate, evolve, expand, improve, perfect. **2** (*to excite gradually, to stir up*) arouse, awaken, excite, foment, generate, inflame, instigate, kindle, prompt, rouse, stimulate, stir up, whet. ANTONYMS: calm down, soothe, stifle, suppress.

workable *a.* (*capable of being worked, practicable*) feasible, possible, practicable, practical, viable. ANTONYMS: impossible, impracticable, impractical, unworkable.

workaday *a.* (*relating to or suitable for workdays, ordinary*) common, everyday, familiar, ordinary, practical, routine, run-of-the-mill, usual. ANTONYMS: extraordinary, special, unusual.

worker *n.* **1** (*a person who works, esp. a member of the working class*) artisan, blue-collar worker, employee, hand, labourer, manual worker, member of the proletariat, member of the workforce, wage earner. ANTONYMS: boss, manager. **2** (*an employee*) employed person, employee, member of staff, member of the workforce, working man, working woman. **3** (*a person who works hard*) busy bee, hard worker, toiler, (*coll.*) workaholic. ANTONYMS: layabout, loafer, shirker, (*coll.*) skiver. **4** (*a performer or doer*) doer, executor, operator, performer, perpetrator.

working *a.* **1** (*engaged in work, esp. manual labour*) employed, in a job, in work, salaried, waged. ANTONYMS: jobless, out of work, unemployed. **2** (*functioning or able to function*) functioning, going, in operation, in working order, operating, running. ANTONYMS: broken, malfunctioning, out of order. **3** (*taking an active part in a business*) active, hands-on, involved.

workman *n.* (*any man employed in manual labour, an operative*) artisan, craftsman, craftswoman, hand, labourer, operative, tradesman, tradeswoman, worker.

workmanlike *a.* (*done in the manner of a good worker*) adept, efficient, expert, masterly, professional, proficient, satisfactory, skilful, skilled. ANTONYMS: amateurish, clumsy, inefficient, unsatisfactory.

workmanship *n.* (*comparative skill or execution shown in making something or in the thing made*) art, artistry, craft, craftsmanship, expertise, handicraft, skill, technique, work.

workout *n.* (*a series of exercises for physical fitness*) (*coll.*) daily dozen, drill, exercise, exercise programme, exercise session, physical exercises, (*coll.*) physical jerks, training.

workshop *n.* **1** (*a building in which manual work, esp. making or repairing things, is carried on*) factory, mill, plant, shop, works. **2** (*a room in which manual work, esp. making or repairing things, is carried on*) atelier, studio, workroom. **3** (*a meeting for discussion, training etc.*) discussion group, seminar, study group.

world *n.* **1** (*the earth with its lands and seas*) earth, globe. **2** (*a celestial body regarded as similar to this*) celestial body, heavenly body, planet, star. **3** (*the human inhabitants of the earth, humankind*) everybody, everyone, human beings, humanity, humankind, mankind, people, people everywhere, the general public, the human race, the public, the whole world. **4** (*the whole system of things, the universe*) cosmos, creation, life, universe. **5** (*a particular section or class of people, animals or things*) division, group, section, sector. **6** (*a particular area of activity, a realm*) area, department, domain, field, province, realm, sphere. **7** (*a vast quantity, number, degree etc.* (*of*)) a great deal, a vast amount. **8** (*any time, state or sphere of existence*) age, epoch, era, period, times. **9** (*secular interest as opposed to spiritual*) secular things, things temporal.

worldly *a.* **1** (*earthly, secular, not spiritual*) carnal, earthly, fleshly, material, physical, secular, temporal. ANTONYMS: heavenly, spiritual. **2** (*sophisticated, worldly-wise*) blasé, experienced, knowing, sophisticated, urbane, worldly-wise. ANTONYMS: innocent, naive, unsophisticated.

worldwide *a.* **1** (*spread over the whole world*) global, international, universal. ANTONYMS: domestic, local, national. **2** (*existing everywhere*) everywhere, general, pandemic, ubiquitous, universal, widespread. ANTONYMS: limited, local, restricted.

worn *a.* **1** (*tired, exhausted*) (*coll.*) done in, exhausted, fatigued, (*coll.*) knackered, played out, (*esp. N Am., coll.*) pooped, spent, tired, tired out, wearied, weary, worn out. ANTONYMS: energetic, fresh, lively. **2** (*well-worn*) frayed, shabby, threadbare, well-worn. ANTONYMS: brand-new, in mint condition. **3** (*haggard, strained*) careworn, drawn, haggard, strained.

worn out *a.* **1** (*thoroughly tired, exhausted*) (*coll.*) done in, exhausted, fatigued, (*coll.*) knackered, played out, (*esp. N Am., coll.*) pooped, spent, tired, tired out, wearied, weary. ANTONYMS: energetic, fresh, lively. **2** (*rendered useless by long wear*) broken-down, (*sl.*) clapped out, done, frayed, on its last legs, ragged, shabby, tatty, threadbare, well-worn. ANTONYMS: brand-new, in mint condition.

worried *a.* (*anxious, troubled*) afraid, agitated, anxious, apprehensive, bothered, concerned, distraught, distressed, disturbed, edgy, fearful, fretful, ill at ease, nervous, on edge, overwrought, tense, troubled, uneasy, upset, (*coll.*) uptight, worked up. ANTONYMS: carefree, tranquil, unconcerned.

worry *v.t.* **1** (*to cause mental distress to*) agitate, be a worry to, bother, cause anxiety to, disquiet, distress, make agitated, make anxious, make distraught, make tense, make uneasy, perturb, put on edge, trouble, upset, work up. ANTONYMS: calm down, comfort, put (someone's) mind at rest. **2** (*to harass or bother*) annoy, badger, bother, disturb, harass, harry, (*coll.*) hassle, importune, irritate, nag, pester, plague, torment, vex. **3** ((*of dogs etc.*) *to bite or keep on biting, to shake or pull about with the teeth*) attack, bite, gnaw at, go for, lacerate, savage, tear at.
~*v.i.* (*to be unduly anxious or troubled, to fret*) be afraid, be agitated, be anxious, be apprehensive, be bothered, be concerned, be distressed, be edgy, be fearful, be ill at ease, be nervous, be on edge, be overwrought, be tense, be troubled, be uneasy, be upset, (*coll.*) be uptight, be worried, fret, get worked up. ANTONYMS: be carefree, relax, (*coll.*) stay cool.
~*n.* **1** (*a cause or source of worry*) bother, irritant, irritation, nuisance, pest, problem, thorn in one's flesh, thorn in one's side, trial, trouble. ANTONYMS: comfort. **2** (*the state of being worried; anxiety, care*) agitation, anxiety, apprehension, bother, concern, disquiet, distress, edginess, fear, misgiving, nervousness, tenseness, trepidation, trouble, unease, upset. ANTONYMS: calmness, peace of mind, serenity.

worsen *v.i.* (*to grow worse*) become worse, decline, degenerate, deteriorate, get worse, go downhill, go from bad to worse, grow worse, retrogress, take a turn for the worse. ANTONYMS: get better, improve, take a turn for the better.
~*v.t.* (*to make worse*) aggravate, exacerbate, intensify, make worse. ANTONYMS: ameliorate, enhance, improve.

worship *v.t.* **1** (*to pay divine honours to*) extol, glorify, honour, laud, praise, pray to, revere, venerate. ANTONYMS: blaspheme. **2** (*to reverence with supreme respect and admiration*) adore, be devoted to, hero-worship, idolize, put (someone) on a pedestal, revere. ANTONYMS: despise, hate.

worth *n.* **1** (*that which a person or thing is worth, value*) price, value. **2** (*usefulness or importance*) avail, benefit, help, importance, merit, usefulness, value. **3** (*high character, excellence*) eminence, excellence, merit, nobility, quality, worthiness. ANTONYMS: worthlessness.

worthless *a.* **1** (*having little or no value in terms of money*) of little value, of no value, valueless, without value. ANTONYMS: valuable. **2** (*having no importance or use*) ineffectual, no

use, of no value, to no avail, useless. ANTO-
NYMS: effectual, important, useful, worthwhile.
3 ((*of a person*) *having no good qualities*) good-
for-nothing, incompetent, (*coll.*) no-good,
useless. ANTONYMS: competent, good.

worthy *a.* **1** (*deserving of or entitled to respect
or honour, respectable*) admirable, decent,
deserving, good, honest, honourable, moral,
reputable, respectable, righteous, upright,
virtuous. ANTONYMS: dishonourable, disreput-
able. **2** (*deserving* (*of, to be etc.*)) deserving (of),
meriting, worth.

wound *n.* **1** (*an injury caused by a cut or blow to
the skin and flesh*) cut, gash, injury, laceration,
lesion, sore. **2** (*any damage or pain to feelings,
reputation etc.*) anguish, distress, hurt, injury,
pain, shock, trauma, upset.
~*v.t.* **1** (*to inflict a wound on*) cause injury to, cut,
damage, gash, hurt, injure, lacerate, pierce.
2 (*to make* (*someone*) *feel very unhappy or
upset*) distress, hurt, hurt (someone's) feelings,
offend, upset.

wrangle *v.i.* (*to argue or quarrel angrily or
noisily, to brawl*) argue, bicker, fight, quarrel,
row, squabble.
~*n.* (*an angry or noisy dispute or quarrel, an
altercation*) altercation, argument, difference
of opinion, disagreement, dispute, fight,
quarrel, row, (*coll.*) set-to, squabble.

wrap *v.t.* **1** (*to fold or arrange so as to cover or
enclose something*) arrange, fold, swathe. **2** (*to
enfold or pack in some soft material*) bind,
bundle up, encase, enfold, envelop, swaddle,
swathe. **3** (*to fold paper round a present*) gift-
wrap, pack, package, parcel up, wrap up.
ANTONYMS: open, unpack, unwrap.
~*n.* (*something intended to wrap, such as a cloak
or shawl*) cape, cloak, scarf, shawl, stole. **to
wrap up 1** (*to fold paper etc. round*) gift-wrap,
pack, package, parcel up, wrap. ANTONYMS:
open, unpack, unwrap. **2** (*to bring to a conclusion*) bring to a close, bring to an end, close,
conclude, finish, wind up.

wrapper *n.* **1** (*that in which anything is
wrapped, esp. an outer covering*) casing, cover,
packaging, paper. **2** (*the outer paper covering of
a book*) cover, dust jacket, jacket.

wrath *n.* (*deep or violent anger, rage*) anger,
exasperation, fury, indignation, ire, passion,
rage, temper.

wreath *n.* **1** (*a band or ring of flowers or leaves
woven or twisted together for wearing on the
head, decorating graves etc.*) circlet, coronet,
crown, festoon, garland, lei. **2** (*a ring, a curl* (*of
cloud, smoke etc.*)) circle, curl, loop, ring.

wreck *v.t.* **1** (*to ruin or destroy*) (*sl.*) cock up,

demolish, destroy, disrupt, play havoc with,
ruin, spoil, undo. **2** (*to destroy or shatter* (*a
vessel etc.*) *by collision, driving ashore etc.*)
demolish, ruin, smash, write off.

wrench *n.* **1** (*a violent twist or sideways pull*)
jerk, pull, rip, tear, tug, twist, wrest, yank.
2 (*an injury caused by twisting, a sprain*) rick,
sprain, strain, twist. **3** (*pain or distress caused
by a parting, loss etc.*) ache, anguish, blow,
hurt, pain, pang, shock, trauma. **4** (*a tool for
twisting or untwisting screws, bolts etc., a
spanner*) monkey wrench, spanner.
~*v.t.* **1** (*to pull or twist with force or violence*)
force, jerk, pull, rip, tear, tug, twist, wrest,
yank. **2** (*to strain, to sprain*) rick, sprain, strain,
twist.

wrest *v.t.* **1** (*to pull or wrench* (*away*) *forcibly*)
pull, snatch, take, twist, wrench. **2** (*to take or
obtain* (*from*) *with force or difficulty*) extract,
force, wring.

wrestle *v.i.* (*to struggle, to strive vehemently
*(*with*)) battle, contend, grapple, strive,
struggle.

wretched *a.* **1** (*miserable, unhappy*) dejected,
depressed, disconsolate, doleful, downhearted, gloomy, miserable, mournful, sad,
unhappy, woebegone. ANTONYMS: cheerful,
happy, merry. **2** (*calamitous, pitiable*) deplorable, dreadful, grim, harsh, miserable,
pitiful, poor, tragic, unfortunate, unhappy.
ANTONYMS: comfortable, fortunate, happy.
3 (*worthless, contemptible*) base, contemptible, inferior, low, miserable, poor, worthless.
ANTONYMS: great, noble. **4** (*extremely unsatisfactory or unpleasant*) bad, inferior, poor,
substandard, unsatisfactory. ANTONYMS: good,
high-grade, superior. **to feel wretched** (*to feel
ill*) be ill, be out of sorts, be sick, be under the
weather, be unwell. ANTONYMS: be well, feel
fine.

wriggle *v.i.* **1** (*to twist or move the body to and
fro with short motions*) jiggle, squirm, twist,
writhe. **2** (*to move or go* (*along, in, out etc.*) *with
writhing contortions or twistings*) crawl, snake,
squirm, turn, twist, twist and turn, worm,
zigzag. **to wriggle out of** (*to evade or shirk*)
avoid, dodge, evade, extricate oneself from,
shirk, talk one's way out of.

wring *v.t.* **1** (*to twist and squeeze or compress*)
squeeze, twist. **2** (*to pain, to distress*) distress,
hurt, pain, pierce, rack, stab, tear at, wound.
3 (*to extract, to extort*) coerce, exact, extort,
extract, force, wrest.

wrinkle *n.* **1** (*a small crease or furrow caused
by the folding or contraction of a flexible
surface*) crease, crinkle, crumple, fold, gather,

pucker, rumple. **2** (*such a crease or furrow in the skin, esp. as a result of age*) crease, crow's foot, furrow, line, pucker.

writ *n.* (*a written command or precept issued by a court*) court order, decree, summons.

write *v.t.* **1** (*to set* (*down*) *or convey by writing*) inscribe, jot down, list, note, note down, put down, put in black and white, put in writing, record, register, scribble down, set down, take down, write down. **2** (*to compose or produce as an author*) be the author of, compose, draft. ~*v.i.* (*to write or send a letter* (*to*)) correspond (with), (*coll.*) drop (someone) a line, send a letter (to), write a letter (to). **to write off 1** (*to consider* (*a loss etc.*) *as irrecoverable*) cancel, disregard, forget about, (*coll.*) give (something) up as a bad job, wipe out. **2** (*to damage* (*a car*) *beyond repair*) demolish, smash, (*N Am., sl.*) total, wreck. **3** (*to discard as useless, insignificant etc.*) dismiss, disregard.

writer *n.* (*an author, a journalist etc.*) author, hack, journalist, novelist, wordsmith.

writhe *v.i.* (*to twist or roll the body about, as in pain*) jerk, squirm, thrash, toss, turn, twist, twist and turn, wriggle.

writing *n.* **1** (*handwriting*) calligraphy, hand, handwriting, penmanship, script. **2** (*a book, article or other literary composition*) book, opus, publication, work.

wrong *a.* **1** (*inaccurate, incorrect*) erroneous, false, imprecise, inaccurate, incorrect, in error, inexact, mistaken, off the beam, wide of the mark. ANTONYMS: accurate, correct, precise, right. **2** (*not that which is required, intended etc.*) inapposite, inappropriate, inapt, incongruous, infelicitous, unsuitable. ANTONYMS: appropriate, proper, right. **3** (*not morally right, contrary to morality*) bad, criminal, (*coll.*) crooked, delinquent, dishonest, dishonourable, evil, illegal, illicit, immoral, sinful, unethical, unlawful, wicked. ANTONYMS: good, lawful, legal, virtuous. **4** (*out of order, in bad condition etc.*) amiss, awry, defective, faulty, not right, out of order. ANTONYMS: all right, in order, in working order, working. ~*n.* **1** (*that which is wrong*) badness, dishonesty, evil, immorality, iniquity, sin, wickedness. ANTONYMS: goodness, right, virtue. **2** (*a wrong act, an injustice*) abuse, crime, evil, infraction, injury, misdeed, offence, sin, transgression. ~*v.t.* **1** (*to treat unjustly, to do wrong to*) abuse, do injury to, harm, hurt, ill-treat, ill-use, injure, maltreat, mistreat. ANTONYMS: aid, help. **2** (*to impute evil motives to unjustly*) (*coll.*) bad-mouth, defame, impugn, libel, malign, misrepresent, slander. ANTONYMS: laud, praise.

wrongdoer *n.* (*a person who does wrong*) criminal, (*coll.*) crook, culprit, delinquent, evildoer, lawbreaker, miscreant, offender, sinner, trangressor, villain.

wrongful *a.* (*injurious, unjust*) illegal, illicit, unethical, unfair, unjust, unlawful, unwarranted, wrong. ANTONYMS: just, lawful, legal, right.

wry *a.* ((*of humour*) *dry or sardonic*) droll, dry, ironic, sarcastic, sardonic.

Y

yank *v.t.* (*to pull sharply*) jerk, jolt, pull, snatch, tug, twitch, wrench.

yap *v.i.* **1** (*to yelp or bark snappishly*) bark, snap, yelp. **2** (*to talk constantly in a shrill, foolish manner*) babble, blather, chatter, gossip, jabber, (*coll.*) jaw, natter, prattle, (*coll.*) rabbit, spout, talk, tattle, (*coll.*) waffle. **3** (*to scold*) nag, scold.

yarn *n.* **1** (*any spun fibre prepared for weaving, knitting etc.*) fibre, strand, thread. **2** (*a long story, esp. one of doubtful truth*) anecdote, cock and bull story, fable, narrative, story, tale, tall story, (*sl.*) whopper.

yearn *v.i.* (*to feel a longing desire* (*for*)) ache (for), covet, crave, desire, fancy, hanker (after), (*coll.*) have a yen (for), hunger (for), itch (for), long (for), lust (after), pant (for), pine (for), set one's heart (on), want, wish.

yell *v.i.* **1** (*to cry out with a loud or inarticulate cry*) caterwaul, cry out, howl, scream, screech, shriek, squeal, yowl. **2** (*to shout*) bawl, bellow, (*esp. N Am., coll. or dial.*) holler, roar, shout. ANTONYMS: murmur, whisper.
~*n.* (*such a cry or shout*) bellow, caterwaul, cry, (*esp. N Am., coll. or dial.*) holler, howl, roar, scream, screech, shout, shriek, squall, whoop, yelp, yowl.

yet *adv.* **1** (*up to this or that time*) hitherto, still, until now, up to now. **2** (*by this or that time*) as yet, so far, thus far. **3** (*in addition, besides*) additionally, as well, besides, further, furthermore, in addition, into the bargain, moreover, over and above, still. **4** (*eventually, at some future time*) eventually, in the future, in time, later. **5** (*with comp.*) (*even*) even, still. **6** (*nevertheless, in spite of that*) anyhow, anyway, despite, even so, however, in spite of, nevertheless, notwithstanding, regardless, still.

yield *v.t.* **1** (*to bring forth as fruit or result*) afford, bear, bring forth, bring in, earn, generate, give, pay, produce, provide, return, supply. **2** (*to give up, to surrender*) abandon, abdicate, admit defeat, bow, capitulate, cave in, cede, concede, forgo, give up, relinquish, resign, succumb, surrender.
~*v.i.* (*to give way, to submit*) accede, agree, allow, assent, bow, concede, consent, give way, go along (with), grant, permit, relent, submit, surrender. ANTONYMS: oppose, resist.
~*n.* (*something that is yielded or produced*) crop, earnings, gain, gate, harvest, income, output, proceeds, produce, production, profit, return, revenue, takings.

yielding *a.* **1** (*compliant*) accommodating, acquiescent, amenable, biddable, complaisant, compliant, docile, easy, flexible, obedient, obliging, pliant, submissive, tractable. ANTONYMS: obdurate, stubborn. **2** (*able to bend, pliable*) bendable, elastic, flexible, plastic, pliable, soft, spongy, springy, supple, unresisting. ANTONYMS: inelastic, rigid.

young *a.* **1** (*being in the early stage of life or development*) adolescent, growing, infant, junior, juvenile, little, minor, teenage, unfledged, youthful. ANTONYMS: adult, old. **2** (*of recent birth or beginning, newly formed*) early, fledgling, new, recent, undeveloped. **3** (*not infirm or decayed with age*) fresh, vigorous. **4** (*immature, inexperienced*) callow, green, immature, inexperienced, innocent, naive, raw, uninitiated. ANTONYMS: experienced, mature.
~*n.* (*offspring*) babies, brood, children, issue, litter, offspring, progeny. ANTONYMS: parent.

youngster *n.* **1** (*a young person*) boy, child, girl, juvenile, (*coll.*) kid, lad, lass, (*sl., derog.*) pup, teenager, toddler, (*coll.*) young 'un, youth. ANTONYMS: adult. **2** (*a young animal*) colt, cub, kitten, pup.

youth *n.* **1** (*the period of life from infancy to manhood or womanhood*) adolescence, boyhood, childhood, early years, girlhood, immaturity, young days. ANTONYMS: adulthood, maturity. **2** (*the vigour, inexperience etc. of this period*) freshness, inexperience, vigour, youthfulness. **3** (*a young man*) adolescent, boy, child, juvenile, (*coll.*) kid, lad, minor, stripling, teenager, young man, youngster. ANTONYMS: adult. **4** (*young men and women collectively*) (*coll.*) kids, teenagers, young, younger generation, young people.

youthful *a.* **1** (*young*) boyish, childish, girlish, immature, inexperienced, juvenile, pubescent, puerile, young. ANTONYMS: adult, aged. **2** (*vigorous*) active, fresh, spry, vigorous, young at heart, young-looking. ANTONYMS: decrepit, senile.

Z

zany *a.* (*comical, absurd*) absurd, bizarre, clownish, comical, (*coll.*) crackpot, crazy, eccentric, foolish, funny, hilarious, (*sl.*) loony, ludicrous, madcap, nonsensical, (*sl.*) nutty, oddball, off the wall, silly, (*sl.*) wacky, weird. ANTONYMS: serious.

zeal *n.* (*ardour, enthusiasm*) ardour, devotion, eagerness, earnestness, enthusiasm, fanaticism, keenness, passion. ANTONYMS: apathy, indifference.

zealot *n.* **1** (*a fanatical partisan*) bigot, extremist, fanatic, militant, partisan, radical. **2** (*a person full of zeal, esp. one carried away by it*) (*coll.*) buff, enthusiast, (*coll.*) fiend, maniac.

zealous *a.* (*very enthusiastic*) ardent, burning, conscientious, dedicated, devoted, eager, earnest, enthusiastic, fanatical, fervent, impassioned, intense, keen, militant, passionate, rabid, spirited, vehement. ANTONYMS: indifferent, unenthusiastic.

zenith *n.* (*the highest or culminating point*) acme, apex, apogee, climax, crest, culmination, height, high point, meridian, peak, pinnacle, summit, top. ANTONYMS: bottom, nadir.

zero *n.* **1** (*the figure 0, nought*) cipher, naught, nil, nothing, nought. **2** (*the lowest point in any scale*) bottom, low point, nadir, nullity.

zest *n.* **1** (*keen enjoyment*) appetite, delectation, eagerness, enjoyment, enthusiasm, exuberance, gusto, hunger, interest, keenness, relish, thirst, zeal. ANTONYMS: aversion, indifference. **2** (*piquancy, relish*) bite, charm, edge, flavour, interest, kick, pepper, piquancy, (*sl.*) pizazz, pungency, relish, savour, smack, spice, tang, taste, zing, (*coll.*) zip. ANTONYMS: blandness.

zone *n.* (*an area sectioned off for a particular function*) area, district, region, section, sector.

zoom *v.i.* (*to move quickly* (*as*) *with a deep loud buzzing noise*) dash, fly, race, rush, shoot, speed, zip.